McGraw–Hill's

Taxation of Individuals and Business Entities

Brian C. Spilker
Brigham Young University
Editor

Benjamin C. Ayers
The University of Georgia

Edmund Outslay
Michigan State University

Connie D. Weaver
Texas A&M University

John A. Barrick
Brigham Young University

John R. Robinson
Texas A&M University

Ron G. Worsham
Brigham Young University

McGRAW-HILL'S TAXATION OF INDIVIDUALS AND BUSINESS ENTITIES, 2017 EDITION, EIGHTH EDITION

Published by McGraw-Hill Education, 2 Penn Plaza, New York, NY 10121. Copyright © 2017 by McGraw-Hill Education. All rights reserved. Printed in the United States of America. Previous editions © 2016, 2015, and 2014. No part of this publication may be reproduced or distributed in any form or by any means, or stored in a database or retrieval system, without the prior written consent of McGraw-Hill Education, including, but not limited to, in any network or other electronic storage or transmission, or broadcast for distance learning.

Some ancillaries, including electronic and print components, may not be available to customers outside the United States.

This book is printed on acid-free paper.

2 3 4 5 6 7 8 9 0 DOW 21 20 19 18 17 16

ISBN   978-1-259-54866-6
MHID   1-259-54866-X
ISSN   1946-7745

Senior Vice President, Products & Markets: *Kurt L. Strand*	Digital Product Developer: *Kevin Moran*
Vice President, General Manager, Products & Markets: *Marty Lange*	Digital Product Analyst: *Xin Lin*
Vice President, Content Design & Delivery: *Kimberly Meriwether David*	Director, Content Design & Delivery: *Linda Avenarius*
Managing Director: *Tim Vertovec*	Program Manager: *Daryl Horrocks*
Senior Brand Manager: *Kathleen Klehr*	Content Project Managers: *Lori Koetters, Brian Nacik*
Director, Product Development: *Rose Koos*	Buyer: *Susan K. Culbertson*
Director of Digital Content: *Peggy Hussey*	Design: *Matt Diamond*
Lead Product Developer: *Kristine Tibbetts*	Content Licensing Specialists: *Melissa Homer, Shannon Manderscheid*
Product Developer: *Danielle Andries*	Cover Image: © *Alija/iStock/Getty Images*
Market Development Manager: *Erin Chomat*	Compositor: *Aptara®, Inc.*
	Printer: *R. R. Donnelley*

mheducation.com/highered

Dedications

We dedicate this book to:

My children, Braxton, Cameron, Ethan, and Lauren, and to my parents, Ray and Janet. Last but not least, to my wife, Kim, for allowing me to take up valuable kitchen space while I was working on the project. I love you all.

Brian Spilker

My wife, Marilyn, daughters Margaret Lindley and Georgia, son Benjamin, and parents Bill and Linda.

Ben Ayers

My wife, Jill, and my children Annika, Corinne, Lina, Mitch, and Connor.

John Barrick

My family, Jane, Mark, Sarah, Chloe, Lily, and Jeff, and to Professor James E. Wheeler, my mentor and friend.

Ed Outslay

JES, Tommy, and Laura.

John Robinson

My family, Dan, Travis, Alix, and Alan.

Connie Weaver

My wife, Anne, sons Matthew and Daniel, and daughters Whitney and Hayley.

Ron Worsham

Brian Spilker (PhD, University of Texas at Austin, 1993) is the Robert Call/Deloitte Professor in the School of Accountancy at Brigham Young University. He teaches taxation in the graduate and undergraduate programs at Brigham Young University. He received both BS (Summa Cum Laude) and MAcc (tax emphasis) degrees from Brigham Young University before working as a tax consultant for Arthur Young & Co. (now Ernst & Young). After his professional work experience, Brian earned his PhD at the University of Texas at Austin. In 1996, he was selected as one of two nationwide recipients of the Price Waterhouse Fellowship in Tax Award. In 1998, he was a winner of the American Taxation Association and Arthur Andersen Teaching Innovation Award for his work in the classroom; he has also been awarded for his use of technology in the classroom at Brigham Young University. Brian researches issues relating to tax information search and professional tax judgment. His research has been published in journals such as *The Accounting Review, Organizational Behavior and Human Decision Processes, Journal of the American Taxation Association, Behavioral Research in Accounting, Journal of Accounting Education, Journal of Corporate Taxation,* and *Journal of Accountancy.*

Ben Ayers (PhD, University of Texas at Austin, 1996) holds the Earl Davis Chair in Taxation and is the dean of the Terry College of Business at the University of Georgia. He received a PhD from the University of Texas at Austin and an MTA and BS from the University of Alabama. Prior to entering the PhD program at the University of Texas, Ben was a tax manager at KPMG in Tampa, Florida, and a contract manager with Complete Health, Inc., in Birmingham, Alabama.

Ben teaches tax planning and research courses in the undergraduate and graduate programs at the University of Georgia. He is the recipient of 11 teaching awards at the school, college, and university levels, including the Richard B. Russell Undergraduate Teaching Award, the highest teaching honor for University of Georgia junior faculty members. His research interests include the effects of taxation on firm structure, mergers and acquisitions, and capital markets and the effects of accounting information on security returns. He has published articles in journals such as the *Accounting Review, Journal of Finance, Journal of Accounting and Economics, Contemporary Accounting Research, Review of Accounting Studies, Journal of Law and Economics, Journal of the American Taxation Association,* and *National Tax Journal.* Ben was the 1997 recipient of the American Accounting Association's Competitive Manuscript Award and the 2003 and 2008 recipient of the American Taxation Association's Outstanding Manuscript Award.

John Barrick (PhD, University of Nebraska at Lincoln, 1998) is currently an associate professor in the Marriott School at Brigham Young University. He served as an accountant at the United States Congress Joint Committee on Taxation for the 110th and 111th Congresses. He teaches taxation in the graduate and undergraduate programs at Brigham Young University. He received both BS and MAcc (tax emphasis) degrees from Brigham Young University before working as a tax consultant for Price Waterhouse (now PricewaterhouseCoopers). After his professional work experience, John earned his PhD at the University of Nebraska at Lincoln. He was the 1998 recipient of the American Accounting Association, Accounting, Behavior, and Organization Section's Outstanding Dissertation Award. John researches issues relating to professional tax judgment and tax information search. His research has been published in journals such as *Organizational Behavior and Human Decision Processes, Contemporary Accounting Research,* and *Journal of the American Taxation Association.*

Ed Outslay (PhD, University of Michigan, 1981) is a professor of accounting and the Deloitte/Michael Licata Endowed Professor of Taxation in the Department of Accounting and Information Systems at Michigan State University, where he has taught since 1981. He received a BA from Furman University in 1974 and an MBA and PhD from the University of Michigan in 1977 and 1981. Ed currently teaches graduate classes in corporate taxation, multiunit enterprises, accounting for income taxes, and international taxation. In February 2003, Ed testified before the Senate Finance Committee on the Joint Committee on Taxation's Report on Enron Corporation. MSU has honored Ed with the Presidential Award for Outstanding Community Service, Distinguished Faculty Award, John D. Withrow Teacher-Scholar Award, Roland H. Salmonson Outstanding Teaching Award, Senior Class Council Distinguished Faculty Award, MSU Teacher-Scholar Award, and MSU's 1st Annual Curricular Service-Learning and Civic Engagement Award in 2008. Ed received the Ray M. Sommerfeld Outstanding Tax Educator Award in 2004 and the lifetime Service Award in 2013 from the American Taxation Association. He has also received the ATA Outstanding Manuscript Award twice, the ATA/Deloitte Teaching Innovations Award, and the 2004 Distinguished Achievement in Accounting Education Award from the Michigan Association of CPAs. Ed has been recognized for his community service by the Greater Lansing Chapter of the Association of Government Accountants, the City of East Lansing (Crystal Award), and the East Lansing Education Foundation. He received a National Assistant Coach of the Year Award in 2003 from AFLAC and was named an Assistant High School Baseball Coach of the Year in 2002 by the Michigan High School Baseball Coaches Association.

John Robinson (PhD, University of Michigan, 1981) is the Patricia '77 and Grant E. Sims '77 Eminent Scholar Chair in Business. Prior to joining the faculty at Texas A&M, John was the C. Aubrey Smith Professor of Accounting at the University of Texas at Austin, Texas, and he taught at The University of Kansas where he was The Arthur Young Faculty Scholar. In 2009-2010 John served as the Academic Fellow in the Division of Corporation Finance at the Securities and Exchange Commission. He is the recipient of the Henry A. Bubb Award for outstanding teaching, the Texas Blazer's Faculty Excellence Award, and the MPA Council Outstanding Professor Award. John also received the 2012 Outstanding Service Award from the American Taxation Association (ATA). John served as the 2014-2015 -President (elect) of the ATA and is the ATA's president for 2015-2016. John conducts research in a broad variety of topics involving financial accounting, mergers and acquisitions, and the influence of taxes on financial structures and performance. His scholarly articles have appeared in *The Accounting Review, The Journal of Accounting and Economics, Journal of Finance, National Tax Journal, Journal of Law and Economics, Journal of the American Taxation Association, The Journal of the American Bar Association*, and *The Journal of Taxation*. John's research was honored with the 2003 and 2008 ATA Outstanding Manuscript Awards. In addition, John was the editor of *The Journal of the American Taxation Association* from 2002 through 2005. Professor Robinson received his J.D. (*Cum Laude*) from The University of Michigan in 1979, and he earned a PhD in accounting from The University of Michigan in 1981. John teaches courses on individual and corporate taxation and advanced accounting.

Connie Weaver Connie Weaver (PhD, Arizona State University, 1997) is the KPMG Professor of Accounting at Texas A&M University. She received a PhD from Arizona State University, an MPA from the University of Texas at Arlington, and a BS (chemical engineering) from the University of Texas at Austin. Prior to entering the PhD Program, Connie was a tax manager at Ernst & Young in Dallas, Texas, where she became licensed to practice as a CPA. She teaches taxation in the graduate and undergraduate programs at Texas A&M University. She has also taught undergraduate and graduate students at the University of Wisconsin-Madison and the University of Texas at Austin. She is the recipient of several teaching awards including the 2006 American Taxation Association/ Deloitte Teaching Innovations, the David and Denise Baggett Teaching, and Association of Former Students Distinguished Achievement awards recognizing innovation in teaching taxation. Connie's current research interests include the effects of tax and financial incentives on corporate decisions and reporting. She has published articles in journals such as the *Accounting Review, Contemporary Accounting Research, Journal of the American Taxation Association, Accounting Horizons, Journal of Corporate Finance,* and *Tax Notes*. She serves on the editorial board of Contemporary Accounting Research and Issues in Accounting Education and was the 1998 recipient of the American Taxation Association/Price Waterhouse Outstanding Dissertation award.

Ron Worsham (PhD, University of Florida, 1994) is an associate professor in the School of Accountancy at Brigham Young University. He teaches taxation in the graduate, undergraduate, MBA, and Executive MBA programs at Brigham Young University. He has also taught as a visiting professor at the University of Chicago. He received both BS and MAcc (tax emphasis) degrees from Brigham Young University before working as a tax consultant for Arthur Young & Co. (now Ernst & Young) in Dallas, Texas. While in Texas, he became licensed to practice as a CPA. After his professional work experience, Ron earned his PhD at the University of Florida. He has been honored for outstanding innovation in the classroom at Brigham Young University. Ron has published academic research in the areas of taxpayer compliance and professional tax judgment. He has also published legal research in a variety of areas. His work has been published in journals such as *Journal of the American Taxation Association, The Journal of International Taxation, The Tax Executive, Journal of Accountancy,* and *Practical Tax Strategies*.

TEACHING THE CODE IN CONTEXT

   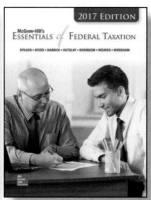

*The basic approach to teaching taxation hasn't changed in decades. **Today's student deserves a new approach.*** McGraw-Hill's Taxation of Individuals and Business Entities *is a bold and innovative series that has been adopted by over 300 schools across the country.*

McGraw-Hill's Taxation is designed to provide a unique, innovative, and engaging learning experience for students studying taxation. The breadth of the topical coverage, **the storyline approach to presenting the material,** the emphasis on the tax and nontax consequences of multiple parties involved in transactions, and the integration of financial and tax accounting topics make this book ideal for the modern tax curriculum.

> "This is the best tax book on the market. It's very readable, student-friendly, and provides great supplements."
>
> – Ann Esarco,
> McHenry County College

> "A lot of thought and planning went into the structure and content of the text, and a great product was achieved. **One of the most unique and helpful features is the common storyline** throughout each chapter."
>
> – Raymond J. Shaffer,
> Youngstown State University

Since the first manuscript was written in 2005, 400 professors have contributed 441 book reviews, in addition to 23 focus groups and symposia. Throughout this preface, their comments on the book's organization, pedagogy, and unique features are a testament to the **market-driven nature of *Taxation*'s development.**

> "The Spilker text, in many ways, is a more logical approach than any other tax textbook. **The text makes great use of the latest learning technologies through Connect and LearnSmart.**"
>
> – Ray Rodriguez, Southern Illinois University–Carbondale

A MODERN APPROACH FOR TODAY'S STUDENT

> "**This text provides a new approach to the teaching of the technical material.** The style of the text material is easier to read and understand. The examples and storyline are interesting and informative. The arrangement makes more sense in the understanding of related topics."
>
> – Robert Bertucelli, Long Island University–Post

Spilker's taxation series was built around the following five core precepts:

1 **Storyline Approach:** Each chapter begins with a storyline that introduces a set of characters or a business entity facing specific tax-related situations. Each chapter's examples are related to the storyline, providing students with opportunities to **learn the code in context.**

2 **Conversational Writing Style:** The authors took special care to write *McGraw-Hill's Taxation* that fosters a friendly dialogue between the content and each individual student. The tone of the presentation is intentionally conversational—creating the impression of *speaking with* **the student,** as opposed to *lecturing to* the student.

3 **Superior Organization of Related Topics:** *McGraw-Hill's Taxation* takes a fresh approach to taxation by providing two alternative topic sequences. In the *McGraw-Hill's Taxation of Individuals and Business Entities,* topics are grouped in **theme chapters,** including separate

> "I believe it **breaks down complex topics in a way that's easy to understand.** Definitely easier than other tax textbooks that I've had experience with."
>
> – Jacob Gatlin, Athens State University

chapters on home ownership, compensation, investments, and retirement savings and deferred compensation. However, in the *Essentials of Federal Taxation,* topics follow a more traditional sequence with topics presented in a life-cycle approach.

4 **Real-World Focus:** Students learn best when they see how concepts are applied in the real world. For that reason, real-world examples and articles are included in **"Taxes in the Real World"** boxes throughout the book. These vignettes demonstrate current issues in taxation and show the relevance of tax issues in all areas of business.

5 **Integrated Examples:** The examples used throughout the chapter relate directly to the storyline presented at the beginning of each chapter, so students become familiar with one set of facts and learn how to apply those facts to different scenarios. In addition to providing in-context

> "**Excellent text; love the story line approach and integrated examples.** It's easy to read and understand explanations. The language of the text is very clear and straightforward."
>
> – Sandra Owen, Indiana University–Bloomington

examples, we provide **"What if"** scenarios within many examples to **illustrate how variations in the facts might or might not change the answers.**

McGraw-Hill Connect®
Learn Without Limits

Connect is a teaching and learning platform that is proven to deliver better results for students and instructors.

Connect empowers students by continually adapting to deliver precisely what they need, when they need it, and how they need it, so your class time is more engaging and effective.

88% of instructors who use Connect require it; instructor satisfaction increases by 38% when Connect is required.

Course outcomes improve with Connect.

Using **Connect** improves passing rates by **10.8%** and retention by **16.4%**.

Analytics

Connect Insight®

Connect Insight is Connect's new one-of-a-kind visual analytics dashboard that provides at-a-glance information regarding student performance, which is immediately actionable. By presenting assignment, assessment, and topical performance results together with a time metric that is easily visible for aggregate or individual results, Connect Insight gives the user the ability to take a just-in-time approach to teaching and learning, which was never before available. Connect Insight presents data that helps instructors improve class performance in a way that is efficient and effective.

Connect helps students achieve better grades

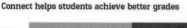

Based on McGraw-Hill Education Connect Effectiveness Study 2013

Adaptive

©Getty Images/iStockphoto

> More students earn **A's** and **B's** when they use McGraw-Hill Education **Adaptive** products.

SmartBook®

Proven to help students improve grades and study more efficiently, SmartBook contains the same content within the print book, but actively tailors that content to the needs of the individual. SmartBook's adaptive technology provides precise, personalized instruction on what the student should do next, guiding the student to master and remember key concepts, targeting gaps in knowledge and offering customized feedback, and driving the student toward comprehension and retention of the subject matter. Available on smartphones and tablets, SmartBook puts learning at the student's fingertips—anywhere, anytime.

> Over **4 billion questions** have been answered, making McGraw-Hill Education products more intelligent, reliable, and precise.

STUDENTS WANT

McGraw Hill Education **SMARTBOOK®**

95% of students reported **SmartBook** to be a more effective way of reading material

100% of students want to use the Practice Quiz feature available within **SmartBook** to help them study

100% of students reported having reliable access to off-campus wifi

90% of students say they would purchase **SmartBook** over print alone

95% reported that **SmartBook** would impact their study skills in a positive way

www.learnsmartadvantage.com

ONLINE ASSIGNMENTS

Connect helps students learn more efficiently by providing feedback and practice material when they need it, where they need it. Connect grades homework automatically and gives immediate feedback on any questions students may have missed. The extensive assignable, gradable end-of-chapter content includes a general journal application that looks and feels more like what you would find in a general ledger software package. Also, select questions have been redesigned to test students' knowledge more fully. They now include tables for students to work through rather than requiring that all calculations be done offline.

Through November, Tex has received gross income of $120,000. For December, Tex is considering whether to accept one more work engagement for the year. Engagement 1 will generate $7,000 of revenue at a cost of $4,000, which is deductible for AGI. In contrast, engagement 2 will generate $7,000 of revenue at a cost of $3,000, which is deductible as an itemized deduction. Tex files as a single taxpayer. (use the tax rate schedules.)

a. Calculate Tex's taxable income assuming he chooses engagement 1 and assuming he chooses engagement 2. Assume he has no itemized deductions other than those generated by engagement 2.

	Description	Engagement 1	Engagement 2
(1)	Gross income before new work engagement	$ 120,000	$ 120,000
(2)	Income from engagement	7,000	7,000
(3)	Additional for AGI deduction	(4,000)	
(4)	Adjusted gross income	$ 123,000	$ 127,000
(5)	Greater		
(6)	Greater of itemized deductions or standard deduction		

End-of-chapter questions in Connect include:

- Discussion Questions
- Problems
- Comprehensive Problems **(Available in the Tax Form Simulation!)**

NEW! Tax Form Simulation

New auto-graded **Tax Form Simulation** provides a much-improved student experience when solving the tax-form based problems. The tax form simulation allows students to apply tax concepts by completing the actual tax forms online with automatic feedback and grading for both students and instructors.

1040 PG1	1040 PG2

Form 1040	Department of the Treasury—Internal Revenue Service (99) U.S. Individual Income Tax Retrun	**2015**	OMB No. 1545-0074	IRS Use Only - Do not write in this space.

For the year Jan. 1–Dec. 31, 2015, or other tax year beginning , 2015, ending , 20

See separate instructions.

Your first name and initial	Your social security number
Mar	111-22-3333
Marc	Spouse's social security number
	222-33-4444

19010 N.W. 135th Street	Apt. no.	▲ Make sure the SSN(s) above and on line 6c are correct.

City, town or post office, state, and ZIP code. If you have a foreign address, also complete spaces below.

Miami, FL 33054

Presidential Election Campaign

Foreign country name	Foreign province	Foreign postal code

Check here if you, or your spouse if filing jointly, want $3 to go to this fund. Checking a box below will not change your tax or refund.

	You	Spouse

Filing Status	1	☐ Single	4	☐ Head of household (with qualifying person). If the qualifying person is a child
Check only one box.	2	☑ Married filing jointly		but not your dependent, enter this child's name here. ▶
	3	☐ Married filing separately. Enter spouse's SSN above and full name here. ▶	5	☐ Qualifying widow(er) with dependent child

NEW! Guided Examples

The Guided Examples in Connect provide a narrated, animated, step-by-step walk-through of select problems similar to those assigned. These short presentations can be turned on or off by instructors and provide reinforcement when students need it most.

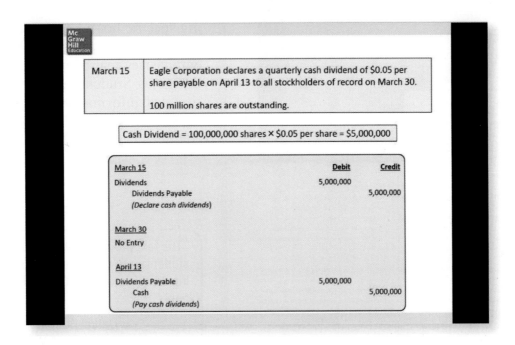

McGraw-Hill Customer Experience Group Contact Information

At McGraw-Hill, we understand that getting the most from new technology can be challenging. That's why our services don't stop after you purchase our products. You can contact our Product Specialists 24 hours a day to get product training online. Or you can search the knowledge bank of Frequently Asked Questions on our support website. For Customer Support, call **800-331-5094**, or visit **www.mhhe.com/support**. One of our Technical Support Analysts will be able to assist you in a timely fashion.

TaxACT®

McGraw-Hill's Taxation can be packaged with tax software from TaxACT, one of the leading preparation software companies in the market today. The 2016 edition includes availability of both Individuals and Business Entities software, including the 1040 forms and TaxACT Preparer's Business 3-Pack (with Forms 1065, 1120, and 1120S).

A STORYLINE APPROACH THAT WILL RESONATE WITH STUDENTS

Each chapter begins with a storyline that introduces a set of characters facing specific tax-related situations. This revolutionary approach to teaching tax emphasizes real people facing real tax dilemmas. Students learn to apply practical tax information to specific business and personal situations. The characters are brought further to life.

© Image Source

Storyline Summary

Taxpayers:	Courtney Wilson, age 40, Courtney's mother Dorothy "Gram" Weiss, age 70
Family description:	Courtney is divorced with a son, Deron, age 10, and a daughter, Ellen, age 20. Gram is currently residing with Courtney.
Location:	Kansas City, Missouri
Employment status:	Courtney works as an architect for EWD. Gram is retired.
Filing status:	Courtney is head of household. Gram is single.
Current situation:	Courtney and Gram have computed their taxable income. Now they are trying to determine their tax liability, tax refund or additional taxes due, and whether they owe any payment-related penalties.

Courtney has already determined her taxable income. Now she's working on computing her tax liability. She knows she owes a significant amount of regular income tax on her employment and business activities. However, she's not sure how to compute the tax on the qualified dividends she received from General Electric. Courtney is worried that she may be subject to the alternative minimum tax this year because she's heard that an increasing number of taxpayers in her income range must pay the tax. Finally, Courtney knows she owes some self-employment taxes on her business income. Courtney would like to determine whether she is eligible to claim any tax credits such as the child tax credit for her two children and education credits because she paid for a portion of her daughter Ellen's tuition at the University of Missouri–Kansas City this year. she has paid enough in taxes during the year to avoid underpayment penalties. She's planning on filing her tax return and paying her taxes on time.

Gram's tax situation is much more straightforward. She needs to determine the regular income tax on her taxable income. Her income is so low she knows she need not worry about the alternative minimum tax, and she believes she doesn't owe any self-employment tax. Gram didn't prepay any taxes this year, so she is concerned that she might be required to pay an underpayment penalty. She also expects to file her tax return and pay her taxes by the upcoming due date.

Examples

Examples are the cornerstone of any textbook covering taxation. For this reason, *McGraw-Hill's Taxation* authors took special care to create clear and helpful examples that relate to the storyline of the chapter. Students learn to refer to the facts presented in the storyline and apply them to other scenarios—in this way, they build a greater base of knowledge through application. Many examples also include "What if?" scenarios that add more complexity to the example or explore related tax concepts.

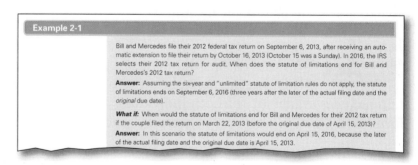

Example 2-1

Bill and Mercedes file their 2012 federal tax return on September 6, 2013, after receiving an automatic extension to file their return by October 16, 2013 (October 15 was a Sunday). In 2016, the IRS selects their 2012 tax return for audit. When does the statute of limitations end for Bill and Mercedes's 2012 tax return?

Answer: Assuming the six-year and "unlimited" statute of limitation rules do not apply, the statute of limitations ends on September 6, 2016 (three years after the later of the actual filing date and the *original* due date).

What if: When would the statute of limitations end for Bill and Mercedes for their 2012 tax return if the couple filed the return on March 22, 2013 (before the original due date of April 15, 2013)?

Answer: In this scenario the statute of limitations would end on April 15, 2016, because the later of the actual filing date and the original due date is April 15, 2013.

THE PEDAGOGY YOUR STUDENTS NEED TO PUT THE CODE IN CONTEXT

Taxes in the Real World

Taxes in the Real World are short boxes used throughout the book to demonstrate the real-world use of tax concepts. Current articles on tax issues, real-world application of chapter-specific tax rules, and short vignettes on popular news about tax are some of the issues covered in Taxes in the Real World boxes.

> "The Spilker text makes tax easy for students to understand. **It integrates great real-world examples so students can see how topics will be applied in practice.** The integration of the tax form and exhibits of the tax forms in the text are outstanding."
>
> – Kristen Bigbee, Texas Tech University

TAXES IN THE REAL WORLD Republicans vs. Democrats

We often boil down the tax policy of our major political parties into its simplest form: Democrats raise taxes to fund social programs, and Republicans lower taxes to benefit big businesses and the wealthy. Both ideas simplify the policy of each party, yet both ideas are essentially true.

Whether you agree with more government spending or tax breaks for corporations, each party's agenda will affect your taxes.

Political Ideology: Republican

"We believe government should tax only to raise money for its essential functions." The Republicans state their case plainly on the Republican National Convention website. That is, Republicans believe government should spend money only to enforce contracts, maintain basic infrastructure and national security, and protect citizens against criminals.

The literature of the House Republican Conference goes on to illuminate the role of the government and how tax policies affect individuals: "The money the government spends does not belong to the government; it belongs to the taxpayers who earned it. Republicans believe Americans deserve to keep more of their own money to save and invest for the future, and low tax policies help drive a strong and healthy economy."

Tax relief is the Republican route to growing the economy. A Republican government would reduce taxes for businesses to allow businesses to grow and thus hire more employees.

Republicans also seek to limit income taxes for individuals so that people can hold on to more disposable income, which they can then spend, save, or invest.

Political Ideology: Democrat

The tax policy for the Democratic Party calls for raising certain taxes to provide money for government spending, which in turn generates business. The party platform asserts that government spending provides "good jobs and will help the economy today."

Many Democrats are adherents to Keynesian economics, or aggregate demand, which holds that when the government funds programs, those programs pump new money into the economy. Keynesians believe that prices tend to stay relatively stable and therefore any kind of spending, whether by consumers or the government, will grow the economy.

Like the Republicans, Democrats believe the government should subsidize vital services that keep cities, states, and the country running: infrastructure such as road and bridge maintenance and repairs for schools. Democrats also call for tax cuts for the middle class. But who benefits most under each platform? The conventional wisdom is that corporations and the wealthy will benefit more with a Republican tax policy, while small businesses and middle-class households will benefit from a Democratic tax policy.

Source: http://www.investopedia.com/articles/economics/09/us-parties-republican-democrat-taxes.asp

The Key Facts

Marginal Key Facts provide quick synopses of the critical pieces of information presented throughout each chapter.

		($100,000 – $75,300).	
(3) Taxable income before additional $60,000 of tax deductions	$160,000.00	Example 1-3.	
(4) Tax on $160,000 taxable income	$ 31,785.50	Example 1-3.	
Marginal tax rate on additional $60,000 of tax deductions	25.41%	$\frac{\Delta Tax}{\Delta Taxable\ income} = [(2)-(4)]/[(1)-(3)]$	

Bill and Mercedes's marginal tax rate on $60,000 of additional deductions (25.41 percent) differs

THE KEY FACTS

Different Ways to Measure Tax Rates

- Marginal tax rate
  - The tax that applies to next increment of income or deduction.
- $= \dfrac{\Delta Tax}{\Delta Taxable\ income}$

Exhibits

Today's students are visual learners, and *McGraw-Hill's Taxation* delivers by making appropriate use of charts, diagrams, and tabular demonstrations of key material.

EXHIBIT 2-2 IRS Appeals/Litigation Process

> "A good textbook that uses **great examples throughout the chapters** to give a student an understanding of the tax theory and how it applies to the taxpayers."
>
> – Jennifer Wright, Drexel University

> "Spilker's use of examples immediately following the concept is a **great way to reinforce the concepts.**"
>
> – Karen Wisniewski, County College of Morris

PRACTICE MAKES PERFECT WITH A ...

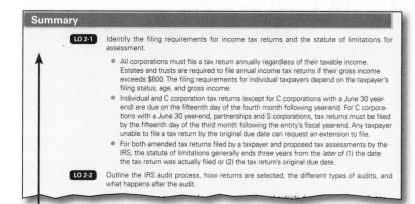

Summary

A unique feature of *McGraw-Hill's Taxation* is the end-of-chapter summary organized around learning objectives. Each objective has a brief, bullet-point summary that covers the major topics and concepts for that chapter, including references to critical exhibits and examples.

All end-of-chapter material is tied to learning objectives:

"You can tell the authors of this textbook are still in the classroom and responsible for the day-to-day education of accounting students. Examples are representative of the end-of-chapter problems, and the end-of-chapter summary is an excellent study tool."

– Debra Petrizzo, Franklin University

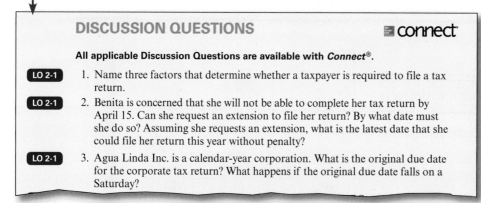

Discussion Questions

Discussion questions, now available in *Connect,* are provided for each of the major concepts in each chapter, providing students with an opportunity to review key parts of the chapter and answer evocative questions about what they have learned.

"This is a very readable text. **Students will understand it on their own,** generally, freeing more class time for application, practice, and student questions."

– Valrie Chambers,
Texas A&M University–Corpus Christi

...WIDE VARIETY OF ASSIGNMENT MATERIAL

Problems Problems are designed to test the comprehension of more complex topics. Each problem at the end of the chapter is tied to one of that chapter's learning objectives, with multiple problems for critical topics.

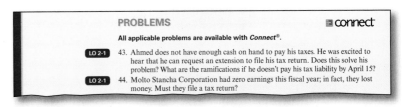

Tax Forms Problems Tax forms problems are a set of requirements included in the end-of-chapter material of the 2017 edition. These problems require students to complete a tax form (or part of a tax form), providing students with valuable experience and practice with filling out these forms. These requirements—and their relevant forms—are also included in *Connect*. Each tax forms problem includes an icon to differentiate it from regular problems.

Research Problems Research problems are special problems throughout the end of the chapter assignment material. These require students to do both basic and more complex research on topics outside of the scope of the book. Each research problem includes an icon to differentiate it from regular problems.

> "The textbook is comprehensive, uses an integrated approach to taxation, contains clear illustrations and examples in each chapter, and has a **wealth of end-of-chapter assignment material**."
>
> – James P. Trebby, Marquette University

Planning Problems Planning problems are another unique set of problems, also located at the end of the chapter assignment material. These require students to test their tax planning skills after covering the chapter topics. Each planning problem includes an icon to differentiate it from regular problems.

Comprehensive and Tax Return Problems Comprehensive and tax return problems address multiple concepts in a single problem. Comprehensive problems are ideal for cumulative topics; for this reason, they are located at the end of all chapters. In the end-of-book Appendix C, we include tax return problems that cover multiple chapters. **Additional tax return problems are also available in the *Connect Library*.**

Four Volumes to Fit...

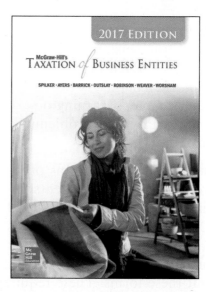

McGraw-Hill's Taxation of Individuals is organized to emphasize topics that are most important to undergraduates taking their first tax course. The first three chapters provide an introduction to taxation and then carefully guide students through tax research and tax planning. Part II discusses the fundamental elements of individual income tax, starting with the tax formula in Chapter 4 and then proceeding to more depth on individual topics in Chapters 5–7. Part III then discusses tax issues associated with business and investment activities. On the business side, it addresses business income and deductions, accounting methods, and tax consequences associated with purchasing assets and property dispositions (sales, trades, or other dispositions). For investments it covers portfolio-type investments such as stocks and bonds and business investments including loss limitations associated with these investments. Part IV is unique among tax textbooks; this section combines related tax issues for compensation, retirement savings, and home ownership.

Part I: Introduction to Taxation
 1. An Introduction to Tax
 2. Tax Compliance, the IRS, and Tax Authorities
 3. Tax Planning Strategies and Related Limitations

Part II: Basic Individual Taxation
 4. Individual Income Tax Overview
 5. Gross Income and Exclusions
 6. Individual Deductions
 7. Individual Income Tax Computation and Tax Credits

Part III: Business- and Investment-Related Transactions
 8. Business Income, Deductions, and Accounting Methods
 9. Property Acquisition and Cost Recovery
10. Property Dispositions
11. Investments

Part IV: Specialized Topics
12. Compensation
13. Retirement Savings and Deferred Compensation
14. Tax Consequences of Home Ownership

McGraw-Hill's Taxation of Business Entities begins with the process for determining gross income and deductions for businesses, and the tax consequences associated with purchasing assets and property dispositions (sales, trades, or other dispositions). Part II provides a comprehensive overview of entities, and the formation, reorganization, and liquidation of corporations. Unique to this series is a complete chapter on accounting for income taxes, which provides a primer on the basics of calculating the income tax provision. Included in the narrative is a discussion of temporary and permanent differences and their impact on a company's book "effective tax rate." Part III provides a detailed discussion of partnerships and S corporations. The last part of the book covers state and local taxation, multinational taxation, and transfer taxes and wealth planning.

Part I: Business- and Investment-Related Transactions
 1. Business Income, Deductions, and Accounting Methods
 2. Property Acquisition and Cost Recovery
 3. Property Dispositions

Part II: Entity Overview and Taxation of C Corporations
 4. Entities Overview
 5. Corporate Operations
 6. Accounting for Income Taxes
 7. Corporate Taxation: Nonliquidating Distributions
 8. Corporate Formation, Reorganization, and Liquidation

Part III: Taxation of Flow-Through Entities
 9. Forming and Operating Partnerships
10. Dispositions of Partnership Interests and Partnership
    Distributions
11. S Corporations

Part IV: Multijurisdictional Taxation and Transfer Taxes
12. State and Local Taxes
13. The U.S. Taxation of Multinational Transactions
14. Transfer Taxes and Wealth Planning

...Four Course Approaches

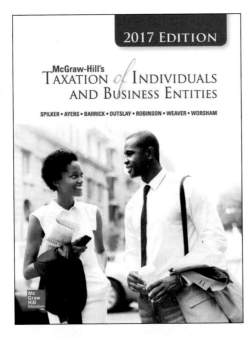

McGraw-Hill's Taxation of Individuals and Business Entities covers all chapters included in the two split volumes in one convenient volume.
See Table of Contents.

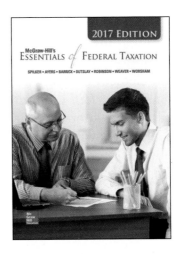

McGraw-Hill's Essentials of Federal Taxation is designed for a one-semester course, covering the basics of taxation of individuals and business entities. To facilitate a one-semester course, *McGraw-Hill's Essentials of Federal Taxation* folds the key topics from the investments, compensation, retirement savings, and home ownership chapters in *Taxation of Individuals* into three individual taxation chapters that discuss gross income and exclusions, for AGI deductions, and from AGI deductions, respectively. The essentials volume also includes a two-chapter C corporation sequence that uses a life-cycle approach covering corporate formations and then corporate operations in the first chapter and nonliquidating and liquidating corporate distributions in the second chapter. This volume is perfect for those teaching a one-semester course and for those who struggle to get through the 25-chapter comprehensive volume.

SUPPLEMENTS FOR INSTRUCTORS

Assurance of Learning Ready

Many educational institutions today are focused on the notion of *assurance of learning*, an important element of many accreditation standards. *McGraw-Hill's Taxation* is designed specifically to support your assurance of learning initiatives with a simple, yet powerful, solution.

Each chapter in the book begins with a list of numbered learning objectives, which appear throughout the chapter as well as in the end-of-chapter assignments. Every test bank question for *McGraw-Hill's Taxation* maps to a specific chapter learning objective in the textbook. Each test bank question also identifies topic area, level of difficulty, Bloom's Taxonomy level, and AICPA and AACSB skill area. You can use our test bank software, *EZ Test Online*, or Connect to easily search for learning objectives that directly relate to the learning objectives for your course. You can then use the reporting features of *EZ Test* to aggregate student results in similar fashion, making the collection and presentation of Assurance of Learning data simple and easy.

AACSB Statement

McGraw-Hill Education is a proud corporate member of AACSB International. Understanding the importance and value of AACSB accreditation, *McGraw-Hill's Taxation* recognizes the curricula guidelines detailed in the AACSB standards for business accreditation by connecting selected questions in the text and the test bank to the general knowledge and skill guidelines in the revised AACSB standards.

The statements contained in *McGraw-Hill's Taxation* are provided only as a guide for the users of this textbook. The AACSB leaves content coverage and assessment within the purview of individual schools, the mission of the school, and the faculty. While *McGraw-Hill's Taxation* and the teaching package make no claim of any specific AACSB qualification or evaluation, we have, within the text and test bank, labeled selected questions according to the eight general knowledge and skill areas.

McGraw-Hill Education's Connect

connect Connect offers a number of powerful tools and features to make managing your classroom easier. Connect with *McGraw-Hill's Taxation* offers enhanced features and technology to help both you and your students make the most of your time inside and outside the classroom.

EZ Test Online

This test bank in Word™ format contains multiple-choice questions, essay questions, and short problems. Each test item is coded for level of difficulty, learning objective, AACSB and AICPA skill area, and Bloom's Taxonomy level.

McGraw-Hill's EZ Test Online is a flexible and easy-to-use electronic testing program that allows instructors to create tests from book-specific items. EZ Test Online accommodates a wide range of question types and allows instructors to add their own questions. Multiple versions of the test can be created and any test can be exported for use with course management systems such as BlackBoard/WebCT. EZ Test Online gives instructors a place to easily administer exams and quizzes online. The program is available for Windows and Macintosh environments.

A HEARTFELT THANKS TO THE MANY COLLEAGUES WHO SHAPED THIS BOOK

The version of the book you are reading would not be the same book without the valuable suggestions, keen insights, and constructive criticisms of the list of reviewers below. Each professor listed here contributed in substantive ways to the organization of chapters, coverage of topics, and the use of pedagogy. We are grateful to them for taking the time to read chapters or attend reviewer conferences, focus groups, and symposia in support of the development for the book:

Previous Edition Reviewers
Kevin Baugess, *ICDC College*
Christopher Becker, *Coastal Carolina University*
Jeanne Bedell, *Keiser University*
Lisa Blum, *University of Louisville*
Cathalene Bowler, *University of Northern Iowa*
Suzon Bridges, *Houston Community College*
Terry Crain, *University of Oklahoma Norman*
Brad Cripe, *Northern Illinois University*
Richard Cummings, *University of Wisconsin-Whitewater*
John Dorocak, *California State University San Berdinado*
Amy Dunbar, *University of Connecticut Storrs*
Lisa Ekmekjian, *William Paterson University*
Ann Esarco, *Columbia College Columbia*
Robert Gary, *University of New Mexico*
Greg Geisler, *University of Missouri St. Louis*
Earl Godfrey, *Gardner Webb University*
Thomas Godwin, *Purdue University*
Brian Greenstein, *University of Delaware*
Marcye Hampton, *University of Central Florida*
Melanie Hicks, *Liberty University*
Mary Ann Hofmann, *Appalachian State University*
Bambi Hora, *University of Central Oklahoma*
Athena Jones, *University of Maryland University College*
Susan Jurney, *University of Arkansas Fayetteville*
Sandra Kemper, *Regis University*
Jack Lachman, *Brooklyn College*
Stacie Laplante, *University of Wisconsin Madison*
Stephanie Lewis, *Ohio State University Columbus*
Troy Lewis, *Brigham Young University*

Teresa Lightner, *University of North Texas*
Robert Lin, *California State University East Bay*
Kate Mantzke, *Northern Illinois University*
Robert Martin, *Kennesaw State University*
Anthony Masino, *East Tennessee State University*
Lisa McKinney, *University of Alabama at Birmingham*
Allison McLeod, *University of North Texas*
Janet Meade, *University of Houston*
Frank Messina, *University of Alabama at Birmingham*
Michelle Moshier, *University at Albany*
Leslie Mostow, *University of Maryland, College Park*
James Motter, *IUPUI Indianapolis*
Jackie Myers, *Sinclair Community College*
Jeff Paterson, *Florida State University*
James Pierson, *Franklin University*
Anthony Pochesci, *Rutgers University*
Joshua Racca, *University of Alabama*
Lucia Smeal, *Georgia State University*
Pamela Smith, *University of Texas at San Antonio*
Jason Stanfield, *Ball State University*
James Stekelberg, *University of Arizona*
Terrie Stolte, *Columbus State Community College*
Erin Towery, *The University of Georgia*
Luke Watson, *University of Florida*
Sarah Webber, *University of Dayton*
Marvin Williams, *University of Houston—Downtown*
Chris Woehrle, *American College*
Massood Yahya-Zadeh, *George Mason University*
James Yang, *Montclair State University*
Scott Yetmar, *Cleveland State University*
Mingjun Zhou, *DePaul University*

Acknowledgments

We would like to thank the many talented people who made valuable contributions to the creation of this eighth edition. William A. Padley of Madison Area Technical College, Deanna Sharpe of the University of Missouri—Columbia, and Troy Lewis of Brigham Young University checked the page proofs, test bank, and solutions manual for accuracy; we greatly appreciate the hours they spent checking tax forms and double-checking our calculations throughout the book. Special thanks to Troy Lewis of Brigham Young University for his sharp eye and valuable feedback throughout the revision process. Sarah Wood from Agate Publishing for managing the supplement process. William A. Padley of Madison Area Technical College, Deanna Sharpe of the University of Missouri, Vivian Paige of Old Dominion University, and Teressa Farough greatly contributed to the accuracy of McGraw-Hill's *Connect* for the 2017 edition.

We also appreciate the expert attention given to this project by the staff at McGraw-Hill Education, especially Tim Vertovec, Managing Director; Kathleen Klehr, Senior Brand Manager; Danielle Andries, Product Developer; Lori Koetters, Brian Nacik, and Jill Eccher, Content Project Managers; Matthew Diamond, Designer; and Sue Culbertson, Senior Buyer.

Changes in *Taxation of Individuals and Business Entities,* 2017 Edition

For the 2017 edition of McGraw Hill's *Taxation of Individuals and Business Entities,* many changes were made in response to feedback from reviewers and focus group participants:

- All **tax forms** have been **updated for the latest available tax form as of January 2016.** In addition, **chapter content** throughout the text has been **updated to reflect tax law changes through January 2016.**

Other notable changes in the 2017 edition include:

Chapter 2

- Updated for 2016 inflation adjustments and legislative changes.
- Updated discussion of tax return due dates.

Chapter 3

- Updated tax rates for 2016.
- Updated Exhibit 3-3 for new tax rates.
- Added new Taxes in the Real World.
- Added new Ethics box.

Chapter 4

- Updated personal exemption amounts for 2016.
- Updated standard deduction amounts for 2016.
- Updated tax rates for 2016.
- Moved rates from back cover of text to new appendix near end of the book.
- Updated tax forms from 2014 to 2015 forms.
- Revised the discussion relating to character of income.
- Revised the opening paragraph in the Personal and Dependency Exemptions section.
- Updated the taxes in the real world on "Tax status for same-sex married couples" to reflect recent developments in the area.

Chapter 5

- Updated for legislative changes.
- Updated for 2016 inflation adjustments.
- Updated for new tax forms.

Chapter 6

- Updated for legislative changes.
- Updated for 2016 inflation adjustments.
- Updated for new tax forms.

Chapter 7

- Updated tax rates for 2016.
- Updated tax forms from 2014 to 2015.

- Revised and streamlined the discussion of capital gains netting process.
- Revised the step-by-step capital gains netting process.
- Revised capital gains examples.
- Clarified Example 7-14 on investment interest expense.

Chapter 8

- Updated for legislative changes.
- Updated for 2016 inflation adjustments.
- Revised Kiddie Tax discussion.
- Updated for new tax forms.

Chapter 9

- Added new standard business mileage.
- Updated for new tax forms.

Chapter 10

- Updated tax rates for 2016.
- Updated tax forms from 2014 to 2015.
- Added new discussion for repair regulations.
- Added example on repair regulations.
- Added new end-of-chapter problems for repair regulations.

Chapter 11

- Updated tax rates for 2016.
- Updated tax forms from 2014 to 2015.
- Added discussion about holding period for dual basis rules.
- Added discussion about holding period for related party losses.
- Updated end-of-chapter problems.

Chapter 13

- Updated inflation adjusted limits for defined benefit plans, defined contribution plans, and individually managed plans.
- Added new taxes in the real world about Jeb Bush's defined benefit plan.
- Updated AGI phase-out thresholds for deductible contributions to traditional IRAs and contributions to Roth IRAs.

- Clarified the tax consequences of nonqualified distributions from Roth type retirement accounts.
- Clarified how the earned income limit applies to nondeductible contributions to IRAs.
- Clarified the contribution limits for Individual 401(k) retirement plans.
- Added a problem comparing the tax consequences of potential early distributions from traditional 401(k) and a Roth 401(k) retirement accounts.
- Updated Saver's credit information.

Chapter 14

- Updated URL in footnote 4.
- Added mortgage insurance deduction to Exhibit 14-1.
- Added new taxes in the real world called "Double take on home-related interest deductions."
- Removed taxes in the real world called "Extreme tax savings strategy" that dealt with how contestants on "Extreme makeover: Home Edition" treated their benefit for tax purposes.
- Updated Example 14-15 dealing with the IRS method vs. Tax court method of allocating rent expense to reflect leap year in 2016.
- Updated tax forms from 2014 forms to 2015 forms.
- Updated settlement statement in Appendix A.

Chapter 15

- Added a footnote highlighting the idea that unincorporated entities taxed as partnerships have more favorable ownership requirements and more favor-

able tax treatment on nonliquidating and liquidating distributions of noncash property than C or S corporations.
- Edited a footnote to point out that when a shareholder receives interest from a loan to the corporation, the interest income is investment income that could be subject to the 3.8% Net Investment Income Tax.
- Edited footnote to point out that shareholders who hold stock until death may avoid while shareholders may escape the shareholder level of the double tax. However, these shareholders may pay estate tax on the value of the stock held at death.
- Added a row to the entity comparison chart in Exhibit 15-3 that compares across entities the tax consequences of nonliquidating distributions of noncash property.

Chapter 18

- Added new Taxes in the Real World.

Chapter 19

Revised and clarified explanations of merger forms.

Chapter 22

- Updated chapter for tax law changes.
- Updated for new tax forms.

Chapter 25

- Revised explanation and computations based on updated exemption equivalent (unified credit).
- Updated tax forms.

As We Go to Press

The 2017 Edition is current through March 4, 2016. You can visit the *Connect Library* for updates that occur after this date.

Table of Contents

8 Individual Income Tax Computation and Tax Credits

9 Business Income, Deductions, and Accounting Methods

12 Compensation

13 Retirement Savings and Deferred Compensation

McGraw-Hill's

Taxation of Individuals and Business Entities

chapter

1 An Introduction to Tax

Learning Objectives

Upon completing this chapter, you should be able to:

LO 1-1 Demonstrate how taxes influence basic business, investment, personal, and political decisions.

LO 1-2 Discuss what constitutes a tax and the general objectives of taxes.

LO 1-3 Describe the different tax rate structures and calculate a tax.

LO 1-4 Identify the various federal, state, and local taxes.

LO 1-5 Apply appropriate criteria to evaluate alternate tax systems.

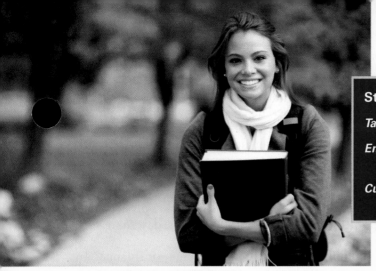
© Andrew Rich/Getty Images

Storyline Summary

Taxpayers:	Margaret
Employment status:	Margaret is a full-time student at the University of Georgia.
Current situation:	She is beginning her first tax class.

Margaret is a junior beginning her first tax course. She is excited about her career prospects as an accounting major but hasn't had much exposure to taxes. On her way to campus she runs into an old friend, Eddy, who is going to Washington, D.C., to protest recent proposed changes to the U.S. tax system. Eddy is convinced the IRS is evil and that the current tax system is blatantly unfair and corrupt. He advocates a simpler, fairer way of taxation. Margaret is intrigued by Eddy's passion but questions whether he has a complete understanding of the U.S. tax system. She decides to withhold all judgments about it (or about pursuing a career in taxation) until the end of her tax course. ∎

LO 1-1 WHO CARES ABOUT TAXES AND WHY?

A clear understanding of the role of taxes in everyday decisions will help you make an informed decision about the value of studying taxation or pursuing a career in taxation. One view of taxation is that it represents an inconvenience every April 15th (the annual due date for filing federal individual tax returns without extensions). However, the role of taxation is much more pervasive than this view suggests. Your study of this subject will provide you a unique opportunity to develop an informed opinion about taxation. As a business student, you can overcome the mystery that encompasses popular impressions of the tax system and perhaps, one day, share your expertise with friends or clients.

What are some common decisions you face that taxes may influence? In this course, we alert you to situations in which you can increase your return on investments by up to one-third! Even the best lessons in finance courses can't approach the increase in risk-adjusted return that smart tax planning provides. Would you like to own your home someday? Tax deductions for home mortgage interest and real estate taxes can reduce the after-tax costs of owning a home relative to renting. Thus, when you face the decision to buy or rent, you can make an informed choice if you understand the relative tax advantages of home ownership. Would you like to retire someday? Understanding the tax-advantaged methods of saving for retirement can increase the after-tax value of your retirement nest egg—and thus increase the likelihood that you can afford to retire, and do so in style. Other common personal financial decisions that taxes influence include: choosing investments, evaluating alternative job offers, saving for education expenses, and doing gift or estate planning. Indeed, taxes are a part of everyday life and have a significant effect on many of the personal financial decisions all of us face.

The role of taxes is not limited to personal finance. Taxes play an equally important role in fundamental business decisions such as the following:

- What organizational form should a business use?
- Where should the business locate?
- How should business acquisitions be structured?
- How should the business compensate employees?
- What is the appropriate mix of debt and equity for the business?
- Should the business rent or own its equipment and property?
- How should the business distribute profits to its owners?

Savvy business decisions require owners and managers to consider all costs and benefits in order to evaluate the merits of a transaction. Although taxes don't necessarily dominate these decisions, they do represent large transaction costs that businesses should factor into the financial decision-making process.

Taxes also play a major part in the political process. U.S. presidential candidates often distinguish themselves from their opponents based upon their tax rhetoric. Indeed, the major political parties generally have very diverse views of the appropriate way to tax the public.[1] Determining who is taxed, what is taxed, and how much is taxed are tough questions with nontrivial answers. Voters must have a basic understanding of taxes to evaluate the merits of alternative tax proposals. Later in this chapter, we'll introduce criteria you can use to evaluate alternative tax proposals.

---

[1]The U.S. Department of the Treasury provides a "history of taxation" on its Web site (www.treasury.gov/resource-center/faqs/Taxes/Pages/historyrooseveltmessage.aspx). You may find it interesting to read this history in light of the various political parties in office at the time.

TAXES IN THE REAL WORLD Republicans vs. Democrats

We often boil down the tax policy of our major political parties into its simplest form: Democrats raise taxes to fund social programs, and Republicans lower taxes to benefit big businesses and the wealthy. Both ideas simplify the policy of each party, yet both ideas are essentially true.

Whether you agree with more government spending or tax breaks for corporations, each party's agenda will affect your taxes.

Political Ideology: Republican

"We believe government should tax only to raise money for its essential functions." The Republicans state their case plainly on the Republican National Convention website. That is, Republicans believe government should spend money only to enforce contracts, maintain basic infrastructure and national security, and protect citizens against criminals.

The literature of the House Republican Conference goes on to illuminate the role of the government and how tax policies affect individuals: "The money the government spends does not belong to the government; it belongs to the taxpayers who earned it. Republicans believe Americans deserve to keep more of their own money to save and invest for the future, and low tax policies help drive a strong and healthy economy."

Tax relief is the Republican route to growing the economy. A Republican government would reduce taxes for businesses to allow businesses to grow and thus hire more employees.

Republicans also seek to limit income taxes for individuals so that people can hold on to more disposable income, which they can then spend, save, or invest.

Political Ideology: Democrat

The tax policy for the Democratic Party calls for raising certain taxes to provide money for government spending, which in turn generates business. The party platform asserts that government spending provides "good jobs and will help the economy today."

Many Democrats are adherents to Keynesian economics, or aggregate demand, which holds that when the government funds programs, those programs pump new money into the economy. Keynesians believe that prices tend to stay relatively stable and therefore any kind of spending, whether by consumers or the government, will grow the economy.

Like the Republicans, Democrats believe the government should subsidize vital services that keep cities, states, and the country running: infrastructure such as road and bridge maintenance and repairs for schools. Democrats also call for tax cuts for the middle class. But who benefits most under each platform? The conventional wisdom is that corporations and the wealthy will benefit more with a Republican tax policy, while small businesses and middle-class households will benefit from a Democratic tax policy.

Source: http://www.investopedia.com/articles/economics/09/us-parties-republican-democrat-taxes.asp

---

> **THE KEY FACTS**
>
> **What Qualifies as a Tax?**
>
> - The general purpose of taxes is to fund government agencies.
> - Unlike fines or penalties, taxes are not meant to punish or prevent illegal behavior; but "*sin taxes*" are meant to discourage some behaviors.
> - The three criteria necessary to be a tax are that the payment is
>   - required
>   - imposed by a government
>   - and not tied directly to the benefit received by the taxpayer.

In summary, taxes affect many aspects of personal, business, and political decisions. Developing a solid understanding of taxation should allow you to make informed decisions in these areas. Thus, Margaret can take comfort that her semester will likely prove useful to her personally. Who knows? Depending on her interest in business, investment, retirement planning, and the like, she may ultimately decide to pursue a career in taxation.

WHAT QUALIFIES AS A TAX? `LO 1-2`

"Taxes are the price we pay for a civilized society."—Oliver Wendell Holmes Jr.

Taxes have been described in many terms: some positive, some negative, some printable, some not. Let's go directly to a formal definition of a tax, which should prove useful in identifying alternative taxes and discussing alternative tax systems.

A **tax** *is a payment required by a government that is unrelated to any specific benefit or service received from the government.* The general purpose of a tax is to fund the operations of the government (to raise revenue). Taxes differ from fines and penalties in that taxes are not intended to punish or prevent illegal behavior. Nonetheless, by allowing deductions from income, our federal tax system does encourage

---

TAXES IN THE REAL WORLD Affordable Care Act

The Affordable Care Act requires individuals to be covered by a health insurance plan or to pay a tax—which is paid on the individual's income tax return. The adult annual dollar amount phased in as follows: $95 in 2014; $325 in 2015; and $695 in 2016. The Congressional Budget Office and the Joint Committee on Taxation jointly estimated that 5.9 million Americans will be subject to the penalty in 2016 and the provision will raise $6.9 billion in revenue in that year.

You may recall that one question the Supreme Court had to rule on was whether this provision was a "penalty" or a "tax." The Supreme Court held that the provision is a tax and answered as follows: "The payment is not so high that there is really no choice but to buy health insurance; the payment is not limited to willful violations, as penalties for unlawful acts often are; and the payment is collected solely by the (Internal Revenue Service) through the normal means of taxation," Chief Justice John Roberts wrote in the decision.

Source: National Federation of Independent Business v. Sebelius, 132 S. Ct. 2566 (2012).

---

certain behaviors like charitable contributions, retirement savings, and research and development. Thus, we can view it as discouraging other legal behavior. For example, **sin taxes** impose relatively high surcharges on alcohol and tobacco products.[2] Another example is the shared-responsibility payment introduced by the Affordable Care Act. This payment was declared to be a "tax" by the Supreme Court. The tax is imposed on those who do not have minimum essential health care coverage.[3]

Key components of the definition of a tax are that

- the payment is required (it is not voluntary),
- the payment is imposed by a government agency (federal, state, or local), and
- the payment is not tied directly to the benefit received by the taxpayer.

This last point is not to say that taxpayers receive no benefits from the taxes they pay. They benefit from national defense, a judicial system, law enforcement, government-sponsored social programs, an interstate highway system, public schools, and many other government-provided programs and services. The distinction is that taxes paid are not *directly* related to any specific benefit received by the taxpayer. For example, the price of admission to Yellowstone National Park is a fee rather than a tax because a specific benefit is received.

Can taxes be assessed for special purposes, such as a 1 percent sales tax for education? Yes. Why is an **earmarked tax,** a tax that *is* assessed for a specific purpose, still considered a tax? Because the payment made by the taxpayer does not directly relate to the specific benefit *received by the taxpayer*.

Example 1-1

Margaret travels to Birmingham, Alabama, where she rents a hotel room and dines at several restaurants. The price she pays for her hotel room and meals includes an additional 2 percent city surcharge to fund roadway construction in Birmingham. Is this a tax?

Answer: Yes. The payment is required by a local government and does not directly relate to a specific benefit that Margaret receives.

---

[2]Sin taxes represent an interesting confluence of incentives. On the one hand, demand for such products as alcohol, tobacco, and gambling is often relatively inelastic because of their addictive quality. Thus, taxing such a product can raise substantial revenues. On the other hand, one of the arguments for sin taxes is frequently the social goal of *reducing* demand for such products.

[3]For details on the computation of the shared responsibility payment see Reg. §1.5000A-4.

Example 1-2

Margaret's parents, Bill and Mercedes, recently built a house and were assessed $1,000 by their county government to connect to the county sewer system. Is this a tax?

Answer: No. The assessment was mandatory and it was paid to a local government. However, the third criterion was not met since the payment directly relates to a specific benefit (sewer service) received by the payees. For the same reason, tolls, parking meter fees, and annual licensing fees are also not considered taxes.

HOW TO CALCULATE A TAX

LO 1-3

In its simplest form, the amount of tax equals the tax base multiplied by the tax rate:

Eq. 1-1   Tax = Tax Base × Tax Rate

The **tax base** defines what is actually taxed and is usually expressed in monetary terms, whereas the **tax rate** determines the level of taxes imposed on the tax base and is usually expressed as a percentage. For example, a sales tax rate of 6 percent on a purchase of $30 yields a tax of $1.80 ($1.80 = $30 × .06).

Federal, state, and local jurisdictions use a large variety of tax bases to collect tax. Some common tax bases (and related taxes) include taxable income (federal and state income taxes), purchases (sales tax), real estate values (real estate tax), and personal property values (personal property tax).

Different portions of a tax base may be taxed at different rates. A single tax applied to an entire base constitutes a **flat tax.** In the case of **graduated taxes,** the base is divided into a series of monetary amounts, or **brackets,** and each successive bracket is taxed at a different (gradually higher or gradually lower) percentage rate.

Calculating some taxes—income taxes for individuals or corporations, for example—can be quite complex. Advocates of flat taxes argue that the process should be simpler. But as we'll see throughout the text, most of the difficulty in calculating a tax rests in determining the tax *base,* not the tax rate. Indeed, there are only three basic tax rate structures (proportional, progressive, and regressive), and each can be mastered without much difficulty.

> **THE KEY FACTS**
>
> **How to Calculate a Tax**
> - Tax = Tax base × Tax rate
> - The tax base defines what is actually taxed and is usually expressed in monetary terms.
> - The tax rate determines the level of taxes imposed on the tax base and is usually expressed as a percentage.
> - Different portions of a tax base may be taxed at different rates.

DIFFERENT WAYS TO MEASURE TAX RATES

Before we discuss the alternative tax rate structures, let's first define three different tax rates that will be useful in contrasting the different tax rate structures: the marginal, average, and effective tax rates.

The **marginal tax rate** is the tax rate that applies to the *next additional increment* of a taxpayer's taxable income (or deductions). Specifically,

Eq. 1-2

$$\text{Marginal Tax Rate} = \frac{\Delta \text{Tax}^*}{\Delta \text{Taxable Income}} = \frac{(\text{New Total Tax} - \text{Old Total Tax})}{(\text{New Taxable Income} - \text{Old Taxable Income})}$$

*Δ means *change in*.

where "old" refers to the current tax and "new" refers to the revised tax after incorporating the additional income (or deductions) in question. In graduated income tax systems, additional income (deductions) can push a taxpayer into a higher (lower) tax bracket, thus changing the marginal tax rate.

Example 1-3

Margaret's parents, Bill and Mercedes, file a joint tax return. They have $160,000 of taxable income this year (after all tax deductions). Assuming the following federal tax rate schedule applies, how much federal income tax will they owe this year?[4]

2016 Federal Married Filing Jointly Tax Rate Schedule

If taxable income is over	But not over	The tax is
$ 0	$ 18,550	10% of taxable income
18,550	75,300	$1,855.00 + 15% of taxable income in excess of $18,550
75,300	151,900	$10,367.50 + 25% of taxable income in excess of $75,300
151,900	231,450	$29,517.50 + 28% of taxable income in excess of $151,900
231,450	413,350	$51,791.50 + 33% of taxable income in excess of $231,450
413,350	466,950	$111,818.50 + 35% of taxable income in excess of $413,350
466,950	no limit	$130,578.50 + 39.6% of taxable income in excess of $466,950

Answer: Bill and Mercedes will owe $31,785.50 computed as follows:

$$\$31,785.50 = \$29,517.50 + 28\% \, (\$160,000 - \$151,900)$$

Note that in this graduated tax rate structure, the first $18,550 of taxable income is taxed at 10 percent, the next $56,750 of taxable income (between $18,550 and $75,300) is taxed at 15 percent, and the next $76,600 of taxable income (between $75,300 and $151,900) is taxed at 25 percent. Bill and Mercedes's last $8,100 of taxable income (between $151,900 and $160,000) is taxed at 28 percent.

Many taxpayers incorrectly believe that all their income is taxed at their marginal rate. This mistake leads people to say, "I don't want to earn any additional money because it will put me in a higher tax bracket." Bill and Mercedes are currently in the 28 percent marginal tax rate bracket, but notice that *not* all their income is taxed at this rate. Their *marginal* tax rate is 28 percent. This means that small increases in income will be taxed at 28 percent, and small increases in tax deductions will generate tax *savings* of 28 percent. If Bill and Mercedes receive a large increase in income (or in deductions) such that they would change tax rate brackets, we cannot identify their marginal tax rate by simply identifying their current tax bracket.

Example 1-4

Bill, a well-known economics professor, signs a publishing contract with an $80,000 royalty advance. Using the rate schedule from Example 1-3, what would Bill and Mercedes's marginal tax rate be on this additional $80,000 of taxable income?

Answer: 28.53 percent, computed as follows:

Description	Amount	Explanation
(1) Taxable income with additional $80,000 of taxable income	$240,000.00	$80,000 plus $160,000 taxable income stated in Example 1-3.
(2) Tax on $240,000 taxable income	$ 54,613.00	Using the rate schedule in Example 1-3, $54,613 = $51,791.50 + 33% × ($240,000 − $231,450).

[4]The tax rate schedules for single, married filing jointly, married filing separately, and head of household are included inside the back cover of the text.

Description	Amount	Explanation
(3) Taxable income before additional $80,000 of taxable income	$160,000.00	Example 1-3.
(4) Tax on $160,000 taxable income	$ 31,785.50	Example 1-3.
Marginal tax rate on additional	28.53%	$\frac{\Delta\text{Tax}}{\Delta\text{Taxable income}} = [(2)-(4)]/[(1)-(3)]$

Note that Bill and Mercedes's marginal tax rate on the $80,000 increase in taxable income rests *between* the 28 percent and 33 percent bracket rates because a portion of the additional income ($231,450 − $160,000 = $71,450) is taxed at 28 percent with the remaining income ($240,000 − $231,450 = $8,550) taxed at 33 percent.

Example 1-5

Assume now that, instead of receiving a book advance, Bill and Mercedes start a new business that *loses* $60,000 this year (it results in $60,000 of additional tax deductions). What would be their marginal tax rate for these deductions?

Answer: 25.41 percent, computed as follows:

Description	Amount	Explanation
(1) Taxable income with additional $60,000 of tax deductions	$100,000.00	$160,000 taxable income stated in Example 1-3 less $60,000.
(2) Tax on $100,000 taxable income	$ 16,542.50	Using the rate schedule in Example 1-3, $16,542.50 = $10,367.50 + 25% × ($100,000 − $75,300).
(3) Taxable income before additional $60,000 of tax deductions	$160,000.00	Example 1-3.
(4) Tax on $160,000 taxable income	$ 31,785.50	Example 1-3.
Marginal tax rate on additional $60,000 of tax deductions	25.41%	$\frac{\Delta\text{Tax}}{\Delta\text{Taxable income}} = [(2)-(4)]/[(1)-(3)]$

Bill and Mercedes's marginal tax rate on $60,000 of additional deductions (25.41 percent) differs from their marginal tax rate on $80,000 of additional taxable income (28.53 percent) in these scenarios because the relatively large increase in deductions causes some of their income to be taxed in a lower tax rate bracket and the relatively large increase in income caused some of their income to be taxed in a higher tax rate bracket. Taxpayers often will face the same marginal tax rates for small changes in income and deductions.

The marginal tax rate is particularly useful in tax planning because it represents the rate of taxation or savings that would apply to additional taxable income (or tax deductions). In Chapter 3, we discuss basic tax planning strategies that use the marginal tax rate.

The **average tax rate** represents a taxpayer's average level of taxation on each dollar of taxable income. Specifically,

Eq. 1-3

$$\text{Average Tax Rate} = \frac{\text{Total Tax}}{\text{Taxable Income}}$$

The average tax rate is often used in budgeting tax expense as a portion of income (what percent of taxable income earned is paid in tax).

THE KEY FACTS

Different Ways to Measure Tax Rates

- Marginal tax rate
  - The tax that applies to next increment of income or deduction.
  - $= \dfrac{\Delta\text{Tax}}{\Delta\text{Taxable income}}$
  - Useful in tax planning.
- Average tax rate
  - A taxpayer's average level of taxation on each dollar of *taxable* income.
  - $= \dfrac{\text{Total tax}}{\text{Total income}}$
  - Useful in budgeting tax expense.
- Effective tax rate
  - A taxpayer's average rate of taxation on each dollar of *total* income (taxable *and* nontaxable income).
  - $= \dfrac{\text{Total tax}}{\text{Total income}}$
  - Useful in comparing the relative tax burdens of taxpayers.

The **effective tax rate** represents the taxpayer's average rate of taxation on each dollar of total income (sometimes referred to as economic income), including taxable *and* nontaxable income. Specifically,

Eq. 1-4
$$\text{Effective Tax Rate} = \frac{\text{Total Tax}}{\text{Total Income}}$$

Relative to the average tax rate, the effective tax rate provides a better depiction of a taxpayer's tax burden because it depicts the taxpayer's total tax paid as a ratio of the sum of both taxable and nontaxable income earned.

Example 1-6

Assuming Bill and Mercedes have $160,000 of taxable income and $10,000 of nontaxable income, what is their average tax rate?

Answer: 19.87 percent, computed as follows:

Description	Amount	Explanation
(1) Taxable income	$160,000.00	
(2) Tax on $160,000 taxable income	$ 31,785.50	Example 1-3.
Average tax rate	19.87%	$\dfrac{\text{Total tax}}{\text{Taxable income}} = (2)/(1)$

We should not be surprised that Bill and Mercedes's average tax rate is lower than their marginal tax rate because, although they are currently in the 28 percent tax rate bracket, not all of their taxable income is subject to tax at 28 percent. The first $18,550 of their taxable income is taxed at 10 percent, their next $56,750 is taxed at 15 percent, their next $76,600 is taxed at 25 percent, and only their last $8,100 of taxable income is taxed at 28 percent. Thus, their average tax rate is considerably lower than their marginal tax rate.

Example 1-7

Again, given the same income figures as in Example 1-6 ($160,000 of taxable income and $10,000 of nontaxable income), what is Bill and Mercedes's effective tax rate?

Answer: 18.70 percent, computed as follows:

Description	Amount	Explanation
(1) Total income	$170,000.00	$160,000 taxable income plus $10,000 in nontaxable income (Example 1-6).
(2) Tax on $160,000 taxable income	$ 31,785.50	Example 1-3.
Effective tax rate	18.70%	$\dfrac{\text{Total tax}}{\text{Total income}} = (2)/(1)$

Should we be surprised that the effective tax rate is lower than the *average* tax rate? No, because except when the taxpayer has more nondeductible expenses (such as fines or penalties) than nontaxable income (such as tax-exempt interest), the effective tax rate will be equal to or less than the average tax rate.

TAX RATE STRUCTURES

There are three basic tax rate structures used to determine a tax: proportional, progressive, and regressive.

Proportional Tax Rate Structure

A **proportional tax rate structure,** also known as a flat tax, imposes a constant tax rate throughout the tax base. As the tax base increases, the taxes paid increase proportionally. Because this rate stays the same throughout all levels of the tax base, the marginal tax rate remains constant and, in fact, equals the average tax rate (see Exhibit 1-1). The most common example of a proportional tax is a sales tax, although Steve Forbes proposed a flat income tax as part of his 1996 and 2000 presidential campaigns.

To calculate the tax owed for a proportional tax, simply use Equation 1-1 to multiply the tax base by the tax rate.

$$\text{Proportional tax} = \text{Tax base} \times \text{Tax rate}$$

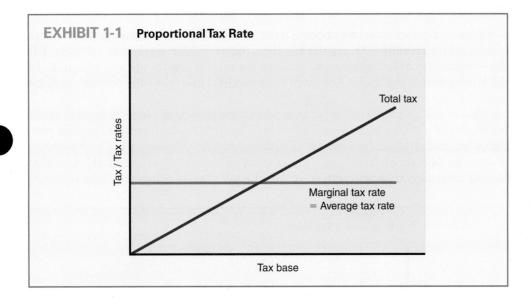

EXHIBIT 1-1   Proportional Tax Rate

> **Example 1-8**

Knowing her dad is a serious Bulldog fan, Margaret buys a $100 sweatshirt in downtown Athens. The city of Athens imposes a sales tax rate of 7 percent. How much tax does Margaret pay on the purchase?

Answer: $100 purchase (tax base) × 7% (tax rate) = $7

Progressive Tax Rate Structure

A **progressive tax rate structure** imposes an increasing marginal tax rate as the tax base increases. Thus as the tax base increases, both the marginal tax rate and the taxes paid increase. Common examples of progressive tax rate structures include federal and most state income taxes. The tax rate schedule in Example 1-3 is a progressive tax rate structure. As illustrated in Exhibit 1-2, the average tax rate in a progressive tax rate structure will always be less than or equal to the marginal tax rate.

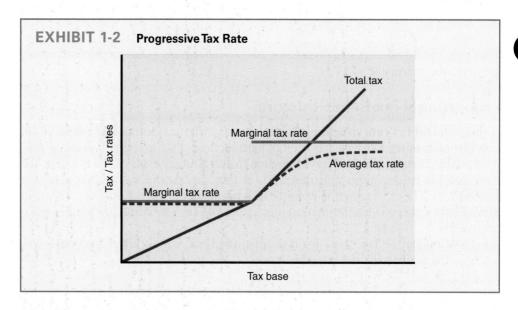

EXHIBIT 1-2   **Progressive Tax Rate**

Regressive Tax Rate Structure

A **regressive tax rate structure** imposes a decreasing marginal tax rate as the tax base increases (see Exhibit 1-3). As the tax base increases, the taxes paid increase, but the marginal tax rate decreases. Regressive tax rate structures are not common. In the United States, the Social Security tax and federal and state unemployment taxes employ a regressive tax rate structure.[5]

However, some taxes are regressive when viewed in terms of effective tax rates. For example, a sales tax is a proportional tax by definition, because as taxable purchases increase, the sales tax rate remains constant.[6] Nonetheless, when you consider that the proportion of your total income spent on taxable purchases likely decreases as your total income increases, you can see the sales tax as a regressive tax.

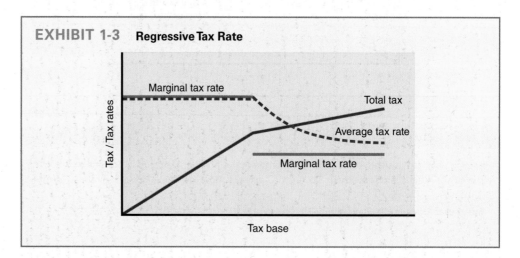

EXHIBIT 1-3   **Regressive Tax Rate**

[5]Wages subject to the Social Security tax (6.2 percent in 2016) are capped each year ($118,500 in 2016). Wages in excess of the cap are not subject to the tax. As might be expected, the maximum Social Security retirement benefit is capped as a function of the maximum wage base. Likewise, the federal and state unemployment tax bases and related unemployment benefits are capped.

[6]For example, a destitute taxpayer likely spends all he makes on food and other items subject to the sales tax; thus, all of his income is subject to a sales tax. In contrast, a wealthy taxpayer likely spends only a small fraction of his income on items subject to sales tax (while saving the rest). Thus, less of wealthy taxpayers' total income is subject to the sales tax, which ultimately results in a lower effective tax rate.

Example 1-9

Bill and Mercedes have two single friends, Elizabeth and Marc, over for dinner. Elizabeth earns $300,000 as CFO of a company and spends $70,000 for purchases subject to the 7 percent sales tax. Marc, who earns $75,000 as a real estate agent, spends $30,000 of his income for taxable purchases. Let's compare their marginal, average, and effective tax rates for the sales tax with Bill and Mercedes, who spend $50,000 of their income for taxable purchases:

	Elizabeth	Bill and Mercedes	Marc
Total income (1)	$300,000	$170,000	$75,000
Total purchases subject to 7% sales tax (2)	$ 70,000	$ 50,000	$30,000
Sales tax paid (3)	$ 4,900	$ 3,500	$ 2,100
Marginal tax rate	7%	7%	7%
Average tax rate (3)/(2)	7%	7%	7%
Effective tax rate (3)/(1)	1.6%	2.1%	2.8%

Is the sales tax regressive?

Answer: Yes. In terms of *effective* tax rates.

When we consider the marginal and average tax rates in Example 1-9, the sales tax has a proportional tax rate structure. But when we look at the *effective* tax rates, the sales tax is a regressive tax. Indeed, Marc, who has the smallest total income, bears the highest effective tax rate, despite all three taxpayers being subject to the same marginal and average tax rates. Why do we see such a different picture when considering the effective tax rate? Because unlike the marginal and average tax rates, the effective tax rate captures the *incidence* of taxation, which relates to the ultimate economic burden of a tax. Thus, a comparison of effective tax rates is more informative about taxpayers' relative tax burdens.

TYPES OF TAXES

LO 1-4

"You can't live with 'em. You can't live without 'em." This statement has often been used in reference to bosses, parents, spouses, and significant others. To some degree, it applies equally as well to taxes. Although we all benefit in multiple ways from tax revenues, and all civilized nations impose them, it would be hard to find someone who *enjoys* paying them. Most people don't object to the idea of paying taxes. Instead, it's the way taxes are levied that many people, like Margaret's friend Eddy, dislike. Hence, the search for the "perfect" tax can be elusive. The following paragraphs describe the major types of taxes currently used by federal, state, and local governments. After this discussion, we describe the criteria for evaluating alternative tax systems.

Federal Taxes

The federal government imposes a variety of taxes to fund federal programs such as national defense, Social Security, an interstate highway system, educational programs, and Medicare. Major federal taxes include the individual and corporate income taxes, employment taxes, estate and gift taxes, and excise taxes (each discussed in detail in the following paragraphs). Noticeably absent from this list are a sales tax (a common tax for most state and local governments) and a **value-added tax** (a type of sales tax also commonly referred to as a VAT). Value-added taxes are imposed on

THE KEY FACTS

Tax Rate Structures

- Proportional tax rate structure
  - Imposes a constant tax rate throughout the tax base.
  - As a taxpayer's tax base increases, the taxpayer's taxes increase proportionally.
  - The marginal tax rate remains constant and always equals the average tax rate.
- Progressive tax rate structure
  - Imposes an increasing marginal tax rate as the tax base increases.
  - As a taxpayer's tax base increases, both the marginal tax rate and the taxes paid increase.
- Regressive tax rate structure
  - Imposes a decreasing marginal tax rate as the tax base increases.
  - As a taxpayer's tax base increases, the marginal tax rate decreases while the total taxes paid increases.

THE KEY FACTS

Federal Taxes

- Income taxes
  - The most significant tax assessed by the U.S. government is the income tax, representing approximately 60 percent of all tax revenues collected in the United States.
  - Levied on individuals, corporations, estates, and trusts.
- Employment and unemployment taxes
  - Second largest group of taxes imposed by the U.S. government.

(continued)

- Employment taxes consist of the Old Age, Survivors, and Disability Insurance (OASDI) tax, commonly called the Social Security tax, and the Medical Health Insurance (MHI) tax known as the Medicare tax.
- Unemployment taxes fund temporary unemployment benefits for individuals terminated from their jobs without cause.
- Excise taxes
  - Third largest group of taxes imposed by the U.S. government.
  - Levied on the *quantity* of products sold.
- Transfer taxes
  - Levied on the fair market values of wealth transfers upon death or by gift.

the producers of goods and services based on the value added to the goods and services at each stage of production. They are quite common in Europe.

Income Tax   The most significant tax assessed by the U.S. government is the individual **income tax,** representing approximately 46.2 percent of all tax revenues collected in the United States in 2014. Despite the magnitude and importance of the federal income tax, its history is relatively short. Congress enacted the first U.S. personal income tax in 1861 to help fund the Civil War. This relatively minor tax (maximum tax rate of 5 percent) was allowed to expire in 1872. In 1892, Congress resurrected the income tax, but not without dissension among the states. In 1895, the income tax was challenged in *Pollock v. Farmers' Loan and Trust Company,* 157 U.S. 429 (1895). The U.S. Supreme Court ruled that the income tax was unconstitutional because direct taxes were prohibited by the Constitution unless the taxes were apportioned across states based upon their populations. This ruling, however, did not deter Congress. In July 1909, Congress sent a proposed constitutional amendment to the states to remove any doubt as to whether income taxes were allowed by the Constitution—and in February 1913, the 16th Amendment was ratified.

Congress then enacted the Revenue Act of 1913, which included a graduated income tax structure with a maximum rate of 6 percent. The income tax has been an important source of tax revenues for the U.S. government ever since. Today, income taxes are levied on individuals (maximum rate of 39.6 percent), corporations (maximum rate of 35 percent), estates (maximum rate of 39.6 percent), and trusts (maximum rate of 39.6 percent). Higher income taxpayers must also pay a 3.8% tax on their net investment income. As Exhibit 1-4 illustrates, the individual income tax and employment taxes represent the largest sources of federal tax revenues. We discuss each of these taxes in greater detail later in the text.

Employment and Unemployment Taxes   Employment and unemployment taxes are the second largest group of taxes imposed by the U.S. government. **Employment taxes** consist of the Old Age, Survivors, and Disability Insurance (OASDI) tax, commonly called the Social Security tax, and the Medical Health Insurance (MHI) tax known as the Medicare tax. The **Social Security tax** pays the monthly retirement, survivor, and disability benefits for qualifying individuals, whereas the **Medicare tax** pays for medical insurance for individuals who are elderly

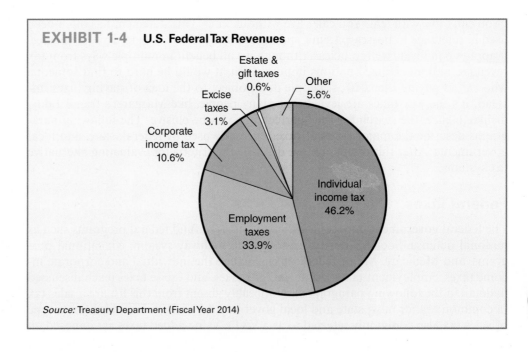

EXHIBIT 1-4   U.S. Federal Tax Revenues

Source: Treasury Department (Fiscal Year 2014)

or disabled. The tax base for the Social Security and Medicare taxes is wages or salary, and the rates are 12.4 percent and 2.9 percent, respectively, in 2016. In 2016, the tax base for the Social Security tax is capped at $118,500. The tax base for the Medicare tax is not capped. Employers and employees split these taxes equally. Self-employed individuals, however, must pay these taxes in their entirety. In this case, the tax is often referred to as the **self-employment tax.** We discuss these taxes in more depth later in the text. There is a 0.9 percent Additional Medicare Tax levied on income earned income by employees (employers are exempt) and self-employed taxpayers on income exceeding a threshold amount (see Chapter 8 for details).

In addition to the Social Security and Medicare taxes, employers are also required to pay federal and state **unemployment taxes,** which fund temporary unemployment benefits for individuals terminated from their jobs without cause. As you might expect, the tax base for the unemployment taxes is also wages or salary. Currently, the Federal Unemployment Tax rate is 6.0 percent. The wage base is the first $7,000 of wages received during the year. The U.S. government allows a credit for state unemployment taxes paid up to 5.4 percent. Thus, the effective Federal Unemployment Tax rate may be as low as 0.6 percent (6.0% − 5.4% = 0.6%).[7]

Excise Taxes **Excise taxes** are taxes levied on the retail sale of particular products. They differ from other taxes in that the tax base for an excise tax typically depends on the *quantity* purchased, rather than a monetary amount. The federal government imposes a number of excise taxes on goods such as alcohol, diesel fuel, gasoline, and tobacco products and on services such as telephone use, air transportation, and tanning beds. In addition, states often impose excise taxes on these same items.

On the drive home from Athens, Georgia, Margaret stops at Gasup-n-Go. On each gallon of gasoline she buys, Margaret pays 18.4 cents of federal excise tax and 7.5 cents of state excise tax (plus 4 percent sales tax). Could Margaret have avoided paying excise tax had she stopped in Florida instead?

Answer: No. Had she stopped in Florida instead, Margaret would have paid the same federal excise tax. Additionally, Florida imposes higher state taxes on gas.

Because the producer of the product pays the government the excise tax, many consumers are not even aware that businesses build these taxes into the prices consumers pay. Nonetheless, consumers bear the incidence of the taxes because of the higher price.

Transfer Taxes Although they are a relatively minor tax compared to the income tax in terms of revenues collected, federal **transfer taxes**—estate and gift taxes—can be substantial for certain individual taxpayers and have been the subject of much debate in recent years. The **estate tax** (labeled the "death tax" by its opponents) and **gift taxes** are based on the fair market values of wealth transfers upon death or by gift, respectively. The estate and gift tax rates have traditionally been high (maximum tax rate through 2009 was 45 percent) compared to income tax rates and can be burdensome without proper planning. In 2016, the maximum rate imposed on gifts is 40 percent. Most taxpayers, however, are not subject to estate and gift taxation because of the annual gift exclusion and gift and estate unified tax credits. The annual gift exclusion allows a taxpayer to transfer $14,000 of gifts per donee (gift recipient) each year without gift taxation. In 2016, the unified tax credit exempts from taxation

THE KEY FACTS

State and Local Taxes

- Sales and use taxes
  - The tax base for a sales tax is the retail sales of goods and some services.
  - The tax base for the use tax is the retail price of goods owned, possessed, or consumed within a state that were *not* purchased within the state.
- Property taxes
  - Property taxes are ad valorem taxes, meaning that the tax base for each is the fair market value of the property.

(continued)

[7]Although employers pay both federal and state unemployment taxes, all unemployment benefits actually are administered and paid by state governments.

- Real property taxes consist of taxes on land, structures, and improvements permanently attached to land.
- Personal property taxes include taxes on all other types of property, both tangible and intangible.
- Income taxes
  - Most state taxable income calculations largely conform to the federal taxable income calculations, with a limited number of modifications.
- Excise taxes
  - States typically impose excise taxes on items subject to federal excise tax.

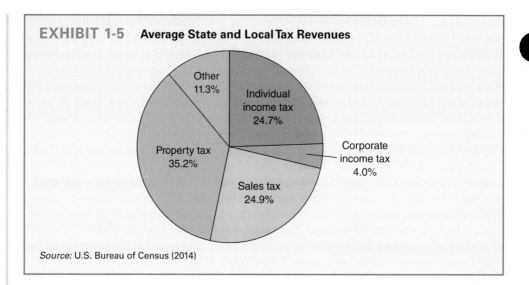

EXHIBIT 1-5   Average State and Local Tax Revenues

- Other 11.3%
- Individual income tax 24.7%
- Corporate income tax 4.0%
- Sales tax 24.9%
- Property tax 35.2%

Source: U.S. Bureau of Census (2014)

$5,450,000 in bequests (transfers upon death) and gifts. Thus, only large transfers are subject to the gift and estate taxes.

State and Local Taxes

Like the federal government, state and local governments (such as counties, cities, and school districts) use a variety of taxes to generate revenues for their programs (such as education, highways, and police and fire departments). Some of the more common **state** and **local taxes** include income taxes, sales and use taxes, excise taxes, and property taxes. Typically, as shown in Exhibit 1-5, the largest state and local revenues are generated by state sales taxes and local property taxes—in contrast to federal revenues which rely primarily on income and employment taxes.

Income Taxes   Currently, most states and the District of Columbia impose income taxes on individuals and corporations who either reside in or earn income within the state.[8] This requires individuals living in these states to file a state tax return in addition to the federal return they already file. Calculations of individual and corporate taxable income vary with state law. Nonetheless, most state taxable income calculations largely conform to the federal taxable income calculations, with a limited number of modifications, although the tax rates are significantly less than the federal rate. The state of California is a notable exception because it has numerous modifications. Certain local governments such as New York City also impose an income tax, and again, the local calculations generally follow the respective state taxable income calculation.

Sales and Use Taxes   Most states, the District of Columbia, and local governments impose sales and use taxes. The tax base for a **sales tax** is the retail sales of goods and some services, and retailers are responsible for collecting and remitting

---

[8]Currently, Alaska, Florida, Nevada, South Dakota, Texas, Washington, and Wyoming have no personal income tax, and New Hampshire and Tennessee only tax individual dividend and interest income. Nevada and Wyoming do not impose taxes on corporate income, and South Dakota only taxes banks. Washington imposes a gross receipts tax instead of a corporate income tax. Texas and Ohio have an activity-based tax that is based on net income or gross receipts.

the tax; typically, sales tax is collected at the point of sale. The tax base for the **use tax** is the retail price of goods owned, possessed, or consumed within a state that were *not* purchased within the state. The purpose of a use tax is to discourage taxpayers from buying goods out of state in order to avoid or minimize the sales tax in their home state. At the same time, by eliminating the incentive to purchase goods out of state, a use tax removes any competitive disadvantage a retailer may incur from operating in a state with a high sales tax. States with a sales tax allow taxpayers to take a use tax credit on goods purchased out of state to mitigate the potential for double taxation on goods subject to sales tax in another state.

Example 1-11

Margaret buys three new Lands' End shirts for her dad for $100. Because Lands' End does not have a business presence in Florida, it does not collect Florida sales tax on the $100 purchase. Does Margaret's purchase escape Florida taxation?

Answer: No. Because Florida has a 6 percent use tax, Margaret is liable for $6 in use tax on the purchase ($6 = $100 × .06).

Despite the potential importance of the use tax as a source of state tax revenue, states have only recently begun to enforce it. Poor compliance is therefore not surprising; indeed, many individuals have never heard of the use tax. While it is relatively easy to enforce it on goods obtained out of state if they are subject to a registration requirement, such as automobiles, it is quite difficult for states to tax most other out-of-state purchases. The state of Florida is not likely to search your closet to look for tax-evaded Lands' End shirts. Note, however, that the majority of states have joined together (www.streamlinedsalestax.org) to try to subject all Internet sales to sales taxes.

Property Taxes   State and local governments commonly use two types of property taxes as sources of revenue: **real property taxes** and **personal property taxes.** Both are **ad valorem taxes**, meaning that the tax base for each is the fair market value of the property, and both are generally collected annually (if imposed at all).

Real property consists of land, structures, and improvements permanently attached to land, whereas *personal property* includes all other types of property, both tangible and intangible. Common examples of tangible personal property potentially subject to state and local taxation include automobiles, boats, private planes, business inventory, equipment, and furniture. Intangible personal property potentially subject to state and local taxation includes stocks, bonds, and intellectual property. Relative to personal property tax, real property taxes are easier to administer because real property is not movable and purchases often have to be registered with the state, thereby making it easy to identify the tax base and taxpayer. Furthermore, the taxing body can estimate market values for real property without much difficulty. In contrast, personal property is generally mobile (easier to hide) and may be more difficult to value, which make personal property taxes difficult to enforce. Accordingly, whereas all states and the District of Columbia provide for a real property tax, only a majority of states currently impose personal property taxes, most of which are assessed at the time of licensing or registration. However, most states collect personal property taxes on business property.

Excise Taxes   We've said that the tax base for excise taxes is typically the quantity of an item or service purchased. States typically impose excise taxes on items subject to federal excise tax. Transactions subject to state excise tax often include the sale of alcohol, diesel fuel, gasoline, tobacco products, and telephone services.

Implicit Taxes

All the taxes discussed above are **explicit taxes;** that is, they are taxes directly imposed by a government and are easily quantified. **Implicit taxes,** on the other hand, are indirect taxes—not paid directly to the government—that result from a tax advantage the government grants to certain transactions to satisfy social, economic, or other objectives. Implicit taxes are defined as the reduced before-tax return that a tax-favored asset produces because of its tax-advantaged status. Let's examine this concept more closely.

First of all, what does it mean to be *tax-favored?* An asset is said to be tax-favored when the income the asset produces is either excluded from the tax base or subject to a lower (preferential) tax rate, or if the asset generates some other tax benefit such as large tax deductions. These tax benefits, *all other things equal,* result in higher after-tax profits (or lower after-tax costs) from investing in the tax-advantaged assets.

Why do tax-advantaged assets bear an implicit tax, or a reduced before-tax return as a result of the tax advantage? The answer is simple economics. The tax benefits associated with the tax-favored asset increase the demand for the asset. Increased demand drives up the price of the asset, which in turn reduces its before-tax return, which is an implicit tax by definition. Consider Example 1-12.

Example 1-12

Consider two bonds, one issued by the Coca-Cola Co. and the other issued by the state of Georgia. Both bonds have similar nontax characteristics (risk, for example), the same face value of $10,000, and the same market interest rate of 10 percent. The only difference between the two bonds is that the interest income from the Coca-Cola Co. bond is subject to a 20 percent income tax rate, whereas the interest income from the State of Georgia bond is tax-exempt with a 0 percent tax rate. Which of the two bonds is a better investment and should therefore have a higher demand?

	Price	Before-Tax* Return	Interest Income	Income† Tax	After-Tax Income	After-Tax† Return
Coca-Cola Bond	$10,000	10%	$1,000	$200	$ 800	8%
State of GA Bond	10,000	10	1,000	0	1,000	10

*Before-tax return is calculated as the before-tax income divided by the price of the bond. Likewise, after-tax return is calculated as the after-tax income divided by the price of the bond.
†Income tax equals the taxable interest income ($1,000) multiplied by the assumed income marginal tax rate (20 percent).

Answer: Compare the after-tax returns of the bonds. Given the difference between the return after taxes (10 percent vs. 8 percent), the better investment—again, all other investment features being equal—is the State of Georgia bond because it provides a higher *after*-tax return. Because all investors in this example should prefer to buy the State of Georgia bond, the demand for the bond will be high, and its price should increase. This increase in price leads to a lower before-tax return due to the bond's tax-favored status (this is an implicit tax).

Example 1-12 is a basic illustration of the need to consider the role of taxes in investment decisions. Without understanding the relative tax effects associated with each bond, we cannot correctly compare their after-tax returns.

At what point in Example 1-12 would you be indifferent between investing in the Coca-Cola Co. bond and the State of Georgia bond? Assuming each bond has the same nontax characteristics, you would be indifferent between them when they both provide the same after-tax rate of return. This could occur if the state of Georgia raised the price of its bond from $10,000 to $12,500 ($1,000 interest/$12,500 price = 8% return). Or the state of Georgia could lower its bond interest payment from $1,000 to $800 ($800 interest/$10,000 price = 8% return). Either way, the state of Georgia benefits from selling the tax-exempt bonds—either at a higher price or at a lower interest rate relative to other bonds. Let's look more closely at this latter option, because it is, in fact, what many tax-exempt bond issuers choose to do.

	Price	Before-Tax Return	Interest Income	Income Tax	After-Tax Income	After-Tax Return
Coca-Cola Bond	$10,000	10%	$1,000	$200	$800	8%
State of GA Bond	10,000	8	800	0	800	8

At this point, assuming each bond has the same nontax characteristics, an investor should be indifferent between the Coca-Cola Co. bond and the State of Georgia bond. What is the tax burden on investors choosing the Coca-Cola Co. bond? Coca-Cola Co. bond investors are paying $200 of income taxes (explicit taxes). What is the tax burden on investors choosing the State of Georgia bond? While it is true they are subject to zero income taxes (explicit taxes), they are subject to implicit taxes in the form of the $200 less in interest income they accept. This $200 reduced interest income (2 percent reduced before-tax rate of return) is an implicit tax. Although the investors in the State of Georgia bond are not paying this tax directly, they are paying it indirectly.

Does this happen in real life? Yes. Municipal bond interest income (interest income paid on bonds issued by state and local governments) generally is not subject to federal income taxation. Because of their tax-advantaged status, municipalities are able to pay a lower interest rate on their bond issuances and investors are willing to accept the lower rate. This type of indirect federal subsidy allows municipalities to raise money at a reduced cost without the need of direct federal subsidy or approval.

Although we were able to quantify the implicit taxes paid in the above example, in reality it is very difficult to estimate the amount of implicit taxes paid. For example, the federal government subsidizes housing by allowing taxpayers to deduct mortgage interest on their principal residence. Does this subsidy result in an implicit tax in the form of higher housing prices? Probably. Nonetheless, it would be difficult to quantify this implicit tax.

Despite the difficulty in quantifying implicit taxes, you should understand the concept of implicit taxes so you can make informed judgments about the attractiveness of alternative investments, and about the relative total tax burdens of tax-advantaged investments (considering both explicit and implicit taxes).

THE KEY FACTS
Implicit Taxes
- Implicit taxes are indirect taxes that result from a tax advantage the government grants to certain transactions to satisfy social, economic, or other objectives.
- Implicit taxes are defined as the reduced before-tax return that a tax-favored asset produces because of its tax-advantaged status.
- Implicit taxes are difficult to quantify, but are important to understand in evaluating the relative tax burdens of tax-advantaged investments.

EVALUATING ALTERNATIVE TAX SYSTEMS   `LO 1-5`

Although it may appear that tax systems are designed without much forethought, in truth lawmakers engage in continuous debate over the basic questions of whom to tax, what to tax, and how much to tax. Margaret's friend Eddy is obviously upset with what he views as an unfair tax system. But fairness, as we will discuss shortly, is often like beauty—it is in the eye of the beholder. What is fair to one may seem blatantly unfair to others. In the following paragraphs, we offer various criteria (sufficiency, equity, certainty, convenience, and economy) you can use to evaluate alternative tax systems.[9] Satisfying everyone at the same time is difficult. Hence, the spirited debate on tax reform.

[9]Adam Smith identified and described the latter four criteria in *The Wealth of Nations.*

Sufficiency

Judging the **sufficiency** of a tax system means assessing the size of the tax revenues it must generate and ensuring that it provides them. For a tax system to be successful, it must provide sufficient revenues to pay for governmental expenditures for a defense system, social services, and so on. This sounds easy enough: Estimate the amount of government expenditures that will be required, and then design the system to generate enough revenues to pay for these expenses. In reality, however, accurately estimating governmental expenditures and revenues is a rather daunting and imprecise process. Estimating governmental expenditures is difficult because it is impossible to predict the unknown. For example, in recent years governmental expenditures have increased due to the terrorist attacks of September 11, 2001, the Afghanistan and Iraq Wars, natural disasters, economic stimulus, and health care. Likewise, estimating governmental revenues is difficult because tax revenues are the result of transactions influenced by these same national events, the economy, and other factors. Thus, precisely estimating and matching governmental expenditures with tax revenues is nearly impossible.

The task of estimating tax revenues becomes even more daunting when the government attempts to make significant changes to the existing tax system or design a new one. Whenever Congress proposes changing who is taxed, what is taxed, or how much is taxed, its members must consider the taxpayer response to the change. That affects the amount of tax collected, and how forecasters predict what taxpayers will do affects how much revenue they estimate.

Static vs. Dynamic Forecasting   One option in forecasting revenue is to ignore how taxpayers may alter their activities in response to a tax law change and to base projected tax revenues on the existing state of transactions, a process referred to as **static forecasting.** However, this type of forecasting may result in a large discrepancy in projected versus actual tax revenues if taxpayers do change their behavior. The other choice is to attempt to account for possible taxpayer responses to the tax law change, a process referred to as **dynamic forecasting.** Dynamic forecasting is ultimately only as good as the assumptions underlying the forecasts and does not guarantee accurate results. Nonetheless, considering how taxpayers may alter their activities in response to a tax law change is a useful exercise to identify the potential ramifications of the change, even if the revenue projections ultimately miss the mark. For more information on the Congressional Revenue Estimating Process, including dynamic scoring, see the Joint Committee on Taxation explanation at https://www.jct.gov/publications.html?func=startdown&id=3720.

In some cases, static forecasting can lead to a tax consequence opposite the desired outcome. In Example 1-13, we might estimate that given Heflin's close proximity to other cities with a $1.00 cigarette tax, the number of packs of cigarettes sold within the city would drop significantly to, say, 50,000. In this case, the tax increase would actually *decrease* tax revenues by $100,000 ($400,000 existing tax − $300,000 new tax), not a good outcome if the goal was to increase tax revenues.

Example 1-13

The city of Heflin would like to increase tax revenues by $2,000,000 to pay for needed roadwork. A concerned taxpayer recently proposed increasing the cigarette excise tax from $1.00 per pack of cigarettes to $6.00 per pack to raise the additional needed revenue. Last year, 400,000 packs of cigarettes were sold in the city. Will the tax be successful in raising the $2,000,000 revenue?

Answer: Not likely. The proposed tax increase of $5, and the assumption that 400,000 packs will still be sold, is an example of static forecasting: It ignores that many taxpayers may respond to the tax change by quitting, cutting down, or buying cheaper cigarettes in the next town.

Income vs. Substitution Effects   The example above described proposed changes in an excise tax, which is a proportional tax. In terms of a progressive tax such as an *income* tax, a tax rate increase or an expansion of the tax base can result in one of two taxpayer responses, both of which are important for dynamic forecasting. The **income effect** predicts that when taxpayers are taxed more (when, say, a tax rate increases from 25 to 28 percent), they will work harder to generate the same after-tax dollars. The **substitution effect** predicts that when taxpayers are taxed more, rather than work more, they will substitute nontaxable activities like leisure pursuits for taxable ones because the marginal value of taxable activities has decreased. Which view is accurate? The answer depends on the taxpayer. Consider the following examples.

Example 1-14

Margaret's friend George, who earns $40,000 taxable income as a mechanic, is taxed at an average rate of 10 percent ($4,000 of tax). If Congress increases the income tax rate such that George's average tax rate increases from 10 percent to 25 percent, how much more income tax will he pay?

Answer: It depends on whether the income effect or the substitution effect is operating. Assuming George is single and cannot afford a net decrease in his after-tax income, he will likely work more (the income effect rules). Prior to the tax rate increase, George had $36,000 of after-tax income ($40,000 taxable income less $4,000 tax). With the increased tax rate, George will have to earn $48,000 of taxable income to keep $36,000 after taxes [$48,000 − ($48,000 × .25) = $36,000]. Thus, if the income effect rules, the government will collect $12,000 of federal income tax from George, or $8,000 more than under the previous lower tax rate. In this scenario, the tax change increases government revenues because of the increased tax rate *and* the increased tax base.

Whether the substitution effect or the income effect will describe any individual taxpayer's reaction to a tax increase is something we can only guess. But some factors—such as having higher disposable income—are likely to correlate with the substitution effect.

Example 1-15

What if: Now let's assume that George is married and has two young children, both he and his wife work, and they file a tax return jointly with a 10 percent average tax rate. Either of their incomes is sufficient to meet necessities, even after the tax rate increase. But fixed child care costs make the marginal wage rate (the after-tax hourly wage less hourly child care cost) more sensitive to tax rate increases. In this case, the lower-earning spouse may choose to work less. Suppose George quits his full-time job and takes a part-time position that pays $10,000 to spend more time with his kids and to pursue his passion, reading sports novels. What are the taxes on George's income?

Answer: In this case, George will owe $2,500 tax ($10,000 × .25 = $2,500). Here, the substitution effect operates, and the government collects much less than it would have if George had maintained his full-time position, because the tax rate increase had a negative effect on the tax base.

As the previous examples illustrate, the response to a tax law change can vary by taxpayer and can greatly affect the magnitude of tax revenues generated by the change. Herein lies one of the challenges in significantly changing an existing tax system or designing a new one: If a tax system fails to generate sufficient revenues, the government must seek other sources to pay for governmental expenditures. The most common source of these additional funds for the federal government is the issuance of debt instruments such as Treasury bonds. This, however, is only a short-term solution to a budget deficit. Debt issuances require both interest and principal payments, which require the federal government to identify even more sources of revenue to service the debt issued, or to cut governmental spending (both of which may be unpopular choices with voters). A third option is for the government to default on its debt obligations. However, the costs of this option are potentially devastating. If the historical examples of Mexico, Brazil, Argentina, and Greece are any guide, a U.S. government default on its debt obligations would likely devalue the U.S. dollar severely and have extreme negative consequences for the U.S. capital markets.

The best option is for the government to match its revenues with its expenses—that is, not to spend more than it collects. State governments seem to be more successful in this endeavor than the U.S. federal government. Indeed, all states except Vermont require a balanced budget each year, whereas the federal government has had deficit spending for most of the last 40 years.

TAXES IN THE REAL WORLD   **National Debt**

How much debt does the U.S. have today? About $17.9 trillion. Over $12.8 trillion of the national debt is held by public investors including: individual bondholders; institutional investors; and foreign governments such as China, the United Kingdom, and Brazil. The almost $5 trillion remaining amount represents intragovernmental holdings—primarily Social Security.

Is $17.9 trillion too much to handle? The key issue is fiscal sustainability: the ability to pay off a debt in the future. Rising debt also has other negative consequences, such as higher interest payments, a need for higher taxes, restricting policymaker's fiscal policy choices, and increasing the probability of a sudden fiscal crisis. If nothing is done to change the national debt tra-

jectory, the debt will grow faster than the economy.

Is the national debt sustainable? The federal government has been recording budget deficits that are a larger share of the economy than any year since the end of World War II. With an aging population, Social Security and other benefits will require larger expenditures. By the end of the current decade, barring any significant policy shifts, the vast majority of federal tax revenue will be consumed by just four expenditures: interest on the debt, Medicare, Medicaid, and Social Security. To finance other government expenditures, including defense and all other discretionary programs, policymakers will have to borrow the money to pay for them.

Equity

We've looked at the challenges of designing a tax system that provides sufficient revenues to pay for governmental expenditures. An equally challenging issue is how the tax burden should be distributed across taxpayers. At the heart of this issue is the concept of **equity** or fairness. Fairness is inherently subject to personal interpretation, and informed minds often disagree about what is fair. There is no "one-size-fits-all" definition of equity or fairness. Nonetheless, it is informative to consider in broad terms what makes a fair or equitable tax system.

In general terms, a tax system is considered fair or equitable if the tax is based on the taxpayer's ability to pay. Taxpayers with a greater ability to pay tax, pay more tax. In broad terms, each of the federal, state, and local taxes we've discussed satisfies this criterion. For example, those individuals with greater taxable income, purchases, property, and estates (upon death) generally pay higher dollar amounts in federal income tax, sales tax, property tax, and estate tax. If this is the case, why is there so much debate over the fairness of the U.S. income tax system? The answer is that equity is more complex than our first definition suggests. Let's take a closer look.

Horizontal vs. Vertical Equity   Two basic types of equity are relevant to tax systems. **Horizontal equity** means that two taxpayers in similar situations pay the same tax. In broad terms, each of the federal, state, and local taxes discussed satisfy this definition. Two individual taxpayers with the same taxable income, same purchases, same value of property, and same estate value pay the same federal income tax, sales tax, property tax, and estate tax. However, on closer inspection we might argue that each of these tax systems is *not* horizontally equitable. Here are some examples:

- Two individual taxpayers with the same income will not pay the same federal income tax if one individual's income was earned as salary and the other individual's income was tax-exempt municipal bond interest income, dividend income, or capital gain(s) income, which can be subject to a lower tax rate.
- Two individuals with the same dollar amount of purchases will not pay the same sales tax if one buys a higher proportion of goods that are subject to a lower sales tax rate, such as groceries.
- Two individuals with real estate of the same value will not pay the same property tax if one individual owns farmland, which is generally subject to a lower property tax rate.
- Finally, two individuals with estates of the same value will not pay the same estate tax if one individual bequeaths more of her property to charity or a spouse, because these transfers are not subject to estate tax.

These failures of horizontal equity are due to what we call *tax preferences.* Governments provide tax preferences for a variety of reasons, such as to encourage investment or further social objectives. Whether we view these tax preferences as appropriate greatly influences whether we consider a tax system to be fair in general and horizontally equitable in particular.

The second type of equity to consider in evaluating a tax system is **vertical equity.** Vertical equity is achieved when taxpayers with greater ability to pay tax, pay more tax than taxpayers with less ability to pay. We can think of vertical equity in terms of tax dollars paid or in terms of tax rates. Proponents of a flat income tax or of a sales tax—both of which are proportional tax rate structures—are more likely to argue that vertical equity is achieved when taxpayers with a greater ability to pay tax, simply pay more in tax *dollars.* Proponents of a progressive tax system are more likely to argue that taxpayers with a greater ability to pay should be subject to a higher tax *rate.* This view is based upon the argument that the *relative* burden of a flat tax rate decreases as a taxpayer's income increases. Which is the correct answer? There is no correct answer. Nonetheless, many feel very strongly regarding one view or the other.

Our discussion has focused on how we can view alternative tax rate structures in terms of vertical equity, ignoring the role that the tax base plays in determining vertical equity. Indeed, focusing on the tax rate structure in evaluating a tax system is appropriate only if the tax base chosen—whether it's taxable income, purchases, property owned, or something else—accurately portrays a taxpayer's ability to pay. This can be a rather strong assumption. Consider the sales tax in Example 1-9. Although taxable purchases in this example increase as the taxpayers' total incomes increase, total incomes increase at a much faster rate than taxable purchases. Thus, the gap between taxable purchases and total income widens as total income increases. The end result is that the effective tax rates for those with a greater ability to pay are *lower* than for those taxpayers with a lesser ability to pay, making this tax regressive. Regressive tax rate structures are generally considered not to satisfy vertical equity, unless you strongly believe that those with a greater ability to pay do so simply by paying more tax dollars, albeit at a lower tax rate. In sum, evaluating vertical equity in terms of effective tax rates may be much more informative than simply evaluating tax rate structures.

THE KEY FACTS

Evaluating Alternative Taxes—Equity

- Equity considers how the tax burden should be distributed across taxpayers.
- Horizontal equity means that two taxpayers in similar situations pay the same tax.
- Vertical equity is achieved when taxpayers with greater ability to pay tax, pay more tax relative to taxpayers with a lesser ability to pay tax.

Certainty

Certainty means that taxpayers should be able to determine when to pay the tax, where to pay the tax, and how to determine the tax. Determining when and where to pay each of the taxes previously discussed is relatively easy. For example, individual federal income tax returns and the remaining balance of taxes owed must be filed with the Internal Revenue Service each year on or before April 15th. Likewise, sales taxes, property taxes, and excise taxes are each determined with relative ease: Sales taxes are based on the value of taxable purchases, property taxes are generally based on assessed property values, and excise taxes are based on the number of taxable units purchased. Indeed, these taxes are calculated for the taxpayer and often charged at regular intervals or at the point of purchase; they do not require a tax return.

In contrast, income taxes are often criticized as being too complex. What are taxable vs. nontaxable forms of income? What are deductible/nondeductible expenses? When should income or expenses be reported? For wage earners with few investments, the answers to these questions are straightforward. For business owners and individuals with a lot of investments, the answers are nontrivial. Yearly tax law changes enacted by Congress can make it more difficult to determine a taxpayer's current tax liability, much less plan for the future.

Convenience

Convenience suggests that a tax system should be designed to facilitate the collection of tax revenues without undue hardship on the taxpayer or the government. Various tax systems meet this criterion by tying the collection of the tax as closely as possible to the transaction that generates (when it is most convenient to pay the tax). For example, retailers collect sales taxes when buyers purchase goods. Thus, it is difficult for the buyer to avoid paying sales tax, assuming she is transacting with an ethical retailer. Likewise, employers withhold federal income and Social Security taxes directly from wage earners' paychecks, which speeds the government's collection of the taxes and makes it difficult for the taxpayer to evade the taxes. If tax withholdings are not sufficient relative to the taxpayer's anticipated income tax liability, the taxpayer is required to make quarterly estimated tax installments. Individual quarterly estimated payments are due on April 15, June 15, September 15, and January 15, whereas corporate estimated tax payments are due on the 15th day of the third, sixth, ninth, and twelfth months of the corporation's fiscal year.

Economy

Economy requires that a good tax system should minimize the compliance and administration costs associated with the tax system. We can view economy from both the taxpayers' and the government's perspectives. Believe it or not, most tax systems fare well in terms of economy, at least from the government's perspective. For example, the current IRS budget represents approximately $\frac{1}{2}$ of a percent of every tax dollar collected. Compared to the typical costs of a collection agency, this is quite low.

How about from the taxpayer's perspective? Here the picture is a bit different. The sales tax imposes no administrative burden on the taxpayer and only small administrative costs on the local retailer. However, out-of-state sellers argue that collecting and remitting use taxes for thousands of state and city jurisdictions would be a substantial burden. Other taxes such as excise taxes and property taxes also impose minimal administrative costs on the taxpayer. In contrast, as we've seen, the income tax is often criticized for the compliance costs imposed on the taxpayer. Indeed, for certain taxpayers, record-keeping costs, accountant fees, attorney fees, and so on can be substantial. Advocates of alternative tax systems often challenge the income tax on this criterion.

THE KEY FACTS

Evaluating Alternative Taxes—Certainty, Convenience, and Economy

- Certainty
  - Means taxpayers should be able to determine when, where, and how much tax to pay.
  - Determining when and where to pay each of the taxes previously discussed is relatively easy.
  - The income tax has been criticized for its complexity in determining how much to pay.
- Convenience
  - Means a tax system should be designed to facilitate the collection of tax revenues without undue hardship on the taxpayer or the government.
  - Various tax systems meet this criterion by tying the collection of the tax as closely as possible to the transaction that generates it.
- Economy
  - Means a tax system should minimize its compliance and administration costs.
  - May be viewed from both the taxpayers' and the government's perspectives.

Evaluating Tax Systems—The Trade-Off

At the heart of any debate on tax reform are fundamental decisions and concessions based on the five criteria we've just discussed. Interestingly enough, much of the debate regarding alternative tax systems reduces to a choice between simplicity and fairness. Those taxes that generally are simpler and easier to administer, such as the sales tax, are typically viewed as less fair. Those taxes that may be viewed as more fair, such as the federal income tax, often are more complex to administer. Thus, Margaret's friend Eddy faces a difficult choice about which type of tax system to advocate, as do all taxpayers. An understanding of the evaluative criteria should be helpful to anyone trying to reconcile the trade-offs among alternative tax proposals.

CONCLUSION

In almost any society, taxes are a part of life. They influence decisions about personal finance, investment, business, and politics. In this chapter, we introduced the basic concepts of why one should study tax, what is a tax, and how to calculate a tax. We also discussed various tax rates, tax rate structures, and different types of taxes imposed by federal, state, and local governments. Finally, we discussed the criteria that one might use to evaluate alternative tax rate systems. To make informed personal finance, investment, business, and political decisions, one must have a basic understanding of these items. In the following chapters we expand the discussion of how taxes influence these decisions while providing a basic understanding of our federal income tax system. Read on and learn more!

Summary

Demonstrate how taxes influence basic business, investment, personal, and political decisions. **LO 1-1**

- Taxes are significant costs that influence many basic business, investment, and personal decisions.
  - *Business decisions:* what organization form to take; where to locate; how to compensate employees; appropriate debt mix; owning vs. renting equipment and property; how to distribute profits, and so forth.
  - *Investment decisions:* alternative methods for saving for education or retirement, and so forth.
  - *Personal finance decisions:* evaluating job offers; gift or estate planning; owning vs. renting home, and so forth.
- Taxes also play a major part in the political process. Major parties typically have very diverse views on whom, what, and how much to tax.

Discuss what constitutes a tax and the general objectives of taxes. **LO 1-2**

- The general purpose of taxes is to fund the government. Unlike fines or penalties, taxes are not meant to punish or prevent illegal behavior; but *"sin taxes"* (on alcohol, tobacco, tanning beds, etc.) are meant to discourage some behaviors.
- The three criteria necessary to be a tax are that the payment is (1) required (it is not voluntary), (2) imposed by a government (federal, state, or local), and (3) not tied directly to the benefit received by the taxpayer.

Describe the different tax rate structures and calculate a tax. **LO 1-3**

- Tax = Tax rate × Tax base, where the tax base is what is taxed and the tax rate is the level of taxes imposed on the base. Different portions of a tax base may be taxed at different rates.

- There are three different tax rates that are useful in contrasting the different tax rate structures, tax planning, and/or assessing the tax burden of a taxpayer: the marginal, average, and effective tax rates.
- The marginal tax rate is the tax that applies to the next increment of income or deduction. The average tax rate represents a taxpayer's average level of taxation on each dollar of taxable income. The effective tax rate represents the taxpayer's average rate of taxation on each dollar of total income (taxable *and* nontaxable income).
- The three basic tax rate structures are proportional, progressive, and regressive.
  - A *proportional tax rate* structure imposes a constant tax rate throughout the tax base. As a taxpayer's tax base increases, the taxpayer's taxes increase proportionally. The marginal tax rate remains constant and always equals the average tax rate. A common example is a sales tax.
  - A *progressive tax rate* imposes an increasing marginal tax rate as the tax base increases. As a taxpayer's tax base increases, both the marginal tax rate and the taxes paid increase. A common example is the U.S. federal income tax.
  - A *regressive tax rate* imposes a decreasing marginal tax rate as the tax base increases. As a taxpayer's tax base increases, the marginal tax rate decreases while the total taxes paid increases.

LO 1-4 Identify the various federal, state, and local taxes.

- Federal taxes include the income tax, employment taxes (Social Security and Medicare taxes), unemployment taxes, excise taxes (levied on quantity purchased), and transfer taxes (estate and gift taxes).
- State and local taxes include the income tax (levied by most states), sales tax (levied on retail sales of goods and some services), use tax (levied on the retail price of goods owned or consumed within a state that were purchased out of state), property taxes (levied on fair market value of real and personal property), and excise taxes.
- Implicit taxes are indirect taxes that result from a tax advantage the government grants to certain transactions to satisfy social, economic, or other objectives. They are defined as the reduced before-tax return that a tax-favored asset produces because of its tax-advantaged status.

LO 1-5 Apply appropriate criteria to evaluate alternate tax systems.

- Sufficiency involves assessing the aggregate size of the tax revenues that must be generated and ensuring that the tax system provides these revenues. Static forecasting ignores how taxpayers may alter their activities in response to a proposed tax law change and bases projected tax revenues on the existing state of transactions. Dynamic forecasting attempts to account for possible taxpayer responses to a proposed tax law change.
- Equity considers how the tax burden should be distributed across taxpayers. Generally, a tax system is considered fair or equitable if the tax is based on the taxpayer's ability to pay—that is, taxpayers with a greater ability to pay tax, pay more tax. Horizontal equity means that two taxpayers in similar situations pay the same tax. Vertical equity is achieved when taxpayers with greater ability to pay tax, pay more tax relative to taxpayers with a lesser ability to pay tax.
- Certainty means taxpayers should be able to determine when, where, and how much tax to pay.
- Convenience means a tax system should be designed to facilitate the collection of tax revenues without undue hardship on the taxpayer or the government.
- Economy means a tax system should minimize its compliance and administration costs.

KEY TERMS

ad valorem tax (1-15)
average tax rate (1-7)
bracket (1-5)
certainty (1-22)

convenience (1-22)
dynamic forecasting (1-18)
earmarked tax (1-4)
economy (1-22)

effective tax rate (1-8)
employment taxes (1-12)
equity (1-20)
estate tax (1-13)

excise taxes (1-13)	Medicare tax (1-12)	static forecasting (1-18)
explicit tax (1-16)	personal property tax (1-15)	substitution effect (1-19)
flat tax (1-5)	progressive tax rate structure (1-9)	sufficiency (1-18)
gift tax (1-13)	proportional tax rate structure (1-9)	tax (1-3)
graduated taxes (1-5)	real property tax (1-15)	tax base (1-5)
horizontal equity (1-21)	regressive tax rate structure (1-10)	tax rate (1-5)
implicit tax (1-16)	sales tax (1-14)	transfer taxes (1-13)
income effect (1-19)	self-employment tax (1-13)	unemployment tax (1-13)
income tax (1-12)	sin taxes (1-4)	use tax (1-15)
local tax (1-14)	Social Security tax (1-12)	value-added tax (1-11)
marginal tax rate (1-5)	state tax (1-14)	vertical equity (1-21)

DISCUSSION QUESTIONS

Discussion Questions are available in *Connect*®.   ■ connect

1. Jessica's friend Zachary once stated that he couldn't understand why someone would take a tax course. Why is this a rather naïve view? **LO 1-1**

2. What are some aspects of business that require knowledge of taxation? What are some aspects of personal finance that require knowledge of taxation? **LO 1-1**

3. Describe some ways in which taxes affect the political process in the United States. **LO 1-1**

4. Courtney recently received a speeding ticket on her way to the university. Her fine was $200. Is this considered a tax? Why or why not? **LO 1-2**

5. Marlon and Latoya recently started building a house. They had to pay $300 to the county government for a building permit. Is the $300 payment a tax? Why or why not? **LO 1-2**

6. To help pay for the city's new stadium, the city of Birmingham recently enacted a 1 percent surcharge on hotel rooms. Is this a tax? Why or why not? **LO 1-2**

7. As noted in Example 1-2, tolls, parking meter fees, and annual licensing fees are not considered taxes. Can you identify other fees that are similar? **LO 1-2**

8. If the general objective of our tax system is to raise revenue, why does the income tax allow deductions for charitable contributions and retirement plan contributions? **LO 1-2**

9. One common argument for imposing so-called sin taxes is the social goal of *reducing* demand for such products. Using cigarettes as an example, is there a segment of the population that might be sensitive to price and for whom high taxes might discourage purchases? **LO 1-2**

10. Dontae stated that he didn't want to earn any more money because it would "put him in a higher tax bracket." What is wrong with Dontae's reasoning? **LO 1-3**

11. Describe the three different tax rates discussed in the chapter and how taxpayers might use them. **LO 1-3**

12. Which is a more appropriate tax rate to use to compare taxpayers' tax burdens—the average or the effective tax rate? Why? **LO 1-3**

13. Describe the differences between a proportional, progressive, and regressive tax rate structure. **LO 1-3**

14. Arnold and Lilly have recently had a heated discussion about whether a sales tax is a proportional tax or a regressive tax. Arnold argues that a sales tax is regressive. Lilly counters that the sales tax is a flat tax. Who is correct? **LO 1-3**

15. Which is the largest tax collected by the U.S. government? What types of taxpayers are subject to this tax? **LO 1-4**

LO 1-4   16. What is the tax base for the Social Security and Medicare taxes for an employee or employer? What is the tax base for Social Security and Medicare taxes for a self-employed individual? Is the self-employment tax in addition to or in lieu of federal income tax?

LO 1-4   17. What are unemployment taxes?

LO 1-4   18. What is the distinguishing feature of an excise tax?

LO 1-4   19. What are some of the taxes that currently are unique to state and local governments? What are some of the taxes that the federal, state, and local governments each utilize?

LO 1-4   20. The state of Georgia recently increased its tax on a pack of cigarettes by $2. What type of tax is this? Why might Georgia choose this type of tax?

LO 1-4   21. What is the difference between a sales tax and a use tax?

LO 1-4   22. What is an ad valorem tax? Name an example of this type of tax.

LO 1-4   23. What are the differences between an explicit and an implicit tax?

LO 1-4   24. When we calculate average and effective tax rates, do we consider implicit taxes? What effect does this have on taxpayers' perception of equity?

LO 1-4   25. Benjamin recently bought a truck in Alabama for his business in Georgia. What different types of federal and state taxes may affect this transaction?

LO 1-5   26. Kobe strongly dislikes SUVs and is appalled that so many are on the road. He proposes to eliminate the federal income tax and replace it with a $50,000 annual tax per SUV. Based on the number of SUVs currently owned in the United States, he estimates the tax will generate exactly the amount of tax revenue currently collected from the income tax. What is wrong with Kobe's proposal? What type of forecasting is Kobe likely using?

LO 1-5   27. What is the difference between the income and substitution effects? For which types of taxpayers is the income effect more likely descriptive? For which types of taxpayers is the substitution effect more likely descriptive?

LO 1-5   28. What is the difference between horizontal and vertical equity? How do tax preferences affect people's view of horizontal equity?

LO 1-3   LO 1-5   29. Montel argues that a flat income tax rate system is vertically equitable. Oprah argues that a progressive tax rate structure is vertically equitable. How do their arguments differ? Who is correct?

LO 1-3   LO 1-5   30. Discuss why evaluating vertical equity simply based on tax rate structure may be less than optimal.

LO 1-4   LO 1-5   31. Compare the federal income tax to sales taxes using the "certainty" criterion.

LO 1-5   32. Many years ago a famous member of Congress proposed eliminating federal income tax withholding. What criterion for evaluating tax systems did this proposal violate? What would likely have been the result of eliminating withholding?

LO 1-5   33. "The federal income tax scores very high on the economy criterion because the current IRS budget is relatively low compared to the costs of a typical collection agency." Explain why this statement may be considered wrong.

PROBLEMS

Select problems are available in *Connect*®.   ![connect logo]

LO 1-3   34. Chuck, a single taxpayer, earns $75,000 in taxable income and $10,000 in interest from an investment in City of Heflin bonds. Using the U.S. tax rate schedule, how much federal tax will he owe? What is his average tax rate? What is his effective tax rate? What is his current marginal tax rate?

35. Using the facts in the previous problem, if Chuck earns an additional $40,000 of taxable income, what is his marginal tax rate on this income? What is his marginal rate if, instead, he had $40,000 of additional deductions? `LO 1-3`

36. In reviewing the tax rate schedule for a single taxpayer, Chuck notes that the tax on $75,000 is $5,183.75 plus 25 percent of the taxable income over $37,650. What does the $5,183.75 represent? `LO 1-3`

37. Campbell, a single taxpayer, earns $400,000 in taxable income and $2,000 in interest from an investment in State of New York bonds. Using the U.S. tax rate schedule, how much federal tax will she owe? What is her average tax rate? What is her effective tax rate? What is her current marginal tax rate? `LO 1-3`

38. Using the facts in the previous problem, if Campbell earns an additional $15,000 of taxable income, what is her marginal tax rate on this income? What is her marginal rate if, instead, she had $15,000 of additional deductions? `LO 1-3`

39. Jorge and Anita, married taxpayers, earn $150,000 in taxable income and $40,000 in interest from an investment in City of Heflin bonds. Using the U.S. tax rate schedule for married filing jointly, how much federal tax will they owe? What is their average tax rate? What is their effective tax rate? What is their current marginal tax rate? `LO 1-3`

40. Using the facts in the previous problem, if Jorge and Anita earn an additional $100,000 of taxable income, what is their marginal tax rate on this income? What is their marginal rate if, instead, they reported an additional $100,000 in deductions? `LO 1-3`

41. In reviewing the tax rate schedule for married filing jointly, Jorge and Anita note that the tax on $155,000 is $29,517.50 plus 28 percent of the taxable income over $151,900. What does the $29,517.50 represent? `LO 1-3`

42. Scot and Vidia, married taxpayers, earn $240,000 in taxable income and $5,000 in interest from an investment in City of Tampa bonds. Using the U.S. tax rate schedule for married filing jointly, how much federal tax will they owe? What is their average tax rate? What is their effective tax rate? What is their current marginal tax rate? `LO 1-3`

43. Using the facts in the previous problem, if Scot and Vidia earn an additional $70,000 of taxable income, what is their marginal tax rate on this income? How would your answer differ if they, instead, had $70,000 of additional deductions? `LO 1-3`

44. Melinda invests $200,000 in a City of Heflin bond that pays 6 percent interest. Alternatively, Melinda could have invested the $200,000 in a bond recently issued by Surething Inc., that pays 8 percent interest with similar risk and other nontax characteristics to the City of Heflin bond. Assume Melinda's marginal tax rate is 25 percent. `LO 1-3` `LO 1-4`
    a) What is her after-tax rate of return for the City of Heflin bond?
    b) How much explicit tax does Melinda pay on the City of Heflin bond?
    c) How much implicit tax does she pay on the City of Heflin bond?
    d) How much explicit tax would she have paid on the Surething Inc. bond?
    e) What is her after-tax rate of return on the Surething Inc. bond?

45. Hugh has the choice between investing in a City of Heflin bond at 6 percent or a Surething bond at 9 percent. Assuming that both bonds have the same nontax characteristics and that Hugh has a 40 percent marginal tax rate, in which bond should he invest? `LO 1-3` `LO 1-4` planning

46. Using the facts in the previous problem, what interest rate does Surething Inc. need to offer to make Hugh indifferent between investing in the two bonds? `LO 1-3` `LO 1-4` planning

LO 1-3 **LO 1-4**
planning

47. Fergie has the choice between investing in a State of New York bond at 5 percent and a Surething bond at 8 percent. Assuming that both bonds have the same nontax characteristics and that Fergie has a 30 percent marginal tax rate, in which bond should she invest?

LO 1-3 **LO 1-4**
planning

48. Using the facts in the previous problem, what interest rate does the state of New York need to offer to make Fergie indifferent between investing in the two bonds?

LO 1-3

49. Given the following tax structure, what minimum tax would need to be assessed on Shameika to make the tax progressive with respect to average tax rates?

Taxpayer	Salary	Muni-Bond Interest	Total Tax
Mihwah	$10,000	$10,000	$600
Shameika	50,000	30,000	???

LO 1-3

50. Using the facts in the previous problem, what minimum tax would need to be assessed on Shameika to make the tax progressive with respect to effective tax rates?

LO 1-3 **LO 1-5**

51. Song earns $100,000 taxable income as an interior designer and is taxed at an average rate of 20 percent (i.e., $20,000 of tax). If Congress increases the income tax rate such that Song's average tax rate increases from 20 percent to 25 percent, how much more income tax will she pay assuming that the income effect is descriptive? What effect will this tax rate change have on the tax base and tax collected?

LO 1-3 **LO 1-5**

52. Using the facts from the previous problem, what will happen to the government's tax revenues if Song chooses to spend more time pursuing her other passions besides work in response to the tax rate change and earns only $75,000 in taxable income? What is the term that describes this type of reaction to a tax rate increase? What types of taxpayers are likely to respond in this manner?

LO 1-5

53. Given the following tax structure, what tax would need to be assessed on Venita to make the tax horizontally equitable?

Taxpayer	Salary	Total Tax
Mae	$10,000	$ 600
Pedro	20,000	1,500
Venita	10,000	???

LO 1-5

54. Using the facts in the previous problem, what is the minimum tax that Pedro should pay to make the tax structure vertically equitable based on the tax rate paid? This would result in what type of tax rate structure?

LO 1-5

55. Using the facts in the previous problem, what is the minimum tax that Pedro should pay to make the tax structure vertically equitable with respect to the amount of tax paid? This would result in what type of tax rate structure?

LO 1-5

56. Consider the following tax rate structure. Is it horizontally equitable? Why or why not? Is it vertically equitable? Why or why not?

Taxpayer	Salary	Total Tax
Rajiv	$10,000	$600
LaMarcus	20,000	600
Dory	10,000	600

57. Consider the following tax rate structure. Is it horizontally equitable? Why or why not? Is it vertically equitable? Why or why not?   **LO 1-5**

Taxpayer	Salary	Total Tax
Marilyn	$10,000	$ 600
Kobe	20,000	3,000
Alfonso	30,000	6,000

58. Consider the following tax rate structure. Is it horizontally equitable? Why or why not? Is it vertically equitable? Why or why not?   **LO 1-5**

Taxpayer	Salary	Total Tax
Rodney	$10,000	$600
Keisha	10,000	600

59. Lorenzo is considering starting a trucking company either in Texas or Oklahoma. He will relocate his family, which includes his wife, children, and parents, to reside in the same state as his business. What types of taxes may influence his decision of where to locate his business?   **LO 1-1**   **LO 1-4**

60. Congress would like to increase tax revenues by 10 percent. Assume that the average taxpayer in the United States earns $65,000 and pays an average tax rate of 15 percent. If the income effect is in effect for all taxpayers, what average tax rate will result in a 10 percent increase in tax revenues? This is an example of what type of forecasting?   **LO 1-3**   **LO 1-5**

61. Locate the IRS Web site at www.irs.gov/. For every $100 the IRS collected, how much was spent on the IRS collection efforts? What tax system criterion does this information help you to evaluate with respect to the current U.S. tax system?   **LO 1-5**   **research**

62. Using the Internet, find a comparison of income tax rates across states. What state currently has the highest income tax rate? In considering individual tax burdens across states, what other taxes should you consider?   **LO 1-4**   **research**

Tax Compliance, the IRS, and Tax Authorities

Upon completing this chapter, you should be able to:

LO 2-1 Identify the filing requirements for income tax returns and the statute of limitations for assessment.

LO 2-2 Outline the IRS audit process, how returns are selected, the different types of audits, and what happens after the audit.

LO 2-3 Evaluate the relative weights of the various tax law sources.

LO 2-4 Describe the legislative process as it pertains to taxation.

LO 2-5 Perform the basic steps in tax research and evaluate various tax law sources when faced with ambiguous statutes.

LO 2-6 Describe tax professional responsibilities in providing tax advice.

LO 2-7 Identify taxpayer and tax professional penalties.

© Jose Luis Pelaez Inc/Blend Images

Storyline Summary

Taxpayers:	Bill and Mercedes
Family description:	Bill and Mercedes are married with one daughter, Margaret.
Employment status:	Bill is an economics professor; Mercedes is a small business owner.
Filing status:	Married, filing jointly
Current situation:	Bill and Mercedes face an IRS audit involving a previous year's interest deductions.

Bill and Mercedes received a notice from the Internal Revenue Service (IRS) that their return is under audit for certain interest deductions. As you might expect, they are quite concerned, especially because it has been several years since they claimed the deductions and they worry that all their supporting documentation may not be in place. Several questions run through their minds. How could the IRS audit a return that was filed so long ago? Why was their tax return selected, and what should they expect during the audit? The interest deductions they reported were based on advice from their CPA. What would cause the IRS and a CPA to interpret the law differently? What is their financial exposure if the deductions are ultimately disallowed?

Will they have to pay interest and penalties in addition to the tax they might owe? ■

Even the most conservative taxpayer is likely to feel anxiety after receiving an IRS notice. This chapter will help answer Bill and Mercedes's questions and provide an overview of the audit process and tax research. While all taxpayers should understand these basics of our tax system, aspiring accountants should be especially familiar with them.

LO 2-1 TAXPAYER FILING REQUIREMENTS

To file or not to file? Unlike Hamlet's "to be or not to be," this question has a pretty straightforward answer. Filing requirements are specified by law for each type of taxpayer. All corporations must file a tax return annually regardless of their taxable income. Estates and trusts are required to file annual income tax returns if their gross income exceeds $600.[1]

The filing requirements for individual taxpayers are a little more complex. Specifically, they depend on the taxpayer's filing status (single, married filing jointly, and so on, discussed in more detail in Chapter 4), age, and gross income (income before deductions). Exhibit 2-1 lists the 2016 gross income thresholds for taxpayers based on their filing status, gross income, and age. As detailed in Exhibit 2-1, the gross income thresholds are calculated as the sum of the standard deduction, additional deductions for taxpayers age 65 or older, and personal exemption(s) that apply to each respective filing status.[2] These amounts are indexed for inflation and thus change each year. For certain taxpayers such as the self-employed and those claimed as dependents by another taxpayer, lower gross income thresholds apply.

EXHIBIT 2-1 2016 Gross Income Thresholds by Filing Status

Filing Status and Age (in 2016)	2016 Gross Income	Explanation
Single	$10,350	$6,300 standard deduction + $4,050 personal exemption
Single, 65 or older	$11,900	$6,300 standard deduction + $1,550 additional deduction + $4,050 personal exemption
Married, filing a joint return	$20,700	$12,600 standard deduction + $8,100 personal exemptions (2)
Married, filing a joint return, one spouse 65 or older	$21,950	$12,600 standard deduction + $1,250 additional deduction (2) + $8,100 personal exemptions (2)
Married, filing a joint return, both spouses 65 or older	$23,200	$12,600 standard deduction + $2,500 additional deductions (2) + $8,100 personal exemptions (2)
Married, filing a separate return	$ 4,050	$4,050 personal exemption
Head of household	$13,350	$9,300 standard deduction + $4,050 personal exemption
Head of household, 65 or older	$14,900	$9,300 standard deduction + $1,550 additional deduction + $4,050 personal exemption
Surviving spouse with a dependent child	$16,650	$12,600 standard deduction + $4,050 personal exemption
Surviving spouse, 65 or older, with a dependent child	$17,900	$12,600 standard deduction + $1,250 additional deduction + $4,050 personal exemption

Whether a taxpayer is due a refund (which occurs when taxes paid exceed tax liability) does *not* determine whether a taxpayer must file a tax return. Gross income determines whether a tax return is required. Further, note that a taxpayer whose gross income falls below the respective threshold is not precluded from filing a tax

[1]Estates file income tax returns during the administration period (i.e., before all of the estate assets are distributed).
[2]IRC §6012. We describe the standard deduction and personal exemptions in detail later in the text.

return. Indeed, taxpayers due a refund *should* file a tax return to receive the refund (or claim a refundable tax credit), even if they are not required to file a tax return.

Tax Return Due Date and Extensions

Like the filing requirements, due dates for tax returns vary based on the type of taxpayer. Individual tax returns are due on the fifteenth day of the fourth month following year-end—that is, April 15 for calendar-year individuals. (Due dates that fall on a Saturday, Sunday, or holidays are automatically extended to the next day that is not a Saturday, Sunday, or holiday.) Similarly, tax returns for taxable corporations ("C" corporations) are generally due on the fifteenth day of the fourth month following the corporation's year-end. The exception is for tax returns for C corporations with a June 30 year-end, which are due on the fifteenth day of the third month (September 15th). For both partnerships and S corporations (generally nontaxable corporations), tax returns must be filed by the fifteenth day of the third month following the entity's year-end (March 15 for calendar-year partnerships or S corporations). Any individual, partnership, or S corporation unable to file a tax return by the original due date can, by that same deadline, request a six-month extension to file, which is granted automatically by the IRS. Similarly, C corporations may request an automatic five-, six-, or seven-month extension to file depending on the corporation's year-end.[3]

An extension allows the taxpayer to delay filing a tax return but does *not* extend the due date for tax payments. Thus, when a taxpayer files an extension, she must estimate how much tax will be owed. If a taxpayer fails to pay the entire balance of tax owed by the original due date of the tax return, the IRS charges the taxpayer interest on the underpayment from the due date of the return until the taxpayer pays the tax.[4] The interest rate charged depends on taxpayer type (individual or corporation) and varies quarterly with the federal short-term interest rate.[5] For example, the interest rate for tax underpayments for individuals equals the federal short-term rate plus three percentage points.[6]

What happens if the taxpayer does not file a tax return by the time required, whether April 15 or an extended deadline? As you might guess, the IRS imposes penalties on taxpayers failing to comply with the tax law. In many cases, the penalties can be quite substantial (see later discussion in this chapter). In the case of failure to file a tax return, the penalty equals 5 percent of the tax due for each month (or partial month) that the return is late. However, the maximum penalty is generally 25 percent of the tax owed, and the failure-to-file penalty does not apply if the taxpayer owes no tax.

Statute of Limitations

Despite the diligent efforts of taxpayers and tax professionals, it is quite common for tax returns to contain mistakes. Some may be to the taxpayer's advantage and others may be to the government's advantage. Regardless of the nature of the mistake, the taxpayer is obligated to file an amended return to correct the error (and request a refund or pay a deficiency) if the statute of limitations has not expired for the tax return. Likewise, the IRS can propose adjustments to the taxpayer's return if the statute of limitations for the return has not expired.

By law, the **statute of limitations** defines the period in which the taxpayer can file an amended tax return or the IRS can assess a tax deficiency for a specific tax year. For both amended tax returns filed by a taxpayer and proposed tax assessments by the IRS, the statute of limitations generally ends three years from the *later* of (1) the date the tax return was actually filed or (2) the tax return's original due date.

---

[3]Calendar year-end C corporations may request a five-month extension, and June 30 year-end C corporations may request a seven-month extension. All other C corporations may request a six-month extension.

[4]The tax law also imposes a penalty for late payment in addition to the interest charged on the underpayment. We briefly discuss this penalty later in the chapter and in Chapter 8.

[5]The federal short-term rate is determined from a one-month average of the market yields from marketable obligations of the United States with maturities of three years or less.

[6]This same interest rate applies to individuals who overpay their taxes (i.e., receive a tax refund and interest payment as a result of an IRS audit or from filing an amended tax return).

The statute of limitations for IRS assessment can be extended in certain circumstances. For example, a six-year statute of limitations applies to IRS assessments if the taxpayer omits items of gross income that exceed 25 percent of the gross income reported on the tax return. For fraudulent returns, or if the taxpayer fails to file a tax return, the news is understandably worse. The statute of limitations remains open indefinitely in these cases.

Example 2-1

Bill and Mercedes file their 2012 federal tax return on September 6, 2013, after receiving an automatic extension to file their return by October 16, 2013 (October 15 was a Sunday). In 2016, the IRS selects their 2012 tax return for audit. When does the statute of limitations end for Bill and Mercedes's 2012 tax return?

Answer: Assuming the six-year and "unlimited" statute of limitation rules do not apply, the statute of limitations ends on September 6, 2016 (three years after the later of the actual filing date and the *original* due date).

What if: When would the statute of limitations end for Bill and Mercedes for their 2012 tax return if the couple filed the return on March 22, 2013 (before the original due date of April 15, 2013)?

Answer: In this scenario the statute of limitations would end on April 15, 2016, because the later of the actual filing date and the original due date is April 15, 2013.

Taxpayers should prepare for the possibility of an audit by retaining all supporting documents (receipts, cancelled checks, etc.) for a tax return until the statute of limitations expires. After the statute of limitations expires, taxpayers can discard the majority of supporting documents but should still keep a copy of the tax return itself, as well as any documents that may have ongoing significance, such as those establishing the taxpayer's *basis* or original investment in existing assets like personal residences and long-term investments.

LO 2-2 IRS AUDIT SELECTION

Why me? This is a recurring question in life and definitely a common taxpayer question after receiving an IRS audit notice. The answer, in general, is that a taxpayer's return is selected for audit because the IRS has data suggesting the taxpayer's tax return has a high probability of a significant understated tax liability. Budget constraints limit the IRS's ability to audit a majority or even a large minority of tax returns. Currently, fewer than 2 percent of all tax returns are audited. Thus, the IRS must be strategic in selecting returns for audit in an effort to promote the highest level of voluntary taxpayer compliance and increase tax revenues.

Specifically, how does the IRS select tax returns for audit? The IRS uses a number of computer programs and outside data sources (newspapers, financial statement disclosures, informants, and other public and private sources) to identify tax returns that may have an understated tax liability. Common computer initiatives include the **DIF (Discriminant Function) system, document perfection program,** and **information matching program.** The most important of these initiatives is the DIF system. The DIF system assigns a score to each tax return that represents the probability the tax liability on the return has been underreported (a higher score = a higher likelihood of underreporting). The IRS derives the weights assigned to specific tax return attributes from historical IRS audit adjustment data from the National Research Program.[7] The DIF system then uses these (undisclosed) weights to score each tax return

[7]Similar to its predecessor, the Taxpayer Compliance Measurement Program, the National Research Program (NRP) analyzes a large sample of tax returns that are randomly selected for audit. From these randomly selected returns, the IRS identifies tax return characteristics (e.g., deductions for a home office, unusually high tax deductions relative to a taxpayer's income) associated with underreported liabilities, weights these characteristics, and then incorporates them into the DIF system. The NRP analyzes randomly selected returns to ensure that the DIF scorings are representative of the population of tax returns.

based on the tax return's characteristics. Returns with higher DIF scores are then reviewed to determine whether an audit is the best course of action.

All returns are checked for mathematical and tax calculation errors, a process referred to as the document perfection program. Individual returns are also subject to the information matching program. This program compares the taxpayer's tax return to information submitted to the IRS from other taxpayers like banks, employers, mutual funds, brokerage companies, and mortgage companies. Information matched includes items such as wages (Form W-2 submitted by employers), interest income (Form 1099-INT submitted by banks), and dividend income (Form 1099-DIV submitted by brokerage companies). For tax returns identified as incorrect via the document perfection and information matching programs, the IRS recalculates the taxpayer's tax liability and sends a notice explaining the adjustment. If the taxpayer owes tax, the IRS will request payment of the tax due. If the taxpayer overpaid tax, the IRS will send the taxpayer a refund of the overpayment.

In addition to computer-based methods for identifying tax returns for audit, the IRS may use a number of other audit initiatives that target taxpayers in certain industries, engaged in certain transactions like the acquisition of other companies, or having specific attributes like home office deductions. Taxpayers of a given size and complexity, such as large publicly traded companies, may be audited every year.

TAXES IN THE REAL WORLD Turning in Your Neighbor Can Pay Big Bucks

The Wall Street Journal reported that in April 2011 the IRS paid its first payment under its new taxpayer whistleblower program that promises large rewards for turning in tax cheats. Under the large-award whistleblower program (where unpaid taxes, interest, and penalties exceed $2 million and the tax cheat, if an individual, had gross income exceeding $200,000 in at least one year), whistleblowers can be paid between 15 and 30 percent of the taxes, interest, and penalties collected by the IRS. Under the small-award whistleblower program (tax, interest, and penalty underpayments of $2 million or less), the IRS may pay whistleblowers up to 15 percent of the unpaid taxes and interest collected. Whistleblowers use IRS Form 211 (www.IRS.gov)

to apply for the program, and as you might expect, all whistleblower payments received are fully taxable. In its first payment, the IRS paid $4.5 million to a former in-house accountant for a large financial services firm. Given the potential windfall to whistleblowers, you might expect a long line of "concerned" citizens applying for the program. You would be correct. As of July 2015, the IRS Commissioner announced that the IRS has paid out more than $238 million in awards in the preceding four years, on collection of more than $1.3 billion based on whistleblower information.

Based on: "Taxes: How to Turn in Your Neighbor to the IRS," *The Wall Street Journal*, WSJ.com, September 3, 2011.

How was Bill and Mercedes's tax return selected for audit? Given the audit focus on certain deductions, the IRS likely selected their return for audit because the amount or type of the deductions resulted in a high DIF score. IRS personnel then determined that the deductions warranted further review and, thus, selected the tax return for audit.

ETHICS

After Bill and Mercedes's tax return was selected for audit, Bill read on the Internet speculation that filing a paper copy tax return (instead of filing electronically) and extending a tax return decrease

the chance of IRS audit. Bill has convinced Mercedes that they need to use these strategies going forward and look for other ways to avoid audit. Has Bill crossed an ethical boundary?

Types of Audits

The three types of IRS audits are correspondence, office, and field examinations. **Correspondence examinations** are the most common. These audits, as the name suggests, are conducted by mail and generally are limited to one or two items on the taxpayer's return. Of the three types of audits, correspondence audits are generally the narrowest in scope and the least complex. The IRS typically requests supporting documentation for one or more items on the taxpayer's return, like charitable contributions deducted, for example. When appropriate documentation is promptly supplied, these audits typically can be concluded relatively quickly. Of course, they can also be expanded to address other issues that arise as a result of the IRS's inspection of taxpayer documents.

Office examinations are the second most common audit. As the name suggests, the IRS conducts them at its local office. These audits are typically broader in scope and more complex than correspondence examinations. Small businesses, taxpayers operating sole proprietorships, and middle- to high-income individual taxpayers are more likely, if audited, to have office examinations. In these examinations, the taxpayer receives a notice that identifies the items subject to audit; requests substantiation for these items as necessary; and notifies the taxpayer of the date, time, and location of the exam. Taxpayers may attend the examination alone, with representation, such as their tax adviser or attorney, or simply let their tax adviser or attorney attend on the taxpayer's behalf.

Field examinations are the least common audit. The IRS conducts these at the taxpayer's place of business or the location where the taxpayer's books, records, and source documents are maintained. Field examinations are generally the broadest in scope and the most complex of the three audit types. They can last months to years and generally are limited to business returns and the most complex individual returns.

What type of exam do you think Bill and Mercedes will have? Because their return is an individual tax return and the audit is restricted to a relatively narrow set of deductions, their return will likely be subject to a correspondence audit. If the audit were broader in scope, an office examination would be more likely.

After the Audit After the examination, the IRS agent provides a list of proposed adjustments (if any) to the taxpayer for review. If he or she agrees to the proposed changes, the taxpayer signs an agreement form (Form 870) and pays the additional tax owed or receives the proposed refund. If the taxpayer disputes the proposed changes, the taxpayer will receive a **30-day letter** giving him or her 30 days to either (1) request a conference with an appeals officer, who is independent and resides in a separate IRS division from the examining agent, or (2) agree to the proposed adjustment. An appeals officer would consider the merits of the unresolved issues as well as the "hazards of litigation"—that is, the probability that the IRS will lose if the case is brought to court and the resulting costs of a taxpayer-favorable ruling. If the taxpayer chooses the appeals conference and reaches an agreement with the IRS there, the taxpayer can then sign Form 870. If the taxpayer and IRS still do not agree on the proposed adjustment at the appeals conference, or the taxpayer chooses not to request an appeals conference, the IRS will send the taxpayer a 90-day letter. See Exhibit 2-2.

The **90-day letter** (also known as a *statutory notice of deficiency*) explains that the taxpayer has 90 days to either (1) pay the proposed deficiency or (2) file a petition in the U.S. Tax Court to hear the case.[8] The **U.S. Tax Court** is a national court whose judges are tax experts and who hear only tax cases. If the taxpayer would like to litigate the case but prefers it to be heard in the local **U.S. District Court** or the **U.S. Court of Federal Claims,** the taxpayer must pay the tax deficiency first, then request a refund from the IRS, and then sue the IRS for refund in the court after the IRS denies the refund claim.

Why would a taxpayer prefer one trial court over others? To understand this, we must appreciate the basic distinguishing factors of each. First and foremost, it is relatively common for the U.S. Tax Court, local U.S. District Court, or the U.S. Court of

---

THE KEY FACTS

IRS Audits

- The three types of IRS audits are correspondence, office, and field examinations.
- After the audit, the IRS will send the taxpayer a 30-day letter, which provides the taxpayer the opportunity to pay the proposed assessment or request an appeals conference.
- If an agreement is not reached at appeals or the taxpayer does not pay the proposed assessment, the IRS will send the taxpayer a 90-day letter.
- After receiving the 90-day letter, the taxpayer may pay the tax or petition the U.S. Tax Court to hear the case.
- If the taxpayer chooses to pay the tax, the taxpayer may then request a refund of the tax and eventually sue the IRS for refund in the U.S. District Court or the U.S. Court of Federal Claims.

---

[8]If the taxpayer lacks the funds to pay the assessed tax, there is legitimate doubt as to whether the taxpayer owes part or all of the assessed tax, or collection of the tax would cause the taxpayer economic hardship or be unfair or inequitable, the taxpayer can request an offer in compromise with the IRS to settle the tax liability for less than the full amount assessed by completing Form 656.

EXHIBIT 2-2   IRS Appeals/Litigation Process

IRS Exam: © Royalty-Free/Corbis, Supreme Court: © McGraw-Hill Education/Jill Braaten, photographer, File Claim: © Michael A. Keller/Corbis

Federal Claims to interpret and rule differently on the same basic tax issue. Given a choice of courts, the taxpayer should prefer the court most likely to rule favorably on his or her particular issues. The courts also differ in other ways. For example, the U.S. District Court is the only court that provides for a jury trial; the U.S. Tax Court is the only court that allows tax cases to be heard *before* the taxpayer pays the disputed liability and the only court with a small claims division (hearing claims involving disputed liabilities of $50,000 or less); the U.S. Tax Court judges are tax experts, whereas the U.S. District Court and U.S. Court of Federal Claims judges are generalists. The taxpayer should consider each of these factors in choosing a trial court. For example, if the taxpayer feels very confident in her tax return position but does not have sufficient funds to pay the disputed liability, she will prefer the U.S. Tax Court. If, instead, the taxpayer is litigating a tax return position that is low on technical merit but high on emotional appeal, a jury trial in the local U.S. District Court may be the best option.

What happens after the taxpayer's case is decided in a trial court? The process may not be quite finished. After the trial court's verdict, the losing party has the right to request one of the 13 **U.S. Circuit Courts of Appeals** to hear the case. Exhibit 2-3 depicts the specific appellant courts for each lower-level court. Both the U.S. Tax Court and local U.S. District Court cases are appealed to the specific U.S. Circuit Court of Appeals based on the taxpayer's residence.[9] Cases litigated in Alabama, Florida, and

[9]Decisions rendered by the U.S. Tax Court Small Claims Division cannot be appealed by the taxpayer or the IRS.

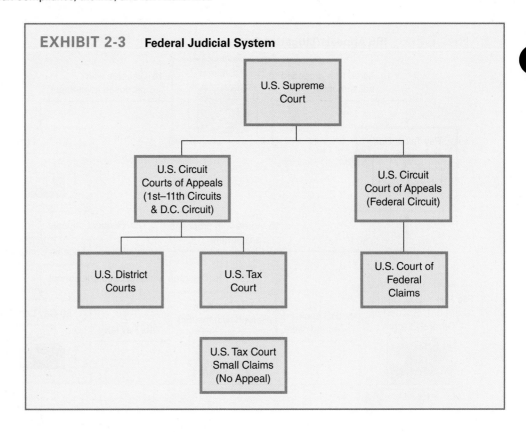

EXHIBIT 2-3   Federal Judicial System

Georgia, for example, appeal to the U.S. Circuit Court of Appeals for the 11th Circuit; whereas those tried in Louisiana, Mississippi, and Texas appeal to the 5th Circuit. In contrast, all U.S. Court of Federal Claims cases appeal to the U.S. Circuit Court of Appeals for the Federal Circuit (located in Washington, D.C.). Exhibit 2-4 depicts the geographic regions for each of the 11 U.S. Circuit Courts of Appeal defined by numerical region. Not depicted are the U.S. Circuit Court of Appeals for the District of Columbia and the U.S. Circuit Court of Appeals for the Federal Circuit.

Through the initial selection of a trial court—U.S. District Court, U.S. Tax Court, or U.S. Court of Federal Claims—the taxpayer has the ability to determine which circuit court would hear an appeal of the case (the U.S. Circuit Court of Appeals based on residence or the U.S. Circuit Court of Appeals for the Federal Circuit). Because alternative circuit courts may interpret the law differently, the taxpayer should consider in choosing a trial-level court the relevant circuit courts' judicial histories to determine which circuit court (and thus, which trial court) would be more likely to rule in his or her favor.

After an appeals court hears a case, the losing party has one last option to receive a favorable ruling: a petition to the **U.S. Supreme Court** to hear the case. However, given the quantity of other cases appealed to the U.S. Supreme Court that are of national importance, the Supreme Court agrees to hear only a few tax cases a year with great significance to a broad cross-section of taxpayers, or cases litigating issues in which there has been disagreement among the circuit courts. For most tax cases, the Supreme Court refuses to hear the case (denies the ***writ of certiorari***) and litigation ends with the circuit court decision.

Although litigation of tax disputes is quite common, taxpayers should carefully consider the pros and cons. Litigation can be very costly financially and emotionally, and thus it is more appropriately used as an option of last resort, after all other appeal efforts have been exhausted.

What is the likely course of action for Bill and Mercedes's audit? It is too soon to tell. Before you can assess the likely outcome of their audit, you need a better understanding of both the audit issue and the relevant tax laws that apply to the

EXHIBIT 2-4 Geographic Boundaries for the U.S. Circuit Courts of Appeal

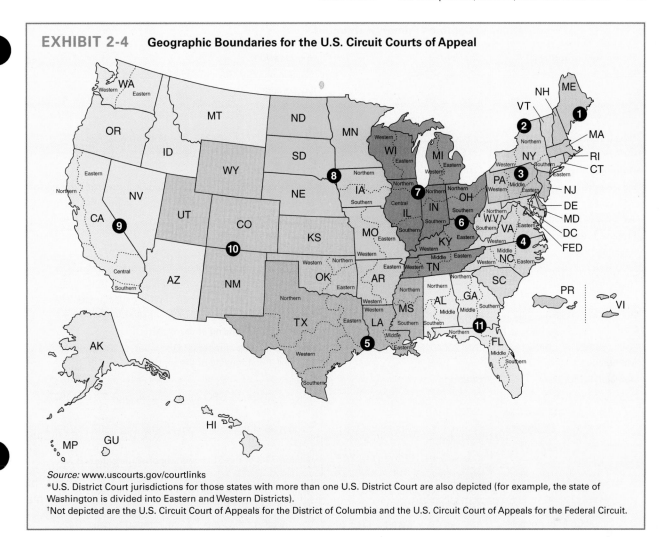

Source: www.uscourts.gov/courtlinks

*U.S. District Court jurisdictions for those states with more than one U.S. District Court are also depicted (for example, the state of Washington is divided into Eastern and Western Districts).

†Not depicted are the U.S. Circuit Court of Appeals for the District of Columbia and the U.S. Circuit Court of Appeals for the Federal Circuit.

issue. The next section explains alternative tax law sources. After we discuss the various sources of our tax laws, we'll describe how Bill and Mercedes (or their CPA) can research the sources to identify the best possible course of action.[10]

TAX LAW SOURCES

LO 2-3 LO 2-4

There are two broad categories of tax authorities: primary authorities and secondary authorities. **Primary authorities** are official sources of the tax law generated by the legislative branch (statutory authority issued by Congress), judicial branch (rulings by the U.S. District Court, U.S. Tax Court, U.S. Court of Federal Claims, U.S. Circuit Court of Appeals, or U.S. Supreme Court), and executive/administrative branch (Treasury and IRS pronouncements). Exhibit 2-5 displays the most common primary sources, their respective citations, and related explanations. We'll discuss each of these authorities below.

Secondary authorities are unofficial tax authorities that interpret and explain the primary authorities, such as tax research services (discussed below), tax articles from professional journals and law reviews, newsletters, and textbooks. For quick questions, practitioners often use the *CCH Master Tax Guide* or *RIA Federal Tax Handbook*.

---

[10]Accountants should be mindful to not engage in the unauthorized practice of law. In years past, several court cases have addressed this issue without providing a clear understanding between practicing tax accounting and the unauthorized practice of law. At present, tax accountants are not likely to overstep their responsibilities if they limit their advice to tax issues and leave the general legal advice and drafting of legal documents to attorneys.

EXHIBIT 2-5 **Citations to Common Primary Authorities**

Statutory Authorities:	Citation:	Explanation:
Internal Revenue Code	IRC Sec. 162(e)(2)(B)(i)	Section number 162, subsection e, paragraph 2, subparagraph B, clause i
Committee Reports: Senate Finance Committee Report	S. Rep. No. 353, 82d Cong., 1st Sess. 14 (1951).	Senate report number 353, Congress number 82, Congressional session 1, page number 14, year 1951
House Ways and Means Committee Report	H. Rep. No. 242, 82d Cong., 1st Sess. 40 (1951)	House report number 242, Congress number 82, Congressional session 1, page number 40, year 1951
Administrative Authorities:	**Citation:**	**Explanation:**
Final Regulation	Reg. Sec. 1.217-2(c)(1)	Type of regulation (1 = income tax), code section 217, regulation number 2, paragraph number c, subparagraph number 1
Temporary Regulation	Temp. Reg. Sec. 1.217-2(c)(1)	Same as final regulation
Proposed Regulation	Prop. Reg. Sec. 1.217-2(c)(1)	Same as final regulation
Revenue Ruling	Rev. Rul. 77-262, 1977-2 C.B. 41	Ruling number 77-262 (262nd ruling of 1977), volume number of cumulative bulletin 1977-2, page number 41
Revenue Procedure	Rev. Proc. 99-10, 1999-1 C.B. 272	Procedure number 99-10 (10th procedure of 1999), volume number of cumulative bulletin 1999-1, page number 272
Private Letter Ruling	PLR 200601001	Year 2006, week number 01 (1st week of 2006), ruling number 001 (1st ruling of the week)
Technical Advice Memorandum	TAM 200402001	Year 2004, week number 02 (2nd week of 2004), ruling number 001 (1st ruling of the week)
Judicial Authorities:	**Citation:**	
U.S. Supreme Court	*Comm. v. Kowalski*, 434 U.S. 77 (S. Ct., 1977)	Volume 434 of the GPO court reporter, page 77, year 1977
	Comm. v. Kowalski, 98 S. Ct. 315 (S. Ct., 1977)	Volume 98 of the West court reporter, page 315, year 1977
	Comm. v. Kowalski, 77-2 USTC par. 9,748 (S. Ct., 1977)	Volume 77-2 of the CCH court reporter, paragraph 9,748, year 1977
	Comm. v. Kowalski, 40 AFTR2d 77-6128 (S. Ct., 1977)	Volume 40 of the RIA AFTR2d court reporter, paragraph 77-6128, year 1977
U.S. Circuit Court of Appeals	*Azar Nut Co. v. Comm.*, 931 F.2d 314 (5th Cir., 1991)	Volume 931 of the West F.2d court reporter, page 314, circuit 5th, year 1991
	Azar Nut Co. v. Comm., 91-1 USTC par. 50,257 (5th Cir., 1991)	Volume 91-1 of the CCH USTC court reporter, paragraph 50,257, circuit 5th, year 1991
	Azar Nut Co. v. Comm., 67 AFTR2d 91-987 (5th Cir., 1991)	Volume 67 of the RIA AFTR2d court reporter, paragraph 77-6128, year 1977
U.S. Tax Court—Regular decision	*L.A. Beeghly*, 36 TC 154 (1962)	Volume 36 of the Tax Court reporter, page 154, year 1962
U.S. Tax Court—Memorandum decision	*Robert Rodriguez*, RIA TC Memo 2005-012	Paragraph number 2005-012 of the RIA Tax Court Memorandum reporter
	Robert Rodriguez, 85 TCM 1162 (2005)	Volume 85 of the CCH Tax Court Memorandum reporter, page 1162, year 2005
U.S. Court of Federal Claims	*J.R. Cohen v. U.S.*, 510 F. Supp. 297 (Fed. Cl., 1993)	Volume 510 of the West F. Supp. court reporter, page 297, year 1993
	J.R. Cohen v. U.S., 72 AFTR2d 93-5124 (Fed. Cl., 1993)	Volume 72 of the RIA AFTR2d court reporter, paragraph 93-5124, year 1993
	J.R. Cohen v. U.S., 93-1 USTC par. 50,354 (Fed. Cl., 1993)	Volume 93-1 of the CCH USTC court reporter, paragraph 50,354, year 1993
U.S. District Court	*Waxler Towing Co., Inc. v. U.S.*, 510 F. Supp. 297 (W.D, TN, 1981)	Volume 510 of the West F. Supp. court reporter, page 297, Western District (W.D.), state Tennessee, year 1981
	Waxler Towing Co., Inc. v. U.S., 81-2 USTC par. 9,541 (W.D., TN, 1981)	Volume 81-2 of the CCH USTC court reporter, paragraph 9,541, Western District (W.D.), state Tennessee, year 1981
	Waxler Towing Co., Inc. v. U.S., 48 AFTR2d 81-5274 (W.D., TN, 1981)	Volume 48 of the RIA AFTR2d court reporter, paragraph 81-5274, Western District (W.D.), state Tennessee, year 1981

EXHIBIT 2-6   Common Secondary Tax Authorities

Tax Research Services:	***Professional Journals:***
BNA Tax Management Portfolios	*Journal of Accountancy*
CCH Standard Federal Tax Reporter	*Journal of Taxation*
CCH Tax Research Consultant	*Practical Tax Strategies*
RIA Federal Tax Coordinator	*Taxes*
RIA United States Tax Reporter	*Tax Adviser*
Newsletters:	***Quick Reference Sources:***
Daily Tax Report	*IRS Publications*
Federal Tax Weekly Alert	*CCH Master Tax Guide*
Tax Notes	*RIA Federal Tax Handbook*
Law Reviews:	***Textbooks:***
Tax Law Review (New York University School of Law)	*McGraw-Hill's Taxation of Individuals and Business Entities*
Virginia Tax Review (University of Virginia School of Law)	*McGraw-Hill's Essentials of Federal Taxation*

Secondary authorities may be very helpful in understanding a tax issue, but they hold little weight in a tax dispute (hence their "unofficial" status). Thus, tax advisers should always be careful to verify their understanding of tax law by examining primary authorities directly and to *never* cite secondary authority in a research memo. Exhibit 2-6 lists some of the common sources of secondary authority.

TAXES IN THE REAL WORLD   Google: Not Authoritative on Tax Matters

While Internet super giant Google may be the king of all cyberspace knowledge, the Tax Court ruled in *Woodard v. Comm.*, TC Summary Opinion 2009-150, that a Google search does not constitute reasonable cause to excuse a Harvard MBA/CPA from taking an incorrect tax return position. The Tax Court noted that although the taxpayer had not worked as an accountant for years before filing his tax return, "his accounting degree, MBA, and CPA training, no matter how stale, undoubtedly taught him what sources could be relied upon as definitive; such as, for example, the Internal Revenue Code and the income tax regulations, both of which are readily available on the Internet."

Legislative Sources: Congress and the Constitution

The three legislative or statutory tax authorities are the U.S. Constitution, the Internal Revenue Code, and tax treaties. The **U.S. Constitution** is the highest authority in the United States, but it provides very little in the way of tax law since it contains no discussion of tax rates, taxable income, or other details. Instead, the 16th Amendment provides Congress the ability to tax income directly, from whatever source derived, without apportionment across the states.

Various attempts to amend the U.S. Constitution with regard to taxation—for example, one effort to repeal the 16th Amendment entirely and one to require a two-thirds majority in both houses to raise taxes—have so far met with failure.

Internal Revenue Code   The second (and main) statutory authority is the **Internal Revenue Code of 1986,** as amended, known as the Code. The Internal Revenue Code has the same authoritative weight as tax treaties and Supreme Court rulings. Thus, a taxpayer should feel very confident in a tax return position, such as taking a deduction that is specifically allowed by the Code. The Internal Revenue Code is unique in that every other authority—all administrative and judicial authorities except tax treaties

EXHIBIT 2-7 **Tax Legislation Process**

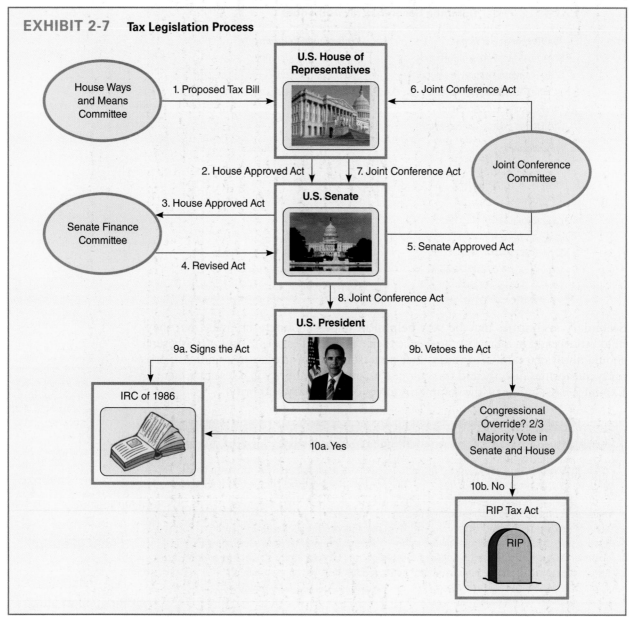

US House: © Dwight Nadig/Getty Images, US Senate: © Brand X Pictures/PunchStock, President: Library of Congress Prints and Photographs Division [LC-DIG-ppbd-00358]

and the Constitution—can be seen as an interpretation of it. Hence, understanding the relevant code section(s) is critical to being an efficient and effective tax professional.

Congress enacts tax legislation virtually every year that changes the Code; 1986 was simply the last major overhaul. Prior to 1986, tax law changes were incorporated into the Internal Revenue Code of 1954, the year a new numbering system and other significant changes were introduced. Before that, tax law changes were incorporated into the Internal Revenue Code of 1939, which was the year the tax law was first codified.

The Legislative Process for Tax Laws Exhibit 2-7 illustrates the legislative process for enacting tax laws. As required by the U.S. Constitution (Article 1, Section 7), "All bills for raising revenue shall originate in the House of Representatives." The Senate may propose tax legislation, but the first to formally consider a bill will be the House, typically within its Ways and Means Committee. After the committee debates the proposed legislation and drafts a bill, the bill goes to the House of Representatives floor for debate and ultimately a vote (either yea or nay without modification). If the bill is approved, it becomes an *act* and is sent to the Senate, which typically refers the act to the Senate Finance Committee. Not to be outdone by the House, the Senate Finance Committee usually amends the act during its deliberations. After the revised act passes the Senate Finance Committee, it goes to the Senate for debate and vote. Unlike representatives, senators may modify the proposed legislation during their debate.

If the Senate passes the act, both the House and Senate versions of the legislation are sent to the Joint Conference Committee, which consists of members of the House Ways and Means Committee and the Senate Finance Committee. During the Joint Conference Committee deliberations, committee members debate the two versions of the proposed legislation. Possible outcomes for any specific provision in the proposed legislation include adoption of the Senate version, the House version, or some compromise version of the two acts. Likewise, the Joint Conference Committee may simply choose to eliminate specific provisions from the proposed legislation or fail to reach a compromise, thereby terminating the legislation.

After the Joint Conference Committee approves the act, the revised legislation is sent to the House and Senate for vote. If both the House and Senate approve it, the act is sent to the president for his or her signature. If the president signs the act, it becomes law and is incorporated into the Internal Revenue Code of 1986 (Title 26 of the U.S. Code, which contains *all* codified laws of the United States). If the president vetoes the legislation, Congress may override the veto with a two-thirds positive vote in both the House and the Senate.

The House Ways and Means Committee, Senate Finance Committee, and Joint Conference Committee each produce a committee report that explains the current tax law, proposed change in the law, and reasons for the change. These committee reports are considered statutory sources of the tax law and may be very useful in interpreting tax law changes and understanding congressional intent. This is especially important after new legislation has been enacted because, with the exception of the Code, there will be very little authority interpreting the new law (i.e., no judicial or administrative authorities because of the time it takes for the new law to be litigated or for the IRS to issue interpretative guidance).

Basic Organization of the Code   The Internal Revenue Code is segregated into subtitles, chapters, subchapters, parts, subparts, and sections. All existing and any new tax laws are placed in the Code within a specific subtitle, chapter, subchapter, part, subpart, and section of the Code. When referencing a tax law, the researcher generally refers to the law simply by its code section. Code sections are numbered from 1 to 9833, with gaps in the section numbers to allow new code sections to be added to the appropriate parts of the Code as needed. Each code section is further segregated into subsections, paragraphs, subparagraphs, and clauses to allow more specific reference or citation. See Exhibit 2-5 for an example code citation and explanation.

Memorizing the various subtitles and chapters of the Code has limited value (except to impress your friends at parties). However, understanding the *organization* of the Code is important, especially for the aspiring tax accountant. (See Exhibit 2-8.) First, you must understand the organization of a code section, its subsections, paragraphs, subparagraphs, and clauses to be able to cite the respective law correctly as, for example, IRC Sec. 162(b)(2). Second, note that many provisions in the Code apply only to specific parts of the Code. For example, it is quite common for a code section to include the phrase "for purposes of this chapter, ..." If you do not understand what laws are encompassed in the chapter, it would be very difficult for you to interpret the code section and determine its applicability to a research question.

Finally, remember that code sections addressing similar transactions, such as deductions, or topics, such as C corporations, are grouped together. Consider a researcher faced with the question of whether an item of income is taxable. If the researcher understands the organization of the Code, she can quickly focus her research on code sections 61–140, which provide a broad definition of gross income, list items specifically included in gross income, and identify items specifically excluded from gross income.

EXHIBIT 2-8   Example of Code Organization

Subtitle A—Income Taxes

Chapter 1—Income Taxes

Subchapter A—Determination of Tax Liability

Part I—Definition of Gross Income, Adjusted Gross Income, Taxable Income, etc. (Sec. 61–68)

Sec. 61—Gross Income Defined

Sec. 62—Adjusted Gross Income Defined

Sec. 63—Taxable Income Defined

Subsection 63(c)—Standard Deduction

Paragraph 63(c)(2)—Basic Standard Deduction

Subparagraph 63(c)(2)(A)

Clause 63(c)(2)(A)(i)

Part II—Items Specifically Included in Gross Income (Sec. 71–90)

Sec. 71—Alimony

Sec. 72—Annuities

Sec. 73—Services of Child

Sec. 74—Prizes & Awards

Part III—Items Specifically Excluded from Gross Income (Sec. 101–140)

Sec. 101—Certain Death Benefits

Sec. 102—Gifts and Inheritances

Sec. 103—Interest on State & Local Bonds

Tax Treaties   **Tax treaties** are negotiated agreements between countries that describe the tax treatment of entities subject to tax in both countries, such as U.S. citizens earning investment income in Spain. The U.S. president has the authority to enter into a tax treaty with another country after receiving the Senate's advice. If you are a U.S. citizen earning income abroad or an accountant with international clients, you need knowledge of U.S. tax laws, the foreign country's tax laws, and the respective tax treaty between the U.S. and the foreign country for efficient tax planning. Because the focus in this text is on U.S. tax laws, we only briefly mention the importance of tax treaties as a statutory authority.

Example 2-2

Bill recently spent a summer in Milan, Italy, teaching a graduate level economics course. While in Italy he earned a $20,000 stipend from Bocconi University and some interest in a temporary banking account that he established for the trip. What tax laws must Bill consider to determine the taxation of his $20,000 stipend?

Answer: U.S. tax laws, Italian tax laws, and the U.S.–Italy tax treaty will determine the tax consequences of the amounts Bill earned in Italy.

THE KEY FACTS

Judicial Authorities

- Our judicial system is tasked with the ultimate authority to interpret the Internal Revenue Code and settle disputes between taxpayers and the IRS.
- The Supreme Court is the highest judicial authority.
- Beneath the Supreme Court, the decisions of the 13 Circuit Courts of Appeal represent the next highest judicial authority.

(continued)

Judicial Sources: The Courts

Our judicial system has the ultimate authority to interpret the Internal Revenue Code and settle disputes between the IRS and taxpayers. As Exhibit 2-3 illustrates, there are five basic sources of judicial authority (three trial-level courts, 13 U.S. Circuit Courts of Appeal, and the Supreme Court). We've noted that the Supreme Court, along with the Code, represents the highest tax-specific authority. An important distinction between the two, however, is that the Supreme Court does not establish law, but instead simply interprets and applies the Code (along with other authorities). Thus, the Code and the Supreme Court should never be in conflict.[11]

[11]The Supreme Court does have the authority to declare a Code provision unconstitutional.

Below the Supreme Court, the decisions of the 13 U.S. Circuit Courts of Appeal represent the next highest judicial authority. The lowest level of judicial authority consists of three different types of trial-level courts (94 U.S. District Courts that hear cases involving taxpayers that reside within their respective district, the U.S. Court of Federal Claims, and the U.S. Tax Court). Given that the U.S. Tax Court hears only tax cases and that its judges are "tax experts," its decisions typically have more weight than those rendered by a district court or the U.S. Court of Federal Claims.[12] Likewise, because the U.S. Court of Federal Claims hears a much narrower set of issues than U.S. District Courts (only monetary claims against the U.S. government), its decisions have more weight than district court decisions.

In rendering court decisions, all courts apply the judicial doctrine of *stare decisis.* This doctrine means that a court will rule consistently with (a) its previous rulings (unless, due to evolving interpretations of the tax law over time, the court decides to overturn an earlier decision) and (b) the rulings of higher courts with appellate jurisdiction (the courts its cases are appealed to). The implication of *stare decisis* is that a circuit court will abide by Supreme Court rulings and its own rulings, whereas a trial-level court will abide by Supreme Court rulings, its respective circuit court's rulings, and its own rulings. For example, a district court in California would follow U.S. 9th Circuit and Supreme Court rulings as well as the court's own rulings.

The doctrine of *stare decisis* presents a special problem for the U.S. Tax Court because it appeals to different circuit courts based on the taxpayer's residence. To implement the doctrine of *stare decisis,* the tax court applies the **Golsen rule.**[13] The Golsen rule simply states that the tax court will abide by rulings of the circuit court that has appellate jurisdiction for a case.

> - The lowest level of judicial authority consists of three different types of trial-level courts (U.S. District Courts, U.S. Court of Federal Claims, and the U.S. Tax Court).
> - U.S. Tax Court decisions typically are considered to have more authoritative weight than decisions rendered by a district court or the U.S. Court of Federal Claims.
> - All courts apply the judicial doctrine of *stare decisis,* which means that a court will rule consistently with its previous rulings and the rulings of higher courts with appellate jurisdiction.

Example 2-3

What if: If Bill and Mercedes opt to litigate their case in the U.S. Tax Court, by which circuit court's rulings will the court abide?

Answer: Because Bill and Mercedes live in Florida, the U.S. Tax Court will abide the circuit court with appellate jurisdiction in Florida, which happens to be the U.S. 11th Circuit Court.

Administrative Sources: The U.S. Treasury

Regulations, Revenue Rulings, and Revenue Procedures   The Treasury Department, of which the IRS is a bureau, is charged with administering and interpreting the tax laws of the United States, among other duties such as printing money and advising the president on economic issues. **Regulations** are the Treasury Department's official interpretation of the Internal Revenue Code, have the highest authoritative weight, and often contain examples of the application of the Code that may be particularly helpful to the tax researcher. Regulations are issued in three different forms: final, temporary, and proposed. The names are very descriptive. **Final regulations** are regulations that have been issued in final form, and thus, unless or until revoked, they represent the Treasury's interpretation of the Code. **Temporary regulations** have a limited life (three years for regulations issued after November 20, 1988). Nonetheless, during their life, they carry the same authoritative weight as final regulations. Finally, all regulations are issued in the form of **proposed regulations** first, to allow public comment on them. Proposed regulations do not carry the same authoritative weight as temporary or final regulations.

In addition to being issued in three different forms, regulations also serve three basic purposes: interpretative, procedural, and legislative. Most regulations are issued as

> **THE KEY FACTS**
>
> **Administrative Authorities**
>
> - The Treasury Department is charged with administering and interpreting the tax laws.
> - Regulations
>   - Regulations are the Treasury Department's official interpretation of the Internal Revenue Code and have the highest authoritative weight.
>   - Regulations are issued in three different forms (proposed, temporary, and final) and serve three basic purposes (interpretative, procedural, and legislative).
>
> *(continued)*

---

[12]The Tax Court renders both "regular" and "memorandum" decisions. Regular decisions involve new or unusual points of law, whereas memorandum decisions involve questions of fact or the application of existing law. Both decisions have similar authoritative weight. Decisions issued by the Tax Court's Small Claims division may not be cited as precedent.

[13]54 TC 742 (1970).

interpretative or procedural regulations. As the names suggest, **interpretative regulations** represent the Treasury's interpretation of the Code. In Bill and Mercedes's case, these might be the regulations issued under IRC Sec. 163, which discuss interest deductions. **Procedural regulations** explain Treasury Department procedures as they relate to administering the Code. Again, for Bill and Mercedes's case, these might be the regulations issued under IRC Sec. 6501 regarding the statute of limitations for IRS assessment and collection. **Legislative regulations,** the rarest type, are issued when Congress specifically directs the Treasury Department to create regulations to address an issue in an area of law. In these instances, the Treasury is actually writing the law instead of interpreting the Code. Because legislative regulations represent tax law instead of interpretation of tax law, legislative regulations generally have been viewed to have more authoritative weight than interpretative and procedural regulations. However, in *Mayo Foundation for Medical Education & Research v. U.S.,* 131 S.Ct. 704 (2011), the Supreme Court held (subject to specific conditions) that all Treasury regulations warrant deference. Accordingly, it is a very difficult process to challenge any regulation and thus, taxpayers are cautioned not to take tax return positions inconsistent with regulations.

Revenue rulings and revenue procedures are second in administrative authoritative weight after regulations. But unlike regulations, revenue rulings address the application of the Code and regulations to a specific factual situation. Thus, while **revenue rulings** have less authoritative weight, they provide a much more detailed interpretation of the Code as it applies to a specific transaction and fact pattern. For example, Rev. Rul. 87-22 discusses the deductions of prepaid interest (points) a taxpayer may claim when refinancing the mortgage for a principal residence, whereas the Code and regulations do not specifically address this issue. Although revenue rulings are binding on the IRS (until revoked, superseded, or modified), courts may agree or disagree with a revenue ruling. Thus, while revenue rulings should be carefully evaluated as they represent the IRS's interpretation, courts may provide a different interpretation of the tax law that a taxpayer might choose to follow. **Revenue procedures** are also much more detailed than regulations. They explain in greater detail IRS practice and procedures in administering the tax law. For example, Rev. Proc. 87-56 provides the specific depreciation lives for depreciable assets (discussed in Chapter 10). As with revenue rulings, revenue procedures are binding on the IRS until revoked, modified, or superseded.

Letter Rulings   Below revenue rulings and revenue procedures in authoritative weight rest letter rulings. As you might guess, letter rulings are less authoritative but more specific than revenue rulings and regulations. Letter rulings generally may not be used as precedent by taxpayers. However, they may be cited as authority to avoid the substantial understatement of tax penalty under IRC Sec. 6662 imposed on taxpayers and the related tax practitioner penalty under IRC Sec. 6694 (discussed later in this chapter). **Private letter rulings** represent the IRS's application of the Code and other tax authorities to a specific transaction and taxpayer. Private letter rulings are issued in response to a taxpayer request and are common for proposed transactions with potentially large tax implications. For example, companies commonly request a private letter ruling to ensure that a proposed corporate acquisition meets the definition of a tax-free exchange. However, the IRS also maintains a list of certain issues on which it refuses to rule, such as the tax consequences of proposed federal tax legislation. Each year, the IRS publishes an updated list of these transactions in a revenue procedure.

Other types of letter rulings include determination letters and technical advice memorandums. **Determination letters,** issued by local IRS directors, are generally not controversial. An example of a determination letter is the request by an employer for the IRS to rule that the taxpayer's retirement plan is a "qualified plan." **Technical advice memorandums** differ from private letter rulings in that they are generated for completed transactions and usually are requested by an IRS agent during an IRS audit.

Is this a comprehensive list of IRS pronouncements? No. In addition to the pronouncements listed above, the IRS issues several less common types, which are beyond the scope of this text. A couple of other pronouncements, however, warrant some discussion. As we mentioned above, the IRS and taxpayers litigate tax cases in a number of courts and jurisdictions. Obviously, the IRS wins some and loses some of these cases. Except for Supreme Court cases, whenever the IRS loses, it may issue an **acquiescence** or **nonacquiescence** as guidance for how the IRS intends to respond to the loss. Although an acquiescence indicates that the IRS has decided to *follow* the court's adverse ruling in the future, it does not mean that the IRS *agrees* with it. Instead, it simply means that the IRS will no longer litigate this issue. A nonacquiescence has the exact opposite implications and alerts taxpayers that the IRS does plan to continue to litigate this issue. Finally, the IRS also issues **actions on decisions,** which explain the background reasoning behind an IRS acquiescence or nonacquiescence.[14] What are noticeably absent from the list of administrative authorities? IRS publications and tax return form instructions. *Neither can be cited as precedent or relied upon to avoid taxpayer or tax practitioner penalties.*

TAX RESEARCH

LO 2-5

Now that you have a basic understanding of the different types of tax authority, why do you think that the IRS and taxpayers disagree with respect to the tax treatment of a transaction? In other words, why would the IRS and Bill and Mercedes's CPA reach different conclusions regarding the deductibility of certain expenses? The answer is that, because the Code does not specifically address the tax consequences of each transaction type or every possible variation of a particular transaction, the application of the tax law is subject to debate and differing interpretations by the IRS, courts, tax professionals, taxpayers, and so on. Tax research, therefore, plays a vital role in allowing us to identify and understand the varying authorities that provide guidance on an issue, to assess the relative weights of differing authorities, to understand the risks associated with different tax return positions, and ultimately to draw an appropriate conclusion regarding the application of the tax law to the issue. The following paragraphs describe the basic process of tax research that tax professionals use to identify and analyze tax authorities to answer tax questions. We will then revisit Bill and Mercedes's issue and view the research memo prepared by their CPA.

Step 1: Understand Facts

To answer a tax question, you must understand the question. To understand the question, you must know the facts. There are two basic types of facts: open facts and closed facts. Open facts have not yet occurred, such as the facts associated with a proposed transaction. Closed facts have already occurred. The distinction between open and closed facts is important because, unlike closed facts, open facts can be altered, and different facts may result in very different tax consequences. Open facts allow the taxpayer to arrange a transaction to achieve the most advantageous outcome. Thus, they are especially important in tax planning.

How do you determine the facts for a research question? Interview clients, speak with third parties such as attorneys and brokers, and review client documents such as contracts, prior tax returns, wills, trust documents, deeds, and corporate minutes. When interviewing clients, remember that not many are tax experts. Thus, it is up to the tax professional to ask the correct initial and follow-up questions to obtain all the relevant facts. Also consider nontax factors, such as a client's personal values or objectives, as these often put constraints on tax planning strategies.

Step 2: Identify Issues

A tax professional's ability to identify issues is largely a function of his or her type of tax expertise. A tax expert in a particular area will typically be able to identify quickly

> **THE KEY FACTS**
>
> **Tax Research**
>
> - The five steps in tax research are (1) understand the facts, (2) identify issues, (3) locate relevant authorities, (4) analyze the tax authorities, and (5) document and communicate research results.
> - The two types of tax services that tax professionals use in tax research are annotated tax services, arranged by code section, and topical services, arranged by topic.
> - Research questions often consist of questions of fact or questions of law.
>   - The answer to a question of fact hinges upon the facts and circumstances of the taxpayer's transaction.
>   - The answer to a question of law hinges upon the interpretation of the law, such as interpreting a particular phrase in a code section.
> - When the researcher identifies that different authorities have conflicting views, she should evaluate the "hierarchy," jurisdiction, and age of the authorities.
> - Once the tax researcher has identified relevant authorities, she must make sure that the authorities are still valid and up to date.
> *(continued)*

---

[14]Actions on decisions have no precedential value but may be cited as authority to avoid the substantial understatement of tax penalty under IRC Sec. 6662 imposed on taxpayers and the related tax practitioner penalty under IRC Sec. 6694 (discussed later in this chapter).

• The most common end product of a research question is a research memo, which has five basic parts: (1) facts, (2) issues, (3) authority list, (4) conclusion, and (5) analysis.

the specific tax issues that relate to transactions in that area. For example, an expert in corporate acquisitions would quickly identify the tax consequences and specific issues of alternative acquisition types. A novice, on the other hand, would likely identify broader issues first and then more specific issues as he or she researched the relevant tax law.

What's the best method to identify tax issues? First of all, get a good understanding of the client's facts. Then, combine your understanding of the facts with your knowledge of the tax law. Let's consider the example of Bill and Mercedes's interest deduction. For an expert in this particular area, the issues will be immediately evident. For a novice, the initial response may take the form of a series of general questions: (1) Is this item of expense deductible? (2) Is that item of income taxable? (3) In what year should the expense be deducted? (4) In what year should the item of income be taxed? After you identify these types of general issues, your research will enable you to identify the more specific issues that ultimately determine the tax ramifications of the transaction.

Example 2-4

Elizabeth, Bill and Mercedes's friend who is a shareholder and the CFO of a company, loaned money to her company to help prevent the company from declaring bankruptcy. Despite Elizabeth's loan, the company did file bankruptcy, and Elizabeth was not repaid the loan. What issues would a researcher consider?

Answer: The first questions to ask are whether Elizabeth can deduct the bad debt expense and, if so, as what type of deduction? As the researcher delves more into the general issue, he would identify that the type of deduction depends on whether Elizabeth's debt is considered a business or nonbusiness bad debt. This more specific issue depends on whether Elizabeth loaned the money to the company to protect her job (business bad debt) or to protect her stock investment in the company (nonbusiness bad debt). Bad debt expenses incurred for nonbusiness debts (investment-related debts) are deducted as capital losses and thus subject to limitations (discussed in Chapter 7), whereas bad debt expenses for business debts (business-related debts) are ordinary deductions and not limited.

Why might this case be a good one to litigate in U.S. District Court?

Answer: Because a jury might be more likely to be convinced to assess Elizabeth's motives favorably.

Step 3: Locate Relevant Authorities

Step three in the research process is to locate the relevant authorities (code sections, regulations, court cases, revenue rulings) that address the tax issue. Luckily, tax services can aid the researcher in identifying relevant authorities. Most, if not all, of these services are available on the Internet (with a subscription), and thus offer the flexibility to conduct research almost anywhere.[15]

There are two basic types of tax services: annotated and topical. **Annotated tax services** are arranged by Internal Revenue Code Section. That is, for each code section, an annotated service includes the code section; a listing of the code section history; copies of congressional committee reports that explain changes to the code section; a copy of all the regulations issued for the specific code section; the service's unofficial explanation of the code section; and brief summaries (called annotations) of relevant court cases, revenue rulings, revenue procedures, and letter rulings that address issues specific to the code section. Two examples of annotated tax services are Commerce Clearing House's (CCH) Standard Federal Tax Reporter and Research Institute of America's (RIA) United States Tax Reporter.

---

[15]www.IRS.gov contains a lot of information (tax forms, IRS publications, etc.) that may be especially useful for answering basic tax questions. In addition, tax publishers, such as CCH and RIA, produce quick reference tax guides (e.g., the *CCH Master Tax Guide* or the *RIA Tax Handbook*) that may be used to answer basic tax questions.

Topical tax services are arranged by topic, such as taxable forms of income, tax-exempt income, and trade or business expenses. For each topic, the services identify tax issues that relate to each topic, and then explain and cite authorities relevant to the issue (code sections, regulations, court cases, revenue rulings, etc.). Beginning tax researchers often prefer topical services, because they generally are easier to read. Some examples of topical federal tax services include BNA's Tax Management Portfolios, CCH's Tax Research Consultant, and RIA's Federal Tax Coordinator.

How does a researcher use these services? An expert would probably go directly to the relevant portions of an annotated or topical service. A novice may conduct a keyword search in the service, use the tax service's topical index, or "browse" the tax service to identify the relevant portions. Some suggestions for identifying keywords: Try to describe the transaction in three to five words. An ideal keyword search typically includes (1) the relevant area of law and (2) a fact or two that describes the transaction. Try to avoid keywords that are too broad (income, deduction, taxable) or that may be too narrow.

Example 2-5

Bill and Mercedes refinanced the mortgage on their principal residence a couple of years ago when their original mortgage's four-year balloon payment came due. Their mortgage institution charged Bill and Mercedes $3,000 of points (prepaid interest) upon the refinancing in order to give them a reduced interest rate. On their CPA's advice, Bill and Mercedes deducted the $3,000 in the year they paid it, but upon audit, the IRS disallowed the deduction. What is the research issue?

Answer: The issue is, should Bill and Mercedes have deducted the $3,000 of points in the year they paid it?

What are some keywords that could identify relevant tax authority?

Answer: Points (area of law), interest (area of law), refinancing (fact that describes the transaction).

Keyword searching is more an art than an exact science. As you gain a better understanding of different areas of the tax law, you'll become much more efficient at using keywords. If keyword searching is not proving beneficial, check your spelling, make sure you're searching within the correct database, rethink your keywords, use another research method, use another tax service, or as a last resort, take a break.

While utilizing keyword searches or other research methods to identify potentially relevant areas of law and tax authorities, constantly ask yourself whether you are indeed in the correct area of law. Once the answer to this question is an authoritative yes, you can delve deeper into the area of law and related authorities to answer the question.

Step 4: Analyze Tax Authorities

Once a researcher identifies relevant authorities, she must read carefully to ensure she fully understands them, as well as their application to the research problem. Two basic types of issues researchers will encounter are questions of fact and questions of law.

The answer to a **question of fact** hinges upon the facts and circumstances of the taxpayer's transaction. For example, whether a trade or business expense is "ordinary," "necessary," "reasonable," and thus deductible, is a question of fact. If you're researching a question of fact, understand *which* facts determine the answer—in this case, which facts make an expense "ordinary," "necessary," and "reasonable" and which do not. In this type of question, the researcher will focus on understanding how various facts affect the research answer and identifying authorities with fact patterns similar to her client's.

The answer to a **question of law** hinges upon the interpretation of the law, such as interpreting a particular phrase in a code section (see the sample research memo in Exhibit 2-9 for an example of a question of law). If a researcher is faced with this type

EXHIBIT 2-9 **Sample Internal Research Memo**

Below is the memo that Bill and Mercedes's CPA drafted after researching their issue.

Date:	July 8, 2016
Preparer:	Joe Staff
Reviewer:	Sandra Miller
Subject:	Deductibility of Points Paid in Refinancing
Facts:	Four years ago Bill and Mercedes's credit union provided them a $250,000 mortgage loan for their new home. The mortgage loan was a four-year interest-only note with a balloon payment at the end of four years. Bill and Mercedes (Floridians residing in the 11th Circuit) chose this type of loan to allow them to minimize their mortgage payment until their previous house was sold. After 18 months, Bill and Mercedes sold their previous house and refinanced their original short-term loan with a 15-year conventional mortgage. The credit union charged Bill and Mercedes $3,000 in points (prepaid interest) upon the refinancing.
Issue:	Can Bill and Mercedes deduct the points in the year they paid them?
Authorities:	IRC Sec. 461(g)
	Rev. Rul. 87-22, 1987-1 CB 146.
	J.R. Huntsman v. Comm. (8 Cir., 1990), 90-2 USTC par. 50,340, rev'g 91 TC 917 (1988).
	AOD 1991-002.
	P.G. Cao v. Comm. (9 Cir., 1996), 96-1 USTC par. 50,167, aff'g 67 TCM 2171 (1994)
Conclusion:	Because Bill and Mercedes's refinancing represents an integrated step in securing permanent financing for their home, substantial authority supports their deduction of the $3,000 in points this year.
Analysis:	IRC Sec. 461(g)(1) provides that cash-method taxpayers (Bill and Mercedes) must amortize prepaid interest (points) over the life of the loan instead of receiving a current deduction. IRC Sec. 461(g)(2) provides an exception to the general rule of Sec. 461(g)(1). Specifically, IRC Sec. 461(g)(2) allows cash-method taxpayers to deduct points in the year paid if the related debt was incurred "in connection with the purchase or improvement of," and secured by, the taxpayer's principal residence. The question whether Bill and Mercedes should amortize or currently deduct the points paid to refinance the mortgage on their principal residence depends upon the interpretation of "in connection with the purchase or improvement of" found in IRC Sec. 461(g)(2).
	There are two basic interpretations of "in connection with the purchase or improvement of." In Revenue Ruling 87-22, the IRS rules that points incurred in refinancing a mortgage on a taxpayer's residence are deductible in the year paid to the extent that the taxpayer uses the loan proceeds to improve the taxpayer's residence. Thus, points paid to simply refinance an existing mortgage without improving the residence must be amortized over the life of the loan.
	In contrast, in *J.R. Huntsman v. Comm.*, the 8th Circuit Court interpreted the phrase "in connection with the purchase or improvement of" much more broadly and held that points incurred to refinance a mortgage on the taxpayer's principal residence are currently deductible if the refinancing represents an *integrated step to secure permanent financing* for the taxpayer's residence. The facts in *J.R. Huntsman v. Comm.* are very similar to Bill and Mercedes's facts. Like Bill and Mercedes, the taxpayers in *J.R. Huntsman v. Comm.* also purchased their principal residence using a short-term loan with a "balloon" payment. When the balloon payment came due, the taxpayers obtained a permanent mortgage on their home (a 30-year conventional mortgage). The 8th Circuit Court held that in this case the permanent mortgage was acquired to extinguish the short-term financing and finalize the purchase of the home. "Thus, where taxpayers purchase a principal residence with a short-term three-year loan secured by a mortgage on the residence, and replace the loan with permanent financing . . . , the permanent mortgage obtained is sufficiently in connection with the purchase of the home to fall within the exception provided for by section 461(g)(2)."
	In Action on Decision 1991-002, the IRS has indicated that it will not follow the *J.R. Huntsman v. Comm.* decision outside the 8th Circuit (in the 11th Circuit where Bill and Mercedes live). Nonetheless, other courts (the 9th Circuit in *P.G. Cao v. Comm.*) have indicated a willingness to apply the 8th Circuit's interpretation of IRC Sec. 461(g)(2). That is, they have allowed deductibility of points incurred in refinancing if the refinancing occurred to secure permanent financing, instead of for some other reason such as to secure a lower interest rate.
	Given the similarity in facts between Bill and Mercedes's refinancing and those in *J.R. Huntsman v. Comm.* (refinancing of a short-term note to secure permanent financing), substantial authority supports a current deduction of the points paid.

of question, she will spend much of her time researching the various interpretations of the code section and take note of which authorities interpret the code differently and why.

For many tax questions, the answer is clear with no opposing interpretations or contrary authorities. For other questions, the researcher may identify that different authorities have conflicting views. In this situation, the tax researcher should evaluate the hierarchical level, jurisdiction, and age of the authorities, placing more weight on higher and newer authorities that have jurisdiction over the taxpayer. A tax researcher will become more adept at this process as she gains experience.

Once the tax researcher has identified relevant authorities, she must make sure the authorities are still valid and up to date. For court cases, a **citator,** which is a research tool that allows you to check the status of several types of tax authorities, will review the history of the case to find out, for example, whether it was subsequently appealed and overturned, and to identify subsequent cases that cite the case. Favorable citations strengthen a case, while unfavorable ones weaken it. Citators can also check the status of revenue rulings, revenue procedures, and other IRS pronouncements. Checking the status of the Code is fairly simple: just locate the current version. Checking the status of regulations is a little more complicated. Most tax services alert researchers if a regulation has not been updated for certain changes in the Code. If this is the case, the researcher should evaluate whether the changes in the Code make the regulation obsolete.

As you will see in the analysis section of the sample research memo drafted by Bill and Mercedes's CPA (see Exhibit 2-9), the question whether they should amortize or currently deduct the points paid to refinance the mortgage on their principal residence is a question of law that ultimately depends upon the interpretation of a particular phrase: "in connection with the purchase or improvement of" found in IRC Sec. 461(g)(2). Is there a correct answer to this question? No. There is no clear-cut answer. Rather, this is a situation where the tax professional must use professional judgment. Because there is substantial authority supporting the current deduction of the points (discussed in detail in the sample memo), Bill and Mercedes should be able to deduct the points currently without risk of penalty. However, Bill and Mercedes should be aware that the IRS has clearly stated in an action on decision that it will fight this issue outside the 8th Circuit—for example, in the 11th Circuit, where Bill and Mercedes live.

Step 5: Document and Communicate the Results

After a researcher finishes her research, the final step of the process is to document and communicate the results. The most common end product of a research question is the internal research memo the researcher drafts for her supervisor's attention. The memo has five basic parts: (1) facts, (2) issues, (3) authority list, (4) conclusion, and (5) analysis. The purpose of the memo is to inform the reader of the answer to a research question, and thus, it should be written in an objective manner by discussing all relevant authorities to the research question, including those authorities that support, as well as those that conflict with, the answer. Below are some suggestions for each part of the memo. Compare these to the execution within the sample internal research memo presented in Exhibit 2-9.

Facts   Discuss facts relevant to the question presented—that is, facts that provide necessary background of the transaction (generally, who, what, when, where, and how much) and those facts that may influence the research answer. Keeping the fact discussion relatively brief will focus the reader's attention on the relevant characteristics of the transaction.

Issues   State the specific issues that the memo addresses. This section confirms that you understand the research question, reminds the reader of the question being analyzed, and allows future researchers to determine whether the analysis in the memo is relevant. Issues should be written as specifically as possible and be limited to one or two sentences per issue.

Authorities In this section, the researcher cites the relevant tax authorities that apply to the issue, such as the IRC, court cases, and revenue rulings. How many authorities should you cite? Enough to provide a clear understanding of the issue and interpretation of the law. Remember, in order to reach an accurate assessment of the strength of your conclusion, you should consider authorities that may support your desired conclusion, as well as those that may go against it.

Conclusion There should be one conclusion per issue. Each conclusion should answer the question as briefly as possible and, preferably, indicate why the answer is what it is.

Analysis The goal of the analysis is for the researcher to provide the reader a clear understanding of the area of law and specific authorities that apply. Typically, an analysis will be organized to discuss the general area(s) of law first (the code section) and then the specific authorities (court cases, revenue rulings) that apply to the research question. How many authorities should you discuss? As many as necessary to provide the reader an understanding of the issue and relevant authorities. After you discuss the relevant authorities, apply the authorities to your client's transaction and explain how the authorities result in your conclusion.

Client Letters In addition to internal research memos, tax professionals often send their clients letters that summarize their research and recommendations. Basic components of the client letter include: (1) research question and limitations, (2) facts, (3) analysis, and (4) closing. Below are some suggestions for each part of the client letter. Compare these to the execution within the sample client letter presented in Exhibit 2-10.

Research Question and Limitations After the salutation (Dear Bill and Mercedes) and social graces (I enjoyed seeing you last week at the Tampa Bay Boys and Girls Clubs charity auction. What a great event for such a worthy cause!), clearly state the research question addressed and any disclaimers related to the work performed. This portion of the letter ensures that the tax professional and client have a mutual understanding of the question researched and any limitations on the research performed. As with a memo, issues should be written as specifically as possible and be limited to one or two sentences. Most accounting firms have standard boilerplate language regarding the limitations on work performed that is included in every client letter.

Facts Briefly summarize the facts relevant to the question presented—that is, facts that provide necessary background of the transaction and those facts that may influence the research answer. Keeping the fact discussion relatively brief will focus the client's attention on the relevant characteristics of the transaction.

Analysis Summarize the relevant authorities (including citations in most situations) and their implications for the client's research question using precise language appropriate for the client's level of tax expertise. The length of this portion of the letter will vary with the complexity of the research question and client's interest in understanding the specific research details.

Closing In this section, summarize the key outcome(s) of the research conducted and any recommended client action, thank the client for requesting your service, and remind the client to contact you with additional questions or for further assistance.

In the case of Bill and Mercedes's interest deduction, their CPA recommended a tax return position that the IRS disallowed upon audit. Did their CPA violate her professional responsibilities by recommending a position the IRS disallowed? Good question. Let's take a look at the rules governing tax professional responsibilities.

EXHIBIT 2-10 **Sample Client Letter**

Below is the client letter that Bill and Mercedes's CPA sent to them.

Dear Bill and Mercedes,

I enjoyed seeing you last week at the Tampa Bay Boys and Girls Clubs charity auction. What a great event for such a worthy cause!

Thank you for requesting my advice concerning the tax treatment of the points paid when refinancing your mortgage.

My research is based upon the federal income tax laws that apply as of the date of this letter and the facts that you have provided as follows: Four years ago your credit union provided you a $250,000 interest-only note on your home that required a balloon payment at the end of four years. You chose this type of loan to minimize your mortgage payment until your previous house sold. After 18 months, you sold your previous house and refinanced the original short-term loan with a 15-year conventional mortgage. The credit union charged you $3,000 in points upon the refinancing.

After a thorough review of the applicable tax authority, there is substantial authority that supports a current deduction of the $3,000 points paid. IRC Sec. 461(g)(2) allows cash-method taxpayers to deduct points in the year paid if the related debt was incurred "in connection with the purchase or improvement of," and secured by, the taxpayer's principal residence. There are two basic interpretations of "in connection with the purchase or improvement of." The IRS has ruled (Revenue Ruling 87-22) that points paid to simply refinance an existing mortgage without improving the residence must be amortized over the life of the loan. In contrast, in *J.R. Huntsman v. Comm.*, the 8th Circuit Court held that points incurred to refinance a mortgage on the taxpayer's principal residence are currently deductible if the refinancing represents an *integrated step to secure permanent financing* for the taxpayer's residence.

The facts in *J.R. Huntsman v. Comm.* are very similar to your facts. Like you, the taxpayers in *J.R. Huntsman v. Comm.* purchased their principal residence using a short-term loan with a "balloon" payment. When the balloon payment came due, the taxpayers obtained a permanent mortgage on their home. The 8th Circuit Court held that in this case the permanent mortgage was acquired to finalize the purchase of the home and allowed the current deduction of the points.

J.R. Huntsman v. Comm. provides substantial authority to support a current deduction of the $3,000 points paid to refinance your initial short-term mortgage. In addition, other courts have applied the 8th Circuit's interpretation of IRC Sec. 461(g)(2), which adds "strength" to the 8th Circuit decision. However, the IRS has indicated that it will not follow the *J.R. Huntsman v. Comm.* decision outside the 8th Circuit (in the 11th Circuit where you live). Accordingly, the IRS would likely disallow the $3,000 deduction upon audit, and thus, while you have substantial authority to deduct the points currently, there is risk in doing so.

I would be happy to discuss this issue with you in more depth as these types of issues are always difficult. Likewise, if you have any other questions or issues with which I may assist you, please do not hesitate to contact me. Thank you again for requesting my advice.

Sincerely,

Sandra Miller, CPA

TAX PROFESSIONAL RESPONSIBILITIES

LO 2-6

Tax practitioners are subject to a variety of statutes, rules, and codes of professional conduct. Some examples include the American Institute of CPAs (AICPA) Code of Professional Conduct, the AICPA **Statements on Standards for Tax Services (SSTS),** the IRS's Circular 230, and statutes enacted by a CPA's specific state board of accountancy. Tax practitioners should absolutely have a working knowledge of these statutes, rules, and guidelines because (1) they establish the professional standards for the practitioner and (2) failure to comply with the standards could result in adverse consequences for the tax professional, such as being admonished, suspended, or barred from practicing before the IRS; being admonished, suspended, or expelled from the AICPA; or suffering suspension or revocation of the CPA license. Given the voluminous nature of applicable statutes, rules, and codes, we will simply provide a brief overview of the major common sources of tax professional standards.

CPAs who are members of the AICPA are bound by the AICPA Code of Professional Conduct and Statements on Standards for Tax Services. Other tax professionals use these provisions as guidance of professional standards. The AICPA Code of Professional Conduct is not specific to tax practice and provides broader professional standards that are especially relevant for auditors—that is, for those independent CPAs charged with examining an entity's financial statements. Provisions included in the Code of Professional Conduct address the importance of a CPA maintaining independence from the client and using due professional care in carrying out responsibilities. Additional provisions limit the acceptance of contingent fees, preclude discreditable acts such as signing a false return, and prohibit false advertising and charging commissions. Most of these provisions rightly fall under the heading of common sense. Nonetheless, a regular review should prove useful to the practicing CPA.

The AICPA's Statements on Standards for Tax Services (SSTS) recommend appropriate standards of practice for tax professionals and are intended to complement other provisions that govern tax practice (e.g., Circular 230 discussed below). One objective of these standards is to encourage increased understanding by the Treasury, IRS, and the public of a CPA's professional standards. Many state boards of accountancy have adopted similar standards, thus making the SSTS especially important. Currently, seven SSTS describe the tax professional standards when recommending a tax return position, answering questions on a tax return, preparing a tax return using data supplied by a client, using estimates on a tax return, taking a tax return position inconsistent with a previous year's tax return, discovering a tax return error, and giving tax advice to taxpayers. Exhibit 2-11 provides a brief summary of each SSTS. Most important from a research perspective, SSTS No. 1 provides that a tax professional must comply with the standards imposed by the applicable tax authority when recommending a tax return position or preparing or signing a tax return. IRC Sec. 6694 provides these standards for federal tax purposes.

IRC Sec. 6694 imposes a penalty on a *tax practitioner* for any position that is not supported by **substantial authority**.[16] A good tax professional evaluates whether supporting authority is substantial based upon the supporting and opposing authorities' weight and relevance. Substantial authority suggests the probability that the taxpayer's position is sustained upon audit or litigation is in the 35 to 40 percent range or above. The tax practitioner can also avoid penalty under IRC Sec. 6694 if the tax return position has at least a reasonable basis (i.e., supported by one or more tax authorities) and the position is disclosed on the taxpayer's return.

Example 2-6

Did Bill and Mercedes's CPA meet her professional standards as provided by SSTS No. 1?

Answer: Yes. Based on *J.R. Huntsman v. Comm.*, it is safe to conclude that there is a 35 to 40 percent or greater probability that the current points deduction will be sustained upon judicial review. Specifically, Bill and Mercedes's facts are very similar to those in *J.R. Huntsman v. Comm.*, and subsequent courts have interpreted the phrase "in connection with" consistently with *J.R. Huntsman v. Comm.*

Circular 230, issued by the IRS, provides regulations governing tax practice and applies to all persons practicing before the IRS. There are five parts of Circular 230: Subpart A describes who may practice before the IRS (CPAs, attorneys, enrolled agents)

---

[16]The "more likely than not" standard, defined as a greater than 50 percent chance of a position being sustained on its merits, applies to tax shelters and other reportable transactions specified by the IRS.

EXHIBIT 2-11   Summary of the AICPA Statements on Standards for Tax Services

SSTS No 1: Tax Return Positions

A tax professional should comply with the standards, if any, imposed by the applicable tax authority for recommending a tax return position, or preparing or signing a tax return. If the tax authority has no written standards (or if they are lower than the following standard), the tax professional may recommend a tax return position or prepare or sign a return when she has a good-faith belief that the position has a realistic possibility of being sustained if challenged, or if there is a reasonable basis for the position and it is *adequately disclosed* on the tax return.

SSTS No. 2: Answers to Questions on Returns

A tax professional should make a reasonable effort to obtain from the taxpayer the information necessary to answer all questions on a tax return.

SSTS No. 3: Certain Procedural Aspects of Preparing Returns

In preparing or signing a tax return, a tax professional may rely without verification on information that a taxpayer or a third party has provided, unless the information appears to be incorrect, incomplete, or inconsistent.

SSTS No. 4: Use of Estimates

Unless prohibited by statute or rule, a tax professional may use taxpayer estimates in preparing a tax return if it is impractical to obtain exact data and if the estimated amounts appear reasonable based on the facts and circumstances known by the professional.

SSTS No. 5: Departure from a Position Previously Concluded in an Administrative Proceeding or Court Decision

A tax professional may sign a tax return that contains a departure from a position previously concluded in an administrative or court proceeding if the tax professional adheres to the standards of SSTS No. 1. This rule does not apply if the taxpayer is bound to a specific tax treatment in the later year, such as by a formal closing agreement with the IRS.

SSTS No. 6: Knowledge of Error: Return Preparation and Administrative Proceedings

A tax professional must advise the taxpayer promptly of an error and its potential consequences when she learns of an error in a previously filed tax return, an administrative hearing (such as an audit), or the taxpayer's failure to file a required return. The tax professional should include a recommendation for appropriate measures the taxpayer should take. The professional is not obligated to inform the IRS of the error, nor may she do so without the taxpayer's permission, except when required by law. However, in an administrative proceeding only, the tax professional should request the taxpayer's agreement to disclose the error to the IRS. If the taxpayer refuses to disclose the error to the IRS, the professional may consider terminating the professional relationship with the taxpayer.

SSTS No. 7: Form and Content of Advice to Taxpayers

In providing advice to taxpayers, tax professionals must use judgment that reflects professional competence and serves the taxpayer's needs. The professional should ensure that the standards under SSTS No. 1 are satisfied for all advice rendered. The professional is not obligated to communicate with a taxpayer when subsequent events affect advice previously provided except when implementing plans associated with the advice provided or when the professional is obligated to do so by specific agreement.

THE KEY FACTS

Tax Professional Responsibilities

- Tax practitioners are subject to a variety of statutes, rules, and codes of professional conduct.
- The AICPA's seven Statements on Standards for Tax Services (SSTS) recommend appropriate standards of practice for tax professionals.
  - Many state boards of accountancy have adopted similar standards to the SSTS standards.
- Circular 230 provides regulations governing tax practice and applies to all persons practicing before the IRS.
  - There is a good bit of overlap between Circular 230 and the AICPA SSTS.

and what practicing before the IRS means (tax return preparation, representing clients before the IRS, and so on).[17] Subpart B describes the duties and restrictions that apply to individuals governed by Circular 230. Included in Subpart B are provisions discussing the submission of records to the IRS, guidelines when a practitioner discovers a tax return error, restrictions on charging contingency fees, prohibition of sharing employment with someone suspended from practicing before the IRS, stringent rules relating

---

[17]Similar to attorneys and CPAs, enrolled agents and registered tax return preparers can represent taxpayers before the IRS. To become an enrolled agent, you must have either worked for the IRS for five years or pass a comprehensive examination. Registered tax return preparers must pay an annual registration fee and complete continuing education requirements designated by the IRS.

to providing advice for tax shelters, and standards for when a practitioner can recommend a tax return position.[18] Subparts C and D explain sanctions and disciplinary proceedings for practitioners violating the Circular 230 provisions. Subpart E concludes with a few miscellaneous provisions (such as the Circular 230 effective date). There is a good bit of overlap between Circular 230 and the AICPA SSTS.

Although Circular 230 provides many rules governing tax practice, the Internal Revenue Code and other Treasury Regulations often contain requirements specific to tax professionals. Thus, it is important for tax professionals to keep abreast of all applicable guidance, regardless of the specific authoritative source. A good example of this is the tax-preparer registration requirement in Reg. §1.6109-2, which requires that all paid tax-return preparers apply for and receive a preparer tax identification number (PTIN) and pay an annual fee, as prescribed by the IRS. Although not a particularly daunting registration requirement, it is important nonetheless as failure to include the tax-return preparer's PTIN on tax returns is subject to a $50 penalty per violation.

LO 2-7 TAXPAYER AND TAX PRACTITIONER PENALTIES

THE KEY FACTS

Taxpayer and Tax Practitioner Penalties

- The IRS can impose both criminal and civil penalties to encourage tax compliance by both tax professionals and taxpayers.
- The standard of conviction is higher in a criminal trial, but the penalties are also much higher.
- A taxpayer will not be subject to an underpayment penalty if there is substantial authority that supports the tax return position.
- A tax practitioner will also not be subject to penalty for recommending a tax return position if there is substantial authority that supports the position.

In addition to motivating good behavior via tax professional standards, the IRS can impose both criminal and civil penalties to encourage tax compliance by both tax professionals and taxpayers. **Civil penalties** are much more common, generally come in the form of monetary penalties, and may be imposed when tax practitioners or taxpayers violate tax statutes without reasonable cause—say, as the result of negligence, intentional disregard of pertinent rules, willful disobedience, or outright fraud. Some common examples of civil penalties are listed in Exhibit 2-12.

Criminal penalties are much less common than civil penalties, although they have been used to incarcerate some of the most notorious criminals. (Notorious mobster Al Capone was convicted and put in prison for tax evasion.) They are commonly charged in tax evasion cases, which include willful intent to defraud the government, but are imposed only after normal due process, including a trial. Compared to civil cases, the standard of conviction is higher in a criminal trial; guilt must be proven beyond a reasonable doubt (versus a "clear and convincing evidence" standard for civil tax fraud). However, the penalties are also much higher, such as fines up to $100,000 for individuals plus a prison sentence.

Assuming the IRS assesses additional tax upon audit, will the taxpayer always be subject to penalty? No. While the taxpayer will have to pay interest on the underpayment, he or she will *not* be subject to an underpayment penalty *if there is* substantial authority *that supports the tax return position.*[19] As previously discussed, substantial authority suggests the probability that the taxpayer's position is sustained upon audit or litigation is in the 35 to 40 percent range or above.

Example 2-7

What is Bill and Mercedes's exposure to penalties in their IRS audit?

Answer: None. Why? Because "substantial tax authority" supports their tax return position and the disputed tax liability is relatively small (the tax savings on a $3,000 tax deduction), Bill and Mercedes have no penalty exposure. Nonetheless, Bill and Mercedes will owe interest on the disputed tax liability unless the IRS recants its position in the audit or appeals process (or if the case is litigated and Bill and Mercedes win).

---

[18]Circular 230 imposes the same tax practitioner standards as in IRC Sec. 6694 for when a tax practitioner generally may recommend a tax return position (substantial authority and no disclosure or reasonable basis with disclosure).

[19]The taxpayer can also avoid penalty if the tax return position has at least a reasonable basis (i.e., supported by one or more tax authorities) and the position is disclosed on the taxpayer's return (IRC Sec. 6662).

EXHIBIT 2-12 **Civil Penalties Imposed for Tax Violations**

Taxpayers		Tax Practitioners	
Failure to file a tax return.	5% of tax due per month (or partial month). Maximum penalty is 25% of net tax due. If the tax return is not filed within 60 days of the due date (including extensions), the minimum penalty is the smaller of $135 or 100% of the unpaid tax.	Failure to provide a copy of the tax return to a taxpayer.	$50 per violation.
Failure to pay tax owed.	0.5% of tax due per month (or partial month). Reduces the failure to file a tax return penalty, if applicable. Maximum combined failure to file and failure to pay tax penalty is 5% of net tax due per month not to exceed 25% of net tax due. Minimum combined penalty if the tax return is not filed within 60 days of the due date (including extensions) is the smaller of $135 or 100% of the unpaid tax.	Failure to sign a tax return.	$50 per violation.
Failure to make estimated payments.	Penalty varies with federal short-term interest rate and underpayment.	Failure to include the tax practitioner's ID number on the tax return.	$50 per violation.
Substantial understatement of tax.	20% of understatement.	Failure to keep a listing of taxpayers or tax returns.	$50 per violation.
Underpayment of tax due to transactions lacking economic substance.	20% or 40% of understatement.		
Providing false withholding information.	$500.	Failure to keep a listing of employees.	$50 per violation.
Fraud.	75% of liability attributable to fraud.	Understatement due to unreasonable position.	Greater of $1,000 or 50% of income derived from preparing the taxpayer's tax return.
		Willful understatement of tax.	Greater of $5,000 or 50% of income derived from preparing the taxpayer's tax return.
		Organizing, promoting, etc. an abusive tax shelter.	Lesser of $1,000 or 100% of gross income derived from tax shelter. If activity is based on fraudulent statements, the penalty equals 50% of gross income derived from tax shelter.
		Aiding and abetting the understatement of a tax liability.	$1,000.

As we explained in Example 2-6, Bill and Mercedes's CPA met her professional standards (as defined currently in SSTS No. 1) by recommending a tax return position that meets the "Substantial Authority" standard. Likewise, because substantial tax authority supports the tax return position, Bill and Mercedes's CPA should also not have penalty exposure under IRC Sec. 6694.

CONCLUSION

Now that we have a full understanding of the issue under audit for Bill and Mercedes, what is their likely outcome? Another good question. The IRS has stated that it will continue to disallow a current deduction for points incurred for refinanced mortgages. Nonetheless, the courts appear to follow *J.R. Huntsman v. Comm.,* and therefore, the IRS stands a strong possibility of losing this case if litigated. In an IRS appeals conference, the appeals officer may consider the hazards of litigation. Accordingly, Bill and Mercedes have a good likelihood of a favorable resolution at the appeals conference.

In this chapter we discussed several of the fundamentals of tax practice and procedure: taxpayer filing requirements, the statute of limitations, the IRS audit process, the primary tax authorities, tax research, tax professional standards, and taxpayer and tax practitioner penalties. For the tax accountant, these fundamentals form the basis for much of her work. Likewise, tax research forms the basis of much of a tax professional's compliance and planning services. Even for the accountant who doesn't specialize in tax accounting, gaining a basic understanding of tax practice and procedure is important, as assisting clients with the IRS audit process is a valued service that accountants provide, and clients expect all accountants to understand basic tax procedure issues and how to research basic tax issues.

Summary

LO 2-1 Identify the filing requirements for income tax returns and the statute of limitations for assessment.

- All corporations must file a tax return annually regardless of their taxable income. Estates and trusts are required to file annual income tax returns if their gross income exceeds $600. The filing requirements for individual taxpayers depend on the taxpayer's filing status, age, and gross income.

- Individual and C corporation tax returns (except for C corporations with a June 30 year-end) are due on the fifteenth day of the fourth month following year-end. For C corporations with a June 30 year-end, partnerships and S corporations, tax returns must be filed by the fifteenth day of the third month following the entity's fiscal year-end. Any taxpayer unable to file a tax return by the original due date can request an extension to file.

- For both amended tax returns filed by a taxpayer and proposed tax assessments by the IRS, the statute of limitations generally ends three years from the *later* of (1) the date the tax return was actually filed or (2) the tax return's original due date.

LO 2-2 Outline the IRS audit process, how returns are selected, the different types of audits, and what happens after the audit.

- The IRS uses a number of computer programs and outside data sources to identify tax returns that may have an understated tax liability. Common computer initiatives include the DIF (Discriminant Function) system, document perfection program, and information matching program.

- The three types of IRS audits consist of correspondence, office, and field examinations.

- After the audit, the IRS will send the taxpayer a 30-day letter, which provides the taxpayer the opportunity to pay the proposed assessment or request an appeals conference. If an agreement is not reached at appeals or the taxpayer does not pay the proposed assessment, the IRS will send the taxpayer a 90-day letter. At this time, the taxpayer may pay the tax or petition the U.S. Tax Court to hear the case. If the taxpayer chooses to pay the tax, the taxpayer may then request a refund of the tax and eventually sue the IRS for a refund in the U.S. District Court or the U.S. Court of Federal Claims.

Evaluate the relative weights of the various tax law sources.   **LO 2-3**

- Primary authorities are official sources of the tax law generated by the legislative branch (statutory authority issued by Congress), judicial branch (rulings by the U.S. District Court, U.S. Tax Court, U.S. Court of Federal Claims, U.S. Circuit Court of Appeals, or U.S. Supreme Court), or executive/administrative branch (Treasury and IRS pronouncements). Secondary authorities are unofficial tax authorities that interpret and explain the primary authorities.

Describe the legislative process as it pertains to taxation.   **LO 2-4**

- Exhibit 2-7 illustrates the legislative process for enacting tax law changes. Bills proceed from the House Ways and Means Committee to the House of Representatives. If approved, the act is sent to the Senate Finance Committee with a revised version then sent to the U.S. Senate. If approved, the Joint Conference Committee considers the acts passed by the House of Representatives and Senate. If a compromise is reached, the revised act is sent to the House of Representatives, if approved then to the Senate, and if approved then to the president. If signed by the president, the act is incorporated into the IRC of 1986. If the president vetoes the legislation, Congress may override the veto with a two-thirds positive vote in both the House of Representatives and Senate.

Perform the basic steps in tax research and evaluate various tax law sources when faced with   **LO 2-5**
ambiguous statutes.

- The five basic steps in tax research are (1) understand the facts, (2) identify issues, (3) locate relevant authorities, (4) analyze the tax authorities, and (5) document and communicate research results.

- When the researcher identifies that different authorities have conflicting views, she should evaluate the "hierarchy," jurisdiction, and age of the authorities, placing more weight on higher and newer authorities that have jurisdiction over the taxpayer.

Describe tax professional responsibilities in providing tax advice.   **LO 2-6**

- Tax practitioners are subject to a variety of statutes, rules, and codes of professional conduct. Some examples include the American Institute of CPAs (AICPA) Code of Professional Conduct, the AICPA Statements on Standards for Tax Services (SSTS), the IRS's Circular 230, and statutes enacted by a CPA's specific state board of accountancy.

- The AICPA's Statements on Standards for Tax Services (SSTS) recommend appropriate standards of practice for tax professionals. Many state boards of accountancy have adopted similar standards, thus making the SSTS especially important. Currently, there are seven SSTS summarized in Exhibit 2-11 that describe the tax professional standards.

- Circular 230 provides regulations governing tax practice and applies to all persons practicing before the IRS. There is a good bit of overlap between Circular 230 and the AICPA SSTS.

Identify taxpayer and tax professional penalties.   **LO 2-7**

- The IRS can impose both criminal and civil penalties to encourage tax compliance by both tax professionals and taxpayers. Civil penalties are much more common, generally come in the form of monetary penalties, and may be imposed when tax practitioners or taxpayers violate tax statutes without reasonable cause. Some common examples of civil penalties are listed in Exhibit 2-12.

- Criminal penalties are much less common than civil penalties and are commonly charged in tax evasion cases. Compared to civil cases, the standard of conviction is higher in a criminal trial, but the penalties are also much higher.

- A taxpayer will not be subject to an underpayment penalty if there is substantial authority that supports the tax return position.

- A tax practitioner will also not be subject to penalty for recommending a tax return position if there is substantial authority that supports the position.

KEY TERMS

30-day letter (2-6)
90-day letter (2-6)
acquiescence (2-17)
action on decision (2-17)
annotated tax service (2-18)
Circular 230 (2-24)
citator (2-21)
civil penalties (2-26)
correspondence examination (2-5)
criminal penalties (2-26)
determination letters (2-16)
DIF (Discriminant Function)
    system (2-4)
document perfection program (2-4)
field examination (2-6)
final regulations (2-15)
Golsen rule (2-15)

information matching program (2-4)
Internal Revenue Code of 1986 (2-11)
interpretative regulations (2-16)
legislative regulations (2-16)
nonacquiescence (2-17)
office examination (2-6)
primary authority (2-9)
private letter rulings (2-16)
procedural regulations (2-16)
proposed regulations (2-15)
question of fact (2-19)
question of law (2-19)
regulations (2-15)
revenue procedures (2-16)
revenue rulings (2-16)
secondary authorities (2-9)
stare decisis (2-15)

Statements on Standards for Tax
    Services (SSTS) (2-23)
statute of limitations (2-3)
substantial authority (2-24)
tax treaties (2-14)
technical advice memorandum (2-16)
temporary regulations (2-15)
topical tax service (2-19)
U.S. Circuit Courts of Appeal (2-7)
U.S. Constitution (2-11)
U.S. Court of Federal Claims (2-6)
U.S. District Court (2-6)
U.S. Supreme Court (2-8)
U.S. Tax Court (2-6)
writ of certiorari (2-8)

DISCUSSION QUESTIONS

connect

All applicable Discussion Questions are available with *Connect*®.

LO 2-1 1. Name three factors that determine whether a taxpayer is required to file a tax return.

LO 2-1 2. Benita is concerned that she will not be able to complete her tax return by April 15. Can she request an extension to file her return? By what date must she do so? Assuming she requests an extension, what is the latest date that she could file her return this year without penalty?

LO 2-1 3. Agua Linda Inc. is a calendar-year corporation. What is the original due date for the corporate tax return? What happens if the original due date falls on a Saturday?

LO 2-2 4. Approximately what percentage of tax returns does the IRS audit? What are the implications of this number for the IRS's strategy in selecting returns for audit?

LO 2-2 5. Explain the difference between the DIF system and the National Research Program. How do they relate to each other?

LO 2-2 6. Describe the differences between the three types of audits in terms of their scope and taxpayer type.

LO 2-2 7. Simon just received a 30-day letter from the IRS indicating a proposed assessment. Does he have to pay the additional tax? What are his options?

LO 2-2 8. Compare and contrast the three trial-level courts.

LO 2-3 9. Compare and contrast the three types of tax law sources and give examples of each.

LO 2-3 10. The U.S. Constitution is the highest tax authority but provides very little in the way of tax laws. What are the next highest tax authorities after the U.S. Constitution?

LO 2-3 11. Jackie has just opened her copy of the Code for the first time. She looks at the table of contents and wonders why it is organized the way it is. She questions whether it makes sense to try and understand the Code's organization. What are some reasons why understanding the organization of the Internal Revenue Code may prove useful?

12. Laura Li, a U.S. resident, worked for three months this summer in Hong Kong. What type of tax authority may be especially useful in determining the tax consequences of her foreign income?   `LO 2-3`

13. What are the basic differences between regulations, revenue rulings, and private letter rulings?   `LO 2-3`

14. Under what circumstance would the IRS issue an acquiescence? A nonacquiescence? An action on decision?   `LO 2-3`

15. Carlos has located a regulation that appears to answer his tax research question. He is concerned because the regulation is a temporary regulation. Evaluate the authoritative weight of this type of regulation. Should he feel more or less confident in his answer if the regulation was a proposed regulation?   `LO 2-3`

16. Tyrone recently read a regulation that Congress specifically requested the IRS to issue. What type of regulation is this? How does this regulation's authoritative weight compare to other regulations?   `LO 2-3`

17. In researching a tax question, you find only one authority (a trial-level court opinion) that is directly on point. Which court would you least prefer to have hear this case and why?   `LO 2-3`

18. What is *stare decisis* and how does it relate to the Golsen rule?   `LO 2-3`

19. Mason was shocked to learn that the current Code is the Internal Revenue Code of 1986. He thought that U.S. tax laws change more frequently. What is wrong with Mason's perception?   `LO 2-4`

20. Describe in general the process by which new tax legislation is enacted.   `LO 2-4`

21. What are the three committees that debate proposed tax legislation? What documents do these committees generate, and how might they be used?   `LO 2-4`

22. The president recently vetoed a tax act passed by the House and Senate. Is the tax act dead? If not, what will it take for the act to be passed?   `LO 2-4`

23. What are the five basic parts of an internal research memo?   `LO 2-5`

24. What is the difference between primary and secondary authorities? Explain the role of each authority type in conducting tax research.   `LO 2-5`

25. Jorge is puzzled that the IRS and his CPA could legitimately reach different conclusions on a tax issue. Why does this happen?   `LO 2-5`

26. What is the difference between open and closed facts? How is this distinction important in conducting tax research?   `LO 2-5`

27. In writing a research memo, what types of facts should be included in the memo?   `LO 2-5`

28. Amber is a tax expert, whereas Rob is a tax novice. Explain how their process in identifying tax issues may differ.   `LO 2-5`

29. Discuss the basic differences between annotated and topical tax services. How are these services used in tax research?   `LO 2-5`

30. In constructing a keyword search, what should the keyword search include?   `LO 2-5`

31. Lindley has become very frustrated in researching a tax issue using keyword searches. What suggestions can you give her?   `LO 2-5`

32. Nola, a tax novice, has a fairly simple tax question. Besides tax services, what are some sources that she can use to answer her question?   `LO 2-5`

33. Armando identifies a tax research question as being a question of fact. What types of authorities should he attempt to locate in his research?   `LO 2-5`

34. How are citators used in tax research?   `LO 2-5`

35. What is the general rule for how many authorities a research memo should discuss?   `LO 2-5`

36. Identify some of the sources for tax professional standards. What are the potential ramifications of failing to comply with these standards?   `LO 2-6`

LO 2-6 37. Levi is recommending a tax return position to his client. What standard must he meet to satisfy his professional standards? What is the source of this professional standard?

LO 2-6 38. What is Circular 230?

LO 2-7 39. What are the basic differences between civil and criminal tax penalties?

LO 2-7 40. What are some of the most common civil penalties imposed on taxpayers?

LO 2-7 41. What are the taxpayer's standards to avoid the substantial understatement of tax penalty?

LO 2-7 42. What are the tax practitioner's standards to avoid a penalty for recommending a tax return position?

PROBLEMS

All applicable problems are available with *Connect*®.

LO 2-1 43. Ahmed does not have enough cash on hand to pay his taxes. He was excited to hear that he can request an extension to file his tax return. Does this solve his problem? What are the ramifications if he doesn't pay his tax liability by April 15?

LO 2-1 44. Molto Stancha Corporation had zero earnings this fiscal year; in fact, they lost money. Must they file a tax return?

LO 2-1 45. The estate of Monique Chablis earned $450 of income this year. Is the estate required to file an income tax return?

LO 2-1 46. Jamarcus, a full-time student, earned $2,500 this year from a summer job. He had no other income this year and will have zero federal income tax liability this year. His employer withheld $300 of federal income tax from his summer pay. Is Jamarcus required to file a tax return? Should Jamarcus file a tax return?

LO 2-1 47. Shane has never filed a tax return despite earning excessive sums of money as a gambler. When does the statute of limitations expire for the years in which Shane has not filed a tax return?

LO 2-1 48. Latoya filed her tax return on February 10 this year. When will the statute of limitations expire for this tax return?

LO 2-1 49. Using the facts from the previous problem, how would your answer change if Latoya understated her income by 40 percent? How would your answer change if Latoya intentionally failed to report as taxable income any cash payments she received from her clients?

LO 2-2 50. Paula could not reach an agreement with the IRS at her appeals conference and has just received a 90-day letter. If she wants to litigate the issue but does not have sufficient cash to pay the proposed deficiency, what is her best court choice?

LO 2-2 51. In choosing a trial-level court, how should a court's previous rulings influence the choice? How should circuit court rulings influence the taxpayer's choice of a trial-level court?

LO 2-2 52. Sophia recently won a tax case litigated in the 7th Circuit. She recently heard that the Supreme Court denied the *writ of certiorari*. Should she be happy or not, and why?

LO 2-2 53. Campbell's tax return was audited because she failed to report interest she earned on her tax return. What IRS audit selection method identified her tax return?

LO 2-2 54. Yong's tax return was audited because he calculated his tax liability incorrectly. What IRS audit procedure identified his tax return for audit?

LO 2-2 55. Randy deducted a high level of itemized deductions two years ago relative to his income level. He recently received an IRS notice requesting documentation for his itemized deductions. What audit procedure likely identified his tax return for audit?

56. Jackie has a corporate client that has recently received a 30-day notice from the IRS with a $100,000 tax assessment. Her client is considering requesting an appeals conference to contest the assessment. What factors should Jackie advise her client to consider before requesting an appeals conference?

LO 2-2

planning

57. The IRS recently completed an audit of Shea's tax return and assessed $15,000 additional tax. Shea requested an appeals conference but was unable to settle the case at the conference. She is contemplating which trial court to choose to hear her case. Provide her a recommendation based on the following alternative facts:

LO 2-2

planning

   a) Shea resides in the 2nd Circuit, and the 2nd Circuit has recently ruled against the position Shea is litigating.

   b) The Federal Circuit Court of Appeals has recently ruled in favor of Shea's position.

   c) The issue being litigated involves a question of fact. Shea has a very appealing story to tell but little favorable case law to support her position.

   d) The issue being litigated is highly technical, and Shea believes strongly in her interpretation of the law.

   e) Shea is a local elected official and would prefer to minimize any local publicity regarding the case.

58. Juanita, a Texas resident (5th Circuit), is researching a tax question and finds a 5th Circuit case ruling that is favorable and a 9th Circuit case that is unfavorable. Which circuit case has more "authoritative weight" and why? How would your answer change if Juanita were a Kentucky resident (6th Circuit)?

LO 2-3

59. Faith, a resident of Florida (11th Circuit) recently found a circuit court case that is favorable to her research question. Which two circuits would she prefer to have issued the opinion?

LO 2-3

60. Robert has found a "favorable" authority directly on point for his tax question. If the authority is a court case, which court would he prefer to have issued the opinion? Which court would he least prefer to have issued the opinion?

LO 2-3

61. Jamareo has found a "favorable" authority directly on point for his tax question. If the authority is an administrative authority, which specific type of authority would he prefer to answer his question? Which administrative authority would he least prefer to answer his question?

LO 2-3

62. For each of the following citations, identify the type of authority (statutory, administrative, or judicial) and explain the citation.

LO 2-3

   a) Reg. Sec. 1.111-1(b)

   b) IRC Sec. 469(c)(7)(B)(i)

   c) Rev. Rul. 82-204, 1982-2 C.B. 192

   d) *Amdahl Corp.*, 108 TC 507 (1997)

   e) PLR 9727004

   f) *Hills v. Comm.*, 50 AFTR2d 82-6070 (11th Cir., 1982)

63. For each of the following citations, identify the type of authority (statutory, administrative, or judicial) and explain the citation.

LO 2-3

   a) IRC Sec. 280A(c)(5)

   b) Rev. Proc. 2004-34, 2004-1 C.B. 911

   c) *Lakewood Associates*, RIA TC Memo 95-3566

   d) TAM 200427004

   e) *U.S. v. Muncy*, 2008-2 USTC par. 50,449 (E.D., AR, 2008)

64. Justine would like to clarify her understanding of a code section recently enacted by Congress. What tax law sources are available to assist Justine?

LO 2-4

65. Aldina has identified conflicting authorities that address her research question. How should she evaluate these authorities to make a conclusion?

LO 2-5

LO 2-5 66. Georgette has identified a 1983 court case that appears to answer her research question. What must she do to determine if the case still represents "current" law?

LO 2-5 67. Sandy has determined that her research question depends upon the interpretation of the phrase "not compensated by insurance." What type of research question is this?

LO 2-5 68. J. C. has been a professional gambler for many years. He loves this line of work and believes the income is tax-free.

research
a) Use an available tax research service to determine whether J. C.'s thinking is correct. Is the answer to this question found in the Internal Revenue Code? If not, what type of authority answers this question?

b) Write a memo communicating the results of your research.

LO 2-5 69. Katie recently won a ceramic dalmatian valued at $800 on a television game show. She questions whether this prize is taxable since it was a "gift" she won on the show.

research
a) Use an available tax research service to answer Katie's question.

b) Write a letter to Katie communicating the results of your research.

LO 2-5 70. Pierre recently received a tax penalty for failing to file a tax return. He was upset to receive the penalty, but he was comforted by the thought that he will get a tax deduction for paying the penalty.

research
a) Use an available tax research service to determine if Pierre is correct.

b) Write a memo communicating the results of your research.

LO 2-5 71. Paris was happy to provide a contribution to her friend Nicole's campaign for mayor, especially after she learned that charitable contributions are tax deductible.

research
a) Use an available tax service to determine whether Paris can deduct this contribution.

b) Write a memo communicating the results of your research.

LO 2-5 72. Matt and Lori recently were divorced. Although grief stricken, Matt was at least partially comforted by his monthly receipt of $10,000 alimony. He was particularly excited to learn from his friend, Denzel, that the alimony was not taxable. Use an available tax service to determine if Denzel is correct. Would your answer change if Matt and Lori continued to live together?

research

LO 2-5 73. Shaun is a huge college football fan. In the past, he has always bought football tickets on the street from ticket scalpers. This year, he decided to join the university's ticket program, which requires a $2,000 contribution to the university for the "right" to purchase tickets. Shaun will then pay $400 per season ticket. Shaun understands that the price paid for the season tickets is not tax deductible as a charitable contribution. However, contributions to a university are typically tax deductible.

research
a) Use an available tax service to determine how much, if any, of Shaun's $2,000 contribution for the right to purchase tickets is tax deductible.

b) Write a letter to Shaun communicating the results of your research.

LO 2-5 74. Latrell recently used his Delta Skymiles to purchase a free round-trip ticket to Milan, Italy (value $1,200). The frequent flyer miles used to purchase the ticket were generated from Latrell's business travel as a CPA. Latrell's employer paid for his business trips, and he was not taxed on the travel reimbursement.

research
a) Use an available tax research service to determine how much income, if any, does Latrell have to recognize as a result of purchasing an airline ticket with Skymiles earned from business travel.

b) Write a memo communicating the results of your research.

75. Benjamin, a new staff accountant for Local Firm CPAs LLC takes a CPA review course to help prepare for the CPA exam. Benjamin is not reimbursed for the cost of the course ($1,500), but his firm expects him to take and pass the exam. **LO 2-5**

    research

    a) Use an available tax research service to determine if Benjamin may deduct the cost of the CPA exam course.

    b) Write a memo communicating the results of your research.

76. Randy has found conflicting authorities that address a research question for one of his clients. The majority of the authorities provide an unfavorable answer for his client. Randy estimates that if the client takes the more favorable position on its tax return that there is approximately a 48 percent chance that the position will be sustained upon audit or judicial proceeding. If the client takes this position on its tax return, will Randy be subject to penalty? Will the client potentially be subject to penalty? **LO 2-6**

77. Using the same facts from the previous problem, how would your answer change if Randy estimates that there is only a 20 percent chance that the position will be sustained upon audit or judicial proceeding? **LO 2-6**

78. Sasha owes additional tax imposed in a recent audit. In addition to the tax, will she be assessed other amounts? If so, how will these amounts be determined? **LO 2-7**

79. Maurice has a client that recently asked him about the odds of the IRS detecting cash transactions not reported on a tax return. What are some of the issues that Maurice should discuss with his client? **LO 2-7**

chapter

3

Tax Planning Strategies and Related Limitations

Learning Objectives

Upon completing this chapter, you should be able to:

LO 3-1 Identify the objectives of basic tax planning strategies.

LO 3-2 Apply the timing strategy and describe its applications and limitations.

LO 3-3 Apply the concept of present value to tax planning.

LO 3-4 Apply the strategy of income shifting, provide examples, and describe its limitations.

LO 3-5 Apply the conversion strategy, provide examples, and describe its limitations.

LO 3-6 Describe basic judicial doctrines that limit tax planning strategies.

LO 3-7 Contrast tax avoidance and tax evasion.

© Cultura RF/Getty Images

Storyline Summary

Taxpayers:	Bill and Mercedes
Family description:	Bill and Mercedes are married with one daughter, Margaret.
Employment status:	Bill is an economics professor; Mercedes is a small-business owner.
Filing status:	Married, filing jointly
Current situation:	Bill and Mercedes want to engage in less risky tax planning strategies.

While working with their CPA during their audit, Bill and Mercedes decide to inquire about less risky tax planning opportunities. Specifically, they would like to gain a better understanding of how to maximize their after-tax returns without increasing their potential for another audit. (Although it was fun and educational, one audit is enough!) Mercedes is convinced that, as a small-business owner (Lavish Interior Designs Inc.), she pays more than her fair share of taxes. Likewise, Bill, an avid investor, wonders whether he is missing the mark by not considering taxes in his investment decisions. ■

Bill and Mercedes have come to the right place. This chapter describes the basic tax planning concepts that form the basis of the simplest to most complex tax planning transactions. In the process we also discuss the judicial doctrines that serve as basic limits on tax planning.

BASIC TAX PLANNING OVERVIEW

LO 3-1

Effective tax planning requires a basic understanding of the roles that taxes and nontax factors play in structuring business, investment, and personal decisions. Although taxes may not be the sole or even the primary determinant of a transaction or its structure, taxes can significantly affect the costs or benefits associated with business, investment, and personal transactions. Thus, the tax implications of competing transactions warrant careful consideration. Likewise, nontax factors, such as the taxpayer's financial goals or legal constraints, are an integral part of every transaction.

In general terms, effective tax planning maximizes the taxpayer's after-tax wealth while achieving the taxpayer's nontax goals. Maximizing after-tax wealth is not necessarily the same as minimizing taxes. Specifically, maximizing after-tax wealth requires us to consider both the tax and nontax costs and benefits of alternative transactions, whereas tax minimization focuses solely on a single cost—taxes. Indeed, if the goal of tax planning were simply to minimize taxes, the simplest way to achieve it would be to earn no income at all. Obviously, this strategy has potential limitations—most notably, the unattractive nontax consequence of poverty. Thus, it is necessary to consider the nontax ramifications of any planning strategy.

Virtually every transaction includes three parties: the taxpayer, the other transacting party, and the uninvited silent party that specifies the tax consequences of the transaction—the government. Astute tax planning requires an understanding of the tax and nontax costs from the taxpayer's *and* the other party's perspective. For example, as discussed in Chapter 12, it would be impossible for an employer to develop an effective compensation plan without considering the tax and nontax costs associated with different compensation arrangements from both the employer's and the employees' perspectives. With sound tax planning, the employer can design a compensation package that generates value for employees while reducing costs for the employer. (One way to achieve this goal is through the use of nontaxable fringe benefits, such as health insurance, which are deductible by the employer but not taxable income to employees.) Throughout the text, we highlight situations where this multilateral approach to tax planning is especially important.

In this chapter we discuss three basic tax planning strategies that represent the building blocks of tax planning:

1. *Timing* (deferring or accelerating taxable income and tax deductions).
2. *Income shifting* (shifting income from high- to low-tax-rate taxpayers).
3. *Conversion* (converting income from high- to low-tax-rate activities).

TIMING STRATEGIES

LO 3-2 **LO 3-3**

LO 3-6

One of the cornerstones of basic tax planning is the idea of *timing. When* income is taxed or an expense is deducted affects the associated "real" tax costs or savings. This is true for two reasons. First, the timing of when income is taxed or an expense is deducted affects the *present value* of the taxes paid on income or the tax savings on deductions. Second, the tax costs of income and tax savings of deductions vary as *tax rates* change. The tax costs on income are higher when tax rates are higher and lower when tax rates are lower. Likewise, the tax savings on deductions are higher when tax rates are higher and lower when tax rates are lower. Let's look at the effects of present value and tax rates on the timing strategy.

Present Value of Money

The concept of **present value**—also known as the time value of money—basically states that $1 today is worth *more* than $1 in the future. Is this true, or is this some type of new math?

It's true. Assuming an investor can earn a positive **after-tax rate of return** such as 5 percent, $1 invested today should be worth $1.05 in one year.[1] Specifically

Eq. 3-1

$$\text{Future Value} = \text{Present Value} \times (1 + r)^n$$
$$= \$1 \times (1 + .05)^1 = \$1.05$$

where $1 is the present value, r is the after-tax rate of return (5 percent), and n is the investment period (1 year). Hence, $1 today is equivalent to $1.05 in one year. The implication of the time value of money for tax planning is that the timing of a cash inflow or a cash outflow affects the present value of the income or expense.

Example 3-1

Bill is given the choice of receiving a $1,000 nontaxable gift today or a $1,000 nontaxable gift in one year. Which would Bill prefer? Assume Bill could invest $1,000 today and earn an 8 percent return after taxes in one year. If he receives the gift today, how much would the $1,000 be worth in one year?

Answer: The $1,000 gift today would be worth $1,080 in one year and thus, Bill should prefer to receive the gift today. Specifically,

$$\text{Future Value} = \text{Present Value} \times (1 + r)^n$$
$$= \$1,000 \times (1 + .08)^1 = \$1,080$$

In terms of *future value,* the choice in the above example of receiving either $1,000 today or $1,000 in one year simplifies to a choice of $1,080 or $1,000. For even the least materialistic individual, choosing $1,080—that is, $1,000 *today*—should be straightforward.

Often tax planners find it useful to consider sums not in terms of future value, but rather in terms of present value. How would we restate the choice in Example 3-1 in terms of present value? Obviously, the present value of receiving $1,000 today is $1,000, but what is the *present value* of $1,000 received in one year? The answer depends on the **discount factor,** which we derive from the taxpayer's expected after-tax rate of return. The discount factor is very useful for calculating the present value of future inflows or outflows of cash. We can derive the discount factor for a given rate of return simply by rearranging the future value equation (Eq. 3-1) from above:

Eq. 3-2

$$\text{Present Value} = \text{Future Value}/(1 + r)^n$$
$$= \$1/(1 + .08)^1 = \$0.926$$
$$\text{Therefore, the discount factor} = 0.926$$

THE KEY FACTS

Present Value of Money

- The concept of present value—also known as the time value of money—states that $1 today is worth *more* than $1 in the future.
- The implication of the time value of money for tax planning is that the timing of a cash inflow or a cash outflow affects the present value of the income or expense.
- Present Value = Future Value/$(1 + r)^n$.
- When considering cash inflows, higher present values are preferred; when considering cash outflows, lower present values are preferred.

[1]Assuming a constant marginal tax rate (t), after-tax rate of return (r) may be calculated as follows: $r = R \times (1 - t)$, where R is the taxpayer's before-tax rate of return.

EXHIBIT 3-1   **Present Value of a Single Payment at Various Annual Rates of Return**

Year	4%	5%	6%	7%	8%	9%	10%	11%	12%
1	.962	.952	.943	.935	.926	.917	.909	.901	.893
2	.925	.907	.890	.873	.857	.842	.826	.812	.797
3	.889	.864	.840	.816	.794	.772	.751	.731	.712
4	.855	.823	.792	.763	.735	.708	.683	.659	.636
5	.822	.784	.747	.713	.681	.650	.621	.593	.567
6	.790	.746	.705	.666	.630	.596	.564	.535	.507
7	.760	.711	.665	.623	.583	.547	.513	.482	.452
8	.731	.677	.627	.582	.540	.502	.467	.434	.404
9	.703	.645	.592	.544	.500	.460	.424	.391	.361
10	.676	.614	.558	.508	.463	.422	.386	.352	.322
11	.650	.585	.527	.475	.429	.388	.350	.317	.287
12	.625	.557	.497	.444	.397	.356	.319	.286	.257
13	.601	.530	.469	.415	.368	.326	.290	.258	.229
14	.577	.505	.442	.388	.340	.299	.263	.232	.205
15	.555	.481	.417	.362	.315	.275	.239	.209	.183

Applying the discount factor, we can see that $1,000 received in one year is worth $926 in today's dollars. Thus, in terms of present value, Bill's choice in Example 3-1 simplifies to a choice between a cash inflow of $1,000 today and a cash inflow worth $926 today. Again, choosing $1,000 today is pretty straightforward.

Exhibit 3-1 provides the discount factors for a lump sum (single payment) received in *n* periods using various rates of return. Tax planners frequently utilize such tables for quick reference in calculating present value for sums under consideration.

Example 3-2

At a recent holiday sale, Bill and Mercedes purchased $1,000 worth of furniture with "no money down and no payments for one year!" How much money is this deal really worth? (Assume their after-tax rate of return on investments is 10 percent.)

Answer: The discount factor of .909 (Exhibit 3-1, 10% Rate of Return column, Year 1 row) means the present value of $1,000 is $909 ($1,000 × .909 = $909)—so Bill and Mercedes save $91 ($1,000 − $909 = $91).

While Example 3-1 considers a $1,000 cash inflow, Example 3-2 addresses a $1,000 cash *outflow*. In terms of present value, a choice between $1,000 paid today and $1,000 paid in a year simplifies to incurring a cash outflow of either $1,000 (by paying today) or $909 (by paying in one year). Most people would prefer to pay $909. Indeed, financial planners always keep the following general rule of thumb in mind: When considering *cash inflows, prefer higher present values;* when considering *cash outflows, prefer lower present values*.

The Timing Strategy When Tax Rates Are Constant

In terms of tax planning, remember that *taxes paid* represent cash *outflows*, while *tax savings* generated from tax deductions are cash *inflows*. This perspective leads us to two basic tax-related timing strategies when tax rates are constant (not changing):

1. Accelerate tax deductions (deduct in an earlier period).
2. Defer recognizing taxable income (recognize in a later period).

Accelerating tax deductions to an earlier period increases the present value of the tax savings from the deduction. That is, tax savings received now have a higher present value than the same amount received a year from now.

Deferring income to a later period decreases the present value of the tax cost of the income. That is, taxes paid a year from now have a lower present value than taxes paid today. These two strategies are summarized in Exhibit 3-2.

EXHIBIT 3-2   The Timing Tax Strategy When Tax Rates Are Constant

Item	Recommendation	Why?
Tax deductions	Accelerate tax deductions into earlier years.	Maximizes the present value of tax savings from deductions.
Taxable income	Defer taxable income into later tax years.	Minimizes the present value of taxes paid.

Example 3-3

Mercedes, a calendar-year taxpayer, uses the cash method of accounting for her small business.[2] On December 28, she receives a $10,000 bill from her accountant for consulting services related to her small business. She can avoid late payment charges by paying the $10,000 bill before January 10 of next year. Let's assume that Mercedes's marginal tax rate is 30 percent *this year and next* and that she can earn an after-tax rate of return of 10 percent on her investments. When should she pay the $10,000 bill—this year or next?

Answer: If Mercedes pays the bill this year, she will receive a tax deduction on this year's tax return.[3] If she pays the bill in January, she will receive a tax deduction on next year's tax return (one year later). She needs to compare the after-tax cost of the accounting service using the present value of the tax savings for each scenario:

Present Value Comparison		
Description	Option 1: Pay $10,000 bill *this year*	Option 2: Pay $10,000 bill *next year*
Tax deduction	$10,000	$10,000
Marginal tax rate	× 30%	× 30%
Tax savings	$ 3,000	$ 3,000
Discount factor	× 1	× .909
Present value tax savings	$ 3,000	$ 2,727
After-tax cost of accounting services:		
Before-tax cost	$10,000	$10,000
Less: Present value tax savings	− 3,000	− 2,727
After-tax cost of accounting services	$ 7,000	$ 7,273

Since Mercedes would surely rather spend $7,000 than $7,273 for accounting services, paying the bill in December is the clear winner.

---

[2]In Chapter 9, we discuss the basic accounting methods (e.g., cash vs. the accrual method), which influence the timing of when income and deductions are recognized for tax purposes.

[3]Accelerating her payment from January 10 to December 31 will increase the present value of the $10,000 cash outflow by 10 days. Thus, there is a minor present value cost associated with accelerating her payment.

In terms of accelerating deductions, the intent of the timing strategy is to accelerate the tax deduction significantly *without* accelerating the actual cash outflow that generates the expense. Indeed, if we assume a marginal rate of 30 percent and an after-tax return of 8 percent, accelerating a $1,000 cash outflow by one year to realize $300 in tax savings actually *increases* the after-tax *cost* of the expense from $648.20 to $700.

Present Value Comparison		
Description	**Present value of net cash outflow *today***	**Present value of net cash outflow in *one year***
Cash outflow	$1,000	$ 1,000.00
Less: Tax savings (outflow × 30% tax rate)	− 300	− 300.00
Net cash outflow	$ 700	$ 700.00
Present value factor	× 1	× .926
Present value of net cash outflow today	$ 700	$ 648.20

Generally speaking, whenever a taxpayer can accelerate a deduction without also accelerating the cash outflow, the timing strategy will be more beneficial.

Is the accelerating deductions strategy utilized in the real world? Yes. While the strategy is particularly effective for cash-method taxpayers who can often control the year in which they pay their expenses, all taxpayers have *some* latitude in timing deductions. Common examples of the timing strategy include accelerating depreciation deductions for depreciable assets, using LIFO instead of FIFO for inventory, and accelerating the deduction of certain prepaid expenses.[4] For large corporations, the benefits associated with this timing strategy can be quite substantial. Thus, tax planners spend considerable time evaluating the proper period in which to recognize expenses and identifying opportunities to accelerate deductions.

Are there certain taxpayer or transaction attributes that enhance the advantages of accelerating deductions? Absolutely. Higher tax rates, higher rates of return, larger transaction amounts, and the ability to accelerate deductions by two or more years all increase the benefits of accelerating deductions. To demonstrate this for yourself, simply rework Example 3-3 and substitute any of the following: 50 percent tax rate, 12 percent after-tax rate of return, $100,000 expense, or a five-year period difference in the timing of the expense deduction. The benefits of accelerating deductions become much more prominent with these changes.

Deferring income recognition is an equally beneficial timing strategy, especially when the taxpayer can defer the recognition of income significantly without deferring the actual receipt of income very much. Consider the following example.

Example 3-4

In early December, Bill decides he would like to sell $100,000 of his Dell Inc. stock, which cost $20,000 10 years ago. Assume Bill's tax rate on the $80,000 gain will be 15 percent and his typical after-tax rate of return on investments is 7 percent. What effect would deferring the sale to January have on Bill's after-tax income on the sale?

[4]See the discussion of accounting methods in Chapter 9.

Answer:

Description	Option 1: Sell the $100,000 stock in *December*[5]	Option 2: Sell the $100,000 stock in *January*[6]
Sales price	$100,000	$100,000
Less: Cost of stock	− 20,000	− 20,000
Gain on sale	$ 80,000	$ 80,000
Marginal tax rate	× 15%	× 15%
Tax on gain	$ 12,000	$ 12,000
Discount factor	× 1	× .935
Present value tax cost	$ 12,000	$ 11,220
After-tax income from sale:		
Before-tax income	$100,000	$100,000
Less: Present value tax cost	− 12,000	− 11,220
After-tax income from sale	$ 88,000	$ 88,780

Present Value Comparison

Bill would doubtlessly prefer to earn $88,780 to $88,000, so from a tax perspective, selling the Dell Inc. stock in January is preferable. An important nontax issue for Bill to consider is the possibility that the stock price may fluctuate between December and January.

Income deferral represents an important aspect of investment planning (Chapter 7), retirement planning (Chapter 13), and certain property transactions (Chapter 11). Income-related timing considerations also affect tax planning for everyday business operations, such as determining the appropriate period in which to recognize sales income (upon product shipment, on delivery, or on customer acceptance).

Do certain taxpayer or transaction attributes enhance the advantages of deferring income? Yes. The list is very similar to that for accelerating deductions: Higher tax rates, higher rates of return, larger transaction amounts, and the ability to defer revenue recognition for longer periods of time increase the benefits of deferral. To demonstrate this for yourself, simply rework Example 3-4 using any of the following: 50 percent tax rate, 12 percent after-tax rate of return on investments, or $200,000 gain.[7]

The Timing Strategy When Tax Rates Change

When tax rates change, the timing strategy requires a little more consideration because the tax costs of income and the tax savings from deductions will now vary. The higher the tax rate, the higher the tax savings for a tax deduction. The

THE KEY FACTS

The Timing Strategy

- The timing of when income is taxed or an expense is deducted affects the *present value* of the taxes paid on income or tax savings on deductions.
- The tax costs of income and tax savings of deductions vary as *tax rates* change.
- When tax rates are constant, tax planners prefer to defer income and accelerate deductions.
- When tax rates are increasing, the taxpayer must calculate the optimal tax strategies for deductions and income.
- When tax rates are decreasing, taxpayers should accelerate tax deductions into earlier years and defer taxable income to later years.

---

[5]This will require Bill to pay the tax on the gain no later than April 15 of the following year (i.e., three months after the sale). If Bill and Mercedes's current-year withholding and estimated payments do not equal or exceed 110 percent of their previous year's tax liability, they will have to make an estimated payment by January 15 to avoid the failure to make estimated tax payment penalty discussed later in Chapter 8. This example assumes that Bill and Mercedes can avoid the underpayment of estimated tax penalty discussed in Chapter 8 by paying 110 percent of their previous year's tax liability in both options 1 and 2. Thus, they can defer paying the tax on the gain until April 15 of the year following the sale.

[6]This will require Bill to pay the tax on the gain no later than April 15 of the following year (i.e., 15 months after the sale).

[7]In Example 3-4, increasing the deferral period (e.g., from one to five years) also increases the benefits of tax deferral but requires additional assumptions regarding the expected five-year return of the Dell Inc. stock (assuming he does not sell the stock for five years) and his new investment (assuming he sells the Dell Inc. stock and immediately reinvests the after-tax proceeds).

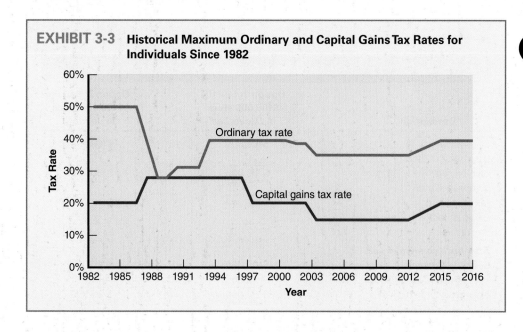

EXHIBIT 3-3   Historical Maximum Ordinary and Capital Gains Tax Rates for Individuals Since 1982

lower the tax rate, the lower the tax costs for taxable income. *All other things being equal, taxpayers should prefer to recognize deductions during high-tax-rate years and income during low-tax-rate years.* The implication is that before a taxpayer implements the timing strategies suggested above (accelerate deductions, defer income), she should consider whether her tax rates are likely to change. In fact, as we discuss below, increasing tax rates may even suggest the taxpayer should *accelerate* income and *defer* deductions.

What would cause a taxpayer's marginal tax rate to change? The taxpayer's taxable income can change, perhaps due to changing jobs, retiring, or starting a new business. Indeed, in Chapter 1, we demonstrated how a taxpayer's marginal tax rate changes as income or deductions change. Marginal tax rates can also change because of tax legislation. We discussed the tax legislative process in Chapter 2 and noted that Congress frequently enacts tax legislation because lawmakers use taxes to raise revenue, stimulate the economy, and so on. In the last 30 years, Congress has changed the maximum statutory tax rates that apply to ordinary income, such as wages and business income, or capital gains, such as gains from the sale of stock, for individual taxpayers no fewer than nine times (see Exhibit 3-3).

Let's take a look at how changing tax rates affect the timing strategy recommendations. Exhibit 3-4 presents recommendations when tax rates are increasing. The taxpayer must actually calculate the optimal tax strategies for deductions and income when tax rates are increasing. Specifically, because accelerating deductions causes them to be recognized in a *lower*-tax-rate year, the taxpayer must

EXHIBIT 3-4   The Timing Tax Strategy When Tax Rates Are Increasing

Item	Recommendation	Why?
Tax deductions	Requires calculation to determine optimal strategy.	The taxpayer must calculate whether the benefit of accelerating deductions outweighs the disadvantage of recognizing deductions in a *lower*-tax-rate year.
Taxable income	Requires calculation to determine optimal strategy.	The taxpayer must calculate whether the benefit of deferring income outweighs the disadvantage of recognizing income in a *higher*-tax-rate year.

calculate whether the benefit of accelerating the deduction outweighs the disadvantage. Likewise, because deferring income causes income to be recognized in a *higher*-tax-rate year, the taxpayer must calculate whether the benefit of deferring it outweighs the disadvantage.

Example 3-5

Having decided she needs new equipment for her business, Mercedes is now considering whether to make the purchase and claim a corresponding $10,000 deduction at year-end or next year. Mercedes anticipates that, with the new machinery, her business income will rise such that her marginal rate will increase from 20 percent this year to 28 percent next year. Assuming her after-tax rate of return is 8 percent, what should Mercedes do?

Answer: Given rising tax rates, Mercedes must calculate the after-tax cost of the equipment for *both* options and compare present values.

Present Value Comparison		
Description	**Option 1: Pay $10,000 bill *this year***	**Option 2: Pay $10,000 bill *next year***
Tax deduction	$10,000	$10,000
Marginal tax rate	× 20%	× 28%
Tax savings	$ 2,000	$ 2,800
Discount factor	× 1	× .926
Present value tax savings	$ 2,000	$ 2,593
After-tax cost of equipment:		
Before-tax cost	$10,000	$10,000
Less: Present value tax savings	− 2,000	− 2,593
After-tax cost of equipment	$ 8,000	$ 7,407

Paying the $10,000 in January is the clear winner.

In the above example, if the choice were either to recognize $10,000 of *income* this year or next, the *amounts* would be exactly the same but the conclusion would be different, and Mercedes would prefer to receive $8,000 of after-tax income this year instead of $7,407. (Remember, when considering cash *inflows,* we prefer the *higher* present value.) Are these always the answers when tax rates are increasing? No, the answer will depend both on the taxpayer's after-tax rate of return and on the magnitude of the tax rate increase.

Now let's consider the recommendations when tax rates are *decreasing*—a common scenario when an individual reaches retirement. Exhibit 3-5 presents the timing strategy recommendations in this case. The recommendations are clear. Taxpayers

EXHIBIT 3-5   The Timing Tax Strategy When Tax Rates Are *Decreasing*

Item	Recommendation	Why?
Tax deductions	Accelerate tax deductions into earlier years.	Maximizes the present value of tax savings from deductions due to the acceleration of the deductions into *earlier* years with a *higher*-tax-rate year.
Taxable income	Defer taxable income into later tax years.	Minimizes the present value of taxes paid due to the deferral of the income to later years with a *lower* tax rate.

should accelerate tax deductions into earlier years to reap the tax savings from *accelerating* deductions to *higher*-tax-rate years. Likewise, taxpayers should defer taxable income to later years to enjoy the tax benefits of *deferring* taxable income to *lower*-tax-rate years.

Limitations to Timing Strategies   Timing strategies contain certain inherent limitations. First, tax laws generally require taxpayers to continue their investment in an asset in order to defer income recognition for tax purposes. In other words, deferral is generally not an option if a taxpayer has "cashed out" of an investment.[8] For example, Bill could not sell his Dell stock in December and then choose not to recognize the income until January. A deferral strategy may not be optimal (1) if the taxpayer has severe cash flow needs, (2) if continuing the investment would generate a low rate of return compared to other investments, or (3) if the current investment would subject the taxpayer to unnecessary risk. For example, the risk that the value of Bill's investment in Dell Inc. will decline from December to January in Example 3-4 may lead Bill to forgo deferring his stock sale until January. Again, the astute taxpayer considers both the tax *and* nontax ramifications of deferring income.

A second limitation results from the **constructive receipt doctrine,** which also restricts income deferral for cash-method taxpayers.[9] Unlike accrual-method taxpayers, cash-method taxpayers report income for tax purposes when the income is *received,* whether it is in the form of cash, property, or services.[10] The cash method affords taxpayers some leeway in determining when to recognize income because such taxpayers can control when they bill their clients. However, the constructive receipt doctrine provides that a taxpayer must recognize income when it is actually *or* constructively received. Constructive receipt is deemed to have occurred if the income has been credited to the taxpayer's account or if the income is unconditionally available to the taxpayer, the taxpayer is aware of the income's availability, and there are no restrictions on the taxpayer's control over the income.

Example 3-6

Mercedes's brother-in-law, Carlos, works for King Acura, which recently instituted a bonus plan that pays year-end bonuses each December to employees rated above average for their customer service. Carlos is expecting a $10,000 bonus this year that will be paid on December 31. Thinking he'd prefer to defer this income until next year, Carlos plans to take a vacation on December 30 so that he will not receive his bonus check until January. Will Carlos's strategy work?

Answer: No, the constructive receipt doctrine applies here. Because Carlos's check was unconditionally available to him on December 31, he was aware of its availability, and there were no restrictions on his control over the income on that date, Carlos must report the income in the current year.

---

[8]See the discussions of like-kind exchanges in Chapter 11, investment planning in Chapter 7, and retirement planning in Chapter 13.

[9]Later in this chapter we discuss other judicial doctrines that apply to all planning strategies.

[10]As we discuss in depth in Chapter 9, accrual-method taxpayers report income when it is earned. In general, income is deemed earned when all events have occurred that fix the taxpayer's right to the income and the income can be estimated with reasonable accuracy. Thus, income recognition for accrual-method taxpayers generally is not tied to payment. Receipt of prepaid income by accrual-method taxpayers may trigger income recognition in certain circumstances. The constructive receipt doctrine may apply in these situations.

What could taxpayers do to avoid Carlos's problem in the future? They could request that their employer institute a company policy of paying bonuses on January 1, which would allow all employees to report the bonus income in that year. However, if the employer is a cash-method taxpayer, this creates a potential conflict with its employees.[11] Such an employer would most likely prefer to deduct the bonus in the current year, which requires the bonuses to be paid in December. This conflict would not exist if the employer were an accrual-method taxpayer, because paying the bonuses in January would not affect its ability to deduct the bonuses in the previous year.[12]

INCOME-SHIFTING STRATEGIES

LO 3-4   LO 3-6

We've seen that the value of a tax deduction, or the tax cost of income, varies with the marginal tax rate. We've also seen that tax rates can vary across time, which leads to basic tax planning strategies regarding when to recognize deductions and income. Tax rates can also vary across *taxpayers* or *jurisdictions* (states, countries), which leads to still other tax planning strategies—for example, shifting income from high-tax-rate taxpayers to low-tax-rate taxpayers or shifting deductions from low-tax-rate taxpayers to high-tax-rate taxpayers.

The type of taxpayers who benefit most from this strategy are (1) related parties, such as family members or businesses and their owners, who have varying marginal tax rates and are willing to shift income for the benefit of the group; and (2) taxpayers operating in multiple jurisdictions with different marginal tax rates. In any case, tax planners should seek only legitimate methods of shifting income that will withstand IRS scrutiny. In the following section we discuss transactions between family members, followed by a discussion of transactions between owners and their businesses, and finally a discussion of income shifting across jurisdictions.

Transactions between Family Members and Limitations

One of the most common examples of income shifting is high-tax-rate parents shifting income to low-tax-rate children. For example, Bill and Mercedes have a 30 percent marginal tax rate, whereas their daughter, Margaret, has a 10 percent marginal tax rate. Assuming their marginal tax rates remain constant with relatively modest changes in income, every $1 of income that Bill and Mercedes shift to Margaret reduces the family's tax liability by 20 cents [$1 × (30% − 10%)]. Thus, if Bill and Mercedes shift $10,000 of taxable income to Margaret, the family's after-tax income will increase by $2,000. Can taxpayers legally do this? Yes and no. As you might expect, there are limitations on this type of income shifting.

The **assignment of income doctrine** requires income to be taxed to the taxpayer who actually earns it.[13] Merely attributing your paycheck or dividend to another

---

[11]Because King Acura carries inventory, the cash method is not allowed for transactions related to its inventory (e.g., cost of goods sold, sales, etc.). However, King Acura is permitted to use the cash method for other transactions. This mixed method is referred to as the "hybrid" method of accounting.

[12]When an employee/shareholder and an employer/corporation are related (i.e., the employee/shareholder owns more than 50 percent of the value of the employer corporation), the corporation is not allowed to deduct the compensation expense until the employee/shareholder includes the payment in income. §267(a)(2).

[13]Later in this chapter we discuss other judicial doctrines that apply to all planning strategies.

taxpayer does not transfer the tax liability associated with the income. The assignment of income doctrine implies that, in order to shift income to a taxpayer, that taxpayer must actually earn the income. For example, if Mercedes would like to shift some of her business income to Margaret, Margaret must actually earn it. One way to accomplish this would be for Mercedes to employ Margaret in her business and pay her a $10,000 salary. The effects of this transaction are to decrease Mercedes's taxable income by $10,000 because of tax-deductible salary expense, and increase Margaret's income by the $10,000 taxable salary. What if Margaret is paid $10,000 to answer Mercedes's business phone one Saturday afternoon every month? Does this seem reasonable? Not likely. The IRS frowns upon this type of aggressive strategy.

Indeed, the IRS closely scrutinizes such **related-party transactions**—that is, financial activities among family members (also among owners and their businesses, or among businesses owned by the same owners). Unlike **arm's-length transactions,** where each transacting party negotiates for his or her own benefit, related-party transactions involve taxpayers who are much more willing to negotiate for their own common good to the detriment of the IRS. For example, would Mercedes pay an unrelated party $10,000 to answer the phone once a month? Doubtful.[14]

Are there other ways to shift income to children? For example, could Bill shift some of his investment income to Margaret? Yes, but there's a catch. The assignment of income applies what is referred to as the "fruit and the tree" analogy [*Lucas v. Earl* (S. Ct., 1930), 8 AFTR 10287]. For the owner to avoid being taxed on the fruit from the tree (the income), the owner must transfer the tree. Thus, to shift investment income, Bill would also have to transfer ownership in the underlying investment assets to Margaret.[15] Is there a problem with this requirement? Not for Margaret. However, Bill would likely prefer to maintain his wealth. The nontax disadvantages of transferring wealth to implement the income-shifting strategy often outweigh the tax benefits of the transfer. For example, most parents either could not afford to or would have serious reservations about transferring significant wealth to their children—a prime example of how nontax costs may override tax considerations.

Transactions between Owners and Their Businesses and Limitations

Income shifting is not limited to transactions within a family unit. One of the most common examples occurs between owners and their businesses. Let's consider Mercedes's interior design business. Currently, Mercedes operates her business as a sole proprietorship. A sole proprietorship (unlike a C corporation) is not a separate reporting entity, and thus, Mercedes reports her business income and deductions on her individual tax return. Shifting income to or from her sole proprietorship offers little benefit, because all of her sole proprietorship income is reported on her tax return regardless of whether it is attributed to her personally or to her business. On the other hand, if Mercedes operated her interior design business as a C corporation, shifting income to or from the C corporation may make good financial sense because the corporation would be a separate entity

---

[14]The Internal Revenue Code also contains specific provisions to curtail benefits from related-party transactions. For example, as we discuss in Chapter 11, §267 disallows a tax deduction for losses on sales to related parties (even if the sale was consummated at the asset's fair market value).

[15]Further, as we discuss in Chapter 8, the "kiddie tax" may apply when parents shift too much investment income to children. The kiddie tax restricts the amount of a child's investment income that can be taxed at the child's (lower) tax rate instead of the parents' (higher) tax rate.

with tax rates distinct from Mercedes's individual tax rate. Shifting income to herself may allow Mercedes to decrease the tax on her business profits, thereby increasing her after-tax income. Example 3-7 illustrates the savings obtainable from this strategy.

In order to shift income from the corporation to the owner, the corporation must create a tax deduction for itself in the process. Compensation paid to employee–owners is the most common method of shifting income from corporations to their owners. Compensation expense is deductible by the corporation and is generally taxable to the employee. (See Chapter 12 for a broader discussion of nontaxable compensation benefits.) Having the business owner rent property to the corporation or loan money to the corporation are also effective income-shifting methods, because both transactions generate tax deductions for the corporation and income for the shareholder. Because corporations don't get a tax deduction for dividends paid, paying dividends is *not* an effective way to shift income. Having a corporation pay dividends actually results in "double taxation"—the profits generating the dividends are taxed first at the corporate level, and then at the shareholder level. Recommending this tax planning strategy may not be a good way to keep your job as a tax consultant.

Example 3-7

Mercedes is considering incorporating her interior design business. She projects $200,000 of business profit next year. Excluding this profit, Bill and Mercedes expect $160,000 of taxable income next year. If Mercedes would like to minimize her current-year tax liability, should she incorporate her business? [Use the married filing jointly and corporate tax rates inside the back cover of the book to answer this question.]

Answer: If Mercedes does not incorporate her business, the first $71,450 of her business profits will be taxed at 28 percent (from $160,000 to $231,450 of taxable income, the marginal tax rate is 28 percent). The remaining $128,550 (from $231,450 to $360,000 of taxable income) would be taxed at 33 percent. Upon reviewing the corporate tax rate schedule, you should note that the first two corporate tax rates (15 and 25 percent) are lower than Bill and Mercedes's current marginal tax rate of 33 percent. Thus, there appears to be some opportunity for Mercedes to reduce her current-year tax exposure by incorporating her business.[16]

After a taxpayer identifies the opportunity and appropriate method to shift income (compensation paid to a related party), he or she can easily determine the optimal amount to shift depending on the taxpayers' marginal tax rates.

Example 3-8

Assuming Mercedes's goal is to minimize her current-year federal income tax liability, how much of the $200,000 business income should her corporation report?

Answer: It should report $75,000. Comparing the two tax rate schedules reveals how to calculate this number.

Step 1: Would Mercedes rather have income taxed at 15 percent (the corporation's marginal tax rate from zero to $50,000 taxable income) or 28 percent (Bill and Mercedes's marginal tax rate

(continued on page 3-14)

---

[16]Note that this is a simplified discussion of one of many tax issues associated with incorporating a business. For example, as discussed later in this chapter, Mercedes must consider the judicial doctrines (economic substance, business purpose, etc.) in making this decision and for further tax planning opportunities described in the following example.

before recognizing any profit from Mercedes's business)? Fifteen percent is the obvious answer. To take advantage of the 15 percent corporate tax bracket, Mercedes should retain $50,000 of the expected $200,000 in profits in the corporation, because $50,000 is the width of the 15 percent corporate tax bracket.

Step 2: Assuming the corporation reports $50,000 of income, its marginal tax rate will now be 25 percent, and thus Mercedes's choice is to have any additional income taxed at 25 percent (the corporation's marginal tax rate) or at 28 percent (Bill and Mercedes's marginal tax rate before recognizing any profit from Mercedes's business). Twenty-five percent is the clear answer. To take advantage of the 25 percent corporate tax bracket, the corporation should retain another $25,000 of the expected $200,000 in profits ($25,000 is the width of the 25 percent corporate tax bracket). The corporation's marginal tax rate will now be 34 percent.

Step 3: Continuing this same decision process, Mercedes should shift the remaining $125,000 of profits ($71,450 taxed at 28 percent and $53,550 taxed at 33 percent) to herself and Bill—via a salary paid to Mercedes—because their marginal tax rates (28 percent and 33 percent) will be lower than the corporation's marginal tax rate (34 percent).

How much current federal income tax does this strategy save Bill and Mercedes? The corporation's and Bill and Mercedes's combined federal income tax liability will be $83,213 ($13,750 for the corporation plus $69,463 for Bill and Mercedes) compared to $94,213 for Bill and Mercedes if the business is operated as a sole proprietorship. Thus, they will save $11,000.[17]

Are there nontax disadvantages of the income-shifting-via-incorporating strategy? Yes. For example, one nontax disadvantage for Mercedes is that her new corporation now has $61,250 of her after-tax profits ($75,000 profits less $13,750 of corporate tax). If Mercedes has personal cash-flow needs that require use of the $61,250, this is not a viable strategy. Indeed, it's advantageous only if the business owner intends to reinvest the business profits into the business. Furthermore, any subsequent transactions between Mercedes and the corporation would clearly be related-party transactions. Thus, Mercedes should be prepared for IRS scrutiny.[18] If the salary, rent, and other costs are deemed to be unreasonable, the IRS may reclassify any excess payments above the value of services and property provided as nondeductible corporate dividends. In this scenario, the corporation and Mercedes would both pay income tax on each dollar of deemed dividend payment. This is not a good outcome for Mercedes or any business owner.

Example 3-9

Upon reviewing Bill and Mercedes's tax return, the IRS reclassifies $65,000 of Mercedes's $125,000 salary in Example 3-8 as a dividend. What are the tax consequences of this reclassification?

Answer: (1) The corporation's taxable income will increase from $75,000 to $140,000 because dividends are not deductible, thereby increasing the corporation's tax liability from $13,750 to $37,850; and (2) Bill and Mercedes's taxable income will remain the same, except $65,000 of

---

[17]This strategy will result in the eventual double taxation of the income retained in Mercedes's corporation. Specifically, Mercedes will eventually have to pay tax on the income retained by the corporation, either in the form of taxable dividends from the corporation or a taxable gain when she sells or liquidates the corporation. The present value of this additional layer of tax reduces the tax savings from this strategy. The longer that the second layer of tax is deferred, the more advantageous this strategy will be. This calculation is beyond the scope of this chapter.

[18]The taxpayer should maintain documentation for related-party transactions (e.g., notes for related-party loans and contemporaneous documentation of reasonable compensation paid to related parties).

their $285,000 of taxable income will be dividends taxed at a preferential 15 percent tax rate.[19] Thus, Bill and Mercedes will have $220,000 of taxable income taxed at their ordinary tax rates ($48,586 of tax) and $65,000 of dividend income taxed at 15 percent ($9,750 of tax), resulting in a tax liability of $58,336.

Under this scenario, the combined tax liabilities of the corporation and Bill and Mercedes will be $96,186, which is $1,973 *higher* than Bill and Mercedes's $94,213 tax liability had they not incorporated Mercedes's business.[20]

As the above examples illustrate, tax-avoiding strategies can be quite beneficial, but they also entail some financial risks if the structure fails to pass muster with the IRS.

ETHICS

Agnes Meher is the owner of LuPat, a profitable construction company that she operates as a sole proprietorship. As a sole proprietor, Agnes reports the business income from LuPat on her individual tax return. Agnes expects the business to generate $400,000 of taxable income this year, which in combination with her other income, will put her in the top tax bracket (39.6%). Agnes has two children named Ellie Mae and Spencer, ages 9 and 11 respectively, who do not currently have any taxable income. Agnes would like to shift some of her income from LuPat to Ellie Mae and Spencer to reduce the overall tax burden from the business income. To shift the income, Agnes hired Ellie Mae and Spencer to perform some janitorial and clerical services for LuPat, paying each child $20,000. What do you think of Agnes's strategy?

Income Shifting across Jurisdictions and Limitations

Taxpayers that operate in multiple jurisdictions (states, countries) also apply the income-shifting strategy. Specifically, income earned in different jurisdictions— whether in the United States or abroad, and for state income tax purposes, income earned in different states—is often taxed very differently. With a proper understanding of the differences in tax laws across jurisdictions, taxpayers can use these differences to maximize their after-tax wealth.

Example 3-10

Carlos's employer, King Acura, has two locations. Its main location is in South Dakota (a state with no corporate tax), with a secondary location in North Dakota (maximum corporate state tax rate of 4.31 percent). What tax planning strategy may save money for King Acura?

Answer: The most obvious strategy is to shift income from the North Dakota location to the South Dakota location, thereby reducing King Acura's state income tax liability by about 4.31 cents for every dollar of income shifted.[21]

---

[19]Bill and Mercedes may also be subject to an additional 3.8% Net Investment Income Tax on some of the reclassified dividends, which would increase the combined tax liabilities if Bill and Mercedes incorporate the business.

[20]Chapter 12 discusses the consequences of unreasonable compensation to employee–owners.

[21]Because state taxes are deductible for federal tax purposes, every dollar of state taxes reduced with this strategy will increase King Acura's federal income tax liability by its federal marginal tax rate (e.g., 35 percent). Thus, the net tax savings for every dollar of income shifted from North Dakota to South Dakota will be 2.94 percent, which equals the state tax savings (4.53 percent) less the federal tax increase resulting from the lost state tax deduction (4.53% × 35%).

A number of possibilities exist to execute a strategy such as King Acura's in Example 3-10. Assuming that the North Dakota and South Dakota locations exchange cars, the firm could shift income via *transfer pricing* (using the price the South Dakota location charges the North Dakota location for cars transferred to North Dakota). Likewise, if the South Dakota location (the corporate headquarters) provides a legitimate support function for the North Dakota location, the firm should allocate a portion of the overhead and administrative expenses from the South Dakota location to the North Dakota location.

What are some of the limitations of income shifting across jurisdictions? First, taxing authorities are fully aware of the tax benefits of strategically structuring transactions across tax borders (across countries or states). Thus, the IRS closely examines transfer pricing on international transactions. Similarly, state tax authorities scrutinize interstate transactions between related taxpayers. Second, when taxpayers locate in low-tax-rate jurisdictions to, in effect, shift income to a tax-advantaged jurisdiction, they may bear **implicit taxes** (i.e., additional costs attributable to the jurisdiction's tax advantage). For example, the demand for workers, services, or property in low-tax-rate jurisdictions, whether a foreign country or a low-tax state, may increase the nontax costs associated with operating a business there enough to offset the tax advantages. Finally, negative publicity from moving operations (and jobs) from the United States to a lower-tax jurisdiction may more than offset any tax benefits associated with these strategies.

LO 3-5

CONVERSION STRATEGIES

We've now seen how tax rates can vary across time and taxpayers. They can also vary across different *activities*. For example, ordinary income such as salary, interest income, and business income received by individual taxpayers is taxed at their ordinary marginal tax rates, whereas long-term capital gains, which are gains from the sale of investment assets held longer than one year, and dividends are taxed at lower tax rates (currently a maximum of 20 percent), and still other forms of income like nontaxable compensation benefits and municipal bond interest are tax-exempt. Expenses from different types of activities may also be treated very differently for tax purposes. Business expenses are generally fully tax deductible, whereas tax deductions for investment expenses may be limited, and tax deductions for personal expenses may be completely disallowed. In sum, the tax law does not treat all types of income or deductions the same. This understanding forms the basis for the conversion strategy—recasting income and expenses to receive the most favorable tax treatment.

To implement the conversion strategy, the taxpayer must be aware of the underlying differences in tax treatment across various types of income, expenses, and activities and have some ability to alter the nature of the income or expense to receive the more advantageous tax treatment. What are some common examples of the conversion strategy? In Chapter 4, we explain character differences in income and deductions. In Chapter 7, we consider investment planning and the advantages of investing in assets that generate preferentially taxed income. In Chapter 9, we explain the basic differences between business and investment activities and what characteristics result in the more favorable "business" designation for expense deductions. In Chapters 12 and 13, we discuss compensation planning and the benefits of restructuring employee compensation from currently taxable compensation to nontaxable or tax-deferred forms of compensation, such as employer-provided health insurance and retirement contributions.

To analyze the benefits of the conversion strategy, you often compare the after-tax returns of alternative investments. Given a stationary marginal tax rate, you can calculate an investment's after-tax rate of return as follows:

Eq. 3-3

$$\text{After-Tax Return} = \text{Before-Tax Return} - (\text{Before-Tax Return} \times \text{Marginal Tax Rate})$$

which simplifies to

Eq. 3-4

$$\text{After-Tax Return} = \text{Before-Tax Return} \times (1 - \text{Marginal Tax Rate})$$

Example 3-11

Bill is contemplating three different investments, each with the same amount of risk:

1. A high-dividend stock that pays 8.5 percent dividends annually but has no appreciation potential.
2. Taxable corporate bonds that pay 9 percent interest annually.
3. Tax-exempt municipal bonds that pay 6 percent interest annually.

Assuming that dividends are taxed at 20 percent and that Bill's marginal tax rate on ordinary income is 30 percent, which investment should Bill choose?

Answer: To answer this question, we must compute Bill's after-tax rate of return for each investment. The after-tax returns for the three investments are

Investment Choice	Computation	After-Tax Return
High-dividend stock	8.5% × (1 − 20%) =	6.8%
Corporate bond	9% × (1 − 30%) =	6.3
Municipal bond	6% × (1 − 0%) =	6.0

Accordingly, Bill should choose the dividend-yielding stock.

What marginal tax rate on ordinary income would make Bill indifferent between the dividend-yielding stock and the corporate bond?

Answer: The dividend-yielding stock has an after-tax rate return of 6.8 percent. For Bill to be indifferent between this stock and the corporate bond, the corporate bond would need a 6.8 percent after-tax rate of return. We can use Eq. 3-4 above to solve for the marginal tax rate.

$$\text{After-Tax Return} = \text{Before-Tax Return} \times (1 - \text{Marginal Tax Rate})$$
$$6.8\% = 9\% \times (1 - \text{Marginal Tax Rate})$$
$$\text{Marginal Tax Rate} = 24.44\%$$

Let's check this answer: After-Tax Return = 9% × (1 − 24.44%) = 6.8%

The example above shows how taxpayers may compare investments when the investment period is one year. However, when taxpayers hold investments for more than a year they potentially receive benefits from combining the timing strategy and the conversion strategy. First, they may be able to defer recognizing gains on the assets until they sell them—the longer the deferral period, the lower the present value of the tax when taxpayers ultimately sell the assets. Second, they may pay taxes on the gains at preferential rates. For example, taxpayers who invest in a corporate stock (capital asset) that does not pay dividends will defer gain on any stock appreciation until they sell the stock; and because it is a capital asset held longer than one year, gains will be taxed at the lower preferential tax rate for long-term capital gains. These tax advantages provide taxpayers with a greater after-tax rate of return on these investments than they would obtain from less tax-favored assets that earn equivalent before-tax rates of return. Investors who quickly sell investments pay taxes on gains at higher, ordinary rates and incur significantly greater transaction costs. Nevertheless, taxpayers should balance the tax benefits available for holding assets with the risk that the asset values will have declined by the time they want to sell the assets.

To enable comparison of investments with differing time horizons, taxpayers use the annualized after-tax rate of return. In general, the after-tax rate of return on any investment is $(FV/I)^{1/n} - 1$ where FV is the future value after taxes, I is the investment, and n is the number of investment periods.[22]

Example 3-12

What if: Assume Bill decides to purchase Intel stock for $50,000 and hold the shares for five years. If the Intel stock grows at a constant 8 percent before-tax rate and does not pay any dividends, how much cash will Bill accumulate after taxes after five years assuming a long-term capital gains tax rate of 20 percent?

Answer: $68,773, computed as follows:

Description	Amount	Explanation
(1) Proceeds from sale	$73,466	[$50,000 × (1 + 0.08)^5]
(2) Basis in shares	50,000	This is the investment in the shares.
(3) Gain realized on sale	$23,466	(1) − (2)
(4) Tax rate on gain	× 20%	Low rate for long-term capital gain*
(5) Tax on gain	$ 4,693	(3) × (4)
After-tax cash after 5 years	**$68,773**	(1) − (5)

*Assumes Bill doesn't have any capital losses.

What annual after-tax rate of return will Bill earn on the money invested?

Answer: 6.58 percent [($68,773/$50,000)$^{1/5}$ − 1].

What if: What would be the after-tax rate of return if Bill held the stock for 18 years?

Answer: 7.03 percent, computed as follows:

Description	Amount	Explanation
(1) Proceeds from sale	$199,801	[$50,000 × (1 + 0.08)^{18}]
(2) Basis in shares	50,000	This is the investment in the shares.
(3) Gain realized on sale	$149,801	(1) − (2)
(4) Tax rate on gain	× 20%	Low rate for long-term capital gain*
(5) Tax on gain	$ 29,960	(3) × (4)
After-tax cash after 18 years	$169,841	(1) − (5)
After-tax rate of return after 18 years	**7.03**	[($169,841/$50,000)$^{1/18}$ − 1]

*Assumes Bill doesn't have any capital losses.

What if: How does Bill's rate of return on the Intel stock held for five years compare to a taxable corporate bond that pays 9 percent interest annually and is held for five years?

Answer: The annualized rate of return on the stock held for five years is 6.58 percent as shown above. Because the interest on the taxable corporate bond is taxed annually, the annual after-tax rate of return does not change with the investment horizon and will equal 6.3 percent as shown in Example 3-11 [9% × (1−30%)]. In this situation, the combined tax benefits from the timing and conversion strategies causes the stock investment to generate a higher annualized after-tax return than the taxable corporate bond even though its pretax return is lower.

[22]Financial calculators designate this calculation as the IRR or internal rate of return.

TAXES IN THE REAL WORLD Deducting Losses on Residences Is Tricky

The conversion tax planning strategy can involve converting ordinary income into capital gains, taxable income into tax-exempt income, or even nondeductible losses into deductible losses. Taxpayers often look to employ this strategy when they sell a home at a loss. The tax law disallows losses on the sale of personal use assets so any loss generated upon the sale of a personal residence is nondeductible. However, the tax law permits deductions for losses on the sale of rental property (including residences).

Suppose that you would like to sell your home but you are facing a large nondeductible loss if you were to sell it. Can you simply move out, convert the home to a rental property, then sell the house and deduct the loss? It seems the answer is yes, subject to a couple of important caveats. First, the law prevents taxpayers from deducting losses that were incurred while the home was used for personal purposes. That is, only the losses generated while the house was a rental property are deductible. Second, if you claim that you converted the house to rental property, you should actually rent the house.

In a recent court case (*Redisch v. Commissioner*, TC Memo 2015-95), the taxpayers had a beachfront condo they used personally for four years and would have realized a large nondeductible loss had they sold it at that time. Instead they decided to convert the condo to a rental. They hired a realtor to help in finding a renter but rather than finding a tenant, the realtor used the condo for a "model" of other units in the community. The following year, the taxpayers listed the home for sale and it sold the next year at a loss. The taxpayers deducted a loss on the sale of the home claiming they had converted the home from personal use to rental. The IRS disagreed and argued that the taxpayers had not successfully converted the home to rental because it was never rented. The Tax Court agreed with the IRS and disallowed the loss on the sale of the home arguing that the taxpayers did not rent the home and, more importantly, did not really even put forth a good effort to rent it.

Drawn from: "Tax Court: In Order to Convert a Home to a Rental, You Should Probably Rent It." *Forbes,* May 20, 2015, http://www.forbes.com/sites/anthonynitti/2015/05/20/tax-court-in-order-to-convert-a-home-to-a-rental-you-should-probably-rent-it/).

Limitations of Conversion Strategies

Like other tax planning strategies, conversion strategies face potential limitations. The Code itself also contains several specific provisions that prevent the taxpayer from changing the nature of expenses, income, or activities to a more tax-advantaged status, including (among many others) the depreciation recapture rules discussed in Chapter 11 and the luxury auto depreciation rules discussed in Chapter 10. In addition, as discussed in Chapter 1, implicit taxes may reduce or eliminate the advantages of tax-preferred investments (such as municipal bonds or any investment taxed at preferential tax rates) by decreasing their before-tax rate of returns. Thus, implicit taxes may reduce the advantages of the conversion strategy.

ADDITIONAL LIMITATIONS TO TAX PLANNING STRATEGIES: JUDICIAL DOCTRINES

LO 3-6

The IRS also has several other doctrines at its disposal for situations where it expects taxpayer abuse. These doctrines apply across a wide variety of transactions and planning strategies (timing, income shifting, and conversion). The **business purpose doctrine,** for instance, allows the IRS to challenge and disallow business expenses for transactions with no underlying business motivation, such as the travel cost of a spouse accompanying a taxpayer on a business trip. The **step-transaction doctrine** allows the IRS to collapse a series of related transactions into one transaction to determine the tax consequences of the transaction. The **substance-over-form doctrine** allows the IRS to consider the transaction's substance regardless of its form, and where appropriate, to reclassify the transaction according to its substance. Finally, the **economic substance doctrine** requires transactions to meet two criteria to obtain tax benefits. First, a transaction must meaningfully change a taxpayer's economic position (excluding any federal income tax effects). Second, the taxpayer must have a substantial purpose (other than tax avoidance) for the transaction. Economic substance is clearly related to several other doctrines such as business purpose, step-transaction, and substance-over-form doctrine; however, its codification standardizes the requirement for transactions to meet both tests. The courts had been inconsistent with the application of the tests with some requiring the transaction to meet either the business purpose or economic substance and others requiring that both tests be met. A key part of the codification is the strict penalty of 40 percent—reduced to 20 percent if the taxpayer makes adequate disclosure—of the underpayment for failing to meet the requirements. In Chapter 2, we noted that the Internal Revenue Code is the ultimate tax authority. The business purpose, step-transaction, substance-over-form, and economic substance doctrines allow the IRS to determine the tax consequences of transactions that follow only the form of the Internal Revenue Code and not the spirit.

You can often assess whether the business purpose, step-transaction, or substance-over-form doctrines apply by using the "smell test." If the transaction "smells bad," one of these doctrines likely applies. (Transactions usually smell bad when the primary purpose is to avoid taxes and not to accomplish an independent business objective.) For example, using the substance-over-form doctrine, the IRS would likely reclassify most of the $10,000 paid to Margaret for answering the phone one Saturday afternoon a month as a gift from Mercedes to Margaret (see the earlier discussion of income shifting and transactions between family members), even though the transaction was structured as compensation and Margaret did do some work for her mother. This recharacterization would unwind the income-shifting benefits for the amount considered to be a gift, as gifts to family members are not tax deductible. In sum, the *substance* of the transaction must be justifiable, not just the form.

LO 3-7   TAX AVOIDANCE VERSUS TAX EVASION

Each of the tax planning strategies discussed in this book falls within the confines of legal **tax avoidance.** Tax avoidance has long been endorsed by the courts and even Congress. For example, remember that Congress specifically encouraged tax avoidance by excluding municipal bond income from taxation, preferentially taxing dividend and capital gain income, and other strategies. Likewise, the courts have often made it quite clear that taxpayers are under no moral obligation to pay more taxes than required by law. As an example, in *Commissioner v. Newman*, 159 F.2d 848 (2 Cir., 1947), which considered a taxpayer's ability to shift income to his children using trusts, Judge Learned Hand included the following statement in his dissenting opinion:

> Over and over again courts have said that there is nothing sinister in so arranging one's affairs as to keep taxes as low as possible. Everybody does so, rich or poor; and all do right, for nobody owes any public duty to pay more than the law demands: taxes are enforced exactions, not voluntary contributions. To demand more in the name of morals is mere cant.

In contrast to tax avoidance, **tax evasion**—that is, the willful attempt to defraud the government—falls outside the confines of legal tax avoidance and thus may land the perpetrator within the confines of a federal prison. (Recall from Chapter 2 that the rewards of tax evasion include stiff monetary penalties and imprisonment.) When does tax avoidance become tax evasion? Very good question. In many cases a clear distinction exists between avoidance (such as not paying tax on municipal bond interest) and evasion (not paying tax on a $1,000,000 game show prize). In other cases, the line is less clear. In these situations, professional judgment, the use of a smell test, and consideration of the business purpose, step-transaction, and substance-over-form doctrines may prove useful.

TAXES IN THE REAL WORLD Cheating the IRS

Few people like to pay taxes, but most of us do so. Some, however, try to cheat the IRS, including the rich and famous (Lindsay Lohan, Nicholas Cage, Willie Nelson). Folks who are trying to escape the reach of the IRS may fail to file tax returns, claim deductions to which they're not entitled, make up fake business expenses, or otherwise try to disguise how much money they really made. These tax evaders cost the government a lot of money. In 2006, the latest year for which statistics are available, the IRS reported a gross "tax gap"—the amount of owed taxes that weren't paid on time—of $450 billion.

The main cause of the tax gap is underreporting income, accounting for $376 billion of the IRS's missing money. Not filing returns and underpaying taxes owed were two other causes. Some of that money fails to make it into the hands of the government through innocent accounting mistakes or because taxpayers want to pay but aren't able to. But some of that money goes missing due to deliberate fraud.

For the past three years, the IRS has launched roughly 5,000 criminal investigations related to tax code violations (these aren't the same as audits, which are much more common—1.4 million people were audited in 2013). The number of criminal investigations is relatively small, especially considering the millions of taxpayers in the U.S. But once the IRS starts an investigation, there's a good chance that it will lead to a conviction and prison time for the offender. Of the 4,297 investigations in 2014, 3,110, or 72%, eventually led to a conviction.

Source: "5 Lessons from Celebrities Who Cheat on Their Taxes." http://www.cheatsheet.com/personal-finance/5-lessons-from-celebrity-tax-cheats. html/?a=viewall April 12, 2015.

As you might expect, tax evasion is a major area of concern and focus for the IRS. While the IRS vigorously prosecutes suspected tax evaders, its actions alone have not been able to solve this problem. Is tax evasion a victimless crime? No. Because the federal government must replace lost tax revenues by imposing higher taxes on others, honest taxpayers are the true victims of tax evasion. Currently, the federal government estimates that tax evasion costs the federal government annually more than $450 billion in lost tax revenues. As citizens and residents of the United States, each of us must recognize our obligation to support our country. As future accountants and business professionals, we also must recognize the inherent value of high ethical standards, which call for us to do the right thing in *all* situations. As business professionals have learned over and over, the costs of doing otherwise far exceed any short-term gains.

CONCLUSION

In this chapter we discussed three basic tax planning strategies—timing, income shifting, and conversion—and their related limitations. Each of these strategies exploits the variation in taxation across different dimensions. The timing strategy exploits the variation in taxation across time: The "real" tax costs of income decrease as taxation is deferred; the "real" tax savings associated with tax deductions increase as tax deductions are accelerated. However, because tax rates may change over time and the tax costs of income and tax savings of deductions vary with tax rates, tax planning should consider the effects of such changes on the timing strategy. The income-shifting strategy exploits the variation in taxation across taxpayers or jurisdictions. The assignment of income doctrine limits aggressive attempts to shift income across taxpayers. In addition, related-party transactions receive close IRS attention given the increased likelihood of taxpayer abuses in these transactions. Finally, the conversion strategy exploits the variation in taxation rates across activities although implicit taxes may reduce the advantages of this strategy. In addition to limitations specific to each planning strategy, the judicial doctrines of business purpose, step-transaction, and substance-over-form broadly apply to a wide range of transactions and planning strategies.

The timing, income-shifting, and conversion strategies represent the building blocks for the more sophisticated tax strategies that tax professionals employ on a daily basis. Combining an understanding of these basic tax planning strategies with knowledge of our tax law will provide you with the tools necessary to identify, evaluate, and implement tax planning strategies. Throughout the remainder of the text, we will discuss how these strategies can be applied to different transactions.

Summary

LO 3-1   Identify the objectives of basic tax planning strategies.

- Effective tax planning maximizes the taxpayer's after-tax wealth while achieving the taxpayer's nontax goals. Maximizing after-tax wealth is not necessarily the same as tax minimization. Maximizing after-tax wealth requires one to consider both the tax and nontax costs and benefits of alternative transactions, whereas tax minimization focuses solely on a single cost (i.e., taxes).

- Virtually every transaction involves three parties: the taxpayer, the other transacting party, and the uninvited silent party that specifies the tax consequences of the transaction (i.e., the government). Astute tax planning requires an understanding of the tax and nontax costs from the taxpayer's *and* the other party's perspectives.

LO 3-2   Apply the timing strategy and describe its applications and limitations.

- One of the cornerstones of basic tax planning involves the idea of *timing*—that is, *when* income is taxed or an expense is deducted affects the associated "real" tax costs or savings. This is true for two reasons. First, the timing of when income is taxed or an expense is deducted affects the *present value* of the taxes paid on income or tax savings on deductions. Second, the tax costs of income and tax savings income vary as *tax rates* change.

- When tax rates are constant, tax planners prefer to defer income (i.e., to reduce the present value of taxes paid) and accelerate deductions (i.e., to increase the present value of tax savings). Higher tax rates, higher rates of return, larger transaction amounts, and the ability to accelerate deductions or defer income by two or more years increase the benefits of the timing strategy.

- When tax rates change, the timing strategy requires a little more consideration because the tax costs of income and the tax savings from deductions vary as *tax rates* change. When tax rates are increasing, the taxpayer must calculate the optimal tax strategies for deductions and income. When tax rates are decreasing, the recommendations are clear. Taxpayers should accelerate tax deductions into earlier years and defer taxable income to later years.

- Timing strategies contain several inherent limitations. Generally speaking, whenever a taxpayer must accelerate a cash outflow to accelerate a deduction, the timing strategy will be less beneficial. Tax law generally requires taxpayers to continue their investment in an asset in order to defer income recognition for tax purposes. A deferral strategy may not be optimal if the taxpayer has severe cash flow needs, if continuing the investment would generate a low rate of return compared to other investments, if the current investment would subject the taxpayer to unnecessary risk, and so on. The constructive receipt doctrine, which provides that a taxpayer must recognize income when it is actually or constructively received, also restricts income deferral for cash-method taxpayers.

Apply the concept of present value to tax planning.

LO 3-3

- The concept of present value—also known as the time value of money—basically states that $1 today is worth *more* than $1 in the future. For example, assuming an investor can earn a positive return (e.g., 5 percent after taxes), $1 invested today should be worth $1.05 in one year. Hence, $1 today is equivalent to $1.05 in one year.
- The implication of the time value of money for tax planning is that the timing of a cash inflow or a cash outflow affects the present value of the income or expense.

Apply the strategy of income shifting, provide examples, and describe its limitations.

LO 3-4

- The income-shifting strategy exploits the differences in tax rates across taxpayers or jurisdictions. Three of the most common examples of income shifting are high-tax-rate parents shifting income to low-tax-rate children, businesses shifting income to their owners, and taxpayers shifting income from high-tax jurisdictions to low-tax jurisdictions.
- The assignment of income doctrine requires income to be taxed to the taxpayer who actually earns the income. In addition, the IRS closely monitors such related-party transactions—that is, financial activities among family members, among owners and their businesses, or among businesses owned by the same owners. Implicit taxes may also limit the benefits of income shifting via locating in tax-advantaged jurisdictions.

Apply the conversion strategy, provide examples, and describe its limitations.

LO 3-5

- Tax law does not treat all types of income or deductions the same. This understanding forms the basis for the conversion strategy—recasting income and expenses to receive the most favorable tax treatment. To implement the conversion strategy, one must be aware of the underlying differences in tax treatment across various types of income, expenses, and activities, and have some ability to alter the nature of the income or expense to receive the more advantageous tax treatment.
- Common examples of the conversion strategy include investment planning to invest in assets that generate preferentially taxed income, compensation planning to restructure employee compensation from currently taxable compensation to nontaxable or tax-deferred forms of compensation, and corporate distribution planning to structure corporate distributions to receive the most advantageous tax treatment.
- The Internal Revenue Code contains specific provisions that prevent the taxpayer from changing the nature of expenses, income, or activities to a more tax-advantaged status. Implicit taxes may also reduce or eliminate the advantages of conversion strategies.

Describe basic judicial doctrines that limit tax planning strategies.

LO 3-6

- The constructive receipt doctrine, which may limit the timing strategy, provides that a taxpayer must recognize income when it is actually *or* constructively received. Constructive receipt is deemed to have occurred if the income has been credited to the taxpayer's account or if the income is unconditionally available to the taxpayer, the taxpayer is aware of the income's availability, and there are no restrictions on the taxpayer's control over the income.
- The assignment of income doctrine requires income to be taxed to the taxpayer who actually earns the income. The assignment of income doctrine implies that, in order to shift income to a taxpayer, that taxpayer must actually earn the income.
- The business purpose, step-transaction, and substance-over-form doctrines apply across a wide variety of transactions and planning strategies (timing, income shifting, and conversion).
- The business purpose doctrine allows the IRS to challenge and disallow business expenses for transactions with no underlying business motivation, such as a travel cost of a spouse accompanying a taxpayer on a business trip.
- The step-transaction doctrine allows the IRS to collapse a series of related transactions into one transaction to determine the tax consequences of the transaction.
- The substance-over-form doctrine allows the IRS to consider the transaction's substance regardless of its form and, where appropriate, reclassify the transaction according to its substance.

- The codified economic substance doctrine requires transactions to have a substantial purpose and to meaningfully change a taxpayer's economic position in order for a taxpayer to obtain tax benefits.

LO 3-7 Contrast tax avoidance and tax evasion.

- Tax avoidance is the legal act of arranging one's transactions, and so on, to minimize taxes paid. Tax evasion is the willful attempt to defraud the government (i.e., by not paying taxes legally owed). Tax evasion falls outside the confines of legal tax avoidance.
- In many cases a clear distinction exists between avoidance (e.g., not paying tax on municipal bond interest) and evasion (e.g., not paying tax on a $1,000,000 game show prize). In other cases, the line between tax avoidance and evasion is less clear. In these situations, professional judgment, the use of a "smell test," and consideration of the business purpose, step-transaction, and substance-over-form doctrines may prove useful.

KEY TERMS

after-tax rate of return (3-3)
arm's-length transaction (3-12)
assignment of income doctrine (3-11)
before-tax rate of return (3-18)
business purpose doctrine (3-19)

constructive receipt doctrine (3-10)
discount factor (3-3)
economic substance doctrine (3-20)
implicit tax (3-16)
present value (3-3)

related-party transaction (3-12)
step-transaction doctrine (3-19)
substance-over-form doctrine (3-19)
tax avoidance (3-20)
tax evasion (3-20)

DISCUSSION QUESTIONS

Discussion Questions are available in *Connect®*.

LO 3-1 1. "The goal of tax planning is to minimize taxes." Explain why this statement is not true.

LO 3-1 2. Describe the three parties engaged in every business transaction and how understanding taxes may aid in structuring transactions.

LO 3-1 3. In this chapter we discuss three basic tax planning strategies. What different features of taxation does each of these strategies exploit?

LO 3-2 4. What are the two basic timing strategies? What is the intent of each?

LO 3-2 5. Why is the timing strategy particularly effective for cash-method taxpayers?

LO 3-2 6. What are some common examples of the timing strategy?

LO 3-2 7. What factors increase the benefits of accelerating deductions or deferring income?

LO 3-2 **LO 3-3** 8. How do changing tax rates affect the timing strategy? What information do you need to determine the appropriate timing strategy when tax rates change?

LO 3-2 **LO 3-6** 9. Describe the ways in which the timing strategy has limitations.

LO 3-3 10. The concept of the time value of money suggests that $1 today is not equal to $1 in the future. Explain why this is true.

LO 3-3 11. Why is understanding the time value of money important for tax planning?

LO 3-3 12. What two factors increase the difference between present and future values?

LO 3-4 13. What factors have to be present for income shifting to be a viable strategy?

LO 3-4 14. Name three common types of income shifting.

LO 3-4 15. What are some ways that a parent could effectively shift income to a child? What are some of the disadvantages of these methods?

LO 3-4 16. What is the key factor in shifting income from a business to its owners? What are some methods of shifting income in this context?

17. Explain why paying dividends is not an effective way to shift income from a corporation to its owners. `LO 3-4`

18. What are some of the common examples of the conversion strategy? `LO 3-5`

19. What is needed to implement the conversion strategy? `LO 3-5`

20. Explain how implicit taxes may limit the benefits of the conversion strategy. `LO 3-5`

21. Clark owns stock in BCS Corporation that he purchased in January of the current year. The stock has appreciated significantly during the year. It is now December of the current year, and Clark is deciding whether or not he should sell the stock. What tax and nontax factors should Clark consider before making the decision on whether to sell the stock now? `LO 3-5` `LO 3-6` planning

22. Do after-tax rates of return for investments in either interest or dividend paying securities increase with the length of the investment? Why or why not? `LO 3-5`

23. Cameron purchases stock in Corporation X and in Corporation Y. Neither corporation pays dividends. The stocks both earn an identical before-tax rate of return. Cameron sells stock in Corporation X after three years and he sells the stock in Corporation Y after five years. Which investment likely earned a greater after-tax return? Why? `LO 3-5`

24. Under what circumstances would you expect the after-tax return from an investment in a capital asset to approach that of tax-exempt assets assuming equal before-tax rates of return? `LO 3-5`

25. Laurie is thinking about investing in one or several of the following investment options: `LO 3-5` planning

    Corporate bonds (ordinary interest paid annually)
    Dividend-paying stock (qualified dividends)
    Life insurance (tax-exempt)
    Savings account
    Growth stock

    a) Assuming all of the options earn similar returns before taxes, rank Laurie's investment options from highest to lowest according to their after-tax returns.

    b) Which of the investments employ the deferral and/or conversion tax planning strategies?

    c) How does the time period of the investment affect the returns from these alternatives?

    d) How do these alternative investments differ in terms of their nontax characteristics?

26. What is an "implicit tax" and how does it affect a taxpayer's decision to purchase municipal bonds? `LO 3-5`

27. Several judicial doctrines limit basic tax planning strategies. What are they? Which planning strategies do they limit? `LO 3-6`

28. What is the constructive receipt doctrine? What types of taxpayers does this doctrine generally affect? For what tax planning strategy is the constructive receipt doctrine a potential limitation? `LO 3-6`

29. Explain the assignment of income doctrine. In what situations would this doctrine potentially apply? `LO 3-6`

30. Relative to arm's-length transactions, why do related-party transactions receive more IRS scrutiny? `LO 3-6`

31. Describe the business purpose, step-transaction, and substance-over-form doctrines. What types of tax planning strategies may these doctrines inhibit? `LO 3-6`

LO 3-7   32. What is the difference between tax avoidance and tax evasion?

LO 3-7   33. What are the rewards of tax avoidance? What are the rewards of tax evasion?

LO 3-7   34. "Tax avoidance is discouraged by the courts and Congress." Is this statement true or false? Please explain.

PROBLEMS

Select problems are available in *Connect*®.

LO 3-2
planning

35. Yong recently paid his accountant $10,000 for elaborate tax planning strategies that exploit the timing strategy. Assuming this is an election year and there could be a power shift in the White House and Congress, what is a potential risk associated with Yong's strategies?

LO 3-2 LO 3-3
planning

36. Billups, a physician and cash-method taxpayer, is new to the concept of tax planning and recently learned of the timing strategy. To implement the timing strategy, Billups plans to establish a new policy that allows all his clients to wait two years to pay their co-pays. Assume that Billups does not expect his marginal tax rates to change. What is wrong with his strategy?

LO 3-2 LO 3-3
planning

37. Tesha works for a company that pays a year-end bonus in January of each year (instead of December of the preceding year) to allow employees to defer the bonus income. Assume Congress recently passed tax legislation that decreases individual tax rates as of next year. Does this increase or decrease the benefits of the bonus deferral this year? What if Congress passed legislation that increased tax rates next year? Should Tesha ask the company to change its policy this year? What additional information do you need to answer this question?

LO 3-2 LO 3-3
planning

38. Isabel, a calendar-year taxpayer, uses the cash method of accounting for her sole proprietorship. In late December she received a $20,000 bill from her accountant for consulting services related to her small business. Isabel can pay the $20,000 bill anytime before January 30 of next year without penalty. Assume her marginal tax rate is 40 percent this year and next year, and that she can earn an after-tax rate of return of 12 percent on her investments. When should she pay the $20,000 bill—this year or next?

LO 3-2 LO 3-3
planning

39. Using the facts from the previous problem, how would your answer change if Isabel's after-tax rate of return were 8 percent?

LO 3-2 LO 3-3
planning

40. Manny, a calendar-year taxpayer, uses the cash method of accounting for his sole proprietorship. In late December he performed $20,000 of legal services for a client. Manny typically requires his clients to pay his bills immediately upon receipt. Assume Manny's marginal tax rate is 40 percent this year and next year, and that he can earn an after-tax rate of return of 12 percent on his investments. Should Manny send his client the bill in December or January?

LO 3-2 LO 3-3
planning

41. Using the facts from the previous problem, how would your answer change if Manny's after-tax rate of return were 8 percent?

LO 3-2 LO 3-3
planning

42. Reese, a calendar-year taxpayer, uses the cash method of accounting for her sole proprietorship. In late December, she received a $20,000 bill from her accountant for consulting services related to her small business. Reese can pay the $20,000 bill anytime before January 30 of next year without penalty. Assume Reese's marginal tax rate is 30 percent this year and will be 40 percent next year, and that she can earn an after-tax rate of return of 12 percent on her investments. When should she pay the $20,000 bill—this year or next?

43. Using the facts from the previous problem, when should Reese pay the bill if she expects her marginal tax rate to be 33 percent next year? 25 percent next year?

   LO 3-2 *LO 3-3*
   planning

44. Hank, a calendar-year taxpayer, uses the cash method of accounting for his sole proprietorship. In late December, he performed $20,000 of legal services for a client. Hank typically requires his clients to pay his bills immediately upon receipt. Assume his marginal tax rate is 30 percent this year and will be 40 percent next year, and that he can earn an after-tax rate of return of 12 percent on his investments. Should Hank send his client the bill in December or January?

   LO 3-2 *LO 3-3*
   planning

45. Using the facts from the previous problem, when should Hank send the bill if he expects his marginal tax rate to be 33 percent next year? 25 percent next year?

   LO 3-2 *LO 3-3*
   planning

46. Geraldo recently won a lottery and chose to receive $100,000 today instead of an equivalent amount in 10 years, computed using an 8 percent rate of return. Today, he learned that interest rates are expected to increase in the future. Is this good news for Geraldo given his decision?

   LO 3-3

47. Assume Rafael can earn an 8 percent after-tax rate of return. Would he prefer $1,000 today or $1,500 in five years?

   LO 3-3
   planning

48. Assume Ellina earns a 10 percent after-tax rate of return, and that she owes a friend $1,200. Would she prefer to pay the friend $1,200 today or $1,750 in four years?

   LO 3-3
   planning

49. Jonah has the choice of paying Rita $10,000 today or $40,000 in 10 years. Assume Jonah can earn a 12 percent after-tax rate of return. Which should he choose?

   LO 3-3
   planning

50. Bob's Lottery Inc. has decided to offer winners a choice of $100,000 in 10 years or some amount currently. Assume that Bob's Lottery Inc. earns a 10 percent after-tax rate of return. What amount should Bob offer lottery winners currently, in order for him to be indifferent between the two choices?

   LO 3-3
   planning

51. Tawana owns and operates a sole proprietorship and has a 40 percent marginal tax rate. She provides her son, Jonathon, $8,000 a year for college expenses. Jonathon works as a pizza delivery person every fall and has a marginal tax rate of 15 percent.

   LO 3-4
   planning

   a) What could Tawana do to reduce her family tax burden?

   b) How much pretax income does it currently take Tawana to generate the $8,000 after-taxes given to Jonathon?

   c) If Jonathon worked for his mother's sole proprietorship, what salary would she have to pay him to generate $8,000 after taxes (ignoring any Social Security, Medicare, or self-employment tax issues)?

   d) How much money would this strategy save?

52. Moana is a single taxpayer who operates a sole proprietorship. She expects her taxable income next year to be $250,000, of which $200,000 is attributed to her sole proprietorship. Moana is contemplating incorporating her sole proprietorship. Using the single individual tax brackets and the corporate tax brackets, find out how much current tax this strategy could save Moana (ignore any Social Security, Medicare, or self-employment tax issues). How much income should be left in the corporation?

   LO 3-4
   planning

53. Orie and Jane, husband and wife, operate a sole proprietorship. They expect their taxable income next year to be $300,000, of which $125,000 is attributed to the sole proprietorship. Orie and Jane are contemplating incorporating their sole proprietorship. Using the married-joint tax brackets and the corporate tax brackets, find out how much current tax this strategy could save Orie and Jane. How much income should be left in the corporation?

   LO 3-4
   planning

LO 3-4
planning

54. Hyundai is considering opening a plant in two neighboring states. One state has a corporate tax rate of 10 percent. If operated in this state, the plant is expected to generate $1,000,000 pretax profit. The other state has a corporate tax rate of 2 percent. If operated in this state, the plant is expected to generate $930,000 of pretax profit. Which state should Hyundai choose? Why do you think the plant in the state with a lower tax rate would produce a lower before-tax income?

LO 3-4 **LO 3-6**
planning

55. Bendetta, a high-tax-rate taxpayer, owns several rental properties and would like to shift some income to her daughter, Jenine. Bendetta instructs her tenants to send their rent checks to Jenine so Jenine can report the rental income. Will this shift the income from Bendetta to Jenine? Why, or why not?

LO 3-4 **LO 3-6**
planning

56. Using the facts in the previous problem, what are some ways that Bendetta could shift some of the rental income to Jenine? What are the disadvantages associated with these income-shifting strategies?

LO 3-5
planning

57. Daniel is considering selling two stocks that have not fared well over recent years. A friend recently informed Daniel that one of his stocks has a special designation, which allows him to treat a loss up to $50,000 on this stock as an ordinary loss rather than the typical capital loss. Daniel figures that he has a loss of $60,000 on each stock. If Daniel's marginal tax rate is 35 percent and he has $120,000 of other capital gains (taxed at 15 percent), what is the tax savings from the special tax treatment?

LO 3-5
planning

58. Dennis is currently considering investing in municipal bonds that earn 6 percent interest, or in taxable bonds issued by the Coca-Cola Company that pay 8 percent. If Dennis's tax rate is 20 percent, which bond should he choose? Which bond should he choose if his tax rate is 30 percent? At what tax rate would he be indifferent between the bonds? What strategy is this decision based upon?

LO 3-5
planning

59. Helen holds 1,000 shares of Fizbo Inc. stock that she purchased 11 months ago. The stock has done very well and has appreciated $20/share since Helen bought the stock. When sold, the stock will be taxed at capital gains rates (long-term rate is 15 percent and short-term rate is the taxpayer's marginal tax rate). If Helen's marginal tax rate is 35 percent, how much would she save by holding the stock an additional month before selling? What might prevent Helen from waiting to sell?

LO 3-5

60. Anne's marginal income tax rate is 30 percent. She purchases a corporate bond for $10,000 and the maturity, or face value, of the bond is $10,000. If the bond pays 5 percent per year before taxes, what is Anne's annual after-tax rate of return from the bond if the bond matures in one year? What is her annual after-tax rate of return if the bond matures in 10 years?

LO 3-5
planning

61. Irene is saving for a new car she hopes to purchase either four or six years from now. Irene invests $10,000 in a growth stock that does not pay dividends and expects a 6 percent annual before-tax return (the investment is tax deferred). When she cashes in the investment after either four or six years, she expects the applicable marginal tax rate on long-term capital gains to be 25 percent.

a) What will be the value of this investment four and six years from now?

b) When Irene sells the investment, how much cash will she have after taxes to purchase the new car (four and six years from now)?

LO 3-5
planning

62. Komiko Tanaka invests $12,000 in LymaBean, Inc. LymaBean does not pay any dividends. Komiko projects that her investment will generate a 10 percent before-tax rate of return. She plans to invest for the long term.

a) How much cash will Komiko retain, after-taxes, if she holds the investment for five years and then she sells it when the long-term capital gains rate is 15 percent?

b) What is Komiko's after-tax rate of return on her investment in part (a)?

c) How much cash will Komiko retain, after-taxes, if she holds the investment for five years and then sells when the long-term capital gains rate is 25 percent?

d) What is Komiko's after-tax rate of return on her investment in part (c)?

e) How much cash will Komiko retain, after taxes, if she holds the investment for 15 years and then she sells when the long-term capital gains rate is 15 percent?

f) What is Komiko's after-tax rate of return on her investment in part (e)?

63. Alan inherited $100,000 with the stipulation that he "invest it to financially benefit his family." Alan and Alice decided they would invest the inheritance to help them accomplish two financial goals: purchasing a Park City vacation home and saving for their son, Cooper's, education.

LO 3-5

🔵 planning

	Vacation Home	Cooper's Education
Initial investment	$50,000	$50,000
Investment horizon	5 years	18 years

Alan and Alice have a marginal income tax rate of 30 percent (capital gains rate of 15 percent) and have decided to investigate the following investment opportunities.

	5 Years	Annual After-Tax Rate of Return	18 Years	Annual After-Tax Rate of Return
Corporate bonds (ordinary interest taxed annually)	5.75%		4.75%	
Dividend-paying stock (no appreciation and dividends are taxed at 15%)	3.50%		3.50%	
Growth stock	Future value is $65,000		Future value is $140,000	
Municipal bond (tax-exempt)	3.20%		3.10%	

Complete the two annual after-tax rates of return columns for each investment and provide investment recommendations for Alan and Alice.

64. Duff is really interested in decreasing his tax liability, and by his very nature he is somewhat aggressive. A friend of a friend told him that cash transactions are more difficult for the IRS to identify and, thus, tax. Duff is contemplating using this "strategy" of not reporting cash collected in his business to minimize his tax liability. Is this tax planning? What are the risks with this strategy?

LO 3-7

65. Using the facts from the previous problem, how would your answer change if instead, Duff adopted the cash method of accounting to allow him to better control the timing of his cash receipts and disbursements?

LO 3-7

66. Using an available tax service or the Internet, identify three basic tax planning ideas or tax tips suggested for year-end tax planning. Which basic tax strategy from this chapter does each planning idea employ?

LO 3-2   **LO 3-4**   **LO 3-5**

🔵 planning

🔴 research

67. Jayanna, an advertising consultant, is contemplating instructing some of her clients to pay her in cash so that she does not have to report the income on her tax return. Use an available tax service to identify the three basic elements of tax evasion and penalties associated with tax evasion. Write a memo to Jayanna explaining tax evasion and the risks associated with her actions.

LO 3-7

🔴 research

68. Using the IRS website (https://www.irs.gov/uac/The-Tax-Gap), how large is the current estimated "tax gap" (i.e., the amount of tax underpaid by taxpayers annually)? What group of taxpayers represents the largest "contributors" to the tax gap?

LO 3-7

🔴 research

Individual Income Tax Overview, Exemptions, and Filing Status

Learning Objectives

Upon completing this chapter, you should be able to:

LO 4-1 Describe the formula for calculating an individual taxpayer's taxes payable or refund and generally explain each formula component.

LO 4-2 Explain the requirements for determining a taxpayer's personal and dependency exemptions.

LO 4-3 Determine a taxpayer's filing status.

© Creatas Images/Getty Images

Tara Hall just completed a unit on individual taxation in her undergraduate tax class at South Dakota State University. She was excited to share her knowledge with her parents, Rodney and Anita Hall, as they prepared their tax return. Rodney and Anita have been married for over 25 years, and they have filed a joint tax return each year. The Halls' 12-year-old son Braxton lives at home but Tara, who is 21, lives nearby in the university dorms. Further, in January of this year, Rodney's younger brother Shawn moved in with the Halls. They expect Shawn to live with them for at least one year and maybe two. Every year Rodney and Anita use tax-preparation software to complete their tax return, but they are not always sure they understand the final result. This year, with Tara's help, they hope that will change. ∎

Storyline Summary	
Taxpayers:	Rodney and Anita Hall
Other household members:	Tara, their 21-year-old daughter, and Braxton, their 12-year-old son. Shawn, Rodney's brother, also lives with the Halls.
Location:	Brookings, South Dakota
Employment status:	Rodney is a manager for a regional grocery chain. His annual salary is $64,000. Anita works part-time as a purchasing-card auditor at South Dakota State University. Her annual salary is $46,000.
Current situation:	Determining their tax liability

This chapter and the next four discuss the fundamental elements of the individual income tax formula. This is the overview chapter; the other chapters provide more depth on individual income tax topics. Here we introduce the individual income tax formula, summarize its components, describe requirements for dependency exemptions, and explain how to determine a taxpayer's filing status. Chapter 5 explains gross income, Chapter 6 describes deductible expenses to determine adjusted gross income and taxable income, and Chapter 7 discusses tax issues associated with investments. Finally, Chapter 8 addresses issues associated with calculating a taxpayer's tax liability and discusses tax return filing concerns.

LO 4-1

THE INDIVIDUAL INCOME TAX FORMULA

Each year, individuals file tax returns to report their **taxable income,** the tax base for the individual income tax, to the Internal Revenue Service.[1] Exhibit 4-1 presents a simplified formula for calculating taxable income.

EXHIBIT 4-1 **Individual Tax Formula**

	Gross income
Minus:	*For* AGI deductions
Equals:	Adjusted gross income (AGI)
Minus:	*From* AGI deductions:
	(1) *Greater* of
	(a) Standard deduction or
	(b) Itemized deductions and
	(2) Personal and dependency exemptions
Equals:	Taxable income
Times:	Tax rates
Equals:	Income tax liability
Plus:	Other taxes
Equals:	Total tax
Minus:	Credits
Minus:	Prepayments
Equals:	Taxes due or (refund)

Beginning with gross income, this formula is embedded in the first two pages of the individual income tax Form 1040, the form individuals generally use to report their taxable income.[2] Exhibit 4-2 presents the first two pages of the form (throughout the text we use 2015 tax forms because 2016 forms were unavailable when the book went to press). The last line on page 1 of Form 1040 is **adjusted gross income (AGI),** an important reference point in the income tax formula.

Let's look at the components of the individual tax formula and provide a brief description of each of the key elements.

Gross Income

The U.S. tax laws are based on the **all-inclusive income concept.** Under this concept, **gross income** generally includes all **realized income** from *whatever source derived.*[3] Realized income is generated in a transaction with a second party in which there is a measurable change in property rights between parties (for example, appreciation in a stock investment would not represent realized income unless the taxpayer sold the

---

[1] See Exhibit 2-1 (in Chapter 2) for a description of who must file a tax return.
[2] To see the 1913 version of the individual tax form, go to http://www.irs.gov/pub/irs-utl/1913.pdf
[3] §61(a).

EXHIBIT 4-2   Form 1040, pages 1 and 2

Form **1040** Department of the Treasury—Internal Revenue Service (99)
U.S. Individual Income Tax Return **2015** OMB No. 1545-0074 IRS Use Only—Do not write or staple in this space.

For the year Jan. 1–Dec. 31, 2015, or other tax year beginning , 2015, ending , 20 | See separate instructions.

Your first name and initial | Last name | Your social security number

If a joint return, spouse's first name and initial | Last name | Spouse's social security number

Home address (number and street). If you have a P.O. box, see instructions. | Apt. no.

▲ Make sure the SSN(s) above and on line 6c are correct.

City, town or post office, state, and ZIP code. If you have a foreign address, also complete spaces below (see instructions).

Presidential Election Campaign
Check here if you, or your spouse if filing jointly, want $3 to go to this fund. Checking a box below will not change your tax or refund. ☐ You ☐ Spouse

Foreign country name | Foreign province/state/county | Foreign postal code

Filing Status
Check only one box.
1 ☐ Single
2 ☐ Married filing jointly (even if only one had income)
3 ☐ Married filing separately. Enter spouse's SSN above and full name here. ▶
4 ☐ Head of household (with qualifying person). (See instructions.) If the qualifying person is a child but not your dependent, enter this child's name here. ▶
5 ☐ Qualifying widow(er) with dependent child

Exemptions
6a ☐ Yourself. If someone can claim you as a dependent, do not check box 6a
b ☐ Spouse
c Dependents:
(1) First name Last name | (2) Dependent's social security number | (3) Dependent's relationship to you | (4) ✓ if child under age 17 qualifying for child tax credit (see instructions)

If more than four dependents, see instructions and check here ▶☐

Boxes checked on 6a and 6b ___
No. of children on 6c who:
• lived with you ___
• did not live with you due to divorce or separation (see instructions) ___
Dependents on 6c not entered above ___
Add numbers on lines above ▶ ___

d Total number of exemptions claimed

Income

Attach Form(s) W-2 here. Also attach Forms W-2G and 1099-R if tax was withheld.

If you did not get a W-2, see instructions.

7 Wages, salaries, tips, etc. Attach Form(s) W-2 | 7
8a Taxable interest. Attach Schedule B if required | 8a
b Tax-exempt interest. Do not include on line 8a | 8b
9a Ordinary dividends. Attach Schedule B if required | 9a
b Qualified dividends | 9b
10 Taxable refunds, credits, or offsets of state and local income taxes | 10
11 Alimony received | 11
12 Business income or (loss). Attach Schedule C or C-EZ | 12
13 Capital gain or (loss). Attach Schedule D if required. If not required, check here ▶☐ | 13
14 Other gains or (losses). Attach Form 4797 | 14
15a IRA distributions | 15a | b Taxable amount | 15b
16a Pensions and annuities | 16a | b Taxable amount | 16b
17 Rental real estate, royalties, partnerships, S corporations, trusts, etc. Attach Schedule E | 17
18 Farm income or (loss). Attach Schedule F | 18
19 Unemployment compensation | 19
20a Social security benefits | 20a | b Taxable amount | 20b
21 Other income. List type and amount | 21
22 Combine the amounts in the far right column for lines 7 through 21. This is your total income ▶ | 22

Adjusted Gross Income

23 Educator expenses | 23
24 Certain business expenses of reservists, performing artists, and fee-basis government officials. Attach Form 2106 or 2106-EZ | 24
25 Health savings account deduction. Attach Form 8889 | 25
26 Moving expenses. Attach Form 3903 | 26
27 Deductible part of self-employment tax. Attach Schedule SE | 27
28 Self-employed SEP, SIMPLE, and qualified plans | 28
29 Self-employed health insurance deduction | 29
30 Penalty on early withdrawal of savings | 30
31a Alimony paid b Recipient's SSN ▶ | 31a
32 IRA deduction | 32
33 Student loan interest deduction | 33
34 Tuition and fees. Attach Form 8917 | 34
35 Domestic production activities deduction. Attach Form 8903 | 35
36 Add lines 23 through 35 | 36
37 Subtract line 36 from line 22. This is your adjusted gross income ▶ | 37

For Disclosure, Privacy Act, and Paperwork Reduction Act Notice, see separate instructions. Cat. No. 11320B Form **1040** (2015)

(continued)

EXHIBIT 4-2 Form 1040, pages 1 and 2 (*continued*)

Form 1040 (2015)   Page **2**

Tax and Credits	38	Amount from line 37 (adjusted gross income)	38	
	39a	Check if: ☐ **You** were born before January 2, 1951, ☐ Blind. ☐ **Spouse** was born before January 2, 1951, ☐ Blind. } Total boxes checked ▶ 39a		
	b	If your spouse itemizes on a separate return or you were a dual-status alien, check here▶ 39b☐		
Standard Deduction for— • People who check any box on line 39a or 39b **or** who can be claimed as a dependent, see instructions. • All others: Single or Married filing separately, $6,300 Married filing jointly or Qualifying widow(er), $12,600 Head of household, $9,250	40	**Itemized deductions** (from Schedule A) **or** your **standard deduction** (see left margin) . .	40	
	41	Subtract line 40 from line 38	41	
	42	**Exemptions.** If line 38 is $154,950 or less, multiply $4,000 by the number on line 6d. Otherwise, see instructions	42	
	43	**Taxable income.** Subtract line 42 from line 41. If line 42 is more than line 41, enter -0- . .	43	
	44	**Tax** (see instructions). Check if any from: **a** ☐ Form(s) 8814 **b** ☐ Form 4972 **c** ☐	44	
	45	**Alternative minimum tax** (see instructions). Attach Form 6251	45	
	46	Excess advance premium tax credit repayment. Attach Form 8962	46	
	47	Add lines 44, 45, and 46 . . . . ▶	47	
	48	Foreign tax credit. Attach Form 1116 if required . . .	48	
	49	Credit for child and dependent care expenses. Attach Form 2441	49	
	50	Education credits from Form 8863, line 19	50	
	51	Retirement savings contributions credit. Attach Form 8880	51	
	52	Child tax credit. Attach Schedule 8812, if required .	52	
	53	Residential energy credits. Attach Form 5695 . . .	53	
	54	Other credits from Form: **a** ☐ 3800 **b** ☐ 8801 **c** ☐	54	
	55	Add lines 48 through 54. These are your **total credits**	55	
	56	Subtract line 55 from line 47. If line 55 is more than line 47, enter -0- . . . . . . ▶	56	
Other Taxes	57	Self-employment tax. Attach Schedule SE	57	
	58	Unreported social security and Medicare tax from Form: **a** ☐ 4137 **b** ☐ 8919 . .	58	
	59	Additional tax on IRAs, other qualified retirement plans, etc. Attach Form 5329 if required . .	59	
	60a	Household employment taxes from Schedule H	60a	
	b	First-time homebuyer credit repayment. Attach Form 5405 if required	60b	
	61	Health care: individual responsibility (see instructions) Full-year coverage ☐	61	
	62	Taxes from: **a** ☐ Form 8959 **b** ☐ Form 8960 **c** ☐ Instructions; enter code(s)	62	
	63	Add lines 56 through 62. This is your **total tax** . . . . ▶	63	
Payments If you have a qualifying child, attach Schedule EIC.	64	Federal income tax withheld from Forms W-2 and 1099 . .	64	
	65	2015 estimated tax payments and amount applied from 2014 return	65	
	66a	**Earned income credit (EIC)**	66a	
	b	Nontaxable combat pay election 66b		
	67	Additional child tax credit. Attach Schedule 8812 . . .	67	
	68	American opportunity credit from Form 8863, line 8 . . .	68	
	69	Net premium tax credit. Attach Form 8962	69	
	70	Amount paid with request for extension to file	70	
	71	Excess social security and tier 1 RRTA tax withheld . . .	71	
	72	Credit for federal tax on fuels. Attach Form 4136	72	
	73	Credits from Form: **a** ☐ 2439 **b** ☐ Reserved **c** ☐ 8885 **d** ☐	73	
	74	Add lines 64, 65, 66a, and 67 through 73. These are your **total payments** . . . . . ▶	74	
Refund Direct deposit? See instructions.	75	If line 74 is more than line 63, subtract line 63 from line 74. This is the amount you **overpaid**	75	
	76a	Amount of line 75 you want **refunded to you.** If Form 8888 is attached, check here . ▶ ☐	76a	
	▶ b	Routing number ▶ c Type: ☐ Checking ☐ Savings		
	▶ d	Account number		
	77	Amount of line 75 you want **applied to your 2016 estimated tax** ▶ 77		
Amount You Owe	78	**Amount you owe.** Subtract line 74 from line 63. For details on how to pay, see instructions ▶	78	
	79	Estimated tax penalty (see instructions) 79		

Third Party Designee	Do you want to allow another person to discuss this return with the IRS (see instructions)? ☐ **Yes.** Complete below. ☐ **No**		
	Designee's name ▶	Phone no. ▶	Personal identification number (PIN) ▶

Sign Here Joint return? See instructions. Keep a copy for your records.	Under penalties of perjury, I declare that I have examined this return and accompanying schedules and statements, and to the best of my knowledge and belief, they are true, correct, and complete. Declaration of preparer (other than taxpayer) is based on all information of which preparer has any knowledge.			
	Your signature	Date	Your occupation	Daytime phone number
	Spouse's signature. If a joint return, **both** must sign.	Date	Spouse's occupation	If the IRS sent you an Identity Protection PIN, enter it here (see inst.)

Paid Preparer Use Only	Print/Type preparer's name	Preparer's signature	Date	Check ☐ if self-employed	PTIN
	Firm's name ▶			Firm's EIN ▶	
	Firm's address ▶			Phone no.	

stock). Certain tax provisions allow taxpayers to permanently exclude specific types of realized income from gross income (the income items are never taxable) and other provisions allow taxpayers to defer including certain types of realized income items in gross income until a subsequent year (the income item is included in gross income in a later year). Realized income items that taxpayers permanently exclude from taxation are referred to as **exclusions.** Realized income items that taxpayers include in gross income in a subsequent year are called **deferrals.** Exhibit 4-3 provides a

EXHIBIT 4-3   Partial Listing of Common Income Items

Income Item	Character	Discussed in More Detail in
Compensation for services including fringe benefits	Ordinary	Chapters 5 and 12
Business income	Ordinary	Chapter 9
Gains from selling property	Ordinary or capital[4]	Chapters 7 and 11
Interest and dividends	Ordinary or qualified dividend	Chapters 5 and 7
Rents and royalties	Ordinary	Chapters 5, 7, and 14
Alimony received and annuities	Ordinary	Chapter 5
Retirement income	Ordinary	Chapter 13
Income from the discharge of indebtedness	Ordinary	Chapter 5

partial listing of common income items included in gross income, their character (discussed below), and where in the text we provide more detail on each income item. Exhibit 4-4 provides a partial listing of common exclusions and deferrals and indicates where in the text we discuss each in more detail.

EXHIBIT 4-4   Partial Listing of Common Exclusions and Deferrals

Exclusion or Deferral Item	Exclusion or Deferral	Discussed in
Interest income from municipal bonds	Exclusion	Chapter 5
Gifts and inheritances	Exclusion	Chapter 5
Gain on sale of personal residence	Exclusion	Chapters 5 and 14
Life insurance proceeds	Exclusion	Chapter 5
Installment sale	Deferral	Chapter 11
Like-kind exchange	Deferral	Chapter 11

Character of Income   While gross income increases taxable income dollar for dollar, it is important to note that certain types of income are treated differently than other types of income for purposes of computing a taxpayer's taxable income and income tax liability. For example, one type of income may be taxed at a different rate than another type of income. The *type* of income is commonly referred to as the **character of income.** The most common characters of income are as follows:

• Ordinary: This is income or loss that is taxed at the ordinary rates provided in the tax rate schedules in Appendix D, or offsets income taxed at these rates, and is not capital in character.

[4]Dispositions of assets used in a trade or business for more than a year generate an intermediate character of income called §1231 gain or loss. Ultimately, §1231 gains and losses are treated as either ordinary or capital on the tax return.

- Capital: These are gains or losses on the disposition or sale of capital assets. In general, capital assets are all assets *other than*

  1. Accounts receivable from the sale of goods or services.
  2. Inventory and other assets held for sale in the ordinary course of business.
  3. Assets used in a trade or business, including supplies.[5]

Nonbusiness assets such as a personal-use automobile or a personal residence and assets held for investment such as stocks and bonds are capital assets.

Capital gains and losses are further characterized as long-term (when the taxpayer owned the capital asset for more than one year before selling it) or as short-term (when the taxpayer owned the capital asset for one year or less before selling it). A gain on a sale of a capital asset is generally included in gross income. If the gain is a long-term capital gain, it is taxed at a 15 percent tax rate (20 percent for high income taxpayers and 0 percent for low income taxpayers). If the gain is a short-term capital gain, the gain is taxed at ordinary income rates. Note that even though a short-term capital gain is taxed at ordinary rates, it is still considered to be a capital gain and not ordinary income.

A loss on the sale of a capital asset (no matter how long the taxpayer held the asset before selling) generates a deduction for the taxpayer in the year of sale (a for AGI deduction as discussed below). However, the deduction for the loss is limited to $3,000 for the year (losses in excess of the limit are carried forward indefinitely). If the taxpayer sells a personal-use asset (like a personal automobile or personal residence) at a loss, the loss is not deductible. When a taxpayer sells more than one capital asset during the year, the gains and losses are netted together. A net loss is subject to the $3,000 annual deduction limit. A net gain may be taxed at 15, 20, or 0 percent or at the ordinary rates depending on the outcome of the netting process and the taxpayer's taxable income. We discuss the netting process in detail in Chapter 7.[6]

- Qualified dividend: Shareholders receiving dividends from corporations include the dividend income in gross income. If the dividend meets the qualified dividend requirements, it is taxed at a rate of 15 percent (20 percent for high income taxpayers and 0 percent for low income taxpayers).[7] If a dividend does not meet the qualified dividend requirement, it is taxed at ordinary rates. Because qualified dividends (and long-term capital gains) are taxed at a preferential rate (a rate lower than the ordinary income rate), qualified dividends (and long-term capital gains) can be referred to as **preferentially taxed income**. While qualified dividends are taxed at the same rate as long-term capital gains, qualified dividends are not included in the capital gain and loss netting process. Therefore, qualified dividend is a separate and distinct character from capital.

Example 4-1

Rodney earned a salary of $64,000, and Anita earned a salary of $46,000 working part-time. The Halls also received $600 of interest income from investments in corporate bonds and $300 of interest income from investments in municipal bonds. This was their only income during the year. What is the Halls' gross income?

[5]See §1221(a) for the definition of a capital asset.
[6]As we discover in Chapter 7, certain capital gains may be taxed at a maximum rate of 28 percent or 25 percent.
[7]A qualified dividend generally includes dividends distributed by a U.S. corporation if the shareholder meets certain holding requirements for the stock. These requirements are discussed in more detail in Chapter 7.

Answer: $110,600, computed as follows:

Description	Amount	Explanation
(1) Rodney's salary	$ 64,000	
(2) Anita's salary	46,000	
(3) Interest from corporate bonds	600	
Gross income	**$110,600***	(1) + (2) + (3).

*The $300 of interest income from municipal bonds is excluded from gross income.

What is the character of the salary, the interest income from the corporate bonds, and the interest income from the investments in municipal bonds?

Answer: The salary and interest income from corporate bonds are ordinary income. The interest income from the municipal bonds is excluded from gross income.

What if: Suppose this year the Halls sold shares of stock in XYZ corporation at a $4,000 gain. They purchased the stock three years ago. What would be the character of the gain? At what rate would the gain be taxed?

Answer: Long-term capital gain because stock is a capital asset and the Halls owned the stock for more than a year before selling. The gain would be taxed at a maximum rate of 15 percent.

What if: Suppose this year the Halls sold stock at a $4,000 loss (their only transaction involving a capital asset). They purchased the stock three years ago. What would be the character of the loss? How much of the loss may the Halls deduct in the current year?

Answer: Long-term capital loss because the stock is a capital asset and the Halls owned the stock for more than a year before selling. The Halls can deduct $3,000 of the loss as a *for* AGI deduction this year. The remaining $1,000 loss is carried over to next year.

What if: Suppose this year the Halls sold a personal automobile at a $4,000 loss. They purchased the automobile three years ago. What is the character of the loss? How much of the loss may the Halls deduct in the current year?

Answer: Long-term capital loss because the automobile is a capital asset and the Halls owned the auto for more than a year before selling. However, the Halls are not allowed to deduct any of the $4,000 loss this year or any year because the automobile is a personal-use asset.

Deductions

Deductions reduce a taxpayer's taxable income. However, they are not necessarily easy to come by because, in contrast to the all-inclusive treatment of income, taxpayers are *not allowed to deduct anything unless a specific tax provision allows them to do so*. Thus, deductions are a matter of **legislative grace.** The tax laws provide for two distinct types of deductions in the individual tax formula: *for adjusted gross income (AGI) deductions* and *from AGI deductions.* As indicated in the individual tax formula, gross income minus *for* **AGI deductions** equals AGI and AGI minus *from* **AGI deductions** equals taxable income. When it enacts new legislation that grants deductions, Congress identifies whether the deductions are *for* or *from* AGI. The distinction between the deduction types is particularly important because AGI is an important reference point that is often used in other tax-related calculations. Specifically, limits on certain *from* AGI deductions depend on AGI (certain *from* AGI deductions are reduced as a taxpayer's AGI increases). Because *for* AGI deductions decrease AGI, they *increase* the deductibility of *from* AGI deductions subject to AGI limitations.

***For* AGI Deductions**   *For* AGI deductions tend to be deductions associated with business activities and certain investing activities. Because *for* AGI deductions are subtracted in determining AGI (deducted on page 1 of Form 1040), they are referred to as **"deductions above the line."** The "line" in this case is AGI, which is the last line on page 1 of Form 1040 (see Exhibit 4-2). Exhibit 4-5 provides a partial listing of common *for* AGI deductions and indicates where in the text we discuss them.

THE KEY FACTS

***For* and *From* AGI Deductions**

- *For* AGI deductions
  - Deduct in determining AGI.
  - Deduction "above the line."
  - Generally more valuable than *from* AGI deductions.
- *From* AGI deductions
  - Deducted *from* AGI to determine taxable income.
  - Deduction "below the line."
  - Generally less valuable than *for* AGI deductions.

EXHIBIT 4-5 **Partial Listing of Common *for* AGI Deductions**

For AGI Deduction	Discussed in
Alimony paid	Chapter 6
Health insurance deduction for self-employed taxpayers	Chapter 6
Moving expenses	Chapter 6
Rental and royalty expenses	Chapters 6 and 14
Capital losses (*net* losses limited to $3,000 for the year)	Chapter 7
One-half of self-employment taxes paid	Chapter 8
Business expenses	Chapter 9
Losses on dispositions of assets used in a trade or business	Chapter 11
Contributions to qualified retirement accounts	Chapter 13

Example 4-2

The Halls paid $5,000 of deductible moving expenses (*for* AGI) when the family relocated due to an employment transfer for Rodney. What is the Halls' adjusted gross income?

Answer: $105,600, computed as follows:

Description	Amount	Explanation
(1) Gross income	$110,600	Example 4-1.
(2) Moving expenses	(5,000)	*For* AGI deduction (see Exhibit 4-5).
Adjusted gross income	**$105,600**	(1) + (2).

***From* AGI Deductions** In contrast to *for* AGI deductions, *from* AGI deductions tend to be personal in nature. *From* AGI deductions are commonly referred to as **"deductions below the line"** because they are deducted after AGI has been determined (deducted on page 2 of Form 1040). *From* AGI deductions include **itemized deductions,** the **standard deduction,** and **exemptions.** In a given year, individuals have the choice of deducting *either* their itemized deductions *or* deducting a fixed amount called the standard deduction. As we discuss in Chapter 6, itemized deductions are partially phased out for taxpayers with AGI over a certain threshold. Taxpayers generally deduct the higher of the standard deduction or itemized deductions (after the itemized deductions phase out, if any). Exhibit 4-6 identifies the primary categories of itemized deductions.

EXHIBIT 4-6 **Primary Categories of Itemized Deductions**

- *Medical and dental expenses:* Deductible to the extent these expenses exceed 10 percent of AGI for taxpayers under age 65 at year-end and 7.5 percent otherwise.
- *Taxes:* State and local income taxes, sales taxes, real estate taxes, personal property taxes, and other taxes.
- *Interest expense:* Mortgage, home equity, and investment interest expense.
- *Gifts to charity (charitable contributions).*
- *Casualty and theft losses:* Deductible to the extent they exceed 10 percent of AGI.
- *Job expenses and certain miscellaneous deductions:* Deductible to the extent the sum of these expenses exceeds 2 percent of AGI.
- *Other miscellaneous deductions:* Gambling losses (to the extent of gambling winnings) and certain other deductions not subject to AGI limitation.

Note: Itemized deductions are detailed on Schedule A of Form 1040. We discuss itemized deductions in more depth in Chapter 6.

The amount of the standard deduction varies by taxpayer filing status (we discuss filing status in more detail later in the chapter); the government indexes this deduction for inflation. Exhibit 4-7 presents the basic standard deduction amounts by filing status for 2015 and 2016. Special rules may alter the allowable standard deduction for certain taxpayers. We discuss these departures from the basic standard deduction amounts in Chapter 6.

EXHIBIT 4-7   **Standard Deduction Amounts by Filing Status***

	2015	2016
Married filing jointly	$12,600	$12,600
Qualifying widow or widower	12,600	12,600
Married filing separately	6,300	6,300
Head of household	9,250	9,300
Single	6,300	6,300

*Married taxpayers 65 years of age or over and/or blind are entitled to an additional standard deduction of $1,250 ($1,250 for age and another $1,250 for blindness); single and head of household taxpayers 65 years of age or over and/or blind are entitled to an additional standard deduction of $1,550 (one for age and another for blindness). (See Chapter 6 for more detail.) For individuals claimed as a dependent on another tax return, the 2016 standard deduction is the greater of (1) $1,050 or (2) $350 plus earned income not to exceed the standard deduction amount for those who are not dependents (see Chapter 8 for more detail).

The final *from* AGI deduction is the deduction for exemptions. An exemption is a flat deduction allowed for the taxpayer, the taxpayer's spouse, and each person who qualifies as a dependent of the taxpayer. The exemptions for the taxpayer(s) filing the tax return are called **personal exemptions,** while the others are referred to as **dependency exemptions.** In 2016, the amount of the exemption deduction is $4,050 for both exemption types. As we discuss in Chapter 6, deductions for exemptions are phased out over a range of AGI for taxpayers with AGI over a certain threshold. We discuss the dependency qualification requirements later in this chapter.

Example 4-3

Rodney and Anita Hall annually file a joint tax return. They paid a total of $14,000 for expenditures that qualify as itemized deductions. Assuming Tara and her younger brother Braxton qualify as Rodney and Anita's dependents, what is the total amount of *from* AGI deductions Rodney and Anita are allowed to deduct on their tax return?

Answer: $30,200, computed as follows:

Description	Amount	Explanation
(1) Standard deduction	$12,600	Married filing joint filing status (see Exhibit 4-7).
(2) Itemized deductions	14,000	
(3) Greater of (1) or (2)	14,000	Itemized deductions exceed the standard deduction.
(4) Personal and dependency exemptions	16,200	($4,050 × 4) One exemption each for Rodney, Anita, Tara, and Braxton.
Total deductions from AGI	**$30,200**	(3) + (4). (Also referred to as deductions "below the line.")

What if: What would be the amount of the Halls' *from* AGI deductions if, instead of the original facts, Rodney and Anita had paid a total of $8,000 in expenditures that qualified as itemized deductions?

(*continued on page 4-10*)

Answer: $28,800, computed as follows:

Description	Amount	Explanation
(1) Standard deduction	$12,600	Married filing joint filing status (see Exhibit 4-7).
(2) Itemized deductions	8,000	
(3) Greater of (1) or (2)	12,600	The standard deduction exceeds itemized deductions.
(4) Personal and dependency exemptions	16,200	($4,050 × 4) One personal exemption each for Rodney, Anita, Tara, and Braxton.
Total deductions from AGI	**$28,800**	(3) + (4).

Income Tax Calculation

After determining taxable income, taxpayers can generally calculate their regular income tax liability using either a **tax table** or a **tax rate schedule,** depending on their filing status and income level (see Appendix D for the regular tax rate schedules). Taxpayers with taxable income under $100,000 generally must use the tax tables.[8] However, as we discussed above, certain types of income that are included in taxable income are taxed at rates different from the rates embedded in the tables or published in the tax rate schedules.

Example 4-4

With Tara's help, the Halls determined their taxable income to be $75,400 as follows:

Description	Amount	Explanation
(1) Adjusted gross income	$105,600	Example 4-2.
(2) *From* AGI deductions	(30,200)	Example 4-3.
Taxable income	$ 75,400	(1) + (2).

They have also determined that all of their income is ordinary income. What is their tax liability (use the tax rate schedule rather than the tax tables to answer the question)?

Answer: $10,392.50. See the married filing jointly tax rate schedule in Appendix D. {$10,367.50 + $25 [25% × ($75,400 − $75,300)]}.

What if: Using the tax rate schedules, what would the Halls' tax liability be if their taxable income was $12,000 (all ordinary income)?

Answer: $1,200 ($12,000 × 10%).

What if: Assume that in addition to the $75,400 of ordinary income, the Halls also reported $5,000 of long-term capital gain subject to a 15 percent tax rate. How much tax would they pay on the additional $5,000 gain?

Answer: $750 ($5,000 × 15%). Long-term capital gains (gains on the sale of a capital asset owned for more than a year) are generally taxed at a 15 percent rate. Note that the Halls' taxable income is $80,400. $75,400 of the income is taxed at ordinary rates and $5,000 is taxed at the preferential 15 percent rate.

Other Taxes

In addition to the individual income tax, individuals may also be required to pay other taxes such as the **alternative minimum tax (AMT)** or **self-employment taxes.** These taxes are imposed on tax bases other than the individual's regular taxable

[8]For administrative convenience and to prevent low- and middle-income taxpayers from making mathematical errors using a rate schedule, the IRS provides tax tables that present the gross tax for various amounts of taxable income. For simplicity, we use the tax rate schedule to determine tax liabilities in the examples presented in this text.

income. Furthermore, taxpayers with relatively high AGI are subject to a 3.8% net investment income tax and a .9% additional Medicare tax on earned income. We discuss these taxes in more detail in Chapter 8.

Tax Credits

Individual taxpayers may reduce their tax liabilities by **tax credits** to determine their total taxes payable. Like deductions, tax credits are specifically granted by Congress and are narrowly defined. Unlike deductions, which reduce *taxable income,* tax credits *directly reduce taxes payable.* Thus, a $1 deduction reduces taxes payable by $1 times the marginal tax rate while a $1 credit reduces taxes payable by $1. Common credits include the child tax credit ($1,000 per child that qualifies for the credit), the child and dependent care credit, the earned income credit, the American opportunity credit, and the lifetime learning credit. We discuss credits in more detail in Chapter 8.

Tax Prepayments

After calculating the total tax and subtracting their available credits, taxpayers determine their taxes due (or tax refund) by subtracting tax prepayments from the total tax remaining after credits. Tax prepayments include (1) **withholdings,** or income taxes withheld from the taxpayer's salary or wages by her employer; (2) **estimated tax payments** the taxpayer makes for the year (paid directly to the IRS), and (3) taxes the taxpayer overpaid on the prior year tax return that the taxpayer elects to apply as an estimated payment for the current tax year instead of receiving the overpayment as a refund.

If tax prepayments exceed the total tax after subtracting credits, the taxpayer receives a tax refund for the difference. If tax prepayments are less than the total tax after credits, the taxpayer owes additional tax and potentially a penalty for the underpayment.

Example 4-5

Based on their calculation in Example 4-4, Rodney and Anita Hall's tax liability is $10,392.50. The Halls had $9,800 of federal income taxes withheld by their employers from their paychecks and are able to claim a $1,000 child tax credit for their 12-year-old son Braxton (Tara is too old to qualify). What is the Halls' tax due or tax refund?

Answer: $407.50 tax refund, computed as follows:

Description	Amount	Explanation
(1) Tax liability	$10,392.50	Example 4-4.
(2) Tax credits	(1,000)	$1,000 child tax credit for 12-year old son Braxton.
(3) Tax prepayments	(9,800)	
Tax refund	**($ 407.50)**	(1) + (2) + (3).

Although not explicitly stated in the individual tax formula, a taxpayer's filing status affects many parts of the tax formula, including the standard deduction amount and the applicable income tax rate schedule among others. Below, we describe the rules for determining a taxpayer's filing status. However, because a taxpayer's filing status may depend on whether the taxpayer has dependents for tax purposes, we discuss how to determine who qualifies as a taxpayer's dependent before we address filing status.

LO 4-2 **PERSONAL AND DEPENDENCY EXEMPTIONS**

Individual taxpayers generally may deduct a personal exemption for themselves. Married couples filing jointly may claim two personal exemptions (one for each spouse).[9] Further, to provide some tax relief for those supporting others, a taxpayer may claim an additional exemption for each person who qualifies as the taxpayer's dependent.[10] In 2016, taxpayers are allowed to deduct $4,050 for each personal and dependency exemption they are entitled to claim. Individuals who qualify as a dependent of another taxpayer may *not* claim a personal exemption for themselves on their own individual tax returns and they may not claim a dependency exemption for someone else.[11,12]

Example 4-6

Assume that Tara (the Halls' 21-year-old daughter who is a full-time college student) qualifies as Rodney and Anita's dependent. Tara earned $9,000 at a summer job this year, and she files her own tax return. Is Tara allowed to claim a personal exemption for herself on her own tax return?

Answer: No. Because Tara qualifies as the Halls' dependent, the Halls may deduct a dependency exemption for Tara, but Tara may *not* deduct a personal exemption for herself.

Dependency Requirements

Taxpayers (who are not dependents of another) may claim exemptions only for persons qualifying as their **dependents.** To qualify as a dependent of another, an individual

1. Must be a citizen of the United States or a resident of the United States, Canada, or Mexico.
2. Must *not* file a joint return with the individual's spouse unless there is no tax liability on the couple's joint return and there would not have been any tax liability on either spouse's tax return if they had filed separately.[13]
3. Must be considered either a **qualifying child** of the taxpayer *or* a **qualifying relative** of the taxpayer.[14]

While the requirements for determining a qualifying child and a qualifying relative have some similarities, the qualifying relative requirements are broader in scope than the qualifying child requirements.

Qualifying Child   To be considered a qualifying child of a taxpayer, an individual must satisfy the following four tests: (1) relationship, (2) age, (3) residence, and (4) support.[15]

---

[9]§151(b).
[10]§151(c).
[11]§151(b).
[12]See Publication 17, "Your Federal Income Tax," for information relating to personal and dependency exemptions.
[13]Rev. Rul. 54-567, 1954-2 C.B. 108.
[14]§152.
[15]Technically, an individual is not eligible to be a qualifying child of another if she filed a joint return with her spouse (other than to claim a refund) [see §151(c)(2)(e)]. However, because this is also a requirement to be claimed as a dependent, we do not discuss the requirement separately here.

Relationship test.   A qualifying child must be an eligible relative of the taxpayer. Eligible relatives include the taxpayer's

- Child or descendant of a child. For this purpose, a child includes a taxpayer's adopted child, stepchild, and eligible foster child.
- Sibling or descendant of sibling. For this purpose, a sibling includes a taxpayer's half-brother, half-sister, stepbrother, or stepsister.

Under this definition, the taxpayer's grandchild would qualify as an eligible relative as would the taxpayer's sister's grandchild.

Age test.   A qualifying child must be younger than the taxpayer and *either* (1) under age 19 at the end of the year or (2) under age 24 at the end of the year *and* a full-time student.[16] A person is a full-time student if she was in school full-time during any part of each of five calendar months during the calendar year.[17] An individual who is permanently and totally disabled is deemed to have met the age test.[18]

Residence test.   A qualifying child must have the same principal residence as the taxpayer for *more* than half the year. Time that a child (or the taxpayer) is temporarily (not permanently) away from the taxpayer's home because the child (or taxpayer) is ill, is pursuing an education, or has other special circumstances is counted as though the child (or taxpayer) were living in the taxpayer's home.[19]

Support test.   A qualifying child must *not* have provided more than half his or her *own* support (living expenses) for the year. Support generally includes

- Food, school lunches, toilet articles, and haircuts.
- Clothing.
- Recreation—including toys, summer camp, horseback riding, entertainment, and vacation expenses.
- Medical and dental care.
- Child care expenses.
- Allowances and gifts.
- Wedding costs.
- Lodging.
- Education—including board, uniforms at military schools, and tuition. When determining who provided the support for a *child* of the taxpayer who is a full-time student, scholarships are excluded from the computation (neither the parent nor the child are treated as providing the support for the child).[20]

Example 4-7

Rodney and Anita have two children: Braxton, age 12, who lives at home and Tara, age 21, who is a full-time student and does not live at home. Tara earned $9,000 in a summer job, but she did *not* provide more than half of her own support during the year. Are Braxton and Tara qualifying children of Rodney and Anita?

(continued on page 4-14)

---

[16]§152(c)(3)(A).

[17]§152(f)(2).

[18]§151(c)(3)(B).

[19]Reg. §1.152-1(b).

[20]§152(f)(5) and §152(f)(1). This provision requires that the student be a son, daughter, stepson, stepdaughter, or an eligible foster child of the taxpayer.

Answer: Yes, see analysis of factors below:

Test	Braxton	Tara
Relationship	Yes, son.	Yes, daughter.
Age	Yes, under age 19 at end of year (and younger than his parents).	Yes, under age 24 at year-end *and* full-time student (and younger than her parents).
Residence	Yes, lived at home entire year.	Yes, time away at college is considered as time at home if Tara plans to live in her parent's home again at some point (it is a temporary absence).
Support	Yes, does not provide more than half of own support.	Yes, does not provide more than half of own support.

Because they both meet all the requirements, Braxton and Tara are qualifying children to the Halls. So, the Halls may claim one dependency exemption for Braxton and one for Tara.

What if: Suppose Tara provided more than half of her own support, would she be considered a qualifying child of her parents?

Answer: No. She would fail the support test.

What if: Assume the original facts except that Tara was age 25. Would Tara be considered a qualifying child of her parents?

Answer: No. She would fail the age test. Note, however, that Tara could still qualify as her parents' dependent as a qualifying relative (see Example 4-9 below).

What if: Assume the original facts except that Braxton was Anita's stepbrother's son. Would Braxton be considered a qualifying child of Rodney and Anita?

Answer: Yes. Braxton meets the relationship test because he is the descendant of Anita's stepbrother (sibling).

Tiebreaking rules. The requirements for determining who is a qualifying child leave open the possibility that one person could be a qualifying child to more than one taxpayer. In these circumstances, the taxpayer who has priority for claiming the dependency exemption is based on the following tiebreaking rules:

1. If the person is a qualifying child of a parent, the parent is entitled to the dependency exemption for the child. This situation could arise, for example, when a child lives with her mother *and* her grandparents. In this case, the mother has priority for claiming the dependency exemption over the grandparents.
2. If the individual is a qualifying child to both parents, the parent with whom the child has resided for the longest period of time during the year has priority for claiming the dependency exemption. This situation may arise in a year when the child lives with both parents for more than half of the year, but the parents divorce in the latter part of the year. Note, however, that the dependency exemption for a child of divorced parents can be claimed by the noncustodial parent if the custodial parent (the parent entitled to claim the exemption) releases the exemption to the noncustodial parent through a written declaration and the noncustodial parent attaches the declaration to his or her tax return.[21]
3. Finally, if the child resides with both parents for the same amount of time during the year or the qualifying child resides with a taxpayer who is not the child's parent, the taxpayer with the *highest AGI* has priority for claiming the dependency exemption for the child.[22]

[21]See §152(e). The custodial parent releases the exemption to the noncustodial parent with a signature on Form 8332.

[22]However, if the parents may claim the child as a qualifying child but no parent does so, another taxpayer may claim the individual as a qualifying child but only if the other individual's AGI is higher than the AGI of any parent of the child [§152(c)(4)(C)].

Example 4-8

In the previous example, we determined that Braxton (Rodney and Anita's son) is Rodney and Anita's qualifying child. Braxton's Uncle Shawn (Rodney's brother) lived in the Halls' home (the same home Braxton lived in) for more than 11 months during the year. Does Braxton meet the requirements to be considered Shawn's qualifying child?

Answer: Yes, see analysis of factors below.

Test	Braxton
Relationship	Yes, son of Shawn's brother.
Age	Yes, under age 19 at end of year (and younger than Shawn).
Residence	Yes, lived in same residence as Shawn for more than half the year.
Support	Yes, does not provide more than half of own support.

Thus, Braxton is considered to be Rodney and Anita's qualifying child *and* he is considered to be Shawn's qualifying child. Under the tiebreaker rules, who is allowed to claim Braxton as a dependent for the year?

Answer: Rodney and Anita. Under the first tiebreaking rule, Rodney and Anita are allowed to claim the dependency exemption for Braxton because they are Braxton's parents.

What if: Suppose that Shawn is Rodney's cousin. Would Braxton be Shawn's qualifying child?

Answer: No, Braxton does not meet the relationship test for Shawn. Braxton is not the descendant of Shawn's sibling.

Qualifying Relative A qualifying relative is a person who is *not* a qualifying child *and* satisfies (1) a relationship test, (2) a support test, and (3) a gross income test.

Relationship test. As you might expect, the relationship test for a qualifying relative is more inclusive than the relationship test for a qualifying child. A person meets the qualifying relative relationship test if the person either 1) has a qualifying family relationship with the taxpayer or 2) meets the qualifying relative "member of the household" test. A qualifying family relationship with the taxpayer includes the following:

- A descendant or ancestor of the taxpayer. For this purpose, a child includes a taxpayer's adopted child, stepchild, and eligible foster child; and a parent includes a stepmother and stepfather.
- A sibling of the taxpayer, including a stepbrother or a stepsister.
- A son or daughter of the brother or sister of the taxpayer (cousins do not qualify).
- A sibling of the taxpayer's mother or father.
- An in-law (mother-in-law, father-in-law, sister-in-law, brother-in-law, son-in-law, or daughter-in-law) of the taxpayer.
- A person meets the qualifying relative "member of the household" test if that person has the same principal place of abode as the taxpayer for the *entire* year (*even if the person does not have a qualifying family relationship with the taxpayer*).[23]

Support test. The support test generally requires that the taxpayer pay more than half the qualifying relative's living expenses (note that this is a different support test than the support test for a qualifying child). As we discussed above, living expenses

[23]A person is considered to live with the taxpayer for the entire year if he or she was either born during the year or died during the year and resided with the taxpayer for the remaining part of the year.

include rent, food, medicine, and clothes, among other things. Just as with the qualifying child support test, scholarships of children of a taxpayer who are full-time students are excluded from the support test.[24] Under a multiple support agreement, taxpayers who don't pay over half of an individual's support may still be allowed to claim the individual as a dependent under the qualifying relative rules if the following apply:[25]

1. No one taxpayer paid over one-half of the individual's support.
2. The taxpayer and at least one other person provided more than half the support of the individual, and the taxpayer and the other person(s) would have been allowed to claim the individual as a dependent except for the fact that they did not provide over half of the support of the individual.
3. The taxpayer contributed *over* 10 percent of the individual's support for the year.
4. Each other person who provided *over* 10 percent of the individual's support (see requirement (2) above) provides a signed statement to the taxpayer agreeing not to claim the individual as a dependent. The taxpayer includes the names, addresses, and Social Security numbers of each other person on Form 2120, which the taxpayer attaches to her Form 1040.

Multiple support agreements are commonly used in situations when siblings support elderly parents.

Gross income test.   The gross income test requires that a qualifying relative's gross income for the year be *less* than the personal exemption amount. As we noted above, the personal exemption amount for 2016 is $4,050.

Example 4-9

What if: Suppose Tara is age 25, is a full-time student, and does not live with her parents. Tara earned $3,000 in a summer job, and her parents provided more than half her support. Does Tara qualify as her parents' dependent?

Answer: Yes, as their qualifying relative. She is too old to be their qualifying child.

Test	Explanation
Relationship	Yes, Rodney and Anita's daughter.
Support	Yes, the Halls provide more than half of Tara's support.
Gross income	Yes, Tara's gross income for the year is less than the exemption amount.

Tara's parents may claim a dependency exemption for Tara. Tara is not allowed to claim a personal exemption for herself. Note that if Tara's gross income exceeded the exemption amount, she would not qualify as her parents' dependent, and she would claim a personal exemption for herself.

Example 4-10

In determining their dependency exemptions for the year, Rodney and Anita evaluated whether Shawn is their *qualifying relative*. Assuming Shawn's gross income for the year is $42,000, the Halls provided food and lodging for Shawn valued at $8,000, and Shawn paid for his other living expenses valued at $14,000, is Shawn a qualifying relative of the Halls?

[24]§152(f)(5) and §152(f)(1). Just as with a qualifying child, this provision requires that the student be a son, daughter, stepson, stepdaughter, or an eligible foster child of the taxpayer.
[25]§152(d)(3).

Answer: No, as analyzed below.

Test	Explanation
Relationship	Yes, Rodney's brother.
Support	No, the Halls provided $8,000 of support to Shawn, but Shawn provided $14,000 of his own support. Because the Halls provided less than half of Shawn's support, Shawn does not pass the support test.
Gross income	No, Shawn's gross income for the year is $42,000, which exceeds the exemption amount, so Shawn fails the gross income test.

Because Shawn fails the support test and the gross income test, he is not a qualifying relative of the Halls. Consequently, they cannot claim a dependency exemption for him. Thus, Shawn can claim a personal exemption for himself on his own tax return.

What if: Assume that Shawn received $5,000 of tax-exempt interest during the year and that this is his only source of income. Does he fail the gross income test?

Answer: No. Because tax-exempt interest is excluded from gross income, Shawn's gross income is $0, so he passes the gross income test.

What if: Assume the original facts in the example except that Shawn paid for his $14,000 of living expenses with interest he had received from tax-exempt bonds. Would Shawn pass the support test?

Answer: No. The Halls would not have provided more than half of Shawn's support. The fact that Shawn received the money he spent on his support from tax-exempt income does not matter. All that matters is that he provided more than half of his own support.

What if: Assume that Anita's 92-year-old grandfather Juan lives in an apartment by himself near the Halls' residence. His gross income for the year is $3,000. Assuming the Halls provide more than half of Juan's living expenses for the year, would Juan be a qualifying relative of the Halls?

Answer: Yes, as analyzed below.

Test	Explanation
Relationship	Yes, Anita's grandfather.
Support	Yes, as assumed in the facts, the Halls provide more than half of Juan's support.
Gross income	Yes, Juan's gross income for the year is $3,000, which is below the exemption amount, so Juan passes the gross income test.

What if: Assume that Anita's 92-year-old grandfather Juan lives in an apartment by himself and reports gross income for the year of $3,000. Anita provided 40 percent of Juan's support, Juan provided 25 percent of his own support, Anita's brother Carlos provides 30 percent of the support, and Anita's sister Kamella provided 5 percent of Juan's support. Who is eligible to claim Juan as a dependent under a multiple support agreement?

Answer: Anita and Carlos. Anita and Carlos are eligible because (1) no one taxpayer provided more than half of Juan's support, (2) Anita and Carlos together provided more than half of Juan's support and Juan would have been both Anita's and Carlos's qualifying relative except for the fact that neither provided over half of Juan's support, and (3) Anita and Carlos each provided over 10 percent of Juan's support (Kamella provided only 5 percent of Juan's support so she is not eligible). Anita and Carlos would need to agree on who would claim the dependency exemption for Juan. Assuming they agree that Anita would claim the exemption, she would need to receive a signed statement from Carlos agreeing not to claim the exemption and she would need to attach Form 2120 to her (and Rodney's) tax return providing Carlos's name, address, and Social Security number.

What if: Assume Juan lived in an apartment by himself and was a friend of the family but was not related to either Rodney or Anita, that his gross income is $3,000, and that the Halls provided over half of his support. Is Juan a qualifying relative of the Halls?

(*continued on page 4-18*)

Answer: No, as analyzed below.

Test	Explanation
Relationship	No, not related to Halls and his principal place of abode was not in the Halls' household for the *entire* year. If the Halls' home was his principal place of abode for the entire year, he would have met the relationship test even though he's not actually related to anyone in the Hall family.
Support	Yes, as assumed in the facts, the Halls provide more than half of Juan's support.
Gross income	Yes, Juan's gross income for the year is $3,000, which is below the exemption amount, so Juan passes the gross income test.

The Halls would not be able to claim an exemption for Juan as a qualifying relative because he fails the relationship test under this set of facts.

The rules for determining who qualifies as a dependent as a qualifying child and who qualifies as a dependent as a qualifying relative overlap to some extent. The primary differences between the two are

1. The relationship requirement is more broadly defined for qualifying relatives than qualifying children.
2. Qualifying children are subject to age restrictions while qualifying relatives are not.
3. Qualifying relatives are subject to a gross income restriction while qualifying children are not.
4. Taxpayers need not provide more than half a qualifying child's support (though the child cannot provide more than half of her own support), but they must provide more than half the support of a qualifying relative.
5. Qualifying children are subject to a residence test (they must have the same primary residence as the taxpayer for more than half the year) while qualifying relatives are not. Exhibit 4-8 summarizes the dependency requirements.

EXHIBIT 4-8 **Summary of Dependency Requirements**

Test	Qualifying Child	Qualifying Relative
Relationship	Taxpayer's child, stepchild, foster child, sibling, half-brother or sister, stepbrother or sister, or a descendant of any of these relatives.	Taxpayer's descendant or ancestor, sibling, stepmother, stepfather, stepbrother or stepsister, son or daughter of taxpayer's sibling, sibling of the taxpayer's mother or father, in-laws, and anyone else who has the same principal place of abode as the taxpayer for the entire year (even if not otherwise related).
Age	Younger than the taxpayer claiming the individual as a qualifying child and under age 19 or a full-time student under age 24. Also anyone totally and permanently disabled.	Not applicable.
Residence	Lives with taxpayer for more than half of the year (includes temporary absences for things such as illness and education).	Not applicable.
Support	The qualifying child must not provide more than half of his or her own support.	Taxpayer must have provided more than half of the support for the qualifying relative.
Gross income	Not applicable.	Gross income less than exemption amount ($4,050 in 2016).
Other	Not applicable.	Not a qualifying child.

Appendix A provides a flowchart for determining whether an individual qualifies as the taxpayer's dependent.

ETHICS

Blake is 21 years of age at the end of the year. During the year, Blake was a full-time college student. He also worked part-time and earned $8,000, which he used to pay all of his $6,000 of living expenses. Blake's parents, Troy and Camille, claimed Blake as a dependent on their joint tax return. After filing the joint tax return, Troy told Blake they owed him $3,001 for his annual living expenses. What do you think of Troy and Camille's strategy to claim a dependency exemption for Blake?

FILING STATUS

`LO 4-3`

Each year taxpayers determine their **filing status** according to their marital status at year-end and whether they have any dependents. A taxpayer's filing status is important because, as we discussed above, it determines

- The applicable tax rate schedule for determining the taxpayer's tax liability.
- The taxpayer's standard deduction amount.
- The AGI threshold for reductions in certain tax benefits such as itemized deductions and certain tax credits, among others.

Each year, all taxpayers filing tax returns file under one of the following five filing statuses:

1. Married filing jointly
2. Married filing separately
3. Qualifying widow or widower (surviving spouse)
4. Single
5. Head of household

Married Filing Jointly and Married Filing Separately

Married couples may file tax returns jointly **(married filing jointly)** or separately **(married filing separately)**. To be married for filing status purposes, taxpayers must be married on the last day of the year. When one spouse dies during the year, the surviving spouse is considered to be *married* to the spouse who died at the end of the year unless the surviving spouse remarries during the year. Married couples filing joint returns combine their income and deductions and agree to share joint and several liability for the resulting tax. That is, they are both ultimately responsible to see that the tax is paid.

When married couples file separately, each spouse reports the income he or she received during the year and the deductions he or she is claiming on a tax return separate from that of the other spouse.[26] So that married taxpayers can't file separately to gain more combined tax benefits than they are entitled to if they filed jointly, tax-related items for married filing separate (MFS) taxpayers—such as tax rate schedules and standard deduction amounts, among others—are generally one-half what they are for married filing joint (MFJ) taxpayers. Also, if one spouse deducts itemized deductions, the other spouse is required to deduct itemized deductions even if his or her standard deduction amount is more than the total itemized deductions. Thus, only in unusual circumstances does it make economic sense for *tax* purposes for married couples to file separately.

---

[26]As we discuss in the next chapter, under community property laws of certain states, one spouse may be treated as receiving income earned by the other spouse.

THE KEY FACTS

Filing Status for Married Taxpayers
- Married filing jointly
  - Taxpayers are legally married as of the last day of the year.
  - When one spouse dies during the year the surviving spouse is still considered to be married for tax purposes during the year of the spouse's death.
  - Both spouses are ultimately responsible for paying the joint tax.
- Married filing separately
  - Taxpayers are legally married as of the last day of the year.
  - Generally no tax advantage to filing separately (usually a disadvantage).
  - Each spouse is ultimately responsible for paying own tax.
  - Couples may choose to file separately (generally for nontax reasons).
- Qualifying widow or widower
  - When a taxpayer's spouse dies, the surviving spouse can file as qualifying widow or widower for two years after the year of the spouse's death if the surviving spouse remains unmarried and maintains a household for a dependent child.

However, it may be wise for married couples to file separately for *nontax* reasons. For example, a spouse who does not want to be liable for the other spouse's income tax liability, or a spouse who is not in contact with the other spouse, may want to file separately (see abandoned spouse discussion below).

Example 4-11

Rodney and Anita Hall are married at the end of the year. What is their filing status?

Answer: Married filing jointly, unless they choose to file separately.

What if: Assume that in 2016 the Halls file a joint return. In 2017, Rodney and Anita divorce and the IRS audits their 2016 tax return and determines that due to overstating their deductions, the Halls underpaid their taxes by $2,000. Who must pay the tax?

Answer: Both Rodney and Anita are responsible for paying. If the IRS can't locate Rodney, it can require Anita to pay the full $2,000 even though Anita earned $46,000 and Rodney earned $64,000.

What if: Assume that in 2016 the Halls file separate tax returns. In 2017, Rodney and Anita divorce and the IRS audits the Halls' separate tax returns. It determines that by overstating deductions, Rodney understated his tax liability by $1,500 and Anita understated her tax liability by $500. Further, the IRS cannot locate Rodney. What is the maximum amount of taxes Anita is liable for?

Answer: $500. Because she filed a separate return, she is responsible for the tax liability associated with her separate tax return, and she is not responsible for the taxes associated with Rodney's tax return.

TAXES IN THE REAL WORLD — Tax Status for Same-Sex Married Couples

In June of 2013, the Supreme Court struck down the federal "Defense of Marriage Act" (DOMA) which meant that same-sex couples that were married in a state that authorized and recognized same-sex marriages would be treated as married for federal income tax purposes. However, couples who were in a registered domestic partnership, civil union, or other similar formal relationship recognized under state law were not recognized as married for federal income tax purposes. In June of 2015, the Supreme Court ruled that the 14th Amendment of the Constitution guarantees a right to same-sex marriage. This ruling unifies marital status at both the federal and state levels. A taxpayer's marital status is important for determining income tax filing status and has implications for other areas of the tax law (estate and gift tax, for example).

See *Obergefell vs. Hodges*, 576 U.S. ____ (2015).

Qualifying Widow or Widower (Surviving Spouse)

When a taxpayer's spouse dies, the taxpayer is no longer legally married. However, to provide tax relief for widows and widowers *with dependents,* taxpayers who meet certain requirements qualify for the **qualifying widow or widower** (also referred to as surviving spouse) filing status for up to two years *after* the end of the year in which the other spouse died (recall that for tax purposes, they are still considered to be married for the year of the spouse's death). Taxpayers are eligible for qualifying widow or widower filing status if they (1) remain unmarried and (2) pay over half the cost of maintaining a household where a dependent child lived for the entire year (except for temporary absences).[27] The dependent child must be a child or stepchild (including an adopted child) for whom the taxpayer may claim an exemption (not a

[27]§2(a).

foster child). A qualifying widow or widower is not considered to be married for tax purposes. Consequently, a qualifying widow or widower is allowed to claim one personal exemption (recall that taxpayers who are married filing jointly are allowed to claim two personal exemptions).

Example 4-12

What if: Assume that last year Rodney passed away, and during the current year Anita did not remarry but maintained a household for Braxton and Tara, her dependent children. Under these circumstances, what would Anita's filing status be?

Answer: Qualifying widow. Last year, the year of Rodney's death, Anita qualified to file a joint return with Rodney. This year, Anita qualifies as a qualifying widow (also referred to as a surviving spouse) because she has not remarried and she maintains a household for the entire year for her dependent children. She will qualify as a surviving spouse next year (two years after Rodney's death) if she does not remarry and she continues to maintain a household for Braxton and/or Tara for the entire year. Anita will claim three exemptions. One personal exemption and two dependency exemptions (for Braxton and Tara).

Single

Unmarried taxpayers who do not qualify for head of household status (discussed below) file as **single** taxpayers. As we discuss below, an unmarried taxpayer generally must be able to claim an exemption for a dependent in order to qualify for head of household status.

Example 4-13

Shawn Hall, Rodney's brother, was divorced in January and is unmarried at the end of the year. Shawn does not claim any dependency exemptions. What is his filing status?

Answer: Single. Because Shawn is unmarried at the end of the year, and he does not have any dependents, his filing status is single.

Head of Household

In terms of tax rate schedules and standard deduction amounts, the **head of household** filing status is less favorable than the married filing jointly and qualifying widow or widower filing statuses. However, it is more favorable than married filing separately and single filing statuses (see tax rates and standard deduction amounts provided in Appendix D). To qualify for head of household filing status, a taxpayer must

- Be unmarried (or considered to be unmarried under the provisions discussed below) at the end of the year.
- Not be a qualifying widow or widower.
- Pay more than half the costs of keeping up a home for the year.
- Have a "qualifying person" live in the taxpayer's home for more than half the year (except for temporary absences such as military service, illness, or schooling). However, if the qualifying person is the taxpayer's *dependent* parent, the parent is not required to live with the taxpayer. A qualifying person may not qualify more than one person for head of household filing status. Exhibit 4-9 describes who is a qualifying person for purposes of head of household filing status.[28]

THE KEY FACTS

Filing Status for Unmarried Taxpayers

- Single
  - Unmarried taxpayers at year-end who do not qualify for head of household.
- Head of household
  - Unmarried taxpayers or taxpayers considered to be unmarried at year end.
  - Must pay more than half of the costs of maintaining a household in which a qualifying person lives for more than half of the tax year or must pay more than half of the costs for maintaining a separate household for a parent who qualifies as taxpayer's dependent.

---

[28]§2(b).

EXHIBIT 4-9 **Who Is a Qualifying Person for Determining Head of Household Filing Status? (Adapted from Table 4 in IRS Publication 501)**

IF the person is the taxpayer's . . .	And . . .	THEN the person is . . .
qualifying child	the person is single.	a qualifying person, whether or not the taxpayer can claim an exemption for the person.*
	the person is married and the taxpayer may claim a dependency exemption for the person.	a qualifying person.*
	the person is married and the taxpayer may not claim a dependency exemption for the person.	not a qualifying person.
qualifying relative who is the taxpayer's mother or father	the taxpayer may claim a dependency exemption for the taxpayer's father or mother.	a qualifying person even if the taxpayer's mother or father did not live with the taxpayer. However, the taxpayer must have paid more than half the costs to maintain the household of the mother or father.
	the taxpayer may not claim a dependency exemption for the mother or father.	not a qualifying person.
qualifying relative other than the taxpayer's mother or father	the person did not live with the taxpayer for more than half the year.	not a qualifying person.
	the taxpayer can claim a dependency exemption for the person, the person lived with the taxpayer for more than half the year and the person is related to the taxpayer through a qualifying family relationship.	a qualifying person.
	the person is the taxpayer's qualifying relative only because the person lived with the taxpayer as a member of the taxpayer's household for the entire year (the person does not have a qualifying family relationship with the taxpayer).	not a qualifying person.
	the taxpayer cannot claim a dependency exemption for the person or the taxpayer can claim a dependency exemption only because of a multiple support agreement.	not a qualifying person.

*If a custodial parent releases the exemption deduction of a qualifying child to a noncustodial parent, the child is still considered to be a qualifying person of the custodial parent not the noncustodial parent for purposes of determining which parents qualifies for head of household filing status.

Example 4-14

What if: Assume Rodney and Anita divorced last year. During the current year, Braxton lives with Anita for the entire year and Anita pays all the costs of maintaining the household for herself and Braxton. Under these circumstances, what is Anita's filing status for the year?

Answer: Head of household. Anita is unmarried at the end of the year, she provides more than half the costs of maintaining her household, Braxton lives with her for more than half the year, and Braxton is her qualifying child.

What if: Assume Rodney and Anita divorced last year. During the current year, Braxton lives with Anita for the entire year, and Anita pays all the costs of maintaining the household for herself and Braxton. Assume that Anita released the dependency exemption to Rodney under the divorce decree. Under these circumstances, what is Anita's filing status for the year?

Answer: Head of household. Braxton is a qualifying person for Anita (the custodial parent) even though Anita is not claiming the dependency exemption for Braxton. Braxton is not a qualifying person for Rodney (the noncustodial parent).

What if: Assume that Rodney and Anita divorced last year, Braxton is Anita's cousin, and Braxton lived with Anita in her home from June 15 through December 31. What is Anita's filing status for the year?

Answer: Single. Anita does not qualify for head of household filing status because Braxton is not Anita's qualifying child (fails relationship test) or qualifying relative (fails relationship test because he did not live in Anita's home for the entire year, and he does not have a qualifying family relationship with Anita because he is Anita's cousin).

What if: Assume that Rodney and Anita divorced last year, Braxton is Anita's cousin, and Braxton lived with Anita in her home for the entire year. What is Anita's filing status for the year?

Answer: Single. Even though Braxton is Anita's qualifying relative, Braxton meets the qualifying relative relationship test only because he lived with Anita for the entire year (not because he had a qualifying family relationship with Anita). Therefore, while Anita may claim a dependency exemption for Braxton, she does not qualify for the head of household filing status.

What if: Assume Shawn (Rodney's brother) lived with the Halls, but Shawn paid more than half the costs of maintaining a separate apartment that is the principal residence of his mother, Sharon, whose gross income is $1,500. Because Shawn provided more than half of Sharon's support during the year, and because Sharon's gross income was only $1,500, she qualifies as Shawn's dependent (as a qualifying relative). In these circumstances, what is Shawn's filing status?

Answer: Head of household. Shawn paid more than half the costs of maintaining a separate household where his mother resides, and his mother qualifies as his dependent.

If Sharon's gross income exceeded the exemption amount she would fail the dependency gross income test and would not qualify as Shawn's dependent. If she did not qualify as his dependent she would not be a qualifying person, and Shawn would not qualify for the head of household filing status. Also, if Sharon were Shawn's grandmother rather than his mother, she would not be a qualifying person (no matter the amount of her gross income) and Shawn would not qualify for head of household status—Sharon must be Shawn's parent in order for her to qualify Shawn as a head of household.

Married Individuals Treated as Unmarried (Abandoned Spouse)   In certain situations a couple may be legally married at the end of the year, but living apart. Although the couple could technically file a joint tax return, this is often not desirable from a nontax perspective, because each spouse would be assuming responsibility for paying tax on income earned by either spouse whether it was reported or not. However, because both spouses are married at the end of the year, their only other option is to file under the tax-unfavorable married filing separately filing status.

To provide tax relief in these situations, the tax laws treat a married taxpayer *as though he or she were unmarried* at the end of the year if the taxpayer meets the following requirements:

- The taxpayer is married at the end of the year (or is not *legally* separated from the other spouse).
- The taxpayer does not file a joint tax return with the other spouse.
- The taxpayer pays *more than half* the costs of maintaining his or her home for the entire year, and this home is the principal residence for a child (who qualifies as the taxpayer's dependent[29]) for *more than half* the year (the child must be a child of the taxpayer, including adopted child, stepchild, or eligible foster child[30]).
- The taxpayer lived apart from the other spouse for the last six months of the year (the other spouse did not live at all in the taxpayer's home during the last six months—temporary absences due to illness, education, business, vacation, or military service count as though the spouse still lived in the taxpayer's home).

If the taxpayer meets these requirements, he or she also meets the head of household filing status requirements and may file as head of household for the year. The primary objective of this tax rule is to provide tax relief to one spouse who has been abandoned by or separated from the other spouse and left to care for a dependent child. Thus, a married taxpayer who qualifies as unmarried under this provision is

---

[29]A taxpayer meets this test if the taxpayer (custodial parent) cannot claim an exemption for the child only because he or she released the exemption to the noncustodial parent under a divorce agreement.
[30]§152(f).

frequently referred to as an **abandoned spouse.** Nevertheless, the provision may still apply even when no spouse has been abandoned. For example, a couple may separate by mutual consent. Further, if both spouses meet the requirements, both spouses may qualify as being unmarried in the same year and thus both may qualify for head of household filing status.

Example 4-15

What if: Assume that last year, Rodney and Anita informally separated (they did not *legally* separate). Rodney moved out of the home and into his own apartment. Anita stayed in the Halls' home with Braxton. During the current year, Anita paid more than half the costs of maintaining the home for herself and Braxton. Even though Rodney and Anita were legally married at the end of the year, they filed separate tax returns. Under these circumstances, is Anita considered to be married or unmarried for tax purposes?

Answer: Unmarried. Anita meets the requirements for being treated as unmarried determined as follows (see requirements above):

- Anita is married to Rodney at the end of the year.
- Anita filed a tax return separate from Rodney's.
- Anita paid more than half the costs of maintaining her home, and her home was the principal residence for Braxton who is her dependent child.
- Rodney did not live in Anita's home for the last six months of the year (in fact, he didn't live there at any time during the entire year).

What if: Given that Anita meets the requirements for being treated as unmarried, what is her filing status?

Answer: Head of household. Since Anita meets the abandoned spouse requirements she also meets the head of household filing status requirements. Without the abandoned spouse rule, Anita would have been required to file as married filing separately. Rodney's filing status, however, is married filing separately. Note, however, that if Rodney's new residence became Tara's principal residence, Rodney would also be treated as unmarried and would be eligible for head of household filing status.

Appendix B includes a flowchart for determining a taxpayer's filing status.

SUMMARY OF INCOME TAX FORMULA

Tara crunched some numbers and put together a summary of her parents' taxable income calculation. She determined that her parents will receive a $407.50 tax refund when they file their tax return. Tara's summary is provided in Exhibit 4-10, and Exhibit 4-11 presents pages 1 and 2 of the Halls' Form 1040.

EXHIBIT 4-10   Taxable Income and Tax Calculation Summary for Rodney and Anita Hall

Description	Amount	Explanation
(1) Gross income	110,600.00	Example 4-1.
(2) For AGI deductions	(5,000.00)	Example 4-2, line (2).
(3) Adjusted gross income	$105,600.00	(1) + (2).
(4) Itemized deductions	(14,000.00)	Example 4-3, line (2).
(5) Personal and dependency exemptions	(16,200.00)	Example 4-3, line (4).
(6) Taxable income	$ 75,400.00	(3) + (4) + (5).
(7) Income tax liability	$ 10,392.50	Example 4-4.
(8) Other taxes	0	
(9) Total tax	$ 10,392.50	(7) + (8).
(10) Credits	(1,000.00)	Example 4-5, line (2).
(11) Prepayments	(9,800.00)	Example 4-5, line (3).
Tax refund	($407.50)	(9) + (10) + (11).

EXHIBIT 4-11

Form **1040** Department of the Treasury—Internal Revenue Service (99)
U.S. Individual Income Tax Return 2015 OMB No. 1545-0074 IRS Use Only—Do not write or staple in this space.

For the year Jan. 1–Dec. 31, 2015, or other tax year beginning , 2015, ending , 20 | See separate instructions.

Your first name and initial	Last name	Your social security number
Rodney	Hall	2 2 4 5 6 1 2 4 5

If a joint return, spouse's first name and initial	Last name	Spouse's social security number
Anita	Hall	3 2 4 4 3 3 4 7 8

Home address (number and street). If you have a P.O. box, see instructions. | Apt. no.

665 Henry Avenue

▲ Make sure the SSN(s) above and on line 6c are correct.

City, town or post office, state, and ZIP code. If you have a foreign address, also complete spaces below (see instructions).

Brookings, SD 57007

Foreign country name | Foreign province/state/county | Foreign postal code

Presidential Election Campaign
Check here if you, or your spouse if filing jointly, want $3 to go to this fund. Checking a box below will not change your tax or refund. ☐ You ☐ Spouse

Filing Status

Check only one box.

1 ☐ Single
2 ☑ Married filing jointly (even if only one had income)
3 ☐ Married filing separately. Enter spouse's SSN above and full name here. ▶
4 ☐ Head of household (with qualifying person). (See instructions.) If the qualifying person is a child but not your dependent, enter this child's name here. ▶
5 ☐ Qualifying widow(er) with dependent child

Exemptions

If more than four dependents, see instructions and check here ▶ ☐

6a ☑ **Yourself.** If someone can claim you as a dependent, **do not** check box 6a .
b ☑ **Spouse** .

c Dependents:	(2) Dependent's social security number	(3) Dependent's relationship to you	(4) ✓ if child under age 17 qualifying for child tax credit (see instructions)
(1) First name Last name			
Tara Hall	2 4 2 6 8 9 9 4 5	Daughter	☐
Braxton Hall	2 4 2 2 3 7 8 4 5	Son	☑
			☐
			☐

d Total number of exemptions claimed .

Boxes checked on 6a and 6b **2**
No. of children on 6c who:
• lived with you **2**
• did not live with you due to divorce or separation (see instructions)
Dependents on 6c not entered above
Add numbers on lines above ▶ **4**

Income

Attach Form(s) W-2 here. Also attach Forms W-2G and 1099-R if tax was withheld.

If you did not get a W-2, see instructions.

7	Wages, salaries, tips, etc. Attach Form(s) W-2 .	7	110,000
8a	**Taxable** interest. Attach Schedule B if required .	8a	600
b	**Tax-exempt** interest. **Do not** include on line 8a .	8b	
9a	Ordinary dividends. Attach Schedule B if required .	9a	
b	Qualified dividends .	9b	
10	Taxable refunds, credits, or offsets of state and local income taxes .	10	
11	Alimony received .	11	
12	Business income or (loss). Attach Schedule C or C-EZ .	12	
13	Capital gain or (loss). Attach Schedule D if required. If not required, check here ▶ ☐	13	
14	Other gains or (losses). Attach Form 4797 .	14	
15a	IRA distributions . 15a	b Taxable amount .	15b	
16a	Pensions and annuities . 16a	b Taxable amount .	16b	
17	Rental real estate, royalties, partnerships, S corporations, trusts, etc. Attach Schedule E	17	
18	Farm income or (loss). Attach Schedule F .	18	
19	Unemployment compensation .	19	
20a	Social security benefits . 20a	b Taxable amount .	20b	
21	Other income. List type and amount	21	
22	Combine the amounts in the far right column for lines 7 through 21. This is your **total income** ▶	22	

Adjusted Gross Income

23	Educator expenses .	23	
24	Certain business expenses of reservists, performing artists, and fee-basis government officials. Attach Form 2106 or 2106-EZ	24	
25	Health savings account deduction. Attach Form 8889 .	25	
26	Moving expenses. Attach Form 3903 .	26	5,000
27	Deductible part of self-employment tax. Attach Schedule SE .	27	
28	Self-employed SEP, SIMPLE, and qualified plans .	28	
29	Self-employed health insurance deduction .	29	
30	Penalty on early withdrawal of savings .	30	
31a	Alimony paid b Recipient's SSN ▶	31a	
32	IRA deduction .	32	
33	Student loan interest deduction .	33	
34	Tuition and fees. Attach Form 8917 .	34	
35	Domestic production activities deduction. Attach Form 8903	35	
36	Add lines 23 through 35 .	36	5,000
37	Subtract line 36 from line 22. This is your **adjusted gross income** ▶	37	105,600

For Disclosure, Privacy Act, and Paperwork Reduction Act Notice, see separate instructions. Cat. No. 11320B Form **1040** (2015)

(continued)

EXHIBIT 4-11 *(continued)*

Form 1040 (2015)   Page **2**

	38	Amount from line 37 (adjusted gross income)	**38**	105,600

Tax and Credits

39a Check if: ☐ **You** were born before January 2, 1951, ☐ Blind. / ☐ **Spouse** was born before January 2, 1951, ☐ Blind. } **Total boxes** checked ▶ **39a** [ ]

b If your spouse itemizes on a separate return or you were a dual-status alien, check here▶ **39b** ☐

Standard Deduction for—
- People who check any box on line 39a or 39b or who can be claimed as a dependent, see instructions.
- All others:
Single or Married filing separately, $6,300
Married filing jointly or Qualifying widow(er), $12,600
Head of household, $9,250

40	**Itemized deductions** (from Schedule A) **or** your **standard deduction** (see left margin) . .	**40**	14,000
41	Subtract line 40 from line 38	**41**	91,600
42	**Exemptions.** If line 38 is $154,950 or less, multiply $4,000 by the number on line 6d. Otherwise, see instructions	**42**	16,200
43	**Taxable income.** Subtract line 42 from line 41. If line 42 is more than line 41, enter -0- . .	**43**	75,400
44	**Tax** (see instructions). Check if any from: **a** ☐ Form(s) 8814 **b** ☐ Form 4972 **c** ☐ _____	**44**	10,393
45	**Alternative minimum tax** (see instructions). Attach Form 6251 . .	**45**	
46	Excess advance premium tax credit repayment. Attach Form 8962 . .	**46**	
47	Add lines 44, 45, and 46 . . . . ▶	**47**	10,393

48	Foreign tax credit. Attach Form 1116 if required . . .	**48**	
49	Credit for child and dependent care expenses. Attach Form 2441	**49**	
50	Education credits from Form 8863, line 19 . . .	**50**	
51	Retirement savings contributions credit. Attach Form 8880	**51**	
52	Child tax credit. Attach Schedule 8812, if required . .	**52**	1,000
53	Residential energy credits. Attach Form 5695 . . .	**53**	
54	Other credits from Form: **a** ☐ 3800 **b** ☐ 8801 **c** ☐ ___	**54**	

55	Add lines 48 through 54. These are your **total credits**	**55**	1,000
56	Subtract line 55 from line 47. If line 55 is more than line 47, enter -0- . . . ▶	**56**	9,393

Other Taxes

57	Self-employment tax. Attach Schedule SE	**57**	
58	Unreported social security and Medicare tax from Form: **a** ☐ 4137 **b** ☐ 8919 . .	**58**	
59	Additional tax on IRAs, other qualified retirement plans, etc. Attach Form 5329 if required . .	**59**	
60a	Household employment taxes from Schedule H	**60a**	
b	First-time homebuyer credit repayment. Attach Form 5405 if required	**60b**	
61	Health care: individual responsibility (see instructions) Full-year coverage ☐	**61**	
62	Taxes from: **a** ☐ Form 8959 **b** ☐ Form 8960 **c** ☐ Instructions; enter code(s) _____	**62**	
63	Add lines 56 through 62. This is your **total tax** . . . . ▶	**63**	9,393

Payments

If you have a qualifying child, attach Schedule EIC.

64	Federal income tax withheld from Forms W-2 and 1099	**64**	9,800	
65	2015 estimated tax payments and amount applied from 2014 return	**65**		
66a	**Earned income credit (EIC)**	**66a**		
b	Nontaxable combat pay election **66b**			
67	Additional child tax credit. Attach Schedule 8812 . . .	**67**		
68	American opportunity credit from Form 8863, line 8 . . .	**68**		
69	Net premium tax credit. Attach Form 8962	**69**		
70	Amount paid with request for extension to file . . .	**70**		
71	Excess social security and tier 1 RRTA tax withheld . .	**71**		
72	Credit for federal tax on fuels. Attach Form 4136 . . .	**72**		
73	Credits from Form: **a** ☐ 2439 **b** ☐ Reserved **c** ☐ 8885 **d** ☐ ___	**73**		
74	Add lines 64, 65, 66a, and 67 through 73. These are your **total payments** . . . . ▶	**74**	9,800	

Refund

Direct deposit? See instructions.

75	If line 74 is more than line 63, subtract line 63 from line 74. This is the amount you **overpaid**	**75**	407
76a	Amount of line 75 you want **refunded to you.** If Form 8888 is attached, check here . ▶ ☐	**76a**	407
▶ **b**	Routing number [ ][ ][ ][ ][ ][ ][ ][ ][ ] ▶**c** Type: ☐ Checking ☐ Savings		
▶ **d**	Account number [ ][ ][ ][ ][ ][ ][ ][ ][ ][ ][ ][ ][ ][ ][ ][ ][ ]		
77	Amount of line 75 you want **applied to your 2016 estimated tax** ▶ **77**		

Amount You Owe

78	**Amount you owe.** Subtract line 74 from line 63. For details on how to pay, see instructions ▶	**78**	
79	Estimated tax penalty (see instructions) **79**		

Third Party Designee

Do you want to allow another person to discuss this return with the IRS (see instructions)? ☐ **Yes.** Complete below. ☐ **No**

Designee's name ▶ _____   Phone no. ▶ _____   Personal identification number (PIN) ▶ [ ][ ][ ][ ][ ]

Sign Here

Joint return? See instructions. Keep a copy for your records.

Under penalties of perjury, I declare that I have examined this return and accompanying schedules and statements, and to the best of my knowledge and belief, they are true, correct, and complete. Declaration of preparer (other than taxpayer) is based on all information of which preparer has any knowledge.

Your signature	Date	Your occupation	Daytime phone number
Spouse's signature. If a joint return, **both** must sign.	Date	Spouse's occupation	If the IRS sent you an Identity Protection PIN, enter it here (see inst.) [ ][ ][ ][ ][ ][ ]

Paid Preparer Use Only

Print/Type preparer's name	Preparer's signature	Date	Check ☐ if self-employed	PTIN
Firm's name ▶			Firm's EIN ▶	
Firm's address ▶			Phone no.	

www.irs.gov/form1040   Form **1040** (2015)

CONCLUSION

This chapter presents an overview of the individual income tax formula and provides rules for determining who qualifies as a taxpayer's dependents and for determining a taxpayer's filing status. In Chapter 5, we turn our attention to determining gross income. In Chapter 6, we describe deductions available to taxpayers when computing their taxable income. In Chapter 8, we conclude our review of the individual income tax formula by determining how to compute a taxpayer's tax liability and her taxes due or tax refund.

Appendix A   Dependency Exemption Flowchart (Part I)

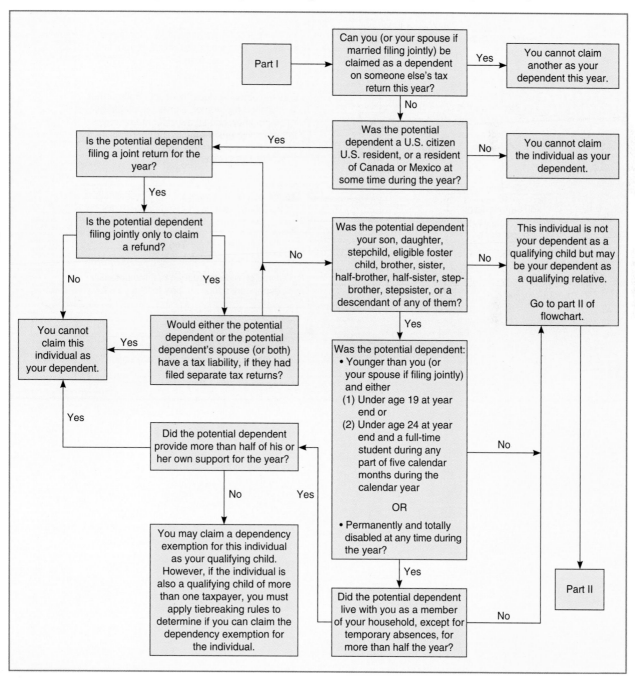

Appendix A   (Part II)

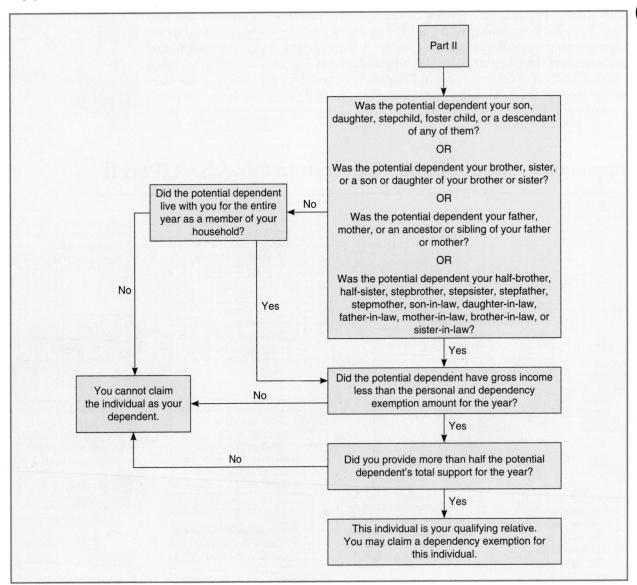

Appendix B   Qualifying Person for Head of Household Filing Status

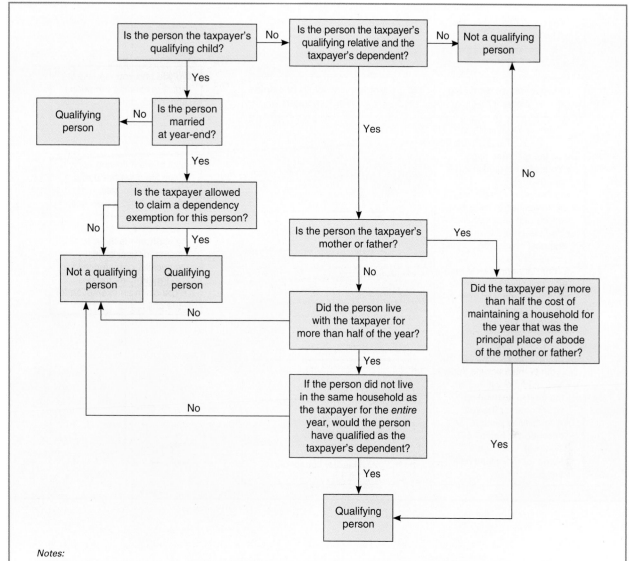

Notes:

- If a custodial parent releases the exemption for the person under a divorce decree the person is still a qualifying person to the custodial parent. The person is not a qualifying person to the noncustodial parent.
- If the taxpayer can claim an exemption for the person only because of a multiple support agreement, that person is not a qualifying person.
- One qualifying person may not qualify more than one person for head of household filing status.

Appendix C   Determination of Filing Status Flowchart

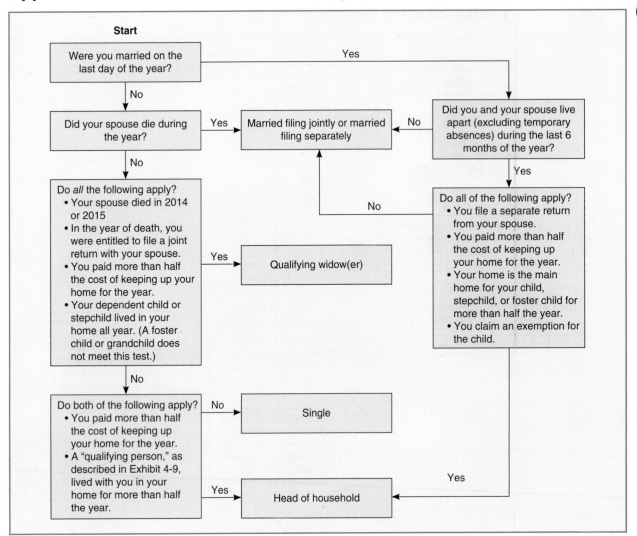

Summary

LO 4-1   Describe the formula for calculating an individual taxpayer's taxes payable or refund and generally explain each formula component.

- Generally, taxpayers are taxed on all income they realize during the year, no matter the source. However, the tax laws allow taxpayers to permanently exclude or to defer to a later year certain types of income they realize during the year.

- Income items that taxpayers are allowed to permanently exclude from income are called exclusions. Realized income items that taxpayers are not taxed on until a future period are called deferrals.

- Taxpayers include gross income on their tax returns.

- The character of the income determines how the income is treated for tax purposes, including, potentially, the rate at which the income is taxed.

- Ordinary income is taxed at the rates provided in the tax rate schedules; long-term capital gains (after a netting process) and qualified dividends are taxed at a maximum rate of 0, 15, or 20 percent, depending on the taxpayer's taxable income.

- Capital gains and losses arise from the sale or disposition of capital assets. In general a capital asset is any asset other than accounts receivable from the sale of goods or services, inventory, and assets used in a trade or business. If a capital asset is owned for more than a year before it is sold, the capital gain or loss is long-term. Otherwise, it is short-term.

- Taxpayers may deduct up to $3,000 of net capital loss for the year (excess of capital losses over capital gains for the year) against ordinary income. The remainder is suspended and carried over to the next year.

- Even though a personal-use asset meets the capital asset definition, a taxpayer is not allowed to deduct a loss on the sale or disposition of a personal-use asset.

- Deductions reduce a taxpayer's taxable income. The two types of deductions are *for* AGI deductions and *from* AGI deductions.

- Gross income minus *for* AGI deductions equals adjusted gross income (AGI). *For* AGI deductions are deductions "above the line," the last line on the front page of the individual tax Form 1040.

- *For* AGI deductions tend to relate to business activities and certain investment activities.

- AGI minus *from* AGI deductions equals taxable income.

- *From* AGI deductions include itemized deductions, the standard deduction, and exemptions. *From* AGI deductions are referred to as "deductions below the line."

- AGI is an important reference point in the individual tax formula because it is often used in other tax-related calculations, including determining limitations on *from* AGI deductions.

- Taxpayers generally deduct itemized deductions when the amount of the itemized deductions exceeds the standard deduction. The standard deduction varies by filing status and is indexed for inflation. Special rules may alter the standard deduction amount for certain taxpayers.

- Taxpayers are allowed to deduct personal exemptions for themselves (and their spouses if they file jointly) and dependency exemptions for those who qualify as their dependents.

- Taxpayers generally calculate the tax on their taxable income by referring to tax tables or tax rate schedules.

- Taxpayers may be required to pay the alternative minimum tax (AMT), self-employment tax, the 3.8% net investment income tax, and/or the .9% additional Medicare tax on earned income in addition to their regular income tax.

- Tax credits reduce taxpayers' tax liability dollar for dollar, while deductions decrease taxable income dollar for dollar.

- Taxpayers prepay taxes during the year through withholdings by employers, estimated tax payments, or prior year overpayments applied toward the current-year tax liability.

- If tax prepayments exceed the taxpayer's total tax after credits, the taxpayer receives a refund. If tax prepayments are less than the total tax after credits, the taxpayer owes additional tax with his or her tax return.

Explain the requirements for determining a taxpayer's personal and dependency exemptions.   **LO 4-2**

- For 2016, taxpayers are allowed to deduct $4,050 for each personal and dependency exemption they are entitled to claim.

- Individuals may claim a personal exemption for themselves (and for their spouses if they are married and file jointly). They may also claim dependency exemptions for each person who qualifies as their dependent.

- If an individual qualifies as a dependent of another taxpayer, the individual may not deduct a personal exemption for him- or herself on his or her individual return. Also, the individual may not claim any dependency exemptions.

- Taxpayers may claim dependency exemptions for those who (1) are citizens of the United States or residents of the United States, Canada, or Mexico and (2) meet the joint tax return test, and are considered either a qualifying child or a qualifying relative of the taxpayer.
- A child must meet a relationship test, an age test, a residence test, and a support test to qualify as a qualifying child.
- A person who is not a qualifying child may be considered a qualifying relative by meeting a relationship test, a support test, and a gross income test.

LO 4-3 Determine a taxpayer's filing status.

- Taxpayers may file their tax returns as married filing jointly, married filing separately, qualifying widow or widower (also referred to as surviving spouse), single, or head of household.
- Married taxpayers may file a joint return or they may file separately. It is generally more advantageous for tax purposes to file jointly, if married. However, for nontax reasons, it may be advantageous to file separately.
- Each spouse is ultimately responsible for paying the tax on a joint return no matter who received the income.
- For two years after the year in which one spouse dies, the surviving spouse may file as a qualifying widow or widower as long as he or she (1) remains unmarried and (2) maintains a household for a dependent child (child, stepchild, or adopted child). However, the surviving spouse is not allowed to claim a dependency exemption for the deceased spouse beyond the year of the spouse's death. That is, a qualifying widow or widower (surviving spouse) may claim only one personal exemption.
- Unmarried taxpayers who do not qualify for head of household status file as single taxpayers.
- An unmarried taxpayer who is not a qualifying widow or widower may file as head of household if the person pays more than half the costs of maintaining a household that is, for *more* than half the taxable year, the principal place of abode for a qualifying person (if the qualifying person is a parent, the parent need not reside with the taxpayer). In general, for an individual to be a qualifying person, the taxpayer must be able to claim an exemption for that individual and the individual must be considered to be related to the taxpayer even if the individual does not live with the taxpayer for the entire year. That is, the taxpayer and the individual must be related through a qualifying family relationship. See Exhibit 4-9 for a flowchart for determining whether an individual is a qualifying person for determining head of household filing status.

KEY TERMS

abandoned spouse (4-24)	exclusions (4-5)	preferentially taxed income (4-6)
adjusted gross income (AGI) (4-2)	exemptions (4-8)	qualifying child (4-12)
all-inclusive income concept (4-2)	filing status (4-19)	qualifying relative (4-12)
alternative minimum tax (AMT) (4-10)	*for* AGI deductions (4-7)	qualifying widow or widower (4-20)
	from AGI deductions (4-7)	realized income (4-2)
character of income (4-5)	gross income (4-2)	single (4-21)
deductions (4-7)	head of household (4-21)	self-employment taxes (4-10)
deductions above the line (4-7)	itemized deductions (4-8)	standard deduction (4-8)
deductions below the line (4-8)	legislative grace (4-7)	taxable income (4-2)
deferrals (4-5)	married filing jointly (4-19)	tax credits (4-11)
dependency exemptions (4-9)	married filing separately (4-19)	tax rate schedule (4-10)
dependent (4-12)	personal exemptions (4-9)	tax tables (4-10)
estimated tax payments (4-11)	preferential tax rate (4-6)	withholdings (4-11)

DISCUSSION QUESTIONS

Discussion Questions are available in *Connect*®.   connect

1. How are realized income, gross income, and taxable income similar, and how are they different?   `LO 4-1`

2. Are taxpayers required to include all realized income in gross income? Explain.   `LO 4-1`

3. All else being equal, should taxpayers prefer to exclude income or to defer it? Why?   `LO 4-1`

4. Why should a taxpayer be interested in the character of income received?   `LO 4-1`

5. Is it easier to describe what a capital asset is or what it is not? Explain.   `LO 4-1`

6. Are all capital gains (gains on the sale or disposition of capital assets) taxed at the same rate? Explain.   `LO 4-1`

7. Are taxpayers allowed to deduct net capital losses (capital losses in excess of capital gains)? Explain.   `LO 4-1`

8. Compare and contrast *for* and *from* AGI deductions. Why are *for* AGI deductions likely more valuable to taxpayers than *from* AGI deductions?   `LO 4-1`

9. What is the difference between gross income and adjusted gross income, and what is the difference between adjusted gross income and taxable income?   `LO 4-1`

10. How do taxpayers determine whether they should deduct their itemized deductions or utilize the standard deduction?   `LO 4-1`

11. Why are some deductions called "above the line" deductions and others are called "below the line" deductions? What is the "line"?   `LO 4-1`

12. What is the difference between a tax deduction and a tax credit? Is one more beneficial than the other? Explain.   `LO 4-1`

13. What types of federal income-based taxes, other than the regular income tax, might taxpayers be required to pay? In general terms, what is the tax base for each of these other taxes on income?   `LO 4-1`

14. Identify three ways taxpayers can pay their income taxes to the government.   `LO 4-1`

15. If a person is considered to be a qualifying child or qualifying relative of a taxpayer, is the taxpayer automatically entitled to claim a dependency exemption for the person?   `LO 4-1`

16. Emily and Tony are recently married college students. Can Emily qualify as her parents' dependent? Explain.   `LO 4-2`

17. Compare and contrast the relationship test requirements for a qualifying child with the relationship requirements for a qualifying relative.   `LO 4-2`

18. In general terms, what are the differences in the rules for determining who is a qualifying child and who qualifies as a dependent as a qualifying relative? Is it possible for someone to be a qualifying child and a qualifying relative of the same taxpayer? Why or why not?   `LO 4-2`

19. How do two taxpayers determine who has priority to claim the dependency exemption for a qualifying child of both taxpayers when neither taxpayer is a parent of the child (assume the child does not qualify as a qualifying child of either parent)? How do parents determine who gets to deduct the dependency exemption for a qualifying child of both parents when the parents are divorced or file separate returns?   `LO 4-2`

20. Isabella provides 30 percent of the support for her father Hastings who lives in an apartment by himself and has no gross income. Is it possible for Isabella to claim a dependency exemption for her father? Explain.   `LO 4-2`

LO 4-3 21. What requirements do an abandoned spouse and qualifying widow or widower have in common?

LO 4-3 22. True or False. For purposes of determining head of household filing status, the taxpayer's mother or father is considered to be a qualifying person of the taxpayer (even if the mother or father does not qualify as the taxpayer's dependent) as long as the taxpayer pays more than half the costs of maintaining the household of the mother or father. Explain.

LO 4-3 23. Is a qualifying relative always a qualifying person for purposes of determining head of household filing status?

LO 4-3 24. For tax purposes, why is the married filing jointly tax status generally preferable to the married filing separately filing status? Why might a married taxpayer prefer *not* to file a joint return with the taxpayer's spouse?

LO 4-3 25. What does it mean to say that a married couple filing a joint tax return has joint and several liability for the taxes associated with the return?

PROBLEMS

Select problems are available in *Connect*®.   📰 **connect**

LO 4-1 26. Jeremy earned $100,000 in salary and $6,000 in interest income during the year. Jeremy has two qualifying dependent children who live with him. He qualifies to file as head of household and has $17,000 in itemized deductions. Neither of his dependents qualifies for the child tax credit.

a) Use the 2016 tax rate schedules to determine Jeremy's taxes due.

b) Assume that in addition to the original facts, Jeremy has a long-term capital gain of $4,000. What is Jeremy's tax liability including the tax on the capital gain?

c) Assume the original facts except that Jeremy had only $7,000 in itemized deductions. What is Jeremy's total income tax liability?

LO 4-1 27. David and Lilly Fernandez have determined their tax liability on their joint tax return to be $1,700. They have made prepayments of $1,500 and also have a child tax credit of $1,000. What is the amount of their tax refund or taxes due?

LO 4-1 28. Rick, who is single, has been offered a position as a city landscape consultant. The position pays $125,000 in cash wages. Assume Rick files single and is entitled to one personal exemption. Rick deducts the standard deduction instead of itemized deductions.

a) What is the amount of Rick's after-tax compensation (ignore payroll taxes)?

b) Suppose Rick receives a competing job offer of $120,000 in cash compensation and nontaxable (excluded) benefits worth $4,000. What is the amount of Rick's after-tax compensation for the competing offer? Which job should he take if taxes were the only concern?

LO 4-1 29. Through November, Tex has received gross income of $120,000. For December, Tex is considering whether to accept one more work engagement for the year. Engagement 1 will generate $7,000 of revenue at a cost of $4,000 which is deductible for AGI. In contrast, engagement 2 will generate $7,000 of revenue at a cost of $3,000, which is deductible as an itemized deduction. Tex files as a single taxpayer.

a) Calculate Tex's taxable income assuming he chooses engagement 1 and assuming he chooses engagement 2. Assume he has no itemized deductions other than those generated by engagement 2.

b) Calculate Tex's taxable income assuming he chooses engagement 1 and assuming he chooses engagement 2. Assume he has $4,500 of itemized deductions other than those generated by engagement 2.

c) Calculate Tex's taxable income assuming he chooses engagement 1 and assuming he chooses engagement 2. Assume he has $7,000 of itemized deductions other than those generated by engagement 2.

30. Matteo, who is single and has no dependents, was planning on spending the weekend repairing his car. On Friday, Matteo's employer called and offered him $500 in overtime pay if he would agree to work over the weekend. Matteo could get his car repaired over the weekend at Autofix for $400. If Matteo works over the weekend, he will have to pay the $400 to have his car repaired but he will earn $500. Assume Matteo pays tax at a flat 15 percent rate.

LO 4-1

planning

a) Strictly considering tax factors, should Matteo work or repair his car if the $400 he must pay to have his car fixed is not deductible?

b) Strictly considering tax factors, should Matteo work or repair his car if the $400 he must pay to have his car fixed is deductible for AGI?

31. Rank the following three single taxpayers in order of the magnitude of taxable income (from lowest to highest) and explain your results.

LO 4-1   LO 4-2

	Ahmed	Baker	Chin
Gross income	$80,000	$80,000	$80,000
Deductions *for* AGI	8,000	4,000	0
Itemized deductions	0	4,000	8,000

32. Aishwarya's husband passed away in 2015. She needs to determine whether Jasmine, her 17-year-old stepdaughter, who is single, qualifies as her dependent in 2016. Jasmine is a resident but not a citizen of the United States. She lived in Aishwarya's home from June 15 through December 31, 2016.

LO 4-2

a) Aishwarya provided more than half of Jasmine's support for 2016. Is Aishwarya allowed to claim a dependency exemption for Jasmine for 2016?

b) Would Aishwarya be allowed to claim a dependency exemption for Jasmine for 2016 if Aishwarya provided more than half of Jasmine's support in 2016, Jasmine lived in Aishwarya's home from July 15 through December 31 of 2016, and Jasmine reported gross income of $5,000 in 2016?

c) Would Aishwarya be allowed to claim a dependency exemption for Jasmine for 2016 if Aishwarya provided more than half of Jasmine's support in 2016, Jasmine lived in Aishwarya's home from July 15 through December 31 of 2016, and Jasmine reported gross income of $2,500 in 2016?

33. The Samsons are trying to determine whether they can claim their 22-year-old adopted son, Jason, as a dependent. Jason is currently a full-time student at an out-of-state university. Jason lived in his parents' home for three months of the year and he was away at school for the rest of the year. He received $9,500 in scholarships this year for his outstanding academic performance and earned $4,800 of income working a part-time job during the year. The Samsons paid a total of $5,000 to support Jason while he was away at college. Jason used the scholarship, the earnings from the part-time job, and the money from the Samsons as his only sources of support.

LO 4-2

a) Can the Samsons claim Jason as their dependent?

b) Assume the original facts except that Jason's grandparents, not the Samsons, provided him with the $5,000 worth of support. Can the Samsons (Jason's parents) claim Jason as their dependent? Why or why not?

c) Assume the original facts except substitute Jason's grandparents for his parents. Determine whether Jason's grandparents can claim Jason as a dependent.

d) Assume the original facts except that Jason earned $5,500 while working part-time and used this amount for his support. Can the Samsons claim Jason as their dependent? Why or why not?

LO 4-2

34. John and Tara Smith are married and have lived in the same home for over 20 years. John's uncle Tim, who is 64 years old, has lived with the Smiths since March of this year. Tim is searching for employment but has been unable to find any—his gross income for the year is $2,000. Tim used all $2,000 toward his own support. The Smiths provided the rest of Tim's support by providing him with lodging valued at $5,000 and food valued at $2,200.

a) Are the Smiths able to claim a dependency exemption for Tim?

b) Assume the original facts except that Tim earned $10,000 and used all the funds for his own support. Are the Smiths able to claim Tim as a dependent?

c) Assume the original facts except that Tim is a friend of the family and not John's uncle.

d) Assume the original facts except that Tim is a friend of the family and not John's uncle and Tim lived with the Smiths for the entire year.

LO 4-2

35. Francine's mother Donna and her father Darren separated and divorced in September of this year. Francine lived with both parents until the separation. Francine does *not* provide more than half of her own support. Francine is 15 years old at the end of the year.

a) Is Francine a qualifying child to Donna?

b) Is Francine a qualifying child to Darren?

c) Assume Francine spends more time living with Darren than Donna after the separation. Who may claim Francine as a dependency exemption for tax purposes?

d) Assume Francine spends an equal number of days with her mother and her father and that Donna has AGI of $52,000 and Darren has AGI of $50,000. Who may claim a dependency exemption for Francine?

LO 4-2

36. Jamel and Jennifer have been married 30 years and have filed a joint return every year of their marriage. Their three daughters, Jade, Lindsay, and Abbi, are ages 12, 17, and 22, respectively, and all live at home. None of the daughters provides more than half of her own support. Abbi is a full-time student at a local university and does not have any gross income.

a) How many personal and dependency exemptions are Jamel and Jennifer allowed to claim?

b) Assume the original facts except that Abbi is married. She and her husband live with Jamel and Jennifer while attending school and they file a joint return. Abbi and her husband reported a $1,000 tax liability on their tax return. If all parties are willing, can Jamel and Jennifer claim Abbi as a dependent on their tax return? Why or why not?

c) Assume the same facts as part (b), except that Abbi and her husband report a $0 tax liability on their joint tax return. Also, if the couple had filed separately, Abbi would have not had a tax liability on her return but her husband would have had a $250 tax liability on his separate return. Can Jamel and Jennifer claim Abbi as a dependent on their tax return? Why or why not?

d) Assume the original facts except that Abbi is married. Abbi files a separate tax return. Abbi's husband files a separate tax return and reports a $250 tax liability on the return. Can Jamel and Jennifer claim Abbi as a dependent?

LO 4-2   LO 4-3

37. Dean Kastner is 78 years old and lives by himself in an apartment in Chicago. Dean's gross income for the year is $2,500. Dean's support is provided as follows: Himself (5 percent), his daughters Camille (25 percent) and Rachel (30 percent), his son Zander (5 percent), his friend Frankie (15 percent), and his niece Sharon (20 percent).

a) Absent a multiple support agreement, of the parties mentioned in the problem, who may claim a dependency exemption for Dean as a qualifying relative?

b) Under a multiple support agreement, who is eligible to claim a dependency exemption for Dean as a qualifying relative? Explain.

c) Assume that Camille is allowed to claim Dean as a dependent under a multiple support agreement. Camille is single, and Dean is her only dependent. What is Camille's filing status?

38. Mel and Cindy Gibson's 12-year-old daughter Rachel was abducted on her way home from school on March 15, 2016. Police reports indicated that a stranger had physically dragged Rachel into a waiting car and sped away. Everyone hoped that the kidnapper and Rachel would be located quickly. However, as of the end of the year, Rachel was still missing. The police were still pursuing several promising leads and had every reason to believe that Rachel was still alive. In 2017, Rachel was returned safely to her parents.

    a) Are the Gibsons allowed to claim an exemption deduction for Rachel in 2016 even though she only lived in the Gibsons' home for two-and-one-half months? Explain and cite your authority.

    b) Assume the original facts except that Rachel is unrelated to the Gibsons but she has been living with them since January 2011. The Gibsons have claimed a dependency exemption for Rachel for the years 2011 through 2015. Are the Gibsons allowed to claim a dependency exemption for Rachel in 2016? Explain and cite your authority.

    LO 4-2

    research

39. Bob Ryan filed his tax return and claimed a dependency exemption for his 16-year-old son Dylan. Both Bob and Dylan are citizens and residents of the United States. Dylan meets all the necessary requirements to be considered a qualifying child; however, when Bob filed the tax return he didn't know Dylan's Social Security number and, therefore, didn't include an identifying number for his son on the tax return. Instead, Bob submitted an affidavit with his tax return stating he had requested Dylan's Social Security number from Dylan's birth state. Is Bob allowed to claim a dependency exemption for Dylan without including Dylan's identifying number on the return?

    LO 4-2

    research

40. Kimberly is divorced and the custodial parent of a 3-year-old girl named Bailey. Kimberly and Bailey live with Kimberly's parents, who pay all the costs of maintaining the household (such as mortgage, property taxes, and food). Kimberly pays for Bailey's clothing, entertainment, and health insurance costs. These costs comprised only a small part of the total costs of maintaining the household. Kimberly does not qualify as her parent's dependent.

    a) Determine the appropriate filing status for Kimberly.

    b) What if Kimberly lived in her own home and provided all the costs of maintaining the household?

    c) Assume Kimberly qualifies as her parents' dependent. How many personal and dependency exemptions may Kimberly claim on her tax return?

    LO 4-2 **LO 4-3**

41. Lee is 30 years old and single. Lee paid all the costs of maintaining his household for the entire year. Determine Lee's filing status in each of the following alternative situations:

    a) Lee is Ashton's uncle. Ashton is 15 years old and has gross income of $5,000. Ashton lived in Lee's home from April 1 through the end of the year.

    b) Lee is Ashton's uncle. Ashton is 20 years old, not a full-time student, and has gross income of $7,000. Ashton lived in Lee's home from April 1 through the end of the year.

    c) Lee is Ashton's uncle. Ashton is 22 years old and was a full-time student from January through April. Ashton's gross income was $5,000. Ashton lived in Lee's home from April 1 through the end of the year.

    LO 4-2 **LO 4-3**

d) Lee is Ashton's cousin. Ashton is 18 years old, has gross income of $3,000, and is not a full-time student. Ashton lived in Lee's home from April 1 through the end of the year.

e) Lee and Ashton are cousins. Ashton is 18 years old, has gross income of $3,000, and is not a full-time student. Ashton lived in Lee's home for the entire year.

LO 4-2 **LO 4-3** 42. Ray Albertson is 72 years old and lives by himself in an apartment in Salt Lake City. Ray's gross income for the year is $3,000. Ray's support is provided as follows: himself (11 percent), his daughters Diane (20 percent) and Karen (15 percent), his sons Mike (20 percent) and Kenneth (10 percent), his friend Milt (14 percent), and his cousin Henry (12 percent).

a) Absent a multiple support agreement, of the parties mentioned in the problem, who may claim a dependency exemption for Ray as a qualifying relative?

b) Under a multiple support agreement, who is eligible to claim a dependency exemption for Ray as a qualifying relative? Explain.

c) Assume that under a multiple support agreement, Diane claims a dependency exemption for Ray. Diane is single with no other dependents. What is her filing status?

LO 4-3 43. Juan and Bonita are married and have two dependent children living at home. This year, Juan is killed in an avalanche while skiing.

a) What is Bonita's filing status this year?

b) Assuming Bonita doesn't remarry and still has two dependent children living at home, what will her filing status be next year?

c) Assuming Bonita doesn't remarry and doesn't have any dependents next year, what will her filing status be next year?

LO 4-3 44. Gary and Lakesha were married on December 31 last year. They are now preparing their taxes for the April 15 deadline and are unsure of their filing status.

a) What filing status options do Gary and Lakesha have for last year?

b) Assume instead that Gary and Lakesha were married on January 1 of this year. What is their filing status for last year (neither has been married before and neither had any dependents last year)?

LO 4-3 45. Elroy, who is single, has taken over the care of his mother Irene in her old age. Elroy pays the bills relating to Irene's home. He also buys all her groceries and provides the rest of her support. Irene has no gross income.

a) What is Elroy's filing status?

b) Assume the original facts except that Elroy has taken over the care of his grandmother, Renae, instead of his mother. What is Elroy's filing status?

c) Assume the original facts except that Elroy's mother, Irene, lives with him and that she receives an annual $4,500 taxable distribution from her retirement account. Elroy still pays all the costs to maintain the household. What is his filing status?

LO 4-3 46. Kano and his wife, Hoshi, have been married for 10 years and have two children under the age of 12. The couple has been living apart for the last two years and both children live with Kano. Kano has provided all the means necessary to support himself and his children. Kano and Hoshi do not file a joint return.

a) What is Kano's filing status?

b) Assume the original facts except that Kano and Hoshi separated in May of the current year. What is Kano's filing status?

c) Assume the original facts except that Kano and Hoshi separated in November of this year. What is Kano's filing status?

d) Assume the original facts except that Kano's parents, not Kano, paid more than half of the cost of maintaining the home in which Kano and his children live. What is Kano's filing status?

47. Horatio and Kelly were divorced at the end of last year. Neither Horatio nor Kelly remarried during the current year and Horatio moved out of state. Determine the filing status of Horatio and Kelly for the current year in the following independent situations: [LO 4-3]

    a) Horatio and Kelly did not have any children and neither reported any dependents in the current year.

    b) Horatio and Kelly had one child, Amy, who turned 10 years of age in the current year. Amy lived with Kelly for all of the current year and Kelly provided all of her support.

    c) Assume the same facts as in part (b), but Kelly released the exemption for Amy to Horatio even though Amy did not reside with him at all during the current year.

    d) Assume the original facts except that during the current year Madison, a 17-year-old friend of the family, lived with Kelly (for the entire year) and was fully supported by Kelly.

    e) Assume the original facts except that during the current year Kelly's mother, Janet, lived with Kelly. For the current year, Kelly was able to claim a dependency exemption for her mother under a multiple support agreement.

48. In each of the following *independent* situations, determine the taxpayer's filing status and the number of personal and dependency exemptions the taxpayer is allowed to claim.   [LO 4-2] [LO 4-3]

    a) Frank is single and supports his 17-year-old brother, Bill. Bill earned $3,000 and did not live with Frank.

    b) Geneva and her spouse reside with their son, Steve, who is a 20-year-old undergraduate student at State University. Steve earned $13,100 at a part-time summer job, but he deposited this money in a savings account for graduate school. Geneva paid all of the $12,000 cost of supporting Steve.

    c) Hamish's spouse died last year and Hamish has not remarried. Hamish supports his father, Reggie, age 78, who lives in a nursing home and had interest income this year of $2,500.

    d) Irene is married but has not seen her spouse since February. She supports her spouse's 18-year-old child, Dolores, who lives with Irene. Dolores earned $4,500 this year.

    e) Assume the same facts as in part (d). Also, assume that Craig is Irene's husband. Craig supports his 12-year-old son Ethan, who lives with Craig. Ethan did not earn any income.

49. In each of the following *independent* cases, determine the taxpayer's filing status and the number of personal and dependency exemptions the taxpayer is allowed to claim.   [LO 4-2] [LO 4-3]

    a) Alexandra is a blind widow (her spouse died five years ago) who provides a home for her 18-year-old nephew, Newt. Newt's parents are dead and so Newt supports himself. Newt's gross income is $5,000.

    b) Bharati supports and maintains a home for her daughter, Daru, and son-in-law, Sam. Sam earned $15,000 and filed a joint return with Daru, who had no income.

    c) Charlie intended to file a joint return with his spouse, Sally. However, Sally died in December. Charlie has not remarried.

    d) Deshi cannot convince his spouse to consent to signing a joint return. The couple has not separated.

    e) Edith and her spouse support their 35-year-old son, Slim. Slim is a full-time college student who earned $5,500 over the summer in part-time work.

50. Jasper and Crewella Dahvill were married in year 0. They filed joint tax returns in years 1 and 2. In year 3, their relationship was strained and Jasper insisted on   [LO 4-3]

filing a separate tax return. In year 4, the couple divorced. Both Jasper and Crewella filed single tax returns in year 4. In year 5, the IRS audited the couple's joint year 2 tax return and each spouse's separate year 3 tax returns. The IRS determined that the year 2 joint return and Crewella's separate year 3 tax return understated Crewella's self-employment income causing the joint return year 2 tax liability to be understated by $4,000 and Crewella's year 3 separate return tax liability to be understated by $6,000. The IRS also assessed penalties and interest on both of these tax returns. Try as it might, the IRS has not been able to locate Crewella, but they have been able to find Jasper.

a) What amount of tax can the IRS require Jasper to pay for the Dahvill's year 2 joint return? Explain.

b) What amount of tax can the IRS require Jasper to pay for Crewella's year 3 separate tax return? Explain.

LO 4-3

 research

51. Janice Traylor is single. She has an 18-year-old son named Marty. Marty is Janice's only child. Marty has lived with Janice his entire life. However, Marty recently joined the Marines and was sent on a special assignment to Australia. During the current year, Marty spent nine months in Australia. Marty was extremely homesick while in Australia, since he had never lived away from home. However, Marty knew this assignment was only temporary, and he couldn't wait to come home and find his room just the way he left it. Janice has always filed as head of household, and Marty has always been considered a qualifying child (and he continues to meet all the tests with the possible exception of the residence test due to his stay in Australia). However, this year Janice is unsure whether she qualifies as head of household due to Marty's nine-month absence during the year. Janice has come to you for advice on whether she qualifies for head of household filing status. What do you tell her?

LO 4-3

research

52. Doug Jones submitted his 2016 tax return on time and elected married filing jointly status with his wife, Darlene. Doug and Darlene did not request an extension for their 2016 tax return. Doug and Darlene owed and paid the IRS $124,000 for their 2016 tax year. Two years later, Doug amended his return and claimed married filing separate status. By changing his filing status, Doug sought a refund for an overpayment for the tax year 2016 (he paid more tax in the original joint return than he owed on a separate return). Is Doug allowed to change his filing status for the 2016 tax year and receive a tax refund with his amended return?

COMPREHENSIVE PROBLEMS

Select problems are available in *Connect®*.

tax forms

53. Marc and Michelle are married and earned salaries this year of $64,000 and $12,000, respectively. In addition to their salaries, they received interest of $350 from municipal bonds and $500 from corporate bonds. Marc and Michelle also paid $2,500 of qualifying moving expenses, and Marc paid alimony to a prior spouse in the amount of $1,500. Marc and Michelle have a 10-year-old son, Matthew, who lived with them throughout the entire year. Thus, Marc and Michelle are allowed to claim a $1,000 child tax credit for Matthew. Marc and Michelle paid $6,000 of expenditures that qualify as itemized deductions and they had a total of $5,500 in federal income taxes withheld from their paychecks during the course of the year.

a) What is Marc and Michelle's gross income?

b) What is Marc and Michelle's adjusted gross income?

c) What is the total amount of Marc and Michelle's deductions *from* AGI?

d) What is Marc and Michelle's taxable income?

e) What is Marc and Michelle's taxes payable or refund due for the year? (Use the tax rate schedules.)

f) Complete the first two pages of Marc and Michelle's Form 1040 (use 2015 forms if 2016 forms are unavailable).

54. Demarco and Janine Jackson have been married for 20 years and have four children who qualify as their dependents (Damarcus, Janine, Michael, and Candice). The couple received salary income of $100,000, and they sold their home this year. They initially purchased the home three years ago for $200,000 and they sold it for $250,000. The gain on the sale qualified for the exclusion from the sale of a principal residence. The Jacksons incurred $16,500 of itemized deductions, and they had $6,250 withheld from their paychecks for federal taxes. They are also allowed to claim a child tax credit for each of their children.

tax forms

a) What is the Jacksons' taxable income, and what is their tax liability or (refund)?

b) Complete the first two pages of the Jacksons' 1040 (use 2015 forms if 2016 forms are unavailable).

c) What would their taxable income be if their itemized deductions totaled $6,000 instead of $16,500?

d) What would their taxable income be if they had $0 itemized deductions and $6,000 of *for* AGI deductions?

e) Assume the original facts except that they also incurred a loss of $5,000 on the sale of some of their investment assets. What effect does the $5,000 loss have on their *taxable income*?

f) Assume the original facts except that the Jacksons owned investments that appreciated by $10,000 during the year. The Jacksons believe the investments will continue to appreciate, so they did not sell the investments during this year. What is the Jacksons' taxable income?

55. Camille Sikorski was divorced last year. She currently provides a home for her 15-year-old daughter, Kaly, and 18-year-old son, Parker. Both children lived in Camille's home, which she owns, for the entire year, and Camille paid for all the costs of maintaining the home. She received a salary of $105,000 and contributed $6,000 of it to a qualified retirement account (a *for* AGI deduction). She also received $10,000 of alimony from her former husband. Finally, Camille paid $5,000 of expenditures that qualified as itemized deductions.

a) What is Camille's taxable income?

b) What would Camille's taxable income be if she incurred $14,000 of itemized deductions instead of $5,000?

c) Assume the original facts except that Camille's daughter, Kaly, is 25 years old and a full-time student. Kaly's gross income for the year was $5,000. Kaly provided $3,000 of her own support, and Camille provided $5,000 of support. What is Camille's taxable income?

56. Tiffany is unmarried and has a 15-year-old qualifying child. Tiffany has determined her tax liability to be $3,525, and her employer has withheld $1,500 of federal taxes from her paycheck. Tiffany is allowed to claim a $1,000 child credit for her qualifying child. What amount of taxes will Tiffany owe (or what amount will she receive as a refund) when she files her tax return?

Gross Income and Exclusions

Learning Objectives

Upon completing this chapter, you should be able to:

LO 5-1 Apply the concept of realization and explain when taxpayers recognize gross income.

LO 5-2 Understand the distinctions between the various sources of income, including income from services and property.

LO 5-3 Apply basic income exclusion provisions to compute gross income.

© Image Source

Storyline Summary

Taxpayers:	Courtney Wilson, age 40 Courtney's mother, Dorothy "Gram" Weiss, age 70
Family description:	Courtney is divorced with a son, Deron, age 10, and a daughter, Ellen, age 20. Gram is currently residing with Courtney.
Location:	Kansas City, Missouri
Employment status:	Courtney works as an architect for EWD. Her salary is $98,000. Gram is unemployed.
Current situation:	Determining what income is taxable

The past year was a year of change for Courtney Wilson. After her divorce from Al Wilson, Courtney assumed sole custody of their 10-year-old son, Deron, and their 20-year-old daughter, Ellen. Looking for a fresh start in January, Courtney quit her job as an architect in Cincinnati, Ohio, and moved to Kansas City, Missouri. Courtney wanted to pursue several promising job opportunities in Kansas City and be close to Ellen while she attends the University of Missouri–Kansas City. Courtney's 70-year-old mother "Gram" also lives in Kansas City and is in relatively good health. However, Courtney's father, "Gramps," passed away last December from cancer. At Courtney's insistence, Gram moved in with Courtney and Deron in April.

In late April, Courtney broke her wrist in a mountain biking accident and was unable to work for two weeks. Thankfully, Courtney's disability insurance paid her for lost wages during her time away from work.

While her personal life has been in disarray, Courtney's financial prospects have been improving. Shortly after arriving in Kansas City, Courtney was fortunate to land a job as an architect with Earth Wise Design (EWD). EWD provided Courtney the following compensation and benefits this year:

- Salary $98,000.
- Medical and life insurance premiums.
- Contribution of 10 percent of her base salary to her qualified retirement account.
- No-interest loan with a promise to forgive the loan principal over time if she continues her employment with EWD.
- Performance bonus for her first year on the job.

Courtney also received other payments unrelated to her employment with EWD as follows:

- Alimony from her ex-husband Al.
- Child support from her ex-husband Al.
- Consulting income.
- Dividend, interest, and rental income.
- Refund of state taxes she paid last year.

Before Gram moved in with Courtney, she lived alone in an apartment in Kansas City. After Gramps died, Gram was dependent on her Social Security benefits. In March, Gram's landlord agreed to allow Gram to babysit his infant son in lieu of paying rent. In early April, Gram received the proceeds from Gramps's life insurance policy. She invested part of the proceeds in an annuity contract that will pay Gram a fixed amount per year. Gram also invested some of the proceeds in the stock of a local corporation. She used the rest of the life insurance proceeds to purchase a certificate of deposit and start a savings account. Gram also spent some of her spare time completing sweepstakes entries. Her hard work paid off when she won a WaveRunner in a sweepstakes contest.

Until their divorce, Courtney's husband always prepared their income tax return. Since EWD hired her, Courtney has become anxious about her income tax and whether her withholding will be sufficient to cover her tax bill. Courtney is also worried about Gram's tax situation, because Gram did not make any tax payments this year. ∎

In the previous chapter, we presented an overview of individual taxation. In this chapter, we begin to dig deeper into the tax formula to determine a taxpayer's gross income. We focus on whether income is included or excluded from a taxpayer's gross income rather than the rate at which the income is taxed. In the next three chapters, we continue to work through the individual tax formula to determine the tax liabilities for Courtney and Gram. Chapter 6 describes deductible expenses to determine adjusted gross income and taxable income, Chapter 7 discusses the taxation of investments, and Chapter 8 addresses issues associated with calculating the tax liability, tax credits, and tax return filing concerns.

LO 5-1 REALIZATION AND RECOGNITION OF INCOME

As we learned in the previous chapter, **gross income** is income that taxpayers realize, recognize, and report on their tax returns for the year. In the previous chapter, we discussed gross income in general terms. In this chapter we explain the requirements for taxpayers to recognize gross income, and we discuss the most common sources of gross income.

What Is Included in Gross Income?

The definition of gross income for tax purposes is provided in §61(a) as follows:

> GENERAL DEFINITION.—Except as otherwise provided in this subtitle, gross income means all income *from whatever source derived* (emphasis added).

In addition to providing this **all-inclusive definition of income,** §61 includes a list of examples of gross income such as compensation for services, business income, rents, royalties, interest, and dividends. However, it is clear that unless a tax provision says otherwise, gross income includes *all* income. Thus, gross income is *broadly* defined. Reg. §1.61-(a) provides further insight into the definition of gross income as follows:

> Gross income means all income from whatever source derived, unless excluded by law. Gross income includes income realized in any form, whether in money, property, or services.

Based on §61(a), Reg. §1.61-(a), and various judicial rulings, taxpayers *recognize* gross income when (1) they receive an economic benefit, (2) they realize the income, *and* (3) no tax provision allows them to exclude or defer the income from gross income for that year.[1] Let's address each of these three requirements for recognizing gross income.

Economic Benefit   Taxpayers must receive an economic benefit (i.e., receive an item of value) to have gross income. Common examples where a taxpayer receives economic benefit include receiving compensation for services (the compensation could be in the form of cash, other property, or even services received), proceeds from property sales (typically cash, property, or debt relief), and income from investments or business activities (such as business income, rents, interest, and dividends). How about when a taxpayer borrows money? Is the economic benefit criterion met? No, because when a taxpayer borrows money, the economic benefit received (the cash received) is completely offset by the liability the taxpayer is required to pay from borrowing the funds (the debt amount).

Realization Principle   As indicated in Reg. §1.61-(a), the tax definition of income adopts the **realization principle.** Under this principle, income is realized when (1) a taxpayer engages in a transaction with another party, and (2) the transaction results in a measurable change in property rights. In other words, assets or services are exchanged for cash, claims to cash, or other assets with determinable value.

The concept of realization for tax purposes closely parallels the concept of realization for financial accounting purposes. Requiring a transaction to trigger realization reduces the uncertainty associated with determining the *amount* of income because a change in rights can typically be traced to a specific moment in time and is generally accompanied by legal documentation.

Example 5-1

In April, Gram used part of the life insurance proceeds she received from Gramps's death to purchase 50 shares in Acme Corporation for $30 per share. From April to the end of December, the value of the shares fluctuated between $40 and $25, but on December 31, the shares were worth $35. If Gram does *not* sell the shares, how much income from her stockholdings in Acme Corporation does she *realize for* the year?

Answer: $0. Unless Gram sells the stock, she does not enter into a transaction resulting in a measurable change of property rights with a second party. Thus, she does not realize income even though she experienced an economic benefit from the appreciation of the stock from $30 per share to $35 per share.

Adopting the realization principle for defining gross income provides two major advantages. First, because parties to the transaction must agree to the value of the exchanged property rights, the transaction allows the income to be measured objectively. Second, the transaction often provides the taxpayer with the **wherewithal to pay** taxes (at least when the taxpayer receives cash in the transaction). That is, the transaction itself provides the taxpayer with the funds to pay taxes on income generated by the transaction. Thus, it reduces the possibility that the taxpayer will be required to sell other assets to pay the taxes on the income from the transaction. Note, however, when taxpayers receive property or services in a transaction (instead of cash), realization has also occurred (despite the absence of wherewithal to pay).

[1]For tax purposes it matters not whether income is obtained through legal or illegal activities (e.g., embezzlement). See *Eugene James v. U.S.* (1961, S. Ct.), 7 AFTR 2d 1361.

Recognition Taxpayers who realize an economic benefit must include the benefit in gross income unless a specific provision of the tax code says otherwise. That is, taxpayers are generally required to *recognize* all realized income by reporting it as gross income on their tax returns. However, as we describe later in this chapter, through exclusions Congress allows taxpayers to permanently exclude certain types of income from gross income and through deferrals they allow taxpayers to defer certain types of income from gross income until a subsequent year. Thus, it is important to distinguish between realized and recognized income.

Other Income Concepts

The tax laws, administrative authority, and judicial rulings have established several other concepts important for determining an individual's gross income.

Form of Receipt A common misperception is that taxpayers must receive cash to realize and recognize gross income. However, Reg. §1.61-(a) indicates that taxpayers realize income whether they receive money, property, *or* services in a transaction. For example, **barter clubs** facilitate the exchange of rights to goods and services between members, many of whom have the mistaken belief that they need not recognize income on the exchanges. However, when members exchange property, they realize and recognize income at the market price, the amount that outsiders are willing to pay for the goods or services. Also, other taxpayers who exchange or trade goods or services with each other must recognize the value of the goods or services as income, even when they do not receive any cash. Indeed, taxpayers have the legal and ethical responsibility to report realized income no matter the form of its receipt or whether the IRS knows the taxpayer received the income.

Example 5-2

During March, Gram paid no rent to her neighbor (also her landlord). Although the neighbor typically charges $350 per month for rent, he allowed Gram to live rent free in exchange for babysitting his infant son. What income must Gram and Gram's neighbor realize and recognize on this exchange?

Answer: $350. Gram and the neighbor each must recognize $350 of income for March. The neighbor recognizes $350 of rental receipts because this is the value of the babysitting services the neighbor received in lieu of a cash payment for rent from Gram (an economic benefit the neighbor realized through the exchange). Gram recognizes $350 of babysitting income, because this is the value of the services provided to her neighbor (an economic benefit was realized because Gram was not required to pay rent).

Return of Capital Principle When taxpayers sell assets, they must determine the extent to which they include the sale proceeds in gross income. Initially, the IRS was convinced that Congress's all-inclusive definition of income required taxpayers to include *all* sale proceeds in gross income. Taxpayers, on the other hand, argued that a portion of proceeds from a sale represented a return of the cost or capital investment in the underlying property (called **tax basis**). The courts determined that when receiving a payment for property, taxpayers are allowed to recover the cost of the property tax free. Consequently, when taxpayers sell property, they are allowed to reduce the sale proceeds by their unrecovered investment in the property to determine the realized gain from the sale.[2] When the tax basis exceeds

---

[2]§1001(a).

the sale proceeds, the **return of capital** principle generally applies to the extent of the sale proceeds. The excess of basis over sale proceeds is generally not considered to be a return of capital, but rather a loss that is deductible only if specifically authorized by the tax code. Below, we revisit the return of capital principle when we discuss asset dispositions.

The return of capital principle gets complicated when taxpayers sell assets and collect the sale proceeds over several periods. In these cases, the principle is usually modified by law to provide that the return of capital occurs pro rata as the proceeds are collected over time. We discuss this issue in more detail later in this chapter when we discuss the taxation of annuities.

Recovery of Amounts Previously Deducted   A refund is not typically included in gross income because it usually represents a return of capital. For example, a refund of $1,000 on an auto purchased for $12,000 simply reduces the net cost of the vehicle to $11,000. Likewise, a $200 refund of a $700 business expense is not included in gross income but instead reduces the net expense to $500. However, if the refund is made for an expenditure deducted in a *previous* year, then under the **tax benefit rule** the refund is included in gross income to the extent that the prior deduction produced a tax benefit.[3] For example, suppose an individual paid a $1,000 business expense claimed as a *for* AGI deduction in 2016, but $250 of the expense was subsequently reimbursed in 2017. Because the $250 business deduction produced a tax benefit in 2016 (reduced taxable income), the $250 refund in 2017 would be included in income.

The application of the tax benefit rule is more complex for individuals who itemize deductions. An itemized deduction only produces a tax benefit to the extent that total itemized deductions exceed the standard deduction. For example, suppose that an individual's total itemized deductions exceeded the standard deduction by $100. A refund of $150 of itemized deductions would cause the individual's itemized deductions to fall $50 beneath the standard deduction. If the refund occurred in the same year as the expense, the individual would have elected the standard deduction, and the refund would have only caused taxable income to increase by $100 (the difference between claiming the standard deduction and the total itemized deductions that would have been claimed in the absence of any refund). If the refund occurs the year after the deduction is claimed, then only $100 of the $150 refund would be included in gross income under the tax benefit rule. The $100 is added to taxable income in the year of the refund because this is the increment in taxable income that would have resulted if the refund was issued in the year the itemized deduction was claimed.

Example 5-3

In 2015 Courtney paid $3,500 in Ohio state income taxes, and she included this payment with her other itemized deductions when she filed her federal income tax return in March of 2016. Courtney filed her 2015 federal return as a head of household and claimed $15,500 of itemized deductions. She also filed an Ohio state income tax return in March of 2016 and discovered she only owed $3,080 in Ohio income tax for 2015. Hence, Courtney received a $420 refund of her Ohio income tax in June of 2016. How much of the $420 refund, if any, is Courtney required to include in her gross income in 2016? The answer depends upon the standard deduction for 2015. Help Courtney apply the tax benefit rule (the standard deduction for head of household filling status in 2015 was $9,250).

Answer: All $420. Courtney is required to include the entire refund in her 2016 gross income because her itemized deduction for the $420 of state income taxes that she overpaid last year reduced her taxable income by $420. Accordingly, because she received a tax benefit (deduction) for the entire

(continued on page 5-6)

---

[3]§111.

$420 overpayment, she must include it all in gross income in 2016. See the following for the calculation of the amount of tax benefit Courtney received from the $420 overpayment of taxes in 2015.

Deduction	Amount	Explanation
(1) Itemized deduction	$15,500	
(2) 2015 standard deduction	9,250	Head of household filing status.
(3) Reduction in taxable income	15,500	Greater of (1) and (2).
(4) Itemized deductions adjusted for the $420 refund	15,080	(1) − $420.
(5) Reduction in taxable income after adjustment for the $420 refund	15,080	Greater of (2) and (4).
Tax benefit due to prior deduction or $420 refund	$ 420	(3) − (5).

What if: Let's consider *alternative* fact patterns provided in Scenarios A and B to further illustrate the application of the tax benefit rule.

Scenario A: In 2015 Courtney's itemized deductions, including $3,500 in state taxes, were $5,500.

Scenario B: In 2015 Courtney's itemized deductions, including $3,500 in state taxes, were $9,450. How much of the $420 refund would Courtney include in her 2016 gross income in Scenarios A and B?

Answer Scenario A: $0. As computed below, Courtney received $0 tax benefit from the $420 tax overpayment in 2015, so she need not include any of the refund in her gross income.

Answer Scenario B: $200. As computed below, Courtney received a $200 tax benefit (reduction in taxable income) from the $420 state tax overpayment in 2015, so she must include $200 of the refund in her 2016 gross income.

Deduction	Scenario A Amount	Scenario B Amount	Explanation
(1) Itemized deductions	$5,500	$9,450	
(2) 2015 standard deduction	9,250	9,250	Head of household filing status.
(3) Reduction in taxable income	9,250	9,450	Greater of (1) and (2).
(4) Itemized deductions adjusted for the $420 refund	5,080	9,030	(1) − $420.
(5) Reduction in taxable income adjusted for the $420 refund	9,250	9,250	Greater of (2) and (4).
Tax benefit due to prior deduction of $420 refund	$ 0	$ 200	(3) − (5).

When Do Taxpayers Recognize Income?

Individual taxpayers generally file tax returns reporting their taxable income for a calendar-year period, whereas corporations often use a fiscal year-end. In either case, the taxpayer's method of accounting generally determines the year in which realized income is recognized and included in gross income.

Accounting Methods Most large corporations use the accrual method of accounting. Under the **accrual method,** income is generally recognized when earned, and expenses are generally deducted in the period when liabilities are incurred. In contrast, most individuals use the **cash method** as their overall method of accounting.[4] Under the cash method, taxpayers recognize income in the period they receive it (in the form of cash, property, or services), rather than when they actually earn it. Likewise,

---

[4]Taxpayers involved in a business may use the accrual or hybrid overall method of accounting. We discuss these methods in Chapter 9.

cash-method taxpayers claim deductions when they make expenditures, rather than when they incur liabilities. The cash method greatly simplifies the computation of income for the overwhelming majority of individuals, many of whom have neither the time nor the training to apply the accrual method. Another advantage of the cash method is that taxpayers may have some control over when income is received and expenses are paid. Because of this control, taxpayers can more easily use the timing tax planning strategy (described in Chapter 3) to lower the present value of their tax bill.

Constructive Receipt Taxpayers using the cash method of accounting may try to shift income from the current year to the next year when they receive payments near year-end. For instance, taxpayers may merely delay cashing a check or avoid picking up a compensation payment until after year-end. The courts responded to this ploy by devising the **constructive receipt doctrine.**[5] The constructive receipt doctrine states that a taxpayer realizes and recognizes income when it is actually or *constructively* received. Constructive receipt is deemed to occur when the income has been credited to the taxpayer's account or when the income is unconditionally available to the taxpayer, the taxpayer is aware of the income's availability, and there are no restrictions on the taxpayer's control over the income.

<table><tr><td>

THE KEY FACTS

Income Recognition

- Cash-method taxpayers recognize income when it is received.
- Income is realized regardless of whether payments are received in money, property, *or* services.
- Income is taxed in the period in which a cash-method taxpayer has a right to receive payment without substantial restrictions.
</td></tr></table>

Example 5-4

Courtney is a cash-method taxpayer. Based on her outstanding performance, Courtney earned a $4,800 year-end bonus. On December 28, Courtney's supervisor told her that her bonus was issued as a separate check and that Courtney could pick up the check in the accounting office anytime. Courtney did not pick up the check until January 2 of the next year, and she did not cash it until late January. When does Courtney realize and recognize the $4,800 income?

Answer: On December 28 of the tax year in question. Courtney *constructively* received the check that year because it was unconditionally available to her on December 28, she was aware of the check's availability, and there were no restrictions on her control over the check. Courtney must include the $4,800 bonus in gross income for that year, even though she did not actually receive the funds until late January of the next year.[6]

Claim of Right The **claim of right doctrine** is another judicial doctrine created to address the timing of income recognition. This doctrine was conceived when a taxpayer received income in one period but was required to return the payment in a subsequent period. The claim of right doctrine states that income has been realized if a taxpayer receives income and there are no restrictions on the taxpayer's use of the income (e.g., the taxpayer does not have an obligation to repay the amount). A common example of the claim of right doctrine is a cash bonus paid to employees based on company earnings. Despite *potentially* having to repay the bonuses (e.g., if there is a "clawback" provision that requires repayment if the company has an earnings restatement), the employees would include the bonuses in gross income in the year received because there are no restrictions on their use of the income.[7]

[5]Justice Holmes summarized this doctrine as follows: "The income that is subject to a man's unfettered command and that he is free to enjoy at his own option may be taxed to him as his income, whether he sees fit to enjoy it or not." *Corliss v. Bowers,* 281 US 378 (1930).

[6]Note also that Courtney's employer would include her bonus on Courtney's W-2 for the year in which it issued the check.

[7]§1341 provides relief for a taxpayer who recognizes taxable income because of the claim of right doctrine and in a later year determines that she does not have a claim of right. Specifically, §1341 provides that if a taxpayer recognizes taxable income because she has a "claim of right" (unrestricted right) to the income received, a deduction is allowable in a later year because she did not have an unrestricted right to the income, and the related tax deduction exceeds $3,000, then the tax imposed in the later year is the lesser of (1) the tax for the taxable year computed with the deduction or (2) the tax for the taxable year computed without the deduction, less a tax credit for the previous tax paid on the item of income.

Who Recognizes the Income?

In addition to determining when taxpayers realize and recognize income, it is important to consider *who* (which taxpayer) recognizes the income. This question often arises when taxpayers attempt to shift income to other related taxpayers through the income-shifting strategy. For example, a father (with a high marginal income tax rate) might wish to assign his paycheck to his baby daughter (with a low marginal income tax rate) to minimize their collective tax burden.

Assignment of Income   The courts developed the **assignment of income doctrine** to prevent taxpayers from arbitrarily transferring the taxation on their income to others. In essence, the assignment of income doctrine holds that the taxpayer who earns income from services must recognize the income. Likewise, income from property, such as dividends and interest, is taxable to the person who actually owns the income-producing property.[8] For example, interest income from a bond is taxable to the person who owns the bond during the time the interest income accrues. Thus, to shift income from property to another person, a taxpayer must also transfer the *ownership* in the property to the other person.

Example 5-5

What if: Courtney would like to begin saving for Deron's college tuition. If Courtney were to direct EWD to deposit part of her salary in Deron's bank account, who would pay tax on the salary income?

Answer: Courtney would be taxed on her entire salary as income because she earned the income.[9] The payment to Deron would be treated as a gift and would not be taxable to him (gifts are excluded from the recipient's income as discussed later in the chapter).

What if: Suppose that Courtney wanted to shift her rental income to Deron. What would Courtney need to do to ensure that her rental income is taxed to Deron?

Answer: Courtney would have to transfer her ownership in the rental property to Deron in order for Deron to be taxed on the rental income.[10]

Community Property Systems   While most states use a common law system, nine states (Arizona, California, Idaho, Louisiana, Nevada, New Mexico, Texas, Washington, and Wisconsin) implement **community property systems.** Under community property systems, the income earned from services by one spouse is treated as though it was earned equally by both spouses. Also, property acquired by either spouse during the marriage is usually community property and is treated as though it is owned equally by each spouse.[11] Property that a spouse brings into a marriage is treated as that spouse's separate property. For federal income tax purposes, the community property system has the following consequences:

- Half of the income earned from the *services* of one spouse is included in the gross income of the other spouse.
- Half of the income from property held as *community* property by the married couple is included in the gross income of each spouse.

---

[8]This rule of thumb is also referred to as the "fruit and the tree" doctrine because of the analogy to fruit belonging to the tree upon which it was grown. See *Lucas v. Earl* (1930) 281 US 111 and *Helvering v. Horst* (1940) 311 US 112.

[9]Note also that EWD has the responsibility of issuing a W-2 to the taxpayer who provided the services—Courtney in this case.

[10]As explained in Chapter 8, the tax savings from such a transfer would be mitigated in the calculation of Deron's tax by the so-called "kiddie" tax. Likewise, Courtney should consider the gift tax implications of this transfer before transferring the property to Deron.

[11]Property acquired during the marriage via gift or inheritance or purchased with a spouse's separate property is considered separate property.

- In five community property states (Arizona, California, Nevada, New Mexico, and Washington), all of the income from property owned *separately* by one spouse is included in that spouse's gross income.
- In Texas, Louisiana, Wisconsin, and Idaho, half of the income from property owned *separately* by one spouse is included in the gross income of each spouse.

In contrast, for federal income tax purposes, the common law system has the following consequences:

- All of the income earned from the *services* of one spouse is included in the gross income of the spouse who earned it.
- For property owned *separately,* all of the income from the separately owned property is included in that spouse's gross income.
- For property owned *jointly* (i.e., not separately), each co-owner is taxed on the income attributable to his or her share of the property. For example, suppose that a parcel of property is jointly owned by husband and wife. One-half would be included in the gross income of each spouse. Similarly, income from property owned by three or more persons would be included in the gross income of each co-owner based on his or her respective ownership share.

Example 5-6

In the year of their divorce, Courtney and Al Wilson lived in Ohio, a common law state. The divorce was finalized on October 1 of that year, and up to that date Al had earned $90,000 of annual salary and Courtney had earned $60,000. How much of the income earned by Al and by Courtney in the year of the divorce did Al report on his individual tax return? How much income did Courtney report on her individual tax return?

Answer: Because they resided in a common law state, Al reports the $90,000 that he earned through September (and all the income he earned through the end of the year) on his own return, and Courtney reports the entire $60,000 she earned through September (and all the income she earned through the rest of the year) on her own tax return.

What if: How much of this income would Al have been required to include on his individual tax return, and how much of this income would Courtney have been required to report on her individual tax return if they lived in California, a community property state?

Answer: If they resided in a community property state, both Al and Courtney would have included $75,000 of the $150,000 the couple had jointly earned through September [(Al's $90,000 + Courtney's $60,000)/2] on their respective individual tax returns. Whether they resided in a community property state or not, Al and Courtney also would have included on their respective individual tax returns the income they individually earned and received from October through December.

  If a couple files a joint tax return, the community property rules do not affect the aggregate taxes payable by the couple, because the income of both spouses is aggregated on the return. However, when couples file separate tax returns, their combined tax liability may depend on whether they live in a common law state, a community property state that shares income from separate property equally between spouses, or a community property state that does not split income from separate property between spouses.[12]

TYPES OF INCOME

LO 5-2

Now that we have a basic understanding of the general definition of gross income and related concepts, let's turn our attention to specific *types* of income subject to taxation. Our discussion is organized around income from services, income from property, and other sources of income.

---

[12]§66 provides rules that allow spouses living apart in community property states to be taxed on his or her own income from services if (1) the taxpayers live apart for the entire year, (2) they do not file a joint tax return with each other, and (3) they do not transfer any of the income from services between each other.

Income from Services

Income from labor is one of the most common sources of gross income, and it is rarely exempt from taxation. Payments for services including salary, wages, and fees that a taxpayer earns through services in a nonemployee capacity are all considered income from services and so is unemployment compensation. Income from services is often referred to as **earned income** because it is generated by the efforts of the taxpayer (this also includes business income earned by a taxpayer even if the taxpayer's business is selling inventory).

Example 5-7

EWD pays Courtney a salary of $98,000. In addition, Courtney earned and received $19,500 of fees from consulting work she did on weekends independent of her employment with EWD. She incurred $1,500 of miscellaneous expenses for supplies and transportation while doing the consulting work. What is Courtney's *income* from services (earned income) from her employment and her self-employment activities?

Answer: $116,000, consisting of her $98,000 of salary and $19,500 of her business income from her consulting activities, less the $1,500 of expenses related to her consulting activities. Note that business deductions are *for* AGI deductions that taxpayers subtract from their gross business income to derive net business income or loss reported on page 1 of Form 1040. We discuss *for* AGI deductions in greater detail in Chapter 6.

Income from Property

Income from property, often referred to as **unearned income,** may take different forms, such as gain or losses from the sale of property, dividends, interest, rents, royalties, and annuities.[13] The tax treatment of unearned income depends upon the type of income and, in some circumstances, the type of the transaction generating the income. For example, as discussed in Chapter 4, qualified dividends and long-term capital gains are taxed at preferential tax rates, whereas other unearned income is generally taxed at ordinary tax rates. Likewise, while gains or losses are typically recognized in the current period, certain types of gains and losses are postponed indefinitely. We discuss annuity income and property dispositions briefly in the following paragraphs. We discuss income from property in more detail in subsequent chapters.

Example 5-8

Courtney owns 1,000 shares of GE stock that she registered in a dividend reinvestment plan. Under this plan, all dividends are automatically used to purchase more shares of the stock. This year, GE declared and paid $700 in dividends on Courtney's stock. Must Courtney include the dividend in her gross income for the year?

Answer: Yes. Courtney includes the $700 of dividends (unearned income) in her gross income. The fact that Courtney chose to reinvest the dividends does not affect their taxability because she received an economic benefit and change in property rights associated with the dividend.

Example 5-9

Gram purchased a $100,000, three-year certificate of deposit (CD) with a portion of the life insurance proceeds she received on Gramps's death. At year-end, her CD account is credited with $4,100 of interest, and her savings account is credited with $300 of interest. Courtney had a total of $567 of interest credited to her savings account and $50 credited to her checking account during the year. How much interest must Gram and Courtney include in their gross income for the year?

---

[13]The tax definition of unearned income is different from the financial accounting definition. Unearned income for financial accounting purposes is a liability that represents advance payments for goods or services.

Answer: Gram must include the $4,100 of interest credited to her CD account and the $300 of interest credited to her savings account this year regardless of whether she withdraws the interest or not. Courtney must include the $567 of interest credited to her savings account and the $50 credited to her checking account regardless of whether she withdraws the interest or not.

Example 5-10

Courtney owns a condo in town that she rents to tenants. This year, the condo generated $14,000 of rental revenue. Courtney incurred $4,000 in real estate taxes, $2,500 in utility expenses, $500 in advertising expenses, and $2,000 of depreciation and other expenses associated with the rental. What effect does the rental have on Courtney's *gross income*? What effect does the rental have on Courtney's *taxable income*?

Answer: The rent increases Courtney's *gross income* by $14,000. However, after considering her allowable deductions for the rental, Courtney will only report $5,000 of *taxable income* from rental activities computed as follows:

Description		Amount
Rental revenue		$14,000
Less allowable deductions:		
Real estate taxes	(4,000)	
Utilities	(2,500)	
Advertising	(500)	
Depreciation and other expenses	(2,000)	
Total rental expenses		(9,000)
Net rental income		$ 5,000

Annuities An **annuity** is an investment that pays a stream of equal payments over time. Individuals often purchase annuities as a means of generating a fixed income stream during retirement. There are two basic types of annuities: (1) annuities paid over a fixed period and (2) annuities paid over a person's life (for as long as the person lives). The challenge from a tax perspective is to determine how much of each annuity payment represents gross income (income taxed at ordinary tax rates) and how much represents a nontaxable *return of capital* (return of the original investment). For both types of annuities, the tax law deems a *portion* of each annuity payment as a nontaxable return of capital and the remainder as gross income. Taxpayers use the annuity *exclusion* ratio to determine the portion of each payment that is a nontaxable return of capital.

$$\text{Annuity exclusion ratio} = \frac{Original\ investment}{Expected\ value\ of\ annuity} = \text{Return of capital } percentage$$

For fixed annuities, the expected value is the number of payments times the amount of the payment. In other words, for an annuity payable over a fixed term the return of capital is simply the original investment divided by the number of payments. The number of payments, however, is uncertain for annuities paid over a person's life. For these annuities, taxpayers must use IRS tables to determine the expected value based upon the taxpayer's life expectancy at the start of the annuity.[14] To calculate the

[14]See Reg. §1.72-9. Special rules under §72(d) apply to annuities from qualified retirement plans. These rules only apply when a taxpayer makes an after-tax contribution to a qualified employer retirement plan (which is uncommon). In most cases, taxpayers only make pretax contributions to qualified retirement plans, which results in fully taxable annuity distributions.

expected value of the annuity, the number of annual payments from the table (referred to as the expected return multiple) is multiplied by the annual payment amount. Taxpayers with an annuity paid over the life of one person (a single-life annuity) use the expected return multiple from the table, a portion of which is presented in Exhibit 5-1.

EXHIBIT 5-1 Table for Expected Return Multiple for Ordinary Single-Life Annuity

Age at Annuity Starting Date	Expected Return Multiple
68	17.6
69	16.8
70	16.0
71	15.3
72	14.6

Some annuities provide payments over the lives of two people. For example, a taxpayer may purchase an annuity that provides an annual payment each year until both the taxpayer *and* the taxpayer's spouse pass away. This type of annuity is called a joint-life annuity. The IRS provides a separate table for determining the expected number of payments from joint-life annuities.

A taxpayer receiving a life annuity who lives longer than his or her estimated life expectancy will ultimately receive more than the expected number of payments. The entire amount of these "extra" payments is included in the taxpayer's gross income because the taxpayer has completely recovered her investment in the annuity by the time she receives them. If the taxpayer dies *before* receiving the expected number of payments, the amount of the unrecovered investment (the initial investment less the amounts received that is treated as a nontaxable return of capital) is deducted on the taxpayer's final income tax return.[15]

Example 5-11

In January of this year, Gram purchased an annuity from UBET Insurance Co. that will pay her $10,000 per year for the next 15 years. Gram received the first $10,000 payment in December. Gram paid $99,000 for the annuity and will receive $150,000 over the life of the annuity (15 years × $10,000 per year). How much of the $10,000 payment Gram receives in December should she include in her gross income?

Answer: $3,400. Because Gram purchased a fixed-payment annuity, the portion of the annuity payment included in gross income is calculated as follows:

Description	Amount	Explanation
(1) Investment in annuity contract	$99,000	
(2) Number of payments	15	
(3) Return of capital per payment	$ 6,600	(1)/(2).
(4) Amount of each payment:	$10,000	
Gross income per payment	**$ 3,400**	(4) − (3).

What if: Assume the annuity Gram purchased pays her $1,000 per month over the remainder of her life. Gram (70 years old) paid $99,000 for the annuity, and she received her first $1,000 payment in December of this year. How much income would she recognize on the $1,000 payment?

[15]The unrecovered cost of the annuity is deducted as a miscellaneous itemized deduction not subject to the 2 percent of AGI floor. See §72(b)(3) and §67(b)(10).

Answer: $484.40, computed as follows:

Description	Amount	Explanation
(1) Investment in annuity contract	$ 99,000	
(2) Expected return multiple	16	Exhibit 5-1, 70 years old.
(3) Amount of each payment	$ 1,000	
(4) Expected return	$192,000	(2) × (3) × 12 months.
(5) Return of capital percentage	51.56%	(1)/(4).
(6) Return of capital per payment	$ 515.60	(3) × (5).
Taxable income per payment	$ 484.40	(3) − (6).

After Gram receives her entire $99,000 as a return of capital, each subsequent $1,000 annuity payment would be fully taxable.

Property Dispositions   Taxpayers can realize a gain or loss when disposing of an asset. Consistent with the return of capital principle we discussed above, taxpayers are allowed to recover their investment in property (tax basis) before they realize any gain. A loss is realized when the proceeds are less than the tax basis in the property. Because the return of capital principle generally applies only to the extent of the sale proceeds, a loss does not necessarily reduce the taxpayer's taxable income. A loss will only reduce the taxpayer's taxable income if the loss is deductible. Exhibit 5-2 presents a general formula for computing the gain or loss from a sale of an asset.

> **THE KEY FACTS**
> **Return of Capital**
> - Taxpayers are allowed to recover the capital invested in property tax free.
> - Payments from purchased annuities are part income and part return of capital.
> - When property is sold or disposed, the realized gain or loss equals the sale proceeds reduced by the tax basis of the property.

EXHIBIT 5-2   **Formula for Calculating Gain (Loss) from Sale of an Asset**

Sales proceeds
Less: Selling expenses
= Amount realized
Less: Basis (investment) in property sold
= Gain (Loss) on sale

The rate at which taxpayers are taxed on *gains* from property dispositions and the extent to which they can deduct *losses* from property dispositions depends on whether the taxpayer used the asset for business purposes, investment purposes, or personal purposes. For example, as we discussed in Chapter 4, long-term capital gains realized by individuals are taxed at preferential tax rates, and deductions for net capital losses realized by individuals are limited to $3,000 per year. In contrast, losses realized on assets used for personal purposes are generally not deductible. We discuss specific rules associated with property dispositions in Chapters 7 and 11.

Example 5-12

On December 31, Gram sold her 50 shares of Acme Corporation stock for $40 per share. Gram also paid $150 in broker's commissions on the sale. Gram originally purchased the shares in April of this year for $30 per share. How much gross income does Gram recognize from the stock sale?

Answer: Gram recognizes $350 gross income on the sale, computed as follows:

Sales proceeds ($40 × 50 shares)	$2,000
Less: Selling expenses	−150
= Amount realized	$1,850
Less: Tax basis (investment) in property sold ($30 × 50 shares)	−1,500
Gain (Loss) on sale	$ 350

Other Sources of Gross Income

Taxpayers may receive income from sources other than their efforts (earned income from wages or business) and their property (unearned income such as dividends and interest). In this section we briefly summarize other common types of gross income. If by chance you encounter other types of income that are not specifically discussed here, remember that the tax law is based upon the all-inclusive income concept. That is, unless a specific provision grants exclusion or deferral, economic benefits that are realized generate gross income. This basic understanding of the structure of our tax law (and research skills to investigate the taxability of specific income types) will serve you well as you evaluate whether realized income should be included in gross income.

Income from Flow-through Entities   Individuals may invest in various business entities. The legal form of the business affects how the income generated by the business is taxed. For example, income earned by a corporation (other than an S corporation) is taxed at the entity level as opposed to the owner level. In contrast, the income and deductions from a **flow-through entity,** such as a partnership or S corporation (a corporation electing S corporation status), "flow through" to the owners of the entity (partners or shareholders). That is, the owners report income or deductions as though they operated a portion of the business personally. Specifically, each partner or S corporation shareholder reports his or her share of the entity's income and deductions, generally in proportion to his or her ownership percentage, on his or her individual tax return.[16]

Because different types of income and deductions may be treated differently for tax purposes (e.g., qualified dividends are eligible for a special low tax rate), each item the partners or shareholders report on their tax returns retains its underlying tax characteristics. That is, the partners are treated as if they personally received their share of each item of the flow-through entity's income. For example, corporate dividend income paid to a partnership is reported and taxed as dividend income on the partners' individual tax returns. Also, it is important to note that owners of flow-through entities are taxed on their share of the entity's income whether or not cash is distributed to them. When owners receive cash distributions from the entity, the distributions are generally treated as a return of capital to the extent of their investment (tax basis) in the entity and, therefore, not included in the owner's gross income. Distributions in excess of basis are taxable. Partnerships and S corporations report to each partner or shareholder, that partner's or shareholder's share of partnership and S corporation income (or loss) on Schedule K-1 filed with the partnership and S corporation's annual information returns (Form 1065 and 1120S, respectively).[17]

Example 5-13

What if: Suppose that Courtney is a 40 percent partner in KJZ partnership. KJZ reported $20,000 of business income and $3,000 of interest income for the year. KJZ also distributed $1,000 of cash to Courtney. What amount of gross income from her ownership in KJZ partnership would Courtney report for the current year?

Answer: $9,200, consisting of $8,000 of business income ($20,000 × 40%) and $1,200 of interest income ($3,000 × 40%). Courtney would not include the $1,000 distribution in her gross income because it was a return of her investment.

Alimony   When couples legally separate or divorce, one spouse may be required to provide financial support to the other in the form of **alimony.** The tax law defines alimony as (1) a transfer of *cash* made under a written separation agreement or divorce decree, (2) the separation or divorce decree does not designate the payment as something

---

[16]The deduction of losses from partnerships and S corporations are subject to several limitations that we discuss in Chapter 7.

[17]See Forms 1065 and 1120S on the IRS website, www.IRS.gov.

other than alimony, (3) in the case of legally separated (or divorced) taxpayers under a separation or divorce decree, the spouses do not live together when the payment is made, and (4) the payments cannot continue after the death of the recipient.[18]

For tax purposes, a transfer between former spouses represents alimony only if it meets this definition. If the payment is alimony, then the amount of the payment is included in the gross income of the person receiving it and is deductible *for* AGI by the person paying it. Thus, alimony shifts income from one spouse to the other.

Example 5-14

In addition to paying child support, under the divorce decree Al is required to pay Courtney $20,000 cash each year until she dies. The decree does not designate the payment as a payment for something other than alimony, and Al and Courtney do not live together. Does this payment qualify as alimony?

Answer: Yes. These payments qualify as alimony for tax purposes because they are (1) cash payments made under a divorce decree, (2) the payments are not designated as something other than alimony, (3) Al and Courtney do not live together, and (4) the payments cease on Courtney's death. In the current year, Al made a $20,000 alimony payment to Courtney. Courtney includes all $20,000 in her gross income. To ensure that the income is taxed only once, Al is allowed to deduct the entire payment as a deduction *for* AGI.

There may be other types of payments that *do not qualify as alimony*. These include (1) property divisions (e.g., who gets the car, house, or china?) and (2) child support payments fixed by the divorce or separation agreement.[19] In any event, if a transfer of property between spouses does *not* meet the definition of alimony, the *recipient* of the transfer *excludes* the value of the transfer from income, and the person transferring the property is not allowed to deduct the value of the property transferred.

Example 5-15

As required by the divorce decree, Al made $10,000 in child support payments during the year to Courtney to help her support Deron. Al is required to make child support payments until Deron is 18 years old. Is the current-year payment considered alimony?

Answer: No. The $10,000 of child support payments are not income to Courtney. The payments are not alimony because the divorce decree specifies that the payments are for child support. Consequently, Courtney does not include these payments in gross income, and Al does not deduct them.

The objective definition of alimony eliminates uncertainty regarding which transfers are treated as alimony. However, it creates a second problem. Since the purpose of the transfer is irrelevant to the tax consequences, it is possible to use alimony transfers to assign income from the (higher tax rate) payer of the alimony to the (lower tax rate) recipient. For example, instead of transferring ownership of an asset to the recipient as a nondeductible/nontaxable property settlement, the payer could claim an alimony deduction by making a transfer that meets the alimony requirements. The spouses can share the tax savings from this transaction if they can agree on structuring the payments to qualify as alimony (although cooperation may be a little difficult for a couple going through a divorce). To address this tax-avoidance opportunity, Congress enacted a complex set of restrictions called the *anti-front loading* rules that make it difficult for taxpayers to disguise property payments as alimony payments. In general terms, when taxpayers attempt to disguise property payments as alimony payments (large alimony payments shortly after the divorce, followed by smaller alimony payments in subsequent

---

[18]§71(b). In addition, certain payments to third parties on behalf of the spouse, such as mortgage payments, can also qualify as payments in cash.

[19]§71(c). A payment that is not specifically designated as child support may nonetheless be treated as child support if the payment is reduced on the happening of a specific contingency related to the child. For example, a payment that ceases once a child reaches the age of 18 would be treated as child support.

years), the tax laws may require the taxpayers to recharacterize (or "recapture") part of the alimony payments as nondeductible property transfers.[20]

Example 5-16

As part of the divorce agreement, Al transferred his interest in their joint residence to Courtney. The couple did not have any outstanding debt on the home. At the time of the divorce, the home was valued at $500,000 and Al's share was valued at $250,000. What are the tax consequences of the home ownership transfer to Courtney?

Answer: Because the transfer is not a cash transfer, it does not qualify as alimony. Consequently, Courtney does not recognize the $250,000 as income, and Al is not allowed to deduct the $250,000 transfer.

What if: Assume that Al's marginal tax rate is 35 percent and Courtney's marginal tax rate is 15 percent. To generate tax savings, in lieu of transferring his share of the ownership in the home, Al and Courtney agreed that Al would make a $250,000 cash transfer to Courtney. The divorce agreement stipulated that this payment was alimony. What are Al and Courtney trying to accomplish under this arrangement? Will they be successful?

Answer: They are trying to convert a property payment into alimony that is deductible by Al (at a high tax rate) and includible in Courtney's income (at a lower tax rate). As we discussed above, under a complex set of alimony recapture rules, it is likely that a portion of this payment will be treated as a nonalimony property settlement.

Prizes, Awards, and Gambling Winnings   Prizes, awards, and gambling winnings, such as raffle or sweepstakes prizes or lottery winnings, are included in gross income.

Example 5-17

After devoting much of her free time during the year to filling out sweepstakes entries, Gram hit the jackpot. She won a WaveRunner worth $7,500 in a sweepstakes sponsored by *Reader's Digest*. How much of the prize, if any, must Gram include in her gross income?

Answer: Gram must include the full $7,500 value of the WaveRunner in her gross income. Note that because she must pay taxes on the winnings, she's not really getting the WaveRunner for "free."

There are two specific, narrowly defined exceptions to this rule. First, awards for scientific, literary, or charitable achievement such as the Nobel Prize are excluded from gross income, *but only if* (1) the recipient was selected without any action on his part to enter the contest or proceeding, (2) the recipient is not required to render substantial future services as a condition to receive the prize or award, and (3) the payer of the prize or award transfers the prize or award to a federal, state, or local governmental unit or qualified charity such as a church, school, or charitable organization designated by the taxpayer.[21] The obvious downside of this exception is that the award recipient does not actually get to receive or keep the cash from the award. However, for tax purposes it is more beneficial for the recipient to exclude the award from income entirely by immediately transferring it to a charitable organization than it is to receive the award, recognize the income, and then contribute funds to a charity for a charitable deduction. Designating the award for payment to a federal, state, or local governmental unit or qualified charity has the same effect as claiming the transfer as a deduction *for* AGI. However, by receiving the award, recognizing the income, and then contributing funds to a charity, the taxpayer is deducting the donation as a deduction *from* AGI. As we discussed in Chapter 4, deductions *for* AGI are likely more advantageous than deductions *from* AGI.

[20]These rules apply when alimony decreases by more than $15,000 between years 1 and 3 after the divorce. See §71(f) for details.
[21]§74(b).

The second exception is for employee *awards for length of service or safety achievement.*[22] These nontaxable awards are limited to $400 of tangible property *other than cash* per employee per year.[23] The award is not excluded from the employee's income if circumstances suggest it is disguised compensation.[24]

TAXES IN THE REAL WORLD   You Get a Car! And You Get a Car!

Remember when Oprah gave out cars like other people give out refrigerator magnets and foam cup holders? Audience members were thrilled with her generosity—until they realized that they had to pay income tax on their newfound luck. That's because there's literally no such thing as a free lunch—unless that lunch is served up with a heap of exceptions that make the IRS happy.

So in her last go-round, Oprah had her ducks in a row. When she gave her entire audience an all-expense-paid trip to Australia in honor of her 25th and final season, she really meant *all* expenses. Including taxes. A CPA was said to be waiting in the wings to settle all of the tax issues associated with the trip. Reportedly, Oprah took care of paying the taxes associated with the fabulous prize.

Source: Kelly Phillips Erb, "The Oprah of Oz," TaxGirl.com, September 18, 2010. Copyright © 2010 by Kelly Phillips Erb. Used with permission.

Taxpayers must include the *gross* amount of their gambling winnings for the year in gross income.[25] Taxpayers are allowed to deduct their gambling losses to the extent of their gambling winnings, but the losses are usually deductible as miscellaneous itemized deductions.[26] For professional gamblers, however, the losses are deductible (to the extent of gambling winnings) *for* AGI.

ETHICS

While vacationing you find a $100 bill on the beach. Nobody saw you find it. Assuming the find meets the definition of gross income, would you report it as taxable income? Why or why not? Would your answer differ if you found $100,000 instead of $100?

Social Security Benefits   Over the last 40 years, the taxation of Social Security benefits has changed considerably. Forty years ago, Social Security benefits were completely excluded from income. Today, taxpayers may be required to include *up to* 85 percent of the benefits in gross income *depending* on the amount of the taxpayer's filing status, Social Security benefits, and *modified* AGI.[27] Modified AGI is regular AGI (excluding Social Security benefits) plus tax-exempt interest income, excluded foreign income (discussed later in the chapter), and certain other deductions *for* AGI.[28] The calculation of the amount of Social Security benefits to be included in income is depicted on the IRS worksheet in the appendix at the end of this chapter.[29]

---

[22]Prizes or awards from an employer-sponsored contest are fully taxable.

[23]§74(c).

[24]The $400 limit is increased to $1,600 for qualified award plans (written plans that do not discriminate in favor of highly compensated employees). However, the *average* cost of all qualified plan awards from an employer is limited to $400. Managers, administrators, clerical employees, or professional employees are not eligible for an exclusion for a safety award.

[25]Subject to de minimis rules, payers of gambling winnings report winnings to recipients and the IRS on Form W-2G.

[26]See Rev. Rul. 83-130, 1983-2 CB 148.

[27]§86(d) applies to monthly benefits under title II of the Social Security Act and tier 1 railroad retirement benefits. The Social Security Administration reports Social Security benefits on Form SSA-1099.

[28]See §86(b)(2).

[29]Because the 2016 worksheet was not available at the time the book went to press, we include the 2015 worksheet in the appendix at the end of the chapter. The 2015 worksheet can be used to determine the taxable portion of Social Security benefits received in 2016.

The calculation is complex, to say the least. However, the taxability of Social Security benefits can be summarized as follows:

Single taxpayers:

1. If modified AGI + 50 percent of Social Security benefits ≤ $25,000, Social Security benefits are not taxable.
2. If $25,000 < modified AGI + 50 percent of Social Security benefits ≤ $34,000, taxable Social Security benefits are the lesser of (a) 50 percent of the Social Security benefits or (b) 50 percent of (modified AGI + 50 percent of Social Security benefits − $25,000).
3. If modified AGI + 50 percent of Social Security benefits > $34,000, taxable Social Security benefits are the lesser of (a) 85 percent of Social Security benefits or (b) 85 percent of (modified AGI + 50 percent of Social Security benefits − $34,000), plus the lesser of (1) $4,500 or (2) 50 percent of Social Security benefits.

Taxpayers filing married separate:

Taxable Social Security benefits are the lesser of (a) 85 percent of the Social Security benefits or (b) 85 percent of the taxpayer's modified AGI + 50 percent of Social Security benefits.

Taxpayers filing married joint:

1. If modified AGI + 50 percent of Social Security benefits ≤ $32,000, Social Security benefits are not taxable.
2. If $32,000 < modified AGI + 50 percent of Social Security benefits ≤ $44,000, taxable Social Security benefits are the lesser of (a) 50 percent of the Social Security benefits or (b) 50 percent of (modified AGI + 50 percent of Social Security benefits − $32,000).
3. If modified AGI + 50 percent of Social Security benefits > $44,000, taxable Social Security benefits are the lesser of (a) 85 percent of Social Security benefits or (b) 85 percent of (modified AGI + 50 percent of Social Security benefits − $44,000), plus the lesser of (1) $6,000 or (2) 50 percent of Social Security benefits.

The implications of the above calculations are that the Social Security benefits of taxpayers with relatively low taxable income are not taxable and that 85 percent of the Social Security benefits of taxpayers with moderate to high taxable income is taxable.

Example 5-18

Gram received $7,200 of Social Security benefits this year. Suppose that Gram's modified AGI is $16,000. What amount of the Social Security benefits must Gram include in her gross income?

Answer: $0. Gram's modified AGI plus one-half of her Social Security benefits is $19,600 [$16,000 modified AGI + ($7,200 Social Security Benefits × 50%)], which is below $25,000. Hence, Gram may *exclude* the entire $7,200 of Social Security income from gross income.

What if: Assume that Gram received $7,200 of Social Security benefits this year and that her modified AGI is $50,000. What amount of benefits must Gram include in her gross income?

Answer: $6,120 ($7,200 × 85%).

What if: Assume that Gram received $7,200 of Social Security benefits this year and that her modified AGI is $26,400. What amount of benefits must Gram include in her gross income?

Answer: $2,500. Gram is single and her modified AGI + 50 percent of Social Security benefits falls between $25,000 and $34,000. Her taxable Social Security benefits are the lesser of (a) 50 percent of the Social Security benefits ($7,200 × 50% = $3,600) or (b) 50 percent of [$26,400 modified AGI + $3,600 (50 percent of Social Security benefits) − $25,000] = $2,500. Thus, her taxable Social Security benefits are $2,500.

What if: Assume that Gram received $7,200 of Social Security benefits this year and that her modi-fied AGI is $31,400. What amount of benefits must Gram include in her gross income?

Answer: $4,450. Gram is single and her modified AGI + 50 percent of Social Security benefits exceeds $34,000. Her taxable Social Security benefits are the lesser of (a) 85 percent of Social Security benefits ($7,200 × 85% = $6,120) or (b) 85 percent of [$31,400 modified AGI + $3,600 (50 percent of Social Security benefits) − $34,000] = $850, plus the lesser of (1) $4,500 or (2) 50 percent of Social Security benefits (50% × $7,200 = $3,600). This calculation simplifies to the lesser of (a) $6,120 or (b) $4,450 ($850 + lesser of (1) $4,500 or (2) $3,600). Thus, Gram's taxable Social Security benefits are $4,450.

Imputed Income   Besides realizing *direct* economic benefits like wages and inter-est, taxpayers sometimes realize *indirect* economic benefits that they must include in gross income as **imputed income.** Bargain purchases (such as an employer selling a good to an employee at a discount) and below-market loans (such as an employer lending an employee money at a zero or unusually low interest rate) are two common examples of taxable indirect economic benefits. Both bargain purchases and be-low-market loans generally result in gross income if the purchase or loan transaction takes place between related parties (such as an employer and employee, owner and entity, or transactions among family members). For bargain purchases, the general rule is that the discount received on the purchase from a related party is taxable, but the tax consequences vary based on the relationship of the parties. For example, a bargain purchase by an employee from an employer results in taxable compensation income to the employee, a bargain purchase by a shareholder from a corporation results in a taxable dividend to the shareholder, and a bargain purchase between family members is deemed to be a gift from one family member to the other (as dis-cussed later in the chapter, gifts are nontaxable for income tax purposes but poten-tially subject to gift tax to be paid by the person making the gift).

Although the general rule is that bargain purchases by an employee from an em-ployer creates taxable compensation income to the employee, the tax law does pro-vide a limited exclusion for employee bargain purchases. Specifically, employees may exclude (a) a discount on employer-provided goods as long as the discount does not exceed the employer's gross profit percentage on all property offered to sale to cus-tomers and (b) up to 20 percent employer-provided discount on services. Discounts in excess of these amounts are taxable as compensation.[30]

Example 5-19

As part of her compensation package, EWD agreed to provide Courtney with EWD architectural design services (to create more space for Gram) at a substantial discount. EWD provided Courtney with services valued at $35,000 but charged her only $22,000 for the services. How much of the discount must Courtney include in gross income?

Answer: $6,000, computed as follows:

Description	Amount	Explanation
(1) Value of services EWD provided to Courtney	$35,000	
(2) Courtney's cost of the services	22,000	
(3) Discount on services	$13,000	(1) − (2).
(4) Excludable discount	7,000	(1) × 20%.
Discount in excess of 20% is included in gross income	**$ 6,000**	(3) − (4).

For below-market loans, the indirect economic benefit conveyed to the borrower (such as an employee, shareholder, or family member) is a function of the amount of the loan and the difference in the market interest rate and the rate actually charged by the lender (such as an employer, corporation, or family member). To eliminate

[30]§132(a)(2).

any tax advantages of below-market loans, the tax law generally requires the lender and borrower to treat the transaction as if

1. The borrower paid the lender the difference between the applicable federal interest rate (compounded semiannually) and the actual interest paid (this difference is called *imputed interest*).
2. The lender then returned the imputed interest to the borrower.

The deemed "payment" of the imputed interest in these transactions is treated as interest income to the lender and interest expense to the borrower. The deductibility of the interest expense for the borrower depends on how she used the loan proceeds (for business, investment, or personal purposes). As we learn in the next chapter, business interest expense is a deduction *for* AGI, investment interest expense is an itemized deduction subject to limitations, and personal interest is generally not deductible. The tax consequences of the "return" of the imputed interest from the lender to the borrower vary based on the relationship of the parties (similar to a bargain purchase). For example, the return of the imputed interest from an employer lender to an employee borrower is treated by both parties as taxable compensation paid to the employee, the return of the imputed interest from a corporation to a shareholder is considered a dividend, and a return of imputed interest by a family member to another family member is considered a gift. The imputed interest rules generally do not apply to aggregate loans of $10,000 or less between the lender and borrower [§7872(c)].[31]

Example 5-20

At the beginning of January, EWD provides Courtney with a $100,000 zero-interest loan. Assume that the applicable federal interest rate (compounded semiannually) is 4 percent. Courtney used the loan proceeds to acquire several personal-use assets (an automobile and other items). What amount is Courtney required to include in gross income in the current year?

Answer: $4,000, computed as follows:

Description	Amount	Explanation
(1) Loan principal	$100,000	
(2) Applicable federal interest rate compounded semiannually	4%	
(3) Interest on loan principal at federal rate	$ 4,000	(1) × (2).
(4) Interest paid by Courtney	0	
Imputed interest included in Courtney's gross income	**$ 4,000**	(3) − (4).

Courtney will include the $4,000 imputed interest in gross income as compensation and will also incur an imputed interest expense of $4,000 for the year. EWD will (a) deduct $4,000 of compensation expense and (b) report $4,000 of interest income. In this example, we assume Courtney used the proceeds for personal purposes so she is not allowed to deduct the interest expense.

What if: Assume the same facts except that EWD had loaned Courtney $10,000 at a zero-interest rate. How much imputed interest income would Courtney be required to include in her gross income for the year?

Answer: $0. The imputed interest rules don't apply because the loan did not exceed $10,000.

Discharge of Indebtedness   In general, when a taxpayer's debt is forgiven by a lender (the debt is discharged), the taxpayer must include the amount of debt relief in gross income.[32]

---

[31] For "gift" loans (loans between family members), the $10,000 de minimis exception is not available for loan proceeds used to purchase or carry income-producing assets. Likewise, the $10,000 de minimis exception is not available for compensation-related loans or corporate-shareholder loans where the principal purpose of the loans is to avoid federal tax. For gift loans of $100,000 or less, the imputed interest is limited to the borrower's net investment income (investment income, such as interest income or other investment income not taxed at preferential rates, less related investment expenses). If the borrower's net investment income is $1,000 or less, the imputed interest rules do not apply. §7872(d). The exception for gift loans of $100,000 or less is not available for loans where the principal purpose of the loans is to avoid federal tax.

[32] §61(a)(12). Income from discharge of indebtedness is also realized when debt is forgiven by lenders other than employers such as banks and credit card companies.

To provide tax relief for insolvent taxpayers—taxpayers with liabilities, including tax liabilities, exceeding their assets—a **discharge of indebtedness** is *not* taxable if the taxpayer is insolvent before *and* after the debt forgiveness.[33] If the discharge of indebtedness makes the taxpayer solvent, the taxpayer recognizes gross income to the extent of his solvency.[34] For example, if a taxpayer is discharged of $30,000 of debt and this causes him to be solvent by $10,000 (after the debt relief, the taxpayer's assets exceed his liabilities by $10,000), the taxpayer must include $10,000 in gross income.[35]

Example 5-21

In the previous example, Courtney borrowed $100,000 from EWD. Because EWD wants to keep Courtney as an employee, it agreed to forgive $10,000 of loan principal at the end of each year that Courtney stays on board. On December 31 of this year, EWD formally cancels $10,000 of Courtney's indebtedness. How much of this debt relief is Courtney required to include in gross income?

Answer: All $10,000 is included in Courtney's gross income.

EXCLUSION PROVISIONS

LO 5-3

So far in this chapter, we've discussed various types of income taxpayers must realize and recognize by reporting it on their tax returns in the current year. However, there are specific types of income that taxpayers realize but are allowed to permanently *exclude* from gross income or temporarily defer from gross income until a subsequent period. As we discussed in the previous chapter, *exclusions* and *deferrals* are the result of *specific congressional action* and are *narrowly defined*. Because taxpayers are not required to recognize income that is excluded or deferred, we refer to tax laws allowing exclusions or deferrals as **nonrecognition provisions.** Nonrecognition provisions result from various policy objectives. In very general terms, Congress allows most exclusions and deferrals for two primary reasons: (1) to subsidize or encourage particular activities or (2) to be fair to taxpayers (such as mitigating the inequity of double taxation). Our discussion in this chapter focuses on exclusions.

Common Exclusions

Because exclusion provisions allow taxpayers to permanently remove certain income items from their tax base, they are particularly taxpayer friendly. We begin by introducing three common exclusion provisions, the exclusions of municipal interest, gain on the sale of a personal residence, and fringe benefits. We continue with a survey of other exclusion provisions based on their underlying purpose: education, double taxation, and sickness and injury.[36]

Municipal Interest   The most common example of an exclusion provision is the exclusion of interest on **municipal bonds.** Municipal bonds include bonds issued by state and local governments located in the United States, and this exclusion is generally recognized as a subsidy to state and local governments (the exclusion allows

[33]§108(a)(1)(B).

[34]§108(a)(3).

[35]Other circumstances in which taxpayers may exclude a discharge of indebtedness are beyond the scope of this chapter. See §108(f)(2) for discussion of the limited exclusion of student loan forgiveness for loans requiring students to work for a specified time in certain professions. See §108(a)(1)(E) for discussion of the exclusion of up to $2,000,000 of home mortgage forgiveness from 2007 through 2016. See §108(i) for a discussion for the deferral of debt forgiveness income for businesses reacquiring debt at a discounted price in 2009 and 2010. This provision allows taxpayer to recognize the debt forgiveness income ratably over the five-year period 2014 through 2018.

[36]Another common exclusion we discuss in detail in Chapter 13 is the exclusion of earnings on "Roth" retirement savings accounts.

state and local governments to offer bonds at a lower before-tax interest rate). In contrast, interest on U.S. government obligations (such as Treasury bills) is taxable for federal tax purposes but is tax-exempt for state and local tax purposes.

Example 5-22

Courtney holds a $10,000 City of Cincinnati municipal bond. The bond pays 5 percent interest annually. Courtney acquired the bond a few years ago. The city used the proceeds from the bond issuance to help pay for renovations on a major league baseball stadium. In late December, Courtney received $500 of interest income from the bond for the year. How much of the $500 interest from the municipal bond may Courtney *exclude* from her gross income?

Answer: All $500 because the interest is from a municipal bond.

Gains on the Sale of Personal Residence   The tax law provides several provisions that encourage or subsidize home ownership, and the exclusion of the gain on the sale of a personal residence is a common example of one such provision. Specifically, taxpayers meeting certain home ownership *and* use requirements can permanently exclude up to $250,000 ($500,000 if married filing jointly) of realized gain on the sale of their principal residence.[37] Gain in excess of the excludable amount generally qualifies as long-term capital gain subject to tax at preferential rates. To satisfy the ownership test, the taxpayer must have owned the residence (house, condominium, trailer, or houseboat) for a total of two or more years during the five-year period ending on the date of the sale. To satisfy the use test, the taxpayer must have *used* the property as her principal residence for a total of two or more years (noncontiguous use is permissible) during the five-year period ending on the date of the sale. The tax law limits each taxpayer to one exclusion every two years. Married couples filing joint returns are eligible for the full $500,000 exclusion if *either* spouse meets the ownership test and *both* spouses meet the principal-use test. However, if *either* spouse is ineligible for the exclusion because he or she personally used the $250,000 exclusion on another home sale during the two years before the date of the current sale, the couple's available exclusion is reduced to $250,000.[38]

Example 5-23

What if: Assume that in October of this year, Courtney sold her prior home in Cincinnati. Courtney and her ex-husband purchased the home four years ago for $400,000, and Courtney received the house in the divorce. Courtney lived in the home until she moved to Kansas City in January. Courtney sold the home for $550,000. How much taxable gain does she recognize on the sale of the home?

Answer: $0. Because Courtney satisfies the two-year ownership and two-year use test, she may exclude up to $250,000 of gain from the sale of her home. Thus, Courtney may exclude the entire $150,000 gain that she realized on the sale ($550,000 sales price less $400,000 basis).

What if: Assume the same facts except Courtney sold the home for $700,000. How much taxable gain does she recognize on the sale of the home?

Answer: $50,000. Because Courtney satisfies the two-year ownership and two-year use test, she may exclude $250,000 of the $300,000 gain from the sale of her home ($700,000 sales price less $400,000 basis). Thus, Courtney recognizes a $50,000 taxable gain on the sale.

[37]§121.

[38]We discuss the rules for sale of principal residence in more detail in Chapter 14, including relief rules for taxpayers who cannot meet the ownership and use test due to unusual or hardship circumstances and the limitation on the gain exclusion for taxpayers using a home for something other than a principal residence for a period (nonqualified *use*) before using the home as a principal residence.

Fringe Benefits   In addition to paying salary and wages, many employers provide employees with **fringe benefits.** For example, an employer may provide an employee with an automobile to use for personal purposes, pay for an employee to join a health club, or pay for an employee's home security. In general, the value of these benefits is *included* in the employee's gross income as compensation for services. However, certain fringe benefits, called "qualifying" fringe benefits, are excluded from gross income.[39] Exhibit 5-3 lists some of the most common fringe benefits that are excluded from an employee's gross income. In addition to excluded fringe benefits, many employers make contributions to retirement plans on behalf of their employees. Subject to specific rules that we discuss in Chapter 13, these contributions (as well as employee contributions from salary) are not currently included in the employee's gross income but are deferred until the employee withdraws the contributions and related earnings from the plan. We discuss fringe benefits in more depth in Chapter 12.

Example 5-24

EWD paid $6,000 this year for Courtney's health insurance premiums and $150 in premiums for her $40,000 group-term life insurance policy. How much of the $6,150 in benefits can Courtney exclude from her gross income?

Answer: Courtney can exclude all $6,150 in benefits from her gross income. All health insurance premiums paid by an employer on an employee's behalf are excluded from the employee's income. In addition, premiums employers pay on an employee's behalf for group-term life insurance (up to $50,000 of coverage) are also excluded from the employee's gross income.

Example 5-25

In December, Courtney mailed a newsletter to several dozen friends and relatives with a recent picture of her son, daughter, and grandmother. Courtney printed both the newsletter and the photos on printers at work (with permission of EWD). Courtney would have paid $55 for the duplicate newsletters and photos at a nearby copy center. How much of this $55 benefit that Courtney received from EWD may Courtney *exclude* from her gross income?

Answer: All $55 is excluded. The $55 benefit is considered a nontaxable de minimis fringe benefit because it is small in amount and infrequent.

TAXES IN THE REAL WORLD   Have Phone, Will Call Tax-Free

In years past, the IRS classified employee cell phones issued by employers as a taxable benefit (i.e., taxable compensation), and required employees to keep detailed records to substantiate business versus personal use of the phone. As you might expect, the classification and record-keeping requirements were not met with great enthusiasm. In 2011, the IRS reversed its course and now considers an employer-issued cell phone as an excludible fringe benefit (both the business and personal use) when the phone is provided primarily for noncompensatory business reasons. Even better, the IRS no longer requires record-keeping to receive the tax-free treatment. See Notice 2011-72.

---

[39]Most nontaxable fringe benefits are listed with "items specifically excluded from gross income" in §§101-140 of the Internal Revenue Code. Employers are generally prohibited from discriminating among employees with respect to nontaxable fringe benefits (i.e., they cannot offer them only to executives).

EXHIBIT 5-3   **Common Qualifying Fringe Benefits** (excluded from employee's gross income)

Item	Description
Medical and dental health insurance coverage (§106)	An employee may exclude from income the cost of medical and insurance coverage and dental health insurance premiums the employer pays on an employee's behalf.[40]
Life insurance coverage (§79)	Employees may exclude from income the value of life insurance premiums the employer pays on an employee's behalf for up to $50,000 of group-term life insurance.
De minimis (small) benefits (§132(a)(4))	As a matter of administrative convenience, Congress allows employees to exclude from income relatively small and infrequent benefits employees receive at work (such as limited use of a business copy machine).
Meals and lodging for the employer's provided convenience (§119)	Employees may exclude employer-provided meals and lodging if they (1) are provided on the employer's business premises to the employee (and spouse and dependents); (2) are provided for the employer's convenience (such as allowing the employee to be on-call 24 hours a day or continue working on-site over lunch); and (3) for lodging only, the employee must accept the lodging as a condition of employment.
Employee educational assistance programs (§127)	Employees may exclude up to $5,250 of employer-provided educational assistance benefits covering tuition, books, and fees for any instruction that improves the taxpayer's capabilities, whether or not job-related or part of a degree program.
No additional cost services (§132(a)(1))	Employees may exclude the value of services provided by an employer that generate no substantial costs to the employer (such as free flight benefits for airline employees on a space-available basis or free hotel service for hotel employees).
Qualified employee discounts (§132(a)(2))	Employees may exclude (a) a discount on employer-provided goods as long as the discount does not exceed the employer's gross profit percentage on all property offered to sale to customers and (b) up to 20 percent employer-provided discount on services. Discounts in excess of these amounts are taxable as compensation. See Example 5-19.
Dependent care benefits (§129)	Employees may exclude up to $5,000 for benefits paid or reimbursed by employers for caring for children under age 13 or dependents or spouses who are physically or mentally unable to care for themselves.
Working condition fringe benefits (§132(a)(3))	Employees may exclude from income any benefit or reimbursement of a benefit provided by an employer that would be deductible as an ordinary and necessary expense by the employee if the employee had paid the expense.
Qualified transportation benefits (§132(a)(5))	Employees may exclude up to $255 per month of employer-provided parking and up to $255 per month of the combined value of employer-provided mass transit passes and the value of a car pool vehicle for employee use.
Qualified moving expenses (§132(a)(6))	Employees may exclude employer reimbursement for qualified moving expenses (cost of moving household items and costs of travel, including lodging, to a new home for employee and dependents) that would otherwise be deductible by the employee. We discuss deductible moving expenses in Chapter 6.
Cafeteria plans (§125)	A plan where employees choose among various nontaxable fringe benefits (such as health insurance and dental insurance) or cash. Tax-free to the extent the taxpayer chooses nontaxable fringe benefits; taxable to the extent the employee receives cash.
Flexible Spending Accounts (§125)	Allow employees to set a portion of their before-tax salary for payment of either health and/or dependent-care benefits. Amounts set aside must be used by the end of the year or within the first two and a half months of the next plan year, or employees forfeit the unused balance. In lieu of the two-and-a-half month grace period each year for health care flexible spending accounts, employers instead can allow employees to carryover up to $500 of unused amounts to be used anytime during the next year (i.e., it is the employer's choice). This option does not apply to dependent-care flexible spending accounts. For 2016, the amount of before-tax salary that an employee may set aside for medical expenses is limited to $2,550 and for dependent-care expenses is limited to $5,000.

[40]The cost of medical coverage paid by an employer and offered through a health insurance exchange is not an excludible benefit unless the employer is a small employer that elects to make all of its full-time employees eligible for plans offered through the small business health options program (SHOP). For this purpose, a small employer is an employer that employed an average of at least one but 100 or fewer employees during business days in the prior year, and employs at least one employee on the first day of the plan year. In 2015, SHOP was open to employers with 50 or fewer full-time equivalent employees. Beginning in 2016, all SHOPs will be open to employers with up to 100 full-time equivalent employees.

Education-Related Exclusions

As an incentive for taxpayers to participate in higher education (education beyond high school), Congress excludes certain types of income if the funds are used for higher education. In the following paragraphs, we discuss exclusions for scholarships and exclusions for certain types of investment plans used to save for college.[41]

Scholarships   College students seeking a degree can exclude from gross income scholarships (including Pell grants) that pay for tuition, fees, books, supplies, and other equipment *required* for the student's courses.[42] Any excess scholarship amounts (such as for room or meals) are fully taxable. The scholarship exclusion applies only if the recipient is *not* required to perform services in exchange for receiving the scholarship. "Scholarships" that represent compensation for past, current, or future services are fully taxable. However, tuition waivers or reductions provided by an educational institution for undergraduate courses for student employees or for graduate courses for teaching or research assistants are not taxable.

What about athletic scholarships? Good question. The IRS has ruled that the value of athletic scholarships—which may not exceed expenses for tuition, fees, room, board, and necessary supplies; are awarded to students by a university that *expects* but *does not require* the students to participate in a particular sport; require no particular activity in lieu of participation; and are not canceled if the student cannot participate—is excludable from gross income.[43]

Example 5-26

Ellen, Courtney's daughter, received a $700 scholarship from the University of Missouri–Kansas City that pays $400 of her tuition and provides $300 cash for books. Ellen spent $350 on books. How much of the scholarship may she exclude from gross income?

Answer: All $700 is excluded. Ellen may exclude all of the scholarship for tuition and she may exclude the $300 cash she received for books because she spent all $300 purchasing her books for school.

What if: How much is Ellen allowed to exclude if she spent only $250 on books?

Answer: $650 is excluded. Ellen excludes all of the scholarship for her tuition and $250 of the $300 in cash payments because she spent $250 on books. She must include the excess cash payment of $50 ($300 − $250) in her gross income.

> **THE KEY FACTS**
>
> **Education Exclusions**
>
> - Students seeking a college degree can exclude scholarships that pay for required tuition, fees, books, and supplies.
> - Taxpayers can elect to exclude interest earned on Series EE savings bonds when the redemption proceeds are used to pay qualified higher education expenses.
> - The exclusion of interest on Series EE savings bonds is restricted to taxpayers with modified AGI below specific limits.

Other Educational Subsidies   Taxpayers are allowed to exclude from gross income earnings on investments in qualified education plans such as 529 plans and Coverdell education savings accounts as long as they use the earnings to pay for qualifying educational expenditures.

529 plans allow parents, grandparents, and other individuals to contribute up to the maximum allowed by state-sponsored 529 plans to fund the qualified educational costs of future *college* students.[44] Earnings in 529 plans are distributed tax-free provided they are used for qualified *higher* education expenses. If, on the other hand, distributions are made to the beneficiary for other purposes, the earnings distributed are taxed to the beneficiary at the beneficiary's tax rate and are subject to an additional 10 percent penalty while distributions of the original investment (contributions) to the

---

[41]A detailed explanation is available in IRS Publication 970 *Tax Benefits for Education* available on the IRS website at www.IRS.gov.

[42]§117(b)(2).

[43]Rev. Rul. 77-263, 1977-2 CB 47.

[44]Contribution limits vary according to the state administering the 529 plan. In addition, more than half the states offer a state tax deduction or credit to residents contributing to the 529 plan sponsored by the state in which the contributors reside.

beneficiary are treated as gifts.[45] Similarly, distributions to contributors (e.g., parents, grandparents) that represent earnings on their contributions are included in contributors' gross income and are also subject to the 10 percent penalty.

With a Coverdell account, yearly contributions to the account are limited to $2,000 for each beneficiary, and distributions may be used to pay for qualified educational costs of kindergarten through 12th grade and qualified higher education expenses such as tuition, books, fees, supplies, and reasonable room and board.[46] The $2,000 contribution limit for Coverdell accounts phases out as AGI (modified to include certain types of excluded foreign income) increases from $190,000 to $220,000 for married filing jointly taxpayers, and from $95,000 to $110,000 for all other taxpayers.

U.S. Series EE bonds   The federal government issues bonds that allow taxpayers to acquire the bonds at a discount and redeem the bonds for a fixed amount over stated time intervals. These bonds don't generate any cash in the form of interest until the taxpayer redeems the bond. At redemption, the amount of the redemption price in excess of the acquisition price is interest included in gross income.[47] U.S. Series EE bonds fall into this category. However, an exclusion is available for interest from Series EE bonds. This exclusion requires that the redemption proceeds be used to pay for higher education expenses of the taxpayer, the taxpayer's spouse, or a dependent of the taxpayer. Qualified higher education expenses include the tuition and fees required for enrollment or attendance at an eligible educational institution. Taxpayers may also exclude the interest income if they contribute the proceeds to a qualified tuition program.

The exclusion is partially reduced or eliminated for taxpayers exceeding a fixed level of modified adjusted gross income (adjusted gross income before the educational savings bond exclusion, the foreign earned income exclusion, and certain other deductions).[48] If the taxpayer's modified AGI exceeds the thresholds in the redemption year, the exclusion is phased out (gradually reduced) until all of the interest from the bonds is taxed.[49]

Exclusions That Mitigate Double Taxation

Congress provides certain exclusions that eliminate the potential double tax that may arise for gifts, inheritances, and life insurance proceeds.

Gifts and Inheritances   Individuals may transfer property to other taxpayers without receiving or expecting to receive value in return. If the *transferor* is alive at the time of the transfer, the property transfer is called a **gift.** If the property is transferred from the decedent's estate (*transferor* is deceased), it is called an **inheritance.** These transfers are generally subject to a federal transfer tax, *not* the income tax. Gifts are typically subject to the federal gift tax and inheritances are typically subject to a federal estate tax.[50] Thus, gift and estate taxes are imposed on *transfer* of the

---

[45]Under §529(c)(3), multiple distributions received under these circumstances are treated as annuities. As a result, a portion of each distribution would be treated as a gift with the remainder treated as income.

[46]§530(b). This definition of qualified higher education expenses is consistent with the definition used in §221(d)(2) to determine if interest paid on education-related loans is deductible (see Chapter 6).

[47]Alternatively, taxpayers can elect to include the annual increase in the redemption value in gross income rather than waiting to recognize all the income on redemption. See §454(a).

[48]§135(c)(4).

[49]In 2016, the phase-out range begins at $116,300 of modified adjusted gross income for married taxpayers filing joint returns. For all other taxpayers, the phase-out range begins at $77,550.

[50]As a general rule, the federal gift tax does not apply to relatively small gifts ($14,000 or less), and the federal estate tax does not apply to transfers from relatively small estates (under $5,450,000).

property and *not included in income by the recipient.* The exclusion of gifts and inheritances from income taxation avoids the potential double taxation (transfer and income taxation) on these transfers.

Example 5-27

Ellen graduated from high school last year. As a graduation present, Gram purchased a $1,500 travel package for Ellen, so that Ellen could go on a Caribbean cruise. Last year, Ellen also received an inheritance of $2,000 from Gramps's estate. How much gross income does Ellen recognize on the $1,500 gift she received from Gram and the $2,000 inheritance she received from Gramps's estate?

Answer: $0. Ellen is allowed to exclude the entire gift and the entire amount of the inheritance from her gross income. Consequently, she does not recognize any gross income from these transactions.

Life Insurance Proceeds   In some ways, life insurance proceeds are similar to inheritances. When the owner of the life insurance policy dies, the beneficiary receives the death benefit proceeds. The decedent (or the decedent's estate) is generally subject to estate taxation on the amount of the insurance proceeds. In order to avoid potential double taxation on the life insurance proceeds, the tax laws allow taxpayers receiving life insurance proceeds to exclude the proceeds from gross income.[51] However, when the insurance proceeds are paid over a period of time rather than in a lump sum, a portion of the payments represents interest and must be included in gross income. In addition, the life insurance proceeds exclusion generally does not apply when a life insurance policy is transferred to another party for valuable consideration. In this case, the eventual life insurance proceeds collected by the purchaser are excluded up to the sum of the purchase price of the policy and any subsequent premiums with remaining proceeds taxable as ordinary income.[52]

What happens if a taxpayer cashes out a policy before death? The tax treatment varies based on the specific facts. Generally, if a taxpayer simply cancels a life insurance contract and is paid the policy's cash surrender value, she would recognize ordinary income to the extent the proceeds received exceed previous premiums paid. If premiums paid exceed the proceeds received, the loss is not deductible. If, however, the taxpayer is terminally ill (medically certified with an illness expected to cause death within 24 months), early receipt of life insurance proceeds **(accelerated death benefits)** are not taxable. If a taxpayer is chronically ill (medically certified to require substantial assistance for daily living activities or due to cognitive impairment), life insurance proceeds are not taxable to the extent they are used to pay for the taxpayer's long-term care.

Example 5-28

What if: Gramps received $200,000 of accelerated death benefits from a life insurance policy last year when he was diagnosed with terminal cancer with an expected life of less than one year. How much gross income would the $200,000 payment generate?

Answer: None, because Gramps was medically certified as terminally ill with an illness expected to cause death within 24 months. (continued on page 5-28)

[51]§101. The exclusion does not apply if the insurance policy is sold by the owner.

[52]This exception to the exclusion does not apply if the recipient of the policy is the insured, a partner of the insured, a partnership in which the insured is a partner, or a corporation in which the insured is an officer or shareholder. This exception also does not apply to policies transferred by gift or tax-free exchange. §101(a)(2).

What if: Due to financial issues, Gramps several years ago transferred a $100,000 life insurance policy on his life to a business associate for $5,000. Since that time, the business associate continued to pay the annual premiums on the policy (totaling $20,000 before Gramps's death). Upon Gramps's death, the life insurance company paid the business associate the policy's $100,000 face value. How much of the $100,000 payment is taxable?

Answer: $75,000. Because the business associate purchased the life insurance policy from Gramps for valuable consideration, she may exclude the $100,000 proceeds up to the sum of the purchase price of the policy ($5,000) and any subsequent premiums ($20,000) with the remaining proceeds ($100,000 − $5,000 − $20,000 = $75,000) taxable as ordinary income.

THE KEY FACTS

Exclusions to Mitigate Double Taxation

- Gifts and inheritances are subject to federal transfer taxes and are, therefore, excluded from the income of the recipient.
- A maximum of $101,300 (2016) of foreign earned income can be excluded from gross income for qualifying individuals.
- To be eligible for the foreign earned income exclusion, the taxpayer must live in the foreign country for 330 days in a consecutive 12-month period.

Foreign-Earned Income U.S. citizens are subject to tax on all income whether it is generated in the United States or in foreign countries. Because most foreign countries also impose tax on income earned within their borders, U.S. citizens could be subject to both U.S. and foreign taxation on income earned abroad. To provide relief from this potential double taxation, Congress allows taxpayers to exclude foreign-earned income (income from foreign sources for personal services performed) up to an annual maximum amount. Income from pensions, annuities, salary paid by the U.S. government, or deferred compensation does not qualify for the exclusion. The maximum exclusion is indexed for inflation, and in 2016 the maximum is $101,300. Rather than claim this exclusion, taxpayers may deduct foreign taxes paid as itemized deductions or they may claim the foreign tax credit for foreign taxes paid on their foreign-earned income.[53] To determine whether claiming the annual exclusion, the deduction, or the foreign tax credit is most advantageous, taxpayers should compare the tax effects of each option. To claim the annual exclusion instead of the foreign tax deduction or credit, the taxpayer must elect to do so using Form 2555. Taxpayers who elect to use the exclusion may revoke the election for later years and use the foreign tax credit or deduct foreign taxes paid. However, once a taxpayer revokes the exclusion election, she may not reelect to use the exclusion before the sixth tax year after the tax year the revocation was made.

As you might expect, individuals must meet certain requirements to qualify for the foreign-earned income exclusion. To be eligible for the annual exclusion, a taxpayer must have her tax home in a foreign country and (1) be considered a resident of the foreign country or (2) live in the foreign country for 330 days in a consecutive 12-month period. However, because the exclusion is computed on a *daily* basis, the *maximum* exclusion is reduced pro rata for each day during the calendar year the taxpayer is not considered to be a resident of the foreign country or does not actually live in the foreign country. Taxpayers meeting the requirement for the foreign-earned income exclusion may also exclude from income reasonable housing costs (provided by an employer) that exceed 16 percent of the statutory foreign-earned income exclusion amount for the year (exceed 16 percent × $101,300 = $16,208 in 2016). The exclusion, however, is limited to a maximum of 14 percent of the statutory exclusion amount (14 percent × $101,300 = $14,182 in 2016). Thus, in 2016, if a taxpayer incurs housing costs (provided by an employer) exceeding $16,208, she may exclude such excess costs up to $14,182 (thus, the first $16,208 of employer-provided housing costs are included in gross income).[54] The housing exclusion limit is also subject to daily proration if the taxpayer is not considered a resident of the foreign country for the entire year or does not actually live in the foreign country the entire year.

---

[53]See §911(b)(2) and Chapters 6 and 8.
[54]§911(c).

Example 5-29

What if: Assume that Courtney is considering a transfer to EWD's overseas affiliate. If Courtney transfers, she anticipates she will earn approximately $120,000 in salary. How much of her expected $120,000 salary will Courtney be allowed to exclude from her gross income assuming she meets the residency requirements?

Answer: She is eligible to exclude $101,300 of her $120,000 of compensation from U.S. taxation in 2016. However, her entire $120,000 salary may be subject to the foreign country's income tax.

What if: Assume that Courtney decides to transfer but she expects to live in the foreign country for only 340 days in the first year. How much of her expected $120,000 salary will she be allowed to exclude from gross income?

Answer: $94,104 [$101,300 full exclusion × 340/366 (days in foreign country/days in year)].

What if: Assume that Courtney expects to live in the foreign country for 340 days in the first year and that she expects her salary to be $60,000. How much of her expected $60,000 salary will she be allowed to exclude from gross income?

Answer: All $60,000. She can exclude up to $94,104 of salary from income (see above computation).

What if: Assume that if Courtney transfers, EWD's overseas affiliate will also pay for her housing while overseas ($25,000). How much of the $25,000 housing payments may Courtney exclude?

Answer: $8,792. Since Courtney meets the requirements for the foreign-earned income exclusion, she may exclude the employer-provided housing costs that exceed $16,208 (16% × $101,300), up to a maximum exclusion of $14,182 (14% × $101,300). Thus, Courtney may exclude $8,792 [the lesser of (a) $8,792 ($25,000 housing cost less $16,208) or (b) $14,182].

Sickness and Injury-Related Exclusions

The tax laws provide several exclusion provisions for taxpayers who are sick or injured. One explanation for these exclusions is that payments for sickness or injury are considered returns of (human) capital.

Workers' Compensation The provision for workers' compensation is relatively straightforward. Taxpayers receive workers' compensation benefits when they are unable to work because of a work-related injury. Any payments a taxpayer receives from a state-sponsored workers' compensation plan are excluded from the taxpayer's income.[55] Note that this treatment is *opposite* that of *unemployment* compensation, which is fully taxable.

Payments Associated with Personal Injury Historically, the question of which payments associated with a personal injury were excludable was controversial. In 1996 Congress settled the matter by deciding that all payments associated with compensating a taxpayer for a *physical* injury (including payments for past, current, and future lost wages) are excluded from gross income. That is, the tax laws specify that any *compensatory damages* on account of a *physical injury* or *physical sickness* are nontaxable. Thus, damages taxpayers receive for emotional distress associated with a physical injury are excluded. In contrast, *punitive damages* are *fully taxable,* because they are intended to punish the harm-doer rather than to compensate the taxpayer for injuries. Likewise, taxpayers receiving damages for emotional distress that are not associated with a physical injury must include those payments in income. In general, all other awards (those that do not relate to physical injury or sickness or are payments for the medical costs of treating emotional distress) are included in gross income.

[55]§104.

Example 5-30

In February, Courtney's cousin, Kelsey, was struck and injured by a bus while walking in a crosswalk. Because the bus driver was negligent, the bus company settled Kelsey's claim by paying her $1,500 for medical expenses and $500 for emotional distress associated with the accident. How much of the $2,000 Kelsey received from the bus company may she *exclude* from her gross income?

Answer: All $2,000. Kelsey may exclude the $1,500 she received for medical expenses and the $500 payment she received for emotional distress because these damages were associated with Kelsey's physical injury.

What if: Assume Kelsey sued the bus company and was awarded $5,000 in punitive damages. How much of the $5,000 would Kelsey be able to exclude from her gross income?

Answer: $0. Payments for punitive damages are not excludable. Kelsey would be required to include the entire $5,000 in her gross income.

THE KEY FACTS

Exclusions Related to Sickness and Injury

- Payments from workers' compensation plans are excluded from gross income.
- Payments received as compensation for a *physical* injury are excluded from gross income, but punitive damages are included in gross income.
- Reimbursements by health and accident insurance policies for medical expenses paid by the taxpayer are excluded from gross income.
- Disability payments received from an *employee-purchased* policy are excluded from gross income.

Health Care Reimbursement   Any reimbursement a taxpayer receives from a health and accident insurance policy for medical expenses paid by the taxpayer during the current year is excluded from gross income. The exclusion applies regardless of whether the taxpayer, her employer, or someone else purchased the health and accident policy for the taxpayer. Of course, the tax benefit rule may require inclusion of reimbursements of medical expenses that were deducted by the taxpayer in a prior year.

Disability Insurance   The exclusion provisions for **disability insurance** are more restrictive than those for workers' compensation payments or reimbursements from a health and accident insurance plan. Disability insurance, sometimes called wage replacement insurance, pays the insured individual for wages lost when the individual misses work due to injury or disability. If an individual purchases disability insurance directly, the cost of the policy is not deductible, but any disability benefits are excluded from gross income.

Disability insurance may also be purchased on an individual's behalf by an employer. When an employer pays disability insurance premiums, the employer may allow employees to choose whether the payments on their behalf are to be considered taxable compensation or a nontaxable fringe benefit. If the premiums paid on the employee's behalf are taxable compensation to the employee, the policy is considered to have been purchased by the employee. If the premium paid for by the employer is a nontaxable fringe benefit to the employee, the policy is considered to have been purchased by the employer. This distinction is important because only payments taxpayers receive from an *employee-purchased* policy are excluded from an employee's gross income. If the employer pays the premiums for an employee as a nontaxable fringe benefit, the employee must include all disability benefits in gross income.

Example 5-31

Courtney purchased disability insurance last year. In late April of this year, she broke her wrist in a mountain biking accident and could not work for two weeks. Courtney's doctor bills totaled $2,000, of which $1,600 were reimbursed by her health insurance purchased by EWD. How much of the $1,600 health insurance reimbursement for medical expenses is Courtney allowed to *exclude* from her gross income?

Answer: All $1,600 is excluded. All medical expense reimbursements from health insurance are excluded from a taxpayer's gross income.

Courtney also received $600 for lost wages due to the accident from her disability insurance policy. How much of the $600 is Courtney allowed to exclude from her gross income?

Answer: All $600 is excluded. Courtney can exclude the entire amount because she paid the premiums on the policy.

What if: How much of the $600 payment for lost wages from the disability insurance policy would Courtney exclude if EWD paid the disability insurance premium on her behalf as a nontaxable fringe benefit?

Answer: $0 is excluded. In this circumstance the policy would be considered to be purchased by the employer, so Courtney would not be allowed to exclude any of the payment from gross income. She would include the payment in gross income and be taxed on the entire $600.

What if: How much of the $600 payment for lost wages from the disability insurance policy would Courtney be allowed to exclude if she paid half the cost of the policy with after-tax dollars and EWD paid the other half as a taxable fringe benefit?

Answer: All $600 is excluded. Because Courtney paid for the entire cost of the policy with after-tax dollars, she is allowed to exclude all of the disability insurance benefit. Note that if EWD had paid for half the cost of the policy as a nontaxable fringe benefit, Courtney would have been able to exclude $300 not $600.

Deferral Provisions

We've described exclusion provisions that allow taxpayers to permanently eliminate certain types of income from their tax base. Other code sections, called *deferral provisions,* allow taxpayers to defer (but not permanently exclude) the recognition of certain types of realized income. Transactions generating deferred income include **installment sales,** like-kind exchanges, involuntary conversions, and contributions to non-Roth **qualified retirement accounts.** We "defer" our detailed discussion of these transactions to subsequent chapters.

INCOME SUMMARY

At the end of the year, Courtney calculated her income and Gram's income. Exhibit 5-4 presents Courtney's income calculation, Exhibit 5-5 displays how this income would be reported on the front page of Courtney's tax return, and Exhibit 5-6 presents Gram's income calculation. Note that Courtney's actual *gross* income equals her total income on page 1 of her Form 1040 plus her $1,500 consulting expenses (see Example 5-7) and her $9,000 deductions for rental expenses (see Example 5-10), which are both *for* AGI deductions. Because Gram doesn't have any business, rental, or royalty deductions, her gross income is equal to her total income on line 22 of page 1 of her tax return.

EXHIBIT 5-4   Courtney's Income

Description	Amount	Reference
(1) Salary (line 7, 1040 page 1)	$ 98,000	Example 5-7.
(2) Employment bonus award (line 7, 1040 page 1)	4,800	Example 5-4.
(3) Discount architectural design services (line 7, 1040 page 1)	6,000	Example 5-19.
(4) Compensation on below market loan from EWD (line 7, 1040 page 1)	4,000	Example 5-20.
(5) Discharge of indebtedness (line 7, 1040 page 1)	10,000	Example 5-21.
(6) Interest income (line 8a, 1040 page 1)	617	Example 5-9.
(7) Dividends (lines 9a and 9b, 1040 page 1)	700	Example 5-8.
(8) State tax refund (line 10, 1040 page 1)	420	Example 5-3.
(9) Alimony (line 11, 1040 page 1)	20,000	Example 5-14.
(10) Net business income (line 12, 1040 page 1)	18,000	Example 5-7.
(11) Net rental income (line 17, 1040 page 1)	5,000	Example 5-10.
Total income as presented on line 22 of front page of 1040 (see Exhibit 5-5)	**$167,537**	Sum of (1) through (11).

EXHIBIT 5-5 **Courtney's Tax Return**

(total income as reported on 1040 page 1, lines 7–22)

								(see instructions)	
If more than four dependents, see instructions and check here ▶ ☐						☐ ☐ ☐		Dependents on 6c not entered above	
	d	Total number of exemptions claimed						Add numbers on lines above ▶	

Income	**7**	Wages, salaries, tips, etc. Attach Form(s) W-2			**7**	122,800
	8a	**Taxable** interest. Attach Schedule B if required			**8a**	617
Attach Form(s) W-2 here. Also attach Forms W-2G and 1099-R if tax was withheld.	**b**	**Tax-exempt** interest. **Do not** include on line 8a . .	**8b**	500		
	9a	Ordinary dividends. Attach Schedule B if required			**9a**	700
	b	Qualified dividends	**9b**	700		
	10	Taxable refunds, credits, or offsets of state and local income taxes			**10**	420
	11	Alimony received			**11**	20,000
	12	Business income or (loss). Attach Schedule C or C-EZ			**12**	18,000
If you did not get a W-2, see instructions.	**13**	Capital gain or (loss). Attach Schedule D if required. If not required, check here ▶ ☐			**13**	
	14	Other gains or (losses). Attach Form 4797			**14**	
	15a	IRA distributions .	**15a**		b Taxable amount . . .	**15b**	
	16a	Pensions and annuities	**16a**		b Taxable amount . . .	**16b**	
	17	Rental real estate, royalties, partnerships, S corporations, trusts, etc. Attach Schedule E			**17**	5,000
	18	Farm income or (loss). Attach Schedule F			**18**	
	19	Unemployment compensation			**19**	
	20a	Social security benefits	**20a**		b Taxable amount . . .	**20b**	
	21	Other income. List type and amount			**21**	
	22	Combine the amounts in the far right column for lines 7 through 21. This is your **total income** ▶			**22**	167,537
Adjusted Gross Income	**23**	Educator expenses	**23**			
	24	Certain business expenses of reservists, performing artists, and fee-basis government officials. Attach Form 2106 or 2106-EZ	**24**			
	25	Health savings account deduction. Attach Form 8889 .	**25**			
	26	Moving expenses. Attach Form 3903	**26**			

EXHIBIT 5-6 **Gram's Income**

Deduction	Amount	Reference
Babysitting services	$ 350	Example 5-2.
Interest income	4,400	Example 5-9.
Annuity income	3,400	Example 5-11.
Gain on stock sale	350	Example 5-12.
Sweepstakes winnings (WaveRunner)	7,500	Example 5-17.
Income for current year	**$16,000**	

CONCLUSION

In this chapter we explained the basic concepts of income realization and recognition, identified and discussed the major types of income, and described the most common income exclusions. We discovered that many exclusions are related to specific congressional objectives, but that absent a specific exclusion, realized income should be included in gross income. In the next chapter, we turn our attention to the deductions available to taxpayers when computing their taxable income. We will continue to follow Courtney and Gram in their quest to determine their taxable income and corresponding tax liability.

Appendix   2015 Social Security Worksheet from Form 1040

2015 Form 1040—Lines 20a and 20b

Social Security Benefits Worksheet—Lines 20a and 20b   *Keep for Your Records*

Before you begin: ✓ Complete Form 1040, lines 21 and 23 through 32, if they apply to you.
       ✓ Figure any write-in adjustments to be entered on the dotted line next to line 36 (see the instructions for line 36).
       ✓ If you are married filing separately and you lived apart from your spouse for all of 2015, enter "D" to the right of the word "benefits" on line 20a. If you do not, you may get a math error notice from the IRS.
       ✓ Be sure you have read the **Exception** in the line 20a and 20b instructions to see if you can use this worksheet instead of a publication to find out if any of your benefits are taxable.

1.	Enter the total amount from **box 5** of **all** your **Forms SSA-1099** and **Forms RRB-1099.** Also, enter this amount on Form 1040, line 20a	**1.** _____
2.	Multiply line 1 by 50% (0.50)	**2.** _____
3.	Combine the amounts from Form 1040, lines 7, 8a, 9a, 10 through 14, 15b, 16b, 17 through 19, and 21	**3.** _____
4.	Enter the amount, if any, from Form 1040, line 8b	**4.** _____
5.	Combine lines 2, 3, and 4	**5.** _____
6.	Enter the total of the amounts from Form 1040, lines 23 through 32, plus any write-in adjustments you entered on the dotted line next to line 36	**6.** _____
7.	Is the amount on line 6 less than the amount on line 5?	
	☐ **No.** (STOP) None of your social security benefits are taxable. Enter -0- on Form 1040, line 20b.	
	☐ **Yes.** Subtract line 6 from line 5	**7.** _____
8.	If you are:	
	• Married filing jointly, enter $32,000	
	• Single, head of household, qualifying widow(er), or married filing separately and you **lived apart** from your spouse for all of 2015, enter $25,000	.... **8.** _____
	• Married filing separately and you lived with your spouse at any time in 2015, skip lines 8 through 15; multiply line 7 by 85% (0.85) and enter the result on line 16. Then go to line 17	
9.	Is the amount on line 8 less than the amount on line 7?	
	☐ **No.** (STOP) None of your social security benefits are taxable. Enter -0- on Form 1040, line 20b. If you are married filing separately and you **lived apart** from your spouse for all of 2015, be sure you entered "D" to the right of the word "benefits" on line 20a.	
	☐ **Yes.** Subtract line 8 from line 7	**9.** _____
10.	Enter: $12,000 if married filing jointly; $9,000 if single, head of household, qualifying widow(er), or married filing separately and you **lived apart** from your spouse for all of 2015	**10.** _____
11.	Subtract line 10 from line 9. If zero or less, enter -0-	**11.** _____
12.	Enter the **smaller** of line 9 or line 10	**12.** _____
13.	Enter one-half of line 12	**13.** _____
14.	Enter the **smaller** of line 2 or line 13	**14.** _____
15.	Multiply line 11 by 85% (0.85). If line 11 is zero, enter -0-	**15.** _____
16.	Add lines 14 and 15	**16.** _____
17.	Multiply line 1 by 85% (0.85)	**17.** _____
18.	**Taxable social security benefits.** Enter the **smaller** of line 16 or line 17. Also enter this amount on Form 1040, line 20b	**18.** _____

(TIP)   *If any of your benefits are taxable for 2015 **and** they include a lump-sum benefit payment that was for an earlier year, you may be able to reduce the taxable amount. See* Lump-Sum Election *in Pub. 915 for details.*

Summary

LO 5-1 Apply the concept of realization and explain when taxpayers recognize gross income.

- Income is typically realized with a transaction that allows economic benefit to be identified and measured.
- Unless realized income is deferred or excluded, it is included in gross income in the period dictated by the taxpayer's accounting method.
- The accrual method of accounting recognizes income in the period it is earned, and this method is typically used by large corporations.
- The cash method of accounting recognizes income in the period received, and this method offers a simple and flexible method of accounting typically used by individuals.
- The return of capital principle, constructive receipt doctrine, and assignment of income doctrine affect how much income is recognized, when income is recognized, and who recognizes income, respectively.

LO 5-2 Understand the distinctions between the various sources of income, including income from services and property.

- Income from services is called earned income, whereas income from property is called unearned income.
- A portion of annuity payments and proceeds from sales of property is a nontaxable return of capital.
- Earned and unearned income generated by flow-through business entities is reported by partners and Subchapter S shareholders.
- Other sources of income include alimony payments, unemployment compensation, Social Security benefits, prizes and awards, bargain purchases, imputed interest on below-market loans, and discharge of indebtedness.

LO 5-3 Apply basic income exclusion provisions to compute gross income.

- Interest received from holding state and local indebtedness (municipal interest) is excluded from gross income.
- A taxpayer satisfying certain home ownership and use requirements can permanently exclude up to $250,000 ($500,000 if married filing jointly) of realized gain on the sale of her principal residence.
- Employment-related nonrecognition provisions include a variety of excludable fringe benefits.
- Gifts, inheritances, life insurance proceeds, and foreign earned income are excluded from gross income in order to mitigate the effects of double taxation.
- Common injury-related nonrecognition provisions include the exclusions for worker's compensation, personal injury payments and reimbursements from health insurance policies, and certain payments from disability policies.

KEY TERMS

accelerated death benefits (5-27)	constructive receipt doctrine (5-7)	installment sale (5-31)
accrual method (5-6)	disability insurance (5-30)	municipal bond (5-21)
alimony (5-14)	discharge of indebtedness (5-21)	nonrecognition provisions (5-21)
all-inclusive definition of income (5-2)	earned income (5-10)	qualified retirement accounts (5-31)
annuity (5-11)	flow-through entity (5-14)	realization principle (5-3)
assignment of income doctrine (5-8)	fringe benefits (5-23)	return of capital (5-5)
barter clubs (5-4)	gift (5-26)	tax basis (5-4)
cash method (5-6)	gross income (5-2)	tax benefit rule (5-5)
claim of right doctrine (5-7)	imputed income (5-19)	unearned income (5-10)
community property systems (5-8)	inheritance (5-26)	wherewithal to pay (5-3)

DISCUSSION QUESTIONS

Discussion Questions are available in *Connect*®.   ■ connect

1. Based on the definition of gross income in §61 and related regulations, what is the general presumption regarding the taxability of income realized?   `LO 5-1`

2. Based on the definition of gross income in §61, related regulations, and judicial rulings, what are the three criteria for recognizing taxable income?   `LO 5-1`

3. Describe the concept of realization for tax purposes.   `LO 5-1`

4. Compare and contrast realization of income with recognition of income.   `LO 5-1`

5. Tim is a plumber who joined a barter club. This year Tim exchanges plumbing services for a new roof. The roof is properly valued at $2,500, but Tim would have only billed $2,200 for the plumbing services. What amount of income should Tim recognize on the exchange of his services for a roof? Would your answer change if Tim would have normally billed $3,000 for his services?   `LO 5-1`

6. Andre constructs and installs cabinets in homes. Blair sells and installs carpet in apartments. Andre and Blair worked out an arrangement whereby Andre installed cabinets in Blair's home and Blair installed carpet in Andre's home. Neither Andre nor Blair believes they are required to recognize any gross income on this exchange because neither received cash. Do you agree with them? Explain.   `LO 5-1`

7. What issue precipitated the return of capital principle? Explain.   `LO 5-1`

8. Compare how the return of capital principle applies when (1) a taxpayer sells an asset and collects the sale proceeds immediately and (2) a taxpayer sells an asset and collects the sale proceeds over several periods (an installment sale). If Congress wanted to maximize revenue from installment sales, how would they have applied the return of capital principle for installment sales?   `LO 5-1`

9. This year Jorge received a refund of property taxes that he deducted on his tax return last year. Jorge is not sure whether he should include the refund in his gross income. What would you tell him?   `LO 5-1`

10. Describe in general how the cash method of accounting differs from the accrual method of accounting.   `LO 5-1`

11. Janet is a cash-method calendar-year taxpayer. She received a check for services provided in the mail during the last week of December. However, rather than cash the check, Janet decided to wait until the following January because she believes that her delay will cause the income to be realized and recognized next year. What would you tell her? Would it matter if she didn't open the envelope? Would it matter if she refused to check her mail during the last week of December? Explain.   `LO 5-1`

12. The cash method of accounting means that taxpayers don't recognize income unless they receive cash or cash equivalents. True or false? Explain.   `LO 5-1`

13. Contrast the constructive receipt doctrine with the claim of right doctrine.   `LO 5-1`

14. Dewey is a lawyer who uses the cash method of accounting. Last year Dewey provided a client with legal services worth $55,000, but the client could not pay the fee. This year Dewey requested that in lieu of paying Dewey $55,000 for the services, the client could make a $45,000 gift to Dewey's daughter. Dewey's daughter received the check for $45,000 and deposited it in her bank account. How much of this income is taxed, if any, to Dewey? Explain.   `LO 5-1`

15. Clyde and Bonnie were married this year. Clyde has a steady job that will pay him about $37,000, while Bonnie does odd jobs that will produce about $28,000 of income. They also have a joint savings account that will pay about $400 of interest. If Clyde and Bonnie reside in a community property state and file married-separate tax returns, how much gross income will Clyde and Bonnie each report? Any difference if they reside in a common law state? Explain.   `LO 5-2`

LO 5-2 16. Distinguish earned income from unearned income, and provide an example of each.

LO 5-2 17. Jim purchased 100 shares of stock this year and elected to participate in a dividend reinvestment program. This program automatically uses dividends to purchase additional shares of stock. This year Jim's shares paid $350 of dividends and he used these funds to purchase additional shares of stock. These additional shares are worth $375 at year-end. What amount of dividends, if any, should Jim declare as income this year? Explain.

LO 5-2 18. Jerry has a certificate of deposit at the local bank. The interest on this certificate was credited to his account on December 31 of last year, but he didn't withdraw the interest until January of this year. When is the interest income taxed?

LO 5-2 19. Conceptually, when taxpayers receive annuity payments, how do they determine the amount of the payment they must include in gross income?

LO 5-2 20. George purchased a life annuity to provide him monthly payments for as long as he lives. Based on IRS tables, George's life expectancy is 100 months. Is George able to recover his cost of the annuity if he dies before he receives 100 monthly payments? Explain. What happens for tax purposes if George receives more than 100 payments?

LO 5-2 21. Brad purchased land for $45,000 this year. At year-end Brad sold the land for $51,700 and paid a sales commission of $450. What effect does this transaction have on Brad's gross income? Explain.

LO 5-2 22. Tomiko is a 50 percent owner (partner) in the Tanaka partnership. During the year, the partnership reported $1,000 of interest income and $2,000 of dividends. How much of this income must Tomiko include in her gross income?

LO 5-2 23. Clem and Ida have been married for several years, but this year they decided to get divorced. In the divorce decree, Clem agreed to deed his car to Ida and pay Ida $10,000 per year for four years. Will either of these transfers qualify as alimony for tax purposes? Explain.

LO 5-2 **planning** 24. Otto and Fiona are negotiating the terms of their divorce. Otto has agreed to transfer property to Fiona over the next two years, but he has reserved the right to make cash payments in lieu of property transfers. Will tax considerations play a role in Otto's decision to transfer property or pay cash? How will Otto's choice affect the combined gross income and income taxes paid by Otto and Fiona? Explain.

LO 5-2 25. Larry Bounds has won the gold bat award for hitting the longest home run in major league baseball this year. The bat is worth almost $35,000. Under what conditions can Larry exclude the award from his gross income? Explain.

LO 5-2 26. Rory and Nicholi, single taxpayers, each annually receive Social Security benefits of $15,000. Rory's taxable income from sources other than Social Security exceeds $200,000. In contrast, the Social Security benefits are Nicholi's only source of income. What percentage of the Social Security benefits must Rory include in his gross income? What percentage of Social Security benefits is Nicholi required to include in his gross income?

LO 5-2 27. Rolando purchases a golf cart from his employer, E-Z-Go Golf Carts, for a sizable discount. Explain the rules for determining if Rolando's purchase results in taxable income for him.

LO 5-2 28. When an employer makes a below-market loan to an employee, what are the tax consequences to the employer and employee?

LO 5-3 29. Explain why an insolvent taxpayer is allowed to exclude income from the discharge of indebtedness if the taxpayer remains insolvent after receiving the debt relief.

LO 5-3 30. What are the basic requirements to exclude the gain on the sale of a personal residence?

31. Cassie works in an office and has access to several professional color printers. Her employer allows Cassie and her fellow employees to use the printers to print color postcards for the holidays. This year Cassie printed out two dozen postcards worth almost $76. Must Cassie include this amount in her gross income this year? Explain your answer.   `LO 5-3`

32. What are some common examples of taxable and tax-free fringe benefits?   `LO 5-3`

33. Explain how state and local governments benefit from the provisions that allow taxpayers to exclude interest on state and local bonds from their gross income.   `LO 5-3`

34. Explain why taxpayers are allowed to exclude gifts and inheritances from gross income even though these payments are realized and clearly provide taxpayers with the wherewithal to pay.   `LO 5-3`

35. Describe the kinds of insurance premiums an employer can pay on behalf of an employee without triggering includible compensation to the employee.   `LO 5-3`

36. How are state-sponsored 529 educational savings plans taxed if investment returns are used for educational purposes? Are the returns taxed differently if they are not ultimately used to pay for education costs?   `LO 5-3`

37. Jim was injured in an accident and his surgeon botched the medical procedure. Jim recovered $5,000 from the doctors for pain and suffering and $2,000 for emotional distress. Determine the taxability of these payments and briefly explain to Jim the apparent rationale for including or excluding these payments from gross income.   `LO 5-3`

38. Tom was just hired by Acme Corporation and has decided to purchase disability insurance. This insurance promises to pay him weekly benefits to replace his salary should he be unable to work because of disability. Disability insurance is also available through Acme as part of its compensation plan. Acme pays these premiums as a nontaxable fringe benefit, but the plan promises to pay about 10 percent less in benefits. If Tom elects to have Acme pay the premiums, then his compensation will be reduced by an equivalent amount. Should tax considerations play a role in Tom's choice to buy disability insurance through Acme or on his own? Explain.   `LO 5-3`

PROBLEMS

Select problems are available in *Connect*®.   ■ **connect**

39. For the following independent cases, determine whether economic income is present and, if so, whether it must be included in gross income (i.e., is it realized and recognized for tax purposes?).   `LO 5-1`

    a) Asia owns stock that is listed on the New York Stock Exchange, and this year the stock increased in value by $20,000.

    b) Ben sold stock for $10,000 and paid a sales commission of $250. Ben purchased the stock several years ago for $4,000.

    c) Bessie is a partner in SULU Enterprises LLC. This year SULU reported that Bessie's share of rental income was $2,700 and her share of municipal interest was $750.

40. Devon owns 1,000 shares of stock worth $10,000. This year he received 200 additional shares of this stock from a stock dividend. His 1,200 shares are now worth $12,500. Must Devon include the dividend paid in stock in income?   `LO 5-1`   ● research

41. XYZ declared a $1 per share dividend on August 15. The date of record for the dividend was September 1 (the stock began selling *ex-dividend* on September 2). The dividend was paid on September 10. Ellis is a cash-method taxpayer. Determine if he must include the dividends in gross income under the following independent circumstances.   `LO 5-1`   ● research

    a) Ellis bought 100 shares of XYZ stock on August 1 for $21 per share. Ellis received $100 on September 10. Ellis still owns the shares at year-end.

b) Ellis bought 100 shares of XYZ stock on August 1 for $21 per share. Ellis sold his XYZ shares on September 5 for $23 per share. Ellis received the $100 dividend on September 10 (note that even though Ellis didn't own the stock on September 10, he still received the dividend because he was the shareholder on the record date).

c) Ellis bought 100 shares of XYZ stock for $22 per share on August 20. Ellis received the $100 dividend on September 10. Ellis still owns the shares at year-end.

LO 5-1

research

42. For the following independent cases, determine whether economic income is present and, if so, whether it must be included in gross income. Identify a tax authority that supports your analysis.

   a) Hermione discovered a gold nugget (valued at $10,000) on her land.

   b) Jay embezzled $20,000 from his employer and has not yet been apprehended.

   c) Keisha found $1,000 inside an old dresser. She purchased the dresser at a discount furniture store at the end of last year and found the money after the beginning of the new year. No one has claimed the money.

LO 5-1

43. Although Hank is retired, he is an excellent handyman and often works part-time on small projects for neighbors and friends. Last week his neighbor, Mike, offered to pay Hank $500 for minor repairs to his house. Hank completed the repairs in December of this year. Hank uses the cash method of accounting and is a calendar-year taxpayer. Compute Hank's gross income for this year from each of the following alternative transactions:

   a) Mike paid Hank $200 in cash in December of this year and promised to pay the remaining $300 with interest in three months.

   b) Mike paid Hank $100 in cash in December of this year and gave him a negotiable promissory note for $400 due in three months with interest. Hank sold the note in January for $350.

   c) Mike gave Hank tickets to the big game in January. The tickets have a face value of $50 but Hank could sell them for $400. Hank went to the game with his son.

   d) Mike bought Hank a new set of snow tires. The tires typically sell for $500, but Mike bought them on sale for $450.

LO 5-1

44. Jim recently joined the Austin Barter Club, an organization that facilitates the exchange of services between its members. This year Jim provided lawn-mowing services to other club members. Jim received the following from the barter club. Determine the amount, if any, Jim should include in his gross income in each of the following situations:

   a) Jim received $275 of car repair services from another member of the club.

   b) Jim received a $150 credit that gave him the option of receiving a season pass at a local ski resort from another member of the club. However, he forgot to request the pass by the end of the ski season and his credit expired.

   c) Jim received a $450 credit that can only be applied for goods or services from club members next year.

LO 5-1

research

45. Last year Acme paid Ralph $15,000 to install a new air-conditioning unit at its headquarters building. The air conditioner did not function properly, and this year Acme requested that Ralph return the payment. Because Ralph could not repair one critical part in the unit, he refunded the cost of the repair, $5,000, to Acme.

   a) Is Ralph required to include the $15,000 payment he received last year in his gross income from last year?

   b) What are the tax implications of the repayment if Ralph was in the 35 percent tax bracket when he received the $15,000 payment from Acme, but was in the 28 percent tax bracket when he refunded $5,000 to Acme?

   c) How would you answer the question in part (b) if Ralph refunded $2,500 to Acme and not $5,000?

46. Louis files as a single taxpayer. In April of this year he received a $900 refund of state income taxes that he paid last year. How much of the refund, if any, must Louis include in gross income under the following independent scenarios? Assume the standard deduction last year was $6,300. **LO 5-1**

   a) Last year Louis claimed itemized deductions of $6,550. Louis's itemized deductions included state income taxes paid of $1,750.

   b) Last year Louis had itemized deductions of $4,800 and he chose to claim the standard deduction. Louis's itemized deductions included state income taxes paid of $1,750.

   c) Last year Louis claimed itemized deductions of $7,740. Louis's itemized deductions included state income taxes paid of $2,750.

47. L. A. and Paula file as married taxpayers. In August of this year, they received a $5,200 refund of state income taxes that they paid last year. How much of the refund, if any, must L. A. and Paula include in gross income under the following independent scenarios? Assume the standard deduction last year was $12,600. **LO 5-1**

   a) Last year L. A. and Paula had itemized deductions of $10,200, and they chose to claim the standard deduction.

   b) Last year L. A. and Paula claimed itemized deductions of $23,200. Their itemized deductions included state income taxes paid of $7,500.

   c) Last year L. A. and Paula claimed itemized deductions of $15,400. Their itemized deductions included state income taxes paid of $10,500.

48. Clyde is a cash-method taxpayer who reports on a calendar-year basis. This year Paylate Corporation has decided to pay Clyde a year-end bonus of $1,000. Determine the amount Clyde should include in his gross income this year under the following circumstances: **LO 5-1**

   a) Paylate Corporation wrote the check and put it in his office mail slot on December 30 of this year, but Clyde did not bother to stop by the office to pick it up until after year-end.

   b) Paylate Corporation mistakenly wrote the check for $100. Clyde received the remaining $900 after year-end.

   c) Paylate Corporation mailed the check to Clyde before the end of the year, (and it was delivered before year-end). Although Clyde expected the bonus payment, he decided not to collect his mail until after year-end.

   d) Clyde picked up the check in December, but the check could not be cashed immediately because it was postdated January 10.

49. Identify the amount, if any, that these individuals must include in gross income in the following independent cases. Assume that the individuals are on the cash method of accounting and report income on a calendar-year basis. **LO 5-2**

   a) Elmer was an extremely diligent employee this year and his employer gave him three additional days off with pay (Elmer's gross pay for the three days totaled $1,200, but his net pay was only $948).

   b) Amax purchased new office furniture and allowed each employee to take home old office furniture valued at $250.

50. Ralph owns a building that he is trying to lease. Ralph is a calendar-year, cash-method taxpayer and is trying to evaluate the tax consequences of three different lease arrangements. Under lease 1, the building rents for $500 per month, payable on the first of the next month, and the tenant must make a $500 security deposit that is refunded at the end of the lease. Under lease 2, the building rents for $5,500 per year, payable at the time the lease is signed, but no security deposit is required. Under lease 3, the building rents for $500 per month, payable at the beginning of each month, and the tenant must pay a security deposit of $1,000 that is to be applied toward the rent for the last two months of the lease. **LO 5-2**

   research

a) What amounts are included in Ralph's gross income this year if a tenant signs lease 1 on December 1 and makes timely payments under that lease?

b) What amounts are included in Ralph's gross income this year if the tenant signs lease 2 on December 31 and makes timely payments under that lease?

c) What amounts are included in Ralph's gross income this year if the tenant signs lease 3 on November 30 and makes timely payments under that lease?

LO 5-2   51. Anne purchased an annuity from an insurance company that promised to pay her $20,000 per year for the next 10 years. Anne paid $145,000 for the annuity, and in exchange she will receive $200,000 over the term of the annuity.

a) How much of the first $20,000 payment should Anne include in gross income?

b) How much income will Anne recognize over the term of the annuity?

LO 5-2   52. Larry purchased an annuity from an insurance company that promises to pay him $1,500 per month for the rest of his life. Larry paid $170,820 for the annuity. Larry is in good health and he is 72 years old. Larry received the first annuity payment of $1,500 this month. Use the expected number of payments in Exhibit 5-1 for this problem.

a) How much of the first payment should Larry include in gross income?

b) If Larry lives more than 15 years after purchasing the annuity, how much of each additional payment should he include in gross income?

c) What are the tax consequences if Larry dies just after he receives the 100th payment?

LO 5-2
research   53. Gramps purchased a joint survivor annuity that pays $500 monthly over his remaining life and that of his wife, Gram. Gramps is 70 years old and Gram is 65 years old. Gramps paid $97,020 for the contract. How much income will Gramps recognize on the first payment?

LO 5-2   54. Lanny and Shirley are recently divorced and do not live together. Shirley has custody of their child, Art, and Lanny pays Shirley $22,000 per year. All property was divided equally.

a) How much should Shirley include in income if Lanny's payments are made in cash but will cease if Shirley dies or remarries?

b) How much should Shirley include in income if $12,000 of Lanny's payments is designated as "nonalimony" in the divorce decree?

c) How much should Shirley include in income if Lanny's payments drop to $15,000 once Art reaches the age of 18?

LO 5-2
planning   55. Todd and Margo are seeking a divorce and no longer live together. Margo has offered to pay Todd $42,000 per year for five years if Margo receives sole title to the art collection. This collection cost them $100,000 but is now worth $360,000. All other property is to be divided equally.

a) If Margo's payments cease in the event of Todd's death, how are the payments treated for tax purposes?

b) How much of the gain would be taxed to Todd if Margo sells the art at the end of five years?

c) Compute the tax cost (benefit) to Todd (Margo) if the payments qualify as alimony. Assume that Todd (Margo) has a marginal tax rate of 15 percent (35 percent), and ignore the time value of money.

d) How much more over the five-year period should Todd demand in order to agree to allow the payments to cease in the event of his death? (How much more will make him indifferent between receiving $42,000 a year in nonalimony payments and receiving higher payments that are considered to be alimony?)

56. For each of the following independent situations, indicate the amount the tax-payer must include in gross income and explain your answer: LO 5-2
    a) Phil won $500 in the scratch-off state lottery. There is no state income tax.
    b) Ted won a compact car worth $17,000 in a TV game show. Ted plans to sell the car next year.
    c) Al Bore won the Nobel Peace Prize of $500,000 this year. Rather than take the prize, Al designated that the entire award should go to Weatherhead Charity, a tax-exempt organization.
    d) Jerry was awarded $2,500 from his employer, Acme Toons, when he was selected most handsome employee for Valentine's Day this year.
    e) Ellen won a $1,000 cash prize in a school essay contest. The school is a tax-exempt entity, and Ellen plans to use the funds to pay her college education.
    f) Gene won $400 in the office March Madness pool.

57. Grady received $8,200 of Social Security benefits this year. Grady also reported salary and interest income this year. What amount of the benefits must Grady include in his gross income under the following five independent situations? LO 5-2
    a) Grady files single and reports salary of $12,100 and interest income of $250.
    b) Grady files single and reports salary of $22,000 and interest income of $600.
    c) Grady files married joint and reports salary of $75,000 and interest income of $500.
    d) Grady files married joint and reports salary of $44,000 and interest income of $700.
    e) Grady files married separate and reports salary of $22,000 and interest income of $600.

58. George and Weezy received $30,200 of Social Security benefits this year ($12,000 for George; $18,200 for Weezy). They also received $5,000 of interest from jointly owned City of Ranburne bonds and dividend income. What amount of the Social Security benefits must George and Weezy include in their gross income under the following independent situations? LO 5-2
    a) George and Weezy file married joint and receive $8,000 of dividend income from stocks owned by George.
    b) George and Weezy file married separate and receive $8,000 of dividend income from stocks owned by George.
    c) George and Weezy file married joint and receive $30,000 of dividend income from stocks owned by George.
    d) George and Weezy file married joint and receive $15,000 of dividend income from stocks owned by George.

59. Nikki works for the Shine Company, a retailer of upscale jewelry. How much taxable income does Nikki recognize under the following scenarios? LO 5-2
    a) Nikki buys a diamond ring from Shine Company for $10,000 (normal sales price, $14,000; Shine Company's gross profit percentage is 40%).
    b) Nikki receives a 25 percent discount on jewelry restoration services offered by Shine Company. This year, Nikki had Shine Company repair a set of antique earrings (normal repair cost $500; discounted price $375).

60. Wally is employed as an executive with Pay More Incorporated. To entice Wally to work for Pay More, the corporation loaned him $20,000 at the beginning of the year at a simple interest rate of 1 percent. Wally would have paid interest of $2,400 this year if the interest rate on the loan had been set at the prevailing federal interest rate. LO 5-2

a) Wally used the funds as a down payment on a speedboat and repaid the $20,000 loan (including $200 of interest) at year-end. Does this loan result in any income to either party, and if so, how much?

b) Assume instead that Pay More forgave the loan and interest on December 31. What amount of gross income does Wally recognize this year? Explain.

LO 5-3 61. Jimmy has fallen on hard times recently. Last year he borrowed $250,000 and added an additional $50,000 of his own funds to purchase $300,000 of undeveloped real estate. This year the value of the real estate dropped dramatically, and Jimmy's lender agreed to reduce the loan amount to $230,000. For each of the following independent situations, indicate the amount Jimmy must include in gross income and explain your answer:

a) The real estate is worth $175,000 and Jimmy has no other assets or liabilities.

b) The real estate is worth $235,000 and Jimmy has no other assets or liabilities.

c) The real estate is worth $200,000 and Jimmy has $45,000 in other assets but no other liabilities.

LO 5-3

research 62. Grady is a 45-year-old employee with AMUCK Garbage Corporation. AMUCK pays group-term life insurance premiums for employees, and Grady chose the maximum face amount of $120,000. What amount, if any, of the premium AMUCK paid on his behalf, must Grady include in his gross income for the year? Provide a tax authority to support your answer.

LO 5-3 63. Fred currently earns $9,000 per month. Fred has been offered the chance to transfer for three to five years to an overseas affiliate. His employer is willing to pay Fred $10,000 per month if he accepts the assignment. Assume that the maximum foreign earned income exclusion for next year is $101,300.

a) How much U.S. gross income will Fred report if he accepts the assignment abroad on January 1 of next year and works overseas for the entire year? If Fred's employer also provides him free housing (cost of $20,000), how much of the $20,000 is excludable from Fred's income?

b) Suppose that Fred's employer has offered Fred a six-month overseas assignment beginning on January 1 of next year. How much U.S. gross income will Fred report next year if he accepts the six-month assignment abroad and returns home on July 1 of next year?

c) Suppose that Fred's employer offers Fred a permanent overseas assignment beginning on March 1 of next year. How much U.S. gross income will Fred report next year if he accepts the permanent assignment abroad? Assume that Fred will be abroad for 305 days out of 365 days next year. If Fred's employer also provides him free housing (cost of $16,000 next year), how much of the $16,000 is excludable from Fred's income?

LO 5-3 64. For each of the following situations, indicate how much the taxpayer is required to include in gross income and explain your answer:

a) Steve was awarded a $5,000 scholarship to attend State Law School. The scholarship pays Steve's tuition and fees.

b) Hal was awarded a $15,000 scholarship to attend State Hotel School. All scholarship students must work 20 hours per week at the school residency during the term.

LO 5-3 65. Cecil cashed in a Series EE savings bond with a redemption value of $14,000 and an original cost of $9,800. For each of the following independent scenarios, calculate the amount of interest Cecil will include in his gross income assuming he files as a single taxpayer:

a) Cecil plans to spend all of the proceeds to pay his son's tuition at State University. Cecil's son is a full-time student, and Cecil claims his son as a dependent. Cecil estimates his modified adjusted gross income at $63,100.

b) Assume the same facts in part (a), except Cecil plans to spend $4,200 of the proceeds to pay his son's tuition at State University, and Cecil estimates his modified adjusted gross income at $60,600.

66. Grady is a member of a large family and received the following payments this year. For each payment, determine whether the payment constitutes realized income and determine the amount of each payment Grady must include in his gross income. **LO 5-3**

a) A gift of $20,000 from Grady's grandfather.

b) One thousand shares of GM stock worth $120 per share inherited from Grady's uncle. The uncle purchased the shares for $25 each, and the shares are worth $125 at year-end.

c) A gift of $50,000 of Ford Motor Bonds. Grady received the bonds on October 31, and he received $1,500 of semiannual interest from the bonds on December 31.

d) A loan of $5,000 for school expenses from Grady's aunt.

67. Bart is the favorite nephew of his aunt Thelma. Thelma transferred several items of value to Bart. For each of the following transactions, determine the effect on Bart's gross income. **LO 5-3**

a) Thelma gave Bart an auto worth $22,000. Thelma purchased the auto three years ago for $17,000.

b) Thelma elects to cancel her life insurance policy, and she gives the cash surrender value of $15,000 to Bart.

c) Bart is the beneficiary of a $100,000 whole life insurance policy on the life of Thelma. Thelma died this year, and Bart received $100,000 in cash.

d) Bart inherited 500 shares of stock from Thelma's estate. Thelma purchased the shares many years ago for $1,200, and the shares are worth $45,000 at her death.

68. Terry was ill for three months and missed work during this period. During his illness, Terry received $4,500 in sick pay from a disability insurance policy. What amounts are included in Terry's gross income under the following independent circumstances? **LO 5-3**

a) Terry has disability insurance provided by his employer as a nontaxable fringe benefit. Terry's employer paid $2,800 in disability premiums for Terry this year.

b) Terry paid $2,800 in premiums for his disability insurance this year.

c) Terry's employer paid the $2,800 in premiums for Terry, but Terry elected to have his employer include the $2,800 as compensation on Terry's W-2.

d) Terry has disability insurance whose cost is shared with his employer. Terry's employer paid $1,800 in disability premiums for Terry this year as a nontaxable fringe benefit, and Terry paid the remaining $1,000 of premiums from his after-tax salary.

69. Tim's parents plan to provide him with $50,000 to support him while he establishes a new landscaping business. In exchange for the support, Tim will maintain the landscape at his father's business. Under what conditions will the transfer of $50,000 be included in Tim's gross income? Explain. Do you have a recommendation for Tim and his parents? **LO 5-3** **planning**

70. What amounts are included in gross income for the following taxpayers? Explain your answers. **LO 5-3**

a) Janus sued Tiny Toys for personal injuries from swallowing a toy. Janus was paid $30,000 for medical costs and $250,000 for punitive damages.

b) Carl was injured in a car accident. Carl's insurance paid him $500 to reimburse his medical expenses and an additional $250 for the emotional distress Carl suffered as a result of the accident.

c) Ajax published a story about Pete and as a result Pete sued Ajax for damage to his reputation. Ajax lost in court and paid Pete an award of $20,000.

d) Bevis was laid off from his job last month. This month he drew $800 in unemployment benefits.

LO 5-3 71. This year, Janelle received $200,000 in life insurance proceeds. Under the following scenarios, how much of the $200,000 is taxable?

a) Janelle received the proceeds upon the death of her father, Julio.

b) Janelle received the $200,000 proceeds because she was diagnosed with colon cancer (life expectancy of six months), and she needed the proceeds for her care.

c) The proceeds related to a life insurance policy she purchased for $35,000 from a friend in need. After purchase, Janelle paid annual premiums that total $22,000.

LO 5-3 72. This year, Leron and Sheena sold their home for $750,000 after all selling costs. Under the following scenarios, how much taxable gain does the home sale generate for Leron and Sheena?

a) Leron and Sheena bought the home three years ago for $150,000 and lived in the home until it sold.

b) Leron and Sheena bought the home one year ago for $600,000 and lived in the home until it sold.

c) Leron and Sheena bought the home five years ago for $500,000. They lived in the home for three years until they decided to buy a smaller home. Their home has been vacant for the past two years.

LO 5-3 73. Dontae's employer has offered him the following employment package. What is Dontae's gross income from his employment?

Salary	$400,000
Health insurance	10,000
Dental insurance	1,500
Membership to Heflin Country Club	20,000
Season tickets to Atlanta Braves games	5,000
Tuition reimbursement for graduate courses	4,000
Housing allowance (for a McMansion in his neighborhood of choice)	40,000

COMPREHENSIVE PROBLEMS

Select problems are available in *Connect*®.　　　**connect**

74. Charlie was hired by Ajax this year as a corporate executive and a member of the board of directors. During the current year, Charlie received the following payments or benefits paid on his behalf.

Salary payments	$92,000
Contributions to qualified pension plan	10,200
Qualified health insurance premiums	8,400
Year-end bonus	15,000
Annual director's fee	10,000
Group-term life insurance premiums (face = $40,000)	750
Whole life insurance premiums (face = $100,000)	1,420
Disability insurance premiums (no special elections)	4,350

a) Charlie uses the cash method and calendar year for tax purposes. Calculate Charlie's gross income for the current year.

b) Suppose that Ajax agrees to pay Charlie an additional $100,000 once Charlie completes five years of employment. Will this agreement alter Charlie's gross income this year relative to your part (a) answer? Explain.

c) Suppose that in exchange for his promise to remain with the firm for the next four years, Ajax paid Charlie four years of director's fees in advance. Will this arrangement alter Charlie's gross income this year relative to your part (a) answer? Explain.

d) Assume that in lieu of a year-end bonus Ajax transferred 500 shares of Bell stock to Charlie as compensation. Further assume that the stock was listed at $35 per share and Charlie would sell the shares by year-end, at which time he expected the price to be $37 per share. Will this arrangement alter Charlie's gross income this year relative to your part (a) answer? Explain.

e) Suppose that in lieu of a year-end bonus Ajax made Charlie's house payments (a total of $23,000). Will this arrangement alter Charlie's gross income this year relative to your part (a) answer? Explain.

75. Irene is disabled and receives payments from a number of sources. The interest payments are from bonds that Irene purchased over past years and a disability insurance policy that Irene purchased herself. Calculate Irene's gross income.

Interest, bonds issued by City of Austin, Texas	$2,000
Social Security benefits	8,200
Interest, U.S. Treasury bills	1,300
Interest, bonds issued by Ford Motor Company	1,500
Interest, bonds issued by City of Quebec, Canada	750
Disability insurance benefits	19,500
Distributions from qualified pension plan	5,400

76. Ken is 63 years old and unmarried. He retired at age 55 when he sold his business, Understock.com. Though Ken is retired, he is still very active. Ken reported the following financial information this year. *Assume* Ken files as a single taxpayer. Determine Ken's gross income and complete page 1 of Form 1040 for Ken.

tax forms

a) Ken won $1,200 in an illegal game of poker (the game was played in Utah, where gambling is illegal).

b) Ken sold 1,000 shares of stock for $32 a share. He inherited the stock two years ago. His tax basis (or investment) in the stock was $31 per share.

c) Ken received $25,000 from an annuity he purchased eight years ago. He purchased the annuity, to be paid annually for 20 years, for $210,000.

d) Ken received $13,000 in disability benefits for the year. He purchased the disability insurance policy last year.

e) Ken decided to go back to school to learn about European history. He received a $500 cash scholarship to attend. He used $300 to pay for his books and tuition, and he applied the rest toward his new car payment.

f) Ken's son, Mike, instructed his employer to make half of his final paycheck of the year payable to Ken as a gift from Mike to Ken. Ken received the check on December 30 in the amount of $1,100.

g) Ken received a $610 refund of the $3,600 in state income taxes his employer withheld from his pay last year. Ken claimed $6,350 in itemized deductions last year (the standard deduction for a single filer was $6,300).

h) Ken received $30,000 of interest from corporate bonds and money market accounts.

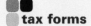

tax forms

77. Consider the following letter and answer Shady's question.

To my friendly student tax preparer:

Hello, my name is Shady Slim. I understand you are going to help me figure out my gross income for the year . . . whatever that means. It's been a busy year and I'm a busy man, so let me give you the lowdown on my life and you can do your thing.

I was unemployed at the beginning of the year and got $2,000 in unemployment compensation. I later got a job as a manager for Roca Cola. I earned $55,000 in base salary this year. My boss gave me a $5,000 Christmas bonus check on December 22. I decided to hold on to that check and not cash it until next year, so I won't have to pay taxes on it this year. Pretty smart, huh? My job's pretty cool. I get a lot of fringe benefits like a membership to the gym that costs $400 a year and all the Roca Cola I can drink, although I can't really drink a whole lot I figure $40 worth this year.

As part of my manager duties, I get to decide on certain things like contracts for the company. My good buddy, Eddie, runs a bottling company. I made sure that he won the bottling contract for Roca Cola for this year (even though his contract wasn't quite the best). Eddie bought me a Corvette this year for being such a good friend. The Corvette cost $50,000 and I'm sure he bought it for me out of the goodness of his heart. What a great guy!

Here's a bit of good luck for the year. Upon leaving my office one day, I found $8,000 lying in the street! Well, one person's bad luck is my good luck, right?

I like to gamble a lot. I won a $22,000 poker tournament in Las Vegas this year. I also won about $5,000 over the year playing the guys at our Friday night poker game. Can you believe that I didn't lose anything this year?

Speaking of the guys, one of them hit me with his car as we were leaving the game one night. He must have been pretty ticked that he lost! I broke my right leg and my left arm. I sued the guy and got $11,000 for my medical expenses, $3,000 to pay my psychotherapist for the emotional problems I had relating to the injuries (I got really depressed!), and I won $12,000 in punitive damages. That'll teach him that he's not so tough without his car!

Another bit of bad luck. My uncle Monty died this year. I really liked the guy, but the $200,000 inheritance I received from him made me feel a little better about the loss. I did the smart thing with the money and invested it in stocks and bonds and socked a little into my savings account. As a result, I received $600 in dividends from the stock, $200 in interest from the municipal bonds, and $300 in interest from my savings account.

My ex-wife, Alice, is still paying me alimony. She's a lawyer who divorced me a few years ago because I was "unethical" or something like that. Since she was making so much money and I was unemployed at the time, the judge ruled that she had to pay ME alimony. Isn't that something? She sent me $3,000 in alimony payments this year. She still kind of likes me, though. She sent me a check for $500 as a Christmas gift this year. I didn't get her anything, though.

So there you go. That's this year in a nutshell. Can you figure out my gross income and complete page 1 of Form 1040 for me? And since you're a student, this is free, right? Thanks, I owe you one! Let me know if I can get you a six-pack of Roca Cola or something.

tax forms

78. Diana and Ryan Workman were married on January 1 of last year. Diana has an eight-year-old son, Jorge, from her previous marriage. Ryan works as a computer programmer at Datafile Inc. (DI) earning a salary of $96,000. Diana is self-employed and runs a day care center. The Workmans reported the following financial information pertaining to their activities during the current year.

a) Ryan earned a $96,000 salary for the year.

b) Ryan borrowed $12,000 from DI to purchase a car. DI charged him 2 percent interest $240 on the loan, which Ryan paid on December 31. DI would have charged Ryan $720 if interest had been calculated at the applicable federal interest rate.

c) Diana received $2,000 in alimony and $4,500 in child support payments from her former husband.

d) Diana won a $900 cash prize at her church-sponsored Bingo game.

e) The Workmans received $500 of interest from corporate bonds and $250 of interest from a municipal bond. Diana owned these bonds before she married Ryan.

f) The couple bought 50 shares of ABC Inc. stock for $40 per share on July 2. The stock was worth $47 a share on December 31. The stock paid a dividend of $1.00 per share on December 1.

g) Diana's father passed away on April 14. She inherited cash of $50,000 from her father and his baseball card collection, valued at $2,000. As the beneficiary of her father's life insurance policy, Diana also received $150,000.

h) The couple spent a weekend in Atlantic City in November and came home with gross gambling winnings of $1,200.

i) Ryan received $400 cash for reaching 10 years of continuous service at DI.

j) Ryan was hit and injured by a drunk driver while crossing a street at a crosswalk. He was unable to work for a month. He received $6,000 from his disability insurance. DI paid the premiums for Ryan, but they reported the amount of the premiums as compensation to Ryan on his year-end W-2.

k) The drunk driver who hit Ryan in part (j) was required to pay his $2,000 medical costs, $1,500 for the emotional trauma he suffered from the accident, and $5,000 for punitive damages.

l) For meeting his performance goals this year, Ryan was informed on December 27 that he would receive a $5,000 year-end bonus. DI (located in Houston, Texas) mailed Ryan's bonus check from its payroll processing center (Tampa, Florida) on December 28. Ryan didn't receive the check at his home until January 2.

m) Diana is a 10 percent owner of MNO Inc., a Subchapter S corporation. The company reported ordinary business income for the year of $92,000. Diana acquired the MNO stock last year.

n) Diana's day care business collected $35,000 in revenues. In addition, customers owed her $3,000 at year-end. During the year, Diana spent $5,500 for supplies, $1,500 for utilities, $15,000 for rent, and $500 for miscellaneous expenses. One customer gave her use of his vacation home for a week (worth $2,500) in exchange for Diana allowing his child to attend the day care center free of charge. Diana accounts for her business activities using the cash method of accounting.

o) Ryan's employer pays the couple's annual health insurance premiums of $5,500 for a qualified plan.

Required:

A) Assuming the Workmans file a joint tax return, determine their gross income.

B) Using your answer in part A, complete page 1 of Form 1040 through line 22 for the Workmans.

C) Assuming the Workmans live in California, a community property state, and that Diana and Ryan file separately, what is Ryan's gross income?

D) Using your answer in part C, complete page 1 of Form 1040 through line 22 for Ryan Workman.

6 Individual Deductions

Learning Objectives

Upon completing this chapter, you should be able to:

LO 6-1 Identify the common deductions necessary for calculating adjusted gross income (AGI).

LO 6-2 Describe the different types of itemized deductions available to individuals and compute itemized deductions.

LO 6-3 Explain the operation of the standard deduction, determine the deduction for personal and dependency exemptions, and compute taxable income.

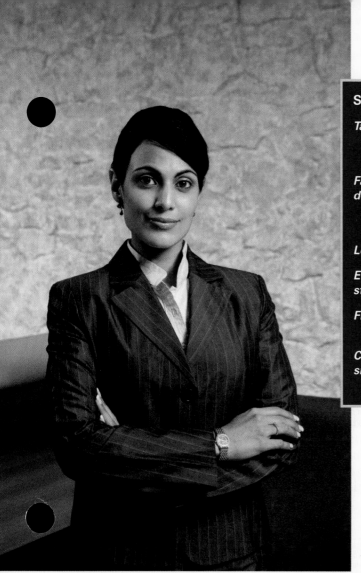

© Image Source

Storyline Summary

Taxpayers:	Courtney Wilson, age 40 Courtney's mother, Dorothy "Gram" Weiss, age 70
Family description:	Courtney is divorced with a son, Deron, age 10, and a daughter, Ellen, age 20. Gram is currently residing with Courtney. Ellen is currently a full-time student.
Location:	Kansas City, Missouri
Employment status:	Courtney works as an architect for EWD. Gram is retired.
Filing status:	Courtney files as head-of-household. Gram files as a single taxpayer.
Current situation:	Courtney and Gram are trying to determine their allowable deductions and compute taxable income.

Now that Courtney has determined her gross income, she still must determine her deductions to compute taxable income. Fortunately, Courtney keeps detailed records of all the expenditures she believes to be deductible. Besides expenses associated with her weekend consulting work and rental property, Courtney incurred some significant costs moving from Cincinnati to Kansas City. She also paid self-employment taxes on her consulting income and paid tuition for Ellen to attend summer school. Courtney is confident most of these items are deductible, but she isn't quite sure about the tuition.

Based on her review of prior-year tax returns, Courtney has a pretty good handle on her itemized deductions. She incurred some extra medical expenses to treat a broken wrist from a mountain biking accident and had additional state income taxes withheld from her paycheck. Courtney paid real estate taxes for her personal residence and investment property and interest expense on loans secured by her new home. She also donated (cash and property) to her favorite charities. Courtney experienced losses when her purse was stolen and when she damaged her car in an accident. She isn't sure if these losses are deductible.

In a push to improve her job performance, Courtney incurred costs to attend motivational seminars and travel to other parts of the country to study different architectural designs. Despite the fact that she was trying to improve her job performance, EWD did not reimburse her for these costs.

Gram wasn't as busy as Courtney this year. Gram paid a penalty for cashing in her certificate of deposit early. She also paid some medical expenses and donated money to her local church. Gram is a little frustrated because she doesn't incur enough itemized deductions to exceed the standard deduction amount. Gram recently heard that she might be able to save taxes by "bunching" her itemized deductions into one year. She's hoping to learn a little bit more about this technique. In any event, Gram didn't pay any taxes during the year and she wants to learn how much she's going to owe. ∎

In the previous chapter, we determined *gross income* for both Courtney and Gram. To compute their taxable income, however, we need to identify their deductions. As emphasized previously, taxpayers are not allowed to deduct expenditures unless there is a specific tax law authorizing the deductions. And as we learn in this chapter, Congress grants many deductions for taxpayers for a variety of reasons.

As we discussed in Chapter 4, deductions appear in one of two places in the individual income tax formula. Deductions "for AGI" (also called deductions "above the line") are subtracted directly from gross income.[1] Next, deductions "from AGI" (also called deductions "below the line" or "itemized" deductions) are subtracted directly from AGI, resulting in taxable income. Deductions for AGI are generally preferred over deductions from AGI because deductions above the line reduce taxable income dollar for dollar. In contrast, deductions from AGI sometimes have no effect on taxable income. Further, because many of the limitations on tax benefits for higher income taxpayers are based upon AGI, deductions for AGI often reduce these limitations thereby increasing potential tax benefits. Thus, it's important to determine both the amount of the deduction and whether it's a deduction *for* AGI or *from* AGI. We begin our discussion of deductions by describing deductions for AGI, and we conclude by tackling itemized deductions, the standard deduction, and exemptions.

LO 6-1 DEDUCTIONS FOR AGI

Congress allows taxpayers to claim a variety of deductions for AGI.[2] To provide an overview, we select a cross section of deductions for AGI and classify them into three categories:

1. Deductions *directly* related to **business activities.**
2. Deductions *indirectly* related to business activities.
3. Deductions subsidizing specific activities.

We've organized our discussion around these categories to illustrate the variety of deductions for AGI and explain why Congress provides preferential treatment for certain deductions.

Deductions Directly Related to Business Activities

As a matter of equity, Congress allows taxpayers involved in business activities to deduct expenses incurred to generate business income. That is, because taxpayers include the revenue they receive from doing business in gross income, they should be allowed to deduct against gross income the expenses they incur to generate those revenues.

To begin, we must define "business activities" and, for reasons we discuss below, we must distinguish business activities from **investment activities.** In general, for tax

---

[1]Most, but not all, deductions for AGI appear on lines 23 through 35 on page 1 of Form 1040. The term "above the line" refers to the placement of deductions for AGI before the last line of the first page of Form 1040. This last line is the taxpayer's AGI.

[2]§62 identifies deductions for AGI.

purposes activities are either *profit-motivated* or motivated by personal objectives. Profit-motivated activities are, in turn, classified as either (1) business activities or (2) investment activities. Business activities are sometimes referred to as a **trade or business,** and these activities require a relatively high level of involvement or effort. For example, if an individual is a full-time employee, the individual is in the business of being an employee. Self-employed individuals are also engaged in business activities. Unlike business activities, investment activities are profit-motivated activities that *don't* require a high degree of involvement or effort.[3] Instead, investment activities involve investing in property for appreciation or for income payments. An individual who occasionally buys land or stock in anticipation of appreciation or dividend payments would be engaged in an investment activity.

Example 6-1

Suppose that Courtney purchased a parcel of land for its appreciation potential. Would her ownership in the land be considered a business or investment activity?

Answer: Courtney's activity would most likely be considered an investment activity, because she acquired the land for its appreciation potential and she does not plan to exercise any special effort to develop the property or to become actively involved in other real estate speculation.

What if: Suppose that Courtney frequently buys and sells land or develops land to sell in small parcels to those wanting to build homes. Would Courtney's activity be considered a business or investment activity?

Answer: Courtney's activity would most likely be considered a business activity because she is actively involved in generating profits from the land by developing it rather than simply holding the land for appreciation.

The distinction between business and investment activities is critical for determining whether a deduction associated with the activity is above the line or below. With one exception, business expenses are deducted for AGI. The lone exception is unreimbursed employee business expenses, which are deductible as miscellaneous itemized deductions (from AGI deduction).[4] In contrast, investment expenses are deductible as itemized deductions, with one exception. Expenses associated with rental and royalty activities are deductible for AGI regardless of whether the activity qualifies as an investment or a business. Exhibit 6-1 summarizes the rules for classifying business and investment expenses as for and from AGI deductions.

EXHIBIT 6-1   **Individual Business and Investment Expense Deductions for AGI and from AGI**

Activity Type	Deduction for AGI	Deduction from AGI (itemized deduction)
Business activities	Self-employed business expenses	Unreimbursed employee business expenses
Investment activities	Rental and royalty expenses	Other investment expenses

[3]§162 authorizes trade or business expense deductions, while §212 authorizes deductions for investment activities. The distinction between these activities is discussed in Chapter 9.

[4]For example, an employee may use her own automobile to make a business delivery for her employer. The expenses she incurs to make the delivery (cost of operating the automobile and parking) are business expenses that are deducted from AGI as miscellaneous itemized deductions.

Trade or Business Expenses Congress limits business deductions to expenses directly related to the business activity and those that are **ordinary and necessary** for the activity.[5] This means that deductible expenses must be appropriate and helpful for generating a profit. Although business deductions are one of the most common deductions for AGI, they are not readily visible on the front page of Form 1040. Instead, these deductions are reported with business revenues on Schedule C of Form 1040. Schedule C, presented in Exhibit 6-2, is essentially an income statement for the business that identifies typical ordinary and necessary business expenses. Taxpayers transfer the *net* income or loss from Schedule C to Form 1040 (page 1), line 12.

EXHIBIT 6-2 **Parts I and II from Schedule C Profit or Loss from Business**

Part I **Income**

1	Gross receipts or sales. See instructions for line 1 and check the box if this income was reported to you on Form W-2 and the "Statutory employee" box on that form was checked . . . . ▶ ☐	1	
2	Returns and allowances	2	
3	Subtract line 2 from line 1	3	
4	Cost of goods sold (from line 42)	4	
5	**Gross profit.** Subtract line 4 from line 3	5	
6	Other income, including federal and state gasoline or fuel tax credit or refund (see instructions)	6	
7	**Gross income.** Add lines 5 and 6 . . . . ▶	7	

Part II **Expenses.** Enter expenses for business use of your home **only** on line 30.

8	Advertising	8		18	Office expense (see instructions)	18	
9	Car and truck expenses (see instructions).	9		19	Pension and profit-sharing plans .	19	
				20	Rent or lease (see instructions):		
10	Commissions and fees .	10		a	Vehicles, machinery, and equipment	20a	
11	Contract labor (see instructions)	11		b	Other business property . . .	20b	
12	Depletion	12		21	Repairs and maintenance . . .	21	
13	Depreciation and section 179 expense deduction (not included in Part III) (see instructions).	13		22	Supplies (not included in Part III) .	22	
				23	Taxes and licenses	23	
				24	Travel, meals, and entertainment:		
14	Employee benefit programs (other than on line 19) . .	14		a	Travel	24a	
15	Insurance (other than health)	15		b	Deductible meals and entertainment (see instructions) .	24b	
16	Interest:			25	Utilities	25	
a	Mortgage (paid to banks, etc.)	16a		26	Wages (less employment credits) .	26	
b	Other	16b		27a	Other expenses (from line 48) . .	27a	
17	Legal and professional services	17		b	**Reserved for future use** . . .	27b	
28	**Total expenses** before expenses for business use of home. Add lines 8 through 27a . . . . . . ▶		28				
29	Tentative profit or (loss). Subtract line 28 from line 7		29				

30	Expenses for business use of your home. Do not report these expenses elsewhere. Attach Form 8829 unless using the simplified method (see instructions). **Simplified method filers only:** enter the total square footage of: (a) your home: _____ and (b) the part of your home used for business: _____. Use the Simplified Method Worksheet in the instructions to figure the amount to enter on line 30	30	
31	**Net profit or (loss).** Subtract line 30 from line 29.		
	• If a profit, enter on both **Form 1040, line 12** (or Form 1040NR, line 13) and on **Schedule SE, line 2.** (If you checked the box on line 1, see instructions). Estates and trusts, enter on **Form 1041, line 3.** • If a loss, you **must** go to line 32.	31	
32	If you have a loss, check the box that describes your investment in this activity (see instructions).		
	• If you checked 32a, enter the loss on both **Form 1040, line 12,** (or **Form 1040NR, line 13**) and on **Schedule SE, line 2.** (If you checked the box on line 1, see the line 31 instructions). Estates and trusts, enter on **Form 1041, line 3.** • If you checked 32b, you **must** attach Form 6198. Your loss may be limited.	32a ☐ All investment is at risk. 32b ☐ Some investment is not at risk.	

For Paperwork Reduction Act Notice, see the separate instructions.   Cat. No. 11334P   Schedule C (Form 1040) 2015

Example 6-2

Besides being employed by EWD, Courtney is also a self-employed consultant (a business activity). This year her consulting activity generated $19,500 of revenue and incurred $1,500 in expenses (primarily travel and transportation expenses). How does she report the revenue and deductions from the activity?

Answer: Courtney reports the $19,500 of revenue and deducts the $1,500 of business expenses for AGI on her Schedule C. Her net income of $18,000 from her consulting activities is included on the front page (line 12) of her individual tax return.

---

[5]§162. In Chapter 9, we address the requirements for deductible business expenses in detail.

Rental and Royalty Expenses   Taxpayers are allowed to deduct their expenses associated with generating rental or royalty income for AGI.[6] Similar to business expenses, rental and royalty expenses do not appear directly on the front page of Form 1040. Instead, rental and royalty deductions are reported with rental and royalty revenues on Schedule E of Form 1040.[7] Schedule E, presented in Exhibit 6-3, is essentially an income statement for the taxpayer's rental or royalty activities. Taxpayers transfer the *net* income or loss from Schedule E to Form 1040 (page 1), line 17.

Rental and royalty endeavors are most commonly considered to be investment activities, but like trade or business expenses, rental and royalty deductions are claimed above the line.[8] Perhaps rental and royalty expenses are deductible for AGI because Congress believed that these activities usually require more taxpayer involvement than other types of investment activities. Despite this preferential treatment, the deductibility of rental losses (where expenses exceed income) are subject to limitations (basis, at-risk, and passive loss rules). We discuss these limitations in Chapter 7 when we discuss similar limitations that apply to investments in flow-through entities.

EXHIBIT 6-3   Page 1 of Schedule E Rental or Royalty Income

Income:	Properties:	A	B	C
3 Rents received	3			
4 Royalties received	4			
Expenses:				
5 Advertising	5			
6 Auto and travel (see instructions)	6			
7 Cleaning and maintenance	7			
8 Commissions	8			
9 Insurance	9			
10 Legal and other professional fees	10			
11 Management fees	11			
12 Mortgage interest paid to banks, etc. (see instructions)	12			
13 Other interest	13			
14 Repairs	14			
15 Supplies	15			
16 Taxes	16			
17 Utilities	17			
18 Depreciation expense or depletion	18			
19 Other (list) ▶	19			
20 Total expenses. Add lines 5 through 19	20			
21 Subtract line 20 from line 3 (rents) and/or 4 (royalties). If result is a (loss), see instructions to find out if you must file **Form 6198**	21			
22 Deductible rental real estate loss after limitation, if any, on **Form 8582** (see instructions)	22 ( )	( )	( )	( )
23a Total of all amounts reported on line 3 for all rental properties	23a			
b Total of all amounts reported on line 4 for all royalty properties	23b			
c Total of all amounts reported on line 12 for all properties	23c			
d Total of all amounts reported on line 18 for all properties	23d			
e Total of all amounts reported on line 20 for all properties	23e			
24 **Income.** Add positive amounts shown on line 21. **Do not** include any losses		24		
25 **Losses.** Add royalty losses from line 21 and rental real estate losses from line 22. Enter total losses here		25 (	)	
26 **Total rental real estate and royalty income or (loss).** Combine lines 24 and 25. Enter the result here. If Parts II, III, IV, and line 40 on page 2 do not apply to you, also enter this amount on Form 1040, line 17, or Form 1040NR, line 18. Otherwise, include this amount in the total on line 41 on page 2		26		

For Paperwork Reduction Act Notice, see the separate instructions.   Cat. No. 11344L   Schedule E (Form 1040) 2015

[6]§212(a)(4).

[7]Rental income and expenses for renting personal property (e.g., equipment, furniture, etc.) instead of real property is generally reported on Schedule C (not Schedule E). If the rental of personal property is not considered a trade or business, the rental income and expenses are reported on lines 21 and 36, respectively, of Form 1040.

[8]Royalties are received for allowing others to use property or rights to property. For example, royalties are paid for allowing others to use or sell copyrighted material such as books or plays, or extract natural resources from property. The amount of the royalty is often a percentage of total revenues derived from the property or rights to property.

Example 6-3

Courtney owns a condominium that she rents to tenants. This year she received $14,000 in rental revenue and incurred $9,000 of expenses associated with the rental, including management fees, maintenance, and depreciation. How does she report the revenue and expenses for tax purposes?

Answer: Courtney reports the $14,000 of rental receipts and deducts the $9,000 of rental expenses for AGI on Schedule E. The net rental income of $5,000 is reported on the front page (line 17) of her individual tax return.

Losses As we discuss in more detail in Chapter 11, taxpayers disposing of business assets at a loss are allowed to deduct the losses for AGI. Also, individual taxpayers selling investment (capital) assets at a loss are allowed to deduct the "capital" losses against other capital gains. If the capital losses exceed the capital gains, they can deduct up to $3,000 as a net capital loss in a particular year. Losses in excess of the $3,000 limit are carried forward indefinitely to subsequent years when they are deductible subject to the same limitations.

Flow-through Entities Income from flow-through entities such as partnerships, LLCs, and S corporations passes through to the owners of those entities and is reported on Schedule E of the tax returns of the owners. Similarly, any expenses and losses incurred by the entity pass through to the entity owners, who typically treat them as deductions for AGI, subject to certain restrictions (basis, at-risk, and passive loss rules) that we discuss in Chapter 7.

Deductions Indirectly Related to Business Activities

Taxpayers can incur expenses in activities that are not directly related to making money but that they would not have incurred if they were not involved in a business activity. Taxpayers are allowed to deduct several of these expenses that are indirectly related to business activities as deductions for AGI. We describe several of these deductions below.

Moving Expenses The cost of moving personal possessions is not a direct cost of doing business or being employed. Nonetheless, individuals qualify for a moving expense deduction if they move *and* change their principal place of work. Specifically, individuals can deduct moving expenses as deductions for AGI if they meet two tests: (1) a distance test and (2) a time test associated with the move.[9]

To satisfy the distance test, the distance from the taxpayer's old residence to the new place of work must be at least 50 miles more than the distance from the old residence to the old place of work. In other words, if the taxpayer were staying in her old home, the new place of work must increase her commute by at least 50 miles, thereby justifying a move to a new residence. To satisfy the time test, the taxpayer must either be employed full-time for 39 of the first 52 weeks after the move or be self-employed for 78 of the first 104 weeks after the move. A taxpayer can deduct moving expenses on her return if she expects to meet the time test but

---

[9]§217. Moving expenses are deducted on Form 3903.

has not yet done so at year-end. If the taxpayer later fails to meet the time test, she must either amend her prior return to eliminate the moving expense deduction or include the previous moving expense deduction as other income on her return in the year the time test was not met.

Individuals need not change employers if they meet both tests. Indeed, taxpayers can qualify for a moving expense deduction by beginning their first job, by beginning a job after a prolonged absence from the workforce, or by changing locations with the same employer. In addition, a taxpayer's reasons for moving may be entirely personal, such as wanting to move to a milder climate; business-related, such as wanting to change jobs or start a new business; or some of both.

Example 6-4

Before moving to Kansas City, Courtney lived in Cincinnati, Ohio, where she commuted 10 miles to her place of work. The distance from Courtney's home in Cincinnati to EWD in Kansas City, her new place of work, is 580 miles. Can Courtney deduct the expenses of moving her residence to Kansas City?

Answer: Yes. Courtney meets both the distance and the time tests because 580 miles is more than 60 miles (her original 10-mile commute from her former residence to her former place of work, plus 50 miles), and because she worked for EWD for the requisite 39 weeks during her first 52 weeks after her move (she worked from mid-January through December 31).

What if: Suppose that Courtney started a new job at an office just outside of Cincinnati and moved into a new residence. The distance from Courtney's former residence to her former place of work was 12 miles. The distance from Courtney's former residence to her new place of work is 55 miles. Does Courtney meet the distance test for moving expenses?

Answer: No, because if she had stayed in her former residence her commute would have increased by only 43 miles. To qualify, the commute from her former residence to her new work must be at least 50 miles longer than her commute from her former residence to her former place of work. Note that the location of her new residence is irrelevant to the distance test.

What if: Suppose that Courtney started a new job at an office just outside of Cincinnati and moved into a new residence. If the distance from Courtney's former residence to her former place of work was 12 miles, and the distance from her former residence to her new work place was 80 miles, would Courtney meet the distance test for moving expenses?

Answer: Yes, the commute from her former residence to her new job is 68 miles longer than the commute from her former residence to her old job.

Deductible moving expenses are limited to reasonable expenses associated with moving personal possessions and traveling to the new residence, including transportation and lodging. Taxpayers are allowed to deduct a mileage rate in lieu of the actual costs of driving their personal automobiles during the move. In 2016, taxpayers are allowed to deduct 19 cents a mile for driving their personal automobiles during a move. Taxpayers may also deduct the cost of moving their personal belongings and the belongings of members of their households. Taxpayers are *not* allowed to deduct costs such as meals during the move or costs associated with house-hunting trips. Taxpayers who are reimbursed by their employers for actual moving expenses exclude the reimbursement from income but do not deduct the reimbursed expenses. However, taxpayers who receive a flat amount as a moving allowance from their employers (i.e., without a requirement to document actual moving expenses to the employer) are required to include the allowance in gross income and can deduct their actual moving expenses for AGI.

THE KEY FACTS

Moving Expenses

- Deductible for AGI for individuals who pass a mileage test and a time test.
- Mileage test: New job site must extend existing commute by at least 50 miles.
- Time test: Taxpayer must be employed at least 39 of 52 weeks or be self-employed for 78 of the 104 weeks following the move.

Example 6-5

Courtney drove 691 miles in her move from Cincinnati to Kansas City and incurred the following expenses related to the move:

Description	Amount
Moving company (personal belongings)	$5,000
Lodging (one night en route)	165
Meals en route	75
House-hunting trip	520

What amount can Courtney deduct as moving expenses?

Answer: Courtney can deduct $5,296 computed as follows:

Description	Deduction
Transportation (19¢ per mile times 691 miles)	$ 131
Moving company (personal belongings)	5,000
Lodging (one night en route)	165
Total deduction	**$5,296**

The meals and house-hunting are not deductible.

What if: Suppose that EWD agreed to reimburse Courtney for moving expenses up to a maximum of $2,000. What amount would Courtney deduct for moving expenses?

Answer: $3,296. Courtney would deduct $3,296 in moving expenses ($5,296 minus $2,000 reimbursement). She would not include the reimbursement in income and would not deduct the $2,000 of expenses for which she was reimbursed.

Health Insurance Deduction by Self-Employed Taxpayers   The cost of health insurance is essentially a personal expense. However, *employers* often pay a portion of health insurance premiums for employees as a qualified fringe benefit. Employers are allowed to deduct health insurance premiums as compensation expense while employees are allowed to *exclude* these premiums from gross income. In contrast to employees, the health insurance fringe benefit does not apply to self-employed taxpayers because they are not "employees." To provide equitable treatment, Congress allows self-employed taxpayers to claim personal health insurance premiums for the taxpayer, the taxpayer's spouse, the taxpayer's dependents, and taxpayer's children under age 27 (regardless of whether or not the child is a dependent of the taxpayer) as deductions for AGI, but only to the extent of the self-employment income derived from the specific trade or business.[10]

This deduction is intended to help self-employed taxpayers who must pay their own insurance premiums. Consequently, self-employed taxpayers are *not* allowed to deduct health care insurance premiums if the taxpayer is *eligible* to participate in an employer-provided health plan. This restriction applies regardless of whether the health plan is sponsored by either an employer of the taxpayer or an employer of the taxpayer's spouse, and it is irrelevant whether the taxpayer actually participates in the plan.[11]

---

[10] §162(l). As we'll explain shortly, health insurance premiums also qualify as itemized deductions as medical expenses, but itemizing these deductions may not produce any tax benefits. To the extent that self-employed taxpayers do not have sufficient self-employment income to deduct all of their health insurance premiums as a for AGI deduction, they may deduct the remaining premiums as an itemized deduction. Finally, subject to certain restrictions, self-employed taxpayers who purchase health insurance through an exchange, have household incomes below 400% of the poverty line, and are not eligible for affordable coverage through an employer health plan that provides at least 60% of the expected costs for covered services can receive a premium tax credit under §36B. Any premiums offset by the tax credit cannot be deducted as either a for AGI or itemized deduction.

[11] §162(l)(2)(B).

Self-Employment Tax Deduction   Employees and employers each pay Social Security and Medicare tax on employee salaries. Employers deduct the Social Security and Medicare taxes they pay on employee salaries. In contrast, because self-employed individuals do not have an employer, these individuals are required to pay self-employment tax. This tax represents both the employee's *and* the employer's share of the Social Security and Medicare taxes. Unfortunately for the self-employed, the self-employment tax is *not* considered a business expense. To put self-employed individuals on somewhat equal footing with other employers who are allowed to deduct the *employer's* share of the Social Security and Medicare taxes, self-employed taxpayers are allowed to deduct the employer portion of the self-employment tax they pay.

Example 6-6

As we indicated in Example 6-2, Courtney reported $18,000 of net income from her self-employed consulting activities. She paid $482 in self-employment taxes on this income, with $241 representing the employer portion of the self-employment tax.[12] What amount of self-employment tax can she deduct this year?

Answer: $241 (the employer portion of the self-employment tax).

Penalty for Early Withdrawal of Savings   This provision allows a deduction for AGI for any interest income an individual forfeits to a bank as a penalty for prematurely withdrawing a certificate of deposit or similar deposit. This deduction reduces the taxpayer's net interest income to the amount she actually received. Otherwise, taxpayers would be required to report the full amount of interest income as taxable income and could deduct only the forfeited interest as an investment-expense miscellaneous itemized deduction. As we discuss below, investment expenses deducted as miscellaneous itemized deductions are subject to limitations that substantially reduce their tax benefits.

Example 6-7

Gram invested $100,000 in a three-year certificate of deposit (CD). On December 31, she decided to cash out the certificate of deposit after holding it for less than a year. She receives the $4,100 of interest income the CD had generated up to the withdrawal date, less a $410 early withdrawal penalty. How will Gram report the interest and early withdrawal for tax purposes?

Answer: Gram reports $4,100 as interest income this year and deducts the $410 early withdrawal penalty as a deduction for AGI.

Deductions Subsidizing Specific Activities

To address specific policy objectives, Congress provides that certain expenditures are deductible for AGI. For example, alimony payments are deductible for AGI to maintain equity and contributions to retirement savings are deductible for AGI to encourage savings.[13] Further, Congress created two important deductions for AGI to encourage and subsidize higher education. Taxpayers are allowed to deduct for AGI, subject to certain limitations, (1) interest expense on **qualified educational loans** and (2) **qualified educational expenses.**[14] As we discuss throughout the text, Congress has

---

[12]In this case, Courtney uses the following equation to determine her total self-employment tax $18,000 × .9235 × .029 (Courtney's business income is subject to the Medicare tax but not the Social Security tax due to the level of her salary). Of the total self-employment tax, the employer portion is calculated as $18,000 × .9235 × .0145 = $241. We discuss how to compute the self-employment tax in detail in Chapter 8.

[13]See Chapter 5 for detailed discussion of alimony and Chapter 13 for detailed discussion of the tax consequences of retirement savings.

[14]See §221 and §222.

also created a number of related provisions, including education tax credits, to encourage and subsidize higher education.

Deduction for Interest on Qualified Education Loans   Qualified education loans are loans whose proceeds are used to pay qualified education expenses.[15] Qualified education expenses encompass expenses paid for the education of the taxpayer, the taxpayer's spouse, or a taxpayer's dependent to attend a postsecondary institution of higher education.[16] These expenses include tuition and fees, books and expenses required for enrollment, room and board, and other necessary supplies and expenses including travel.

The deduction for interest expense on qualified education loans is the amount of interest paid up to $2,500. However, the deduction is reduced (phased-out) for taxpayers depending on the taxpayer's filing status and **modified AGI.** Modified AGI for this purpose is AGI *before* deducting interest expense on the qualified education loans and *before* deducting qualified education expenses (discussed below). Married individuals who file separately are not allowed to deduct this expense under any circumstance. The deduction limitations for other taxpayers are summarized in Exhibit 6-4 as follows:

EXHIBIT 6-4   Summary of Limitations on Deduction of Interest on Education Loans

Panel A: AGI Limitations	
Modified AGI Level	**Deduction**
Not over $65,000 ($130,000 for married filing jointly)	Amount paid up to $2,500
Above $65,000 ($130,000 for married filing jointly) but below $80,000 ($160,000 for married filing jointly)	Amount paid up to $2,500 reduced by the phase-out amount. The phase-out amount is the amount paid up to $2,500 times the phase-out percentage (see Panel B for the phase-out percentage computation).
Equal to or above $80,000 ($160,000 for married filing jointly)	Zero

Panel B: Phase-Out Percentage*	
Filing Status	**Phase-out Percentage**
Single or head of household	(Modified AGI − $65,000)/$15,000
Married filing jointly	(Modified AGI − $130,000)/$30,000

*Married taxpayers filing separately are ineligible for the deduction.

Example 6-8

What if: Assume that Courtney's brother Jason paid interest on a qualified education loan that he used to pay the tuition and fees for his three daughters to attend State University. In 2016, Jason was married and filed a joint return, paid $2,000 of interest expense on the loan, and reported modified AGI of $142,000. What amount of interest expense on the education loan is Jason allowed to deduct as a for AGI deduction?

---

[15]Home equity loans cannot qualify as education loans regardless of how the loan proceeds are spent.

[16]Postsecondary education includes courses at a university, college, or vocational school including internship programs leading to a degree or certificate. Qualifying costs claimed as deductions for AGI cannot be reimbursed by scholarships or Coverdell education savings accounts and are also ineligible for American opportunity and lifetime learning credit purposes.

Answer: $1,200, computed as follows:

Description	Amount	Explanation
(1) Modified AGI	$142,000	AGI before higher education deductions.
(2) Amount of interest paid up to $2,500	2,000	Lesser of amount paid ($2,000) or $2,500.
(3) Phase-out (reduction) percentage	40%	[(1) − $130,000]/30,000).
(4) Phase-out amount (reduction in maximum)	800	(2) × (3).
Deductible interest expense	$ 1,200	(2) − (4).

Deduction for Qualified Education Expenses This deduction subsidizes tuition payments for higher education. For purposes of this deduction, qualified education expenses are limited to the tuition and fees required for enrollment at a postsecondary institution of higher education. Thus, the definition of qualifying expenses is more restrictive for the qualified education expense deduction than it is for the education loan interest expense deduction. However, similar to the education interest expense deduction, the amount of the maximum education expense deduction depends on filing status and level of modified AGI. For purposes of the qualified education expense deduction, modified AGI is AGI *after* deducting the education loan interest expense but *before* deducting qualified education expenses. Just as with the qualified education loan interest deduction, married individuals filing separately are ineligible for the qualified education expense deduction. The rules for determining the allowable education expense deduction for taxpayers who qualify for the deduction are summarized in Exhibit 6-5.[17]

EXHIBIT 6-5 **Summary of 2016 Limitations on Qualified Education Expenses**

Modified AGI Level	Deduction
Not over $65,000 ($130,000 for married filing jointly)	Amount paid up to $4,000
Above $65,000 ($130,000 for married filing jointly) but less than or equal to $80,000 ($160,000)	Lesser of amount paid or $2,000
Above 80,000 ($160,000 for married filing jointly)	Zero

A taxpayer generally may only deduct the qualified education expenses that he or she pays. To deduct a dependent's education expense, the taxpayer must actually pay the expense and claim the student as a dependent. If a student pays his or her own education expenses and is eligible to be claimed as another taxpayer's dependent, no taxpayer (including the dependent) may deduct the education expense. In contrast, if another taxpayer pays a student's education expenses and the student is not considered the taxpayer's dependent, the payment of the student's education expense is considered a gift and the student can deduct the expenses.

There are two important differences between the AGI limits on the interest on education loans deduction (summarized in Exhibit 6-4) and the AGI limits on the educational expense deduction (summarized in Exhibit 6-5). First, the definition of modified AGI for qualified education expenses in Exhibit 6-5 includes the deduction for interest on education loans. Second, the interest expense on education loans is phased out gradually over a range of AGI but the deduction for qualified education expenses is phased out in specific AGI increments (the phase-out applies in steps).

[17]The deduction for qualified education expenses is scheduled to expire after 2016.

Example 6-9

Courtney paid $2,100 of tuition for Ellen to attend the University of Missouri–Kansas City during the summer. How much of this payment can Courtney deduct as a qualifying education expense?

Answer: None. The cost of the tuition is a qualified education expense, but Courtney's modified AGI exceeds $80,000. (Courtney files as a head of household.) Hence, Courtney is not allowed to deduct any of the cost of the tuition she paid for Ellen.

What if: Assume the same facts except that Courtney is married filing jointly and her modified AGI is $57,000. What amount can Courtney deduct as a qualifying education expense in this situation?

Answer: $2,100. She can deduct the full amount of the expenditure (limited to $4,000) because she is married filing jointly and her modified AGI is less than $130,000.

What if: Assume the original facts except that Courtney's modified AGI is $77,000. How much of the $2,100 tuition for Ellen would Courtney be allowed to deduct as a *for AGI* qualified education expense?

Answer: $2,000. Because Courtney's AGI is greater than $65,000 but not greater than $80,000 (she files as head of household) her deduction is the lesser of (1) her actual qualified education expenditures and (2) $2,000. Since Courtney's actual education expenditures were $2,100, her deduction is $2,000.

Because there are several education-related tax incentives, individuals can sometimes select among different tax benefits. For example, certain education expenses that qualify as deductions for AGI may also qualify for an education tax credit (see Chapter 8) or employee business expenses (deductible as miscellaneous itemized deductions discussed later in the chapter). Likewise, as shown in Chapter 5, up to $5,250 of education expenses paid by an employer's educational assistance program may be excluded from an employee's gross income (but not deducted or claimed as a credit by the employee). Typically, a single expenditure *cannot* generate multiple tax benefits. Consequently, individuals should select the tax provision to apply to the expenses that generates the most benefit.

Summary: Deductions for AGI

Business expenses and rental and royalty expenses are two of the most important deductions for AGI. There are other important deductions for AGI that are indirectly related to business or provided to subsidize certain activities. After we have determined the deductions for AGI, we can compute AGI. Exhibits 6-6 and 6-7 summarize the computation of AGI for Courtney and Gram. Exhibit 6-8 shows Courtney's AGI calculation as presented on the front page of her Form 1040.

EXHIBIT 6-6   Courtney's Adjusted Gross Income

Description	Amount	Reference
Gross income for current year	$178,037	Exhibit 5-4.
Deductions for AGI:		
Business expenses	(1,500)	Example 6-2.
Rental expenses	(9,000)	Example 6-3.
Moving expenses	(5,296)	Example 6-5.
Employer-portion of self-employment taxes	(241)	Example 6-6.
Adjusted gross income	**$162,000**	

EXHIBIT 6-7   Gram's Adjusted Gross Income

Description	Amount	Reference
Gross income for current year	$16,000	Exhibit 5-6.
Deduction for AGI:		
Penalty for early withdrawal of savings	(410)	Example 6-7.
Adjusted gross income	**$15,590**	

EXHIBIT 6-8   Courtney's AGI Computation on Form 1040, Page 1

			Amount
Income	7	Wages, salaries, tips, etc. Attach Form(s) W-2	122,800
	8a	Taxable interest. Attach Schedule B if required	617
Attach Form(s) W-2 here. Also attach Forms W-2G and 1099-R if tax was withheld.	b	Tax-exempt interest. Do not include on line 8a **8b** 500	
	9a	Ordinary dividends. Attach Schedule B if required	700
	b	Qualified dividends **9b** 700	
	10	Taxable refunds, credits, or offsets of state and local income taxes	420
	11	Alimony received	20,000
If you did not get a W-2, see instructions.	12	Business income or (loss). Attach Schedule C or C-EZ	18,000
	13	Capital gain or (loss). Attach Schedule D if required. If not required, check here ▶ ☐	
	14	Other gains or (losses). Attach Form 4797	
	15a	IRA distributions **15a** b Taxable amount	
	16a	Pensions and annuities **16a** b Taxable amount	
	17	Rental real estate, royalties, partnerships, S corporations, trusts, etc. Attach Schedule E	5,000
	18	Farm income or (loss). Attach Schedule F	
	19	Unemployment compensation	
	20a	Social security benefits **20a** b Taxable amount	
	21	Other income. List type and amount	
	22	Combine the amounts in the far right column for lines 7 through 21. This is your **total income** ▶	167,537
Adjusted Gross Income	23	Educator expenses **23**	
	24	Certain business expenses of reservists, performing artists, and fee-basis government officials. Attach Form 2106 or 2106-EZ **24**	
	25	Health savings account deduction. Attach Form 8889 **25**	
	26	Moving expenses. Attach Form 3903 **26** 5,296	
	27	Deductible part of self-employment tax. Attach Schedule SE **27** 241	
	28	Self-employed SEP, SIMPLE, and qualified plans **28**	
	29	Self-employed health insurance deduction **29**	
	30	Penalty on early withdrawal of savings **30**	
	31a	Alimony paid b Recipient's SSN ▶ **31a**	
	32	IRA deduction **32**	
	33	Student loan interest deduction **33**	
	34	Tuition and fees. Attach Form 8917 **34**	
	35	Domestic production activities deduction. Attach Form 8903 **35**	
	36	Add lines 23 through 35	5,537
	37	Subtract line 36 from line 22. This is your **adjusted gross income** ▶	162,000

For Disclosure, Privacy Act, and Paperwork Reduction Act Notice, see separate instructions.   Cat. No. 11320B   Form **1040** (2015)

Once we have determined AGI, we calculate taxable income by identifying deductions *from* AGI. These deductions consist of (1) the greater of itemized deductions or the standard deduction and (2) personal and dependency exemption deductions. We address itemized deductions next.

DEDUCTIONS FROM AGI: ITEMIZED DEDUCTIONS   LO 6-2

There is a variety of itemized deductions, a few of which relate to profit-motivated activities (employee business expenses and investment expenses that are unrelated to rental or royalty activities). Many itemized deductions are personal in nature but are allowed to subsidize desirable activities such as home ownership and charitable giving. Other itemized deductions, such as medical expenses and casualty losses, provide relief for taxpayers whose ability to pay taxes has been involuntarily reduced. We discuss itemized deductions in the order they appear on the individual tax return, Form 1040, Schedule A.

Medical Expenses

The medical expense deduction is designed to provide relief for taxpayers whose ability to pay taxes is seriously hindered by health-related circumstances. Qualifying medical expenses include any payments for the care, prevention, diagnosis, or cure of injury, disease, or bodily function that are not reimbursed by health insurance or are not paid for through a "flexible spending account."[18] Taxpayers may also deduct medical expenses incurred to treat their spouses and their dependents.[19] Common medical expenses include

- Prescription medication, insulin, and medical aids such as eyeglasses, contact lenses, and wheelchairs. Over-the-counter medicines are generally not deductible.

[18]Taxpayers participating in flexible spending accounts are allowed to direct that a fixed amount of their salary be placed in an account to pay for medical expenses. The salary paid into these accounts is excluded from gross income and used to pay for medical expenses. See Chapter 12.

[19]For the purpose of deducting medical expenses, a dependent need not meet the gross income test [§213(a)], and a child of divorced parents is considered a dependent of both parents [§213(d)(5)]. We discuss the general requirements for dependency in Chapter 4.

- Payments to medical care *providers* such as doctors, dentists, and nurses and medical care *facilities* such as hospitals.
- Transportation for medical purposes.
- Long-term care facilities.
- Health insurance premiums (if not deducted for AGI by self-employed taxpayers) and insurance for long-term care services.[20],[21]

Example 6-10

In April, Courtney broke her wrist in a mountain biking accident. She paid $2,000 for a visit to the hospital emergency room and follow-up visits with her doctor. While she recuperated, Courtney paid $300 for prescription medicine and $700 to a therapist for rehabilitation. Courtney's insurance reimbursed her $1,840 for these expenses. What is the amount of Courtney's qualifying medical expenses?

Answer: $1,160, computed as follows:

Description	Deduction
Emergency room and doctor visits	$2,000
Prescription medication	300
Physical therapy	700
Total qualifying medical expenses	$3,000
Less insurance reimbursement	−1,840
Qualifying medical expenses from the accident	**$1,160**

Medical expenses for cosmetic surgery or other similar procedures are not deductible unless the surgery or procedure is necessary to ameliorate a deformity arising from, or directly related to, a congenital abnormality, a personal injury resulting from an accident or trauma, or disfiguring disease.[22]

TAXES IN THE REAL WORLD Are Discretionary Medical Expenses Deductible?

While cosmetic surgery is generally not deductible, discretionary medical costs may be deducted where the procedure affects the structure or function of the body. Take, for example, procedures that facilitate pregnancy by overcoming infertility. In IRS Letter Ruling 200318017, the IRS ruled that egg donor fees and expenses related to obtaining a willing donor, paid by a taxpayer who could not conceive using her own eggs, qualified as deductible medical expenses because they were incurred in preparation of the taxpayer's medical procedure (the implantation of a donated egg). Deductible expenses included the donor's fee for her time and expense in following the procedures to ensure successful egg retrieval, the agency's fee for procuring the donor and coordinating the transaction, expenses for medical and psychological testing and assistance of the donor before and after the procedure, and legal fees for preparing a contract between the taxpayer and the donor.

What about the same type of expenses paid by a single male to father a child through a surrogate? Are those expenses deductible? No, because in that situation, the expenses are not related to an underlying medical condition or defect of the taxpayer nor are they affecting any structure or function of his body. See *William Magdalin,* TC Memo 2008-293.

---

[20]This includes the annual cost of Medicare and prescription insurance withheld from Social Security recipient's benefits checks.

[21]The portion of any premiums for health insurance purchased through an exchange and offset by a premium tax credit under §36B is not deductible as an itemized deduction.

[22]§213(d)(9)(A).

Transportation and Travel for Medical Purposes   Taxpayers traveling for the primary purpose of receiving essential and deductible medical care may deduct the cost of lodging while away from home overnight (with certain restrictions) and transportation.[23] Taxpayers using personal automobiles for medical transportation purposes may deduct a standard mileage allowance in lieu of actual costs. For 2016, the mileage rate is 19 cents a mile.

Example 6-11

Gram drove Courtney, *in Courtney's car,* 110 miles back and forth from the doctor's office and the physical therapist's facility during the period Courtney was being treated for her broken wrist. What is the amount of Courtney's qualifying medical expense for her trips to the doctor's office?

Answer: $21 (110 × $0.19, rounded).

Hospitals and Long-Term Care Facilities   Taxpayers may deduct the cost of meals and lodging at hospitals. However, the cost of meals and lodging at other types of facilities such as nursing homes are deductible only when the principal purpose for the stay is medical care rather than convenience.[24] Of course, taxpayers may deduct the costs of actual medical care whether the care is provided at hospitals or other long-term care facilities.

Example 6-12

Gram considered moving into a long-term care facility before she decided she would move in with Courtney. The facility was not primarily for medical care and would have cost Gram $36,000 a year. During discussions with facility administrators, Gram learned that typically 20 percent of the total cost for the facility is allocable to medical care. If Gram were to stay in the facility for an entire year, what amount of the long-term care costs would qualify as a medical expense for Gram?

Answer: $7,200 ($36,000 × 20% allocable to medical care).

Medical Expense Deduction Limitation   The deduction for medical expenses is limited to the amount of unreimbursed qualifying medical expenses paid during the year (no matter when the services were provided) *reduced* by 10 percent of the taxpayer's AGI. If a taxpayer or his or her spouse is age 65 or older at the end of the tax year, the 10 percent AGI floor is reduced to 7.5 percent of AGI through 2016. This restriction is called a **floor limitation** because it eliminates any deduction for amounts below the floor. The purpose of a floor limitation is to restrict a deduction to taxpayers with substantial qualifying expenses. Because this floor limitation is set at a high percentage of AGI, unreimbursed medical expenses rarely produce tax benefits, especially for high income taxpayers.

---

[23]The cost of travel for and essential to medical care, including lodging (with certain limitations) is also deductible if the expense is not extravagant and the travel has no significant element of personal pleasure. However, under §213(d)(2) the deduction for the cost of lodging is limited to $50 per night per individual.

[24]Taxpayers may deduct the cost of long-term care facilities if they are chronically ill under a prescribed plan of care. A taxpayer is deemed to be chronically ill, generally, if she or he cannot perform at least two daily living tasks (eating, bathing, dressing, toileting, transferring, continence) for 90 days or more. §7702B. Taxpayers may also deduct long-term care insurance premiums, which are limited annually based on the age of the taxpayer.

Example 6-13

This year Courtney incurred $2,400 in unreimbursed qualifying medical expenses (including the $1,160 of qualifying medical expenses associated with the accident and the $21 transportation deduction for mileage). Given that Courtney's AGI is $162,000, what is the amount of Courtney's itemized medical expense deduction?

Answer: $0 computed as follows:

Description	Expense
Total unreimbursed qualifying medical expenses	$ 2,400
Minus: 10% of AGI ($162,000 × 10%)	(16,200)
Medical expense itemized deduction	**$ 0**

What if: What amount of medical expenses would Courtney be allowed to deduct if her AGI was $20,000?

Answer: $400, computed as follows:

Description	Expense
Total unreimbursed qualifying medical expenses	$ 2,400
Minus: 10% of AGI ($20,000 × 10%)	(2,000)
Medical expense itemized deduction	**$ 400**

Taxes

Individuals may deduct as itemized deductions payments made during the year for the following taxes:

- State, local, and foreign *income* taxes, including state and local taxes paid during the year through employer withholding, estimated tax payments, and overpayments on the prior year return that the taxpayer applies to the current year (the taxpayer asks the state to keep the overpayment rather than refund it).
- Real estate taxes on property held for personal or investment purposes.
- Personal property taxes that are assessed on the *value* of the specific property.[25]

Taxpayers may elect to deduct state and local sales taxes *instead* of deducting state and local income taxes. This election is particularly advantageous for taxpayers in states that don't have an individual state income tax.[26]

Example 6-14

During the year, Courtney paid $6,700 of state income taxes through withholding from her paycheck. She also paid $2,700 of real estate taxes on her personal residence and $980 of real estate taxes on an investment property she owns in Oklahoma. Finally, Courtney paid $180 as a registration fee for her automobile (the fee is based on the year the automobile was manufactured, not its value). What amount of these payments can Courtney deduct as itemized deductions?

---

[25]§164.

[26]The deduction can be based upon either the amount paid or the amount published in the IRS tables (IRS Publication 600) based upon the state of residence, income, and number of exemptions. The states with no income tax are Alaska, Florida, Nevada, South Dakota, Texas, Washington, and Wyoming. Tennessee and New Hampshire have no state income tax on wages, but do impose a tax on unearned income.

Answer: $10,380 ($6,700 state taxes + $2,700 real estate taxes on residence + $980 real estate taxes on investment property). Courtney is not allowed to deduct the registration fee for her car because the fee is not based on the value of the automobile.

What if: Suppose that on April 1, 2016, Courtney filed her 2015 state tax return and was due a refund from the state in the amount of $420. However, Courtney elected to have the state keep the overpayment and apply it to her 2016 tax payments. What amount of state income taxes is Courtney allowed to deduct as an itemized deduction in 2016?

Answer: $7,120 ($6,700 withholding + $420 overpayment applied to 2016). The treatment of the overpayment is the same as if Courtney had received the refund in 2016 and then remitted it to the state as payment of 2016 taxes. Because she paid the tax in 2016, she is allowed to deduct the tax in 2016. Recall that under the tax benefit rule (see Chapter 5), Courtney was required to include the $420 in her 2016 gross income.

Interest

There are two itemized deductions for interest expense.[27] First, subject to limitations described in more detail in Chapter 14, individuals can deduct interest paid on acquisition indebtedness and home-equity indebtedness secured by a qualified residence (the taxpayer's principal residence and one other residence).[28] Acquisition indebtedness is any debt secured by a qualified residence that is incurred in acquiring, constructing, or substantially improving the residence.[29] Home-equity indebtedness is any other debt secured by the taxpayer's qualified residence. Two rules limit the mortgage interest deduction: (1) Taxpayers may only deduct mortgage interest on up to $1,000,000 of acquisition indebtedness and (2) The amount of qualified home-equity indebtedness is limited to the *lesser* of (a) the fair market value of the qualified residence(s) in excess of the acquisition debt related to the residence(s) (determined when the home-equity loan is executed) and (b) $100,000 ($50,000 for married filing separately). In combination, these limitations allow taxpayers to deduct interest on up to $100,000 of home-equity debt (no matter what the taxpayer does with the proceeds from the home-equity loan) plus interest on up to $1,000,000 acquisition debt.[30]

As we discuss in more detail in Chapter 7, individuals can also deduct interest paid on loans used to purchase investment assets such as stocks, bonds, or land (investment interest expense). The deduction of investment interest is limited to a taxpayer's net investment income (investment income minus investment expenses). Any investment interest in excess of the net investment income limitation carries forward to the subsequent year. Taxpayers are not allowed to deduct interest on personal credit card debt or on loans to acquire (and secured by) personal-use automobiles.

---

[27]Interest paid on loans where the proceeds are used in a trade or business is fully deductible as a business expense deduction for AGI.

[28]In Chapter 8, we note that interest expense on home-equity loans not used to purchase or substantially improve the home is not deductible for AMT purposes.

[29]Subject to rules discussed in Chapter 14, points paid on indebtedness incurred in acquiring a home are also generally deductible as mortgage interest expense in the year the loan originates and points to refinance a home mortgage are typically amortized and deducted over the life of the loan (but see research memo in Chapter 2 for an exception).

[30]Taxpayers can also deduct premiums paid or accrued on mortgage insurance (insurance premiums paid by the borrower to protect the lender against the borrower defaulting on the loan) as qualified residence interest expense. The deduction for mortgage insurance premiums is scheduled to expire after 2016.

Example 6-15

Courtney acquired her home in Kansas City in January of this year for $300,000 (also its value throughout the year). She purchased it by paying $40,000 as a down payment and borrowing $260,000 from a credit union. Her home is the collateral for the loan. During the year, Courtney paid $15,800 in interest on the loan. How much of this interest may Courtney deduct?

Answer: $15,800. Because Courtney's home mortgage is secured by her home, she is allowed to deduct the interest expense on the home as an itemized deduction.

What if: Suppose Courtney paid $3,000 in interest this year on a $60,000 home-equity loan. When Courtney secured the home-equity loan her house was worth $450,000 and her acquisition indebtedness was $250,000. How much of the $3,000 interest is deductible?

Answer: $3,000. Because the $60,000 home-equity loan does not exceed the lesser of (a) the fair market value of the residence in excess of the acquisition debt ($450,000 − $250,000 = $200,000) or (b) $100,000, Courtney may deduct the $3,000 interest paid.

What if: Suppose Courtney paid $6,000 in interest this year on a $120,000 home-equity loan (the average balance for the year). When Courtney secured the home-equity loan her house was worth $450,000 and her acquisition indebtedness was $250,000. How much of the $6,000 interest is deductible?

Answer: $5,000. Courtney is limited to deducting interest on $100,000 of the home-equity debt, which is the lesser of (a) the fair market value of the residence in excess of the acquisition debt ($450,000 − $250,000 = $200,000) or (b) $100,000. The deductible interest on the home-equity debt is calculated as: $6,000 interest paid × ($100,000 home-equity limit/$120,000 home-equity debt) = $5,000.

What if: Suppose that Courtney borrowed $26,000 to purchase a new car (the loan was secured by the car). Would she be allowed to deduct the interest on the loan?

Answer: No, the loan was not used to purchase a personal residence or investment assets.

Charitable Contributions

Congress encourages donations to charities by allowing taxpayers to deduct contributions of money and other property to *qualified* domestic charitable organizations. Qualifying charitable organizations include organizations that engage in educational, religious, scientific, governmental, and other public activities.[31] Political and campaign contributions are not deductible even though they arguably indirectly support the government (contributions to which are generally deductible).

Example 6-16

This year Courtney donated $1,700 to the Red Cross. She also gave $200 in cash to various homeless people she met on the streets during the year. What amount of these donations is Courtney allowed to deduct as a charitable contribution?

Answer: $1,700. Because the Red Cross is a public charity recognized by the IRS, Courtney may deduct her $1,700 charitable contribution to it as an itemized deduction. However, despite Courtney's charitable intent, her donations to the homeless are not deductible as charitable contributions because individuals do not qualify as charitable organizations.

What if: Suppose that instead of transferring cash to homeless people on the streets, Courtney donated $200 cash to a local food bank that is listed in the IRS Exempt Organizations Select Check as a qualified charity. The food bank provides meals to those in need. Would Courtney be allowed to deduct this contribution?

Answer: Yes, because the food bank is a qualified charity.

---

[31]§170(c). The IRS Exempt Organizations Select Check (http://www.irs.gov/Charities-&-Non-Profits/Exempt-Organizations-Select-Check) lists the organizations that the IRS has determined to be qualified charities.

The *amount* of the charitable contribution deduction depends on whether the taxpayer contributes money or other property to the charity. Note that in virtually all circumstances, donations are only deductible if the contribution is substantiated by written records.[32]

Contributions of Money Cash contributions are deductible in the year paid, including donations of cash or by check, electronic funds transfers, credit card charges, and payroll deductions.[33] Taxpayers are also considered as making monetary contributions for the cost of transportation and travel for charitable purposes if there is no significant element of pleasure or entertainment in the travel. When taxpayers use their personal vehicles for charitable transportation purposes, they may deduct, as a cash contribution, a standard mileage allowance for each mile driven (14 cents a mile in 2016). While taxpayers are allowed to deduct their transportation costs and other out-of-pocket costs of providing services for charities, they are not allowed to deduct the value of the services they provide for charities.

Example 6-17

Once a month, Courtney does volunteer work at a Goodwill Industries outlet about 20 miles from her home. Altogether, Courtney traveled 500 miles during the year driving to and from the Goodwill outlet. Courtney has determined that the services she provided during the year are reasonably valued at $1,500. What amount is Courtney allowed to deduct for her volunteer work with Goodwill Industries?

Answer: $70. Courtney is *not* allowed to deduct the value of the services she provides to Goodwill. However, she is allowed to deduct the $70 cost of her transportation to and from the Goodwill outlet (500 miles × 14 cents per mile).

Taxpayers receiving goods or services from a charity in exchange for a contribution may only deduct the amount of the contribution *in excess of the fair market value of the goods or services they receive* in exchange for their contribution.[34]

Contributions of Property Other Than Money When a taxpayer donates *property* to charity, the *amount* the taxpayer is allowed to deduct depends on whether the property is **capital gain property** or **ordinary income property.**

Capital gain property. In general, taxpayers are allowed to deduct the *fair market value* of capital gain property on the date of the donation. Capital gain property is

---

[32]For example, to deduct monetary donations, taxpayers must keep a bank record or a written communication from the charity showing the name of the charity and the date and amount of the contribution. In addition, to deduct charitable contributions for cash or noncash contributions of $250 or more, a taxpayer must receive a written acknowledgment from the charity that shows the amount of cash and a description of any property contributed. The acknowledgment must also state whether the donee organization provided any goods or services to the donor for the contribution and if so, either include a description and estimate of the value of the goods or services provided by the donee organization or, if applicable, a statement that the goods or services provided by the donee organization consist entirely of intangible religious benefits. See Publication 526 for more information.

[33]When individual taxpayers mail a contribution, they are allowed to deduct the contribution when they place the payment in the mail. When they pay via credit card, they are allowed to deduct the contribution on the day of the charge. Rev. Rul. 78-38, 1978-1 CB 67.

[34]Reg. §1.170A-1(h). To help with this determination, a charity that provides goods or services in return for a contribution of more than $75 must provide contributors with a written statement estimating the value of goods and services that the charity has provided to the donor.

any appreciated asset that would have generated a *long-term* capital gain if the taxpayer had sold the property for its fair market value instead of contributing the asset to charity. To qualify as long-term, the taxpayer must have held the asset for more than a year. Capital assets include the following assets:

- Investment assets (stocks, bonds, land held for investment, paintings, etc.).
- Business assets (to the extent that gain on the sale of the business asset would *not* have been considered ordinary income).[35]
- Personal-use assets.

Contributing capital gain property is a particularly tax-efficient way to make charitable contributions, because taxpayers are allowed to deduct the fair market value of the property, and they are *not* required to include the appreciation on the asset in gross income.

Example 6-18

In December of the current year, Courtney donated 100 shares of stock in JBD Corp. to her church, a qualified charity. Courtney purchased the stock several years ago for $2,600, but the shares were worth $10,600 at the time of the donation. What is the amount of Courtney's charitable deduction for donating the stock?

Answer: $10,600. Because the stock is an appreciated investment asset held for more than a year, it qualifies as capital gain property. Hence, Courtney is allowed to deduct the $10,600 fair market value of the stock, and she is *not* required to recognize any of the $8,000 realized gain ($10,600 − $2,600).

Certain contributions of capital gain property do not qualify for a fair market value deduction. The deduction for capital gain property that is *tangible personal property* is limited to the *adjusted basis* of the property if the charity uses the property for a purpose that is *unrelated* to its charitable purpose.[36] That is, this restriction applies to capital gains property that is (1) tangible, (2) personal property (not realty), and (3) unrelated to the charity's operations. The third requirement does not apply if, at the time of the donation, the taxpayer reasonably anticipates that the charity will put the property to a related use.

Example 6-19

What if: Suppose that Courtney donated a religious-themed painting to her church. Courtney purchased the painting several years ago for $2,600, but the painting was worth $10,600 at the time of the donation. When Courtney contributed the painting, she reasonably expected the church to hang the painting in the church chapel. What would be the amount of Courtney's charitable contribution deduction?

Answer: $10,600. Because Courtney reasonably expected the church to use the painting in a manner related to its tax-exempt purpose, Courtney is allowed to deduct the full fair market value of the painting without recognizing the $8,000 realized gain.

---

[35]These assets are considered to be §1231(b) assets. We discuss the tax treatment of dispositions of business assets in Chapter 11.

[36]Reg. §1.170A-4(b)(2). The taxpayer's deduction for donating capital gain property is also limited to basis if the taxpayer contributes capital gain property other than publicly traded stock to a private non-operating foundation. There are also other exceptions in which capital gain property might not otherwise qualify for deduction at value such as the subsequent sales of donated property by the charity. These exceptions are beyond the scope of this text.

What if: Suppose that Courtney was told at the time she donated the painting that the church intended to sell it and use the cash to help fund expansion of the church building. What would be Courtney's charitable contribution deduction?

Answer: $2,600, the adjusted basis of the property. Because the church expects to sell it, the painting is being used for a purpose unrelated to the charitable purpose of the church. Thus, Courtney may deduct only the tax basis of the painting.

What if: Suppose that Courtney donated stock to her church ($10,600 current fair market value, originally purchased several years ago for $2,600) and the church informed her that it intended to immediately sell the stock. What would be the amount of Courtney's charitable contribution deduction?

Answer: $10,600. Stock is intangible property, not tangible personal property. Hence, Courtney would deduct the fair market value of the stock.

Ordinary income property.   Taxpayers contributing ordinary income property can only deduct the *lesser* of (1) the property's fair market value or (2) the property's adjusted basis. Ordinary income property consists of all assets other than capital gain property. That is, ordinary income property is property that if sold would generate income taxed at ordinary rates. This includes the following types of assets:

- Assets the taxpayer has held for a year or less.
- Inventory the taxpayer sells in a trade or business.
- Business assets held for more than a year to the extent the taxpayer would recognize ordinary income under the depreciation recapture rules if the taxpayer had sold the property.[37]
- Assets, including investment assets and personal-use assets, with a value *less than* the taxpayer's basis in the assets (assets that have declined in value).

Example 6-20

Before her move from Cincinnati, Courtney decided to donate her excess possessions to Goodwill Industries. Courtney estimated that she paid over $900 for these items, including clothing, a table, and a couch. However, although the items were in excellent condition, they were worth only $160. What amount can Courtney deduct for her donation of these items?

Answer: $160. Because Courtney's possessions have declined in value, they are considered to be ordinary income property. Consequently, Courtney may deduct the lesser of (1) the fair market value of $160 or (2) her tax basis in the property of $900.

Charitable Contribution Deduction Limitations   The amount of a taxpayer's charitable contribution deduction for the year is limited to a **ceiling** or maximum deduction. The ceiling depends upon the type of property the taxpayer donates and the nature of the charity receiving the donation; donations to public charities (charities that are publicly supported such as churches and schools) and **private operating foundations** (privately sponsored foundations that actually fund and conduct charitable activities) are subject to less stringent restrictions than other charities. In general, cash and property donations to public charities and private operating foundations are limited to 50 percent of the taxpayer's AGI. Deductions for contributions of capital gain property to public charities and private operating foundations are generally limited to 30 percent of the taxpayer's AGI. Deductions for cash and property contributions to **private nonoperating foundations** (privately sponsored foundations that disburse funds to other charities, such as the Bill and Melinda Gates Foundation) are limited to 30 percent of the taxpayer's AGI. Finally, deductions for

[37]We discuss depreciation recapture in Chapter 11.

contributions of capital gain property to private nonoperating foundations are limited to 20 percent of the taxpayer's AGI. Exhibit 6-9 summarizes the charitable contribution limitations for individual taxpayers.

When taxpayers make contributions that are subject to different percentage limitations, they apply the AGI limitations in the following sequence:

Step 1: Determine the limitation for the 50 percent contributions.

Step 2: Apply the limitations to the 30 percent contributions. The 30 percent contribution limit is the *lesser* of (a) AGI × 30% or (b) AGI × 50% minus the contributions subject to the 50 percent limit.

Step 3: Apply the limitations to the 20 percent contributions. The 20 percent contribution limit is the *lesser* of (a) AGI × 20%, (b) AGI × 30% minus contributions subject to 30 percent limit, or (c) AGI × 50% minus the contributions subject to 50 percent and the contributions subject to the 30 percent limit.

EXHIBIT 6-9   Summary of Charitable Contribution Limitation Rules

Contribution Type	Public Charity and Private Operating Foundation	Private Nonoperating Foundation
Cash:		
Amount	Cash amount	Cash amount
AGI limit	50%	30%
Capital gain property:		
Amount	FMV	Basis*
AGI limit	30%	20%
Ordinary income property:		
Amount	Lesser of Basis or FMV	Lesser of Basis or FMV
AGI limit	50%	30%

*FMV if the stock is publicly traded [§170(e)(5)].

When a taxpayer's contributions exceed the AGI ceiling limitation for the year, the excess contribution is treated as though it were made in the subsequent tax year and is subject to the same AGI limitations in the next year. The excess contribution can be carried forward for five years before it expires. If a charitable contribution deduction is carried forward, the current year contributions must first be considered when applying the AGI percentage limitations. However, because the ceiling limitations are fairly generous, taxpayers exceed the ceiling limitations only in unusual circumstances.

Example 6-21

This year Courtney made the following contributions to qualified charities:

Organization	Amount	Type	AGI Limitation	Reference
Red Cross	$ 1,700	Cash	50%	Example 6-16.
Goodwill Industries	70	Cash-mileage	50	Example 6-17.
Goodwill	160	Ordinary income property	50	Example 6-20.
Church	10,600	Capital gain property	30	Example 6-18.
Total contributions	$12,530			

After applying the AGI limitations, how much of the $12,530 in contributions is Courtney allowed to deduct?

Answer: $12,530, computed as follows:

Description	Amount	Explanation
(1) AGI	$162,000	Exhibit 6-6.
(2) 50% contributions	1,930	($1,700 + 70 + 160).
(3) 50% AGI contribution limit	81,000	(1) × 50%.
(4) Allowable 50% deductions	**1,930**	Lesser of (2) or (3).
(5) 30% contributions	10,600	
(6) 30% AGI contribution limit	48,600	(1) × 30%.
(7) Remaining 50% AGI limitation	79,070	(3) − (4).
(8) Allowable 30% deductions	**10,600**	Least of (5), (6), or (7).
Deductible charitable contributions	**$ 12,530**	(4) + (8).

What if: Suppose that Courtney's AGI was $30,000. After applying the AGI limitations, how much of the $12,530 in contributions would Courtney be allowed to deduct?

Answer: $10,930, computed as follows:

Description	Amount	Explanation
(1) AGI	$30,000	
(2) 50% contributions	1,930	
(3) 50% AGI contribution limit	15,000	(1) × 50%.
(4) Allowable 50% deductions	**1,930**	Lesser of (2) and (3).
(5) 30% contributions	10,600	
(6) 30% AGI contribution limit	9,000	(1) × 30%.
(7) Remaining 50% AGI limitation	13,070	(3) − (4).
(8) Allowable 30% deductions	**9,000**	Least of (5), (6), or (7).
Deductible charitable contributions	**$10,930**	(4) + (8).

Courtney would not be allowed to deduct this year $1,600 of her $10,600 capital gain property contribution to her church. However, she will carry forward the $1,600 to next year (and up to four years after that, if necessary) and treat it as though she made a $1,600 contribution next year subject to the 30 percent of AGI limitation.

ETHICS

Sabrina loves the latest fashions, but she is also very charitable. Every year she donates her previous year's clothing to Goodwill to make room in her closet for this year's fashion. Sabrina estimates the value of her donation to be approximately $6,000. Sabrina recently learned that because her donation exceeds $5,000, she must support her donation with an appraisal and signed statement by the appraiser on Form 8283. Sabrina decides to claim a charitable deduction of $4,900 to avoid the appraisal requirement. What do you think of Sabrina's decision? Do you think nationally that there is an abnormally large number of charitable contributions valued just under $5,000?

Casualty and Theft Losses on Personal-Use Assets

Individuals cannot deduct losses they realize when they sell or dispose of assets used for personal purposes (personal-use assets as opposed to business or investment assets). However, individuals *are* allowed to deduct casualty and theft losses realized on personal-use assets.[38] A **casualty loss** is defined as a loss arising from a *sudden, unexpected,* or *unusual* event such as a "fire, storm, or shipwreck" or loss from theft.[39] Taxpayers may deduct casualty losses in the year the casualty occurs or in the year the theft of an asset is discovered.

Tax Loss from Casualties   Congress allows deductions for unreimbursed casualty and theft losses because these losses may substantially reduce a taxpayer's ability to pay taxes. However, limitations on the deduction generally ensure that taxpayers receive a tax benefit from such losses only when the losses are relatively large. The *amount* of the tax loss from any *specific casualty event* (including theft) is the *lesser* of (1) the decline in value of the property caused by the casualty or (2) the taxpayer's tax basis in the damaged or stolen asset. The loss is reduced by any reimbursements the individual is eligible to receive, such as insurance reimbursements. Likewise, any deductible loss reduces the taxpayer's basis in the underlying asset.

Example 6-22

In June, Courtney had a bad day at a nearby lake. Her purse containing $200 in cash was stolen, and she wrecked her car on the way home. Courtney purchased her purse for $150 and it was worth $125 at the time of the theft ($325 in total value was stolen). Courtney purchased her car earlier in the year for $22,000 and had to pay $2,000 to have it repaired. Courtney's insurance company reimbursed her $1,400 for the repairs. What is the amount of Courtney's casualty tax loss before considering deductibility limitations?

Answer: $925 ($325 theft + $600 accident). The theft and the automobile accident are considered to be two separate casualty events generating two different casualty losses. The amount of each casualty loss, before considering deductibility limitations, is computed as follows:

	Theft	Accident
Fair market value (FMV) before casualty	$325	
FMV after the casualty	−0	
(1) Decline in FMV (cost to repair)	325	$ 2,000
(2) Tax basis in property before casualty	350	22,000
Loss before reimbursement [lesser of (1) or (2)]	325	2,000
Insurance reimbursement	−0	−1,400
Unreimbursed casualty losses	$325	$ 600

Casualty Loss Deduction Floor Limitations   Casualty losses must exceed two separate floor limitations to qualify as itemized deductions. The first floor is $100 for *each* casualty event during the year. This floor eliminates deductions for small losses. The second floor limitation is 10 percent of AGI, and it applies to the sum of all casualty losses for the year (after applying the $100 floor). In other words, the itemized deduction is the aggregate amount of casualty losses that exceeds 10 percent of AGI.

---

[38]§165. As we discuss in more detail in Chapter 9, businesses may deduct casualty and theft losses of business property as a deduction for AGI. Further, casualty or theft losses on investment assets are deductible as a miscellaneous itemized deduction not subject to the 2 percent of AGI floor.

[39]§165(c)(3). See also IRS Publication No. 547.

Example 6-23

Courtney's total casualty loss before applying the deduction limitations is $925. What amount of the $925 loss is Courtney allowed to deduct after applying the two floor limitations?

Answer: $0, computed as follows:

	Theft	Accident	Total
Losses before limitations	$325	$600	
Less $100 per casualty floor	−100	−100	
Casualty loss before AGI limit	$225	$500	$ 725
Less 10% of $162,000			−16,200
Casualty loss deduction after AGI limit			$ 0

What if: Suppose that Courtney's automobile was worth $20,000, and that it was completely destroyed in the accident. What would be Courtney's casualty loss deduction if she received only $3,100 of insurance reimbursement for her loss?

Answer: $825, computed as follows:

	Theft	Accident	Total
Fair market value (FMV) before casualty	$325	$20,000	
FMV after the casualty	0	0	
(1) Decline in FMV (cost to repair)	$325	$20,000	
(2) Tax basis in property before casualty	$350	$22,000	
Loss before reimbursement [lesser of (1) or (2)]	$325	$20,000	
Less Insurance reimbursement	−0	−3,100	
Less $100 per casualty floor	−100	−100	
Unreimbursed casualty losses	$225	$16,800	$17,025
Less 10% of $162,000			−16,200
Casualty loss deduction after AGI limit			$ 825

TAXES IN THE REAL WORLD   "The Trilogy of the Rings"

In order to qualify for a casualty loss deduction, a taxpayer's personal loss must be sudden or unexpected. Taxpayers and the IRS sometimes disagree about what is a casualty. Consider the following three case summaries (sometimes called the "trilogy of the rings") and, for each case, see whether you can determine whether the taxpayer or the IRS was victorious.

Case 1

Nancy Carpenter cleaned her wedding ring by placing it in some ammonia near the kitchen sink. Nancy's husband, William, later emptied the ammonia into the drain along with the ring while doing the dishes. He then turned on the garbage disposal, destroying the ring [*William H. Carpenter,* decided by the Tax Court in 1966, 25 TCM 1186].

Case 2

John lovingly helped his wife Agnes from the car and started to shut the door. Agnes, upon realizing she had left something on the seat, reached her hand back toward the car only to have the door shut directly on her engagement ring. The setting of the ring broke on impact and the diamond was flung into the leaf-covered driveway as she retracted her hand. Despite all their efforts, John and Agnes never found the stone [*John P. White,* decided by the Tax Court in 1967, 48 TC 430].

Case 3

Mr. and Mrs. Keenan spent the night at a hotel. Mr. Keenan, who was suffering from a stuffy nose, used tissues he had placed near his bed throughout the night. During the night

(continued on page 6-26)

Mrs. Keenan removed her rings and placed them within a tissue at the bedside. Mr. Keenan awoke before his wife the following morning, and he gathered the tissues, including the ring, and flushed them down the toilet [*Keenan v. Bowers,* decided in 1950 by the South Carolina District Court, 50-2 USTC ¶9444].

So, what do you think?
The taxpayers won Case 1 and Case 2 because the losses were deemed to be "sudden and unexpected" in nature. However, the taxpayer lost Case 3 because the loss was due to a "chain of events on the parts of Mrs. Keenan and Mr. Keenan." Thus, the loss was not considered to be sudden in nature.

Miscellaneous Itemized Deductions Subject to AGI Floor

There are a variety of deductions that address specific objectives but do not fit easily into any category. Congress called these deductions **miscellaneous itemized deductions** and subjected most of these deductions to an AGI floor (only amounts over the floor are deductible). Miscellaneous itemized deductions subject to the floor limitation include employee business expenses, investment expenses, and certain other expenses. These miscellaneous deductions are summed together and are deductible only to the extent that their sum *exceeds* 2 percent of the taxpayer's AGI.

Employee Business Expenses While most business expenses are typically deductible as deductions for AGI, employee business expenses are deductible as miscellaneous itemized deductions. Expenses that qualify include those that are appropriate and helpful for the employee's work such as the cost of professional dues, uniforms (unless suitable as normal attire), union dues, and subscriptions to publications related to employment.

Example 6-24

Courtney subscribes to several architectural publications at an annual cost of $410. She finds these publications helpful, and it is certainly appropriate that an architect read current publications to keep up with new trends. Her employer does not reimburse Courtney for the cost of the subscriptions. What amount, if any, qualifies as a deductible employee business expense?

Answer: All $410 qualifies as a deductible employee business expense because the expense is appropriate and helpful to Courtney's employment.

Several types of employee expenses are restricted. For example, the costs of job hunting qualify if the job is in the employee's current trade or business, but not for the individual's first job. In addition, the cost of education qualifies if it serves to maintain or improve the employee's skill in the business, but not if the education is *required* to qualify for a new business or profession.[40] Thus, a high school teacher would not be able to deduct the cost of attending law school because a law degree would qualify him for a different profession.

Example 6-25

During the year, Courtney paid $1,529 to attend motivational seminars sponsored by a continuing education provider. Courtney has found these seminars helpful, and her employer has encouraged Courtney to attend. How much of the cost of the seminars qualifies as a deductible employee business expense?

Answer: All $1,529. The cost qualifies as an employee business expense because the courses are appropriate and helpful and do not qualify Courtney for a new business.

[40]If a taxpayer is self-employed (instead of an employee), the cost of education that maintains or improves his or her skills (but is not required for a new business or profession) is deductible on Schedule C (not on Schedule A as a miscellaneous itemized deduction).

TAXES IN THE REAL WORLD   Is the Cost of an MBA Deductible?

Is the cost of an MBA deductible? That is a very good question with differing answers depending on the taxpayer's specific facts. The nature of an MBA degree lends itself to vigorous disputes as to whether the degree qualifies a taxpayer to engage in a new trade or business. On the one hand, an MBA degree is typically not a foundational requirement to practice in a profession. On the other hand, the knowledge and skills obtained in an MBA program may be stepping stones to opportunities that otherwise may have been out of reach to the taxpayer. As a result, the determination of whether MBA expenditures are deductible is fact intensive. From a purely objective standpoint, an MBA degree surely qualifies its recipient for a new trade or business somewhere and someplace. The

courts, however, have not focused on this fact. Instead, the courts have focused on the relationship of the MBA curriculum to the taxpayer's duties and responsibilities in his or her profession *before* and *after* he or she receives the degree. Thus, in the typical situation where students enter an MBA program to change career paths, the deductibility of the education is not likely to pass muster. For a taxpayer working in the same profession before and after the MBA degree (the more typical situation for an executive MBA program), the result is much more favorable.

Source: Matthew A. Melone, "Tax Court Upholds Deduction for MBA Tuition," *Practical Tax Strategies,* March 2010.

Travel and transportation. The cost of travel and transportation associated with the employee's work responsibilities may also qualify as miscellaneous itemized deductions. The cost of travel is deductible if the primary purpose of the trip is business. However, the cost of **commuting**—traveling from a residence to the place of business—is personal and never deductible.[41] When employees drive their personal automobiles for business purposes, they may deduct a standard mileage rate in lieu of deducting actual costs.[42] In 2016, the standard business mileage rate is 54 cents per mile. When employees travel on business trips long enough to be away from home overnight, meals and lodging also qualify as employee business expenses. Although meals and lodging are deductible employee business expenses, employees are allowed to deduct only half the cost of the meals. When the travel has both business and personal aspects, the deductibility of transportation costs depends on the primary purpose of the trip. If the primary purpose is business, the transportation costs to arrive at the location are fully deductible. If the primary purpose is personal, the transportation costs to arrive at the location are not deductible. For travel with both business and personal aspects, the meals (50 percent), lodging, transportation while at the location, and incidental expenses are deductible for the business portion of the trip (that is, for the business days of the trip).

Example 6-26

Because Courtney is extremely motivated to reach her potential as an architect (the seminars are doing wonders), she spent a week in September, at her own expense, driving her personal car to several large cities to study different architectural designs. During the trip, she drove a total of
(continued on page 6-28)

---

[41]Costs of commuting to and from a temporary place of work are deductible and costs of commuting from a first job to a second job are deductible. Employees may take *temporary* business trips that last for months. For these trips, the costs of the travel, including meals and lodging, are deductible for the duration of the trip. However, because trips in excess of one year are deemed to be *permanent,* the cost of travel on indefinite trips is *not* deductible.

[42]If an employee chooses to deduct actual automobile costs instead, she would deduct the automobile depreciation or lease payments (see Chapter 10 for applicable depreciation limits), gas, oil, repairs, license, and insurance attributable to business use. Expenses are allocated to business use based on the proportion of business miles to total miles driven for the year. Once a taxpayer chooses the actual cost method, she cannot switch to using the standard business mileage rate.

2,134 miles, spent $828 on lodging, and paid $500 for meals. What amount can Courtney deduct as unreimbursed employee business expenses before considering the 2 percent of AGI floor?

Answer: $2,230, computed as follows:

Description	Expense	Calculation
Transportation	$1,152	2,134 miles × 54 cents
Lodging	828	
Meals	250	$500 × 50%
Total employee business expense from trip	$2,230	

Employee expense reimbursements.   Many employees are reimbursed for their business expenses by their employers. As a general rule, employees *include* reimbursements in gross income and deduct employee business expenses as miscellaneous itemized deductions. However, if an employee is required to submit documentation supporting expenses to receive reimbursement and the employer reimburses only legitimate business expenses, then the employer's reimbursement plan qualifies as an **accountable plan.** Under an accountable plan (which is the most common method for reimbursement) employees *exclude* expense reimbursements from gross income and do *not* deduct the reimbursed expenses. If the expenses exceed the reimbursements, the excess (unreimbursed) portion of each expense is deductible as an employee business expense. Thus, miscellaneous itemized deductions for employee business expenses are commonly referred to as deductions for *unreimbursed* employee business expenses.

Example 6-27

In November, Courtney went on a business trip to Los Angeles to meet with a prospective client and spent $1,700 on business travel including meals and lodging. EWD reimbursed Courtney for the entire $1,700 cost of the trip under an accountable plan. What amount can Courtney deduct?

Answer: $0. Because EWD's reimbursement is made under an accountable plan, Courtney ignores the reimbursement and the expenses for tax purposes; the reimbursement and expenses completely offset each other.

What if: Suppose that EWD provided Courtney with a flat amount of $2,000 to cover her expenses for the trip and did not require her to account for expenditures. How would Courtney treat the reimbursement and the expenses for tax purposes?

Answer: Courtney would include the $2,000 in gross income and claim the $1,700 from the trip from AGI as an employee business expense, miscellaneous itemized deduction subject to the 2 percent of AGI floor (and 50 percent meals limitation). The reimbursement was not made under an accountable plan because Courtney was not required to substantiate her expenses.

Investment Expenses   As previously explained, investment expenses are itemized deductions. These expenses are classified as miscellaneous itemized deductions and include expenditures necessary for the production or collection of income, or for the management, conservation, or maintenance of property held for the production of income.[43] Common investment expenses include

- Expenses associated with investment income or property.
- Investment advisory fees.
- Safe-deposit box fees.
- Subscriptions to investment-related publications.

---

[43]§212. As we discussed earlier in the chapter, rental and royalty expenses are the only investment expenses that qualify as a deduction for AGI.

Tax Preparation Fees Ordinary and necessary expenses incurred in connection with determining tax obligations imposed by federal, state, municipal, or foreign authorities are also deductible as miscellaneous itemized deductions subject to the 2 percent of AGI floor.[44] While the most common tax preparation fees are the costs of preparing taxpayers' tax returns, taxpayers may also deduct other related expenses such as the cost of property appraisals for tax purposes and the costs of contesting tax liabilities.

Example 6-28

In 2016, Courtney paid Quick Taxes Inc. $250 to prepare her 2015 income tax return. What amount of this expenditure can Courtney deduct before considering the 2 percent of AGI floor?

Answer: $250. The entire amount qualifies as a miscellaneous itemized deduction for 2016.

Hobby Losses As stated previously, individuals engaged in *business* activities are allowed to deduct their business expenses as deductions for AGI. However, taxpayers may engage in certain activities for primarily personal enjoyment but these activities may also generate revenue. For tax purposes, this type of activity is considered a **hobby** rather than a business. Hobby expenses are deductible only to the extent of the revenue generated by the hobby. Sometimes referred to as the *hobby loss limitation,* this limit is less taxpayer-friendly for a hobby than the limits on business expenses. Thus, it's important to determine whether an activity should be considered a business or a hobby for tax purposes. This determination hinges upon whether the taxpayer is engaged in the activity *primarily* to make a profit or *primarily* for personal enjoyment.

To help make this subjective determination, the regulations provide a list of the following factors to consider:[45]

- The manner in which the taxpayer carries on the activity.
- The expertise of the taxpayer or his advisors.
- The time and effort expended by the taxpayer in carrying on the activity.
- The expectation that assets used in the activity may appreciate in value.
- The success of the taxpayer in carrying on other, similar activities.
- The taxpayer's history of income or losses with respect to the activity.
- The amount of occasional profits, if any.
- The financial status of the taxpayer.
- The elements of personal pleasure or recreation.

One of the most important factors is the taxpayer's history of income or loss in the activity. In fact, the tax law explicitly presumes that an activity is a business if it generates a profit in three of five consecutive years.[46] This presumption is difficult for the IRS to overcome in disputes with taxpayers.

If an activity is determined to be a hobby, the taxpayer must *include* the revenue from the activity in gross income and may deduct the expenses, to the extent of the gross income from the activity, as itemized deductions (mortgage interest, real estate taxes, and *miscellaneous itemized deductions*). When hobby expenses exceed revenue, the expenses must be deducted in a particular sequence. Taxpayers first deduct

[44]§212.
[45]See Reg. §1.183-2.
[46]For activities involving breeding, training, or racing horses, the taxpayer need show a profit in only two of seven years for the activity to be presumed to be a business.

expenses that are deductible anyway, such as mortgage interest or property taxes. Second, taxpayers deduct all other hobby expenses except depreciation expense (deducted as miscellaneous itemized deductions). Finally, they deduct depreciation expense (also deducted as a miscellaneous itemized deduction). As discussed below, miscellaneous itemized deductions are only deductible to the extent they exceed 2 percent of AGI. Thus, the revenue from the activity increases the taxpayer's AGI (and taxable income) dollar for dollar. However, the hobby deductions may or may not decrease taxable income depending on whether and the extent to which the taxpayer's itemized deductions exceed her standard deduction and her miscellaneous itemized deductions exceed the 2 percent of AGI floor.

Example 6-29

Courtney's cousin, Phil T. Thrill, played golf at Arizona State University. He turned pro and tried to qualify for the PGA tour when he graduated from college. Unfortunately, he couldn't support his family playing golf and is currently employed as a high school physical education instructor. Every summer, Phil plays in several local and a few regional professional golf tournaments. His only source of revenue from golf is the prize money he wins in these tournaments. Phil has managed to earn prize money in excess of his expenses in only one of the previous five years. This year Phil received golf revenues of $3,200 and incurred golf-related expenses of $8,800 consisting of tournament entry fees, equipment, food, transportation, clothing, and lodging. For tax purposes, are Phil's golf activities considered to be a business or a hobby? If Phil's golfing activities are determined to be a *hobby*, how does Phil account for his revenues and expenses for tax purposes?

Answer: It could go either way. We need more facts regarding his golf activities to make a more clear determination. See *Donald C. Kimbrough,* TC Memo 1988-185, for an example of the Tax Court ruling in a somewhat similar setting that the golfer was engaged in a business. Nonetheless, because Phil has only generated golf revenue in excess of expenses in one of the past five years, the activity is not presumed to be a business activity. To qualify as a business, Phil would have to convince the IRS that he is primarily engaging in golf activities to make a profit rather than for personal enjoyment. If the activity is determined to be a hobby, Phil includes the $3,200 of revenue in gross income as miscellaneous income. He is allowed to deduct $3,200 of his expenses as miscellaneous itemized deductions subject to the 2 percent floor (the deduction is limited to gross income from the activity).

What if: Suppose that Phil's golfing activities are determined to be a hobby and (1) his AGI is $70,000 before considering the effects of his golfing activity, (2) he has itemized deductions of $10,000 that are unrelated to the golf activity, (3) the applicable standard deduction is $6,300, and (4) he has no miscellaneous itemized deductions other than his golfing expenses. What is the effect of his golfing activities on his AGI and taxable income this year?

Answer: The golfing activities will increase Phil's AGI by $3,200 and his taxable income by $1,464 because the full amount of the revenue is included in gross income but his expense deductions are limited. Phil's AGI and taxable income are computed as follows:

Description	Amounts without Hobby	Amounts with Hobby	Explanation
(1) AGI before activity	$70,000	$70,000	
(2) Golf revenue (increase in AGI)		3,200	
(3) AGI after activity	70,000	73,200	(1) + (2).
(4) Golf expenses	0	8,800	
(5) Golf expenses after revenue limit	0	3,200	Lesser of (2) or (4).
(6) 2% of AGI floor	0	1,464	(3) × 2%.
(7) Deductible golf expenses (as miscellaneous itemized deduction)	0	1,736	(5) − (6).
(8) Other itemized deductions	10,000	10,000	
(9) Total itemized deductions	10,000	11,736	(7) + (8).
(10) Taxable income (ignoring exemptions)	60,000	61,464	(3) − (9).
Increase in taxable income		**$ 1,464**	Difference in line (10).

What if: Suppose the same preceding facts, except that Phil does not have the $10,000 of item-ized deductions unrelated to the golf activity. What is the effect of his golfing activities on his AGI and taxable income this year?

Answer: The golfing activities will increase Phil's AGI and taxable income by $3,200 because the full amount of the revenue is included in gross income but none of his expense deductions are deductible because his itemized deductions (including the $1,736 of golf expenses that exceed 2 percent of AGI) do not exceed the standard deduction. Thus, the $3,200 golf revenue increases his AGI and taxable income, but he gets no tax deduction for his related expenses because his itemized deductions do not exceed the standard deduction.

Limitation on Miscellaneous Itemized Deductions (2 percent of AGI Floor)   To apply the 2 percent floor limit and determine the miscellaneous itemized deduction, the sum of all deductions subject to the 2 percent floor limitation is re-duced by 2 percent of AGI. If the 2 percent floor equals or exceeds the sum of mis-cellaneous itemized deductions, the deductions do not increase the taxpayer's itemized deductions (they don't provide any tax benefit). The 2 percent floor limita-tion makes it likely that most taxpayers will receive limited, if any, tax benefit from the deductions subject to the floor.

Example 6-30

What amount is Courtney's deduction for miscellaneous itemized deductions that are subject to the 2 percent floor?

Answer: $1,179, computed as follows:

Description	Amount	Reference
Subscriptions to publications	$ 410	Example 6-24.
Educational costs	1,529	Example 6-25.
Business trip to observe architecture	2,230	Example 6-26.
Tax preparation fees	250	Example 6-28.
Total deductions subject to 2% floor	$4,419	
2% of AGI floor (162,000 × 2%)	−3,240	
Total miscellaneous itemized deductions	$1,179	

Courtney incurred a total of $4,419 of miscellaneous itemized deductions, but she can deduct only $1,179 of them due to the 2 percent of AGI restriction.

Miscellaneous Itemized Deductions *Not* Subject to AGI Floor

Several deductions are considered to be miscellaneous itemized deductions but are not subject to the 2 percent of AGI floor. Perhaps because gambling includes a significant element of personal enjoyment (losers may think otherwise), individuals include all gambling winnings for the year in gross income but may also deduct gam-bling losses *to the extent of gambling winnings* for the year.[47] The deductible gambling losses are miscellaneous itemized deductions; therefore, *losses don't directly offset*

THE KEY FACTS

Miscellaneous Itemized Deductions

- Employee business expenses not reimbursed by an accountable plan.
- Investment expenses if not in a rental or royalty activity.
- Tax preparation fees and allowable hobby expenses.
- Total miscellaneous itemized deductions are subject to a 2 percent of AGI floor limit.

[47]§165(d).

winnings.[48] However, unlike other miscellaneous itemized deductions, gambling losses are *not* subject to the 2 percent of AGI floor. Casualty and theft losses on property held for investment and the unrecovered cost of a life annuity (the taxpayer died before recovering the full cost of the annuity) also qualify as miscellaneous itemized deductions not subject to the AGI floor.

Phase-Out of Itemized Deductions

In addition to limits on specific deductions, the amount of a taxpayer's *total* itemized deductions *other than* medical expenses, casualty losses, investment *interest* expense, and gambling losses is subject to a phase-out. That is, when AGI exceeds a certain threshold, itemized deductions are reduced. In 2016, the threshold begins at $311,300 for married taxpayers filing jointly, $285,350 for heads of household, $259,400 for single taxpayers, and $155,650 for married taxpayers filing separately. We provide the computation details of the phase-out in Appendix A to this chapter.

Summary of Itemized Deductions

This part of the chapter examined the various itemized deductions (deductions from AGI). We found that both medical expense and casualty loss deductions are designed to reduce the tax burden on individuals whose ability to pay has been involuntarily impaired, but because of large floor limitations these itemized deductions are unlikely to produce tax benefits. Most miscellaneous itemized deductions, including unreimbursed employee business expense and investment expenses (excluding rental and royalty expenses), are likewise hampered by a relatively large floor limitation.

Example 6-31

Given Courtney's current year AGI of $162,000, what is the amount of her total itemized deductions she may claim on her tax return?

Answer: Courtney's itemized deductions for the year are $39,889 calculated as follows:

Description	Amount	Reference
Taxes	$10,380	Example 6-14.
Interest on loans secured by residence	15,800	Example 6-15.
Charitable contributions	12,530	Example 6-21.
Miscellaneous itemized deductions	+1,179	Example 6-30.
Total itemized deductions	$39,889	

*Because Courtney's AGI of $162,000 is below the phase-out threshold of $285,350 for taxpayers filing as a head of household, none of her itemized deductions is phased-out.

Exhibit 6-10 presents Courtney's itemized deductions on Form 1040, Schedule A.

---

[48]If gambling is deemed to be a business activity (see *Linda M. Myers,* TC Summary Opinion 2007-194), then the taxpayer reports gambling winnings and losses on Schedule C (not as a miscellaneous itemized deduction). However, gambling losses remain only deductible to the extent of gambling winnings.

EXHIBIT 6-10   Courtney's Form 1040, Schedule A

SCHEDULE A (Form 1040)	Itemized Deductions	OMB No. 1545-0074
Department of the Treasury Internal Revenue Service (99)	▶ Information about Schedule A and its separate instructions is at *www.irs.gov/schedulea*. ▶ Attach to Form 1040.	20**15** Attachment Sequence No. **07**

Name(s) shown on Form 1040				Your social security number
Courtney Wilson				123-45-6789

Medical and Dental Expenses	**Caution:** Do not include expenses reimbursed or paid by others.			
	1 Medical and dental expenses (see instructions)	**1**	2,400	
	2 Enter amount from Form 1040, line 38 **2** 162,000			
	3 Multiply line 2 by 10% (.10). But if either you or your spouse was born before January 2, 1951, multiply line 2 by 7.5% (.075) instead	**3**	16,200	
	4 Subtract line 3 from line 1. If line 3 is more than line 1, enter -0-		**4**	0

Taxes You Paid	5 State and local (**check only one box**):
	    a ☐ Income taxes, **or**
	    b ☐ General sales taxes
		5	6,700	

	6 Real estate taxes (see instructions)	**6**	3,680	
	7 Personal property taxes	**7**		
	8 Other taxes. List type and amount ▶ _____	**8**		
	9 Add lines 5 through 8		**9**	10,380
Interest You Paid **Note:** Your mortgage interest deduction may be limited (see instructions).	10 Home mortgage interest and points reported to you on Form 1098	**10**	15,800	
	11 Home mortgage interest not reported to you on Form 1098. If paid to the person from whom you bought the home, see instructions and show that person's name, identifying no., and address ▶ _____ _____	**11**		
	12 Points not reported to you on Form 1098. See instructions for special rules	**12**		
	13 Mortgage insurance premiums (see instructions)	**13**		
	14 Investment interest. Attach Form 4952 if required. (See instructions.)	**14**		
	15 Add lines 10 through 14		**15**	15,800
Gifts to Charity If you made a gift and got a benefit for it, see instructions.	16 Gifts by cash or check. If you made any gift of $250 or more, see instructions	**16**	1,770	
	17 Other than by cash or check. If any gift of $250 or more, see instructions. You **must** attach Form 8283 if over $500 . . .	**17**	10,760	
	18 Carryover from prior year	**18**		
	19 Add lines 16 through 18		**19**	12,530
Casualty and Theft Losses	20 Casualty or theft loss(es). Attach Form 4684. (See instructions.)		**20**	
Job Expenses and Certain Miscellaneous Deductions	21 Unreimbursed employee expenses—job travel, union dues, job education, etc. Attach Form 2106 or 2106-EZ if required. (See instructions.) ▶ _____	**21**	3,759	
	22 Tax preparation fees	**22**	250	
	23 Other expenses—investment, safe deposit box, etc. List type and amount ▶ _____ Subscription to Business Publications	**23**	410	
	24 Add lines 21 through 23	**24**	4,419	
	25 Enter amount from Form 1040, line 38 **25** 162,000			
	26 Multiply line 25 by 2% (.02)	**26**	3,240	
	27 Subtract line 26 from line 24. If line 26 is more than line 24, enter -0-		**27**	1,179
Other Miscellaneous Deductions	28 Other—from list in instructions. List type and amount ▶ _____ _____		**28**	

Total Itemized Deductions	29 Is Form 1040, line 38, over $154,950?
	   ☐ **No.** Your deduction is not limited. Add the amounts in the far right column for lines 4 through 28. Also, enter this amount on Form 1040, line 40.
	   ☑ **Yes.** Your deduction may be limited. See the Itemized Deductions Worksheet in the instructions to figure the amount to enter.
			29	39,889

	30 If you elect to itemize deductions even though they are less than your standard deduction, check here . . . . ▶ ☐			

For Paperwork Reduction Act Notice, see Form 1040 instructions.	Cat. No. 17145C	Schedule A (Form 1040) 2015

LO 6-3 **THE STANDARD DEDUCTION AND EXEMPTIONS**

Standard Deduction

The **standard deduction** is a flat amount that most individuals can elect to deduct *instead* of deducting their itemized deductions (if any). That is, taxpayers generally *deduct the greater of their standard deduction or their itemized deductions.*

The amount of the standard deduction varies according to the taxpayer's filing status, age, and eyesight. The basic standard deduction is greater for married taxpayers filing jointly and those supporting a family (head of household) than it is for married taxpayers filing separately and unmarried taxpayers not supporting a family. Taxpayers who are at least 65 years of age on the last day of the year or blind are entitled to additional standard deduction amounts above and beyond their basic standard deduction.[49] Exhibit 6-11 summarizes the standard deduction amounts.[50]

EXHIBIT 6-11 Standard Deduction Amounts*

2015 Amounts		
Filing Status	Basic Standard Deduction	Additional Standard Deduction for Age and/or Blindness at End of Year
Married filing jointly	$12,600	$1,250
Head of household	9,250	1,550
Single	6,300	1,550
Married filing separately	6,300	1,250

2016 Amounts		
Filing Status	Basic Standard Deduction	Additional Standard Deduction for Age and/or Blindness at End of Year
Married filing jointly	$12,600	$1,250
Head of household	9,300	1,550
Single	6,300	1,550
Married filing separately	6,300	1,250

*For individuals claimed as a dependent on another return, the 2016 standard deduction is the greater of (1) $1,050 or (2) $350 plus earned income not to exceed the standard deduction amount of those who are not dependents.

For 2016, the additional standard deduction for either age and/or blindness is $1,250 for married taxpayers and $1,550 for taxpayers who are not married. Thus, a blind individual who is 65 years old and single is entitled to a standard deduction of $9,400 (6,300 + 1,550 + 1,550). A married couple filing a joint return with one spouse over age 65 and one spouse considered legally blind is entitled to a standard deduction of $15,100 (12,600 + 1,250 + 1,250). Finally, for an individual who is eligible to be claimed as a dependent on another's return, the standard deduction is the greater of (1) $1,050 or (2) $350 plus the individual's earned income limited to the regular standard deduction. The additional standard deduction amounts for age and blindness, if any, are not impacted by the preceding limitation for eligible dependents.

[49]Taxpayers are considered 65 on the day before their 65th birthday. Taxpayers are considered to be blind if they have a certified statement from their eye doctor or registered optometrist that their corrected vision of their better eye is no better than 20/200 or their field of vision is 20 degrees or less.
[50]The standard deduction amount is indexed for inflation.

What is Courtney's standard deduction for the year?

Answer: $9,300. Because Courtney is unmarried at the end of the year and she maintains a household for more than six months for Deron and Ellen who both qualify as her dependents (as qualifying children), Courtney's filing status is head of household, which allows her to claim a standard deduction of $9,300.

Given that Courtney's itemized deductions are $39,889, will Courtney deduct her itemized deductions or her standard deduction?

Answer: She will deduct her itemized deductions because they exceed her standard deduction.

What if: Suppose that Courtney's 10-year-old son, Deron, earned $600 this summer by mowing lawns for neighbors. If Courtney claims a dependency exemption for Deron, what amount of standard deduction can Deron claim on his individual return?

Answer: Deron claims a minimum standard deduction of $1,050 because he is claimed as a dependent on Courtney's return. Hence, Deron would not pay any income tax because his taxable income is reduced to zero by the standard deduction.[51]

What if: Any difference in amount of the standard deduction if Deron earned $2,100?

Answer: Because of the amount of his earnings, Deron claims a standard deduction in the amount of his earned income plus $350. Hence, Deron claims a standard deduction of $2,450 and he would not pay any income tax.[52]

What if: Suppose that Deron earned $8,600?

Answer: Again, Deron claims a standard deduction in the amount of his earned income plus $350. However, Deron's standard deduction is limited to $6,300, the maximum allowable standard deduction for a taxpayer filing single and claimed as a dependent on another return. Hence, Deron would report taxable income of $2,300.

From the government's standpoint, the standard deduction serves two purposes. First, to help taxpayers with lower income, it automatically provides a minimum amount of income that is not subject to taxation. Second, it eliminates the need for the IRS to verify and audit itemized deductions for those taxpayers who chose to deduct the standard deduction. From the taxpayers' perspective, the standard deduction allows them to avoid taxation on a portion of their income, and for those not planning to itemize deductions, it eliminates the need to substantiate and collect information about them. The standard deduction, however, is a double-edged sword. While it reduces taxes by offsetting income with an automatic deduction, it eliminates the tax benefits of itemized deductions up to the amount of the standard deduction. This is a very important point to consider when evaluating the tax benefits of itemized deductions.

In Example 6-31, we determined that Courtney is entitled to deduct $39,889 of itemized deductions this year. How much do Courtney's itemized deductions reduce her taxable income relative to a situation in which she had $0 itemized deductions?

Answer: $30,589. Because Courtney files as a head of household, she would have been able to deduct $9,300 as a standard deduction even if she had not incurred *any* itemized deductions. Consequently, her itemized deductions reduce her taxable income by only $30,589 ($39,889 − $9,300) beyond what her taxable income would have been if she did not itemize deductions.

---

[51]Deron will need to file a tax return because his self-employment income exceeds $400 and, as explained in Chapter 8, he will likely owe self-employment tax.

[52]As mentioned previously, Deron will need to file a tax return because his self-employment income exceeds $400 and, as explained in Chapter 8, he will likely owe self-employment taxes.

Bunching Itemized Deductions   Some taxpayers may deduct the standard deduction every year because their itemized deductions always fall just short of the standard deduction amount and thus never produce any tax benefit. They may gain some tax benefit from their itemized deductions by implementing a simple timing tax planning strategy called **bunching itemized deductions.** The basic strategy consists of shifting itemized deductions into one year such that the amount of itemized deductions exceeds the standard deduction for the year, and then deducting the standard deduction in the next year (or vice versa).

Because individuals are cash-method taxpayers, they may shift certain itemized deductions by accelerating payment into the current year. For example, a taxpayer could make charitable contributions at the end of December rather than at the beginning of January in the following year. Taxpayers' ability to shift itemized deductions is limited because the timing of these payments is not completely discretionary. For example, real estate taxes have due dates, state taxes are generally paid throughout the year via withholding, and employees may incur and be required to pay business expenses throughout the year. However, taxpayers who annually make a certain amount of charitable contributions, for example, may consider lumping contributions for two years into one year and not contributing in the next year.[53]

Example 6-34

What if: Gram is 70 years old and files as a single taxpayer. Last year Gram paid deductible medical expenses (after the AGI floor limitation) of $4,000. She also contributed $3,000 to her local church. Last year her total itemized deductions were $7,000 ($4,000 medical + 3,000 charitable). Assuming Gram has similar expenditures this year, what amount of additional deductions would Gram have been able to deduct last year if she had bunched her deductions by making her 2015 and 2016 charitable contributions in 2016?

Answer: $2,150, computed as follows:

	No Bunching		Bunching	
	2015	**2016**	**2015**	**2016**
(1) Standard deduction*	$7,850	$7,850	$7,850	$ 7,850
(2) Itemized deductions	7,000	7,000	4,000	10,000
Greater of (1) and (2)	$7,850	$7,850	$7,850	$10,000
Total deductions (combined years)	$15,700 ($7,850 + $7,850)		$17,850 ($7,850 + $10,000)	
Deductions gained through bunching	$2,150 ($17,850 bunching deductions − $15,700 nonbunching deductions)			

*For 2015 and 2016, her standard deduction is the $6,300 standard deduction for single taxpayers plus an additional $1,550 standard deduction amount for age.

Deduction for Personal and Dependency Exemptions

As we learned in Chapter 4, taxpayers are generally allowed to deduct $4,050 in 2016 for each **personal** and **dependency exemption.** In general, then, a taxpayer's *from AGI* deduction for personal and dependency exemptions is $4,050 multiplied by the number of the taxpayer's **exemptions.** However, just as with itemized deductions, a taxpayer's total exemption deduction is phased out based on AGI for relatively high income taxpayers. The AGI threshold for the beginning of the phase-out and the AGI for the maximum phase-out depends on the taxpayer's filing status. The amounts for 2016 are presented in Exhibit 6-12. We discuss the computational details of the phase-out in Appendix B to this chapter.

[53]Of course, as we discussed in Chapter 3, taxpayers adopting this strategy must also consider the time value of money for the contributions amounts they pay in advance to determine whether a tax planning strategy designed to save taxes makes economic sense.

EXHIBIT 6-12 **Maximum Phase-Out Range for Personal and Dependency Exemptions for 2016**

Filing Status	Threshold	AGI Maximum Phase-out
Married filing jointly	$311,300	$433,801
Head of household	285,350	407,851
Single	259,400	381,901
Married filing separately	155,650	216,901

Example 6-35

This year, Courtney is allowed to claim a personal exemption for herself and dependency exemptions for her daughter Ellen and her son Deron. Courtney's filing status is head of household. What amount is Courtney allowed to deduct for her personal and dependency exemptions?

Answer: $12,150 ($4,050 × 3). Because Courtney's AGI is $162,000 and she files as a head of household, her AGI is below the $285,350 threshold for the exemption phase-out. Thus, she is allowed to deduct her full exemption amounts without phase-out.

Taxable Income Summary

We now have enough information to calculate Courtney's and Gram's taxable income. Exhibit 6-13 shows Courtney's taxable income calculation and Exhibit 6-14 illustrates how this information would be displayed on page 2 of Courtney's Form 1040.

Exhibit 6-15 provides Gram's taxable income calculation.

EXHIBIT 6-13   **Courtney's Taxable Income**

Description	Amount	Reference
AGI	$162,000	Exhibit 6-6.
Less: Greater of (1) itemized deductions ($39,889) or (2) standard deduction ($9,300)	(39,889)	Example 6-31.
Less: Personal and dependency exemptions	(12,150)	Example 6-35.
Taxable income	$109,961	

EXHIBIT 6-14   **Courtney's Taxable Income Computation as Presented on Form 1040, Page 2**

Form 1040 (2015)   Page **2**

Tax and Credits	38	Amount from line 37 (adjusted gross income)	38		162,000
	39a	Check if: ☐ **You** were born before January 2, 1951, ☐ Blind. ☐ **Spouse** was born before January 2, 1951, ☐ Blind. } Total boxes checked ▶ 39a			
	b	If your spouse itemizes on a separate return or you were a dual-status alien, check here ▶ 39b ☐			
Standard Deduction for— • People who check any box on line	40	**Itemized deductions** (from Schedule A) **or** your **standard deduction** (see left margin) . .	40		39,889
	41	Subtract line 40 from line 38	41		122,111
	42	**Exemptions.** If line 38 is $154,950 or less, multiply $4,000 by the number on line 6d. Otherwise, see instructions	42		12,150
	43	**Taxable income.** Subtract line 42 from line 41. If line 42 is more than line 41, enter -0- . .	43		109,961

EXHIBIT 6-15   **Gram's Taxable Income**

Description	Amount	Explanation
(1) AGI	$15,590	Exhibit 6-7.
(2) Greater of (a) itemized deductions ($7,000) or (b) standard deduction ($7,850)	(7,850)	Example 6-34.
(3) Personal and dependency exemptions	(4,050)	One exemption.
Taxable income	$ 3,690	(1) + (2) + (3).

Note that because Gram's gross income of $16,000 (Exhibit 5-6) is more than the sum of her basic standard deduction amount plus her personal and dependency exemption ($11,900), she is required to file a tax return.

CONCLUSION

We started this chapter with Courtney's and Gram's gross incomes. In this chapter, we first identified the duo's separate *deductions for AGI* and we computed their AGI. We then determined their *from* AGI deductions. Courtney deducted her itemized deductions because they exceeded her standard deduction. Gram, on the other hand, deducted her standard deduction. Finally, Courtney deducted three exemptions: a personal exemption for herself and dependency exemptions for each of her two children, Deron and Ellen. Gram deducted one personal exemption for herself. By subtracting their *from* AGI deductions from their AGI, we determined taxable income for both Courtney and Gram. With this knowledge, we proceed to the next two chapters and address issues relating to investments and determining the amount of tax Courtney and Gram are required to pay on their taxable income.

Appendix A   Calculation of Itemized Deduction Phase-Out for 2016

The amount of the itemized deduction phase-out for 2016 is the lesser of

(1) 3 percent × [AGI minus $311,300 ($285,350 for heads of household, $259,400 for single taxpayers, and $155,650 for married taxpayers filing separately)] or

(2) 80 percent of the total itemized deductions subject to phase-out.

Example 6-1A

What if: Suppose Courtney's AGI was $320,000. What would be the amount of her total itemized deductions she may claim on her tax return after computing the itemized deduction phase-out?

Answer: Courtney's itemized deductions for the year are $38,849, calculated as follows:

Description	Amount	Reference
Interest on loans secured by residence	$15,800	Example 6-15.
Charitable contributions	12,530	Example 6-21.
Miscellaneous itemized deductions	1,179	Example 6-30.
Total itemized deductions subject to phase-out	$39,889	
Less phase-out of itemized deductions	−1,040	See calculation below.
Total itemized deductions	$38,849	

Calculation of the phase-out:

Lesser of

(1) 3 percent × (AGI minus $285,350) = 3 percent × ($320,000 − $285,350) = $1,040 or

(2) 80 percent of the total itemized deductions subject to phase-out ($39,889) = $31,911

Appendix B   Personal Exemption Phase-out Computation for 2016

The process of determining the amount of the phase-out involves the following five steps:

Step 1: Subtract the taxpayer's AGI from the AGI threshold based on the taxpayer's filing status. If the threshold equals or exceeds the taxpayer's AGI, the taxpayer deducts her full personal and dependency exemption.

Step 2: Divide the excess AGI (the amount from Step 1) by 2,500. If the result is not a whole number (i.e., the excess AGI is not evenly divisible by 2,500), round *up* to the next whole number. (For married filing separate taxpayers, replace the 2,500 amount with 1,250.)

Step 3: Multiply the outcome of Step 2 by 2 percent, but limit the product to 100 percent.

Step 4: Multiply the percentage determined in Step 3 by the taxpayer's total personal and dependency exemptions (i.e., number of personal and dependency exemptions times $4,050 in 2016). The product is the amount of personal and dependency exemption that is phased-out (i.e., the taxpayer is *not* allowed to deduct this amount).

Step 5: Subtract the Step 4 result from the taxpayer's total personal and dependency exemptions that would be deductible without any phase-out (i.e., number of personal and dependency exemptions times $4,050 in 2016).

Example 6-1B

What if: Suppose that Courtney's AGI was $340,850 and her personal and dependency exemptions total $12,150 ($4,050 × 3). What amount of personal and dependency exemptions would she be allowed to deduct with the phase-out?

Answer: $6,561, computed as follows:

	Amount	Explanation
Step 1:	$55,500	$340,850 − $285,350 (Excess AGI).
Step 2:	23	Divide $55,500 by 2,500 and round up to nearest whole number $55,500/2,500 = 22.2 = 23 (rounded).
Step 3:	46%	Multiply the amount in Step 2 by 2% (i.e., 23 × 2%).
Step 4:	$ 5,589	Multiply the Step 3 result by the total exemption amount (i.e., $12,150 × 46%). This is the amount of the phase-out.
Step 5:	$ 6,561	Subtract the Step 4 result from the total exemption amount (i.e., $12,150 − $5,589). This is the deductible exemption amount.

Summary

Identify the common deductions necessary for calculating adjusted gross income (AGI).

LO 6-1

- Deductions for AGI may be categorized into those that are directly or indirectly business-related and those that address specific policy issues.
- The business-related deductions for AGI include business expenses, rent and royalty expenses, self-employment taxes, moving expenses, medical and health insurance by self-employed taxpayers, and forfeited interest.
- Other common deductions for AGI include the deductions for alimony, interest on student loans, qualified education expenses, and early withdrawal penalties.

LO 6-2   Describe the different types of itemized deductions available to individuals and compute itemized deductions.

- The medical expense and casualty loss deductions are designed to provide tax benefits to needy individuals but both are subject to significant floor limitations.
- The itemized deduction for interest is limited to interest related to a personal residence and investment interest, and the latter is limited by net investment income.
- The deduction for charitable contributions extends to contributions of money and property to qualifying charities. The charitable deduction is subject to ceiling limitations, which are more restrictive for donations of property.
- The deduction for taxes includes state income and property taxes. Sales taxes can be deducted in lieu of deducting state and local income taxes.
- Employee business expenses and investment expenses (except rental and royalty expenses) are miscellaneous itemized deductions subject to a 2 percent of AGI floor limitation.

LO 6-3   Explain the operation of the standard deduction, determine the deduction for personal and dependency exemptions, and compute taxable income.

- Itemized deductions do not produce any tax benefit unless the total itemized deductions exceed the standard deduction.
- Certain itemized deductions are subject to a phase-out for high income taxpayers.
- Personal exemptions are allowed for the taxpayer and spouse (if married filing jointly).
- Personal and dependency exemptions are subject to a phase-out for high income taxpayers.

KEY TERMS

accountable plan (6-28)
bunching itemized deductions (6-36)
business activities (6-2)
capital gain property (6-19)
casualty loss (6-24)
ceiling (6-21)
commuting (6-27)
dependency exemption (6-36)

exemption (6-36)
floor limitation (6-15)
hobby (6-29)
investment activities (6-2)
miscellaneous itemized deductions (6-26)
modified AGI (6-10)
ordinary and necessary (6-4)

ordinary income property (6-19)
personal exemption (6-36)
private nonoperating foundations (6-21)
private operating foundations (6-21)
qualified educational expenses (6-9)
qualified educational loans (6-9)
standard deduction (6-34)
trade or business (6-3)

DISCUSSION QUESTIONS

Discussion Questions are available in *Connect®*.   **connect**

LO 6-1   1. It has been suggested that tax policy favors deductions for AGI compared to itemized deductions. Describe two ways in which deductions for AGI are treated more favorably than itemized deductions.

LO 6-1   2. How is a business activity distinguished from an investment activity? Why is this distinction important for the purpose of calculating federal income taxes?

LO 6-1   3. Describe how a business element is reflected in the requirements to deduct moving expenses and how Congress limited this deduction to substantial moves.

LO 6-1   4. Explain why Congress allows self-employed taxpayers to deduct the cost of health insurance above the line (for AGI) when employees can only itemize this cost as a medical expense. Would a self-employed taxpayer ever prefer to claim health insurance premiums as an itemized deduction rather than a deduction for AGI? Explain.

5. Explain why Congress allows self-employed taxpayers to deduct the employer portion of their self-employment tax.

   LO 6-1

6. Using the Internal Revenue Code, describe two deductions for AGI that are not discussed in this chapter.

   LO 6-1

   research

7. Explain why Congress allows taxpayers to deduct interest forfeited as a penalty on the premature withdrawal from a certificate of deposit.

   LO 6-1

8. Describe the mechanical limitation on the deduction for interest on qualified educational loans.

   LO 6-1

9. Explain why the medical expense and casualty loss provisions are sometimes referred to as "wherewithal" deductions and how this rationale is reflected in the limits on these deductions.

   LO 6-2

10. Describe the type of medical expenditures that qualify for the medical expense deduction. Does the cost of meals consumed while hospitalized qualify for the deduction? Do over-the-counter drugs and medicines qualify for the deduction?

    LO 6-2

11. Under what circumstances can a taxpayer deduct medical expenses paid for a member of his family? Does it matter if the family member reports significant amounts of gross income and cannot be claimed as a dependent?

    LO 6-2

12. What types of taxes qualify to be deducted as itemized deductions? Would a vehicle registration fee qualify as a deductible tax?

    LO 6-2

13. Compare and contrast the limits on the deduction of interest on home acquisition indebtedness versus home equity loans. Are these limits consistent with horizontal equity? Explain.

    LO 6-2

14. Explain the argument that the deductions for charitable contributions and home mortgage interest represent indirect subsidies for these activities.

    LO 6-2

15. Cash donations to charity are subject to a number of very specific substantiation requirements. Describe these requirements and how charitable gifts can be substantiated. Describe the substantiation requirements for property donations.

    LO 6-2

    research

16. Describe the conditions in which a donation of property to a charity will result in a charitable contribution deduction of fair market value and when it will result in a deduction of the tax basis of the property.

    LO 6-2

17. Describe the type of event that qualifies as a casualty for tax purposes.

    LO 6-2

18. A casualty loss from the complete destruction of a personal asset is limited to the lesser of fair market value or the property's adjusted basis. Explain the rationale for this rule as opposed to just allowing a deduction for the basis of the asset.

    LO 6-2

19. This week Jim's residence was heavily damaged by a storm system that spread destruction throughout the region. While Jim's property insurance covers some of the damage, there is a significant amount of uninsured loss. The governor of Jim's state has requested that the president declare the region a federal disaster area and provide federal disaster assistance. Explain to Jim the income tax implications of such a declaration and any associated tax planning possibilities.

    LO 6-2

    research

20. Describe the types of expenses that constitute miscellaneous itemized deductions and explain why these expenses rarely produce any tax benefits.

    LO 6-2

21. Explain why the cost of commuting from home to work is not deductible as a business expense.

    LO 6-2

22. When is the cost of education deductible as an employee business expense?

    LO 6-2

23. How might the reimbursement of a portion of an employee expense influence the deductibility of the expense for the employee?

    LO 6-2

LO 6-2 24. Explain why an employee should be concerned about whether his employer reimburses business expenses using an "accountable" plan?

LO 6-2 25. Jake is a retired jockey who takes monthly trips to Las Vegas to gamble on horse races. Jake also trains racehorses part time at his Louisville ranch. So far this year, Jake has won almost $47,500 during his trips to Las Vegas while spending $27,250 on travel expenses and incurring $62,400 of gambling losses. Jake also received $60,000 in revenue from his training activities and he incurred $72,000 of associated costs. Explain how Jake's gambling winnings and related costs will be treated for tax purposes. Describe the factors that will influence how Jake's ranch expenses are treated for tax purposes.

LO 6-2
research 26. Frank paid $3,700 in fees for an accountant to tabulate business information (Frank operates as a self-employed contractor and files a Schedule C). The accountant also spent time tabulating Frank's income from his investments and determining Frank's personal itemized deductions. Explain to Frank whether or not he can deduct the $3,700 as a business expense or as an itemized deduction, and provide a citation to an authority that supports your conclusion.

LO 6-2 27. Contrast ceiling and floor limitations, and give an example of each.

LO 6-2 28. Identify which itemized deductions are subject to floor limitations, ceiling limitations, or some combination of these limits.

LO 6-3 29. Describe the tax benefits from "bunching" itemized deductions in one year. Describe the characteristics of the taxpayers who are most likely to benefit from using bunching and explain why this is so.

LO 6-3 30. Explain how the standard deduction is rationalized and why the standard deduction might be viewed as a floor limit on itemized deductions.

LO 6-3 31. Explain how the calculation of the standard deduction limits the ability to shift income to a dependent.

LO 6-3 32. Explain why the overall phase-out of itemized deductions has been described as a "haircut" of itemized deductions. Explain whether it is possible for taxpayers to lose all their itemized deductions under the phase-out rules.

LO 6-3 33. Describe the mechanism for phasing out exemptions. Can a taxpayer lose the benefit of all of her personal and dependency exemptions?

LO 6-3
research 34. Determine whether a taxpayer can change his or her election to itemize deductions once a return is filed. (*Hint:* Read about itemization under Reg. §1.63-1.)

LO 6-3
research 35. Determine whether a taxpayer who is claimed as a dependent on another return is entitled to an addition to the standard deduction for age or blindness. (*Hint:* Read the calculation of the standard deduction under IRC §63.)

PROBLEMS

Select problems are available in *Connect*®. **connect**

LO 6-1 36. Clem is married and is a skilled carpenter. Clem's wife, Wanda, works part-time as a substitute grade school teacher. Determine the amount of Clem's expenses that are deductible *for AGI* this year (if any) under the following independent circumstances:

a) Clem is self-employed and this year he incurred $525 in expenses for tools and supplies related to his job. Since neither were covered by a qualified health plan, Wanda paid health insurance premiums of $3,600 to provide coverage for herself and Clem (not through an exchange).

b) Clem and Wanda own a garage downtown that they rent to a local business for storage. This year they incurred expenses of $1,250 in utilities and $780 in depreciation.

c) Clem paid self-employment tax of $15,300 (the employer portion is $7,650), and Wanda had $3,000 of Social Security taxes withheld from her pay.

d) Clem paid $45 to rent a safe deposit box to store his coin collection. Clem has collected coins intermittently since he was a boy, and he expects to sell his collection when he retires.

37. Clyde currently commutes 55 miles to work in the city. He is considering a new assignment in the suburbs on the other side of the city that would increase his commute considerably. He would like to accept the assignment, but he thinks it might require that he move to the other side of the city. Determine if Clyde's move qualifies for a moving expense deduction and calculate the amount (if any) under the following circumstances: **LO 6-1**

a) Clyde estimates that unless he moves across town, his new commute would be almost 70 miles. He also estimates the costs of a move as follows:

Lodging while searching for an apartment	$ 126
Transportation—auto (100 miles @ 19 cents/mile)	19
Mover's fee (furniture and possessions)	1,500
Meals while en route	35

b) Same as part (a), except Clyde estimates that unless he moves across town, his new commute would be almost 115 miles.

c) Same as part (a), except Clyde's new commute would be almost 150 miles and the movers intend to impose a $450 surcharge on the moving fee for the additional distance.

38. Smithers is a self-employed individual who earns $30,000 per year in self-employment income. Smithers pays $2,200 in annual health insurance premiums (not through an exchange) for his own medical care. In each of the following situations, determine the amount of the deductible health insurance premium for Smithers before any AGI limitation. **LO 6-1**

a) Smithers is single and the self-employment income is his only source of income.

b) Smithers is single, but besides being self-employed, Smithers is also employed part-time by SF Power Corporation. This year Smithers elected not to participate in SF's health plan.

c) Smithers is self-employed and he is also married. Smithers's spouse, Samantha, is employed full-time by SF Power Corporation and is covered by SF's health plan. Smithers is not eligible to participate in SF's health plan.

d) Smithers is self-employed and he is also married. Smithers's spouse, Samantha, is employed full-time by SF Power Corporation and is covered by SF's health plan. Smithers elected not to participate in SF's health plan.

39. Hardaway earned $100,000 of compensation this year. He also paid (or had paid for him) $3,000 of health insurance (not through an exchange). What is Hardaway's AGI in each of the following situations (ignore the effects of Social Security and self-employment taxes)? **LO 6-1**

a) Hardaway is an employee and his employer paid Hardaway's $3,000 of health insurance for him as a nontaxable fringe benefit. Consequently, Hardaway received $97,000 of taxable compensation and $3,000 of nontaxable compensation.

b) Hardaway is a self-employed taxpayer, and he paid $3,000 of health insurance himself. He is not eligible to participate in an employer-sponsored plan.

LO 6-1

tax forms

40. Betty operates a beauty salon as a sole proprietorship. Betty also owns and rents an apartment building. This year Betty had the following income and expenses. Determine Betty's AGI and complete page 1 of Form 1040 for Betty. You may assume that Betty will owe $2,502 in self-employment tax on her salon income.

Interest income	$11,255
Salon sales and revenue	86,360
Salaries paid to beauticians	45,250
Beauty salon supplies	23,400
Alimony paid to her ex-husband, Rocky	6,000
Rental revenue from apartment building	31,220
Depreciation on apartment building	12,900
Real estate taxes paid on apartment building	11,100
Real estate taxes paid on personal residence	6,241
Contributions to charity	4,237

LO 6-1

41. Lionel is an unmarried law student at State University Law School, a qualified educational institution. This year Lionel borrowed $24,000 from County Bank and paid interest of $1,440. Lionel used the loan proceeds to pay his law school tuition. Calculate the amounts Lionel can deduct for higher education expenses and interest on higher education loans under the following circumstances:

a) Lionel's AGI before deducting interest on higher education loans is $50,000.

b) Lionel's AGI before deducting interest on higher education loans is $74,000.

c) Lionel's AGI before deducting interest on higher education loans is $90,000.

LO 6-1

planning

42. This year Jack intends to file a married-joint return with two dependents. Jack received $162,500 of salary and paid $5,000 of interest on loans used to pay qualified tuition costs for his dependent daughter, Deb. This year Jack has also paid qualified moving expenses of $4,300 and $24,000 of alimony.

a) What is Jack's adjusted gross income? Assume that Jack will opt to treat tax items in a manner to minimize his AGI.

b) Suppose that Jack also reported income of $8,800 from a half share of profits from a partnership. Disregard any potential self-employment taxes on this income. What AGI would Jack report under these circumstances? Again, assume that Jack will opt to treat tax items in a manner to minimize his AGI.

LO 6-1   **LO 6-2**

43. In each of the following independent cases, indicate the amount (1) deductible *for* AGI, (2) deductible *from* AGI, and (3) neither deductible for nor from AGI before considering income limitations or the standard deduction.

a) Ted paid $8 rent on a safety deposit box at the bank. In this box he kept the few shares of stock that he owned.

b) Tyler paid $85 for minor repairs to the fence at a rental house he owned.

c) Timmy paid $545 for health insurance premiums this year (not through an exchange and not with pretax dollars). Timmy is employed full-time and his employer paid the remaining premiums as a qualified fringe benefit.

d) Tess paid $1,150 of state income taxes on her consulting income.

44. In each of the following independent cases, indicate the amount (1) deductible *for* AGI, (2) deductible *from* AGI, and (3) neither deductible *for* nor deductible *from* AGI before considering income limitations or the standard deduction. **LO 6-1** **LO 6-2**

    a) Fran spent $90 for uniforms for use on her job. Her employer reimbursed her for $75 of this amount under an accountable plan (and did not report the reimbursement as wages).

    b) Timothy, a plumber employed by ACE Plumbing, spent $65 for small tools to be used on his job, but he was not reimbursed by ACE.

    c) Jake is a perfume salesperson. Because of his high pay, he receives no allowance or reimbursement from his employer for advertising expenses even though his position requires him to advertise frequently. During the year, he spent $2,200 on legitimate business advertisements.

    d) Trey is a self-employed special-duty nurse. He spent $120 for uniforms.

    e) Mary, a professor at a community college, spent $340 for magazine subscriptions. The magazines were helpful for her research activities, but she was not reimbursed for the expenditures.

    f) Wayne lost $325 on the bets he made at the race track, but he won $57 playing slot machines.

45. Ted is a successful attorney, but when he turned 50 years old he decided to retire from his law practice and become a professional golfer. Ted has been a very successful amateur golfer, so beginning this year, Ted began competing in professional golf tournaments. At year-end, Ted reported the following expenses associated with competing in 15 professional events: **LO 6-2**

Transportation from his home to various tournaments	$25,000
Lodging for the 15 weeks on the road	18,200
Meals while traveling and during golf tournaments	5,200
Entry fees	7,500
Lessons from various golf teachers	12,500
Golf supplies (balls, tees, etc.)	783
Total expenses	$69,183

    a) Suppose that Ted reports $175,000 in gross income from his pension and various investments. Describe the various considerations that will dictate the extent to which Ted can deduct the expenses associated with professional golf.

    b) Calculate Ted's deduction for golf expenses assuming that the IRS and the courts are convinced that Ted engages in competitive golf primarily for enjoyment rather than the expectation of making a profit. Assume Ted wins $10,000 this year and his AGI is $185,000 (including the golf revenues).

46. Penny, a full-time biochemist, loves stock car racing. To feed her passion, she bought a used dirt-track car and has started entering some local dirt-track races. The prize money is pretty small ($1,000 for the winner), but she really is not in it for the money. Penny reported the following income and expenses from her nights at the track: **LO 6-2**

Prize money	$2,500
Expenses:	
Transportation from her home to the races	1,000
Depreciation on the dirt-track car	4,000
Entry fees	3,500
Oil, gas, supplies, repairs for the dirt-track car	2,050

Calculate Penny's deduction for the racing expenses assuming that the racing activity is a hobby, and Penny's AGI is $97,500 *before* considering the prize money.

LO 6-2 47. Simpson is a single individual who is employed full-time by Duff Corporation. This year Simpson reports AGI of $50,000 and has incurred the following medical expenses:

Dentist charges	$ 900
Physician's charges	1,800
Optical charges	500
Cost of eyeglasses	300
Hospital charges	2,100
Prescription drugs	250
Over-the-counter drugs	450
Medical insurance premiums (not through an exchange)	775

a) Calculate the amount of medical expenses that will be included with Simpson's itemized deductions after any applicable limitations.

b) Suppose that Simpson was reimbursed for $250 of the physician's charges and $1,200 for the hospital costs. Calculate the amount of medical expenses that will be included with Simpson's itemized deductions after any applicable limitations.

LO 6-2
 research 48. This year Tim is age 45 and is considering enrolling in an insurance program that provides for long-term care insurance. He is curious about whether the insurance premiums are deductible as a medical expense and, if so, what the maximum amount is that can be deducted in any year.

LO 6-2
 research 49. Doctor Bones prescribed physical therapy in a pool to treat Jack's broken back. In response to this advice (and for no other reason), Jack built a swimming pool in his backyard and strictly limited use of the pool to physical therapy. Jack paid $25,000 to build the pool, but he wondered if this amount could be deducted as a medical expense. Determine if a capital expenditure such as the cost of a swimming pool qualifies for the medical expense deduction.

LO 6-1 LO 6-2 50. Charles has AGI of $50,000 and has made the following payments related to (1) land he inherited from his deceased aunt and (2) a personal vacation taken last year. Calculate the amount of taxes Charles may include in his itemized deductions for the year under the following circumstances:

State inheritance tax on the land	$1,200
County real estate tax on the land	1,500
School district tax on the land	690
City special assessment on the land (replacing curbs and gutters)	700
State tax on airline tickets (paid on vacation)	125
Local hotel tax (paid during vacation)	195

a) Suppose that Charles holds the land for appreciation.

b) Suppose that Charles holds the land for rent.

c) Suppose that Charles holds the land for appreciation and that the vacation was actually a business trip.

LO 6-2 51. Dan has AGI of $50,000 and paid the following taxes during this tax year. Calculate how much Dan can deduct for taxes as an itemized deduction this year.

State income tax withholding	$1,400
State income tax estimated payments	750
Federal income tax withholding	3,000
Social Security tax withheld from wages	2,100
State excise tax on liquor	400
Automobile license (based on the car's weight)	300
State sales tax paid	475

52. Tim is a single, cash-method taxpayer with one personal exemption and an AGI of $50,000. In April of this year, Tim paid $1,020 with his state income tax return for the previous year. During the year, Tim had $5,400 of state income tax and $18,250 of federal income tax withheld from his salary. In addition, Tim made estimated payments of $1,360 and $1,900 of state and federal income taxes, respectively. Finally, Tim expects to receive a refund of $500 for state income taxes when he files his state tax return for this year in April next year. What is the amount of taxes that Tim can deduct as an itemized deduction?   `LO 6-1` `LO 6-2`

53. This year Randy paid $28,000 of interest. (Randy borrowed $450,000 to buy his residence, which is currently worth $500,000.) Randy also paid $2,500 of interest on his car loan and $4,200 of margin interest to his stockbroker (investment interest expense). How much of this interest expense can Randy deduct as an itemized deduction under the following circumstances?   `LO 6-2`

    a) Randy received $2,200 of interest this year and no other investment income or expenses. His AGI is $75,000.

    b) Randy had no investment income this year, and his AGI is $75,000.

54. This year, Major Healy paid $40,000 of interest on a mortgage on his home (Major Healy borrowed $800,000 to buy the residence; $900,000 original purchase price and value at purchase; $1,000,000 current worth), $6,000 of interest on a $120,000 home equity loan on his home (loan proceeds were used to buy antique cars), and $10,000 of interest on a mortgage on his vacation home (loan of $200,000; home purchased for $500,000). Major Healy's AGI is $220,000.   `LO 6-2`

    a) How much interest expense can Major Healy deduct as an itemized deduction?

    b) Assume the original facts, except that Major Healy's home had a fair market value of $1,000,000 when he purchased the home and took out the home equity debt, but now the home is worth $500,000. How much interest expense can Major Healy deduct as an itemized deduction?

55. Ray Ray made the following contributions this year.   `LO 6-2`

Charity	Property	Cost	FMV
Athens Academy School	cash	$ 5,000	$ 5,000
United Way	cash	4,000	4,000
American Heart Association	antique painting	15,000	75,000
First Methodist Church	Coca-Cola stock	12,000	20,000

Determine the maximum amount of charitable deduction for each of these contributions *ignoring* the AGI ceiling on charitable contributions and assuming that the American Heart Association plans to sell the antique painting to fund its operations. Ray Ray has owned the painting and Coca-Cola stock since 1990.

56. Calvin reviewed his cancelled checks and receipts this year for charitable contributions. He has owned the IBM stock and painting since 2005. Calculate Calvin's charitable contribution deduction and carryover (if any) under the following circumstances.   `LO 6-2`

Donee	Item	Cost	FMV
Hobbs Medical Center	IBM stock	$5,000	$22,000
State Museum	painting	5,000	3,000
A needy family	food and clothes	400	250
United Way	cash	8,000	8,000

a) Calvin's AGI is $100,000.

b) Calvin's AGI is $100,000 but the State Museum told Calvin that it plans to sell the painting.

c) Calvin's AGI is $50,000.

d) Calvin's AGI is $100,000 and Hobbs is a nonoperating private foundation.

e) Calvin's AGI is $100,000 but the painting is worth $10,000.

LO 6-2 57. In addition to cash contributions to charity, Dean decided to donate shares of stock and a portrait painted during the earlier part of the last century. Dean purchased the stock and portrait many years ago as investments. Dean reported the following recipients:

Charity	Property	Cost	FMV
State University	cash	$15,000	$15,000
Red Cross	cash	14,500	14,500
State History Museum	painting	5,000	82,000
City Medical Center	Dell stock	28,000	17,000

a) Determine the maximum amount of charitable deduction for each of these contributions *ignoring* the AGI ceiling on charitable contributions.

b) Assume that Dean's AGI this year is $150,000. Determine Dean's itemized deduction for his charitable contributions this year and any carryover.

c) Assume that Dean's AGI this year is $240,000. Determine Dean's itemized deduction for his charitable contributions this year and any carryover.

d) Suppose Dean is a dealer in antique paintings and had held the painting for sale before the contribution. What is Dean's charitable contribution deduction for the painting in this situation (ignoring AGI limitations)?

e) Suppose that Dean's objective with the donation to the museum was to finance expansion of the historical collection. Hence, Dean was not surprised when the museum announced the sale of the portrait because of its limited historical value. What is Dean's charitable contribution deduction for the painting in this situation (ignoring AGI limitations)?

LO 6-2 58. Tim suffered greatly this year. In January a freak storm damaged his sailboat and in July Tim's motorcycle was stolen from his vacation home. Tim originally paid $27,000 for the boat, but he was able to repair the damage for $6,200. Tim paid $15,500 for the motorcycle, but it was worth $17,000 before it was stolen. Insurance reimbursed $1,000 for the boat repairs and the cycle was uninsured.

a) Calculate Tim's deductible casualty loss if his AGI is $50,000.

b) Calculate Tim's deductible casualty loss if his AGI is $150,000.

c) How would you answer (a) if Tim received an additional $65,000 in interest from municipal bonds this year?

LO 6-2
planning
59. Trevor is a single individual who is a cash-method calendar-year taxpayer. For each of the next two years (year 1 and year 2), Trevor expects to report AGI of $80,000, contribute $3,500 to charity, and pay $2,500 in state income taxes.

a) Estimate Trevor's taxable income for year 1 and year 2 using the 2016 amounts for the standard deduction and personal exemption for both years.

b) Now assume that Trevor combines his anticipated charitable contributions for the next two years and makes the combined contribution in December of year 1. Estimate Trevor's taxable income for each of the next two years using the 2016 amounts for the standard deduction and personal exemption. Reconcile the total taxable income to your solution to part (a).

c) Trevor plans to purchase a residence next year, and he estimates that additional property taxes and residential interest will each cost $4,000 annually ($8,000 in total annually). Estimate Trevor's taxable income for each of the next two years (year 1 and year 2) using the 2016 amounts for the standard deduction and personal exemption and also assuming Trevor makes the charitable contribution of $3,500 and state tax payments of $2,500 in each year.

d) Assume that Trevor makes the charitable contribution for year 2 and pays the real estate taxes for year 2 in December of year 1. Estimate Trevor's taxable income for year 1 and year 2 using the 2016 amounts for the standard deduction and personal exemption. Reconcile the total taxable income to your solution to part (c).

e) Explain the conditions in which the bunching strategy in part (d) will generate tax savings for Trevor.

60. Baker paid $775 for the preparation of his tax return and incurred $375 of employee business expenses, of which $60 was reimbursed by his employer through an accountable plan. Baker also paid a $100 fee for investment advice. Calculate the amount of these expenses that Baker is able to deduct assuming he itemizes his deductions in each of the following situations: `LO 6-2`

a) Baker's AGI is $50,000.

b) Baker's AGI is $100,000.

61. Simon lost $5,000 gambling this year on a trip to Las Vegas. In addition, he paid $2,000 to his broker for managing his $200,000 portfolio and $1,500 to his accountant for preparing his tax return. In addition, Simon incurred $2,500 in transportation costs commuting back and forth from his home to his employer's office, which were not reimbursed. Calculate the amount of these expenses that Simon is able to deduct, assuming he itemizes his deductions, in each of the following situations: `LO 6-2`

a) Simon's AGI is $40,000.

b) Simon's AGI is $200,000.

62. Zack is employed as a full-time airport security guard. This year Zack's employer transferred him from Dallas to Houston. At year-end, Zack discovered a number of unreimbursed expenses related to his employment in Dallas prior to his move to Houston. Identify which expenses are deductible and whether the deductions are *for* or *from* AGI. `LO 6-2`

Cost of bus transportation from his home to the airport	$ 150
Subscription to *Journal of Security Guards*	52
Lunch with colleagues	195
Cost of self-defense course at local community center	500
Cost of lunch with supervisor during evaluations	383
Total	$1,280

63. Stephanie is a 12-year-old who often assists neighbors on weekends by babysitting their children. Calculate the 2016 standard deduction Stephanie will claim under the following independent circumstances (assume that Stephanie's parents will claim her as a dependent). `LO 6-3`

a) Stephanie reported $850 of earnings from her babysitting.

b) Stephanie reported $1,500 of earnings from her babysitting.

c) Stephanie reported $8,000 of earnings from her babysitting.

LO 6-1 LO 6-2 LO 6-3

research

64. Tammy teaches elementary school history for the Metro School District. In 2016 she has incurred the following expenses associated with her job:

Noncredit correspondence course on history	$ 900
Teaching cases for classroom use	1,800
Tuition for university graduate course in physics	1,200
Transportation between school and home	750
Photocopying class materials	100
Transportation from school to extracurricular activities	110
Cost of lunches eaten during study halls	540

Tammy receives a base salary of $45,000 and a $200 salary supplement to help her cover expenses associated with her school extracurricular activities.

a) Identify the amount and type (*for* AGI or *from* AGI) of deductible expenses.

b) Calculate Tammy's AGI and taxable income for 2016 assuming she files single with one personal exemption.

LO 6-3

65. In 2016, Jeff, who is single, is entitled to the following deductions before phase-outs:

State income taxes	$7,850
Real estate taxes	1,900
Home mortgage interest	8,200
Charitable contributions	1,700

a) Assume that Jeff's AGI is $280,000. Calculate Jeff's itemized deductions after considering the overall phase-out of itemized deductions.

b) Suppose that Jeff's AGI increases to $1,280,000. Calculate Jeff's itemized deductions after considering the overall phase-out of itemized deductions.

LO 6-3

66. Jim files single and has three dependent children. Calculate his deductible total personal and dependency exemptions under the following independent conditions:

a) Jim has AGI of $150,000.

b) Jim has AGI of $303,000.

c) Jim has AGI of $450,000.

COMPREHENSIVE PROBLEMS

Select problems are available in *Connect*®.   connect

67. This year Evan graduated from college and took a job as a deliveryman in the city. Evan was paid a salary of $68,500 and he received $700 in hourly pay for part-time work over the weekends. Evan summarized his expenses below:

Cost of moving his possessions to the city (125 miles away)	$1,200
Interest paid on accumulated student loans	2,800
Cost of purchasing a delivery uniform	1,400
Contribution to State University deliveryman program	1,300

Calculate Evan's AGI and taxable income if he files single with one personal exemption. Assume that interest payments were initially required on Evan's student loans this year.

68. Read the following letter and help Shady Slim with his tax situation. Please assume that his gross income is $172,900 (which consists only of salary) for purposes of this problem.

tax forms

December 31, 2016

To the friendly student tax preparer:

Hi, it's Shady Slim again. I just got back from my 55th birthday party, and I'm told that you need some more information from me in order to complete my tax return. I'm an open book! I'll tell you whatever I think you need to know.

Let me tell you a few more things about my life. As you may recall, I am divorced from my wife, Alice. I know that it's unusual, but I have custody of my son, Shady, Jr. The judge owed me a few favors and I really love the kid. He lives with me full-time and my wife gets him every other weekend. I pay the vast majority of my son's expenses. I think Alice should have to pay some child support, but she doesn't have to pay a dime. The judge didn't owe me that much, I guess.

I had to move this year after getting my job at Roca Cola. We moved on February 3 of this year, and I worked my job at Roca Cola for the rest of the year. I still live in the same state, but I moved 500 miles away from my old house. I left a little bit early to go on a house-hunting trip that cost me a total of $450. I hired a moving company to move our stuff at a cost of $2,300, and I drove Junior in my car. Junior and I got a hotel room along the way that cost us $65 (I love Super 8!). We spent $35 on meals on the way to our new home. Oh yeah, I took Junior to a movie on the way and that cost $20.

Can you believe I'm still paying off my student loans, even after 15 years? I paid a total of $900 in interest on my old student loans this year.

Remember when I told you about that guy that hit me with his car? I had a bunch of medical expenses that were not reimbursed by the lawsuit or by my insurance. I incurred a total of $20,000 in medical expenses, and I was only reimbursed for $11,000. Good thing I can write off medical expenses, right?

I contributed a lot of money to charity this year (and have receipt documentation for all contributions). I'm such a nice guy! I gave $1,000 in cash to the March of Dimes. I contributed some of my old furniture to the church. It was some good stuff! I contributed a red velvet couch and my old recliner. The furniture is considered vintage and is worth $5,000 today (the appraiser surprised me!), even though I only paid $1,000 for it back in the day. When I contributed the furniture, the pastor said he didn't like the fabric and was going to sell the furniture to pay for some more pews in the church. Oh well, some people just have no taste, right? Roca Cola had a charity drive for the United Way this year and I contributed $90. Turns out, I don't even miss it, because Roca Cola takes it right off my paycheck every month . . . $15 a month starting in July. My pay stub verifies that I contributed the $90 to the United Way. Oh, one other bit of charity from me this year. An old buddy of mine was down on his luck. He lost his job and his house. I gave him $500 to help him out.

I paid a lot of money in interest this year. I paid a total of $950 in personal credit card interest. I also paid $13,000 in interest on my home mortgage. I also paid $2,000 in real estate taxes for my new house.

A few other things I want to tell you about this year. Someone broke into my house and stole my kid's brand new bicycle and my set of golf clubs. The total loss from theft was $900. I paid $125 in union dues this year. I had to pay $1,200 for new suits for my job. Roca Cola requires its managers to wear suits every day on the job. I spent a total of $1,300 to pay for gas to commute to my job this year.

Oh, this is pretty cool. I've always wanted to be a firefighter. I spent $1,400 in tuition to go to the local firefighter's school. I did this because someone told me that I can deduct the tuition as an itemized deduction, so the money would be coming back to me.

That should be all the information you need right now. Please calculate my taxable income and complete pages 1 and 2 of Form 1040 (through taxable income, line 43) and Schedule A. You're still doing this for free, right?

69. Jeremy and Alyssa Johnson have been married for five years and do not have any children. Jeremy was married previously and has one child from the prior

marriage. He is self-employed and operates his own computer repair store. For the first two months of the year, Alyssa worked for Office Depot as an employee. In March, Alyssa accepted a new job with Super Toys Inc. (ST), where she worked for the remainder of the year. This year, the Johnsons received $255,000 of gross income. Determine the Johnsons' AGI given the following information:

a) Expenses associated with Jeremy's store include $40,000 in salary (and employment taxes) to employees, $45,000 of supplies, and $18,000 in rent and other administrative expenses.

b) As a salesperson, Alyssa incurred $2,000 in travel expenses related to her employment that were not reimbursed by her employer.

c) The Johnsons own a piece of raw land held as an investment. They paid $500 of real property taxes on the property and they incurred $200 of expenses in travel costs to see the property and to evaluate other similar potential investment properties.

d) The Johnsons own a rental home. They incurred $8,500 of expenses associated with the property.

e) The Johnsons' home was only five miles from the Office Depot store where Alyssa worked in January and February. The ST store was 60 miles from their home, so the Johnsons decided to move to make the commute easier for Alyssa. The Johnsons' new home was only 10 miles from the ST store. However, their new home was 50 miles from their former residence. The Johnsons paid a moving company $2,002 to move their possessions to the new location. They also drove the 50 miles to their new residence. They stopped along the way for lunch and spent $60 eating at Denny's. None of the moving expenses were reimbursed by ST.

f) Jeremy paid $4,500 for health insurance coverage for himself (not through an exchange). Alyssa was covered by health plans provided by her employer, but Jeremy is not eligible for the plan until next year.

g) Jeremy paid $2,500 in self-employment taxes ($1,250 represents the employer portion of the self-employment taxes).

h) Jeremy paid $5,000 in alimony and $3,000 in child support from his prior marriage.

i) Alyssa paid $3,100 of tuition and fees to attend night classes at a local university. The Johnsons would like to deduct as much of this expenditure as possible rather than claim a credit.

j) The Johnsons donated $2,000 to their favorite charity.

tax forms

70. Shauna Coleman is single. She is employed as an architectural designer for Streamline Design (SD). Shauna wanted to determine her taxable income for this year. She correctly calculated her AGI. However, she wasn't sure how to compute the rest of her taxable income. She provided the following information with hopes that you could use it to determine her taxable income.

a) Shauna paid $4,680 for medical expenses for care from a broken ankle. Also, Shauna's boyfriend, Blake, drove Shauna (in her car) a total of 115 miles to the doctor's office so she could receive care for her broken ankle.

b) Shauna paid a total of $3,400 in health insurance premiums during the year (not through an exchange). SD did not reimburse any of this expense. Besides the health insurance premiums and the medical expenses for her broken ankle, Shauna had Lasik eye surgery last year and she paid $3,000 for the surgery (she received no insurance reimbursement). She also incurred $450 of other medical expenses for the year.

c) SD withheld $1,800 of state income tax, $7,495 of Social Security tax, and $14,500 of federal income tax from Shauna's paychecks throughout the year.

d) In 2016, Shauna was due a refund of $250 for overpaying her 2015 state taxes. On her 2015 state tax return that she filed in April 2016, she applied the overpayment toward her 2016 state tax liability. She estimated that her state tax liability for 2016 will be $2,300.

e) Shauna paid $3,200 of property taxes on her personal residence. She also paid $500 to the developer of her subdivision, because he had to replace the sidewalk in certain areas of the subdivision.

f) Shauna paid a $200 property tax based on the state's estimate of the value of her car.

g) Shauna has a home mortgage loan in the amount of $220,000 that she secured when she purchased her home. The home is worth about $400,000. Shauna paid interest of $12,300 on the loan this year.

h) Shauna made several charitable contributions throughout the year. She contributed stock in ZYX Corp. to the Red Cross. On the date of the contribution, the fair market value of the donated shares was $1,000 and her basis in the shares was $400. Shauna originally bought the ZYX Corp. stock in 2008. Shauna also contributed $300 cash to State University and religious artifacts she has held for several years to her church. The artifacts were valued at $500 and Shauna's basis in the items was $300. Shauna had every reason to believe the church would keep them on display indefinitely. Shauna also drove 200 miles doing church-related errands for her minister. Finally, Shauna contributed $1,200 of services to her church last year.

i) Shauna's car was totaled in a wreck in January. The car was worth $14,000 and her cost basis in the car was $16,000. The car was a complete loss. Shauna received $2,000 in insurance reimbursements for the loss.

j) Shauna paid $300 for architectural design publications, $100 for continuing education courses to keep her up to date on the latest design technology, and $200 for professional dues to maintain her status in a professional designer's organization.

k) Shauna paid $250 in investment advisory fees and another $150 to have her tax return prepared (that is, she paid $150 in 2016 to have her 2015 tax return prepared).

l) Shauna is involved in horse racing as a hobby. During the year, she won $2,500 in prize money and incurred $10,000 in expenses. She has never had a profitable year with her horse racing activities, so she acknowledges that this is a hobby for federal income tax purposes.

m) Shauna sustained $2,000 in gambling losses over the year (mostly horse-racing bets) and only had $200 in winnings.

Required

A) Determine Shauna's taxable income and complete page 2 of Form 1040 (through taxable income, line 43) and Schedule A assuming her AGI is $107,000.

B) Determine Shauna's taxable income and complete page 2 of Form 1040 (through taxable income, line 43) and Schedule A assuming her AGI is $207,000.

71. Joe and Jessie are married and have one dependent child, Lizzie. Lizzie is currently in college at State University. Joe works as a design engineer for a manufacturing firm while Jessie runs a craft business from their home. Jessie's craft business consists of making craft items for sale at craft shows that are held periodically at various locations. Jessie spends considerable time and effort on her craft business and it has been consistently profitable over the years. Joe and

Jessie own a home and pay interest on their home loan (balance of $220,000) and a personal loan to pay for Lizzie's college expenses (balance of $35,000). Neither Joe nor Jessie is blind or over age 65, and they plan to file as married joint. Based on their estimates, determine Joe and Jessie's AGI and taxable income for the year and complete pages 1 and 2 of Form 1040 (through taxable income, line 43) and Schedule A. Assume that the employer portion of the self-employment tax on Jessie's income is $808. Joe and Jessie have summarized the income and expenses they expect to report this year as follows:

Income:

Joe's salary	$119,100
Jessie's craft sales	18,400
Interest from certificate of deposit	1,650
Interest from Treasury bond funds	727
Interest from municipal bond funds	920

Expenditures:

Federal income tax withheld from Joe's wages	$13,700
State income tax withheld from Joe's wages	6,400
Social Security tax withheld from Joe's wages	7,482
Real estate taxes on residence	6,200
Automobile licenses (based on weight)	310
State sales tax paid	1,150
Home mortgage interest	14,000
Interest on Masterdebt credit card	2,300
Medical expenses (unreimbursed)	1,690
Joe's employee expenses (unreimbursed)	2,400
Cost of Jessie's craft supplies	4,260
Postage for mailing crafts	145
Travel and lodging for craft shows	2,230
Meals during craft shows	670
Self-employment tax on Jessie's craft income	1,615
College tuition paid for Lizzie	5,780
Interest on loans to pay Lizzie's tuition	3,200
Lizzie's room and board at college	12,620
Cash contributions to the Red Cross	525

7 Investments

Upon completing this chapter, you should be able to:

LO 7-1 Explain how interest income and dividend income are taxed.

LO 7-2 Compute the tax consequences associated with the disposition of capital assets, including the netting process for calculating gains and losses.

LO 7-3 Calculate the deduction for portfolio investment-related expenses, including investment expenses and investment interest expense.

LO 7-4 Understand the distinction between portfolio investments and passive investments and apply tax basis, at-risk, and passive activity loss limits to losses from passive investments.

© Image Source

Storyline Summary

Taxpayers:	Courtney Wilson, age 40 Courtney's uncle, Jeb Landers, age 65
Family description:	Courtney is divorced with a son, Deron, age 10, and a daughter, Ellen, age 20. Jeb is single.
Location:	Kansas City, Missouri
Employment status:	Courtney works as an architect for EWD. Her salary is $98,000. Jeb is recently retired.
Current situation:	Courtney is deciding how to invest her inheritance. Jeb is concerned about the tax effects of selling investment assets.

Courtney has settled into her new Kansas City location and is now focusing on her investment portfolio. When her father, "Gramps," passed away last December, he left Courtney an inheritance of $100,000 with the stipulation that she "invest it to financially benefit her family." After considerable thought, Courtney decided to invest the inheritance to accomplish two financial goals. First, she wants to save for her son Deron's college education. She figures that if she immediately invests $50,000 of the inheritance for his college education, she should have a significant sum accumulated when Deron starts college in eight years. Second, she decided that she will immediately invest the remaining $50,000 for five years and use the accumulation to make a significant down payment on a vacation home in Park City, Utah, a town she fell in love with during a college ski trip. Courtney is concerned about how different investment choices will be taxed and how this might affect her ability to meet her financial goals.

Courtney's Uncle Jeb, who is single, has sold several investments during the year with the hope that he could use the proceeds to fulfill his lifelong dream of owning a sailboat. He is uncertain about how much tax he will owe after selling the assets. ∎

INVESTMENTS OVERVIEW

Investors are attracted to certain investments according to their investment philosophy and their appetite for risk, among other things. Some prefer investments that provide a consistent income stream. Others prefer investments that have significant appreciation potential but provide no current cash flows. These investment attributes affect the before-tax returns on investments. However, taxes are levied on **investment income,** and thus, it would be unwise to make an investment without considering the tax cost. For example, it is possible that two investments with identical before-tax rates of return will generate different after-tax rates of return because the investments are taxed differently. Indeed, it is possible that an investment with a lower before-tax rate of return compared to an alternative investment will have a higher after-tax rate of return because income from the investment is taxed at a later date or taxed at a lower rate than the alternative investment.

Two key tax characteristics that affect after-tax returns from investments are (1) the timing of tax payments or tax benefits and (2) the rate at which investment income or gains are taxed or deductible expenses or losses generate tax savings. Not surprisingly, these variables are directly related to the timing and conversion tax planning strategies introduced in Chapter 3.

Income from **portfolio investments** (investments producing **dividends,** interest, royalties, annuities, or capital gains) may be taxed at ordinary rates, preferential rates, or may be exempt from taxation. Further, depending on the type of investment, tax on income from a portfolio investment may be imposed annually or may be deferred until the taxpayer sells the investment. Losses from portfolio investments are deferred until the investment is sold and are typically subject to limitations.

In contrast to portfolio investments, **passive investments** generate **operating income** and **operating losses.** Operating income is always taxed annually at ordinary rates while operating losses are either deducted annually at ordinary rates or deferred and deducted later at ordinary rates depending on the investor's circumstances. Losses from passive investments are also subject to limitations.

This chapter explores several common portfolio and passive investments, discusses important tax and nontax considerations relevant for those investments, and compares investment returns on an after-tax basis.

LO 7-1

PORTFOLIO INCOME: INTEREST AND DIVIDENDS

Taxpayers who desire current cash flows from their investments may choose investments that generate interest or regular dividends. Investments generating interest income include **certificates of deposit** (CDs), savings accounts, corporate **bonds,** and governmental bonds. Investments generating dividend income include direct equity investments in corporate stocks or investments in **mutual funds** that invest in corporate stock.[1] Although all of these investments generate current cash flows, they differ significantly in terms of their economic and tax consequences.

By lending money to banks, governmental entities, or corporations, investors essentially become debt holders. As such, they are legally entitled to receive periodic interest payments *and* to recover the amount of principal loaned (in the case of bonds, principal is the **maturity value** or **face value** of the bonds). Interest payments and the time and manner of repayment of the loan principal are defined either contractually for CDs and savings accounts or by bond covenants for loans made either to governments or corporations. In contrast, investors who purchase stocks become shareholders (also called equity holders) of a corporation. As shareholders, they are

---

[1]Mutual funds are portfolios of investment assets managed by professional money managers. Generally, the income earned by mutual funds flows through to the owners of mutual fund shares who pay the resulting taxes due. The nature of the assets held by the mutual fund determines the character of the income.

entitled to receive dividends if the company declares dividends and to *indirectly* share in either the future appreciation or depreciation in the value of a corporation through stock ownership. Unlike debt holders, shareholders are not legally entitled to receive dividend payments or to recover their initial investment. Thus, from an investor's perspective, debt tends to be less risky than equity.

For tax purposes, individual investors typically are taxed on both interest and dividend income when they receive it. However, interest income is taxed at ordinary rates while dividend income is generally taxed at lower capital gains rates.

- Dividends
  - Dividends are taxed annually.
  - Qualified dividends are taxed at preferential rates.

Interest

In general, taxpayers recognize interest income from investments when they receive the interest payments.[2] Taxpayers investing in savings accounts, money market accounts, CDs, and most bonds receive interest payments based on a stated annual rate of return at yearly or more frequent intervals.

Special rules apply for determining the timing and amount of interest from bonds when there is a **bond discount** (bonds are issued at an amount below the maturity value) or a **bond premium** (bonds are issued at an amount above the maturity value). Below we discuss these rules as they apply to corporate, U.S. Treasury bonds, and **U.S. savings bonds.**

Corporate and U.S. Treasury Bonds

Both corporations and the U.S. Treasury raise money from debt markets by issuing bonds.[3] Corporate bonds, **Treasury bonds,** and **Treasury notes** are issued at maturity value, at a discount, or at a premium, depending on prevailing interest rates.[4] Treasury bonds and Treasury notes pay a stated rate of interest semiannually.[5] However, corporate bonds may pay interest at a stated "coupon" rate or they may not provide any periodic interest payments. Corporate bonds that do not pay periodic interest are called **zero-coupon bonds.** Overall, the consequences of holding corporate or Treasury bonds are very similar. The two primary differences are that (1) interest from Treasury bonds is exempt from *state* taxation while interest from corporate bonds is not and (2) Treasury bonds always pay interest periodically while corporate bonds may or may not. The tax rules for determining the timing and amount of interest income from corporate and U.S. Treasury bonds are as follows:

- Taxpayers include the actual interest payments they receive in gross income.
- If the bond was issued at a discount, special **original issue discount** (OID) rules apply. Taxpayers are required to amortize the discount and include the amount of the current year **amortization** in gross income in addition to any interest payments the taxpayer actually receives.[6] In the case of corporate zero-coupon bonds, this means taxpayers must report and pay taxes on income related to the bonds even though they did not receive *any* payments from the bonds. Bond issuers or brokers are responsible for calculating the yearly amortization of original issue discount and providing this information to investors using Form 1099-OID.

[2]Interest income is reported on Part I of Schedule B filed with taxpayers' Form 1040.

[3]Investors in corporate bonds assume more risk than investors in Treasury securities because they are relying on the creditworthiness of the corporation issuing the bonds. To compensate bondholders for this additional risk, corporate bonds usually yield higher before-tax rates of return than Treasury securities.

[4]The bonds are issued at a discount (premium) if the market interest rate is higher (lower) than the stated rate on the bonds.

[5]Treasury notes and bonds differ in terms of their maturities. Treasury notes are issued with 2-, 5-, and 10-year maturities. In contrast, Treasury bonds are issued with maturities greater than 10 years. From this point forward, we use the term Treasury bonds to refer to both Treasury notes and Treasury bonds.

[6]§1272. Original issue discount is amortized semiannually under the constant yield method, which is consistent with the approach used to amortize bond discount under GAAP.

- If the bond was issued at a premium, taxpayers may *elect* to amortize the premium.[7] Taxpayers or their advisors are responsible for determining the yearly amortization of bond premium if the election to amortize the premium has been made. The amount of the current year amortization offsets a portion of the actual interest payments that taxpayers must include in gross income. The original tax basis of the bond includes the premium and is reduced by any amortization of bond premium over the life of the bond.

- If the bond is purchased in the secondary bond market at a discount, the taxpayer treats some of or all of the **market discount** as interest income *when she sells the bond or the bond matures.*[8] If the bond is sold prior to **maturity,** a ratable amount of the market discount (based on the number of days the bond is held over the number of days until maturity when the bond is purchased), called the **accrued market discount,** is treated as interest income on the date of sale.[9] If the bond is held to maturity, the entire bond discount is treated as interest income at maturity.

- If the bond is purchased in the secondary bond market at a premium, the premium is treated exactly like original issue bond premiums. As a result, the taxpayer may elect to amortize the **market premium** to reduce the annual interest income received from the bond. Otherwise, the premium remains as part of the tax basis of the bond and affects the capital gain or loss the taxpayer recognizes when the taxpayer sells or redeems the bond.

U.S. Savings Bonds   U.S. savings bonds such as Series EE or Series I bonds are issued at either face value or at a discount. These bonds do not pay periodic interest; rather, interest accumulates over the term of the bonds and is paid when investors redeem them at maturity or earlier.[10] That is, the amount of interest income taxpayers recognize *when they redeem* the bonds is the excess of the bond proceeds over the taxpayer's **basis** (purchase price) in the bonds. Taxpayers may elect to include the increase in the bond redemption value in income each year, but this is generally not advisable because it accelerates the income from the bond without providing any cash to pay the taxes.[11] Finally, interest from Series EE and Series I bonds may be excluded from gross income to the extent the bond proceeds are used to pay qualifying educational expenses. However, this exclusion benefit is subject to phase-out based on the taxpayer's AGI.

Example 7-1

What if: Assume that Courtney was deciding whether to invest the $50,000 earmarked for the Park City vacation home in (1) Series EE savings bonds that mature in exactly five years, (2) original issue AMD Corporation zero-coupon bonds that mature in exactly five years, or (3) U.S. Treasury bonds that pay $46,250 at maturity in five years trading in the secondary bond market with a stated annual interest rate of 10 percent. Further, assume that all bonds yield 8 percent annual before-tax returns compounded semiannually. At the end of the first year, the redemption value of the EE savings bond would be $54,080, or Courtney would receive a Form 1099-OID from AMD reporting

---

[7]§171. Like an original issue discount, a bond premium is amortized semiannually under the constant yield method—the same method used to amortize bond premiums under GAAP. Unlike premiums on taxable bonds, premiums on tax-exempt bonds must always be amortized.

[8]§1276(a). Under §1278(b)(1), taxpayers may elect to include the amortization of market discount in their income annually. However, this election accelerates the recognition of income from the market discount and is therefore usually not advisable.

[9]§1276(b).

[10]Series EE savings bonds are issued at a discount and Series I savings bonds are issued at maturity value. EE bonds provide a constant rate of return while Series I bonds provide a return that is indexed for inflation and thus increases over time.

[11]§454(a). Investors that make this election report the annual increase in the redemption value of their savings bonds using savings bond redemption tables published by the Treasury Department.

$4,080 of OID amortization for the year, or she would receive two semiannual interest payments of $2,312.50 from the Treasury bonds. Under the general rules, how much interest income from each bond would Courtney report at the end of the first year?

Answer: $0 from the Series EE savings bonds, $4,080 from the AMD bonds, and $4,625 (two semiannual payments of $2,312.50) from the Treasury bonds. Note, however, that Courtney could *elect* to include the $4,080 increase in redemption value of the Series EE bond in interest income even though she did not receive any interest payments on the bond (probably not optimal). She also could *elect* to amortize $637.50 of the $3,750 premium ($50,000 purchase price less the $46,250 maturity value) on the Treasury bond to offset the $4,625 in actual interest payments she received on the bond (probably a good idea). The calculations required to amortize the premium on the Treasury bond for the first year are reflected in the following table:

Semiannual Period	(A) Adjusted Basis of Bond at Beginning of Semiannual Period	(B) Interest Received and Reported ($46,250 × 10% × .5)	(C) Interest Earned (A) × 8% × .5	Premium Amortization (B) − (C)
1	$50,000.00	$2,312.50	$2,000.00	$312.50
2	49,687.50	2,312.50	1,987.50	325.00
Yearly Total		4,625.00	3,987.50	637.50

Intuitively, would Courtney be better or worse off purchasing the Series EE savings bonds rather than a corporate bond to save for the Park City home?

Answer: She would be better off in two respects. First, she wouldn't have to pay state income taxes on the interest earned from the savings bonds. Second, she would be able to defer paying taxes on the accumulated interest from the savings bonds until the savings bonds are cashed in at maturity. This will increase the after-tax returns from the savings bonds relative to a corporate bond.

Intuitively, would Courtney be better or worse off purchasing the AMD zero-coupon bonds rather than a corporate bond to save for the Park City home?

Answer: She will be worse off because she will have to pay taxes currently from the OID amortization on the AMD bonds without receiving any cash flow from the bonds to pay the taxes due. This will reduce the after-tax returns from the AMD bonds relative to a corporate bond.

Example 7-2

What if: Assume that on January 1, Courtney used the $50,000 earmarked for the Park City vacation home to purchase AMD zero-coupon bonds in the *secondary bond market* almost immediately after they were originally issued. If the bonds mature in exactly five years and have a maturity value of $74,000, how much interest income will Courtney report at the end of the first year and in the year the bonds mature?

Answer: $0 in the first year and $24,000 in the year the bonds mature. Because the AMD zero-coupon bonds were not purchased at original issue, the entire $24,000 market discount on the bonds will be reported as interest income when the bonds mature. Thus, Courtney will not report any income related to the AMD bonds until the year the bonds mature.

What if: Assume the same facts as above, except Courtney purchased a U.S. Series EE bond instead of an AMD zero-coupon bond to fund the Park City vacation home in five years. How much interest income will she report at the end of the first year and in the year the bonds mature?

Answer: $0 in the first year and $24,000 in the year the EE savings bonds mature; exactly the same outcome as the investment in the AMD zero-coupon bonds.

As our discussion suggests, for certain types of investments such as savings accounts, money market accounts, and CDs, computing the annual taxable interest income is relatively straightforward. However, for investments in bonds, the process is much more involved. Exhibit 7-1 summarizes the general rule and exceptions for the timing of interest payments and related tax payments.

EXHIBIT 7-1 **Timing of Interest Payments and Taxes**

General Rule	Exception	Exception
Interest Received Annually and Taxed Annually	**Interest Received at Sale or Maturity and Taxed at Sale or Maturity**	**Interest Received at Sale or Maturity but Taxed Annually**
• Savings accounts • CDs • Money market accounts • Bond interest payments actually received in the year	• Accrued market discount on bonds • Interest earned on U.S. savings bonds	• Original issue discount (OID) on corporate and Treasury bonds

Dividends

Historically, dividends received by investors have been taxed at the same rate as interest income; however, in 2003 Congress changed the law for dividends to mitigate the so-called "double tax" on dividend income.[12] Consistent with the general rule for taxing interest income, dividend payments (including reinvested dividends) are taxed annually.[13] However, as we discuss in Chapter 8, **qualified dividends** are taxed at a preferential rate: 0, 15, or 20 percent, depending on the rate at which the dividends would be taxed if they were ordinary income.[14] Qualified dividends are those paid by domestic or certain qualified foreign corporations provided investors hold the dividend-paying stock for *more than* 60 days during the 121-day period that begins 60 days before the **ex-dividend date** (the first day on which the purchaser of the stock would not be entitled to receive a declared dividend on the stock).[15] Exhibit 7-2 illustrates the 121-day period surrounding the ex-dividend date. Nonqualified dividends are not eligible for the reduced rate and are therefore taxed at ordinary rates. Corporations report the amounts of the dividends and indicate whether the dividends are potentially eligible for the preferential rate when they send Form 1099-DIV to shareholders after year-end. However, shareholders ultimately must determine if they qualify for the preferential rate by confirming they held the stock for the required number of days around the ex-dividend date.

EXHIBIT 7-2 **Holding Period for Qualified Dividends**

[12]Because corporations pay income taxes, dividends are taxed once at the corporate level when the income used to pay dividends is earned by the corporation, and a second time when dividends are received by investors.

[13]Dividends are reported on Part II of Schedule B filed with taxpayers' Form 1040.

[14]Qualified dividends that would have been taxed at 10 or 15 percent if they were ordinary income are taxed at 0 percent, qualified dividends that would have been taxed at 39.6 percent as ordinary income are taxed at 20 percent, and all other qualified dividends are taxed at 15 percent.

[15]Qualified foreign corporations are those incorporated in a U.S. possession (e.g., Puerto Rico, U.S. Virgin Islands), those eligible for the benefits of a comprehensive income tax treaty with the United States, or those whose shares are readily traded on an established U.S. securities market.

Example 7-3

What if: Assume Courtney decides to purchase dividend-paying stocks to achieve her financial objectives. She invests $50,000 in Xerox stock, which she intends to hold for five years and then sell it to fund the Park City home down payment. She invests another $50,000 in Coca-Cola stock, which she intends to hold for eight years and then sell it to fund her son's education. How much dividend income will Courtney report at the end of the first year if the dividend payments provide an 8 percent return on her investments?[16]

Answer: Courtney will report $4,000 ($50,000 × .08) of dividend income from the Xerox stock for the first year of her investment and $4,000 ($50,000 × .08) of dividend income from the Coca-Cola stock for a total of $8,000 of dividend income.

What if: Assume Courtney's ordinary marginal tax rate is 30 percent. How much tax would Courtney owe on her dividend income if the dividends are nonqualified?

Answer: Courtney would owe $2,400 ($8,000 × 30%) of tax if the dividends are nonqualified because the income would be taxed at her ordinary income tax rate.

What if: What amount of tax would Courtney owe if the dividends are qualified?

Answer: Courtney would owe $1,200 ($8,000 × 15%) of tax if the dividends are qualified because qualified dividends are taxed at preferential rates. Courtney's dividends are taxed at 15 percent because her ordinary tax rate is more than 15 percent but less than 39.6 percent.

Because dividend income is taxed generally at lower rates than interest income, it appears that taxpayers seeking current cash flows from their investments should favor dividend-paying investments over interest-paying investments. This raises the question of why anyone would ever prefer investments paying interest over those paying dividends. Remember, though, that savvy investors also should consider nontax factors such as before-tax rates of return, risk, and liquidity needs when choosing among alternative investments. These fundamental differences explain why investors may continue to seek out interest income in spite of the associated tax disadvantages.

PORTFOLIO INCOME: CAPITAL GAINS AND LOSSES   LO 7-2

Investors who don't need annual cash flows from their investments may prefer to invest in assets with the expectation that the investments will appreciate in value over time, providing cash at some point in the future when they sell the assets. Investors also may be willing to assume greater risk in exchange for greater returns than those provided by interest or dividend-paying investments. For example, they might purchase raw land, fine art, rare coins, precious gems or metals, growth stocks (stock in corporations that reinvest their earnings to grow the company as opposed to distributing earnings to shareholders in the form of dividends), mutual fund shares, or even vintage automobiles. Purchasing any such asset is not without risk. Indeed, investments held solely for appreciation potential *may* actually decline in value.

When taxpayers buy and hold assets with appreciation potential, they typically are investing in **capital assets.** As we discussed in Chapter 4, capital assets are typically investment-type assets and personal-use assets.[17] Thus, artwork, corporate stock, bonds, your personal residence, and even your iPhone are capital assets.

---

[16]Annual returns from dividend-paying stocks are typically lower than the return from taxable bonds. However, it is assumed here that the returns are equal for the sake of comparability.

[17]§1221 defines capital assets in the negative. This code section excludes inventory, depreciable property or real property used in a trade or business, certain self-created intangibles, accounts or notes receivable, U.S. government publications, certain commodities derivative financial instruments, certain hedging transactions, and supplies from the definition of a capital asset.

While it may be enjoyable to view collectible fine art in your home or watch a stock portfolio grow in value on quarterly brokerage statements, from a tax perspective the real advantages of investing in capital assets are (1) gains are deferred for tax purposes until the taxpayer sells or otherwise disposes of the assets[18] and (2) gains generally are taxed at preferential rates relative to ordinary income.[19] Why the favorable treatment? One reason is that taxpayers may not have the wherewithal (cash) to pay the tax on their gains until they sell the investment. Another is that the preferential tax rate provides an incentive for taxpayers to invest in assets that may stimulate the economy. Investors can capture these tax benefits when they sell capital assets at a gain. However, when they sell capital assets at a loss, their ability to deduct the loss may be limited.

When a taxpayer sells a capital asset for more than its **tax basis,** the taxpayer recognizes a capital gain; if a taxpayer sells a capital asset for less than its tax basis, the taxpayer recognizes a capital loss (to the extent the loss is deductible).[20] The amount realized or selling price of a capital asset includes the cash and fair market value of other property received, less broker's fees and other selling costs. The basis of any asset, including a capital asset, is generally the taxpayer's "cost" of acquiring the asset, including the initial purchase price and other costs incurred to purchase or improve the asset.[21] Thus, the tax basis of corporate stock purchased from a stockbroker includes the cost of the stock and any additional brokerage fees paid by the taxpayer to acquire the stock. Also, the tax basis in a personal residence includes the initial purchase price plus the cost of subsequent improvements to the home.

TAXES IN THE REAL WORLD Creative Genius

The tax code defines capital assets by listing assets that are *not* capital assets in §1221. Listed among the assets not to be treated as capital are copyrights and literary, musical, and artistic compositions. This placed those who create intangible products on par with those who produce tangible products because §1221 also defines inventory as not a capital asset. Back in 2005, Congress passed temporary legislation (later made permanent in 2006) that permits musicians to treat the sale of their creative works as the sale of capital assets. In 2011, the IRS issued final regulations on making this election. As a result of making this election, a composer who sells copyrighted material will pay tax on any gain at the lower capital gains tax rates.

Source: Federal Tax Updates on Checkpoint Newsstand tab, February 7, 2011.

Because a taxpayer cannot accurately compute the gain or loss on the sale of a capital asset without knowing its basis, it is important for taxpayers to maintain accurate records to track their basis in capital assets. This process is relatively

---

[18]Similarly, interest related to market discount on bonds and the original issue discount on U.S. EE savings bonds accumulates free of tax until the bonds mature or are sold. However, ordinary rather than capital gains rates apply when the tax must finally be paid.

[19]Mutual funds that generate current income by regularly selling capital assets or by holding income-producing securities are an exception to this general rule. However, tax-efficient mutual funds that only buy and hold growth stocks are treated more like other capital assets for tax purposes (capital gains are deferred until mutual fund shares are sold).

[20]As discussed below, losses on personal assets are not deductible for tax purposes.

[21]For stocks acquired on or after January 1, 2011, brokers are required to report to the IRS the tax basis of securities their customers sell. Starting January 1, 2012, brokers are required to report cost basis information for sales associated with shares of mutual funds and dividend reinvestment plans that were purchased on or after January 1, 2012. Finally, for all other securities not previously mentioned, starting for sales after January 1, 2013, cost basis information must be reported if the securities were purchased on or after January 1, 2013.

straightforward for unique assets such as a taxpayer's personal residence or individual jewels in a taxpayer's jewelry collection. However, capital assets such as shares of stock are much more homogeneous and difficult to track. For example, a taxpayer may purchase blocks of stock in a given corporation at different times over a period of several years, paying a different price per share for each block of stock acquired. When the taxpayer sells shares of this stock in subsequent years, what basis does she use to compute gain or loss? By default, taxpayers are required to use the **first-in first-out (FIFO) method** of determining the basis of the shares they sell.[22] However, if they (or their broker) track the basis of their stock, taxpayers can sell (or instruct their broker to sell) specific shares using the **specific identification method** to determine the basis of the shares they sell. Taxpayers using the specific identification method can choose to sell their high-basis stock first, minimizing their gains or increasing their losses on stock dispositions.

Example 7-4

After Courtney's car broke down, she decided to buy a new one. To fund the down payment, she sold 200 shares of Cisco stock at the current market price of $40 per share for a total amount realized of $8,000. Courtney held the following blocks of Cisco stock at the time of the sale:

Cisco Corporation Stock Ownership					
Holding Period	(1) Cost per Share	(2) Shares	(1) × (2) Basis	Basis of 200 Shares Sold	Explanation
5 years	$25	250	$6,250	$5,000	FIFO basis ($25 × 200)
2 years	32	250	8,000	6,400	Specific ID basis ($32 × 200)

How much capital gain will Courtney recognize if she uses the FIFO method of computing the basis in the Cisco shares sold?

Answer: $3,000. $8,000 amount realized ($40 × 200) minus $5,000 FIFO basis ($25 × 200). As indicated in the table above, under the FIFO (oldest first) method, they are treated as though she sold the stock held for five years.

What if: How much capital gain will Courtney recognize if they use the specific identification method of computing the basis in the shares sold to minimize the taxable gain on the sale?

Answer: $1,600. $8,000 amount realized ($40 × 200) minus $6,400 ($32 × 200). To minimize her gain on the sale under the specific identification method, Courtney would choose to sell the 200 shares with the highest basis. As indicated in the table above, the shares with the higher basis are those acquired and held two years for $32 per share.

Note in the above example that Courtney receives $8,000 from the stock sale ($40 per share × 200 shares sold) regardless of the method she uses to compute the basis of the shares she sells. The difference between the FIFO and specific identification methods lies in the amount of taxable gain on the *current* sale. Over time, as taxpayers sell all of their stock, both methods will ultimately allow taxpayers to fully recover their cost in the investments. However, applying the specific identification method will result in lower capital gains taxes currently and thereby minimize the present value of the taxes paid on stock sales.

[22]Reg. §1.1012-1(c)(1).

Types of Capital Gains and Losses

Taxpayers selling capital assets that they hold for a year or less recognize **short-term capital gains or losses.**[23] Alternatively, taxpayers selling capital assets they hold for more than a year recognize **long-term capital gains or losses.** Short-term capital gains are taxed at ordinary rather than preferential rates. In contrast, long-term capital gains are taxed at preferential rates. However, not all long-term capital gains are created equal. Just like dividends, most long-term capital gains are taxed at either 0 percent, 15 percent, or 20 percent depending on the rate at which the gains would be taxed if they were ordinary income. Long-term capital gains that would be taxed at 10 or 15 percent as ordinary income are taxed at 0 percent, gains that would be taxed at 39.6 percent as ordinary income are taxed at 20 percent, and other long-term capital gains are taxed at 15 percent. However, certain long-term capital gains are taxed at a maximum rate of 25 percent **(unrecaptured §1250 gain)** and others are taxed at a maximum 28 percent rate **(collectibles and qualified small business stock)** for tax policy reasons.

25 Percent Gain   When individuals sell depreciable real property held more than one year at a gain, a portion (or even all) of the gain may be taxed at a maximum rate of 25 percent (the unrecaptured §1250 gain portion) and a portion may be taxed as a 0/15/20 percent gain. In Chapter 11, we discuss the details of how to compute the amount of 25 percent gain and the amount of 0/15/20 percent gain when an individual sells depreciable real property; however, we include a brief discussion in this chapter because the amount of 25 percent gain affects the capital gain and loss netting process we discuss in this chapter.

Example 7-5

What if: Assume Jeb Landers (single), Courtney's uncle, recently sold a rental home for $160,000. He originally acquired the home many years ago for $100,000, and he has fully depreciated it for tax purposes. Assume that $100,000 of the gain (the unrecaptured §1250 gain portion) is taxed at a maximum rate of 25 percent. If Jeb's marginal ordinary tax rate is 35 percent, what tax does he owe on the gain if he did not sell any other property during the year?

Answer: $34,000. Because Jeb's tax basis in the home is $0 (he has fully depreciated it), his gain on the sale is $160,000. Jeb owes 25 percent tax on the $100,000 resulting in $25,000 of tax on this portion of the gain ($100,000 × 25%). The remaining $60,000 of gain is taxed at 15 percent, so he owes $9,000 of tax on this portion ($60,000 × 15%). In total, he owes $34,000 of tax on the gain ($25,000 + $9,000).

What if: Suppose Jeb's marginal ordinary tax rate is 39.6 percent rather than 35 percent. What tax does he owe on the gain?

Answer: $37,000. The $100,000 is taxed at 25 percent for a tax of $25,000. The remaining $60,000 of gain is taxed at 20 percent because it would have been taxed at 39.6 percent if it were ordinary income. Consequently, he owes $12,000 of tax on this portion ($60,000 × 20%). In total, Jeb owes $37,000 of tax on the gain ($25,000 + $12,000).

---

28 Percent Gains   Gains from two types of capital assets are taxable at a maximum 28 percent rate. The first type, **collectibles,** consists of works of art, any rug or antique, any metal or gem, any stamp or coin, any alcoholic beverage, or other

---

[23]Nonbusiness bad debt is treated as a short-term capital loss no matter how long the debt was outstanding before it became worthless. Whether a bad debt is considered to be a business bad debt for individuals depends on the facts and circumstances. In general, if the taxpayer experiencing the loss is in the business of loaning money, the bad debt should be considered to be business bad debt; otherwise, the bad debt will likely be considered nonbusiness bad debt.

similar items held for more than one year.[24] The second type is qualified small business stock held for *more than five years*.[25] In general, §1202 defines qualified small business stock as stock received at *original issue* from a C corporation with a gross tax basis in its assets both before and after the issuance of no more than $50,000,000 and with at least 80 percent of the value of its assets used in the active conduct of certain qualified trades or businesses. Under this definition, many investors and employees who hold stock in closely held corporations are likely to hold qualified small business stock. When taxpayers sell qualified small business stock after holding it for more than five years, they may exclude a portion of the gain on the sale from regular taxation. The excluded portion depends on the date the taxpayer acquired the stock.

EXHIBIT 7-3   Exclusion for §1202 Stock Held More Than Five Years

Acquisition Date	Exclusion	Effective Capital Gains Tax Rate
After December 31, 2014	100%	04%
After December 31, 2013, and before January 1, 2015	50	14
After September 27, 2010, and before January 1, 2014	100	0
After February 17, 2009, and before September 28, 2010	75	7
After August 10, 1993, and before February 18, 2009	50	14

The capital gain not excluded from income is taxed at 28 percent. For example, using the minimum exclusion percentage of 50 percent, the effective capital gains tax rate is 14 percent.[26]

Example 7-6

What if: Assume that Jeb sold his stock in Gangbusters Inc., a qualified small business stock, for $200,000 on December 12, 2016. He acquired the stock on November 8, 2010, and his basis in the stock is $50,000. How much tax will he owe on the sale if his ordinary marginal rate is 35 percent?

Answer: $0. Because Jeb held the qualified small business stock for more than five years and because he acquired the stock when the exclusion percentage was 100 percent, he will exclude the entire $150,000 gain from income.

What if: Assume instead that Jeb sold his Gangbusters stock on December 12, 2016, but had acquired the stock on February 17, 2013. How much tax will he owe on the sale?

Answer: $22,500. Because Jeb didn't hold the stock for more than five years, he must recognize all $150,000 of long-term capital gain. This gain is taxed at 15 percent, yielding a total tax due of $22,500.

Exhibit 7-4 presents the maximum tax rates applicable to capital gains.

[24]§408(m).

[25]§1(h)(7).

[26]The maximum exclusion is the greater of $10,000,000 ($5,000,000 for married taxpayers filing separately) or 10 times the adjusted basis of the stock [see §1202(b)(1)]. Generally, the amount of gain excluded from the sale of qualified small business stock is an AMT preference item. Consequently, the gain otherwise excludable for regular tax purposes may be taxed under the AMT system. However, gain excluded from the sale of qualified small business stock acquired after September 27, 2010, and before January 1, 2014, is not an AMT preference item.

EXHIBIT 7-4 **Classification of Capital Gains by Maximum Applicable Tax Rates**

Short-Term or Long-Term	Type	Maximum Rate
Short-term	All	39.6%*
Long-term	Collectibles	28*
Held > 5 years	Qualified small business stock	14%**
Long-term	Unrecaptured §1250 gain from depreciable realty	25*
Long-term	All remaining capital (and §1231 gains) gain not included elsewhere	20†,‡

*Lower rates will apply when the taxpayer's ordinary rate is less than the rates reflected in this exhibit.
**The maximum rate of 15% applies when the lowest exclusion percentage of 50% is in effect.
†This gain is taxed at 0 percent to the extent it would have been taxed at a rate of 15 percent or less if it were ordinary income, taxed at 20 percent to the extent it would have been taxed at 39.6 percent as ordinary income, and taxed at 15 percent otherwise.
‡High income taxpayers may also be subject to an additional 3.8% net investment income tax on capital gains.

Netting Process for Gains and Losses To this point, our discussion of applicable tax rates for capital gains hasn't considered situations in which taxpayers recognize both capital gains and capital losses in the same year. To determine the appropriate tax treatment for the capital gains and losses recognized during the year, the taxpayer must complete a netting process. This netting process can be complex when taxpayers recognize capital losses and long-term capital gains subject to different maximum tax rates. In essence, the netting process separates capital gains and losses into short-term and three different long-term categories (based on the maximum rate applicable to the long-term gains). Although the process is complex, the underlying intuition is to have taxpayers net all long-term gains and losses together allowing long-term losses to offset the highest rate long-term gains first. Then, taxpayers use net long-term losses to offset short-term gains or short-term losses to offset long-term gains.

After completing the netting process, taxpayers must calculate the tax consequences of the resulting outcomes. Net short-term capital gains are taxed at the same rate as ordinary income. Net long-term capital gains are taxed at a maximum of 28 percent if from the collectible and §1202 category, a maximum of 25 percent if from the unrecaptured §1250 gain category, or 0/15/20 percent for all other long-term capital gains. In the 0/15/20 percent category, net long-term gains are taxed at 20 percent to the extent the gains would have been taxed at 39.6 percent if they were ordinary income, at 15 percent to the extent the gains would have been taxed between 15 and 39.6 percent if they were ordinary income, and at 0 percent to the extent they would have been taxed at a rate of 15 percent or lower if they were ordinary income.

Taxpayers can deduct up to $3,000 ($1,500 if married filing separately) of net capital losses against ordinary income. Net capital losses in excess of $3,000 ($1,500 if married filing separately) retain their short- or long-term character and are carried forward and treated as though they were incurred in the subsequent year. Short-term losses are applied first to reduce ordinary income when the taxpayer recognizes both short- and long-term net capital losses. Capital loss carryovers for individuals never expire.

The following provides a step-by-step guide to the capital gains and losses netting process.

Step 1: Net all short-term capital gains and short-term capital losses, including any short-term capital loss carried forward from the prior year. A net positive amount is a **net short-term capital gain.** A net negative amount is a **net short-term capital loss.** If there are no long-term capital gains or losses, the netting process is complete. Otherwise, continue to step 2.

Step 2: Separate long-term capital gains and losses into three separate rate groups (28%, 25%, and 0/15/20%). Place any net long-term capital loss carried over from the prior year into the 28% rate group. Sum the gains and losses within each group. The outcome will be a net 28% gain or loss, a 25% gain (there are no 25% losses), and/or a net 0/15/20% gain or loss. Proceed to step 3.

Step 3: (A) If none of the long-term rate groups from step 2 nets to a gain, transfer the net loss (if any) in the 0/15/20% rate group to the 28% rate group, combine it with the loss in that group (if any) and proceed to step 4.

(B) If none of the long-term rate groups from step 2 nets to a loss, proceed to step 6.

(C) Combining net gains and losses in long-term rate groups:

1. If step 2 results in net losses in both the 28% and 0/15/20% rate groups, combine the net losses and then apply them to offset gains in the 25% rate group. If the losses exceed the gain, the result is a net long-term capital loss. Proceed to step 4. If the gain exceeds the losses, the result is a net long-term capital gain. Proceed to step 6.

2. If the step 2 outcomes include a net loss in the 28% rate group and net gains in the other rate groups, apply the net loss from the 28% rate group to the gain in the 25% rate group until the 25% rate group gain is reduced to zero. Then offset any remaining 28% rate group loss against the net gain in the 0/15/20% rate group. If the net loss from the 28% rate group exceeds the net gains from the other rate groups, the net loss is a net long-term capital loss. Proceed to step 4. If gain remains in the 25% and/or 0/15/20% rate groups after applying the loss, the result is a net long-term capital gain. Proceed to step 6.

3. If the amounts from step 2 include a net loss in the 0/15/20% rate group and net gains in the 28% and/or the 25% rate groups, apply the net loss from the 0/15/20% rate group to the net gain in the 28% rate group until the net gain is reduced to zero. Then offset any remaining loss against the gain in the 25% rate group. If the net loss from the 0/15/20% rate group exceeds the net gains from the other rate groups, the net loss is a net long-term capital loss. Proceed to step 4. If gain remains in the 28% and/or 25% rate groups after applying the loss, the result is a net long-term capital gain. Proceed to step 6.

Step 4: If there is no net short-term capital gain or loss from step 1, the netting process is complete; apply the net capital loss deduction limitations as described previously and ignore the remaining steps. If the result from step 1 is a net short-term capital loss *and* the result from step 3 is a net long-term capital loss, the netting process is complete: apply the net capital loss deduction limitations described previously and ignore the remaining steps. Otherwise, continue on to step 5.

Step 5: If step 1 produces a net short-term capital gain *and* step 3 produces a net long-term capital loss, sum the net short-term capital gain and the net long-term capital loss.

(a) If the outcome is a net loss, the netting process is complete. Apply the net capital loss deduction limitations described previously.

(b) If the outcome is a net gain, the net gain is treated the same as a net short-term capital gain and is taxed at ordinary rates. The netting process is complete.

Step 6: If there is no net short-term capital gain or loss from step 1, the netting process is complete. The tax on the net long-term capital gain remaining in each long-term group is determined as described in the next section. If the step 1 outcome is a net short-term capital gain, skip to step 7. If the step 1 outcome is a net short-term capital loss *and* step 3 results in a net gain in any (or all) of the long-term rate groups, first use the short-term capital loss to offset the gain in the 28% rate group (if any), then the gain in the 25% rate group (if any), and finally the gain in 0/15/20% rate group (if any).

(a) If the net short-term capital loss exceeds all gains in the long-term rate groups, the netting process is complete. Apply the net capital loss deduction limitations described previously.

(b) If the net short-term capital loss does not offset all of the gain in any (or all) of the long-term rate groups, the netting process is complete. The tax on the gain remaining in each long-term group is determined as described in the next section.

Step 7: If step 1 produces a net short-term capital gain *and* step 3 produces a net long-term capital gain(s), the netting process is complete. The tax on the remaining gains is determined as described in the next section.

Example 7-7

Jeb Landers has recently retired and now wants to pursue his life-long dream of owning a sailboat. To come up with the necessary cash, he sells the following investments:

Stock	Market Value	Basis	Capital Gain/Loss	Scenario 1 Type	Scenario 2 Type
A	$40,000	$ 5,000	$35,000	Long	Short
B	20,000	30,000	(10,000)	Long	Short
C	20,000	12,000	8,000	Short	Long
D	17,000	28,000	(11,000)	Short	Long

What is the amount and nature of Jeb's capital gains and losses (Scenario 1)?

Answer: $22,000 net capital gain (treated as long-term capital gain), computed as follows:

Step 1: Net short-term gains and short-term losses. The $8,000 short-term gain on stock C is netted against the $11,000 short-term loss on stock D, yielding an NSTCL of $3,000.

Step 2: Separate long-term gains and losses into rate groups and sum within group. Both long-term transactions are 0/15/20% types. The $35,000 long-term gain on stock A is netted against the $10,000 long-term loss on stock B, producing a gain of $25,000.

Step 3: 3(A) does not apply. 3(B) applies and requires skipping to step 6.

Step 4: Not required.

Step 5: Not required.

Step 6: Combine the net long-term capital gain of $25,000 with the net short-term capital loss of $3,000. This step results in a net capital gain of $22,000. The netting process is complete.

What if: Consider the original facts, except that Scenario 2 dictates the long- and short-term capital gains. What is the amount and character of Jeb's net gain (or loss) on the sale of the shares in this situation?

Answer: $22,000 net short-term capital gain computed as follows:

Step 1: The gain from stock A would first be netted with the loss from stock B to produce a $25,000 NSTCG [$35,000 + ($10,000)]

Step 2: The loss from stock D and the gain from stock C are both 0/15/20% types and are combined to provide a $3,000 loss [($11,000) + $8,000].

Step 3: 3(A) applies as the loss from step 2 is the only long-term amount and we proceed to step 4.

Step 4: Continue to step 5.

Step 5: 5(b) applies. The results from step 1 and step 2 are netted to reach a $22,000 net short-term capital gain [$25,000 NSTCG + ($3,000) NLTCL].

Example 7-7 included long-term capital gains and losses only in the 0/15/20% group. Example 7-8 shows the netting process when taxpayers also sell long-term capital assets and recognize gains subject to the 25 percent and/or 28 percent capital gains rates.

Example 7-8

What if: Assume that in addition to selling stocks, Jeb sold gold coins and a rental home as follows:

Capital Asset	Market Value	Tax Basis	Capital Gain/Loss	Scenario 1 Type
A stock	$ 40,000	$ 5,000	$ 35,000	Long 0/15/20%
B stock	20,000	30,000	(10,000)	Long 0/15/20%
C stock	20,000	12,000	8,000	Short
D stock	17,000	28,000	(11,000)	Short
Gold coins	4,000	3,000	1,000	Long 28%
Rental home	200,000	80,000	120,000	Long 25% and 0/15/20%*
Overall gain			$143,000	

*$50,000 of the gain is 25 percent gain and the remaining $70,000 is 0/15/20 percent gain.

Assuming Jeb did not sell any other capital assets during the year, he recognizes an overall capital gain of $143,000. What is (are) the maximum tax rate(s) applicable to this gain?

Answer: $95,000 of gain subject to a 0/15/20 percent maximum rate and $48,000 of gain is subject to a 25 percent rate, computed as follows:

Step 1: $3,000 net short-term capital loss [$8,000 + ($11,000)].

Step 2: Stock A and Stock B are placed in 0/15/20% group, the gold coins are placed in the 28% group, $50,000 of the gain from the sale of the rental home is placed in the 25% group and the remaining $70,000 gain from the rental home is placed in the 0/15/20% group. The sum of the gains and losses in each group results in a net 28% gain of $1,000, a 25% gain of $50,000, and a net $95,000 gain in the 0/15/20% group.

Step 3: 3(A) does not apply. 3(B) applies because all of the long-term rate groups have a net gain from step 2. We proceed to step 6.

Step 4: Not required.

Step 5: Not required.

Step 6: Move the $3,000 loss from step 1 into the 28 percent group to offset the $1,000 gain. Next, move the remaining $2,000 loss [$1,000 gain on gold + ($3,000) short-term loss from step 1] into the 25% group to offset the $50,000 gain. The netting process is complete at this point because the net short-term capital loss does not offset all of the gains in the long-term rate groups (step 6(b)) and only gains remain in the long-term rate groups.

Step 7: Not required.

(continued on page 7-16)

Jeb's netting process is reflected in the following table:

Description	Short-Term	Long-Term 28%	Long-Term 25%	Long-Term 0/15/20%
Stock C	$8,000			
Stock D	(11,000)			
Step 1:	(3,000)			
Coins		$1,000		
Unrecaptured §1250 Gain			$50,000	
Remaining Gain from Rental Property				$70,000
Stock A				35,000
Stock B				(10,000)
Step 2:		$1,000	$50,000	$95,000
Step 6:	(3,000) ———→	(3,000)		
		(2,000) ———→	(2,000)	
			$48,000	
Summary			$48,000	$95,000
Applicable Rate			25%	0/15/20%

Reporting capital gains and losses   When taxpayers sell capital assets, they report the details of their sales on Form 8949 (dates of sale and purchase are additional items provided on Form 8949). After listing their sales on Form 8949, taxpayers then use Schedule D to summarize the sales and apply the basic capital gains netting process. Exhibits 7-5 and 7-6 illustrate how Jeb would report his stock sales in Example 7-7, Scenario 1.

Calculating Tax Liability on Net Capital Gains   So, we've learned how to determine the *maximum* tax rates applicable to different types of capital gains. How do we go about actually calculating the effect these gains have on the taxpayer's tax liability? Follow these basic guidelines:

- If the long-term capital gains would have been taxed at a rate of 39.6 percent if they were ordinary income, the gain is taxed at the maximum rate for their group (0/15/20 percent, 25 percent, or 28 percent).
- To the extent the long-term capital gains would have been taxed at a rate of 15 percent or lower if they were ordinary income, the 0/15/20 percent gains are taxed at 0 percent, and the 25 percent and 28 percent gains are taxed at the taxpayer's ordinary rate.
- For other situations, use the following steps to determine the tax on the gains:[27]

  Step 1: Fill up the 10, 15, 25, 28, 35, and 39.6 percent tax rate brackets with taxable income, exclusive of long-term capital gains subject to preferential rates.

  Step 2: Next, if there is any remaining space in the 10 or 15 percent brackets, add any 25 percent rate capital gains to these brackets to the extent room remains in either of these brackets after step 1. Twenty-five percent rate capital gains included in these brackets are taxed at the ordinary rates applicable to these brackets.

[27]§1(h).

EXHIBIT 7-5   **Jeb's Form 8949**

Form **8949**	**Sales and Other Dispositions of Capital Assets**	OMB No. 1545-0074

Department of the Treasury
Internal Revenue Service

▶ Information about Form 8949 and its separate instructions is at *www.irs.gov/form8949.*
▶ File with your Schedule D to list your transactions for lines 1b, 2, 3, 8b, 9, and 10 of Schedule D.

2015

Attachment
Sequence No. **12A**

Name(s) shown on return

Jeb Landers

Social security number or taxpayer identification number

Before you check Box A, B, or C below, see whether you received any Form(s) 1099-B or substitute statement(s) from your broker. A substitute statement will have the same information as Form 1099-B. Either will show whether your basis (usually your cost) was reported to the IRS by your broker and may even tell you which box to check.

Part I   **Short-Term.** Transactions involving capital assets you held 1 year or less are short term. For long-term transactions, see page 2.

Note: You may aggregate all short-term transactions reported on Form(s) 1099-B showing basis was reported to the IRS and for which no adjustments or codes are required. Enter the totals directly on Schedule D, line 1a; you aren't required to report these transactions on Form 8949 (see instructions).

You *must* check Box A, B, *or* C below. Check only one box. If more than one box applies for your short-term transactions, complete a separate Form 8949, page 1, for each applicable box. If you have more short-term transactions than will fit on this page for one or more of the boxes, complete as many forms with the same box checked as you need.

- ☑ **(A)** Short-term transactions reported on Form(s) 1099-B showing basis was reported to the IRS (see **Note** above)
- ☐ **(B)** Short-term transactions reported on Form(s) 1099-B showing basis was **not** reported to the IRS
- ☐ **(C)** Short-term transactions not reported to you on Form 1099-B

1	(a) Description of property (Example: 100 sh. XYZ Co.)	(b) Date acquired (Mo., day, yr.)	(c) Date sold or disposed of (Mo., day, yr.)	(d) Proceeds (sales price) (see instructions)	(e) Cost or other basis. See the **Note** below and see *Column (e)* in the separate instructions	Adjustment, if any, to gain or loss. If you enter an amount in column (g), enter a code in column (f). See the separate instructions.		(h) Gain or (loss). Subtract column (e) from column (d) and combine the result with column (g)
						(f) Code(s) from instructions	(g) Amount of adjustment	
	Stock C	3/01/15	11/15/15	20,000	12,000			8,000
	Stock D	2/01/15	6/09/15	17,000	28,000			(11,000)
2 Totals. Add the amounts in columns (d), (e), (g), and (h) (subtract negative amounts). Enter each total here and include on your Schedule D, **line 1b** (if **Box A** above is checked), **line 2** (if **Box B** above is checked), or **line 3** (if **Box C** above is checked) ▶				37,000	40,000			(3,000)

Note: If you checked Box A above but the basis reported to the IRS was incorrect, enter in column (e) the basis as reported to the IRS, and enter an adjustment in column (g) to correct the basis. See *Column (g)* in the separate instructions for how to figure the amount of the adjustment.

For Paperwork Reduction Act Notice, see your tax return instructions.   Cat. No. 37768Z   Form **8949** (2015)

EXHIBIT 7-5 **Jeb's Form 8949** (*continued*)

Form 8949 (2015)   Attachment Sequence No. **12A**   Page **2**

Name(s) shown on return. Name and SSN or taxpayer identification no. not required if shown on other side	Social security number or taxpayer identification number
Jeb Landers	

Before you check Box D, E, or F below, see whether you received any Form(s) 1099-B or substitute statement(s) from your broker. A substitute statement will have the same information as Form 1099-B. Either will show whether your basis (usually your cost) was reported to the IRS by your broker and may even tell you which box to check.

Part II   **Long-Term.** Transactions involving capital assets you held more than 1 year are long term. For short-term transactions, see page 1.

> **Note:** You may aggregate all long-term transactions reported on Form(s) 1099-B showing basis was reported to the IRS and for which no adjustments or codes are required. Enter the totals directly on Schedule D, line 8a; you aren't required to report these transactions on Form 8949 (see instructions).

You *must* **check Box D, E,** *or* **F below. Check only one box.** If more than one box applies for your long-term transactions, complete a separate Form 8949, page 2, for each applicable box. If you have more long-term transactions than will fit on this page for one or more of the boxes, complete as many forms with the same box checked as you need.

- ☑ **(D)** Long-term transactions reported on Form(s) 1099-B showing basis was reported to the IRS (see **Note** above)
- ☐ **(E)** Long-term transactions reported on Form(s) 1099-B showing basis was **not** reported to the IRS
- ☐ **(F)** Long-term transactions not reported to you on Form 1099-B

1 **(a)** Description of property (Example: 100 sh. XYZ Co.)	**(b)** Date acquired (Mo., day, yr.)	**(c)** Date sold or disposed of (Mo., day, yr.)	**(d)** Proceeds (sales price) (see instructions)	**(e)** Cost or other basis. See the **Note** below and see *Column (e)* in the separate instructions	Adjustment, if any, to gain or loss. If you enter an amount in column (g), enter a code in column (f). **See the separate instructions.**		**(h)** Gain or (loss). Subtract column (e) from column (d) and combine the result with column (g)
					(f) Code(s) from instructions	**(g)** Amount of adjustment	
Stock A	11/07/13	3/06/15	40,000	5,000			35,000
Stock B	7/09/12	9/01/15	20,000	30,000			(10,000)
2 Totals. Add the amounts in columns (d), (e), (g), and (h) (subtract negative amounts). Enter each total here and include on your Schedule D, **line 8b** (if **Box D** above is checked), **line 9** (if **Box E** above is checked), or **line 10** (if **Box F** above is checked) ▶			60,000	35,000			25,000

Note: If you checked Box D above but the basis reported to the IRS was incorrect, enter in column (e) the basis as reported to the IRS, and enter an adjustment in column (g) to correct the basis. See *Column (g)* in the separate instructions for how to figure the amount of the adjustment.

Form **8949** (2015)

EXHIBIT 7-6   Jeb's Schedule D

SCHEDULE D (Form 1040)	**Capital Gains and Losses**	OMB No. 1545-0074

Department of the Treasury
Internal Revenue Service (99)

► **Attach to Form 1040 or Form 1040NR.**
► **Information about Schedule D and its separate instructions is at *www.irs.gov/scheduled*.**
► **Use Form 8949 to list your transactions for lines 1b, 2, 3, 8b, 9, and 10.**

2015

Attachment Sequence No. **12**

Name(s) shown on return
Jeb Landers

Your social security number

Part I   Short-Term Capital Gains and Losses—Assets Held One Year or Less

See instructions for how to figure the amounts to enter on the lines below. This form may be easier to complete if you round off cents to whole dollars.	(d) Proceeds (sales price)	(e) Cost (or other basis)	(g) Adjustments to gain or loss from Form(s) 8949, Part I, line 2, column (g)	(h) Gain or (loss) Subtract column (e) from column (d) and combine the result with column (g)
1a Totals for all short-term transactions reported on Form 1099-B for which basis was reported to the IRS and for which you have no adjustments (see instructions). However, if you choose to report all these transactions on Form 8949, leave this line blank and go to line 1b .				
1b Totals for all transactions reported on Form(s) 8949 with **Box A** checked	37,000	40,000		(3,000)
2 Totals for all transactions reported on Form(s) 8949 with **Box B** checked				
3 Totals for all transactions reported on Form(s) 8949 with **Box C** checked				

4 Short-term gain from Form 6252 and short-term gain or (loss) from Forms 4684, 6781, and 8824 .	**4**	
5 Net short-term gain or (loss) from partnerships, S corporations, estates, and trusts from Schedule(s) K-1	**5**	
6 Short-term capital loss carryover. Enter the amount, if any, from line 8 of your **Capital Loss Carryover Worksheet** in the instructions	**6** ( )	
7 **Net short-term capital gain or (loss).** Combine lines 1a through 6 in column (h). If you have any long-term capital gains or losses, go to Part II below. Otherwise, go to Part III on the back	**7**	(3,000)

Part II   Long-Term Capital Gains and Losses—Assets Held More Than One Year

See instructions for how to figure the amounts to enter on the lines below. This form may be easier to complete if you round off cents to whole dollars.	(d) Proceeds (sales price)	(e) Cost (or other basis)	(g) Adjustments to gain or loss from Form(s) 8949, Part II, line 2, column (g)	(h) Gain or (loss) Subtract column (e) from column (d) and combine the result with column (g)
8a Totals for all long-term transactions reported on Form 1099-B for which basis was reported to the IRS and for which you have no adjustments (see instructions). However, if you choose to report all these transactions on Form 8949, leave this line blank and go to line 8b .				
8b Totals for all transactions reported on Form(s) 8949 with **Box D** checked	60,000	35,000		25,000
9 Totals for all transactions reported on Form(s) 8949 with **Box E** checked				
10 Totals for all transactions reported on Form(s) 8949 with **Box F** checked.				

11 Gain from Form 4797, Part I; long-term gain from Forms 2439 and 6252; and long-term gain or (loss) from Forms 4684, 6781, and 8824	**11**	
12 Net long-term gain or (loss) from partnerships, S corporations, estates, and trusts from Schedule(s) K-1	**12**	
13 Capital gain distributions. See the instructions	**13**	
14 Long-term capital loss carryover. Enter the amount, if any, from line 13 of your **Capital Loss Carryover Worksheet** in the instructions	**14** ( )	
15 **Net long-term capital gain or (loss).** Combine lines 8a through 14 in column (h). Then go to Part III on the back	**15**	25,000

For Paperwork Reduction Act Notice, see your tax return instructions.   Cat. No. 11338H   **Schedule D (Form 1040) 2015**

Step 3: Next, if there is any remaining space in the 10 or 15 percent brackets, add any 28 percent rate capital gains to these brackets to the extent room remains in either of these brackets after step 2. Twenty-eight percent rate capital gains included in these brackets are taxed at the ordinary rates applicable to these brackets.

Step 4: Next, add any 0/15/20 percent rate capital gains to either the 10 percent or 15 percent brackets to the extent room remains in either of these brackets after step 3. 0/15/20 percent rate capital gains included in these brackets are taxed at 0 percent.

Step 5: Add any remaining 0/15/20 percent rate capital gains (those not taxed in step 4) to the 25, 28, 33, 35, and 39.6) percent brackets. The 0/15/20 percent rate capital gains included in brackets below 39.6 percent are taxed at 15 percent. The 0/15/20 percent rate capital gains included in the 39.6 percent bracket are taxed at 20 percent.

Step 6: Any remaining 25 percent rate capital gains (those not taxed in step 2) are taxed at 25 percent. Any remaining 28 percent rate capital gains are taxed at 28 percent. [This means that 28 percent rate capital gains that would have been taxed at 25 percent if they were ordinary income are taxed at the higher 28 percent rate. If, however, a taxpayer's tax liability would be lower using the regular tax rates for all ordinary income and capital gains (which is possible but not typical), the taxpayer would simply owe tax based on the regular tax rates.]

Example 7-9

What if: Let's return to the facts of the previous example where Jeb recognized a $48,000 25 percent net capital gain and a $95,000 0/15/20 percent net capital gain. Also, assume that Jeb's taxable income before considering the net capital gains is $10,000. Jeb's filing status is single. What is Jeb's gross tax liability for the year?

Answer: $24,521.25, computed as follows:

Amount and Type of Income	Applicable Rate	Tax	Explanation
$9,275; ordinary	10%	$ 927.50	$9,275 × 10%. The first $9,275 of Jeb's $10,000 of ordinary income is taxed at 10 percent (see single tax rate schedule for this and other computations).
$725	15	108.75	$725 × 15%. Jeb's remaining $725 of ordinary income ($10,000 − $9,275) is taxed at 15 percent.
$27,650; 25 percent rate capital gains	15	4,147.50	$27,650 × 15%. The end of the 15 percent bracket is $37,650 minus $10,000 ($9,275 + $725) already taxed.
$20,350; 25 percent rate capital gains	25	5,087.50	$20,350 × 25%. $48,000 total 25% gain minus $27,650 25 percent gain already taxed at 15 percent.
$95,000; 15 percent rate capital gains	15	14,250.00	$95,000 × 15%. All of the 15 percent gain would have been taxed at a rate higher than 15 percent but less than 39.6%, so it is all taxed at 15 percent.
Gross tax liability		**$24,521.25**	

What if: Suppose Jeb's 0/15/20 percent capital gain was $400,000 rather than $95,000. What is Jeb's gross tax liability for the year?

Answer: $72,418.75, computed as follows:

Amount and Type of Income	Applicable Rate	Tax	Explanation
$9,275; ordinary	10%	$ 927.50	$9,275 × 10%. The first $9,275 of Jeb's $10,000 of ordinary income is taxed at 10 percent (see single tax rate schedule for this and other computations).
$725	15	108.75	$725 × 15%. Jeb's remaining $725 of ordinary income ($10,000 − $9,275) is taxed at 15 percent.
$27,650; 25 percent rate capital gains	15	4,147.50	$27,650 × 15%. The end of the 15 percent bracket is $37,650 minus $10,000 ($9,275 + $725) already taxed.
$20,350; 25 percent rate capital gains	25	5,087.50	$20,350 × 25%. $48,000 total 25% gain minus $27,650 25 percent gain already taxed at 15 percent.
$357,050; 0/15/20 percent rate capital gains	15	53,557.50	$357,050 × 15%. $357,050 represents the 0/15/20 percent gain that would have been taxed at 25, 28, 33, or 35 percent if it were ordinary. This gain is taxed at 15 percent.
$42,950; 0/15/20 percent rate capital gains	20	8,590.00	$42,950 × 20%. The remaining 0/15/20 percent gain that would have been taxed at 39.6 percent had it been ordinary is taxed at the maximum 20 percent.
Gross tax liability		**$72,418.75**	

Limitations on Capital Losses

We've previously discussed the general rule that taxpayers may deduct capital losses against capital gains in the netting process and that individual taxpayers may deduct up to $3,000 ($1,500 if married filing separately) of net capital losses against ordinary income in a given year. This general rule, however, is subject to certain exceptions as described below.

Losses on the Sale of Personal-Use Assets   As previously described, personal-use assets fall within the category of capital assets. When taxpayers sell personal-use assets, what are the tax consequences? Consider an engaged taxpayer who calls off the wedding plans. After getting the ring back from his former fiancée, the taxpayer sells the engagement ring for more than its purchase price. Does he recognize a taxable gain? Absolutely—the gain from the sale of a personal-use asset is taxable even though it was not purchased for its appreciation potential. The tax rate on the gain depends on the amount of time between the date the taxpayer purchased the ring and the date he sold it and on the netting process involving the seller's other capital gains and losses during the year. What if a taxpayer sold her car for less than she paid for it? Does she get to deduct the capital loss? Unfortunately, no—losses on the sale of personal-use assets are *not* deductible, and therefore never become part of the netting process.

Capital Losses on Sales to Related Parties When taxpayers sell capital assets at a loss to related parties, they are not able to deduct the loss.[28] As we described in detail in Chapter 11, the related party acquiring the asset may eventually be allowed to deduct all, a portion, or none of the disallowed loss on a subsequent sale.

Wash Sales Consider the case of a taxpayer attempting to do some tax planning near the end of the year: She has invested in the stock of several corporations; some of these investments have appreciated while others have declined in value. The taxpayer wants to capture the tax benefit of the stock losses in the current year to offset ordinary income (up to $3,000) or to offset other capital gains she has already recognized during the year. However, she can't deduct the losses until she sells the stock. Why might this be a problem? If the taxpayer believes that the stocks with unrealized losses are likely to appreciate in the near future, she may prefer *not* to sell those stocks but rather to keep them in her investment portfolio. What might this taxpayer do to deduct the losses while continuing to hold the investment in the stocks? For one, she might be tempted to sell the stocks and then immediately buy them back. Or, she might buy more of the same stock and then sell the stock she originally held to recognize the losses. With this strategy, she hopes to realize (and then recognize or deduct) the losses and, at the end of the day, still hold the stocks in her investment portfolio.

Although this might sound like a great plan, certain **wash sale** tax rules prevent this strategy from accomplishing the taxpayer's objective. A wash sale occurs when an investor sells or trades stock or securities at a loss *and* within 30 days *either before or after* the day of sale buys substantially identical stocks or securities.[29] Because the day of sale is included, the 30 days before and after period creates a 61-day window during which the wash sale provisions may apply.[30] When the wash sale provisions apply to a sale of stock, realized losses are not recognized; instead, the amount of *the unrecognized loss is added to the basis of the newly acquired stock.* Congress created this rule to prevent taxpayers from accelerating losses on securities that have declined in value without actually altering their investment in the securities. The 61-day period ensures that taxpayers cannot deduct losses from stock sales without exposing themselves to the risk that the stock they sold will subsequently increase in value.

Example 7-10

What if: Suppose Courtney owns 100 shares of Cisco stock that she purchased in June 2014 for $50 a share. On December 21, 2016, Courtney sells the shares for $40 a share to generate cash for the holidays. This sale generates a capital loss of $1,000 [$4,000 sale proceeds (100 × $40) − $5,000 tax basis ($50 × 100)]. Later, however, Courtney decides that Cisco might be a good long-term investment. On January 3, 2017 (13 days later), Courtney purchases 100 shares of Cisco stock for $41 a share ($4,100). Does Courtney *realize* a short- or long-term capital loss on the December 21 sale?

Answer: Long-term capital loss. She held the stock for more than one year (June 2014 to December 2016) before selling.

How much of the realized $1,000 long-term capital loss can Courtney recognize or deduct on her 2016 tax return?

[28]§267(a).

[29]Substantially identical stocks or securities include contracts or options to buy substantially identical securities. However, corporate bonds and preferred stock are not generally considered substantially identical to common stock of the same corporation.

[30]§1091.

Answer: Zero. Because Courtney sold the stock at a loss and purchased the same stock within the 61-day period centered on the date of sale (30 days before December 21, and 30 days after December 21), the wash sale rules disallow the loss in 2016. Had Courtney waited just another 18 days to repurchase the Cisco shares, she could have avoided the wash sale rules. In that case, under the general rules for capital loss deductibility, Courtney *would* be able to deduct the $1,000 capital loss from the sale against her ordinary income on her 2016 income tax return.

What tax basis will Courtney have in the Cisco stock she purchased (or repurchased) on January 3, 2017?

Answer: $5,100. Under the wash sale rules, Courtney adds the $1,000 disallowed loss to the basis of the stock she purchased on January 3. Thus, she now owns 100 shares of Cisco stock with a $5,100 basis in the shares, which is $1,000 more than she paid for it.

What if: How much of the $1,000 realized loss would Courtney have recognized if she had only purchased 40 shares of Cisco stock instead of 100 shares on January 3, 2017?

Answer: $600. The wash sale rules disallow the loss to the extent taxpayers acquire other shares in the 61-day window. In this situation, Courtney only acquired 40 percent (40 of 100) of the shares she sold at a loss within the window. Consequently, she must disallow 40 percent, or $400, of the loss, and she is allowed to deduct the remaining $600 loss.

ETHICS

In December, T. D. Weber evaluated his stock portfolio and found that his DLW Inc. common stock had declined in value since T. D. purchased it. He strategizes to sell the DLW stock on December 15. However, T. D. figures that he'd like to retain an interest in the company. So, knowing that he needs to avoid the wash sale rules, when he sells the common stock on December 15th he simultaneously purchased an equivalent amount of preferred stock in DLW Inc. On January 17 of the next year, T. D. sells the preferred stock and repurchases DLW common stock. What do you think of his strategy?

THE KEY FACTS

Capital Gains and Losses

- Tax on the appreciation of capital assets is deferred until the asset is sold.
  - The longer the holding period, the greater the after-tax rate of return for a given before-tax rate of return.
- Tracking the basis of stock sold.
  - FIFO method is the default.
  - Specific identification is allowed.
- Capital gains and losses.
  - Long-term capital gain if the asset is held more than a year before sold; short-term otherwise.
  - Net long-term capital gains are taxed at the maximum 0/15/20 percent rate.
  - ($3,000) net capital loss is deductible annually against ordinary income.
  - Losses on personal-use assets are not deductible.
  - Losses on wash sales are not deductible but are added to the basis of new shares acquired.
- Basic tax planning strategies.
  - Hold capital assets for more than a year before selling.
  - Sell loss capital assets to offset gains.

Balancing Tax Planning Strategies for Capital Assets with Other Goals

When taxpayers invest in capital assets and hold the assets for more than a year, they receive at least two benefits. First, they are able to defer recognizing gains on the assets until they sell them—the longer the deferral period, the lower the present value of the capital gains tax when taxpayers ultimately sell the assets. Second, they pay taxes on the gains at preferential rates. These tax advantages provide taxpayers with a greater after-tax rate of return on these investments than they would obtain from less tax-favored assets that earn equivalent before-tax rates of return. Investors who quickly sell investments pay taxes on gains at higher, ordinary rates and incur significantly greater transaction costs. Nevertheless, taxpayers should balance the tax benefits available for holding assets with the risk that the asset values will have declined by the time they want to sell the assets.

Example 7-11

What if: Assume Courtney decides to purchase Intel stock for $100,000 and hold half of the shares for 5 years to purchase the Park City home and the other half for 18 years to pay for Deron's education. If the Intel stock grows at a constant 8 percent before-tax rate and does not pay any dividends, how much cash will Courtney accumulate after taxes for the Park City home?

(*continued on page 7-24*)

Answer: $69,946, computed as follows:

Description	Amount	Explanation
1. Proceeds from sale	$73,466	$[\$50,000 \times (1 + .08)^5]$.
2. Basis in fund shares	50,000	This is the nondeductible investment in the shares.
3. Gain realized on sale	$23,466	(1) − (2).
4. Tax rate on gain	× 15%	Low rate for long-term capital gain.*
5. Tax on gain	$ 3,520	(3) × (4).
After-tax cash for Park City home	**$69,946**	(1) − (5).

*Assumes Courtney doesn't have any capital losses.

How much cash will Courtney accumulate after taxes for Deron's education?

Answer: $177,331, computed as follows:

Description	Amount	Explanation
1. Proceeds from sale	$199,801	$[\$50,000 \times (1 + .08)^{18}]$.
2. Basis in fund shares	50,000	This is the nondeductible investment in the shares.
3. Gain realized on sale	$149,801	(1) − (2).
4. Tax rate on gain	× 15%	Low rate for long-term capital gain.*
5. Tax on gain	$ 22,470	(3) × (4).
After-tax cash for education goal	**$177,331**	(1) − (5).

*Assumes Courtney doesn't have capital losses.

TAXES IN THE REAL WORLD Turning Losses into Gains

Many investors have seen their investments plummet in value in recent years due to the economic downturn. However, financial advisers remind us that even in the midst of such seemingly bad news, there is good news. The tax code allows individuals to reduce or eliminate tax on their current gains using these losses, which in turn raises overall returns. Using capital losses to offset capital gains (or even up to $3,000 of ordinary income) is a term investment advisers call *tax-loss harvesting*. Tax advisers encourage investors to take advantage of the available capital loss offset and many investors do. For example, New York's billionaire mayor, Michael Bloomberg, disclosed that he would declare no net capital gains on his 2010 tax return. So, how much can loss harvesting improve your returns? Investment advisers have differing predictions but claim that loss harvesting can add up to 2 percentage points over a 10-year period. Pretty good considering that the Standard & Poor's 500 stock index's annualized total return for the period has been under 2 percent.

Source: The Wall Street Journal, Laura Saunders, August 20, 2011.

When investing in capital assets, taxpayers run the risk that some of their investments may decline in value. Thus, a productive strategy for managing investments in capital assets is to sell investments with built-in losses. This strategy is commonly referred to as "loss harvesting." By selectively selling loss assets, taxpayers can reduce their taxes by deducting up to $3,000 against their ordinary income and by reducing the amount of capital gains that would otherwise be subject to tax during the year. This is particularly beneficial for taxpayers who have short-term capital gains that will be taxed at higher ordinary rates absent offsetting capital losses. Note, however, that taxpayers should not sell investments to gain tax benefits if they believe that the potential economic benefit of holding the investment outweighs the tax benefits of selling the stock. Also, keep in mind that capital losses on stock sales may not be deductible due to the wash sale rules discussed above.

PORTFOLIO INCOME SUMMARY

As we've discussed the tax consequences of various investments up to this point in the chapter, we have proceeded from the least tax-advantaged (taxed annually at ordinary rates) to more tax-advantaged (capital gains). By moving along this continuum from investments taxed annually at ordinary rates (corporate bonds[31]) to investments taxed annually at capital gains rates (dividend-paying stock), investors are in essence employing the conversion planning strategy referred to repeatedly throughout this text. As taxpayers move from dividend-paying stock to growth stock, which provides tax deferral in addition to preferential tax rates, taxpayers combine the conversion strategy with the basic strategy of shifting income from one time period to another.

In this chapter and elsewhere in this text, we emphasize that tax planning must not be done in a vacuum without considering all relevant parties and taxpayers' economic and personal objectives. Because investments typically are not designed to accommodate the specific needs of each individual investor, considering the other party in the deal is not as relevant when investing as it is in other transactions. However, it is vital that investors carefully balance the tax characteristics of their investment options with the other attributes of their investment options such as risk and liquidity.

PORTFOLIO INVESTMENT EXPENSES

LO 7-3

Now that we've discussed how *income* from various forms of investments is taxed, let's explore the deductibility of expenses taxpayers incur to acquire or maintain their investments. We first discuss tax consequences associated with **investment expenses,** and we conclude by discussing the deductibility of **investment interest expense.** Even though the names of these two deductions sound very similar, investment expenses and investment interest expense are two different deductions with different deductibility limitations. So, when you are reading about an investment-related expense, pay careful attention to whether the expense is an *investment expense* or *investment interest expense.* Exhibit 7-7 provides a description of these expenses and the limitations on the deductibility of the expenses.

EXHIBIT 7-7 Summary of Investment-Related Expenses

Item	Investment Expense	Investment *Interest* Expense
Description	Expenses (other than interest) incurred to generate investment income.	Interest expense on loans used to acquire investments.
Deduction type	Miscellaneous itemized deduction (subject to 2 percent of AGI floor).	Interest expense itemized deduction.
Deduction limitations	Deductible only when investment expenses and other miscellaneous itemized deductions exceed 2 percent of AGI floor.	Deduction limited to taxpayer's net investment income for the year. Net investment income is gross investment income reduced by *deductible investment expenses.*
Nondeductible amounts due to limitations	Deduct it in the year incurred or lose it.	Carryover indefinitely.

Investment Expenses

Just as taxpayers can deduct ordinary and necessary business expenditures when conducting business activities, individual taxpayers are allowed to deduct ordinary and necessary expenses they incur in investment activities to produce or collect income

---

[31]We refer here to corporate bonds issued or acquired at face value.

THE KEY FACTS

Investment-Related Expenses

- Investment expenses deducted as miscellaneous itemized deductions are subject to the 2 percent of AGI floor.
  - Expenses other than interest incurred to generate investment income.
  - No carryover of amounts not currently deductible.

and for expenses they pay or incur to manage property held for producing income—such as safe deposit box rental fees, attorney and accounting fees that are necessary to produce investment income, and expenses for investment advice, among other things.[32]

The arrangement makes sense if you think about it: The government taxes investment income, so it is willing to allow taxpayers to deduct expenses they incur to generate investment income. Conversely, to the extent taxpayers incur expenses to produce tax-exempt income, such as municipal bond interest, they are not allowed to deduct the related expenses.[33] For example, a taxpayer who keeps a fully taxable corporate bond in a safe deposit box would be allowed an investment expense deduction for the cost of renting the box, but one who keeps a tax-exempt municipal bond in a safe deposit box would not.

The bad news here for taxpayers is that investment expenses are treated as miscellaneous itemized deductions subject to the 2 percent of AGI floor.[34] Thus, taxpayers with investment expenses will only realize tax benefits from these expenses if they itemize deductions *and* their total miscellaneous itemized deductions (fees for investment advice, tax return preparation fees, an employee's job-related magazine subscriptions, and other unreimbursed employee business expenses—see Chapter 6)—including investment expenses—exceed 2 percent of their AGI. Consequently, it is likely that taxpayers with taxable investments and investment expenses will receive little tax benefit, if any, from the expenses.

Example 7-12

What if: Suppose Courtney met with a financial planner who advised her about her investment decisions. Courtney paid the advisor $500 for her services. Also, during the year Courtney paid a CPA $250 to prepare her tax return. Courtney had no other miscellaneous itemized deductions for the year. Does Courtney gain any tax benefit from the $500 she paid to the financial planner (her AGI is $162,000)?

Answer: No. The $500 payment is a deductible investment expense for Courtney. However, to receive any tax benefit from the payment, her total miscellaneous itemized deductions must exceed 2 percent of her AGI. The computation for her deductible investment expense is as follows:

Description	Amount
Investment expenses	$ 500
Tax return preparation fees	250
Total miscellaneous itemized deductions	750
Less: 2 percent of AGI ($162,000 × 2%)	3,240
Miscellaneous itemized deductions over 2 percent of AGI floor	0

Because her miscellaneous itemized deductions are less than 2 percent of her AGI, Courtney does not gain any tax benefit from the $500 investment expense (it does not reduce taxable income).

In fact, Courtney could have paid another $2,490 of investment expenses before she would have exceeded the 2 percent of AGI threshold and received any tax benefit from the payment ($3,240 − $750).

Investment Interest Expense

When taxpayers borrow money to acquire investments, the interest expense they pay on the loan is investment interest expense. For example, if you borrow funds to buy stock, any interest you pay on the loan would be considered investment interest

---

[32]IRC §212. Rental expenses are also deductible under §212 as we discuss in Chapter 6.

[33]§265.

[34]See Chapter 6 for a discussion of the tax treatment of miscellaneous itemized deductions. Also note that as we discussed in Chapter 6, investment expenses from rental and royalty-related activities are deductible as *for* AGI and not as itemized deductions.

expense. Investment interest expense may be deductible as an itemized deduction.[35] Unlike investment expenses, the investment interest expense deduction is *not* a miscellaneous itemized deduction subject to the 2 percent of AGI floor. It is, however, subject to a different limitation. A taxpayer's investment interest expense deduction for the year is limited to the taxpayer's **net investment income** for the year.[36]

Net Investment Income   Net investment income is gross investment income reduced by *deductible* investment expenses. Deductible investment expenses are investment expenses that actually reduce taxable income *after* applying the 2 percent of AGI floor.[37] Gross investment income includes interest, annuity, and royalty income not derived in the ordinary course of a trade or business. It also includes net *short*-term capital gains, and nonqualified dividends. However, investment income generally does not include net long-term capital gains and qualified dividends because this income is taxed at a preferential rate.

Example 7-13

What if: Suppose that during the year, Courtney recognized the following income from investments: $3,000 of qualified dividends and $500 of taxable interest. What is Courtney's gross investment income?

Answer: $500. The taxable interest is included, and the qualified dividends are excluded because they are taxed at a preferential rate.

What is Courtney's *net* investment income?

Answer: $500. Recall that net investment income is gross investment income minus deductible (taxable income reducing) investment expenses. In Example 7-12, we found that Courtney's deductible investment expenses were $0. Thus, her net investment income is $500 ($500 – $0).

Taxpayers may deduct their investment interest expense up to the amount of their net investment income. Any investment interest expense in excess of net investment income is carried over and treated as though it was incurred in the next year when it is subject to the same limitations. The carryover amount never expires. That is, taxpayers can carry over the excess investment interest expense until they generate sufficient net investment income to deduct it.

Example 7-14

What if: Continuing with Example 7-13 suppose that in July of this year, Courtney purchased a parcel of undeveloped land as an investment for $120,000. She made a $20,000 down payment and financed the remaining $100,000 with a loan from her local credit union. The interest rate on the loan was 9 percent, payable annually. During the year, Courtney paid $4,500 in interest expense on the loan. Because the loan was used to purchase an investment, the interest expense is investment interest expense. What amount of this investment interest expense is Courtney allowed to deduct this year?

Answer: $500. Although she incurred $4,500 of investment interest expense, her deduction for the current year is limited to her $500 net investment income (see Example 7-13). The $4,000 of investment interest expense that is not deductible this year is carried forward until Courtney generates enough net investment income to deduct it.

---

[35]§163.

[36]The investment interest expense limitation is calculated on Form 4952. Note that taxpayers can avoid the limitations on investment interest expense by acquiring the investment assets with funds from a qualified home equity loan. As we discuss in Chapter 14, interest on home equity loans is generally fully deductible.

[37]When taxpayers have both investment expenses and other miscellaneous itemized deductions subject to the 2 percent of AGI floor, deductible amounts in excess of the 2 percent of AGI floor are considered to first come from investment expenses up to the total amount of investment expenses and then from other miscellaneous itemized deductions.

Congress allows taxpayers to *elect to include* preferentially taxed income in investment income if they are willing to subject this income to tax at the ordinary (not preferential) tax rates. Taxpayers who make this election benefit from increasing their net investment income and thus increasing their current year investment interest expense deduction. But, this additional deduction comes at a price because they must subject their net long-term capital gains and qualified dividends included in investment income to ordinary tax rates.[38]

Example 7-15

In Examples 7-13 and 7-14, we discovered that Courtney paid $4,500 of investment interest expense during the year but was only able to deduct $500 of the interest expense because her net investment income was only $500. However, as indicated in Example 7-13, Courtney also received $3,000 of qualified dividends that were *excluded* from the net investment income computation. Courtney may elect to increase her investment income by the amount of the qualified dividends (and increase her investment interest expense deduction), but by doing so, she must subject the qualified dividends to her ordinary tax rate (30 percent) instead of the preferential rate (15 percent). Thus, Courtney is faced with a choice of whether to include the $3,000 dividend in investment income and tax it at ordinary rates (Alternative 1) or to exclude it from investment income and tax it at preferential rates (Alternative 2). How much more investment interest expense is she allowed to deduct under Alternative 1 than Alternative 2?

Answer: $3,000 more under Alternative 1, computed as follows:

Alternative 1: *Include the $3,000 dividends in investment income.*

Description	Amount	Explanation
1. Increase in net investment income	$3,000	Elect to include dividends in net investment income.
2. Increase in investment interest expense deduction	**3,000**	Investment interest expense deduction increased from $500 to $3,500.
3. Tax benefit from additional deduction	900	(2) × 30%.
4. Tax cost of taxing dividends at ordinary rate	450	(1) × (30% − 15%).
5. Current savings from election to include dividends in net investment income	450	(3) − (4).
Investment interest expense carryforward	$1,000	$4,500 total − $3,500 deducted.

Alternative 2: *Exclude the $3,000 dividends from investment income.*

Description	Amount	Explanation
Forgone tax benefit available *this year* under Alternative 1	$ 450	Under Alternative 2, Courtney doesn't receive the tax savings available under Alternative 1.
1. Increase in investment interest expense carryforward	3,000	Investment interest expense not deducted under Alternative 2.
Total investment interest expense carryforward	$4,000	(1) + $1,000 investment interest expense carryforward under Alternative 1.

Whether or not it makes sense to elect to include net long-term capital gains and qualified dividends in investment income depends on the taxpayers' circumstances and their personal preferences. As we see in Example 7-15, Courtney could save $450

[38]Note that the election is not an all-or-nothing proposition. Taxpayers can elect to include all or only a portion of their net long-term capital gains and qualifying dividends in investment income. However, the amount they include in investment income is subject to tax at ordinary tax rates.

this year by electing to include this income in investment income. However, by doing so, she is forgoing $3,000 of investment interest expense carryforward ($4,000 − $1,000) that would be available to offset ordinary income in future years.

Net Investment Income Tax

A net investment income tax is imposed on net investment income. The tax imposed is 3.8 percent of the lesser of (a) net investment income or (b) the excess of modified adjusted gross income over $250,000 for married-joint filers and surviving spouses, $125,000 for married separate filers, and $200,000 for other taxpayers. Modified adjusted gross income equals adjusted gross income increased by income excluded under the foreign earned income exclusion less any disallowed deductions associated with the foreign earned income exclusion. The tax is calculated and reported on Form 8960. Additional details and examples of the tax are provided in Chapter 8.

PASSIVE ACTIVITY INCOME AND LOSSES   LO 7-4

Thus far we have discussed how taxpayers may invest in business- and income-producing activities and earn various forms of income that are taxed as *portfolio income*. For example, taxpayers acquiring stock in a **C corporation** that files tax returns and pays taxes or purchasing bonds issued by a taxable corporation are taxed on the portfolio income these investments generate in the form of dividends and interest. On the other hand, a taxpayer may invest directly in an income-producing enterprise by purchasing rental property or by forming a business as a sole proprietor. Similarly, a taxpayer could invest in a partial interest in a trade or business or rental activity by acquiring an ownership interest in a **flow-through entity** that doesn't pay taxes such as a partnership, limited liability company (taxed as a partnership), or an S corporation (taxed similar to a partnership by shareholders' election). No matter whether an investor makes a direct investment in rental property or in a sole proprietorship or makes an indirect investment in a business or rental activity through a partnership, limited liability company, or S corporation, the *actual operating income or loss* from these investments flows through to the taxpayer as it is earned and is treated as ordinary income or ordinary loss. If trade or business or rental activities (held either directly or indirectly through flow-through entities) generate ordinary operating income, taxpayers report it on their tax returns and it is taxed at ordinary rates. However, if these activities generate operating losses, the operating losses must clear three hurdles to be deductible currently. The three loss limits are the tax basis, at-risk, and the passive loss limits.

The tax basis hurdle limits a taxpayer's deductible operating losses to the taxpayer's tax basis in the business or rental activity. This limitation is very similar to loss limitations that apply when a taxpayer sells an investment asset such as corporate stock or other similar capital asset. Recall that the formula for determining gain or loss on an exchange is the amount realized less the taxpayer's adjusted basis in the property. If a taxpayer were to sell an asset for nothing, the loss would be the amount of her tax basis in the property, but no more.

Obviously, in order to apply the tax basis loss limitation, we must first determine the taxpayer's tax basis in the activity. Very generally speaking, the tax basis is the taxpayer's investment in the activity adjusted for certain items (namely, income, debt, and investments). The adjustments are beyond the scope of this chapter; however, tax basis is discussed in later chapters relating to flow-through entities.

When a loss from a business or business-related activity clears the tax basis hurdle, it next must clear an **at-risk** hurdle on its journey toward deductibility.[39] The at-risk rules are meant to limit the ability of investors to deduct "artificial" ordinary

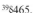

[39]§465.

losses produced with certain types of debt. These rules serve to limit ordinary losses to a taxpayer's economic risk in an activity. Generally, a taxpayer is considered to be at risk in an activity to the extent of any cash personally contributed to the activity and certain other adjustments similar (but not identical) to those for tax basis.[40] Because the computation of tax basis and at-risk amount are so similar, a taxpayer's tax basis and her at-risk amount in the activity are frequently the same so that when she clears the tax basis hurdle for deducting a loss, she also clears the at-risk hurdle. If the at-risk amount does differ from the tax basis, the at-risk amount will be less than the tax basis. Losses that do not clear the at-risk hurdle are suspended until the taxpayer generates more at-risk amounts to absorb the loss or until the activity is sold, when they may offset the seller's gain from the disposition of the activity.

Example 7-16

What if: Assume that instead of investing solely in assets that generate portfolio income, Courtney used $10,000 of the inheritance from "Gramps" to acquire a 5 percent interest in a limited partnership (a flow-through entity) called Color Comfort Sheets (CCS). Courtney's share of CCS's loss for the year is $15,000. What amount of this loss is Courtney allowed to deduct after applying the tax basis and at-risk limitations?

Answer: $10,000. Since Courtney's tax basis and at-risk amount in her CCS interest are both $10,000 (the amount of cash invested), the tax basis and at-risk amount limitations result in the same limitation. Thus, Courtney may deduct $10,000 of the $15,000 loss before considering the passive activity loss limits discussed below.

Even when a taxpayer has sufficient tax basis and sufficient amounts at risk to absorb a loss from a business-related activity, the loss may still be limited by the passive activity loss rules. Prior to 1986, investors were able to use ordinary losses from certain passive activities to offset portfolio income (interest, dividends, and capital gains), salary income, and self-employment income, including income from other trades or businesses they were actively involved in managing. During this time, a **tax shelter** industry thrived by marketing investments to wealthy investors designed primarily to generate ordinary losses that could be used to shield other income from tax. To combat this practice, Congress introduced the passive activity loss rules.[41] Specifically, these rules limit the ability of investors in certain passive activities involving interests in trade or businesses and in rental property, including real estate, to use their ordinary losses from these activities currently to reduce taxable income from other sources.[42] The passive activity loss rules are applied to any losses remaining *after* applying the tax basis and at-risk loss limits.

Passive Activity Definition

The **passive activity loss rules** define a passive activity as "any activity which involves the conduct of a trade or business, and in which the taxpayer does not materially participate." According to the tax code, participants in rental activities, including rental real estate, and limited partners in partnerships are generally deemed to be passive participants, and participants in all other trade or business activities are passive unless

---

[40]A detailed discussion of these adjustments is beyond the scope of this chapter.

[41]§469.

[42]Before passage of the passive activity loss rules, the "at-risk rules" in §465 were adopted in an attempt to limit the ability of investors to deduct "artificial" ordinary losses. Given the similarity of the at-risk and tax basis computations, especially for real estate investments, the at-risk rules were not entirely successful at accomplishing this objective. The passive activity loss rules were adopted as a backstop to the at-risk rules and both sets of rules may potentially apply to a given activity.

their involvement in an activity is "regular, continuous, and substantial." Clearly, these terms are quite subjective and difficult to apply. Fortunately, regulations provide more certainty in this area by listing seven separate tests for material participation.[43] An individual, other than a limited partner, can be classified as a material participant in an activity by meeting any one of the seven tests in Exhibit 7-8. Therefore, investors who purchase rental property or an interest in a trade or business without intending to be involved in the management of the trade or business are classified as passive participants, and these activities are classified as passive activities with respect to them.

EXHIBIT 7-8   **Tests for Material Participation**

Individuals are generally considered material participants for the activity if they meet any *one* of these tests:

1. The individual participates in the activity more than 500 hours during the year.

2. The individual's activity constitutes substantially all of the participation in such activity by all individuals including nonowners.

3. The individual participates more than 100 hours during the year, and the individual's participation is not less than any other individual's participation in the activity.

4. The activity qualifies as a "significant participation activity" (more than 100 hours spent during the year) and the aggregate of all "significant participation activities" is greater than 500 hours for the year.

5. The individual materially participated in the activity for any 5 of the preceding 10 taxable years.

6. The individual materially participated for any three preceding years in any personal service activity (personal services in health, law, accounting, architecture, etc.)

7. Taking into account all the facts and circumstances, the individual participates on a regular, continuous, and substantial basis during the year.

Income and Loss Categories

Under the passive activity loss rules, each item of a taxpayer's income or loss for the year is placed in one of three categories. Losses from *the passive category* cannot offset income from other categories. The three different categories are as follows (see Exhibit 7-9):

1. *Passive activity income or loss*—income or loss from an activity in which the taxpayer is not a material participant.

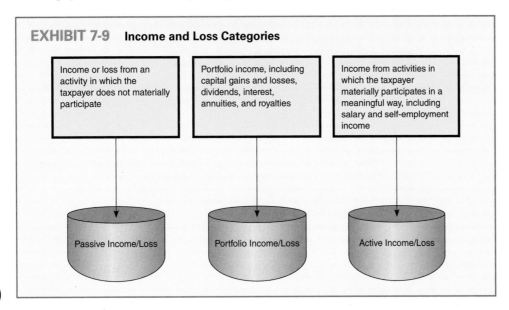

EXHIBIT 7-9   **Income and Loss Categories**

Income or loss from an activity in which the taxpayer does not materially participate	Portfolio income, including capital gains and losses, dividends, interest, annuities, and royalties	Income from activities in which the taxpayer materially participates in a meaningful way, including salary and self-employment income
Passive Income/Loss	Portfolio Income/Loss	Active Income/Loss

[43]§1.469-5T.

2. *Portfolio income*—income from investments including capital gains and losses, dividends, interest, annuities, and royalties.
3. *Active business income*—income from sources in which the taxpayer is a material participant. For individuals, this includes salary and self-employment income. Thus, an individual with income in this category is no longer an investor with respect to this source of income given that we define investors in this chapter as individuals with portfolio and/or passive income and losses.

The impact of segregating taxpayers' income in these categories is to limit their ability to apply passive activity losses against income in the other two categories. In effect, passive activity losses are suspended and remain in the passive income or loss category until the taxpayer generates passive income, either from the passive activity producing the loss or from some other passive activity, or until the taxpayer sells the entire activity that generated the passive loss in a taxable transaction. On the sale, current and suspended passive losses from the activity are first applied to reduce gain from the sale of the activity, then to reduce net passive income from other passive activities, and then to reduce nonpassive income.[44]

Example 7-17

What if: Let's return to the facts in the previous example where Courtney's share of CCS loss was $15,000, her tax basis in their CCS interest is $10,000, and her at-risk amount in the activity is also $10,000. Further assume that Courtney received $170,000 in combined salary, $4,000 of taxable interest income from corporate bonds, $3,000 of dividends, and $5,000 of long-term capital gains. Finally, assume that Courtney also owned a rental condominium that generated $8,000 of net income. How would each of these income or loss items be allocated among the passive, portfolio, and active income and loss categories?

Answer: Courtney's $10,000 loss from CCS remaining after applying the tax basis and at-risk loss limits is placed in the passive category because, as a limited partner, Courtney did not materially participate in the activity. Further, her $8,000 of net income from her rental property is included in the passive category because rental activities are generally considered to be passive. The $4,000 of taxable interest income, $3,000 of dividends, and $5,000 of long-term capital gains are all included in the portfolio income category. Finally, the $170,000 of salary is included in the active income category.

What if: What is Courtney's AGI for the year assuming, other than the items described above, no other items affect her AGI?

Answer: $182,000, computed as follows:

Description	Amount	Explanation
1. Active income	$170,000	Salary
2. Portfolio income	12,000	Interest of $4,000; dividends of $3,000; $5,000 of long-term capital gains.
3. Passive income	0	$10,000 passive loss that clears tax basis and at-risk hurdles and $8,000 of passive income. However, the passive loss clearing the basis and at-risk hurdles is deductible only to the extent of passive income. The suspended passive loss is ($2,000).
AGI	$182,000	(1) + (2) + (3).

What if: Assume the facts above and that at the beginning of next year Courtney sells her limited partnership interest for $12,000. If Courtney's tax basis on the date of sale is $0, what effect does the sale have on her AGI?

THE KEY FACTS

Passive Activities

- Ordinary losses from flow-though entities and other enterprises will be classified as passive if the taxpayer is not a material participant.
- Losses from limited partnerships and from rental activities, including rental real estate, are generally deemed to be passive losses.
- Passive loss rules limit losses from passive activities to passive income from other sources.
  - Active business income such as salary and self-employment income is not passive income.
  - Investment-type income such as interest and dividends is portfolio income, not passive income.

(*continued*) [44]§469(g).

Answer: $10,000 increase in AGI, computed as follows:

Description	Amount	Explanation
1. Capital gain	$12,000	Gain recognized = $12,000 – $0 tax basis.
2. Ordinary loss	0	The ($5,000) loss that was suspended at the basis level is not deductible on the sale. This loss expires unused. There was no loss suspended at the at-risk level or it would have been deductible on the sale.
3. Ordinary loss	(2,000)	This is the loss that was suspended at the passive loss level last year.
Increase in AGI	$10,000	(1) + (2) + (3).

Rental Real Estate Exception to the Passive Activity Loss Rules

Tax laws are renowned for exceptions to rules and, not surprisingly, the general rule that passive activity losses cannot be used to offset nonpassive types of income is subject to a few important exceptions. The one we choose to discuss here applies to lower-to-middle income individuals with rental real estate.[45] A taxpayer who is an **active participant in a rental activity** may be allowed to deduct up to $25,000 of the rental loss against other types of income. To be considered an active participant, the taxpayer must (1) own at least 10 percent of the rental property, and (2) participate in the process of making management decisions such as approving new tenants, deciding on rental terms, and approving repairs and capital expenditures.

Consistent with a number of tax benefits, the exception amount for active owners is phased out as adjusted gross income increases: The $25,000 maximum exception amount is phased out by 50 cents for every dollar the taxpayer's adjusted gross income (before considering the rental loss) exceeds $100,000. Consequently, the entire $25,000 deduction is phased out when the taxpayer's adjusted gross income reaches $150,000.

THE KEY FACTS

Rental Real Estate Losses

• Rental real estate exception to passive loss rules.
  • Applies to active participants in rental property.
  • Deduct up to $25,000 of rental real estate loss against ordinary income.
• $25,000 maximum deduction phased out by 50 cents for every dollar of AGI over $100,000 (excluding the rental loss deduction).
• Fully phased out at $150,000 of AGI.

Example 7-18

What if: Assume that Jeb Landers, Courtney's uncle, owns and rents a condominium. Jeb is involved in approving new tenants for the rental home and in managing its maintenance. During the year, he reported a net loss of $5,000 from the rental activity, and he had sufficient tax basis and at-risk amounts to absorb the loss. Further, his only sources of income during the year were $126,000 of salary and $22,000 of long-term capital gains. Given Jeb's $5,000 loss from his rental home, how much of the loss could he deduct currently and what would be his passive loss carryforward?

Answer: $1,000. Because Jeb meets the definition of an "active participant" and has adjusted gross income of less than $150,000, before considering his rental loss, he may deduct a portion of the loss against his other income. His $1,000 deduction is computed as follows:

Description	Amount	Explanation
1. Maximum deduction available before phase-out	$25,000	
2. Phase-out of maximum deduction	24,000	[($148,000 – 100,000) × .5].
3. Maximum deduction in current year	$ 1,000	(1) – (2).
4. Rental loss in current year	5,000	
5. Rental loss deductible in current year	**1,000**	Lesser of (3) or (4).
Passive loss carryforward	**$ 4,000**	(4) – (3).

(continued on page 7-34)

[45]§469(b)(7) provides another important exception to the general rule that all real estate activities are passive. To overcome this presumption, taxpayers must spend more than half their time working in real estate trades or businesses and for more than 750 hours during the year. This exception benefits individuals that spend a substantial amount of time in activities like real estate development and construction.

> **What if:** Assume that Jeb's salary for the year had been $50,000 and he reported $22,000 from the sale of his stock. How much of his rental loss could he deduct currently?
>
> **Answer:** Because Jeb's adjusted gross income would only be $72,000 under this scenario, he could deduct his entire $5,000 rental loss during the year.

Net Investment Income Tax on Net Passive Income

Earlier in this chapter we noted that taxpayers with modified AGI over certain thresholds are required to pay a 3.8 percent tax on their net investment income (in addition to the income tax). In calculating net investment income for this tax, taxpayers must include their net passive income.

Example 7-19

What if: Suppose Courtney has income from her salary of $170,000. Assume that in addition to this income, Courtney also owns 50 percent of an S corporation in which she does not materially participate. The S corporation is profitable and generates $100,000 of flow-through income to her this year. How much net investment income tax will Courtney owe?

Answer: $2,660, calculated as follows:

Description	Amount	Explanation
1. Net investment income	$100,000	Income from passive investment.
2. Modified AGI	270,000	$170,000 salaries + $100,000 LLC income.
3. Modified AGI threshold	200,000	
4. Excess modified AGI above threshold	70,000	(2) − (3).
5. Net investment income tax base	70,000	Lesser of (1) or (4).
Net investment income tax	2,660	(5) × 3.8%.

What if: Assume that Courtney spends 525 hours participating in the activity during the year. How much net investment income tax will she owe?

Answer: $0. Because Courtney materially participates in the S corporation, the flow-through income is no longer passive income and she will not be subject to the net investment income tax.

CONCLUSION

Investors and their advisors face numerous tax rules that apply to investment income and expenses. Understanding these rules is important, not only to comply with the tax law, but also to make wise investment choices. Investments differ in terms of their potential for implementing the conversion and shifting tax planning strategies. Failing to consider these strategies when investing will lead to less than optimal results. By carefully weighing nontax investment objectives along with the tax characteristics of different investment options, informed investors will be better equipped to select investments appropriate for them.

Summary

Explain how interest income and dividend income are taxed.   **LO 7-1**

- Investors seeking current income invest in interest-bearing securities or dividend-paying stocks.
- Interest income received from certificates of deposit, U.S. Treasury securities, corporate bonds, and other similar investments is typically taxed annually at ordinary rates.
- Accrued market discount on bonds and interest earned on U.S. savings bonds is taxed at sale or maturity, while original issue discount on bonds is taxed annually.
- Bond premiums increase the tax basis of bonds and affect the amount of capital gains or losses investors report.
- Taxpayers may elect to amortize bond premiums to reduce the amount of annual interest reported on bonds purchased at a premium.
- Dividend income, like interest income, is taxed annually when it is received. However, most dividend income currently is taxed at preferential capital gains rates.

Compute the tax consequences associated with the disposition of capital assets, including the netting process for calculating gains and losses.   **LO 7-2**

- When taxpayers sell stock, they may determine the basis of the stock using the specific identification method or the FIFO method.
- Capital assets held for more than one year generate long-term capital gains or losses on sale or disposition. Other capital assets generate short-term capital gains or losses on sale or disposition.
- Generally, net long-term capital gains in excess of net short-term losses are taxed at a maximum 20 percent tax rate.
- Unrecaptured §1250 gain is taxed at a maximum 25 percent rate, and gains from collectibles and §1202 stock are taxed at a maximum 28 percent rate.
- Up to $3,000 of net capital losses are deductible against ordinary income for the year.
- A taxpayer's capital gains and losses for the year are reported on Schedule D of Form 1040.
- Wash sale provisions prevent taxpayers from selling stock at a loss, deducting the loss, and replacing the stock sold with the same stock or substantially identical securities within 30 days either before or after the day of sale.
- Losses on the disposition of property held for personal use are not deductible.
- Because of the deferral of the capital gains tax, after-tax returns from capital assets will increase as an investor's investment horizon increases.

Calculate the deduction for portfolio investment-related expenses, including investment expenses and investment interest expense.   **LO 7-3**

- Investment expenses are miscellaneous itemized deductions subject to the 2 percent of AGI floor.
- Investment interest expense is deductible to the extent of net investment income.
- Net investment income is investment income minus deductible investment expenses.
- Net long-term capital gains and qualified dividends are not included in investment income unless the taxpayer elects to tax them as ordinary income.

Understand the distinction between portfolio investments and passive investments and apply tax basis, at-risk, and passive activity loss limits to losses from passive investments.   **LO 7-4**

- A taxpayer's share of operating losses from flow-through entities and other trade or business activities are deductible to the extent they clear the tax basis, at-risk, and passive activity loss hurdles.
- A taxpayer's ordinary losses from flow-through entities and other trade or business activities may be classified as passive if the taxpayer's involvement is not regular, continuous, and substantial.
- A taxpayer's operating losses from rental activities are, with limited exceptions, deemed to be passive regardless of taxpayer's activity level.

- A taxpayer's passive losses from an activity are limited to passive income from all other sources until disposition of the activity. On disposition, current and prior passive losses from an activity can be used without limitation.
- A rental real estate exception allows taxpayers to deduct up to $25,000 of operating losses from rental real estate annually provided they are actively involved in managing the rental real estate and have adjusted gross income of less than $150,000.

KEY TERMS

accrued market discount (7-4)	first-in first-out (FIFO) method (7-9)	original issue discount (7-3)
active participant in a rental activity (7-33)	flow-through entity (7-29)	passive activity loss rules (7-30)
amortization (7-3)	investment expenses (7-25)	passive investments (7-2)
at-risk (7-29)	investment income (7-2)	portfolio investments (7-2)
basis (7-4)	investment interest expense (7-25)	qualified dividends (7-6)
bond (7-2)	long-term capital gains or losses (7-10)	qualified small business stock (7-10)
bond discount (7-3)	market discount (7-4)	short-term capital gains or losses (7-10)
bond premium (7-3)	market premium (7-4)	specific identification method (7-9)
C corporation (7-29)	maturity (7-4)	tax basis (7-8)
capital asset (7-7)	maturity value (7-2)	tax shelter (7-30)
certificate of deposit (7-2)	mutual fund (7-2)	Treasury bond (7-3)
collectibles (7-10)	net investment income (7-27)	Treasury note (7-3)
dividend (7-2)	net short-term capital gain (7-12)	unrecaptured §1250 gain (7-10)
ex-dividend date (7-6)	net short-term capital loss (7-12)	U.S. savings bonds (7-3)
face value (7-2)	operating income (7-2)	wash sale (7-22)
	operating loss (7-2)	zero-coupon bonds (7-3)

DISCUSSION QUESTIONS

Discussion Questions are available in *Connect*®.

LO 7-1   1. Describe how interest income and dividend income are taxed. What are the similarities and differences in their tax treatment?

LO 7-1   2. What is the underlying policy rationale for the current tax rules applicable to interest income and dividend income?

LO 7-1   3. Compare and contrast the tax treatment of interest from a Treasury bond and qualified dividends from corporate stock.

LO 7-1   4. How are Treasury notes and Treasury bonds treated for federal and state income tax purposes?

LO 7-1   5. Why would taxpayers generally prefer the tax treatment of market discount to the treatment of original issue discount on corporate bonds?

LO 7-1   6. In what ways are U.S. savings bonds treated more favorably for tax purposes than corporate bonds?

research   **LO 7-1**   7. When should investors consider making an election to amortize market discount on a bond into income annually? [*Hint:* See §1278(b).]

planning   **LO 7-1**   8. Why might investors purchase interest-paying securities rather than dividend-paying stocks?

LO 7-1   9. Compare and contrast the tax treatment of dividend-paying stocks and growth stocks.

LO 7-2   10. What is the definition of a capital asset? Give three examples of capital assets.

LO 7-2   11. Why does the tax law allow a taxpayer to defer gains accrued on a capital asset until the taxpayer actually sells the asset?

12. Why does the tax law provide preferential rates on certain capital gains?   **LO 7-2**

13. What is the deciding factor in determining whether a capital gain is a short-term or long-term capital gain?   **LO 7-2**

14. What methods may taxpayers use to determine the adjusted basis of stock they have sold?   **LO 7-2**

15. What tax rate applies to net short-term capital gains?   **LO 7-2**

16. What limitations are placed on the deductibility of capital losses for individual taxpayers?   **LO 7-2**

17. What happens to capital losses that are not deductible in the current year?   **LO 7-2**

18. Are all long-term capital gains taxable at the same maximum rate? If not, what rates may apply to long-term capital gains?   **LO 7-2**

19. This year, David, a taxpayer in the highest tax rate bracket, has the option to purchase either stock in a Fortune 500 company or qualified small business stock in his friend's corporation. All else equal, which of the two will he prefer from a tax perspective if he intends to hold the stock for six years? Which would he prefer if he only plans to hold the stock for two years?   **LO 7-2** **planning**

20. What is a "wash sale"? What is the purpose of the wash sale tax rules?   **LO 7-2**

21. Nick does not use his car for business purposes. If he sells his car for less than he paid for it, does he get to deduct the loss for tax purposes? Why or why not?   **LO 7-2**

22. Describe three basic tax planning strategies available to taxpayers investing in capital assets.   **LO 7-2**

23. Clark owns stock in BCS Corporation that he purchased in January of the current year. The stock has appreciated significantly during the year. It is now December of the current year, and Clark is deciding whether or not he should sell the stock. What tax and nontax factors should Clark consider before making the decision on whether to sell the stock now?   **LO 7-2** **planning**

24. Are dividends and capital gains considered to be investment income for purposes of determining the amount of a taxpayer's deductible investment interest expense for the year?   **LO 7-3**

25. How is the amount of net investment income determined for a taxpayer with investment expenses and other noninvestment miscellaneous itemized deductions?   **LO 7-3**

26. What limitations are placed on the deductibility of investment interest expense? What happens to investment interest expense that is not deductible because of the limitations?   **LO 7-3**

27. When taxpayers borrow money to buy municipal bonds, are they allowed to deduct interest expense on the loan? Why or why not?   **LO 7-3**

28. What types of losses may potentially be characterized as passive losses?   **LO 7-3**

29. What are the implications of treating losses as passive?   **LO 7-4**

30. What tests are applied to determine if losses should be characterized as passive?   **LO 7-4**

31. All else being equal, would a taxpayer with passive losses rather have wage income or passive income?   **LO 7-4** **planning**

PROBLEMS

Select problems are available in *Connect*®.   connect

32. Matt recently deposited $20,000 in a savings account paying a guaranteed interest rate of 4 percent for the next 10 years. If Matt expects his marginal tax rate to be 20 percent for the next 10 years, how much interest will he earn after-tax for the first year of his investment? How much interest will he earn after-tax for the second year of his investment if he withdraws enough cash every year to pay the tax on the interest he earns? How much will he have in the account after 4 years? How much will he have in the account after 7 years?   **LO 7-1**

LO 7-1   33. Dana intends to invest $30,000 in either a Treasury bond or a corporate bond. The Treasury bond yields 5 percent before tax and the corporate bond yields 6 percent before tax. Assuming Dana's federal marginal rate is 25 percent and her marginal state rate is 5 percent, which of the two options should she choose? If she were to move to another state where her marginal state rate would be 10 percent, would her choice be any different? Assume that Dana itemizes deductions.

LO 7-1   34. At the beginning of his current tax year, David invests $12,000 in original issue U.S. Treasury bonds with a $10,000 face value that mature in exactly 10 years. David receives $700 in interest ($350 every six months) from the Treasury bonds during the current year, and the yield to maturity on the bonds is 5 percent.

a) How much interest income will he report this year if he elects to amortize the bond premium?

b) How much interest will he report this year if he does not elect to amortize the bond premium?

LO 7-1   35. Seth invested $20,000 in Series EE savings bonds on April 1. By December 31, the published redemption value of the bonds had increased to $20,700. How much interest income will Seth report from the savings bonds in the current year absent any special election?

LO 7-1   36. At the beginning of her current tax year, Angela purchased a zero-coupon corporate bond at original issue for $30,000 with a yield to maturity of 6 percent. Given that she will not actually receive any interest payments until the bond matures in 10 years, how much interest income will she report this year assuming semiannual compounding of interest?

LO 7-1   37. At the beginning of his current tax year, Eric bought a corporate bond with a maturity value of $50,000 from the secondary market for $45,000. The bond has a stated annual interest rate of 5 percent payable on June 30 and December 31, and it matures in five years on December 31. Absent any special tax elections, how much interest income will Eric report from the bond this year and in the year the bond matures?

LO 7-1   38. Hayley recently invested $50,000 in a public utility stock paying a 3 percent annual dividend. If Hayley reinvests the annual dividend she receives net of any taxes owed on the dividend, how much will her investment be worth in four years if the dividends paid are qualified dividends? (Hayley's marginal income tax rate is 28 percent.) What will her investment be worth in four years if the dividends are nonqualified?

LO 7-1
planning   39. Five years ago, Kate purchased a dividend-paying stock for $10,000. For all five years, the stock paid an annual dividend of 4 percent before tax and Kate's marginal tax rate was 25 percent. Every year Kate reinvested her after-tax dividends in the same stock. For the first two years of her investment, the dividends qualified for the 15 percent capital gains rate; however, for the last three years the 15 percent dividend rate was repealed and dividends were taxed at ordinary rates.

a) What is the current value (at the beginning of year 6) of Kate's investment assuming the stock has not appreciated in value?

b) What will Kate's investment be worth three years from now (at the beginning of year 9) assuming her marginal tax rate increases to 35 percent for the next three years?

LO 7-2   40. John bought 1,000 shares of Intel stock on October 18, 2013, for $30 per share plus a $750 commission he paid to his broker. On December 12, 2016, he sells the shares for $42.50 per share. He also incurs a $1,000 fee for this transaction.

a) What is John's adjusted basis in the 1,000 shares of Intel stock?

b) What amount does John realize when he sells the 1,000 shares?

c) What is the gain/loss for John on the sale of his Intel stock? What is the character of the gain/loss?

41. Dahlia is in the 28 percent tax rate bracket and has purchased the following shares of Microsoft common stock over the years:

Date Purchased	Shares	Basis
7/10/2006	400	$12,000
4/20/2007	300	10,750
1/29/2008	500	12,230
11/02/2010	250	7,300

If Dahlia sells 800 shares of Microsoft for $40,000 on December 20, 2016, what is her capital gain or loss in each of the following assumptions?

a) She uses the FIFO method.

b) She uses the specific identification method and she wants to minimize her current year capital gain.

42. Karyn loaned $20,000 to her co-worker to begin a new business several years ago. If her co-worker declares bankruptcy on June 22 of the current year, is Karyn allowed to deduct the bad debt loss this year? If she can deduct the loss, what is the character of the loss?

43. Sue has 5,000 shares of Sony stock that has an adjusted basis of $27,500. She sold the 5,000 shares of stock for cash of $10,000, and she also received a piece of land as part of the proceeds. The land was valued at $20,000 and had an adjusted basis to the buyer of $12,000. What is Sue's gain or loss on the sale of 5,000 shares of Sony stock?

44. Matt and Meg Comer are married. They do not have any children. Matt works as a history professor at a local university and earns a salary of $64,000. Meg works part-time at the same university. She earns $21,000 a year. The couple does not itemize deductions. Other than salary, the Comers' only other source of income is from the disposition of various capital assets (mostly stocks).

a) What is the Comers' tax liability for 2016 if they report the following capital gains and losses for the year?

Short-term capital gains	$ 9,000
Short-term capital losses	(2,000)
Long-term capital gains	15,000
Long-term capital losses	(6,000)

b) What is the Comers' tax liability for 2016 if they report the following capital gains and losses for the year?

Short-term capital gains	$ 1,500
Short-term capital losses	0
Long-term capital gains	13,000
Long-term capital losses	(10,000)

45. Grayson is in the 25 percent tax rate bracket and has the sold the following stocks in 2016:

	Date Purchased	Basis	Date Sold	Amount Realized
Stock A	1/23/1992	$ 7,250	7/22/2016	$ 4,500
Stock B	4/10/2016	14,000	9/13/2016	17,500
Stock C	8/23/2014	10,750	10/12/2016	15,300
Stock D	5/19/2006	5,230	10/12/2016	12,400
Stock E	8/20/2016	7,300	11/14/2016	3,500

a) What is Grayson's net short-term capital gain or loss from these transactions?

b) What is Grayson's net long-term gain or loss from these transactions?

c) What is Grayson's overall net gain or loss from these transactions?

d) What amount of the gain, if any, is subject to the preferential rate for certain capital gains?

LO 7-2 46. George bought the following amounts of Stock A over the years:

	Date Purchased	Number of Shares	Adjusted Basis
Stock A	11/21/1990	1,000	$24,000
Stock A	3/18/1996	500	9,000
Stock A	5/22/2005	750	27,000

On October 12, 2016, he sold 1,200 of his shares of Stock A for $38 per share.

a) How much gain/loss will George have to recognize if he uses the FIFO method of accounting for the shares sold?

b) How much gain/loss will George have to recognize if he specifically identifies the shares to be sold by telling his broker to sell all 750 shares from the 5/22/2005 purchase and 450 shares from the 11/21/1990 purchase?

LO 7-2 47. During the current year, Ron and Anne sold the following assets:

Capital Asset	Market Value	Tax Basis	Holding Period
L stock	$ 50,000	$41,000	> 1 year
M stock	28,000	39,000	> 1 year
N stock	30,000	22,000	< 1 year
O stock	26,000	33,000	< 1 year
Antiques	7,000	4,000	> 1 year
Rental home	300,000*	90,000	> 1 year

*$30,000 of the gain is 25 percent gain (from accumulated depreciation on the property).

a) Given that Ron and Anne have taxable income of only $20,000 (all ordinary) before considering the tax effect of their asset sales, what is their gross tax liability for 2016 assuming they file a joint return?

b) Given that Ron and Anne have taxable income of $400,000 (all ordinary) before considering the tax effect of their asset sales, what is their gross tax liability for 2016 assuming they file a joint return?

LO 7-2 48. In 2016, Tom and Amanda Jackson (married filing jointly) have $200,000 of taxable income before considering the following events:

a) On May 12, 2016, they sold a painting (art) for $110,000 that was inherited from Grandma on July 23, 2014. The fair market value on the date of Grandma's death was $90,000 and Grandma's adjusted basis of the painting was $25,000.

b) Applied a long-term capital loss carryover from 2015 of $10,000.

c) Recognized a $12,000 loss on 11/1/2016 sale of bonds (acquired on 5/12/2006).

d) Recognized a $4,000 gain on 12/12/2016 sale of IBM stock (acquired on 2/5/2016).

e) Recognized a $17,000 gain on the 10/17/2016 sale of rental property (the only §1231 transaction) of which $8,000 is reportable as gain subject to the 25 percent maximum rate and the remaining $9,000 is subject to the 10/15/20 percent maximum rates (the property was acquired on 8/2/2010).

f) Recognized a $12,000 loss on 12/20/2016 sale of bonds (acquired on 1/18/2016).

g) Recognized a $7,000 gain on 6/27/2016 sale of BH stock (acquired on 7/30/2007).

h) Recognized an $11,000 loss on 6/13/2016 sale of QuikCo stock (acquired on 3/20/2009).

i) Received $500 of qualified dividends on 7/15/2016.

Complete the required capital gains netting procedures and calculate the Jacksons' 2016 tax liability.

49. For 2016, Sherri has a short-term loss of $2,500 and a long-term loss of $4,750.   **LO 7-2**

a) How much loss can Sherri deduct in 2016?

b) How much loss will Sherri carryover to 2017, and what is the character of the loss carryover?

50. Three years ago, Adrian purchased 100 shares of stock in X Corp. for $10,000. On December 30 of year 4, Adrian sells the 100 shares for $6,000.   **LO 7-2**

a) Assuming Adrian has no other capital gains or losses, how much of the loss is Adrian able to deduct on her year 4 tax return?

b) Assume the same facts as in part (a), except that on January 20 of year 5, Adrian purchases 100 shares of X Corp. stock for $6,000. How much loss from the sale on December 30 of year 4 is deductible on Adrian's year 4 tax return? What basis does Adrian take in the stock purchased on January 20 of year 5?

51. Christopher sold 100 shares of Cisco stock for $5,500 in the current year. He purchased the shares several years ago for $2,200. Assuming his ordinary income tax rate is 28 percent, and he has no other capital gains or losses, how much tax will he pay on this gain?   **LO 7-2**

52. Christina, who is single, purchased 100 shares of Apple Inc. stock several years ago for $3,500. During her year-end tax planning, she decided to sell 50 shares of Apple for $1,500 on December 30. However, two weeks later, Apple introduced its latest iPhone, and she decided that she should buy the 50 shares (cost of $1,600) of Apple back before prices skyrocket.   **LO 7-2**

a) What is Christina's deductible loss on the sale of 50 shares? What is her basis in the 50 new shares?

b) Assume the same facts, except that Christina repurchased only 25 shares for $800. What is Christina's deductible loss on the sale of 50 shares? What is her basis in the 25 new shares?

53. Arden purchased 300 shares of AMC common stock several years ago for $1,500. On April 30, Arden sold the shares of AMC common for $500 and then purchased 250 shares of AMC preferred stock two days later for $700. The AMC preferred stock is not convertible into AMC common stock. What is Arden's deductible loss from the sale of the 300 shares of AMC common stock?   **LO 7-2**   **research**

54. Shaun bought 300 shares of Dental Equipment Inc. several years ago for $10,000. Currently the stock is worth $8,000. Shaun's marginal tax rate this year is 25 percent, and he has no other capital gains or losses. Shaun expects to have a marginal rate of 30 percent next year, but also expects to have a long-term capital gain of $10,000. To minimize taxes, should Shaun sell the stock on December 31 of this year or January 1 of next year (ignore the time value of money)?   **LO 7-2**   **planning**

55. Becky recently discovered some high-tech cooking technology that has advantages over microwave and traditional ovens. She received a patent on the technology that gives her exclusive rights to the technology for 20 years. Becky   **LO 7-2**   **research**

would prefer to retain the patent, but she doesn't want to deal with the manufacturing and marketing of the technology. She was able to reach a compromise. A little over a year after she secured the patent, Becky signed a contract with DEF Company giving DEF control to manufacture and market the technology. In exchange, Becky is to receive a royalty based on the sales of the technology. For tax purposes, Becky is not sure how to treat her arrangement with DEF. If the exchange with DEF is treated as a sale, she will recognize long-term capital gain because the patent is a capital asset held for more than a year. If the exchange is not treated as a sale, Becky will recognize ordinary income as she receives the royalties. (*Hint:* IRC §1235 and http://www.aicpa.org/publications/taxadviser/2013/december/pages/kelley_dec2013.aspx)

a) Is it possible for Becky to treat the exchange with DEF as a sale even though she never relinquishes actual title of the patent? If so, what requirements must she meet to treat the contract as a sale for tax purposes?

b) Does your answer to the question above change if Becky's contract with DEF gave DEF Company control over the income from the patent for the next 10 years of the patent's remaining 19-year life?

LO 7-3   56. Rich and Shauna Nielson file a joint tax return, and they itemize deductions. Assume their marginal tax rate on ordinary income is 25 percent. The Nielsons incur $2,000 in miscellaneous itemized deductions, excluding investment expenses. They also incur $1,000 in noninterest investment expenses during the year. What tax savings do they receive from the investment expenses under the following assumptions:

a) Their AGI is $90,000.

b) Their AGI is $130,000.

LO 7-3   57. Mickey and Jenny Porter file a joint tax return, and they itemize deductions. The Porters incur $2,000 in employment-related miscellaneous itemized deductions. They also incur $3,000 of investment interest expense during the year. The Porters' income for the year consists of $150,000 in salary, and $2,500 of interest income.

a) What is the amount of the Porters' investment interest expense deduction for the year?

b) What would their investment interest expense deduction be if they also had a ($2,000) long-term capital loss?

LO 7-3
planning   58. On January 1 of year 1, Nick and Rachel Sutton purchased a parcel of undeveloped land as an investment. The purchase price of the land was $150,000. They paid for the property by making a down payment of $50,000 and borrowing $100,000 from the bank at an interest rate of 6 percent per year. At the end of the first year, the Suttons paid $6,000 of interest to the bank. During year 1, the Suttons' only source of income was salary. On December 31 of year 2, the Suttons paid $6,000 of interest to the bank and sold the land for $210,000. They used $100,000 of the sale proceeds to pay off the $100,000 loan. The Suttons itemize deductions and are subject to a marginal ordinary income tax rate of 35 percent.

a) Should the Suttons treat the capital gain from the land sale as investment income in year 2 in order to minimize their year 2 tax bill? If so, how much?

b) How much does this cost or save them in year 2?

LO 7-3
research   59. George recently received a great stock tip from his friend, Mason. George didn't have any cash on hand to invest, so he decided to take out a $20,000 loan to facilitate the stock acquisition. The loan terms are 8 percent interest with interest-only payments due each year for five years. At the end of the

five-year period the entire loan principal is due. When George closed on the loan on April 1, 2016, he decided to invest $16,000 in stock and to use the remaining $4,000 to purchase a four-wheel recreation vehicle. George is unsure how he will treat the interest paid on the $20,000 loan. In 2016, George paid $1,200 interest expense on the loan. For tax purposes, how should he treat the 2016 interest expense? (*Hint:* Visit www.irs.gov and consider IRS Publication 550.)

60. Larry recently invested $20,000 (tax basis) in purchasing a limited partnership interest. His at-risk amount is also $20,000. In addition, Larry's share of the limited partnership loss for the year is $2,000, his share of income from a different limited partnership was $1,000, and he had $3,000 of dividend income from the stock he owns. How much of Larry's $2,000 loss from the limited partnership can he deduct in the current year?   `LO 7-4`

61. Rubio recently invested $20,000 (tax basis) in purchasing a limited partnership interest. His at-risk amount is $15,000. In addition, Rubio's share of the limited partnership loss for the year is $22,000, his share of income from a different limited partnership was $5,000, and he had $40,000 in wage income and $10,000 in long-term capital gains.   `LO 7-4`

    a) How much of Rubio's $22,000 loss is allowed considering only the tax basis loss limitations?

    b) How much of the loss from part (a) is allowed under the at-risk limitations?

    c) How much of Rubio's $22,000 loss from the limited partnership can he deduct in the current year considering all limitations?

62. Molly Grey (single) acquired a 30 percent limited partnership interest in Beau Geste LLP several years ago for $48,000. At the beginning of year 1, Molly has tax basis and an at-risk amount of $20,000. In year 1, Beau Geste incurs a loss of $180,000 and does not make any distributions to the partners.   `LO 7-4`

    • In year 1, Molly's AGI (excluding any income or loss from Beau Geste) is $60,000. This includes $10,000 of passive income from other passive activities.

    • In year 2, Beau Geste earns income of $30,000. In addition, Molly contributes an additional $30,000 to Beau Geste during year 2. Molly's AGI in year 2 is $63,000 (excluding any income or loss from Beau Geste). This amount includes $8,000 in income from her other passive investments.

    a) Based on the above information, determine the following amounts:

       • At-risk amount at the end of year 1
       • At-risk amount at the end of year 2
       • Losses allowed under the at-risk rules in year 2
       • Total suspended passive losses at the end of year 1
       • Total suspended at-risk losses at the end of year 2
       • Deductible losses in year 1
       • Year 2 AGI after considering Beau Geste events

    b) Briefly describe actions Molly Grey could undertake in year 2 to utilize any suspended passive losses from year 1.

63. Anwar owns a rental home and is involved in maintaining it and approving renters. During the year he has a net loss of $8,000 from renting the home. His other sources of income during the year were a salary of $111,000 and $34,000 of long-term capital gains. How much of Anwar's $8,000 rental loss can he deduct currently if he has no sources of passive income?   `LO 7-4`

COMPREHENSIVE PROBLEMS

Select problems are available in *Connect*®.

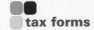

64. During 2016, your clients, Mr. and Mrs. Howell, owned the following investment assets:

Investment Assets	Date Acquired	Purchase Price	Broker's Commission Paid at Time of Purchase
300 shares of IBM common	11/22/13	$ 10,350	$ 100
200 shares of IBM common	4/3/14	43,250	300
3,000 shares of Apple preferred	12/12/14	147,000	1,300
2,100 shares of Cisco common	8/14/15	52,500	550
420 shares of Vanguard mutual fund	3/2/16	14,700	No load fund*

*No commissions are charged when no load mutual funds are bought and sold.

Because of the downturn in the stock market, Mr. and Mrs. Howell decided to sell most of their stocks and mutual fund in 2016 and to reinvest in municipal bonds. The following investment assets were sold in 2016:

Investment Assets	Date Sold	Sale Price	Broker's Commission Paid at Time of Sale
300 shares of IBM common	5/6/16	$ 13,700	$ 100
3,000 shares of Apple preferred	10/5/16	221,400	2,000
2,100 shares of Cisco common	8/15/16	63,250	650
451 Shares of Vanguard mutual fund	12/21/16	15,700	No load fund*

*No commissions are charged when no load mutual funds are bought and sold.

The Howells' broker issued them a Form 1099 showing the sales proceeds net of the commissions paid. For example, the IBM sales proceeds were reported as $13,600 on the Form 1099 they received.

In addition to the sales reflected in the table above, the Howells provided you with the following additional information concerning 2016:

- The Howells received a Form 1099 from the Vanguard mutual fund reporting a $900 long-term capital gain distribution. This distribution was reinvested in 31 additional Vanguard mutual fund shares on 6/30/2016.
- In 2011, Mrs. Howell loaned $6,000 to a friend who was starting a new multilevel marketing company called LD3. The friend declared bankruptcy in 2016, and Mrs. Howell has been notified she will not be receiving any repayment of the loan.
- The Howells have a $2,300 short-term capital loss carryover and a $4,800 long-term capital loss carryover from prior years.
- The Howells did not instruct their broker to sell any particular lot of IBM stock.
- The Howells earned $3,000 in municipal bond interest, $3,000 in interest from corporate bonds, and $4,000 in qualified dividends.
- Assume the Howells have $130,000 of wage income during the year.

a) Go to the IRS website (www.IRS.gov) and download the most current version of Form 8949 and Schedule D. Use Form 8949 and page 1 of Schedule D to compute net long-term and short-term capital gains. Then, compute the Howells' tax liability for the year (ignoring the alternative

minimum tax and any phase-out provisions) assuming they file a joint
return, they have no dependents, they don't make any special tax elections,
and their itemized deductions total $25,000. Assume that asset bases are
reported to the IRS.

b) Are there any tax planning recommendations related to the stock sales that
you should have shared with the Howells before their decision to sell?

c) Assume the Howells' short-term capital loss carryover from prior years is
$82,300 rather than $2,300 as indicated above. If this is the case, how much
short-term and long-term capital loss carryover remains to be carried beyond
2016 to future tax years?

Individual Income Tax Computation and Tax Credits

Learning Objectives

Upon completing this chapter, you should be able to:

LO 8-1 Determine a taxpayer's regular tax liability and identify tax issues associated with the process.

LO 8-2 Compute a taxpayer's alternative minimum tax liability and describe the tax characteristics of taxpayers most likely to owe the alternative minimum tax.

LO 8-3 Calculate a taxpayer's employment and self-employment taxes payable and explain tax considerations relating to whether a taxpayer is considered to be an employee or a self-employed independent contractor.

LO 8-4 Describe the different general types of tax credits, identify specific tax credits, and compute a taxpayer's allowable child tax credit, child and dependent care credit, American opportunity credit, lifetime learning credit, and earned income credit.

LO 8-5 Explain taxpayer filing and tax payment requirements and describe in general terms how to compute a taxpayer's underpayment, late filing, and late payment penalties.

© Image Source

Storyline Summary

Taxpayers:	Courtney Wilson, age 40, Courtney's mother Dorothy "Gram" Weiss, age 70
Family description:	Courtney is divorced with a son, Deron, age 10, and a daughter, Ellen, age 20. Gram is currently residing with Courtney.
Location:	Kansas City, Missouri
Employment status:	Courtney works as an architect for EWD. Gram is retired.
Filing status:	Courtney is head of household. Gram is single.
Current situation:	Courtney and Gram have computed their taxable income. Now they are trying to determine their tax liability, tax refund or additional taxes due, and whether they owe any payment-related penalties.

Courtney has already determined her taxable income. Now she's working on computing her tax liability. She knows she owes a significant amount of regular income tax on her employment and business activities. However, she's not sure how to compute the tax on the qualified dividends she received from General Electric. Courtney is worried that she may be subject to the alternative minimum tax this year because she's heard that an increasing number of taxpayers in her income range must pay the tax. Finally, Courtney knows she owes some self-employment taxes on her business income. Courtney would like to determine whether she is eligible to claim any tax credits such as the child tax credit for her two children and education credits because she paid for a portion of her daughter Ellen's tuition at the University of Missouri–Kansas City this year. Courtney is hoping that she has paid enough in taxes during the year to avoid underpayment penalties. She's planning on filing her tax return and paying her taxes on time.

Gram's tax situation is much more straight-forward. She needs to determine the regular income tax on her taxable income. Her income is so low she knows she need not worry about the alternative minimum tax, and she believes she doesn't owe any self-employment tax. Gram didn't prepay any taxes this year, so she is concerned that she might be required to pay an underpayment penalty. She also expects to file her tax return and pay her taxes by the looming due date.

to be continued...

In prior chapters we've learned how to compute taxable income for taxpayers such as Courtney and Gram. This chapter describes how to determine a taxpayer's tax liability for the year. We discover that the process is not as easy as simply applying taxable income to the applicable tax rate schedule or tax table. Taxpayers may generate taxable income that is taxed at rates not provided in the tax rate schedules or tax tables. We will learn that they may also be required to pay taxes in addition to the regular income tax. We also describe tax credits taxpayers may use to reduce their gross taxes payable. We conclude the chapter by describing taxpayer filing requirements and identifying certain penalties taxpayers may be required to pay when they underpay or are late paying their taxes. We start our coverage by explaining how to compute one's regular tax liability.

LO 8-1 REGULAR FEDERAL INCOME TAX COMPUTATION

When taxpayers have determined their taxable income, they are ready to compute their gross tax from a series of progressive tax rates called a **tax rate schedule.**

Tax Rate Schedules

Congress has constructed four different tax rate schedules for individuals. The applicable tax rate schedule is determined by the taxpayer's filing status, which we discussed in depth in Chapter 4. Recall that a taxpayer's filing status is one of the following:

1. Married filing jointly.
2. Qualifying widow or widower, also referred to as surviving spouse.
3. Married filing separately.
4. Head of household.
5. Single.

As we described in Chapter 1, a tax rate schedule is composed of several ranges of income taxed at different (increasing) rates. Each separate range of income subject to a different tax rate is referred to as a **tax bracket.** While each filing status has its own tax rate schedule (married filing jointly and qualifying widow or widower use the same rate schedule), all tax rate schedules consist of tax brackets taxed at 10 percent, 15 percent, 25 percent, 28 percent, 33 percent, 35 percent, and 39.6 percent. However, the width or range of income within each bracket varies by filing status. In general, the tax brackets are widest and higher levels of income are taxed at the lowest rates for the married filing jointly filing status, followed by the head of household filing status, single filing status, and finally, the married filing separately filing status.

The tax rate schedule for each filing status is provided inside the back cover of this book. Notice that the married filing separately schedule is the same as the married filing jointly schedule except that the taxable income levels listed in the schedule are exactly one-half the taxable income levels for married filing jointly.

Example 8-1

As we determined in Chapter 6, Courtney files under the head of household filing status and her 2016 taxable income is $109,961 (see Exhibit 6-14).

What if: For now, let's *assume* that all of Courtney's income is taxed as ordinary income. That is, assume that none of her income is taxed at a preferential rate (some is, but we'll address this in a bit). What is the tax on her taxable income?

Answer: $21,788. Using the head of household tax rate schedule, her taxable income falls in the 25 percent marginal tax rate bracket, in between $50,400 and $130,150, so her tax is computed as follows:

Description	Amount	Explanation
(1) Base tax	$ 6,897.50	From head of household tax rate schedule for taxpayer with taxable income in 25% bracket.
(2) Income taxed at marginal tax rate	59,561	$109,961 − 50,400 from head of household tax marginal tax rate rate schedule.
(3) Marginal tax rate	25%	From head of household tax rate schedule.
(4) Tax on income at marginal tax rate	14,890.25	(2) × (3).
Tax on taxable income	**$21,788**	(1) + (4), rounded.

Example 8-2

As we determined in Chapter 6, Gram files under the single filing status. In Chapter 6 we calculated her 2016 taxable income to be $3,690 (see Exhibit 6-15). None of her income is taxed at a preferential rate. What is the tax on her taxable income using the tax rate schedules?

Answer: $369 ($3,690 × 10%)

For administrative convenience and to prevent low- and middle-income taxpayers from making mathematical errors using a tax rate schedule, the IRS provides **tax tables** that present the gross tax for various amounts of taxable income under $100,000 and filing status (it's impractical to provide a table for essentially unlimited amounts of income). Taxpayers with taxable income less than $100,000 generally must use the tax tables to determine their tax liability.[1]

Because the tax tables generate nearly the same tax as calculated from the tax rate schedule, we use the tax rate schedules throughout this chapter.

Marriage Penalty or Benefit

An interesting artifact of the tax rate schedules is that they can impose what some refer to as a **marriage penalty,** but they may actually produce a **marriage benefit.** A marriage penalty (benefit) occurs when, for a given level of income, a married couple has a greater (lesser) tax liability when they use the married filing jointly tax rate schedule to determine the tax on their joint income than they would have owed (in total) if each spouse would have used the single tax rate schedule to compute the tax on each spouse's individual income. Exhibit 8-1 explores the marriage penalty in a scenario in which both spouses earn income and another in which only one spouse earns income. As the exhibit illustrates, the marriage penalty applies to couples with two wage earners, but a marriage benefit applies to couples with single breadwinners.

Exceptions to the Basic Tax Computation

In certain circumstances, taxpayers cannot completely determine their final tax liability from their tax rate schedule or tax table. Taxpayers must perform additional computations to determine their tax liability (1) when they recognize long-term capital gains or receive dividends that are taxed at preferential (lower) rates, (2) when they receive investment income subject to the net investment income tax, or (3) when the taxpayer is a child and the child's unearned income is taxed at her parent's **marginal tax rate.** We describe these additional computations in detail below.

[1]Exceptions to this requirement include taxpayers subject to the kiddie tax, with qualified dividends or capital gains, or claiming the foreign earned income exclusion. You may view the tax tables in the instructions for Form 1040 located at www.irs.gov/.

EXHIBIT 8-1   2016 Marriage Penalty (Benefit) Two Income vs. Single Income Married Couple*

Married Couple	Taxable Income	Tax if File Jointly (1)	Tax if File Single[†] (2)	Marriage Penalty (Benefit) (1) – (2)
Scenario 1: *Two wage-earners*				
Wife	$100,000		$21,036.75	
Husband	100,000		$21,036.75	
Combined	$200,000	$42,985.50	$42,073.50	$912
Scenario 2: *One wage-earner*				
Wife	$200,000		$49,529.25	
Husband	0		0	
Combined	$200,000	$42,985.50	$49,529.25	($6,543.75)

*This analysis assumes the taxpayers do not owe any alternative minimum tax (discussed below).
[†]Married couples do not actually have the option of filing as single. If they choose not to file jointly they must file as married filing separately.

Preferential Tax Rates for Capital Gains and Dividends

As we described in detail in Chapter 7, certain capital gains and certain dividends are taxed at a lower or **preferential tax rate** relative to other types of income. In general, the preferential tax rate is 0 percent, 15 percent, or 20 percent. The preferential tax rate is 0 percent *to the extent* the income would have been taxed in the 10 percent or 15 percent tax rate bracket if it were ordinary income, 20 percent to the extent the income would have been taxed in the 39.6 percent tax rate bracket if it were ordinary income, and 15 percent for all other taxpayers.[2] The tax rate tables and tax rate schedules allow taxpayers to compute their tax on ordinary but not **preferentially taxed income.** This is true even though preferentially taxed income is included in adjusted gross income (AGI) and in taxable income. Taxpayers with income subject to the preferential rate (long-term capital gains and qualified dividends) can use the following three-step process to determine their tax liability.

Step 1: Split taxable income into the portion that is subject to the preferential rate and the portion taxed at the ordinary rates.

Step 2: Compute the tax separately on each type of income. Note that the income that is not taxed at the preferential rate is taxed at the ordinary tax rates using the tax rate schedule for the taxpayer's filing status.

Step 3: Add the tax on the income subject to the preferential tax rates and the tax on the income subject to the ordinary rates. This is the taxpayer's regular tax liability.

Example 8-3

Courtney's taxable income of $109,961 includes $700 of qualified dividends from GE (Exhibit 5-4). What is her tax liability on her taxable income?

Answer: $21,718, computed at head of household rates as follows:

Description	Amount	Explanation
(1) Taxable income	$109,961	Exhibit 6-14.
(2) Preferentially taxed income	700	Exhibit 5-4.
(3) Income taxed at ordinary rates	$109,261	(1) – (2).

---

[2]As we discovered in Chapter 7, some types of income may be taxed at a preferential rate of 28 percent or 25 percent. In addition, as we discuss later in this chapter, dividends and capital gains for higher income taxpayers are subject to the 3.8% net investment income tax.

Description	Amount	Explanation
(4) Tax on income taxed at ordinary rates	21,612.75	[$6,897.50 + (109,261 − 50,400) × 25%], rounded.
(5) Tax on preferentially taxed income	105	(2) × 15% [Note that if (2) were ordinary income it would have been taxed at 25 percent.]
Tax on taxable income	**$ 21,718**	(4) + (5), rounded.

In this example, what is Courtney's tax savings from having the dividends taxed at the preferential rate rather than the ordinary rate?

Answer: $70. $700 × (25% − 15%). This is the amount of the dividend times the difference in the ordinary and preferential tax rate.

What if: Assume that Courtney's taxable income is $451,000 including $15,000 of qualified dividends taxed at the preferential rate. What would be Courtney's tax liability under these circumstances?

Answer: $126,936, computed using the head of household tax rate schedule as follows:

Description	Amount	Explanation
(1) Taxable income	$451,000	
(2) Preferentially taxed income	15,000	
(3) Income taxed at ordinary rates	436,000	(1) − (2).
(4) Tax on income at ordinary tax rates	124,186	$116,258.50 + [($436,000 − $413,350) × 35%] (see tax rate schedule for head of household).
(5) Tax on preferentially taxed income	2,750	[($5,000 × 15%) + ($10,000 × 20%)].*
Tax	**$126,936**	(4) + (5).

*Courtney had $15,000 of preferentially taxed income. If this income was ordinary income, $5,000 would have been taxed at 35 percent [$441,000 (end of 35 percent bracket) − $436,000 (ordinary taxable income)] and the remaining $10,000 would have been taxed at 39.6 percent [$451,000 (total taxable income) − $441,000 (end of 35 percent bracket)]. Consequently, $5,000 of the preferential income is taxed at 15 percent and the remaining $10,000 is taxed at 20 percent.

Net Investment Income Tax   Higher-income taxpayers are required to pay a 3.8 percent tax on net investment income. For purposes of this tax, net investment income equals the sum of

1. Gross income from interest, dividends, annuities, royalties, and rents (unless these items are derived in a trade or business to which the net investment income tax does not apply).
2. Income from a trade or business that is a passive activity or a trade or business of trading financial instruments or commodities.
3. Net gain from disposing of property (other than property held in a trade or business in which the net investment income tax does not apply).[3]
4. Less the allowable deductions that are allocable to items 1, 2, and 3.

Tax-exempt interest, veterans' benefits, excluded gain from the sale of a principal residence, distributions from qualified retirement plans, and any amounts subject to self-employment tax are not subject to the net investment income tax.

The tax imposed is 3.8 percent of the lesser of (1) net investment income or (2) the excess of modified adjusted gross income over $250,000 for married joint filers and surviving spouses, $125,000 for married separate filers, and $200,000 for

[3]However, the income, gain, or loss attributable to invested working capital of a trade or business is subject to the net investment income tax. §1411(c)(3).

other taxpayers. Modified adjusted gross income equals adjusted gross income increased by income excluded under the foreign earned income exclusion less any disallowed deductions associated with the foreign earned income exclusion.[4]

Example 8-4

Courtney's AGI (and modified AGI) is $162,000, and her investment income consists of $617 of taxable interest, $700 of dividends, and $5,000 of rental income. How much net investment income tax will Courtney owe?

Answer: $0. Because Courtney's modified AGI ($162,000) is less than the $200,000 threshold for the net investment income tax for a taxpayer filing as head of household, she will not be subject to the tax.

What if: Assume that Courtney's AGI (and modified AGI) is $225,000. How much net investment income tax will Courtney owe?

Answer: $240, calculated as follows:

Description	Amount	Explanation
(1) Net investment income	$ 6,317	$617 interest + $700 dividends + $5,000 rental income.
(2) Modified AGI	225,000	
(3) Modified AGI threshold	200,000	
(4) Excess modified AGI above threshold	25,000	(2) − (3).
(5) Net investment income tax base	6,317	Lesser of (1) or (4).
Net investment income tax	**240**	(5) × 3.8%.

Kiddie Tax Parents can reduce their family's income tax bill by shifting income that would otherwise be taxed at their higher tax rates to their children whose income is taxed at lower rates. However, as we described in Chapter 5, under the assignment of income doctrine, taxpayers cannot simply assign or transfer income to other parties. Earned income, or income from services or labor, is taxed to the person who earns it. Thus, it's difficult for a parent to shift *earned* income to a child. However, unearned income or income from property such as dividends from stocks or interest from bonds is taxed to the *owner* of the property. Thus, a parent can shift unearned income to a child by transferring actual ownership of the income-producing property to the child. By transferring ownership, the parent runs the risk that the child will sell the asset or use it in a way unintended by the parent. However, this risk is relatively small for parents transferring property ownership to younger children.

The tax laws reduce parents' ability to shift unearned income to children through the so-called **kiddie tax.** The kiddie tax provisions apply (or potentially apply) to a child if (1) the child is under 18 years old at year-end, (2) the child is 18 at year-end but her earned income does *not* exceed half of her support, or (3) the child is over age 18 but under age 24 at year-end, is a full-time student during the year, and her earned income does not exceed half of her support (excluding scholarships).[5] The kiddie tax does not apply to a child filing a joint tax return or to a child without living parents.

In general terms, if the kiddie tax applies, children must pay tax on a certain amount of their unearned income (their **net unearned income,** discussed below) at their parents' marginal tax rate rather than at their own marginal tax rate, unless the parents' marginal tax rate on the income (the preferential tax rate if the income is long-term capital gain or qualified dividends) would be lower than the child's marginal tax rate.[6] When the parents of the child are not married, this

---

[4]Taxpayers compute the net investment income tax using Form 8960.

[5]§1(g)(2)(A).

[6]§1(g).

provision applies to the custodial parent.[7] That is, the kiddie tax will never allow children to pay less tax than they would have been required to pay without the kiddie tax provision.

The kiddie tax base is the child's net unearned income. Net unearned income is the *lesser* of (1) the child's gross *unearned income* minus $2,100[8] or (2) the child's taxable income (the child is not taxed on more than her taxable income).[9] Consequently, the kiddie tax does not apply unless the child has *unearned* income in *excess* of $2,100.[10] Thus the kiddie tax significantly limits, but does not eliminate, the tax benefit gained by a family unit when parents transfer income-producing assets to children.

Example 8-5

What if: Suppose that during 2016, Deron received $1,100 in interest from the IBM bond, and he received another $2,200 in interest income from a money market account that his parents have been contributing to over the years. Is Deron potentially subject to the kiddie tax?

Answer: Yes, Deron is younger than 18 years old at the end of the year and his net unearned income exceeds $2,100.

What is Deron's taxable income and corresponding tax liability?

Answer: $2,250 taxable income and $405 tax liability, calculated as follows:

Description	Amount	Explanation
(1) Gross income/AGI	$3,300	$1,100 interest from IBM bond + $2,200 interest. All unearned income.
(2) Standard deduction	1,050	Minimum for taxpayer claimed as a dependent on another return (no earned income, so must use minimum). See Chapter 6.
(3) Personal exemption	0	Claimed as a dependent on Courtney's return.
(4) Taxable income	**$2,250**	(1) − (2) − (3).
(5) Gross unearned income minus $2,100	1,200	(1) − 2,100.
(6) Net unearned income	$1,200	Lesser of (4) or (5).
(7) Courtney's ordinary marginal rate	25%	See Example 8-3 (use Courtney's rate because she is the custodial parent).
(8) Kiddie tax	$ 300	(6) × (7) (Deron's income taxed at Courtney's marginal rate.)
(9) Taxable income taxed at Deron's rate	1,050	(4) − (6).
(10) Tax on taxable income using Deron's tax rates	$ 105	(9) × 10% (See single filing status, $1,050 taxable income.)
Deron's total tax liability	**$ 405**	(8) + (10).

What if: Assume Deron's only source of income is qualified dividends of $2,200 (unearned income). What is his taxable income and tax liability?

(continued on page 8-8)

THE KEY FACTS

Tax Rates

- Regular tax rates
  - Schedule depends on filing status.
  - Progressive tax rate schedules with tax rates ranging from 10 percent to 39.6 percent.
  - Marriage penalty (benefit) occurs because dual earning spouses pay more (less) combined tax than if they each filed single.
- Preferential tax rates
  - Net long-term capital gains and qualified dividends generally taxed at 0 percent, 15 percent, or 20 percent.
- Net investment income tax
  - 3.8 percent tax on lesser of (a) net investment income or (b) excess of modified AGI over applicable threshold based on filing status.
- Kiddie tax
  - Unearned income in excess of $2,100 is taxed at parent's marginal tax rate if child is (1) under age 18, (2) 18 but earned income does not exceed one-half of support, or (3) over 18 and under 24, full-time student, and earned income does not exceed one-half of support.

---

[7]§1(g)(5).

[8]The $2,100 consists of $1,050 of the child's standard deduction (even if the child is entitled to a larger standard deduction) plus an *extra* $1,050. See Chapter 6 for a discussion of the standard deduction for the dependent of another taxpayer. If the child itemizes deductions, then the calculation becomes more complex and is beyond the scope of this text.

[9]§1(g)(4).

[10]Under §1(g)(7), subject to certain requirements, parents may elect to include their child's unearned income on their own tax return (on Form 8814).

Answer: Taxable income is $1,150; tax liability is $15, computed as follows:

Description	Amount	Explanation
(1) Gross income/(AGI)	$2,200	Qualified dividends, all unearned income.
(2) Minimum standard	1,050	Minimum for taxpayer claimed as a dependent deduction on another return (all unearned income, so must use minimum). See Chapter 6.
(3) Personal exemption	0	Claimed as a dependent on Courtney's return.
(4) Taxable income	**$1,150**	(1) − (2) − (3).
(5) Gross unearned income minus $2,100	100	(1) − $2,100.
(6) Net unearned income	$ 100	Lesser of (4) or (5).

Description	Amount	Explanation
(7) Courtney's marginal tax rate on qualified dividend income	15%	See Example 8-3 (her marginal rate on ordinary income is 25%, so her marginal rate on preferentially taxed income is 15%).
(8) Kiddie tax	$ 15	(6) × (7) (Deron's income taxed at Courtney's marginal rate on the dividend income.)
(9) Taxable income taxed at Deron's rate	1,050	(4) − (6).
(10) Tax on taxable income using Deron's tax rates	$ 0	(9) × 0% (Deron's marginal rate on the dividend would be 10% if it were ordinary income, so he qualifies for 0% rate on dividend.)
Deron's total tax liability	**$ 15**	(8) + (10).

As we've just described, all individual taxpayers must pay federal income taxes on their federal taxable income. However, taxpayers may be liable for other federal taxes in addition to the regular tax liability. Many taxpayers are also required to pay the alternative minimum tax, and some working taxpayers are required to pay employment or self-employment taxes. We delve into these additional taxes below.

LO 8-2 ALTERNATIVE MINIMUM TAX

Each year, a number of taxpayers are required to pay the **alternative minimum tax (AMT)** in *addition to* their *regular* tax liability. The **alternative minimum tax system** was implemented in 1986 (earlier variations date back to the late 1960s) to ensure that taxpayers generating income pay some *minimum* amount of income tax each year. The tax was originally targeted at higher-income taxpayers who were benefiting from or were perceived by the public to be benefiting from the *excessive* use (more than Congress intended) of tax preference items such as exclusions, deferrals, and deductions to reduce or even eliminate their tax liabilities. However, as currently structured, the tax forces many taxpayers who don't fit this description to pay the tax.

In general terms, the alternative minimum tax is a tax on an *alternative* tax base meant to more closely reflect economic income than the regular income tax base. Thus the **AMT base** is more inclusive (or more broadly defined) than is the regular income tax base. To compute their AMT, taxpayers first compute their regular income tax liability. Then, they compute the AMT base and multiply the base by the applicable alternative tax rate.[11] They must pay the AMT only when the tax on the AMT base exceeds their regular tax liability.

---

[11]The rate of the alternative minimum tax (AMT) was set below that of the income tax with the objective of avoiding the perception that the AMT was an additional assessment.

Alternative Minimum Tax Formula

Regular taxable income is the starting point for determining the alternative minimum tax. As the AMT formula in Exhibit 8-2 illustrates, taxpayers make several "plus" and "minus" adjustments to regular taxable income to compute alternative minimum taxable income (AMTI). They then arrive at the AMT base by subtracting an AMT exemption from AMTI. Taxpayers multiply the AMT base by the AMT rate to determine their **tentative minimum tax.** Finally, to determine their alternative minimum tax, taxpayers subtract their regular tax liability from the tentative minimum tax. The alternative minimum tax is the *excess* of the tentative minimum tax over the regular tax. If the regular tax liability equals or exceeds the tentative minimum tax, taxpayers need not pay any AMT. Individual taxpayers compute their AMT on Form 6251 (see Exhibit 8-3).

Alternative Minimum Taxable Income (AMTI)   In order to compute alternative minimum taxable income (AMTI), taxpayers make several **alternative minimum tax adjustments** to regular taxable income. Many of these are plus adjustments that are added to regular taxable income to reach AMTI and some are minus adjustments that are subtracted from regular taxable income to determine AMTI. Consequently, these adjustments tend to expand the regular income tax base to more closely reflect economic income.

Exemptions, standard deduction, and itemized deduction phase-out.   Taxpayers first add back to regular taxable income the amount of personal and dependency exemptions they actually deducted, after considering phase-outs, in determining their regular taxable income. The exemption deduction is added back because it does not represent an actual economic outflow. Next, taxpayers add back the standard deduction amount, but only *if they deducted it* in determining taxable income. Again, just like exemptions, taxpayers add back the standard deduction because it is a deduction that does not reflect an actual economic outflow from the taxpayer.[12] Finally, taxpayers *subtract* the amount of itemized deductions they incurred but did not deduct because the deductions were phased-out or reduced for regular tax purposes (see discussion in Chapter 6). The phase-out is subtracted because it represents an economic outflow that did not reduce taxable income.

EXHIBIT 8-2   Formula for Computing the Alternative Minimum Tax

	Regular Taxable Income
Plus:	Personal exemptions and standard deduction if taxpayer deducted the standard deduction in computing regular taxable income
Minus:	Phase-out of itemized deductions for regular tax purposes (if applicable)
Plus or *Minus:*	Other adjustments*
	Alternative minimum taxable income
Minus:	AMT exemption amount (if any)
Equals:	Tax base for AMT
Times:	AMT rate
Equals:	Tentative minimum tax
Minus:	Regular tax
Equals:	Alternative minimum tax

*Technically, some of these adjustments are referred to as preference items and some are referred to as adjustments. We refer to all of these items as adjustments for simplicity's sake.

---

[12]The AMT add back of personal and dependency exemptions and the standard deduction is accomplished on Form 6251 by beginning with taxable income before personal and dependency exemptions (and before the standard deduction if the taxpayer does not itemize).

EXHIBIT 8-3 2015 Form 6251 (Page 1 of 2)

Form **6251**

Department of the Treasury
Internal Revenue Service (99)

Alternative Minimum Tax—Individuals

▶ Information about Form 6251 and its separate instructions is at *www.irs.gov/form6251*.
▶ Attach to Form 1040 or Form 1040NR.

OMB No. 1545-0074

20**15**

Attachment
Sequence No. **32**

Name(s) shown on Form 1040 or Form 1040NR

Your social security number

Part I   Alternative Minimum Taxable Income (See instructions for how to complete each line.)

1	If filing Schedule A (Form 1040), enter the amount from Form 1040, line 41, and go to line 2. Otherwise, enter the amount from Form 1040, line 38, and go to line 7. (If less than zero, enter as a negative amount.)	**1**
2	Medical and dental. If you or your spouse was 65 or older, enter the **smaller** of Schedule A (Form 1040), line 4, **or** 2.5% (.025) of Form 1040, line 38. If zero or less, enter -0-	**2**
3	Taxes from Schedule A (Form 1040), line 9	**3**
4	Enter the home mortgage interest adjustment, if any, from line 6 of the worksheet in the instructions for this line	**4**
5	Miscellaneous deductions from Schedule A (Form 1040), line 27.	**5**
6	If Form 1040, line 38, is $154,950 or less, enter -0-. Otherwise, see instructions	**6** ( )
7	Tax refund from Form 1040, line 10 or line 21	**7** ( )
8	Investment interest expense (difference between regular tax and AMT).	**8**
9	Depletion (difference between regular tax and AMT)	**9**
10	Net operating loss deduction from Form 1040, line 21. Enter as a positive amount	**10**
11	Alternative tax net operating loss deduction	**11** ( )
12	Interest from specified private activity bonds exempt from the regular tax	**12**
13	Qualified small business stock, see instructions	**13**
14	Exercise of incentive stock options (excess of AMT income over regular tax income)	**14**
15	Estates and trusts (amount from Schedule K-1 (Form 1041), box 12, code A)	**15**
16	Electing large partnerships (amount from Schedule K-1 (Form 1065-B), box 6)	**16**
17	Disposition of property (difference between AMT and regular tax gain or loss)	**17**
18	Depreciation on assets placed in service after 1986 (difference between regular tax and AMT)	**18**
19	Passive activities (difference between AMT and regular tax income or loss)	**19**
20	Loss limitations (difference between AMT and regular tax income or loss)	**20**
21	Circulation costs (difference between regular tax and AMT)	**21**
22	Long-term contracts (difference between AMT and regular tax income)	**22**
23	Mining costs (difference between regular tax and AMT)	**23**
24	Research and experimental costs (difference between regular tax and AMT)	**24**
25	Income from certain installment sales before January 1, 1987	**25** ( )
26	Intangible drilling costs preference	**26**
27	Other adjustments, including income-based related adjustments	**27**
28	**Alternative minimum taxable income.** Combine lines 1 through 27. (If married filing separately and line 28 is more than $246,250, see instructions.)	**28**

Part II   Alternative Minimum Tax (AMT)

29 Exemption. (If you were under age 24 at the end of 2015, see instructions.)

IF your filing status is . . .	AND line 28 is not over . . .	THEN enter on line 29 . . .	
Single or head of household	$119,200	$53,600	
Married filing jointly or qualifying widow(er)	158,900	83,400	
Married filing separately	79,450	41,700	**29**

If line 28 is **over** the amount shown above for your filing status, see instructions.

30	Subtract line 29 from line 28. If more than zero, go to line 31. If zero or less, enter -0- here and on lines 31, 33, and 35, and go to line 34	**30**
31	• If you are filing Form 2555 or 2555-EZ, see instructions for the amount to enter. • If you reported capital gain distributions directly on Form 1040, line 13; you reported qualified dividends on Form 1040, line 9b; **or** you had a gain on both lines 15 and 16 of Schedule D (Form 1040) (as refigured for the AMT, if necessary), complete Part III on the back and enter the amount from line 64 here. • **All others:** If line 30 is $185,400 or less ($92,700 or less if married filing separately), multiply line 30 by 26% (.26). Otherwise, multiply line 30 by 28% (.28) and subtract $3,708 ($1,854 if married filing separately) from the result.	**31**
32	Alternative minimum tax foreign tax credit (see instructions)	**32**
33	Tentative minimum tax. Subtract line 32 from line 31	**33**
34	Add Form 1040, line 44 (minus any tax from Form 4972), and Form 1040, line 46. Subtract from the result any foreign tax credit from Form 1040, line 48. If you used Schedule J to figure your tax on Form 1040, line 44, refigure that tax without using Schedule J before completing this line (see instructions)	**34**
35	**AMT.** Subtract line 34 from line 33. If zero or less, enter -0-. Enter here and on Form 1040, line 45	**35**

For Paperwork Reduction Act Notice, see your tax return instructions.   Cat. No. 13600G   Form **6251** (2015)

Example 8-6

Courtney started the process of determining whether she owed any AMT by adjusting her regular taxable income for her exemptions. What is Courtney's AMTI before other adjustments?

Answer: $122,111, computed as follows:

Description	Amount	Explanation
(1) Taxable income	$109,961	Exhibit 6-14.
(2) Exemptions	12,150	Exhibit 6-14.
AMTI before other adjustments	**$122,111**	(1) + (2).

Other adjustments.   Taxpayers are required to make several other adjustments to compute AMTI. Exhibit 8-4 describes the most common of these adjustments.

EXHIBIT 8-4   Common AMT Adjustments

Adjustment	Description
Plus adjustments:	
Tax-exempt interest from private activity bonds	Taxpayers must add back interest income that was excluded for activity bonds' regular tax purposes if the bonds were used to fund private activities (privately owned baseball stadium or private business subsidies) and not for the public good (build or repair public roads). However, taxpayers do not add back interest income from private if the bonds were issued in either 2009 or 2010.
Real property and personal property taxes deducted as itemized deductions	Deductible for regular tax purposes, but not for AMT purposes.
State income or sales taxes	Deductible for regular tax purposes, but not for AMT purposes.
Home-equity interest expense	This is *not deductible* for AMT purposes if the proceeds from the loan are used for *purposes other than to acquire or substantially improve the home.*
Miscellaneous itemized deductions (subject to the 2 percent floor) in excess of the 2 percent floor	Deductible for regular tax purposes but not for AMT purposes.
Plus or Minus adjustment:	
Depreciation	Taxpayers must compute their depreciation expense for AMT purposes. For certain types of assets, the regular tax method is more accelerated than the AMT method. In any event, if the regular tax depreciation exceeds the AMT depreciation, this is a plus adjustment. If the AMT depreciation exceeds the regular tax depreciation, this is a minus adjustment.
Minus adjustments:	
State income tax refunds included in regular taxable income	Because state income taxes paid are not deductible for AMT purposes, refunds are not taxable (they do not increase the AMT base).
Gain or loss on sale of depreciable assets	Due to differences in regular tax and AMT depreciation methods, taxpayers may have a different adjusted basis (cost minus accumulated depreciation) for regular tax and for AMT purposes. Thus, they may have a different gain or loss for regular tax purposes than they do for AMT purposes. If regular tax gain exceeds AMT gain, this is a minus adjustment. Because AMT accumulated depreciation will never exceed regular tax accumulated depreciation, this would never be a plus adjustment.

As Exhibit 8-4 indicates, several itemized deductions are not deductible for AMT purposes. The major itemized deductions that are deductible for both regular tax and AMT purposes using the *same limitations* are

- Casualty and theft losses.
- Charitable contributions.
- Home mortgage interest expenses.
- Gambling losses.

Deductions that are deductible for regular tax and AMT purposes but have *different limitations* are

- Medical expenses [10 percent of AGI floor for AMT purposes rather than 7.5 percent for regular tax purposes if the taxpayer (or his or her spouse) is age 65 or older]. Note that for regular tax and AMT purposes, all other taxpayers have a 10 percent AGI floor for medical expenses.
- Home-equity interest (interest not deductible for AMT purposes unless loan proceeds used to acquire or substantially improve the home).
- Investment interest expense (interest income that is tax exempt for regular tax purposes but included in the AMT base is included in investment income for determining the AMT investment interest expense deduction).

Example 8-7

Courtney continued to work on her AMT computation by determining the other adjustments she needs to make to determine her alternative minimum taxable income (AMTI). What is Courtney's AMTI?

Answer: $133,750, computed as follows:

Description	Amount	Explanation
(1) AMTI before other adjustments	$ 122,111	Example 8-6.
Plus adjustments:		
(2) Tax-exempt interest on Cincinnati bond used to pay for renovations to major league baseball stadium (Private activity bond: issued in 2005)	500	Example 5-22.
(3) Real estate property taxes	3,680	Example 6-14.
(4) State income taxes	6,700	Example 6-14.
(5) Miscellaneous itemized deductions in excess of 2 percent floor	1,179	Example 6-30.
Minus adjustments:		
(6) State income tax refund	(420)	Example 5-3.
Alternative minimum taxable income	$133,750	Sum of (1) through (6).

AMT Exemption To help ensure that low-income taxpayers aren't required to pay the alternative minimum tax, Congress allows taxpayers to deduct an **alternative minimum tax (AMT) exemption** amount to determine their alternative minimum tax base.[13] The amount of the exemption depends on the taxpayer's filing status. The exemption is phased-out (reduced) by 25 cents for every dollar the AMTI exceeds the threshold amount. Exhibit 8-5 identifies, by filing status, the base exemption amount, the phase-out threshold, and the range of AMTI over which the exemption is phased out for 2016.

[13]Similar to exemption and standard deduction amounts, the AMT exemption is indexed for inflation. The phase-out threshold amounts are also indexed annually for inflation.

EXHIBIT 8-5   2016 AMT Exemptions

Filing Status	Exemption	Phase-out Begins at This Level of AMTI	Phase-out Complete for This Level of AMTI
Married filing jointly	$83,800	$159,700	$494,900
Married filing separately	41,900	79,850	247,450
Head of household and Single	53,900	119,700	335,300

What is Courtney's AMT base?

Answer: $83,363 computed by subtracting her allowable exemption amount from her AMTI as follows:

Description	Amount	Explanation
(1) AMTI	$133,750	Example 8-7.
(2) Full AMT exemption (head of household):	53,900	Exhibit 8-5.
(3) Exemption phase-out threshold	119,700	
(4) AMTI in excess of exemption phase-out threshold	14,050	(1) – (3).
(5) Exemption phase-out percentage	25%	
(6) Exemption phase-out amount	3,513	(4) × (5), rounded.
(7) Deductible exemption amount	50,387	(2) – (6).
AMT base	**$ 83,363**	(1) – (7).

Tentative Minimum Tax and AMT Computation   Taxpayers compute the tentative minimum tax by multiplying the AMT base by the applicable AMT rates. The 2016 AMT rate schedule consists of just two regular brackets as follows:

- 26 percent on the first $186,300 (indexed for inflation annually) of AMT base for all taxpayers other than married taxpayers filing separately ($93,150, indexed for inflation annually, for married taxpayers filing separately).
- 28 percent on AMT base in excess of $186,300 (indexed for inflation annually) for all taxpayers other than married taxpayers filing separately ($93,150, indexed for inflation annually, for married taxpayers filing separately).

However, for AMT purposes long-term capital gains and dividends are taxed at the same preferential rate as they were taxed for regular tax purposes (generally 0 percent, 15 percent, or 20 percent).

Courtney's AMT base is $83,363. However, Courtney also received $700 in dividends that are included in the base but are subject to a tax rate of 15 percent even under the AMT system. The remaining $82,663 ($83,363 – $700) is taxed at the normal AMT rates. What is Courtney's tentative minimum tax?

Answer: $21,597, computed as follows:

Description	Amount	Explanation
(1) AMT base	$83,363	Example 8-8.
(2) Dividends taxed at preferential rate	700	Example 8-3.
(3) Tax rate applicable to dividends	15%	
(4) Tax on dividends	105	(2) × (3).
(5) AMT base taxed at regular AMT rates	82,663	(1) – (2).
(6) Regular AMT tax rate	26%	For AMT base below $186,300.
(7) Tax on AMT base taxed at regular AMT rates	21,492	(5) × (6), rounded.
Tentative minimum tax	**$21,597**	(4) + (7).

Taxpayers subtract their regular tax liability from their tentative minimum tax to determine their AMT.[14] If the taxpayer's regular tax liability is equal to or exceeds the tentative minimum tax liability, the taxpayer does not owe any AMT.

Example 8-10

THE KEY FACTS

Alternative Minimum Tax (AMT)

- Implemented to ensure taxpayers pay some minimum level of income tax.
- AMT base
  - More broad than regular income tax base.
  - No deductions for exemptions, standard deduction, state income taxes, property taxes, and others.
- AMT exemption amounts for 2016
  - $83,800 married filing jointly.
  - $41,900 married filing separately.
  - $53,900 other.
  - Phased-out by 25 cents for each dollar of AMTI over threshold.
- AMT rates
  - 26 percent on first $186,300 of AMT base.
  - 28 percent on AMT base in excess of $186,300.
  - Net long-term capital gains and qualified dividends taxed at same preferential rates used for regular tax purposes.
- AMT is the excess of tentative minimum tax (tax on AMT base) over regular tax liability.

What is Courtney's alternative minimum tax liability?

Answer: $0, computed as follows:

Description	Amount	Reference
(1) Tentative minimum tax	$21,597	Example 8-9.
(2) Regular tax liability	21,718	Example 8-3.
Alternative minimum tax	$ 0	(1) − (2), $0 if negative.

Courtney does not owe alternative minimum tax because her regular tax liability exceeds her tentative minimum tax.

In some situations, taxpayers who pay the AMT are entitled to a **minimum tax credit** to use when the regular tax exceeds the tentative minimum tax. They can use the credit to offset regular tax but not below the tentative minimum tax for that year.[15]

General AMT Planning Strategies Based on the nature of the adjustments we've explained, it's clear that the taxpayers who tend to get hit the hardest by AMT are taxpayers who (1) have many dependents, (2) live in a high-income-tax state (they deduct state taxes for regular tax purposes but not AMT purposes), (3) pay high real estate or other property taxes, and/or (4) have relatively high capital gains (the capital gains increase AMTI, which reduces the exemption amount and thus exposes more income to the AMT). In certain circumstances, taxpayers can implement tax planning strategies to mitigate the impact of the AMT. For example, consistent with the tax rate timing strategy we discussed in Chapter 3, taxpayers who pay AMT at 26 percent (or 28 percent) one year and expect to pay regular tax at 35 percent in the next year may want to consider accelerating income into the AMT year to ensure that it is taxed at a lower rate than it would be in a regular tax year. In any event, taxpayers who either pay or may pay the AMT should consider their tax situation to determine whether and how to use timing tax planning strategies to reduce their combined tax burden (regular tax and AMT) given their circumstances.

LO 8-3 EMPLOYMENT AND SELF-EMPLOYMENT TAXES

As we discussed in Chapter 1, employees and self-employed taxpayers must pay employment (or self-employment) taxes known as FICA taxes.[16] The FICA tax consists of a Social Security and a Medicare component that are payable by both employees and employers. The **Social Security tax** is intended to provide basic pension coverage for the retired and disabled. The **Medicare tax** helps pay medical costs for qualifying

[14]As might be expected, self-employment taxes and the 3.8 percent net investment income tax are not considered as part of a taxpayer's regular tax liability in determining whether a taxpayer owes AMT.

[15]The credit applies only when the taxpayer has positive adjustments that will reverse and become negative adjustments in the future. For example, depreciation, gain or loss on asset sales, and incentive stock option bargain element adjustments (see Chapter 12) fall into this category. Due to the nature of her adjustments, Courtney does not qualify for the minimum tax credit.

[16]FICA stands for Federal Insurance Contributions Act.

individuals. Because Social Security and Medicare taxes are paid by working taxpayers but received by retired taxpayers, Social Security and Medicare taxes represent intergenerational transfers. The Social Security tax rate is 12.4 percent on the tax base (limited to $118,500 in 2016). The Medicare tax rate is 2.9 percent on the tax base up to $200,000 ($125,000 for married filing separately; $250,000 for married filing jointly) and is 3.8 percent on the tax base in excess of $200,000 ($125,000 for married filing separately; $250,000 for married filing jointly). The party responsible for paying the tax and the tax base depends on whether the taxpayer is an employee or whether the taxpayer is self-employed.

Employee FICA Taxes Payable

Both employees and employers have to pay **FICA taxes** on employee salary, wages, and other compensation paid by employers. The Social Security tax rate for employees is 6.2 percent of their salary or wages (wage base limited to $118,500 in 2016). The Medicare tax rate for employees is 1.45 percent on salary or wages up to $200,000 ($125,000 for married filing separate; $250,000 of combined salary or wages for married filing joint) and is 2.35 percent on salary or wages in excess of $200,000 ($125,000 for married filing separate; $250,000 of combined salary or wages for married filing joint). Employers withhold the employees' FICA tax liabilities from the employees' paychecks for both the Social Security tax and the Medicare tax. For the Medicare tax, employers are required to withhold the tax at a rate of 1.45 percent on salary or wages up to $200,000 and at a rate of 2.35 percent for any salary or wages above $200,000, irrespective of the taxpayer's filing status (e.g., single, married filing separate, married filing joint, or head of household).[17] Taxpayers use Form 8959 to determine their liability for the .9 percent additional Medicare tax and report all of the .9 percent additional Medicare tax withheld as a tax payment on Form 1040 (line 62).

Employers must also pay their portion of the Social Security tax (6.2 percent of employee salary or wages) and Medicare tax (1.45 percent of employee salary or wages, regardless of the amount of salary or wages). In contrast to employees, employers are not subject to the .9 percent additional Medicare tax on employee salary or wages.

THE KEY FACTS

Employee FICA Tax

- Social Security tax
  - 6.2 percent rate on wage base.
  - 2016 wage base limit is $118,500.
- Medicare tax
  - 1.45 percent rate on wage base up to $200,000 ($125,000 for married filing separately; $250,000 for married filing jointly). 2.35 percent rate on excess wage base.
  - Wage base unlimited.

Example 8-11

While she was attending school full-time, Ellen received $15,000 in wages working part-time for an off-campus employer during 2016. How much in FICA taxes should Ellen's employer have withheld from her paychecks during the year?

Answer: $1,148, computed as follows:

Description	Amount	Reference
(1) Wages	$15,000	
(2) Social Security tax rate	6.2%	
(3) Social Security tax	930	(1) × (2).
(4) Medicare tax rate	1.45%	
(5) Medicare tax	218	(1) × (4).
FICA taxes withheld	$ 1,148	(3) + (5).

The wage base for Social Security taxes is limited to an annually determined amount, reflecting the fact that the benefits the employee may ultimately receive are also capped. The limits apply to *each* taxpayer's wages regardless of marital or tax filing status. That is, the earnings of each spouse are subject to a *separate* limit. The 2016

---

[17]To avoid potential underpayment penalty, taxpayers can request additional income tax withholding or make estimated tax payments to pay any Medicare tax that otherwise would have been owed upon filing their tax return.

limit is $118,500. There is no wage base limit for the Medicare component of the FICA tax, but as previously discussed, the Medicare tax rate varies with the taxpayer's salary or wages (or combined salary or wages for married filing joint taxpayers).

Example 8-12

During 2016, Courtney received a total of $122,800 in employee compensation from EWD. Recall that the compensation consisted of $98,000 in wages, $4,800 performance bonus, $6,000 discount for architectural design services, $4,000 compensation for a below-market loan, and $10,000 forgiveness of debt (see Exhibit 5-4). What is her FICA tax liability on this income?

Answer: $9,128, computed as follows:

Description	Amount	Reference
(1) Compensation subject to FICA tax	$122,800	
(2) Social Security tax base limit for 2016	118,500	
(3) Compensation subject to Social Security tax	118,500	Lesser of (1) or (2).
(4) Social Security tax rate	6.2%	
(5) Social Security tax	7,347	(3) × (4).
(6) Medicare tax rate on compensation up to $200,000	1.45%	
(7) Medicare tax	1,781	(1) × (6).
FICA taxes	**$ 9,128**	(5) + (7).

What amount of FICA taxes for the year must EWD pay on Courtney's behalf?

Answer: $9,128, which includes $7,347 of Social Security tax ($118,500 × 6.2%) and $1,781 of Medicare tax ($122,800 × 1.45%).

What if: Courtney received a total of $220,000 in employee compensation. What is her FICA tax liability on this income?

Answer: $10,717, computed as follows:

Description	Amount	Reference
(1) Compensation subject to FICA tax	$220,000	
(2) Social Security tax base limit for 2016	118,500	
(3) Compensation subject to Social Security tax	118,500	Lesser of (1) or (2).
(4) Social Security tax rate	6.2%	
(5) Social Security tax	7,347	(3) × (4).
(6) Medicare tax rate on compensation up to $200,000	1.45%	
(7) Compensation subject to 1.45% Medicare tax	200,000	Lesser of (1) or $200,000.
(8) Medicare tax rate on compensation in excess of $200,000	2.35%	
(9) Compensation subject to 2.35% Medicare tax	20,000	Greater of [((1) − $200,000) or $0].
(10) Medicare tax	3,370	[(6) × (7)] + [(8) × (9)].
FICA taxes	**10,717**	(5) + (10).

What amount of FICA taxes for the year must EWD pay on Courtney's behalf?

Answer: $10,537, which includes $7,347 of Social Security tax ($118,500 × 6.2%) and $3,190 of Medicare tax ($220,000 × 1.45%).

Employees who work for multiple employers within a calendar year may receive aggregate compensation that exceeds the Social Security wage base. Because each employer is required to withhold Social Security taxes on the employee's wages until the employee has reached the wage base limit *with that employer,* the employee may end up paying Social Security tax in *excess* of the required maximum. Similar to situations in which excess Medicare tax has been withheld, the IRS treats the excess Social Security tax paid through withholding as an additional federal income tax payment (or credit) on Page 2 of Form 1040 (line 71). The government refunds the excess withholding to the employee through either lower taxes payable with the tax return or a greater tax refund. Employers, on the other hand, are *not* able to recover excess Social Security taxes paid on behalf of their employees.

Example 8-13

What if: Suppose that Courtney worked for her former employer Landmark Architects Inc. (LA), in Cincinnati for two weeks in January 2016 before moving to Kansas City. During those two weeks, Courtney would have earned $4,000 in salary. LA would have withheld $306 in FICA taxes from her final paycheck consisting of $248 of Social Security taxes ($4,000 × 6.2%) and $58 of Medicare taxes ($4,000 × 1.45%). How much excess Social Security tax would have been withheld from Courtney's combined salaries from LA and EWD during 2016?

Answer: $248 ($4,000 wages earned with LA × 6.2% Social Security rate). Due to the $118,500 Social Security tax wage base for the year, Courtney's Social Security tax liability is limited to $7,347 ($118,500 × 6.2%). However, through employer withholding, she would have paid a total of $7,595 in Social Security taxes, consisting of $248 withheld by LA ($4,000 × 6.2%) and $7,347 withheld by EWD ($118,500 × 6.2%). Thus, given these facts, Courtney's *excess* Social Security tax withheld was $248 ($7,595 – $7,347). Courtney would get this amount back from the government through either lower taxes payable with her tax return or a greater tax refund.

Self-Employment Taxes

While employees share their FICA (Social Security and Medicare) tax burden with employers, self-employed taxpayers must pay the *entire* FICA tax burden on their self-employment earnings.[18] Just as it is with FICA taxes for employees, self-employment taxes consist of both Social Security and Medicare taxes. Because their FICA taxes are based on their self-employment earnings, FICA taxes for self-employed taxpayers are referred to as **self-employment taxes.** Just as it is with employees, the base for the Social Security component of the self-employment tax is limited to $118,500. The base for the Medicare portion of the self-employment tax is unlimited. Taxpayers use Schedule SE to determine their Social Security tax and 2.9% Medicare tax on self-employment earnings and Form 8959 to determine the .9 percent additional Medicare tax on self-employment earnings. The process for determining the taxpayer's self-employment taxes payable requires the following steps:

Step 1: Compute the amount of the taxpayer's net income from self-employment activities (this is generally the taxpayer's net income from **Schedule C** of Form 1040 Schedule C reports the taxpayers self-employment-related income and expenses) that is subject to self-employment taxes.

Step 2: Multiply the amount from Step (1) by 92.35 percent. The product is called **net earnings from self-employment.** Because self-employed taxpayers are responsible for paying the *entire* amount of their FICA taxes, they are allowed an implicit deduction for the 7.65 percent "employer's portion" of the taxes, leaving 92.35 percent (100% – 7.65%) of the full amount subject to self-employment taxes. Note that the 7.65 percent consists of

---

[18]As we discussed in Chapters 5 and 6, self-employed taxpayers report their self-employment earnings on Schedule C of Form 1040. Individuals who are partners in partnerships and who are actively involved in the partnerships' business activities may be required to pay self-employment taxes on the income they are allocated from the partnerships. They would report these earnings on Schedule E of Form 1040.

the 6.2 percent Social Security tax and 1.45 percent Medicare tax. Net earnings from self-employment is the base for the self-employment tax. If net earnings from self-employment is less than $400, the taxpayer is not subject to self-employment tax (but the taxpayer is still subject to income tax on the earnings).

Step 3: **Social Security tax.** The Social Security tax component of the self-employment tax equals 12.4 percent [the combined Social Security tax rate for employer and employee (6.2% + 6.2% = 12.4%)] multiplied by the lesser of (a) the taxpayer's net earnings from self-employment (from step 2) or (b) $118,500 (the maximum tax base for the Social Security tax).

Step 4: **Medicare tax.** The Medicare tax component of the self-employment tax equals 2.9 percent [the combined Medicare tax rate for employer and employee (1.45% + 1.45% = 2.9%)] multiplied by the net earnings from self-employment (from Step 2).

Step 5: **.9 Percent Additional Medicare tax.** The .9 percent additional Medicare tax due on net self-employment earnings equals .9 percent multiplied by the greater of (1) zero or (2) net earnings from self-employment (from Step 2) less $200,000 ($125,000 for married filing separately; $250,000 for married filing jointly). The .9 percent additional Medicare tax is considered an "employee" tax.

Note that as we discussed in Chapter 6, taxpayers are allowed to deduct the employer portion of their self-employment taxes as a *for* AGI deduction. For years prior to 2011, the employer and employee portions of self-employment tax were equal. Since 2011, the employer and employee portions potentially vary based on the level of self-employment earnings. Nonetheless, the employer portion is simple to calculate if you know the Social Security and Medicare tax rates that apply to employers.

Example 8-14

What if: Assume that Courtney's only income for the year is her $18,000 in net self-employment income from her weekend consulting business. What amount of self-employment taxes would Courtney be required to pay on this income?

Answer: $2,543, computed as follows:

Step 1: $18,000 of net self-employment income subject to self-employment taxes.

Step 2: $18,000 × .9235 = $16,623. This is net earnings from self-employment.

Step 3: $16,623 × 12.4% = $2,061. This is Courtney's Social Security tax payable for her self-employment income.

Step 4: $16,623 × 2.9% = $482. This is Courtney's Medicare tax payable for self-employment income.

Step 5: $2,543. The sum of the Social Security and Medicare taxes in Steps 3 and 4.

Under these circumstances, Courtney would be able to deduct $1,272 as a *for* AGI deduction for the employer portion of self-employment taxes she paid [i.e., $16,623 × (6.2% + 1.45%)].

When a taxpayer receives *both* employee compensation and self-employment earnings in the same year, the calculation of self-employment tax is a bit more complicated. For the Social Security tax component, the taxpayer's *total earnings* subject to the Social Security tax are capped at $118,500. In these situations, the taxpayer's Social Security tax liability on the employee compensation is determined as if the employee had no self-employment income. The taxpayer then computes her Social Security tax on her net self-employment earnings. This ordering is favorable for taxpayers because it allows them to use up all or a portion of the Social Security wage base limit with their employee income (taxed at 6.2 percent) before they determine the Social Security tax on their net earnings from self-employment (taxed at 12.4 percent). Consequently, if an employee's wages exceed the Social Security tax wage base limitation, she would not be required to pay any Social Security tax on her self-employment earnings.

Likewise, the Medicare tax calculation is more complicated when (1) the taxpayer receives both employee compensation and self-employment earnings or (2) the taxpayer files married jointly with a spouse receiving employee compensation or net self-employment earnings. Specifically, while the employer portion of the Medicare tax is 1.45 percent regardless of the level of net self-employment earnings, the employee portion of the Medicare tax varies based on the combined amount of employee compensation and net self-employment earnings for the taxpayer (or the taxpayer and his or her spouse, if they file married jointly). For taxpayers not filing married jointly, the employee portion of the Medicare tax rate is 1.45 percent on the taxpayer's salary or wages and net self-employment earnings up to $200,000 ($125,000 for married filing separately) and is 2.35 percent on salary or wages and net self-employment earnings in excess of $200,000 ($125,000 for married filing separately). For married filing jointly taxpayers, the employee portion of the Medicare tax rate is 1.45 percent on the taxpayer's and his or her spouse's salary or wages and net self-employment earnings up to $250,000 and is 2.35 percent on the taxpayer's and his or her spouse's salary or wages and net self-employment earnings in excess of $250,000.

The calculation of the taxpayer's FICA taxes on self-employment earnings in these settings can be determined as follows:[19]

Social Security Tax:

Step 1: Determine the limit on the Social Security portion of the self-employment tax base by subtracting the employee compensation from the Social Security wage base ($118,500 in 2016) (not below $0).

Step 2: Determine the net earnings from self-employment (self-employment earnings times 92.35 percent).

Step 3: Multiply the lesser of Steps (1) and (2) by 12.4 percent. This is the amount of Social Security taxes due on the self-employment income.

Medicare Tax:

Step 4: Multiply the amount from Step (2) by 2.9 percent, the combined Medicare tax rate for employer and employee.

.9 Percent Additional Medicare Tax:

Step 5: Add the amount from Step (2) and the taxpayer's compensation. If married filing jointly, also add the spouse's compensation and net earnings from self-employment (spouse's self-employment earnings times 92.35 percent).

Step 6: Multiply the greater of [(a) zero or (b) the amount from Step (5) minus $200,000 ($125,000 for married filing separately; $250,000 for married filing jointly)] by .9 percent.

Step 7: Take the amount from Step 6 and subtract the amount of the .9 percent additional Medicare tax withheld by the taxpayer's employer (and his or her spouse's employer if married filing jointly). This is the .9 percent additional Medicare tax due on the self-employment income.

[19]If net earnings from self-employment is less than $400, the taxpayer is *not* subject to self-employment tax (but the taxpayer is still subject to income tax on the earnings).

Example 8-15

In 2016, Courtney received $122,800 in taxable compensation from EWD (see Example 8-12) and $18,000 in self-employment income from her weekend consulting activities (see Example 6-2). What are Courtney's *self-employment taxes* payable on her $18,000 of income from self-employment? Assume that Courtney's employer correctly withheld $7,347 of Social Security tax and $1,781 of Medicare tax.

Answer: $482, computed as follows:

Description	Amount	Explanation
(1) Social Security wage base limit less employee compensation subject to Social Security tax	$ 0	$118,500 – $122,800, limited to $0.
(2) Net earnings from self-employment	16,623	$18,000 × 92.35%.
(3) Social Security portion of self-employment tax	0	[Lesser of Step (1) or (2)] × 12.4%.
(4) Medicare tax	482	Step (2) × 2.9%.
(5) Sum of taxpayer's compensation and net earnings from self-employment	139,423	$122,800 + Step (2).
(6) [Greater of (a) zero or (b) the amount from Step (5) minus $200,000] × 0.9%.	0	0 × 0.9%.
(7) Step (6) less any .9 percent additional Medicare tax withheld by Courtney's employer.	0	0 – 0.
(8) Steps (3) + (4) + (7)	482	0 + 482 + 0.

As we reported in Chapter 6, Courtney is entitled to a $241 *for* AGI deduction for the employer portion of the $482 self-employment taxes she incurred during the year ($16,623 × 1.45% employer portion of the Medicare tax rate = $241).

Example 8-16

What if: Let's change the facts and assume that Courtney received $100,000 of taxable compensation from EWD in 2016, and she received $180,000 in self-employment income from her weekend consulting activities. What amount of self-employment taxes is Courtney required to pay on her $180,000 of business income? Assume that Courtney's employer correctly withheld $6,200 of Social Security tax, $1,450 of Medicare tax, and $0 of .9 percent additional Medicare tax.

Answer: $7,711, computed as follows:

Description	Amount	Explanation
(1) Social Security wage base limit less employee compensation subject to Social Security tax	$ 18,500	$118,500 – $100,000, limited to $0.
(2) Net earnings from self-employment	166,230	$180,000 × 92.35%.
(3) Social Security portion of self-employment tax	2,294	[Lesser of Step (1) or (2)] × 12.4%.
(4) Medicare tax	4,821	Step (2) × 2.9%.

Description	Amount	Explanation
(5) Sum of taxpayer's compensation and net earnings from self-employment	266,230	$100,000 + Step (2).
(6) [Greater of (a) zero or (b) the amount from Step (5) minus $200,000] × 0.9%.	596	66,230 × 0.9%.
(7) Step (6) less any .9 percent additional Medicare tax withheld by Courtney's employer.	596	596 − 0.
(8) Steps (3) + (4) + (7)	7,711	2,294 + 4,821 + 596.

What if: Now let's assume that Courtney is married and files jointly. Assume that Courtney received $100,000 of taxable compensation from EWD in 2016 and $180,000 in self-employment income from her weekend consulting activities. In addition, her husband received $75,000 of taxable compensation from his employer. What amount of self-employment taxes is Courtney required to pay on her $180,000 of business income? Assume that Courtney's employer correctly withheld $6,200 of Social Security tax, $1,450 of Medicare tax, and $0 of .9 percent additional Medicare tax and that her husband's employer correctly withheld $4,650 of Social Security tax, $1,088 of Medicare tax, and $0 of .9 percent additional Medicare tax.

Answer: $7,936, computed as follows:

Description	Amount	Explanation
(1) Social Security wage base limit less employee compensation subject to Social Security tax	$ 18,500	$118,500 − $100,000, limited to $0.
(2) Net earnings from self-employment	166,230	$180,000 × 92.35%.
(3) Social Security portion of self-employment tax	2,294	[Lesser of Step (1) or (2)] × 12.4%.
(4) Medicare tax	4,821	Step (2) × 2.9%.
(5) Sum of taxpayer's and spouse's compensation and net earnings from self-employment	341,230	$100,000 + $75,000 + Step (2).
(6) [Greater of (a) zero or (b) the amount from Step (5) minus $250,000] × 0.9%.	821	91,230 × 0.9%.
(7) Step (6) less any .9 percent additional Medicare tax withheld by Courtney's employer and her husband's employer.	821	821 − 0.
(8) Steps (3) + (4) + (7)	7,936	2,294 + 4,821 + 821.

Unlike employees, whose employers withhold tax throughout the year on their behalf, self-employed taxpayers must satisfy their self-employment tax obligations through periodic, usually quarterly, estimated tax payments. Taxpayers who are employed and self-employed (an employee with a business on the side, like Courtney) may have their employers withhold enough taxes to cover both their income and self-employment tax obligations. Any self-employment taxes not paid through these mechanisms must be paid with the self-employed taxpayer's individual tax return.

continued from page 8-1...

Courtney was enjoying her work with EWD but she also really liked her weekend consulting work. A couple of months ago, after Courtney had played an integral part in completing a successful project, Courtney's boss jokingly mentioned that, if Courtney ever decided to leave EWD to work for herself as a full-time consultant, EWD would love to hire her back for contract work. This caused Courtney to start thinking about the possibilities of starting her own consulting business. She's always had some interest in working for herself, but she is not at a point in her life where she can take significant financial risks even if it might mean a more satisfying career. Courtney knew that before making such a move she would need to seriously consider the nontax issues associated with self-employment and she would need to learn more about the tax consequences of working as an independent contractor. She was particularly interested in the tax consequences of working for EWD as an independent contractor (contract worker) relative to working for EWD as an employee. ∎

Employee vs. Self-Employed (Independent Contractor)

Determining whether an individual is taxed as an **employee** or as an **independent contractor** can be straightforward or quite complex, depending on the specific arrangement between the parties. In its published guidance, the IRS stipulates that an employer/employee relationship exists when the party for whom services are performed has the right to direct or control the individual performing services.[20] To assist taxpayers in deciding whether the party receiving services has the requisite amount of control over the individual providing services, the IRS has published a list of 20 factors to consider.[21] A few of the factors suggesting independent contractor rather than employee status include the contractor's ability to

1. Set her own working hours.
2. Work part-time.
3. Work for more than one firm.
4. Realize either a profit or a loss from the activities.
5. Perform work somewhere other than on an employer's premises.
6. Work without frequent oversight.

When these factors are absent, individuals are more likely to be classified as employees. Rather than simply summing the number of factors in favor of independent contractor status and those in favor of employee status, however, taxpayers and their advisors should use the factors as guides in determining the overall substance of the contractual relationship.

Whether a taxpayer is classified as an employee or as an independent contractor (self-employed) has both tax and nontax consequences to the employer and the taxpayer. The best classification for the taxpayer is situation specific.

Employee vs. Independent Contractor Comparison   The two primary *tax* differences between independent contractors and employees relate to (1) the amount of their FICA taxes payable and (2) the deductibility of their business expenses.[22] However, there are several nontax factors to consider as well. In the previous section,

[20]IRS Publication 1779. Independent Contractor or Employee brochure.
[21]Rev. Rul. 87-41, 1987-1 CB 296.
[22]Also, independent contractors generally receive a Form 1099 from each client reporting the gross income they received from the client during the year. Employees receive Form W-2 reporting the compensation the employee received from the employer during the year.

we detailed how to determine the FICA taxes payable for employees and independent contractors (self-employed taxpayers). In terms of the deductibility of business expenses, as we discussed in Chapter 6, *employees* who incur unreimbursed business expenses relating to their employment can deduct these expenses as miscellaneous itemized deductions subject to a 2 percent of AGI floor. This floor means, in many cases, that employees receive little or no tax benefit for their employee business expenses. In contrast, as we also described in Chapter 6, self-employed independent contractors are able to deduct expenses relating to their business activities as *for* AGI deductions, which they can deduct without restriction. While these factors appear to favor independent contractor status over employee status, note that employees generally don't incur many unreimbursed expenses relating to their employment. Thus, even though independent contractors may be able to deduct more expenses than employees, they typically incur more costs in doing business.

When taxpayers are classified as independent contractors rather than employees, they are not eligible for nontaxable fringe benefits available to employees, such as health care insurance, retirement plan benefits, and other fringe benefits provided to employees. Further, independent contractors are responsible for paying their estimated tax liability throughout the year through estimated tax payments because the employer does not withhold taxes from an independent contractor's pay. However, as we mentioned above, taxpayers are allowed to deduct the employer portion of the self-employment taxes they pay.

From the employer's perspective, it is generally less costly to hire an independent contractor than an employee because the employer need not provide these benefits and the employer need not withhold or pay any FICA taxes on behalf of an independent contractor. As a result, an employer may be willing to offer an apparently higher level of taxable compensation to an independent contractor than a similarly situated employee. However, after considering all relevant factors, the taxpayer may do better receiving less compensation as an employee than slightly higher compensation as an independent contractor.

ETHICS

Sudipta is an accounting major who works during the day and takes classes in the evening. He was excited to finally land his first accounting job doing the books for a local dry cleaners. In his new job, Sudipta works 30 hours a week at the dry cleaners' main office. His excitement quickly dampened when he realized that his new employer was not withholding any income taxes or FICA taxes from his paycheck. Apparently, Sudipta's employer is treating him as an independent contractor. Sudipta likes his job, loves the money that he is earning, but recognizes that he should be treated as an employee instead of an independent contractor. What would you do if you were Sudipta?

Example 8-17

What if: Let's compare Courtney's compensation as an employee with EWD to her compensation if she were to work for EWD as an independent contractor. *Assume* that Courtney works an average of 40 hours per week for 50 weeks per year to earn a salary of $100,000; in addition she receives fringe benefits including a 5 percent contribution to her retirement plan, life insurance coverage, and health insurance coverage. Would Courtney be "made whole" in terms of her hourly rate if EWD agreed to pay her $55 an hour for her contract work (10 percent more than her hourly rate as an employee)?

Answer: Not very likely. As an independent contractor, Courtney must pay more costly self-employment taxes (at nearly twice the rate of employment taxes) under the new arrangement. In addition, she will be ineligible for the nontaxable fringe benefits (retirement plan contributions, life insurance, and health coverage) she was receiving as an employee and will not receive as a contractor.

THE KEY FACTS

Employee vs. Independent Contractor

- Employees
  - Less control over how, when, and where to perform duties.
  - Pay 6.2 percent Social Security tax subject to limit.

(continued)

- Pay Medicare tax from 1.45 percent to 2.35 percent.
- Independent contractors
  - More control over how, when, and where to perform duties.
  - Report income and expenses on Form 1040, Schedule C.
  - Pay 12.4 percent self-employment (Social Security) tax subject to limit.
  - Pay self-employment (Medicare tax) tax from 2.9 percent to 3.8 percent.
  - Self-employment tax base is 92.35 percent of net self-employment income.
  - Deduct the employer portion of self-employment taxes paid for AGI.

We've described how to calculate a taxpayer's regular tax liability, alternative minimum tax liability, and self-employment tax liability. These tax liabilities sum to a taxpayer's gross tax liability. While Gram's gross tax is simply her regular income tax liability of $369 (see Example 8-2), Courtney's gross tax includes other taxes. Courtney's gross tax liability is calculated in Exhibit 8-6.

EXHIBIT 8-6 **Courtney's Gross Tax**

Description	Amount	Explanation
(1) Regular federal income tax	$ 21,718	Example 8-3.
(2) Alternative minimum tax	0	Example 8-10.
(3) Self-employment tax	482	Example 8-15.
Gross tax	$ 22,200	(1) + (2) + (3).

Taxpayers reduce their gross tax by tax credits and tax prepayments (withholding and estimated tax payments) for the year. As indicated in Exhibit 8-7, if the gross tax exceeds the tax credits and prepayments, the taxpayer owes additional

EXHIBIT 8-7 **Formula for Computing Net Tax Due or Refund**

> **Gross tax**
> Minus: Tax credits
> Minus: Prepayments
> **Net tax due (refund)**

taxes when she files her tax return. In contrast, if the prepayments exceed the gross tax after applying tax credits, the taxpayer is entitled to a tax refund. We next explore available tax credits and conclude the chapter by dealing with taxpayer prepayments.

LO 8-4

TAX CREDITS

Congress provides a considerable number of credits for taxpayers. **Tax credits** reduce a taxpayer's *tax liability* dollar for dollar. In contrast, deductions reduce *taxable income* dollar for dollar, but the tax savings deductions generated depend on the taxpayer's marginal tax rate. Because tax credits generate tax savings *independent of* a taxpayer's marginal tax rate, they are a popular tax policy tool for avoiding the perception that tax benefits for certain tax policies are distributed disproportionately to taxpayers with higher incomes and corresponding higher marginal tax rates. Further, tax credits are powerful tax policy tools because they directly affect taxes due. By using tax credits, policy makers can adjust the magnitude of the tax effects of tax policy without changing tax rates.

Tax credits may be either nonrefundable or refundable. A **nonrefundable credit** may reduce a taxpayer's gross tax liability to zero, but if the amount of the credit exceeds the amount of the taxpayer's gross tax liability, the credit in excess of the gross tax liability is not refunded to the taxpayer and expires without ever providing tax benefits (unless the unused credit can be carried over to a different year). Refundable credits in excess of a taxpayer's gross tax liability are refunded to the taxpayer.

Tax credits are generally classified into one of three categories: nonrefundable personal, refundable personal, or business credits, depending on the nature of the credit. The primary exception to this general rule is the foreign tax credit. The foreign tax credit is a hybrid between personal and business credits because, like nonrefundable personal credits, it reduces the taxpayer's liability before business credits but, like business credits, unused foreign tax credits can be carried over to use in other years.

Nonrefundable Personal Credits

Congress provides many nonrefundable personal tax credits to generate tax relief for certain groups of individuals. For example, the child tax credit (partially refundable) provides tax relief for taxpayers who provide a home for dependent children and the child and dependent care credit provides tax relief for taxpayers who incur expenses to care for their children and other dependents in order to work. The American opportunity credit (partially refundable) and the lifetime learning credit help taxpayers pay for the cost of higher education. Because the child tax credit, the child and dependent care credit, and the American opportunity and lifetime learning credits are some of the most common nonrefundable personal credits, we discuss them in detail.

Child Tax Credit   Taxpayers may claim a $1,000 **child tax credit** for *each qualifying child* (same definition for dependency exemption purposes—see §152(c) and Chapter 4) who is under age 17 at the end of the year and who is claimed as their dependent.[23] The credit is subject to phase-out based on the taxpayer's AGI. The phase-out threshold depends on the taxpayer's filing status and is provided in Exhibit 8-8.

> **THE KEY FACTS**
>
> **Child Tax Credit**
>
> - Taxpayers may claim a $1,000 credit for each qualifying child under age 17.
> - Credit is phased out for taxpayers with AGI above threshold.
>   - Lose $50 for every $1,000 or portion thereof that AGI exceeds threshold.

EXHIBIT 8-8   **Child Tax Credit Phase-Out Threshold**

Filing Status	Phase-Out Threshold
Married filing jointly	$110,000
Married filing separately	55,000
Head of household and single	75,000

The total amount of the credit ($1,000 × number of qualifying children) is phased-out, but not below zero, by $50 for each $1,000 *or portion thereof* by which the taxpayer's AGI exceeds the applicable threshold. Taxpayers can determine their allowable child tax credit after the phase-out by using the following four steps:

Step 1: Determine the excess AGI by subtracting the threshold amount (see Exhibit 8-8) from the taxpayer's AGI.

Step 2: Divide the excess AGI from step (1) by 1,000 and round up to the next whole number.

Step 3: Multiply the amount from step (2) by $50. This is the amount of the total credit that is phased-out or disallowed.

Step 4: Subtract the amount from step (3) from the total credit before phase-out (limited to $0) to determine the allowable child tax credit.

Because the phase-out is based upon a fixed amount ($50) rather than a percentage, the phase-out range varies according to the amount of credit claimed.[24]

---

[23]§24(a).

[24]The child tax credit is partially refundable. The refundable portion of the credit is the lesser of (1) the taxpayer's earned income in excess of $3,000 times 15 percent, or (2) the amount of the unclaimed portion of the otherwise nonrefundable credit. Thus, if a taxpayer has enough tax liability to absorb the nonrefundable portion of the credit, the refundable portion is reduced to zero. The computation is modified for taxpayers with three or more qualifying children. See IRS Publication 972 for more information percent relating to the child tax credit.

Example 8-18

Both Ellen and Deron are Courtney's qualifying children. Courtney may claim a child tax credit for Deron but she may *not* claim a child tax credit for Ellen because Ellen is not under age 17 at the end of the year. What amount of child tax credit is Courtney allowed to claim for Deron after accounting for the credit phase-out?

Answer: $0. Because Courtney's AGI of $162,000 exceeds the $75,000 AGI phase-out threshold, she must determine her credit after the phase-out. Her phase-out is computed as follows:

1. $162,000 AGI (Exhibit 6-6) – $75,000 head of household threshold (Exhibit 8-8) = $87,000.
2. $87,000 excess AGI divided by 1,000 = 87 (if her AGI was $87,001, this would be 88).
3. 87 × $50 = $4,350. This is the amount of the phase-out.
4. $1,000 allowable credit minus $4,350 = $0 (limited to $0).

Courtney is *not able to claim any child tax credit* because the entire amount is phased out.

What if: How much child tax credit would Courtney be able to claim after the phase-out if she had claimed five qualifying children under the age of 17 as dependents?

Answer: $650. Her total child tax credit before phase-outs would be $5,000 ($1,000 × 5). Assuming the same AGI of $162,000, she would be required to phase-out $4,350 of the credit. Consequently, she would still be able to reduce her taxes by the $650 portion of the credit that was not phased-out ($5,000 – $4,350).

Child and Dependent Care Credit   The child and dependent care credit is a tax subsidy to help taxpayers pay the cost of providing care for their dependents to allow taxpayers to work or look for work. The amount of the credit is based on the amount of the taxpayer's expenditures to provide care for one or more qualifying persons. A qualifying person includes (1) a dependent under the age of 13, and (2) a dependent or spouse who is physically or mentally incapable of caring for herself or himself and who lives in the taxpayer's home for more than half the year.

The amount of expenditures eligible for the credit is the *least* of the following three amounts:

1. The total amount of dependent care expenditures for the year.
2. $3,000 for one qualifying person or $6,000 for two or more qualifying persons.
3. The taxpayer's earned income including wage, salary, or other taxable employee compensation, or net earnings from self-employment. Married taxpayers must file a joint tax return and the amount of earned income for purposes of the dependent care credit limitation is the earned income of the lesser-earning spouse.[25]

Expenditures for care qualify whether the care is provided outside or within the home. But, expenditures for care do *not* qualify if the caregiver is a dependent relative or child of the taxpayer.[26] The amount of the credit is calculated by multiplying qualifying expenditures by the appropriate credit percentage. The credit percentage is based upon the taxpayer's AGI level and begins at 35 percent for taxpayers with AGI of $15,000 or less. The minimum dependent care credit is 20 percent for taxpayers with AGI over $43,000. Exhibit 8-9 provides the dependent care credit percentage for different levels of AGI.

THE KEY FACTS

Child and Dependent Care Credit

- Designed to help taxpayers who work or seek work when they must provide care for dependents.
- Nonrefundable.
- Based on maximum qualifying expenditures multiplied by the rate based on AGI.
  - Maximum expenditures are $3,000 for one qualifying person or $6,000 for two or more qualifying persons.
  - Rate is 35 percent for the lowest AGI taxpayers and 20 percent for the highest.

[25]If the lesser-earning spouse cannot work due to a disability or is a full-time student, the lesser-earning spouse is *deemed* to have earned $250 a month if the couple is computing the credit for one qualifying person or $500 a month if the couple is computing the credit for more than one qualifying person.

[26]§21(e)(6). Also, the regulations indicate that the costs of summer school and tutoring programs are indistinguishable from general education and, therefore, do not qualify for the credit [See Reg. §1.21-1(b)].

EXHIBIT 8-9 **Child and Dependent Care Credit Percentage**

If AGI is over	but not over	then the percentage is
$ 0	15,000	35%
15,000	17,000	34
17,000	19,000	33
19,000	21,000	32
21,000	23,000	31
23,000	25,000	30
25,000	27,000	29
27,000	29,000	28
29,000	31,000	27
31,000	33,000	26
33,000	35,000	25
35,000	37,000	24
37,000	39,000	23
39,000	41,000	22
41,000	43,000	21
43,000	No limit	20

Example 8-19

What if: Suppose that this year, Courtney paid a neighbor $3,200 to care for her 10-year-old son, Deron, so Courtney could work. Would Courtney be allowed to claim the child and dependent care credit for the expenditures she made for Deron's care?

Answer: Yes. (1) Courtney paid for Deron's care to allow her to work, and (2) Deron is a qualifying person for purposes of the credit because (a) he is Courtney's dependent and (b) he is under 13 years of age at the end of the year.

What amount of child and dependent care credit, if any, would Courtney be allowed to claim for the $3,200 she spent to provide Deron's care given her AGI is $162,000?

Answer: $600, computed as follows:

Description	Amount	Explanation
(1) Dependent care expenditures	$ 3,200	
(2) Limit on qualifying expenditures for one dependent	3,000	
(3) Courtney's earned income	140,800	$122,800 compensation from EWD + $18,000 business income (see Example 8-15).
(4) Expenditures eligible for credit	3,000	Least of (1), (2), and (3).
(5) Credit percentage rate	20%	AGI over $43,000 (see Exhibit 8-9).
Dependent care credit	**$ 600**	(4) × (5).

What if: If Courtney's AGI (and her earned income) was only $31,500, what would be her child and dependent care credit?

Answer: $780, computed as follows:

Description	Amount	Explanation
(1) Dependent care expenditures	$ 3,200	
(2) Limit on qualifying expenditures for one dependent	3,000	
(3) Courtney's earned income	31,500	
(4) Expenditures eligible for credit	3,000	Least of (1), (2), and (3).
(5) Credit percentage rate	26%	See table for AGI between $31,000 and $33,000.
Dependent care credit	**$ 780**	(4) × (5).

Education Credits Congress provides the American opportunity credit (AOC) (formerly called the Hope scholarship credit) and the lifetime learning credit to encourage taxpayers and their dependents to obtain higher education by reducing the costs of the education. In contrast to the payment rules discussed in Chapter 6 for the deduction for Qualified Education Expense, taxpayers may claim credits for eligible expenditures made by them personally, their dependents, and third parties on behalf of the taxpayers' dependents.[27] If a student is claimed as a dependent of another taxpayer, only that taxpayer may claim the education credits (even if the dependent or another third party actually pays the education expenses).[28] Married taxpayers filing separate returns are not eligible for the AOC or the lifetime learning credit.

The AOC is available for students in their *first four years* of postsecondary (post high school) education. To qualify, students must be enrolled in a qualified postsecondary educational institution at least half time.[29] The amount of the credit is 100 percent of the first $2,000 of eligible expenses paid by the taxpayer (or another person) plus 25 percent of the next $2,000 of eligible expenses paid by the taxpayer (or another person). Thus, the maximum AOC for eligible expenses paid for any one person is $2,500 [$2,000 + (25% × $2,000)]. To be eligible for the 2016 credit, taxpayers must pay the eligible expenses in 2016 for any academic period beginning in 2016 or in the first three months of 2017.[30] Eligible expenses for the AOC include tuition, fees, and course materials (cost of books and other materials) needed for courses of instruction at an eligible educational institution.[31] The AOC is applied on a *per student* basis. Consequently, a taxpayer with three eligible dependents can claim a maximum AOC of $2,500 for *each* dependent. The AOC is subject to phase-out based on the taxpayer's AGI. The credit is phased out pro rata for taxpayers with AGI between $80,000 and $90,000 ($160,000 – $180,000 for married taxpayers filing jointly).[32] Forty percent of a taxpayer's allowable AOC is refundable.[33]

Example 8-20

THE KEY FACTS

Education Credits

- American opportunity credit
  - Qualifying expenses include tuition for a qualifying student incurred during the first four years at a qualifying institution of higher education.
  - Maximum credit of $2,500 per student calculated as percentage of maximum of $4,000 qualifying expenses.

(continued)

Courtney paid $2,000 of tuition and $300 for books for Ellen to attend the University of Missouri–Kansas City during the summer at the end of her freshman year. What is the maximum American opportunity credit (AOC) (before phase-out) Courtney may claim for these expenses?

Answer: $2,075. Because the cost of tuition and books is an eligible expense Courtney may claim a maximum AOC before phase-out of $2,075 [($2,000 × 100%) + ($2,300 – $2,000) × 25%].

How much AOC is Courtney allowed to claim on her 2016 tax return (how much can she claim after applying the phase-out)?

Answer: $0. Because Courtney's AGI exceeds the head of household limit of $90,000, she is not allowed to claim any AOC.

[27]§25A(g)(3).

[28]If a third party pays the education expenses of a student claimed as a dependent by another taxpayer, the dependent is deemed to have paid the education expenses and the taxpayer claiming the student as a dependent is allowed to claim the credit for the expenses.

[29]§25A(b). Generally, eligible institutions are those eligible to participate in the federal student loan program [§25A(f)(2)].

[30]Reg. §1.25A-3(e).

[31]§25A(i)(3). Eligible expenses for both the AOC and the lifetime learning credit must be reduced by scholarships received to pay for these expenses or other amounts received as reimbursements for the expenses (Pell grants, employer-sponsored reimbursement plans, Educational IRAs, 529 plans, and the like). The cost of room and board or other personal expenses do not qualify as eligible expenses for either the AOC or the lifetime learning credit.

[32]§25A(i)(4).

[33]§25A(i)(5). The refundability of the tax credit is not applicable to a taxpayer that is a child subject to the "kiddie tax" rules—i.e., a child (a) who does not file a joint return, (b) has at least one living parent, and who is either (1) under 18 years old at year-end, (2) 18 at year-end with earned income that does not exceed half of her support, or (3) over age 18 but under age 24 at year-end, is a full-time student during the year, and has earned income that does not exceed half of her support.

What if: How much AOC would Courtney have been allowed to claim on her 2016 tax return if she were married and filed a joint return with her husband (assuming the couple's AGI is $162,000)?

Answer: $1,867, computed as follows:

Description	Amount	Explanation
(1) AOC before phase-out	$ 2,075	
(2) AGI	162,000	
(3) Phase-out threshold	160,000	
(4) Excess AGI	2,000	(2) – (3).
(5) Phase-out range for taxpayer filing for married filing jointly	20,000	$180,000 – 160,000.
(6) Phase-out percentage	10%	(4)/(5).
(7) Phase-out amount	208	(1) × (6).
AOC after phase-out	$ 1,867	(1) – (7).

What if: Suppose Courtney could claim a $1,867 AOC in 2016 (after phase-out). How much of this credit would be refundable?

Answer: $747 ($1,867 × 40%).

- Subject to phase-out for taxpayers with AGI in excess of $80,000 ($160,000 MFJ).
- Lifetime learning credit
    - Qualifying expenses include costs at a qualifying institution associated with acquiring or improving job skills.
    - Maximum credit of $2,000 per taxpayer calculated as percentage of maximum of $10,000 in annual expenses.
    - Subject to phase-out for taxpayers with AGI in excess of $55,000 ($111,000 MFJ).

The lifetime learning credit is a nonrefundable credit that applies to the cost of tuition and fees (but generally not books) for any course of instruction to acquire or improve a taxpayer's job skills.[34] This includes the cost of professional or graduate school tuition (expenses are not limited to those incurred in the first four years of postsecondary education). The credit is equal to 20 percent of eligible expenses up to an annual maximum of $10,000 of eligible expenses (maximum of $2,000). The credit for a year is based on the amount paid during that year for an academic period beginning in that year or the first three months of the following year. In contrast to the American opportunity credit, the lifetime learning credit limit applies to the taxpayer (a married couple filing a joint return may claim only $2,000 of lifetime learning credit). Thus, a taxpayer with multiple eligible dependents can claim a maximum lifetime learning credit of only $2,000. Finally, the credit is phased out pro rata for taxpayers with AGI between $55,000 and $65,000 ($111,000 and $131,000) for married taxpayers filing jointly).[35]

Example 8-21

Courtney paid $1,550 to attend motivational seminars to help her improve her job skills. Courtney could elect to claim the lifetime learning credit for these expenses instead of deducting them as miscellaneous itemized deductions. If Courtney decided to claim a credit for these expenditures, what would be her maximum lifetime learning credit (before phase-out)?

Answer: $310 ($1,550 × 20%)

How much lifetime learning credit is Courtney allowed to claim on her 2016 tax return (how much can she claim after applying the phase-out)?

Answer: $0. Because Courtney's AGI exceeds the head of household limit of $65,000 she is not allowed to claim any lifetime learning credit.

For expenses that qualify for both the AOC and lifetime learning credit (tuition and fees during the first four years of postsecondary education), taxpayers may

[34]§25A(f)(1).
[35]§25A(d).

choose which credit to use, but they may not claim both credits for the same student in the same year. In addition, taxpayers may choose to *either* (1) deduct qualifying education expenses of an individual as a *for* AGI deduction (see discussion of this *for* AGI deduction in Chapter 6) or claim an education credit for the individual's expenses. However, if a taxpayer claims *any* educational credit for an individual's educational expenditures, the taxpayer may not claim *any for* AGI deduction for that individual's qualifying expenditures (and vice versa).[36]

Example 8-22

What if: Suppose Courtney paid $5,000 of tuition for Ellen to attend the University of Missouri–Kansas City during the summer at the end of her freshman year. Further assume that Courtney's AGI is $45,000, so her education credits are not subject to phase-out. Courtney would be allowed to claim the maximum AOC of $2,500 on the first $4,000 of the qualifying educational expenditures. Assuming Courtney used $4,000 of the educational expenses to claim the maximum AOC, would she be allowed to deduct (or claim the lifetime credit on) the remaining $1,000 of tuition costs ($5,000 total expenses – $4,000 maximum AOC expenses)?

Answer: No. If Courtney claims any AOC for Ellen's expenditures, she is not allowed to deduct or claim a lifetime learning credit for Ellen's expenditures (even for the expenses not used in computing the AOC).

What if: Assume that both Ellen and Deron were in their first year of college, and that Courtney paid tuition for both Ellen and Deron. Further, assume that Courtney's AGI is below the phase-out threshold. Is Courtney allowed to claim an AOC for Ellen's expenses and claim a *for* AGI educational expense deduction for Deron's expenses?

Answer: Yes. Courtney may claim an AOC or a deduction for Ellen's expenses, and she may claim an AOC or a deduction for Deron's expenses.

Example 8-23

What if: Assume that Courtney paid $8,000 tuition for Ellen to attend graduate school at the University of Missouri–Kansas City (assume this is her fifth year at the university and that Ellen still qualifies as Courtney's dependent). Further assume that Courtney's AGI is $60,000, so her potential lifetime learning credit for Ellen would be phased out by 50 percent (assume Courtney did not claim the credit for herself). Before phase-out, Courtney would be allowed to claim a $1,600 lifetime learning credit ($8,000 tuition × 20% credit percentage). After the phase-out, however, Courtney would be able to claim an $800 lifetime learning credit ($1,600 full credit × 1–50% phase-out percentage). If Courtney claims the $800 lifetime learning credit for Ellen's tuition, is she allowed to claim any *for* AGI deduction for Ellen's tuition since half of the lifetime learning credit is phased out based on Courtney's AGI?

Answer: No. As we discussed above, if Courtney claims *any* lifetime learning credit for Ellen's expenditures, she is not allowed to deduct any *for* AGI deduction for Ellen's expenditures (even the portion of the expenses that provided no tax benefit because the credit was partially phased out).

What if: Assume the same facts as above and that Courtney's marginal tax rate is 15%. Would Courtney be better off claiming an $800 lifetime learning credit or a $4,000 *for* AGI qualified education expense deduction for the cost of Ellen's tuition?

Answer: The $800 lifetime learning credit. The credit saves Courtney $800 while the qualified education expense deduction would save her $600 ($4,000 × 15%).

---

[36]§222(c)(2)(A).

Refundable Personal Credits

Several personal credits are refundable, the most common of which is the earned income credit, which we discuss in this chapter.

Earned Income Credit   The **earned income credit** is a refundable credit that is designed to help offset the effect of employment taxes on compensation paid to low-income taxpayers and to encourage lower-income taxpayers to seek employment. Because it is refundable (if the credit exceeds the tax after considering nonrefundable credits the taxpayer receives a refund for the excess), it is sometimes referred to as a *negative income tax.* The credit is available for qualified individuals who have earned income for the year.[37] Qualified individuals generally include (1) any individual who has at least one qualifying child (same definition of qualifying child for dependent purposes—see Chapter 4) or (2) any individual who does not have a qualifying child for the taxable year, but who lives in the United States for more than half the year, is at least 25 years old but younger than 65 years old at the end of the year, and is not a dependent of another taxpayer. Earned income includes wages, salaries, tips, and other employee compensation included in gross income and net earnings from self-employment. Taxpayers with investment income such as interest, dividends, and capital gains in excess of $3,400 are ineligible for the credit.[38]

The amount of the credit depends on the taxpayer's filing status, the number of the taxpayer's qualifying children who live in the home for more than half of the year, and the amount of the taxpayer's earned income. To be eligible for the credit, married taxpayers must file a joint tax return. The credit is computed by multiplying the appropriate credit percentage times the taxpayer's earned income up to a maximum amount. The credit percentage depends upon the number of qualifying children in the home and is subject to a phase-out based upon AGI (or earned income if greater). As summarized in Exhibit 8-10, the earned income credit increases as taxpayers receive earned income up to the maximum amount of earned income eligible for the credit. However, as taxpayers earn more income, the credit begins to phase out and is completely eliminated once taxpayers' earned income reaches established levels.

EXHIBIT 8-10   2016 Earned Income Credit Table

Qualifying Children	(1) Maximum Earned Income Eligible for Credit	(2) Credit %	(3) Maximum Credit (1) × (2)	(4) Credit Phase-Out for AGI (or earned income if greater) Over This Amount	(5) Phase-Out Percentage	No Credit When AGI (or earned income if greater) Equals or Exceeds This Amount (4) + [(3)/(5)]
		Married taxpayers filing joint returns				
0	$ 6,610	7.65%	$ 506	$13,820	7.65%	$20,434
1	9,920	34	3,373	23,740	15.98	44,848
2	13,930	40	5,572	23,740	21.06	50,198
3+	13,930	45	6,269	23,740	21.06	53,507
		All taxpayers *except* married taxpayers filing joint returns				
0	$ 6,610	7.65%	$ 506	$ 8,270	7.65%	$14,884
1	9,920	34	3,373	18,190	15.98	39,298
2	13,930	40	5,572	18,190	21.06	44,648
3+	13,930	45	6,269	18,190	21.06	47,957

[37]§32.
[38]§32(i).

Example 8-24

Courtney's earned income for the year is $140,800 (Example 8-19) and her AGI is $162,000 (Exhibit 6-6). Deron and Ellen both qualify as Courtney's qualifying children. What amount of earned income credit is Courtney entitled to claim on her 2016 tax return?

Answer: $0. Courtney's AGI (which is greater than her earned income) exceeds the $44,648 limit for unmarried taxpayers with two or more qualifying children. Consequently, Courtney is not allowed to claim any earned income credit.

What if: Assume that Courtney's only source of income for the year was $30,000 in salary. Also assume Courtney's AGI for the year was $30,000. What would be Courtney's earned income credit in these circumstances?

Answer: $3,085, computed as follows

Description	Amount	Explanation
(1) Earned income	$30,000	
(2) Maximum earned income eligible for earned income credit for taxpayers filing as head of household with two qualifying children	13,930	Exhibit 8-10.
(3) Earned income eligible for credit	13,930	Lesser of (1) and (2).
(4) Earned income credit percentage for taxpayer with two qualifying children	40%	
(5) Earned income credit before phase-out	5,572	(3) × (4).
(6) Phase-out threshold begins at this level of AGI (or earned income if greater)	18,190	See Exhibit 8-11 for head of household filing status and two qualifying children.
(7) Greater of (a) AGI or (b) earned income, less the phase-out threshold	11,810	(1) – (6). In this example AGI equals earned income.
(8) Phase-out percentage	21.06%	See Exhibit 8-11.
(9) Credit phase-out amount	2,487	(7) × (8).
Earned income credit after phase-out	**$ 3,085**	(5) – (9).

TAXES IN THE REAL WORLD *Taking a Bite Out of Earned Income Tax Credit Abuse*

The IRS has special reporting requirements (Form 8867) for tax professionals filing tax returns that include an earned income tax credit. Form 8867, the Paid Preparer's Earned Income Credit Checklist, is intended to ensure that tax professionals use appropriate due diligence in determining a taxpayer's eligibility for, and the amount of, the earned income tax credit.

Why the extra concern with the earned income tax credit? Because the earned income tax credit is a refundable tax credit, the potential for abuse (fraudulent claim) is quite high. Only paid tax preparers are required to complete the form, and failure to do so could result in a $500 penalty for each failure. See Form 8867 and IRC Sec. 6695(g).

Other Refundable Personal Credits Other refundable personal tax credits include a portion of the child tax credit (discussed above), excess FICA withholdings (see discussion above under FICA taxes), and taxes withheld on wages and estimated tax payments. We address withholdings and estimated taxes below when we discuss tax prepayments.

Business Tax Credits

Business tax credits are designed to provide incentives for taxpayers to hire certain types of individuals or to participate in certain business activities. For example, Congress provides the employment tax credit to encourage businesses to hire certain unemployed individuals, and it provides the research and development credit to encourage businesses to expend funds to develop new technology. Business tax credits are *nonrefundable* credits. However, when business credits other than the foreign tax credit (discussed below), exceed the taxpayer's gross tax for the year, the credits are carried *back* one year and forward 20 years to use in years when the taxpayer has sufficient gross tax liability to use the credits.

Why discuss business credits in an individual tax chapter? We discuss business credits here because self-employed individuals may qualify for these credits. Also, individuals may be allocated business credits from flow-through entities (partnerships, LLCs, and S corporations). Finally, individuals working as employees overseas or receiving dividends from investments in foreign securities may qualify for the foreign tax credit.

Foreign Tax Credit   U.S. citizens must pay U.S. tax on their worldwide income. However, when they generate some or all of their income in other countries, they generally are required to pay income taxes to the foreign country where they earned their income. Without some form of tax relief, taxpayers earning income overseas would be double-taxed on this income. When taxpayers pay income taxes to foreign countries, for U.S. tax purposes, they may treat the payment in one of three ways: (1) as we discussed in Chapter 5 when we introduced the foreign earned income exclusion, taxpayers may exclude the foreign earned income from U.S. taxation (in which case they would *not* deduct or receive a credit for any foreign taxes paid); (2) taxpayers may include the foreign income in their gross income and deduct the foreign taxes paid as itemized deductions; or (3) taxpayers may include foreign income in gross income and claim a foreign tax credit for the foreign taxes paid. Here, we discuss the foreign tax credit.

The foreign tax credit helps reduce the double tax taxpayers may pay when they pay income taxes on foreign earned income to the United States and to foreign countries. Taxpayers are allowed to claim a foreign tax credit, against their U.S. tax liability, for the income taxes they pay to foreign countries.[39] In certain situations, taxpayers may not be able to claim the full amount of foreign tax paid as a credit. This restriction may apply when the taxpayer's effective foreign tax rate is higher than the effective U.S. tax rate on the foreign earnings. Taxpayers generally benefit from claiming credits rather than deductions for foreign taxes paid because credits reduce their liabilities dollar for dollar. However, in circumstances when the foreign tax credit is restricted (see above), taxpayers may benefit by claiming deductions for the taxes paid instead of credits.

As we discussed above, the foreign tax credit may be limited in circumstances where a taxpayer's effective foreign tax rate exceeds her U.S. tax rate. In addition, as a nonrefundable credit, it may only reduce the taxpayer's tax liability to zero. When the use of a foreign tax credit is limited, taxpayers may carry back their unused credits one year and carry forward the credits up to 10 years.[40]

---

[39]§904.

[40]See IRS Publication 514 "Foreign Tax Credit for Individuals" for more information about the foreign tax credit.

Tax Credit Summary

Exhibit 8-11 identifies several tax credits and for each credit identifies the credit type, notes the IRC section allowing the credit, and describes the credit.

EXHIBIT 8-11 **Summary of Selected Tax Credits**

Credit	Type of Credit	IRC	Description
Child and dependent care credit	Nonrefundable personal	§21	Credit for taxpayers who pay dependent care expenses due to their employment activities.
Credit for elderly and disabled	Nonrefundable personal	§22	Credit for elderly low-income taxpayers who retired because of a disability.
Adoption expense credit	Nonrefundable personal	§23	Credit for qualified adoption-related expenses.
Child tax credit	Nonrefundable and refundable personal	§24	Credit for providing home for dependent children under the age of 17.
American opportunity credit	Nonrefundable and refundable personal	§25A	Credit for higher education expenses for the first four years of postsecondary education.
Lifetime learning credit	Nonrefundable personal	§25A	Credit for higher education expenses.
Saver's credit	Nonrefundable personal	§25B	Credit for contributing to qualified retirement plans.
Residential energy	Nonrefundable personal	§25D	Credit for qualified expenditures for efficient property credit solar water heating property, fuel cell property, wind energy property, and qualified geothermal heat pump property.
Earned income credit	Refundable personal	§32	Credit to encourage low-income taxpayers to work.
Premium tax credit	Refundable personal	§36B	Credit for health insurance purchased through an exchange for individuals and families with household incomes between 100% and 400% of the poverty line.
Credit for increasing research activities	Business	§41	Credit to encourage research and development.
Employer-provided child care credit	Business	§45F	Credit for providing child care for employees.
Small employer health insurance credit	Business	§45R	Credit to encourage employer-provided health insurance.
Rehabilitation credit	Business	§47	Credit for expenditures to renovate or restore older business buildings.
Energy credit	Business	§48	Credit for businesses that invest in energy conservation measures.
Work opportunity credit	Business	§51	Credit for hiring certain qualified veterans.
Foreign tax credit	Hybrid business and personal	§904	Credit to reduce effects of double taxation of foreign income.

Credit Application Sequence

As we've discussed, credits are applied against a taxpayer's gross tax. However, we still must describe what happens when the taxpayer's allowable credits exceed the taxpayer's gross tax. To set up this discussion, it is important to understand that nonrefundable personal credits and business credits may be used to reduce a tax-payer's gross tax to zero, but not below zero.[41] In contrast, by definition, a refundable credit may reduce a taxpayer's gross tax below zero. This excess refundable credit generates a tax refund for the taxpayer.

When a nonrefundable personal credit exceeds the taxpayer's gross tax, it reduces the gross tax to zero, but the excess credit (credit in excess of the taxpayer's gross tax) disappears. That is, the taxpayer may *not* carry over any excess nonrefundable personal credits to use in other years. However, when a business credit or foreign tax credit exceeds the gross tax, it reduces the taxpayer's gross tax to zero, but the excess credit may be carried forward or back to be used in other years when the taxpayer has sufficient gross tax to use the credit (subject to certain time restrictions discussed above).

Because the tax treatment of excess credits depends on the type of credit, it is important to identify the sequence in which taxpayers apply the credits when they have more than one type of credit for the year. When taxpayers have multiple credit types in the same year, they apply the credits against their gross tax in the following order: (1) non-refundable personal credits, (2) business credits, and (3) refundable credits. This sequence maximizes the chances that taxpayers will receive full benefit for their tax credits.

Because, as we discuss above, the foreign tax credit is a hybrid credit subject to a unique set of application rules, we exclude it from our general discussion on applying credits. Exhibit 8-12 summarizes the order in which the credits are applied against gross tax and indicates the tax treatment of any excess credits.

EXHIBIT 8-12   Credit Application

Credit Type	Order Applied	Excess Credit
Nonrefundable personal	First	Lost
Business	Second	Carryback and carryover
Refundable personal	Last	Refunded

Example 8-25

What if: As we describe in Example 8-2, Gram's gross tax liability is $369. For illustrative purposes, let's *assume* that Gram is entitled to an $800 nonrefundable personal tax credit, a $700 business tax credit, and a $600 refundable personal tax credit. What is the amount of Gram's refund or taxes due?

Answer: $600 refund. Gram would apply these credits as follows:

Description	Amount	Treatment of Excess Credit
Gross tax liability	$ 369	Example 8-2.
Nonrefundable personal credits	(369)	$431 ($800 – $369) excess credit expires unused.
Business credits	0	$700 carried back one year or forward 20 years (10 years for foreign tax credit).
Refundable personal credits	**(600)**	**Generates $600 tax refund to Gram.**

TAXPAYER PREPAYMENTS AND FILING REQUIREMENTS   LO 8-5

Even after determining their tax liabilities, taxpayers must still file a tax return and pay any additional tax due or receive a refund. When taxpayers don't pay enough taxes during the year or when they are late filing their tax return or late paying their taxes due, they may be subject to certain penalties.

[41]In general, nonrefundable personal credits can offset a taxpayer's regular tax and AMT (§26) but not self-employment tax. The limitation on business credits is more complex. We limit our discussion here to basic concepts. See §38(c) for the detailed limitations.

Prepayments

The income tax must be paid on a *pay-as-you-go* basis. This means that the tax must be prepaid via **withholding** from salary or through periodic **estimated tax payments** during the tax year. Employees pay tax through withholding, and self-employed taxpayers generally pay taxes through estimated tax payments. Employers are required to withhold taxes from an employee's wages based upon the employee's marital status, exemptions, and estimated annual pay. Wages include both cash and noncash remuneration for services, and employers remit withholdings to the government on behalf of employees. At the end of the year employers report the amounts withheld to each employee via Form W-2. Estimated tax payments are required only if withholdings are insufficient to meet the taxpayer's tax liability. For calendar-year taxpayers, estimated tax payments are due on April 15, June 15, and September 15 of the current year and January 15 of the following year. If the due date falls on a Saturday, Sunday, or holiday, it is automatically extended to the next day that is not a Saturday, Sunday, or holiday.

Example 8-26

Courtney's gross tax liability for the year including federal income tax, alternative minimum tax, and self-employment taxes is $22,200 (see Exhibit 8-6). However, because she had only $19,400 withheld from her paycheck by EWD, she underpaid $2,800 for the year ($22,200 – $19,400). Because Courtney did not pay in her full tax liability, she is potentially subject to underpayment penalties discussed below. If she had been aware that her withholding would be insufficient, she could have increased her withholding at any time during the year (even in her December paycheck) or made estimated tax payments of $700 on April 18, June 15, and September 15 in 2016 and January 16, 2017 ($2,800/4).

What if: If Courtney was self-employed (instead of employed by EWD) and thus had no tax withholdings by an employer, she would be *required* to pay quarterly estimated tax payments. In this scenario, she would need to pay $5,550 ($22,200/4 = $5,550) by April 18, June 15, and September 15 of 2016 and $5,550 by January 16 of 2017 to cover her gross tax liability of $22,200.

Underpayment Penalties   When taxpayers like Courtney fall behind on their tax prepayments, they may be subject to an **underpayment penalty.**[42] Taxpayers with unpredictable income streams may be particularly susceptible to this penalty because it is difficult for them to accurately estimate their tax liability for the year. To help taxpayers who may not be able to predict their earnings for the year and to provide some margin of error for those who can, the tax laws provide some **safe-harbor provisions.** Under these provisions taxpayers can avoid underpayment penalties if their withholdings and estimated tax payments equal or exceed one of the following two safe harbors: (1) 90 percent of their *current tax liability* or (2) 100 percent of their *previous year tax liability* (110 percent for individuals with AGI greater than $150,000).

These two safe harbors determine on a quarterly basis the minimum tax prepayments that a taxpayer must have made to avoid the underpayment penalty. The first safe harbor requires that a taxpayer must have paid at least 22.5 percent (90 percent/4 = 22.5 percent) of the *current*-year liability via withholdings or estimated tax payments by April 15 to avoid the underpayment penalty for the first quarter. Similarly by June 15, September 15, and January 15, the taxpayer must have paid 45 percent (22.5 percent × 2), 67.5 percent (22.5 percent × 3), and 90 percent (22.5 percent × 4), respectively, of the current-year liability via withholding or estimated tax payments to avoid the underpayment penalty in the second, third, and fourth

---

[42]§6654.

quarters.[43] In determining taxpayers' prepayments for a quarter, tax withholdings are generally treated as though they are withheld evenly through the year. In contrast, estimated tax payments are credited to the taxpayer's account when they are remitted.

Example 8-27

Because all of Courtney's prepayments were made through withholding by EWD, the payments are treated as though they were made evenly throughout the year. What are Courtney's actual and required withholdings under the 90 percent safe-harbor provision throughout the year?

Answer: See the following table:

Dates	(1) Actual Withholding	(2) Required Withholding	(1) – (2) Over (Under) Withheld
April 18, 2016	$4,850 ($19,400 × .25)	$4,995 ($22,200 × .9 × .25)	($145)
June 15, 2016	$9,700 ($19,400 × .50)	$9,990 ($22,200 × .9 × .50)	(290)
September 15, 2016	$14,550 ($19,400 × .75)	$14,985 ($22,200 × .9 × .75)	(435)
January 16, 2017	$19,400	$19,980 ($22,200 × .9 × 1)	(580)

It looks like Courtney is underwithheld in each quarter.

The second safe harbor requires that by April 15, June 15, September 15, and January 15, the taxpayer must have paid 25 percent, 50 percent (25 percent × 2), 75 percent (25 percent × 3), and 100 percent (25 percent × 4), respectively, of the *previous* year tax liability (110 percent of the previous year tax liability for individuals with AGI greater than $150,000) via withholding or estimated tax payments to avoid the underpayment penalty in the first, second, third, and fourth quarters.

If the taxpayer does not satisfy either of the safe-harbor provisions, the taxpayer can compute the underpayment penalty owed using Form 2210. The underpayment penalty is determined by multiplying the **federal short-term interest rate** plus 3 percentage points by the amount of tax underpayment per quarter. For purposes of this computation, the quarterly tax underpayment is the difference between the taxpayer's quarterly withholding and estimated tax payments and the required minimum tax payment under the first or second safe harbor (whichever is less). If the taxpayer does not complete Form 2210 and remit the underpayment penalty with the taxpayer's tax return, the IRS will compute and assess the penalty for the taxpayer.

Example 8-28

In the previous example, we discovered that Courtney was underwithheld in each quarter based on the first (90 percent of current year) safe-harbor provision. Assuming Courtney was underwithheld by even more under the second (100 percent of prior year) safe-harbor provision, she is required to pay an underpayment penalty based on the underpayments determined using the first safe harbor. Assuming the federal short-term rate is 5 percent, what is Courtney's underpayment penalty for 2016?

(continued on page 8-38)

---

[43]As an alternative method of estimating safe harbor, (1) taxpayers can compute 90 percent of the current liability using the seasonal method. This method allows the taxpayer to estimate 90 percent of their current tax liability by annualizing their taxable income earned through the month prior to the payment date (e.g., through March for April 15, May for June 15, and August for September 15). Taxpayers with uneven taxable income throughout the year with smaller taxable income earlier in the year benefit from this method.

Answer: $30, computed as follows:

Description	First Quarter	Second Quarter	Third Quarter	Fourth Quarter
Underpayment	$ 145	$290	$435	$ 580
Times: federal rate + 3% (5% + 3%)	× 8%	× 8%	× 8%	× 8%
	$ 12	$ 23	$ 35	$ 46
Times one quarter of a year[44]	× 25%	× 25%	× 25%	× 25%
Underpayment penalty per quarter	$ 3	$ 6	$ 9	$ 12

That's a lot of work to figure out a $30 penalty: (3 + 6 + 9 + 12 = $30)

As a matter of administrative convenience, taxpayers who either (1) had no tax liability in the previous year or (2) whose tax payable after subtracting their withholding amounts (but not estimated payments) is less than $1,000 are not subject to underpayment penalties.

Example 8-29

Gram's tax liability for the year is $369 (Example 8-2), but she did not have any taxes withheld during the year, and she did not make any estimated tax payments. What is Gram's underpayment penalty?

Answer: $0. Because Gram's $369 tax payable after subtracting her withholding amounts ($369 tax – $0 withholding) is less than $1,000, she is not subject to an underpayment penalty.

Filing Requirements

Individual taxpayers are required to file a tax return only if their *gross income* exceeds certain thresholds, which vary based on the taxpayer's filing status and age. However, a taxpayer may prefer to file a tax return even when she is not required to do so. For example, a taxpayer with gross income less than the threshold may want to file a tax return to receive a refund of income taxes withheld. In general, the thresholds are simply the applicable standard deduction amount for the different filing statuses plus the personal exemption amount (twice the personal exemption amount of married taxpayers filing jointly).[45]

Individual tax returns are due on April 15 for calendar-year individuals (the fifteenth day of the fourth month following year-end). If the due date falls on a Saturday, Sunday, or holiday, it is automatically extended to the next day that is not a Saturday, Sunday, or holiday. Taxpayers unable to file a tax return by the original due date can request (by that same deadline) a six-month extension to file, which is granted automatically by the IRS. The extension gives the taxpayer additional time to file the tax return, but does *not* extend the due date for paying the tax.

Late Filing Penalty   The tax law imposes a penalty on taxpayers that do not file a tax return by the required date (the original due date plus extension).[46] The penalty

---

[44]Form 2210 actually computes the penalty per quarter based on the number of days in the quarter divided by the number of days in the year. For simplicity, we assume this ratio is per quarter.

[45]§6012. Filing requirements for individuals who are dependents of other taxpayers are subject to special rules that consider the individual's unearned income, earned income, and gross income. See IRS Publication 17 "Your Federal Income Tax."

[46]§6651.

equals 5 percent of the amount of tax owed for each month (or fraction thereof) that the tax return is late, with a maximum penalty of 25 percent. For fraudulent failure to file, the penalty is 15 percent of the amount of tax owed per month with a maximum penalty of 75 percent. If the taxpayer owes no tax as of the due date of the tax return (plus extension), the tax law does not impose a **late filing penalty.**

Late Payment Penalty An extension allows the taxpayer to delay filing a tax return but does *not* extend the due date for tax payments. If a taxpayer fails to pay the entire balance of tax owed by the original due date of the tax return, the tax law imposes a **late payment penalty** from the due date of the return until the taxpayer pays the tax.[47] The late payment penalty equals .5 percent of the amount of tax owed for each month (or fraction thereof) that the tax is not paid.

The *combined* maximum penalty that may be imposed for late payment and late filing (nonfraudulent) is 5 percent per month (25 percent in total). For late payment and filing due to fraud, the combined maximum penalty for late payment and late filing is 15 percent per month (75 percent in total).

Example 8-30

Courtney filed her tax return on April 10 and included a check with the return for $2,830 made payable to the United States Treasury. The $2,830 consisted of her underpaid tax liability of $2,800 (Example 8-26) and her $30 underpayment penalty (Example 8-28).

What if: If Courtney had waited until May 1 to file her return and pay her taxes, what late filing and late payment penalties would she owe?

Answer: Her combined *late filing penalty* and *late payment penalty* would be $140 ($2,800 late payment × 5 percent × 1 month or portion thereof—the combined penalty is limited to 5 percent per month).

TAX SUMMARY

Courtney's and Gram's net taxes due, including an underpayment penalty for Courtney, are provided in Exhibits 8-13 and 8-15, respectively. Exhibit 8-14 illustrates how this information would be presented on Courtney's tax return by providing Courtney's Form 1040, page 2.

EXHIBIT 8-13 Courtney's Net Tax Payable

Description	Amount	Reference
(1) Regular federal income tax	$21,718	Example 8-3.
(2) Alternative minimum tax	0	Example 8-10.
(3) Self-employment tax	482	Example 8-15.
(4) Gross tax	$22,200	(1) + (2) + (3).
(5) Tax credits	0	Examples 8-18, 8-20, 8-21, and 8-24.
(6) Prepayments	($19,400)	Example 8-27.
(7) Underpayment penalties	30	Example 8-28.
Tax and penalties due with tax return	$ 2,830	

THE KEY FACTS

Filing Requirements and Filing-Related Penalties

- Filing requirements vary based on the taxpayer's filing status, age, and gross income.
- Individual tax returns are due on April 15 for calendar-year individuals.
- Taxpayers unable to file a tax return by the original due date can request a six-month extension to file.
- The tax law imposes penalties on taxpayers who do not file a tax return (by the original due date plus extension) or pay the tax owed (by the original due date).

[47]§6651. As we discussed in Chapter 2, the tax law also assesses interest on any tax underpayments until the tax is paid (§6601).

EXHIBIT 8-14 Courtney's Net Tax Payable (as presented on her Form 1040, page 2)

Form 1040 (2015)   Page **2**

Tax and Credits	38	Amount from line 37 (adjusted gross income)	38	162,000
	39a	Check { You were born before January 2, 1951, [ ] Blind. } Total boxes if: { Spouse was born before January 2, 1951, [ ] Blind. } checked ▶ 39a		
	b	If your spouse itemizes on a separate return or you were a dual-status alien, check here ▶ 39b [ ]		
Standard Deduction for— • People who check any box on line 39a or 39b **or** who can be claimed as a dependent, see instructions. • All others: Single or Married filing separately, $6,300 Married filing jointly or Qualifying widow(er), $12,600 Head of household, $9,250	40	**Itemized deductions** (from Schedule A) **or** your **standard deduction** (see left margin)	40	39,889
	41	Subtract line 40 from line 38	41	122,111
	42	**Exemptions.** If line 38 is $154,950 or less, multiply $4,000 by the number on line 6d. Otherwise, see instructions	42	12,150
	43	**Taxable income.** Subtract line 42 from line 41. If line 42 is more than line 41, enter -0-	43	109,961
	44	**Tax** (see instructions). Check if any from: **a** [ ] Form(s) 8814 **b** [ ] Form 4972 **c** [ ]	44	21,718
	45	**Alternative minimum tax** (see instructions). Attach Form 6251	45	0
	46	Excess advance premium tax credit repayment. Attach Form 8962	46	
	47	Add lines 44, 45, and 46 ▶	47	21,718
	48	Foreign tax credit. Attach Form 1116 if required [48]		
	49	Credit for child and dependent care expenses. Attach Form 2441 [49]		
	50	Education credits from Form 8863, line 19 [50]		
	51	Retirement savings contributions credit. Attach Form 8880 [51]		
	52	Child tax credit. Attach Schedule 8812, if required [52]		
	53	Residential energy credits. Attach Form 5695 [53]		
	54	Other credits from Form: **a** [ ] 3800 **b** [ ] 8801 **c** [ ] [54]		
	55	Add lines 48 through 54. These are your **total credits**	55	
	56	Subtract line 55 from line 47. If line 55 is more than line 47, enter -0- ▶	56	21,718
Other Taxes	57	Self-employment tax. Attach Schedule SE	57	482
	58	Unreported social security and Medicare tax from Form: **a** [ ] 4137 **b** [ ] 8919	58	
	59	Additional tax on IRAs, other qualified retirement plans, etc. Attach Form 5329 if required	59	
	60a	Household employment taxes from Schedule H	60a	
	b	First-time homebuyer credit repayment. Attach Form 5405 if required	60b	
	61	Health care: individual responsibility (see instructions) Full-year coverage [ ]	61	
	62	Taxes from: **a** [ ] Form 8959 **b** [ ] Form 8960 **c** [ ] Instructions; enter code(s)	62	
	63	Add lines 56 through 62. This is your **total tax** ▶	63	22,200
Payments If you have a qualifying child, attach Schedule EIC.	64	Federal income tax withheld from Forms W-2 and 1099 [64] 19,400		
	65	2015 estimated tax payments and amount applied from 2014 return [65]		
	66a	**Earned income credit (EIC)** [66a]		
	b	Nontaxable combat pay election [66b]		
	67	Additional child tax credit. Attach Schedule 8812 [67]		
	68	American opportunity credit from Form 8863, line 8 [68]		
	69	Net premium tax credit. Attach Form 8962 [69]		
	70	Amount paid with request for extension to file [70]		
	71	Excess social security and tier 1 RRTA tax withheld [71]		
	72	Credit for federal tax on fuels. Attach Form 4136 [72]		
	73	Credits from Form: **a** [ ] 2439 **b** [ ] Reserved **c** [ ] 8885 **d** [ ] [73]		
	74	Add lines 64, 65, 66a, and 67 through 73. These are your **total payments** ▶	74	19,400
Refund Direct deposit? See instructions.	75	If line 74 is more than line 63, subtract line 63 from line 74. This is the amount you **overpaid**	75	
	76a	Amount of line 75 you want **refunded to you.** If Form 8888 is attached, check here . ▶ [ ]	76a	
	▶ b	Routing number [ ] ▶ **c** Type: [ ] Checking [ ] Savings		
	▶ d	Account number [ ]		
	77	Amount of line 75 you want **applied to your 2016 estimated tax** ▶ [77]		
Amount You Owe	78	**Amount you owe.** Subtract line 74 from line 63. For details on how to pay, see instructions ▶	78	2,830
	79	Estimated tax penalty (see instructions) [79] 30		

Third Party Designee
Do you want to allow another person to discuss this return with the IRS (see instructions)? [ ] **Yes. Complete below.** [ ] **No**
Designee's name ▶   Phone no. ▶   Personal identification number (PIN) ▶

Sign Here
Joint return? See instructions. Keep a copy for your records.
Under penalties of perjury, I declare that I have examined this return and accompanying schedules and statements, and to the best of my knowledge and belief, they are true, correct, and complete. Declaration of preparer (other than taxpayer) is based on all information of which preparer has any knowledge.
Your signature | Date | Your occupation | Daytime phone number
Spouse's signature. If a joint return, **both** must sign. | Date | Spouse's occupation | If the IRS sent you an Identity Protection PIN, enter it here (see inst.)

Paid Preparer Use Only
Print/Type preparer's name | Preparer's signature | Date | Check [ ] if self-employed | PTIN
Firm's name ▶   Firm's EIN ▶
Firm's address ▶   Phone no.

www.irs.gov/form1040   Form **1040** (2015)

EXHIBIT 8-15 Gram's Tax Payable

Description	Amount	Reference
(1) Gross tax	$369	Example 8-2.
(2) Alternative minimum tax	0	
(3) Self-employment tax	0	
(4) Gross tax	$369	(1) + (2) + (3).
(5) Tax credits	0	
(6) Prepayments	0	
(7) Penalties	0	
Tax due with return	$369	(4) − (5) − (6) − (7).

CONCLUSION

This chapter reviewed the process for determining an individual's gross and net tax liability. We discovered that taxpayers may be required to pay regular federal income tax, alternative minimum tax, and employment-related tax. Taxpayers are able to offset their gross tax liability dollar for dollar with various types of tax credits and by the amount of tax they prepay during the year. Taxpayers must pay additional taxes with their tax return or they may receive a refund when they file their tax return depending on their gross tax liability and their available tax credits and tax prepayments. The prior three chapters have covered the basic individual tax formula. The next three chapters (9–11) address issues relevant for taxpayers involved in business activities. In Chapters 12–14, we dig a little deeper into certain individual income taxation issues.

Summary

Determine a taxpayer's regular tax liability and identify tax issues associated with the process. **LO 8-1**

- Individual income is taxed using progressive tax rate schedules with rates ranging from 10 percent to 39.6 percent.
- Marginal tax rates depend on filing status and amount of taxable income.
- Progressive tax rate schedules may lead to either a marriage penalty or a marriage benefit for married taxpayers.
- Long-term capital gains and qualified dividends are taxed at either 0 percent, 15 percent, or 20 percent depending on the amount of taxable income.
- A 3.8 percent tax is levied on net investment income for higher income taxpayers.
- Strategies to shift investment income from parents to children are limited by the "kiddie tax" whereby children's investment income is taxed at the parents' marginal tax rate.

Compute a taxpayer's alternative minimum tax liability and describe the tax characteristics of taxpayers most likely to owe the alternative minimum tax. **LO 8-2**

- The AMT was designed to ensure that higher-income taxpayers pay some minimum level of income tax.
- The AMT base is broader than the regular income tax base. The AMT base is designed to more closely reflect economic income than is regular taxable income.
- The starting point for calculating AMT is regular taxable income. To compute AMTI, taxpayers add back items not deductible for AMT purposes. In some cases, taxpayers may subtract items not includible in AMTI and items deductible for AMT but not for regular tax purposes. Taxpayers then subtract the allowable AMT exemption to generate the AMT base. They then apply the AMT rates and compare the product (the tentative minimum tax) to their regular tax liability. They owe AMT if the tentative minimum tax exceeds the regular tax liability.
- The AMT exemption depends on the taxpayer's filing status and is subject to phase-out of 25 cents for each dollar of AMTI over the specific thresholds based on filing status.
- The 2016 AMT tax rates are 26 percent up to $186,300 of AMT base ($93,150 of AMT base for married taxpayers filing separately) and 28 percent thereafter. However, long-term capital gains and qualified dividends are subject to the same preferential rate they are taxed at for regular tax purposes.
- The amount of the AMT is the excess of the tentative minimum tax over the taxpayer's regular tax liability.

Calculate a taxpayer's employment and self-employment taxes payable and explain tax considerations relating to whether a taxpayer is considered to be an employee or a self-employed independent contractor. **LO 8-3**

- Employees' wages are subject to FICA tax. The Social Security component is 6.2 percent and the Medicare component ranges from 1.45 percent to 2.35 percent for employees.

For employers, the Social Security component is 6.2 percent and the Medicare component is 1.45 percent. The Social Security tax applies to the first $118,500 of salary or wages in 2016. The wage base on the Medicare tax is unlimited.

- Self-employed taxpayers pay self-employment tax on their net self-employment income (92.35 percent of their net Schedule C income). They pay Social Security tax of 12.4 percent and Medicare tax of 2.9 percent to 3.8 percent on their net self-employment income. The Social Security tax applies to the first $118,500 of net Schedule C income in 2016. The base for the Medicare tax is unlimited.

- The determination as to whether to treat a worker as an independent contractor or as an employee for tax purposes is a subjective test based in large part on the extent of control the worker has over things such as the nature, timing, and location of work performed.

- Independent contractors are able to deduct ordinary and necessary business expenses as *for* AGI deductions. Employees incurring unreimbursed business expenses must deduct the items as miscellaneous itemized deductions subject to the 2 percent of AGI floor.

- Independent contractors may deduct the employer portion of their self-employment taxes paid during the year. Employees may not deduct their FICA taxes.

- Independent contractors are required to pay self-employment tax, which represents the employer and employee portions of FICA taxes. Further, independent contractors must pay estimated taxes on their income because the employer does not withhold taxes from the independent contractor's paychecks.

- Hiring independent contractors is generally less costly for employers than is hiring employees. Employers do not pay FICA taxes, withhold taxes, or provide fringe benefits for independent contractors.

LO 8-4 Describe the different general types of tax credits, identify specific tax credits, and compute a taxpayer's allowable child tax credit, child and dependent care credit, American opportunity credit, lifetime learning credit, and earned income credit.

- Tax credits are generally classified into one of three categories: business, nonrefundable personal, or refundable personal credits.

- Nonrefundable personal tax credits provide tax relief to specified groups of individuals.

- The child tax credit is a $1,000 credit for low-income taxpayers who provide a home for dependent children under the age of 17.

- The child and dependent care credit is provided to help taxpayers pay the cost of providing care for their dependents to allow taxpayers to work or to look for work.

- The American opportunity credit provides a credit for a percentage of the costs of the first four years of a student's college education. Forty percent of the credit is refundable.

- The lifetime learning credit provides a credit for a percentage of the costs for instruction in a postsecondary degree program, or to acquire or improve a taxpayer's job skills.

- Nonrefundable credits are first used to reduce a taxpayer's gross tax but cannot reduce the gross tax below zero. Any excess credit is lost unless it is allowed to be carried to a different tax year.

- The earned income credit is refundable but subject to a very complex calculation.

- Business credits reduce the tax after applying nonrefundable credits. Any credit in excess of the remaining tax is generally allowed to be carried over or back to be used in other years.

- Refundable credits are the last credit applied to the tax after applying nonrefundable and business credits. Any refundable credit in excess of the remaining tax is treated as an overpayment and refunded to the taxpayer.

LO 8-5 Explain taxpayer filing and tax payment requirements and describe in general terms how to compute a taxpayer's underpayment, late filing, and late payment penalties.

- The income tax must be prepaid via withholding from salary or through periodic estimated tax payments during the tax year. Estimated tax payments are required only if withholdings are insufficient to meet the taxpayer's tax liability. For calendar-year taxpayers, estimated tax payments are due on April 15, June 15, and September 15 of the current year and January 15 of the following year.

- Taxpayers can avoid an underpayment penalty if their withholdings and estimated tax payments equal or exceed one of two safe harbors: (1) 90 percent of current-year tax or (2) 100 percent of previous year tax (110 percent if AGI exceeds $150,000). If the tax-payer does not satisfy either of the safe-harbor provisions, the underpayment penalty is determined by multiplying the federal short-term interest rate plus 3 percentage points by the amount of tax underpayment per quarter.
- Individual taxpayers are required to file a tax return only if their *gross income* exceeds certain thresholds, which vary based on the taxpayer's filing status, age, and gross income.
- Individual tax returns are due on April 15 for calendar-year individuals. Taxpayers unable to file a tax return by the original due date can request a six-month extension to file.
- The tax law imposes penalties on taxpayers that do not file a tax return (by the original due date plus extension) or pay the tax owed (by the original due date). The failure-to-file penalty equals 5 percent of the amount of tax owed for each month (or fraction thereof) that the tax return is late with a maximum penalty of 25 percent. The late payment penalty equals .5 percent of the amount of tax owed for each month (or fraction thereof) that the tax is not paid. The combined maximum penalty that may be imposed for late filing and late payment is 5 percent per month (25 percent in total). The late filing and late payment penalties are higher if fraud is involved.

KEY TERMS

alternative minimum tax (AMT) (8-8)
alternative minimum tax adjustments (8-9)
alternative minimum tax base (AMT base) (8-8)
alternative minimum tax (AMT) exemption (8-12)
alternative minimum tax system (8-8)
business tax credits (8-33)
child tax credits (8-25)
earned income credit (8-31)
employee (8-22)
estimated tax payments (8-36)
federal short-term interest rate (8-37)

FICA taxes (8-15)
independent contractor (8-22)
kiddie tax (8-6)
late filing penalty (8-39)
late payment penalty (8-39)
marginal tax rate (8-3)
marriage benefit (8-3)
marriage penalty (8-3)
Medicare tax (8-14)
minimum tax credit (8-14)
net earnings from self-employment (8-17)
net investment income tax (8-6)
net unearned income (8-6)

nonrefundable credit (8-24)
preferential tax rate (8-4)
preferentially taxed income (8-4)
safe-harbor provisions (8-36)
Schedule C (8-17)
self-employment taxes (8-17)
Social Security tax (8-14)
tax bracket (8-2)
tax credits (8-24)
tax rate schedule (8-2)
tax tables (8-3)
tentative minimum tax (8-9)
underpayment penalty (8-36)
withholding (8-36)

DISCUSSION QUESTIONS

Discussion Questions are available in *Connect*®.

1. What is a tax bracket? What is the relationship between filing status and the width of the tax brackets in the tax rate schedule? **LO 8-1**
2. In 2016, for a taxpayer with $50,000 of taxable income, without doing any actual computations, which filing status do you expect to provide the lowest tax liability? Which filing status provides the highest tax liability? **LO 8-1**
3. What is the tax marriage penalty and when does it apply? Under what circum-stances would a couple experience a tax marriage benefit? **LO 8-1**
4. Once they've computed their taxable income, how do taxpayers determine their regular tax liability? What additional steps must taxpayers take to compute their tax liability when they have preferentially taxed income? **LO 8-1**

LO 8-1

research

5. Are there circumstances in which preferentially taxed income (long-term capital gains and qualified dividends) is taxed at the same rate as ordinary income? Explain.

LO 8-1

6. Augustana received $10,000 of qualified dividends this year. Under what circumstances would all $10,000 be taxed at the same rate? Under what circumstances might the entire $10,000 of income not be taxed at the same rate?

LO 8-1

7. What is the difference between earned and unearned income?

LO 8-1

8. Does the kiddie tax eliminate the tax benefits gained by a family when parents transfer income-producing assets to children? Explain.

LO 8-1

9. Does the kiddie tax apply to all children no matter their age? Explain.

LO 8-1

10. What is the kiddie tax and on whose tax return is the kiddie tax liability reported? Explain.

LO 8-1

11. Lauren is 17 years old. She reports earned income of $3,000 and unearned income of $2,200. Is it likely that she is subject to the kiddie tax? Explain.

LO 8-2

12. In very general terms, how is the alternative minimum tax system different from the regular income tax system? How is it similar?

LO 8-2

13. Describe, in general terms, why Congress implemented the AMT.

LO 8-2

14. Do taxpayers always add back the standard deduction when computing alternative minimum taxable income? Explain.

LO 8-2

15. The starting point for computing alternative minimum taxable income is regular taxable income. What are some of the plus adjustments, plus or minus adjustments, and minus adjustments to regular taxable income to compute alternative minimum taxable income?

LO 8-2

16. Describe what the AMT exemption is and who is and isn't allowed to deduct the exemption. How is it similar to the standard deduction and how is it dissimilar?

LO 8-1 LO 8-2

17. How do the AMT tax rates compare to the regular income tax rates?

LO 8-2

18. Is it possible for a taxpayer who pays AMT to have a marginal tax rate higher than the stated AMT rate? Explain.

LO 8-2

19. What is the difference between the tentative minimum tax (TMT) and the AMT?

LO 8-2

planning

20. Lee is single and he runs his own business. He uses the cash method of accounting to determine his business income. Near the end of the year, Lee performed work that he needs to bill a client for. The value of his services is $5,000. Lee figures that if he immediately takes the time to put the bill together and send it out, the client will pay him before year-end. However, if he doesn't send out the bill for one week, he won't receive the client's payment until the beginning of next year. Lee expects that he will owe AMT this year and that his AMT base will be around $200,000 before counting any of the additional business income. Further, Lee anticipates that he will not owe AMT next year. He anticipates his regular taxable income next year will be in the $200,000 range. Would you advise Lee to immediately bill his client or to wait? What factors would you consider in making your recommendation?

LO 8-3

21. Are an employee's entire wages subject to the FICA tax? Explain.

LO 8-3

22. Bobbie works as an employee for Altron Corp. for the first half of the year and for Betel Inc. for the rest of the year. She is relatively well paid. What FICA tax

issues is she likely to encounter? What FICA tax issues do Altron Corp. and Betel Inc. need to consider?

23. Compare and contrast an employee's FICA tax payment responsibilities with those of a self-employed taxpayer. **LO 8-3**

24. When a taxpayer works as an employee and as a self-employed independent contractor during the year, how does the taxpayer determine her employment and self-employment taxes payable? **LO 8-3**

25. What are the primary factors to consider when deciding whether a worker should be considered an employee or a self-employed taxpayer for tax purposes? **LO 8-3**

26. How do the tax consequences of being an employee differ from those of being self-employed? **LO 8-3**

27. Mike wanted to work for a CPA firm but he also wanted to work on his father's farm in Montana. Because the CPA firm wanted Mike to be happy, they offered to let him work for them as an independent contractor during the fall and winter and let him return to Montana to work for his father during the spring and summer. He was very excited to hear that they were also going to give him a 5 percent higher "salary" for the six months he would be working for the firm over what he would have made over the same six-month period if he worked full-time as an employee (i.e., an increase from $30,000 to $31,500). Should Mike be excited about his 5 percent raise? Why or why not? What counteroffer could Mike reasonably suggest? **LO 8-3**   **planning**

28. How are tax credits and tax deductions similar? How are they dissimilar? **LO 8-4**

29. What are the three types of tax credits, and explain why it is important to distinguish between the different types of tax credits. **LO 8-4**

30. Explain why there is such a large number and variety of tax credits. **LO 8-4**

31. What is the difference between a refundable and nonrefundable tax credit? **LO 8-4**

32. Is the child tax credit a refundable or nonrefundable credit? Explain. **LO 8-4**

33. Diane has a job working three-quarter time. She hired her mother to take care of her two small children so Diane could work. Do Diane's child care payments to her mother qualify for the child and dependent care credit? Explain. **LO 8-4**

34. The amount of the child and dependent care credit is based on the amount of the taxpayer's expenditures to provide care for one or more qualifying persons. Who is considered to be a qualifying person for this purpose? **LO 8-4**

35. Compare and contrast the lifetime learning credit with the American opportunity credit. **LO 8-4**

36. Jennie's grandfather paid her tuition this fall to State University (an eligible educational institution). Jennie is claimed as a dependent by her parents, but she also files her own tax return. Can Jennie claim an education credit for the tuition paid by her grandfather? What difference would it make, if any, if Jennie did not qualify as a dependent of her parents (or anyone else)? **LO 8-4**   **research**

37. Why is the earned income credit referred to as a negative income tax? **LO 8-4**

38. Under what circumstances can a college student qualify for the earned income credit? **LO 8-4**

39. How are business credits similar to personal credits? How are they dissimilar? **LO 8-4**

40. Is the foreign tax credit a personal credit or a business credit? Explain. **LO 8-4**

LO 8-4 41. When a U.S. taxpayer pays income taxes to a foreign government, what options does the taxpayer have when determining how to treat the expenditure on her U.S. individual income tax return?

LO 8-4 42. Describe the order in which different types of tax credits are applied to reduce a taxpayer's tax liability.

LO 8-5 43. Describe the two methods that taxpayers use to prepay their taxes.

LO 8-5 44. What are the consequences of a taxpayer underpaying his or her tax liability throughout the year? Explain the safe-harbor provisions that may apply in this situation.

LO 8-5 45. Describe how the underpayment penalty is calculated.

LO 8-5 46. What determines if a taxpayer is required to file a tax return? If a taxpayer is not required to file a tax return, does this mean that the taxpayer should not file a tax return?

LO 8-5 47. What is the due date for individual tax returns? What extensions are available?

LO 8-5 48. Describe the consequences for failing to file a tax return and for paying tax owed late.

PROBLEMS

Select problems are available in *Connect*®.

LO 8-1 49. Whitney received $75,000 of taxable income in 2016. All of the income was salary from her employer. What is her income tax liability in each of the following alternative situations?
   a) She files under the single filing status.
   b) She files a joint tax return with her spouse. Together their taxable income is $75,000.
   c) She is married but files a separate tax return. Her taxable income is $75,000.
   d) She files as a head of household.

LO 8-1 50. In 2016, Lisa and Fred, a married couple, have taxable income of $300,000. If they were to file separate tax returns, Lisa would have reported taxable income of $125,000 and Fred would have reported taxable income of $175,000. What is the couple's marriage penalty or benefit?

LO 8-1 51. In 2016, Jasmine and Thomas, a married couple, have taxable income of $150,000. If they were to file separate tax returns, Jasmine would have reported taxable income of $140,000 and Thomas would have reported taxable income of $10,000. What is the couple's marriage penalty or benefit?

LO 8-1 52. Lacy is a single taxpayer. In 2016, her taxable income is $40,000. What is her tax liability in each of the following alternative situations?
   a) All of her income is salary from her employer.
   b) Her $40,000 of taxable income includes $1,000 of qualified dividends.
   c) Her $40,000 of taxable income includes $5,000 of qualified dividends.

LO 8-1 53. Henrich is a single taxpayer. In 2016, his taxable income is $425,000. What is his income tax and net investment income tax liability in each of the following alternative scenarios?
   a) All of his income is salary from his employer.

b) His $425,000 of taxable income includes $2,000 of long-term capital gain that is taxed at preferential rates.

c) His $425,000 of taxable income includes $55,000 of long-term capital gain that is taxed at preferential rates.

d) Henrich has $195,000 of taxable income, which includes $50,000 of long-term capital gain that is taxed at preferential rates. Assume his modified AGI is $210,000.

54. In 2016, Sheryl is claimed as a dependent on her parents' tax return. Her parents' ordinary income marginal tax rate is 35 percent. Sheryl did not provide more than half her own support. What is Sheryl's tax liability for the year in each of the following alternative circumstances? `LO 8-1`

a) She received $7,000 from a part-time job. This was her only source of income. She is 16 years old at year-end.

b) She received $7,000 of interest income from corporate bonds she received several years ago. This is her only source of income. She is 16 years old at year-end.

c) She received $7,000 of interest income from corporate bonds she received several years ago. This is her only source of income. She is 20 years old at year-end and is a full-time student.

d) She received $7,000 of qualified dividend income. This is her only source of income. She is 16 years old at year-end.

55. In 2016, Carson is claimed as a dependent on his parent's tax return. His parents' ordinary income marginal tax rate is 28 percent. Carson's parents provided most of his support. What is Carson's tax liability for the year in each of the following alternative circumstances? `LO 8-1`

a) Carson is 17 years old at year-end and earned $12,000 from his summer job and part-time job after school. This was his only source of income.

b) Carson is 23 years old at year-end. He is a full-time student and earned $12,000 from his summer internship and part-time job. He also received $5,000 of qualified dividend income.

56. Brooklyn files as a head of household for 2016 and claims a total of three exemptions (3 × $4,050 = $12,150). She claimed the standard deduction of $9,300 for regular tax purposes. Her regular taxable income was $80,000. What is Brooklyn's AMTI? `LO 8-2`

57. Sylvester files as a single taxpayer during 2016 and claims one personal exemption. He itemizes deductions for regular tax purposes. He paid charitable contributions of $7,000, real estate taxes of $1,000, state income taxes of $4,000, and interest on a home-equity loan of $2,000. Sylvester's regular taxable income is $100,000. `LO 8-2`

a) What is Sylvester's AMTI if he used the home-equity proceeds to purchase a car?

b) What is Sylvester's AMTI if he used the home-equity loan proceeds to build a new garage next to his home?

58. In 2016, Nadia has $100,000 of regular taxable income. She itemizes her deductions as follows: real property taxes of $1,500, state income taxes of $2,000, and mortgage interest expense of $10,000 (not a home-equity loan). In addition, she receives tax-exempt interest of $1,000 from a municipal bond (issued in 2006) that was used to fund a new business building for a (formerly) out-of-state employer. Finally, she received a state tax refund of $300 from the prior year. `LO 8-2` **tax forms**

a) What is Nadia's AMTI this year if she deducted $15,000 of itemized deductions last year (she did not owe any AMT last year)? Complete Form 6251 (through line 28) for Nadia.

b) What is Nadia's AMTI this year if she deducted the standard deduction last year (she did not owe any AMT last year)? Complete Form 6251 (through line 28) for Nadia.

LO 8-2

tax forms

59. In 2016, Sven is single and has $120,000 of regular taxable income. He itemizes his deductions as follows: real property tax of $2,000, state income tax of $4,000, mortgage interest expense of $15,000 (not a home-equity loan). He also paid $2,000 in tax preparation fees and has a positive AMT depreciation adjustment of $500. What is Sven's alternative minimum taxable income (AMTI)? Complete Form 6251 (through line 28) for Sven.

LO 8-2

60. Olga is married and files a joint tax return with her husband. What amount of AMT exemption may she deduct under each of the following alternative circumstances?

a) Her AMTI is $90,000.

b) Her AMTI is $180,000.

c) Her AMTI is $500,000.

LO 8-2

61. Corbett's AMTI is $130,000. What is his AMT exemption under the following alternative circumstances?

a) He is married and files a joint return.

b) He is married and files a separate return.

c) His filing status is single.

d) His filing status is head of household.

LO 8-2

62. In 2016, Juanita is married and files a joint tax return with her husband. What is her tentative minimum tax in each of the following alternative circumstances?

a) Her AMT base is $100,000, all ordinary income.

b) Her AMT base is $250,000, all ordinary income.

c) Her AMT base is $100,000, which includes $10,000 of qualified dividends.

d) Her AMT base is $250,000, which includes $10,000 of qualified dividends.

LO 8-2

63. Steve's tentative minimum tax (TMT) for 2016 is $15,000. What is his AMT if

a) His regular tax is $10,000?

b) His regular tax is $20,000?

LO 8-2

tax forms

64. In 2016, Janet and Ray are married filing jointly. They have five dependent children under 18 years of age. Janet and Ray's taxable income is $140,000, and they itemize their deductions as follows: real property taxes of $5,000, state income taxes of $9,000, and mortgage interest expense of $15,000 (not a home-equity loan). What is Janet and Ray's AMT? Complete Form 6251 for Janet and Ray.

LO 8-2

tax forms

65. In 2016, Deon and NeNe are married filing jointly. They have three dependent children under 18 years of age. Deon and NeNe's AGI is $811,300, their taxable income is $720,250, and they itemize their deductions as follows: real property taxes of $10,000, state income taxes of $40,000, miscellaneous itemized deductions of $4,000 (subject to but in excess of 2 percent AGI floor), charitable contributions of $11,050, and mortgage interest expense of $41,000 ($11,000 of which is attributable to a home-equity loan used to buy a new car). What is Deon and NeNe's AMT? Complete Form 6251 for Deon and NeNe.

LO 8-3

66. Brooke works for Company A for all of 2016, earning a salary of $50,000.

a) What is her FICA tax obligation for the year?

b) Assume Brooke works for Company A for half of 2016, earning $50,000 in salary, and she works for Company B for the second half of 2016, earning $70,000 in salary. What is Brooke's FICA tax obligation for the year?

67. Rasheed works for Company A, earning $350,000 in salary during 2016. Assuming he has no other sources of income, what amount of FICA tax will Rasheed pay for the year?   `LO 8-3`

68. Alice is self-employed in 2016. Her net business profit on her Schedule C for the year is $140,000. What is her self-employment tax liability for 2016?   `LO 8-3`

69. Kyle worked as a free-lance software engineer for the first three months of 2016. During that time, he earned $44,000 of self-employment income. On April 1, 2016, Kyle took a job as a full-time software engineer with one of his former clients, Hoogle Inc. From April through the end of the year, Kyle earned $178,000 in salary. What amount of FICA taxes (self-employment and employment related) does Kyle owe for the year?   `LO 8-3`

70. Eva received $60,000 in compensation payments from JAZZ Corp. during 2016. Eva incurred $5,000 in business expenses relating to her work for JAZZ Corp. JAZZ did not reimburse Eva for any of these expenses. Eva is single and she deducts a standard deduction of $6,300 and a personal exemption of $4,050. Based on these facts answer the following questions: `LO 8-3`

    a) Assume that Eva is considered to be an *employee*. What amount of FICA taxes is she required to pay for the year?

    b) Assume that Eva is considered to be an *employee*. What is her regular income tax liability for the year?

    c) Assume that Eva is considered to be a *self-employed contractor*. What is her self-employment tax liability for the year?

    d) Assume that Eva is considered to be a *self-employed contractor*. What is her regular tax liability for the year?

71. Terry Hutchison worked as a self-employed lawyer until two years ago when he retired. He used the cash method of accounting in his business for tax purposes. Five years ago, Terry represented his client ABC corporation in an antitrust lawsuit against XYZ corporation. During that year, Terry paid self-employment taxes on all of his income. ABC won the lawsuit but Terry and ABC could not agree on the amount of his earnings. Finally, this year, the issue got resolved and ABC paid Terry $90,000 for the services he provided five years ago. Terry plans to include the payment in his gross income, but because he spends most of his time playing golf and absolutely no time working on legal matters, he does not intend to pay self-employment taxes on the income. Is Terry subject to self-employment taxes on this income?   `LO 8-3`   **research**

72. Trey claims a dependency exemption for both of his daughters, ages 14 and 17, at year-end. Trey files a joint return with his wife. What amount of child credit will Trey be able to claim for his daughters under each of the following alternative situations?   `LO 8-4`

    a) His AGI is $100,000.

    b) His AGI is $120,000.

    c) His AGI is $122,100, and his daughters are ages 10 and 12.

73. Julie paid a day care center to watch her two-year-old son while she worked as a computer programmer for a local start-up company. What amount of child and dependent care credit can Julie claim in each of the following alternative scenarios?   `LO 8-4`

    a) Julie paid $2,000 to the day care center and her AGI is $50,000 (all salary).

b) Julie paid $5,000 to the day care center and her AGI is $50,000 (all salary).

c) Julie paid $4,000 to the day care center and her AGI is $25,000 (all salary).

d) Julie paid $2,000 to the day care center and her AGI is $14,000 (all salary).

e) Julie paid $4,000 to the day care center and her AGI is $14,000 ($2,000 salary and $12,000 unearned income).

LO 8-4   74. In 2016, Elaine paid $2,800 of tuition and $600 for books for her dependent son to attend State University this past fall as a freshman. Elaine files a joint return with her husband. What is the maximum American opportunity credit that Elaine can claim for the tuition payment and books in each of the following alternative situations?

a) Elaine's AGI is $80,000.

b) Elaine's AGI is $168,000.

c) Elaine's AGI is $184,000.

LO 8-4   75. In 2016, Laureen is currently single. She paid $2,800 of qualified tuition and related expenses for each of her twin daughters Sheri and Meri to attend State

planning   University as freshmen ($2,800 each for a total of $5,600). Sheri and Meri qualify as Laureen's dependents. Laureen also paid $1,900 for her son Ryan's (also Laureen's dependent) tuition and related expenses to attend his junior year at State University. Finally, Laureen paid $1,200 for herself to attend seminars at a community college to help her improve her job skills. What is the maximum amount of education credits Laureen can claim for these expenditures in each of the following alternative scenarios?

a) Laureen's AGI is $45,000. If Laureen claims education credits for her three children and herself, how much credit is she allowed to claim in total? If she claims education credits for her children, how much of her children's tuition costs that do not generate credits may she deduct as *for* AGI expenses?

b) Laureen's AGI is $95,000. What options does Laureen have for deducting her continuing education costs to the extent the costs don't generate a credit?

c) Laureen's AGI is $45,000 and Laureen paid $12,000 (not $1,900) for Ryan to attend graduate school (his fifth year not his junior year).

LO 8-4   76. In 2016, Amanda and Jaxon Stuart have a daughter who is one year old. The Stuarts are full-time students and they are both 23 years old. Their only sources of income are gains from stock they held for three years before selling and wages from part-time jobs. What is their earned income credit in the following alternative scenarios if they file jointly?

a) Their AGI is $15,000, consisting of $5,000 of capital gains and $10,000 of wages.

b) Their AGI is $15,000, consisting of $10,000 of lottery winnings (unearned income) and $5,000 of wages.

c) Their AGI is $25,000, consisting of $20,000 of wages and $5,000 of lottery winnings (unearned income).

d) Their AGI is $25,000, consisting of $5,000 of wages and $20,000 of lottery winnings (unearned income).

e) Their AGI is $10,000, consisting of $10,000 of lottery winnings (unearned income).

77. In 2016, Zach is single with no dependents. He is not claimed as a dependent on another's return. All of his income is from salary and he does not have any *for* AGI deductions. What is his earned income credit in the following alternative scenarios? `LO 8-4`

    a) Zach is 29 years old and his AGI is $5,000.

    b) Zach is 29 years old and his AGI is $10,000.

    c) Zach is 29 years old and his AGI is $19,000.

    d) Zach is 24 years old and his AGI is $5,000.

78. This year Luke has calculated his gross tax liability at $1,800. Luke is entitled to a $2,400 nonrefundable personal tax credit, a $1,500 business tax credit, and a $600 refundable personal tax credit. In addition, Luke has had $2,300 of income taxes withheld from his salary. What is Luke's net tax due or refund? `LO 8-4`

79. This year Lloyd, a single taxpayer, estimates that his tax liability will be $10,000. Last year, his total tax liability was $15,000. He estimates that his tax withholding from his employer will be $7,800. `LO 8-5` `planning`

    a) Is Lloyd required to increase his withholding or make estimated tax payments this year to avoid the underpayment penalty? If so, how much?

    b) Assuming Lloyd does not make any additional payments, what is the amount of his underpayment penalty? Assume the federal short-term rate is 5 percent.

80. This year, Paula and Simon (married filing jointly) estimate that their tax liability will be $200,000. Last year, their total tax liability was $170,000. They estimate that their tax withholding from their employers will be $175,000. Are Paula and Simon required to increase their withholdings or make estimated tax payments this year to avoid the underpayment penalty? If so, how much? `LO 8-5` `planning`

81. This year, Santhosh, a single taxpayer, estimates that his tax liability will be $100,000. Last year, his total tax liability was $15,000. He estimates that his tax withholding from his employer will be $35,000. Is Santhosh required to increase his withholding or make estimated tax payments this year to avoid the underpayment penalty? If so, how much? `LO 8-5` `planning`

82. For the following taxpayers, determine if they are required to file a tax return in 2016. `LO 8-5`

    a) Ricko, single taxpayer, with gross income of $12,000.

    b) Fantasia, head of household, with gross income of $17,500.

    c) Ken and Barbie, married taxpayers with no dependents, with gross income of $12,000.

    d) Dorothy and Rudolf, married taxpayers, both age 68, with gross income of $19,000.

    e) Janyce, single taxpayer, age 73, with gross income of $12,500.

83. For the following taxpayers, determine the due date of their tax returns. `LO 8-5`

    a) Jerome, a single taxpayer, is not requesting an extension this year. Assume the due date falls on a Tuesday.

    b) Lashaunda, a single taxpayer, requests an extension this year. Assume the extended due date falls on a Wednesday.

    c) Barney and Betty, married taxpayers, do not request an extension this year. Assume the due date falls on a Sunday.

    d) Fred and Wilma, married taxpayers, request an extension this year. Assume the extended date falls on a Saturday.

LO 8-5

planning

84. Determine the amount of the late filing and late payment penalties that apply for the following taxpayers.

a) Jolene filed her tax return by its original due date but did not pay the $2,000 in taxes she owed with the return until one and a half months later.

b) Oscar filed his tax return and paid his $3,000 tax liability seven months late.

c) Wilfred, attempting to evade his taxes, did not file a tax return or pay his $10,000 in taxes for several years.

COMPREHENSIVE PROBLEMS

All applicable problems are available with _Connect_®.

85. In 2016, Jack and Diane Heart are married with two children, ages 10 and 12. Jack works full-time and earns an annual salary of $80,000, while Diane works as a substitute teacher and earns approximately $25,000 per year. Jack and Diane expect to file jointly and do not itemize their deductions. In the fall of this year, Diane was offered a full-time teaching position that would pay her an additional $20,000.

a) Calculate the marginal tax rate on the additional income, _excluding employment taxes,_ to help Jack and Diane evaluate the offer.

b) Calculate the marginal tax rate on the additional income, _including employment taxes,_ to help Jack and Diane evaluate the offer.

c) Calculate the marginal tax rate on the additional income, _including self-employment taxes,_ if Diane earned an additional $20,000 as a self-employed contractor ($20,000 self-employment income in addition to the $25,000 as an employee).

planning

86. Matt and Carrie are married, have two children, and file a joint return. Their daughter Katie is 19 years old and was a full-time student at State University. During 2016, she completed her freshman year and one semester as a sophomore. Katie's expenses while she was away at school during the year were as follows:

Tuition	$5,000
Class fees	300
Books	500
Room and board	4,500

Katie received a half-tuition scholarship that paid for $2,500 of her tuition costs. Katie's parents paid the rest of these expenses. Matt and Carrie are able to claim Katie as a dependent on their tax return.

Matt and Carrie's 23-year-old son Todd also attended graduate school (fifth year of college) full time at a nearby college. Todd's expenses while away at school were as follows:

Tuition	$3,000
Class fees	0
Books	250
Room and board	4,000

Matt and Carrie paid for Todd's tuition, books, and room and board.

Since Matt and Carrie still benefit from claiming Todd as a dependent on their tax return, they decided to provide Todd with additional financial assistance by making the payments on Todd's outstanding student loans. Besides paying off some of the loan principal, Matt and Carrie paid a total of $900 of interest on the loan.

This year Carrie decided to take some classes at the local community college to help improve her skills as a schoolteacher. The community college is considered to be a qualifying postsecondary institution of higher education. Carrie spent a total of $1,300 on tuition for the classes, and she was not reimbursed by her employer. Matt and Carrie's AGI for 2016 before any education-related tax deductions is $121,000 and their taxable income before considering any education-related tax benefits is $80,000. Matt and Carrie incurred $500 of miscellaneous itemized deductions subject to the 2 percent floor not counting any education-related expenses.

Required:

Determine the mix of tax benefits that maximize tax savings for Matt and Carrie. Their options for credits for each student are as follows:

 a) They may claim either a credit or a qualified education deduction for Katie's expenses.

 b) They may claim either a credit or a qualified education deduction for Todd.

 c) They may claim (1) a credit or (2) a qualified education deduction for Carrie. They may deduct any amount not included in (1) or (2) as a miscellaneous itemized deduction subject to the 2 percent of AGI floor.

Remember to apply any applicable limits or phase-outs in your computations.

87. Reba Dixon is a fifth-grade schoolteacher who earned a salary of $38,000 in 2016. She is 45 years old and has been divorced for four years. She received $1,200 of alimony payments each month from her former husband. Reba also rents out a small apartment building. This year Reba received $30,000 of rental payments from tenants and she incurred $19,500 of expenses associated with the rental.

tax forms

Reba and her daughter Heather (20 years old at the end of the year) moved to Georgia in January of this year. Reba provides more than one-half of Heather's support. They had been living in Colorado for the past 15 years, but ever since her divorce, Reba has been wanting to move back to Georgia to be closer to her family. Luckily, last December, a teaching position opened up and Reba and Heather decided to make the move. Reba paid a moving company $2,010 to move their personal belongings, and she and Heather spent two days driving the 1,426 miles to Georgia. During the trip, Reba paid $200 for lodging and $85 for meals. Reba's mother was so excited to have her daughter and granddaughter move back to Georgia that she gave Reba $3,000 to help out with the moving costs.

Reba rented a home in Georgia. Heather decided to continue living at home with her mom, but she started attending school full-time in January at a nearby university. She was awarded a $3,000 partial tuition scholarship this year, and Reba helped out by paying the remaining $500 tuition cost. If possible, Reba thought it would be best to claim the education credit for these expenses.

Reba wasn't sure if she would have enough items to help her benefit from itemizing on her tax return. However, she kept track of several expenses this year that she thought might qualify if she was able to itemize. Reba paid $2,800 in state income taxes and $6,500 in charitable contributions during the year. She also paid the following medical-related expenses for her and Heather:

Insurance premiums	$4,795
Medical care expenses	1,100
Prescription medicine	350
Nonprescription medicine	100
New contact lenses for Heather	200

Shortly after the move, Reba got distracted while driving and she ran into a street sign. The accident caused $900 in damage to the car and gave her whiplash. Because the repairs were less than her insurance deductible, she paid the entire cost of the repairs. Reba wasn't able to work for two months after the accident. Fortunately, she received $2,000 from her disability insurance. Her employer, the Central Georgia School District, paid 60 percent of the premiums on the policy as a nontaxable fringe benefit and Reba paid the remaining 40 percent portion.

A few years ago, Reba acquired several investments with her portion of the divorce settlement. This year she reported the following income from her investments: $2,200 of interest income from corporate bonds and $1,500 interest income from City of Denver municipal bonds. Overall, Reba's stock portfolio appreciated by $12,000 but she did not sell any of her stocks.

Heather reported $3,200 of interest income from corporate bonds she received as gifts from her father over the last several years. This was Heather's only source of income for the year.

Reba had $10,000 of federal income taxes withheld by her employer. Heather made $500 of estimated tax payments during the year. Reba did not make any estimated payments. Reba had qualifying insurance for purposes of the Affordable Care Act (ACA).

Required:

a) Determine Reba's federal income taxes due or taxes payable for the current year. Complete pages 1 and 2 of Form 1040 for Reba.

b) Is Reba allowed to file as a head of household or single?

c) Determine the amount of FICA taxes Reba was required to pay on her salary.

d) Determine Heather's federal income taxes due or payable.

tax forms

88. John and Sandy Ferguson got married eight years ago and have a seven-year-old daughter Samantha. In 2016, John worked as a computer technician at a local university earning a salary of $52,000, and Sandy worked part-time as a receptionist for a law firm earning a salary of $29,000. John also does some Web design work on the side and reported revenues of $4,000 and associated expenses of $750. The Fergusons received $800 in qualified dividends and a $200 refund of their state income taxes. The Fergusons always itemize their deductions and their itemized deductions were well over the standard deduction amount last year. The Fergusons had qualifying insurance for purposes of the Affordable Care Act (ACA).

The Fergusons reported making the following payments during the year:

- State income taxes of $4,400. Federal tax withholding of $4,000.
- Alimony payments to John's former wife of $10,000.
- Child support payments for John's child with his former wife of $4,100.
- $3,200 of real property taxes.

- Sandy was reimbursed $600 for employee business expenses she incurred. She was required to provide documentation for her expenses to her employer.
- In addition to the $750 of Web design expenses, John attended a conference to improve his skills associated with his Web design work. His trip was for three days and he incurred the following expenses: airfare $370, total taxi fares for trip $180, meals $80, and conference fee of $200.
- $3,600 to Kid Care day care center for Samantha's care while John and Sandy worked.
- $14,000 interest on their home mortgage.
- $3,000 interest on a $40,000 home-equity loan. They used the loan to pay for a family vacation and new car.
- $6,000 cash charitable contributions to qualified charities.
- Donation of used furniture to Goodwill. The furniture had a fair market value of $400 and cost $2,000.

Required:

What is the Fergusons' 2016 federal income taxes payable or refund, including any self-employment tax and AMT, if applicable? Complete pages 1 and 2 of Form 1040 and Form 6251 for John and Sandy.

Business Income, Deductions, and Accounting Methods

Upon completing this chapter, you should be able to:

LO 9-1 Describe the general requirements for deducting business expenses and identify common business deductions.

LO 9-2 Apply the limitations on business deductions to distinguish between deductible and nondeductible business expenses.

LO 9-3 Identify and explain special business deductions specifically permitted under the tax laws.

LO 9-4 Explain the concept of an accounting period and describe accounting periods available to businesses.

LO 9-5 Identify and describe accounting methods available to businesses and apply cash and accrual methods to determine business income and expense deductions.

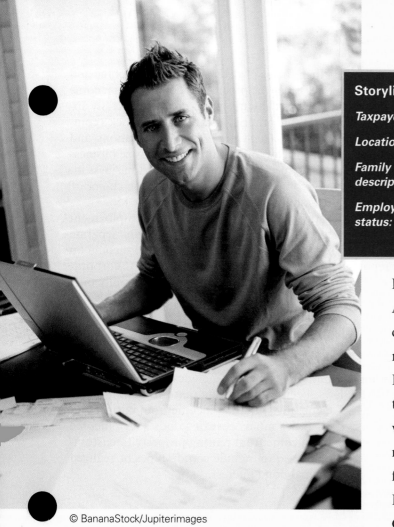

© BananaStock/Jupiterimages

Rick Grime graduated from Texas A&M University with a degree in agronomy, and for the past few years he has been employed by a landscape architect in Dallas. Nearly every day that Rick went to work, he shared ideas with his employer about improving the business. Rick finally decided to take his ideas and start his own landscaping business in his hometown of San Antonio, Texas. In mid-April,

Rick left his job and moved his belongings to San Antonio. Once in town, Rick discovered he had to do a lot of things to start his business. First, he registered his new business name (Green Acres Landscaping) and established a bank account for the business. Next, he rented a used sport utility vehicle (SUV) and a shop for his place of business. Rick didn't know much about accounting for business activities, so he hired a CPA, Jane Bronson, to help him. Jane and Rick decided that Green Acres would operate as a sole proprietorship, but Jane suggested that as the business grew, he might want to consider organizing it as a different type of legal entity. Operating as a corporation, for instance, would allow him to invite new investors or business partners to help fund future expansion. Rick formally started his business on May 1. He spent a lot of time attracting new customers, and he figured he would hire employees as he needed them.

to be continued . . .

In previous chapters, we've emphasized the process of determining gross income and deductions for *individuals*. This chapter describes the process for determining income for *businesses*. Keep in mind that the concepts we discuss in this chapter generally apply to all types of business entities including sole proprietorships (such as Rick's company, Green Acres), partnerships, hybrid entities (such as LLCs), S corporations, and C corporations.[1] Because Rick is a sole proprietor, our examples emphasize business income and deductions from his personal perspective. Proprietors report business income on Schedule C of their individual income tax returns. However, the choice of the organizational form is a complex decision that is described in Chapter 15.

Schedule C income is subject to both individual income and self-employment taxes. Entities other than sole proprietorships report income on tax forms separate from the owners' tax returns. For example, partnerships report taxable income on Form 1065, S corporations report taxable income on Form 1120S, and C corporations report taxable income on Form 1120. Of all these entity types, generally only C corporations pay taxes on their income.

BUSINESS GROSS INCOME

In most respects, the rules for determining business gross income are the same as for determining gross income for individuals. Gross income includes "all income from whatever source derived."[2] The tax laws specifically indicate that this definition includes gross income from "business." Generally speaking, income from business includes gross profit from inventory sales (sales minus cost of goods sold), income from services provided to customers, and income from renting property to customers. Just like individuals, businesses are allowed to exclude certain types of realized income from gross income, such as municipal bond interest.

LO 9-1

BUSINESS DEDUCTIONS

Because Congress intended for taxable income to reflect the *net* increase in wealth from a business, it is only fair that businesses be allowed to deduct expenses incurred to generate business income. Typically, Congress provides *specific* statutory rules authorizing deductions. However, as you can see from the following excerpt from IRC §162, the provision authorizing business deductions is relatively broad and ambiguous:

> There shall be allowed as a deduction all the ordinary and necessary expenses paid or incurred during the taxable year in carrying on any trade or business . . .

This provision authorizes taxpayers to deduct expenses for "trade or business" activities.[3] The tax code does not define the phrase "trade or business," but it's clear that the objective of business activities is to make a profit. Thus, the law requires that a business expense be made in the pursuit of profits rather than the pursuit of other, presumably personal, motives.

When a taxpayer's activity does not meet the "for profit" requirement, it is treated as a hobby, an activity motivated by personal objectives. A taxpayer engaged in a hobby that generates revenues includes all revenues from the activity in gross

---

[1]Both S corporations and C corporations are incorporated for state law purposes. However, S corporations are taxed as flow-through entities (S corporation income is taxed to its owners) while C corporations (or taxable corporations) are taxed as separate taxable entities. Hybrid entities may opt to be taxed as either flow-through entities or taxable corporations.

[2]§61(a).

[3]§212 contains a sister provision to §162 allowing deductions for ordinary and necessary expenses incurred for the production of income ("investment expenses") and for the management and maintenance of property (including expenses incurred in renting property in situations when the rental activity is not considered to be a trade or business). Recall from Chapter 6 that a business activity, sometimes referred to as a trade or business, requires a relatively high level of involvement or effort from the taxpayer. Unlike business activities, investments are profit-motivated activities that don't require a high degree of taxpayer involvement or effort.

income and deducts associated expenses to the extent of gross income from the activity as *miscellaneous itemized deductions* (subject to the 2 percent of AGI floor).

Ordinary and Necessary

Business expenditures must be both **ordinary and necessary** to be deductible. An *ordinary* expense is an expense that is normal or appropriate for the business under the circumstances.[4] An expense is *not* necessarily required to be typical or repetitive in nature to be considered ordinary. For example, a business could deduct the legal fees it expends to defend itself in an antitrust suit. Although an antitrust suit would be atypical and unusual for most businesses, defending the suit would probably be deemed ordinary because it would be expected under the circumstances. A *necessary* expense is an expense that is helpful or conducive to the business activity, but the expenditure need not be essential or indispensable. For example, a deduction for metric tools would qualify as ordinary and necessary even if there was only a small chance that a repairman might need these tools. The "ordinary and necessary" requirements are applied on a case-by-case basis, and while the deduction depends on individual circumstances, the IRS is often reluctant to second-guess business decisions. Exhibit 9-1 presents examples of expenditures that are ordinary and necessary for typical businesses.

EXHIBIT 9-1 Examples of Typical Ordinary and Necessary Business Expenses

- Advertising
- Car and truck expenses
- Depreciation
- Employee compensation and benefits
- Insurance
- Interest
- Legal fees
- Office expenses
- Rent
- Repairs
- Supplies
- Travel
- Utilities
- Wages

Example 9-1

Outside Rick's office is a small waiting room for clients. Rick paid $50 for several books to occupy clients while waiting for appointments. These are hardcover books with photographs and illustrations of landscape designs. Rick believes that the books will inspire new designs and will alleviate boredom for potential clients, and he deducted the $50 cost as a business expense. Is he correct?

Answer: Under the code and regulations, expenses directly connected to a business are deductible if the expenditure is ordinary and necessary. The phrase *ordinary and necessary* is interpreted as *helpful or conducive to business activity*. In Rick's situation, it seems highly unlikely that the IRS or a court would conclude that the cost of these books is not ordinary and necessary. What do you think?

What if: Suppose that Rick's hobby was pre-Columbian Maya civilization. Do you think Rick would be able to deduct the cost of a new treatise on translating Maya script if he placed the book in his waiting room? Why or why not?

ETHICS

Sheri is a lawyer who operates as a sole practitioner. Despite her busy schedule, in the past Sheri found time for her family. This year Sheri took on two new important clients, and she hired a personal assistant to help her manage her schedule and make timely court filings. Occasionally, Sheri asked her assistant to assist her with personal tasks such as having her car serviced or buying groceries. Do you think that Sheri should treat her assistant's entire salary as a business expense? Would your answer be any different if personal assistants commonly perform these tasks for busy attorneys?

[4]*Welch v. Helvering* (1933), 290 US 111.

Reasonable in Amount

Ordinary and necessary business expenses are deductible only *to the extent* they are also **reasonable in amount.** The courts have interpreted this requirement to mean that an expenditure is not reasonable when it is extravagant or exorbitant.[5] If the expenditure is extravagant in amount, the courts presume the excess amount is spent for personal rather than business reasons and is not deductible.

Determining whether an expenditure is reasonable is not an exact science, and not surprisingly, taxpayers and the IRS may have different opinions. Generally, the courts and the IRS test for extravagance by comparing the amount of the expense to a market price or an **arm's-length amount.** If the amount of the expense is the amount typically charged in the market by unrelated parties, the amount is considered to be reasonable. The underlying issue is *why* a profit-motivated taxpayer would pay an extravagant amount. Hence, reasonableness is most likely to be an issue when a payment is made to an individual related to the taxpayer, or the taxpayer enjoys some incidental benefit from the expenditure, such as entertainment value.

Example 9-2

During the busy part of the year, Rick could not keep up with all the work. Therefore, he hired four part-time employees and paid them $10 an hour to mow lawns and pull weeds for an average of 20 hours a week. When things finally slowed down in late fall, Rick released his four part-time employees. Rick paid a total of $22,000 in compensation to the four employees. He still needed some extra help now and then, so he hired his brother, Tom, on a part-time basis. Tom performed the same duties as the prior part-time employees (his quality of work was about the same). However, Rick paid Tom $25 per hour because Tom is a college student and Rick wanted to provide some additional support for Tom's education. At year-end, Tom had worked a total of 100 hours and received $2,500 from Rick. What amount can Rick deduct for the compensation he paid to his employees?

Answer: $23,000. Rick can deduct the $22,000 paid to part-time employees. However, he can only deduct $10 an hour for Tom's compensation because the extra $15 per hour Rick paid Tom is unreasonable in amount.[6] The remaining $15 per hour is considered a personal (nondeductible) gift from Rick to Tom. Hence, Rick can deduct a total of $23,000 for compensation expense this year [$22,000 + ($10 × 100)].

TAXES IN THE REAL WORLD What Qualifies as a "Business"?

Richard Bagley earned an MS in accounting from UCLA and was the chief financial manager for TRW's space and technology group. Bagley became aware of false claims made by TRW to the government and discussed these false claims with supervisors. Bagley was subsequently fired. Bagley retained attorneys to help him file a False Claims Act (FCA) suit against his employer.

Over a nine-year period, Bagley exclusively worked on his FCA prosecution activity. Bagley maintained a contemporaneous log of hours that showed he spent over 21,000 hours prosecuting the FCA suits. Besides numerous meetings, Bagley drafted and/or edited at least 73 documents in furtherance of the FCA litigation activity. According to Bagley, he was actively involved with the litigation because the lawyers "weren't accountants and . . . didn't have an in-depth understanding of TRW's accounting system."

Bagley considered himself to be in a trade or business as a "Private Attorney General," but Bagley never filed any business registration or

---

[5]§162(a) and *Comm. v. Lincoln Electric Co.* (CA-6, 1949), 176 F.2d 815.

[6]In practice, this distinction is rarely cut and dried. Rick may be able to argue for various reasons that Tom's work is worth more than $10 an hour but perhaps not as much as $25 per hour. We use this example to illustrate the issue of reasonable expenses and not to discuss the merits of what actually is reasonable compensation to Tom.

notice anywhere with a city or the state. Furthermore, Bagley did not advertise his business nor did he keep accounting books, but he ultimately received an award of $36,651,295. On his amended federal tax refund claim, Bagley reported the income as attributable to his "trade or business" and deducted $18,477,815 in attorney's fees as ordinary and necessary business expenses. The IRS denied Bagley's refund claim.

The District Court, however, rejected the government's claim that a one-time pursuit of an FCA claim with a large payout was not indic-

ative of a for-profit business. The court held that Bagley's litigation activities, and the regular, continuous way he undertook them, combined with skill and a good-faith effort to make a profit, indicated a trade or business. Further, the individual's litigation expenses were ordinary and necessary expenses paid in relation to his trade or business of prosecuting the FCA lawsuits. Without hiring the attorneys, the individual could not have engaged in his business.

Source: Richard D. Bagley v. U.S. (DC CA), 2013-2 U.S.T.C. 50,462.

LIMITATIONS ON BUSINESS DEDUCTIONS

LO 9-2

For a variety of reasons, Congress specifically prohibits or limits a business's ability to deduct certain expenditures that appear to otherwise meet the general business expense deductibility requirements.

Expenditures against Public Policy

Businesses occasionally incur fines and penalties and may even pay illegal bribes and kickbacks. However, these payments are not deductible for tax purposes.[7] Congress disallows these expenditures under the rationale that allowing them would subsidize illegal activities and frustrate public policy. Interestingly enough, businesses conducting illegal activities (selling stolen goods or conducting illegal gambling activities) are allowed to deduct their cost of goods sold and their ordinary and necessary business expenses in conducting the business activities (note, however, that they are not allowed to deduct fines, penalties, illegal bribes, or illegal kickbacks).[8] Of course, the IRS is probably more concerned that many illegal businesses fail to report *any* income than that illegal businesses overstate deductions.[9]

Political Contributions and Lobbying Costs

Perhaps to avoid the perception that the federal government subsidizes taxpayer efforts to influence politics, the tax laws disallow deductions for political contributions and most lobbying expenses.[10] An exception exists to the prohibition of lobbying expenses. Under §162(e), deductions are allowed for reasonable costs incurred in conjunction with the submission of statements to a local council with respect to proposed legislation of direct interest to the taxpayer.

THE KEY FACTS

Limitations on Business Deductions

- No business deductions are allowable for expenditures against public policy (bribes) or political contributions.
- Expenditures that benefit a period longer than 12 months generally must be capitalized.
- No deductions are allowable for expenditures associated with the production of tax-exempt income.
- Personal expenditures are not deductible.

---

[7]§162(c) and Reg. §1.162-21. This prohibition applies to fines and penalties imposed by a government or governmental unit. Fines and penalties imposed by other organizations, such as a NASCAR fine, would be fully deductible if the payment otherwise qualified as an ordinary and necessary business expense.

[8]*Comm. v. Sullivan* (1958), 356 US 27.

[9]§280E explicitly prohibits drug dealers from deducting any business expenses associated with this "business" activity. However, drug dealers are able to deduct cost of goods sold because cost of goods sold is technically a reduction in gross income and not a business expense. See Reg. §1.61-3(a).

[10]§162(e).

Example 9-3

In July, the city fined Rick $200 for violating the city's watering ban when he watered a newly installed landscape. Later, Rick donated $250 to the mayor's campaign for reelection. Can Rick deduct these expenditures?

Answer: No. Rick cannot deduct either the fine or the political contribution as a business expense because the tax laws specifically prohibit deductions for these expenditures.

What if: Suppose that Rick had paid $250 for an economist to help Rick prepare a presentation to the city council on a proposed ordinance restricting water usage. Rick's presentation demonstrated to the council how the ordinance on water restrictions could affect area landscapers.

Answer: It is likely that this expenditure would qualify for deduction as a business expense under the exception in §162(e)(2).

Capital Expenditures

Whether a business uses the cash or the accrual method of accounting, it must capitalize expenditures for *tangible* assets such as buildings, machinery and equipment, furniture and fixtures, and similar property that have useful lives of more than one year (12 months).[11] For tax purposes, businesses recover the cost of capitalized tangible assets (other than land) through depreciation.

Businesses also capitalize the cost to create or acquire *intangible* assets such as patents, goodwill, start-up costs, and organizational expenditures.[12] They recover the costs of capitalized intangible assets either through amortization (when the tax laws allow them to do so) or upon disposition of the assets. Prepaid expenses are also subject to capitalization, but there is a special exception that we discuss under accounting methods later in this chapter.[13]

Expenses Associated with the Production of Tax-Exempt Income

Expenses that do not help businesses generate *taxable* income are not allowed to offset taxable income. For example, this restriction disallows interest expense deductions for businesses that borrow money and invest the loan proceeds in municipal (tax-exempt) bonds. It also disallows deductions for life insurance premiums businesses pay on policies that cover the lives of officers or other key employees and compensate the business for the disruption and lost income they may experience due to a key employee's death. Because the death benefit from the life insurance policy is not taxable, the business is not allowed to deduct the insurance premium expense associated with this nontaxable income.

Example 9-4

Rick employs Joan, an arborist who specializes in trimming trees and treating local tree ailments. Joan generates a great deal of revenue for Rick's business, but is in her mid-60s and suffers from diabetes. In November, Rick purchased a "key-employee" term life-insurance policy on Joan's life. The policy cost Rick $720 and will pay Rick (Green Acres) a $20,000 death benefit if Joan passes away during the next 12 months. What amount of life insurance policy premium can Rick deduct?

Answer: $0. Rick cannot deduct the $720 premium on the life insurance policy because the life insurance proceeds from the policy are tax-exempt.

---

[11]Reg. §1.263(a)-2(d)(4). The act of recording the asset is sometimes referred to as *capitalizing* the expenditure.

[12]Reg. §1.263(a)-4(b). The extent to which expenditures for intangible assets must be capitalized is explored in *Indopco v. Comm.* (1992), 503 US 79.

[13]See §195, §197, and §248 for provisions that allow taxpayers to amortize the cost of certain intangible assets.

What if: Suppose Rick purchased the life insurance policy on Joan's life and allowed Joan to name the beneficiary. The policy cost Rick $720 and will pay the beneficiary a $20,000 death benefit if Joan passes away during the next 12 months. What amount of life insurance policy premium can Rick deduct?

Answer: $720. In this scenario, Rick can deduct the entire premium of $720 as a *compensation* expense because the benefit of the policy inures to Joan and not to Rick's business.

Personal Expenditures

Taxpayers are not allowed to deduct **personal expenses** unless the expenses are "expressly" authorized by a provision in the law.[14] While the tax laws do not define personal expenses, they imply the scope of personal expenses by stating that "personal, living, or family expenses" are not deductible. Therefore, at a minimum, the costs of food, clothing, and shelter are assumed to be personal and nondeductible. Of course, there are the inevitable exceptions when otherwise personal items are specially adapted to business use. For example, taxpayers may deduct the cost of uniforms or special clothing they purchase for use in their business, if the clothing is not appropriate to wear as ordinary clothing outside the place of business. When the clothing is adaptable as ordinary clothing, the cost of the clothing is a nondeductible personal expenditure.[15]

Example 9-5

Rick spent $500 to purchase special coveralls that identify his landscaping service and provide a professional appearance. How much of the cost for the clothing can Rick deduct as a business expense?

Answer: All $500. While the cost of clothing is inherently personal, Rick can deduct the $500 cost of the coveralls because, due to the design and labeling on the coveralls, they are not suitable for ordinary use.

Many business owners, particularly small-business owners such as sole proprietors, may be in a position to use business funds to pay for items that are entirely personal in nature. For example, a sole proprietor could use the business checking account to pay for family groceries. These expenditures, even though funded by the business, are not deductible.

Expenditures made by a taxpayer for education, such as tuition and books, are often related to a taxpayer's business aspirations. However, educational expenditures are not deductible as business expenses unless the education: (1) maintains or improves skills required by the individual in his employment or other trade or business, or (2) meets the express requirements of the individual's employer, or the requirements of applicable law or regulations, imposed as a condition to the retention by the individual of an established employment relationship, status, or rate of compensation. Education necessary to meet minimum requirements for an occupation are not deductible. For example, tuition payments for courses to satisfy the education requirement to sit for the CPA exam are not deductible. This is an example of education that qualifies the taxpayer for a new trade or business rather than improving his skills in an existing trade or business.

[14]§262(a).

[15]An employee who purchases clothing for work would go through a similar analysis to determine if the cost of the clothing qualifies as an employee business expense.

Mixed-Motive Expenditures

Business owners in general, and owners of small or closely held businesses in particular, often make expenditures that are motivated by *both* business and personal concerns. These **mixed-motive expenditures** are of particular concern to lawmakers and the IRS because of the tax incentive to disguise nondeductible personal expenses as deductible business expenses. Thus, deductions for business expenditures with potential personal motives are closely monitored and restricted. The rules for determining the amount of *deductible* mixed-motive expenditures depend on the type of the expenditure. Here we review the rules for determining the deductible portion of mixed-motive expenditures for meals and entertainment, travel and transportation, and the use of property for both business and personal purposes.

Meals and Entertainment   Because everyone needs to eat, even business meals contain a significant personal element. To allow for this personal element, taxpayers may only deduct 50 percent of actual business meals. In addition, to deduct any portion of the cost of a meal as a business expense, (1) the amount must be reasonable under the circumstances, (2) the taxpayer (or an employee) must be present when the meal is furnished, and (3) the meal must be directly associated with the active conduct of the taxpayer's business.

Similar to business meals, entertainment associated with business activities contains a significant element of enjoyment. Hence, only 50 percent of allowable business entertainment may be deducted as a business expense.[16] Further, entertainment deductions are allowable only if (1) "business associates" are entertained, (2) the amounts paid are reasonable in amount, and (3) the entertainment is either "directly related" or "associated with" the active conduct of business.

Business associates are individuals with whom the taxpayer reasonably expects to do business, such as customers, suppliers, employees, or advisors. Entertainment is directly related to business if there is an active discussion aimed at generating revenue or fees or the discussion occurs in a clear business setting (such as a hospitality room). The cost of entertainment that occurs in a setting with little possibility of conducting a business discussion, such as a theater or sports venue, will only be deductible if the entertainment directly precedes or follows a substantial business discussion, thereby satisfying the "associated with" test. In addition, to deduct the cost of meals and entertainment, taxpayers generally must meet strict record-keeping requirements we discuss below.[17]

Example 9-6

Rick went out to dinner with a prospective client to discuss Rick's ideas for landscaping the homeowner's yard. After dinner, Rick and the prospective client attended the theater. Rick paid $190 for the meal and $350 for the tickets, amounts that were reasonable under the circumstances. What amount of these expenditures can Rick deduct as a business expense?

Answer: Rick can deduct $270 [($190 + $350) × 50%], representing half the cost of the meal and entertainment, as a business expense, as long as Rick can substantiate the business purpose and substantial nature of the dinner discussion.

---

[16]§274 also provides some exceptions to the 50 percent reduction for meals and entertainment, such as meals and entertainment provided for special events or as employee compensation. Taxpayers can also use a *per diem* rate (an automatic, flat amount per meal) in lieu of actual expenditures to determine the amount of the deduction. There are special limits placed on entertainment expenses associated with spouses.

[17]Under §274, there are special limits placed on certain entertainment expenditures, such as those related to spouses; club dues and entertainment facilities; skyboxes; and entertainment associated with corporate officers, directors, and large shareholders.

What if: Suppose that Rick did not discuss business with the client either before, during, or after the meal. What amount of the expenditures can Rick deduct as a business expense?

Answer: $0. In this scenario, Rick cannot deduct the costs of the meal or entertainment because the activity was not directly related to or associated with a substantial business discussion.

Travel and Transportation Under certain conditions, sole proprietors and self-employed taxpayers may deduct the cost of travel and transportation for business purposes. Transportation expenses include the direct cost of transporting the taxpayer to and from business sites. However, the cost of commuting between the taxpayer's home and regular place of business is personal and, therefore, not deductible. If the taxpayer uses a vehicle for business, the taxpayer can deduct the costs of operating the vehicle plus depreciation on the vehicle's tax basis. Alternatively, in lieu of deducting these costs, the taxpayer may simply deduct a standard amount for each business mile driven. The standard mileage rate represents the per-mile cost of operating an automobile (including depreciation or lease payments).[18] For 2016 the standard mileage rate has been set at 54 cents per mile. To be deductible, the transportation must be for business reasons. If the transportation is primarily for personal purposes, the cost is not deductible.

Example 9-7

Rick leases an SUV to drive between his shop and various work sites. Rick carefully documents the business use of the SUV (8,100 miles this year) and his $5,335 of operating expenses ($3,935 for gas, oil, and repairs and $1,400 for lease payments). At no time does Rick use the SUV for personal purposes. What amount of these expenses may Rick deduct as business expenses?

Answer: $5,335. Since Rick uses the SUV in his business activities, he can deduct (1) the $5,335 cost of operating and leasing the SUV or (2) $4,374 for the 8,100 business miles he drove (54 cents per mile × 8,100 miles). Assuming Rick chooses to deduct operating expenses and lease payments in lieu of using the mileage rate, he can deduct $5,335.

In contrast to transportation expenses, travel expenses are only deductible if the taxpayer is *away from home* overnight while traveling. This distinction is important because, besides the cost of transportation, the deduction for **travel expenses** includes meals (50 percent), lodging, and incidental expenses. A taxpayer is considered to be away from home overnight if the travel is away from the primary place of business and of sufficient duration to require sleep or rest (typically this will be overnight). When a taxpayer travels solely for business purposes, *all* of the costs of travel are deductible (but only 50 percent of meals). When the travel has both business and personal aspects, the deductibility of the transportation costs depends upon whether business is the *primary* purpose for the trip. If the primary purpose of a trip is business, the transportation costs are fully deductible, but meals (50 percent), lodging, and incidental expenditures are limited to those incurred during the business portion of the travel.[19] If the taxpayer's primary purpose for the trip is personal, the taxpayer may not deduct *any* transportation costs to arrive at the location but may deduct meals (50 percent), lodging, transportation, and incidental expenditures for the *business* portion of the trip. The primary purpose of a trip depends upon facts and circumstances and is often the subject of dispute.

[18]This mileage rate is updated periodically (sometimes two or three times within a year) to reflect changes in the cost of operating a vehicle. The mileage option is only available for vehicles not previously depreciated, vehicles previously depreciated on the straight-line method, or leased vehicles where this method has been used throughout the term of the lease.

[19]Note that travel days are considered business days. Also, special limitations apply to a number of travel expenses that are potentially abusive, such as luxury water travel, foreign conventions, conventions on cruise ships, and travel expenses associated with taking a companion.

The rule for business travel is modified somewhat if a trip abroad includes both business and personal activities. Like the rule for domestic travel, if foreign travel is primarily for personal purposes, then only those expenses directly associated with business activities are deductible. However, unlike the rule for domestic travel, when foreign travel is primarily for business purposes, a portion of the round-trip transportation costs is not deductible. The nondeductible portion is typically computed based on a time ratio such as the proportion of personal days to total days (travel days count as business days).[20]

Example 9-8

Rick paid a $300 registration fee for a three-day course in landscape design. The course was held in upstate New York (Rick paid $700 for airfare to attend) and he spent four days away from home. He spent the last day sightseeing. During the trip, Rick paid $150 a night for three nights' lodging, $50 a day for meals, and $70 a day for a rental car. What amount of these travel-related expenditures may Rick deduct as business expenses?

Answer: $1,435 for business travel and $300 for business education. The primary purpose for the trip appears to be business because Rick spent three days on business activities versus one personal day. He can deduct travel costs, computed as follows:

Deductible Travel Costs		
Description	**Amount**	**Explanation**
Airfare	$ 700	Primary purpose is business.
Lodging	450	3 business days × $150 a day.
Meals	75	3 business days × $50 a day × 50% limit.
Rental car	210	3 business days × $70 a day.
Total business travel expenses	$1,435	

What if: Assume Rick stayed in New York for 10 days, spending 3 days at the seminar and seven days sightseeing. What amount could he deduct?

Answer: In this scenario Rick can deduct $735 for business travel and $300 for business education. Rick would not be able to deduct the $700 cost of airfare because the trip is primarily personal, as evidenced by the seven days of personal activities compared to only three days of business activities.

Deductible Travel Costs		
Description	**Amount**	**Explanation**
Airfare	$ 0	Primary purpose is personal.
Lodging	450	3 business days × $150 a day.
Meals	75	3 business days × $50 a day × 50% limit.
Rental car	210	3 business days × $70 a day.
Total business travel expenses	$735	

What if: Assume the original facts in the example except Rick traveled to London (rather than upstate New York) for 10 days spending 6 days at the seminar and 4 days sightseeing. What amount could he deduct?

Answer: In this scenario Rick can deduct $1,890 for travel (computed below) and $300 for business education.

---

[20]Foreign transportation expense is deductible without prorating under special circumstances authorized in §274(c). For example, the cost of getting abroad is fully deductible if the travel is for one week or less or if the personal activity constitutes less than one-fourth of the travel time.

Deductible Travel Costs		
Description	**Amount**	**Explanation**
Airfare to London	$ 420	6 business days/10 total days × $700.
Lodging in London	900	6 business days × $150 a day.
Meals	150	6 business days × $50 a day × 50% limit.
Rental car	420	6 business days × $70 a day.
Total business travel expenses	$1,890	

Rick is allowed to deduct $420 of the $700 airfare (60 percent) because he spent 6 of the 10 days on the trip conducting business activities.

Property Use   Several types of property may be used for both business and personal purposes. For example, business owners often use automobiles, computers, or cell phones for both business and personal purposes.[21] However, because expenses relating to these assets are deductible only to the extent the assets are used for business purposes, taxpayers must allocate the expenses between the business and personal use portions. The calculation of depreciation on mixed-use assets is discussed in the next chapter and with specific topics, such as the office in the home deduction.

Example 9-9

Rick occasionally uses his personal auto (a BMW) to drive to interviews with prospective clients and to drive back and forth between his shop and various work sites. This year Rick carefully recorded that the BMW was driven 567 miles for business activities and 10,500 miles in total. What expenses associated with the BMW may Rick deduct?

Answer: $306. Based on the standard mileage rate of 54 cents per mile, Rick can deduct $306 (567 × 54 cents) for business use of his BMW. Alternatively, Rick can track the operating expenses of the BMW (including depreciation) and deduct the business portion [based upon the percentage of business miles driven to total miles driven (567 business miles/10,500 total miles)].

When taxpayers use other business assets for both business and personal purposes, the deductible business expense is determined by prorating the expenses based upon the percentage of the time the asset is used for business purposes. For example, if a full year's expense for a business asset is $1,000, but the asset is only used for business purposes 90 percent of the time, then only $900 of expense can be deducted ($1,000 × 90%). Special rules apply when the business usage for an asset drops below 50 percent. We discuss these issues in the next chapter.

Record Keeping and Other Requirements   Because distinguishing business purposes from personal purposes is a difficult and subjective task, the tax laws include provisions designed to help the courts and the IRS determine the business element of mixed-motive transactions. Under these provisions, taxpayers must maintain specific, written, contemporaneous records (of time, amount, and business purpose) for mixed-motive expenses. For example, as we discussed above, the tax laws prohibit any deductions for business meals and entertainment unless substantial business discussions accompany the entertainment activity. Consequently, when taxpayers incur

[21]These types of assets are referred to as "listed property." Note that cell phones are specifically exempted from the definition of listed property [§280F(d)(4)(A), as amended by the 2010 Small Business Act §2043(a)].

meals and entertainment expenses, they must document the business purpose and the extent of the discussion to deduct any of the expenditures.[22]

LO 9-3 SPECIFIC BUSINESS DEDUCTIONS

As we discussed above, the tax code provides general guidelines for determining whether business expenditures are deductible. We learned that to be deductible, business expenditures must be ordinary, necessary, and reasonable in amount. In some cases, however, the tax laws identify specific items businesses are allowed to deduct. We discuss several of these deductions below.

Domestic Production Activities Deduction

Businesses that manufacture goods are allowed to deduct an *artificial* business deduction for tax purposes called the U.S. **domestic production activities deduction (DPAD).** This deduction is designed to reduce the tax burden on domestic manufacturers to make investments in domestic manufacturing facilities more attractive. The DPAD provides a special tax deduction for businesses, large and small, that "manufacture, produce, grow or extract" tangible products entirely or in significant part within the United States.[23] This deduction is artificial because it does not represent an expenditure per se, but merely serves to reduce the income taxes the business must pay and thereby increase the after-tax profitability of domestic manufacturing.

The formula for computing the DPAD is 9 percent times the *lesser* of (1) the business's taxable income before the deduction (or modified AGI for individuals) or (2) **qualified production activities income (QPAI).**[24] Generally speaking, QPAI is the *net* income from selling or leasing property that was manufactured in the United States. Thus, to compute QPAI, businesses need to determine the amount of revenues, cost of goods sold, and expenses attributable to U.S. production activities. Obviously, the calculation of the income allocable to domestic production can be exceedingly complex, especially in the case of large multinational businesses. The final deduction cannot exceed 50 percent of the wages the business paid to employees for working in qualifying production activities during the year.[25]

Example 9-10

This fall Rick constructed a greenhouse that qualified for the domestic production activities deduction. Rick received $5,000 for the construction project from his client and allocated $4,000 in expenses to the project. These expenses included $2,000 of qualified wages. Thus, the greenhouse project generated $1,000 of qualified production activity income (QPAI) for Rick ($5,000 minus $4,000). What is Rick's domestic production activities deduction for this project?

Answer: $90. Assuming Rick's QPAI of $1,000 is less than his modified AGI, the DPAD is $90, calculated by multiplying 9 percent times $1,000 of QPAI. The entire computation is summarized as follows:

---

[22]§274 requires substantiation of all elements of travel and entertainment including sufficient corroborating evidence. Although there are a few exceptions to this rule, approximations and estimates are generally not sufficient. Also, taxpayers must maintain records to deduct the business portion of mixed-use assets such as cars used for both business and personal purposes. Note that when the taxpayer is unable to substantiate other deductions, the court may estimate the deductible amount under the Cohan rule (*George Cohan v. Com.*, (1930, CA2), 39 F2d 540).

[23]§199 also allows this deduction for qualifying taxpayers in the domestic film and sound recording industries, those engaged in a construction business in the United States, and engineering and architectural firms providing services for U.S. construction projects. Because the domestic production activities deduction does not represent a real expenditure, the deduction is not an expense for financial accounting purposes.

[24]See §199(d)(2). Modified AGI is AGI before the DPAD and certain other specified deductions.

[25]Taxpayers report the deduction computations on Form 8903.

DPAD Calculation		
Description	**Amount**	**Explanation**
Qualified domestic gross receipts	$5,000	Must be a qualified activity.
Allocable costs and expenses	−4,000	Allocate to qualified activity.
Qualified production activity income	$1,000	Limited to modified AGI.
Statutory percentage	× 9%	
Domestic production activities deduction	$ 90	Limited to 50% of wages.

The 50 percent wage limitation is $1,000 (50% × $2,000 in wages Rick paid to employees working on the project). Thus, Rick is allowed to deduct the entire $90 domestic production activities deduction even though the $90 deduction doesn't represent a specific liability or payment to anyone.

TAXES IN THE REAL WORLD   Decorative Packaging as a Manufacturing Process

Houdini, Inc. designs, assembles, and sells gift baskets and gift "towers" (stacked decorative boxes of food). Houdini has two facilities and maintains about 300 employees and additional temporary workers during the holidays. Houdini selects gift baskets and the items to be placed inside, such as candy or wine, as well as the "void fill" that holds everything together. Houdini's Packaging Department takes food items that are in small, food-safe containers and places them in other packaging, such as a small, colorful box.

Houdini claimed the domestic production activities deduction contending that designing a gift basket is a complicated process that involves steps like determining appropriate container sizes and colors, selecting materials, ensuring quality control, and reviewing packaging. The IRS filed to recover the taxes relating to the DPAD deductions asserting that Houdini merely packaged the items in its gift baskets and towers. To qualify for the deduction, the gift baskets must be items

that are "manufactured, produced, grown, or extracted" (MPGE). The regulations hold that "packaging, repackaging, labeling, or minor assembly" doesn't qualify as MPGE but only if the taxpayer engages in no other MPGE activity.

The court determined that Houdini's production qualifies as manufacturing or producing, but also qualifies as packaging or repackaging. To reconcile this contradiction, the court found that Houdini's production process changes "the form of an article" under the regulations. Houdini uses assembly line workers and machines and ultimately produces a final product (i.e., a gift) that is distinct in form and purpose from the individual items inside (i.e., grocery-type items). The court rejected the IRS's argument that Houdini's packaging and repackaging are mere services. The court held that, rather than merely enhancing an existing product, Houdini creates a new product with a different demand.

U.S. v. Dean (DC CA), 112 AFTR 2d 2013-5164.

Losses on Dispositions of Business Property

Besides operating expenses, businesses are generally allowed to deduct losses incurred when selling or disposing of business assets.[26] The calculation of losses from business property dispositions can be complex, but the main idea is that businesses realize and recognize a loss when the asset's tax basis exceeds the sale proceeds. We will discuss the rules governing the tax treatment of gains and losses on asset disposition in more detail in Chapter 11.

[26]In most circumstances businesses may *not* deduct losses on assets sold to related parties. We describe who qualifies as a related party later in this chapter.

Example 9-11

What if: Assume that in late October, Rick purchased a used trailer to transport equipment to work sites. Rick bought the trailer for what he thought was a bargain price of $1,000. However, shortly after Rick acquired it, the axle snapped and was not repairable. Rick was forced to sell the trailer to a parts shop for $325. What amount can Rick deduct as a loss from the trailer sale?

Answer: $675, because the trailer was a business asset (amount realized of $325 minus adjusted basis of $1,000). (Note, as we discuss in the next chapter, Rick is not allowed to deduct depreciation on the trailer because he disposed of it in the same year he acquired it.)

Business Casualty Losses

Besides selling assets, businesses can incur losses when their assets are stolen, damaged, or completely destroyed by a force outside the control of the business. These events are called casualties.[27] Businesses may deduct **casualty losses** in the year the casualty occurs or in the year the theft of an asset is discovered. The amount of the loss deduction depends on whether the asset is (1) completely destroyed or stolen or (2) only partially destroyed. When its asset is *completely* destroyed or stolen, the business calculates the amount of the loss as though it sold the asset for the insurance proceeds, if any. That is, the loss is the amount of insurance proceeds minus the adjusted tax basis of the asset. If the asset is damaged but not completely destroyed, the amount of the loss is the amount of the insurance proceeds minus the *lesser* of (1) the asset's tax basis or (2) the decline in the value of the asset due to the casualty. While individuals deduct business casualty losses and casualty losses associated with rentals and royalties as deductions *for* AGI, casualty and theft losses of assets used for the production of income (investments) and personal-use assets are generally deductible as itemized deductions.[28] We summarize the casualty and theft loss rules for business, production of income, and personal-use assets in Exhibit 9-2, which appears on the following page.

Example 9-12

What if: Suppose Rick acquired a personal-use asset several years ago for $9,000. Suppose further that a casualty event destroyed the asset, and at that time the asset was worth $1,000 and insured for $250. What is the amount of Rick's casualty loss (before applying the per casualty floor and the AGI restriction)?

Answer: $750, computed as follows:

Insurance proceeds		$250
Minus the *lesser* of:		
(1) adjusted tax basis or	$9,000	
(2) value at time of casualty	1,000	−1,000
Casualty loss deduction (before limitations)		($750)

Suppose instead that Rick's asset was a business-use asset and Rick had deducted $4,000 of depreciation expense against the asset. Hence, the asset's tax basis was $5,000 ($9,000 − $4,000). What would be the amount of his business casualty loss?

Answer: $4,750, computed as follows:

Insurance proceeds	$ 250
Minus adjusted tax basis	−5,000
Casualty loss deduction	($4,750)

---

[27]Casualties are unexpected events driven by forces outside the control of the taxpayer that damage or destroy a taxpayer's property. Section 165 lists "fire, storm, and shipwreck" as examples of casualties.

[28]For example, a taxpayer with a coin collection that is stolen or valuable antique collection that burns is potentially eligible for a casualty loss deduction on assets used for the production of income. Under §165(h)(5), personal casualty losses are allowed to offset personal casualty gains in computing AGI.

EXHIBIT 9-2   **Comparison of Casualty and Theft Loss Rules for Property Used in Business, for Production of Income, and for Personal Purposes**

	Property Used in Business (including losses from rental and royalty property)	Property Used for the Production of Income	Property Used for Personal Purposes
Amount of loss if property completely destroyed or stolen	Insurance proceeds minus adjusted basis	Same as business	
Amount of loss if property is not completely destroyed	Insurance proceeds minus lesser of (1) adjusted basis or (2) decline in asset's value	Same as business	Same as business
Loss limitation	None	None	A per casualty floor limitation and 10 percent of AGI floor for total casualty losses for year.
Type of deduction	For AGI	Miscellaneous itemized deduction (not subject to 2 percent floor)	Itemized deduction

ACCOUNTING PERIODS

LO 9-4

So far we've discussed how to determine a business's income and how to determine its deductible business expenses. In this section, we will discuss accounting periods, which affect when taxpayers determine their income and deductions. Businesses must report their income and deductions over a fixed **accounting period** or **tax year.** A full tax year consists of 12 full months. A tax year can consist of a period less than 12 months (a short tax year) in certain circumstances. For instance, a business may report income for such a short year in its first year of existence (for example, it reports income on a calendar year-end and starts business after January 1) or in its final year of existence (for example, a calendar-year business ends its business before December 31). Short tax years in a business's initial or final year are treated the same as full years. A business may also have a short year when it changes its tax year, and this can occur when the business is acquired by new owners. In these situations, special rules may apply for computing the tax liability of the business.[29]

There are three types of tax years, each with different year-ends:

1. A calendar year ends on December 31.
2. A **fiscal year** that ends on the last day of a month other than December.
3. A 52/53-week year. This is a fiscal year that ends on the same day of the week every year. In other words, a 52/53-week fiscal year could end on the same day of the week that is the last such day in the month or on the same day of the week nearest the end of the month. For example, a business could adopt a 52/53-week fiscal year that (1) ends on the last Saturday in July each year or (2) ends on the Saturday closest to the end of July (although this Saturday might be in August rather than July).[30]

---

[29]§443. Discussion of tax consequences associated with these short years is beyond the scope of this text.

[30]Businesses with inventories may benefit from 52/53-week year-ends to facilitate an inventory count when the store is closed (e.g., over a weekend).

Not all types of tax years are available to all types of businesses. The rules for determining the tax years available to the business depends on whether the business is a sole proprietorship, a **flow-through entity,** or a C corporation. These rules are summarized as follows:

- *Sole proprietorships:* Because individual proprietors must report their business income on their individual returns, proprietorships use a calendar year-end to report their business income.[31]
- *Flow-through entities:* Partnerships and S corporations are flow-through entities (partners and S corporation owners report the entity's income directly on their own tax returns), and these entities generally must adopt tax years consistent with the owners' tax years.[32] Because owners are allocated income from flow-through entities on the last day of the entity's taxable year, the tax laws impose the tax year consistency requirement to minimize income tax deferral opportunities for the owners.
- *C corporations:* C corporations are generally allowed to select a calendar, fiscal, or 52/53-week year-end.

A business adopts a calendar year-end or fiscal year-end by filing its initial tax return. In contrast, a business adopts a 52/53-week year-end by filing a special election with the IRS. Once a business establishes its tax year, it generally must receive permission from the IRS to change.

Example 9-13

Rick is a calendar-year taxpayer. What tax year must Rick use to report income from his business Green Acres?

Answer: Calendar year. This is true even though Rick began his business in May of this year. He will calculate income and expense for his landscaping business over the calendar year and include the net business income from May through December of this year on Schedule C of his individual tax return.

What if: Suppose that Rick incorporated Green Acres at the time he began his business. What tax year could Green Acres adopt?

Answer: If Green Acres was operated as a C corporation, it could elect a calendar year-end, a fiscal year-end, or a 52/53-week year-end. If it were an S corporation, it likely would use a calendar year-end.

LO 9-5 ## ACCOUNTING METHODS

Once a business adopts a tax year, it must determine which items of income and deduction to recognize during a particular year. Generally speaking, the taxpayer's **accounting methods** determine the tax year in which a business recognizes a particular item of income or deduction. Because accounting methods affect the *timing* of when a taxpayer reports income and deductions, these methods are very important for taxpayers using a timing tax strategy to defer income or accelerate deductions.[33]

---

[31]Virtually all individual taxpayers use a calendar-year tax year.

[32]See §706 for the specific restrictions on year-ends for partnerships and §1378 for restrictions on S corporations. If they can show a business purpose (not easy to do), both partnerships and S corporations may adopt year-ends other than those used by their owners.

[33]Accounting methods do not determine *whether* an item of income is taxable or an expense is deductible. Accordingly, accounting methods generally do not affect the total income or deductions recognized over the lifetime of the business.

Financial and Tax Accounting Methods

Many businesses are required to generate financial statements for nontax reasons. For example, publicly traded corporations must file financial statements with the Securities and Exchange Commission (SEC) based on generally accepted accounting principles (GAAP). Also, privately owned businesses borrowing money from banks are often required to generate financial statements under GAAP, so that the lender can evaluate the business's creditworthiness. In reporting financial statement income, businesses have incentives to select accounting methods permissible under GAAP that accelerate income and defer deductions. In contrast, for tax planning purposes, businesses have incentives to choose accounting methods that *defer income* and *accelerate deductions*. This natural tension between financial reporting incentives and tax reporting incentives may be the reason the tax laws sometimes require businesses to use the same accounting methods for tax purposes that they use for financial accounting purposes. In other words, in many circumstances, if businesses want to defer taxable income, they must also defer book income.[34]

Sometimes the tax laws require businesses to use different, presumably more appropriate, accounting methods for tax purposes. Consequently, for policy and administrative reasons, the tax laws also identify several circumstances when businesses must use specific tax accounting methods to determine taxable income no matter what accounting method they use for financial reporting purposes. We will now turn our attention to accounting methods prescribed by the tax laws. With certain restrictions, businesses are able to select their *overall* accounting method and accounting methods for *specific* items or transactions. We will cover each of these in turn.

Overall Accounting Method

Businesses must choose an overall method of accounting to track and report their business activities for tax purposes. The overriding requirement for any tax accounting method is that the method must "clearly reflect income" and be applied consistently.[35] The two primary overall methods are the cash method and the accrual method. Businesses may also choose a hybrid method (some accounts on the cash method and others on the accrual method).

Cash Method A taxpayer (or business) using the cash method of accounting recognizes revenue when property or services are actually or constructively received. This is generally true no matter when the business sells the good or performs the service that generates the revenue. Likewise, a business adopting the cash method generally recognizes deductions when the expense is paid. Thus, the timing of the liability giving rise to the expense is usually irrelevant.

Keep in mind that a cash-method business receiving payments in *noncash* form (as property or services) must recognize the noncash payments as gross income. Also, in certain circumstances, a business expending cash on ordinary and necessary business expenses may not be allowed to *currently* deduct the expense at the time of the payment. For example, cash-method taxpayers (and accrual-method taxpayers) are not allowed to deduct prepaid interest expense and cannot usually deduct prepaid expenses or payments that create a tangible or intangible asset.[36] However, the regulations provide a **12-month rule** for prepaid business expenses to simplify the process of determining whether to capitalize or immediately expense payments that create benefits for a relatively brief period of time, such as insurance, security, rent, and

[34]§446(a). Businesses that use different accounting methods for book and tax must typically file a form M-1 that reconciles the results from the two accounting methods.
[35]§446(b).
[36]§461(g).

warranty service contracts. When a business prepays business expenses, it may *immediately* deduct the prepayment if (1) the contract period does not last more than a year *and* (2) the contract period does not extend beyond the end of the taxable year following the tax year in which the taxpayer makes the payment.[37] If the prepaid expense does not meet both of these criteria, the business must capitalize the prepaid amount and amortize it over the length of the contract whether the business uses the cash or accrual method of accounting.[38]

Example 9-14

On July 1 of this year, Rick paid $1,200 for a 12-month insurance policy that covers his business property from accidents and casualties from July 1 of this year, through June 30 of next year. How much of the $1,200 expenditure may Rick deduct this year if he uses the cash method of accounting for his business activities?

Answer: $1,200. Because the insurance coverage does not exceed 12 months and does not extend beyond the end of next year, Rick is allowed to deduct the entire premium payment under the 12-month rule.

What if: Suppose the insurance policy was for 12 months but the policy ran from February 1 of next year, through January 31 of the following year. How much of the expenditure may Rick deduct this year if he uses the cash method of accounting for his business activities?

Answer: $0. Even though the contract period is 12 months or less, Rick is required to capitalize the cost of the prepayment for the insurance policy because the contract period extends beyond the end of next year.

What if: Suppose Rick had paid $1,200 for an *18-month* policy beginning July 1 of this year and ending December 31 of next year. How much may he deduct this year if he uses the cash method of accounting for his business activities?

Answer: $400. In this scenario, because the policy exceeds 12 months, Rick is allowed to deduct the portion of the premium pertaining to this year. Hence, this year, he would deduct $400 [(6 months/18 months) × $1,200]. He would deduct the remaining $800 in the next year.

Accrual Method Businesses using the accrual method to determine taxable income follow rules similar to GAAP with two basic differences. First, as we discuss below, requirements for recognizing taxable income tend to be structured to recognize income earlier than the recognition rules for financial accounting. Second, requirements for accruing tax deductions tend to be structured to recognize less accrued expenses than the recognition rules for financial reporting purposes. These differences reflect the underlying objectives of financial accounting income and taxable income. The objective of financial accounting is to provide useful information to stakeholders such as creditors, prospective investors, and shareholders. Because financial accounting methods are designed to guard against businesses overstating their profitability to these users, financial accounting tends to bias against *overstating* income. In contrast, the government's main objective for writing tax laws is to collect revenues. Thus, tax accounting rules for accrual-method businesses tend to bias against *understating* income. These differences will become apparent as we describe tax accounting rules for businesses.

---

[37]This 12-month rule applies to both cash-method and accrual-method taxpayers. However, for accrual-method taxpayers to deduct prepaid expenses, they must meet both the 12-month rule requirements and the economic performance requirements that we discuss in the next section.

[38]Reg. §1.263(a)-4(f).

continued from page 9-1...

Rick's CPA, Jane, informed him that he needs to select an overall method of accounting for Green Acres to compute its taxable income. Jane advised Rick to use the cash method. However, Rick wanted to prepare GAAP financial statements and use the accrual method of accounting. He decided that if Green Acres was going to become a big business, it needed to act like a big business. Finally, after much discussion, Rick and Jane reached a compromise. For the first year, they would track Green Acres's business activities using both the cash *and* the accrual methods. In addition, they would also keep GAAP-based books for financial purposes. When filing time comes, Rick would decide which method to use in reporting taxable income. Jane told Rick that he could wait until he filed his tax return to select the accounting method for tax purposes. ■

Accrual Income

Businesses using the accrual method of accounting generally recognize income when they meet the all-events test.

All-Events Test for Income   The all-events test requires that businesses recognize income when (1) all events have occurred that determine or fix their right to receive the income and (2) the amount of the income can be determined with reasonable accuracy.[39] Assuming the amount of income can be determined with reasonable accuracy, businesses meet the all-events requirement on the *earliest* of the following three dates:

1. When they complete the task required to earn the income. Businesses earn income for services as they provide the services, and they generally earn income from selling property when the title of the property passes to the buyer.
2. When the payment for the task is due from the customer.
3. When the business receives payment for the task.

Example 9-15

In early fall, Rick contracted with a dozen homeowners to landscape their yards. Rick agreed to do the work for an aggregate of $11,000. Rick and his crew started in the fall and completed the jobs in December of this year. However, he didn't mail the bills until after the holidays and didn't receive any payments until the following January. When must Rick recognize the income from this work?

Answer: Under the accrual method, Rick must recognize the entire $11,000 as income this year because his right to the income is fixed when Rick and his crew had completed the work by year-end. Under the cash method, however, Rick would not recognize the $11,000 as income until next year when he received it.

Taxation of Advance Payments of Income (Unearned Income)

In some cases, businesses receive income payments *before* they actually earn the income (they receive a prepayment). *When* the business must recognize a prepayment as income depends on the type of income. The rule for interest and rental income is

[39]Reg. §1.451-1(a). The all-events test is sometimes called the "fixed and determinable" test because the right to payment must be fixed and the amount determinable with reasonable accuracy.

relatively strict. Businesses must recognize unearned rental and unearned interest income *immediately* upon receipt (the income is recognized before it is earned). However, businesses are not required to recognize security deposits received from rental customers because they incur a liability to return the deposits when they receive the payments.[40] The income recognition rules are less strict when businesses receive advance payments for services or goods.

Unearned Service Revenue   For financial reporting purposes, a business does not immediately recognize income on payments it receives for services to be provided in the future. For financial reporting purposes, an advance payment for services is recorded as a debit for cash received and a credit to a liability account (unearned income). The business then recognizes the *financial* income from the services as it performs the services. In contrast, for tax purposes, the all-events test generally requires businesses receiving *advance* payments for services to recognize the income when they receive the payment, rather than when they perform the services.

The IRS provides an exception to this immediate recognition general rule. Specifically, businesses receiving advance payments for services may *defer* recognizing the *prepayment* as income until the tax year *following* the year they receive the payment.[41] This one-year deferral does *not* apply (1) if (or the extent to which) the income is actually earned by the end of the year of receipt, (2) if the prepayment was included in financial reporting income, or (3) if the prepayment was for interest or rent (taxpayers must recognize unearned interest and rental income on receipt).

Advance Payment for Goods   When an accrual-method business receives an advance payment for *goods* it will provide to customers in the future, the business may account for the prepayment for tax purposes under the **full-inclusion method** or the **deferral method**.[42] A business electing the full-inclusion method will *immediately* recognize an advance payment as income. In contrast, a business using the deferral method will recognize advance payments for goods by the earlier of (1) when the business would recognize the income for tax purposes if it had not received the *advance* payment or (2) when it recognizes the income for financial reporting purposes. Thus, the deferral method is comparable to the deferral allowed for advance payments received for future services. However, unlike the treatment of advance payments for services, advance payments for goods could be deferred for more than a year if the business defers the income for financial reporting purposes for more than a year.

Example 9-16

In late November 2016, Rick received a $7,200 payment from a client for monthly landscaping services from December 1, 2016, through November 30, 2018 ($300 a month for 24 months). When must Rick recognize the income from the advance payment for services?

Answer: Under the accrual method, Rick would initially recognize the $300 income he earned in December 2016. In 2017, he would recognize the remaining $6,900 (rather than only the $3,600

---

[40]*Comm. v. Indianapolis Power & Light Co.* (1990), 493 US 203. Customer deposits required by a public utility weren't taxable income because the right to keep the deposits depended on events outside of the taxpayer's control, such as the decision to have the deposit applied to future bills.

[41]Rev Proc. 2004-34, 2004-1 CB 991.

[42]Reg. §1.451-5. This exception does not apply to goods held for sale in the ordinary course of business (inventory).

related to 2017) because he is not allowed to defer the prepayments for services for more than a year. Under the cash method, Rick must recognize the entire prepayment, $7,200, as income upon receipt in 2016.

What if: Suppose the $7,200 prepayment was for the delivery of 15 pallets of sod (not inventory) at a cost to Rick of $1,800. Suppose further that five pallets were to be delivered in 2017 and the remainder was to be delivered in 2018. When would Rick recognize the income from the advance payment of goods under the accrual method?

Answer: If Rick elected the full-inclusion method, then he would recognize the entire prepayment of $7,200 as income (minus his cost of goods sold of $1,800) in 2016. However, if Rick elected the deferral method, then he would recognize the income as the sod is delivered, $2,400 in 2017 (minus $600 cost of goods sold) and $4,800 in 2018 (minus $1,200 cost of goods sold).

Inventories

Many businesses generate income by selling products they acquire for resale or products they manufacture. When selling inventory is a material income-producing factor, a business generally must account for gross profit (sales minus cost of goods sold) using the accrual method, even if they are a cash-method taxpayer.

An exception to this general rule is that a cash-method business is allowed to use the cash method to account for gross profit if the average annual gross receipts for the three-year period prior to the current year do not exceed $10 million. In addition, the primary business activity must be to provide services to customers and the sales of products is a secondary or small part of its services.[43] However, the business is not allowed to deduct the cost of the inventory to the extent it has the product at the end of the year. How does this exception benefit a cash-method business if the business is not allowed to fully deduct the cost of inventory until it sells the inventory? It may be beneficial because it allows the business to use the cash method to account for sales revenue. Without the exception, cash-method service businesses would be required to account for sales revenue from inventory sales on the accrual method, which means they may be required to recognize revenue before they actually receive it. With the exception, they are allowed to defer the revenue recognition until they receive the payments from customers.

Businesses selling inventory must determine their inventory costs to accurately compute taxable income. This requires businesses to maintain records of balances for finished goods inventory and, if applicable, for partially finished goods and raw materials. Inventory costs include the purchase price of raw materials (minus any discounts), shipping costs, and any indirect costs it allocates to the inventory under the **uniform cost capitalization rules (UNICAP rules).**[44]

Uniform Capitalization   The tax laws require businesses to capitalize certain direct and indirect costs associated with inventories.[45] Congress enacted these rules primarily for two reasons. First, the rules accelerate tax revenues for the government by deferring deductions for the capitalized costs until the business sells the associated inventory. Thus, there is generally a one-year lag between when businesses initially capitalize the costs and when they deduct them. Second, Congress

> **THE KEY FACTS**
>
> **Inventories**
>
> - Businesses must use the accrual method to account for substantial inventories.
> - The UNICAP rules require capitalization of most indirect costs of production.
> - The LIFO method is allowed if also used for financial reporting purposes.

---

[43]Rev. Proc. 2002-28, 2002-1 CB 815. There are other exceptions to this general rule. For example, certain cash-method taxpayers (average annual receipts of $1 million or less) can qualify to account for merchandise for sale as materials and supplies under Rev. Proc. 2001-10, 2001-1 CB 272.

[44]Inventory valuation allowances are generally not allowed, but taxpayers can adopt the lower of cost or market method of inventory valuation. In addition, under certain conditions specific goods not salable at normal prices can be valued at bona fide selling prices less direct cost of disposition.

[45]§263A(a).

designed the "uniform" rules to reduce variation in the costs businesses include in inventory. Congress intended the UNICAP provisions to apply to manufacturers and large resalers. Consequently, businesses that resell personal property are not required to use the UNICAP rules if they report average annual gross receipts of $10 million or less over the three-year period ending with the taxable year prior to the current year.

Under these uniform cost capitalization rules, large businesses are generally required to capitalize more costs to inventory for tax purposes than they capitalize under financial accounting rules. Under GAAP, businesses generally include in inventory only those costs incurred within their production facility. In contrast, the UNICAP rules require businesses to allocate to inventory the costs they incur inside the production facility and the costs they incur outside the facility to support production (or inventory acquisition) activities. For example, under the UNICAP provisions, a business must capitalize at least a portion of the compensation paid to employees in its purchasing department, general and administrative department, and even its information technology department, to the extent these groups provide support for the production process. In contrast, businesses immediately expense these items as period costs for financial accounting purposes. The regulations provide guidance on the costs that must be allocated to inventory. Selling, advertising, and research are specifically identified as costs that do not have to be allocated to inventory under the UNICAP provisions.[46]

Example 9-17

What if: Green Acres sells trees but Rick anticipates selling flowers, shrubs, and other plants in future years. Ken is Rick's employee in charge of purchasing inventory. Ken's compensation this year is $30,000, and Rick estimates that Ken spends about 5 percent of his time acquiring inventory and the remaining time working on landscaping projects. How would Rick allocate Ken's compensation under the UNICAP rules?

Answer: If the UNICAP rules applied to Green Acres, Rick would allocate $1,500 ($30,000 × 5%) of Ken's compensation to the cost of the inventory Green Acres acquired this year. In contrast, Ken's entire salary would be expensed as a period cost for financial accounting purposes. (Note, however, because Green Acres's gross receipts for the year are under $10,000,000, it is not *required* to apply the UNICAP rules.)

Inventory Cost-Flow Methods   Once a business determines the cost of its inventory, it must use an inventory cost-flow method to determine its cost of goods sold. Three primary cost-flow methods are (1) first-in, first-out (**FIFO**), (2) last-in, first-out (**LIFO**), and (3) **specific identification.** Businesses might be inclined to use FIFO or LIFO methods when they sell similar, relatively low-cost, high-volume products such as cans of soup or barrels of oil. These methods simplify inventory accounting because the business need not track the individual cost of each item it sells. In contrast, businesses that sell distinct, relatively high-cost, low-volume products might be more likely to adopt the specific identification method. For example, jewelry and used-car businesses would likely use the specific identification method to account for their cost of sales. In general terms, when costs are increasing, a business using the FIFO method will report a higher gross margin than if it used the LIFO method. The opposite is true if costs are decreasing.

---

[46]Reg. §1.263A–1(e)(3)(iii).

Example 9-18

In late August, Rick purchased 10 oak saplings (immature trees) for a total purchase price of $3,000. In September, he purchased 12 more for a total price of $3,900, and in late October, he purchased 15 more for $5,000. The total cost of each lot of trees was determined as follows:

Purchase Date	Trees	Direct Cost	Other Costs	Total Cost
August 20	10	$ 3,000	$200	$ 3,200
September 15	12	3,900	300	4,200
October 22	15	5,000	400	5,400
Totals	37	$11,900	$900	$12,800

Before the end of the year, Green Acres sold 20 of the oak saplings (5 from the August lot, 5 from the September lot, and 10 from the October lot) for cash. What is Green Acres's gross profit from sales of oak saplings if the sales revenue totaled $14,000 (all collected by year-end), and what is its ending oak sapling inventory under the accrual and the cash method of accounting?

Answer: Under the accrual method, Green Acres's gross profit from sapling sales and its ending inventory balance for the remaining oak saplings under the FIFO, LIFO, and specific identification cost-flow methods is as follows:

	FIFO	LIFO	Specific ID
Sales	$14,000	$14,000	$14,000
Cost of goods sold	−6,700	−7,150	−6,950
Gross profit	$ 7,300	$ 6,850	$ 7,050
Ending inventory:			
August 20 trees	$ 0	$ 3,200	$ 1,600
September 15 trees	700	2,450	2,450
October 22 trees	5,400	0	1,800
Total ending inventory	$ 6,100	$ 5,650	$ 5,850

Using the cash method, the answer is the same as it is under the accrual method. Green Acres is not allowed to deduct the cost of its ending inventory even if it qualifies to use the cash method to account for gross profit under the small business ($10M) exception.

What if: Assume the same original facts except that Green Acres received $10,000 sales revenue from customers this year and the remaining $4,000 early next year. Assuming Green Acres qualifies to use the cash method to account for gross profit under the small business ($10M) exception, what is the amount of Green Acres's gross profit this year if it uses the specific identification method of accounting for its ending inventory?

Answer: $3,050 ($10,000 revenue minus $6,950 cost of goods sold). In this situation Green Acres would be allowed to defer $4,000 of the sales revenue until it collected it next year.

    When costs are subject to inflation over time, a business would get the best of both worlds if it adopted the FIFO method for financial reporting purposes and the LIFO method for tax purposes. Not surprisingly, the tax laws require that a business can use LIFO for tax purposes only if it also uses LIFO for financial reporting purposes.[47] While this "conformity" requirement may not matter to entities not required to generate financial reports, it can be very restrictive to publicly traded corporations.

[47]§472(c).

Accrual Deductions

Generally, when accrual-method businesses incur a liability relating to a business expense, they account for it by crediting a liability account (or cash if they pay the liability at the time they incur it) and debiting an expense account. However, to record an expense and the corresponding deduction for tax purposes, the business must meet (1) an **all-events test** for the liability *and* (2) an **economic performance test** with respect to the liability.[48] While the all-events test for recognizing deductions is similar to the all-events test for recognizing income, the additional economic performance requirement makes the deduction recognition rules more stringent than the income recognition rules. The deduction rules generally preclude businesses from deducting estimated expenses or reserves.

All-Events Test for Deductions   For a business to recognize a deduction, all events that establish its liability giving rise to the deduction must have occurred, and it must be able to determine the amount of the liability with reasonable accuracy.[49]

Example 9-19

On November of this year, Rick agreed to a one-year $6,000 contract with Ace Advertising to produce a radio ad campaign. Ace agreed that Rick would owe nothing under the contract unless his sales increase a minimum of 25 percent over the next six months. What amount, if any, may Rick deduct this year for this contract under the accrual and cash methods?

Answer: Under the accrual method, Green Acres is not allowed to recognize *any* deduction this year for the liability. Even though Ace will have completed two months of advertising for Green Acres by the end of the year, its guarantee means that Rick's liability is not fixed until and unless his sales increase by 25 percent. Under the cash method, Rick would not deduct any of the cost of the campaign this year because he has not paid anything to Ace.

Economic Performance   Even when businesses meet the all-events test, they still must clear the economic performance hurdle to recognize the tax deduction. Congress added the economic performance requirement because in some situations taxpayers claimed current deductions and delayed paying the associated cash expenditures for years. Thus, the delayed payment reduced the real (present value) cost of the deduction. This requirement specifies that businesses may not recognize a deduction for an expense until the underlying activity generating the associated liability has occurred. Thus, an accrual-method business would not be allowed to deduct a prepaid business expense even if it qualified to do so under the 12-month rule (discussed above) unless it also met the economic performance test with respect to the liability associated with the expense.

The specific requirements for the economic performance test differ based on whether the liability arose from

- Receiving goods or services *from* another party.
- Use of property.
- Providing goods or services *to* another party.
- Certain activities creating **payment liabilities.**

THE KEY FACTS

Accrual of Business-Expense Deductions

- Both all-events and economic performance are required for deducting accrued business expenses.
- The all-events test requires that the business be liable for the payment.
- Economic performance generally requires that underlying activity generating liability has occurred in order for the associated expense to be deductible.

[48]§461(h).
[49]§461.

Receiving goods and (or) services from another party. When a business agrees to pay another party for goods or services the other party will provide, the business deducts the expense associated with the liability only when the other party provides the goods or services (assuming the all-events test is met for the liability). An exception to this general rule occurs when a business hires another party to provide goods or services, and the business actually *pays* the liability before the other party provides the goods or services. In this circumstance, the business may treat the *actual payment* as economic performance as long as it *reasonably expects* the other party to provide the goods or all of the services within three and one-half months after the payment.[50]

Example 9-20

On December 15, 2016, Rick hires Your New Fence LLC (YNF) to install a concrete wall for one of his clients by paying $1,000 of the cost as a down payment and agreeing to pay the remaining $7,000 when YNF finishes the wall. YNF was not going to start building the wall until early 2017, so as of the end of the year Rick has not billed his client for the wall. Rick expects YNF to finish the wall by the end of April. What amount associated with his liability to YNF is Rick allowed to deduct in 2016 and 2017?

Answer: Under the accrual method, Rick is not entitled to a deduction in 2016. Rick will deduct his full $8,000 cost of the wall in 2017 when YNF builds the wall, because economic performance occurs as YNF provides the services, even though Rick paid for part of the goods and services in 2016. Under the cash method, Rick would deduct $1,000 (his down payment) in 2016 and the remainder in 2017 when he pays the remainder on the contract.

What if: Assume that Rick expected YNF to finish building the wall by the end of January 2017. What amount associated with this liability to YNF is Rick allowed to deduct in 2016 and 2017?

Answer: Under the accrual method, Rick is allowed to deduct $1,000 in 2016 because Rick actually paid this amount in 2016 and he reasonably expected YNF to finish its work on the wall within 3½ months after he made the payment to YNF on December 15. Rick would deduct the remaining $7,000 cost of the wall in 2017 when YNF builds the wall. Under the cash method, Rick deducts the $1,000 down payment in 2016 and the remaining $7,000 when he makes the payment in 2017.

Renting or leasing property from another party. When a business enters into an agreement to rent or lease property from another party, economic performance occurs over the rental period. Thus, the business is allowed to deduct the rental expense over the lease.

Example 9-21

On May 1, 2016, Rick paid $7,200 in advance to rent his shop for 12 months ($600 per month). What amount may Rick deduct for rent in 2016 if he accounts for his business activities using the accrual method?

Answer: $4,800 ($600 × 8 months use). Even though the rent is a prepaid business expense under the 12-month rule (the contract period is for 12 months and the contract period does not extend beyond 2017), he must deduct the rent expense over the term of the lease because that is when economic performance occurs.

What if: Assuming the original facts, what amount of the $7,200 rental payment may Rick deduct in 2016 if he is using the cash method of accounting for his business?

Answer: $7,200. In this case, Rick may deduct the expense under the 12-month rule. He does not have to meet the economic performance requirement to deduct the expense because the economic performance requirements apply to accrual—not cash-method taxpayers.

[50]Reg. §1.461-4(d)(6).

Example 9-22

On November 1, 2016, Rick paid $2,400 to rent a trailer for 24 months. What amount of this payment may Rick deduct and when may he deduct it?

Answer: Under the accrual method, even though Rick paid the entire rental fee in advance, economic performance occurs over the 24-month rental period. Thus, Green Acres deducts $200 for the trailer rental in 2016, $1,200 in 2017, and $1,000 in 2018. Because the rental period exceeds 12 months, the amount and timing of the deductions are the same under the cash method.

Providing goods and services to another party. Businesses liable for providing goods and services to other parties meet the economic performance test as they provide the goods or services that satisfy the liability.

Example 9-23

In the summer, Rick landscaped a city park. As part of this service, Rick agreed to remove a fountain from the park at the option of the city parks committee. In December 2016, the committee decided to have Rick remove the fountain. Rick began the removal in December and completed the removal in the spring of 2017. Rick paid a part-time employee $850 for the removal work in December and an additional $685 to complete the removal the following spring. What is the amount and timing of Rick's deductions for the removal project?

Answer: Under the accrual method, Rick is allowed to deduct his costs as he provides the services. Consequently, in 2016 Rick can deduct $850 for the cost of the services provided by his employee in 2016. In 2017, Rick can deduct the remaining $685 cost of the services provided by his employee in 2017. Under the cash method, the amount and timing of his deductions would be the same as it is under the accrual method.

Payment liabilities. Economic performance occurs for certain liabilities only when the business actually *pays* the liability. Thus, accrual-method businesses incurring payment liabilities are essentially on the *cash method* for deducting the associated expenses. Exhibit 9-3 describes different categories of these payment liabilities.

EXHIBIT 9-3   Categories of Payment Liabilities

Economic performance occurs when taxpayer pays liability associated with

- Worker's compensation, tort, breach of contract, or violation of law.
- Rebates and refunds.
- Awards, prizes, and jackpots.
- Insurance, warranties, and service contracts provided *to* the business. (Note: This is insurance, warranties, and product service contracts that cover the taxpayer and *not* a warranty that the taxpayer provides to others.)
- Taxes.[51]
- Other liabilities not provided for elsewhere.

Recurring item exception. One of the most common exceptions to economic performance is the **recurring item** exception. This exception is designed to minimize the cost of applying economic performance to relatively small expenses that occur on a regular basis. Under §461(h)(3), accrual method taxpayers can deduct certain accrued

---

[51]While taxes are generally not deducted until they are paid, §461(c) allows businesses to elect to accrue the deduction for real property taxes ratably over the tax period instead of deducting them when they actually pay them.

expenses even if economic performance has not occurred by year-end. A recurring item is a liability that is expected to persist in future years, and is either not material in amount or deducting the expense currently matches with revenue. In addition, the all-events test must be satisfied at year-end and actual economic performance must occur within a reasonable time after year-end (but prior to the filing of the tax return which could be up to 8½ months with an extension). As a final note, the recurring item exception does not apply to worker's compensation or tort liabilities.

Example 9-24

If clients are not completely satisfied with Green Acres's landscaping work, Rick offers a $200 refund with no questions asked. Near the end of 2016, Rick had four clients request refunds. Rick incurred the liability for the refunds this year. However, Rick was busy during the holiday season, so he didn't pay the refunds until January 2017. When should Rick deduct the customer refunds?

Answer: Because refunds are payment liabilities, economic performance does not occur until Rick actually pays the refunds. Consequently, Rick deducts the $800 of refunds in 2017 even though the liability for the refunds met the all-events test in 2016. Under the cash method, Rick would not deduct the refunds until he paid them in 2017.

What if: Suppose that Rick expected that $800 of refunds would typically be accrued at year-end. Under what conditions could Rick deduct the refunds in 2016 if he elects to use accrual accounting?

Answer: If the accrued refunds are not material in amount and Rick expects actual economic performance within a reasonable time after year-end (but not longer than 8½ months or filing of the tax return), then Rick can elect to deduct the refunds in 2016 using the recurring item exception.

Accrual-method taxpayers that prepay business expenses for *payment liabilities* (insurance contracts, warranties, and product service contracts provided to the taxpayer) are allowed to immediately deduct the prepayments subject to the 12-month rule for prepaid expenses. Thus, the deductible amounts for Rick's prepaid insurance contracts in Example 9-14 are the same for both the cash method and accrual method of accounting. Exhibit 9-4 describes the requirements for economic performance for the different types of liabilities.

EXHIBIT 9-4   **Economic Performance**

Taxpayer incurs liability from	Economic performance occurs
Receiving goods and services *from* another party	When the goods or services are provided to the taxpayer or with payment if the taxpayer reasonably expects actual performance within 3½ months.
Renting or leasing property *from* another party	Ratably over the time period during which the taxpayer is entitled to use the property or money.
Providing goods and services *to* another party	When the taxpayer incurs costs to satisfy the liability or provide the goods and services.
Activities creating "payment" liabilities	When the business actually makes payment.
Interest expense	As accrued. This technically does not fall within the economic performance rules but it is a similar concept.

Bad Debt Expense   When accrual method businesses sell a product or a service on credit, they debit accounts receivable and credit sales revenue for both financial and tax purposes. However, because businesses usually are unable to collect the full amount of their accounts receivable, they incur bad debt expense (a customer owes them a debt that the customer will not pay). For financial reporting purposes, the business estimates the amount of the bad debt, debits bad debt expense, and credits an allowance for doubtful accounts. However, for tax purposes, businesses are allowed to deduct bad debt expense only when the debt actually becomes worthless within the taxable year.[52] Consequently, for tax purposes, businesses determine which debts are uncollectible and write them off by debiting bad debt expense and *directly* crediting the actual account receivable account that is uncollectible. This required method of determining bad debt expense for tax purposes is called the **direct write-off method.** In contrast, the method used for financial reporting purposes is called the **allowance method.** Businesses reporting taxable income on the cash method of accounting are *not* allowed to deduct bad debt expenses, because they do not include receivables in taxable income (they do not credit revenue until they actually receive payment).

Example 9-25

At year-end, Rick estimates that about $900 of the receivables from his landscaping services will be uncollectible, but he has identified only one client, Jared, who will definitely not pay his bill. Jared, who has skipped town, owes Rick $280 for landscaping this fall. What amount of bad debt expense may Rick deduct for the year?

Answer: For financial reporting purposes, Rick recognizes a $900 bad debt expense. However, for tax purposes, under the accrual method, Rick can only deduct $280—the amount associated with specifically writing off Jared's receivable. Under the cash method, Rick would not be able to claim any deduction, because he did not receive a payment from Jared and thus did not recognize income on the amount Jared owed him.

Limitations on Accruals to Related Parties   To prevent businesses and related parties from working together to defer taxes, the tax laws prevent an accrual-method business from accruing (and deducting) an expense for a liability owed to a related party using the cash method until the related party recognizes the income associated with the payment.[53] For this purpose, related parties include

- Family members including parents, siblings, and spouses.
- Shareholders and C corporations when the shareholder owns more than 50 percent of the corporation's stock.[54]
- Owners of partnerships and S corporations no matter the ownership percentage.[55]

This issue frequently arises in situations in which a business employs the owner or a relative of an owner. The business is not allowed to deduct compensation expense owed to the related party until the year in which the related party includes the compensation in income. However, this related-party limit extends beyond compensation to *any* accrued expense the business owes to a related cash-method taxpayer.

Example 9-26

In December, Rick asked his retired father, Henry, to help him finish a landscaping job. By the end of 2016, Rick owed Henry $2,000 of (reasonable) compensation for his efforts, which he paid in January 2017. What amount of this compensation may Rick deduct and when may he deduct it?

Answer: If Rick uses the accrual method and Henry the cash method, Rick will not be able to deduct the $2,000 compensation expense until 2017. Rick is Henry's son, so Rick and Henry are "related" parties for tax purposes. Consequently, Rick can deduct the compensation only when Henry includes the payment in his taxable income in 2017. If Rick uses the cash method, he will deduct the expense when he pays it in January 2017.

---

[52]§166(a).

[53]§267(a).

[54]Certain constructive ownership rules apply in determining ownership percentages for this purpose. See §267(c).

[55]See §267(b) for related-party definitions.

Comparison of Accrual and Cash Methods

From a business perspective, the two primary advantages of adopting the cash method over the accrual method are that (1) the cash method provides the business with more flexibility to time income and deductions by accelerating or deferring payments (timing tax planning strategy) and (2) bookkeeping for the cash method is easier. For example, a cash-method taxpayer could defer revenue by waiting to bill clients for goods or services until after year-end, thereby increasing the likelihood that customers would send payment after year-end. There are some concerns with this tax strategy. For example, delaying the bills might increase the likelihood that the customers will not pay their bills at all.

The primary advantage of the accrual method over the cash method is that it better matches revenues and expenses. For that reason, external financial statement users who want to evaluate a business's financial performance prefer the accrual method. Consistent with this idea, the cash method is not allowed for financial reporting under GAAP.

Although the cash method is by far the predominate accounting method among sole proprietors, it is less common in other types of businesses. In fact, tax laws generally prohibit C corporations and partnerships with corporate partners from using the cash method of accounting.[56] Exhibit 9-5 details the basic differences in accounting for income and deductions under the accrual and the cash method of accounting.

EXHIBIT 9-5   **Comparison of Cash and Accrual Methods**

Income or Expense Item	Cash Method	Accrual Method
Income recognition	Actually or constructively received.	Taxable once the all-events test is satisfied.
Unearned rental and interest income	Taxable on receipt.	Taxable on receipt.
Advance payment for services	Taxable on receipt.	Taxed when received or under the deferral method in the following year of receipt if not earned by end of year of receipt.
Advance payment for goods	Taxable on receipt.	Full-inclusion is taxed on receipt but deferral election allows taxation when earned.
Deduction recognition	Deduct when paid; economic performance does not apply.	Deduct once all-events test and economic performance test are both satisfied.
Expenditures for tangible assets with a useful life more than one year	Capitalize and apply cost recovery.	Same as the cash method.
Expenditures for intangible assets other than prepaid business expenses	Capitalize and amortize if provision in code allows it.	Same as the cash method.
Prepaid business expenses	Immediately deductible unless contract period exceeds 12 months or extends beyond the end of the next taxable year.	Same as cash method for payment liabilities; otherwise, apply all-events and economic performance tests to ascertain when to capitalize and amortize.
Prepaid interest expense	Not deductible until interest accrues.	Same as the cash method.
Bad debt expense	Not deductible because sales on account not included in income.	Deduct under direct write-off method.

[56]These entities are able to adopt the cash method if their average annual gross receipts for the three tax years ending with the prior tax year do not exceed $5 million (see §448).

Example 9-27

At year-end, Rick determined that Green Acres had collected a total of $71,000 of service revenue (not described elsewhere in examples). Rick is debating whether to adopt the cash or accrual method. To help him resolve his dilemma, Jane includes these revenues in a calculation of Green Acres's taxable income under the cash and accrual methods (Exhibit 9-6). What are the differences between the two calculations?

Answer: Jane provided the following summary of the differences between taxable income under the cash method and taxable income under the accrual method:

Description	(1) Cash	(2) Accrual	(1) – (2) Difference	Example
Revenue:				
Credit sales	0	11,000	−11,000	9-15
Prepaid revenue	7,200	300	+6,900	9-16
Expenses:				
Prepaid services	−1,000	0	−1,000	9-20
Prepaid rent expense	−7,200	−4,800	−2,400	9-21
Bad debts	0	−280	+280	9-25
Total difference (accrual income > cash income)			−7,220	

Jane explains that by comparing the revenue and expenses recognized under the two accounting methods, the selection of the accrual method for Green Acres means that Rick will be taxed on an additional $7,220 of income this year than if Green Acres adopts the cash method.

The business income for Green Acres under the accrual and cash methods is summarized in Exhibit 9-6. After reflecting on these numbers and realizing that he would recognize $7,220 more taxable income (and self-employment income subject to self-employment tax) this year under the accrual method than under the cash method, Rick determined it made sense to adopt the cash method of accounting for Green Acres's first tax return. Meanwhile, he knew he had to include Green Acres's business income on Schedule C of his individual tax return. Exhibit 9-7 presents Rick's Schedule C for Green Acres using the cash method of accounting.

Adopting an Accounting Method

We've seen that businesses use overall accounting methods (cash, accrual, or hybrid) and many specific accounting methods (inventory cost-flow assumption, methods of accounting for prepaid income for goods, and methods for accounting for prepaid expenses, among other methods) to account for their business activities. For tax purposes, it's important to understand how and when a business technically *adopts* an accounting method because once it does so, it must get the IRS's permission to change the method.

Businesses generally elect their accounting methods by using them on their tax returns. However, *when* the business technically adopts a method depends on whether it is a **permissible accounting method** or an **impermissible accounting method.** So far, our discussion has emphasized accounting methods permissible under the tax laws. A business adopts a permissible accounting method by using and reporting the tax results of the method for at least one year. However, businesses may

EXHIBIT 9-6   **Green Acres's Net Business Income**

Description	Cash	Accrual	Example
Income			
Service revenue:			
Greenhouse construction	$ 5,000	$ 5,000	9-10
December landscape service	0	11,000	9-15
Prepaid landscape services	7,200	300	9-16
Landscaping revenue	71,000	71,000	9-27
Sales of inventory:			
Tree sales	14,000	14,000	9-18
Cost of goods sold (LIFO method)	−7,150	−7,150	9-18
Gross Profit	**$90,050**	**$94,150**	
Car and truck expense:			
SUV operating expense	$ 5,335	$ 5,335	9-7
BMW operating expense	306	306	9-9
Insurance	1,200	1,200	9-14
Rent			
Shop	7,200	4,800	9-21
Trailer	200	200	9-22
Travel, meals, and entertainment:			
Travel to NY seminar	1,435	1,435	9-8
Dinner and theater with client	270	270	9-6
Wages and subcontractor fees:			
Part-time employees	23,000	23,000	9-2
Full-time employee (Ken)	30,000	30,000	9-17
Fountain removal (part-time employee)	850	850	9-23
Fence installation (prepaid subcontractor)	1,000	0	9-20
Other expenses:			
Education—meditation class	50	50	9-1
Education—seminar	300	300	9-8
Domestic production activities deduction	90	90	9-10
Uniforms	500	500	9-5
Bad debts	0	280	9-25
Other expenses not in examples:			
Advertising	1,100	1,100	
Depreciation	4,000	4,000	
Interest	300	300	
Legal and professional services	1,100	1,100	
Office expense	1,500	1,500	
Repairs and maintenance	1,975	1,975	
Taxes and licenses	400	400	
Utilities	2,200	2,200	
Total deductions	**$84,311**	**$81,191**	
Net Business Income	**$ 5,739**	**$12,959**	

unwittingly (or intentionally) use impermissible accounting methods. For example, a business using the allowance method for determining bad debt expense for tax purposes is using an impermissible accounting method because the tax laws prescribe the use of the direct write-off method for determining bad debt expense. A business *adopts* an *impermissible* method by using and reporting the results of the method for *two consecutive years*.

EXHIBIT 9-7 **Green Acres Schedule C**

SCHEDULE C (Form 1040) Department of the Treasury Internal Revenue Service (99)	**Profit or Loss From Business** (Sole Proprietorship) ▶ Information about Schedule C and its separate instructions is at *www.irs.gov/schedulec*. ▶ **Attach to Form 1040, 1040NR, or 1041; partnerships generally must file Form 1065.**	OMB No. 1545-0074 20**15** Attachment Sequence No. **09**

Name of proprietor	Social security number (SSN)
RICK GRIME	000-00-0000

A	Principal business or profession, including product or service (see instructions)	**B** Enter code from instructions
	LANDSCAPER	▶ 5 7 1 6 3 0
C	Business name. If no separate business name, leave blank.	**D** Employer ID number (EIN), (see instr.)
	GREEN ACRES LANDSCAPING	4 6 0 0 0 0 0 0 0
E	Business address (including suite or room no.) ▶ BUCKSNORT STREE	
	City, town or post office, state, and ZIP code SAN ANTONIO, TEXAS 78208 ▶	

F	Accounting method: **(1)** ☑ Cash **(2)** ☐ Accrual **(3)** ☐ Other (specify) ▶ _____
G	Did you "materially participate" in the operation of this business during 2015? If "No," see instructions for limit on losses . ☑ Yes ☐ No
H	If you started or acquired this business during 2015, check here . . . . ▶ ☑
I	Did you make any payments in 2015 that would require you to file Form(s) 1099? (see instructions) . . . . . . ☐ Yes ☑ No
J	If "Yes," did you or will you file required Forms 1099? . . . . ☐ Yes ☐ No

Part I **Income**

1	Gross receipts or sales. See instructions for line 1 and check the box if this income was reported to you on Form W-2 and the "Statutory employee" box on that form was checked . . . . ▶ ☐	**1**	97,200
2	Returns and allowances	**2**	
3	Subtract line 2 from line 1	**3**	97,200
4	Cost of goods sold (from line 42)	**4**	7,150
5	**Gross profit.** Subtract line 4 from line 3	**5**	90,050
6	Other income, including federal and state gasoline or fuel tax credit or refund (see instructions)	**6**	
7	**Gross income.** Add lines 5 and 6 . . . . ▶	**7**	90,050

Part II **Expenses. Enter expenses for business use of your home only on line 30.**

8	Advertising	**8**	1,100	**18**	Office expense (see instructions)	**18**	1,500
9	Car and truck expenses (see instructions)	**9**	5,641	**19**	Pension and profit-sharing plans .	**19**	
				20	Rent or lease (see instructions):		
10	Commissions and fees .	**10**		**a**	Vehicles, machinery, and equipment	**20a**	7,400
11	Contract labor (see instructions)	**11**	1,000	**b**	Other business property . . .	**20b**	
12	Depletion	**12**		**21**	Repairs and maintenance . . .	**21**	1,975
13	Depreciation and section 179 expense deduction (not included in Part III) (see instructions)	**13**	4,000	**22**	Supplies (not included in Part III) .	**22**	
				23	Taxes and licenses	**23**	400
				24	Travel, meals, and entertainment:		
14	Employee benefit programs (other than on line 19) . .	**14**		**a**	Travel	**24a**	1,435
15	Insurance (other than health)	**15**	1,200	**b**	Deductible meals and entertainment (see instructions)	**24b**	270
16	Interest:			**25**	Utilities	**25**	2,200
a	Mortgage (paid to banks, etc.)	**16a**	300	**26**	Wages (less employment credits) .	**26**	53,850
b	Other	**16b**		**27a**	Other expenses (from line 48) . .	**27a**	940
17	Legal and professional services	**17**	1,100	**b**	**Reserved for future use** . . .	**27b**	

28	**Total expenses** before expenses for business use of home. Add lines 8 through 27a . . . . . . ▶	**28**	84,311
29	Tentative profit or (loss). Subtract line 28 from line 7	**29**	5,739
30	Expenses for business use of your home. Do not report these expenses elsewhere. Attach Form 8829 unless using the simplified method (see instructions). **Simplified method filers only:** enter the total square footage of: (a) your home: _____ and (b) the part of your home used for business: _____ . Use the Simplified Method Worksheet in the instructions to figure the amount to enter on line 30	**30**	
31	**Net profit or (loss).** Subtract line 30 from line 29. • If a profit, enter on both **Form 1040, line 12** (or **Form 1040NR, line 13**) and on **Schedule SE, line 2.** (If you checked the box on line 1, see instructions). Estates and trusts, enter on **Form 1041, line 3.** • If a loss, you **must** go to line 32.	**31**	5,739
32	If you have a loss, check the box that describes your investment in this activity (see instructions). • If you checked 32a, enter the loss on both **Form 1040, line 12,** (or **Form 1040NR, line 13**) and on **Schedule SE, line 2.** (If you checked the box on line 1, see the line 31 instructions). Estates and trusts, enter on **Form 1041, line 3.** • If you checked 32b, you **must** attach **Form 6198.** Your loss may be limited.	**32a** ☐ All investment is at risk. **32b** ☐ Some investment is not at risk.	

For Paperwork Reduction Act Notice, see the separate instructions.	Cat. No. 11334P	Schedule C (Form 1040) 2015

Changing Accounting Methods

Once a business has adopted an accounting method, it must receive permission to change the method, regardless of whether it is a permissible or an impermissible method. A taxpayer requests permission to change accounting methods by filing Form 3115 with the IRS. The IRS automatically approves certain types of accounting method changes, but for others the business must provide a good business purpose for the change and pay a fee. The IRS also requires permission when a business must change from using an impermissible method; this requirement helps the IRS to certify that the business properly makes the transition to a permissible method. In essence, the IRS requires the business to report its own noncompliance. Why would a business do so? Besides complying with the tax laws, a business might report its own noncompliance to receive leniency from the IRS. Without getting into the details, the IRS is likely to assess fewer penalties and less interest expense for noncompliance when the business reports the noncompliance before the IRS discovers it on its own.

Tax Consequences of Changing Accounting Method   When a business changes from one accounting method to another, the business determines its taxable income for the year of change using the new method. Furthermore, the business must make an adjustment to taxable income that effectively represents the *cumulative difference,* as of the beginning of the tax year, between the amount of income (or deductions) recognized under the old accounting method and the amount that would have been recognized for all prior years if the new method had been applied. This adjustment is called a **§481 adjustment.** The §481 adjustment prevents the duplication or omission of items of income or deduction due to a change in accounting method. If the §481 adjustment *increases* taxable income, the taxpayer recognizes it over *four years* beginning with the year of the change (25 percent of the full adjustment each year).[57] If the adjustment *decreases* taxable income, the taxpayer recognizes it *entirely in the year of change.*

Example 9-28

What if: Suppose that at the end of 2016, Green Acres has $24,000 of accounts receivable. Assuming Green Acres uses the cash method of accounting in 2016, it would not include the $24,000 of receivables in income in determining its 2016 taxable income. Suppose further that Rick decides to switch Green Acres to the accrual method of accounting in 2017 by filing a Form 3115 and receiving permission from the IRS. What is Rick's §481 adjustment for his change in accounting method from the cash to the accrual method?

Answer: $24,000 increase to income ($6,000 in 2017 and each of the subsequent three years). Since Rick would use the accrual method in 2017, he would *not* include payments he receives for the $24,000 receivables as income because he earned this income in 2016 (not 2017). Instead, Rick would be required to make a §481 adjustment to ensure that he does not *omit* these items from taxable income. His total §481 adjustment is to increase net income by $24,000. Because this is an income-increasing adjustment, Rick includes $6,000 of the adjustment (25 percent) in Green Acres's taxable income in 2017. He would likewise include a $6,000 §481 adjustment in each of the subsequent three years.

What if: Suppose that at the end of 2016, Green Acres has $4,000 of accounts payable instead of $24,000 of accounts receivable. What is Rick's §481 adjustment for his change in accounting method from the cash to the accrual method?

Answer: In this instance Green Acres would have a negative (income-decreasing) §481 adjustment of $4,000 because the $4,000 of expenses would have accrued in 2016 but would not have been deducted. Hence, Green Acres would be entitled to deduct the full $4,000 as a negative §481 adjustment amount in 2017.

---

[57]Taxpayers with positive §481 adjustments less than $25,000 can elect to recognize the entire amount in the year of change. Rev. Proc. 2002-19, 2002 IRB 696.

CONCLUSION

This chapter discussed issues relating to business income and deductions. We learned that the income rules for businesses are very similar to those for individuals, and that businesses may deduct only ordinary and necessary business expenses and other business expenses specifically authorized by law. We also described several business expense limitations and discussed the accounting periods and methods businesses may use in reporting taxable income to the IRS. The issues described in this chapter are widely applicable to all types of business entities including sole proprietorships, partnerships, S corporations, and C corporations. In the next chapter, we determine how businesses recover the costs of assets they use in their business activities.

Summary

LO 9-1 Describe the general requirements for deducting business expenses and identify common business deductions.

- Ordinary and necessary business expenses are allowed as deductions to calculate net income from activities entered into with a profit motive.
- Only reasonable amounts are allowed as business expense deductions. Extravagant or excessive amounts are likely to be characterized by personal motives and are disallowed.

LO 9-2 Apply the limitations on business deductions to distinguish between deductible and nondeductible business expenses.

- The law specifically prohibits deducting expenses against public policy (such as fines or bribes) and expenses that produce tax-exempt income.
- Expenses benefiting multiple periods must be capitalized and special limits and record-keeping requirements are applied to business expenses that may have personal benefits, such as entertainment and meals.

LO 9-3 Identify and explain special business deductions specifically permitted under the tax laws.

- Special calculations are necessary for deductions such as bad debt expenses, the domestic production activities deduction, and casualty losses.

LO 9-4 Explain the concept of an accounting period and describe accounting periods available to businesses.

- Accounting periods and methods are chosen at the time of filing the first tax return.
- There are three types of tax years—calendar year, fiscal year, and 52/53-week year—and each tax year is distinguished by year-end.

LO 9-5 Identify and describe accounting methods available to businesses and apply cash and accrual methods to determine business income and expense deductions.

- Under the cash method, taxpayers recognize revenue when they actually or constructively receive property or services and recognize deductions when they actually pay the expense.
- Under the accrual method, the all-events test requires that income be recognized when all the events have occurred that are necessary to fix the right to receive payments and the amount of the payments can be determined with reasonable accuracy.
- The accrual method must be used to account for sales and purchases for businesses where inventories are an income-producing factor.
- Under the accrual method, accrued expenses can only be deducted once both the all-events test and the economic performance tests are met. The application of the economic performance test depends, in part, on the type of business expense.
- Changes in accounting method or accounting period typically require the consent of the IRS and a §481 adjustment to taxable income. A negative adjustment is included in income for the year of change whereas a positive adjustment is spread over four years.

KEY TERMS

12-month rule (9-17)	economic performance test (9-24)	personal expenses (9-7)
accounting method (9-16)	FIFO (9-22)	qualified production activities income
accounting period (9-15)	fiscal year (9-15)	(QPAI) (9-12)
all-events test (9-24)	flow-through entities (9-16)	reasonable in amount (9-4)
allowance method (9-28)	full-inclusion method (9-20)	recurring item (9-26)
arm's-length amount (9-4)	impermissible accounting method (9-30)	§481 adjustment (9-33)
casualty losses (9-14)	LIFO (9-22)	specific identification (9-22)
deferral method (9-20)	mixed-motive expenditures (9-8)	tax year (9-15)
direct write-off method (9-28)	ordinary and necessary (9-3)	travel expenses (9-9)
domestic production activities	payment liabilities (9-24)	uniform cost capitalization rules
deduction (DPAD) (9-12)	permissible accounting method (9-30)	(UNICAP rules) (9-21)

DISCUSSION QUESTIONS

Discussion Questions are available in *Connect*®.   connect

1. What is an "ordinary and necessary" business expenditure?   `LO 9-1`

2. Is cost of goods sold deductible as a business expense for a business selling inventory? Explain.   `LO 9-1`

3. Tom is an attorney who often represents individuals injured while working (worker liability claims). This year Tom spent $50 on a book entitled *Plumbing for Dummies* and paid $500 to take a course on plumbing residences and rental housing. Can you imagine circumstances in which these expenditures would be deductible as "ordinary and necessary" for an attorney? Explain.   `LO 9-1`

4. Jake is a professional dog trainer who purchases and trains dogs for use by law enforcement agencies. Last year Jake purchased 500 bags of dog food from a large pet food company at an average cost of $30 per bag. This year, however, Jake purchased 500 bags of dog food from a local pet food company at an average cost of $45 per bag. Under what circumstances would the IRS likely challenge the cost of Jake's dog food as unreasonable?   `LO 9-1`

5. What kinds of deductions are prohibited as a matter of public policy? Why might Congress deem it important to disallow deductions for expenditures against public policy?   `LO 9-2`

6. Provide an example of an expense associated with the production of tax-exempt income, and explain what might happen if Congress repealed the prohibition against deducting expenses incurred to produce tax-exempt income.   `LO 9-2`

7. Jerry is a self-employed rock star and this year he expended $1,000 on special "flashy" clothes and outfits. Jerry would like to deduct the cost of these clothes as work-related because the clothes are not acceptable to Jerry's sense of fashion. Under what circumstances can Jerry deduct the cost of these work clothes?   `LO 9-2`   research

8. Jimmy is a sole proprietor of a small dry-cleaning business. This month Jimmy paid for his groceries by writing checks from the checking account dedicated to the dry-cleaning business. Why do you suppose Jimmy is using his business checking account rather than his personal checking account to pay for personal expenditures?   `LO 9-2`

9. Tim employs three sales representatives who often take clients to dinner and provide entertainment in order to increase sales. This year Tim reimbursed the representatives $2,500 for the cost of meals and $8,250 for the cost of   `LO 9-2`

entertaining clients. Describe the conditions under which Tim can claim deductions for meals and entertainment.

LO 9-2 10. Jenny uses her car for both business and personal purposes. She purchased the auto this year and drove 11,000 miles on business trips and 9,000 miles for personal transportation. Describe how Jenny will determine the amount of deductible expenses associated with the auto.

LO 9-1 **LO 9-2** 11. What expenses are deductible when a taxpayer combines both business and personal activities on a trip? How do the rules for international travel differ from the rules for domestic travel?

LO 9-2 12. Clyde lives and operates a sole proprietorship in Dallas, Texas. This year Clyde found it necessary to travel to Fort Worth (about 25 miles away) for legitimate business reasons. Is Clyde's trip likely to qualify as "away from home," and why would this designation matter?

LO 9-2 13. Describe the record-keeping requirements for business deductions expenses including mixed-motive expenditures.

LO 9-3 14. Explain why the domestic production activities deduction is sometimes described as an "artificial" expense and the apparent rationale for this deduction. How might a business begin to determine the domestic portion of revenues and expenses for products that are assembled in the United States from parts made overseas?

LO 9-3 15. Describe the calculation of the domestic production activities deduction.

LO 9-3 16. Describe the limits placed on the domestic production activities deduction, and explain the apparent reason for each limitation.

LO 9-3 17. Explain the difference between calculating a loss deduction for a business asset that was partially damaged in an accident and a loss deduction for a business asset that was stolen or completely destroyed in an accident.

LO 9-3 18. How do casualty loss deductions differ when a business asset is completely destroyed as opposed to the destruction of a personal-use asset?

LO 9-4 19. What is the difference between a full tax year and a short tax year? Describe circumstances in which a business may have a short tax year.

LO 9-4 20. Explain why a taxpayer might choose one tax year over another if given a choice.

LO 9-4 21. Compare and contrast the different year-ends available to sole proprietorships, flow-through entities, and C corporations.

LO 9-4 22. Why does the law generally require partnerships to adopt a tax year consistent with the year used by the partners?

LO 9-4 23. How does an entity choose its tax year? Is it the same process no matter the type of tax year-end the taxpayer adopts?

LO 9-5 24. Explain when an expenditure should be "capitalized" rather than expensed based upon accounting principles. From time to time, it is suggested that all business expenditures should be expensed for tax purposes. Do you agree with this proposition, and if so, why?

LO 9-5 25. Describe the 12-month rule for determining whether and to what extent businesses should capitalize or immediately deduct prepaid expenses such as insurance or security contracts. Explain the apparent rationale for this rule.

LO 9-5 26. Explain why Congress sometimes mandates that businesses use particular accounting methods while other times Congress is content to require businesses to use the same accounting methods for tax purposes that they use for financial accounting purposes.

LO 9-5 27. Why is it not surprising that specific rules differ between tax accounting and financial accounting?

28. Fred is considering using the accrual method for his next business venture. Explain to Fred the conditions for recognizing income for tax purposes under the accrual method. **LO 9-5**

29. Describe the all-events test for determining income and describe how to determine the date on which the all-events test has been met. **LO 9-5**

30. Compare and contrast the tax treatment for rental income received in advance and advance payments for services. **LO 9-5**

31. Compare and contrast the rules for determining the tax treatment of advance payments for services versus advance payments for goods. **LO 9-5**

32. Jack operates a plumbing business as a sole proprietorship on the cash method. Besides providing plumbing services, Jack also sells plumbing supplies to homeowners and other plumbers. The sales of plumbing supplies constitute less than $20,000 per year, and this is such a small portion of Jack's income that he does not keep physical inventories for the supplies. Describe the conditions in which Jack must account for sales and purchases of plumbing supplies on the accrual method. **LO 9-5** **research**

33. Explain why Congress enacted the UNICAP rules and describe the burdens these rules place on taxpayers. **LO 9-5**

34. Compare and contrast financial accounting rules with the tax rules under UNICAP (§263A). Explain whether the UNICAP rules tend to accelerate or defer income relative to the financial accounting rules. **LO 9-5**

35. Compare and contrast the tests for accruing income and those for accruing deductions for tax purposes. **LO 9-5**

36. Compare and contrast when taxpayers are allowed to deduct amounts for warranties provided by others to the taxpayer and when taxpayers are allowed to deduct expenses associated with warranties they provide to others. **LO 9-5**

37. Describe when economic performance occurs for the following expenses: **LO 9-5**
    Worker's compensation
    Rebates and refunds
    Insurance, warranties, and service contracts provided *to* the business
    Taxes

38. On December 31 of the current year, a taxpayer prepays an advertising company to provide advertising services for the next 10 months. Using the 12-month rule and the economic performance rules, contrast when the taxpayer would be able to deduct the expenditure if the taxpayer uses the cash method of accounting versus if the taxpayer uses the accrual method of accounting. **LO 9-5**

39. Compare and contrast how bad debt expense is determined for financial accounting purposes and how the deduction for bad debts is determined for accrual-method taxpayers. How do cash-method taxpayers determine their bad debt expense for accounts receivable? **LO 9-5**

40. Describe the related-party limitation on accrued deductions. What tax savings strategy is this limitation designed to thwart? **LO 9-5**

41. What are the relative advantages of the cash and accrual methods of accounting? **LO 9-5**

42. Describe how a business adopts a permissible accounting method. Explain whether a taxpayer can adopt an impermissible accounting method. **LO 9-5**

43. Describe why the IRS might be skeptical of permitting requests for changes in accounting method without a good business purpose. **LO 9-5**

44. What is a §481 adjustment and what is its purpose? **LO 9-5**

PROBLEMS

Select problems are available in *Connect*®.　■connect

LO 9-1 45. Manny hired his brother's firm to provide accounting services to his business. During the current year, Manny paid his brother's firm $82,000 for services even though other firms were willing to provide the same services for $40,000. How much of this expenditure, if any, is deductible as an ordinary and necessary business expenditure?

LO 9-1 LO 9-2 46. Indicate the amount (if any) that Michael can deduct as ordinary and necessary business deductions in each of the following situations and explain your solution.
a) From time to time, Michael rents a dump truck for his business. While hauling gravel to a job site, Michael was stopped for speeding. He paid a fine of $125 for speeding and a fine of $80 for carrying an overweight load.
b) Michael paid a part-time employee $750 to drive his rented dump truck. Michael reimbursed the employee $35 for gasoline for the truck.
c) Michael gave a member of the city council a new watch, which cost $200. He hopes that the city councilman will "throw" some contracts to his business.

LO 9-1 LO 9-2 47. Indicate the amount (if any) that Josh can deduct as ordinary and necessary business deductions in each of the following situations and explain your solution.
a) Josh borrowed $50,000 from the First State Bank using his business assets as collateral. He used the money to buy City of Blanksville bonds. Over the course of a year, Josh paid interest of $4,200 on the borrowed funds, but he received $3,500 of interest on the bonds.
b) Josh purchased a piece of land for $45,000 in order to get a location to expand his business. He also paid $3,200 to construct a new driveway for access to the property.
c) This year Josh paid $15,000 to employ the mayor's son in the business. Josh would typically pay an employee with these responsibilities about $10,000 but the mayor assured Josh that after his son was hired, some city business would be coming his way.
d) Josh paid his brother, a mechanic, $3,000 to install a robotic machine for Josh's business. The amount he paid to his brother is comparable to what he would have paid to an unrelated party to do the same work. Once the installation was completed by his brother, Josh began calibrating the machine for operation. However, by the end of the year, he had not started using the machine in his business.

LO 9-2 48. Ralph invited a potential client to dinner and the theater. Ralph paid $250 for the dinner and $220 for the theater tickets in advance. They first went to dinner and then they went to the theater.
a) What amount can Ralph deduct if, prior to the dinner, he met with the potential client to discuss future business prospects?
b) What amount can Ralph deduct if he and the client only discussed business during the course of the dinner?
c) What amount can Ralph deduct if he and the potential client tried to discuss business during the course of the theater performance but did not discuss business at any other time?
d) What amount can Ralph deduct if the potential client declined Ralph's invitation, so Ralph took his accountant to dinner and the theater to reward his accountant for a hard day at work? At dinner, they discussed the accountant's workload and upcoming assignments.

49. Melissa recently paid $400 for round-trip airfare to San Francisco to attend a business conference for three days. Melissa also paid the following expenses: $250 fee to register for the conference, $300 per night for three nights' lodging, $200 for meals, and $150 for cab fare.

    LO 9-2

    a) What amount of the travel costs can Melissa deduct as business expenses?

    b) Suppose that while Melissa was on the coast, she also spent two days sightseeing the national parks in the area. To do the sightseeing, she paid $1,000 for transportation, $800 for lodging, and $450 for meals during this part of her trip, which she considers personal in nature. What amount of the travel costs can Melissa deduct as business expenses?

    c) Suppose that Melissa made the trip to San Francisco primarily to visit the national parks and only attended the business conference as an incidental benefit of being present on the coast at that time. What amount of the airfare can Melissa deduct as a business expense?

    d) Suppose that Melissa's permanent residence and business was located in San Francisco. She attended the conference in San Francisco and paid $250 for the registration fee. She drove 100 miles over the course of three days and paid $90 for parking at the conference hotel. In addition, she spent $150 for breakfast and dinner over the three days of the conference. She bought breakfast on the way to the conference hotel and she bought dinner on her way home each night from the conference. What amount of the travel costs can Melissa deduct as business expenses?

50. Kimberly is a self-employed taxpayer. She recently spent $1,000 for airfare to travel to Italy. What amount of the airfare is deductible in each of the following alternative scenarios?

    LO 9-2

    a) Her trip was entirely for personal purposes.

    b) On the trip, she spent eight days on personal activities and two days on business activities.

    c) On the trip, she spent seven days on business activities and three days on personal activities.

    d) Her trip was entirely for business purposes.

51. Ryan is self-employed. This year Ryan used his personal auto for several long business trips. Ryan paid $1,500 for gasoline on these trips. His depreciation on the car if he was using it fully for business purposes would be $3,000. During the year, he drove his car a total of 12,000 miles (a combination of business and personal travel).

    LO 9-2

    a) Ryan can provide written documentation of the business purpose for trips totaling 3,000 miles. What business expense amount can Ryan deduct (if any) for these trips?

    b) Ryan estimates that he drove approximately 1,300 miles on business trips, but he can only provide written documentation of the business purpose for trips totaling 820 miles. What business expense amount can Ryan deduct (if any) for these trips?

52. Christopher is a cash-method, calendar-year taxpayer, and he made the following cash payments related to his business this year. Calculate the after-tax cost of each payment assuming he has a 30 percent marginal tax rate.

    LO 9-1   LO 9-2

    a) $500 fine for speeding while traveling to a client meeting.

    b) $240 of interest on a short-term loan incurred in September and repaid in November. Half of the loan proceeds were used immediately to pay salaries and the other half was invested in municipal bonds until November.

c) $600 for office supplies in May of this year. He used half of the supplies this year and he will use the remaining half by February of next year.

d) $450 for several pairs of work boots. Christopher expects to use the boots about 80 percent of the time in his business and the remainder of the time for hiking. Consider the boots to be a form of clothing.

LO 9-2

research

53. Heather paid $15,000 to join a country club in order to meet potential clients. This year she paid $4,300 in greens fees when golfing with clients. Under what circumstances, if any, can Heather deduct the $15,000 cost of country club dues and the costs of the golf played with clients?

LO 9-1 **LO 9-2**

54. Assume Sarah is a cash-method, calendar-year taxpayer, and she is considering making the following cash payments related to her business. Calculate the after-tax cost of each payment assuming she has a 25 percent marginal tax rate.

a) $2,000 payment for next year's property taxes on her place of business.

b) $800 to reimburse the cost of meals incurred by employees while traveling for the business.

c) $1,200 for football tickets to entertain out-of-town clients during contract negotiations.

d) $500 contribution to the mayor's re-election campaign.

LO 9-3

55. Renee manufactured and sold a "gadget," a specialized asset used by auto manufacturers that qualifies for the domestic production activities deduction. Renee incurred $15,000 in direct expenses in the project, which includes $2,000 of wages Renee paid to employees in the manufacturing of the gadget. What is Renee's domestic production activities deduction for the gadget in each of the following alternative scenarios?

a) Renee sold the gadget for $25,000 and she reported AGI of $75,000 before considering the manufacturing deduction.

b) Renee sold the gadget for $25,000 and she reported AGI of $5,000 before considering the manufacturing deduction.

c) Renee sold the gadget for $40,000 and she reported AGI of $50,000 before considering the manufacturing deduction.

LO 9-3

planning

56. Andrew is considering starting a business of constructing and selling pre-fabricated greenhouses. There are three very different methods to constructing these greenhouses, and each method results in different revenue and cost projections. Below, Andrew has projected the qualifying revenue and costs for each method. The selling price includes qualifying receipts. The allocable expenses include wages and allocable expenses are included in total costs.

Method	Selling Price	Qualifying Receipts	Total Cost	Allocable Expenses	Allocable Wages
#1	$13,000	$ 9,000	$6,500	$2,500	$2,000
#2	14,000	9,000	7,400	5,500	1,500
#3	15,000	14,000	8,600	2,000	1,000

a) Estimate the tax benefit from the domestic production activities deduction for each construction technique. You may assume that Andrew has sufficient AGI to utilize the deduction and that his marginal tax rate is 30 percent.

b) Which construction technique should Andrew use if his marginal tax rate is 30 percent?

57. This year Amy purchased $2,000 of equipment for use in her business. However, the machine was damaged in a traffic accident while Amy was transporting the equipment to her business. Note that because Amy did not place the equipment into service during the year, she does not claim any depreciation expense for the equipment.   `LO 9-3`

    a) After the accident, Amy had the choice of repairing the equipment for $1,800 or selling the equipment to a junk shop for $300. Amy sold the equipment. What amount can Amy deduct for the loss of the equipment?

    b) After the accident, Amy repaired the equipment for $800. What amount can Amy deduct for the loss of the equipment?

    c) After the accident, Amy could not replace the equipment so she had the equipment repaired for $2,300. What amount can Amy deduct for the loss of the equipment?

58. In July of this year, Stephen started a proprietorship called ECR (which stands for electric car repair). ECR uses the cash method of accounting and Stephen has produced the following financial information for this year: `LO 9-3`

    tax forms

    • ECR collected $81,000 in cash for repairs completed during the year and an additional $3,200 in cash for repairs that will commence after year-end.

    • Customers owe ECR $14,300 for repairs completed this year, and while Stephen isn't sure which bills will eventually be paid, he expects to collect all but about $1,900 of these revenues next year.

    ECR has made the following expenditures:

Interest expense	$ 1,250
Shop rent ($1,500 per month)	27,000
Utilities	1,075
Contract labor	8,250
Compensation	21,100
Liability insurance premiums ($350 per month)	4,200
Term life insurance premiums ($150 per month)	1,800

    The interest paid relates to interest accrued on a $54,000 loan made to Stephen in July of this year. Stephen used half of the loan to pay for 18 months of shop rent, and the remainder he used to upgrade his personal wardrobe. In July, Stephen purchased 12 months of liability insurance to protect against liability should anyone be injured in the shop. ECR has only one employee (the remaining workers are contract labor), and this employee thoroughly understands how to repair an electric propulsion system. On November 1 of this year, Stephen purchased a 12-month term-life policy that insures the life of this "key" employee. Stephen paid Gecko Insurance Company $1,800; in return, Gecko promises to pay Stephen a $40,000 death benefit if this employee dies any time during the next 12 months.

    Fill out a draft of the front page of Stephen's Schedule C.

59. Nicole is a calendar-year taxpayer who accounts for her business using the cash method. On average, Nicole sends out bills for about $12,000 of her services at the first of each month. The bills are due by the end of the month, and typically 70 percent of the bills are paid on time and 98 percent are paid within 60 days.   `LO 9-5`

    planning

    a) Suppose that Nicole is expecting a 2 percent reduction in her marginal tax rate next year. Ignoring the time value of money, estimate the tax savings for Nicole if she postpones mailing of bills for December until January 1 of next year.

    b) Describe how the time value of money affects your calculations.

    c) Would this tax savings strategy create any additional business risks? Explain.

LO 9-5

60. Jeremy is a calendar-year taxpayer who sometimes leases his business equipment to local organizations. He recorded the following receipts this year. Indicate the extent to which these payments are taxable income to Jeremy this year if Jeremy is (1) a cash-method taxpayer and (2) he is an accrual-method taxpayer.

a) $1,000 deposit from the Ladies' Club, which wants to lease a trailer. The club will receive the entire deposit back when the trailer is returned undamaged.

b) $800 from the Ladies' Club for leasing the trailer from December of this year through March of next year ($200 per month).

c) $300 lease payment received from the Men's Club this year for renting Jeremy's trailer last year. Jeremy billed the club last year but recently he determined that the Men's Club would never pay him, so he was surprised when he received the check.

LO 9-5

61. Brown Thumb Landscaping is a calendar-year, accrual-method taxpayer. In September, Brown Thumb negotiated a $14,000 contract for services it would provide to the city in November of the current year. The contract specifies that Brown Thumb will receive $4,000 in October as a down payment for these services and it will receive the remaining $10,000 in January of next year.

a) How much income from this $14,000 contract will Brown Thumb recognize in the current year? Explain.

b) How much income from this $14,000 contract will Brown Thumb recognize in the current year if it uses the cash method of accounting?

c) Suppose that the total amount to be paid under the contract with the city is estimated at $14,000 but may be adjusted to $12,000 next year during the review of the city budget. What amount from the contract, if any, should Brown Thumb recognize as income this year? Explain.

d) Suppose that in addition to the basic contract, Brown Thumb will be paid an additional $3,000 if its city landscape design wins the annual design competition next year. Should Brown Thumb accrue $3,000 revenue this year? Why or why not?

LO 9-5

62. In January of year 0, Justin paid $4,800 for an insurance policy that covers his business property for accidents and casualties. Justin is a calendar-year taxpayer who uses the cash method of accounting. What amount of the insurance premium may Justin deduct in year 0 in each of the following alternative scenarios?

a) The policy covers the business property from April 1 of year 0 through March 31 of year 1.

b) The policy begins on February 1 of year 1 and extends through January 31 of year 2.

c) Assume Justin paid $6,000 for a 24-month policy that covers from April 1, year 0 through March 31, year 2.

d) Assume that instead of paying an insurance premium, Justin paid $4,800 to rent his business property from April 1 of year 0 through March 31 of year 1.

LO 9-5

tax forms

63. Ben teaches golf lessons at a country club under a business called Ben's Pure Swings (BPS). He operates this business as a sole proprietorship on the accrual basis of accounting. Ben's trusty accountant, Brian, has produced the following accounting information for BPS:

This year BPS billed clients for $86,700 and collected $61,000 in cash for golf lessons completed during the year. In addition, BPS collected an additional $14,500 in cash for lessons that will commence after year-end. Ben hopes to collect about half of the outstanding billings next year but the rest will likely be written off.

Besides providing private golf lessons, BPS also contracted with the country club to staff the driving range. This year, BPS billed the country club $27,200 for the service. The club paid $17,000 of the amount but disputed the remainder. By year-end, the dispute had not been resolved, and while Ben believes he is entitled to the money, he has still not collected the remaining $10,200.

BPS has accrued the following expenses (explained below):

Advertising (in the clubhouse)	$13,150
Pro golf teachers membership fees	860
Supplies (golf tees, balls, etc.)	4,720
Club rental	6,800
Malpractice insurance	2,400
Accounting fees	8,820

The expenditures were all paid for this calendar year with several exceptions. First, Ben initiated his golfer's malpractice insurance on June 1 of this year. The $2,400 insurance bill covers the last six months of this calendar year and the first six months of next year. At year-end, Ben had only paid $600, but he has assured the insurance agent he would pay the remaining $1,800 early next year. Second, the amount paid for club rental ($100 per week) represents rental charges for the last 6 weeks of the previous year, for the 52 weeks in this calendar year, and the first 10 weeks of next year. Ben has also mentioned that BPS only pays for supplies that are used at the club. Although BPS could buy the supplies for half the cost elsewhere, Ben likes to "throw some business" to the golf pro shop because it is operated by his brother.

Fill out a draft of the front page of a Schedule C for BPS.

64. On April 1 of year 0 Stephanie received a $9,000 payment for full payment on a three-year service contract (under the contract Stephanie is obligated to provide advisory services for the next three years).   **LO 9-5**

   a) What amount of income should Stephanie recognize in year 0 if she uses the accrual method of accounting (she recognized $2,250 for financial accounting purposes)?

   b) What amount of income will Stephanie recognize in year 1 if she uses the accrual method of accounting?

   c) What amount of income will Stephanie recognize in year 2 if she uses the accrual method of accounting?

   d) What amount of income will Stephanie recognize in year 0 if she recognizes $5,000 of income from the contract for financial statement purposes?

65. In October of year 0, Janine received a $6,000 payment from a client for 25 months of security services she will provide starting on November 1 of year 0. This amounts to $240 per month.   **LO 9-5**

   a) When must Janine recognize the income from the $6,000 advance payment for services if she uses the cash method of accounting?

   b) When must Janine recognize the income from the $6,000 advance payment for services if she uses the accrual method of accounting?

   c) Suppose that instead of services, Janine received the payment for a security system (inventory) that she will deliver and install in year 2. When would Janine recognize the income from the advance payment for inventory sale if she uses the accrual method of accounting and she uses the deferral method for reporting income from advance payments? For financial accounting purposes, she reports the income when the inventory is delivered.

   d) Suppose that instead of services, Janine received the payment for the delivery of inventory to be delivered next year. When would Janine recognize the income from the advance payment for sale of goods if she uses the accrual method of accounting and she uses the full-inclusion method for advance payments?

LO 9-5   66. Nicole's business uses the accrual method of accounting and accounts for inventory with specific identification. In year 0, Nicole received a $4,500 payment with an order for inventory to be delivered to the client early next year. Nicole has the inventory ready for delivery at the end of year 0 (she purchased the inventory in year 0 for $2,300).

a) When does Nicole recognize the $2,200 of gross profit ($4,500 revenue minus $2,300 cost of the inventory) if she uses the full-inclusion method?

b) When does Nicole recognize the $2,200 of gross profit from the inventory sale if she uses the deferral method?

c) How would Nicole account for the inventory-related transactions if she uses the cash method of accounting and her annual sales are usually less than $100,000?

d) How would Nicole account for the inventory-related transactions if she uses the cash method of accounting and her annual sales are usually over $2,000,000 per year?

LO 9-5   67. This year Amber opened a factory to process and package landscape mulch. At the end of the year, Amber's accountant prepared the following schedule for allocating manufacturing costs to the mulch inventory, but her accountant is unsure of what costs need to be allocated to the inventory under UNICAP. Approximately 20 percent of management time, space, and expenses are spent on this manufacturing process.

		Costs	Tax Inventory
Material:	Mulch and packaging	$ 5,000	?
	Administrative supplies	250	?
Salaries:	Factory labor	12,000	?
	Sales & advertising	3,500	?
	Administration	5,200	?
Property taxes:	Factory	4,600	?
	Offices	2,700	?
Depreciation:	Factory	8,000	?
	Offices	1,500	?

a) At the end of the year, Amber's accountant indicated that the business had processed 10,000 bags of mulch but only 1,000 bags remained in the ending inventory. What is Amber's tax basis in her ending inventory after applying the UNICAP rules to allocate indirect costs to inventory? (Assume direct costs are allocated to inventory according to the level of ending inventory. In contrast, indirect costs are first allocated by time spent and then according to level of ending inventory.)

b) Under what conditions could Amber's business avoid having to apply UNICAP to allocate indirect costs to inventory for tax purposes?

LO 9-5   68. Suppose that David adopted the last-in, first-out (LIFO) inventory-flow method for his business inventory of widgets (purchase prices below).

Widget	Purchase Date	Direct Cost	Other Costs	Total Cost
#1	August 15	$2,100	$100	$2,200
#2	October 30	2,200	150	2,350
#3	November 10	2,300	100	2,400

In late December, David sold widget #2 and next year David expects to purchase three more widgets at the following estimated prices:

Widget	Purchase Date	Estimated Cost
#4	Early spring	$2,600
#5	Summer	2,260
#6	Fall	2,400

a) What cost of goods sold and ending inventory would David record if he elects to use the LIFO method this year?

b) If David sells two widgets next year, what will be his cost of goods sold and ending inventory next year under the LIFO method?

c) How would you answer (a) and (b) if David had initially selected the first-in, first-out (FIFO) method instead of LIFO?

d) Suppose that David initially adopted the LIFO method, but wants to apply for a change to FIFO next year. What would be his §481 adjustment for this change, and in what year(s) would he make the adjustment?

69. On November 1 of year 0, Jaxon borrowed $50,000 from Bucksnort Savings and Loan for use in his business. In December, Jaxon paid interest of $4,500 relating to the 12-month period from November of year 0 through October of year 1.   **LO 9-5**

a) How much interest, if any, can Jaxon deduct in year 0 if his business uses the cash method of accounting for tax purposes?

b) How much interest, if any, can Jaxon deduct in year 0 if his business uses the accrual method of accounting for tax purposes?

70. Matt hired Apex Services to repair his business equipment. On November 1 of year 0, Matt paid $2,000 for the repairs that he expects to begin in early March of year 1.   **LO 9-5**

a) What amount of the cost of the repairs can Matt deduct in year 0 if he uses the cash method of accounting for his business?

b) What amount of the cost of the repairs can Matt deduct in year 0 if he uses the accrual method of accounting for his business?

c) What amount of the cost of the repairs can Matt deduct in year 0 if he uses the accrual method and he expects the repairs to be done by early February?

d) What amount of the cost of the repairs can Matt deduct in year 0 if he uses the cash method of accounting and he expects the repairs to be done by early February?

71. Circuit Corporation (CC) is a calendar-year, accrual-method taxpayer. CC manufactures and sells electronic circuitry. On November 15, year 0, CC enters into a contract with Equip Corp (EC) that provides CC with exclusive use of EC's specialized manufacturing equipment for the five-year period beginning on January 1 of year 1. Pursuant to the contract, CC pays EC $100,000 on December 30, year 0. How much of this expenditure is CC allowed to deduct in year 0 and in year 1?   **LO 9-5**

72. This year (year 0) Elizabeth agreed to a three-year service contract with an engineering consulting firm to improve efficiency in her factory. The contract requires Elizabeth to pay the consulting firm $1,500 for each instance that Elizabeth requests their assistance. The contract also provides that Elizabeth only pays the consultants if its advice increases efficiency as measured 12 months from the date of service. This year Elizabeth requested advice on three occasions and she has not yet made any payments to the consultants.   **LO 9-5**

a) How much should Elizabeth deduct in year 0 under this service contract if she uses the accrual method of accounting?

b) How much should Elizabeth deduct in year 0 under this service contract if she uses the cash method of accounting?

LO 9-5

73. Travis is a professional landscaper. He provides his clients with a one-year (12-month) warranty for retaining walls he installs. In June of year 1, Travis installed a wall for an important client, Sheila. In early November, Sheila informed Travis that the retaining wall had failed. To repair the wall, Travis paid $700 cash for additional stone that he delivered to Sheila's location. Travis also offered to pay a mason $800 to repair the wall on November 20 of year 1. Due to some bad weather and the mason's work backlog, the mason agreed to finish the work by the end of January of year 2. Even though Travis expected the mason to finish the project by the end of February, Travis informed the mason that he would pay the mason the $800 when he completed the job.

a) Assuming Travis is an accrual-method taxpayer, how much can he deduct in year 1 from these activities?

b) Assuming Travis is a cash-method taxpayer, how much can he deduct in year 1 from these activities?

LO 9-5

research

74. Adam elects the accrual method of accounting for his business. What amount of deductions does Adam recognize in year 0 for the following transactions?

a) Adam guarantees that he will refund the cost of any goods sold to a client if the goods fail within a year of delivery. In December of year 0, Adam agreed to refund $2,400 to clients, and he expects to make payment in January of year 1.

b) On December 1 of year 0, Adam paid $480 for a one-year contract with CleanUP Services to clean his store. The agreement calls for services to be provided on a weekly basis.

c) Adam was billed $240 for annual personal property taxes on his delivery van. Because this was the first time Adam was billed for these taxes, he did not make payment until January. However, he considers the amounts immaterial.

LO 9-5

75. Rebecca is a calendar-year taxpayer who operates a business. She made the following business-related expenditures in December of year 0. Indicate the amount of these payments that she may deduct in year 0 under both the cash method of accounting and the accrual method of accounting.

a) $2,000 for an accountant to evaluate the accounting system of Rebecca's business. The accountant spent three weeks in January of year 1 working on the evaluation.

b) $2,500 for new office furniture. The furniture was delivered on January 15, year 1.

c) $3,000 for property taxes payable on her factory.

d) $1,500 for interest on a short-term bank loan relating to the period from November 1, year 0 through March 31, year 1.

LO 9-5

76. BCS Corporation is a calendar-year, accrual-method taxpayer. BCS was formed and started its business activities on January 1, year 0. It reported the following information for year 0. Indicate BCS's deductible amount for year 0 in each of the following alternative scenarios.

a) BCS provides two-year warranties on products it sells to customers. For its year 0 sales, BCS estimated and accrued $200,000 in warranty expense for financial accounting purposes. During year 0, BCS actually spent $30,000 repairing its product under the warranty.

b) BCS accrued an expense for $50,000 for amounts it anticipated it would be required to pay under the workers' compensation act. During year 0, BCS actually paid $10,000 for workers' compensation–related liabilities.

c) In June of year 0, a display of BCS's product located in its showroom fell on and injured a customer. The customer sued BCS for $500,000. The case is scheduled to go to trial next year. BCS anticipates that it will lose the case and accrued a $500,000 expense on its financial statements.

d) Assume the same facts as in (c) except that BCS was required to pay $500,000 to a court-appointed escrow fund in year 0. If BCS loses the case in year 1, the money from the escrow fund will be transferred to the customer suing BCS.

e) On December 1 of year 0, BCS acquired equipment from Equip Company. As part of the purchase, BCS signed a warranty agreement with Equip so that Equip would warranty the equipment for two years (from December 1 of year 0 through November 30 of year 2). The cost of the warranty was $12,000. BCS paid Equip for the warranty in January of year 1.

77. This year William provided $4,200 of services to a large client on credit. Unfortunately, this client has recently encountered financial difficulties and has been unable to pay William for the services. Moreover, William does not expect to collect for his services. William has "written off" the account and would like to claim a deduction for tax purposes. **LO 9-5**

a) What amount of deduction for bad debt expense can William claim this year if he uses the accrual method?

b) What amount of deduction for bad debt expense can William claim this year if he uses the cash method?

78. Dustin has a contract to provide services to Dado Enterprises. In November of year 0, Dustin billed Dado $10,000 for the services he rendered during the year. Dado is an accrual-method proprietorship that is owned and operated by Dustin's father. **LO 9-5**

a) What amount of revenue must Dustin recognize in year 0 if Dustin uses the cash method and Dado remits payment for the services in December of year 0? What amount can Dado deduct in year 0?

b) What amount of revenue must Dustin recognize in year 0 if Dustin uses the accrual method and Dado remits payment for the services in December of year 0? What amount can Dado deduct in year 0?

c) What amount of revenue must Dustin recognize in year 0 if Dustin uses the cash method and Dado remits payment for the services in January of year 1? What amount can Dado deduct in year 0?

d) What amount of revenue must Dustin recognize in year 0 if Dustin uses the accrual method and Dado remits payment for the services in January of year 1? What amount can Dado deduct in year 0?

79. Nancy operates a business that uses the accrual method of accounting. In December, Nancy asked her brother, Hank, to provide her business with consulting advice. Hank billed Nancy for $5,000 of consulting services in year 0 (a reasonable amount), but Nancy was only able to pay $3,000 of the bill by the end of year 0. However, Nancy paid the remainder of the bill in year 1. **LO 9-5**

a) How much of the $5,000 consulting services will Hank include in his income in year 0 if he uses the cash method of accounting? What amount can Nancy deduct in year 0 for the consulting services?

b) How much of the $5,000 consulting services will Hank include in his income in year 0 if he uses the accrual method of accounting? What amount can Nancy deduct in year 0 for the consulting services?

LO 9-5 80. Erin is considering switching her business from the cash method to the accrual method at the beginning of next year (year 1). Determine the amount and timing of her §481 adjustment assuming the IRS grants Erin's request in the following alternative scenarios.

  a) At the end of year 0/beginning of year 1, Erin's business has $15,000 of accounts receivable and $18,000 of accounts payable that have not been recorded for tax purposes.

  b) At the end of year 0/beginning of year 1, Erin's business reports $25,000 of accounts receivable and $9,000 of accounts payable that have not been recorded for tax purposes.

COMPREHENSIVE PROBLEMS

Select problems are available in *Connect*®.

81. Joe operates a business that locates and purchases specialized assets for clients, among other activities. Joe uses the accrual method of accounting but he doesn't keep any significant inventories of the specialized assets that he sells. Joe reported the following financial information for his business activities during year 0. Determine the effect of each of the following transactions on the taxable business income.

  a) Joe has signed a contract to sell gadgets to the city. The contract provides that sales of gadgets are dependent upon a test sample of gadgets operating successfully. In December, Joe delivers $12,000 worth of gadgets to the city that will be tested in March. Joe purchased the gadgets especially for this contract and paid $8,500.

  b) Joe paid $180 for entertaining a visiting out-of-town client. The client didn't discuss business with Joe during this visit, but Joe wants to maintain good relations to encourage additional business next year.

  c) On November 1, Joe paid $600 for premiums providing for $40,000 of "key man" insurance on the life of Joe's accountant over the next 12 months.

  d) At the end of year 0, Joe's business reports $9,000 of accounts receivable. Based upon past experience, Joe believes that at least $2,000 of his new receivables will be uncollectible.

  e) In December of year 0, Joe rented equipment to complete a large job. Joe paid $3,000 in December because the rental agency required a minimum rental of three months ($1,000 per month). Joe completed the job before year-end, but he returned the equipment at the end of the lease.

  f) Joe hired a new sales representative as an employee and sent her to Dallas for a week to contact prospective out-of-state clients. Joe ended up reimbursing his employee $300 for airfare, $350 for lodging, $250 for meals, and $150 for entertainment (Joe provided adequate documentation to substantiate the business purpose for the meals and entertainment). Joe requires the employee to account for all expenditures in order to be reimbursed.

  g) Joe uses his BMW (a personal auto) to travel to and from his residence to his factory. However, he switches to a business vehicle if he needs to travel after he reaches the factory. Last month, the business vehicle broke down and he was forced to use the BMW both to travel to and from the factory and to visit work sites. He drove 120 miles visiting work sites and 46 miles driving to and from the factory from his home. Joe uses the standard mileage rate to determine his auto-related business expenses.

  h) Joe paid a visit to his parents in Dallas over the Christmas holidays. While he was in the city, Joe spent $50 to attend a half-day business symposium. Joe paid $200 for airfare, $50 for meals during the symposium, and $20 on cab fare to the symposium.

82. Jack, a geologist, had been debating for years whether or not to venture out on his own and operate his own business. He had developed a lot of solid relationships with clients and he believed that many of them would follow him if he were to leave his current employer. As part of a New Year's resolution, Jack decided he would finally do it. Jack put his business plan together and, on January 1 of this year, Jack opened his doors for business as a C corporation called Geo-Jack (GJ). Jack is the sole shareholder. Jack reported the following financial information for the year (assume GJ reports on a calendar year and uses the accrual method of accounting).

    a) In January, GJ rented a small business office about 12 miles from Jack's home. GJ paid $10,000 which represented a damage deposit of $4,000 and rent for two years ($3,000 annually).

    b) GJ earned and collected $290,000 performing geological-related services and selling its specialized digging tool [see part (i)].

    c) GJ received $50 interest from municipal bonds and $2,100 interest from other investments.

    d) GJ purchased some new equipment in February for $42,500. It claimed depreciation on these assets during the year in the amount of $6,540.

    e) GJ paid $7,000 to buy luxury season tickets for Jack's parents for State U football games.

    f) GJ paid Jack's father $10,000 for services that would have cost no more than $6,000 if Jack had hired any other local business to perform the services. While Jack's dad was competent, he does not command such a premium from his other clients.

    g) In an attempt to get his name and new business recognized, GJ paid $7,000 for a one-page ad in the Geologic Survey. It also paid $15,000 in radio ads to be run through the end of December.

    h) GJ leased additional office space in a building downtown. GJ paid rent of $27,000 for the year.

    i) In August, GJ began manufacturing a special geological digging tool that it sells to wholesalers. QPAI from the activity for the year is $100,000 [included in revenues reported in part (b)]. GJ paid $10,000 of wages to the employees working on the project during the year and its cost of goods sold on the sales is $15,000. (Assume that taxable income does not limit the amount of the DPAD, and that no wages should be included in cost of goods sold.) Remember that cost of goods sold and wages reduce taxable income.

    j) In November, Jack's office was broken into and equipment valued at $5,000 was stolen. The tax basis of the equipment was $5,500. Jack received $2,000 of insurance proceeds from the theft.

    k) GJ incurred a $4,000 fine from the state government for digging in an unauthorized digging zone.

    l) GJ contributed $3,000 to lobbyists for their help in persuading the state government to authorize certain unauthorized digging zones.

    m) On July 1, GJ paid $1,800 for an 18-month insurance policy for its business equipment. The policy covers the period July 1 of this year through December 31 of next year.

    n) GJ borrowed $20,000 to help with the company's initial funding needs. GJ used $2,000 of funds to invest in municipal bonds. At the end of the year, GJ paid the $1,200 of interest expense that accrued on the loan during the year.

    o) Jack lives 12 miles from the office. He carefully tracked his mileage and drove his truck 6,280 miles between the office and his home. He also drove an additional 7,200 miles between the office and traveling to client sites. Jack did not use the truck for any other purposes. He did not keep track of the specific expenses associated with the truck. However, while traveling to a client site, Jack received a $150 speeding ticket. GJ reimbursed Jack for business mileage and for the speeding ticket.

p) GJ purchased two season tickets (20 games) to attend State U baseball games for a total of $1,100. Jack took existing and prospective clients to the games to maintain contact and find further work. This was very successful for Jack as GJ gained many new projects through substantial discussions with the clients following the games.

q) GJ reimbursed employee-salespersons $3,500 for meals involving substantial business discussion.

r) GJ had a client who needed Jack to perform work in Florida. Because Jack had never been to Florida before, he booked an extra day and night for sightseeing. Jack spent $400 for airfare and booked a hotel for three nights ($120/night). (Jack stayed two days for business purposes and one day for personal purposes.) He also rented a car for $45 per day. The client arranged for Jack's meals while Jack was doing business. GJ reimbursed Jack for all expenses.

Required:

A) What is GJ's net business income for tax purposes for the year?

B) As a C corporation, does GJ have a required tax year? If so, what would it be?

C) If GJ were a sole proprietorship, would it have a required tax year-end? If so, what would it be?

D) If GJ were an S corporation, would it have a required tax year-end? If so, what would it be?

83. Rex loves to work with his hands and is very good at making small figurines. Three years ago, Rex opened Bronze Age Miniatures (BAM) for business as a sole proprietorship. BAM produces miniature characters ranging from sci-fi characters (his favorite) to historical characters like George Washington (the most popular). Business has been going very well for him, and he has provided the following information relating to his business. Calculate the business taxable income for BAM.

a) Rex received approval from the IRS to switch from the cash method of accounting to the accrual method of accounting effective January 1 of this year. At the end of last year, BAM reported accounts receivable that had not been included in income under the accrual method of $14,000 and accounts payable that had not been deducted under the accrual method of $5,000.

b) In March, BAM sold 5,000 miniature historical figures to History R Us Inc. (HRU), a retailer of historical artifacts and figurines, for $75,000.

c) HRU was so impressed with the figurines that it purchased in March that it wanted to contract with BAM to continue to produce the figurines for them for the next three years. HRU paid BAM $216,000 ($12 per figurine) on October 30 of this year, to produce 500 figurines per month for 36 months beginning on November 1 of this year. BAM delivered 500 figurines on November 30 and again on December 30. Rex elects to use the deferral method to account for the transaction.

d) Though the sci-fi figurines were not quite as popular, BAM sold 400 figurines at a sci-fi convention in April. Rex accepted cash only and received $11,000 for these sales.

e) In January, BAM determined that it would not be able to collect on $2,000 of its beginning-of-the-year receivables, so it wrote off $2,000 of specific receivables. BAM sold 100,000 other figurines on credit for $120,000. BAM estimates that it will be unable to collect 5 percent of the sales revenue from these sales but it has not been able to specifically identify any accounts to write off.

f) Assume that BAM correctly determined that its cost of goods sold this year is $54,000.

g) The sci-fi convention in April was held in Chicago, Illinois. Rex attended the convention because he felt it was a good opportunity to gain new customers and to get new ideas for figurines. He paid $350 round-trip airfare, $100 for entrance to the convention, $210 for lodging, $65 for cab fare, and $110 for meals during the trip. He was busy with business activities the entire trip.

h) On August 1, BAM purchased a 12-month insurance policy that covers its business property for accidents and casualties through July 31 of next year. The policy cost BAM $3,600.

i) BAM reported depreciation expense of $8,200 for this year.

j) Rex had previously operated his business out of his garage, but in January he decided to rent a larger space. He entered into a lease agreement on February 1 and paid $14,400 ($1,200 per month) to possess the space for the next 12 months (February of this year through January of next year).

k) Before he opened his doors for business, Rex spent $30,000 investigating and otherwise getting ready to do business. He expensed $5,000 immediately and is amortizing the remainder using the straight-line method over 180 months.

l) In December, BAM agreed to a 12-month $8,000 contract with Advertise-With-Us (AWU) to produce a radio ad campaign. BAM paid $3,000 up front (in December of this year) and AWU agreed that BAM would owe the remaining $5,000 only if BAM's sales increased by 15 percent over the nine-month period after the contract was signed.

m) In November of this year, BAM paid $2,500 in business property taxes (based on asset values) covering the period December 1 of this year through November 30 of next year. In November of last year, BAM paid $1,500 for business property taxes (based on asset values) covering the period December 1 of last year through November 30 of this year.

84. Bryan followed in his father's footsteps and entered into the carpet business. He owns and operates I Do Carpet (IDC). Bryan prefers to install carpet only, but in order to earn additional revenue, he also cleans carpets and sells carpet-cleaning supplies. Compute his taxable income for the current year considering the following items:

a) IDC contracted with a homebuilder in December of last year to install carpet in 10 new homes being built. The contract price of $80,000 includes $50,000 for materials (carpet). The remaining $30,000 is for IDC's service of installing the carpet. The contract also stated that all money was to be paid up front. The homebuilder paid IDC in full on December 28 of last year. The contract required IDC to complete the work by January 31 of this year. Bryan purchased the necessary carpet on January 2 and began working on the first home January 4. He completed the last home on January 27 of this year.

b) IDC entered into several other contracts this year and completed the work before year-end. The work cost $130,000 in materials. Bryan billed out $240,000 but only collected $220,000 by year-end. Of the $20,000 still owed to him, Bryan wrote off $3,000 he didn't expect to collect as a bad debt from a customer experiencing extreme financial difficulties.

c) IDC entered into a three-year contract to clean the carpets of an office building. The contract specified that IDC would clean the carpets monthly from July 1 of this year through June 30 three years hence. IDC received payment in full of $8,640 ($240 a month for 36 months) on June 30 of this year.

d) IDC sold 100 bottles of carpet stain remover this year for $5 per bottle (it collected $500). Rex sold 40 bottles on June 1 and 60 bottles on November 2.

IDC had the following carpet-cleaning supplies on hand for this year and it uses the LIFO method of accounting for inventory under a perpetual inventory system:

Purchase Date	Bottles	Total Cost
November last year	40	$120
February this year	35	112
July this year	25	85
August this year	40	140
Totals	140	$457

e) On August 1 of this year, IDC needed more room for storage and paid $900 to rent a garage for 12 months.

f) On November 30 of this year, Bryan decided it was time to get his logo on the sides of his work van. IDC hired We Paint Anything Inc. (WPA) to do the job. It paid $500 down and agreed to pay the remaining $1,500 upon completion of the job. WPA indicated it wouldn't be able to begin the job until January 15 of next year, but the job would only take one week to complete. Due to circumstances beyond its control, WPA wasn't able to complete the job until April 1 of next year, at which time IDC paid the remaining $1,500.

g) In December, Bryan's son, Aiden, helped him finish some carpeting jobs. IDC owed Aiden $600 (reasonable) compensation for his work. However, Aiden did not receive the payment until January of next year.

h) IDC also paid $1,000 for interest on a short-term bank loan relating to the period from November 1 of this year through March 31 of next year.

85. Hank started a new business in June of last year, Hank's Donut World (HW for short). He has requested your advice on the following specific tax matters associated with HW's first year of operations. Hank has estimated HW's income for the first year as follows:

Revenue:		
Donut sales	$252,000	
Catering revenues	71,550	$323,550
Expenditures:		
Donut supplies	$124,240	
Catering expense	27,910	
Salaries to shop employees	52,500	
Rent expense	40,050	
Accident insurance premiums	8,400	
Other business expenditures	6,850	−259,950
Net Income		$ 63,600

HW operates as a sole proprietorship and Hank reports on a calendar year. Hank uses the cash method of accounting and plans to do the same with HW (HW has no inventory of donuts because unsold donuts are not salable). HW does not purchase donut supplies on credit nor does it generally make sales on credit. Hank has provided the following details for specific first-year transactions.

• A small minority of HW clients complained about the catering service. To mitigate these complaints, Hank's policy is to refund dissatisfied clients 50 percent of the catering fee. By the end of the first year, only two HW clients had complained but had not yet been paid refunds. The expected refunds amount to $1,700, and Hank reduced the reported catering fees for the first year to reflect the expected refund.

• In the first year, HW received a $6,750 payment from a client for catering a monthly breakfast for 30 consecutive months beginning in December. Because the payment didn't relate to last year, Hank excluded the entire amount when he calculated catering revenues.

- In July, HW paid $1,500 to ADMAN Co. for an advertising campaign to distribute fliers advertising HW's catering service. Unfortunately, this campaign violated a city code restricting advertising by fliers, and the city fined HW $250 for the violation. HW paid the fine, and Hank included the fine and the cost of the campaign in "other business" expenditures.

- In July, HW also paid $8,400 for a 24-month insurance policy that covers HW for accidents and casualties beginning on August 1 of the first year. Hank deducted the entire $8,400 as accident insurance premiums.

- On May of the first year, Hank signed a contract to lease the HW donut shop for 10 months. In conjunction with the contract, Hank paid $2,000 as a damage deposit and $8,050 for rent ($805 per month). Hank explained that the damage deposit was refundable at the end of the lease. At this time, Hank also paid $30,000 to lease kitchen equipment for 24 months ($1,250 per month). Both leases began on June 1 of the first year. In his estimate, Hank deducted these amounts ($40,050 in total) as rent expense.

- Hank signed a contract hiring WEGO Catering to help cater breakfasts. At year-end, WEGO asked Hank to hold the last catering payment for the year, $9,250, until after January 1 (apparently because WEGO didn't want to report the income on its tax return). The last check was delivered to WEGO in January after the end of the first year. However, because the payment related to the first year of operations, Hank included the $9,250 in last year's catering expense.

- Hank believes that the key to the success of HW has been hiring Jimbo Jones to supervise the donut production and manage the shop. Because Jimbo is such an important employee, HW purchased a "key-employee" term-life insurance policy on his life. HW paid a $5,100 premium for this policy and it will pay HW a $40,000 death benefit if Jimbo passes away any time during the next 12 months. The term of the policy began on September 1 of last year and this payment was included in "other business" expenditures.

- In the first year, HW catered a large breakfast event to celebrate the city's anniversary. The city agreed to pay $7,100 for the event, but Hank forgot to notify the city of the outstanding bill until January of this year. When he mailed the bill in January, Hank decided to discount the charge to $5,500. On the bill, Hank thanked the mayor and the city council for their patronage and asked them to "send a little more business our way." This bill is not reflected in Hank's estimate of HW's income for the first year of operations.

Required:

A) Hank files his personal tax return on a calendar year, but he has not yet filed last year's personal tax return nor has he filed a tax return reporting HW's results for the first year of operations. Explain when Hank should file the tax return for HW and calculate the amount of taxable income generated by HW last year.

B) Determine the taxable income that HW will generate if Hank chooses to account for the business under the accrual method.

C) Describe how your solution might change if Hank incorporated HW before he commenced business last year.

86. R.E.M., a calendar-year corporation and Athens, Georgia, band, recently sold tickets ($20,000,000) for concerts scheduled in the United States for next year and the following year. For financial statement purposes, R.E.M. will recognize the income from the ticket sales when it performs the concerts. For tax purposes, it uses the accrual method and would prefer to defer the income from the ticket sales until after the concerts are performed. This is the first time that it has sold tickets one or two years in advance. Michael Stipe has asked your advice. Write a memo to Michael explaining your findings.

research

chapter

10 Property Acquisition and Cost Recovery

Learning Objectives

Upon completing this chapter, you should be able to:

LO 10-1 Explain the concept of basis and adjusted basis and describe the cost recovery methods used under the tax law to recover the cost of personal property, real property, intangible assets, and natural resources.

LO 10-2 Determine the applicable cost recovery (depreciation) life, method, and convention for tangible personal and real property and calculate the deduction allowable under basic MACRS.

LO 10-3 Explain the additional special cost recovery rules (§179, bonus, listed property) and calculate the deduction allowable under these rules.

LO 10-4 Explain the rationale behind amortization, describe the four categories of amortizable intangible assets, and calculate amortization expense.

LO 10-5 Explain cost recovery of natural resources and the allowable depletion methods.

© Brand X Pictures/SuperStock

Storyline Summary

Taxpayer:	Teton Mountaineering Technology, LLC (Teton)—a calendar-year single-member LLC (treated as a sole proprietorship for tax purposes)
Location:	Cody, Wyoming
President/ Founder:	Steve Dallimore
Current situation:	Teton must acquire property to start manufacturing operations and wants to understand the tax consequences of property acquisitions.

Two years ago while climbing the Black Ice Couloir (pronounced "cool-wahr") in Grand Teton National Park, Steve Dallimore and his buddy got into a desperate situation. The climbers planned to move fast and light and to be home before an approaching storm reached the Teton. But just shy of the summit, climbing conditions forced them to turn back. Huddled in a wet sleeping bag in a dark snow cave waiting for the tempest to pass, Steve had an epiphany—a design for a better ice-climbing tool. Since that moment, Steve has been quietly consumed with making his dream—designing and selling his own line of climbing equipment—a reality. Although his current sales career is challenging and financially rewarding, Steve has too often found himself watching the clock and dreaming of a more fulfilling and adventurous career based upon his early training as a mechanical engineer. Steve decided to exercise his stock options, leave his current position, and start Teton. The only problem is that Steve has no employees, no business location, and no manufacturing equipment.

to be continued . . .

Steve obviously has many issues to resolve and decisions to make. In this chapter, we focus on the tax issues relating to the assets Steve will acquire for use in his new business. In particular, we explain how Teton will determine its cost recovery (depreciation, amortization, and depletion) deductions for the assets in the year the business begins and in subsequent years.[1] These deductions can generate significant tax savings for companies in capital-intensive industries.

This chapter explores the tax consequences of acquiring new or used property, depreciation methods businesses may use to recover the cost of their assets, and other special cost recovery incentives. Along the way, we compare and contrast the process of computing depreciation for tax purposes and for financial accounting purposes. We also address the tax consequences of using intangible assets and natural resources in business activities.

LO 10-1 COST RECOVERY AND BASIS FOR COST RECOVERY

Most businesses make a significant investment in property, plant, and equipment that is expected to provide benefits over a number of years. For both financial accounting and tax accounting purposes, businesses must capitalize the cost of assets with a useful life of more than one year (on the balance sheet) rather than expense the cost immediately. Businesses are allowed to use various methods to allocate the cost of these assets over time because the assets are subject to wear, tear, and obsolescence.

The method of **cost recovery** depends on the nature of the underlying asset. **Depreciation** is the method of deducting the cost of *tangible* personal and real property (other than land) over a specific time period. **Amortization** is the method of deducting the cost of **intangible assets** over a specific time period. Finally, **depletion** is the method of deducting the cost of natural resources over time. Exhibit 10-1 summarizes these concepts.

Generally, a significant portion of a firm's assets comprises property, plant, equipment, intangibles, or even natural resources. In most cases, this holds true for small businesses like Teton and also for large publicly traded companies. For example, Exhibit 10-2 describes the assets held by Weyerhaeuser, a publicly traded timber company. As indicated in Exhibit 10-2, Weyerhaeuser has almost $3 billion in property and equipment (net of depreciation) and $6 billion in timber (net of depletion), comprising roughly 60 percent of its assets.

Businesses must choose accounting methods for the assets acquired during the year from among the allowable cost recovery alternatives we describe in this chapter. Attention to detail is important because the basis of an asset must be reduced by the

EXHIBIT 10-1 Assets and Cost Recovery

Asset Type	Cost Recovery Method
Personal property comprises tangible assets such as automobiles, equipment, and machinery.	Depreciation
Real property comprises buildings and land (although land is nondepreciable).	Depreciation
Intangible assets are nonphysical assets such as goodwill and patents.	Amortization
Natural resources are commodities that are considered valuable in their natural form such as oil, coal, timber, and gold.	Depletion

[1]Cost recovery is the common term used to describe the process by which businesses allocate the cost of their fixed assets over the time period in which they are used.

EXHIBIT 10-2   **Weyerhaeuser Assets**

Assets (in millions) per 2014 10-K Statement	2013	2014
Total current assets	$ 2,326	$ 3,033
Property and equipment, net (Note 7)	2,689	2,623
Construction in progress	112	131
Timber and timberlands at cost, less depletion charged to disposals	6,580	6,580
Investments in and advances to equity affiliates (Note 8)	190	188
Goodwill	42	40
Deferred tax assets (Note 20)	5	8
Restricted assets held by special purpose entities (Note 10)	615	615
Other (Note 3)	2,018	289
Total assets	$14,577	$13,457

cost recovery deductions allowed or *allowable*.[2] This means that if a business fails to deduct (by mistake or error) the allowable amount of depreciation expense for the year, the business must still reduce the asset's basis by the depreciation expense the taxpayer could have deducted under the method the business is using to depreciate the asset (this reduces the future depreciation deductions for the asset).

Basis for Cost Recovery

Businesses may begin recouping the cost of purchased business assets (cost basis) once they begin using the asset in their business (place it in service).[3] Once the business establishes its cost basis in an asset, the basis is reduced as the business recovers the cost of the asset through cost recovery deductions such as depreciation, amortization, or depletion. The amount of an asset's cost that has yet to be recovered through cost recovery deductions is called the asset's **adjusted basis** or **tax basis.** An asset's adjusted basis can be computed by subtracting the accumulated depreciation (or amortization or depletion) from the asset's initial cost or historical basis.[4]

For most assets, the initial basis is the cost plus all of the expenses to purchase, prepare it for use, and begin using the asset. These expenses include sales tax, shipping costs, and installation costs. The financial accounting and tax rules for computing an asset's basis are very similar. Thus, a purchased asset's initial basis for both tax and book purposes is generally the same.[5] So how do taxpayers know if they should immediately deduct the cost of an asset or capitalize and depreciate it? The Treasury has issued regulations that are quite lengthy (over 200 pages) and complex to guide taxpayers in answering this question.[6] The regulations provide a de minimis safe harbor that allows taxpayers to deduct low-cost personal property items used in their business. The definition of low-cost depends on whether the taxpayer has an applicable financial statement, which generally means a certified, audited financial statement. If taxpayers have an applicable financial statement, they may use the de minimis safe harbor to deduct amounts paid for tangible property up to $5,000 per

> **THE KEY FACTS**
>
> **Cost Basis**
>
> - An asset's cost basis includes all costs needed to purchase the asset, prepare it for use, and begin using it.
> - Cost basis is usually the same for book and tax purposes.
> - Special basis rules apply when personal-use assets are converted to business use and when assets are acquired through nontaxable transactions, gifts, or inheritances.

---

[2]If a business discovers that it failed to claim allowable depreciation in a previous year, it cannot currently deduct the depreciation attributable to prior years. Rather, the business must file amended returns—assuming the statute of limitations is still open—to claim the depreciation expense. Additionally, Reg. §1.446-1 indicates other situations that will result in an accounting method change.

[3]Cost basis is defined under §1012. The mere purchase of an asset does not trigger cost recovery deductions. A business must begin using the asset for business purposes (place it in service) in order to depreciate the asset. However, because businesses generally acquire and place assets in service at the same time, we refer to these terms interchangeably throughout the chapter.

[4]§1011.

[5]However, special basis rules apply when an asset is acquired through a nontaxable transaction. See discussion in Chapter 11.

[6]Reg. §1.263(a)-1, -2, and -3.

invoice or item.[7] If taxpayers don't have an applicable financial statement, they may use the safe harbor to deduct amounts up to $2,500 per invoice or item. Taxpayers generally use the invoice amount to determine whether they meet the safe harbor; however, if the total invoice amount exceeds the $5,000/$2,500 threshold and the invoice provides detailed cost information about each item, taxpayers may immediately deduct individual items that are less than the threshold amount. Taxpayers must capitalize the cost of personal property that does not fall under the de minimis safe harbor provision.[8]

When a business acquires multiple assets for one purchase price, the tax laws require the business to determine a cost basis for each separate asset. For example, if Teton were to acquire land and a building on the land, Teton must treat the building and land as separate assets. In these types of acquisitions, businesses determine the cost basis of each asset by allocating a portion of the purchase price to each asset based on that asset's value relative to the total value of all the assets the business acquired in the same purchase. The asset values are generally determined by an appraisal.[9]

Example 10-1

Steve determined that he needed machinery and office furniture for a manufacturing facility and a design studio (located in Cody, Wyoming). During the year, Steve purchased the following assets and incurred the following costs to prepare the assets for business use. His cost basis in each asset is determined as follows:

Asset	Date Acquired	(1) Purchase Price	(2) Business Preparation Costs	(1) + (2) Cost Basis
Office furniture	2/3/16	$ 10,000		$ 10,000
Warehouse	5/1/16	270,000*	$5,000 (minor modifications)	275,000
Land (10 acres)	5/1/16	75,000*		75,000
Machinery	7/22/16	500,000	$10,000 (delivery and setup)	510,000
Delivery truck (used)	8/17/16	15,000		15,000

*Note that the warehouse and the land were purchased together for $345,000. Steve and the seller determined that the value (and cost) of the warehouse was $270,000 and the value (and cost) of the land was $75,000.

What if: Assume Steve acquired a printer for $800 on July 9. Would he immediately deduct the cost of the printer or capitalize it?

Answer: Assuming that Steve has a policy to expense items costing $2,500 or less for nontax purposes, he would be able to immediately deduct the cost of the printer under the de minimis safe harbor.

When a business incurs additional costs associated with an asset after the asset has been placed in service, are these costs immediately expensed or are they capitalized? In general, the answer depends on whether the expense constitutes routine maintenance on the asset or whether it results in a "betterment, restoration, or new or different use for the property."[10] Taxpayers can immediately deduct the costs if

---

[7]Taxpayers must have accounting procedures in place at the beginning of the year treating items as an expense for nontax purposes amounts costing less than a specified dollar figure.

[8]Separate rules apply when taxpayers purchase materials and supplies to be used in their business (Reg. §1.162-3).

[9]Reg. §1.167(a)-5.

[10]Reg. §1.263(a)-3.

they meet the routine maintenance safe harbor rules provided in the Treasury regulations.[11] Routine maintenance is defined as preventative or cyclical maintenance that is an essential part of the ongoing care and upkeep of a building or building system. Costs related to the replacement of damaged or worn parts with comparable and commercially available replacement parts arising from inspecting, cleaning, and testing of the property are immediately deductible if two conditions are met. First, the taxpayer must fully expect to perform the activity more than once during a 10-year period (for buildings and structures related to buildings), or more than once during the property's class life (for property other than buildings). Second, the safe harbor cannot be used to deduct expenses incurred from major renovations, restorations, or improvements.

Example 10-2

What if: Suppose that Steve's business requires an annual safety certification on all its equipment and machinery. As a result of a required inspection of the machinery, Steve finds a defect in the engine of one of his machines and must replace the engine at a cost of $3,000. Can Steve immediately deduct the cost of the new engine?

Answer: Steve's business requires an annual safety certification inspection, thus Steve meets the requirement of reasonably expecting to perform the activity more than once during the machinery's class life. Assuming that Steve replaces the engine with a comparable, commercially available engine, he may immediately deduct the $3,000 cost of the new engine.

If the routine maintenance safe harbor rules do not apply, then taxpayers must determine whether the costs result in a betterment, restoration, or adaptation for a new or different use for the property.[12] If so, they must capitalize the costs; if not, they may immediately deduct the costs.[13] For example, if the roof of Teton's warehouse was completely replaced because it was leaking, Steve would be required to capitalize the costs to replace the roof as a restoration because a significant portion (100 percent) of a major component was replaced. If Teton needed to replace only 10 percent of the roof, Steve would most likely be able to immediately deduct the costs.

Special rules apply when determining the tax basis of assets converted from personal to business use or assets acquired through a nontaxable exchange, gift, or inheritance. If an asset is used for personal purposes and is later converted to business (or rental) use, the basis for cost recovery purposes is the *lesser* of (1) the cost basis of the asset or (2) the fair market value of the asset on the date of conversion to business use.[14] This rule prevents taxpayers from converting a nondeductible personal loss into a deductible business loss. For example, if Steve had purchased a

---

[11]The routine maintenance safe harbor is discussed in Reg. 1.263(a)-3(i). In addition to the routine maintenance safe harbor, the regulations provide an additional safe harbor for small taxpayers (SHST). This safe harbor allows taxpayers with average annual gross receipts over the last three years of $10 million or less to immediately deduct amounts paid for maintenance and improvement on buildings with an unadjusted basis of $1 million or less if the amounts expended are less than the lesser of 2 percent of the building's unadjusted basis or $10,000 [Reg. §1.263(a)-3(h)].

[12]Reg. §1.263(a)-3.

[13]The regulations provide detailed guidelines for taxpayers to use to establish when they have expenses related to these three distinct concepts that are beyond the scope of this chapter. See Reg. §1.263(a)-3 for details.

[14]Reg. §§1.167(g)-1 and 1.168(i)-4(b). However, this rule creates an interesting situation when selling converted assets. The taxpayer uses the lower of the adjusted basis or the fair market value at the time of the conversion for computing loss but uses the adjusted basis to compute a gain when selling converted assets.

truck for $20,000 several years ago for personal use but decided to use it as a delivery truck when its value had declined to $15,000, his basis in the truck for cost recovery purposes would be $15,000. The $5,000 decline in the truck's value from $20,000 to $15,000 would be a nondeductible personal loss to Steve, and the reduction in basis ensures that he will not be allowed to deduct the loss as a business loss. Assets acquired through a nontaxable exchange such as a like-kind exchange generally take the same basis the taxpayer had in the property the taxpayer transferred in the transaction. Assets acquired by gift have a carryover basis. This means that the taxpayer's basis in property received through a gift is generally the same basis the transferor had in the property.[15] For example, if Steve's parents gave him equipment worth $45,000 to help him start his business and his parents had purchased the equipment 10 years earlier for $25,000, Steve's basis in the equipment would be $25,000 (the same basis his parents had in the equipment). Assets acquired through inheritance generally receive a basis equal to the fair market value on the transferor's date of death.[16] For example, if Steve inherited a building worth $90,000 from his grandfather who originally paid $3,500 for it, Steve's basis would be $90,000 (its fair market value at date of death) because Steve acquired it through an inheritance.

ETHICS

Catherine Travis is starting a new business. She has several assets that she wants to use in her business that she has been using personally. Since she plans to convert several assets from personal to business use, she will need to find out how much each asset is worth so she can determine her basis for depreciating the assets. Catherine has decided that getting an appraisal would be too costly so she simply uses her cost basis for the assets. What do you think of Catherine's strategy for determining her business asset bases?

LO 10-2   DEPRECIATION

THE KEY FACTS

Tax Depreciation

- To depreciate an asset, a business must determine:
  - Original basis
  - Depreciation method
  - Recovery period
  - Depreciation convention

Before 1981, tax depreciation methods closely resembled financial accounting methods. For both financial accounting and tax purposes, businesses were allowed to choose from among a wide range of depreciation methods and **recovery periods.** Computing both tax and financial accounting depreciation required businesses to determine the assets' useful lives and "salvage values." In 1981, tax and financial accounting depreciation methods parted ways when Congress introduced the **Accelerated Cost Recovery System (ACRS)** for computing depreciation expense. Under ACRS, businesses used accelerated depreciation methods to depreciate assets over predetermined, fixed recovery periods.

Today, businesses calculate their tax depreciation using the **Modified Accelerated Cost Recovery System (MACRS)**—which is pronounced "makers" by tax accountants.[17] Compared to financial (book) depreciation, MACRS tax depreciation is quite simple. To compute MACRS depreciation for an asset, the business need only know the asset's *original cost,* the applicable *depreciation method,* the asset's *recovery*

---

[15]§1015. The basis may be increased if the transferor is required to pay gift tax on the transfer [see §1015(d)]. In addition, special dual basis rules apply if the basis in the gifted property at the gift date is greater than its fair market value.

[16]§1014. In certain circumstances, the estate can elect an alternative valuation date six months after death.

[17]IRS Publication 946 provides a useful summary of MACRS depreciation.

period (or depreciable "life"), and the applicable depreciation *convention* (the amount of depreciation deductible in the year of acquisition and the year of disposition). The method, recovery, period, and convention vary based on whether the asset is **personal property** or **real property.** The tax depreciation laws also include several special rules, which we discuss following the basic MACRS rules. We first turn our attention to determining depreciation expense for personal property.

Personal Property Depreciation

Personal property includes all tangible property, such as computers, automobiles, furniture, machinery, and equipment, other than real property. Note that personal property and *personal-use* property are *not* the same thing. Personal property denotes any property that is not real property (e.g., building and land) while personal-use property is any property used for personal purposes (e.g., a personal residence is personal-use property even though it is real property). Personal property is relatively short-lived and subject to obsolescence as compared to real property.

Depreciation Method   MACRS provides three acceptable methods for depreciating personal property: 200 percent (double) declining balance (DB), 150 percent declining balance, and straight-line.[18] The 200 percent declining balance method is the default method. This method takes twice the straight-line amount of depreciation in the first year and continues to take twice the straight-line percentage on the asset's declining basis until switching to the straight-line method in the year that the straight-line method over the remaining life provides a greater depreciation expense. Fortunately, as we describe below, the IRS provides depreciation tables to simplify the calculations.

Profitable businesses with relatively high marginal tax rates generally choose to use the 200 percent declining balance method because it generates the largest depreciation expense in the early years of the assets' lives and, thus, the highest current-year after-tax cash flows. For tax planning purposes, companies that currently have lower marginal tax rates but expect their marginal tax rates to increase in the near future may elect the straight-line method because that method generates less depreciation expense in the early years of the asset's life, relatively, and more depreciation expense in the later years when their marginal tax rates may increase.

Example 10-3

If Teton wants to accelerate its current depreciation deductions to the extent possible, what method should it use to depreciate its office furniture, machinery, and delivery truck?

Answer: The 200 percent declining balance method (default). Teton could elect to use either the 150 percent declining balance or the straight-line method, if it wants a less accelerated method for determining its depreciation deductions.

Each year, businesses elect the depreciation method for the assets placed in service during *that year*. Specifically, businesses elect one depreciation method for all similar assets they acquired that year.[19] Thus, if a business acquires several different machines during the year, it must use the same method to depreciate all of the machines. However, the methods may differ for machines acquired in different tax years.

[18]For personal property, the 200 percent DB is often referred to as the general depreciation system (GDS) while the 150 percent DB or straight-line methods are referred to as the alternative depreciation system (ADS).

[19]Technically, similar assets are assets in the same asset class. We discuss asset classes below.

EXHIBIT 10-3 Excerpt from Revenue Procedure 87-56

Description of Assets Included		Years	
Specific depreciable assets used in all business activities, except as noted:	Class Life	General Recovery Period	Alternative Recovery Period
00.11 Office Furniture, Fixtures, and Equipment: Includes furniture and fixtures that are not a structural component of a building. Includes such assets as desks, files, safes, and communications equipment. Does not include communications equipment that is included in other classes.	10	7	10
00.241 Light General Purpose Trucks: Includes trucks for use over the road (actual unloaded weight less than 13,000 pounds) . . .	4	5	5
34.0 Manufacture of Fabricated Metal Products Special Tools: Includes assets used in the production of metal cans, tinware . . .	12	7	12

Depreciation Recovery Period For financial accounting purposes, an asset's recovery period (depreciable life) is based on its taxpayer-determined estimated useful life. In contrast, for tax purposes an asset's recovery period is predetermined by the IRS in Rev. Proc. 87-56. This revenue procedure helps taxpayers categorize each of their assets based upon the property's description. Once the business has determined the appropriate categories for its assets, it can use the Revenue Procedure to identify the recovery period for all assets in a particular category. For example, Teton placed office furniture in service during the year. By examining the excerpt from Rev. Proc. 87-56 provided in Exhibit 10-3, you can see that Category or Asset Class 00.11 includes office furniture and that assets in this category, including Teton's office furniture, have a recovery period of seven years (emphasis in excerpt added through bold text).[20]

While even this small excerpt from Rev. Proc. 87-56 may seem a bit intimidating, you can classify the vast majority of business assets acquired by knowing a few common recovery periods. Exhibit 10-4 lists the most commonly purchased assets and their recovery periods.

To this point, our discussion has emphasized computing depreciation for new assets. Does the process change when businesses acquire used assets? No, it is exactly the same. For example, Teton purchased a *used* delivery truck. The fact that the truck is used does not change its MACRS recovery period. No matter how long the previous owner used the truck, Teton will restart the five-year recovery period for light general-purpose trucks (see Exhibit 10-4).

EXHIBIT 10-4 Recovery Period for Most Common Business Assets

Asset Description (summary of Rev. Proc. 87-56)	Recovery Period
Cars, light general-purpose trucks, and computers and peripheral equipment.	5 years
Office furniture, fixtures, and equipment.	7 years

[20]The "alternative" recovery period in Rev. Proc. 87-56 refers to an asset's life under the alternative depreciation system (which was discussed earlier under depreciation methods). The class life referred to in Rev. Proc. 87-56 refers to the midpoint of asset depreciation range (ADR) applicable under pre-ACRS and has little or no meaning under MACRS.

EXHIBIT 10-5   Teton Personal Property Summary (Base Scenario)

Asset	Date Acquired	Quarter Acquired	Cost Basis	Recovery Period	Reference
Office furniture	2/3/16	1st	$ 10,000	7	Example 10-1; Exhibit 10-3.
Machinery	7/22/16	3rd	510,000	7	Example 10-1; Exhibit 10-3.
Delivery truck	8/17/16	3rd	15,000	5	Example 10-1; Exhibit 10-3.
Total personal property			**$535,000**		

Under MACRS, the tax recovery period for machinery and equipment is seven years. Using Rev. Proc. 87-56, Teton has determined the cost recovery periods for the personal property it purchased and placed in service during the year. Exhibit 10-5 summarizes this information.

Depreciation Conventions   Once a business has determined the depreciation methods and recovery periods for the assets it placed in service during the year, it must also determine the applicable depreciation conventions. The depreciation convention specifies the portion of a full year's depreciation the business can deduct for an asset in the year the asset is first placed in service *and* in the year the asset is sold. For *personal property,* taxpayers must use either the **half-year convention** or the **mid-quarter convention.** But, as we discuss below, taxpayers are *not* free to choose between the two conventions. The half-year convention applies most of the time; however, under certain conditions taxpayers will be required to use the mid-quarter convention.

Half-year convention.   The half-year convention allows one-half of a full year's depreciation in the year the asset is placed in service, regardless of when it was actually placed in service. For example, when the half-year convention applies to a calendar-year business, an asset placed in service on either February 3 or August 17 is treated as though it was placed in service on July 1, which is the middle of the calendar year. Thus, under this convention, Teton would deduct one-half of a year's worth of depreciation for the machinery, office furniture, and delivery truck even though it acquired the machinery, delivery truck, and office furniture at various times during the year (see Exhibit 10-5). The half-year convention is built into the depreciation tables provided by the IRS, which simplifies the depreciation calculation for the year the asset is placed into service.

The original ACRS system required the use of the half-year convention for all personal property placed in service during the year. However, Congress believed that many businesses took unfair advantage of the half-year convention by purposely acquiring assets at the end of the year that they otherwise would have acquired at the beginning of the next taxable year. Thus, businesses received one-half of a year's worth of depreciation for assets that they only used for a small portion of the year. Even though the half-year convention is the default convention, policy makers introduced the *mid-quarter convention* under MACRS to limit or prevent this type of opportunistic behavior.

Calculating Depreciation for Personal Property   Once a business has identified the applicable method, recovery period, and convention for personal property, tax depreciation is relatively easy to calculate because the Internal Revenue Service provides depreciation percentage tables in Rev. Proc. 87-57. The percentages in the depreciation tables for tangible personal property incorporate the method and

> **THE KEY FACTS**
>
> **Half-Year Convention**
>
> - One-half of a year's depreciation is allowed in the first and the last year of an asset's life.
> - The IRS depreciation tables automatically account for the half-year convention in the acquisition year.
> - If an asset is disposed of before it is fully depreciated, only one-half of the table's applicable depreciation percentage is allowed in the year of disposition.

convention. Accordingly, there are separate tables for each combination of depreciation method (200 percent declining balance, 150 percent declining balance, and straight-line) and convention (half-year and mid-quarter; each quarter has its own table). To determine the depreciation for an asset for the year, use the following three steps:

Step 1: Locate the applicable table provided in Rev. Proc. 87-57.
Step 2: Select the column that corresponds with the asset's recovery period.
Step 3: Find the row identifying the year of the asset's recovery period.

The tables are constructed so that the intersection of the row and column provides the percentage of the asset's *original basis* that is deductible as depreciation expense for the particular year. Thus, depreciation expense for a particular asset is the product of the percentage from the table and the asset's *original basis*.

Applying the Half-Year Convention   Consider Table 1 in the appendix at the end of the chapter that shows the depreciation percentages for MACRS 200 percent declining balance using the half-year convention. If a seven-year asset is placed into service during the current year, the depreciation percentage is 14.29 percent [the intersection of row 1 (year 1) and the seven-year property column].

Notice from Table 1 that the depreciation percentages for five-year property extend for six years and the percentages for seven-year property extend for eight years. Why does it take six years to fully depreciate an asset with a five-year recovery period and eight years for a seven-year asset? Because the business does not deduct a full year's depreciation in the first year (businesses must use either the half-year or mid-quarter convention), an entire year of depreciation is effectively split between the first and last year. For example, when the half-year convention applies to a five-year asset, the taxpayer deducts one-half of a year's depreciation in year 1 and one-half of a year's depreciation in year 6.

Example 10-4

Teton is using the 200 percent declining balance method and half-year convention to compute depreciation expense on its current-year personal property additions. What is Teton's depreciation expense for these assets?

Answer: $77,308, computed as follows:

Asset	Date Placed in Service	(1) Original Basis	(2) Rate	(1) × (2) Depreciation
Office furniture	February 3	$ 10,000	14.29%	$ 1,429
Machinery	July 22	510,000	14.29	72,879
Used delivery truck	August 17	15,000	20.00	3,000
Total				**$77,308**

Because the office furniture and machinery have a seven-year recovery period and it is the first year for depreciation, the depreciation rate is 14.29 percent (see Table 1). The depreciation rate for the used delivery truck (five-year property) is determined in a similar manner.

Calculating depreciation for assets in years after the year of acquisition is also relatively simple. Again, using Table 1 to compute depreciation for the second year, the taxpayer would multiply the asset's original basis times the rate factor in the *year 2* row and the *year 3* row in the following year and so on.

Example 10-5

What if: Assume that Teton holds the tangible personal property it acquired and placed in service this year until the assets are fully depreciated. Using the IRS provided tables (see Table 1), how would Teton determine its depreciation expense for years 1 through 8?

Answer: See the following table:

	Depreciation Over Asset Recovery Period			
Year	7-Year Office Furniture	7-Year Machinery	5-Year Delivery Truck	Yearly Total
1	$ 1,429	$ 72,879	$ 3,000	$ 77,308
2	2,449	124,899	4,800	132,148
3	1,749	89,199	2,880	93,828
4	1,249	63,699	1,728	66,676
5	893	45,543	1,728	48,164
6	892	45,492	864	47,248
7	893	45,543	N/A	46,436
8	446	22,746	N/A	23,192
Accumulated Depreciation	$10,000	$510,000	$15,000	$535,000

Half-year convention for year of disposition. Businesses often sell or dispose of assets before they fully depreciate them. Recall that the half-year convention applies in both the year of acquisition and the year of disposition. Note, however, that the tables can't anticipate when a business may dispose of an asset. Accordingly, the tables only provide depreciation percentages for assets assuming the asset won't be disposed of before it is fully depreciated. That is, for each year in the asset's recovery period, the tables provide a percentage for an entire year's worth of depreciation. So, to calculate the depreciation for the year of disposition, the business first calculates depreciation for the *entire year* as if the property had not been disposed of. Then the business applies the half-year convention by multiplying the full year's depreciation by 50 percent (one-half of a year's depreciation). Note, however, that if a business acquires and disposes of an asset in the same tax year, it is not allowed to claim any depreciation on the asset.[21]

Example 10-6

What if: Assume that Teton sells all of its office furniture in year 2 (the year after it buys it). What is Teton's depreciation for the office furniture in the year of disposition (year 2)?

Answer: $1,225, calculated using the MACRS Half-Year Convention Table as follows:

Asset	Amount	Explanation
(1) Office furniture	$10,000	Original basis.
(2) Depreciation percentage	24.49%	Seven-year property, year 2.
(3) Full year of depreciation	$ 2,449	(1) × (2).
(4) Half-year convention percentage	50%	Depreciation limit in year of disposal.
Depreciation in year of disposal	$ 1,225	(3) × (4).

(continued on page 10-12)

[21]Suppose Teton sells the 5-year delivery truck in year 6 on January 5. What depreciation percentage should Teton use for purposes of determining year 6 depreciation? Teton should take one-half year's depreciation on the truck. The percentage shown in Table 1 for year 6 already reflects the half-year convention, so Teton would take $864 of depreciation regardless of when during year 6 the truck was sold.

What if: Assume that Teton sold all of its office furniture in year 1 (the year it bought it and placed it in service). How much depreciation expense can Teton deduct for the office furniture in year 1?

Answer: $0. A business is not allowed to claim any depreciation expense for assets it acquires and disposes of in the same year.

Mid-quarter convention. Under the mid-quarter convention, businesses treat assets *as though* they were placed in service during the middle of the *quarter* in which the business actually placed the assets into service. For example, when the mid-quarter convention applies, if a business places an asset in service on December 1 (in the fourth quarter) it must treat the asset as though it was placed in service on November 15, which is the middle of the fourth quarter. Consequently, the business would only be able to deduct one-half of a quarter's worth of depreciation in the year the asset was placed in service (depreciation for the second half of November and the entire month of December). In addition, if the mid-quarter convention applies, businesses must use the convention for all tangible personal property placed in service during the year. The IRS depreciation tables have built in the mid-quarter convention to simplify the calculations.

Businesses must use the mid-quarter convention when *more* than 40 percent of their total *tangible personal property* that they place in service during the year is placed in service during the *fourth* quarter. Thus, the steps to determine whether the mid-quarter convention applies are the following:

Step 1: Sum the total basis of the tangible personal property that was placed in service during the year.

Step 2: Sum the total basis of the tangible personal property that was placed in service in the fourth quarter.

Step 3: Divide the outcome of Step 2 by the outcome of Step 1. If the quotient is greater than 40 percent, the business must use the mid-quarter convention to determine the depreciation for all tangible personal property the business placed in service during the year. Otherwise, the business uses the half-year convention for depreciating this property.

In accordance with Reg. §1.168(d)-1(b)(4), property expensed under §179 is not included in the numerator or denominator of the mid-quarter test. The mid-quarter test is applied after the §179 expense but before bonus depreciation (discussed later in the chapter).

Example 10-7

The following excerpt from the base scenario in Exhibit 10-5 provides the information we need to determine if Teton must use the mid-quarter convention to compute depreciation:

Asset	Date Acquired	Quarter Acquired	Cost Basis
Office furniture	2/3/16	First	$ 10,000
Machinery	7/22/16	Third	510,000
Delivery truck	8/17/16	Third	15,000
Total personal property			**$535,000**

Is Teton required to use the mid-quarter convention to depreciate its personal property?

Answer: No. See computation below.

Description	Amount	Explanation
(1) Total basis of tangible personal property placed in service during year	$535,000	
(2) Total basis of tangible personal property placed in service in fourth quarter	0	
(3) Percentage of basis of total tangible personal property placed in service during fourth quarter	0%	(2)/(1).

Teton is not required to use the mid-quarter convention because it did not place more than 40 percent of its assets in service during the fourth quarter. (In fact, Teton did not place any assets in service in the fourth quarter.) Consequently, Teton will use the half-year convention to calculate its depreciation expense.

Example 10-8

What if: Let's replace the facts from the base scenario presented in Exhibit 10-5 with the following alternative scenario 1 facts. In this alternative set of facts, we assume the machinery was acquired during the fourth quarter on October 25 as follows:

Asset	Date Acquired	Quarter Acquired	Cost Basis
Office furniture	2/3/16	First	$ 10,000
Delivery truck	8/17/16	Third	15,000
Machinery	10/25/16	Fourth	510,000
Total personal property			**$535,000**

Under alternative scenario 1, is Teton required to use the mid-quarter convention?

Answer: Yes. Of the personal property it placed in service during the year, it placed 95.3 percent in service in the last quarter (this is greater than 40 percent). See the calculations below:

Description	Amount	Explanation
(1) Cost of all personal property placed in service during current year.	$535,000	
(2) Cost of personal property placed in service in the fourth quarter during current year.	510,000	
(3) Percentage of all personal property placed in service during current year that was placed in service in the fourth quarter.	95.3%	(2)/(1).

What if: Assume that Teton also placed in service on July 1 a building costing $1,000,000. Is Teton subject to the mid-quarter convention?

Answer: Yes. Because the building is real property (not personal property), it is not included in the mid-quarter calculation. The calculation is exactly the same as the calculation in alternative scenario 1 above.

Applying the Mid-Quarter Convention   When the mid-quarter convention applies, the process for computing depreciation is the same as it is when the half-year convention applies, except that businesses use a different set of depreciation tables (a separate table for each quarter). After categorizing the assets by recovery period and grouping them into quarters, businesses consult the Mid-Quarter Convention

Tables 2a–d in the appendix to this chapter to determine the depreciation rate for each asset group.

The depreciation expense for an asset is the product of the asset's original basis and the percentage from the table.

Example 10-9

What if: For this example, we assume the facts from alternative scenario 1 presented in Example 10-8 (see table below). What is Teton's year 1 depreciation expense for its personal property additions under the alternative scenario 1 presented in Example 10-8?

Answer: $22,957, computed as follows:

Asset	Purchase Date	Quarter	Original Basis	Rate	Depreciation
Office furniture (7-year)	February 3	First	$ 10,000	25.00%	$ 2,500
Delivery truck (5-year)	August 17	Third	15,000	15.00%	2,250
Machinery (7-year)	October 25	Fourth	510,000	3.57%	18,207
					$22,957

The office furniture factor of 25.00 percent is located in Table 2a. See the columns for property placed into service during the first quarter (first two columns); select the 7-year recovery period column (last column), and the year 1 row. The process for determining the rate factor for the delivery truck and machinery follows the same methodology using Tables 2c and 2d, respectively.

Teton's $77,308 depreciation expense under the half-year convention (see Example 10-3) is significantly higher than its $22,957 depreciation expense under the mid-quarter convention (see Example 10-8). Why the big disparity? Because the (high cost) machinery was placed into service during the fourth quarter and thus generated significantly less current depreciation expense (one-half of one quarter's depreciation) than it would have under the half-year convention. It is important to note, however, that when using the mid-quarter convention, assets placed in service in the first or second quarter will generate more depreciation than they would have under the half-year convention (10.5/12 and 7.5/12 of a full year, respectively). However, because the mid-quarter convention only applies when a large percentage of the cost of the assets was placed in service in the fourth quarter, the mid-quarter convention tends to generate less overall depreciation expense for new additions than the half-year convention.

The process for calculating depreciation for assets in years after the year of acquisition under the mid-quarter convention is nearly identical to the process we described for making this computation under the half-year convention. The only difference is that the business looks to the MACRS Mid-Quarter Convention Table (Table 2 in the chapter appendix) for the appropriate quarter rather than the MACRS Half-Year Convention Table (Table 1 in the chapter appendix).

Example 10-10

What if: Assume that Teton held and fully depreciated the tangible personal property it placed in service this year under the mid-quarter convention (alternative scenario 1). What would be Teton's depreciation expense for its personal property additions for years 1 through 8 using the mid-quarter tables provided in the appendix at the end of this chapter?

Answer: See table below:*

Year	7-Year Office Furniture 1st Quarter	5-Year Delivery Truck 3rd Quarter	7-Year Machinery Year 4th Quarter	Yearly Total
1	$ 2,500	$ 2,250	$ 18,207	$ 22,957
2	2,143	5,100	140,505	147,748
3	1,531	3,060	100,368	104,959
4	1,093	1,836	71,706	74,635
5	875	1,695	51,204	53,774
6	874	1,059	44,523	46,456
7	875	N/A	44,523	45,398
8	109	N/A	38,964	39,073
	$10,000	$15,000	$510,000	$535,000

*See Table 2; the depreciation is calculated by multiplying the applicable rate by the cost basis.

Mid-quarter convention for year of disposition.   Calculating depreciation expense in the year of sale or disposition is a bit more involved when the mid-quarter convention applies than when it does not. When the mid-quarter convention applies, the asset is treated as though it is sold in the middle of the quarter of which it was actually sold. The process for calculating mid-quarter convention depreciation for the year of sale is exactly the same as the process for using the half-year convention, except that *instead of* multiplying the full year's depreciation by 50 percent, the business multiplies the amount of depreciation it would have been able to claim on the asset if it had not sold the asset (a full year's depreciation) by the applicable percentage in Exhibit 10-6.[22]

EXHIBIT 10-6   **Mid-Quarter Convention Percentage of Full Year's Depreciation in Year of Disposition**

Quarter of Disposition	Percentage	Calculation*
First	12.5%	1.5/12
Second	37.5	4.5/12
Third	62.5	7.5/12
Fourth	87.5	10.5/12

*The calculation is the number of months the taxpayer held or is deemed to have held the asset in the year of disposition divided by 12 months in the year.

Example 10-11

What if: Assume that Teton depreciates its personal property under the mid-quarter convention (alternative scenario 1, see Example 10-5) and that it sells its office furniture in the third quarter of year 2. The office furniture ($10,000 original basis) was placed into service during the first quarter of year 1 and has a seven-year recovery period. What depreciation expense can Teton deduct for the office furniture in year 2, the year of sale?

(continued on page 10-16)

[22]Suppose Teton sells the 5-year delivery truck in year 6 on January 5 after using the mid-quarter convention as in Example 10-9. What depreciation percentage should Teton use for purposes of determining year 6 depreciation? Teton should be allowed 1/2 of a quarter's depreciation in year 6. The calculation of this amount is complicated by the mid-quarter convention because the 3rd quarter depreciation percentage for a 5-year asset in year 6 using Table 2c shows 7.06 percent. This amount, however, is the depreciation rate for 2 1/2 quarters representing the remaining depreciation in the final year of the asset's recovery period. Teton will be allowed $212 of depreciation in the year of disposition determined as $15,000 multiplied by 1.412 percent (7.06%/2.5 quarters × .5 quarters = 1.412%).

Answer: $1,339, computed as follows:

Description	Amount	Explanation
(1) Original basis	$10,000	Example 10-8.
(2) Year 2 depreciation percentage	21.43%	Table 2a, mid-quarter, first quarter table, 7-year property, year 2.
(3) Full year 2 depreciation	2,143	(1) × (2).
(4) Percentage of full year's depreciation in year of disposition if mid-quarter convention applies	62.5%	From Exhibit 10-6; asset disposed of in third quarter.
Depreciation in year of disposition	**$ 1,339**	(3) × (4).

What if: Assume Teton disposed of the office furniture on January 2 of year 2. How much depreciation expense would it be able to claim on the furniture in year 2?

Answer: $268 ($2,143 full year's depreciation × 12.5% from Exhibit 10-6).

Real Property

For depreciation purposes, real property is classified as land, *residential rental* property, or *nonresidential property*. Land is nondepreciable. Residential rental property consists of dwelling units such as houses, condominiums, and apartment complexes. Residential property has a 27.5-year recovery period. Nonresidential property consists of all other buildings (office buildings, manufacturing facilities, shopping malls, and the like). Nonresidential property placed in service on or after May 13, 1993, has a 39-year recovery period and nonresidential property placed in service after December 31, 1986, and before May 13, 1993, has a 31.5-year recovery period. Exhibit 10-7 summarizes the recovery periods for real property.

If a building is substantially improved (not a minor repair) at some point after the initial purchase, the building addition is treated as a new asset with the same recovery period of the original building. For example, if Teton expanded its warehouse 10 years after the building was placed in service, the expansion or building addition would be depreciated as a *new, separate* asset over 39 years because it is nonresidential property.

An important area of tax practice related to real property is cost segregation. This practice attempts to partition or divide the costs of a building into two or more categories. The first category is the building itself, which has a recovery period as noted in Exhibit 10-7. The second category is building components (tangible personal property associated with the building such as electrical and plumbing fixtures that have a shorter recovery period and accelerated depreciation method). Cost segregation utilizes engineers and construction experts who divide the costs between real and tangible personal property. This can generate significant tax savings due to the difference in the present value of the tax savings from the accelerated depreciation deductions associated with personal property relative to real property.

EXHIBIT 10-7 **Recovery Period for Real Property**

Asset Description (summary from Rev. Proc. 87-57)	Recovery Period
Residential	27.5 years
Nonresidential property placed in service on or after May 13, 1993	39 years
Nonresidential property placed in service before May 13, 1993	31.5 years

Applicable Method   All depreciable real property is depreciated for tax purposes using the straight-line method. This is generally consistent with depreciation methods used for financial accounting purposes.

Applicable Convention   All real property is depreciated using the mid-month convention. The **mid-month convention** allows the owner of real property to expense one-half of a month's depreciation for the month in which the property was placed in service (and in the month of the year it is sold as well). This is true regardless of whether the asset was placed in service at the beginning or at the end of the month. For example, if Teton placed its warehouse into service on May 1 (or on *any* other day in May), it would deduct *one-half* a month's depreciation for May and then full depreciation for the months June through December.

Depreciation Tables   Just as it does for personal property, the IRS provides depreciation tables for real property. The depreciation tables for 27.5 years, 31.5 years, and 39 years real property are reproduced as Tables 3, 4, and 5, respectively, in this chapter's appendix. The percentage of the asset's original basis that is depreciated in a particular year is located at the intersection of the month the asset was placed in service (column) and the year of depreciation (row—first, second, etc.).

Example 10-12

As indicated in Example 10-1, Teton's basis in the warehouse it purchased on May 1 of year 1 is $275,000. What is Teton's year 1 depreciation on its warehouse?

Answer: $4,414, computed as follows:

Asset	Method	Recovery Period	Date Placed in Service	(1) Basis	(2) Rate*	(1) × (2) Depreciation
Warehouse	SL	39	May 1	$275,000	1.605%	**$4,414**

What if: What would be Teton's year 1 depreciation expense if the building was not a warehouse but was an apartment building that it rented to Teton's employees?

Answer: $6,251, computed as follows:

Asset	Method	Recovery Period	Date Placed in Service	(1) Basis	(2) Rate†	(1) × (2) Depreciation
Apt. Bldg.	SL	27.5	May 1	$275,000	2.273%	**$6,251**

*The 1.605 percent tax rate factor for the year is found in the 39-year table (Table 5, in the appendix to this chapter) in the fifth column (fifth month) and first row (first year).
† The 2.273 percent tax rate factor for the year is found in the 27.5-year table (Table 4, in the appendix to this chapter) in the fifth column (fifth month) and first row (first year).

When using depreciation tables for real property it is important to stay in the month column corresponding with the month the property was originally placed in service.[23] Thus, to calculate depreciation for a piece of real property placed in service in May (the fifth month), businesses will *always* (for each year of depreciation) find the current-year rate factor in the fifth column for that asset. This is true even if the asset is sold in a subsequent year in July (it's easy to make the mistake of using the seventh column to calculate the depreciation for the year of disposition in this situation).

---

[23]Failure to do so will result in the wrong depreciation expense and is technically a change in accounting method (which requires filing of a Form 3115 with the IRS).

Mid-month convention for year of disposition.   Businesses deduct one-half of a month's depreciation in the month they sell or otherwise dispose of real property. For example, if Teton sold its warehouse on March 5 of year 2, it would deduct two and one-half months of depreciation in that year for the warehouse (depreciation for January, February, and one-half of March). Calculating depreciation expense in the year of sale or disposition for mid-month convention assets is similar to the calculation under the mid-quarter convention. When the mid-month convention applies, the asset is treated as though it is sold in the *middle of the month* of which it was actually sold. The simplest process for calculating mid-month convention depreciation for the year of sale consists of the following four steps:

> **Step 1:** Determine the amount of depreciation expense for the asset as if the asset was held for the entire year.
>
> **Step 2:** Subtract one-half of a month from the month in which the asset was sold (if sold in third month, subtract .5 from 3 to get 2.5). (Subtract half of a month because the business is treated as though the asset was disposed of in the middle of the third month—not the end.)
>
> **Step 3:** Divide the amount determined in Step 2 by 12 months (2.5/12). This is the fraction of the full year's depreciation the business is eligible to deduct.
>
> **Step 4:** Multiply the Step 3 outcome by the full depreciation determined in Step 1.

These steps are summarized in the following formula:

$$\text{Mid-month depreciation for year of disposition}$$
$$= \text{Full year's depreciation} \times \frac{(\text{Month in which asset was disposed of} - .5)}{12}$$

Example 10-13

What if: Assume that Teton sells its warehouse on March 5 in year 2 (the year after Teton buys it). What is Teton's depreciation for the warehouse in the year of disposition (year 2)?

Answer: $1,469, computed using the four-step procedure outlined above as follows.

> **Step 1:** Determine full year's depreciation: $275,000 × 2.564%* = $7,051
>
> **Step 2:** 3 (month sold) − .5 = 2.5
>
> **Step 3:** 2.5/12
>
> **Step 4:** $7,051 × 2.5/12 = $1,469 (see formula above).

*The 2.564 percent rate factor (full-year percentage) in Step 1 is obtained from the MACRS Mid-Month Table for 39-year property (Table 5) placed in service during the fifth month (year 2 row).

LO 10-3   ## Special Rules Relating to Cost Recovery

In addition to the basic MACRS rules, several additional provisions may affect the cost recovery of tangible personal property. Congress often uses these special rules for economic stimulus or to curb perceived taxpayer abuses. On December 18, 2015, Congress passed the Protecting Americans from Tax Hikes (PATH) Act of 2015, which modifies, extends and in some cases, makes permanent several of these special rules relating to depreciation. We discuss these rules below.

Immediate Expensing   Policy makers created an important tax incentive designed to help small businesses purchasing new or used tangible personal property. This incentive is commonly referred to as the **§179 expense** or *immediate expensing* election.[24] As discussed earlier in the chapter, businesses must generally depreciate assets over the assets' recovery periods. However, under §179, businesses may elect to immediately expense up to $500,000 of tangible personal property placed in service during 2016.[25,26] Businesses can also use immediate expensing (up to $250,000) for qualified real property (qualified leasehold improvements, qualified retail improvements, and qualified restaurant property). They may also elect to deduct less than the maximum. When businesses elect to deduct a certain amount of §179 expense, they immediately expense all or a portion of an asset's basis or several assets' bases. To reflect this immediate depreciation expense, they must reduce the basis of the asset or assets (to which they applied the expense) *before* they compute the MACRS depreciation expense (from the tables).

Example 10-14

What if: Assume Teton is eligible for and elects to immediately deduct $80,000 of §179 expense against the basis of the machinery. (Note that Teton could have elected to deduct up to $500,000.) What is the amount of Teton's current year depreciation expense, including regular MACRS depreciation and the §179 expense on its machinery (assuming half-year convention applies)?

Answer: $141,447, computed as follows:

Description	Amount	Explanation
(1) Machinery	$510,000	Example 10-1.
(2) §179 expense	80,000	
(3) Remaining basis in machinery	$430,000	(1) – (2).
(4) MACRS depreciation rate for 7-year machinery	14.29%	Rate from Table 1.
(5) MACRS depreciation expense on machinery	$ 61,447	(3) × (4).
Total depreciation on machinery	**$141,447**	(2) + (5).

What if: Assume that Teton was eligible for and elected to claim the maximum amount of §179 expense. What would be its total current-year depreciation expense, including MACRS depreciation and §179 expense (assuming half-year convention applies)?

Answer: $501,429, computed as follows:

Description	Amount	Explanation
(1) Machinery	$510,000	Example 10-1.
(2) §179 expense	500,000	Maximum expense in 2016.
(3) Remaining basis in machinery	$ 10,000	(1) – (2).
(4) MACRS depreciation rate for 7-year machinery	14.29%	Rate from Table 1.
(5) MACRS depreciation expense on machinery	$ 1,429	(3) × (4).
Total depreciation on machinery	**$501,429**	(2) + (5).

[24]Intangibles and tangible personal property that are used less than 50 percent for business and most real property are not eligible for immediate expensing.

[25]The maximum allowable expense under §179 is indexed for inflation beginning with years after 2015. For 2016, the maximum §179 amount remains the same as the 2015 maximum of $500,000. (Rev. Proc. 2016-14)

[26]These maximum amounts are per tax return. Thus, if an individual has multiple businesses with asset acquisitions, the taxpayer may only deduct up to these maximum amounts for the combined businesses.

Limits on immediate expensing. The maximum amount of §179 expense a business may elect to claim for the year is subject to a phase-out limitation. Under the phase-out limitation, businesses must reduce the $500,000 maximum available expense dollar for dollar for the amount of *tangible personal property* purchased and placed in service during 2016 *over* a $2,010,000 threshold.[27] Thus if a business places $2,510,000 ($2,010,000 threshold plus $500,000) or more of tangible personal property into service during 2016, its maximum available §179 expense for the year is $0. The phased-out portion of the maximum expense disappears and does *not* carry over to another year.

Example 10-15

What if: Let's assume that during 2016, Teton placed into service $2,100,000 of machinery (up from the base scenario amount of $510,000), $10,000 of office furniture, and a $15,000 truck for a total of $2,125,000 tangible *personal* property placed in service for the year. What is Teton's maximum §179 expense after applying the phase-out limitation?

Answer: $385,000, computed as follows:

Description	Amount	Explanation
(1) Property placed in service in 2016	$2,125,000	
(2) Threshold for §179 phase-out	2,010,000	2016 amount [§179(b)(1)].
(3) Phase-out of maximum §179 expense	$ 115,000	(1) − (2) (permanently disallowed).
(4) Maximum §179 expense before phase-out	$ 500,000	§179(b)(2).
(5) Phase-out of maximum §179 expense	115,000	From (3).
Maximum §179 expense after phase-out*	**$ 385,000**	(4) − (5).

*Note that this is the maximum expense after phase-out but *before* the taxable income limitation we discuss next.

What if: Assume further that Teton acquired and placed in service a warehouse costing $275,000. Taking the warehouse into account, what is Teton's maximum §179 expense after the phase-out?

Answer: $385,000. The same answer as above. The phase-out is based on the amount of tangible personal property placed in service during the year. Because the warehouse is *real property* (not qualified), its acquisition has no effect on Teton's maximum §179 expense.

Businesses may elect to claim the §179 expense for the year up to the maximum amount available (after computing the phase-out—see the previous example). When a business elects to claim a certain amount of §179 expense, it must reduce the basis of the asset(s) to which the expense is applied. It then computes regular depreciation on the remaining basis after reducing the basis of the asset(s) for the §179 expense.

The business's *deductible* §179 expense is limited to the taxpayer's business income after deducting all expenses (including regular depreciation expense) except the §179 expense. Consequently, the §179 expense cannot create or extend a business's net operating loss. Taxpayers' business income includes income from all businesses. For example, a sole-proprietor's business income for purposes of §179 would include not only the income from all Schedules C but also from regular wages. If a business claims more §179 expense than it is allowed to deduct due to the taxable income limitation, it carries the excess forward (indefinitely) and deducts it in a subsequent year, subject to the taxable income limitation (but not the phase-out limitation) in the subsequent year.[28]

---

[27]The threshold under §179 is indexed for inflation beginning with years after 2015. The threshold for 2016 was increased to $2,010,000 from the 2015 amount of $2,000,000. (Rev. Proc. 2016-14)

[28]Businesses typically elect only to expense the currently deductible amount since the taxable income limitation may also limit their §179 expense in future years just as it does for the current year.

Example 10-16

What if: Let's assume the facts of the previous example, where Teton's maximum §179 expense after applying the phase-out limitation is $385,000. Also assume that Teton elects to claim the entire $385,000 expense and it chooses to apply it against the machinery. Further assume that Teton reports $296,503 of taxable income before deducting any §179 expense and depreciation. What amount of total depreciation (including §179 expense) is Teton able to deduct on the machinery for the year?

Answer: $296,503 computed as follows:

Description	Amount	Explanation
(1) Machinery	$2,100,000	Example 10-15.
(2) Elected §179 expense	385,000	
(3) Remaining basis	$1,715,000	(1) – (2).
(4) MACRS depreciation rate for 7-year machinery, year 1	14.29%	See Table 1.
(5) MACRS deprecation expense on machinery	$245,074	(3) × (4).
(6) Deductible §179 expense	51,429	Taxable income limitation ($296,503 – $245,074).
(7) Total depreciation expense on machinery for the year	**$ 296,503**	(5) + (6).
(8) Excess §179 expense	$333,571	(2) – (6).

What is the amount of Teton's excess §179 expense (elected expense in excess of the deductible amount due to the taxable income limitation), and what does it do with it for tax purposes?

Answer: $333,571. See the above table for the computation (line 8). Teton carries this $333,571 excess §179 expense forward to future years and may deduct it subject to the taxable income limitation. Note that the depreciable basis of the machinery remaining after the §179 expense is $1,715,000 because the depreciable basis is reduced by the full $385,000 of §179 expense claimed even though the deductible §179 expense was limited to $51,429 in the current year.

THE KEY FACTS

§179 Expenses

- $500,000 of tangible personal property can be immediately expensed in 2016.
- Businesses are eligible for the full amount of this expense when tangible personal property placed in service is less than $2,010,000. Beginning at $2,010,000, the §179 expense is phased out, dollar-for-dollar. When assets placed in service reach $2,510,000, no §179 expense can be taken.
- §179 expenses are also limited to a business's taxable income before the §179 expense. §179 expenses cannot create losses.

Choosing the assets to immediately expense. Businesses qualifying for immediate expensing are allowed to choose the asset or assets (from tangible personal property placed in service during the year) they immediately expense under §179. If a business's objective is to maximize its current depreciation expense and the half-year convention applies, it should immediately expense the asset with the lowest first-year cost recovery percentage including bonus depreciation (discussed in the next section). For example, looking at Tables 2a and 2c in the chapter appendix, if a business had to choose between immediately expensing seven-year property placed in service in the first quarter or five-year property placed in service in the third quarter, which asset should it elect to expense under §179 if it wanted to maximize its current-year depreciation expense? The five-year asset because its first-year depreciation percentage is 15 percent, while the seven-year asset's first-year depreciation percentage is 25 percent. Finally, it is important to note that businesses reduce the basis of the assets for the §179 expense before computing whether the mid-quarter convention applies.[29]

Example 10-17

What if: Let's assume that Teton placed into service on June 1, five-year property costing $600,000 and seven-year property costing $600,000. Further assume that Teton is not subject to the taxable income limitation for the §179 expense. What is Teton's depreciation expense (including §179 expense) if it elects to apply the full §179 expense against the five-year property (Scenario A)? What is its depreciation expense if it applies it against its seven-year property (Scenario B)?

(continued on page 10-22)

[29]Treasury Regulation §1.168(d)-1(b)(4)(i).

Answer: $605,740 if it applies the §179 to the five-year property (Scenario A) and $634,290 if it applies it to the seven-year property (Scenario B). See the computations below:

Description	(Scenario A) §179 Expense on 5-Year Property	(Scenario B) §179 Expense on 7-Year Property	Explanation
(1) Original basis	$600,000	$600,000	
(2) Elected §179 expense	500,000	500,000	Maximum expense.
(3) Remaining basis	100,000	100,000	(1) − (2).
(4) MACRS depreciation rate	20%	14.29%	See Table 1.
(5) MACRS depreciation expense	$ 20,000	$ 14,290	(3) × (4).
(6) Deductible §179 expense	500,000	500,000	Example 10-15.
(7) MACRS depreciation on other property	85,740	120,000	This is the depreciation on the $600,000 seven-year property in the five-year column and on the $600,000 five-year property in the seven-year column.
Total depreciation expense	$605,740	$634,290	(5) + (6) + (7).

Note that Teton deducts $28,550 more in depreciation expense if it applies the §179 expense to the seven-year property.

What if: Assume the same facts, except that Teton placed the five-year property in service on December 1. Absent any §179 expense, Teton would be subject to the mid-quarter convention because 50 percent of its tangible personal property was placed in service in the fourth quarter. Assuming Teton wanted to avoid the mid-quarter convention, how should it apply its §179 expense?

Answer: It should apply the §179 expense against the five-year property. By doing so, the basis of the assets placed in service in the fourth quarter is $100,000 ($600,000 minus $500,000 §179 expense) and the basis of the assets placed in service in total is $700,000 ($600,000 7-year property + $100,000 5-year property). Thus, the percentage of tangible personal property placed in service in the fourth quarter is 14.3 percent ($100,000/$700,000) and the mid-quarter convention does not apply. If, however, it applies the §179 expense against the seven-year property, the mid-quarter convention would apply because the percentage of tangible personal property placed in service in the fourth quarter increases to 85.7 percent ($600,000/$700,000). Because this exceeds 40 percent, the mid-quarter convention applies. Teton could also expense just enough five-year property to avoid the mid-quarter convention and elect the rest of the §179 expense against the seven-year property to maximize its total depreciation.

Bonus depreciation. To stimulate the economy, policy makers occasionally implement **bonus depreciation.**[30] On December 18, 2015, Congress extended the bonus depreciation provision with the passage of the Protecting Americans from Tax Hikes (PATH) Act of 2015. Bonus depreciation allows taxpayers to immediately expense 50 percent of qualified property. Qualified property must have a recovery period of 20 years or less (no real property) and the original use of the property must commence with the taxpayer (the property must be new rather than used), and the property must be placed in service during 2016.[31] Bonus depreciation is calculated after the §179 expense but before regular MACRS depreciation.[32] Taxpayers may elect not to take bonus depreciation by attaching a statement to their tax return indicating they are electing to not claim bonus depreciation.

---

[30]§168(k)(2)(6). Bonus depreciation, if applicable, is also allowable for purposes of the AMT.
[31]§168(k)(2)(A)(iv).
[32]Reg. §1.168(k)-1(a)(2)(iii) and Reg. §1.168(k)-1(d)(3) Example (2).

Example 10-18

What if: Assume that Teton elected bonus depreciation for the tangible personal property acquired in Exhibit 10-5.

Asset	Date Acquired	Quarter Acquired	Cost Basis	Recovery Period
Office furniture	2/3/16	1st	$ 10,000	7
Machinery	7/22/16	3rd	510,000	7
Delivery truck	8/17/16	3rd	15,000	5
Total			$535,000	

Assuming Teton elects no §179 expense, what is Teton's bonus depreciation?

Answer: $260,000 computed as follows:

Description	Amount	Explanation
(1) Qualified property	$520,000	
(2) Bonus depreciation rate	50%	§168(k)(1)(A).
Bonus depreciation	$260,000	(1) × (2).

Note that the delivery truck is not eligible for bonus depreciation because it is used property.

What if: Assuming Teton elects the maximum §179 expense, what is Teton's bonus depreciation?

Answer: $17,500 computed as follows:

Description	Amount	Explanation
(1) §179 qualified property	$535,000	
(2) §179 expense	500,000	Maximum expense.
(3) Remaining basis	35,000	(1) − (2).
(4) Remaining amount eligible for bonus depreciation	35,000	Remaining amount relates to the office furniture and machinery. Since the truck is used and not eligible for bonus depreciation, we would apply the §179 expense to the truck to maximize the current year depreciation deduction.
(5) Bonus depreciation rate	50%	§168(k)(1)(A).
(6) Bonus depreciation	$ 17,500	(4) × (5).

TAXES IN THE REAL WORLD   What a Difference a Day (or Few) Makes

Taxpayers may begin taking depreciation deductions on their tax returns for business assets "placed in service" during the taxable year. As one taxpayer recently found out, determining when an asset is placed in service is not as simple as purchasing and using an asset. Michael Brown, a wealthy insurance salesman, purchased a $22 million Bombardier Challenger 604 airplane for use in his business. He took possession of the plane on December 30, 2003, and flew the plane across the country on business trips before the end of the year. Accordingly, Brown claimed about $11 million of bonus depreciation on his 2003 tax return. In January 2004, the plane was grounded for a period of time while a conference table and a display screen were added at an additional cost of $500,000. These improvements were "needed" and "required" for his insurance business according to Brown.

The IRS challenged Brown's bonus depreciation deduction claiming that the plane was not "placed in service" in 2003. The issue is when the plane was regularly available for use in its specifically intended function. Per Brown's testimony, he insisted on having the conference table and display screen so he could conduct business on the plane. Because of this testimony that determined the plane's specifically intended function, the Tax Court denied the bonus depreciation deduction for 2003.

THE KEY FACTS

Listed Property

- When an asset is used for both personal and business use, calculate the business-use percentage.
- If the business-use percentage is above 50 percent, the allowable depreciation is limited to the business-use percentage.
- If a listed property's business-use percentage ever falls below 50 percent, depreciation for all previous years is retroactively restated using MACRS straight-line method.

The outcome of this case illustrates the importance of determining the specific function for an asset and whether seemingly minor (2 percent) upgrades can make the asset substantially unavailable for its specifically intended function. It seems the taxpayer's own testimony of the plane's specifically intended function drove the Tax Court's decision to disallow the bonus depreciation deduction.

Source: Brown, T. C. Memo. 2013-275.

Listed Property   Most business-owned assets are used for business rather than personal purposes. For example, Weyerhaeuser employees probably have little or no personal interest in using Weyerhaeuser's timber-harvesting equipment during their free time. In contrast, business owners and employees may find some business assets, such as company automobiles or laptop computers, conducive for personal use.

Business assets that tend to be used for both business and personal purposes are referred to as **listed property.** For example, automobiles, other means of transportation (planes, boats, and recreation vehicles), computer equipment, and even digital cameras are considered to be listed property. The tax law limits the allowable depreciation on listed property to the portion of the asset used for business purposes.

How do taxpayers compute depreciation for listed property? First, they must determine the percentage of business vs. personal use of the asset for the year. If the business-use percentage for the year *exceeds* 50 percent, the deductible depreciation is limited to the full annual depreciation multiplied by the *business-use* percentage for the year. Listed property used in trade or business more than 50 percent is eligible for the §179 expensing election and bonus depreciation (if bonus depreciation is applicable for year asset was placed into service).

Example 10-19

What if: Assume that, in addition to the assets Teton purchased in the base scenario presented in Exhibit 10-5, it also purchased a new computer projector for $2,000 that its employees use for business presentations on weekdays. On weekends, Steve uses the projector as an integral part of his high-definition home theater system. Since the computer projector is listed property, Teton must assess the business-use percentage to properly calculate its deductible depreciation for the projector. Assuming that Teton determines the business-use percentage to be 75 percent, what is Teton's depreciation deduction on the projector for the year (ignoring bonus depreciation and §179 expensing)?

Answer: $300, computed as follows:

Description	Amount	Explanation
(1) Original basis of projector	$2,000	
(2) MACRS depreciation rate	20%	5-year property, year 1, half-year convention.
(3) Full MACRS depreciation expense	$ 400	(1) × (2).
(4) Business-use percentage	75%	
Depreciation deduction for year	$ 300	(3) × (4).

When the business-use percentage of an asset is 50 percent or less, the business must compute depreciation for the asset using the MACRS *straight-line* method over the MACRS ADS (alternative depreciation system) recovery period.[33] For five-year assets such as automobiles and computers, the assets on which the personal-use limitation is most common, the MACRS ADS recovery period is also 5 years. However, for seven-year assets, the ADS recovery period is generally 10 years.[34]

---

[33]This is the alternative recovery period listed in Rev. Proc. 87-56. See §168(g)(3)(C) and Reg. §1.280F-3T(d)(1).

[34]However, there are exceptions to this general rule. For example, the ADS recovery period for certain machinery for food and beverages is 12 years and the ADS recovery period for machinery for tobacco products is 15 years. Thus, it is important to check Rev. Proc. 87-56 to verify the ADS recovery period in these situations.

If a business initially uses an asset more than 50 percent of the time for business (and appropriately adopts the 200 percent declining balance method) but subsequently its business use drops to 50 percent or below, the *depreciation expense for all prior years must be recomputed* as if it had been using the straight-line depreciation over the ADS recovery period the entire time. It must then recapture any excess accelerated depreciation it deducted over the straight-line depreciation it should have deducted by adjusting the current year depreciation. In practical terms, the business can use the following five steps to determine its current depreciation expense for the asset:

Step 1: Compute depreciation for the year it drops to 50 percent or below using the straight-line method (this method also applies to all subsequent years).

Step 2: Compute the amount of depreciation the taxpayer would have deducted if the taxpayer had used the straight-line method over the ADS recovery period for all prior years (recall that depreciation is limited to the business-use percentage in those years).

Step 3: Compute the amount of depreciation the taxpayer had actually deducted on the asset for all prior years.

Step 4: Subtract the amount from Step 2 from the amount in Step 3. The difference is the prior year accelerated depreciation in excess of straight-line depreciation.

Step 5: Subtract the excess accelerated depreciation determined in Step 4 from the current-year straight-line depreciation in Step 1. This is the business's allowable depreciation expense on the asset for the year. If the prior-year excess depreciation from Step 4 exceeds the current-year straight-line depreciation in Step 1, the business is not allowed to deduct any depreciation on the asset for the year and must actually recognize additional ordinary income for the amount of the excess.

This five-step process is designed to place the business in the same position it would have been in if it had used straight-line depreciation during all years of the asset's life.

Example 10-20

What if: Assume that, consistent with the previous example, in year 1 Teton used the projector 75 percent of the time for business purposes and deducted $300 depreciation expense on the projector. However, in year 2, Teton's business-use percentage falls to 40 percent. What is Teton's depreciation deduction for the projector in year 2?

Answer: $10, computed using the five-step process described above as follows:

Description	Amount	Explanation*
(1) Straight-line depreciation in current year	$160	$2,000/5 years × 40 percent business-use percentage (Step 1).
(2) Prior-year straight-line depreciation	150	$2,000/5 × 50 percent (half-year convention) × 75 percent business-use percentage (Step 2).
(3) Prior-year accelerated depreciation	300	Example 10-19 (prior example) (Step 3).
(4) Excess accelerated depreciation	150	(3) − (2) (Step 4).
Allowable current-year depreciation	**$ 10**	(1) − (4) (Step 5).

*Note that the MACRS ADS recovery period (five years) for computers and peripherals (qualified technological equipment) is the same as the standard MACRS recovery period (five years).

(continued on page 10-26)

What if: Now assume that, in year 1 Teton used the projector 85 percent of the time for business purposes and deducted $340 depreciation expense on the projector. However, in year 2, Teton's business-use percentage falls to 40 percent. What is Teton's depreciation deduction for the projector in year 2?

Answer: $0 depreciation deduction and $10 of ordinary income because excess accelerated depreciation exceeds current-year straight-line depreciation, computed as follows:

Description	Amount	Explanation
(1) Straight-line depreciation in current year	$160	$2,000/5 years × 40 percent business use.
(2) Prior-year straight-line depreciation	170	$2,000/5 × 50 percent (half-year convention) × 85 percent business-use percentage.
(3) Prior-year accelerated depreciation	340	Example 10-19 (prior example, if 85%).
(4) Excess accelerated depreciation	170	(3) − (2).
Allowable current-year depreciation (income)	**($10)**	(1) − (4).

TAXES IN THE REAL WORLD   Do Depreciation Tax Incentives Work?

U.S. companies have been hoarding cash to the tune of $1.64 trillion as of the 2013 year-end according to a Moody's Investors Services report. One way the government tries to stimulate business spending is through generous depreciation provisions such as bonus depreciation and §179 immediate expensing provisions. So do these provisions really work?

A survey conducted by Bloomberg BNA, a tax and accounting software vendor, says not really. The survey found that just 10 percent of CFOs, controllers, and tax directors of companies with average revenues of $7.5 billion per year expect their 2014 capital expenditures to change because of the expiration of the bonus depreciation and §179 incentives. A majority of respondents to the survey were even more specific by saying that even if the currently available tax incentives could reduce their total cost of capital by 10 percent, their companies would not increase their capital expenditures.

Bloomberg BNA concludes that "Bonus depreciation and Section 179 expensing, while welcomed by the business community, is not viewed by a majority of that same community as an economic stimulus that drives business decisions."

Source: Bloomberg BNA "US Corporate Capital Expenditures: Consciously Uncoupled from Federal Tax Incentives," http://forms.bnasoftware.com/MTC_Common/mtcURLSrv.aspx?ID=13723&Key=ECEDF59D-C244-4682-B6EF-8278126A6F67&URLID=30222&mtc Promotion=20490

THE KEY FACTS

Luxury Vehicles

- Depreciation on automobiles weighing less than 6,000 lbs. is subject to luxury auto provisions.
- Luxury automobiles have a maximum depreciation limit for each year.
- Listed property rules are also applicable to luxury automobiles.

Luxury Automobiles   As we discussed in Chapter 9, §162 limits business deductions to those considered to be "ordinary, necessary, and reasonable" to prevent subsidizing (giving a tax deduction for) unwarranted business expenses. Although these terms are subject to interpretation, most taxpayers agree that for purposes of simply transporting passengers for business-related purposes, the cost of acquiring and using a Ford Focus is more likely to be ordinary, necessary, and reasonable than the cost of acquiring and using a Ferrari California—although perhaps not as exhilarating. Since either vehicle should be able to transport an employee or business owner from the office to a business meeting, the Ford Focus should be just as effective at accomplishing the business purpose as

EXHIBIT 10-8   Automobile Depreciation Limits

Recovery Year	Year Placed in Service			
	2016	**2015**	**2014**	**2013**
1	3,160*	3,160*	3,160*	3,160*
2	5,100	5,100	5,100	5,100
3	3,050	3,050	3,050	3,050
4 and after	1,875	1,875	1,875	1,875

*$8,000 additional depreciation is allowed when bonus depreciation is elected.

the Ferrari. If this is true, why should the government help taxpayers pay for expensive cars with tax savings from large depreciation deductions associated with automobiles? Congress decided it shouldn't. Therefore, with certain exceptions we discuss below, the tax laws generally limit the annual depreciation expense for automobiles.[35] Each year, the IRS provides a maximum depreciation schedule for automobiles placed in service during that particular year.[36] For 2013 through 2016, taxpayers are allowed to expense $8,000 of bonus depreciation above the otherwise allowable maximum depreciation (maximum depreciation of $11,160).[37] Exhibit 10-8 summarizes these schedules for automobiles placed in service for each year from 2016 back to 2013.

Businesses placing automobiles into service during the year determine depreciation expense for the automobiles by first computing the regular MACRS depreciation expense (using the appropriate convention). They then compare it to the maximum depreciation amount for the first year of the recovery period based on the IRS-provided tables. Businesses are allowed to deduct the lesser of the two. If the automobile depreciation limits apply in the first year, the taxpayer must use the IRS maximum automobile depreciation table to compute depreciation for the asset(s) in all subsequent years. In 2016, if the half-year convention applies, the table limits the depreciation on automobiles placed in service during the year costing more than $15,800.[38] Automobiles to which the depreciation limits apply are commonly referred to as **luxury automobiles.**[39] For any two such luxury cars—say, a 2017 Honda Civic and a 2017 Porsche 911—the annual depreciation limit is the same, regardless of the cost of the vehicles. The only difference is the length of time it will take to fully depreciate the vehicle.

[35]The passenger automobile definition excludes vehicles that charge for transportation such as taxi cabs, limousines, and hearses. It also excludes delivery trucks and vans. The tax law also limits the deduction for leased autos, which closed the leasing loophole that circumvented the luxury auto depreciation rules.

[36]These limitations are indexed for inflation and change annually. Revenue Procedure 2015-19 includes the 2015 limitations for automobiles and also provides slightly higher limits for hybrids, trucks, and SUVs. As of press date, the IRS had not released the 2016 limitations for automobiles, so we assume the same limitations as in 2015.

[37]§168(k)(2)(F)(i).

[38]In 2016, the full first-year depreciation on an automobile costing $15,800 is $3,160 ($15,800 × 20%). This is the amount of the first-year limit for automobiles placed in service in 2016.

[39]Correspondingly, the depreciation limits on automobiles are commonly referred to as the *luxury auto depreciation limits.*

Example 10-21

What is the maximum annual depreciation expense available for 2015 (year 1) on a 2017 Honda Civic costing $15,860 and a 2017 Porsche 911 costing $97,400 (ignoring bonus depreciation)?

Answer: $3,160 for both. See the following depreciation schedules for each automobile.

Luxury Auto Depreciation		
Year/Make	**2017 Honda Civic**	**2017 Porsche 911**
Model	DX 2dr Coupe	Carrera 4S
Price	$15,860	$97,400
Depreciation		
Year 1	$ 3,160	$ 3,160
Year 2	5,100	5,100
Year 3	3,050	3,050
Year 4	1,875	1,875
Year 5	1,875	1,875
Year 6	800	1,875
Years 7–48		1,875
Year 49		1,715

Given the maximum deduction limitations, the depreciation of the Honda and Porsche are identical in years 1–5. However, beginning in year 6 the Porsche is depreciated at a maximum of $1,875 per year until fully depreciated in year 49—however, it is unlikely the business will actually hold the Porsche through year 49.

The luxury automobile limitations don't apply to vehicles weighing more than 6,000 pounds. Thus, businesses owning these vehicles are allowed to claim §179, bonus, and regular MACRS depreciation expense for these vehicles.[40]

Just like businesses using other types of listed property, businesses using luxury automobiles for business and personal purposes may only deduct depreciation on the asset to the extent of business use. Business use is determined by miles driven for business purposes relative to total miles driven for the year.[41] Consequently, if a business places a luxury automobile into service in 2016 and uses the automobile 90 percent of the time for business purposes during the year (9,000 miles for business and 1,000 miles of personal use), the owner's depreciation (ignoring bonus depreciation) on the auto for the year is limited to $2,844 (year 1 full depreciation of $3,160 × 90 percent business use—see Exhibit 10-8).[42] Further, if the business use falls to 50 percent or less in any subsequent year, just as with other listed property, the taxpayer must use the straight-line method of depreciation and reduce depreciation expense by the amount of excess accelerated depreciation (see Example 10-19). However, because straight-line depreciation is also limited by the luxury auto depreciation limits, it may turn out that the business doesn't have any excess accelerated depreciation.

[40]§280F(d)(5)(A).

[41]As an alternative to deducting depreciation expense and other costs of operating an automobile, taxpayers using automobiles for both personal and business purposes may deduct a standard mileage rate for each mile of business use. In 2016 the business mileage rate is 54 cents per mile.

[42]Even if the business-use percentage multiplied by the MACRS depreciation is greater than the $3,160 maximum, the depreciation amount is limited to the maximum depreciation amount times the business-use percentage.

Are businesses allowed to deduct §179 expensing on luxury automobiles? Yes, but the maximum depreciation *including* §179 expense (but excluding the additional $8,000 bonus depreciation) is subject to the luxury auto limits ($3,160 for 2016). Thus, using the §179 expense on a luxury auto is unlikely to provide any tax benefit beyond the regular depreciation for most automobiles. However, businesses may deduct $25,000 of §179 expense for trucks and SUVs weighing over 6,000 pounds. This $25,000 is part of the overall $500,000 maximum §179 amount. Some companies use tax benefits to sell customers on purchasing these types of automobiles.

Depreciation for the Alternative Minimum Tax

Both individuals and corporations are subject to tax under the alternative minimum tax (AMT) system. In determining their alternative minimum taxable income, individuals and corporations may be required to recalculate their depreciation expense. For AMT purposes, the allowable recovery period and conventions are the same for all depreciable assets as they are for regular tax purposes.[43] However, for AMT purposes, businesses are not allowed to use the 200 percent declining balance method to depreciate tangible personal property. Rather, they must choose from the 150 percent declining balance method or the straight-line method to depreciate the property for AMT purposes. The difference between regular tax depreciation and AMT depreciation is an adjustment that is either added to or subtracted from regular taxable income in computing the alternative minimum tax base.[44] In contrast, the §179 expense is equally deductible for both regular tax and AMT purposes. Depreciation of real property is the same for both regular tax and AMT purposes.

Depreciation Summary

Teton's depreciation for the year is summarized in Exhibit 10-9, and Exhibit 10-10 presents Teton's depreciation expense as it would be reported on its tax return on Form 4562 (this assumes Teton elected out of bonus depreciation).

EXHIBIT 10-9 **Tax Depreciation Expense Summary**

Asset	Original Basis	§179 Expense	Remaining Basis*	Depreciation Expense	Reference
Machinery	$510,000	$80,000	$430,000	$ 61,447	Example 10-14 (What-if scenario).
Office furniture	10,000		10,000	1,429	Example 10-4.
Delivery truck	15,000	0	15,000	3,000	Example 10-4.
Warehouse	275,000	N/A	275,000	4,414	Example 10-12.
Land	75,000	N/A	75,000	0	N/A.
§179 Expense				80,000	Example 10-14.
Total Depreciation Expense				$150,290	

*Note that Teton's remaining basis is the original cost less the §179 expense.

[43]This is true for assets placed in service after 1998.

[44]If the taxpayer elected either the 150 percent declining balance or the straight-line method for regular tax depreciation of tangible personal property, then there is no AMT adjustment with respect to that property.

EXHIBIT 10-10 Teton's Form 4562 Parts I–IV for Depreciation (Assumes $100,000 of taxable income before the §179 expense)

Form **4562**

Department of the Treasury
Internal Revenue Service (99)

Depreciation and Amortization
(Including Information on Listed Property)
▶ Attach to your tax return.
▶ Information about Form 4562 and its separate instructions is at *www.irs.gov/form4562.*

OMB No. 1545-0172

2015

Attachment
Sequence No. **179**

Name(s) shown on return | Business or activity to which this form relates | Identifying number

Part I Election To Expense Certain Property Under Section 179
Note: If you have any listed property, complete Part V before you complete Part I.

1	Maximum amount (see instructions)	**1**	500,000
2	Total cost of section 179 property placed in service (see instructions)	**2**	535,000
3	Threshold cost of section 179 property before reduction in limitation (see instructions)	**3**	2,000,000
4	Reduction in limitation. Subtract line 3 from line 2. If zero or less, enter -0-	**4**	0
5	Dollar limitation for tax year. Subtract line 4 from line 1. If zero or less, enter -0-. If married filing separately, see instructions	**5**	500,000

6	(a) Description of property	(b) Cost (business use only)	(c) Elected cost	
	Machinery	510,000	80,000	

7	Listed property. Enter the amount from line 29	**7**		
8	Total elected cost of section 179 property. Add amounts in column (c), lines 6 and 7	**8**	80,000	
9	Tentative deduction. Enter the **smaller** of line 5 or line 8	**9**	80,000	
10	Carryover of disallowed deduction from line 13 of your 2014 Form 4562	**10**		
11	Business income limitation. Enter the smaller of business income (not less than zero) or line 5 (see instructions)	**11**	100,000	
12	Section 179 expense deduction. Add lines 9 and 10, but do not enter more than line 11	**12**	80,000	
13	Carryover of disallowed deduction to 2016. Add lines 9 and 10, less line 12 ▶	**13**		

Note: Do not use Part II or Part III below for listed property. Instead, use Part V.

Part II Special Depreciation Allowance and Other Depreciation (Do not include listed property.) (See instructions.)

14	Special depreciation allowance for qualified property (other than listed property) placed in service during the tax year (see instructions)	**14**	
15	Property subject to section 168(f)(1) election	**15**	
16	Other depreciation (including ACRS)	**16**	

Part III MACRS Depreciation (Do not include listed property.) (See instructions.)

Section A

17	MACRS deductions for assets placed in service in tax years beginning before 2015	**17**	
18	If you are electing to group any assets placed in service during the tax year into one or more general asset accounts, check here ▶ ☐		

Section B—Assets Placed in Service During 2015 Tax Year Using the General Depreciation System

(a) Classification of property	(b) Month and year placed in service	(c) Basis for depreciation (business/investment use only—see instructions)	(d) Recovery period	(e) Convention	(f) Method	(g) Depreciation deduction
19a 3-year property						
b 5-year property		15,000	5-year	HY	DDB	3,000
c 7-year property		440,000	7-year	HY	DDB	62,876
d 10-year property						
e 15-year property						
f 20-year property						
g 25-year property			25 yrs.		S/L	
h Residential rental property			27.5 yrs.	MM	S/L	
			27.5 yrs.	MM	S/L	
i Nonresidential real property	May 2015	275,000	39 yrs.	MM	S/L	4,414
				MM	S/L	

Section C—Assets Placed in Service During 2015 Tax Year Using the Alternative Depreciation System

20a Class life					S/L	
b 12-year			12 yrs.		S/L	
c 40-year			40 yrs.	MM	S/L	

Part IV Summary (See instructions.)

21	Listed property. Enter amount from line 28	**21**	
22	**Total.** Add amounts from line 12, lines 14 through 17, lines 19 and 20 in column (g), and line 21. Enter here and on the appropriate lines of your return. Partnerships and S corporations—see instructions	**22**	150,290
23	For assets shown above and placed in service during the current year, enter the portion of the basis attributable to section 263A costs	**23**	

For Paperwork Reduction Act Notice, see separate instructions.   Cat. No. 12906N   Form **4562** (2015)

AMORTIZATION

Businesses recover the cost of intangible assets through amortization rather than depreciation expense. Intangible assets in the form of capitalized expenditures, such as capitalized **research and experimentation (R&E) costs** or **covenants not to compete,** do not have physical characteristics. Nonetheless, they may have determinable lives. While research and experimentation costs may have an indeterminate life, a covenant not to compete, for example, would have a life equal to the stated term of the contractual agreement. When the life of intangible assets cannot be determined, taxpayers recover the cost of the assets when they dispose of them—unless they are assigned a specific tax recovery period.

For tax purposes, an intangible asset can be placed into one of the following four general categories:

1. §197 purchased intangibles.
2. Start-up expenditures and organizational costs.
3. Research and experimentation costs.
4. Patents and copyrights.

Businesses amortize all intangible assets in these categories using the straight-line method for both book and tax purposes.

Section 197 Intangibles

When a business purchases the *assets* of another business for a single purchase price, the business must determine the basis of each of the assets it acquired in the transaction. To determine basis, the business must allocate a portion of the purchase price to each of the individual assets acquired in the transaction. Generally, under this approach, each asset acquired in the purchase (cash, machinery, and real property, for example) takes a basis equal to its fair market value. However, some of the assets acquired in the transaction may not appear on the seller's balance sheet. In fact, a substantial portion of a business's value may exist in the form of intangible assets such as customer lists, patents, trademarks, trade names, goodwill, going-concern value, covenants not to compete, and so forth. Nearly all of these assets are amortized according to §197 of the Internal Revenue Code—hence, they are often referred to as **§197 purchased intangibles**. According to §197, these assets have a recovery period of 180 months (15 years), *regardless of their actual life.*[45] For example, when a business buys an existing business, the owner selling the business often signs a covenant not to compete for a specified period such as 5 years.[46] Even though a five-year covenant not to compete clearly has a fixed and determinable life, it must be amortized over 180 months (15 years). The **full-month convention** applies to the amortization of purchased intangibles. This convention allows taxpayers to deduct an entire month's worth of amortization for the month of purchase and all subsequent months in the year. The full-month convention also applies in the month of sale or disposition.[47]

> **THE KEY FACTS**
>
> **§197 Intangible Assets**
> - Purchased intangibles are amortized over a period of 180 months, regardless of their explicitly stated lifetimes.
> - The full-month convention applies to amortizable assets.

[45]§197 was Congress's response to taxpayers manipulating the valuation and recovery periods assigned to these purchased intangibles.

[46]A covenant not to compete is a contract between the seller of a business and its buyer that the seller will not operate a similar business that would compete with the previous business for a specified period of time.

[47]Reg. §1.197-2(g)(l)(i) illustrates the special rules that apply when a taxpayer sells a §197 intangible or the intangible becomes worthless and the taxpayer's basis in the asset exceeds the sale proceeds (if any). A business may recognize a loss on the sale or disposition only when the business does not hold any other §197 assets that the business acquired in the *same initial transaction.* Otherwise, the taxpayer may not deduct the loss on the sale or disposition until the business sells or disposes of *all* of the other §197 intangibles that it purchased in the same initial transaction. The same loss disallowance rule applies if a §197 intangible expires before it is fully amortized.

Example 10-22

What if: Assume that at the beginning of year 1, Teton acquires a competitor's assets for $350,000.[48] Of the $350,000 purchase price, $125,000 is allocated to tangible assets and $225,000 is allocated to §197 intangible assets (patent, goodwill, and a customer list with a three-year life).[49] For each of the first three years, Teton would deduct one-fifteenth of the basis of each asset as amortization expense. What is Teton's accumulated amortization and remaining basis in each of these §197 intangibles after three years?

Answer: See the table below:

Description	Patent	Goodwill	Customer List
Basis	$25,000	$150,000	$50,000
Accumulated amortization (3/15 of original basis)	(5,000)	(30,000)	(10,000)
Remaining basis	$20,000	$120,000	$40,000

When a taxpayer sells a §197 intangible for more than its basis, the taxpayer recognizes gain. We describe how to characterize this type of gain in the next chapter.

Organizational Expenditures and Start-Up Costs

Organizational expenditures include expenditures to form and organize a business in the form of a corporation or a partnership.[50] Organizational expenditures typically include costs of organizational meetings, state fees, accounting service costs incident to organization, and legal service expenditures such as document drafting, taking minutes of organizational meetings, and creating terms of the original stock certificates. These costs are generally incurred prior to the starting of business (or shortly thereafter) but relate to creating the business entity. The costs of selling or marketing stock do *not* qualify as organizational expenditures and cannot be amortized.[51]

Example 10-23

What if: Suppose Teton was organized as a corporation rather than a sole proprietorship (recall that sole proprietorships cannot expense organizational expenditures). Steve paid $35,000 of legal costs to Scott, Tang, and Malan to draft the corporate charter and articles of incorporation; $10,000 to Harvey and Stratford for accounting fees related to the organization; and $7,000 for organizational meetings, $5,000 for stock issuance costs, and $1,000 for state fees related to the incorporation. What amounts of these expenditures qualify as organizational costs?

Answer: $53,000 computed as follows (with the exception of the stock issuance costs, each of Teton's expenses qualify as amortizable organizational expenditures):

---

[48]If a business acquires another business's stock (rather than assets) there is no goodwill assigned for tax purposes, and the purchase price simply becomes the basis of the stock purchased.

[49]A customer base is the value assigned to current customers (i.e., the lists that will allow the new owner to capture future benefits from the current customers).

[50]§248 for corporations and §709 for partnerships. Sole proprietorships cannot deduct organizational expenditures.

[51]These syndication costs are capitalized and deducted on the final tax return.

Description	Qualifying Organizational Expenditures
Legal drafting of corporate charter and articles of incorporation	$35,000
Accounting fees related to organization	10,000
Organizational meetings	7,000
Stock issuance costs	0
State incorporation fees	1,000
Totals	**$53,000**

Businesses may *immediately expense* up to $5,000 of organizational expenditures.[52] However, businesses incurring more than $50,000 in organizational expenditures must phase-out (reduce) the $5,000 immediate expense amount dollar for dollar for expenditures exceeding $50,000. Thus, businesses incurring at least $55,000 of organizational expenditures are not allowed to immediately expense any of the expenditures.

Example 10-24

What if: Suppose Teton is a corporation and it wants to maximize its current-year organizational expenditure deduction. As described in Example 10-24, Teton incurred $53,000 of organizational expenditures in year 1. How much of the organizational expenditures can Teton immediately expense in year 1?

Answer: $2,000, computed as follows:

Description	Amount	Explanation
(1) Maximum immediate expense	$ 5,000	§248(a)(1).
(2) Total organizational expenditures	53,000	Example 10-23.
(3) Phase-out threshold	50,000	§248(a)(1)(B).
(4) Immediate expense phase-out	3,000	(2) − (3).
(5) Allowable immediate expense	**2,000**	(1) − (4), but not below zero.
Remaining organizational expenditures	$51,000*	(2) − (5).

What if: Assuming that Teton is a corporation and that it incurred $41,000 of organizational expenditures in year 1, how much of the organizational expenditures could Teton immediately expense in year 1?

Answer: $5,000, computed as follows:

Description	Amount	Explanation
(1) Maximum immediate expense	$ 5,000	§248(a)(1).
(2) Total organizational expenditures	41,000	
(3) Phase-out threshold	50,000	§248(a)(1)(B).
(4) Immediate expense phase-out	0	(2) − (3), limit to zero.
(5) Allowable immediate expense	**5,000**	(1) − (4).
Remaining organizational expenditures	$36,000*	(2) − (5).

(continued on page 10-34)

[52]§248(a)(1) for corporations or §709 for partnerships.

What if: Assuming that Teton is a corporation and it incurred $60,000 of organizational expenditures in year 1, how much of the organizational expenditures could Teton immediately expense in year 1?

Answer: $0, computed as follows:

Description	Amount	Explanation
(1) Maximum immediate expense	$ 5,000	§248(a)(1).
(2) Total organizational expenditures	60,000	
(3) Phase-out threshold	50,000	§248(a)(1)(B).
(4) Immediate expense phase-out	10,000	(2) − (3).
(5) Allowable immediate expense	**0**	(1) − (4).
Remaining organizational expenditures	$60,000*	(2) − (5).

*As we discuss below, Teton amortizes the remaining organizational costs.

Businesses amortize organizational expenditures that they do not immediately expense using the straight-line method over a recovery period of 15 years (180 months).

Example 10-25

What if: Assume Teton is a corporation and it amortizes the $51,000 of organizational expenditures remaining after it immediately expenses $2,000 of the costs (see Example 10-25). If Teton began business on February 1 of year 1, how much total cost recovery expense for the organizational expenditures is Teton able to deduct in year 1?

Answer: $5,117, computed as follows:

Description	Amount	Explanation
(1) Total organizational expenditures	$53,000	Example 10-23.
(2) Amount immediately expensed	2,000	Example 10-24.
(3) Expenditures subject to straight-line amortization	$51,000	(1) − (2).
(4) Recovery period in months	180	15 years §248(a)(2).
(5) Monthly straight-line amortization	283.33	(3)/(4).
(6) Teton business months during year 1	× 11	February through December.
(7) Year 1 straight-line amortization	3,117	(5) × (6).
Total year 1 cost recovery expense for organizational expenditures.	**$ 5,117**	(2) + (7).

Start-up costs are costs businesses incur to, not surprisingly, start up a business.[53] Start-up costs apply to all types of business forms.[54] These costs include costs associated with investigating the possibilities of and actually creating or acquiring a trade or business. For example, costs Teton incurs in deciding whether to locate the business in Cody, Wyoming, or Bozeman, Montana, are start-up costs. Start-up costs also include costs that would normally be deductible as ordinary business expenses except that they don't qualify as business expenses because they are incurred before the trade or business activity actually begins. For example, costs Teton incurs to train its employees before the business begins are start-up costs. The rules for immediately expensing and amortizing start-up costs are the same as those for immediately expensing and amortizing organizational expenditures. Consequently, businesses incurring at least $55,000 of start-up costs are not allowed to immediately expense any of the costs. The limitations are computed separately for organizational expenditures and for start-up costs. Consequently, a business could immediately expense $5,000 of organizational expenditures and $5,000 of start-up costs in its first year of business.

[53]§195.

[54]Recall that rules for amortizing organizational expenditures apply only to corporations and partnerships.

Example 10-26

What if: Assume that in January of year 1 (before it began business on February 1) Teton spent $4,500 investigating the climbing hardware market, creating company logos, and determining the locations for both the office and manufacturing facility. The $4,500 of expenditures qualifies as start-up costs. How much of the $4,500 of start-up costs is Teton allowed to immediately expense?

Answer: All $4,500. Teton is allowed to immediately expense the entire $4,500 because its total start-up costs do not exceed $50,000. Teton could have immediately expensed up to $5,000 of start-up costs as long as its total start-up costs did not exceed $50,000.

Exhibit 10-11 illustrates the timing of organizational expenditures, start-up costs, and normal trade or business expenses.

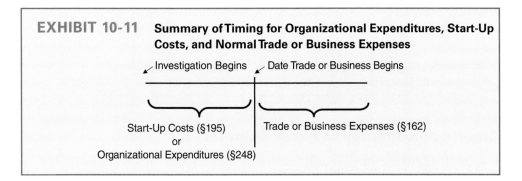

EXHIBIT 10-11   Summary of Timing for Organizational Expenditures, Start-Up Costs, and Normal Trade or Business Expenses

Research and Experimentation Expenditures

To stay competitive, businesses often invest in activities they believe will generate innovative products or significantly improve their current products or processes. These research and experimentation costs include expenditures for research laboratories including salaries, materials, and other related expenses. Businesses may immediately expense these costs or they may *elect* to capitalize these costs and amortize them using the straight-line method over the determinable useful life or, if there is no determinable useful life, over a period of not less than 60 months, beginning in the month benefits are first derived from the research.[55] However, if a business elects to capitalize and amortize the costs, it must stop amortizing the costs if and when the business receives a patent relating to the expenditures. When the business obtains a patent, it adds any remaining basis in the costs to the basis of the patent and it amortizes the basis of the patent over the patent's life (see discussion below).

Patents and Copyrights

The manner in which a business amortizes a patent or copyright depends on whether the business directly purchases the patent or copyright or whether it self-creates the intangibles. Businesses directly purchasing patents or copyrights (not in an asset acquisition to which §197 applies) amortize the cost over the remaining life of the patents or copyrights.[56] Businesses receiving "self-created" patents or copyrights amortize the cost or basis of the self-created intangible assets over their legal lives. The costs included in the basis of a self-created patent or copyright include legal costs, fees, and, as we discussed above, unamortized research and experimentation

[55]See §174. High tax rate taxpayers may choose to deduct these costs while low tax rate taxpayers may prefer to capitalize and amortize them so that they will have more future deductions when they generate more income. There is also the research and experimentation credit which is available to some businesses.
[56]§167(f).

expenditures associated with the creation of the patent or copyright. However, because the patent approval process is slow, the unamortized research and experimentation costs included in the patent's basis are likely to be relatively small because, with a five-year recovery period, the research and experimentation costs would likely be mostly or even fully amortized by the time the patent is approved.

Example 10-27

In September of year 1, Teton purchased a patent with a remaining life of 10 years from Chouinard Equipment for $60,000. What amount of amortization expense is Teton allowed to deduct for the patent in year 1?

Answer: $2,000, computed as follows:

Description	Amount	Explanation
(1) Cost of patent	$60,000	
(2) Remaining life of patent in months	120	10 years.
(3) Monthly amortization	$ 500	(1)/(2).
(4) Months in year 1 Teton held patent	× 4	September through December.
(5) Monthly straight-line amortization	**$ 2,000**	(3) × (4).
Unamortized cost of patent at end of year 1	$58,000	(1) − (5).

Amortizable Intangible Asset Summary

Exhibit 10-12 summarizes the different types of amortizable intangible assets, identifies the recovery period of these assets, and describes the applicable amortization method for each asset. Exhibit 10-12 also identifies the applicable convention for each type of amortizable intangible asset and identifies the financial accounting treatment for recovering the cost of the intangible assets under GAAP.

EXHIBIT 10-12 Summary of Amortizable Assets

Asset Description	Recovery Period (months)	Applicable Method	Applicable Convention	Financial Accounting Treatment
§197 purchased intangibles including goodwill, trademarks, patents, and covenants not to compete.[57]	180	Straight-line	Full-month beginning with month of purchase.	ASC 350 tests for annual impairment.
Organizational expenditures and start-up costs are required to be capitalized.	180	Straight-line	Full-month in month business begins.	AICPA SOP 98-5.
Research and experimentation costs that are capitalized.	Determinable useful life, or 60 (not less than); ceases when patent is issued.	Straight-line	Full-month in first month that benefits from research are obtained.	Expensed.
Self-created patents and copyrights.	Actual life.	Straight-line	Full-month in month intangible is obtained.	Expensed.
Purchased patents and copyrights.	Remaining life.	Straight-line	Full-month in month intangible is obtained.	Expensed.

[57]A patent or copyright that is part of a basket purchase (several assets together) is treated as a §197 intangible. A patent or copyright that is purchased separately is simply amortized over its remaining life (§167(f)).

Exhibit 10-13 presents Teton's amortization expense as it would be reported on its tax return on Form 4562 (the exhibit assumes that Teton is a corporation so it can amortize organizational expenditures).

EXHIBIT 10-13   Teton Form 4562, Part VI Amortization of Organizational Expenditures and Patent

Part VI Amortization

(a) Description of costs	(b) Date amortization begins	(c) Amortizable amount	(d) Code section	(e) Amortization period or percentage	(f) Amortization for this year
42 Amortization of costs that begins during your 2015 tax year (see instructions):					
Organizational expenditures	2/1/2016	53,000	243	15 years	5,117
Patents	9/1/2016	60,000	167	10 years	2,000
43 Amortization of costs that began before your 2015 tax year				43	
44 Total. Add amounts in column (f). See the instructions for where to report				44	7,117

Form **4562** (2015)

---

continued from page 10-1 . . .
Teton was developing some additional employee parking on a lot adjacent to the warehouse when the excavation crew discovered a small gold deposit. Steve called his friend Ken, who had some experience in mining precious metals, to see what Ken thought of the find. Ken was impressed and offered Steve $150,000 for the rights to the gold. Steve accepted the offer on Teton's behalf. ■

DEPLETION

LO 10-5

Depletion is the method taxpayers use to recover their capital investment in natural resources. Depletion is a particularly significant deduction for businesses in the mining, oil and gas, and forestry industries. These businesses generally incur depletion expense as they use the natural resource. Specifically, businesses compute annual depletion expense under both the cost and percentage depletion methods and they deduct the larger of the two.[58]

Under **cost depletion,** taxpayers must estimate or determine the number of units or reserves (tons of coal, barrels of oil, board feet of timber, for example) that remain at the beginning of the year and allocate a pro rata share of that basis to each unit that is extracted during the year.[59]

Example 10-28

Ken's cost basis in the gold is the $150,000 he paid for it. Based on a mining engineer's estimate that the gold deposit probably holds 1,000 ounces of gold, Ken can determine his cost depletion. What is Ken's cost depletion for year 1 and year 2, assuming he extracts 300 and 700 ounces of gold in year 1 and year 2, respectively?

(continued on page 10-38)

---

[58]Depletion of timber and major integrated oil companies must be calculated using only the cost depletion method (no percentage depletion is available).

[59]§612.

THE KEY FACTS

Depletion

- Cost depletion involves estimating resource reserves and allocating a pro-rata share of basis based on the number of units extracted.
- Percentage depletion is determined by a statutory percentage of gross income that is permitted to be expensed each year. Different resources have different statutory percentages (i.e., gold, tin, coal).
- Taxpayers may expense the larger of cost or percentage depletion.

Answer: $45,000 in year 1 and $105,000 in year 2, computed as follows:

Description	Amount	Explanation
(1) Cost basis in gold	$150,000	
(2) Estimated ounces of gold	1,000	
(3) Per ounce cost depletion rate	150	(1)/(2).
(4) Year 1 ounces extracted	300	
(5) Year 1 cost depletion	**$ 45,000**	(3) × (4).
(6) Basis remaining after year 1 depletion	105,000	(1) − (5).
(7) Year 2 ounces extracted	700	
(8) Year 2 cost depletion	**$105,000**	(7) × (3).
Basis remaining after year 2 depletion	$ 0	(6) − (8).

Ken is not eligible for cost depletion after year 2 because as of the end of year 2, his cost basis has been reduced to $0.

Because the cost depletion method of depletion requires businesses to estimate the number of units of the resource they will actually extract, it is possible that their estimate will prove to be inaccurate. If they underestimate the number of units, they will fully deplete the cost basis of the resource before they have fully extracted the resource. Once they have recovered the entire cost basis of the resource, businesses are not allowed to use cost depletion to determine depletion expense. Businesses, however, may continue to use percentage depletion (see discussion below). If a business overestimates the number of units to be extracted, it will still have basis remaining after the resource has been fully extracted. In these situations, the business would deduct the unrecovered basis once it had sold all the remaining units.

The amount of **percentage depletion** for a natural resource business activity is determined by multiplying the *gross income* from the resource extraction activity by a fixed percentage based on the type of natural resource as indicated in Exhibit 10-14.[60]

EXHIBIT 10-14   Applicable Percentage Depletion Rates

Statutory Percentage	Natural Resources (Partial list)
5 percent [§613(b)(6)]	Gravel, pumice, and stone.
14 percent [§613(b)(3)]	Asphalt rock, clay, and other metals.
15 percent [§613(b)(2)]	Gold, copper, oil shale, and silver.
15 percent [§613A(c)(1)]	Domestic oil and gas.
22 percent [§613(b)(1)]	Platinum, sulfur, uranium, and titanium.

In many cases, percentage depletion may generate *larger* depletion deductions than does cost depletion. Recall that taxpayers are allowed to deduct the greater of cost or percentage depletion. Businesses reduce their cost basis in the resource when they deduct percentage depletion. However, once the cost basis is exhausted, they are allowed to continue to deduct percentage (but not cost) depletion. This provides a potentially significant governmental subsidy to extraction businesses that have completely recovered their costs in a natural resource.[61]

It is important to note that businesses deduct percentage depletion when they *sell* the natural resource and they deduct cost depletion in the year they *produce* or extract the natural resource. Also, percentage depletion cannot exceed 50 percent (100 percent in the case of oil and gas properties) of the *taxable income* from the

[60]§613.
[61]Percentage depletion in excess of basis is an AMT preference item.

natural resource business activity before considering the depletion expense, while cost depletion has no such limitation.

Example 10-29

In Example 10-28, Ken determined his cost depletion expense for the gold. However, because he is allowed to deduct the greater of cost or percentage depletion each year, he set out to determine his percentage depletion for year 2. Assuming that Ken has gross (taxable) income from the gold mining activity before depletion expense of $200,000 ($50,000), $600,000 ($450,000), and $600,000 ($500,000) in year 1, year 2, and year 3, respectively, what is his percentage depletion expense for each of these three years?

Answer: $25,000, $90,000, and $90,000 for years 1, 2, and 3, respectively, computed as follows:

	Year 1	Year 2	Year 3	Explanation
(1) Taxable income from activity (before depletion expense)	$ 50,000	$450,000	$500,000	
(2) Gross income	$200,000	$600,000	$600,000	
(3) Percentage	× 15%	× 15%	× 15%	Exhibit 10-14.
(4) Percentage depletion expense before limit	$ 30,000	$ 90,000	$ 90,000	(2) × (3).
(5) 50 percent of taxable income limitation	$ 25,000	$225,000	$250,000	(1) × 50%.
Allowable percentage depletion	**$ 25,000**	**$ 90,000**	**$ 90,000**	Lesser of (4) or (5).

Finally, as we discussed above, a business's depletion expense deduction is the greater of either the annual cost or percentage depletion.

Example 10-30

Based on his computations of cost depletion and percentage depletion, Ken was able to determine his deductible depletion expense. Using the cost and percentage depletion computations from Examples 10-28 and 10-29, what is Ken's deductible depletion expense for years 1, 2, and 3?

Answer: $45,000 for year 1, $105,000 for year 2, and $90,000 for year 3, computed as follows:

Tax Depletion Expense	Year 1	Year 2	Year 3	Explanation
(1) Cost depletion	$45,000	$105,000	$ 0	Example 10-28.
(2) Percentage depletion	25,000	90,000	90,000	Example 10-29.
Allowable expense	45,000	105,000	90,000	Greater of (1) or (2).

CONCLUSION

This chapter describes and discusses how businesses recover the costs of their tangible and intangible assets. Cost recovery expenses are important because they represent a significant tax deduction for many businesses. Businesses must routinely make choices that affect the amount and timing of these deductions. Further understanding cost recovery basics helps businesses determine how to compute and characterize gain and loss they recognize when they sell or otherwise dispose of business assets. We address the interaction between cost recovery expenses and gain and loss on property dispositions in the next chapter.

Appendix   MACRS Tables

TABLE 1   MACRS Half-Year Convention

	Depreciation Rate for Recovery Period					
Year	3-Year	5-Year	7-Year	10-Year	15-Year	20-Year
1	33.33%	20.00%	14.29%	10.00%	5.00%	3.750%
2	44.45	32.00	24.49	18.00	9.50	7.219
3	14.81	19.20	17.49	14.40	8.55	6.677
4	7.41	11.52	12.49	11.52	7.70	6.177
5		11.52	8.93	9.22	6.93	5.713
6		5.76	8.92	7.37	6.23	5.285
7			8.93	6.55	5.90	4.888
8			4.46	6.55	5.90	4.522
9				6.56	5.91	4.462
10				6.55	5.90	4.461
11				3.28	5.91	4.462
12					5.90	4.461
13					5.91	4.462
14					5.90	4.461
15					5.91	4.462
16					2.95	4.461
17						4.462
18						4.461
19						4.462
20						4.461
21						2.231

TABLE 2a   MACRS Mid-Quarter Convention: *For property placed in service during the first quarter*

	Depreciation Rate for Recovery Period	
Year	5-Year	7-Year
1	35.00%	25.00%
2	26.00	21.43
3	15.60	15.31
4	11.01	10.93
5	11.01	8.75
6	1.38	8.74
7		8.75
8		1.09

TABLE 2b   **MACRS Mid-Quarter Convention:** *For property placed in service during the second quarter*

Depreciation Rate for Recovery Period		
Year	5-Year	7-Year
1	25.00%	17.85%
2	30.00	23.47
3	18.00	16.76
4	11.37	11.97
5	11.37	8.87
6	4.26	8.87
7		8.87
8		3.34

TABLE 2c   **MACRS Mid-Quarter Convention:** *For property placed in service during the third quarter*

Depreciation Rate for Recovery Period		
Year	5-Year	7-Year
1	15.00%	10.71%
2	34.00	25.51
3	20.40	18.22
4	12.24	13.02
5	11.30	9.30
6	7.06	8.85
7		8.86
8		5.53

TABLE 2d   **MACRS-Mid Quarter Convention:** *For property placed in service during the fourth quarter*

Depreciation Rate for Recovery Period		
Year	5-Year	7-Year
1	5.00%	3.57%
2	38.00	27.55
3	22.80	19.68
4	13.68	14.06
5	10.94	10.04
6	9.58	8.73
7		8.73
8		7.64

TABLE 3   Residential Rental Property Mid-Month Convention Straight Line—27.5 Years

Year	*Month Property Placed in Service											
	1	2	3	4	5	6	7	8	9	10	11	12
1	3.485%	3.182%	2.879%	2.576%	2.273%	1.970%	1.667%	1.364%	1.061%	0.758%	0.455%	0.152%
2–9	3.636	3.636	3.636	3.636	3.636	3.636	3.636	3.636	3.636	3.636	3.636	3.636
10	3.637	3.637	3.637	3.637	3.637	3.637	3.636	3.636	3.636	3.636	3.636	3.636
11	3.636	3.636	3.636	3.636	3.636	3.636	3.637	3.637	3.637	3.637	3.637	3.637
12	3.637	3.637	3.637	3.637	3.637	3.637	3.636	3.636	3.636	3.636	3.636	3.636
13	3.636	3.636	3.636	3.636	3.636	3.636	3.637	3.637	3.637	3.637	3.637	3.637
14	3.637	3.637	3.637	3.637	3.637	3.637	3.636	3.636	3.636	3.636	3.636	3.636
15	3.636	3.636	3.636	3.636	3.636	3.636	3.637	3.637	3.637	3.637	3.637	3.637
16	3.637	3.637	3.637	3.637	3.637	3.637	3.636	3.636	3.636	3.636	3.636	3.636
17	3.636	3.636	3.636	3.636	3.636	3.636	3.637	3.637	3.637	3.637	3.637	3.637
18	3.637	3.637	3.637	3.637	3.637	3.637	3.636	3.636	3.636	3.636	3.636	3.636
19	3.636	3.636	3.636	3.636	3.636	3.636	3.637	3.637	3.637	3.637	3.637	3.637
20	3.637	3.637	3.637	3.637	3.637	3.637	3.636	3.636	3.636	3.636	3.636	3.636
21	3.636	3.636	3.636	3.636	3.636	3.636	3.637	3.637	3.637	3.637	3.637	3.637
22	3.637	3.637	3.637	3.637	3.637	3.637	3.636	3.636	3.636	3.636	3.636	3.636
23	3.636	3.636	3.636	3.636	3.636	3.636	3.637	3.637	3.637	3.637	3.637	3.637
24	3.637	3.637	3.637	3.637	3.637	3.637	3.636	3.636	3.636	3.636	3.636	3.636
25	3.636	3.636	3.636	3.636	3.636	3.636	3.637	3.637	3.637	3.637	3.637	3.637
26	3.637	3.637	3.637	3.637	3.637	3.637	3.636	3.636	3.636	3.636	3.636	3.636
27	3.636	3.636	3.636	3.636	3.636	3.636	3.637	3.637	3.637	3.637	3.637	3.637
28	1.97	2.273	2.576	2.879	3.182	3.485	3.636	3.636	3.636	3.636	3.636	3.636
29							0.152	0.455	0.758	1.061	1.364	1.667

TABLE 4 Nonresidential Real Property Mid-Month Convention Straight Line—31.5 Years (for assets placed in service before May 13, 1993)

Year	*Month Property Placed in Service* 1	2	3	4	5	6	7	8	9	10	11	12
1	3.042%	2.778%	2.513%	2.249%	1.984%	1.720%	1.455%	1.190%	0.926%	0.661%	0.397%	0.132%
2–7	3.175	3.175	3.175	3.175	3.175	3.175	3.175	3.175	3.175	3.175	3.175	3.175
8	3.175	3.174	3.175	3.174	3.175	3.174	3.175	3.175	3.175	3.175	3.175	3.175
9	3.174	3.175	3.174	3.175	3.174	3.175	3.174	3.174	3.174	3.174	3.174	3.174
10	3.175	3.174	3.175	3.174	3.175	3.174	3.175	3.175	3.175	3.175	3.175	3.175
11	3.174	3.175	3.174	3.175	3.174	3.175	3.174	3.174	3.174	3.174	3.174	3.174
12	3.175	3.174	3.175	3.175	3.175	3.174	3.175	3.175	3.175	3.175	3.175	3.175
13	3.174	3.175	3.174	3.174	3.174	3.175	3.174	3.174	3.174	3.174	3.174	3.174
14	3.175	3.174	3.175	3.175	3.175	3.174	3.175	3.175	3.175	3.175	3.175	3.175
15	3.174	3.175	3.174	3.174	3.174	3.175	3.174	3.174	3.174	3.174	3.174	3.174
16	3.175	3.174	3.175	3.175	3.175	3.174	3.175	3.175	3.175	3.175	3.175	3.175
17	3.174	3.175	3.174	3.174	3.174	3.175	3.174	3.174	3.174	3.174	3.174	3.174
18	3.175	3.174	3.175	3.175	3.175	3.174	3.175	3.175	3.175	3.175	3.175	3.175
19	3.174	3.175	3.174	3.174	3.174	3.175	3.174	3.174	3.174	3.174	3.174	3.174
20	3.175	3.174	3.175	3.175	3.175	3.174	3.175	3.175	3.175	3.175	3.175	3.175
21	3.174	3.175	3.174	3.174	3.174	3.175	3.174	3.174	3.174	3.174	3.174	3.174
22	3.175	3.174	3.175	3.175	3.175	3.174	3.175	3.175	3.175	3.175	3.175	3.175
23	3.174	3.175	3.174	3.174	3.174	3.175	3.174	3.115	3.174	3.174	3.174	3.174
24	3.175	3.174	3.175	3.175	3.175	3.174	3.175	3.175	3.175	3.175	3.175	3.175
25	3.174	3.175	3.174	3.174	3.174	3.175	3.174	3.174	3.174	3.174	3.174	3.174
26	3.175	3.174	3.175	3.175	3.175	3.174	3.175	3.175	3.175	3.175	3.175	3.175
27	3.174	3.175	3.174	3.174	3.174	3.175	3.174	3.174	3.174	3.174	3.174	3.174
28	3.175	3.174	3.175	3.175	3.175	3.174	3.175	3.175	3.175	3.175	3.175	3.175
29	3.174	3.175	3.174	3.174	3.174	3.175	3.174	3.174	3.174	3.174	3.174	3.174
30	3.175	3.174	3.175	3.175	3.175	3.174	3.175	3.175	3.175	3.175	3.175	3.175
31	3.174	3.175	3.174	3.174	3.174	3.175	3.174	3.174	3.174	3.174	3.174	3.174
32	3.174	3.174	3.175	3.175	3.175	3.174	3.175	3.175	3.175	3.175	3.175	3.174
33	1.720	1.984	2.249	2.513	2.778	3.042	0.132	0.397	0.661	0.926	1.190	1.455

TABLE 5 Nonresidential Real Property Mid-Month Convention Straight Line—39 Years (for assets placed in service on or after May 13, 1993)

Year	*Month property placed in service* 1	2	3	4	5	6	7	8	9	10	11	12
1	2.461%	2.247%	2.033%	1.819%	1.605%	1.391%	1.177%	0.963%	0.749%	0.535%	0.321%	0.107%
2–39	2.564	2.564	2.564	2.564	2.564	2.564	2.564	2.564	2.564	2.564	2.564	2.564
40	0.107	0.321	0.535	0.749	0.963	1.177	1.391	1.605	1.819	2.033	2.247	2.461

Summary

LO 10-1 Explain the concept of basis and adjusted basis and describe the cost recovery methods used under the tax law to recover the cost of personal property, real property, intangible assets, and natural resources.

- Tangible personal and real property (depreciation), intangibles (amortization), and natural resources (depletion) are all subject to cost recovery.
- An asset's basis is the amount that is subject to cost recovery. Generally, an asset's initial basis is its purchase price, plus the cost of any other expenses incurred to get the asset in working condition.
- The taxpayer's basis of assets acquired in a nontaxable exchange is the same basis the taxpayer transferred to acquire the property received.
- Expenditures on an asset are either expensed currently or capitalized as a new asset. Expenditures for routine or general maintenance of the asset are expensed currently. Expenditures that better, restore, or adapt an asset to a new use are capitalized.
- When acquiring a business and purchasing a bundle of property, the basis of each asset is determined as the fair market value of the asset.

LO 10-2 Determine the applicable cost recovery (depreciation) life, method, and convention for tangible personal and real property and calculate the deduction allowable under basic MACRS.

- Tax depreciation is currently calculated under the Modified Accelerated Cost Recovery System (MACRS).
- MACRS for tangible personal property is based upon recovery period (Rev. Proc. 87-56), method (200 percent declining balance, 150 percent declining balance, and straight-line), and convention (half-year or mid-quarter).
- Real property is divided into two groups for tax purposes: residential rental and non-residential. The recovery period is 27.5 years for residential property and 31.5 years or 39 years for nonresidential property, depending on when the property was placed in service. The depreciation method is straight-line and the convention is mid-month.

LO 10-3 Explain the additional special cost recovery rules (§179, bonus, listed property) and calculate the deduction allowable under these rules.

- §179 allows taxpayers to expense tangible personal property. The expense is limited by the amount of property placed in service and taxable income.
- Bonus depreciation allows taxpayers to immediately expense 50 percent of qualified property in the year of acquisition.
- Listed property includes automobiles, other means of transportation, and computer equipment. Depreciation is limited to the expense multiplied by business-use percentage. Special rules apply if business use is less than 50 percent.
- Additional limitations apply to luxury automobiles.

LO 10-4 Explain the rationale behind amortization, describe the four categories of amortizable intangible assets, and calculate amortization expense.

- Intangible assets (such as patents, goodwill, and trademarks) have their costs recovered through amortization.
- Intangible assets are amortized (straight-line method) using the full-month convention.
- Intangibles are divided into four types (§197 purchased intangibles, start-up costs and organizational expenditures, research and experimentation, and self-created intangibles).

LO 10-5 Explain cost recovery of natural resources and the allowable depletion methods.

- Depletion allows a taxpayer to recover his or her capital investment in natural resources.
- Two methods of depletion are available, and the taxpayer must calculate both and take the one that results in the larger depletion deduction each year.
- Cost depletion allows taxpayers to estimate number of units and then allocate a pro rata share of the basis to each unit extracted during the year.
- Percentage depletion allows the taxpayer to take a statutory determined percentage of gross income as an expense. Deductions are not limited to basis.

KEY TERMS

Accelerated Cost Recovery System (ACRS) (10-6)
adjusted basis (10-3)
amortization (10-2)
bonus depreciation (10-22)
cost depletion (10-37)
cost recovery (10-2)
covenant not to compete (10-31)
depletion (10-2)
depreciation (10-2)

full-month convention (10-31)
half-year convention (10-9)
intangible assets (10-2)
listed property (10-24)
luxury automobile (10-27)
mid-month convention (10-15)
mid-quarter convention (10-9)
Modified Accelerated Cost Recovery System (MACRS) (10-6)
organizational expenditures (10-32)

percentage depletion (10-38)
personal property (10-7)
real property (10-7)
recovery period (10-6)
research and experimentation (R&E) costs (10-31)
§179 expense (10-18)
§197 purchased intangibles (10-31)
start-up costs (10-34)
tax basis (10-3)

DISCUSSION QUESTIONS

Discussion Questions are available in *Connect*®.

1. Explain why the tax laws require the cost of certain assets to be capitalized and recovered over time rather than immediately expensed. `LO 10-1`

2. Explain the differences and similarities between personal property, real property, intangible property, and natural resources. Also, provide an example of each type of asset. `LO 10-1`

3. Explain the similarities and dissimilarities between depreciation, amortization, and depletion. Describe the cost recovery method used for each of the four asset types (personal property, real property, intangible property, and natural resources). `LO 10-1`

4. Is an asset's initial or cost basis simply its purchase price? Explain. `LO 10-1`

5. Compare and contrast the basis of property acquired via purchase, conversion from personal use to business or rental use, a nontaxable exchange, gift, and inheritance. `LO 10-1`

6. Explain why the expenses incurred to get an asset in place and operable should be included in the asset's basis. `LO 10-1`

7. Graber Corporation runs a long-haul trucking business. Graber incurs the following expenses: replacement tires, oil changes, and a transmission overhaul. Which of these expenditures may be deducted currently and which must be capitalized? Explain. `LO 10-1`

8. MACRS depreciation requires the use of a recovery period, method, and convention to depreciate tangible personal property assets. Briefly explain why each is important to the calculation. `LO 10-2`

9. Can a taxpayer with very little current year income choose to not claim any depreciation expense for the current year and thus save depreciation deductions for the future when the taxpayer expects to be more profitable? `LO 10-2`

10. What depreciation methods are available for tangible personal property? Explain the characteristics of a business likely to adopt each method. `LO 10-2` planning

11. If a business places several different assets in service during the year, must it use the same depreciation method for all assets? If not, what restrictions apply to the business's choices of depreciation methods? `LO 10-2`

12. Describe how you would determine the MACRS recovery period for an asset if you did not already know it. `LO 10-2`

research   LO 10-2   13. Compare and contrast the recovery periods used by MACRS and those used under generally accepted accounting principles (GAAP).

LO 10-2   14. What are the two depreciation conventions that apply to tangible personal property under MACRS? Explain why Congress provides two methods.

LO 10-2   15. A business buys two identical tangible personal property assets for the same identical price. It buys one at the beginning of the year and one at the end of the year. Under what conditions would the taxpayer's depreciation on each asset be exactly the same? Under what conditions would it be different?

LO 10-2   16. AAA Inc. acquired a machine in year 1. In May of year 3, it sold the asset. Can AAA find its year 3 depreciation percentage for the machine on the MACRS table? If not, what adjustment must AAA make to its full-year depreciation percentage to determine its year 3 depreciation?

LO 10-2   17. There are two recovery period classifications for real property. What reasons might Congress have to allow residential real estate a shorter recovery period than nonresidential real property?

LO 10-2   18. Discuss why Congress has instructed taxpayers that real property be depreciated using the mid-month convention as opposed to the half-year or mid-quarter conventions used for tangible personal property.

LO 10-2   19. If a taxpayer has owned a building for 10 years and decides that it should make significant improvements to the building, what is the recovery period for the improvements?

research   LO 10-2   20. Compare and contrast the differences between computing depreciation expense for tangible personal property and depreciation expense for real property under both the regular tax and alternative tax systems.

LO 10-3   21. Discuss why a small business might be able to deduct a greater percentage of the assets it places in service during the year than a larger business.

LO 10-3   22. Explain the two limitations placed on the §179 deduction. How are they similar? How are they different?

LO 10-3   23. Compare and contrast the types of businesses that would benefit from and those that would not benefit from the §179 expense.

LO 10-3   24. What strategies will help a business maximize its current depreciation deductions (including §179)? Why might a taxpayer choose not to maximize its current depreciation deductions?

LO 10-3   25. Why might a business elect only the §179 expense it can deduct in the current year rather than claiming the full amount available?

LO 10-3   26. Describe assets that are considered to be listed property. Why do you think the Internal Revenue Service requires them to be "listed"?

LO 10-3   27. Are taxpayers allowed to claim depreciation expense on assets they use for both business and personal purposes? What are the tax consequences if the business use drops from above 50 percent in one year to below 50 percent in the next?

LO 10-3   28. Discuss why Congress limits the amount of depreciation expense businesses may claim on certain automobiles.

LO 10-3   29. Compare and contrast how a Land Rover SUV and a Mercedes Benz sedan are treated under the luxury auto rules. Also include a discussion of the similarities and differences in available §179 expense.

LO 10-4   30. What is a §197 intangible? How do taxpayers recover the costs of these intangibles? How do taxpayers recover the cost of a §197 intangible that expires (such as a covenant not to compete)?

31. Compare and contrast the tax and financial accounting treatment of goodwill. Are taxpayers allowed to deduct amounts associated with self-created goodwill? `LO 10-4`

32. Compare and contrast the similarities and differences between organizational expenditures and start-up costs for tax purposes. `LO 10-4`

33. Discuss the method used to determine the amount of organizational expenditures or start-up costs that may be immediately expensed in the year a taxpayer begins business. `LO 10-4`

34. Explain the amortization convention applicable to intangible assets. `LO 10-4`

35. Compare and contrast the recovery periods of §197 intangibles, organizational expenditures, start-up costs, and research and experimentation expenses. `LO 10-4`

36. Compare and contrast the cost and percentage depletion methods for recovering the costs of natural resources. What are the similarities and differences between the two methods? `LO 10-5`

37. Explain why percentage depletion has been referred to as a government subsidy. `LO 10-5`

PROBLEMS

Select problems are available in *Connect*®.   connect

38. Jose purchased a delivery van for his business through an online auction. His winning bid for the van was $24,500. In addition, Jose incurred the following expenses before using the van: shipping costs of $650; paint to match the other fleet vehicles at a cost of $1,000; registration costs of $3,200, which included $3,000 of sales tax and a registration fee of $200; wash and detailing for $50; and an engine tune-up for $250. What is Jose's cost basis for the delivery van? `LO 10-1`

39. Emily purchased a building to store inventory for her business. The purchase price was $760,000. Beyond this, Emily incurred the following necessary expenses to get the building ready for use: $2,000 to repair minor leaks in the roof, $5,000 to make the interior suitable for her finished goods, and $300 in legal fees. What is Emily's cost basis in the new building? `LO 10-1` research

40. In January, Prahbu purchases a new machine for use in an existing production line of his manufacturing business for $90,000. Assume that the machine is a unit of property and is not a material or supply. Prahbu pays $2,500 to install the machine, and after the machine is installed, he pays $1,300 to perform a critical test on the machine to ensure that it will operate in accordance with quality standards. On November 1, the critical test is complete, and Prahbu places the machine in service on the production line. On December 3, Prahbu pays another $3,300 to perform periodic quality control testing after the machine is placed in service. How much will Prahbu be required to capitalize as the cost of the machine? `LO 10-1` research

41. Dennis contributed business assets to a new business in exchange for stock in the company. The exchange did not qualify as a nontaxable exchange. The fair market value of these assets was $287,000 on the contribution date. Dennis's original basis in the assets he contributed was $143,000, and the accumulated depreciation on the assets was $78,000. `LO 10-1`

    a) What is the business's basis in the assets it received from Dennis?

    b) What would be the business's basis if the transaction qualified as a nontaxable exchange?

42. Brittany started a law practice as a sole proprietor. She owned a computer, printer, desk, and file cabinet she purchased during law school (several years ago) that she is planning to use in her business. What is the depreciable basis `LO 10-1`

that Brittany should use in her business for each asset, given the following information?

Asset	Purchase Price	FMV at Time Converted to Business Use
Computer	$2,500	$ 800
Printer	300	150
Desk	1,200	1,000
File cabinet	200	225

LO 10-1 43. Meg O'Brien received a gift of some small-scale jewelry manufacturing equipment that her father had used for personal purposes for many years. Her father originally purchased the equipment for $1,500. Because the equipment is out of production and no longer available, the property is currently worth $4,000. Meg has decided to begin a new jewelry manufacturing trade or business. What is her depreciable basis for depreciating the equipment?

LO 10-1 44. Gary inherited a Maine summer cabin on 10 acres from his grandmother. His grandparents originally purchased the property for $500 in 1950 and built the cabin at a cost of $10,000 in 1965. His grandfather died in 1980 and when his grandmother recently passed away, the property was appraised at $500,000 for the land and $700,000 for the cabin. Since Gary doesn't currently live in New England, he decided that it would be best to put the property to use as a rental. What is Gary's basis in the land and in the cabin?

LO 10-1 45. Wanting to finalize a sale before year-end, on December 29, WR Outfitters sold to Bob a warehouse and the land for $125,000. The appraised fair market value of the warehouse was $75,000, and the appraised value of the land was $100,000.
a) What is Bob's basis in the warehouse and in the land?
b) What would be Bob's basis in the warehouse and in the land if the appraised value of the warehouse is $50,000, and the appraised value of the land is $125,000?
c) Which appraisal would Bob likely prefer?

LO 10-2 46. At the beginning of the year, Poplock began a calendar-year dog boarding business called Griff's Palace. Poplock bought and placed in service the following assets during the year:

Asset	Date Acquired	Cost Basis
Computer equipment	3/23	$ 5,000
Dog-grooming furniture	5/12	7,000
Pickup truck	9/17	10,000
Commercial building	10/11	270,000
Land (one acre)	10/11	80,000

Assuming Poplock does not elect §179 expensing or bonus depreciation, answer the following questions:
a) What is Poplock's year 1 depreciation expense for each asset?
b) What is Poplock's year 2 depreciation expense for each asset?

LO 10-2 47. DLW Corporation acquired and placed in service the following assets during the year:

Asset	Date Acquired	Cost Basis
Computer equipment	2/17	$ 10,000
Furniture	5/12	17,000
Commercial building	11/1	270,000

Assuming DLW does not elect §179 expensing or bonus depreciation, answer the following questions:

a) What is DLW's year 1 cost recovery for each asset?

b) What is DLW's year 3 cost recovery for each asset if DLW sells all of these assets on 1/23 of year 3?

48. At the beginning of the year, Dee began a calendar-year business and placed in service the following assets during the year: `LO 10-2`

Asset	Date Acquired	Cost Basis
Computer equipment	3/23	$ 5,000
Furniture	5/12	7,000
Pickup truck	11/15	10,000
Commercial building	10/11	270,000

Assuming Dee does not elect §179 expensing or bonus depreciation, answer the following questions:

a) What is Dee's year 1 cost recovery for each asset?

b) What is Dee's year 2 cost recovery for each asset?

49. Evergreen Corporation (calendar-year-end) acquired the following assets during the current year (ignore §179 expense and bonus depreciation for this problem):   `LO 10-2`

Asset	Placed in Service Date	Original Basis
Machinery	October 25	$ 70,000
Computer equipment	February 3	10,000
Used delivery truck*	August 17	23,000
Furniture	April 22	150,000

*The delivery truck is not a luxury automobile.

a) What is the allowable MACRS depreciation on Evergreen's property in the current year?

b) What is the allowable MACRS depreciation on Evergreen's property in the current year if the machinery had a basis of $170,000 rather than $70,000?

50. Convers Corporation (June 30 year-end) acquired the following assets during the current tax year (ignore §179 expense and bonus depreciation for this problem):   `LO 10-2`

Asset	Placed in Service Date	Original Basis
Machinery	October 25	$ 70,000
Computer equipment	February 3	10,000
Used delivery truck*	March 17	23,000
Furniture	April 22	150,000
Total		$253,000

*The delivery truck is not a luxury automobile.

What is the allowable MACRS depreciation on Convers's property in the current year?

LO 10-2

51. Harris Corp. is a technology start-up and is in its second year of operations. The company didn't purchase any assets this year but purchased the following assets in the prior year:

Asset	Placed in Service	Basis
Office equipment	August 14	$10,000
Manufacturing equipment	April 15	68,000
Computer system	June 1	16,000
Total		$94,000

Harris did not know depreciation was tax deductible until it hired an accountant this year and didn't claim any depreciation expense in its first year of operation.

a) What is the maximum amount of depreciation expense Harris Corp. can deduct in its second year of operation (ignore bonus and §179 expense)?

b) What is the basis of the office equipment at the end of the second year?

LO 10-2

planning

52. Parley needs a new truck to help him expand Parley's Plumbing Palace. Business has been booming and Parley would like to accelerate his tax deductions as much as possible (ignore §179 expense and bonus depreciation for this problem). On April 1, Parley purchased a new delivery van for $25,000. It is now September 26 and Parley, already in need of another vehicle, has found a deal on buying a truck for $22,000 (all fees included). The dealer tells him if he doesn't buy the truck (Option 1), it will be gone tomorrow. There is an auction (Option 2) scheduled for October 5 where Parley believes he can get a similar truck for $21,500, but there is also a $500 auction fee.

a) Which option allows Parley to generate more depreciation expense deductions this year (the vehicles are not considered to be luxury autos)?

b) Assume the original facts, except that the delivery van was placed in service one day earlier on March 31 rather than April 1. Which option generates more depreciation expense?

LO 10-2

53. Way Corporation disposed of the following tangible personal property assets in the current year. Assume that the delivery truck is not a luxury auto. Calculate Way Corporation's 2016 depreciation expense (ignore §179 expense and bonus depreciation for this problem).

Asset	Date Acquired	Date Sold	Convention	Original Basis
Furniture (7-year)	5/12/12	7/15/16	HY	$ 55,000
Machinery (7-year)	3/23/13	3/15/16	MQ	72,000
Delivery truck (5-year)	9/17/14	3/13/16	HY	20,000
Machinery (7-year)	10/11/15	8/11/16	MQ	270,000
Computer (5-year)	10/11/16	12/15/16	HY	80,000

LO 10-2

54. On November 10 of year 1 Javier purchased a building, including the land it was on, to assemble his new equipment. The total cost of the purchase was $1,200,000; $300,000 was allocated to the basis of the land and the remaining $900,000 was allocated to the basis of the building.

a) Using MACRS, what is Javier's depreciation expense on the building for years 1 through 3?

b) What would be the year 3 depreciation expense if the building was sold on August 1 of year 3?

c) Answer the question in part (a), except assume the building was purchased and placed in service on March 3 instead of November 10.

d) Answer the question in part (a), except assume that the building is residential property.

e) What would be the depreciation for 2016, 2017, and 2018 if the property were nonresidential property purchased and placed in service November 10, 1999 (assume the same original basis)?

55. Carl purchased an apartment complex for $1.1 million on March 17 of year 1. $300,000 of the purchase price was attributable to the land the complex sits on. He also installed new furniture into half of the units at a cost of $60,000. **LO 10-2**

a) What is Carl's allowable depreciation expense for his real property for years 1 and 2?

b) What is Carl's allowable depreciation expense for year 3 if the real property is sold on January 2 of year 3?

56. AMP Corporation (calendar-year-end) has 2016 taxable income of $900,000 before the §179 expense. During 2016, AMP acquired the following assets: **LO 10-3** **LO 10-2**

Asset	Placed in Service	Basis
Machinery	September 12	$1,550,000
Computer equipment	February 10	365,000
Office building	April 2	480,000
Total		$2,395,000

a) What is the maximum amount of §179 expense AMP may deduct for 2016?

b) What is the maximum total depreciation expense, including §179 expense, that AMP may deduct in 2016 on the assets it placed in service in 2016 assuming no bonus depreciation?

57. Assume that TDW Corporation (calendar-year-end) has 2016 taxable income of $650,000 before the §179 expense and acquired the following assets during 2016: **LO 10-3** **LO 10-2**

Asset	Placed in Service	Basis
Machinery	October 12	$1,270,000
Computer equipment	February 10	263,000
Furniture	April 2	880,000
Total		$2,413,000

a) What is the maximum amount of §179 expense TDW may deduct for 2016?

b) What is the maximum total depreciation expense, including §179 expense, that TDW may deduct in 2016 on the assets it placed in service in 2016 assuming no bonus depreciation?

58. Assume that Timberline Corporation has 2016 taxable income of $240,000 before the §179 expense. **LO 10-3** **LO 10-2**

Asset	Purchase Date	Basis
Furniture (7-year)	December 1	$350,000
Computer equipment (5-year)	February 28	90,000
Copier (5-year)	July 15	30,000
Machinery (7-year)	May 22	480,000
Total		$950,000

a) What is the maximum amount of §179 expense Timberline may deduct for 2016? What is Timberline's §179 carryforward to 2017, if any?

b) What would Timberline's maximum depreciation expense be for 2016 assuming no bonus depreciation?

c) What would Timberline's maximum depreciation expense be for 2016 if the furniture cost $2,000,000 instead of $350,000 and assuming no bonus depreciation?

LO 10-3 **LO 10-2**

planning

59. Dain's Diamond Bit Drilling purchased the following assets this year. Assume its taxable income for the year was $53,000 before deducting any §179 expense (assume no bonus depreciation).

Asset	Purchase Date	Original Basis
Drill bits (5-year)	January 25	$ 90,000
Drill bits (5-year)	July 25	95,000
Commercial building	April 22	220,000

a) What is the maximum amount of §179 expense Dain may deduct for the year?

b) What is Dain's maximum depreciation expense for the year (including §179 expense)?

c) If the January drill bits' original basis was $2,375,000, what is the maximum amount of §179 expense Dain may deduct for the year?

d) If the January drill bits' basis was $2,495,000, what is the maximum amount of §179 expense Dain may deduct for the year?

LO 10-3 **LO 10-2**

research

60. Assume that ACW Corporation has 2016 taxable income of $1,000,000 before the §179 expense and acquired the following assets during 2016 (assume no bonus depreciation).

Asset	Placed in Service	Basis
Machinery	September 12	$ 470,000
Computer equipment	February 10	70,000
Delivery truck	August 21	93,000
Qualified leasehold improvements	April 2	380,000
Total		$1,013,000

a) What is the maximum amount of §179 expense ACW may deduct for 2016?

b) What is the maximum *total* depreciation expense that ACW may deduct in 2016 on the assets it placed in service in 2016?

LO 10-3 **LO 10-2**

61. Chaz Corporation has taxable income in 2016 of $312,000 before the §179 expense and acquired the following assets during the year:

Asset	Placed in Service	Basis
Office furniture	September 12	$1,280,000
Computer equipment	February 10	930,000
Delivery truck	August 21	68,000
Total		$2,278,000

What is the maximum *total* depreciation expense that Chaz may deduct in 2016?

62. Woolard Inc. has taxable income in 2016 of $150,000 before any depreciation deductions (§179, bonus, or MACRS) and acquired the following assets during the year:

Asset	Placed in Service	Basis
Office furniture (used)	March 20	$600,000

LO 10-3 LO 10-2

planning

research

a) If Woolard elects $50,000 of §179, what is Woolard's total depreciation deduction for the year?
b) If Woolard elects the maximum amount of §179 for the year, what is the amount of deductible §179 expense for the year? What is the *total* depreciation expense that Woolard may deduct in 2016? What is Woolard's §179 carryforward amount to next year, if any?
c) Woolard is concerned about future limitations on its §179 expense. How much §179 expense should Woolard expense this year if it wants to maximize its depreciation this year and avoid any carryover to future years?

63. Assume that Sivart Corporation has 2016 taxable income of $750,000 before the §179 expense and acquired the following assets during 2016:

LO 10-3 LO 10-2

planning

Asset	Placed in Service	Basis
Machinery	October 12	$1,440,000
Computer equipment	February 10	70,000
Delivery truck—used	August 21	93,000
Furniture	April 2	310,000
Total		$1,913,000

a) What is the maximum amount of §179 expense Sivart may deduct for 2016?
b) What is the maximum *total* depreciation expense (§179, bonus, MACRS) that Sivart may deduct in 2016 on the assets it placed in service in 2016?

64. Acorn Construction (calendar year-end C-corporation) has had rapid expansion during the last half of the current year due to the housing market's recovery. The company has record income and would like to maximize its cost recovery deduction for the current year. Acorn provided you with the following information:

LO 10-3 LO 10-2

planning

Asset	Placed in Service	Basis
New equipment and tools	August 20	$ 800,000
Used light duty trucks	October 17	1,200,000
Used machinery	November 6	525,000
Total		$2,525,000

a) What is Acorn's maximum cost recovery deduction in the current year?
b) What planning strategies would you advise Acorn to consider?

65. Phil owns a ranch business and uses four-wheelers to do much of his work. Occasionally, though, he and his boys will go for a ride together as a family activity. During year 1, Phil put 765 miles on the four-wheeler that he bought on January 15 for $6,500. Of the miles driven, only 175 miles were for personal use. Assume four-wheelers qualify to be depreciated according to the five-year MACRS schedule and the four-wheeler was the only asset Phil purchased this year.

LO 10-3

a) Calculate the allowable depreciation for year 1 (ignore the §179 expense and bonus depreciation).

b) Calculate the allowable depreciation for year 2 if total miles were 930 and personal use miles were 400 (ignore the §179 expense and bonus depreciation).

LO 10-3 66. Assume that Ernesto purchased a laptop computer on July 10 of year 1 for $3,000. In year 1, 80 percent of his computer usage was for his business and 20 percent was for computer gaming with his friends. This was the only asset he placed in service during year 1. Ignoring any potential §179 expense and bonus depreciation, answer the questions for each of the following alternative scenarios:

a) What is Ernesto's depreciation deduction for the computer in year 1?

b) What would be Ernesto's depreciation deduction for the computer in year 2 if his year 2 usage was 75 percent business and 25 percent for computer gaming?

c) What would be Ernesto's depreciation deduction for the computer in year 2 if his year 2 usage was 45 percent business and 55 percent for computer gaming?

d) What would be Ernesto's depreciation deduction for the computer in year 2 if his year 2 usage was 30 percent business and 70 percent for computer gaming?

LO 10-3 67. Lina purchased a new car for use in her business during 2016. The auto was the only business asset she purchased during the year and her business was extremely profitable. Calculate her maximum depreciation deductions (including §179 expense unless stated otherwise) for the automobile in 2016 and 2017 (Lina doesn't want to take bonus depreciation for 2016 or 2017) in the following alternative scenarios (assuming half-year convention for all):

a) The vehicle cost $15,000 and business use is 100 percent (ignore §179 expense).

b) The vehicle cost $40,000, and business use is 100 percent.

c) The vehicle cost $40,000, and she used it 80 percent for business.

d) The vehicle cost $40,000, and she used it 80 percent for business. She sold it on March 1 of year 2.

e) The vehicle cost $40,000, and she used it 20 percent for business.

f) The vehicle cost $40,000, and is an SUV that weighed 6,500 pounds. Business use was 100 percent.

LO 10-3 **LO 10-2** 68. Burbank Corporation (calendar-year end) acquired the following property this year:

Asset	Placed in Service	Basis
Used copier	February 12	$ 7,800
New computer equipment	June 6	14,000
Furniture	July 15	32,000
New delivery truck	October 28	19,000
Luxury auto	December 31	70,000
Total		$142,800

a) Assuming no bonus or §179 expense, what is Burbank's maximum cost recovery deduction for this year?

b) Assuming Burbank would like to maximize its cost recovery deductions by electing bonus and §179 expense, which assets should Burbank immediately expense?

c) What is Burbank's maximum cost recovery deduction this year assuming it elects §179 expense and bonus depreciation?

69. Paul Vote purchased the following assets this year (ignore §179 expensing and bonus depreciation when answering the questions below):

LO 10-3

 research

Asset	Purchase Date	Basis
Machinery	May 12	$ 23,500
Computers	August 13	20,000
Warehouse	December 13	180,000

a) What is Paul's allowable MACRS depreciation expense for the property?

b) What is Paul's allowable alternative minimum tax (AMT) depreciation expense for the property? You will need to find the AMT depreciation tables to compute the depreciation.

70. After several profitable years running her business, Ingrid decided to acquire the assets of a small competing business. On May 1 of year 1, Ingrid acquired the competing business for $300,000. Ingrid allocated $50,000 of the purchase price to goodwill. Ingrid's business reports its taxable income on a calendar-year basis.

LO 10-4

a) How much amortization expense on the goodwill can Ingrid deduct in year 1, year 2, and year 3?

b) In lieu of the original facts, assume that Ingrid purchased only a phone list with a useful life of 5 years for $10,000. How much amortization expense on the phone list can Ingrid deduct in year 1, year 2, and year 3?

71. Juliette formed a new business to sell sporting goods this year. The business opened its doors to customers on June 1. Determine the amount of start-up costs Juliette can immediately expense (not including the portion of the expenditures that are amortized over 180 months) this year in the following alternative scenarios:

LO 10-4

a) She incurred start-up costs of $2,000.

b) She incurred start-up costs of $45,000.

c) She incurred start-up costs of $53,500.

d) She incurred start-up costs of $63,000.

e) How would you answer parts (a) through (d) if she formed a partnership or a corporation and she incurred the same amount of organizational expenditures rather than start-up costs (how much of the organizational expenditures would be immediately deductible)?

72. Nicole organized a new corporation. The corporation began business on April 1 of year 1. She made the following expenditures associated with getting the corporation started:

LO 10-4

Expense	Date	Amount
Attorney fees for articles of incorporation	February 10	$32,000
March 1–March 30 wages	March 30	4,500
March 1–March 30 rent	March 30	2,000
Stock issuance costs	April 1	20,000
April 1–May 30 wages	May 30	12,000

a) What is the total amount of the start-up costs and organizational expenditures for Nicole's corporation?

b) What amount of the start-up costs and organizational expenditures may the corporation immediately expense in year 1 (excluding the portion of the expenditures that are amortized over 180 months)?

c) What amount can the corporation deduct as amortization expense for the organizational expenditures and for the start-up costs for year 1 (not including the amount determined in part b)?

d) What would be the total allowable organizational expenditures, if Nicole started a sole proprietorship instead?

LO 10-4 73. Bethany incurred $20,000 in research and experimental costs for developing a specialized product during July of year 1. Bethany went through a lot of trouble and spent $10,000 in legal fees to receive a patent for the product in August of year 3. Bethany expects the patent to have a remaining useful life of 10 years.

    a) What amount of research and experimental expenses for year 1, year 2, and year 3 may Bethany deduct if she elects to amortize the expenses over 60 months?

    b) How much *patent* amortization expense would Bethany deduct in year 3 assuming she elected to amortize the research and experimental costs over 60 months?

    c) If Bethany chose to capitalize but *not* amortize the research and experimental expenses she incurred in year 1, how much patent amortization expense would Bethany deduct in year 3?

LO 10-5 74. Last Chance Mine (LC) purchased a coal deposit for $750,000. It estimated it would extract 12,000 tons of coal from the deposit. LC mined the coal and sold it, reporting gross receipts of $1 million, $3 million, and $2 million for years 1 through 3, respectively. During years 1–3, LC reported net income (loss) from the coal deposit activity in the amount of ($20,000), $500,000, and $450,000, respectively. In years 1–3, LC actually extracted 13,000 tons of coal as follows:

(1) Tons of Coal	(2) Basis	Depletion (2)/(1) Rate	Tons Extracted per Year		
			Year 1	Year 2	Year 3
12,000	$750,000	$62.50	2,000	7,200	3,800

    a) What is Last Chance's cost depletion for years 1, 2, and 3?

    b) What is Last Chance's percentage depletion for each year (the applicable percentage for coal is 10 percent)?

    c) Using the cost and percentage depletion computations from the previous parts, what is Last Chance's actual depletion expense for each year?

COMPREHENSIVE PROBLEMS

Select problems are available in *Connect®*.

tax forms

75. Back in Boston, Steve has been busy creating and managing his new company, Teton Mountaineering (TM), which is based out of a small town in Wyoming. In the process of doing so, TM has acquired various types of assets. Below is a list of assets acquired during 2015:

Asset	Cost	Date Placed in Service
Office furniture	$ 10,000	02/03/2015
Machinery	560,000	07/22/2015
Used delivery truck*	15,000	08/17/2015

*Not considered a luxury automobile, thus not subject to the luxury automobile limitations.

During 2015, TM had huge success (and had no §179 limitations) and Steve acquired more assets the next year to increase its production capacity. These are the assets acquired during 2016:

Asset	Cost	Date Placed in Service
Computers & info. system	$ 40,000	03/31/2016
Luxury auto†	80,000	05/26/2016
Assembly equipment	475,000	08/15/2016
Storage building	400,000	11/13/2016

†Used 100% for business purposes.

TM generated a taxable income in 2016 before any §179 expense of $732,500.

Required

a) Compute the maximum 2015 depreciation deductions including §179 expense (ignoring bonus depreciation).

b) Compute the maximum 2016 depreciation deductions including §179 expense (ignoring bonus depreciation).

c) Compute the maximum 2016 depreciation deductions including §179 expense, but now assume that Steve would like to take bonus depreciation.

d) Ignoring part (c), now assume that during 2016, Steve decides to buy a competitor's assets for a purchase price of $350,000. Compute the maximum 2016 cost recovery including §179 expense (ignoring bonus depreciation). Steve purchased the following assets for the lump-sum purchase price.

Asset	Cost	Date Placed in Service
Inventory	$ 20,000	09/15/2016
Office furniture	30,000	09/15/2016
Machinery	50,000	09/15/2016
Patent	98,000	09/15/2016
Goodwill	2,000	09/15/2016
Building	130,000	09/15/2016
Land	20,000	09/15/2016

Complete Part I of Form 4562 for part (b) (use the most current form available).

76. While completing undergraduate school work in information systems, Dallin Bourne and Michael Banks decided to start a business called ISys Answers, which was a technology support company. During year 1, they bought the following assets and incurred the following fees at start-up:

tax forms

Year 1 Assets	Purchase Date	Basis
Computers (5-year)	October 30, Y1	$15,000
Office equipment (7-year)	October 30, Y1	10,000
Furniture (7-year)	October 30, Y1	3,000
Start-up costs	October 30, Y1	17,000

In April of year 2, they decided to purchase a customer list from a company started by fellow information systems students preparing to graduate who provided virtually the same services. The customer list cost $10,000 and the sale was completed on April 30. During their summer break, Dallin and Michael passed on internship opportunities in an attempt to really grow their business into something they could do full-time after graduation. In the summer, they purchased a small van (for transportation, not considered a luxury auto) and a pinball machine (to help attract new employees). They bought the van on June 15, Y2, for $15,000 and spent $3,000 getting it ready to put into service. The pinball machine cost $4,000 and was placed in service on July 1, Y2.

Year 2 Assets	Purchase Date	Basis
Van	June 15, Y2	$18,000
Pinball machine (7-year)	July 1, Y2	4,000
Customer list	April 30, Y2	10,000

Assume that ISys Answers does not claim any §179 expense or bonus depreciation.

a) What are the maximum cost recovery deductions for ISys Answers for Y1 and Y2?

b) Complete ISys Answers' Form 4562 (use the most current form available).

c) What is ISys Answers' basis in each of its assets at the end of Y2?

77. Diamond Mountain was originally thought to be one of the few places in North America to contain diamonds, so Diamond Mountain Inc. (DM) purchased the land for $1,000,000. Later, DM discovered that the only diamonds on the mountain had been planted there and the land was worthless for mining. DM engineers discovered a new survey technology and discovered a silver deposit estimated at 5,000 pounds on Diamond Mountain. DM immediately bought new drilling equipment and began mining the silver.

In years 1–3 following the opening of the mine, DM had net (gross) income of $200,000 ($700,000), $400,000 ($1,100,000), and $600,000 ($1,450,000), respectively. Mining amounts for each year were as follows: 750 pounds (year 1), 1,450 pounds (year 2), and 1,800 pounds (year 3). At the end of year 2, engineers used the new technology (which had been improving over time) and estimated there was still an estimated 6,000 pounds of silver deposits.

DM also began a research and experimentation project with the hopes of gaining a patent for its new survey technology. Diamond Mountain Inc. chooses to capitalize research and experimentation expenditures and amortize the costs over 60 months or until it obtains a patent on its technology. In March of year 1, DM spent $95,000 on research and experimentation. DM spent another $75,000 in February of year 2 for research and experimentation. In September of year 2, DM paid $20,000 of legal fees and was granted the patent in October of year 2 (the entire process of obtaining a patent was unusually fast).

Answer the following questions regarding DM's activities (assume that DM tries to maximize its deductions if given a choice).

a) What is DM's depletion expense for years 1–3?

b) What is DM's research and experimentation amortization for years 1 and 2?

c) What is DM's basis in its patent and what is its amortization for the patent in year 2?

chapter

11 Property Dispositions

Upon completing this chapter, you should be able to:

LO 11-1 Calculate the amount of gain or loss recognized on the disposition of assets used in a trade or business.

LO 11-2 Describe the general character types of gain or loss recognized on property dispositions.

LO 11-3 Explain the rationale for and calculate depreciation recapture.

LO 11-4 Describe the tax treatment of unrecaptured §1250 gains and determine the character of gains on property sold to related parties.

LO 11-5 Describe the tax treatment of §1231 gains or losses, including the §1231 netting process.

LO 11-6 Explain common exceptions to the general rule that realized gains and losses are recognized currently.

Storyline Summary

Taxpayer:	Teton Mountaineering Technologies LLC (Teton)—a calendar-year, single-member LLC (treated as a sole proprietorship for tax purposes)
President:	Steve Dallimore
Location:	Cody, Wyoming

By most measures, Teton Mountaineering Technologies LLC (Teton) has become a success with sponsored climbers summiting the world's highest peaks, satisfied customers creating brand loyalty, and profitability improving steadily. However, after several years of operation, some of Teton's machinery is wearing out and must be replaced. Further, because Teton has outgrown its manufacturing capacity, Steve is considering whether to expand the company's current facility or sell it and build a new one in a different location. Steve would like to know how any asset dispositions will affect Teton's tax bill.

Steve has found a willing buyer for Teton's machinery, and he has options for trading the equipment. For tax purposes, does it matter whether he sells or trades the equipment? Steve also has questions about how to best manage Teton's acquisitions and dispositions of real property. It all seems a bit overwhelming. . . . He picks up the phone and dials his tax accountant's number. ■

You can imagine why Steve might be eager to reach his accountant. Tax accounting widely impacts business decisions: What are the tax consequences of selling, trading, or even abandoning business assets? Are the tax consequences the same whether taxpayers sell machinery, inventory, or investment assets? Does it matter for tax purposes whether Teton is structured as a sole proprietorship or a corporation when it sells its warehouse? If Steve sells his personal sailboat, car, or furniture, what are the tax consequences?

In the previous chapter we explained the tax consequences associated with purchasing assets and recovering the cost of the assets through depreciation, amortization, or depletion. This chapter explores fundamental tax issues associated with property dispositions (sales, trades, or other dispositions). We focus on the disposition of tangible assets, but the same principles apply to the sale of intangible assets and natural resources.

LO 11-1   DISPOSITIONS

Taxpayers can dispose of assets in many ways. For example, a taxpayer could sell an asset, donate it to charity, trade it for a similar asset, take it to the landfill, or have it destroyed in a natural disaster. No matter how it is accomplished, every asset disposition triggers a realization event for tax purposes. To calculate the amount of gain or loss taxpayers realize when they sell assets, they must determine the amount realized on the sale and the *adjusted basis* of each asset they are selling.

Amount Realized

Simply put, the **amount realized** by a taxpayer from the sale or other disposition of an asset is everything of *value* received from the buyer *less* any selling costs.[1] Although taxpayers typically receive cash when they sell property, they may also accept marketable securities, notes receivable, similar assets, or any combination of these items as payment. Additionally, taxpayers selling assets such as real property subject to loans or mortgages may receive some debt relief and would increase their amount realized by the amount of debt relief (the buyer's assumption of the seller's liability increases the seller's amount realized). The amount realized computation is captured in the following formula:

$$\text{Amount realized} = \text{Cash received} + \text{Fair market value of other property} + \text{Buyer's assumption of liabilities} - \text{Seller's expenses}$$

Example 11-1

Teton wants to upgrade its old manufacturing machinery that is wearing out. On November 1 of the current year, Teton sells the old machinery for $130,000 cash and marketable securities valued at $70,500. Teton paid a broker $500 to find a buyer. What is Teton's amount realized on the sale of the machinery?

Answer: $200,000, computed as follows:

Description	Amount	Explanation
(1) Cash received	$130,000	
(2) Marketable securities received	70,500	
(3) Broker commission paid	(500)	
Amount realized	$200,000	(1) + (2) + (3).

[1]*S. C. Chapin*, CA-8, 50-1 USTC ¶9171.

Determination of Adjusted Basis

In the previous chapter, we discussed the basis for cost recovery and focused on purchased assets in which the initial basis is the asset's cost. However, taxpayers may acquire assets without purchasing them. For example, a taxpayer may acquire an asset as a gift or as an inheritance. In either case, the taxpayer does not purchase the asset, so the taxpayer's initial basis in the asset must be computed as something other than purchase price. Although there are many situations when an asset's initial basis is not the asset's cost, we focus on three cases: gifts, inherited assets, and property converted from personal use to business use.

Gifts. A gift is defined as a transfer of property proceeding from a detached and disinterested generosity, out of affection, respect, admiration, charity, or like impulses.[2] The initial basis of gift property to a recipient (donee) depends on whether the value of the asset exceeds the donor's basis on the date of the gift. If the fair market value of the asset on the date of the gift is greater than the donor's basis, then the asset's initial basis to the recipient of the gift will be the same as the donor's basis.[3] That is, the donor's basis carries over to the donee.

If the asset has declined in value since the donor acquired it (fair market value at the date of the gift is less than the donor's basis), then special dual basis rules apply. A dual basis means that the gift property has one basis to the donee for determining gains and a different basis for determining losses when the donee disposes of the property. Thus, the basis of gifted property that has declined in value depends on the sales price of the asset subsequent to the gift. The donee uses the carryover basis if the asset is sold for a gain, whereas the donee uses the fair market value at the date of the gift if the asset sells for a loss. If the asset sells at a price between the donor's basis and the fair market value at the date of the gift, then the donee's basis at the time of the sale is to equal the selling price and the donee does not recognize gain or loss on the sale. The dual basis rule prevents the transfer of unrealized losses from one taxpayer to another by gift.

When the dual basis rules apply, the holding period of the asset depends on whether the gift property subsequently sells for a gain or loss. If the donor's basis is used to determine the gain, the holding period includes that of the donor. If the fair market value at the date of the gift is used to figure the loss, the holding period starts on the date of the gift. If the asset subsequently sells at a price between the donor's basis and the fair market value at the date of the gift, the holding period is irrelevant because there is no recognized gain or loss.

Inherited Property. For inherited property, the general rule is that the heir's basis in property passing from a decedent to the heir is the fair market value on the date of the decedent's death.[4] The holding period of inherited property is deemed to be long-term regardless of how long the heir owns the property.[5]

Property Converted from Personal Use to Business Use. In order to prevent taxpayers from converting nondeductible personal losses to business losses, special basis rules apply when property is converted from personal use to business use. The basis for determining the gain or loss on the sale of converted property depends on whether the property appreciated or declined in value during the time the property was used personally. That is, if the fair market value at the date of the conversion is greater than the taxpayer's basis in the property, then the taxpayer will use the lower taxpayer basis to calculate gain or loss at disposition. However, if the fair market value at the date of conversion is below the taxpayer's basis, the basis for calculating loss will be the fair market value at the date of conversion. After conversion, the taxpayer adjusts the loss

---

[2]*Comr. v. Duberstein,* 363 U.S. 278 (1960), rev'g 265 F.2d 28 (6th Cir. 1959), rev'g T. C. Memo 1958–4.

[3]§1015(a). The basis to the donee may be increased if the donor is required to pay gift tax on the gift.

[4]§1014(a)(1). An alternate valuation date may be used to determine the basis to the heirs if elected by the estate.

[5]§1223(9).

basis and the gain basis for depreciation deductions from the date of conversion to the date of disposition. As discussed in Chapter 10, the taxpayer uses the basis for loss in calculating depreciation deductions. If the property later sells for an amount that falls between the basis for gain and the basis for loss, the basis for the sale is treated as the sales price so that the taxpayer does not recognize gain or loss on the sale.[6]

Example 11-2

Assume that Steve received 100 shares of FZL stock from his grandfather on January 8. On the date of the gift, the stock was worth $15,000. Steve's grandfather originally purchased the stock 10 years earlier for $10,000. What is Steve's initial basis in the stock?

Answer: Since the stock had appreciated in value while Steve's grandfather owned it, Steve's initial basis is a carryover basis of $10,000.

What if: Assume that on the date of the gift, the fair market value of the stock was $8,000. What is Steve's initial basis in the stock?

Answer: Steve's initial basis depends on the price for which he later sells the stock. If Steve sells the stock six months later at a price greater than $10,000, his basis is the $10,000 carryover basis. He will recognize a long-term capital gain because his holding period is ten and a half years (includes the time his grandfather owned the stock). If he sells the stock six months later at a price less than $8,000, his basis is $8,000, the fair market value at the date of the gift. He will recognize a short-term capital loss because his holding period is only six months (begins on the date of the gift). If he sells the stock for a price in between $10,000 and $8,000, his basis is the sales price and he recognizes no gain or loss (his holding period does not matter).

What if: Assume that Steve inherited the stock from his grandfather on January 8. What is Steve's initial basis if the fair market value was (a) $15,000 and (b) $8,000 at the time of his grandfather's death?

Answer: Steve's initial basis is the fair market value at the date of his grandfather's death regardless of whether the value is greater or less than his grandfather's original cost. If the fair market value was $15,000, Steve's initial basis is $15,000. If the fair market value is $8,000, Steve's initial basis is $8,000. Steve's holding period is long-term regardless of how long he actually holds the stock because it is inherited property.

What if: Assume Steve owns some mountaineering equipment that he uses personally and purchased two years ago for $4,000. On March 20, he converts the equipment into business use property when the fair market value of the equipment is $5,000. What is Steve's initial basis in the equipment for business purposes?

Answer: Because the equipment appreciated in value before Steve converted it to business use, his basis is his original cost of $4,000. Steve uses the $4,000 as his initial basis for calculating cost recovery and determining his adjusted basis when he sells or otherwise disposes of the equipment.

What if: Assume that the equipment that Steve converts from personal to business use has a fair market value of $3,000 at the date of conversion. What is Steve's initial basis in the equipment for business purposes?

Answer: The equipment declined in value before Steve converted it to business use. In order to prevent Steve from converting his $1,000 personal loss into a business loss, his initial basis for business purposes will depend on whether he subsequently sells the equipment at a gain or loss. His initial basis for loss (and cost recovery) is the $3,000 fair market value at the conversion date. His initial basis for gain is his $4,000 original cost.

What if: Assume that the equipment that Steve converts from personal to business use has a fair market value of $3,000 at the date of conversion. Two years later, after taking $500 of depreciation deductions, he sells the equipment for $3,300. What is Steve's adjusted basis in the equipment for purposes of determining the gain or loss on the disposition?

[6]Reg. §1.165-9(b)(2) and Reg. §1.167(g)-1.

Answer: Steve's initial basis for loss was the $3,000 fair market value at the conversion date, and his initial basis for gain was $4,000 original cost. At the time of the sale, the adjusted basis for loss is $2,500, and the adjusted basis for gain is $3,500. Because the sales price falls between the adjusted basis for gain and the adjusted basis for loss, the adjusted basis is assumed to be equal to the sales price of $3,300.

The **adjusted basis** for determining the gain or loss on the sale of an asset is the initial basis (however determined) reduced by depreciation or other types of cost recovery deductions allowed (or allowable) on the property. The adjusted basis of an asset can be determined using the following formula:

Adjusted basis = Initial basis − Cost recovery allowed (or allowable)

Example 11-3

To determine its realized gain or loss on the sale, Teton must calculate the adjusted basis of the machinery it sold in Example 11-1 for $200,000. Teton originally purchased the machinery for $510,000 three years ago. For tax purposes, Teton depreciated the machinery using MACRS (seven-year recovery period, 200 percent declining balance method, and half-year convention). The machinery's adjusted basis at the time of the sale is $191,173, computed as follows:

Description	Tax	Explanation
(1) Original basis	$510,000	Example 10-1.
(2) Year 1	(72,879)	Example 10-4.
(3) Year 2	(124,899)	Example 10-4.
(4) Year 3	(89,199)	Example 10-4.
(5) Year 4	(31,850)	$63,699 (Example 10-4) × 50% (half-year convention).
(6) Accumulated depreciation	(318,827)	(2) + (3) + (4) + (5).
Adjusted basis	$191,173	(1) + (6).

Because businesses generally use more highly accelerated depreciation methods for tax purposes than they do for book purposes, the tax-adjusted basis of a particular asset is likely to be lower than the book-adjusted basis.

Realized Gain or Loss on Disposition

The amount of gain or loss taxpayers realize on a sale or other disposition of assets is simply the amount they realize minus their adjusted basis in the disposed assets.[7] The formula for computing **realized gain or loss** is as follows:

Gain or (loss) realized = Amount realized − Adjusted basis

Example 11-4

In Example 11-1, we learned that Teton sold machinery for a total amount realized of $200,000, and in Example 11-3 we learned that its basis in the machinery was $191,173. What is Teton's realized gain or loss on the sale of the machinery?

(continued on page 11-6)

[7]§1001(a).

Answer: $8,827, computed as follows:

Description	Amount	Explanation
(1) Amount realized	$200,000	Example 11-1.
(2) Adjusted basis	(191,173)	Example 11-3.
Gain realized	**$ 8,827**	(1) + (2).

Exhibit 11-1 details the important formulas necessary to determine realized tax gains and losses.

EXHIBIT 11-1   Summary of Formulas for Computing Gain or Loss Realized on an Asset Disposition

- Gain (loss) realized = Amount realized − Adjusted basis; where
  - Amount realized = Cash received + Fair market value of other property + Buyer's assumption of seller's liabilities − Seller's expenses
  - Adjusted basis = Initial basis − Cost recovery deductions

So far, our examples have used one of Teton's asset sales to demonstrate how to compute gain or loss realized when property is sold. However, as we describe in Exhibit 11-2, Teton disposed of several assets during the year. We refer to this exhibit throughout the chapter as a reference point for discussing the tax issues associated with property dispositions.

EXHIBIT 11-2   Teton's Asset Dispositions* Realized Gain (Loss) for Tax Purposes

Assets	(1) Amount Realized	(2) Initial Basic	(3) Accumulated Depreciation	(4) [(2) − (3)] Adjusted Basic	(5) [(1) − (4)] Gain (Loss) Realized
Machinery	$200,000	$510,000	$318,827	$191,173	$ 8,827
Office furniture	12,000	10,000	7,000	3,000	9,000
Delivery truck	2,000	15,000	10,500	4,500	(2,500)
Warehouse	350,000	275,000	15,000	260,000	90,000
Land	175,000	75,000	0	75,000	100,000
Total gain realized					$205,327

*These are the assets initially purchased by Teton in Example 10-1. Chapter 11 generally assumes that Teton has been in business for four years. For simplicity, this chapter assumes Teton did not previously elect any §179 immediate expensing or bonus depreciation.

Recognized Gain or Loss on Disposition

As a general rule, taxpayers realizing gains and losses during a year must recognize the gains or losses. **Recognized gains or losses** are gains (losses) that increase (decrease) taxpayers' gross income.[8] Thus, taxpayers must report recognized gains and losses on their tax returns. Although taxpayers must immediately recognize the vast majority of realized gains and losses, in certain circumstances they may be allowed to defer recognizing gains to subsequent periods, or they may be allowed to

[8]Recall under the return of capital principle we discussed in Chapter 5, when a taxpayer sells an asset, the taxpayer's adjusted basis is a return of capital and not a deductible expense.

permanently exclude the gains from taxable income. However, taxpayers may also be required to defer losses to later periods and, in more extreme cases, they may have their realized losses permanently disallowed. We address certain nonrecognition provisions later in the chapter.

CHARACTER OF GAIN OR LOSS

In order to determine how a recognized gain or loss affects a taxpayer's income tax liability, the taxpayer must determine the *character* or type of gain or loss recognized. Ultimately, every gain or loss is characterized as either ordinary or capital (long-term or short-term). As described below, businesses may recognize certain gains or losses (known as §1231) on property dispositions that require some intermediary steps, but even the §1231 gains or losses are eventually characterized as ordinary or capital (long-term). The character of a gain or loss is important because gains and losses of different characters are treated differently for tax purposes. For example, ordinary income (loss) is generally taxed at ordinary rates (fully deductible against ordinary income). However, capital gains may be taxed at preferential (lower) rates while deductions for capital losses are subject to certain restrictions. The character of the gains or losses taxpayers recognize when they sell assets depends on the character of the assets they are selling. The character of an asset depends on how the taxpayer used the asset and how long the taxpayer owned the asset (the holding period) before selling it.

In general terms, property may be used in a trade or business, treated as inventory or accounts receivable of a business, held for investment, or used for personal purposes. The holding period may be short-term (one year or less) or long-term (more than a year). Exhibit 11-3 provides a matrix of the character of assets (ordinary, capital, or §1231) depending on how taxpayers used the assets and the length of time they held the property before selling it.

THE KEY FACTS
Character of Assets
- Ordinary assets
  - Assets created or used in a taxpayer's trade or business.
  - Business assets held for one year or less.
- Capital assets
  - Assets held for investment purposes.
  - Assets held for personal-use purposes.
- §1231 assets
  - Depreciable assets and land used in a trade or business held for *more* than one year.

EXHIBIT 11-3 **Character of Assets Depending on Property Use and Holding Period**

Holding Period	Trade or Business	Investment or Personal-Use Assets*	Inventory and Accounts Receivable
Short-term (one year or less)	Ordinary	Short-term capital	Ordinary
Long-term (more than one year)	§1231†	Long-term capital	Ordinary

*Gains on the sale of personal-use assets are taxable capital gains, but losses on the sale of personal-use assets are not deductible.
†As we describe later in the chapter, gain or loss is eventually characterized as ordinary or capital (long-term).

Ordinary Assets

Ordinary assets are generally assets created or used in a taxpayer's trade or business. For example, inventory is an **ordinary asset** because it is held for sale to customers in the ordinary course of business. Accounts receivable are ordinary assets because receivables are generated from the sale of inventory or business services. Other assets used in a trade or business such as machinery and equipment are also considered to be ordinary assets if they have been used in a business for *one year or less*. For example, if Teton purchased a forklift for the warehouse but sold it six months later, the gain or loss would be ordinary. When taxpayers sell ordinary assets at a gain, they recognize an ordinary gain that is taxed at ordinary rates. When taxpayers sell ordinary assets at a loss, they deduct the loss against other ordinary income.

Capital Assets

A **capital asset** is generally something held for investment (stocks and bonds), for the **production of income** (a for-profit activity that doesn't rise to the level of a trade or business), or for personal use (your car, house, or personal computer).[9] Whether an asset qualifies as a capital asset depends on the purpose for which the taxpayer uses the asset. Thus, the same asset may be considered a capital asset to one taxpayer and an ordinary asset to another taxpayer. For example, a piece of land held as an investment because it is expected to appreciate in value over time is a capital asset to that taxpayer. However, the same piece of land held as inventory by a real estate developer would be an ordinary asset. Finally, the same piece of land would be a §1231 asset if the taxpayer held it for more than one year and used it in a trade or business (e.g., as a parking lot).

Individual taxpayers generally prefer capital gains to ordinary income because certain capital gains are taxed at lower rates and capital gains may offset capital losses that cannot be deducted against ordinary income. Individuals also prefer ordinary losses to capital losses because ordinary losses are deductible without limit, while individuals may deduct only $3,000 of net capital losses against ordinary income each year. Corporate taxpayers may prefer capital gains to ordinary income because capital gains may offset capital losses that they would not be allowed to offset otherwise. Corporations are not allowed to offset any net capital losses, but they are allowed to carry capital losses back three years and forward five years. Exhibit 11-4 reviews the treatment of capital gains and losses for individuals and corporations.

EXHIBIT 11-4   Review of Capital Gains and Losses

Taxpayer Type	Preferential Rates	Loss Limitations
Individuals	• Net capital gains on assets held more than one year are taxed at 15 percent (0 percent to the extent the gain would have been taxed at a 15 percent or lower rate if it were ordinary income and 20 percent to the extent the gain would have been taxed at 39.6 percent if it were ordinary income). • Unrecaptured §1250 gains on real property held more than one year are taxed at a maximum rate of 25 percent. • Net gains on collectibles held for more than a year are taxed at a maximum rate of 28 percent. • Net capital gains on assets held one year or less are taxed at ordinary rates.	• Individuals may annually deduct up to $3,000 of net capital losses against ordinary income. • Losses can be carried forward indefinitely but not carried back.
Corporations	• No preferential rates; taxed at ordinary rates.	• No offset against ordinary income. • Net capital losses can generally be carried back three years and forward five years to offset net capital gains in those years.

[9]§1221 defines what is not a capital asset. Broadly speaking, a *capital asset* is any property *other than* property used in a trade or business (e.g., inventory, manufacturing equipment) or accounts (or notes) receivable acquired in a business from the sale of services or property.

§1231 Assets

Section 1231 assets are depreciable assets and land used in a trade or business (including rental property) held by taxpayers for *more* than one year.[10] At a general level, when a taxpayer sells a §1231 asset, the taxpayer recognizes a §1231 gain or loss. As discussed above, however, ultimately §1231 gains or losses are characterized as ordinary or capital on a taxpayer's return. When taxpayers sell multiple §1231 assets during the year, they combine or "net" their §1231 gains and §1231 losses together. If the netting results in a net §1231 gain, the net gain is treated as a long-term capital gain. If the netting results in a net §1231 loss, the net loss is treated as an ordinary loss. Because net §1231 gains are treated as capital gains and §1231 losses are treated as ordinary losses, §1231 assets are tax favored relative to other types of assets.

As we discuss below, §1231 gains on individual depreciable assets may be recharacterized as ordinary income under the depreciation recapture rules. However, because land is not depreciable, when taxpayers sell or otherwise dispose of land that qualifies as §1231 property, the gain or loss from the sale is always characterized as §1231 gain or loss. Thus, we refer to land as a pure §1231 asset.

Example 11-5

In order to acquire another parcel of land to expand its manufacturing capabilities, Teton sold five acres of land that it has been using in its trade or business for $175,000. Teton purchased the land several years ago for $75,000. What is the amount and character of Teton's gain recognized on the land?

Answer: $100,000 §1231 gain, calculated as follows:

Description	Amount	Explanation
(1) Amount realized	$175,000	
(2) Original basis and current adjusted basis	75,000	
Gain (Loss) realized and recognized	**$100,000**	(1) − (2) §1231 gain.

What if: Assume that Teton sold the land for $50,000. What would be the character of the ($25,000) loss it would recognize?

Answer: §1231 loss.

What if: Assume that the land was the only asset Teton sold during the year. How would the §1231 gain or §1231 loss on the sale ultimately be characterized on its tax return?

Answer: If Teton recognized a §1231 gain on the sale, it would be characterized as a long-term capital gain on its return. If Teton recognized a §1231 loss on the sale, it would be characterized as an ordinary loss.

DEPRECIATION RECAPTURE

LO 11-3

Although Congress intended for businesses to receive favorable treatment on economic gains from the economic *appreciation* of §1231 assets, it did not intend for this favorable treatment to apply to gains that were created artificially through depreciation deductions that offset ordinary income. For example, if a taxpayer purchases an asset for $100 and sells it three years later for the same amount, we would generally agree that there is no economic gain on the disposition of the asset. However, if the taxpayer claimed depreciation deductions of $70 during the three years of ownership, the taxpayer would recognize a $70 gain on the disposition simply because the depreciation deductions reduced the asset's adjusted basis. Depreciation is an ordinary deduction that offsets income that would otherwise be taxed at ordinary rates. Absent tax rules to

---

[10]As noted above, property used in a trade or business and held for *one year or less* is ordinary income property.

the contrary, the gain recognized by the taxpayer upon the sale of the asset would be treated as long-term capital gain and would be taxed at a preferential rate (for individuals). Thus, depreciation deductions save taxes at the ordinary rate but the gains created by depreciation would generate income taxed at a preferential rate. This potential asymmetrical treatment led Congress to implement the concept of **depreciation recapture.** Depreciation recapture potentially applies to gains (but not losses) on the sale of depreciable or amortizable business property. When depreciation recapture applies, it changes the character of the gain on the sale of a §1231 asset (all or a portion of the gain) from §1231 gain into ordinary income. Note, however, that depreciation recapture does not affect losses recognized on the disposition of §1231 assets.

The method for computing the amount of depreciation recapture depends on the type of §1231 asset the taxpayer is selling (personal property or real property). As presented in Exhibit 11-5, §1231 assets can be categorized as pure §1231 assets (land), §1245 assets (personal property), or §1250 assets (real property). Whether personal or real property is sold, it is important to understand that depreciation recapture changes only the *character* but not the *amount* of gain recognized.

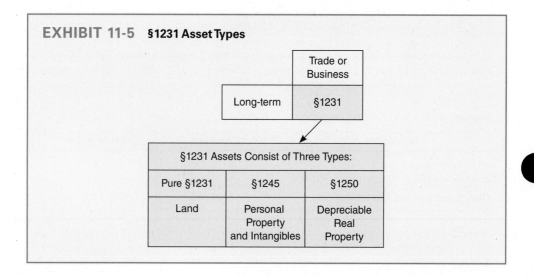

EXHIBIT 11-5   §1231 Asset Types

§1245 Property

Tangible personal property (machinery, equipment, and automobiles) and amortizable intangible property (patents, copyrights, and purchased goodwill) are a subset of §1231 property known as **§1245 property.**[11] The gain from the sale of §1245 property is characterized as ordinary income to the extent the gain was created by depreciation or amortization deductions. The amount of *ordinary income* (§1245 depreciation recapture) taxpayers recognize when they sell §1245 property is the lesser of (1) recognized gain on the sale *or* (2) total accumulated depreciation (or amortization) on the asset.[12] The remainder of any recognized gain is characterized as §1231 gain.[13] The sum of the ordinary income (due to depreciation recapture) and the §1231 gain on the sale equals the *total* gain recognized because depreciation recapture changes only the character of the gain, not the amount.

[11]An exception in the law is that §1245 property also includes nonresidential real property placed in service between 1981 and 1986 (ACRS) for which the taxpayer elected accelerated depreciation.

[12]§1245 recapture is commonly referred to as "full" depreciation recapture because it may cause a taxpayer to recapture the entire accumulated depreciation amount as ordinary income. §1245 recapture applies notwithstanding any other provision of the Internal Revenue Code (depreciation recapture trumps all other tax rules).

[13]As a practical matter, taxpayers are unlikely to recognize any §1231 gain on the disposition of personal property because the real economic value of most tangible personal property does not increase over time as the property is used.

When taxpayers sell or dispose of §1245 property, they encounter one of the following three scenarios involving gain or loss:

Scenario 1: They recognize a gain created solely through depreciation deductions.

Scenario 2: They recognize a gain created through both depreciation deductions and actual asset appreciation.

Scenario 3: They recognize a loss.

The following discussion considers each of these scenarios.

Scenario 1: Gain Created Solely through Cost Recovery Deductions

Most §1231 assets that experience wear and tear or obsolescence generally do not appreciate in value. Thus, when a taxpayer sells these types of assets at a gain, the gain is usually created because the taxpayer's depreciation deductions associated with the asset reduced the asset's adjusted basis faster than the real decline in the asset's economic value. In other words, the entire gain is artificially generated through depreciation the taxpayer claims before disposing of the asset. That is, absent depreciation deductions, the taxpayer would recognize a loss on the sale of the asset. Therefore, the entire gain on the disposition is recaptured (or characterized) as ordinary income under §1245 (recall that without depreciation recapture the gain would be §1231 gain, which can generate long-term capital gain and could create a double benefit for the taxpayer: ordinary depreciation deductions and capital gain upon disposition).

Example 11-6

As indicated in Exhibit 11-2, Teton sold machinery for $200,000. What is the amount and character of the gain Teton recognizes on the sale?

Answer: $8,827 of ordinary income under the §1245 depreciation recapture rules and $0 of §1231 gain, computed as follows:

Machinery Sale: Scenario 1 (Original scenario sales price = $200,000)		
Description	**Amount**	**Explanation**
(1) Amount realized	$200,000	Exhibit 11-2.
(2) Original basis	510,000	Exhibit 11-2.
(3) Accumulated depreciation	318,827	Exhibit 11-2.
(4) Adjusted basis	191,173	(2) − (3).
(5) Gain (loss) recognized	8,827	(1) − (4).
(6) Ordinary income (**§1245 depreciation recapture**)	**$ 8,827**	Lesser of (3) or (5).
§1231 gain	0	(5) − (6).

Note that in this situation, because Teton's entire gain is created through depreciation deductions, the entire gain is treated as ordinary income under §1245.

What if: What would be the amount and character of Teton's gain without the depreciation recapture rules?

Answer: $8,827 of §1231 gain. Note that the recapture rules change the character of the gain but not the amount of the gain.

Scenario 2: Gain Due to Both Cost Recovery Deductions and Asset Appreciation

Assets subject to cost recovery deductions may actually *appreciate* in value over time. When these assets are sold, the recognized gain must be divided into ordinary gain from depreciation recapture and §1231 gain. The portion of the gain created through cost recovery deductions is **recaptured** as ordinary income. The remaining gain (the gain due to economic appreciation) is §1231 gain.

Example 11-7

What if: Let's assume the same facts as in the previous example and in Exhibit 11-2, except that Teton sells the machinery for $520,000. What is the amount and character of the gain Teton would recognize on this sale?

Answer: $318,827 of ordinary income under the §1245 depreciation recapture rules and $10,000 of §1231 gain due to the asset's economic appreciation, computed as follows:

Machinery Sale: Scenario 2 (Assumed sales price = $520,000)		
Description	**Amount**	**Explanation**
(1) Amount realized	$520,000	
(2) Original basis	510,000	Exhibit 11-2.
(3) Accumulated depreciation	$318,827	Exhibit 11-2.
(4) Adjusted basis	191,173	(2) − (3).
(5) Gain (loss) recognized	328,827	(1) − (4).
(6) Ordinary income (§1245 depreciation recapture)	**$318,827**	Lesser of (3) or (5).
§1231 gain	$ 10,000	(5) − (6).

Note that taxpayers can quickly determine their §1231 gain (if any) when they sell §1245 property by subtracting the asset's *original* basis from the amount realized. In Scenario 2, presented above (Example 11-7), the §1231 gain is $10,000 ($520,000 amount realized less the $510,000 original basis).

Scenario 3: Asset Sold at a Loss   Many §1231 assets, such as computer equipment or automobiles, tend to decline in value faster than the corresponding depreciation deductions reduce the asset's adjusted basis. When taxpayers sell or dispose of these assets before the assets are fully depreciated, they recognize a loss on the disposition. Because the depreciation recapture rules don't apply to losses, taxpayers selling §1245 property at a loss recognize §1231 loss.

Example 11-8

What if: Let's assume the same facts as in Example 11-6 and in Exhibit 11-2, except that Teton sells the machinery for $180,000. What is the amount and character of the gain or loss Teton would recognize on this sale?

Answer: A $11,173 §1231 loss, computed as follows:

Machinery Sale: Scenario 3 (Assumed sales price = $180,000)		
Description	**Amount**	**Explanation**
(1) Amount realized	$180,000	
(2) Original basis	510,000	Exhibit 11-2.
(3) Accumulated depreciation	318,827	Exhibit 11-2.
(4) Adjusted basis	191,173	(2) − (3).
(5) Gain (loss) recognized	(11,173)	(1) − (4).
(6) Ordinary income (§1245 depreciation recapture)	0	Lesser of (3) or (5) (limited to $0).
§1231 (loss)	($11,173)	(5) − (6).

Exhibit 11-6 graphically illustrates the §1245 depreciation recapture computations for the machinery sold in Scenarios 1, 2, and 3, presented in Examples 11-6, 11-7, and 11-8, respectively.[14]

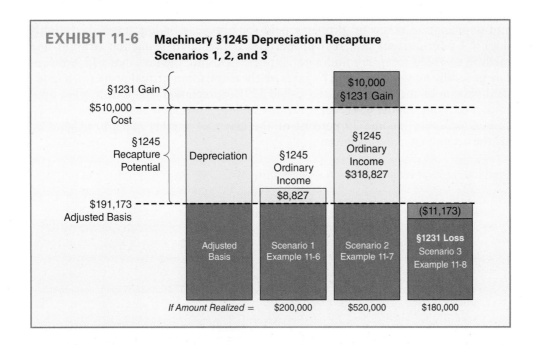

EXHIBIT 11-6   **Machinery §1245 Depreciation Recapture Scenarios 1, 2, and 3**

Example 11-9

In Example 11-6 (Scenario 1), we characterized the gain Teton recognized when it sold its machinery. For completeness, let's characterize the gain or loss Teton recognized on the other two §1245 assets it sold during the year (see Exhibit 11-2). Teton sold its office furniture for $12,000 and its delivery truck for $2,000. What is the amount and character of gain or loss Teton recognizes on the sales of the office furniture and delivery truck?

Answer: Office furniture: $7,000 ordinary income and $2,000 §1231 gain. Delivery truck: $2,500 §1231 loss. The computations supporting the answers are as follows:

Description	Office Furniture	Delivery Truck	Explanation
(1) Amount realized	$12,000	$ 2,000	Exhibit 11-2.
(2) Original basis	10,000	15,000	Exhibit 11-2.
(3) Accumulated depreciation	7,000	10,500	Exhibit 11-2.
(4) Adjusted basis	3,000	4,500	(2) − (3).
(5) Gain (loss) recognized	9,000	(2,500)	(1) − (4).
(6) Ordinary income (**§1245 depreciation recapture**)	**7,000**	**0**	Lesser of (3) or (5), limited to $0.
§1231 gain (loss)	2,000	(2,500)	(5) − (6).

§1250 Depreciation Recapture for Real Property

Depreciable real property, such as an office building or a warehouse, sold at a gain is *not* subject to §1245 depreciation recapture. Rather, it is subject to a different type of recapture called §1250 depreciation recapture. Thus, depreciable real property is

[14]The authors thank PwC for allowing us to use these figures.

frequently referred to as **§1250 property.** Under §1250, when depreciable real property is sold at a gain, the amount of gain recaptured as ordinary income is limited to *additional* depreciation, defined as the excess of *accelerated* depreciation deductions on the property over the amount that would have been deducted if the taxpayer had used the straight-line method of depreciation to depreciate the asset and depreciation taken on property held for one year or less (even if straight-line).[15] Under current law, real property is depreciated using the straight-line method so §1250 recapture no longer applies.[16] Despite the fact that *§1250 recapture* generally no longer applies to gains on the disposition of real property, a modified version of the recapture rules called **§291 depreciation recapture** applies only to corporations. Under §291, corporations selling depreciable real property recapture as ordinary income 20 percent of the lesser of the (1) recognized gain or (2) the accumulated depreciation.

Example 11-10

What if: Suppose that Teton was organized as a corporation and that, as described in Exhibit 11-2, it sold its existing warehouse. Let's assume the same facts: that Teton sold the warehouse for $350,000, that it initially purchased the warehouse for $275,000, and that it has deducted $15,000 of straight-line depreciation deductions as of the date of the sale. What is Teton's recognized gain on the sale and what is the character of its gain on the sale?

Answer: $90,000 gain recognized; $3,000 ordinary income and $87,000 §1231 gain, computed as follows:

Description	Amount	Explanation
(1) Amount realized	$350,000	Exhibit 11-2.
(2) Original basis	275,000	Exhibit 11-2.
(3) Accumulated depreciation	15,000	Exhibit 11-2.
(4) Adjusted basis	260,000	(2) − (3).
(5) Gain (Loss) recognized	**90,000**	(1) − (4).
(6) Lesser of accumulated depreciation or recognized gain	15,000	Lesser of (3) or (5).
(7) §291 recapture (ordinary income)	**$ 3,000**	20% × (6).
§1231 gain	**$ 87,000**	(5) − (7).

LO 11-4   ## OTHER PROVISIONS AFFECTING THE RATE AT WHICH GAINS ARE TAXED

Other provisions, other than depreciation recapture, may affect the rate at which taxpayer gains are taxed. The first potentially applies when individuals sell §1250 property at a gain, and the second potentially applies when taxpayers sell property to related parties at a gain.

Unrecaptured §1250 Gain for Individuals

Except for assets held 12 months or less, neither corporations nor individuals recognize §1250 recapture on the sale of §1250 property when sold at a gain. Instead,

---

[15]§1250 recapture is commonly referred to as *partial depreciation recapture.*

[16]Accelerated depreciation was allowed for real property placed in service before 1987. Such property had a maximum recovery period of 19 years, which means that as of 2005 all of this property is now fully depreciated under both the accelerated and straight-line depreciation methods.

corporations recognize §291 recapture as ordinary income on the sale of these assets. Individuals, however, do not recognize ordinary income from the sale of §1250 property when held long term. Rather, individual taxpayers treat a gain resulting from the disposition of §1250 property as a §1231 gain and combine it with other §1231 gains and losses to determine whether a net §1231 gain or a net §1231 loss results for the year.

After the §1231 netting process (described below), if the gain on the sale of the §1250 property is ultimately determined to be a long-term capital gain, the taxpayer must determine the rate at which the gain will be taxed. Tax policy makers determined that the portion of the gain caused by depreciation deductions reducing the basis (called **unrecaptured §1250 gain**) should be taxed at a maximum rate of 25 percent (taxed at the ordinary rate if the ordinary rate is lower than 25 percent) and not the 0/15/20 percent rate generally applicable to other types of long-term capital gains. Consequently, when an individual sells §1250 property at a gain, the amount of the gain taxed at a maximum rate of 25 percent is the *lesser* of the (1) recognized gain or (2) the accumulated depreciation on the asset.[17] The remainder of the gain is taxed at a maximum rate of 0/15/20 percent.[18]

Example 11-11

Teton bought its warehouse for $275,000, depreciated it $15,000, and sold it for $350,000. What is the amount and character of the gain Teton (and thus Steve) reports on the sale (recall that income of sole proprietorships is taxed directly to the owner of the business)?

Answer: $90,000 of §1231 gain, which includes $15,000 of unrecaptured §1250 gain, computed as follows:

Description	Amount	Explanation
(1) Amount realized	$350,000	
(2) Original basis	275,000	
(3) Accumulated depreciation	15,000	
(4) Adjusted basis	260,000	(2) − (3).
(5) Gain (Loss) recognized	90,000	(1) − (4).
(6) Unrecaptured §1250 gain	15,000	Lesser of (3) or (5).
(7) Remaining §1231 gain	75,000	(5) − (6).
Total §1231 gain	**$ 90,000**	(6) + (7).

What if: Suppose Steve's marginal ordinary tax rate is 35 percent. What amount of tax will he pay on the gain (assuming no other asset dispositions)?

Answer: $15,000, computed as follows:

Description	(1) Gain	(2) Rate	(1) × (2) Tax	Explanation
Long-term capital gain (unrecaptured §1250 gain portion)	$15,000	25%	$ 3,750	This is the gain due to depreciation deductions.
Long-term capital gain (15 percent portion)	75,000	15%	11,250	Taxed at 15 percent because Steve is in the 35% tax bracket.
Totals	$90,000		$15,000	

Because Steve did not sell any other §1231 assets during the year, the entire §1231 gain is treated as a long-term capital gain that is split into a portion taxed at 25 percent and a portion taxed at 15 percent.

THE KEY FACTS

Unrecaptured §1250 Gains

- Depreciable real property sold at a gain is §1250 property but is no longer subject to §1250 recapture unless it is held 12 months or less.
- The lesser of the (1) recognized gain or (2) accumulated depreciation on the assets is called *unrecaptured* §1250 gain.
- Unrecaptured §1250 gain is §1231 gain that, if ultimately characterized as a long-term capital gain, is taxed at a maximum rate of 25 percent.

[17]The amount taxed at a maximum rate of 25 percent cannot exceed the amount of the taxpayer's net §1231 gain.

[18]These rates (25 or 0/15/20 percent) apply to net §1231 gains after a netting process for capital gains, which we discussed in Chapter 7.

Characterizing Gains on the Sale of Depreciable Property to Related Persons

Under §1239, when a taxpayer sells property to a *related person* and the property is depreciable property to the *buyer,* the entire gain on the sale is characterized as ordinary income to the *seller*.[19] Without this provision, related taxpayers could create tax savings by currently generating capital or §1231 gains through selling appreciated assets to related persons who would receive future ordinary deductions through depreciation expense on the basis of the property (stepped up to fair market value through the sale) acquired in the transaction.

The §1239 recapture provision is different from depreciation recapture in the sense that the seller is required to recognize ordinary income *for depreciation deductions the buyer will receive in the future,* while depreciation recapture requires taxpayers to recognize ordinary income *for depreciation deductions they have received in the past.* In both cases, however, the tax laws are designed to provide symmetry between the character of deductions an asset generates and the character of income the asset generates when it is sold. When depreciation recapture and the §1239 recapture provision apply to the same gain, the depreciation recapture rule applies first.

For purposes of §1239, a related person includes an individual and his or her controlled (more than 50 percent owned) corporation or partnership or a taxpayer and any trust in which the taxpayer (or spouse) is a beneficiary.[20]

Example 11-12

What if: Suppose that Teton is organized as a corporation and Steve is the sole shareholder. Steve sells equipment that he was using for personal purposes to Teton for $90,000 (he originally purchased the equipment for $80,000). The equipment was a capital asset to Steve because he had been using it for personal purposes (he did not depreciate it). What is the amount and character of the gain Steve would recognize on the sale?

Answer: $10,000 of ordinary income (amount realized $90,000 − $80,000 adjusted basis). Even though Steve is selling what is a capital asset to him, because it is a depreciable asset to Teton and because Steve and Teton are considered to be related persons, Steve is required to characterize the entire amount of gain as ordinary under §1239. Without the §1239 provision, Steve would have recognized a capital gain.

Exhibit 11-7 provides a flowchart for determining the character of gains and losses on the taxable sale of assets used in a trade or business.

LO 11-5   CALCULATING NET §1231 GAINS OR LOSSES

Once taxpayers determine the amount and character of gain or loss they recognize on *each* §1231 asset they sell during the year, they still have work to do to determine whether the gains or losses will be treated as ordinary or capital. After recharacterizing §1231 gain as ordinary income under the §1245 and §291 (if applicable) depreciation recapture rules and the §1239 related-person rules, the remaining §1231 gains and losses are netted together.[21] If the gains exceed the

---

[19]§1239. §707(b)(2) contains a similar provision for partnerships.

[20]Additional related persons for purposes of §1239 include two corporations that are members of the same controlled group, a corporation and a partnership if the same person owns more than 50 percent of both entities, two S corporations controlled by the same person, and an S corporation and a C corporation controlled by the same person.

[21]If any of the §1231 gains and losses result from casualty or theft, these gains and losses are netted together first. If a net loss results, the net loss from §1231 casualty and theft events are treated as ordinary loss. Net gains from casualty and theft are treated as other §1231 gains and continue through the normal §1231 netting process.

EXHIBIT 11-7

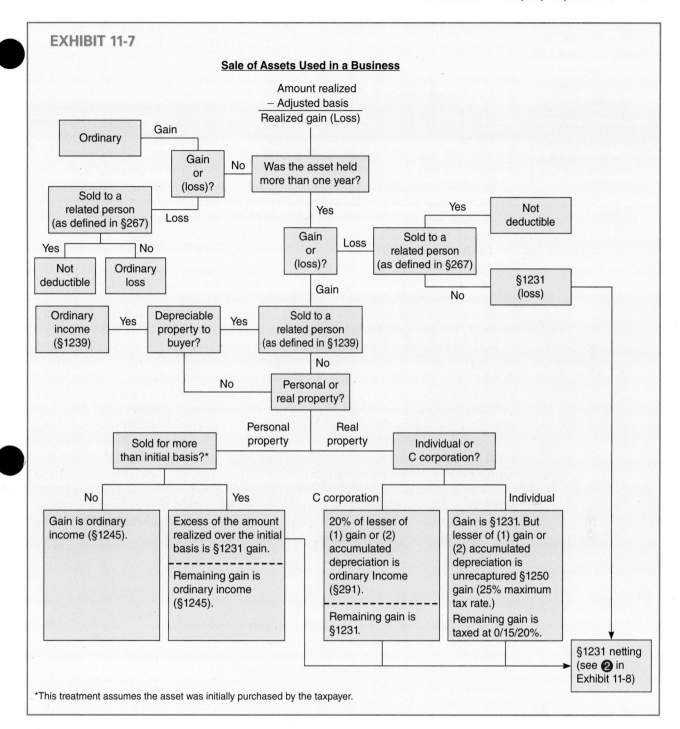

Sale of Assets Used in a Business

$$\frac{\text{Amount realized}}{\text{Realized gain (Loss)}}$$

*This treatment assumes the asset was initially purchased by the taxpayer.

losses, the net gain becomes a long-term capital gain (a portion of which may be taxed at the maximum rate of 25 percent). If the losses exceed the gains, the net loss is treated as an ordinary loss.

A taxpayer could gain significant tax benefits by discovering a way to have all §1231 gains treated as long-term capital gains and all §1231 losses treated as ordinary losses. The *annual* netting process makes this task impossible for a *particular* year. However, a taxpayer who owns multiple §1231 assets could sell the §1231 loss assets at the end of year 1 and the §1231 gain assets at the beginning of year 2. The taxpayer could benefit from this strategy in three ways: (1) accelerating losses into year 1, (2) deferring gains until year 2, and (3) characterizing the gains and losses due to the §1231 netting process. The **§1231 look-back rule** prevents this strategy.

§1231 Look-Back Rule

The §1231 look-back rule is a *nondepreciation* recapture rule that applies in situations like the one we just described to turn what would otherwise be §1231 gain into ordinary income. That is, the rule affects the character but not the amount of gains on which a taxpayer is taxed. In general terms, the §1231 look-back rule is designed to require taxpayers who recognize net §1231 gains in the current year to recapture (recharacterize) current year gains as ordinary to the extent the taxpayer recognized ordinary net §1231 losses in prior years. Without the look-back rule, taxpayers could carefully time the year in which the §1231 assets are sold to maximize the tax benefits.

In specific terms, the §1231 look-back rule indicates that when a taxpayer recognizes a net §1231 gain for a year, the taxpayer must "look-back" to the *five-year* period preceding the current tax year to determine if, during that period, the taxpayer recognized any **nonrecaptured net §1231 losses** (losses that were deducted as ordinary losses that have not caused subsequent §1231 gains to be recharacterized as ordinary income). The taxpayer starts the process by looking back to the year five years prior to the beginning of the current year. If the taxpayer recognized a net §1231 loss in that period and had not previously recaptured the loss (by causing a subsequent §1231 gain to be recharacterized as ordinary) in a subsequent year (but prior to the current year), the taxpayer must recharacterize the *current year* net §1231 gain as ordinary income to the extent of that prior year nonrecaptured net §1231 loss. The prior year loss is then "recaptured," to the extent it caused the current year gain to be treated as ordinary income. If the current year net §1231 gain exceeds the nonrecaptured net §1231 loss from the year five-years prior, the taxpayer repeats the process for the year four-years prior, and then three-years prior, and so on. It is important to note that a prior year's nonrecaptured net losses are not netted against the current year's gains (they don't offset the current year gains); rather, they cause the taxpayer to recharacterize a net §1231 gain or a portion of that gain (that would otherwise be characterized as a long-term capital gain) as ordinary income.[22]

Example 11-13

What if: Suppose that Teton began business in year 1 and that it recognized a $7,000 net §1231 loss in year 1. Assume that the current year is year 6 and that Teton reports a *net* §1231 gain of $25,000 for the year. Teton did not recognize any §1231 gains or losses in years 2–5. For year 6, what would be the ultimate character of the $25,000 net §1231 gain?

Answer: $7,000 ordinary income and $18,000 long-term capital gain. Because it recognized a net §1231 loss in year 1, it must recharacterize $7,000 of its net §1231 gain in year 6 as ordinary income. The remaining $18,000 §1231 gain is taxed as long-term capital gain.

What if: Assume the same facts as above, except that Teton also recognized a $2,000 net §1231 loss in year 5. For year 6, what would be the ultimate character of the $25,000 net §1231 gain?

Answer: $9,000 ordinary income and $16,000 long-term capital gain. Note that the overall gain is still $25,000, but to the extent of the $7,000 loss in year 1 and the $2,000 loss in year 5, the §1231 gain is recharacterized as ordinary income under the §1231 look-back rule.

---

[22]If the taxpayer's net §1231 gains include unrecaptured §1250 gains and other 0/15/20 percent long-term capital gains, the nonrecaptured net §1231 losses first recharacterize the unrecaptured §1250 gains as ordinary income.

Emma Bean operates a yoga studio and wants to sell some of her business equipment and a piece of land that is used as a parking lot. She expects to realize a $10,000 loss on the equipment and a $15,000 gain on the land. Emma has talked to her accountant and has learned about the look-back rule for §1231 property. To thwart any negative effects, she has decided to game the system and sell the land this year and then sell the equipment early next year. What do you think about her strategy to avoid the look-back rule?

As we've mentioned before, ultimately, all of a taxpayer's §1231 gains and losses must be characterized as ordinary or capital for purposes of determining a taxpayer's tax liability. Exhibit 11-8 summarizes the process of characterizing §1231 gains and losses as ordinary or capital.

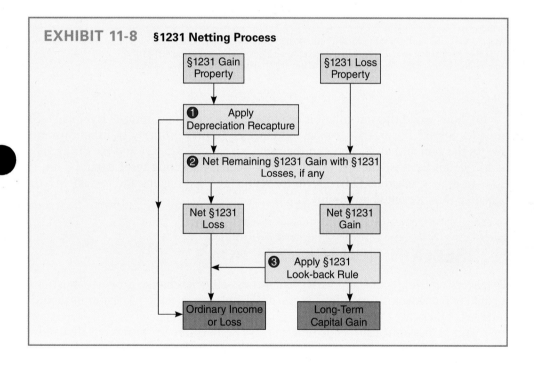

EXHIBIT 11-8 §1231 Netting Process

The following provides details on Steps 1–3 from Exhibit 11-8:

Step 1: Apply the *depreciation* recapture rules (and the §1239 recapture rules) to §1231 assets sold at a gain (any recaptured amounts become ordinary).

Step 2: Net the remaining §1231 gains with the §1231 losses. If the netting process yields a §1231 loss, the net §1231 loss becomes an ordinary loss.

Step 3: If the netting process produces a net §1231 gain, the taxpayer applies the §1231 look-back rule to determine if any of the remaining §1231 gain should be recharacterized as ordinary gain. Any gain remaining after applying the look-back rule is treated as long-term capital gain (including unrecaptured §1250 gain). This gain is included in the capital gains netting process, which is discussed in Chapter 7.

GAIN OR LOSS SUMMARY

As indicated in Exhibit 11-2, Teton sold several assets during the year. Exhibit 11-9 summarizes the character of the gain or loss Teton (and thus Steve) recognized on each asset sale.

EXHIBIT 11-9 **Summary of Teton Gains and Losses on Property Dispositions**

Asset	(1) §1245 Ordinary Gain	(2) Total Ordinary Gain	(3) §1231 Gain (Loss)	(2) + (3) Total Gain
Machinery	$ 8,827	$ 8,827	$ 0	$ 8,827
Office furniture	7,000	7,000	2,000	9,000
Delivery truck	0	0	(2,500)	(2,500)
Warehouse	0	0	90,000*	90,000
Land	0	0	100,000	100,000
§1231 look-back		10,000	(10,000)†	0
Totals	$15,827	$25,827	$179,500*	$205,327

*Because the warehouse is §1231 property, the $90,000 gain is included in the §1231 gain (loss) column. Further, $15,000 of the $90,000 gain is considered unrecaptured §1250 gain (see Example 11-11).
†This exhibit assumes that Teton had $10,000 of net §1231 losses in the prior five years.

So, how would this information be reported on Steve's tax return? Exhibit 11-10 provides Steve's Form 4797, which summarizes Teton's property transactions and divides the gain and losses between the ordinary gain of $25,827 and the §1231 gain of $179,500. Because the net §1231 gain is treated as a long-term capital gain, it flows to Steve's Schedule D (the form for reporting capital gains and losses). Steve's Schedule D is presented in Exhibit 11-11.

LO 11-6 ## NONRECOGNITION TRANSACTIONS

Taxpayers realizing gains and losses when they sell or exchange property must immediately recognize the gain for tax purposes unless a specific provision in the tax code says otherwise. Under certain tax provisions, taxpayers defer or delay recognizing a gain or loss until a subsequent period. We first explore tax provisions that allow taxpayers to defer recognizing realized gains. Congress allows taxpayers to defer recognizing gains in certain types of exchanges because the exchange itself does not provide the taxpayers with the wherewithal (cash) to pay taxes on the realized gain if the taxpayers were required to immediately recognize the gain. In particular, we discuss common **nonrecognition transactions** such as like-kind exchanges, involuntary conversions, installment sales, and other business-related transactions such as business formations and reorganizations.

Like-Kind Exchanges

Taxpayers involved in a business may have valid reasons to trade business assets to others for similar business assets. For example, to increase productivity a taxpayer may want to trade machinery used in the business for the latest model. As we discussed earlier in this chapter, taxpayers exchanging property *realize* gains (or losses) on exchanges just as taxpayers do by selling property for cash. However,

EXHIBIT 11-10   Teton's (On Steve's return) Form 4797

Form **4797**	**Sales of Business Property** (Also Involuntary Conversions and Recapture Amounts Under Sections 179 and 280F(b)(2)) ▶ Attach to your tax return. ▶ Information about Form 4797 and its separate instructions is at *www.irs.gov/form4797.*	OMB No. 1545-0184 **2015** Attachment Sequence No. **27**

Department of the Treasury
Internal Revenue Service

Name(s) shown on return: **Steve Dallimore (Teton Mountaineering Technologies, LLC)**   Identifying number

1 Enter the gross proceeds from sales or exchanges reported to you for 2015 on Form(s) 1099-B or 1099-S (or substitute statement) that you are including on line 2, 10, or 20 (see instructions) . . . . | **1** |

Part I   Sales or Exchanges of Property Used in a Trade or Business and Involuntary Conversions From Other Than Casualty or Theft—Most Property Held More Than 1 Year (see instructions)

2 (a) Description of property	(b) Date acquired (mo., day, yr.)	(c) Date sold (mo., day, yr.)	(d) Gross sales price	(e) Depreciation allowed or allowable since acquisition	(f) Cost or other basis, plus improvements and expense of sale	(g) Gain or (loss) Subtract (f) from the sum of (d) and (e)
Delivery truck	Yr 0	Yr 4	2,000	10,500	15,000	(2,500)
Land	Yr 0	Yr 4	175,000	0	75,000	100,000

3 Gain, if any, from Form 4684, line 39	**3**	
4 Section 1231 gain from installment sales from Form 6252, line 26 or 37	**4**	
5 Section 1231 gain or (loss) from like-kind exchanges from Form 8824	**5**	
6 Gain, if any, from line 32, from other than casualty or theft.	**6**	92,000
7 Combine lines 2 through 6. Enter the gain or (loss) here and on the appropriate line as follows:	**7**	189,500

Partnerships (except electing large partnerships) and S corporations. Report the gain or (loss) following the instructions for Form 1065, Schedule K, line 10, or Form 1120S, Schedule K, line 9. Skip lines 8, 9, 11, and 12 below.

Individuals, partners, S corporation shareholders, and all others. If line 7 is zero or a loss, enter the amount from line 7 on line 11 below and skip lines 8 and 9. If line 7 is a gain and you did not have any prior year section 1231 losses, or they were recaptured in an earlier year, enter the gain from line 7 as a long-term capital gain on the Schedule D filed with your return and skip lines 8, 9, 11, and 12 below.

8 Nonrecaptured net section 1231 losses from prior years (see instructions)	**8**	10,000
9 Subtract line 8 from line 7. If zero or less, enter -0-. If line 9 is zero, enter the gain from line 7 on line 12 below. If line 9 is more than zero, enter the amount from line 8 on line 12 below and enter the gain from line 9 as a long-term capital gain on the Schedule D filed with your return (see instructions)	**9**	179,500

Part II   Ordinary Gains and Losses (see instructions)

10 Ordinary gains and losses not included on lines 11 through 16 (include property held 1 year or less):

11 Loss, if any, from line 7	**11** ( )	
12 Gain, if any, from line 7 or amount from line 8, if applicable	**12**	10,000
13 Gain, if any, from line 31	**13**	15,827
14 Net gain or (loss) from Form 4684, lines 31 and 38a	**14**	
15 Ordinary gain from installment sales from Form 6252, line 25 or 36	**15**	
16 Ordinary gain or (loss) from like-kind exchanges from Form 8824.	**16**	
17 Combine lines 10 through 16	**17**	25,827

18 For all except individual returns, enter the amount from line 17 on the appropriate line of your return and skip lines a and b below. For individual returns, complete lines a and b below:

a If the loss on line 11 includes a loss from Form 4684, line 35, column (b)(ii), enter that part of the loss here. Enter the part of the loss from income-producing property on Schedule A (Form 1040), line 28, and the part of the loss from property used as an employee on Schedule A (Form 1040), line 23. Identify as from "Form 4797, line 18a." See instructions . . | **18a** |

b Redetermine the gain or (loss) on line 17 excluding the loss, if any, on line 18a. Enter here and on Form 1040, line 14 | **18b** | 25,827 |

For Paperwork Reduction Act Notice, see separate instructions.   Cat. No. 13086I   Form **4797** (2015)

EXHIBIT 11-10   Teton's (On Steve's return) Form 4797 (*continued*)

Form 4797 (2015)   Page **2**

Part III   Gain From Disposition of Property Under Sections 1245, 1250, 1252, 1254, and 1255 (see instructions)

19	(a) Description of section 1245, 1250, 1252, 1254, or 1255 property:		(b) Date acquired (mo., day, yr.)	(c) Date sold (mo., day, yr.)
A	Machinery		Yr 0	Yr 4
B	Office furniture		Yr 0	Yr 4
C	Warehouse		Yr 0	Yr 4
D				

	These columns relate to the properties on lines 19A through 19D. ▶		Property A	Property B	Property C	Property D
20	Gross sales price (**Note:** *See line 1 before completing.*) .	20	200,000	12,000	350,000	
21	Cost or other basis plus expense of sale	21	510,000	10,000	275,000	
22	Depreciation (or depletion) allowed or allowable. . .	22	318,827	7,000	15,000	
23	Adjusted basis. Subtract line 22 from line 21. . . .	23	191,173	3,000	260,000	
24	Total gain. Subtract line 23 from line 20	24	8,827	9,000	90,000	
25	**If section 1245 property:**					
a	Depreciation allowed or allowable from line 22 . . .	25a	318,827	7,000		
b	Enter the **smaller** of line 24 or 25a	25b	8,827	7,000		
26	**If section 1250 property:** If straight line depreciation was used, enter -0- on line 26g, except for a corporation subject to section 291.					
a	Additional depreciation after 1975 (see instructions) .	26a				
b	Applicable percentage multiplied by the **smaller** of line 24 or line 26a (see instructions)	26b				
c	Subtract line 26a from line 24. If residential rental property **or** line 24 is not more than line 26a, skip lines 26d and 26e	26c				
d	Additional depreciation after 1969 and before 1976. .	26d				
e	Enter the **smaller** of line 26c or 26d	26e				
f	Section 291 amount (corporations only)	26f				
g	Add lines 26b, 26e, and 26f.	26g			0	
27	**If section 1252 property:** Skip this section if you did not dispose of farmland or if this form is being completed for a partnership (other than an electing large partnership).					
a	Soil, water, and land clearing expenses	27a				
b	Line 27a multiplied by applicable percentage (see instructions)	27b				
c	Enter the **smaller** of line 24 or 27b	27c				
28	**If section 1254 property:**					
a	Intangible drilling and development costs, expenditures for development of mines and other natural deposits, mining exploration costs, and depletion (see instructions)	28a				
b	Enter the **smaller** of line 24 or 28a	28b				
29	**If section 1255 property:**					
a	Applicable percentage of payments excluded from income under section 126 (see instructions)	29a				
b	Enter the **smaller** of line 24 or 29a (see instructions) .	29b				

Summary of Part III Gains. Complete property columns A through D through line 29b before going to line 30.

30	Total gains for all properties. Add property columns A through D, line 24	30	107,827
31	Add property columns A through D, lines 25b, 26g, 27c, 28b, and 29b. Enter here and on line 13	31	15,827
32	Subtract line 31 from line 30. Enter the portion from casualty or theft on Form 4684, line 33. Enter the portion from other than casualty or theft on Form 4797, line 6	32	92,000

Part IV   Recapture Amounts Under Sections 179 and 280F(b)(2) When Business Use Drops to 50% or Less (see instructions)

			(a) Section 179	(b) Section 280F(b)(2)
33	Section 179 expense deduction or depreciation allowable in prior years.	33		
34	Recomputed depreciation (see instructions)	34		
35	Recapture amount. Subtract line 34 from line 33. See the instructions for where to report . .	35		

Form **4797** (2015)

EXHIBIT 11-11 Steve's Schedule D (Assumes Steve had no other capital gains and losses other than those incurred by Teton)

SCHEDULE D	**Capital Gains and Losses**	OMB No. 1545-0074
(Form 1040)	▶ Attach to Form 1040 or Form 1040NR.	
Department of the Treasury Internal Revenue Service (99)	▶ Information about Schedule D and its separate instructions is at *www.irs.gov/scheduled*. ▶ Use Form 8949 to list your transactions for lines 1b, 2, 3, 8b, 9, and 10.	**20**15 Attachment Sequence No. **12**

Name(s) shown on return: **Steve Dallimore**   Your social security number

Part I   Short-Term Capital Gains and Losses—Assets Held One Year or Less

See instructions for how to figure the amounts to enter on the lines below. This form may be easier to complete if you round off cents to whole dollars.	(d) Proceeds (sales price)	(e) Cost (or other basis)	(g) Adjustments to gain or loss from Form(s) 8949, Part I, line 2, column (g)	(h) Gain or (loss) Subtract column (e) from column (d) and combine the result with column (g)
1a Totals for all short-term transactions reported on Form 1099-B for which basis was reported to the IRS and for which you have no adjustments (see instructions). However, if you choose to report all these transactions on Form 8949, leave this line blank and go to line 1b .				
1b Totals for all transactions reported on Form(s) 8949 with **Box A** checked				
2 Totals for all transactions reported on Form(s) 8949 with **Box B** checked				
3 Totals for all transactions reported on Form(s) 8949 with **Box C** checked				

4 Short-term gain from Form 6252 and short-term gain or (loss) from Forms 4684, 6781, and 8824 .	**4**	
5 Net short-term gain or (loss) from partnerships, S corporations, estates, and trusts from Schedule(s) K-1	**5**	
6 Short-term capital loss carryover. Enter the amount, if any, from line 8 of your **Capital Loss Carryover Worksheet** in the instructions	**6** ( )	
7 **Net short-term capital gain or (loss).** Combine lines 1a through 6 in column (h). If you have any long-term capital gains or losses, go to Part II below. Otherwise, go to Part III on the back	**7**	

Part II   Long-Term Capital Gains and Losses—Assets Held More Than One Year

See instructions for how to figure the amounts to enter on the lines below. This form may be easier to complete if you round off cents to whole dollars.	(d) Proceeds (sales price)	(e) Cost (or other basis)	(g) Adjustments to gain or loss from Form(s) 8949, Part II, line 2, column (g)	(h) Gain or (loss) Subtract column (e) from column (d) and combine the result with column (g)
8a Totals for all long-term transactions reported on Form 1099-B for which basis was reported to the IRS and for which you have no adjustments (see instructions). However, if you choose to report all these transactions on Form 8949, leave this line blank and go to line 8b .				
8b Totals for all transactions reported on Form(s) 8949 with **Box D** checked				
9 Totals for all transactions reported on Form(s) 8949 with **Box E** checked				
10 Totals for all transactions reported on Form(s) 8949 with **Box F** checked.				

11 Gain from Form 4797, Part I; long-term gain from Forms 2439 and 6252; and long-term gain or (loss) from Forms 4684, 6781, and 8824	**11**	179,500
12 Net long-term gain or (loss) from partnerships, S corporations, estates, and trusts from Schedule(s) K-1	**12**	
13 Capital gain distributions. See the instructions	**13**	
14 Long-term capital loss carryover. Enter the amount, if any, from line 13 of your **Capital Loss Carryover Worksheet** in the instructions	**14** ( )	
15 **Net long-term capital gain or (loss).** Combine lines 8a through 14 in column (h). Then go to Part III on the back	**15**	179,500

For Paperwork Reduction Act Notice, see your tax return instructions.   Cat. No. 11338H   Schedule D (Form 1040) 2015 taxpayers exchanging property for property are in a different situation than taxpayers selling the same property for cash. Taxpayers exchanging one piece of business property for another haven't changed their relative economic position in the sense that both before and after the exchange they hold an asset for use in their business. Further, exchanges of property do not generate the wherewithal (cash) for the taxpayers to pay taxes on the gain they realize on the exchanges. While taxpayers selling property for cash must immediately recognize gain on the sale, taxpayers exchanging property for assets other than cash must defer recognizing gain (or loss) realized on the exchange if they meet certain requirements. This type of deferred gain (or loss) transaction is commonly referred to as a **like-kind exchange** or §1031 exchange.[23]

Like-kind exchange treatment can provide taxpayers with significant tax advantages by allowing them to defer gain (and current taxes payable) that would otherwise be recognized immediately.[24] For an exchange to qualify as a like-kind exchange for tax purposes, the transaction must meet the following three criteria:

1. The property is exchanged "solely for like-kind" property.
2. Both the property given up and the property received in the exchange by the taxpayer are either "used in a trade or business" or are "held for investment," by the taxpayer.
3. The "exchange" must meet certain time restrictions.

Below, we discuss each of these requirements in detail.

Definition of Like-Kind Property

The definition of like-kind property depends on whether the property exchanged is real property or tangible personal property. Generally, the definition of like-kind *real* property is much less restrictive than it is for like-kind *personal* property.

Real Property   All real property is considered to be "like-kind" with any other type of real property as long as the real property is used in a trade or business or held for investment. For example, from Teton's perspective, its warehouse on 10 acres would be considered to be like-kind with a nearby condominium complex, a 20-acre parcel of raw land for sale across town, or even a Manhattan skyscraper.

Personal Property   Determining what qualifies as like-kind property for tangible personal property is a little more involved. The Treasury regulations explain that tangible personal property qualifies as "like-kind" if the property transferred and the property received in the exchange is in the same general asset class in Rev. Proc. 87-56 (this is the concept we used in the previous chapter to determine the recovery period for MACRS depreciation).[25] In simpler terms, for personal property to qualify as like-kind property, the property given in the exchange and the property received in the exchange must have the same general use to the taxpayer. For example, if Teton were to trade some machinery used in its manufacturing operations for some new machinery to be used in its manufacturing process, the transaction would qualify as a like-kind exchange. However, if Teton were to trade some machinery used in its manufacturing operations for a new delivery truck, the exchange would not qualify as a like-kind exchange.

[23]Like-kind exchanges are defined in §1031 of the Internal Revenue Code.

[24]In contrast, financial accounting rules require businesses to recognize (for financial accounting purposes) any gain they realize in a like-kind exchange transaction.

[25]Like-kind is defined in Reg. §1.1031(a)-2(b).

THE KEY FACTS

Like-Kind Property

- Real property
  - All real property used in a trade or business or held for investment is considered "like-kind" with other real property used in a trade or business or held for investment.
- Personal property
  - Personal property is considered "like-kind" if it has the same general use and is used in a business or held for investment.
- Ineligible property
  - Inventory.
  - Most financial instruments.
  - Partnerships interests.
  - Domestic property exchanged for property used in a foreign country and all property used in a foreign country.

Property Ineligible for Like-Kind Treatment Certain types of property are, by definition, excluded from the definition of like-kind property and thus are not eligible for like-kind treatment.[26] This property includes inventory held for resale (including land held by a developer), most financial instruments (such as stocks, bonds, or notes), domestic property exchanged for foreign property, and partnership interests.[27]

Property Use

Even when property meets the definition of like-kind property, taxpayers can only exchange the property in a qualifying like-kind exchange if the taxpayer used the transferred property in a trade or business or for investment *and* the taxpayer will use the property received in the exchange in a trade or business or for investment. For example, Teton could exchange its warehouse on 10 acres for a 200-acre parcel of land it intends to hold as an investment in a qualifying like-kind exchange because Teton was using the warehouse in its business and it would hold the land as an investment. However, if Steve exchanged his personal-use cabin in Maine for a personal residence in Wyoming, the exchange would not qualify because Steve used the residence for personal purposes, and he would be using the Wyoming property for personal rather than business or investment purposes. In fact, even if Steve was renting his Maine cabin (it qualifies as investment property) when he exchanged it for his principal residence in Wyoming, the exchange would not qualify for like-kind exchange treatment because *both* properties (the property the taxpayer is giving up and the property the taxpayer is receiving in the exchange) must meet the use test (the personal residence does not qualify as business or investment property). Likewise, if Teton exchanged a business computer for Steve's personal use computer, Teton would qualify for like-kind exchange treatment because Teton was using its computer equipment in its business and it will use Steve's computer in its business. However, the exchange would not qualify as a like-kind exchange for Steve because Steve used the computer for personal (not business or investment) purposes. A key takeaway here is that due to the use and other requirements, one party to an exchange may qualify for like-kind treatment and the other party may not. Each party to the exchange must individually determine whether or not the exchange qualifies as a like-kind exchange to her.

Timing Requirements for a Like-Kind Exchange

Many like-kind exchanges involve a simultaneous exchange of like-kind assets. For example, Teton could take its used machinery to a dealer and pick up its new machinery at the same time. However, a simultaneous exchange may not be practical or possible. For example, taxpayers may not always be able to immediately (or even eventually) find another party who is willing to exchange properties with the taxpayer. In these situations taxpayers often use **third-party intermediaries** to facilitate like-kind exchanges. When a third party is involved, the taxpayer transfers the like-kind property to the intermediary and the intermediary sells the property and uses the proceeds to acquire the new property for the taxpayer.[28] Because the third party must sell the taxpayer's old property and locate and purchase suitable replacement property, this process is subject to delay. In these types of situations, does a delay in

> **THE KEY FACTS**
>
> **Timing Requirements**
>
> - Like-kind property exchanges may involve intermediaries.
> - Taxpayers must identify replacement like-kind property within 45 days of giving up their property.
> - Like-kind property must be received within 180 days of when the taxpayer transfers property in a like-kind exchange.

---

[26]§1031(a)(2).

[27]Property used more than 50 percent of the time in a foreign country is not like-kind with domestic or with other foreign property.

[28]Exchanges involving third-party intermediaries are very common with real estate exchanges. For real estate, taxpayers must use a "qualified exchange intermediary," such as a title company, and cannot use a personal attorney (because attorneys are considered to be the taxpayer's agent).

the completion of the exchange disqualify an otherwise allowable like-kind exchange? Not necessarily. The tax laws do not require a simultaneous exchange of assets, but they do impose some timing requirements to ensure that a transaction is completed within a reasonable time in order to qualify as a **deferred** (not simultaneous) **like-kind exchange**—often referred to as a *Starker exchange*.[29]

The two timing rules applicable to like-kind exchanges are (1) the taxpayer must *identify* the like-kind replacement property within 45 days after transferring the property given up in the exchange, and (2) the taxpayer must receive the replacement like-kind property within 180 days (or the due date of the tax return including extensions) after the taxpayer initially transfers property in the exchange.[30] The time limits force the taxpayer to close the transaction within a specified time period, so that the taxpayers can report the tax consequences of the transaction. Exhibit 11-12 provides a diagram of a like-kind exchange involving a third-party intermediary.

EXHIBIT 11-12   Diagram of Deferred or Starker Exchange

When a taxpayer fails to meet the timing requirements, the exchange fails to qualify for like-kind treatment and is thus fully taxable.

Example 11-14

What if: Suppose that on July 1 of year 1 Steve transferred a parcel of real property that he was holding as an investment to a third-party intermediary with the intention of exchanging the property for another suitable investment property. By what date does Steve need to identify the replacement property?

Answer: August 16 of year 1, which is 45 days after Steve transferred the property to the intermediary.

Assuming Steve identifies the replacement property within the 45-day time period, by what date does he need to receive the replacement property in order to qualify for like-kind exchange treatment?

Answer: December 28 of year 1, which is 180 days from July 1, the date he transferred the property to the intermediary.

---

[29]The term *Starker exchange* refers to a landmark court case that first allowed deferred exchanges (*T.J. Starker, Appellant v. United States of America*, 79-2 USTC ¶9541). The rules for deferred exchanges are found in §1031(a)(3). The tax laws also allow for reverse like-kind exchanges where replacement property is acquired before the taxpayer transfers the like-kind property.

[30]The taxpayer must identify at least one like-kind asset; however, since failure to obtain the asset disqualifies the transaction from having deferred like-kind exchange status, the taxpayer may identify up to three alternatives to hedge against the inability to obtain the first identified asset. Generally, a taxpayer must obtain only one to facilitate the exchange [see Reg. §1.1031(k)-1(c)(4)].

Tax Consequences When Like-Kind Property Is Exchanged Solely for Like-Kind Property

As we've discussed, when taxpayers exchanging property meet the like-kind exchange requirements, they do not recognize gain or loss on the exchange. They also establish or receive an **exchanged basis** in the like-kind property they receive. That is, they exchange the basis they had in the property given up and transfer it to the basis of the property received.[31]

Example 11-15

Teton would like to trade machinery worth $29,500 (adjusted basis of $18,742), for new machinery worth $29,500. How much gain does Teton recognize on this exchange?

Answer: $0. Teton's exchange qualifies as a like-kind exchange and the $10,758 realized gain ($29,500 amount realized minus $18,742 adjusted basis) is deferred.

What is Teton's basis in the new machinery?

Answer: $18,742, the basis it had in the old machinery it traded in.

Tax Consequences of Transfers Involving Like-Kind and Non-Like-Kind Property (Boot)

A practical problem with like-kind exchanges is that the value of the like-kind property the taxpayer transfers may differ from the value of the like-kind property the taxpayer receives in the exchange. In these situations the party transferring the lesser-valued asset must also transfer additional property to the other party to equate the values. When this additional property or **"boot"** (non-like-kind property) is transferred, the party receiving it apparently fails the first like-kind exchange requirement that like-kind property be exchanged solely for like-kind property. Nevertheless, if a taxpayer receives boot in addition to like-kind property, the transaction can still qualify for like-kind exchange treatment, but the taxpayer is required to recognize realized gain *to the extent of the boot received*.[32] As a practical matter, this means the taxpayer's recognized gain is the *lesser of* (1) gain realized or (2) boot received.

The reason a taxpayer must recognize gain is that the taxpayer is essentially selling a portion of the like-kind property for the boot in a taxable exchange. The receipt of boot triggers taxable gain (but not a taxable loss) in an otherwise qualifying like-kind exchange. If the taxpayer transfers loss property (adjusted basis is greater than fair market value) in a qualifying like-kind exchange, the taxpayer defers recognition of the loss until the taxpayer sells or disposes of the loss property in a taxable transaction—so it may be important for tax planning purposes to avoid the like-kind exchange rules if the taxpayer wishes to currently recognize the loss.[33] When a taxpayer recognizes gain in a like-kind exchange, the character of the gain depends on the character of the asset transferred by the taxpayer (the depreciation recapture rules apply when characterizing gains).

THE KEY FACTS

Like-Kind Exchanges Involving Boot

- Non-like-kind property is known as boot.
- When boot is given as part of a like-kind transaction:
  - The asset received is recorded in two parts: property received in exchange for like-kind property and property received in a sale (bought by the boot).
- When boot is received:
  - Boot received usually creates recognized gain.
  - Gain recognized is lesser of gain realized or boot received.

---

[31]If the asset is a depreciable asset, the taxpayer continues to depreciate the new asset as if it were the old asset.

[32]§1031(b).

[33]§1031(a) states that no gain or loss is recognized in a qualifying like-kind exchange.

Example 11-16

What if: Suppose that Teton trades its used machinery with a value of $29,500 and an adjusted basis of $18,742 ($30,615 historical cost less $11,873 of accumulated depreciation) to the dealer for new machinery valued at $27,500. To equate the value of the property exchanged, the dealer also pays Teton $2,000. What gain or loss does Teton realize on the exchange and what gain or loss does Teton recognize on the exchange?

Answer: $10,758 realized gain and $2,000 recognized gain, calculated as follows:

Description	Amount	Explanation
(1) Amount realized from machine	$27,500	
(2) Amount realized from boot (cash)	2,000	
(3) Total amount realized	29,500	(1) + (2).
(4) Adjusted basis	18,742	
(5) Gain realized	**10,758**	(3) − (4).
Gain recognized	**$ 2,000**	Lesser of (2) or (5).

What is the character of Teton's $2,000 gain?

Answer: Ordinary income. Because Teton's accumulated depreciation on the asset exceeds its $2,000 gain, Teton must treat the gain as ordinary gain under the §1245 depreciation recapture rules discussed earlier.

What if: Suppose the same facts as above, except that Teton's adjusted basis in the machinery was $29,000. What amount of gain would Teton recognize on the exchange?

Answer: $500. Teton recognizes the lesser of (1) $500 gain realized ($29,500 minus $29,000) or (2) $2,000 boot received.

When taxpayers receive like-kind property and boot in a like-kind exchange, their basis in the like-kind property is computed under §1031(d) using the following formula:

> Adjusted basis of like-kind property surrendered
>
> + Adjusted basis of boot given
> + Gain recognized
> − Fair market value of boot received
> − Loss recognized
> _____
> = Basis of like-kind property received

An alternative and simplified method for checking the basis calculation is to begin with the fair market value of the like-kind property received and subtract any deferred gain or add any deferred loss.

The basis of boot received in the exchange is always the boot's fair market value. This formula for computing basis ensures that the taxpayer's deferred gain or loss on the exchange (the gain or loss realized that is not recognized) is captured in the difference between the value and the basis of the new property received. Consequently, taxpayers defer realized gain or loss on qualifying like-kind exchanges; they do not exclude them. Taxpayers will ultimately recognize the gain or loss when they dispose of the new asset in a taxable transaction.[34]

[34]Additionally, the deferred gain is subject to depreciation recapture when the asset is eventually disposed of in a taxable disposition.

Example 11-17

What if: Assume the facts in the previous example where Teton traded its used machinery with a value of $29,500 and an adjusted basis of $18,742 to the dealer for new machinery valued at $27,500 and $2,000 cash. Teton recognized $2,000 on the exchange. What is Teton's basis in the new machinery it received from the dealer?

Answer: $18,742, computed as follows:

Description	Amount	Explanation
(1) Amount realized from machine	$27,500	Fair market value of new machine.
(2) Amount realized from boot (cash)	2,000	
(3) Total amount realized	29,500	(1) + (2).
(4) Adjusted basis of used machinery	18,742	
(5) Gain realized	10,758	(3) − (4).
(6) Gain recognized	$ 2,000	Lesser of (2) or (5).
(7) Deferred gain	8,758	(5) − (6).
Adjusted basis in new property	**$18,742**	(1) − (7).

It is important to note that anything a taxpayer receives in an exchange other than like-kind property is considered boot. This includes cash, other property, or even the amount of a taxpayer's liability transferred to (assumed by) the other party in the exchange. For example, let's return to the previous example. If instead of paying Teton $2,000 of cash, the dealer assumed Teton's $2,000 liability secured by Teton's old machinery, the tax consequences would have been identical. The dealer relieved Teton of $2,000 of debt and the debt relief is treated the same as if the dealer had paid Teton cash and Teton had paid off its $2,000 liability. Generally, when a taxpayer both transfers and receives boot in an otherwise qualifying like-kind exchange, the taxpayer must recognize any realized gain to the extent of the boot received. That is, the taxpayer is not allowed to offset boot received with boot paid.[35] However, when the taxpayer gives and receives boot in the form of liabilities, the taxpayer is allowed to net the boot received and the boot paid.[36]

Reporting Like-Kind Exchanges

Like-kind exchange transactions are reported on Form 8824. Exhibit 11-13 presents the computations from Form 8824 reflecting the like-kind exchange of the machinery in Example 11-15.

Involuntary Conversions

Usually, when taxpayers sell, exchange, or abandon property they intend to do so. However, sometimes taxpayers may involuntarily dispose of property due to circumstances beyond their control. Thus, the tax law refers to these types of property dispositions as **involuntary conversions.**[37] Involuntary conversions occur when property is partially or wholly destroyed by a natural disaster or accident, stolen, condemned, or seized via eminent domain by a governmental agency. Tragic examples of this include the results of the September 11, 2001, terrorist attacks and the Hurricane Katrina-related events in 2005. Even in situations

[35]However, Reg. §1.1031(j)-1 provides an exception where multiple like-kind exchanges are made in a single exchange.

[36]Further details of this important exception are beyond the scope of our discussion. See the examples provided in Reg. §1.1031(d)-2 for further guidance.

[37]§1033.

EXHIBIT 11-13 Form 8824, Part III (From machine exchange in Example 11-15)

Form 8824 (2015)   Page **2**

Name(s) shown on tax return. Do not enter name and social security number if shown on other side. | Your social security number

Steve Dallimore (Teton Mountaineering Technologies LLC)

Part III Realized Gain or (Loss), Recognized Gain, and Basis of Like-Kind Property Received

Caution: *If you transferred and received (a) more than one group of like-kind properties or (b) cash or other (not like-kind) property, see* **Reporting of multi-asset exchanges** *in the instructions.*

Note: *Complete lines 12 through 14* **only** *if you gave up property that was not like-kind. Otherwise, go to line 15.*

12	Fair market value (FMV) of other property given up	12	
13	Adjusted basis of other property given up	13	
14	Gain or (loss) recognized on other property given up. Subtract line 13 from line 12. Report the gain or (loss) in the same manner as if the exchange had been a sale	14	
	Caution: *If the property given up was used previously or partly as a home, see* **Property used as home** *in the instructions.*		
15	Cash received, FMV of other property received, plus net liabilities assumed by other party, reduced (but not below zero) by any exchange expenses you incurred (see instructions) . .	15	0
16	FMV of like-kind property you received	16	29,500
17	Add lines 15 and 16	17	29,500
18	Adjusted basis of like-kind property you gave up, net amounts paid to other party, plus any exchange expenses **not** used on line 15 (see instructions)	18	18,742
19	**Realized gain or (loss).** Subtract line 18 from line 17	19	10,758
20	Enter the smaller of line 15 or line 19, but not less than zero	20	
21	Ordinary income under recapture rules. Enter here and on Form 4797, line 16 (see instructions)	21	
22	Subtract line 21 from line 20. If zero or less, enter -0-. If more than zero, enter here and on Schedule D or Form 4797, unless the installment method applies (see instructions)	22	
23	**Recognized gain.** Add lines 21 and 22	23	0
24	Deferred gain or (loss). Subtract line 23 from line 19. If a related party exchange, see instructions	24	10,758
25	**Basis of like-kind property received.** Subtract line 15 from the sum of lines 18 and 23 . .	25	18.742

when taxpayers experience a loss of property due to theft, disaster, or other circumstances, they might realize a gain for tax purposes if they receive replacement property or insurance proceeds in excess of their basis in the property that was stolen or destroyed.

Taxpayers may experience a tremendous financial hardship if they were required to recognize the realized gain in these circumstances. For example, let's consider a business that acquired a building for $100,000. The building appreciates in value and when the building is worth $150,000 it is destroyed by fire. The building is fully insured at its replacement cost, so the business receives a check from the insurance company for $150,000. The problem for the business is that it realizes a $50,000 gain on this involuntary conversion ($150,000 insurance proceeds minus $100,000 basis in property without considering depreciation). Assuming the business's income is taxed at a 30 percent marginal rate, it must pay $15,000 of tax on the insurance money it receives. This leaves the business with only $135,000 to replace property worth $150,000. This hardly seems equitable. Congress provides special tax laws to allow taxpayers to defer the gains on such *involuntary* conversions.

Taxpayers may defer realized gains on both direct and indirect involuntary conversions. **Direct conversions** involve taxpayers receiving a direct property replacement for the involuntarily converted property. For example, a municipality that is widening its streets may seize land from a taxpayer through its eminent domain and compensate the taxpayer with another parcel of similar value. In this case, the taxpayer would not recognize gain on the exchange of property and would take an adjusted basis in the new parcel of land equal to the taxpayer's basis in the land that was claimed by the municipality. Just as with like-kind exchanges, an exchanged basis

(basis of old property exchanged for basis of new property) ensures that the gain built into the new property (fair market value minus adjusted basis) includes the same gain that was built into the old property.

Indirect conversions involve taxpayers receiving money for the involuntarily converted property through insurance reimbursement or some other type of settlement. Taxpayers meeting the involuntary conversion requirements may *elect* to either recognize or defer realized gain on the conversions. Indirect conversions are more common than direct conversions. Taxpayers can defer realized gains on indirect conversions *if* they acquire **qualified replacement property** within a prescribed time limit, which is generally two years (three years in case of condemnation) after the close of the tax year in which they receive the proceeds.[38]

For both personal and real property, qualified replacement property for an involuntary conversion is defined more narrowly than is like-kind property in a like-kind exchange. The property must be similar *and* related in service or use to qualify.[39] For example, a bowling alley is not qualified replacement property for a pool hall, even though both are real properties used for entertainment purposes. This is stricter than the like-kind exchange rules that would allow the bowling alley to be exchanged for any other real property including a pool hall. Taxpayers recognize realized gain to the extent that they do not reinvest the reimbursement proceeds in qualified property. However, just as in like-kind exchanges, taxpayers do not recognize more gain than they realize on involuntary conversions. That is, a taxpayer's recognized gain on an involuntary conversion can be determined by the following formula: Recognized gain on involuntary conversion = the *lesser of* (1) the gain realized on the conversion or (2) the amount of reimbursement the taxpayer does *not reinvest* in qualified property.

The character of any gain recognized in an involuntary conversion depends on the nature of the asset that was converted—including depreciation recapture if applicable. The basis of the replacement property in an involuntary conversion is calculated in the same way it is for like-kind exchange property. That is, the basis of the replacement property is the fair market value of the new property minus the deferred gain on the conversion.

Example 11-18

What if: Assume that one of Teton's employees was involved in a traffic accident while driving a delivery van. The employee escaped without serious injury but the van was totally destroyed. Before the accident, Teton's delivery van had a fair market value of $15,000 and an adjusted basis of $11,000 (the cost basis was $15,000 and accumulated depreciation on the van was $4,000). Teton received $15,000 of insurance proceeds to cover the loss. Teton was considering two alternatives for replacing the van: Alternative 1 was to purchase a new delivery van for $20,000 and Alternative 2 was to purchase a used delivery van for $14,000. What gain or loss does Teton recognize under Alternative 1 and Alternative 2?

Answer: $0 gain recognized under Alternative 1 and $1,000 gain recognized under Alternative 2 (see computations below). Teton qualifies for a deferral because the new property (delivery van) has a similar and related use to the old property (delivery van). But it must recognize gain under Alternative 2 because it did not reinvest all of the insurance proceeds in a replacement van.

(continued on page 11-32)

---

[38]§1033(a)(2)(B). The time period varies depending on the type of property converted. Additionally, the IRS may consent to an extension of the time period for replacement.

[39]The similar and related-use test has been developed through a variety of administrative pronouncements and judicial law.

What is Teton's basis in the replacement property it acquired under Alternative 1 and Alternative 2?

Answer: $16,000 in Alternative 1 and $11,000 in Alternative 2, computed as follows:

Description	Alternative 1 Amount	Alternative 2 Amount	Explanation
(1) Amount realized	$15,000	$15,000	
(2) Adjusted basis	11,000	11,000	
(3) Gain realized	4,000	4,000	(1) − (2).
(4) Insurance proceeds	15,000	15,000	
(5) Proceeds reinvested	15,000	14,000	
(6) Amount not reinvested	0	1,000	(4) − (5).
(7) Gain recognized	**0**	**1,000**	Lesser of (3) or (6).*
(8) Deferred gain	4,000	3,000	(3) − (7).
(9) Value of replacement property	20,000	14,000	
Basis of replacement property	**16,000**	**11,000**	(9) − (8).

*The character of the $1,000 recognized gain is ordinary income under §1245 (lesser of gain recognized or accumulated depreciation).

Involuntary conversions share several similar concepts with like-kind exchanges such as the concept of qualified property, time period restrictions, the method of computing gain recognized (lesser of realized gain or cash received in addition to qualifying property), and basis calculation (gain or loss from old property remains built into new property). However, one important difference between the two is that taxpayers experiencing a loss from involuntary conversion may immediately deduct the loss as a casualty loss (either personal or business depending on the nature of the loss).

TAXES IN THE REAL WORLD   Weather Break

Weather conditions across the country have caused hardship to many cattle farmers. Drought in the Southwest or floods in the Plains could cause cattle farmers to sell more of their herds than normal because they may not have enough crops to feed the livestock. To aid these farmers, the IRS offers relief in the form of an election to postpone recognizing gain from the sale of livestock sold due to weather-related conditions. What's the catch? The livestock must be replaced within a two-year period. In essence, the IRS allows cattle farmers to take advantage of the §1033 (involuntary conversion) rules.

As an alternative, if a taxpayer sells livestock because of weather conditions, he or she may be able to defer reporting the sale of the livestock for a one-year period. As a result of these two possibilities, cattle farmers may need to consider whether they will replace the livestock to take advantage of the involuntary conversion provision or whether the one-year deferral will better suit their plans.

Installment Sales

In general, when taxpayers sell property for cash and collect the entire sale proceeds in one lump-sum payment, they immediately recognize gain or loss for tax purposes. However, taxpayers selling property don't always collect the sale proceeds in one lump sum from the buyer. For example, the buyer may make a down payment in the year of sale and then agree to pay the remainder of the sale proceeds over a period of time. This type of arrangement is termed an **installment sale.** Technically, an installment sale is any sale of property where the seller receives at least one payment in a taxable year subsequent to the year of disposition of the property.[40] Taxpayers selling property via an installment sale realize gains to the extent the selling price (the amount realized) exceeds their adjusted basis in the property sold. The installment

[40]§453(b)(1).

sale rules stay true to the wherewithal-to-pay concept and allow taxpayers selling property in this manner to use the installment method of recognizing *gain* on the sale over time.[41] The installment method does not apply to property sold at a loss. Under the installment method taxpayers determine the amount of realized gain on the transaction, and they recognize the gain pro rata as they receive the installment payments. So, by the time they have received all of the installment payments, they will have recognized all of the initial realized gain.[42] For financial accounting purposes, businesses selling property on an installment basis generally immediately recognize the realized gain on their financial statements.[43]

To determine the amount of gain the taxpayer (seller) must recognize on each installment payment received, the seller must compute the gross profit percentage on the transaction. The gross profit percentage is calculated as follows:

$$\text{Gross profit percentage} = \frac{\text{Gross profit}}{\text{Contract price}}$$

The gross profit percentage indicates the percentage of the contract price that will ultimately be recognized as gain. Gross profit is calculated as the sales price minus the adjusted basis of the property being sold. The contract price is the sales price less the seller's liabilities that are assumed by the buyer. To determine the portion of a particular payment that is currently recognized as gain, the seller multiplies the amount of the payments received during the year (including the year of sale) by the gross profit percentage (note that once established, the gross profit percentage does not change). Similar to fully taxable transactions, the character of gain taxpayers recognize using the installment method is determined by the character of the asset sold.

Example 11-19

What if: Suppose Teton decides to sell 5 acres of land adjacent to the warehouse for $100,000. The cost basis for the land is $37,500. Teton agrees to sell the property for four equal payments of $25,000—one now (in year 1) and the other three on January 1 of the next three years—plus interest. What amount of gain does Teton realize on the sale and what amount of gain does it recognize in year 1?

Answer: The realized gain on the transaction is $62,500 ($100,000 amount realized less $37,500 adjusted basis), and the year 1 recognized gain is $15,625, computed as follows:

Description	Amount	Explanation
(1) Sales price	$100,000	
(2) Adjusted basis	37,500	
(3) Gross profit	$ 62,500	(1) − (2).
(4) Contract price	$100,000	(1) − assumed liabilities (-0-).
(5) Gross profit percentage	62.5%	(3)/(4).
(6) Payment received in year 1	$ 25,000	
Gain recognized in year 1	**$ 15,625**	(5) × (4).

Because Teton used the land in its trade or business and it held the land for more than a year, the character of the gain is §1231 gain.

---

[41]Technically, a taxpayer selling property on an installment basis at a gain is required to use the installment method of reporting the recognized gain from the transaction. However, taxpayers are allowed to *elect* out of using the installment method §453(d).

[42]Because the seller in an installment sale is essentially lending money to the buyer, the buyer makes the required installment payments to the seller and the buyer pays interest to the seller for the money the buyer is borrowing. Any interest income received by the seller is immediately taxable as ordinary income. Special rules apply regarding interest for installment sales of more than $150,000 (see §453A).

[43]One exception is that the installment sale method similar to the tax installment method is used for financial accounting purposes when there is doubt that the business will collect the receivable.

The formula for determining the basis of an installment note receivable is (1 − gross profit percentage) × remaining payments on note. Because the gross profit percentage reflects the percentage of the installment payments that will be recognized as gain, (1 − gross profit percentage) is the percentage that is not recognized as gain because it reflects a return of capital (basis).

Gains Ineligible for Installment Reporting

Not all gains are eligible for installment sale reporting. Taxpayers selling marketable securities or inventory on an installment basis may not use the installment method to report gain on the sales. Similarly, any depreciation recapture (including §1245, §1250, and §291 depreciation recapture) is not eligible for installment reporting and must be recognized in the year of sale.[44] However, the §1231 gain remaining after the depreciation recapture can be recognized using the installment method. To ensure that any depreciation recapture is not taxed twice (once immediately and then a second time as payments are received), immediately taxable recapture-related gains are *added to* the adjusted basis of the property sold to determine the gross profit percentage. The increase in basis reduces the gain realized, which also reduces the gross profit percentage and the amount of future gain that will ultimately be recognized as the taxpayer receives the installment payments.

Example 11-20

What if: Assume that Teton agrees to sell some of its machinery for $90,000 for two equal payments of $45,000 plus interest. Teton's original basis was $80,000 and accumulated depreciation on the machinery was $30,000. Teton will receive one payment in year 1 (the current year) and the other payment in year 2. What is the amount and character of the gain Teton recognizes on the sale in year 1?

Answer: $30,000 ordinary income and $5,000 of §1231 gain, computed as follows:

Description	Amount	Explanation
(1) Sales price	$90,000	
(2) Original basis	80,000	
(3) Accumulated depreciation	(30,000)	
(4) Adjusted basis	50,000	(2) + (3).
(5) Realized gain (loss)	$40,000	(1) − (4).
(6) Ordinary income from depreciation recapture (not eligible for installment reporting)	**$30,000**	Ordinary income. Lesser of (3) or (5).
(7) Gain eligible for installment reporting	$10,000	(5) − (6).
(8) Contract price	$90,000	(1) − assumed liabilities (-0-)
(9) Gross profit percentage	11.11%	(7)/(8)
(10) Payment received in year 1	$45,000	
Installment gain recognized in year 1	**$ 5,000**	(10) × (9) §1231 gain.

What is the amount and character of the gain Teton recognized upon receipt of the payment in year 2?

Answer: $5,000 of §1231 gain ($45,000 payment received times the gross profit percentage of 11.11 percent).

Other Nonrecognition Provisions

There are several tax law provisions that allow businesses to change the form or organization of their business while deferring the realized gains for tax purposes. For

[44]§453(i).

example, a sole proprietor can form his business as a corporation or contribute assets to an existing corporation and defer the gain realized on the exchange of assets for an ownership interest in the business entity.[45] Without the nonrecognition provision, the tax cost of forming a corporation may be large enough to deter taxpayers from doing so. Nonrecognition rules also apply to taxpayers forming partnerships or contributing assets to partnerships.[46] In still other corporate transactions, such as mergers, divisions (spin-offs or split-ups), or reorganizations, corporations can often do so in tax deferred transactions.[47] While these transactions generally result in deferred gain or loss for the involved parties, the specific details of these topics can easily fill chapters worth of material, and are not considered further in this chapter.

Related-Person Loss Disallowance Rules

Taxpayers selling business or investment property at a loss to unrelated persons are generally able to deduct the loss.[48] This makes sense in most situations because taxpayers are selling the property for less than their remaining investment (adjusted basis) in the property, and after the sale, the taxpayer's investment in the property is completely terminated. In contrast, when a taxpayer sells property at a loss to a related person, she effectively retains some element of control over the property through the related person. Consistent with this idea, §267(a) disallows recognition of losses on sales to related persons. Under §267, related persons include individuals with family relationships including siblings, spouses, ancestors, and lineal descendants. Related persons also include an individual and a corporation if the individual owns more than 50 percent of the stock of the corporation.[49]

THE KEY FACTS

Related-Person Losses

- Related persons are defined in §267 and include certain family members, related corporations, and other entities.
- Losses on sales to related persons are not deductible by the seller.
- The related person may deduct the previously disallowed loss *to the extent of the gain* on the sale to the unrelated third person.

Example 11-21

What if: Suppose Teton is formed as a corporation and Steve is its sole shareholder. Teton is looking to make some long-term investments to fund its anticipated purchase of a new manufacturing facility. Steve currently owns 1,000 shares of stock in his previous company, Northeastern Corp., which he intends to sell in the near future. Steve initially paid $40 a share for the stock but the stock is currently valued at $30 a share. While Steve believes the stock has good long-term potential, he needs cash now to purchase a personal residence in Cody, Wyoming. Steve believes selling the shares to Teton makes good sense because he can deduct the loss and save taxes now and Teton can benefit from the expected long-term appreciation of the stock. If Steve sells 1,000 shares of Northeastern Corp. stock to Teton for $30 per share, what amount of loss will he realize and what amount of loss will he recognize for tax purposes?

Answer: $10,000 loss realized and $0 loss recognized, determined as follows:

Description	Amount	Explanation
(1) Amount realized on sale	$ 30,000	(1,000 × $30).
(2) Adjusted basis in stock	40,000	(1,000 × $40).
(3) Loss realized on sale	**(10,000)**	(1) – (2).
Loss recognized on sale	**$ 0**	Losses on sales to related persons are disallowed.

Because Steve owns more than 50 percent of Teton (he owns 100 percent), Steve and Teton are considered to be related persons. Consequently, Steve is not allowed to recognize any loss on the sale.

[45]§351.
[46]§721.
[47]§368 contains the numerous variations and requirements of these tax-deferred reorganizations.
[48]Capital losses are subject to certain limitations for individuals and corporate taxpayers (§1211).
[49]§267(a). The related-person rules include both direct ownership as well as indirect ownership (ownership attributed to the taxpayer from related persons). See §267(c) for a description of the indirect ownership rules.

Although taxpayers are not allowed to immediately deduct losses when they sell property to the related person, the related-person buyer may be able to subsequently deduct the disallowed loss by selling the property to an *unrelated* third party at a gain. The rules follow:

- If the related buyer sells the property at a gain (the related-person buyer sells it for more than she purchased it for) greater than the disallowed loss, the entire loss that was disallowed for the related-person seller is deductible by the buyer.
- If the related-person buyer subsequently sells the property and the related-person seller's disallowed loss exceeds the related person's gain on the subsequent sale, the related-person buyer may only deduct or offset the previously disallowed loss *to the extent of the gain* on the sale to the unrelated third party—the remaining disallowed loss expires unused.
- If the related-person buyer sells the property for less than her purchase price from the related seller, the disallowed loss expires unused.
- The holding period for the related-person buyer begins on the date of the sale between the related parties.[50]

Example 11-22

What if: Let's return to the previous example where Steve sold 1,000 shares of Northeastern Corp. stock to Teton (a corporation) for $30,000. As we discovered in that example, Steve realized a $10,000 loss on the sale, but he was not allowed to deduct it because Steve and Teton are related persons. Let's assume that a few years after Teton purchased the stock from Steve, Teton sells the Northeastern Corp. stock to an unrelated third party. What gain or loss does *Teton* recognize when it sells the stock in each of three scenarios, assuming it sells the stock for $37,000 in Scenario 1, $55,000 in Scenario 2, and $25,000 in Scenario 3?

Answer: $0 gain or loss in Scenario 1, $15,000 gain in Scenario 2, and $5,000 loss in Scenario 3, computed as follows:

Description	Scenario 1	Scenario 2	Scenario 3	Explanation
(1) Amount realized	$ 37,000	$ 55,000	$25,000	
(2) Adjusted basis	30,000	30,000	30,000	Example 11-21 (Teton's purchase price).
(3) Realized gain (loss)	7,000	25,000	(5,000)	(1) − (2).
(4) Benefit of Steve's ($10,000) disallowed loss	(7,000)	(10,000)	0	Loss benefit limited to realized gain.
Recognized gain (loss)	$ 0	$ 15,000	**($5,000)**	(3) + (4).

In Scenario 1 $3,000 of Steve's $10,000 remaining disallowed loss expires unused. In Scenario 3, Steve's entire $10,000 disallowed loss expires unused.

CONCLUSION

This chapter describes and discusses the tax consequences associated with sales and other types of property dispositions. We've learned how to determine the amount of gain or loss taxpayers recognize when they sell or otherwise dispose of property, and we've learned how to determine the character of these gains and losses. Tax accountants who understand the rules and concepts of property dispositions are able to comply with the tax law and advise clients of potential tax planning opportunities and avoid pitfalls associated with various nonrecognition provisions.

[50]Reg. §1.267(d)-1(c)(3).

Summary

Calculate the amount of gain or loss recognized on the disposition of assets used in a trade or business.

`LO 11-1`

- Dispositions occur in the form of sales, trades, or other realization events.
- Gain realized is the amount realized less the adjusted basis of an asset.
- Amount realized is everything of value received in the transaction less any selling costs.
- Adjusted basis is the historical cost or basis of an asset less any cost recovery deductions applied against the asset.
- Gain realized on asset dispositions is not always recognized.

Describe the general character types of gain or loss recognized on property dispositions.

`LO 11-2`

- Recognized gains must be characterized as ordinary, capital, or §1231. An asset's character is a function of the asset's use and holding period.
- Ordinary assets are derived from normal transactions of the business (revenues and accounts receivable), sale of short-term trade or business assets, and depreciation recapture.
- Capital assets are assets that are held either for investment or for personal use (a taxpayer's principal residence).
- §1231 assets consist of property used in a taxpayer's trade or business that has been held for more than one year.
- Net §1231 gains are treated as long-term capital gains and net §1231 losses are treated as ordinary losses.

Explain the rationale for and calculate depreciation recapture.

`LO 11-3`

- §1231 assets, other than land, are subject to cost recovery deductions (depreciation), which generate ordinary deductions.
- Gains that are created through depreciation deductions are subject to depreciation recapture. Any remaining gain is §1231 gain.
- Depreciation recapture does not change the amount of the gain but simply converts or recharacterizes the gain from §1231 to ordinary.
- Different recapture rules apply to tangible personal property (§1245) and real property (§291 for corporations only and §1250).

Describe the tax treatment of unrecaptured §1250 gains and determine the character of gains on property sold to related parties.

`LO 11-4`

- When individuals sell §1250 property at a gain, the portion of the gain generated by depreciation deductions is called unrecaptured §1250 gain.
- This gain is a §1231 gain that, if treated as a capital gain after the §1231 netting process, flows into the capital gain/loss process (Chapter 11) and is taxed at a maximum rate of 25 percent.
- If a taxpayer sells an asset at a gain to a related person and the asset is a depreciable asset to the related person, the seller must characterize the entire gain as ordinary income.

Describe the tax treatment of §1231 gains or losses, including the §1231 netting process.

`LO 11-5`

- After applying the depreciation recapture rules, taxpayers calculate the net §1231 gain or loss.
- If a net §1231 loss results, the loss will become ordinary and offset ordinary income.
- If a net §1231 gain results, the §1231 look-back rule must be applied.
- After applying the look-back rule, any remaining net §1231 gain is a long-term capital gain.

Explain common exceptions to the general rule that realized gains and losses are recognized currently.

`LO 11-6`

- Like-kind exchanges involve trading or exchanging business assets for similar business assets. The gain is deferred unless boot or non-like-kind property is received.

- Involuntary conversions are the losses on property through circumstances beyond tax-payers' control. Reasons include natural disasters, accidents, theft, or condemnation.
- Installment sales occur when any portion of the amount realized is received in a year subsequent to the disposition.
- §267 related-person losses are disallowed but the related-person buyer may be able to deduct the disallowed loss if she subsequently sells the property at a gain.

KEY TERMS

adjusted basis (11-5)	installment sale (11-32)	recapture (11-11)
amount realized (11-2)	involuntary conversion (11-29)	recognized gain or loss (11-6)
boot (11-27)	like-kind exchange (11-24)	§291 depreciation recapture (11-14)
capital asset (11-8)	nonrecaptured net §1231 losses (11-18)	§1231 assets (11-9)
deferred like-kind exchange (11-26)	nonrecognition transaction (11-20)	§1231 look-back rule (11-18)
depreciation recapture (11-10)	ordinary asset (11-7)	§1245 property (11-10)
direct conversion (11-30)	production of income (11-8)	§1250 property (11-14)
exchanged basis (11-27)	qualified replacement property (11-31)	third-party intermediaries (11-25)
indirect conversion (11-31)	realized gain or loss (11-5)	unrecaptured §1250 gain (11-15)

DISCUSSION QUESTIONS

Discussion Questions are available in *Connect®*.   ■ connect

LO 11-1   1. Compare and contrast different ways in which a taxpayer triggers a realization event by disposing of an asset.

LO 11-1   2. Potomac Corporation wants to sell a warehouse that it has used in its business for 10 years. Potomac is asking $450,000 for the property. The warehouse is subject to a mortgage of $125,000. If Potomac accepts Wyden Inc.'s offer to give Potomac $325,000 in cash and assume full responsibility for the mortgage on the property, what amount does Potomac realize on the sale?

LO 11-1   3. Montana Max sells a 2,500-acre ranch for $1,000,000 in cash, a note receivable of $1,000,000, and debt relief of $2,400,000. He also pays selling commissions of $60,000. In addition, Max agrees to build a new barn on the property (cost $250,000) and spend $100,000 upgrading the fence on the property before the sale. What is Max's amount realized on the sale?

LO 11-1   4. Hawkeye sold farming equipment for $55,000. It bought the equipment four years ago for $75,000, and it has since claimed a total of $42,000 in depreciation deductions against the asset. Explain how to calculate Hawkeye's adjusted basis in the farming equipment.

LO 11-1   5. When a taxpayer sells an asset, what is the difference between realized and recognized gain or loss on the sale?

LO 11-2   6. What does it mean to characterize a gain or loss? Why is characterizing a gain or loss important?

LO 11-2   7. Explain the difference between ordinary, capital, and §1231 assets.

LO 11-2   8. Discuss the reasons why individuals generally prefer capital gains over ordinary gains. Explain why corporate taxpayers might prefer capital gains over ordinary gains.

LO 11-2   9. Dakota Conrad owns a parcel of land he would like to sell. Describe the circumstances in which the sale of the land would generate §1231 gain or loss, ordinary gain or loss, or capital gain or loss. Also, describe the circumstances where Dakota would not be allowed to deduct a loss on the sale.

10. Lincoln has used a piece of land in her business for the past five years. The land qualifies as §1231 property. It is unclear whether Lincoln will have to recognize a gain or loss when she eventually sells the asset. She asks her accountant how the gain or loss would be characterized if she decides to sell. Her accountant said that selling §1231 assets gives sellers "the best of both worlds." Explain what her accountant means by "the best of both worlds." `LO 11-2`

11. Explain Congress's rationale for depreciation recapture. `LO 11-3`

12. Compare and contrast §1245 recapture and §1250 recapture. `LO 11-3`

13. Why is depreciation recapture not required when assets are sold at a loss? `LO 11-3`

14. What are the similarities and differences between the tax benefit rule and depreciation recapture? `LO 11-3`

15. Are both corporations and individuals subject to depreciation recapture when they sell depreciable real property at a gain? Explain. `LO 11-3` `LO 11-4`

16. How is unrecaptured §1250 gain for individuals similar to depreciation recapture? How is it different? `LO 11-4`

17. Explain why gains from depreciable property sold to a related taxpayer are treated as ordinary income under §1239. `LO 11-4`

18. Bingaman Resources sold two depreciable §1231 assets during the year. One asset resulted in a large gain (the asset was sold for more than it was purchased for) and the other in a small loss. Describe the §1231 netting process for Bingaman. `LO 11-5`

19. Jeraldine believes that when the §1231 look-back rule applies, the taxpayer deducts a §1231 loss in a previous year against §1231 gains in the current year. Explain whether Jeraldine's description is correct. `LO 11-5`

20. Explain the purpose behind the §1231 look-back rule. `LO 11-5`

21. Does a taxpayer apply the §1231 look-back rule in a year when the taxpayer recognizes a net §1231 loss? Explain. `LO 11-5`

22. Describe the circumstances in which an individual taxpayer with a net §1231 gain will have different portions of the gain taxed at different rates. `LO 11-4` `LO 11-5`

23. Rocky and Bullwinkle Partnership sold a parcel of land during the current year and realized a gain of $250,000. Rocky and Bullwinkle did not recognize gain related to the sale of the land on its tax return. Is this possible? Explain how a taxpayer could realize a gain but not recognize it. `LO 11-6`

24. Why does the tax code allow taxpayers to defer gains on like-kind exchanges? How do the tax laws ensure that the gains (or losses) are deferred and not permanently excluded from a taxpayer's income? `LO 11-6`

25. Compare and contrast the like-kind property requirements for real property and for personal property for purposes of qualifying for a like-kind exchange. Explain whether a car held by a corporation for delivering documents will qualify as like-kind property with a car held by an individual for personal use. `LO 11-6`

26. Salazar Inc., a Colorado company, is relocating to a nearby town. It would like to trade its real property for some real property in the new location. While Salazar has found several prospective buyers for its real property and has also located several properties that are acceptable in the new location, it cannot find anyone that is willing to trade Salazar Inc. for its property in a like-kind exchange. Explain how a third-party intermediary could facilitate Salazar's like-kind exchange. `LO 11-6`

27. Minuteman wants to enter into a like-kind exchange by exchanging its old New England manufacturing facility for a ranch in Wyoming. Minuteman is using a third-party intermediary to facilitate the exchange. The purchaser of the manufacturing facility wants to complete the transaction immediately but, for various reasons, the ranch transaction will not be completed for three to four months. Will this delay cause a problem for Minuteman's desire to accomplish this through a like-kind exchange? Explain. `LO 11-6`

LO 11-6   28. Olympia Corporation, of Kittery, Maine, wants to exchange its manufacturing machinery for Bangor Company's machinery. Both parties agree that Olympia's machinery is worth $100,000 and that Bangor's machinery is worth $95,000. Olympia would like the transaction to qualify as a like-kind exchange. What could the parties do to equalize the value exchanged but still allow the exchange to qualify as a like-kind exchange? How would the necessary change affect the tax consequences of the transaction?

LO 11-6   29. Compare and contrast the similarities and differences between like-kind exchanges and involuntary conversions for tax purposes.

LO 11-6   30. What is an installment sale? How do the tax laws ensure that taxpayers recognize all the gain they realize on an installment sale? How is depreciation recapture treated in an installment sale? Explain the gross profit ratio and how it relates to gains recognized under installment method sales.

LO 11-6   31. Mr. Kyle owns stock in a local publicly traded company. Although the stock price has declined since he purchased it two years ago, he likes the long-term prospects for the company. If Kyle sells the stock to his sister because he needs some cash for a down payment on a new home, is the loss deductible? If Kyle is right and the stock price increases in the future, how is his sister's gain computed if she sells the stock?

PROBLEMS

Select problems are available in *Connect*®.   ▇ connect

LO 11-1   32. Rafael sold an asset to Jamal. What is Rafael's amount realized on the sale in each of the following alternative scenarios?
  a) Rafael received $80,000 of cash and a vehicle worth $10,000. Rafael also pays $5,000 in selling expenses.
  b) Rafael received $80,000 of cash and was relieved of a $30,000 mortgage on the asset he sold to Jamal. Rafael also paid a commission of $5,000 on the transaction.
  c) Rafael received $20,000 of cash, a parcel of land worth $50,000, and market-able securities of $10,000. Rafael also paid a commission of $8,000 on the transaction.

LO 11-1   33. Alan Meer inherits a hotel from his grandmother, Mary, on February 11 of the current year. Mary bought the hotel for $730,000 three years ago. Mary deducted $27,000 of cost recovery on the hotel before her death. The fair market of the hotel in February is $725,000. (Assume that the alternative valuation date is not used.)
  a) What is Alan's adjusted basis in the hotel?
  b) If the fair market value of the hotel at the time of Mary's death was $500,000, what is Alan's basis?

LO 11-1   34. Shasta Corporation sold a piece of land to Bill for $45,000. Shasta bought the land two years ago for $30,600. What gain or loss does Shasta realize on the transaction?

LO 11-1   35. Lassen Corporation sold a machine to a machine dealer for $25,000. Lassen bought the machine for $55,000 and has claimed $15,000 of depreciation expense on the machine. What gain or loss does Lassen realize on the transaction?

LO 11-1   LO 11-2   36. Hannah Tywin owns 100 shares of MM Inc. stock. She sells the stock on December 11 for $25 per share. She received the stock as a gift from her Aunt Pam on March 20 of this year when the fair market value of the stock was $18 per share. Aunt Pam originally purchased the stock seven years ago at a price of $12 per share. What is the amount and character of Hannah's recognized gain on the stock?

37. On September 30 of last year, Rex received some investment land from Holly as a gift. Holly's adjusted basis was $50,000 and the land was valued at $40,000 at the time of the gift. Holly acquired the land five years ago. What is the amount and character of Rex's recognized gain (loss) if he sells the land on May 12 this year at the following prices? `LO 11-1` `LO 11-2`
    a) $32,000
    b) $70,000
    c) $45,000

38. Franco converted a building from personal to business use in May 2014 when the fair market value was $55,000. He purchased the building in July 2011 for $80,000. On December 15 of this year, Franco sells the building for $40,000. On the date of sale, the accumulated depreciation on the building was $5,565. What is Franco's recognized gain or loss on the sale? `LO 11-1` `LO 11-2`

39. Identify each of White Corporation's following assets as an ordinary, capital, or §1231 asset. `LO 11-2`
    a) Two years ago, White used its excess cash to purchase a piece of land as an investment.
    b) Two years ago, White purchased land and a warehouse. It uses these assets in its business.
    c) Manufacturing machinery White purchased earlier this year.
    d) Inventory White purchased 13 months ago but is ready to be shipped to a customer.
    e) Office equipment White has used in its business for the past three years.
    f) 1,000 shares of stock in Black corporation that White purchased two years ago because it was a good investment.
    g) Account receivable from a customer with terms 2/10 net 30.
    h) Machinery White held for three years and then sold at a loss of $10,000.

40. In year 0, Canon purchased a machine to use in its business for $56,000. In year 3, Canon sold the machine for $42,000. Between the date of the purchase and the date of the sale, Canon depreciated the machine by $32,000. `LO 11-3` `LO 11-4`
    a) What is the amount and character of the gain Canon will recognize on the sale, assuming that it is a partnership?
    b) What is the amount and character of the gain Canon will recognize on the sale, assuming that it is a corporation?
    c) What is the amount and character of the gain Canon will recognize on the sale, assuming that it is a corporation and the sale proceeds were increased to $60,000?
    d) What is the amount and character of the gain Canon will recognize on the sale, assuming that it is a corporation and the sale proceeds were decreased to $20,000?

41. In year 0, Longworth Partnership purchased a machine for $40,000 to use in its business. In year 3, Longworth sold the machine for $35,000. Between the date of the purchase and the date of the sale, Longworth depreciated the machine by $22,000. `LO 11-3` `LO 11-4`
    a) What is the amount and character of the gain (loss) Longworth will recognize on the sale?
    b) What is the amount and character of the gain (loss) Longworth will recognize on the sale if the sale proceeds were increased to $45,000?
    c) What is the amount and character of the gain (loss) Longworth will recognize on the sale if the sale proceeds were decreased to $15,000?

LO 11-3 **LO 11-4** 42. On August 1 of year 0, Dirksen purchased a machine for $20,000 to use in its business. On December 4 of year 0, Dirksen sold the machine for $18,000.

a) What is the amount and character of the gain or loss Dirksen will recognize on the sale?

b) What is the amount and character of the gain or loss Dirksen will recognize on the sale if the machine was sold on January 15 of year 1 instead?

LO 11-3 **LO 11-4** 43. Rayburn Corporation has a building that it bought during year 0 for $850,000. It sold the building in year 5. During the time it held the building Rayburn depreciated it by $100,000. What is the amount and character of the gain or loss Rayburn will recognize on the sale in each of the following alternative situations?

a) Rayburn receives $840,000.

b) Rayburn receives $900,000.

c) Rayburn receives $700,000.

LO 11-3 **LO 11-4** 44. Moran owns a building he bought during year 0 for $150,000. He sold the building in year 6. During the time he held the building he depreciated it by $32,000. What is the amount and character of the gain or loss Moran will recognize on the sale in each of the following alternative situations?

a) Moran received $145,000.

b) Moran received $170,000.

c) Moran received $110,000.

LO 11-3 **LO 11-4** **LO 11-5** planning 45. Hart, an individual, bought an asset for $500,000 and has claimed $100,000 of depreciation deductions against the asset. Hart has a marginal tax rate of 30 percent. Answer the questions presented in the following alternative scenarios (assume Hart had no property transactions other than those described in the problem):

a) What is the amount and character of Hart's recognized gain if the asset is tangible personal property sold for $450,000? What effect does the sale have on Hart's tax liability for the year?

b) What is the amount and character of Hart's recognized gain if the asset is tangible personal property sold for $550,000? What effect does the sale have on Hart's tax liability for the year?

c) What is the amount and character of Hart's recognized gain if the asset is tangible personal property sold for $350,000? What effect does the sale have on Hart's tax liability for the year?

d) What is the amount and character of Hart's recognized gain if the asset is a nonresidential building sold for $450,000? What effect does the sale have on Hart's tax liability for the year?

e) Now assume that Hart is a corporation. What is the amount and character of its recognized gain if the asset is a nonresidential building sold for $450,000? What effect does the sale have on Hart's tax liability for the year (assume the same 30 percent marginal tax rate)?

f) Now assuming that the asset is real property, which entity type should be used to minimize the taxes paid on real estate gains?

LO 11-4 46. Luke sold a building and the land on which the building sits to his wholly owned corporation, Studemont Corp. at fair market value. The fair market value of the building was determined to be $325,000; Luke built the building several years ago at a cost of $200,000. Luke had claimed $45,000 of depreciation expense on the building. The fair market value of the land was determined to be $210,000 at the time of the sale; Luke purchased the land many years ago for $130,000.

a) What is the amount and character of Luke's recognized gain or loss on the building?

b) What is the amount and character of Luke's recognized gain or loss on the land?

47. Buckley, an individual, began business two years ago and has never sold a §1231 asset. Buckley owned each of the assets since he began the business. In the current year, Buckley sold the following business assets:

LO 11-5

Asset	Original Cost	Accumulated Depreciation	Gain/Loss
Computers	$ 6,000	$ 2,000	$(3,000)
Machinery	10,000	4,000	(2,000)
Furniture	20,000	12,000	7,000
Building	100,000	10,000	(1,000)

Assuming Buckley's marginal ordinary income tax rate is 35 percent, answer the questions for the following alternative scenarios:

a) What is the character of Buckley's gains or losses for the current year? What effect do the gains and losses have on Buckley's tax liability?

b) Assume that the amount realized increased so that the building was sold at a $6,000 gain instead. What is the character of Buckley's gains or losses for the current year? What effect do the gains and losses have on Buckley's tax liability?

c) Assume that the amount realized increased so that the building was sold at a $15,000 gain instead. What is the character of Buckley's gains or losses for the current year? What effect do the gains and losses have on Buckley's tax liability?

48. Lily Tucker (single) owns and operates a bike shop as a sole proprietorship. This year, she sells the following long-term assets used in her business:

LO 11-3   LO 11-4
LO 11-5

Asset	Sales Price	Cost	Accumulated Depreciation
Building	$230,000	$200,000	$52,000
Equipment	80,000	148,000	23,000

Lily's taxable income before these transactions is $160,500. What are Lily's taxable income and tax liability for the year?

49. Shimmer Inc. is a calendar-year-end, accrual-method corporation. This year, it sells the following long-term assets:

LO 11-3   LO 11-4
LO 11-5

Asset	Sales Price	Cost	Accumulated Depreciation
Building	$650,000	$642,000	$37,000
Sparkle Corporation stock	130,000	175,000	n/a

Shimmer does not sell any other assets during the year, and its taxable income before these transactions is $800,000. What are Shimmer's taxable income and tax liability for the year?

50. Aruna, a sole proprietor, wants to sell two assets that she no longer needs for her business. Both assets qualify as §1231 assets. The first is machinery and will generate a $10,000 §1231 loss on the sale. The second is land that will generate a $7,000 §1231 gain on the sale. Aruna's ordinary marginal tax rate is 30 percent.

LO 11-5

a) Assuming she sells both assets in December of year 1 (the current year), what effect will the sales have on Aruna's tax liability?

b) Assuming that Aruna sells the land in December of year 1 and the machinery in January of year 2, what effect will the sales have on Aruna's tax liability for each year?

c) Explain why selling the assets in separate years will result in greater tax savings for Aruna.

LO 11-5 51. Bourne Guitars, a corporation, reported a $157,000 net §1231 gain for year 6.

 a) Assuming Bourne reported $50,000 of nonrecaptured net §1231 losses during years 1–5, what amount of Bourne's net §1231 gain for year 6, if any, is treated as ordinary income?

 b) Assuming Bourne's nonrecaptured net §1231 losses from years 1–5 were $200,000, what amount of Bourne's net §1231 gain for year 6, if any, is treated as ordinary income?

LO 11-5

planning

52. Tonya Jefferson, a sole proprietor, runs a successful lobbying business in Washington, DC. She doesn't sell many business assets, but she is planning on retiring and selling her historic townhouse, from which she runs her business, in order to buy a place somewhere sunny and warm. Tonya's townhouse is worth $1,000,000 and the land is worth another $1,000,000. The original basis in the townhouse was $600,000, and she has claimed $250,000 of depreciation deductions against the asset over the years. The original basis in the land was $500,000. Tonya has located a buyer that would like to finalize the transaction in December of the current year. Tonya's marginal ordinary income tax rate is 35 percent.

 a) What amount of gain or loss does Tonya recognize on the sale? What is the character of the gain or loss? What effect does the gain or loss have on her tax liability?

 b) In addition to the original facts, assume that Tonya reports the following nonrecaptured net §1231 loss:

Year	Net §1231 Gains/(Losses)
Year 1	($200,000)
Year 2	0
Year 3	0
Year 4	0
Year 5	0
Year 6 (current year)	?

 What amount of gain or loss does Tonya recognize on the sale? What is the character of the gain or loss? What effect does the gain or loss have on her year 6 (the current year) tax liability?

 c) As Tonya's tax advisor, you suggest that Tonya sell the townhouse in year 7 in order to reduce her taxes. What amount of gain or loss does Tonya recognize on the sale in year 7?

LO 11-5 53. Morgan's Water World (MWW), an LLC, opened several years ago and reports the following net §1231 gains and losses since it began business.

Year	Net §1231 Gains/(Losses)
Year 1	($11,000)
Year 2	5,000
Year 3	(21,000)
Year 4	(4,000)
Year 5	17,000
Year 6	(43,000)
Year 7 (current year)	113,000

 What amount, if any, of the year 7 $113,000 net §1231 gain is treated as ordinary income?

54. Hans runs a sole proprietorship. Hans reported the following net §1231 gains and losses since he began business:

Year	Net §1231 Gains/(Losses)
Year 1	($65,000)
Year 2	15,000
Year 3	0
Year 4	0
Year 5	10,000
Year 6	0
Year 7 (current year)	50,000

LO 11-5

   a) What amount, if any, of the year 7 (current year) $50,000 net §1231 gain is treated as ordinary income?

   b) Assume that the $50,000 net §1231 gain occurs in year 6 instead of year 7. What amount of the gain would be treated as ordinary income in year 6?

55. Independence Corporation needs to replace some of the assets used in its trade or business and is contemplating the following exchanges:

LO 11-6

Exchange	Asset Given Up by Independence	Asset Received by Independence
a	Band saw	Band saw
b	Machinery used in textiles	Machinery used for wood working
c	Passenger automobile used for deliveries	Heavy duty van that seats two and has a large cargo box
d	Large warehouse on two acres	Small warehouse on twenty-two acres
e	Office building in Green Bay, WI, used in the business	Apartment complex in Newport Beach, CA, that will be held as an investment

   Determine whether each exchange qualifies as a like-kind exchange. Also, explain the rationale for why each qualifies or does not qualify as a like-kind exchange.

56. Kase, an individual, purchased some property in Potomac, Maryland, for $150,000 approximately 10 years ago. Kase is approached by a real estate agent representing a client who would like to exchange a parcel of land in North Carolina for Kase's Maryland property. Kase agrees to the exchange. What is Kase's realized gain or loss, recognized gain or loss, and basis in the North Carolina property in each of the following alternative scenarios?

LO 11-6

   a) The transaction qualifies as a like-kind exchange and the fair market value of each property is $675,000.

   b) The transaction qualifies as a like-kind exchange and the fair market value of each property is $100,000.

57. Longhaul Trucking traded two small trucks (each had a 10,000-pound gross weight) for one large truck (18,000-pound gross weight). Do the trucks qualify as like-kind property? (*Hint:* Because the trucks are tangible personal property they must be the same asset class to be like-kind assets. Use Rev. Proc. 87-56 to determine the asset classes for the trucks.)

LO 11-6

research

58. Twinbrook Corporation needed to upgrade to a larger manufacturing facility. Twinbrook first acquired a new manufacturing facility for $2,100,000 cash, and then transferred the facility it was using (building and land) to White Flint Corporation for $2,000,000 three months later. Does the exchange qualify for like-kind exchange treatment? (*Hint:* Examine Revenue Procedures 2000-37 and 2004-51.) If not, can you propose a change in the transaction that will allow it to qualify?

LO 11-6

research

LO 11-6

research

59. Woodley Park Corporation currently owns two parcels of land (parcel 1 and parcel 2). It owns a warehouse facility on parcel 1. Woodley needs to acquire a new and larger manufacturing facility. Woodley was approached by Blazing Fast Construction (who specializes in prefabricated warehouses) about acquiring Woodley's existing warehouse on parcel 1. Woodley indicated that it prefers to exchange its existing facility for a new and larger facility in a qualifying like-kind exchange. Blazing Fast indicated that it could construct a new manufacturing facility on parcel 2 to Woodley's specification within four months. Woodley and Blazing Fast agreed to the following arrangement. First, Blazing Fast would construct the new warehouse on parcel 2 and then relinquish the property to Woodley within four months. Woodley would then transfer the warehouse facility and land parcel 1 to Blazing Fast. All of the property exchanged in the deal was identified immediately and the construction was completed within 180 days. Does the exchange of the new building for the old building and parcel 1 qualify as a like-kind exchange (see *DeCleene v. Commissioner,* 115 TC 457)?

LO 11-6

60. Metro Corp. traded machine A for machine B. Metro originally purchased machine A for $50,000 and machine A's adjusted basis was $25,000 at the time of the exchange. What is Metro's realized gain or loss, recognized gain or loss, and adjusted basis in machine B in each of the following alternative scenarios?

a) The fair market value of machine A and of machine B is $40,000 at the time of the exchange. The exchange does not qualify as a like-kind exchange.

b) The fair market value of machine A and of machine B is $40,000. The exchange qualifies as a like-kind exchange.

c) The fair market value of machine A is $35,000 and machine B is valued at $40,000. Metro exchanges machine A and $5,000 cash for machine B. Machine A and machine B are like-kind property.

d) The fair market value of machine A is $45,000 and Metro trades machine A for machine B valued at $40,000 and $5,000 cash. Machine A and machine B are like-kind property.

LO 11-6

61. Prater Inc. enters into an exchange in which it gives up its warehouse on 10 acres of land and receives a tract of land. A summary of the exchange is as follows:

Transferred	FMV	Original Basis	Accumulated Depreciation
Warehouse	$300,000	$225,000	$45,000
Land	50,000	50,000	
Mortgage on warehouse	30,000		
Cash	20,000	20,000	

Assets received	FMV
Land	$340,000

What is Prater's realized and recognized gain on the exchange and its basis in the assets it received in the exchange?

LO 11-6

62. Baker Corporation owned a building located in Kansas. Baker used the building for its business operations. Last year a tornado hit the property and completely destroyed it. This year, Baker received an insurance settlement. Baker had originally purchased the building for $350,000 and had claimed a total of $100,000 of depreciation deductions against the property. What is Baker's realized and recognized gain or (loss) on this transaction and what is its basis in the new building in the following alternative scenarios?

a) Baker received $450,000 in insurance proceeds and spent $450,000 rebuilding the building during the current year.

b) Baker received $450,000 in insurance proceeds and spent $500,000 rebuilding the building during the current year.

c) Baker received $450,000 in insurance proceeds and spent $400,000 rebuilding the building during the current year.

d) Baker received $450,000 in insurance proceeds and spent $450,000 rebuilding the building during the next three years.

63. Russell Corporation sold a parcel of land valued at $400,000. Its basis in the land was $275,000. For the land, Russell received $50,000 in cash in year 0 and a note providing that Russell will receive $175,000 in year 1 and $175,000 in year 2 from the buyer.

    a) What is Russell's realized gain on the transaction?

    b) What is Russell's recognized gain in year 0, year 1, and year 2?

`LO 11-6`

64. In year 0, Javens Inc. sold machinery with a fair market value of $400,000 to Chris. The machinery's original basis was $317,000 and Javens's accumulated depreciation on the machinery was $50,000, so its adjusted basis to Javens was $267,000. Chris paid Javens $40,000 immediately (in year 0) and provided a note to Javens indicating that Chris would pay Javens $60,000 a year for six years beginning in year 1. What is the amount and character of the gain that Javens will recognize in year 0? What amount and character of the gain will Javens recognize in years 1 through 6?

`LO 11-6`

65. Ken sold a rental property for $500,000. He received $100,000 in the current year and $100,000 each year for the next four years. $400,000 of the sales price was allocated to the building and the remaining $100,000 was allocated to the land. Ken purchased the property several years ago for $300,000. When he initially purchased the property, he allocated $225,000 of the purchase price to the building and $75,000 to the land. Ken has claimed $25,000 of depreciation deductions over the years against the building. Ken had no other sales of §1231 or capital assets in the current year. For the year of the sale, determine Ken's recognized gain or loss, the character of Ken's gain, and calculate Ken's tax due because of the sale (assuming his marginal ordinary tax rate is 35 percent). (*Hint:* See the examples in Reg. §1.453-12.)

`LO 11-6`

`research`

66. Hillary is in the leasing business and faces a marginal tax rate of 35 percent. She has leased equipment to Whitewater Corporation for several years. Hillary bought the equipment for $50,000 and claimed $20,000 of depreciation deductions against the asset. The lease term is about to expire and Whitewater would like to acquire the equipment. Hillary has been offered two options to choose from:

`LO 11-6`

`research`

Option	Details
Like-kind exchange	Whitewater would provide Hillary with like-kind equipment. The like-kind equipment has a fair market value of $35,000.
Installment sale	Whitewater would provide Hillary with two payments of $19,000. She would use the proceeds to purchase equipment that she could also lease.

Ignoring time value of money, which option provides the greatest after-tax value for Hillary, assuming she is indifferent between the proposals based on nontax factors?

67. Deirdre sold 100 shares of stock to her brother, James, for $2,400. Deirdre purchased the stock several years ago for $3,000.

    a) What gain or loss does Deirdre recognize on the sale?

    b) What amount of gain or loss does James recognize if he sells the stock for $3,200?

    c) What amount of gain or loss does James recognize if he sells the stock for $2,600?

    d) What amount of gain or loss does James recognize if he sells the stock for $2,000?

`LO 11-6`

COMPREHENSIVE PROBLEMS

Select problems are available in *Connect*®.

68. Two years ago, Bethesda Corporation bought a delivery truck for $30,000 (not subject to the luxury auto depreciation limits). Bethesda used MACRS 200 percent declining balance and the half-year convention to recover the cost of the truck, but it did not elect §179 expensing or any eligible bonus depreciation. Answer the questions for the following alternative scenarios.

    a) Assuming Bethesda used the truck until it sold it in March of year 3, what depreciation expense can it claim on the truck for years 1 through 3?

    b) Assume that Bethesda claimed $18,500 of depreciation expense on the truck before it sold it in year 3. What is the amount and character of the gain or loss if Bethesda sold the truck in year 3 for $17,000, and incurred $2,000 of selling expenses on the sale?

    c) Assume that Bethesda claimed $18,500 of depreciation expense on the truck before it sold it in year 3. What is the amount and character of the gain or loss if Bethesda sold the truck in year 3 for $35,000, and incurred $3,000 of selling expenses on the sale?

69. Hauswirth Corporation sold (or exchanged) some manufacturing equipment in year 0. Hauswirth bought the machinery several years ago for $65,000 and it has claimed $23,000 of depreciation expense against the equipment.

    a) Assuming that Hauswirth receives $50,000 in cash for the equipment, compute the amount and character of Hauswirth's recognized gain or loss on the sale.

    b) Assuming that Hauswirth receives like-kind equipment with a fair market value of $50,000 in exchange for its equipment, compute Hauswirth's gain realized, gain recognized, deferred gain, and basis in the new equipment.

    c) Assuming that Hauswirth receives $20,000 in cash in year 0 and a $50,000 note receivable that is payable in year 1, compute the amount and character of Hauswirth's gain in year 0 and in year 1.

research

70. Fontenot Corporation sold some machinery to its majority owner Gray (an individual who owns 60 percent of Fontenot). Fontenot purchased the machinery for $100,000 and has claimed a total of $40,000 of depreciation expense deductions against the property. Gray will provide Fontenot with $10,000 of cash today and provide a $100,000 note that will pay Fontenot $50,000 one year from now and $50,000 two years from now.

    a) What gain does Fontenot realize on the sale?

    b) What is the amount and character of the gain that Fontenot must recognize in the year of sale (if any) and each of the two subsequent years? (*Hint:* Use the Internal Revenue Code and start with §453; please give appropriate citations.)

tax forms

71. Moab Inc. manufactures and distributes high-tech biking gadgets. It has decided to streamline some of its operations so that it will be able to be more productive and efficient. Because of this decision it has entered into several transactions during the year.

    Part (1) Determine the gain/loss realized and recognized in the current year for each of these events. Also determine whether the gain/loss recognized will be §1231, capital, or ordinary.

    a) Moab Inc. sold a machine that it used to make computerized gadgets for $27,300 cash. It originally bought the machine for $19,200 three years ago and has taken $8,000 depreciation.

    b) Moab Inc. held stock in ABC Corp., which had a value of $12,000 at the beginning of the year. That same stock had a value of $15,230 at the end of the year.

    c) Moab Inc. sold some of its inventory for $7,000 cash. This inventory had a basis of $5,000.

d) Moab Inc. disposed of an office building with a fair market value of $75,000 for another office building with a fair market value of $55,000 and $20,000 in cash. It originally bought the office building seven years ago for $62,000 and has taken $15,000 in depreciation.

e) Moab Inc. sold some land held for investment for $28,000. It originally bought the land for $32,000 two years ago.

f) Moab Inc. sold another machine for a note payable in four annual installments of $12,000. The first payment was received in the current year. It originally bought the machine two years ago for $32,000 and has claimed $9,000 in depreciation expense against the machine.

g) Moab Inc. sold stock it held for eight years for $2,750. It originally purchased the stock for $2,100.

h) Moab Inc. sold another machine for $7,300. It originally purchased this machine six months ago for $9,000 and has claimed $830 in depreciation expense against the asset.

Part (2) From the recognized gains/losses determined in part 1, determine the net §1231 gain/loss and the net ordinary gain/loss Moab will recognize on its tax return. Moab Inc. also has $2,000 of nonrecaptured net §1231 losses from previous years.

Part (3) Complete Moab Inc.'s Form 4797 for the year. Use the most current form available.

72. Vertovec Inc., a large local consulting firm in Utah, hired several new consultants from out of state last year to help service their expanding list of clients. To aid in relocating the consultants, Vertovec Inc. purchased the consultants' homes in their prior location if the consultants were unable to sell their homes within 30 days of listing them for sale. Vertovec Inc. bought the homes from the consultants for 5 percent less than the list price and then continued to list the homes for sale. Each home Vertovec Inc. purchased was sold at a loss. By the end of last year, Vertovec had suffered a loss totaling $250,000 from the homes. How should Vertovec treat the loss for tax purposes? Write a memo to Vertovec Inc. explaining your findings and any planning suggestions that you may have if Vertovec Inc. continues to offer this type of relocation benefit to newly hired consultants.

 research

73. WAR (We Are Rich) has been in business since 1983. WAR is an accrual method sole proprietorship that deals in the manufacturing and wholesaling of various types of golf equipment. Hack & Hack CPAs have filed accurate tax returns for WAR's owner since WAR opened its doors. The managing partner of Hack & Hack (Jack) has gotten along very well with the owner of WAR—Mr. Someday Woods (single). However, in early 2016, Jack Hack and Someday Woods played a round of golf and Jack, for the first time ever, actually beat Mr. Woods. Mr. Woods was so upset that he fired Hack & Hack and has hired you to compute his 2016 taxable income. Mr. Woods was able to provide you with the following information from prior tax returns. The taxable income numbers reflect the results from all of Mr. Wood's activities *except for the items separately stated*. You will need to consider how to handle the separately stated items for tax purposes. Also, note that the 2011–2015 numbers do not reflect capital loss carryovers.

 tax forms

	2011	2012	2013	2014	2015
Ordinary taxable income	$4,000	$2,000	$94,000	$170,000	$250,000
Other items not included in ordinary taxable income					
Net gain (loss) on disposition of §1231 assets	3,000	10,000		(6,000)	
Net long-term capital gain (loss) on disposition of capital assets	(15,000)	1,000	(7,000)		(7,000)

In 2016, Mr. Woods had taxable income in the amount of $460,000 *before* considering the following events and transactions that transpired in 2016:

a) On January 1, 2016, WAR purchased a plot of land for $100,000 with the intention of creating a driving range where patrons could test their new golf equipment. WAR never got around to building the driving range; instead, WAR sold the land on October 1, 2016, for $40,000.

b) On August 17, 2016, WAR sold its golf testing machine, "Iron Byron" and replaced it with a new machine "Iron Tiger." "Iron Byron" was purchased and installed for a total cost of $22,000 on February 5, 2012. At the time of sale, "Iron Byron" had an adjusted tax basis of $4,000. WAR sold "Iron Byron" for $25,000.

c) In the months October through December 2016, WAR sold various assets to come up with the funds necessary to invest in WAR's latest and greatest invention—the three dimple golf ball. Data on these assets are provided below:

Asset	Placed in Service (or purchased)	Sold	Initial Basis	Accumulated Depreciation	Selling Price
Someday's black leather sofa (used in office)	4/4/15	10/16/16	$ 3,000	$ 540	$ 2,900
Someday's office chair	3/1/14	11/8/16	8,000	3,000	4,000
Marketable securities	2/1/13	12/1/16	12,000	0	20,000
Land held for investment	7/1/15	11/29/16	45,000	0	48,000
Other investment property	11/30/14	10/15/16	10,000	0	8,000

d) Finally, on May 7, 2016, WAR decided to sell the building where they tested their plutonium shaft, lignite head drivers. WAR purchased the building on January 5, 2004, for $190,000 ($170,000 for the building, $20,000 for the land). At the time of the sale, the accumulated depreciation on the building was $50,000. WAR sold the building (with the land) for $300,000. The fair market value of the land at the time of sale was $45,000.

Part 1: Compute Mr. Woods's taxable income *after* taking into account the transactions described above.
Part 2: Compute Mr. Woods's tax liability for the year. (Ignore any net investment income tax for the year.)
Part 3: Complete Mr. Woods's Form 8949, Schedule D, and Form 4797 (use the most current version of these schedules) to be attached to his Form 1040. Assume that asset bases are not reported to the IRS.

74. Fizbo Corporation is in the business of breeding and racing horses. Fizbo has taxable income of $5,000,000 other than from these transactions. It has nonrecaptured §1231 losses of $10,000 from 2012 and $13,000 from 2010.

Consider the following transactions that occur during 2016:

a) A building with an adjusted basis of $300,000 is totally destroyed by fire. Fizbo receives insurance proceeds of $400,000, but does not plan to replace the building. The building was built 12 years ago at a cost of $420,000 and was used to provide lodging for employees.

b) Fizbo sells four acres of undeveloped farmland (used for grazing) for $50,000. Fizbo purchased the land 15 years ago for $15,000.

c) Fizbo sells a racehorse for $250,000. The racehorse was purchased four years ago for $200,000. Total depreciation taken on the racehorse was $160,000.

d) Fizbo exchanges equipment that was purchased three years ago for $300,000 for $100,000 of IBM common stock. The adjusted basis of the equipment is

$220,000. If straight-line depreciation had been used, the adjusted basis would be $252,000.

e) On November 1, Fizbo sold XCON stock for $50,000. Fizbo had purchased the stock on December 12, 2015 for $112,000.

Part 1: After ALL netting is complete, what is Fizbo's total amount of income from these transactions to be treated as ordinary income or loss? What is its capital gain or loss?

Part 2: What is Fizbo's taxable income for the year after including the effects of these transactions?

chapter
12

Compensation

Upon completing this chapter, you should be able to:

LO 12-1 Discuss and explain the tax implications of compensation in the form of salary and wages from the employee's and employer's perspectives.

LO 12-2 Describe and distinguish the tax implications of various forms of equity-based compensation from the employee's and employer's perspectives.

LO 12-3 Compare and contrast taxable and nontaxable fringe benefits and explain the employee and employer tax consequences associated with fringe benefits.

© Alija/iStock/Getty Images

Storyline Summary

Taxpayers:	Julie and Ethan Clark
Location:	San Diego, California
Employment status:	Julie—mid-level executive for Premier Computer Corporation (PCC); current salary $240,000 Ethan—mechanical engineer; current salary $70,000
Filing status:	Married filing jointly
Dependents:	Two children
Marginal ordinary tax rate:	40 percent
Current situation:	Julie is considering an offer for the vice president of marketing position with Technology Products Inc (TPI).

Julie and Ethan Clark and their two children have been settled into their life in San Diego, California, for some time. Julie has decided her career is at a crossroads. On the one hand, her employment as a mid-level executive for Premier Computer Corporation (PCC) is going well, but the work is not as challenging as it used to be. She suspects that, given her skills and abilities, she could put her career on the fast track with the right opportunity, engaging in more fulfilling work and gaining a significant increase in compensation.

Julie was sitting at her desk contemplating her career when she received yet another call from a corporate headhunter. While she usually quickly dismisses such calls, this time her interest and curiosity were piqued and she gave her full attention. He asked if she had any interest in a vice president of marketing position with a publicly traded company located nearby. After the headhunter answered a few of her questions, Julie gave him the go-ahead to set up an interview.

A couple of weeks later, Julie had been through two rounds of interviews for the marketing VP position when she received a call informing her that she was the one Technology Products Inc. (TPI) wanted for the job and that an offer letter with the details was on its way. The letter indicated TPI was offering a $280,000 salary (a significant increase from her current salary). TPI was also offering her a choice of certain types of equity-based compensation and some attractive fringe benefits. While excited by the letter, Julie knew she needed to learn more about the equity-based compensation alternatives and the other forms of compensation TPI was offering before she could adequately evaluate the offer and reach her decision.

to be continued . . .

As TPI's letter to Julie illustrates, employers are able to offer many different forms of compensation to employees. They can also pay some compensation now and defer some to the future. Each type of compensation has unique tax and nontax consequences.

This chapter addresses the tax and nontax consequences of *current* compensation packages from both the employee's and the employer's perspective. The next chapter addresses *future* or *deferred* compensation.

LO 12-1 ## SALARY AND WAGES

Current compensation paid to **employees** in the form of **salary** and **wages,** usually paid in cash, has tax consequences to both employees and employers. Below, we address the tax (and nontax) considerations of salary and wages from the employee's perspective followed by the employer's perspective.

Emwployee Considerations for Salary and Wages

Employees receiving salary generally earn a fixed amount of compensation for the year no matter how many hours they work. In addition, salaried employees may be eligible for bonuses based on satisfying certain criteria. In contrast, employees receiving wages generally get paid by the hour. Salary, bonus, and wages are taxed to employees as ordinary income. Employees generally report income from salary and wages as they receive it.[1] As we discussed in detail in Chapter 8, employees must pay **FICA taxes** on their wages.[2] FICA tax consists of both a Social Security and a Medicare component.

At the end of each year, employees receive a **Form W-2** (see Exhibit 12-1) from their employers summarizing their salary or wage compensation and the various withholding amounts made during the year.[3] Employees simply report their wages on Page 1, line 7 of the 1040 federal tax return and report their federal income taxes withheld on line 64 of Page 2. Self-employed taxpayers receive a Form 1099 indicating the compensation they received, which they report on Schedule C.

Tax Withholding When employees begin employment with a firm, they complete a **Form W-4** to supply the information the firm needs in order to withhold the correct amount of tax from each paycheck. Specifically, employees use Form W-4 to indicate (1) whether to withhold at the single rate or at the lower married rate, (2) the number of withholding allowances the employee chooses to claim (the more withholding allowances claimed, the less the withholding amount), and (3) whether the employee wants an additional amount of tax withheld each period above the amount based on the number of allowances claimed.

Employer Considerations for Salary and Wages

> **THE KEY FACTS**
>
> **Employment-Related Forms**
>
> - **Form W-2**
>   - Summarizes an employee's taxable salary and wages.
>   - Provides annual federal and state withholding information.
>   - Generated by employer on an annual basis.
> - **Form W-4**
>   - Supplies an employee's withholding information to employer.
>   - Generated by employee.
>   - Numbers reported on form remain constant unless employee makes changes.
> - **Form 1099**
>   - Summarizes an independent contractor's or nonemployee's taxable compensation.
>   - Generated by person or entity paying the compensation.

Storyline Summary	
Taxpayer:	TPI Corporation
Location:	San Diego, California
Ownership:	Publicly traded corporation
Industry:	Manufacturer of high-technology products
CEO:	Daniel Hewitt
Marginal tax rate:	35 percent
Current Situation:	Recruiting Julie Clark for VP of marketing position

[1]Reg. §1.451-1(a).

[2]FICA stands for Federal Insurance Contributions Act.

[3]Compensation received by taxpayers who are self-employed is not considered to be salary and wages.

EXHIBIT 12-1   **The 2016 Form W-2 was unavailable at press time. Please visit the IRS website (www.irs.gov) for the final 2015 form.**

a Employee's social security number	OMB No. 1545-0008	Safe, accurate, FAST! Use IRS e-file Visit the IRS website at www.irs.gov/efile
b Employer identification number (EIN)		**1** Wages, tips, other compensation / **2** Federal income tax withheld
c Employer's name, address, and ZIP code		**3** Social security wages / **4** Social security tax withheld
		5 Medicare wages and tips / **6** Medicare tax withheld
		7 Social security tips / **8** Allocated tips
d Control number		**9** / **10** Dependent care benefits
e Employee's first name and initial Last name Suff.		**11** Nonqualified plans / **12a** See instructions for box 12
	13 Statutory employee Retirement plan Third-party sick pay	**12b**
	14 Other	**12c**
		12d
f Employee's address and ZIP code		

15 State Employer's state ID number	**16** State wages, tips, etc.	**17** State income tax	**18** Local wages, tips, etc.	**19** Local income tax	**20** Locality name

Form **W-2** Wage and Tax Statement   **2015**   Department of the Treasury—Internal Revenue Service

Copy B—To Be Filed With Employee's FEDERAL Tax Return.
This information is being furnished to the Internal Revenue Service.

Deductibility of Salary Payments   Employers computing taxable income under the cash method of accounting generally deduct salary and wages when they pay the employee.[4] Employers computing taxable income under the accrual method generally deduct wages payable to employees as the employees earn the wages.[5] This general rule holds even in situations when the employer accrues compensation expense in one year but actually pays the employee in the subsequent year, as long as the company makes the payment within 2½ months after the employer's year-end. If the employer pays the employee more than 2½ months after the employer's year-end, the wages are considered deferred compensation and are not deductible by the employer until the employee recognizes the salary as income (receives payment).[6] Because most employers pay regular salary and wages to employees each month (or more frequently), the 2½-month rule is likely to be more of an issue for accrued compensation, such as one-time year-end bonuses, than it is for normal wages.

In situations when the employer and employee are "related" parties, special rules apply. In this context, the definition of related parties includes an employee/shareholder who owns more than 50 percent of the value of the employer corporation.[7] When the corporation and employee/shareholder are related parties, a

> **THE KEY FACTS**
>
> **Compensation Deductibility for Accrual-Basis Taxpayers**
>
> - Compensation expense accrued at end of year is deductible in year accrued if
>   - Paid to an *unrelated* party within 2½ months of year-end.
> - Compensation expense accrued at end of year is not *deductible when paid* if
>   - Paid to *related* party owning > 50 percent of corporate employer.

[4]Reg. §1.461-1(a)(1).

[5]Reg. §1.461-1(a)(2). See Chapter 9 for a detailed discussion of the cash and accrual accounting methods.

[6]Reg. §1.404(b)-1T(A-2). We discuss tax issues and consequences relating to deferred compensation in Chapter 13.

[7]See §267(b) for the complete definition of "related" parties.

corporation is not allowed to deduct the compensation expense until the employee/shareholder (related party) includes the payment in income.[8] Therefore, for an accrual-method company paying compensation, such as wages or a bonus, to a related employee, the 2½-month rule does not apply. Because related parties are theoretically considered to be the same taxpayer to some extent, the tax laws limit the corporation's ability to accelerate deductions and enjoy the immediate tax benefits, while at the same time permitting the employee a deferral of income and delaying the payment of taxes.

The after-tax cost of providing this salary is generally much less than the before-tax cost.[9] The formula for computing the after-tax cost of the salary (the cost after subtracting the tax savings from the deduction), or any deductible expense, for that matter, is as follows:

$$\text{Deductible expenditure} \times (1 - \text{Marginal tax rate})$$

Example 12-1

What is PCC's before-tax and after-tax costs of paying Julie a $240,000 salary? (Note that PCC's marginal tax rate is 35 percent.)

Answer: $240,000 before taxes and $156,000 after taxes, computed as follows:

Description	Amount	Explanation
Before tax cost of salary:		
(1) Compensation	$240,000	
(2) (1 − marginal tax rate)	× 65%	(1 − 35%).
After-tax cost of salary	**$156,000**	(1) × (2).

TAXES IN THE REAL WORLD Are CEOs Rewarded for Tax Dodging?

In 2011, the Institute for Policy Studies reported that 25 U.S. companies paid their CEOs more than they paid the U.S. government in taxes. The list of companies includes: International Paper, General Electric, Verizon, Boeing, and Ford Motor Company. On average, the companies reported $1.6 billion in profits and $16.7 million in executive compensation. In total, the companies also reported 556 subsidiaries located in tax havens, $12.6 million in campaign contributions, and $129 million in lobbying expenditures (campaign contributions and lobbying expenditures are nondeductible for tax). On average, these CEOs were paid $5.9 million more than the average of CEOs comprising the S&P 500.

Limits on salary deductibility. Employers are generally allowed to deduct reasonable compensation paid to employees.[10] Determining whether compensation is reasonable in amount is a **facts and circumstances test** that involves considering the duties of the employee, the complexities of the business, and the amount of salary

---

[8]§267(a)(2).

[9]As discussed in Chapter 8, employers are required to pay FICA taxes on employees' compensation. Employers may also be required to pay other expenses based on employee wages such as workers' compensation insurance.

[10]As we discussed in Chapter 9, all business expenses (not just compensation) must be reasonable in amount to be fully deductible.

compared with the income of the business among other things. The amount of salary in excess of the amount considered reasonable is not deductible. The reasonable compensation limit typically applies to closely held businesses where the employee is also an owner of the company or the employee is a relative of the business owner. For publicly traded corporations, another limitation applies that is generally more restrictive than the reasonableness limitation.

Responding to a growing public perception that executives of publicly traded corporations were being overpaid at the expense of shareholders and that the government was subsidizing (paying a part of) the excess by allowing corporations to deduct the high salaries, in 1993 Congress enacted §162(m) of the Internal Revenue Code.[11] This provision limits the deduction for compensation paid by publicly traded corporations to covered employees to $1 million per year. Covered employees include the principal executive officer (CEO) and the next three highest paid officers [not including the principal financial officer (CFO)].[12] However, certain exceptions allow companies to pay and deduct compensation in excess of the $1 million limit. For example, the limit does not apply to compensation based on (1) performance (this is the most significant of the exceptions in terms of dollars and frequency of application), (2) commissions, (3) contributions to qualified retirement plans, or (4) other tax-free benefits.

While most publicly traded corporations are aware of and are sensitive to the limitation, they may take different approaches in dealing with it. For example, as described in the excerpt from its proxy statement (see Exhibit 12-2), Callaway Golf attempts to maximize its compensation deduction, yet it acknowledges that there are situations when, in order to achieve its nontax goals, it may provide compensation to executives that is not deductible.

THE KEY FACTS

Limits on Salary Deductibility of Publicly Traded Corporations
- $1,000,000 maximum annual compensation deduction per person.
  - Limit applies to CEO and three other highest compensated officers (not including the CFO).
  - Does not apply to performance-based compensation.

EXHIBIT 12-2   Excerpt from Callaway Golf's 2015 Proxy Statement

The tax deductibility of compensation should be maximized where appropriate.
In designing and approving the Company's executive compensation plans, the Compensation Committee considers the effect of all applicable tax regulations, including Section 162(m) of the Internal Revenue Code of 1986, as amended (the "Code"), which generally disallows a tax deduction to public corporations for nonqualifying compensation in excess of $1.0 million paid to the chief executive officer or certain of the Company's other executive officers. Although maximizing the tax deductibility of compensation is an important consideration, the Compensation Committee may from time to time approve compensation that does not qualify for deductibility where it is appropriate to do so in light of other compelling interests or objectives. In addition, because of ambiguities and uncertainties as to the application and interpretation of Section 162(m) and related regulations, and the fact that such regulations and interpretations may change from time to time (with potentially retroactive effect), no assurance can be given that compensation intended to satisfy the requirements for deductibility under Section 162(m) will in fact do so.

In contrast, State Street Corporation takes a slightly different approach. As indicated in the following excerpt from its proxy statement (see Exhibit 12-3), State Street caps its salaries at $1 million. Apparently, the firm wants to make sure salaries paid to executives are fully deductible.

[11]Daniel Nelson, "Section 162(m) Revisited," *Tax Notes Today,* January 10, 2005, pp. 8–22.
[12]Notice 2007-49. Section 162(m) defines "covered employees" as the CEO and the four most highly compensated officers (as of the end of the year). In providing this definition, Section 162(m) references and relies on executive compensation rules provided in the Securities Exchange Act of 1934. In September of 2006, the SEC modified the executive compensation disclosure rules referenced in Section 162(m). Nevertheless, Section 162(m) has not been updated to reflect this change. To resolve the inconsistency in the definition of "covered employee" between the language in Section 162(m) and the modified executive compensation rules, the IRS issued Notice 2007-49.

EXHIBIT 12-3 **Excerpt from State Street Bank's 2015 Proxy Statement**

Tax Deductibility of Executive Compensation

Section 162(m) of the U.S. Internal Revenue Code, or Section 162(m), generally limits to $1 million the U.S. federal income tax deductibility of compensation paid in one year to any one of a group of specified employees, including our NEOs (other than our chief financial officer). Performance-based compensation is not subject to the limits on deductibility of Section 162(m), provided such compensation meets specified requirements, including shareholder approval of material terms of compensation. The Compensation Committee considers tax deductibility in making compensation decisions, to the extent deductibility is reasonably practicable and consistent with our other compensation objectives.

The difference in philosophy between Callaway and State Street may be driven by nontax considerations. To be deductible, compensation to executives in excess of $1 million generally must be performance-based. This means that the executives bear the risk that they won't receive the additional compensation if certain performance benchmarks, like stock-price targets, aren't met. Some companies may decide they don't want their executives to shoulder this risk, so they pay them salaries in excess of the deductible amount to guarantee a certain level of compensation. Companies may also decide to cap executive salaries at $1 million just to avoid the public perception that they are being fiscally irresponsible by paying more than the deductibility limits.

Example 12-2

Several years ago, TPI was actively searching for a new CEO. The board of directors eventually chose Daniel Hewitt. During negotiations, Daniel indicated he wanted a $2 million salary (Option 1) in addition to the equity-based compensation the board was offering. While this level of salary could be considered reasonable, the board of directors was concerned about the $1 million limitation on deductible salary, so the board offered an alternative proposal. Under this proposal, TPI would pay Daniel a $1 million salary and offer him an additional $1.2 million bonus, contingent on achieving realistic financial performance goals for TPI (Option 2). Confident he could meet the financial goals, Daniel accepted the offer. Assuming the performance goals are met, what is TPI's after-tax cost of providing the current-year compensation under Option 1 and Option 2?

Answer: $1,650,000 under Option 1 and $1,430,000 under Option 2, computed as follows:

	Option 1 ($2,000,000 salary $0 bonus)	Option 2 ($1,000,000 salary $1,200,000 bonus)	Explanation
Before-tax cost:			
(1) Total compensation	$2,000,000	$2,200,000	Salary + bonus.
(2) Deductible amount	$1,000,000	$2,200,000	Option 1: $1M salary not deductible.
(3) Marginal tax rate	× 35%	× 35%	
(4) Tax savings from compensation deduction	$ 350,000	$ 770,000	(2) × (3).
After-tax cost	$1,650,000	$1,430,000	(1) − (4).

Assuming the performance goals are met, both parties benefit from the arrangement. Daniel prefers Option 2 because it provides him with $200,000 more of before-tax compensation ($2.2M − $2M). TPI also prefers Option 2 because it costs $220,000 less after taxes than Option 1 ($1,650,000 − $1,430,000). Of course, Daniel is the one who must bear the risk of the contingent compensation in Option 2, so he must consider this risk before accepting the offer.

As this example illustrates, the $1 million deduction limitation can have a considerable impact on the after-tax cost of providing compensation to corporate executives. However, employers frequently utilize the options described above to craft offers that meet the needs of both parties.

EQUITY-BASED COMPENSATION   LO 12-2

continued from page 12-1 . . .

As she read TPI's offer letter more carefully, Julie discovered that on the first day of January following her acceptance of the offer, she would be granted 10,000 shares of restricted stock, 50 incentive stock options (ISOs), and 200 nonqualified options (NQOs). Each stock option gives her the right to purchase 100 shares of stock (50 ISOs allows up to 5,000 shares and 200 NQOs allows up to 20,000 shares) at a fixed price equal to the market value of TPI stock on the date of grant. As she read on, Julie noticed that she would not be able to exercise either type of stock option (i.e., purchase TPI stock for the exercise price stated in the options) until the options vested (the options become hers when they vest), which will be 2 years from the grant date. Further, Julie understood that, after the restricted stock vests (one year from the grant date on January 1), she would be free to do what she wanted with it. The last detail Julie noticed when reading this part of the offer letter was that both types of options will expire 10 years from the grant date. She understood this to mean that if she did not exercise her options sometime before their expiration date, she would lose them.

Although it was obvious to Julie that the value of the options and restricted stock would increase as the share price of TPI increased from the current share price of $5 per share, she remained unsure about the terminology used in this section of the letter, and she realized she needed to know more about the economic and tax implications of stock options and restricted stock before making her decision.

to be continued . . .

Equity-based compensation such as stock options and restricted stock provides risks and potential rewards not available with other forms of compensation. If the employer's stock price increases after it grants options and restricted stock, employees can be rewarded handsomely. On the other hand, if employer stock prices don't increase, the value of restricted stock will be limited and stock options will expire worthless.

Employers use equity-based compensation, in part, to motivate their employees to take ownership in their companies. When employees hold employer options and stock, their compensation is more directly tied to the fortunes of their employer and its shareholders—employees' compensation increases in tandem with their employer's stock price. This philosophy is reflected in an excerpt from Adobe's proxy statement presented in Exhibit 12-4.

EXHIBIT 12-4   **Excerpt from Adobe's 2015 Proxy Statement**

Goals of Equity Compensation

We use equity compensation to motivate and reward strong corporate performance and to retain valued executive officers. We also use equity incentive awards as a means to attract and recruit qualified executives. We believe that equity awards serve to align the interest of our named executive officers (NEOs) with those of our stockholders by rewarding them for stock price growth. By having a significant majority of our NEOs' target TDC payable in the form of multiyear equity and, thus, subject to higher risk and longer vesting than cash compensation, our NEOs are motivated to align themselves with our stockholders by taking actions that will benefit Adobe and its stockholders in the long term.

In addition to its motivational effects, equity-based compensation has traditionally brought employers cash flow benefits as well. How? Unless employers purchase their own stock in a market transaction to satisfy option exercises and stock grants, there are no cash outflows associated with this form of compensation. In fact, employers actually *receive* cash from their employees in the amount of the exercise price on the options exercised. There are a couple of downsides to this benefit, however. First, employers experience the opportunity cost of selling shares at a discounted price to employees rather than selling the shares at fair market value on the open market. Second, because employers must issue new shares to satisfy option exercises and stock grants, the total number of shares outstanding increases, and therefore, earnings per share are diluted, which is a detriment to existing shareholders. The only way for employers to mitigate this problem without increasing earnings is to use their cash reserves to acquire their own shares to satisfy the options exercise.[13] However, from a cash-flow perspective, this is no different than paying cash compensation.

Stock Options

As a form of equity-based compensation, stock options have two important characteristics: (1) employees must use cash to purchase the employer's stock once they are allowed to exercise the options and (2) employees often never exercise options when share prices are depressed. When stock options **vest,** employees are legally entitled to buy or exercise employer stock at a stipulated price, referred to as the **exercise price** or **strike price.** Options may be exercised anytime between the vesting date and the expiration date of the options.[14] If the share price does not go above the exercise price at some point during this interval,

[13]Because earnings per share is calculated by dividing earnings by the number of shares of stock outstanding, for a given level of earnings, earnings per share could even increase when new shares are issued to satisfy option exercises if earnings increase by an amount that more than offsets the effect of issuing new shares into the market.

[14]Vesting dates are frequently specified as future calendar dates or they may be triggered when certain events occur (i.e., predefined performance objectives are met, or the company has been sold).

EXHIBIT 12-5 Sample Timeline for Incentive and Nonqualified Options

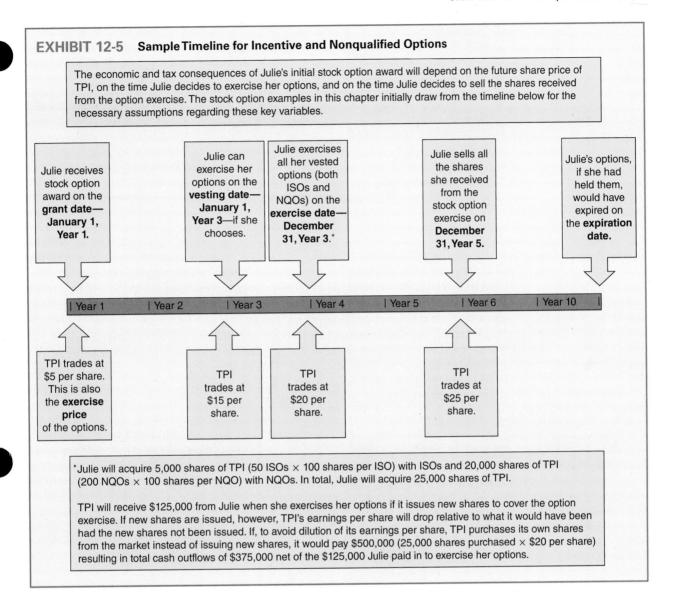

The economic and tax consequences of Julie's initial stock option award will depend on the future share price of TPI, on the time Julie decides to exercise her options, and on the time Julie decides to sell the shares received from the option exercise. The stock option examples in this chapter initially draw from the timeline below for the necessary assumptions regarding these key variables.

Julie receives stock option award on the **grant date—January 1, Year 1.**

Julie can exercise her options on the **vesting date—January 1, Year 3**—if she chooses.

Julie exercises all her vested options (both ISOs and NQOs) on the **exercise date—December 31, Year 3.***

Julie sells all the shares she received from the stock option exercise on **December 31, Year 5.**

Julie's options, if she had held them, would have expired on the **expiration date.**

| Year 1 | Year 2 | Year 3 | Year 4 | Year 5 | Year 6 | Year 10 |

TPI trades at $5 per share. This is also the **exercise price** of the options.

TPI trades at $15 per share.

TPI trades at $20 per share.

TPI trades at $25 per share.

*Julie will acquire 5,000 shares of TPI (50 ISOs × 100 shares per ISO) with ISOs and 20,000 shares of TPI (200 NQOs × 100 shares per NQO) with NQOs. In total, Julie will acquire 25,000 shares of TPI.

TPI will receive $125,000 from Julie when she exercises her options if it issues new shares to cover the option exercise. If new shares are issued, however, TPI's earnings per share will drop relative to what it would have been had the new shares not been issued. If, to avoid dilution of its earnings per share, TPI purchases its own shares from the market instead of issuing new shares, it would pay $500,000 (25,000 shares purchased × $20 per share) resulting in total cash outflows of $375,000 net of the $125,000 Julie paid in to exercise her options.

employees will not exercise their options and the options will expire without providing them any benefit.

As suggested in Exhibit 12-5, the future value of stock option awards will depend on the exercise price, the company's future share price, the exercise date of the options, and the timing for selling the shares received from the **option exercise.**

Example 12-3

Given the assumptions in the stock option timeline shown in Exhibit 12-5 (above), how much will it cost Julie to exercise all of her options at the end of year 3 (before taxes), and how much will she have if she were to immediately sell the acquired shares (before taxes)?[15]

(continued on page 12-10)

[15]According to the facts presented in Exhibit 12-5, Julie could have exercised her options as early as the vesting date for her options at the end of year 2. We assume she waits one year to exercise her options to better illustrate the implications of deferring the option exercise beyond the vesting date. In reality, it is quite common for employees to exercise their stock options on the vesting date.

Answer: $125,000 cost to exercise; $375,000 remaining after sale before taxes, calculated as follows:

Description	Amount	Explanation
(1) Shares acquired	25,000	(20,000 NQOs and 5,000 ISOs).
(2) Exercise price	$ 5	Exhibit 12-5.
(3) Cash needed to exercise	$125,000	(1) × (2).
(4) Market price	$ 20	Exhibit 12-5.
(5) Market value of shares	$500,000	(1) × (4).
Net proceeds upon sale	$375,000	(5) − (3).

If, in the prior example, Julie didn't have enough cash on hand to cover the $125,000 cost of exercising the options, she could simultaneously exercise the options and sell the stock, using $125,000 of the proceeds from the stock sale to pay for exercising the options. This so-called **cashless exercise** is typically facilitated using the services of an employer-provided stockbroker.

An employee who uses options to purchase shares experiences an increase in net worth equal to the difference between the exercise price and the market value of the acquired shares on the date of exercise. This difference is called the **bargain element.** In Example 12-3, the bargain element is $15 per share and the total bargain element is $375,000 (25,000 shares × $15 per share).

Example 12-4

What if: What is Julie's economic loss from her stock options if the TPI shares fall to $3 per share and remain there after the options are granted?

Answer: Zero. If TPI's stock price never increases above the $5 per share exercise price before the expiration date of the options, Julie would never exercise her options to purchase TPI shares, and those options would expire worthless.

Employee Considerations for Stock Options   Stock options are classified for tax purposes as either **nonqualified stock options** (NQOs) or **incentive stock options** (ISOs). They differ in terms of when and how the bargain element is taxed. To appreciate these differences, it's important to understand what happens on the **grant date,** the **vesting date,** the **exercise date,** and the date the shares are ultimately sold.

For either type of option, employees experience no tax consequences on the grant date and vesting date. However, when they exercise *nonqualified* stock options, employees report ordinary income equal to the total bargain element on the shares of stock acquired (as if they were sold)—whether they hold the shares or sell them immediately.[16] A taxpayer's basis in nonqualified stock options acquired is the fair market value on the date of exercise. Thus the basis includes the exercise price plus the ordinary income the taxpayer recognizes on the exercise (the bargain element). In contrast, when *incentive* stock options are exercised, employees don't report any income for regular tax purposes (as long as they don't immediately sell

---

[16]The bargain element income is reflected on employees' Form W-2 and the applicable income and payroll taxes are withheld.

their shares). Their basis in shares acquired with ISOs is the exercise price. The holding period for stock shares acquired with NQOs and ISOs begins on the exercise date.

When taxpayers exercise incentive stock options, the bargain element is added to their alternative minimum taxable income. This increases the likelihood that taxpayers exercising incentive stock options will be required to pay the alternative minimum tax—this is almost always true if the bargain element is large. We discuss the alternative minimum tax in Chapter 8.

Example 12-5

On the date Julie exercises her options (Example 12-3), she acquires 20,000 shares of TPI with NQOs (200 NQOs × 100 shares per NQO) and 5,000 shares with ISOs (50 ISOs × 100 shares per ISO). Given that the bargain element for each share she purchased is $15, how much income will Julie report on the day she exercises the options?

Answer: $300,000 ordinary income from the NQOs, calculated below, and $0 for the ISOs (she must include the bargain element of $75,000 on the 5,000 ISOs in her AMT calculation).

Description	Amount	Explanation
(1) Shares acquired with NQOs	20,000	
(2) Market price per share	$ 20	Exhibit 12-5.
(3) Exercise price	5	Exhibit 12-5.
(4) Bargain element per share	$ 15	(2) − (3).
Bargain element (ordinary income)	$300,000	(1) × (4).

What is Julie's basis in the 20,000 shares she acquired with NQOs?

Answer: $400,000. [$100,000 (20,000 shares × $5 per share exercise price) + $300,000 (bargain element taxed as ordinary income).]

What is Julie's basis in the 5,000 shares she acquired through ISOs?

Answer: $25,000 is the regular tax basis (5,000 shares acquired × $5 per share exercise price). $100,000 is the AMT basis ($25,000 regular tax basis + the $75,000 bargain element).

Once they've exercised their stock options, employees face different choices depending on the type of option. Employees who purchase stock with NQOs and retain the stock are in the same position for tax purposes as any other investor: Their basis in the stock is the fair market value on the date they exercised the options (this is the exercise price of the stock plus the bargain element), and any *future* appreciation or depreciation of the stock will be treated for tax purposes as either short-term or long-term capital gain(s) or loss(es) depending on the holding period, which begins on the date of exercise. Moreover, employees using NQOs to purchase employer stock are also in the same economic position as any other investor in that the value of the stock is subject to investment risk (the risk that the value of the stock will go down). To avoid overweighting their investment portfolios with a single stock, employees exercising NQOs often immediately sell all or a significant portion of the shares acquired on the exercise date, a practice referred to as a cashless exercise or **same-day sale.**[17]

---

[17]In addition to limiting investment risk, employees also engage in same-day sales to cover all or a portion of the exercise price associated with the options exercised, to pay the taxes triggered when nonqualified options are exercised, and to fund planned purchases.

Example 12-6

THE KEY FACTS

Nonqualified Stock Options (NQOs)

- No tax consequences on grant date.
- On exercise date, bargain element is treated as ordinary (compensation) income to employee.
  - Employee holds stock with holding period beginning on date of exercise.
- Employers deduct bargain element as compensation expense on exercise date.

What if: Suppose that five years after Julie exercised her NQOs and acquired 20,000 TPI shares with a basis of $20 per share, she sold all of the shares for $25 per share. What is the amount and character of the gain she will recognize on the sale?

Answer: $100,000 long-term capital gain, calculated as follows:

Description	Amount	Explanation
(1) Amount realized (sale proceeds)	$500,000	(20,000 × $25).
(2) Tax basis	400,000	Example 12-5.
Long-term capital gain recognized	$100,000	(1) − (2).

What if: If Julie sold the shares for $25 per share six months after she exercised them, what is the character of the $100,000 gain she recognized on the sale?

Answer: Short-term capital gain because she held the shares for one year or less before selling.

Employees who acquire shares through the exercise of ISOs also have an additional tax benefit: If they hold such shares *for at least two years after the grant date and one year after the exercise date,* they will not be taxed until they sell the stock.[18] When they sell, employees will treat the difference between the sale proceeds and the tax basis (the exercise price) as a long-term capital gain in the year of disposition. Thus, employees prefer ISOs to NQOs.

Example 12-7

What if: Suppose that five years after Julie exercised her ISOs and acquired 5,000 TPI shares with a basis of $5 per share, she sold all of the shares for $25 per share. What is the amount and character of the gain she will recognize on the sale?

Answer: Julie will recognize a $100,000 long-term capital gain, calculated as follows:

Description	Amount	Explanation
(1) Amount realized	$125,000	(5,000 × $25).
(2) Tax basis	25,000	Example 12-5.
Long-term capital gain recognized	$100,000	(1) − (2).

If the two-year and one-year requirements are not met, the premature sale of stock is classified as a **disqualifying disposition,** and the bargain element is taxed at the time of sale *as if* the option had been an NQO. Thus, when holders of ISOs execute same-day sales, they forgo the benefit of taxing the bargain element at lower capital gains rates—but they do so in order to eliminate the investment risk they would otherwise have to bear if they attempted to satisfy the two-year from grant date and one-year from exercise holding period requirements.

Example 12-8

What if: Assume that Julie exercised her ISOs and executed a same-day sale of the 5,000 shares on the vesting date (January 1, year 3) when the share price was $15. What is the amount and character of income she will recognize on these transactions?

[18]§422(a)(1).

Answer: $50,000 ordinary income. Because Julie's sale is a disqualifying disposition, the transactions are recast as though she exercised nonqualified options. See computations below.

Description	Amount	Explanation
(1) Shares acquired with ISOs that were disqualified (became NQOs)	5,000	
(2) Market price per share	$ 15	
(3) Exercise price	5	Exhibit 12-5.
(4) Bargain element per share	$ 10	(2) − (3).
Bargain element (ordinary income)	$50,000	(1) × (4).

TAXES IN THE REAL WORLD   Stock Options

Sometimes, stock option compensation is the icing on the cake. Other times, options are the entire cake. According to Oracle Corporation's 2015 proxy statement, it paid founder and CEO Larry Ellison an annual salary of $1 in cash ($1 is not a misprint) and stock options worth more than $63 million. No need to pay taxes on the compensation now; once the shares vest, Mr. Ellison can choose when to exercise the shares and, consequently, time his tax payments as well.

Source: Oracle Corporation 2015 Proxy Statement.

Employer Considerations for Stock Options   As is true for employees, an employer's tax treatment of stock options depends on whether the options are NQOs or ISOs.

Nonqualified options.   With NQOs, employers deduct the bargain element that employees recognize as income when the employees exercise the NQOs. From the employer's perspective, no other date is relevant for tax purposes.

Example 12-9

What if: Suppose that in year 3, Julie exercises NQOs to acquire 20,000 shares of TPI, and she reports $300,000 of ordinary income for the bargain element of the exercise (see Example 12-5). How much compensation expense for Julie's stock option exercise can TPI deduct in year 3?

Answer: $300,000. TPI can deduct the bargain element of Julie's exercise.

Note that this tax deduction is not tied to a cash payment. Thus, unless employers purchase their own shares to satisfy their employees' stock option exercises, they'll be entitled to a tax deduction without incurring any cash outflow.

Another important tax benefit associated with NQOs derives from the fact that income from NQOs is usually viewed as performance-based compensation. As a result, employers frequently use these options to circumvent the $1,000,000 deduction limitation imposed by §162(m). In fact, the stock option income of key executives at publicly traded companies usually dwarfs their cash salaries.

Incentive stock options.   Employers typically don't view incentive stock options as favorably as NQOs, because (1) ISOs don't provide them with the same tax benefits (no tax deduction) and (2) the IRS regulatory requirements for ISOs can be cumbersome. That is, as long as the employee doesn't sell the stock in a disqualifying disposition, the employer does not get a tax deduction for ISOs. For this reason, employers with high marginal tax rates may lose significant tax benefits by issuing ISOs rather than NQOs. On the other hand, start-up companies or employers with net operating losses may actually benefit by issuing ISOs instead of NQOs. Due to their low or nonexistent marginal tax rates, companies in this position may not lose tax benefits by granting ISOs; however, because of the potential tax benefits ISOs provide to their employees relative to NQOs, they may be able to persuade their employees to accept relatively fewer ISOs.

ETHICS

Many companies use stock options as a form of equity compensation—to motivate executives and key employees. Some stock option issuers have either backdated and/or repriced stock options. Backdating is an illegal practice where a company, after-the-fact, chooses a date (timed retroactively) where the stock price was at its lowest point in order to maximize executive compensation. Stock option repricing is used when stock options are underwater (the market price is below the strike price). Repricing simply resets the strike price to a price below the current market price. While backdating options is illegal and obviously unethical, what do you think about the practice of repricing stock options?

Accounting issues. Historically, a major reason that companies used stock options to compensate their employees was the favorable accounting treatment stock options were afforded. Before 2006, companies were not required to reflect stock options as an expense in their financial statements. Thus, before 2006, companies that used stock options in lieu of cash salaries typically reported higher earnings than equally situated firms that were not heavy users of stock options. To increase the comparability of financial statements as well as to ensure that the true cost of stock options would be reflected in the financial statements, the FASB mandated the expensing of stock options for financial accounting purposes for years beginning on or after January 1, 2006.[19] Firms must measure the economic value of options on the grant date and then amortize this cost on a straight-line basis over the vesting period of the options.[20]

Example 12-10

THE KEY FACTS

Stock Option Expense: GAAP vs. Tax

- For tax purposes, employers deduct the bargain element of NQOs on exercise date but receive no tax deduction for ISOs unless they become disqualified.
- For GAAP purposes, employers expense the estimated value of the option pro rata over the vesting period.

What if: Assume that an accounting employee benefits specialist calculated the economic value of Julie's stock option grant (NQOs and ISOs) to be $32,000. Also assume that Julie's options vest 50 percent in year 1 (the year of the grant) and 50 percent in year 2. What compensation expense for book purposes would TPI report for Julie's stock options in year 1 and year 2?

Answer: $16,000 ($32,000 × 50%) in year 1 and $16,000 in year 2.

As you probably realize by now, the tax rules governing the treatment of stock options differ markedly from generally accepted accounting principles in terms of both the amount and the timing of the stock option expense. To compare the tax and book treatment, we present TPI's book expense and tax deduction resulting from its stock option grant to Julie (given prior assumptions) in Exhibit 12-6.

The tremendous difference between the book and tax numbers presented in Exhibit 12-6 is driven by the increase in TPI's share price, from $5 on the date of

[19]Accounting Standards Codification (ASC) 718, Stock Compensation.

[20]Although the exercise price of compensatory stock options typically equals the stock price on the date of grant, compensatory options are, nevertheless, economically valuable on the grant date. They have economic value because the stock price may eventually exceed the exercise price before the options expire. To determine economic value, firms typically use either the Black-Scholes option pricing model or the binomial option pricing model.

EXHIBIT 12-6 TPI's Tax Deductions and Book Expense from Stock Option Grant to Julie

	Tax Deduction if Stock Price Increases	Tax Deduction if Stock Price Decreases	Book Expense
Year 1	$ 0	$0	$16,000
Year 2	0	0	16,000
Year 3	300,000	0*	0

*There would be no exercise because the exercise price exceeds the stock price.

grant to $20 on the date of exercise. The economic valuation of the stock options used to determine the book expense did not anticipate the extent of the stock appreciation before exercise.

Restricted Stock

Like stock options described above, **restricted stock** can't be sold or otherwise treated as owned by employees until they legally have the right to sell the shares on the vesting date. However, unlike the stock acquired through options exercises, employees receive restricted stock on the vesting date *without having to pay for it,* after which they can either sell it immediately or retain it.

As indicated in the timeline in Exhibit 12-7, the initial value of an employee's restricted stock award depends on the share price of the stock on the vesting date.

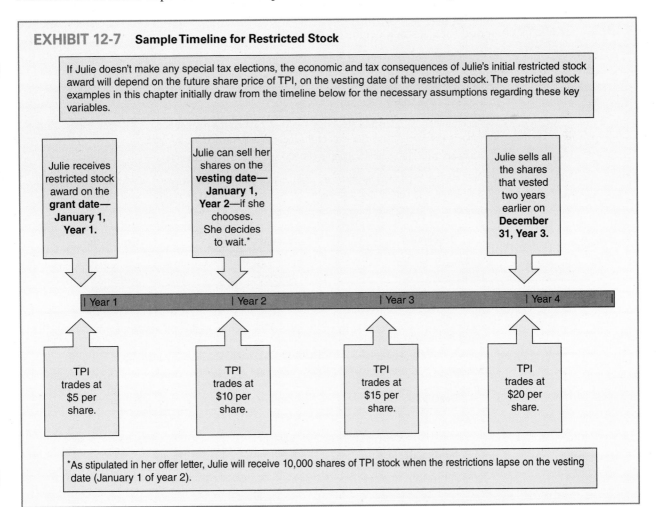

EXHIBIT 12-7 Sample Timeline for Restricted Stock

If Julie doesn't make any special tax elections, the economic and tax consequences of Julie's initial restricted stock award will depend on the future share price of TPI, on the vesting date of the restricted stock. The restricted stock examples in this chapter initially draw from the timeline below for the necessary assumptions regarding these key variables.

Julie receives restricted stock award on the **grant date— January 1, Year 1.**

Julie can sell her shares on the **vesting date— January 1, Year 2**—if she chooses. She decides to wait.*

Julie sells all the shares that vested two years earlier on **December 31, Year 3.**

| Year 1 | Year 2 | Year 3 | Year 4 |

TPI trades at $5 per share.

TPI trades at $10 per share.

TPI trades at $15 per share.

TPI trades at $20 per share.

*As stipulated in her offer letter, Julie will receive 10,000 shares of TPI stock when the restrictions lapse on the vesting date (January 1 of year 2).

Example 12-11

Given the assumptions regarding the restricted stock in Exhibit 12-7, by how much would Julie's wealth increase on the vesting date?

Answer: Julie's wealth would increase by $100,000 (10,000 shares × $10 per share).

What if: Assuming that the stock decreased to $3 per share on the vesting date, by how much would Julie's wealth increase or decrease on the vesting date?

Answer: $30,000 increase ($3 × 10,000). Until the vesting date, Julie was not entitled to any economic benefit from the restricted stock. On the vesting date, however, she is entitled to stock valued at $30,000. Thus, the vesting of Julie's restricted stock increases her wealth even if the stock price decreases between the grant date and vesting date (unlike options that would be worthless).

Employee Considerations for Restricted Stock Restricted stock is taxed like NQOs with two important distinctions: While employees receiving NQOs are taxed at ordinary rates on the bargain element of the shares when they exercise their options, employees receiving restricted stock are taxed on the *full fair market value* of the shares *on the date the restricted stock vests.* They are taxed on the fair market value of the stock because they are entitled to receive the stock without any payment requirements (contrast this with the exercise price paid for stock options). Any subsequent appreciation in the value of the stock is taxed as either long-term or short-term capital gain(s) or loss(es) when the taxpayer sells the stock, depending on the holding period and future movement of the stock price. The employee's holding period for the stock begins on the vesting date.

Example 12-12

Assume that the restricted stock vests in year 2 when the market price is $10 (see Exhibit 12-7). What is the amount and character of the income Julie recognizes in year 2?

Answer: $100,000 ordinary income (10,000 shares × $10 per share).

Assume the same facts as above and that Julie sells the shares in year 4 when the market price is $20? What is the amount and character of the income she will recognize on the sale?

Answer: $100,000 long-term capital gain, calculated as follows:

Description	Amount	Explanation
(1) Amount realized	$200,000	10,000 shares × $20 per share.
(2) Tax basis	100,000	Gain recognized on vesting date.
Long-term capital gain	$100,000	(1) − (2).

What if: Assume the original facts except that Julie sells the shares in year 4 when the market price is $4. What is the amount and character of the gain or loss she recognizes on the sale?

Answer: $60,000 long-term capital loss, calculated as follows:

Description	Amount	Explanation
(1) Amount realized	$ 40,000	10,000 shares × $4 per share.
(2) Adjusted basis	100,000	Gain recognized on vesting date.
Long-term capital loss	($60,000)	(1) − (2).

§83(b) election.   The tax laws allow employees who receive restricted stock to make a tax election that can significantly change the tax consequences by treating the stock nearly the same as vested stock. Up until 30 days after the grant date, employees can make what is known as an **§83(b) election**; once made, however, this election is irrevocable. If the employee makes the §83(b) election, the value of the restricted stock is taxed on the grant date rather than the date on which the stock vests. The effect of the election is to accelerate the tax on the market value of the restricted shares—which, you'll recall from Chapter 3, is usually not desirable from a tax planning perspective. However, if the employee expects the share price to increase after the grant date, making the election converts subsequent stock value appreciation from ordinary income into long-term capital gain (which, assuming the shares are held for more than one year after the grant date, results in a preferential tax rate when the taxpayer sells the shares). Without the §83(b) election, the employee reports no income when the shares are granted, but is taxed on their fair market value at ordinary rates when the stock vests. With the §83(b) election, the employee simply pays tax at ordinary rates on the market value of the shares at the grant date.

> **THE KEY FACTS**
>
> **Restricted Stock *with* Section §83(b) Election**
>
> - On grant date, employee recognizes market value of stock as ordinary income.
> - Employee takes fair market value basis in stock.
> - Holding period for stock begins on grant date.
> - If employee never vests, no deduction for basis in stock.
> - Employer deducts value of stock on grant date.

Example 12-13

What if: How much tax on the restricted stock would Julie pay in year 1 if she does not make an §83(b) election?

Answer: $0. The stock has not vested yet so she has no income.

What if: How much tax on the restricted stock would Julie pay in year 1 if she makes an §83(b) election?

Answer: $20,000 [$50,000 ordinary income (10,000 shares × $5 per share) × 40 percent marginal ordinary tax rate].

What if: How much tax would Julie pay in year 2 on the restricted stock (the year the restricted stock vests) if she did *not* make an §83(b) election in year 1 (the stock is trading at $10 a share on the vesting date)?

Answer: $40,000 [$100,000 ordinary income (10,000 shares × $10 per share) × 40 percent marginal ordinary tax rate].

What if: How much tax would Julie pay in year 2 on the restricted stock if she made the §83(b) election in year 1?

Answer: $0. With the §83(b) election, Julie treated the stock as though it vested in year 1, not year 2, so she does not have a taxable event in year 2 when the stock actually vests.

What if: How much tax would Julie pay in year 4 on the restricted stock when she sells the stock for $20 a share (on December 31) if she did *not* make the §83(b) election in year 1?

Answer: $20,000 [$200,000 (10,000 × $20) – $100,000 tax basis (fair market value on vesting date in year 2) – $100,000. $100,000 × 20 percent long-term capital gains rate = $20,000].

What if: How much tax would Julie pay in year 4 on the restricted stock when she sells the stock for $20 a share (on December 31) if she made the §83(b) election in year 1?

Answer: $30,000 [$200,000 (10,000 × $20) – $50,000 tax basis (fair market value in year 1 when made §83(b) election) = $150,000. $150,000 × 20 percent long-term capital gains rate = $30,000].

Given the analyses above, what amount of taxes would Julie save by making the §83(b) election (ignore time value of money)?

(continued on page 12-18)

Answer: $10,000 ($50,000 with election; $60,000 without), computed as follows:

	Taxes Payable	
Description	**With Election**	**Without Election**
Year 1 taxes on ordinary income	$20,000	$ 0
Year 2 taxes on ordinary income	0	40,000
Year 4 taxes on long-term capital gains	30,000	20,000
Total taxes	**$50,000**	**$60,000**

Note that Julie reduces her taxable income because the election allowed her to convert $50,000 in income from ordinary income taxed at 40 percent into long-term capital gain taxed at 20 percent.

Also note that this computation overstates to some degree the benefits of making the §83(b) election because it ignores the time value of money. In order to have a greater portion of her gains taxed at the preferential capital gain rates, Julie gave up some tax deferral when she accelerated $50,000 of income from year 4 into year 1.

Employees making the §83(b) election essentially trade off some additional current tax now in order to convert ordinary income into a long-term capital gain later. Accordingly, the §83(b) election is advisable when the potential for growth in the stock value is high and the amount of additional current tax is manageable. If an employee makes an §83(b) election and then forfeits the stock for any reason, the employee cannot deduct the loss on the forfeiture.[21] Thus, the risk of making the election is that if the employee forfeits the stock, tax would have been paid on value never received.

Employer Considerations for Restricted Stock   Like the tax treatment of NQOs, the employer's deduction for restricted stock equals the amount of ordinary income reported by its employees. The timing of the deduction is determined by the employee's decision regarding the §83(b) election. If the employee makes an §83(b) election, the employer claims the deduction in the year the restricted stock is granted. Otherwise, the employer claims a deduction when the restrictions lapse. Some employers believe that restricted stock is a superior form of compensation to stock options. See Apple Inc.'s proxy statement in Exhibit 12-8.

EXHIBIT 12-8   **Excerpt from Apple Inc.'s 2015 Proxy Statement**

The Role of Long-Term Equity Awards

Emphasis on restricted stock units (RSUs). The Company has traditionally believed that long-term equity awards in the form of RSUs are the most effective way to attract and retain a talented executive team and align executives' interests with those of shareholders. Accordingly, the Company's executive compensation program in recent years has been weighted considerably toward long-term equity awards rather than cash compensation. The Company believes RSUs create incentives for performance and further align executives' interests with those of shareholders because an RSU's value increases or decreases in conjunction with the Company's stock price. As explained in more detail above, the Company is committed to including performance criteria in a portion of the equity awards it grants to executive officers in the future. At Mr. Cook's request, the Compensation Committee began this initiative in 2013 by amending his 2011 RSU award to include performance-based vesting conditions.

The accounting treatment for restricted stock is similar to the accounting treatment for stock options.[22] If restricted stock grants vest over time, the value of restricted stock on the *date of grant* is expensed pro rata over the vesting period.

[21]Reg. §1.83-2(a).
[22]ASC 718.

Example 12-14

What if: Given the assumptions in Exhibit 12-7, what amount can TPI deduct for tax purposes in year 1 and in year 2 assuming Julie does *not* make an §83(b) election?

Answer: $0 in year 1 and $100,000 in year 2 (10,000 shares of restricted stock vested × $10 per share market price at vesting date).

What if: What amount can TPI deduct in year 1 and in year 2 if Julie *does* make an §83(b) election?

Answer: $50,000 in year 1 (10,000 shares of restricted stock awarded × $5 per share market price on the grant date) and $0 in year 2.

What amount is TPI's compensation expense for financial accounting purposes for Julie's restricted stock in year 1 and in year 2?

Answer: $50,000 book expense in year 1. Because the value of Julie's restricted stock award on the date of grant is $50,000, TPI expenses the award on its books over the vesting period, which in this case is just one year (it has a one-year vesting period).

Equity-Based Compensation Summary

To summarize our discussion of the tax treatment of equity-based compensation, Exhibit 12-9 highlights the general tax treatment of NQOs, ISOs, and restricted stock on a per share basis from both employee and employer perspectives given an arbitrary time series of share prices. In addition to future share prices, the exhibit assumes options are exercisable for the share price on the grant date.

THE KEY FACTS

Restricted Stock Expense: GAAP vs. Tax

- For tax purposes, employers deduct the market value of stock when the employee recognizes income. For GAAP purposes, employers deduct the grant date value over the vesting period.

EXHIBIT 12-9   Reportable Income and Deductions from Equity-Based Compensation (for given time frame and stock prices)

	Party Affected	NQOs	ISOs	Restricted Stock
Grant date–year 1 Stock (exercise) price = $1/share	Employee Employer	No effect No effect	No effect No effect	No effect No effect
Vesting date–year 4 Stock price = $6/share	Employee Employer	No effect No effect	No effect No effect	$6/share ordinary income $6/share ordinary deduction
Exercise date for options–year 6 Stock price = $11/share	Employee Employer	$10/share ordinary income $10/share ordinary deduction	No effect* No effect	N/A N/A
Sale date–year 8 Stock price = $16/share	Employee Employer	$5/share LT capital gain No effect	$15/share LT capital gain No effect	$10/share Capital gain No effect

*$10 per share is included in alternative minimum taxable income.

FRINGE BENEFITS

LO 12-3

continued from page 12-7...
The final section of TPI's offer letter indicated Julie would receive fringe benefits in the form of health and dental insurance (value of $18,000), $750,000 of group-term life insurance, a biennial $30,000 automobile allowance, monthly parking, and a flexible spending account for medical expenses. ■

Employees generally receive most of their compensation in the form of cash salary or wages. However, employers often provide noncash benefits to employees in addition to their cash compensation. These **fringe benefits** range from the common (health insurance) to the exotic (use of a corporate aircraft). As a general rule, because fringe benefits are employee compensation, they are taxable to the employee on receipt. In fact, fringe benefits are specifically mentioned in the definition of gross income. As we indicated in Chapter 5, IRC §61(a) indicates that, "gross income means all income from whatever source derived, including . . . (1) Compensation for services, including fees, commissions, *fringe benefits,* and similar items (emphasis added)." This definition of income notwithstanding, the tax laws specifically *exclude* certain fringe benefits from an employee's gross income. Thus, some fringe benefits are taxable and others are not.

Taxable Fringe Benefits

Taxable fringe benefits are fringe benefits not specifically excluded from gross income. Congress views many of the taxable fringe benefits as luxuries and chooses not to subsidize them. Taxable fringe benefits include such things as below-market interest rate loans (see discussion in Chapter 5), gym memberships, season tickets to the local NBA team, an automobile allowance for a personal automobile, or anything else not specifically excluded by the tax laws. Employers generally provide taxable fringe benefits to executives and higher-salaried employees rather than to the rank-and-file employees.

Employee Considerations for Taxable Fringe Benefits   From an employee's perspective, taxable fringe benefits are treated just like cash. Employees recognize ordinary compensation income when they receive taxable benefits and, just as they do with salary, pay FICA taxes on the value of the benefit. As a result, taxable fringe benefits cost employees the amount of tax they must pay on the benefits.

Example 12-15

Julie's offer includes a biennial auto allowance of up to $30,000. That is, every other year, TPI will reimburse Julie for an automobile purchase up to $30,000. TPI provides this benefit to executives that interact with the public on a regular basis. Julie purchases a Toyota 4Runner with a retail price of $35,000. What tax is Julie required to pay if she uses the allowance to apply toward the purchase? What is Julie's after-tax cost of the automobile if her marginal tax rate is 40 percent (ignoring FICA taxes)?

Answer: $12,000 in income taxes and $17,000 after-tax cost, computed as follows:

Description	Amount	Explanation
(1) Fair market value of Toyota	$35,000	
(2) Automobile allowance	30,000	Taxable fringe benefit.
(3) Julie's additional cost	5,000	(1) − (2).
(4) Income tax on allowance	12,000	(2) × 40%.
Total after-tax cost	$17,000	(3) + (4).

From Julie's perspective, this is a pretty good deal—particularly if she was willing to pay the market price for the car.

Employees may prefer a taxable benefit to an equivalent amount of cash when they benefit from employer-provided quantity or group discounts associated with the benefit. For example, many companies provide (pay premiums for) **group-term life insurance** as a fringe benefit, in part, because they can purchase the insurance at a lower rate than employees can purchase it individually. However, employees must recognize a certain amount of gross income when employers pay life insurance premiums for the employee for policies with a death benefit in excess of $50,000.[23] Consequently, a portion of the group-term life insurance benefit is taxable and a portion is nontaxable. In these circumstances, the employer determines the employee's taxable amount using a table provided in the Treasury Regulations. An excerpt of this table is provided in Exhibit 12-10.[24] To compute the annual taxable benefit, taxpayers use the following steps:

Step 1: Subtract $50,000 from the death benefit of their employer-provided group-term life insurance policy.

Step 2: Divide the Step 1 result by $1,000.

Step 3: Multiply the result from Step 2 by the cost per $1,000 of protection for one month from the table (Exhibit 12-10) based on the taxpayer's age.

Step 4: Multiply the outcome of Step 3 by the number of months the benefit was received during the taxable year.

EXHIBIT 12-10 Uniform Premiums for $1,000 of Group-Term Life Insurance Protection

5-Year Age Bracket	Cost per $1,000 of Protection for One Month
Under 25	$0.05
25 to 29	.06
30 to 34	.08
35 to 39	.09
40 to 44	.10
45 to 49	.15
50 to 54	.23
55 to 59	.43
60 to 64	.66
65 to 69	1.27
70 and above	2.06

Example 12-16

Julie's offer from TPI includes $750,000 of group-term life insurance. TPI's cost to provide Julie the insurance is $500 per year. If Julie were to purchase the insurance herself she would pay $2,000 per year. Assume that Julie is 37 years old. Based on the Treasury's table (see Exhibit 12-10), the monthly premium per $1,000 of insurance is $.09. What is Julie's taxable compensation from receiving the group-term life benefit? What does this benefit cost Julie (ignoring FICA taxes)?

(continued on page 12-22)

[23]§79.
[24]Reg. §1.79-3(d)(2) provides an age-based table and instructions to calculate the employee's includable amount.

Answer: $756 of taxable compensation and $302 cost (all taxes). Julie's cost is the income and Medicare taxes she must pay on the compensation, calculated as follows:

Group-Term Life Insurance Description	Amount	Explanation
(1) Insurance coverage	$750,000	Provided by employer.
(2) Excluded coverage	(50,000)	Nontaxable portion.
(3) Taxable benefit	$700,000	(1) + (2) (Step 1).
(4) Divide by 1,000	1,000	Divide by 1,000 (Step 2).
(5) Result of Step 2	700	(3)/(4).
(6) Monthly cost per $1,000	× 0.09	Taxable portion per $1,000 from Exhibit 12-10.
(7) Monthly benefit	$ 63	(5) × (6), (Step 3).
(8) Months	× 12	Annualize monthly taxable amount.
(9) Annual taxable benefit	$ 756	(7) × (8), (Step 4).
Income taxes	$ 302	(9) × 40%.

Note that Julie's income is not based on TPI's actual cost ($500) of providing the policy.

Taxpayers receiving taxable fringe benefits may experience some financial strain because they must pay the tax on the benefits. Frequently, when corporations provide taxable fringe benefits to senior executives, they also provide the executives enough cash to cover the taxes so the benefit(s) costs the executive nothing.[25] This is commonly referred to as a *gross-up.* For example, GE's 2015 proxy statement reveals that it made payments of $1,048,864 to John G. Rice, its vice chairman, and indicates that the additional cash is for "Expatriate Tax Benefits."[26] Employees can choose to forgo a benefit if they prefer not to pay taxes on it.

Employer Considerations for Taxable Fringe Benefits   Like employees, employers treat taxable fringe benefits just like cash compensation. That is, the employer has an outlay for the cost of the benefit and deducts its *cost* of the benefit, *not the value* of the benefit to the employee.[27] As we mention above, employers are often able to purchase fringe benefits at a lower cost than individual employees can. For example, employers may receive a group discount for purchasing life insurance, automobiles, financial or tax planning services, or accident insurance.

Example 12-17

In Example 12-16, TPI provided Julie with $750,000 of group-term life insurance. Its cost of providing the entire $750,000 of coverage is $500 per year. If Julie were to purchase the policy herself, it would cost her $2,000 per year. Assuming TPI's marginal tax rate is 35 percent, what is TPI's after-tax cost of the partially taxable group-term life insurance benefit it provided to Julie?

[25]Companies generally choose a formula to determine how much cash (gross-up) they need to pay the employee in addition to the taxable benefit to ensure the benefit costs the employee nothing.

[26]This amount represents the tax gross-up payments made on behalf of Mr. Heintzelman in connection with his nonpermanent relocation, at the company's request, to Florence, Italy, consistent with the company's policy for all employees

[27]The employer also has an outlay for the cost of the employer's share of FICA taxes on the taxable portion of benefits it provides to employees and receives a deduction for the FICA taxes paid.

Answer: TPI's after-tax cost of the benefit provided is $325, calculated as follows:

Description	Amount	Explanation
(1) Cost of policy	$500	
(2) Income tax benefit	(175)	(1) × 35%.
Total after-tax cost	$325	(1) + (2).

Finally, employers may discriminate between employees when providing taxable benefits. That is, they can select which employees receive the taxable benefits and which do not. Not surprisingly, the more highly compensated employees tend to receive these benefits. For example, as described in an excerpt from Walmart's proxy statement in Exhibit 12-11, Walmart's perquisite and supplemental benefits provide certain officers with use of the company aircraft and home security systems. Walmart is unlikely to offer these same benefits to its hourly sales associates.

EXHIBIT 12-11   Excerpt from Walmart's 2015 Proxy Statement

What perquisites and other benefits do our NEOs receive?

Our Named Executive Officers (NEOs) receive a limited number of perquisites and supplemental benefits. We cover the cost of annual physical examinations for our NEOs and provide each NEO with personal use of our aircraft for a limited number of hours each year. Our NEOs also receive company-paid life and accidental death and dismemberment insurance. Additionally, our NEOs are entitled to benefits available to officers generally, such as participation in the Deferred Compensation Matching Plan, and benefits available to Associates generally, including a Walmart discount card, a limited 15 percent match of purchases of Shares through our Stock Purchase Plan, participation in our 401(k) Plan, medical insurance, and foreign business travel insurance. We provide these perquisites and supplemental benefits to attract talented executives to our company and to retain our current executives, and we believe their limited cost is outweighed by these benefits to our company.

TAXES IN THE REAL WORLD   Fringe Benefits

Google Takes Off

Google's stock price isn't the only thing that has taken off; its executive usage of aircraft paid for by the company has as well.

According to two excerpts from Google's 2015 Proxy Statement this amount exceeds $1 million:

In 2014, we paid for personal security for Eric and incremental costs related to the personal use of non-commercial aircraft for Eric, David, and Omid. Pursuant to our Non-Commercial Aircraft Policy, executives and their guests may use company aircraft with appropriate approvals and pay tax on any associated imputed income.

Corporate Use of Personal Aircraft

Eric E. Schmidt beneficially owns 100% of one aircraft and 33% of another aircraft, both of which are used by Eric and our other executive officers from time to time for business trips. The reimbursement rate for use of these aircraft is $7,500 per hour. The board of directors approved this hourly reimbursement rate based upon a competitive analysis of comparable chartered aircraft that, as our board of directors determined, is at or below market rates for the charter of similar aircraft. In 2014, we used these aircraft for business-related travel services for certain of our executive officers, including Eric, and we reimbursed Eric approximately $1,318,500. Due to the fact that the $7,500 hourly rate paid for the use of these aircraft is less than the actual operational costs incurred by Eric as owner of these aircraft, Eric does not profit from the use of these aircraft.

Nontaxable Fringe Benefits

For policy reasons, Congress specifically excludes certain fringe benefits, such as health insurance, from employees' gross income to encourage employers to provide the benefits.[28] We refer to excluded benefits as **nontaxable fringe benefits.** Other nontaxable fringe benefits enable taxpayers to become or stay employed, including meals or lodging for the convenience of the employer, educational assistance, dependent-care benefits, moving expense benefits, and transportation-related benefits. Finally, some benefits are excluded for simplicity's sake, such as no-additional-cost services, qualified employee discounts, and *de minimis* (small) fringe benefits. Exhibit 12-12 provides a partial list of nontaxable fringe benefits, and in the text that follows, we discuss these benefits in more detail.

EXHIBIT 12-12   **Common Forms of Nontaxable Fringe Benefits**

Benefit	Description
Group-term life insurance (§79)	Employer-paid premiums on up to $50,000 group-term life insurance policy are excluded from employees' income.
Health benefits (§§105–106)	Employer-paid premiums covering health, medical, and dental insurance and the benefits provided through the insurance.
Meals or lodging for the convenience of the employer (§119)*	Meals provided on employer's premises and lodging provided by the employer as a condition of employment.
Employee educational assistance (§127)	Up to $5,250 exclusion for tuition, books, and fees. See IRS Publication 970, *Tax Benefits for Education.*
Dependent care benefits (§129)	Up to $5,000 exclusion for cost of providing care for a dependent who is under 13 years old or a dependent who is disabled.
No-additional-cost services [§132(a)(1)]	Benefits that don't cost the employer a material amount.
Qualified employee discounts [§132(a)(2)]	Reduced prices on employer's product within certain limits.
Working condition fringe benefits [§132(a)(3)]*	A benefit provided by an employer that would be deductible as an ordinary and necessary business expense by the employee if the employee rather than the employer paid the expense.
De minimis fringe benefits [§132(a)(4)]*	Relatively small and infrequently provided benefits.
Qualified transportation fringe benefits [§132(a)(5)]*	Mass transit passes up to monthly limit of $255, qualified parking is also up to monthly limit of $255, or use of company-owned carpool vehicles (vans).
Qualified moving expense reimbursement [§132(a)(6)]*	Reimbursement for allowable moving expenses such as moving household goods and travel.
Cafeteria plans (§125)	A plan where employees can choose from among various nontaxable fringe benefits or cash. Taxable to the extent employees receive cash.

*Employer may discriminate in providing this benefit.

Group-Term Life Insurance   As we mentioned in the taxable benefits section, employees may exclude from income the employer-provided benefit for the first $50,000 of group-term life insurance.[29] Any remaining group-term life insurance

[28]The nontaxable fringe benefits are listed with "items specifically excluded from gross income" in §§101–140 of the Internal Revenue Code. Employers are generally prohibited from discriminating among employees with respect to nontaxable fringe benefits (they cannot offer them only to executives). This chapter indicates whether or not discrimination for a particular benefit is allowed. However, the discrimination rules are complex and vary from benefit to benefit in ways too numerous to explain in detail in this text.
[29]§79.

benefit is taxable (see Example 12-16). An employer may not discriminate between employees in providing nontaxable group-term life insurance benefits.

Health and Accident Insurance and Benefits   When employers pay for **health and accident insurance** for an employee and the employee's spouse and dependents, the employee excludes the benefit from her gross income.[30] For example, if TPI pays health premiums of $18,000 for Julie and her family, Julie is not required to include this $18,000 fringe benefit in her gross income.[31] Further, when employees receive cash reimbursements for medical care, they can exclude the reimbursement from gross income.[32] For example, if TPI reimburses Julie for $450 of medical co-payments she makes during the year, Julie excludes the $450 from gross income. Generally, employers may not discriminate between employees when providing health and accident insurance benefits.[33]

TAXES IN THE REAL WORLD   Free Lunch

Apple, Google, and Facebook are famous for their cafeterias, which have been chronicled in Bon Appetit and other foodie magazines. These cafeterias are light years ahead of the dorm cafeteria you ate in as a college freshman. And better yet, they are either free or almost free for employees. However, the secret is out—and now the IRS is questioning whether these benefits are taxable or nontaxable. To be considered nontaxable, the benefit has to be provided "for the convenience of the employer" rather than as a way to attract and compensate employees. These companies are arguing that without these cafeterias employees will be away from the company premises more and lose the opportunity to talk together, both of which are detrimental to the employer. The IRS has made this issue an administrative priority; that could be bad news for those companies that have relied on such perks to lure the best and brightest employees. The result may also cost the companies and employees back taxes in the future.

Meals and Lodging for the Convenience of the Employer   The value of certain meals and lodging the employer provides to an employee may be excluded from an employee's gross income if the benefit meets two criteria: (1) the meals and lodging are provided on the employer's business premises to the employee (and the employee's spouse and dependents, if any) and (2) the meals and lodging are provided for the convenience of the employer.[34] For example, employers may provide meals at their place of business so employees can continue working efficiently without taking time off to go out to eat. Accounting firms frequently provide meals to tax professionals working late during tax season. Employers are allowed to deduct the full cost of meals provided to employees for the convenience of the employer. That is, the cost is not subject to the 50 percent deductibility limitation on meals we discussed in Chapter 9.[35] Employers may generally discriminate between employees **for the convenience of the employer benefits.**

Example 12-18

What if: Assume that last year Julie purchased 25 meals, at a cost of $500, on evenings when she worked late. Julie turned in expense reports and receipts for the meals totaling $500, which PCC reimbursed. What is the amount Julie must include in income?

Answer: Julie will not include the value of any of the overtime meals into income because they were provided for PCC's convenience.

[30]§106.
[31]If Julie were to purchase the health insurance with after-tax dollars the equivalent would be $30,000 [$18,000/(1 − .4 marginal tax rate)].
[32]§105(b). Although, reimbursement in excess of costs is included in income.
[33]However, employers may exclude part-time employees from participation.
[34]§119(a)(1).
[35]§274(n).

In some situations, employers may provide lodging for employees and require employees to live on the business premises as a condition of their employment. In these cases, employees may exclude the value of the lodging from gross income.[36] For example, an employer may require an apartment complex manager to live in an apartment in the complex (free of charge) so the employee can respond to tenant needs, provide security, and handle emergencies. The apartment manager can exclude the value of the lodging from gross income.

Employee Educational Assistance Employees can exclude from income up to $5,250 of employee **educational assistance benefits** covering tuition, books, and fees.[37] Amounts received in excess of this limit are taxed as compensation to the employee. (See IRS Publication 970 for details related to education benefits.) This includes amounts employers provide for employee undergraduate- or graduate-level courses or for courses that lead to a professional degree. Amounts excluded from income cannot qualify for educational deductions or credits (such as the American opportunity and lifetime learning credits).

Dependent Care Benefits Employees can exclude up to $5,000 for benefits paid or reimbursed by employers for caring for children under age 13 or dependents or spouses who are physically or mentally unable to care for themselves.[38] Excluded amounts do not qualify for the child and dependent care credit (see Chapter 8).

No-Additional-Cost Services Employees can exclude the value of **no-additional-cost services.** These are any services employers provide to employees in the ordinary course of business that generate no substantial costs to the employer (including opportunity costs).[39] For example, airline companies can provide employees with free flight benefits on a space-available basis, hoteliers can allow employees to use vacant hotel rooms, and telephone companies can provide free basic phone service to their employees—all without the employees recognizing gross income. Exhibit 12-13 describes no-cost benefits that airline companies like JetBlue provide to their employees.[40]

EXHIBIT 12-13 Flight Benefits

JetBlue, like most other airlines, offers the following flight benefits to employees:
- It's our favorite perk! JetBlue crew members enjoy the benefit of free standby travel on JetBlue, as well as reduced-rate standby travel on some other airlines.

Example 12-19

What if: Assume that Julie's current employer, PCC, has a division that provides wireless Internet service and virus protection software. Because PCC has such a large contract with a national provider, its contract has sufficient bandwidth to allow employees to use the service without incurring additional cost. The market value of the services is $1,080 per year. What amount of this benefit must Julie include in her gross income?

Answer: $0. Julie may exclude the value of the wireless Internet from her income because it qualifies as a no-additional-cost service under §132.

[36]§119(a)(2).
[37]§127(a)(2). The discrimination and eligibility rules are provided in §127(b)(2).
[38]§129.
[39]§132(a)(1).
[40]See http://www.jetblue.com/work-here/benefits.aspx

Qualified Employee Discounts   Employers frequently allow employees to purchase their goods and services at a discount. Employees may exclude **qualified employee discounts** from income as long as they don't acquire *goods* at a discount greater than the average gross profit percentage for the employer's goods.[41] Employees may also exclude qualified employee discounts on *services* as long as the discount is not more than 20 percent of the price of the services that are offered to customers. This can be a fairly significant nontaxable benefit to employees, particularly for higher priced products. For example, Ford Motor Company could allow employees a substantial discount on its Ford, Lincoln, and Mercury brand cars. Also, Exhibit 12-14 presents an excerpt from the IBM Web site describing the IBM employee product purchase plan that allows employees to acquire home appliances at a significant discount.

EXHIBIT 12-14   **Excerpt from IBM's Web site**

Employee Purchase Program

Discounted pricing for IBM U.S. and employees, their family and friends.

See www-304.ibm.com/shop/americas/content/home/store_eppus/en_US/epplogin.html

From a nontax perspective, employers can use this qualified fringe benefit to entice and retain employees who would otherwise purchase the employer's brand or product.

Example 12-20

What if: Assume that Julie's current employer, PCC, allows all employees to purchase computers (both laptops and desktops) from its retail stores at a discount. Julie purchased two computers during the current year: a laptop for $1,600 (retails for $2,100, with a cost to PCC of $1,500) and a desktop for $1,300 (retails for $1,800, with a cost of $1,250). Julie saved $500 ($2,100 – $1,600) on the laptop and $500 ($1,800 – $1,300) on the desktop. Assume that PCC's average gross profit percentage is 25 percent. What amount of the savings must Julie include in her gross income?

Answer: Julie must include $50 into her gross income. The $50 of income is from the desktop because the employee discount of $500 ($1,800 retail price less the $1,300 purchase price) exceeds the $450 discount allowed ($1,800 retail price x 25% average gross profit percentage). The $500 savings on the laptop may be excluded from her income because the savings are less than the $525 ($2,100 x 25%) qualified employee discount under §132.

What if: Suppose that the laptop Julie purchased for $1,600 has a cost of $1,700 (instead of $1,500 as stated above). What amount of the tax savings on the laptop must Julie include in her gross income?

Answer: Zero for the laptop. Because Julie's employee discount of $500 is still less than the allowable qualified employee discount of $525 ($2,100 x 25%). The qualified discount is tied to PCC's gross profit percentage, not the purchase price of a specific item.

What if: Assume that Julie's current employer, PCC, allows all employees to receive one free computer each year. Julie selected the laptop (retails for $2,100, with a cost to PCC of $1,500) as her free computer. What amount must PCC include in Julie's gross income?

Answer: $1,575. Julie's cost of the computer ($0) is $1,575 less than PCC's sales price ($2,100) less its gross profit percentage $525 ($2,100 × 25%). Therefore, she must include $1,575 in income. Employee discounts only qualify as a qualified employee discount under §132 to the extent they don't exceed the employer's gross profit percentage.

[41]§132(a)(2).

Working Condition Fringe Benefits   Employees may exclude from income any benefit or reimbursement of a benefit provided by an employer that would be deductible as an ordinary and necessary expense by the employee if the employee rather than the employer paid the expense (or the employer did not reimburse the employee). For example, if a company or firm reimburses its employees for professional licensing costs or dues (CPA or bar fees or AICPA dues), the reimbursement may be excluded from an employee's income.[42] Additionally, telephones or computers provided to employees for business use may be excluded. Employers may discriminate between employees with respect to **working condition fringe benefits.**

Example 12-21

What if: Assume that Julie's employer reimburses executives for business-related continuing education courses as well as travel costs related to such education. Julie attended a certificate (nondegree program) course at the University of Chicago this year. Her costs were as follows: $2,500 for the course, $600 for airfare, $800 for hotels, and $200 for books and course materials. PCC reimbursed Julie for the entire $4,100 ($2,500 + $600 + $800 + $200). What amount of the reimbursement must Julie include in her gross income?

Answer: $0. The reimbursement qualifies as a working condition fringe benefit under §132.

What if: Assume that Ethan's employer allows all of its engineers to take home products for consumer testing and evaluation. For example, Ethan is currently designing a new disc brake system for mountain bikes. So Ethan is allowed to check out up to three mountain bikes at a time to see how various different brake systems work. The annual rental value of products Ethan uses is $2,500. What amount of the annual rental value must Ethan include in his gross income?

Answer: $0. The value of the consumer testing products is an excludible working condition fringe benefit under §132.

De Minimis Fringe Benefits   Employees can also exclude from income occasional or incidental *de minimis* **fringe benefits** (very small).[43] These typically include occasional personal use of a copy machine, company-sponsored picnics, noncash traditional holiday gifts (Thanksgiving turkey or Christmas ham), and occasional tickets to sporting or theatrical events. Employers are allowed to discriminate between employees when providing *de minimis* fringe benefits. Who do you think gets to use a company's NBA tickets—the new employee or the boss?

Qualified Transportation Fringe   Employees may exclude from income the value of certain transportation benefits they receive from employers, whether employers pay for these benefits directly or reimburse employees for the transportation costs.[44] These **qualified transportation fringe benefits** eligible for exclusion include the value of company-owned car pool vehicles for commuting to and from work, the cost of mass transit passes, and the cost of qualified parking near the work place. In 2016, the maximum exclusion for the car pool vehicle and mass transit pass is $255 per month and the maximum exclusion for the qualified parking benefit is also up to $255 per month.

Qualified Moving Expense Reimbursement   Employees receiving payments (or reimbursements) from employers for **qualified moving expense reimbursements** may exclude the payments from gross income to the extent that they do not deduct the moving expenses.[45] As we discussed in Chapter 6, qualified moving expenses

---

[42]Employees can exclude reimbursements from their income if they properly document their expenses through expense reports, mileage logs, and receipts.

[43]§132(a)(4).

[44]§132(f)(1).

[45]§132(a)(6).

include the cost of moving household items and travel, including lodging, for the employee and dependents as long as the employee's move meets certain distance and length of employment tests. Employees are, however, taxed on payments they receive from employers for house-hunting trips, temporary housing allowances, and reimbursements for expenses related to the sale of their prior residence.

Cafeteria Plans and Flexible Spending Accounts (FSAs)

Employers choose the benefits they make available to employees. Some employers offer a standard package of benefits that employees can either take or leave. Standard benefits typically include health and dental insurance for the employee and family, dependent care benefits, and group-term life insurance for the employee. However, a standard benefit plan is not optimal for all employees because each employee has individual needs. So how can employers tailor their benefits to the needs of employees? The answer is cafeteria plans and flexible spending accounts.

Under a **cafeteria plan,** employers determine the total cost of benefits they are willing to provide for each employee. Each employee then either chooses (or buys) benefits up to the determined amount from a menu of nontaxable fringe benefits or may receive a cash equivalent in lieu of forgone benefits.[46] However, cash received from a cafeteria plan is taxable compensation to employees. Cafeteria plans are popular because each employee may desire different types of nontaxable fringe benefits. For example, if an employer provides $3,000 of dependent care benefits to every employee, the benefits would be worthless to employees without dependents. Through a cafeteria plan, employees can select the benefits best suited to their needs. For example, instead of selecting dependent care benefits, an employee with no dependents could choose any combination of nontaxable benefits such as dental insurance, educational benefits, or cash if none of the benefits are desirable.

Employers can also offer **flexible spending accounts (FSAs),** which allow employees to set aside a portion of their before-tax salary for payment of either health and/ or dependent-care benefits. These plans allow employees to set aside either employee contributions (on a before-tax basis) or employer contributions (a leftover cafeteria plan amount) to pay for medical-related expenses (such as co-payments and prescriptions) or dependent care. The Patient Protection and Affordable Care Act reduces the limit for medical-related expenses to $2,550 in 2016. Generally, amounts placed in flexible spending accounts must be used for qualifying benefits during the FSA plan year (which is often the calendar year). However, employers may allow employees to use the remaining balance from one year within the first two and a half months of the next FSA plan year.[47] Any remaining balance is forfeited by the employee.

Employee and Employer Considerations for Nontaxable Fringe Benefits

Nontaxable fringe benefits are very attractive to employees because their after-tax cost of these benefits is zero.[48] They do not pay for the benefits and they are not taxed on the value of the benefits they receive. In contrast to taxable fringe benefits, nontaxable fringe benefits cannot, with a few exceptions noted above, be provided on a discriminatory basis (may be provided to some employees and not others). Employers deduct the cost of providing the benefits, which (thanks to group or quantity discounts) can be considerably lower than the cost to the employee of

---

THE KEY FACTS

Nontaxable Fringe Benefits

- Specifically identified in the Code.
- Employee excludes benefit from taxable income.
- Employer deducts cost when benefit is paid.

---

[46]§125.

[47]Employers can elect to allow employees to use funds set aside for one year until March 15 of the following year under Notice 2005-42. If employers don't make the election, employees must use their account balance by December 31 of the current year or they lose it after year-end.

[48]Furthermore, there are nontax reasons for employees to value nontaxable benefits, such as the fact that many employer-provided group health insurance plans allow for preexisting health conditions, whereas employees may not be able to obtain health insurance plans that cover preexisting health conditions on their own.

purchasing the benefit(s) separately. IRS publication 15-B "Employer's Tax Guide to Fringe Benefits" (available at www.IRS.gov) provides tax guidance for employers providing fringe benefits.

Tax Planning with Fringe Benefits

The fact that employees can exclude nontaxable fringe benefits from gross income, while employers can deduct the cost of providing them (just as they deduct the cost of taxable fringe benefits), gives rise to compensation-related tax-planning opportunities that may benefit both employee and employer.

Example 12-22

TPI proposed to reimburse Julie $200 a month for her parking costs. What amount of this reimbursement would be a nontaxable qualified transportation fringe to Julie?

Answer: All $2,400. Julie can exclude up to $255 per month ($3,060 per year) as a qualified transportation fringe.

What if: Assume that TPI would not reimburse Julie's parking costs unless Julie is willing to accept a reduction in salary. Assuming Julie is subject to a 40 percent marginal tax rate, how much salary should Julie be willing to forgo to receive the $2,400 of nontaxable parking benefits?

Answer: $4,000, computed as follows:

Description	Amount	Explanation
(1) Annual fringe benefit	$2,400	
(2) Marginal ordinary tax rate	40%	
Before-tax compensation required to pay for annual fringe benefit	$4,000	(1)/[1 − (2)].

Example 12-23

What if: Assume that instead of a parking benefit, TPI would pay Julie $4,000 of salary that she would use to pay for her parking. What would be TPI's after-tax cost of paying $4,000 of salary to Julie assuming its marginal tax rate is 35 percent?

Answer: $2,600, calculated as follows:

Description	Amount	Explanation
(1) Taxable salary paid	$4,000	
(2) Income tax benefit	(1,400)	(1) × 35%.
Total after-tax cost of salary	$2,600	(1) + (2).

What if: Assume that TPI were to provide Julie $2,400 of qualified transportation fringe benefits in the form of parking. What would be its after-tax cost of paying the $2,400 nontaxable fringe benefit to Julie assuming its marginal tax rate is 35 percent?

Answer: $1,560, calculated as follows:

Description	Amount	Explanation
(1) Nontaxable fringe benefit paid	$2,400	
(2) Income tax benefit	(840)	(1) × 35%
Total after-tax cost of nontaxable benefit	$1,560	(1) + (2).

Can an employer and an employee work together to implement the conversion tax planning strategy to make both the employee and employer better off by substituting desired nontaxable fringe benefits for taxable salary in the compensation package? The answer is yes!

What if: As shown in Example 12-22, Julie is indifferent between receiving (1) $4,000 in salary or (2) $2,400 in nontaxable parking benefits. Consequently, if TPI paid Julie $2,400 in nontaxable benefits and any amount of additional salary, she would be better off than she would be by receiving no parking and $4,000 in salary. As shown in Example 12-23, TPI would be better off after taxes by providing Julie with (1) $2,400 in nontaxable benefits (cost of $1,560) rather than (2) salary of $4,000 (after-tax cost of $2,600). What amount of salary could TPI provide in addition to the $2,400 of nontaxable benefits to make it indifferent between providing the parking and the additional salary or providing salary of $4,000?

Answer: $1,600 additional salary for indifference, calculated as follows:

Description	Amount	Explanation
(1) After-tax cost of salary	$2,600	Example 12-23.
(2) After-tax cost of fringe benefit	1,560	Example 12-23.
(3) After-tax cost of additional salary	$1,040	(1) − (2).
(4) After-tax cost percentage	65%	(1 − .35).
Additional before-tax salary	$1,600	(3)/(4).

To summarize, if TPI pays Julie's parking costs and provides her with additional salary of any amount below $1,600, it will be better off than it would be by not providing the parking and paying her $4,000 in salary. Julie is better off if TPI pays her parking and gives her any additional salary than she is if it doesn't pay her parking but pays her $4,000 of salary.

Fringe Benefits Summary

Fringe benefits, both taxable and nontaxable, can make up a significant portion of an employee's compensation. Fringe benefits are taxable unless the tax laws specifically exclude them from gross income. Taxable fringe benefits usually represent a luxury perk, while nontaxable fringe benefits are generally excluded for public policy reasons. At this point, you should be able to distinguish between taxable and nontaxable fringe benefits. Exhibit 12-15 presents an excerpt from Disney Company's proxy statement. Read through the excerpt and see if you can determine which of the benefits Mr. Iger received are taxable and which are nontaxable.

Mr. Iger's taxable benefits include the personal air travel, security, health club membership, annual physical exam, reimbursement for financial consulting, and perhaps part of the group-term life insurance. Mr. Iger's nontaxable benefits include theme park access (a no-additional-cost service), merchandise discounts (qualified employee discount), occasional sporting events (*de minimis* fringe benefit), educational expense reimbursements, health insurance, and group-term life insurance (some of this coverage may be taxable).

Recall the fringe benefits included in Julie's offer letter: health insurance (valued at $18,000), $750,000 of group-term life insurance, and a flexible spending account (no amounts given—assume she elects $1,500). She also received an annual parking benefit of $2,400. Which benefits are taxable and which are nontaxable? Exhibit 12-16 summarizes how each of these benefits is classified for tax purposes, Julie's after-tax benefit, and TPI's after-tax cost.

EXHIBIT 12-15 **Excerpt from Disney Company's 2015 Proxy Statement Dealing with Fringe Benefits**

The following table identifies the incremental cost of each perquisite or personal benefit that exceeded the greater of $25,000 or 10% of the total amount of perquisites and personal benefits for a named executive officer in fiscal 2014.

	Fiscal 2014 Perquisites and Personal Benefits				
Executive	**Year**	**Personal Air Travel**	**Security**	**Other**	**Total**
Robert A. Iger	2014	$391,411	$614,582	$82,349	$1,088,342

The incremental cost to the Company of the items specified above was determined as follows:

- Personal air travel: the actual catering costs, landing and ramp fees, fuel costs and lodging costs incurred by flight crew plus a per hour charge based on the average hourly maintenance costs for the aircraft during the year for flights that were purely personal in nature, and a pro rata portion of catering costs where personal guests accompanied a named executive officer on flights that were business in nature. Where a personal flight coincided with the positioning of an aircraft following a business flight, only the incremental costs of the flight compared to an immediate repositioning of the aircraft are included. As noted on page 24, above, Mr. Iger is required for security reasons to use corporate aircraft for all of his personal travel.
- Security: the actual costs incurred by the Company for providing security equipment and services.

The "Other" column in the table above includes, to the extent a named executive officer elected to receive any of these benefits, the incremental cost to the Company of the vehicle benefit, personal air travel where the cost to the Company was less than $25,000, reimbursement of up to $1,000 for wellness-related purchases such as fitness, nutrition, and stress management, and reimbursement of expenses for financial consulting. With respect to Mr. Iger, the "Other" column also includes the filing fee and related legal fees incurred in connection with a filing by Mr. Iger under the Hart-Scott Rodino Antitrust Improvements Act that was required as a result of Mr. Iger's participation in the Company's equity compensation program.

The named executive officers also were eligible to receive the other benefits described in *Compensation Discussion and Analysis* under the discussion of *"Benefits and Perquisites"* in the *"Compensation Program Elements"* section, which involved no incremental cost to the Company or are offered through group life, health, or medical reimbursement plans that are available generally to all of the Company's salaried employees.

EXHIBIT 12-16 **Summary of Julie's Nonsalary Benefits from TPI**

Benefit	Nontaxable Fringe	Taxable Fringe	Employee After-Tax Benefit	Employer After-Tax Cost
Auto allowance		X	**$18,000** ($30,000 − $12,000) (Example 12-15)	**$19,500** [$30,000 × (1 − .35)]
Health and dental insurance	X		**$18,000** [$18,000 × (1 − .0)]	**$11,700** [$18,000 × (1 − .35)]
Flexible spending account	X		**$1,500** [$1,500 × (1 − .0)]	**$975** [$1,500 × (1 − .35)]
Parking reimbursement	X		**$2,400** [$2,400 × (1 − .0)] (Example 12-22)	**$1,560** [$2,400 × (1 − .35)] (Example 12-23)
Group-term life insurance	X	X	**$1,698** ($2,000 − $302)* (Examples 12-16, 17)	**$325** [$500 × (1 − .35)] (Example 12-17)
Total			**$41,598**	**$34,060**

*This is the fair market value of the benefit less the actual taxes payable by Julie.

CONCLUSION

Individuals and employers routinely make choices involving compensation issues. As they do so, they must understand how alternative forms of compensation are taxed. In this chapter, we have discussed the tax compliance and planning implications associated with common types of payment including salary and wages, equity-based compensation (such as stock options and restricted stock), and taxable and nontaxable fringe benefits from both employee and employer perspectives. Throughout, we have emphasized that both tax and nontax issues must be considered in the broader context of compensation planning. Armed with the information provided in this chapter, future employees and employers can approach the compensation decisions they will undoubtedly face with more confidence and insight.

Summary

Discuss and explain the tax implications of compensation in the form of salary and wages from the employee's and employer's perspectives.   **LO 12-1**

- Employees are taxed on salary at ordinary income rates.
- Employees use Form W-4 to supply their employer with withholding information. Employees can use the W-4 to manage withholding throughout the year because withholding is treated as though it is withheld evenly throughout the year for estimated tax purposes.
- Cash-method employers deduct wages when paid. Accrual-method employers deduct wages when accrued as long as the wages are paid within 2.5 months of year-end. If paid after 2.5 months of year-end, wages are deductible when the employee recognizes the income (when paid). When an employer accrues wages to a related-party employee (more than 50 percent ownership), the wages are not deductible until the employee recognizes the income (when paid).
- Employers' after-tax cost of wages is the cost of the wages minus the tax benefit of the deduction for the wages.
- For publicly traded corporations, the tax deduction for nonperformance-based compensation paid to the CEO and the three other most highly compensated officers, not including the CFO, is limited to $1,000,000 per year per individual.

Describe and distinguish the tax implications of various forms of equity-based compensation from the employee's and employer's perspectives.   **LO 12-2**

- Stock options and restricted stock are common forms of equity-based compensation. Although both reward employees for increases in the stock price of their employers, there are fundamental economic differences between them.
- Stock options are treated as either nonqualified or incentive stock options for tax purposes.
- Employees recognize ordinary income equal to the bargain element on NQOs when they are exercised. Employers are able to deduct the bargain element when NQOs are exercised. Any appreciation in the value of shares subsequent to the exercise of NQOs is treated as capital gain by employees when the shares are sold.
- If certain holding period requirements are met, employees exercising ISOs don't recognize any income until the shares received from the exercised options are sold. When the shares are sold, the difference between the exercise price and the share price is long-term capital gain (assuming appreciation). Employers are not permitted a deduction for ISOs.
- Generally, employees prefer ISOs and employers prefer NQOs because of differences in the way the two types of options are taxed.
- Employers treat stock options differently for book and tax purposes.

- Employees recognize ordinary income from restricted stock equal to the fair market value of the stock on the vesting date. Employers receive a corresponding tax deduction.
- Employees may elect to recognize taxable income from restricted stock on the date it is received rather than on the vesting date if they make an §83(b) election. Although this election accelerates the recognition of income, it gives the employee the ability to convert ordinary income from further appreciation into a capital gain.

LO 12-3 Compare and contrast taxable and nontaxable fringe benefits and explain the employee and employer tax consequences associated with fringe benefits.

- Fringe benefits are taxable to the employee unless the Code specifically excludes the benefit from gross income. Taxable fringe benefits are generally luxury perks, such as corporate air travel and security.
- Nontaxable fringe benefits include up to $50,000 of group-term life insurance, health benefits, meals and lodging for the convenience of the employer, educational assistance, dependent care benefits, qualified employee discounts, and qualified transportation benefits (among others).

KEY TERMS

bargain element (12-10)
cafeteria plan (12-29)
cashless exercise (12-10)
de minimis fringe benefit (12-28)
disqualifying disposition (12-12)
educational assistance benefit (12-26)
employee (12-2)
exercise date (12-10)
exercise price (12-8)
facts and circumstances test (12-4)
FICA taxes (12-2)
flexible spending account (FSA) (12-29)
for the convenience of the employer benefits (12-25)

Form W-2 (12-2)
Form W-4 (12-2)
fringe benefits (12-20)
grant date (12-10)
group-term life insurance (12-21)
health and accident insurance (12-25)
incentive stock option (12-10)
no-additional-cost services (12-26)
nonqualified stock option (12-10)
nontaxable fringe benefit (12-24)
option exercise (12-9)
qualified employee discount (12-27)
qualified moving expense reimbursement (12-28)

qualified transportation fringe benefit (12-28)
restricted stock (12-15)
salary (12-2)
same-day sale (12-11)
§83(b) election (12-17)
strike price (12-8)
taxable fringe benefit (12-20)
vest (12-8)
vesting date (12-10)
wages (12-2)
working condition fringe benefit (12-28)

DISCUSSION QUESTIONS

Discussion Questions are available in *Connect*®.   ■ connect

LO 12-1 1. Nicole and Braxton are each 50 percent shareholders of NB Corporation. Nicole is also an employee of the corporation. NB is a calendar-year taxpayer and uses the accrual method of accounting. The corporation pays its employees monthly on the first day of the month after the salary is earned by the employees. What issues must NB consider with respect to the deductibility of the wages it pays to Nicole if Nicole is Braxton's sister? What issues arise if Nicole and Braxton are unrelated?

LO 12-1 2. Holding all else equal, does an employer with a higher marginal tax rate or lower marginal tax rate have a lower after-tax cost of paying a particular employee's salary? Explain.

LO 12-1 3. What are nontax reasons for why a corporation may choose to cap its executives' salaries at $1 million?

4. What are tax reasons why a corporation may choose to cap its executives' salaries at $1 million? `LO 12-1`

5. Lea is a highly paid executive with MCC Inc., a publicly traded corporation. What are the circumstances under which MCC will be able to deduct more than $1 million of compensation paid to Lea during the year? `LO 12-1`

6. From an *employee* perspective, how are ISOs treated differently than NQOs for tax purposes? In general, for a given number of options, which type of stock option should employees prefer? `LO 12-2`

7. From an *employer* perspective, how are ISOs treated differently than NQOs for tax purposes? In general, for a given number of options, which type of stock option should employers prefer? `LO 12-2`

8. Why do employers use stock options in addition to salary to compensate their employees? For employers, are stock options treated more favorably than salary for tax purposes? Explain. `LO 12-2`

9. What is a "disqualifying disposition" of ISOs, and how does it affect employees who have exercised ISOs? `LO 12-2`

10. Compare and contrast how employers record book and tax expense for stock options. `LO 12-2`

11. How is the tax treatment of restricted stock different from that of NQOs? How is it similar? `LO 12-2`

12. Matt just started work with Boom Zoom Inc., a manufacturer of credit-card-sized devices for storing and playing back music. Due to the popularity of its devices, analysts expect Boom Zoom's stock price to increase dramatically. In addition to his salary, Matt received Boom Zoom restricted stock. How will Matt's restricted stock be treated for tax purposes? Should Matt consider making the §83(b) election? What are the factors he should consider in making this decision? From a tax perspective, would this election help or hurt Boom Zoom? `LO 12-2`

13. What risks do employees making an §83(b) election on a restricted stock grant assume? `LO 12-2`

14. Explain the differences and similarities between fringe benefits and salary as forms of compensation. `LO 12-3`

15. When an employer provides group-term life insurance to an employee, what are the tax consequences to the employee? What are the tax consequences for the employer? `LO 12-3`

16. Compare and contrast the employer's tax consequences of providing taxable versus nontaxable fringe benefits. `LO 12-3`

17. Mike is working his way through college and trying to make ends meet. Tara, a friend, is graduating soon and tells Mike about a really great job opportunity. She is the onsite manager for an apartment complex catering to students. The job entails working in the office for about 10 hours a week, collecting rent each month, and answering after-hours emergency calls. The owner of the apartment complex requires the manager to live onsite as a condition of employment. The pay is $10 per hour, plus a rent-free apartment (worth about $500 per month). Tara then tells him the best part: the rent-free apartment is tax-free. Knowing that you are a tax student, Mike asks you if the rent-free apartment is really tax-free or if Tara is mistaken. Explain to Mike whether the compensation for the apartment is really a nontaxable fringe benefit. `LO 12-3`

18. Assume that your friend has accepted a position working as an accountant for a large automaker. As a signing bonus, the employer provides the traditional cash incentive but also provides the employee with a vehicle not to exceed a retail price of $25,000. Explain to your friend whether the value of the vehicle is included, excluded, or partially included in the employee's gross income. `LO 12-3`

LO 12-3   19. Explain why an employee might accept a lower salary to receive a nontaxable fringe benefit. Why might an employee not accept a lower salary to receive a nontaxable fringe benefit?

LO 12-3   20. Describe a cafeteria plan and discuss why an employer would provide a cafeteria plan for its employees.

LO 12-3   21. Explain why Congress allows employees to receive certain fringe benefits tax-free but others are taxable.

LO 12-3   22. Explain the policy reason for including the value of country club memberships provided to an executive as a taxable fringe benefit.

LO 12-3   23. Describe the circumstances in which an employee may not value a nontaxable fringe benefit.

PROBLEMS

Select problems are available in *Connect*®.

LO 12-1   24. North Inc. is a calendar-year C corporation, accrual-basis taxpayer. At the end of year 1, North accrued and deducted the following bonuses for certain employees for financial accounting purposes.

- $7,500 for Lisa Tanaka, a 30 percent shareholder.
- $10,000 for Jared Zabaski, a 35 percent shareholder.
- $12,500 for Helen Talanian, a 20 percent shareholder.
- $5,000 for Steve Nielson, a 0 percent shareholder.

Unless stated otherwise, assume these shareholders are unrelated.

How much of the accrued bonuses can North Inc. deduct in year 1 under the following alternative scenarios?

a) North paid the bonuses to the employees on March 1 of year 2.

b) North paid the bonuses to the employees on April 1 of year 2.

c) North paid the bonuses to employees on March 1 of year 2 and Lisa and Jared are related to each other, so they are treated as owning each other's stock in North.

d) North paid the bonuses to employees on March 1 of year 2 and Lisa and Helen are related to each other, so they are treated as owning each other's stock in North.

LO 12-1   25. Jorgensen High Tech Inc. is a calendar-year, accrual-method taxpayer. At the end of year 1, Jorgensen accrued and deducted the following bonuses for certain employees for financial accounting purposes.

- $40,000 for Ken.
- $30,000 for Jayne.
- $20,000 for Jill.
- $10,000 for Justin.

How much of the accrued bonuses can Jorgensen deduct in year 1 under the following alternative scenarios?

a) Jorgensen paid the bonuses to the employees on March 1 of year 2.

b) Jorgensen paid the bonuses to the employees on April 1 of year 2.

c) Jorgensen paid the bonuses to employees on March 1 of year 2, and there is a requirement that the employee remain employed with Jorgensen on the payment date to receive the bonus.

d) Jorgensen paid the bonuses to employees on March 1 of year 2, and there is a requirement that the employee remain employed with Jorgensen on the payment date to receive the bonus; if not, the forfeited bonus is reallocated to the other employees.

26. Lynette is the CEO of publicly traded TTT Corporation and earns a salary of $200,000 in the current year. Assume TTT has a 35 percent marginal tax rate.   `LO 12-1`

    a) What is TTT Corporation's after-tax cost of paying Lynette's salary?

27. Marcus is the CEO of publicly traded ABC Corporation and earns a salary of $1,500,000. Assume ABC has a 35 percent marginal tax rate.   `LO 12-1`

    a) What is ABC's after-tax cost of paying Marcus's salary?

    b) Now assume that Marcus, in addition to the $1.5 million salary, earns a performance-based bonus of $500,000. What is ABC's after-tax cost of paying Marcus's salary?

28. Ramon has finally arrived. He has interviewed for the CEO position with MMM Corporation. They have presented him with two alternative compensation offers. Alternative 1 is for a straight salary of $2,500,000. Option 2 is for a salary of $1,000,000 and performance-based compensation of up to $2,000,000. Assume that Ramon has a marginal tax rate of 40 percent, MMM has a marginal tax rate of 35 percent. Answer the questions under each of the following alternative scenarios.   `LO 12-1`   `planning`

    a) If Ramon is 100 percent certain he can meet the qualifications for the full performance-based compensation, which offer should he choose?

    b) If Ramon believes there is only a 20 percent chance that he can meet the performance-based requirements, which offer should he choose (assume he is risk neutral)?

    c) What is MMM's after-tax cost of providing Ramon with Option 1?

    d) What is MMM's expected after-tax cost of providing Ramon with Option 2 if it believes there is a 40 percent chance Ramon will qualify for the performance-based compensation?

29. Cammie received 100 NQOs (each option provides a right to purchase 10 shares of MNL stock for $10 per share) at the time she started working for MNL Corporation (5/1/Y1) four years ago when MNL's stock price was $8 per share. Now (8/15/Y5) that MNL's stock price is $40 per share, she intends to exercise all of her options. After acquiring the 1,000 MNL shares with her options, she held the shares for over one year (10/1/Y6) and sold them at $60 per share.   `LO 12-2`   `tax forms`

    a) What are Cammie's taxes due on the grant date (5/1/Y1), exercise date (8/15/Y5) , and sale date (10/1/Y6), assuming her ordinary marginal rate is 30 percent and her long-term capital gains rate is 15 percent?

    b) What are MNL Corporation's tax savings on grant date (5/1/Y6), exercise date (8/15/Y5), and sale date (10/1/Y6), assuming its marginal tax rate is 35 percent?

    c) Complete Cammie's Form 8949 and Schedule D for the year of sale. Also assume that the sale transaction of the MNL Corporation stock was not reported to Cammie on a Form 1099-B.

30. Yost received 300 NQOs (each option gives Yost the right to purchase 10 shares of Cutter Corporation stock for $15 per share) at the time he started working for Cutter Corporation three years ago. Cutter's stock price was $15 per share. Yost exercises all of his options when the share price is $26 per share. Two years after acquiring the shares, he sold them at $47 per share.   `LO 12-2`   `planning`

    a) What are Yost's taxes due on the grant date, exercise date, and sale date, assuming his ordinary marginal rate is 35 percent and his long-term capital gains rate is 15 percent?

b) What are Cutter Corporation's tax consequences (amount of deduction and tax savings from deduction) on the grant date, the exercise date, and the date Yost sells the shares assuming its marginal tax rate is 25 percent?

c) Assume that Yost is "cash poor" and needs to engage in a same-day sale in order to buy his shares. Due to his belief that the stock price is going to increase significantly, he wants to maintain as many shares as possible. How many shares must he sell in order to cover his purchase price and taxes payable on the exercise?

d) Assume that Yost's options were exercisable at $20 and expired after five years. If the stock only reached $18 dollars during its high point during the five-year period, what are Yost's tax consequences on the grant date, the exercise date, and the date the shares are sold, assuming his ordinary marginal rate is 35 percent and his long-term capital gains rate is 15 percent?

LO 12-2   31. Haven received 200 NQOs (each option gives him the right to purchase 20 shares of Barlow Corporation stock for $7 per share) at the time he started working for Barlow Corporation three years ago when its stock price was $7 per share. Now that Barlow's share price is $50 per share, he intends to exercise all of his options. After acquiring the 4,000 Barlow shares with his options, he intends to hold the shares for more than one year and then sell the shares when the price reaches $75 per share.

a) What are Haven's taxes due on the grant date, exercise date, and sale date, assuming his ordinary marginal rate is 30 percent and his long-term capital gains rate is 15 percent?

b) What are the cash flow effects for Barlow Corporation resulting from Haven's option exercise if Barlow's marginal tax rate is 35 percent?

LO 12-2   32. Mark received 10 ISOs (each option gives him the right to purchase 10 shares of Hendricks Corporation stock for $5 per share) at the time he started working for Hendricks Corporation five years ago when Hendricks's stock price was $5 per share. Now that Hendricks's share price is $35 per share, he intends to exercise all options and hold all of his shares for more than one year. Assume that more than a year after exercise, Mark sells the stock for $35 a share.

a) What are Mark's taxes due on the grant date, the exercise date, and the date he sells the shares, assuming his ordinary marginal rate is 30 percent and his long-term capital gains rate is 15 percent?

b) What are Hendricks's tax consequences on the grant date, the exercise date, and the date Mark sells the shares assuming its marginal tax rate is 25 percent?

LO 12-2   33. Antonio received 40 ISOs (each option gives him the right to purchase 20 shares of Zorro stock for $3 per share) at the time he started working for Zorro Corporation six years ago. Zorro's stock price was $3 per share at the time. Now that Zorro's stock price is $50 per share, he intends to exercise all of his options and immediately sell all the shares he receives from the options exercise.

a) What are Antonio's taxes due on the grant date, the exercise date, and the date the shares are sold, assuming his ordinary marginal rate is 30 percent and his long-term capital gains rate is 15 percent?

b) What are Zorro's tax consequences on the grant date, the exercise date, and the date Antonio sells the shares, assuming its marginal tax rate is 25 percent?

c) What are the cash flow effects of these transactions to Antonio, assuming his ordinary marginal rate is 25 percent and his long-term capital gains rate is 15 percent?

d) What are the cash flow effects to Zorro Corporation resulting from Antonio's option exercise if Zorro's marginal tax rate is 35 percent?

34. Harmer Inc. is now a successful company. In the early days (before it became profitable), it issued ISOs to its employees. Now Harmer is trying to decide whether to issue NQOs or ISOs to its employees. Initially, Harmer would like to give each employee 20 options (each option allows the employee to acquire one share of Harmer stock). For purposes of this problem, assume that the options are exercised in three years (*three years from now*) and that the underlying stock is sold in five years (*five years from now*). Assume that taxes are paid at the same time the income generating the tax is recognized. Also assume the following facts:

LO 12-2

planning

   - The after-tax discount rate for both Harmer Inc. and its employees is 10 percent.
   - Corporate tax rate is 35 percent.
   - Personal (employee) ordinary income rate is 40 percent.
   - Personal (employee) long-term capital gains rate is 20 percent.
   - Exercise price of the options is $7.
   - Market price of Harmer at date of grant is $5.
   - Market price of Harmer at date of exercise is $25.
   - Market price of Harmer at date of sale is $35.

   Answer the following questions:

   a) Considering these facts, which type of option plan, NQO or ISO, should Harmer Inc. prefer? Explain.
   b) Assuming Harmer issues NQOs, what is Harmer's tax benefit from the options for each employee in the year each employee exercises the NQOs?
   c) Assuming Harmer issues ISOs, what is the tax benefit to Harmer in the year the ISOs are exercised?
   d) Which type of option plan should Harmer's employees prefer?
   e) What is the present value of each employee's after-tax cash flows from year 1 through year 5 if the employees receive ISOs?
   f) What is the present value of each employee's after-tax cash flows from year 1 through year 5 if the employees receive NQOs?
   g) How many NQOs would Harmer have to grant to keep its employees indifferent between NQOs and 20 ISOs?

35. On January 1, year 1, Dave received 1,000 shares of restricted stock from his employer, RRK Corporation. On that date, the stock price was $7 per share. Dave's restricted shares will vest at the end of year 2. He intends to hold the shares until the end of year 4 when he intends to sell them to help fund the purchase of a new home. Dave predicts the share price of RRK will be $30 per share when his shares vest and will be $40 per share when he sells them.

LO 12-2

   a) If Dave's stock price predictions are correct, what are the taxes due on these transactions to Dave if his ordinary marginal rate is 30 percent and his long-term capital gains rate is 15 percent?
   b) If Dave's stock price predictions are correct, what are the tax consequences of these transactions to RRK if its marginal rate is 35 percent?

36. On January 1, year 1, Dave received 1,000 shares of restricted stock from his employer, RRK Corporation. On that date, the stock price was $7 per share. On receiving the restricted stock, Dave made the §83(b) election. Dave's restricted shares will vest at the end of year 2. He intends to hold the shares until the end of year 4 when he intends to sell them to help fund the purchase of a new home. Dave predicts the share price of RRK will be $30 per share when

LO 12-2

his shares vest and will be $40 per share when he sells them. Assume that Dave's price predictions are correct and answer the following questions:

a) What are Dave's taxes due if his ordinary marginal rate is 30 percent and his long-term capital gains rate is 15 percent?

b) What are the tax consequences of these transactions to RRK if its marginal rate is 35 percent?

LO 12-2 37. On January 1, year 1, Jessica received 10,000 shares of restricted stock from her employer, Rocket Corporation. On that date, the stock price was $10 per share. On receiving the restricted stock, Jessica made the §83(b) election. Jessica's restricted shares will all vest at the end of year 4. After the shares vest, she intends to sell them immediately to fund an around-the-world cruise. Unfortunately, Jessica decided that she couldn't wait four years and she quit her job to start her cruise on January 1, year 3.

a) What are Jessica's taxes due in year 1 assuming her marginal tax rate is 33 percent and her long-term capital gains rate is 15 percent?

b) What are Jessica's taxes due in year 3 assuming her marginal tax rate is 33 percent and her long-term capital gains rate is 15 percent?

LO 12-2 38. On May 1, year 1, Anna received 5,000 shares of restricted stock from her employer, Jarbal Corporation. On that date, the stock price was $5 per share. On receiving the restricted stock, Anna made the §83(b) election. Anna's restricted shares will all vest on May 1, year 3. After the shares vest, she intends to sell them immediately to purchase a condo. True to her plan, Anna sold the shares immediately after they were vested.

a) What is Anna's ordinary income in year 1?

b) What is Anna's gain or loss in year 3 if the stock is valued at $1 per share on the day the shares vest?

c) What is Anna's gain or loss in year 3 if the stock is valued at $9 per share on the day the shares vest?

d) What is Anna's gain or loss in year 3 if the stock is valued at $5 per share on the day the shares vest?

LO 12-2

planning

39. On January 1, year 1, Tyra started working for Hatch Corporation. New employees must choose immediately between receiving seven NQOs (each NQO provides the right to purchase for $5 per share 10 shares of Hatch stock) or 50 restricted shares. Hatch's stock price is $5 on Tyra's start date. Either form of equity-based compensation will vest in two years. Tyra believes that the stock will be worth $15 per share in two years and $25 in four years when she will sell the stock. Tyra's marginal tax rate is 30 percent and her long-term capital gains rate is 15 percent. Assuming that Tyra's price predictions are correct, answer the following questions (ignore present value, use nominal dollars):

a) What are the cash-flow effects to Tyra in the year she receives the options, the year the options vest and she exercises the options, and in the year she sells the stock if she chooses the NQOs?

b) What are the cash-flow effects to Tyra in the year she receives the restricted stock, in the year the stock vests, and in the year she sells the stock if Tyra chooses the restricted stock?

c) What are the cash-flow effects to Tyra in the year she receives the restricted stock, the year the stock vests, and the year she sells the stock if she makes an §83(b) election?

d) What recommendation would you give Tyra? Explain.

40. Nicole's employer, Poe Corporation, provides her with an automobile allowance of $20,000 every other year. Her marginal tax rate is 30 percent. Poe Corporation has a marginal tax rate of 35 percent. Answer the following questions relating to this fringe benefit.

    a) What is Nicole's after-tax benefit if she receives the allowance this year?

    b) What is Poe's after-tax cost of providing the auto allowance?

    LO 12-3

41. Bills Corporation runs a defense contracting business that requires security clearance. To prevent unauthorized access to its materials, Bills requires its security personnel to be on duty except for a 15-minute break every two hours. Since the nearest restaurants are a 25-minute round trip, Bills provides free lunches to its security personnel. Bills has never included the value of these meals in its employees' compensation. Bills is currently under audit, and the IRS agent wants to deny Bills a deduction for past meals. The agent also wants Bills to begin including the value of the meals in employee compensation starting with the current year. As Bills's tax advisor, give it a recommendation on whether to appeal the agent's decision. (*Hint:* See *Boyd Gaming Corp.*, CA-9, 99-1 USTC ¶50,530 (Acq.), 177 F3d 1096.)

    LO 12-3
    research

42. Lars Osberg, a single taxpayer with a 35 percent marginal tax rate, desires health insurance. The health insurance would cost Lars $8,500 to purchase if he pays for it himself (Lars's AGI is too high to receive any tax deduction for the insurance as a medical expense). Volvo, Lars's employer, has a 40 percent marginal tax rate. Answer the following questions about this benefit.

    LO 12-3
    planning

    a) What is the maximum amount of before-tax salary Lars would give up to receive health insurance from Volvo?

    b) What would be the after-tax cost to Volvo to provide Lars with health insurance if it could purchase the insurance through its group plan for $5,000?

    c) Assume that Volvo could purchase the insurance for $5,000. Lars is interested in getting health insurance and he is willing to receive a lower salary in exchange for the health insurance. What is the least amount by which Volvo would be willing to reduce Lars's salary while agreeing to pay his health insurance?

    d) Will Volvo and Lars be able to reach an agreement by which Volvo will provide Lars with health insurance?

43. Seiko's current salary is $85,000. Her marginal tax rate is 30 percent and she fancies European sports cars. She purchases a new auto each year. Seiko is currently a manager for an office equipment company. Her friend, knowing of her interest in sports cars, tells her about a manager position at the local BMW and Porsche dealer. The new position pays only $75,000 per year, but it allows employees to purchase one new car per year at a discount of $15,000. This discount qualifies as a nontaxable fringe benefit. In an effort to keep Seiko as an employee, her current employer offers her a $10,000 raise. Answer the following questions about this analysis.

    LO 12-3
    planning

    a) What is the annual after-tax cost to her current employer (office equipment company that has a 35 percent marginal tax rate) to provide Seiko with the $10,000 increase in salary?

    b) Financially, which offer is better for Seiko on an after-tax basis and by how much? (Assume that Seiko is going to purchase the new car whether she switches jobs or not.)

    c) What salary would Seiko need to receive from her current employer to make her financially indifferent (after taxes) between receiving additional salary from her current employer and accepting a position at the auto dealership?

LO 12-1 LO 12-3   44. JDD Corporation provides the following benefits to its employee, Ahmed (age 47):

Salary	$300,000
Health insurance	10,000
Dental insurance	2,000
Life insurance	3,000
Dependent care	5,000
Professional dues	500
Personal use of company jet	200,000

Assume the life insurance is a group-term life insurance policy that provides $200,000 of coverage for Ahmed.

a) Assuming Ahmed is subject to a marginal tax rate of 30 percent, what is his after-tax benefit of receiving each of these benefits?

LO 12-3   45. Gray's employer is now offering group-term life insurance. The company will provide each employee with $100,000 of group-term life insurance. It costs Gray's employer $300 to provide this amount of insurance to Gray each year. Assuming that Gray is 52 years old, determine the monthly premium that Gray must include in gross income as a result of receiving the group-term life benefit.

LO 12-3   46. Brady graduated from SUNY New Paltz with his bachelor's degree recently. He works for Makarov & Company CPAs. The firm pays his tuition ($10,000 per year) for him so that he can receive his Master of Science in Taxation, which will qualify him to sit for the CPA exam. How much of the $10,000 tuition benefit does Brady need to include in gross income?

LO 12-3   47. Meg works for Freedom Airlines in the accounts payable department. Meg and all other employees receive free flight benefits (for the employee, family, and 10 free buddy passes for friends per year) as part of its employee benefits package. If Meg uses 30 flights with a value of $12,350 this year, how much must she include in her compensation this year?

LO 12-3   48. Sharmilla works for Shasta Lumber, a local lumber supplier. The company an-
research   nually provides each employee with a Shasta Lumber shirt so that employees look branded and advertise for the business while wearing the shirts. Are Shasta's employees required to include the value of the shirts in income?

LO 12-3   49. LaMont works for a company in downtown Chicago. The firm encourages em-
research   ployees to use public transportation (to save the environment) by providing them with transit passes at a cost of $260 per month.

a) If LaMont receives one pass (worth $260) each month, how much of this benefit must he include in his gross income each year?

b) If the company provides each employee with $260 per month in parking benefits, how much of the parking benefit must LaMont include in his gross income each year?

LO 12-3   50. Jasmine works in Washington, D.C. She accepts a new position with her current firm in Los Angeles. Her employer provides the following moving benefits:

- Temporary housing for one month—$3,000.
- Transportation for her household goods—$4,500.
- Flight and hotel for a house-hunting trip—$1,750.
- Flights to Los Angeles for her and her family—$2,000.

What amount of these benefits must Jasmine include in her gross income?

LO 12-3   51. Jarvie loves to bike. In fact, he has always turned down better paying jobs to work in bicycle shops where he gets an employee discount. At Jarvie's current shop, Bad Dog Cycles, each employee is allowed to purchase four bicycles a year at a discount. Bad Dog has an average gross profit percentage on bicycles of 25 percent. During the current year, Jarvie bought the following bikes:

Description	Retail Price	Cost	Employee Price
Specialized road bike	$3,200	$2,000	$2,240
Rocky Mountain mountain bike	3,800	3,200	3,040
Trek road bike	2,700	2,000	1,890
Yeti mountain bike	3,500	2,500	2,800

a) What amount is Jarvie required to include in taxable income from these purchases?

b) What amount of deductions is Bad Dog allowed to claim from these transactions?

52. Matt works for Fresh Corporation. Fresh offers a cafeteria plan that allows each employee to receive $15,000 worth of benefits each year. The menu of benefits is as follows: `LO 12-1` `LO 12-3`

Benefit	Cost
Health insurance—single	$ 5,000
Health insurance—with spouse	$ 8,000
Health insurance—with spouse and dependents	$11,000
Dental and vision	$ 1,500
Dependent care—any specified amount up to $5,000	Variable
Adoption benefits—any specified amount up to $5,000	Variable
Educational benefits—any specified amount (no limit)	Variable
Cash—any specified amount up to $15,000 plan benefit	Variable
401(k)—any specified amount up to $10,000	Variable

For each of the following independent circumstances, determine the amount of income Matt must recognize and the amount of deduction Fresh may claim:

a) Matt selects the single health insurance and places $10,000 in his 401(k).

b) Matt selects the single health insurance, is reimbursed $5,000 for MBA tuition, and takes the remainder in cash.

c) Matt selects the single health insurance and is reimbursed for MBA tuition of $10,000.

d) Matt gets married and selects the health insurance with his spouse and takes the rest in cash to help pay for the wedding.

e) Matt elects to take all cash.

COMPREHENSIVE PROBLEMS

Select problems are available in *Connect®*.   connect

53. Pratt is ready to graduate and leave College Park. His future employer (Ferndale Corp.) offers the following four compensation packages from which Pratt may choose. Pratt will start working for Ferndale on January 1, year 1.   **tax forms**

Benefit Description	Option 1	Option 2	Option 3	Option 4
Salary	$60,000	$50,000	$45,000	$45,000
Health insurance	No coverage	5,000	5,000	5,000
Restricted stock	0	0	1,000 shares	0
NQOs	0	0	0	100 options

Assume that the restricted stock is 1,000 shares that trade at $5 per share on the grant date (January 1, year 1) and are expected to be worth $10 per share on the vesting date at the end of year 1. Assume that the NQOs (100 options that each allow the employee to purchase 10 shares at $5 strike price). The stock trades at $5 per share on the grant date (January 1, year 1) and is expected to be worth $10 per share on the vesting date at the end of year 1. Also assume that Pratt spends on average $3,000 on health-related costs that would be covered by insurance if he has coverage. Assume that Pratt's marginal tax rate is 35 percent. Assume that Pratt spends $3,000 in after-tax dollars for health expenses when he doesn't have health insurance coverage (treat this as an outflow), and that there is no effect when he has health insurance coverage. (Ignore FICA taxes and time value of money considerations).

a) What is the after-tax value of each compensation package for year 1?

b) If Pratt's sole consideration is maximizing after-tax value for year 1, which scheme should he select?

c) Assuming Pratt chooses Option 3 and sells the stock on the vesting date (on the last day of year 1), complete Pratt's Schedule D for the sale of the restricted stock.

54. Santini's new contract for 2016 indicates the following compensation and benefits:

Benefit Description	Amount
Salary	$130,000
Health insurance	9,000
Restricted stock grant	2,500
Bonus	5,000
Hawaii trip	4,000
Group-term life insurance	1,600
Parking ($285 per month)	3,420

Santini is 54 years old at the end of 2016. He is single and has no dependents. Assume that the employer matches $1 for $1 for the first $6,000 that the employee contributes to his 401(k) during the year. The 100 ISOs each allow the purchase of 10 shares of stock at a strike price of $5 (also the market price on the date of grant). The ISOs vest in two years when the stock price is expected to be $15 and Santini expects to sell the shares in three years when the market price is $20. The restricted stock grant is 500 shares granted when the market price was $5 per share. Assume that the stock vests on December 31, 2016, and that the market price on that date is $7.50 per share. Also assume that Santini is willing to make any elections to reduce equity-based compensation taxes. The Hawaii trip was given to him as the outstanding sales person for 2015. The group-term life policy gives him $150,000 of coverage. Assume that Santini does not itemize deductions for the year. Determine Santini's taxable income and income tax liability for 2016.

planning 55. Sylvana is given a job offer with two alternative compensation packages to choose from. The first package offers her $250,000 annual salary with no qualified fringe benefits. The second package offers $235,000 annual salary plus health and life insurance benefits. If Sylvana were required to purchase the health and life insurance benefits herself, she would need to pay $10,000 annually after taxes. Assume her marginal tax rate is 33 percent.

a) Which compensation package should she choose and by how much would she benefit in after-tax dollars by choosing this package?

b) Assume the second package offers $240,000 plus benefits instead of $235,000 plus benefits. Which compensation package should she choose and by how much would she benefit in after-tax dollars by choosing this package?

56. In 2016, Jill, age 35, received a job offer with two alternative compensation packages to choose from. The first package offers her $90,000 annual salary with no qualified fringe benefits, requires her to pay $3,500 a year for parking, and will purchase life insurance at a cost of $1,000. The second package offers $80,000 annual salary, employer-provided health insurance, annual free parking (worth $310 per month), $200,000 of life insurance (purchasing on her own would have been $1,000 annually), and free flight benefits (she figures that it will save her $5,000 per year). If Jill chooses the first package, she would purchase the health and life insurance benefits herself at a cost of $5,000 annually after taxes and spend another $5,000 in flights while traveling. Assume her marginal tax rate is 28 percent.

   a) Which compensation package should she choose, and by how much would she benefit in after-tax dollars by choosing this compensation package instead of the other compensation package?

   b) Assume the first package offers $100,000 salary with no qualified benefits instead of $90,000 salary plus benefits. Which compensation package should she choose, and by how much would she benefit in after-tax dollars by choosing this package?

planning

chapter

13 Retirement Savings and Deferred Compensation

Learning Objectives

Upon completing this chapter, you should be able to:

LO 13-1 Describe the tax and nontax aspects of employer-provided defined benefit plans from both the employer's and employee's perspective.

LO 13-2 Explain and determine the tax consequences associated with employer-provided defined contribution plans, including traditional 401(k) and Roth 401(k) plans.

LO 13-3 Describe the tax implications of deferred compensation from both the employer's and employee's perspective.

LO 13-4 Determine the tax consequences of traditional and Roth Individual Retirement Accounts and explain the differences between them.

LO 13-5 Describe retirement savings options available to self-employed taxpayers and compute the limitations for deductible contributions to retirement accounts for self-employed taxpayers.

LO 13-6 Compute the saver's credit.

© Paul Bradbury/age fotostock

Storyline Summary

Taxpayer:	Tina Hillman
Location:	Chicago, Illinois
Employment status:	Graduating student about to begin career in the tax department of Corporate Business Associates
Starting salary:	$60,000 per year
Filing status:	Single
Dependents:	None
Marginal tax rate:	Current year 15 percent, next year 25 percent
Taxpayer:	Lisa Whitlark
Location:	Chicago, Illinois
Employment status:	Recently promoted to chief financial officer (CFO) for Corporate Business Associates
Salary:	$400,000
Filing status:	Married, filing jointly
Marginal tax rate:	33 percent
Dependents:	Spouse and three children
Taxpayer:	Dave Allan
Location:	Chicago, Illinois
Employment status:	Recently retired as CFO for Corporate Business Associates after 20 years of employment with the company
Salary at retirement:	$450,000
Retirement benefits:	Participant in Corporate Business Associates' defined benefit plan, 401(k) plan, and nonqualified deferred compensation plan
Filing status:	Married filing jointly
Dependents:	Spouse
Marginal tax rate:	35 percent for current year
Taxpayer:	Corporate Business Associates (CBA)
Location:	Chicago, Illinois
Marginal tax rate:	35 percent
Status:	Publicly traded corporation

Tina Hillman

Tina Hillman just completed her last exam, finally fulfilling the requirements for a bachelor's degree in accounting. It was the end of June and she would finally have some time to vacation and see her family before September when she will start her professional career working in the tax department of Corporate Business Associates (CBA). While Tina was looking forward to the time off, she was also eager to start making money instead of just spending it. She had a great experience during her internship at CBA last year. She had some challenging but enjoyable work assignments and she got along very well with the staff. Overall, she was excited about the work opportunities she would get at CBA.

Tina recently received an information packet on the benefits available to her as a CBA employee. The information indicated that Tina would be eligible to participate in CBA's 401(k) retirement plan on January 1 of next year. Tina plans on contributing to the plan as soon as she is eligible because CBA matches employee contributions to the plan such that for every dollar contributed by the employee (up to 4 percent of the employee's salary) CBA contributes two dollars. In the meantime, Tina wonders if she has any retirement savings options during the current year while waiting to become eligible to participate in CBA's plan.

Lisa Whitlark

Lisa Whitlark is finally getting used to her new responsibilities. She was recently promoted to the position of chief financial officer (CFO) for CBA. Lisa threw her name into the ring a few months ago when CBA announced that Dave Allan, the former CFO, would be retiring. Lisa had been working as CBA's tax director for the last 10 years. As a top executive of the company, Lisa is now eligible to participate in CBA's nonqualified deferred compensation program. She didn't have this option as a tax director. Lisa knows she should consider both tax and nontax factors when deciding whether and to what extent she will participate in the plan.

Dave Allan

Dave Allan couldn't believe that he was actually retiring at the end of this year. Looking back, his successful career had passed so quickly. At age 72, he is now ready to move on and spend time seeing the world with his wife. Dave's retirement plans are going to be quite expensive. Fortunately, he has accumulated substantial retirement benefits during his CBA career. Dave will be receiving retirement benefits from CBA's defined benefit plan, 401(k) plan, and nonqualified deferred compensation plan. He knows he has some choices about the timing and amounts of his distributions from these plans. Dave wants to be sure to evaluate both the tax and nontax considerations before making these decisions. ∎

At different stages in their careers, taxpayers are likely to face issues similar to those confronting Tina, Lisa, and Dave. Saving for retirement is not always easy to do because it requires forgoing cash now in order to receive benefits at some point in the future. However, not saving for retirement can be a costly mistake because it's not likely that government-promised Social Security benefits alone will satisfy most taxpayers' retirement needs.[1] Many employers help employees save for retirement by sponsoring retirement plans on behalf of their employees. These plans may be "qualified" retirement plans or "nonqualified" deferred compensation plans. Qualified plans are subject to certain restrictions not applicable to nonqualified plans. Both qualified and nonqualified plans are useful tools through which employers can

---

[1] Under current law, the projected cost of Social Security generally increases faster than projected income because of the aging of the baby-boom generation, continuing low fertility since the baby-boom period, and increasing life expectancy. Social Security's total expenditures have exceeded noninterest income of its combined trust funds since 2010. The 2015 Social Security Trustees report projects that the Social Security Trust fund reserves will be depleted in 2034. See http://www.socialsecurity.gov/oact/TRSUM/index.html

achieve various compensation-related goals. In this chapter, we discuss the tax and nontax consequences of qualified retirement plans and nonqualified plans to both employers and to employees, including issues relating to contributions to and distributions from these plans. We also discuss individually managed retirement savings plans available to certain individual taxpayers and qualified retirement plans available to self-employed taxpayers.

EMPLOYER-PROVIDED QUALIFIED PLANS

Traditional **qualified retirement plans** grew from a congressional concern that, if unregulated, employers might not adequately fund and protect employee pension benefits and that they might be tempted to provide lavish retirement plans to highly compensated employees such as executives and business owners to the detriment of rank-and-file employees. To address these concerns, Congress mandated that employer-provided plans only receive tax-favored qualified plan status if they meet certain requirements ensuring the plan does not discriminate against rank-and-file employees and if promised benefits are secure. Over the years, the rules addressing these issues have evolved, but the concept of a qualified plan eligible for favorable tax treatment remains the same.

Employer-provided qualified plans can be generally classified as **defined benefit plans** or **defined contribution plans.** As the name suggests, defined benefit plans spell out the specific benefit the employee will receive on retirement. In contrast, defined contribution plans specify the maximum annual contributions that employers and employees may contribute to the plan. While we explore both basic plan types below, we emphasize defined contribution plans because they are much more common than defined benefit plans.

DEFINED BENEFIT PLANS

LO 13-1

Defined benefit plans are traditional pension plans used by many older and more established companies and tax-exempt organizations. These plans provide standard retirement benefits to employees based on a fixed formula. The formula to determine the standard retirement benefit is usually a function of years of service and employees' compensation levels as they near retirement. For employees who retire in 2016, the maximum annual benefit an employee can receive is the *lesser* of (1) 100 percent of the average of the employee's three highest years of compensation or (2) $210,000.[2]

Example 13-1

CBA provides a defined benefit plan for its employees. The plan uses a fixed formula to determine employee benefits. The formula specifies a benefit of 2 percent for each year of service, up to a maximum of 50 percent (25 years of service), of the average of the employee's three highest years of salary. In 2016, Dave retires from CBA. On the date of retirement, Dave had been a CBA employee for 20 years. The average of his three highest years of salary was $420,000. What is Dave's annual benefit from the defined benefit plan?

Answer: $168,000 a year. The benefit is calculated by multiplying 40 percent (2 percent for each of his 20 years of service) by $420,000 (the average of his highest three years of salary).

What if: Assume the same facts except that the average of Dave's three highest years of salary was $600,000. What is the annual benefit he will receive from the plan?

Answer: $210,000. The lesser of (1) $240,000 ($600,000 × 40%) or (2) $210,000.

---

[2]§415(b)(1). The maximum benefit is adjusted annually for inflation.

Vesting

We've discussed the idea that an employee's benefit is based on the number of years she works for an employer. When an employee works for an employer for only a short time before leaving, her benefit depends on her salary, the number of full years she worked for the employer, and the employer's vesting schedule. **Vesting** is the process of becoming legally entitled to a certain right or property. Thus, a taxpayer vests in retirement benefits (becomes legally entitled to retirement benefits) as she meets certain requirements set forth by the employer. The most restrictive vesting requirements an employer can impose on a qualified defined benefit plan is either a five-year "cliff" or seven-year graded vesting schedule.[3] Under the **cliff vesting** option, after a certain period of time, benefits vest all at once. With a **graded vesting** schedule, the employee's vested benefit increases each full year she works for the employer. Exhibit 13-1 features the five-year cliff and seven-year graded minimum vesting schedules for defined benefit plans.

EXHIBIT 13-1   Defined Benefit Plans Minimum Vesting Schedules*

Full Years of Service	5-Year Cliff	7-Year Graded
1	0%	0%
2	0	0
3	0	20
4	0	40
5	100	60
6	N/A	80
7	N/A	100

*Percent of employee benefit no longer subject to forfeiture.

Example 13-2

What if: CBA provides a defined benefit plan to its employees. Under the plan, employees earn a benefit equal to 2 percent for every year of service of their average salary for their three highest years of compensation. CBA implements a seven-year graded vesting schedule as part of the plan. If Tina works for CBA for four years, earning annual salaries of $60,000, $65,000, $70,000, and $75,000, and then leaves to work for another employer, what annual benefit would she be entitled to receive (her vested benefit)?

Answer: $2,240, computed as follows:

Description	Amount	Explanation
(1) Average of three highest years of salary	$70,000	($65,000 + 70,000 + 75,000)/3.
(2) Benefit percentage	× 8%	Four years of service × 2 percent per year.
(3) Full annual benefit	$ 5,600	(1) × (2).
(4) Vesting percentage	× 40%	Four years of service on 7-year graded vesting schedule (see Exhibit 13-1).
Vested benefit	$ 2,240	(3) × (4) Amount that she is allowed to keep.

Tina would forfeit her unvested benefit of $3,360 ($5,600 − $2,240 vested benefit).

What if: Assume the same facts except that CBA uses a five-year cliff schedule. What would be Tina's vested benefit?

Answer: $0. She did not work for CBA for five years so she would not vest in her benefits in CBA's defined benefit plan.

---

[3]§411(a) specifies maximum vesting periods for employer contributions to qualified plans. Employers are allowed to adopt more generous vesting requirements such as immediate vesting if they choose.

Distributions

When their benefits have vested, employees are entitled to receive future distributions according to the provisions of the plan—these distributions are taxable as ordinary income in the year received.[4] Distributions from defined benefit plans (and defined contribution plans) are subject to early distribution requirements and to minimum distribution requirements. Distributions violating these requirements are penalized. However, because defined benefit plans typically don't permit payout arrangements that would trigger the early distribution or minimum distribution penalties, these penalties are of greater concern to participants in defined contribution plans. Consequently, we address these penalties in more detail when we discuss distributions from defined contribution plans.

Nontax Considerations

From a nontax perspective, a defined benefit plan imposes administrative burdens and risks on the employer sponsoring the plan. A significant amount of work is required to track employee benefits and to compute required contributions to the plan. Because defined benefit plans require employers to provide particular benefits to employees on retirement, the employer bears the investment risk associated with investments within the plan. Beyond the additional administrative costs and risk, defined benefit plans impose significant funding costs on employers relative to alternative retirement plans. Consequently, in recent years, many employers have begun replacing defined benefit plans with defined contribution plans.

> **THE KEY FACTS**
> **Defined Benefit Plans**
> - Employer, not employee, bears investment risk of plan.
> - Early and minimum distribution rules apply, but usually not restrictive.

TAXES IN THE REAL WORLD   Define Your Benefit and Deduct It While You're at It

Because defined benefit plans create significantly more administrative burdens and economic risks for employers than defined contribution plans, defined benefit plans are losing popularity with employers. However, self-employed taxpayers and taxpayers running family businesses may be able to use defined benefit plans to contribute significantly more to qualified retirement plans on behalf of themselves and working family members than they would be able to otherwise contribute to a defined contribution plan. Former Florida governor (and presidential candidate at the time he released his tax returns) Jeb Bush provides Exhibit A for this strategy. Mr. Bush released his tax returns in July 2015. His tax returns reported that he claimed deductions for payments to "pension and profit-sharing plans" that averaged $350,000 a year for the previous five years. Mr. Bush's (completely legal) defined benefit plan was set up for two people working for his consulting firm Jeb Bush & Associates LLC. Those in the know believe the plan likely covered Mr. Bush and his son, Jeb Bush Jr. The $350,000 annual contribution average is more than three times the contribution limit otherwise allowable to be made to a defined contribution plan. Why was he able to contribute so much more to a defined benefit than he could have contributed to a defined contribution plan? Under a defined benefit plan, the business is allowed to contribute as much as required to fund the expected benefit it must pay to the recipient. Because Mr. Bush started the plan when he was nearing retirement age, the business was allowed to contribute (and deduct) significantly more to fund Mr. Bush's retirement than if he had started the plan when he had a longer time-horizon to work before retirement. In contrast, contributions to defined contribution plans are limited to $59,000 per year (in 2016) for taxpayers who are at least 50 years of age ($53,000 to those who are not), no matter when the taxpayer is planning to retire.

Based on: "Pension Plan Cut Jeb Bush's Taxes," by Mark Maremont, updated July 2, 2015, *The Wall Street Journal*, http://www.wsj.com/articles/jeb-bushs-pension-cut-his-taxes-1435858574

---

[4]Distributions of both defined benefit plans and defined contribution plans are reported to taxpayers on Form 1099-R.

LO 13-2 DEFINED CONTRIBUTION PLANS

Defined contribution plans provide an alternative approach for employers to help employees save for retirement. While defined contribution plans and defined benefit plans have similar overall objectives, they are different in important ways. First, employers maintain separate accounts for *each* employee participating in a defined contribution plan. Second, defined contribution plans specify the up-front contributions the employer will make to the employee's separate account rather than specifying the ultimate benefit the employee will receive from the plan. Third, employees are often allowed to contribute to their own defined contribution plans, and in many instances they contribute more than their employers. Finally, employees are generally free to choose how amounts in their retirement accounts are invested. If investments in the plan perform well, employees benefit; if the investments perform poorly, employees suffer the financial consequences. Thus, relative to defined benefit plans, defined contribution plans shift the funding responsibility and investment risk from the employer to the employee.

Employers may provide different types of defined contribution plans such as 401(k) plans (used by for-profit companies), 403(b) plans (used by nonprofit organizations, including educational institutions), and 457 plans (used by government agencies), profit sharing plans, and money purchase pension plans.[5] Employers may even offer multiple defined contribution plans. Because of their popularity, we use 401(k) plans here to represent the general category of defined contribution plans. However, no matter what defined contribution plan(s) employers provide, employers must ensure that their plans meet certain requirements relating to annual contribution limits and vesting requirements. Also, to a greater extent than with defined benefit plans, *participants* in defined contribution plans should be careful to avoid the penalties associated with either early distributions or insufficient minimum distributions from these plans (discussed later in the chapter).

Employer Matching

Employers, but not employees, typically contribute to certain defined contribution plan types such as profit-sharing plans (contributions may be made based on a fixed formula based on profits or may be at the employer's discretion) and money-purchase plans (contributions are a fixed percentage of the employee's compensation). In contrast, employees contribute to 401(k) type plans. Many employers also "match" employee contributions to these plans. When deciding whether to contribute to a 401(k) plan, employees should take into account the matching policies of their employers. For companies matching employee contributions, the match can range from a small percentage (25 cents on the dollar) to a multiple of the employee's contribution. A dollar-for-dollar match gives employees a 100 percent immediate return on their contributions. Therefore, whenever possible, employees should contribute enough to receive the full match from the employer because, subject to the plan's vesting requirements, the match represents an immediate, no-risk return on the amount contributed.

Example 13-3

Tina's offer from CBA includes participation in its 401(k) plan effective the beginning of next year. The plan's formula provides that CBA will match employee contributions on a two-for-one basis up to employee contributions of 4 percent of the employee's annual salary. Next year when she's eligible, Tina will contribute 4 percent of her salary to the plan. Assuming a $60,000 salary for next year, how much will Tina contribute and how much will CBA contribute to Tina's 401(k) account?

Answer: Tina will contribute $2,400 ($60,000 × 4%) to her 401(k) account and CBA will contribute $4,800 ($2,400 × 2).

---

[5]401(k), 403(b), and 457 plans reflect the Code sections describing the plans.

Contribution Limits

For 2016, the sum of employer *and* employee contributions to an employee's defined contribution account(s) is limited to the *lesser* of (1) $53,000 ($59,000 for employees who are at least 50 years of age by the end of the year) or (2) 100 percent of the employee's compensation for the year.[6] *Employee* contributions to an employee's 401(k) account are limited to $18,000 (or $24,000 for employees that reach age 50 by the end of the year).[7] While this limit applies only to employee contributions, the $53,000 (or $59,000) limit still applies to the sum of employer and employee contributions. For example, if an employee under age 50 contributes the maximum $18,000 to her employer-sponsored 401(k) plan in 2016, the employer's contribution would be limited to $35,000 ($53,000 − $18,000).[8] Because of this limit on employer contributions, highly compensated employees may not be able to receive the full employer match available to other employees.

- Lesser of $53,000 ($59,000 for employees 50 years old by year-end) or 100 percent of employee's annual compensation.
- 2016 employee contribution limit to 401(k) plan:
  - $18,000 or
  - $24,000 for employees 50 years old by year-end.

Example 13-4

Before Dave retires at the end of 2016 he continues to contribute to his CBA-sponsored 401(k) account. CBA matches employee contributions on a two-for-one basis up to 4 percent of the employee's salary. Dave is 72 years old at the end of the year and he earned a salary of $450,000 during the year. Dave contributed $24,000 to his 401(k) account. How much would CBA contribute to Dave's 401(k) account?

Answer: $35,000 [$59,000 (Dave is 50+ years old) minus $24,000 (Dave's contribution)]. Without the limitation, CBA would have contributed $36,000 ($450,000 × 4% × 2) to Dave's account.

What if: Assume Dave contributed $23,000 to his 401(k) account. How much would CBA contribute to his account?

Answer: $36,000. Note that this is a better deal for Dave because $59,000 ends up in his account either way, but he funded $23,000 of the contribution instead of $24,000.

Vesting

When employees contribute to defined contribution plans, they are fully vested in the accrued benefit from those contributions (employee contributions plus earnings on their contributions). However, employees vest in the accrued benefit from employer contributions (employer contributions plus earnings on the contributions) based on the plan's vesting schedule. When separate employee accounts are not maintained, the accrued benefit from employee contributions is determined by multiplying the total accrued benefit in the account by the ratio of employee contributions to total contributions (employee plus employer) to the account.[9] The accrued benefit from employer contributions is the difference between the total accrued benefit and the accrued benefit from employee contributions. The minimum vesting requirements for defined contribution plans are a bit more accelerated than the five-year cliff and seven-year graded vesting schedules applicable to defined benefit

---

[6]§415(c)(1). The amount is indexed for inflation under §415(d)(1)(C). Note that the increase in the limit for taxpayers age 50 and older increases the amount the employee can contribute but does not affect the limit the employer can contribute.

[7]§402(g)(1). The amount is indexed for inflation under §402(g)(4).

[8]If an employee participates in more than one defined contribution plan, these limits apply to the total employee and employer contributions to all defined contribution plans. Thus, in a situation where the employee participates in more than one defined contribution plan, the contribution limits for any one defined contribution plan may be less than the overall contribution limits described here.

[9]§411(c).

plans. For defined contribution plans, employers have the option of providing three-year cliff or six-year graded vesting. These minimum vesting schedules are presented in Exhibit 13-2.

EXHIBIT 13-2   **Defined Contribution Plans Minimum Vesting Schedules***

Full Years of Service with Employer	3-Year Cliff	6-Year Graded
1	0%	0%
2	0	20
3	100	40
4	N/A	60
5	N/A	80
6	N/A	100

*Percent of employer contributions no longer subject to forfeiture.

Example 13-5

THE KEY FACTS

Traditional Defined Contribution Plans: Vesting and After-Tax Cost

- Employee must vest to be entitled to employer contributions (and earnings on those contributions) using:
  - 3-year cliff vesting schedule.
  - 6-year graded vesting schedule.
- Employee contributes before-tax amounts (contributions are deductible).
- After-tax cost is before-tax contribution minus tax savings from contribution.

What if: Suppose that in three and one-half years the balance in Tina's 401(k) account is $33,000. In total, Tina had contributed $9,000 to the account and CBA had contributed $18,000. Also assume that Tina was 40 percent vested in her accrued benefit from CBA contributions. What is Tina's vested benefit?

Answer: $19,800 [$11,000 accrued benefit from her contributions + $8,800, which is 40 percent of the $22,000 accrued benefit from CBA contributions]. Tina is fully vested in the $11,000 accrued benefit from her contributions ($33,000 total accrued benefit in account × $9,000 employee contributions/$27,000 total contributions to her account) and 40 percent vested in the $22,000 accrued benefit from CBA contributions ($33,000 total accrued benefit in account minus $11,000 accrued benefit from her contributions).

After-Tax Cost of Contributions to Traditional (non-Roth) Defined Contribution Plans

Employer sponsored traditional defined contribution plans include all plans except Roth 401(k) plans (discussed below). Employees effectively deduct their contributions to traditional defined contribution plans [defined contribution plans other than Roth 401(k) plans (discussed below)], because contributions are removed from their taxable salary (they are, however, still subject to FICA taxes).[10] Consequently, the after-tax cost of a contribution to a traditional defined contribution plan is the contribution amount minus the tax savings generated by the deduction from the contribution.

Example 13-6

Tina contributed $2,400 to her CBA-sponsored traditional 401(k) account in her first full calendar year with CBA. Given Tina's marginal tax rate of 25 percent, what is the after-tax cost of her $2,400 contribution?

Answer: $1,800 computed as follows:

Description	Amount	Explanation
(1) Contribution amount	$2,400	Cost of contribution before tax savings.
(2) Tax savings from contribution	(600)	$2,400 deduction × 25 percent marginal tax rate.
After-tax cost of contribution	$1,800	(1) + (2).

[10]Employees pay the same FICA taxes no matter how much they contribute to defined contribution plans.

Distributions From Traditional Defined Contribution Plans

When employees receive distributions from traditional defined contribution plans, the distributions are taxed as ordinary income. However, when employees receive distributions (or take withdrawals) from traditional defined contribution plans either too early or too late, they must pay a penalty in addition to the ordinary income taxes they owe on the distributions. Generally, employees who receive distributions before they reach

- 59½ years of age or
- 55 years of age *and* have separated from service (retired or employment terminated by employer)

are subject to a 10 percent nondeductible penalty on the amount of the early distributions.

Example 13-7

What if: Assume that when she reaches 60 years of age, Lisa Whitlark retires from CBA and receives a $60,000 distribution from her traditional 401(k) account in the year she retires. Assuming her marginal ordinary tax rate is 33 percent, what amount of tax and penalty will Lisa pay on the distribution?

Answer: $19,800 taxes ($60,000 × 33%) + $0 penalty (she is over 59½ years of age on date of distribution).

What if: Assume that when Lisa is 57 years of age and still employed by CBA, she requests and receives a $60,000 distribution from her traditional 401(k) account. What amount of tax and penalty is Lisa required to pay on the distribution?

Answer: $19,800 taxes ($60,000 × 33%) + $6,000 penalty ($60,000 × 10%).

What if: Assume that Lisa's employment is terminated by CBA when she is 57 years old. In that same year, she requests and receives a $60,000 distribution from her traditional 401(k) account. What amount of tax and penalty is Lisa required to pay on the distribution?

Answer: $19,800 taxes ($60,000 × 33%) + $0 penalty (she is over 55 years of age and has separated from service with CBA).

> **THE KEY FACTS**
>
> **Traditional Defined Contribution Plans: Distributions**
>
> - Taxed at ordinary rates.
> - 10 percent penalty on early distributions.
>   - Before 59½ years of age if not retired or
>   - Before 55 years of age if retired.
> - Minimum distribution requirements:
>   - Must receive by April 1 of the later of (1) the year after the year in which taxpayer reaches 70½ years of age or (2) the year after the year in which the employee retires.
>   - If retired employee waits until year after 70½ to begin receiving distributions, must receive two distributions in year of first distribution.
> - 50 percent penalty on excess of required minimum distribution amounts and amount actually distributed.

Taxpayers who fail to receive a minimum distribution for (pertaining to) a particular year are also penalized. The year for which taxpayers must receive their *first* minimum distribution is the *later* of

- The year in which the employee reaches 70½ years of age.
- The year in which the employee retires.

Taxpayers must receive their first required minimum distribution no later than April 1 of the year after the year to which the distribution pertains.[11] Taxpayers generally must receive minimum distributions for subsequent years by the end of the years to which they pertain. Thus, a retired taxpayer who turns 70½ years of age in 2015 must receive a minimum distribution for 2016 by April 1, 2017. The same taxpayer must also receive a minimum distribution for 2017 by December 31, 2017.

The amount of the minimum required distribution for a particular year is the taxpayer's account balance at the end of the year *prior to* the year to which the distribution pertains multiplied by a percentage from an IRS Uniform Lifetime

---

[11]The amount of the required minimum distribution *for the year* in which a retired employee turns 70½ is the same whether the employee receives the distribution in the year she turns 70½ or whether she defers receiving the distribution until the next year (no later than April 1).

Table. The percentage is based on the distribution period (in years) which depends on the taxpayer's age at the end of the year to which the distribution pertains. An abbreviated version of the table is presented in Exhibit 13-3.[12]

EXHIBIT 13-3   Abbreviated Uniform Lifetime Table

Age of Participant	Distribution Period	Applicable Percentage*
70	27.4	3.65%
71	26.5	3.77
72	25.6	3.91
73	24.7	4.05
74	23.8	4.20
75	22.9	4.37
76	22.0	4.54
77	21.2	4.72

*The applicable percentage is calculated by dividing one by the relevant distribution period.

Example 13-8

What if: Suppose that Dave retires from CBA in 2016 at age 72 (also 72 at year-end). When must he receive his minimum distribution for 2016 from his traditional 401(k) account?

Answer: By April 1, 2017.

What if: Assuming Dave retires in 2016 and that his traditional 401(k) account balance on December 31, 2015, was $3,500,000, what is the amount of the minimum distribution Dave must receive by April 1, 2017?

Answer: $136,850 ($3,500,000 × 3.91%). The percentage from the IRS table for determining this minimum distribution is based on Dave's age at the end of 2016, which is 72 years old.

What if: Assuming Dave's traditional 401(k) account balance on December 31, 2016, is $3,700,000, what is the minimum distribution for 2017 Dave must receive sometime during 2017 (in addition to the $136,850 distribution by April 1)?

Answer: $149,850 ($3,700,000 × 4.05%) for 2017 to be received in 2017.

The consequences for failing to receive timely minimum distributions from defined contribution plans are even more severe than receiving distributions too early. Taxpayers incur a 50 percent nondeductible penalty on the amount of a minimum distribution the employee should have received but did not (the penalty is payable as an additional tax for the calendar year containing the last day by which the amount is required to be distributed). For this reason, it is vital that payouts from defined contribution plans be monitored to avoid not only the 10 percent premature distribution penalty, but also the 50 percent penalty for failing to receive timely required minimum distributions.

Example 13-9

What if: In the previous example, we determined that Dave must receive a minimum distribution of $136,850 from his traditional 401(k) account by April 1, 2017. If Dave does not receive any distribution before April 1, 2017, what penalty will he be required to pay?

Answer: $68,425 ($136,850 × 50%). Dave will pay this penalty as an other tax on his 2017 tax return. This nondeductible penalty is a strong incentive to take the required minimum distributions or at least to take the penalty into consideration when developing a distribution plan.

[12]See Reg. §1.401(a)(9)-9 Q&A 2 to reference the full version of the table. The table provided in this exhibit applies in most circumstances.

What if: Assume that Dave received his first distribution from his traditional 401(k) account on March 1, 2017, in the amount of $100,000. But, he did not receive any other distributions before April 1, 2017. What penalty is Dave required to pay?

Answer: $18,425 [($136,850 − $100,000) × 50%]

In contrast to defined benefit plans, defined contribution plans often provide distribution options that could trigger the penalty for premature distributions for the uninformed or unwary. For example, an employee who retires (or is fired) and takes a lump-sum distribution from her defined contribution account in a year before the year in which she turns 55 will be subject to a 10 percent early distribution penalty on the entire amount of the distribution. Employees who receive such lump-sum distributions may avoid the 10 percent penalty by electing to "roll over" (deposit) the distributions into one of the individually managed retirement plans we discuss later in this chapter.

After-Tax Rates of Return for Traditional Defined Contribution Plans

For a given before-tax rate of return and a constant tax rate, the longer the taxpayer defers distributions from a traditional defined contribution plan, the greater the taxpayer's after-tax rate of return on the retirement account, because deferring the distribution reduces the present value of the taxes paid on the distribution. A taxpayer's after-tax rate of return also depends on the taxpayer's marginal tax rate at the time she contributes to the plan and at the time she receives distributions from the plan. All else being equal, the higher her marginal tax rate at the time she contributes to the plan, the higher the after-tax rate of return (the higher tax rate increases the tax savings from the deduction), and the lower her marginal tax rate at the time she receives distributions from the plan the higher the after-tax rate of return (the lower rate reduces the taxes from the distribution).

Of course, any employer contributions to an employee's account, such as CBA's two-for-one matching contributions to Tina's account, significantly increases the after-tax rate of return (and after-tax accumulation) because the contributions increase the employee's after-tax proceeds, but the employee's cost of these contributions is zero.

Exhibit 13-4 summarizes the tax aspects of defined benefit and defined contribution plans.

Roth 401(k) Plans

Employers that provide **traditional 401(k)** plans to employees may also provide **Roth 401(k)** plans. As we discuss below, employee tax consequences for Roth 401(k) plans differ from tax consequences of other traditional defined contribution plans.

When employers provide a Roth 401(k) plan, *employees* may elect to contribute to the Roth 401(k) *instead of or in addition to* contributing to a traditional 401(k) plan. However, *employer* contributions to an employee's 401(k) account must go to the employee's *traditional* 401(k) account rather than the employee's Roth 401(k) account. Consequently, the balance in an employee's Roth 401(k) account must consist of only the employee's contributions and the earnings on those contributions. Because employers providing Roth 401(k) plans to employees are not allowed to contribute to the Roth plans, these employers are required to maintain traditional 401(k) accounts for each employee participating in the Roth 401(k) plan.

In contrast to contributions to traditional 401(k) plans, employee contributions to Roth 401(k) accounts are *not* deductible and, therefore, do not produce any im-

THE KEY FACTS

Roth 401(k) Defined Contribution Plans

- Employees but not employers may contribute.
  - Employers contribute to traditional 401(k).
- Contributions are not deductible.
- Same contribution limits as traditional 401(k) plans.

EXHIBIT 13-4   Defined Benefit Plan vs. Defined Contribution Plan Summary

	Defined Benefit Plan	Defined Contribution Plan
Benefits	• Specifies benefit employee receives on retirement. • Maximum benefit in 2016 lesser of (1) 100 percent of average of highest three years' compensation or (2) $210,000.	• Specifies the amounts employer and employee contribute to the account. • Ultimate benefit depends on earnings on contributions.
Payout type	• Life annuity. • Lump sum distribution of the present value of standard benefit.	• Life annuity. • Lump sum. • Fixed number of years.
Funding requirements	• Employers fund increase in expected future liability each year.	• No funding requirement other than to make required contributions to employee accounts.
Employer's contributions tax deductible?	• Yes.	• Yes, but limited to 25 percent of aggregate employee annual compensation.
Employee's contributions tax deductible?	• No employee contributions.	• Yes, subject to limitations on the amount that can be contributed [$18,000 ($24,000 if 50 or older) maximum contribution to 401(k) plan in 2016].
Contribution limits	• Not applicable.	• In 2016, lesser of (1) $53,000 ($59,000 for taxpayers at least 50 years of age at end of year) and (2) 100 percent of the employee's compensation for year.
Other factors	• All employees paid from same account. • Heavy administrative burden. • Employees make investment choices.	• Separate accounts for each employee. • Employees assume investment risk. • Employees assume investment risk.
Vesting requirements	• 5-year cliff or • 7-year graded	• 3-year cliff or • 6-year graded • Employee contributions vest immediately.
Distributions	• Taxed as ordinary income. • No 10 percent penalty if 59½ years of age or 55 years of age and retired. • Minimum distributions required by April 1 of year after the later of (1) year employee reaches 70½ or (2) year employee retires.	• Taxed as ordinary income (except Roth type accounts). • No 10 percent penalty if either 59½ years of age or 55 years of age and retired. • Minimum distributions requirements same as for defined benefit plan.

mediate tax savings for employees. Therefore, employees wanting to contribute a certain amount to a Roth 401(k) plan must earn more than that specified amount in order to have the desired contribution amount remaining *after* paying taxes on the amount they earn. For example, assume an employee with a 20 percent marginal tax rate wants to contribute $2,000 to a Roth 401(k) account. To earn the funds to make this contribution, the employee must earn $2,500 before taxes. The tax on the $2,500 of income is $500 ($2,500 × 20%). This leaves the taxpayer with $2,000 after taxes ($2,500 before taxes minus $500 in taxes) to contribute to the Roth 401(k) account.

Example 13-10

What if: Let's assume that CBA offers a Roth 401(k) plan in addition to its traditional 401(k) plan. In her first full calendar year of employment with CBA, Tina elects to contribute 4 percent of her $60,000 salary to CBA's Roth 401(k) plan instead of CBA's traditional 401(k) plan. What is Tina's after-tax cost of this $2,400 contribution (her marginal tax rate is 25 percent)?

Answer: $2,400. Her after-tax cost is her $2,400 contribution because the contribution does not generate any tax savings.

What is Tina's before-tax cost of the contribution? That is, how much did Tina need to earn before taxes to fund the $2,400 after-tax contribution?

Answer: $3,200. Because her marginal tax rate is 25 percent, she needs to earn $3,200 before taxes [$2,400/(1 − .25)] to have $2,400 to contribute to the Roth 401(k) after taxes [$3,200 × (1 − .25)]. When she contributes $2,400 *after taxes* to the Roth 401(k), she is contributing $3,200 *before taxes*.

THE KEY FACTS

Roth 401(k) Defined Contribution Plans

- Qualified distributions not taxable.
  - Account open for five years.
  - Employee at least 59½ at time of distribution.
- Nonqualified distributions.
  - Distributions of account earnings taxable and subject to 10 percent penalty if taxpayer is not either 59½ years of age or 55 years of age and retired.
  - Distributions of contributions not taxed or penalized.
  - Distribution × ratio of contributions to account balance is nontaxable. The remainder of distribution is out of account earnings.
- After-tax return equals before-tax return.

While contributions to Roth 401(k) accounts are not deductible and, as a result, do not generate any current tax savings, *qualified* distributions from Roth 401(k) accounts are excluded from gross income. Because contributions to Roth 401(k) accounts are not deductible and qualified distributions from Roth 401(k) accounts are not taxable, the before-tax rate of return equals the after-tax rate of return on Roth 401(k) accounts. Note also that because qualified Roth 401(k) distributions are excluded from income, in contrast to traditional 401(k) distributions, they do not increase AGI and thus do not cause AGI-based tax benefit phase-outs (e.g., certain itemized deductions and tax credits) and they do not cause an increase in the taxation of the recipient's Social Security benefits (see Chapter 5 for discussion of taxation of Social Security benefits).

Example 13-11

What if: In the previous example, Tina contributed $2,400 to her Roth 401(k) account in her first calendar year on the job with CBA. Let's assume that Tina leaves this contribution in the account until she retires in 40 years at the age of 63, that her contribution earns an annual 8 percent before-tax rate of return, and that her marginal tax rate will be 30 percent when she receives the distribution. How much will Tina have accumulated after taxes if she withdraws the initial contribution and all the earnings on the contribution when she retires?

Answer: $52,139 ($2,400 × 1.08^{40}).

Tina's after-tax rate of return on her $2,400 after-tax contribution is exactly 8 percent, the same as the before-tax rate of return. With a Roth 401(k) the after-tax rate of return should always equal the before-tax rate of return because the contributions are not deductible and distributions are not taxable.

Qualified distributions from Roth 401(k) accounts are those made after the employee's account has been open for five taxable years *and* the employee is at least 59½ years of age. All other distributions are nonqualified distributions. When a taxpayer receives a *non*qualified distribution from a Roth 401(k) account, the tax consequences of the distribution depend on the extent to which the distribution is from the account earnings and the extent to which it is from the employee's contributions to the account. Nonqualified distributions of account *earnings* are fully taxable. Nonqualified distributions of account earnings are also subject to a 10 percent early distribution penalty unless the taxpayer is either 59½ years of age at the time of the distribution or at least 55 years of age and retired at the time of the distribution. Nonqualified distributions of the taxpayer's account *contributions* are not subject to tax because the taxpayer did not deduct these amounts. If less than the entire balance in the plan is distributed, the non-taxable portion of the distribution is determined by multiplying the amount of the distribution by the ratio of account contributions to the total account balance.

Example 13-12

What if: In the previous example, Tina contributed $2,400 to CBA's Roth 401(k) plan, her account generated an 8 percent before-tax rate of return, and she withdrew the entire balance 40 years after the contribution. Let's assume that at the end of year 6, Tina needs cash, so she withdraws $1,000 from the account when the account balance is $3,808 and her marginal tax rate is 28 percent. How much tax and penalty, if any, is Tina required to pay on this nonqualified distribution?

Answer: $104 tax and $37 penalty, computed as follows:

Description	Amount	Explanation
(1) Contribution to Roth 401(k) (nondeductible)	$2,400	Beginning of year 1.
(2) Account balance end of year 6	3,808	$2,400 × 1.08^6.
(3) Nonqualified distribution end of year 6	1,000	
(4) Percentage of distribution that is not taxable	63.03%	(1)/(2).
(5) Nontaxable portion of distribution	630	(3) × (4).
(6) Taxable portion of distribution	370	(3) − (5).
(7) Marginal tax rate in year 6	28%	
(8) Regular income tax on distribution	**104**	**(6) × (7).**
(9) Penalty tax percentage for early distributions	10%	
(10) Penalty tax on early distribution	**37**	**(6) × (9).**
Total tax and penalty on early distribution	$ 141	(8) + (10).

Finally, it is important to note that the minimum distribution requirements applicable to traditional 401(k) accounts also apply to Roth 401(k) accounts.

Comparing Traditional Defined Contribution Plans and Roth 401(k) Plans

We've described and discussed the tax consequences associated with participating in traditional and Roth 401(k) plans. So which is better for employees? If given a choice, which type of 401(k) plan should you contribute to? While many factors should be considered in making this decision, perhaps the most important is the taxpayer's current marginal tax rate (the rate in the year of contributions) compared to the taxpayer's expected future marginal tax rate (the expected rate in the year of distributions). Taxpayers generally should prefer traditional 401(k) plans when their current marginal rate is higher (greater tax savings derived from deductions) than their expected future marginal rate (lower tax cost on income from distributions) and they should prefer Roth 401(k) plans when their current marginal rate is lower than their expected future tax rate. When future rates are higher than current rates, taxpayers should generally prefer Roth 401(k) plans because the forgone tax savings from a nondeductible contribution is smaller when the marginal tax rate is lower and the tax savings from excluding the distribution from income is greater when the marginal tax rate is higher. While current and expected future marginal tax rates are important to consider, other factors relevant to this decision include, among others, the uncertainty of future tax rates and the taxpayer's risk tolerance for this uncertainty and how a taxpayer reinvests the tax savings from contributions to traditional 401(k) plans. A detailed discussion of all factors relevant to this decision is beyond the scope of this text. Exhibit 13-5 summarizes and compares the tax consequences of traditional 401(k) plans and Roth 401(k) plans.

EXHIBIT 13-5   **Traditional 401(k) Plan vs. Roth 401(k) Plan Summary**

	Traditional 401(k) Plans	Roth 401(k) Plans
Employer contributions allowed	• Yes.	• No.
Tax consequences to employer	• Contributions deductible when paid.	• Not applicable.
Tax consequences to employee	• Contributions are deductible.	• Contributions are not deductible.
Distributions	• Taxed as ordinary income. • No 10 percent penalty if the taxpayer is at least 59½ years of age or at least 55 years of age and retired at time of distribution. • If life annuity or joint and survivor annuity no penalty even if not 55 years of age. • Minimum distributions required by April 1 of the later of (1) the year after the year in which the employee reaches 70½ or (2) the year after the year in which the employee retires. • Failure to meet minimum distribution timing and amount requirements triggers 50 percent penalty.	• Qualified distributions not taxed. • Qualified distributions when account is open for at least 5 years and employee has reached age 59½. • No 10 percent penalty on taxable part of nonqualified distribution if the taxpayer is at least 59½ years of age or at least 55 years of age and retired at time of distribution. • If life annuity or joint and survivor annuity, no penalty even if not 55 years of age. • Minimum distribution requirements and penalties are the same as for traditional 401(k) plans. • If nonqualified distribution, nontaxable percentage of distribution is the ratio of contributions to total account value.

NONQUALIFIED DEFERRED COMPENSATION   `LO 13-3`

So far, our discussion has emphasized the tax and nontax aspects of employer-provided *qualified* defined benefit and defined contribution plans. In addition to or perhaps in lieu of these types of qualified plans, employers may offer **nonqualified deferred compensation** plans to certain employees.

Nonqualified Plans vs. Qualified Defined Contribution Plans

Deferred compensation plans permit employees to defer (or contribute) current salary in exchange for a future payment from the employer. From an employee's perspective, the tax consequences of contributions to and distributions from nonqualified plans are similar to the tax consequences of contributions to and distributions from qualified defined contribution plans. For example, just as with defined contribution plans, employee contributions to nonqualified deferred compensation plans (NQDC) reduce an employee's taxable income in the year of contribution.[13] Also, just as with qualified plans, employees are not taxed on the balance in their accounts until they receive distributions. Finally, like distributions from qualified plans, distributions from nonqualified deferred compensation plans are taxed as ordinary income.

[13]Technically, employees participating in NQDC plans defer the receipt of current salary and employers credit the employee's account for the amount of the deferral. This has the same effect as if the employee had actually made a deductible contribution (for AGI) to her account as an employee participating in a defined contribution plan would do.

Example 13-13

CBA provides a nonqualified deferred compensation plan under which executives may elect to defer up to 10 percent of their salary. Dave Allan has been participating in the plan by deferring a portion of his salary each year for the last 15 years. The balance in his deferred compensation account is currently $2,000,000. In keeping with a fixed payment schedule Dave elected under the plan, he receives a $50,000 distribution. What amount of tax must Dave pay on the distribution (recall that his marginal tax rate is 35 percent)?

Answer: $17,500 ($50,000 × .35).

For employers, NQDC plans are treated differently than qualified plans. For example, because nonqualified plans are not subject to the same restrictive requirements pertaining to qualified plans, employers may discriminate in terms of whom they allow to participate in the plan. In fact, employers generally restrict participation in nonqualified plans to more highly compensated employees. Also, employers are not required to "fund" nonqualified plans. That is, employers are not required to formally set aside and accumulate funds specifically to pay the deferred compensation obligation when it comes due. Rather, employers typically retain funds deferred by employees under the plan, use the funds for business operations, and pay the deferred compensation out of their general funds when it becomes payable. Because employers retain, control, and generate income on funds deferred by employees under nonqualified plans, employers are allowed to *deduct only actual payments* of deferred compensation to employees. That is, employers cannot deduct the amount of deferred compensation they accrue each year. Thus, for tax purposes, an employer may not deduct the deferred compensation when an employee initially earns the compensation even though the employer becomes liable for the deferred compensation payment. In contrast, for financial accounting purposes, companies generally expense deferred compensation in the year employees earn it and record a corresponding deferred compensation liability.[14]

THE KEY FACTS

Nonqualified Deferred Compensation Plans

- Employees defer current income in exchange for future payment.
  - Employee is taxed when payment received.
  - Employee generally selects deemed investment choices up front to determine return on deferral.
  - Just like traditional deferred compensation plans, after-tax rate of return depends on before-tax rate of return, marginal tax rate at time of deferral, and marginal tax rate at time of distribution.
  - Payment is not guaranteed. If employer doesn't pay, employee becomes unsecured creditor.

Employee Considerations

Should employees participate in nonqualified plans when given the chance? The decision obviously involves several considerations. First, employees must decide if the benefits they expect to receive from qualified retirement plans (or other sources) will be adequate to provide for their expected costs during retirement. Next, employees should consider whether they can afford to defer current salary. This may not be a significant concern for most eligible participants, however, because nonqualified plans are generally available only to highly compensated employees who likely may not have the liquidity concerns that lower-compensated employees may face. Also, employees should consider the expected after-tax rate of return on the deferred salary relative to what they could earn on the salary by receiving it currently and personally investing it.

Generally, larger employers allow employees participating in nonqualified plans to choose how their deferred compensation will be invested from among alternative investments provided under the plan (money market, various bond funds, and stock funds among others). However, because employers *do not actually invest* compensation deferred under the plan on the employee's behalf, the employer credits the employee's account "as if" the employee's contributions had been invested in the employee's *deemed* investment choices. The description of

[14]Employers record additional expense and liability as earnings on the deferred compensation accumulate.

Coca-Cola Company's nonqualified retirement plan, presented in Exhibit 13-6, illustrates this concept:

EXHIBIT 13-6   **Description of Nonqualified Retirement Plan**
Excerpt from Coca-Cola Company's proxy statement

Deferred Compensation Plan. The Deferred Compensation Plan is a nonqualified and unfunded deferred compensation program offered to approximately 945 U.S. based Company employees in 2014. International Service Associates do not participate in the Deferred Compensation Plan. Eligible participants may defer up to 80% of base salary and up to 95% of their annual incentive. The Company has the benefit of full unrestricted use of all amounts deferred under the Deferred Compensation Plan until such amounts are required to be distributed to the plan participants. Gains and losses are credited based on the participant's election of a variety of deemed investment choices. The Company does not match any employee deferral or guarantee a return. Participants' accounts may or may not appreciate and may depreciate depending on the performance of their deemed investment choices. None of the deemed investment choices provide returns at above-market or preferential rates. All deferrals are paid out in cash upon distribution. Participants may schedule a distribution during employment or may opt to receive their balance after separation from service.

Just as with qualified defined contribution plans, other than Roth 401(k) plans, an employee's after-tax rate of return on deferred compensation depends on the employee's investment choices *and* on the employee's marginal tax rates at the time of the contribution and at the time of the distribution.

Example 13-14

As a new executive with CBA, Lisa Whitlark is eligible to participate in CBA's nonqualified deferred compensation plan. Recall that CBA provides a nonqualified deferred compensation plan under which executives may elect to defer up to 10 percent of their salary. In her first year with CBA, Lisa elects to defer $40,000 of salary ($400,000 × 10%) under the plan. Because her current marginal income tax rate is 33 percent, she saves $13,200 in taxes by deferring the salary ($40,000 × 33%). Consequently, her after-tax cost of deferring the compensation is $26,800 ($40,000 − $13,200). She plans to receive a distribution from the nonqualified plan in 20 years when she expects her marginal tax rate to be 28 percent. Lisa selects a stock index fund as her "deemed" investment choice. She expects the fund to provide an 8 percent before-tax rate of return on her $40,000 deferral. What will Lisa receive after taxes from her $40,000 deferral?

Answer: $134,235 after-tax accumulation, computed as follows:

Description	Amount	Explanation
Contribution to plan	$ 40,000	Deferral of 10 percent of her current salary.
Times future value factor	× 1.08^{20}	8 percent annual rate of return for 20 years.
Future value of deferred compensation	186,438	Value of deferral/distribution 20 years after deferral.
Minus: taxes payable on distribution	(52,203)	$186,438 value of account × 28 percent marginal tax rate.
After-tax proceeds from distributions	**$134,235**	Value of account minus taxes payable on distribution.

Deferring salary to a future period is potentially an effective tax planning technique, particularly when the employee anticipates her marginal tax rate to be lower in the year she will receive the deferred compensation than it is in the year she defers the salary. In fact, if employees had complete flexibility as to when they could receive distributions from deferred compensation plans, they would likely accelerate distributions from deferred compensation plans into years they knew with certainty would have relatively low marginal tax rates. This strategy is limited, however, by rules requiring employees to specify the timing of the future payments at the time they decide to participate in deferred compensation plans.[15]

Employees considering participating in nonqualified deferred compensation plans should also consider potential financial risks of doing so. Recall that employers are not required to fund nonqualified plans. So, there's always the possibility that the employer becomes bankrupt and will not have the funds to pay the employee on the scheduled distribution dates. If the employer is not able to make the payments, the employee becomes an unsecured creditor of the company and may never receive the full compensation owed to her. Consequently, the employee should evaluate the financial stability of the company when deciding whether to defer compensation under the employer's plan.

Employer Considerations

It's pretty clear that nonqualified plans can provide significant benefits to employees. How might employers benefit from providing nonqualified plans? First, employers may benefit if they are able to earn a better rate of return on the deferred compensation than the rate of return they are required to pay employees participating in the plan. In addition, employers can use nonqualified plans to achieve certain compensation objectives. For example, nonqualified plans could be a component of a compensation package a company may use to attract prospective executives. Also, because deferred compensation is not deductible until it is paid, deferred compensation plans provide a potentially effective way for employers to circumvent the $1 million salary deduction limitation for executives of publicly traded corporations imposed by the **§162(m) limitation** (see Chapter 12 discussion of the limitation). That is, an employer may pay an executive $1 million of current compensation and defer compensation over $1 million to a future period. By doing this, the employer is able to deduct the full $1 million of salary and the entire amount of the deferred compensation as long as the employee has retired at the time the employer pays the deferred compensation. This is because the $1 million deductibility limitation on compensation does not apply if the executive is no longer employed by the company when the company pays the deferred compensation. However, if the executive is still an employee when the deferred compensation is paid, it is subject to the $1 million deduction limit.

Likewise, deferring compensation may be an important tax planning tool for employers in situations where their current marginal tax rates are low (employers currently experiencing net operating losses) and they expect their future marginal tax rates when deferred compensation is paid to be significantly higher (employers expect to return to profitability). In effect, deferring compensation into a year with a higher marginal tax rate increases the tax benefit of the compensation deduction, which reduces the after-tax cost of the compensation to the employer.

THE KEY FACTS

Nonqualified Deferred Compensation Plans

- Employer promises to pay deferred compensation at some point in future.
  - Deduct when paid to employee.
  - Not required to fund obligation.
  - Use to accomplish compensation objectives like avoid $1M deductibility and to provide more deferred compensation to employees who are over contribution limits on qualified plans.
  - Employer's marginal tax rates at time of deferral relative to those at time of payment affect after-tax cost of providing deferred compensation relative to current compensation.

[15]§409A. These rules do provide, however, that specified payments from deferred compensation plans may commence while employees are still employed.

Exhibit 13-7 summarizes and compares qualified retirement plans and nonqualified deferred compensation plans.

EXHIBIT 13-7   Qualified Plan vs. Nonqualified Plan Summary

	Qualified Plans	Nonqualified Plans
Types	• Defined benefit (Pension). • Defined contribution [401(k)].	• Deferred compensation.
Requirements	• May not discriminate against "rank and file" employees of the company. • Funding or contribution requirements. • Vesting requirements.	• May discriminate. • Generally provided to executives and highly compensated. • No formal funding requirements (employee essentially unsecured creditor). • No formal vesting requirements.
Tax consequences to employers	• Immediately deduct contributions to plan (amount funded).	• No deduction until paid to employee.
Tax consequences to employees	• Employee contributions deductible unless to Roth-type account. • Earnings deferred until distributed to employee. • Employer contributions not immediately taxed. • Distributions from non-Roth plans treated as ordinary income.	• Employee contributions (or deferrals) deductible. • Taxed as ordinary income when received. • Earnings deferred until distributed to employee.

INDIVIDUALLY MANAGED QUALIFIED RETIREMENT PLANS

We've covered tax and nontax issues relating to both qualified and nonqualified employer-sponsored retirement savings plans. However, not all employers provide retirement savings plans, and when they do, some employees may not be eligible to participate, while others who are eligible may elect to not participate in these plans. The tax laws provide opportunities for these taxpayers to provide for their own retirement security through individually managed retirement plans. The **individual retirement account (IRA)** is the most common of the individually managed retirement plans. Other types of individually managed plans are available to self-employed taxpayers.

INDIVIDUAL RETIREMENT ACCOUNTS   LO 13-4

Taxpayers who meet certain eligibility requirements can contribute to **traditional IRAs,** to **Roth IRAs,** or to both. Just like traditional and Roth 401(k) plans, traditional IRAs and Roth IRAs have different tax characteristics. In fact, in most respects, the tax characteristics of traditional 401(k) plans mirror those of traditional IRAs and tax characteristics of Roth 401(k) plans mirror those of Roth IRA accounts. To minimize redundancy, we focus on the tax characteristics that differ between employer-sponsored 401(k) plans and self-managed IRAs.

Traditional IRAs

Contributions   Deductible contributions to IRAs are for AGI deductions. The maximum deductible contribution for a taxpayer in 2016 depends on the taxpayer's age as follows:

- $5,500 deduction limit if the taxpayer is less than 50 years of age at year-end.[16,17]
- $6,500 deduction limit if the taxpayer is at least 50 years of age at year-end.[18]
- $0 deduction if the taxpayer is at least 70½ years of age at year-end.

The deductible contribution limit may be further restricted depending on the following factors:

- Whether the taxpayer is an active participant in an employer-sponsored retirement plan.
- The taxpayer's filing status.
- The amount of the taxpayer's earned income.
- The taxpayer's AGI.

Unmarried taxpayers not participating in an employer-sponsored retirement plan may deduct IRA contributions up to the *lesser* of

- $5,500 ($6,500 for taxpayers 50+ years of age).
- Earned income.

As we discuss in Chapter 5, earned income generally includes income actually earned through the taxpayer's efforts such as wages, salaries, tips, and other employee compensation plus the amount of the taxpayer's net earnings from self-employment. Alimony income is also considered as earned income for this purpose.

Example 13-15

In the year she graduated from college, Tina earned $25,000. She earned $5,000 in salary working part-time while she was in school and she earned $20,000 in salary working for CBA from September through December. To get an early start saving for retirement, she contributed $5,000 to a *traditional* IRA (recall that Tina is not eligible to participate in CBA's 401(k) retirement plan until January of next year). How much of this contribution may Tina deduct?

Answer: $5,000. Because Tina is not participating in an employer-sponsored retirement plan during the current year, Tina may deduct the full $5,000 contribution as a *for* AGI deduction, reducing her AGI from $25,000 to $20,000.

For *unmarried taxpayers* who actively participate in an employer-sponsored retirement plan, the deduction limits are the same as for those who do not participate except that the maximum deduction is phased out based on the taxpayer's AGI as follows:

- No phase-out if AGI is equal to or less than $61,000.
- Proportional phase-out of full limit for AGI between $61,000 and $71,000 [The phase-out percentage is computed as follows: (AGI minus $61,000) divided by ($71,000 − $61,000), for example, if AGI is $63,000, taxpayer loses 20 percent of contribution limit].
- Full phase-out (no deduction) if AGI is equal to or greater than $71,000.

---

[16]Lump-sum distributions from qualified plans other than Roth 401(k)s received prior to retirement are frequently rolled over into traditional IRA accounts to avoid the 10 percent premature distribution penalty and current taxation. Rollover contributions are not subject to normal contribution limits for traditional IRAs.

[17]The IRA contribution limit is indexed for inflation.

[18]The $1,000 increase in the deduction limit for older taxpayers is granted to allow taxpayers nearing retirement age to "catch up" on contributions they may have not made in previous years.

Married taxpayers can make deductible contributions to separate IRAs (IRA for each spouse), subject to limitations. If the married couple files jointly, before considering any AGI-based phase-out amounts (discussed below), the maximum deduction for the spouse with the *higher* amount of earned income is the same as it is for unmarried taxpayers [$5,500 ($6,500 if at least 50 years of age at year-end) or earned income if it is less]. However, the maximum deduction for the spouse with the *lesser* amount of earned income, is limited to the lesser of

- $5,500 ($6,500 if this spouse is age 50+) or
- Total earned income of both spouses reduced by deductible and nondeductible contributions to the higher-earning spouse's traditional IRA and by contributions to the higher-earning spouse's Roth IRA.[19]

The contribution to the lesser-earning spouse's IRA is called a **spousal IRA.** The money in the account belongs to the lesser-earning spouse no matter where the funds for the contribution came from.

If either spouse is an active participant in an employer's retirement plan, and the couple files jointly, the maximum deduction for each spouse is phased out based on the *couple's* AGI as follows:

- No phase-out if the couple's AGI is equal to or less than $98,000.
- Proportional phase-out of full limit for AGI between $98,000 and $118,000 (for example, if AGI is $110,000, taxpayer loses 60 percent of deductible contribution limit).
- Full phase-out (no deduction) if AGI is equal to or greater than $118,000.

If one spouse is an active participant in an employer's retirement plan and the other is not, and the couple files jointly, the deduction for the spouse who is not an active participant is phased out based on the couple's AGI as follows (the phase-out applies whether the spouse is the higher- or lesser-earning spouse):

- No phase-out if the couple's AGI is equal to or less than $184,000.
- Proportional phase-out of full limit for AGI between $184,000 and $194,000.
- Full phase-out (no deduction) if AGI is equal to or greater than $194,000.

Married taxpayers who file separately may also make deductible contributions to an IRA. The maximum deduction is the lesser of

- $5,500 ($6,500 if taxpayer is 50+).
- The taxpayer's earned income.

However, if either spouse is an active participant in an employer's retirement plan, and they file separately, then each spouse's deductible contribution (including the nonactive participant spouse) is phased out over the spouse's AGI as follows:

- No phase-out if the taxpayer's AGI is $0 (also no tax benefit of deducting).
- Proportional phase-out of full limit for AGI between $0 and $10,000.
- Full phase-out (no deduction) if AGI is equal to or greater than $10,000.

If the couple files separate tax returns and did not live with each other at any time during the year, both spouses will be treated as unmarried taxpayers for purposes of the IRA deduction limitations. Appendix A to this chapter provides a flowchart for determining traditional IRA deduction limitations.

> **THE KEY FACTS**
>
> **Traditional IRAs**
>
> - If taxpayer does not participate in employer provided plan but spouse does
>   - Deduction limit phased out for AGI between $184,000 and $194,000.
> - Distribution taxed as ordinary income
>   - If distribution before taxpayer is 59½, 10 percent penalty generally applies.

[19]§219(c).

Example 13-16

In her first full calendar year working for CBA, Tina earns $60,000. Because she contributes $2,400 of her salary to CBA's 401(k) plan, her AGI is $57,600 ($60,000 − $2,400). Tina would like to make the maximum deductible contribution to her IRA. Assuming the 2016 limitations apply, how much is she allowed to deduct?

Answer: $5,500. Because Tina is a participant in CBA's retirement plan, the $5,500 deduction limit is subject to phase-out. However, because Tina's AGI is less than the beginning of the phase-out threshold ($61,000), she is allowed to deduct the maximum contribution.

What if: Assume that in her first full calendar year working for CBA, Tina earns $65,000. Because she contributes $2,400 of her salary to CBA's 401(k) plan, her AGI is $62,600 ($65,000 − $2,400). Tina would like to make the maximum deductible contribution to her IRA. How much is she allowed to deduct?

Answer: $4,620. The deductible amount before considering AGI limitations is $5,500. However, because Tina is a participant in CBA's retirement plan, the $5,500 deduction limit is subject to phase-out. Because Tina's AGI is 16 percent of the way through the $61,000 − $71,000 phase-out range for a single taxpayer [($62,600 − $61,000)/($71,000 − $61,000)], the $5,500 deductible contribution limit is reduced by 16 percent to $4,620 [$5,500 × (1 − .16)]. So, $4,620 is the maximum deductible contribution she can make to her traditional IRA.

What if: Assume that Tina is married and files a joint return with her spouse Steve. Tina participates in CBA's 401(k) plan and she receives $60,000 in salary from CBA for the year. Steve is a full-time student and is unemployed. The couple's AGI before considering IRA contributions is $60,000. What is Tina's maximum deductible IRA contribution for the year? What is Steve's maximum deductible IRA contribution for the year?

Answer: Tina's maximum deductible contribution for the year is $5,500. Because Tina is married, files a joint return, and reports AGI under $98,000 with her husband, her contribution is not phased out at all even though she is an active participant in CBA's retirement plan.

Steve's maximum deductible contribution for the year is also $5,500. Because Steve reports less earned income than Tina (in fact he doesn't report any earned income for the year), his deductible IRA contribution is limited to the lesser of (1) $5,500 or (2) $54,500 ($60,000 − $5,500) which is the couple's earned income minus Tina's deductible IRA contribution.

What if: Assume the same facts as the previous what-if example, except that Tina and Steve file separately. What is each spouse's maximum deductible IRA contribution for the year?

Answer: $0 for Tina and $0 for Steve. Tina is ineligible to make a deductible IRA contribution because her AGI of $60,000 exceeds the $10,000 phase-out limit and Steve may not make a deductible contribution to the IRA because he does not report any earned income.

Nondeductible Contributions For all taxpayers, to the extent the maximum deductible contribution is phased out based on AGI, taxpayers can still make *nondeductible* contributions of up to $5,500 per year ($6,500 for taxpayers are at least 55 years of age at year end). Taxpayers who have reached age 70½ by year-end are not allowed to contribute at all to an IRA. Earned income limitations (including the spousal IRA limits) that apply to deductible IRA contributions also apply to nondeductible contributions. That is, a taxpayer must have earned income in order to make nondeductible contributions to a traditional IRA (with the exception of a spouse who is contributing to a spousal IRA). The earnings on nondeductible contributions grow tax-free until the taxpayer receives distributions from the IRA. On distribution, the taxpayer is taxed on the earnings generated by the nondeductible contributions but not on the actual nondeductible contributions. When taxpayers take partial distributions from an IRA to which they have made deductible and nondeductible contributions, each distribution consists of a taxable and nontaxable component. The portion of the distribution that is nontaxable is the ratio of the nondeductible contributions to the total account balance at the time of the distribution.

This is exactly the same formula used in Example 13-12 to determine the nontaxable portion of nonqualified distributions from Roth 401(k) accounts. Most taxpayers exceeding the deductibility limits on traditional IRAs would likely do better by contributing to a Roth IRA, if eligible, instead of making nondeductible contributions to traditional IRAs.

Taxpayers who are eligible to contribute to an IRA may contribute to the IRA up to the unextended tax return due date (generally, April 15 of the subsequent year). That is, as long as the taxpayer makes a contribution to the IRA by April 15 of year 2, the contribution counts as though it were made during year 1 (the prior calendar year).

Distributions   Just as with traditional 401(k) plans, distributions from traditional IRAs are taxed as ordinary income to the taxpayer. Also, taxpayers withdrawing funds from traditional IRAs before reaching the age of 59½ are subject to a 10 percent early distribution penalty on the amount of the withdrawal. The IRA rules exempt certain distributions from the 10 percent penalty for early withdrawal. Among others, these distributions include proceeds distributed in the form of a life annuity (fixed payment each month or year over the taxpayer's life) and proceeds used for qualifying medical expenses, health insurance premiums for the owner, qualified higher education expenses, or first-time home purchases (limited to $10,000).[20] Taxpayers must receive their first required minimum distribution by April 1 of the year following the year in which the taxpayer reaches 70½ years of age. Because the distribution rules for traditional IRAs are so similar to the rules for traditional 401(k) accounts, taxpayers with traditional IRAs face virtually the same issues as participants in traditional 401(k) plans when planning for distributions. Thus, they should be careful to avoid the 10 percent penalty while at the same time taking similar steps to maximize the tax deferral on their traditional IRA account balances.

Roth IRAs

As an alternative to traditional IRAs, taxpayers meeting certain requirements can contribute to Roth IRAs. Contributions to Roth IRAs are *not* deductible and *qualifying* distributions from Roth IRAs are *not* taxable.

Contributions   Roth IRAs are subject to the same annual contribution limits as traditional IRAs [the lesser of $5,500 ($6,500 if at least age 50 at year-end) or earned income]. Further, the same spousal IRA rules that apply to traditional IRAs apply to Roth IRA contributions. These limits apply to the sum of a taxpayer's contributions to deductible IRAs, nondeductible IRAs, and Roth IRAs.

Whether or not they participate in an employer-sponsored retirement plan, the Roth IRA contribution limitation phases out as follows:

Unmarried taxpayers

- No phase-out if the taxpayer's AGI is $117,000 or below.
- Proportional phase-out of full limit for AGI between $117,000 and $132,000.
- Full phase-out (no contribution) if AGI is $132,000 or higher.

Married taxpayer filing jointly

- No phase-out if the taxpayer's AGI is $184,000 or below.
- Proportional phase-out of full limit for AGI between $184,000 and $194,000.
- Full phase-out (no contribution) if AGI is $194,000 or higher.

Married taxpayers filing separately

- No phase-out if the taxpayer's AGI is $0.
- Proportional phase-out of full limit if taxpayer's AGI between $0 and $10,000.
- Full phase-out (no contribution) if taxpayer's AGI is equal to or greater than $10,000.

Appendix B to this chapter provides a flowchart for determining Roth IRA contribution limits.

THE KEY FACTS

Roth IRAs

- Contributions not deductible.
- Same contribution limits as traditional IRAs but
  - For 2016, contribution phases out for AGI between $117,000 and $132,000 for unmarried taxpayers and between $184,000 and $194,000 for married filing jointly taxpayers.
- Qualified distributions not taxable.
  - To qualify, account must be open for at least five years before distribution and distribution made after taxpayer reaches 59½ years of age (among others).
- Nonqualified distributions of account earnings
  - Taxed at ordinary rates and subject to 10 percent penalty if the taxpayer is not at least 59½ years of age at the time of the distribution.
- Distributions first from contributions and then from account earnings.

---

[20]§72(t). A first-time homebuyer is someone who did not own a principal residence in the two years before acquiring the new home [see §72(t)(8)(D)].

Distributions   *Qualified* distributions from Roth IRAs are not taxable. A qualified distribution is a distribution from funds or earnings from funds in a Roth IRA *if the distribution is at least five years after the taxpayer opened the Roth IRA*[21] and the distribution meets one of the following requirements:

- Distribution is made on or after the date the taxpayer reaches 59½ years of age,
- Distribution is made to a beneficiary (or to the estate of the taxpayer) on or after the death of the taxpayer,
- Distribution is attributable to the taxpayer being disabled, or
- Distribution is used to pay qualified acquisition costs for first-time homebuyers (limited to $10,000).[22]

All other distributions are considered to be *nonqualified* distributions.

Nonqualified distributions are not necessarily taxable, however. Because taxpayers do not deduct Roth IRA contributions, they are able to withdraw the contributions tax-free at any time. However, *nonqualified* distributions of the *earnings* of a Roth IRA are taxable as ordinary income. The distributed earnings are also subject to a 10 percent penalty unless the taxpayer is 59½ years of age at the time of the distribution.[23] Nonqualified distributions are deemed to come

- First from the taxpayer's contributions (nontaxable).
- Then from account earnings after the total contributions have been distributed (note that this is different than the equivalent rule for Roth 401(k) plans).

Thus, taxpayers can treat the Roth IRA as an emergency savings account to the extent of their contributions without incurring any penalties.

ETHICS

Ryan had just finished a finance class and had learned about the importance of the time value of money. With this knowledge, he wanted to start saving for retirement. Last year Ryan had a job and earned $2,000. After paying his expenses, he placed the remaining $500 in a savings account in the bank. This year, however, Ryan decided to focus on his studies so he did not earn any income. He paid his living expenses through student loans. At the end of the current year, Ryan contributed $400 to a Roth IRA. On his tax return for the year, Ryan reported $400 of self-employment income (even though he didn't earn any). Why did Ryan report this "phantom" income? What do you think of his strategy?

Example 13-17

What if: Assume that when Tina started working for CBA, she made a one-time contribution of $4,000 to a Roth IRA. Years later, she retired at the age of 65 when the value of her Roth account was $60,000. If Tina receives a $10,000 distribution from her Roth IRA, what amount of taxes (and penalty, if applicable) must she pay on the distribution (assume her ordinary marginal rate is 30 percent)?

Answer: $0 taxes and $0 penalty. Qualified Roth IRA distributions are not taxable.

What if: Assume the same facts as above, except that Tina received a $10,000 distribution when she was 57 years of age. What amount of taxes (and penalty, if applicable) is she required to pay on the distribution (assume a 30 percent ordinary marginal rate)?

Answer: $2,400 in total consisting of $1,800 in taxes ($6,000 earnings distributed × 30 percent marginal tax rate) and $600 penalty ($6,000 earnings × 10 percent penalty rate). Because Tina has not reached age 59½ at the time of the distribution, this is a nonqualified distribution.

---

[21]The five-year period starts on January 1 of the year in which the contribution was made and ends on the last day of the fifth taxable year. See Reg §1.408A-6, Q&A2 and Q&A-5(b).

[22]§408A(d)(2).

[23]See §72(t)(2) for other exceptions to the penalty.

Consequently, she is taxed on the $6,000 distribution of earnings ($10,000 distribution minus $4,000 contribution). She is penalized on the distribution of earnings because she is not 59½ years of age at the time of the distribution.

What if: Assume that when Tina was 62 years old, she opened a Roth IRA, contributing $4,000. Three years later, Tina withdrew the entire account balance of $5,000. What amount of taxes (and penalty, if applicable) must Tina pay on the distribution (assume her marginal tax rate is 30 percent)?

Answer: $300 of taxes ($1,000 earnings × 30 percent marginal tax rate) but zero penalty. The distribution is a nonqualified distribution because Tina did not have the Roth IRA open for five years before receiving the distribution. Consequently, she must pay tax on the $1,000 earnings portion of the distribution ($5,000 − $4,000) but she is not penalized on the distribution because she was over 59½ years of age at the time of the distribution.

In contrast to taxpayers with traditional IRAs, taxpayers are *not* required to take minimum distributions from Roth IRAs. Thus, taxpayers can minimize distributions from Roth IRAs to maintain a source of tax-free income during their lifetime.

Rollover from Traditional to Roth IRA

Many taxpayers made contributions to traditional IRAs before Roth IRAs were available. Some taxpayers may have contributed to traditional IRAs and then later decided they should have contributed to Roth IRAs. The tax laws accommodate these taxpayers by allowing them to transfer funds from a traditional IRA (and other qualified defined contribution plans) to a Roth IRA.[24] This transfer of funds is called a **rollover.** When taxpayers do this, however, the entire amount taken out of the traditional IRA is taxed at ordinary rates but is not subject to the 10 percent penalty tax as long as the taxpayer contributes the *full amount* to a Roth IRA within 60 days of the withdrawal from the traditional IRA.[25]

Example 13-18

What if: Let's assume that in the year she graduated from college and began working for CBA, Tina made a fully deductible $4,000 contribution to a *traditional* IRA. Three years later, when her marginal tax rate is 25 percent, she rolls over the entire $5,000 account balance into a Roth IRA. What amount of taxes is she required to pay on the rollover?

Answer: $1,250 ($5,000 × 25%). The entire $5,000 transferred from the IRA to the Roth IRA is taxed at 25 percent but is not subject to the 10 percent early withdrawal penalty. Even though Tina pays $1,250 in taxes on the transfer, she is required to contribute $5,000 to the Roth IRA within 60 days from the time she withdraws the money from the traditional IRA.

What if: What are the tax consequences if Tina pays the $1,250 tax bill and contributes only $3,750 to the Roth IRA account?

Answer: She must pay a $125 penalty. The penalty is 10 percent of the $1,250 that she withdrew from the IRA and did not contribute to the Roth IRA ($5,000 − $3,750).

THE KEY FACTS

Roth IRAs

- Rollovers from traditional IRAs to Roth IRAs.
  - Amount withdrawn from traditional IRA fully taxable but not penalized.
  - Must contribute full amount withdrawn to Roth IRA account within 60 days of withdrawal.
  - Amounts withdrawn but not contributed subject to tax and 10 percent penalty.

Why would anyone be willing to pay taxes currently in order to avoid paying taxes later? Typically, a rollover from a traditional to a Roth IRA makes sense when a taxpayer's marginal tax rate is currently low (when the tax cost of the rollover is low) and expected to be significantly higher in the future (when the expected benefit of the rollover is high). Note that high-income taxpayers may not be allowed to contribute to Roth IRAs due to the AGI restrictions on contribution limits. However, because currently there is no AGI restriction on who may rollover funds from a traditional

---

[24]See Notice 2009-75, 2009-39 IRB.

[25]§408(d)(3). Taxpayers who roll over funds from a traditional IRA (or other traditional retirement account) to a Roth must wait at least five years from the date of the rollover to withdraw the funds from the rollover in order to avoid a 10 percent penalty on the distribution [§408(d)(3)(F)].

IRA (or other qualified defined contribution plan) into a Roth IRA, high-income taxpayers who would like to fund a Roth IRA may do so through a rollover.[26]

Comparing Traditional and Roth IRAs

So, which type of IRA is better for taxpayers? The tax considerations are very similar to those we already discussed when we compared traditional and Roth 401(k) plans. In general, after-tax rates of return from traditional IRAs will exceed those from Roth IRAs when marginal tax rates decline. However, after-tax rates of return from Roth IRAs will exceed those from traditional IRAs when tax rates increase.

Unrelated to marginal tax rates, Roth IRAs have other advantages relative to traditional IRAs as follows:

- Taxpayers can contribute to Roth IRAs at any age. In contrast, taxpayers are not allowed to make deductible contributions to traditional IRAs once they have reached 70½ years of age.
- The minimum distribution requirements for traditional IRAs do not apply to Roth IRAs. This provision permits owners of Roth IRAs to use their accounts to generate tax-free returns long after retirement.
- Taxpayers can withdraw their Roth contributions tax free at any time without paying tax or paying a penalty. Taxpayers who withdraw their traditional IRA contributions are taxed on the distribution and potentially penalized.

Exhibit 13-8 summarizes tax-related requirements for traditional and Roth IRAs.

EXHIBIT 13-8   Traditional IRA vs. Roth IRA Summary

	Traditional IRA	Roth IRA
Contributions requirements	• Taxpayer must not be a participant in an employer-sponsored plan or, if participating in an employer-provided plan, must meet certain income thresholds. Those above the threshold will have deductible portion of contribution phased out.	• No deduction allowed for contributions. Must meet certain income requirements to be able to contribute to a Roth IRA.
Contributions	• Deductible unless participant in employer plan and high AGI. • Nondeductible contributions allowed.	• Not deductible. • May not contribute if high AGI.
Maximum contribution	• Lesser of $5,500 per taxpayer ($6,500 for taxpayers over 50 years old) or earned income. • The contribution limits apply to the sum of contributions to traditional deductible IRAs, nondeductible IRAs, and Roth IRAs for the year. • For married couples filing jointly, contributions for the lesser earning spouse may not exceed the total earned income of both spouses reduced by deductible and nondeductible contributions to the other spouse's traditional IRA and by contributions to the other spouse's Roth IRA.	• Same as traditional IRA. • Same as traditional IRA. • Same as traditional IRA.
Contribution dates	• Can contribute up to unextended tax return due date, generally April 15.	• Same as traditional IRA.
Distributions	• Generally taxed as ordinary income. • If made before 59½, generally subject to 10 percent penalty. • If nondeductible contribution made, allocate distribution between taxable and nontaxable amounts similar to annuity rules. • Minimum distributions required by April 1 of the year after the year in which the taxpayer reaches 70½. • Failure to meet minimum distribution timing and amount requirements triggers 50 percent penalty.	• Qualified distributions not taxed. • Generally, distributions are qualified after account open for five years and employee has reached the age of 59½. • Nonqualified distributions not taxed to extent of prior contributions. • Nonqualified distributions of earnings subject to tax at ordinary rates and are also subject to a 10 percent penalty if the taxpayer is not at least 59½ years of age at the time of the distribution. • No minimum distribution requirements.

[26]§408A(c)(3).

SELF-EMPLOYED RETIREMENT ACCOUNTS

LO 13-5

We've discussed retirement savings opportunities available to employees. However, many taxpayers are self-employed small business owners who do not have access to employer-sponsored plans.[27] Moreover, individually managed retirement plans such as traditional and Roth IRAs are not particularly attractive to self-employed taxpayers due to the relatively low contribution limits on these plans. What retirement savings options, then, are available to the self-employed?

Congress created a number of retirement savings plans targeted toward self-employed taxpayers. Two of the more popular plans for the self-employed are SEP IRAs and individual (or "self-employed") 401(k) plans. These are defined contribution plans that generally work the same as employer-provided plans. That is, amounts set aside in these plans are deducted from income, earnings are free from tax until distributed, and distributions from the plans are fully taxable.[28] As we discuss below, these plans differ in terms of their annual contribution limits. They also have different nontax characteristics including their suitability for businesses with employees other than the owner and their administration costs. As you might expect, these factors come into play when self-employed small business owners choose a retirement plan.[29] We describe SEP IRAs and individual 401(k) plans below.[30]

Simplified Employee Pension (SEP) IRA

A simplified employee pension (SEP) can be administered through an individual retirement account (IRA) called a **SEP IRA**.[31] The owner of a sole proprietorship can

> **THE KEY FACTS**
>
> **Self-Employed Retirement Accounts**
> - Popular plans include SEP IRAs and individual 401(k)s.
> - Similar to (non-Roth) qualified defined contribution plans.
>   - Contributions deductible, distributions taxable.

---

[27]Because sole proprietorships with self-employment income are very common, we assume in our examples and explanations here that any self-employment income originates from a sole proprietorship. In some cases, however, partners and LLC members may also have self-employment income from a partnership or LLC.

[28]"Keogh" self-employed defined benefit plans are also an option. Generally, defined benefit plans are attractive to older, self-employed individuals with profitable businesses because they allow for greater deductible contributions. However, they are usually more costly to maintain than the defined contribution plans we mention here.

[29]Many investment firms provide comparisons to help taxpayers select self-employed retirement plans. One particularly good comparison is provided by Fidelity Investments at www.fidelity.com/retirement/small-business/compare-plans-chart

[30]A Savings Incentive Match Plans for Employees (SIMPLE) IRA is another popular form of retirement plan for the self-employed. For those earning lower amounts of self-employment income, the contribution limits for a SIMPLE IRA tend to be higher than contribution limits for SEP IRAs.

[31]§408(k).

make annual contributions directly to her SEP IRA. For 2016, the annual contribution is limited to the *lesser* of

- $53,000.
- 20 percent of Schedule C net income after reducing Schedule C net income by the deduction for the employer's portion of self-employment taxes paid (50 percent of the self-employment taxes paid).[32]

Contributions can be made up to the extended due date of the tax return.[33]

Example 13-19

What if: Dave (age 64) reports Schedule C net income of $40,000 during the current year. If he sets up a SEP IRA for himself, what is the maximum contribution he may make to the plan (assuming he has no other source of employee or self-employment income)?

Answer: $7,435, computed as follows:

Description	Amount	Explanation
(1) First limit on contribution	$53,000	
(2) Schedule C net income minus the self-employment tax deduction	37,174	$40,000 – ($40,000 × .9235 × 15.3% × 50%).
(3) Percentage for limitation based on (2)	20%	
(4) Second limit on contribution	7,435	(2) × (3).
Maximum contribution	**$ 7,435**	Lesser of (1) or (4).

What if: Assume Dave is 48 years old at the end of the year. What is his maximum deductible contribution?

Answer: $7,435. Dave's maximum deductible contribution for a SEP IRA does not depend on his age.

What if: Suppose Dave reports $310,000 of Schedule C net income rather than $40,000. What is his maximum deductible contribution to his SEP IRA account?

Answer: $53,000, the lesser of (1) $53,000 or (2) $59,700 [20% × ($310,000 – (((310,000 × .9235 – $118,500) × 2.9% × 50%) + ($118,500 × 15.3% × 50%)))].

THE KEY FACTS

Self-Employed Retirement Accounts

- SEP IRA 2016 contribution limit.
  - Lesser of (1) $53,000 or (2) 20 percent of Schedule C net income (after reducing Schedule C net income by the deduction for the employer's portion of self-employment taxes paid).

Nontax Considerations If a sole proprietor has hired employees, the sole proprietor *must* contribute to the employees' respective SEP IRAs based on their compensation. Because owners may view this requirement as being too favorable to employees, this plan is best suited for sole proprietors who do not have employees or for situations where owners are willing to provide generous benefits to their employees. From an administrative perspective, SEP IRAs are easy to set up and have relatively low administrative costs from year to year.

Individual 401(k)s

Individual 401(k) plans are strictly for sole proprietors (and the spouse of the sole proprietor) who do not have employees. Under this type of plan, for 2016, the sole proprietor can contribute the lesser of

- $53,000.
- 20 percent of Schedule C net income after reducing Schedule C net income by the deduction for the employer's portion of self-employment taxes paid (50 percent of self-employment taxes paid) (employer's contribution) plus an additional $18,000 (employee's contribution).

---

[32]Chapter 8 addresses self-employment taxes in more detail. Also note that for SEP IRAs no catch-up contributions are allowed for taxpayers 50 years and older.

[33]§404(h). This is September 15 for a calendar-year taxpayer.

Further, if the sole proprietor is at least 50 years of age by the end of the tax year, she may contribute an *additional* $6,000 as a catch-up contribution. Thus, a self-employed taxpayer with sufficient self-employment earnings and who is at least 50 years of age at year-end could contribute up to $59,000 to an individual 401(k) for 2016 ($53,000 + $6,000).

Finally, even though the individual 401(k) contribution limits provide for taxpayers to contribute an additional $18,000 or $24,000 (this includes the additional $6,000 for taxpayers at least 50 years of age at year-end) relative to a SEP IRA, a taxpayer's individual 401(k) contributions for the year are not allowed to exceed the taxpayer's Schedule C net income minus the self-employment tax deduction. Consequently, a taxpayer with limited self-employment income may not be able to take advantage of the additional $18,000 ($24,000) of contributions that individual 401(k)s allow relative to SEP IRAs.

Example 13-20

What if: Suppose that Dave is 64 years old at the end of the year, reports $40,000 of Schedule C net income, and has no other sources of income. What is the maximum amount he can contribute to an individual 401(k) account?

Answer: $31,435, computed as follows:

Description	Amount	Explanation
(1) First limit on contribution	$53,000	
(2) Schedule C net income minus the self-employment tax deduction	37,174	$40,000 − ($40,000 × .9235 ×15.3% × 50%).
(3) Percentage for limitation based on (2)	20%	
(4) Limit on employer's contribution	7,435	(2) × (3).
(5) Limit on employee's contribution	18,000	
(6) Second limitation	25,435	(4) + (5).
(7) Maximum contribution before catch-up contribution	25,435	Lesser of (1) or (6).
(8) Catch-up contribution	6,000	Dave is 64 years old at year-end.
Maximum contribution	**$31,435**	(7) + (8), not to exceed (2).

THE KEY FACTS

Self-Employed Retirement Accounts

- Individual 401(k) 2016 contribution limit.
  - Lesser of (1) $53,000 or (2) 20 percent of Schedule C net income (after reducing Schedule C net income by the deduction for the employer's portion of self-employment taxes paid) plus $18,000.
- Taxpayers who are at least 50 years old at the end of the year may contribute an additional $6,000 per year (maximum of $59,000, if self-employment earnings are sufficient).
- Contribution cannot exceed Schedule C net income minus self-employment tax deduction.

Example 13-21

What if: Assume Dave is 48 years old at the end of the year, reports $40,000 of Schedule C net income, and has no other sources of income. What is his maximum deductible contribution to his individual 401(k) account?

Answer: $25,435. This is the same as the amount he could contribute as a 64-year-old (see prior example), minus the $6,000 catch-up adjustment ($31,435 − $6,000).

What if: Assume the same facts as above except that Dave (age 64) earned $10,000 of Schedule C net income rather than $40,000. What is his maximum deductible contribution to his individual 401(k)?

(continued on page 13-30)

Answer: $9,294, computed as follows (Dave's contribution is limited to his Schedule C net income minus self-employment tax deduction):

Description	Amount	Explanation
(1) First limit on contribution	$53,000	
(2) Schedule C net income minus self-employment tax deduction	9,294	$10,000 − ($10,000 × .9235 × 15.3% × 50%).
(3) Percentage for limitation based on (2)	20%	
(4) Limit on employer's contribution	1,859	(2) × (3).
(5) Limit on employee's contribution	18,000	
(6) Second limitation	19,859	(4) + (5).
(7) Maximum contribution before catch-up contribution	19,859	Lesser of (1) or (6).
(8) Catch-up contribution	6,000	Dave is 64 years old at year-end.
Maximum contribution	**$ 9,294**	(7) + (8), not to exceed (2).

Example 13-22

What if: Assume Dave (age 64) earned $400,000 of Schedule C net income. What is his maximum deductible contribution to his individual 401(k)?

Answer: $59,000, computed as follows:

Description	Amount	Explanation
(1) First limit on contribution	$ 53,000	
(2) Schedule C net income minus self-employment tax deduction	387,297	$400,000 − [((400,000 × .9235 − 118,500) × 2.9% × 50%) + (118,500 × 15.3% × 50%)].
(3) Percentage for limitation based on (2)	20%	
(4) Limit on employer's contribution	77,459	(2) × (3).
(5) Limit on employee's contribution	18,000	
(6) Second limitation	95,459	(4) + (5).
(7) Maximum contribution before catch-up contribution	53,000	Lesser of (1) or (6).
(8) Catch-up contribution	6,000	Dave is 64 years old at year-end.
Maximum contribution	**$ 59,000**	(7) + (8), not to exceed (2).

Nontax Considerations   As we mentioned above, the individual 401(k) plan is not available for sole proprietors with employees, so providing benefits to employees under the plan is not a concern. However, the administrative burden of establishing, operating, and maintaining a 401(k) plan is potentially higher than it is for the other self-employed plans.

LO 13-6   SAVER'S CREDIT

To encourage middle- and low-income taxpayers to take advantage of the retirement savings opportunities discussed in this chapter, Congress provides an additional saver's credit for an individual's elective contribution of up to $2,000 to any of the qualified retirement plans discussed in this chapter including employer-sponsored qualified plans, traditional and Roth IRA plans, and self-employed qualified plans. The credit is provided *in addition to* any deduction the taxpayer is allowed for contributing to a retirement account. It is calculated by multiplying the taxpayer's contribution, up to a maximum of $2,000, by the applicable percentage depending on the taxpayer's filing status and AGI. The credit is nonrefundable.[34] Exhibit 13-9 provides the applicable percentages for 2016 according to a taxpayer's filing status and AGI.[35]

EXHIBIT 13-9 **2016 Applicable Percentages for Saver's Credit by Filing Status and AGI**

Applicable Percentage	Joint Filers AGI	Heads of Household AGI	All Other Filers AGI
50%	0 to $37,000	0 to $27,750	0 to $18,500
20	$37,001 to $40,000	$27,751 to $30,000	$18,501 to $20,000
10	$40,001 to $61,500	$30,001 to $46,125	$20,001 to $30,750
No credit available	Above $61,500	Above $46,125	Above $30,750

In addition to restricting the credit to taxpayers with AGI below a certain threshold, the credit is also restricted to individuals who are 18 years of age or older, are not claimed as dependents by another taxpayer, and are not full-time students at a qualified educational organization during each of five calendar months of the taxpayer's tax year.[36] Although limited in scope, the saver's credit provides some tax benefits for those taxpayers who qualify.

Example 13-23

What if: Tina earned $24,000 during the year she began working for CBA. She earned $4,000 in salary working part-time while she was in school and $20,000 in salary working for CBA from September through December. To get an early start saving for retirement, assume she contributed $4,000 to a traditional IRA. Because Tina did not participate in an employer-sponsored retirement plan during the current year she may deduct the full $4,000 contribution as a *for* AGI deduction, reducing her AGI from $24,000 to $20,000. What amount of saver's credit, if any, is Tina allowed to claim, assuming she was a full-time student during four months of the year (if she were a full-time student during five months of the year she would be ineligible for the saver's credit)?

Answer: $400 ($2,000 × 20 percent applicable credit).

What if: What saver's credit may Tina claim if her AGI was $15,000?

Answer: $1,000 ($2,000 × 50 percent applicable credit).

CONCLUSION

The decisions that employees like Tina, Lisa, and Dave must deal with highlight the role that tax issues play in this important area. Employers, like their employees, must also pay careful attention to tax considerations when deciding on retirement savings vehicles to offer their employees. Further, as has been a recurring theme throughout this book, nontax issues play an equal, if not more important, role in the retirement savings decisions of both employees and employers.

[34]According to §25B(g), the saver's credit is applied to the taxpayer's remaining tax liability after the application of certain other tax credits including the child tax credit and the American opportunity and lifetime learning credits.

[35]For this purpose, AGI is determined without considering the foreign earned income exclusion provided for U.S. residents living abroad under §911.

[36]§152(f)(2).

Appendix A   (Page 1) Traditional IRA Deduction Limitations

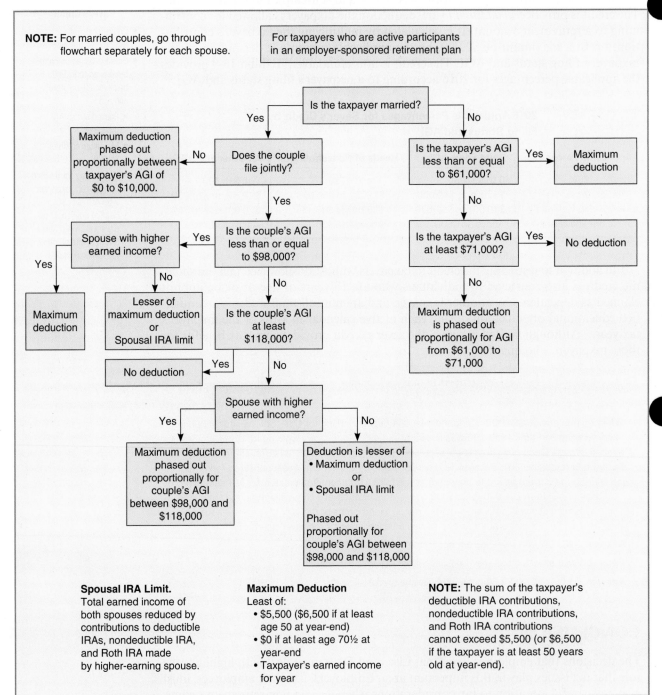

NOTE: For married couples, go through flowchart separately for each spouse.

For taxpayers who are active participants in an employer-sponsored retirement plan

Is the taxpayer married?

Spousal IRA Limit.
Total earned income of both spouses reduced by contributions to deductible IRAs, nondeductible IRA, and Roth IRA made by higher-earning spouse.

Maximum Deduction
Least of:
- $5,500 ($6,500 if at least age 50 at year-end)
- $0 if at least age 70½ at year-end
- Taxpayer's earned income for year

NOTE: The sum of the taxpayer's deductible IRA contributions, nondeductible IRA contributions, and Roth IRA contributions cannot exceed $5,500 (or $6,500 if the taxpayer is at least 50 years old at year-end).

(Page 2) Traditional IRA Deduction Limitations

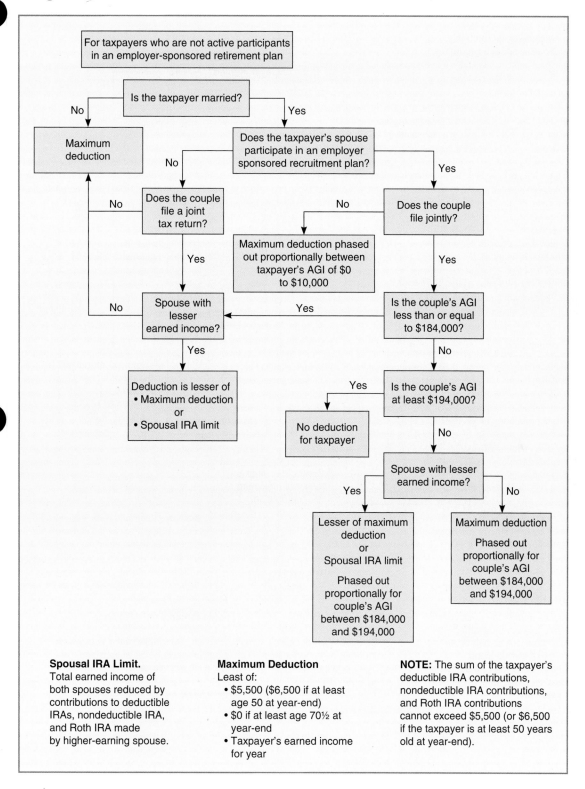

Spousal IRA Limit.
Total earned income of both spouses reduced by contributions to deductible IRAs, nondeductible IRA, and Roth IRA made by higher-earning spouse.

Maximum Deduction
Least of:
- $5,500 ($6,500 if at least age 50 at year-end)
- $0 if at least age 70½ at year-end
- Taxpayer's earned income for year

NOTE: The sum of the taxpayer's deductible IRA contributions, nondeductible IRA contributions, and Roth IRA contributions cannot exceed $5,500 (or $6,500 if the taxpayer is at least 50 years old at year-end).

Appendix B   Roth IRA Contribution Limits

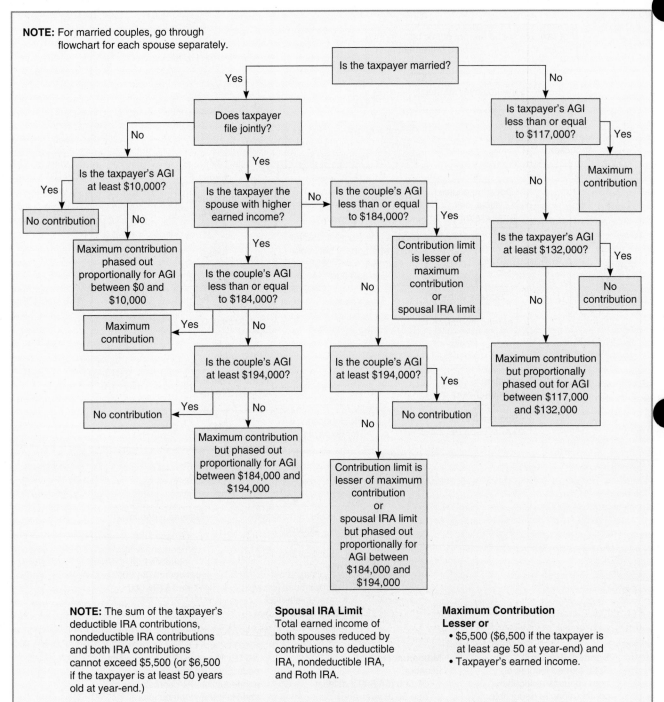

NOTE: For married couples, go through flowchart for each spouse separately.

NOTE: The sum of the taxpayer's deductible IRA contributions, nondeductible IRA contributions and both IRA contributions cannot exceed $5,500 (or $6,500 if the taxpayer is at least 50 years old at year-end.)

Spousal IRA Limit
Total earned income of both spouses reduced by contributions to deductible IRA, nondeductible IRA, and Roth IRA.

Maximum Contribution
Lesser or
• $5,500 ($6,500 if the taxpayer is at least age 50 at year-end) and
• Taxpayer's earned income.

Summary

Describe the tax and nontax aspects of employer-provided defined benefit plans from both the employer's and employee's perspective.

LO 13-1

- Benefits are determined based on years of service and salary. The maximum annual benefit is capped and adjusted upward annually for inflation.
- Benefits vest over time using either a five-year cliff or seven-year graded vesting schedule.
- Employers deduct cash contributions to fund the plan and employees treat cash distributions as ordinary income in the year received.
- Employers bear investment risk with defined benefit plans.
- Premature distribution and minimum distribution penalties don't typically apply to defined benefit distributions.
- Because of the high cost of funding and maintaining defined benefit plans, they are waning in popularity.

Explain and determine the tax consequences associated with employer-provided defined contribution plans, including traditional 401(k) and Roth 401(k) plans.

LO 13-2

- Employers specify the amount they will contribute to defined contribution plans instead of the annual benefit. However, employers are not permitted to contribute to Roth 401(k) plans.
- Employees may contribute to either a traditional 401(k) or Roth 401(k) account, and they determine how employer and employee contributions are invested. Employees bear investment risk with defined contribution plans.
- Annual employer and employee contributions are limited and maximum contribution amounts are adjusted annually for inflation.
- Employer contributions to traditional plans vest over time using either a three-year cliff or six-year graded vesting schedule.
- Employers deduct their contributions to traditional defined contribution plans.
- Employee contributions to traditional defined contribution plans are excluded from their taxable wages on Form W-2. Employee contributions to Roth 401(k) plans are not excluded.
- Distributions from traditional 401(k) plans are taxable at ordinary rates and qualified distributions from Roth 401(k) plans are not taxable.
- Distributions from both traditional 401(k) and Roth 401(k) plans are subject to premature and minimum distribution penalties.
- After-tax rates of return from Roth 401(k) plans are generally superior to those from traditional 401(k) plans when marginal tax rates are increasing.

Describe the tax implications of deferred compensation from both the employer's and employee's perspective.

LO 13-3

- Employees elect to defer current salary in exchange for promised future payments from the employer.
- Because the employer's promise of future payment is unsecured, employees recognize ordinary income when future payments are received. Employers wait to deduct payments until cash is actually paid.
- The after-tax rates of return and costs from deferred compensation arrangements to employees and employers depend on the current and future marginal tax rates of both the employee and employer.
- Deferred compensation can be used used to overcome deductibility constraints imposed on salary and qualified pension plans.
- Employees bear more risk with deferred compensation relative to other forms of retirement savings because employees are unsecured creditors of their employers and because the investments upon which their compensation is based have risk.

LO 13-4 Determine the tax consequences of traditional and Roth Individual Retirement Accounts and explain the differences between them.

- The same inflation-adjusted annual contribution limits apply to both traditional IRAs and Roth IRAs.
- The deduction for traditional IRA contributions is phased out for taxpayers covered by a retirement plan at work and with AGI above certain inflation-adjusted amounts. Special rules pertain for spouses not covered by an employer plan.
- The ability to contribute to a Roth IRA is phased out for individuals with AGI above certain inflation-adjusted amounts.
- Distributions from traditional IRAs are taxed at ordinary rates. A 10 percent premature distribution penalty generally applies to distributions from traditional IRAs received before age 59½.
- Distributions from Roth IRAs received after a Roth IRA account has been open for at least five years and after the recipient reaches age 59½ are not taxable. The earnings component of any distributions not meeting these requirements is generally taxable and subject to the 10 percent premature distribution penalty.
- Taxpayers generally prefer Roth IRAs to traditional IRAs when they expect their marginal tax rates to increase.

LO 13-5 Describe retirement savings options available to self-employed taxpayers and compute the limitations for deductible contributions to retirement accounts for self-employed taxpayers.

- Self-employed individuals may set up their own qualified pension plans such as SEP IRAs and individual 401(k)s.
- Contribution limits generally parallel those for employer-sponsored plans, allowing self-employed individuals to have the same access to qualified plans that employees have.
- Self-employed individuals with employees may have to incur the cost of covering their employees when they establish a qualified retirement plan.

LO 13-6 Compute the saver's credit.

- Individuals may receive up to a $1,000 tax credit for contributions they make to IRAs and employer-sponsored qualified plans.
- The amount of the credit is a function of the taxpayer's filing status and AGI.

KEY TERMS

cliff vesting (13-4)
defined benefit plan (13-3)
defined contribution plan (13-3)
graded vesting (13-4)
Individual Retirement Account (IRA) (13-19)

nonqualified deferred compensation (13-15)
qualified retirement plans (13-3)
rollover (13-25)
Roth 401(k) (13-11)
Roth IRA (13-19)

§162(m) limitation (13-18)
SEP IRA (13-27)
spousal IRA (13-21)
traditional 401(k) (13-11)
traditional IRA (13-19)
vesting (13-4)

DISCUSSION QUESTIONS

Discussion Questions are available in *Connect*®.

LO 13-1 LO 13-2 1. How are defined benefit plans different from defined contribution plans? How are they similar?

LO 13-1 2. Describe how an employee's benefit under a defined benefit plan is computed.

LO 13-1 LO 13-2 3. What does it mean to vest in a defined benefit or defined contribution plan?

LO 13-1 LO 13-2 4. Compare and contrast the minimum vesting requirements for defined benefit plans and defined contribution plans.

LO 13-1 LO 13-2 5. What are the nontax advantages and disadvantages of defined benefit plans relative to defined contribution plans?

6. Describe the maximum annual benefit that taxpayers may receive under defined benefit plans. `LO 13-1`

7. Describe the distribution or payout options available to taxpayers participating in qualified defined benefit plans. How are defined benefit plan distributions to recipients taxed? `LO 13-1`

8. Describe the minimum distribution requirements for defined benefit plans. Are these requirements typically an item of concern for taxpayers? `LO 13-1` `LO 13-2`

9. Compare and contrast the employer's responsibilities for providing a defined benefit plan to employees relative to providing a defined contribution plan. `LO 13-1` `LO 13-2`

10. Describe how an employee's benefit under a defined contribution plan is determined. `LO 13-2`

11. Is there a limit to how much an employer and/or employee may contribute to an employee's defined contribution account(s) for the year? If so, describe the limit. `LO 13-2`

12. Cami (age 52 and married) was recently laid off as part of her employer's reduction in force program. Cami's annual AGI was usually around $50,000. Shortly after Cami's employment was terminated, her employer distributed the balance of her employer-sponsored 401(k) account to her. What could Cami do to avoid being assessed the 10 percent early distribution penalty? `LO 13-2`

13. When may employees begin to receive defined contribution plan distributions without penalty? `LO 13-2`

14. Describe the circumstances under which distributions from defined contribution plans are penalized. What are the penalties? `LO 13-2`

15. Brady Corporation has a profit-sharing plan that allocates 10 percent of all after-tax income to employees. The profit sharing is allocated to individual employees based on relative employee compensation. The profit-sharing contributions vest to employees under a six-year graded plan. If an employee terminates his or her employment before fully vesting, the plan allocates the forfeited amounts among the remaining participants according to their account balances. Is this forfeiture allocation policy discriminatory, and will it cause the plan to lose its qualified status? Use Rev. Rul. 81-10 to help formulate your answer. `LO 13-2` research

16. What does it mean if an employer "matches" employee contributions to 401(k) plans? `LO 13-2`

17. What nontax factor(s) should an employee consider when deciding whether and to what extent to participate in an employer's 401(k) plan? `LO 13-2` planning

18. What are the differences between a traditional 401(k) and Roth 401(k) plan? `LO 13-2`

19. Can employers match employee contributions to Roth 401(k) plans? Explain. `LO 13-2`

20. Describe the annual limitation on employer and employee contributions to traditional 401(k) and Roth 401(k) plans. `LO 13-2`

21. When a company is limited by the tax laws in the amount it can contribute to an employee's 401(k) plan, what will it generally do to make the employee whole? Is this likely an issue for rank-and-file employees? Why or why not? `LO 13-2` `LO 13-3`

22. From a tax perspective, how would taxpayers determine whether they should contribute to a traditional 401(k) or a Roth 401(k)? `LO 13-2` planning

23. Could a taxpayer contributing to a traditional 401(k) plan earn an after-tax return *greater* than the before-tax return? Explain. `LO 13-2`

24. Explain the *tax* similarities and differences between qualified defined contribution plans and nonqualified deferred compensation plans from an *employer's* perspective. `LO 13-2` `LO 13-3`

25. Explain the *tax* similarities and differences between qualified defined contribution plans and nonqualified deferred compensation plans from an *employee's* perspective. `LO 13-2` `LO 13-3`

LO 13-2 **LO 13-3** 26. Explain the *nontax* similarities and differences between qualified defined contribution plans and nonqualified deferred compensation plans from an *employer's* perspective.

LO 13-2 **LO 13-3** 27. Explain the *nontax* similarities and differences between qualified defined contribution plans and nonqualified deferred compensation plans from an *employee's* perspective.

LO 13-3
planning 28. From a *tax* perspective, what issues does an employee need to consider in deciding whether to defer compensation under a nonqualified deferred compensation plan or to receive it immediately?

LO 13-3
planning 29. From a *nontax* perspective, what issues does an employee need to consider in deciding whether to defer compensation under a nonqualified deferred compensation plan or to receive it immediately?

LO 13-3 30. What are reasons why companies provide nonqualified deferred compensation plans for certain employees?

planning **LO 13-2** 31. How can companies use deferred compensation to avoid the §162(m) limitation on salary deductibility?

LO 13-3 32. Are companies allowed to decide who can and who cannot participate in nonqualified deferred compensation plans? Briefly explain.

LO 13-1 **LO 13-2**
LO 13-3 33. How might the ultimate benefits to an employee who participates in a qualified retirement plan of a company differ from an employee who participates in a nonqualified deferred compensation plan of the company if the company experiences bankruptcy before the employee is scheduled to receive the benefits?

LO 13-4 34. What are the primary tax differences between traditional IRAs and Roth IRAs?

planning **LO 13-4** 35. Describe the circumstances in which it would be more favorable for a taxpayer to contribute to a traditional IRA rather than a Roth IRA and vice versa.

LO 13-4 36. What are the requirements for a taxpayer to make a deductible contribution to a traditional IRA? Why do the tax laws impose these restrictions?

LO 13-4 37. What is the limitation on a deductible IRA contribution for 2016?

LO 13-4 38. Compare the minimum distribution requirements for traditional IRAs to those of Roth IRAs.

LO 13-4 39. How are qualified distributions from Roth IRAs taxed? How are nonqualified distributions taxed?

LO 13-4 40. Explain when a taxpayer will be subject to the 10 percent penalty when receiving distributions from a Roth IRA.

LO 13-4 41. Is a taxpayer who contributed to a traditional IRA able to transfer or "roll over" the money into a Roth IRA? If yes, explain the tax consequences of the transfer.

LO 13-4 42. Assume a taxpayer makes a nondeductible contribution to a traditional IRA. How does the taxpayer determine the taxability of distributions from the IRA on reaching retirement?

LO 13-4 43. When a taxpayer takes a nonqualified distribution from a Roth IRA, is the entire amount of the distribution treated as taxable income?

LO 13-5 44. What types of retirement plans are available to self-employed taxpayers?

LO 13-5 45. Compare and contrast the annual limitations on deductible contributions for self-employed taxpayers to SEP IRAs, and individual 401(k) accounts.

planning **LO 13-5** 46. What are the nontax considerations for self-employed taxpayers deciding whether to set up a SEP IRA or an individual 401(k)?

LO 13-6 47. What is the saver's credit and who is eligible to receive it?

LO 13-6 48. What is the maximum saver's credit available to taxpayers? What taxpayer characteristics are relevant to the determination?

LO 13-6 49. How is the saver's credit computed?

PROBLEMS

Select problems are available in *Connect*®.

50. Javier recently graduated and started his career with DNL Inc. DNL provides
    a defined benefit plan to all employees. According to the terms of the plan, for
    each full year of service working for the employer, employees receive a benefit
    of 1.5 percent of their average salary over their highest three years of compen-
    sation from the company. Employees may accrue only 30 years of benefit under
    the plan (45 percent). Determine Javier's annual benefit on retirement, before
    taxes, under each of the following scenarios: `LO 13-1`

    a) Javier works for DNL for three years and three months before he leaves for
       another job. Javier's annual salary was $55,000, $65,000, $70,000, and $72,000
       for years 1, 2, 3, and 4, respectively. DNL uses a five-year cliff vesting schedule.

    b) Javier works for DNL for three years and three months before he leaves for
       another job. Javier's annual salary was $55,000, $65,000, $70,000, and
       $72,000 for years 1, 2, 3, and 4, respectively. DNL uses a seven-year graded
       vesting schedule.

    c) Javier works for DNL for six years and three months before he leaves for
       another job. Javier's annual salary was $75,000, $85,000, $90,000, and
       $95,000 for years 4, 5, 6, and 7, respectively. DNL uses a five-year cliff
       vesting schedule.

    d) Javier works for DNL for six years and three months before he leaves for
       another job. Javier's annual salary was $75,000, $85,000, $90,000, and
       $95,000 for years 4, 5, 6, and 7, respectively. DNL uses a seven-year graded
       vesting schedule.

    e) Javier works for DNL for 32 years and three months before retiring. Javier's
       annual salary was $175,000, $185,000, $190,000, and $195,000 for his final
       four years of employment.

51. Alicia has been working for JMM Corp. for 32 years. Alicia participates in
    JMM's defined benefit plan. Under the plan, for every year of service for JMM
    she is to receive 2 percent of the average salary of her three highest years of
    compensation from JMM. She retired on January 1, 2016. Before retirement,
    her annual salary was $570,000, $600,000, and $630,000 for 2013, 2014, and
    2015. What is the maximum benefit Alicia can receive in 2016?   `LO 13-1`

52. Kim has worked for one employer her entire career. While she was working, she
    participated in the employer's defined contribution plan [traditional 401(k)]. At
    the end of 2016, Kim retires and the balance in her defined contribution plan
    was $2,000,000 at the end of 2015.   `LO 13-2`

    a) What is Kim's minimum required distribution for 2016 in 2017 if she is
       68 years old at the end of 2016?

    b) What is Kim's minimum required distribution for 2016 if she turns 70½
       during 2016 and she has not turned 71 years old by the end of 2016?
       When must she receive this distribution?

    c) What is Kim's minimum required distribution for 2016 in 2017 if she is
       73 years old at the end of 2016?

    d) Assuming that Kim is 75 years old at the end of 2016 and that her marginal
       tax rate is 33 percent, what amount of her distribution will she have remain-
       ing after taxes if she receives only a distribution of $50,000 for 2016?

    e) Complete Form 5329, page 2, to report the minimum distribution penalty in
       part (d). Use the most recent form available.

53. Matthew (48 at year-end) develops cutting-edge technology for SV Inc., located
    in Silicon Valley. In 2016, Matthew participates in SV's money purchase pension   `LO 13-2`

plan (a defined contribution plan) and in his company's 401(k) plan. Under the money purchase pension plan, SV contributes 15 percent of an employee's salary to a retirement account for the employee up to the amount limited by the tax code. Because it provides the money purchase pension plan, SV does not contribute to the employee's 401(k) plan. Matthew would like to maximize his contribution to his 401(k) account after SV's contribution to the money purchase plan.

a) Assuming Matthew's annual salary is $400,000, what amount will SV contribute to Matthew's money purchase plan? What can Matthew contribute to his 401(k) account in 2016?

b) Assuming Matthew's annual salary is $240,000, what amount will SV contribute to Matthew's money purchase plan? What can Matthew contribute to his 401(k) account in 2016?

c) Assuming Matthew's annual salary is $60,000, what amount will SV contribute to Matthew's money purchase plan? What amount can Matthew contribute to his 401(k) account in 2016?

d) Assume the same facts as part (c), except that Matthew is 54 years old at the end of 2016. What amount can Matthew contribute to his 401(k) account in 2016?

LO 13-2

planning

54. In 2016, Maggy (34 years old) is an employee of YBU Corp. YBU provides a 401(k) plan for all its employees. According to the terms of the plan, YBU contributes 50 cents for every dollar the employee contributes. The maximum employer contribution under the plan is 15 percent of the employee's salary (if allowed, YBU contributes until the employee has contributed 30 percent of her salary).

a) Maggy has worked for YBU corporation for 3½ years before deciding to leave. Maggy's annual salary during this time was $45,000, $52,000, $55,000, and $60,000 (she only received half of her final year's salary). Assuming Maggy contributed 8 percent of her salary (including her 2016 salary) to her 401(k) account, what is Maggy's vested account balance when she leaves YBU (exclusive of account earnings)? Assume YBU uses three-year cliff vesting.

b) Same question as part (a), except YBU uses six-year graded vesting.

c) Maggy wants to maximize YBU's contribution to her 401(k) account in 2016. How much should Maggy contribute to her 401(k) account assuming her annual salary is $100,000 (she works for YBU for the entire year)?

d) Same question as part (c), except Maggy is 55 years old rather than 34 years old at the end of the year.

LO 13-2

55. In 2016, Nina contributes 10 percent of her $100,000 annual salary to her 401(k) account. She expects to earn a 7 percent before-tax rate of return. Assuming she leaves this (and any employer contributions) in the account until she retires in 25 years, what is Nina's after-tax accumulation from her 2016 contributions to her 401(k) account?

a) Assume Nina's marginal tax rate at retirement is 30 percent.

b) Assume Nina's marginal tax at retirement is 20 percent.

c) Assume Nina's marginal tax rate at retirement is 40 percent.

LO 13-2

56. Kathleen, age 56, works for MH, Inc. in Dallas, Texas. Kathleen contributes to a Roth 401(k) and MH contributes to a traditional 401(k) on her behalf. Kathleen has contributed to $30,000 to her Roth 401(k) over the past six years. The current balance in her Roth 401(k) account is $50,000 and the balance in her traditional 401(k) is $40,000. Kathleen needs cash because she is taking a month of vacation to travel the world. Answer the following questions relating to distributions

from Kathleen's retirement accounts assuming her marginal tax rate for ordinary income is 28 percent.

a) If Kathleen receives a $10,000 distribution from her traditional 401(k) account, how much will she be able to keep after paying taxes and penalties, if any, on the distribution?

b) If Kathleen receives a $10,000 distribution from her Roth 401(k) account, how much will she be able to keep after paying taxes and penalties, if any, on the distribution?

c) If Kathleen retires from MH and then she receives a $10,000 distribution from her traditional 401(k), how much will she be able to keep after paying taxes and penalties, if any, on the distribution?

d) If Kathleen retires from MH and then she receives a $10,000 distribution from her Roth 401(k), how much will she be able to keep after paying taxes and penalties, if any, on the distribution?

e) Assume the original facts except that Kathleen is 60 years of age not 56. If Kathleen receives a $10,000 distribution from her Roth 401(k) (without retiring), how much will she be able to keep after paying taxes and penalties, if any, on the distribution?

57. In 2016, Nitai (age 40) contributes 10 percent of his $100,000 annual salary to a Roth 401(k) account sponsored by his employer, AY Inc. AY Inc. matches employee contributions dollar for dollar up to 10 percent of the employee's salary to the employee's traditional 401(k) account. Nitai expects to earn a 7 percent before-tax rate of return. Assume he leaves the contributions in the Roth 401(k) and traditional 401(k) accounts until he retires in 25 years and that he makes no additional contributions to either account. What are Nitai's after-tax proceeds from the Roth 401(k) and traditional 401(k) accounts after he receives the distributions assuming his marginal tax rate at retirement is 30 percent? `LO 13-2`

58. Marissa participates in her employer's nonqualified deferred compensation plan. For 2016, she is deferring 10 percent of her $320,000 annual salary. Assuming this is her only source of income and her marginal income tax rate is 30 percent, how much *tax* does Marissa save in 2016 by deferring this income (ignore payroll taxes)? `LO 13-3` `planning`

59. Paris participates in her employer's nonqualified deferred compensation plan. For 2016, she is deferring 10 percent of her $320,000 annual salary. Assuming this is her only source of income and her marginal income tax rate is 30 percent, how much does deferring Paris's income save her employer (after taxes) in 2016? Paris's employer's marginal tax rate is 35 percent (ignore payroll taxes). `LO 13-3`

60. Leslie participates in IBO's nonqualified deferred compensation plan. For 2016, she is deferring 10 percent of her $300,000 annual salary. Based on her deemed investment choice, Leslie expects to earn a 7 percent before-tax rate of return on her deferred compensation, which she plans to receive in 10 years. Leslie's marginal tax rate in 2016 is 30 percent. IBO's marginal tax rate is 35 percent (ignore payroll taxes in your analysis). `LO 13-3` `planning`

a) Assuming Leslie's marginal tax rate in 10 years when she receives the distribution is 33 percent, what is Leslie's after-tax accumulation on the deferred compensation?

b) Assuming Leslie's marginal tax rate in 10 years when she receives the distribution is 20 percent, what is Leslie's after-tax accumulation on the deferred compensation?

c) Assuming IBO's cost of capital is 8 percent after taxes, how much deferred compensation should IBO be willing to pay Leslie that would make it indifferent between paying 10 percent of Leslie's current salary or deferring it for 10 years?

LO 13-3

planning

61. XYZ Corporation has a deferred compensation plan under which it allows certain employees to defer up to 40 percent of their salary for five years. For purposes of this problem, ignore payroll taxes in your computations.

a) Assume XYZ has a marginal tax rate of 35 percent for the foreseeable future and earns an after-tax rate of return of 8 percent on its assets. Joel Johnson, XYZ's VP of finance, is attempting to determine what amount of deferred compensation XYZ should be willing to pay in five years that would make XYZ indifferent between paying the current salary of $10,000 and paying the deferred compensation. What amount of deferred compensation would accomplish this objective?

b) Assume Julie, an XYZ employee, has the option of participating in XYZ's deferred compensation plan. Julie's marginal tax rate is 40 percent and she expects the rate to remain constant over the next five years. Julie is trying to decide how much deferred compensation she will need to receive from XYZ in five years to make her indifferent between receiving the current salary of $10,000 and receiving the deferred compensation payment. If Julie takes the salary, she will invest it in a taxable corporate bond paying interest at 5 percent annually (after taxes). What amount of deferred compensation would accomplish this objective?

LO 13-4

62. John (age 51 and single) has earned income of $3,000. He has $30,000 of unearned (capital gain) income.

a) If he does not participate in an employer-sponsored plan, what is the maximum deductible IRA contribution John can make in 2016?

b) If he does participate in an employer-sponsored plan, what is the maximum deductible IRA contribution John can make in 2016?

c) If he does not participate in an employer-sponsored plan, what is the maximum deductible IRA contribution John can make in 2016 if he has earned income of $10,000?

LO 13-4

63. William is a single writer (age 35) who recently decided that he needs to save more for retirement. His 2016 AGI is $65,000 (all earned income).

a) If he does not participate in an employer-sponsored plan, what is the maximum deductible IRA contribution William can make in 2016?

b) If he does participate in an employer-sponsored plan, what is the maximum deductible IRA contribution William can make in 2016?

c) Assuming the same facts as in part (b), except his AGI is $75,000, what is the maximum deductible IRA contribution William can make in 2016?

LO 13-4

64. In 2016, Susan (44 years old) is a highly successful architect and is covered by an employee-sponsored plan. Her husband, Dan (47 years old), however, is a Ph.D. student and is unemployed. Compute the maximum deductible IRA contribution for each spouse in the following alternative situations.

a) Susan's salary and the couple's AGI is $190,000. The couple files a joint tax return.

b) Susan's salary and the couple's AGI is $120,000. The couple files a joint tax return.

c) Susan's salary and the couple's AGI is $80,000. The couple files a joint tax return.

d) Susan's salary and her AGI is $80,000. Dan reports $5,000 of AGI (earned income). The couple files separate tax returns.

LO 13-4

tax forms

65. In 2016, Rashaun (62 years old) retired and planned on immediately receiving distributions (making withdrawals) from his traditional IRA account. The balance of his IRA account is $160,000 (before reducing it for withdrawals/distributions described below). Over the years, Rashaun has contributed

$40,000 to the IRA. Of his $40,000 contributions, $30,000 was *nondeductible* and $10,000 was *deductible*. Assume Rashaun did not make any contributions to the account during 2016.

a) If Rashaun currently withdraws $20,000 from the IRA, how much tax will he be required to pay on the withdrawal if his marginal tax rate is 25 percent?

b) If Rashaun currently withdraws $70,000 from the IRA, how much tax will he be required to pay on the withdrawal if his marginal tax rate is 28 percent?

c) Using the information provided in part (b), complete Form 8606, Part I, to report the taxable portion of the $70,000 distribution (withdrawal). Use 2015 forms if 2016 forms are unavailable.

66. Brooklyn has been contributing to a traditional IRA for seven years (all deductible contributions) and has a total of $30,000 in the account. In 2016, she is 39 years old and has decided that she wants to get a new car. She withdraws $20,000 from the IRA to help pay for the car. She is currently in the 25 percent marginal tax bracket. What amount of the withdrawal, after tax considerations, will Brooklyn have available to purchase the car? `LO 13-4`

67. Jackson and Ashley Turner (both 45 years old) are married and want to contribute to a Roth IRA for Ashley. In 2016, their AGI is $186,000. Jackson and Ashley each earned half of the income. `LO 13-4`

a) How much can Ashley contribute to her Roth IRA if they file a joint return?

b) How much can Ashley contribute if she files a separate return?

c) Assume that Ashley earned all of the couple's income and that she contributed the maximum amount she is allowed to contribute to a Roth IRA. What amount can be contributed to Jackson's Roth IRA?

68. Harriet and Harry Combs (both 37 years old) are married and both want to contribute to a Roth IRA. In 2016, their AGI is $50,000. Harriet earned $46,000 and Harry earned $4,000. `LO 13-4`

a) How much can Harriet contribute to her Roth IRA if they file a joint return?

b) How much can Harriet contribute if she files a separate return?

c) How much can Harry contribute to his Roth IRA if they file separately?

69. Michael is single and 35 years old. He is a participant in his employer's sponsored retirement plan. How much can Michael contribute to a Roth IRA in each of the following alternative situations? `LO 13-4`

a) Michael's AGI is $50,000 after he contributed $3,000 to a traditional IRA.

b) Michael's AGI is $80,000 before any IRA contributions.

c) Michael's AGI is $135,000 before any IRA contributions.

70. George (age 42 at year-end) has been contributing to a traditional IRA for years (all deductible contributions) and his IRA is now worth $25,000. He is planning on transferring (or rolling over) the entire balance into a Roth IRA account. George's marginal tax rate is 25 percent. `LO 13-4`

a) What are the tax consequences to George if he takes $25,000 out of the traditional IRA and puts the entire amount into a Roth IRA?

b) What are the tax consequences to George if he takes $25,000 out of the traditional IRA, pays the taxes due from the IRA distribution, and contributes the remaining distribution to the Roth IRA?

c) What are the tax consequences to George if he takes $25,000 out of the traditional IRA, keeps $10,000 to pay taxes and to make a down payment on a new car, and contributes the remaining distribution to the Roth IRA?

71. Jimmer has contributed $15,000 to his Roth IRA and the balance in the account is $18,000. In the current year, Jimmer withdrew $17,000 from the Roth IRA to pay for a new car. If Jimmer's marginal ordinary income tax rate is 25 percent, `LO 13-4`

what amount of tax and penalty, if any, is Jimmer required to pay on the withdrawal in each of the following alternative situations?

a) Jimmer opened the Roth account 44 months before he withdrew the $17,000 and Jimmer is 62 years of age.

b) Jimmer opened the Roth account 44 months before he withdrew the $17,000 and Jimmer is age 53.

c) Jimmer opened the Roth account 76 months before he withdrew the $17,000 and Jimmer is age 62.

d) Jimmer opened the Roth account 76 months before he withdrew the $17,000 and Jimmer is age 53.

LO 13-4

planning

72. John is trying to decide whether to contribute to a Roth IRA or a traditional IRA. He plans on making a $5,000 contribution to whichever plan he decides to fund. He currently pays tax at a 30 percent marginal income tax rate but he believes that his marginal tax rate in the future will be 28 percent. He intends to leave the money in the Roth IRA or traditional IRA accounts for 30 years and he expects to earn a 6 percent before-tax rate of return on the account.

a) How much will John accumulate after taxes if he contributes to a Roth IRA (consider only the funds contributed to the Roth IRA)?

b) How much will John accumulate after taxes if he contributes to a traditional IRA (consider only the funds contributed to the Roth IRA)?

c) Without doing any computations, explain whether the traditional IRA or the Roth IRA will generate a greater after-tax rate of return.

LO 13-4

73. Sherry, who is 52 years of age, opened a Roth IRA three years ago. She has contributed a total of $12,000 to the Roth IRA ($4,000 a year). The current value of the Roth IRA is $16,300. In the current year, Sherry withdraws $14,000 of the account balance to purchase a car. Assuming Sherry is in a 25 percent marginal tax bracket, how much of the $14,000 withdrawal will she retain after taxes to fund her car purchase?

LO 13-4

74. Seven years ago, Halle (currently age 41) contributed $4,000 to a Roth IRA account. The current value of the Roth IRA is $9,000. In the current year Halle withdraws $8,000 of the account balance to use as a down payment on her first home. Assuming Halle is in a 25 percent marginal tax bracket, how much of the $8,000 withdrawal will she retain after taxes to fund her house down payment?

LO 13-4

research

planning

75. Yuki (age 45 at year-end) has been contributing to a traditional IRA for years (all deductible contributions), and her IRA is now worth $50,000. She is trying to decide whether she should roll over her traditional IRA into a Roth IRA. Her current marginal tax rate is 25 percent. She plans to withdraw the entire balance of the account in 20 years and she expects to earn a before-tax rate of return of 5 percent on her retirement accounts and a 4 percent after-tax rate of return on all investments outside of her retirement accounts. For each of the following alternative scenarios, indicate how much more or less Yuki will accumulate after taxes in 20 years if she rolls over her traditional IRA into a Roth IRA. Be sure to include the opportunity cost of having to pay taxes on the rollover.

a) When she withdraws the retirement funds in 20 years, she expects her marginal tax rate to be 35 percent.

b) When she withdraws the retirement funds in 20 years, she expects her marginal tax rate to be 20 percent.

c) Assume the same facts as in part (b), except that she earns a 3 percent after-tax rate of return on investments outside of the retirement accounts.

d) In general terms, reconcile your answer from part (b) with your answer to part (c) (no numbers required).

76. Sarah was contemplating making a contribution to her traditional individual retirement account for 2016. She determined that she would contribute $5,500 to her IRA and she deducted $5,500 for the contribution when she completed and filed her 2016 tax return on February 15, 2017. Two months later, on April 15, Sarah realized that she had not yet actually contributed the funds to her IRA. On April 15, she went to the post office and mailed a $5,500 (for all) check to the bank holding her IRA. The bank received the payment on April 18. In which year is Sarah's $5,500 contribution deductible?

LO 13-4

research

77. Elvira is a self-employed taxpayer who turns 42 years old at the end of the year (2016). In 2016, her net Schedule C income was $120,000. This was her only source of income. This year, Elvira is considering setting up a retirement plan. What is the maximum amount Elvira may contribute to the self-employed plan in each of the following situations?

    a) She sets up a SEP IRA.

    b) She sets up an individual 401(k).

LO 13-5

planning

78. Hope is a self-employed taxpayer who turns 54 years old at the end of the year (2016). In 2016, her net Schedule C income was $120,000. This was her only source of income. This year, Hope is considering setting up a retirement plan. What is the maximum amount Hope may contribute to the self-employed plan in each of the following situations?

    a) She sets up a SEP IRA.

    b) She sets up an individual 401(k).

LO 13-5

planning

79. Rita is a self-employed taxpayer who turns 39 years old at the end of the year (2016). In 2016, her net Schedule C income was $300,000. This was her only source of income. This year, Rita is considering setting up a retirement plan. What is the maximum amount Rita may contribute to the self-employed plan in each of the following situations?

    a) She sets up a SEP IRA.

    b) She sets up an individual 401(k).

LO 13-5

80. Reggie is a self-employed taxpayer who turns 59 years old at the end of the year (2016). In 2016, his net Schedule C income was $300,000. This was his only source of income. This year, Reggie is considering setting up a retirement plan. What is the maximum amount he may contribute to the self-employed plan in each of the following situations?

    a) He sets up a SEP IRA.

    b) He sets up an individual 401(k).

LO 13-5

81. Desmond is 25 years old and he participates in his employer's 401(k) plan. During the year, he contributed $3,000 to his 401(k) account. What is Desmond's 2016 saver's credit in each of the following alternative scenarios?

    a) Desmond is not married and has no dependents. His AGI after deducting his 401(k) contribution is $34,000.

    b) Desmond is not married and has no dependents. His AGI after deducting his 401(k) contribution is $17,500.

    c) Desmond files as a head of household and has an AGI of $44,000.

    d) Desmond and his wife file jointly and report an AGI of $30,000 for the year.

LO 13-6

82. Penny is 57 years old and she participates in her employer's 401(k) plan. During the year, she contributed $2,000 to her 401(k) account. Penny's AGI is $29,000 after deducting her 401(k) contribution. What is Penny's 2016 saver's credit in each of the following alternative scenarios?

    a) Penny is not married and has no dependents.

    b) Penny files as a head of household and she has three dependents.

LO 13-6

c) Penny files as a head of household and she has one dependent.

d) Penny is married and files a joint return with her husband. They have three dependents.

e) Penny files a separate tax return from her husband. She claims two dependent children on her return.

COMPREHENSIVE PROBLEMS

Select problems are available in *Connect*®.

83. Jacquiline is unmarried and age 32. Even though she participates in an employer-sponsored retirement plan, Jacquiline contributed $3,000 to a traditional IRA during the year. Jacquiline files as a head of household, her AGI before the contribution is $43,000, and her marginal tax rate is 15 percent. What is the after-tax cost of her $3,000 traditional IRA contribution?

84. Ian retired in June 2015 at the age of 69 (he turned 70 in August 2015). Ian's retirement account was valued at $490,000 at the end of 2014 and $500,000 at the end of 2015. He has had all of his retirement accounts open for 15 years. What is Ian's required minimum distribution for 2016 under each of the following alternative scenarios?

a) Ian's retirement account is a traditional 401(k) account.

b) Ian's retirement account is a Roth 401(k) account.

c) Ian's retirement account is a traditional IRA.

d) Ian's retirement account is a Roth IRA.

85. Alex is 31 years old and has lived in Los Alamos, New Mexico, for the last four years where he works at the Los Alamos National Laboratory (LANL). LANL provides employees with a 401(k) plan and for every $1 an employee contributes (up to 9 percent of the employee's salary) LANL contributes $3 (a 3-to-1 match). The plan provides a six-year graded vesting schedule. Alex is now in his fifth year working for LANL, and his current year salary is $150,000. Alex's marginal tax rate is 28 percent in 2016. Answer the following questions relating to Alex's retirement savings in 2016.

a) Assume that over the past four years, Alex has contributed $45,000 to his 401(k) and his employer has contributed $115,000 to the plan. The plan has an account balance of $175,000. What is Alex's vested account balance in his 401(k)?

b) Because Alex considers his employer's matching contributions "free money," he wants to maximize the amount of LANL's contributions. What is the least amount Alex can contribute and still maximize LANL's contribution?

c) In need of cash to build a home theater, Alex withdrew $30,000 from his traditional 401(k) account. What amount of the withdrawal, after taxes and penalties, will Alex have available to complete his project?

d) Assume that Alex contributes $10,000 to his traditional 401(k) account this year. Also assume that in 30 years, Alex retires (at age 61) and withdraws the $10,000 contribution made this year *and* all the earnings generated by the contribution. Also assume that his marginal tax rate at the time he retires is 25 percent. Ignore any prior or subsequent contributions to his plan. If Alex earns a 6 percent annual before-tax rate of return, what are his after-tax proceeds from the distribution?

e) Assume that Alex is 74 years old at the end of the year, retired, and that his marginal tax rate is 25 percent. His account balance in his traditional 401(k) was $1,250,000 at the end of last year. What is the minimum distribution Alex must receive from his 401(k) account for this year? If Alex receives a $43,000 distribution from his 401(k) account (his only distribution during the year), what amount will he be able to keep after taxes and penalties (if any)?

86. Tommy (age 47) and his wife, Michelle (age 49), live in Columbus, Ohio, where Tommy works for Callahan Auto Parts (CAP) as the vice president of the brakes division. Tommy's 2016 salary is $360,000. CAP allows Tommy to participate in its nonqualified deferred compensation plan in which participants can defer 15 percent of their salary for five years. Tommy also participates in CAP's qualified 401(k) plan. Tommy's current marginal tax rate is 28 percent and CAP's current marginal tax rate is 34 percent.

   a) Assuming Tommy earns a 6 percent *after-tax* rate of return and he expects his marginal tax rate to be 30 percent in five years, what before-tax deferred compensation payment in five years would make him indifferent between receiving the deferred compensation payment or 15 percent of his salary now (ignore payroll taxes)?

   b) Assuming CAP has an 8 percent *after-tax* rate of return and expects its marginal tax rate to be 35 percent in five years, how much would it be willing to pay in five years to be indifferent between paying the deferred compensation or paying 15 percent of Tommy's salary now (ignore payroll taxes)?

   c) Will Tommy and CAP be able to come to an agreement on deferring Tommy's salary?

   d) Assume that Tommy and Michelle have an AGI of $99,000 before IRA deductions by either spouse. The AGI includes $10,000 that Michelle earned working part-time (but she does not participate in an employer-sponsored retirement plan). Tommy and Michelle file a joint return. What is the maximum deductible contribution Tommy and Michelle may make to a traditional IRA?

   e) Tommy has a balance of $55,000 in his traditional IRA. Due to some recent tax cuts, his marginal tax rate is 20 percent, so he would like to roll his traditional IRA into a Roth IRA. What are the tax consequences to Tommy if he takes $55,000 out of the IRA, pays the taxes due from the traditional IRA distribution, and contributes the remaining distribution to the Roth IRA?

87. Gerry (age 56) and Elaine (age 54) have been married for 12 years and file a joint tax return. The couple lives in an apartment in downtown Manhattan. Gerry's father, Mortey, recently retired from Del Boca Vista Corporation (DBVC) where he worked for many years. Mortey participated in DBVC's defined benefit plan. Elaine is an editor and works for Pendent Publishing earning an annual $150,000 salary in 2016. Gerry is a self-employed stand-up comedian and had net business income of $46,000 in 2016. At the advice of their neighbor, Gerry and Elaine have come to you to for help in answering several retirement savings-related questions.

   a) The DBVC defined benefit plan specifies a benefit of 1.5 percent for each year of service, up to a maximum of 30 percent (20 years of service), of the average of the employee's three highest years of salary. Mortey worked for the company for 25 years and earned $75,000, $78,000, and $84,000 over his final three years of service. What is Mortey's annual benefit from DBVC's defined benefit plan?

   b) Elaine has worked at Pendent Publishing since January 1, 2011. The company offers a defined contribution plan. It matches 100 percent of employee contributions to the plan up to 6 percent of her salary. Prior to 2016, Elaine had contributed $40,000 to the plan and her employer had contributed $28,000 to the plan. In 2016, Elaine contributed $17,000 to her traditional 401(k). What is the amount of her employer's matching contribution for 2016? Assuming the company uses a six-year graded vesting schedule, what is Elaine's vested balance in the plan at the end of 2016 (for simplicity, disregard the plan's earnings)?

c) Elaine tells you that her employer has offered her $30,000 in 10 years to defer 10 percent of her current salary (defer $15,000). Assuming that the couple's marginal tax rate is currently 30 percent, they earn an after-tax rate of return of 8 percent, and they expect their marginal tax rate to be 25 percent in 10 years, should Elaine accept her company's offer? What is the minimum amount she should be willing to accept (ignoring nontax factors and payroll taxes)?

d) Gerry has a SEP IRA and would like to contribute as much as possible to this account. What is the maximum contribution Gerry can make to his SEP IRA in 2016?

e) Assuming Gerry had an individual 401(k), what is the maximum amount he could contribute to the plan in 2016?

f) Gerry also has a traditional IRA with an account balance of $42,000. He would like to convert the traditional IRA to a Roth IRA. Gerry would like to pay the least amount of tax possible in rolling the account over. What is the least amount of tax Gerry will be required to pay on the rollover?

g) Assume that Gerry rolled over his traditional IRA into a Roth IRA six years ago (rather than in 2016) and that the account now has a balance of $78,000. The couple is considering buying their first home and would like to pay as much down as possible. They have heard from their friends that they can take the funds from their Roth IRA and use it to buy their first home. Are their friends correct? What would you advise them to do?

h) Assume that Gerry and Elaine made total contributions of $20,000 to their qualified retirement accounts in 2016. Also assume that their AGI is $38,000. What would be the amount of their saver's credit for 2016?

chapter

14 Tax Consequences of Home Ownership

Learning Objectives

Upon completing this chapter, you should be able to:

LO 14-1 Determine whether a home is considered a principal residence, a residence (not principal), or a nonresidence for tax purposes.

LO 14-2 Compute the taxable gain on the sale of a residence and explain the requirements for excluding gain on the sale.

LO 14-3 Determine the amount of allowable interest expense deductions on loans secured by a residence.

LO 14-4 Discuss the deductibility of real property taxes.

LO 14-5 Explain the tax issues and consequences associated with rental use of the home, including determining the deductibility of residential rental real estate losses.

LO 14-6 Describe the requirements necessary to qualify for home office deductions and compute the deduction limitations on home office deductions.

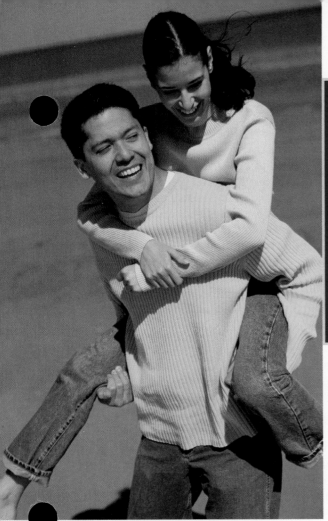

© Purestock/SuperStock

With the extra income Tyler Jefferson is earning in his new VP of sales position for GLO Corporation, his family now has greater financial flexibility, but with the money come new possibilities. For one, Tyler and Jasmine Jefferson would like to sell their current home and purchase a larger one closer to Tyler's work. Fortunately, the value of their home has increased considerably since they purchased it, which should allow them to make a substantial down payment on a new home. Still, they would need to acquire financing to make the purchase. Jasmine likes the idea of buying a vacation home in Scottsdale, Arizona. Besides the great weather (she and Tyler both love golf), Scottsdale has the added benefit of being near Jasmine's family. She is trying to sell the second-home idea to Tyler by suggesting that, to help defray the costs, they could rent the house when they're not there. Finally, Jasmine is seriously considering a transition to self-employment as a graphic designer. She believes that, with her experience and contacts, she can find enough clients to keep busy most of the time—and she very much likes the idea of setting aside a room in their primary home as her workplace. ■

When making these decisions, the Jeffersons should consider the tax consequences of their actions. Will the gain on the sale of their current home be taxable? Will the interest expense on the new home be fully deductible? Should they pay points to obtain a lower interest rate on the home loan? What will be the after-tax cost of the loan payments? If they use a home-equity loan to cover personal expenses, is the interest expense deductible? If they borrow money to buy a vacation home, can they deduct interest on the loan? If they rent out the vacation home for part of the year, how do they account for the related income and expenses for tax purposes? If the rental of the second home generates losses, are these losses deductible? If Jasmine sets up a home office, will the Jeffersons be allowed any tax deductions for expenses relating to their home? This chapter answers these and other relevant questions for the Jeffersons and for others interested in the tax consequences of home ownership.

LO 14-1

The starting point for determining the tax consequences of home ownership is first determining whether the taxpayer owns a **dwelling unit.** A dwelling unit is property that provides a place suitable for people to occupy (live and sleep). For tax purposes, a dwelling unit includes the following:

- House
- Condominium
- Mobile home
- Boat
- Other similar property[1]

A taxpayer may acquire a dwelling unit solely for personal use, for some mixture of personal and rental use, or solely for rental use. Each year, the dwelling unit is classified as either a residence or a nonresidence (rental property) based on how the taxpayer used the unit. The dwelling unit is considered to be a residence if the taxpayer's number of personal-use days of the home is more than the greater of

1. 14 days or
2. 10 percent of the number of rental days during the year.[2]

Thus, to determine whether a dwelling unit is a residence or not, the taxpayer needs to calculate the number of days the home (dwelling unit) was used for personal use during the year and the number of days the home was rented out during the year. So what counts as a day of personal use and what counts as a day of rental use? The rules for determining the days of personal use are

- The taxpayer (owner) or any other owner of the home stays in the home.
- A relative of an owner stays in the home, even if the relative pays full fair market value rent unless the home is the relative's principal residence (discussed below).
- A nonowner stays in the home under a vacation home exchange or swap arrangement.
- The taxpayer rents out the property for less than fair market value.[3]

Rental use includes the following:

- Days when the taxpayer rents out the property at fair market value.
- Days spent repairing or maintaining the home for rental use.

Days when the home is available for rent, but not actually rented out, *do not count* as either personal or rental days.

When a dwelling unit is determined to be a residence, the taxpayer must determine whether the residence is the taxpayer's **principal residence** in order to determine

---

[1]§280A(f)(1). A dwelling unit does not include a hotel, motel, inn, or similar establishment.
[2]§280A(d)(1).
[3]§280A(d)(2).

certain tax consequences associated with the property (for certain purposes, the taxpayer need only determine whether the property is a residence). What makes a residence a "principal" residence? When a taxpayer lives in more than one residence during the year, the determination of which residence is the principal residence depends on the facts and circumstances such as

- The amount of time the taxpayer spends at each residence during the year.
- The proximity of each residence to the taxpayer's place of employment.
- The principal place of abode (living and sleeping) of the taxpayer's immediate family.
- The taxpayer's mailing address for bills and correspondence.

Note that a taxpayer can have only one principal residence during a particular year, and the principal residence may change from year to year.

To summarize, with respect to a particular taxpayer for a particular year, a dwelling unit or home can be classified as either a

- Principal residence,
- Residence (not principal), or a
- Nonresidence (rental property).

We refer to these property classifications throughout the chapter as we describe the tax consequences of home ownership. Exhibit 14-1 lists deductions and other tax provisions available for each property type. We discuss each of these tax provisions, including limitations, throughout the chapter. Also, Appendix B at the end of this chapter provides a flowchart for determining the tax status of a dwelling unit.

EXHIBIT 14-1   **Tax Provisions by Property Type**

	Property Type		
Tax Provision	**Principal Residence**	**Residence (not principal)**	**Nonresidence**
Home mortgage interest deductions (*from* AGI)	X	X	
Home-equity interest deduction (*from* AGI)	X	X	
Home mortgage insurance (*from* AGI deduction)	X	X	
Real property taxes (*from* AGI deduction)	X	X	X
Deductions associated with rental use, if any (*for* AGI)	X	X	X
Exclusion of gain on sale of home	X	X*	X*
Forgiveness of debt on home foreclosure (income exclusion)	X		

*Must have previously been a principal residence to qualify.

We begin our discussion by considering the tax consequences associated with personal use of the home. We then discuss the tax consequences of rental use of the home, and we conclude the chapter by discussing the tax consequences of business use of the home.

PERSONAL USE OF THE HOME

To buy or to rent? This is a difficult question with no single answer. The decision to purchase a home is a significant one that involves both nontax and tax considerations. Primary nontax factors favoring home ownership include the appreciation potential for the home as an investment. As the value of the home increases, so does

THE KEY FACTS

Tax and Nontax Consequences of Home Ownership

- Nontax Consequences
  - Large investment.
  - Potential for big return (or loss) on investment with use of leverage.
  - Risk of default on home loan.
  - Time and costs of maintenance.
  - Limited mobility.
- Tax Consequences
  - Interest expense deductible.
  - Gain on sale excludable.
  - Real property taxes on home deductible.
  - Rental and business-use possibilities.

the homeowner's net worth. A home is frequently an individual's most significant investment. Therefore, home ownership also involves significant potential risk. When real estate values decline, the owner's net worth declines as well. Homeowners borrowing funds to purchase their home can potentially achieve large returns on their investment due to the power of leverage, but a home is by no means a liquid asset. Furthermore, homeowners must assume the risk associated with the possible default on the loan. If the owner does not make the mortgage payments required by the terms of the loan, the lender may repossess the home. Homeowners also are responsible for the cost or effort required to repair, maintain, and landscape the home. Finally, because building, buying, or selling a home and moving in or out of a home are expensive and time-consuming tasks, home ownership reduces one's ability to relocate to take advantage of new opportunities.

On the tax side, the government clearly smiles on home ownership given the deductions available to homeowners that are unavailable to renters. In fact, the deductibility of mortgage interest on owner-occupied homes is ranked number two in the government's listing of projected "tax expenditures" (tax breaks provided to taxpayers) for the years 2015–2024.[4] The projections indicate that in 2016, homeowners are expected to save over $75 billion in tax payments due to the mortgage interest deduction. Besides the deduction for interest payments made on home-related loans, other tax benefits of home ownership include deducting real estate taxes paid on the home, excluding gain on the sale of the home, and deducting expenses relating to business offices in the home. Homeowners also may gain tax benefits associated with owning and renting a vacation home. We address the tax consequences of home ownership throughout the remainder of the chapter.

LO 14-2   Exclusion of Gain on Sale of Personal Residence

When a taxpayer sells a personal residence, she *realizes* a gain or a loss determined by subtracting the basis of the home from the amount the taxpayer receives from the buyer (minus selling costs). The basis of the residence depends on how the taxpayer acquired the home. The general rules for determining the basis of the home are as follows:

- Purchase: the cost of the home.
- Inheritance: the fair market value of the home on the date of death.
- Gift: the donor's basis.
- Conversion of rental home to residence: the taxpayer's basis in the rental home at the time of the conversion.

Because a personal residence is a capital asset, the gain or loss a taxpayer realizes by selling the residence is a capital gain or loss. However, because a personal residence is a personal-use asset, the loss on the sale of a personal residence is a nondeductible personal loss.[5] This is an important limitation to many taxpayers when the housing market is depressed. When a taxpayer sells a personal residence at a gain, the tax consequences are generally more favorable. In fact, taxpayers meeting certain requirements are allowed to exclude a certain amount of realized gain on the sale. The maximum exclusion depends on filing status as follows:

- $500,000 for married filing jointly taxpayers.
- $250,000 for other taxpayers.

Gain in excess of the excludable amount generally qualifies as long-term capital gain subject to tax at preferential rates. Further, gain in excess of the exclusion amount is considered to be investment income for purposes of determining the 3.8% net investment income tax discussed in Chapter 8.

[4]Number one on the list is the gross income exclusion for employer-paid medical insurance premiums and medical care. See www.whitehouse.gov/sites/default/files/omb/budget/fy2016/assets/teb2016.xls (Table 3).
[5]§165(c).

Requirements   To qualify for the exclusion, the taxpayer must meet both ownership and use tests for the residence:

Ownership test: The taxpayer must have owned the property for a total of two or more years during the five-year period ending on the date of the sale. The ownership test prevents a taxpayer from purchasing a home, fixing it up, and soon thereafter selling it and excluding the gain—a real estate investment practice termed **flipping.** In these circumstances, the gain is primarily due to the taxpayer's efforts in remodeling the home, not to general appreciation in the value of the property.

Use test: The taxpayer must have *used* the property as her principal residence (see earlier discussion) for a total of two or more years during the five-year period ending on the date of the sale. The exclusion provision was designed to provide tax benefits to homeowners rather than investors or landlords. The use test helps ensure that taxpayers using the exclusion have realized gains from selling the home they actually live in as opposed to selling an investment or rental property.

Note that the periods of ownership and use need not be continuous nor do they need to cover the same two-year period. In fact, a taxpayer could rent a home and live in it as her principal residence during 2011 and then again during 2013, purchase the home and rent it to someone else during 2014 and 2015, and then sell the home at the beginning of 2016—and *still* meet the ownership and use tests!

Example 14-1

The Jeffersons sold their home in Denver, Colorado, before moving to Chicago. They sold the Denver home for $350,000. The Jeffersons initially purchased the home for $250,000. They owned and lived in the home (as their principal residence) for four years before selling. How much of the $100,000 gain realized on the sale ($350,000 − $250,000) are they allowed to exclude?

Answer: All $100,000. The Jeffersons qualified for the full exclusion available to married couples filing jointly because they met the ownership and use tests. Consequently, they are allowed to exclude the entire $100,000 of gain and could have excluded up to $500,000 of gain on the sale.

How do the ownership and use tests apply to married couples filing joint returns? Married couples filing joint returns are eligible for the full $500,000 exclusion if *either* spouse meets the ownership test and *both* spouses meet the principal-use test. If one only spouse meets both the ownership and the principal use test, the couple is eligible to claim the $250,000 exclusion on the couple's joint tax return.

Example 14-2

What if: Suppose that when Tyler and Jasmine were married, Jasmine moved into Tyler's home located in Denver, Colorado. Tyler had purchased the home two years before the marriage. After the marriage, the couple lived in the home together as their principal residence for four years before selling the home to move to Chicago. Tyler was the sole owner of the home for the entire six years he resided in the home. Would gain on the sale of the home qualify for the $500,000 exclusion available to married couples filing jointly even though Jasmine was never an owner of the home?

Answer: Yes. Gain on the sale qualifies for the full $500,000 exclusion available to married couples filing jointly because Tyler met the ownership test, and both Tyler and Jasmine met the use test.

What if: Suppose that Tyler and Jasmine lived in the home together for only one year before selling it. Would the couple be allowed to exclude any gain on the sale?

Answer: Yes, but because only Tyler meets the ownership and use tests, they would qualify only for the $250,000 exclusion even if they file a joint return.

If a widow or widower sells a home that the surviving spouse owned and occupied with the decedent spouse (the spouse who died), the surviving spouse is entitled to the full $500,000 exclusion provided that the surviving spouse sells the home within two years after the date of death of the decedent spouse. Finally, once a taxpayer claims a home sale exclusion, she is not eligible to claim another exclusion until at least two years pass from the time of the first sale (see the unforseen circumstances discussion for an exception to this general rule).

General rule exceptions for nonqualified use, unforseen circumstances and depreciation. In certain circumstances, taxpayers who otherwise meet the ownership and use requirements may have their exclusion limited under a "nonqualified use" provision. In other circumstances, taxpayers who fail the ownership and/or use tests are allowed to exclude gain on the sale of their residence under an "unforseen" circumstances provision. Finally, taxpayers who have claimed depreciation deductions on their home for rental or business use (see discussion later in the chapter) may be required to recognize gain on the sale of their residence that would have otherwise been excluded. Let's first discuss the nonqualified use provision.

Under the general rules for the home sale exclusion, taxpayers could exclude gain on the sale of a vacation home or rental property (including gain accrued while it was not a principal residence) simply by moving into the property and using it as their principal residence for two years before selling it. To limit a taxpayer's ability to benefit from this strategy, the nonqualified use provision reduces the taxpayer's otherwise excludable gain on the home sale if, on or after January 1, 2009, the taxpayer used or uses the home for something other than a principal residence (termed *nonqualified use*).[6] The period of nonqualified use does not include any portion of the five-year period ending on the date of the sale that is after the last date that such property is used as the principal residence of the taxpayer or the taxpayer's spouse. This exception allows the taxpayer time to sell the principal residence after moving out of use (if it were considered to be nonqualified use it, without having to count the time the house is available for sale as nonqualified it would increase the amount of gain the taxpayer would be required to recognize on the sale).

If the nonqualified use limitation applies, the percentage of the realized gain that must be recognized is the ratio of the period of nonqualified use divided by the period of time the taxpayer owned the home (acquisition date through date of sale). Note that this provision does not reduce the maximum exclusion; it reduces the amount of realized gain eligible for exclusion.

Example 14-3

What if: Suppose the Jeffersons purchased home 1 on January 1, 2013, for $250,000. They lived in home 1 as their principal residence until January 1, 2016, when they moved into a new principal residence (home 2). They finally sold home 1 on January 1, 2018, for $350,000. What amount of the $100,000 gain on the sale of home 1 ($350,000 amount realized minus $250,000 basis) may the Jeffersons exclude from gross income?

Answer: All $100,000. The Jeffersons meet the ownership and use tests (they owned and used home 1 as their principal residence for at least two of the five years prior to January 1, 2018), so they qualify for a maximum exclusion of $500,000. Further, the gain eligible for the exclusion is *not* reduced because the Jeffersons stopped using home 1 as a principal residence after January 1, 2016, and they sold the home within five years of this date.

What if: Assume the same facts as above, except that on January 1, 2017, the Jeffersons moved back into home 1 and used it as their principal residence until they sold it for $350,000 on January 1, 2018. What amount of the $100,000 gain on the sale of home 1 may the Jeffersons exclude from income?

Answer: $80,000. The Jeffersons meet the ownership and use tests for home 1 and therefore qualify for the maximum $500,000 exclusion. However, because they stopped using the home as their principal residence for a period on or after January 1, 2009 (nonqualified use from January 1, 2016–January 1, 2017), and they used the home as their principal residence immediately before selling (January 1, 2017–January 1, 2018), the gain eligible for exclusion must be reduced. The percentage of the gain that is not eligible for exclusion is 20 percent, which is the period of nonqualified use (one year: January 1, 2017–January 1, 2018) divided by the total period of time the Jeffersons owned the home (five years: January 1, 2013–January 1, 2018). Therefore, the Jeffersons must reduce their gain eligible for exclusion by $20,000 ($100,000 gain × 20% reduction percentage), allowing them to exclude $80,000 of the $100,000 gain from gross income.

[6]§121(b) (4)[(5)].

Sometimes taxpayers are unable to meet the two-year requirements for the ownership and use tests due to unforseen circumstances. For example, a taxpayer may be forced to sell his home before he meets the ownership and use requirements due to a change in employment, significant health issues, or other unforeseen financial difficulties. In such cases, the *maximum* exclusion amount ($500,000 for married filing jointly, $250,000 otherwise) is reduced based on the amount of time the taxpayer owned and used the home as a principal residence before selling. For example, if a single taxpayer owned and used a home as principal residence for six months before selling due to unforseen circumstances, the maximum exclusion would be $62,500, which is one-fourth of what it would be otherwise (6 months of ownership and use divided by 24 months required under general rule multiplied by the full $250,000 exclusion for single taxpayers). The maximum exclusion available to a taxpayer selling under these circumstances is expressed in the formula presented in Exhibit 14-2.

THE KEY FACTS

Exclusion of Gain on Sale of Personal Residence

- Exclusion Amount
  - $500,000 for married couples filing joint returns.
  - $250,000 for other taxpayers.
- Unforseen circumstances provision *maximum exclusion* = full exclusion × months of qualifying ownership and use/24 months.
- Gain eligible for exclusion may be reduced for period of nonqualified use.

EXHIBIT 14-2   **Formula for Determining Maximum Home Sale Exclusion in Unforseen Circumstances**

Maximum exclusion in unforseen circumstances = Full exclusion × Qualifying months/24 months, where

Full exclusion = $250,000 for single taxpayers or $500,000 for taxpayers filing a joint return.

Qualifying months = the number of months the taxpayer met the ownership and use requirements for the home before *selling* it.

24 months = the number of months taxpayer must own and use home as principal residence to qualify for the full exclusion.[7]

Example 14-4

What if: Let's assume that when the Jeffersons moved from Denver, they purchased a home in Chicago for $275,000 and moved into the home on July 1, 2015. In January of 2016, Tyler accepted a work opportunity with a different employer located in Miami, Florida. On February 1, 2016, the Jeffersons sold their home for $295,000 and permanently relocated to Miami. How much of the $20,000 realized gain ($295,000 − $275,000) on their Chicago home sale can the Jeffersons exclude from taxable income?

Answer: All $20,000. The Jeffersons lived in the home for only seven months (July 1, 2015, to February 1, 2016), so they do not meet either the ownership or the use test to qualify for the maximum exclusion. However, under the unforseen circumstances provision, they are eligible for a reduced maximum exclusion computed as follows: $500,000 (maximum exclusion) × 7 (qualifying months)/24 = $145,833. Because the amount they are able to exclude ($145,833) exceeds the $20,000 gain they realized on the sale, they are able to exclude all $20,000.

What if: Assume the same facts, except that the Jeffersons realized a $150,000 gain on the sale of their home. How much of the realized gain would they recognize and at what rate would this gain be taxed?

Answer: $150,000 gain realized minus $145,833 exclusion = $4,167 short-term capital gain (the home is a capital asset that the Jeffersons owned for one year or less). Assuming the Jeffersons did not recognize any other capital gains during the year, the $4,167 would be taxed at the Jeffersons' 28 percent marginal tax rate (see storyline summary at beginning of chapter).

Note, as the previous example illustrates, that under the so-called unforseen circumstances, it is the *full exclusion* that is reduced, not necessarily the excludable gain. Consequently, if a taxpayer's gain on the sale of a residence is less than the maximum exclusion, the taxpayer may exclude the full amount of the gain.

---

[7]Taxpayers may choose to use the number of days the taxpayer fully qualified for the exclusion divided by 730 days. See Reg §1.121-3(g).

Finally, taxpayers who used their home for business purposes (home office expense) or rental purposes are not allowed to exclude gain attributable to depreciation deductions incurred after May 6, 1997. Rather, this gain is treated as unrecaptured §1250 gain and is subject to a maximum 25 percent tax rate (see Chapter 11 for detailed discussion of unrecaptured §1250 gain)

Exclusion of Gain from Debt Forgiveness on Foreclosure of Home Mortgage

Prior to 2007, if a lender foreclosed (took possession of) a taxpayer's principal residence, sold the home for less than the taxpayer's outstanding mortgage, and forgave the taxpayer of the remainder of the debt, the taxpayer was required to include the debt forgiveness in her gross income. However, through December 31, 2016, taxpayers who realize income from this situation are allowed to exclude up to $2 million of debt forgiveness if the debt is secured by the taxpayer's principal residence (the principal residence is collateral for the loan) and the debt was incurred to acquire, construct, or substantially improve the home.[8] The taxpayer must apply the excluded amount of debt forgiveness income to reduce the basis of the principal residence, but not below zero.

LO 14-3   Interest Expense on Home-Related Debt

A major tax benefit of owning a home is that taxpayers are generally allowed to deduct the interest they pay on their home mortgage loans as itemized (*from* AGI) deductions. Taxpayers report these itemized deductions on Schedule A of their individual tax Form 1040. For taxpayers who itemize deductions, the mortgage interest expense can generate significant tax savings and reduce the after-tax cost of mortgage payments. Often, this deduction alone exceeds the standard deduction, thus allowing taxpayers to claim other itemized deductions.[9]

Example 14-5

During the current year, Tyler and Jasmine own a home with an average mortgage balance of $300,000. They pay interest at 6 percent annually on the loan, and they qualify to deduct the interest expense as an itemized deduction. The Jeffersons' marginal income tax rate is 28 percent, and before counting mortgage interest, their itemized deductions exceed the standard deduction. What is the before- and after-tax cost of their mortgage interest expense for the year?

Answer: $18,000 before-tax cost and $12,960 after-tax cost, computed as follows:

Description	Amount	Explanation
(1) Before-tax interest expense	$18,000	$300,000 × 6%. All deductible.
(2) Marginal tax rate	× 28%	
(3) Tax savings from interest expense	5,040	(1) × (2).
After-tax cost of interest expense	**$12,960**	(1) − (3).

Note that the $5,040 tax savings generated by the mortgage interest expense deduction reduces the after-tax cost of their monthly mortgage payment by $420 ($5,040/12).

What if: Assume that instead of buying a home, the Jeffersons rented a home and paid $1,500 a month for rent expense. What would be the before- and after-tax cost of the $18,000 annual rental payments?

[8]§108(a)(1)(E) and §108(h). The exclusion also applies to qualifying debt forgiven in 2017 if the debt is forgiven pursuant to a written agreement that was entered into in 2016.

[9]Note that home mortgage interest deductions (including deductions for home equity interest and points) are subject to the itemized deduction phase-out for high income taxpayers. See Chapter 6 for a detailed discussion.

Answer: $18,000 before- and after-tax cost of rental payments. Because rental payments are not deductible, they do not generate any tax savings, so the before- and after-tax cost of the rental payments is the same.

Despite the apparent tax savings from buying versus renting a home, it is important to consider that nontax factors could favor renting over purchasing a home.

Taxpayers are allowed to deduct only "qualified" residence interest as an itemized deduction.[10] Qualified residence interest is interest paid on the principal amount of **acquisition indebtedness** and on the principal amount of **home-equity indebtedness.** Both types of indebtedness must be **secured** by a **qualified residence** to qualify. To understand what this means exactly, we need to define a few terms.

Loan secured by residence: The residence is the collateral for the loan. If the owner does not make the payments on the loan, the lender may take possession of the home to satisfy the owner's responsibility for the loan.

Qualified residence: The taxpayer's principal residence *and* one other residence (see previous discussion for definition of principal residence and of residence). For a taxpayer with *more* than two residences, which property is treated as the second qualified residence is an annual election—that is, the taxpayer can choose to deduct interest related to a particular second home one year and a different second home the next. The second residence is often a vacation home where the taxpayer resides part time.

Acquisition indebtedness: Any debt secured by a qualified residence that is incurred in acquiring, constructing, or substantially improving the residence (limited to $1,000,000, as discussed below).

Home-equity indebtedness: Any debt, except for acquisition indebtedness, secured by the taxpayer's qualified residence to *the extent it does not exceed the fair market value of the residence minus the acquisition indebtedness* (limited to $100,000, as discussed below). That is, for purposes of deducting interest, total qualifying home-related debt cannot exceed the total value of the home. The determination of the amount of home-equity debt is made at the time the loan is executed, so a subsequent decline in a home's value does not reduce the interest expense deduction.

Limitations on Home-Related Debt   The tax laws *limit the amount of debt* on which taxpayers can deduct interest expense. Two separate considerations limit the amount of debt that generates qualifying residence (and thus deductible) interest: a limitation on the amount of acquisition indebtedness and a limitation on the amount of home-equity indebtedness.

Limitation on amount of acquisition indebtedness.   Interest expense on up to $1,000,000 of acquisition indebtedness is deductible as qualified residence interest. Once acquisition indebtedness is established for a qualifying residence (or for the sum of two qualifying residences), only principal payments on the loan(s) can reduce it and only additional indebtedness, secured by the residence(s) *and* incurred to substantially improve the residence(s), can increase it. (Notice the requirements to use funds to *acquire or improve the residence,* a stipulation that markedly differentiates acquisition indebtedness from home-equity indebtedness.)

When a taxpayer **refinances** a mortgage, how does the tax law treat the new loan? Assuming the taxpayer does not use the proceeds from the refinance to substantially improve her residence, the refinanced loan is treated as acquisition debt *only to the*

THE KEY FACTS

Home-Related Interest Deduction

- Deduction allowed for qualified residence interest.
  - Principal residence and one other residence.
- Acquisition Indebtedness
  - Proceeds used to acquire or substantially improve home.
  - Limited to $1,000,000.
  - Principal payments permanently reduce amount.

---

[10]§163(h).

extent that the principal amount of the refinancing does not exceed the amount of the acquisition debt immediately before the refinancing. Consequently, any amount borrowed in excess of the remaining principal on the original loan does not qualify as acquisition indebtedness. Interest on the "excess" part of this loan can only be deducted if it qualifies as home-equity indebtedness (described below).

Example 14-6

What if: Assume the Jeffersons purchased a home in Chicago costing $330,000 by making a down payment of $30,000 and taking out a $300,000 loan secured by the home. What is the Jeffersons' acquisition indebtedness?

Answer: $300,000. This is debt secured by a qualified residence that is incurred in acquiring, constructing, or substantially improving the residence.

What if: Assume that when they moved to Chicago, the Jeffersons purchased a home costing $330,000 by making a down payment of $300,000, and taking out a $30,000 loan secured by the home. During the next few years, the Jeffersons paid $10,000 of principal on the loan, thereby reducing the loan balance to $20,000. Last year, due to a decrease in interest rates and a need for cash, the Jeffersons refinanced their mortgage by taking out a loan, secured by their residence, for $150,000. With the $150,000 they paid off the $20,000 balance on the original loan and used the $130,000 of extra cash for purposes unrelated to the home. After the refinance, what is the Jeffersons' acquisition indebtedness?

Answer: $20,000, the same amount as before the refinance. The only way to increase acquisition indebtedness is to borrow money to substantially improve the home. Thus, the Jeffersons' interest deductions on the home will be limited to the interest expense on the $20,000 acquisition indebtedness plus a limited amount of home-equity indebtedness.

What if: Assume the same facts as the previous what-if example except that the Jeffersons used $40,000 of the cash from the loan to build a new garage on their property. After the refinance, what is the Jeffersons' acquisition indebtedness?

Answer: $60,000 ($20,000 original loan principal + $40,000 used to substantially improve home).

THE KEY FACTS
Home-Related Interest Deduction

- Home-equity indebtedness
- Can use proceeds for any purpose.
- Loan must be secured by equity in home (FMV > Debt).
- $100,000 limit.

Limitation on amount of home-equity indebtedness. As noted earlier, interest on home-equity indebtedness is deductible as qualified residence interest. However, the amount of qualified home-equity indebtedness is limited to the *lesser* of (1) the fair market value of the qualified residence(s) in excess of the acquisition debt related to the residence(s) and (2) $100,000 ($50,000 for each spouse if married filing separately). Thus, a taxpayer can deduct interest on up to $100,000 of home-related debt above and beyond acquisition debt (acquisition debt is limited to $1,000,000) as long as the debt is secured by the equity in the home(s), no matter what the taxpayer does with the proceeds from the home-equity loan. However, as we note in Chapter 8, interest expense on home-equity loans not used to purchase or substantially improve the home is not deductible for AMT purposes. When deciding whether to borrow money through a home-equity loan, the taxpayer must weigh the advantage of the interest deductibility against the risk of losing her home if she does not repay the loan.

Example 14-7

What if: Assume that the Jeffersons' home is worth $400,000 and they have a balance of $290,000 on their original home loan. The Jeffersons are interested in purchasing a $50,000 Chevy Suburban. Wanting to finance the full purchase price, they ask you, their financial planner, whether they should borrow the money with a 6 percent automobile loan from their local credit union or use a home-equity loan at 8 percent to fund the purchase. Assuming their marginal tax rate is 28 percent, and that they itemize deductions, what is the after-tax interest rate for the automobile loan, and what is the after-tax interest rate for the home-equity loan?

Answer: 6 percent for the automobile loan (same as the before-tax rate because the interest is not deductible) and 5.76 percent for the home equity loan [8% × (1 − 28%)]. After taxes, the home-equity loan appears to be a much better deal than the automobile loan. Before taking out the home-equity loan, however, the Jeffersons should consider the economic consequences if they are not able to repay the loan. If they don't make the payments on the automobile loan, they may lose the automobile; if they don't make the payments on the home-equity loan, they may lose their home.

What if: If the Jeffersons wanted to borrow $110,000 from their home-equity loan so that they could buy two automobiles, would they be allowed to deduct the interest on the entire loan?

Answer: No. Even though the home has $110,000 of equity ($400,000 fair market value minus $290,000 acquisition indebtedness), the cap on qualifying home-equity debt is $100,000. Consequently, the Jeffersons would be able to deduct interest on only $100,000 of the $110,000 home-equity loan. Note, however, that they wouldn't be able to deduct any of the interest expense for AMT purposes.

Combined limitation on qualifying debt. What is the maximum amount of debt on which a taxpayer can deduct qualified residence interest? Because the acquisition indebtedness limit of $1,000,000 and the home-equity indebtedness limit of $100,000 are two separate limits, the maximum amount of debt on which a taxpayer may deduct qualified residence interest is $1,100,000—provided, of course, that the value of the taxpayer's qualified residence (or residences) is at least $1,100,000.

When a taxpayer's home-related debt exceeds the limitations, the amount of deductible interest can be determined in one of two ways. First, the deductible interest can be computed as the product of (1) total interest expense on debt secured by the home and (2) the ratio of **qualified debt** to total debt outstanding on the home. This average interest expense option is summarized as follows:

$$\text{Total interest expense} \times \frac{\text{Qualified debt}}{\text{Total debt}} = \text{Deductible interest}$$

The second method is based on the chronological order of when the loans were executed, rather than as a weighted average. A taxpayer can choose to deduct all interest on earlier loans up to the limit on qualifying debt. Once the limit on qualifying debt is reached, interest on debt above the limit is not deductible. Why might taxpayers opt for this ordering method? This method generates a higher deduction when the earlier loans have a higher interest rate than subsequent loans.[11]

Example 14-8

What if: Assume the Jeffersons purchased a home for $1,550,000 by paying $150,000 down and borrowing $1,400,000 with a loan secured by the home. During the year, the Jeffersons paid $84,000 in interest on the loan. What amount of interest can the Jeffersons deduct as qualified residence interest?

Answer: $66,000. The Jefferson's qualifying debt is $1,100,000. The $1,100,000 consists of $1,000,000 of acquisition indebtedness (the limit) and $100,000 of home-equity indebtedness [the Jeffersons have $150,000 of equity in their home ($1,550,000 fair market value minus $1,400,000 loan on their home). Note that the same loan can include acquisition indebtedness and home equity indebtedness. Inserting the numbers into the formula for determining deductible interest expense when total debt exceeds the qualifying debt (see above) yields the following:

$84,000 × $1,100,000/$1,400,000 = $66,000

Where the total interest expense is $84,000, the qualifying debt is $1,100,000, and total debt on the home is $1,400,000.

(continued on page 14-12)

[11]The Treasury Regulations refer to the average interest expense method as the "simplified method" and the chronological method as the "exact method." See Treas. Reg §1.163-10T(c) and (d).

What if: Assume the Jeffersons moved to Chicago several years ago and purchased a home valued at $330,000 by paying $30,000 down and funding the remaining balance with a 30-year mortgage fixed at 6 percent. By the beginning of last year the value of their home had increased to $400,000, and the principal amount of their original loan had been paid down to $290,000. In need of extra cash for anticipated expenditures unrelated to their home, the Jeffersons borrowed $70,000 at a fixed interest rate of 7 percent with a loan secured by their home. As of the beginning of this year, the value of the Jeffersons' home had increased to $420,000. With a need for still more cash, the Jeffersons took out a third loan secured by their home at the beginning of the year. The Jeffersons borrowed $50,000 on the third mortgage at an annual interest rate of 9 percent. During the year, they made interest-only payments on all three loans. The interest they paid on these loans is summarized as follows:

Loan	Balance	Rate	Interest Paid
Acquisition indebtedness:			
Original home loan	$290,000	6%	$17,400
Home equity indebtedness:			
Home-equity loan 1	70,000	7	4,900
Home-equity loan 2	50,000	9	4,500
Totals	$410,000		$26,800

How much of the $26,800 interest expense can the Jeffersons deduct this year using the average interest expense option?

Answer: $25,493. Inserting the numbers into the formula for this option (see above) yields the following:

$$\$26,800 \times \frac{\$390,000}{\$410,000} = \$25,493$$

Where the total interest expense is $26,800, the qualifying debt is $390,000 ($290,000 acquisition indebtedness + $100,000 limit on home-equity indebtedness), and the total debt is $410,000 ($290,000 + $70,000 + $50,000).

How much of the $26,800 interest expense can the Jeffersons deduct this year using the chronological order method of determining interest expense?

Answer: $25,000. The first loan is the original home loan. Because the loan is acquisition debt and is under the $1,000,000 acquisition debt limit, the entire $17,400 interest on this loan is deductible. The second mortgage of $70,000 was executed next. Because this loan is a home-equity loan and is under the $100,000 home-equity limit, the entire $4,900 interest on this loan is deductible. Finally, the third mortgage of $50,000 was executed last. However, because only $30,000 of this debt is qualifying home-equity debt ($100,000 limit minus $70,000 second mortgage) only $2,700 of interest on this loan is deductible ($30,000 × 9%). Thus, under the chronological order option, the Jeffersons can deduct $25,000 of the interest expense ($17,400 + $4,900 + $2,700).

Note that the $25,493 interest deduction under the first option is higher than the $25,000 interest expense under the second option because the interest rate on the second home equity loan is higher than the rates on the original loan and on the first home equity loan.

Finally, even though there are separate limits on acquisition indebtedness and home-equity indebtedness, both limits can apply to the same loan.

Example 14-9

Refer back to Example 14-6 where we assumed the Jeffersons refinanced their $20,000 home loan by borrowing $150,000 against their home and paying off the original $20,000 loan. Of course, the Jeffersons can deduct interest on the $20,000 acquisition debt on the loan. How much interest on the remaining $130,000 of the loan are the Jeffersons allowed to deduct?

Answer: The Jeffersons can deduct interest on $100,000 of the remaining $130,000 loan because this is the amount that qualifies as home-equity indebtedness. Interest on the other $30,000 of loan principal is not deductible.

Assuming they paid $9,000 of interest expense on these loans during the year, the Jeffersons could deduct $7,200 of the interest, computed under the average interest rate option as follows:

$$\$9,000 \times \frac{\$120,000}{\$150,000} = \$7,200$$

Note that because in this example the Jeffersons have only one loan (part acquisition debt and part home-equity debt, and part neither), the second (chronological order) method of deducting interest expense does not apply.

TAXES IN THE REAL WORLD Double Take on Home-Related Interest Deductions

Taxpayers (other than married taxpayers filing separately) are allowed to deduct interest paid on up to $1,000,000 of acquisition indebtedness + $100,000 of home-equity indebtedness on their principal residence (and one other residence). In 2012, the Tax Court concluded that the indebtedness limit for interest deductions is a per-residence(s) limit and not a per-taxpayer limit. For example, if two unmarried taxpayers jointly own and reside in a home, the qualifying debt limit for both taxpayers combined would be $1,100,000. However, at least for some taxpayers residing within the 9th Circuit boundaries, this limit has recently become considerably more generous. The 9th Circuit Court recently overruled the the 2012 Tax Court decision and concluded that the qualifying debt limit applies on a per-taxpayer basis and not a per-residence(s) basis. Consequently, two unmarried taxpayers who live within the 9th Circuit boundaries and who jointly own a home can each deduct interest on up to $1,100,000 of qualified debt ($2,200,000 of qualified debt in total). If the two taxpayers were married, together, they would be able to deduct interest on up to only $1,100,000 of qualified debt. Now, that's a marriage penalty!

Source: *Voss v. Comm.* No. 12-73257(9 Cir. 8/27/2015), rev'g *Sophy*, 138 TC 204, (2012).

Mortgage Insurance   Taxpayers are allowed to deduct as qualified residence interest expense premiums paid or accrued on mortgage insurance (insurance premiums paid by the borrower to protect the lender against the borrower defaulting on the loan). To qualify, the premiums for the mortgage insurance must be paid or accrued in connection with acquisition indebtedness on a qualified residence and must be paid by December 31, 2016. The deduction does not apply to mortgage insurance contracts issued before January 1, 2007. The (itemized) deduction is phased out by 10 percent for every $1,000 ($500 for married taxpayers filing separately), or fraction thereof, that the taxpayer's AGI exceeds $100,000 ($50,000 for married taxpayers filing separately).

Points   A home buyer arranging financing for a home typically incurs several loan-related fees or expenses including charges for "points." A **point** is 1 percent of the principal amount of the loan. In general, borrowers pay points to lenders in exchange for reduced interest rates on loans. However, borrowers may also pay lenders for other purposes (e.g., to compensate lenders for the service of providing the loan). In order for taxpayers to deduct points, the points must be paid for a reduced interest rate (rather than for the service of providing the loans).[12] However, to minimize possible disputes regarding the deductibility of points and as a matter of administrative convenience, the IRS will treat points as deductible **qualified residence interest** if the following requirements are met:[13]

1. The **settlement statement** (see Appendix A at the end of this chapter—the settlement statement details the monies paid out and received by the buyer and seller

---

[12]§461(g)(2).
[13]Rev. Proc. 94-27 1994-1 C.B. 613.

as part of the loan transaction) must clearly designate the amounts as points payable in connection with the loan, for example as "loan origination fees," "loan discount," or "discount points." (These amounts are typically provided on lines 801 and 802 of the settlement statement.)

2. The amounts must be computed as a percentage of the stated principal amount of the loan.

3. The amounts paid must conform to an established business general practice of charging points for loans in the area in which the residence is located, and the amount of the points paid must not exceed the amount generally charged in that area.

4. The amounts must be paid in connection with the acquisition of the taxpayer's *principal residence* and the loan *must be secured by that residence* (the deduction for points is not available for points paid in connection with a loan for a second home).

5. The buyer must provide enough funds in the down payment on the home to at least equal the cost of the points (the buyer is not allowed to borrow from the lender to pay the points). However, points paid by the *seller* to the lender in connection with the taxpayer's loan are treated as paid directly by the taxpayer. Consequently, such points are generally deductible by the buyer.

Note that points paid in *refinancing* a home loan are not immediately deductible by the homeowner. These points must be amortized and deducted on a straight-line basis over the life of the loan.[14]

Now that we understand how the tax laws treat points, let's consider the home buyer's decision of whether or not to pay points to obtain a lower interest rate on a home loan. From an economic standpoint, the buyer must choose between (1) paying extra money up front and having lower monthly mortgage payments or (2) paying less initially and having larger monthly payments.

When the taxpayer can afford to pay points, deciding whether or not to do so generally requires a "break-even" analysis. Essentially, the taxpayer determines how long it will take to recoup the after-tax cost of the point(s) through the after-tax interest savings on the loan. Generally speaking, the longer the taxpayer plans on staying in the home and maintaining the loan (not refinancing it), the more likely it is financially beneficial to pay points to obtain a lower interest rate. However, paying points can be costly if, after too short a time, the taxpayer sells the home or refinances the home loan. In these situations, the taxpayer may not reach the break-even point.

Example 14-10

Tyler and Jasmine are seeking financing for their new $800,000 home. They are paying $500,000 down and borrowing the remaining $300,000 to be paid back over 30 years. They have the choice of paying two discount points ($6,000) and getting a fixed interest rate of 5 percent or paying no discount points and getting a fixed interest rate of 6 percent. Assuming the points meet the immediate deductibility requirements, the Jeffersons' marginal tax rate is 28 percent, and they pay interest only for the first three years of the loan, what is the Jeffersons' break-even point for paying the points?

Answer: Two years, calculated as follows:

Loan summary: $300,000; 6 percent rate with no points. 5 percent rate with two points ($6,000). Assume the Jeffersons pay interest only (no principal) for the first three years.

---

[14]See Chapter 2 research memo and *J.R. Huntsman v. Comm.* (8 Cir., 1990), 90-2 USTC par. 50,340, rev'g 91 TC 917 (1988) for a limited exception to this rule.

Description	Amounts	Calculation
(1) Initial cash outflow from paying points	($6,000)	$300,000 × 2%.
(2) Tax benefit from deducting points	1,680	(1) × 28%.
(3) After-tax cost of points	(4,320)	(1) + (2).
(4) Before-tax *savings per year* from 5% vs. 6% interest rate	3,000	$300,000 × (6% − 5%).
(5) *Forgone tax benefit per year* of higher interest rate	(840)	(4) × 28%.
(6) After-tax savings per year of 5% vs. 6% interest rate	$2,160	(4) + (5).
Break-even point in years	2 years	(3)/(6).

The break-even analysis in Example 14-10, while a useful exercise, oversimplifies the calculations a bit. Why? It oversimplifies because it doesn't take into account the present value of the tax savings, nor does it take into account the increasing principal that would be paid on a traditional principal-and-interest-type loan. In reality, the cost of the points is immediate while the savings comes later—so the break-even point on a present value basis is likely a little longer than two years. Also, the more principal paid on the loan, the less the amount of interest paid each month—so savings from the lower interest rate declines over time, which would also extend the break-even point.

Because points paid on a refinancing are deducted over the life of the loan, the break-even point for paying points on a refinanced mortgage is longer than the break-even point for an original mortgage of the same amount.

Example 14-11

What if: Assume that, due to recent interest rate declines, the Jeffersons have decided to refinance the $300,000 mortgage on their home with a new 30-year loan. The Jeffersons have the option of paying two discount points ($6,000) and obtaining a 5 percent interest rate or obtaining a 6 percent interest rate with no discount points. Assuming the Jeffersons' marginal tax rate is 28 percent and they pay interest only for the first three years of the loan, what is the Jeffersons' approximate break-even point for paying the points on the refinance?

Answer: 2.71 years, calculated as follows:

Loan summary: $300,000; 6 percent rate with no points. 30 years or 5 percent rate with two points ($6,000). Assume the Jeffersons pay interest only for the first three years.

Description	Points	Notes
(1) Initial cash outflow from paying points	($6,000)	$300,000 × 2%.
(2) Tax benefit from deducting points	0	
(3) After-tax cost of points	(6,000)	(1) + (2).
(4) Before-tax savings per year from 5% vs. 6% interest rate	3,000	$300,000 × (6% − 5%).
(5) Forgone tax benefit per year of higher interest payments	(840)	(4) × 28%.
(6) After-tax savings per year of 5% vs. 6% interest rate	2,160	(4) + (5).
(7) Annual tax savings from amortizing points	56	(1)/30 years × 28%.
(8) Annual after-tax cash flow benefit of paying points	$2,216	(6) + (7).
Break-even point in years	2.71 years	(3)/(8).

The reason for the longer break-even point is that the points effectively cost more because they are not immediately deductible in a refinance.

Real Property Taxes

LO 14-4

Owners of personal residences and other types of real estate such as land, rental properties, business buildings, and other types of real property are generally required to pay **real property taxes.** These taxes are assessed by local governments and are based on the fair market value of the property.[15] Real property taxes support general public welfare by providing funding for public needs such as schools and roads.

Local governments set the tax rates applied to the value of the property annually based on financial needs for the year. The applicable rates may depend on the type of real estate. For example, the tax rate for real estate used in a business may be higher than the rates for residential real property. Real property tax payments are deductible by taxpayers conducting self-employment activities against business income as *for* AGI deductions, by landlords against rental income as *for* AGI deductions, and by other individuals as itemized deductions.[16]

Taxpayers are not allowed to deduct fees paid for setting up water and sewer services, and assessments for local benefits such as streets and sidewalks.[17] Taxpayers generally add these expenditures to the basis of their property.

Frequently, homeowners pay their real estate taxes through an **escrow** (holding) **account** with their mortgage lender. Each monthly payment to the lender includes an amount that represents roughly one-twelfth of the anticipated real property taxes for the year. The actual tax payment (or payments if the taxes are due more than once a year) is made by the mortgage company with funds accumulated in the escrow account. When does the homeowner get to deduct the property taxes? The homeowner gets to deduct the property taxes when the actual taxes are paid to the taxing jurisdiction, not when the homeowner makes payments for taxes to the escrow account.

Because property taxes are generally payable to the government only once or twice a year, who is responsible for paying the taxes when an owner sells a personal residence or another type of real estate during the year? Is the owner at the time the taxes are due responsible for paying the full amount of the taxes? Does the person who makes the tax payment also receive the corresponding tax deduction? In most situations, the buyer and seller divide the responsibility for the tax payments based on the portion of the property tax year that each party held the property. This allocation of taxes between buyer and seller is generally spelled out on the settlement statement when the sale becomes final (see Appendix A to this chapter for a sample settlement statement for the Jeffersons). For tax purposes, it doesn't matter who actually pays the tax, although generally the current owner has the responsibility to do so. As long as the taxes are paid, the tax deduction is based on the relative amount of time each party owned the property during the year (or period over which the property taxes are payable).[18]

Example 14-12

On February 1, Tyler and Jasmine purchased a new home for $800,000. At the time of the purchase, it was estimated that the property tax bill on the home for the year would be $12,000 ($800,000 × 1.5%). Assuming the tax bill is paid and that the property tax bill is based on a calendar year, how much will the Jeffersons *deduct* in property taxes for the year?

Answer: $11,000. Because the seller lived in the home for one-twelfth of the year (January) and the Jeffersons lived in the home for eleven-twelfths of the year (February through December), the seller will deduct $1,000 of the property taxes (one-twelfth) and the Jeffersons will deduct $11,000 (eleven-twelfths) as an itemized deduction.

---

[15]Local governments tend to understate the fair market value of property when appraising it to minimize the chances that the taxpayer will contest the appraisal.

[16]Note that real property taxes that are itemized deductions are subject to the overall itemized deduction phase-out discussed in Chapter 6.

[17]Reg. §1.164-4(a).

[18]The seller gets a deduction for the taxes allocable for the period of time up to and including the day *before* the date of the sale. The taxes allocable to the day of the sale through the end of the property tax year are deductible by the buyer. See §164(d).

RENTAL USE OF THE HOME

A taxpayer with the financial wherewithal to do so may purchase a second home as a vacation home, a rental property, or a combination of the two. A taxpayer may own a second home outright or may share ownership with others through a time-share or fractional ownership arrangement. The nontax benefits of owning a second home include a fixed vacation destination, the ability to trade the use of the home with an owner of a home in a different destination, the opportunity for generating income through rentals, and the potential appreciation of the second home as an investment. The nontax costs of owning a second home include the initial cost of the home, the extra cost of maintaining the home, the hassle of dealing with renters or property managers, and the downside risk associated with holding the second home as an investment.

The tax consequences of owning a second home depends on whether the home qualifies as a residence (see discussion at the beginning of the chapter) and on the number of days the taxpayer rents out the home. The home is categorized in one of three ways:

1. Residence with minimal rental use (rents home for 14 or fewer days).
2. Residence with significant rental use (rents home for 15 or more days).
3. Nonresidence.

Recall that, as we discussed earlier in the chapter, a property is considered a "residence" for tax purposes if the taxpayer uses the home for personal purposes for *more than* the greater of 14 days or 10 percent of the number of rental days during the year. For example, if a taxpayer rents her home for 200 days and uses it for personal purposes for 21 days or more, the home is considered to be a residence for tax purposes. If the same taxpayer used the home for personal purposes for 20 days, the home would be considered a nonresidence for tax purposes.

Residence with Minimal Rental Use

The law is simple for homeowners who rent a home that qualifies as a residence for a minimal amount of time during the year. That is, they live in it for at least 15 days and they rent it for 14 or fewer days. Taxpayers are not required to include the gross receipts in rental income and are not allowed to deduct any expenses related to the rental.[19] The owner is, however, allowed to deduct qualified residence interest and real property taxes on the second home as itemized deductions.

> **THE KEY FACTS**
> **Rental Use of the Home**
> - Tax treatment depends on amount of personal and rental use. The three categories are:
>   1) Residence with minimal rental use (personal residence)
>   2) Residence with significant rental use (vacation home)
>   3) Nonresidence (rental property)

> **THE KEY FACTS**
> **Rental Use of the Home**
> - Residence with minimal rental use.
>   - Taxpayer lives in the home at least 15 days and rents it 14 days or fewer.
>   - Exclude all rental income.
>   - Don't deduct rental expenses.

Example 14-13

The Jeffersons purchased a vacation home in a golf community in Scottsdale, Arizona, in January. They spent 10 days vacationing in the home in early March and another 15 days vacationing in the home in mid-December. In early February, they rented the home for 14 days to a group of golfers who were in town to attend a PGA Tour golf tournament and to play golf. The Jeffersons received $6,000 in rent from the group, and the Jeffersons incurred $1,000 of expenses relating to the rental home. The Jeffersons did not rent the property again for the rest of the year. How much will the $5,000 net income from the rental increase their taxable income?

Answer: Zero! Because the Jeffersons lived in the home for at least 15 days (25 days) and rented the home for 14 or fewer days (14) during the year, they do not report the rental income to the IRS, and they do not deduct expenses associated with the rental. The Jeffersons saved $1,400 in taxes by excluding the $5,000 of net rental income ($5,000 net income × 28 percent marginal tax rate). Note that the Jeffersons can also deduct the mortgage interest and real property taxes on the property for the *full year* as itemized deductions.

[19]§280A(g).

ETHICS

Carey and Pat were good friends and neighbors in an upscale neighborhood near several highly rated golf courses in Arizona. During the winter, both Carey and Pat decided to rent their homes (at a premium) to groups of golfers from the New York area who want to get out of the snow and enjoy sunshine and golf for a couple of weeks during the winter. While their homes were rented, Carey and Pat vacationed together in Cancun. In January 2016, Carey rented his home for 14 days and received $14,000 in rent. Pat also rented his home for the same 14 days and received $16,000 in rent. Near the end of the 14-day rental period, Pat got a call from the renters who wanted to extend their stay for one day. Pat agreed to the extension and charged the group $2,000 for the extra day. When preparing his 2016 tax return, Pat discovered that taxpayers who rent their home for more than 14 days are required to report all of their rental income on their tax returns. Pat didn't think it was fair that he had to pay taxes on the rental income while Carey did not just because Pat rented his home for one more day than Carey in 2016. Consequently, Pat decided that he rented his property for 14 days and gave the renters the last day for free. What do you think about Pat's approach to solving his tax problem?

A taxpayer with a strategically located second (or even first) home can take advantage of this favorable tax rule by renting the property and excluding potentially large rental payments from those in town to attend high-profile events such as the Olympics, the Masters golf tournament, the Super Bowl, and Mardi Gras.

Residence with Significant Rental Use (Vacation Home)

When a home qualifies as a residence and the taxpayer rents out the home for 15 days or more, the rental revenue is included in gross income, expenses to obtain tenants (advertising and realtor commissions) are fully deductible as direct rental expenses, and expenses relating to the home are allocated between personal and rental use. The expenses allocated to personal use are not deductible unless they are deductible under nonrental tax provisions as itemized deductions. (The most common of these deductions are mortgage interest and real property taxes but this also includes casualty losses on the home.)

When the gross rental revenue exceeds the sum of the direct rental expenses and the expenses allocated to the rental use of the home, the taxpayer is allowed to deduct the expenses in full. However, when these expenses exceed the rental revenue, the deductibility of the expenses is limited. In these situations, taxpayers divide the rental expenses into one of three categories or "tiers." The tier 1, 2, and 3 expenses for rental property are described in Exhibit 14-3.

The taxpayer first deducts tier 1 expenses (expenses to obtain tenants and mortgage interest and real property taxes allocated to rental use[20]) in full. This is true even when tier 1 expenses exceed the gross rental revenue.[21] Second, the taxpayer deducts tier 2 expenses.[22] However, the tier 2 expense deductions are limited to the gross rental revenue in excess of tier 1 expenses. Any tier 2 expenses not deducted in the current year due to the income limitation are suspended and carried forward to the next year. Finally, the taxpayer deducts tier 3 expense (depreciation calculated using

[20]Technically, expenses to obtain tenants (advertising and realtor commissions) are a reduction in gross rental income for tax purposes. However, we classify them as tier 1 expenses to simplify the discussion.

[21]The rental activity associated with a home falling into the residence with significant rental use category is not considered to be a passive activity, so income or loss generated from the activity is not considered to be passive income or passive loss [§469(j)]. See discussion of passive loss rules below.

[22]§280A(c)(5). Also see IRS Publication 527, "Residential Rental Property (Including Rental of Vacation Homes)."

EXHIBIT 14-3   Rental Expenses by Tier and Deduction Sequence

> **Tier 1**
> Expenses for obtaining tenants (such as advertising expense and realtor commissions) and expenses allocated to the rental use of the home that would be deductible as itemized deductions even if the home were not rented (mortgage interest expense and real property taxes).

> **Tier 2**
> All other expenses allocated to the rental activity except depreciation expense, including payments for utilities, maintenance, and other direct expenses

> **Tier 3**
> Depreciation expense

the straight-line method over 27.5 years). The tier 3 expense deduction is limited to the gross rental revenue in excess of tier 1 and tier 2 expenses. Any tier 3 expenses not deductible because of the income limitation are suspended and carried forward to the subsequent year. The nondeductible tier 3 expense does not reduce the basis in the home. In general terms, this deduction sequence is unfavorable for taxpayers, because it is designed to maximize taxpayer deductions for expenses that would be deductible even without any rental use of the home (most commonly mortgage interest and real property taxes) and to minimize the allowable depreciation deductions for the home.

As we mentioned above, expenses associated with the rental use of the home must be allocated between rental use and personal use of the home. These expenses are *generally* allocated to rental use based on the ratio of the number of days of rental use to the total number of days the property was used for rental and personal purposes (see Exhibit 14-4). All expenses not allocated to rental use are allocated to personal use.

The only potential exception to the general allocation rule involves the allocation of mortgage interest expense and real property taxes (both tier 1 expenses). The IRS and the Tax Court disagree on how to allocate these particular expenses. The IRS allocates these expenses the same way as all other expenses. However, the Tax Court allocates *interest* and *taxes* to rental use based on the ratio of days that the property was rented over the *number of days in the year*, rather than the number of days the

EXHIBIT 14-4   Tax Court vs. IRS Method of Allocating Expenses

Rental Allocation	IRS Method	Tax Court Method
Mortgage interest and property taxes (tier 1 expenses)	$\text{Expense} \times \dfrac{\text{Total rental days}}{\text{Total days used}}$	$\text{Expense} \times \dfrac{\text{Total rental days}}{\text{Days in year}}$
All other expenses	$\text{Expense} \times \dfrac{\text{Total rental days}}{\text{Total days used}}$	$\text{Expense} \times \dfrac{\text{Total rental days}}{\text{Total days used}}$

property was used for any purpose during the year.[23] The **IRS** and **Tax Court allocation methods** are described in Exhibit 14-4.

The Tax Court justifies its approach by pointing out that interest expense and property taxes accrue over the entire year regardless of the level of personal or rental use. Taxpayers generally choose the approach that is most beneficial to them. The Tax Court method generally favors the taxpayer because it tends to allocate less interest expense and real property taxes to the rental use, which reduces the tier 1 expenses and allows more tier 2 and tier 3 expenses to be deducted when the gross income limitation applies. That is, the sum of the taxpayer's deductible personal (*from* AGI) and rental expenses (*for* AGI) associated with the rental home under the Tax Court method generally will exceed the sum of personal (*from* AGI) and rental expenses (*for* AGI) associated with the home under the IRS method when the gross income limitation applies. This is because the taxpayer does not lose deductions for the extra interest and real property taxes allocated to personal use under the Tax Court method because these expenses are allowed as itemized deductions on Schedule A. Note, however, that use of the Tax Court method likely involves more risk of IRS scrutiny than use of the IRS method.

Example 14-14

At the beginning of the year, the Jeffersons purchased a vacation home in Scottsdale, Arizona, for $500,000 ($400,000 for the building and $100,000 for the land). They paid $200,000 down and financed the remaining $300,000 with a 6 percent mortgage secured by the home. During the year, the Jeffersons used the home for personal purposes for 30 days and rented the home for 200 days. Thus, the home falls in the residence with significant rental use category. They received $37,500 of rental revenue and incurred $500 of rental advertising expenses. How are their expenses allocated to the rental use under the IRS and Tax Court methods? Note that the current year is leap year.

Answer: See the following summary of allocation of expenses associated with the home:

Allocation Method to Rental Use				
Expense	**Amount**	**Tier**	**IRS Method (200/230)**	**Tax Court Method (200/366 Tier 1 200/230 other)**
Advertising*	$ 500	1	$ 500	$ 500
Interest	18,000	1	15,652	9,836
Real estate taxes	5,000	1	4,348	2,732
Total tier 1 expenses	**$23,500**	1	**$20,500**	**$13,068**
Utilities	4,500	2	3,913	3,913
Repairs	1,800	2	1,565	1,565
Insurance	3,500	2	3,043	3,043
Maintenance	3,200	2	2,783	2,783
Total tier 2 expenses	**$13,000**	2	**$11,304**	**$11,304**
Tier 3: Depreciation	13,939	3	**$12,121**	**$12,121**
Total expenses	$50,439			

*Advertising is a direct expense of the rental so it is fully deductible against rental revenue.

[23]The Tax Court method of allocating these expenses is also referred to as the Bolton method after the taxpayer in the court case in which the Tax Court approved this method of allocating deductions. While the court case initially was tried in the Tax Court, the decision in favor of the taxpayer was appealed to the Ninth Circuit Court that also ruled in favor of the taxpayer and sanctioned the use of the Tax Court or Bolton method of allocating interest expense. *Bolton v. Commissioner*, 82-2 USTC §9699 (CA 9), Affirming Tax Court, 77 TC 104.

Net income from rental	IRS Method	Tax Court Method
Rental receipts	$ 37,500	$ 37,500
Less tier 1 expenses	(20,500)	(13,068)
Income after tier 1 expenses	17,000	24,432
Less tier 2 expenses	(11,304)	(11,304)
Income after tier 2 expenses	5,696	13,128
Less tier 3 expenses	(5,696)	(12,121)
Taxable rental income	**$ 0**	**$ 1,007**
Deductible personal expenses (interest and property taxes)	$ 3,000	$10,432
Deductible rental expenses (sum of tier 1, 2, and 3 expenses)	37,500	36,493
Total personal and rental expenses	**$40,500**	**$46,925**

Note that under the Tax Court method, the Jeffersons are able to deduct $7,432 ($10,432 minus $3,000) more in itemized deductions for interest and real property taxes than they do under the IRS method, and they deduct $1,007 ($37,500 minus $36,493) fewer rental expenses (*for* AGI) under the Tax Court method relative to the IRS method. In total, the Jeffersons are allowed to deduct $6,425 more in total deductions under the Tax Court method than the IRS method in the current year ($46,925 minus $40,500). However, under the IRS method, the Jeffersons are allowed to carry forward to next year the $6,425 in depreciation expense that they were not allowed to deduct in the current year ($12,121 – $5,696). Under the Tax Court method, they were able to deduct all of their expenses so they do not carry forward any expenses to future years.

Taxpayers would report their rental activities on Schedule E of Form 1040. The deductible tier 1, tier 2, and tier 3 expenses are *for* AGI deductions. Exhibit 14-5 displays the completed Schedule E for the Jefferson's Scottsdale vacation home using the Tax Court method. Note that net rental income is considered to be investment income for purposes of determining the 3.8% net investment income tax discussed in Chapter 8.

Nonresidence (Rental Property)

For property in this category, the taxpayer includes the rental revenue in gross income and deducts all rental expenses *allocated to the rental use* of the property as *for* AGI deductions (all on Schedule E). When the property is used for even a day for personal purposes, the expenses must be allocated between the rental usage and the personal usage.[24] In this situation, however, the law does *not allow* the taxpayer to deduct mortgage interest not allocated to rental use because the taxpayer does not meet the minimum amount of personal use required for the deduction (the home is not a qualified residence—see prior discussion). However, the taxpayer is still allowed to deduct, as an itemized deduction, real property taxes not allocated to the rental. In contrast to the residence with significant rental use category, if the rental expenses exceed the gross income from the home in this category, the deductibility of the loss is not subject to a gross income limitation but it is subject to the passive activity restrictions discussed below.[25]

> **THE KEY FACTS**
>
> **Rental Use of the Home**
>
> - Nonresidence.
>   - Rental use is at least one day and personal use is no more than the *greater* of (1) 14 days or (2) 10 percent of rental days.
>   - Allocate expenses to rental and personal use.
>   - Rental deductions in excess of rental income are deductible subject to passive loss limitation rules.
>   - Interest expense allocated to personal use not deductible.

[24]§280A(e).

[25]If the home rental is deemed to be a not-for-profit activity, the loss is subject to the hobby loss rules in §183.

EXHIBIT 14-5 Jeffersons' Schedule E for Vacation Home Rental

SCHEDULE E (Form 1040) Department of the Treasury Internal Revenue Service (99)	**Supplemental Income and Loss** (From rental real estate, royalties, partnerships, S corporations, estates, trusts, REMICs, etc.) ▶ Attach to Form 1040, 1040NR, or Form 1041. ▶ Information about Schedule E and its separate instructions is at *www.irs.gov/schedulee.*	OMB No. 1545-0074 20**15** Attachment Sequence No. **13**

Name(s) shown on return	Your social security number
Tyler and Jasmine Jefferson	321-54-9876

Part I Income or Loss From Rental Real Estate and Royalties   **Note:** If you are in the business of renting personal property, use **Schedule C** or **C-EZ** (see instructions). If you are an individual, report farm rental income or loss from **Form 4835** on page 2, line 40.

A Did you make any payments in 2015 that would require you to file Form(s) 1099? (see instructions) ☐ Yes ☑ No
B If "Yes," did you or will you file required Forms 1099? ☐ Yes ☐ No

1a Physical address of each property (street, city, state, ZIP code)

A Hole-in-One Blvd. Scottsdale, Arizona 85262
B
C

1b	Type of Property (from list below)	2	For each rental real estate property listed above, report the number of fair rental and personal use days. Check the **QJV** box only if you meet the requirements to file as a qualified joint venture. See instructions.		Fair Rental Days	Personal Use Days	QJV
A	1			A	200	30	☐
B				B			☐
C				C			☐

Type of Property:
1 Single Family Residence   3 Vacation/Short-Term Rental   5 Land   7 Self-Rental
2 Multi-Family Residence   4 Commercial   6 Royalties   8 Other (describe)

Income:	Properties:		A	B	C
3	Rents received	3	37,500		
4	Royalties received	4			
Expenses:					
5	Advertising	5	500		
6	Auto and travel (see instructions)	6			
7	Cleaning and maintenance	7	2,783		
8	Commissions.	8			
9	Insurance	9	3,043		
10	Legal and other professional fees	10			
11	Management fees	11			
12	Mortgage interest paid to banks, etc. (see instructions)	12	9,836		
13	Other interest.	13			
14	Repairs.	14	1,565		
15	Supplies	15			
16	Taxes	16	2,732		
17	Utilities.	17	3,913		
18	Depreciation expense or depletion	18	12,121		
19	Other (list) ▶ _____	19			
20	Total expenses. Add lines 5 through 19	20	36,493		
21	Subtract line 20 from line 3 (rents) and/or 4 (royalties). If result is a (loss), see instructions to find out if you must file **Form 6198**	21	1,007		
22	Deductible rental real estate loss after limitation, if any, on **Form 8582** (see instructions)	22	( )	( )	( )

23a	Total of all amounts reported on line 3 for all rental properties	23a	37,500	
b	Total of all amounts reported on line 4 for all royalty properties	23b		
c	Total of all amounts reported on line 12 for all properties	23c	9,836	
d	Total of all amounts reported on line 18 for all properties	23d	12,121	
e	Total of all amounts reported on line 20 for all properties	23e	36,493	
24	**Income.** Add positive amounts shown on line 21. **Do not** include any losses		24	1,007
25	**Losses.** Add royalty losses from line 21 and rental real estate losses from line 22. Enter total losses here		25	( )
26	**Total rental real estate and royalty income or (loss).** Combine lines 24 and 25. Enter the result here. If Parts II, III, IV, and line 40 on page 2 do not apply to you, also enter this amount on Form 1040, line 17, or Form 1040NR, line 18. Otherwise, include this amount in the total on line 41 on page 2		26	1,007

For Paperwork Reduction Act Notice, see the separate instructions.   Cat. No. 11344L   Schedule E (Form 1040) 2015

Example 14-15

What if: Suppose that at the beginning of the year, the Jeffersons purchased a vacation home in Scottsdale, Arizona, for $400,000. They paid $100,000 down and financed the remaining $300,000 with a 6 percent mortgage secured by the home. During the year, the Jeffersons *did not use the home for personal purposes* and they rented the home for 200 days. They received $37,500 in gross rental revenue for the year and incurred $50,439 of expenses relating to the rental property. How much can the Jeffersons deduct in this situation?

Answer: The good news is that the deductions are not limited to gross income from the rental so they can deduct all $50,439, generating a $12,939 loss on the property ($37,500 − $50,439). The bad news is that, as we discuss below, the loss may not be immediately deductible due to the passive activity loss limitations.

Exhibit 14-6 summarizes the tax rules relating to a home used for rental purposes depending on the extent of rental (and personal use). Appendix B to this chapter provides a flowchart summarizing the implementation of these rules.

Losses on Rental Property   A rental property can be a great investment that gets the best of all worlds. It could (1) appreciate in value, (2) produce annual positive cash flow (rental receipts exceed expenses other than depreciation), and (3) generate tax losses that reduce the taxes the owner is required to pay on other sources of income. Consider the Jeffersons' second-home property, purchased for $400,000 and used primarily as a rental home (see previous example), which we'll assume has appreciated to $440,000 by the end of 2016. The property has appreciated by $40,000, produced a positive cash flow of $1,000 [$37,500 rental income minus expenses other than depreciation of $36,500 ($50,439 total expenses minus depreciation expense of $13,939)], and generated a net tax loss of $12,939. This tax loss apparently saves the Jeffersons $3,623 in taxes [($12,939) × 28% marginal tax rate].

Thus, the increase in the Jeffersons' wealth from their second-home investment for the year appears to be $44,623 ($40,000 appreciation + $1,000 rental cash flow + $3,623 tax savings). But as noted elsewhere in this text, when a tax outcome seems too good to be true, it usually is. Read on.

Passive activity loss rules.   In Chapter 7, we introduced the **passive activity loss** rules that indicate taxpayers may only deduct passive losses for a year to the extent of their passive income. We also learned that, by definition, a rental activity (including a second home rental that falls in the nonresidence category) is considered to be a passive activity.[26] Because they are passive losses, losses from rental property are generally not allowed to offset other ordinary or investment type income. However, as we also discussed in Chapter 7, a taxpayer who is an **active participant in a rental activity** may be allowed to deduct up to $25,000 of the rental loss against nonpassive income.[27] Consistent with a number of tax benefits, the exception amount for active owners is phased out as income increases: the $25,000 maximum exception amount is phased out by 50 cents for every dollar the taxpayer's adjusted gross income (before considering the rental loss) exceeds $100,000. Consequently, the entire $25,000 is phased out when the taxpayer's adjusted gross income reaches $150,000.

[26]Recall that second homes falling in the significant personal and rental use category are not passive activities. See §469(j).

[27]§469(i).

EXHIBIT 14-6 **Summary of Tax Rules Relating to Home Used for Rental Purposes**

	Residence with Minimal Rental Use	Residence with Significant Rental Use	Nonresidence
Classification test	Reside in home for at least 15 days and rent home for 14 or fewer days during the year.	Rent home for 15 days or more and use home for personal purposes for more than the greater of (1) 14 days or (2) 10 percent of the total rental days.	Rent home for at least one day, and personal use does not exceed the greater of (1) 14 days or (2) 10 percent of the rental days.
Rental revenue	Exclude from gross income	Include in gross income.	Include in gross income.
Direct rental expenses unrelated to home use	Not deductible.	Fully deductible for AGI (loss not subject to passive activity loss rules).	Deductible for AGI but subject to passive activity loss rules.
Treatment of mortgage interest and real property taxes	Deductible as itemized deductions.	Allocate between personal-use days and rental days; interest and taxes allocated to rental days are deductible as rental expenses; interest and taxes allocated to personal-use days are deductible as itemized deductions.	Allocated between personal-use days and rental days; interest and taxes allocated to rental days are deductible as rental expenses; taxes allocated to personal-use days are deductible as itemized deductions; interest allocated to personal-use days is not deductible.
Treatment of all other expenses	Not deductible.	Allocate between personal-use days and rental days; expenses allocated to personal-use days are not deductible; expenses allocated to rental days are deductible as rental expenses to the extent of rental revenue minus the sum of direct rental expenses, rental mortgage interest, and real property taxes; when expenses allocated to rental days exceed the rental income.	Allocated between personal-use days and rental days; expenses allocated to personal-use days are not deductible; expenses allocated to rental days are deductible and can generate loss but loss is subject to passive activity loss rules.
Excess expenses	Not applicable.	Rental expenses in excess of rental income minus the sum of direct rental expenses, rental mortgage interest, and real property taxes are carried forward to the next year.	Not applicable; rental expenses are deductible, even if they create a rental loss.

Example 14-16

Suppose the Jeffersons incurred a $12,939 passive loss from their Scottsdale rental home (described in the previous example), and they did not receive any passive income during the year. Assuming their current-year AGI is $250,000 and that they are considered to be active participants in the rental activity, how much of the rental loss are the Jeffersons allowed to deduct this year under the rental real estate exception to the passive activity loss rules?

Answer: $0. Because their adjusted gross income exceeds $150,000, the $25,000 deduction exception to the passive activity loss rules is completely phased out. Consequently, the Jeffersons are not allowed to deduct any of the $12,939 rental loss for the year.

What if: How much of the $12,939 loss could the Jeffersons deduct for the year if their adjusted gross income (before considering the rental loss) were $120,000?

Answer: They could deduct the entire $12,939 loss. The $25,000 exception amount would be reduced by a $10,000 phase-out [50 cents × ($120,000 − $100,000)]. The maximum amount of the rental loss that can offset ordinary income would therefore be reduced from $25,000 to $15,000 ($25,000 − $10,000 phased out). However, because their loss is less than $15,000, they may deduct the entire $12,939 rental loss against their other sources of income for the year.

Are passive losses from rental real estate activities that taxpayers are not allowed to deduct in the current year permanently disallowed? No, these losses are suspended until the taxpayer generates passive income or until the taxpayer sells the property that generated the passive loss. On the sale, in addition to reporting gain or loss from the sale of the property, the taxpayer will be allowed to deduct suspended passive losses against ordinary income.

BUSINESS USE OF THE HOME   LO 14-6

Because a personal residence is a personal use asset, utility payments and depreciation due to wear and tear are not deductible expenses. However, taxpayers who use their home—or at least part of their home—for business purposes may be able to deduct expenses associated with their home use if they meet certain stringent requirements.[28]

To qualify for **home office deductions,** a taxpayer must use her home—or part of her home—*exclusively and regularly* as either

1. The principal place of business for any of the taxpayer's trade or businesses, or
2. As a place to meet with patients, clients, or customers in the normal course of business.

Taxpayers fail the exclusive use test if they use the area of the home in question for both business and personal purposes.

Example 14-17

What if: Jasmine recently quit her job as an employee for an advertising firm because, with the move to the new home, the commute was too long. She has decided to go it alone as a self-employed graphic designer. She uses a large room in the basement of the Jeffersons' new home as her office. The room has been wired for all of her office needs. Once or twice a week, Tyler sits at the desk in the room and surfs the web to read up on his favorite sports teams. Is the office space eligible for a home office deduction?

Answer: No. The office is not used exclusively for Jasmine's business.

[28]§280A. If taxpayers rent the home they occupy and they meet the requirements for business use of the home, they can deduct part of the rent they pay. To determine the amount of the deduction, multiply the rental payment by the percentage of the home used for business purposes.

The exclusive use rule does not apply if the taxpayer either

- Uses part of the home for the storage of inventory or product samples.
- Uses part of the home as a day care facility.

When a taxpayer has more than one business location, including the home, which is her principal place of business? This is a facts-and-circumstances determination based upon

- The relative importance of the activities performed at each place where the taxpayer conducts business (more income from an activity generally means it's a more important activity) and
- The total time spent doing work at each location.

However, by definition, a taxpayer's principal place of business also includes the place of business used by the taxpayer for the administrative or management activities of the taxpayer's trade or business if there is no other fixed location of the trade or business where the taxpayer conducts substantial administrative or management activities of the trade or business.[29]

If a taxpayer meets with clients or patients in her home during the normal course of business, she qualifies for the home office deduction even if the home is not her principal place of business. However, the clients or patients must visit the taxpayer's home *in person*. Communication through telephone calls or other types of communication technology does not qualify.

Example 14-18

What if: Jasmine recently quit her job as an employee for an advertising firm because, with the move to the new home, the commute was too long. She has decided to go it alone as a self-employed graphic designer. She uses a large room in the basement of the Jeffersons' new home as her office. The room has been wired for all of her office needs. The Jeffersons use the room exclusively for Jasmine's graphic design business use. Does this space qualify for the home office deduction?

Answer: Yes. While Jasmine will spend a good deal of time meeting with clients on location, she has no other fixed location for her trade or business. Further, the office is used exclusively for business purposes. Consequently, the Jeffersons qualify for the home office deduction subject to certain limitations described below.

THE KEY FACTS

Home Office Deduction

- Deductibility limits on expenses allocated to office.
  - If employee, expenses deducted as unreimbursed employee business expenses.
  - If self-employed, deducted *for* AGI but deductions may be subject to income limitation.
  - If deduction is limited by income limitation, apply the same tiered system as used for rental property when tier 2 and tier 3 deductions are limited to gross rental income minus tier 1 expenses.

Finally, note that an *employee* (not a self-employed taxpayer) who otherwise meets these requirements qualifies for home office deductions only if

- The employee's use of the home is considered to be for the convenience of the employer and not just something that is helpful or useful for the employer, and
- The employee does not rent part of the home to the employer.

Generally, with such strict requirements, only self-employed taxpayers and employees such as outside salespersons or full-time telecommuters who have no office space anywhere except at home can qualify for the deductions.[30]

---

[29]§280A(c)(1).

[30]IRS Publication 587 Business Use of Your Home, page 4, provides a flowchart for determining whether taxpayers are allowed to deduct home office expenses.

> **TAXES IN THE REAL WORLD** If You Want The Bathroom to Qualify as a Home Office, You Better Lock It and Keep the Key
>
> The IRS and a taxpayer with seven years of IRS work experience recently did battle over home office expenses in the Tax Court. The taxpayer operates an accounting business, and he uses a bedroom in his residence exclusively for his accounting business. The taxpayer included the bathroom adjacent to the bedroom in his home office square footage. However, because the taxpayer testified that his children and personal guests occasionally used the bathroom, the Tax Court determined that the bathroom was not used exclusively for business purposes (the children and personal guests may beg to differ), and it disallowed the expenses associated with the bathroom square footage. See *Luis Bulas*, T.C. Memo. 2011-201 (2011).

- Taxpayers can elect simplified method to report home office expenses.
  - Business use square footage (limited to 300 sq. feet) × $5 per square foot.
  - Deduction limited to gross business revenue (minus business expenses unrelated to home).
  - No carryover of excess deduction to subsequent year.
  - Deduct all property taxes and mortgage interest as itemized deductions.
  - Do not deduct depreciation expense so basis in home is unaffected by home office expense deduction (under the simplified method).
- Depreciation expense
  - Reduces basis in home.
  - Gain on sale due to depreciation deductions after 5/6/1997 is ineligible for exclusion.
  - This gain is taxed at a maximum 25 percent rate as unrecaptured §1250 gain.

Direct vs. Indirect Expenses

When a taxpayer qualifies for home office deductions, they are allowed to deduct only actual expenses that are related—either directly or indirectly—to the business. Direct expenses are expenses incurred in maintaining the room or part of the home that is set aside for business use. Direct expenses include painting or costs of other repairs to the area of the home used for business.[31] These expenses are deductible in full as home office expenses. Indirect expenses are expenses incurred in maintaining and using the home. Indirect expenses include insurance, utilities, interest, real property taxes, general repairs, and depreciation on the home as if it were used entirely for business purposes. Depreciation on the home is calculated using nonresidential real property depreciation tables (straight-line depreciation over 39 years). In contrast to direct expenses, only indirect expenses *allocated* to the home office space are deductible.

How do taxpayers allocate indirect expenses to the home office space? If the rooms in the home are roughly of equal size, the taxpayer may allocate the indirect expenses to the business portion of the home based on the number of rooms. In a 10-room home, a taxpayer using one room for qualifying business use is allowed to deduct 10 percent of the indirect expenses. Alternatively, the taxpayer may allocate indirect expenses based on the amount of the space or square footage of the business-use room relative to the total square footage in the home. If the home is 5,000 square feet and the home office is 250 square feet, the taxpayer may deduct 5 percent of the indirect expenses. Unrelated expenses such as painting a room not used for business purposes are not deductible.

In lieu of allocating actual expenses to home office use, the IRS allows taxpayers to use an optional simplified method for computing home office expenses.[32] Under the simplified method, taxpayers are not allowed to deduct any *actual* expenses relating to qualified business use of the home (including depreciation). Instead, taxpayers electing the simplified method deduct, subject to limitations described below, the allowable business use square footage of the office (not to exceed 300 square feet) multiplied by $5 per square foot. Thus, this method generates a maximum deduction of $1,500 (300 square feet × $5 per square foot). In addition, taxpayers using this method are allowed to deduct all of their home mortgage interest and real property taxes as itemized deductions on Schedule A. Taxpayers may choose from year to year whether to use the simplified method or the actual expense method.

---

[31] The basic local telephone service charge, including taxes, for the first telephone line into a home is a nondeductible personal expense. However, charges for business long-distance phone calls on that line, as well as the cost of a second line into the home used exclusively for business, are deductible business expenses. However, these expenses are not deducted as home office expenses. Rather, these expenses are deducted separately on the appropriate form or schedule. Taxpayers filing Schedule C (Form 1040), would deduct these expenses as utilities.

[32] Rev. Proc. 2013-13.

Example 14-19

The Jeffersons moved into their new $800,000, 6,000-square-foot home on February 1 (The home building was valued at $600,000, and the land was valued at $200,000.) Jasmine quit her job and set up a 420-square-foot home office in the basement on that same date. Through the end of the calendar year, the Jeffersons incurred several expenses relating to their home (see table below). Assuming they qualify for the home office deduction, they would sum the direct expenses and the indirect expenses allocated to the office. They would allocate the indirect expenses based on the square footage of the office compared to the rest of the home. Using the actual expense method, what amount of home-related expenses would qualify as home office expenses?

Answer: $4,575. See allocation below. All direct expenses and 7 percent of the indirect expenses would be allocated to the home office (420 office square footage/6,000 home square footage). The Jeffersons would allocate the expenses as follows:

Total Expense	Type	(A) Amount	(B) Office %	(A) × (B) Home Office Expense
Painting office	Direct	$ 200	100%	$ 200
Real property taxes	Indirect	11,000	7	770
Home interest expense	Indirect	27,917	7	1,954
Electricity	Indirect	2,600	7	182
Gas and other utilities	Indirect	2,500	7	175
Homeowner's insurance	Indirect	5,000	7	350
Depreciation	Indirect	13,482	7	944
Total expenses		$62,699		$4,575

The expenses attributable to the home office are deductible subject to the limitations discussed below. Also, as discussed below, the Jeffersons are able to deduct the real property taxes and home interest expense not allocated to the home office as itemized deductions.

What if: Suppose Jasmine elects to use the simplified method for determining home office expenses. What would be the amount of their home office expenses?

Answer: $1,500 (300 square feet × $5 per square foot). Even though the Jeffersons' home office is 420 square feet, for purposes of the home office expense under the simplified method, the square footage is limited to 300 square feet.

What if: Suppose the Jeffersons elect to use the simplified method for home office expenses. What amount of home mortgage interest expenses and real property taxes would they be able to deduct on Schedule A as itemized deductions?

Answer: Home mortgage interest expense $27,917; real property taxes $11,000. They are allowed to deduct all of these expenses as itemized deductions.

Limitations on Deductibility of Expenses

The process for determining the home office expense deduction using the actual expense method is similar to the process used to determine deductions for vacation homes. When net business income (net Schedule C income) exceeds total home office expenses (before applying any limitations), the full amount of the expenses are deductible. However, when home office expenses exceed net Schedule C income (before the home office deduction), the deduction is potentially limited. In these situations, taxpayers first divide home office expenses into one of three categories or "tiers." Tier 1 expenses consist of mortgage interest and real property taxes allocated to the business use of the home. Tier 2 expenses consist of all other expenses allocated to the business use of the home except for depreciation. Tier 3 expense consists of depreciation. Taxpayers first deduct tier 1 expenses in full even when tier 1 expenses exceed net Schedule C income before the home office deduction.[33] Second, taxpayers

[33]§280A(c)(5).

deduct tier 2 expenses. However, deductible tier 2 expenses are limited to net Schedule C income before home office deductions minus tier 1 expenses (that is, deducting tier 2 expenses cannot create a net Schedule C loss). Any tier 2 expenses not deductible due to the income limitation are suspended and carried forward to the next year, subject to the same limitations. Finally, taxpayers deduct tier 3 expense. The deductible tier 3 expense is limited to net Schedule C income before the home office deduction minus tier 1 and deductible tier 2 expenses (tier 3 expense cannot create a net Schedule C loss). The nondeductible portion of tier 3 expense is carried forward to the next year, subject to the same limitations.

Under the simplified method, the expense, as calculated by multiplying the square footage by the $5 application rate, is limited to net Schedule C income before home office deductions. Further, taxpayers using the simplified method in a particular year may not carryover expenses disallowed by the income limitation and they may not deduct expenses carried over to that year under the actual expense method. However, disallowed expenses under the actual expense method can be carried over to a subsequent year in which the taxpayer uses the actual expense method for determining the home office expense deduction.

Example 14-20

For the year, Jasmine generated $4,000 of net business income before the home office deduction from her graphic design business. Her home office expenses before limitation total $4,575 (see previous example). The expenses consist of painting office $200, real property taxes $770, home interest expense $1,954, electricity $182, gas and other utilities $175, homeowner's insurance $350, and depreciation $944. What is the total amount of tier 1, tier 2, and tier 3 expenses?

Answer: Tier 1 expenses $2,724 (real property taxes $770 and home interest expense of $1,954); tier 2 expenses $907 (painting office $200, electricity $182, gas and other utilities $175, and homeowner's insurance $350); tier 3 expense $944 (depreciation).

What is Jasmine's net income from the business after claiming the home office deduction and what expenses, if any, will she carry over to next year?

Answer: $0 net income and carry over $575 of depreciation expense, determined as follows:

	Net Income from Business
Gross business receipts	$4,000
Less tier 1 expenses	(2,724)
Income after tier 1 expenses	1,276
Less tier 2 expenses	(907)
Income after tier 2 expenses	369
Less tier 3 expense	(369)
Taxable business income	$ 0

Due to the income limitation, Jasmine was allowed to deduct only $369 of the $944 depreciation expense. She will carry over the remaining $575 ($944 minus $369) to next year to deduct as a home office expense subject to the same limitations.

What if: Suppose Jasmine uses the simplified method of determining home office expenses. What amount of the $1,500 expense (300 square feet × $5 application rate) would she be allowed to deduct?

Answer: All $1,500, because the home office expense is less than the $4,000 net business income before the home office deduction.

What if: Assume the same facts as in the previous what-if example except that net business income before the home office deduction was $1,200. What amount of the $1,500 home office expense would Jasmine be allowed to deduct?

Answer: $1,200. The home office expense deduction under the simplified method is limited to net business income before the home office deduction. Jasmine is not allowed to carry over the $300 nondeductible portion of the expense to a subsequent year ($1,500 total expense minus $1,200 deductible expense).

It is important to note that, when a taxpayer deducts depreciation as a home office expense, the depreciation expense reduces the basis of the taxpayer's home. Consequently, when the taxpayer sells the home, the gain on the sale will be greater than it would have been had the taxpayer not deducted depreciation expense. Further, the gain on the sale of the home attributable to the depreciation deductions (incurred after 5/6/1997) is not eligible to be excluded under the home sale exclusion provision. Rather, the gain is treated as unrecaptured §1250 gain and is subject to a maximum 25 percent tax rate (See Chapter 11 for detailed discussion of unrecaptured §1250 gain).

Example 14-21

At the beginning of the year, the Jeffersons' basis in their home was $800,000. Jasmine's first-year home office deductions included $369 in depreciation expense. What is their adjusted basis in the home at the end of the year?

Answer: The depreciation deduction reduces the basis to $799,631 ($800,000 minus $369).

What if: Now, suppose that after the Jeffersons meet the ownership and use tests for the home sale exclusion, they sell the home for $900,000. Assume the only depreciation expense the Jeffersons have deducted is the $369 they deducted in the year they bought the home. Consequently, their adjusted basis in the home on the date of sale was $799,631 and they realize a gain of $100,369 on the sale. How much of the gain are they allowed to exclude?

Answer: They can exclude $100,000 of gain. However, they are not allowed to exclude the remaining $369 gain caused by the depreciation expense for the home office. The Jeffersons must pay $92 of tax on the gain ($369 × 25% unrecaptured §1250 gain).

Taxpayers using the simplified method are not allowed to deduct depreciation expense. Consequently, the simplified method does not affect the taxpayer's adjusted basis in the home. However, if a taxpayer switches from the simplified method in one year to the actual expense method in a subsequent year, the taxpayer is required to use modified depreciation tables to compute depreciation expense under the actual expense method.

Allowing taxpayers to deduct part of their home-related expenses as business expenses creates temptations for taxpayers to deduct home-related expenses that don't meet the requirements. Not surprisingly, the IRS is very concerned about taxpayers inappropriately deducting expenses relating to their home. Consequently, expenses for business use of the home are some of the most highly scrutinized deductions available to taxpayers. Self-employed taxpayers claiming home office deductions must file a Form 8829 "Expenses for Business Use of Your Home" when deducting home office expenses on a tax return. With the high level of scrutiny applied to home office expenses, taxpayers should be sure to have documentation available to support their deductions. Exhibit 14-7 includes Form 8829 for Jasmine taken from Examples 14-19 and 14-20.

CONCLUSION

When deciding whether to invest in a home as a primary residence, a vacation home, or even a rental home, prospective owners should consider both nontax and tax factors relating to the ownership of the property. The tax code includes several provisions favorable to homeowners. This chapter is intended to provide current and prospective homeowners with enough insight on tax and nontax consequences of home ownership to allow them to make informed investment and compliance decisions when applicable.

EXHIBIT 14-7

Form **8829**

Department of the Treasury
Internal Revenue Service (99)

Expenses for Business Use of Your Home

▶ File only with Schedule C (Form 1040). Use a separate Form 8829 for each home you used for business during the year.
▶ Information about Form 8829 and its separate instructions is at www.irs.gov/form8829.

OMB No. 1545-0074

20**15**

Attachment Sequence No. **176**

Name(s) of proprietor(s): Jasmine Jefferson

Your social security number: 674-65-6564

Part I   Part of Your Home Used for Business

1 Area used regularly and exclusively for business, regularly for daycare, or for storage of inventory or product samples (see instructions)	1	420
2 Total area of home	2	6,000
3 Divide line 1 by line 2. Enter the result as a percentage	3	7 %

For daycare facilities not used exclusively for business, go to line 4. All others, go to line 7.

4 Multiply days used for daycare during year by hours used per day	4	hr.
5 Total hours available for use during the year (365 days x 24 hours) (see instructions)	5	8,760 hr.
6 Divide line 4 by line 5. Enter the result as a decimal amount	6	
7 Business percentage. For daycare facilities not used exclusively for business, multiply line 6 by line 3 (enter the result as a percentage). All others, enter the amount from line 3 ▶	7	7 %

Part II   Figure Your Allowable Deduction

8 Enter the amount from Schedule C, line 29, **plus** any gain derived from the business use of your home, **minus** any loss from the trade or business not derived from the business use of your home (see instructions)		8	4,000

See instructions for columns (a) and (b) before completing lines 9–21.

	(a) Direct expenses	(b) Indirect expenses		
9 Casualty losses (see instructions)				
10 Deductible mortgage interest (see instructions)		27,917		
11 Real estate taxes (see instructions)		11,000		
12 Add lines 9, 10, and 11		38,917		
13 Multiply line 12, column (b) by line 7		13	2,724	
14 Add line 12, column (a) and line 13			14	2,724
15 Subtract line 14 from line 8. If zero or less, enter -0-			15	1,276
16 Excess mortgage interest (see instructions)				
17 Insurance		5,000		
18 Rent				
19 Repairs and maintenance	200			
20 Utilities		5,100		
21 Other expenses (see instructions)				
22 Add lines 16 through 21	200	10,100		
23 Multiply line 22, column (b) by line 7		23	707	
24 Carryover of prior year operating expenses (see instructions)		24		
25 Add line 22, column (a), line 23, and line 24			25	907
26 Allowable operating expenses. Enter the **smaller** of line 15 or line 25			26	907
27 Limit on excess casualty losses and depreciation. Subtract line 26 from line 15			27	369
28 Excess casualty losses (see instructions)	28			
29 Depreciation of your home from line 41 below	29	944		
30 Carryover of prior year excess casualty losses and depreciation (see instructions)	30			
31 Add lines 28 through 30			31	944
32 Allowable excess casualty losses and depreciation. Enter the **smaller** of line 27 or line 31			32	369
33 Add lines 14, 26, and 32			33	4,000
34 Casualty loss portion, if any, from lines 14 and 32. Carry amount to **Form 4684** (see instructions)			34	
35 **Allowable expenses for business use of your home.** Subtract line 34 from line 33. Enter here and on Schedule C, line 30. If your home was used for more than one business, see instructions ▶			35	4,000

Part III   Depreciation of Your Home

36 Enter the **smaller** of your home's adjusted basis or its fair market value (see instructions)	36	800,000
37 Value of land included on line 36	37	200,000
38 Basis of building. Subtract line 37 from line 36	38	600,000
39 Business basis of building. Multiply line 38 by line 7	39	42,000
40 Depreciation percentage (see instructions)	40	2.247 %
41 Depreciation allowable (see instructions). Multiply line 39 by line 40. Enter here and on line 29 above	41	944

Part IV   Carryover of Unallowed Expenses to 2016

42 Operating expenses. Subtract line 26 from line 25. If less than zero, enter -0-	42	
43 Excess casualty losses and depreciation. Subtract line 32 from line 31. If less than zero, enter -0-	43	575

For Paperwork Reduction Act Notice, see your tax return instructions.   Cat. No. 13232M   Form **8829** (2015)

Appendix A   Sample Settlement Statement for the Jeffersons (page 1)

A. **Settlement Statement**	U.S. Department of Housing and Urban Development	OMB Approval No. 2502-0265

B. Type of Loan

1. ☐ FHA 2. ☐ FmHA 3. ☑ Conv. Unins. 4. ☐ VA 5. ☐ Conv. Ins.	6. File Number: 1355	7. Loan Number: 6788	8. Mortgage Insurance Case Number:

C. Note: This form is furnished to give you a statement of actual settlement costs. Amounts paid to and by the settlement agent are shown. Items marked "(p.o.c.)" were paid outside the closing; they are shown here for informational purposes and are not included in the totals.

D. Name & Address of Borrower:	E. Name & Address of Seller:	F. Name & Address of Lender:
Tyler Jefferson Jasmine Jefferson 225 El Tejon Dr. Chicago, IL 60612	Ian Sabin 525 Roberts Ln. Glencoe, IL 60022	125 Decatur St. Chicago, IL 60612

G. Property Location:	H. Settlement Agent: Beardsley Settlement Group	
225 El Tejon Dr. Chicago, IL 60612 Lot 1, Block 2, Dozier Estates Cook County, Illinois	Place of Settlement: 425 McCray St. Chicago, IL 60612	I. Settlement Date: 1/31/2016

J. Summary of Borrower's Transaction		K. Summary of Seller's Transaction	
100. Gross Amount Due From Borrower		**400. Gross Amount Due To Seller**	
101. Contract sales price	800,000.00	401. Contract sales price	800,000.0
102. Personal property		402. Personal property	
103. Settlement charges to borrower (line 1400)	28,116.00	403.	
104.		404.	
105.		405.	
Adjustments for items paid by seller in advance		Adjustments for items paid by seller in advance	
106. City/town taxes to		406. City/town taxes to	
107. County taxes to		407. County taxes to	
108. Assessments to		408. Assessments to	
109.		409.	
110.		410.	
111.		411.	
112.		412.	
120. Gross Amount Due From Borrower	828,116.00	**420. Gross Amount Due To Seller**	800,000.00
200. Amounts Paid By Or In Behalf Of Borrower		**500. Reductions In Amount Due To Seller**	
201. Deposit or earnest money	20,000.00	501. Excess deposit (see instructions)	
202. Principal amount of new loan(s)	300,000.00	502. Settlement charges to seller (line 1400)	48,260.00
203. Existing loan(s) taken subject to		503. Existing loan(s) taken subject to	
204.		504. Payoff of first mortgage loan	
205.		505. Payoff of second mortgage loan	
206.		506.	
207.		507.	
208.		508.	
209.		509.	
Adjustments for items unpaid by seller		Adjustments for items unpaid by seller	
210. City/town taxes to		510. City/town taxes to	
211. County taxes 1/1/2016 to 1/31/2016	1,000.00	511. County taxes 1/1/2016 to 1/31/2016	1,000.00
212. Assessments to		512. Assessments to	
213.		513.	
214.		514.	
215.		515.	
216.		516.	
217.		517.	
218.		518.	
219.		519.	
220. Total Paid By/For Borrower	321,000.00	**520. Total Reduction Amount Due Seller**	49,260.00
300. Cash At Settlement From/To Borrower		**600. Cash At Settlement To/From Seller**	
301. Gross Amount due from borrower (line 120)	828,116.00	601. Gross amount due to seller (line 420)	800,000.00
302. Less amounts paid by/for borrower (line 220)	(321,000.00)	602. Less reductions in amt. due seller (line 520)	(49,260.00)
303. Cash ☑ From ☐ To Borrower	507,116.00	**603. Cash** ☑ To ☐ From Seller	750,740.00

Section 5 of the Real Estate Settlement Procedures Act (RESPA) requires the following: • HUD must develop a Special Information Booklet to help persons borrowing money to finance the purchase of residential real estate to better understand the nature and costs of real estate settlement services; • Each lender must provide the booklet to all applicants from whom it receives or for whom it prepares a written application to borrow money to finance the purchase of residential real estate; • Lenders must prepare and distribute with the Booklet a Good Faith Estimate of the settlement costs that the borrower is likely to incur in connection with the settlement. These disclosures are manadatory.

Section 4(a) of RESPA mandates that HUD develop and prescribe this standard form to be used at the time of loan settlement to provide full disclosure of all charges imposed upon the borrower and seller. These are third party disclosures that are designed to provide the borrower with pertinent information during the settlement process in order to be a better shopper.

The Public Reporting Burden for this collection of information is estimated to average one hour per response, including the time for reviewing instructions, searching existing data sources, gathering and maintaining the data needed, and completing and reviewing the collection of information.

This agency may not collect this information, and you are not required to complete this form, unless it displays a currently valid OMB control number.

The information requested does not lend itself to confidentiality.

(page 2)

L. Settlement Charges

700. Total Sales/Broker's Commission based on price $ 800,000.00 @ 6.000 % = 48,000.00	Paid From Borrowers Funds at Settlement	Paid From Seller's Funds at Settlement
Division of Commission (line 700) as follows:		
701. $ 24,000.00 to Selling Agent Co.		
702. $ 24,000.00 to Listing Agent Co.		
703. Commission paid at Settlement		48,000.00
704.		
800. Items Payable In Connection With Loan		
801. Loan Origination Fee 1.000 %	3,000.00	
802. Loan Discount 2.000 %	6,000.00	
803. Appraisal Fee to Drumgoole Apraisal Co.	400.00	
804. Credit Report to O'Brien Credit Check Inc.	40.00	
805. Lender's Inspection Fee		
806. Mortgage Insurance Application Fee to		
807. Assumption Fee		
808.		
809.		
810.		
811.		
900. Items Required By Lender To Be Paid In Advance		
901. Interest from 1/31/2016 to 2/10/2016 @$ 41.10 /day	411.00	
902. Mortgage Insurance Premium for months to		
903. Hazard Insurance Premium for years to		
904. years to		
905.		
1000. Reserves Deposited With Lender		
1001. Hazard insurance 2 months@$ 100.00 per month	200.00	
1002. Mortgage insurance months@$ per month		
1003. City property taxes months@$ per month		
1004. County property taxes 11 months@$ 1,000.00 per month	11,000.00	
1005. Annual assessments months@$ per month		
1006. months@$ per month		
1007. months@$ per month		
1008. months@$ per month		
1100. Title Charges		
1101. Settlement or closing fee to Beardsley Settlement Group	300.00	
1102. Abstract or title search to		
1103. Title examination to Title Examination Inc.	250.00	
1104. Title insurance binder to		
1105. Document preparation to Buckles & Pitts, L.L.P		200.00
1106. Notary fees to		
1107. Attorney's fees to		
(includes above items numbers:)		
1108. Title insurance to Title Insurance Co.	3,250.00	
(includes above items numbers:)		
1109. Lender's coverage $		
1110. Owner's coverage $		
1111.		
1112.		
1113.		
1200. Government Recording and Transfer Charges		
1201. Recording fees: Deed $ 40.00 ; Mortgage $ 50.00 ; Releases $	90.00	
1202. City/county tax/stamps: Deed $ 450.00 ; Mortgage $ 350.00	800.00	
1203. State tax/stamps: Deed $ 1,250.00 ; Mortgage $ 1,000.00	2,250.00	
1204.		
1205.		
1300. Additional Settlement Charges		
1301. Survey to Beardsley Settlement Group	125.00	
1302. Pest inspection to Clark's Pest Control		60.00
1303.		
1304.		
1305.		
1400. Total Settlement Charges (enter on lines 103, Section J and 502, Section K)	28,116.00	48,260.00

Appendix B   Flowchart of Tax Rules Relating to Home Used for Rental Purposes (page 1)

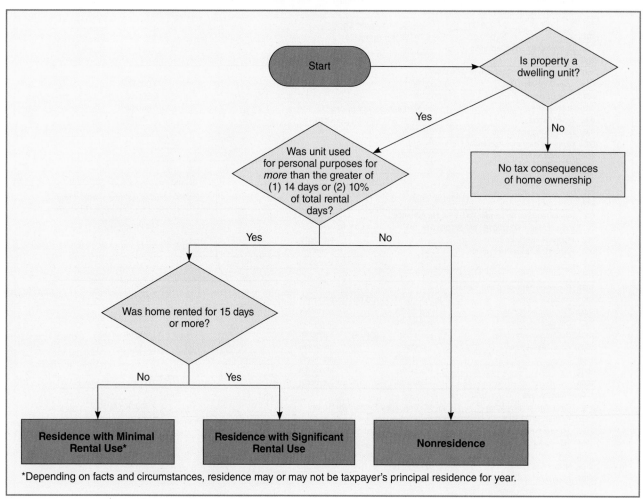

*Depending on facts and circumstances, residence may or may not be taxpayer's principal residence for year.

(page 2)

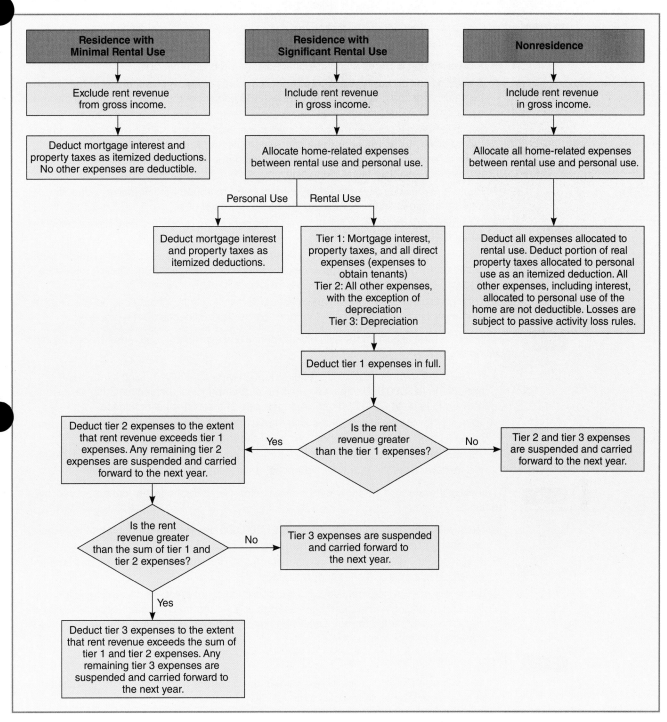

Summary

LO 14-1 Determine whether a home is considered a principal residence, a residence (not principal), or a nonresidence for tax purposes.

- A dwelling unit includes a house, condominium, mobile home, boat, or similar property.
- A dwelling unit is considered to be a residence if the taxpayer's personal use of the unit or home exceeds the greater of (1) 14 days or (2) 10 percent of the rental days during the year.
- Personal use includes days when the taxpayer or other owners stay in the home, a relative of the owner stays in the home, even if the relative pays full fair market value unless the relative is using the home as a principal residence, a nonowner stays in the home under a vacation home exchange or swap arrangement, or the taxpayer rents out the property for less than fair market value.
- Rental use includes days the taxpayer rents out the property at fair market value and days spent repairing or maintaining the home for rental use.
- Days when the home is available for rent but not rented out do not count as personal or rental days.
- When a taxpayer owns more than one residence, the principal residence is determined based on the facts and circumstances such as total time spent living in each residence. A taxpayer can have only one principal residence for a given year.
- For a particular taxpayer for a particular year, a dwelling unit or home can be classified as a principal residence, residence (not principal), or nonresidence (rental property).

LO 14-2 Compute the taxable gain on the sale of a residence and explain the requirements for excluding gain on the sale.

- If they meet ownership and use requirements, married taxpayers filing jointly may exclude up to $500,000 of gain on the sale of their principal residence. Other taxpayers may exclude up to $250,000 of gain on the sale of their principal residence.
- To qualify for the exclusion on the sale of real estate, taxpayers must own and use the home as their principal residence for two of the five years preceding the sale.
- The amount of gain eligible for exclusion may be reduced if on or after January 1, 2009, the taxpayer uses the home for a purpose other than as a principal residence.

LO 14-3 Determine the amount of allowable interest expense deductions on loans secured by a residence.

- Taxpayers may deduct interest on up to $1,000,000 of acquisition indebtedness of their principal residence and one other residence.
- Taxpayers may deduct interest on up to $100,000 of home-equity indebtedness on their principal residence and one other residence.
- Taxpayers may immediately deduct points paid (discount points and loan origination fees) on qualifying home mortgages used to acquire the taxpayer's principal residence if certain requirements are met. Qualifying points paid on a loan refinancing are deductible over the life of the loan.

LO 14-4 Discuss the deductibility of real property taxes.

- Taxpayers deduct real property taxes when the taxes are paid to the taxing jurisdiction and not when the taxes are paid to an escrow account.
- When a piece of real property is sold during the year, the property tax deduction for the property is allocated to the buyer and seller based on the portion of the year that each held the property no matter who pays the taxes.

LO 14-5 Explain the tax issues and consequences associated with rental use of the home, including determining the deductibility of residential rental real estate losses.

- Taxpayers who live in a home for 15 days or more and rent the home out for 14 days or less (a residence with minimal rental use) do not include gross rental receipts in taxable income and do not deduct rental expenses.
- Taxpayers who both reside in and rent out a home for a significant portion of the year (a residence with significant rental use) include rental revenue in gross income, deduct

direct rental expenses not relating to the home (expenses to obtain tenants), and allocate home-related expenses between personal use and rental use of the home. They deduct mortgage interest expense and real property taxes allocated to the rental use of the home as *for* AGI deductions and the mortgage interest expense and real property taxes allocated to the personal use of the home as itemized deductions. The remaining deductions allocated to the rental use of the home are deductible in a particular sequence and the amount of these deductions cannot exceed rental revenue in excess of direct rental expenses and rental mortgage interest and real property taxes.

- Net rental income reported on Schedule E is subject to the 3.8% net investment income tax discussed in Chapter 8. This tax applies to net investment income for high income taxpayers.
- Taxpayers who rent a home with minimal or no personal use (nonresidence) include rental receipts in income and deduct all rental expenses. In this situation expenses exceeding income are subject to the passive activity loss rules.
- Taxpayers may be able to deduct up to $25,000 of passive loss on their rental home if they are active participants with respect to the property. This deduction is phased out for taxpayers with adjusted gross income between $100,000 and $150,000.

Describe the requirements necessary to qualify for home office deductions and compute the deduction limitations on home office deductions. **LO 14-6**

- To deduct expenses relating to a home office, the taxpayer must use the home office exclusively and regularly for business purposes.
- Home-related expenses are allocated between business expenses and personal expenses based on the size of the office relative to the size of the home.
- Mortgage interest and real property taxes allocated to business use of the home are deductible in full without regard to the income of the business.
- Other expenses allocated to the business use of the home are deducted in a particular sequence. The deduction for these expenses cannot exceed the taxpayer's net Schedule C income (before home office expenses) minus the mortgage interest and real property taxes allocated to business use of the home.
- Taxpayers electing the simplified method for claiming home office expenses may deduct $5 per square foot up to 300 square feet.

KEY TERMS

acquisition indebtedness (14-9)
active participant in a rental
    activity (14-23)
dwelling unit (14-2)
escrow account (14-15)
flipping (14-5)
home-equity indebtedness (14-9)

home office deductions (14-25)
IRS allocation method (14-20)
passive activity income or
    loss (14-23)
point (14-13)
principal residence (14-2)
qualified debt (14-11)

qualified residence (14-9)
qualified residence interest (14-13)
real property taxes (14-16)
refinance (14-9)
secured loan (14-9)
settlement statement (14-13)
Tax Court allocation method (14-20)

DISCUSSION QUESTIONS

Discussion Questions are available in *Connect*®.   connect

1. How does a taxpayer determine whether a dwelling unit is treated as a residence or nonresidence for tax purposes? **LO 14-1**

2. Does a residence for tax purposes need to be situated at a fixed location? Explain. **LO 14-1**

3. When determining whether a dwelling unit is treated as a residence or a non-residence for tax purposes, what constitutes a day of personal use and what constitutes a day of rental use? **LO 14-1**

4. A taxpayer owns a home in Salt Lake City, Utah, and a second home in St. George, Utah. How does the taxpayer determine which home is her principal residence for tax purposes? **LO 14-1**

LO 14-2   5. What are the ownership and use requirements a taxpayer must meet to qualify for the exclusion of gain on the sale of a residence?

LO 14-2   6. Under what circumstances, if any, can a taxpayer fail to meet the ownership and use requirements but still be able to exclude all of the gain on the sale of a principal residence?

LO 14-2   7. Under what circumstances can a taxpayer meet the ownership and use requirements for a residence but still not be allowed to exclude all realized gain on the sale of the residence?

LO 14-2   8. A taxpayer purchases and lives in a home for a year. The home appreciates in value by $50,000. The taxpayer sells the home and purchases a new home. What information do you need to obtain to determine whether the taxpayer is allowed to exclude the gain on the sale of the first home?

LO 14-3   9. Juanita owns a principal residence in New Jersey, a cabin in Montana, and a houseboat in Hawaii. All of these properties have mortgages on which Juanita pays interest. What limits, if any, apply to Juanita's mortgage interest deductions? Explain whether deductible interest is deductible *for* AGI or *from* AGI.

LO 14-3   10. Barbi really wants to acquire an expensive automobile (perhaps more expensive than she can really afford). She has two options. Option 1: finance the purchase with an automobile loan from her local bank at a 7 percent interest rate, or Option 2: finance the purchase with a home-equity loan at a rate of 7 percent. Compare and contrast the tax and nontax factors Barbi should consider before deciding which loan to use to pay for the automobile. Barbi typically has more itemized deductions than the standard deduction amount.

LO 14-3   11. Lars and Leigha saved up for years before they purchased their dream home. They were considering (1) using all of their savings to make a large down payment on the home (90 percent of the value of the home) and barely scraping by without the backup savings, or (2) making a more modest down payment (50 percent of the value of the loan) and holding some of the savings in reserve as needed if funds get tight. They decided to go with the large down payment because they figured they could always refinance the home to pull some equity out of the home if things got tight. What advice would you give them about the tax consequences of their decision?

LO 14-3   12. How are acquisition indebtedness and home-equity indebtedness similar? How are they dissimilar?

LO 14-3   13. Why might it be good advice from a tax perspective to think hard before deciding to quickly pay down mortgage debt?

LO 14-3   14. Can portions of one loan secured by a residence consist of both acquisition indebtedness and home-equity indebtedness? Explain.

LO 14-3   15. When a taxpayer has multiple loans secured by her residence that in total exceed the limits for deductibility, how does the taxpayer determine the amount of the deductible interest expense?

LO 14-3   16. Compare and contrast the characteristics of a deductible point from a non-deductible point on a first home mortgage.

LO 14-3   17. Is the break-even period generally longer for points paid to reduce the interest rate on initial home loans or points paid for the same purpose on a refinance? Explain.

planning **LO 14-3**   18. Under what circumstances is it likely economically beneficial to pay points to reduce the interest rate on a home loan?

LO 14-3   19. Harry decides to finance his new home with a 30-year fixed mortgage. Because he figures he will be in this home for a long time, he decides to pay a fully deductible discount point on his mortgage to reduce the interest rate. Assuming Harry itemizes deductions and has a constant marginal tax rate over time, will the time required to recover the cost of the discount point be shorter or longer if Harry makes extra principal payments starting in the first year than it would be if he does not make any extra principal payments? Explain.

20. Consider the settlement statement in Appendix A to this chapter. What amounts on the statement are the Jeffersons allowed to deduct on their 2016 tax return? Indicate the settlement statement line number for each deductible amount (discuss any issues that must be addressed to determine deductibility) and label each deduction as a *for* AGI deduction or as a *from* AGI deduction.   **LO 14-3** **LO 14-4**

21. A taxpayer sold a piece of real property in year 1. The amount of year 1 real property taxes was estimated at the closing of the sale and the amounts were allocated between the buyer and the taxpayer. At the end of year 1, the buyer receives a property tax bill that turns out to be higher than the estimate. After paying the tax bill, the buyer contacts the taxpayer at the beginning of year 2 and asks the taxpayer to pay the taxpayer's share of the shortfall. The taxpayer sends a check to the buyer. Should the taxpayer be concerned that she won't get to deduct the extra tax payment because it was paid to the buyer and not to the taxing jurisdiction? Explain.   **LO 14-4**

22. Is a homeowner allowed a property tax deduction for amounts included in the monthly mortgage payment that are earmarked for property taxes? Explain.   **LO 14-4**

23. Is it possible for a taxpayer to receive rental income that is not subject to taxation? Explain.   **LO 14-5** planning

24. Halle just acquired a vacation home. She plans on spending several months each year vacationing in the home and on renting the property for the rest of the year. She is projecting tax losses on the rental portion of the property for the year. She is not too concerned about the losses because she is confident she will be able to use the losses to offset her income from other sources. Is her confidence misplaced? Explain.   **LO 14-5**

25. A taxpayer stays in a second home for the entire month of September. He would like the home to fall into the residence with significant rental use category for tax purposes. What is the maximum number of days he can rent out the home and have it qualify?   **LO 14-5** planning

26. Compare and contrast the IRS method and the Tax Court method for allocating expenses between personal use and rental use for vacation homes. Include the Tax Court's justification for departing from the IRS method in your answer.   **LO 14-5**

27. In what circumstances is the IRS method for allocating expenses between personal use and rental use for second homes more beneficial to a taxpayer than the Tax Court method?   **LO 14-5**

28. Under what circumstances would a taxpayer who generates a loss from renting a home that is not a residence be able to fully deduct the loss? What potential limitations apply?   **LO 14-5**

29. Describe the circumstances in which a taxpayer acquires a home and rents it out and is not allowed to deduct a portion of the interest expense on the loan the taxpayer used to acquire the home.   **LO 14-5**

30. Is it possible for a rental property to generate a positive annual cash flow and at the same time produce a loss for tax purposes? Explain.   **LO 14-5**

31. How are the tax issues associated with home offices and vacation homes used as rentals similar? How are the tax issues or requirements dissimilar?   **LO 14-5** **LO 14-6**

32. Are employees or self-employed taxpayers more likely to qualify for the home office deduction? Explain.   **LO 14-6**

33. Compare and contrast the manner in which employees and employers report home office deductions on their tax returns.   **LO 14-6**

34. For taxpayers qualifying for home office deductions, what are considered to be indirect expenses of maintaining the home? How are these expenses   **LO 14-6**

allocated to personal and home office use? Can taxpayers choose to calculate home office expenses without regard to actual expenses allocated to the home office? Explain.

LO 14-6 35. What limitations exist for self-employed taxpayers in deducting home office expenses, and how does the taxpayer determine which expenses are deductible and which are not in situations when the overall amount of the home office deduction is limited?

LO 14-2 LO 14-6 36. A self-employed taxpayer deducts home office expenses including depreciation expense. The taxpayer then sells the home at a $100,000 gain. Assuming the taxpayer meets the ownership and use tests, does the full gain qualify for exclusion? Explain.

PROBLEMS

Select problems are available in *Connect*®. ■ connect

LO 14-1 37. Several years ago, Junior acquired a home that he vacationed in part of the time and rented out part of the time. During the current year Junior:

- Personally stayed in the home for 22 days.
- Rented it to his favorite brother at a discount for 10 days.
- Rented it to his least favorite brother for 8 days at the full market rate.
- Rented it to his friend at a discounted rate for 4 days.
- Rented the home to third parties for 58 days at the market rate.
- Did repair and maintenance work on the home for 2 days.
- Marketed the property and made it available for rent for 150 days during the year (in addition to the days mentioned above).

How many days of personal use and how many days of rental use did Junior experience on the property during the year?

LO 14-1 38. Lauren owns a condominium. In each of the following alternative situations, determine whether the condominium should be treated as a residence or non-residence for tax purposes.
a) Lauren lives in the condo for 19 days and rents it out for 22 days.
b) Lauren lives in the condo for 8 days and rents it out for 9 days.
c) Lauren lives in the condo for 80 days and rents it out for 120 days.
d) Lauren lives in the condo for 30 days and rents it out for 320 days.

LO 14-2 39. Steve and Stephanie Pratt purchased a home in Spokane, Washington, for $400,000. They moved into the home on February 1 of year 1. They lived in the home as their primary residence until June 30 of year 5, when they sold the home for $700,000.
a) What amount of gain on the sale of the home are the Pratts required to include in taxable income?
b) Assume the original facts, except that Steve and Stephanie lived in the home until January 1 of year 3 when they purchased a new home and rented out the original home. They finally sell the original home on June 30 of year 5 for $700,000. Ignoring any issues relating to depreciation taken on the home while it was being rented, what amount of realized gain on the sale of the home are the Pratts required to include in taxable income?
c) Assume the same facts as in part (b), except that the Pratts lived in the home until January of year 4 when they purchased a new home and rented out the first home. What amount of realized gain on the sale of the home will the Pratts include in taxable income if they sell the first home on June 30 of year 5 for $700,000?

d) Assume the original facts, except that Stephanie moved in with Steve on March 1 of year 3 and the couple was married on March 1 of year 4. Under state law, the couple jointly owned Steve's home beginning on the date they were married. On December 1 of year 3, Stephanie sold her home that she lived in before she moved in with Steve. She excluded the entire $50,000 gain on the sale on her individual year 3 tax return. What amount of gain must the couple recognize on the sale in June of year 5?

40. Steve and Stephanie Pratt purchased a home in Spokane, Washington, for $400,000. They moved into the home on February 1 of year 1. They lived in the home as their primary residence until November 1 of year 1, when they sold the home for $500,000. The Pratts' marginal ordinary tax rate is 35 percent. **LO 14-2**

  a) Assume that the Pratts sold their home and moved because they don't like their neighbors. How much gain will the Pratts recognize on their home sale? At what rate, if any, will the gain be taxed?

  b) Assume the Pratts sell the home because Stephanie's employer transfers her to an office in Utah. How much gain will the Pratts recognize on their home sale?

  c) Assume the same facts as in part (b), except that the Pratts sell their home for $700,000. How much gain will the Pratts recognize on the home sale?

  d) Assume the same facts as part (b), except that on December 1 of year 0 the Pratts sold their home in Seattle and excluded the $300,000 gain from income on their year 0 tax return. How much gain will the Pratts recognize on the sale of their Spokane home?

41. Steve Pratt, who is single, purchased a home in Spokane, Washington, for $400,000. He moved into the home on February 1 of year 1. He lived in the home as his primary residence until June 30 of year 5, when he sold the home for $700,000. **LO 14-2**

  a) What amount of gain will Steve be required to recognize on the sale of the home?

  b) Assume the original facts, except that the home is Steve's vacation home and he vacations there four months each year. Steve does not ever rent the home to others. What gain must Steve recognize on the home sale?

  c) Assume the original facts, except that Steve married Stephanie on February 1 of year 3 and the couple lived in the home until they sold it in June of year 5. Under state law, Steve owned the home by himself. How much gain must Steve and Stephanie recognize on the sale (assume they file a joint return in year 5).

42. Celia has been married to Daryl for 52 years. The couple has lived in their current home for the last 20 years. In October of year 0, Daryl passed away. Celia sold their home and moved into a condominium. What is the maximum exclusion Celia is entitled to if she sells the home on December 15 of year 1? **LO 14-2**

43. Sarah (single) purchased a home on January 1, 2008, for $600,000. She eventually sold the home for $800,000. What amount of the $200,000 gain on the sale does Sarah recognize in each of the following alternative situations? (Assume accumulated depreciation on the home is zero.) **LO 14-2**

  a) Sarah used the home as her principal residence through December 31, 2014. She used the home as a vacation home from January 1, 2015, until she sold it on January 1, 2017.

  b) Sarah used the property as a vacation home through December 31, 2014. She then used the home as her principal residence from January 1, 2015, until she sold it on January 1, 2017.

  c) Sarah used the home as a vacation home from January 1, 2008, until January 1, 2016. She used the home as her principal residence from January 1, 2016, until she sold it on January 1, 2017.

  d) Sarah used the home as a vacation home from January 1, 2008, through December 31, 2010. She used the home as her principal residence from January 1, 2011, until she sold it on January 1, 2016.

LO 14-2
44. Troy (single) purchased a home in Hopkinton, MA, on January 1, 2007, for $300,000. He sold the home on January 1, 2016, for $320,000. How much gain must Troy recognize on his home sale in each of the following alternative situations?

a) Troy rented the home out from January 1, 2007, through November 30, 2008. He lived in the home as his principal residence from December 1, 2008, through the date of sale. Assume accumulated depreciation on the home at the time of sale was $7,000.

b) Troy lived in the home as his principal residence from January 1, 2007, through December 31, 2011. He rented the home from January 1, 2012, through the date of the sale. Assume accumulated depreciation on the home at the time of sale was $2,000.

c) Troy lived in the home as his principal residence from January 1, 2007, through December 31, 2013. He rented out the home from January 1, 2014, through the date of the sale. Assume accumulated depreciation on the home at the time of sale was $0.

d) Troy rented the home from January 1, 2007, through December 31, 2011. He lived in the home as his principal residence from January 1, 2012, through December 31, 2012. He rented out the home from January 1, 2013, through December 31, 2013, and lived in the home as his principal residence from January 1, 2014, through the date of the sale. Assume accumulated depreciation on the home at the time of sale was $0.

LO 14-3
45. Javier and Anita Sanchez purchased a home on January 1, 2016, for $500,000 by paying $200,000 down and borrowing the remaining $300,000 with a 7 percent loan secured by the home. The loan requires interest-only payments for the first five years. The Sanchezes would itemize deductions even if they did not have any deductible interest. The Sanchezes' marginal tax rate is 30 percent.

a) What is the after-tax cost of the interest expense to the Sanchezes in 2016?

b) Assume the original facts, except that the Sanchezes rent a home and pay $21,000 in rent during the year. What is the after-tax cost of their rental payments in 2016?

c) Assuming the interest expense is their only itemized deduction for the year and that Javier and Anita file a joint return, have great eyesight, and are under 60 years of age, what is the after-tax cost of their 2016 interest expense?

LO 14-3
46. Javier and Anita Sanchez purchased a home on January 1 of year 1 for $500,000 by paying $50,000 down and borrowing the remaining $450,000 with a 7 percent loan secured by the home. The loan requires interest-only payments for the first five years. The Sanchezes would itemize deductions even if they did not have any deductible interest.

a) Assume the Sanchezes also took out a second loan (on the same day as the first loan) secured by the home for $80,000 to fund expenses unrelated to the home. The interest rate on the second loan is 8 percent. The Sanchezes make interest-only payments on the loan in year 1. What is the maximum amount of their deductible interest expense (on both loans combined) in year 1?

b) Assume the original facts and that the Sanchezes take out a second loan (on the same day as the first loan) secured by the home in the amount of $50,000 to fund expenses unrelated to the home. The interest rate on the second loan is 8 percent. The Sanchezes make interest-only payments during the year. What is the maximum amount of their deductible interest expense in year 1 on both loans combined?

LO 14-3
47. Javier and Anita Sanchez purchased a home on January 1 of year 1 for $500,000 by paying $200,000 down and borrowing the remaining $300,000 with a 7 percent loan secured by the home. The loan requires interest-only payments for the first

five years. The Sanchezes would itemize deductions even if they did not have any deductible interest. On January 1, the Sanchezes also borrowed money on a second loan secured by the home for $75,000. The interest rate on the loan is 8 percent and the Sanchezes make interest-only payments in year 1 on the second loan.

a) Assuming the Sanchezes use the second loan to landscape the yard to their home, what is the maximum amount of interest expense (on both loans combined) they are allowed to deduct in year 1?

b) Assume the original facts and that the Sanchezes use the $75,000 loan proceeds for an extended family vacation. What is the maximum amount of interest expense (on both loans combined) they are allowed to deduct in year 1?

c) Assume the original facts, except that the Sanchezes borrow $120,000 on the second loan and they use the proceeds for an extended family vacation and other personal expenses. What is the maximum amount of interest expense (on both loans combined) they are allowed to deduct in year 1?

48. Lewis and Laurie are married and jointly own a home valued at $240,000. They recently paid off the mortgage on their home. In need of cash for personal purposes unrelated to the home, the couple borrowed money from the local credit union. How much interest may the couple deduct in each of the following alternative situations? (Assume they itemize deductions no matter the amount of interest.)   `LO 14-3`

a) The couple borrows $40,000, and the loan is secured by their home. The couple pays $1,600 interest on the loan during the year, and the couple files a joint return.

b) The couple borrows $10,000 unsecured from the credit union. The couple pays $900 interest on the loan during the year, and the couple files a joint return.

c) The couple borrows $110,000, and the loan is secured by their home. The couple pays $5,200 interest on the loan during the year, and the couple files a joint return.

d) The couple borrows $110,000, and the loan is secured by their home. The couple pays $5,200 interest on the loan during the year, and the couple files separate tax returns.

49. On January 1 of year 1, Arthur and Aretha Franklin purchased a home for $1.5 million by paying $200,000 down and borrowing the remaining $1.3 million with a 7 percent loan secured by the home.   `LO 14-3`

a) What is the amount of the interest expense the Franklins may deduct in year 1?

b) Assume that in year 2, the Franklins pay off the entire loan but at the beginning of year 3, they borrow $300,000 secured by the home at a 7 percent rate. They make interest-only payments on the loan during the year. What amount of interest expense may the Franklins deduct in year 3 on this loan (the Franklins do not use the loan proceeds to improve the home)?

c) Assume the same facts as in (b), except that the Franklins borrow $80,000 secured by their home. What amount of interest expense may the Franklins deduct in year 3 on this loan (the Franklins do not use the loan proceeds to improve the home)?

50. In year 0, Eva took out a $50,000 home-equity loan from her local credit union. At the time she took out the loan, her home was valued at $350,000. At the time of the loan, Eva's original mortgage on the home was $265,000. At the end of year 1, her original mortgage is $260,000. Unfortunately for Eva, during year 1, the value of her home dropped to $280,000. Consequently, as of the end of year 1, Eva's home secured $310,000 of home-related debt but her home is only valued at $280,000. Assuming Eva paid $15,000 of interest on the original mortgage and $3,500 of interest on the home-equity loan during the year, how much qualified residence interest can Eva deduct in year 1?   `LO 14-3`

LO 14-3

51. On January 1 of year 1, Jason and Jill Marsh acquired a home for $500,000 by paying $400,000 down and borrowing $100,000 with a 7 percent loan secured by the home. On January 1 of year 2, the Marshes needed cash so they refinanced the original loan by taking out a new $250,000 7 percent loan. With the $250,000 proceeds from the new loan, the Marshes paid off the original $100,000 loan and used the remaining $150,000 to fund their son's college education.

a) What amount of interest expense on the refinanced loan may the Marshes deduct in year 2?

b) Assume the original facts, except that the Marshes use the $150,000 cash from the refinancing to add two rooms and a garage to their home. What amount of interest expense on the refinanced loan may the Marshes deduct in year 2?

LO 14-3

planning

52. On January 1 of year 1 Brandon and Alisa Roy purchased a home for $1.5 million by paying $500,000 down and borrowing the remaining $1 million with a 7 percent loan secured by the home. Later the same day, the Roys took out a second loan, secured by the home, in the amount of $300,000.

a) Assuming the interest rate on the second loan is 8 percent, what is the maximum amount of interest expense the Roys may deduct on these two loans (combined) in year 1?

b) Assuming the interest rate on the second loan is 6 percent, what is the maximum amount of interest expense the Roys may deduct on these two loans (combined) in year 1?

LO 14-3

research

53. Jennifer has been living in her current principal residence for three years. Six months ago Jennifer decided that she would like to purchase a second home near a beach so she can vacation there for part of the year. Despite her best efforts, Jennifer has been unable to find what she is looking for. Consequently, Jennifer recently decided to change plans. She purchased a parcel of land for $200,000 with the intention of building her second home on the property. To acquire the land, she borrowed $200,000 secured by the land. Jennifer would like to know whether the interest she pays on the loan before construction on the house is completed is deductible as mortgage interest.

a) How should Jennifer treat the interest if she has begun construction on the home and plans to live in the home in 12 months from the time construction began?

b) How should Jennifer treat the interest if she hasn't begun construction on the home but plans to live in the home in 15 months?

c) How should Jennifer treat the interest if she has begun construction on the home but doesn't plan to live in the home for 37 months from the time construction began?

LO 14-3

planning

54. Rajiv and Laurie Amin are recent college graduates looking to purchase a new home. They are purchasing a $200,000 home by paying $20,000 down and borrowing the other $180,000 with a 30-year loan secured by the home. The Amins have the option of (1) paying no discount points on the loan and paying interest at 8 percent or (2) paying one discount point on the loan and paying interest of 7.5 percent. Both loans require the Amins to make interest-only payments for the first five years. Unless otherwise stated, the Amins itemize deductions irrespective of the amount of interest expense. The Amins are in the 25 percent marginal ordinary income tax bracket.

a) Assuming the Amins *do not itemize deductions,* what is the break-even point for paying the point to get a lower interest rate?

b) Assuming the Amins do itemize deductions, what is the break-even point for paying the point to get a lower interest rate?

c) Assume the original facts, except that the amount of the loan is $300,000. What is the break-even point for the Amins for paying the point to get a lower interest rate?

d) Assume the original facts, except that the $180,000 loan is a refinance instead of an original loan. What is the break-even point for paying the point to get a lower interest rate?

e) Assume the original facts, except that the amount of the loan is $300,000 and the loan is a refinance and not an original loan. What is the break-even point for paying the point to get a lower interest rate?

55. In year 1, Peter and Shaline Johnsen moved into a home in a new subdivision.   `LO 14-4`
    Theirs was one of the first homes in the subdivision. In year 1, they paid $1,500
    in real property taxes to the state government, $500 to the developer of the sub-
    division for an assessment to pay for the sidewalks, and $900 for real property
    taxes on land they hold as an investment. What amount of property taxes are
    the Johnsens allowed to deduct assuming their itemized deductions exceed the
    standard deduction amount before considering any property tax deductions?

56. Jesse Brimhall is single. In 2016, his itemized deductions were $4,000 before   `LO 14-4`
    considering any real property taxes he paid during the year. Jesse's adjusted
    gross income was $70,000 (also before considering any property tax deduc-
    tions). In 2016, he paid real property taxes of $3,000 on property 1 and $1,200
    of real property taxes on property 2.

    a) If property 1 is Jesse's primary residence and property 2 is his vacation home
       (he does not rent it out at all), what is his taxable income after taking prop-
       erty taxes into account?

    b) If property 1 is Jesse's business building (he owns the property) and property
       2 is his primary residence, what is his taxable income after taking property
       taxes into account?

    c) If property 1 is Jesse's primary residence and property 2 is a parcel of land
       he holds for investment, what is his taxable income after taking property
       taxes into account?

57. Craig and Karen Conder purchased a new home on May 1 of year 1 for   `LO 14-4`
    $200,000. At the time of the purchase, it was estimated that the real property
    tax rate for the year would be 1 percent of the property's value. How much in
    property taxes on the new home are the Conders allowed to deduct under each
    of the following circumstances (the Conders' itemized deductions exceed the
    standard deduction before considering property taxes)?

    a) The property tax estimate proves to be accurate. The seller and the Conders
       paid their share of the tax. The full property tax bill is paid to the taxing
       jurisdiction by the end of the year.

    b) The actual property tax bill turns out to be 1.05 percent of the property's
       value. The Conders' paid their share of the estimated tax bill and the entire
       difference between the 1 percent estimate and the 1.05 percent actual tax bill
       and the seller paid the rest. The full property tax bill is paid to the taxing
       jurisdiction by the end of the year.

    c) The actual property tax bill turns out to be .95 percent of the property's
       value. The seller paid their share of taxes based on the 1 percent estimate
       and the Conders paid the difference between what the seller paid and the
       amount of the final tax bill. The full property tax bill is paid to the taxing
       jurisdiction by the end of the year.

58. Kirk and Lorna Newbold purchased a new home on August 1 of year 1 for   `LO 14-4`
    $300,000. At the time of the purchase, it was estimated that the real property
    tax rate for the year would be .5 percent of the property's value. Because the

taxing jurisdiction collects taxes on a July 1 year-end, it was estimated that the Newbolds would be required to pay $1,375 in property taxes for the property tax year relating to August through June of year 2 ($300,000 × .005 × 11/12). The seller would be required to pay the $125 for July of year 1. Along with their monthly payment of principal and interest, the Newbolds paid $125 to the mortgage company to cover the property taxes. The mortgage company placed the money in escrow and used the funds in the escrow account to pay the property tax bill in July of year 2. The Newbolds' itemized deductions exceed the standard deduction before considering real property taxes.

a) How much in real property taxes can the Newbolds deduct for year 1?

b) How much in real property taxes can the Newbolds deduct for year 2?

c) Assume the original facts, except that the Newbolds were not able to collect $125 from the seller for the property taxes for July of year 1. How much in real property taxes can the Newbolds deduct for year 1 and year 2?

d) Assume the original facts, except that the tax bill for July 1 of year 1 through June 30 of year 2 turned out to be $1,200 instead of $1,500. How much in real property taxes can the Newbolds deduct in year 1 and year 2?

LO 14-4

research

59. Jenae and Terry Hutchings own a parcel of land as tenants by entirety. That is, they both own the property but when one of them dies the other becomes the sole owner of the property. For nontax reasons, Jenae and Terry decide to file separate tax returns for the current year. Jenae paid the entire $3,000 property tax bill for the land. How much of the $3,000 property tax payment is each spouse entitled to deduct in the current year?

LO 14-5

60. Dillon rented his personal residence at Lake Tahoe for 14 days while he was vacationing in Ireland. He resided in the home for the remainder of the year. Rental income from the property was $6,500. Expenses associated with use of the home for the entire year were as follows:

Real property taxes	$ 3,100
Mortgage interest	12,000
Repairs	1,500
Insurance	1,500
Utilities	3,900
Depreciation	13,000

a) What effect does the rental have on Dillon's AGI?

b) What effect does the rental have on Dillon's itemized deductions?

Use the following facts to answer problems 61 and 62.
Natalie owns a condominium near Cocoa Beach in Florida. This year, she incurs the following expenses in connection with her condo:

Insurance	$1,000
Advertising expense	500
Mortgage interest	3,500
Property taxes	900
Repairs & maintenance	650
Utilities	950
Depreciation	8,500

During the year, Natalie rented out the condo for 75 days, receiving $10,000 of gross income. She personally used the condo for 35 days during her vacation.

LO 14-5

tax forms

61. Assume Natalie uses the IRS method of allocating expenses to rental use of the property.

a) What is the total amount of *for* AGI (rental) deductions Natalie may deduct in the current year related to the condo?

b) What is the total amount of itemized deductions Natalie may deduct in the current year related to the condo?

c) If Natalie's basis in the condo at the beginning of the year was $150,000, what is her basis in the condo at the end of the year?

d) Assume that gross rental revenue was $2,000 (rather than $10,000). What amount of *for* AGI deductions may Natalie deduct in the current year related to the condo?

e) Using the original facts, complete Natalie's Form 1040, Schedule E, for this property. Also, partially complete Natalie's 1040, Schedule A, to include her *from* AGI deductions related to the condo.

62. Assume Natalie uses the Tax Court method of allocating expenses to rental use of the property.   `LO 14-5`

a) What is the total amount of *for* AGI (rental) deductions Natalie may deduct in the current year related to the condo?

b) What is the total amount of itemized deductions Natalie may deduct in the current year related to the condo?

c) If Natalie's basis in the condo at the beginning of the year was $150,000, what is her basis in the condo at the end of the year?

d) Assume that gross rental revenue was $2,000 (rather than $10,000). What amount of *for* AGI deductions may Natalie deduct in the current year related to the condo?

Use the following facts to answer problems 63, 64, and 65.

Alexa owns a condominium near Cocoa Beach in Florida. This year, she incurs the following expenses in connection with her condo:

Insurance	$ 2,000
Mortgage interest	6,500
Property taxes	2,000
Repairs & maintenance	1,400
Utilities	2,500
Depreciation	14,500

During the year, Alexa rented out the condo for 100 days. She did not use the condo at all for personal purposes during the year. Alexa's AGI from all sources other than the rental property is $200,000. Unless otherwise specified, Alexa has no sources of passive income.

63. Assume Alexa receives $30,000 in gross rental receipts.   `LO 14-5`

a) What effect do the expenses associated with the property have on her AGI?

b) What effect do the expenses associated with the property have on her itemized deductions?

64. Assuming Alexa receives $20,000 in gross rental receipts, answer the following questions: `LO 14-5`

a) What effect does the rental activity have on her AGI for the year?

b) Assuming that Alexa's AGI from other sources is $90,000, what effect does the rental activity have on Alexa's AGI? Alexa makes all decisions with respect to the property.

c) Assuming that Alexa's AGI from other sources is $120,000, what effect does the rental activity have on Alexa's AGI? Alexa makes all decisions with respect to the property.

d) Assume that Alexa's AGI from other sources is $200,000. This consists of $150,000 salary, $10,000 of dividends, and $25,000 of long-term capital gain, and net rental income from another rental property in the amount of $15,000. What effect does the Cocoa Beach Condo rental activity have on Alexa's AGI?

LO 14-5

planning

65. Assume that in addition to renting the condo for 100 days, Alexa uses the condo for 8 days of personal use. Also assume that Alexa receives $30,000 of gross rental receipts. Answer the following questions:

   a) What is the total amount of *for* AGI deductions relating to the condo that Alexa may deduct in the current year? Assume she uses the IRS method of allocating expenses between rental and personal days.

   b) What is the total amount of *from* AGI deductions relating to the condo that Alexa may deduct in the current year? Assume she uses the IRS method of allocating expenses between rental and personal days.

   c) Would Alexa be better or worse off after taxes in the current year if she uses the Tax Court method of allocating expenses?

LO 14-6

tax forms

66. Brooke owns a sole proprietorship in which she works as a management consultant. She maintains an office in her home where she meets with clients, prepares bills, and performs other work-related tasks. The home office is 300 square feet and the entire house is 4,500 square feet. Brooke incurred the following home-related expenses during the year. Unless indicated otherwise, assume Brooke uses the actual expense method to compute home office expenses.

Real property taxes	$ 3,600
Interest on home mortgage	14,000
Operating expenses of home	5,000
Depreciation	12,000
Repairs to home theater room	1,000

   a) What amount of each of these expenses is allocated to the home office?

   b) What are the total amounts of tier 1, tier 2, and tier 3 expenses, respectively, allocated to the home office?

   c) If Brooke reported $2,000 of Schedule C net income before the home office expense deduction, what is the amount of her home office expense deduction and what home office expenses, if any, would she carry over to next year?

   d) Assuming Brooke reported $2,000 of Schedule C income before the home office expense deduction, complete Form 8829 for Brooke's home office expense deduction. Also assume the value of the home is $500,000 and the adjusted basis of the home (exclusive of land) is $468,019.

   e) Assume that Brooke uses the simplified method for computing home office expenses. If Brooke reported $2,000 of Schedule C net income before the home office expense deduction, what is the amount of her home office expense deduction and what home office expenses, if any, would she carry over to next year?

Use the following facts to answer problems 67 and 68.

Rita owns a sole proprietorship in which she works as a management consultant. She maintains an office in her home (500 square feet) where she meets with clients, prepares bills, and performs other work-related tasks. Her business expenses, other than home office expenses, total $5,600. The following home-related expenses have been allocated to her home office under the actual expense method for calculating home office expenses.

Real property taxes	$1,600
Interest on home mortgage	5,100
Operating expenses of home	800
Depreciation	1,600

Also, assume that not counting the sole proprietorship, Rita's AGI is $60,000.

67. Assume Rita's consulting business generated $15,000 in gross income.

   a) What is Rita's home office deduction for the current year?

   b) What would Rita's home office deduction be if her business generated $10,000 of gross income instead of $15,000? (Answer for both the actual expense method and the simplified method.)

   c) Given the original facts, what is Rita's AGI for the year?

   d) Given the original facts, what types and amounts of expenses will she carry over to next year?

LO 14-6
planning

68. Assume Rita's consulting business generated $13,000 in gross income for the current year. Further, assume Rita uses the actual expense method for computing her home office expense deduction.

   a) What is Rita's home office deduction for the current year?

   b) What is Rita's AGI for the year?

   c) Assume the original facts, except that Rita is an employee and not self-employed. (She uses the home office for the convenience of her employer.) Consequently, she does not receive any gross income from the (sole proprietorship) business and she does not incur any business expenses unrelated to the home office. Finally, her AGI is $60,000 consisting of salary from her work as an employee. What effect do her home office expenses have on her itemized deductions?

   d) Assuming the original facts, what types and amounts of expenses will she carry over to next year?

LO 14-6

69. Alisha, who is single, owns a sole proprietorship in which she works as a management consultant. She maintains an office in her home where she meets with clients, prepares bills, and performs other work-related tasks. She purchased the home at the beginning of year 1 for $400,000. Since she purchased the home and moved into it she has been able to deduct $10,000 of depreciation expenses to offset her consulting income. At the end of year 3, Alisha sold the home for $500,000. What is the amount of taxes Alisha will be required to pay on the gain from the sale of the home? Alisha's ordinary marginal tax rate is 30 percent.

LO 14-2   LO 14-6

COMPREHENSIVE PROBLEMS

Select problems are available in *Connect*®.

📘 connect

70. Derek and Meagan Jacoby recently graduated from State University and Derek accepted a job in business consulting while Meagan accepted a job in computer programming. Meagan inherited $75,000 from her grandfather who recently passed away. The couple is debating whether they should buy or rent a home. They located a rental home that meets their needs. The monthly rent is $2,250. They also found a three-bedroom home that would cost $475,000 to purchase. The Jacobys could use Meagan's inheritance for a down payment on the home. Thus, they would need to borrow $400,000 to acquire the home. They have the option of paying two discount points to receive a fixed interest rate of 4.5 percent on the loan or paying no points and receiving a fixed interest rate of 5.75 percent for a 30-year fixed loan.

   Though anything could happen, the couple expects to live in the home for no more than five years before relocating to a different region of the country. Derek and Meagan don't have any school-related debt, so they will save the $75,000 if they don't purchase a home. Also, consider the following information:

planning

- The couple's marginal tax rate is 25 percent.
- Regardless of whether they buy or rent, the couple will itemize their deductions.

- If they buy, the Jacobys would purchase and move into the home on January 1, 2016.
- If they buy the home, the property taxes for the year are $3,600.
- Disregard loan-related fees not mentioned above.
- If the couple does not buy a home, they will put their money into their savings account where they earn 5 percent annual interest.
- Assume that all unstated costs are equal between the buy and rent option.

Required:

Help the Jacobys with their decisions by answering the following questions:

a) If the Jacobys decide to rent the home, what is their after-tax cost of the rental for the first year (include income from the savings account in your analysis)?

b) What is the approximate break-even point in years (or months) for paying the points to receive a reduced interest rate (to simplify this computation, assume the Jacobys will make interest-only payments, and ignore the time value of money)?

c) What is the after-tax cost (in interest and property taxes) of living in the home for 2016? Assume that the Jacobys' interest rate is 5.75 percent, they do not pay discount points, they make interest-only payments for the first year, and the value of the home does not change during the year.

d) Assume that on March 1, 2016, the Jacobys sold their home for $525,000, so that Derek and Meagan could accept job opportunities in a different state. The Jacobys used the sale proceeds to (1) pay off the $400,000 principal of the mortgage, (2) pay a $10,000 commission to their real estate broker, and (3) make a down payment on a new home in the different state. However, the new home cost only $300,000. What gain or loss do the Jacobys realize and recognize on the sale of their home and what amount of taxes must they pay on the gain, if any (assume they make interest-only payments on the loan)?

e) Assume the same facts as in part (d), except that the Jacobys sell their home for $450,000 and they pay a $7,500 commission. What effect does the sale have on their 2016 income tax liability? Recall that the Jacobys are subject to an ordinary marginal tax rate of 25 percent and assume that they do not have any other transactions involving capital assets in 2016.

71. James and Kate Sawyer were married on New Year's Eve of 2015. Before their marriage, Kate lived in New York and worked as a hair stylist for one of the city's top salons. James lives in Atlanta where he works for a public accounting firm earning an annual salary of $100,000. After their marriage, Kate left her job in New York and moved into the couple's newly purchased 3,200-square-foot home in Atlanta. Kate incurred $2,200 of qualified moving expenses. The couple purchased the home on January 3, 2016, by paying $100,000 down and obtaining a $240,000 mortgage for the remainder. The interest rate on this loan was 7 percent and the Sawyers made interest-only payments on the loan through June 30, 2016 (assume they paid exactly one-half of a year's worth of interest on this loan by June 30). On July 1, 2016, because the value of their home had increased to $400,000, the Sawyers were in need of cash, and interest rates had dropped, the Sawyers refinanced their home loan. On the refinancing, they borrowed $370,000 at 6 percent interest. They made interest-only payments on the home loan through the end of the year and they spent $20,000 of the loan proceeds improving their home (assume they paid exactly one-half of a year's worth of interest on this loan by year-end).

Kate wanted to try her hand at making it on her own in business, and with James's help, she started Kate's Beauty Cuts LLC. She set up shop in a

384-square-foot corner room of the couple's home and began to get it ready for business. The room conveniently had a door to the outside providing customers direct access to the shop. Kate paid $2,100 to have the carpet replaced with a tile floor. She also paid $1,200 to have the room painted with vibrant colors, and $650 to have the room rewired for appropriate lighting. Kate ran an ad in the local newspaper and officially opened her shop on January 24, 2016. By the end of the year, Kate's Beauty Cuts LLC generated $40,000 of *net* income before considering the home office deduction. The Sawyers incurred the following home-related expenditures during 2016:

- $4,200 of real property taxes.
- $2,000 for homeowner's insurance.
- $2,400 for electricity.
- $1,500 for gas and other utilities.

They determined depreciation expense for their entire house was $8,364.

Also, on March 2, Kate was able to finally sell her one-bedroom Manhattan condominium for $478,000. She purchased the condo, which she had lived in for six years prior to her marriage, for $205,000.

Kate owns a vacation home in Myrtle Beach, South Carolina. She purchased the home several years ago, largely as an investment opportunity. To help cover the expenses of maintaining the home, James and Kate decided to rent the home out. They rented the home for a total of 106 days at fair market value (this included 8 days that they rented the home to James's brother Jack). In addition to the 106 days, Kate allowed a good friend and customer, Clair, to stay in the home for half-price for 2 days. James and Kate stayed in the home for 6 days for a romantic getaway and another 3 days in order to do some repair and maintenance work on the home. The rental revenues from the home in 2016 were $18,400. The Sawyers incurred the following expenses associated with the home:

- $9,100 of interest expense.
- $3,400 of real property taxes.
- $1,900 for homeowner's insurance.
- $1,200 for electricity.
- $1,600 for gas, other utilities, and landscaping.
- $5,200 for depreciation.

Required:

Determine the Sawyer's taxable income for 2016. Disregard self-employment taxes for Kate. Assume the couple paid $4,400 in state income taxes and files a joint return. The Sawyers would like to use the method for determining deductible home office expenses and the method for allocating expenses to the rental that minimize their overall taxable income for the year.

chapter
15 Entities Overview

Learning Objectives

Upon completing this chapter, you should be able to:

LO 15-1 Discuss the legal and nontax characteristics of different types of legal entities.

LO 15-2 Describe the different types of entities for tax purposes.

LO 15-3 Identify fundamental differences in tax characteristics across entity types.

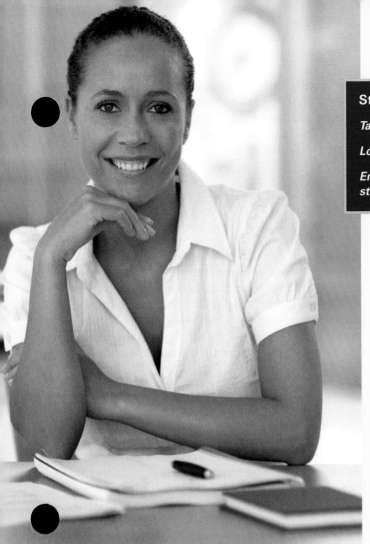

© PhotoAlto

Storyline Summary

Taxpayer: Nicole Johnson

Location: Salt Lake City, Utah

Employment status: State government employee with entrepreneurial ambitions

Nicole Johnson is currently employed by the Utah Chamber of Commerce in Salt Lake City, Utah. While she enjoys the relatively short workweeks, she eventually would like to work for herself rather than for an employer. In her current position, she deals with a lot of successful entrepreneurs who have become role models for her. Nicole has also developed an extensive list of contacts that should serve her well when she starts her own business. It has taken a while, but Nicole believes she has finally developed a viable new business idea. Her idea is to design and manufacture bed sheets that have various colored patterns and are made of unique fabric blends. The sheets look great and

are extremely comfortable whether the bedroom is warm or cool. She has had several friends try out her prototype sheets and they have consistently given the sheets rave reviews. With this encouragement, Nicole started giving serious thought to making "Color Comfort Sheets" a moneymaking enterprise.

Nicole has enough business background to realize that she is embarking on a risky path, but one, she hopes, with significant potential rewards in the future. After creating some initial income projections, Nicole realized that it will take a few years for the business to become profitable.

While Nicole's original plan was to start the business by herself, she is considering seeking out another equity owner for the business so that she can add financial resources and business experience to the venture. Nicole felt like she had a grasp on her business plan, but she still needed to determine how to organize the business for tax purposes. After doing some research, Nicole learned that she should consider many factors in order to determine the "best" entity type for her business. Each type of entity has advantages and disadvantages from both tax and nontax perspectives, and the best entity for a business depends on the goals, outlook, and strategy for that particular business and its owners. She realized she had more work to do to make an informed decision.

to be continued . . .

This chapter explores various types of legal entities and then discusses entities available for tax purposes. We outline some of the pros and cons of each entity type, emphasizing both nontax and tax perspectives as we help Nicole determine how she will organize her business to best accomplish her goals. Subsequent chapters provide additional detail concerning the tax characteristics of each entity type.

LO 15-1 ENTITY LEGAL CLASSIFICATION AND NONTAX CHARACTERISTICS

When forming new business ventures, entrepreneurs can choose to house their operations under one of several basic entity types. These entities differ in terms of their legal and tax considerations. In fact, as we discuss in more depth below, the legal classification of a business may be different from its tax classification. These entities differ in terms of the formalities that entrepreneurs must follow to create them, the legal rights and responsibilities conferred on the entities and their owners, and the tax rules that determine how the entities and owners will be taxed on income generated by the entities. CPAs are frequently asked to help clients determine the best entity choice for their businesses.

Legal Classification

Generally, a business entity may be classified as a **corporation,** a **limited liability company** (LLC), a **general partnership** (GP), a **limited partnership** (LP), or a **sole proprietorship** (not formed as an LLC).[1] Under state law, corporations are recognized as legal entities separate from their owners (shareholders). Business owners legally form corporations by filing **articles of incorporation** with the state in which they organize the business. State laws also recognize limited liability companies (LLCs) as legal entities separate from their owners (members). Business owners create limited liability companies by filing **articles of organization** with the state in which they are organizing the businesses.

Partnerships are formed under state partnership statutes and the degree of formality required depends on the type of partnership being formed. General partnerships may be formed by written agreement among the partners, called a **partnership agreement,** or may be formed informally without a written agreement when two or more owners join together in an activity to generate profits. Although general partners are not required to file partnership agreements with the state, general partnerships are still considered to be legal entities separate from their owners under state laws. Unlike general partnerships, limited partnerships are usually organized by written agreement and must typically file a **certificate of limited partnership** to be recognized by the state.[2]

Finally, for state law purposes, sole proprietorships are *not* treated as legal entities separate from their individual owners. As a result, sole proprietors are not required to formally organize their businesses with the state, and they hold title to business assets in their own names rather than in the name of their businesses.

Nontax Characteristics

The different legal entity types may differ from or share similarities with other legal entity types with respect to certain nontax characteristics. Rather than identify and discuss all possible nontax entity characteristics, we compare and contrast several prominent characteristics across the different legal entity types.

[1] Variations of these entities include limited liability partnerships (LLPs), limited liability limited partnerships (LLLPs), professional limited liability companies (PLLCs), and professional corporations (PCs).

[2] Similar to limited partnerships, LLPs, LLLPs, PLLCs, and PCs must register with the state to receive formal recognition.

Responsibility for Liabilities   Whether the entity or the owner(s) is ultimately responsible for paying the liabilities of the business depends on the type of entity. Under state law, a corporation is solely responsible for its liabilities.[3] Similarly, LLCs and not their members are responsible for the liabilities of the business.[4] For entities formed as partnerships, all general partners are ultimately responsible for the liabilities of the partnership. In contrast, limited partners are not responsible for the partnership's liabilities.[5] However, limited partners are not allowed to actively participate in the activities of the business.

Finally, if a business is conducted as a sole proprietorship, the individual owner is responsible for the liabilities of the business. It is important to note, however, that individual business owners may also organize their businesses as single-member LLCs. In exchange for observing the formalities of organizing as an LLC, they receive the liability protection afforded LLC members.[6]

Rights, Responsibilities, and Legal Arrangement among Owners   State corporation laws specify the rights and responsibilities of corporations and their shareholders. For example, to retain limited liability protection for shareholders, corporations must create, regularly update, and comply with their bylaws (internal rules governing how the corporation is run). They must have a board of directors. They must have regular board meetings and regular (at least annual) shareholder meetings, and they must keep minutes of these meetings. They must also issue shares of stock to owners (shareholders) and maintain a stock ledger reflecting stock ownership. They must comply with annual filing requirements specified by the state of incorporation, pay required filing fees, and pay required corporate taxes, if any. Consequently, shareholders have no flexibility to alter their legal treatment with respect to one another, with respect to the corporation, and with respect to outsiders. In contrast, while state laws provide *default* provisions specifying rights and responsibilities of LLCs and their members, members have the *flexibility to alter* their arrangement by spelling out, through an operating agreement, the management practices of the entity and the rights and responsibilities of the members consistent with their wishes. Thus, LLCs allow more flexible business arrangements than do corporations.

Similar to LLC statutes, state partnership laws provide default provisions specifying the partners' legal rights and responsibilities for dealing with each other absent an agreement to the contrary. Because partners have the flexibility to depart from the default provisions, they frequently craft partnership agreements that are consistent with their preferences.

Although in many instances having the flexibility to customize business arrangements is desirable, sometimes inflexible governance rules mandated by state statute are needed to limit the participation of owners in management when their participation becomes impractical. For example, when businesses decide to "go public" with an **initial public offering** (IPO) on one of the public securities exchanges, they usually solicit a vast pool of potential investors to become *corporate*

---

[3]Payroll tax liabilities are an important exception to this general rule. Shareholders of closely held corporations may be held responsible for these liabilities.

[4]When closely held corporations and LLCs borrow from banks or other lenders, shareholders or members are usually asked to personally guarantee the debt. To the extent they do this, they become personally liable to repay the loan in the event the corporation or LLC is unable to repay it.

[5]Limited liability limited partnerships (LLLPs) are limited partnerships in which the general partners are protected from the liabilities of the entity. Also, professional service businesses such as accounting firms and law firms are generally not allowed to operate as corporations, LLCs, or limited partnerships. These businesses are frequently organized as limited liability partnerships (LLPs), professional limited liability companies (PLLCs), or as professional corporations (PCs). An owner of PLLCs and PCs are protected from liabilities other than liabilities stemming from the owner's negligence. LLPs do not provide protection against liabilities stemming from a partner's own malpractice or from the LLP's contractual liabilities.

[6]Shareholders of corporations and LLC members are responsible for liabilities stemming from their own negligence.

shareholders.[7] As shareholders, state corporation laws prohibit them from directly amending corporate governance rules and from directly participating in management—they only have the right to vote for corporate directors or officers. In comparison, LLC members generally have the right to amend the LLC operating agreement, provide input, and manage LLCs. Obviously, managing a publicly traded business would be next to impossible if thousands of owners had the legal right to change operating rules and to directly participate in managing the enterprise.

Exhibit 15-1 summarizes several nontax characteristics of different types of legal entities.

EXHIBIT 15-1 Business Types: Legal Entities and Nontax Characteristics

Nontax Characteristics	Corporation	LLC	General Partnership	Limited Partnership	Sole Proprietorship
Must formally organize with state	Yes	Yes	No	Yes	No*
Responsibility for liabilities of business	Entity	Entity	General partner(s)	General partner(s)	Owner†
Legal arrangement among owners	Not flexible	Flexible	Flexible	Flexible	Not applicable
Suitable for initial public offering	Yes	No	No	No	No

*Sole proprietor must organize with state if she forms a single-member LLC.
†Owner is not responsible for the liabilities of the business if sole proprietorship is organized as an LLC. However, owner is responsible for liabilities stemming from her own negligence.

As summarized in Exhibit 15-1, corporations and LLCs have the advantage in liability protection, LLCs and partnerships have an advantage over other entities in terms of legal flexibility, and corporations have the advantage when owners want to take a business public.

continued from page 15-1...

As an initial step in the process of selecting an entity to house CCS, Nicole began to research nontax issues that might be relevant to her decision. Early on in her research she realized that the nontax benefits unique to traditional corporations were relevant primarily to large, publicly traded corporations. Although Nicole was very optimistic about CCS's prospects, she knew it would likely be a long time, if ever, before it went public. However, she remained concerned about limiting her own and other potential investors' liability in the new venture so she began to dig a little deeper. As she perused the Utah state Web site, she learned that corporations and LLCs are the only legal entities that can completely shield her and future investors from liabilities. Although Nicole doesn't anticipate any trouble from her future creditors, she decides to limit her choice of legal entity to either a corporation or LLC.

At this point in her information-gathering process, Nicole is leaning toward the LLC option because she is not sure if she wants to deal with board meetings and all the other formalities of operating a corporation; however, she decides to assemble a five-year forecast of CCS's expected operating results and to learn a little more about the way corporations and LLCs are taxed before narrowing her options any further.

to be continued...

---

[7]The vast majority of IPOs involve corporate shares; however, limited partnership interests are occasionally sold in IPOs. Like shareholders, limited partners are typically not allowed to participate in management. Limited partnerships are used for public offerings in lieu of corporations when they qualify for favorable partnership tax treatment available to some publicly traded partnerships.

ENTITY TAX CLASSIFICATION

A business's legal form may be different from its tax form. We discussed the legal form of business entities above. We now discuss the tax form of business entities. In general terms, for tax purposes business entities can be classified as either separate taxpaying entities or as **flow-through entities.** Separate taxpaying entities pay tax on their own income. In contrast, flow-through entities generally don't pay taxes because income from these entities flows through to their business owners who are responsible for paying tax on the income.

How do we determine whether a particular business entity is treated as a separate taxpaying entity or as a flow-through entity for tax purposes? According to Treasury Regulations, commonly referred to as the "check-the-box" regulations, entities that are legal corporations under state law are, by default, treated as **C corporations** for tax purposes. These corporations and their shareholders are subject to tax provisions in Subchapter C (and not Subchapter S) of the Internal Revenue Code.[8] C corporations report their taxable income to the IRS on Form 1120. However, shareholders of *legal* corporations may qualify to make a special tax election known as an "S" election permitting the corporation to be taxed as a flow-through entity called an **S corporation.**[9] S corporations and their shareholders are subject to tax provisions in Subchapter S of the Internal Revenue Code. S corporations report the results of their operations to the IRS on Form 1120S.

Also under the check-the-box regulations, unincorporated entities are, by default, treated as flow-through entities.[10] However, owners of an unincorporated entity can still elect to have their business taxed as a C corporation instead of as the default flow-through entity.[11] In fact, the owner(s) of an unincorporated entity could elect to have the business taxed as a C corporation and then make a second election to have the "C corporation" taxed as an S corporation (provided that it meets the S corporation eligibility requirements).[12] Before making such elections, however, the business owner(s) would need to be convinced that the move makes sense from a tax perspective.[13] The nontax considerations do not change because these elections do not affect the legal classification of the entity.

Finally, unincorporated flow-through entities (all flow-through entities except S corporations) are treated (for tax purposes) as either partnerships, sole proprietorships, or **disregarded entities** (an entity that is considered to be the same entity as the owner).[14] Unincorporated entities (including LLCs) with more than one owner are treated as partnerships.[15] Partnerships report their operating results to the IRS on Form 1065. Unincorporated entities (including LLCs) with only one *individual* owner such as sole proprietorships and **single-member LLCs** are treated as sole proprietorships.[16] Income from businesses taxed as sole proprietorships is reported on Schedule C of Form 1040. Similarly, unincorporated entities with only one *corporate* owner, typically a single-member LLC, are disregarded for tax purposes. Thus, income and losses from this single, corporate-member LLC is reported as if it had originated from a division of the corporation and is reported directly on the single-member corporation's return. Exhibit 15-2 provides a flowchart for determining the tax form of a business entity under the check the box regulations. Taxpayers check the box by filing Form 8832.

THE KEY FACTS

Tax Classification of Legal Entities

- Corporations are C corporations unless they make a valid S election.
- Unincorporated entities are taxed as partnerships if they have more than one owner.
- Unincorporated entities are taxed as sole proprietorships if held by a single individual or as disregarded entities if held by a single entity.
- Unincorporated entities may elect to be treated as C corporations. They then could make an S election if eligible.

---

[8]Reg. §301.7701-3(a).

[9]§1362(a). Because §1361 limits the number and type of shareholders of corporations qualifying to make an S election, some corporations are ineligible to become S corporations.

[10]Reg. §301.7701-3(b). However, §7704 mandates that unincorporated publicly traded entities be taxed as corporations unless their income predominately consists of certain types of passive income.

[11]Reg. §301.7701-3(a).

[12]In general, a noncorporate entity that is eligible to elect to be treated as a corporation can elect to be treated as a corporation for tax purposes and as an S corporation in one step by filing a timely S corporation election.

[13]As presented in Exhibit 15-3, compared to corporations, unincorporated entities taxed as partnerships have more favorable ownership requirements and more favorable tax treatment on nonliquidating and liquidating distributions of noncash property.

[14]Reg. §301.7701-3(a).

[15]Reg. §301.7701-3(b)(i).

[16]Reg. §301.7701-3(b)(ii).

EXHIBIT 15-2

```
                          ┌──────────────────┐
                          │ Is the entity a  │
                          │ legal corporation?│
                          └──────────────────┘
        No                                        Yes
┌──────────────────────┐              ┌──────────────────────┐
│ Does the entity elect│     Yes      │ Does the entity      │
│ to be treated as a C │ ───────────► │ qualify for and elect│
│ corporation for tax  │              │ S corporation status?│
│ purposes?            │              │ Election made on     │
└──────────────────────┘              │ Form 2553.           │
        No                            └──────────────────────┘
┌──────────────────────┐              No                Yes
│ Does the entity have │     ┌──────────────────┐ ┌──────────────────┐
│ more than one owner? │     │ C corporation for│ │ S corporation for│
└──────────────────────┘     │ tax purposes.    │ │ tax purposes.    │
  Yes            No           │ Files Form 1120  │ │ Files Form 1120S │
┌────────────┐ ┌────────────┐└──────────────────┘ └──────────────────┘
│Partnership │ │ Is the     │
│for tax     │ │ owner an   │
│purposes.   │ │ Individual?│
│Files Form  │ └────────────┘
│1065        │  Yes        No
└────────────┘┌──────────┐ ┌──────────────────────┐
              │Sole      │ │Treated the same as   │
              │proprietor│ │the owner (not a      │
              │for tax   │ │separate entity from  │
              │purposes. │ │the owner). Income or │
              │Files Form│ │loss is included on   │
              │1040,     │ │the owner's tax return.│
              │Schedule C│ └──────────────────────┘
              └──────────┘
```

To summarize, although there are other types of legal entities, there are really only four categories of business entities recognized by the U.S. tax system, as follows:

1. C corporation (separate taxpaying entity; income reported on Form 1120)
2. S corporation (flow-through entity; income reported on Form 1120S)
3. Partnership (flow-through entity; income reported on Form 1065)
4. Sole proprietorship (flow-through entity; income reported on Form 1040, Schedule C)

Example 15-1

What if: Assume Nicole legally forms CCS as a corporation (with only common stock) by filing articles of incorporation with the state. What are Nicole's options for classifying CCS for tax purposes if she is the only shareholder of CCS?

Answer: Nicole may treat CCS as either a C corporation or as an S corporation. The default tax classification of legal corporations is as a C corporation for tax purposes. In addition, certain eligible corporations may elect to be treated as S corporations. Given the facts provided, CCS is eligible to make an S election.[17]

[17]§1361(b).

What if: Assume Nicole legally forms CCS as an LLC (with only one class of ownership rights) by filing articles of organization with the state. What are Nicole's options for classifying CCS for tax purposes if she is the only member of CCS?

Answer: The default classification for CCS is a sole proprietorship because CCS is unincorporated with one individual member. However, Nicole may elect to have CCS treated as a C corporation or as an S corporation. CCS can be treated as a C corporation because unincorporated entities may elect to be taxed as corporations. Further, eligible entities taxed as corporations can elect to be treated as S corporations. Given the facts provided, CCS is eligible to elect to be treated as a corporation and to be treated as an S corporation.

What if: Assume Nicole legally forms CCS as an LLC and allows other individuals or businesses to become members in return for contributing their cash, property, or services to CCS. What is the default tax classification of CCS under these assumptions?

Answer: Partnership. The default tax classification for unincorporated entities with more than one owner is a partnership.

It might seem at this point that owners of businesses classified as flow-through entities would be treated the same for tax purposes; however, that is only true in a general sense. We see in this and in other chapters that there are some subtle, and some not so subtle, differences in how the owners of ventures classified as S corporations, partnerships, and sole proprietorships are taxed.[18]

ENTITY TAX CHARACTERISTICS

LO 15-3

In deciding among the available options for taxing business ventures, owners and their advisors must carefully consider whether tax rules that apply to a particular tax classification would be either more or less favorable than tax rules under other alternative tax classifications. The specific tax rules they must compare and contrast are unique to their situations; however, certain key differences in the tax rules tend to be relevant in many scenarios. We turn our attention to the taxation (or double taxation) of entity

TAXES IN THE REAL WORLD   Comparing Entities Selected

In its Statistics of Income Tax report for 2008 (the most recent report posted when this book went to press), the Internal Revenue Service reported the following information relating to tax entity selection by business owners. Sole proprietorships are most common but C corporations by far generate the most business receipts and net income.

	Number of Entities	Business Receipts	Net Income (including deficits)
Totals for all entities	31,607,710	$30,379,435,786	$1,784,099,872
Entity Type	**Percentage**	**Percentage**	**Percentage**
C corporations	5.64%	61.57%	21.79%
S corporations	12.81	19.79	17.77
General partnerships	2.26	2.07	9.46
Limited partnerships	1.69	4.51	3.07
LLCs (taxed as partnerships)	6.01	7.72	14.07
Sole proprietorships (nonfarm)	71.55	4.34	14.83
Other*	.05	0	19.93

*Other includes Real Estate Investment Trusts (REITs) and Regulated Investment Companies (RICs). Neither type of entity has business receipts.

Source: http://www.irs.gov/uac/SOI-Tax-Stats-Integrated-Business-Data Table 3: Selected financial data on businesses Tax Year 2008.

---

[18]Chapter 9 explains how sole proprietors are taxed, and Chapters 20 through 22 explain how partners and S corporation shareholders are taxed.

income and the tax treatment of entity losses because these are two of the most important tax characteristics to consider when selecting how to organize a business for tax purposes. Later in the chapter we preview other tax factors that differ between entities and we identify the chapters where each factor is discussed in detail.

Double Taxation

Under our current system of tax rates, flow-through entities are generally considered to be superior to corporations for tax purposes because they generate income that is taxed only once while corporations produce income that is taxed twice. Flow-through entity income retains its character (such as ordinary, short-term capital gain, or long-term capital gain) and is allocated to or "flows through" to entity owners. The owners include their share of the income on their own tax returns and pay tax on the income as if they had earned it themselves.

C corporations (or entities taxed as C corporations) pay the first level of tax on their taxable income. The marginal rate for the first level of tax depends on where the corporation's taxable income falls in the corporate tax rate schedule (provided in Appendix D).[19] The current lowest marginal tax rate for corporations is 15 percent and the top marginal rate is 39 percent. The most profitable corporations are taxed at a flat 35 percent rate.

Corporate taxable income is subject to **double taxation** because shareholders pay a second level of tax on corporate income. The applicable rate for the second level of tax depends on whether corporations retain their after-tax earnings and on the type of shareholder(s). We first discuss the second level of tax that shareholders pay if corporations distribute their after-tax earnings and then we discuss the second level of tax if they retain the earnings.

After-Tax Earnings Distributed   Assuming a C corporation distributes its after-tax earnings, the second level of tax depends on whether the corporation's shareholders are individuals, other corporations, **institutional shareholders,** tax-exempt, or foreign entities.

Individual shareholders.   Individual shareholders receiving distributions from C corporations pay the second tax on the dividends they receive generally at a 15 percent tax rate. However, to the extent the dividends would be taxed at 39.6 percent if they were ordinary income, they are taxed at 20 percent and to the extent they would be taxed at 15 percent or less as ordinary income, they are taxed at 0 percent. Also, taxpayers with (modified) AGI in excess of a threshold amount pay an additional 3.8 percent net investment income tax on dividends. The threshold amount is $250,000 for married taxpayers filing jointly and surviving spouses, $125,000 for married taxpayers filing separately, and $200,000 for all other taxpayers.[20,21]

Example 15-2

What if: Assume that Nicole did some income projections to help her in her quest to determine the taxable form of her business. She makes the following assumptions:

- CCS earns taxable income of $335,000.
- CCS will pay out all of its after-tax earnings annually as a dividend.
- Her ordinary marginal tax rate is 33 percent and her dividend rate is 18.8 percent (including the 3.8 percent net investment income tax).

---

[19]C corporations that qualify as personal service corporations (PSCs) are taxed at a flat 35 percent rate (not eligible for graduated corporate rates). In general, a personal service corporation is a corporation whose shareholders perform professional services such as law, engineering, and accounting. See §448(d)(2) for more detail.

[20]Distributions to shareholders of C corporations are taxed as dividends to the extent they come from the "earnings and profits" (similar to economic income) of corporations.

[21]See §1(h) and §1411.

Given these assumptions, if Nicole organizes CCS as a C corporation, what would be the overall tax rate on CCS's income [(corporate-level tax + shareholder-level tax)/taxable income]?

Answer: 46.41 percent, computed as follows:

Description	Amount	Explanation
(1) Taxable income	$335,000	
(2) Corporate tax rate	34%	From tax rate schedule in Appendix D.
(3) Corporate-level tax	**$113,900**	(1) × (2) [first level of tax].
(4) Income remaining after taxes and distributed as a dividend	$221,100	(1) − (3).
(5) Dividend tax rate	18.8%	
(6) Shareholder-level tax on dividend	**$ 41,567**	(4) × (5) [second level of tax].
(7) Total tax paid on corporate taxable income	**$155,467**	(3) + (6).
Overall tax rate on corporate taxable income	**46.41%**	(7)/(1).

Note that the overall rate is not 52.8 percent (34 percent corporate rate + 18.8 percent shareholder rate) because the amount of corporate-level tax ($113,900) is not taxed twice (it is paid to the government, not to the shareholders).

What if: Given the same assumptions, what would be the overall tax rate on CCS's income if Nicole forms CCS as an S corporation (a flow-through entity)?

Answer: 33 percent, computed as follows:

Description	Amount	Explanation
(1) Taxable income	$335,000	
(2) Nicole's marginal individual tax rate	33%	
(3) Owner-level tax	$110,550	(1) × (2) [first and only level of tax].
Overall tax rate on CCS income	**33%**	(3)/(1).

Under these assumptions, CCS's income is subject to a 13.41 percent higher overall tax rate if it is organized as a C corporation rather than as an S corporation (46.41% − 33%).

Although corporate income is subject to a double tax, there may be circumstances in which the overall tax rate for corporate income is lower than the tax rate for flow-through income. With recent increases in individual tax rates, including the net investment income tax, and proposed legislation to reduce corporate tax rates, this situation may become increasingly more common.

Example 15-3

What if: Assume that Nicole made the following assumptions when projecting CCS's income:
- CCS's taxable income is $50,000.
- CCS pays out all of its after-tax earnings.
- Nicole's ordinary marginal tax rate is 33 percent and her dividend tax rate is 18.8 percent (including the 3.8 percent net investment income tax).

Given these assumptions, if Nicole organizes CCS as a C corporation, what would be the overall tax rate on CCS's income?

Answer: 30.98 percent, computed as follows:

(*continued on page 15-10*)

Description	Amount	Explanation
(1) Taxable income	$50,000	
(2) Corporate tax rate	15%	From tax rate schedule in Appendix D.
(3) Corporate-level tax	$ 7,500	(1) × (2) [first level of tax].
(4) Income remaining after taxes and amount distributed as a dividend	$42,500	(1) − (3).
(5) Dividend tax rate	18.8%	
(6) Shareholder-level tax on dividend	$ 7,990	(4) × (5) [second level of tax].
(7) Total tax paid on corporate taxable income	$15,490	(3) + (6).
Overall tax rate on corporate taxable income	**30.98%**	(7)/(1).

What if: Under the revised assumptions presented in this example, if Nicole forms CCS as an S corporation (flow-through entity), what would be the overall tax rate on CCS's income?

Answer: 33 percent. CCS's income would flow through to Nicole and be taxed at her 33 percent marginal ordinary income tax rate. Under the assumptions provided in this example, CCS's income is subject to a 2.02 percent *lower* overall tax rate if it is organized as a C corporation rather than as an S corporation (33% − 30.98%).

Examples 15-2 and 15-3 highlight the importance for business owners to accurately estimate their corporate marginal tax rate and their own individual marginal tax rates when deciding whether to have an entity taxed as a corporation or flow-through entity. These examples also suggest that individual business owners' overall tax rates will be higher with a corporation when the corporation's marginal tax rate is expected to be higher than or equal to the owners' marginal tax rates. Moreover, they suggest that overall tax rates may be lower with corporations when corporate marginal rates are substantially lower than individual shareholder marginal rates.

Corporate shareholders. Corporate shareholders receiving dividends are not entitled to the reduced dividend tax rate available to individual shareholders. That is, dividends received by a C corporation are subject to the corporation's ordinary tax rates. Further, dividends received by a corporation are potentially subject to another (third) level of tax when the corporation receiving the dividend distributes its earnings as dividends to its shareholders. This potential for more than two levels of tax on the same before-tax earnings prompted Congress to allow corporations to claim the **dividends received deduction** (DRD). In the next chapter, we discuss the DRD in detail, but the underlying concept is that a corporation *receiving* a dividend is allowed to deduct a certain percentage of the dividend from its taxable income to offset the potential for additional layers of taxation on the dividend when the dividend-receiving corporation distributes the dividend to its shareholders. The dividends received deduction percentage is 70, 80, or 100 percent of the dividend received depending on the extent of the recipient corporation's ownership in the dividend-paying corporation. Thus, the DRD partially mitigates the tax burden associated with *more than two levels* of tax on corporate income.

Example 15-4

What if: Assume that Nicole invites a corporation with a 35 percent marginal tax rate to invest in exchange for a 10 percent share in CCS. Nicole makes the following assumptions as part of her calculations:

- CCS is a C corporation.
- CCS earns taxable income of $335,000.
- CCS will pay out all of its after-tax earnings annually as a dividend.

Given these assumptions, what would be the overall tax rate on the corporate investor's share of CCS's income [(corporate-level tax + shareholder-level tax)/taxable income] given that the corporation would be eligible for a 70 percent dividends received deduction?

Answer: 40.9 percent, computed as follows:

Description	Amount	Explanation
(1) Taxable income	$335,000	
(2) Corporate tax rate	34%	From tax rate schedule in Appendix D.
(3) Entity-level tax	$113,900	(1) × (2) [first level of tax].
(4) After-tax income	$221,100	(1) − (3).
(5) Corporate investor's dividend	$ 22,110	(4) × 10%.
(6) Taxable dividend	$ 6,633	(5) × (1 − 70% DRD).
(7) Corporate investor's share of entity-level tax	$ 11,390	(3) × 10% investor's share.
(8) Corporate investor's tax on dividend	$ 2,322	(6) × 35% assumed investor tax rate [second level of tax].
(9) Total tax paid on corporate taxable income	$ 13,712	(7) + (8).
Overall tax rate on corporate taxable income	**40.9%**	(9)/[(1) × 10% investor's share].

Institutional shareholders. Pension and retirement funds are some of the largest institutional shareholders of corporations. However, these entities do not pay shareholder-level tax on the dividends they receive. Ultimately, retirees pay the second tax on this income when they receive retirement distributions from these funds. While retirees pay the second tax at ordinary rates, not the reduced dividend rates, they are able to defer the tax until they receive fund distributions.

Tax-exempt and foreign shareholders. Tax-exempt organizations such as churches and universities are exempt from tax on their investment income, including dividend income from investments in corporate stock. Similarly, foreign investors may be eligible for reduced rates on dividend income depending on the tax treaty, if any, their country of residence has signed with the United States.

Some or All After-Tax Earnings Retained We've already determined that a double tax on corporate income arises when corporations pay tax on their income, and shareholders pay a second level of tax when they receive dividends. Can corporations avoid the second level of tax entirely by not paying dividends? The answer is no for two reasons. First, corporations that retain earnings may be required to pay a penalty tax in addition to income tax on their earnings. With certain exceptions, unless corporations have a business reason to retain earnings, they are subject to a 20 percent **accumulated earnings tax** on the retained earnings.[22] Also, **personal holding companies** (closely held corporations generating primarily investment income) are subject to a 20 percent **personal holding company tax** on their undistributed income.[23] These penalty taxes remove the tax incentive for corporations to retain earnings. Second, shareholders also pay a second level of tax when corporations *retain* their after-tax earnings. Keep in mind that shareholders should experience an increase in the value of their shares to reflect any undistributed earnings (increase in assets). Individual shareholders generally pay the second tax at capital gains rates on this undistributed income when they realize the appreciation in their stock (from the retained earnings) by selling their shares. These long-term capital gains are generally taxed at 15 percent, However, to the extent the (long-term) capital gains would be taxed at 39.6 percent if they were ordinary income, they are taxed at 20 percent and to the extent they would be taxed at 15 percent or less as ordinary income, they are

[22]See §531 and §532.
[23]See §541.

taxed at 0 percent. Also, taxpayers with (modified) AGI in excess of a threshold amount pay an additional 3.8 percent net investment income tax on net capital gains. The threshold amount is $250,000 for married taxpayers filing jointly and surviving spouses, $125,000 for married taxpayers filing separately, and $200,000 for all other taxpayers.[24] Because shareholders *defer* paying this portion of the second tax until they sell their shares, taxes on capital gains must be discounted to reflect their present value.

Note, however, that other types of shareholders will face different tax consequences when they sell their shares. If a corporation with corporate shareholders retains after-tax earnings, corporate shareholders are taxed on capital gains at ordinary rates (there is no preferential tax rate on capital gains for corporations) when they eventually sell the stock. Consequently, a corporate shareholder's income from capital appreciation may be subject to *more* than two levels of taxation because income from capital appreciation doesn't qualify for the dividends received deduction. Also, institutional shareholders don't pay tax when they sell their stock and recognize capital gains. However, retirees generally pay tax on the gains at ordinary rates when they receive distributions from their retirement accounts. Finally, tax-exempt shareholders do not pay tax on capital gains from selling stock and foreign investors are generally not subject to U.S. tax on their capital gains from selling corporate stock.

Mitigating the Double Tax   While corporate taxable income is subject to double taxation, corporations and shareholders have options for mitigating the double tax by taking steps to reduce the corporate-level tax and/or the shareholder-level tax. These options are particularly relevant when corporations are not eligible to make an S election or when the tax and nontax costs of converting to some other legal entity are prohibitive. Let's first focus on strategies to reduce the corporate-level tax.

Reducing the corporate-level tax.   When a C corporation's marginal tax rate exceeds its *individual* shareholders' marginal tax rates, the overall tax rate on corporate income will exceed the flow-through tax rate even if shareholders can defer the second tax indefinitely. In these situations, it makes sense for closely held corporations and their shareholders to consider strategies to shift income from the corporation to shareholders. These strategies are all designed to move earnings out of the corporations and to shareholders with payments that are *deductible* (dividends are not deductible payments) by the corporation and (generally) taxable to shareholders. Making tax-deductible payments to shareholders accomplishes two objectives. First, it shifts income away from (relatively) high tax rate corporations to (relatively) low tax rate shareholders. Second, the deduction shields income from the corporate-level tax. Strategies that shift income from corporations to shareholders include:

- Paying salaries to shareholders (salaries are deductible only to the extent they are reasonable).
- Paying fringe benefits to shareholders (generally taxable to shareholders unless benefits are specifically excluded from taxation).[25]
- Leasing property from shareholders.
- Paying interest on loans from shareholders.[26]

[24]See §1(h) and §1411.

[25]Common fringe benefits excluded from taxation are medical insurance, group-term life insurance, dependent care assistance, tuition benefits, and so forth.

[26]For individual shareholders, depending on their income level, salaries and taxable fringe benefits may be be subject to the .9 percent additional Medicare tax while rental income and interest income may be subject to the 3.8 percent net investment income tax.

Example 15-5

What if: Assume Nicole uses her own funds to purchase the equipment required to manufacture the color comfort sheets. She leases the equipment to CCS corporation for $12,000 per year, the fair rental value for the equipment. What are the tax consequences to CCS and to Nicole of this leasing arrangement?

Answer: CCS deducts the $12,000 paid to Nicole each year for the use of the equipment, shielding $12,000 of its earnings from the corporate-level tax. Nicole is taxed on the $12,000 lease payments at her ordinary rate. In the end, Nicole and the corporation have achieved their objective of getting earnings out of CCS and into Nicole's hands with only one level of tax on the earnings.

THE KEY FACTS
Double Taxation

- Most profitable C corporations are taxed at a 35 percent rate.
- Individual C corporation shareholders are generally taxed at a 15 percent rate on dividends when received (20 percent for high income taxpayers). Further, certain taxpayers may be charged a 3.8 percent net investment income tax on dividends and capital gains.
- C corporation shareholders that are C corporations are generally eligible to receive a 70 percent or greater dividends received deduction.
- C corporation shareholders who are individuals generally pay capital gains taxes when shares are sold at a gain.
- The double tax is mitigated when income is shifted from C corporations to shareholders and when dividends are deferred or not paid.

ETHICS

Troy is the CEO and sole shareholder of BQT. BQT is a very profitable C corporation. Until this year, Troy's salary was in line with the salaries of other comparable CEOs. However, early this year it came to Troy's attention that another CEO for a similarly sized firm in the same industry was receiving a salary almost two times what Troy was receiving. Wanting to mitigate the double tax on his corporation's income, Troy decided to give himself a 75 percent raise. Do you think Troy's decision is ethical? Why or why not?

Reducing the shareholder-level tax. Shareholders generally pay the second tax immediately when they receive dividends or in the future when they sell their stock and pay capital gains tax. For *individual* shareholders, the tax rate applicable to both dividend income and (long-term) capital gains is generally 15 or 20 percent depending on the taxpayer's income level. Further, high-income taxpayers may be charged an additional 3.8 percent net investment income tax on dividends and capital gains. However, because individual shareholders defer paying the second tax on capital gains until they sell their stock, the present value of the second tax is a function of the (1) percentage of after-tax earnings the corporation retains rather than currently distributing as dividends and (2) the length of time shareholders hold the stock before selling. By retaining after-tax earnings, corporations defer the second level of tax until the shareholder sells the stock. The longer a shareholder holds stock in a corporation that retains earnings, the lower the present value of the shareholder-level tax on the corporation's earnings. Individuals who make lifetime gifts of appreciated stock to their children utilize this basic strategy. The concept is that by deferring the second level of tax until children sell the shares many years into the future, the double tax becomes very small on a present value basis.[27] Alternatively, the donor could have sold the shares, paid the resulting capital gains tax, and given the remainder to her children, but this would have immediately triggered the shareholder tax leaving her children with less after-tax wealth on a present value basis.

It is important to note that the length of time a shareholder holds stock before selling and the percentage of earnings retained are not always under the shareholder's or corporation's control. For example, a shareholder may need cash for reasons unrelated to the business and therefore may need to sell the stock before recognizing the deferral benefits of holding the stock. Also, as we discussed above,

---

[27]Shareholders who wait until death to bequeath stock along with their heirs escape the shareholder tax entirely because the tax basis of inherited shares is stepped up to fair market value on the date of death. These shareholders may pay estate tax on the value of the shares held at death, however.

the accumulated earnings tax and personal holding company tax may force corporations to distribute rather than retain earnings.

In spite of the fact that the double tax can be reduced by careful planning at both the corporate and shareholder level, some element of the double tax will likely remain, leaving corporations disadvantaged relative to flow-through entities under our current system of individual and corporate tax rates.

Deductibility of Entity Losses

When C corporations are reporting losses for tax purposes, double taxation (or even single taxation) is not a concern. Losses generated by C corporations are called **net operating losses** (NOLs). While NOLs provide no tax benefit to a corporation in the year the corporation experiences the NOL, they may be used to reduce corporate taxes in other years. Generally, C corporations with an NOL for the year can carry back the loss to offset the taxable income reported in the two preceding years and carry it forward for up to 20 years.

Under this approach, losses from C corporations are *not* available to offset their shareholders' personal income. In contrast, losses generated by flow-through entities are generally available to offset the owners' personal income, subject to certain restrictions. For example, the owner of a flow-through entity may only deduct losses from the entity to the extent of the owner's basis in her ownership interest in the flow-through entity. In addition, deductibility of losses from flow-through entities may be further limited by the "at-risk" and passive activity loss limitations. The at-risk limitation is similar to the basis limitation but slightly more restrictive. The passive activity loss limitations typically apply to individual investors who do little, if any, work for the business activities of the flow-through entity (referred to as "passive" activities to the individual investors). In these circumstances, the taxpayer can only deduct such losses to the extent they have income from other passive activities. Due to the complex nature of these limitations, we defer detailed discussion of these limitations until we discuss partnerships in Chapter 20. The ability to deduct flow-through losses against other sources of income can be a significant issue for owners of new businesses because new businesses tend to report losses early on as the businesses get established. If owners form a new business as a C corporation, the corporate-level losses provide no current tax benefits to the shareholders. The fact that C corporation losses are trapped at the corporate level effectively imposes a higher tax cost for shareholders initially doing business as a C corporation relative to a flow-through entity such as an S corporation or partnership because the flow-through entity owners, subject to the limits mentioned above, can use the losses to offset other sources of income.

Example 15-6

What if: Assume that Nicole organizes CCS as a C corporation and that, in spite of her best efforts as CEO of the company, CCS reports a tax loss of $50,000 in its first year of operation (year 1). Also, assume Nicole's marginal tax rate is 33 percent and assume she will have ordinary taxable income of $200,000 from her husband's salary in year 1. How much tax will CCS pay in year 1 and how much tax will Nicole (and her husband) pay on the $200,000 of other taxable income if CCS is organized as a C corporation?

Answer: CCS will pay $0 in taxes because it reports a loss for tax purposes. Because Nicole may not use the CCS loss to offset her other income, she must pay $66,000 in taxes. See the computations in the table below.

What if: Suppose CCS is organized as an S corporation and Nicole's stock basis in CCS before the year 1 loss is $100,000. How much tax will CCS pay in year 1, and how much tax will Nicole (and her husband) pay on the $200,000 of other income?

Answer: CCS pays $0 taxes (S corporations are not taxpaying entities) and Nicole pays $49,500 in taxes. See the computations in the table below:

Description	C Corporation	S Corporation (flow-through)	Explanation
(1) Taxable income (loss)	($50,000)	($50,000)	
(2) CCS corporate-level tax	$ 0	$ 0	No taxable income.
(3) Nicole's other income	$200,000	$200,000	
(4) CCS loss available to offset Nicole's other income	$ 0	($50,000)	$0 if C corp. (1) if flow-through entity (S corporation).
(5) Nicole's other income reduced by entity loss	$200,000	$150,000	(3) + (4).
(6) Nicole's marginal ordinary tax rate	33%	33%	
Nicole's tax on other income	**$ 66,000**	**$ 49,500**	(5) × (6).

What if: Suppose CCS is organized as an S corporation and Nicole's stock basis before the $50,000 year 1 loss is $100,000. Further, assume that Nicole does not participate in CCS's business activities; that is, assume she is a passive investor in the business entity. How much tax will Nicole (and her husband) pay on the $200,000 of other income?

Answer: $66,000. Because Nicole is a passive investor, she is not allowed to deduct the loss allocated to her this year. She must carry it over and use it in future years (this assumes neither Nicole nor her husband have income from other investments in which they are passive investors).

As the example above illustrates, owners' ability to immediately use start-up losses from flow-through entities to offset income from other sources further enhances the tax advantages of flow-through entities relative to corporations in many situations.

OTHER TAX CHARACTERISTICS

The taxation of entity income and the tax treatment of entity losses are two important factors to consider when comparing tax entities. There are many other tax characteristics that differ across entities and could influence the entity selection decision. Factors that are most important to the decision also depend on the facts and circumstances of the particular situation. Exhibit 15-3 provides an overview of many of these tax characteristics. The exhibit describes the general rules for each tax characteristic as it relates to C corporations, S corporations, entities taxed as partnerships, and sole proprietorships and it ranks the entities on each characteristic (1 is most tax favorable). Finally, the exhibit indicates the chapters where detail on these tax characteristics can be found. Because this is an overview chapter, details on each factor are provided elsewhere in the text.

Converting to Other Entity Types

As we discussed previously, C corporations can take steps to mitigate the double tax. For example, deductible compensation, rent, and interest payments, to the extent they are reasonable, provide a mechanism for shifting income to their shareholders. Depending on the total amount of these deductible shareholder payments relative to a corporation's income before the payments, they effectively convert or partially

EXHIBIT 15-3 Comparison of Tax Characteristics across Entities

Tax Characteristic	C Corporation	Entity Taxed as Partnership	S Corporation	Sole Proprietorship	Detail in Chapter	Summary
Owner limits	At least one shareholder.	At least two owners.	Not more than 100; no corporations, partnerships, nonresident aliens, or certain trusts.	N/A	22	Limitations are least strict for C corporations and most strict for S corporations. S corporations are the only entity with significant owner limitations.
Rank[1]	1	2	3	N/A		
Owner contributions of appreciated property to entity	Nontaxable to shareholder if certain requirements are met.	Nontaxable to owner.	Nontaxable to shareholder if certain requirements are met.	N/A	19, 20, and 22	This factor favors entities taxed as partnerships because partners are not required to meet special requirements in order to avoid recognizing gain on the contribution of appreciated property to the partnership, but shareholders of both C and S corporations are required to meet certain requirements to avoid recognizing gain on such contributions to the corporation.
Rank	2	1	2	N/A		
Accounting periods	Generally, any tax year that ends on the last day of any month.[2]	Generally, must use tax year that matches tax year of owners (special rules when not all owners have same tax year-end).	Calendar year.	Generally a calendar year.	9, 20, and 22	C corporations generally have the most flexibility to select their year-end. But because C corporations are not flow-through entities, this is not a real advantage or disadvantage from a tax perspective. Partnerships generally are not free to choose their year-end but they can have a year-end that is a different year-end from some of the owners. Because this allows some partners to defer reporting income, this factor favors partnerships over S corporations. S corporations generally have the same calendar year-end as their shareholders.
Rank	N/A	1	2	N/A		
Overall accounting method	Generally, must use accrual method unless smaller corporation.[3]	Generally, allowed to use cash or accrual method.	Generally, allowed to use cash or accrual method.	Cash or accrual method.	9, 16, 20, and 22	Entities taxed as partnerships, S corporations, and sole proprietorships generally have more flexibility to choose their overall accounting method than do C corporations. The cash method makes it easier for these entities to plan the timing of income and expenses than does the accrual method.
Rank	4	1	2	1		
Allocation of income or loss items to owners	N/A	Allocations based on partnership agreement (can differ from ownership percentages).	Allocations based on stock ownership percentages.	N/A	20 and 22	This factor applies to partnerships and S corporations only. Partnerships have more flexibility than S corporations to determine how to allocate income and loss items to entity owners.
Rank	N/A	1	2	N/A		

(continued on page 15-17)

Characteristic					Research	Factor tending to favor one entity type over others[1]
FICA and self-employment tax	Employee-owners pay FICA tax on salary.	Compensation received by owners (guaranteed payments) is subject to self-employment tax. Business (operating) income allocation is generally subject to self-employment tax if owner is actively involved in business. It is not otherwise.[4]	Employee-owners pay FICA on salary. But they do not pay FICA/self-employment tax on business income allocations. Owners providing services for the S corporation must receive a reasonable salary for their efforts.[5]	Net income is subject to self-employment tax, including the .9 percent additional Medicare tax depending on the proprietor's income level (see §1401 for details).	20 and 22	This factor tends to favor S corporations because S corporation owners can work for the business and yet receive business income allocations that are not subject to FICA/self-employment tax or the .9 percent additional Medicare tax. In contrast, business income allocations to partners working for partnerships are subject to self-employment tax and potentially the .9 percent additional Medicare tax. Congress is currently considering proposals to reduce this discrepancy in tax treatment between entities.
Rank	2	3	1	4		
Share of flow-through entity debt included in basis of owner's equity interest	N/A	Increase basis in ownership interest by owner's share of entity's debt.	No increase in stock basis for debt of entity (special rules if shareholder lends money to S corporation).	N/A	20 and 22	Partners are allowed to increase the basis in their ownership interest by their share of the partnership's debt; S corporation shareholders generally are not. This factor favors partnerships over S corporations.
Rank	N/A	1	2	N/A		
Nonliquidating distributions of noncash property	Gains recognized on distributions of appreciated property and losses disallowed on distributions of appreciated property.	Generally no gain or loss recognized on noncash property distributions.	Same as C corporation.	N/A	18, 21, and 22	This factor favors partnerships for distributions of appreciated and depreciated property.
Rank	2	1	2	N/A		
Liquidating distributions	Gain and loss (certain losses disallowed).	Generally no gain or loss.	Gain and loss (certain losses disallowed).	N/A	19, 21, and 22	This factor tends to favor partnerships if the liquidating entities have gain assets, and it tends to favor corporations if the entities have loss assets.
Rank	1	1	1	N/A		

[1]"Rank" orders the entities based on the particular characteristic (1 is most favorable).

[2]C corporations that qualify as personal service corporations (PSCs) are generally required to use a calendar year. In general, a personal service corporation is a corporation whose shareholders perform professional services such as law, engineering, and accounting. See §448(d)(2) for more detail.

[3]C corporations that qualify as personal service corporations (PSCs) are required to use the cash method.

[4]Guaranteed payments and income allocations (if the partner is involved in the business) may be subject to a .9 percent additional Medicare tax depending on the partner's income level (see §1401 for details). If the partner is not involved in the business, income allocations may be subject to the 3.8 percent net investment income tax, depending on the partner's income level.

[5]An S corporation shareholder receiving salary may be required to pay the .9 percent additional Medicare tax on some or all of the salary depending on the shareholder's income level and other sources of earned income (see §1401 for details). Further, if the S corporation shareholder does not materially participate in the business, business income allocations may be subject to the 3.8 percent net investment income tax, depending on the shareholder's income level.

convert C corporations into flow-through entities in the sense that these payments are taxed at the owner level and not at the corporate level. If this is true, why not avoid the constraints associated with deductible shareholder payments and accomplish the same result more directly by converting an existing corporation into a flow-through entity?

Besides making deductible payments to their shareholders, existing corporations really only have two options for converting into flow-through entities. First, shareholders of C corporations could make an S election to treat the corporation as an S corporation (flow-through entity), if they are eligible to do so. This option is not available for many corporations due to the tax rule restrictions prohibiting certain corporations from operating as S corporations. The only other option is for the shareholders to liquidate the corporation and form the business as a partnership or LLC. This may not be a viable option, however, because the taxes imposed on liquidating corporations with appreciated assets can be very punitive. As described in Exhibit 15-3, liquidating corporations are taxed on the appreciation in the assets they distribute to their shareholders as part of the liquidation. Further, shareholders of liquidating corporations are also taxed on the difference between the fair market value of the assets they receive from the liquidating corporation and their tax basis in their stock. Effectively, the total double-tax cost of liquidating a corporation can swamp the expected tax savings from operating as a flow-through entity.

Example 15-7

What if: Assume we are years down the road and that Nicole is the sole shareholder of CCS (a C corporation). CCS's assets have a fair market value of $10 million and adjusted tax basis of $6 million ($4 million built-in gain). Further assume that CCS has a 34 percent marginal tax rate, Nicole's stock basis in CCS is $2 million, and her marginal tax rate on long-term capital gains is 23.8 percent (20 percent capital gains rate + 3.8 percent net investment income tax). How much tax would the CCS and Nicole be required to pay if CCS were to liquidate in order to form an LLC?

Answer: $2,940,320. This is a steep tax price to pay for changing from C corporation to LLC.

Description	Amount	Explanation
(1) FMV of CCS assets	$10,000,000	
(2) Adjusted basis of CCS assets	$ 6,000,000	
(3) CCS taxable income on liquidation	$ 4,000,000	(1) − (2).
(4) Corporate tax rate	34%	
(5) Entity-level tax	$ 1,360,000	(3) × (4).
(6) After-tax assets distributed to Nicole.	$ 8,640,000	(1) − (5).
(7) Nicole's stock basis	$ 2,000,000	
(8) Nicole's long-term capital gain on distribution	$ 6,640,000	(6) − (7).
(9) Nicole's marginal tax rate on gain	23.8%	
(10) Shareholder-level tax	$ 1,580,320	(8) × (9).
Total entity and shareholder-level tax on liquidation	**$ 2,940,320**	(5) + (10).

When feasible, S elections or corporate liquidations, like deductible payments to shareholders, are used to convert *existing* corporations into flow-through entities. Why then, didn't shareholders of *existing* corporations initially form the entities as flow-through entities? Perhaps at the time of formation the corporate form was optimal from purely a tax perspective because corporate marginal tax rates were significantly lower than shareholder marginal tax rates at that time. Or, maybe, the corporations were willing to be treated as C corporations in order to go public but then became closely held when all their outstanding shares were purchased by a small number of shareholders.

As costly as it can be to convert corporations to flow-through entities, it is equally as easy and inexpensive to convert entities taxed as partnerships or sole proprietorships into corporations. Typically, converting entities taxed as partnerships or sole proprietorships into corporations can be accomplished in a tax-deferred transaction without any special tax elections.[28] For this reason, many businesses that plan to eventually go public will operate for a time as entities taxable as partnerships to receive the associated tax benefits and then convert to C corporations when they finally decide to go public.

continued from page 15-4 . . .

Nicole's five-year forecast of CCS's expected operating results showed that CCS would generate losses for the first three years and then become very profitable after. With these projections in hand, Nicole then considered the basic question of whether a C corporation or a flow-through entity would minimize her overall tax liability. Nicole's marginal tax rate and CCS's expected marginal tax rate after three years, if it were to operate as a C corporation, led her to conclude that she needed to avoid the double tax by operating CCS as a flow-through entity from the start. Given her initial desire to limit her choice of legal entity to either a corporation or LLC, this left her with the option of operating CCS as either an S corporation or as an LLC taxed as a partnership.

After narrowing her choice down to either an LLC or S corporation, Nicole compared the specific tax rules applicable to LLCs and S corporations before making her final decision. As she compared them, she identified four differences that could sway her decision one way or the other. Supporting a decision to select an LLC, Nicole learned she would likely be able to deduct the projected start-up losses from CCS more quickly with an LLC compared with an S corporation because she could include a share of the LLC's debt in her tax basis (but she would not be able to include a share of the S corporation's debt in the tax basis of her ownership interest). Moreover, she learned that LLC profits and losses can be specially allocated while S corporation profits and losses must be allocated pro rata to the shareholders. Nicole was hoping to have the ability to be a little more creative with profit and loss allocations. Finally, she had hoped to possibly attract corporate investors, but discovered that S corporations are not permitted to have corporate shareholders. She did find, however, that S corporations appear to have a compelling advantage over LLCs in reducing the self-employment tax of owners active in managing their businesses.

Ultimately, Nicole decided that she would be willing to incur additional self-employment taxes with an LLC in exchange for the ability to deduct her losses sooner, for the flexibility she might need one day to specially allocate profits or losses, and for the freedom to solicit corporate investors. Given these considerations, she decided to organize CCS as an LLC in the state of Utah.

With this big decision out of the way, Nicole could now focus on applying for a small-business loan from her local bank and on having her attorney take the necessary steps to formally organize CCS as a limited liability company. ∎

[28]§351 and Rev. Rul. 84-111 1984-2 CB 88.

TAXES IN THE REAL WORLD Best Entity Choice for Small Businesses?

Small businesses generally have the option to be taxed as a flow-through entity (S corporation or partnership). Historically, the obvious tax benefit of a flow-through entity is that the entity's income is taxed once at the owner level. Nevertheless, a recently published study from economists at the Treasury Department indicates that more than 1.6 million small businesses forgo flow-through entity status and are taxed as Subchapter C corporations, subjecting their income to both entity-level and shareholder level tax (Matthew Knittel, Susan Nelson, Jason DeBacker, John Kitchen, James Pearce, and Richard Prisinzano, "Methodology to Identify Small Businesses and Their Owners," Office of Tax Analysis, Technical Paper 4, Aug. 2011, *Doc 2011–17260, 2011 TNT 154-18*). Despite a C corporation's historically bad tax reputation, there are good tax reasons for small businesses to subject themselves to double tax under Subchapter C. For example, graduated corporate rates, the low effective tax rate on corporate dividends (due to the dividends received deduction), and an exemption from payroll taxes (that is, a C corporation is not subject to FICA or self-employment tax on its own earnings) combine to make Subchapter C the most advantageous choice for a lot of small business profits. This is particularly true when a business owner can afford to defer the shareholder level tax by leaving profits inside the corporation. Further, now that the top marginal individual tax rate is higher than the top corporate tax rate, even more small businesses may choose to be taxed as C corporations.

CONCLUSION

Any time a new business is formed and periodically thereafter as circumstances change, business owners must carefully evaluate what type of business entity will maximize the after-tax profits from their business ventures. Many of the key factors to consider in the entity selection decision-making process are outlined in this chapter. When making the entity selection decision, owners must carefully balance the tax and nontax characteristics unique to the entities available to them. This chapter explains how various legal entities are treated for tax purposes and how certain tax characteristics differ between entity types. Moreover, it also identifies some of the more important nontax issues that come to bear on the choice of entity decision. With this understanding, taxpayers and their advisors will be better prepared to face this frequently encountered business decision. In Chapter 20, we return to Nicole and Color Comfort Sheets LLC to examine the tax rules that apply to Nicole and other members in CCS as they form the entity for tax purposes and begin business operations.

Summary

LO 15-1 Discuss the legal and nontax characteristics of different types of legal entities.

- Entities that differ in terms of their legal characteristics include corporations, limited liability companies, general partnerships, limited partnerships, and sole proprietorships.
- Corporations are formally organized by filing articles of incorporation with the state. They are legally separate entities and protect their shareholders from the liabilities of the corporation. State corporation laws dictate interactions between corporations and shareholders. As a result, shareholders have limited flexibility to customize their business arrangements with the corporation and other shareholders. State corporate governance rules do, however, facilitate initial public offerings.
- Limited liability companies are formally organized by filing articles of organization with the state. Like corporations, they are separate legal entities that shield their members from liabilities. In contrast to corporations, state LLC statutes give members a great deal of latitude in customizing their business arrangements with the LLC and other members.

- General partnerships may be organized informally without state approval, but limited partnerships must file a certificate of limited partnership with the state to organize. Although they are considered to be legally separate entities, they provide either limited or no liability protection for partners. While limited partners in limited partnerships have liability protection, general partners are fully exposed to the liabilities of the partnership. General and limited partnerships are given a great deal of latitude in customizing their partnership agreements.

- Sole proprietorships are businesses legally indistinguishable from their sole individual owners. As such, they are very flexible but provide no liability protection. Sole proprietors can obtain liability protection by converting to a single-member LLC.

Describe the different types of entities for tax purposes.   **LO 15-2**

- The four categories of business entities recognized by our tax system include: C corporations, S corporations, partnerships, and sole proprietorships.

- Legal corporations that don't make the S election are treated as C corporations and therefore pay taxes. All other entities recognized for tax purposes are flow-through entities.

- Legal corporations that qualify for and make the S election are treated as S corporations.

- Unincorporated entities with more than one owner are treated as partnerships.

- Unincorporated entities with one owner are treated as sole proprietorships where the sole owner is an individual or as a disregarded entity otherwise.

Identify fundamental differences in tax characteristics across entity types.   **LO 15-3**

- Because C corporations and their shareholders pay taxes, C corporation income is double taxed. Corporations that retain earnings may be subject to the accumulated earnings tax or the personal holding company tax. These taxes eliminate the tax incentive for corporations to retain earnings.

- Shareholders in C corporations are taxed either when they receive dividends or when they sell their shares.

- Tax planning strategies applied at the corporate level to mitigate the double taxation of C corporations include paying salary to shareholder-employees, paying fringe benefits to shareholder-employees, leasing property from a shareholder, and borrowing money from and paying interest to shareholders. All of these strategies provide deductions to the corporation, which reduces corporate-level taxes. Shareholders are generally taxed when they receive these payments except when they receive qualified fringe benefits. In addition, corporations also mitigate the double tax by retaining income rather than paying dividends.

- Shareholders can mitigate the double tax by increasing the time they hold shares before selling.

- C corporation losses are referred to as net operating losses (NOLs). Generally, C corporations may carry an NOL back 2 years and forward up to 20 years to offset taxable income in those years. C corporation losses do not flow through to shareholders.

- Operating losses from S corporations and partnerships flow through to the owners. Owners may deduct these losses only to the extent of the basis in their ownership interest. The losses must also clear "at-risk" limitations and passive activity loss limitations in order for the owners to deduct the loss.

- The at-risk limitation is similar to the basis limitation. The passive activity loss limitations typically apply to individual investors who do little, if any, work relating to the business activities of the flow-through entity (referred to as *passive* activities to the individual investors). In these circumstances, the taxpayer can only deduct such losses to the extent they have income from other passive activities.

- C corporations may have one or many shareholders. S corporations may have one shareholder and as many as 100 unrelated shareholders; but corporations, nonresident aliens, partnerships, and certain trusts may not be S corporation shareholders. Partnerships must have at least two partners but are not restricted to a maximum number of partners. Sole proprietorships may have only one owner.

- Gains and income from contributing appreciated property to business entities are more easily deferred with partnerships compared to C and S corporations.

- S corporations, partnerships, and sole proprietorships are generally required to use tax year-ends conforming to the tax year-ends of their owners. C corporations may use any tax year-end.
- C corporations generally must use the accrual method unless they are a smaller corporation. S corporations may use either the cash or accrual method of accounting. Partnerships generally may use either the cash or accrual method. Sole proprietorships may use either the cash or accrual method.
- Income and losses may be specially allocated to partners based on the partnership agreement. This gives partnerships a great deal of flexibility in determining how the risks and rewards of the enterprise are shared among partners. In contrast, income and losses must be allocated pro rata to S corporation shareholders consistent with their ownership percentages.
- Shareholder-employees of C corporations or S corporations must pay FICA tax on their wages. However, shareholders of S corporations are not required to pay self-employment tax on business income allocated to them from S corporations. Owners providing services for an S corporation must receive a reasonable salary for their efforts.
- Owners of entities taxed as partnerships must pay self-employment taxes on compensation (guaranteed payments) they receive from the entity. Owners of entities taxed as a partnership generally must pay self-employment tax on business (operating) income allocated to them if the owner is actively involved in business.
- Partners, but not S corporation shareholders, may add their share of entity debt to their basis.
- Generally, distributions of appreciated property trigger gain at both the corporate and shareholder level when made to shareholders of C corporations, trigger gain at the corporate level when made to S corporation shareholders, and don't trigger any gain at all when made to partners.
- On liquidation, C and S corporations will generally recognize gains and losses on distributed assets. In contrast, partnerships and their partners generally do not recognize gains or losses on liquidating distributions.
- C corporations wanting to convert to a flow-through entity have two options. They may elect to become an S corporation if eligible, or they may liquidate the corporation and organize as a new entity. Taxes from liquidating C corporations are typically prohibitive when C corporations have appreciated assets.

KEY TERMS

accumulated earnings tax (15-11)
articles of incorporation (15-2)
articles of organization (15-2)
C corporation (15-5)
corporation (15-2)
certificate of limited partnership (15-2)
disregarded entities (15-5)

dividends received deduction (15-10)
double taxation (15-8)
flow-through entities (15-5)
general partnership (15-2)
initial public offering (15-3)
institutional shareholders (15-8)
limited liability company (15-2)
limited partnership (15-2)

net operating losses (15-14)
partnership agreement (15-2)
personal holding company (15-11)
personal holding company tax (15-11)
S corporation (15-5)
single-member LLCs (15-5)
sole proprietorship (15-2)

DISCUSSION QUESTIONS

Discussion Questions are available in *Connect®*.

LO 15-1
1. What are the most common legal entities used for operating a business? How are these entities treated similarly and differently for state law purposes?

LO 15-1
2. How do business owners create legal entities? Is the process the same for all entities? If not, what are the differences?

LO 15-1
3. What is an operating agreement for an LLC? Are operating agreements required for limited liability companies? If not, why might it be important to have one?

4. Explain how legal entities differ in terms of the liability protection they afford their owners. `LO 15-1`

5. Why are C corporations still popular despite the double tax on their income? `LO 15-1`

6. Why is it a nontax advantage for corporations to be able to trade their stock on the stock market? `LO 15-1`

7. How do corporations protect shareholders from liability? If you formed a small corporation, would you be able to avoid repaying a bank loan from your community bank if the corporation went bankrupt? Explain. `LO 15-1`

8. Other than corporations, are there other legal entities that offer liability protection? Are any of them taxed as flow-through entities? Explain. `LO 15-1` `LO 15-2`

9. In general, how are unincorporated entities classified for tax purposes? `LO 15-2`

10. Can unincorporated legal entities ever be treated as corporations for tax purposes? Can corporations ever be treated as flow-through entities for tax purposes? Explain. `LO 15-2`

11. What are the differences, if any, between the legal and tax classification of business entities? `LO 15-2`

12. What types of business entities does the U.S. tax system recognize? `LO 15-2`

13. Who pays the first level of tax on a C corporation's income? What is the tax rate applicable to the first level of tax? `LO 15-3`

14. Who pays the second level of tax on a C corporation's income? What is the tax rate applicable to the second level of tax and when is it levied? `LO 15-3`

15. Is it possible for shareholders to defer or avoid the second level of tax on corporate income? Briefly explain. `LO 15-3`

16. How does a corporation's decision to pay dividends affect its overall tax rate [(corporate level tax + shareholder level tax)/taxable income]? `LO 15-3`

17. Is it possible for the overall tax rate on corporate taxable income to be lower than the tax rate on flow-through entity taxable income? If so, under what conditions would you expect the overall corporate tax rate to be lower? `LO 15-3`

18. Assume Congress increases individual tax rates on ordinary income while leaving all other tax rates unchanged. How would this change affect the overall tax rate on corporate taxable income? How would this change affect overall tax rates for owners of flow-through entities? `LO 15-3`

19. Assume Congress increases the dividend tax rate to the ordinary tax rate while leaving all other tax rates unchanged. How would this change affect the overall tax rate on corporate taxable income? `LO 15-3`

20. Evaluate the following statement: "When dividends and long-term capital gains are taxed at the same rate, the overall tax rate on corporate income is the same whether the corporation distributes its after-tax earnings as a dividend or whether it reinvests the after-tax earnings to increase the value of the corporation." `LO 15-3`

21. If XYZ corporation is a shareholder of BCD corporation, how many levels of tax is BCD's before-tax income potentially subject to? Has Congress provided any tax relief for this result? Explain. `LO 15-3`

22. How many times is income from a C corporation taxed if a retirement fund is the owner of the corporation's stock? Explain. `LO 15-3`

23. List four basic tax planning strategies that corporations and shareholders can use to mitigate double taxation of a C corporation's taxable income. `LO 15-3`

24. Explain why paying a salary to an employee-shareholder is an effective way to mitigate the double taxation of corporate income. `LO 15-3`

LO 15-3 25. What limits apply to the amount of deductible salary a corporation may pay to an employee-shareholder?

LO 15-3 26. Explain why the IRS would be concerned that a closely held C corporation only pay its shareholders reasonable compensation.

LO 15-3 27. When a corporation pays salary to a shareholder-employee beyond what is considered to be reasonable compensation, how is the salary in excess of what is reasonable treated for tax purposes? Is it subject to double taxation? [*Hint:* See Reg. §1.162-7(b)(1).]

research

LO 15-3 28. How can fringe benefits be used to mitigate the double taxation of corporate income?

LO 15-3 29. How many levels of taxation apply to corporate earnings paid out as qualified fringe benefits? Explain.

LO 15-3 30. How many levels of taxation apply to corporate earnings paid out as nonqualified fringe benefits? Explain.

LO 15-3 31. How can leasing property to a corporation be an effective method of mitigating the double tax on corporate income?

LO 15-3 32. When a corporation leases property from a shareholder and pays the shareholder at a higher than market rate, how is the excess likely to be classified by the IRS?

LO 15-3 33. How do shareholder loans to corporations mitigate the double tax of corporate income?

LO 15-3 34. Conceptually, what is the overall tax rate imposed on interest paid on loans from shareholders to corporations?

LO 15-3 35. If a corporation borrows money from a shareholder and pays the shareholder interest at a greater than market rate, how will the interest in excess of the market rate be treated by the IRS?

LO 15-3 36. When a C corporation reports a loss for the year, can shareholders use the loss to offset their personal income? Why or why not?

LO 15-3 37. Is a current-year net operating loss of a C corporation available to offset income from the corporation in other years? Explain.

LO 15-3 38. A C corporation has a current year loss of $100,000. The corporation had paid estimated taxes for the year of $10,000 and expects to have this amount refunded when it files its tax return. Is it possible that the corporation may receive a refund larger than $10,000? If so, how is it possible? If not, why not?

LO 15-3 39. What happens to a C corporation's net operating loss carryover after 20 years?

LO 15-3 40. Does a C corporation gain more tax benefit by carrying forward a net operating loss to offset other taxable income two years after the NOL arises or by carrying the NOL back two years? Explain.

LO 15-3 41. In its first year of existence, KES, an S corporation, reported a business loss of $10,000. Kim, KES's sole shareholder, reports $50,000 of taxable income from sources other than KES. What must you know to determine whether she can deduct the $10,000 loss against her other income? Explain.

LO 15-3 42. Why are S corporations less favorable than C corporations and entities taxed as partnerships in terms of owner-related limitations?

LO 15-3 43. Are C corporations or flow-through entities (S corporations and entities taxed as partnerships) more flexible in terms of selecting a tax year-end? Why are the tax rules in this area different for C corporations and flow-through entities?

LO 15-3 44. Which entity types are generally allowed to use the cash method of accounting?

LO 15-3 45. According to the tax rules, how are profits and losses allocated to LLC members? How are they allocated to S corporation shareholders? Which entity permits greater flexibility in allocating profits and losses?

46. Compare and contrast the FICA tax burden of S corporation shareholder-employees and LLC members receiving compensation for working for the entity (guaranteed payments) and business income allocations to S corporation shareholders and LLC members assuming the owners are actively involved in the entity's business activities. How does your analysis change if the owners are not actively involved in the entity's business activities? `LO 15-3`

47. Explain how liabilities of an LLC or an S corporation affect the amount of tax losses from the entity that limited liability company members and S corporation shareholders may deduct. Do the tax rules favor LLCs or S corporations? `LO 15-3`

48. Compare the entity level tax consequences for C corporations, S corporations, and partnerships for both nonliquidating and liquidating distributions of noncash property. Do the tax rules tend to favor one entity type more than the others? Explain. `LO 15-3`

49. If limited liability companies and S corporations are both taxed as flow-through entities for tax purposes, why might an owner prefer one form over the other for tax purposes? List separately the tax factors supporting the decision to operate as either an LLC or S corporation. `LO 15-3`

50. What are the tax advantages and disadvantages of converting a C corporation into an LLC? `LO 15-3`

PROBLEMS

Select problems are available in *Connect*®.   connect

51. Visit your state's official Web site and review the information there related to forming and operating business entities in your state. Write a short report explaining the steps for organizing a business in your state and summarizing any tax-related information you found. `LO 15-1` **research**

52. Evon would like to organize SHO as either an LLC or as a C corporation generating an 11 percent annual before-tax return on a $200,000 investment. Assume individual and corporate tax rates are both 35 percent and individual capital gains and dividend tax rates are 15 percent. SHO will pay out its after-tax earnings every year as a dividend if it is formed as a C corporation. Assume Evon is the sole owner of the entity. Ignore self-employment taxes, the additional Medicare tax, and the net investment income tax. `LO 15-3`

    a) How much would Evon keep after taxes if SHO is organized as either an LLC or as a C corporation?

    b) What are the overall tax rates if SHO is organized as either an LLC or as a C corporation?

53. Evon would like to organize SHO as either an S corporation or as a C corporation generating a 9 percent annual before-tax return on a $200,000 investment. Assume individual and corporate tax rates are both 35 percent and individual capital gains and dividend tax rates are 23.8 percent (including the net investment income tax). SHO will pay out its after-tax earnings every year as a dividend if it is formed as a C corporation. Assume Evon is the sole owner of the entity and she materially participates in the business. `LO 15-3`

    a) How much would Evon keep after taxes if SHO is organized as either an S corporation or as a C corporation?

    b) What are the overall tax rates if SHO is organized as either an S corporation or as a C corporation?

LO 15-3

54. Jack would like to organize PPS as either an LLC or as a C corporation generating an 11 percent annual before-tax return on a $100,000 investment. Assume Jack's marginal tax rate on earned income is 38 percent (including the .9 percent additional Medicare tax and 2.9 percent self-employment tax), corporate rates are 15 percent, and individual capital gains and dividends tax rates are 23.8 percent (including the 3.8 percent net investment income tax). PPS will distribute its after-tax earnings every year as a dividend if it is formed as a C corporation. Assume Jack is the sole owner of the entity and materially participates in the business.

a) How much would Jack keep after taxes if PPS is organized as either an LLC or as a C corporation?

b) What are the overall tax rates if PPS is organized as either an LLC or as a C corporation?

LO 15-3

research

55. Using the Web as a research tool, determine which countries levy a double tax on corporate income. Based on your research, what seem to be the pros and cons of the double tax?

LO 15-3

tax forms

56. Marathon Inc. (a C corporation) reported $1,000,000 of taxable income in the current year. During the year, it distributed $100,000 as dividends to its shareholders as follows:

- $5,000 to Guy, a 5 percent individual shareholder.
- $15,000 to Little Rock Corp., a 15 percent shareholder (C corporation).
- $80,000 to other shareholders.

a) How much of the dividend payment did Marathon deduct in determining its taxable income?

b) Assuming Guy's marginal ordinary tax rate is 35 percent, how much tax will he pay on the $5,000 dividend he received from Marathon Inc. (including the net investment income tax)?

c) Assuming Little Rock Corp.'s marginal tax rate is 34 percent, what amount of tax will it pay on the $15,000 dividend it received from Marathon Inc. (70 percent dividends received deduction)?

d) Complete Form 1120 Schedule C for Little Rock Corp. to reflect its dividends received deduction.

e) On what line of Little Rock Corp.'s Form 1120 page 1 is the dividend from Marathon Inc. reported, and on what line of Little Rock Corp.'s Form 1120 is its dividends received deduction reported?

LO 15-3

research

57. After several years of profitable operations, Javell, the sole shareholder of JBD Inc., a C corporation, sold 18 percent of her JBD stock to ZNO Inc., a C corporation in a similar industry. During the current year JBD reports $1,000,000 of after-tax income. JBD distributes all of its after-tax earnings to its two shareholders in proportion to their shareholdings. Assume ZNO's marginal tax rate is 35 percent. How much tax will ZNO pay on the dividend it receives from JBD? What is ZNO's overall tax rate on its dividend income? [*Hint:* See IRC §243(a).]

LO 15-3

58. For the current year, Custom Craft Services Inc. (CCS), a C corporation, reports taxable income of $200,000 before paying salary to Jaron the sole shareholder. Jaron's marginal tax rate on ordinary income is 35 percent and 15 percent on dividend income. Assume CCS's tax rate is 35 percent.

a) How much total income tax will Custom Craft Services and Jaron pay (combining both corporate and shareholder level taxes) on the $200,000 taxable income for the year if CCS doesn't pay any salary to Jaron and instead distributes all of its after-tax income to Jaron as a dividend (assume Jaron is not subject to the net investment income tax or the additional Medicare tax)?

b) How much total income tax will Custom Craft Services and Jaron pay (combining both corporate and shareholder level taxes) on the $200,000 of income if CCS pays Jaron a salary of $150,000 and distributes its remaining after-tax earnings to Jaron as a dividend (assume Jaron is not subject to the net investment income tax or the additional Medicare tax)?

c) Why is the answer to part (b) lower than the answer to part (a)?

59. For the current year, Maple Corporation, a C corporation, reports taxable income of $200,000 before paying salary to its sole shareholder Diane. Diane's marginal tax rate on ordinary income is 35.9 percent (including the additional Medicare tax) and 18.8 percent on dividend income (including the 3.8% net investment income tax). If Maple pays Diane a salary of $150,000 but the IRS determines that Diane's salary in excess of $80,000 is unreasonable compensation, what is the amount of the overall tax (corporate level + shareholder level) on Maple's $200,000 pre-salary income? Assume Maple's tax rate is 35 percent and it distributes all after-tax earnings to Diane. `LO 15-3`

60. Sandy Corp. projects that it will have taxable income of $150,000 for the year before paying any fringe benefits. Assume Karen, Sandy's sole shareholder, has a marginal tax rate of 35 percent on ordinary income and 15 percent on dividend income. Assume Sandy's tax rate is 35 percent. `LO 15-3`

    a) What is the amount of the overall tax (corporate level + shareholder level) on Sandy's $150,000 of pre-benefit income if Sandy Corp. does not pay out any fringe benefits and distributes all of its after-tax earnings to Karen (ignore the net investment income tax)?

    b) What is the amount of the overall tax on Sandy's $150,000 of pre-benefit income if Sandy Corp. pays Karen's adoption expenses of $10,000 and the payment is considered to be a nontaxable fringe benefit (ignore the net investment income tax)? Sandy Corp. distributes all of its after-tax earnings to Karen.

    c) What is the amount of the overall tax on Sandy's $150,000 of pre-benefit income if Sandy Corp. pays Karen's adoption expenses of $10,000 and the payment is considered to be a taxable fringe benefit (ignore the net investment income tax and the additional Medicare tax)? Sandy Corp. distributes all of its after-tax earnings to Karen.

61. Jabar Corporation, a C corporation, projects that it will have taxable income of $300,000 before incurring any lease expenses. Jabar's tax rate is 35 percent. Abdul, Jabar's sole shareholder, has a marginal tax rate of 39.6 percent on ordinary income and 20 percent on dividend income. Jabar always distributes all of its after-tax earnings to Abdul. `LO 15-3`

    a) What is the amount of the overall tax (corporate level + shareholder level) on Jabar Corp.'s $300,000 pre-lease expense income if Jabar Corp. does not lease property from Abdul and it distributes all of its after-tax earnings to its sole shareholder Abdul (include the net investment income tax in your calculations)?

    b) What is the amount of the overall tax on Jabar Corp.'s $300,000 pre-lease expense income if Jabar leases equipment from Abdul at a cost of $30,000 for the year (include the net investment income tax on the dividend and on the rental income received by Abdul)?

    c) What is the amount of the overall tax on Jabar Corp.'s $300,000 pre-lease expense income if Jabar Corp. leases equipment from Abdul at a cost of $30,000 for the year but the IRS determines that the fair market value of the lease payments is $25,000 (include the net investment income tax on the dividend and rental income received by Abdul)?

62. Nutt Corporation projects that it will have taxable income for the year of $400,000 before incurring any interest expense. Assume Nutt's tax rate is 35 percent. `LO 15-3`

    a) What is the amount of the overall tax (corporate level + shareholder level) on the $400,000 of preinterest expense earnings if Hazel, Nutt's sole shareholder, lends Nutt Corporation $30,000 at the beginning of the year, Nutt pays Hazel $8,000 of interest on the loan (interest is considered to be reasonable), and Nutt distributes all of its after-tax earnings to Hazel (ignore the net investment income tax)? Assume her ordinary marginal rate is 35 percent and dividend tax rate is 15 percent.

b) Assume the same facts as in part (a) except that the IRS determines that the fair market value of the interest should be $6,000. What is the amount of the overall tax on Nutt Corporation's preinterest expense earnings (ignore the net investment income tax)?

LO 15-3

research

63. Ultimate Comfort Blankets Inc. has had a great couple of years and wants to distribute its earnings while avoiding double taxation on its income. It decides to give its sole shareholder, Laura, a salary of $1,500,000 in the current year. What factors would the courts examine to determine if Laura's salary is reasonable? [*Hint:* See *Elliotts, Inc. v. Commissioner,* 716 F.2d 1241 (9th Cir. 1983)].

LO 15-3

64. Alice, the sole shareholder of QLP, decided that she would purchase a building and then lease it to QLP. She leased the building to QLP for $1,850 per month. However, the IRS determined that the fair market value of the lease payment should only be $1,600 per month. How would the lease payment be treated with respect to both Alice and QLP?

LO 15-3

65. In its first year of existence (year 1), SCC Corporation (a C corporation) reported a loss for tax purposes of $30,000. Using the corporate tax rate table, determine how much tax SCC will pay in year 2 if it reports taxable income from operations of $20,000 in year 2 before any loss carryovers.

LO 15-3

66. In its first year of existence (year 1), Willow Corp. (a C corporation) reported a loss for tax purposes of $30,000. In year 2 it reports a $40,000 loss. For year 3, it reports taxable income from operations of $100,000 before any loss carryovers. Using the corporate tax rate table, determine how much tax Willow Corp. will pay for year 3.

LO 15-3

research

planning

67. In its first year of existence (year 1), WCC Corporation (a C corporation) reported taxable income of $170,000 and paid $49,550 of federal income tax. In year 2, WCC reported a net operating loss of $40,000. WCC projects that it will report $800,000 of taxable income from its year 3 activities.

a) Based on its projections, should WCC carry back its year 2 NOL to year 1, or should it forgo the carryback and carry the year 2 NOL forward to year 3?

b) Assuming WCC corporation carries back its year 2 NOL to year 1, prepare a Form 1139 "Corporation Application for Tentative Refund" for WCC Corporation to reflect the NOL carryback. Use reasonable assumptions to fill in missing information.

LO 15-3

68. Damarcus is a 50 percent owner of Hoop (a business entity). In the current year, Hoop reported a $100,000 business loss. Answer the following questions associated with each of the following alternative scenarios.

a) Hoop is organized as a C corporation and Damarcus works full-time as an employee for Hoop. Damarcus has a $20,000 basis in his Hoop stock. How much of Hoop's loss is Damarcus allowed to deduct this year?

b) Hoop is organized as an LLC. Fifty percent of Hoop's loss is allocated to Damarcus. Damarcus works full-time for Hoop (he is not considered to be a passive investor in Hoop). Damarcus has a $20,000 basis in his Hoop ownership interest and he also has a $20,000 at-risk amount in his investment in Hoop. Damarcus does not report income or loss from any other business activity investments. How much of the $50,000 loss allocated to him by Hoop is Damarcus allowed to deduct this year?

c) Hoop is organized as an LLC. Fifty percent of Hoop's loss is allocated to Damarcus. Damarcus does not work for Hoop at all (he is a passive investor in Hoop). Damarcus has a $20,000 basis in his Hoop ownership interest and he also has a $20,000 at-risk amount in his investment in Hoop. Damarcus does not report income or loss from any other business activity investments. How much of the $50,000 loss allocated to him by Hoop is Damarcus allowed to deduct this year?

d) Hoop is organized as an LLC. Fifty percent of Hoop's loss is allocated to Damarcus. Damarcus works full-time for Hoop (he is not considered to be a passive investor in Hoop). Damarcus has a $70,000 basis in his Hoop ownership interest and he also has a $70,000 at-risk amount in his investment in Hoop. Damarcus does not report income or loss from any other business activity investments. How much of the $50,000 loss allocated to him by Hoop is Damarcus allowed to deduct this year?

e) Hoop is organized as an LLC. Fifty percent of Hoop's loss is allocated to Damarcus. Damarcus does not work for Hoop at all (he is a passive investor in Hoop). Damarcus has a $70,000 basis in his Hoop ownership interest and he also has a $70,000 at-risk amount in his investment in Hoop. Damarcus does not report income or loss from any other business activity investments. How much of the $50,000 loss allocated to him by Hoop is Damarcus allowed to deduct this year?

f) Hoop is organized as an LLC. Fifty percent of Hoop's loss is allocated to Damarcus. Damarcus does not work for Hoop at all (he is a passive investor in Hoop). Damarcus has a $20,000 basis in his Hoop ownership interest and he also has a $20,000 at-risk amount in his investment in Hoop. Damarcus reports $10,000 of income from a business activity in which he is a passive investor. How much of the $50,000 loss allocated to him by Hoop is Damarcus allowed to deduct this year?

69. Mickey, Mickayla, and Taylor are starting a new business (MMT). To get the business started, Mickey is contributing $200,000 for a 40 percent ownership interest, Mickayla is contributing a building with a value of $200,000 and a tax basis of $150,000 for a 40 percent ownership interest, and Taylor is contributing legal services for a 20 percent ownership interest. What amount of gain is each owner required to recognize under each of the following alternative situations? [*Hint:* Look at §351 and §721.]

LO 15-3

research

a) MMT is formed as a C corporation.

b) MMT is formed as an S corporation.

c) MMT is formed as a LLC.

70. Dave and his friend Stewart each own 50 percent of KBS. During the year, Dave receives $75,000 compensation for services he performs for KBS during the year. He performed a significant amount of work for the entity and he was heavily involved in management decisions (he was not a passive investor in KBS). After deducting Dave's compensation, KBS reports taxable income of $30,000. How much FICA and/or self-employment tax is Dave required to pay on his compensation and his share of the KBS income if KBS is formed as a C corporation, S corporation, or a limited liability company (ignore the .9 percent additional Medicare tax)?

LO 15-3

research

71. Rondo and his business associate, Larry, are considering forming a business entity called R&L but they are unsure about whether to form it as a C corporation, an S corporation, or as an LLC. Rondo and Larry would each invest $50,000 in the business. Thus, each owner would take an initial basis in his ownership interest of $50,000 no matter which entity type was formed. Shortly after the formation of the entity, the business borrowed $30,000 from the bank. If applicable, this debt is shared equally between the two owners.

LO 15-3

research

a) After taking the loan into account, what is Rondo's tax basis in his R&L stock if R&L is formed as a C corporation?

b) After taking the loan into account, what is Rondo's tax basis in his R&L stock if R&L is formed as an S corporation?

c) After taking the loan into account, what is Rondo's tax basis in his R&L ownership interest if R&L is formed as an LLC?

72. Kevin and Bob have owned and operated SOA as a C corporation for a number of years. When they formed the entity, Kevin and Bob each contributed $100,000 to SOA. They each have a current basis of $100,000 in their SOA ownership interest. Information on SOA's assets at the end of year 5 is as follows (SOA does not have any liabilities):

Assets	FMV	Adjusted Basis	Built-in Gain
Cash	$200,000	$200,000	$ 0
Inventory	80,000	40,000	40,000
Land and building	220,000	170,000	50,000
Total	$500,000		

At the end of year 5, SOA liquidated and distributed half of the land, half of the inventory, and half of the cash remaining after paying taxes (if any) to each owner. Assume that, excluding the effects of the liquidating distribution, SOA's taxable income for year 5 is $0. Also, assume that if SOA is required to pay tax, it pays at a flat 30 percent tax rate.

a) What is the amount and character of gain or loss SOA will recognize on the liquidating distribution?

b) What is the amount and character of gain or loss Kevin will recognize when he receives the liquidating distribution of cash and property? Recall that his stock basis is $100,000 and he is treated as having sold his stock for the liquidation proceeds.

COMPREHENSIVE PROBLEMS

Select problems are available with *Connect*®.

73. Dawn Taylor is currently employed by the state Chamber of Commerce. While she enjoys the relatively short workweeks, she eventually would like to work for herself rather than for an employer. In her current position, she deals with a lot of successful entrepreneurs who have become role models for her. Dawn has also developed an extensive list of contacts that should serve her well when she starts her own business.

It has taken a while but Dawn believes she has finally developed a viable new business idea. Her idea is to design and manufacture cookware that remains cool to the touch when in use. She has had several friends try out her prototype cookware and they have consistently given the cookware rave reviews. With this encouragement, Dawn started giving serious thoughts to making "Cool Touch Cookware" (CTC) a moneymaking enterprise.

Dawn has enough business background to realize that she is embarking on a risky path, but one, she hopes, with significant potential rewards down the road. After creating some initial income projections, Dawn realized that it will take a few years for the business to become profitable. After that, she hopes the sky's the limit. She would like to grow her business and perhaps at some point "go public" or sell the business to a large retailer. This could be her ticket to the rich and famous.

Dawn, who is single, decided to quit her job with the state Chamber of Commerce so that she could focus all of her efforts on the new business. Dawn had some savings to support her for a while but she did not have any other source of income. Dawn was able to recruit Linda and Mike to join her as initial equity investors in CTC. Linda has an MBA and a law degree. She was employed as a business consultant when she decided to leave that job and work with Dawn and Mike. Linda's husband earns around $300,000 a year as an engineer (employee). Mike owns a *very* profitable used car business. Because buying and selling used cars takes all his time, he is interested in becoming only a passive investor in CTC. He wanted to get in on the ground floor because he really likes the product and believes CTC will be wildly successful. While CTC originally has three investors, Dawn and Linda have plans to grow the business and seek more owners and capital in the future.

The three owners agreed that Dawn would contribute land and cash for a 30 percent interest in CTC, Linda would contribute services (legal and business advisory) for the first two years for a 30 percent interest, and Mike would contribute cash for a 40 percent interest. The plan called for Dawn and Linda to be actively involved in managing the business while Mike would not be. The three equity owners' contributions are summarized as follows:

Dawn Contributed	FMV	Adjusted Basis	Ownership Interest
Land (held as investment)	$120,000	$70,000	30%
Cash	30,000		
Linda Contributed			
Services	150,000		30
Mike Contributed			
Cash	200,000		40

Working together, Dawn and Linda made the following five-year income and loss projections for CTC. They anticipate the business will be profitable and that it will continue to grow after the first five years.

Cool Touch Cookware 5-Year Income and Loss Projections	
Year	Income (Loss)
1	$(200,000)
2	(80,000)
3	(20,000)
4	60,000
5	180,000

With plans for Dawn and Linda to spend a considerable amount of their time working for and managing CTC, the owners would like to develop a compensation plan that works for all parties. Down the road, they plan to have two business locations (in different cities). Dawn would take responsibility for the activities of one location and Linda would take responsibility for the other. Finally, they would like to arrange for some performance-based financial incentives for each location.

To get the business activities started, Dawn and Linda determined CTC would need to borrow $800,000 to purchase a building to house its manufacturing facilities and its administrative offices (at least for now). Also, in need of additional cash, Dawn and Linda arranged to have CTC borrow $300,000 from a local bank and to borrow $200,000 cash from Mike. CTC would pay Mike a market rate of interest on the loan but there was no fixed date for principal repayment.

Required:

Identify significant tax and nontax issues or concerns that may differ across entity types and discuss how they are relevant to the choice of entity decision for CTC.

research 74. Cool Touch Cookware (CTC) has been in business for about 10 years now. Dawn and Linda are each 50 percent owners of the business. They initially established the business with cash contributions. CTC manufactures unique cookware that remains cool to the touch when in use. CTC has been fairly profitable over the years. Dawn and Linda have both been actively involved in managing the business. They have developed very good personal relationships with many customers (both wholesale and retail) that, Dawn and Linda believe, keep the customers coming back.

On September 30 of the current year, CTC had all of its assets appraised. Below is CTC's balance sheet, as of September 30, with the corresponding appraisals of the fair market value of all of its assets. Note that CTC has several depreciated assets. CTC uses the hybrid method of accounting. It accounts for its gross margin-related items under the accrual method and it accounts for everything else using the cash method of accounting.

Assets	Adjusted Tax Basis	FMV
Cash	$150,000	$150,000
Accounts receivable	20,000	15,000
Inventory*	90,000	300,000
Equipment	120,000	100,000
Investment in XYZ stock	40,000	120,000
Land (used in the business)	80,000	70,000
Building	200,000	180,000
Total assets	$700,000	$935,000[†]
Liabilities		
Accounts payable	$ 40,000	
Bank loan	60,000	
Mortgage on building	100,000	
Equity	500,000	
Total liabilities and equity	$700,000	

*CTC uses the LIFO method for determining the adjusted basis of its inventory. Its basis in the inventory under the FIFO method would have been $110,000.
[†]In addition, Dawn and Linda had the entire business appraised at $1,135,000, which is $200,000 more than the value of the identifiable assets.

From January 1 of the current year through September 30, CTC reported the following income:

Ordinary business income	$530,000
Dividends from XYZ stock	12,000
Long-term capital losses	15,000
Interest income	3,000

Dawn and Linda are considering changing the business form of CTC.

Required:

a) Assume CTC is organized as a C corporation. Identify significant tax and nontax issues associated with converting CTC from a C corporation to an S corporation. [*Hint:* See IRC §1374 and §1363(d).]

b) Assume CTC is organized as a C corporation. Identify significant tax and nontax issues associated with converting CTC from a C corporation to an LLC. Assume CTC converts to an LLC by distributing its assets to its shareholders who then contribute the assets to a new LLC. [*Hint:* See IRC §§331, 336, and 721(a).]

c) Assume that CTC is a C corporation with a net operating loss carryforward as of the beginning of the year in the amount of $2,000,000. Identify significant tax and nontax issues associated with converting CTC from a C corporation to an LLC. Assume CTC converts to an LLC by distributing its assets to its shareholders who then contribute the assets to a new LLC. [*Hint:* See IRC §§172(a), 331, 336, and 721(a).]

16 Corporate Operations

Learning Objectives

Upon completing this chapter, you should be able to:

LO 16-1 Describe the corporate income tax formula, compare and contrast the corporate tax formula to the individual tax formula, and discuss tax considerations relating to corporations' accounting periods and accounting methods.

LO 16-2 Identify common book–tax differences, distinguish between permanent and temporary differences, and compute a corporation's taxable income and regular tax liability.

LO 16-3 Describe a corporation's tax return reporting and estimated tax payment obligations.

LO 16-4 Calculate a corporation's alternative minimum tax liability.

© Sam Edwards/age fotostock

Storyline Summary

Premiere Computer Corporation (PCC)
Medium-sized publicly traded company
Manufactures and sells computer-related equipment
Calendar-year taxpayer

Elise Brandon
Newly hired tax associate for a large public accounting firm
Currently assigned to prepare the federal income tax return for PCC

Today was Elise's first day on the job as a tax associate for a public accounting firm. Shortly after she arrived, Darryl, a tax manager, introduced himself and took Elise around the office to meet some of the people with whom she would be working. After the introductions, Darryl told Elise he would like her to work with him to prepare the tax return for Premiere Computer Corporation (PCC).

PCC is a medium-sized publicly traded taxable corporation (C corporation) that manufactures computers and computer equipment. It has been a client of the firm for several years. Overall, PCC has been a fairly profitable company, but last year it experienced a bit of a setback, incurring its first tax loss in many years.

Elise was excited about her opportunity, and she was confident her accounting education had adequately prepared her to successfully complete the assignment. In fact, her tax class was her favorite class. She had studied hard and learned all about computing corporate taxable income. When Elise spoke with Darryl about the assignment, he advised her to first review PCC's tax return and tax return workpapers from last year to get an idea how to prepare the return. Next, she should start with the audited numbers on the income statement and make book-to-tax adjustments for the items that are accounted for differently for book and tax purposes. Once she makes these adjustments, Elise should input the numbers into the firm's tax preparation software package to produce the return. Because Darryl would be reviewing the return, he encouraged Elise to stay in close contact and let him know if she had any questions.

to be continued . . .

This chapter explores computing and reporting taxable income for taxable corporations (also known as *C corporations*). As we discussed in the previous chapter, C corporations are legal and taxpaying entities separate from their owners. Each year, C corporations are required to compute their taxable income and pay tax on the income. In contrast to individuals, C corporations generally compute their taxable income by starting with their book (financial accounting) income and making adjustments for book–tax differences.

LO 16-1

CORPORATE TAXABLE INCOME FORMULA

The formula for computing corporate taxable income and individual taxable income is similar in some respects and different in others. Exhibit 16-1 presents the corporate income tax formula along with the individual tax formula for comparison purposes.

EXHIBIT 16-1   Corporate and Individual Tax Formulas

	Corporate Tax Formula	Individual Tax Formula
	Gross income	Gross income
Minus:	Deductions	*For AGI* deductions
Equals		Adjusted gross income
Minus:		*From AGI deductions*
		(1) *Greater* of:
		(a) Standard deduction or
		(b) Itemized deductions and
		(2) Personal and dependency exemptions
Equals	Taxable income	Taxable income
Times	Tax rates	Tax rates
Equals	Regular income tax liability	Regular income tax liability
Add	Other taxes	Other taxes
Equals	Total tax	Total tax
Minus	Credits	Credits
Minus	Prepayments	Prepayments
Equals	Taxes due (or refund)	Taxes due (or refund)

Corporations compute gross income as do other types of business entities and individual taxpayers. However, in contrast to individual taxpayers, corporations do not report adjusted gross income (AGI). Similar to other businesses, corporations are allowed to deduct ordinary and necessary business expenditures (see discussion in Chapter 9). In contrast to individual taxpayers, corporations treat all deductions as related to a trade or business and do not compute adjusted gross income. Corporations do not receive a standard deduction or exemptions. Consequently, the "formula" to compute a corporation's taxable income is relatively straightforward.

Accounting Periods and Methods

In Chapter 9, we discussed accounting periods and methods for all types of business entities. We learned that corporations measure their taxable income over a tax year and that their tax year must be the same as their financial accounting year. Corporations generally elect their tax year when they file their first income tax returns.

The timing of when corporations recognize income and deductions depends on their accounting methods. As we discussed in Chapter 9, accounting methods

---

THE KEY FACTS

Corporate Taxable Income Formula and Accounting Periods and Methods

- The corporate tax formula is similar to the individual tax formula, but corporations don't itemize deductions or deduct personal and dependency exemptions.
- Corporations with average gross receipts of $5 million or less over the three prior tax years (or a shorter period for new corporations) may use the cash method.

include overall methods of accounting (accrual method, cash method, or hybrid method) and accounting methods for individual items such as inventory (LIFO vs. FIFO) or depreciation (accelerated vs. straight line). For tax purposes, corporations have some flexibility in choosing methods of accounting for individual items or transactions. However, corporations generally are required to use the accrual over-all method of accounting.[1] For tax purposes, corporations with average gross receipts of $5 million or less for the three years prior to the current tax year may use the cash method of accounting.[2] Corporations that have not been in existence for at least three years compute their average gross receipts over the prior periods they have been in existence to determine if they are allowed to use the cash method of accounting.

TAXES IN THE REAL WORLD   Choosing Tax Accounting Methods

For certain transaction types, corporations face an interesting choice when choosing between permissible accounting methods. A corporation could choose an accounting method that tends to defer income or accelerate deductions from certain types of transactions or it could choose a method that tends to accelerate income or defer deductions. A research study by accounting professors provides evidence that when faced with this decision, publicly traded corporations tend to select income *accelerating* methods while privately held corporations tend to select income *deferring* methods.[3] Why the difference? Recall that generally speaking, the tax treatment of a transaction follows the book treatment. Publicly traded corporations are generally more concerned with increasing financial statement income to satisfy stockholders and potential investors. If corporations have to report higher levels of taxable income and pay more taxes as a result, that's OK. Privately held corporations are just the opposite. They don't need to impress the shareholders with accelerated earnings. They would rather reap the benefits of paying less current taxes even if it means reporting lower book income. This research illustrates the fact that nontax considerations may be more important than tax factors in the decision-making process. *After all, a business's objective should not be to minimize taxes but rather to maximize after-tax cash-flows.*

COMPUTING CORPORATE REGULAR TAXABLE INCOME   `LO 16-2`

To compute taxable income, most corporations begin with **book (financial reporting) income** and then make adjustments for book–tax differences to reconcile to the tax numbers.[4]

Book–Tax Differences

Many items of income and expense are accounted for differently for book and tax purposes. The following discussion describes several common **book–tax differences** applicable to corporations. Each book–tax difference can be considered to be

---

[1]See Chapter 9 for a detailed discussion of determining the timing of taxable income and tax deductions under the accrual method.

[2]§448. Other special types of corporations such as qualified family farming corporations and qualified personal service corporations may use the cash method of accounting.

[3]See C. B. Cloyd, J. Pratt, and T. Stock, "The Use of Financial Accounting Choice to Support Aggressive Tax Positions: Public and Private Firms," *Journal of Accounting Research* 34 (Spring 1996), pp. 23–43.

[4]This chapter generally assumes that GAAP is used to determine book income numbers.

"unfavorable" or "favorable" depending on its effect on taxable income relative to book income. Any book–tax difference that requires an add back to book income to compute taxable income is an **unfavorable book–tax difference** because it requires an adjustment that increases taxable income (and taxes payable) relative to book income. Any book–tax difference that requires corporations to subtract the difference from book income in computing taxable income is a **favorable book–tax difference** because it decreases taxable income (and taxes payable) relative to book income.

In addition to the favorable/unfavorable distinction, book–tax differences also can be categorized as permanent or temporary differences. **Permanent book–tax differences** arise from items that are income or deductions during the year for either book purposes or for tax purposes but not both. Permanent differences *do not reverse* over time, so over the long-term, the *total* amount of income or deductions for the items is different for book and tax purposes. In contrast, **temporary book–tax differences** are those book–tax differences that reverse over time such that over the long-term, corporations recognize the same amount of income or deductions for the items on their financial statements as they recognize on their tax returns. Temporary book–tax differences arise because the income or deduction items are included in financial accounting income in one year and in taxable income in a different year. It also is important to note that temporary book–tax differences that are *initially* favorable (unfavorable) subsequently will become unfavorable (favorable) in future years when they reverse.

Distinguishing between permanent and temporary book–tax differences is important for at least two reasons. First, as we discuss later in the chapter, large corporations are *required to disclose* their permanent and temporary book–tax differences on their tax returns. Second, the distinction is useful for those responsible for computing and tracking book–tax differences. For temporary book–tax differences, it is important to understand how the items were accounted for in previous years to appropriately account for current year reversals. In contrast, for permanent book–tax differences, corporations need only consider current year amounts to determine book–tax differences. Although small corporations often report only a few book–tax differences, large corporations frequently report hundreds. Below we describe some of the most common book–tax differences.

Common Permanent Book–Tax Differences

As we previously described in Chapter 9, businesses, including corporations, are allowed to exclude certain income items from gross income, and they are not allowed to deduct certain expenditures for tax purposes. Because these income items are included in book income, and the expenditures are deductible for financial reporting purposes, they generate permanent book–tax differences. Exhibit 16-2 identifies several permanent book–tax differences associated with items we discuss in Chapter 9, explains their tax treatment, and identifies whether the items create favorable or unfavorable book–tax differences.

Example 16-1

Elise reviewed PCC's prior-year tax return and its current-year trial balance. She discovered that PCC earned $12,000 of interest income from City of San Diego municipal bonds (bonds issued in 2013), expensed $34,000 for premiums on key employee life insurance policies, expensed $28,000 in meals and entertainment expenses for the year, and reported a domestic production activities deduction of $465,000. What amount of permanent book–tax differences does PCC report from these transactions? Are the differences favorable or unfavorable?

Answer: See Elise's summary of these items below:

Item	Adjustment (Favorable) Unfavorable	Notes
Interest income from City of San Diego municipal bonds (bonds issued in 2013)	($12,000)	Income excluded from gross income. Bond proceeds used to help fund *privately owned* baseball stadium.
Premiums paid for key employee life insurance policies	34,000	Premiums paid to insure lives of key company executives are not deductible for tax purposes.
Meals and entertainment	14,000	$28,000 expense for book purposes, but only 50 percent deductible for tax purposes.
Domestic production activities deduction	(465,000)	$5,166,667 qualified production activities income (QPAI) × 9%.

EXHIBIT 16-2   **Common Permanent Book–Tax Differences Associated with Items Discussed in Chapter 9**

Description	Explanation	Difference
Interest income from municipal bonds	Income included in book income, excluded from taxable income	Favorable
Death benefit from life insurance on key employees	Income included in book income, excluded from taxable income	Favorable
Interest expense on loans to acquire investments generating tax-exempt income	Deductible for books, but expenses incurred to generate tax-exempt income are not deductible for tax	Unfavorable
Life insurance premiums for which corporation is beneficiary	Deductible for books, but expenses incurred to generate tax-exempt income (life insurance death benefit) are not deductible for tax	Unfavorable
Meals and entertainment expenses	Fully deductible for books but only 50 percent deductible for tax	Unfavorable
Fines and penalties and political contributions	Deductible for books but not for tax	Unfavorable
Domestic production activities deduction (DPAD)	Deduction for businesses involved in manufacturing activities in the U.S. equal to the lesser of 9 percent of the company's qualified production activities income (QPAI) or taxable income computed without the DPAD (i.e., the DPAD cannot create a NOL)	Favorable

Federal income tax expense. Corporations deduct federal income tax expense (called a provision for income taxes) in determining their book income [determined under ASC (Accounting Standards Codification) 740 (the codification of FAS 109)]. However, they are not allowed to deduct federal income tax expense for tax purposes.[5] The book–tax provision acts as a permanent difference if the corporation is reconciling after-tax book income with taxable income.

[5]§275(a)(1).

Example 16-2

What if: Assume that PCC's audited financial reporting income statement indicates that its federal income tax provision (expense) is $2,000,000.[6] What is PCC's book–tax difference for the year associated with this expense? Is the difference favorable or unfavorable? Is it permanent or temporary?

Answer: $2,000,000 unfavorable, permanent book–tax difference because PCC is not allowed to deduct federal income tax expense for tax purposes.

Common Temporary Book–Tax Differences   Corporations experience temporary book–tax differences because the accounting methods they apply to determine certain items of income and expense for financial reporting purposes differ from those they use for tax purposes. Unlike permanent book–tax differences, temporary book–tax differences balance out over time so that corporations eventually recognize the same amount of income or deduction for the particular item. Exhibit 16-3

EXHIBIT 16-3   Common Temporary Book–Tax Differences Associated with Items Discussed in Other Chapters

Description	Explanation	Initial Difference*
Depreciation expense (Chapter 10)	Difference between accelerated depreciation expense for tax purposes and straight-line depreciation expense for book purposes.	Favorable
Gain or loss on disposition of depreciable assets (Chapter 11)	Difference between gain or loss for tax and book purposes when corporation sells or disposes of depreciable property. Difference generally arises because depreciation expense, and thus the adjusted basis of the asset, is different for tax and book purposes. This difference is essentially the reversal of the book–tax difference for the depreciation expense on the asset sold or disposed of.	Unfavorable
Bad debt expense (Chapter 9)	Direct write-off method for tax purposes, allowance method for book purposes.	Unfavorable
Unearned rent revenue (Chapter 9)	Taxable on receipt but recognized when earned for book purposes.	Unfavorable
Deferred compensation (Chapter 9)	Deductible when accrued for book purposes, but deductible when paid for tax purposes if accrued but not paid within 2.5 months after year-end. Also, accrued compensation to shareholders owning more than 50 percent of the corporation is not deductible until paid.	Unfavorable
Organizational expenses and start-up costs (Chapter 10)	Immediately deducted for book purposes but capitalized and amortized for tax purposes (limited immediate expensing allowed for tax).	Unfavorable
Warranty expense and other estimated expenses (Chapter 9)	Estimated expenses deducted for book purposes, but actual expenses deducted for tax purposes.	Unfavorable
UNICAP (§263A) (Chapter 9)	Certain expenditures deducted for book purposes, but capitalized to inventory for tax purposes. Difference reverses when inventory is sold.	Unfavorable

*Note that each of the initial book–tax differences will reverse over time [the initially favorable (unfavorable) book–tax differences will reverse to become unfavorable (favorable) book–tax differences in the future].

[6]Note that this example is presented in what-if form because this is not the income tax expense PCC will report in its financial statements. We compute PCC's actual income tax expense in Chapter 17.

identifies common book–tax differences associated with items we discuss in other chapters. Exhibit 16-4 summarizes PCC's temporary book–tax differences described in Exhibit 16-3.

EXHIBIT 16-4 PCC's Temporary Book–Tax Differences Associated with Items Discussed in Other Chapters

Item	(1) Books (Dr) Cr	(2) Tax (Dr) Cr	(2) – (1) Difference (Favorable) Unfavorable
Depreciation expense	($2,400,000)	($3,100,000)	($700,000)
Gain on fixed asset disposition	54,000	70,000	16,000
Bad debt expense	(165,000)	(95,000)	70,000
Warranty expense	(580,000)	(410,000)	170,000
Deferred compensation	(300,000)	(450,000)	(150,000)

Dividends. Corporations receiving dividends from other corporations may account for the dividends in different ways for book and tax purposes. For tax purposes, corporations receiving dividends include the dividends in gross income.[7] For financial reporting purposes, accounting for the dividend (and investment in the corporation) depends on the level of ownership in the distributing corporation. The *general* rules for such investments are summarized as follows:

- If the receiving corporation owns less than 20 percent of the stock of the distributing corporation, the receiving corporation includes the dividend in income (same as tax; no book–tax difference).
- If the receiving corporation owns at least 20 percent but not more than 50 percent of the distributing corporation's stock, the receiving corporation usually includes a pro rata portion of the distributing corporation's earnings in its book income under the "equity method of accounting" (ASC 323) and does not include the dividend in its income (temporary favorable or unfavorable book–tax difference for the difference between the pro rata share of income and the dividend amount).
- If the receiving corporation owns more than 50 percent of the distributing corporation's stock, the receiving corporation and the distributing corporation usually consolidate their financial reporting books (ASC 810) and the intercompany dividend is eliminated (book–tax difference beyond the scope of the text).[8]

Example 16-3

What if: Assume that PCC owns 30 percent of the stock of BCS corporation and applies the equity method of accounting for book purposes. During 2016, BCS distributed a $40,000 dividend to PCC. BCS reported $100,000 of net income for 2016. Based on this information, what is PCC's 2016 book–tax difference relating to the dividend and its investment in BCS (ignore the dividends received deduction)? Is the difference favorable or unfavorable?

(continued on page 16-8)

---

[7]As we discuss later in the chapter, corporations are entitled to deduct a certain percentage of the dividends received based on the level of the receiving corporation's ownership in the distributing corporation.

[8]Note that 80 percent ownership is required to file a consolidated tax return.

Answer: $10,000 unfavorable book–tax difference, computed as follows:

Description	Amount	Explanation
(1) Dividend received in 2016 (included in 2016 taxable income but not in book income)	$ 40,000	
(2) BCS 2016 net income	$100,000	
(3) PCC's ownership in BCS stock	30%	
(4) PCC's book income from BCS investment	$ 30,000	(2) × (3).
Unfavorable book–tax difference associated with dividend	**$ 10,000**	(1) – (4).

What if: Assume the same facts as above, except that PCC owns 10 percent of BCS rather than 30 percent. What would be PCC's 2016 book–tax difference relating to the dividend and its investment in BCS (ignore the dividends received deduction)?

Answer: $0. PCC includes the $40,000 dividend in income for both book and tax purposes.

Goodwill acquired in an asset acquisition. When a corporation acquires the *assets* of another business in a taxable transaction, and it allocates part of the purchase price to goodwill (excess purchase price over the fair market value of identifiable assets acquired), the corporation is allowed to amortize this purchased goodwill on a straight-line basis over 15 years (180 months) for tax purposes.[9] For book purposes, corporations acquiring the assets of another business also allocate part of the purchase price to goodwill. Generally speaking in these asset acquisitions, the amount of goodwill corporations recognize for tax purposes can be the same as or different from the amount they recognize for book purposes. Corporations recover the cost of goodwill for book purposes only when and only to the extent the goodwill is impaired. Thus, to determine the *temporary* book–tax difference associated with purchased goodwill, corporations generally compare the amount of goodwill they amortize for tax purposes with the goodwill impairment expense for book purposes. If the tax amortization exceeds the book impairment expense, corporations report favorable book–tax differences. If the book impairment expense exceeds the goodwill tax amortization, corporations report unfavorable book–tax differences for goodwill.[10]

Example 16-4

What if: Suppose that on July 1, 2016, PCC acquired the assets of another business in a taxable acquisition. As part of the transaction, PCC recognized $180,000 of goodwill for both financial accounting and tax purposes. During 2016, PCC amortized $6,000 of the goodwill for tax purposes ($180,000/180 months × 6 months during year) and did not impair any of the goodwill for financial accounting purposes. What was PCC's book–tax difference associated with this goodwill in 2016? Is it a favorable or unfavorable difference? Is the difference permanent or temporary?

Answer: $6,000 favorable, temporary book–tax difference. The amount of capitalized goodwill is the same for book and tax purposes and PCC deducted $6,000 of the goodwill for tax purposes and none for book purposes.

What if: Assume that at the end of 2017, PCC determined that the carrying value of the goodwill had been reduced to $150,000. That is, PCC experienced a $30,000 impairment expense to its goodwill. What is PCC's book–tax difference associated with its goodwill during 2017? Is the difference favorable or unfavorable? Is the difference permanent or temporary?

---

[9]§197. Self-created goodwill is not amortizable for tax purposes.

[10]When corporations acquire the stock of another corporation, they often recognize book goodwill but do not recognize any tax goodwill. When this book goodwill is written off as impaired, it generates a permanent unfavorable book–tax difference. Beginning in 2016, private companies can elect to amortize book goodwill over 10 years or less.

Answer: $18,000 unfavorable, temporary book–tax difference, computed as follows:

Description	Amount	Explanation
(1) Goodwill initially recorded on 7/1/16 acquisition	$180,000	
(2) Goodwill impairment recorded in 2017	$ 30,000	This write-down is expensed for book purposes.
(3) Months over which goodwill amortized for tax purposes.	180	15 years × 12 months = 180 months.
(4) Tax goodwill amortization expense for 2017	$ 12,000	[(1)/(3)] × 12 months.
Unfavorable book–tax temporary difference associated with goodwill in 2017.	**$ 18,000**	(2) – (4).

Corporate-Specific Deductions and Associated Book–Tax Differences

Certain deductions and corresponding limitations apply specifically to corporations. In this section, we introduce these deductions and identify book–tax differences associated with the deductions.

Stock Options Corporations often compensate executives and other employees with stock options. Stock options allow recipients to acquire stock in the corporation issuing the options at a predetermined price over a specified period of time. To acquire the stock, employees exercise the options and pay the **exercise price.** The exercise price is usually at or above the stock price on the day the options are issued to the employee. For example, at a time when a corporation's stock is trading for $10 per share, a corporation might issue (or grant) 100 stock options to an employee that allow the employee to purchase up to 100 shares of the corporation's stock for $10 a share. In most cases, employees must wait a certain amount of time (requisite service period) between when they receive the options and when they are able to exercise them (i.e., they must wait until the options **vest** before they can exercise them). If employees quit working for the corporation before the options vest, they forfeit the options.

Stock options are valuable to employees when the stock price appreciates above the exercise price because, when the options vest, employees can use the options to purchase the stock at a price below the market price. Stock options are a popular form of compensation because they provide incentives for employees receiving the options to work to increase the value of the corporation and thereby benefit themselves and the other stockholders.

For tax purposes, the tax treatment to the corporation (and the employee[11]) depends on whether the options are **incentive stock options** (ISOs) (less common, more administrative requirements for the corporation to qualify) or **nonqualified stock options** (NQOs) (more common, options that don't qualify as ISOs).[12] Corporations issuing incentive stock options do not deduct compensation expense associated with the options for tax purposes unless the employee "disqualifies" (intentionally fails one of the administrative requirements), in which case the exercised option becomes deductible. In contrast, for nonqualified options, corporations deduct the difference between the fair market value of the stock and the exercise price of the option (the **bargain element**) as compensation expense in the year in which employees exercise the stock options.

[11]Employees do not recognize any income when they exercise incentive stock options. However, for nonqualified options, they recognize ordinary income for the difference between the value of the stock and the exercise price on the date of exercise. This chapter emphasizes the tax treatment of the options from the corporation's perspective.

[12]Requirements for options to qualify as incentive stock options are more restrictive than for nonqualified stock options. The formal requirements for incentive stock options are beyond the scope of this chapter.

For financial accounting purposes, corporations generally were not required to expense stock options until 2006. Consequently, corporations do not report a book–tax difference for *incentive* stock options granted before 2006, and they report favorable, *permanent* book–tax differences for the bargain element of *nonqualified* stock options they granted *before* 2006 (when the options are exercised).

Under ASC 718, corporations are required to recognize *book expense* for stock options they grant after 2005.[13] Corporations granting stock options *after 2005* are required to estimate the fair value of the options at the time they issue them (i.e., the **grant date**). They deduct the estimated fair value of the options as the employee services are received **(requisite service period),** which is presumed to be the **vesting period.** Book–tax differences for options granted after 2005 may be permanent, temporary, or a combination of both. For incentive stock options, the amount of the permanent difference is the estimated value of the stock option that is expensed pro rata over the vesting period during the year. The book–tax difference associated with incentive stock options is always unfavorable.

Example 16-5

What if: Assume that on January 1, 2016, PCC issued 10,000 incentive stock options (ISOs) with an estimated fair value of $6 per option. Each option entitles the owner to purchase one share of PCC stock for $15 a share (the per share price of PCC stock on January 1, 2016, when the options were granted). The options vest at the end of four years. What would be PCC's 2016 book–tax difference associated with the incentive stock options? Would the difference be favorable or unfavorable? Would the difference be permanent or temporary?

Answer: $15,000 unfavorable, permanent difference (10,000 options × $6 estimated fair value = $60,000 / 4-year service period). This is the book deduction for the ISOs. PCC does not deduct compensation expense relating to the ISOs for tax purposes.

Nonqualified options (NQOs) generate temporary book–tax differences. Corporations *initially* recognize *temporary* book–tax differences associated with stock options for the fair value of options spread over the employees' requisite service period. This initial temporary difference is always *unfavorable* because the corporation deducts the fair value of the options over the requisite service period for book purposes but does not deduct compensation expense for tax purposes until the employees exercise the stock option. This initial unfavorable temporary book–tax difference *generally* becomes a favorable temporary book-tax difference when employees *actually exercise* the stock options (assuming the amount of the tax deduction at the exercise date exceeds the estimated fair value of the NQOs at the grant date).

When an employee exercises the NQO, the tax deduction, which is the difference between the fair market value of the stock purchased less the option price, likely will differ from the compensation expense recorded on the income statement over the requisite service period. If the tax deduction exceeds the previously recorded book deduction, the tax benefit from the excess deduction (called a *"windfall tax benefit"*) is recorded in shareholders' equity as an addition to paid-in capital (APIC). If the tax deduction is less than the previously recorded book deduction, the tax detriment from the excess book deduction (called a *"shortfall"*) reduces the existing windfall tax benefit pool in APIC with any excess charged to the income statement. The tax windfall or shortfall from an NQO exercise acts as a permanent difference, although it generally does not impact the income statement. In November 2015, the FASB affirmed its intention to require all excess tax benefits and tax deficiencies to be recognized as income tax expense or benefit in the income statement in the period in which the stock option was exercised. A full discussion of this complicated topic is beyond the scope of this chapter.

---

[13]ASC 718 is effective for years beginning after June 15, 2005, for large publicly traded corporations and for years beginning after December 15, 2005, for small publicly traded corporations and nonpublicly traded entities. Corporations could have elected to expense stock options for book purposes before the effective date of ASC 718.

Example 16-6

On January 1, 2016, PCC granted 20,000 nonqualified options with an estimated $10 fair value per option ($200,000 total fair value). Each option entitled the recipient to purchase one share of PCC stock for $20 a share (the per share price of PCC stock on January 1, 2016, when the options were granted). The options vested at the end of the day on December 31, 2017 (employees could not exercise options in 2016 or 2017). What is PCC's book–tax difference associated with the nonqualified options in 2016? in 2017? Is the difference favorable or unfavorable? Is it permanent or temporary?

Answer: $100,000 unfavorable, temporary book–tax difference in both 2016 and 2017. PCC reports $100,000 of compensation expense for book purposes in 2016 and 2017 ($200,000 / 2-year vesting period) and $0 for tax purposes (the options were not exercised in 2016 or 2017).

What if: Assume the same facts as above and that on March 1, 2018, employees exercised all 20,000 options at a time when the PCC stock was trading at $30 per share. What is PCC's book–tax difference associated with the stock options in 2018? Is it a permanent difference or a temporary difference? Is it favorable or unfavorable?

Answer: $200,000 favorable, temporary book–tax difference in 2018. PCC gets a $200,000 tax deduction in 2018, equal to the number of shares exercised times the bargain element of $10 per option exercised ($30 - $20). The favorable book–tax difference is a complete reversal of the unfavorable book–tax differences in 2016 and 2017.

What if: Assume that on March 1, 2017, employees exercised all 20,000 options at a time when the PCC stock was trading at $35 per share. What is PCC's book–tax difference associated with the stock options in 2018? Is it a permanent difference or a temporary difference? Is it favorable or unfavorable?

Answer: $300,000 favorable book–tax difference in 2018. The $300,000 difference consists of a $200,000 favorable, temporary difference (the reversal of the prior years' unfavorable, temporary differences) and a $100,000 "*windfall tax benefit*" that is recorded as an increase in PCC's additional paid-in capital. The *windfall tax benefit* is the bargain element on the 20,000 options in excess of the estimated value of the options for book purposes [($15 – $10) × 20,000 options]. Under the FASB's expected change to ASC 718, the $100,000 excess tax benefit will be treated as a permanent difference in the computation of PCC's income tax provision.

Exhibit 16-5, which appears on the next page, summarizes the book and tax treatment of stock options both before and after ASC 718 became effective.

TAXES IN THE REAL WORLD   Facebook's Billion Dollar NQO Tax Benefit

When Facebook filed its Registration Statement for its Initial Public Offering in February 2012, it was revealed that CEO Mark Zuckerberg had been granted nonqualifying stock options (NQOs) to purchase 120 million additional shares of the company for 6 cents per share. The company also informed potential investors that Mr. Zuckerberg intended to exercise these options when the company became a publicly traded company. Mr. Zuckerberg subsequently exercised his option to purchase 60 million additional Facebook shares prior to the IPO at a time when the value of the shares was $2,276,677,500. This transaction simultaneously created a tax deduction for Facebook and compensation income to Mr. Zuckerberg of approximately $2,273 million (fair value of the Facebook stock on the exercise date less the exercise price)! The company's tax

benefit of $800 million also created an $800 million tax bill to Mr. Zuckerberg. In total, employees of Facebook exercised 135.5 million NQOs in 2012, resulting in a tax benefit to the company of more than $1 billion, of which $451 million was recovered as a refund for taxes paid in 2010–2011. The cash proceeds received by the company from the employees exercise of the NQOs was only $17 million.

The publicity surrounding the stock option exercise by Mr. Zuckerberg and the subsequent deduction granted to Facebook did not go unnoticed in Congress. Then Senator Carl Levin of Michigan expressed outrage that a "profitable" U.S. company could eliminate its tax liability because of the tax deduction granted (legally) by the U.S. tax laws. Senator Levin emphasized that Facebook's actions were within the tax

(*continued on page 16-12*)

law, but exclaimed that "As with so much of our tax code, it's not the law-breaking that shocks the conscience, it's the stuff that's perfectly legal." Of course, Senator Levin neglected to mention that the income taxes saved by Facebook were offset by the income taxes paid by Mr. Zuckerberg.

In 2014, executives from Facebook continued to exercise their stock options and provided the company with excess tax benefits of more than $1.8 billion dollars! Under current accounting rules, these excess benefits were recorded in shareholders equity and did not reduce the company's income tax provision. As a result, Facebook reported an accounting effective tax rate of 40.1%. If these tax benefits had reduced the company's income tax expense, as the FASB has proposed, the company's accounting effective tax rate would have been 3.5%! Which effective tax rate do you think better represents the company's tax status?

Source: All of the information is publicly available on Facebook's Form 10-K and Proxy Statement for 2012 and 2014.

EXHIBIT 16-5 **Book and Tax Treatment of Stock Options Before and After ASC 718 Effective Date**

Description	Book Deduction	Tax Deduction	Book–Tax Difference
Pre ASC 718			
Incentive stock option	No deduction	No deduction	None
Nonqualified stock option	No deduction	Bargain element*	Favorable, permanent
Under ASC 718			
Incentive stock option	Initial estimated fair value of stock options / requisite service period	No deduction	Unfavorable, permanent
Nonqualified stock option (in years before exercise)	Initial estimated fair value of stock options / requisite service period	No deduction until exercise	Unfavorable, temporary
Nonqualified stock option (in year of exercise)	Initial estimated fair value of stock options / requisite service period	Bargain element*	Favorable, temporary reversing unfavorable, temporary difference in prior years
			Favorable, permanent difference if the bargain element exceeds the initial estimated value of stock options, unfavorable permanent difference otherwise

*The bargain element is the difference between the fair market value of the stock and the exercise price on the date the employee exercises the stock options.

Net Capital Losses For corporations, all net capital gains (long- and short-term) are taxed at ordinary income rates. Yet, corporations still generally prefer capital gains to ordinary income because corporations can only deduct capital losses *to the extent they recognize capital gains* in a particular year.[14] That is, corporations cannot deduct net capital losses. In contrast, individuals can deduct up to $3,000 of net capital losses in a year against ordinary income.[15]

When corporations recognize net capital losses for a year, they are permitted to carry the capital losses back three years (called a **net capital loss carryback**) and forward five years (called a **net capital loss carryover**) to offset net capital gains in the three years

---

[14]§1211(a).

[15]§1211(b). Individuals are also allowed to carry net capital losses forward indefinitely.

preceding the current tax year and then to offset net capital gains in the five years subsequent to the current tax year.[16] The capital loss carrybacks and carryovers must be applied in a particular order. If a corporation reports a net capital loss in year 4, it must first carry back the loss to year 1, then year 2, and then year 3. If the net capital loss remains after the carryback period, the corporation carries the loss forward to year 5 first, then year 6, year 7, year 8, and finally year 9. If the capital loss carryover has not been fully absorbed by the end of the fifth year after it was incurred (year 9), the carryover expires unused.

Although corporations may carry back net capital losses, they may not *carry back* a capital loss to a year if doing so creates or increases the net operating loss of the corporation (excess of deductions over income) in the year to which it is carried back (see discussion of net operating losses in the next section).[17]

For financial reporting purposes, corporations deduct net capital losses in the year they are incurred. Thus, corporations recognizing net capital losses report unfavorable book–tax differences in the year they recognize the losses and favorable book–tax differences in the year they use capital loss carrybacks or carryovers.

Example 16-7

During 2016, PCC sold Intel stock at a $12,000 gain and also reported a $40,000 capital loss on the disposition of land held for investment. PCC has not recognized a net capital gain or loss since 2011. PCC has a net operating loss carryover from 2015. What is PCC's net capital loss for the year?

Answer: $28,000 loss; [$12,000 + ($40,000)]. Because PCC had not recognized any net capital gains in 2013, 2014, and 2015 it may not carry back the loss (note that PCC could not carry back the loss to 2016 in any event because it recognized a net operating loss in that year as evidenced by its net operating loss carryover from 2015).

What amount of book–tax difference does this loss trigger? Is the difference favorable or unfavorable? Is it temporary or permanent?

Answer: $28,000 unfavorable, temporary book tax difference.

What if: Assume that in 2016, PCC reported a net capital loss of $28,000 and that it reported a $7,000 net capital gain in 2013, no net capital gain or loss in 2014, and a $4,000 net capital gain in 2015. What is the amount of its net capital loss carryover to 2017? PCC reported a net operating loss in 2015 but did not report a net operating loss in either 2013 or 2014.

Answer: $21,000. PCC first carries back the $28,000 loss to 2013, offsetting the $7,000 net capital gain in that year. PCC then carries the remaining $21,000 loss [($28,000) + $7,000] back to 2015. However, because PCC reported a net operating loss in 2015, it is not allowed to offset the $4,000 net capital gain with the capital loss carryback. Consequently, the $21,000 unused capital loss carryover is carried forward to 2017.

What if: Suppose PCC did not recognize any net capital gains in prior years but that next year (2017) it recognizes a net capital gain of $5,000 (before considering any capital loss carryovers). What will be its book–tax difference associated with capital gains and losses next year? Is it favorable or unfavorable? Is it temporary or permanent?

Answer: Next year, PCC would report a $5,000 favorable, temporary book–tax difference because it would be allowed to deduct $5,000 of its $28,000 capital loss carryover for tax purposes. This is a reversal of $5,000 of the unfavorable $28,000 book–tax difference from the prior year.

Net Operating Losses   Compare the tax burden of Corporation A and Corporation B. Corporation A reports $1,000,000 of taxable income and pays $340,000 of tax in year 1 and again in year 2 (see corporate tax rate schedule inside of the back cover). In contrast, Corporation B reports $4,000,000 of taxable income in year 1 and a $2,000,000 loss in year 2. Absent any special tax provisions, Corporation B would pay

---

[16]§1212(a).

[17]§1212(a)(1)(A)(ii). To allow a corporation to carry back a net capital loss to absorb capital gains in a net operating loss year would increase the NOL carry forward by the amount of the net capital loss used to offset the capital gain. This freed-up NOL would have a 20-year carryover rather than the 5-year carryover of the net capital loss.

$1,360,000 of tax in year 1 and no tax in year 2. Over the same two-year period both Corporation A and Corporation B reported $2,000,000 of (net) taxable income, yet Corporation B paid twice the tax Corporation A paid ($1,360,000 vs. $680,000). The inequity for Corporation B is that, because it is required to report taxable income on an annual basis, it would receive no tax benefit for its $2,000,000 loss (deductions in excess of gross income) in year 2. To ease the tax burden on corporations that aren't consistently profitable (for tax purposes), the tax laws allow corporations that report deductions in excess of gross income in a particular year to carry back or carry over the excess deductions to reduce taxable income and taxes payable in years when gross income exceeds deductions. This excess of deductions over gross income is referred to as a **net operating loss (NOL).** A corporation's net operating loss for the current year is the excess of its deductions over its gross income with the following adjustments:

- A corporation does not deduct an NOL generated in another year in determining its current year NOL.
- A corporation may deduct a capital loss carryover against a net capital gain arising in the current year in determining its NOL but it may not deduct a capital loss carryback against a net capital gain in determining its NOL.
- A corporation does not deduct the domestic production activities deduction in determining its NOL.

Corporations can carry current year net operating losses back **(net operating loss carrybacks)** 2 years and forward **(net operating loss carryovers)** 20 years to offset taxable income and reduce taxes payable (or already paid) in those years. Corporations that carry back losses to offset taxable income in prior years can file for and receive an immediate refund of taxes they paid on this income using Form 1139. When corporations carry a loss back, they must first carry it back to the year 2 years before the current year.

Example 16-8

What if: Assume that in 2016 PCC reported a $300,000 net operating loss. In addition, PCC reported the following taxable income from 2013 through 2015:

	2013	2014	2015
Taxable income	$90,000	$45,000	$250,000

If PCC carries back its NOL, what is its NOL carryover to 2017?

Answer: $5,000 carryover. PCC first carries the 2016 NOL back to 2014 reducing its 2014 taxable income to $0 and reducing the NOL carryback/over to $255,000 ($300,000 − $45,000). PCC receives a refund for taxes it paid in 2014. It then carries the remaining $255,000 NOL back to 2015 reducing 2015 taxable income to $0. PCC receives a refund for tax it paid in 2015. This leaves a $5,000 NOL carryover (from 2016) to 2017 ($255,000 − $250,000).

What if: Assume that in 2016 PCC reported $120,000 of deductions and $90,000 of gross income (including $6,000 of net capital gain). PCC also has a $15,000 NOL carryover from 2015 and an $8,000 net capital loss carryover from 2015. What are PCC's net operating loss and capital loss carryovers to 2017 and when do they expire?

Answer: $15,000 net operating loss carryover from 2015 that expires at the end of 2035 if unused, a $36,000 net operating loss carryover from 2016 that expires at the end of 2036 if unused, and a $2,000 net capital loss carryover from 2015 that expires at the end of 2020 if unused. PCC's 2015 NOL is unused in 2016 because PCC reports an NOL in 2016 and it does not deduct NOL carryovers in determining its 2016 NOL. In 2016, PCC is able to offset the $6,000 net capital gain included in gross income with $6,000 of the $8,000 net capital loss carryover from 2015. This reduces PCC's gross income to $84,000 ($90,000 − $6,000) and increases its deductions in excess of gross income (its current year NOL) to $36,000 ($120,000 − $84,000). Finally, PCC's 2015 capital loss carryover is reduced by the $6,000 absorbed portion to $2,000 ($8,000 minus $6,000 used in 2016).

A corporation with a current net operating loss can elect to forgo the carryback option and instead carry the net operating loss forward to future years. From a tax-planning perspective, why would a corporation elect to forgo the carryback if it had taxable income in previous years? In deciding whether to forgo the carryback, corporations must evaluate the tax savings the NOL will generate if they carry the losses back and the tax savings they will generate if they carry them forward. If a carryback will offset income that was taxed at a low marginal tax rate, it may make sense for the corporation to forgo the carryback and carry the NOL forward to offset income that would otherwise be taxed at a higher rate in upcoming years. Tax savings notwithstanding, corporations carrying back losses receive immediate cash while corporations forgoing the carryback do not.

Example 16-9

What if: Suppose that PCC generates a $50,000 net operating loss in the current year (year 1) and that last year (year 0) it reported taxable income of $50,000 and paid $7,500 in taxes. Next year, PCC expects to earn $335,000 of taxable income. How much more tax savings will PCC realize by electing to forgo the NOL carryback (ignore the time value of money)?

Answer: $12,000 [$50,000 × (39% − 15%)]. If PCC carries the loss back, it offsets $50,000 of income that was taxed at 15%. If it decides to forgo the carryback, the carryover to next year will offset $50,000 of income that would be taxed at 39%. Note, however, that PCC will immediately receive the $7,500 if it carries the loss back. It will have to wait to get its tax savings if it elects to forgo the carryback.

For financial reporting purposes, corporations report losses in the year they incur them. Consequently corporations report unfavorable temporary book–tax difference in the year they generate NOLs. However, because corporations do not deduct NOL carrybacks or NOL carryovers in determining book income, they report favorable *temporary* book–tax differences in the year they deduct the NOL carrybacks or carryovers for tax purposes. A corporation reports its NOL carryforwards on Schedule K to Form 1120.

Example 16-10

What if: Assume that last year PCC incurred a $24,000 net operating loss. Last year's NOL becomes an NOL carryover to this year that is available to reduce its current-year taxable income. What is PCC's current-year book–tax difference associated with its NOL carryover? Is the difference favorable or unfavorable? Is it permanent or temporary?

Answer: $24,000 favorable, temporary book–tax difference. The net operating loss carryover from the prior year is deductible for tax purposes but not for book purposes.

Charitable Contributions Similar to individuals, corporations are allowed to deduct charitable contributions to qualified charitable organizations.[18] However, the deduction and timing limitations are a little different for corporations than they are for individual taxpayers. Generally, corporations are allowed to deduct the amount of money they contribute, the fair market value of **capital gain property** they donate (property that would generate long-term capital gain if sold), and the adjusted basis of **ordinary income property** they donate (property that if sold would generate income taxed at ordinary rates). This chapter emphasizes the tax consequences of cash donations by corporations to qualified charities.[19] Generally, corporations are allowed

[18]The IRS has a database of qualifying charities on its Web site (http://www.irs.gov/Charities-&-Non-Profits/Organizations-Eligible-to-Receive-Tax-Deductible-Charitable-Contributions). Qualifying organizations tend to be those engaging in educational, scientific, governmental, and other public activities.

[19]For more details on the tax consequences of charitable contributions, see §170.

to deduct charitable contributions at the time they make payment to charitable organizations (subject to an overall taxable income limitation we discuss below). However, corporations using the accrual method of accounting can deduct contributions in the year *before* they actually pay the contribution when (1) their board of directors approves the payment and (2) they actually pay the contributions within three and one-half months of their tax year (beginning for tax years after 2015).[20]

Example 16-11

On December 1, 2016, the PCC board of directors approved a $110,000 cash contribution to the American Red Cross (ARC). For financial reporting purposes, PCC accrued and expensed the donation in 2016. PCC transferred the cash to the ARC on March 1, 2017. Does PCC report a book–tax difference associated with the charitable contribution (assume the taxable income limitation does not apply)?

Answer: No book–tax difference. For tax purposes, as an accrual-method taxpayer PCC may deduct the $110,000 contribution in 2016 because it paid the donation to the ARC within three and one-half months after year-end.

What if: Assume the same facts as above, except that PCC transferred the cash to the ARC on April 31, 2017. Does PCC report a book–tax difference associated with the charitable contribution (assume the taxable income limitation does not apply)?

Answer: Yes, PCC reports a $110,000 unfavorable, temporary book–tax difference in 2016. Beginning in 2016, a calendar year-end corporation such as PCC must pay the charitable contribution by the 15th day of the fourth month after its year-end (April 15). This book-tax difference will reverse and become a $110,000 favorable, temporary book–tax difference in 2017 when PCC deducts the contribution for tax purposes.

THE KEY FACTS

Charitable Contributions

- Charitable contribution deductions
  - Deductible when they accrue if approved by board of directors and paid within 3.5 months of year-end (2.5 months for corporations with a June 30 year-end and taxable years before 2016).
- Deductions limited to 10 percent of charitable contribution deduction modified taxable income.
- Contributions in excess of 10 percent limit carried forward up to five years.

A corporation's deductible charitable contributions for the year may not exceed 10 percent of its **charitable contribution limit modified taxable income**. A corporation's charitable contribution limit modified taxable income is its taxable income *before* deducting the following:

1. *Any* charitable contributions.
2. The dividends received deduction (DRD) (discussed below).
3. NOL *carrybacks.*
4. The domestic production activities deduction (DPAD).
5. Capital loss *carrybacks.*

Note that capital loss and NOL *carryovers are deductible* in determining charitable contribution limit modified taxable income. Capital loss and NOL *carrybacks* are *not deductible* for charitable contribution limitation purposes because they are unknown when corporations must determine the limitation (they arise in a future year).

Due to the 10 percent limitation, a corporation's charitable contribution deduction for the year is the *lesser* of (1) the amount of charitable contributions to qualifying charities (including charitable contribution carryovers—discussed below) or (2) 10 percent of charitable contribution limit modified taxable income.

Example 16-12

What if: Assume that PCC's 2016 taxable income before considering the charitable contribution limitation was $100,000. The taxable income computation includes an $18,000 charitable contribution deduction, an $11,000 DRD, a $9,000 DPAD, a $24,000 NOL carryover, a $4,000 capital loss carryover (offsets $4,000 of capital gain), and $25,000 of depreciation expense. Under these circumstances, what would be PCC's 2016 deductible charitable contribution?

---

[20]§170(a)(2). For tax years before 2016 and for corporations with a June 30 year-end from 2016–2025, the charitable contribution must be paid within two and one-half months after the year-end to be deductible in the year authorized. This exception was enacted by Congress in the "Surface Transportation and Veterans Heath Care Choice Improvement Act of 2015."

Answer: $13,800 deductible charitable contribution, computed as follows:

Description	Amount	Explanation
(1) Taxable income before charitable contribution limitation	$100,000	
(2) Charitable contribution deduction before limitation	$ 18,000	Not deductible in computing limitation
(3) Dividends received deduction	$ 11,000	Not deductible in computing limitation.
(4) Domestic production activities deduction	$ 9,000	Not deductible in computing limitation
(5) Charitable contribution limit modified taxable income*	**$138,000**	Sum of (1) through (4).
(6) Tax deduction limitation percentage	10%	§170(b)(2)(A).
(7) Charitable contribution deduction limitation	$ 13,800	(5) × (6).
(8) Charitable contribution deduction for year	**$ 13,800**	Lesser of (2) or (7).
Charitable contribution carryover	$ 4,200	(2) – (8).

*Note that the NOL and capital loss carryover are not added back to compute line (5) because they are deductible in determining the charitable contribution limit modified taxable income.

Corporations making current year charitable contributions in excess of the 10 percent modified taxable limitation may carry forward the excess for up to five years after the year in which the carryover arises. Carryforwards are absorbed on a first-in first-out (FIFO) basis and are applied after the current year contribution deduction. Corporations can deduct the carryover in future years to the extent the 10 percent limitation does not restrict deductions for charitable contributions corporations actually make in those years. Unused carryovers expire after five years.

Example 16-13

What if: Under the assumptions provided in the previous example, we determined that PCC had a $4,200 charitable contribution carryover (it was not able to deduct $4,200 of its $18,000 contribution). Assume that in 2017, PCC contributed $10,000 to charity, and its charitable contribution limit modified taxable income was $110,000. What would be PCC's deductible charitable contribution in 2017? What would its charitable contribution carryover be at the end of 2017? When would it expire?

Answer: $11,000 charitable contribution deduction. This is the lesser of the charitable contribution limit of $11,000 ($110,000 × 10%) or $14,200 ($10,000 current year contribution plus $4,200 carryover from prior year). The carryover is $3,200 ($14,200 – $11,000). Because the current year contribution uses the limit first, the $3,200 carryover is from the excess contribution in 2016 and it will expire if it has not been used by the end of 2021.

Corporations report *unfavorable, temporary* book–tax differences to the extent the 10 percent modified taxable income limitation restricts the amount of their charitable contribution tax deduction. That is, they recognize unfavorable, temporary book–tax differences in the amount of the charitable contribution *carryover* they generate for the year. Conversely, corporations report *favorable, temporary* book–tax differences when they deduct charitable contribution carryovers because they deduct the carryovers for tax purposes, but not book purposes.

Example 16-14

In 2016, PCC donated a total of $700,000 of cash to the American Red Cross. Elise knew she had to apply the 10 percent taxable income limitation to determine the amount PCC could deduct for tax purposes. She had determined that PCC's taxable income before the charitable contribution deduction, NOL carryover ($24,000), DRD ($21,000) (see Example 16-15 below), and DPAD ($465,000) was $6,287,000. What is PCC's charitable contribution deduction for the year? What is its charitable contribution carryover to next year, if any?

Answer: $626,300 charitable contribution deduction and $73,700 charitable contribution carryover, computed as follows:

Description	Amount	Explanation
(1) Taxable income before *any* charitable contribution, NOL carryover from previous year, DRD, and DPAD	$ 6,287,000	Exhibit 16-7.
(2) NOL *carryover* from previous year	(24,000)	Deductible in determining taxable income limit.
(3) Charitable contribution limit modified taxable income	$6,263,000	(1) + (2).
(4) Total charitable contributions for year	$ 700,000	
(5) Tax deduction limitation percentage	10%	§170(b)(2)(A)
(6) Charitable contribution deduction limitation	$ 626,300	(3) × (5).
(7) Charitable contribution deduction for year	**$ 626,300**	Lesser of (4) or (6).
Charitable contribution carryover*	**$ 73,700**	(4) − (7).

*As we discuss above, the carryover expires if it has not been used during the five-year period after the current year.

What is PCC's book–tax difference associated with its charitable contribution? Is the difference favorable or unfavorable? Is it permanent or temporary?

Answer: $73,700 unfavorable, temporary book–tax difference.

THE KEY FACTS

Dividends Received Deduction

- Dividends received deduction
  - Generally lesser of deduction percentage (70 percent, 80 percent, or 100 percent) based on ownership times DRD modified taxable income.
  - Limitation doesn't apply if full DRD creates or increases a corporation's NOL.
  - Generates favorable permanent difference.

Dividends Received Deduction   When corporations receive dividends from other corporations they are taxed on the dividends at their ordinary tax rate, not the preferential tax rates available to individual taxpayers. Unlike individuals, corporations are allowed a dividends received deduction (DRD) that reduces the actual tax they pay on the dividends.[21] The DRD is designed to mitigate the extent to which corporate earnings are subject to three (or perhaps even more) levels of taxation. Corporate taxable income is subject to triple taxation when a corporation pays tax on its income and then distributes its after-tax income to shareholders that are corporations. Corporate shareholders are taxed on the dividends, creating the second tax. When corporate shareholders distribute their after-tax earnings as dividends to their shareholders the income is taxed for a third time. The dividends received deduction reduces the amount of the second-level tax and thus mitigates the impact of triple taxation (or more) of earnings that corporations distribute as dividends.

Corporations generally compute their dividends received deduction by multiplying the dividend amount by 70 percent, 80 percent, or 100 percent, depending on their level of ownership in the distributing corporation's stock. Exhibit 16-6

---

[21]§243. Also, §246(c) describes certain dividends that are ineligible for the dividends received deduction.

EXHIBIT 16-6   **Stock Ownership and Dividends Received Deduction Percentage**

Receiving Corporation's Stock Ownership in Distributing Corporation's Stock	Dividends Received Deduction Percentage
Less than 20 percent	70%
At least 20 percent but less than 80 percent	80
80 percent or more[22]	100

summarizes the stock ownership thresholds and the corresponding dividends received deduction percentage. Only dividends received from domestic corporations are eligible for the DRD. Dividends received from non-U.S. corporations may be eligible for a foreign tax credit, which is discussed in Chapter 24.

Example 16-15

During 2016, PCC received a $30,000 dividend from Apple. PCC owns less than 1 percent of the Apple stock. What is PCC's DRD associated with the dividend?

Answer: $21,000 ($30,000 × 70%).

What if: Assume PCC's marginal tax rate on the dividend *before* considering the effect of the dividends received deduction is 34 percent. What is PCC's marginal tax rate on the Apple dividend income *after* considering the dividends received deduction?

Answer: 10.2 percent marginal tax rate on dividend income, computed as follows:

Description	Amount	Explanation
(1) Dividend from Apple	$30,000	
(2) The percentage DRD	70%	Less than 20 percent ownership in Apple.
(3) Dividends received deduction	**$21,000**	(1) × (2).
(4) Dividend subject to taxation after DRD	$ 9,000	(1) − (3).
(5) Marginal ordinary tax rate	34%	
(6) Taxes payable on dividend *after* DRD	$ 3,060	(4) × (5).
Marginal tax rate on dividend *after* DRD	**10.20%**	(6)/(1).

Deduction limitation.   The dividends received deduction is limited to the product of the applicable dividends received deduction percentage (see Exhibit 16-6) and **DRD modified taxable income.**[23] DRD modified taxable income is the dividend receiving corporation's taxable income *before* deducting the following:

- The DRD.
- *Any* NOL deduction (carryover or carryback).
- Capital loss *carrybacks.*
- The domestic production activities deduction (DPAD).[24]

[22]To qualify for the 100 percent dividends received deduction, the receiving and distributing corporations must be in the same affiliated group as described in §1504. The 80 percent ownership requirement is the minimum ownership level required for inclusion in the same affiliated group.

[23]When corporations receive dividends from multiple corporations with different deduction percentages, according to §246(b)(3), the limitations first apply to the 80 percent dividends received deduction and then the 70 percent dividends received deduction.

[24]§246(b)(1).

Example 16-16

What if: Suppose that during 2016, PCC received a $30,000 dividend from Apple and that PCC owns less than 1 percent of the Apple stock. Further assume that PCC's taxable income before the dividends received deduction was $50,000 in Scenario A and $25,000 in Scenario B. To arrive at the taxable income under both scenarios (before the DRD), PCC deducted a $2,000 NOL carryover, a $4,000 capital loss carryover, and a $1,000 DPAD. What is PCC's dividends received deduction associated with the dividend in Scenario A and in Scenario B?

Answer: $21,000 in Scenario A and $19,600 in Scenario B, computed as follows:

Description	Scenario A	Scenario B	Explanation
(1) Taxable income before the dividends received deduction (includes dividend income)	$50,000	$25,000	
(2) NOL carryover	2,000	2,000	
(3) The DPAs	1,000	1,000	
(4) DRD modified taxable income	$53,000	$28,000	(1) + (2) + (3).
(5) Dividend income	$30,000	$30,000	
(6) Dividends received deduction percentage based on ownership	70%	70%	§243(a).
(7) Dividends received deduction before limitation	$21,000	$21,000	(5) × (6).
(8) Dividends received deduction limitation	$ 37,100	$19,600	(4) × (6).
DRD deductible	**$21,000**	**$19,600**	Lesser of (7) or (8).

Note that the capital loss carryover is deductible in determining the DRD modified taxable income so it is not added back to taxable income to arrive at DRD modified taxable income.

The modified taxable income limitation *does not apply* if after deducting the *full* dividends received deduction (dividend × DRD percentage) a corporation reports a current year net operating loss. That is, if after deducting the full dividends received deduction, the corporation has a net operating loss, the corporation is allowed to deduct the *full* dividends received deduction no matter what the modified taxable income limitation is.[25] As the following example illustrates, this rule can cause some unusual results.

Example 16-17

What if: Let's assume that PCC reports gross income of $80,000, *including* $30,000 of dividend income from TOU Corp. PCC owns 25 percent of TOU Corp. stock so its applicable DRD percentage is 80 percent (see Exhibit 16-6). Finally, let's consider two alternative scenarios. In Scenario A, PCC reports $56,000 of business expenses deductible in determining its DRD modified taxable income. In Scenario B, PCC reports $57,000 of business expenses deductible in determining its DRD modified taxable income. For each scenario, what is PCC's DRD modified taxable income? For each scenario, what is PCC's dividends received deduction?

[25]§246(b)(2).

Scenario A Answer: $24,000 DRD modified taxable income; $19,200 dividends received deduction (see computation below).

Scenario B Answer: $23,000 DRD modified taxable income; $24,000 dividends received deduction, computed as follows:

Description	Scenario A	Scenario B	Explanation
(1) Gross income other than dividends	$50,000	$50,000	
(2) Dividend income	30,000	30,000	
(3) Gross income	$80,000	$80,000	(1) + (2).
(4) Business expenses deductible in determining the DRD modified taxable income	56,000	57,000	
(5) DRD modified taxable income (note this is taxable income before the DRD)	**$24,000**	**$23,000**	(3) − (4).
(6) Full dividends received deduction	$24,000	$24,000	(2) × 80%.
(7) DRD modified taxable income limitation	19,200	18,400	(5) × 80%.
(8) Taxable income (loss) after deducting full DRD	0	(1,000)	(5) − (6).
DRD deductible	**19,200**	**24,000**	Lesser of (6) or (7) unless (8) is negative, then (6).

Compare the results in Scenario A and Scenario B in the previous example. In Scenario B, PCC's DRD is $4,800 larger than it is in Scenario A ($24,000 − $19,200) despite the fact that the only difference in the two scenarios is that PCC reports $56,000 of business expenses in Scenario A and $57,000 of business expenses in Scenario B. Interestingly, the tax laws allow a corporation to increase its DRD by $4,800 for a $30,000 dividend simply by incurring $1,000 more in expenses (or even $1 more).

Because the dividends received deduction is strictly a tax deduction and not a book deduction, *any* dividends received deduction creates a *favorable, permanent* book–tax difference.

Example 16-18

From her review of PCC's dividend income computations, Elise discovered that the only dividend PCC received during the year was a $30,000 dividend from Apple, a U.S. corporation. Because PCC owns a very small percentage of Apple stock (less than 1 percent) Elise determined that PCC was entitled to a 70 percent dividends received deduction. What is PCC's book–tax difference associated with its dividends received deduction? Is the difference favorable or unfavorable? Is it permanent or temporary?

(*continued on page 16-22*)

Answer: $21,000 favorable, permanent book–tax difference, computed as follows:

Description	Amount	Explanation
(1) Taxable income before NOL, DRD, and DPAD (DRD modified taxable income)	$5,660,700	Exhibit 16-7 ($5,636,700 + 24,000 NOL).
(2) Dividend income	$ 30,000	Exhibit 16-7.
(3) Applicable DRD percentage	70%	Own less than 20 percent of Apple.
(4) Full dividends received deduction	$ 21,000	(2) × (3).
(5) Dividends received deduction taxable income limitation	$3,962,490	(1) × (3).
(6) Book deductible dividends received deduction	0	No book DRD.
(7) Tax deductible dividends received deduction	$ 21,000	Lesser of (4) or (5).
(Favorable) permanent book–tax difference	**($21,000)**	(6) − (7).

Taxable Income Summary

Exhibit 16-7 presents Elise's template for reconciling PCC's book and its taxable income. Note that the template does not follow the typical financial accounting format because it organizes the information to facilitate the taxable income computation. In particular, it puts the deductions in the *sequence they are deducted for tax purposes.*

Regular Tax Liability

When corporations determine their taxable income, they can compute their tax liability from the corporate tax rate schedule. The corporate tax rate schedule is not indexed for inflation like the individual tax rate schedules are. Consequently, unlike the individual tax rate schedules, the corporate tax rate schedule does not change every year. The lowest marginal corporate tax rate bracket is 15 percent and the highest marginal tax rate bracket is 39 percent. Corporations with over $18,333,333 of taxable income pay tax at a flat 35 percent rate.

Example 16-19

Elise determined that PCC's taxable income is $5,150,700. What is its regular income tax liability?

Answer: $1,751,238, computed as follows:

Description	Amount	Explanation
(1) Taxable income	$5,150,700	Exhibit 16-7.
(2) Tax on first $335,000	$ 113,900	Corporate tax rate schedule (for taxable income between $335K and $10M).
(3) Taxable income above $335,000	$4,815,700	(1) − $335,000.
(4) Marginal tax rate for fifth bracket	34%	Tax rate schedule.
(5) Tax on income above $335,000	$ 1,637,338	(3) × (4).
Regular tax liability	**$1,751,238**	(2) + (5).

EXHIBIT 16-7   PCC Book–Tax Reconciliation Template

Description	Book Income (Dr) Cr	Book–Tax Adjustments (Dr)[†]		Taxable Income (Dr) Cr
Revenue from sales	$60,000,000			$60,000,000
Cost of goods sold	(38,000,000)			(38,000,000)
Gross profit	$22,000,000			$22,000,000
Other income:				
Dividend income	30,000			30,000
Interest income	120,000	(12,000)[ex. 1]		108,000
Capital gains (losses)	(28,000)		28,000[ex. 7]	0
Gain on fixed asset dispositions	54,000		16,000 [Exh. 4]	70,000
Gross income	$ 22,176,000			$22,208,000
Expenses:				
Compensation	(9,868,000)			(9,868,000)
Deferred compensation	(300,000)	(150,000) [Exh. 4]		(450,000)
Stock option compensation	(100,000)		100,000[ex. 6]	0
Bad debt expense	(165,000)		70,000 [Exh. 4]	(95,000)
Charitable contributions	Moved below			
Depreciation	(2,400,000)	(700,000) [Exh. 4]		(3,100,000)
Advertising	(1,920,000)			(1,920,000)
Warranty expenses	(580,000)		170,000 [Exh. 4]	(410,000)
Meals and entertainment	(28,000)		14,000[ex. 1]	(14,000)
Life insurance premiums	(34,000)		34,000[ex. 1]	0
Other expenses	(64,000)			(64,000)
Federal income tax expense	(2,000,000)*		2,000,000[ex. 2]	0
Total expenses *before* charitable contribution, NOL, DRD, and DPAD	(17,459,000)			(15,921,000)
Income *before* charitable contribution, NOL, DRD, and DPAD	4,717,000			$ 6,287,000
NOL carryover from prior year		(24,000)[ex. 10]		(24,000)
Taxable income for charitable contribution limitation purposes				6,263,000
Charitable contributions	(700,000)		73,700[ex. 14]	(626,300)
Taxable income before DRD and DPAD				5,636,700
Dividends received deduction (DRD)		(21,000)[ex. 18]		(21,000)
Domestic production activities deduction (DPAD)		(465,000)[ex. 1]		(465,000)
Book/taxable income	**$ 4,017,000**			**$ 5,150,700**

*This number is used only for illustrative purposes. In Chapter 17, we compute the correct federal income tax expense (also referred to as the federal income tax provision).

[†]Note that the superscript by each book–tax difference identifies the example (Ex) or exhibit (Exh) where the adjustment is calculated. Also note that the numbers in the debit column are favorable book–tax adjustments while numbers in the credit column are unfavorable book–tax adjustments.

Why do corporate marginal tax rates increase from 15 percent to 25 percent to 34 percent to 39 percent and then drop to 34 percent and then increase again to 35 percent and then to 38 percent before settling in at 35 percent? This doesn't really look like a truly progressive tax rate schedule, does it? It turns out that the rate schedule is progressive with some modifications. When the apparent marginal rate increases to 39 percent, the marginal tax rate is really 34 percent but the tax laws impose a 5 percent add-on tax that is designed to eliminate the benefit of the rates lower than 34 percent (15 percent and 25 percent). Consequently, by the time the marginal rate from the schedule drops back down to 34 percent at \$335,000 of taxable income, the entire amount of taxable income is taxed at a flat 34 percent rate. Therefore, taxable income between \$335,000 and \$10,000,000 is taxed at a flat 34 percent rate (verify this by referring to the previous example and dividing PCC's tax liability by its taxable income). The marginal rate then jumps to 35 percent and then to 38 percent. The 3 percent increase from 35 percent to 38 percent is also an add-on tax designed to phase-out the benefit of the 34 percent tax rate relative to the 35 percent rate. As a result, by the time taxable income hits \$18,333,333, a corporation's taxable income is taxed at a flat 35 percent tax rate. In effect, the 15 percent and 25 percent rate brackets are reserved for "small" corporations.

Controlled Groups   Corporate shareholders interested in reducing a corporation's overall tax burden may be tempted to split up an existing profitable corporation into several smaller corporations. By doing this, the group of corporations may earn the same taxable income in the aggregate but will pay less in taxes because each corporation will benefit from the low end of the corporate tax rate schedule. In the extreme, shareholders could split a corporation into enough separate corporations such that each separate corporation will report taxable income of \$50,000 or lower and, consequently, pay tax on all of its income at the lowest marginal tax rate of 15 percent. Congress was concerned about this possibility and other similar abuses so they implemented special rules for **controlled groups.**

Essentially, a controlled group is a group of corporations that is controlled or owned by the same taxpayer or group of taxpayers. A controlled group could be a **parent-subsidiary controlled group,** a **brother-sister controlled group,** or a **combined controlled group.**[26] Exhibit 16-8 summarizes, in general terms, the definition of each of these controlled group types.

EXHIBIT 16-8   Controlled Group Definitions

Type	Definition	Reference
Parent-Subsidiary	One corporation (the parent) owns at least 80 percent of the voting power or stock value of another corporation (the subsidiary) on the last day of the year.	§1563(a)(1)
Brother-Sister	Two or more corporations of which five or fewer individuals collectively own more than 50 percent of the voting power or stock value of each corporation on the last day of the year, taking into account each individual's minimum ownership in each corporation in the group.	§1563(a)(2)
Combined	Three or more corporations, each of which is a member of either a parent-subsidiary or brother-sister controlled group and one of the corporations is the parent in the parent-subsidiary controlled group and also is in a brother-sister controlled group.	§1563(a)(3)

The tax laws impose complex rules for determining whether corporations meet the stock ownership requirements for controlled groups described in Exhibit 16-8.[27]

[26]§1563(a). The definition of a controlled group also includes certain insurance companies [§1563(a)].

[27]The ownership rules include direct and indirect (or constructive) ownership and the concept of identical ownership in each corporation in a brother-sister controlled group. For example, an individual is treated as owning the stock owned by a spouse, children under age 21, and parents, grandparents, and children age 21 or older, but only if the individual owns more than 50 percent of the corporation's stock. The details of these rules are beyond the scope of this text. See §1563 for more detail.

No matter the type, a controlled group of corporations may use only one 15 percent tax bracket and one 25 percent tax bracket among all the corporations in the group. That is, the controlled group is treated as one corporation for purposes of using the tax rate schedules.[28] In general, the tax provisions associated with controlled groups are designed to eliminate the benefit of splitting large corporations into smaller commonly controlled entities to take advantage of multiple tax benefits allowable to smaller corporations because the controlled group rules treat the entire group as though it is one entity.[29]

Example 16-20

What if: Assume that PCC and ACC are privately held corporations with calendar year-ends. On December 31, Jordan Michaels owns 50 percent of the stock of PCC and 50 percent of the stock of ACC. Sally Perkins owns the remaining shares of PCC and ACC. Are PCC and ACC a controlled group?

Answer: Yes, two individuals (Jordan and Sally) own more than 50 percent of the stock of both PCC and ACC on the last day of the year (they own 100 percent of the stock of both corporations).

Assuming PCC reported $45,000 of taxable income for the year and ACC reported $40,000 of taxable income, what is the combined tax liability of PCC and ACC (given that they comprise a controlled group)?

Answer: $17,150 [$13,750 + 34% × (85,000 − 75,000)].

What if: Assume the same taxable income for PCC and for ACC but that PCC and ACC have the same 10 owners and that each owner owns 10 percent of each corporation. What would be the combined tax liability of PCC and ACC?

Answer: $12,750 [PCC: $6,750 ($45,000 × 15%) + ACC: $6,000 ($40,000 × 15%)]. PCC and ACC are *not* part of a controlled group, so both corporations are allowed to take advantage of the 15 percent corporate tax bracket.

In this example, the controlled group rules would extract an additional $4,400 of tax ($17,150 − $12,750) from the entities because the rules essentially treat the two entities as one.

COMPLIANCE   LO 16-3

Corporations report their taxable income on Form 1120. Exhibit 16-9 presents the front page of PCC's current year Form 1120 through the tax liability.

Form 1120 includes a schedule for corporations to report their book–tax differences and reconcile their book and taxable income. Corporations with total assets of less than $10,000,000 report their book–tax differences on Schedule M-1. Corporations with total assets of $10,000,000 or more are required to report their book–tax differences on Schedule M-3.[30] Because corporations report book–tax differences as adjustments to book income to compute taxable income on either Schedule M-1 or M-3, these book-to-tax adjustments are often referred to as **Schedule M adjustments, M adjustments,** and even "Ms" (plural version of M).

---

[28]§1561(a).

[29]The controlled group provisions require corporations in the group to share other tax benefits such as the AMT exemption discussed below. A potential benefit of having a controlled group is that if the group files a consolidated tax return, the losses of one corporation in the group can offset income from other corporations in the group. The apportionment of tax benefits between a controlled group is reported on Schedule O to Form 1120.

[30]Corporations with at least $10 million but less than $50 million in total assets at tax year-end are permitted to file Schedule M-1 in place of Schedule M-3, Parts II and III. Schedule M-3, Part I, lines 1–12 continue to be required for these taxpayers. Corporations with $10 million to $50 million in total assets may voluntarily file Schedule M-3 Parts II and III rather than Schedule M-1.

EXHIBIT 16-9   **PCC Form 1120 page 1, through tax refund**

Form **1120**		**U.S. Corporation Income Tax Return**				OMB No. 1545-0123

Department of the Treasury
Internal Revenue Service

For calendar year 2015 or tax year beginning _____ , 2015, ending _____ , 20 ____

20 15

▶ Information about Form 1120 and its separate instructions is at *www.irs.gov/form1120.*

A Check if:
1a Consolidated return (attach Form 851) . ☐
  b Life/nonlife consolidated return . . ☐
2 Personal holding co. (attach Sch. PH) . ☐
3 Personal service corp. (see instructions) . ☐
4 Schedule M-3 attached ☐

TYPE OR PRINT

Name: **Premier Computer Corporation**
Number, street, and room or suite no. If a P.O. box, see instructions.
1533 East Crown Drive
City or town, state, or province, country, and ZIP or foreign postal code
Denver, CO 80239

B Employer identification number
12-3456789

C Date incorporated
01/01/1998

D Total assets (see instructions)
$ 9,500,000

E Check if: **(1)** ☐ Initial return **(2)** ☐ Final return **(3)** ☐ Name change **(4)** ☐ Address change

Income	1a	Gross receipts or sales	1a 60,000,000	
	b	Returns and allowances	1b	
	c	Balance. Subtract line 1b from line 1a	1c	60,000,000
	2	Cost of goods sold (attach Form 1125-A)	2	38,000,000
	3	Gross profit. Subtract line 2 from line 1c	3	22,000,000
	4	Dividends (Schedule C, line 19)	4	30,000
	5	Interest	5	108,000
	6	Gross rents	6	
	7	Gross royalties	7	
	8	Capital gain net income (attach Schedule D (Form 1120)) .	8	
	9	Net gain or (loss) from Form 4797, Part II, line 17 (attach Form 4797)	9	70,000
	10	Other income (see instructions—attach statement) . .	10	
	11	**Total income.** Add lines 3 through 10 . . . . ▶	11	22,208,000
Deductions (See instructions for limitations on deductions.)	12	Compensation of officers (see instructions—attach Form 1125-E) . ▶	12	1,500,000
	13	Salaries and wages (less employment credits) . . .	13	8,818,000
	14	Repairs and maintenance	14	
	15	Bad debts	15	95,000
	16	Rents	16	
	17	Taxes and licenses	17	
	18	Interest	18	
	19	Charitable contributions	19	626,000
	20	Depreciation from Form 4562 not claimed on Form 1125-A or elsewhere on return (attach Form 4562) . .	20	3,100,000
	21	Depletion	21	
	22	Advertising	22	1,920,000
	23	Pension, profit-sharing, etc., plans	23	
	24	Employee benefit programs	24	
	25	Domestic production activities deduction (attach Form 8903) .	25	465,000
	26	Other deductions (attach statement)	26	488,000
	27	**Total deductions.** Add lines 12 through 26 . . . ▶	27	17,012,300
	28	Taxable income before net operating loss deduction and special deductions. Subtract line 27 from line 11.	28	5,195,700
	29a	Net operating loss deduction (see instructions) . . .	29a 24,000	
	b	Special deductions (Schedule C, line 20)	29b 21,000	
	c	Add lines 29a and 29b	29c	45,000
Tax, Refundable Credits, and Payments	30	**Taxable income.** Subtract line 29c from line 28 (see instructions) .	30	5,150,700
	31	Total tax (Schedule J, Part I, line 11)	31	1,751,238
	32	Total payments and refundable credits (Schedule J, Part II, line 21) .	32	1,813,333
	33	Estimated tax penalty (see instructions). Check if Form 2220 is attached ▶ ☐	33	
	34	**Amount owed.** If line 32 is smaller than the total of lines 31 and 33, enter amount owed	34	
	35	**Overpayment.** If line 32 is larger than the total of lines 31 and 33, enter amount overpaid . . .	35	62,095
	36	Enter amount from line 35 you want: **Credited to 2016 estimated tax** ▶ _____ **Refunded** ▶	36	62,095

Sign Here ▶

Under penalties of perjury, I declare that I have examined this return, including accompanying schedules and statements, and to the best of my knowledge and belief, it is true, correct, and complete. Declaration of preparer (other than taxpayer) is based on all information of which preparer has any knowledge.

Signature of officer _____ Date _____ ▶ Title _____

May the IRS discuss this return with the preparer shown below (see instructions)? ☐ Yes ☐ No

Paid Preparer Use Only

Print/Type preparer's name	Preparer's signature	Date	Check ☐ if self-employed	PTIN

Firm's name ▶ _____ Firm's EIN ▶ _____
Firm's address ▶ _____ Phone no. _____

For Paperwork Reduction Act Notice, see separate instructions.   Cat. No. 11450Q   Form **1120** (2015)

EXHIBIT 16-10   Form 1120, Schedule M-1

Schedule M-1	**Reconciliation of Income (Loss) per Books With Income per Return**

Note: The corporation may be required to file Schedule M-3 (see instructions).

1	Net income (loss) per books	4,017,000	7	Income recorded on books this year not included on this return (itemize):	
2	Federal income tax per books	2,000,000			
3	Excess of capital losses over capital gains .	28,000		Tax-exempt interest $ _____ 12,000	
4	Income subject to tax not recorded on books this year (itemize): _____			----------------------------	
	_____ gain on disposition of fixed assets	16,000		----------------------------	12,000
5	Expenses recorded on books this year not deducted on this return (itemize):		8	Deductions on this return not charged against book income this year (itemize):	
a	Depreciation . . . . $ _____		a	Depreciation . . $ _____ 700,000	
b	Charitable contributions . $ _____ 73,700		b	Charitable contributions $ _____	
c	Travel and entertainment . $ _____ 14,000			_____ deferred comp. 150,000	
	_____ other (see statement)	461,700		_____ dom. prod. act. ded. 465,000	1,315,000
			9	Add lines 7 and 8	1,327,000
6	Add lines 1 through 5	6,522,700	10	Income (page 1, line 28)—line 6 less line 9	5,195,700

Schedule M-1
Statement 1
Other expenses recorded on books this year not deducted on this return

Compensation expense (stock options)	$100,000
Bad debt expense	70,000
Warranty expense	170,000
Life insurance premiums	34,000
Total other expenses	$374,000

Because PCC's total assets are $9,500,000 (see Exhibit 16-9, line D), it may complete a Schedule M-1 rather than a Schedule M-3. Exhibit 16-10 presents PCC's completed Schedule M-1 based on the information provided in Exhibit 16-7 (the 2015 form is used because the 2016 form was unavailable at the time the book went to press). Schedule M-1 is a relatively short schedule, and it does not require corporations to provide much detail about the nature of their book–tax differences.

The schedule begins on line 1 with book income after taxes. The left-hand column includes all unfavorable book–tax differences (add-backs to book income to arrive at taxable income). In general, the top part of the left column is for income items and the bottom part is for expense items. The right-hand column consists of all favorable book–tax differences. The top part of the right column is for income items and the bottom part includes expense items.

Finally, note that Schedule M-1 (and Schedule M-3) reconcile to taxable income *before* the net operating loss deduction and the dividends received deduction.[31] Consequently, to fully reconcile book and taxable income, corporations must deduct net operating loss carryovers and dividends received deductions from line 10 on Schedule M-1 (or the amount on line 30d on Schedule M-3).

Example 16-21

In reviewing her work on PCC's tax return, Elise wanted to check to make sure that she could reconcile from the bottom line of the Schedule M-1 to PCC's taxable income. She noted that line 10 of PCC's Schedule M-1 was $5,195,700. How should Elise reconcile from this number to PCC's taxable income? *(continued on page 16-28)*

[31]Schedule M-1 (and the Schedule M-3) reconcile to line 28 on Form 1120. Line 28 is taxable income before the net operating loss and special deductions (the dividends received deduction).

Answer: Start with the amount on line 10 and subtract PCC's NOL carryover and its DRD, as illustrated below:

Description	Amount	Explanation
(1) Schedule M-1 taxable income reconciliation total	$5,195,700	Form 1120, Schedule M-1, line 10.
(2) Net operating loss deduction	(24,000)	Exhibit 16-7.
(3) Dividends received deduction	(21,000)	Exhibit 16-7.
Taxable income	**$5,150,700**	(1) + (2) + (3).

Schedule M-3 requires corporations to report significantly more information than Schedule M-1 does. For example, Schedule M-3 includes more than 60 specific types of book–tax differences, while Schedule M-1 includes only 10 summary lines. Furthermore, Schedule M-3 requires corporations to identify each book–tax difference as either temporary or permanent. The IRS created Schedule M-3 in hopes of providing a better and more efficient starting point for agents to identify and scrutinize large dollar compliance issues.

Form 1120 also requires corporations to complete Schedule M-2, which provides a reconciliation of the corporation's beginning and ending balance in its unappropriated retained earning from its financial accounting balance sheet (reported on Schedule L). Corporations with total receipts and total assets less than $250,000 are not required to complete Schedules L, M-1, and M-2.

ETHICS

Elizabeth (Liz) Young, senior manager in the tax group in the Cleveland office of Tics & Tax, an international professional services firm, was reviewing the work papers related to the tax return to be filed by her biggest client, General Inertia. She was intrigued by one of the items listed under *"other deductions"* (line 26 of Form 1120), which was described as a *"settlement amount"* of $100 million. After consulting with the director of taxes at General Inertia, Dee Ductit, Liz discovered the amount related to a settlement with the Department of Justice (DOJ) for violation of the False Claims Act. Dee described the settlement as a *"penalty"* (her words) the firm had to pay to the federal government because one of its divisions billed the Department of Defense (DOD) for work that was not performed in relation to a contract to provide helicopters to the DOD.

Dee's use of the term *"penalty"* caused Liz to question whether such a payment was deductible for tax purposes (the company also deducted the payment on its financial statements). In particular, she remembered that Code §162(f) specifically prohibits the deduction of *"any fine or similar penalty paid to a government for the violation of any law."* When Liz asked to see the settlement letter from the DOJ, she was told that the client's legal department considered the terms of the letter to be confidential, but that the company's reason for deducting the amount was that the letter did not describe the settlement as a *"penalty"* and specifically stated that *"nothing in the agreement characterizes the payments for federal income tax purposes."*

General Inertia is a long-term client that provides the firm with $10 million in audit and tax fees annually. Dee informed Liz that the company was willing to take the *"risk"* in deducting the full amount of the settlement payment because its IRS auditors were unlikely to question the item and the *"tax refund"* from deducting the settlement ($35 million) would help alleviate some short-term cash flow problems the company was having. In fact, the company hoped to use the *"refund"* to pay off parts suppliers that were threatening to take the company to court over nonpayment. The company also preferred not to provide any further disclosure or description of the deduction in the tax return so as not to alert the IRS to a potential tax audit issue.

What do you think of the tax director's approach to filing the company's tax return? What would you do if you were in Liz's position?[32]

[32]See S. Convery and E. Outslay, "Assessing Professional Ethics in Tax: A Case on Uncertain Tax Positions," *Journal of Accounting Education* 30 (March 2012), pp. 80–99.

Consolidated Tax Returns   An affiliated group of corporations may elect to file a **consolidated tax return** in which the group files a tax return as if it were one entity for tax purposes. An **affiliated group** exists when one corporation owns at least 80 percent of (1) the total voting power and (2) the total stock value of another corporation.[33] Filing a consolidated tax return allows the losses of one group member to offset income of other members. Further, income from certain intercompany transactions is deferred until realized through a transaction outside of the affiliated group. However, losses from certain intercompany transactions are deferred until realized through a transaction outside of the affiliated group.

Affiliated groups cannot file a consolidated tax return unless they elect to do so. Because the election is binding on subsequent years, it should be made with care. Consolidated tax returns may impose additional administrative and compliance costs on the taxpayers. The consolidated tax return laws are very complex and beyond the scope of this text. Further, the rules for consolidated reporting for financial statement purposes are different from the tax rules.

Corporate Tax Return Due Dates and Estimated Taxes

Beginning in 2016, the tax return due date for most C corporations (those with a tax year-end other than June 30) is three and one-half months after the corporation's year-end. Thus, a calendar-year corporation's unextended tax return due date is April 15. Corporations requesting an extension can extend the due date for filing their tax returns (not for paying the taxes) for five months (September 15 for calendar-year corporations). Prior to 2016, a corporation's unextended tax due date was two and one-half months after the corporation's year-end.

Corporations with a federal income tax liability of $500 or more (including the alternative minimum tax—discussed below) are required to pay their tax liability for the year in quarterly estimated installments.[34] For 2015, the installments are due on the 15th day of the 4th, 6th, 9th, and 12th months of their tax year.[35] When corporations file their tax returns, they determine whether they must pay estimated tax underpayment penalties. Generally, corporations are subject to underpayment penalties if they did not pay in 25 percent, 50 percent, 75 percent, and 100 percent of their *required annual payment* with their first, second, third, and fourth installment payments, respectively.[36] The required annual payment is the *least* of:

1. 100 percent of the tax liability on the prior year's return, but only if there was a positive tax liability on the return and the prior-year return covered a 12-month period (however, see discussion of "large" corporations below).
2. 100 percent of the current-year tax liability (corporations usually don't rely on this method to determine the required payment because they won't know what this is until they complete their tax returns—after the estimated tax due dates).
3. 100 percent of the estimated current-year tax liability using the annualized income method (discussed below).[37]

From a cash management perspective (time value of money) it generally makes sense for corporations to make the *minimum* required estimated payment installments for each quarter. Thus, as each estimated tax due date approaches, corporations will generally compute the required estimated payment under the prior-year tax method (if available) and under the annualized method and pay the lesser of the two.

> **THE KEY FACTS**
>
> **Tax Compliance**
>
> - Corporations report taxable income on Form 1120.
> - Corporations with total assets of less than $10M report book–tax differences on Schedule M-1 of Form 1120. Otherwise, they are required to report book–tax differences on Schedule M-3.
> - Beginning in 2016, the tax return due date is 3.5 months after year-end.
>   - Extensions of filing return (not paying taxes) for five additional months after year-end.
> - An affiliated group may file a consolidated tax return.
> - Corporations pay expected annual tax liability through estimated tax payments.
>   - Installments due in 4th, 6th, 9th, and 12th months of their taxable year.
> - Underpayment penalties apply if estimated tax payments are inadequate.

---

[33]§1504(a).

[34]§6655; §6655(e).

[35]§6655(c).

[36]§6665(d).

[37]§6655(e). Corporations may also use the adjusted seasonal income method of determining their required estimated tax payments. This method is similar in concept to the annualized method but is less common and is beyond the scope of this text.

The **annualized income method** is perhaps the most popular method of determining estimated tax payments (particularly for corporations that can't use the prior-year tax liability to determine their current-year estimated tax payment obligations) because corporations can use this method as a safe harbor to avoid estimated payment penalties. Under this method, corporations determine their taxable income as of the end of each quarter and then annualize (project) the amounts to determine their estimated taxable income and tax liability for the year. The estimated annual tax liability is used at the end of each quarter to determine the minimum required estimated payment for that quarter. Corporations use the first quarter taxable income to project their annual tax liability for the *first and second quarter* estimated tax payments. They use taxable income at the end of the second quarter to determine the third quarter estimated tax payment requirement, and taxable income at the end of the third quarter to determine their fourth quarter payment requirement. Exhibit 16-11 shows the formula for computing estimated taxable income under the annualized income method.

EXHIBIT 16-11   **Estimated Taxable Income Computation under Annualized Income Method**

Installment	(1) Taxable Income (first __ months of year)	(2) Annualization Factor	(1) × (2) Annual Estimated Taxable Income
First quarter	3	12/3 = 4	
Second quarter	3	12/3 = 4	
Third quarter	6	12/6 = 2	
Fourth quarter	9	12/9 = 1.3333	

Example 16-22

PCC determined its taxable income at the close of the first, second, and third quarters as follows:

Quarter-End	Cumulative Taxable Income
First	$1,000,000
Second	3,200,000
Third	4,000,000

What is its annual estimated taxable income for estimated tax purposes as of the end of the first, second, third, and fourth quarters respectively?

Answer: $4,000,000 for the first and second quarters, $6,400,000 for the third quarter, and $5,333,333 for the fourth quarter, computed as follows:

Installment	(1) Taxable Income	(2) Annualization Factor	(1) × (2) Annual Estimated Taxable Income
First quarter	$1,000,000	12/3 = 4	**$4,000,000**
Second quarter	1,000,000	12/3 = 4	**4,000,000**
Third quarter	3,200,000	12/6 = 2	**6,400,000**
Fourth quarter	4,000,000	12/9 = 1.333	**5,333,333**

Once corporations have determined their annual estimated taxable income for each quarter, they can use the formulas in Exhibit 16-12 to compute the required estimated tax installments for each quarter under the annualized income method.

EXHIBIT 16-12   Estimated Taxable Income Computation under Annualized Income Method

Installment	(1) Annual Estimated Taxable Income	(2) Tax on Estimated Taxable Income	(3) Percentage of Tax Required to Be Paid	(4) (2) × (3) Required Cumulative Payment	(5) Prior Cumulative Payment	(4) − (5) Required Estimated Tax Payment
First quarter			25%			
Second quarter			50			
Third quarter			75			
Fourth quarter			100			

Example 16-23

Based on the estimated taxable income in the previous example, what are PCC's required estimated tax payments for the year under the annualized income method?

Answer: $340,000 for the first and second quarters, $952,000 for the third quarter, and $181,333 for the fourth quarter, computed as follows:

Installment	(1) Annual Estimated Taxable Income	(2) Tax on Estimated Taxable Income (flat 34 percent)	(3) Percentage of Tax Required to Be Paid	(4) (2) × (3) Required Cumulative Payment	(5) Prior Cumulative Payments	(4) − (5) Required Estimated Tax Payment
First quarter	$4,000,000	$1,360,000	25%	$ 340,000	$ 0	**$340,000**
Second quarter	4,000,000	1,360,000	50	680,000	340,000	**340,000**
Third quarter	6,400,000	2,176,000	75	1,632,000	680,000	**952,000**
Fourth quarter	5,333,333	1,813,333	100	1,813,333	1,632,000	**181,333**

Can PCC use its prior-year tax liability to determine its current-year estimated tax payments?

Answer: No. PCC reported a net operating loss last year and did not pay taxes so it may not use its prior-year tax liability to determine its current-year estimated tax payments.

Can PCC use its current-year tax liability to determine its current-year estimated tax payments?

Answer: Yes. As we determined in Example 16-19, PCC's actual tax liability for the year is $1,751,238. So, PCC could have avoided estimated tax penalties by paying in $437,810 each quarter ($1,751,238 × 25%). However, it did not know this amount when it was required to make its estimated tax payments so it would likely have used the annualized income method of determining its estimated tax payments to protect itself from penalties.

"Large" corporations, defined as corporations with over $1,000,000 of taxable income in *any* of the three years prior to the current year,[38] may use the prior-year tax liability to determine their *first quarter* estimated tax payments only. If they use the prior-year tax liability to determine their first quarter payment, their second quarter payment must "catch up" their estimated payments. That is, the second quarter payment must be large enough for the sum of their first and second quarter payments to equal or exceed 50 percent of their projected current-year tax liability.[39]

[38]§6655(g)(2).
[39]§6655(d).

Example 16-24

What if: Assume that last year PCC reported taxable income of $2,000,000 and a tax liability of $680,000. Further, PCC determined its required estimated tax payments under the annualized method as described in the previous example. What would be PCC's required minimum estimated tax payments for each quarter for the current year (ignore the current-year tax requirement because PCC is unsure what its current-year tax will be)?

Answer: $170,000 for the first quarter, $510,000 for the second quarter, $952,000 for the third quarter, and $181,333 for the fourth quarter, computed as follows:

Installment	(1) Estimated Tax Payment under Prior Year Tax Exception	(2) Estimated Tax Payment under Annualized Method	(3) Required Cumulative Payment for Quarter × [sum of the lesser of (1) or (2) through quarter]	(4) Prior Cumulative Payments	(5) (3) − (4) Required Estimated Tax Payment
First quarter	$170,000*	$340,000	$ 170,000	$ 0	**$170,000**
Second quarter	Not applicable*	340,000	680,000	170,000	**510,000**
Third quarter	Not applicable*	952,000	1,632,000	680,000	**952,000**
Fourth quarter	Not applicable*	181,333	1,813,333	$1,632,000	**181,333**

*Because PCC is a large corporation, it may determine its first quarter estimated tax payment using its prior-year liability ($680,000 × 25% = $170,000). However, it must use the annualized method to determine its second, third, and fourth quarter required payments.

With its second installment, PCC must have paid in $680,000. Because it only paid in $170,000 with the first quarter installment, it must pay $510,000 with its second quarter payment.

What if: Assume the same facts as above, except that last year PCC paid $200,000 in tax and PCC is not a large corporation. What would be PCC's required minimum estimated tax payments for each quarter (ignore the current-year tax requirement)?

Answer: $50,000 for the first quarter, $50,000 for the second quarter, $50,000 for the third quarter, and $50,000 for the fourth quarter, computed as follows:

Installment	(1) Estimated Tax Payment under Prior Year Tax Exception ($200,000/4)	(2) Estimated Tax Payment under Annualized Method	(3) Required Cumulative Payment for Quarter × [sum of the lesser of (1) or (2) through quarter ×]	(4) Prior Cumulative Payments	(5) (3) − (4) Required Estimated Tax Payment
First quarter	$50,000	$340,000	$ 50,000	$ 0	**$50,000**
Second quarter	50,000	340,000	100,000	50,000	**50,000**
Third quarter	50,000	952,000	150,000	100,000	**50,000**
Fourth quarter	50,000	181,333	200,000	150,000	**50,000**

PCC can use the prior-year tax to determine its minimum required estimated tax payments.

Corporations that have underpaid their estimated taxes for any quarter must pay an underpayment penalty determined on Form 2220. The amount of the penalty is based on the underpayment rate (or interest rate), the amount of the underpayment, and the period of the underpayment. The interest rate is generally the federal short-term interest rate plus 3 percent. The period of the underpayment is the due date for the installment through the earlier of (1) the date the payment is made or (2) the due date of the tax return without extensions. The penalties are not deductible.[40]

[40]§6655(b)(2).

continued from page 16-1...

Elise figured she was done when she sat down to discuss PCC's tax return with Darryl. Darryl only had a few review comments. One of the comments sounded pretty important, though. Darryl asked Elise if PCC owed any alternative minimum tax. Elise told Darryl she would get back to him on that one. She left Darryl's office and immediately started researching the alternative minimum tax. ■

CORPORATE ALTERNATIVE MINIMUM TAX

In the early 1980s Congress became concerned that many large corporations were reporting positive financial income to shareholders, but reporting tax losses or minimal taxable income to the IRS and, as a result, not paying what the voting public perceived as their fair share of taxes. A common perception was that big businesses (and wealthy individuals) had the ability and sophistication to avoid paying taxes while middle-class taxpayers were carrying a disproportionate amount of the country's tax burden. Congress addressed this perceived inequity by enacting the corporate (and individual) **alternative minimum tax** as part of the Tax Reform Act of 1986. The alternative minimum tax is a tax on a base broader than the regular tax base. The alternative minimum tax is designed to require corporations to pay some minimum level of tax even when they have low or no regular taxable income due to certain tax breaks they gain from the tax code.

Small corporations are exempt from the AMT. For this purpose, small corporations are those with average annual gross receipts *less than* $7.5 million for the three years prior to the current tax year. New corporations are automatically exempt from the AMT in their first year of existence, and they are exempt from the AMT for their first three years of existence as long as their average annual gross receipts are below $5 million during the three-year period. Once a corporation fails the AMT gross-receipts test, it is no longer exempt from the AMT.

Corporations compute their alternative minimum tax by multiplying their AMT base by the 20 percent AMT rate and then subtracting their regular tax liability from the product of the base and rate.[41] To determine their AMT base, corporations start with regular taxable income, add preference items, add or subtract certain adjustments, and then subtract an exemption amount. Exhibit 16-13 presents the corporate AMT formula.

Preference Items

When computing alternative minimum taxable income, corporations *add* preference items to taxable income. These items represent tax breaks that corporations received for regular tax purposes, but that Congress chose to eliminate for alternative minimum tax purposes. Common preference items include percentage depletion in excess of cost basis and tax-exempt interest income from a **private activity bond** (a municipal bond used to fund a nonpublic activity—if the bond is for a public purpose, the interest is not a preference item). Tax exempt interest on private activity bonds issued in 2009 or 2010 is not an AMT tax preference item.[42]

---

[41]§55(a).
[42]§56(a)(5)(C)(vi).

EXHIBIT 16-13 **Corporate AMT Formula**

Taxable income or loss before NOL deduction
Add: Preference items
Add or subtract: Adjustments
Preadjustment AMT income
Add or subtract: ACE adjustment
Subtract: AMT NOL deduction
Alternative minimum taxable income (AMTI)
Subtract: Exemption
AMT base
× 20%
Gross AMT
− AMT foreign tax credit
Tentative minimum tax
Subtract: Regular income tax
Alternative minimum tax if positive

Example 16-25

Elise reviewed PCC's book–tax reconciliation provided in Exhibit 16-7 to determine if it had any preference items during the year. What preference items if any should PCC report for alternative minimum tax purposes?

Answer: $12,000 tax-exempt interest income from the San Diego municipal bond issued in 2014. The bond is a private activity bond because proceeds from the bond were used to fund a privately owned and used baseball stadium.

What if: Assume the San Diego municipal bond proceeds were used to construct public roads. Would the interest represent an AMT preference item?

Answer: No, because the bond was not a private activity bond.

Adjustments

Corporations may add or subtract alternative minimum tax adjustments to regular taxable income in computing alternative minimum taxable income.[43] Whether the adjustment is positive (unfavorable) or negative (favorable) for a particular item depends on the way the corporation accounts for the item for regular taxable income purposes and the way it accounts for the item for AMT purposes. In general, the most common AMT adjustments for corporations are (1) depreciation, (2) gain or loss on sale of depreciable assets, and (3) adjusted current earnings (ACE).

Depreciation Adjustment Corporations with fixed assets may benefit from the highly accelerated depreciation methods allowed under the regular taxable income system. For alternative minimum tax purposes, assets aren't depreciated as quickly.[44] Consequently, in the early years of an asset's depreciable life, regular tax depreciation exceeds alternative minimum tax depreciation, and corporations must make positive adjustments to regular taxable income to compute the AMT base. However,

---

[43]§56.

[44]Chapter 10 describes the regular tax and alternative minimum tax depreciable lives and methods.

after corporations fully depreciate assets for regular tax purposes they may still have basis left to depreciate for AMT purposes. In these situations, corporations make negative AMT depreciation adjustments to regular taxable income to compute the AMT base.

Example 16-26

Elise reviewed the tax depreciation calculations. She discovered that although PCC deducted $3,100,000 of depreciation expense for regular tax purposes, it was entitled to deduct only $2,500,000 for AMT purposes. What is the amount of PCC's depreciation AMT adjustment? Is the adjustment positive or negative?

Answer: $600,000 positive or unfavorable adjustment, computed as follows:

Description	Amount	Explanation
(1) Regular tax depreciation	$3,100,000	Exhibit 16-7.
(2) AMT depreciation	2,500,000	
Positive or unfavorable AMT adjustment	**$ 600,000**	(1) – (2).

Gain or Loss on Disposition of Depreciable Assets   Depreciation differences for regular tax and AMT purposes cause differences in the adjusted basis of the assets for regular tax purposes and AMT purposes. Consequently, when corporations sell or dispose of depreciable assets before they completely depreciate them, they will likely recognize a different gain or loss for regular tax purposes than they recognize for AMT purposes. If the regular tax gain is greater than the AMT gain, due to accelerated depreciation, corporations make negative adjustments to regular taxable income to compute the AMT base.

Example 16-27

Elise discovered that while PCC's regular tax gain on fixed asset dispositions for the year was $70,000, its AMT gain on fixed asset dispositions was only $55,000. What is the amount of PCC's fixed asset dispositions AMT adjustment? Is the adjustment positive or negative?

Answer: $15,000 negative (favorable), computed as follows:

Description	Amount	Explanation
(1) AMT gain on fixed asset dispositions	$55,000	
(2) Regular tax gain on fixed asset dispositions	70,000	Exhibit 16-7.
Negative or (favorable) AMT adjustment	**($15,000)**	(1) – (2).

THE KEY FACTS

Alternative Minimum Tax

- Corporations with average annual gross receipts less than $7.5M for three years prior to the current year are exempt from tax.
  - Corporations are exempt from tax in their first year of existence.
  - For first three years, exempt if annual average gross receipts are below $5M.
  - Once fail gross receipts test, no longer exempt.

(continued)

ACE Adjustment   The ACE **(adjusted current earnings)** adjustment is designed to capture various sources of economic income not otherwise included in the alternative minimum tax base. Consequently, unlike other adjustments, the ACE adjustment is not tied to any one item. To calculate the ACE adjustment, a corporation must first compute its adjusted current earnings. Adjusted current earnings is computed by making certain modifications (designed to reflect economic income) to AMTI (discussed below). Once the corporation has computed its ACE it determines

- Common preference items are tax-exempt interest from private activity bonds (unless issued in 2009 or 2010) and percentage depletion in excess of cost basis.
- Common adjustments are for depreciation, gain or loss on sale of depreciable assets, and adjusted current earnings.
  - ACE adjustment is sum of ACE adjustment items times 75 percent.

its ACE *adjustment* by subtracting AMTI (before the ACE adjustment) from ACE and multiplying the difference by 75 percent [(ACE – AMTI) × 75%].[45] Exhibit 16-14 describes several of the more common modifications to AMTI in computing ACE and indicates whether each modification is added to or subtracted from AMTI to determine ACE.

EXHIBIT 16-14 **Common Modifications to AMTI to Determine ACE**

Description	Modification to AMTI
Tax-exempt interest income from tax-exempt bond that funds a public *activity* (as opposed to private activity). If bond was issued in 2009 or 2010 it is not a modification.[46]	+
Death benefit from life insurance contracts	+
70 percent dividends received deduction (not the 80 percent or 100 percent deduction)	+
Organizational expenditures that were expensed during the year	+
Difference between gain reported under the installment method and gain otherwise reported (installment method not allowed for ACE purposes)	+ or −

As a practical matter, the amount of the ACE adjustment can be determined by multiplying the sum of the modifications to AMTI in computing ACE by 75 percent. If the sum of the modifications is negative, the ACE adjustment may also be negative. However, negative ACE adjustments in excess of cumulative positive prior-year ACE adjustments are not allowed.[47]

Example 16-28

Finally, Elise focused on the ACE adjustment. She discovered that the only modification to AMTI for computing ACE was the $21,000 (70 percent) dividends received deduction. What is PCC's ACE adjustment?

Answer: $15,750, positive adjustment, computed as follows:

Description	Amount	Explanation
(1) Dividends received deduction	$21,000	70 percent dividends received deduction is not deductible in determining ACE.
(2) ACE adjustment percentage	75%	§56(g)(1).
Positive or unfavorable ACE adjustment	**$15,750**	(1) × (2).

What if: Assume that PCC did not receive any dividends and that the San Diego bond generating $12,000 of tax-exempt interest is *not* a private activity bond. Further, assume that PCC reported $5,000 of organizational expenses this year and it reported $20,000 of gain this year from an installment sale it executed two years ago. Assuming PCC's cumulative ACE adjustment as of the beginning of the year is $100,000, what is its current-year ACE adjustment under these circumstances?

[45]§56(g)(1).
[46]§56(g)(4)(B)(iv).
[47]§56(g)(2).

Answer: $2,250 negative ACE adjustment.

Description	Amount	Explanation
(1) Tax-exempt interest	$12,000	Public activity bond.
(2) Organizational expenses	5,000	Not deductible for ACE.
(3) Installment gain	(20,000)	Negative modification because all gain was already included in ACE in year of sale (prior year).
(4) Total modification items	($3,000)	(1) + (2) + (3).
(5) ACE adjustment percentage	75%	§56(g)(1).
Negative or favorable ACE adjustment	**($2,250)**	(4) × (5). Not limited because prior-year cumulated ACE adjustment is positive $100,000.

What if: Assume the same facts as above except that PCC's cumulative positive ACE adjustment at the beginning of the year was $1,000 rather than $100,000. What would be PCC's ACE adjustment in these circumstances?

Answer: $1,000 negative ACE adjustment. PCC's current-year negative ACE adjustment is limited to the cumulative positive ACE adjustment at the beginning of the year.

AMT NOL Deduction (ATNOLD)   If the deductions allowed in computing AMTI exceed the income included in AMTI, the excess becomes an AMT net operating loss (ATNOL). The ATNOL can be carried back 2 years (elective) and carried forward 20 years, similar to a regular tax NOL. The AMT NOL deduction (AMTNOLD) is limited to 90 percent of AMTI computed without regard to the ATNOLD and the domestic production activities deduction.

Alternative Minimum Taxable Income (AMTI)   Corporations compute their alternative minimum taxable income by adding their preference items and adding or subtracting their adjustments from regular taxable income. The alternative minimum taxable income is an important number because corporations use it to determine the amount of the AMT exemption (discussed next) they are allowed to deduct to compute their AMT base.

Example 16-29

After computing PCC's preference items and adjustments Elise had all the information she needed to compute PCC's AMTI. What is PCC's AMTI?

Answer: $5,763,450, computed as follows:

Description	Amount	Explanation
(1) Regular taxable income	$5,150,700	Exhibit 16-7.
(2) Preference items	12,000	Example 16-25.
(3) Depreciation adjustment	600,000	Example 16-26.
(4) Fixed asset disposition adjustment	(15,000)	Example 16-27.
(5) ACE adjustment	15,750	Example 16-28.
Alternative minimum taxable income (AMTI)	$5,763,450	Sum of (1) through (5).

Note, PCC's NOL deduction of $24,000 to 2016 (Exhibit 16-7) is less than the 90 percent limitation applied to modified AMTI. The limitation is $5,627,205, computed as 90 percent × (5,763,450 + 24,000 + 465,000 DPAD). As a result, the full amount of the NOL carryforward can be deducted in computing AMTI.

AMT Exemption   Much like individual taxpayers are allowed to deduct standard deductions and personal exemptions in computing their taxable income, corporations are allowed to deduct a certain exemption amount in computing their alternative minimum tax base. The exemption is subject to an AMTI-based phase-out. The full exemption amount for corporations is $40,000. The exemption is phased out by 25 percent of the amount that AMTI exceeds $150,000 and is completely phased out for corporations with AMTI of at least $310,000.[48] Thus, the exemption is fully phased out for only moderately profitable large corporations. However, the exemption protects many small corporations from paying the alternative minimum tax.

Example 16-30

Because PCC's AMTI exceeds $310,000, Elise determined that PCC's deductible AMT exemption amount is $0.

What if: If PCC's AMTI was $200,000, what exemption amount would it deduct?

Answer: $27,500, computed as follows:

Description	Amount	Explanation
(1) Full exemption amount	$ 40,000	§55(d)(2).
(2) Assumed AMTI	200,000	
(3) Exemption phase-out threshold	150,000	§55(d)(3).
(4) AMTI over exemption threshold	$ 50,000	(2) − (3).
(5) Phase-out percentage	25%	§55(d)(3).
(6) Exemption phase-out amount	$ 12,500	(4) × (5).
Deductible exemption	**$ 27,500**	(1) − (6).

THE KEY FACTS
Alternative Minimum Tax
- AMT full exemption amount is $40,000.
  - Phase-out 25 percent for each $1 of AMTI in excess of $150,000.
- AMT rate is 20 percent.
- AMT equals excess of TMT over regular tax liability.
- Tentative minimum tax credit reduces regular tax down to TMT in year corporation doesn't owe AMT.

Alternative Minimum Tax   To determine their alternative minimum tax, corporations next compute their **tentative minimum tax** (TMT) by multiplying their AMT base (AMTI minus exemption amount) by a flat 20 percent rate. Then they compare their TMT to their regular tax liability. If a corporation's regular tax liability is greater than the TMT, it does not owe any alternative minimum tax. If its TMT is greater than its regular tax liability, it must pay its regular tax liability and the excess of the TMT over its regular tax liability. This excess is the alternative minimum tax. Corporations are allowed to reduce the gross AMT by any foreign tax credits they have for regular tax purposes.

Example 16-31

Elise had enough information to compute PCC's alternative minimum tax. She knew the tax software would compute the AMT but she wanted to calculate it independent from the program to ensure the results were accurate. What is PCC's alternative minimum tax, if any?

Answer: $0, computed as follows:

Description	Amount	Explanation
(1) AMTI	$5,763,450	Example 16-29.
(2) Deductible exemption	0	Example 16-30.
(3) AMT base	$5,763,450	(1) + (2).
(4) AMT rate	20%	§55(b)(3)(D).
(5) Tentative minimum tax	$1,152,690	(3) × (4).
(6) Regular tax	$1,751,238	Example 16-19.
Alternative minimum tax	**$ 0**	(5) − (6), but not less than $0.

[48]§55(d)(2).

What if: If PCC's regular tax liability had been $1,000,000, what would be the amount of its AMT?

Answer: $152,690, which is the excess of the $1,152,690 TMT over the $1,000,000 regular tax liability. PCC would pay its $1,000,000 regular tax liability and $152,690 of AMT.

When corporations owe the alternative minimum tax, they generate a **minimum tax credit** that they can carry forward *indefinitely* to offset their regular tax liability down to their tentative minimum tax in years when their regular tax exceeds their tentative minimum tax. That is, they can use the tentative minimum tax credit in years when they do not owe the alternative minimum tax.

Example 16-32

What if: Assume that in year 1, PCC has a TMT of $1,152,690 and a regular tax liability of $1,000,000. PCC would owe $152,690 of AMT and $1,000,000 of regular tax. It would also generate a $152,690 minimum tax credit. Further, assume that in year 2 PCC reports a tentative minimum tax of $900,000 and a regular tax liability of $1,000,000. What is PCC's tax liability after applying the minimum tax credit?

Answer: $900,000 tax liability and $52,690 minimum tax credit carryover, computed as follows:

Description	Amount	Explanation
(1) Year 1 minimum tax credit	$ 152,690	
(2) Year 2 tentative minimum tax	900,000	
(3) Year 2 regular tax liability	1,000,000	
(4) Year 2 AMT	0	(2) − (3), but not less than $0.
(5) Limit on year 2 minimum tax credit	100,000	(3) − (2).
(6) Year 2 minimum tax credit	100,000	Lesser of (1) and (5).
(7) Total tax liability for year	**900,000**	(3) − (6).
Minimum tax credit carryover	**52,690**	(1) − (6).

Exhibit 16-15 presents PCC's Form 4626: Alternative Minimum Tax—Corporations.

CONCLUSION

A taxable or C corporation is a separate legal and taxpaying entity from its stockholders. Consequently, it must determine and report its own taxable income to the IRS. This chapter discussed and described the process of computing a corporation's taxable income and the associated tax liability for C corporations. We learned that book income is the starting point for determining taxable income. Corporations adjust their book income for book–tax differences that arise because they account for many items of income and deduction differently for book purposes than they do for tax purposes. Some of these book–tax differences are temporary (the differences balance out over time) and some are permanent in nature (they don't balance out over the long-term). As we discover in the next chapter, the distinction between temporary and permanent book–tax differences is critical for corporations computing their income tax expense or benefit for financial accounting purposes.

EXHIBIT 16-15 PCC's Form 4626

Form **4626**	**Alternative Minimum Tax—Corporations**	OMB No. 1545-0123
Department of the Treasury Internal Revenue Service	▶ Attach to the corporation's tax return. ▶ Information about Form 4626 and its separate instructions is at *www.irs.gov/form4626.*	20**15**

Name	Employer identification number
Premier Computer Corporation	12-3456789

Note: *See the instructions to find out if the corporation is a small corporation exempt from the alternative minimum tax (AMT) under section 55(e).*

1	Taxable income or (loss) before net operating loss deduction	**1**	5,150,700
2	**Adjustments and preferences:**		
a	Depreciation of post-1986 property	**2a**	600,000
b	Amortization of certified pollution control facilities.	**2b**	
c	Amortization of mining exploration and development costs	**2c**	
d	Amortization of circulation expenditures (personal holding companies only)	**2d**	
e	Adjusted gain or loss	**2e**	(15,000)
f	Long-term contracts	**2f**	
g	Merchant marine capital construction funds.	**2g**	
h	Section 833(b) deduction (Blue Cross, Blue Shield, and similar type organizations only) . .	**2h**	
i	Tax shelter farm activities (personal service corporations only)	**2i**	
j	Passive activities (closely held corporations and personal service corporations only)	**2j**	
k	Loss limitations	**2k**	
l	Depletion	**2l**	
m	Tax-exempt interest income from specified private activity bonds	**2m**	12,000
n	Intangible drilling costs	**2n**	
o	Other adjustments and preferences	**2o**	
3	Pre-adjustment alternative minimum taxable income (AMTI). Combine lines 1 through 2o.	**3**	5,747,700

4	**Adjusted current earnings (ACE) adjustment:**			
a	ACE from line 10 of the ACE worksheet in the instructions	**4a**	5,768,700	
b	Subtract line 3 from line 4a. If line 3 exceeds line 4a, enter the difference as a negative amount (see instructions).	**4b**	21,000	
c	Multiply line 4b by 75% (.75). Enter the result as a positive amount	**4c**	15,750	
d	Enter the excess, if any, of the corporation's total increases in AMTI from prior year ACE adjustments over its total reductions in AMTI from prior year ACE adjustments (see instructions). **Note:** *You* **must** *enter an amount on line 4d (even if line 4b is positive).*	**4d**		
e	ACE adjustment. • If line 4b is zero or more, enter the amount from line 4c • If line 4b is less than zero, enter the **smaller** of line 4c or line 4d as a negative amount	} . . .	**4e**	15,750
5	Combine lines 3 and 4e. If zero or less, stop here; the corporation does not owe any AMT	**5**		5,763,450
6	Alternative tax net operating loss deduction (see instructions).	**6**		
7	**Alternative minimum taxable income.** Subtract line 6 from line 5. If the corporation held a residual interest in a REMIC, see instructions	**7**		5,763,450
8	**Exemption phase-out** (if line 7 is $310,000 or more, skip lines 8a and 8b and enter -0- on line 8c):			
a	Subtract $150,000 from line 7 (if completing this line for a member of a controlled group, see instructions). If zero or less, enter -0-	**8a**		
b	Multiply line 8a by 25% (.25).	**8b**		
c	Exemption. Subtract line 8b from $40,000 (if completing this line for a member of a controlled group, see instructions). If zero or less, enter -0-	**8c**		0
9	Subtract line 8c from line 7. If zero or less, enter -0-	**9**		5,763,450
10	Multiply line 9 by 20% (.20)	**10**		1,152,690
11	Alternative minimum tax foreign tax credit (AMTFTC) (see instructions)	**11**		
12	Tentative minimum tax. Subtract line 11 from line 10	**12**		1,562,690
13	Regular tax liability before applying all credits except the foreign tax credit	**13**		1,751,238
14	**Alternative minimum tax.** Subtract line 13 from line 12. If zero or less, enter -0-. Enter here and on Form 1120, Schedule J, line 3, or the appropriate line of the corporation's income tax return . . .	**14**		0

For Paperwork Reduction Act Notice, see separate instructions.   Cat. No. 12955I   Form **4626** (2015)

Summary

Describe the corporate income tax formula, compare and contrast the corporate to the individual tax formula, and discuss tax considerations relating to corporations' accounting periods and accounting methods.   **LO 16-1**

- A corporation's taxable income is gross income minus deductions.
- The corporate tax formula is similar to the individual formula except that corporations don't itemize deductions or deduct standard deductions. Corporations also don't deduct personal and dependency exemptions.
- Corporations may generally elect any tax year for reporting their taxable income, but the year must coincide with their financial accounting year.
- The timing of a corporation's income and deductions depends on the corporation's overall accounting method and its methods for specific transactions.
- Corporations are generally required to use the accrual overall method of accounting. However, smaller corporations may be allowed to use the cash method.

Identify common book–tax differences, distinguish between permanent and temporary differences, and compute a corporation's taxable income and regular tax liability.   **LO 16-2**

- Corporations typically compute taxable income by starting with book income and adjusting for book–tax differences.
- Book–tax differences are favorable when they reduce taxable income relative to book income and unfavorable when they increase it.
- Book–tax differences are permanent when the amount of income or deduction items is different for book and tax purposes and the amount will not reverse in the future.
- Book–tax differences are temporary when the amount of income or deduction item is different for book and tax purposes in the current year but the same for book and tax purposes over the long-term. That is, temporary book–tax differences reverse over time.
- Common permanent book–tax differences include interest from municipal bonds (favorable), life insurance premiums on policies covering key employees (unfavorable), and one-half of meals and entertainment expense, among others.
- Nonqualified stock options granted before ASC 718's effective date generate favorable permanent book–tax differences when employees exercise them. The amount of the difference is the bargain element of the options that is deductible for tax but not for books.
- Common temporary book–tax differences include depreciation expense, gain or loss on sale of depreciable assets, bad-debt expense, purchased goodwill amortization, and warranty expense, among others.
- Stock options granted when ASC 718 applies can generate temporary and permanent book–tax differences.
- Corporations may not deduct net capital losses for tax purposes. However, they may carry them back three years and forward five years to offset capital gains in those other years.
- When computing their net operating losses for the year, corporations may not deduct net operating losses from other years or net capital losses from other years.
- Subject to limitation, corporations can deduct as the amount of money, the fair market value of capital gain property, and the adjusted basis of ordinary income property they donate to charity.
- The charitable contribution deduction for the year is limited to 10 percent of taxable income before deducting the charitable contribution, the dividends received deduction, NOL carrybacks, the domestic production activities deduction, and capital loss carrybacks. Amounts in excess of the limitation can be carried forward for up to five years.
- Corporations are allowed a deduction for dividends received to help mitigate potential triple taxation of the income distributed as a dividend. The amount of the deduction depends on the corporation's ownership in the distributing corporation. The deduction is 70 percent if the ownership is less than 20 percent; the deduction is 80 percent if the ownership is at least 20 percent but less than 80 percent; and finally, the deduction is 100 percent if the ownership is 80 percent or more.

- The dividends received deduction (DRD) is subject to a taxable income limitation. This limitation does not apply if the full DRD extends or creates a net operating loss for the corporation in the current year.

- A corporation's marginal tax rates range from 15 percent to 39 percent. High-income corporations are taxed at a flat 35 percent tax rate.

- Controlled groups are groups of corporations with common ownership. Special rules apply to limit the tax benefits (including lower marginal tax rates) of splitting large corporations into smaller corporations. Controlled groups can be parent-subsidiary controlled groups, brother-sister controlled groups, or combined groups.

LO 16-3   Describe a corporation's tax return reporting and estimated tax payment obligations.

- Corporations file their tax returns on Form 1120, which are due three and one-half months after the corporation's year-end beginning in 2016 (two and one-half months for years prior to 2016 and for corporations with a June 30 year-end through 2025). Corporations can apply for an extension of the due date for filing the return for five months.

- Small corporations report their book–tax differences on Schedule M-1 of Form 1120. Large corporations (assets of $10 million or more) report them on Schedule M-3. Schedule M-3 requires much more detail than Schedule M-1.

- Corporations pay income taxes through estimated tax payments. Each payment should be 25 percent of their required annual payment. The installments are due on the 15th day of the 4th, 6th, 9th, and 12th months of the corporation's taxable year.

- Corporations' required annual payment is the least of (1) 100 percent of their current-year tax liability, (2) 100 percent of their prior-year tax liability (but only if they had a positive tax liability in the prior year), or (3) 100 percent of the estimated current year tax liability using the annualized income method. Large corporations may rely on (2) only to compute their first quarter estimated payment requirement.

LO 16-4   Calculate a corporation's alternative minimum tax liability.

- The alternative minimum tax is a tax on a broader base than the regular tax. It ensures that corporations are not able to avoid taxes entirely by receiving tax-advantaged treatment for regular income tax items. The alternative minimum tax rate is a flat 20 percent for corporations.

- To compute alternative minimum taxable income, corporations start with regular taxable income and add preferences, add or subtract adjustments, and subtract an exemption amount. The AMT base is taxed at 20 percent to provide a tentative minimum tax. The AMT is the excess of the tentative minimum tax over the regular tax.

- Corporations receive a minimum tax credit in the amount of the alternative minimum tax they pay for the year. This credit can offset the corporation's regular tax liability to the extent it exceeds the tentative minimum tax in a future year.

KEY TERMS

adjusted current earnings (ACE) (16-35)
affiliated group (16-29)
alternative minimum tax (16-33)
annualized income method (16-30)
bargain element (16-9)
book (financial reporting) income (16-3)
book–tax differences (16-3)
brother-sister controlled group (16-24)
capital gain property (16-15)
charitable contribution limit modified taxable income (16-16)
combined controlled group (16-24)

controlled groups (16-24)
consolidated tax return (16-29)
DRD modified taxable income (16-19)
exercise price (16-9)
favorable book–tax difference (16-4)
grant date (16-10)
incentive stock options (16-9)
M adjustments (16-25)
minimum tax credit (16-39)
net capital loss carryback (16-12)
net capital loss carryover (16-12)
net operating loss (NOL) (16-14)
net operating loss carryback (16-14)

net operating loss carryover (16-14)
nonqualified stock options (16-9)
ordinary income property (16-15)
parent-subsidiary controlled group (16-24)
permanent book–tax differences (16-4)
private activity bond (16-33)
Schedule M adjustments (16-25)
temporary book–tax differences (16-4)
tentative minimum tax (16-38)
unfavorable book–tax difference (16-4)
vest (16-9)
vesting period (16-10)

DISCUSSION QUESTIONS

Discussion Questions are available in *Connect*®.   **connect**

1. In general terms, identify the similarities and differences between the corporate taxable income formula and the individual taxable income formula.   `LO 16-1`

2. Is a corporation's choice of its tax year independent from its year-end for financial accounting purposes?   `LO 16-1`

3. Can C corporations use the cash method of accounting? Explain.   `LO 16-1`

4. Briefly describe the process of computing a corporation's taxable income assuming the corporation must use GAAP to determine its book income. How might the process differ for corporations not required to use GAAP for book purposes?   `LO 16-2`

5. What role does a corporation's audited financial statements play in determining its taxable income?   `LO 16-2`

6. What is the difference between favorable and unfavorable book–tax differences?   `LO 16-2`

7. What is the difference between permanent and temporary book–tax differences?   `LO 16-2`

8. Why is it important to be able to determine whether a particular book–tax difference is permanent or temporary?   `LO 16-2`

9. Describe the relation between the book–tax differences associated with depreciation expense and with gain or loss on disposition of depreciable assets.   `LO 16-2`

10. When a corporation receives a dividend from another corporation, does the dividend generate a book–tax difference to the dividend-receiving corporation (ignore the dividends received deduction)? Explain.   `LO 16-2`

11. Describe how goodwill recognized in an asset acquisition leads to temporary book–tax differences.   `LO 16-2`

12. Describe the book–tax differences that arise from incentive stock options and nonqualified stock options granted before ASC 718 became effective.   `LO 16-2`

13. Describe the book–tax differences that arise from incentive stock options granted after ASC 718 became effective.   `LO 16-2`

14. Describe the book–tax differences that arise from nonqualified stock options granted after ASC 718 became effective.   `LO 16-2`

15. How do corporations account for capital gains and losses for tax purposes? How is this different from the way individuals account for capital gains and losses?   `LO 16-2`

16. What are the common book–tax differences relating to accounting for capital gains and losses? Do these differences create favorable or unfavorable book-to-tax adjustments?   `LO 16-2`

17. What is the carryback and carryover period for a net operating loss? Does it depend on the size of the corporation? Explain.   `LO 16-2`

18. Is a corporation allowed to carry a net operating loss forward if it has income in prior years that it could offset with a carryback? Explain.   `LO 16-2`

19. What must a decision maker consider when deciding whether to carry back a net operating loss or to elect to forgo the carryback?   `LO 16-2`

20. A corporation commissioned an accounting firm to recalculate the way it accounted for leasing transactions. With the new calculations, the corporation was able to file amended tax returns for the past few years that increased the corporation's net operating loss carryover from $3,000,000 to $5,000,000. Was the corporation wise to pay the accountants for their work that led to the increase in the NOL carryover? What factors should be considered in making this determination?   `LO 16-2`

21. Compare and contrast the general rule for determining the amount of the charitable contribution if the corporation contributes capital gain property versus ordinary income property.   `LO 16-2`

LO 16-2 22. Which limitations might restrict a corporation's deduction for a cash charitable contribution? Explain how to determine the amount of the limitation.

LO 16-2 23. For tax purposes, what happens to a corporation's charitable contributions that are not deducted in the current year because of the taxable income limitation?

LO 16-2 24. What are common book–tax differences relating to corporate charitable contributions? Are these differences favorable or unfavorable?

LO 16-2 25. Why does Congress provide the dividends received deduction for corporations receiving dividends?

LO 16-2 26. How does a corporation determine the percentage for its dividends received deduction? Explain.

LO 16-2 27. What limitations apply to the amount of the allowable dividends received deduction?

LO 16-2 28. Why do the marginal rates in the corporate tax rate schedule increase and then decrease before increasing again?

LO 16-2 29. Explain the controlled group rules in very general terms and indicate what type of behavior the rules are attempting to prevent in terms of computing a corporation's tax liability.

LO 16-2 30. Describe the three types of controlled groups.

LO 16-3 31. How is the Schedule M-1 similar to and different from a Schedule M-3? How does a corporation determine whether it must complete Schedule M-1 or Schedule M-3 when it completes its tax return?

LO 16-3 32. What is the due date for a calendar year corporation tax return Form 1120 for 2016? Is it possible to extend the due date? Explain.

LO 16-3 33. How does a corporation determine the minimum amount of estimated tax payments it must make to avoid underpayment penalties? How are these rules different for large corporations than they are for other corporations?

LO 16-3 34. Describe the annualized income method for determining a corporation's required estimated tax payments. What advantages does this method have over other methods?

LO 16-4 35. Are any corporations exempt from the AMT? Briefly explain.

LO 16-4 36. Briefly describe the process of computing a corporation's AMT.

LO 16-4 37. What is the conceptual difference between adjustments and preference items for AMT purposes?

LO 16-4 38. What does the ACE adjustment attempt to capture? How does a corporation determine its ACE adjustment?

LO 16-4 39. What is the corporate AMT exemption? Is it available to all corporations? Briefly explain.

LO 16-4 40. How is it possible that a corporation's marginal AMT rate is greater than 20 percent if the stated AMT rate is 20 percent?

LO 16-4 41. Does a corporation pay the AMT in addition to or instead of the regular tax? Briefly explain.

LO 16-4 42. How does a corporation compute its minimum tax credit? How does a minimum tax credit benefit a corporation?

LO 16-4
planning 43. What basic tax planning strategies might a corporation that is expected to owe AMT this year but not next year engage in? How would those strategies change if the corporation expected to be in AMT next year but not in the current year?

PROBLEMS

Select problems are available in *Connect*®.

🔲 connect

44. LNS corporation reports book income of $2,000,000. Included in the
$2,000,000 is $15,000 of tax-exempt interest income. LNS reports $1,345,000 in
ordinary and necessary business expenses. What is LNS corporation's taxable
income for the year?

LO 16-1

45. ATW corporation currently uses the FIFO method of accounting for its inventory
for book and tax purposes. Its beginning inventory for the current year was
$8,000,000. Its ending inventory for the current year was $7,000,000. If ATW
had been using the LIFO method of accounting for its inventory, its beginning
inventory would have been $7,000,000 and its ending inventory would have been
$5,500,000. Assume ATW corporation's marginal tax rate is 34 percent.

LO 16-1

   a) How much more in taxes did ATW corporation pay for the current year
   because it used the FIFO method of accounting for inventory than it would
   have paid if it had used the LIFO method?

   b) Why would ATW use the FIFO method of accounting if doing so causes it to
   pay more taxes on a present value basis? (Note that the tax laws don't allow
   corporations to use the LIFO method of accounting for inventory unless they
   also use the LIFO method of accounting for inventory for book purposes.)

46. ELS corporation is about to begin its sixth year of existence. Assume that ELS
reported gross receipts for each of its first five years of existence for Scenarios
A, B, and C as follows:

LO 16-1

Year of Existence	Scenario A	Scenario B	Scenario C
1	$4,000,000	$3,000,000	$5,500,000
2	5,000,000	5,000,000	5,000,000
3	5,900,000	7,500,000	4,750,000
4	6,000,000	6,000,000	5,000,000
5	4,500,000	4,500,000	5,250,000

   a) In what years is ELS allowed to use the cash method of accounting under
   Scenario A?

   b) In what years is ELS allowed to use the cash method of accounting under
   Scenario B?

   c) In what years is ELS allowed to use the cash method of accounting under
   Scenario C?

47. On its year 1 financial statements, Seatax Corporation, an accrual-method taxpayer,
reported federal income tax expense of $570,000. On its year 1 tax return, it reported
a tax liability of $650,000. During year 1, Seatax made estimated tax payments of
$700,000. What book–tax difference, if any, associated with its federal income tax
expense should Seatax have reported when computing its year 1 taxable income? Is
the difference favorable or unfavorable? Is it temporary or permanent?

LO 16-2

48. Assume Maple Corp. has just completed the third year of its existence (year 3).
The table below indicates Maple's ending book inventory for each year and the
additional §263A costs it was required to include in its ending inventory. Maple
immediately expensed these costs for book purposes. In year 2, Maple sold all of
its year 1 ending inventory, and in year 3 it sold all of its year 2 ending inventory.

LO 16-2

	Year 1	Year 2	Year 3
Ending book inventory	$2,400,000	$2,700,000	$2,040,000
Additional §263A costs	60,000	70,000	40,000
Ending tax inventory	$2,460,000	$2,770,000	$2,080,000

a) What book–tax difference associated with its inventory did Maple report in year 1? Was the difference favorable or unfavorable? Was it permanent or temporary?

b) What book–tax difference associated with its inventory did Maple report in year 2? Was the difference favorable or unfavorable? Was it permanent or temporary?

c) What book–tax difference associated with its inventory did Maple report in year 3? Was the difference favorable or unfavorable? Was it permanent or temporary?

LO 16-2 49. JDog corporation owns stock in Oscar Inc. JDog received a $10,000 dividend from Oscar Inc. What temporary book–tax difference associated with the dividend will JDog report for the year in the following alternative scenarios (income difference only—ignore the dividends received deduction)?

a) JDog owns 5 percent of the Oscar Inc. stock. Oscar's income for the year was $500,000.

b) JDog owns 40 percent of the Oscar Inc. stock. Oscar's income for the year was $500,000.

LO 16-2 50. On July 1 of year 1, Riverside Corp. (RC), a calendar-year taxpayer, acquired the assets of another business in a taxable acquisition. When the purchase price was allocated to the assets purchased, RC determined it had purchased $1,200,000 of goodwill for both book and tax purposes. At the end of year 1, RC determined that the goodwill had not been impaired during the year. In year 2, however, RC concluded that $200,000 of the goodwill had been impaired, and they required RC to write down the goodwill by $200,000 for book purposes.

a) What book–tax difference associated with its goodwill should RC report in year 1? Is it favorable or unfavorable? Is it permanent or temporary?

b) What book–tax difference associated with its goodwill should RC report in year 2? Is it favorable or unfavorable? Is it permanent or temporary?

LO 16-2 51. Assume that on January 1, year 1, ABC Inc. issued 5,000 stock options with an estimated value of $10 per option. Each option entitles the owner to purchase one share of ABC stock for $25 a share (the per share price of ABC stock on January 1, year 1, when the options were granted). The options vest at the end of the day on December 31, year 2. All 5,000 stock options were exercised in year 3 when the ABC stock was valued at $31 per share. Identify ABC's year 1, 2, and 3 tax deductions and book–tax differences (indicate whether permanent and/or temporary) associated with the stock options under the following alternative scenarios:

a) The stock options are incentive stock options and ASC 718 does not apply to the options.

b) The stock options are nonqualified stock options and ASC 718 does not apply to the options.

c) The stock options are incentive stock options and ASC 718 applies to the options.

d) The stock options are nonqualified stock options and ASC 718 applies to the options.

LO 16-2 52. Assume that on January 1, year 1, XYZ Corp. issued 1,000 nonqualified stock options with an estimated value of $4 per option. Each option entitles the owner to purchase one share of XYZ stock for $14 a share (the per share price of XYZ stock on January 1, year 1, when the options were granted). The options vest 25 percent a year (on December 31) for four years (beginning with year 1). All 500 stock options that had vested to that point were exercised in year 3 when the XYZ stock was valued at $20 per share. No other options were exercised in year 3 or year 4. Identify XYZ's year 1, 2, 3, and 4 tax deductions and book–tax difference (identify as permanent and/or temporary) associated with the stock options under the following alternative scenarios:

a) ASC 718 does not apply to the stock options.

b) ASC 718 applies to the stock options.

53. What book–tax differences in year 1 and year 2 associated with its capital gains and losses would ABD Inc. report in the following alternative scenarios? Identify each book–tax difference as favorable or unfavorable and as permanent or temporary.   **LO 16-2**

a)

	Year 1	Year 2
Capital gains	$20,000	$ 5,000
Capital losses	8,000	0

b)

	Year 1	Year 2
Capital gains	$ 8,000	$ 5,000
Capital losses	20,000	0

c)

	Year 1	Year 2
Capital gains	$ 0	$50,000
Capital losses	25,000	30,000

d)

	Year 1	Year 2
Capital gains	$ 0	$40,000
Capital losses	25,000	0

e) Answer for year 6 only.

	Year 1	Years 2–5	Year 6
Capital gains	$ 0	$ 0	$15,000
Capital losses	10,000	0	0

f) Answer for year 7 only.

	Year 1	Years 2–6	Year 7
Capital gains	$ 0	$ 0	$15,000
Capital losses	10,000	0	0

54. What book–tax differences in year 1 and year 2 associated with its capital gains and losses would DEF Inc. report in the following alternative scenarios? Identify each book–tax difference as favorable or unfavorable and as permanent or temporary.   **LO 16-2**

a) In year 1, DEF recognized a loss of $15,000 on land that it had held for investment. In year 1, it also recognized a $30,000 gain on equipment it had purchased a few years ago. The equipment sold for $50,000 and had an adjusted basis of $20,000. DEF had deducted $40,000 of depreciation on the equipment. In year 2, DEF recognized a capital loss of $2,000.

b) In year 1, DEF recognized a loss of $15,000 on land that it had held for investment. It also recognized a $20,000 gain on equipment it had purchased a few years ago. The equipment sold for $50,000 and had an adjusted basis of $30,000. DEF had deducted $15,000 of tax depreciation on the equipment.

LO 16-2   55. MWC Corp. is currently in the sixth year of its existence (2016). In 2011–2015, it reported the following income and (losses) (before net operating loss carryovers or carrybacks).

2011	($ 70,000)
2012	(30,000)
2013	60,000
2014	140,000
2015	(25,000)
2016	300,000

a) Assuming the original facts and that MWC elects to not carry back NOLs, what was MWC's 2014 taxable income?

b) If MWC does not elect to forgo any NOL carrybacks, what is its 2016 taxable income after the NOL deduction?

c) If MWC always elects to forgo NOL carrybacks, what is its 2016 taxable income after the NOL deduction? What is its 2016 book–tax difference associated with its NOL? Is it favorable or unfavorable? Is it permanent or temporary?

LO 16-2   56. WCC Inc. has a current year (2016) net operating loss of $100,000. It is trying to determine whether it should carry back the loss or whether it should elect to forgo the carryback. How would you advise WCC in each of the following alternative situations (ignore the time value of money in your computations)?

a)

	2014	2015	2017
Taxable income	$ 30,000	$ 0	$ 300,000

b)

	2014	2015	2017
Taxable income	$900,000	$60,000	$ 100,000

c)

	2014	2015	2017
Taxable income	$900,000	$60,000	$5,000,000

d)

	2014	2015	2017
Taxable income	$ 50,000	$20,000	$2,000,000

LO 16-2   57. Assume that in year 1 Hill Corporation reported a net operating loss of $10,000 that it carried forward to year 2. In year 1, Hill also reported a net capital loss of $3,000 that it carried forward to year 2. In year 2, ignoring any carryovers from other years, Hill reported a loss for tax purposes of $50,000. The current-year loss includes a $12,000 net capital gain. What is Hill's year 2 net operating loss?

LO 16-2   58. Golf Corp. (GC), a calendar-year accrual-method corporation, held its directors' meeting on December 15 of year 1. During the meeting the board of directors authorized GC to pay a $75,000 charitable contribution to the World Golf Foundation, a qualifying charity.

a) If GC actually pays $50,000 of this contribution on January 15 of year 2 and the remaining $25,000 on March 15 of year 2, what book–tax difference will it report associated with the contribution in year 1 (assume the 10 percent limitation does not apply)? Is it favorable or unfavorable? Is it permanent or temporary?

b) Assuming the same facts as in part (a), what book–tax difference will GC report in year 2 (assuming the 10 percent limitation does not apply)? Is it favorable or unfavorable?

c) If GC actually pays $50,000 of this contribution on January 15 of year 2 and the remaining $25,000 on May 15 of year 2, what book–tax difference will it report associated with the contribution in year 1 (assume the 10 percent limitation does not apply)? Is it favorable or unfavorable? Is it permanent or temporary?

d) Assuming the same facts as in part (c), what book–tax difference will GC report in year 2 (assuming the 10 percent limitation does not apply)? Is it favorable or unfavorable?

59. In year 1 (the current year), OCC Corp. made a charitable donation of $200,000 to the Jordan Spieth Family Foundation (a qualifying charity). For the year, OCC reported taxable income of $1,500,000 before deducting any charitable contributions, before deducting its $20,000 dividends received deduction, and before deducting its $40,000 NOL carryover from last year.   **LO 16-2**

   a) What amount of the $200,000 donation is OCC allowed to deduct for tax purposes in year 1?

   b) In year 2, OCC did not make any charitable contributions. It reported taxable income of $300,000 before any charitable contribution deductions and before a $15,000 dividends received deduction. What book–tax difference associated with the charitable contributions will OCC report in year 2? Is the difference favorable or unfavorable? Is it permanent or temporary?

   c) Assume the original facts and those provided in part (b). In years 3, 4, and 5, OCC reported taxable losses of $50,000. Finally, in year 6 it reported $1,000,000 in taxable income before any charitable contribution deductions. It did not have any dividends received deduction. OCC did not actually make any charitable donations in year 6. What book–tax difference associated with charitable contributions will OCC report in year 6?

60. In year 1 (the current year), LAA Inc. made a charitable donation of $100,000 to the American Red Cross (a qualifying charity). For the year, LAA reported taxable income of $550,000, which included a $100,000 charitable contribution deduction (before limitation), a $50,000 dividends received deduction, a $20,000 domestic production activities deduction, and a $10,000 net operating loss carryover from year 0. What is LAA Inc.'s charitable contribution deduction for year 1?   **LO 16-2**

61. Coattail Corporation (CC) manufactures and sells women's and children's coats. This year, CC donated 1,000 coats to a qualified public charity. The charity distributed the coats to needy women and children throughout the region. At the time of the contribution, the fair market value of each coat was $80. Determine the amount of CC's charitable contribution (the taxable income limitation does not apply) for the coats assuming the following: **LO 16-2**   **research**

   a) CC's adjusted basis in each coat was $30.

   b) CC's adjusted basis in each coat was $10.

62. Maple Corp. owns several pieces of highly valued paintings that are on display in the corporation's headquarters. This year, it donated one of the paintings valued at $100,000 (adjusted basis of $25,000) to a local museum for the museum to display. What is the amount of Maple Corp.'s charitable contribution deduction for the painting (assuming income limitations do not apply)? What would be Maple's deduction if the museum sold the painting one month after it received it from Maple?   **LO 16-2**   **research**

63. Riverbend Inc. received a $200,000 dividend from stock it held in Hobble Corporation. Riverbend's taxable income is $2,100,000 before deducting the dividends received deduction (DRD), a $40,000 NOL carryover, a $10,000 domestic production activities deduction, and a $100,000 charitable contribution.   **LO 16-2**

   a) What is Riverbend's deductible DRD assuming it owns 10 percent of Hobble Corporation?

   b) Assuming the facts in part (a), what is Riverbend's marginal tax rate on the dividend?

   c) What is Riverbend's DRD assuming it owns 60 percent of Hobble Corporation?

d) Assuming the facts in part (c), what is Riverbend's marginal tax rate on the dividend?

e) What is Riverbend's DRD assuming it owns 85 percent of Hobble Corporation (and is part of the same affiliated group)?

f) Assuming the facts in part (e), what is Riverbend's marginal tax rate on the dividend?

LO 16-2 64. Wasatch Corp. (WC) received a $200,000 dividend from Tager Corporation (TC). WC owns 15 percent of the TC stock. Compute WC's deductible DRD in each of the following situations:

a) WC's taxable income (loss) without the dividend income or the DRD is $10,000.

b) WC's taxable income (loss) without the dividend income or the DRD is ($10,000).

c) WC's taxable income (loss) without the dividend income or the DRD is ($59,000).

d) WC's taxable income (loss) without the dividend income or the DRD is ($61,000).

e) WC's taxable income (loss) without the dividend income or the DRD is ($500,000).

f) What is WC's book–tax difference associated with its DRD in part (a)? Is the difference favorable or unfavorable? Is it permanent or temporary?

LO 16-2 65. Compute SWK Inc.'s tax liability for each of the following scenarios:

a) SWK's taxable income is $60,000.

b) SWK's taxable income is $275,000.

c) SWK's taxable income is $15,500,000.

d) SWK's taxable income for the year is $50,000,000.

LO 16-2 66. ABC's taxable income for the year is $200,000 and CBA's taxable income for the year is $400,000. Compute the combined tax liability of the two corporations assuming the following:

a) Amanda, Jermaine, and O'Neil each own one-third of the stock of ABC and CBA.

b) Amanda, Jermaine, and O'Neil each own one-third of the stock of ABC and Amanda and Dustin each own 50 percent of the stock of CBA.

c) ABC owns 85 percent of CBA's stock on the last day of the year. ABC and CBA file separate (as opposed to consolidated) tax returns.

LO 16-2 67. ABC's taxable income for the year is $25,000 and CBA's taxable income for the year is $10,000,000. Compute the combined tax liability of the two corporations assuming the following:

a) Amanda, Jermaine, and O'Neil each own one-third of the stock of ABC and CBA.

b) Amanda, Jermaine, and O'Neil each own one-third of the stock of ABC and Amanda and Dustin each own 50 percent of the stock of CBA.

LO 16-3 68. Last year, TBA Corporation, a calendar-year taxpayer, reported a tax liability of $100,000. TBA confidently anticipates a current-year tax liability of $240,000. What minimum estimated tax payments should TBA make for the first, second, third, and fourth quarters respectively (ignore the annualized income method), assuming the following:

a) TBA is not considered to be a large corporation for estimated tax purposes.

b) TBA is considered to be a large corporation for estimated tax purposes.

69. Last year, BTA Corporation, a calendar-year taxpayer, reported a net operating loss of $10,000 and a $0 tax liability. BTA confidently anticipates a current-year tax liability of $240,000. What minimum estimated tax payments should BTA make for the first, second, third, and fourth quarters, respectively (ignore the annualized income method), assuming the following: `LO 16-3`

   a) BTA is not considered to be a large corporation for estimated tax purposes.

   b) BTA is considered to be a large corporation for estimated tax purposes.

70. For the current year, LNS corporation reported the following taxable income at the end of its first, second, and third quarters. What are LNS's minimum first, second, third, and fourth quarter estimated tax payments determined using the annualized income method?   `LO 16-3`

Quarter-End	Cumulative Taxable Income
First	$1,000,000
Second	1,600,000
Third	2,400,000

71. Last year, JL Corporation's tax liability was $900,000. For the current year, JL Corporation reported the following taxable income at the end of its first, second, and third quarters (see table below). What are JL's minimum required first, second, third, and fourth quarter estimated tax payments (ignore the actual current-year tax safe harbor)?   `LO 16-3` `planning`

Quarter-End	Cumulative Taxable Income
First	$ 500,000
Second	1,250,000
Third	2,250,000

72. Last year, Cougar Corp. (CC) reported a net operating loss of $25,000. In the current year, CC expected its current-year tax liability to be $440,000 so it made four equal estimated tax payments of $110,000 each. Cougar closed its books at the end of each quarter. The following schedule reports CC's taxable income at the end of each quarter: `LO 16-3`

Quarter-End	Cumulative Taxable Income
First	$ 300,000
Second	700,000
Third	1,000,000
Fourth	1,470,588

    CC's current-year tax liability on $1,470,588 of taxable income is $500,000. Does CC owe underpayment penalties on its estimated tax payments? If so, for which quarters does it owe the penalty?

73. For the current year, CCP Inc. received the following interest income: `LO 16-2` `LO 16-4`
    - $12,000 interest from Irvine City bonds: Bonds issued in 2012 and proceeds used to fund public schools.
    - $20,000 interest from Fluor Corporation bonds.
    - $8,000 interest from Mission Viejo City: Bonds issued in 2013 and proceeds used to lure new business to the area.
    - $6,000 interest from U.S. Treasury notes.

    a) What amount of this interest income is taxable to CCP?

    b) What amount of interest should CCP report as a preference item when calculating its alternative minimum tax liability?

LO 16-4

74. On January 2 of year 1, XYZ Corp. acquired a piece of machinery for $50,000. The recovery period for the assets is seven years for both regular tax and AMT purposes. XYZ uses the double declining balance method to compute its tax depreciation on this asset, and it uses 150 percent declining balance to determine its depreciation for AMT purposes. The following schedule projects the tax and AMT depreciation on the asset until it is fully depreciated:

	Tax		AMT	
Year	Depreciation	Basis at End of Year	Depreciation	Basis at End of Year
1	$ 7,145	$42,855	$5,355	$44,645
2	12,245	30,610	9,565	35,080
3	8,745	21,865	7,515	27,565
4	6,245	15,620	6,125	21,440
5	4,465	11,155	6,125	15,315
6	4,460	6,695	6,125	9,190
7	4,465	2,230	6,125	3,065
8	2,230	0	3,065	0

a) What AMT adjustment relating to depreciation on the equipment will XYZ make for year 1? Is the adjustment positive (unfavorable) or negative (favorable)?

b) What AMT adjustment relating to depreciation on the equipment will XYZ make for year 5? Is the adjustment positive or negative?

c) If XYZ sells the equipment for $30,000 at the beginning of year 3, what AMT adjustment will it make in year 3 to reflect the difference in the gain or loss for regular tax and for AMT purposes on the sale (assume no year 3 depreciation)? Is the adjustment positive or negative?

LO 16-4

75. During the current year, CRS Inc. reported the following tax-related information:

- $10,000 tax-exempt interest from public activity bonds issued in 2014.
- $16,000 tax-exempt interest from private activity bonds issued in 2014.
- $150,000 death benefit from life insurance policies on officers' lives.
- $6,000 70 percent dividends received deduction.
- $12,000 80 percent dividends received deduction.
- $50,000 bad debt expense.
- $20,000 tax amortization expense relating to organizational expenditures.
- $80,000 gain included in taxable income under the installment method (sale occurred in previous year).

What is CRS's current year ACE adjustment?

LO 16-4

76. During the current year, ELS Corporation reported the following tax-related information:

- $5,000 tax-exempt interest from public activity bonds issued in 2008.
- $45,000 gain included in taxable income under the installment method. The installment sale occurred two years ago.

a) What is ELS Corp.'s current year ACE adjustment, assuming its cumulative ACE adjustment as of the beginning of the year is a positive $12,000?

b) What is ELS Corp.'s current year ACE adjustment, assuming its cumulative ACE adjustment as of the beginning of the year is a positive $80,000?

77. During the current year, FTP Corporation reported regular taxable income of $500,000. FTP used the following information in its tax-related computations:

    - $12,000 interest from Irvine City bonds: Bonds issued in 2013 and proceeds used to fund public schools.
    - $20,000 interest from Fluor Corporation bonds.
    - $8,000 interest from Mission Viejo City bonds: Bonds issued in 2012 and proceeds used to lure new business to the area.
    - $6,000 interest from U.S. Treasury notes.
    - $30,000 dividends received from General Electric Corporation (FTP owns less than 1 percent of GE stock).
    - $10,000 dividends received from Hobble Inc. (FTP owns 25 percent of Hobble Inc.).
    - $25,000 charitable contribution to the World Golf Foundation.
    - $60,000 AMT depreciation (regular tax depreciation was $70,000).
    - $50,000 ACE depreciation.
    - $7,000 AMT gain on disposition of assets (regular tax gain on the disposition of assets was $8,000).
    - $5,000 ACE gain on disposition of assets.
    a) What is FTP's ACE adjustment for the current year? Is it positive or negative?
    b) What is FTP's alternative minimum tax base?
    c) What is FTP's alternative minimum tax liability, if any?

78. What is WSS Corporation's AMT base in each of the following alternative scenarios?

    a) WSS's AMTI is $50,000.
    b) WSS's AMTI is $175,000.
    c) WSS's AMTI is $300,000.
    d) WSS's AMTI is $1,000,000.

79. Assume CDA corporation must pay the AMT for the current year. It is considering entering into a transaction that will generate $20,000 of income for the current year. What is CDA's after-tax benefit of receiving this income in each of the following alternative scenarios?

    a) CDA's AMTI before the transaction is $50,000.
    b) CDA's AMTI before the transaction is $140,000.
    c) CDA's AMTI before the transaction is $200,000.
    d) CDA's AMTI before the transaction is $1,000,000.

80. Assume JJ Inc. must pay the AMT for the current year. Near the end of the year, JJ is considering making a charitable contribution of $20,000. What is its after-tax cost of the contribution under each of the following alternative scenarios?

    a) JJ's AMTI before the transaction is $50,000.
    b) JJ's AMTI before the transaction is $160,000.
    c) JJ's AMTI before the transaction is $200,000.
    d) JJ's AMTI before the transaction is $1,000,000.

LO 16-4

planning

81. Compute ACC Inc.'s tentative minimum tax (TMT), alternative minimum tax (AMT), and minimum tax credit (MTC) in each of the following alternative scenarios:

    a) ACC's alternative minimum tax base is $500,000 and its regular tax liability is $80,000.

    b) ACC's alternative minimum tax base is $300,000 and its regular tax liability is $80,000.

    c) ACC's alternative minimum tax base is $1,000,000 and its regular tax liability is $250,000.

LO 16-4

82. In year 1, GSL Corp.'s alternative minimum tax base was $2,000,000 and its regular tax liability is $350,000.

    a) What is GSL's total tax liability for years 1, 2, 3, and 4 (by year) assuming the following?

       Year 2: AMT base $600,000; Regular tax liability $100,000.

       Year 3: AMT base $500,000; Regular tax liability $160,000.

       Year 4: AMT base $1,000,000; Regular tax liability $150,000.

    b) What, if any, minimum tax credit does GSL have at the end of year 4?

LO 16-4

research

83. In year 1, Lazy Corporation reported a $500,000 net operating loss for regular tax purposes and a $450,000 net operating loss for alternative minimum tax purposes (called an *alternative tax net operating loss*). In year 2, Lazy reported $450,000 of taxable income before deducting its net operating loss carryover from year 1 (it elected to forgo the net operating loss carryback). It also reported $450,000 of alternative minimum taxable income before taking the alternative tax net operating loss carryover into account (it did not report any preference or adjustments in year 2). (Note that, subject to certain limitations, alternative tax NOLs are deducted from AMTI in the process of determining the alternative minimum tax.) What is Lazy Corporation's year 2 tax liability? Assume Lazy did not have any MTC carryover from a prior year.

COMPREHENSIVE PROBLEMS

Select problems are available in *Connect*®.

connect

84. Compute MV Corp.'s 2016 taxable income given the following information relating to its year 1 activities. Also, compute MV's Schedule M-1 assuming that MV's federal income tax expense for book purposes is $100,000.

    • Gross profit from inventory sales of $500,000 (no book–tax differences).

    • Dividends MV received from 25 percent-owned corporation of $100,000 (assume this is also MV's pro rata share of the distributing corporation's earnings).

    • Expenses *other than* DRD, charitable contribution (CC), net operating loss (NOL), and domestic production activities deduction (DPAD) are $350,000 (no book–tax differences).

    • NOL carryover from prior year of $10,000.

    • Cash charitable contribution of $120,000.

    • Domestic production activities deduction of $5,000 (wage limitation does not apply).

85. Compute HC Inc.'s current year taxable income given the following information relating to its 2016 activities. Also, compute HC's Schedule M-1 assuming that HC's federal income tax expense for book purposes is $30,000.

   - Gross profit from inventory sales of $310,000 (no book–tax differences).
   - Dividends HC received from 28 percent-owned corporation of $120,000 (this is also HC's pro rata share of the corporation's earnings).
   - Expenses *other than* DRD, charitable contribution (CC), net operating loss (NOL), and domestic production activities deduction (DPAD) are $300,000 (no book–tax differences).
   - NOL carryover from prior year of $12,000.
   - Cash charitable contribution of $50,000.
   - Domestic production activities deduction of $4,000 (wage limitation does not apply).

86. Timpanogos Inc. is an accrual-method calendar-year corporation. For 2016, it reported financial statement income after taxes of $1,152,000. Timpanogos provided the following information relating to its 2016 activities:

tax forms

Life insurance proceeds as a result of CEO's death	$ 200,000
Revenue from sales (for both book and tax purposes)	2,000,000
Premiums paid on the key-person life insurance policies. The policies have no cash surrender value.	21,000
Charitable contributions	180,000
Overhead costs that were expensed for book purposes but are included in ending inventory for tax purposes under §263A	50,000
Overhead costs that were expensed for book purposes in 2015 but were included in 2015 ending inventory. All 2015 ending inventory was sold in 2016.	60,000
Cost of goods sold for book purposes	300,000
Interest income on private activity tax-exempt bonds issued in 2015	40,000
Interest paid on loan obtained to purchase tax-exempt bonds	45,000
Rental income payments received and earned in 2016	15,000
Rental income payments received in 2015 but earned in 2016	10,000
Rental income payments received in 2016 but not earned by year-end	30,000
MACRS depreciation	55,000
Book depreciation	25,000
Alternative minimum tax depreciation	50,000
Net capital loss	42,000
Federal income tax expense for books in 2016	500,000

Timpanogos did not qualify for the domestic production activities deduction.

Required

   a) Reconcile book income to taxable income for Timpanogos Inc. Be sure to start with book income and identify all of the adjustments necessary to arrive at taxable income.
   b) Identify each book–tax difference as either permanent or temporary.
   c) Complete Schedule M-1 for Timpanogos.
   d) Compute Timpanogos Inc.'s regular tax liability for 2016.
   e) Determine Timpanogos's alternative minimum tax, if any.

tax forms

87. XYZ is a calendar-year corporation that began business on January 1, 2016. For 2016, it reported the following information in its current-year audited income statement. Notes with important tax information are provided below.

Required

Identify the book-to-tax adjustments for XYZ.

a) Reconcile book income to taxable income and identify each book–tax difference as temporary or permanent.

b) Compute XYZ's regular income tax liability.

c) Complete XYZ's Schedule M-1.

d) Complete XYZ's Form 1120, page 1 (use the 2015 form if the 2016 form is unavailable). Ignore estimated tax penalties when completing this form.

e) Compute XYZ's alternative minimum tax, if any.

f) Complete Form 4626 for XYZ (use the 2015 form if the 2016 form is unavailable).

g) Determine the quarters for which XYZ is subject to underpayment of estimated taxes penalties (see estimated tax information below).

XYZ Corp. Income Statement for Current Year	Book Income	Book to Tax Adjustments (Dr.)	Cr.	Taxable Income
Revenue from sales	$40,000,000			
Cost of goods sold	(27,000,000)			
Gross profit	$13,000,000			
Other income:				
Income from investment in corporate stock	300,000[1]			
Interest income	20,000[2]			
Capital gains (losses)	(4,000)			
Gain or loss from disposition of fixed assets	3,000[3]			
Miscellaneous income	50,000			
Gross income	$13,369,000			
Expenses:				
Compensation	(7,500,000)[4]			
Stock option compensation	(200,000)[5]			
Advertising	(1,350,000)			
Repairs and maintenance	(75,000)			
Rent	(22,000)			
Bad debt expense	(41,000)[6]			
Depreciation	(1,400,000)[7]			
Warranty expenses	(70,000)[8]			
Charitable donations	(500,000)[9]			
Meals and entertainment	(18,000)			
Goodwill impairment	(30,000)[10]			
Organizational expenditures	(44,000)[11]			
Other expenses	140,000[12]			
Total expenses	($11,390,000)			
Income before taxes	$ 1,979,000			
Provision for income taxes	(720,000)[13]			
Net Income after taxes	$ 1,259,000[14]			

Notes

1. XYZ owns 30 percent of the outstanding Hobble Corp. (HC) stock. Hobble Corp. reported $1,000,000 of income for the year. XYZ accounted for its investment in HC under the equity method and it recorded its pro rata share of HC's earnings for the year. HC also distributed a $200,000 dividend to XYZ.
2. Of the $20,000 interest income, $5,000 was from a City of Seattle bond (issued in 2014) that was used to fund public activities, $7,000 was from a Tacoma City bond (issued in 2014) used to fund private activities, $6,000 was from a fully taxable corporate bond, and the remaining $2,000 was from a money market account.
3. This gain is from equipment that XYZ purchased in February and sold in December (i.e., it does not qualify as §1231 gain).
4. This includes total officer compensation of $2,500,000 (no one officer received more than $1,000,000 compensation).
5. This amount is the portion of incentive stock option compensation that was expensed during the year (recipients are officers).
6. XYZ actually wrote off $27,000 of its accounts receivable as uncollectible.
7. Regular tax depreciation was $1,900,000 and AMT (and ACE) depreciation was $1,700,000.
8. In the current year, XYZ did not make any actual payments on warranties it provided to customers.
9. XYZ made $500,000 of cash contributions to qualified charities during the year.
10. On July 1 of this year XYZ acquired the assets of another business. In the process it acquired $300,000 of goodwill. At the end of the year, XYZ wrote off $30,000 of the goodwill as impaired.
11. XYZ expensed all of its organizational expenditures for book purposes. XYZ expensed the maximum amount of organizational expenditures allowed for tax purposes.
12. The other expenses do not contain any items with book–tax differences.
13. This is an estimated tax provision (federal tax expense) for the year. (In a subsequent class period, we will learn how to compute the correct tax provision.) Assume that XYZ is not subject to state income taxes.
14. XYZ calculated that its domestic production activities deduction (DPAD) is $90,000. This amount is not included on the audited income statement numbers.

Estimated Tax Information

XYZ made four equal estimated tax payments totaling $480,000. Assume for purposes of estimated tax liabilities, XYZ was in existence in 2015 and it reported a tax liability of $800,000. During 2016, XYZ determined its taxable income at the end of each of the four quarters as follows:

Quarter-End	Cumulative Taxable Income (Loss)
First	$ 350,000
Second	800,000
Third	1,000,000

Finally, assume that XYZ is not a large corporation for purposes of estimated tax calculations.

Accounting for Income Taxes

Learning Objectives

Upon completing this chapter, you should be able to:

LO 17-1 Explain the objectives behind FASB ASC Topic 740, *Income Taxes,* and the income tax provision process.

LO 17-2 Calculate the current and deferred income tax expense or benefit components of a company's income tax provision.

LO 17-3 Recall what a valuation allowance represents and describe the process by which it is determined.

LO 17-4 Explain how a company accounts for its uncertain income tax positions under FASB ASC Topic 740.

LO 17-5 Recognize the different components of a company's disclosure of its income tax accounts in the financial statements and footnotes, and comprehend how a company computes and discloses the components of its "effective tax rate."

© Sam Edwards/age fotostock

Storyline Summary

Elise Brandon

Employment status:	Tax associate for a large public accounting firm.

Assigned to prepare the federal income tax provision and income-tax-related balance sheet accounts and footnote disclosures for Premiere Computer Corporation, a nonaudit client.

Premiere Computer Corporation

Medium-sized publicly traded company.
Manufactures and sells computer-related equipment.
Calendar-year taxpayer.

Marginal tax rate:	34 percent, unless otherwise stated.

Elise felt a great sense of accomplishment when she completed the federal income tax return for Premiere Computer Corporation (PCC). She was glad the return was filed on time and did not need to be extended. With the tax return filed, Elise was assigned to help the PCC tax department compute the federal income tax provision for the company's soon to be published income statement and to determine the correct amounts in the company's income-tax-related balance sheet accounts. She also was given the responsibility to help prepare the income tax note to the financial statements.[1]

Elise was aware that, as a result of more stringent independence requirements imposed by the Sarbanes-Oxley Act, her colleagues in the tax group were getting a lot of engagements to help prepare the income tax provision for nonaudit clients. In fact, her firm now considered accounting for income taxes to be a "core competency" for all tax staff. Elise had heard that individuals who understood the nuances of accounting for income taxes were being called the new "rock stars" of accounting.[2] Having recently attended firm training on accounting for income taxes, which was now required of all tax staff, Elise was eager to apply her new knowledge to an actual client situation. She knew that developing her skill set in this complex topic would make her more valuable to her firm and her clients.[3]

to be continued . . .

---

[1]Publicly traded companies usually file their financial statements (Form 10-K) with the Securities and Exchange Commission well before they file their income tax returns with the Internal Revenue Service, often by as much as six months. The company must estimate its current year income tax liability when it files its financial statements and then adjust for any "provision to return" differences in the quarter (Form 10-Q) in which the tax return is filed. In today's post–Sarbanes-Oxley environment, staff from public accounting firms that are not a company's auditors often are hired to help prepare the company's income tax provision under ASC 740 because many companies do not have staff with the expertise to make this calculation.

[2]Kris Frieswick, "Too Taxing," *CFO Magazine* (November 1, 2005).

[3]An international tax services partner at a major public accounting firm recently testified before members of Congress that her firm spent more than 7,000 hours auditing a client's accounting for income taxes for its 2011 Form 10-K. See Beth Carr, "Written Testimony for Senate Permanent Subcommittee on Investigations," September 20, 2012, available at http://www.hsgac.senate.gov/

As you learned in computing PCC's taxable income in the previous chapter, many of the items of income (revenue) and deductions (expenses) that are included in a company's taxable income also are included in the company's net income before taxes. Not all of these items are included in the computations in the same accounting period, however, which creates "temporary" differences between taxable income and net income. Other items affect only one of the computations, which creates "permanent" differences between taxable income and pretax net income. A company must take these differences into account in computing its income tax provision on the income statement and its "deferred" income taxes payable (liabilities) or refundable (assets) on the balance sheet.

FASB Accounting Standards Codification Topic 740, *Income Taxes* (hereafter, ASC 740), governs the computation and disclosure of a company's income tax provision (expense or benefit) and its expected future income tax liabilities or benefits related to "events" that have been recorded on either the financial statement or the tax return. ASC 740 codifies the majority of accounting and reporting guidance related to income taxes, primarily FAS 109. Accounting for income taxes guidance related to accounting for investments under the equity method, stock compensation, business combinations, foreign currency translation, and industry subtopics such as real estate, entertainment, and oil and gas is embedded within the ASC topic that deals with that issue. The Emerging Issues Task Force (EITF)[4] and the Securities and Exchange Commission continue to provide guidance on issues related to accounting for income taxes.

A company's failure to accurately compute the income tax provision and related balance sheet accounts can lead to the issuance of a material weakness statement by the auditor and, in some cases, a restatement of the financial statements. Not surprisingly, individuals who understand these complex and sometimes counterintuitive rules are in great demand by public accounting firms and industry.

This chapter discusses the basic rules for how a company computes and discloses its current year income tax provision and its future income taxes payable or refundable using the facts related to Premiere Computer Corporation in the previous chapter. We focus on the portion of the provision that relates to federal income taxes.

LO 17-1 OBJECTIVES OF ACCOUNTING FOR INCOME TAXES AND THE INCOME TAX PROVISION PROCESS

In addition to filing its federal, state and local, and non-U.S. income tax returns, Premiere Computer Corporation, along with all other U.S. publicly traded corporations and many privately held corporations, must prepare financial statements in accordance with generally accepted accounting principles (GAAP) issued by the FASB. Under GAAP, a company must include as part of its income statement a "provision" for the income tax expense or benefit that is associated with the pretax net income or loss reported on the income statement. The income tax provision includes not only current-year taxes payable or refundable, but also any changes to future income taxes payable or refundable that result from differences in the timing of when an item is reported on the tax return compared to the financial statement. The company records these future income taxes payable or refundable on its balance sheet as the amount the company expects to pay (**deferred tax liability**) or recover (**deferred tax asset**) in a future accounting period.

---

[4]The Emerging Issues Task Force is a committee of accounting practitioners who assist the FASB in providing timely guidance on emerging issues and the implementation of existing standards.

On March 1, 2011, Weatherford International informed its shareholders that it would be late in issuing its Form 10-K because of a material weakness in internal control over the company's financial reporting for income taxes. As a result, management cautioned its investors not to rely on any of its financial statements issued for the years 2007–2010. Management estimated the total financial reporting error to be around $500 million. At a press conference the next day, the CEO made the following statement:

> To a degree, the discipline of tax within our Company is a two-headed animal—one, planning, and two, process. Both pieces must work well in order for us to be able to maximize the value of our multinational status. This mistake, the embarrassment of which is difficult, if not impossible to quantify, highlights that we have work to do on strengthening the process piece. We will work hard to make sure this happens with all appropriate speed and effectiveness.[1]

The company remediated the deficiencies during 2013, although the SEC and the U.S. Department of Justice are now investigating the circumstances surrounding the material weakness and restatements of the company's financial statements. The company restated its 2009–2011 financial statements in December 2012. During 2012, the company hired a new vice president of taxes and 25 additional

"qualified tax professionals." In addition, the company spent considerable resources engaging third-party tax advisors and consultants to assist with enhancing internal controls over financial reporting for income taxes and developing and implementing a remediation plan; revising the process for the quarterly and annual tax provisions; recruiting positions within the tax and financial reporting departments; and providing income tax accounting training to tax and financial personnel. The magnitude of these expenditures was published in the company's Proxy Statement in June 2013. The company's outside advisors provided more than 272,000 hours of time to the restatement and remediation as a cost of over $100 million.

The remediation was completed by the end of December 2013, to management's great relief. However, the company announced that the SEC and the Department of Justice were investigating the circumstances surrounding the material weakness and the weaknesses in the company's internal controls that led to restatement. In addition, shareholders have filed a lawsuit charging the company with providing misleading financial statements. Out of the frying pan and into the fire!

[1]Final transcript of Weatherford International to adjust 2007–2010 results due to "material weakness" in its income tax reporting—Conference Call. Available at http://www.sec.gov.

Why Is Accounting for Income Taxes So Complex?

ASC 740 provides the general rules that apply to the computation of a company's income tax provision. The basic principles that underlie these rules are fairly straightforward, but the application of the rules themselves can be very complex. Much of the complexity is due to the fact that the U.S. tax laws are complex and often ambiguous. In addition, companies frequently prepare their financial statements (Form 10-K) much earlier than when they file their corresponding tax returns. For example, a calendar-year corporation generally files its Form 10-K with the SEC in February or early March, but the company might not file its federal income tax return (Form 1120) with the Internal Revenue Service (IRS) until August or September.[5] As a result, a company often must exercise a high degree of judgment in estimating its income tax return positions currently and in future years when a tax return position might be challenged by the tax authorities. After the tax return is filed, it may take five years or more before the tax

[5]The due date for a federal income tax return filed by a calendar-year corporation is March 15, but corporations can request a six-month extension to September 15 by filing Form 7004 and paying any remaining tax liability.

return is audited by the IRS and the final tax liability is determined.[6] For example, General Electric (GE) mentions in its Form 10-K for 2014 that the IRS currently was auditing its U.S. income tax returns for 2010–2011. GE also notes that it files more than 5,500 income tax returns in over 250 global taxing jurisdictions!

Objectives of ASC 740

ASC 740 applies only to *income* taxes levied by the U.S. federal government, U.S. state and local governments, and non-U.S. ("foreign") governments. The FASB defines an *income tax* as a tax *based on income.* This definition excludes property taxes, excise taxes, sales taxes, and value-added taxes. Companies report nonincome taxes as expenses in the computation of their net income before taxes.

ASC 740 has two primary objectives. One objective is to "recognize the amount of taxes payable or refundable in the current year" (referred to as the **current tax liability or asset**).[7] A second objective is to "recognize deferred tax liabilities and assets for the future tax consequences of events that have been recognized in an entity's financial statements or tax returns."[8] Both objectives relate to reporting a company's income tax amounts on the *balance sheet,* not the *income statement.* The FASB refers to this method as the "asset and liability approach" to accounting for income taxes.[9] The FASB chose this approach because it felt it is most consistent with the definitions in FASB Concepts Statement No. 6, *Elements of Financial Statements,* and produces the most useful and understandable information.[10]

To compute the deferred tax liability or asset, a company must calculate the future tax effects attributable to temporary differences and **tax carryforwards.**[11] As you learned in the previous chapter, temporary differences generally can be thought of as revenue (income) or expenses (deductions) that will appear on both the income statement and the tax return but in different accounting periods. Temporary differences that are cumulatively favorable create deferred tax liabilities, while temporary differences that are cumulatively unfavorable create deferred tax assets.

Example 17-1

Before she began the income tax provision process, Elise knew she needed to get the ending balances in PCC's deferred tax accounts from the prior year. Accordingly, she retrieved PCC's prior year balance sheet (Exhibit 17-1) and the deferred tax component of the company's income tax note (Exhibit 17-2).

Looking at Exhibit 17-1, what income tax accounts appear on PCC's balance sheet from the prior year?

Answer: There are three deferred tax accounts on PCC's prior-year balance sheet: current deferred tax assets of $271,660, noncurrent deferred tax assets of $408,000, and noncurrent deferred tax liabilities of $3,400,000.

Looking at Exhibit 17-2, is PCC in a net deferred tax asset or net deferred tax liability position at the end of the prior year (gross deferred tax assets less gross deferred tax liabilities)?

Answer: PCC ended the prior year with a net deferred tax liability of $2,720,340.

Since its inception, has PCC had net favorable or unfavorable temporary differences (i.e., has PCC's cumulative pretax net income been greater or less than its taxable income)?

Answer: PCC's net deferred tax liability indicates that the company has had net cumulative favorable temporary differences, which indicates its cumulative pretax net income has exceeded its cumulative taxable income.

---

[6]Although the statute of limitations for a filed income tax return is three years, large corporations often agree to extend the statute for a longer period of time to allow the IRS to audit the return. As a result, a corporation's tax return may not be audited for five or more years from the date it is filed.

[7]ASC 740-10-10-1(a).

[8]ASC 740-10-10-1(b).

[9]FAS 109, ¶63. (This paragraph was not codified in ASC 740.)

[10]FAS 109, ¶63.

[11]ASC 740-10-25-2(b).

EXHIBIT 17-1   PCC Balance Sheet at 12/31/2015

Assets

Current Assets

Cash	$ 10,722,380
Municipal bonds	300,000
Accounts receivable	17,250,000
Less: Allowance for bad debts	(345,000)
Accounts receivable (net)	16,905,000
Inventory	4,312,500
Deferred tax assets	271,660
Total current assets	$ 32,511,540

Noncurrent Assets

Fixed assets	$60,000,000
Less: Accumulated depreciation	(12,000,000)
Fixed assets (net)	48,000,000
Life insurance (cash surrender value)	1,100,000
Investments	497,960
Goodwill	180,000
Deferred tax assets	408,000
Total noncurrent assets	50,185,960
Total assets	$ 82,697,500

Liabilities and Shareholders' Equity

Current Liabilities

Accounts payable	$ 20,013,000
Reserve for warranties	430,000
Deferred tax liabilities	—
Total current liabilities	$20,443,000

Noncurrent Liabilities

Long-term debt	$40,000,000
Deferred compensation	1,200,000
Deferred tax liabilities	3,400,000
Total noncurrent liabilities	$44,600,000
Total liabilities	$65,043,000

Shareholders' Equity

Common stock (par value = $1)	$ 500,000
Additional paid-in-capital	5,000,000
Retained earnings	12,154,500
Total shareholders' equity	$ 17,654,500
Total liabilities and shareholders' equity	$ 82,697,500

EXHIBIT 17-2   PCC Deferred Tax Accounts at 12/31/2015

Deferred Tax Assets

Allowance for bad debts	$ 117,300
Reserve for warranties	146,200
Net operating loss carryforward	8,160
Current deferred tax assets	$ 271,660
Deferred compensation	408,000
Capital loss carryforward	—
Contribution carryforward	—
Noncurrent deferred tax assets	$ 408,000
Total deferred tax assets	$ 679,660
Valuation allowance for deferred tax assets	—
Deferred tax assets, net of valuation allowance	$ 679,660

Deferred Tax Liabilities

Depreciation	(3,400,000)
Total deferred tax liabilities	($3,400,000)
Net deferred tax liabilities	($2,720,340)

The Income Tax Provision Process

A company computes the two components of its income tax provision (current and deferred) separately (independently) for each category of income tax (U.S. federal, U.S. state and local, and international) and then combines the components to produce the total income tax provision. The "formula" to compute a company's total income tax provision can be summarized as:

> Total income tax provision = Current income tax expense (benefit)
> + Deferred income tax expense (benefit)

There are six steps in the computation of a company's federal income tax provision. These steps are:

1. Adjust pretax net income or loss for all permanent differences.
2. Identify all temporary differences and tax carryforward amounts.
3. Calculate the current income tax expense or benefit (refund).
4. Determine the ending balances in the balance sheet deferred tax asset and liability accounts.
5. Evaluate the need for a valuation allowance for gross deferred tax assets.
6. Calculate the deferred income tax expense or benefit.

CALCULATING THE CURRENT AND DEFERRED INCOME TAX EXPENSE OR BENEFIT COMPONENTS OF A COMPANY'S INCOME TAX PROVISION

continued from page 17-1 . . .

Elise gathered the financial statement and tax return data she needed to get started beginning with the workpaper template she used to compute PCC's taxable income. (Exhibit 17-3 reproduces the book–tax reconciliation template from Exhibit 16-7, excluding the book federal income tax expense of $2,000,000.) She identified each of the book–tax adjustments as being either permanent (P) or temporary (T). Elise was ready to begin the process of computing PCC's federal income tax provision using the six-step method she had learned at firm training.

to be continued . . .

Step 1: Adjust Pretax Net Income for All Permanent Differences

As you learned in the previous chapter, not all book–tax differences meet the definition of a temporary difference. Some differences will appear only on the income statement or the tax return, but not on both. Examples of the former include tax-exempt interest income and nondeductible fines. Examples of the latter include the dividends received deduction and the domestic production activities deduction. Although not defined as such in ASC 740, most accounting professionals refer to these types of book–tax differences as **permanent differences.**

A company does not take permanent differences into account in computing its balance sheet deferred tax assets and liabilities (and consequently, the deferred component of its income tax provision). Permanent differences enter into the company's computation of taxable income, and thus affect the current tax expense or benefit,

EXHIBIT 17-3 PCC Book–Tax Reconciliation Template for 2016

Income Statement for Current Year	Book Income	Book–Tax Adjustments (Dr)	Cr	Taxable Income
Revenue from sales	$60,000,000			$60,000,000
Cost of goods sold	(38,000,000)			(38,000,000)
Gross profit	$22,000,000			$22,000,000
Other income:				
Dividend income	30,000			30,000
Interest income (P)	120,000	(12,000)		108,000
Capital gains (losses) (T)	(28,000)		28,000	0
Gain on fixed asset dispositions (T)	54,000		16,000	70,000
Gross income	$22,176,000			$22,208,000
Expenses:				
Compensation	(9,868,000)			(9,868,000)
Deferred compensation (T)	(300,000)	(150,000)		(450,000)
Stock option compensation (T)	(100,000)		100,000	0
Bad debt expense (T)	(165,000)		70,000	(95,000)
Charitable contributions (T)	(700,000)		73,700	(626,300)
Depreciation (T)	(2,400,000)	(700,000)		(3,100,000)
Advertising	(1,920,000)			(1,920,000)
Warranty expenses (T)	(580,000)		170,000	(410,000)
Meals and entertainment (P)	(28,000)		14,000	(14,000)
Life insurance premiums (P)	(34,000)		34,000	0
Other expenses	(64,000)			(64,000)
Total expenses *before* NOL, DRD, DPAD	$(16,159,000)			$16,547,300
Income *before* NOL, DRD, DPAD	$ 6,017,000			$ 5,660,700
NOL carryforward from prior year (T)	0	(24,000)		(24,000)
Dividends received deduction (P)	0	(21,000)		(21,000)
Domestic production activities deduction (P)	0	(465,000)	0	(465,000)
Book/taxable income	**$ 6,017,000**	**(1,372,000)**	**505,700**	**$ 5,150,700**

either increasing or decreasing it. As a result, permanent differences usually affect a company's **effective tax rate** (income tax provision/pretax net income) and appear as part of the company's reconciliation of its effective tax rate with its statutory U.S. tax rate (34 percent in PCC's case).[12] We discuss ASC 740 disclosure requirements in a subsequent section of this chapter.

Exhibit 17-4 provides a list of common permanent differences you will encounter in practice.

EXHIBIT 17-4 Common Permanent Differences

Life insurance proceeds	Disallowed meals and entertainment expenses
Tax-exempt interest income	Disallowed premiums on officers' life insurance
Nondeductible tax penalties and fines	Dividends received deduction
Tax credits	Domestic production activities deduction
Political contributions	

[12]The windfall tax benefit from a nonqualified stock option deduction that is not treated as a temporary difference is recorded in additional paid-in capital (refer back to the previous discussion of stock option deductions in Chapter 16).

Example 17-2

Elise went back to the template she used to compute PCC's taxable income and identified the book–tax adjustments that were considered permanent in nature. What are PCC's permanent differences and are they favorable or unfavorable?

Answer: A net favorable permanent difference of $450,000, computed as follows:

Permanent Differences	(Favorable) Unfavorable
Tax-exempt interest income	$ (12,000)
Meals and entertainment	14,000
Life insurance premiums	34,000
Dividends received deduction	(21,000)
Domestic production activities deduction	(465,000)
Net favorable permanent difference	$(450,000)

Example 17-3

Elise used the net favorable permanent difference of $450,000 to adjust PCC's pretax net income. What is PCC's pretax net income adjusted for permanent differences?

Answer: $5,567,000, computed as follows:

PCC pretax net income	$6,017,000
Net favorable permanent difference	(450,000)
PCC pretax net income adjusted for permanent differences	$5,567,000

Elise remembered that her instructor at ASC 740 training referred to this intermediate computation as a company's **book equivalent of taxable income.** That is, this amount represents the book income that ultimately will be taxable, either currently or in the future.

Step 2: Identify All Temporary Differences and Tax Carryforward Amounts

ASC 740 formally defines a *temporary difference* as

> A difference between the tax basis of an asset or liability . . . and its reported amount in the financial statements that will result in taxable or deductible amounts in future years when the reported amount of the asset or liability is recovered or settled, respectively.[13]

As you learned in Chapter 16, temporary differences commonly arise in four instances:

Revenues or Gains That Are Taxable after They Are Recognized in Financial Income   An example of such a "favorable" book–tax adjustment is gain from an installment sale that is recognized for financial accounting purposes in the year of sale but is recognized over the collection period for tax purposes.[14]

Expenses or Losses That Are Deductible after They Are Recognized in Financial Income   Examples of such "unfavorable" book–tax adjustments include bad debt expenses, warranty expenses, and accrued compensation and vacation pay that are recorded using the reserve method for financial accounting purposes but

[13]ASC 740-10-20 Glossary.

[14]Consistent with the terminology introduced in Chapter 16, a "favorable" book–tax adjustment is one that reduces current-year taxable income compared to current-year net income.

can only be deducted when paid on the tax return.[15] Capitalized inventory costs under §263A also fall into this category, as do nonqualified stock option compensation expenses that are recorded at the grant date for financial reporting purposes under ASC 718 but do not become tax deductible until the exercise date.

Revenues or Gains That Are Taxable before They Are Recognized in Financial Income   An example of such an "unfavorable" book–tax adjustment is a prepayment of income that is recognized in the year received for tax purposes but is not recognized for financial accounting purposes until the revenue is earned.

Expenses or Losses That Are Deductible before They Are Recognized in Financial Income   A common example of such a "favorable" book–tax adjustment is the excess of tax depreciation over financial reporting depreciation.

Temporary differences also can arise from items that cannot be associated with a particular asset or liability for financial accounting purposes but produce revenue (income) or expense (deduction) that has been recognized in the financial statement and will result in taxable or deductible amounts in future years. For example, a net operating loss carryover and a net capital loss carryover create unfavorable temporary differences in the year they arise without being associated with a specific asset or liability.

Exhibit 17-5 lists common temporary differences.

EXHIBIT 17-5   **Common Temporary Differences**

Depreciation	Reserves for bad debts (uncollectible accounts)
Accrued vacation pay	Inventory costs capitalized under §263A
Prepayments of income	Warranty reserves
Installment sale income	Stock option expense under ASC 718
Pension plan deductions	Accrued bonuses and other compensation
Accrued contingency losses	Net operating loss and net capital loss carryovers

Identifying Taxable and Deductible Temporary Differences

Taxable Temporary Difference   A temporary difference that is cumulatively *favorable* (i.e., an item that has cumulatively decreased taxable income relative to book income) gives rise to what ASC 740 refers to as a **taxable temporary difference.**[16] This category of temporary difference gets its name from the fact that when the difference reverses in a future period it will *increase taxable income* relative to book income.

Taxable temporary differences generally arise when (1) revenues or gains are taxable *after* they are recognized in net income (e.g., gross profit from an installment sale) and (2) expenses or losses are deductible on the tax return *before* they reduce net income (e.g., excess tax depreciation over financial accounting depreciation). From a balance sheet perspective, a taxable temporary difference generally arises when the financial reporting (book) basis of an asset exceeds its corresponding tax basis or when the financial reporting (book) basis of a liability is less than its corresponding tax basis. Subsequent "recovery" of the financial statement balance sheet basis of the asset or "payment" of the balance sheet liability will cause taxable income to exceed book income, either by creating a tax gain or reducing a tax deduction. The future tax cost associated with a taxable temporary difference is recorded on the balance sheet as a deferred tax liability.

Deductible Temporary Difference   A temporary difference that is cumulatively *unfavorable* (i.e., an item that has cumulatively increased taxable income relative to book income) gives rise to what ASC 740 refers to as a **deductible temporary**

---

[15]Consistent with the terminology introduced in Chapter 16, an "unfavorable" book–tax adjustment is one that increases current year taxable income compared to current year net income.

[16]ASC 740-10-25-23.

THE KEY FACTS

Identifying Taxable and Deductible Temporary Differences

- ASC 740 defines a temporary difference as a difference between the financial reporting and tax basis of an asset or liability that will create a future tax liability or benefit when the difference reverses.

- A temporary difference that cumulatively is *favorable* gives rise to a net taxable temporary difference.

- The future tax cost associated with a taxable temporary difference is recorded on the balance sheet as a deferred tax liability.

- A temporary difference that cumulatively is *unfavorable* gives rise to a net deductible temporary difference.

- The future tax benefit associated with a deductible temporary difference is recorded on the balance sheet as a deferred tax asset.

difference.[17] This category of temporary difference gets its name from the fact that when the difference reverses in a future period it will *decrease taxable income* relative to book income.

Deductible temporary differences generally arise when (1) revenues or gains are taxable *before* they are recognized in net income (e.g., prepayments of subscriptions) and (2) expenses or losses are deductible on the tax return *after* they reduce net income (e.g., reserves for product warranty or uncollectible accounts). From a balance sheet perspective, a deductible temporary difference generally arises when the financial reporting (book) basis of an asset is less than its corresponding tax basis or the financial reporting (book) basis of a liability exceeds its corresponding tax basis. Subsequent "recovery" of the financial reporting balance sheet basis of the asset or "payment" of the balance sheet liability will cause taxable income to be less than book income, either by creating a tax loss or increasing a tax deduction. The future tax benefit associated with a deductible temporary difference is recorded on the balance sheet as a deferred tax asset.

Unfavorable temporary differences that do not have balance sheet accounts, such as net operating loss carryovers, net capital loss carryovers, and charitable contribution carryovers, must be tracked to ensure that the appropriate adjustment is made to a company's deferred tax asset accounts when the carryover is used on a future tax return.

Example 17-4

Elise decided to separate PCC's temporary differences as being cumulatively favorable or cumulatively unfavorable (see Exhibit 17-3). What are PCC's taxable (cumulatively favorable) temporary differences?

Answer: PCC has one taxable temporary difference that arises in the current year—the excess of tax depreciation over book depreciation in the amount of $684,000. The gain on the sale of the fixed asset appears as an unfavorable difference, but it actually represents the reversal of a previously recorded favorable difference, the excess of tax over book depreciation. This "drawdown" of a previously recorded taxable temporary difference reduces the cumulatively favorable temporary differences arising in the current year. Elise summarized the taxable temporary differences as follows:

Taxable Temporary Differences	Amount
Excess of tax over book depreciation	($700,000)
Gain on fixed asset dispositions	16,000
Total taxable temporary differences	($684,000)

What are PCC's deductible (cumulatively unfavorable) temporary differences?

Answer: The deduction of previously accrued deferred compensation and PCC's use of its net operating loss carryover appear as favorable temporary differences in 2016, but they are actually reversals of prior year unfavorable temporary differences and reduce the cumulatively unfavorable temporary differences. PCC has net deductible temporary differences of $267,700, computed as follows:

Deductible Temporary Differences	Amount
Net capital loss carryforward	$ 28,000
Deferred compensation	(150,000)
Stock option compensation	100,000
Bad debt expense	70,000
Charitable contribution carryforward	73,700
Warranty expense	170,000
NOL carryforward from prior year	(24,000)
Total deductible temporary differences	$ 267,700

For the year, PCC has a net taxable (favorable) temporary difference of $(416,300) [($684,000) + $267,700].

---

[17]ASC 740-10-25-23.

Step 3: Compute the Current Income Tax Expense or Benefit

In many respects, the computation of the current portion of a company's tax provision appears to be straightforward. ASC 740 defines the **current income tax expense or benefit** as

> The amount of income taxes paid or payable (or refundable) for a year as determined by applying the provisions of the enacted tax law to the taxable income or excess of deductions over revenues for that year.[18]

In most cases, the major component of a company's current income tax expense or benefit is the income tax liability or refund from its current-year operations. However, there are other items that enter into the computation that do not appear on the company's income tax return (Form 1120), which adds to the complexity of the computation.

In practice, the computation of a company's current income tax expense or benefit rarely equals the actual taxes paid on the company's current-year tax returns. In particular, the current component of PCC's income tax provision also can be impacted by prior-year income tax refunds from current-year carrybacks of a net operating loss or net capital loss,[19] IRS audit adjustments from prior-year tax returns,[20] windfall tax benefits from the exercise of nonqualified stock options, and changes in the company's **uncertain tax positions** (a company's reserve for taxes it has not paid but could pay in the future for positions taken on the current- and prior-year income tax returns).[21]

Example 17-5

Elise used her summary of permanent and temporary differences to verify her previous computation of PCC's taxable income. Does using Elise's summary of PCC's permanent and temporary differences verify her previous computation of PCC's taxable income?

Answer: Yes!

PCC pretax net income	$6,017,000
Net favorable permanent differences (from Example 17-2)	(450,000)
Net favorable temporary differences (from Example 17-4)	(416,300)
PCC taxable income	$5,150,700

What is PCC's current income tax expense, assuming a tax rate of 34 percent?

Answer: $1,751,238, computed as follows:

PCC taxable income	$5,150,700
	× 34%
PCC federal income tax payable	$1,751,238

What tax accounting journal entry does PCC make to record its current tax expense?

Answer:

Current income tax expense	1,751,238	
Current income taxes payable (or cash)		1,751,238

THE KEY FACTS

Computing the Deferred Income Tax Expense or Benefits

- Identify current-year changes in taxable and deductible temporary differences.
- Determine ending balances in each deferred tax asset and liability balance sheet account.
- Identify carryovers (net operating loss, capital loss, charitable contributions) not on the balance sheet.
- The current-year deferred income tax expense or benefit is the difference between the deferred tax asset and liability balances at the beginning of the year to the end of the year as well as changes in tax carryovers.

---

[18]ASC 740-10-20 Glossary.

[19]Requested on Form 1139 or Form 1120X.

[20]Agreed to on Form 5701.

[21]Calculated in the uncertain tax position workpapers.

Step 4: Determine the Ending Balances in the Balance Sheet Deferred Tax Asset and Liability Accounts

continued from page 17-6 . . .

Having calculated the current portion of PCC's income tax provision, Elise turned her attention to computing the deferred component of PCC's income tax provision. She knew from training that the technically correct method to compute PCC's deferred tax provision would be to compare the financial accounting (book) basis of each asset and liability with its corresponding tax basis. Elise had the financial accounting basis of each account from the balance sheet but, like most companies, PCC did not keep a formal **tax accounting balance sheet**.[22] She would need to use an alternative method to calculate the change in the cumulative book–tax basis differences for each account she identified as being a temporary difference.

to be continued . . .

The FASB could have decided that a company report only the "as-paid" income taxes on its income statement. Investors and policymakers might favor this approach because it would disclose the actual income taxes paid or refunded (cash outflow or inflow) in the current year. Reporting only income taxes currently payable ignores one of the basic premises underlying financial accounting, which is that the accrual method of accounting provides more relevant information to investors and creditors than the cash method of accounting.[23]

The deferred income tax expense or benefit portion of a company's income tax provision reflects the change during the year in a company's balance sheet deferred tax liabilities or assets.[24] This information provides investors and other interested parties with a measure of a company's expected future income tax-related cash inflows or outflows resulting from book–tax differences that are *temporary* in nature or from tax carryovers.

ASC 740 takes an "asset and liability" or balance sheet approach to the computation of the deferred tax expense or benefit. The computations are based on the change in the *cumulative* differences between the financial accounting (book) basis of an asset or liability and its corresponding tax basis from the beginning of the year to the end of the year. Under GAAP, the company is presumed to recover these basis differences over time, resulting in future sacrifices of a company's resources (in the case of liabilities) or future recoveries of a company's resources (in the case of assets). These expected future recoveries of assets or future sacrifices of assets to settle liabilities give rise to future (deferred) tax payments or refunds that are recorded in the income tax provision in the year the differences arise rather than in the year in which the future taxes are paid or recovered.

The future tax cost of a taxable (cumulatively favorable) temporary difference is recorded on the balance sheet as a deferred tax liability. The company computes the deferred tax liability using the **enacted tax rate** that is expected to apply to taxable income in the period(s) in which the deferred tax liability is expected to be settled.[25]

---

[22]Schedule L to Form 1120 requests that the taxpayer report its financial statement balance sheet. An increasing number of corporations are finding that a "best practice" is to maintain a tax basis balance sheet separate from the financial accounting balance sheet.

[23]ASC 230, *Statement of Cash Flows,* requires an enterprise to separately disclose income taxes paid as part of the statement itself or in a note to the financial statements (usually the income taxes note or a supplemental cash flow note).

[24]ASC 740-10-20 Glossary.

[25]ASC 740-10-30-2. For federal income tax provision purposes, a corporation applies the regular tax rate in computing its deferred tax assets and liabilities. The alternative minimum tax is treated as a prepaid income tax and reported as a deferred tax asset on the balance sheet.

Example 17-6

Lacking a formal tax-basis balance sheet, Elise identified the current-year temporary differences and adjusted ("rolled forward") the cumulative differences at the beginning of the year to get the end-of-the-year cumulative book–tax basis differences. She used this change in the cumulative book–tax basis difference to compute the deferred tax expense or benefit for the current year. Elise reviewed her schedules of favorable and unfavorable temporary differences (from Example 17-3). She identified one favorable temporary difference related to an asset recorded on the balance sheet—the excess of tax depreciation over book depreciation. Elise retrieved the fixed asset work-papers and recorded the changes in the financial accounting and tax accumulated depreciation balances of PCC's fixed assets from the beginning of the year to the end of the year related to current year depreciation.

Financial accounting change in accumulated depreciation	
Beginning of the year	$12,000,000
End of the year	14,400,000
Net change	$ 2,400,000
*Tax accounting change in accumulated depreciation**	
Beginning of the year	$22,000,000
End of the year	25,100,000
Net change	$ 3,100,000

*Not given in the original facts; assumed for purposes of this example.

The net increase in tax accounting accumulated depreciation over the corresponding financial accounting depreciation created a current-year $700,000 favorable (taxable) temporary difference (i.e., the difference between the financial accounting basis of the fixed assets increased by $700,000 over their corresponding tax basis). This increase in the cumulative favorable temporary difference requires an *increase* in PCC's deferred tax liabilities.

By what amount will PCC increase its deferred tax liabilities as a result of the increase in the book over tax basis in these assets from the beginning of the year to the end of the year?

Answer: $238,000, computed as $700,000 × 34 percent.

What tax accounting journal entry does PCC record related to this transaction?

Answer:

Deferred income tax expense	238,000	
Deferred income tax liability		238,000

What if: Assume current-year book depreciation exceeded current-year tax depreciation by $700,000. What adjustment to the balance sheet would PCC be required to make?

Answer: PCC would *decrease* its deferred tax liability on the balance sheet by $238,000.

Example 17-7

Elise also saw that accumulated depreciation decreased as a result of PCC's sale of a fixed asset during the year (see Exhibit 17-3). She observed from the workpapers that PCC sold the fixed asset for $100,000, its original cost (not given in the original facts, assumed for purposes of this example). The book basis of the asset was $46,000, resulting in a book gain of $54,000. The tax gain on the sale was $70,000, which corresponds to a decrease in accumulated tax depreciation of $70,000 (i.e., the tax basis of the asset was $30,000). The excess of the reduction in accumulated tax

(*continued on page 17-14*)

depreciation over accumulated book depreciation of $16,000 corresponds to the excess of the tax gain over the book gain on the sale.

Financial accounting change in accumulated depreciation on the fixed asset sold	
Beginning of the year	$54,000
End of the year	0
Net change	$54,000

Tax accounting change in accumulated depreciation on the fixed asset sold	
Beginning of the year	$70,000
End of the year	0
Net change	$70,000

By what amount will PCC *decrease* its deferred tax liabilities as a result of the decrease in the tax over book basis in this asset from the beginning of the year to the end of the year?

Answer: $5,440, computed as $16,000 × 34%

What tax accounting journal entry does PCC record *related to this transaction*?

Answer:

Deferred income tax liability	5,440	
Deferred income tax benefit		5,440

This drawdown of the excess of tax accumulated depreciation over book accumulated depreciation requires a reduction in the previously recorded deferred tax liability that resulted from the book–tax difference created by the excess of tax depreciation over book depreciation in prior periods.

By what amount will PCC increase its current income tax expense as a result of this transaction (the tax gain was $70,000)?

Answer: $23,800, computed as $70,000 × 34%

What tax accounting journal entry does PCC record *related to this transaction*?

Answer:

Current income tax expense	23,800	
Income taxes payable		23,800

What is the net impact of this transaction on PCC's income tax provision?

Answer: A net increase of $18,360, computed as:

Current income tax expense	$23,800
Deferred income tax benefit	(5,440)
Net increase in PCC's income tax provision	$18,360

What do these journal entries accomplish?

Answer: The $18,360 provision reflects the tax expense related to the book gain of $54,000, computed as follows:

Book gain on sale of the fixed asset	$54,000
	× 34%
Net increase in PCC's income tax provision	$18,360

The recording of a deferred tax liability for years in which tax depreciation exceeded book depreciation anticipated the difference in the book and tax gain that would result when the fixed asset eventually was recovered, either through sale or depreciation of the entire basis.

Example 17-8

Using her cumulative temporary differences template, Elise recorded the cumulative taxable temporary differences and the corresponding deferred tax liability at the beginning of the year (BOY) and the end of the year (EOY) to determine the change in the deferred tax liability related to accumulated depreciation.

Premiere Computer Corporation Temporary Difference Scheduling Template					
Taxable Temporary Differences	**BOY Cumulative T/D**	**Beginning Deferred Taxes (@ 34%)**	**Current- Year Change**	**EOY Cumulative T/D**	**Ending Deferred Taxes (@ 34%)**
Noncurrent Accumulated Depreciation	(10,000,000)*	**(3,400,000)**	(684,000)	(10,684,000)	**(3,632,560)**

*$22,000,000 − $12,000,000, from Example 17-6.

What is the net increase in PCC's deferred tax liability related to fixed assets for 2016?

Answer: $232,560, the change in the cumulative deferred tax liability from the beginning of the year ($3,400,000) to the end of the year ($3,632,560).

This amount corresponds to the increase in the deferred tax liability due to the current-year change in the book–tax difference related to depreciation ($700,000) less the reduction in the deferred tax liability due to the change in the book–tax difference related to accumulated depreciation written off on the sale of the fixed asset ($16,000).

What tax accounting journal entry does PCC record related to the change in total deferred tax liabilities from the beginning of the year to the end of the year?

Answer:

Deferred income tax expense	232,560	
Deferred income tax liability		232,560

Using a template that tracks the cumulative changes in the book–tax differences related to balance sheet accounts becomes especially important when a company's enacted tax rate changes. For example, if PCC's federal income tax rate increased from 34 percent to 35 percent as a result of an increase in its taxable income, and PCC expects to maintain that tax rate in future periods, the company would tax-effect its year-end cumulative book–tax difference related to fixed assets at the new tax rate, 35 percent. The increase in the deferred tax expense related to adjusting the balance sheet will reflect the current-year change in the book–tax difference and also an adjustment to revalue the cumulative book–tax difference at the beginning of the year. This discussion points to the fact that the focus of ASC 740 is to have the balance sheet deferred tax accounts reflect the tax that will be due or refunded when the underlying temporary differences reverse in a future period.

Example 17-9

What if: Assume PCC's tax rate increased from 34 percent in 2015 to 35 percent in 2016. By what amount would PCC increase or decrease its balance sheet deferred tax liability related to the fixed asset account?

(continued on page 17-16)

Answer: PCC *increases* its deferred tax liability related to fixed assets by $339,400, calculated as follows:

Taxable Temporary Differences	BOY Cumulative T/D	Beginning Deferred Taxes (@ 34%)	Current-Year Change	EOY Cumulative T/D	Ending Deferred Taxes (@ 35%)
Premiere Computer Corporation Temporary Difference Scheduling Template					
Noncurrent					
Accumulated Depreciation	(10,000,000)	(3,400,000)	(684,000)	(10,684,000)	**(3,739,400)**

PCC would use a tax rate of 35 percent to compute the ending balance in its deferred tax liability related to fixed assets. The net increase in the deferred tax liability related to accumulated depreciation is now $339,400 ($3,739,400 − $3,400,000).

What tax accounting journal entry does PCC record *related to fixed assets*?

Answer:

Deferred income tax expense	339,400	
Deferred income tax liability		339,400

This amount no longer corresponds to the increase in the deferred income tax liability due to the current-year net change in the book–tax difference related to depreciation of $684,000 times the new applicable tax rate of 35 percent ($684,000 × 35% = $239,400). The $100,000 difference results from increasing the beginning of the year cumulative temporary difference of $10,000,000 times the change in the tax rate of 1 percent ($10,000,000 × 1% = $100,000).

Example 17-10

Returning to her temporary differences template, Elise recorded the deductible (cumulatively unfavorable) temporary differences and the corresponding deferred tax assets at the beginning of the year (BOY) and the end of the year (EOY) to determine the change in PCC's deferred tax assets during the current year.

Deductible Temporary Differences	BOY Cumulative T/D	Beginning Deferred Taxes (@ 34%)	Current-Year Change	EOY Cumulative T/D	Ending Deferred Taxes (@ 34%)
Premiere Computer Corporation Temporary Difference Scheduling Template					
Current					
Allowance for bad debts	$ 345,000	$ 117,300	$ 70,000	$ 415,000	$ 141,100
Reserve for warranties	430,000	146,200	170,000	600,000	204,000
Net operating loss	24,000	8,160	(24,000)	0	0
Total current	**$ 799,000**	**$271,660**	**$ 216,000**	**$1,015,000**	**$345,100**
Noncurrent					
Deferred compensation	$1,200,000	$408,000	($150,000)	$1,050,000	$357,000
Stock option compensation	0	0	100,000	100,000	34,000
Net capital loss carryover	0	0	28,000	28,000	9,520
Contribution carryover	0	0	73,700	73,700	25,058
Total noncurrent	**$1,200,000**	**$408,000**	**$ 51,700**	**$1,251,700**	**$425,578**
Total	**$1,999,000**	**$679,660**	**$ 267,700**	**$2,266,700**	**$770,678**

What is the net increase in PCC's total deferred income tax assets for 2016?

Answer: $91,018, the change in the cumulative deferred tax asset from the beginning of the year balance of $679,660 to the end of the year balance of $770,678.

What tax accounting journal entry does PCC record *related to deferred tax assets*?

Answer:

Deferred income tax assets	91,018	
Deferred income tax benefit		91,018

Example 17-11

What if: Assume PCC's tax rate increased from 34 percent in 2015 to 35 percent in 2016. By what amount would PCC increase or decrease its *total* balance sheet deferred income tax assets?

Answer: PCC *increases* its total deferred tax asset balance by $113,685, calculated as follows:

Premiere Computer Corporation Temporary Difference Scheduling Template					
Deductible Temporary Differences	**BOY Cumulative T/D**	**Beginning Deferred Taxes (@ 34%)**	**Current- Year Change**	**EOY Cumulative T/D**	**Ending Deferred Taxes (@ 35%)**
Current					
Allowance for bad debts	$ 345,000	$ 117,300	$ 70,000	$ 415,000	$145,250
Reserve for warranties	430,000	146,200	170,000	600,000	210,000
Net operating loss	24,000	8,160	(24,000)	0	0
Total current	**$ 799,000**	**$271,660**	**$ 216,000**	**$1,015,000**	**$355,250**
Noncurrent					
Deferred compensation	$1,200,000	$408,000	($150,000)	$1,050,000	$367,500
Stock option compensation	0	0	100,000	100,000	35,000
Net capital loss carryover	0	0	28,000	28,000	9,800
Contribution carryover	0	0	73,700	73,700	25,795
Total noncurrent	**$1,200,000**	**$408,000**	**$ 51,700**	**$1,251,700**	**$438,095**
Total	**$1,999,000**	**$679,660**	**$ 267,700**	**$2,266,700**	**$793,345**

PCC would use a tax rate of 35 percent to compute the ending balance in each of its deferred tax asset accounts. The net increase in total deferred tax assets is now $113,685 ($793,345 − $679,660).

What tax accounting journal entry does PCC record to reflect the change in its *total* deferred tax assets?

Answer:

Deferred income tax assets	113,685	
Deferred income tax benefit		113,685

This amount no longer corresponds to the increase in total deferred tax assets due to the current-year change in cumulative deductible temporary differences of $267,700 times the new applicable tax rate of 35 percent ($267,700 × 35% = $93,695). The $19,990 difference results from increasing the beginning of the year cumulative temporary difference of $1,999,000 times the change in the tax rate of 1 percent ($1,999,000 × 1% = $19,990).

LO 17-3 # DETERMINING WHETHER A VALUATION ALLOWANCE IS NEEDED

Step 5: Evaluate the Need for a Valuation Allowance for Gross Deferred Tax Assets

ASC 740 specifically precludes PCC or any company from discounting (recording the present value of) the deferred income tax liability or asset related to a temporary difference based on when the asset is expected to be recovered or the liability settled. The FASB debated whether discounting deferred income tax assets and liabilities would provide more relevant information to investors, but ultimately it decided that the complexity and cost of making the computation outweighed any benefits investors and creditors might receive from the computation.[26]

In lieu of discounting, ASC 740 requires that a company evaluate each of its gross deferred income tax assets on the balance sheet and assess the likelihood the expected tax benefit will be *realized* in a future period. The income tax benefits reflected in the deferred tax assets can only be realized (converted into cash) if the company expects to have sufficient taxable income or tax liability in the future or carryback period to absorb the unused tax deductions or credits before they expire.

Determining the Need for a Valuation Allowance

Under ASC 740, if a company determines that it is *more likely than not* (a likelihood greater than 50 percent) that some portion or all of the deferred tax assets will not be realized in a future period, it must offset the deferred tax assets with a **valuation allowance** to reflect the amount the company does not expect to realize in the future.[27] Valuation allowances operate as *contra accounts* to the deferred income tax assets on the balance sheet, much like the allowance for bad debts a company must estimate for its accounts receivable. Companies usually disclose the amount of the valuation allowance in the income tax footnote to the financial statements.

Management must assess whether it is more likely than not that a deferred income tax asset will *not* be realized in the future based on all available evidence, both positive and negative. ASC 740 identifies four sources of potential future taxable income, two of which are objective and two of which are subjective (i.e., determined by management judgment).[28] The objective sources include (1) future reversals of existing taxable temporary differences and (2) taxable income in prior carryback year(s). The subjective sources include (1) expected future taxable income exclusive of reversing temporary differences and carryforwards and (2) tax planning strategies.

Future Reversals of Existing Taxable Temporary Differences Existing taxable (cumulatively favorable) temporary differences provide taxable income when they are recovered in a future period. For example, the recovery of the excess of an asset's financial accounting (book) basis over its tax basis, whether through sale or depreciation, will cause taxable income to be higher than pretax net income in the periods in which the excess financial accounting basis is recovered. If the reversing taxable temporary differences provide sufficient future taxable income to absorb the

---

[26]FAS 109, ¶¶198–199. (These paragraphs were not codified in ASC 740.)
[27]ASC 740-10-30-5(e).
[28]ASC 740-10-30-18.

reversing deductible temporary differences, the company does not record a valuation allowance against the deferred tax asset.

Taxable Income in Prior Carryback Year(s)   The company does not record a valuation allowance if the tax benefit from the realization of a deferred income tax asset can be carried back to a prior year that has sufficient taxable income (or capital gain net income in the case of a net capital loss carryback) to absorb the realized tax benefit.

Expected Future Taxable Income Exclusive of Reversing Temporary Differences and Carryforwards   ASC 740 allows a company to consider taxable income it expects to earn in future periods in determining whether a valuation allowance is necessary. The company might support its predictions of future taxable income with evidence of existing contracts or a sales backlog that will produce enough taxable income to realize the deferred tax asset when it reverses. In addition, the company could demonstrate that it has a strong earnings history if a deferred tax asset arises from a loss that could be considered out of the ordinary and not from a continuing condition. Cyclical industries such as automobile manufacturers, builders, and airlines traditionally have cited a history of past income as evidence of expected future income.

Tax Planning Strategies   The most subjective source of future taxable income to support the realization of a deferred income tax asset involves the company's ability and willingness to employ tax strategies in those future periods to create the taxable income needed to absorb the deferred tax asset. ASC 740 allows a company to consider actions it might take to create sufficient taxable income to absorb a deferred income tax asset, provided such actions (1) are prudent and feasible; (2) are actions an enterprise might not take, but would take to prevent an operating loss or tax credit carryforward from expiring unused; and (3) would result in realization of the deferred tax assets. The company does not have to implement the strategy to avoid recording a valuation allowance, but management must be willing and able to execute the strategy if the need arises. Tax planning strategies could include (1) selling and leasing back operating assets, (2) changing inventory accounting methods (e.g., from LIFO to FIFO), (3) refraining from making voluntary contributions to the company pension plan, (4) electing to capitalize certain expenditures (e.g., research and development costs) rather than deduct them currently, (5) selling noncore assets, (6) converting tax-exempt investments into taxable investments, and (7) electing the alternative depreciation system (straight line instead of declining balance).

Negative Evidence That a Valuation Allowance Is Needed   ASC 740 requires that a company consider *negative evidence* as well as *positive evidence* in determining whether it is more likely than not that a deferred income tax asset will not be realized in the future. Negative evidence includes (1) cumulative (book) losses in recent years, (2) a history of net operating (capital) losses and credits expiring unused, (3) an expectation of losses in the near future, and (4) unsettled circumstances that, if resolved unfavorably, will result in losses from continuing operations in future years (e.g., the loss of a patent on a highly profitable drug).[29] As a general rule, public accounting firms interpret "recent years" with regard to cumulative book losses as a rolling 12 quarters (i.e., 36 months). As with all general rules, there are exceptions depending on the industry.

[29]ASC 740-10-30-21.

TAXES IN THE REAL WORLD   AIG's $17.7 Billion "Fantasy" Profit

On February 23, 2012, American International Group, Inc. (AIG) announced net income of $19.8 billion for the full year 2011. Closer inspection of the announcement revealed that $17.7 billion of the amount was due to the company's release of a portion of its valuation allowance related to its deferred tax assets. The company's CEO stated that, "In 2011, we began to prosper once again. We have a high degree of confidence in our future earnings prospects, which is a critical element in our assessment supporting the release of the deferred tax asset valuation allowance."[a] In its Form 10-K, the company explained the rationale for releasing the valuation allowance as follows:

> The evaluation of the recoverability of the deferred tax asset and the need for a valuation allowance requires AIG to weigh all positive and negative evidence to reach a conclusion that it is more likely than not that all or some portion of the deferred tax asset will not be realized. The weight given to the evidence is commensurate with the extent to which it can be objectively verified. The more negative evidence that exists, the more positive evidence is necessary and the more difficult it is to

support a conclusion that a valuation allowance is not needed. During 2011, AIG's level of profitability, excluding the $3.3 billion loss on extinguishment of debt in January confirmed its return to sustainable operating profit for the full year. This, together with the emergence from cumulative losses in recent years and projections of sufficient future taxable income, represent significant positive evidence. As of December 31, 2011, the cumulative positive evidence outweighed the historical negative evidence regarding the likelihood that the deferred tax asset for AIG's U.S. consolidated income tax group (other than the life-insurance-business capital loss carryforwards) will be realized.[b]

Not everyone was impressed with AIG's "whopping" profit. A writer for *The New York Times* referred to the profit as "pure fantasy." What do you think?[c]

[a]Form 8-K, issued 2/23/12. Available at http://www.sec.gov.
[b]Form 10-K, page 357. Available at http://www.sec.gov.
[c]Andrew Ross Sorkin, "Bending the Tax Code, and Lifting A.I.G.'s Profit," *The New York Times*, February 23, 2012, (blog).

Example 17-12

Elise created a workpaper that listed PCC's ending balances in its deferred tax assets and liabilities at December 31, 2016 (from Examples 17-8 and 17-10), as follows:

PCC Deferred Tax Accounts at 12/31/2016

Deferred Tax Assets	
Allowance for bad debts	$ 141,100
Reserve for warranties	204,000
Net operating loss carryforward	0
Deferred compensation	357,000
Stock option compensation	34,000
Capital loss carryforward	9,520
Contribution carryforward	25,058
Total deferred tax assets	**$ 770,678**
Deferred tax liabilities	
Depreciation	(3,632,560)
Total deferred tax liabilities	$(3,632,560)
Net deferred tax liabilities	**$(2,861,882)**

What *positive* evidence should Elise consider in her evaluation as to whether PCC should record a valuation allowance against some or all of the deferred tax assets?

Answer: PCC has an excess of deferred tax liabilities over deferred tax assets of $2,861,882. When the book–tax depreciation difference reverses in the future, this will provide PCC with enough taxable income to absorb the reversing deferred tax assets.

What *negative* evidence should Elise consider in her evaluation as to whether PCC should record a valuation allowance against some or all of the deferred tax assets?

Answer: The deferred tax asset related to the charitable contribution carryover has a short carry-over expiration date (five years). Elise may need to schedule out when the depreciation differences will reverse to determine if the reversals alone will provide PCC with enough taxable income to absorb the contribution carryover within the next five years.

  More problematic, the net capital loss carryover has both a short carryover expiration date (five years) and requires PCC to recognize net capital gains in future periods to absorb the net capital loss. A reversal of the book–tax depreciation temporary difference will not provide PCC with net capital gain to absorb the net capital loss carryover.

What other sources of *positive* evidence should Elise consider in her evaluation as to whether PCC should record a valuation allowance against the deferred tax asset related to the net capital loss carryover?

Answer: Two additional sources of positive evidence are management's projections of future taxable income from sources other than reversing taxable temporary differences and future tax-able income from tax planning strategies. Because PCC is in the business of manufacturing and selling computer-related equipment, any additional taxable income it generates from selling ad-ditional equipment will produce ordinary income. The company likely will have to rely on an asser-tion that management has a "prudent" *tax planning strategy* it would be willing to use to generate net capital gain in the future. An example of such a strategy might be management's willingness to sell a parcel of land held for investment to generate a capital gain sufficient to absorb the net capital loss.

Example 17-13

What if: Assume PCC has had net book losses of $5,000,000 and $2,500,000 in 2014 and 2015, respectively. How might this additional fact influence Elise's assessment about the need for a valu-ation allowance?

Answer: PCC would have a cumulative book loss of $1,483,000 over the past 36 months at December 31, 2016 (combined book losses of $7,500,00 in excess of 2016 book income of $6,017,000 from Exhibit 17-3). ASC 740 states that a cumulative loss "in recent years" is considered objective negative evidence that may be hard to overcome. Elise would have to consider other sources of positive evidence that will outweigh the "significant" negative evidence in this situation. Often, the national office of the firm will make the determination as to whether a valuation allowance is required.

Example 17-14

What if: Assume PCC just lost a big account to its competitor, but the company had reported cu-mulative net income in the current and prior two years. How might this additional fact influence Elise's assessment about the need for a valuation allowance?

Answer: Expectations of future events can outweigh historic results. In this case, Elise would have to seriously consider whether a valuation allowance would be required to the extent that re-versing taxable temporary differences would not absorb expected future losses.

Step 6: Calculate the Deferred Income Tax Expense or Benefit

Example 17-15

After discussing with management its assessment of the company's sources of future taxable income, Elise concurred with management that the company did not need to record a valuation allowance for 2016. Elise now had the pieces to determine PCC's deferred income tax expense or benefit for 2016. What is PCC's deferred income tax provision for 2016 (use the solutions from Examples 17-8 and 17-10)?

Answer: $141,542 net deferred tax expense, computed as follows:

Gross deferred tax expense	$232,560	[Example 17-8]
Gross deferred tax benefit	(91,018)	[Example 17-10]
Net deferred tax expense	$141,542	

What is PCC's total income tax provision for 2016 (also use the solution from Example 17-5)?

Answer: $1,892,780 income tax expense, computed as follows:

Current tax expense	$1,751,238	[Example 17-5]
Gross deferred tax expense	232,560	
Gross deferred tax benefit	(91,018)	
Income tax expense	$1,892,780	

There is a straightforward "back-of-the-envelope" method of verifying the ASC 740 approach to calculating PCC's total tax provision. Under the assumption that all temporary differences will appear on a tax return in a current or future period, the total tax provision should reflect the tax that ultimately will be paid on pretax net income adjusted for *permanent differences*. Remember from Example 17-3 that this amount is sometimes referred to as a company's *book equivalent of taxable income*. The total income tax provision should equal the company's tax rate times its book equivalent of taxable income. We would emphasize that this approach to computing a company's income tax provision is not in accordance with GAAP and will not provide the correct answer when there are changes in a company's income tax rate.

Example 17-16

Elise retrieved her computation of PCC's book equivalent of taxable income (from Example 17-3), as follows:

PCC pretax net income	$6,017,000	
Net favorable permanent difference	(450,000)	
PCC book equivalent to taxable income	$5,567,000	

What is PCC's total tax provision using book equivalent of taxable income as a base?

Answer: $1,892,780, computed as follows:

PCC book equivalent to taxable income	$5,567,000	
	× 34%	
PCC book equivalent to taxable income	$1,892,780	

This computation confirms the computation made under ASC 740 from Example 17-15.

ACCOUNTING FOR UNCERTAINTY IN INCOME TAX POSITIONS

LO 17-4

continued from page 17-12...

Elise recalled from her calculation of PCC's taxable income that there had been some discussion about the appropriate tax treatment of certain items on the tax return. In particular, she and PCC's tax director had debated whether certain income qualified for the domestic production activities deduction. In particular, there was some uncertainty as to whether $1,000,000 of the company's QPAI would be allowed by the IRS on audit. This amount of QPAI provided the company with a domestic production activities deduction of $90,000 (9% × $1,000,000). The tax director felt "comfortable" in taking the tax return position that the income met the definition of qualified production activity income (QPAI). Elise decided she needed to know more about how to deal with accounting for this tax uncertainty. ■

As you have learned in your study of the U.S. income tax laws, the answer to every tax question is not always certain. Taxpayers and the IRS can differ in their opinions as to whether an expenditure is deductible or must be capitalized or whether income is taxable or is deferred or exempt from taxation. When irresolvable disputes arise, the taxpayer can petition the courts to resolve the tax treatment of a transaction. Taxpayers and the IRS can appeal decisions of the lower courts to the appellate courts and ultimately to the U.S. Supreme Court. Taxpayers also take tax positions that can be disputed by state and local taxing authorities and international tax authorities. For example, the taxpayer and a state (international) tax authority may differ on whether the taxpayer has earned income in that jurisdiction and should pay tax on such income. The courts may not resolve this issue for many years after the original transaction takes place. If the courts do not resolve the issue in the taxpayer's favor, the taxpayer will be subject to interest and possible penalties on the tax owed.

For financial accounting purposes, a company must determine whether it can record the current or future tax benefits from an "uncertain" tax position in its financial statement for the period in which the transaction takes place, knowing that the ultimate resolution of the tax position may not be known until some time in the future.

FAS 109 as originally written provided no specific guidance on how to deal with uncertain tax positions. As a result, companies generally applied the principles of FAS 5, *Accounting for Contingencies* (codified as ASC 450), to uncertain tax positions. The FASB became concerned that companies were not applying FAS 5 uniformly, leading to diversity in practice and financial statements that were not comparable. After much debate, the FASB issued FASB Interpretation (FIN) No. 48, *Accounting for Uncertainty in Income Taxes—An Interpretation of FASB Statement No. 109,* in July 2006, effective for years beginning after December 15, 2006. FIN 48 has been codified in ASC 740. The objective of FIN 48 is to provide a uniform approach to recording and disclosing tax benefits resulting from tax positions that are considered to be uncertain.

ASC 740 (FIN 48) applies a two-step process to evaluating tax positions. ASC 740 refers to the first step as *recognition.*[30] A company must determine whether it is *more likely than not* (a greater than 50 percent probability) that a tax position will be sustained on examination by the IRS or other taxing authority, including resolution of any appeals within the court system, based on the technical merits of the position. In making this determination, the company must presume that the taxing authority (IRS) will examine the tax position with full knowledge of all relevant information.

THE KEY FACTS

Accounting for Uncertain Tax Positions

- ASC 740 requires a two-step process in determining if a tax benefit can be recognized in the financial statements.
  - A company first determines if it is more likely than not that its tax position on a particular account will be sustained on IRS examination based on its technical merits.
  - A company then determines the amount it expects to be able to recognize.
- The measurement process requires the company to make a cumulative probability assessment of all likely outcomes of the audit and litigation process.
  - The company recognizes the amount that has a greater than 50 percent probability of being sustained on examination and subsequent litigation.
  - The amount not recognized is recorded as a liability on the balance sheet.

---

[30]ASC 740-10-25-5 through 25-7.

In other words, the company cannot take into account the possibility that the taxing authority will not audit the uncertain tax position (play the "audit lottery").

The second step is referred to as *measurement*.[31] If the tax position meets the more-likely-than-not threshold (a subjective determination), the company must determine the amount of the benefit to record in the financial statements, or from an ASC 740 perspective, how much of its claimed tax benefit the company is not allowed to recognize. (ASC 740 refers to this unclaimed amount as "unrecognized tax benefits.") Under ASC 740, the company records the largest amount of the benefit, as calculated on a cumulative probability basis, which is more likely than not to be realized on the ultimate settlement of the tax position.

Application of ASC 740 to Uncertain Tax Positions

ASC 740 applies to all *tax positions* dealing with income taxes. As a result, ASC 740 pertains to tax positions taken on a current or previously filed tax return or a tax position that will be taken on a future tax return that is reflected in the financial statements as a deferred tax asset or liability. ASC 740 also applies to tax positions that result in permanent differences (e.g., the domestic production activities deduction and credits) and to decisions not to file a tax return in a particular jurisdiction. For example, assume a company deducts an expenditure on its current tax return, which the IRS may challenge on audit in a future period. The deduction produces a net operating loss that will be carried forward and offset against future taxable income. ASC 740 addresses whether the company can *recognize* the deferred tax asset related to the NOL carryforward on its balance sheet. Once the recognition hurdle is overcome, the company must then evaluate whether it is more likely than not that the deferred tax asset will be *realized* in the future period (i.e., whether a valuation allowance should be recorded).

Step 1: Recognition A company first must determine if it is more likely than not that its tax position on a particular account will be sustained on IRS examination based on its technical merits. If the company believes this threshold has been met, the company can record (recognize) the tax benefit of the tax position on its financial statements as a reduction in its current tax expense or an increase in its deferred tax benefit. The company must presume that the IRS will examine this tax position with full knowledge of all relevant information. However, in determining if the more-likely-than-not threshold has been met, the company can take into account how the tax position might be resolved if litigated. This requires the company to evaluate the sources of authority that address this issue (i.e., the tax law, regulations, legislative history, IRS rulings, and court opinions).

Step 2: Measurement After the company determines that the more-likely-than-not recognition threshold has been met, it must compute the amount of the tax benefit to recognize in its financial statements. ASC 740 states that the tax position is to be measured as

> the largest amount of tax benefit that is greater than 50 percent likely of being realized upon ultimate settlement with a taxing authority that has full knowledge of all relevant information.[32]

This measurement process requires the company to make a cumulative probability assessment of all likely outcomes of the audit and litigation process. The company then recognizes the amount that has a greater than 50 percent probability of being sustained on examination and subsequent litigation.

The amount of the tax benefit that is not recognized ("unrecognized tax benefit") is recorded as a liability on the balance sheet (usually labeled as "Income Taxes

[31]ASC 740-10-30-7.
[32]ASC 740-10-30-7.

Payable"). The corresponding "debit" to record the balance sheet liability is to *current* income tax expense (or a decrease in income tax benefit). If the company expects the uncertain tax position to be resolved in the next 12 months, the balance sheet payable is characterized as current. Otherwise, the payable is characterized as being noncurrent. The increase in tax expense is added to the current portion of the provision under the theory that this is an on-demand liability.

Example 17-17

Elise saw in the domestic production activities deduction (DPAD) workpapers that PCC claimed $465,000 of DPAD on its tax return, computed as 9 percent times $5,166,667 of qualified production activity income (from Example 16-1). She noted that there was mention in the uncertain tax position (UTP) workpapers that there was uncertainty as to whether $1,000,000 of the $5,166,667 met the definition of qualified production activity income (QPAI). This tax position provided PCC with a current-year tax benefit of $30,600 ($1,000,000 × 9% × 34%).

What threshold must be met before PCC can *recognize* any of the tax benefit from the "uncertain" portion of the DPAD on its financial statements?

Answer: PCC must determine that it is more likely than not that its tax position on the DPAD will be sustained by the IRS on examination based on its technical merits.

Example 17-18

PCC determined that it was more likely than not that the tax position would be sustained on audit and litigation. The tax department calculated the probability of receiving a full or partial benefit after resolution of the issue as follows:

Potential Estimated Tax Benefit	Individual Probability of Being Realized (%)	Cumulative Probability of Being Realized (%)
$30,600	60	60
22,500	25	85
18,000	10	95
0	5	100

Based on these probabilities, how much of the uncertain tax benefit of $30,600 can PCC recognize?

Answer: $30,600. PCC can recognize all $30,600 of the DPAD tax benefit because this amount is the largest amount that has a greater than 50 percent cumulative probability of being realized on the ultimate settlement of the tax position.

Example 17-19

What if: Assume PCC's tax department had assessed the cumulative probabilities of sustaining the DPAD tax benefit as follows:

Potential Estimated Tax Benefit	Individual Probability of Being Realized (%)	Cumulative Probability of Being Realized (%)
$30,600	40	40
22,500	30	70
18,000	20	90
0	10	100

Based on these probabilities, how much of the uncertain tax benefit of $30,600 can PCC recognize?

(continued on page 17-26)

> **Answer:** $22,500. PCC can recognize $22,500 of the DPAD tax benefit because this amount is the largest amount that has a greater than 50 percent cumulative probability of being realized on the ultimate settlement of the tax position. This translates into management believing that $735,294 of the uncertain DPAD will be sustained on audit ($22,500/.09/.34).
>
> What would be PCC's journal entry to record the portion of the tax benefit that cannot be recognized?
>
> **Answer:** PCC would establish a liability for the $8,100 difference between the amount of the benefit received on the current-year tax return ($30,600) and the amount the company ultimately expects to receive ($22,500). PCC would record the following journal entry:
>
> | | | |
> |---|---|---|
> | Current income tax expense | 8,100 | |
> | Income taxes payable | | 8,100 |
>
> The income taxes payable account is characterized as noncurrent on the balance sheet if PCC does not expect the UTP to be resolved within the next 12 months. The uncertain tax benefit is recorded as a current tax expense because this is the additional amount of taxes PCC would pay if it prepared its tax return by deducting only $735,294 of the uncertain DPAD instead of $1,000,000.

Subsequent Events

ASC 740 requires a company to monitor subsequent events (e.g., the issuance of new regulations, rulings, court opinions) that might change the company's assessment that a tax position will be sustained on audit and litigation. As facts and circumstances change, a company must reevaluate the tax benefit amount they expect to realize in the future. For example, the Treasury might issue a regulation or ruling that clarifies its tax position on a particular item. This regulation could change a company's assessment that its tax position meets the more-likely-than-not threshold required for recognition.

In its 2009 Annual Report, Cisco Systems Inc. disclosed that it took a tax charge of approximately $174 million in the fourth quarter of fiscal 2009 after the U.S. Court of Appeals for the Ninth Circuit overturned a 2005 U.S. Tax Court ruling in *Xilinx, Inc. v. Commissioner.* The company increased its unrecognized tax benefits even though it was not named as a party to the case because it had the same issue on its tax returns (the deduction of share-based compensation expenses for the purpose of determining intangible development costs under a company's research and development cost-sharing arrangement). This increase in the company's prior-period unrecognized tax benefits increased its effective tax rate by 2.3 percentage points in fiscal 2009.

In its 2010 Annual Report, Cisco reported that the Ninth Circuit withdrew its prior holding and reaffirmed the 2005 U.S. Tax Court ruling in *Xilinx, Inc. v. Commissioner.* As a result of this final decision, the company decreased the amount of gross unrecognized tax benefits by approximately $220 million and decreased the amount of accrued interest by $218 million. This adjustment decreased Cisco's effective tax rate by 1.7 percentage points.

Interest and Penalties

ASC 740 requires a company to accrue interest and any applicable penalties on liabilities it establishes for potential future tax obligations. The interest (net of the tax benefit from deducting it on a future tax return when paid) and penalties (which are not tax deductible) can be treated as part of the company's UTP-related income tax expense and income tax payable or can be recognized as interest or penalties separate from the UTP-related income tax expense. ASC 740 only requires that the company apply its election consistently from period to period.

This election creates the potential for diversity in practice. For example, General Motors Corporation treats accrued interest and penalties on its uncertain tax positions as part of its selling, general, and administrative expenses, while Ford Motor Company treats accrued interest and penalties on its uncertain tax positions as part of its income tax provision.

Disclosures of Uncertain Tax Positions

One of the most controversial aspects of ASC 740 is its expansion of the disclosure requirements related to liabilities recorded due to uncertain tax positions. ASC 740 requires the company to roll forward all unrecognized tax benefits (UTBs) on a worldwide aggregated basis. Specific line items must disclose (1) the gross amounts of increases and decreases in liabilities related to uncertain tax positions as a result of tax positions taken during a prior period, (2) the gross amounts of increases and decreases in liabilities related to uncertain tax positions as a result of tax positions taken during the current period, (3) the amounts of decreases in liabilities related to uncertain tax positions relating to settlements with taxing authorities, and (4) reductions in liabilities related to uncertain tax positions as a result of a lapse of the applicable statute of limitations (the taxing authority can no longer audit the tax return on which the tax position was taken). The UTP disclosure by Microsoft Corporation is illustrated in Exhibit 17-6.

EXHIBIT 17-6 **The UTP Disclosure of Microsoft Corporation**

The aggregate changes in the balance of unrecognized tax benefits were as follows:

Year Ended June 30	(In millions)		
	2015	2014	2013
Balance, beginning of year	$8,714	$8,648	$7,202
Decreases related to settlements	(50)	(583)	(30)
Increases for tax positions related to the current year	1,091	566	612
Increases for tax positions related to prior years	94	217	931
Decreases for tax positions related to prior years	(144)	(95)	(65)
Decreases due to lapsed statutes of limitations	(106)	(39)	(2)
Balance, end of year	$9,599	$8,714	$8,648

FIN 48 became effective for years beginning after December 15, 2006. The FASB required adopters to record their initial FIN 48 cumulative effect adjustment (in the first quarter after adoption) to retained earnings or other balance sheet account rather than to the income tax provision. Subsequent adjustments must be reported as part of the income tax provision.

Opponents of FIN 48 worried that the FIN 48 disclosures would provide a "roadmap" to the IRS to a company's uncertain tax positions.[33] The FIN 48 disclosures have not provided the IRS with the hoped-for details because the UTP disclosure does not identify the tax jurisdictions to which the uncertain tax positions relate.

Schedule UTP (Uncertain Tax Position Statement)

In January 2010, Commissioner Shulman announced that the IRS would begin asking large corporations to report their financial statement uncertain tax positions

---

[33]Jesse Drucker, "Lifting the Veil on Tax Risk—New Accounting Rule Lays Bare a Firm's Liability if Transaction Is Later Disallowed by the IRS," *The Wall Street Journal,* May 25, 2007.

on new Schedule UTP beginning in tax year 2010. The commissioner stated that the goals of the new schedule would be to increase transparency and efficiency in identifying audit issues and help the IRS prioritize the selection of issues and taxpayers for audit. Schedule UTP requires corporations to report any federal income tax position for which an unrecognized tax benefit has been recorded in an audited financial statement. A corporation must identify the IRC section or sections relating to the position, indicate whether the position involves a temporary or permanent difference, identify whether the tax position is a major tax position (10 percent or more of the total), rank the tax positions by size, and provide a "concise" description of the UTP. Corporations with assets of $10 million or more must file Schedule UTP. An analysis of the tax year 2013 filed Schedule UTPs revealed that 2,090 taxpayers filed the schedule and reported 5,110 issues. The top three issues involved the research credit (32%), transfer pricing (18%), and the domestic production activities deduction (5%).[34]

ETHICS

Pete Cooper, senior manager in the tax group in the Boston office of Bean Counters LLP, an international professional services firm, was reviewing the workpapers related to the uncertain tax positions prepared by his biggest client, Pro Vision Inc. Pete noticed that the client took the position that it did not need to record an uncertain tax benefit for a significant transaction because it had a "should level" opinion from its law firm. (A "should level" tax opinion means that the law firm believes there is a 70 to 90 percent probability that the tax benefit from the transaction will be allowed if litigated.) When Pete asked to see the tax opinion, he was told by the firm's tax director that the company did not want to disclose the item for fear the IRS also would ask to see the opinion. Pete has always had a good working relationship with the tax staff at Pro Vision and trusts their integrity.

Should Pete take the tax director's word when auditing the company's reserve for uncertain tax positions? What would you do if you were in Pete's position?

LO 17-5 FINANCIAL STATEMENT DISCLOSURE AND THE COMPUTATION OF A CORPORATION'S EFFECTIVE TAX RATE

Balance Sheet Classification

For years beginning before December 16, 2016 (December 16, 2017, for all business entities other than public companies), ASC 740 requires publicly traded and privately held companies to disclose their deferred tax assets and liabilities on their balance sheets and classify them as either current or noncurrent.[35] A business entity classifies its deferred tax assets and liabilities based on the classification of the asset or liability to which the deferred tax account relates. For example, a deferred tax liability related to a long-term asset (e.g., depreciation of a fixed asset) is classified as noncurrent because the related asset is classified as noncurrent on the balance sheet. Deferred tax liabilities and assets not related to a specific asset (e.g., a net operating loss carryover or organizational expenditures capitalized for tax purposes) are classified based on the expected reversal date of the temporary difference.

ASC 740 requires business entities to net deferred tax assets and liabilities based on their classification (current with current, noncurrent with noncurrent) and present the net amount on the balance sheet.[36] ASC 740 does not permit netting of

---

[34]https://www.irs.gov/Businesses/Corporations/UTPFilingStatistics

[35]ASC 740-10-45-4.

[36]ASC 740-10-45-6. The FASB has proposed simplifying ASC 740 by treating all deferred tax accounts as noncurrent beginning in 2017.

deferred tax assets and liabilities that are attributable to different tax jurisdictions. For example, PCC cannot offset a noncurrent deferred tax asset related to a net operating loss incurred in Germany against a noncurrent deferred tax liability arising from depreciation of fixed assets within the United States. Exhibit 17-7 provides the balance sheet classification for common deferred tax assets and liabilities.

In November 2015, the FASB issued Accounting Standards Update (ASU) No. 2015-17 to ASC 740, which requires classification of all deferred tax assets and liabilities as noncurrent for financial statements issued by public business entities for annual periods beginning after December 15, 2016, (December 15, 2017, for all other entities) and interim periods issued within those annual periods. The FASB made this change to reduce complexity and to respond to stakeholders who informed the Board that the current rules provided little or no benefit to users of financial statements relative to the costs to comply with the rules. The FASB will permit early adoption of the new rules, which most public companies likely will choose.

EXHIBIT 17-7 **Classification of Common Deferred Tax Assets and Liabilities**

Current Deferred Account	Related Balance Sheet Account
Allowance for Bad Debts	Accounts Receivable
Reserve for Warranties	Warranty Payable (liability)
Inventory §263A Adjustment	Inventory
Revenue Recognition	Unearned Revenue (liability)

Noncurrent Deferred Account	Related Balance Sheet Account
Accumulated Depreciation	Fixed Assets
Amortization	Goodwill or Other Intangible
Deferred Compensation	Deferred Compensation (liability)

Deferred tax assets related to net operating loss carryovers, net capital loss carryovers, and charitable contribution are classified based on when the temporary difference is expected to reverse (be deducted on a future tax return).

Example 17-20

Elise reviewed her temporary difference templates (see Examples 17-8 and 17-10). What will be the ending balance in PCC's net current deferred tax assets or liabilities at December 31, 2016, assuming PCC does not early adopt ASU No. 2015-17?

Answer: $345,100 net current deferred tax assets. PCC does not have any current deferred tax liabilities to offset against its current deferred tax assets.

What will be the ending balance in PCC's net noncurrent deferred tax assets or liabilities at December 31, 2016?

Answer: ($3,206,982) net noncurrent deferred tax liability.

Because PCC's deferred tax accounts relate to the same tax jurisdiction (United States), PCC can net the noncurrent deferred tax liabilities of $3,632,560 with the noncurrent deferred tax assets of $425,578, resulting in a net noncurrent deferred tax liability of $3,206,982.

Example 17-21

What if: Assume the noncurrent deferred tax asset related to deferred compensation arose in Canada. What will be the ending balance in PCC's net noncurrent deferred tax assets or liabilities at December 31, 2016?

Answer: $357,000 noncurrent deferred tax asset and $3,563,982 net noncurrent deferred tax liability ($3,632,560 − $68,578).

PCC cannot net the deferred tax asset that relates to Canada with the other noncurrent deferred tax accounts that relate to the United States.

Income Tax Footnote Disclosure

In addition to the above balance sheet disclosure requirements, ASC 740 mandates that a company disclose the components of the net deferred tax assets and liabilities reported on its balance sheet and the total valuation allowance recognized for deferred tax assets.[37] Most companies provide this information in a footnote to the financial statements (often referred to as the *income tax footnote*). Publicly traded companies must disclose the approximate "tax effect" of each type of temporary difference and carryforward that gives rise to a *significant* portion of the net deferred tax liabilities and deferred tax assets.[38] Privately held (nonpublic) companies only need to disclose the types of significant temporary differences without disclosing the tax effects of each type. ASC 740 does not define the term *significant,* although the SEC requires a publicly traded company to disclose separately the components of its total deferred tax assets and liabilities that are 5 percent or more of the total balance.[39] Exhibit 17-8 provides the disclosure of PCC's deferred tax accounts in its income tax footnote.

ASC 740 also requires publicly traded companies to disclose the significant components of its income tax provision (expense or benefit) attributable to continuing operations in either the financial statements or a note thereto.[40] These components include the (1) current tax expense or benefit, (2) deferred tax expense or benefit, (3) the benefits of operating loss carryforwards, (4) adjustments of a deferred tax liability or asset for enacted changes in tax laws or rates, and (5) adjustments of the beginning-of-the-year balance of a valuation allowance because of a change in circumstances that causes a change in management's judgment about the realizability of the recognized deferred tax assets.

Computation and Reconciliation of the Income Tax Provision with a Company's *Hypothetical* Tax Provision

ASC 740 requires a company to reconcile its (a) reported income tax provision attributable to continuing operations with (b) the amount of income tax expense that would result from applying its U.S. statutory tax rate to its pretax net income or loss from continuing operations.[41] Alternatively, a company can present the reconciliation in terms of tax rates, comparing its statutory tax rate with its effective tax rate (income tax provision/pretax income from continuing operations).

Differences between a company's income tax provision and its hypothetical tax provision can arise from several sources. Income taxes paid to a state or municipality increase a company's total income tax provision over its hypothetical income tax expense. Income taxes paid to a jurisdiction outside the United States can increase or decrease a company's total income tax provision over its hypothetical income tax expense depending on whether the jurisdiction taxes the company's income at more or less than the U.S. statutory rate. Permanent differences also affect the computation of PCC's income tax provision. Favorable permanent differences (e.g., tax-exempt income) decrease the income tax provision relative to the hypothetical income tax provision. Unfavorable permanent differences (e.g., nondeductible fines and penalties) increase the income tax provision relative to the hypothetical income tax provision.

---

[37]ASC 740-10-50-2.

[38]ASC 740-10-50-6.

[39]ASC 740-10-50-8 and SEC Regulation S-X, §210.4-08(h).

[40]ASC 740-10-50-9.

[41]ASC 740-10-50-12. The income tax provision computed using the statutory tax rate is often referred to as the *hypothetical* income tax expense.

EXHIBIT 17-8 **PCC's Income Tax Note to Its Financial Statements**

NOTE 5 INCOME TAXES

The Company's income (loss) from continuing operations before the income tax provision by taxing jurisdiction is as follows:

	2016
United States	$6,017,000

The provision (benefit) for income taxes is as follows:

Current tax provision (benefit)	
Federal (U.S.)	$1,751,238
Deferred tax expense (benefit)	
Federal (U.S.)	141,542
Income tax provision	$1,892,780

Deferred tax assets and liabilities are classified as current or noncurrent according to the classification of the related asset or liability. The significant components of the Company's deferred tax assets and liabilities as of December 31, 2016, are as follows:

	2016
Deferred tax *assets*	
Allowance for bad debts	$ 141,100
Reserve for warranties	204,000
Deferred compensation	357,000
Stock option compensation	34,000
Capital loss carryover	9,520
Contribution carryforward	25,058
Total deferred tax assets	$ 770,678
Valuation allowance	0
Deferred tax assets net of valuation allowance	$ 770,678
Deferred tax *liabilities*	
Depreciation	$(3,632,560)
Total deferred tax liabilities	(3,632,560)
Net deferred tax liabilities	$(2,861,882)

The capital loss carryforward and the contribution carryforward expire in 2021 if unused.

A reconciliation of income taxes computed by applying the statutory U.S. income tax rate to the Company's income before income taxes to the income tax provision is as follows:

	2016
Amount computed at the statutory U.S. tax rate (34%)	$2,045,780
Tax-exempt income	(4,080)
Nondeductible meals and entertainment	4,760
Nondeductible life insurance premiums	11,560
Dividends received deduction	(7,140)
Domestic production activities deduction	(158,100)
Income tax provision	$1,892,780

Cash amounts paid during 2016 for income taxes, net of refunds, was $1,751,238.

ASC 740 requires a publicly traded company to disclose the estimated amount and nature of each significant reconciling item, which the SEC defines as an amount equal to or greater than 5 percent of the hypothetical provision. The SEC requires nonpublicly traded companies to disclose the nature of significant reconciling items but not the reconciling amount.

Example 17-22

Elise used her schedule of permanent differences (from Example 17-2) to reconcile PCC's income tax provision ($1,892,780, from Example 17-15) with the company's hypothetical income tax provision. The permanent differences from Example 17-2 are reproduced below:

Permanent Differences	(Favorable) Unfavorable
Tax exempt interest income	$ (12,000)
Meals and entertainment	14,000
Life insurance premiums	34,000
Dividends received deduction	(21,000)
Domestic production activities deduction	(465,000)

PCC's pretax net income from continuing operations in 2016 is $6,017,000.

What is PCC's *hypothetical* income tax provision for 2016?
Answer: $2,045,780, computed as $6,017,000 × 34 percent.

What is PCC's *effective tax rate* for 2016?
Answer: 31.5 percent, computed as $1,892,780/$6,017,000.

Provide a reconciliation of PCC's hypothetical income tax provision with its actual income tax provision in 2016. The tax cost or benefit from each permanent difference is computed by multiplying the permanent difference (from above) times 34 percent.
Answer:

	2016
Amount computed at statutory U.S. tax rate (34%)	$2,045,780
Tax-exempt income	(4,080)
Nondeductible meals and entertainment	4,760
Nondeductible life insurance premiums	11,560
Dividends received deduction	(7,140)
Domestic production activities deduction	(158,100)
Income tax provision	$1,892,780

The SEC requires its registrants to separately disclose only those components of their effective tax rate reconciliations that equal or exceed 5 percent of the "hypothetical" tax expense. In the above reconciliation, PCC would only be required to separately disclose the items that equal or exceed $102,289 ($2,045,780 × 5%), which, in this example, would be the domestic production activities deduction. The other items could be netted in the reconciliation.

Provide a reconciliation of PCC's statutory income tax rate (34 percent) with its actual effective tax rate (31.5 percent) in 2016. The percentage effect of each permanent difference is computed by dividing the tax cost or benefit from the item (from above) by PCC's pretax net income ($6,017,000).
Answer:

	2016
Statutory U.S. tax rate	34.0%
Tax-exempt income	(0.0)
Nondeductible meals and entertainment	0.0
Nondeductible life insurance premiums	0.2
Dividends received deduction	(0.1)
Domestic production activities deduction	(2.6)
Effective tax rate	31.5%

Exhibit 17-8 provides the disclosure of PCC's reconciliation of its effective tax rate in its income tax footnote.

Importance of a Corporation's Effective Tax Rate The effective tax rate often serves as a benchmark for companies in the same industry. However, nonrecurring events can sometimes have a significant impact on the effective tax rate. To mitigate the impact of such aberrational events, companies and their investors may use (at least for internal purposes) a different measure of effective tax rate that backs out one-time and nonrecurring events. This effective tax rate is referred to as the company's **structural tax rate.** The structural effective tax rate often is viewed as more representative of the company's effective tax rate from its normal (recurring) operations. In our example, PCC does not appear to have any nonrecurring reconciling items, which would make its effective tax rate and its structural tax rate the same.

Analysts often compute a company's **cash tax rate** (cash taxes paid divided by pretax book income) in their evaluation of the company's tax status. As the name implies, the cash tax rate excludes deferred taxes. PCC's cash tax rate in 2016 is 29.1 percent ($1,751,238/$6,017,000). Companies earning income in low-tax jurisdictions outside the United States or that have significant favorable permanent differences can have a cash tax rate that is much lower than their accounting effective tax rate. For example, Amazon.com Inc. reported an accounting effective tax rate of 31.1 percent and a cash tax rate of 3.5 percent in 2011!

Interim Period Effective Tax Rates

In addition to annual reports (Form 10-K), PCC also must report earnings on a quarterly basis (Form 10-Q). ASC 740-270, *Interim Reporting,* governs the preparation of these quarterly statements. ASC 740-270-30-6, states that *"at the end of each interim period the entity should make its best estimate of the effective tax rate expected to be applicable for the full fiscal year"* and apply this rate to the income reported in the quarterly statement. A company must reconsider its estimate of the annual rate each quarter. When the estimate changes, the company must adjust the cumulative tax provision for the year-to-date earnings to reflect the new expected annual rate. The adjusting amount becomes the company's income tax provision for the quarter.

FASB PROJECTS RELATED TO ACCOUNTING FOR INCOME TAXES

The FASB has been deliberating making "simplification" changes to disclosures related to uncertain tax benefits and to expanding disclosures in other areas. In particular, the FASB has discussed and decided to increase the disclosure related to a company's international operations and valuation allowances. With respect to international operations, the FASB has decided to require entities to disclose taxes paid as either domestic (U.S.) or foreign and reporting income before taxes by individual countries that are significant in relation to total income before taxes. The FASB also wants increased disclosure regarding the nature and amounts of the valuation allowance recorded and released during the reporting period. The board also decided to require all entities to disclose the rate reconciliation currently required only for public companies. No formal Accounting Statement Updates have been issued on these topics to date.

CONCLUSION

In this chapter we discussed the basic rules that govern the computation of a company's U.S. income tax provision. As a result of increased SEC and PCAOB scrutiny, the need for individuals who understand these rules has increased dramatically. The FASB requires a company to take a balance sheet approach to computing its current and future (deferred) tax liabilities or benefits (assets). The income tax provision that appears on a company's income statement becomes the amount necessary to adjust the beginning balances of these accounts to their appropriate ending balances. The FASB and SEC also impose disclosure requirements for how a company reports its tax accounts in the financial statement amounts and notes to the financial statements.

Summary

LO 17-1 Explain the objectives behind FASB ASC Topic 740, *Income Taxes,* and the income tax provision process.

- Objectives of ASC 740:
  - To recognize a current income tax liability or asset for the company's taxes payable or refundable in the current year.
  - To recognize a deferred income tax liability or asset for the income tax effects of the company's temporary differences and carryovers.
- The income tax provision process consists of six steps:
  - Adjust net income before income taxes for all permanent differences.
  - Identify all temporary differences and tax carryforward amounts.
  - Calculate the current income tax expense or benefit (refund).
  - Determine the ending balances in the balance sheet deferred tax asset and liability accounts.
  - Evaluate the need for a valuation allowance for gross deferred tax assets.
  - Calculate the deferred income tax expense or benefit.

LO 17-2 Calculate the current and deferred income tax expense or benefit components of a company's income tax provision.

- The company first adjusts its pretax net income or loss for permanent and temporary book–tax differences to compute taxable income or loss. The company then applies the appropriate tax rate to taxable income (loss) to compute the tax return current tax expense or benefit.
- The company adjusts its tax return income tax liability or benefit for audit refunds or deficiencies from prior-year tax returns, and income tax benefits from stock option exercises treated as permanent differences.
- A company computes its deferred income tax expense or benefit by applying the applicable tax rate to the change in the cumulative balance sheet temporary differences between the financial accounting basis of an asset or liability and its corresponding tax basis from the beginning of the year to the end of the year.
- The future tax benefits from deductible (cumulatively unfavorable) temporary differences are recorded as deferred tax assets.
- The future tax costs of favorable taxable (cumulatively favorable) temporary differences are recorded as deferred tax liabilities.

LO 17-3 Recall what a valuation allowance represents and describe the process by which it is determined.

- If a company determines that it is more likely than not (a greater than 50 percent probability) that some portion or all of the deferred tax assets will not be realized in a future period, it must offset the deferred tax assets with a valuation allowance to reflect the amount the company does not expect to realize in the future.

- The determination as to whether it is more likely than not that a deferred tax asset will not be realized in the future must be based on all available evidence, both positive and negative.
- ASC 740 identifies four sources of prior and future taxable income to consider: (1) future reversals of existing taxable temporary differences, (2) taxable income in prior carryback year(s), (3) expected future taxable income exclusive of reversing temporary differences and carryforwards, and (4) expected income from tax strategies.

Explain how a company accounts for its uncertain income tax positions under FASB ASC 740.   **LO 17-4**

- A company must determine whether it can record the tax benefits from an "uncertain" tax position in its financial statement for the period in which the transaction takes place, knowing that the ultimate resolution of the tax position may not be known until some future period.
- ASC 740 applies a two-step process to evaluating uncertain tax positions:
  - Recognition: A company must determine whether it is more likely than not (a greater than 50 percent probability) that a tax position will be sustained upon examination by the IRS or other taxing authority, including resolution of any appeals within the court system, based on the technical merits of the position.
  - Measurement: If the tax position meets the more-likely-than-not threshold (a subjective determination), the company must determine the amount of the benefit to record in the financial statements.
- Under ASC 740, the amount to be recorded is the largest amount of the benefit, as calculated on a cumulative probability basis, which is more likely than not to be realized on the ultimate settlement of the tax position.

Recognize the different components of a company's disclosure of its income tax accounts in the financial statements and footnotes, and comprehend how a company computes and discloses the components of its "effective tax rate."   **LO 17-5**

- For annual periods beginning before December 16, 2016, ASC 740 requires a business entity to disclose and separate its deferred tax liabilities and assets into a current amount and a noncurrent amount on its balance sheet.
- A company also is required to present the "significant" components of the income tax provision (expense or benefit) attributable to continuing operations.
- ASC 740 requires publicly traded companies to reconcile their reported income tax expense (benefit) from continuing operations with the *hypothetical* tax expense that would have resulted from applying the domestic federal statutory rate to pretax income from continuing operations. Alternatively, the company can compute an *effective tax rate* from its continuing operations and reconcile it with the domestic federal statutory rate (34 percent or 35 percent).
- A company computes its effective tax rate by dividing its income tax provision (benefit) from continuing operations by its pretax net income from continuing operations.
- Items that cause the effective tax rate to differ from the statutory tax rate include permanent differences, audit adjustments, state and local taxes, and international taxes.

KEY TERMS

book equivalent of taxable income (17-8)

cash tax rate (17-33)

corporate effective tax rate (17-33)

current income tax expense or benefit (17-11)

current tax liability or asset (17-4)

deductible temporary difference (17-9)

deferred tax asset (17-2)

deferred tax liability (17-2)

effective tax rate (17-7)

enacted tax rate (17-12)

permanent differences (17-6)

structural tax rate (17-33)

tax accounting balance sheet (17-12)

tax carryforwards (17-4)

taxable temporary difference (17-9)

uncertain tax positions (17-11)

valuation allowance (17-18)

DISCUSSION QUESTIONS

Discussion Questions are available in *Connect*®.

LO 17-1 1. Identify some of the reasons why accounting for income taxes is complex.

LO 17-1 2. True or False: ASC 740 applies to all taxes paid by a corporation. Explain.

LO 17-1 3. True or False: ASC 740 is the sole source for the rules that apply to accounting for income taxes. Explain.

LO 17-1 4. How does the fact that most corporations file their financial statements several months before they file their income tax returns complicate the income tax provision process?

LO 17-1 5. What distinguishes an *income tax* from other taxes?

LO 17-1 6. Briefly describe the six-step process by which a company computes its income tax provision.

LO 17-2 7. What are the two components of a company's income tax provision? What does each component represent about a company's income tax provision?

LO 17-2 8. True or False: All differences between book and taxable income, both permanent and temporary, affect a company's effective tax rate. Explain.

LO 17-2 9. When does a temporary difference resulting from an expense (deduction) create a taxable temporary difference? A deductible temporary difference?

LO 17-2 10. When does a temporary difference resulting from income create a taxable temporary difference? A deductible temporary difference?

LO 17-2 11. Briefly describe what is meant by the *asset and liability* or *balance sheet* approach taken by ASC 740 with respect to computing a corporation's deferred tax provision.

LO 17-2 12. Why are cumulatively favorable temporary differences referred to as taxable temporary differences?

LO 17-2 13. Why are cumulatively unfavorable temporary differences referred to as deductible temporary differences?

LO 17-2 14. In addition to the current-year tax return taxes payable or refundable, what other transactions can affect a company's current income tax provision?

LO 17-2 **LO 17-4** 15. What is an unrecognized tax benefit and how does it affect a company's current income tax expense?

LO 17-2 16. True or False: When Congress changes the corporate tax rates, only the current year book–tax temporary differences are measured using the new rates. Explain.

LO 17-2 17. True or False: All temporary differences have a financial accounting basis. Explain.

LO 17-3 18. What is the purpose behind a valuation allowance as it applies to deferred tax assets?

LO 17-3 19. What is the difference between *recognition* and *realization* as it applies to the recording of a deferred tax asset on a balance sheet?

LO 17-3 20. Briefly describe the four sources of taxable income a company evaluates in determining if a valuation allowance is necessary.

LO 17-3 21. Which of the four sources of taxable income are considered objective and which are considered subjective? Which of these sources generally receives the most weight in analyzing whether a valuation allowance is necessary?

LO 17-3 22. What are the elements that define a tax planning strategy as it applies to determining if a valuation allowance is necessary? Provide an example where a tax planning strategy may be necessary to avoid recording a valuation allowance.

LO 17-3 23. When does a company remove a valuation allowance from its balance sheet?

24. What is a company's *book equivalent of taxable income* and how does this computation enter into the income tax provision process? `LO 17-3`

25. What motivated the FASB to issue FIN 48? `LO 17-4`

26. Briefly describe the two-step process a company must undertake when it evaluates whether it can record the tax benefit from an uncertain tax position under ASC 740. `LO 17-4`

27. Distinguish between *recognition* and *measurement* as they relate to the computation of unrecognized tax benefits under ASC 740. `LO 17-4`

28. What is a *tax position* as it relates to the application of ASC 740 to uncertain tax positions? `LO 17-4`

29. True or False: A company determines its unrecognized tax benefits with respect to a transaction only at the time the transaction takes place; subsequent events are ignored. Explain. `LO 17-4`

30. True or False: ASC 740 requires that a company treat potential interest and penalties related to an unrecognized tax benefit as part of its income tax provision. Explain. `LO 17-4`

31. Where on the balance sheet does a company report its unrecognized tax benefits? `LO 17-4`

32. Why did many companies oppose FIN 48 when it was first proposed? `LO 17-4`

33. How does a company determine if a deferred tax asset or liability should be classified as current or noncurrent on its balance sheet? `LO 17-5`

34. Under what conditions can a company net its current deferred tax assets with its current deferred tax liabilities on the balance sheet? `LO 17-5`

35. True or False: A publicly traded company must disclose all of the components of its deferred tax assets and liabilities in a footnote to the financial statements. Explain. `LO 17-5`

36. What is a company's *hypothetical* income tax provision and what is its importance in a company's disclosure of its income tax provision in the tax footnote? `LO 17-5`

37. Briefly describe the difference between a company's effective tax rate, cash tax rate, and structural tax rate. `LO 17-5`

PROBLEMS

Select problems are available in *Connect*. ▪ connect

38. Which of the following taxes is *not* accounted for under ASC 740? `LO 17-1`
   a) Income taxes paid to the U.S. government.
   b) Income taxes paid to the French government.
   c) Income taxes paid to the city of Detroit.
   d) Property taxes paid to the city of Detroit.
   e) All of the above taxes are accounted for under ASC 740.

39. Which of the following organizations can issue rules that govern accounting for income taxes? `LO 17-1`
   a) FASB.
   b) SEC.
   c) IRS.
   d) (a) and (b) above.
   e) All of the above organizations.

LO 17-1

research

40. Find the paragraph(s) in ASC 740 that deal with the following items (you can access ASC 740 on the FASB Web site, www.fasb.org, and then clicking on "Standards"). You will need a password from your instructor.

a) The objectives and basic principles that underlie ASC 740.

b) Examples of book–tax differences that create temporary differences.

c) The definition of a *tax planning strategy.*

d) Examples of positive evidence in the valuation allowance process.

e) Rules relating to financial statement disclosure.

LO 17-2

41. Woodward Corporation reported pretax book income of $1,000,000. Included in the computation were favorable temporary differences of $200,000, unfavorable temporary differences of $50,000, and favorable permanent differences of $100,000. Assuming a tax rate of 34 percent, compute the company's current income tax expense or benefit.

LO 17-2

42. Cass Corporation reported pretax book income of $10,000,000. During the current year, the reserve for bad debts increased by $100,000. In addition, tax depreciation exceeded book depreciation by $200,000. Cass Corporation sold a fixed asset and reported book gain of $50,000 and tax gain of $75,000. Finally, the company received $250,000 of tax-exempt life insurance proceeds from the death of one of its officers. Assuming a tax rate of 34 percent, compute the company's current income tax expense or benefit.

LO 17-2

43. Grand Corporation reported pretax book income of $600,000. Tax depreciation exceeded book depreciation by $400,000. In addition, the company received $300,000 of tax-exempt municipal bond interest. The company's prior-year tax return showed taxable income of $50,000. Assuming a tax rate of 34 percent, compute the company's current income tax expense or benefit.

LO 17-2

44. Chandler Corporation reported pretax book income of $2,000,000. Tax depreciation exceeded book depreciation by $500,000. During the year the company capitalized $250,000 into ending inventory under §263A. Capitalized inventory costs of $150,000 in beginning inventory were deducted as part of cost of goods sold on the tax return. Assuming a tax rate of 34 percent, compute the company's taxes payable or refundable.

LO 17-2

45. Davison Company determined that the book basis of its office building exceeded the tax basis by $800,000. This basis difference is properly characterized as

a) A permanent difference.

b) A taxable temporary difference.

c) A deductible temporary difference.

d) A favorable book–tax difference.

e) Both (b) and (d) above are correct.

LO 17-2

46. Abbot Company determined that the book basis of its allowance for bad debts is $100,000. There is no corresponding tax basis in this account. The basis difference is properly characterized as

a) A permanent difference.

b) A taxable temporary difference.

c) A deductible temporary difference.

d) A favorable book–tax difference.

e) Both (b) and (d) above are correct.

LO 17-2

47. Which of the following items is *not* a temporary book–tax basis difference?

a) Warranty reserve accruals.

b) Accelerated depreciation.

c) Capitalized inventory costs under §263A.

d) Nondeductible stock option compensation from exercising an ISO.

e) All of the above are temporary differences.

48. Which of the following book–tax differences does *not* create a favorable temporary book–tax basis difference? `LO 17-2`

a) Tax depreciation for the period exceeds book depreciation.

b) Bad debts charged off in the current period exceed the bad debts accrued in the current period.

c) Inventory costs capitalized under §263A deducted as part of current-year tax cost of goods sold are less than the inventory costs capitalized in ending inventory.

d) Vacation pay accrued for tax purposes in a prior period is deducted in the current period.

e) All of the above create a favorable temporary book–tax difference.

49. Lodge Inc. reported pretax book income of $5,000,000. During the year, the company increased its reserve for warranties by $200,000. The company deducted $50,000 on its tax return related to warranty payments made during the year. What is the impact on taxable income compared to pretax book income of the book–tax difference that results from these two events? `LO 17-2`

a) Favorable (decreases taxable income).

b) Unfavorable (increases taxable income).

c) Neutral (no impact on taxable income).

50. Which of the following book–tax basis differences results in a deductible temporary difference? `LO 17-2`

a) Book basis of a fixed asset exceeds its tax basis.

b) Book basis of a pension-related liability exceeds its tax basis.

c) Prepayment of income included on the tax return but not on the income statement (the transaction is recorded as a liability on the balance sheet).

d) All of the above result in a deductible temporary difference.

e) Both (b) and (c) result in a deductible temporary difference.

51. Shaw Corporation reported pretax book income of $1,000,000. Included in the computation were favorable temporary differences of $200,000, unfavorable temporary differences of $50,000, and favorable permanent differences of $100,000. Assuming a tax rate of 34 percent, compute the company's deferred income tax expense or benefit. `LO 17-2`

52. Shaw Inc. reported pretax book income of $10,000,000. During the current year, the reserve for bad debts increased by $100,000. In addition, tax depreciation exceeded book depreciation by $200,000. Shaw Inc. sold a fixed asset and reported book gain of $50,000 and tax gain of $75,000. Finally, the company received $250,000 of tax-exempt life insurance proceeds from the death of one of its officers. Assuming a tax rate of 34 percent, compute the company's deferred income tax expense or benefit. `LO 17-2`

53. Harrison Corporation reported pretax book income of $600,000. Tax depreciation exceeded book depreciation by $400,000. In addition, the company received $300,000 of tax-exempt municipal bond interest. The company's prior-year tax return showed taxable income of $50,000. Assuming a tax rate of 34 percent, compute the company's deferred income tax expense or benefit. `LO 17-2`

LO 17-2 54. Identify the following items as creating a temporary book–tax difference, permanent book–tax difference, or no book–tax difference.

Item	Temporary Difference	Permanent Difference	No Difference
Reserve for warranties			
Accrued pension liability			
Goodwill not amortized for tax purposes but subject to impairment under ASC 350			
Meal and entertainment expenses			
Life insurance proceeds			
Net capital loss carryover			
Nondeductible fines and penalties			
Accrued vacation pay liability paid within the first two and one-half months of the next tax year			

LO 17-2 55. Which of the following items is *not* a permanent book–tax difference?
   a) Tax-exempt interest income.
   b) Tax-exempt insurance proceeds.
   c) Domestic production activities deduction.
   d) Nondeductible meals and entertainment expense.
   e) First-year expensing under §179.

LO 17-2 56. Ann Corporation reported pretax book income of $1,000,000. Included in the computation were favorable temporary differences of $200,000, unfavorable temporary differences of $50,000, and favorable permanent differences of $100,000. Compute the company's book equivalent of taxable income. Use this number to compute the company's total income tax provision or benefit, assuming a tax rate of 34 percent.

LO 17-2 57. Burcham Corporation reported pretax book income of $600,000. Tax depreciation exceeded book depreciation by $400,000. In addition, the company received $300,000 of tax-exempt municipal bond interest. The company's prior-year tax return showed taxable income of $50,000. Compute the company's book equivalent of taxable income. Use this number to compute the company's total income tax provision or benefit, assuming a tax rate of 34 percent.

LO 17-3 58. Adams Corporation has total deferred tax assets of $3,000,000 at year-end. Management is assessing whether a valuation allowance must be recorded against some or all of the deferred tax assets. What level of assurance must management have, based on the weight of available evidence, that some or all of the deferred tax assets will not be realized before a valuation allowance is required?
   a) Probable.
   b) More likely than not.
   c) Realistic possibility.
   d) Reasonable.
   e) More than remote.

LO 17-3 59. Which of the following evidence would *not* be considered positive in determining whether Adams Corporation needs to record a valuation allowance for some or all of its deferred tax assets?
   a) The company forecasts future taxable income because of its backlog of orders.
   b) The company has unfavorable temporary differences that will create future taxable income when they reverse.
   c) The company has tax-planning strategies that it can implement to create future taxable income.

d) The company has cumulative net income over the current and prior two years.

e) The company had a net operating loss carryover expire in the current year.

60. As of the beginning of the year, Gratiot Company recorded a valuation allowance of $200,000 against its deferred tax assets of $1,000,000. The valuation allowance relates to a net operating loss carryover from the prior year. During the year, management concludes that the valuation allowance is no longer necessary because it forecasts sufficient taxable income to absorb the NOL carryover. What is the impact of management's reversal of the valuation allowance on the company's effective tax rate?   `LO 17-3`

   a) Increases the effective tax rate.

   b) Decreases the effective tax rate.

   c) No impact on the effective tax rate.

61. Which of the following evidence would be considered negative in determining whether Gratiot Corporation needs to record a valuation allowance for some or all of its deferred tax assets?   `LO 17-3`

   a) The company forecasts future taxable income because of its backlog of orders.

   b) The company has a cumulative net loss over the current and prior two years.

   c) The company has unfavorable temporary differences that will create future taxable income when they reverse.

   d) The company had a net operating loss carryover expire in the current year.

   e) Both (b) and (d) constitute negative evidence in assessing the need for a valuation allowance.

62. Saginaw Inc. completed its first year of operations with a pretax loss of $500,000. The tax return showed a net operating loss of $600,000, which the company will carry forward. The $100,000 book–tax difference results from excess tax depreciation over book depreciation. Management has determined that they should record a valuation allowance equal to the net deferred tax asset. Assuming the current tax expense is zero, prepare the journal entries to record the deferred tax provision and the valuation allowance.   `LO 17-3`

63. Access Ford Motor Company's Annual Report for 2011 from the company's Web site. What amount of valuation allowance against its deferred tax assets did the company release in 2011? What reasons did management give for releasing the valuation allowance? (*Hint:* Read Management's Discussion and Analysis section and the Income Taxes footnote.) What impact, if any, did release of the valuation allowance have on the company's effective tax rate for 2011? Why did the valuation allowance release affect (or not affect) the company's ETR?   `LO 17-3`   **research**

64. Montcalm Corporation has total deferred tax assets of $3,000,000 at year-end. Of that amount, $1,000,000 results from the current expensing of an expenditure that the IRS might assert must be capitalized on audit. Management is trying to determine if it should not recognize the deferred tax asset related to this item under ASC 740. What confidence level must management have that the item will be sustained on audit before it can recognize any portion of the deferred tax asset under ASC 740?   `LO 17-4`

   a) Probable.

   b) More likely than not.

   c) Realistic possibility.

   d) Reasonable.

   e) More than remote.

LO 17-4 65. Which of the following statements about uncertain tax positions (UTP) is correct?

   a) UTP applies only to tax positions accounted for under ASC 740 taken on a filed tax return.

   b) UTP applies to all tax positions accounted for under ASC 740, regardless of whether the item is taken on a filed tax return.

   c) UTP deals with both the recognition and realization of deferred tax assets.

   d) If a tax position meets the more-likely-than-not standard, the entire amount of the deferred tax asset or current tax benefit related to the tax position can be recognized under ASC 740.

   e) Statements (b), (c), and (d) are correct.

LO 17-4 66. Cadillac Square Corporation determined that $1,000,000 of its domestic production activities deduction (DPAD) on its current year tax return was uncertain, but that it was more likely than not to be sustained on audit. Management made the following assessment of the company's potential tax benefit from the deduction and its probability of occurring.

Potential Estimated Benefit (000s)	Individual Probability of Occurring (%)	Cumulative Probability of Occurring (%)
$340,000	40	40
272,000	25	65
170,000	20	85
0	15	100

What amount of the tax benefit related to the uncertain tax position from the domestic production activities deduction can Cadillac Square Corporation recognize in calculating its income tax provision in the current year?

LO 17-4 67. How would your answer to problem 66 change if management determined that there was only a 50/50 chance any portion of the $1,000,000 DPAD would be sustained on audit?

LO 17-4 68. As part of its UTP assessment, Penobscot Company records interest and penalties related to its unrecognized tax benefit of $500,000. Which of the following statements about recording this amount is most correct?

   a) Penobscot must include the amount in its income tax provision.

   b) Penobscot must record the amount separate from its income tax provision.

   c) Penobscot can elect to allocate a portion of the amount to both its income tax provision and its general and administrative expenses provided the company discloses which option it chose.

   d) Penobscot can elect to record the entire amount as part of its income tax provision or separate from its income tax provision, provided the company discloses which option it chose.

   e) Statements (c) and (d) above are both correct.

LO 17-5 69. What was IBM's accounting effective tax rate for 2014? What items caused the company's accounting effective tax rate to differ from the "hypothetical" tax rate of 35 percent? What was the company's cash effective tax rate for 2014? What factors cause a company's cash tax rate to differ from its accounting effective tax rate? You can access IBM's annual report for 2014 at http://www.ibm.com/investor/financials/financial-reporting.html.

research

LO 17-5 70. Beacon Corporation recorded the following deferred tax assets and liabilities:

Current deferred tax assets	$ 650,000
Current deferred tax liabilities	(400,000)
Noncurrent deferred tax assets	1,000,000
Noncurrent deferred tax liabilities	(2,500,000)
Net deferred tax liabilities	$(1,250,000)

All of the deferred tax accounts relate to temporary differences that arose as a result of the company's U.S. operations. Which of the following statements describes how Beacon should disclose these accounts on its balance sheet? Assume Beacon has not adopted ASU 2015–17.

a) Beacon reports a net deferred tax liability of $1,250,000 on its balance sheet.

b) Beacon nets the deferred tax assets and the deferred tax liabilities and reports a net deferred tax asset of $1,650,000 and a net deferred tax liability of $2,900,000 on its balance sheet.

c) Beacon can elect to net the current deferred tax accounts and the noncurrent tax accounts and report a net current deferred tax asset of $250,000 and a net deferred tax liability of $1,500,000 on its balance sheet.

d) Beacon is required to net the current deferred tax accounts and the noncurrent deferred tax accounts and report a net current deferred tax asset of $250,000 and a net deferred tax liability of $1,500,000 on its balance sheet.

71. ASC 740 requires a company to disclose those components of its deferred tax assets and liabilities that are considered `LO 17-5`
    a) Relevant.
    b) Significant.
    c) Important.
    d) Major.

72. Which of the following temporary differences creates a current deferred tax asset? `LO 17-5`
    a) Allowance for bad debts.
    b) Goodwill amortization.
    c) Accumulated depreciation.
    d) Inventory capitalization under §263A.
    e) Both (a) and (d) above create a current deferred tax asset.

73. Which formula represents the calculation of a company's effective tax rate? `LO 17-5`
    a) Income taxes paid/Taxable income.
    b) Income taxes paid/Pretax income from continuing operations.
    c) Income tax provision/Taxable income.
    d) Income tax provision/Pretax income from continuing operations.

74. Which of the following items is *not* a reconciling item in the income tax footnote? `LO 17-5`
    a) State income taxes.
    b) Foreign income taxes.
    c) Accrued pension liabilities.
    d) Dividends received deduction.
    e) Tax-exempt municipal bond interest.

75. Randolph Company reported pretax net income from continuing operations of $800,000 and taxable income of $500,000. The book–tax difference of $300,000 was due to a $200,000 favorable temporary difference relating to depreciation, an unfavorable temporary difference of $80,000 due to an increase in the reserve for bad debts, and a $180,000 favorable permanent difference from the receipt of life insurance proceeds. Randolph Company's applicable tax rate is 34 percent. `LO 17-5`
    a) Compute Randolph Company's current income tax expense.
    b) Compute Randolph Company's deferred income tax expense or benefit.

c) Compute Randolph Company's effective tax rate.

d) Provide a reconciliation of Randolph Company's effective tax rate with its hypothetical tax rate of 34 percent.

LO 17-5 76. Which of the following pronouncements should a company consult in computing its quarterly income tax provision?

a) ASC 740.

b) ASC 230.

c) ASC 718.

d) ASC 810.

e) SarbOX 404.

COMPREHENSIVE PROBLEMS

All applicable problems are available with *Connect*®.   connect

77. You have been assigned to compute the income tax provision for Motown Memories Inc. (MM) as of December 31, 2016. The company's federal income tax rate is 34 percent. The company's income statement for 2016 is provided below:

Motown Memories Inc. Statement of Operations at December 31, 2016	
Net sales	$50,000,000
Cost of sales	28,000,000
Gross profit	$22,000,000
Compensation	$ 2,000,000
Selling expenses	1,500,000
Depreciation and amortization	4,000,000
Other expenses	500,000
Total operating expenses	$ 8,000,000
Income from operations	$14,000,000
Interest and other income	1,000,000
Income before income taxes	$15,000,000

You identified the following permanent differences:

Interest income from municipal bonds	$ 50,000
Nondeductible meals and entertainment expenses	20,000
Domestic production activities deduction:	250,000
Nondeductible fines	5,000

MM prepared the following schedule of temporary differences from the beginning of the year to the end of the year:

Motown Memories Inc. Temporary Difference Scheduling Template					
Taxable Temporary Differences	BOY Cumulative T/D	Beginning Deferred Taxes (@ 34%)	Current Year Change	EOY Cumulative T/D	Ending Deferred Taxes (@ 35%)
Noncurrent					
Accumulated depreciation	(8,000,000)	(2,720,000)	(1,000,000)	(9,000,000)	(3,060,000)

Deductible Temporary Differences	BOY Cumulative T/D	Beginning Deferred Taxes (@ 34%)	Current Year Change	EOY Cumulative T/D	Ending Deferred Taxes (@ 34%)
Current					
Allowance for bad debts	200,000	68,000	50,000	250,000	85,000
Reserve for warranties	100,000	34,000	20,000	120,000	40,800
Inventory §263A adjustment	240,000	81,600	60,000	300,000	102,000
Total current	**540,000**	**183,600**	**130,000**	**670,000**	**227,800**
Noncurrent					
Deferred compensation	50,000	17,000	10,000	60,000	20,400
Accrued pension liabilities	3,000,000	1,020,000	250,000	3,250,000	1,105,000
Total noncurrent	**3,050,000**	**1,037,000**	**260,000**	**3,310,000**	**1,125,400**
Total	**3,590,000**	**1,220,600**	**390,000**	**3,980,000**	**1,353,200**

Required:

a) Compute MM's current income tax expense or benefit for 2016.

b) Compute MM's deferred income tax expense or benefit for 2016.

c) Prepare a reconciliation of MM's total income tax provision with its hypothetical income tax expense in both dollars and rates.

78. You have been assigned to compute the income tax provision for Tulip City Flowers Inc. (TCF) as of December 31, 2016. The company's federal income tax rate is 34 percent. The company's income statement for 2016 is provided below:

Tulip City Flowers Inc. Statement of Operations at December 31, 2016	
Net sales	$20,000,000
Cost of sales	12,000,000
Gross profit	$ 8,000,000
Compensation	$ 500,000
Selling expenses	750,000
Depreciation and amortization	1,250,000
Other expenses	1,000,000
Total operating expenses	$ 3,500,000
Income from operations	$ 4,500,000
Interest and other income	25,000
Income before income taxes	$ 4,525,000

You identified the following permanent differences:

Interest income from municipal bonds	$10,000
Nondeductible stock compensation	5,000
Domestic production activities deduction (DPAD)	8,000
Nondeductible fines	1,000

TCF prepared the following schedule of temporary differences from the beginning of the year to the end of the year:

Tulip City Flowers Inc. Temporary Difference Scheduling Template					
Taxable Temporary Differences	**BOY Cumulative T/D**	**Beginning Deferred Taxes (@ 34%)**	**Current Year Change**	**EOY Cumulative T/D**	**Ending Deferred Taxes (@ 34%)**
Noncurrent					
Accumulated depreciation	(5,000,000)	(1,700,000)	(500,000)	(5,500,000)	(1,870,000)

Deductible Temporary Differences	**BOY Cumulative T/D**	**Beginning Deferred Taxes (@ 34%)**	**Current Year Change**	**EOY Cumulative T/D**	**Ending Deferred Taxes (@ 34%)**
Current					
Allowance for bad debts	100,000	34,000	10,000	110,000	37,400
Prepaid income	0	0	20,000	20,000	6,800
Total current	**100,000**	**34,000**	**30,000**	**130,000**	**44,200**
Noncurrent					
Deferred compensation	50,000	17,000	10,000	60,000	20,400
Accrued pension liabilities	500,000	170,000	100,000	600,000	204,000
Total noncurrent	**550,000**	**187,000**	**110,000**	**660,000**	**224,400**
Total	**650,000**	**221,000**	**140,000**	**790,000**	**268,600**

Required:

a) Compute TCF's current income tax expense or benefit for 2016.

b) Compute TCF's deferred income tax expense or benefit for 2016.

c) Prepare a reconciliation of TCF's total income tax provision with its hypothetical income tax expense in both dollars and rates.

d) Assume TCF's tax rate increased to 35 percent in 2016. Recompute TCF's deferred income tax expense or benefit for 2016 using the following template:

Tulip City Flowers Inc. Temporary Difference Scheduling Template					
Taxable Temporary Differences	**BOY Cumulative T/D**	**Beginning Deferred Taxes (@ 34%)**	**Current Year Change**	**EOY Cumulative T/D**	**Ending Deferred Taxes (@ 35%)**
Noncurrent					
Accumulated depreciation	(5,000,000)	(1,700,000)	(500,000)	(5,500,000)	

Deductible Temporary Differences	BOY Cumulative T/D	Beginning Deferred Taxes (@ 34%)	Current Year Change	EOY Cumulative T/D	Ending Deferred Taxes (@ 35%)
Current					
Allowance for bad debts	100,000	34,000	10,000	110,000	
Prepaid income	0	0	20,000	20,000	
Total current	**100,000**	**34,000**	**30,000**	**130,000**	
Noncurrent					
Deferred compensation	50,000	17,000	10,000	60,000	
Accrued pension liabilities	500,000	170,000	100,000	600,000	
Total noncurrent	**550,000**	**187,000**	**110,000**	**660,000**	
Total	**650,000**	**221,000**	**140,000**	**790,000**	

79. Access the 2014 Annual Report for Google and answer the following questions. **research**

Required:

   a) Using information from the company's Income Statement and Income Taxes footnote, what was the company's effective tax rate for 2014? Show how the rate is calculated.

   b) Using information from the Statement of Cash Flows, calculate the company's cash tax rate.

   c) What does the company's Income Taxes note tell you about where the company earns its international income? Why does earning income in these countries cause the effective tax rate to decrease?

   d) What item creates the company's largest deferred tax asset? Explain why this item creates a deductible temporary difference.

   e) What item creates the company's largest deferred tax liability? Explain why this item creates a taxable temporary difference.

   f) How does the company classify its income taxes payable related to its unrecognized tax benefits on the balance sheet?

   g) How does the company treat interest and penalties related to its unrecognized tax benefits?

80. Spartan Builders Corporation is a builder of high-end housing with locations in major metropolitan areas throughout the Midwest. At June 30, 2016, the company has deferred tax assets totaling $10 million and deferred tax liabilities of $5 million, all of which relate to U.S. temporary differences. Reversing taxable temporary differences and taxable income in the carryback period can be used to support approximately $2 million of the $10 million gross deferred tax asset. The remaining $8 million of gross deferred tax assets will have to come from future taxable income.

   The company has historically been profitable. However, significant losses were incurred in fiscal years 2014 and 2015. These two years reflect a cumulative loss of $10 million, with losses of $3 million expected in 2016. $7 million of the losses was due to a write-down of inventory. Beginning in fiscal 2017, management decided to get out of the metropolitan Chicago market, which had become oversaturated with new houses.

   Evaluate the company's need to record a valuation allowance for the $10 million of gross deferred tax assets. What positive and negative evidence would you weigh?

chapter

18 Corporate Taxation: Nonliquidating Distributions

© Jupiterimages Corporation

Storyline Summary

Taxpayer:	Jim Wheeler
Location:	East Lansing, Michigan
Employment status:	Co-owner of Spartan Cycle and Repair (75 percent)
Filing status:	Married filing jointly
Dependents:	One child
Marginal tax rate:	30 percent
Taxpayer:	Ginny Gears
Location:	East Lansing, Michigan
Employment status:	Co-owner of Spartan Cycles and Repair (25 percent)
Filing status:	Unmarried
Marginal tax rate:	25 percent

Jim Wheeler and Ginny Gears are old friends who met at the Mid-Michigan Cycling Club. They often discussed their shared dream of owning and operating a high-end bicycle shop in East Lansing, Michigan. Many of their friends in the club often remarked how difficult it was to get parts and have their bicycles repaired locally. Jim found himself repairing his friends' bicycles using the knowledge he gained while working at a bicycle shop during his undergraduate days at the University of Colorado. Ginny majored in marketing at Michigan State University (MSU) and was eager to put her marketing and management skills to work in her own business.

A few years ago, Jim and Ginny fulfilled their dream by launching Spartan Cycles and Repair (SCR). Their business had humble beginnings, as most start-up companies do. They raised the $50,000 capital they needed to purchase inventory and the necessary repair tools by borrowing from Jim's father, Walt. They also leased a vacant building on Grand River Avenue. On the advice of their accountant and lawyer, Jim and Ginny organized their company as a C corporation, with Jim owning 75 percent of the corporation's stock and Ginny owning the remaining 25 percent. Jim's responsibilities include doing the bicycle repairs and deciding which bicycle brands to carry, while Ginny is responsible for managing and marketing the business. Jim works approximately 10 hours per week at the store, and he currently receives a modest salary of $15,000 per year. Ginny works half-time at the store and currently receives a salary of $25,000 per year.

Since the company's inception, Jim and Ginny used most of the company's profits to pay back the loan to Jim's father and expand the store's inventory and marketing activities. By the end of this year, SCR had become very successful, as evidenced by the significant amount of cash ($300,000) in the company's bank accounts. Jim and Ginny made many sacrifices, both financially and socially, to make the business successful. Over a café latte at the local gourmet coffee shop, Jim and Ginny decided it was time to think about distributing some of the company's profits to reward their hard work. Jim admitted he had his eye on a dark green BMW 528i Sedan, which retailed for approximately $48,000, fully loaded. Ginny was a bit more restrained, hoping she could put a down payment on a condominium in the newly developed Evergreen Commons being constructed near their store. She estimated she would need approximately $16,000 for the down payment.

Jim and Ginny considered several options for distributing cash from SCR. One alternative was to increase their salaries. Another option was to pay a year-end bonus, while a third alternative was for SCR to pay a $64,000 dividend at year-end ($48,000 to Jim and $16,000 to Ginny). They decided to call their tax accountant, Louis Tully, to ask for his recommendation.

to be continued . . .

At some point during the life of a company, especially in the case of a closely held business, the shareholders will likely want to distribute some of the company's accumulated profits. If the business is operated as a C corporation, the company can distribute its *after-tax* profits to its shareholders in the form of a **dividend, stock redemption,** or, in rare cases, a **partial liquidation.** Alternatively, if a shareholder also serves in some other capacity in the business (e.g., as an employee, creditor, or lessor), the company may be able to distribute its *before-tax* profits to this person in the form of compensation (salary or bonus), interest, or rent.

This chapter addresses the tax consequences to the corporation and its shareholders when making distributions to its shareholders in these various ways. Because Jim and Ginny have chosen to operate through a C corporation, they must confront the potential of double taxation if the company's earnings are distributed as a dividend. If Jim and Ginny elected to operate their business through an S corporation or partnership, the entity-level taxation of the company's earnings would be eliminated. The tax consequences of these two flow-through entity choices are discussed in more detail in subsequent chapters.

LO 18-1 TAXATION OF PROPERTY DISTRIBUTIONS

The characterization of a distribution from a corporation to a shareholder has important tax consequences to both the shareholders and the corporation. If the tax law characterizes the distribution as a dividend, the corporation may not deduct the amount paid in computing its taxable income. In addition, the shareholder must include the gross amount of the dividend received in gross income. The nondeductibility of the distribution by the corporation, coupled with the taxation of the distribution to the shareholder, creates *double taxation* of the corporation's income, first at the corporate level and then at the shareholder level. The double taxation of distributed corporate income has been a fundamental principle of the U.S. income tax since 1913.

Historically, tax planning focused on eliminating or mitigating the second level of taxation on C corporation earnings.[1] For example, if the distribution can instead be characterized as salary, bonus, interest, or rent, the corporation can deduct the amount paid in computing its taxable income. However, the Internal Revenue Service (IRS) can assert that the distribution is a **constructive dividend.** In such a case, the corporation cannot deduct the amount recharacterized as a dividend.

DETERMINING THE DIVIDEND AMOUNT FROM EARNINGS AND PROFITS

`LO 18-2`

Overview

When a corporation distributes property to shareholders *in their capacity as shareholders,* the shareholders will characterize the distribution either as dividend income or a return of capital. They include the portion characterized as dividend income in their gross income. In contrast, a return of capital is not considered income, but rather a reduction in the shareholder's tax basis in the stock. If the return of capital exceeds the tax basis of the stock, then the excess distribution (above basis) is taxed as a capital gain from the sale of the shares.[2]

Corporate distributions of "property" usually take the form of cash, but distributions can also consist of other tangible or intangible property. Special rules apply when a corporation distributes its own stock **(stock dividends)** to its shareholders.[3]

Dividends Defined

A dividend is any distribution of property made by a corporation to its shareholders out of its earnings and profits (E&P) account. Congress intended earnings and profits to be a measure of the corporation's *economic earnings* available for distribution to its shareholders. Hence, earnings and profits is similar in concept to financial accounting retained earnings, but the computation of E&P can be very different.

Corporations keep two separate E&P accounts: one for the current year **(current earnings and profits)** and one for undistributed earnings and profits accumulated in all prior years **(accumulated earnings and profits).** Distributions are designated as dividends in the following order:

1. Distributions are dividends up to the balance of current E&P.
2. Distributions in excess of current E&P are dividends up to the balance in accumulated E&P.

Current E&P not distributed to shareholders is added to accumulated E&P at the beginning of the next taxable year. Distributions reduce E&P but cannot produce (or extend) a deficit (negative balance) in E&P. That is, dividend treatment requires positive E&P, but E&P can have a deficit balance if losses exceed income. In other words, a corporation cannot distribute E&P if there is a deficit in E&P, and only losses can create a deficit in E&P. A corporation that makes a distribution in excess of its total E&P (i.e., a return of capital) must report the distribution on Form 5452 and include a calculation of its E&P balance to support the tax treatment.

---

[1]Taxable corporations are referred to as *C corporations* because Subchapter C (§§301–385) describes the tax consequences of distributions between a corporation and its shareholders.
[2]§301(c).
[3]§317.

Example 18-1

Jim owns 75 percent of the SCR stock, while Ginny owns the remaining 25 percent. Jim has a tax basis in his Spartan Cycles and Repair (SCR) stock of $24,000. Ginny's tax basis in her SCR stock is $10,000.

What if: Assume SCR has current earnings and profits (CE&P) of $30,000, and no accumulated earnings and profits. At year-end, SCR makes a $64,000 distribution, a $48,000 distribution to Jim and a $16,000 distribution to Ginny.

What is the tax treatment of the distribution to Jim and Ginny?

Answer: Only $30,000 of the $64,000 distribution is treated as a dividend. The distribution in excess of E&P is treated as a return of capital.

Jim treats the $48,000 distribution for tax purposes as follows:
- $22,500 is treated as a dividend (to the extent of his 75 percent share of current E&P).
- $24,000 is a nontaxable reduction in his stock tax basis (return of capital).
- $1,500 is treated as gain from the deemed sale of his stock (capital gain).

Note that a distribution cannot reduce a shareholder's stock basis below zero.

Ginny treats the $16,000 distribution for tax purposes as follows:
- $7,500 is treated as a dividend (to the extent of her 25 percent share of current E&P).
- $8,500 is a nontaxable reduction in her stock tax basis (return of capital).

What is Jim and Ginny's tax basis in their SCR stock after the distribution?

Answer: Jim has a zero basis in his SCR stock, while Ginny has a remaining tax basis of $1,500 ($10,000 − $8,500) in her SCR stock.

Computing Earnings and Profits

Earnings and profits has been part of the tax laws since 1916, but Congress has never provided a precise definition of this term. Hence, the calculation of E&P is somewhat counterintuitive. For example, E&P includes both taxable and nontaxable income indicating that Congress intended E&P to represent a corporation's economic income. As a result, shareholders may be taxed on distributions of income that is not taxable income to the corporation.

A corporation begins the computation of current E&P with taxable income or loss. It then makes adjustments required by the IRC or the accompanying regulations and IRS rulings. These adjustments fall into four broad categories:

1. Certain nontaxable income is included in E&P.
2. Certain deductions do not reduce E&P.
3. Certain nondeductible expenses reduce E&P.
4. The timing of certain items of income and deduction is modified for E&P calculations because separate accounting methods are required for E&P purposes.[4]

Nontaxable Income Included in E&P   Tax exempt income has economic value when distributed to shareholders and, thus, increases E&P. Common examples of tax-exempt income included in E&P are tax-exempt municipal interest and tax-exempt life insurance proceeds. Other types of exempt income, such as gifts, bequests, and contributions to capital, are not included in E&P.

Example 18-2

SCR reported current earnings and profits of $100,000 related to taxable income. The company also earned $5,000 of tax-exempt interest from its investment in City of East Lansing municipal bonds. If SCR distributes all of its current year E&P to Jim and Ginny, what amount will they report as dividend income in the current year?

[4]§312 and the related regulations describe these adjustments.

Answer: $105,000. SCR must include the $5,000 of tax-exempt interest in the computation of current E&P. The portion of the E&P that represents the tax-exempt interest will be treated as a taxable dividend even though Jim and Ginny would not have included the interest in gross income had they earned it directly.

What if: Assume Jim and Ginny operated SCR as a partnership. How would that have changed your answer to the previous example?

Answer: Jim and Ginny would have reported their share of the tax-exempt interest on their individual tax returns as being tax-exempt and would not have been taxed on the amount.

Deductible Expenses That Do Not Reduce E&P   Deductions that require no cash outlay by the corporation or are carryovers from another tax year do not represent current economic outflows and cannot be used to reduce E&P. Examples include the dividends received deduction, the domestic production activities deduction, net capital loss carryovers from a different tax year, net operating loss carryovers from a different tax year, and charitable contribution carryovers from a prior tax year. Note, however, that the deduction allowed for employee exercises of nonqualified stock options reduces E&P even though no cash flow is required.

Nondeductible Expenses That Reduce E&P   A corporation reduces its current E&P for certain items that are not deductible in computing its taxable income but require a cash outflow. Examples of such expenses include:

- Federal income taxes (regular or alternative minimum tax) paid or accrued (depending on the corporation's method of accounting).
- Expenses incurred in earning tax-exempt income (such income is included in E&P).
- Current year charitable contributions in excess of 10 percent of taxable income (there is no 10 percent limitation for E&P purposes).
- Premiums on life insurance contracts in excess of the increase in the policy's cash surrender value.
- Current year net capital loss (there is no limit on capital losses).
- Meals and entertainment expenses disallowed (generally 50 percent of the total).
- Nondeductible lobbying expenses and political contributions.
- Penalties and fines.

Timing Items Requiring Separate Accounting Methods for E&P Purposes
A corporation must generally use the same accounting method for computing E&P and taxable income. For example, a gain or loss deferred for tax purposes under the like-kind exchange rules (§1031) or the involuntary conversion rules is also deferred for E&P purposes. A corporation using the accrual method for regular income tax purposes generally must use the accrual method for E&P purposes. However, some types of income deferred from inclusion in the computation of current year taxable income must be included in the computation of current E&P in the year in which the transaction occurs. For example, if a corporation uses the installment sales method for tax purposes, the deferred gain from current year sales must be included in current E&P.

In addition, certain expenses currently deducted in the computation of taxable income are deferred in computing E&P.[5] Organizational expenditures, which can be

---

[5]§312(n). Section 312(n) was added in 1984 to "ensure that a corporation's earnings and profits more closely conform to its economic income."

deducted currently or amortized for income tax purposes, must be capitalized for E&P purposes. Depreciation must be computed using the prescribed E&P method. For property acquired after 1986, the alternative depreciation system must be used. This system requires that assets be depreciated using a straight-line method over the asset's *"mid-point class life"* (40 years in the case of realty).[6] Amounts expensed under §179 (first year expensing) must be amortized over five years for E&P purposes.

The IRC does not impose a statute of limitations on the computation of earnings and profits. Hence, for many corporations (public and private), the initial computation of E&P only comes after years of operations and often requires significant resources because the annual adjustments to taxable income were not well documented. Exhibit 18-1 provides a summary of common adjustments made to compute current E&P.

EXHIBIT 18-1 Template for Computing Current Earnings and Profits

Taxable Income (Net Operating Loss)

Add: **Exclusions from Taxable Income**
- Tax-exempt bond interest.
- Life insurance proceeds.
- Federal tax refunds (if a cash-basis taxpayer).

Add: **Deductions Allowed for Tax Purposes but Not for E&P**
- Dividends received deduction.
- NOL deduction carrybacks and carryforwards.
- Net capital loss carrybacks and carryforwards.
- Contribution carryforwards.
- Domestic production activities deduction.

Add: **Income Deferred for Tax Purposes but Not for E&P**
- Deferred gain on installment sales.
- Deferred gain on completed contract method of accounting.
- Increase in cash surrender value of corporate-owned life insurance policies.

Add: **Deductions Deferred for E&P Purposes**
- Regular tax depreciation in excess of E&P depreciation.
- Percentage depletion in excess of cost depletion.
- Capitalized construction period interest, taxes, and carrying charges.
- Amortized intangible costs of oil and gas wells over 60 months.
- Amortized mineral exploration and development costs over 120 months.
- Capitalized circulation expenditures and organizational expenditures.
- Capitalized first-year expensing and amortize over five years.
- Increases in the LIFO recapture amount (FIFO over LIFO ending inventory).

Less: **Deductions Allowed for E&P Purposes but Not for Tax**
- Gain recognized this year on prior-year installment sales.
- Federal income taxes paid or accrued.
- Expenses of earning tax-exempt income.
- Current-year charitable contributions in excess of the 10 percent limitation.
- Nondeductible premiums on life insurance policies.
- Current-year net capital loss.
- E&P depreciation in excess of regular tax depreciation.
- Penalties and fines.
- Decreases in the LIFO recapture amount (LIFO over FIFO ending inventory).
- Disallowed entertainment expenses.
- Disallowed lobbying expenses, dues, and political contributions.

Equals: **Current Earnings and Profits**

[6]§168(g)(2).

Example 18-3

This year, SCR reported taxable income of $500,000 and paid federal income tax of $170,000. SCR reported the following items of income and expense:

- $50,000 of depreciation.
- $7,000 dividends received deduction.
- $10,000 net operating loss from the prior year.
- $5,000 of tax-exempt interest.
- $6,000 of nondeductible meals and entertainment expense.
- $4,000 net capital loss from the current year.

For E&P purposes, depreciation computed under the alternative depreciation method is $30,000.

What is SCR's current E&P?

Answer: $362,000, computed as follows:

Taxable income	$500,000
Add:	
Tax-exempt interest	5,000
Dividends received deduction	7,000
NOL carryover	10,000
Excess of regular tax deprecation over E&P depreciation	20,000
Subtract:	
Federal income taxes	(170,000)
Nondeductible meals and entertainment	(6,000)
Net capital loss for the current year	(4,000)
Current E&P	**$362,000**

What if: Assume SCR also reported a tax-deferred gain of $100,000 as the result of a §1031 exchange and deferred $75,000 of gain from an installment sale during the year. What is SCR's current E&P under these circumstances?

Answer: Current E&P would equal $437,000 ($362,000 + $75,000). Deferred gains from §1031 (like-kind) exchanges are not included in the computation of current E&P, but all gain from current-year installment sales is included in current E&P. In future years, SCR would back out any deferred gain recognized in taxable income from the installment sale in its computation of current E&P.

What if: Assume SCR did not report any gains from the sale of property and instead reported a $400,000 loss from a sale of property. What is SCR's current E&P under these circumstances?

Answer: Current E&P would be a deficit balance of $38,000 ($362,000 − $400,000). The balance of E&P can be negative, but E&P cannot be driven below zero by distributions.

Ordering of E&P Distributions

As we noted above, a corporation must maintain two separate E&P accounts: current E&P and accumulated E&P. Whether a distribution is characterized as a dividend depends on whether the balances in these accounts are positive or negative. There are four possible scenarios:

1. Positive current E&P, positive accumulated E&P.
2. Positive current E&P, negative accumulated E&P.
3. Negative current E&P, positive accumulated E&P.
4. Negative current E&P, negative accumulated E&P.

Positive Current E&P and Positive Accumulated E&P Corporate distributions are deemed to be paid out of current E&P first. If distributions exceed current E&P, the amount distributed out of current E&P is allocated pro rata to all of the distributions made during the year. Any distribution out of accumulated E&P is allocated to the recipients in the chronological order in which the distributions were made.[7] This ordering of distributions is necessary only when distributions exceed current E&P and either the identity of the shareholders receiving the distributions changes or a shareholder's percentage ownership changes during the year.

Example 18-4

What if: Assume SCR reported current E&P of $40,000, and the balance in accumulated E&P was $16,000. On December 31, SCR distributed $48,000 to Jim and $16,000 to Ginny. What amount of dividend income do Jim and Ginny report, and what is the balance of E&P for SCR at the beginning of next year?

Answer: $42,000 and $14,000 of dividend income to Jim and Ginny, respectively. The distribution is first deemed to be paid from current E&P to each shareholder in proportion to their ownership interests on the date of the distribution: $30,000 to Jim (equal to $40,000 × 75%) and $10,000 to Ginny (equal to $40,000 × 25%). The distribution in excess of current E&P ($64,000 − $40,000 equals $24,000) is then deemed to be paid from accumulated E&P ($16,000) in proportion to ownership interests ($12,000 to Jim and $4,000 to Ginny). The remaining distribution of $8,000 ($64,000 total minus $40,000 current E&P and $16,000 accumulated E&P) is a return of capital. Hence, Jim will reduce his stock basis by $6,000 and Ginny will reduce her stock basis by $2,000.

SCR has a zero balance in accumulated E&P at the beginning of the next year because all current and accumulated E&P was distributed during the year.

What if: Assume that SCR's current E&P is $40,000 and its accumulated E&P is $15,000. Also, assume that Jim was the sole shareholder of SCR and he received a $45,000 distribution on June 1. Assume that after the June distribution Jim sold all his SCR shares to Ginny who received a $15,000 dividend on December 31. What is the amount and the character of each distribution?

Answer: Jim has a $45,000 dividend. Ginny has a $10,000 dividend and a $5,000 return of capital. Of the $40,000 of current E&P, $30,000 is allocated to Jim's distribution and $10,000 is allocated to Ginny's distribution. Current E&P is allocated between the two distributions in proportion to the total distributions (the calculation for June 1 is $40,000 × [$45,000/$60,000]). However, because Jim's distribution took place before Ginny's distribution, the accumulated E&P is allocated to Jim's distribution ($15,000), leaving $0 in remaining accumulated E&P to be allocated to Ginny's distribution. Ginny is allocated only $10,000 of E&P, leaving her with an excess distribution of $5,000 ($15,000 − $10,000). This excess distribution is treated as a nontaxable reduction of her basis in the SCR stock. Current E&P is determined on the last day of the tax year before deduction for current year distributions.

Positive Current E&P and Negative Accumulated E&P Distributions deemed paid out of current E&P are taxable as dividends. Distributions in excess of current E&P in this scenario would first be treated as nontaxable reductions in the shareholders' tax basis in their stock. Any excess received over their stock basis would be treated as a (capital) gain from sale of the stock.

Example 18-5

What if: Assume SCR reported current E&P of $60,000. The balance in accumulated E&P at the beginning of the year was negative $20,000. On December 31, SCR distributed $48,000 to Jim and $16,000 to Ginny. Jim has a tax basis in his SCR stock of $24,000. Ginny's tax basis in her SCR stock is $10,000. What amount of income will Jim and Ginny report?

Answer: $45,000 and $15,000 of dividend income to Jim and Ginny, respectively. The distribution is first deemed to be paid from current E&P ($45,000 to Jim and $15,000 to Ginny). No additional amount is treated as a dividend because SCR has negative accumulated E&P.

---

[7]Reg. §1.316-2(b) and Rev. Rul. 74-164, 1974-1 C.B. 74.

What tax basis will Jim and Ginny have in their SCR stock after the distribution?

Answer: The amount in excess of current E&P ($3,000 to Jim, $1,000 to Ginny) would be treated as a nontaxable return of capital because Jim and Ginny have enough tax basis in their SCR stock to absorb the amount paid in excess of E&P. Jim's tax basis in his SCR stock after the distribution would be $21,000 ($24,000 − $3,000), and Ginny's tax basis in her SCR stock after the distribution would be $9,000 ($10,000 − $1,000).

What is SCR's remaining balance in accumulated E&P at the end of the year?

Answer: SCR has a $20,000 deficit (negative) balance in accumulated E&P.

Negative Current E&P and Positive Accumulated E&P

When current E&P is negative, the tax status of a dividend is determined by total E&P on the *date of the distribution*. This requires the corporation to prorate the negative current E&P to the distribution date and add it to accumulated E&P at the beginning of the year to determine total E&P at the distribution date. Distributions in excess of total E&P in this scenario are treated as reductions in the shareholders' tax basis in their stock. Any excess over their stock basis would be treated as a capital gain.

Example 18-6

What if: Assume SCR reported current E&P of negative $20,000. The balance in accumulated E&P at the beginning of the year was $60,000. On June 30, SCR distributed $48,000 to Jim and $16,000 to Ginny. Jim has a tax basis in his SCR stock of $24,000. Ginny's tax basis in her SCR stock is $10,000. What amount of dividend income do Jim and Ginny report?

Answer: $37,500 to Jim and $12,500 to Ginny. Because current E&P is negative, SCR must determine its total E&P on the distribution date. SCR prorates the full-year negative current E&P to June 30 [6 months/12 months × ($20,000) = ($10,000)]. The negative current E&P of $10,000 is added to the beginning balance in accumulated E&P of $60,000 to get total E&P as of July 1 of $50,000. Because their distributions were made at the same time, Jim is allocated 75 percent of the total E&P and Ginny is allocated the remaining 25 percent.

What tax basis do Jim and Ginny have in their SCR stock after the distribution?

Answer: $13,500 for Jim and $6,500 for Ginny. The amount in excess of total E&P ($10,500 to Jim, $3,500 to Ginny) is treated first as a nontaxable return of capital. Jim reduces the basis in his SCR stock to $13,500 ($24,000 − $10,500). Ginny reduces the basis in her SCR stock to $6,500 ($10,000 − $3,500).

What is SCR's remaining balance in accumulated E&P at the end of the year?

Answer: Negative $10,000, computed as follows:

Beginning balance	$ 60,000
Prorated negative current E&P, 1/1–6/30	(10,000)
Dividends	(50,000)
Prorated negative current E&P, 7/1–12/31	(10,000)
Ending balance (deficit)	$(10,000)

Negative Current E&P and Negative Accumulated E&P

When current E&P and accumulated E&P are both negative, none of the distribution is treated as a dividend. Distributions in this scenario would first be treated as reductions in the shareholders' tax basis in their stock. Any excess over their stock basis would be treated as a capital gain.

Example 18-7

What if: Assume SCR reported current E&P of negative $50,000. The balance in accumulated E&P at the beginning of the year was negative $60,000. Jim has a tax basis in his SCR stock of $24,000. Ginny's tax basis in her SCR stock is $10,000. On December 31 of this year, SCR distributed $48,000 to Jim and $16,000 to Ginny. What amount of dividend income do Jim and Ginny report this year?

Answer: $0 to Jim and $0 to Ginny. Because current E&P and accumulated E&P are negative, the entire distribution would be treated as either a return of capital or capital gain.

What is the tax basis in the SCR stock for Jim and Ginny?

Answer: The amount in excess of total E&P ($48,000 to Jim, $16,000 to Ginny) is treated first as a nontaxable return of capital. Jim reduces the basis in his SCR stock to $0 ($24,000 − $48,000, limited to $0). Ginny reduces the basis in her SCR stock to $0 ($10,000 − $16,000, limited to $0).

What amount of capital gain do Jim and Ginny report as a result of the distribution?

Answer: Jim has a capital gain of $24,000, the amount by which the distribution exceeds the tax basis in his SCR stock ($48,000 − $24,000). Ginny has a capital gain of $6,000, the amount by which the distribution exceeds the tax basis in her SCR stock ($16,000 − $10,000).

What is SCR's remaining balance in accumulated E&P at the end of the year?

Answer: A deficit (negative) balance of $110,000, the sum of accumulated E&P deficit of $60,000 plus current E&P deficit of $50,000.

Exhibit 18-2 summarizes the rules for determining whether a distribution represents dividend income. When both balances are negative, the distribution is treated as a return of capital (tax-free to the extent of the shareholder's tax basis in their stock and capital gain in excess of this amount), and the deficits in E&P are unaffected. When both balances are positive, the distribution is treated as a dividend to the extent of current E&P at year-end and then to the extent of the balance of accumulated E&P. A distribution in excess of current and accumulated E&P is treated as a return of capital. When current E&P is negative and accumulated E&P is positive, distributions are dividend income to the extent of accumulated E&P after netting against deficit in current E&P (up to the date of the distribution). The distribution reduces accumulated E&P but not below zero. Finally, when accumulated E&P is negative and current E&P is positive, distributions are dividend income to the extent of current E&P.

EXHIBIT 18-2   **Summary of E&P Status and Taxability of Cash Distributions**

Balance in Current E&P at the Time of the Distribution	Balance in Accumulated E&P at the Time of the Distribution	
	Negative	**Positive**
Negative	Distributions are a return of capital.	Distributions are dividend income to extent of accumulated E&P after netting against deficit in current E&P.
Positive	Distributions are dividend income to extent of current E&P.	Distributions are dividend income to extent of current E&P and the balance of accumulated E&P.

Distributions of Noncash Property to Shareholders

On occasion, a shareholder will receive property other than cash in the form of a dividend. When noncash property is received, the shareholder determines the amount distributed as follows:

> Money received
> + Fair market value of other property received
> − Liabilities assumed by the shareholder on property received
> Amount distributed[8]

Example 18-8

What if: Assume Ginny elected to receive $15,000 in cash and a Fuji custom touring bike that had a fair market value of $1,000. SCR has current E&P of $100,000 and no accumulated E&P. What amount of dividend income will Ginny report this year?

Answer: $16,000. Ginny would include the $15,000 plus the $1,000 fair market value of the bicycle in her gross income as a dividend.

As a general rule, a shareholder's tax basis in noncash property received as a dividend equals the property's fair market value.[9] No downward adjustment is made for liabilities assumed by the shareholder (these are considered part of the property's cost). The shareholder determines fair market value as of the date of the distribution.

Example 18-9

What is Ginny's tax basis in the bicycle she received as a dividend in the previous example?

Answer: $1,000. Ginny has a tax basis in the bicycle of $1,000, the bicycle's fair market value. Ginny would pay an income tax of $150 on receipt of the bicycle (assuming the dividend qualifies for the preferential 15 percent tax rate).

Example 18-10

What if: Assume that, instead of cash, Jim elected to receive a parcel of land SCR had previously purchased for possible expansion. The land has a fair market value of $60,000 and a remaining mortgage of $12,000 attached to it. SCR has a tax basis in the land of $20,000. Jim will assume the mortgage on the land. SCR has current E&P of $100,000 and no accumulated E&P. How much dividend income does Jim recognize on the distribution?

Answer: $48,000. Jim recognizes dividend income in an amount equal to the land's fair market value of $60,000 less the mortgage he assumes on the land in the amount of $12,000.

What is Jim's tax basis in the land he receives?

Answer: $60,000. Jim receives a tax basis equal to the land's fair market value. Jim has a $60,000 basis in the land because he recognized $48,000 of income and assumed $12,000 of debt.

---

[8]§301(b).
[9]§301(d).

Corporate Tax Consequences of Noncash Distributions   Gains (but not losses) are recognized by a corporation on the distribution of noncash property.[10] Specifically, to the extent the fair market value of property distributed exceeds the corporation's tax basis in the property, the corporation recognizes a taxable gain on the distribution. This gain increases current E&P because it increases taxable income. In contrast, if the fair market value of the property distributed is less than the corporation's tax basis in the property, the corporation does not recognize a deductible loss on the distribution. E&P is subsequently reduced by the distributed property's fair market value if the property is appreciated (gain is recognized) and by the property's E&P basis if the property is depreciated (loss is not recognized).

Example 18-11

What if: Assume SCR had a tax basis of $650 in the Fuji custom touring bike that it distributed to Ginny (see the facts in Example 18-8). How much gain, if any, does SCR recognize when it distributes the bicycle to Ginny as a dividend?

Answer: $350. SCR recognizes a taxable gain of $350 on the distribution of the bicycle to Ginny ($1,000 − $650). Because the bike is considered inventory, SCR would characterize the gain as ordinary income. Assuming a tax rate of 34 percent, SCR would pay a corporate level tax of $119 on the distribution (34% × $350). The total tax paid by SCR and Ginny would be $269 ($150 + $119). This is a high tax cost to pay to transfer the $1,000 bicycle to Ginny in the form of a dividend.

What if: Assume SCR had a tax basis of $1,200 in the Fuji custom touring bike that it distributed to Ginny. The bicycle's fair market value declined to $1,000 because it was an outdated model. How much loss, if any, does SCR recognize when it distributes the bicycle to Ginny as a dividend?

Answer: $0. SCR is not permitted to recognize a loss on the distribution of the bicycle to Ginny.

What if: Suppose SCR *sold* the bicycle to Ginny for $1,000. How much loss, if any, could SCR recognize if it sold the bicycle to Ginny?

Answer: $200. SCR is permitted to recognize a loss on the sale of property to a shareholder provided it does not run afoul of the related-person loss rules found in §267. To be a related person, Ginny must own *more than* 50 percent of SCR, which she does not in this scenario.

Liabilities   If the property's fair market value is less than the amount of the liability assumed, the property's fair market value is deemed to be the amount of the liability assumed by the shareholder.[11] If the liability assumed is less than the property's fair market value, the gain recognized on the distribution is the excess of the property's fair market value over its tax basis (i.e., the liability is ignored).

Example 18-12

What if: Assume Jim received a parcel of land the company had previously purchased for possible expansion. The land has a fair market value of $60,000 and a remaining mortgage of $12,000 attached to it. SCR has a tax basis in the land of $20,000. Jim will assume the mortgage on the land. SCR has current E&P of $100,000 and no accumulated E&P. How much gain, if any, does SCR recognize when it distributes the land to Jim as a dividend?

Answer: $40,000 ($60,000 − $20,000). Because the mortgage assumed by Jim is less than the land's fair market value, SCR recognizes gain in an amount equal to the excess of the land's fair market value of $60,000 over its tax basis of $20,000.

---

[10]§311. Congress made distributions of appreciated property taxable to the distributing corporation in 1986 to prevent corporations from avoiding the double taxation of corporate income by distributing appreciated property to shareholders in the form of a dividend.

[11]§311(b)(2) refers to §336(b).

Effect of Noncash Property Distributions on E&P

Gain recognized by a corporation on a distribution of appreciated property increases current E&P because it increases taxable income. In contrast, if the fair market value of the property distributed is less than the corporation's tax basis in the property, the corporation does not recognize a deductible loss on the distribution. E&P is subsequently reduced by the distributed property's fair market value if the property is appreciated (gain is recognized) and by the property's E&P basis if the property is depreciated (loss is not recognized).[12]

When appreciated property is distributed by the corporation, the corporation recognizes gain to the extent the property's fair market value exceeds the corporation's E&P tax basis in the property. The corporation then reduces E&P by the property's fair market value and adds back any mortgage or other liability assumed by the shareholders in the distribution.

Exhibit 18-3 provides a template for computing the effect of distributions on current E&P.

EXHIBIT 18-3   **Template to Compute the Effect of Distributions on E&P**

	Current E&P (computed before any distributions but including gain recognized on distribution of appreciated property)
−	Money distributed
−	E&P adjusted basis of unappreciated property distributed
−	Fair market value of appreciated property distributed
+	Liabilities assumed by the shareholders
−	Tax on gain recognized
	Undistributed current E&P (added to accumulated E&P from prior years)

In the case where a property's fair market value or E&P basis exceeds current E&P, the excess amount reduces any accumulated E&P at the beginning of the year. Note, however, that a distribution of property can only reduce E&P to the extent E&P is positive. Recall that a distribution cannot create negative E&P or increase already existing negative E&P that results from operations.

Example 18-13

What if: Assume the same facts as in Example 18-12. SCR distributed land to Jim that has a fair market value of $60,000 and a remaining mortgage of $12,000 attached to it. SCR has a tax and E&P basis in the land of $20,000. Jim assumed the mortgage on the land. SCR has current E&P of $100,000, which includes the net gain of $26,400 from distribution of the land ($40,000 gain less a related tax liability of $13,600 assuming a tax rate of 34 percent), and accumulated E&P at the beginning of the year of $500,000. What is SCR's beginning balance in accumulated E&P at January 1 of next year, as a result of the distribution of the land to Jim?

(continued on page 18-14)

THE KEY FACTS

Adjustments to Taxable Income (Loss) to Compute Current E&P

- A corporation makes the following adjustments to taxable income to compute current E&P:
  - Include certain income that is excluded from taxable income.
  - Disallow certain expenses that are deducted in computing taxable income.
  - Deduct certain expenses that are excluded from the computation of taxable income.
  - Defer deductions or accelerate income due to separate accounting methods required for E&P purposes.
- The amount distributed as a dividend equals:
  - Cash received.
  - Fair market value of noncash property received.
  - Reduced by any liabilities assumed by the shareholder on property received.
- E&P is reduced by distributions treated as dividends as follows:
  - Cash distributed.
  - E&P basis of noncash property with a fair market value less than or equal to its E&P basis.
  - Fair market value of noncash appreciated property reduced by any liabilities assumed by the shareholder on property received.

[12]§312.

Answer: $552,000, computed as follows:

Accumulated E&P, this year	$500,000
Current E&P	100,000
Fair market value of land distributed	(60,000)
Liability assumed by Jim	12,000
Beginning balance, AE&P, next year	$552,000

What if: Assume SCR has current E&P of $40,000, which includes the net gain of $26,400 from distribution of the land ($40,000 gain less a related tax liability of $13,600 assuming a tax rate of 34 percent), and accumulated E&P of $500,000. What is SCR's beginning balance in accumulated E&P at January 1 of next year, as a result of the distribution of the land to Jim?

Answer: $492,000, computed as follows:

Accumulated E&P, this year	$500,000
Current E&P	40,000
Fair market value of land distributed	(60,000)
Liability assumed by Jim	12,000
Beginning balance, AE&P, next year	$492,000

What if: Assume the land distributed to Jim had a tax and E&P basis to SCR of $75,000 instead of $20,000. SCR has current E&P of $100,000, which does not include the disallowed loss of $15,000 on the distribution ($60,000 fair market value less $75,000 tax basis). SCR has accumulated E&P at the beginning of the year of $500,000. What is SCR's beginning balance in accumulated E&P at January 1 of next year, as a result of the distribution of the land to Jim?

Answer: $537,000, computed as follows:

Accumulated E&P, this year	$500,000
Current E&P	100,000
E&P basis of land distributed	(75,000)
Liability assumed by Jim	12,000
Beginning balance, AE&P, next year	$537,000

TAXES IN THE REAL WORLD   Visteon's Special Distribution

Visteon Corporation is a global automotive supplier that manufactures vehicle information and controls. During 2008 and 2009, weakened economic conditions triggered a global economic recession that severely impacted the automotive sector. Visteon filed voluntary petitions for reorganization relief in 2009, and the company has been profitable since it emerged from bankruptcy in 2010.

Visteon currently has two technology-focused core businesses: vehicle cockpit electronics and thermal energy management. The company's vehicle cockpit electronics product line includes audio systems, infotainment systems, driver information systems, and electronic control modules. In order to focus its operations on automotive cockpit electronics, Visteon sold a subsidiary that generated a pre-tax gain of approximately $2.3 billion. The sale was completed on June 9, 2015, and Visteon received net cash proceeds of approximately $2.7 billion. The company then announced a plan to return $2.5 billion–$2.75 billion of cash to shareholders through a series of actions including a special distribution.

Based on the tax disclosures in Visteon's annual report, it appears that the company had about a $1 billion deficit in accumulated E&P entering 2015. If Visteon's operations and gain on the sale of the subsidiary generates current E&P of $1.5 billion, then a distribution of $2.5 billion by year-end will generate a taxable dividend of $1.5 billion. Despite the deficit in accumulated E&P, the distribution would come from current E&P. The distribution in excess of current E&P ($1 billion) would be a return of capital to shareholders.

In contrast, if Visteon waits until 2016 to distribute the 2.5 billion, the distribution would only generate a dividend of $500 million. Assuming Visteon doesn't generate any additional E&P in 2016, the current E&P from 2015 would be offset by the deficit in accumulated E&P ($1.5 billion minus $1 billion equals $500 million).

Sources: Visteon Corporation 2014 Form 10-K filed February 26, 2015, and Form 8-K filed September 11, 2015.

CONSTRUCTIVE DIVIDENDS

LO 18-3

Dividend distributions result in double taxation to the parties to the transaction because the corporation making the distribution cannot deduct dividends paid in computing its taxable income. Corporations can avoid this second level of taxation by making a distribution to a shareholder in a nonshareholder capacity. For example, the corporation might characterize the distribution as a payment of salary, interest, or rent to a shareholder who also is an employee, creditor, or lessor to the corporation, respectively. The corporation can deduct these types of payments, thus eliminating the double tax imposed on the distribution at the corporate level. From the recipient's perspective, the amount included in gross income no longer qualifies for preferential tax rates and would be taxed at the recipient's marginal tax rate. Payments designated as compensation are subject to Social Security and Medicare payroll taxes.

> **THE KEY FACTS**
>
> **Examples of Disguised Dividends**
> - Unreasonable compensation.
> - Bargain sales to shareholders.
> - Shareholder use of corporate assets without an arm's-length payment.
> - Loans from shareholders at unreasonable interest rates.
> - Corporate payments made on behalf of the shareholder.

The incentive for a corporation to make payments to shareholders that are deductible typically arises in closely held corporations, where the shareholders act in other capacities, such as managers, creditors, and lessors. In this setting, the shareholders are likely to consider the combined taxes to be paid by the corporation and themselves rather than just the tax they pay individually.

The IRS has the ability to recharacterize the form of a transaction between a corporation and its shareholders into what the IRS considers to be the transaction's substance. In effect, the IRS can recharacterize what the corporation calls a deductible payment (e.g., compensation) into a nondeductible *constructive* dividend distribution. Common examples of constructive dividends include

- Excess (*unreasonable*) compensation paid to shareholder/employees.
- Bargain sales of property by the corporation to shareholders.
- A bargain lease or uncompensated use of corporate property by a shareholder (e.g., a company car or corporate jet used for personal reasons).
- Excess rent paid to a shareholder/lessor by the corporation.
- Payments to a shareholder/creditor where the corporation is undercapitalized or the loan has an unreasonably high rate of interest.
- Corporate payments on a shareholder's behalf (e.g., legal fees paid to defend a sole shareholder of criminal charges).

The most frequent causes of disputes between corporations and the IRS over the characterization of deductible payments made to shareholders involve compensation and interest payments. To determine if compensation paid to a shareholder/employee is *reasonable,* the IRS usually looks to factors that include the individual's duties and responsibilities, what individuals performing in comparable capacities at other corporations are paid, whether the corporation has a formal compensation policy, and what the individual's return on his or her investment is as a shareholder of the company.[13]

Corporate payments made on behalf of shareholders are often the subject of litigation. In one case, the Tax Court held that a corporation's payment of a seat license fee to purchase season tickets to Houston Texans football games, to be used exclusively by the sole shareholder, was a constructive dividend to the shareholder.[14]

---

[13]*Thomas A. Curtis, M.D., Inc.,* 67 T.C.M. 1958 (1994).

[14]*Kerns v. Comm.,* T.C. Memo 2004-63. See also *U.S. vs. Boulware* (9th CA, 2009) 558 F.3d. 971, and *William F. Bruecher III,* TC Summary 2005-52.

Example 18-14

What if: Assume SCR has current E&P of $200,000. Jim and Ginny would like to withdraw $48,000 and $16,000, respectively, from the company to fulfill some personal dreams (a BMW and a condominium, respectively). If SCR pays the amounts to Jim and Ginny as dividends, it will not be able to deduct the payments in computing its taxable income. What is the total tax cost (entity and shareholder level) of distributing a dividend to Jim and Ginny?

Answer: $31,360. The nondeductibility of the dividend payments will increase SCR's tax liability by $21,760 ($64,000 × 34%). Jim and Ginny will be eligible for a reduced dividend tax rate of 15 percent on the distributions, causing them to pay a shareholder-level tax of $7,200 ($48,000 × 15%) and $2,400 ($16,000 × 15%), respectively. The total tax cost to this strategy will be $31,360 ($21,760 + $7,200 + $2,400).

What if: Assume SCR declared a year-end bonus (additional compensation) of $48,000 and $16,000 to Jim and Ginny, respectively, to reward them for their hard work as employees. What is the total income tax cost (entity and shareholder level) of paying a bonus to Jim and Ginny?

Answer: $18,400. By converting the dividend into compensation, SCR can deduct the $64,000 payment in computing its taxable income, saving $21,760 in taxes in the process ($64,000 × 34%). However, Jim and Ginny will no longer be eligible for the preferential dividend tax rate and will have to pay tax at their marginal tax rates (30 percent and 25 percent, respectively). Jim's tax cost will increase to $14,400 ($48,000 × 30%) while Ginny's tax cost will increase to $4,000 ($16,000 × 25%), for a combined tax cost of $18,400. This is still $12,960 less than the combined cost of the dividend strategy ($31,360).

What other tax costs will SCR and Jim and Ginny incur as a result of converting the dividend into a bonus?

Answer: Social Security and Medicare taxes. SCR and Jim and Ginny will have to pay Social Security and Medicare taxes on the $64,000 of compensation payments.

What if: If Jim and Ginny go through with the bonus compensation alternative, would the strategy be vulnerable to IRS scrutiny?

Answer: Possibly. The IRS could argue that the bonus is really a constructive dividend. Key facts in the determination would be Jim and Ginny's contribution to the business, the compensation paid to individuals doing similar jobs at comparable businesses, whether SCR paid any dividends, whether SCR had a formal compensation policy for determining year-end bonuses, and whether payments are correlated to ownership interests. For example, would Jim, who works only part-time, be able to justify why his contributions as an employee are valued at four times the bonus paid to Ginny, who works full-time?

Example 18-15

What if: Assume SCR sold Ginny a Fuji custom touring bike for its cost of $650. The selling price of the bicycle to customers was $1,000. What tax issues might arise in this transaction?

Answer: Two tax issues arise here. The transaction by Ginny meets the definition of a *bargain purchase* of the bicycle. The IRS could argue that Ginny received property worth $1,000 for $650 and thus had a constructive dividend of $350. Because the bicycle is inventory to SCR, the sale could qualify as a nontaxable fringe benefit under the employee discount rules.[15] Assuming this "discount" is available to all SCR employees, Ginny would not have taxable income (compensation) for the bargain portion of the sale in an amount equal to SCR's gross profit percentage times the price it normally charges nonemployee customers for the bicycle. SCR's gross profit percentage is 35 percent ($350/$1,000). The maximum employee discount that would be tax-free is $350 (35% × $1,000). Ginny would not have to report any compensation in this bargain purchase under the fringe benefit rules.

What if: Assume SCR sold the bicycle to Ginny for $500 (i.e., below cost). How might your answer change?

Answer: Ginny would now have taxable compensation of $150 at the very least. Depending on the circumstances, the IRS could assert that she had a constructive dividend of $500.

[15]§132(c).

The Motivation to Pay Dividends

Many publicly traded corporations regularly pay out a portion of their earnings to shareholders as a dividend. Why corporate managers would willingly pay out cash that could be reinvested in the corporation has long intrigued corporate finance theorists. Several possible reasons have been offered to explain this "dividend puzzle" such as signaling earnings persistence.

Most closely held corporations are the alter egos of their shareholders. As a result, their dividend policies are much less likely to be structured. Rather, dividends may be a function of the shareholders' cash needs. The double taxation of corporate earnings plus the higher corporate tax rates provide an incentive for closely held corporations to pay out earnings in tax deductible ways, the additional payroll tax cost of a compensation strategy might outweigh the double tax imposed on the dividend. It makes sense to retain earnings in the corporation if the after-tax rate of return earned by the corporation exceeds the rate that could be earned by the individual shareholders. Paying dividends rather than salary can be a way to avoid Social Security taxes (in which case, the IRS may argue the dividend is really compensation). Most closely held corporations also run the risk of paying a penalty tax called the *accumulated earnings tax* if they accumulate earnings in excess of $250,000 without having a documented business purpose for retaining the excess.[16]

ETHICS

Karla Heyne is the sole shareholder of XYZ Corporation. This past year Karla paid her retired father, Paul, $10,000 from the company's checking account because he was having financial trouble. XYZ files as a C corporation, and Karla noticed that her accountant erroneously deducted this payment as salary on XYZ's return. What would you do with this information if you were in Karla's position?

STOCK DIVIDENDS

LO 18-4

Rather than distribute cash to its shareholders, a corporation may instead distribute additional shares of its own stock (or rights to acquire additional shares) to shareholders as a stock dividend. Publicly held corporations are likely to declare a stock dividend to promote shareholder goodwill (i.e., a stock dividend allows the corporation to retain cash and still provide shareholders with tangible evidence of their interest in corporate earnings) or reduce the market price of its outstanding shares. A stock dividend increases the number of shares outstanding and thereby reduces the price per share and makes the stock more accessible to a wider range of shareholders. For example, a 5 percent stock dividend would increase the number of shares outstanding by 5 percent. Hence, a shareholder holding 100 shares would own 105 shares after a 5 percent stock dividend. Corporations may also declare a **stock split,** where the number of shares outstanding is increased by the ratio of the split. For example, a 2-for-1 stock split would double the number of shares outstanding. Hence, a shareholder holding 100 shares would own 200 shares after a 2-for-1 stock split. Stock splits are used by many firms to keep stock prices accessible to a diverse group of investors.

---

[16]§§531–535. Under certain conditions, accumulated earnings can also trigger the personal holding company tax. See §§541–547.

Tax Consequences to Shareholders Receiving a Stock Distribution

Nontaxable Stock Distributions   Stock dividends and stock splits generally do not provide shareholders with any increase in value. In other words, the shareholders' interest in the corporation remains unchanged except that they now own more pieces of paper (stock) than before. As a result, these distributions are generally not included in the shareholders' gross income.[17]

For the nontaxable general rule to apply, however, the stock distribution must meet two conditions: (1) it must be made with respect to the corporation's common stock, and (2) it must be pro rata with respect to all shareholders (i.e., the shareholders' relative equity positions do not change as a result of the distribution).

The recipient of a nontaxable stock distribution allocates a portion of the tax basis from the stock on which the distribution was issued to the newly issued stock based on the relative fair market values (FMV) of the stock.[18] In the case of a simple dividend of common stock or stock split where the stock distributed is identical to the stock from which the distribution is made (same class and same fair market value), the new per share tax basis is the original tax basis divided by the total number of shares held (including the new shares).

For example, assume a shareholder owns 100 shares of Acme Corporation stock, for which she paid $3,000. Acme declares a 100 percent stock dividend and sends the shareholder an additional 100 shares of stock. The shareholder will now own 200 shares of stock with the same tax basis of $3,000. The basis of each share of stock decreases from its original $30 per share ($3,000/100) to $15 per share ($3,000/200). The holding period of the new stock includes the holding period for which the shareholder held the old stock.[19]

Example 18-16

Jim has a tax basis in his SCR stock of $24,000. Ginny's tax basis in her SCR stock is $10,000. Jim owns 75 of the 100 shares of outstanding SCR stock, while Ginny owns the remaining 25 shares.

What if: Assume for estate and gift tax purposes, their tax accountant, Louis Tully, suggested that SCR declare a 100 percent stock dividend. As a result, Jim would own 150 shares of SCR stock and Ginny would own the remaining 50 shares.

Is the stock dividend taxable to Jim and Ginny?

Answer: No. The stock dividend to Jim and Ginny is nontaxable because it is made equally (pro rata) to the shareholders.

What is the tax basis of each share of SCR stock now held by Jim and Ginny?

Answer: Jim's original tax basis of $24,000 is divided among 150 shares. Hence, each one of Jim's shares has a basis of $160. Ginny's original tax basis of $10,000 is divided among 50 shares. Hence, each one of Ginny's shares has a basis of $200.

THE KEY FACTS

Tax Consequences of Stock Distributions

- Pro rata stock distributions generally are nontaxable.
- Shareholders allocate basis from the "old" stock to the "new" stock based on relative fair market value.
- Non-pro rata stock distributions usually are taxable as dividends.

Taxable Stock Distributions   Non-pro rata stock distributions usually are included in the shareholder's gross income as taxable dividends to the extent of the distributing corporation's E&P.[20] This makes sense because the recipient has now received something of value: an increase in the shareholder's claim on the

---

[17]§305(a).

[18]§307. Technically, the shares received in the distribution are allocated a portion of the original basis determined by the ratio of FMVs. This computation is necessary when the stock dividend includes a different class of shares (e.g., preferred stock).

[19]§1223(4).

[20]§305(b).

corporation's income and assets. For example, a corporation may give its shareholders the choice between a cash dividend or a stock dividend. In this case, shareholders who elect the stock dividend in lieu of money will have a taxable dividend equal to the fair market value of the stock received. Because the stock dividend is taxable, the recipient will have a tax basis in the stock equal to its fair market value. A technical discussion of all of the rules that apply to determine if a stock dividend is taxable is beyond the scope of this text.

STOCK REDEMPTIONS   LO 18-5

continued from page 18-2...

In the original storyline, Jim and Ginny raised some of the initial capital they needed to start SCR by borrowing $50,000 from Jim's father, Walt. An alternative strategy would have been to issue 25 additional shares of SCR stock to Walt in return for $50,000. This change in facts would reduce Jim's ownership percentage in SCR to 60 percent (75 shares/125 shares). Ginny's ownership percentage would decrease to 20 percent (25 shares/125 shares). Walt would own the remaining 20 percent. We will assume this change in facts to continue the storyline.

Walt does not participate in the management of the company. In fact, Walt was hoping to cash out of SCR when it became profitable and use the money to put a down payment on a condominium in The Villages, a retirement community near Orlando, Florida. With the SCR stock valued at $5,000 per share ($125,000 in total), Walt saw this as an opportunity to realize his retirement dream. Jim and Ginny saw this as an opportunity to own all of the company's stock, eliminating a potential source of discord should Jim's father disapprove of the way Jim and Ginny were managing the company.

By the end of this year, the company expects to have sufficient cash to buy back some or all of Walt's shares of SCR stock. Jim and Ginny were wondering about the potential tax consequences to SCR and Walt under various redemption plans. In particular, Jim and Ginny wanted to know if there was a tax difference in (1) buying back five of Walt's shares this year, and the remaining 20 shares equally over the next four years (five shares per year), or (2) buying back all 25 shares this year using an installment note that would pay him 20 percent of the purchase price in each of the next five years plus interest. Once again, they turned to their trusted tax accountant, Louis Tully, for advice. ■

Publicly held corporations buy back (redeem) their stock from existing shareholders for many and varied reasons. For example, a corporation may have excess cash and limited investment opportunities, or management may feel the stock is undervalued. Management may see a large redemption as a way to get analysts to take a closer look at their company (this action sometimes is referred to as *signaling*). Reducing the number of outstanding shares also increases earnings per share (by reducing the number of shares in the denominator of the calculation) and potentially increases the stock's market price. Moreover, corporations are not taxed on gains or losses resulting from transactions in their own stock.[21] Stock redemptions can also be used to selectively buy out dissenting shareholders who have become disruptive to the company.

[21]§1032.

Privately held corporations engage in stock redemptions for reasons that are different from publicly traded corporations. These corporations often use stock redemptions to shift ownership control between family members (usually the older generation to the younger generation) when the acquiring family members do not have the resources to purchase shares directly from the other family members. They also use redemptions to buy out dissatisfied, disinterested, or deceased shareholders (e.g., a child who does not want to continue in the family business or a family member who has become disruptive in the management of the company). In addition, redemptions of an ex-spouse's stock can provide liquidity in a divorce agreement and eliminate the individual from management or ownership in the company. Finally, redemptions can be used to provide cash to satisfy estate taxes imposed on the estate of a deceased shareholder of the company.

The Form of a Stock Redemption

A stock redemption is an acquisition by a corporation of its stock from a shareholder in exchange for property, whether or not the stock so acquired is cancelled, retired, or held as treasury stock.[22] The term *property* has the same meaning as it did for dividend transactions (i.e., cash and noncash property).

Stock redemptions take the form of an *exchange* where the shareholders exchange their stock in the corporation for property, usually cash. If the *form* of the transaction is respected, shareholders compute gain or loss (usually capital) by comparing the amount realized (money and the fair market value of other property received) with their tax basis in the stock exchanged.

Without any tax law restrictions, a sole shareholder of a corporation could circumvent the dividend rules by structuring distributions to have the form of an exchange (i.e., a stock redemption). For example, rather than have the corporation make a $100,000 dividend distribution, the shareholder could have the corporation buy back $100,000 of stock from the shareholder. If the shareholder had a tax basis of $60,000 in the stock redeemed, the amount of income reported on the shareholder's tax return would decrease from $100,000 (dividend) to $40,000 (capital gain). At present, both amounts would be taxed at the same preferential tax rate (generally 15 percent), assuming the shareholder held the stock for more than a year. Similar to a dividend, however, the sole shareholder would continue to own 100 percent of the corporation before and after the stock redemption.

Form is not always respected in a redemption, however. The tax law may determine (or the IRS may argue that) the transaction is, in substance, a property distribution, the tax consequences of which should be determined under the previously discussed dividend rules.

The IRC provides both "bright line" and subjective tests to distinguish when a redemption should be treated as an exchange or a potential dividend.[23] The result is an intricate set of rules that must be navigated carefully by the corporation and its shareholders to ensure that the shareholders receive the tax treatment they desire.[24] This is especially true in closely held, family corporations, where the majority of stock is held by people related to each other through birth or marriage.

While individual shareholders prefer sale treatment, corporate shareholders generally have more incentive for dividend treatment. Dividends from domestic corporations are eligible for the dividends received deduction (usually 70 or 80 percent),

---

[22]§317(b).

[23]§302. The IRC also defines when sale treatment is appropriate in some special circumstances. For example, §303 defines when sale treatment is allowed for redemptions of stock to pay death taxes.

[24]Not all taxpayers have the same tax incentives in a redemption. Corporate shareholders may desire dividend treatment to capture the dividends received deduction. Individuals, on the other hand, may desire exchange treatment to lessen the amount of gain recognized (by reducing the amount received by the basis of the stock exchanged) or to report a capital loss.

whereas a capital gain is taxed at the corporation's marginal tax rate (as high as 39 percent). Again, a corporation might prefer exchange treatment if the redemption results in a loss or its stock tax basis as a percentage of the redemption price exceeds the dividends received deduction ratio.

Redemptions That Reduce a Shareholder's Ownership Interest

The IRC allows a shareholder to treat a redemption as an exchange if the transaction meets one of three change-in-stock-ownership tests.[25] These stock ownership tests look at the redemption from the shareholder's perspective.

Redemptions That Are Substantially Disproportionate   The IRC states in §302(b)(2) that a redemption will be treated as an exchange if the redemption is *"substantially disproportionate with respect to the shareholder."* A shareholder meets this requirement by satisfying all three mechanical ("bright line") *stock ownership tests:*

1. Immediately after the exchange, the shareholder owns less than 50 percent of the total combined voting power of all classes of stock entitled to vote.
2. The shareholder's percentage ownership of voting stock after the redemption is less than 80 percent of his or her percentage ownership before the redemption.
3. The shareholder's percentage ownership of the aggregate fair market value of the corporation's common stock (voting and nonvoting) after the redemption is less than 80 percent of his or her percentage ownership before the redemption.

For example, suppose a shareholder owns 60 of 100 shares (60 percent) of a corporation's stock prior to a redemption. He must own less than 48 shares of the stock after a redemption to have the redemption treated as an exchange ($60\% \times 80\% = 48\%$ and 48% is less than 50 percent). In contrast, suppose the same shareholder owns 70 shares of stock before a redemption (70 percent). In this case, a redemption must reduce his ownership below 50 percent to qualify as an exchange. In this example an 80% reduction in the percentage owned ($70\% \times 80\% = 56\%$) will not satisfy the 50 percent test.

The determination as to whether a shareholder meets both the 50 percent and 80 percent tests is evaluated on a shareholder-by-shareholder basis. As a result, some shareholders can satisfy the test while others do not. If a shareholder owns multiple classes (voting and nonvoting) of common stock, the less-than-80-percent of fair market value test is applied to the shareholder's aggregate ownership of the common stock rather than on a class-by-class basis.

Example 18-17

What if: Assume Walt is not related to either Jim or Ginny. This year, SCR redeemed five shares of his stock in exchange for $25,000. Walt has a tax basis in the five shares of SCR stock of $10,000 ($2,000 per share). What is the tax treatment of the stock redemption to Walt under §302(b)(2)?

Answer: $25,000 dividend. Prior to the redemption, Walt owned 20 percent of SCR (25/125 shares). After the redemption, his ownership percentage in SCR drops to 16.67 percent (20/120 shares). This redemption does not satisfy the substantially disproportionate test. After the redemption, Walt owns less than 50 percent of SCR stock, but his ownership percentage after the redemption (16.67 percent) does not fall below 80 percent of their ownership percentage prior to the redemption ($80\% \times 20\% = 16\%$). Walt will not be able to treat the redemption as an exchange

(continued on page 18-22)

---

[25]§302(b)(1), (b)(2), and (b)(3).

under this change-in-ownership test. Unless he can satisfy one of the other change-in-ownership tests, Walt will have a $25,000 dividend, assuming SCR has sufficient E&P, rather than a $15,000 capital gain ($25,000 − $10,000).

How many shares of stock would SCR have to redeem from Walt to guarantee exchange treatment under the substantially disproportionate test?

Answer: Six shares. For Walt to meet the 80 percent test, SCR must redeem six shares of stock. The computation is made as follows:

$$\frac{25 - x}{125 - x} < 16\%, \text{ where } x \text{ is the number of shares to be redeemed}$$

Using some algebra, we can compute x to be 5.95, rounded up to six shares.[26] If SCR redeems six shares from Walt, his ownership percentage after the redemption will be 15.97 percent (19/119 shares), which now meets the 80 percent test. The redemption of this one additional share transforms the transaction from a $30,000 dividend (6 shares × $5,000) to an $18,000 capital gain ($30,000 − $12,000).

TAXES IN THE REAL WORLD   An (Un)Fortunate Redemption

There are many reasons that companies choose to redeem stock, but sometimes the timing of the transactions is questionable. For example, Netflix (the online movie company, symbol NFLX) is a company that has a policy of returning "excess" cash to shareholders in the form of buybacks. However, in September 2011, Netflix proposed a rate change that was supposed to increase average revenue per subscriber. Netflix proposed to separate its DVD-by-mail service from movie streaming and increase fees. This proposal would have required subscribers who wanted both DVDs and movie streaming to have separate accounts for each service.

This proposal made finding entertainment more complicated and triggered a revolt by subscribers. Instead of paying more, an estimated 800,000 Netflix subscribers dropped their subscription. More bad news followed when, in late October, Netflix announced that the expected costs of expanding into Ireland and the United Kingdom were likely to generate a quarterly deficit rather than the $7 per share earnings expected in the first-quarter 2012. Altogether, these changes caused shares in Netflix to plummet from $300 to around $42.

Unfortunately during the third quarter Netflix continued to redeem shares, spending $39.6 million to repurchase approximately 182,000 shares at an average cost of $218 per share. Without more information, it is difficult to determine if any single sale would qualify as substantially disproportionate under §302(b)(2). However, because Netflix is publicly held (no individual or corporation owns more than 5 percent of the stock), it is likely that these redemptions were treated as sales because they would meet the not essentially equivalent to a dividend test under §302(b)(1). Hence, many former shareholders benefited from participating in redemptions at historically high prices and having the redemptions taxed as sales. However, Netflix could not recognize any of the losses associated with transactions in its own stock.

Source: Netflix Shareholder letter Q3 2011, October 24, 2011.

In determining whether Walt meets the 50 percent and 80 percent tests, he must take into account the **constructive ownership** (stock attribution) rules found in subchapter C.[27] Under certain circumstances, these tax rules treat stock owned by other persons (individuals and entities) that are related to the redeeming shareholder as being owned by the redeeming shareholder for purposes of determining whether the shareholder has met the change-in-stock-ownership tests. The purpose of the attribution rules is to prevent shareholders from dispersing stock ownership to either

---

[26]Multiply both sides by (125 − x), we get 25 − x = 20 − .16x. Moving x to the right side of the equation and the integers to the left side of the equation, we get 5 = .84x. Solving for x, we get x = 5.95.

[27]§318.

family members who have similar economic interests or entities controlled by the shareholder to avoid having a stock redemption characterized as a dividend.

Family attribution. Individuals are treated as owning the shares of stock owned by their spouse, children, grandchildren, and parents. Stock owned constructively through the family attribution rule cannot be reattributed to another family member through the family attribution rule (this rule is sometimes referred to as *reattribution* or *double attribution*).

Example 18-18

Return to the original storyline facts, where Walt is Jim's father. This year, SCR redeemed six shares of stock from them in exchange for $30,000. Walt has a tax basis in the six shares of stock redeemed of $12,000 ($2,000 per share). What is the tax treatment of the stock redemption to Walt under §302(b)(2)?

Answer: $30,000 dividend.

Prior to the redemption, Walt owned 20 percent of SCR (25/125 shares) directly. Under the family attribution rules, he is treated as constructively owning the shares of SCR stock owned by his son Jim (75 shares). In applying the substantially disproportionate change-in-stock-ownership tests, Walt is treated as owning 100 shares of SCR stock (25 + 75), or 80 percent of the SCR stock (100/125 shares). After the redemption, his ownership percentage in SCR drops to 79 percent (94/119 shares). This redemption does not satisfy the substantially disproportionate test because Walt is deemed to own more than 50 percent of the SCR stock after the redemption. As a result, he will have a $30,000 dividend, assuming SCR has sufficient E&P, rather than an $18,000 capital gain ($30,000 − $12,000).

An interesting question arises as to what happens to the tax basis of stock redeemed that is not used in determining the shareholder's tax consequences. This occurs in a redemption treated as a dividend, where the tax basis of the stock redeemed is not subtracted from the amount received from the corporation. Under the current rules, the tax basis of the stock redeemed is added back to the tax basis of any shares still held by the shareholder.[28] If the shareholder no longer holds any shares, the tax basis transfers to the stock held by those persons who caused the shareholder to have dividend treatment under the attribution rules.

Example 18-19

In the prior example, SCR redeemed six shares of stock from Walt for $30,000, and the transaction was treated as a dividend because of the application of the family attribution rules. Walt had a tax basis in the six shares of stock redeemed of $12,000 ($2,000 per share), but this tax basis was not used in determining their taxable income from the transaction.

What is Walt's tax basis in the remaining 19 shares of SCR stock?

Answer: $50,000. Walt adds back the unused $12,000 tax basis in the six shares redeemed to the tax basis of their remaining 19 shares. The tax basis in these remaining shares increases to $50,000, the original tax basis of the 25 shares.

Attribution from entities to owners or beneficiaries. Owners or beneficiaries of entities can be deemed to own shares of stock owned by the entity itself. Under these rules, partners are deemed to own a pro rata share of their partnership's stock holdings (i.e., a partner who has a 10 percent interest in a partnership is deemed to own

---

[28]Reg. §1.302-2.

10 percent of any stock owned by the partnership). Beneficiaries are deemed to own a pro rata share of the stock owned by the trust or estate of which they are a beneficiary. Shareholders are deemed to own a pro rata share of their corporation's stock holdings, but only if they own at least 50 percent of the value of the corporation's stock. Other attribution rules, such as family attribution, apply in determining if this 50 percent test is met.

For example, assume an individual owns 100 shares of a corporation's stock directly. In addition, she is a 50 percent partner in a partnership that owns 100 shares of stock in the same corporation. Under the entity-to-owner attribution rules, the individual is deemed to own 50 percent of the partnership's 100 shares in the corporation. She is deemed to own 150 shares of stock in the corporation (100 + 50) for purposes of applying any of the change-in-stock-ownership tests in a stock redemption.

Example 18-20

What if: Assume that Walt is not Jim's father, and he is a 50 percent partner in a partnership that owns 25 shares in SCR. The other 50 percent of the partnership is owned by his neighbors, Fred and Ethel, who are unrelated to Walt. How many shares of SCR is treated as constructively owning through the partnership?

Answer: 12.5 shares. Walt is treated as owning a pro rata share of stock owned by the partnership; in this example, 50 percent times 25 shares.

Attribution from owners or beneficiaries to entities. Entities can be deemed to own other stock owned by their owners or beneficiaries. Under these rules, a partnership is deemed to own 100 percent of the shares owned by its partners. A trust or estate is deemed to own 100 percent of the shares owned by its beneficiaries. A corporation is deemed to own 100 percent of the shares owned by its shareholders, but only if the shareholder owns at least 50 percent of the value of the corporation's stock. Stock that is deemed owned by an entity cannot be reattributed to the other owners in the entity under the entity-to-owner rules previously discussed (this is known as *sideways attribution*).

For example, assume an individual owns 100 shares of a corporation's stock directly. In addition, she is a 50 percent partner in a partnership that owns 100 shares of stock in the same corporation. Under the owner-to-entity attribution rules, the partnership is deemed to own 100 percent of the partner's 100 shares in the corporation. The partnership is treated as owning 200 shares of stock in the corporation (100 + 100) for purposes of applying any of the change-in-stock-ownership tests in a stock redemption.

Option attribution. A person having an option to purchase stock is deemed to own the stock that the option entitles the person to purchase.

Complete Redemption of the Stock Owned by a Shareholder

The IRC holds that a redemption will be treated as an exchange if the redemption is in *"complete redemption of all of the stock of the corporation owned by the shareholder."*[29] This test seems redundant with the substantially disproportionate test discussed previously; after all, a complete redemption automatically satisfies the 50 percent and 80 percent tests. The difference relates to the application of the stock attribution rules that apply to this form of redemption.

The stock attribution rules previously discussed also apply to a complete redemption. This presents a potential problem in family-owned corporations in which the only (or majority) shareholders are parents, children, and grandchildren. Parents who have all of their stock redeemed will be treated as having received a dividend if

[29] §302(b)(3).

their children or grandchildren continue to own the remaining stock in the corporation because of the operation of the family attribution rules. To provide family members with relief in these situations, the IRC allows shareholders to waive (ignore) the family attribution rules in a complete redemption of their stock.[30] As usual, there are some strings attached.

The first requirement is that the shareholder has no interest in the corporation immediately after the exchange as a *"shareholder, employee, director, officer or consultant."*[31] These relations to the corporation are referred to as prohibited interests. The second requirement is that the shareholder does not acquire a prohibited interest within 10 years after the redemption, unless by inheritance (this is known as the *10-year look-forward rule*). Finally, the shareholder must agree to notify the IRS district director within 30 days if he or she acquires a prohibited interest within 10 years after the redemption. These agreements are referred to as **triple i agreements.**[32] The shareholder can still be a creditor of the corporation (i.e., the parents can receive a corporate note in return for their stock if the corporation does not have the cash on hand to finance the redemption).

Example 18-21

Return to the original storyline facts, where Walt is Jim's father. Assume SCR redeemed all of his 25 shares this year for $125,000. Walt's tax basis in the SCR shares is $50,000 (25 × $2,000). Under the family attribution rules, Walt would still be treated as constructively owning 75 percent of the SCR stock (Jim would own 75 of the remaining 100 shares in SCR). The $125,000 payment would be treated as a taxable dividend.

What happens to the unused $50,000 tax basis in the SCR stock redeemed?

Answer: The tax basis transfers to Jim's stock, giving him a new tax basis in his SCR stock of $74,000 ($24,000 + $50,000).

How can Walt change the tax treatment of the complete redemption?

Answer: Because Walt has all of their shares redeemed, he can waive the family attribution rules, provided they file a triple i agreement with the IRS, and does not retain a prohibited interest in SCR (e.g., as an employee or consultant). By waiving the family attribution rules, Walt will be able to treat the redemption as an exchange and report a capital gain of $75,000 ($125,000 − $50,000).

Redemptions That Are Not Essentially Equivalent to a Dividend   The IRC provides that a redemption will be treated as an exchange if the redemption is *"not essentially equivalent to a dividend."*[33] This is a subjective determination that turns on the facts and circumstances of each case. To satisfy this requirement, there must be a "meaningful" reduction in the shareholder's ownership interest in the corporation as a result of the redemption. Neither the IRS nor the courts provide any mechanical tests to make this determination. As a result of the potential for litigation, shareholder reliance on this test is typically a last resort.[34]

Although the courts have held that a shareholder's interest can include the right to vote and exercise control, participate in current and accumulated earnings, or share in net assets on liquidation, the IRS generally looks at the change in voting power as the key factor. The shareholder's voting power must decrease and be below

---

[30]§302(c)(2).

[31]§302(c).

[32]The agreement gets its name from the clause in which it is described [§302(c)(2)(A)(iii)].

[33]§302(b)(1).

[34]The Supreme Court has held in *United States v. Davis*, 397 U.S. 301, at 313 (1970), that the only way for a shareholder to qualify under this test is for the redemption to "result in a meaningful reduction of the shareholder's proportionate interest in the corporation."

50 percent as a result of the exchange before this test can be considered.[35] As before, the stock attribution rules apply to these types of redemptions. Shareholders generally turn to this test to provide exchange treatment for redemptions when they cannot meet the "bright line" tests discussed previously.

Example 18-22

What if: Assume Walt is not related to Jim or Ginny. This year, SCR redeemed five shares of his stock in exchange for $25,000. Walt has a tax basis in the five shares of SCR stock of $10,000 ($2,000 per share).

What is the tax treatment of the stock redemption to Walt under the *not essentially equivalent to a dividend* test?

Answer: $15,000 capital gain.

Prior to the redemption, Walt owned 20 percent of SCR (25/125 shares). After the redemption, his ownership percentage in SCR drops to 16.67 percent (20/120 shares). This redemption does not satisfy the substantially disproportionate test, which would treat the redemption as an exchange. Walt likely has a case that the redemption should be treated as an exchange because it was *not essentially equal to a dividend*. After all, his ownership percentage decreased (20 percent to 16.67 percent) and is below 50 percent after the redemption. However, the result Walt seeks (exchange treatment) is not guaranteed. For peace of mind, he might prefer having SCR redeem one additional share and have the certainty that the redemption will be treated as an exchange.

Example 18-23

What if: Assume Walt is Jim's father, and SCR redeemed five shares of his stock in exchange for $25,000. Walt has a tax basis in the five shares of SCR stock of $10,000 ($2,000 per share). What is the tax treatment of the stock redemption to Walt under the *not essentially equivalent to a dividend* test?

Answer: $25,000 dividend.

Prior to the redemption, Walt is treated as owning 80 percent of SCR (25 shares directly and 75 shares through Jim). After the redemption, his ownership percentage in SCR drops to 79 percent (95/120 shares). This redemption does not satisfy the *not essentially equal to a dividend* test because Walt is treated as owning more than 50 percent of the SCR stock.

Tax Consequences to the Distributing Corporation

The corporation distributing property to shareholders in a redemption generally recognizes gain on distributions of appreciated property, but is not permitted to recognize loss on distribution of property with a fair market value less than its tax basis.[36]

If the shareholder treats the redemption as a *dividend,* the corporation reduces its current E&P by the cash distributed and the fair market value of other property

---

[35]In Rev. Rul. 76-385, 1976-2 C.B. 92, the IRS held that in the case of a "small, minority shareholder, whose relative stock interest is minimal and who exercises no control over the affairs of the corporation," any reduction in proportionate interest is "meaningful." In this ruling, the shareholder's ownership percentage decreased from .0001118% to .0001081%, which would not be considered a "meaningful" reduction by most standards. Because the reduction in stock ownership did not meet the substantially disproportionate tests of §302(b)(2), the shareholder's only hope for exchange treatment was to qualify under §302(b)(1).

[36]§311(a) and (b).

distributed as described in Exhibit 18-3.[37] If the shareholder treats the redemption as an *exchange,* the corporation reduces current and accumulated E&P at the date of distribution by the percentage of stock redeemed (i.e., if 60 percent of the stock is redeemed, E&P is reduced by 60 percent), not to exceed the fair market value of the property distributed.[38] The distributing corporation reduces its current E&P by any dividend distributions made during the year before reducing its E&P for redemptions treated as exchanges.[39]

The distributing corporation cannot deduct expenses incurred in a stock redemption.[40] The corporation can deduct interest on debt incurred to finance a redemption, however.

Example 18-24

What if: Assume SCR redeemed all of the 25 shares owned by Walt in exchange for $125,000. The stock redeemed represents 20 percent of the total stock outstanding. Walt has a tax basis in his SCR shares of $50,000. Further assume that Walt treated the redemption as an exchange because he waived the family attribution rules and filed a triple i agreement with the IRS.[41] As a result, Walt recognized a capital gain of $75,000 ($125,000 − $50,000). The redemption took place on December 31, on which date SCR had total E&P of $500,000. SCR did not make any dividend payments during the year.

By what amount does SCR reduce its E&P as a result of this redemption?

Answer: $100,000. SCR reduces total E&P by the lesser of (1) $100,000 (20% × $500,000) or (2) $125,000, the amount paid to Walt in the redemption.

What if: Assume total E&P was $1,000,000 at the end of the year. By what amount does SCR reduce its E&P as a result of this redemption?

Answer: $125,000. SCR reduces total E&P by the lesser of (1) $200,000 (20% × $1,000,000) or (2) $125,000, the amount paid to Walt in the redemption.

What if: Assume SCR paid a dividend of $100,000 to its shareholders on June 1. Total E&P was $500,000 at the end of the year, before taking into account the dividend and redemption. By what amount does SCR reduce its E&P as a result of this redemption?

Answer: $80,000. SCR first reduces total E&P by the dividend paid during the year to $400,000 ($500,000 − $100,000). SCR then reduces its E&P for the redemption by the lesser of (1) $80,000 (20% × $400,000) or (2) $125,000, the amount paid to Walt in the redemption.

THE KEY FACTS

Stock Redemptions Treated as Exchanges

- A stock redemption is treated as an exchange if it meets one of the following three tests:
  - Not essentially equivalent to a dividend.
  - Substantially disproportionate with respect to the shareholders.
  - In complete termination of the shareholder's interest.
- The following attribution rules are used to determine if one of the three tests is met:
  - Family attribution.
  - Entity-to-owner attribution (pro rata).
  - Owner-to-entity attribution (100 percent).
  - Options.
- A corporation reduces its E&P as a result of a stock redemption as follows:
  - If the distribution is treated as an exchange, E&P is reduced by the lesser of (1) the amount distributed or (2) the percentage of stock redeemed times AE&P at the redemption date.
  - If the distribution is treated as a dividend, E&P is reduced using the dividend rules.

Trends in Stock Redemptions by Publicly Traded Corporations

Traditionally, publicly traded corporations viewed stock redemptions as a tax-efficient means to return cash to their shareholders. Redemptions allow shareholders to "declare their own dividends" by voluntarily selling shares back to the corporation. Many companies increased their dividends after Congress decreased the dividend tax rate to 15 percent or 5 percent (now 0 percent) for individuals in 2003. On the other hand, the impending dividend tax increase at the end of 2012 motivated other companies, such as Costco, to declare special dividends to avoid the anticipated higher shareholder tax.

---

[37]§312(a), and note that E&P cannot be reduced by more than the pro rata percentage of E&P allocated to the redeemed shares.

[38]§312(n)(7).

[39]Rev. Rul. 74-338, 1974-2 C.B. 101 and Rev. Rul. 74-339, 1974-2 C.B. 103.

[40]§162(k).

[41]The requirements for filing the triple i agreement are found in Reg. §1.302-4T.

TAXES IN THE REAL WORLD   Changing Distribution Strategies
in Light of Tax Law Changes

Costco Board of Directors Declares Special Cash Dividend

November 29, 2012—Costco (NASDAQ: COST) announced today that its Board of Directors has declared a special $7.00 per share cash dividend, payable on December 18, 2012, to stockholders of record as of the close of business on December 10, 2012. The total dividend payout is expected to be approximately $3 billion, based on the current shares outstanding. When paid, these

dividends could be taxed at the top rate of 15%. However, had the dividend been paid two weeks later, the top tax rate would have been 20%.

Richard Galanti, Executive VP and CFO, stated, that the special dividend is "our latest effort in returning capital to our shareholders while maintaining our conservative capital structure." Maybe the CFO should have added that Costco was returning capital in a tax-efficient manner?

Source: Costco Form 8-K filed November 29, 2012.

Individuals have a tax incentive to participate in a redemption because gain recognized as a result of the redemption is usually capital gain (which is reduced by the basis of the stock redeemed and can absorb capital losses from other investments). Losses produced by the buyback generally can be deducted against capital gains.

PARTIAL LIQUIDATIONS

Corporations can contract their operations by either distributing the stock of a subsidiary to their shareholders or by selling the business. In the case of a sale, the corporation may distribute the proceeds from the sale to its shareholders in partial liquidation of their ownership interests. The distribution may require the shareholders to tender shares of stock back to the corporation or may be pro rata to all the shareholders without an actual exchange of stock.

The tax treatment of a distribution received in a partial liquidation depends on the identity of the shareholder receiving the distribution.[42] All *noncorporate* shareholders receive exchange treatment. This entitles the individual to capital gain treatment with respect to gain or loss recognized on the actual or deemed exchange. If the shareholder is not required to tender stock to the corporation in return for the property received, the shareholder computes gain or loss recognized on the exchange by calculating the tax basis of the shares that would have been transferred to the corporation had the transaction been a stock redemption.

All *corporate* shareholders are subject to the change-in-stock-ownership rules that apply to stock redemptions. This usually results in dividend treatment because partial liquidations almost always involve pro rata distributions. Corporate shareholders generally prefer dividend treatment because of the availability of the dividends received deduction.

For a distribution to be in partial liquidation of the corporation, it must either be *"not essentially equivalent to a dividend"* (as determined at the corporate level) or the result of the termination of a *"qualified trade or business."*[43] The technical requirements to meet these requirements are beyond the scope of this text.

Partial liquidations can be a tax-efficient way for a corporation to satisfy both its corporate and individual shareholders. For example, in the 1990s, General Dynamics Corporation sold off several of its divisions and distributed the proceeds ($20 per share) to its shareholders in partial liquidation of the corporation. As a result, the company's largest corporate shareholder treated the distribution as a dividend and received a 70 percent dividends received deduction. The company's largest individual

THE KEY FACTS

Tax Consequences to Shareholders in a Partial Liquidation of a Corporation

- Noncorporate shareholders receive exchange treatment.
- Corporate shareholders determine their tax consequences using the change-in-stock ownership rules that apply to stock redemptions.

[42]§302(b)(4).
[43]§302(e).

shareholders treated the redemption as an exchange and received preferential taxation at the capital gain tax rate. The corporation was able to distribute cash from the sale of its assets in a manner that was tax-efficient to its diverse set of shareholders. Despite their beneficial tax results, partial liquidations are rare in practice.

CONCLUSION

In this chapter we learned that a corporation can distribute cash and other property to its shareholders in alternative ways. The most common forms are dividend distributions and stock buybacks (redemptions). The form chosen to make such a distribution affects the tax consequences to the recipients (shareholders) as well as the corporation itself. In some cases, the tax laws or the tax administrators can ignore the form of the transaction and assess tax based on the substance of the transaction. This is common in the case of stock redemptions that can be taxed as dividend payments or deductible payments (compensation, interest, rent) that can be treated as constructive dividends (with no deduction for the corporation). The tax rules that apply to make this distinction often are complex and must be evaluated carefully by taxpayers and their tax advisers prior to making a decision.

Summary

Explain the framework that applies to the taxation of property distributions from a corporation to a shareholder. **LO 18-1**

- Subchapter C of the Internal Revenue Code provides guidelines and rules for determining the tax status of distributions from a taxable ("C") corporation to its shareholders.
- When a corporation distributes property to persons in their capacity as shareholders without receiving any property or services in return, the shareholder must determine if the amount received is a dividend.
- If the distribution is of property other than cash, the distributing corporation recognizes gain but not loss on the distribution.

Compute a corporation's earnings and profits and a shareholder's dividend income. **LO 18-2**

- The IRC defines a dividend as any distribution of property made by a corporation to its shareholders out of its current or accumulated earnings and profits (E&P).
- Earnings and profits is the tax equivalent of financial accounting retained earnings, although the computations can be significantly different.
- A corporation must keep two E&P accounts: current E&P and accumulated E&P.
- The IRC and the related regulations list four basic types of adjustments that a corporation must make to its taxable income to compute current E&P.
  - Inclusion of income that is excluded from taxable income.
  - Disallowance of certain expenses that are deducted in computing taxable income.
  - Deduction of certain expenses that are excluded from the computation of taxable income.
  - Deferral of deductions or acceleration of income due to separate accounting methods required for E&P purposes.
- The shareholder computes the dividend amount to include in gross income as the sum of cash received plus the fair market value of property received less any liabilities assumed.
- The distributing corporation recognizes gain, but not loss, on the distribution of noncash property in a dividend distribution.

- A corporation reduces its E&P by the amount of cash distributed, the E&P basis of unappreciated property distributed, and the fair market value of appreciated property distributed, net of any liability assumed by the shareholders.

LO 18-3 Identify when a corporation may be deemed to have paid a "constructive dividend" to a shareholder.

- A transaction between a shareholder and a corporation that does not take the form of a dividend may be treated by the IRS as a constructive dividend. Examples include:
  - Unreasonable compensation paid to shareholder/employees.
  - A bargain lease or uncompensated use of corporate property by a shareholder.
  - An excess purchase/lease price paid to a shareholder.
  - "Loans" to a shareholder who has no intent to repay the loan.
  - Corporate payments on a shareholder's behalf.
  - Unlawful diversions of corporate income to shareholders.

LO 18-4 Explain the taxation of stock dividends.

- The general rule is that a stock dividend is not taxable.
- The basis of the "new" stock received is computed by allocating basis from the existing stock based on relative fair market value.
- The holding period of the new stock includes the holding period of the existing stock on which the new stock was distributed.
- Non-pro rata stock dividends usually are treated as taxable dividends to the recipients.

LO 18-5 Comprehend the tax consequences of stock redemptions.

- If a redemption is treated as an exchange, the shareholder computes gain or loss by comparing the amount realized (money and property received) with the tax-adjusted basis of the stock surrendered.
  - The character of the gain or loss is capital.
  - The basis of noncash property received is its fair market value.
  - The holding period of the property received begins at the date of receipt.
- If the transaction is treated as a dividend, the shareholder has gross income in an amount equal to the cash and fair market value of other property received to the extent of the corporation's E&P.
  - The basis of the property received is its fair market value.
- The IRC treats redemptions as exchanges in transactions in which the shareholder's ownership interest in the corporation has been "meaningfully" reduced relative to other shareholders as a result of the redemption.
- There are three change-in-stock-ownership tests that entitle the shareholder to exchange treatment in a redemption.
- The IRC states that a redemption will be treated as an exchange if the redemption is "not essentially equivalent to a dividend."
  - This is a facts and circumstances determination (subjective).
  - To satisfy this requirement, the courts or IRS must conclude that there has been a "meaningful" reduction in the shareholder's ownership interest in the corporation as a result of the redemption (usually below 50 percent stock ownership).
- The IRC states that a redemption will be treated as an exchange if the redemption is "substantially disproportionate with respect to the shareholder," defined as follows:
  - Immediately after the exchange the shareholder owns less than 50 percent of the total combined voting power of all classes of stock entitled to vote.
  - The shareholder's percentage ownership of voting stock after the redemption is less than 80 percent of his or her percentage ownership before the redemption.
  - The shareholder's percentage ownership of the aggregate fair market value of the corporation's common stock (voting and nonvoting) after the redemption is less than 80 percent of his or her percentage ownership before the redemption.
- The IRC holds that a redemption will be treated as an exchange if the redemption is in "complete redemption of all of the stock of the corporation owned by the shareholder."

- In determining whether the change-in-stock-ownership tests are met, each shareholder's percentage change in ownership in the corporation before and after a redemption must take into account constructive ownership (attribution) rules.
- The attribution rules cause stock owned by other persons to be treated as owned by (attributed to) the shareholder for purposes of determining whether the shareholder has met any of the change-in-stock-ownership tests to receive exchange treatment.
  - Family attribution. Individuals are treated as owning the shares of stock owned by their spouse, children, grandchildren, and parents.
  - Attribution from entities to owners or beneficiaries.
    - Partners are deemed to own a pro rata share of their partnership's stock holdings (i.e., a partner who has a 10 percent interest in a partnership is deemed to own 10 percent of any stock owned by the partnership).
    - Shareholders are deemed to own a pro rata share of their corporation's stock holdings, but only if they own at least 50 percent of the value of the corporation's stock.
  - Attribution from owners or beneficiaries to entities.
    - Partnerships are deemed to own 100 percent of stock owned by partners (i.e., a partnership is deemed to own 100 percent of stock owned by a 10 percent partner).
    - Attribution to a corporation only applies to shareholders owning 50 percent or more of the value of the corporation's stock.
  - Option attribution. A person having an option to purchase stock is deemed to own the stock that the option entitles the person to purchase.
- Shareholders can waive the family attribution rules in a complete redemption of their stock if certain conditions are met.
  - The shareholder has not retained a prohibited interest in the corporation immediately after the exchange (e.g., as a shareholder, employee, director, officer, or consultant).
  - The shareholder does not acquire a prohibited interest within 10 years after the redemption, unless by inheritance (the 10-year look-forward rule).
  - The shareholder agrees to notify the IRS district director within 30 days if she acquires a prohibited interest within 10 years (sign a triple i agreement).
- If the redemption is treated as a dividend by the shareholder, the corporation generally reduces its E&P by the cash distributed and the fair market value of other property distributed.
- If the redemption is treated as an exchange by the shareholder, the corporation reduces E&P at the date of distribution by the percentage of stock redeemed (i.e., if 50 percent of the stock is redeemed, E&P is reduced by 50 percent), not to exceed the fair market value of the property distributed.

Describe the tax consequences of a partial liquidation to the corporation and its shareholders.   **LO 18-6**

- For a distribution to be a partial liquidation, it must either be "not essentially equivalent to a dividend" (as determined at the corporate level, not the shareholder level) or is the result of the termination of a "qualified trade or business."
- The tax treatment of a distribution received in partial liquidation of a corporation depends on the identity of the shareholder receiving it.
  - All noncorporate shareholders get exchange treatment.
  - All corporate shareholders are subject to the stock redemption change in ownership rules, which usually results in dividend treatment because partial liquidations are almost always pro rata distributions.

KEY TERMS

accumulated earnings and profits (18-3)

constructive dividend (18-3)

constructive ownership (18-22)

current earnings and profits (18-3)

dividend (18-2)

partial liquidation (18-2)

stock dividend (18-17)

stock redemption (18-2)

stock split (18-17)

triple i agreement (18-25)

DISCUSSION QUESTIONS

Discussion Questions are available in *Connect*®.

LO 18-1   1. What is meant by the term *double taxation of corporate income*?

LO 18-1   2. How does the issue of double taxation arise when a corporation decides between making a distribution to a shareholder-employee as a dividend or compensation?

LO 18-1   3. Why might a shareholder who is also an employee prefer receiving a dividend instead of compensation from a corporation?

LO 18-2   4. What are the three potential tax treatments of a cash distribution to a shareholder? Are these potential tax treatments elective by the shareholder?

LO 18-2   5. In general, what is the concept of earnings and profits designed to represent?

LO 18-2   6. How does *current earnings and profits* differ from *accumulated earnings and profits*? Is there any congressional logic for keeping the two accounts separate?

LO 18-2   7. True or False: A calendar-year corporation has positive current E&P of $100 and an accumulated deficit (negative) E&P of $200. A cash distribution of $100 to the corporation's sole shareholder at year-end will not be treated as a dividend because total E&P is negative $100. Explain.

LO 18-2   8. True or False: A calendar-year corporation has a deficit (negative) current E&P of $100 and accumulated E&P of $100. A cash distribution of $100 to the corporation's sole shareholder on June 30 will not be treated as a dividend because total E&P at December 31 is $0. Explain.

LO 18-2   9. List the four basic adjustments that a corporation makes to taxable income or net loss to compute current E&P. What is the rationale for making these adjustments?

LO 18-2   10. What must a shareholder consider in computing the amount of a noncash distribution to include in gross income?

LO 18-2   11. What income tax issues must a corporation consider before it makes a noncash distribution to a shareholder?

LO 18-2   12. Will the shareholder's tax basis in noncash property received equal the amount included in gross income as a dividend? Under what circumstances will the amounts be different, if any?

LO 18-2   13. A shareholder receives appreciated noncash property in a corporate distribution and assumes a liability attached to the property. How does the assumption of a liability affect the amount of dividend reported in gross income?

LO 18-2   14. A shareholder receives appreciated noncash property in a corporate distribution and assumes a liability attached to the property. How does this assumption affect the amount of gain the corporation recognizes? From the corporation's perspective, does it matter if the liability assumed by the shareholder exceeds the property's gross fair market value?

LO 18-2   15. A corporation distributes appreciated noncash property to a shareholder as a dividend. What impact does the distribution have on the corporation's earnings and profits?

LO 18-3   16. Amy is the sole shareholder of a corporation. Rather than have the corporation pay her a dividend, Amy decides to have the corporation declare a "bonus" at year-end and pay her tax-deductible compensation. What potential tax issue may arise in this situation? Which parties, Amy or the corporation or both, are affected by the classification of the payment?

LO 18-4   17. Why might a corporation issue a stock dividend to its shareholders?

LO 18-4   18. What tax issue arises when a shareholder receives a nontaxable stock dividend?

LO 18-4   19. In general, what causes a stock dividend to be taxable to the recipient?

20. What are the potential tax consequences to a shareholder who participates in a stock redemption? `LO 18-5`

21. What stock ownership tests must be met before a shareholder receives exchange treatment under the substantially disproportionate change-in-stock-ownership test in a stock redemption? Why is a change-in-stock-ownership test used to determine the tax status of a stock redemption? `LO 18-5`

22. What are the criteria to meet the "not essentially equivalent to a dividend" change-in-stock-ownership test in a stock redemption? `LO 18-5`

23. When might a shareholder have to rely on the not essentially equivalent to a dividend test in arguing that a stock redemption should be treated as an exchange for tax purposes? `LO 18-5`

24. Why do you think the tax law imposes constructive stock ownership rules on stock redemptions? `LO 18-5`

25. Which members of a family are included in the family attribution rules? Is there any rationale for the family members included in the test? `LO 18-5`

26. Ilya and Olga are brother and sister. Ilya owns 200 shares of stock in Parker Corporation. Is Olga deemed to own Ilya's 200 shares under the family attribution rules that apply to stock redemptions? `LO 18-5`

27. Maria has all of her stock in Mayan Corporation redeemed. Under what conditions will Maria treat the redemption as an exchange and recognize capital gain or loss? `LO 18-5`

28. What must a shareholder do to waive the family attribution rules in a complete redemption of stock? `LO 18-5`

29. How does a corporation's computation of earnings and profits differ based on the tax treatment of a stock redemption to the shareholder (i.e., as either a dividend or exchange)? `LO 18-5`

30. How does the tax treatment of a partial liquidation differ from a stock redemption? `LO 18-6`

31. Bevo Corporation experienced a complete loss of its mill as the result of a fire. The company received $2 million from the insurance company. Rather than rebuild, Bevo decided to distribute the $2 million to its two shareholders. No stock was exchanged in return. Under what conditions will the distribution meet the requirements to be a partial liquidation and not a dividend? Why does it matter to the shareholders? `LO 18-6`

PROBLEMS

Select problems are available in *Connect*®.   ☒ connect

32. Gopher Corporation reported taxable income of $500,000 this year. Gopher paid a dividend of $100,000 to its sole shareholder, Sven Anderson. Gopher Corporation is subject to a flat-rate tax of 34 percent. The dividend meets the requirements to be a qualified dividend, and Sven is subject to a tax rate of 15 percent on the dividend. What is the income tax imposed on the corporate income earned by Gopher and the income tax on the dividend distributed to Sven? `LO 18-1`

33. Bulldog Corporation reported taxable income of $500,000 this year, before any deduction for any payment to its sole shareholder and employee, Georgia Brown. Bulldog chose to pay a bonus of $100,000 to Georgia at year-end. Bulldog Corporation is subject to a flat-rate tax of 34 percent. The bonus meets the requirements to be "reasonable" and is therefore deductible by Bulldog. Georgia is subject to a marginal tax rate of 35 percent on the bonus. What is the income tax imposed on the corporate income earned by Bulldog and the income tax on the bonus paid to Georgia? `LO 18-1`

LO 18-2 34. Hawkeye Company reports current E&P of $300,000 this year and accumulated E&P at the beginning of the year of $200,000. Hawkeye distributed $400,000 to its sole shareholder, Ray Kinsella, on December 31 of this year. Ray's tax basis in his Hawkeye stock is $75,000.

a) How much of the $400,000 distribution is treated as a dividend to Ray?

b) What is Ray's tax basis in his Hawkeye stock after the distribution?

c) What is Hawkeye's balance in accumulated E&P as of January 1 of next year?

LO 18-2 35. Jayhawk Company reports current E&P of $300,000 and accumulated E&P of negative $200,000. Jayhawk distributed $400,000 to its sole shareholder, Christine Rock, on the last day of the year. Christine's tax basis in her Jayhawk stock is $75,000.

a) How much of the $400,000 distribution is treated as a dividend to Christine?

b) What is Christine's tax basis in her Jayhawk stock after the distribution?

c) What is Jayhawk's balance in accumulated E&P on the first day of next year?

LO 18-2 36. This year, Sooner Company reports current E&P of negative $300,000. Its accumulated E&P at the beginning of the year was $200,000. Sooner distributed $400,000 to its sole shareholder, Boomer Wells, on June 30 of this year. Boomer's tax basis in his Sooner stock is $75,000.

a) How much of the $400,000 distribution is treated as a dividend to Boomer?

b) What is Boomer's tax basis in his Sooner stock after the distribution?

c) What is Sooner's balance in accumulated E&P on the first day of next year?

LO 18-2 37. Blackhawk Company reports current E&P of negative $300,000. Its accumulated E&P at the beginning of the year was a negative $200,000. Blackhawk distributed $400,000 to its sole shareholder, Melanie Rushmore, on June 30 of this year. Melanie's tax basis in her Blackhawk stock is $75,000.

a) How much of the $400,000 distribution is treated as a dividend to Melanie?

b) What is Melanie's tax basis in her Blackhawk stock after the distribution?

c) What is Blackhawk's balance in accumulated E&P on the first day of next year?

LO 18-2 38. This year, Jolt Inc. reported $40,000 of taxable income before any charitable contribution deduction. Jolt contributed $10,000 this year to Goodwill Industries, a public charity. Compute the company's current E&P.

LO 18-2 39. Boilermaker Inc. reported taxable income of $500,000 this year and paid federal income taxes of $170,000. Not included in the company's computation of taxable income is tax-exempt income of $20,000, disallowed meals and entertainment expenses of $30,000, and disallowed expenses related to the tax-exempt income of $1,000. Boilermaker deducted depreciation of $100,000 on its tax return. Under the alternative (E&P) depreciation method, the deduction would have been $60,000. Compute the company's current E&P.

LO 18-2 40. Gator Inc. reported taxable income of $1,000,000 this year and paid federal income taxes of $340,000. Included in the company's computation of taxable income is gain from the sale of a depreciable asset of $50,000. The income tax basis of the asset was $100,000. The E&P basis of the asset using the alternative depreciation system was $175,000. Compute the company's current E&P.

LO 18-2 41. Paladin Inc. reported taxable income of $1,000,000 this year and paid federal income taxes of $340,000. The company reported a capital gain from sale of investments of $150,000, which was partially offset by a $100,000 net capital loss carryover from last year, resulting in a net capital gain of $50,000 included in taxable income. Compute the company's current E&P.

LO 18-2 42. Volunteer Corporation reported taxable income of $500,000 from operations this year. The company paid federal income taxes of $170,000 on this taxable income. During the year, the company made a distribution of land to its sole shareholder, Rocky Topp. The land's fair market value was $75,000 and its tax and E&P basis to Volunteer was $25,000. Rocky assumed a mortgage attached to the land of $15,000. Any gain from the distribution will be taxed at 34 percent. The company had accumulated E&P of $750,000 at the beginning of the year.

a) Compute Volunteer's total taxable income and federal income tax.

b) Compute Volunteer's current E&P.

c) Compute Volunteer's accumulated E&P at the beginning of next year.

d) What amount of dividend income does Rocky report as a result of the distribution?

e) What is Rocky's income tax basis in the land received from Volunteer?

43. Tiger Corporation reported taxable income of $500,000 from operations this year. The company paid federal income taxes of $170,000 on this taxable income. During the year, the company made a distribution of land to its sole shareholder, Mike Woods. The land's fair market value was $75,000 and its tax and E&P basis to Tiger was $125,000. Mike assumed a mortgage attached to the land of $15,000. Any gain from the distribution will be taxed at 34 percent. The company had accumulated E&P of $750,000 at the beginning of the year.   `LO 18-2`

a) Compute Tiger's total taxable income and federal income tax.

b) Compute Tiger's current E&P.

c) Compute Tiger's accumulated E&P at the beginning of next year.

d) What amount of dividend income does Mike report as a result of the distribution?

e) What is Mike's tax basis in the land he received from Tiger?

44. Illini Corporation reported taxable income of $500,000 from operations for this year. The company paid federal income taxes of $170,000 on this taxable income. During the year, the company made a distribution of an automobile to its sole shareholder, Carly Urbana. The auto's fair market value was $30,000 and its tax basis to Illini was $0. The auto's E&P basis was $15,000. Any gain from the distribution will be taxed at 34 percent. Illini had accumulated E&P of $1,500,000.   `LO 18-2`

a) Compute Illini's total taxable income and federal income tax.

b) Compute Illini's current E&P.

c) Compute Illini's accumulated E&P at the beginning of next year.

d) What amount of dividend income does Carly report as a result of the distribution?

e) What is Carly's tax basis in the auto she received from Illini?

45. Beaver Corporation reported taxable income of $500,000 from operations this year. The company paid federal income taxes of $170,000 on this taxable income. During the year, the company made a distribution of land to its sole shareholder, Eugenia VanDam. The land's fair market value was $20,000 and its tax and E&P basis to Beaver was $50,000. Eugenia assumed a mortgage on the land of $25,000. Any gain from the distribution will be taxed at 34 percent. Beaver Corporation had accumulated E&P of $1,500,000.   `LO 18-2`

a) Compute Beaver's total taxable income and federal income tax.

b) Compute Beaver's current E&P.

c) Compute Beaver's accumulated E&P at the beginning of next year.

d) What amount of dividend income does Eugenia report as a result of the distribution?

46. Tiny and Tim each own half of the 100 outstanding shares of Flower Corporation. This year, Flower reported taxable income of $6,000 and was subject to a 25 percent tax rate. In addition, Flower received $20,000 of life insurance   `LO 18-2`

 research

 tax forms

proceeds due to the death of an employee (Flower paid $500 in life insurance premiums this year). Flower had $5,000 of accumulated E&P at the beginning of the year.

a) What is Flower's current E&P?

b) Flower distributed $6,000 on February 15 and $30,000 on August 1. What total amount of dividends will Tiny and Tim report?

c) What amount of capital gain (if any) would Tiny and Tim report on the distributions in part (b) if their stock basis is $2,000 and $10,000, respectively?

d) What form would Flower use to report nondividend distributions?

e) On what form (line) would Tiny and Tim report nondividend distributions?

LO 18-3 47. Nittany Company pays its sole shareholder, Tammy Lion, a salary of $100,000. At the end of each year, the company pays Tammy a "bonus" equal to the difference between the corporation's taxable income for the year (before the bonus) and $75,000. In this way, the company hopes to keep its taxable income at amounts that are taxed at either 15 percent or 25 percent. This year Nittany reported pre-bonus taxable income of $675,000 and paid Tammy a bonus of $600,000. On audit, the IRS determined that individuals working in Tammy's position earned on average $300,000 per year. The company had no formal compensation policy and never paid a dividend.

a) How much of Tammy's bonus might the IRS recharacterize as a dividend?

b) What arguments might Tammy make to counter this assertion?

c) Assuming the IRS recharacterizes $200,000 of Tammy's bonus as a dividend, what additional income tax liability does Nittany Company face?

LO 18-4 48. Hoosier Corporation declared a 2-for-1 stock split to all shareholders of record on March 25 of this year. Hoosier reported current E&P of $600,000 and accumulated E&P of $3,000,000. The total fair market value of the stock distributed was $1,500,000. Barbara Bloomington owned 1,000 shares of Hoosier stock with a tax basis of $100 per share.

a) What amount of taxable dividend income, if any, does Barbara recognize this year? Assume the fair market value of the stock was $150 per share on March 25 of this year.

b) What is Barbara's income tax basis in the new and existing stock she owns in Hoosier Corporation, assuming the distribution is tax-free?

c) How does the stock dividend affect Hoosier's accumulated E&P at the beginning of next year?

LO 18-4 49. Badger Corporation declared a stock dividend to all shareholders of record on March 25 of this year. Shareholders will receive one share of Badger stock for each 10 shares of stock they already own. Madison Cheeseman owns 1,000 shares of Badger stock with a tax basis of $100 per share. The fair market value of the Badger stock was $110 per share on March 25 of this year.

a) What amount of taxable dividend income, if any, does Madison recognize this year?

b) What is Madison's income tax basis in her new and existing stock in Badger Corporation, assuming the distribution is nontaxable?

c) How would you answer parts (a) and (b) if Madison was offered the choice between one share of stock in Badger for each 10 shares she owned or $100 cash for each 10 shares she owned in Badger?

LO 18-5 50. Wildcat Company is owned equally by Evan Stone and his sister Sara, each of whom hold 1,000 shares in the company. Sara wants to reduce her ownership in the company, and it was decided that the company will redeem 500 of her shares for $25,000 per share on December 31 of this year. Sara's income tax basis in each share is $5,000. Wildcat has current E&P of $10,000,000 and accumulated E&P of $50,000,000.

a) What is the amount and character (capital gain or dividend) recognized by Sara as a result of the stock redemption?

b) What is Sara's income tax basis in the remaining 500 shares she owns in the company?

c) Assuming the company did not make any dividend distributions during this year, by what amount does Wildcat reduce its E&P as a result of the redemption?

51. Flintstone Company is owned equally by Fred Stone and his sister Wilma, each of whom hold 1,000 shares in the company. Wilma wants to reduce her ownership in the company, and it was decided that the company will redeem 250 of her shares for $25,000 per share on December 31 of this year. Wilma's income tax basis in each share is $5,000. Flintstone has current E&P of $10,000,000 and accumulated E&P of $50,000,000. `LO 18-5`

a) What is the amount and character (capital gain or dividend) recognized by Wilma as a result of the stock redemption, assuming only the "substantially disproportionate with respect to the shareholder" test is applied?

b) Given your answer to part (a), what is Wilma's income tax basis in the remaining 750 shares she owns in the company?

c) Assuming the company did not make any dividend distributions this year, by what amount does Flintstone reduce its E&P as a result of the redemption?

d) What other argument might Wilma make to treat the redemption as an exchange?

52. Acme Corporation has 1,000 shares outstanding. Joan and Bill are married, and they each own 20 shares of Acme. Joan's daughter, Shirley, also owns 20 shares of Acme. Joan is an equal partner with Jeri in the J&J partnership, and this partnership owns 60 shares of Acme. Jeri is not related to Joan or Bill. How many shares of Acme is Shirley deemed to own under the stock attribution rules? `LO 18-5`

53. Bedrock Inc. is owned equally by Barney Rubble and his wife Betty, each of whom hold 1,000 shares in the company. Betty wants to reduce her ownership in the company, and it was decided that the company will redeem 500 of her shares for $25,000 per share on December 31 of this year. Betty's income tax basis in each share is $5,000. Bedrock has current E&P of $10,000,000 and accumulated E&P of $50,000,000. `LO 18-5`

a) What is the amount and character (capital gain or dividend) recognized by Betty as a result of the stock redemption, assuming only the "substantially disproportionate with respect to the shareholder" test is applied?

b) Given your answer to part (a), what is Betty's income tax basis in the remaining 500 shares she owns in the company?

c) Assuming the company did not make any dividend distributions this year, by what amount does Bedrock reduce its E&P as a result of the redemption?

d) Can Betty argue that the redemption is "not essentially equivalent to a dividend" and should be treated as an exchange?

54. Assume in problem 53 that Betty and Barney are not getting along and have separated due to marital discord (although they are not legally separated). In fact, they cannot even stand to talk to each other anymore and communicate only through their accountant. Betty wants to argue that she should not be treated as owning any of Barney's stock in Bedrock because of their hostility toward each other. Can family hostility be used as an argument to void the family attribution rules? Consult Rev. Rul. 80-26, 1980-1 C.B. 66, *Robin Haft Trust v. Comm.*, 510 F.2d 43 (CA-1 1975), *Metzger Trust v. Comm.*, 693 F.2d 459 (CA-5 1982), and *Cerone v. Comm.*, 87 TC 1 (1986). `LO 18-5`

`research`

LO 18-5 55. Boots Inc. is owned equally by Frank Albert and his daughter Nancy, each of whom hold 1,000 shares in the company. Frank wants to retire from the company, and it was decided that the company will redeem all 1,000 of his shares for $25,000 per share on December 31 of this year. Frank's income tax basis in each share is $500. Boots Inc. has current E&P of $1,000,000 and accumulated E&P of $5,000,000.

    a) What must Frank do to ensure that the redemption will be treated as an exchange?

    b) If Frank remained as the chairman of the board after the redemption, what is the amount and character (capital gain or dividend) of income that Frank will recognize this year?

    c) If Frank treats the redemption as a dividend, what happens to his stock basis in the 1,000 shares redeemed?

LO 18-5

research

56. In the previous problem, Nancy would like to have Frank stay on as a consultant after all of his shares are redeemed. She would pay him a modest amount of $500 per month. Nancy wants to know if there is any *de minimus* rule such that Frank would not be treated as having retained a prohibited interest in the company because he is receiving such a small amount of money. Consult *Lynch v. Comm.*, 801 F.2d 1176 (CA-9 1986), *reversing* 83 T.C. 597 (1984), *Seda*, 82 T.C. 484 (1984), and *Cerone*, 87 T.C. 1 (1986).

LO 18-5

planning

57. Limited Brands recently repurchased 68,965,000 of its shares, paying $29 per share. The total number of shares outstanding before the redemption was 473,223,066. The total number of shares outstanding after the redemption was 404,258,066. Assume your client owned 20,000 shares of stock in The Limited. What is the minimum number of shares she must tender to receive exchange treatment under the "substantially disproportionate with respect to the shareholder" change-in-ownership rules?

LO 18-5 58. Cougar Company is owned equally by Cat Stevens and a partnership that is owned equally by his father and two unrelated individuals. Cat and the partnership each own 3,000 shares in the company. Cat wants to reduce his ownership in the company, and it is decided that the company will redeem 1,500 of his shares for $25,000 per share. Cat's income tax basis in each share is $5,000. What are the income tax consequences to Cat as a result of the stock redemption, assuming the company has earnings and profits of $10 million?

LO 18-5

planning

59. Oriole Corporation, a privately held company, has one class of voting common stock, of which 1,000 shares are issued and outstanding. The shares are owned as follows:

Larry Byrd	400
Paul Byrd (Larry's son)	200
Lady Byrd (Larry's daughter)	200
Cal Rifkin (unrelated)	200
Total	1,000

Larry is considering retirement and would like to have the corporation redeem all of his shares for $400,000.

    a) What must Larry do or consider if he wants to guarantee that the redemption will be treated as an exchange?

    b) Could Larry act as a consultant to the company and still have the redemption treated as an exchange?

LO 18-5

research

60. Using the facts from the previous problem, Oriole Corporation proposes to pay Larry $100,000 and give him an installment note that will pay him $30,000 per year for the next 10 years plus a market rate of interest. Will this

arrangement allow Larry to treat the redemption as an exchange? Consult §453(k)(2)(A).

61. EG Corporation redeemed 200 shares of stock from one of its shareholders in exchange for $200,000. The redemption represented 20 percent of the corporation's outstanding stock. The redemption was treated as an exchange by the shareholder. By what amount does EG reduce its total E&P as a result of the redemption under the following E&P assumptions? `LO 18-5`

    a) EG's total E&P at the time of the distribution was $2,000,000.

    a) EG's total E&P at the time of the distribution was $500,000.

62. Spartan Corporation redeemed 25 percent of its shares for $2,000 on July 1 of this year, in a transaction that qualified as an exchange under §302(a). Spartan's accumulated E&P at the beginning of the year was $2,000. Its current E&P is $12,000. Spartan made dividend distributions of $1,000 on June 1 and $4,000 on August 31. Determine the beginning balance in Spartan's accumulated E&P at the beginning of the next year. See Rev. Rul. 74-338, 1974-2 C.B. 101 and Rev. Rul. 74-339, 1974-2 C.B. 103 for help in making this calculation. `LO 18-5` **planning**

63. Bonnie and Clyde are the only two shareholders in Getaway Corporation. Bonnie owns 60 shares with a basis of $3,000, and Clyde owns the remaining 40 shares with a basis of $12,000. At year-end, Getaway is considering different alternatives for redeeming some shares of stock. Evaluate whether each of the following stock redemption transactions will qualify for sale and exchange treatment. `LO 18-5`

    a) Getaway redeems 10 of Bonnie's shares for $2,000. Getaway has $20,000 of E&P at year-end and Bonnie is unrelated to Clyde.

    b) Getaway redeems 25 of Bonnie's shares for $4,000. Getaway has $20,000 of E&P at year-end and Bonnie is unrelated to Clyde.

    c) Getaway redeems 10 of Clyde's shares for $2,500. Getaway has $20,000 of E&P at year-end and Clyde is unrelated to Bonnie.

64. Aggie Corporation made a distribution of $500,000 to Rusty Cedar in partial liquidation of the company on December 31 of this year. Rusty, an individual, owns 100 percent of Aggie Corporation. The distribution was in exchange for 50 percent of Rusty's stock in the company. At the time of the distribution, the shares had a fair market value of $200 per share. Rusty's income tax basis in the shares was $50 per share. Aggie had total E&P of $8,000,000 at the time of the distribution. `LO 18-6`

    a) What is the amount and character (capital gain or dividend) of any income or gain recognized by Rusty as a result of the partial liquidation?

    b) Assuming Aggie made no other distributions to Rusty during the year, by what amount does Aggie reduce its total E&P as a result of the partial liquidation?

65. Wolverine Corporation made a distribution of $500,000 to Jim Har Inc. in partial liquidation of the company on December 31 of this year. Jim Har Inc. owns 100 percent of Wolverine Corporation. The distribution was in exchange for 50 percent of Jim Har Inc.'s stock in the company. At the time of the distribution, the shares had a fair market value of $200 per share. Jim Har Inc.'s income tax basis in the shares was $50 per share. Wolverine had total E&P of $8,000,000 at the time of the distribution. `LO 18-6`

    a) What is the amount and character (capital gain or dividend) of any income or gain recognized by Jim Har Inc. as a result of the partial liquidation?

    b) Assuming Wolverine made no other distributions to Jim Har Inc. during the year, by what amount does Wolverine reduce its total E&P as a result of the partial liquidation?

COMPREHENSIVE PROBLEMS

Select problems are available in *Connect*®.

66. Lanco Corporation, an accrual-method corporation, reported taxable income of $1,460,000 this year. Included in the computation of taxable income were the following items:

   - MACRS depreciation of $200,000. Straight-line depreciation would have been $120,000.
   - A net capital loss carryover of $10,000 from last year.
   - A net operating loss carryover of $25,000 from last year.
   - $65,000 capital gain from the distribution of land to the company's sole shareholder (see below).

   Not included in the computation of taxable income were the following items:

   - Tax-exempt income of $5,000.
   - Life insurance proceeds of $250,000.
   - Excess current year charitable contribution of $2,500 (to be carried over to next year).
   - Tax-deferred gain of $20,000 on a like-kind exchange.
   - Federal income tax refund from last year of $35,000.
   - Nondeductible life insurance premium of $3,500.
   - Nondeductible interest expense of $1,000 on a loan used to buy tax-exempt bonds.

   Lanco paid federal income taxes this year of $496,400. The company's accumulated E&P at the beginning of the year was $2,400,000. During the year, Lanco made the following distributions to its sole shareholder, Luigi (Lug) Nutt:

   - June 30: $50,000.
   - September 30: Parcel of land with a fair market value of $75,000. Lanco's tax basis in the land was $10,000. Lug assumed an existing mortgage on the property of $15,000.

Required:

   a) Compute Lanco's current E&P for this year.
   b) Compute the amount of dividend income reported by Lug Nutt this year as a result of the distributions.
   c) Compute Lanco's accumulated E&P at the beginning of next year.

67. Petoskey Stone Quarry Inc. (PSQ), a calendar-year, accrual-method C corporation, provides landscaping supplies to local builders in northern Michigan. PSQ has always been a family-owned business and has a single class of voting common stock outstanding. The 500 outstanding shares are owned as follows:

Nick Adams	150
Amy Adams (Nick's sister)	150
Abigail Adams (Nick's daughter)	50
Charlie Adams (Nick's son)	50
Sandler Adams (Nick's father)	100
Total shares	500

   Nick Adams serves as president of PSQ, and his father Sandler serves as chairman of the board. Amy is the company's CFO, and Abigail and Charlie work as employees of the company. Sandler would like to retire and sell his shares back to the company. The fair market value of the shares is $500,000. Sandler's tax basis is $10,000. The redemption is tentatively scheduled to take place on December 31 of this year. At the beginning of the year, PSQ had accumulated earnings and profits of $2,500,000. The company projects current E&P of $200,000. The company intends to pay pro rata cash dividends of $300 per share to its shareholders on December 1 of this year.

Required:

a) Assume the redemption takes place as planned on December 31 and no elections are made by the shareholders.

  1. What amount of dividend or capital gain will Sandler recognize as a result of the stock redemption?

  2. How will the tax basis of Sandler's stock be allocated to the remaining shareholders?

b) What must Sandler and the other shareholders do to change the tax results you calculated in part (a)?

c) Compute PSQ's accumulated earnings and profits on January 1 of next year, assuming the redemption is treated as an exchange.

68. Thriller Corporation has one class of voting common stock, of which 1,000 shares are issued and outstanding. The shares are owned as follows:

Joe Jackson	400
Mike Jackson (Joe's son)	200
Jane Jackson (Joe's daughter)	200
Vinnie Price (unrelated)	200
Total	1,000

Thriller Corporation has current E&P of $300,000 for this year and accumulated E&P at January 1 of this year of $500,000. During this year, the corporation made the following distributions to its shareholders:

03/31: Paid a dividend of $10 per share to each shareholder ($10,000 in total).

06/30: Redeemed 200 shares of Joe's stock for $200,000. Joe's basis in the 200 shares redeemed was $100,000.

09/30: Redeemed 60 shares of Vinnie's stock for $60,000. His basis in the 60 shares was $36,000.

12/31: Paid a dividend of $10/share to each shareholder ($7,400 in total).

Required:

a) Determine the tax status of each distribution made this year. (*Hint:* First, consider if the redemptions are treated as dividend distributions or exchanges.)

b) Compute the corporation's accumulated E&P at January 1 of next year.

c) Joe is considering retirement and would like to have the corporation redeem all of his shares for $100,000 plus a 10-year note with a fair market value of $300,000.

  1. What must Joe do or consider if he wants to ensure that the redemption will be treated as an exchange?

  2. Could Joe still act as a consultant to the company?

d) Thriller Corporation must pay attorney's fees of $5,000 to facilitate the stock redemptions. Is this fee deductible?

Corporate Formation, Reorganization, and Liquidation

© Purestock/Superstock

Storyline Summary

Spartan Cycle and Repair

Privately held company located in East Lansing, Michigan, that sells and repairs high-end bicycles

Jim Wheeler

Co-owner of Spartan Cycle and Repair (75 percent)

Filing status: Married filing jointly

Dependents: One child

Marginal tax rate: 40 percent

Ginny Gears

Co-owner of Spartan Cycles and Repair (25 percent)

Filing status: Unmarried

Marginal tax rate: 25 percent

360 Air

Privately held company in East Lansing, Michigan, that sells snowboarding equipment

Al Pine

Owner of 360 Air

Filing status: Unmarried

Marginal tax rate: 35 percent

Jim Wheeler and Ginny Gears were excited about the growth of their business, Spartan Cycles and Repair (SCR). The business had a solid base of loyal customers and was showing a healthy profit. Jim and Ginny were ready for some new challenges. They have considered expanding the bicycle business to a new geographic region and branching out into a new line of business. Given the seasonal nature of the demand for bicycle products and repair in Michigan, Jim and Ginny favor a complementary line of business that would provide them with a source of income during the winter months. Ginny was impressed with the growing popularity of snowboarding, especially among young people. Factors that contributed to this growth included low equipment costs (especially compared to skiing), easily attained skills, a "coolness" attractive

to young people, and the sport's inclusion in the Olympic games.

Jim and Ginny were aware of a small snowboarding store in East Lansing called 360 Air that was named after a daring snowboarding maneuver. The business was owned and operated by Al Pine, a rather free-spirited individual whose enthusiasm for the sport was not matched by his business acumen.

Jim and Ginny feel that with some additional capital investment and marketing effort, they could turn Al's snowboarding business into a profitable operation. They set up a meeting with Al to discuss how they could become partners in his business enterprise.

After some negotiation, Jim, Ginny, and Al agreed to jointly operate the snowboarding business through a C corporation. Al had been operating his business as a sole proprietorship. As part of the incorporation process, each of the three individuals will make a contribution of property or services to the corporation in return for stock. Al will contribute his existing inventory as well as the building and land on which the building was situated in return for 50 percent

of the stock in 360 Air. The corporation would assume the existing mortgage on the property. Jim will contribute cash in exchange for 40 percent of the stock, and Ginny will contribute her marketing services in return for 10 percent of the stock.

Each of the parties wants to know the income tax implications of incorporating Al's ongoing business. In addition, Jim is wondering if the manner in which they are intending to create the corporation is tax efficient, and whether there are other issues they should consider that would lessen the tax burdens of both the corporation and its new shareholders. They turned to their trusted tax accountant, Louis Tully, for his expertise.

to be continued...

When creating a business, the owners must choose the organizational form for operating the business. The choice of legal entity affects how (whether) the income or loss generated by the business is taxed at the entity level and the owner level. At some point during the life of a business, the owners may decide to change its tax status. In the case of an ongoing business, such as 360 Air, the decision to change to a corporate tax status will involve the transfer of assets and liabilities by one or more of the owners in return for stock in the corporation. These property transfers raise several tax questions. A transfer of assets or liabilities to a corporation in exchange for stock triggers realization of gains and losses and may cause shareholders to recognize gains in the year of the transfer. In addition, shareholders will need to calculate the tax basis of their stock and the corporation will need to determine the basis of the assets and liabilities received in the transfer.

LO 19-1 REVIEW THE TAXATION OF PROPERTY DISPOSITIONS

This section provides a brief review of tax rules that apply to transfers of property to a corporation in the incorporation process. Before gain or loss is *recognized* (included in taxable income), it must first be *realized*. **Realization** generally occurs when a *transaction* takes place (i.e., an exchange of property rights between two persons).

Exhibit 19-1 provides a template for computing gain or loss realized by a party to a property transaction.

EXHIBIT 19-1 **Computing Gain or Loss Realized in a Property Transaction[1]**

	Amount realized (received)
−	Adjusted tax basis of the property transferred
	Gain (+) or loss (−) realized

The **amount realized** is computed using the template in Exhibit 19-2.

EXHIBIT 19-2 **Computing the Amount Realized in a Property Transaction[2]**

	Cash received
+	Fair market value of other property received
+	Liabilities assumed by the transferee on the transferred property
−	Selling expenses incurred in the transaction
−	Liabilities assumed by the transferor on any property received in the exchange
	Amount realized

A property's **adjusted tax basis** is calculated using the template in Exhibit 19-3.

EXHIBIT 19-3 **Computing a Property's Adjusted Tax Basis in a Property Transaction[3]**

	Acquisition basis
+	Capital improvements
−	Depreciation
	Adjusted tax basis

The entire amount of gain or deductible loss realized is recognized unless *otherwise provided* by the Internal Revenue Code.[4] Gain or loss is not recognized if (1) the gain or loss is *excluded* from gross income (the gain or loss will never be recognized) or (2) the gain or deductible loss is *deferred* from gross income (recognition of the gain or deductible loss is postponed to a future period). Transfers of property to a corporation are transactions in which realized gain or loss may be deferred if certain requirements are met.[5] Recognition of a deferred gain or loss is postponed until the property received in the exchange is subsequently disposed of (e.g., recognition of Al's realized gain will be postponed until he sells his stock in 360 Air).

---

[1]§1001(a).

[2]§1001(b).

[3]§1011.

[4]§1001(c). Realized losses must be deductible to be recognized. Nondeductible losses are never recognized.

[5]§351.

LO 19-2   TAX-DEFERRED TRANSFERS OF PROPERTY TO A CORPORATION

In the formation of a corporation, or in subsequent transfers of property to an existing corporation, shareholders transfer cash and noncash property to the corporation in return for stock in the corporation. The stock can be common or preferred, voting or nonvoting.[6]

Example 19-1

As part of the incorporation of 360 Air, Al Pine will transfer inventory, a building, and land to the corporation in return for 50 percent of the corporation's stock (50 shares). The property has the following fair market values and adjusted bases:

	FMV	Adjusted Basis
Inventory	$ 25,000	$ 15,000
Building	150,000	60,000
Land	200,000	100,000
Total	$375,000	$175,000

The corporation will assume a mortgage of $75,000 attached to the building and land. The fair market value of the 360 Air stock Al will receive in the exchange is $300,000. How much net gain or loss does Al *realize* in the exchange?

Answer: Al realizes a net gain of $200,000 on this transfer, computed as follows:

	Fair market value of 360 Air stock received	$300,000
+	Mortgage assumed by 360 Air	75,000
	Amount realized	$375,000
−	Adjusted tax basis of the property transferred	175,000
	Gain realized	$200,000

THE KEY FACTS

Requirements for Tax Deferral in a Corporate Formation

- Tax deferral only applies to transfers of property to a corporation.
- The persons transferring property to a corporation must receive solely stock in the corporation in return.
- The persons transferring property to a corporation must collectively control the corporation after the transaction.
- Control is defined as ownership of 80 percent or more of the corporation's voting stock and 80 percent or more of each class of nonvoting stock.
- Generally, all stock received by the transferor counts for the control test whether received in exchange for services or property.

Gain or loss deferred in the transfer of property to a corporation in return for stock is reflected in the shareholder's *tax basis* in the stock received in exchange for the transferred property.[7] A deferred gain *decreases* the shareholder's tax basis in the stock to an amount equal to the stock's fair market value less the gain deferred. A deferred loss *increases* the shareholder's tax basis in the stock to an amount equal to the stock's fair market value plus the loss deferred. In essence, the shareholder's tax basis in the stock received reflects the deferred gain or loss.

Congress provides for the deferral of gain or loss on the transfer of property to a corporation in exchange for stock to remove tax consequences as an impediment to forming a corporation and to provide taxpayers with flexibility in choosing their preferred form of doing business. Congress justified tax deferral because shareholders maintained an interest in the property transferred through a different form of ownership (from direct ownership to indirect ownership through stock).

[6]A category of stock with different rights (e.g., voting rights, dividend rights, liquidation rights) is referred to as a *class* of stock.
[7]§358.

Example 19-2

Assume Al meets the tax law requirements to defer recognizing the $200,000 gain realized in the property transfer to 360 Air. The fair market value of the 360 Air stock he receives in the exchange is $300,000. What is Al's tax basis in the stock received?

Answer: $100,000. To reflect the deferral of the gain in his tax basis in the stock, Al's tax basis must be $100,000 ($300,000 − $200,000 gain deferred). If he subsequently sells the stock for $300,000, Al will recognize the $200,000 gain deferred previously ($300,000 − $100,000).

What if: Assume Al realized a $100,000 loss on the exchange of his property for stock in 360 Air. What would be his tax basis in the stock received?

Answer: $400,000. To reflect the deferral of the loss in his tax basis in the stock, Al's tax basis must be $400,000 ($300,000 + $100,000 loss deferred). If he subsequently sells the stock for $300,000, Al will recognize the $100,000 loss deferred previously ($300,000 − $400,000).

Transactions Subject to Tax Deferral

For shareholders to receive tax deferral in a transfer of property to a corporation, the transferors must meet the requirements of IRC §351. Section 351 applies to those transactions in which one or more shareholders transfer property to a corporation in return for stock, and immediately after the transfer, these same shareholders, in the aggregate, control the corporation to which they transferred the property. When the requirements are met, deferral of gain or loss in a §351 transaction is mandatory. Section 351 applies to transfers of property to both C corporations and S corporations.

Section 351 applies only to those **persons** who transfer property to the corporation in exchange for stock (i.e., shareholders). The IRC defines a person for tax purposes as including individuals, corporations, partnerships, and fiduciaries (estates and trusts).[8] Thus, §351 allows individuals like Al to form a corporation and also allows existing corporations such as General Electric to create a subsidiary. The corporation receiving the property in exchange for its own stock is not subject to tax when it receives property.[9]

Meeting the Section 351 Tax Deferral Requirements

The shareholders transferring property to a corporation must meet several requirements for the transfer to be tax deferred. Some of these requirements are not precisely defined in either the IRC or the regulations. As a result, much of what we understand about the parameters of §351 has developed over time as the IRS and the courts have attempted to discern congressional intent. This incremental approach to understanding the parameters within which §351 operates is prevalent throughout Subchapter C of the Internal Revenue Code.[10]

Section 351 Applies Only to the Transfer of Property to the Corporation
Most assets (tangible and intangible) meet the definition of property for purposes of §351. Property includes money, tangible assets, and intangible assets

[8]§7701(a)(1).
[9]§1032. Note, however, that under GAAP a corporation will record contributed property at fair value for book purposes. Hence, a contribution of property under §351 will give rise to book–tax differences because different amounts of depreciation will be recorded for book and tax purposes.
[10]Subchapter C encompasses IRC §§301–385 and provides the tax rules for the corporate transactions discussed in this chapter. Tax advisers who specialize in structuring corporate transactions often are referred to as "subchapter C experts."

(e.g., company name, patents, customer lists, trademarks, and logos). Services are excluded from the definition of property. Thus, a person who receives stock in return for services generally has compensation equal to the fair market value of the stock received.[11]

Example 19-3

As part of the incorporation, Ginny received 10 percent of the stock in 360 Air valued at $60,000 in exchange for her services in setting up the corporation. Will Ginny defer recognition of the $60,000 "gain" she realizes on the transaction?

Answer: No. Ginny must report compensation income of $60,000 as a result of this exchange because services are not considered property under §351.

What if: Suppose Ginny received 10 percent of the stock in 360 Air valued at $60,000 in exchange for a catchphrase she created to provide the company with a distinctive logo. Assume her tax basis in the catchphrase is zero because she created it. Will Ginny defer recognition of the $60,000 gain she realizes on the transfer of the catchphrase?

Answer: Yes. Ginny defers recognition of the $60,000 gain realized because intangibles are considered property under §351.

The Property Transferred to the Corporation Must Be Exchanged for Stock of the Corporation When property is transferred to a corporation in exchange for stock and other property, only the portion of the transfer exchanged for stock will qualify for tax deferral. The portion of the transfer relating to other property is referred to as **boot.** The term *boot* derives from a trading expression where a party to an exchange might throw in additional property "*to boot*" to equalize the exchange. The receipt of boot will cause the transferor to recognize gain, but not loss, realized on the exchange. We will discuss the details of this computation later in the chapter.

The type of stock a shareholder can receive in a §351 exchange is quite flexible and includes voting or nonvoting, common or preferred stock. Stock for purposes of §351 does not include stock warrants, rights, or options.[12] Property transferred in exchange for debt of the corporation is not eligible for deferral under §351.

Example 19-4

What if: Suppose Ginny received a five-year note (debt) in 360 Air valued at $60,000 in exchange for machinery. The original cost of the machinery was $70,000 and Ginny has depreciated it to a basis of zero. Will Ginny defer recognition of the $60,000 gain she realizes on the transfer of the machinery?

Answer: No. Section 351 provides for deferral only when the transferor of property receives stock in return. Ginny must recognize the entire $60,000 gain.

The Transferor(s) of Property to the Corporation Must Be in Control, in the Aggregate, of the Corporation Immediately after the Transfer Control for purposes of §351 is defined as the ownership of 80 percent or more of the

---

[11]An individual who receives stock subject to "restrictions" (e.g., she remains with the company for a certain number of years) does not report compensation income until the restrictions attached to the stock are lifted (§83) unless she elects to value the stock at the date received and report that amount as income (called a "§83(b) election").

[12]§351 precludes nonqualified preferred stock from qualifying as equity eligible for deferral. Nonqualified preferred stock generally has characteristics that cause it to more resemble debt than equity.

total combined *voting power* of all voting stock that is issued and outstanding, and 80 percent or more of the total number of shares of *each class* of nonvoting stock.[13]

Whether the control test is met is based on the collective ownership of the shareholders transferring property to the corporation immediately after the transfer. It is important to reiterate that this group of shareholders is only composed of those who have transferred property (not services) in exchange for stock and the aggregate ownership (not the change in ownership) of these shareholders immediately after the transfer must meet the 80 percent threshold.

ETHICS

Michelle owns appreciated property and she wants to use this property to start a business with her son, Lance. Michelle is considering making a contribution of the property to a newly organized corporation in exchange for 100 percent of the corporate stock. She then contemplates giving half of the stock to Lance in exchange for his promise to manage the business. Do you think this transaction will qualify for §351 treatment? Suppose that Michelle promises that she won't transfer the stock for a month after making the contribution of property. Any difference? Compare Rev. Rul. 54-96, 1954-1 CB 111 with *Intermountain Lumber Co.*, 65 TC 1025 (1976).

Example 19-5

What if: Assume Ginny was hesitant to join with Jim and Al in the incorporation of 360 Air. After six months, she changed her mind and received a 10 percent interest in 360 Air stock in exchange for intangibles that qualified as property under §351. The stock was valued at $60,000, and Ginny's tax basis in the intangibles was zero. Will Ginny defer recognition of the $60,000 gain she realized on the exchange under §351?

Answer: No. Ginny is the only transferor and does not control (80 percent or more) 360 Air immediately after the transfer. As a result, she must recognize the $60,000 gain.

Example 19-6

What if: Suppose Ginny joined with Jim and Al in the incorporation of 360 Air and received 25 percent of the corporation's stock in exchange for services. The stock was valued at $150,000. Al and Jim received the remaining 75 percent of the stock in the company in exchange for appreciated property. Will Al and Jim defer recognition of gain they realize on the exchange of the appreciated property under §351?

Answer: No. Taking into account only the stock received in exchange for property, Al and Jim do not collectively control 360 Air immediately after the transaction. Al and Jim own only 75%, not 80%. Consequently, the transaction is not eligible for deferral under §351, and all gain realized is recognized.

Generally when a shareholder transfers services and property to the corporation in exchange for stock, that shareholder is considered to be a transferor of property for purposes of the control test. However, if the primary purpose for the shareholder's transfer of property to the corporation is to qualify the exchange of another person under §351, that shareholder would be considered to be a transferor of property only if the value of the stock received for property is not of "relatively small value" compared to the value of the stock received for services.[14] The IRS has stated that for ruling purposes, property will not be of *"relatively small value"* if it equals at least 10 percent of the value of the services provided.[15]

[13]§368(c). Voting power is generally defined as the ability of the shareholders to elect members of the corporation's board of directors.

[14]Reg. §1.351-1(a)(1)(ii). Note that this is a factual issue.

[15]Rev. Proc. 77-37, 1977-2 C.B. 568.

Example 19-7

What if: Let's say Ginny joined with Jim and Al in the incorporation of 360 Air and received 25 percent of the corporation's stock in exchange for services and intangibles treated as property. The stock was valued at $150,000. The services were valued at $125,000 and the intangibles were valued at $25,000. Al and Jim received the remaining 75 percent of the stock in the company in exchange for appreciated property. Will Al and Jim defer recognition of gain they realize on the exchange of the appreciated property under §351?

Answer: Yes. The stock Ginny received in exchange for the intangibles exceeds 10 percent of the value of the services ($25,000/$125,000 = 20%). For purposes of determining control, Ginny will treat all of the stock she received in 360 Air as having been received for property. Al, Jim, and Ginny will be treated as collectively receiving 100 percent of the 360 Air stock in exchange for property. Hence, Al and Jim will defer gain realized on their exchanges of property for stock. Ginny will recognize compensation of $125,000 on the exchange, but she will defer recognizing any gain realized on the transfer of the intangibles.

What if: Assume Ginny's services were valued at $140,000 and the intangibles were valued at $10,000. Will Al and Jim defer recognition of gain they realize on the exchange of the appreciated property under §351?

Answer: No. It appears that the primary purpose for Ginny transferring the intangible property was to qualify the transfer for deferral. The fair market value of the intangibles is less than 10 percent of the fair market value of the services ($10,000/$140,000 = 7.14%). As a result, only the stock Ginny receives in exchange for the intangibles is counted in the control test ($10,000/$150,000 × 25% = 1.67%). Al, Jim, and Ginny are treated as having received collectively only 76.67 percent of 360 Air stock in exchange for property. Consequently, §351 does not apply to any of the transferors of the property to 360 Air.

This same rule applies to subsequent transfers of property by an existing shareholder to "accommodate" a new shareholder's transfer of property to an established corporation. The regulations state that stock received for property that is of "relatively small value" in comparison to the value of the stock already owned will not be considered issued in return for property (i.e., the shareholder making the contribution will not be included in the control test) if the "primary purpose" of the transfer is to qualify the exchanges of another person under §351. The IRS has stated that for ruling purposes, an existing shareholder must contribute property that has a fair market value of at least 10 percent of the value of the stock already owned to be included in the control test.[16]

Example 19-8

What if: Assume Jim and Ginny were 100 percent shareholders of SCR and wanted to bring Al on board as a 20 percent shareholder. Al will transfer appreciated property to SCR in return for stock in SCR valued at $100,000. Will Al defer recognizing any gain realized on the transfer under §351?

Answer: No. Al does not control SCR "immediately after" the exchange, taking into account only the stock he owns in SCR.

What if: Suppose Jim agreed to make an additional property contribution to SCR at the same time as Al's transfer in order to help Al qualify his transfer under §351. Jim's 75 percent ownership interest in SCR was valued at $300,000 at the time of Al's transfer. How much property (fair market value) must Jim contribute to SCR to have his ownership of stock in SCR counted in determining if Al qualifies for deferral under §351?

Answer: $30,000. For this "accommodation transfer" by Jim to be respected by the IRS, he must contribute property with a fair market value of 10 percent or more of the fair market value of his existing stock in SCR (10% × $300,000).

[16]Rev. Proc. 77-37, 1977-2 C.B. 568.

Tax Consequences to Shareholders

The tax basis of stock received in a tax-deferred §351 exchange equals the tax basis of the property transferred less any liability assumed by the corporation.[17] The stock is said to have a **substituted basis** (i.e., the basis of the property transferred is substituted for the basis of the property received).[18] Exhibit 19-4 provides a template for computing the tax basis of stock received in a tax-deferred §351 transaction.

EXHIBIT 19-4   **Computing the Tax Basis of Stock Received in a Tax-Deferred Section 351 Transaction**

	Cash contributed
+	Tax basis of other property contributed
−	Liabilities assumed by the corporation on property contributed
	Tax basis of stock received

Example 19-9

As part of the incorporation of 360 Air, Al transferred inventory, a building, and land to the corporation in return for 50 percent of the corporation's stock (50 shares). The property transferred to the corporation had the following fair market values and adjusted bases:

	FMV	Adjusted Basis
Inventory	$ 25,000	$ 15,000
Building	150,000	60,000
Land	200,000	100,000
Total	$375,000	$175,000

In addition, the corporation assumed a mortgage of $75,000 attached to the building and land. The fair market value of the 360 Air stock Al received in the exchange was $300,000. As we computed in Example 19-1, Al realizes a gain of $200,000 on the transfer, computed as follows:

	Fair market value of 360 Air stock received	$300,000
+	Mortgage assumed by 360 Air	75,000
	Amount realized	$375,000
−	Adjusted tax basis of the property transferred	175,000
	Gain realized	$200,000

Assuming Al meets the requirements under §351 to defer recognizing the $200,000 gain realized, what is his tax basis in the 50 shares of 360 Air stock he receives in the exchange?

Answer: $100,000. Al's tax basis in his stock must reflect the gain he defers in the exchange. He computes his tax basis in his 360 Air stock as follows:

	Adjusted basis of property contributed	$175,000
−	Mortgage assumed by 360 Air	75,000
	Tax basis of 360 Air stock received	$100,000

(continued on page 19-10)

---

[17]§358(a).

[18]§7701(a)(44) uses the term *exchanged basis property* for this type of property.

If Al subsequently sells his 360 Air stock for its fair market value of $300,000, he would recognize a capital gain of $200,000 ($300,000 − $100,000), an amount equal to the gain he deferred previously. In determining whether the gain is long or short term, Al includes the holding periods of capital assets and §1231 property transferred in exchange for the stock.[19]

Example 19-10

What if: Assume Al did not meet the requirements under §351 and was required to recognize the $200,000 gain realized. What is his tax basis in the 50 shares of 360 Air stock he receives in the exchange?

Answer: $300,000. Al's tax basis in his stock equals its fair market value. If Al subsequently sells his 360 Air stock for its fair market value of $300,000, he would not recognize any further gain.

Tax Consequences When a Shareholder Receives Boot

A shareholder who receives property other than stock (boot) recognizes gain (*but not loss*) in an amount not to exceed the *lesser of* (1) gain realized or (2) the fair market value of the boot received. The amount of gain recognized when boot is received in a §351 transaction is determined by allocating the boot received pro rata to each property using the relative fair market values of the properties.[20] The character of gain recognized (capital gain, §1231 gain, ordinary income) is determined by the type of property to which the boot is allocated.

Example 19-11

What if: Suppose Al received 40 shares of 360 Air stock with a fair market value of $315,000 plus $60,000 in return for his transfer of inventory, a building, and land to the corporation. The property transferred to the corporation had the following fair market values and adjusted bases:

	FMV	Adjusted Basis	Gain Realized
Inventory	$ 25,000	$ 15,000	$ 10,000
Building	150,000	60,000	90,000
Land	200,000	100,000	100,000
Total	$375,000	$175,000	$200,000

What amount of gain does Al recognize on his receipt of the $60,000 boot and what is its character (ordinary or §1231)?

Answer: The $60,000 received by Al constitutes boot received and causes him to recognize some or all of the gain realized on the transfer. He apportions the $60,000 to each of the properties transferred to the corporation based on their relative fair market values. Al recognizes gain on each property transferred in an amount equal to the lesser of the gain realized or the fair market

[19]§1223(1).

[20]Rev. Rul. 68-55, 1968-1 C.B. 140 and Rev. Rul. 85-164, 1985-2 C.B. 117.

value of the boot apportioned to the property. The computation is made for each property separately as follows:

	Inventory	
	Fair market value of 360 Air stock and cash received	$ 25,000
–	Less adjusted basis of the inventory transferred	−15,000
	(1) Gain realized	$ 10,000
	(2) Boot apportioned (25/375 × $60,000)	4,000
	Gain recognized: lesser of (1) or (2)	$ 4,000
	Character of gain recognized: ordinary	
	Building	
	Fair market value of 360 Air stock and cash received	$150,000
–	Less adjusted basis of the building transferred	− 60,000
	(1) Gain realized	$ 90,000
	(2) Boot apportioned (150/375 × $60,000)	24,000
	Gain recognized: lesser of (1) or (2)	$ 24,000
	Character of gain recognized: §1231[21]	
	Land	
	Fair market value of 360 Air stock and cash received	$200,000
–	Less adjusted basis of the building transferred	−100,000
	(1) Gain realized	$100,000
	(2) Boot apportioned (200/375 × $60,000)	32,000
	Gain recognized: lesser of (1) or (2)	$ 32,000
	Character of gain recognized: §1231	

Al recognizes total gain of $60,000 on this transfer and defers recognition of $140,000 of the $200,000 gain realized ($200,000 − $60,000).

What if: Let's say the land had an adjusted basis of $250,000. What amount of gain or loss does Al now recognize?

Answer: The $60,000 of boot received by Al still must be apportioned among the assets based on relative fair market values. However, Al cannot recognize any of the realized loss on the land because boot only causes gain realized to be recognized. The recomputation for the land is as follows:

	Land	
	Fair market value of 360 Air stock and cash received	$ 200,000
–	Less adjusted basis of the building transferred	− 250,000
	(1) Loss realized	$ (50,000)
	(2) Boot apportioned (200/375 × $60,000)	32,000
	No loss is recognized	

Al recognizes total gain of $28,000 from receipt of the building and inventory ($24,000 + $4,000). Al defers recognition of $72,000 of gain realized ($6,000 + $66,000) from receipt of the building and inventory and all of the $50,000 loss realized from receipt of the land.

Boot received in a §351 transaction receives a tax basis equal to its fair market value.[22] Al must adjust the tax basis in his 360 Air stock to take into account the boot received and the gain recognized. Exhibit 19-5 provides a template for computing stock basis when boot is received in a §351 transaction.

[21]If Al owned more than 50 percent of 360 Air after the transfer, the gain would be treated as ordinary income under §1239(a). Section 1239 converts §1231 gain to ordinary income if the transferor of the property owns more than 50 percent of the corporation and the property is depreciable in the hands of the transferee. The gain also could be unrecaptured §1250 gain subject to a maximum tax rate of 25 percent.

[22]§358(a)(2).

EXHIBIT 19-5 **Computing the Tax Basis of Stock in a Section 351 Transaction When Boot Is Received**

	Cash contributed
+	Tax basis of other property contributed
+	Gain recognized on the transfer
−	Fair market value of boot received
−	Liabilities assumed by the corporation on property contributed
	Tax basis of stock received

Example 19-12

Return to the original facts in Example 19-11, in which Al received $60,000 and recognized $60,000 gain in the exchange. What is Al's tax basis in his 360 Air stock?

Answer: $175,000. Al computes his tax basis in the 360 Air stock as follows:

	Adjusted basis of property contributed	$175,000
+	Gain recognized on the exchange	60,000
−	Fair market value of boot (cash) received	60,000
	Tax basis of stock received	$175,000

If Al subsequently sells his 360 Air stock for its current fair market value of $315,000, he would recognize a gain of $140,000 ($315,000 − $175,000), an amount equal to the gain he deferred in the exchange.

Assumption of Shareholder Liabilities by the Corporation

When an unincorporated business (e.g., Al's sole proprietorship) is incorporated, the newly created corporation frequently assumes the outstanding liabilities of the business (e.g., accounts payable or mortgages). An important tax issue is whether the assumption of these liabilities by the newly created corporation constitutes boot received by the shareholder transferring the liabilities to the corporation. After all, the shareholder does receive something other than stock in the transaction—that is, relief from debt.

Under the general rule, the corporation's assumption of a shareholder's liability attached to property transferred (e.g., the mortgage attached to the building and land transferred by Al to 360 Air) is *not* treated as boot received by the shareholder.[23] However, there are two important exceptions to this rule.

Tax-Avoidance Transactions If *any* of the liabilities assumed by the corporation are contributed with the purpose of avoiding the federal income tax or if there is no corporate business purpose for the assumption, *all* of the liabilities assumed are treated as boot to the shareholder.[24] The "avoidance" motive may be present where the corporation assumes debt created by the shareholders immediately prior to the contribution of the encumbered assets. This transaction is essentially equivalent to having the corporation pay the shareholder cash in exchange for the property. The "no business purpose" motive can also be present where shareholders have the corporation assume the shareholder's personal liabilities (e.g., grocery bills or alimony).

Liabilities in Excess of Basis Even when liabilities are not treated as boot, the taxpayer is required to recognize gain to the extent the liabilities assumed by the corporation exceed the aggregate tax basis of the properties transferred by the shareholder.[25]

[23]§357(a).

[24]§357(b).

[25]§357(c). A liability assumed by the corporation cannot reduce stock basis below zero.

Lisa is the sole proprietor of a business that manufactures solar panels. This week Lisa was approached to exchange her business assets for shares in Burns Power. As part of the exchange, Lisa is requiring Burns Power to assume the home equity loan on her home. Do you think that Lisa should argue that there is no tax-avoidance motive in this arrangement? Suppose that Lisa established her business five years ago by investing funds from a home equity loan. Any difference?

Example 19-13

What if: Assume Al transferred inventory, a building, and land to 360 Air in return for 50 percent of the corporation's stock (50 shares) with a fair market value of $175,000. The corporation will assume a mortgage of $200,000 attached to the land and building. The properties transferred have fair market values and tax bases as follows:

	FMV	Adjusted Basis
Inventory	$ 25,000	$ 15,000
Building	150,000	60,000
Land	200,000	100,000
Total	$375,000	$175,000

Al realizes a gain of $200,000 on the transfer, computed as follows:

	Fair market value of 360 Air stock received	$175,000
+	Mortgage assumed by 360 Air	200,000
	Amount realized	$375,000
−	Adjusted tax basis of the property transferred	175,000
	Gain realized	$200,000

What amount of gain, if any, does Al recognize on the transfer, assuming all of the other requirements of §351 are met?

Answer: $25,000, the excess of the mortgage assumed by 360 Air ($200,000) over the total tax-adjusted basis of the property Al transferred to the corporation ($175,000). Al defers gain of $175,000.

What is Al's tax basis in the 360 Air stock?

Answer: $0, computed as follows:

	Adjusted basis of property contributed	$175,000
+	Gain recognized on the exchange	25,000
−	Mortgage assumed by 360 Air	200,000
	Tax basis of stock received	$ 0

If Al sold his 360 Air stock for $175,000 (its current fair market value), he would recognize a gain of $175,000 ($175,000 − $0), an amount equal to the gain he deferred in the exchange.

There is a special exception for the assumption of liabilities the payment of which would give rise to a deduction. The assumption of such liabilities is disregarded in determining if the liabilities assumed exceed basis.[26] Examples would be where a corporation assumes the accounts payable of a cash-method sole proprietorship or where a subsidiary assumes "payment liabilities" (e.g., accrued vacation pay) of an accrual-method corporation.

[26]357(c)(3). Note that this exception is not available when the liabilities are used to create basis in assets, such as payables related to the purchase of tools.

Example 19-14

What if: Suppose Al transferred inventory, a building, and land to 360 Air in return for 50 percent of the corporation's stock (50 shares) with a fair market value of $175,000. The corporation will assume cash-method accounts payable of $200,000. The properties transferred have fair market values and tax bases as follows:

	FMV	Adjusted Basis
Inventory	$ 25,000	$ 15,000
Building	150,000	60,000
Land	200,000	100,000
Total	$375,000	$175,000

Al realizes a gain of $200,000 on the transfer, computed as follows:

	Fair market value of 360 Air stock received	$175,000
+	Payables assumed by 360 Air	200,000
	Amount realized	$375,000
−	Adjusted tax basis of the property transferred	175,000
	Gain realized	$200,000

What amount of gain, if any, does Al recognize in the transfer, assuming all of the other requirements of §351 are met?

Answer: $0. Al defers recognition of the entire gain of $200,000. The assumption of the cash-method payables is disregarded in computing whether the liabilities assumed exceed the aggregate tax basis of the property transferred.

What is Al's tax basis in the 360 Air stock?

Answer: $175,000, computed as follows:

	Adjusted basis of property contributed	$175,000
+	Gain recognized on the exchange	0
−	Payables assumed by 360 Air	0
	Tax basis of stock received	$175,000

If Al subsequently sells his 360 Air stock for $175,000 (its current fair market value), he would recognize a gain of $0 ($175,000 − $175,000). This result seems odd at first glance because the gain deferred previously was $200,000. However, by transferring the payables to 360 Air, Al is forgoing a $200,000 deduction that he would have received if he paid off the liabilities while operating as a sole proprietorship. This $200,000 "loss" exactly offsets the $200,000 gain he realized when 360 Air assumed the payables, resulting in a net gain of $0.

Tax Consequences to the Transferee Corporation

The corporation receiving property in exchange for its stock does not recognize gain or loss realized on the transfer.[27] In transactions that do not qualify for §351, the corporation will have a fair market value tax basis in the property. In a §351 transaction the corporation will have a tax basis in the property that equals the property's tax basis in the transferor's hands.[28] The transferred property is said to have a **carryover basis** (i.e., the corporation "carries over" the shareholder's basis and holding period in the transferred property).[29] To the extent the shareholder's tax basis carries over to the

---

[27]§1032.

[28]§362(a).

[29]See §1223(2) and note that §7701(a)(43) refers to this type of property as *transferred basis property*.

corporation and the property is §1231 property or a capital asset, the shareholder's holding period also carries over (it *tacks* to the property).[30] This could be important in determining if subsequent gain or loss recognized on the disposition of the property qualifies as a §1231 gain or loss or a long-term capital gain or loss.

If the shareholder recognizes gain as a result of the property transfer (e.g., because boot is received), the corporation increases its tax basis in the property by the gain recognized. Exhibit 19-6 provides a template for computing the tax basis of property received by the corporation in a §351 transaction.

EXHIBIT 19-6   Computing the Tax Basis of Property Received by the Corporation in a Section 351 Transaction

	Cash contributed by the shareholder
+	Tax basis of other property contributed by the shareholder
+	Gain recognized on the transfer by the shareholder
	Tax basis of property received

Example 19-15

Let's return to the facts in Example 19-11 where Al received 40 shares of 360 Air stock with a fair market value of $315,000 and $60,000 in return for his transfer of inventory, a building, and land to the corporation. The $60,000 received by Al constituted boot received and caused him to recognize gain on the transfer. The $60,000 was allocated to each of the properties transferred to the corporation based on their relative fair market values. Al recognized gain on each property transferred in an amount equal to the lesser of the gain realized or the fair market value of the boot allocated to the property. Al's tax results from this transaction can be summarized as follows:

	Tax Basis	Gain Recognized
Inventory	$ 15,000	$ 4,000
Building	60,000	24,000
Land	100,000	32,000
Total	$175,000	$60,000

What tax basis does 360 Air get in each of the properties it receives from Al in the exchange?

Answer: 360 Air will carry over Al's tax basis in the property transferred and will increase the tax basis by gain recognized by Al on the transfer. The corporation's tax basis in each of the three properties is as follows:

	Tax Basis	Gain Recognized	360 Air Tax Basis
Inventory	$ 15,000	$ 4,000	$ 19,000
Building	60,000	24,000	84,000
Land	100,000	32,000	132,000
Total	$175,000	$60,000	$235,000

360 Air also will carry over Al's holding period in the building and land transferred because they are §1231 assets.

The tax law limits the ability of a shareholder to transfer a "built-in loss" to a corporation in a §351 transaction. In particular, if the *aggregate* adjusted tax basis of property transferred to a corporation by a shareholder in a §351 transfer exceeds the aggregate fair market value of the assets, the aggregate tax basis of the assets in the

[30]§1223(1).

hands of the transferee corporation cannot exceed their aggregate fair market value.[31] The aggregate reduction in tax basis is allocated among the assets transferred in proportion to their respective built-in losses immediately before the transfer. As an alternative, the transferor and transferee can elect to have the transferor reduce her stock basis to fair market value (i.e., the duplicate loss is eliminated at either the corporate or shareholder level).

Example 19-16

What if: Assume Al transferred a building and land to the corporation in return for 50 percent of the corporation's stock (50 shares). The property transferred to the corporation had the following fair market values and adjusted bases:

	FMV	Adjusted Basis
Building	$ 75,000	$100,000
Land	200,000	100,000
Total	$275,000	$200,000

The fair market value of the 360 Air stock Al received in the exchange was $275,000.

Assuming the transfer meets the requirements under §351 to defer recognizing the $75,000 net gain realized, what is Al's tax basis in the 50 shares of 360 Air stock he receives in the exchange?

Answer: $200,000. In this case, the aggregate fair market value of the property transferred to the corporation exceeds the aggregate adjusted basis of the property. As a result, Al's tax basis in the stock he receives equals the aggregate adjusted bases of the property transferred.

What is the adjusted basis of the building and land held by 360 Air?

Answer: The building has a carryover basis of $100,000, and the land has a carryover basis of $100,000. Because the aggregate fair market value of the assets transferred to the corporation exceeds the aggregate adjusted basis of the property, 360 Air applies the general basis carryover rules. The building retains its built-in loss of $25,000 at the corporate level.

Example 19-17

What if: Suppose Al transferred a building and land to the corporation in return for 50 percent of the corporation's stock (50 shares). The property transferred to the corporation had the following fair market values and adjusted bases:

	FMV	Adjusted Basis
Building	$ 75,000	$200,000
Land	200,000	100,000
Total	$275,000	$300,000

The fair market value of the 360 Air stock Al received in the exchange was $275,000.

Assuming the transfer meets the requirements under §351 to defer recognizing the $25,000 net loss realized, what is Al's tax basis in the 50 shares of 360 Air stock he receives in the exchange?

Answer: $300,000. In this case, the aggregate adjusted basis of the property transferred to the corporation exceed the aggregate fair market value of the property. Assuming he doesn't elect to reduce his stock basis to fair market value, Al's tax basis in the stock he receives will equal the adjusted basis of the assets transferred.

---

[31]§362(e)(2).

What is the adjusted basis of the building and land held by 360 Air?

Answer: An aggregate adjusted basis of $275,000. Because the aggregate fair market value of the property transferred to the corporation is less than the aggregate adjusted bases of the property, 360 Air must reduce the aggregate adjusted bases of the property to their aggregate fair market value. The allocation is made to those assets that have a built-in loss; in this example, only the building. The adjusted basis of the building will be reduced to $175,000 ($200,000 − $25,000 net built-in loss). The adjusted basis of the land will retain its carryover basis of $100,000. This adjustment eliminates the net $25,000 built-in loss at the corporate level.

What alternative election can Al and 360 Air make with respect to these basis reduction rules?

Answer: Al and the corporation can jointly elect to have Al reduce his stock basis to its fair market value of $275,000. The corporation would take a carryover basis of $200,000 in the building and a carryover basis of $100,000 in the land.

Other Issues Related to Incorporating an Ongoing Business

Depreciable Assets Transferred to a Corporation   To the extent a property's tax-adjusted basis carries over from the shareholder, the corporation *steps into the shoes* of the shareholder and continues to depreciate the *carryover basis* portion of the property's tax basis using the shareholder's depreciation schedule.[32] Any additional basis (from recognition of gain due to boot received) is treated as a separate asset and is subject to a separate depreciation election (i.e., this one physical asset is treated as two tax assets for depreciation purposes).

Example 19-18

Let's return to the facts in Example 19-15. Recall that Al received 40 shares of 360 Air stock with a fair market value of $315,000 and $60,000 in return for his transfer of inventory, a building, and land to the corporation. The cash received by Al constituted boot received and caused him to recognize $60,000 of gain on the transfer. 360 Air takes Al's tax basis in the property and increases it by the gain recognized by Al on the transfer. The corporation's tax basis in each of the three properties is as follows:

	Tax Basis	Gain Recognized	360 Air Tax Basis
Inventory	$ 15,000	$ 4,000	$ 19,000
Building	60,000	24,000	84,000
Land	100,000	32,000	132,000
Total	$175,000	$60,000	$235,000

360 Air also will carry over Al's holding period in the building and land transferred because they are §1231 assets. How will 360 Air compute the depreciation deduction on the building for the year of the transfer? For this problem, let's assume that the transfer occurs on January 1. Furthermore, let's assume that Al originally purchased the building for $67,400 in September five years ago and has claimed $7,400 of depreciation using straight-line and mid-month conventions over a 39-year recovery period.

(*continued on page 19-18*)

[32] §168(i)(7)(B)(ii).

Answer: 360 Air carries over Al's depreciation schedule for the building with respect to the $60,000 original basis, but 360 Air depreciates the additional $24,000 as a new asset. With respect to the carryover basis portion of the building, 360 Air uses Al's original cost of $67,400 in the building to calculate the depreciation computation. Al is entitled to .5 month of depreciation on the building in the year of transfer ($67,400 × .02564 × .5/12 = $72), and the corporation is entitled to the remaining 11.5 months of depreciation of $1,656 ($67,400 × .02564 × 11.5/12 = $1,656). The corporation treats the additional $24,000 of basis as a new asset and applies the proper depreciation rate to calculate the additional depreciation. Because the transfer took place in January, 360 Air would be entitled to 11.5 months of depreciation (recall the mid-month convention). Hence, 360 Air would claim additional depreciation of $591 ($24,000 × .02461 = $591) for a total depreciation deduction of $2,247. This bifurcated computation often is ignored or overlooked in practice.

Practitioners often advise against transferring appreciated property (especially real estate) into a closely held corporation. By transferring the property into the corporation, the shareholder creates two assets with the same built-in gain as the original property (the stock received in the hands of the shareholder and the building owned by the corporation). The federal government can now collect taxes twice on the same gain; once when the corporation sells the property received and a second time when the shareholder sells the stock. You will notice that Congress is not concerned by a duplication of gain result, only a duplication of loss result. By retaining the property outside the corporation, the shareholder can lease the property to the corporation, thereby reducing the corporation's taxable income through rent deductions. Note, however, that there may be valid state tax reasons to own the property inside a corporation, such as lower property taxes.

Contributions to Capital

A **contribution to capital** is a transfer of property to a corporation by a shareholder or nonshareholder for which no stock or other property is received in return. The corporation receiving the property is not taxed on the receipt of the property.[33] If the property is contributed by a shareholder, the corporation takes a carryover tax basis in the property.[34] If the property is contributed by a nonshareholder (e.g., a city contributes land to induce a corporation to locate its operations there), the corporation's tax basis in the property is zero.[35]

A capital contribution generally is not a taxable event to the shareholder because the shareholder does not receive any additional consideration in return for the transfer. A shareholder making a capital contribution gets to increase the tax basis in her existing stock in an amount equal to the tax basis of the property contributed.

Section 1244 Stock

Stock is generally a capital asset in the hands of the shareholders, and gains or losses from sale or exchange are capital in nature. For individuals, long-term capital gains are taxed at a maximum tax rate of 20 percent. Losses can only offset capital gains plus $3,000 of ordinary income per year. Section 1244 allows a shareholder to treat a *loss* on the sale or exchange of stock that qualifies as §1244 stock as an *ordinary* loss.

[33]§118.

[34]§362(a)(2).

[35]§362(c)(1).

Section 1244 applies only to individual shareholders who are the original recipients of the stock. The maximum amount of loss that can be treated as an ordinary loss under §1244 is $50,000 per year ($100,000 in the case of married, filing jointly shareholders). To qualify for this tax benefit, the corporation from which the stock was received must be a "small business corporation" when the stock was issued. The IRC defines a small business corporation as one in which the aggregate amount of money and other property received in return for the stock or as a contribution to capital did not exceed $1 million. In our storyline, 360 Air would qualify as a small business corporation. There is an additional requirement that for the five taxable years preceding the year in which the stock was sold, the corporation must have derived more than 50 percent of its aggregate gross receipts from an *active* trade or business. 360 Air meets this test as well. Section 1244 provides a tax benefit to entrepreneurs who create a risky start-up company that ultimately fails rather than succeeds.

Example 19-19

What if: Assume Al received 50 shares of 360 Air stock (50 percent of the outstanding stock) with a fair market value of $300,000 in return for his transfer of a building and land to the corporation in a transaction that qualified under §351. As a result of the transfer, Al received a tax basis in the 50 shares of $200,000 ($4,000 per share). Suppose that over time, the snowboarding business declined due to a change in weather patterns in Michigan. As a result, Al's 50 shares were worth $50,000 ($1,000 per share). Needing some cash, Al sold all 50 of his shares to Jim for $50,000 and recognized a $150,000 loss [$50,000 − ($4,000 × 50 shares)]. 360 Air qualifies as a small business corporation under §1244. Al has no capital gains in the year of the sale. How much of the loss can Al deduct if he held his stock at least five years, assuming current tax rules and he is married, filing a joint tax return? What is the character of the loss (capital or ordinary)?

Answer: $103,000, $100,000 of which is ordinary loss and $3,000 of which is capital loss that can reduce up to $3,000 of ordinary income. The remaining $47,000 loss is carried forward as a capital loss.

What tax planning advice would you give Al to maximize the tax treatment of his loss from sale of the stock?

Answer: §1244 imposes an annual limit on the amount of the loss that can be treated as ordinary. To maximize the tax value of his loss, Al should sell enough shares of 360 Air stock to generate a $100,000 loss this year and sell the remaining amount to generate a $50,000 loss next year. In that way, the entire $150,000 loss will be treated as ordinary loss. Of course, delaying the sale of shares is risky because the stock could continue to lose value. Al would need to weigh the tax benefits of the delay against the risk of additional loss.

A special rule applies when §1244 stock is issued by a corporation in exchange for property that, immediately before the exchange, has an adjusted basis (for determining loss) in excess of its fair market value (i.e., a "built-in loss"). If §1244 stock is issued in exchange for such property and the taxpayer has elected not to reduce the stock's basis by the built-in loss, then for purposes of §1244 only, the basis of the stock is reduced by an amount equal to the built-in loss at the time of the exchange. For example, assume a taxpayer transfers property with an adjusted basis of $1,000 and a fair market value of $250 in exchange for 10 shares of §1244 stock in a §351 transaction. The total basis of the stock is $1,000, but, solely for purposes of §1244, the total basis of the stock must be reduced by $750, the excess of the adjusted basis of the property exchanged over its fair market value. The total basis of such stock for purposes of §1244 is $250. If the taxpayer sells her 10 shares for $250, she will recognize a loss of $750, all of which must be treated as a capital loss. If she sells the 10 shares for $200, then $50 of her total loss of $800 will be treated as an ordinary loss under §1244 and the remaining $750 will be a capital loss.

LO 19-3
TAXABLE AND TAX-DEFERRED CORPORATE ACQUISITIONS

Storyline Summary

Spartan Cycle and Repair

Privately held company located in East Lansing, Michigan, that sells and repairs high-end bicycles

Jim Wheeler

Co-owner of Spartan Cycle and Repair (75 percent)

Filing status: Married filing jointly

Dependents: One child

Marginal tax rate: 40 percent

Ginny Gears

Co-owner of Spartan Cycles and Repair (25 percent)

Filing status: Unmarried

Marginal tax rate: 25 percent

Wolverine Cycles and Repair

Privately held company in Ann Arbor, Michigan

Sells and repairs high-end bicycles

Pam Peloton

Owner of Wolverine Cycles and Repair

Filing status: Unmarried

Marginal tax rate: 31 percent

continued from page 19-2...

Jim Wheeler and Ginny Gears were excited about their new business venture with Al Pine. This seemed to solve their need to find a source of revenues during the winter months, when the demand for bicycles declined significantly. With that challenge met, Jim and Ginny turned their attention to expanding their bicycle business to a new geographic region. At the recent Tour de Gaslight race sponsored by the Michigan Bicycle Racing Association, Jim struck up a conversation with Pam Peloton, owner of Wolverine Cycles and Repair (WCR) in Ann Arbor, Michigan. Pam mentioned she was planning to move to Colorado and was looking to sell her business. Jim could see lots of synergies in buying her business. He and Ginny were familiar with the biking community in Ann Arbor, and they understood the economics of operating a business in a college town. Ginny was excited about the possibility of expanding their business to Ann Arbor. Both communities had a large network of bike paths and avid biking clubs.

A meeting was set up with Pam to explore the possible acquisition of her business. Pam operated her business through a C corporation, which gave Jim and Pam the opportunity to consider buying the assets of the business directly or buying Pam's stock in the corporation. If the stock acquisition route is taken, Jim and Ginny need to consider whether they want to operate their new company as a subsidiary of Spartan Cycles and Repair or in a lateral ownership arrangement ("brother-sister" corporations). Operating WCR as a subsidiary of SCR would allow Jim and Ginny to file a consolidated tax return with SCR. Pam is concerned about the tax consequences of each of these options, as are Jim and Ginny. They know they are in over their heads, so a call was made to their faithful tax accountant, Louis Tully, for help in sorting out their options.

to be continued...

At some point in the life of a successful business, the owners likely will consider expanding the scope or geographic locations of their business. Businesses can grow internally through expansion or externally by acquiring an existing business. Jim and Ginny prefer to buy Pam's existing business to expand in a new geographic location. Because Pam operates the business through a C corporation, Jim and Ginny have multiple options. Jim and Ginny first need to consider whether they will personally acquire the stock or assets of WCR or whether SCR will make the acquisition. Second, Jim and Ginny then need to decide whether they should acquire Pam's stock or WCR's assets. Third, Jim and Ginny need to decide what consideration should be used to make the acquisition (e.g., SCR stock or cash). Each of these options can result in different tax consequences to the buyer and the seller. Thus, Jim and Ginny will also need to negotiate the form of the transaction with Pam.

In this section of the chapter, we consider the *basic* ways in which a corporation or its shareholders can acquire the stock or assets of another corporation and the tax consequences that follow the form of the acquisition. This is an extremely complicated and technical area of the tax law. A thorough discussion of all of the variations in which an acquisition can take place likely would take up most or all of a semester. As a result, our discussion is limited to the basic types of corporate acquisitions.

The Acquisition Tax Model

When negotiating an acquisition, management of the acquiring corporation must decide whether to acquire the target corporation's assets or stock and what consideration to use (equity, debt, and/or cash). The *form* of the transaction and the consideration paid will jointly determine the *tax status* of the transaction.[36] Nontax considerations, such as the ease of transferring stock or the existence of contingent liabilities, often dictate the form of an acquisition by a publicly traded corporation. In contrast, privately held corporations are more likely to make tax considerations a priority.

The shareholders of the target company also must decide what consideration to accept in return for their stock or assets in the company. Cash provides liquidity and does not decline in value after the acquisition is announced, but it also causes the transaction to be fully or partially taxable to the seller. Receiving stock in the acquiring corporation may allow shareholders to defer paying tax on gain realized on the exchange, but the sellers must accept the risk that the acquiring corporation's stock will decline in value after the merger is announced or consummated.

The technical tax (and accounting) rules that apply to mergers and acquisitions are extremely complex. Because the statutory language governing reorganizations is sparse, the IRS and courts often must decide whether the *form* of a reorganization transaction meets both the literal language of the statute and the *substance* of the judicial principles that underlie the reorganization provisions. As a result, the reorganization area is heavily laden with administrative and judicial pronouncements. Our goal is to provide you with a basic overview of the most common types of corporate acquisitions that you will see discussed in the business press.

Exhibit 19-7 summarizes the four basic types of transactions that can be used to effect an acquisition of another company. The *buyer* can purchase either stock or assets in a transaction that is either taxable or tax-deferred (in whole or in part) to the seller. Both sides to the transaction must decide which category they desire to be in after the transaction.

> ### THE KEY FACTS
> **Tax Model for Corporate Acquisitions**
> - The acquiring corporation can acquire the target corporation through either a stock or asset acquisition.
> - The acquisition can be structured as either taxable or tax-deferred.
> - Taxable asset acquisitions allow the acquiring corporation to step-up the tax basis of the assets acquired to fair value.
> - In stock acquisitions and tax-deferred asset acquisitions, the tax basis of the target corporation's assets remain at their carryover basis (generally, cost less accumulated depreciation).

EXHIBIT 19-7   Types of Corporate Acquisitions

	Asset Purchase from WCR	Stock Purchase from Pam
Taxable	Any consideration (Cell 1)	Any consideration (Cell 2)
Tax Deferred Reorganization	Type A reorganization using SCR equity (Cell 3)	Type B reorganization using SCR voting equity (Cell 4)

[36]The form of the transaction and the consideration paid to shareholders does not affect the financial accounting treatment of the acquisition—ASC 805-10-25-1 requires that all business combinations be accounted for using the purchase method.

Often the buyer and seller have different tax incentives (i.e., they each want to be in a different cell), which requires both sides to negotiate a compromise arrangement that satisfies both parties. For example, the buyer likely prefers to acquire the target corporation's assets in a taxable transaction (cell 1). By purchasing the target corporation's assets directly, the acquiring corporation gets a "stepped-up" tax basis in the assets equal to fair market value (cost). To the extent the acquiring corporation can allocate the purchase price to depreciable or amortizable assets, this increases future depreciation or amortization deductions on the acquiring corporation's tax return. It is not uncommon in an acquisition involving publicly traded corporations for goodwill to comprise 80 percent to 90 percent of the purchase price. If the acquiring corporation can achieve a tax basis in the goodwill, the basis can be amortized over 15 years.[37] If the acquiring corporation makes the acquisition using a tax-deferred technique, then the tax basis of the acquired assets will not be stepped up to fair value and goodwill will have a zero tax basis. Hence, the acquiring company will be ineligible for increased depreciation deductions, and there is no amortization deduction for goodwill.

The seller likely prefers to sell stock in a tax-deferred transaction (cell 1 or cell 4) because any tax on the appreciation in the stock will be postponed. Alternatively, the seller would prefer to sell the stock in a taxable transaction (cell 2) because any gain on the stock would be taxed at a capital gains tax rate. However, neither of these options provides the acquiring corporation with a stepped-up tax basis in the assets, greatly reducing the future value of the acquisition to the buyer. The seller would likely be reluctant to sell the assets of the corporation in a taxable transaction (cell 1) because the seller would be required to pay both the corporate tax on appreciation of the assets and the individual capital gains tax on the appreciation of the stock. Of course, the buyer might be able to overcome the seller's reluctance by offering a sufficiently high purchase price.

LO 19-4   TAX CONSEQUENCES TO A CORPORATE ACQUISITION

continued from page 19-20...

As part of their negotiations with Pam, Jim and Ginny had their tax accountant, Louis Tully, look over WCR's **tax accounting balance sheet** along with a recent valuation of the assets' fair market values. Pam held the WCR stock for 10 years and her tax basis in the stock is $50,000. WCR is an accrual-method taxpayer, and as a result, the payables have a tax basis. That is, the corporation deducted the expenses related to the payables when the expenses were accrued. These facts are summarized as follows:

	FMV	Adjusted Basis	Appreciation
Cash	$ 10,000	$ 10,000	
Receivables	5,000	5,000	
Inventory	20,000	10,000	$ 10,000
Building	80,000	50,000	30,000
Land	120,000	60,000	60,000
Total	$235,000	$135,000	$100,000
Payables	4,000	4,000	
Mortgage*	31,000	31,000	
Total	$ 35,000	$ 35,000	

*The mortgage was attached to the building and land.

---

[37]§197.

Jim and Ginny agreed to pay Pam $300,000 for her business, an amount that is $100,000 more than the net fair market value of the assets less the liabilities listed on the balance sheet ($235,000 − $35,000). The additional $100,000 reflects an amount to be paid for the company's customer list valued at $25,000, with the remaining $75,000 allocated to goodwill.

With the price settled, Jim, Ginny, and Pam now must agree on the form the transaction will take. Jim and Ginny asked Louis to develop some computations for each of the different ways in which the transaction could take place.

to be continued . . .

Taxable Acquisitions

A corporation can acquire an ongoing business through the purchase of its stock or assets in return for cash, debt, or equity or a combination thereof. Cash purchases of stock are the most common form of acquisition of publicly held corporations. Using cash to acquire another company has several nontax advantages; most notably, the acquiring corporation does not "acquire" the target corporation's shareholders in the transaction and does not increase the denominator in its calculation of earnings per share. There are disadvantages to using cash, particularly if the acquiring corporation incurs additional debt to fund the purchase.

If SCR purchases the assets directly from WCR in return for cash (cell 1), WCR will recognize gain or loss on the sale of each asset individually. WCR may cease to exist as a separate corporation and might completely liquidate by transferring the net after-tax proceeds received from SCR to its shareholder. If WCR liquidates, Pam recognizes gain or loss on the exchange of her WCR stock for the cash received.

Example 19-20

What if: Assume SCR will purchase WCR's assets for $300,000 and assume the company's liabilities of $35,000. WCR will realize $335,000 ($300,000 + $35,000), which it will allocate to each of the assets sold, as follows:

	Allocation	Adjusted Basis	Gain Realized
Cash	$ 10,000	$ 10,000	$ 0
Receivables	5,000	5,000	0
Inventory	20,000	10,000	10,000
Building	80,000	50,000	30,000
Land	120,000	60,000	60,000
Customer list	25,000	0	25,000
Goodwill	75,000	0	75,000
Total	$335,000	$135,000	$200,000

What amount of gain or loss does WCR recognize on the sale of its assets, and what is the character of the gain or loss (ordinary, §1231, or capital)?

(continued on page 19-24)

Answer: WCR recognizes total gain of $200,000, and WCR pays a corporate-level tax of $68,000 (assuming a tax rate of 34 percent). The character of the gain will be as follows:

	Gain Recognized	Character
Inventory	$ 10,000	Ordinary
Building	30,000	Ordinary (§291) and §1231
Land	60,000	§1231
Customer list	25,000	§1231
Goodwill	75,000	§1231
Total	$200,000	

What if: Suppose that WRC opts to go out of existence (liquidate) by exchanging the $232,000 net amount realized after taxes ($300,000 − $68,000) to Pam in return for her WCR stock.

What amount of gain or loss will Pam recognize on the exchange of her WCR stock for the after-tax proceeds from the sale ($232,000)?

Answer: Pam recognizes a long-term capital gain of $182,000 ($232,000 − $50,000 stock basis) and pays a shareholder-level tax of $27,300 ($182,000 × 15% assuming Pam's income is not above the trigger for the 20% capital gains tax rate). The total tax paid using this form of acquisition is $95,300. Pam is left with $204,700 after taxes ($300,000 − $68,000 − $27,300).

Although unattractive to Pam, this deal provides SCR (Jim and Ginny) with the maximum tax benefits. The building will have an increased tax basis of $30,000, which SCR can depreciate over 39 years. The customer list and goodwill will have a tax basis of $25,000 and $75,000, respectively, which SCR can amortize over 15 years on a straight-line basis.[38]

If SCR acquires WCR by acquiring Pam's stock for cash (cell 2), WCR retains its tax and legal identity (unless SCR liquidates WCR into itself or merges it into an existing subsidiary). The tax basis of WCR's assets, which will carry over, will not reflect SCR's tax basis (purchase price) in WCR's stock.

Example 19-21

What if: Suppose instead that SCR purchases the WCR stock from Pam for $300,000. What amount of gain or loss does WCR recognize in this transaction?

Answer: WCR will not recognize gain on this form of acquisition because it has not sold any assets directly to SCR.

What amount and character of gain or loss does Pam recognize in this transaction?

Answer: Pam recognizes long-term capital gain of $250,000 ($300,000 − $50,000 stock basis) and pays a shareholder-level tax of $37,500 ($250,000 × 15%). Pam will be left with $262,500 after taxes ($300,000 − $37,500), which is $57,800 more than a direct asset sale ($262,500 − $204,700).

Although attractive to Pam, this deal will not be as attractive to SCR (Jim and Ginny). The building will retain its carryover tax basis of $50,000, and the customer list and goodwill will have a tax basis of zero. The customer list and goodwill have a zero tax basis to WCR because they are self-created assets. The inside tax bases of WCR's assets remain at $135,000. SCR has an outside tax basis in the WCR stock equal to the purchase price of $300,000.

[38]§197. Note that goodwill is not amortized for financial accounting purposes, and the determination of goodwill for accounting purposes under ASC 805-30-30-1 differs from the determination of goodwill for tax purposes under §1060. Hence, even a taxable acquisition can give rise to a book–tax difference because different amounts of goodwill exist for tax and book purposes.

Tax nirvana would be achieved if Pam can treat the transaction as a stock sale and pay a single level of capital gains tax on the gain recognized from the sale, while SCR can treat the transaction as an asset purchase and receive a step-up in basis of the assets to fair market value. This best of both tax worlds is sometimes available in transactions where a corporate taxpayer purchases 80 percent or more of another corporation's stock within a 12-month period. In such cases, SCR can make a **§338 election** to treat the stock purchase as a *deemed asset purchase*.

As with most things that appear too good to be true, this election does not come without some tax costs. The calculation of these costs is extremely technical and beyond the scope of this text. In big-picture terms, WCR is treated as selling its assets prior to the transaction and then repurchasing them at fair market value. This deemed sale of assets causes WCR to recognize gain on assets that have appreciated in value. SCR, as the buyer, bears this tax cost because the fair market value of WCR will be reduced by the tax paid. In almost all cases, this tax cost negates the tax benefits of getting a step-up in basis in WCR's assets and is rarely ever elected. For example, it rarely makes economic sense to pay income taxes on a $100 gain just to increase the basis of an asset by $100. The additional tax on the $100 gain would very likely outweigh the present value of the savings from an additional $100 of future depreciation deductions. However, this election might be tax-efficient if WCR has net operating losses or net capital losses that can be used to offset gain from the deemed sale of its assets.

If the target corporation is a subsidiary of the seller, the acquiring corporation and seller can make a joint **§338(h)(10) election** and have the seller report the gain from the deemed sale of the target corporation's assets on its tax return in lieu of reporting the actual gain from the sale of the target corporation stock. The technical rules that apply to §338(h)(10) elections are beyond the scope of this text. These elections, which are more common than a regular §338 election, often achieve tax savings to both parties to the transaction. For example, the Wm. Wrigley Jr. Company purchased Life Savers® and Altoids® from Kraft Foods. The buyer and seller made a joint §338(h)(10) election, which allowed Wrigley to record a tax basis for the intangibles and goodwill acquired in the transaction. As you can see from the announcement reproduced below, this provided Wrigley with an estimated $300 million in cash tax benefits from being able to amortize the step-up in basis.

TAXES IN THE REAL WORLD   Wrigley's "Curiously Refreshing" Tax Benefits from Acquiring Altoids

Wm. Wrigley Jr. Company entered into an agreement to purchase certain confectionery assets of Kraft Foods for $1.48 billion. In order to complete this all-cash transaction, the Company announced that it had received a commitment for $1.5 billion in credit. Of the estimated $1.5 billion in borrowing to complete the Kraft transaction, the Company issued approximately $1.35 billion of long-term debt, with the balance to be funded primarily with commercial paper. At December 31, 2005, indefinite-lived intangible assets totaled $368 million consisting of brand names purchased as part of the acquisitions of certain confectionery assets from Kraft Foods. Wrigley was looking for additional diversification in key categories of mints and hard and chewy candy including such brands as Life Savers, Altoids, Creme Savers, and Sugus brands. The goodwill from these brands produced over $19 million of amortization deductions in 2005.

Source: Wrigley 2005 Form 10-K dated February 16, 2006.

Tax-Deferred Acquisitions

As you learned previously in this chapter, the tax law allows taxpayers to organize a corporation in a tax-deferred manner under §351. The tax laws also allow taxpayers to *reorganize* their corporate structure in a tax-deferred manner. For tax purposes, **reorganizations** encompass acquisitions and dispositions of corporate assets (including the stock of subsidiaries) and a corporation's restructuring of its capital structure, place of incorporation, or company name. The IRC provides tax deferral to the corporation(s) involved in the reorganization (the *parties to the reorganization*) and the shareholders if the transaction meets one of seven statutory definitions[39] and satisfies the judicial principles that underlie the reorganization statutes. As before, tax deferral in corporate reorganizations is predicated on the seller receiving a continuing ownership interest in the assets transferred through the receipt of equity in the acquiring corporation.

The statutory language governing corporate reorganizations is rather sparse. It should not be surprising, then, that the IRS and the courts frequently must interpret how changes in the facts related to a transaction's form affect its tax status. The end result has been the development of a complex and confusing legacy of IRS rulings and court decisions that dictate how a reorganization transaction will be taxed. Corporate reorganizations are best left to the tax experts who have devoted much of their professional lives to understanding their intricacies. Our goal is to acquaint you with the basic principles that underlie all corporate reorganizations and provide you with an understanding of the most common forms of corporate acquisitions that are tax-deferred.

Judicial Principles That Underlie All Tax-Deferred Reorganizations

Continuity of Interest (COI) Tax deferral in a reorganization is based on the presumption that the shareholders of the acquired (target) corporation retain a continuing ownership (equity) interest in the target corporation's assets or historic business through ownership of stock in the acquiring corporation. The IRC does not provide a **bright line test** for when **continuity of interest (COI)** is met, although the regulations provide an example that states that COI is satisfied when the shareholders of the target corporation, in the aggregate, receive equity equal to 40 percent or more of the total value of the consideration received.[40] The proposed acquisition of Marvel Entertainment by The Walt Disney Company involved a combination of cash and equity and was designed to be a tax-deferred reorganization. As you can see by the announcement below, the amount of cash was restricted to 60 percent of the total consideration so as to not violate the continuity of interest rules.

TAXES IN THE REAL WORLD Disney to Acquire Marvel Entertainment

In 2009 Disney agreed to exchange stock and cash for Marvel Entertainment. Under the agreement, Marvel shareholders would receive cash of $30 and approximately 0.745 Disney shares for each Marvel share. The ratio of cash and stock was to be adjusted so that the total value of the Disney stock issued would not be less than 40% of the total merger consideration. According to SEC filings, this adjustment was necessary to qualify the transaction as a "reorganization" within the meaning of Section 368(a) of the Internal Revenue Code of 1986.

Continuity of Business Enterprise (COBE) For a transaction to qualify as a tax-deferred reorganization, the acquiring corporation must continue the target corporation's historic business or continue to use a *significant* portion of the target corporation's historic business assets. Whether the historic business assets retained are "significant" is a facts and circumstances test, which adds to the administrative and judicial rulings that are part and parcel of the reorganization landscape.

[39]The "forms" of corporate reorganizations are defined in §368(a)(1).
[40]Reg. §1.368-1T(e)(2)(v), Example 10.

Continuity of business enterprise (COBE) does not apply to the historic business or assets of the acquiring corporation; the acquiring corporation can sell off its assets after the reorganization without violating the COBE requirement.

Business Purpose Test   As early as 1935, the Supreme Court stated that transactions with "no business or corporate purpose" should not receive tax deferral even if they comply with the statutory requirements.[41] To meet the business purpose test, the acquiring corporation must be able to show a significant nontax avoidance purpose for engaging in the transaction.

Type A Asset Acquisitions

Type A reorganizations (cell 3) are statutory **mergers** or **consolidations**.[42] In a merger, either the acquired corporation or the acquiring corporation will cease to exist. For example, SCR could acquire the assets and liabilities of WCR by transferring SCR shares to Pam in exchange for her WCR stock, and WCR would no longer exist. This type of merger is an *upstream* or *forward* acquisition because the acquired company is merged into the acquiring company. Alternatively, the acquired company could be the surviving entity, and this type of acquisition is a *downstream* or *reverse* acquisition. In a consolidation, SCR and WCR will transfer their assets and liabilities to a newly formed corporation in return for stock in the new corporation, after which SCR and WCR will both cease to exist.

In a Type A reorganization, the target corporation shareholders defer recognition of gain or loss realized on the receipt of stock of the acquiring corporation. Similar to a §351 transaction, if a target corporation shareholder receives money or other property (boot) from the acquiring corporation or its acquisition subsidiary, the shareholder recognizes *gain* to the extent of the money and fair market value of other property received (not to exceed the gain realized). The shareholder's tax basis in the stock received is a *substituted basis* of the stock transferred plus any gain recognized less any money and the fair market value of other property received. The target corporation's assets remain at their carryover (historic) tax basis in a Type A merger.

Exhibit 19-8 provides an illustration of a Type A merger. The consideration that can be paid to Pam is very flexible in a Type A merger; the only limitation being that the transaction satisfy the COI requirement (i.e., at least 40 percent of the consideration must be SCR stock). The stock used to satisfy the COI test can be voting or nonvoting, common or preferred.

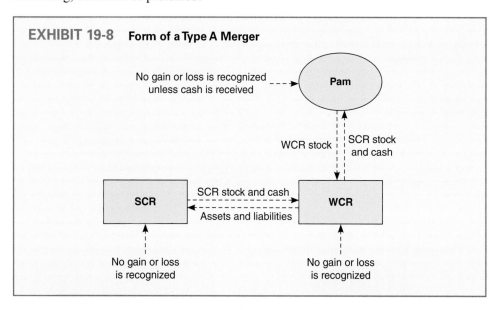

EXHIBIT 19-8   Form of a Type A Merger

No gain or loss is recognized unless cash is received → Pam

WCR stock | SCR stock and cash

SCR ← SCR stock and cash / Assets and liabilities → WCR

No gain or loss is recognized

No gain or loss is recognized

---

[41]*Gregory v. Helvering,* 293 U.S. 465 (1935).

[42]"A reorganizations" are so named because they are described in §368(a)(1)(*A*). Likewise, B and C reorganizations are described in subparagraphs (B) and (C).

Example 19-22

What if: Assume WCR will merge into SCR in a Type A reorganization. Under the terms of the deal, SCR will pay Pam $300,000 in SCR stock, after which WCR will merge into SCR. Pam's tax basis in her WCR stock is $50,000. What amount of gain will Pam realize on the exchange of her WCR stock for SCR stock?

Answer: $250,000 ($300,000 − $50,000)

What amount of gain will Pam recognize on the exchange of her WCR stock for SCR stock?

Answer: $0. Because Pam receives only SCR stock, she defers the entire $250,000 gain realized.

What is Pam's tax basis in her SCR stock?

Answer: $50,000. Because Pam defers the entire gain, her tax basis in the SCR stock is a substituted basis from her WCR stock. This preserves the gain deferred for future recognition if Pam sold her SCR stock in the future for its fair market value of $300,000.

What are SCR's tax bases in the assets it receives from WCR in the merger?

Answer: SCR receives a carryover tax basis in each of the assets received (e.g., the tax basis of the goodwill and customer list will be zero).

Example 19-23

What if: Suppose instead Pam wants some cash as well as SCR stock in the transaction. What is the maximum amount of cash Pam can receive from SCR and not violate the COI rule as illustrated in the regulations?

Answer: $180,000 ($300,000 × 60%). Pam can receive a maximum of 60 percent of the consideration in cash and not violate the COI rule under the regulations.

What if: Assume Pam receives $100,000 plus $200,000 in SCR stock in exchange for all of her WCR stock in a Type A merger. What amount of gain will Pam *realize* on the exchange?

Answer: $250,000 ($300,000 − $50,000)

What amount of gain will Pam *recognize* on the exchange?

Answer: $100,000. Pam must recognize gain in an amount that is the lesser of the gain realized or the boot received. Pam defers recognizing $150,000 gain.

What is Pam's tax basis in her SCR stock?

Answer: $50,000, computed as follows:

	Adjusted basis of WCR stock exchanged	$ 50,000
+	Gain recognized on the exchange	100,000
−	Fair market value of boot (cash) received	100,000
	Tax basis of stock received	$ 50,000

This calculation preserves the gain deferred for future recognition if Pam sold her SCR stock in the future for its fair market value of $200,000 ($200,000 − $50,000 = $150,000).

There are several potential disadvantages to structuring the transaction as a statutory merger. Pam will become a shareholder of SCR, and the historic tax basis of WCR's assets and liabilities will carry over to SCR. Going back to the original set of facts in the above example, Pam will not owe any tax on the transaction but she will not receive any cash. Finally, WCR will cease to exist as a separate corporation. Jim

EXHIBIT 19-9   Form of a Type A Forward Triangular Merger

and Ginny expressed a desire to operate WCR as an independent company. To accomplish this, SCR will have to transfer the WCR assets and liabilities to a newly created subsidiary under §351. SCR will incur the additional cost to retitle the assets a second time and pay any state transfer tax on the transfer of the assets. This latter cost can be avoided by employing a variation of a Type A reorganization called a *forward (upstream) triangular merger.*

Forward Triangular Type A Merger   In a forward triangular merger, SCR creates a subsidiary corporation (called, perhaps, SCR Acquisition Subsidiary) that holds SCR stock. WCR then merges into the subsidiary with Pam receiving the SCR stock in exchange for her WCR stock. When the dust clears, WCR assets and liabilities are isolated in a wholly owned subsidiary of SCR. Exhibit 19-9 provides an illustration of the "fictional" form of a forward triangular Type A merger for determining the tax consequences to the parties to the transaction.

This type of merger is a common vehicle for effecting mergers when the parent corporation stock is publicly traded or the parent corporation is a holding company. For a forward triangular merger to be effective, the transaction must satisfy the requirements to be a straight Type A merger and one additional requirement: SCR's acquisition subsidiary must acquire "substantially all" of WCR's properties in the exchange. The IRS interprets "substantially all" to mean 90 percent of the fair market value of WCR's net properties ($300,000), and 70 percent of the fair market value of WCR's gross properties ($335,000). The technical tax rules that apply to determine the tax basis of WCR's assets after the merger are complex and beyond the scope of this text.

Reverse Triangular Type A Merger   Another variation of a Type A reorganization is the *reverse (downstream) triangular merger.* Suppose that WCR holds valuable assets that cannot be easily transferred to another corporation (perhaps employment contracts or licenses). In this scenario, it would not be prudent to dissolve WCR because these valuable assets would be lost. In a reverse triangular merger, SCR still creates a subsidiary corporation that holds SCR stock. However, it is the acquisition subsidiary that merges into WCR with Pam receiving the SCR stock in exchange for her WCR stock. When the dust clears, WCR is still intact, albeit as a wholly owned subsidiary of SCR. Reverse triangular Type A mergers are desirable because the transaction preserves the target corporation's existence. Exhibit 19-10 provides an illustration of the "fictional" form of a reverse triangular Type A merger for determining the tax consequences to the parties to the transaction.

EXHIBIT 19-10   Form of a Type A Reverse Triangular Merger

There are three additional requirements that must be met to satisfy the requirements for tax deferral in a reverse triangular merger. First, WCR must hold "substantially all" of the properties of both WCR and the SCR Acquisition Subsidiary. Second, Pam must transfer in the exchange an amount of stock in WCR that constitutes control of WCR (80 percent or more of WCR stock). Finally, Pam must receive SCR *voting stock* in return for her WCR stock that constitutes control of WCR in the exchange. For example, if the SCR Acquisition Subsidiary acquires 100 percent of WCR's stock in the exchange, at least 80 percent of the consideration the SCR Acquisition Subsidiary pays Pam must be in the form of SCR voting stock.

This last requirement often presents too difficult a hurdle to overcome in acquisitions in which the acquiring corporation wants to use a combination of cash and stock to acquire the target corporation. Publicly traded companies are very sensitive to the amount of stock they use in an acquisition because of the potential negative effect it can have on the company's earnings per share (i.e., issuing additional stock increases the denominator in the earnings per share computation). The technical tax rules that apply to determine the tax basis of WCR's assets after the merger are complex and beyond the scope of this text.

The Walt Disney Company acquired Pixar in a reverse triangular merger. Disney's acquisition subsidiary merged into Pixar, after which the former shareholders of Pixar received Disney stock in exchange for their Pixar stock.

Type B Stock-for-Stock Reorganizations

Type B reorganizations (cell 2) often are referred to as **stock-for-stock acquisitions.** The requirements to meet a tax-deferred Type B reorganization are very restrictive. In particular, SCR must acquire *control* (80 percent or more ownership) of WCR using *solely* SCR *voting* stock. Additional consideration of as little as $1 can taint the transaction and cause it to be fully taxable to Pam. Not surprisingly, Type B reorganizations are rare among publicly traded companies. Exhibit 19-11 provides an illustration of the form of a Type B merger.

In a Type B reorganization, Pam will defer recognition of any gain or loss realized and take a substituted basis in the SCR stock she receives. SCR takes a *carryover basis* (from Pam) in the WCR stock received. In the case of publicly traded companies, this requires the acquiring corporation to determine the tax basis of each share of stock it receives from thousands or even millions of shareholders of the target corporation. In such cases, the IRS allows the acquiring corporation to determine its stock basis using statistical sampling.

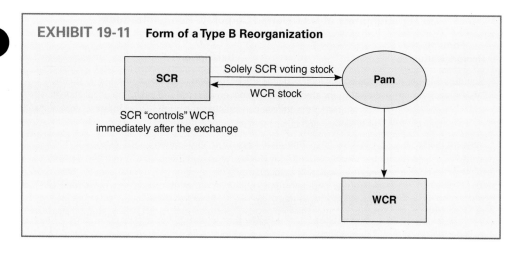

EXHIBIT 19-11   Form of a Type B Reorganization

Solely SCR voting stock

WCR stock

SCR "controls" WCR
immediately after the exchange

Example 19-24

What if: Let's say SCR will exchange SCR voting stock for all of Pam's WCR stock in a Type B stock-for-stock reorganization. Pam's tax basis in her WCR stock is $50,000. The fair market value of the SCR stock is $300,000. What amount of gain will Pam *realize* on the exchange of her WCR stock for SCR stock?

Answer: $250,000 ($300,000 − $50,000)

What amount of gain will Pam *recognize* on the exchange of her WCR stock for SCR stock?

Answer: $0. Because Pam receives only SCR stock, she defers the entire $250,000 gain realized.

What is Pam's tax basis in her SCR stock?

Answer: $50,000. Because Pam defers the entire gain, her tax basis in the SCR stock is a substituted basis from her WCR stock. This preserves the gain deferred for future recognition if Pam sold her SCR stock in the future for its fair market value of $300,000.

What is SCR's tax basis in the WCR stock received in the exchange?

Answer: SCR receives a substituted tax basis equal to Pam's basis in her WCR stock.

What is WCR's tax basis in the assets after the exchange?

Answer: WCR retains a carryover tax basis in each of the assets (e.g., the tax basis of the goodwill and customer list will be zero).

What if: Suppose Pam received $10,000 plus $290,000 of SCR stock in the transaction. How does this change in facts affect Pam's tax consequences?

Answer: The entire realized gain of $250,000 is recognized. For a Type B reorganization to be tax-deferred, Pam cannot receive any cash. Given her desire to move to Colorado, this limitation likely will be a deal breaker.

There are many variations of Type A and Type B acquisitions and other tax-deferred asset-type acquisitions that we do not discuss in this chapter because of complexity. Suffice it to say that tax experts in mergers and acquisitions have a toolbox of ideas and alternatives that allow for a multiplicity of ways to structure a transaction and achieve tax deferral to the parties to the reorganization. For the novice entering this field of taxation, this can be both exhilarating and exasperating. Our goal in this section is to provide you with a glimpse of this intricate area of taxation. A summary of the tax-deferred reorganizations discussed above along with the other forms of tax-deferred reorganizations is provided in Exhibit 19-12.

EXHIBIT 19-12 **Summary of Tax-Deferred Corporate Reorganizations**

Form of Reorganization	Description
Statutory Merger Type A	One corporation acquires the assets and liabilities of another corporation in return for stock or a combination of stock and cash. The acquisition is tax-deferred if the transaction satisfies the continuity of interest, continuity of business, and business purpose requirements.
Forward Triangular Type A	The acquiring corporation uses stock of its *parent* corporation to acquire the target corporation's stock, after which the target corporation merges into the acquiring corporation. To be tax-deferred, the transaction must meet the requirements to be a Type A merger. In addition, the acquiring corporation must use *solely* the stock of its parent corporation and acquire "substantially all" of the target corporation's property in the transaction.
Reverse Triangular Type A	The acquiring corporation uses stock of its parent corporation to acquire the target corporation's stock, after which the acquiring corporation merges into the target corporation (which becomes a subsidiary of the parent corporation). To be tax-deferred, the transaction must satisfy three requirements: (1) the surviving corporation must hold "substantially all" of the properties of both the surviving and the merged corporations; (2) the target shareholders must transfer in the exchange an amount of stock in the target that constitutes control of the target (80 percent or more of the target's stock); and (3) the target shareholders must receive parent corporation voting stock in return.
Type B	The acquiring corporation uses its voting stock (or the voting stock of its parent corporation) to acquire control (80 percent voting power and 80 percent of nonvoting stock) of the target corporation. To be tax-deferred, the target shareholders must receive *solely* voting stock of the acquiring corporation.
Type C	The acquiring corporation uses its voting stock (or voting stock of its parent corporation) to acquire "substantially all" of the target corporation's assets. The end result of a Type C reorganization resembles a Type A reorganization. The major difference between a Type C reorganization and a Type A reorganization is that state law governs the form of the Type A merger, while the Internal Revenue Code governs the form of the Type C reorganization.
Type D	A corporation transfers all or part of its assets to another corporation, and immediately after the transfer the shareholders of the transferor corporation own at least 50 percent of the voting power or value of the transferee corporation (nondivisive Type D). A corporation transfers all or part of its assets to another corporation, and immediately after the transfer the shareholders of the transferor corporation own at least 80 percent of the transferee corporation (divisive Type D).
Type E	Type E reorganizations are often referred to as recapitalizations. Stock in the corporation (e.g., common) is exchanged for a different class of stock (e.g., preferred) or securities (debt). Recapitalizations can range from an amendment in the corporate charter to a change in the redemption price or liquidating value of stock to an actual exchange of stock between the corporation and its shareholder(s).
Type F	Type F reorganizations are described as a "mere change in identity, form, or place of organization" of a single corporation. A corporation uses a Type F reorganization to change its corporate name or its state (country) of incorporation.
Type G	Type G reorganizations are often referred to as bankruptcy reorganizations. In a Type G reorganization, the corporation transfers all or a part of its assets to another corporation in a Title 11 case, and the stock of the corporation receiving the assets is distributed in a transaction that is tax-deferred.

The tax law also allows corporations to divide by transferring stock of a subsidiary to shareholders in a pro rata distribution (spin-off) or a non-pro rata distribution (split-off).[43] The technical details of these transactions are beyond the scope of this text.

COMPLETE LIQUIDATION OF A CORPORATION   `LO 19-5`

continued from page 19-23...
After several years of trying to get 360 Air off the ground, it became clear to Jim, Ginny, and even Al that there was not enough demand for snowboarding products in East Lansing to make their business venture profitable. Reluctantly, the three owners decided to liquidate the corporation. Once again, they summoned their trusty tax adviser, Louis Tully, to help them understand the tax consequences of liquidating the corporation. Louis constructed the company's tax accounting balance sheet, which is reproduced below.

	FMV	Adjusted Basis	Difference
Cash	$138,000	$138,000	
Receivables	2,000	2,000	
Inventory	10,000	12,000	$ (2,000)
Building	150,000	48,000	102,000
Land	200,000	100,000	100,000
Total	$500,000	$300,000	$200,000

The parties agreed that 360 Air would sell off the inventory, land, and building, and collect the remaining receivables. After the sale, 360 Air would pay taxes of $70,000 (assuming a tax rate of 35 percent) on the gains and divide the remaining $430,000 in cash pro rata between the three shareholders (50 percent to Al, 40 percent to Jim, and 10 percent to Ginny). ■

The owners of a corporation may decide at some point to discontinue the corporation's business activities. This decision may be made because the corporation is not profitable, the officers and shareholders wish to change the organizational form of the business (e.g., to a flow-through entity), or the owners want to consolidate operations (e.g., a subsidiary is liquidated into the parent corporation).

A complete liquidation occurs when a corporation acquires all of its stock from all of its shareholders in exchange for "all" of its net assets, after which time the corporation ceases to do business. For tax purposes, a corporation files Form 966 to inform the IRS of its intention to liquidate its tax existence. The form should be filed within 30 days after the owners (board of directors) resolve to liquidate the corporation.

[43]§355.

Tax Consequences to the Shareholders in a Complete Liquidation

The tax consequences to the shareholders in a complete liquidation depend on (1) whether the shareholder is incorporated and (2) what percentage of the corporation the shareholder owns. In general, all *noncorporate* shareholders receiving liquidating distributions have a fully taxable transaction.[44] The shareholders treat the property received as in "full payment in exchange for the stock" transferred. The shareholder computes capital gain or loss by subtracting the stock's tax basis from the money and fair market value of property received in return. If a shareholder assumes the corporation's liabilities on property received as a liquidating distribution, the amount realized in the computation of gain or loss is reduced by the amount of the liabilities assumed. The shareholder's tax basis in the property received equals the property's fair market value.

Example 19-25

Ginny received cash of $43,000 representing her 10 percent ownership in the company after all debts were paid. Ginny's tax basis in the 360 Air stock is $60,000.

What amount of gain or loss will Ginny *realize* on the exchange of her 360 Air stock for 360 Air assets?
Answer: $17,000 capital loss ($43,000 − $60,000).

What amount of loss will Ginny *recognize* on the exchange?
Answer: $17,000. The entire amount could be deductible to the extent of Ginny's capital gains.

Example 19-26

What if: Suppose that rather than sell the land, 360 Air distributed the land with $15,000 cash to Al, representing his 50 percent interest in the net fair market value of the company. Al's tax basis in the 360 Air stock is $100,000.

What amount of gain or loss will Al *realize* on the exchange of his 360 Air stock for 360 Air assets?
Answer: $115,000 capital gain [($200,000 + $15,000) − $100,000].

What amount of gain will Al *recognize* on the exchange?
Answer: $115,000. The entire amount is taxable.

What is Al's tax basis in the cash and land he receives in the liquidation?
Answer: $215,000. Al receives a tax basis in the assets he receives equal to their fair market values.

Example 19-27

As a result of the complete liquidation of 360 Air, Jim received $172,000 cash representing his 40 percent ownership. His tax basis in 360 Air is $240,000, an amount equal to the cash he contributed when the corporation was formed.

---

[44]§331.

What amount of gain or loss will Jim *realize* on the exchange of his 360 Air stock for 360 Air assets?

Answer: $68,000 net capital loss ($172,000 − $240,000).

What amount of loss will Jim *recognize* on the exchange?

Answer: $68,000. The entire amount could be deductible to the extent of Jim's capital gains. Otherwise, Jim can deduct a maximum of $3,000 of net capital loss and carry the unused capital loss forward.

Corporate shareholders are also taxed on liquidating distributions unless the corporation owns 80 percent or more of the stock (voting power and value). Corporate shareholders owning 80 percent or more of the stock of the liquidating corporation do not recognize gain or loss on the receipt of liquidating distributions.[45] This nonrecognition treatment is mandatory. The tax basis in the property transferred carries over to the recipient.[46] This deferral provision allows a group of corporations under common control to reorganize their organizational structure without tax consequences.

Example 19-28

What if: Suppose 360 Air was a 100 percent-owned subsidiary of SCR, and SCR liquidated the company into itself. SCR has a tax basis in its 360 Air stock of $300,000.

What amount of gain or loss will SCR *realize* on the complete liquidation of 360 Air stock for 360 Air assets?

Answer: $200,000 net capital gain ($500,000 − $300,000).

What amount of gain will SCR *recognize* on the exchange?

Answer: $0. The gain is not recognized because SCR owns 80 percent or more of 360 Air.

What is SCR's tax basis in the assets and liabilities it receives in the liquidation?

Answer: 360 Air's tax basis in the assets and liabilities will not change. SCR will inherit a carryover tax basis in 360 Air's assets and liabilities.

> **THE KEY FACTS**
>
> **Tax Consequences of a Complete Liquidation**
>
> - Shareholders other than corporations that own 80 percent or more of the liquidating corporation's stock recognize gain and usually loss in a complete liquidation of the corporation.
> - Corporations that own 80 percent or more of the liquidating corporation's stock (vote and value) do not recognize gain and usually loss in a complete liquidation of the corporation.
> - Shareholders recognizing gain or loss take a tax basis in property received in the complete liquidation equal to its fair market value.
> - Corporate shareholders that defer recognizing gain or loss take a tax basis in property received in the complete liquidation equal to its carryover basis.

Tax Consequences to the Liquidating Corporation in a Complete Liquidation

The tax consequences to the liquidating corporation depend on the tax treatment applied to the shareholder to whom the property was distributed.

Taxable Liquidating Distributions   Typically, a liquidating corporation recognizes all gains and certain losses on taxable distributions of property to shareholders.[47] The liquidating corporation does not recognize *loss* if the property is distributed to a *related party* and either (1) the distribution is non-pro rata, or (2) the asset distributed is *disqualified property*.[48] A *related person* generally is defined as a shareholder

---

[45]§332(a).
[46]§334(b)(1).
[47]§336(a).
[48]§336(d)(1).

who owns more than 50 percent of the stock of the liquidating corporation. *Disqualified property* is property acquired within five years of the date of distribution in a tax-deferred §351 transaction or as a nontaxable contribution to capital.

Example 19-29

360 Air made taxable liquidating distributions to Jim, Ginny, and Al during the current year. Jim owns 50 percent of the stock, Ginny owns 10 percent, and Al owns 40 percent. Assume for purposes of this example that 360 Air made a pro rata distribution of all of the assets to its three shareholders. The company's tax accounting balance sheet at the time of the distribution is reproduced below:

	FMV	Adjusted Basis	Difference
Cash	$138,000	$138,000	
Receivables	2,000	2,000	
Inventory	10,000	12,000	$ (2,000)
Building	150,000	48,000	102,000
Land	200,000	100,000	100,000
Total	$500,000	$300,000	$200,000

What amount of gain or loss does 360 Air recognize as a result of the distribution?

Answer: $200,000. 360 Air recognizes all gains and losses on the distribution of its assets in the following amounts and character:

	Gain (Loss) Recognized	Character
Inventory	$ (2,000)	Ordinary
Building	102,000	Ordinary (§291) and §1231
Land	100,000	§1231
Net gain	$200,000	

Note that the gain or loss on the complete liquidation is identical to gains and losses that would result if 360 Air had sold all of its assets at fair market value.

Example 19-30

What if: Assume Jim owned 60 percent of the stock, and 360 Air distributed all of the inventory to Jim in a non-pro rata distribution. The company's tax accounting balance sheet at the time of the distribution is reproduced below:

	FMV	Adjusted Basis	Difference
Cash	$138,000	$138,000	
Receivables	2,000	2,000	
Inventory	10,000	12,000	$ (2,000)
Building	150,000	48,000	102,000
Land	200,000	100,000	100,000
Total	$500,000	$300,000	$200,000

What amount of gain or loss does 360 Air recognize as a result of the distribution?

Answer: $202,000 gain. 360 Air recognizes all gains but cannot recognize the inventory loss because the distribution is non-pro rata and the loss property is distributed to a related person (Jim owns more than 50 percent of the stock).

	Gain (Loss) Recognized	Character
Inventory	$ 0	
Building	102,000	Ordinary (§291) and §1231
Land	100,000	§1231
Net gain	$202,000	

What if: Assume 360 Air distributed all of the inventory to Ginny in a non-pro rata distribution. What amount of gain or loss does 360 Air recognize as a result of the distribution?

Answer: $200,000. 360 Air can now recognize the $2,000 loss on the distribution of the inventory because the property was not distributed to a related person.

A second loss disallowance rule applies to built-in loss that arises with respect to property acquired in a §351 transaction or as a contribution to capital. A loss on the complete liquidation of such property is not recognized if the property distributed was acquired in a §351 transaction or as a contribution to capital, and a *principal purpose* of the contribution was to recognize a loss by the liquidating corporation.[49] This rule prevents a built-in loss existing at the time of the distribution (basis in excess of fair market value) from being recognized by treating the basis of the property distributed as being its fair market value at the time it was contributed to the corporation. This prohibited tax avoidance purpose is presumed if the property transfer occurs within two years of the liquidation. This presumption can be overcome if the corporation can show that there was a corporate business purpose for contributing the property to the corporation.

This provision is designed as an *anti-stuffing* provision to prevent shareholders from contributing property with built-in losses to a corporation shortly before a liquidation to offset gain property distributed in the liquidation. Earlier in this chapter you learned that Congress added a similar built-in loss disallowance rule that applies to §351 transfers.[50] Under this provision, if the *aggregate* adjusted tax basis of property transferred to a corporation by a shareholder in a §351 transfer exceeds the aggregate fair market value of the assets, the aggregate tax basis of the assets in the hands of the transferee corporation cannot exceed their aggregate fair market value. The loss disallowance rule that relates to liquidating distributions of built-in loss property received in a §351 transaction applies on an asset by asset basis to those assets that retained their built-in loss when contributed to the corporation.

Example 19-31

What if: Suppose Al transferred a building and land to 360 Air in return for 50 percent of the corporation's stock (50 shares) in a transaction that qualified under §351. The property transferred to the corporation had the following fair market values and adjusted bases:

	FMV	Adjusted Basis
Building	$ 75,000	$100,000
Land	200,000	100,000
Total	$275,000	$200,000

(continued on page 19-38)

[49]§336(d)(2).
[50]§362(e)(2).

In this case, the aggregate fair market value of the property transferred to the corporation exceeds the aggregate adjusted basis of the property. As a result, the building will retain its carryover basis of $100,000 and subsequent built-in loss of $25,000.

If the building and land are distributed to Al in complete liquidation of his ownership of 360 Air stock within two years of the §351 transaction, will 360 Air be able to deduct the $25,000 loss on the distribution of the building?

Answer: It depends. Because the liquidating distribution is made within two years of the §351 transaction, the presumption is that Al contributed the property to 360 Air for tax avoidance purposes (i.e., to allow the corporation to deduct the loss). The corporation can rebut this presumption by demonstrating that the contribution of the property by Al had a corporate business purpose at the time of the §351 transaction.

Nontaxable Liquidating Distributions   The liquidating corporation does not recognize gain or loss on tax-free distributions of property to an 80 percent corporate shareholder.[51] If any one of the shareholders receives tax deferral in the liquidation, the liquidating corporation cannot recognize any *loss*, even on distributions to shareholders who receive taxable distributions.[52] There are exceptions to this rule that are beyond the scope of this text.

Example 19-32

What if: Assume 360 Air was a 100 percent-owned subsidiary of SCR, and SCR liquidated the company into itself. SCR has a tax basis in its 360 Air stock of $300,000. The company's tax accounting balance sheet at the time of the distribution is reproduced below:

	FMV	Adjusted Basis	Difference
Cash	$138,000	$138,000	
Receivables	2,000	2,000	
Inventory	10,000	12,000	$ (2,000)
Building	150,000	48,000	102,000
Land	200,000	100,000	100,000
Total	$500,000	$300,000	$200,000

What amount of gain or loss does 360 Air *recognize* as a result of the liquidation?

Answer: $0.   360 Air does not recognize any gain or loss on the liquidation because SCR is not taxed on the liquidating distribution.

What if: Suppose 360 Air was 80 percent owned by SCR and 20 percent owned by Jim. 360 Air distributed the inventory plus $90,000 to Jim in complete liquidation of his stock. Can 360 Air recognize the $2,000 inventory loss?

Answer: No. 360 Air cannot recognize the loss even though Jim is not a related party and has a taxable distribution. When one shareholder is not taxable on a liquidating distribution (SCR), the liquidating corporation cannot recognize any losses on the distribution of property to any shareholder.

Liquidation-related expenses, including the cost of preparing and effectuating a plan of complete liquidation, are deductible by the liquidating corporation on its final Form 1120. Deferred or capitalized expenditures such as organizational expenditures also are deductible on the final tax return.

---

[51]§337(a).

[52]§336(d)(3).

CONCLUSION

In this chapter we discussed some of the important tax rules that apply during the life cycle of a C corporation. As the storyline indicates, forming a corporation generally does not create any tax to any of the parties to the transaction. Gain or loss realized by the shareholders on the transfer of property to the corporation is deferred until a later date, either when the shareholder sells his ownership interest or the corporation liquidates. Subsequent acquisitions of new businesses or dispositions of existing businesses also can be achieved in a tax-deferred manner. However, failure to meet all of the requirements can convert a tax-deferred transaction into a taxable transaction. A complete liquidation of a corporation generally is a fully taxable transaction to the shareholders and the liquidating corporation, except in the case where a subsidiary is liquidated into its parent corporation.

Summary

Review the taxation of property dispositions.   **LO 19-1**

- A person realizes gain or loss as a result of engaging in a transaction, which is defined as an exchange of property rights with another person.
- Gain or loss realized is computed by subtracting the adjusted basis of property transferred in the exchange from the amount realized in the exchange.
- The amount realized is computed as cash received plus the fair market value of other property received plus any liabilities assumed by the transferee on the property transferred, reduced by selling expenses and any liabilities assumed by the transferor on property received in the exchange.
- The general tax rule is that gain or loss realized is recognized (included in the computation of taxable income) unless a specific tax rule exempts the gain or loss from being recognized (permanently) or defers such recognition until a future date.

Compute the tax consequences to the parties to a tax-deferred corporate formation.   **LO 19-2**

- Section 351 applies to transactions in which one or more persons transfer property to a corporation in return for stock, and immediately after the transfer, these same persons control the corporation to which they transferred the property.
- If a transaction meets these requirements, the transferors of property (shareholders) do not recognize (defer) gain or loss realized on the transfer of the property to the corporation.
  - Shareholders contributing property to a corporation in a §351 transaction compute gain or loss realized by subtracting the adjusted basis of the property they contribute to the corporation from the fair market value of the consideration they receive in return (amount realized).
  - Gain, but not loss, is recognized when property other than the corporation's stock (boot) is received in the exchange.
  - Gain is recognized in an amount equal to the *lesser of* the gain realized or the fair market value of boot received.
  - The tax basis of stock received in the exchange equals the tax basis of the property transferred, less any liabilities assumed by the corporation on the property contributed (substituted basis).
  - The shareholder's stock basis is increased by any gain recognized and reduced by the fair market value of any boot received.
- The corporation receiving property for its stock in a §351 exchange does not recognize (excludes) gain or loss realized on the transfer.
  - The tax basis of the property received by the corporation equals the property's tax basis in the transferor's hands (carryover basis).
  - The asset's tax basis is increased by any gain recognized by the shareholder on the transfer of the property to the corporation.

LO 19-3 Identify the different forms of taxable and tax-deferred acquisitions.

- Corporations can be acquired in taxable asset or stock purchases.
- Corporations can be acquired in tax-deferred asset or stock purchases.
- To be tax-deferred, an acquisition must meet certain IRC and judicial requirements to be a reorganization.
  - The judicial requirements, now summarized in the regulations, require continuity of interest, continuity of business enterprise, and business purpose.
- In a Type A tax-deferred acquisition, the target corporation's assets and liabilities are merged into the acquiring corporation (stock-for-assets exchange).
  - Type A acquisitions involving publicly traded corporations often use an acquisition subsidiary (triangular merger) to acquire the target corporation's assets and liabilities.
- In a Type B tax-deferred acquisition, the shareholders of the target corporation exchange their stock for stock of the acquiring corporation (stock-for-stock exchange).
  - Type B acquisitions prohibit the use of cash in the exchange.

LO 19-4 Determine the tax consequences to the parties to a corporate acquisition.

- Shareholders participating in a taxable asset or stock transaction compute gain or loss realized by subtracting the adjusted basis of the stock they surrender to the acquiring corporation from the fair market value of the consideration they receive in the exchange.
- Shareholders participating in a tax-deferred reorganization defer gain and loss realized in the exchange unless cash (boot) is received.
  - Shareholders receiving boot recognize gain, but not loss, in an amount equal to the lesser of the gain realized or the fair market value of the boot received.
- The corporation does not recognize gain on the distribution of its own stock in exchange for property in a reorganization.
- The stock received in return for stock in a tax-deferred reorganization has a tax basis equal to the tax basis of the stock surrendered in the exchange (substituted basis).
- The shareholder's stock basis is increased by any gain recognized and reduced by cash or other boot received.
- The assets transferred to the corporation in a tax-deferred reorganization carry over the tax basis of the shareholders contributing the property (carryover basis).

LO 19-5 Calculate the tax consequences that apply to the parties to a complete liquidation of a corporation.

- Noncorporate shareholders receiving a distribution in complete liquidation of their corporation recognize gain and (usually) loss in the exchange.
- Tax deferral is extended to corporate shareholders owning 80 percent or more of the liquidating corporation.
- The liquidating corporation recognizes gain and (usually) loss on the distribution of property to those shareholders who are taxable on the distribution.
- The liquidating corporation cannot deduct losses on property distributed in the following three situations:
  - The loss property is distributed to a related person and is non-pro rata.
  - The loss property was contributed to the corporation in a §351 transaction and the principle purpose of the contribution was tax avoidance.
  - One of the persons receiving a liquidating distribution was not taxable on the distribution (an 80 percent or more corporate shareholder).
- The liquidating corporation does not recognize gain or loss on the distribution of property to a corporate shareholder that is not taxable on the distribution.
- The tax basis of each asset received by the shareholder in a taxable complete liquidation equals the asset's fair market value on the date of the distribution.
- The tax basis of each asset received by an 80 percent or more corporate shareholder in a tax-deferred complete liquidation carries over from the liquidating corporation.

KEY TERMS

adjusted tax basis (19-3)	continuity of business enterprise (COBE) (19-27)	reorganization (19-26)
amount realized (19-3)		§338 election (19-25)
boot (19-6)	continuity of interest (COI) (19-26)	§338(h)(10) election (19-25)
bright line tests (19-26)	contribution to capital (19-18)	stock-for-stock acquisition (19-30)
carryover basis (19-14)	merger (19-27)	substituted basis (19-9)
consolidation (19-27)	person (19-5)	tax accounting balance sheet (19-22)
	realization (19-2)	

DISCUSSION QUESTIONS

Discussion Questions are available in *Connect*®.

1. Discuss the difference between gain realization and gain recognition in a property transaction. `LO 19-1`

2. What information must a taxpayer gather to determine the *amount realized* in a property transaction? `LO 19-1`

3. Distinguish between exclusion and deferral as it relates to a property transaction. `LO 19-1`

4. Contrast how a taxpayer's tax basis in property received in a property transaction will be affected if the transaction results in gain exclusion versus gain deferral. `LO 19-1`

5. What information must a taxpayer gather to determine the *adjusted basis* of property exchanged in a property transaction? `LO 19-1`

6. Why does Congress allow tax deferral on the formation of a corporation? `LO 19-2`

7. List the key statutory requirements that must be met before a corporate formation is tax-deferred under §351. `LO 19-2`

8. What is the definition of *control* for purposes of §351? Why does Congress require the shareholders to control a corporation to receive tax deferral? `LO 19-2`

9. What is a *substituted basis* as it relates to stock received in exchange for property in a §351 transaction? What is the purpose of attaching a substituted basis to stock received in a §351 transaction? `LO 19-2`

10. Explain whether the receipt of boot by a shareholder in a §351 transaction causes the transaction to be fully taxable. `LO 19-2`

11. Explain whether a corporation's assumption of shareholder liabilities will always constitute boot in a §351 transaction. `LO 19-2`

12. How does the tax treatment differ in cases where liabilities are assumed with a tax avoidance purpose versus where liabilities assumed exceed basis? When would this distinction cause a difference in the tax consequences of the transactions? `LO 19-2`

13. What is a *carryover basis* as it relates to property received by a corporation in a §351 transaction? What is the purpose of attaching a carryover basis to property received in a §351 transaction? `LO 19-2`

14. Under what circumstances does property received by a corporation in a §351 transaction not receive a carryover basis? What is the reason for this rule? `LO 19-2`

15. How does a corporation depreciate an asset received in a §351 transaction in which no gain or loss is recognized by the transferor of the property? `LO 19-2`

16. Are the tax consequences the same whether a shareholder contributes property to a corporation in a §351 transaction or as a capital contribution? Explain. `LO 19-2`

17. Why might a corporation prefer to characterize an instrument as debt rather than equity for tax purposes? Are the holders of the instrument indifferent as to its characterization for tax purposes? `LO 19-2`

18. Under what conditions is it advantageous for a shareholder to hold §1244 stock? Why did Congress bestow these tax benefits on holders of such stock? `LO 19-2`

LO 19-3   19. Why does the acquiring corporation usually prefer to buy the target corporation's assets directly in an acquisition?

LO 19-3   20. Why do the shareholders of the target corporation usually prefer to sell the stock of the target corporation to the acquiring corporation?

LO 19-3   21. What is the congressional purpose for allowing tax deferral on transactions that meet the definition of a corporate reorganization?

LO 19-3   22. Why do publicly traded corporations use a triangular form of Type A reorganization in acquiring other corporations?

LO 19-3   23. What are the key differences in the tax law requirements that apply to forward versus reverse triangular mergers?

LO 19-3   24. What are the key differences in the tax law requirements that apply to a Type A stock-for-assets acquisition versus a Type B stock-for-stock acquisition?

LO 19-4   25. How does the form of a regular §338 election compare and contrast to a §338(h)(10) election?

LO 19-4   26. What tax benefits does the buyer hope to obtain by making a §338 or §338(h)(10) election?

LO 19-4   27. In a stock acquisition, why is there a difference between the *tax basis of assets* held by an acquired corporation and the *tax basis of the shares* held by a corporate acquirer? Why is this difference important?

LO 19-4   28. What is the presumption behind the continuity of ownership interest (COI) requirement in a tax-deferred acquisition? How do the target shareholders determine if COI is met in a Type A reorganization?

LO 19-4   29. W Corporation will acquire all of the assets and liabilities of Z Corporation in a Type A merger, after which W Corporation will sell off all of its assets and liabilities and focus solely on Z Corporation's business. Explain whether the transaction will be taxable because W Corporation fails the *continuity of business enterprise test.*

LO 19-4   30. Compare how a shareholder computes her tax basis in stock received from the acquiring corporation in a straight Type A merger versus a Type B merger.

LO 19-5   31. Explain whether all shareholders receive the same tax treatment in a complete liquidation of a corporation.

LO 19-5   32. Explain whether a corporate shareholder recognizes gains and losses on the receipt of distributions of property from the complete liquidation of a subsidiary corporation.

LO 19-5   33. Under what circumstances does a corporate shareholder receive tax deferral in a complete liquidation?

LO 19-5   34. Under what circumstances will a liquidating corporation be allowed to recognize loss in a non-pro rata distribution?

LO 19-5   35. Compare and contrast the built-in loss duplication rule as it relates to §351 with the built-in loss disallowance rule as it applies to a complete liquidation.

PROBLEMS

Select problems are available in *Connect*®.   ▣ connect

LO 19-2   36. Ramon incorporated his sole proprietorship by transferring inventory, a building, and land to the corporation in return for 100 percent of the corporation's stock. The property transferred to the corporation had the following fair market values and adjusted bases:

	FMV	Adjusted Basis
Inventory	$ 10,000	$ 4,000
Building	50,000	30,000
Land	100,000	50,000
Total	$160,000	$84,000

The fair market value of the corporation's stock received in the exchange equaled the fair market value of the assets transferred to the corporation by Ramon.

a) What amount of gain or loss does Ramon *realize* on the transfer of the property to his corporation?

b) What amount of gain or loss does Ramon *recognize* on the transfer of the property to his corporation?

c) What is Ramon's basis in the stock he receives in his corporation?

37. Carla incorporated her sole proprietorship by transferring inventory, a building, and land to the corporation in return for 100 percent of the corporation's stock. The property transferred to the corporation had the following fair market values and adjusted bases:

`LO 19-2`

 planning

	FMV	Adjusted Basis
Inventory	$ 20,000	$ 10,000
Building	150,000	100,000
Land	250,000	300,000
Total	$420,000	$410,000

The corporation also assumed a mortgage of $120,000 attached to the building and land. The fair market value of the corporation's stock received in the exchange was $300,000.

a) What amount of gain or loss does Carla *realize* on the transfer of the property to the corporation?

b) What amount of gain or loss does Carla *recognize* on the transfer of the property to her corporation?

c) What is Carla's basis in the stock she receives in her corporation?

d) Would you advise Carla to transfer the building and land to the corporation? What tax benefits might she and the corporation receive if she kept the building and land and leased it to the corporation?

38. Ivan incorporated his sole proprietorship by transferring inventory, a building, and land to the corporation in return for 100 percent of the corporation's stock. The property transferred to the corporation had the following fair market values and adjusted bases:

`LO 19-2`

	FMV	Adjusted Basis
Inventory	$ 10,000	$15,000
Building	50,000	40,000
Land	60,000	30,000
Total	$120,000	$85,000

The fair market value of the corporation's stock received in the exchange equaled the fair market value of the assets transferred to the corporation by Ivan. The transaction met the requirements to be tax-deferred under §351.

a) What amount of gain or loss does Ivan *realize* on the transfer of the property to his corporation?

b) What amount of gain or loss does Ivan *recognize* on the transfer of the property to his corporation?

c) What is Ivan's basis in the stock he receives in his corporation?

d) What is the corporation's adjusted basis in each of the assets received in the exchange?

e) Would the stock held by Ivan qualify as §1244 stock? Why would this fact be important if he sold his stock at a loss at some future date?

LO 19-2

39. Zhang incorporated her sole proprietorship by transferring inventory, a building, and land to the corporation in return for 100 percent of the corporation's stock. The property transferred to the corporation had the following fair market values and adjusted bases:

	FMV	Adjusted Basis
Inventory	$ 20,000	$ 10,000
Building	150,000	100,000
Land	230,000	300,000
Total	$400,000	$410,000

The corporation also assumed a mortgage of $100,000 attached to the building and land. The fair market value of the corporation's stock received in the exchange was $300,000. The transaction met the requirements to be tax-deferred under §351.

a) What amount of gain or loss does Zhang *realize* on the transfer of the property to her corporation?

b) What amount of gain or loss does Zhang *recognize* on the transfer of the property to her corporation?

c) What is Zhang's tax basis in the stock she receives in the exchange?

d) What is the corporation's adjusted basis in each of the assets received in the exchange?

Assume the corporation assumed a mortgage of $500,000 attached to the building and land. Assume the fair market value of the building is now $250,000 and the fair market value of the land is $530,000. The fair market value of the stock remains $300,000.

e) How much, if any, gain or loss does Zhang recognize on the exchange assuming the revised facts?

f) What is Zhang's tax basis in the stock she receives in the exchange?

g) What is the corporation's adjusted basis in each of the assets received in the exchange?

LO 19-2

40. Sam and Devon agree to go into business together selling college-licensed clothing. According to the agreement, Sam will contribute inventory valued at $100,000 in return for 80 percent of the stock in the corporation. Sam's tax basis in the inventory is $60,000. Devon will receive 20 percent of the stock in return for providing accounting services to the corporation (these qualified as organizational expenditures). The accounting services are valued at $25,000.

a) What amount of income gain or loss does Sam *realize* on the formation of the corporation? What amount, if any, does he *recognize*?

b) What is Sam's tax basis in the stock he receives in return for his contribution of property to the corporation?

c) What amount of income gain or loss does Devon *realize* on the formation of the corporation? What amount, if any, does he *recognize*?

d) What is Devon's tax basis in the stock he receives in return for his contribution of services to the corporation?

Assume Devon received 25 percent of the stock in the corporation in return for his services.

e) What amount of gain or loss does Sam *recognize* on the formation of the corporation?

f) What is Sam's tax basis in the stock he receives in return for his contribution of property to the corporation?

g) What amount of income, gain, or loss does Devon *recognize* on the formation of the corporation?

h) What is Devon's tax basis in the stock he receives in return for his contribution of services to the corporation?

i) What tax advice could you give Sam and Devon to change the tax consequences?

41. Jekyll and Hyde formed a corporation (Halloween Inc.) on October 31 to develop a drug to address split personalities. Jekyll will contribute a patented formula valued at $200,000 in return for 50 percent of the stock in the corporation. Hyde will contribute an experimental formula worth $120,000 and medical services in exchange for the remaining stock. Jekyll's tax basis in the patented formula is $125,000, whereas Hyde has a basis of $15,000 in his experimental formula.

LO 19-2

tax forms

research

a) Describe the tax consequences of the transaction.

b) Prepare the §351 statement that must be included with the return.

42. Ron and Hermione formed Wizard Corporation on January 2. Ron contributed cash of $200,000 in return for 50 percent of the corporation's stock. Hermione contributed a building and land with the following fair market values and adjusted bases in return for 50 percent of the corporation's stock:

LO 19-2

	FMV	Tax-Adjusted Basis
Building	$ 75,000	$ 20,000
Land	175,000	80,000
Total	$250,000	$100,000

To equalize the exchange, Wizard Corporation paid Hermione $50,000 in addition to her stock.

a) What amount of gain or loss does Ron *realize* on the formation of the corporation? What amount, if any, does he *recognize*?

b) What is Ron's tax basis in the stock he receives in return for his contribution of property to the corporation?

c) What amount of gain or loss does Hermione *realize* on the formation of the corporation? What amount, if any, does she *recognize*?

d) What is Hermione's tax basis in the stock she receives in return for her contribution of property to the corporation?

e) What adjusted basis does Wizard Corporation take in the land and building received from Hermione?

Assume Hermione's adjusted basis in the land was $200,000.

f) What amount of gain or loss does Hermione *realize* on the formation of the corporation? What amount, if any, does she *recognize*?

g) What adjusted basis does Wizard Corporation take in the land and building received from Hermione?

Assume Hermione's adjusted basis in the land was $250,000.

h) What amount of gain or loss does Hermione *realize* on the formation of the corporation? What amount, if any, does she *recognize*?

i) What adjusted basis does Wizard Corporation take in the land and building received from Hermione?

j) What election can Hermione and Wizard Corporation make to allow Wizard Corporation to take a carryover basis in the land?

LO 19-2

planning

43. This year, Jack O. Lantern incurred a $60,000 loss on the worthlessness of his stock in the Creepy Corporation (CC). The stock, which Jack purchased in 2005, met all of the §1244 stock requirements at the time of issue. In December of this year, Jack's wife, Jill, also incurred a $75,000 loss on the sale of Eerie Corporation (EC) stock that she purchased in July 2005 and which also satisfied all of the §1244 stock requirements at the time of issue. Both corporations are operating companies.

a) How much of the losses incurred on the two stock sales can Jack and Jill deduct this year, assuming they do not have capital gains in the current or prior years?

b) Assuming they did not engage in any other property transactions this year, how much of a net capital loss will carry over to next year for Jack and Jill?

c) What would be the tax treatment for the losses if Jack and Jill reported only $60,000 of taxable income this year, excluding the securities transactions?

d) What tax planning suggestions can you offer the Lanterns to increase the tax benefits of these losses?

LO 19-2

44. Breslin Inc. made a capital contribution of investment property to its 100 percent owned subsidiary, Crisler Company. The investment property had a fair market value of $3,000,000 and a tax basis to Breslin of $2,225,000.

a) What are the tax consequences to Breslin Inc. on the contribution of the investment property to Crisler Company?

b) What is the tax basis of the investment property to Crisler Company after the contribution to capital?

LO 19-3

research

45. On February 4, 2013, Verint Systems Inc. acquired Comverse Technology Inc. in a tax-deferred acquisition. The Form 8-K for Comverse (ticker CMVT, cik 803014) describes the transaction and was filed with the SEC on August 13, 2012. You can access the Form 8-K at the SEC's Investor website (http://www.sec.gov/edgar/searchedgar/webusers.htm). Read "Item 1.01, Entry into a Material Definitive Agreement," and determine which form of merger was used to affect the acquisition.

LO 19-3

research

46. On March 1, 2013, Leucadia National Corporation acquired Jefferies Group LLC. in a tax-deferred acquisition. The Form 8-K for Jefferies (ticker JEF, cik 1084580) describes the transaction and was filed with the SEC on November 13, 2012. You can access the Form 8-K at the SEC's Investor Web site (http://www.sec.gov/edgar/searchedgar/webusers.htm). Read "Item 1.01, Entry into a Material Definitive Agreement," and determine which form of merger was used to affect the acquisition.

LO 19-4

47. Amy and Brian were investigating the acquisition of a tax accounting business, Bottom Line Inc. (BLI). As part of their discussions with the sole shareholder of the corporation, Ernesto Young, they examined the company's tax accounting balance sheet. The relevant information is summarized as follows:

	FMV	Adjusted Basis	Appreciation
Cash	$ 10,000	$ 10,000	
Receivables	15,000	15,000	
Building	100,000	50,000	$ 50,000
Land	225,000	75,000	150,000
Total	$350,000	$150,000	$200,000
Payables	$ 18,000	$ 18,000	
Mortgage*	112,000	112,000	
Total	$130,000	$130,000	

*The mortgage is attached to the building and land.

Ernesto was asking for $400,000 for the company. His tax basis in the BLI stock was $100,000. Included in the sales price was an unrecognized customer list valued at $100,000. The unallocated portion of the purchase price ($80,000) will be recorded as goodwill.

a) What amount of gain or loss does BLI recognize if the transaction is structured as a direct asset sale to Amy and Brian? What amount of corporate-level tax does BLI pay as a result of the transaction, assuming a tax rate of 34 percent?

b) What amount of gain or loss does Ernesto recognize if the transaction is structured as a direct asset sale to Amy and Brian and BLI distributes the after-tax proceeds (computed in question a) to Ernesto in liquidation of his stock?

c) What are the tax benefits, if any, to Amy and Brian as a result of structuring the acquisition as a direct asset purchase?

48. Using the same facts in problem 47, assume Ernesto agrees to sell his stock in BLI to Amy and Brian for $400,000.   **LO 19-4**

a) What amount of gain or loss does BLI recognize if the transaction is structured as a stock sale to Amy and Brian? What amount of corporate-level tax does BLI pay as a result of the transaction, assuming a tax rate of 34 percent?

b) What amount of gain or loss does Ernesto recognize if the transaction is structured as a stock sale to Amy and Brian?

c) What are the tax benefits, if any, to Amy and Brian as a result of structuring the acquisition as a stock sale?

49. Rather than purchase BLI directly (as in problems 47 and 48), Amy and Brian will have their corporation, Spartan Tax Services (STS), acquire the business from Ernesto in a tax-deferred Type A merger. Amy and Brian would like Ernesto to continue to run BLI, which he agreed to do if he could obtain an equity interest in STS. As part of the agreement, Amy and Brian propose to pay Ernesto $200,000 plus voting stock in STS worth $200,000. Ernesto will become a 10 percent shareholder in STS after the transaction.   **LO 19-4**

a) Will the continuity of ownership interest (COI) requirements for a straight Type A merger be met? Explain.

b) What amount of gain or loss does BLI recognize if the transaction is structured as a Type A merger? What amount of corporate-level tax does BLI pay as a result of the transaction, assuming a tax rate of 34 percent?

c) What amount of gain or loss does Ernesto recognize if the transaction is structured as a Type A merger?

d) What is Ernesto's tax basis in the STS stock he receives in the exchange?

e) What are the tax bases of the BLI assets held by STS after the merger?

50. Robert and Sylvia propose to have their corporation, Wolverine Universal (WU), acquire another corporation, EMU Inc., in a tax-deferred triangular Type A merger using an acquisition subsidiary of WU. The sole shareholder of EMU, Edie Eagle, will receive $250,000 plus $150,000 of WU voting stock in the transaction.   **LO 19-4**

a) Can the transaction be structured as a forward triangular Type A merger? Explain why or why not.

b) Can the transaction be structured as a reverse triangular Type A merger? Explain why or why not.

51. Robert and Sylvia propose to have their corporation, Wolverine Universal (WU), acquire another corporation, EMU Inc., in a stock-for-stock Type B   **LO 19-4**

acquisition. The sole shareholder of EMU, Edie Eagle, will receive $400,000 of WU voting stock in the transaction. Edie's tax basis in her EMU stock is $100,000.

a) What amount of gain or loss does Edie recognize if the transaction is structured as a stock-for-stock Type B acquisition?

b) What is Edie's tax basis in the WU stock she receives in the exchange?

c) What is the tax basis of the EMU stock held by WU after the exchange?

LO 19-5 52. Shauna and Danielle decided to liquidate their jointly owned corporation, Woodward Fashions Inc. (WFI). After liquidating its remaining inventory and paying off its remaining liabilities, WFI had the following tax accounting balance sheet:

	FMV	Adjusted Basis	Appreciation
Cash	$200,000	$200,000	
Building	50,000	10,000	$ 40,000
Land	150,000	90,000	60,000
Total	$400,000	$300,000	$100,000

Under the terms of the agreement, Shauna will receive the $200,000 cash in exchange for her 50 percent interest in WFI. Shauna's tax basis in her WFI stock is $50,000. Danielle will receive the building and land in exchange for her 50 percent interest in WFI. Danielle's tax basis in her WFI stock is $100,000. Assume for purposes of this problem that the cash available to distribute to the shareholders has been reduced by any tax paid by the corporation on gain recognized as a result of the liquidation.

a) What amount of gain or loss does WFI recognize in the complete liquidation?

b) What amount of gain or loss does Shauna recognize in the complete liquidation?

c) What amount of gain or loss does Danielle recognize in the complete liquidation?

d) What is Danielle's tax basis in the building and land after the complete liquidation?

LO 19-5 53. Tiffany and Carlos decided to liquidate their jointly owned corporation, Royal Oak Furniture (ROF). After liquidating its remaining inventory and paying off its remaining liabilities, ROF had the following tax accounting balance sheet:

	FMV	Adjusted Basis	Appreciation (Depreciation)
Cash	$200,000	$200,000	
Building	50,000	10,000	$ 40,000
Land	150,000	200,000	(50,000)
Total	$400,000	$410,000	$(10,000)

Under the terms of the agreement, Tiffany will receive the $200,000 cash in exchange for her 50 percent interest in ROF. Tiffany's tax basis in her ROF stock is $50,000. Carlos will receive the building and land in exchange for his 50 percent interest in ROF. His tax basis in the ROF stock is $100,000. Assume for purposes of this problem that the cash available to distribute to the shareholders has been reduced by any tax paid by the corporation on gain recognized as a result of the liquidation.

a) What amount of gain or loss does ROF recognize in the complete liquidation?

b) What amount of gain or loss does Tiffany recognize in the complete liquidation?

c) What amount of gain or loss does Carlos recognize in the complete liquidation?

d) What is Carlos's tax basis in the building and land after the complete liquidation?

Assume Tiffany owns 40 percent of the ROF stock and Carlos owns 60 percent. Tiffany will receive $160,000 in the liquidation and Carlos will receive the land and building plus $40,000.

e) What amount of gain or loss does ROF recognize in the complete liquidation?

f) What amount of gain or loss does Tiffany recognize in the complete liquidation?

g) What amount of gain or loss does Carlos recognize in the complete liquidation?

h) What is Carlos's tax basis in the building and land after the complete liquidation?

54. Jefferson Millinery Inc. (JMI) decided to liquidate its wholly owned subsidiary, 8 Miles High Inc. (8MH). 8MH had the following tax accounting balance sheet: `LO 19-5`

	FMV	Adjusted Basis	Appreciation
Cash	$200,000	$200,000	
Building	50,000	10,000	$ 40,000
Land	150,000	90,000	60,000
Total	$400,000	$300,000	$100,000

a) What amount of gain or loss does 8MH recognize in the complete liquidation?

b) What amount of gain or loss does JMI recognize in the complete liquidation?

c) What is JMI's tax basis in the building and land after the complete liquidation?

55. Jones Mills Inc. (JMI) decided to liquidate its wholly owned subsidiary, Most Help, Inc. (MH). MH had the following tax accounting balance sheet: `LO 19-5`

	FMV	Adjusted Basis	Appreciation
Cash	$200,000	$200,000	
Building	50,000	10,000	40,000
Land	150,000	200,000	(50,000)
Total	$400,000	$410,000	$(10,000)

a) What amount of gain or loss does MH recognize in the complete liquidation?

b) What amount of gain or loss does JMI recognize in the complete liquidation?

c) What is JMI's tax basis in the building and land after the complete liquidation?

COMPREHENSIVE PROBLEMS

Select problems are available in *Connect*®.   connect

56. Several years ago, your client, Brooks Robinson, started an office cleaning service. His business was very successful, owing much to his legacy as the greatest defensive third baseman in major league history and his nickname, "The Human Vacuum Cleaner." Brooks operated his business as a sole proprietorship and used the cash method of accounting. Brooks was advised by his attorney that it is too risky to operate his business as a sole proprietorship and that he should incorporate to limit his liability. Brooks has come to you for advice on the tax implications of incorporation. His balance sheet is presented below. Under the terms of the incorporation, Brooks would transfer the assets to the corporation in return for 100 percent of the company's common stock. The corporation would also assume the company's liabilities (payables and mortgage).

Balance Sheet		
	Adjusted Basis	**FMV**
Assets		
Accounts receivable	$ 0	$ 5,000
Cleaning equipment (net)	25,000	20,000
Building	50,000	75,000
Land	25,000	50,000
Total assets	$100,000	$150,000
Liabilities		
Accounts payable	$ 0	$ 10,000
Salaries payable	0	5,000
Mortgage on land and building	35,000	35,000
Total liabilities	$ 35,000	$ 50,000

a) How much gain or loss does Brooks *realize* on the transfer of each asset to the corporation?

b) How much, if any, gain or loss (on a per asset basis) does Brooks *recognize*?

c) How much gain or loss, if any, must the corporation recognize on the receipt of the assets of the sole proprietorship in exchange for the corporation's stock?

d) What tax basis does Brooks have in the corporation's stock?

e) What is the corporation's tax basis in each asset it receives from Brooks?

f) How would you answer the question in part (b) if Brooks had taken back a 10-year note worth $25,000 plus stock worth $75,000 plus the liability assumption?

g) Will Brooks be able to transfer the accounts receivable to the corporation and have the corporation recognize the income when the receivable is collected?

h) Brooks was depreciating the equipment (200 percent declining balance) and building (straight-line) using MACRS when it was held inside the proprietorship. How will the corporation depreciate the equipment and building? Assume Brooks owned the equipment for four years (seven-year property) and the building for six years.

i) Will the corporation be able to deduct the liabilities when paid? Will it matter which accounting method (cash or accrual) the corporation uses?

j) Would you advise Brooks to transfer the land and building to the corporation? What other tax strategy might you suggest to Brooks with respect to the realty?

57. Your client, Midwest Products Inc. (MPI), is a closely held, calendar-year, accrual-method corporation located in Fowlerville, Michigan. MPI has two operating divisions. One division manufactures lawn and garden furniture and decorative objects (furniture division), while the other division manufactures garden tools and hardware (tool division). MPI's single class of voting common stock is owned as follows:

	Shares	Adjusted Basis	FMV
Iris Green	300	$2,000,000	$3,000,000
Rose Ruby	100	1,200,000	1,000,000
Lily White	100	800,000	1,000,000
Totals	500	$4,000,000	$5,000,000

The three shareholders are unrelated.

Outdoor Living Company (OLC), a publicly held, calendar-year corporation doing business in several midwestern states, has approached MPI about acquiring its furniture division. OLC has no interest in acquiring the tool division, however. OLC's management has several strong business reasons for the acquisition, the most important of which is to expand the company's market into Michigan. Iris, Rose, and Lily are amenable to the acquisition provided it can be accomplished in a tax-deferred manner.

OLC has proposed the following transaction for acquiring MPI's furniture division. On April 30 of this year, OLC will create a 100 percent-owned subsidiary, OLC Acquisition Inc. (OLC-A). OLC will transfer to the subsidiary 60,000 shares of OLC voting common stock and $2,000,000. The current fair market value of the OLC voting stock is $50 per share ($3,000,000 in total). Each of the three MPI shareholders will receive a pro rata amount of OLC stock and cash.

As part of the agreement, MPI will sell the tool division before the acquisition, after which MPI will merge into OLC-A under Michigan and Ohio state laws (a forward triangular Type A merger). Pursuant to the merger agreement, OLC-A will acquire all of MPI's assets, including 100 percent of the cash received from the sale of the tool division ($2,000,000), and will assume all of MPI's liabilities. The cash from the sale of the tool division will be used to modernize and upgrade much of the furniture division's production facilities. OLC's management is convinced that the cash infusion, coupled with new management, will make MPI's furniture business profitable. OLC management has no plans to liquidate OLC-A into OLC at any time subsequent to the merger. After the merger, OLC-A will be renamed Michigan Garden Furniture Inc.

a) Determine whether the proposed transaction meets the requirements to qualify as a tax-deferred forward triangular Type A merger. Consult Rev. Rul. 88-48 and Rev. Rul. 2001-25 in thinking about the premerger sale of the tool division assets.

b) Could the proposed transaction qualify as a reverse triangular Type A merger if OLC-A merged into MPI? If not, how would the transaction have to be restructured to meet the requirements to be a reverse triangular merger?

58. Rex and Felix are the sole shareholders of the Dogs and Cats Corporation (DCC). After several years of operations, they decided to liquidate the corporation and operate the business as a partnership. Rex and Felix hired a lawyer to draw up the legal papers to dissolve the corporation, but they need some tax advice from you, their trusted accountant. They are hoping you will find a way for them to liquidate the corporation without incurring any corporate-level tax liability.

The DCC's tax accounting balance sheet at the date of liquidation is as follows:

	Adjusted Basis	FMV
Assets		
Cash	$ 30,000	$ 30,000
Accounts receivable	10,000	10,000
Inventory	10,000	20,000
Equipment	30,000	20,000
Building	15,000	30,000
Land	5,000	40,000
Total assets	$100,000	$150,000
Liabilities		
Accounts payable		$ 5,000
Mortgage payable—Building		10,000
Mortgage payable—Land		10,000
Total liabilities		$ 25,000
Shareholders' Equity		
Common stock—Rex (80%)	$ 60,000	$100,000
Common stock—Felix (20%)	30,000	25,000
Total shareholders' equity	$ 90,000	$125,000

a) Compute the gain or loss recognized by Rex, Felix, and DCC on a complete liquidation of the corporation assuming each shareholder receives a pro rata distribution of the corporation's assets and assumes a pro rata amount of the liabilities.

b) Compute the gain or loss recognized by Rex, Felix, and DCC on a complete liquidation of the corporation assuming Felix receives $25,000 in cash and Rex receives the remainder of the assets and assumes all of the liabilities.

Assume Felix received the accounts receivable and equipment and assumed the accounts payable.

c) Will Felix recognize any income when he collects the accounts receivable?

d) Will Felix be able to take a deduction when he pays the accounts payable?

Assume Rex is a corporate shareholder of DCC.

e) Compute the gain or loss recognized by Rex, Felix, and DCC on a complete liquidation of the corporation assuming each shareholder receives a pro rata distribution of the corporation's assets and assumes a pro rata amount of the liabilities.

f) Compute the gain or loss recognized by Rex, Felix, and DCC on a complete liquidation of the corporation assuming Felix receives $25,000 in cash and Rex receives the remainder of the assets and assumes all of the liabilities.

Assume the equipment was contributed by Rex to DCC in a §351 transaction two months prior to the liquidation. At the time of the contribution, the property's fair market value was $25,000.

g) Would the tax result change if the property was contributed one year ago? Two years ago? Three years ago?

tax forms

research

59. Cartman Corporation owns 90 shares of SP Corporation. The remaining 10 shares are owned by Kenny (an individual). After several years of operations, Cartman decided to liquidate SP Corporation by distributing the assets to Cartman and Kenny. SP reported the following balance sheet at the date of liquidation:

	Adjusted Basis	FMV
Cash	$12,000	$ 12,000
Accounts receivable	8,000	8,000
Stock investment	2,000	10,000
Land	40,000	70,000
Total assets	$62,000	$100,000
Common stock—Cartman (90%)	$10,000	$ 90,000
Common stock—Kenny (10%)	7,000	10,000
Total shareholder equity	$17,000	$100,000

a) Compute the gain or loss recognized by SP, Cartman, and Kenny on a complete liquidation of the corporation, where SP distributes $10,000 of cash to Kenny and the remaining assets to Cartman.

b) Compute the gain or loss recognized by SP and Kenny on a complete liquidation of the corporation, where SP distributes the stock investment to Kenny and the remaining assets to Cartman. Assume that SP's tax rate is zero.

c) What form needs to be filed with the liquidation of SP?

chapter
20 Forming and Operating Partnerships

Learning Objectives

Upon completing this chapter, you should be able to:

LO 20-1 Determine whether a flow-through entity is taxed as a partnership or S corporation, and distinguish the entity approach from the aggregate approach for taxing partnerships.

LO 20-2 Resolve tax issues applicable to partnership formations and other acquisitions of partnership interests, including gain recognition to partners and tax basis for partners and partnerships.

LO 20-3 Determine the appropriate accounting periods and methods for partnerships.

LO 20-4 Calculate and characterize a partnership's ordinary business income or loss and its separately stated items, and demonstrate how to report these items to partners.

LO 20-5 Explain the importance of a partner's tax basis and the adjustments that affect it.

LO 20-6 Apply the basis, at-risk, and passive activity loss limits to losses from partnerships.

© PhotoAlto

In Chapter 15, we introduced you to Nicole Johnson, who decided to turn her sheet-making hobby into a full-time business called Color Comfort Sheets (CCS). Early in 2015, after deciding to organize her new enterprise as a limited liability company (LLC), she turned her attention to raising capital for the business from other investors and a bank loan. Although Nicole's limited savings would clearly not be enough to get CCS started, she was willing to contribute a parcel of land in the industrial section of town that she had inherited five years ago from her grandfather. Her friend and mentor, Sarah Walker, offered to contribute both her time and money to help CCS get off the ground.

With Sarah on board, things seemed to be coming together nicely for Nicole. However, the amount her bank was willing to loan was not enough to fully capitalize CCS, and Nicole and Sarah were unable to invest any more cash into the business to make up the shortfall. Hoping to obtain the additional funding they needed, Nicole and Sarah visited Chance Armstrong, a successful local sports-team owner who had a reputation for being willing to take a chance on new ventures. After listening to Nicole and Sarah's proposal, Chance

Storyline Summary

Nicole Johnson

Location:	Salt Lake City, Utah
Status:	Managing member of Color Comfort Sheets LLC
Filing status:	Married to Tom Johnson
Marginal tax rate:	35 percent unless otherwise stated

Sarah Walker

Location:	Salt Lake City, Utah
Status:	Managing member of Color Comfort Sheets LLC
Filing status:	Married to Blaine Walker
Marginal tax rate:	28 percent unless otherwise stated

Chanzz Inc.

Location:	Salt Lake City, Utah
Business:	Managing sports franchises
Status:	Nonmanaging member of Color Comfort Sheets LLC
Filing status:	C Corporation with a June 30 year-end
Marginal tax rate:	35 percent

agreed to invest the additional cash needed to fully fund CCS. Rather than use his personal funds, however, Chance planned to have his closely held corporation, Chanzz Inc., invest in CCS. Unlike Nicole and Sarah, who would take an active role in managing CCS, Chanzz Inc., with everyone's agreement, would not play a part in running the company. By the end of March, CCS had cash, land on which to build its manufacturing facility and offices, and owners who were excited and willing to work hard to make it a successful company.

to be continued . . .

In this chapter, we review the options for operating a business with multiple owners as a **flow-through entity.** In addition, we explain the basic tax consequences of forming and operating business entities taxed as partnerships by examining the specific tax consequences of forming and operating Color Comfort Sheets as a limited liability company (LLC).

LO 20-1 FLOW-THROUGH ENTITIES OVERVIEW

Income earned by flow-through entities is usually not taxed at the entity level. Instead, the *owners* of flow-through entities are taxed on the share of entity-level income allocated to them. Thus, unlike income earned by **C corporations,** income from flow-though entities is taxed only once—when it "flows through" to owners of these entities.[1]

Flow-through entities with multiple owners are governed by two somewhat different sets of rules in our tax system.[2] Unincorporated business entities such as **general partnerships, limited partnerships,** and **limited liability companies (LLC)** are generally treated as partnerships under the rules provided in **Subchapter K** of the Internal Revenue Code.[3] In contrast, corporations whose owners elect to treat them as flow-through entities are classified as such under the rules in **Subchapter S.** These corporations are called **S corporations.** See Chapter 15 for further detail regarding the tax treatment of different entity types.

There are many similarities and a few important differences between the tax rules for partnerships and S corporations. Our focus in this chapter and the next is on the tax rules for partnerships. Then, in Chapter 22, we turn our attention to the tax treatment of S corporations and their shareholders.

TAXES IN THE REAL WORLD   **Hedge Funds**

One can scarcely read the financial press these days without encountering some reference to hedge funds. Hedge funds are private investment funds that have grown in popularity in recent years to the point where they were estimated to have $1.5 trillion in assets under management at the beginning of 2009.[4] According to a study by the Joint Committee on Taxation, most hedge funds are organized as partnerships and their investors are taxed as limited partners.[5]

Aggregate and Entity Concepts

When Congress adopted Subchapter K in 1954, it had to decide whether to follow an **entity approach** and treat tax partnerships as entities separate from their partners, or to apply an **aggregate approach** and treat partnerships simply as an aggregation of the partners' separate interests in the assets and liabilities of the partnership. In the end, Congress decided to apply both concepts in formulating partnership tax law. For instance, one of the most basic tenets of partnership tax law—that partnerships don't pay taxes—reflects the aggregate approach. However, Congress also adopted

---

[1]The "check the box" rules determine how various legal entities should be classified for tax purposes. See the discussion in Chapter 15 for a more detailed explanation of these rules.

[2]Unincorporated entities with one individual owner are taxed as *sole proprietorships.* The tax rules relevant to sole proprietorships are discussed in Chapter 9. In addition to sole proprietorships, other specialized forms of flow-through entities such as real estate investment trusts and regulated investment companies are authorized by the Code. A discussion of these entities is beyond the scope of this chapter.

[3]Publicly traded partnerships may be taxed as corporations. The tax treatment of publicly traded partnerships is more fully developed in Chapter 15.

[4]*"Hedge Funds 2009,"* International Financial Services London (www.ifsl.org.uk), July 4, 2009.

[5]*"Present Law and Analysis Relating to Tax Treatment of Partnership Carried Interests and Related Issues, Part I"* (JCX-62-07), September 4, 2007.

other partnership tax rules that fall more squarely on the side of the entity approach. For example, the requirement that partnerships, rather than partners, make most tax elections represents the entity concept. Throughout this chapter and the following chapter, we highlight examples where one or the other basic approaches underlies a specific partnership tax rule.

PARTNERSHIP FORMATIONS AND ACQUISITIONS OF PARTNERSHIP INTERESTS

LO 20-2

Acquiring Partnership Interests When Partnerships Are Formed

When a partnership is formed, and afterwards, partners may transfer cash, other tangible or intangible property, and services to it in exchange for an equity interest called a **partnership interest.** Partnership interests represent the bundle of economic rights granted to partners under the partnership agreement (or operating agreement for an LLC).[6] These rights include the right to receive a share of the partnership net assets if the partnership were to liquidate, called a **capital interest,** and the right or obligation to receive a share of *future* profits *or future* losses, called a **profits interest.**[7] It is quite common for partners contributing property to receive both capital and profits interests in the exchange. Partners who contribute services instead of property frequently receive only profits interests. The distinction between capital and profits interests is important because the tax rules for partnerships are sometimes applied to them differently.

Contributions of Property   Partnership formations are similar to other tax-deferred transactions such as like-kind exchanges and corporate formations, because realized gains and losses from the exchange of contributed property for partnership interests are either fully or partially deferred for tax purposes depending on the specifics of the transaction. The rationale for permitting taxpayers to defer realized gains or losses on property contributed to partnerships is identical to the rationale for permitting tax deferral when corporations are formed.[8] From a practical perspective, the tax rules in this area allow entrepreneurs to organize their businesses without having to pay taxes. In addition, these rules follow the aggregate theory of partnership taxation because they recognize that partners contributing property to a partnership still own the contributed property, albeit a smaller percentage, since other partners will also indirectly own the contributed property through their partnership interests.

Gain and loss recognition.   As a general rule, neither partnerships nor partners recognize gain or loss when they contribute property to partnerships.[9] This applies to property contributions when a partnership is initially formed and to subsequent property contributions. In this context, the term *property* is defined broadly to include a wide variety of both tangible and intangible assets but not services. The general rule facilitates contributions of property with **built-in gains** (fair market value is greater than tax basis) but discourages contributions of property with **built-in losses** (fair market value is less than tax basis). In fact, partners holding property with built-in losses are usually better off selling the property, recognizing the related tax loss, and contributing the cash from the sale to the partnership so it can acquire property elsewhere.

---

[6]The partnership books reflect partners' shares of the partnership's net assets in their individual capital accounts.

[7]An interest in the future profits or losses of a partnership is customarily referred to as a profits interest rather than a profits/loss interest.

[8]Chapter 19 discusses the tax rules related to corporate formations.

[9]§721.

THE KEY FACTS

Property Contributions

- Partners don't generally recognize gain or loss when they contribute property to partnerships.
- Initial tax basis for partners contributing property = basis of contributed property – debt securing contributed property + partnership debt allocated to contributing partner + gain recognized.
- Contributing partner's holding period in a partnership interest depends on the type of property contributed.

Example 20-1

What if: Assume Nicole contributes land to CCS with a fair market value of $120,000 and an adjusted basis of $20,000. What amount of gain or loss would she recognize on the contribution?

Answer: None. Under the general rule for contributions of appreciated property, Nicole will not recognize any of the $100,000 built-in gain from her land.

What if: Suppose Chanzz Inc. contributed equipment with a fair market value of $120,000 and a tax basis of $220,000 to CCS. What amount of the gain or loss would Chanzz Inc. recognize on the contribution?

Answer: None. Chanzz Inc. would not recognize any of the $100,000 built-in loss on the equipment. However, if Chanzz Inc. sold the property to an unrelated party and contributed $120,000 in cash instead of the equipment, it could recognize the $100,000 built-in tax loss. If, for some reason, the equipment Chanzz planned to contribute was uniquely suited to CCS's operations, Chanzz could obtain the same result by selling the equipment to Sarah, who would then contribute the equipment to CCS rather than her planned $120,000 cash contribution.

Partner's initial tax basis.   Among other things, partners need to determine the tax basis in their partnership interests to properly compute their taxable gains and losses when they sell their partnership interests. A partner's tax basis in her partnership interest is her **outside basis.** In contrast, the partnership's basis in its assets is its **inside basis.** As we progress through this and the next chapter, you'll see other important reasons for calculating a partner's outside tax basis.

Determining a partner's initial tax basis in a partnership interest acquired by contributing property and/or cash is relatively straightforward if the partnership doesn't have any debt. Partners will simply have a basis in their partnership interest equivalent to the tax basis of the property and cash they contributed.[10] This rule ensures that realized gains and losses on contributed property are merely deferred until either the contributing partner sells her partnership interest or the partnership sells the contributed property.

Example 20-2

What if: Assume that Sarah contributed $120,000 in cash to CCS in exchange for her partnership interest and that CCS had no liabilities. What is Sarah's outside basis in her partnership interest after the contribution?

Answer: Sarah's basis is $120,000, the amount of cash she contributed to CCS.

What if: Assume Nicole contributed land with a fair market value of $120,000 and an adjusted basis of $20,000 and CCS had no liabilities. What is Nicole's initial tax basis in CCS?

Answer: Nicole's basis is $20,000, the basis of the property she contributed to CCS. If Nicole immediately sold her interest in CCS for $120,000 (the value of the land she contributed), she would recognize gain of $100,000—exactly the amount she would have recognized if she had sold the land instead of contributing it to CCS.

When partnerships have debt, a few additional steps are required to determine a partner's tax basis in her partnership interest. First, each partner must include her share of the partnership's debt in calculating the tax basis in her partnership interest because partnership tax law treats each partner as borrowing her proportionate share of the partnership's debt and then contributing the borrowed cash to acquire her partnership interest.[11] You can understand the necessity for this basis increase by recalling that the basis of any purchased asset increases by the amount of any borrowed funds used to purchase it.

[10]§722.

[11]§752(a).

Partnerships may have either **recourse debt** or **nonrecourse debt** or both, and the specific approach to allocating partnership debt to individual partners differs for each. The fundamental difference between the two types of debt lies in the legal responsibility partners assume for ultimately paying the debt. Recourse debts are those for which partners have economic risk of loss—that is, they may have to legally satisfy the debt with their own funds. For example, the unsecured debts of general partnerships, such as payables, are recourse debt because general partners are legally responsible for the debts of the partnership. Recourse debt is usually allocated to the partners who will ultimately be responsible for paying it.[12] The partners must consider their partner guarantees, other agreements, and state partnership or LLC statutes in making this determination.

Nonrecourse debts, in contrast, don't provide creditors the same level of legal recourse against partners. Nonrecourse debts such as mortgages are typically secured by real property and only give lenders the right to obtain the secured property in the event the partnership defaults on the debt. Because partners are responsible for paying nonrecourse debts only to the extent the partnership generates sufficient profits, such debts are generally allocated according to partners' profit-sharing ratios. (We discuss an exception to this general rule later in the chapter.[13]) The *basic* rules for allocating recourse and nonrecourse debt are summarized in Exhibit 20-1.

EXHIBIT 20-1   **Basic Rules for Allocating Partnership Debt to Partners**

Type of Debt	Allocation Method
Recourse	Allocated to partners with ultimate responsibility for paying debt
Nonrecourse	Allocated according to partners' profit-sharing ratios

The legal structure of entities taxed as partnerships also influences the way partners characterize and allocate partnership debt. Recourse debts in limited partnerships are typically allocated only to general partners, because, as we discuss in Chapter 15, limited partners are legally protected from a limited partnership's recourse debt holders.[14] Limited partners, however, may be allocated recourse debt if they forgo their legal protection by guaranteeing some or all of the recourse debt. Similarly, LLC members generally treat LLC debt as nonrecourse because they, like corporate shareholders, are shielded from the LLC's creditors. However, like limited partners, LLC members may treat debt as recourse debt to the extent they contractually assume risk of loss by agreeing to be legally responsible for paying the debt.[15]

Example 20-3

In reality, Sarah and Chanzz Inc. initially each contributed $120,000 and CCS borrowed $60,000 from a bank when CCS was formed. The bank required Nicole, Sarah, and Chanzz Inc. to personally guarantee the bank loan. The terms were structured so the members would each be responsible for a portion of the debt equal to the percentage of CCS losses allocated to each member (one-third

(continued on page 20-6)

[12]Reg. §1.752-2. Under the regulations, partners' obligations for paying recourse debt are determined by assuming a hypothetical, worst-case scenario where partnership assets (including cash) become worthless, and the resulting losses are then allocated to partners. The partners who legally would be responsible for partnership recourse debts under this scenario must be allocated the recourse debt. A detailed description of this approach for allocating recourse debt is beyond the scope of this book.

[13]Reg. §1.752-3 provides the rules for allocating nonrecourse debt, some of which are beyond the scope of this text.

[14]Recall from Chapter 15 that, in limited partnerships, general partners' liability is unlimited, whereas limited partners' liability is usually limited to the amount they have invested.

[15]It's actually quite common for banks and other lenders to require LLC members to personally guarantee loans made to LLCs.

each) and would have no right of reimbursement from either CCS or the other members of CCS. How much of the $60,000 bank debt was allocated to each member?

Answer: Each member was allocated $20,000. The debt is treated as recourse debt because the members are personally guaranteeing it. Because each guarantees one-third of the debt, the $60,000 debt is allocated equally among them.

What if: Assuming the $60,000 bank loan is CCS's only debt, what is Sarah's initial basis in her CCS interest after taking her share of CCS's bank debt into account?

Answer: Sarah's basis is $140,000 ($120,000 + $20,000) and consists of her cash contribution plus her share of CCS's $60,000 bank loan.

Another step is needed to determine a partner's outside basis when the partnership assumes *debt of the partner* secured by property the partner contributes to the partnership. Essentially, the contributing partner must treat her debt relief as a deemed cash distribution from the partnership that reduces her outside basis.[16] If the debt securing the contributed property is nonrecourse debt, the amount of the debt in excess of the basis of the contributed property is allocated solely to the contributing partner, and the remaining debt is allocated to all partners according to their profit-sharing ratios.[17]

Example 20-4

Assume Nicole contributed $10,000 of cash and land with a fair market value of $150,000 and adjusted basis of $20,000 to CCS when it was formed. The land was encumbered by a $40,000 nonrecourse mortgage executed three years before. Recalling that CCS already had $60,000 in bank debt before Nicole's contribution, what tax bases do Nicole, Sarah, and Chanzz Inc. *initially* have in their CCS interests?

Answer: Their bases are $36,666, $146,666, and $146,666, respectively. Nicole, Sarah, and Chanzz Inc. would determine their initial tax bases as illustrated in the table below:

Description	Nicole	Sarah	Chanzz Inc.	Explanation
(1) Basis in contributed land	$20,000			
(2) Cash contributed	10,000	$120,000	$120,000	Example 20-3.
(3) Members' share of $60,000 recourse bank loan	20,000	20,000	20,000	Example 20-3.
(4) Nonrecourse mortgage in excess of basis in contributed land	20,000			Nonrecourse debt > basis is allocated only to Nicole.
(5) Remaining nonrecourse mortgage	6,666	6,666	6,666	33.33% × [$40,000 − (4)].
(6) Relief from mortgage debt	(40,000)			
The member's initial tax basis in CCS	36,666	146,666	146,666	Sum of (1) through (6).

Although in many instances partners don't recognize gains on property contributions, there is an important exception to the general rule that may apply when property secured by debt is contributed to a partnership. In these situations, the contributing partner recognizes gain *only if* the cash deemed to have been received from

[16]§752(b).
[17]Reg. §1.752-3(a)(2).

a partnership distribution exceeds the contributing partner's tax basis in her partnership interest prior to the deemed distribution.[18] Any gain recognized is generally treated as capital gain.[19]

Example 20-5

What if: Assume Sarah and Chanzz Inc., but *not* Nicole, personally guarantee all $100,000 of CCS's debt ($60,000 bank loan + $40,000 mortgage on land). How much gain, if any, would Nicole recognize on her contribution to CCS and what would be the basis in her CCS interest?

Answer: Nicole would recognize $10,000 gain and have a $0 basis, computed as follows:

Description	Amount	Explanation
(1) Basis in contributed land	$20,000	Example 20-4.
(2) Cash contributed	10,000	Example 20-4.
(3) Nicole's share of debt	0	Sarah and Chanzz guaranteed all of CCS's liabilities, including the mortgage on land, thereby turning them into recourse liabilities that should only be allocated to Sarah and Chanzz.
(4) Debt relief	(40,000)	Nicole was relieved of mortgage on land.
(5) Debt relief in excess of basis in contributed land and cash	(10,000)	Sum of (1) through (4).
(6) Capital gain recognized	10,000	(5) with opposite sign.
Nicole's initial tax basis in CCS	0	(5) + (6).

Partner's holding period in partnership interest. Because a partnership interest is a capital asset, its holding period determines whether gains or losses from the disposition of the partnership interest are short-term or long-term capital gains or losses. The length of a partner's holding period for a partnership interest acquired by contributing property depends on the nature of the assets the partner contributed. When partners contribute capital assets or §1231 assets (assets used in a trade or business and held for more than one year), the holding period of the contributed property "tacks on" to the partnership interest.[20] Otherwise, it begins on the day the partnership interest is acquired.

Example 20-6

What if: Assume Nicole contributed land (no cash) that she had held for five years in exchange for her partnership interest. One month after contributing the property, she sold her partnership interest and recognized a capital gain. Is the gain long-term or short-term?

Answer: The gain is long-term because the five-year holding period of the land is tacked on to Nicole's holding period for her partnership interest. She is treated as though she held the partnership interest for five years and one month at the time she sold it.

Partnership's tax basis and holding period in contributed property. Just as partners must determine their initial outside basis in their partnership interests after contributing

---

[18]§731(a). However, §707(a)(2)(B) provides that deemed cash received from the relief of debt should be considered as sale proceeds rather than a distribution when circumstances indicate the relief of debt constitutes a disguised sale. Further discussion of disguised sale transactions is beyond the scope of this book.

[19]§731(a). This is equivalent to increasing what would have been a negative basis by the recognized gain to arrive at a zero basis. This mechanism ensures that partners will be left with an initial tax basis of zero any time they recognize gain from a property contribution.

[20]Reg. §1.1223-1(a).

property, partnerships must establish their inside basis in the contributed property. Measuring both the partner's outside basis and the partnership's inside basis is consistent with the entity theory of partnership taxation. To ensure built-in gains and losses on contributed property are ultimately recognized if partnerships sell contributed property, partnerships generally take a basis in the property equal to the contributing partner's basis in the property at the time of the contribution.[21] Like the adjusted basis of contributed property, the holding period of contributed assets also carries over to the partnership.[22] In fact, the only tax attribute of contributed property that *doesn't* carry over to the partnership is the character of contributed property. Whether gains or losses on dispositions of contributed property are capital or ordinary usually depends on the manner in which the partnership uses contributed property.[23]

Example 20-7

What if: Assume CCS used the land Nicole contributed in its business for one month and then sold it for its fair market value of $150,000. What is the amount and character of the gain CCS would recognize on the sale (see Example 20-4)?

Answer: CCS recognizes $130,000 of §1231 gain. Nicole's basis in the land prior to the formation of CCS was $20,000. Because CCS receives a carryover basis in the land of $20,000, it recognizes $130,000 of gain when the land is sold for $150,000 ($110,000 in cash and $40,000 of debt relief minus $20,000 basis in land). Also, because CCS used the land in its business and because Nicole's five-year holding period carries over to CCS, the land qualifies as a §1231 asset to CCS, and CCS recognizes §1231 gain when the land is sold. Note that $130,000 of gain is recognized regardless of whether Nicole sells the land and contributes cash to CCS, or CCS sells the land shortly after it is contributed.

In addition to tracking the inside basis of its assets for tax purposes, partnerships not required to produce GAAP financial statements may decide to use inside tax basis, as well as tax income and expense recognition rules, to maintain their books. Under this approach, a new partnership would prepare its initial balance sheet using the tax basis for its assets. In addition, it would create a **tax capital account** for each new partner, reflecting the tax basis of any property contributed (net of any debt securing the property) and cash contributions. Because each new partner's tax capital account measures that partner's equity in the partnership using tax accounting rules, it will later be adjusted to include the partner's share of earnings and losses, contributions, and distributions.

Besides satisfying bookkeeping requirements, a partnership's tax basis balance sheet can provide useful tax-related information. For example, we can calculate each partner's share of the inside basis of partnership assets by adding the partner's share of debt to her **capital account.** Interestingly, partners who acquire their interests by contributing property (without having to recognize any gain) will have an *outside basis* equal to their share of the partnership's total inside basis. However, as we discuss more fully in the next chapter, partners' inside and outside bases will likely be different when they purchase existing partnership interests.

As another alternative to maintaining **GAAP capital accounts,** partnerships may also maintain their partner's capital accounts using accounting rules prescribed in the §704(b) tax regulations.[24] Partners set up **§704(b) capital accounts** in much the same way as tax capital accounts, except that §704(b) capital accounts reflect the fair

---

[21]§723.

[22]§1223(2).

[23]§702(b). However, §724 provides some important exceptions to this general rule for certain receivables, inventory, and capital loss property.

[24]Reg. §1.704-1(b)(2)(iv).

market value rather than the tax basis of contributed assets. Once a partnership begins operations, it can adjust §704(b) capital accounts so they continue to reflect the fair market value of partners' capital interests as accurately as possible. Partnerships may prefer this approach over simply maintaining tax capital accounts because §704(b) capital accounts may be a better measure of the true value of partners' capital interests.

continued from page 20-1...

Before forming CCS, its members agreed to keep its books using the tax basis of contributed assets and tax income and expense recognition rules. After receiving the cash and property contributions from its members and borrowing $60,000 from Nicole's bank, CCS prepared the tax basis balance sheet in Exhibit 20-2.

to be continued...

EXHIBIT 20-2   Color Comfort Sheets LLC

	Balance Sheet March 31, 2015	
	Tax Basis	**§704(b)/FMV***
Assets:		
Cash	$310,000	$310,000
Land	20,000	150,000
Totals	$330,000	$460,000
Liabilities and Capital:		
Long-term debt	$100,000	$100,000
Capital—Nicole	(10,000)	120,000
Capital—Sarah	120,000	120,000
Capital—Chanzz Inc.	120,000	120,000
Totals	$330,000	$460,000

*The §704(b)/FMV balance sheet is also provided to illustrate the difference in the two approaches to maintaining partners' capital accounts.

Contribution of Services   So far we've assumed partners receive their partnership interests in exchange for contributed property. They may also receive partnership interests in exchange for services they provide to the partnership. For example, an attorney or other service provider might accept a partnership interest in lieu of cash payment for services provided as part of a partnership formation. Similarly, ongoing partnerships may compensate their employees with partnership interests, to reduce compensation-related cash payments and to motivate employees to behave more like owners. Unlike property contributions, services contributed in exchange for partnership interests may create immediate tax consequences to both the contributing partner *and* the partnership, depending on the nature of the partnership interest received.[25]

---

[25]Rev. Proc. 93-27, 1993-2 CB 343 and Rev. Proc. 2001-43, 2001-2 CB 191. In 2005, the IRS issued Prop. Reg. §1.704-1, which will change certain elements of current tax law when it is adopted as a final regulation. The concepts and examples discussed here are consistent with both current law and the proposed regulation.

continued from page 20-9...

Once CCS was organized in March 2015, it built a small production facility on the commercial land Nicole had contributed, purchased and installed the equipment needed to produce sheets, and hired and trained workers—all before the actual production and marketing of the sheets. After production began on July 1, 2015, CCS started selling its sheets to local specialty bedding stores, but the local market was limited. To create additional demand for their product, the members of CCS decided to draw on Sarah's marketing expertise to develop an advertising campaign targeted at home and garden magazines. All members of CCS agreed Sarah would receive, on December 31, 2015, an additional *capital interest* in CCS with a liquidation value of $20,000 *and* an increase in her profit-and-loss-sharing ratio from 33.33 percent to 40 percent (leaving the other members each with a 30 percent share of profits and losses), to compensate her for the time she would spend on this additional project. At this point, CCS's debt remained at $100,000.

to be continued...

Capital interests.   Partners who receive unrestricted capital interests in exchange for services have the right to receive a share of the partnership's capital if it liquidates.[26] Because capital interests represent a current economic entitlement amenable to measurement, partners receiving capital interests for services must treat the amount they would receive if the partnership were to liquidate, or **liquidation value**[27] of the capital interest, as ordinary income.[28] In addition, the **service partner's** tax basis in the capital interest he receives will equal the amount of ordinary income he recognizes, and his holding period will begin on the date he receives the capital interest. The partnership either deducts or capitalizes the value of the capital interest, depending on the nature of the services the partner provides. For example, a real estate partnership would capitalize the value of a capital interest compensating a partner for architectural drawings used for a real estate development project.[29] Conversely, the same partnership would deduct the value of a capital interest compensating a partner for providing property management services. When the partnership deducts the value of capital interests used to compensate partners for services provided, it allocates the deduction only to the partners not providing services, or **nonservice partners,** because the deduction is related to the segment of the partnership tax year ending immediately before the admission of the new service partner.[30]

Example 20-8

What if: What are the tax consequences to Sarah and CCS if Sarah receives a capital interest (no profits interest) with a $20,000 liquidation value for her services?

Answer: As summarized below, Sarah has $20,000 of ordinary income, and CCS receives a $20,000 ordinary deduction. However, this deduction must be split equally between Nicole and Chanzz Inc. because, in effect, they transferred a portion of their capital to Sarah.

---

[26]Certain restrictions, such as vesting requirements, may be placed on partnership interests received for services. We limit our discussion here to unrestricted partnership interests.

[27]The proposed regulations in this area also allow the parties in this transaction to use the fair market value of partnership interests as a measure of value rather than liquidation value.

[28]The ordinary income recognized by the service partner is treated as a "guaranteed payment" by the service partner. Guaranteed payments are discussed more fully later in this chapter.

[29]§263(a).

[30]The preamble to Prop. Reg. §1.721-1(b) applies the varying interest rule of §706(d)(1) to the admission of a service partner.

Description	Sarah	Nicole	Chanzz Inc.	Explanation
(1) Ordinary income	$20,000			Liquidation value of capital interest.
Ordinary deduction		($10,000)	($10,000)	Capital shift from nonservice partners. (1) × .5

Profits interests.   It's fairly common for partnerships to compensate service partners with profits rather than capital interests. Profits interests are fundamentally different from capital interests, because the only economic benefit they provide is the right to share in the future profits of the partnership. Unlike capital interests, profits interests have no liquidation value at the time they are received. Nonservice partners generally prefer to compensate service partners with profits interests because they don't have to forgo their current share of capital in the partnership and may not ever have to give up anything if the partnership is ultimately unprofitable. Thus, a profits interest is more risky than a capital interest from the perspective of the service partner.

The tax rules applicable to profits interests differ from those pertaining to capital interests due to the fundamental economic differences between them. Because there is no immediate liquidation value associated with a profits interest, the service partner typically will not recognize income and the nonservice partners will not receive deductions.[31] However, future profits and losses attributable to the profits interest are allocated to the service partner (and away from the nonservice partners) as they are generated. In addition, the partnership must adjust debt allocations based on profit-and-loss-sharing ratios to reflect the service partner's new or increased share of profits and losses.

Example 20-9

What if: Assuming Sarah received only a profits interest for her services instead of the capital interest she received in Example 20-8, what are the tax consequences to Sarah, Nicole, Chanzz Inc., and CCS?[32]

Answer: Sarah would not be required to recognize any income, and CCS would not deduct or capitalize any costs. As CCS generates future profits, Sarah will receive a greater share of the profits than she would have otherwise received, and the other two members will receive a correspondingly smaller share. In addition, with the increase in Sarah's profit-and-loss-sharing ratios from 33.33 percent to 40 percent, debt allocations among the partners will change to reflect Sarah's additional entitlement. Note that the debt allocations affect each partner's outside basis. The change in debt allocations is reflected in the table below:

Description	Sarah	Nicole	Chanzz Inc.	Explanation
(1) Increase in debt allocation	$5,334			Loss-sharing ratio increases from 33.33 percent to 40 percent or 6.67 percent [$60,000 recourse bank loan × 6.67% increase in loss-sharing ratio] + [$20,000 nonrecourse mortgage not allocated solely to Nicole × 6.67% increase in profit-sharing ratio].
Decrease in debt allocation		($2,666)	($2,666)	(1) × .5

[31]Rev. Proc. 93-27 indicates that income is recognized by the service partner "if the profits interest relates to a substantially certain and predictable stream of income," if the partner disposes of the profits interest within two years, or "the profits interest is a limited partnership interest in a publicly traded partnership."

[32]It is common for partnerships to grant a profits interest without an accompanying capital interest.

Example 20-10

What are the tax consequences to Sarah, Nicole, and Chanzz Inc. associated with the capital interest (liquidation value of $20,000) and profits interest Sarah receives for her services?

Answer: The tax consequences associated with giving Sarah *both* a capital and profits interest are summarized in the table below:

Description	Sarah	Nicole	Chanzz Inc.	Explanation
(1) Ordinary income	$20,000			Liquidation value of capital interest.
Ordinary deduction		($10,000)	($10,000)	Capital shift from nonservice partners. (1) × .5
(2) Increase in debt allocation	5,334			Loss-sharing ratio increases from 33.33 percent to 40 percent or 6.67 percent ($60,000 recourse bank loan × 6.67% increase in loss-sharing ratio) + ($20,000 nonrecourse mortgage not allocated solely to Nicole × 6.67% increase in profit-sharing ratio).
Decrease in debt allocation		($2,666)	($2,666)	(2) × .5

TAXES IN THE REAL WORLD   Carried Interests

In debates over tax policy, politicians in the news have frequently discussed carried interests as if everyone within earshot understands the term. However, judging from the public's confusion over the issue, not everyone does.

Carried interests are nothing more than profits interests granted to managing partners and key employees of private equity and other similar investment partnerships. Industry norms suggest that typical carried interests provide managing partners with a 20 percent (and sometimes greater) share of profits when partnership investments are eventually sold. Because these investments are typically corporate shares that have been held more than one year, any income from their sale is treated as long-term capital gain.

The benefits of these types of carried interest arrangements are twofold: any income managing partners receive is deferred until partnership investments are sold, and, when the income is finally recognized, it is taxed at favorable, long-term capital gains rates. To some politicians and their supporters, this result seems unfair given that salary income is taxed at higher ordinary rates.

For a more detailed description of carried interests, see: "Business Taxation: What Is Carried Interest and How Should It Be Taxed?" in *The Tax Policy Briefing Book* at www.taxpolicycenter.org

Organization, Start-Up, and Syndication Costs   When partnerships are formed, they typically incur some costs that must be capitalized rather than expensed for tax purposes, because they will benefit the partnership over its entire lifespan. This category of expenses includes **organization costs** associated with legally forming a partnership (such as attorneys' and accountants' fees), **syndication costs** to promote and sell partnership interests, and **start-up costs** that would normally be deducted as operating expenses except that they are incurred before the start of active trade or business. However, with the exception of syndication costs,[33] which are not

---

[33]Syndication costs are typically incurred by partnerships whose interests are marketed to the public. Thus, syndication expenses are unusual in closely held partnerships.

deductible, the partnership may elect to amortize these costs. Chapter 10 provides additional detail about immediately expensing or amortizing business organization and start-up costs.

Acquisitions of Partnership Interests

After a partnership is formed and begins operating, new or existing partners can acquire partnership interests in exchange for contributing property and/or services, in which case the tax rules previously discussed in the context of forming a partnership still apply. Or new partners may purchase partnership interests from existing partners. Partners who purchase their partnership interests don't have to be concerned with recognizing taxable income when they receive their interests. However, in each of these scenarios they must still determine the initial tax basis and holding period in their partnership interests. Exhibit 20-3 summarizes the rules for determining the tax basis of partnership interests when they are received in exchange for contributed property or services, or when they are purchased.

EXHIBIT 20-3   **Summary of Partner's Outside Basis and Holding Period by Acquisition Method**

Acquisition Method	Outside Basis	Holding Period
Contribute Property	Equals basis of contributed property − debt relief + debt allocation + gain recognized.	If property contributed is a capital or §1231 asset, holding period includes holding period of contributed property; otherwise begins on date interest received.
Contribute Services	Equals liquidation value of capital interest + debt allocation. Equals debt allocation if only profits interest received.	Begins on date interest received.
Purchase	Equals cost basis[34] + debt allocation.	Begins on date interest purchased.

Example 20-11

CCS had overall operating losses from July 1, 2015 (when it began operating), through June 30, 2016. Because of the losses, Chanzz Inc. decided to sell its 30 percent interest in CCS (Chanzz Inc.'s original 33.33 percent interest in CCS was reduced to 30 percent at the end of 2015 when Sarah's interest was increased to compensate her for services provided) on July 1, 2016, to Greg Randall who, like Chanzz Inc., will be a nonmanaging member and guarantee a portion of CCS debt. Greg paid Chanzz Inc. $100,000 for its interest in CCS and was allocated a 30 percent share of CCS debt (CCS's debt remained at $100,000 on July 1, 2016). What is Greg's basis and holding period in CCS?

Answer: Greg's basis of $124,000 in CCS includes the $100,000 amount he paid to purchase the interest plus his $24,000 share of CCS's total $80,000 debt available to be allocated to all members ($60,000 recourse bank loan and $20,000 of nonrecourse mortgage remaining after allocating the first $20,000 to Nicole). Greg's holding period in his CCS interest begins on July 1, 2016.

PARTNERSHIP ACCOUNTING PERIODS, METHODS, AND TAX ELECTIONS

LO 20-3

A newly formed partnership must adopt its required tax year-end and decide whether it intends to use either the cash or accrual method as its overall method of accounting. As discussed in Chapter 9, an entity's tax year-end determines the cutoff date for

[34]§742.

including income and deductions in a particular return, and its overall accounting method determines when income and deductions are recognized for tax purposes. Partnerships must frequently make other tax-related elections as well.

Tax Elections

New partnerships determine their accounting periods and make tax elections including the election of overall accounting method, the election to expense a portion of organization and start-up costs, and the election to expense tangible personal property. Who formally makes all these elections? In theory, either the partnership or the partners themselves could do so. With just a few exceptions, the partnership tax rules rely on the entity theory of partnership taxation and make the partnership responsible for tax elections.[35] In many instances, the partnership does so in conjunction with filing its annual return. For example, it selects an accounting method and determines whether to elect to amortize start-up or organization costs by simply applying its elections in calculating ordinary business income on its first return. The partnership makes other tax elections by filing a separate document with the IRS, such as Form 3115 when it elects to change an accounting method.

Example 20-12

How will CCS elect its overall accounting method after it begins operations?

Answer: Nicole, Sarah, and Chanzz Inc. may jointly decide on an overall accounting method or, in their LLC operating agreement, they may appoint one of the members to be responsible for making this and other tax elections. Once they have made this decision, CCS makes the election by simply using the chosen accounting method when preparing its first information return.

Accounting Periods

Required Year-Ends Because partners include their share of partnership income or loss in their taxable year ending with the partnership taxable year, or within which the partnership taxable year falls, any partnership tax year other than that of the partners will result in some degree of tax deferral for some or all of the partners.[36] Exhibit 20-4 reflects the tax deferral a partner with a calendar year-end would receive if the corresponding partnership had a January 31 year-end.

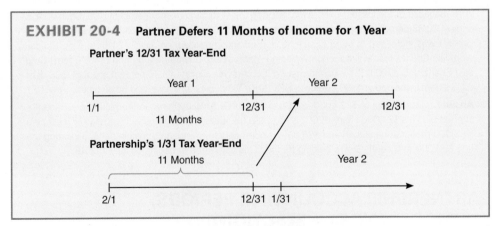

EXHIBIT 20-4 **Partner Defers 11 Months of Income for 1 Year**

Because the partner reports the partnership's year 1 income earned from February 1 until January 31 in the partner's second calendar year (the year within which the partnership's January 31 year-end falls), the partner defers reporting for one year

---

[35]§703(b). Certain elections are made at the partner level.
[36]§706(a).

the 11 months of income she was allocated from February 1 through December 31 of her first calendar year.

The government's desire to reduce the aggregate tax deferral of partners (the sum of the deferrals for each individual partner) provides the underlying rationale behind the rules requiring certain partnership taxable year-ends. Partnerships are generally required to use one of three possible tax year-ends.[37] As illustrated in Exhibit 20-5, they must follow a series of steps to determine the appropriate year-end.

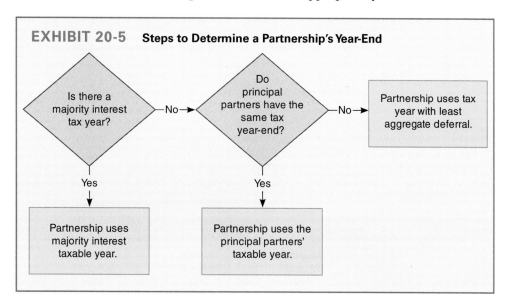

EXHIBIT 20-5   Steps to Determine a Partnership's Year-End

The first potential required tax year is the **majority interest taxable year,** the taxable year of one or more partners who together own more than 50 percent of the capital and profits interests in the partnership.[38] However, there may not be a majority interest taxable year when several partners have different year-ends. For example, if a partnership has two partners with 50 percent capital and profits interests and each has a different tax year, there will be no majority interest taxable year. In that case, the partnership next applies the principal partners test to determine its year-end.

Under the **principal partners** test, the required tax year is the taxable year the principal partners *all* have in common. For this purpose, principal partners are those who have 5 percent or more interest in the partnership profits and capital.[39] Consider a partnership with two calendar-year partners, each with a 20 percent capital and profits interest, and 30 additional fiscal year-end partners, each with less than a 5 percent capital and profits interest. In this scenario, the required taxable year of the partnership is a calendar year corresponding with the taxable year of the partnership's only two principal partners. If, as in the earlier example, the partnership had two 50 percent capital and profits partners with different tax years, it would then use the tax year providing the "least aggregate deferral" to the partners, unless it is eligible to elect an alternative year-end.[40]

The tax year with the **least aggregate deferral** is the one among the tax years of the partners that provides the partner group as a whole with the smallest amount of aggregate tax deferral. Under this approach, we measure the total tax deferral achieved under each potential tax year mathematically by weighting each partner's months of deferral under the potential tax year by each partner's *profits* percentage and then summing the weighted months of deferral for all the partners.

---

[37]Under certain circumstances, other alternative taxable years may be available to partnerships. See Rev. Proc. 2002-38, 2002-1 CB 1037 and §444 for additional information concerning these options.
[38]§706(b)(1)(B)(i).
[39]§706(b)(3).
[40]Reg. §1.706-1(b)(3).

Example 20-13

When CCS began operating in 2015, it had two calendar year-end members, Nicole and Sarah, and one member with a June 30 year-end, Chanzz Inc. What tax year-end must CCS use for 2015?

Answer: CCS was required to use the calendar year as its taxable year unless it was eligible for an alternative year-end. Although Chanzz Inc. had a June 30 taxable year, Nicole and Sarah both had calendar year-ends. Because Nicole and Sarah each initially own 33.33 percent of the capital and profits of CCS, and together they own greater than 50 percent of the profits and capital of CCS, the calendar year is the required taxable year for CCS because it is the majority interest taxable year.

What if: Assume CCS initially began operating with three members: Nicole, a calendar year-end member with a 20 percent profits and capital interest; Chanzz Inc., a June 30 year-end member with a 40 percent profits and capital interest; and Telle Inc., a September 30 year-end member with a 40 percent profits and capital interest. What tax year-end must CCS use for 2015?

Answer: CCS would be required to use a June 30 year-end unless it was eligible for an alternative year-end. CCS does not have a majority interest taxable year because no partner or group of partners with the same year-end owns more than 50 percent of the profits and capital interests in CCS. Also, because all three principal partners in CCS have different year-ends, the principal partner test is not met. As a result, CCS must decide which of three potential year-ends, June 30, September 30, or December 31, will provide its members the least aggregate deferral. The table below illustrates the required computations:

Possible Year-Ends			12/31 Year-End		6/30 Year-End		9/30 Year-End	
Members	%	Tax Year	Months Deferral* (MD)	% × (MD)	Months Deferral* (MD)	% × (MD)	Months Deferral* (MD)	% × (MD)
Nicole	20%	12/31	0	0	6	1.2	3	.6
Chanzz Inc.	40	6/30	6	2.4	0	0	9	3.6
Telle Inc.	40	9/30	9	3.6	3	1.2	0	0
Total aggregate deferral				6		**2.4**		4.2

*Months deferral equals number of months between the proposed year-end and partner's year-end.

June 30 is the required taxable year-end because it provides members with the least aggregate tax deferral (2.4 is less than 6 and 4.2).

Accounting Methods

Although partnerships may use the accrual method freely, they may not use the cash method under certain conditions because it facilitates the deferral of income and acceleration of deductions. For example, partnerships with C corporation partners are generally not eligible to use the cash method[41] unless their average annual gross receipts for the three prior taxable years do not exceed $5 million and they otherwise qualify.[42] It should also be noted that entities generally eligible to use the overall cash method of accounting must nevertheless use the accrual method to account for the purchase and sale of inventory unless they meet certain exceptions provided by the IRS.[43]

---

[41]§448(a)(2). In addition, §448(a)(3) prohibits partnerships classified as "tax shelters" from electing the cash method.

[42]§448(b)(3). If a partnership has not been in existence for at least three years, this test is applied based on the number of years it has been in existence.

[43]For example, Rev. Proc. 2001-10 2001-1 CB 272 exempts taxpayers with average annual gross receipts of $1 million or less from having to use the accrual method to account for the purchase and sale of inventory.

Example 20-14

When CCS began operations, its members decided it should elect the cash method of accounting if eligible to do so. Would having a corporate member—Chanzz Inc.—prevent it from electing the cash method?

Answer: No. Although Chanzz Inc. was a founding member of CCS, its ownership share didn't affect the partnership's eligibility to use the cash method since CCS's average annual gross receipts were less than $5 million. If Chanzz Inc. had remained a member of CCS, the cash method might have been unavailable in future years if average annual gross receipts exceeded $5 million.

REPORTING THE RESULTS OF PARTNERSHIP OPERATIONS

LO 20-4

The first section in the Internal Revenue Code dealing with partnerships states emphatically that partnerships are flow-through entities: "A partnership as such shall not be subject to the income tax imposed by this chapter. Persons carrying on business as partners shall be liable for income tax only in their separate or individual capacities."[44] This feature of partnership taxation largely explains the popularity of partnerships over corporations, whose shareholders are subject to a double tax—once when the income is earned and again when it is distributed to shareholders as a dividend or when the shares are sold.

TAXES IN THE REAL WORLD   Publicly Traded Partnerships

Would it surprise you to know that many private equity firms are organized as partnerships for tax purposes? Even more surprising may be the fact that several well-known private equity funds—including Fortress, KKR, and Blackstone—are publicly traded. Publicly traded firms are typically taxed as corporations even if they are legally structured as partnerships or, in the case of these private equity firms, as limited partnerships. However, relying on a provision in the tax code, they were able to maintain their tax status as partnerships after their public offerings.[45] Thus, investors purchasing shares in these private equity funds are buying investments subject to only one level of taxation but that, like shares in a corporation, can be readily traded in a public securities market.

Ordinary Business Income (Loss) and Separately Stated Items

Although partnerships are not taxpaying entities, they are required to file information returns annually. They also distribute information to each partner detailing the amount *and* character of items of income and loss flowing through the partnership.[46] Partners must report these income and loss items on their tax returns even if they don't receive cash distributions from the partnership during the year.

When gathering this information for their partners, partnerships must determine each partner's share of **ordinary business income (loss)** and **separately stated items.** Partnership ordinary business income (loss) is all partnership income (loss) exclusive of any separately stated items of income (loss). Separately stated items share one common characteristic—they are treated differently from a partner's share of ordinary business income (loss) for tax purposes. To better understand why certain items must be separately disclosed to partners, consider how two particular separately stated items, dividend income and capital losses, might affect an individual partner's tax liability. Qualified dividend income allocated to individual partners is taxed at either a 0 percent, 15 percent, or 20 percent rate, depending on individual partners' tax brackets.[47]

THE KEY FACTS

Reporting the Results of Partnership Operations

- Partnerships file annual information returns reporting their ordinary business income (loss) and separately stated items.
- Ordinary business income (loss) = partnership overall income or loss exclusive of separately stated items.
- Separately stated items change partners' tax liabilities when they are separately stated.

---

[44]§701.

[45]§7704.

[46]Other items, such as tax credits, may also flow through the partnership to partners.

[47]§1(h).

In a similar vein, individual partners without capital gains during the year may deduct up to $3,000 in capital losses against their ordinary income, while other individual partners with capital gains may deduct more.[48] If a partnership's dividends and capital losses were simply buried in the computation of its overall income or loss for the year, the partner would be unable to apply these specific tax rules to her unique situation and determine her correct tax liability.

The Code specifically enumerates several common separately stated items, including short-term capital gains and losses, long-term capital gains and losses, §1231 gains and losses, charitable contributions, and dividends.[49] Many more items are considered under regulations issued by the IRS.[50] Exhibit 20-6 lists several other common separately stated items.

EXHIBIT 20-6 Common Separately Stated Items

- Interest income
- Guaranteed payments
- Net earnings (loss) from self-employment
- Tax-exempt income
- Net rental real estate income
- Investment interest expense
- Charitable contributions
- §179 deduction

Example 20-15

After constructing a building and purchasing equipment in its first year of operations ending on December 31, 2015, CCS invested $15,000 of its remaining idle cash in stocks and bonds. CCS's books reflected an overall loss for the year of $80,000. Included in the $80,000 loss were $2,100 of dividend income, $1,200 of short-term capital gains, and a $20,000 deduction for the capital interest given to Sarah at the end of 2015 (see Example 20-10). How much ordinary business loss and what separately stated items are allocated to the CCS members for the taxable year ended December 31, 2015?

Answer: As reflected in the table below, CCS has $63,300 of ordinary business loss. In addition, it has $2,100 of dividend income, $1,200 in short-term capital gains, and $20,000 of ordinary deduction (related to the capital interest Sarah received) that are separately stated items. To Nicole, Sarah, and Chanzz Inc., CCS would report $21,100 of ordinary business loss, $700 of dividend income, and $400 of short-term capital gain. In addition, CCS would report $20,000 of ordinary income to Sarah for the capital interest she received, and a $10,000 deduction to Nicole and Chanzz Inc. reflecting the amount of partnership capital they relinquished.

Description	CCS	Nicole $\left(\frac{1}{3}\right)$	Sarah $\left(\frac{1}{3}\right)$	Chanzz Inc. $\left(\frac{1}{3}\right)$
2015 overall net loss	($80,000)			
Less:				
Dividends	2,100			
Short-term capital gains	1,200			
Ordinary deduction for Sarah's capital interest	(20,000)			
Ordinary business loss	(63,300)	(21,100)	(21,100)	(21,100)
Separately stated Items				
Dividends	2,100	700	700	700
Short-term capital gains	1,200	400	400	400
Ordinary income for capital interest to Sarah	20,000		20,000	
Ordinary deduction for capital interest to Sarah	(20,000)	(10,000)		(10,000)

[48]§1211.

[49]§702.

[50]Reg. §1.702-1(a).

Nicole and Sarah will treat their shares of CCS's ordinary business loss as an *ordinary* loss and include it along with their shares of dividend income and short-term capital gain in their individual tax returns for the year.[51] Chanzz Inc. will also include its share of these items in its annual tax return. But because Chanzz is a corporation, different tax rules apply to its share of dividend income and short-term capital gains. For example, Chanzz will be entitled to the dividends received deduction, while Nicole and Sarah will pay tax on their share of dividend income at a 15 percent rate since their marginal rates on ordinary income are above 15 percent but below 39.6 percent.

Notice that the character of separately stated items is determined at the partnership level rather than at the partner level.[52] This treatment reflects the entity theory.

Example 20-16

What if: Assume Chanzz Inc. is an investments dealer rather than a sports franchise operator. How would Chanzz Inc. classify its share of the $1,200 gain from the securities sold by CCS during 2015?

Answer: Chanzz Inc. would classify the $1,200 as short-term capital gains. Because the securities CCS sold were capital assets to it, the gain on the sale is a capital gain even though the securities are inventory (an ordinary asset) to Chanzz Inc. That is, we determine the character of the income at the partnership level, not the partner level.

Guaranteed Payments   In addition to dividends, capital gains, and other routine separately stated items, **guaranteed payments** are also very common items reported separately to the partners who receive them. As their name suggests, guaranteed payments are fixed amounts paid to partners regardless of whether the partnership shows a profit or loss for the year.[53] We can think of them—and some partnerships treat them—as economically equivalent to cash salary payments made to partners for services provided.[54] Specifically, they are typically deducted in computing a partnership's ordinary income or loss for the year. Though included in a partnership's ordinary business income (loss) computation, guaranteed payments must, nevertheless, be separately stated to the partners who receive them. This separate reporting serves the same purpose as providing W-2 forms to employees. Because guaranteed payments are similar to salary payments, partners treat them as ordinary income.

continued from page 20-10...

Because Sarah received an additional capital interest for marketing services she provided at the end of 2015, she held a 40 percent capital and profits interest, and Nicole and Chanzz Inc. each held a 30 percent capital and profits interest at the beginning of 2016. After Sarah's initial work in formulating a marketing strategy in 2015, Nicole suggested they hire a permanent employee to oversee product marketing. However, because they were unable to find a suitable candidate, Sarah continued to shoulder the product marketing responsibilities in addition to her normal role as a managing member of CCS. To compensate Sarah for her additional workload, all members of CCS agreed to pay Sarah a $10,000 guaranteed payment for her marketing efforts in 2016. Exhibit 20-7 provides CCS's income statement for 2016. ∎

[51]Nicole and Sarah would report their share of ordinary business loss on Schedule E, their share of dividend income on Schedule B, and their share of short-term capital gain on Schedule D of Form 1040.

[52]§702(b).

[53]§707(c).

[54]Fringe benefits that partners receive for services provided such as medical insurance and group-term life insurance are also treated as guaranteed payments. In addition to compensating partners for services provided, guaranteed payments are also made to partners for the use of capital.

EXHIBIT 20-7   Color Comfort Sheets LLC

Income Statement December 31, 2016	
Sales revenue	$ 40,000
Cost of goods sold	(20,000)
Employee wages	(50,000)
Depreciation expense	(18,000)
Guaranteed payments	(10,000)
Miscellaneous expenses	(2,800)
Dividend income	500
Long-term capital gains	300
Overall net loss	$(60,000)

Example 20-17

Given CCS's operating results for *2016* presented in Exhibit 20-7, how much ordinary business loss and what separately stated items will it report on its return for the year? How will it allocate these amounts to its members?

Answer: The table below displays CCS's ordinary business loss and separately stated items and the allocation of these amounts to CCS's members:

Description	CCS	Nicole 30%	Sarah 40%	Chanzz Inc. 30% × 6/12*	Greg 30% × 6/12*
Sales revenue	$40,000				
Cost of goods sold	(20,000)				
Employee wages	(50,000)				
Depreciation expense	(18,000)				
Guaranteed payment to Sarah	(10,000)				
Miscellaneous expenses	(2,800)				
Ordinary business loss	(60,800)	$(18,240)	$(24,320)	$(9,120)	($9,120)
Separately stated to partners					
Dividends	500	150	200	75	75
Long-term capital gains	300	90	120	45	45
Guaranteed payment			10,000		

*As we noted in Example 20-11, Chanzz Inc. sold out to Greg Randall on July 1, 2016. Therefore, the items related to Chanzz Inc.'s original 30 percent interest must be allocated between Chanzz Inc. and Greg Randall.[55]

Self-Employment Tax   Individual partners, like sole proprietors, may be responsible for paying **self-employment taxes** in addition to income taxes on their share of earned income from partnerships.[56] The degree to which partners are responsible for self-employment taxes depends on their legal status as general partners, limited partners, or LLC members and their business activities. General partners report guaranteed payments for services they provide and their share of ordinary business income (loss) as self-employment income (loss) because they are actively involved in managing the partnership. Limited partners, on the other hand, are generally not allowed under state law to participate in the management of limited partnerships. Therefore, their share of ordinary business income (loss) is conceptually more like investment income than trade or business income. As a result, it is not subject to self-employment

[55]We assume here that the items are allocated based on the number of months the interest was held. See Chapter 21 for additional detail regarding methods to account for partners' varying interests in a partnership when a partnership interest is sold.

[56]Chapters 8 and 15 more fully discuss earned income and related self-employment taxes.

tax. However, if limited partners receive guaranteed payments for services provided to the partnership, they treat those payments as self-employment income.

Because LLC members may either be managing or nonmanaging members, the approach to taxing their share of ordinary business income (loss) for self-employment tax purposes ought to depend to some degree on their level of involvement in the LLC.[57] Tax rules in this area were developed before the popularity of LLCs, however, so no authoritative rules currently exist to help LLCs decide whether to characterize their members' shares of ordinary business income (loss) as self-employment income (loss). However, a proposed regulation issued by the IRS and later withdrawn can assist partnerships in drawing the line between aggressive and conservative positions in this area.[58] It provides that LLC members who have personal liability for the debts of the LLC by reason of being an LLC member, who have authority to contract on behalf of the LLC, *or* who participate more than 500 hours in the LLC's trade or business during the taxable year should be classified as general partners when applying the self-employment tax rules.

The lack of authoritative guidance in this area has resulted in a predictable diversity of practice. Some taxpayers and their advisers ignore the proposed regulation and claim that managing members of LLCs are similar to limited partners and shouldn't have to pay self-employment taxes at all.[59] Others follow the spirit of the proposed regulation and take the approach that managing members are similar to general partners and should pay self-employment tax on part or all of their share of ordinary business income (loss), depending on their level of involvement in the LLC.[60]

Example 20-18

For *2016*, should CCS classify Sarah's $10,000 guaranteed payment as self-employment income?

Answer: Yes. The law is clear with respect to guaranteed payments to LLC members—they are always treated as self-employment income.

Using the proposed regulation, will CCS classify Sarah's $24,320 (see Example 20-17) share of ordinary business loss for *2016* as a self-employment loss?

Answer: Yes. Under the proposed regulations, an LLC member who has personal liability for LLC debts or the ability to contract on behalf of the LLC, or who spends more than 500 hours participating in the business of the LLC, is classified as a general partner when applying the self-employment tax rules. Given Sarah's status as a managing member of CCS, at least one but probably all three criteria for classifying her share of CCS's ordinary business loss as self-employment loss will apply. Although these rules have not been finalized and are therefore not authoritative, the IRS would likely follow them because they represent its current thinking on the matter. Applying the law this way, CCS will report a $14,320 self-employment loss [($24,320) share of ordinary business loss + $10,000 guaranteed payment] as a separately stated item to Sarah so she can properly compute her self-employment tax liability on her individual return.

Example 20-19

Using the proposed regulation, will CCS classify Nicole's $18,240 (see Example 20-17) share of ordinary business loss for *2016* as self-employment loss?

Answer: Yes. Because Nicole, like Sarah, is involved in the day-to-day management of CCS, it will classify her entire share of ordinary business loss as self-employment loss, consistent with its classification of Sarah's share of ordinary business loss, and report the amount as a separately stated item to Nicole.

(*continued on page 20-22*)

[57]Guaranteed payments to LLC members are clearly subject to self-employment tax because they are similar to salary payments.

[58]Proposed Reg. §1.1402(a)-2.

[59]This argument may be difficult to sustain for professional service firms. The Tax Court, in *Renkemeyer, Campbell & Weaver, LLP, et al. v. Commissioner,* 136 TC 137 (2011), decided to treat law partners in a law firm organized as an LLP as subject to self-employment taxes.

[60]Nonmanaging LLC members are so similar to limited partners that taxpayers and their advisers typically treat them as if they were limited partners for self-employment tax purposes.

> Under the proposed regulation, will CCS treat Greg's $9,120 share of ordinary business loss for *2016* as self-employment loss?
>
> **Answer:** Yes. CCS will treat Greg's share of ordinary business loss as self-employment loss because he has guaranteed a portion of CCS's debt. CCS's total self-employment loss is $41,680 consisting of Sarah's $14,320 self-employment loss, Nicole's $18,240 self-employment loss, and Greg's $9,120 self-employment loss.

Net Investment Income Tax

An individual partner's share of gross income from interest, dividends, annuities, royalties, or rents is included in the partner's net investment income when calculating the net investment income tax.[61] In addition, the partner's share of income from a trade or business that is a passive activity, income from a trade or business of trading financial instruments or commodities, and any net gain from disposing of property (other than property used in a trade or business that is not a passive activity) is also included in the partner's net investment income.[62]

Allocating Partners' Shares of Income and Loss

Partnership tax rules provide partners with tremendous flexibility in allocating overall profit and loss as well as specific items of profit and loss to partners, as long as partners agree to the allocations and they have "substantial economic effect." Partnership allocations designed to accomplish business objectives other than reducing taxes will generally have substantial economic effect.[63] If they are not defined in the partnership agreement or do not have substantial economic effect, allocations to partners must be made in accordance with the "partners' interests in the partnership."[64] According to tax regulations, the partners' interests in the partnership are a measure of the partners' economic arrangement, and should be determined by considering factors such as their capital contributions, distribution rights, and interests in economic profits and losses (if different from their interests in taxable income and loss). Partnership allocations inconsistent with partners' capital interests or overall profit-and-loss-sharing ratios are called **special allocations.**

Although special allocations are made largely at the discretion of partners, certain special allocations of gains and losses from the sale of partnership property are mandatory. Specifically, when property contributed to a partnership with built-in gains (fair market value greater than tax basis) or built-in losses (tax basis greater than fair market value) is subsequently sold, the partnership must allocate, to the extent possible, the built-in gain or built-in loss (at the time of the contribution) solely to the contributing partner and then allocate any remaining gain or loss to all the partners in accordance with their profit-and-loss-sharing ratios.[65] This rule prevents contributing partners from shifting their built-in gains and built-in losses to other partners.

---

[61]The tax imposed is 3.8 percent of the lesser of (a) net investment income or (b) the excess of modified adjusted gross income over $250,000 for married-joint filers and surviving spouses, $125,000 for married separate filers, and $200,000 for other taxpayers. Modified adjusted gross income equals adjusted gross income increased by income excluded under the foreign earned income exclusion less any disallowed deductions associated with the foreign earned income exclusion. §1411.

[62]For purposes of computing the net investment income tax, a partner's status as either active or passive with respect to an activity is determined according to the §469 passive activity loss rules explained later in this chapter. §1411(c)(2)(A).

[63]Reg. §1.704-1 defines the requirements allocations must satisfy to have substantial economic effect.

[64]§704(b).

[65]§704(c). In addition to requiring built-in gains and losses to be specially allocated to contributing partners, §704(c) also requires depreciation to be specially allocated to noncontributing partners. Tax regulations permit partners to choose among several methods for making these required special allocations. Further discussion of these methods is beyond the scope of this book.

Example 20-20

What if: Assume that at the beginning of 2016, Nicole and Sarah decide to organize CCS's marketing efforts by region. Nicole will take responsibility for marketing in the western United States, and Sarah will take responsibility for marketing in the eastern United States. All members agree that CCS's provision for allocating profits and losses in the operating agreement should be amended to provide Nicole and Sarah with better incentives. Specifically, CCS would like to allocate the first 20 percent of profits or losses from each region to Nicole and Sarah. Then, it will allocate any remaining profits or losses from each region among the members in proportion to their capital interests and profits interests at the end of 2016—40 percent to Sarah and 30 percent each to Nicole and Greg. Will CCS's proposed special allocation of profits and losses be accepted by the IRS?

Answer: Yes. Since CCS is a partnership for federal income tax purposes, it can make special allocations to members, and because they are designed to accomplish a business objective other than tax reduction, the IRS will accept them.[66]

What if: Assume the land Nicole contributed to CCS with a fair market value of $150,000 and tax basis of $20,000 was sold by CCS for $150,000 of consideration almost immediately after it was contributed. How would the resulting $130,000 gain be allocated among the members of CCS?

Answer: Nicole's built-in gain of $130,000 at the time of contribution must be allocated exclusively to her to prevent it from being shifted to other CCS members. Shifting the gain to other members could lower the overall tax liability of the CCS members if Sarah and Greg's marginal tax rates are lower than Nicole's marginal tax rate.

What if: Suppose CCS held the land Nicole contributed for one year and then sold it on March 31, 2016, for $180,000 instead of $150,000. How should the resulting $160,000 gain be allocated to Nicole, Sarah, and Chanzz Inc.?

Answer: The allocations are $139,000 to Nicole, $12,000 to Sarah, and $9,000 to Chanzz Inc., as reflected in the table below:

Description	CCS	Nicole 30%	Sarah 40%	Chanzz Inc. 30%
Total gain from sale of land	$160,000			
Less:				
Special allocation to Nicole of built-in gain	(130,000)	$130,000		
Post-contribution appreciation in land	30,000	9,000	$12,000	$9,000
Total gain allocations		139,000	12,000	9,000

Partnership Compliance Issues

Although partnerships don't pay taxes, they are required to file **Form 1065,** U.S. Return of Partnership Income (shown in Exhibit 20-8), with the IRS by the 15th day of the 4th month after their year-end for partnerships with tax years ending on or before December 31, 2015, or by the 15th day of the 3rd month after their year-end for partnerships with tax years ending after December 31, 2015. (April 15 for a calendar year-end partnership ending in 2015 and March 15 for a calendar year partnership ending after 2015). Partnerships with tax years ending on or before December 31, 2015, may receive an automatic five-month extension to file or partnerships with tax years ending after December 31, 2015, may receive an automatic six-month extension to file by filing **Form 7004** with the IRS before the original due date of the return.[67] Page 1 of Form 1065 details the calculation of the partnership's ordinary

[66]Reg. §1.704-1(b)(5), Example 10, suggests that this type of special allocation would not violate the substantial economic effect rules.

[67]Under §6698, late filing penalties apply if the partnership fails to file by the normal or extended due date for the return. The penalty is $195 times the number of partners in the partnership times the number of months (or fraction thereof) the return is late up to a maximum of 12 months.

EXHIBIT 20-8 (PART I) Page 1 Form 1065
CCS's 2016 Ordinary Business Loss (on 2015 forms)

Form **1065**		**U.S. Return of Partnership Income**			OMB No. 1545-0123	
Department of the Treasury Internal Revenue Service		For calendar year 2015, or tax year beginning _____, 2015, ending _____, 20 ____. ▶ Information about Form 1065 and its separate instructions is at *www.irs.gov/form1065.*			**2015**	

A Principal business activity **Manufacturing**	Name of partnership **Color Comfort Sheets**		D Employer identification number **00072359**
B Principal product or service **Textile Products**	Type or Print	Number, street, and room or suite no. If a P.O. box, see the instructions. **375 East 450 South**	E Date business started **April 1, 2015**
C Business code number **31400**		City or town, state or province, country, and ZIP or foreign postal code **Salt Lake City, UT 84608**	F Total assets (see the instructions) $ **370,000**

G Check applicable boxes: (1) ☐ Initial return (2) ☐ Final return (3) ☐ Name change (4) ☐ Address change (5) ☐ Amended return
(6) ☐ Technical termination - also check (1) or (2)

H Check accounting method: (1) ☑ Cash (2) ☐ Accrual (3) ☐ Other (specify) ▶ _____

I Number of Schedules K-1. Attach one for each person who was a partner at any time during the tax year ▶ **4** _____

J Check if Schedules C and M-3 are attached . . . . ☐

Caution. *Include only trade or business income and expenses on lines 1a through 22 below. See the instructions for more information.*

Income	1a	Gross receipts or sales	1a	40,000	
	b	Returns and allowances	1b		
	c	Balance. Subtract line 1b from line 1a		1c	40,000
	2	Cost of goods sold (attach Form 1125-A)		2	20,000
	3	Gross profit. Subtract line 2 from line 1c		3	20,000
	4	Ordinary income (loss) from other partnerships, estates, and trusts (attach statement) . .		4	
	5	Net farm profit (loss) (attach Schedule F (Form 1040))		5	
	6	Net gain (loss) from Form 4797, Part II, line 17 (attach Form 4797)		6	
	7	Other income (loss) (attach statement)		7	
	8	**Total income (loss).** Combine lines 3 through 7		8	20,000
Deductions (see the instructions for limitations)	9	Salaries and wages (other than to partners) (less employment credits)		9	50,000
	10	Guaranteed payments to partners		10	10,000
	11	Repairs and maintenance		11	
	12	Bad debts		12	
	13	Rent		13	
	14	Taxes and licenses		14	
	15	Interest		15	
	16a	Depreciation (if required, attach Form 4562)	16a	18,000	
	b	Less depreciation reported on Form 1125-A and elsewhere on return	16b		16c 18,000
	17	Depletion **(Do not deduct oil and gas depletion.)**		17	
	18	Retirement plans, etc.		18	
	19	Employee benefit programs		19	
	20	Other deductions (attach statement)		20	2,800
	21	**Total deductions.** Add the amounts shown in the far right column for lines 9 through 20 .		21	80,800
	22	**Ordinary business income (loss).** Subtract line 21 from line 8		22	(60,800)

Sign Here	Under penalties of perjury, I declare that I have examined this return, including accompanying schedules and statements, and to the best of my knowledge and belief, it is true, correct, and complete. Declaration of preparer (other than general partner or limited liability company member manager) is based on all information of which preparer has any knowledge.	May the IRS discuss this return with the preparer shown below (see instructions)? ☐ Yes ☐ No
	▶ _____ Signature of general partner or limited liability company member manager	▶ _____ Date

Paid Preparer Use Only	Print/Type preparer's name	Preparer's signature	Date	Check ☐ if self-employed	PTIN
	Firm's name ▶			Firm's EIN ▶	
	Firm's address ▶			Phone no.	

For Paperwork Reduction Act Notice, see separate instructions. Cat. No. 11390Z Form **1065** (2015)

business income (loss) for the year, and page 3, **Schedule K,** lists the partnership's ordinary business income (loss) and separately stated items. In addition to preparing Form 1065, the partnership is also responsible for preparing a Schedule K-1 for each partner detailing her individual share of the partnership's ordinary business income (loss) and separately stated items for the year. Once prepared, Schedule K-1s are included with Form 1065 when it is filed, and Schedule K-1s are also separately

EXHIBIT 20-8 (PART II)   Page 3 Form 1065
CCS's 2016 Schedule K (on 2015 forms)

Form 1065 (2015)   Page **4**

Schedule K		Partners' Distributive Share Items					Total amount
Income (Loss)	1	Ordinary business income (loss) (page 1, line 22)				1	(60,800)
	2	Net rental real estate income (loss) (attach Form 8825)				2	
	3a	Other gross rental income (loss)	3a				
	b	Expenses from other rental activities (attach statement)	3b				
	c	Other net rental income (loss). Subtract line 3b from line 3a				3c	
	4	Guaranteed payments				4	10,000
	5	Interest income				5	
	6	Dividends: a Ordinary dividends				6a	500
		b Qualified dividends	6b	500			
	7	Royalties				7	
	8	Net short-term capital gain (loss) (attach Schedule D (Form 1065))				8	
	9a	Net long-term capital gain (loss) (attach Schedule D (Form 1065))				9a	300
	b	Collectibles (28%) gain (loss)	9b				
	c	Unrecaptured section 1250 gain (attach statement) . .	9c				
	10	Net section 1231 gain (loss) (attach Form 4797)				10	
	11	Other income (loss) (see instructions) Type ▶				11	
Deductions	12	Section 179 deduction (attach Form 4562)				12	
	13a	Contributions				13a	
	b	Investment interest expense				13b	
	c	Section 59(e)(2) expenditures: (1) Type ▶_____ (2) Amount ▶				13c(2)	
	d	Other deductions (see instructions) Type ▶				13d	
Self-Employment	14a	Net earnings (loss) from self-employment				14a	(41,680)
	b	Gross farming or fishing income				14b	
	c	Gross nonfarm income				14c	20,000
Credits	15a	Low-income housing credit (section 42(j)(5))				15a	
	b	Low-income housing credit (other)				15b	
	c	Qualified rehabilitation expenditures (rental real estate) (attach Form 3468, if applicable)				15c	
	d	Other rental real estate credits (see instructions) Type ▶_____				15d	
	e	Other rental credits (see instructions) Type ▶_____				15e	
	f	Other credits (see instructions) Type ▶_____				15f	
Foreign Transactions	16a	Name of country or U.S. possession ▶_____					
	b	Gross income from all sources				16b	
	c	Gross income sourced at partner level				16c	
		Foreign gross income sourced at partnership level					
	d	Passive category ▶_____ e General category ▶_____ f Other ▶				16f	
		Deductions allocated and apportioned at partner level					
	g	Interest expense ▶_____ h Other . . . . ▶				16h	
		Deductions allocated and apportioned at partnership level to foreign source income					
	i	Passive category ▶_____ j General category ▶_____ k Other ▶				16k	
	l	Total foreign taxes (check one): ▶ Paid ☐ Accrued ☐				16l	
	m	Reduction in taxes available for credit (attach statement)				16m	
	n	Other foreign tax information (attach statement)					
Alternative Minimum Tax (AMT) Items	17a	Post-1986 depreciation adjustment				17a	
	b	Adjusted gain or loss				17b	
	c	Depletion (other than oil and gas)				17c	
	d	Oil, gas, and geothermal properties—gross income				17d	
	e	Oil, gas, and geothermal properties—deductions				17e	
	f	Other AMT items (attach statement)				17f	
Other Information	18a	Tax-exempt interest income				18a	
	b	Other tax-exempt income				18b	
	c	Nondeductible expenses				18c	
	19a	Distributions of cash and marketable securities				19a	
	b	Distributions of other property				19b	
	20a	Investment income				20a	500
	b	Investment expenses				20b	
	c	Other items and amounts (attach statement)					

Form **1065** (2015)

EXHIBIT 20-8 (PART III) **2016 Schedule K-1 for Sarah Walker (on 2015 forms)**
CCS Operates as an LLC

651113

☐ Final K-1	☐ Amended K-1

OMB No. 1545-0123

Schedule K-1
(Form 1065)

Department of the Treasury
Internal Revenue Service

20**15**

For calendar year 2015, or tax
year beginning _____, 2015
ending _____, 20 _____

Partner's Share of Income, Deductions,
Credits, etc. ▶ See back of form and separate instructions.

Part I	**Information About the Partnership**

A Partnership's employer identification number
00072359

B Partnership's name, address, city, state, and ZIP code

Color Comfort Sheets
375 East 450 South
Salt Lake City, UT 84608

C IRS Center where partnership filed return
Ogden

D ☐ Check if this is a publicly traded partnership (PTP)

Part II	**Information About the Partner**

E Partner's identifying number
429-88-3426

F Partner's name, address, city, state, and ZIP code

Sarah Walker
549 Laurel Lane
Holladay, UT 84609

G ☒ General partner or LLC member-manager ☐ Limited partner or other LLC member

H ☒ Domestic partner ☐ Foreign partner

I1 What type of entity is this partner? Individual

I2 If this partner is a retirement plan (IRA/SEP/Keogh/etc.), check here ☐

J Partner's share of profit, loss, and capital (see instructions):

	Beginning	Ending
Profit	40 %	40 %
Loss	40 %	40 %
Capital	40 %	40 %

K Partner's share of liabilities at year end:

Nonrecourse	$	12,000
Qualified nonrecourse financing	$	8,000
Recourse	$	24,000

L Partner's capital account analysis:

Beginning capital account	$
Capital contributed during the year	$
Current year increase (decrease)	$
Withdrawals & distributions	$ ( )
Ending capital account	$

☐ Tax basis ☐ GAAP ☐ Section 704(b) book
☐ Other (explain)

M Did the partner contribute property with a built-in gain or loss?
☐ Yes ☒ No
If "Yes," attach statement (see instructions)

Part III	**Partner's Share of Current Year Income, Deductions, Credits, and Other Items**

No.	Item	Amount	No.	Item	Amount
1	Ordinary business income (loss)	(24,320)	15	Credits	
2	Net rental real estate income (loss)				
3	Other net rental income (loss)		16	Foreign transactions	
4	Guaranteed payments	10,000			
5	Interest income				
6a	Ordinary dividends	200			
6b	Qualified dividends	200			
7	Royalties				
8	Net short-term capital gain (loss)				
9a	Net long-term capital gain (loss)	120	17	Alternative minimum tax (AMT) items	
9b	Collectibles (28%) gain (loss)				
9c	Unrecaptured section 1250 gain				
10	Net section 1231 gain (loss)		18	Tax-exempt income and nondeductible expenses	
11	Other income (loss)				
12	Section 179 deduction		19	Distributions	
13	Other deductions		20	Other information	
			A		200
14	Self-employment earnings (loss)				
A		(14,320)			
C		8,000			

*See attached statement for additional information.

For IRS Use Only

provided to all partners (each partner receives a Schedule K-1 with her income and loss allocations). Exhibit 20-8, parts I through III, displays CCS's information return, showing the operating results we summarized in Example 20-17 and Sarah's actual Schedule K-1, reflecting the facts and conclusions in Examples 20-17 and 20-18.[68]

PARTNER'S ADJUSTED TAX BASIS IN PARTNERSHIP INTEREST

LO 20-5

Earlier in this chapter, we discussed how partners measure their initial tax basis in their partnership interests when they contribute property or services to partnerships in exchange for their partnership interests, or when they purchase partnership interests from an existing partner. Unlike the basis in a stock or other similar investment, which is usually fixed, the basis in a partnership is dynamic and must be *adjusted* as the partnership generates income and losses, changes its debt levels, and makes distributions to partners. These annual adjustments to a partner's tax basis are required to ensure partners don't double-count taxable income/gains and deductible expenses/ losses, either when they sell their partnership interests or when they receive partnership distributions. They also ensure tax-exempt income and nondeductible expenses are not ultimately taxed or deducted.

Partners make the following adjustments to the basis in their partnership interests, annually:

- Increase for actual and deemed cash contributions to the partnership during the year.[69]
- Increase for partner's share of ordinary business income and separately stated income/gain items.
- Increase for partner's share of tax-exempt income.
- Decrease for actual and deemed[70] cash distributions[71] during the year.
- Decrease for partner's share of nondeductible expenses (fines, penalties, etc.).
- Decrease for partner's share of ordinary business loss and separately stated expense/loss items.

Partners first adjust their bases for items that increase basis, then for distributions, then by nondeductible expenses, and then by deductible expenses and losses to the extent any basis remains after prior adjustments.[72] Basis adjustments that decrease basis may never reduce a partner's tax basis below zero.[73]

Example 20-21

Given the events that affected CCS and its members during *2015,* what tax basis did Nicole, Sarah, and Chanzz Inc. have in their ownership interests at the end of 2015?

(continued on page 20-28)

[68]We use 2015 forms because 2016 forms were unavailable at the time the book was published.

[69]Recall that partners are deemed to have made a cash contribution to the partnership when they are allocated an additional share of partnership debt.

[70]Recall that partners are deemed to have received a cash distribution from the partnership when they are relieved of partnership debt.

[71]Property distributions to partners are also treated as basis reductions. We discuss property distributions at length in Chapter 21.

[72]Reg. §1.704-1(d)(2).

[73]§705(a)(2).

Answer: Their bases in CCS were $4,000, $152,000, and $114,000, respectively. Their individual tax basis calculations at the end of 2015 are illustrated in the table below:

Description	Nicole	Sarah	Chanzz Inc.	Explanation
(1) Initial tax basis (including debt)	$36,666	$146,666	$146,666	Example 20-4.
(2) Dividends	700	700	700	Example 20-15.
(3) Short-term capital gains	400	400	400	Example 20-15.
(4) Debt reallocation (deemed cash contribution/distribution)	(2,666)	5,334	(2,666)	Example 20-10.
(5) Sarah's capital interest	(10,000)	20,000	(10,000)	Examples 20-10, 20-15.
(6) CCS's ordinary business loss	(21,100)	(21,100)	(21,100)	Example 20-15.
Tax basis on 12/31/15	$ 4,000	$152,000	$114,000	Sum of (1) through (6).

What if: Suppose Sarah sold her LLC interest but forgot to include her share of short-term capital gains when computing her basis to determine her gain on the sale. What are the tax consequences of Sarah's mistake?

Answer: Sarah would be double-taxed on the amount of the short-term capital gain. She was initially taxed on her share of the short-term capital gain allocation, and she would be taxed a second time when she recognized $400 more gain on the sale than had she included her share of the gain in her basis.

What if: Assume Sarah was allocated $700 of tax-exempt municipal bond income instead of dividend income. What would happen if she neglected to increase her basis in CCS by the $700 tax-exempt income?

Answer: If Sarah were to sell her interest in CCS for a price reflecting the tax-exempt income received, she would, in effect, be converting tax-exempt income into taxable income.

Example 20-22

In addition to the other events of *2016,* CCS increased its debt from $100,000 to $130,000 in the second half of the year. The $30,000 increase was attributable to accounts payable owed to suppliers. Unlike the case of the $60,000 bank loan, the members did not guarantee any of the accounts payable. Therefore, the accounts payable are considered nonrecourse debt because CCS is an LLC. Given this information, what are Nicole's, Sarah's, and Greg's tax bases in CCS at the end of *2016?*

Answer: Their bases are $0, $140,000, and $124,000, respectively. Nicole, Sarah, and Greg would determine their tax basis in CCS at the end of *2016* as illustrated in the table below:

Description	Nicole 30%	Sarah[74] 40%	Greg 30%	Explanation
(1) Tax basis on 1/1/16	$4,000	$152,000		Example 20-21.
(1) Greg's purchase of Chanzz Inc.'s interest			$124,000	Example 20-11.
(2) Dividends	150	200	75	Example 20-17.
(3) Long-term capital gains	90	120	45	Example 20-17.
(4) Increase in nonrecourse debt from accounts payable (deemed cash contribution)	9,000	12,000	9,000	$30,000 × member's profit-sharing ratio.
(5) CCS's ordinary business loss	(18,240)	(24,320)	(9,120)	Example 20-17.
Preliminary tax basis	(5,000)	140,000	124,000	Sum of (1) through (5).
Tax basis on 12/31/16	0*	140,000	124,000	*Nicole's basis can't go below zero.

[74]Recall that Sarah received a $10,000 cash guaranteed payment for services she performed in 2016. Cash guaranteed payments generally don't have a direct impact on the recipient partner's tax basis because they are similar to salary payments.

Cash Distributions in Operating Partnerships

Even after a partnership has been formed, partners are likely to continue to receive actual and deemed cash distributions. For example, excess cash may be distributed to partners to provide them with cash flow to pay their taxes or simply for consumption, and deemed cash distributions occur as partnerships pay down their debts. The principles underlying the calculation of a partner's tax basis highlight the fact that partners are taxed on income as the partnership earns it instead of when it distributes it. If cash is distributed when partners have a positive tax basis in their partnership interests, the distribution effectively represents a distribution of profits that have been previously taxed, a return of capital previously contributed by the partner to the partnership, a distribution of cash the partnership has borrowed, or some combination of the three. Thus, as long as a cash distribution does not exceed a partner's tax basis before the distribution, it reduces the partner's tax basis but is not taxed. However, as we highlighted in our discussion of property contributions earlier in this chapter, cash distributions (deemed or actual) in excess of a partner's basis are taxable gains and are generally treated as capital gains.[75]

Example 20-23

What if: In Example 20-22, we determined that Sarah's basis in her partnership interest was $140,000. Assume that in addition to the facts provided in that example, Sarah received a $10,000 distribution in *2016*. What will her tax basis be at the end of the year?

Answer: Sarah's tax basis will be $130,000. After making only her positive adjustments for the year (positive adjustments come before negative adjustments such as distributions), she has a basis of $164,320, which is greater than the $10,000 distribution. Thus, the distribution would not have been taxable because it did not exceed her basis. Sarah would have also reduced her basis by the $10,000 distribution in addition to the $24,320 reduction for her share of the ordinary business loss, leaving her with an ending basis of $130,000 ($164,320 − $10,000 − $24,320).

What problem would be created if Sarah did not reduce her basis by the $10,000 distribution?

Answer: After she receives a $10,000 distribution, the value of Sarah's interest will decrease by $10,000. If she didn't reduce her tax basis by the distribution, selling her interest would produce a $10,000 artificial tax loss.

LOSS LIMITATIONS

While partners generally prefer not to invest in partnerships with operating losses, these losses generate current tax benefits when partners can deduct them against other sources of taxable income. Unlike capital losses, which are of limited usefulness if taxpayers don't also have capital gains, ordinary losses from partnerships are deductible against any type of taxable income. However, they are deductible on the partner's tax return only when they clear three separate hurdles: (1) tax basis, (2) at-risk amount, and (3) passive activity loss hurdles. We discuss each hurdle below.

Tax-Basis Limitation

A partner's basis limits the amount of partnership losses the partner can use to offset other sources of income. In theory, a partner's basis represents the amount a partner has invested in a partnership (or may have to invest to satisfy her debt obligations). As a result, partners may not utilize partnership losses in excess of their investment or outside basis in their partnership interests. Any losses allocated in excess of their basis must be suspended and carried forward indefinitely until they have sufficient basis to utilize the losses.[76] Any suspended losses remaining when partners sell or otherwise

[75]§731.
[76]§704(d).

dispose of their interests are lost forever. Among other things, partners may create additional tax basis in the future by making capital contributions, by guaranteeing more partnership debt, and by helping their partnership to become profitable.

Example 20-24

In Example 20-22 we discovered Nicole was allocated $5,000 of ordinary loss in excess of her tax basis for 2016, leaving her with a basis of zero at the end of 2016. What does Nicole do with this loss?

Answer: Nicole will carry forward all $5,000 of ordinary loss in excess of her tax basis indefinitely until her tax basis in CCS becomes positive. To the extent her tax basis increases in the future, the tax-basis limitation will no longer apply to her ordinary loss. Even then, however, the at-risk and/or passive activity loss hurdles may ultimately apply to constrain her ability to deduct the loss on her future tax returns.

What if: Assuming Nicole is allocated $4,000 of income from CCS in 2017, how much of her $5,000 suspended loss will clear the tax basis hurdle in *2017*?

Answer: Nicole's basis will initially increase by $4,000. Then she can apply $4,000 of her suspended loss against this basis increase, leaving her tax basis at zero and holding a remaining suspended loss of $1,000. The $4,000 loss clearing the tax basis hurdle must still clear the at-risk and passive activity loss hurdles before Nicole can deduct it on her return.

At-Risk Limitation

THE KEY FACTS

Loss Limitations

- Partnership losses in excess of a partner's tax basis are suspended and carried forward until additional basis is created.
- Remaining partnership losses are further suspended by the at-risk rules to the extent a partner is allocated nonrecourse debt not secured by real property.
- If a partner is not a material participant or the partnership is involved in rental activities, losses remaining after application of the tax basis and at-risk limitations may be used only against other passive income or when the partnership interest is sold.

The at-risk hurdle or limitation is more restrictive than the tax-basis limitation, because it excludes a type of debt normally included in a partner's tax basis. We have already highlighted the distinction between recourse and nonrecourse debt and noted that partners allocated recourse debt have economic risk of loss, while partners allocated nonrecourse debt have no risk of loss. Instead, the risk of loss on nonrecourse debt is borne by lenders. The **at-risk rules** in §465 were adopted to limit the ability of partners to use nonrecourse debt as a means of creating tax basis to use losses from tax shelter partnerships expressly designed to generate losses for the partners. The at-risk rules limit partners' losses to their amount "at risk" in the partnership—their **at-risk amount.** Generally, a partner's at-risk amount is the same as her tax basis except that, with one exception, the partner's share of certain nonrecourse debts is not included in the at-risk amount. Specifically, the only nonrecourse debts considered to be at risk are nonrecourse real estate mortgages from commercial lenders that are unrelated to borrowers. This type of debt is called **qualified nonrecourse financing.**[77] In addition to qualified nonrecourse financing, partners are considered to be at risk to the extent of cash and the tax basis of property contributed to the partnership. Further, partners are at risk for any partnership recourse debt allocated to them.

Partners apply the at-risk limitation after the tax-basis limitation. Any partnership losses that would otherwise have been allowed under the tax basis limitation are further limited to the extent they exceed a partner's at-risk amount. Losses limited under the at-risk rules are carried forward indefinitely until the partner generates additional at-risk amounts to utilize the losses, or until they are applied to reduce any gain from selling the partnership interest.

Example 20-25

In Example 20-22, we discovered Nicole was allocated an ordinary business loss of $18,240. In Example 20-24, we learned that of this loss, $13,240 cleared the tax basis hurdle and $5,000 did not. How much of the $13,240 ordinary business loss that clears the tax basis hurdle will clear the at-risk hurdle?

Answer: $4,240. The table below summarizes and compares Nicole's calculations to determine her tax basis and at-risk limitations for *2016:*

[77]§465(b)(6).

Example	Description	Tax Basis	At-Risk Amount	Explanation
20-22	(1) Nicole's tax basis on 1/1/16	$ 4,000	$ 4,000	Nicole's tax basis and at-risk amount are the same because she was only allocated recourse debt and qualified nonrecourse financing.
20-22	(2) Dividends	150	150	
20-22	(3) Long-term capital gains	90	90	
20-22	(4) Nonrecourse accounts payable	9,000	0	
	(5) Tax basis and at-risk amount before ordinary business loss	13,240	4,240	Sum of (1) through (4).
20-22	(6) Ordinary business loss	(18,240)		
	(7) Loss clearing the tax basis hurdle	(13,240)		Loss limited to (5).
	Loss suspended by tax basis hurdle	(5,000)		(6) – (7).
	(8) Loss clearing tax basis hurdle		(13,240)	(7).
	(9) Loss clearing at-risk hurdle		**(4,240)**	Loss limited to (5).
	Loss suspended by at-risk hurdle		(9,000)	(8) – (9).

Although Nicole's $9,000 share of the nonrecourse accounts payable added in *2016* and her investment income of $240 allow her to create enough tax basis in *2016* to get $13,240 of her $18,240 ordinary business loss past the tax-basis limitation, she is not at risk with respect to her $9,000 share of accounts payable because an LLC's accounts payable are general nonrecourse debt. Therefore, $9,000 of the $13,240 ordinary business loss clearing the tax basis hurdle is suspended under the at-risk limitation. As a result, Nicole has two separate losses to carry forward: a $5,000 ordinary loss limited by her tax basis and a $9,000 ordinary loss limited by the at-risk rules, leaving $4,240 of ordinary loss that may be deducted on her *2016* return.

Passive Activity Loss Limitation

Prior to 1986, partners with sufficient tax basis and at-risk amounts were able to utilize ordinary losses from their partnerships to offset portfolio income (i.e., interest, dividends, and capital gains), salary income, and self-employment income from partnerships and other trades or businesses. During this time, a partnership tax shelter industry thrived by marketing to wealthy investors partnership interests designed primarily to generate ordinary losses they could use to shield other income from tax. To combat this practice, Congress introduced the **passive activity loss (PAL) rules.**[78] These rules were enacted as a backstop to the at-risk rules and are applied after the tax-basis and at-risk limitations. Thus, depending on their situation, partners may have to overcome *three separate hurdles* before finally reporting partnership ordinary losses on their returns. In a nutshell, the passive activity loss rules limit the ability of partners in rental real estate partnerships and other partnerships they don't actively manage (passive activities) from using their ordinary losses from these activities (remaining after the application of the tax-basis and at-risk limitations) to reduce other sources of taxable income.

[78]§469. The passive activity loss rules apply primarily to individuals but also to estates, trusts, closely held C corporations, and personal service corporations.

Passive Activity Defined The passive activity rules define a passive activity as "any activity which involves the conduct of a trade or business,[79] and in which the taxpayer does not materially participate." According to the Code and Treasury regulations, participants in rental activities, including rental real estate[80] and limited partners without management rights, are automatically deemed to be passive participants. In addition, participants in all other activities are passive unless their involvement in an activity is "regular, continuous, and substantial." Clearly, these terms are quite subjective and difficult to apply. Fortunately, regulations provide more certainty in this area by enumerating seven separate tests for material participation.[81] An individual other than a limited partner can be classified as a material participant in an activity by meeting any *one* of the seven tests in Exhibit 20-9.

EXHIBIT 20-9 **Tests for Material Participation**

1. The individual participates in the activity more than 500 hours during the year.
2. The individual's activity constitutes substantially all the participation in such activity by individuals.
3. The individual participates more than 100 hours during the year and the individual's participation is not less than any other individual's participation in the activity.
4. The activity qualifies as a "significant participation activity" (individual participates for more than 100 hours during the year) and the aggregate of all other "significant participation activities" is greater than 500 hours for the year.
5. The individual materially participated in the activity for any 5 of the preceding 10 taxable years.
6. The activity involves personal services in health, law, accounting, architecture, and so on, and the individual materially participated for any three preceding years.
7. Taking into account all the facts and circumstances, the individual participates on a regular, continuous, and substantial basis during the year.

Income and Loss Baskets Under the passive activity loss rules, each item of a partner's income or loss from all sources for the year is placed in one of three categories or "baskets." Losses from *the passive basket* are not allowed to offset income from other baskets. The three baskets are (see Exhibit 20-10):

1. *Passive activity income or loss*—income or loss from an activity, including partnerships, in which the taxpayer is not a material participant.
2. *Portfolio income*—income from investments, including capital gains and losses, dividends, interest, annuities, and royalties.
3. *Active business income*—income from sources, including partnerships, in which the taxpayer is a material participant. For individuals, this includes salary and self-employment income.

The impact of segregating a partner's income in these baskets is to limit her ability to apply passive activity losses against income in the other two baskets. In effect, passive activity losses are suspended and remain in the passive income or loss basket until the taxpayer generates current-year passive income, either from the passive activity producing the loss or from some other passive activity, or until the taxpayer sells the activity that generated the passive loss. On the sale, in addition to reporting gain or loss from the sale of the property, the taxpayer will be allowed to deduct suspended passive losses as ordinary losses.

[79]The term *trade or business* is also deemed to include property held for the production of income such as rental property.

[80]§469(b)(7) provides an important exception to the general rule that all real estate activities are passive. To overcome this presumption, taxpayers must spend more than half their time working in trades or businesses materially participating in real estate activities and more than 750 hours materially participating in real estate activities during the year. This exception benefits partners that spend a substantial amount of time in partnership activities like real estate development and construction. Moreover, §469(i) permits individual taxpayers to treat up to $25,000 of losses from rental real estate as active losses each year.

[81]Reg. §1.469-5T.

EXHIBIT 20-10   Income and Loss Baskets

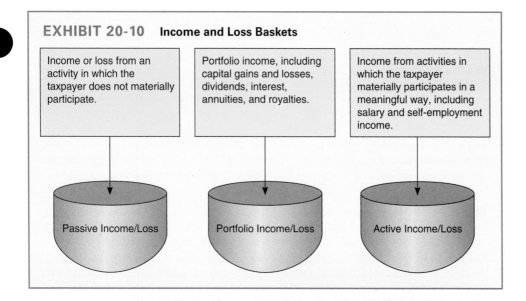

| Income or loss from an activity in which the taxpayer does not materially participate. | Portfolio income, including capital gains and losses, dividends, interest, annuities, and royalties. | Income from activities in which the taxpayer materially participates in a meaningful way, including salary and self-employment income. |

Passive Income/Loss   Portfolio Income/Loss   Active Income/Loss

ETHICS

Several years ago, Lou, together with his friend Carlo, opened an Italian restaurant in their neighborhood. The venture was formed as an LLC with Lou receiving a 75 percent ownership interest and Carlo receiving the remaining 25 percent ownership interest. While Lou was primarily responsible for operating the restaurant, Carlo only came in on weekends because he held a full-time job elsewhere. To document the time he spent in the restaurant, Carlo recorded the number of hours he had worked in a logbook at the end of every shift. This year, because of a downturn in the local economy, the restaurant showed a loss for the first time ever.

To be able to deduct his share of this loss when he files his tax return, Carlo would like to establish that he worked more than 500 hours during the year and is therefore a material participant in the restaurant. His logbook shows that he worked for 502 hours during the year; however, he rounded up to the nearest hour at the end of every shift to simplify his recordkeeping. For example, if he worked 4 hours and 25 minutes during a shift, he would have written 5 hours in the logbook. Should Carlo claim that he is a material participant on the basis of the hours recorded in his logbook and deduct his share of the loss? What would you do?

Example 20-26

As indicated in Example 20-22, Greg was allocated a $9,120 ordinary loss for *2016* and had a $124,000 tax basis at year-end *after* adjusting his tax basis for the loss. Given that Greg was allocated $9,000 of nonrecourse debt from accounts payable during *2016,* what is Greg's at-risk amount at the end of the year?

Answer: $115,000. Greg's at-risk amount is calculated by subtracting his $9,000 share of nonrecourse debt from his $124,000 tax basis.

Given Greg's status as a silent or nonmanaging member of CCS, how much of his $9,120 ordinary loss can he deduct in *2016* if he has no other sources of passive income?

Answer: None. Because Greg's tax basis and at-risk amount are large relative to his $9,120 ordinary loss, the tax basis and at-risk hurdles don't limit his loss. However, Greg's $9,120 loss would be classified as a passive loss and suspended until Greg received passive income from another source—hopefully CCS—or until he disposes of his interest in CCS.

What could Greg do to deduct any losses from CCS in the future?

Answer: He could satisfy one of the seven tests in Exhibit 20-9 to be classified as a material participant in CCS, thereby converting his future CCS losses from passive to active losses. Or he could become a passive participant in some other activity producing trade or business income that could be offset by any future passive losses from CCS.

Example 20-27

From Example 20-25 we learned that Nicole would report $150 of dividend income and $90 of long-term capital gains from CCS on her *2016* tax return. Further, we learned that $4,240 of her $18,240 *2016* ordinary loss allocation from CCS cleared both the tax basis and at-risk hurdles, leaving a total of $14,000 ordinary loss suspended and carried forward. How much of the $4,240 of ordinary loss can Nicole actually deduct on her tax return, given her status as a managing member of CCS?

Answer: Because Nicole is a managing member of CCS, it is likely she will satisfy at least one of the seven tests for material participation in Exhibit 20-9. As a result, she will treat the $4,240 ordinary loss clearing the tax basis and at-risk hurdles as an active loss and deduct it all on her tax return.

What if: Assume Nicole was not a managing member of CCS during *2016* and could not satisfy one of the seven material participation tests in Exhibit 20-9. How much of the $4,240 ordinary loss can she deduct on her tax return, assuming she has no other sources of passive income?

Answer: None. Under this assumption, the $4,240 is a passive activity loss and suspended until Nicole either receives some passive income from CCS (or some other source) or sells her interest in CCS. In the end, her entire $18,240 loss from *2016* would be suspended: $5,000 due to the tax basis limitation, $9,000 due to the at-risk limitation, and $4,240 due to the passive activity loss limitation.

CONCLUSION

This chapter explained the relevant tax rules pertaining to forming and operating partnerships. Specifically, we introduced important tax issues arising from partnership formations, including partner gain or loss recognition and calculating inside and outside basis. In addition, we explained accounting periods and methods, allocations of partners' ordinary income (loss) and separately stated items, basis adjustments, and loss limitation rules in the context of an operating partnership. Although it would seem that partnership tax law should be relatively straightforward given that partnerships don't pay taxes, by now you may have come to realize quite the opposite is true. The next chapter continues our discussion of partnership tax law with a focus on dispositions of partnership interests and partnership distributions.

Summary

 LO 20-1 Determine whether a flow-through entity is taxed as a partnership or S corporation, and distinguish the entity approach from the aggregate approach for taxing partnerships.

- Unincorporated business entities with more than one owner are taxed as partnerships.
- Shareholders of certain corporations may elect to have them treated as flow-through entities by filing an S election with the IRS.
- Though partnerships and S corporations are both flow-through entities, the tax rules that apply to them differ.
- Partnership tax rules reflect both the aggregate and entity concepts.

LO 20-2 Resolve tax issues applicable to partnership formations and other acquisitions of partnership interests, including gain recognition to partners and tax basis for partners and partnerships.

- As a general rule, partners don't recognize gain or loss when they contribute property to partnerships in exchange for a partnership interest.

- Partnership recourse debt is allocated to partners with ultimate responsibility for paying the debt, and nonrecourse debt is allocated to partners using profit-sharing ratios.

- Partners contributing property encumbered by debt may have to recognize gain, depending on the basis of the property and the amount of the debt.

- Partners contributing property to a partnership will have an initial tax basis in their partnership interest equal to the basis of contributed property less any debt relief plus their share of any partnership debt and any gain they recognize.

- Partners receiving partnership interests by contributing capital assets or §1231 assets have a holding period in their partnership interest that includes the holding period of the contributed property. If they contribute any other type of property instead, their holding period begins on the date the partnership interest is received.

- Partnerships with contributed property have a tax basis and holding period in the property equal to the contributing partner's tax basis and holding period.

- Partners who receive capital interests in exchange for services must report the liquidation value of the capital interest as ordinary income, and the partnership either deducts or capitalizes an equivalent amount depending on the nature of the services provided.

- Partners who receive profits interests in exchange for services don't report any income. However, they share in any subsequent partnership profits and losses.

- Partners who purchase partnership interests have a tax basis in their interests equal to the purchase price plus their shares of partnership debt, and their holding periods begin on the date of purchase.

Determine the appropriate accounting periods and methods for partnerships.   **LO 20-3**

- Partnerships, rather than individual partners, are responsible for making most tax elections.

- The Code mandates that partners include their share of income (loss) or other partnership items for "any taxable year of the partnership ending within or with the taxable year of the partner."

- Partnerships must use a tax year-end consistent with the majority interest taxable year, the taxable year of the principal partners, or the year-end providing the least aggregate deferral for the partners.

- Partnerships with average annual gross receipts over $5 million that have corporate partners may not use the cash method of accounting. Otherwise, partnerships may use either the cash or accrual method of accounting.

Calculate and characterize a partnership's ordinary business income or loss and its separately stated items, and demonstrate how to report these items to partners.   **LO 20-4**

- Partnerships must file Form 1065, U.S. Return of Partnership Income, with the IRS annually and must provide each partner with a Schedule K-1 detailing the partner's share of ordinary business income (loss) and separately stated items.

- Separately stated items include short-term and long-term capital gains and losses, dividends, §1231 gains and losses, and other partnership items that may be treated differently at the partner level.

- The character of separately stated items is determined at the partnership rather than at the partner level.

- Guaranteed payments are typically fixed payments made to partners for services provided to the partnership. They are treated as ordinary income by partners who receive them and are either deducted or capitalized by the partnership depending on the nature of services provided.

- Guaranteed payments to any type of partner (or LLC member) and general partners' shares of ordinary business income (loss) are treated as self-employment income (loss).

- Limited partners' shares of ordinary business income (loss) are not treated as self-employment income (loss).

- Though the tax law is uncertain in this area, all or a portion of LLC members' shares of ordinary business income (loss) should be classified as self-employment income (loss) if members are significantly involved in managing the LLC.

- Partnerships provide a great deal of flexibility because they may specially allocate their income, gains, expenses, losses, and other partnership items, as long as the allocations have "substantial economic effect" or are consistent with partners' interests in the partnership. Special allocations of built-in gain or loss on contributed property to contributing partners are mandatory.

LO 20-5   Explain the implications of a partner's tax basis and the adjustments that affect it.

- Partners must make specified annual adjustments to the tax basis in their partnership interests to ensure that partnership taxable income/gain or deductible expense/loss items are not double taxed or deducted twice, and that partnership tax-exempt income or nondeductible expense is not taxed or deducted.
- Partners increase the tax basis in their interests by their actual or deemed cash contributions, shares of ordinary business income, separately stated income/gain items, and shares of tax-exempt income.
- Partners decrease the tax basis in their interests by their actual or deemed cash distributions, shares of ordinary business loss, separately stated expense/loss items, and shares of nondeductible expenses.
- A partner's tax basis may never be reduced below zero.
- Cash distributions that are less than a partner's tax basis immediately before the distribution are not taxable. However, cash distributions in excess of a partner's tax basis immediately before the distribution are generally taxable as capital gain.

LO 20-6   Apply the basis, at-risk, and passive activity loss limits to losses from partnerships.

- In order for losses to provide tax benefits to partners, partnership losses must clear the tax-basis, at-risk, and passive activity loss hurdles (in that order).
- Partnership losses in excess of a partner's tax basis are suspended and may be utilized only when additional tax basis is created.
- Losses clearing the tax basis hurdle may be utilized only to the extent of the partner's at-risk amount. A partner's at-risk amount generally equals her tax basis (before any reduction for current year losses) less her share of nonrecourse debt that is not secured by real estate.
- If a partner is not a material participant in the partnership or if the partnership is involved in rental activities, losses clearing the basis and at-risk hurdles may be reported on the partner's tax return only when she has passive income from the partnership (or other sources) or when she sells her partnership interest.

KEY TERMS

aggregate approach (20-2)	least aggregate deferral (20-15)	profits interest (20-3)
at-risk amount (20-30)	limited liability companies	qualified nonrecourse
at-risk rules (20-30)	(LLC) (20-2)	financing (20-30)
built-in gain (20-3)	limited partnership (20-2)	recourse debt (20-5)
built-in loss (20-3)	liquidation value (20-10)	S corporations (20-2)
C corporations (20-2)	majority interest taxable year (20-15)	Schedule K (20-24)
capital account (20-8)	nonrecourse debt (20-5)	§704(b) capital accounts (20-8)
capital interest (20-3)	nonservice partner (20-10)	self-employment taxes (20-20)
entity approach (20-2)	ordinary business income	separately stated items (20-17)
flow-through entities (20-2)	(loss) (20-17)	service partner (20-10)
Form 1065 (20-23)	organization costs (20-12)	special allocations (20-22)
Form 7004 (20-23)	outside basis (20-4)	start-up costs (20-12)
GAAP capital accounts (20-8)	partnership interest (20-3)	Subchapter K (20-2)
general partnership (20-2)	passive activity loss (PAL)	Subchapter S (20-2)
guaranteed payments (20-19)	rules (20-31)	syndication costs (20-12)
inside basis (20-4)	principal partner (20-15)	tax capital accounts (20-8)

DISCUSSION QUESTIONS

Discussion Questions are available in *Connect*®.   ■ connect

1. What is a *flow-through entity,* and what effect does this designation have on how business entities and their owners are taxed?   `LO 20-1`

2. What types of business entities are taxed as flow-through entities?   `LO 20-1`

3. Compare and contrast the aggregate and entity concepts for taxing partnerships and their partners.   `LO 20-1`

4. What is a partnership interest, and what specific economic rights or entitlements are included with it?   `LO 20-2`

5. What is the rationale for requiring partners to defer most gains and all losses when they contribute property to a partnership?   `LO 20-2`

6. Under what circumstances is it possible for partners to recognize gain when contributing property to partnerships?   `LO 20-2`

7. What is *inside basis* and *outside basis,* and why are they relevant for taxing partnerships and partners?   `LO 20-2`

8. What is recourse and nonrecourse debt, and how is each generally allocated to partners?   `LO 20-2`

9. How does the amount of debt allocated to a partner affect the amount of gain a partner recognizes when contributing property secured by debt?   `LO 20-2`

10. What is a tax basis capital account, and what type of tax-related information does it provide?   `LO 20-2`

11. Distinguish between a capital interest and a profits interest, and explain how partners and partnerships treat each when exchanging them for services provided.   `LO 20-2`

12. How do partners who purchase a partnership interest determine the tax basis and holding period of their partnership interests?   `LO 20-2`

13. Why do you think partnerships, rather than the individual partners, are responsible for making most of the tax elections related to the operation of the partnership?   `LO 20-3`

14. If a partner with a taxable year-end of December 31 is in a partnership with a March 31 taxable year-end, how many months of deferral will the partner receive? Why?   `LO 20-3`

15. In what situation will there be a common year-end for the principal partners when there is no majority interest taxable year?   `LO 20-3`

16. Explain the least aggregate deferral test for determining a partnership's year-end and discuss when it applies.   `LO 20-3`

17. When are partnerships eligible to use the cash method of accounting?   `LO 20-3`

18. What is a partnership's ordinary business income (loss) and how is it calculated?   `LO 20-4`

19. What are some common separately stated items, and why must they be separately stated to the partners?   `LO 20-4`

20. Is the character of partnership income/gains and expenses/losses determined at the partnership or partner level? Why?   `LO 20-4`

21. What are guaranteed payments and how do partnerships and partners treat them for income and self-employment tax purposes?   `LO 20-4`

22. How do general and limited partners treat their share of ordinary business income for self-employment tax purposes?   `LO 20-4`

23. What challenges do LLCs face when deciding whether to treat their members' shares of ordinary business income as self-employment income?   `LO 20-4`

24. How much flexibility do partnerships have in allocating partnership items to partners?   `LO 20-4`

LO 20-4   25. What are the basic tax-filing requirements imposed on partnerships?

LO 20-5   26. In what situations do partners need to know the tax basis in their partnership interests?

LO 20-5   27. Why does a partner's tax basis in her partnership interest need to be adjusted annually?

LO 20-5   28. What items will increase a partner's basis in her partnership interest?

LO 20-5   29. What items will decrease a partner's basis in her partnership interest?

LO 20-6   30. What hurdles (or limitations) must partners overcome before they can ultimately deduct partnership losses on their tax returns?

LO 20-6   31. What happens to partnership losses allocated to partners in excess of the tax basis in their partnership interests?

LO 20-6   32. In what sense is the at-risk loss limitation rule more restrictive than the tax basis loss limitation rule?

LO 20-6   33. How do partners measure the amount they have at risk in the partnership?

LO 20-6   34. In what order are the loss limitation rules applied to limit partner's losses from partnerships?

LO 20-6   35. How do partners determine whether they are passive participants in partnerships when applying the passive activity loss limitation rules?

LO 20-6   36. Under what circumstances can partners with passive losses from partnerships deduct their passive losses?

PROBLEMS

Select problems are available in *Connect*®.

LO 20-2   37. Joseph contributed $22,000 in cash and equipment with a tax basis of $5,000 and a fair market value of $11,000 to Berry Hill Partnership in exchange for a partnership interest.

a) What is Joseph's tax basis in his partnership interest?

b) What is Berry Hill's basis in the equipment?

LO 20-2   38. Lance contributed investment property worth $500,000, purchased three years ago for $200,000 cash, to Cloud Peak LLC in exchange for an 85 percent profits and capital interest in the LLC. Cloud Peak owes $300,000 to its suppliers but has no other debts.

a) What is Lance's tax basis in his LLC interest?

b) What is Lance's holding period in his interest?

c) What is Cloud Peak's basis in the contributed property?

d) What is Cloud Peak's holding period in the contributed property?

LO 20-2   39. Laurel contributed equipment worth $200,000, purchased 10 months ago for $250,000 cash and used in her sole proprietorship, to Sand Creek LLC in exchange for a 15 percent profits and capital interest in the LLC. Laurel agreed to guarantee all $15,000 of Sand Creek's accounts payable, but she did not guarantee any portion of the $100,000 nonrecourse mortgage securing Sand Creek's office building. Other than the accounts payable and mortgage, Sand Creek does not owe any debts to other creditors.

a) What is Laurel's initial tax basis in her LLC interest?

b) What is Laurel's holding period in her interest?

c) What is Sand Creek's initial basis in the contributed property?

d) What is Sand Creek's holding period in the contributed property?

40. Harry and Sally formed the Evergreen Partnership by contributing the following assets in exchange for a 50 percent capital and profits interest in the partnership:

LO 20-2

planning

	Basis	Fair Market Value
Harry:		
Cash	$ 30,000	$ 30,000
Land	100,000	120,000
Totals	$130,000	$150,000
Sally:		
Equipment used in a business	200,000	150,000
Totals	$200,000	$150,000

a) How much gain or loss will Harry recognize on the contribution?

b) How much gain or loss will Sally recognize on the contribution?

c) How could the transaction be structured a different way to get a better result for Sally?

d) What is Harry's tax basis in his partnership interest?

e) What is Sally's tax basis in her partnership interest?

f) What is Evergreen's tax basis in its assets?

g) Following the format in Exhibit 20-2, prepare a tax basis balance sheet for the Evergreen partnership showing the tax capital accounts for the partners.

41. Cosmo contributed land with a fair market value of $400,000 and a tax basis of $90,000 to the Y Mountain Partnership in exchange for a 25 percent profits and capital interest in the partnership. The land is secured by $120,000 of non-recourse debt. Other than this nonrecourse debt, Y Mountain Partnership does not have any debt.

LO 20-2

a) How much gain will Cosmo recognize from the contribution?

b) What is Cosmo's tax basis in his partnership interest?

42. When High Horizon LLC was formed, Maude contributed the following assets in exchange for a 25 percent capital and profits interest in the LLC:

LO 20-2

	Basis	Fair Market Value
Maude:		
Cash	$ 20,000	$ 20,000
Land*	100,000	360,000
Totals	$120,000	$380,000

*Nonrecourse debt secured by the land equals $160,000

James, Harold, and Jenny each contributed $220,000 in cash for a 25 percent profits and capital interest.

a) How much gain or loss will Maude and the other members recognize?

b) What is Maude's tax basis in her LLC interest?

c) What tax basis do James, Harold, and Jenny have in their LLC interests?

d) What is High Horizon's tax basis in its assets?

e) Following the format in Exhibit 20-2, prepare a tax basis balance sheet for the High Horizon LLC showing the tax capital accounts for the members.

LO 20-2

43. Kevan, Jerry, and Dave formed Albee LLC. Jerry and Dave each contributed $245,000 in cash. Kevan contributed the following assets:

	Basis	Fair Market Value
Kevan:		
Cash	$ 15,000	$ 15,000
Land*	120,000	440,000
Totals	$135,000	$455,000

*Nonrecourse debt secured by the land equals $210,000

Each member received a one-third capital and profits interest in the LLC.

a) How much gain or loss will Jerry, Dave, and Kevan recognize on the contributions?

b) What is Kevan's tax basis in his LLC interest?

c) What tax basis do Jerry and Dave have in their LLC interests?

d) What is Albee LLC's tax basis in its assets?

e) Following the format in Exhibit 20-2, prepare a tax basis balance sheet for the Albee LLC showing the tax capital accounts for the members. What is Kevan's share of the LLC's inside basis?

f) If the lender holding the nonrecourse debt secured by Kevan's land required Kevan to guarantee 33.33 percent of the debt and Jerry to guarantee the remaining 66.67 percent of the debt when Albee LLC was formed, how much gain or loss will Kevan recognize?

g) If the lender holding the nonrecourse debt secured by Kevan's land required Kevan to guarantee 33.33 percent of the debt and Jerry to guarantee the remaining 66.67 percent of the debt when Albee LLC was formed, what are the members' tax bases in their LLC interests?

LO 20-2

research

44. Jim has decided to contribute some equipment he previously used in his sole proprietorship in exchange for a 10 percent profits and capital interest in Fast Choppers LLC. Jim originally paid $200,000 cash for the equipment. Since then, the tax basis in the equipment has been reduced to $100,000 because of tax depreciation, and the fair market value of the equipment is now $150,000.

a) Must Jim recognize any of the potential §1245 recapture when he contributes the machinery to Fast Choppers? [*Hint:* See §1245(b)(3).]

b) What cost recovery method will Fast Choppers use to depreciate the machinery? [*Hint:* See §168(i)(7).]

c) If Fast Choppers were to immediately sell the equipment Jim contributed for $150,000, how much gain would Jim recognize and what is its character? [*Hint:* See §1245 and 704(c).]

LO 20-2

research

45. Ansel purchased raw land three years ago for $200,000 to hold as an investment. After watching the value of the land drop to $150,000, he decided to contribute it to Mountainside Developers LLC in exchange for a 5 percent capital and profits interest. Mountainside plans to develop the property and will treat it as inventory, like all the other real estate it holds.

a) If Mountainside sells the property for $150,000 after holding it for one year, how much gain or loss does it recognize and what is the character of the gain or loss? [*Hint:* See §724.]

b) If Mountainside sells the property for $125,000 after holding it for two years, how much gain or loss does it recognize and what is the character of the gain or loss?

c) If Mountainside sells the property for $150,000 after holding it for six years, how much gain or loss does it recognize and what is the character of the gain or loss?

46. Claude purchased raw land three years ago for $1,500,000 to develop into lots and sell to individuals planning to build their dream homes. Claude intended to treat this property as inventory, like his other development properties. Before completing the development of the property, however, he decided to contribute it to South Peak Investors LLC when it was worth $2,500,000, in exchange for a 10 percent capital and profits interest. South Peak's strategy is to hold land for investment purposes only and then sell it later at a gain.

    LO 20-2

    research

    a) If South Peak sells the property for $3,000,000 four years after Claude's contribution, how much gain or loss is recognized and what is its character? [*Hint:* See §724.]

    b) If South Peak sells the property for $3,000,000 five and one-half years after Claude's contribution, how much gain or loss is recognized and what is its character?

47. Reggie contributed $10,000 in cash and a capital asset he had held for three years with a fair market value of $20,000 and tax basis of $10,000 for a 5 percent capital and profits interest in Green Valley LLC.

    LO 20-2

    research

    a) If Reggie sells his LLC interest 13 months later for $30,000 when the tax basis in his partnership interest is still $20,000, how much gain does he report and what is its character?

    b) If Reggie sells his LLC interest two months later for $30,000 when the tax basis in his partnership interest is still $20,000, how much gain does he report and what is its character? [*Hint:* See Reg. §1.1223-3.]

48. Connie recently provided legal services to the Winterhaven LLC and received a 5 percent interest in the LLC as compensation. Winterhaven currently has $50,000 of accounts payable and no other debt. The current fair market value of Winterhaven's capital is $200,000.

    LO 20-2

    a) If Connie receives a 5 percent capital interest only, how much income must she report and what is her tax basis in the LLC interest?

    b) If Connie receives a 5 percent profits interest only, how much income must she report and what is her tax basis in the LLC interest?

    c) If Connie receives a 5 percent capital and profits interest, how much income must she report and what is her tax basis in the LLC interest?

49. Mary and Scott formed a partnership that maintains its records on a calendar-year basis. The balance sheet of the MS Partnership at year-end is as follows:

    LO 20-2

	Basis	Fair Market Value
Cash	$ 60	$ 60
Land	60	180
Inventory	72	60
	$192	$300
Mary	$ 96	$150
Scott	96	150
	$192	$300

At the end of the current year, Kari will receive a one-third capital interest only in exchange for services rendered. Kari's interest will not be subject to a substantial risk of forfeiture and the costs for the type of services she provided are typically not capitalized by the partnership. For the current year, the income and expenses from operations are equal. Consequently, the only tax consequences for the year are those relating to the admission of Kari to the partnership.

a) Compute and characterize any gain or loss Kari may have to recognize as a result of her admission to the partnership.

b) Compute Kari's basis in her partnership interest.

c) Prepare a balance sheet of the partnership immediately after Kari's admission showing the partners' tax capital accounts and capital accounts stated at fair market value.

d) Calculate how much gain or loss Kari would have to recognize if, instead of a capital interest, she received a profits interest.

LO 20-2 50. Dave LaCroix recently received a 10 percent capital and profits interest in Cirque Capital LLC in exchange for consulting services he provided. If Cirque Capital had paid an outsider to provide the advice, it would have deducted the payment as compensation expense. Cirque Capital's balance sheet on the day Dave received his capital interest appears below:

	Basis	Fair Market Value
Assets:		
Cash	$150,000	$ 150,000
Investments	200,000	700,000
Land	150,000	250,000
Totals	$500,000	$1,100,000
Liabilities and capital:		
Nonrecourse debt	100,000	100,000
Lance*	200,000	500,000
Robert*	200,000	500,000
Totals	$500,000	$1,100,000

*Assume that Lance's basis and Robert's basis in their LLC interests equal their tax basis capital accounts plus their respective shares of nonrecourse debt.

a) Compute and characterize any gain or loss Dave may have to recognize as a result of his admission to Cirque Capital.

b) Compute each member's tax basis in his LLC interest immediately after Dave's receipt of his interest.

c) Prepare a balance sheet for Cirque Capital immediately after Dave's admission showing the members' tax capital accounts and their capital accounts stated at fair market value.

d) Compute and characterize any gain or loss Dave may have to recognize as a result of his admission to Cirque Capital if he receives only a profits interest.

e) Compute each member's tax basis in his LLC interest immediately after Dave's receipt of his interest if Dave receives only a profits interest.

LO 20-2 51. Last December 31, Ramon sold the 10 percent interest in the Del Sol Partnership that he had held for two years to Garrett for $400,000. Prior to selling his interest, Ramon's basis in Del Sol was $200,000, which included a $100,000 share of nonrecourse debt allocated to him.

a) What is Garrett's tax basis in his partnership interest?

b) If Garrett sells his partnership interest three months after receiving it and recognizes a gain, what is the character of his gain?

LO 20-3 52. Broken Rock LLC was recently formed with the following members:

Name	Tax Year-End	Capital/Profits %
George Allen	December 31	33.33%
Elanax Corp.	June 30	33.33
Ray Kirk	December 31	33.34

What is the required taxable year-end for Broken Rock LLC?

53. Granite Slab LLC was recently formed with the following members:

Name	Tax Year-End	Capital/Profits %
Nelson Black	December 31	22.0%
Brittany Jones	December 31	24.0
Lone Pine LLC	June 30	4.5
Red Spot Inc.	October 31	4.5
Pale Rock Inc.	September 30	4.5
Thunder Ridge LLC	July 31	4.5
Alpensee LLC	March 31	4.5
Lakewood Inc.	June 30	4.5
Streamside LLC	October 31	4.5
Burnt Fork Inc.	October 31	4.5
Snowy Ridge LP	June 30	4.5
Whitewater LP	October 31	4.5
Straw Hat LLC	January 31	4.5
Wildfire Inc.	September 30	4.5

LO 20-3

What is the required taxable year-end for Granite Slab LLC?

54. Tall Tree LLC was recently formed with the following members:

LO 20-3

Name	Tax Year-End	Capital/Profits %
Eddie Robinson	December 31	40%
Pitcher Lenders LLC	June 30	25
Perry Homes Inc.	October 31	35

What is the required taxable year-end for Tall Tree LLC?

55. Rock Creek LLC was recently formed with the following members:

LO 20-3

Name	Tax Year-End	Capital/Profits %
Mark Banks	December 31	35%
Highball Properties LLC	March 31	25
Chavez Builders Inc.	November 30	40

What is the required taxable year-end for Rock Creek LLC?

56. Ryan, Dahir, and Bill have operated Broken Feather LLC for the last four years using a calendar year-end. Each has a one-third interest. Since they began operating, their busy season has run from June through August, with 35 percent of their gross receipts coming in July and August. The members would like to change their tax year-end and have asked you to address the following questions:

LO 20-3

research

a) Can they change to an August 31 year-end and, if so, how do they make the change? [*Hint:* See Rev. Proc. 2002-38, 2002-1 CB 1037.]

b) Can they change to a September 30 year-end and, if so, how do they make the change? [*Hint:* See §444.]

57. Ashlee, Hiroki, Kate, and Albee LLC each own a 25 percent interest in Tally Industries LLC, which generates annual gross receipts of over $10 million. Ashlee, Hiroki, and Kate manage the business, but Albee LLC is a nonmanaging member. Although Tally Industries has historically been profitable, for the last three years losses have been allocated to the members. Given these facts, the members want to know whether Tally Industries can use the cash method of accounting. Why or why not? [*Hint:* See §448(b)(3).]

LO 20-3

research

LO 20-4

58. Turtle Creek Partnership had the following revenues, expenses, gains, losses, and distributions:

Sales revenue	$ 40,000
Long-term capital gains	2,000
Cost of goods sold	(13,000)
Depreciation—MACRS	(3,000)
Amortization of organization costs	(1,000)
Guaranteed payments to partners for general management	(10,000)
Cash distributions to partners	(2,000)

a) Given these items, what is Turtle Creek's ordinary business income (loss) for the year?

b) What are Turtle Creek's separately stated items for the year?

LO 20-4

59. Georgio owns a 20 percent profits and capital interest in Rain Tree LLC. For the current year, Rain Tree had the following revenues, expenses, gains, and losses:

Sales revenue	$ 70,000
Gain on sale of land (§1231)	11,000
Cost of goods sold	(26,000)
Depreciation—MACRS	(3,000)
§179 deduction*	(10,000)
Employee wages	(11,000)
Fines and penalties	(3,000)
Municipal bond interest	6,000
Short-term capital gains	4,000
Guaranteed payment to Sandra	(3,000)

*Assume the §179 property placed in service limitation does not apply.

a) How much ordinary business income (loss) is allocated to Georgio for the year?

b) What are Georgio's separately stated items for the year?

LO 20-4

research

60. Richard Meyer and two friends from law school recently formed Meyer and Associates as a limited liability partnership (LLP). Income from the partnership will be split equally among the partners. The partnership will generate fee income primarily from representing clients in bankruptcy and foreclosure matters. While some attorney friends have suggested that partners' earnings will be self-employment income, other attorneys they know from their local bar association meetings claim just the opposite. After examining relevant authority, explain how you would advise Meyer and Associates on this matter. [*Hint:* See §1402(a)(13) and *Renkemeyer, Campbell & Weaver LLP v. Commissioner,* 136 T.C. 137 (2011).]

LO 20-4

61. The partnership agreement of the G&P general partnership states that Gary will receive a guaranteed payment of $13,000, and that Gary and Prudence will share the remaining profits or losses in a 45/55 ratio. For year 1, the G&P partnership reports the following results:

Sales revenue	$ 70,000
Gain on sale of land (§1231)	8,000
Cost of goods sold	(38,000)
Depreciation—MACRS	(9,000)
Employee wages	(14,000)
Cash charitable contributions	(3,000)
Municipal bond interest	2,000
Other expenses	(2,000)

a) Compute Gary's share of ordinary income (loss) and separately stated items to be reported on his year 1 Schedule K-1, including his self-employment income (loss).

b) Compute Gary's share of self-employment income (loss) to be reported on his year 1 Schedule K-1, assuming G&P is a limited partnership and Gary is a limited partner.

c) What do you believe Gary's share of self-employment income (loss) to be reported on his year 1 Schedule K-1 should be, assuming G&P is an LLC and Gary spends 2,000 hours per year working there full time?

62. Hoki Poki, a cash-method general partnership, recorded the following items for its current tax year:

LO 20-4

research

Rental real estate income	$ 2,000
Sales revenue	70,000
§1245 recapture income	8,000
Interest income	2,000
Cost of goods sold	(38,000)
Depreciation—MACRS	(9,000)
Supplies expense	(1,000)
Employee wages	(14,000)
Investment interest expense	(1,000)
Partner's medical insurance premiums paid by Hoki Poki	(3,000)

As part of preparing Hoki Poki's current year return, identify the items that should be included in computing its ordinary business income (loss) and those that should be separately stated. [*Hint:* See Schedule K-1 and related preparer's instructions at www.irs.gov.]

63. On the last day of its current tax year, Buy Rite LLC received $300,000 when it sold a machine it had purchased for $200,000 three years ago to use in its business. At the time of the sale, the basis in the equipment had been reduced to $100,000 due to tax depreciation taken. How much did the members' self-employment earnings from Buy Rite increase when the equipment was sold? [*Hint:* See §1402(a)(3).]

LO 20-4

research

64. Jhumpa, Stewart, and Kelly are all one-third partners in the capital and profits of Firewalker general partnership. In addition to their normal share of the partnership's annual income, Jhumpa and Stewart receive an annual guaranteed payment of $10,000 to compensate them for additional services they provide. Firewalker's income statement for the current year reflects the following revenues and expenses:

LO 20-4

Sales revenue	$340,000
Interest income	3,300
Long-term capital gains	1,200
Cost of goods sold	(120,000)
Employee wages	(75,000)
Depreciation expense	(28,000)
Guaranteed payments	(20,000)
Miscellaneous expenses	(4,500)
Overall net income	$ 97,000

a) Given Firewalker's operating results, how much ordinary business income (loss) and what separately stated items [including the partners' self-employment earnings (loss)] will it report on its return for the year?

b) How will it allocate these amounts to its partners?

c) How much self-employment tax will each partner pay assuming none has any other source of income or loss?

LO 20-4

65. This year, Darrel's distributive share from Alcove Partnership includes $6,000 of interest income, $3,000 of dividend income, and $70,000 ordinary business income.

a) Assume that Darrel materially participates in the partnership. How much of his distributive share from Alcove Partnership is potentially subject to the net investment income tax?

b) Assume that Darrel does not materially participate in the partnership. How much of his distributive share from Alcove Partnership is potentially subject to the net investment income tax?

LO 20-4

66. This year, Alex's distributive share from Eden Lakes Partnership includes $8,000 of interest income, $4,000 of net long-term capital gains, $2,000 net §1231 gain from the sale of property used in the partnership's trade or business, and $83,000 of ordinary business income.

a) Assume that Alex materially participates in the partnership. How much of his distributive share from Eden Lakes Partnership is potentially subject to the net investment income tax?

b) Assume that Alex does not materially participate in the partnership. How much of his distributive share from the Eden Lakes partnership is potentially subject to the net investment income tax?

LO 20-4

research

67. Lane and Cal each own 50 percent of the profits and capital of HighYield LLC. HighYield owns a portfolio of taxable bonds and municipal bonds, and each year the portfolio generates approximately $10,000 of taxable interest and $10,000 of tax-exempt interest. Lane's marginal tax rate is 35 percent while Cal's marginal tax rate is 15 percent. To take advantage of the difference in their marginal tax rates, Lane and Cal want to modify their operating agreement to specially allocate all of the taxable interest to Cal and all of the tax-exempt interest to Lane. Until now, Lane and Cal had been allocated 50 percent of each type of interest income.

a) Is HighYield's proposed special allocation acceptable under current tax rules? Why or why not? [*Hint:* See Reg. §1.704-1(b)(2)(iii)(b) and §1.704-1(b)(5) Example (5).]

b) If the IRS ultimately disagrees with HighYield's special allocation, how will it likely reallocate the taxable and tax-exempt interest among the members? [*Hint:* See Reg. §1.704-1(b)(5) Example (5)(ii).]

LO 20-5

68. Larry's tax basis in his partnership interest at the beginning of the year was $10,000. If his share of the partnership debt increased by $10,000 during the year and his share of partnership income for the year is $3,000, what is his tax basis in his partnership interest at the end of the year?

LO 20-5

69. Carmine was allocated the following items from the Piccolo LLC for last year:

> Ordinary business loss
> Nondeductible penalties
> Tax-exempt interest income
> Short-term capital gain
> Cash distributions

Rank these items in terms of the order they should be applied to adjust Carmine's tax basis in Piccolo for the year (some items may be of equal rank).

LO 20-5

70. Oscar, Felix, and Marv are all one-third partners in the capital and profits of Eastside General Partnership. In addition to their normal share of the partnership's annual income, Oscar and Felix receive annual guaranteed payments of $7,000 to compensate them for additional services they provide. Eastside's

income statement for the current year reflects the following revenues and expenses:

Sales revenue	$420,000
Dividend income	5,700
Short-term capital gains	2,800
Cost of goods sold	(210,000)
Employee wages	(115,000)
Depreciation expense	(28,000)
Guaranteed payments	(14,000)
Miscellaneous expenses	(9,500)
Overall net income	$ 52,000

In addition, Eastside owed creditors $120,000 at the beginning of the year but managed to pay down its debts to $90,000 by the end of the year. All partnership debt is allocated equally among the partners. Finally, Oscar, Felix, and Marv had a tax basis of $80,000 in their interests at the beginning of the year.

a) What tax basis do the partners have in their partnership interests at the end of the year?

b) Assume the partners began the year with a tax basis of $10,000 and all the debt was paid off on the last day of the year. How much gain will the partners recognize when the debt is paid off? What tax basis do the partners have in their partnership interests at the end of the year?

71. Pam, Sergei, and Mercedes are all one-third partners in the capital and profits of Oak Grove General Partnership. Partnership debt is allocated among the partners in accordance with their capital and profits interests. In addition to their normal share of the partnership's annual income, Pam and Sergei receive annual guaranteed payments of $20,000 to compensate them for additional services they provide. Oak Grove's income statement for the current year reflects the following revenues and expenses: `LO 20-5`

Sales revenue	$476,700
Dividend income	6,600
§1231 losses	(3,800)
Cost of goods sold	(245,000)
Employee wages	(92,000)
Depreciation expense	(31,000)
Guaranteed payments	(40,000)
Miscellaneous expenses	(11,500)
Overall net income	$ 60,000

In addition, Oak Grove owed creditors $90,000 at the beginning of the year and $150,000 at the end, and Pam, Sergei, and Mercedes had a tax basis of $50,000 in their interests at the beginning of the year. Also, on December 31 of the current year, Sergei and Mercedes agreed to increase Pam's capital and profits interest from 33.33 percent to 40 percent in exchange for additional services she provided to the partnership. The current liquidation value of the additional capital interest Pam received is $40,000.

a) What tax basis do the partners have in their partnership interests at the end of the year?

b) If, in addition to the expenses listed above, the partnership donated $12,000 to a political campaign, what tax basis do the partners have in their partnership interests at the end of the year assuming the liquidation value of the additional capital interest Pam received at the end of the year remains at $40,000?

LO 20-6

research

72. Laura Davis is a member in a limited liability company that has historically been profitable but is expecting to generate losses in the near future because of a weak local economy. In addition to the hours she works as an employee of a local business, she currently spends approximately 150 hours per year helping to manage the LLC. Other LLC members each work approximately 175 hours per year in the LLC, and the time Laura and other members spend managing the LLC has remained constant since she joined the company three years ago. Laura's tax basis and amount at-risk are large compared to her share of projected losses; however, she is concerned that her ability to deduct her share of the projected losses will be limited by the passive activity loss rules.

a) As an LLC member, will Laura's share of losses be presumed to be passive as they are for limited partners? Why or why not? [*Hint:* See §469(h)(2), *Garnett v. Commissioner,* 132 T.C. 368 (2009), and Prop. Reg. § 1.469-5(e)(3)(i).]

b) Assuming Laura's losses are not presumed to be passive, is she devoting sufficient time to the LLC to be considered a material participant? Why or why not?

c) What would you recommend to Laura to help her achieve a more favorable tax outcome?

LO 20-6

73. Alfonso began the year with a tax basis in his partnership interest of $30,000. His share of partnership debt at the beginning and end of the year consists of $4,000 of recourse debt and $6,000 of nonrecourse debt. During the year, he was allocated $40,000 of partnership ordinary business loss. Alfonso does not materially participate in this partnership and he has $1,000 of passive income from other sources.

a) How much of Alfonso's loss is limited by his tax basis?

b) How much of Alfonso's loss is limited by his at-risk amount?

c) How much of Alfonso's loss is limited by the passive activity loss rules?

LO 20-6

74. Jenna began the year with a tax basis of $45,000 in her partnership interest. Her share of partnership debt consists of $6,000 of recourse debt and $10,000 of nonrecourse debt at the beginning of the year and $6,000 of recourse debt and $13,000 of nonrecourse debt at the end of the year. During the year, she was allocated $65,000 of partnership ordinary business loss. Jenna does not materially participate in this partnership and she has $4,000 of passive income from other sources.

a) How much of Jenna's loss is limited by her tax basis?

b) How much of Jenna's loss is limited by her at-risk amount?

c) How much of Jenna's loss is limited by the passive activity loss rules?

LO 20-5 **LO 20-6**

research

75. Juan Diego began the year with a tax basis in his partnership interest of $50,000. During the year, he was allocated $20,000 of partnership ordinary business income, $70,000 of §1231 losses, $30,000 of short-term capital losses, and received a cash distribution of $50,000.

a) What items related to these allocations does Juan Diego actually report on his tax return for the year? [*Hint:* See Reg. §1.704-1(d)(2) and Rev. Rul. 66-94.]

b) If any deductions or losses are limited, what are the carryover amounts and what is their character? [*Hint:* See Reg. §1.704-1(d).]

LO 20-6

76. Farell is a member of Sierra Vista LLC. Although Sierra Vista is involved in a number of different business ventures, it is not currently involved in real estate either as an investor or as a developer. On January 1, year 1, Farell has a $100,000 tax basis in his LLC interest that includes his $90,000 share of Sierra Vista's general debt obligations. By the end of the year, Farell's share of Sierra Vista's general debt obligations has increased to $100,000. Because of the time

he spends in other endeavors, Farell does not materially participate in Sierra Vista. His share of the Sierra Vista losses for year 1 is $120,000. As a partner in the Riverwoods Partnership, he also has year 1, Schedule K-1 passive income of $5,000.

a) Determine how much of the Sierra Vista loss Farell will currently be able to deduct on his tax return for year 1, and list the losses suspended due to tax basis, at-risk, and passive activity loss limitations.

b) Assuming Farell's Riverwoods K-1 indicates passive income of $30,000, determine how much of the Sierra Vista loss he will ultimately be able to deduct on his tax return for year 1, and list the losses suspended due to tax basis, at-risk, and passive activity loss limitations.

c) Assuming Farell is deemed to be an active participant in Sierra Vista, determine how much of the Sierra Vista loss he will ultimately be able to deduct on his tax return for year 1, and list the losses suspended due to tax basis, at-risk, and passive activity loss limitations.

77. Jenkins has a one-third capital and profits interest in the Maverick General Partnership. On January 1, year 1, Maverick has $120,000 of general debt obligations and Jenkins has a $50,000 tax basis (including his share of Maverick's debt) in his partnership interest. During the year, Maverick incurred a $30,000 nonrecourse debt that is not secured by real estate. Because Maverick is a rental real estate partnership, Jenkins is deemed to be a passive participant in Maverick. His share of the Maverick losses for year 1 is $75,000. Jenkins is not involved in any other passive activities, and this is the first year he has been allocated losses from Maverick.

LO 20-6

research

a) Determine how much of the Maverick loss Jenkins will currently be able to deduct on his tax return for year 1, and list the losses suspended due to tax basis, at-risk, and passive activity loss limitations.

b) If Jenkins sells his interest on January 1, year 2, what happens to his suspended losses from year 1? [*Hint:* See §706(c)(2)(A), Reg. §1.704-1(d)(1), Prop. Reg. §1.465-66(a), and *Sennett v. Commissioner* 80 TC 825 (1983).]

78. Suki and Steve own 50 percent capital and profits interests in Lorinda LLC. Lorinda operates the local minor league baseball team and owns the stadium where the team plays. Although the debt incurred to build the stadium was paid off several years ago, Lorinda owes its general creditors $300,000 (at the beginning of the year) that is not secured by firm property or guaranteed by any of the members. At the beginning of the current year, Suki and Steve had a tax basis of $170,000 in their LLC interests, including their share of debt owed to the general creditors. Shortly before the end of the year they each received a $10,000 cash distribution, even though Lorinda's ordinary business loss for the year was $400,000. Because of the time commitment to operate a baseball team, both Suki and Steve spent more than 1,500 hours during the year operating Lorinda.

LO 20-6

research

a) Determine how much of the Lorinda loss Suki and Steve will each be able to deduct on their current tax returns, and list their losses suspended by the tax basis, at-risk, and passive activity loss limitations.

b) Assume that some time before receiving the $10,000 cash distribution, Steve is advised by his tax adviser that his marginal tax rate will be abnormally high during the current year because of an unexpected windfall. To help Steve utilize more of the losses allocated from Lorinda in the current year, his adviser recommends refusing the cash distribution and personally guaranteeing $100,000 of Lorinda's debt, without the right to be reimbursed by Suki. If Steve follows his adviser's recommendations, how much additional

Lorinda loss can he deduct on his current tax return? How does Steve's decision affect the amount of loss Suki can deduct on her current return and the amount and type of her suspended losses?

LO 20-6

research

79. Ray and Chuck own 50 percent capital and profits interests in Alpine Properties LLC. Alpine builds and manages rental real estate, and Ray and Chuck each work full time (over 1,000 hours per year) managing Alpine. Alpine's debt (both at the beginning and end of the year) consists of $1,500,000 in nonrecourse mortgages obtained from an unrelated bank and secured by various rental properties. At the beginning of the current year, Ray and Chuck each had a tax basis of $250,000 in his LLC interest, including his share of the nonrecourse mortgage debt. Alpine's ordinary business losses for the current year totaled $600,000, and neither member is involved in other activities that generate passive income.

a) How much of each member's loss is suspended because of the tax-basis limitation?

b) How much of each member's loss is suspended because of the at-risk limitation?

c) How much of each member's loss is suspended because of the passive activity loss limitation? [*Hint:* See §469(b)(7).]

COMPREHENSIVE PROBLEMS

Select problems are available in *Connect*®.

tax forms

80. Aaron, Deanne, and Keon formed the Blue Bell General Partnership at the beginning of the current year. Aaron and Deanne each contributed $110,000 and Keon transferred an acre of undeveloped land to the partnership. The land had a tax basis of $70,000 and was appraised at $180,000. The land was also encumbered with a $70,000 nonrecourse mortgage for which no one was personally liable. All three partners agreed to split profits and losses equally. At the end of the first year, Blue Bell made a $7,000 principal payment on the mortgage. For the first year of operations, the partnership records disclosed the following information:

Sales revenue	$470,000
Cost of goods sold	410,000
Operating expenses	70,000
Long-term capital gains	2,400
§1231 gains	900
Charitable contributions	300
Municipal bond interest	300
Salary paid as a guaranteed payment to Deanne (not included in expenses)	3,000

a) Compute the adjusted basis of each partner's interest in the partnership immediately after the formation of the partnership.

b) List the separate items of partnership income, gains, losses, and deductions that the partners must show on their individual income tax returns that include the results of the partnership's first year of operations.

c) Using the information generated in answering parts (a) and (b), prepare Blue Bell's page 1 and Schedule K to be included with its Form 1065 for its first year of operations, along with Schedule K-1 for Deanne.

d) What are the partners' adjusted bases in their partnership interests at the end of the first year of operations?

81. The TimpRiders LP has operated a motorcycle dealership for a number of years. Lance is the limited partner, Francesca is the general partner, and they share capital and profits equally. Francesca works full-time managing the partnership. Both the partnership and the partners report on a calendar-year basis. At the start of the current year, Lance and Francesca had bases of $10,000 and $3,000, respectively, and the partnership did not carry any debt. During the current year, the partnership reported the following results from operations:

tax forms

Net sales	$650,000
Cost of goods sold	500,000
Operating expenses	160,000
Short-term capital loss	2,000
Tax-exempt interest	2,000
§1231 gain	6,000

On the last day of the year, the partnership distributed $3,000 each to Lance and Francesca.

a) What outside basis do Lance and Francesca have in their partnership interests at the end of the year?

b) How much of their losses are currently not deductible by Lance and Francesca because of the tax-basis limitation?

c) To what extent does the passive activity loss limitation apply in restricting their deductible losses for the year?

d) Using the information provided, prepare TimpRiders' page 1 and Schedule K to be included with its Form 1065 for the current year. Also, prepare a Schedule K-1 for Lance and Francesca.

82. LeBron, Dennis, and Susan formed the Bar T LLC at the beginning of the current year. LeBron and Dennis each contributed $200,000 and Susan transferred several acres of agricultural land she had purchased two years earlier to the LLC. The land had a tax basis of $50,000 and was appraised at $300,000. The land was also encumbered with a $100,000 nonrecourse mortgage (i.e., qualified nonrecourse financing) for which no one was personally liable. The members plan to use the land and cash to begin a cattle-feeding operation. Susan will work full time operating the business, but LeBron and Dennis will devote less than two days per year to the operation.

   All three members agree to split profits and losses equally. At the end of the first year, Bar T had accumulated $40,000 of accounts payable jointly guaranteed by LeBron and Dennis and had made a $9,000 principal payment on the mortgage. None of the members have passive income from other sources.

   For the first year of operations, the partnership records disclosed the following information:

Sales revenue	$620,000
Cost of goods sold	380,000
Operating expenses	670,000
Dividends	1,200
Municipal bond interest	300
Salary paid as a guaranteed payment to Susan (not included in expenses)	10,000
Cash distributions split equally among the members at year-end	3,000

a) Compute the adjusted basis of each member's interest immediately after the formation of the LLC.

b) When does each member's holding period for his or her LLC interest begin?

c) What is Bar T's tax basis and holding period in its land?

d) What is Bar T's required tax year-end?

e) What overall methods of accounting were initially available to Bar T?

f) List the separate items of partnership income, gains, losses, deductions, and other items that will be included in each member's Schedule K-1 for the first year of operations. Use the proposed self-employment tax regulations to determine each member's self-employment income or loss.

g) What are the members' adjusted bases in their LLC interests at the end of the first year of operations?

h) What are the members' at-risk amounts in their LLC interests at the end of the first year of operations?

i) How much loss from Bar T, if any, will the members be able to deduct on their individual returns from the first year of operations?

chapter

21

Dispositions of Partnership Interests and Partnership Distributions

Learning Objectives

Upon completing this chapter, you should be able to:

LO 21-1 Determine the tax consequences to the buyer and seller of the disposition of a partnership interest, including the amount and character of gain or loss recognized.

LO 21-2 List the reasons for distributions, and compare operating and liquidating distributions.

LO 21-3 Determine the tax consequences of proportionate operating distributions.

LO 21-4 Determine the tax consequences of proportionate liquidating distributions.

LO 21-5 Explain the significance of disproportionate distributions.

LO 21-6 Explain the rationale for special basis adjustments, determine when they are necessary, and calculate the special basis adjustment for dispositions and distributions.

Taxpayer:	Color Comfort Sheets LLC
Location:	Salt Lake City, Utah
Owners and interests:	Nicole Johnson, managing member—30 percent interest
	Sarah Walker, managing member—40 percent interest
	Greg Randall, nonmanaging member—30 percent interest

In January 2017,* Nicole and Sarah sit in the Color Comfort Sheets LLC (CCS), office discussing the current state of business affairs over a cup of coffee. They both agree they are not doing as well as they had hoped after two years of running the business. Their main topic of discussion this morning is how to turn the business around. Both women know the viability of the business is at stake if they can't figure out how to make it profitable . . . and soon.

As Nicole and Sarah brainstorm various ideas, Nicole's administrative assistant interrupts to announce a phone call from Noprah Winsted, the media mogul. Nicole takes the call. On her top-rated television talk show Noprah occasionally promotes products to her viewers based on her successful experience with the product. Apparently, one of Noprah's viewers sent her a set of Color Comfort sheets. Noprah is so happy with the product that she wants to promote the sheets on her show in about two weeks. Nicole and Sarah are, of course, thrilled with this news. Products Noprah has endorsed in the past have become wildly successful. The focus of Nicole and Sarah's meeting changes dramatically. Now they have to figure out how they can gear up for an immediate increase in production. Nicole and Sarah's analysis of the accounting records reveals that CCS is in a precarious cash position—the business is down to its last $10,000.

Nicole and Sarah immediately call Greg to fill him in on the news. Greg is as thrilled as they are to hear that Noprah will promote their sheets and agrees to kick in an additional $30,000. Nicole

---

*To allow the storyline to continue from the previous example, this chapter begins in 2017. We assume the 2016 tax laws apply for 2017 and subsequent years.

says that she will contribute $30,000 and Sarah antes up another $40,000.

The following couple of weeks fly by in a whirlwind of work—phone calls, meetings with bankers, and production scheduling. After the show airs, Nicole and Sarah sit down to talk about the show and the CCS product promotion. Noprah's special guest for the show had been popular film star, Tom Hughes, promoting his soon-to-be-released movie *Global Warfare*. Tom had been good-natured and actually shown interest in the sheets. During the show, he announced he would order a set as soon as the broadcast was over. Nicole and Sarah anticipate orders will roll in. Sure enough, before Noprah had even said goodbye to her studio audience, CCS's Web site traffic picked up and the phone lines were hopping with new orders.

By the end of 2017, CCS's financial situation has completely turned around; business is booming, the accounting records show a healthy profit, and the partners feel comfortable the trend will continue. Greg decides it is time to talk to Nicole and Sarah about cashing out his investment.

to be continued . . .

This chapter explores the tax consequences associated with selling partnership interests and with distributing partnership assets to partners.

LO 21-1 BASICS OF SALES OF PARTNERSHIP INTERESTS

As we've seen in previous chapters, owners of various business entities receive returns on their investments, either when the business makes distributions or upon the sale of their business interest. Corporate shareholders may sell their stock to other investors or back to the corporation. Likewise, partners may dispose of their interest in several ways: sell to a third party, sell to another partner, or transfer the interest back to the partnership. The payments in a disposition (sale) can come from either another owner of the partnership or a new investor; in either case, the sale proceeds come from outside the partnership.

Selling a **partnership interest** raises unique issues because of the flow-through nature of the entity. For example, is the interest a separate asset, or does the disposition represent the sale of the partner's share of each of the partnership's assets? (See Chapter 20 for a discussion of the entity and aggregate approaches to taxation of flow-through entities.) If the tax rules follow an entity approach, the interest is considered a separate asset and a sale of the partnership interest would be very similar to the sale of corporate stock. That is, the partner would simply recognize capital gain or loss on the sale, based on the difference between the sales price and the partner's tax basis in the partnership interest.

Alternatively, if the tax rules use the aggregate approach, the disposition represents a sale of the partner's share of each of the partnership's assets. This approach adds some complexity because of the differing character and holding periods of the partnership assets—ordinary, capital, and §1231. The selling partner also has the additional task of allocating the sales proceeds among the underlying assets in order to determine the gain or loss on each.

Rather than strictly following one approach, the tax rules end up being a mixture of the two approaches. When feasible, the entity approach controls; however, if the result distorts the amount or character of income, then the aggregate approach dominates. We discuss the tax consequences of sales of partnership interests by first taking the perspective of the seller (partner), then of the buyer (new investor).

Seller Issues

The seller's primary tax concern in a partnership interest sale is calculating the amount and character of gain or loss on the sale. The selling partner determines the gain or loss as the difference between the amount realized and her **outside basis** in the partnership.[1] Because the selling partner is no longer responsible for her share of the partnership liabilities, any debt relief increases the amount the partner *realizes* from the sale under general tax principles.

Example 21-1

Last year Chanzz Inc. sold its 30 percent interest in CCS on June 30 to Greg Randall, a wealthy local businessman, to limit its exposure to any further losses. Greg anticipated that CCS would become profitable in the near future and paid Chanzz Inc. $100,000 for its interest in CCS. Chanzz's share of CCS liabilities as of June 30 was $24,000. Chanzz Inc.'s basis in its CCS interest at the sale date was $105,000 (including its share of CCS's liabilities). What amount of gain did Chanzz recognize on the sale?

Answer: $19,000 gain, computed as follows:

Description	Amount	Explanation
(1) Cash and fair market value of property received	$100,000	
(2) Debt relief	24,000	
(3) Amount realized	$124,000	(1) + (2).
(4) Basis in CCS interest	105,000	
Recognized gain	$ 19,000	(3) − (4).

> **THE KEY FACTS**
>
> **Sale of Partnership Interest**
>
> • **Seller issues**
>   Gain or loss calculation
>   Amount realized:
>   Cash and fair market value of property received plus
>   Debt relief
>   Less: Basis in partnership interest
>   Equals: Realized gain or loss
> • Tax year closes with respect to selling partner.
> • **Buyer issues**
>   • Outside basis—cost of the partnership interest plus share of partnership's liabilities.
>   • Inside basis—selling partner's inside basis at sale date.
>   • No changes to partnership asset bases (unless §754 election is in effect).

The character of the gain or loss from a sale of a partnership interest is generally capital, because partnership interests are capital assets.[2] However, a portion of the gain or loss will be ordinary if a seller realizes any gain or loss attributable to **unrealized receivables** or **inventory items**.[3] Practitioners often refer to these assets that give rise to ordinary gains and losses as **hot assets**.[4] Let's discuss that term further, because these assets are central to determining the tax treatment of many transactions in this chapter.

Hot Assets   As you might expect, unrealized receivables include the right to receive payment for (1) "goods delivered, or to be delivered"[5] or (2) "services rendered, or to be rendered."[6] For cash-method taxpayers, unrealized receivables include amounts earned but not yet received (accounts receivable). Accrual-method taxpayers,

---

[1]Partners determine their outside basis as discussed in the previous chapter. Importantly, the outside basis includes the selling partner's share of distributive income for the year to the date of the sale.

[2]§731 and §741.

[3]§751(a). Partnerships are required to provide Form 8308 to all the parties to the sale as well as to the IRS. Selling partners include with their tax returns this form as well as a statement detailing the calculation of any ordinary gain from the sale of their interest.

[4]There are actually two definitions of *inventory items* in §751. Section 751(a) inventory items are defined in §751(d) to include *all* inventory items. However, under §751(b), the definition includes only *substantially appreciated* inventory. For purposes of determining the character of gain or loss from the sale of partnership interests, the term *inventory items* includes all inventory as in §751(a). However, these two definitions have created some confusion when using the term *hot assets*. In this chapter, we use the term *hot assets* to refer to unrealized receivables and all inventory items as in §751(a). The definition under §751(b) becomes more relevant when determining the tax treatment in a disproportionate distribution (discussed only briefly later in the chapter).

[5]§751(c)(1).

[6]§751(c)(2).

however, do not consider accounts receivable as unrealized receivables because they have already realized and recognized these items as ordinary income. Unrealized receivables also include items the partnership would treat as ordinary income if it sold the asset for its fair market value, such as depreciation recapture under §1245.[7]

Inventory items include classic inventory, defined as property held for sale to customers in the ordinary course of business, but also, more broadly, any assets that are *not* capital assets or §1231 assets.[8] Under this definition, assets such as equipment or real estate used in the business but not held for more than a year and all accounts receivable are considered inventory. This broad definition means cash, capital assets, and §1231 assets are the only properties not considered inventory.[9]

Example 21-2

CCS's balance sheet as of the date of Chanzz's sale of its CCS interest to Greg follows:

Color Comfort Sheets LLC
June 30, 2016

	Tax Basis	FMV
Assets:		
Cash	$ 27,000	$ 27,000
Accounts receivable	0	13,000
Investments	15,000	12,000
Inventory	1,000	1,000
Equipment (cost = $100,000)	80,000	86,000
Building	97,000	97,000
Land	20,000	150,000
Totals	$240,000	$386,000
Liabilities and capital:		
Long-term debt	$100,000*	
Capital—Nicole	(49,000)	
—Sarah	108,000	
—Chanzz	81,000	
Totals	$240,000	

*Of the $100,000 of long-term debt, $20,000 is allocated solely to Nicole. The remaining $80,000 is allocated to all three owners according to their profit-sharing ratios.

Which of CCS's assets are considered hot assets under §751(a)?

Answer: The hot assets are accounts receivables of $13,000 and $6,000 depreciation recapture (§1245) potential ($86,000 – $80,000) in the equipment. The accounts receivable is an unrealized receivable because CCS has not included it in income for tax purposes under CCS's cash accounting method. The depreciation recapture is also considered an unrealized receivable under §751(a). Inventory would be considered a hot asset; however, because the tax basis and fair market value are equal, it will not affect the character of any gain recognized on the sale.

---

[7]§751(c).

[8]§751(d)(1).

[9]This broad definition of inventory includes all unrealized receivables except for recapture. Recapture items are excluded from the definition of inventory items simply because recapture is not technically an asset; rather, it is merely a portion of gain that results from the sale of property. Recapture is, however, considered an unrealized receivable (i.e., hot asset) under §751(a). This idea is important in determining whether inventory is substantially appreciated for purposes of determining the §751 assets for distributions as we discuss later in the chapter.

Example 21-3

Review CCS's balance sheet as of the end of 2017.

Color Comfort Sheets LLC December 31, 2017		
	Tax Basis	**FMV**
Assets:		
Cash	$390,000	$ 390,000
Accounts receivable	0	40,000
Inventory	90,000	200,000
Investments	60,000	105,000
Equipment (cost = $200,000)	150,000	200,000
Building (cost = $100,000)	90,000	100,000
Land—original	20,000	160,000
Land—investment	140,000	270,000
Totals	$940,000	$1,465,000
Liabilities and capital:		
Accounts payable	$ 80,000	
Long-term debt		
Mortgage on original land	40,000	
Mortgage on investment land	120,000	
Capital—Nicole	119,000	
—Sarah	332,000	
—Greg	249,000	
Totals	$940,000	

What amount of CCS's assets are considered to be hot assets as of December 31, 2017?

Answer: The hot assets include inventory with a fair market value of $200,000, unrealized receivables of $50,000 of depreciation recapture potential on the equipment, and $40,000 of accounts receivable.

When a partner sells her interest in a partnership that holds hot assets, she modifies her calculation of the gain or loss to ensure the portion that relates to hot assets is properly characterized as ordinary income. The process for determining the gain or loss follows:

Step 1: Determine the total gain or loss by subtracting outside basis from the amount realized.

Step 2: Calculate the partner's share of gain or loss from hot assets as if the partnership sold these assets at their fair market value. This represents the ordinary portion of the gain or loss.

Step 3: Finally, subtract the ordinary portion of the gain or loss obtained in Step 2 from the total gain or loss from Step 1. This remaining amount is the capital gain or loss from the sale.[10,11]

---

[10]The partner must also determine if any portion of the capital gain or loss relates to collectibles (28 percent capital gain property) or to unrecaptured §1250 gains. This is typically referred to as the *look-through rule.*

[11]Any capital gain from the sale of a partnership interest is subject to the 3.8% net investment income tax unless the gain is allocable to trade or business assets held by the partnership that generate trade or business income not subject to the tax. See Prop. Reg. §1.1411-7 for a detailed discussion of this concept.

Example 21-4

In Example 21-1, Chanzz sold its interest in CCS to Greg Randall for $100,000 cash on June 30, 2016. As a result, Chanzz recognized a gain of $19,000 on the sale. What is the character of Chanzz's gain?

Answer: $5,700 of ordinary income and $13,300 of capital gain, determined as follows:

Step 1: Determine the total gain or loss: $19,000 from Example 21-1.

Step 2: Determine the ordinary gain or loss from hot assets:

Asset	(1) Basis	(2) FMV	(3) Gain/Loss (2) − (1)	Chanzz's Share 30% × (3)
Accounts receivable	$ 0	$13,000	$13,000	$3,900
Equipment	80,000	86,000	6,000	1,800
Total ordinary income				$5,700

Step 3: Determine the capital gain or loss:

Description	Amount	Explanation
(1) Total gain	$19,000	From Step 1.
(2) Ordinary income from §751(a)	5,700	From Step 2.
Capital gain	$13,300	(1) − (2).

Example 21-5

What if: Assume the same facts as in Example 21-4, except Greg is willing to pay Chanzz only $82,800 cash for its interest in CCS. What is the amount and character of Chanzz's gain or loss?

Answer: $5,700 of ordinary income and capital loss of $3,900, determined as follows:

Step 1: Determine the total gain or loss:

Description	Amount	Explanation
(1) Cash and fair market value of property received	$ 82,800	
(2) Debt relief	24,000	Chanzz's share of CCS's allocable debt (30% × $80,000).
(3) Amount realized	$106,800	(1) + (2).
(4) Basis in CCS interest	105,000	
Gain recognized	$ 1,800	(3) − (4).

Step 2: Determine the ordinary gain or loss from hot assets:

Asset	(1) Basis	(2) FMV	(3) Gain/Loss (2) − (1)	Chanzz's Share 30% × (3)
Accounts receivable	$ 0	$13,000	$13,000	$3,900
Equipment	80,000	86,000	6,000	1,800
Total ordinary income				$5,700

Step 3: Determine the capital gain or loss:

Description	Amount	Explanation
(1) Total gain	$ 1,800	From Step 1.
(2) Ordinary income from §751(a)	5,700	From Step 2.
Capital loss	$(3,900)	(1) − (2).

ETHICS

Sarah recently sold her partnership interest for significantly more than her tax basis in the interest. Two separate appraisals were commissioned at the time of the sale to estimate the value of the partnership's hot assets and other assets. The first appraisal estimates the value of the hot assets at approximately $750,000, while the second appraisal estimates the value of these assets at approximately $500,000. Given that the partnership's inside basis for its hot assets is $455,000, Sarah intends to use the second appraisal to determine the character of the gain from the sale of her partnership interest. Is it appropriate for Sarah to ignore the first appraisal when determining her tax liability from the sale of her partnership interest?

Buyer and Partnership Issues

A new investor in a partnership is of course concerned with determining how much to pay for the partnership interest. However, his primary tax concerns are about his inside and outside bases in the partnership. In general, for a sale transaction, the new investor's outside basis will be equal to his cost of the partnership interest.[12] To the extent that the new investor shares in the partnership liabilities, his share of partnership liabilities increases his outside basis.

Example 21-6

When Greg Randall acquired Chanzz's 30 percent interest in CCS for $100,000 on June 30, 2016 (see Example 21-1), he guaranteed his share of CCS's debts just as Chanzz had done. As a result, Greg will be allocated his share of CCS's allocable debt in accordance with his 30 percent profit-sharing ratio. What is the outside basis of Greg's acquired interest?

Answer: $124,000, determined as follows:

Description	Amount	Explanation
(1) Initial tax basis	$100,000	Cash paid to Chanzz.
(2) Share of CCS's liabilities	24,000	30% × CCS's allocable debt of $80,000.
Outside basis	$124,000	(1) + (2).

The partnership experiences very few tax consequences when a partner sells her interest.[13] The sale does not generally affect a partnership's **inside basis** in its assets.[14] The new investor typically "steps into the shoes" of the selling partner to determine his share of the partnership's inside basis of the partnership assets. Consequently, the new

---

[12]§1012. The outside basis will depend, in part, on how the new investor obtains the interest. For example, a gift generally results in a carryover basis whereas an inherited interest typically results in a basis equal to the fair market value as of the date of the decedent's death.

[13]Later in the chapter, we discuss situations in which the new investor's share of the partnership's asset bases are adjusted after a sale of a partnership interest under §754. Throughout this section, we assume that the partnership does not have a §754 election in effect.

[14]§743.

investor's share of inside basis is equal to the selling partner's share of inside basis at the sale date. Recall from the preceding chapter that each partner has a tax capital account that reflects the tax basis of property and cash contributed by the partner, the partner's share of earnings and losses, and distributions to the partner. In a sale of a partnership interest, the selling partner's tax capital account carries over to the new investor.[15]

Example 21-7

Refer to Example 21-2 for CCS's balance sheet as of June 30, 2016. What is Greg's share of CCS's inside basis immediately after purchasing Chanzz's 30 percent interest in CCS?

Answer: Greg's share is $105,000: the sum of Chanzz's tax capital account of $81,000 and its share of CCS's liabilities of $24,000. Greg simply steps into Chanzz's place after the acquisition. In the preceding example, we determined Greg's outside basis to be $124,000. A sale of a partnership interest often results in a difference between the new investor's inside and outside bases because the outside basis is the price paid based on fair market value and the inside basis is the share of tax basis in the partnership assets.

Varying Interest Rule If a partner's interest in a partnership increases or decreases during the partnership's tax year, the partnership income or loss allocated to the partner for the year must be adjusted to reflect her *varying interest* in the partnership.[16] Partners' interests increase when they contribute property or cash to a partnership[17] or purchase a partnership interest. Conversely, partners' interests decrease when they receive partnership distributions[18] or sell all or a portion of their partnership interests. Upon the sale of a partnership interest, the partnership tax year closes for the *selling* partner only. Regulations allow partners to choose between two possible methods for allocating income or loss to partners when their interests change during the year.[19] The first method allows the partnership to prorate income or loss to partners with varying interests, while the second method sanctions an interim closing of the partnership's books.[20]

Example 21-8

CCS had a $60,000 overall operating loss for the 2016 calendar year. The issue of how to allocate the 2016 loss between Chanzz Inc. and Greg was easily resolved because CCS's operating agreement specifies the proration method to allocate income or loss when members' interests in CCS change during the year. How much of CCS's 2016 loss will Chanzz be allocated under the proration method?

Answer: Chanzz takes a loss of $9,000, which includes its share of CCS's loss but for only one-half the year ($60,000 × 30% share × 6/12 months) and will report it on its tax return.[21] On the sale date, Chanzz decreases its basis in CCS by the $9,000 loss to determine its adjusted basis to use in calculating its gain or loss on the sale of its interest.

[15]An exception occurs when the selling partner contributed property with a built-in loss to the partnership. Only the contributing partner is entitled to that loss [see Chapter 20 and §704(c)(1)(C)]. Therefore, when a new investor buys a partnership interest from a partner that contributed built-in loss property, the new investor reduces his inside basis by the amount of the built-in loss at the contribution date.

[16]§706(d)(1).

[17]If all partners simultaneously contribute property or cash with a value proportionate to their interests, their relative interests will not change.

[18]If all partners receive distributions with a value proportionate to their interests, their relative interests will not change.

[19]Reg. §1.706-1(c).

[20]If within a 12-month period, there is a sale of 50 percent or more of the total capital and profits interest in the partnership, the partnership is terminated. When this occurs, the partnership tax year is closed for all partners, not just the selling partners. See §708(b).

[21]Prop. Reg. §1.706-1(c) requires the calendar-day convention when using the proration method. For the sake of mathematical simplicity, we use number of months here and elsewhere in the chapter when applying the proration method.

Example 21-9

What if: If CCS's overall loss through June 30 was $20,000, how much of the $60,000 overall loss for 2016 will Chanzz and Greg Randall be allocated under an interim closing of the books?

Answer: CCS will allocate $6,000 of loss (30% × $20,000) to Chanzz and $12,000 of loss (30% × $40,000) to Greg.

TAXES IN THE REAL WORLD Changing the Way Companies Dispose of a Business

Corporate takeovers seemed to be the transaction du jour during the 1990s, but many practitioners are predicting joint ventures will be the defining deal for the current decade. We see regular articles in *The Wall Street Journal* describing how firms are starting up joint ventures or strategic alliances—or exiting them. For example, McGraw-Hill and the CME Group recently brought the S&P 500 index and the Dow Jones Industrial Average under the same roof by forming a new LLC called S&P/Dow Jones Indices. To form the new joint venture, McGraw-Hill contributed its Standard & Poor's index

business and CME group contributed its Dow Jones index business. In the end, McGraw-Hill owned 73 percent and the CME Group owned 27 percent of the new venture.

The increase in the number of joint ventures and their possible dissolution or disposition brings an increasing need to understand the partnership tax rules and regulations. More than ever before, corporate tax executives find they must advise senior management on the opportunities and pitfalls of structuring joint ventures and investments as partnerships or LLCs under Subchapter K of the Internal Revenue Code.

BASICS OF PARTNERSHIP DISTRIBUTIONS

LO 21-2

Like shareholders receiving corporate dividend distributions, partners often receive distributions of the partnership profits, known as **operating distributions.** Recall that owners of flow-through entities are taxed currently on their business income regardless of whether the business distributes it. As a result, partners may require cash distributions in order to make quarterly estimated tax payments on their share of business income. Usually, the general partners (or managing members of LLCs) determine the amount and timing of distributions; however, the partnership (operating) agreement may stipulate some distributions.

Partners may also receive **liquidating distributions.** Because the market for partnership interests is much smaller than for publicly traded stock, partners may have a difficult time finding buyers for their interests. Partnership agreements also often limit purchasers of an interest to the current partner group, to avoid adding an unwanted partner. If the current partner group either cannot or does not want to purchase the interest, the partnership can instead distribute assets to terminate a partner's interest. These liquidating distributions are similar to corporate redemptions of a shareholder's stock. They can also terminate the partnership. We first explore the tax consequences of operating distributions, and then examine the tax treatment for liquidating distributions.

LO 21-3

Operating Distributions

A distribution from a partnership is an operating distribution when the partners continue their interests afterwards. Operating distributions are usually paid to distribute the business profits to the partners but can also reduce a partner's ownership. The partnership may distribute money or other assets. Let's look at the tax consequences of distributions of money, and then the tax consequences of property other than money.

Operating Distributions of Money Only   The general rule for operating distributions states that the partnership does not recognize gain or loss on the distribution of

---

THE KEY FACTS

Operating Distributions

- **Gain or loss recognition:** Partners generally do not recognize gain or loss. One exception occurs when the partnership distributes money only and the amount is greater than the partner's outside basis.

(continued)

property or money.[22,23] Nor do the general tax rules require a partner to recognize gain or loss when she receives distributed property or money.[24] The partner simply reduces her (outside) basis in the partnership interest by the amount of the distribution. In doing so, she retains any gain or loss on her share of partnership assets represented by her outside basis.[25] In general, the partnership's basis in its remaining assets remains unchanged.[26]

Example 21-10

- **Basis of distributed assets:** Partners generally take a carryover basis in the distributed assets. If the partnership distribution includes other property and the combined inside bases is greater than the partner's outside basis, the bases of the other property distributed will be reduced.
- **Remaining outside basis:** In general, partners reduce outside basis by money and other property distributed.

What if: Suppose CCS makes its first distribution to the owners on December 31, 2017: $250,000 each to Nicole and Greg and $333,333 to Sarah. After taking into account their distributive share of CCS's income for the year, the owners have the following predistribution bases in their CCS interests:

Owner	Outside Basis
Nicole	$205,000
Sarah	420,000
Greg	334,000

What are the tax consequences (gain or loss and basis in CCS interest) of the distribution to Sarah?

Answer: Sarah does not recognize any gain or loss on the distribution. She reduces her outside basis from $420,000 to $86,667 ($420,000 − $333,333) after the distribution.

The general rule of no gain is impractical when the partner receives a greater amount of money than her outside basis. She cannot defer gain to the extent of the excess amount because the outside basis is insufficient for a full reduction. Therefore, the partner reduces her outside basis to zero[27] and recognizes gain (generally capital) to the extent the amount of money distributed is greater than her outside basis.[28] A partner *never* recognizes a loss from an *operating* distribution.

Example 21-11

What if: Suppose that in the December 31, 2017, distribution Nicole's distribution consists of $250,000 cash. Her outside basis is $205,000 before the distribution. What are Nicole's gain or loss and basis in her CCS interest after the distribution?

Answer: Nicole has $45,000 capital gain and $0 basis in CCS. Because she receives only money in the distribution, she decreases her outside basis to $0 and must recognize a $45,000 capital gain ($250,000 distribution less $205,000 basis). She recognizes gain because she receives a cash distribution in excess of her outside basis.

Operating Distributions That Include Property Other Than Money   If a partnership makes a distribution that includes property *other than money,* the partners face the problem of reallocating their outside basis between the distributed assets

[22]For distribution purposes, money includes cash, deemed cash from reductions in a partner's share of liabilities, and the fair market value of marketable securities.

[23]§731(b).

[24]§731.

[25]The basis adjustment is a primary mechanism used to meet the overall tax objective of maintaining the partner's economic interest in the underlying partnership assets. We will see its use many times throughout this chapter.

[26]However, if the partnership has a §754 election in effect or if there is a substantial basis reduction, the partnership basis of its remaining assets must be adjusted following a distribution according to §734(a) and §755.

[27]§733.

[28]§731(a)(1).

(including money) and their continuing partnership interests.[29] Under the general rule, the partner takes a basis in the distributed property equal to the partnership basis in the property. This is called a **carryover basis.**[30] The tax rules define the order in which to allocate outside basis to the bases of distributed assets. First, the partner allocates the outside basis to any money received and then to other property as a carryover basis. The remainder is the partner's outside basis after the distribution.

Example 21-12

What if: Suppose CCS's December 31, 2017, distribution to Sarah consists of $133,333 cash and investments (other than marketable securities), with a fair market value of $200,000 and an adjusted basis of $115,000. Sarah has a predistribution outside basis of $420,000. What are the tax consequences (Sarah's gain or loss, basis of distributed assets, and outside basis of CCS interest, and CCS's gain or loss) of the distribution?

Answer: Sarah recognizes no gain or loss on the distribution. To determine her bases in the distributed assets, she first allocates $133,333 to the cash and then takes a carryover basis in the investments so her basis in the investments is $115,000. Sarah reduces her outside basis by $248,333 ($133,333 cash + $115,000 basis of investments). Her outside basis after the distribution is $171,667 ($420,000 − $248,333). CCS does not recognize any gain or loss on the distribution.

When the partnership distributes property (other than money) with a basis that exceeds the remaining outside basis (after the allocation to any money distributed), the partner assigns the remaining outside basis to the distributed assets,[31] and the partner's outside basis is reduced to zero.[32] The first allocation of outside basis goes to money, then to hot assets, and finally to other property.[33] In this case, the partner's basis in the property received in the distribution will be less than the property's basis in the hands of the partnership.

Example 21-13

What if: Suppose Nicole's December 31, 2017, distribution consists of $150,000 cash and investments (other than marketable securities) with a fair market value of $100,000 and an adjusted basis of $90,000. Her outside basis is $205,000 before the distribution. What are Nicole's tax consequences (gain or loss, basis of distributed assets, outside basis in CCS interest) of the distribution?

Answer: Nicole recognizes no gain or loss and takes a basis of $55,000 in the investments. Her outside basis in CCS is $0, computed as follows:

Description	Amount	Explanation
(1) Nicole's outside basis	$205,000	
(2) Cash distribution	150,000	
(3) Remaining basis	55,000	(1) − (2); remaining outside basis to be allocated to the distributed investments.
(4) Inside basis of investments	90,000	
(5) Basis in investments	55,000	Lesser of (3) or (4).
Nicole's outside basis in CCS	0	(3) − (5).

---

[29]In this context, money includes marketable securities [§731(c)(1)(A)]. The special rules in §731(c) for the treatment of distributed marketable securities are beyond the scope of this book.

[30]§732(a).

[31]§732(a)(2).

[32]§733.

[33]If multiple assets are distributed, then the outside basis will be allocated in accordance with §732(c). We discuss these rules later in conjunction with liquidating distributions.

Because a partner's outside basis includes her share of the partnership liabilities, the outside basis must reflect any changes in a partner's share of partnership debt resulting from a distribution. In essence, a partner treats a reduction of her share of debt as a distribution of money.[34] If the partner increases her share of debt, the increase is treated as a cash contribution to the partnership.

Example 21-14

What if: Suppose Greg receives land held for investment with a fair market value of $250,000 (adjusted basis is $140,000) as his distribution from CCS on December 31, 2017. He agrees to assume the $120,000 mortgage on the land after the distribution. His outside basis is $334,000 before considering the distribution. What are the tax consequences (gain or loss, basis of distributed assets, outside basis in his CCS interest) of the distribution to Greg?

Answer: Greg does not recognize any gain or loss on the distribution. His basis in the land is $140,000 and his outside basis in CCS is $278,000, determined as follows:

Description	Amount	Explanation
(1) Greg's predistribution outside basis	$334,000	
(2) Mortgage assumed by Greg	120,000	
(3) Greg's predistribution share of mortgage	36,000	(2) × 30% ownership.
(4) Deemed cash contribution from debt assumption	84,000	(2) − (3).
(5) Greg's outside basis after debt changes	418,000	(1) + (4).
(6) Greg's basis in distributed land	140,000	Carryover basis from CCS.
Greg's post-distribution outside basis	278,000	(5) − (6).

Greg must first consider the effects of changes in debt before determining the effects of the distribution. The tax rules treat him as making a net contribution of $84,000 cash to the partnership, the difference between the full mortgage he assumes and his predistribution share of the debt. Greg then allocates $140,000 of his outside basis to the land and reduces his outside basis accordingly.

LO 21-4 Liquidating Distributions

In contrast to operating distributions in which the partners retain a continuing interest in the partnership, liquidating distributions terminate a partner's interest in the partnership. If the current partners do not have sufficient cash or inclination to buy out the terminating partner, the partnership agreement usually allows the partnership to close out the partner's interest. At some point, all the partners may agree to terminate the partnership, either because they have lost interest in continuing it or it has not been profitable. In such cases, the partnership may distribute all its assets to the partners in complete partnership liquidation. This process is analogous to a complete corporate liquidation (discussed in Chapter 19).

The tax issues in liquidating distributions for partnerships are basically twofold: (1) to determine whether the terminating partner recognizes gain or loss and (2) to reallocate his or her entire outside basis to the distributed assets. The rationale behind the rules for liquidating distributions is simply to replace the partner's outside basis with the underlying partnership assets distributed to the terminating partner. Ideally, there would be no gain or loss on the distribution, and the asset bases would be the same in the partner's hands as they were inside the partnership. Of course, this case rarely occurs. The rules therefore are designed to determine when gain or loss must be recognized and to allocate the partner's outside basis to the distributed assets.

[34]§752(b).

Gain or Loss Recognition in Liquidating Distributions   In general, neither partnerships nor partners recognize gain or loss from liquidating distributions. However, there are exceptions. For example, when a terminating partner receives more money in the distribution than her outside basis, she will recognize gain.[35] See Example 21-11 for an illustration in the context of operating distributions.

In contrast to operating distributions, a partner may recognize a *loss* from a liquidating distribution, but only when two conditions are met. These conditions are (1) the distribution includes only cash, unrealized receivables, and/or inventory; *and* (2) the partner's outside basis is greater than the sum of the *inside bases* of the distributed assets.[36] The loss on the distribution is a capital loss to the partner.

Commonly, the terminating partner's share of partnership debt decreases after a liquidating distribution. Any reduction in the partner's share of liabilities is considered a distribution of money to the partner and reduces the outside basis available for allocation of basis to other assets, including inventory and unrealized receivables.

Example 21-15

What if: Suppose on January 1, 2018, CCS liquidates Greg's interest in the LLC by distributing to him cash of $206,000 and inventory with a fair market value of $96,000 (adjusted basis is $43,000). Greg's share of CCS's liabilities as of the liquidation is $66,000. On January 1, 2018, Greg's outside basis in CCS is $334,000, including his share of CCS's liabilities. What is Greg's gain or loss on the liquidation of his CCS interest?

Answer: Greg recognizes a capital loss of $19,000 on the liquidation, computed as follows:

Description	Amount	Explanation
(1) Outside basis before distribution	$334,000	
(2) Debt relief	66,000	Deemed cash distribution.
(3) Outside basis after considering debt relief	$268,000	(1) – (2).
(4) Basis of property distributed (cash + inventory)	249,000	
Gain (loss) on distribution	$(19,000)	(4) – (3).

Greg recognizes a loss because he meets the two necessary conditions: (1) he receives only cash and inventory in the distribution *and* (2) the sum of the adjusted bases of the distributed assets is less than his basis in his CCS interest ($249,000 asset bases versus $268,000 CCS basis).

THE KEY FACTS

Gain or Loss Recognition in Liquidating Distributions

- **Generally:** Partners and partnerships do not recognize gain or loss.
- **Exceptions:**
  - **Gain:** Partner recognizes gain when partnership distributes money and the amount exceeds the partner's outside basis in the partnership interest.
  - **Loss:** Partner recognizes loss when two conditions are met: (1) Distribution consists of only cash and hot assets, and (2) the partner's outside basis exceeds the sum of the bases of the distributed assets.

Basis in Distributed Property   A key theme of the partnership tax rules is the idea that the partnership acts merely as a conduit for the partners' business activities. Thus, the rules attempt to keep the basis of the assets the same regardless of whether the partner or the partnership has possession of them. Moving assets in and out of the partnership should therefore have few tax consequences. The primary objective of the basis rules in liquidating distributions is to allocate the partner's entire outside basis in the partnership to the assets the partner receives in the liquidating distribution. The allocation essentially depends on two things: (1) the partnership's bases in distributed assets relative to the partner's outside basis and (2) the type of property distributed—whether it is money, hot assets, or other property. For purposes of distributions, hot assets include unrealized receivables and inventory, as we've previously defined. We discuss each of the possible scenarios in Exhibit 21-1 in turn.

---

[35]These rules are very similar to those for operating distributions. When a partner receives money only in complete termination of the partnership interest, any gain on distribution cannot be deferred through a basis adjustment. Therefore, the partner recognizes the gain.

[36]§731(a)(2).

EXHIBIT 21-1 **Alternative Scenarios for Determining Basis in Distributed Property**

Type of Property Distributed	Partner's outside basis is *greater* than inside bases of distributed assets	Partner's outside basis is *less* than inside bases of distributed assets
Money only	Scenario 1	Scenario 3
Money and hot assets	Scenario 1	Scenario 4
Other property included in distribution[37]	Scenario 2	Scenario 5

Partner's Outside Basis Is Greater Than Inside Basis of Distributed Assets

Scenario 1: Distributions of money, inventory, andlor unrealized receivables. If the partnership distributes only money, inventory, and/or unrealized receivables (ordinary income property) and the partner's outside basis is greater than the sum of the inside bases of the distributed assets, the partner recognizes a capital loss.[38] The partner assigns a basis to the assets equal to the partnership basis in the assets and the remaining outside basis determines the recognized loss. To prevent a partner from converting a capital loss from her investment into an ordinary loss, the tax law prohibits increasing her basis in unrealized receivables and inventory and requires the partner to recognize a capital loss.[39]

Example 21-16

What if: Suppose Greg has an outside basis of $334,000, including his share of liabilities of $66,000. In a liquidating distribution, he receives $159,000 cash and inventory with a fair market value and basis of $49,000. Will Greg recognize a gain or loss? Why or why not?

Answer: Yes, Greg will recognize a capital loss of $60,000 on the liquidation computed as follows:

Description	Amount	Explanation
(1) Outside basis before distribution	$334,000	
(2) Debt relief	66,000	Deemed cash distribution.
(3) Outside basis after considering debt relief	$268,000	(1) − (2).
(4) Basis of property distributed (cash + inventory)	208,000	
Gain (loss) on distribution	$ (60,000)	(4) − (3).

In this case, Greg is unable to defer his loss without changing its character. Greg clearly cannot adjust the basis in the cash to defer the loss. *If* he increases his basis in the distributed inventory, he could defer the loss. However, this would produce an ordinary loss of $60,000 when Greg sells the inventory.[40] To prevent the conversion of a capital loss to an ordinary loss, Greg recognizes a $60,000 capital loss.

Scenario 2: Other property included in distributions. Recall that in this scenario the liquidating partner must reallocate all her outside basis to the distributed assets. We determined in Scenario 1 that when the partnership distributes only money and/or

---

[37]This category includes distributions that include other property in addition to or instead of either money or unrealized receivables or inventory. For example, the distributions in this category can include any combination of money, unrealized receivables, and inventory as long as other property is also distributed.

[38]§731(a)(2).

[39]§732(c)(1) and §731(a)(2).

[40]If the inventory distributed to Greg is also considered inventory in his hands, the eventual sale of the inventory will generate ordinary income. If the inventory is a capital asset to Greg, a sale of the asset within five years of the distribution will generate ordinary income. After five years, the gain or loss would be capital.

hot assets and the distributed asset bases are less than the partner's outside basis, it was impossible to allocate the entire outside basis to the distributed assets without changing the character of a resulting loss. Thus, a partner never increases the bases of hot assets. However, when the partnership distributes other property, in addition to money and/or hot assets, the partner can adjust the basis of the *other* property without converting ordinary gains and losses to capital, and the liquidating partner will not recognize any gain or loss from the distribution.

Example 21-17

What if: Suppose CCS has no liabilities or hot assets and distributes $50,000 in cash and land with a fair market value of $160,000 and an adjusted basis of $20,000 to Greg in complete liquidation of his CCS interest. Greg has an outside basis of $268,000 prior to the distribution. What is Greg's recognized gain or loss on the distribution?

Answer: Greg does not recognize any gain or loss. He receives money and other property with a total basis of $70,000, which is less than his outside basis of $268,000. Greg first reduces his outside basis by the amount of money he receives, and he assigns his remaining outside basis to the land as follows:

Description	Amount	Explanation
(1) Outside basis before distribution	$268,000	
(2) Basis allocated to money distributed	50,000	
Remaining outside basis assigned to land	$218,000	(1) − (2).

Note that Greg increases the basis of the other property received in liquidation (land) from $20,000 to $218,000 in order to allocate his entire outside basis to the distributed assets. In some cases, "other" property might include personal assets for which the partner may never be able to recover the basis increase.

Example 21-17 illustrates the required basis increase in a very simple situation. In reality, liquidating distributions may include several types of assets. In these situations, to allocate the outside basis to the distributed assets, the partner completes the following, more detailed process:[41]

Step 1: The partner first assigns a basis to any money, inventory, and unrealized receivables equal to the partnership's basis in these assets. The partner also assigns a basis to the other distributed property in an amount equal to the partnership's basis in those assets.

Step 2: The partner then allocates the remaining outside basis (full outside basis less the amounts assigned in Step 1) to the other distributed property that has unrealized appreciation to the extent of that appreciation. Thus, if an asset has an adjusted basis to the partnership of $500 and a fair market value of $700, the partner will allocate the first $200 of remaining basis to that asset.[42]

Step 3: The partner allocates any remaining basis to all other property in proportion to the relative *fair market values* of the other property.

$$\text{Basis allocation} = \text{Remaining basis} \times \frac{\text{FMV}_{asset}}{\text{Sum of FMV}_{distributed\ other\ property}}$$

---

[41]§732(c)(2).

[42]If the remaining outside basis is insufficient to allocate the full amount of appreciation to the distributed assets in this step, then the partner will allocate the remaining basis in this step to the appreciated assets based on their relative appreciation.

Example 21-18

What if: Suppose CCS makes the following distribution to Greg in liquidation of his CCS interest:

Asset	CCS Tax Basis	Fair Market Value
Cash	$181,000	$181,000
Investment A	5,000	12,000
Investment B	10,000	13,000
Inventory	43,000	96,000

Greg's basis in his CCS interest as of the liquidation is $334,000, including his $66,000 share of CCS's liabilities. What is Greg's recognized gain or loss on the distribution? What is Greg's basis in the distributed assets following the liquidation?

Answer: Greg recognizes no gain or loss on the distribution. Greg's bases in the distributed assets are:

Cash	$181,000
Investment A	21,120
Investment B	22,880
Inventory	43,000
Total	$268,000

Because Greg receives other property in the distribution and the distributed asset bases are less than Greg's outside basis (Scenario 2), he will allocate his outside basis as follows:

First, Greg determines his allocable basis:

Description	Amount	Explanation
(1) Basis in CCS before distribution	$334,000	
(2) Debt relief	66,000	Greg's 30 percent share of CCS's debt.
Allocable basis	$268,000	(1) – (2).

Next, Greg allocates his remaining CCS basis of $268,000 to the distributed assets by following the three-step allocation process.

Description	Amount	Explanation
Step 1:		
(1) Allocable basis	$268,000	See above.
(2) Basis assigned to cash	181,000	
(3) Basis assigned to inventory	43,000	
(4) Initial basis assigned to investment A	5,000	
(5) Initial basis assigned to investment B	10,000	
(6) Remaining allocable CCS basis	$ 29,000	(1) – (2) – (3) – (4) – (5).
Step 2:		
(7) Additional basis assigned to investment A	$ 7,000	Unrealized appreciation on investment A from example. FMV of $12,000 less basis of $5,000.
(8) Additional basis assigned to investment B	3,000	Unrealized appreciation on investment B from example. FMV of $13,000 less basis of $10,000.
(9) Remaining allocable CCS basis after Step 2	$ 19,000	(6) – (7) – (8).

Step 3:

(10) Additional basis allocated to other property: investment A.	$9,120	Basis allocation = $19,000 × ($12,000/$25,000) = $9,120.
(11) Additional basis allocated to other property: investment B.	$9,880	Basis allocation = $19,000 × ($13,000/$25,000) = $9,880.

In Step 3, Greg allocates the remaining basis to the distributed investments based on their relative fair market values using:

$$\text{Basis allocation} = \text{Remaining basis} \times \frac{\text{FMV}_{\text{asset}}}{\text{Sum of FMV}_{\text{distributed other property}}}$$

Thus, Greg's bases in the investments are:

Description	Inv. A	Explanation	Inv. B	Explanation
(12) Initial basis assignment	$ 5,000	From (4) above	$10,000	From (5) above.
(13) Basis assigned in Step 2	7,000	From (7) above	3,000	From (8) above.
(14) Basis assigned in Step 3	9,120	From (10) above	9,880	From (11) above.
Greg's bases in investments	$21,120	(12) + (13) + (14).	$22,880	(12) + (13) + (14).

Partner's Outside Basis Is Less Than Inside Basis of Distributed Assets

Scenario 3: Distributions of money only.   A partner recognizes a gain (generally capital) if the partnership distributes money (only) that exceeds the partner's outside basis. The gain equals the excess amount received over the outside basis. Example 21-11 illustrates the tax consequences for this scenario in the context of an operating distribution.

Scenario 4: Distributions of money, inventory, and/or unrealized receivables.   In liquidating distributions where the partner's outside basis is less than the inside basis of the distributed assets and the partnership distributes money and any property other than money, the partner reduces the basis in the distributed assets other than money but does not recognize gain or loss. Because the tax law does not restrict *reducing* bases of ordinary income assets, distributions of hot assets and other property will cause reductions in basis. However, the tax law does prescribe a particular sequence for the required reductions.

If the partnership distributes only money, inventory, and unrealized receivables, the partner reduces the basis of the hot assets distributed (assuming money doesn't exceed basis). The required decrease in the basis of the distributed assets is equal to the difference between the partner's outside basis and the partnership's inside basis in the distributed assets. The partner first assigns her outside basis to the assets received in an amount equal to the assets' inside bases (allocating to money first). Then the partner allocates the required *decrease* to the assets with unrealized depreciation, to eliminate any existing losses built into the distributed assets.[43] Finally, the partner allocates any remaining required decrease to the distributed assets in proportion to their *adjusted bases* (AB), after considering the previous steps using the following equation:

$$\text{Basis allocation} = \text{Required decrease} \times \frac{\text{AB}_{\text{asset}}}{\text{Sum of AB}_{\text{distributed assets}}}$$

[43]If the required decrease is insufficient to allocate the full amount of depreciation to the distributed assets in this step, then the partner will allocate the remaining required decrease in this step to the depreciated assets based on their relative unrealized depreciation.

Example 21-19

What if: Suppose CCS makes the following distribution to Greg in liquidation of his CCS interest:

Asset	CCS Tax Basis	Fair Market Value
Cash	$256,000	$256,000
Inventory A	50,000	129,000
Inventory B	25,000	17,000
Total	$331,000	

Greg's basis in his CCS interest as of the liquidation is $334,000, including his $66,000 share of CCS's liabilities. What is Greg's recognized gain or loss on the distribution? What is Greg's basis in the distributed assets following the liquidation?

Answer: Greg does not recognize any gain or loss. His basis in the cash is $256,000 and his basis in inventory A is $8,955 and his basis in inventory B is $3,045, computed as follows:

First, Greg reduces his outside basis in CCS by his $66,000 debt relief, such that his outside basis allocable to distributed assets is $268,000 ($334,000 − $66,000). He must allocate this remaining basis to the distributed assets using the following steps:

Description	Amount	Explanation
Step 1:		
(1) Allocable basis	$268,000	Basis in CCS of $334,000 − debt relief of $66,000.
(2) Basis assigned to cash	256,000	
(3) Initial basis assigned to inventory A	50,000	
(4) Initial basis assigned to inventory B	25,000	
(5) Required decrease	63,000	(2) + (3) + (4) − (1). Initial assignment of basis exceeds Greg's allocable CCS basis.
Step 2:		
(6) Required decrease to inventory B	8,000	Unrealized depreciation on inventory B from example. FMV of $17,000 less basis of $25,000.
(7) Remaining required decrease	55,000	(5) − (6).
(8) Interim adjusted basis of inventory B	17,000	(4) − (6).
Step 3:		
(9) Required decrease to inventory A	41,045	Basis reduction = $55,000 × ($50,000/$67,000).
(10) Required decrease to inventory B	13,955	Basis reduction = $55,000 × ($17,000/$67,000).
Final basis of inventory A	8,955	(3) − (9).
Final basis of inventory B	3,045	(8) − (10).

In Step 3, Greg decreases the basis of the inventory in proportion to its relative adjusted bases determined in Step 2 using the following allocation:

$$\text{Basis allocation} = \text{Required decrease} \times \frac{AB_{asset}}{\text{Sum of } AB_{distributed\ assets}}$$

Example 21-20

What if: Suppose CCS makes the following distribution to Greg in liquidation of his CCS interest:

Asset	CCS Tax Basis	Fair Market Value
Cash	$242,000	$242,000
Accounts receivable	0	12,000
Inventory	74,000	120,000
Total	$316,000	

Greg's basis in his CCS interest as of the liquidation is $334,000, including his share ($66,000) of CCS's liabilities. What is Greg's recognized gain or loss on the distribution? What is Greg's basis in the assets he receives in the liquidating distribution?

Answer: Greg does not recognize any gain or loss on the liquidation. His asset bases are:

Cash	$242,000
Accounts receivable	0
Inventory	26,000
Total	$268,000

Greg computes the basis as follows:

As a preliminary step to the allocation, he reduces his outside basis in CCS by his $66,000 debt relief, leaving an allocable outside basis of $268,000 ($334,000 − $66,000). He allocates this basis to the distributed assets using the following steps:

Description	Amount	Explanation
Step 1:		
(1) Allocable basis	$268,000	Basis in CCS of $334,000 − debt relief of $66,000.
(2) Basis assigned to cash	242,000	
(3) Initial basis assigned to accounts receivable	0	
(4) Initial basis assigned to inventory	74,000	
(5) Required decrease	48,000	(2) + (3) + (4) − (1). Initial assignment of basis exceeds Greg's allocable CCS basis.

Step 2: N/A because no assets have unrealized depreciation.

Description	Amount	Explanation
Step 3:		
(6) Required decrease to accounts receivable	0	Basis reduction = $48,000 × ($−0−/$74,000).
(7) Required decrease to inventory	48,000	Basis reduction = $48,000 × ($74,000/$74,000).
Final basis of accounts receivable	0	(3) − (6).
Final basis of inventory	26,000	(4) − (7).

In Step 3, Greg decreases the basis of the accounts receivable and inventory in proportion to their relative adjusted bases using the following reduction:

$$\text{Basis allocation} = \text{Required decrease} \times \frac{AB_{asset}}{\text{Sum of } AB_{distributed\ assets}}$$

Note that in this scenario, the tax rules re-characterize a portion ($48,000) of Greg's ultimate gain from capital gain to ordinary income. The sum of the bases of the distributed assets ($316,000) exceeds Greg's allocable outside basis ($268,000) by $48,000. Absent the allocation rules illustrated in Example 21-20, this would have been a capital gain to Greg. Instead, as we discuss below, the basis decrease to the hot assets will cause Greg to recognize any gain as ordinary upon sale of these assets.

Scenario 5: Other property included in distributions. In our final scenario, the partnership distributes other property in addition to or instead of money and/or inventory and unrealized receivables, and the partner's outside basis is less than the combined inside bases of the distributed property. The terminating partner does not recognize gain or loss; rather, he decreases the basis in the other property distributed. The process for assigning basis to the distributed assets is similar to the method we described above, although the required basis decrease is focused on the other property rather than the hot assets.[44] The procedure is as follows:

Step 1: The partner first assigns a basis to any money, inventory, and unrealized receivables equal to the partnership's basis in these assets. The partner also assigns a basis to any other property equal to the partnership's basis in the other property distributed.

Step 2: The partner then allocates the required decrease (outside basis less partnership adjusted basis in distributed assets) to the other property that has unrealized depreciation to the extent of that depreciation to eliminate inherent losses. Thus, if an asset has an adjusted basis to the partnership of $700 and a fair market value of $600, the asset's basis is first reduced by $100 (unrealized depreciation).

Step 3: If any required decrease remains after accounting for the inherent losses in the distributed assets, the partner then allocates it to all other property in proportion to their *adjusted bases*. The adjusted bases used in this step are the bases from Step 2. We can determine the allocation as follows:

$$\text{Basis reduction} = \text{Required decrease} \times \frac{AB_{asset}}{\text{Sum of } AB_{\text{all distributed other property}}}$$

Example 21-21

What if: Suppose CCS makes the following distribution to Greg in liquidation of his CCS interest:

Asset	CCS Tax Basis	Fair Market Value
Cash	$187,000	$187,000
Investment A	10,000	7,000
Investment B	10,000	18,000
Inventory	70,000	102,000
Total	$277,000	

Greg's basis in his CCS interest as of the liquidation is $334,000, including his $66,000 share of CCS's liabilities. What is Greg's recognized gain or loss on the distribution? What is Greg's basis in the distributed assets following the liquidation?

---

[44] §732(c)(3).

Answer: Greg does not recognize any gain or loss. His asset bases are as follows:

Cash	$187,000
Investment A	4,530
Investment B	6,470
Inventory	70,000
Total	$268,000

Greg's basis in these assets is determined as follows:

Greg first determines his allocable basis of $268,000 by reducing his CCS basis ($334,000) for the deemed cash distribution relating to his $66,000 share of the reduction in CCS's debt.

Description	Amount	Explanation
Step 1:		
(1) Allocable basis	$268,000	Basis in CCS of $334,000 − debt relief of $66,000.
(2) Basis assigned to cash	187,000	
(3) Initial basis assigned to investment A	10,000	
(4) Initial basis assigned to investment B	10,000	
(5) Initial basis assigned to inventory	70,000	
(6) Required decrease	9,000	(2) + (3) + (4) + (5) − (1). Initial assignment of basis exceeds Greg's allocable CCS basis.
Step 2:		
(7) Required decrease to investment A	3,000	Unrealized depreciation on investment A from example. FMV of $7,000 less basis of $10,000.
(8) Remaining required decrease	6,000	(6) − (7).
(9) Interim basis of investment A	7,000	(3) − (7).
Step 3:		
(10) Required decrease to investment A	2,470	Basis reduction = $6,000 × ($7,000/$17,000).
(11) Required decrease to investment B	3,530	Basis reduction = $6,000 × ($10,000/$17,000).
Final basis of investment A	4,530	(9) − (10).
Final basis of investment B	6,470	(4) − (11).

In Step 3, Greg decreases the basis of the other property (investments A and B) in proportion to their relative adjusted bases using the following allocation:

$$\text{Basis reduction} = \text{Required decrease} \times \frac{AB_{asset}}{\text{Sum of } AB_{\text{all distributed other property}}}$$

Character and Holding Period of Distributed Assets   For both operating and liquidating distributions, the character of the distributed assets usually stays the same for the partner as it was in the partnership, in order to prevent conversion of ordinary income to capital gain for both operating and liquidating distributions. The principal purpose of these rules is to prevent the partner from converting partnership ordinary income into capital gain simply by distributing assets. Thus, if a partner sells certain assets with ordinary character after the distribution, the partner will recognize ordinary income from the sale.[45] These assets include inventory [§751(d)] and unrealized receivables [§751(c)]. For inventory items, the ordinary income "taint" will remain for five years after the distribution. For unrealized receivables, a subsequent sale at any time after the distribution will result in ordinary income. The reverse is not true, however. If a partnership distributes a capital asset that will be inventory to a terminating partner, the partner will have ordinary income from an eventual sale, not capital gain or loss. To ensure the character of any distributed long-term capital gain property retains its character to the partner, the partner's holding period generally includes the partnership's holding period.[46]

Example 21-22

Greg has decided to cash out his investment in CCS in order to invest in another project in which he can more actively participate. After speaking to Nicole and Sarah about the options, the three owners decide Greg can cash out using one of two options.

Option 1: CCS will liquidate Greg's interest by distributing cash of $242,000; accounts receivable worth $12,000 (adjusted basis is $0); and inventory worth $120,000 (adjusted basis is $74,000).

Option 2: Nicole and Sarah will purchase Greg's interest in CCS. Nicole agrees to purchase two-thirds of Greg's interest for $249,333 cash and Sarah purchases the remaining one-third for $124,667 cash.

Greg's basis in his 30 percent CCS interest is $334,000, including his share of CCS's liabilities of $66,000. Either event would occur on January 1, 2018, when CCS's balance sheet is as follows:

Color Comfort Sheets LLC January 1, 2018		
	Tax Basis	**FMV**
Assets:		
Cash	$390,000	$ 390,000
Accounts receivable	0	40,000
Inventory	90,000	200,000
Investments	60,000	105,000
Equipment (cost = $200,000)	150,000	200,000
Building (cost = $100,000)	90,000	100,000
Land—original	20,000	160,000
Land—investment	140,000	270,000
Totals	$940,000	$1,465,000
Liabilities and capital:		
Accounts payable	$ 80,000	
Long-term debt	0	
Mortgage on original land	40,000	
Mortgage on investment land	120,000	
Capital—Nicole	119,000	
—Sarah	332,000	
—Greg	249,000	
Totals	$940,000	

---

[45]§735(a).
[46]§735(b).

What are the tax consequences (amount and character of recognized gain or loss, basis in assets) for Greg under each option?

Answer: *Option 1:* Greg recognizes no gain or loss on the liquidation. His bases in the distributed assets are:

Cash	$242,000
Accounts receivable	0
Inventory	26,000
Total	$268,000

Option 2: Greg recognizes ordinary income of $60,000 and a capital gain of $46,000.

We determine these tax consequences as follows:

Option 1: The distribution allows Greg to defer recognizing any gain or loss on the liquidation. Example 21-20 provides the details of the analysis. Greg has debt relief in an amount equal to his share of CCS's liabilities ($66,000). The debt relief is treated as a distribution of cash, so Greg reduces his outside basis by this amount from $334,000 to $268,000. The difference between the sum of the adjusted bases of the distributed property and his outside basis is $48,000 ($316,000 − $268,000) and represents a required *decrease* to the bases of assets distributed in liquidation. Greg follows the prescribed method illustrated in Example 21-20 to determine his asset bases.

The basis reduction for these assets allows Greg to defer recognizing a $48,000 gain on the liquidation. The cost to accomplish the deferral is that if Greg sells the inventory and the accounts receivable immediately after the distribution, he will recognize ordinary income of $106,000 as follows:

Amount realized:		
Cash (equal to FMV of accounts receivable	$ 12,000	
and inventory)	120,000	$132,000
Less: Adjusted basis		
Accounts receivable	0	
Inventory	26,000	26,000
Ordinary Income		$106,000

The $106,000 ordinary income is $48,000 greater than the inherent gain on these assets of $58,000 ($132,000 − $74,000) had the partnership sold the assets. If Greg selects Option 1, he will not recognize income on the liquidation until he sells the inventory and collects (or sells) the accounts receivable, thereby leaving himself flexibility on the timing of gain recognition.

Option 2: In this option, Greg sells his CCS interest to Nicole and Sarah and receives cash of $374,000. Greg determines his total gain or loss as follows:

Amount realized:		
Cash	$374,000	
Debt relief	66,000	$440,000
Less: Basis in CCS interest		334,000
Realized and recognized gain		$106,000

Next, Greg determines the character of the gain from the sale by first identifying the gain related to hot assets.

Hot Asset − CCS	(1) Basis	(2) FMV	(3) Gain/Loss (2) − (1)	Greg's Share 30% × (3)
Accounts receivable	$ 0	$ 40,000	$ 40,000	$12,000
Inventory	90,000	200,000	110,000	33,000
Equipment	150,000	200,000	50,000	15,000
Total ordinary income				$60,000

(*continued on page 21-24*)

The final step for Greg is to determine the capital gain or loss by subtracting the ordinary portion from the total gain.

Total gain	$106,000
Less: ordinary income from §751(a)	(60,000)
Capital gain	$ 46,000

If he chooses Option 2, Greg will recognize $60,000 of ordinary income and $46,000 of capital gain in 2018.

Example 21-23

Given the tax consequences to Greg in the previous example, should he have CCS liquidate his interest (Option 1) or sell his interest (Option 2)?

Answer: Under Option 1 (the liquidation), Greg is able to defer all recognition of gain until he later sells the distributed assets. This provides him flexibility in when he pays tax on the liquidation. However, when he recognizes any income upon subsequent sales, the character of the income will be ordinary and taxed at ordinary rates. Under Option 2, Greg must recognize income immediately upon the sale: $60,000 of ordinary income and $46,000 of capital gain. He has no future tax liability related to the transaction. The capital gain will be taxed at a maximum of 15 percent (the regular maximum tax rate for long-term capital gains). An additional consideration is that under Option 2 Greg receives cash, rather than a mixture of cash and other assets. If he wants to immediately invest the proceeds in another venture, he may prefer a pure cash payment.

---

continued from page 21-2 . . .
Greg takes the liquidation option (Option 1) offered by CCS to avoid recognizing a gain currently. Although this option doesn't give him as much cash as a sale would have, Greg figures it is enough for another investment and he can avoid paying tax this year.

For the first time, CCS has only two owners—Nicole and Sarah. After liquidating Greg's interest, Nicole's interest has increased to 43 percent and Sarah's to 57 percent. Both women are happy with that outcome, though sorry to lose Greg's interest in the business. ∎

LO 21-5 DISPROPORTIONATE DISTRIBUTIONS

Up to this point in the chapter, all our distribution examples have represented the partner's pro rata share of the partnership's ordinary assets and other property, as specified in the partnership agreement based on the partner's capital interests. In practice, distributions may not always reflect each partner's proportionate share.[47] Both operating and liquidating distributions can be **disproportionate distributions.** Without going into all the details of these complex rules, let's briefly discuss the implications of distributions in which partners receive either more or less of their share of the so-called hot assets [assets defined in IRC §751(b) as **substantially appreciated inventory**

---

[47]A thorough discussion of these issues is beyond the scope of this chapter. Therefore, we will abbreviate our discussion just to give a flavor for the issues and consequences of these disproportionate distributions.

and unrealized receivables].[48] Note that the definition of hot assets for purposes of disproportionate distributions includes only *substantially appreciated* inventory, not all inventory as is the case under §751(a), the definition we used to characterize the gain in dispositions of partnership interests. Inventory is considered substantially appreciated if its fair market value is more than 120 percent of its basis.

Suppose a partner receives less than her share of hot assets in a liquidating distribution. This may occur, for example, if a partner receives only cash in a liquidating distribution from a partnership with hot assets. Rather than applying the rules we discussed above, the disproportionate distribution rules require the partner to treat the distribution as a sale or exchange.[49] Basically, the rules treat the partner as having sold her share of hot assets to the partnership in exchange for "cold" [non-§751(b)] assets. This deemed sale generates an ordinary gain or loss to the partner on the deemed sale, essentially equal to her share of the appreciation or depreciation in the portion of hot assets not distributed to her. On the other hand, the partnership is deemed to have purchased the hot assets from the partner in exchange for cold assets. Therefore, the *partnership* recognizes a capital or §1231 gain or loss equal to the remaining partners' inherent gain or loss in the distributed cold assets. The effects are reversed if a partner receives more than her share of the partnership's hot assets.[50] The rules guarantee that partners cannot convert ordinary income into capital gain through distributions. Thus, they require that partners will ultimately recognize their share of the partnership ordinary income regardless of the form of their distributions.

THE KEY FACTS

Disproportionate Distributions

- **When?**
  When distribution changes a partner's relative ownership of partnership hot assets.
- **Why?**
  To prevent partners from converting ordinary income into capital gains through distributions.
- **How?**
  Partner and partnership must treat distribution as a sale or exchange, which may result in recognition of gain (or loss).

Example 21-24

What if: Suppose CCS distributes $270,000 in cash to Greg Randall on January 1, 2018, in complete liquidation of Greg's 30 percent interest in CCS. Greg's basis in his CCS interest before the distribution is $334,000. Assume CCS's balance sheet is as follows:

Color Comfort Sheets LLC
December 31, 2017

	Tax Basis	FMV
Assets:		
Cash	$700,000	$ 700,000
Inventory	240,000	440,000
Totals	$940,000	$1,140,000
Liabilities and capital:		
Liabilities	$240,000	
Capital—Nicole	119,000	
—Sarah	332,000	
—Greg	249,000	
Totals	$940,000	

(continued on page 21-26)

[48]Unrealized receivables include the accounts receivable of a cash-method taxpayer, the excess of the fair market value over basis of accounts receivable for accrual-method taxpayers, and recapture of depreciation under §1245. The definition of substantially appreciated inventory is broader than simply goods primarily held for sale to customers. It also includes property that would not be classified as capital assets or §1231 assets if sold by the partnership. As a result, receivables are included as "inventory."
[49]§751(b).
[50]The partner would generally recognize capital gain on the deemed sale and the partnership would recognize ordinary income.

Is this distribution disproportionate? What are the implications of the distribution?

Answer: From CCS's balance sheet as of December 31, 2017, the fair market value of Greg's share of hot assets for purposes of disproportionate distributions [§751(b)] is $132,000 ($72,000 adjusted basis). This figure includes 30 percent of the fair market value of CCS's inventory of $440,000. Since Greg receives only cash in the distribution, he has not received a proportionate share of CCS's hot assets. Thus, the distribution will be a disproportionate one.

The tax law treats Greg as having sold his share of the hot assets for cold assets, and he will recognize ordinary income equal to his share of the appreciation on the hot assets not distributed, $60,000 ($132,000 − $72,000). CCS does not recognize any gain or loss because it has no appreciation in the assets (cash) used to "purchase" the hot assets.

LO 21-6   # SPECIAL BASIS ADJUSTMENTS

Recall that when a partner sells her partnership interest, the partnership's inside basis is generally unaffected by the sale. This creates a discrepancy between the new investor's outside basis (cost) and her share of the partnership's inside basis, which artificially changes the potential income or loss at the partnership level. For example, earlier in the chapter Greg Randall purchased Chanzz's 30 percent interest in CCS for $82,800 (Example 21-5). Greg's outside basis after the acquisition is $106,800, reflecting the cash payment of $82,800 and his share of CCS's debt at the time of the acquisition, $24,000. However, Greg's share of CCS's inside basis in its assets is $105,000 (see Example 21-7). This is the outcome because the sale does not affect CCS's inside basis and Greg simply steps into Chanzz's shoes for determining his share of the inside basis. The discrepancy reflects Chanzz's unrecognized share of appreciation of CCS's assets (that Greg paid full value for) as of the sale date and causes Greg to be temporarily overtaxed when CCS sells these appreciated assets.

Example 21-25

What if: Suppose that immediately after Greg acquires his 30 percent interest in CCS for $82,800, CCS sells its accounts receivable for their fair market value of $13,000 (adjusted basis is $0). (See Example 21-2 for CCS's balance sheet as of June 30, 2016, the acquisition date.) What is the amount and character of gain that Greg recognizes on the sale?

Answer: When CCS sells the accounts receivable, it recognizes $13,000 of ordinary income, of which $3,900 (30 percent) is allocated to Greg. However, when Chanzz sold its interest to Greg, Chanzz was already taxed on the $3,900 allocated portion of that ordinary income under §751(a), and Greg paid full value for his interest in the receivables when he acquired his 30 percent interest in CCS. This means Greg will be taxed on the $3,900 again in 2016, and his outside basis increases by $3,900. Because Greg paid fair market value for his share of the receivables, he should not have any income when they are sold at fair market value. Eventually, when Greg disposes of his CCS interest, his ultimate gain (or loss) on the disposition will be $3,900 less, because of the increase to his outside basis from this additional income; meanwhile, he is overtaxed on the receivables. Greg must report ordinary income today for an offsetting capital loss (or reduced capital gain) in the future when he disposes of his interest.

The tax rules allow the partnership to make an election for a **special basis adjustment** to eliminate discrepancies between the inside and outside bases and correct the artificial income or loss at the partnership level.[51] For the most part, basis discrepancies arise in two situations: following *sales* of partnership interests, and following *distributions* where a partner receives more (and in cases of a liquidating distribution,

---

[51]§754. The election is made by including a written statement with the partnership return when filed for the year the election is to take effect.

less) than her share of the inside basis in the partnership property and the partner recognizes a gain or loss on the distribution. Once a partnership makes a §754 election, the partnership is required to make the special basis adjustment for all subsequent sales of partnership interest and partnership distributions. The election can be revoked only with permission from the IRS.

Even without a §754 election in effect, the partnership must adjust its bases if the partnership has a **substantial built-in loss** at the time a partner sells her partnership interest. A substantial built-in loss exists if the partnership's aggregate adjusted basis in its property exceeds the property's fair market value by more than $250,000 when a transfer of an interest occurs.[52] An analogous event—a **substantial basis reduction**—may occur for distributions, which also triggers a mandatory basis adjustment.

Although the election is made under §754, the actual authorization of the special basis adjustment is governed by two separate code sections depending on which situation gives rise to the adjustment: (1) sale of partnership interest [§743(b)], or (2) distributions [§734(b)]. These two sections determine how much of an adjustment will be made, and §755 then stipulates how the adjustment is allocated among the partnership assets. The relationships among these code sections are depicted in Exhibit 21-2 below.

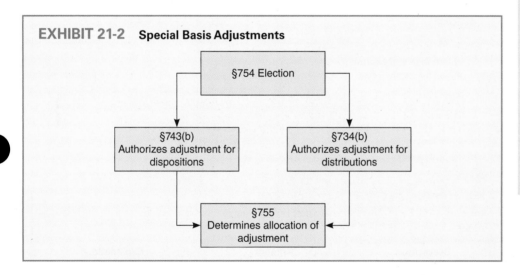

EXHIBIT 21-2 Special Basis Adjustments

Special Basis Adjustments for Dispositions

The special basis adjustment the partnership makes when a partner sells her partnership interest is designed to give the new investor a share in the partnership assets equal to his outside basis. The basis adjustment in these cases applies *only* to the new investor. The inside bases of the continuing partners remain unchanged, so their income and losses will continue to be accurately allocated. The adjustment is equal to the difference between the new investor's outside basis and his share of inside basis.[53] The new investor's outside basis is generally equal to the cost of his partnership interest plus his share of partnership liabilities.[54] The special basis adjustment must

---

[52]§743(d)(1). In this context, a transfer generally refers to sales, exchanges, or transfers at death, not gift transfers.

[53]§743(b).

[54]A partner's share of inside basis is also labeled *previously taxed capital* [§1.743-1(d)]. The technical calculation is determined as follows (but generally equals the partner's tax capital account):

(1) the amount of cash the partner would receive on liquidation after a hypothetical sale of all the partnership assets for their fair market value after the sale of the partnership interest, plus

(2) the amount of taxable loss allocated to the partner from the hypothetical sale, less

(3) the amount of taxable gain allocated to the partner from the hypothetical sale.

then be allocated to the assets under allocation rules in §755, which are beyond the scope of this text.

Example 21-26

On June 30, 2016, Greg acquired Chanzz's 30 percent interest in CCS for $82,800. CCS's balance sheet as of the sale date is as follows:

Color Comfort Sheets LLC June 30, 2016		
	Tax Basis	**FMV**
Assets:		
Cash	$ 27,000	$ 27,000
Accounts receivable	0	13,000
Investments	15,000	12,000
Inventory	1,000	1,000
Equipment (cost = $100,000)	80,000	86,000
Building	97,000	97,000
Land	20,000	150,000
Totals	$240,000	$386,000
Liabilities and capital:		
Long term debt	$100,000	
Capital—Nicole	(49,000)	
—Sarah	108,000	
—Chanzz	81,000	
Totals	$240,000	

What is the special basis adjustment for Greg's purchase, assuming CCS had a §754 election in effect at the sale date?

Answer: $1,800, the difference between Greg's outside basis and inside basis, is calculated as follows:

Description	Amount	Explanation
(1) Cash purchase price	$ 82,800	
(2) Greg's share of CCS debt	24,000	$80,000 × 30%.
(3) Initial basis in CCS	$106,800	(1) + (2).
(4) Greg's inside basis	105,000	Chanzz's tax capital ($81,000) plus share of CCS debt ($24,000) (See Example 21-7).
Special basis adjustment	$ 1,800	(3) − (4).

When a new investor's special basis adjustment is allocated to depreciable or amortizable assets, the new investor will benefit from additional depreciation or amortization. In some cases, the amounts can be quite substantial, and a new investor may be willing to pay more for a partnership interest when the partnership has a §754 election in place than for one without it.

Special Basis Adjustments for Distributions

A similar potential problem exists when the partnership distributes assets to the partners that represent more (or, in some cases, less) than their share of the inside basis in the partnership assets. This usually occurs when a partner recognizes a gain or loss on a distribution or when a partner's basis in the distributed property is different from the partnership's basis in the property. In contrast to the special basis adjustment for sales of partnership interests, the special basis adjustment for distributions affects the common basis of *partnership* property and not merely one partner's basis.

The special basis adjustment can either increase or decrease the basis in the partnership assets. A **positive basis adjustment** will *increase* the basis in the partnership assets (1) when a partner receiving distributed property recognizes a gain on the distribution (for instance, in operating distributions where the partner receives money in excess of her outside basis), and (2) when a partner receiving distributed property takes a basis in the property less than the partnership's basis in the property. The positive adjustment will equal the sum of the gain recognized by the partners receiving distributed property and the amount of the basis reduction.

In Example 21-11, CCS distributed $250,000 cash to Nicole on December 31, 2017, as part of an operating distribution. Because Nicole's outside basis before the distribution was $205,000 and she received only money in the distribution, Nicole was required to recognize a $45,000 gain on the distribution. If CCS had a §754 election in effect, it would have a positive special basis adjustment from the distribution of $45,000.

A **negative basis adjustment** will *decrease* the basis in partnership assets (1) when a partner receiving distributed property in a liquidating distribution recognizes a loss on the distribution, and (2) when a partner receiving distributed property takes a basis in the property greater than the partnership's basis in the property.

The negative adjustment will equal the sum of the recognized loss and the amount of the basis increase made by the partners receiving the distribution. Recall from our previous discussion of distributions that negative adjustments can occur only in liquidating distributions. Only then does a partner recognize a loss or increase the distributed property basis from that of the partnership's basis.

In Example 21-15, CCS liquidated Greg's 30 percent interest by distributing cash of $206,000 and inventory with a fair market value of $96,000 (adjusted basis is $43,000). Because Greg's outside basis after considering his debt relief ($268,000) was greater than the sum of the bases of the property distributed ($249,000), Greg recognized a loss of $19,000 on the liquidation. If CCS had a §754 election in effect at the time of this liquidation, CCS would have a negative basis adjustment of $19,000.

As in the case of partnership dispositions, the allocation of the special basis adjustment among the partnership's assets for distributions is intended to offset any inequitable gain or loss the partners would have realized absent the adjustment. The process of allocating the adjustment for distributions is prescribed in §755, and these procedures are beyond the scope of this text.

CONCLUSION

The tax rules for partnership dispositions and distributions are among the most complex in the Internal Revenue Code. This chapter provided an overview of these rules and in some cases plunged into the complexity. We discussed the calculation of gains and losses from the sale of a partnership interest, as well as the basis implications of the purchase to a new investor. In doing so, we discussed how *hot assets* might affect the gain or loss. The chapter also explained the basic rules for determining the tax treatment of partnership distributions.

We illustrated how partnership elections might affect the partnership's basis in assets following partnership interest dispositions or distributions. In general, the tax rules are designed to avoid having business owners make decisions based on tax rules rather than on business principles; however, making this goal a reality provides for some challenging applications.

Summary

LO 21-1 Determine the tax consequences to the buyer and seller of the disposition of a partnership interest, including the amount and character of gain or loss recognized.

- Sellers are primarily concerned about their realized and recognized gain or loss on the sale of their partnership interest.
- Sellers' debt relief is included in the amount realized from the sale.
- Buyers' main tax concerns are determining their basis in the partnership interest they acquire and their inside bases of the partnership assets.
- A buyer's outside basis after an acquisition is generally his cost plus his share of partnership liabilities. A buyer's inside basis is generally the same as the seller's inside basis at the sale date.
- The sale of a partnership interest does not generally affect a partnership's inside basis.
- A partnership's tax year closes for the selling partner upon the sale of a partnership interest.
- Hot assets include unrealized receivables and inventory items.
- Unrealized receivables include the rights to receive payment for goods delivered or to be delivered, or services rendered or to be rendered, as well as items that would generate ordinary income if the partnership sold the asset for its fair market value, such as depreciation recapture.
- There are actually two definitions of inventory items. The first under §751(a) applies to sales of partnership interests and includes all classic inventory items and assets that are *not* capital or §1231 assets. The second definition of inventory [§751(b)] applies primarily to distributions and includes only substantially appreciated inventory.
- Sellers classify gains and losses from the sale of partnership interests as ordinary to the extent the gain relates to hot assets.
- Hot assets are also important to determine whether a distribution is proportionate or disproportionate.

LO 21-2 List the reasons for distributions, and compare operating and liquidating distributions.

- Distributions from a flow-through entity are one mechanism to return business profits or capital to the owners of the entity.
- Distributions may also be used to liquidate an owner's interest in the business or to completely terminate the business.
- Operating distributions include distributions in which the owner retains an interest in the business.
- The purpose of liquidating distributions is to terminate an owner's interest in the business.

LO 21-3 Determine the tax consequences of proportionate operating distributions.

- Partnerships do not generally recognize gain or loss on the distribution of property.
- Most operating distributions do not result in gain or loss to the partner receiving the distribution. Gains and losses are deferred through basis adjustments to the distributed assets and basis of the partnership interest.
- A partner recognizes a gain from an operating distribution if she receives a distribution of money that exceeds the basis in her partnership interest.
- Partners never recognize losses from operating distributions.

LO 21-4 Determine the tax consequences of proportionate liquidating distributions.

- The tax issues in liquidating distributions are primarily twofold: (1) determining whether the liquidating partner recognizes a gain or loss, and (2) allocating the liquidating partner's basis in her partnership interest to the distributed assets.
- A partner recognizes a gain only when the partnership distributes more money than her basis in the partnership interest.
- A partner recognizes a loss only when the partnership distributes cash and hot assets and the partner's basis in the partnership interest is greater than the sum of the bases of the distributed assets.

- In all other cases, a partner does not recognize gains or losses from a liquidating distribution; rather, she will simply reallocate her basis in the partnership interest to the distributed assets.
- The key to the allocation process is to focus on two factors: (1) the type of property distributed, and (2) whether the total basis in distributed assets is larger or smaller than the partner's basis in the partnership interest.
- The character of the distributed assets usually stays the same to the partner as in the partnership.

Explain the significance of disproportionate distributions.   **LO 21-5**

- Disproportionate distributions occur when the assets distributed in either operating or liquidating distributions do not represent the partner's proportionate share of the partnership's hot and cold assets.
- A disproportionate distribution causes a shift in the proportion of ordinary income and capital gain income from the partnership. Therefore, the rules require the partner to treat a disproportionate distribution as a sale or exchange.
- If a partner receives more cold assets than her proportionate share in a distribution, she will generally recognize ordinary income in an amount equal to the appreciation of hot assets not distributed to her. If a partner receives more hot assets than her proportionate share, she will recognize capital gain equal to the appreciation of cold assets not distributed to her.
- The disproportionate distribution rules ensure that partners cannot convert ordinary income into capital gain through distributions.

Explain the rationale for special basis adjustments, determine when they are necessary, and calculate the special basis adjustment for dispositions and distributions.   **LO 21-6**

- Discrepancies between a partner's inside and outside basis may cause a partner to be overtaxed or undertaxed, at least temporarily. Special basis adjustment rules allow the partnership to eliminate discrepancies between inside and outside bases to correct the artificial income or loss at the partnership level.
- Basis discrepancies may occur following the acquisition of a partnership interest and following distributions where a partner receives more or less than her share of the inside basis in the partnership property.
- When a new investor purchases a partnership interest, she may make a special basis adjustment equal to the difference between her outside basis and her share of inside basis if the partnership has a §754 election in effect.
- A special basis adjustment is mandatory even without a §754 election in effect when a partner sells a partnership interest and the partnership has a substantial built-in loss at the time of the sale.
- When a partner recognizes a gain from a distribution or takes a basis in distributed property less than the partnership's basis in the property, the partnership will have a positive special basis adjustment to increase the partnership asset bases.
- When a partner recognizes a loss from a liquidating distribution or takes a basis in distributed property greater than the partnership's basis in the property, the partnership will have a negative special basis adjustment to decrease the partnership asset bases.

KEY TERMS

carryover basis (21-11)

disproportionate distributions (21-24)

hot assets (21-3)

inside basis (21-7)

inventory items (21-3)

liquidating distributions (21-9)

negative basis adjustment (21-29)

operating distributions (21-9)

outside basis (21-3)

partnership interest (21-2)

positive basis adjustment (21-29)

special basis adjustment (21-26)

substantial basis reduction (21-27)

substantial built-in loss (21-27)

substantially appreciated inventory (21-24)

unrealized receivables (21-3)

DISCUSSION QUESTIONS

Discussion Questions are available in Connect®.

LO 21-1 1. Joey is a 25 percent owner of Loopy LLC. He no longer wants to be involved in the business. What options does Joey have to exit the business?

LO 21-1 2. Compare and contrast the aggregate and entity approaches for a sale of a partnership interest.

LO 21-1 3. What restrictions might prevent a partner from selling his partnership interest to a third party?

LO 21-1 4. Explain how a partner's debt relief affects his amount realized in a sale of partnership interest.

LO 21-1 5. Under what circumstances will the gain or loss on the sale of a partnership interest be characterized as ordinary rather than capital?

LO 21-1 6. What are *hot assets* and why are they important in the sale of a partnership interest?

LO 21-1 7. For an accrual-method partnership, are accounts receivable considered unrealized receivables? Explain.

LO 21-1 8. Can a partnership have unrealized receivables if it has no accounts receivable?

LO 21-1 9. How do hot assets affect the character of gain or loss on the sale of a partnership interest?

LO 21-1 10. Under what circumstances can a partner recognize both gain and loss on the sale of a partnership interest?

LO 21-1 11. Absent any special elections, what effect does a sale of partnership interest have on the partnership?

research **LO 21-1** 12. Generally, a selling partner's capital account carries over to the purchaser of the partnership interest. Under what circumstances will this not be the case?

LO 21-2 13. What distinguishes operating from liquidating distributions?

LO 21-3 14. Under what circumstances will a partner recognize a gain from an operating distribution?

LO 21-3 15. Under what circumstances will a partner recognize a loss from an operating distribution?

LO 21-3 16. In general, what effect does an operating distribution have on the partnership?

LO 21-3 17. If a partner's outside basis is less than the partnership's inside basis in distributed assets, how does the partner determine his basis of the distributed assets in an operating distribution?

LO 21-4 18. Under what conditions will a partner recognize gain in a liquidating distribution?

LO 21-4 19. Under what conditions will a partner recognize loss in a liquidating distribution?

LO 21-4 20. Describe how a partner determines his basis in distributed assets in cases in which a partnership distributes only money, inventory, and/or unrealized receivables in a liquidating distribution.

LO 21-4 21. How does a partner determine his basis in distributed assets when the partnership distributes other property in addition to money and hot assets?

LO 21-5 22. SBT partnership distributes $5,000 cash and a parcel of land with a fair market value of $40,000 and a $25,000 basis to the partnership to Sam (30 percent partner). What factors must Sam and SBT consider in determining the tax treatment of this distribution?

planning

LO 21-5 23. Discuss the underlying concern to tax policymakers in distributions in which a partner receives more or less than his share of the partnership hot assets.

LO 21-5 24. In general, how do the disproportionate distribution rules ensure that partners recognize their share of partnership ordinary income?

planning **LO 21-6** 25. Why would a new partner who pays more for a partnership interest than the selling partner's outside basis want the partnership to elect a special basis adjustment?

26. List two common situations that will cause a partner's inside and outside basis to differ.   `LO 21-6`

27. Explain why a partnership might not want to make a §754 election to allow special basis adjustments.   `LO 21-6`

28. When might a new partner have an upward basis adjustment following the acquisition of a partnership interest?   `LO 21-6`

29. Are special basis adjustments mandatory? If so, when?   `LO 21-6`

PROBLEMS

Select problems are available in Connect®.

30. Jerry is a 30 percent partner in the JJM Partnership when he sells his entire interest to Lucia for $56,000 cash. At the time of the sale, Jerry's basis in JJM is $32,000. JJM does not have any debt or hot assets. What is Jerry's gain or loss on the sale of his interest?   `LO 21-1`

31. Joy is a 30 percent partner in the JOM Partnership when she sells her entire interest to Hope for $72,000 cash. At the time of the sale, Joy's basis in JOM is $44,000 (which includes her $6,000 share of JOM liabilities). JOM does not have any hot assets. What is Joy's gain or loss on the sale of her interest?   `LO 21-1`

32. Allison, Keesha, and Steven each own equal interests in KAS Partnership, a calendar-year-end, cash-method entity. On January 1 of the current year, Steven's basis in his partnership interest is $27,000. During January and February, the partnership generates $30,000 of ordinary income and $4,500 of tax-exempt income. On March 1, Steven sells his partnership interest to Juan for a cash payment of $45,000. The partnership has the following assets and no liabilities at the sale date: `LO 21-1`

	Tax Basis	FMV
Cash	$30,000	$30,000
Land held for investment	30,000	60,000
Totals	$60,000	$90,000

a) Assuming KAS's operating agreement provides for an interim closing of the books when partners' interests change during the year, what is Steven's basis in his partnership interest on March 1 just prior to the sale?

b) What is the amount and character of Steven's recognized gain or loss on the sale?

c) What is Juan's initial basis in the partnership interest?

d) What is the partnership's basis in the assets following the sale?

33. Grace, James, Helen, and Charles each own equal interests in GJHC Partnership, a calendar-year-end, cash-method entity. On January 1 of the current year, James's basis in his partnership interest is $62,000. For the taxable year, the partnership generates $80,000 of ordinary income and $30,000 of dividend income. For the first five months of the year, GJHC generates $25,000 of ordinary income and no dividend income. On June 1, James sells his partnership interest to Robert for a cash payment of $70,000. The partnership has the following assets and no liabilities at the sale date: `LO 21-1`

	Tax Basis	FMV
Cash	$ 27,000	$ 27,000
Land held for investment	80,000	100,000
Totals	$107,000	$127,000

a) Assuming GJHC's operating agreement provides that the proration method will be used to allocate income or loss when partners' interests change during the year, what is James's basis in his partnership interest on June 1 just prior to the sale?

b) What is the amount and character of James's recognized gain or loss on the sale?

c) If GJHC uses an interim closing of the books, what is the amount and character of James's recognized gain or loss on the sale?

LO 21-1   34. At the end of last year, Lisa, a 35 percent partner in the five-person LAMEC Partnership, has an outside basis of $60,000, including her $30,000 share of LAMEC debt. On January 1 of the current year, Lisa sells her partnership interest to MaryLynn for a cash payment of $45,000 and the assumption of her share of LAMEC's debt.

a) What is the amount and character of Lisa's recognized gain or loss on the sale?

b) If LAMEC has $100,000 of unrealized receivables as of the sale date, what is the amount and character of Lisa's recognized gain or loss?

c) What is MaryLynn's initial basis in the partnership interest?

LO 21-1   35. Marco, Jaclyn, and Carrie formed Daxing Partnership (a calendar-year-end entity) by contributing cash 10 years ago. Each partner owns an equal interest in the partnership. Marco, Jaclyn, and Carrie each have an outside basis in his/her partnership interest of $104,000. On January 1 of the current year, Marco sells his partnership interest to Ryan for a cash payment of $137,000. The partnership has the following assets and no liabilities as of the sale date:

	Tax Basis	FMV
Cash	$ 18,000	$ 18,000
Accounts receivable	0	12,000
Inventory	69,000	81,000
Equipment	180,000	225,000
Stock investment	45,000	75,000
Totals	$312,000	$411,000

The equipment was purchased for $240,000, and the partnership has taken $60,000 of depreciation. The stock was purchased seven years ago.

a) What are the *hot assets* [§751(a)] for this sale?

b) What is Marco's gain or loss on the sale of his partnership interest?

c) What is the character of Marco's gain or loss?

d) What are Ryan's inside and outside bases in the partnership on the date of the sale?

LO 21-1   36. Franklin, Jefferson, and Washington formed the Independence Partnership (a calendar-year-end entity) by contributing cash 10 years ago. Each partner owns an equal interest in the partnership. Franklin, Jefferson, and Washington each have an outside basis in his partnership interest of $104,000. On January 1 of the current year, Franklin sells his partnership interest to Adams for a cash payment of $122,000. The partnership has the following assets and no liabilities as of the sale date:

	Tax Basis	FMV
Cash	$ 18,000	$ 18,000
Accounts receivable	0	12,000
Inventory	69,000	81,000
Equipment	180,000	225,000
Stock investment	45,000	30,000
Totals	$312,000	$366,000

The equipment was purchased for $240,000, and the partnership has taken $60,000 of depreciation. The stock was purchased seven years ago.
a) What is Franklin's overall gain or loss on the sale of his partnership interest?
b) What is the character of Franklin's gain or loss?

37. Travis and Alix Weber are equal partners in the Tralix Partnership, which does not have a §754 election in place. Alix sells one-half of her interest (25 percent) to Michael Tomei for $30,000 cash. Just before the sale, Alix's basis in her entire partnership interest is $75,000, including her $30,000 share of the partnership liabilities. Tralix's assets on the sale date are as follows: **LO 21-1**

	Tax Basis	FMV
Cash	$ 40,000	$ 40,000
Inventory	30,000	90,000
Land held for investment	80,000	50,000
Totals	$150,000	$180,000

a) What is the amount and character of Alix's recognized gain or loss on the sale?
b) What is Alix's basis in her remaining partnership interest?
c) What is Michael's basis in his partnership interest?
d) What is the effect of the sale on the partnership's basis in the assets?

38. Newton is a one-third owner of ProRite Partnership. Newton has decided to sell his interest in the business to Betty for $50,000 cash plus the assumption of his share of ProRite's liabilities. Assume Newton's inside and outside basis in ProRite are equal. ProRite shows the following balance sheet as of the sale date: **LO 21-1**

	Tax Basis	FMV
Assets:		
Cash	$ 80,000	$ 80,000
Receivables	25,000	25,000
Inventory	40,000	85,000
Land	30,000	20,000
Totals	$175,000	$210,000
Liabilities and capital:		
Liabilities	$ 60,000	
Capital—Newton	38,333	
—Barbara	38,334	
—Liz	38,333	
Totals	$175,000	

What is the amount and character of Newton's recognized gain or loss?

39. Coy and Matt are equal partners in the Matcoy Partnership. Each partner has a basis in his partnership interest of $28,000 at the end of the current year, prior to any distribution. On December 31 they each receive an operating distribution. Coy receives $10,000 cash. Matt receives $3,000 cash and a parcel of land with a $7,000 fair market value and a $4,000 basis to the partnership. Matcoy has no debt or hot assets. **LO 21-3**
a) What is Coy's recognized gain or loss? What is the character of any gain or loss?
b) What is Coy's ending basis in his partnership interest?
c) What is Matt's recognized gain or loss? What is the character of any gain or loss?
d) What is Matt's basis in the distributed property?
e) What is Matt's ending basis in his partnership interest?

LO 21-3   40. Justin and Lauren are equal partners in the PJenn Partnership. The partners formed the partnership seven years ago by contributing cash. Prior to any distributions, the partners have the following bases in their partnership interests:

Partner	Outside Basis
Justin	$22,000
Lauren	22,000

On December 31 of the current year, the partnership makes a pro rata operating distribution of:

Partner	Distribution
Justin	Cash $25,000
Lauren	Cash $18,000
	Property $7,000 (FMV)
	($2,000 basis to partnership)

a) What is the amount and character of Justin's recognized gain or loss?
b) What is Justin's remaining basis in his partnership interest?
c) What is the amount and character of Lauren's recognized gain or loss?
d) What is Lauren's basis in the distributed assets?
e) What is Lauren's remaining basis in her partnership interest?

LO 21-3   41. Adam and Alyssa are equal partners in the PartiPilo Partnership. The partners formed the partnership three years ago by contributing cash. Prior to any distributions, the partners have the following bases in their partnership interests:

Partner	Outside Basis
Adam	$12,000
Alyssa	12,000

On December 31 of the current year, the partnership makes a pro rata operating distribution of:

Partner	Distribution
Adam	Cash $16,000
Alyssa	Cash $8,000
	Property $8,000 (FMV)
	($6,000 basis to partnership)

a) What is the amount and character of Adam's recognized gain or loss?
b) What is Adam's remaining basis in his partnership interest?
c) What is the amount and character of Alyssa's recognized gain or loss?
d) What is Alyssa's basis in the distributed assets?
e) What is Alyssa's remaining basis in her partnership interest?

LO 21-3   42. Karen has a $68,000 basis in her 50 percent partnership interest in the KD Partnership before receiving a current distribution of $6,000 cash and land with a fair market value of $35,000 and a basis to the partnership of $18,000.
a) What is the amount and character of Karen's recognized gain or loss?
b) What is Karen's basis in the land?
c) What is Karen's remaining basis in her partnership interest?

LO 21-3   43. Pam has a $27,000 basis (including her share of debt) in her 50 percent partnership interest in the Meddoc Partnership before receiving any distributions. This year Meddoc makes a current distribution to Pam of a parcel of land with a $40,000 fair market value and a $32,000 basis to the partnership. The land is encumbered with a $15,000 mortgage (the partnership's only liability).

a) What is the amount and character of Pam's recognized gain or loss?

b) What is Pam's basis in the land?

c) What is Pam's remaining basis in her partnership interest?

44. Two years ago, Kimberly became a 30 percent partner in the KST Partnership with a contribution of investment land with a $10,000 basis and a $16,000 fair market value. On January 2 of this year, Kimberly has a $15,000 basis in her partnership interest and none of her precontribution gain has been recognized. On January 2 Kimberly receives an operating distribution of a tract of land (not the contributed land) with a $12,000 basis and an $18,000 fair market value.

LO 21-3

research

a) What is the amount and character of Kimberly's recognized gain or loss on the distribution?

b) What is Kimberly's remaining basis in KST after the distribution?

c) What is KST's basis in the land Kimberly contributed after Kimberly receives this distribution?

45. Rufus is a one-quarter partner in the Adventure Partnership. On January 1 of the current year, Adventure distributes $13,000 cash to Rufus in complete liquidation of his interest. Adventure has only capital assets and no liabilities at the date of the distribution. Rufus's basis in his partnership interest is $18,500.

LO 21-4

a) What is the amount and character of Rufus's recognized gain or loss?

b) What is the amount and character of Adventure's recognized gain or loss?

c) If Rufus's basis is $10,000 at the distribution date rather than $18,500, what is the amount and character of Rufus's recognized gain or loss?

46. The Taurin Partnership (calendar-year-end) has the following assets as of December 31 of the current year:

LO 21-4

	Tax Basis	FMV
Cash	$ 45,000	$ 45,000
Accounts receivable	15,000	30,000
Inventory	81,000	120,000
Totals	$141,000	$195,000

On December 31 Taurin distributes $15,000 of cash, $10,000 (FMV) of accounts receivable, and $40,000 (FMV) of inventory to Emma (a one-third partner) in termination of her partnership interest. Emma's basis in her partnership interest immediately prior to the distribution is $40,000.

a) What is the amount and character of Emma's recognized gain or loss on the distribution?

b) What is Emma's basis in the distributed assets?

c) If Emma's basis before the distribution was $55,000 rather than $40,000, what is Emma's recognized gain or loss and what is her basis in the distributed assets?

47. Melissa, Nicole, and Ben are equal partners in the Opto Partnership (calendar-year-end). Melissa decides she wants to exit the partnership and receives a proportionate distribution to liquidate her partnership interest on January 1. The partnership has no liabilities and holds the following assets as of January 1:

LO 21-4

	Tax Basis	FMV
Cash	$18,000	$18,000
Accounts receivable	0	24,000
Stock investment	7,500	12,000
Land	30,000	36,000
Totals	$55,500	$90,000

Melissa receives one-third of each of the partnership assets. She has a basis in her partnership interest of $25,000.

a) What is the amount and character of any recognized gain or loss to Melissa?

b) What is Melissa's basis in the distributed assets?

c) What are the tax implications (amount and character of gain or loss and basis of assets) to Melissa if her outside basis is $11,000 rather than $25,000?

d) What is the amount and character of any recognized gain or loss from the distribution to Opto?

LO 21-4

planning

48. Lonnie Davis has been a general partner in the Highland Partnership for many years and is also a sole proprietor in a separate business. To spend more time focusing on his sole proprietorship, he plans to leave Highland and will receive a liquidating distribution of $50,000 in cash and land with a fair market value of $100,000 (tax basis of $120,000). Immediately before the distribution, Lonnie's basis in his partnership interest is $350,000, which includes his $50,000 share of partnership debt. The Highland Partnership does not hold any hot assets.

a) What is the amount and character of any gain or loss to Lonnie?

b) What is Lonnie's basis in the land?

c) What is the amount and character of Lonnie's gain or loss if he holds the land for 13 months as investment property and then sells it for $100,000?

d) What is the amount and character of Lonnie's gain or loss if he places the land into service in his sole proprietorship and then sells it 13 months later for $100,000?

e) Do your answers to parts (c) and (d) suggest a course of action that would help Lonnie to achieve a more favorable tax outcome?

LO 21-4

49. AJ is a 30 percent partner in the Trane Partnership, a calendar-year-end entity. On January 1, AJ has an outside basis in his interest in Trane of $73,000, which includes his share of the $50,000 of partnership liabilities. Trane generates $42,000 of income during the year and does not make any changes to its liabilities. On December 31, Trane makes a proportionate distribution of the following assets to AJ to terminate his partnership interest:

	Tax Basis	FMV
Inventory	$55,000	$65,000
Land	30,000	25,000
Totals	$85,000	$90,000

a) What are the tax consequences (gain or loss, basis adjustments) of the distribution to Trane?

b) What is the amount and character of any recognized gain or loss to AJ?

c) What is AJ's basis in the distributed assets?

d) If AJ sells the inventory four years after the distribution for $70,000, what is the amount and character of his recognized gain or loss?

LO 21-4

50. David's basis in the Jimsoo Partnership is $53,000. In a proportionate liquidating distribution, David receives cash of $7,000 and two capital assets: (1) land 1 with a fair market value of $20,000 and a basis to Jimsoo of $16,000 and (2) land 2 with a fair market value of $10,000 and a basis to Jimsoo of $16,000. Jimsoo has no liabilities.

a) How much gain or loss will David recognize on the distribution? What is the character of any recognized gain or loss?

b) What is David's basis in the distributed assets?

c) If the two parcels of land had been inventory to Jimsoo, what are the tax consequences to David (amount and character of gain or loss and basis in distributed assets)?

51. Megan and Matthew are equal partners in the J & J Partnership (calendar-year-end entity). On January 1 of the current year, they decide to liquidate the partnership. Megan's basis in her partnership interest is $100,000 and Matthew's is $35,000. The two partners receive identical distributions, with each receiving the following assets: `LO 21-4`

	Tax Basis	FMV
Cash	$30,000	$30,000
Inventory	5,000	6,000
Land	500	1,000
Totals	$35,500	$37,000

   a) What is the amount and character of Megan's recognized gain or loss?

   b) What is Megan's basis in the distributed assets?

   c) What is the amount and character of Matthew's recognized gain or loss?

   d) What is Matthew's basis in the distributed assets?

52. Bryce's basis in the Markit Partnership is $58,000. In a proportionate liquidating distribution, Bryce receives the following assets: `LO 21-4`

	Tax Basis	FMV
Cash	$ 8,000	$ 8,000
Land A	20,000	45,000
Land B	20,000	25,000

   a) How much gain or loss will Bryce recognize on the distribution? What is the character of any recognized gain or loss?

   b) What is Bryce's basis in the distributed assets?

53. Danner Inc. has a $395,000 capital loss carryover that will expire at the end of the current tax year if it is not used. Also, Danner Inc. has been a general partner in the Talisman Partnership for three years and plans to end its involvement with the partnership by receiving a liquidating distribution. Initially, all parties agreed that Danner Inc.'s liquidating distribution would include $50,000 in cash and land with a fair market value of $400,000 (tax basis of $120,000). Immediately before the distribution, Danner's basis in its partnership interest is $150,000, which includes its $100,000 share of partnership debt. The Talisman Partnership does not hold any hot assets. `LO 21-4` `planning`

   a) What is the amount and character of any gain or loss to Danner Inc.?

   b) What is Danner Inc.'s basis in the land?

   c) Can you suggest a course of action that would help Danner Inc. avoid the expiration of its capital loss carryover?

54. Bella Partnership is an equal partnership in which each of the partners has a basis in his partnership interest of $10,000. Bella reports the following balance sheet: `LO 21-1` `LO 21-5` `planning`

	Tax Basis	FMV
Assets:		
Inventory	$20,000	$30,000
Land	10,000	15,000
Totals	$30,000	$45,000
Liabilities and capital:		
Capital—Toby	$10,000	
—Kaelin	10,000	
—Andrew	10,000	
Totals	$30,000	

a) Identify the *hot assets* if Toby decides to sell his partnership interest. Are these assets "hot" for purposes of distributions?

b) If Bella distributes the land to Toby in complete liquidation of his partnership interest, what tax issues should be considered?

LO 21-1 **LO 21-6**   55. Michelle pays $120,000 cash for Brittany's one-third interest in the Westlake Partnership. Just prior to the sale, Brittany's basis in Westlake is $96,000. Westlake reports the following balance sheet:

	Tax Basis	FMV
Assets:		
Cash	$ 96,000	$ 96,000
Land	192,000	264,000
Totals	$288,000	$360,000
Liabilities and capital:		
Capital—Amy	$ 96,000	
—Brittany	96,000	
—Ben	96,000	
Totals	$288,000	

a) What is the amount and character of Brittany's recognized gain or loss on the sale?

b) What is Michelle's basis in her partnership interest? What is Michelle's inside basis?

c) If Westlake were to sell the land for $264,000 shortly after the sale of Brittany's partnership interest, how much gain or loss would the partnership recognize?

d) How much gain or loss would Michelle recognize?

e) Suppose Westlake has a §754 election in place. What is Michelle's special basis adjustment? How much gain or loss would Michelle recognize on a subsequent sale of the land in this situation?

LO 21-4 **LO 21-6**   56. Cliff's basis in his Aero Partnership interest is $11,000. Cliff receives a distribution of $22,000 cash from Aero in complete liquidation of his interest. Aero is an equal partnership with the following balance sheet:

	Tax Basis	FMV
Assets:		
Cash	$22,000	$22,000
Investment	8,800	8,800
Land	2,200	35,200
Totals	$33,000	$66,000
Liabilities and capital:		
Capital—Chris	$11,000	
—Cliff	11,000	
—Cooper	11,000	
Totals	$33,000	

a) What is the amount and character of Cliff's recognized gain or loss? What is the effect on the partnership assets?

b) If Aero has a §754 election in place, what is the amount of the special basis adjustment?

57. Erin's basis in her Kiybron Partnership interest is $3,300. Erin receives a distribution of $2,200 cash from Kiybron in complete liquidation of her interest. Kiybron is an equal partnership with the following balance sheet: **LO 21-4** **LO 21-6**

	Tax Basis	FMV
Assets:		
Cash	$2,200	$2,200
Stock (investment)	1,100	2,200
Land	6,600	2,200
Totals	$9,900	$6,600
Liabilities and capital:		
Capital—Erin	$3,300	
—Carl	3,300	
—Grace	3,300	
Totals	$9,900	

a) What is the amount and character of Erin's recognized gain or loss? What is the effect on the partnership assets?

b) If Kiybron has a §754 election in place, what is the amount of the special basis adjustment?

58. Helen's basis in Haywood Partnership is $270,000. Haywood distributes all the land to Helen in complete liquidation of her partnership interest. The partnership reports the following balance sheet just before the distribution: **LO 21-4** **LO 21-6**

	Tax Basis	FMV
Assets:		
Cash	$220,000	$220,000
Stock (investment)	480,000	220,000
Land	110,000	220,000
Totals	$810,000	$660,000
Liabilities and capital:		
Capital—Charles	$270,000	
—Esther	270,000	
—Helen	270,000	
Totals	$810,000	

a) What is the amount and character of Helen's recognized gain or loss? What is the effect on the partnership assets?

b) If Haywood has a §754 election in place, what is the amount of the special basis adjustment?

COMPREHENSIVE PROBLEMS

Select problems are available in Connect®.   connect

59. Simon is a 30 percent partner in the SBD Partnership, a calendar-year-end entity. As of the end of this year, Simon has an outside basis in his interest in SBD of $188,000, which includes his share of the $60,000 of partnership liabilities. On December 31, SBD makes a proportionate distribution of the following assets to Simon:

	Tax Basis	FMV
Cash	$ 40,000	$ 40,000
Inventory	55,000	65,000
Land	30,000	45,000
Totals	$125,000	$150,000

a) What are the tax consequences (amount and character of recognized gain or loss, basis in distributed assets) of the distribution to Simon if the distribution is an operating distribution?

b) What are the tax consequences (amount and character of recognized gain or loss, basis in distributed assets) of the distribution to Simon if the distribution is a liquidating distribution?

c) Compare and contrast the results from parts (a) and (b).

planning   60. Paolo is a 50 percent partner in the Capri Partnership and has decided to terminate his partnership interest. Paolo is considering two options as potential exit strategies. The first is to sell his partnership interest to the two remaining 25 percent partners, Giuseppe and Isabella, for $105,000 cash and the assumption of Paolo's share of Capri's liabilities. Under this option, Giuseppe and Isabella would each pay $52,500 for half of Paolo's interest. The second option is to have Capri liquidate his partnership interest with a proportionate distribution of the partnership assets. Paolo's basis in his partnership interest is $110,000, including Paolo's share of Capri's liabilities. Capri reports the following balance sheet as of the termination date:

	Tax Basis	FMV
Assets:		
Cash	$ 80,000	$ 80,000
Receivables	40,000	40,000
Inventory	50,000	80,000
Land	50,000	60,000
Totals	$220,000	$260,000
Liabilities and capital:		
Liabilities	$ 50,000	
Capital—Paolo	85,000	
—Giuseppe	42,500	
—Isabella	42,500	
Totals	$220,000	

a) If Paolo sells his partnership interest to Giuseppe and Isabella for $105,000, what is the amount and character of Paolo's recognized gain or loss?

b) Giuseppe and Isabella each have a basis in Capri of $55,000 before any purchase of Paolo's interest. What are Giuseppe's and Isabella's basis in their partnership interests following the purchase of Paolo's interest?

c) If Capri liquidates Paolo's partnership interest with a proportionate distribution of the partnership assets ($25,000 deemed cash from debt relief, $15,000 of actual cash, and half of the remaining assets), what is the amount and character of Paolo's recognized gain or loss?

d) If Capri liquidates Paolo's interest, what is Paolo's basis in the distributed assets?

e) Compare and contrast Paolo's options for terminating his partnership interest. Assume Paolo's marginal tax rate is 35 percent, and his capital gains rate is 15 percent.

tax forms   61. Carrie D'Lake, Reed A. Green, and Doug A. Divot share a passion for golf and decide to go into the golf club manufacturing business together. On January 2, 2016, D'Lake, Green, and Divot form the Slicenhook Partnership, a general partnership. Slicenhook's main product will be a perimeter-weighted titanium driver with a patented graphite shaft. All three partners plan to actively participate in the business. The partners contribute the following property to form Slicenhook:

Partner	Contribution
Carrie D'Lake	Land, FMV $460,000
	Basis $460,000, Mortgage $60,000
Reed A. Green	$400,000
Doug A. Divot	$400,000

Carrie had recently acquired the land with the idea that she would contribute it to the newly formed partnership. The partners agree to share in profits and losses equally. Slicenhook elects a calendar-year-end and the accrual method of accounting.

In addition, Slicenhook received a $1,500,000 recourse loan from BigBank at the time the contributions were made. Slicenhook uses the proceeds from the loan and the cash contributions to build a state-of-the-art manufacturing facility ($1,200,000), purchase equipment ($600,000), and produce inventory ($400,000). With the remaining cash, Slicenhook invests $45,000 in the stock of a privately owned graphite research company and retains $55,000 as working cash.

Slicenhook operates on a just-in-time inventory system so it sells all inventory and collects all sales immediately. That means that at the end of the year, Slicenhook does not carry any inventory or accounts receivable balances. During 2016, Slicenhook has the following operating results:

Sales		$1,126,000
Cost of goods sold		400,000
Interest income from tax-exempt bonds		900
Qualified dividend income from stock		1,500
Operating expenses		126,000
Depreciation (tax)		
§179 on equipment	$39,000	
Equipment	81,000	
Building	24,000	144,000
Interest expense on debt		120,000

The partnership is very successful in its first year. The success allows Slicenhook to use excess cash from operations to purchase $15,000 of tax-exempt bonds (you can see the interest income already reflected in the operating results). The partnership also makes a principal payment on its loan from Big Bank in the amount of $300,000 and a distribution of $100,000 to each of the partners on December 31, 2016.

The partnership continues its success in 2017 with the following operating results:

Sales		$1,200,000
Cost of goods sold		420,000
Interest income from tax-exempt bonds		900
Qualified dividend income from stock		1,500
Operating expenses		132,000
Depreciation (tax)		
Equipment	147,000	
Building	30,000	177,000
Interest expense on debt		96,000

The operating expenses include a $1,800 trucking fine that one of its drivers incurred for reckless driving and speeding and meals and entertainment expense of $6,000.

By the end of 2017, Reed has had a falling out with Carrie and Doug and has decided to leave the partnership. He has located a potential buyer for his partnership interest, Indie Ruff. Indie has agreed to purchase Reed's interest in Slicenhook for $730,000 in cash and the assumption of Reed's share of Slicenhook's debt. Carrie and Doug, however, are not certain that admitting Indie to the partnership is such a good idea. They want at least to consider having Slicenhook liquidate Reed's interest on January 1, 2018. As of January 1, 2018, Slicenhook has the following assets:

	Tax Basis	FMV
Cash	$ 876,800	$ 876,800
Investment—tax exempts	15,000	18,000
Investment stock	45,000	45,000
Equipment—net of dep.	333,000	600,000
Building—net of dep.	1,146,000	1,440,000
Land	460,000	510,000
Total	$2,875,800	$3,489,800

Carrie and Doug propose that Slicenhook distribute the following to Reed in complete liquidation of his partnership interest:

	Tax Basis	FMV
Cash	$485,000	$485,000
Investment stock	45,000	45,000
Equipment—$200,000 cost net of dep.	111,000	200,000
Total	$641,000	$730,000

Slicenhook has not purchased or sold any equipment since its original purchase just after formation.

a) Determine each partner's recognized gain or loss upon formation of Slicenhook.

b) What is each partner's initial tax basis in Slicenhook on January 2, 2016?

c) Prepare Slicenhook's opening tax basis balance sheet as of January 2, 2016.

d) Using the operating results, what are Slicenhook's ordinary income and separately stated items for 2016 and 2017? What amount of Slicenhook's income for each period would each of the partner's receive?

e) Using the information provided, prepare Slicenhook's page 1 and Schedule K to be included with its Form 1065 for 2016. Also, prepare a Schedule K-1 for Carrie.

f) What are Carrie's, Reed's, and Doug's bases in their partnership interest at the end of 2016 and 2017?

g) If Reed sells his interest in Slicenhook to Indie Ruff, what is the amount and character of his recognized gain or loss? What is Indie's basis in the partnership interest?

h) What is Indie's inside basis in Slicenhook? What effect would a §754 election have on Indie's inside basis?

i) If Slicenhook distributes the assets proposed by Carrie and Doug in complete liquidation of Reed's partnership interest, what is the amount and character of Reed's recognized gain or loss? What is Reed's basis in the distributed assets?

j) Compare and contrast Reed's options for terminating his partnership interest. Assume Reed's marginal ordinary rate is 35 percent, and his capital gains rate is 15 percent.

22 S Corporations

Learning Objectives

Upon completing this chapter, you should be able to:

LO 22-1 Describe the requirements and process to elect S corporation status.

LO 22-2 Explain the events that terminate the S corporation election.

LO 22-3 Describe operating issues relating to S corporation accounting periods and methods, and explain income and loss allocations and separately stated items.

LO 22-4 Explain stock-basis calculations, loss limitations, determination of self-employment income, and fringe benefit rules that apply to S corporation shareholders.

LO 22-5 Apply the tax rules for S corporation operating distributions and liquidating distributions.

LO 22-6 Describe the taxes that apply to S corporations, estimated tax requirements, and tax return filing requirements.

© PhotoAlto

Storyline Summary

Nicole Johnson, Sarah Walker, and Chance Armstrong

Location: Salt Lake City, Utah

Status: Shareholders of newly formed Color Comfort Sheets Inc. (CCS)

Situation: Formed CCS as a corporation and have elected to have the entity taxed as an S corporation.

In Chapter 15, we met Nicole Johnson, who turned her sheet-making hobby into a full-time business called Color Comfort Sheets (CCS). In this chapter, we assume Nicole formed CCS as a corporation, intending to elect S corporation tax status.

When starting the business, Nicole had cash to contribute to CCS but not enough to meet initial needs. She convinced her friend Sarah Walker to invest in CCS and, fortunately, after listening to Nicole and Sarah's proposal, local sports team owner Chance Armstrong also agreed to invest.

Nicole and Sarah would take an active role in managing CCS; Chance would not. Nicole contributed a parcel of land and cash in exchange for one-third of CCS's stock. Sarah and Chance each contributed cash for one-third of the stock. With funding in place, CCS began operating on January 1, 2015. However, with the excitement (and turmoil) of starting the new business, it took Nicole, Sarah, and Chance a while to talk with their accountant about electing S corporation status. After several discussions, they filed their S election on May 1, 2015. ∎

In this chapter, we discuss the tax and nontax characteristics of an **S corporation,** a hybrid entity that shares some characteristics with C corporations and some with partnerships.[1] S corporations are incorporated under state law and thus have the same legal protections as C corporations. They are governed by the same corporate tax rules that apply in the organization, liquidation, and reorganization of C corporations. However, unlike a C corporation, an S corporation is a flow-through entity and shares many tax similarities with partnerships. For example, basis calculations for S corporation shareholders and partners are similar, the income or loss of an S corporation flows through to its owners, and distributions are generally not taxed to the extent of the owner's basis.

Throughout this chapter, we highlight the tax similarities between S corporations and C corporations and between S corporations and partnerships, while focusing on the unique rules that apply to S corporations. These are more complex for S corporations that were once C corporations with previously undistributed **earnings and profits (E&P).**

LO 22-1

THE KEY FACTS

S Corporation Qualification Requirements

- Only U.S. citizens or residents, estates, certain trusts, and certain tax-exempt organizations may be S corporation shareholders.
- S corporations may have no more than 100 shareholders.
- For purposes of the 100-shareholder limit, family members and their estates count as only one shareholder.

S CORPORATION ELECTIONS

Formations

The same rules for forming and contributing property govern S and C corporations. As discussed in Chapter 19, §351 and related provisions apply when one or more persons transfer property to a corporation (C or S) in return for stock, and immediately after the transfer, these persons control the corporation. These rules allow shareholders meeting the requirements to defer gains they realize when they transfer appreciated property to the corporation in exchange for stock. Note that similar rules apply to formations and property contributions to partnerships under §721. One important difference, however, is that partnership tax rules do not impose a control requirement to defer gains (see Chapter 20 for partnership contributions).

S Corporation Qualification Requirements

Unlike C corporations and partnerships, S corporations are limited as to type and number of owners (shareholders).[2] Only U.S. citizens or residents, estates, certain trusts, and certain tax-exempt organizations may be shareholders. No corporations or partnerships can be shareholders.[3] S corporations may have no more than 100 shareholders; family members and their estates count as one shareholder. Family members include a common ancestor and her lineal descendants and their spouses (or former spouses). Thus, great-grandparents, grandparents, parents, children, grandchildren, great-grandchildren, and the respective spouses are family members for this purpose. A practical implication of these limits is that large, publicly traded corporations cannot elect to be treated as S corporations.

[1]S corporations get their name from **Subchapter S** of the Internal Revenue Code, which includes code sections 1361–1379.

[2]§1361.

[3]Grantor trusts, qualified Subchapter S trusts, electing small business trusts, certain testamentary trusts, and voting trusts can own S corporation stock. A discussion of these trusts is beyond the scope of this chapter. Eligible tax-exempt shareholders include qualified retirement plan trusts or charitable, religious, educational, etc., organizations that are tax-exempt under §501.

Example 22-1

What if: Suppose CCS was formed with Nicole Johnson, Sarah Walker, and Chanzz Inc., a corporation owned by Chance Armstrong, as shareholders. Would CCS be eligible to elect S corporation status?

Answer: No. Because one of its shareholders is a corporation (Chanzz Inc.), CCS would not be eligible to elect S corporation status.

What if: Suppose Nicole, Sarah, and Chance recruited 97 U.S. residents to become shareholders of CCS. Meanwhile, Nicole gave several of her CCS shares to her grandfather and his bride as a wedding gift. After the transfer, CCS had 102 shareholders. Can CCS elect S corporation status?

Answer: Yes. Nicole (descendant of common ancestor), her grandfather (common ancestor), and her grandfather's wife (spouse of common ancestor) are treated as *one* shareholder for purposes of the 100-shareholder limit.

S Corporation Election

An eligible corporation must make an affirmative election to be treated as an S corporation.[4] In addition to meeting the shareholder requirements above, it must:

- Be a domestic corporation (created or organized in the United States or under U.S. law or the law of any state in the United States).
- Not be a specifically identified ineligible corporation.[5]
- Have only one class of stock.

A corporation is considered to have only one class of stock if all of its outstanding shares provide identical distribution and liquidation rights. Differences in voting powers are permissible. In general, debt instruments do not violate the single class of stock requirement unless they are treated as equity elsewhere under the tax law.[6] In addition, §1361 provides safe-harbor rules to ensure that debt obligations are not recharacterized as a second class of stock.[7]

THE KEY FACTS

S Corporation Election
- An eligible corporation must make an affirmative election to be treated as an S corporation.
- Eligible corporations meet the type and number of shareholder requirements, are domestic corporations, are not specifically identified as ineligible corporations, and have only one class of stock.
- To elect S corporation status, the corporation makes a formal election using Form 2553.

Example 22-2

What if: Suppose Nicole was a resident of Toronto, Canada, and while she formed CCS in Canada under Canadian law, she still planned to do business in the United States. Is CCS eligible to elect S corporation status in the United States?

Answer: No. CCS would not be eligible for S corporation treatment because it was neither organized in the United States nor formed under U.S. laws.

What if: Suppose Nicole resided in Seattle and formed CCS under the state laws of Washington but planned to do a significant amount of business in Canada. Would CCS be eligible to elect S corporation status?

Answer: Yes, because CCS was formed under the laws of a U.S. state.

---

[4]§1362(a).

[5]Ineligible corporations include financial institutions using the reserve method of accounting under §585, insurance companies, corporations allowed a tax credit for income from Puerto Rico and from U.S. possessions under §936, corporations previously electing Domestic International Sales Corporation status, and corporations treated as a taxable mortgage pool.

[6]See §385 for factors considered in determining whether debt should be considered as equity for tax purposes.

[7]§1361(c)(5)(A) provides that straight debt issued during an S corporation year (i.e., not during a C corporation year) will not be treated as a second class of stock. §1361(c)(5)(A) defines straight debt as debt characterized by a written unconditional promise to pay on demand or on a specified date a sum certain in money if (1) the interest rate and interest payment dates are not contingent on profits, the borrower's discretion, or similar factors; (2) the debt is not convertible into stock; and (3) the creditor is an individual (other than a nonresident alien), an estate, a qualified trust, or a person who is actively and regularly engaged in the business of lending money.

To formally elect S corporation status effective as of the beginning of the current tax year, the corporation uses **Form 2553,** either in the prior tax year or on or before the 15th day of the third month of the current tax year.[8] Elections made after the 15th day of the third month of a year are effective at the beginning of the following year. All shareholders on the date of the election must consent to the election.

Example 22-3

> *What if:* Suppose Nicole formed CCS as a C corporation in 2015 with a calendar tax year and finally got around to electing S corporation status on February 20, 2016. What is the earliest effective date of the S election?
>
> **Answer:** January 1, 2016.
>
> *What if:* Suppose Nicole formed CCS as a C corporation in 2015 with a calendar tax year and made the S election on March 20, 2016. When is the S election effective?
>
> **Answer:** It is effective January 1, 2017, because Nicole made the election after March 15, 2016.

Even when the corporation makes the election on or before the 15th day of the third month of its tax year, the election will not be effective until the subsequent year if (1) the corporation did not meet the S corporation requirements for each day of the current tax year before it made the S election, or (2) one or more shareholders who held the stock in the corporation during the current year and before the S corporation election was made did not consent to the election (e.g., a shareholder disposes of his stock in the corporation in the election year before the election is made and fails to consent to the S election).[9]

Example 22-4

> *What if:* Suppose in 2015 Nicole formed CCS as a C corporation (calendar tax year) with Nicole, Sarah, and Chanzz Inc. (a corporation) as shareholders. On January 2, 2016, Chanzz Inc. sold all its shares to Chance Armstrong. On January 31, 2016, CCS filed an S corporation election, with Nicole, Sarah, and Chance all consenting to the election. What is the earliest effective date of the S election?
>
> **Answer:** January 1, 2017. Because CCS had an ineligible shareholder (Chanzz Inc.) during 2016, the election is not effective until the beginning of 2017.
>
> *What if:* Suppose in 2015 Nicole formed CCS as a C corporation (calendar tax year) with Nicole, Sarah, and Chance as shareholders. On January 30, 2016, Chance sold his shares to Nicole. On February 15, 2016, CCS filed an S election, with Nicole and Sarah consenting to the election. Chance, however, did not consent to the election. What is the earliest effective date of the S election?
>
> **Answer:** January 1, 2017. Because Chance was a shareholder until January 30, 2016, and he did not consent to the S election in 2016, the S election is not effective until the beginning of 2017, the year after the election.

The timing of the election may be especially important for C corporations with net operating losses. The reason: Net operating losses attributable to C corporation years generally cannot be carried over to the S corporation. Thus, it may be beneficial to delay the S election until the corporation has utilized its net operating losses.[10]

---

[8]§1362(b). When the IRS determines that taxpayers have reasonable cause for making late elections, it has the authority to treat late elections as timely [§1362(b)(5)]. Rev. Proc. 2013-30 provides a simplified method to provide relief for late elections by submitting the Form 2553 to the IRS with a statement that explains (a) that there was either reasonable cause for the late election or the late election was inadvertent and (b) that the taxpayer acted diligently to correct the mistake upon discovery.

[9]§1362(b)(2). Requiring all shareholders who own stock in an S corporation during the year to consent to the election ensures that shareholders who dispose of their stock before the election do not suffer adverse tax consequences from an election to which they did not consent.

[10]Later in this chapter we discuss one exception to the rule that disallows net operating loss carryovers from C corporation to S corporation years. See the discussion of the S corporation built-in gains tax.

S CORPORATION TERMINATIONS

Once the S election becomes effective, the corporation remains an S corporation until the election is terminated. The termination may be voluntary or involuntary.

Voluntary Terminations

The corporation can make a *voluntary revocation* of the S election if shareholders holding more than 50 percent of the S corporation stock (including nonvoting shares) agree.[11] The corporation files a statement with the IRS revoking the election made under §1362(a) and stating the effective date of the revocation and the number of shares issued and outstanding. In general, voluntary revocations made on or before the 15th day of the third month of the year are effective as of the beginning of the year. A revocation after this period is effective the first day of the following tax year. Alternatively, a corporation may specify the termination date as long as the date specified is on or after the date the revocation is made.[12]

Example 22-5

What if: Suppose CCS was initially formed as an S corporation with a calendar year-end. After a couple of years, things were going so well that Nicole and Sarah (each one-third shareholders) wanted to terminate the S election and take CCS public. However, Chance (also a one-third shareholder) was opposed to the S election termination. Can Nicole and Sarah terminate the S election without Chance's consent?

Answer: Yes. To revoke the election, Nicole and Sarah need to own more than 50 percent of the shares, and together they own 66.7 percent.

What if: If Nicole and Sarah file the revocation on February 15, 2017, what is the effective date of the S corporation termination (assuming they do not specify one)?

Answer: January 1, 2017. If they file the S corporation revocation after March 15, 2017, it becomes effective January 1, 2018. Alternatively, CCS could have specified an effective date of the S corporation's termination (in 2017 or after) as long as it was on or after the date the revocation was made.

ETHICS

Suppose Chance Armstrong is a French citizen but U.S. resident. Chance's mother has recently been diagnosed with a terminal illness, and Chance has decided to move back to France to take care of his mother and her affairs. Chance anticipates that he will live in France for several years and that he no longer would be considered a U.S. resident. If you were Sarah or Nicole, how would you react to Chance's decision to move? Would you ignore the impact Chance's move may have on CCS's S corporation status? Would you pressure Chance to sell his CCS stock to you?

Involuntary Terminations

Involuntary terminations can result from failure to meet requirements (by far the most common reason) or from an excess of passive investment income.

Failure to Meet Requirements   A corporation's S election is automatically terminated if the corporation fails to meet the requirements. The termination is effective on the date it fails the S corporation requirements. If the IRS deems the termination inadvertent, it may allow the corporation to continue to be treated as an S corporation if, within a reasonable period after the inadvertent termination, the corporation takes the necessary steps to meet the S corporation requirements.[13]

---

[11]§1362(d)(1)(B).

[12]§1362(d)(1)(D).

[13]§1362(f). Because the restrictions on S corporation ownership are so specific and exact, many S corporations require their shareholders, as a condition of stock ownership, to enter into a shareholder's agreement. These agreements generally restrict the ability of a shareholder to transfer her stock ownership to any disqualified shareholder.

Example 22-6

What if: Suppose CCS was formed as a calendar-year S corporation with Nicole Johnson, Sarah Walker, and Chance Armstrong as equal shareholders. On June 15, 2016, Chance sold his CCS shares to his solely owned C corporation, Chanzz Inc. Is CCS's S election still in effect at the beginning of 2017? If not, when was it terminated?

Answer: No, the election was automatically terminated on June 15, 2016, when Chanzz Inc. became a shareholder because S corporations may not have corporate shareholders.

Excess of Passive Investment Income   If an S corporation has *earnings and profits* from a previous C corporation year (or through a reorganization with a corporation that has earnings and profits), its election is terminated if the S corporation has passive investment income in excess of 25 percent of gross receipts for three consecutive years. If the S corporation never operated as a C corporation or does not have C corporation earnings and profits (either by prior distribution of C corporate earnings and profits, or simply by not having earnings and profits at the effective date of the S election), this provision does not apply.

For purposes of the passive investment income test, **gross receipts** is the total amount of revenues received [including net capital gains from the sale of capital assets and gain (not offset by losses) from the sale of stock and securities] or accrued under the corporation's accounting method, *not* reduced by returns, allowances, cost of goods sold, or deductions. **Passive investment income (PII)** includes royalties, rents, dividends, interest, annuities, and gains from the sales or exchanges of stock or securities.[14] S corporation election terminations due to excess passive investment income are effective on the first day of the year following the third consecutive tax year with excess passive investment income.

Example 22-7

What if: Suppose CCS was initially formed as an S corporation with a calendar year-end. During its first three years, it reported passive investment income in excess of 25 percent of its gross receipts. Is CCS's S election terminated under the excess passive investment income test? If so, what is the effective date of the termination?

Answer: No, the excess passive investment income test does not apply to CCS in this situation because CCS has never operated as a C corporation; consequently, it does not have C corporation earnings and profits.

What if: Suppose CCS was initially formed as a C corporation with a calendar year-end. After its first year of operations (very profitable), CCS elected S corporation status, effective January 1, 2016. During 2017, 2018, and 2019, it reported passive investment income in excess of 25 percent of its gross receipts and had earnings and profits from its C corporation year. Is CCS's S election terminated under the excess passive investment income test? If so, what is the effective date of the termination?

Answer: Yes, it is terminated. Because CCS has C corporation earnings and profits from 2015 and excess passive investment income for three consecutive years as an S corporation, its S election is terminated effective on January 1, 2020.

Short Tax Years

S corporation election terminations frequently create an S corporation *short tax year* (a reporting year less than 12 months) and a C corporation short tax year. The corporation must then allocate its income for the full year between the S and the C corporation years, using the number of days in each short year (the daily method). Or it may use the

[14]PII excludes certain rents (e.g., rents derived from the active trade or business of renting property, produced film rents, income from leasing self-produced tangible property, temporary parking fees, etc.).

corporation's normal accounting rules to allocate income to the actual period in which it was earned (the specific identification method).[15] Both short tax year returns are due on the corporation's customary tax return due date (with normal extensions available).

What if: Suppose CCS was formed as a calendar-year S corporation with Nicole Johnson, Sarah Walker, and Chance Armstrong as equal shareholders. On June 15, 2016, Chance sold his CCS shares (one-third of all shares) to his solely owned C corporation, Chanzz Inc., terminating CCS's S election on June 15, 2016. Assume CCS reported the following business income for 2016:

Period	Income
January 1 through June 14 (166 days)	$100,000
June 15 through December 31 (200 days)	266,000
January 1 through December 31, 2016 (366 days)	$366,000

If CCS uses the daily method of allocating income between the S corporation short tax year (January 1–June 14) and the C corporation short tax year (June 15–December 31), how much income will it report on its S corporation short tax year return and its C corporation short tax year return for 2016?

Answer: S corporation short tax year = $166,000 ($366,000/366 days × 166 days); C corporation short tax year = $200,000 ($366,000/366 days × 200 days).

What if: If CCS uses the specific identification method to allocate income, how much will it allocate to the S corporation short year and C corporation short year?

Answer: S corporation short tax year, $100,000; C corporation short tax year, $266,000.

Note that if the entity wanted to minimize the income subject to taxation as a C corporation, it would use the daily method of allocating income.

S Corporation Reelections

After terminating or voluntarily revoking S corporation status, the corporation may elect it again, but it generally must wait until the beginning of the fifth tax year *after* the tax year in which it terminated the election.[16] Thus, if the election was terminated effective the first day of the tax year, the corporation must wait five full years to again become an S corporation.

What if: Let's return to the facts of the previous example. CCS was formed as a calendar-year S corporation with Nicole Johnson, Sarah Walker, and Chance Armstrong as equal shareholders. On June 15, 2016, Chance sold his CCS shares (one-third of all shares) to his solely owned C corporation, Chanzz Inc., terminating CCS's S election on June 15, 2016. Absent permission from the IRS (see text below), what is the earliest date CCS may again elect to be taxed as an S corporation?

Answer: January 1, 2021. This is the fifth tax year after the year in which the termination became effective.

What if: Assume on February 1, 2016, CCS voluntarily elected to revoke its S corporation status effective January 1, 2017. Absent IRS permission, what is the earliest CCS may again elect to be taxed as an S corporation?

Answer: January 1, 2022. This is the fifth year after the year in which the termination became effective.

[15]Use of the specific identification method requires that all shareholders at any time during the S corporation short year and the shareholders on the first day of the C corporation short year consent to the election using the specific identification method [§1362(e)(3)(A)]. However, an S corporation must use the specific identification method to allocate income between the short years (the per day allocation method is not allowed) if there is a sale or exchange of 50 percent or more of the corporation's stock during the year [§1362(e)(6)(D)].

[16]§1362(g).

The IRS may consent to an earlier election under a couple of conditions: (1) if the corporation is now owned more than 50 percent by shareholders who were not owners at the time of termination, or (2) if the termination was not reasonably within the control of the corporation or shareholders with a substantial interest in the corporation and was not part of a planned termination by the corporation or shareholders. Given the potential adverse consequences of an S election termination, the corporation should carefully monitor compliance with the S corporation requirements.

LO 22-3

OPERATING ISSUES

Accounting Methods and Periods

Like partnerships, S corporations determine their accounting periods and make accounting method elections at the entity level. An S corporation makes most of its elections (like the §179 election) in conjunction with filing its annual tax return, and some by filing a separate request with the IRS. (For example, an application to change accounting methods is filed on Form 3115, separate from the S corporation's tax return.) For an S corporation previously operating as a C corporation, all prior accounting methods carry over to the S corporation.

Recall that both C corporations and partnerships face restrictions on using the cash method. S corporations do not. They may choose the cash, accrual, or hybrid method unless selling inventory is a material income-producing factor for them. In that case they must account for gross profit (sales minus cost of goods sold) using the accrual method, even if they are otherwise cash-method taxpayers. Hence, they would use the hybrid method.

Tax laws also specify permissible tax years for S corporations, but they are a little less cumbersome than for partnerships. S corporations must use a calendar year-end unless they can establish a business purpose for an alternative year-end or a natural business year-end. (For example, a business that receives 25 percent or more of gross receipts for the previous three years in the last two months of the year-end requested would qualify for a noncalendar year-end.)[17]

Income and Loss Allocations

S corporations, like partnerships, are flow-through entities, and thus their profits and losses flow through to their shareholders annually for tax purposes. As we discussed in Chapter 20, partnerships have considerable flexibility in making special profit and loss allocations to their partners. In contrast, S corporations must allocate profits and losses pro rata, based on the number of outstanding shares each shareholder owns on each day of the tax year.[18]

An S corporation generally allocates income or loss items to shareholders on the last day of its tax year.[19] If a shareholder sells her shares during the year, she will report her share of S corporation income and loss allocated to the days she owned the stock (including the day of sale) using a pro rata allocation. If *all shareholders with changing ownership percentages* during the year agree, the S corporation can instead use its normal accounting rules to allocate income and loss (and other separately stated items, discussed below) to the specific periods in which it realized income and losses.

---

[17]§1378(b). In addition, S corporations, like partnerships, have the option of electing an alternative taxable year under §444.

[18]§1366(a), §1377(a).

[19]§1366(a).

Example 22-10

What if: Assume CCS was formed as a calendar-year S corporation with Nicole Johnson, Sarah Walker, and Chance Armstrong as equal (one-third) shareholders. On June 14, 2016, Chance sold his CCS shares to Nicole. CCS reported the following business income for 2016:

Period	Income
January 1 through June 14 (166 days)	$100,000
June 15 through December 31 (200 days)	266,000
January 1 through December 31, 2016 (366 days)	$366,000

How much 2016 income is allocated to each shareholder if CCS uses the daily method of allocating income?

Answer: Nicole's allocation is $188,667; Sarah's is $122,000; and Chance's is $55,333, calculated as follows.

	(1) **January 1–June 14**	(2) **June 15–December 31**	(1) + (2) **Total 2016 Allocation**
Nicole	$55,334 ($366,000/366 × 166 × 1/3)	$133,333 ($366,000/366 × 200 × 2/3)	**$188,667**
Sarah	$55,333 ($366,000/366 × 166 × 1/3)	$66,667 ($366,000/366 × 200 × 1/3)	**122,000**
Chance	$55,333 ($366,000/366 × 166 × 1/3)	$0	**55,333**
Totals	$166,000	$200,000	$366,000

How much 2016 income is allocated to each shareholder if CCS uses its normal accounting rules to allocate income to the specific periods in which it was actually earned?

Answer: Nicole's allocation is $210,667 ($100,000 × 1/3 + $266,000 × 2/3); Sarah's is $122,000 ($366,000 × 1/3); and Chance's is $33,333 ($100,000 × 1/3).

Separately Stated Items

Like partnerships, S corporations are required to file tax returns (Form 1120S) annually. In addition, on Form 1120S, Schedule K-1, they supply information to each shareholder detailing the amount *and* character of items of income and loss flowing through the S corporation.[20] Shareholders must report these income and loss items on their tax returns even if they do not receive cash distributions during the year.

S corporations determine each shareholder's share of ordinary business income (loss) and separately stated items. Like partnerships, **ordinary business income (loss)** (also referred to as non-separately stated income or loss) is all income (loss) exclusive of any separately stated items of income (loss). **Separately stated items** are tax items that are treated differently from a shareholder's share of ordinary business income (loss) for tax purposes. The character of each separately stated item is determined at the S corporation level rather than at the shareholder level. The list of common separately stated items for S corporations is similar to that for partnerships, with a couple of exceptions. (For example, S corporations do not report self-employment income and do not have guaranteed payments.) Exhibit 22-1 lists several common separately stated items. See Form 1120S, Schedule K-1 (and related instructions) for a comprehensive list of separately stated items.

---

[20]Other items, such as tax credits and informational items such as AMT adjustments, also flow through from the S corporation to its shareholders and are reported to shareholders on Form 1120S, Schedule K-1.

EXHIBIT 22-1   **Common Separately Stated Items**

- Short-term capital gains and losses
- Long-term capital gains and losses
- Section 1231 gains and losses
- Dividends
- Interest income
- Charitable contributions
- Tax-exempt income
- Net rental real estate income
- Investment interest expense
- Section 179 deduction
- Foreign taxes

S corporations may hold stock in C corporations, and any dividends S corporations receive will flow through to their shareholders. However, S corporations are not entitled to claim the dividends received deduction (see Chapter 16 for a discussion of the dividends received deduction).

Assuming CCS operated as a C corporation in 2015 and an S corporation in 2016, Exhibit 22-2 presents the results of operations. CCS's S election was not effective until January 1, 2016, because the shareholders filed the S election after the required date for it to be effective in 2015.

EXHIBIT 22-2

Color Comfort Sheets Income Statement December 31, 2015 and 2016		
	2015, C Corporation	**2016, S Corporation**
Sales revenue	$220,000	$520,000
Cost of goods sold	(50,000)	(115,000)
Salary to owners Nicole and Sarah	(70,000)	(90,000)
Employee wages	(45,000)	(50,000)
Depreciation expense	(15,000)	(20,000)
Miscellaneous expenses	(4,000)	(5,000)
Interest income	3,000	6,000
Dividend income	1,000	3,000
Overall net income	$ 40,000	$249,000

Example 22-11

Assume CCS was a C corporation for tax purposes in 2015 and an S corporation for 2016. Based on its operating results in Exhibit 22-2, how much ordinary business income and separately stated items are allocated to CCS's shareholders for 2015?

Answer: $0 ordinary business income and $0 separately stated items. Because CCS is a C corporation in 2015, its income does *not* flow through to its shareholders.

Based on the information in Exhibit 22-2, how much ordinary business income and separately stated items are allocated to CCS's shareholders for 2016?

Answer: See the following table for the allocations:

Description	CCS	Nicole 1/3	Sarah 1/3	Chance 1/3
			Allocations	
2016 overall net income	$249,000			
Less:				
Dividends	3,000			
Interest income	6,000			
Ordinary business income	240,000	**$80,000**	**$80,000**	**$80,000**
Separately Stated Items:				
Interest income	6,000	**2,000**	**2,000**	**2,000**
Dividends	3,000	**1,000**	**1,000**	**1,000**

Nicole, Sarah, and Chance will treat their shares of CCS's ordinary business income as *ordinary* income and include it, along with their shares of interest and dividend income, in their individual tax returns for the year.[21]

Shareholder's Basis

LO 22-4

Just as partners must determine their bases in their partnership interests, S corporation shareholders must determine their bases in the S corporation stock to determine the gain or loss they recognize when they sell the stock, the taxability of distributions, and the deductibility of losses.

Initial Basis   An S corporation shareholder calculates his *initial basis* upon formation of the corporation, like C corporation shareholders. (See Chapter 19 for a review.) Specifically, the shareholder's basis in stock received in the exchange equals the tax basis of the property transferred, less any liabilities assumed by the corporation on the property contributed (*substituted basis*). The shareholder's stock basis is increased by any gain recognized; it is reduced by the fair market value of any property received other than stock.[22] If, on the other hand, the shareholder purchased the S corporation stock from another shareholder or the corporation, the new shareholder's basis is simply the purchase price of the stock.[23]

Example 22-12

At the beginning of 2015, Nicole contributed $30,000 of cash and land with a fair market value of $130,000 and an adjusted basis of $125,000 to CCS. The land was encumbered by a $40,000 mortgage executed three years before. Sarah and Chance each contributed $120,000 of cash to CCS. What tax bases do Nicole, Sarah, and Chance have in their CCS stock at the beginning of 2015?

Answer: Nicole's basis is $115,000 ($30,000 cash + $125,000 adjusted basis of land − $40,000 mortgage assumed); Sarah's basis is $120,000; and Chance's is $120,000.

[21]Nicole, Sarah, and Chance would report their share of ordinary business income on Schedule E and their share of interest and dividend income on Schedule B of Form 1040.

[22]§358. This assumes the shareholder meets the §351 requirements. If the shareholder's exchange with the corporation does not meet these requirements, the shareholder's basis in the stock is its fair market value.

[23]If the shareholder acquires the stock by gift, her basis in the stock is the lesser of the donor's basis (increased for any gift taxes paid on the stock's appreciation) or the fair market value of the stock. In contrast, if the shareholder acquires the stock by bequest, her basis in the stock is the stock's fair market value on the date of the decedent's death adjusted to reflect any income in respect of the decedent.

Annual Basis Adjustments While C corporation rules govern the initial stock basis of an S corporation shareholder, subsequent calculations more closely resemble the partnership rules. Specifically, an S corporation shareholder's stock basis is dynamic and must be *adjusted* annually to ensure that (1) taxable income/gains and deductible expenses/losses are *not* double-counted by shareholders either when they sell their shares or receive S corporation distributions (e.g., because shareholders are taxed on the S corporation's income annually, they should not be taxed again when they receive distributions of the income) and (2) tax-exempt income and nondeductible expenses are not ultimately taxed or deducted.

S corporation shareholders make the following adjustments to their stock basis annually, in the order listed:

- Increase for any contributions to the S corporation during the year.
- Increase for shareholder's share of ordinary business income and separately stated income/gain items (including tax-exempt income).
- Decrease for distributions during the year.
- Decrease for shareholder's share of nondeductible expenses (fines, penalties).
- Decrease for shareholder's share of ordinary business loss and separately stated expense/loss items.[24]

As with a partnership, adjustments that decrease basis may never reduce an S corporation shareholder's tax basis below zero.[25]

S corporation shareholders are not allowed to include any S corporation debt in their stock basis. Recall that partners *are* allowed to include their share of partnership debt in their basis. One implication of this difference is that, everything else equal, an S corporation shareholder's basis will be lower than a partner's basis, due to the exclusion of debt (however, see the discussion of *debt basis* for S corporation shareholders below).

THE KEY FACTS

S Corporation Shareholder's Basis Adjustments

- A shareholder will increase the tax basis in her stock for:
  - Contributions.
  - Share of ordinary business income.
  - Separately stated income/gain items.
  - Tax-exempt income.
- A shareholder will decrease the tax basis in her stock for:
  - Cash distributions.
  - Share of nondeductible expenses.
  - Share of ordinary business loss.
  - Separately stated expense/loss items.
- A shareholder's tax basis may not be negative.

Example 22-13

Given the shareholders' 2015 bases in their CCS stock from the previous example (Nicole, $115,000; Sarah, $120,000; and Chance, $120,000), what basis does each have at the end of 2016, after taking into account the information in Exhibit 22-2 (but before taking into account any distributions, which are discussed below)?

Answer: Nicole, $198,000; Sarah, $203,000; and Chance, $203,000, computed as follows:

Description	Nicole	Sarah	Chance	Explanation
(1) Initial tax basis	$115,000	$120,000	$120,000	Example 22-12.
(2) Ordinary business income	80,000	80,000	80,000	Example 22-11.
(3) Interest income	2,000	2,000	2,000	Example 22-11.
(4) Dividends	1,000	1,000	1,000	Example 22-11.
Tax basis in stock at end of 2016	$198,000	$203,000	$203,000	(1) + (2) + (3) + (4).

Note the shareholders do not include any portion of CCS's debt in their stock basis.

What if: Suppose that, in addition to the amounts in Exhibit 22-2, CCS also recognized $1,200 of tax-exempt interest income in 2016. Nicole's share of this separately stated item is $400. Taking this allocation into account, what is Nicole's stock basis at the end of 2016?

Answer: It is $198,400 ($198,000 + $400). The tax-exempt income allocated to Nicole as a separately stated item increases her tax basis to ensure that she is never taxed on her share of the tax-exempt income.

---

[24]Reg. §1.1367-1(g) allows a shareholder to elect to decrease basis by ordinary business losses and separately stated expense/loss items *before* decreasing basis by nondeductible expenses by attaching a statement to the shareholder's tax return. This election is advantageous because loss/expense deductions are limited to a shareholder's basis, and this election results in a higher basis limitation for deductible loss/expense items.

[25]§1367(a)(2).

Loss Limitations

S corporations have loss-limitation rules similar to those for partnerships. For an S corporation shareholder to deduct it, a loss must clear three separate hurdles: (1) tax-basis, (2) at-risk amount, and (3) passive activity.[26]

Tax-Basis Limitation   S corporation shareholders may not deduct losses in excess of their stock basis. Recall they are not allowed to include debt in their basis; partners are. This restriction makes it more likely that the tax-basis limitation will apply to S corporation shareholders than to similarly situated partners. Losses not deductible due to the tax-basis limitation are not necessarily lost. Rather, they are suspended until the shareholder generates additional basis. The carryover period for the suspended loss is indefinite. However, if the shareholder sells the stock before creating additional basis, the suspended loss disappears unused.

Example 22-14

What if: Suppose at the beginning of 2017, Nicole's basis in her CCS stock was $14,000. During 2017, CCS reported a $60,000 ordinary business loss and no separately stated items. How much of the ordinary loss is allocated to Nicole?

Answer: The loss allocation is $20,000 ($60,000 × 1/3).

How much of the $20,000 loss clears the tax-basis hurdle for deductibility in 2017?

Answer: The amount of Nicole's basis in her CCS stock, or $14,000. The remaining $6,000 of loss does not clear the tax-basis hurdle; it is suspended until Nicole generates additional basis.

Shareholders can mitigate the disadvantage of not including S corporation debt in their stock basis—by loaning money directly to their S corporations. These loans create **debt basis,** separate from the stock basis. Losses are limited first to the shareholders' tax bases in their shares *and then* to their bases in any direct loans made to their S corporations.[27] Specifically, if the total amount of items (besides distributions) that decrease the shareholder's basis for the year exceeds the shareholder's stock basis, the excess amount decreases the shareholder's debt basis. Like stock basis, debt basis cannot be decreased below zero. In subsequent years, any net increase in basis for the year *first restores the shareholder's debt basis* (up to the outstanding debt amount) and then the shareholder's stock basis. If the S corporation repays the debt owed to the shareholder before the shareholder's debt basis is restored, any loan repayment in excess of the shareholder's debt basis will trigger a taxable gain to the shareholder.

Example 22-15

What if: Suppose at the beginning of 2017, Nicole's basis in her CCS stock was $14,000. During 2017, Nicole loaned $8,000 to CCS, and CCS reported a $60,000 ordinary business loss and no separately stated items. How much of the $20,000 ordinary loss allocated to Nicole clears the tax-basis hurdle for deductibility in 2017?

Answer: All $20,000. The first $14,000 of the loss reduces her stock basis to $0, and the remaining $6,000 reduces her debt basis to $2,000 ($8,000 − $6,000).

(continued on page 22-14)

---

[26]S corporations are also subject to the hobby loss rules in §183 that limit loss deductions for activities not engaged in for profit.

[27]§1366(d)(1)(B). These must be direct loans to the corporation. Thus, shareholders do not get debt basis when they guarantee a loan of the S corporation, although they would to the extent they had to "make good" on their guarantee obligation. At that point, the shareholders would get stock basis (if they have no right to repayment from the S corporation) or debt basis (if they have a right to repayment from the S corporation).

What if: Suppose in 2018, CCS allocated $9,000 of ordinary business income to Nicole and no separately stated items. What are Nicole's CCS stock basis and debt basis at the end of 2018?

Answer: Her stock basis is $3,000; her debt basis is $8,000. The income first restores debt basis to the outstanding debt amount and then increases her stock basis.

At-Risk Limitation   Like partners in partnerships, S corporation shareholders are subject to the *at-risk* rules. They may deduct S corporation losses only to the extent of their **at-risk amount** in the S corporation, as defined in §465. With one notable exception, an S corporation shareholder's at-risk amount is the sum of her stock and debt basis. The primary exception relates to nonrecourse loans and is designed to ensure that shareholders only are deemed at risk when they have an actual risk of loss. Specifically, an S corporation shareholder taking out a nonrecourse loan to make a capital contribution (either cash or other property) to the S corporation generally creates stock basis (equal to the basis of property contributed) in the S corporation but only increases her amount at risk by the net fair market value of her property, if any, used as collateral to secure the nonrecourse loan.[28] The collateral's net fair market value is determined at the loan date. Likewise, if the shareholder takes out a nonrecourse loan to make a direct *loan* to the S corporation, the loan creates debt basis, but only increases her amount at risk by the net fair market value of her property, if any, used as collateral to secure the nonrecourse loan. When the stock basis plus debt basis is different from the at-risk amount, S corporation shareholders apply the tax-basis loss limitation first, and then the at-risk limitation. Losses limited under the at-risk rules are carried forward indefinitely until the shareholder generates additional at-risk amounts to utilize them or sells the S corporation stock.

Post-Termination Transition Period Loss Limitation   The voluntary or involuntary termination of a corporation's S election creates a problem for shareholders with suspended losses due to the basis and at-risk rules. The reason: These losses are generally not deductible after the S termination date. Shareholders can obtain some relief provided by §1366(d)(3), which allows them to treat any suspended losses existing at the S termination date as occurring on the last day of the **post-termination transition period (PTTP).** In general, the PTTP begins on the day after the last day of the corporation's last taxable year as an S corporation and ends on the later of (a) one year after the last S corporation day or (b) the due date for filing the return for the last year as an S corporation (including extensions).[29]

This rule allows the shareholder to create additional stock basis (by making additional capital contributions) during the PTTP and to utilize suspended losses based on her *stock* basis (not her debt basis) at the end of the period. Any suspended losses utilized at the end of the PTTP reduce the shareholder's basis in her stock. Any losses not utilized at the end of the period are lost forever.

Example 22-16

What if: Suppose CCS terminated its S election on July 17, 2017. At the end of the S corporation's short tax year ending on July 17, Nicole's stock basis and at-risk amounts were both zero (she has never had debt basis), and she had a suspended loss of $15,000. In 2018, Nicole made additional capital contributions of $10,000 on February 20, 2018, and $7,000 on September 6, 2018. When does the PTTP end for CCS? How much loss may Nicole deduct, and what is her basis in the CCS stock at the end of the PTTP?

[28]§465(b)(2)(B). In some circumstances (beyond the scope of this text), shareholders do not create stock basis (or debt basis) for contributions (or shareholder loans to the S corporation) that are funded by nonrecourse loans.

[29]§1377(b)(1)(A). §1377(b) indicates that the PTTP also includes the 120-day period beginning on the date of a determination (not the date of the actual termination) that the corporation's S election had terminated for a previous taxable year.

Answer: For loss deduction purposes, CCS's PTTP ends on September 17, 2018. That date represents (b) in the "later of (a) or (b)" alternative—(a) one year after the last S corporation day, which would be July 17, 2018, or (b) the due date for filing the return for the last year as an S corporation, including extensions, which would be September 17, 2018 (September 15th falls on a Saturday), assuming CCS extends its tax return. (Note the short tax year S corporation return is due the same time as the short tax year C corporation return.) Nicole may deduct the entire $15,000 suspended loss because her basis at the end of the PTTP and before the loss deduction is $17,000. (That amount is calculated as a carryover basis of $0 on the last S corporation day plus $17,000 capital contributions during the PTTP.) Nicole's basis in CCS stock after the loss deduction is $2,000 ($17,000 basis at the end of the PTTP less the $15,000 loss deduction).

What if: Suppose Nicole made her second capital contribution on October 22, 2018, instead of September 6, 2018. How much loss can Nicole deduct, and what is her basis in CCS stock at the end of the PTTP?

Answer: The loss deduction is $10,000: Nicole's stock basis at the end of the PTTP and before her loss deduction is only $10,000 because the $7,000 contribution occurred after the end of the PTTP. Nicole's basis in the CCS stock at the end of the PTTP and after the loss deduction is zero ($10,000 basis less $10,000 loss deduction). Her basis then increases to $7,000 on October 22, but the $5,000 suspended loss is lost forever.

Passive Activity Loss Limitation   S corporation shareholders, just like partners, are subject to the **passive activity loss rules.** There are no differences in the application of these rules for S corporations; the definition of a passive activity, the tests for material participation, the income and loss baskets, and the passive activity loss carryover rules described in Chapter 20 are exactly the same. Thus, as in partnerships, the passive activity loss rules limit the ability of S corporation shareholders to deduct losses unless they are involved in actively managing the business.[30]

Example 22-17

What if: Suppose in 2018, CCS incurred an ordinary business loss and allocated the loss equally to its shareholders. Assuming Nicole, Sarah, and Chance all had adequate stock basis and at-risk amounts to absorb the losses, which of the three shareholders would be least likely to deduct the loss due to the passive activity limitation rules?

Answer: Chance. Because he is not actively involved in managing CCS's business activities, any loss allocated to him is a passive activity loss.

Self-Employment Income

You might wonder whether an S corporation shareholder's allocable share of ordinary business income (loss) is classified as self-employment income for tax purposes. The answer is no, even when the shareholder actively works for the S corporation.[31]

When a shareholder does work as an employee of and receives a salary from an S corporation, the S corporation treats this salary payment like that made to any other employee: For Social Security taxes, it withholds 6.2% of the shareholder's salary or wages subject to the wage limitation ($118,500 in 2016), and for Medicare taxes, it withholds 1.45% of the shareholder's salary or wages up to $200,000 and 2.35% (1.45% plus .9% additional Medicare tax) on any shareholder salary or wages above $200,000.[32] In addition, the S corporation must pay its portion of the Social Security tax (6.2% of the shareholder's salary or wages) and Medicare tax (1.45% of the shareholder's salary or wages, regardless of the amount of salary or wages).

Because of this stark contrast in the treatment of ordinary business income and shareholder salaries, S corporation shareholders may desire to avoid payroll taxes by

---

[30]§469.

[31]Rev. Rul. 59-221, 1955-1 CB 225.

[32]Although employee liability for the .9% additional Medicare tax varies based on filing status ($250,000 combined salary or wages for married filing joint; $125,000 salary or wages for married filing separate; $200,000 salary or wages for all other taxpayers), employers are required to withhold the additional .9% Medicare tax on salary or wages above $200,000 irrespective of the taxpayer's filing status.

limiting or even eliminating their salary payments. However, if they work as employees, they are required to pay themselves a reasonable salary for the services they perform. If they pay themselves an unreasonably low salary, the IRS may attempt to reclassify some or all of the S corporation's ordinary business income as shareholder salary!

TAXES IN THE REAL WORLD   S Corporation Salary in Question

In 2011, *The Wall Street Journal* reported that over the past 15 years when executive pay skyrocketed, the salaries of S corporation owners declined from 52 percent of the corporation's income in 1995 to 39 percent of the corporation's income in 2007. Over the same period, S corporation income doubled, while S corporation owner salary increased only 26 percent to an average salary of $38,400. Why the low pay? To avoid payroll taxes on salary, of course. The IRS, however, is wise to this strategy and has made this issue a top priority in auditing S corporations. In a recent 8th Circuit Court case, *Watson P.C. v. U.S.*, the IRS argued that the $24,000 salary to a 20-year CPA/S corporation owner was far too low. In this case, Mr. Watson received a $24,000 salary for his work for his CPA firm while receiving profit distributions of $203,651 and $175,470

from his S corporation in 2003 and 2004, respectively. The IRS contended that Mr. Watson's true pay was $91,044 for each year—and the 8th Circuit Court agreed with the IRS and district court, ruling that Mr. Watson owed extra tax plus interest and penalties. Factors indicating that Mr. Watson's salary was too low included the following: he was an exceedingly qualified accountant with an advanced degree and 20 years of experience; he worked 35 to 45 hours per week as a primary earner in a reputable firm, which had earnings much greater than comparable firms; the firm had significant gross earnings; and his salary was unreasonably low compared to other accountants and to the distributions he received.

Source: Watson, P.C. v. U.S. (8 Cir., 2012) 109 AFTR 2d 2012–1059; Laura Saunders, "The IRS Targets Income Tricks," *WSJ.com*, January 22, 2011.

3.8 Percent Net Investment Income Tax

Just like partners in a partnership, S corporation shareholders are subject to the 3.8 percent net investment income tax on their share of an S corporation's gross income from interest, dividends, annuities, royalties, rents, a trade or business that is a passive activity or a trade or business of trading financial instruments or commodities, and any net gain from disposing of property (other than property held in a trade or business in which the net investment income tax does not apply), less any allowable deductions from these items.[33,34] Likewise, any gain from the sale of S corporation stock (or distributions in excess of basis) is subject to the net investment income tax to the extent it is allocable to assets held by the S corporation that would have generated a net gain subject to the net investment income tax if all S corporation assets were sold at fair market value.[35]

Fringe Benefits

True to their hybrid status, S corporations are treated in part like C corporations and in part like partnerships with respect to tax deductions for qualifying employee fringe benefits.[36] For shareholder-employees who own 2 percent or less of the entity, the S corporation receives C corporation tax treatment. That is, it gets a tax deduction for qualifying fringe benefits, and the benefits are nontaxable to *all* employees. For

---

[33]Interest, dividend, annuity, royalty, and rent income derived in the *ordinary* course of a trade or business that is not passive and does not involve financial instrument or commodity trading is exempt from the Net Investment Income tax.

[34]The tax imposed is 3.8 percent of the lesser of (a) net investment income or (b) the excess of modified adjusted gross income over $250,000 for married-joint filers and surviving spouses, $125,000 for married separate filers, and $200,000 for other taxpayers. Modified adjusted gross income equals adjusted gross income increased by income excluded under the foreign earned income exclusion less any disallowed deductions associated with the foreign earned income exclusion.

[35]See Prop. Reg. §1.1411-7.

[36]Qualifying fringe benefits are nontaxable to the employee. Other fringe benefits (nonqualifying) are taxed as compensation to employees.

shareholder-employees who own more than 2 percent of the S corporation, it receives partnership treatment.[37] That is, it gets a tax deduction, but the otherwise qualifying fringe benefits are taxable to the shareholder-employees who own more than 2 percent.[38]

Fringe benefits taxable to this group include employer-provided health insurance[39] (§106), group-term life insurance (§79), meals and lodging provided for the convenience of the employer (§119), and benefits provided under a cafeteria plan (§125). Examples of benefits that are nontaxable to more than 2 percent shareholder-employees (and partners in a partnership) include employee achievement awards (§74), qualified group legal services plans (§120), educational assistance programs (§127), dependent care assistance programs (§129), no-additional-cost services (§132), qualified employee discounts (§132), working condition fringe benefits (§132), *de minimis* fringe benefits (§132), on-premises athletic facilities (§132), and medical savings accounts (§220).

DISTRIBUTIONS

LO 22-5

S corporations face special rules when accounting for distributions (operating distributions of cash or other property and liquidating distributions).[40]

Operating Distributions

The rules for determining the shareholder-level tax consequences of operating distributions depend on the S corporation's history; specifically whether, at the time of the distribution, it has accumulated *earnings and profits* from a previous year as a C corporation. (See Chapter 18 for a discussion of C corporation earnings and profits.) We consider both situations—with and without accumulated earnings and profits.

S Corporation with No C Corporation Accumulated Earnings and Profits

Two sets of historical circumstances could apply here: (1) An entity may have been an S corporation since inception, or (2) it may have been converted from a C corporation but does not have C corporation accumulated earnings and profits at the time of the distribution. In both cases, as long as there are no C corporation accumulated earnings and profits, the rules for accounting for the distribution are very similar to those applicable to distributions to partners. That is, shareholder distributions are tax-free to the extent of the shareholders' stock basis (determined after increasing the stock basis for income allocations for the year[41]). If a distribution exceeds the shareholder's stock basis, the shareholder has a capital gain equal to the excess distribution amount.

Example 22-18

What if: Suppose CCS has been an S corporation since its inception. On June 1, 2018, CCS distributed $30,000 to Nicole. Her basis in her CCS stock on January 1, 2018, was $20,000. For 2018, Nicole was allocated $15,000 of ordinary income from CCS and no separately stated items. What is the amount and character of income Nicole recognizes on the distribution, and what is her basis in her CCS stock after the distribution?

Answer: Nicole has $0 income from the distribution and $5,000 basis in stock after the distribution ($35,000 − $30,000). Her stock basis for determining the taxability of the distribution was $35,000, or her beginning basis of $20,000 plus the $15,000 income allocation for the year (which is taxable to Nicole).

(continued on page 22-18)

[37]§1372(a).

[38]The §318 attribution rules apply (see Chapter 18) for purposes of determining which shareholders own more than 2 percent.

[39]Note, however, that shareholders who own more than 2 percent are allowed to deduct their insurance costs as *for* AGI deductions [§162(l)].

[40]The §302 stock redemption rules that determine whether a distribution in redemption of a shareholder's stock should be treated as a distribution or a sale or exchange apply to both C corporations and S corporations. See discussion on redemptions in Chapter 18.

[41]§1368(d).

What if: Assume the same facts except that CCS distributed $40,000 to Nicole rather than $30,000. What is the amount and character of income Nicole recognizes on the distribution, and what is her basis in her CCS stock after the distribution?

Answer: Nicole has a $5,000 long-term capital gain (she has held her CCS stock more than one year) and $0 basis in her stock (the distribution reduced her stock basis to $0).

What if: Suppose CCS began in 2015 as a C corporation and elected to be taxed as an S corporation in its second year of operations. In 2015, it distributed all its earnings and profits as a dividend, so it did not have any earnings and profits at the end of 2015. In 2016, it distributed $30,000 to Nicole when her basis in her stock was $35,000. What is the amount and character of income she recognizes on the distribution, and what is her basis in her CCS stock after the distribution?

Answer: Nicole has $0 income on the distribution and $5,000 basis in stock after the distribution ($35,000 − $30,000). Because CCS did not have C corporation earnings and profits at the time of the distribution, her outcome is the same as if CCS had been taxed as an S corporation since inception.

S Corporations with C Corporation Accumulated Earnings and Profits

When an S corporation has accumulated earnings and profits (E&P) from prior C corporation years, the distribution rules are a bit more complex. These rules are designed to ensure that shareholders cannot avoid the dividend tax on dividend distributions out of C corporation accumulated E&P by simply electing S corporation status and then distributing the accumulated E&P. For S corporations in this situation, the tax laws require the corporation to maintain an **accumulated adjustments account (AAA)** to determine the taxability of S corporate distributions. The AAA represents the cumulative income or losses *for the period the corporation has been an S corporation.* It is calculated as:

> The beginning of year AAA balance
> + Separately stated income/gain items (excluding tax-exempt income)
> + Ordinary income
> − Separately stated losses and deductions
> − Ordinary losses
> − Nondeductible expenses that are not capital expenditures (except deductions related to generating tax-exempt income)
> − Distributions out of AAA[42]
> = End of year AAA balance

Unlike a shareholder's stock basis, the AAA may have a negative balance. However, the *reduction for distributions* may not cause the AAA to go negative or to become more negative. Also, unlike stock basis, the AAA is a corporate-level account rather than a shareholder-specific account.

Example 22-19

CCS was originally formed as a C corporation and reported 2015 taxable income (and earnings and profits) of $40,000 (see Exhibit 22-2). Effective the beginning of 2016, it elected to be taxed as an S corporation. In 2016, CCS reported $249,000 of overall income (including separately stated items—see Exhibit 22-2). What is the amount of CCS's AAA for 2016 before considering the effects of distributions?

---

[42]If the current year income and loss items net to make a negative adjustment to the AAA, the net negative adjustments from these items is made to the AAA *after* any AAA reductions for distributions (i.e., the reduction in AAA for distributions is made before the net negative adjustment for current year income and loss items). §1368(e)(1)(C).

Answer: $249,000, computed as follows:

Description	Amount	Explanation
(1) Separately stated income	$ 9,000	$6,000 interest income + $3,000 dividend (see Exhibit 22-2).
(2) Ordinary business income	240,000	Example 22-11.
AAA before distributions	$249,000	(1) + (2).

What if: Assume that during 2016, CCS distributed $300,000 to its shareholders. What is CCS's AAA at the end of 2016?

Answer: AAA is $0, because the distribution cannot cause AAA to be negative.

What if: Instead of reporting $249,000 of income during 2016, assume that during 2016 CCS reported an ordinary business loss of $45,000, a separately stated charitable contribution of $5,000, and a $6,000 distribution to its shareholders. What is CCS's AAA at the end of 2016?

Answer: AAA is negative $50,000. CCS decreases its AAA by the $45,000 business loss and the $5,000 charitable contribution. AAA before distributions is negative $50,000. CCS does not decrease AAA by the $6,000 distribution because the distribution cannot cause AAA to be negative or make it more negative.

S corporation distributions are deemed to be paid from the following sources in the order listed:[43]

1. The AAA account (to the extent it has a positive balance).[44]
2. Existing accumulated earnings and profits from years when the corporation operated as a C corporation.
3. The shareholder's stock basis.[45]

S corporation distributions from the AAA (the most common distributions) are treated the same as distributions when the S corporation does not have E&P. They are nontaxable to the extent of the shareholder's basis, and they create capital gains if they exceed the shareholder's stock basis. If an S corporation makes a distribution from accumulated E&P, the distribution is taxable to shareholders as a dividend. (See Chapter 18 for the calculation of corporate E&P.) Once an S corporation's accumulated E&P is fully distributed, the remaining distributions reduce the shareholder's remaining basis in the S corporation stock (if any) and are nontaxable. Any excess distributions are treated as capital gain.

[43]S corporations may elect to have distributions treated as being first paid out of existing accumulated earnings and profits from C corporation years to avoid the excess net passive income tax. We discuss the excess net passive income tax later in the chapter.

[44]Prior to 1983, S corporations' shareholders were taxed on undistributed taxable income as a deemed distribution. This undistributed income is referred to as *previously taxable income (PTI)*. For S corporations with PTI, distributions are considered to be paid out of PTI (if there is any remaining that has not been distributed) after any distributions out of their AAA. These distributions are also nontaxable to the extent of basis and reduce both the shareholder's basis and PTI.

[45]Technically, the distributions come from the Other Adjustments Account (OAA) and then any remaining shareholder equity accounts (e.g., common stock, paid-in capital). The OAA starts at zero at the S corporation's inception; is increased for tax-exempt income; and is decreased by expenses related to tax-exempt income, any federal taxes paid that are attributable to a C corporation tax year, and any S corporate distributions after the AAA and accumulated E&P have been reduced to zero. As with the AAA, the reduction for distributions may not cause the OAA to go negative or to increase a negative balance. Because from the shareholder's perspective distributions out of the OAA and equity accounts both reduce the shareholder's stock basis, we do not discuss the OAA or other equity accounts in detail.

Example 22-20

What if: Assume at the end of 2016, before considering distributions, CCS's AAA was $24,000 and its accumulated E&P from 2015 was $40,000. Also assume Nicole's basis in her CCS stock is $80,000. If CCS distributes $60,000 on July 1 ($20,000 to each shareholder), what is the amount and character of income Nicole must recognize on her $20,000 distribution, and what is her stock basis in CCS after the distribution?

Answer: $12,000 dividend income and $72,000 stock basis after the distribution, computed as follows:

Description	Amount	Explanation
(1) Total distribution	$60,000	
(2) CCS's AAA beginning balance	24,000	
(3) Distribution from AAA	24,000	Lesser of (1) or (2).
(4) Distribution in excess of AAA	36,000	(1) − (3).
(5) Nicole's share of AAA distribution	8,000	(3) × 1/3 (nontaxable reduction of stock basis).
(6) Nicole's beginning stock basis	80,000	
(7) Nicole's ending stock basis	**72,000**	(6) − (5).
(8) CCS's E&P balance	40,000	
(9) Dividend distribution (from E&P)	36,000	Lesser of (4) or (8).
Nicole's share of dividend	**12,000**	(9) × 1/3.

Property Distributions At times, S corporations distribute appreciated property to their shareholders. When they do so, S corporations recognize gain as though they had sold the appreciated property for its fair market value just prior to the distribution.[46] (This rule contrasts with the partnership provisions for property distributions but is consistent with the C corporation rules.) Shareholders who receive the distributed property recognize their distributive share of the deemed gain and increase their stock basis accordingly. On the other hand, S corporations do not recognize losses on distributions of property whose value has declined.

For the shareholder, the amount of a property distribution is the fair market value of the property received (minus any liabilities the shareholder assumes on the distribution). The rules we described above apply in determining the extent to which the amount of the distribution is a tax-free reduction of basis, a capital gain for a distribution in excess of basis, or a taxable dividend to the shareholder.[47] (See the rules for the taxability of distributions for S corporations with and without C corporation accumulated earnings and profits.) Shareholders take a fair market value basis in the property received in the distribution.

Example 22-21

What if: Assume that at the end of 2017, CCS distributes long-term capital gain property (fair market value of $24,000, basis of $15,000) to each shareholder (aggregate property distribution of $72,000 with an aggregate basis of $45,000). At the time of the distribution, CCS has no corporate E&P and Nicole has a basis of $10,000 in her CCS stock. How much gain, if any, does CCS recognize on the distribution? How much income does Nicole recognize as a result of the distribution?

---

[46]§311(b). In addition, the S corporation may incur entity-level tax if the distributed property had built-in gains related to when the corporation converted to an S corporation. We discuss the built-in gains tax later in the chapter.

[47]Note that while S corporation shareholders reduce their stock basis by the fair market value of the property received, partners receiving property distributions from partnerships generally reduce the basis in their partnership interests by the adjusted basis of the distributed property.

Answer: CCS recognizes $27,000 of long-term capital gain and Nicole recognizes $14,000 of long-term capital gain, computed as follows:

Description	Amount	Explanation
(1) FMV of distributed property	$72,000	
(2) CCS's basis in distributed property	45,000	
(3) CCS's LTCG gain on distribution	**27,000**	(1) − (2).
(4) Nicole's share of LTCG from CCS	9,000	(3) × 1/3.
(5) Nicole's stock basis after gain allocation	19,000	$10,000 beginning basis + (4).
(6) Distribution to Nicole	24,000	(1) × 1/3.
(7) Nicole's stock basis after distribution	0	(5) − (6) limited to $0.
(8) LTCG to Nicole on distribution in excess of stock basis	5,000	(6) in excess of (5).
Nicole's total LTCG on distribution	**14,000**	(4) + (8).

Post-Termination Transition Period Distributions Recall the special tax rules relating to suspended losses at the S corporation termination date. Similarly, §1371(e) provides for special treatment of any S corporation distribution *in cash* after an S election termination and during the post-termination transition period (PTTP). Such cash distributions are tax-free to the extent they do not exceed the corporation's AAA balance and the individual shareholder's basis in the stock.

The PTTP for post-termination distributions is generally the same as the PTTP for deducting suspended losses, discussed above. For determining the taxability of distributions, the PTTP generally begins on the day after the last day of the corporation's last taxable year as an S corporation; it ends on the later of (a) one year after the last S corporation day or (b) the due date for filing the return for the last year as an S corporation (including extensions).[48]

Liquidating Distributions

Liquidating distributions of a shareholder interest in an S corporation follow corporate tax rules rather than partnership rules. For a complete liquidation of the S corporation, the rules under §§331 and 336 (discussed in Chapter 19) govern the tax consequences. S corporations generally recognize gain *or* loss on each asset they distribute in liquidation (recall that S corporations recognize gain but not loss on operating distributions of noncash property). These gains and losses are allocated to the S corporation shareholders, increasing or decreasing their stock basis. In general, shareholders recognize gain on the distribution if the value of the property exceeds their stock basis; they recognize loss if their stock basis exceeds the value of the property.

Example 22-22

What if: Assume that at the end of 2018, CCS liquidates by distributing long-term capital gain property (fair market value of $20,000, basis of $12,000) to each shareholder (aggregate property distribution of $60,000 with an aggregate basis of $36,000). At the time of the distribution, CCS has no corporate E&P and Nicole has a basis of $25,000 in her CCS stock. How much gain or loss, if any, does CCS recognize on the distribution? How much gain or loss does Nicole recognize as a result of the distribution?

(*continued on page 22-22*)

---

[48]§1377(b)(1)(A). For purposes of the taxability of distributions, the PTTP also includes: (1) the 120-day period that begins on the date of any determination (court decision, closing agreement, and so on) from an IRS audit that occurs after the S election has been terminated and adjusts the corporation's income, loss, or deduction during the S period; and (2) the 120-day period beginning on the date of a determination (not the date of the actual termination) that the corporation's S election had terminated for a previous taxable year [§1377(b)(1)(B) and (C)].

LO 22-6

Answer: CCS recognizes $24,000 of long-term capital gain and Nicole recognizes $5,000 of net long-term capital loss, computed as follows:

Description	Amount	Explanation
(1) FMV of distributed property	$60,000	
(2) CCS's basis in distributed property	36,000	
(3) CCS's LTCG gain on distribution	24,000	(1) − (2).
(4) Nicole's share of LTCG from CCS	8,000	(3) × 1/3.
(5) Nicole's stock basis after gain allocation	33,000	$25,000 beginning basis + (4).
(6) Distribution to Nicole	20,000	(1) × 1/3.
(7) Nicole's LTCL on liquidating distribution	(13,000)	(6) − (5).
Nicole's NLTCL on distribution	(5,000)	(4) + (7).

THE KEY FACTS

Built-in Gains Tax

- The built-in gains tax applies only to S corporations that have a net unrealized built-in gain at the time they converted from C corporations and that recognize net built-in gains during the built-in gains tax recognition period.

- The net unrealized built-in gain represents the net gain (if any) that the corporation would recognize if it sold each asset at its fair market value.

- Recognized built-in gains (losses) include the gain (loss) for any asset sold during the year [limited to the unrealized gain (loss) for the specific asset at the S conversion date].

- The net recognized built-in gain is limited to the lesser of (a) the net recognized built-in gain less any NOL and capital loss carryovers, (b) the net unrealized built-in gain not yet recognized, and (c) the corporation's taxable income for the year using the C corporation tax rules.

S CORPORATION TAXES AND FILING REQUIREMENTS

Although S corporations are flow-through entities generally not subject to tax, three potential taxes apply to S corporations that previously operated as C corporations: the **built-in gains tax, excess net passive income tax,** and **LIFO recapture tax.** The built-in gains tax is the most common of the three and will be our starting point.

Built-in Gains Tax

Congress enacted the built-in gains tax to prevent C corporations from avoiding corporate taxes on sales of appreciated property by electing S corporation status. The built-in gains tax applies only to an S corporation that has a *net unrealized built-in gain* at the time it converts from a C corporation. Further, for the built-in gains tax to apply, the S corporation must subsequently *recognize* net built-in gains during the **built-in gains tax recognition period.**[49] The built-in gains tax recognition period is the first five years a corporation operates as an S corporation.

What exactly is a **net unrealized built-in gain?** Measured on the first day of the corporation's first year as an S corporation, it represents the net gain (if any) the corporation would recognize if it sold each asset at its fair market value. For this purpose, we net gains and losses to determine whether indeed there is a net unrealized gain at the conversion date. The corporation's accounts receivable and accounts payable are also part of the computation: Under the cash method, accounts receivable are gain items and accounts payable are loss items. If the S corporation has a net unrealized gain at conversion, it must compute its net recognized built-in gains for each tax year during the applicable built-in gain recognition period to determine whether it is liable for the built-in gains tax.

Example 22-23

CCS uses the accrual method of accounting. At the beginning of 2016, it owned the following assets (but leased its manufacturing facility and its equipment):

Asset	Fair Market Value (FMV)	Adjusted Basis (AB)	Built-in Gain (Loss)
Cash	$ 80,000	$ 80,000	$ 0
Accounts receivable	20,000	20,000	0
Inventory (FIFO)	130,000	110,000	20,000
Land	100,000	125,000	(25,000)
Totals	$330,000	$335,000	$ (5,000)

[49]§1374.

What is CCS's net unrealized built-in gain when it converts to an S corporation on January 1, 2016?

Answer: CCS has $0 net unrealized built-in gain. It has a net unrealized built-in loss, so it is not subject to the built-in gains tax.

What if: Suppose CCS's inventory is valued at $155,000 instead of $130,000. What is its net unrealized built-in gain?

Answer: It is $20,000. The $45,000 built-in gain on the inventory is netted against the $25,000 built-in loss on the land.

Recognized built-in gains for an S corporation year include (1) the gain for any asset sold during the year (limited to the unrealized gain for the specific asset at the S conversion date) and (2) any income received during the current year attributable to pre-S corporation years (such as collection on accounts receivable for cash-method S corporations). Likewise, recognized built-in losses for a year include (1) the loss for any asset sold during the year (limited to the unrealized loss for the specific asset at the S conversion date) and (2) any deduction during the current year attributable to pre-S corporation years (such as deductions for accounts payable for cash-method S corporations). The net recognized built-in gain for any year is limited to *the least of:*

1. The net of the recognized built-in gains and losses for the year.
2. The net unrealized built-in gains as of the S election date less the net recognized built-in gains in previous years. (This restriction ensures the net recognized built-in gains during the recognition period do not exceed the net unrealized gain at the S conversion date.)
3. The corporation's taxable income for the year, using the C corporation tax rules exclusive of the dividends received deduction and net operating loss deduction.

If taxable income limits the net recognized built-in gain for any year [item (3) above], we treat the excess gain as a recognized built-in gain in the next tax year, *but only if* the next tax year is in the built-in gains tax recognition period. After the net recognized built-in gain to be taxed has been determined using the limitations above, it should be reduced by any net operating loss (NOL) or capital loss carryovers from prior C corporation years.[50] This base is then multiplied by the highest corporate tax rate (currently 35 percent) to determine the built-in gains tax. The built-in gains tax paid by the S corporation is allocated to the shareholders as a loss. The character of the allocated loss (ordinary, capital, §1231) depends on the nature of assets that give rise to the built-in gain tax. Specifically, the loss is allocated proportionately among the character of the recognized built-in gains resulting in the tax.[51] For planning purposes, it is important to consider when to recognize built-in losses to reduce the S corporation's exposure to the built-in gains tax. That is, the S corporation could seek to recognize built-in losses in years with recognized built-in gains, in order to avoid the built-in gains tax.

Example 22-24

What if: Suppose CCS had a net unrealized built-in gain of $20,000. In addition to other transactions in 2016, CCS sold inventory it owned at the beginning of the year; that inventory had built-in gain at the beginning of the year of $40,000 (FMV $150,000; cost basis $110,000). If CCS had been a C corporation in 2016, its taxable income would have been $200,000. How much built-in gains tax must CCS pay in 2016?

Answer: It must pay $7,000 ($20,000 × 35%) in built-in gains tax. CCS must pay a 35 percent tax on the least of (a) $40,000 (recognized built-in gain on inventory), (b) $20,000 (initial net unrealized gain), and (c) $200,000 (taxable income computed as if CCS were a C corporation for 2016). It will reduce the amount of ordinary business income it would otherwise allocate to its shareholders by $7,000— the amount of the built-in gains tax—because the entire amount of the tax is due to inventory sales.

What if: Assume the same facts as above (an initial net unrealized gain of $20,000) except CCS sold two assets that had built-in gains at the time CCS became an S corporation. CCS sold a capital asset with a
(continued on page 22-24)

---

[50]Capital loss carryovers only reduce built-in gains that are capital gains.
[51]§1366(f)(2).

built-in gain of $10,000 and inventory with a built-in gain of $40,000. CCS would still pay a $7,000 built-in gains tax. This tax would be allocated as a loss to its shareholders. What is the character of the $7,000 loss?

Answer: It is a $1,400 capital loss [$7,000 × (10,000 capital gain/$50,000 total recognized built-in gain)] and a $5,600 ordinary loss [$7,000 × ($40,000 ordinary income from inventory sale/$50,000 total recognized built-in gain)].

What if: Assume that in addition to the initial facts in the example, CCS also had a net operating loss from 2015 (the year it operated as a C corporation) of $15,000. How much built-in gains tax will CCS have to pay in 2016?

Answer: It will pay $1,750 ($5,000 × 35%). CCS is allowed to offset $15,000 of the $20,000 recognized portion of the initial net unrealized gain by its $15,000 net operating loss carryover from 2015.

What if: Suppose CCS had a net unrealized built-in gain of $20,000. In addition to other transactions in 2016, CCS sold inventory it owned at the beginning of the year; that inventory had built-in gain at the beginning of the year of $40,000 (FMV $150,000; AB $110,000). If CCS had been a C corporation in 2016, its taxable income would have been $4,000. How much built-in gains tax would CCS have to pay in 2016?

Answer: $1,400 ($4,000 × 35%). CCS must pay a 35 percent tax on the least of (a) $40,000 (recognized built-in gain on inventory), (b) $20,000 (initial net unrealized gain), and (c) $4,000 (taxable income computed as if CCS were a C corporation for 2016). Because the tax was limited due to the taxable income limitation, the excess gain of $16,000 ($20,000 recognized built-in gain minus $4,000 gain on which CCS paid tax) is treated as a recognized built-in gain in 2017.

Excess Net Passive Income Tax

THE KEY FACTS

Excess Net Passive Income Tax

- The excess net passive income tax applies only to S corporations that previously operated as C corporations *and* at the end of the year have accumulated earnings and profits from a prior C corporation year.
- This tax applies when passive investment income exceeds 25 percent of gross receipts.
- Passive investment income includes royalties, rents, dividends, interest (including tax-exempt interest), and annuities.

If an S corporation previously operated as a C corporation *and* has accumulated earnings and profits at the end of the year from a prior C corporation year, it may be subject to the *excess net passive income tax.*[52] Congress created this tax to encourage S corporations to distribute their accumulated earnings and profits from prior C corporation years. It does not apply to S corporations that never operated as a C corporation, or to S corporations without earnings and profits from prior C corporation years.

The tax is levied on the S corporation's **excess net passive income,** computed as follows:

$$\text{Excess net passive income} = \frac{\text{Net passive}}{\text{investment income}} \times \frac{\text{Passive investment income} - (25\% \times \text{Gross receipts})}{\text{Passive investment income}}$$

Note that an S corporation has excess net passive income only when (1) it has net passive investment income and (2) its passive investment income exceeds 25 percent of its gross receipts. For purposes of determining excess net passive income, *gross receipts* is the total amount of revenues (including passive investment income) received or accrued under the corporation's accounting method, and not reduced by returns, allowances, cost of goods sold, or deductions. Gross receipts include net capital gains from the sales or exchanges of capital assets and gains from the sales or exchanges of stock or securities (losses do not offset gains). As defined previously in the chapter, passive investment income includes royalties, rents, dividends, interest (including tax-exempt interest), annuities, and gains from the sales or exchanges of stock or securities. **Net passive investment income** is passive investment income decreased by any expenses connected with producing that income.

The excess net passive income tax is imposed on excess net passive income at the highest corporate tax rate (currently 35 percent). For purposes of computing the tax, excess net passive income is limited to taxable income computed as if the corporation were a C corporation (excluding net operating losses). The formula for determining the tax is:

$$\text{Excess net passive income tax} = 35\% \times \text{Excess net passive income}$$

---

[52]§1375.

Each item of passive investment income that flows through to shareholders is reduced by an allocable share of the excess net passive income tax. The portion of the tax allocated to each item of passive investment income is the amount of the item divided by the total amount of passive investment income.

The IRS may waive the excess net passive income tax in some circumstances, for example if the S corporation determined in good faith it did not have accumulated earnings and profits at the end of the tax year and within a reasonable period distributed earnings and profits it identified later.[53]

Example 22-25

During 2016 CCS reported the following income (see Exhibit 22-2):

	2016 (S Corporation)
Sales revenue	$520,000
Cost of goods sold	(115,000)
Salary to owners Nicole and Sarah	(90,000)
Employee wages	(50,000)
Depreciation expense	(20,000)
Miscellaneous expenses	(5,000)
Interest income	6,000
Dividend income	3,000
Overall net income	$249,000

What are CCS's passive investment income, net passive investment income, and gross receipts for 2016?

Answer: The amounts are $9,000 passive income ($6,000 interest income + $3,000 dividends); $9,000 net passive investment income (because CCS has $0 expenses in producing passive investment income); and $529,000 gross receipts ($520,000 sales revenue + $3,000 dividends + $6,000 interest income).

What is CCS's excess net passive income tax in 2016, if any?

Answer: Zero. CCS has accumulated earnings and profits from 2015 (see Exhibit 22-2), but it owes zero excess net passive income tax because its passive investment income is less than 25 percent of its gross receipts [$9,000 < $132,250 ($529,000 × 25%)].

What if: Suppose CCS has passive investment income of $180,000 ($120,000 interest + $60,000 dividends), expenses associated with the passive investment income of $20,000, and gross receipts of $700,000 ($520,000 + $180,000). Also, if CCS were a C corporation, its taxable income would have been $249,000; assume it had accumulated earnings and profits of $40,000. What is CCS's excess net passive income tax, if any? What effect, if any, would the excess net passive income tax have on interest and dividends allocated to the shareholders?

Answer: The base for the tax is limited to the lesser of (a) excess net passive income of $4,444 [($180,000 passive investment income minus $20,000 expenses associated with passive investment income) × ($180,000 − 25% × $700,000)/$180,000] or $249,000 (CCS's taxable income if it had been a C corporation). Thus, the base for the tax is limited to $4,444, and the tax is $1,555 (35% × $4,444).

Interest and dividends allocated to the shareholders will be reduced by the excess net passive income tax. The interest income allocated to shareholders will be reduced by $1,037 [$1,555 tax × ($120,000 interest/$180,000 total passive investment income)], and dividend income will be reduced by $518 [$1,555 tax × ($60,000 dividend/$180,000)].

What if: Suppose CCS has passive investment income of $180,000, expenses associated with the passive investment income of $20,000, and gross receipts of $700,000 ($520,000 + $180,000). Also, if CCS were a C corporation, its taxable income would have been $2,000; assume it had accumulated earnings and profits of $40,000. What is CCS's excess net passive income tax, if any?

(*continued on page 22-26*)

---

[53]§1375(d).

Answer: The base for the tax is limited to the lesser of (a) excess net passive investment income of $4,444 [$160,000 × ($180,000 − 25% × $700,000)/$180,000] or (b) $2,000 (taxable income if CCS had been a C corporation). So the tax is $700 (35% × $2,000).

Remember, if an S corporation pays the net excess passive income tax for three years in a row, its S election will be terminated by the excess passive income test.

LIFO Recapture Tax

C corporations that elect S corporation status and use the LIFO inventory method are subject to the *LIFO recapture tax*. The purpose of this tax is to prevent former C corporations from avoiding built-in gains tax by using the LIFO method of accounting for their inventories. Specifically, a LIFO method corporation would not recognize built-in gains unless the corporation invaded its LIFO layers during the built-in gains tax recognition period.

The LIFO recapture tax requires the C corporation to include the **LIFO recapture amount** in its gross income in the last year it operates as a C corporation.[54] That amount equals the excess of the inventory basis computed using the FIFO method over the inventory basis computed using the LIFO method at the end of the corporation's last tax year as a C corporation. In addition to being included in gross income (and taxed at the C corporation's marginal tax rate), the LIFO recapture amount also increases the corporation's adjusted basis in its inventory at the time it converts to an S corporation. The basis increase reduces the amount of net unrealized gain subject to the built-in gains tax.

The corporation pays the LIFO recapture tax (technically a C corporation tax) in four annual installments. The first installment is due on or before the due date (not including extensions) of the corporation's last *C corporation* tax return. The final three annual installments are due each year on or before the due date (not including extensions) of the *S corporation's* tax return.

The LIFO recapture tax does not preclude the S corporation from using the LIFO method, but it obviously does accelerate the gain attributable to differences between LIFO and FIFO for inventory existing at the time of the S corporation election.

Example 22-26

What if: Suppose CCS uses the LIFO method of accounting for its inventory and elected S corporation status effective January 1, 2017. Assume that at the end of 2016, the basis of the inventory under the LIFO method was $90,000. Under the FIFO method, the basis of the inventory would have been $100,000. Finally, regular taxable income in 2016 was $40,000. What amount of LIFO recapture tax must CCS pay?

Answer: CCS must pay $1,500 [($100,000 FIFO inventory basis − $90,000 LIFO inventory basis) × 15 percent]. The 15 percent tax rate is the marginal rate at which the additional $10,000 of income would have been taxed in 2016 under the corporate tax rate schedule. CCS would increase its basis in its inventory by $10,000 to $100,000 as of the end of 2016, its last year as a C corporation. This would reduce the unrealized net built-in gain on the inventory.

When is CCS required to pay the tax?

Answer: CCS must pay $375 by April 15, 2017 (the unextended due date of the C corporation tax return); March 15, 2018; March 15, 2019; and March 15, 2020. March 15 is the annual tax return due date for calendar year-end S corporation returns without extensions (see discussion below).

What if: Assume the same facts as above except CCS's regular taxable income from 2016 was $700,000. What amount of LIFO recapture tax is CCS required to pay?

Answer: CCS must pay $3,400 [($100,000 FIFO inventory basis − $90,000 LIFO inventory basis) × 34 percent]. The 34 percent tax rate is the marginal rate at which the additional $10,000 of income would have been taxed in 2016 under the corporate tax rate schedule. CCS must pay $850 by April 15, 2017; March 15, 2018; March 15, 2019; and March 15, 2020.

[54]§1363(d).

EXHIBIT 22-3, PART I   CCS's Form 1120S, page 1

Form **1120S**

Department of the Treasury
Internal Revenue Service

U.S. Income Tax Return for an S Corporation

▶ Do not file this form unless the corporation has filed or is attaching Form 2553 to elect to be an S corporation.
▶ Information about Form 1120S and its separate instructions is at *www.irs.gov/form1120s.*

OMB No. 1545-0123

20**15**

For calendar year 2015 or tax year beginning _____ , 2015, ending _____ , 20 ____

A S election effective date **January 1, 2016**	
B Business activity code number (see instructions) **314000**	
C Check if Sch. M-3 attached ☐	

TYPE OR PRINT

Name
Color Comfort Sheets

Number, street, and room or suite no. If a P.O. box, see instructions.
375 East 450 South

City or town, state or province, country, and ZIP or foreign postal code
Salt Lake City, UT 84103

D Employer identification number
24-4681012

E Date incorporated
January 1, 2015

F Total assets (see instructions)
$ 370,000

G Is the corporation electing to be an S corporation beginning with this tax year? ☑ Yes ☐ No   If "Yes," attach Form 2553 if not already filed
H Check if: **(1)** ☐ Final return **(2)** ☐ Name change **(3)** ☐ Address change **(4)** ☐ Amended return **(5)** ☐ S election termination or revocation
I Enter the number of shareholders who were shareholders during any part of the tax year . . . . ▶

Caution: Include **only** trade or business income and expenses on lines 1a through 21. See the instructions for more information.

Income

1a	Gross receipts or sales	**1a**	520,000	
b	Returns and allowances	**1b**		
c	Balance. Subtract line 1b from line 1a			**1c** 520,000
2	Cost of goods sold (attach Form 1125-A)			**2** 115,000
3	Gross profit. Subtract line 2 from line 1c			**3** 405,000
4	Net gain (loss) from Form 4797, line 17 (attach Form 4797)			**4**
5	Other income (loss) (see instructions—attach statement)			**5**
6	**Total income (loss).** Add lines 3 through 5 . . . . ▶			**6** 405,000

Deductions (see instructions for limitations)

7	Compensation of officers (see instructions—attach Form 1125-E) . . .	**7**	90,000
8	Salaries and wages (less employment credits)	**8**	50,000
9	Repairs and maintenance	**9**	
10	Bad debts	**10**	
11	Rents	**11**	
12	Taxes and licenses	**12**	
13	Interest	**13**	
14	Depreciation not claimed on Form 1125-A or elsewhere on return (attach Form 4562)	**14**	20,000
15	Depletion (**Do not deduct oil and gas depletion.**)	**15**	
16	Advertising	**16**	
17	Pension, profit-sharing, etc., plans	**17**	
18	Employee benefit programs	**18**	
19	Other deductions (attach statement)	**19**	5,000
20	**Total deductions.** Add lines 7 through 19 . . . . ▶	**20**	165,000
21	**Ordinary business income (loss).** Subtract line 20 from line 6	**21**	240,000

Tax and Payments

22a	Excess net passive income or LIFO recapture tax (see instructions) . .	**22a**		
b	Tax from Schedule D (Form 1120S)	**22b**		
c	Add lines 22a and 22b (see instructions for additional taxes) . . .			**22c**
23a	2015 estimated tax payments and 2014 overpayment credited to 2015	**23a**		
b	Tax deposited with Form 7004	**23b**		
c	Credit for federal tax paid on fuels (attach Form 4136)	**23c**		
d	Add lines 23a through 23c			**23d**
24	Estimated tax penalty (see instructions). Check if Form 2220 is attached . . . . . . ▶ ☐			**24**
25	**Amount owed.** If line 23d is smaller than the total of lines 22c and 24, enter amount owed . .			**25**
26	**Overpayment.** If line 23d is larger than the total of lines 22c and 24, enter amount overpaid . .			**26**
27	Enter amount from line 26 **Credited to 2016 estimated tax** ▶ _____ **Refunded** ▶			**27**

Sign Here

Under penalties of perjury, I declare that I have examined this return, including accompanying schedules and statements, and to the best of my knowledge and belief, it is true, correct, and complete. Declaration of preparer (other than taxpayer) is based on all information of which preparer has any knowledge.

▶ _____ _____ ▶ _____
Signature of officer   Date   Title

May the IRS discuss this return with the preparer shown below (see instructions)? ☐ Yes ☐ No

Paid Preparer Use Only

Print/Type preparer's name	Preparer's signature	Date	Check ☐ if self-employed	PTIN
Firm's name ▶			Firm's EIN ▶	
Firm's address ▶			Phone no.	

For Paperwork Reduction Act Notice, see separate instructions.   Cat. No. 11510H   Form **1120S** (2015)

EXHIBIT 22-3, PART II CCS's 2016 partial Schedule K (on 2015 forms)

Schedule K	Shareholders' Pro Rata Share Items			Total amount
Income (Loss)	**1** Ordinary business income (loss) (page 1, line 21)		**1**	240,000
	2 Net rental real estate income (loss) (attach Form 8825)		**2**	
	3a Other gross rental income (loss)	**3a**		
	b Expenses from other rental activities (attach statement) . .	**3b**		
	c Other net rental income (loss). Subtract line 3b from line 3a		**3c**	
	4 Interest income		**4**	6,000
	5 Dividends: **a** Ordinary dividends		**5a**	3,000
	b Qualified dividends	**5b**	3,000	
	6 Royalties		**6**	
	7 Net short-term capital gain (loss) (attach Schedule D (Form 1120S))		**7**	
	8a Net long-term capital gain (loss) (attach Schedule D (Form 1120S))		**8a**	
	b Collectibles (28%) gain (loss)	**8b**		
	c Unrecaptured section 1250 gain (attach statement)	**8c**		
	9 Net section 1231 gain (loss) (attach Form 4797)		**9**	
	10 Other income (loss) (see instructions) . . Type ▶		**10**	

Estimated Taxes

The estimated tax rules for S corporations generally follow the rules for C corporations: S corporations with a federal income tax liability of $500 or more due to the built-in gains tax or excess net passive income tax must estimate their tax liability for the year and pay it in four quarterly estimated installments. However, an S corporation is not required to make estimated tax payments for the LIFO recapture tax.[55]

Filing Requirements

S corporations are required to file **Form 1120S,** U.S. Income Tax Return for an S Corporation, with the IRS by the 15th day of the third month after the S corporation's year-end (e.g., March 15 for a calendar-year-end S corporation). S corporations may receive an automatic, six-month extension by filing **Form 7004** with the IRS prior to the original due date of the return.[56] Thus, the extended due date of an S corporation tax return is generally September 15.

Exhibit 22-3 presents page 1 of CCS's Form 1120S (for its 2016 activities), CCS's partial Schedule K, and Nicole's K-1 (we use 2015 forms because 2016 forms were unavailable at the time this book went to press). Note the K-1 from the 1120S is different from the K-1 of the 1065. In contrast to the 1065 Schedule K-1, the 1120S Schedule K-1 does not report self-employment income, does not allocate entity-level debt to shareholders, and does not allow for shareholders to have profit-and-loss-sharing ratios that are different from shareholders' percentage of stock ownership.

---

[55]Rev. Proc. 94-61, IRB 1994-38,56.

[56]Under §6698, late-filing penalties apply if the S corporation fails to file by the normal or extended due date for the return.

EXHIBIT 22-3, PART III   Nicole's 2016 Schedule K-1 (on 2015 forms)

671113

☐ Final K-1	☐ Amended K-1	OMB No. 1545-0123

Schedule K-1
(Form 1120S)
Department of the Treasury
Internal Revenue Service

20**15**

For calendar year 2015, or tax
year beginning _____ , 2015
ending _____ , 20

Shareholder's Share of Income, Deductions, Credits, etc.   ▶ See back of form and separate instructions.

Part I	**Information About the Corporation**

A Corporation's employer identification number
24-4681012

B Corporation's name, address, city, state, and ZIP code

Color Comfort Sheets
375 East 450 South
Salt Lake City, UT 84103

C IRS Center where corporation filed return
Ogden UT

Part II	**Information About the Shareholder**

D Shareholder's identifying number
123-45-8976

E Shareholder's name, address, city, state, and ZIP code

Nicole Johnson
811 East 8320 South
Sandy, UT 84094

F Shareholder's percentage of stock
ownership for tax year . . . .   33.333333 %

For IRS Use Only

Part III	**Shareholder's Share of Current Year Income, Deductions, Credits, and Other Items**	
1 Ordinary business income (loss) 80,000	13	Credits
2 Net rental real estate income (loss)		
3 Other net rental income (loss)		
4 Interest income 2,000		
5a Ordinary dividends 1,000		
5b Qualified dividends 1,000	14	Foreign transactions
6 Royalties		
7 Net short-term capital gain (loss)		
8a Net long-term capital gain (loss)		
8b Collectibles (28%) gain (loss)		
8c Unrecaptured section 1250 gain		
9 Net section 1231 gain (loss)		
10 Other income (loss)	15	Alternative minimum tax (AMT) items
11 Section 179 deduction	16	Items affecting shareholder basis
12 Other deductions		
	17	Other information
	A	3,000

* See attached statement for additional information.

COMPARING C AND S CORPORATIONS AND PARTNERSHIPS

Exhibit 22-4 compares tax consequences for C corporations, S corporations, and partnerships discussed in this chapter.

EXHIBIT 22-4   Comparison of Tax Consequences for C and S Corporations and Partnerships

Tax Characteristic	C Corporation	S Corporation	Partnership/LLC
Forming or contributing property to an entity	No gain or loss on contribution of appreciated or depreciated property if transferors of property have control (as defined in §351) after transfer.	Same as C corporation.	Same as C and S corporations except no control requirement (§721 applies to partnerships).
Type of owner restrictions	No restrictions	Only individuals who are U.S. citizens or residents, certain trusts, and tax-exempt organizations.	No restrictions
Number of owner restrictions	No restrictions	Limited to 100 shareholders. (Family members and their estates count as one shareholder.)	Must have more than one owner.
Election	Default status if corporation under state law.	Must formally elect to have corporation taxed as S corporation.	Default status if unincorporated and have more than one owner.
Income and loss allocations	Not allocated to shareholders.	Income and loss flow through to owners based on ownership percentages.	Income and loss flow through to owners but may be allocated based on something other than ownership percentages (special allocations).
Entity debt included in stock (or partnership interest) basis	No	Generally no. However, loans made from shareholder to corporation create debt basis. Losses may be deducted to extent of stock basis and then debt basis.	Yes. All entity liabilities are allocated to basis of partners.
Loss limitations	Losses remain at corporate level.	Losses flow through but subject to basis limitation, at-risk limitation, and passive activity limitations.	Same as S corporations.
Self-employment income status of ordinary income allocations	Not applicable	Not self-employment income.	May be self-employment income depending on partner's status.

EXHIBIT 22-4 (*concluded*)

Tax Characteristic	C Corporation	S Corporation	Partnership/LLC
Salary to owners permitted	Yes	Yes	Generally no. Salary-type payments are guaranteed payments subject to self-employment tax.
Fringe benefits	Can pay nontaxable fringe benefits to owners.	Can pay nontaxable fringe benefits to owners who own 2 percent or less of stock.	May not pay nontaxable fringe benefits to owners.
Operating distributions: owner tax consequences	Taxable as dividends to extent of earnings and profits.	Generally not taxable to extent of owner's basis.	Same as S corporations.
Operating distributions: Entity tax consequences	Gain on distribution of appreciated property; no loss on distribution of depreciated property.	Same as C corporations.	Generally no gain or loss on distribution of property.
Liquidating distributions	Corporation and shareholders generally recognize gain or loss on distributions.	Same as C corporations.	Partnership and partners generally do not recognize gain or loss on liquidating distributions.
Entity-level taxes	Yes, based on corporate tax rate schedule.	Generally no, but may be required to pay built-in gains tax, excess passive investment income tax, or LIFO recapture tax if converting from C to S corporation.	No
Tax year	Last day of any month or 52/53-week year.	Generally calendar year.	Based on tax year of owners.

CONCLUSION

This chapter highlighted the rules specific to S corporations and compared S corporations to C corporations and partnerships. S corporations are a true hybrid entity: They share characteristics with C corporations (the legal protection of a corporation and the tax rules that apply in organizing and liquidating a corporation). They also share characteristics with partnerships (the flow through of the entity's income and loss to its owners, ability to make tax-free distributions to the extent of the owner's basis, and basis calculations for owners).

Although many S corporation attributes follow from the C corporation or partnership rules, several specific attributes unique to S corporations may be particularly important in choosing an entity form or operating an S corporation in a tax-efficient manner. These attributes include unique S corporation taxes, the rules for how debt enters into the basis calculations and loss limitation rules for S corporations, and the rules for how distributions are taxed for S corporations previously operating as C corporations.

Summary

LO 22-1 Describe the requirements and process to elect S corporation status.

- Shareholders of S corporations are able to defer realized gains when they contribute property to the corporation if they have control of the corporation after the contribution.

- S corporations are limited in the type of owners they may have. Only individuals who are U.S. citizens or residents, certain trusts, and certain tax-exempt organizations may be shareholders of S corporations.

- S corporations may have no more than 100 shareholders. For this purpose, family members and their estates count as one shareholder. Family members include a common ancestor and her lineal descendants and their spouses (or former spouses).

- S corporations may have only one class of stock. The stock may have differences in voting rights between shares, but all stock must have identical rights with respect to corporate distribution and liquidation proceeds.

- The S corporation election is made on Form 2553. All shareholders on the date of the election must consent to the election.

- To be effective for the current year, the election must be filed in the prior tax year or on or before the 15th day of the third month of the year. Even then, the election may not be effective in certain circumstances.

LO 22-2 Explain the events that terminate the S corporation election.

- The S corporation election may be voluntarily revoked by shareholders owning more than 50 percent of the S corporation stock. In general, revocations made on or before the 15th day of the third month of the year are effective as of the beginning of the year and revocations after that date are effective on the first day of the next year. Alternatively, the shareholders may choose an alternate date that is not before the revocation election is filed.

- An S corporation's election is automatically terminated on the date it fails to meet the S corporation requirements.

- If an S corporation has earnings and profits from a previous C corporation year, its S election is terminated if it has passive investment income in excess of 25 percent of gross receipts for three consecutive years.

- When an S corporation election is terminated mid-year, the corporation files a short-year tax return for the period it was an S corporation and a short-year tax return for the portion of the year it was a C corporation. It can allocate the income on a per day basis or it may specifically identify the income to each period.

- When an S corporation's S election is terminated, it may not reelect S status until the beginning of the fifth tax year after the tax year in which the election was terminated.

LO 22-3 Describe operating issues relating to S corporation accounting periods and methods, and explain income and loss allocations and separately stated items.

- When C corporations elect to become S corporations, all prior accounting methods carry over to the S corporation.

- S corporations are generally required to use a calendar tax year.

- Income and losses are allocated to S corporation shareholders pro rata based on the number of outstanding shares each shareholder owns on each day of the tax year or, with shareholder consent, it may use its normal accounting rules to allocate income and loss to the shareholders.

- S corporations determine their ordinary business income and separately stated items for the year and allocate these to the shareholders during the year.

- Separately stated items are tax items treated differently at the shareholder level than a shareholder's share of ordinary business income.

Explain stock-basis calculations, loss limitations, determination of self-employment income, and fringe benefit rules that apply to S corporation shareholders. **LO 22-4**

- An S corporation's shareholder's initial basis in her stock is generally the basis of the property contributed to the corporation minus liabilities assumed by the corporation on the contribution.

- S corporation shareholders adjust their stock basis annually. They increase it for (in this order) contributions to the S corporation during the year and the shareholder's share of ordinary business income and separately stated income/gain items. They decrease it for distributions during the year, the shareholder's share of nondeductible expenses, and the shareholder's share of ordinary business loss and separately stated expense/loss items. The basis may not be reduced below zero.

- S corporation shareholders are not allowed to include the S corporation's debt in their stock basis. However, they are allowed to create *debt basis* for the amount of loans they make directly to the S corporation. Debt basis can absorb S corporation losses (see below).

- For an S corporation shareholder to deduct them, S corporation losses must clear three separate hurdles: (1) tax-basis limitation in stock (and debt), (2) at-risk amount limitation, and (3) passive activity loss limitation.

- Losses suspended at a particular level remain suspended until the shareholder creates additional tax-basis or at-risk amounts, clears the passive loss hurdle, or sells her stock in the S corporation.

- If a shareholder's stock and debt basis is reduced by loss allocations and then increased by subsequent income allocations, the income allocation first increases the debt basis to the debt's outstanding amount before increasing the stock basis.

- When an S corporation's S election is terminated, S shareholders can deduct their share of S corporation losses on the last day of the post-termination transition period as long as the losses are able to clear the three loss limitation hurdles.

- Allocation of ordinary business income is not self-employment income to S corporation shareholders.

- If S corporation shareholders are employees of the corporation, their wages are subject to employment taxes.

- S corporation shareholders are subject to the net investment income tax on their share of an S corporation's gross income from interest, dividends, annuities, royalties, rents, a trade or business that is a passive activity or a trade or business of trading financial instruments or commodities, and generally any net gain from disposing of property, less any allowable deductions from these items.

- Many fringe benefits that are nontaxable to other S corporation employees are taxable to employees who own more than 2 percent of the S corporation.

Apply the tax rules for S corporation operating distributions and liquidating distributions. **LO 22-5**

- Operating distributions from S corporations without accumulated earnings and profits from C corporation years are nontaxable to the extent of the shareholder's basis and then taxable as capital gain to the extent they exceed the shareholder's stock basis.

- Operating distributions from S corporations with accumulated earnings and profits from C corporation years are a nontaxable reduction in stock basis to the extent of the S corporation's accumulated adjustments account, a dividend to the extent of the corporation's earnings and profits, and then a nontaxable return of capital to the extent of the stock basis. Amounts in excess of the stock basis are capital gain.

- The accumulated adjustments account represents the cumulative income or losses for the period the corporation has been an S corporation.

- When S corporations distribute appreciated property to shareholders they must recognize gain on the distribution (the gain is allocated to the shareholders). When they distribute loss property, they are not allowed to deduct the losses. In either case, the fair market value of the property (reduced by liabilities) is the amount of the distribution to the shareholders.

- When an S election is terminated, cash distributions during the post-termination transition period are tax-free to the shareholder to the extent of the S corporation's accumulated adjustments account and the shareholder's stock basis.
- S corporations making liquidating distributions recognize gain or loss on the distributions. The gains or losses are allocated to the shareholders. The shareholders compare the amount received in the liquidating distribution to their stock basis to determine if they recognize gain or loss on the distributions.

LO 22-6   Describe the taxes that apply to S corporations, estimated tax requirements, and tax return filing requirements.

- S corporations that were formerly C corporations may be required to pay the built-in gains tax. The tax applies if the S corporation had a net unrealized built-in gain at the time it converted to an S corporation. It must pay the tax when it recognizes these net built-in gains during its first five years operating as an S corporation.
- The base for the tax is limited to the least of (1) the net of the recognized built-in gains and losses for the year, (2) the net unrealized built-in gains as of the date of the S election date less the net recognized built-in gains in previous years, and (3) the corporation's taxable income for the year using the C corporation tax rules (excluding the dividends received deduction and NOL deduction). The base is then reduced by any net operating loss (NOL) or capital loss carryovers from prior C corporation years.
- S corporations that were formerly C corporations and have C corporation earnings and profits must pay the excess net passive income tax when their passive investment income exceeds 25 percent of their gross receipts.
- The formula for the tax is 35 percent (the highest corporate tax rate) × {net passive investment income × [passive investment income − (25% × gross receipts)]/passive investment income}.
- C corporations that elect to be taxed as S corporations and that use the LIFO method of accounting for inventories must pay the LIFO recapture tax. The tax is the C corporation's marginal tax rate times the excess of the inventory valued under the LIFO method over the inventory valued under the FIFO method at the time the S election became effective. The corporation pays one-quarter of the tax on its final C corporation tax return and the final three installments on its S corporation tax return for the first three years it is an S corporation.
- S corporations that must pay the built-in gains tax or the excess passive income tax generally must pay estimated taxes in four quarterly installments. They are not required to make estimated tax payments for the LIFO recapture tax.
- S corporations file Form 1120S by the 15th day of the third month after the tax year-end (generally March 15).
- S corporations may receive a six-month extension by filing Form 7004.
- On Form 1120S, S corporations report ordinary business income and separately stated items on Schedule K. Each shareholder's portion of items on the Schedule K is reported to the shareholder on her Schedule K-1.

KEY TERMS

accumulated adjustments account (AAA) (22-18)
at-risk amount (22-14)
built-in gains tax (22-22)
built-in gains tax recognition period (22-22)
debt basis (22-13)
earnings and profits (E&P) (22-2)
excess net passive income (22-24)

excess net passive income tax (22-24)
Form 1120S (22-28)
Form 2553 (22-4)
Form 7004 (22-28)
gross receipts (22-6)
LIFO recapture amount (22-26)
LIFO recapture tax (22-22)
net passive investment income (22-24)
net unrealized built-in gain (22-22)

ordinary business income (loss) (22-9)
passive activity loss rules (22-15)
passive investment income (PII) (22-6)
post-termination transition period (PTTP) (22-14)
S corporation (22-2)
separately stated items (22-9)
Subchapter S (22-2)

DISCUSSION QUESTIONS

Discussion Questions are available in *Connect*®·   connect

1. In general terms, how are C corporations different from and similar to S corporations? `LO 22-1`

2. What are the limitations on the number and type of shareholders an S corporation may have? How are these limitations different from restrictions on the number and type of shareholders C corporations or partnerships may have? `LO 22-1`

3. Why can't large, publicly traded corporations be treated as S corporations? `LO 22-1`

4. How do the tax laws treat family members for purposes of limiting the number of owners an S corporation may have? `LO 22-1`

5. Super Corp. was organized under the laws of the state of Montana. It issued common voting stock and common nonvoting stock to its two shareholders. Is Super Corp. eligible to elect S corporation status? Why or why not? `LO 22-1`

6. Karen is the sole shareholder of a calendar year-end C corporation she formed last year. If she elects S corporation status this year on February 20, when will the election become effective and why? What if she had made the election on March 20? `LO 22-1`

7. JB Corporation is a C corporation owned 80 percent by Jacob and 20 percent by Bauer. Jacob would like JB to make an S election but Bauer is opposed to the idea. Can JB elect to be taxed as an S corporation without Bauer's consent? Explain. `LO 22-1`

8. In what circumstances could a calendar-year C corporation make an election on February 1, year 1, to be taxed as an S corporation in year 1 but not have the election effective until year 2? `LO 22-1`

9. Theodore, Alvin, and Simon are equal shareholders of Timeless Corp. (an S corporation). Simon wants to terminate the S election, but Theodore and Alvin disagree. Can Simon unilaterally elect to have the S election terminated? If not, what would Simon need to do to have the S election terminated? `LO 22-2`

10. Juanita is the sole shareholder of Belize Corporation (a calendar-year S corporation). She is considering revoking the S election. It is February 1, year 1. What options does Juanita have for timing the effective date of the S election revocation? `LO 22-2`

11. Describe the circumstances in which an S election may be involuntarily terminated. `LO 22-2`

12. Describe a situation in which a former C corporation that elected to be taxed as an S corporation may have its S election automatically terminated, but a similarly situated corporation that has always been taxed as an S corporation would not. `LO 22-2`

13. When a corporation's S election is terminated mid-year, what options does the corporation have for allocating the annual income between the S corporation short year and the C corporation short year? `LO 22-2`

14. On June 1, year 1, Jasper Corporation's S election was involuntarily terminated. What is the earliest Jasper may be taxed as an S corporation again? Are there any exceptions to the general rule? Explain. `LO 22-2`

15. Apple Union (AU), a C corporation with a March 31 year-end, uses the accrual method of accounting. If AU elects to be taxed as an S corporation, what will its year-end and method of accounting be (assuming no special elections)? `LO 22-3`

16. Compare and contrast the method of allocating income or loss to owners for partnerships and for S corporations. `LO 22-3`

17. Why must an S corporation report separately stated items to its shareholders? How is the character of a separately stated item determined? How does the S corporation report this information to each shareholder? `LO 22-3`

18. How do S corporations report dividends they receive? Are they entitled to a dividends received deduction? Why or why not? `LO 22-3`

LO 22-4   19. Shawn receives stock in an S corporation when it is formed by contributing land with a tax basis of $50,000 and encumbered by a $20,000 mortgage. What is Shawn's initial basis in his S corporation stock?

LO 22-4   20. Why is a shareholder's basis in an S corporate stock adjusted annually?

LO 22-4   21. What adjustments are made annually to a shareholder's basis in S corporation stock and in what order? What impact do these adjustments have on a subsequent sale of stock?

LO 22-4   22. Can a shareholder's basis in S corporation stock ever be adjusted to a negative number? Why or why not?

LO 22-4   23. Describe the three hurdles a taxpayer must pass if he wants to deduct a loss from his share in an S corporation.

LO 22-4   24. Is a shareholder allowed to increase her basis in her S corporation stock by her share of the corporation's liabilities, as partners are able to increase the basis of their ownership interest by their share of partnership liabilities? Explain.

LO 22-4   25. How does a shareholder create *debt basis* in an S corporation? How is debt basis similar and dissimilar to stock basis?

LO 22-4   26. When an S corporation shareholder has suspended losses due to the tax-basis or at-risk limitation, is he allowed to deduct the losses if the S corporation status is terminated? Why or why not?

LO 22-4   27. When considering C corporations, the IRS checks to see whether salaries paid are too large. In S corporations, however, it usually must verify that salaries are large enough. Account for this difference.

LO 22-4   28. How does the tax treatment of employee fringe benefits reflect the hybrid nature of the S corporation?

LO 22-4   29. If a corporation has been an S corporation since inception, describe how its operating distributions to its shareholders are taxed to the shareholders.

LO 22-4   30. How are the tax consequences of a cash distribution different from those of a noncash property distribution to both the corporation and the shareholders?

LO 22-5   31. What role does debt basis play in determining the taxability of operating distributions to shareholders?

LO 22-5   32. What does the accumulated adjustments account represent? How is it adjusted year by year? Can it have a negative balance?

LO 22-5   33. If an S corporation with accumulated E&P makes a distribution, from what accounts (and in what order) is the distribution deemed to be paid from?

LO 22-5   34. Under what circumstances could a corporation with earnings and profits make a tax-free distribution to its shareholders after the S election termination?

LO 22-5   35. How do the tax consequences of S corporation liquidating distributions differ from the tax consequences of S corporation operating distributions at both the corporate and shareholder levels?

LO 22-6   36. When is an S corporation required to pay a built-in gains tax?

LO 22-6   37. When is an S corporation required to pay the excess net passive income tax?

LO 22-6   38. Is the LIFO recapture tax a C corporation tax or an S corporation tax? Explain.

LO 22-6   39. When must an S corporation make estimated tax payments?

LO 22-6   40. On what form does an S corporation report its income to the IRS? When is the tax return due? What information does the S corporation provide to shareholders to allow them to complete their tax returns?

LO 22-6   41. Compare and contrast S corporations, C corporations, and partnerships in terms of tax consequences at formation, shareholder restrictions, income allocation, basis calculations, compensation to owners, taxation of distributions, and accounting periods.

PROBLEMS

Select problems are available in *Connect*®.   connect

42. Julie wants to create an S corporation called J's Dance Shoes (JDS). Describe   `LO 22-1`
    how the items below affect her eligibility for an S election.

    a) Because Julie wants all her shareholders to have an equal say in the future of
    JDS, she gives them equal voting rights and decides shareholders who take a
    more active role in the firm will have priority in terms of distribution and
    liquidation rights.

    b) Julie decides to incorporate under the state laws of Utah, since that is where
    she lives. Once she gets her business up and running, however, she plans on
    doing extensive business in Mexico.

43. Lucy and Ricky Ricardo live in Los Angeles, California. After they were married,   `LO 22-1`
    they started a business named ILL Corporation (a C corporation). For state law
    purposes, the shares of stock in ILL Corp. are listed under Ricky's name only.   research
    Ricky signed the Form 2553 electing to have ILL taxed as an S corporation for
    federal income tax purposes, but Lucy did not sign. Given that California is a
    community property state, is the S election for ILL Corp. valid?

44. Jane has been operating Mansfield Park as a C corporation and decides she   `LO 22-1`
    would like to make an S election. What is the earliest the election will become
    effective under each of these alternative scenarios?

    a) Jane is on top of things and makes the election on January 1, 2016.

    b) Jane is mostly on top of things and makes the election on January 15,
    2016.

    c) Jane makes the election on February 10, 2016. She needed a little time to
    convince a C corporation shareholder to sell its stock to a qualifying
    shareholder. That process took all of January, and she was glad to have
    it over with.

    d) Jane makes the election on March 14, 2016.

    e) Jane makes the election on February 5, 2016. One of the shareholders
    refused to consent to the S election. He has since sold his shares (on
    January 15, 2016) to another shareholder who consented to the election.

45. Missy is one of 100 unrelated shareholders of Dalmatian, an S corporation.   `LO 22-2`
    She is considering selling her shares. Under the following alternative scenarios,
    would the S election be terminated? Why or why not?

    a) Missy wants to sell half her shares to a friend, a U.S. citizen, so they can
    rename their corporation 101 Dalmatians.

    b) Missy's mother's family wants to be involved with the corporation. Missy
    splits half her shares evenly among her aunt, uncle, grandfather, and two
    cousins.

    c) Missy sells half her Dalmatian stock to her husband's corporation.

46. Cathy, Heathcliff, and Isabelle are equal shareholders in Wuthering Heights   `LO 22-2`
    (WH), an S corporation. Heathcliff has decided he would like to terminate the
    S election. In the following alternative scenarios, indicate whether the termination
    will occur and indicate the date if applicable (assume no alternative termination
    dates are selected).

    a) Cathy and Isabelle both decline to agree to the termination. Heathcliff files
    the termination election anyway on March 14, 2016.

    b) Isabelle agrees with the termination, but Cathy strongly disagrees. The
    termination is filed on February 16, 2016.

c) The termination seems to be the first thing all three could agree on. They file the election to terminate on March 28, 2016.

d) The termination seems to be the first thing all three could agree on. They file the election to terminate on February 28, 2016.

e) Knowing the other two disagree with the termination, on March 16, 2016, Heathcliff sells one of his 50 shares to his maid, who recently moved back to Bulgaria, her home country.

LO 22-2 47. Assume the following S corporations and gross receipts, passive investment income, and corporate E&P. Will any of these corporations have its S election terminated due to excessive passive income? If so, in what year? All became S corporations at the beginning of year 1.

a) Clarion Corp.

Year	Gross Receipts	Passive Investment Income	Corporate Earnings and Profits
1	$1,353,458	$250,000	$321,300
2	1,230,389	100,000	321,300
3	1,139,394	300,000	230,000
4	1,347,039	350,000	100,000
5	1,500,340	400,000	0

b) Hanson Corp.

Year	Gross Receipts	Passive Investment Income	Corporate Earnings and Profits
1	$1,430,000	$247,000	$138,039
2	700,380	200,000	100,000
3	849,000	190,000	100,000
4	830,000	210,000	80,000
5	1,000,385	257,390	80,000

c) Tiffany Corp.

Year	Gross Receipts	Passive Investment Income	Corporate Earnings and Profits
1	$1,000,458	$250,000	$0
2	703,000	300,480	0
3	800,375	400,370	0
4	900,370	350,470	0
5	670,000	290,377	0

d) Jonas Corp.

Year	Gross Receipts	Passive Investment Income	Corporate Earnings and Profits
1	$1,100,370	$250,000	$500
2	998,000	240,000	400
3	800,350	230,000	300
4	803,000	214,570	200
5	750,000	200,000	100

48. Hughie, Dewey, and Louie are equal shareholders in HDL, an S corporation. HDL's S election terminates under each of the following alternative scenarios. When is the earliest it can again operate as an S corporation?   **LO 22-2**

    a) The S election terminates on August 1, year 2, because Louie sells half his shares to his uncle Walt, a citizen and resident of Scotland.

    b) The S election terminates effective January 1, year 3, because on August 1, year 2, Hughie and Dewey vote (2 to 1) to terminate the election.

49. Winkin, Blinkin, and Nod are equal shareholders in SleepEZ, an S corporation. In the conditions listed below, how much income should each report from SleepEZ for 2016 under both the daily allocation and the specific identification allocation method? Refer to the following table for the timing of SleepEZ's income.   **LO 22-3**

Period	Income
January 1 through March 15 (75 days)	$125,000
March 16 through December 31 (291 days)	345,500
January 1 through December 31, 2016 (366 days)	$470,500

    a) There are no sales of SleepEZ stock during the year.

    b) On March 15, 2016, Blinkin sells his shares to Nod.

    c) On March 15, 2016, Winkin and Nod each sell their shares to Blinkin.

Use the following information to complete problems 50 and 51:

UpAHill Corporation (an S Corporation) Income Statement December 31, Year 1 and Year 2		
	Year 1	Year 2
Sales revenue	$175,000	$310,000
Cost of goods sold	(60,000)	(85,000)
Salary to owners Jack and Jill	(40,000)	(50,000)
Employee wages	(15,000)	(20,000)
Depreciation expense	(10,000)	(15,000)
Miscellaneous expenses	(7,500)	(9,000)
Interest income	2,000	2,500
Dividend income	500	1,000
Overall net income	$ 45,000	$134,500

50. Jack and Jill are owners of UpAHill, an S corporation. They own 25 and 75 percent, respectively.   **LO 22-3**

    tax forms

    a) What amount of ordinary income and separately stated items are allocated to them for years 1 and 2 based on the information above?

    b) Complete UpAHill's Form 1120S, Schedule K, for year 1.

    c) Complete Jill's 1120S, Schedule K-1, for year 1.

51. Assume Jack and Jill, 25 and 75 percent shareholders in UpAHill Corporation, have tax bases in their shares at the beginning of year 1 of $24,000 and $56,000, respectively. Also assume no distributions were made. Given the income statement above, what are their tax bases in their shares at the end of year 1?   **LO 22-3** **LO 22-4**

Use the following information to complete problems 52 and 53:

Falcons Corporation (an S Corporation) Income Statement December 31, Year 1		
	Year 1	**Year 2**
Sales revenue	$300,000	$430,000
Cost of goods sold	(40,000)	(60,000)
Salary to owners Julio and Milania	(40,000)	(80,000)
Employee wages	(25,000)	(50,000)
Depreciation expense	(20,000)	(40,000)
Section 179 expense	(30,000)	(50,000)
Interest income	12,000	22,500
Municipal bond income	1,500	4,000
Government fines	0	(2,000)
Overall net income	$158,500	$174,500
Distributions	$ 30,000	$ 50,000

LO 22-3

 tax forms

52. Julio and Milania are owners of Falcons Corporation, an S corporation. They each own 50 percent of Falcons Corporation. In year 1, Julio and Milania each received distributions of $15,000 from Falcons Corporation.

    a) What amount of ordinary income and separately stated items are allocated to them for year 1 based on the information above?

    b) Complete Falcons's Form 1120S, Schedule K for year 1.

    c) Complete Julio's 1120S, Schedule K-1 for year 1.

LO 22-3

tax forms

53. In year 2, Julio and Milania each received distributions of $25,000 from Falcons Corporation.

    a) What amount of ordinary income and separately stated items are allocated to them for year 2 based on the information above?

    b) Complete Falcons's Form 1120S, Schedule K for year 2.

    c) Complete Milania's 1120S, Schedule K-1 for year 2.

LO 22-4

54. Harry, Hermione, and Ron formed an S corporation called Bumblebore. Harry and Hermione both contributed cash of $25,000 to get things started. Ron was a bit short on cash but had a parcel of land valued at $60,000 (basis of $50,000) that he decided to contribute. The land was encumbered by a $35,000 mortgage. What tax bases will each of the three have in his or her stock of Bumblebore?

LO 22-4

55. Jessica is a one-third owner in Bikes-R-Us, an S corporation that experienced a $45,000 loss this year (year 1). If her stock basis is $10,000 at the beginning of the year, how much of this loss clears the hurdle for deductibility (assume at-risk limitation equals the tax-basis limitation)? If she cannot deduct the whole loss, what happens to the remainder? Is she able to deduct her entire loss if she sells her stock at year-end?

LO 22-4

56. Assume the same facts as in the previous problem, except that at the beginning of year 1 Jessica loaned Bikes-R-Us $3,000. In year 2, Bikes-R-Us reported ordinary income of $12,000. What amount is Jessica allowed to deduct in year 1? What are her stock and debt bases in the corporation at the end of year 1? What are her stock and debt bases in the corporation at the end of year 2?

57. Birch Corp., a calendar-year corporation, was formed three years ago by
    its sole shareholder, James, who has operated it as an S corporation since its
    inception. Last year, James made a direct loan to Birch Corp. in the amount
    of $5,000. Birch Corp. has paid the interest on the loan but has not yet paid
    any principal. (Assume the loan qualifies as debt for tax purposes.) For the
    year, Birch experienced a $25,000 business loss. What amount of the loss
    clears the tax-basis limitation, and what is James's basis in his Birch
    Corp. stock and Birch Corp. debt in each of the following alternative
    scenarios?

    LO 22-4

    a) At the beginning of the year, James's basis in his Birch Corp. stock was
       $45,000 and his basis in his Birch Corp. debt was $5,000.

    b) At the beginning of the year, James's basis in his Birch Corp. stock was
       $8,000 and his basis in his Birch Corp. debt was $5,000.

    c) At the beginning of the year, James's basis in his Birch Corp. stock was $0
       and his basis in his Birch Corp. debt was $5,000.

58. Timo is the sole owner of Jazz Inc., an S corporation. On October 31, 2016,
    Timo executed an unsecured demand promissory note of $15,000 and trans-
    ferred the note to Jazz (Jazz could require Timo to pay it $15,000 on demand).
    When Timo transferred the note to Jazz, his tax basis in his Jazz stock was zero.
    On January 31, 2017, Timo paid the $15,000 to Jazz as required by the promis-
    sory note. For the taxable year ending December 31, 2016, Jazz incurred a
    business loss of $12,000. How much of the loss clears the stock and debt basis
    hurdles for deductibility?

    LO 22-4

    🔴 **research**

59. Chandra was the sole shareholder of Pet Emporium that was originally formed
    as an S corporation. When Pet Emporium terminated its S election on August
    31, 2015, Chandra had a stock basis and an at-risk amount of zero. Chandra
    also had a suspended loss from Pet Emporium of $9,000. What amount of the
    suspended loss is Chandra allowed to deduct, and what is her basis in her Pet
    Emporium stock at the end of the post-termination transition period under the
    following alternative scenarios (assume Pet Emporium files for an extension to
    file its tax returns)?

    LO 22-4

    a) Chandra makes capital contributions of $7,000 on August 30, 2016, and
       $4,000 on September 14, 2016.

    b) Chandra makes capital contributions of $5,000 on September 1, 2016, and
       $5,000 on September 30, 2016.

    c) Chandra makes a capital contribution of $10,000 on August 31, 2016.

    d) Chandra makes a capital contribution of $10,000 on October 1, 2016.

60. Neil owns stock in two S corporations, Blue and Green. He actively partici-
    pates in the management of Blue but maintains ownership in Green only as
    a passive investor. Neil has no other business investments. Both Blue and
    Green anticipate a loss this year, and Neil's basis in his stock of both corpo-
    rations is zero. All else equal, if Neil plans on making a capital contribution
    to at least one of the corporations this year, to which firm should he contrib-
    ute in order to increase his chances of deducting the loss allocated to him
    from the entity? Why?

    LO 22-4

    🔵 **planning**

61. In the past several years, Shakira had loaned money to Shakira Inc. (an
    S corporation) to help the corporation keep afloat in a downturn. Her stock
    basis in the S corporation is now zero, and she had deducted $40,000 in losses
    that reduced her debt basis from $100,000 to $60,000. Things appear to be turn-
    ing around this year, and Shakira Inc. repaid Shakira $20,000 of the $100,000
    outstanding loan. What is Shakira's income, if any, on the partial loan
    repayment?

    LO 22-4

    🔵 **planning**

LO 22-4

62. Adam Fleeman, a skilled carpenter, started a home improvement business with Tom Collins, a master plumber. Adam and Tom are concerned about the payroll taxes they will have to pay. Assume they form an S corporation and each earns a salary of $80,000 from the corporation; in addition, they expect their share of business profits to be $60,000 each. How much Social Security tax and Medicare tax (or self-employment tax) will Adam, Tom, and their corporation have to pay on their salary and profits?

planning   LO 22-4

63. Using the facts in problem 62, could Adam and Tom lower their payroll tax exposure if they operated their business as a partnership? Why or why not?

LO 22-4

64. This year, Justin B.'s share of S corporation income includes $4,000 of interest income, $5,000 of dividend income, and $40,000 of net income from the corporation's professional service business activity.

a) Assume that Justin B. materially participates in the S corporation. How much of his S corporation income is potentially subject to the net investment income tax?

b) Assume that Justin B. does not materially participate in the S corporation. How much of his S corporation income is potentially subject to the net investment income tax?

LO 22-4

65. Friends Jackie (0.5 percent owner), Jermaine (1 percent owner), Marlon (2 percent owner), Janet (86 percent owner), and Tito (10.5 percent owner) are shareholders in Jackson 5 Inc. (an S corporation). As employees of the company, they each receive health insurance ($10,000 per year benefit), dental insurance ($2,000 per year benefit), and free access to a workout facility located at company headquarters ($500 per year benefit). What are the tax consequences of these benefits for each shareholder and for Jackson 5 Inc.?

LO 22-5

66. Maple Corp., a calendar-year corporation, was formed three years ago by its sole shareholder, Brady, who immediately elected S corporation status. On December 31 of the current year, Maple distributed $30,000 cash to Brady. What is the amount and character of gain Brady must recognize on the distribution in each of the following alternative scenarios?

a) At the time of the distribution, Brady's basis in his Maple Corp. stock was $35,000.

b) At the time of the distribution, Brady's basis in his Maple Corp. stock was $8,000.

c) At the time of the distribution, Brady's basis in his Maple Corp. stock was $0.

LO 22-5

67. Oak Corp., a calendar-year corporation, was formed three years ago by its sole shareholder, Glover, and has always operated as a C corporation. However, at the beginning of this year, Glover made a qualifying S election for Oak Corp., effective January 1. Oak Corp. did not have any C corporation earnings and profits on that date. On June 1, Oak Corp. distributed $15,000 to Glover. What is the amount and character of gain Glover must recognize on the distribution, and what is his basis in his Oak Corp. stock in each of the following alternative scenarios?

a) At the time of the distribution, Glover's basis in his Oak Corp. stock was $35,000.

b) At the time of the distribution, Glover's basis in his Oak Corp. stock was $8,000.

c) At the time of the distribution, Glover's basis in his Oak Corp. stock was $0.

68. Janna has a tax basis of $15,000 in her Mimikaki stock (Mimikaki has been an S corporation since inception). In 2016, Janna was allocated $20,000 of ordinary income from Mimikaki. What is the amount and character of gain she recognizes from end of the year distributions in each of the following alternative scenarios, and what is her stock basis following each distribution?

    a) Mimikaki distributes $10,000 to Janna.
    b) Mimikaki distributes $20,000 to Janna.
    c) Mimikaki distributes $30,000 to Janna.
    d) Mimikaki distributes $40,000 to Janna.

LO 22-5

69. Assume the following year 2 income statement for Johnstone Corporation, which was a C corporation in year 1 and elected to be taxed as an S corporation beginning in year 2. Johnstone's earnings and profits at the end of year 1 were $10,000. Marcus is Johnstone's sole shareholder, and he has a stock basis of $40,000 at the end of year 1. What is Johnstone's accumulated adjustments account at the end of year 2, and what amount of dividend income does Marcus recognize on the year 2 distribution in each of the following alternative scenarios?

LO 22-5

Johnstone Corporation
Income Statement
December 31, Year 2

	Year 2 (S Corporation)
Sales revenue	$150,000
Cost of goods sold	(35,000)
Salary to owners	(60,000)
Employee wages	(50,000)
Depreciation expense	(4,000)
Miscellaneous expenses	(4,000)
Interest income	10,000
Overall net income	$ 7,000

    a) Johnstone distributed $6,000 to Marcus in year 2.
    b) Johnstone distributed $10,000 to Marcus in year 2.
    c) Johnstone distributed $16,000 to Marcus in year 2.
    d) Johnstone distributed $26,000 to Marcus in year 2.

70. At the end of the year, before distributions, Bombay (an S corporation) has an accumulated adjustments account balance of $15,000 and accumulated E&P of $20,000 from a previous year as a C corporation. During the year, Nicolette (a 40 percent shareholder) received a $20,000 distribution (the remaining shareholders received $30,000 in distributions). What is the amount and character of gain Nicolette must recognize from the distribution? What is her basis in her Bombay stock at the end of the year (assume her stock basis is $40,000 after considering her share of Bombay's income for the year but before considering the effects of the distribution)?

LO 22-5

71. Pine Corp., a calendar-year corporation, was formed three years ago by its sole shareholder, Connor, who has always operated it as a C corporation. However, at the beginning of this year, Connor made a qualifying S election for Pine Corp., effective January 1. Pine Corp. reported $70,000 of C corporation earnings and profits on the effective date of the S election. This year (its first

LO 22-5

S corporation year), Pine reported business income of $50,000. Connor's basis in his Pine Corp. stock at the beginning of the year was $15,000. What is the amount and character of gain Connor must recognize on the following alternative distributions, and what is his basis in his Pine Corp. stock at the end of the year?

a) Connor received a $40,000 distribution from Pine Corp. at the end of the year.

b) Connor received a $60,000 distribution from Pine Corp. at the end of the year.

c) Connor received a $130,000 distribution from Pine Corp. at the end of the year.

d) Connor received a $150,000 distribution from Pine Corp. at the end of the year.

LO 22-5 72. Carolina Corporation, an S corporation, has no corporate E&P from its years as a C corporation. At the end of the year, it distributes a small parcel of land to its sole shareholder, Shadiya. The fair market value of the parcel is $70,000 and its tax basis is $40,000. Shadiya's basis in her stock is $14,000. Assume Carolina Corporation reported zero taxable income before considering the tax consequences of the distribution.

a) What amount of gain or loss, if any, does Carolina Corporation recognize on the distribution?

b) How much gain must Shadiya recognize (if any) as a result of the distribution, what is her basis in her Carolina Corporation stock after the distribution, and what is her basis in the land?

c) What is your answer to part (a) if the fair market value of the land is $25,000 rather than $70,000?

d) What is your answer to part (b) if the fair market value of the land is $25,000 rather than $70,000?

LO 22-5 73. Last year, Miley decided to terminate the S corporation election of her solely owned corporation on October 17, 2015 (effective immediately), in preparation for taking it public. At the time of the election, the corporation had an accumulated adjustments account balance of $150,000 and $450,000 of accumulated E&P from prior C corporation years, and Miley had a basis in her S corporation stock of $135,000. During 2016, Miley's corporation reported $0 taxable income or loss. Also, during 2016 the corporation made distributions to Miley of $80,000 and $60,000. How are these distributions taxed to Miley assuming the following?

a) Both distributions are in cash, and the first was paid on June 15 and the second on November 15.

b) Both distributions are in cash, and the first was paid on June 15 and the second on September 30.

c) The same facts in part (b) except the June 15 distribution was a property (noncash) distribution (fair market value of distributed property equal to basis).

LO 22-6 74. Alabama Corporation, an S corporation, liquidates this year by distributing a parcel of land to its sole shareholder, Mark Ingram. The fair market value of the parcel is $50,000 and its tax basis is $30,000. Mark's basis in his stock is $25,000.

a) What amount of gain or loss, if any, does Alabama Corporation recognize on the distribution?

b) How much gain must Mark recognize (if any) as a result of the distribution and what is his basis in the land?

c) What is your answer to part (a) if the fair market value of the land is $20,000 rather than $50,000?

d) What is your answer to part (b) if the fair market value of the land is $20,000 rather than $50,000?

75. Rivendell Corporation uses the accrual method of accounting and has the following assets as of the end of 2015. Rivendell converted to an S corporation on January 1, 2016.

Asset	Adjusted Basis	FMV
Cash	$ 40,000	$ 40,000
Accounts receivable	30,000	30,000
Inventory	130,000	60,000
Land	100,000	125,000
Totals	$300,000	$255,000

   a) What is Rivendell's net unrealized built-in gain at the time it converted to an S corporation?

   b) Assuming the land was valued at $200,000, what would be Rivendell's net unrealized gain at the time it converted to an S corporation?

   c) Assuming the land was valued at $125,000 but that the inventory was valued at $85,000, what would be Rivendell's net unrealized gain at the time it converted to an S corporation?

76. Virginia Corporation is a calendar-year corporation. At the beginning of 2016, its election to be taxed as an S corporation became effective. Virginia Corp.'s balance sheet at the end of 2015 reflected the following assets (it did not have any earnings and profits from its prior years as a C corporation).

Asset	Adjusted Basis	FMV
Cash	$ 20,000	$ 20,000
Accounts receivable	40,000	40,000
Inventory	90,000	200,000
Land	150,000	175,000
Totals	$300,000	$435,000

In 2016, Virginia reported business income of $50,000 (this would have been its taxable income if it were still a C corporation). What is Virginia's built-in gains tax in each of the following alternative scenarios?

   a) During 2016, Virginia sold inventory it owned at the beginning of the year for $100,000. The basis of the inventory sold was $55,000.

   b) Assume the same facts as part (a), except Virginia had a net operating loss carryover of $24,000 from its time as a C corporation.

   c) Assume the same facts as part (a), except that if Virginia were a C corporation, its taxable income would have been $1,500.

77. Tempe Corporation is a calendar-year corporation. At the beginning of 2016, its election to be taxed as an S corporation became effective. Tempe Corp.'s balance sheet at the end of 2015 reflected the following assets (it did not have any earnings and profits from its prior years as a C corporation):

Asset	Adjusted Basis	FMV
Cash	$ 20,000	$ 20,000
Accounts receivable	40,000	40,000
Inventory	160,000	200,000
Land	150,000	120,000
Totals	$370,000	$380,000

LO 22-6

LO 22-6

LO 22-6

Tempe's business income for the year was $40,000 (this would have been its taxable income if it were a C corporation).

a) During 2016, Tempe sold all of the inventory it owned at the beginning of the year for $210,000. What is its built-in gains tax in 2016?

b) Assume the same facts as in part (a), except that if Tempe were a C corporation, its taxable income would have been $7,000. What is its built-in gains tax in 2016?

c) Assume the original facts except the land was valued at $140,000 instead of $120,000. What is Tempe's built-in gains tax in 2016?

LO 22-6   78. Wood Corporation was a C corporation in 2015 but elected to be taxed as an S corporation in 2016. At the end of 2015, its earnings and profits were $15,500. The following table reports Wood's (taxable) income for 2016 (its first year as an S corporation).

Wood Corporation Income Statement December 31, 2016	
Sales revenue	$150,000
Cost of goods sold	(35,000)
Salary to owners	(60,000)
Employee wages	(50,000)
Depreciation expense	(4,000)
Miscellaneous expenses	(4,000)
Interest income	8,000
Dividend income	2,000
Overall net income	$ 7,000

What is Wood Corporation's excess net passive income tax for 2016?

LO 22-6   79. Calculate Anaheim Corporation's excess net passive income tax in each of the following alternative scenarios:

a) Passive investment income, $100,000; expenses associated with passive investment income, $40,000; gross receipts, $120,000; taxable income if C corporation, $40,000; corporate E&P, $30,000.

b) Passive investment income, $100,000; expenses associated with passive investment income, $70,000; gross receipts, $120,000; taxable income if C corporation, $1,200; corporate E&P, $30,000.

c) Passive investment income, $100,000; expenses associated with passive investment income, $40,000; gross receipts, $120,000; taxable income if C corporation, $40,000; corporate E&P, $0.

LO 22-5 **LO 22-6**   80. Mark is the sole shareholder of Tex Corporation. Mark first formed Tex as a

C corporation. However, in an attempt to avoid having Tex's income double taxed, Mark elected S corporation status for Tex several years ago. On December 31, 2016, Tex reports $5,000 of earnings and profits from its years as a C corporation and $50,000 in its accumulated adjustments account from its activities as an S corporation (including its 2016 activities). Mark discovered that for the first time Tex was going to have to pay the excess net passive income tax. Mark wanted to avoid having to pay the tax but he determined the only way to avoid the tax was to eliminate Tex's E&P by the end of 2016. He determined that, because of the distribution ordering rules (AAA first), he would need to have Tex immediately (in 2016) distribute $55,000 to him. This would clear out

Tex's accumulated adjustments account first and then eliminate Tex's C corporation earnings and profits in time to avoid the excess net passive income tax. Mark was not sure Tex could come up with $55,000 of cash or property in time to accomplish his objective. Does Mark have any other options to eliminate Tex's earnings and profits without first distributing the balance in Tex's accumulated adjustments account?

81. Farve Inc. recently elected S corporation status. At the time of the election, the company had $10,000 of accumulated earnings and profits, and a net unrealized gain of $1,000,000 associated with land it had invested in (although some parcels had an unrealized loss). In the next couple of years, most of the income the company expects to generate will be in the form of interest and dividends (approximately $200,000 per year). However, in the future, the company will want to liquidate some of its current holdings in land and possibly reinvest in other parcels. What strategies can you recommend for Farve Inc. to help reduce its potential tax liability as an S corporation?   LO 22-6   planning

82. Until the end of year 0, Magic Carpets (MC) was a C corporation with a calendar year. At the beginning of year 1 it elected to be taxed as an S corporation. MC uses the LIFO method to value its inventory. At the end of year 0, under the LIFO method, its inventory of rugs was valued at $150,000. Under the FIFO method, the rugs would have been valued at $170,000. How much LIFO recapture tax must MC pay, and what is the due date of the first payment under the following alternative scenarios?   LO 22-6

   a) Magic Carpets' regular taxable income in year 0 was $65,000.

   b) Magic Carpets' regular taxable income in year 0 was $200,000.

COMPREHENSIVE PROBLEMS

Select problems are available in *Connect*®.   connect

83. Knowshon, sole owner of Moreno Inc., is contemplating electing S status for the corporation (Moreno, Inc. is currently taxed as a C corporation). Provide recommendations related to Knowshon's election under the following alternative scenarios: planning

   a) At the end of the current year, Moreno Inc. has a net operating loss of $800,000 carryover. Beginning next year, the company expects to return to profitability. Knowshon projects that Moreno will report profits of $400,000, $500,000, and $600,000 over the next three years. What suggestions do you have regarding the timing of the S election? Explain.

   b) How would you answer part (a) if Moreno Inc. had been operating profitably for several years and thus had no net operating loss?

   c) While several of Moreno Inc.'s assets have appreciated in value (to the tune of $2,000,000), the corporation has one property—some land in a newly identified flood zone—that has declined in value by $1,500,000. Knowshon plans on selling the loss property in the next year or two. Assume that Moreno does not have a net operating loss. What suggestions do you have for timing the sale of the flood zone property and why?

84. Barry Potter and Winnie Weasley are considering making an S election on March 1, 2017, for their C corporation, Omniocular. However, first they want to consider the implications of the following information: planning

   • Winnie is a U.S. citizen and resident.

   • Barry is a citizen of the United Kingdom, but a resident of the United States.

- Barry and Winnie each own 50 percent of the voting power in Omniocular. However, Barry's stock provides him with a claim on 60 percent of the Omniocular assets in liquidation.
- Omniocular was formed under Arizona state law, but it plans on eventually conducting some business in Mexico.

  a) Is Omniocular eligible to elect S corporation status? If so, when is the election effective?

For the remainder of the problem, assume Omniocular made a valid S election effective January 1, 2017. Barry and Winnie each own 50 percent of the voting power and have equal claim on Omniocular's assets in liquidation. In addition, consider the following information:

- Omniocular reports on a calendar tax year.
- Omniocular's earnings and profits as of December 31, 2016, were $55,000.
- Omniocular's 2016 taxable income was $15,000.
- Omniocular's assets at the end of 2016 are as follows:

Omniocular Assets December 31, 2016		
Asset	**Adjusted Basis**	**FMV**
Cash	$ 50,000	$ 50,000
Accounts receivable	20,000	20,000
Investments in stocks and bonds	700,000	700,000
Investment in land	90,000	100,000
Inventory (LIFO)	80,000*	125,000
Equipment	40,000	35,000
Totals	$980,000	$1,030,000

*$110,000 under FIFO accounting.

- On March 31, 2017, Omniocular sold the land for $42,000.
- In 2017, Omniocular sold all the inventory it had on hand at the beginning of the year. This was the only inventory it sold during the year.

Other Income/Expense Items for 2017	
Sales revenue	$155,000
Salary to owners	(50,000)
Employee wages	(10,000)
Depreciation expense	(5,000)
Miscellaneous expenses	(1,000)
Gain on sale of machinery	12,000
Interest income	40,000
Dividend income	65,000

- Assume that if Omniocular were a C corporation for 2017, its taxable income would have been $88,500.

  b) How much LIFO recapture tax is Omniocular required to pay and when is it due?

  c) How much built-in gains tax, if any, is Omniocular required to pay?

  d) How much excess net passive income tax, if any, is Omniocular required to pay?

  e) Assume Barry's basis in his Omniocular stock was $40,000 on January 1, 2017. What is his stock basis on December 31, 2017?

For the following questions, assume that after electing S corporation status Barry and Winnie had a change of heart and filed an election to terminate Omniocular's S election, effective August 1, 2018.

- In 2018, Omniocular reported the following income/expense items:

	January 1—July 31, 2018 (212 days)	August 1—December 31, 2018 (153 days)	January 1—December 31, 2018
Sales revenue	$ 80,000	$185,000	$265,000
Cost of goods sold	(40,000)	(20,000)	(60,000)
Salaries to Barry and Winnie	(60,000)	(40,000)	(100,000)
Depreciation expense	(7,000)	(2,000)	(9,000)
Miscellaneous expenses	(4,000)	(3,000)	(7,000)
Interest income	6,000	5,250	11,250
Overall net income (loss)	$(25,000)	$125,250	$100,250

f) For tax purposes, how would you recommend Barry and Winnie allocate income between the short S corporation year and the short C corporation year if they would like to minimize double taxation of Omniocular's income?

g) Assume in part (f) that Omniocular allocates income between the short S and C corporation years in a way that minimizes the double taxation of its income. If Barry's stock basis in his Omniocular stock on January 1, 2018, is $50,000, what is his stock basis on December 31, 2018?

h) When is the earliest tax year in which Omniocular can be taxed as an S corporation again?

85. Abigail, Bobby, and Claudia are equal owners in Lafter, an S corporation that was a C corporation several years ago. While Abigail and Bobby actively participate in running the company, Claudia has a separate day job and is a passive owner. Consider the following information for 2016:

- As of January 1, 2016, Abigail, Bobby, and Claudia each have a basis in Lafter stock of $15,000 and a debt basis of $0. On January 1, the stock basis is also the at-risk amount for each shareholder.
- Bobby and Claudia also are passive owners in Aggressive LLC, which allocated business income of $14,000 to each of them in 2016. Neither has any other source of passive income (besides Lafter, for Claudia).
- On March 31, 2016, Abigail lends $5,000 of her own money to Lafter.
- Anticipating the need for basis to deduct a loss, on April 4, 2016, Bobby takes out a $10,000 loan to make a $10,000 contribution to Lafter. Bobby uses his automobile ($12,000 fair market value) as the sole collateral for his loan (nonrecourse).
- Lafter has an accumulated adjustments account balance of $45,000 as of January 1, 2016.
- Lafter has C corporation earnings and profits of $15,000 as of January 1, 2016.
- During 2016, Lafter reports a business loss of $75,000, computed as follows:

Sales revenue	$90,000
Cost of goods sold	(85,000)
Salary to Abigail	(40,000)
Salary to Bobby	(40,000)
Business (loss)	($75,000)

- Lafter also reported $12,000 of tax-exempt interest income.

  a) What amount of Lafter's 2016 business loss of $75,000 are Abigail, Bobby, and Claudia allowed to deduct on their individual tax returns? What are each owner's stock basis and debt basis (if applicable) and each owner's at-risk amount with respect to the investment in Lafter at the end of 2016?

- During 2017, Lafter made several changes to its business approach and reported $18,000 of business income, computed as follows:

Sales revenue	$208,000
Cost of goods sold	(90,000)
Salary to Abigail	(45,000)
Salary to Bobby	(45,000)
Marketing expense	(10,000)
Business income	$ 18,000

- Lafter also reported a long-term capital gain of $24,000 in 2017.
- Lafter made a cash distribution on July 1, 2017, of $20,000 to each shareholder.

  b) What amount of gain/income does each shareholder recognize from the cash distribution on July 1, 2017?

tax forms

86. While James Craig and his former classmate Paul Dolittle both studied accounting at school, they ended up pursuing careers in professional cake decorating. Their company, Good to Eat (GTE), specializes in custom-sculpted cakes for weddings, birthdays, and other celebrations. James and Paul formed the business at the beginning of 2016, and each contributed $50,000 in exchange for a 50 percent ownership interest. GTE also borrowed $200,000 from a local bank. Both James and Paul had to personally guarantee the loan. Both owners provide significant services for the business. The following information pertains to GTE's 2016 activities:

- GTE uses the cash method of accounting (for both book and tax purposes) and reports income on a calendar-year basis.
- GTE received $450,000 of sales revenue and reported $210,000 of cost of goods sold (it did not have any ending inventory).
- GTE paid $30,000 compensation to James, $30,000 compensation to Paul, and $40,000 of compensation to other employees (assume these amounts include applicable payroll taxes if any).
- GTE paid $15,000 of rent for a building and equipment, $20,000 for advertising, $14,000 in interest expense, $4,000 for utilities, and $2,000 for supplies.
- GTE contributed $5,000 to charity.
- GTE received a $1,000 qualified dividend from a great stock investment (it owned 2 percent of the corporation distributing the dividend), and it recognized $1,500 in short-term capital gain when it sold some of the stock.
- On December 1, 2016, GTE distributed $20,000 to James and $20,000 to Paul.

Required:

a) Assume James and Paul formed GTE as an S corporation.
   - Complete GTE's Form 1120S, page 1; Form 1120 S, Schedule K; and Paul's Form 1120S, Schedule K-1 (note that you should use 2015 tax forms).
   - Compute the tax basis of Paul's stock in GTE at the end of 2016.
   - What amount of Paul's income from GTE is subject to FICA or self-employment taxes?

- What amount of income, including its character, will Paul recognize on the $20,000 distribution he receives on December 1?
- What amount of tax does GTE pay on the $1,000 dividend it received?

b) Assume James and Paul formed GTE as an LLC.

- Complete GTE's Form 1065, page 1; Form 1065, Schedule K; and Paul's Form 1065, Schedule K-1 (note that you should use 2015 tax forms).
- Compute the tax basis of Paul's ownership interest in GTE at the end of 2016.
- What amount of Paul's income from GTE is subject to FICA or self-employment taxes?
- What amount of income, including its character, will Paul recognize on the $20,000 distribution he receives on December 1?
- What amount of tax does GTE pay on the $1,000 dividend it received?

c) Assume James and Paul formed GTE as a C corporation.

- Complete GTE's Form 1120, page 1 (note that you should use the 2015 tax form).
- Compute the tax basis of Paul's stock in GTE at the end of 2016.
- What amount of Paul's income from GTE is subject to FICA or self-employment taxes?
- What amount of income, including its character, will Paul recognize on the $20,000 distribution he receives on December 1?
- What amount of tax does GTE pay on the $1,000 dividend it received?

23 State and Local Taxes

Upon completing this chapter, you should be able to:

LO 23-1 Describe the primary types of state and local taxes.

LO 23-2 Determine whether a business has sales and use tax nexus and calculate its sales tax withholding responsibilities.

LO 23-3 Identify whether a business has income tax nexus and determine its state income tax liabilities.

© Design Pics/Monkey Business

Storyline Summary

Ken Brody

Location: Idaho

Status: Sole owner of Wild West River Runners

Situation: Ken owns retail stores in Idaho and Wyoming that sell merchandise locally; a Wyoming-based Internet store; and provides services in Idaho, Tennessee, Washington, and Wyoming. He must determine the company's state and local tax liabilities.

Ken Brody owns Wild West River Runners Incorporated (Wild West), an Idaho corporation. Wild West offers both guided white-water rafting adventures and retail sales of related equipment. It provides white-water rafting adventures in Idaho, Tennessee, Washington, and Wyoming; operates retail stores in Idaho and Wyoming; and runs an Internet-based retail store from Wyoming. Wild West's retail stores sell only locally (they never ship merchandise), but the salesclerks often refer customers to the Internet store (www .wildwestriverrunners.com). Most employees are seasonal (i.e., teachers or college students). During the off-season, a few guides make sales visits with Ken and operate the retail stores. Also during the off-season, Ken attends the annual Raft and River show for 10 days each year in Phoenix, Arizona, and travels the country promoting Wild West's guided river adventures.

Wild West's federal taxable income for the current year is $53,289, and it must determine its state and local tax liabilities. Because Wild West operates a multistate business, it must determine its sales and use tax withholding responsibilities and identify the states in which it must file returns. Once it makes these determinations, it must also compute taxable income for each relevant state. ■

Like a lot of other businesses, Wild West is a multistate operation. From a business perspective, multistate businesses have access to a larger economic base than those operating in a single state. However, with this economic opportunity comes complexity and additional tax burdens.

LO 23-1   STATE AND LOCAL TAXES

The primary purpose of state and local taxes is to raise revenue to finance state governments. All 50 states and the District of Columbia have some combination of three primary revenue sources: sales and use tax, income or franchise tax, and property tax.[1]

This chapter focuses on sales and use taxes (excise taxes levied on the sale or use of tangible personal property within a state) and taxes based on *net* income (income taxes).[2]

Like federal tax law, state tax law includes the following:

- Legislative law (state constitution and tax code).
- Administrative law (regulations and rulings).
- Judicial law (state and federal tax cases).

While taxpayers deal with a single federal tax code, there are different tax codes for each state in which they are required to pay taxes. This makes state tax research particularly challenging. State tax agencies (such as the California Franchise Tax Board and New York Department of Finance and Taxation) administer the law and promulgate regulations for their particular states.[3] State and federal courts interpret the law when a state's tax authority and taxpayers cannot agree on its interpretation or constitutionality. Because of constitutionality questions, judicial law plays a significantly more important role in state tax law than in federal tax law.

It is impractical, if not impossible, to study each individual state statute in one text. Instead, this chapter addresses the most important state and local tax principles at a conceptual level.

The most important question Wild West, or any other taxpayer, must answer is whether it is subject to a state's taxing regime. The answer depends on the taxpayer's state of commercial domicile and whether the taxpayer has nexus in that state. **Commercial domicile** is the state where a business is headquartered and directs its operations; this location may be different from the place of incorporation.[4] A business must always collect sales tax and pay income tax in the state where it is domiciled. **Nondomiciliary businesses** (businesses not domiciled or headquartered in a state) are subject to tax only where they have nexus. **Nexus** is the sufficient (or minimum) connection between a business and a state that subjects the business to the state's tax system. The requirement for establishing nexus with a state depends on whether the tax is a sales and use tax, an income tax, or a nonincome-based tax. The nexus standard varies because the financial and administrative burdens vary across taxes. Sellers collect sales tax out of administrative convenience, but the sales tax burden belongs to the buyer in most states. In contrast, income tax is both owed and paid by the taxpayer earning the income.

---

[1]State and local jurisdictions may also tax or levy the following: personal property, capital stock, business licensing, transfer taxes, incorporation, excise, severance, payroll, disability, unemployment, fuel, and telecommunication.

[2]This chapter discusses income and franchise taxes interchangeably. Franchise taxes are imposed for the right to conduct business within a state. Most franchise taxes (such as the California Franchise Tax) are net income based.

[3]A great resource for guidance and forms from specific states can be found on the Federation of Tax Administrator's Web site: http://www.taxadmin.org/state-tax-forms.

[4]Some companies (e.g., Hewlett-Packard) are incorporated in one state (e.g., Delaware) but domiciled or headquartered in another (e.g., California). These companies pay taxes in both states (although sometimes just a capital stock tax applies in the state of incorporation if there are no activities other than incorporation within a state).

Wild West's commercial domicile is Idaho because it is headquartered there, and it must collect and remit Idaho sales tax and pay Idaho income tax. Yet, as detailed in Exhibit 23-1, it has activities and sales in other states, and therefore must collect sales and use tax and pay income tax in the states in which it has nexus.

EXHIBIT 23-1   Wild West's Activities and Sales by State

Wild West In-State Activities					
State	Sale of Goods	Sale of Services	Employees	Property	Commercial Domicile
Arizona	✓				
California	✓				
Colorado	✓				
Idaho	✓	✓	✓	✓	✓
Tennessee	✓	✓	✓	✓	
Washington	✓	✓	✓	✓	
Wyoming	✓	✓	✓	✓	

Wild West Sales			
State	Goods	Services	Total
Arizona	$ 89,242	$ 0	$ 89,242
California	132,045	0	132,045
Colorado	75,002	0	75,002
Idaho	167,921	625,003	792,924
Tennessee	45,331	357,061	402,392
Washington	41,982	377,441	419,423
Wyoming	185,249	437,755	623,004
Totals	$736,772	$1,797,260	$2,534,032

When a business sells tangible personal property, which is included in a state's sales tax base, in a state, it must collect and remit the **sales tax** on a periodic basis if it has nexus in that state.[5] Exhibit 23-2 provides an overview of who bears the burden

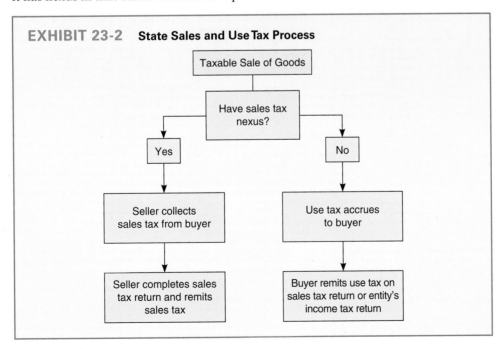

EXHIBIT 23-2   State Sales and Use Tax Process

[5]Businesses remit their sales and use tax liability on a monthly, quarterly, or annual basis depending on the size of the liability and the state law thresholds.

(who must pay and who must collect and remit the tax) of sales and use taxes. Sales tax liability accrues on certain sales of tangible personal property within the state. For example, Wild West's Idaho retail store collects sales tax on goods sold in Idaho stores and remits the tax to the Idaho Department of Revenue. **Use tax** liability accrues in the state where purchased property will be used when no sales tax was paid. The use tax only occurs when a seller in one state ships goods to a customer in a different state and the seller is not required to collect the sales tax (the seller does not have sales and use tax nexus in the state in which the goods are shipped to). For example, Colorado customers ordering through Wild West's Wyoming Internet store (which has no Colorado sales tax nexus) are required to accrue and remit the Colorado use tax (usually through their personal income tax returns).[6] Businesses with sales and use tax nexus in a state are responsible for remitting the sales tax even when they fail to collect it.

Businesses engaged in **interstate commerce** must also deal with income-tax related issues. If a business meets certain requirements creating income tax nexus, it may be required to remit income tax to that state. The general process of determining a business's state income tax liability is highlighted in Exhibit 23-3. We compute the **state tax base** by making adjustments to federal taxable income. The adjustments are necessary to account for differences between federal income tax laws and state income tax laws. Then we divide the state tax base into **business income** and **nonbusiness income.** Business income (income from business activities) is subject to **apportionment** among states where nexus exists, based on the extent of the business's activities and property in various states. Nonbusiness income (all income except business income—generally investment income) is subject to **allocation** (assignment) directly to the business's state of commercial domicile. For states in which the business has nexus, state taxable income is the sum of the business income apportioned to that state plus the nonbusiness income allocated to that state. The business computes its state tax liability for that particular state by multiplying state taxable income by the state's tax rate.

Let's now look in more depth at sales and use tax and net income-based taxes, the nexus requirements, and the calculation of each tax.

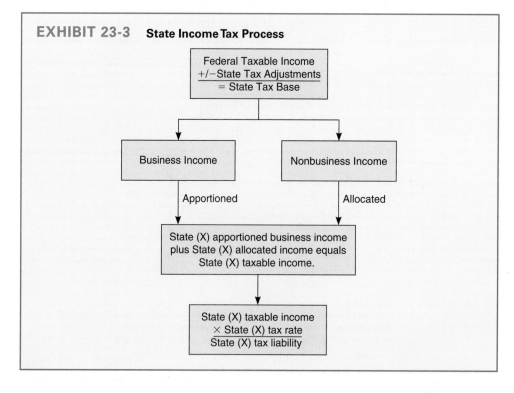

EXHIBIT 23-3   State Income Tax Process

---

[6]Use tax is paid by individuals completing the use tax liability line on their individual tax return. Alternatively, business entities collecting and remitting sales tax include the use tax on their sales tax return.

SALES AND USE TAXES

LO 23-2

Forty-five states and the District of Columbia impose sales and use taxes; Alaska, Delaware, Montana, New Hampshire, and Oregon do not. Sales tax must be collected on the state's sales tax base. Generally, sales of tangible personal property are subject to the tax. Most states also tax restaurant meals, rental car usage, hotel room rentals (often at higher tax rates than general sales), and some services (which vary by state). Purchases of inventory for resale are exempt from the sales tax. For example, Wild West's rafting equipment purchases for resale are exempt from sales tax because inventory is taxed when sold, but its office furniture purchases for use in the business are taxable because they represent final sales. Taxable items that are included in the sales tax base vary from state to state. Many states exempt food (except prepared restaurant food) because taxing food is considered to be regressive; that is, it imposes a proportionally higher tax burden on lower-income taxpayers that spend a greater proportion of their income on food and other necessities. Most states also exempt sales of real property, intangible property, and services. However, many states are expanding the types of services subject to sales tax in order to increase their sales tax revenue.[7]

> ### THE KEY FACTS
> **Sales Tax Nexus**
> - Nexus is the sufficient connection between a business and a state that allows a state to levy a tax on the business.
> - Sales tax nexus is established through physical presence of salespeople or property within a state.

TAXES IN THE REAL WORLD Is It Candy or Is It Food?

Items subject to the sales and use tax vary from state to state. Historically, New York taxed the sale of large marshmallows but exempted the sale of small marshmallows. Large and small marshmallows were treated differently because large marshmallows were considered to be candy, which was included in the sales tax base, while small marshmallows were considered to be a food ingredient and therefore excluded from the sales tax base.

The Washington state legislature passed a law subjecting candy to sales taxes in 2010. Any item containing flour is considered a food item, not candy. As a result, Twix bars were exempt while Starburst candy was subject to sales tax. Within the year, Washington voters repealed the tax on candy through a ballot initiative.

Sales and Use Tax Nexus

Have you ever wondered why sometimes you pay tax on goods purchased over the Internet and sometimes you don't? The answer is nexus. A business is required to collect sales tax from customers in a state only if it has sales and use tax nexus with that state. For example, if you purchased this textbook from your local campus bookstore you paid tax (unless your state exempts educational materials), but if you purchased the book from Amazon.com you didn't pay sales tax unless you live in Washington and a few other states.[8] Exhibit 23-4 explains Amazon's position on sales tax collection and indicates that they could have a substantial sales tax liability if a state successfully asserts that the position was wrong.

Businesses that establish sales and use tax nexus with a state but fail to properly collect sales tax can create significant liabilities that may need to be disclosed for financial reporting purposes.[9] As a result, understanding when a business has nexus can be extremely important for profitability, business modeling, and compliance.

---

[7]For example, Connecticut taxes services such as tax preparation.

[8]Items sold by Amazon.com LLC or its subsidiaries and shipped to destinations in the following states are subject to sales tax withholding: Arizona, California, Connecticut, Florida, Georgia, Indiana, Kansas, Kentucky, Maryland, Massachusetts, Minnesota, Nevada, New Jersey, New York, North Carolina, North Dakota, Pennsylvania, Tennessee, Texas, Virginia, Washington, West Virginia, and Wisconsin. http://www.amazon.com/gp/help/customer/display.html/ref=help_search_1-2?ie=UTF8&nodeId=468512&qid=1414725266&sr=1-2, accessed October 30, 2014.

[9]Sales tax liabilities are ASC 450 contingencies. Amazon indicated a $407 million potential liability associated with sales taxes.

EXHIBIT 23-4   **Excerpt from Amazon's 2014 Annual Report**

From the Form 10-K

We Do Not Collect Sales or Consumption Taxes in Some Jurisdictions

U.S. Supreme Court decisions restrict the imposition of obligations to collect state and local sales taxes with respect to remote sales. However, an increasing number of states have considered or adopted laws that attempt to impose obligations on out-of-state retailers to collect taxes on their behalf. We support a Federal law that would allow states to require sales tax collection under a nationwide system. More than half of our revenue is already earned in jurisdictions where we collect sales tax or its equivalent. A successful assertion by one or more states or foreign countries requiring us to collect taxes where we do not do so could result in substantial tax liabilities, including for past sales, as well as penalties and interest.

Businesses create sales tax nexus (the sufficient connection with a state that requires them to collect sales tax) when they have a *physical presence* in the state. Businesses have a physical presence in the state if (1) salespeople (or independent contractors representing a business) enter a state to obtain sales or if (2) tangible property (such as a company-owned truck making deliveries) is located within a state.[10] One important planning strategy is that, because nexus is determined on a legal entity basis, nexus can be limited by creating a separate legal entity.

The physical presence requirement is a judicial interpretation of the Commerce Clause of the U.S. Constitution. Designed to encourage interstate commerce, this clause gives Congress power "To regulate Commerce with foreign Nations, and among the several States, and with the Indian Tribes." Because Congress has never exercised its right, the courts have determined the sales tax nexus threshold. In *National Bellas Hess,* the Supreme Court held that an out-of-state mail-order company did not have a sales tax collection responsibility because it lacked physical presence (even though it mailed catalogs and advertised in the state).[11] The mail-order industry used this decision as a competitive advantage for several decades. In *Quill,* the Supreme Court reaffirmed that out-of-state (nondomiciliary) businesses must have a physical presence in the state before the state may require a business to collect sales tax from in-state customers.[12]

Example 23-1

Wild West sends promotional brochures from Idaho to its Colorado clients. Wild West generated sales of $75,002 to Colorado customers, but it has never collected Colorado sales and use tax or filed a Colorado sales and use tax return. Wild West has neither employees nor property in Colorado. Does it have sales and use tax nexus in Colorado?

Answer: No. Wild West lacks the physical presence required for Colorado nexus and therefore doesn't have Colorado sales and use tax collection responsibility.

What if: Assume that in addition to mailing promotional brochures, Ken visits Colorado on promotional trips. Does Wild West have sales and use tax nexus in Colorado under these circumstances?

Answer: Yes. The physical presence of Wild West's representatives, even for promotional trips, creates Colorado sales and use tax nexus.

---

[10] *Scripto, Inc. v. Carson, Sherriff,* et al., 362 U.S. 207 (1960). Scripto hired independent salesmen to represent the company in Florida. The Supreme Court held that these salesmen were agents of Scripto, who established the physical presence necessary to create nexus.

[11] *National Bellas Hess, Inc. v. Department of Revenue of the State of Illinois,* 386 U.S. 753 (1967).

[12] *Quill Corporation, Petitioner v. North Dakota,* 504 U.S. 298 (1992).

What if: Assume Wild West's representatives (independent contractors), rather than employees, visit Colorado retail stores to solicit additional sales orders. Does Wild West have sales and use tax nexus in Colorado under these circumstances?

Answer: Yes. The physical presence of Wild West's representatives creates Colorado sales and use tax nexus. Thus, the result is the same for employees or independent contractors.

TAXES IN THE REAL WORLD   E-Commerce Sales and Use Tax

Businesses selling products over the Internet have been able to avoid collecting sales and use tax because sales tax nexus is created through physical presence in the state of the buyer. In fact, Internet sales represent billions of dollars annually. As a result, the physical presence nexus standard has cost states substantial sales tax revenue. In 2008, New York implemented the so-called Amazon rule that requires Internet-based retailers to collect and remit New York sales tax if they have in-state affiliates referring customers to Web sites; the rule is estimated to increase state revenues by $50 million per year. As you might expect, because this law—often referred to as *click-through nexus*—is potentially inconsistent with the Supreme Court's decision in *Quill,* Amazon has filed suit against the state of New York. During 2011, 15 states considered legislation to expand sales and use taxes beyond physical presence. Eight states have now implemented similar laws.

In 2010, Colorado took a different strategy by requiring out-of-state retailers to provide the names, addresses, and taxable purchases of Colorado residents rather than requiring the retailer to collect the sales and use tax. In 2012, this law was determined to be unconstitutional.

Congress is also currently considering three bills that would change the sales and use tax nexus requirements: the Main Street Fairness Act (S. 1452 and H.R. 2701), the Marketplace Equity Act (H.R. 3179), and the Marketplace Fairness Act (S. 1832).

Notwithstanding *Quill* (discussed earlier), it appears that large retailers are losing ground in the nexus fight. In 2011, Amazon agreed to start collecting sales tax in California beginning in 2013. While Amazon originally led the fight against sales and use tax nexus, it has changed its position by announcing it would support a federal law implementing a nationwide system. One question is whether Amazon has changed its policy because it believes the legal position to be unsupportable, because it is changing its business model and no longer seeks the competitive advantage of not collecting sales and use taxes, or whether it wishes to prevent others from entering its markets now that it has established itself as the market leader in online sales. Only time will tell how this story will end.

Sales and Use Tax Liability

Typically, sellers with nexus collect customers' sales tax liabilities. For example, Wild West collects sales tax on river rafting equipment it sells from its retail store but not on river guiding *services* it provides. If the seller doesn't have nexus, then the customer is responsible for remitting a use tax (at the same tax rate as sales tax) to the state in which the property is used. If the buyer is charged a sales tax in another state, the buyer will have a use tax liability for an incremental amount if the state where the property is used has a higher sales tax rate.

Example 23-2

Wild West received $3,500 from a customer named Casey Jarvie residing in Sacramento, California. Of this amount, $500 was for personal rafting equipment shipped to Sacramento, where the sales tax rate is 7.75 percent. The remaining $3,000 was payment for a four-day river raft adventure on the Salmon River in Idaho. Wild West has neither salespeople nor property in California. Does Wild West have a responsibility to collect sales tax from Casey?

Answer: No. Wild West lacks physical presence and does not have sales and use tax nexus in California; therefore, it has no California sales tax collection requirement.

(*continued on page 23-8*)

Because Wild West has no sales tax collection responsibility, does Casey have a use tax liability to the state of California? If so, in what amount?

Answer: Yes. Casey is responsible for remitting $38.75 of use tax ($500 × 7.75%) on his personal California state income tax return for the purchase and use of the personal rafting equipment in California. He is not required to pay California use tax on the river raft adventure purchase because Wild West provided out-of-state *services* (no sales tax is due on the services in Idaho either).

What if: If Casey had Wild West hold the goods until he arrived in Burley, Idaho, to pick them up at the time of the trip (assume the sales tax rate in Burley, Idaho, is 6 percent), would Wild West have sales tax collection responsibility? If so, what is the sales tax amount?

Answer: Yes. Because Wild West has physical presence in Idaho, it is required to collect $30 ($500 × 6%) of sales tax and remit it to Idaho. Casey would also have an $8.75 California use tax liability ($38.75 reduced by the $30.00 remitted to Idaho) in this scenario.

ETHICS

Jill is a Virginia resident who purchased $1,500 of personal property items from Overstock.com and other Internet retailers during the year. While completing her personal tax return using a popular software package, Jill was asked to report her online purchases. After entering these purchases, she noticed that $75 of "use tax" was added to her state tax liability. Jill has never paid this in the past. She decided to delete the online purchase information she had previously entered. What do you think of Jill's failure to report her Virginia use tax?

Large companies must often file sales and use tax returns in all 45 states that have sales and use taxes and the District of Columbia.[13] This administrative burden is further complicated by the fact that there are over 7,500 tax jurisdictions (including counties, cities, school districts, and other divisions) imposing sales and use taxes, and several hundred rates change annually at various times during the year.[14] The sales and use tax administrative burden can also be large for small businesses. For example, a local pizzeria that delivers can sometimes be subject to a half-dozen sales tax rates if its delivery services cross city, county, or school district boundaries.

ETHICS

In 2010, Colorado became the first state to require nondomiciliary businesses without sales tax nexus to report all the necessary information to the Colorado Department of Revenue so that Colorado can collect its use tax from its resident individuals and domiciliary businesses. Assume you are responsible for sales tax issues for an online retailer from another state. You believe that the Colorado tax is unconstitutional based on a seminar you attended and the advice of your accounting firm. Would you recommend that your company comply with the Colorado law? Would your opinion change if the court placed an injunction prohibiting the state from enforcing the new law?

---

[13]Some counties or political subdivisions of states without state sales taxes (such as Kenal Peninsula Borough in Alaska) impose a county or local sales tax.

[14]Software companies provide sales and use tax solutions that help companies with the administrative burden. However, they generally fail to indemnify or compensate businesses against errors in their software that result in uncollected sales taxes, which creates a liability for the business.

Example 23-3

Recall from Exhibit 23-1 that Wild West has sales in Arizona, California, Colorado, Idaho, Tennessee, Washington, and Wyoming. Also, recall that it has property and employees in Idaho, Tennessee, Washington, and Wyoming. In which states does Wild West have sales and use tax nexus and, therefore, sales tax collection responsibility?

Answer: Wild West's physical presence of employees and real and personal property creates sales and use tax nexus in Idaho, Tennessee, Washington, and Wyoming.

How much sales and use tax must Wild West remit? Assume the following sales tax rates: Idaho (6.00 percent); Tennessee (9.25 percent); Washington (7.70 percent); and Wyoming (6.00 percent).

Answer: It must remit $28,616, computed as follows:

State	(1) Taxable Sales	(2) Rate	(1) × (2) Sales Tax Due
Idaho	$167,921	6.00%	$10,075
Tennessee	45,331	9.25	4,193
Washington	41,982	7.70	3,233
Wyoming	185,249	6.00	11,115
Totals	$440,483		$28,616

Remember, services are not generally subject to sales tax.

TAXES IN THE REAL WORLD   Groupon

Have you ever bought a restaurant meal from Groupon? Did you know there is a tax issue complicating these types of purchases? Suppose you pay $25 for a $50 voucher good at your favorite restaurant. You just scored a great deal. Groupon collects the $25 and pays the restaurant $12.50. You show up, order $50 worth of food, and the server brings you the bill. How much sales tax should the restaurant collect from you on the prepared food (which is a taxable item)? You received $50 worth of prepared foods (one possible tax base), but you only paid $25 (another possible tax base), and the restaurant only received $12.50 (a third possible tax base). What is the nature of the $12.50 retained by Groupon? Did they provide a good (taxable) or a service (not taxable)? Most restaurants currently collect tax on the entire $50 benefit you received. They probably collected too much tax, but only time will tell.

INCOME TAXES

LO 23-3

Forty-six states impose an income tax on corporations; Nevada, South Dakota, Washington, and Wyoming do not.[15] Forty-three states tax income from partnerships and S corporations. This chapter focuses on corporations, but the same principles apply to flow-through entities.[16] Businesses must pay income tax in their state of commercial domicile (where they are headquartered). For example, Wild West is both incorporated and domiciled in Idaho and is therefore subject to Idaho's income tax regime. Until a few decades ago, many businesses believed they were virtually exempt from state income taxes in states other than their state of commercial

---

[15]Several states (such as California and New York) impose a franchise tax rather than an income tax. Since franchise taxes are generally based upon net income, they are essentially the same as income taxes.

[16]Actually, these states tax individuals, including the income that flows through from partnerships and S corporations (although New Hampshire and Tennessee tax only dividends and interest); Alaska, Florida, Nevada, South Dakota, Texas, Washington, and Wyoming do not.

domicile. However, in *Complete Auto Transit,* the Supreme Court spelled out four criteria for determining whether states can tax nondomiciliary companies and whether the tax imposed is discriminatory against nondomiciliary (domiciled in another state) businesses.[17] First, a sufficient connection or nexus must exist between the state and the business. Second, a state may tax only a fair portion of a business's income. Businesses must be able to divide or apportion income among the states where nexus exists. Third, the tax cannot be constructed to discriminate against nonresident businesses. For example, states cannot impose a higher tax rate on nondomiciliary businesses than domiciliary businesses. Fourth, the taxes paid must be fairly related to the services the state provides. For example, businesses have access to a state's courts, economic base, infrastructure, and so forth.

To determine their state income tax liabilities, businesses must answer the following questions:

- In which states is the business required to file tax returns (in which states does it have nexus)?
- If the business is related to other entities, should it file separate state tax returns, or should it include the activities of the related entities on its state tax returns?
- What adjustments to federal taxable income must the business make to determine state taxable income for each state in which it is required to file?
- If income is taxable (nexus exists) in more than one state, how is income divided among the various states in which the business is required to file tax returns?

Income Tax Nexus

Businesses must file income tax returns in states where they have income tax nexus. However, the determination of whether the business has established income tax nexus within a state depends on the nature of its business's activities in the state. Thus, the rules for determining income tax nexus are not necessarily the same as those for determining sales and use tax nexus. Physical presence creates income tax nexus for service providers, sellers of real property, and businesses licensing intangibles. However, physical presence does not necessarily create nexus for sellers of tangible personal property if their activities within a state are limited to "protected" activities as described by **Public Law 86-272.**

Public Law 86-272   In *Northwestern States Portland Cement,* the Supreme Court allowed Minnesota to tax an Iowa-based business.[18] By passing Public Law 86-272, Congress placed limits on states' power to impose income taxes on nondomiciliary businesses. Businesses are protected from income tax nexus in a particular state if (and only if) *all* the following apply:

- The tax is based on net income (not gross receipts or revenue).
- The taxpayer sells only tangible personal property in that state.
- The taxpayer's in-state activities are limited to solicitation of sales (see next page for the definition of *solicitation*).
- The taxpayer participates in interstate commerce.
- The taxpayer is nondomiciliary.
- The taxpayer approves orders outside the state.
- The taxpayer delivers goods from outside the state.

---

[17]*Complete Auto Transit, Inc. v. Brady,* 430 U.S. 274 (1977).

[18]*Northwestern Cement Co. v. Minnesota,* 358 U.S. 450 (1959). Widespread alarm from the business community following the case led to an intense lobbying effort, and seven months later Congress enacted Public Law 86-272.

Businesses wishing to avoid nexus for taxes based on net income must sell only tangible personal property within the state.[19] Providing services along with property violates the criteria and creates nexus. For example, providing installation services with tangible personal property exceeds solicitation; in-state activities must be limited to solicitation of sales (discussed further in the next section). Only nondomiciliary companies engaging in interstate commerce are protected. Orders taken or received in-state must be sent out of state—say to regional sales offices or headquarters—for approval. The acceptance of orders in the state, or even the power to accept orders, exceeds the protection of Public Law 86-272 and would result in the business being subject to an income tax. Accepted orders must be delivered by common carrier.[20] Delivery using the seller's truck violates the criteria and creates nexus, except as permitted by state law (New Jersey, Rhode Island, and South Carolina are among the states that list delivery by private vehicles as a protected activity).

Example 23-4

What if: Assume that Wild West sends employees to Oregon to visit retail stores and solicit orders of rafting equipment only. Does the presence of Wild West's employees in Oregon create income tax nexus in Oregon?

Answer: No. The physical presence of representatives soliciting sales of tangible personal property is a protected activity under Public Law 86-272. Thus, no income tax nexus for Wild West in Oregon is created. Note, however, that this physical presence *would* create sales and use tax nexus for any sales generated by Wild West in Oregon, unless they have a valid reseller's certificate.

What if: Assume that Ken or other Wild West sales representatives entered Oregon to solicit customers for both rafting equipment and white-water adventures. Does the presence of Wild West's employees create income tax nexus in Oregon?

Answer: Yes. Solicitation of *services* is not a protected activity under Public Law 86-272. Thus, soliciting services creates income tax nexus for Wild West in Oregon and creates an income tax filing requirement.

Solicitation.   Public Law 86-272 protects **solicitation** of tangible personal property but doesn't clearly define solicitation. In *Wisconsin v. Wrigley,* however, the Supreme Court addressed the definition.[21] Wrigley had sales representatives and a regional manager in Wisconsin. Sales meetings were held both in the manager's basement and in a rented hotel space. The sales reps had company cars, a stock of gum, display racks, and promotional literature. The sales activities included handing out promotional materials, free samples, and free display racks; replacing stale gum; handling billing disputes; and occasionally filling orders from their stock of gum and issuing an agency stock check (a bill) to customers. All other orders were sent to Illinois for acceptance and were filled by common carrier from outside the state. The Supreme Court determined the following activities meet the definition of solicitation:

- Soliciting by any form of advertising.
- Carrying samples and promotional materials for display or distribution without charge.
- Passing inquiries or complaints to the home office.
- Checking customer's inventory for reorder.

---

[19]Taxes calculated based on gross receipts or other bases are not protected by Public Law 86-272.

[20]*Common carrier* is a general term referring to delivery businesses (such as FedEx, UPS, DHL, or USPS).

[21]*Wisconsin Department of Revenue v. William Wrigley, Jr. Co.,* 505 US 214 (1992).

- Maintaining a sample room for two weeks or less; this is known as the **trade show rule.**
- Recruiting, training, and evaluating sales reps using homes or hotels.
- Owning or furnishing personal property and autos used in sales activities.

The Supreme Court held the following activities do *not* meet the definition of solicitation and, therefore, create income tax nexus with the state in which they take place:

- Making repairs.
- Collecting delinquent accounts.
- Investigating creditworthiness.
- Installing or supervising the installation of property.
- Training for employees other than sales reps.
- Approving or accepting orders.
- Repossessing property.
- Securing deposits.
- Maintaining an office other than in-home.

TAXES IN THE REAL WORLD Warranty

One of the biggest current issues for out-of-state retailers is the manner in which warranty work is performed. For example, assume you buy a new laptop for school from an online retailer because the price is unbeatable. Two months later you are told by customer support that the hard drive needs to be replaced and you need to ship the computer to Austin, Texas, for repair. You respond that you cannot go a week without your computer, so the retailer agrees to have a local shop do the repair for you. Many companies wrongly assume that hiring an independent representative to do in-state warranty work does not create nexus. The hiring of the independent contractor is an agency relationship that creates nexus for the out-of-state retailer. The Multistate Tax Commission issued guidance (MTC Nexus Bulletin 95-1) on this issue more than a decade ago—and taxpayers challenging this ruling have lost time and time again. Retailers with these issues quickly find themselves liable for both current and past income as well as sales and use taxes.

If sales reps know and understand these solicitation rules, they can help businesses avoid nexus in states where they want to avoid it.

Example 23-5

Assume that Wild West's Oregon sales reps give store employees free white-water gloves and pass on complaints to the home office. Do these activities create nexus for Wild West in Oregon?

Answer: No. Giving samples (without charge) and passing on complaints, suggestions, and customer inquiries are protected sales activities under Public Law 86-272. Therefore, Wild West is protected from Oregon income tax nexus.

What if: While in Oregon, several sales reps accepted checks for down payments on merchandise, repaired faulty merchandise, and performed credit checks. Do these activities create nexus in Oregon for Wild West?

Answer: Yes. Each of these activities is an unprotected sales activity, and any or all will create Oregon income tax nexus for Wild West.

Does a one-time sales activity violation create income tax nexus? Technically, yes. However, the *Wrigley* decision indicates that *de minimis* (immaterial) activities may be excluded. The determination of whether an activity is *de minimis* is a subjective one, based on relevant facts and circumstances.

Example 23-6

Assume that Wild West's sales reps occasionally investigate creditworthiness and occasionally re-possess property in Oregon. Can Wild West avoid income tax nexus?

Answer: Possibly. Wild West must argue that these unprotected activities are *de minimis* because they were not material to its overall operations within Oregon.

Income Tax Nexus for Other Business Types or Nonincome-Based Taxes

Public Law 86-272 does not protect service providers, sellers of real property, or businesses licensing intangibles. Further, it does not protect businesses from nonincome-based taxes. Establishing income tax nexus for nonprotected activities, and nexus for nonincome-based taxes, requires a physical presence just like establishing sales and use tax nexus. The two most notable nonincome-based taxes are the Texas Margin Tax and the Washington Business and Occupation (B&O) tax. While nonincome-based taxes are beyond the scope of this chapter, a realization that a different nexus standard exists is vitally important.

Example 23-7

What if: Assume that Ken and other Wild West employees visit Colorado retail stores and hold slideshows about summer rafting trips. After the slideshows, Ken and the other guides interact with and gather information from potential white-water rafting customers. Do these solicitation activities create income tax nexus?

Answer: Yes. Because white-water rafting trips are services rather than tangible personal property, the physical presence of Wild West employees creates income tax nexus in Colorado.

Example 23-8

What if: Assume that Wild West sends employees into Texas to visit retail stores and solicit orders of rafting equipment. Texas instituted a new tax, the Margin Tax, beginning in 2008. The tax is calculated on the lesser of gross margin or 70 percent of sales revenue. Would the presence of Wild West employees create nexus for the Texas Margin Tax?

Answer: Yes. Because the tax is nonincome-based (it is not based on *net* income), Wild West is not protected by Public Law 86-272. Therefore, physical presence of salespeople soliciting sales of tangible personal property creates nexus (but it would *not* have created nexus if the tax were based on net income).

THE KEY FACTS

Income Tax Nexus

- Income tax nexus requirements vary depending on whether the business sells tangible personal property, services, or intangibles.
- Sellers of tangible personal property are protected from nexus under Public Law 86-272.
  - Physical presence is protected as long as in-state activities are limited to solicitation.
- Sellers of intangibles, real property, and services establish nexus through physical presence of sales personnel or property.
- Several states are now asserting economic nexus.

Economic Income Tax Nexus   As we have discussed, businesses generally must have a physical presence in a state to establish income tax nexus with that state (Public Law 86-272 is the exception). However, many states currently asserting a business without a physical presence in the state may establish income tax nexus if it has an economic presence in the state.[22] South Carolina was the first state to pursue economic nexus. South Carolina disallowed the royalty expenses of Toys 'R' Us South Carolina to Geoffrey (a related Delaware holding company) rather than subject

[22]The Supreme Court's *Quill* decision created doubt on the standard for income tax nexus because in defining sales tax nexus it said that "nexus for other taxes may be different," which the states have interpreted as meaning that physical presence may not be required for other types of taxes. Several recent cases have given de facto income tax nexus to businesses without the requisite physical presence [*Geoffrey, Inc. v. South Carolina Tax Commission*, S.C. Sup. Ct., 313 S.C. (1992); *Lanco, Inc. v. Director, Division of Taxation*, NJ Sup. Ct., Dkt. No.A-89-05 (2006); and *Tax Commissioner of West Virginia v. MBNA America Bank, N.A.*, 640 SE 2d 226 (WV 2006)].

Geoffrey to the South Carolina income tax. States asserting **economic nexus** claim they provide an infrastructure of phone and Internet connections to consumers (an economic base) that nonresident companies use to solicit business (this claim is analogous to providing roads for salespeople to visit the state's customers). For example, West Virginia asserted an income tax liability on a business (MBNA Bank) that merely solicited credit card customers through advertising and phone calls without having physical presence (employees or property) in the state. The West Virginia Supreme Court upheld the assertion, and the U.S. Supreme Court denied MBNA's *writ of certiorari*. However, most experts believe West Virginia's law to be unconstitutional, and the U.S. Supreme Court's refusal to hear the case was designed to urge Congress to resolve the uncertainty surrounding nexus issues.

Example 23-9

What if: Assume that Wild West's Internet store receives and fills an order from a West Virginia customer. Wild West has no physical presence in West Virginia. Does Wild West have West Virginia income tax nexus?

Answer: Perhaps. West Virginia's assertion of economic nexus does not require physical presence. Therefore, Wild West could have economic income tax nexus, which would require it to file an income tax return in West Virginia.

TAXES IN THE REAL WORLD Factor Presence

While several states have asserted economic nexus through state courts, the Multistate Tax Commission adopted the Factor Presence Nexus Standard in 2002 (MTC Policy Statement 02-02). This policy asserts that if any taxpayer exceeds any of the following criteria, substantial nexus is established:

- $50,000 of property
- $50,000 of payroll

- $500,000 of sales, or
- 25 percent of total property, payroll, or sales

A number of states have recently asserted this standard (or a variation) through either legislation or regulation: California, Colorado, Ohio, Oklahoma, and Washington. If upheld, this standard will change the game by making Public Law 86-272 irrelevant, and it should make all companies not filing income tax returns in a state nervous.

Now that we've explored income tax nexus, let's determine Wild West's income tax nexus and filing requirements.

Example 23-10

Wild West is domiciled in Idaho and has physical presence through property and employees whose activities exceed protected solicitation in Idaho, Tennessee, Washington, and Wyoming. Recall from Exhibit 23-1 that Wild West has sales in the following states: Arizona, California, Colorado, Idaho, Tennessee, Washington, and Wyoming. Where does Wild West have income tax nexus?

Answer: Wild West has income tax nexus in Idaho, Tennessee, Washington, and Wyoming. Nexus in Idaho because of commercial domicile, physical presence of retail stores (where orders are accepted), and provision of services. Nexus in Tennessee, Washington, and Wyoming because of physical presence of retail stores (where orders are accepted) or provision of services. Where does Wild West have an income tax filing requirement?

Answer: Wild West will be required to file income tax returns in Idaho and Tennessee. Washington and Wyoming do not have a corporate income tax. Instead, Washington has a gross receipts tax (Business & Occupation tax). Wyoming does not tax corporations. As a result, Wild West will also file a Washington gross receipts return, as we discuss later.

Entities Included on Income Tax Return

When a business operates as more than one legal entity, how it files its tax return(s) becomes an issue. Some states require a **separate tax return** for each entity with income tax nexus in the state, and others require a **unitary tax return** (one return) for a group of related entities.[23]

Separate Tax Returns   "Separate-return" states require only those businesses with nexus in a state to file an income tax return. This is generally true even when a group of companies file a federal consolidated tax return.[24] Traditionally, most states east of the Mississippi River (except Illinois) were separate-return states.

Example 23-11

Wild West has nexus in Tennessee (a separate-return state) because its employees provide services within the state and it owns property there. Must Wild West file a separate Tennessee income tax return?

Answer: Yes. Wild West must file a separate Tennessee income tax return because it has nexus in Tennessee.

What if: Assume that Wild West splits into two separate corporations: one that runs retail stores (Wild West Retail) and one that provides the guided rafting services (Wild West Services). How would the split affect Wild West's Tennessee income tax filing requirements?

Answer: Wild West would file two separate income tax returns: one for Wild West Retail and one for Wild West Services. Both companies would have nexus in Tennessee because Wild West Retail's stores do more than solicit sales of tangible personal property and Wild West Service's activities are not protected activities under Public Law 86-272.

THE KEY FACTS

Entities Included on a Tax Return

- Separate-return states require a separate return for each entity that has nexus in the state.
- Unitary states require members of a unitary group to file a single tax return reflecting the combined income of the unitary group.
  - Any of three factors determine a unitary group: functional integration, centralization of management, and economies of scale.

While separate tax returns are simple, the income reported on separate tax returns is potentially subject to manipulation through related-entity transactions (transfer pricing, for example). Another important planning technique is the use of *passive investment companies* (PICs). A company simply creates a subsidiary and transfers ownership of its trademarks and patents to a state that does not tax royalties, interest, and other similar types of intangible income. Then the new PIC charges a royalty for use of the intangible, which generates a deductible business expense in the state used and creates income in a little or no taxed state like Delaware or Nevada. States have implemented laws to fight this type of planning, but seven states have adopted unitary filing to avoid this issue. These "tax planning" opportunities are not available if the related entities are required to file a unitary tax return.

Unitary Tax Returns   States west of the Mississippi River (and Illinois) are unitary return states. However, since 2004, Massachusetts, Michigan, New York, Ohio, Texas, Vermont, and Wisconsin have adopted unitary returns. Whether a business must file one tax return with other businesses or entities depends on whether these businesses are considered to be a "unitary" group of entities.

---

[23]The separate versus unitary discussion is a complex and controversial discussion even at the graduate tax level. However, a basic understanding of the terminology and concepts can be useful for all accounting professionals.

[24]Some states allow combined reporting, a setting where more than one corporation files together on the same income tax return. However, the tax is calculated as if each corporation filed a separate return and was taxed separately.

In *Mobil,* the Supreme Court identified the following three factors that can be used to determine whether a group of businesses is unitary:

- Functional integration (vertical or horizontal integration or knowledge transfer).
- Centralization of management (interlocking directors, common officers, or rotation of management between companies).
- Economies of scale (group discounts or other efficiencies due to size).[25]

The unitary concept considers the integration and flow of value, rather than the business's legal form and ownership structure, in determining which companies file a tax return together. Taxpayers must consider each of the three factors to determine whether two (or more) businesses will be treated as one for state tax purposes.

The important concept here is that companies filing a federal consolidated tax return can be separated, and companies not filing a federal consolidated tax return can become a unitary group.[26] A unitary tax return group includes all members meeting the unitary criteria—whether they have nexus or not.[27] Unitary businesses usually have a flow of value between the various businesses. For example, raw materials or components can flow between businesses or one entity may borrow funds from another. The unitary concept pervades activities in the entire income tax system, including computing taxable income, computing apportionment percentages (discussed later in the chapter), and determining tax return filing requirements. The primary difference between separate and unitary states is that separate states tax the entire apportioned income of each separate business unit with nexus while unitary states tax the entire unitary group using a smaller apportioned percentage.

Example 23-12

What if: As in the previous example, assume that Wild West is divided into two separate corporations: Wild West Retail (WWR) and Wild West Services (WWS). Ken owns and manages both companies. The rafting services company purchases all of its rafting equipment from the retail stores company. Guides for the rafting company stop at the retail store before trips so customers can purchase any necessary gear, and the store refers customers looking for guided rafting to the rafting company. Assume the two companies use the same marketing and accounting firms and receive discounts for having multiple bank accounts and insurance policies. Using the *Mobil* factors (functional integration, centralization of management, and economies of scale), are WWR and WWS part of a unitary group?

Answer: Yes. WWR and WWS would likely be considered a unitary group and thus would combine income and file a single tax return. The two companies likely share some integration in that their customer bases have significant overlap, and WWR purchases its equipment from WWS. They share centralization of management in that both are owned and operated by the same individual (Ken). The two companies have some economies of scale because they receive discounts for using the same accounting, banking, insurance, and marketing vendors. Businesses do not have to meet all three factors to be considered a unitary group, but WWR and WWS probably do. As a result, WWR and WWS would likely file a unitary (single) Idaho income tax return.

State Taxable Income

Companies doing business in multiple states must determine tax return due dates, procedures for filing tax return extensions, and other administrative requirements

---

[25]In *Mobil Oil Corp. v. Vermont Tax Commissioner,* 445 U.S. 425 (1980), the U.S. Supreme Court held that the income of a multistate business can be apportioned if its intrastate and out-of-state activities form a part of a unitary business.

[26]In some cases, different divisions of a single corporation can be separated and in others a partnership and corporation can be joined.

[27]Entities without nexus usually have apportionment factors that are zero. While their incomes increase the unitary group's income, their zero apportionment factors decrease the apportionment factors to the state. Therefore, the inclusion of entities without nexus is usually considered to be nondiscriminatory.

specific to each state. Businesses must also calculate state taxable income for each state in which they must file tax returns. Federal taxable income is generally the starting point for computing state taxable income. Just as corporations reconcile from book income to taxable income (see Chapter 16), businesses must reconcile from federal taxable income to state taxable income. This requires them to identify **federal/state adjustments** (differences) for *each specific state* before apportioning the income to a particular state where they have income tax nexus.

Rather than starting from scratch, many states conform to the federal tax law in some way. Most states "piggyback" their state tax laws on the federal tax laws (state tax codes generally follow the Internal Revenue Code).[28] Idaho generally conforms to the current Code. Consequently, Wild West will not report many federal/state adjustments. Other states adopt a specific version of the Code (the Code as of a specific date). California recently adopted the Code as of January 1, 2009 (previously it used the Code as of January 1, 2006), and Texas uses the Code as of January 1, 2007. This method requires more federal/state adjustments, because every subsequent change to the Internal Revenue Code results in less conformity between the state law and the federal tax law.

Because states cannot tax federal interest income (interest from Treasury notes, for example), all states require a negative adjustment (reduction in federal income in adjusting to state income) for federal interest income. Most states require a positive adjustment for state income taxes, because they *do not* allow businesses to deduct state income taxes, and they require a positive adjustment for state and local bond interest income if the bond is from another state (they tax out-of-state bond interest income).[29]

States' tax instruction booklets generally describe common federal/state tax adjustments applicable for that state, but these descriptions are often incomplete, and particularly problematic for states with low federal tax conformity. While it is impractical to identify all potential federal/state adjustments, Exhibit 23-5 provides a list of common federal/state adjustments and identifies each as positive adjustments (state income increasing) or negative adjustments (state income decreasing).

EXHIBIT 23-5 **Common Federal/State Adjustments**

Positive Adjustments (Increasing Taxable Income)
State and local income taxes
State and local bond interest income from bonds in other states
Federal dividends received deduction
Federal income tax refunds (only in states where federal tax is allowed as a deduction)
Intercompany expenses associated with related parties (for separate-return states)*
MACRS depreciation over state depreciation
Federal bonus depreciation
Federal domestic production activities deduction

Negative Adjustments (Decreasing Taxable Income)
U.S. obligation interest income (T-bills, notes, and bonds)
State dividends received deduction
Foreign dividend gross up
Subpart F income
State income tax refunds included on federal return
State depreciation over federal depreciation

*Approximately 20 separate-return states require a positive adjustment of intercompany royalties, interest, and other expenses between related parties. The disallowance prevents companies from extracting profits from high-tax states and placing them in low- or no-tax states.

[28]Also, states may conform or not conform to administrative authority such as Treasury Regulations, Revenue Procedures, and Revenue Rulings.
[29]Thirty-three of the 46 states with an income tax require a positive adjustment for state and local expenses deducted on the federal return.

Example 23-13

Wild West properly included, deducted, or excluded the following items on its federal tax return in the current year:

Item	Amount	Federal Treatment
Idaho income tax	$27,744	Deducted on federal return.
Tennessee income tax	18,152	Deducted on federal return.
Washington gross receipts tax	6,201	Deducted on federal return.
Idaho bond interest income	5,000	Excluded from federal return.
Federal T-note interest income	1,500	Included on federal return.
Domestic production activities deduction (DPAD)	7,304	Deducted on federal return.

Given federal taxable income of $53,289, what is Wild West's state tax base for Idaho and for Tennessee?

Answer: The Idaho state tax base is $97,685; for Tennessee it is $109,989. Bases are calculated as follows:

Federal Taxable Income	Idaho	Tennessee	Source
Wild West	$53,289	$ 53,289	Storyline
Positive Adjustments			
Idaho income tax	$ 27,744	$ 27,744	Idaho tax is not deducted.
Tennessee income tax	18,152	18,152	Tennessee tax is not deducted.
Washington gross receipts tax	0	0	Washington tax is not a positive adjustment because it is not an income-based tax.
State bond interest	0	5,000	States exempt their own interest only.
DPAD	0	7,304	Idaho conforms to federal law, Tennessee does not.
Total positive adjustments	$45,896	$ 58,200	
Negative Adjustments			
Federal interest	$ 1,500	$ 1,500	Federal interest is not taxable for state purposes.
Total negative adjustments	$ 1,500	$ 1,500	
State tax base	$ 97,685	$109,989	Federal + Positive − Negative.

Dividing State Tax Base among States

All state taxable income is taxed in the state of commercial domicile unless the business is taxable in more than one state. An interstate business must separate its business income (earned from business operations) from nonbusiness income (primarily from investments, including rents and royalties). The business must fairly *apportion* its business income among the states in which it conducts business, whereas it *allocates* or assigns nonbusiness income to a specific state (usually the state of commercial domicile).[30]

---

[30]The Multistate Tax Commission has provided guidance on the division of income between states in Article IV of its Compact. The Compact can be found at www.mtc.gov. Also, see the Uniform Division of Income Tax Purposes Act that many states have adopted.

Business Income Business income includes all revenues earned in the ordinary course of business—sales less cost of goods sold and other expenses. Business income is fairly apportioned or divided across the states with nexus.[31] If a business has nexus with a state, it may apportion income to that state—even if the state does not actually impose a tax.[32]

Example 23-14

Recall from the preceding example that Idaho and Tennessee state tax bases were $97,685 and $109,989, respectively. Wild West's federal tax return shows the following items of investment income: dividends of $6,000, interest income of $16,005 (which includes $14,505 of bank interest and $1,500 of federal government interest but excludes $5,000 from Idaho bond interest), and rental income of $18,000. What is Wild West's business income for Idaho and Tennessee?

Answer: Idaho and Tennessee business income amounts are $59,180 and $66,484, respectively, and calculated as follows:

	Idaho	Tennessee	Explanation
(1) State tax base	$97,685	$109,989	Example 23-13.
(2) Dividends	$ 6,000	$ 6,000	Federal tax return.
(3) Interest income	14,505	19,505	$14,505 (bank interest) + $5,000 of Idaho bond interest (for Tennessee only).
(4) Rental income	18,000	18,000	Federal tax return.
(5) Nonbusiness income	$38,505	$ 43,505	(2) + (3) + (4).
Business income	$59,180	$ 66,484	(1) − (5).

Apportionment formula. States determine the apportionment formula for income, and most rely on three factors: sales, payroll, and property. For each state in which it establishes income tax nexus, the business determines the factors as the ratio of (1) total sales, payroll, or property in a specific state to (2) total sales, payroll, or property everywhere. For example, the sales factor is

$$\text{Sales factor in state } X = \frac{\text{Total sales in state } X}{\text{Total sales in all states}}$$

The sales factor includes all gross business receipts net of returns, allowances, and discounts.[33] The general rules for determining the amount of sales to include in the sales factor calculation are:

- Sales of tangible personal property are sourced (included) to the destination state (the location where the property is delivered to and used in).
- If the business does not have nexus in the destination state, sales are generally "thrown back" to the state from which the property is shipped; this is called the **throwback rule**.[34] For example, if Wild West ships goods from Idaho to

---

[31] *Complete Auto Transit, Inc. v. Brady*, 430 U.S. 274 (1977).

[32] Creating nexus in states without an income tax creates "nowhere income"—income that is not taxed anywhere.

[33] There is some variation in the sales factor among states.

[34] Some states don't have a throwback rule and some states such as California have a double-throwback rule. This rule applies to drop shipments from a state without nexus. For example, if a California company ships goods from Arizona into Colorado and has nexus in neither Arizona nor Colorado, the sales are thrown back from Colorado into Arizona and then thrown back again from Arizona to California.

Montana where it does not have nexus the sales are treated as if they are Idaho sales.

- Dock sales should be sourced to the good's ultimate destination (sales picked up by an out-of-state buyer at the seller's in-state dock rather than being shipped to the buyer's out-of-state location).
- Sales of services are sourced in the state where the services are performed (Illinois is an exception to this rule, but the list of market states is growing).
- Government sales are sourced in the state from which they were shipped.

TAXES IN THE REAL WORLD   The Complexities in Sourcing Receipts from the Sale of Other Than Tangible Personal Property

The last 10 to 15 years have seen a shift from the equally weighted three-factor formula to adopting a single sales factor formula for apportionment purposes. As a result, the computation of the sales factor has gained importance for taxpayers and tax administrators alike. The increased significance of the sales factor coupled with an economic shift towards intangibles and services has shifted the focus of apportionment to sourcing receipts from sales other than sales of tangible personal property. Sales of other than the sale of tangible personal property historically have not been sourced on a destination basis. Rather, most states have generally adopted a method that assigns the sales to the state in which the income producing activity/cost of performance was performed. . . . Recently, states have moved towards a market state or destination approach for sourcing such receipts.

Source: Marilyn A. Wethekam, *Journal of State Taxation,* September–October 2010, p. 39.

Example 23-15

Recall from Exhibit 23-1 that Wild West reported sales of $2,534,032. The sales are split between goods and services and sourced by state as follows:

State	Goods	Services	Total
AZ	$ 89,242	$ 0	$ 89,242
CA	132,045	0	132,045
CO	75,002	0	75,002
ID	**167,921**	**625,003**	**792,924**
TN	**45,331**	**357,061**	**402,392**
WA	41,982	377,441	419,423
WY	185,249	437,755	623,004
Totals	**$736,772**	**$1,797,260**	**$2,534,032**

Table title: Wild West Sales

Recall from Example 23-10 that Wild West has nexus in Idaho, Tennessee, Washington, and Wyoming. Washington has a gross receipts tax and Wyoming does not tax corporations. What are the sales apportionment factors for Idaho and Tennessee?

Answer: The apportionment factors for Idaho and Tennessee are 31.29 percent and 15.88 percent, respectively, calculated from figures in the Total column in the sales table above:

$$\text{Idaho} \quad \frac{\$792,924}{\$2,534,032} = 31.29\%$$

$$\text{Tennessee} \quad \frac{\$402,392}{\$2,534,032} = 15.88\%$$

Note the AZ, CA, and CO sales are thrown back to Wyoming because the sales were made through the Internet store.

Payroll is generally defined as total compensation paid to employees.[35] The payroll factor is calculated as follows:

- Payroll includes salaries, commissions, bonuses, and other forms of compensation.
- Payroll does not include amounts paid to independent contractors.
- Payroll for each employee is apportioned to a single state (payroll for employees who work in more than one state is sourced to the state where they perform the majority of services).

Example 23-16

Wild West's payments for wages are $737,021, sourced to the states as follows:

Payroll State	Wild West Wages
Idaho	**$201,032**
Tennessee	**148,202**
Washington	115,021
Wyoming	272,766
Total	**$737,021**

What are the payroll apportionment factors for Idaho and Tennessee?

Answer: The payroll apportionment factors for Idaho and Tennessee are 27.28 percent and 20.11 percent, respectively, calculated from the payroll table above:

$$\text{Idaho} \quad \frac{\$201,032}{\$737,021} = 27.28\%$$

$$\text{Tennessee} \quad \frac{\$148,202}{\$737,021} = 20.11\%$$

Property generally includes both real and tangible personal property, but not intangible property.[36] The general rules for determining the property factors are

- Use the average property values for the year [(beginning + ending)/2].
- Value property at historical cost rather than adjusted basis (do not subtract accumulated depreciation in determining value).

[35]The payroll definition varies by state.
[36]Property definitions may vary slightly by state.

- Include property in transit (such as inventory) in the state of destination.
- Include only business property (values of rented investment properties are excluded).
- Include rented or leased property by multiplying the annual rent by 8 and adding this value to the average owned-property factor.[37]

Example 23-17

The historical cost of Wild West's property (before subtracting accumulated depreciation) owned at the beginning and end of the year and rented during the year, by state, is as follows:

	Property		
State	**Beginning**	**Ending**	**Rented**
Idaho	$1,042,023	$1,203,814	$36,000
Tennessee	502,424	531,984	0
Washington	52,327	65,829	60,000
Wyoming	1,420,387	1,692,373	0
Total	$ 3,017,161	$3,494,000	$96,000

What are the property apportionment factors for Idaho and Tennessee?

Answer: The property apportionment factors for Idaho and Tennessee are 35.07 percent and 12.85 percent, respectively, computed as follows:

	Property and Rents Total				
	Owned Property			**Rented**	
State	**Beginning**	**Ending**	**Average**	**Rents × 8**	**Total**
Idaho	**$1,042,023**	**$1,203,814**	**$1,122,919**	**$288,000**	**$1,410,919**
Tennessee	**502,424**	**531,984**	**517,204**		**517,204**
Washington	52,327	65,829	59,078	$480,000	539,078
Wyoming	1,420,387	1,692,373	1,556,380		1,556,380
Total	**$ 3,017,161**	**$3,494,000**	**$3,255,581**		**$4,023,581**

$$\text{Idaho} \quad \frac{\$1,410,919}{\$4,023,581} = 35.07\%$$

$$\text{Tennessee} \quad \frac{\$517,204}{\$4,023,581} = 12.85\%$$

The average amount for each state from the subtotal property table is added to the inclusion amount from the subtotal rent table to reach the total property numerator for each state.

Historically, most states have used an equally weighted three-factor apportionment formula. This method adds together the sales, payroll, and property factors and divides the total by three to arrive at the apportionment factor (percentages) for each state. In recent years, many states have shifted to a double-weighted sales factor (doubling the sales factor, adding the payroll and property factors, and dividing the total by four). Both Idaho and Tennessee use the double-weighted sales factor for apportionment. Recently, some states have moved to a single-weighted sales factor that eliminates the payroll and property factors altogether. California requires

---

[37]The annual rent is multiplied by 8 to approximate the value of the rental property.

corporations to use a single-weighted sales factor beginning in 2013. All else equal, increasing the weight of the sales factor in the apportionment formula tends to decrease taxes on in-state businesses and increase taxes on out-of-state businesses. The reason is that in-state businesses tend to have higher payroll and property factors relative to their sales factor in the state, and out-of-state businesses tend to have higher sales factors than payroll and property factors.

TAXES IN THE REAL WORLD Apportionment: The Gillette Decision

The California Supreme Court on January 16, 2013, agreed to review the California Court of Appeal decision in *Gillette Co. v. Franchise Tax Board.*

In *Gillette,* the California Court of Appeal held that a taxpayer could apportion its income to California using the Multistate Tax Compact's evenly weighted three-factor formula, despite statutory language mandating the use of a three-factor, double-weighted sales formula for most corporations for the years at issue.

The court's ruling was based entirely on case law regarding interstate compacts and its view that when California became a signatory to the Multistate Tax Compact, it entered into a binding agreement with other signatory states that—absent repeal of the Compact in its entirety—obligated it to offer multistate taxpayers the option of using the Compact's allocation and apportionment provisions.

Oral arguments were heard on October 6, 2015. The court's ruling will have a large impact on whether companies are forced to use unfavorable state laws that typically require out-of-state companies to apportion income based solely on the sales factor or to choose a more favorable three-factor methodology that reduces the tax burden. The Michigan Supreme Court ruled for IBM in a similar case. Oregon and Minnesota courts have recently ruled against taxpayers in similar cases. The California decision in *Gillette Co. v. Franchise Tax Board* is highly anticipated.

Example 23-18

Wild West must apportion its business income to Idaho and Tennessee. Its Idaho sales, payroll, and property factors are 31.29 percent, 27.28 percent, and 35.07 percent, respectively. Its Tennessee sales, payroll, and property factors are 15.88 percent, 20.11 percent, and 12.85 percent, respectively. These factors are aggregated from Examples 23-15 through 23-17. What are Wild West's apportionment factors in both states if they use a double-weighted sales factor?

Answer: The apportionment factors for Idaho and Tennessee are 31.23 percent and 16.18 percent, respectively.

Factor	Idaho	Tennessee	Explanation
(1) Sales	31.29%	15.88%	Exhibit 23-15
(2) Sales	31.29	15.88	Exhibit 23-15
(3) Payroll	27.28	20.11	Exhibit 23-16
(4) Property	35.07	12.85	Exhibit 23-17
Apportionment factor	31.23	16.18	[(1) + (2) + (3) + (4)]/4.

What if: Assume Tennessee uses an equally weighted three-factor apportionment formula. What are Wild West's apportionment factors?

Answer: The apportionment factor for Tennessee is 16.28 percent. Tennessee's apportionment factor would now be calculated as follows:

Factor	Tennessee	Explanation
(1) Sales	15.88%	
(2) Payroll	20.11	
(3) Property	12.85	
Apportionment factor	16.28	[(1) + (2) + (3)]/3.

Nonbusiness Income We've said nonbusiness income is all income except business income. Here are common types of nonbusiness income, and the rules for allocating them to specific states:[38]

- Allocate interest and dividends to the state of commercial domicile (except interest on working capital, which is business income).
- Allocate rental income to the state where the property generating the rental income is located.
- Allocate royalties to the state where the property is used (if the business has nexus in that state; if not, allocate royalties to the state of commercial domicile).
- Allocate capital gains from investment property to the state of commercial domicile.
- Allocate capital gains from selling rental property to the state where the rental property was located.

Example 23-19

Wild West reports nonbusiness income as follows:

Wild West			
	Idaho	**Tennessee**	
Dividends	$ 6,000	$ 6,000	From Example 23-14.
Interest	14,505	19,505	From Example 23-14.
Rental income	18,000	18,000	From Example 23-14.
Allocable total	$38,505	$43,505	

Wild West's commercial domicile is in Idaho. Its rental income is for real property located in Wyoming. To which state(s) should the firm allocate its nonbusiness income?

Answer: Wild West should allocate its nonbusiness income as follows:

Wild West		
Idaho	$20,505	$6,000 dividends + $14,505 interest income.
Nevada	0	
Tennessee	0	
Washington	0	
Wyoming	18,000	Rental income.
Total	$38,505	

State Income Tax Liability

It is relatively easy to calculate a business's state taxable income and state tax after separating business and nonbusiness income, apportioning business income, and allocating nonbusiness income. Specifically, calculate state taxable income by multiplying business income by the apportionment factor and then adding any nonbusiness income allocated to the state.

---

[38]Multistate Tax Compact, Article IV, Division of Income, Paragraph 4.

Example 23-20

What if: Assume Idaho and Tennessee have a flat income tax rate of 7.6 percent and 6.5 percent, respectively. What is Wild West's income tax liability for Idaho and Tennessee?

Answer: Its liabilities are $2,963 and $699 in Idaho and Tennessee, respectively, computed as follows:

Description	Idaho	Tennessee	Explanation
(1) State tax base	$ 97,685	$109,989	Example 23-14.
(2) Allocable income	$(38,505)	$ (43,505)	Example 23-19.
(3) Business income	$ 59,180	$ 66,484	(1) – (2).
(4) Apportionment factor	31.23%	16.18%	Example 23-18.
(5) Apportioned income	$ 18,482	$ 10,757	(3) × (4).
(6) Allocable income	$ 20,505	$ 0	Example 23-19.
(7) State taxable income	$ 38,987	$ 10,757	(5) + (6).
(8) Tax rate	7.6%	6.5%	
Tax liability	$ 2,963	$ 699	(7) × (8).

THE KEY FACTS

Dividing Income among States with Nexus

- Business income is apportioned based on some combination of the following factors:
  - Sales
  - Payroll
  - Property
- Nonbusiness income is allocated.
  - Investment income is allocated to the state of commercial domicile.
  - Rents and royalties are generally allocated to the state where the property is used.

Non (Net) Income-Based Taxes

Several states have nonincome-based taxes. Washington has the Business & Occupation Tax, which is a gross receipts tax. Texas has the Margin Tax (many states are treating the Texas Margin Tax as a tax based on net income), the lesser of a gross margin tax or gross receipts tax. As we discussed earlier, Public Law 86-272 doesn't apply to nexus for nonincome-based taxes such as gross receipts taxes or property taxes; these are deductible for calculating taxable income for net income-based taxes.

Example 23-21

Wild West has nexus in Washington and is subject to that state's business and occupation (B&O) tax. The tax is .471 percent of gross receipts for retailers and 1.5 percent of gross receipts on services. Wild West's gross receipts from retail sales and services are $41,982 and $377,441, respectively (from Exhibit 23-1). Calculate Wild West's B&O tax.

Answer: Wild West's B&O tax is $5,860, calculated as follows:

Activity	(1) Receipts	(2) Rate	(1) × (2) Tax
Retailing	$ 41,982	0.471%	$ 198
Services	377,441	1.500	5,662
B&O tax			$5,860

CONCLUSION

In this chapter we discussed the fundamentals of state and local taxation with an emphasis on nexus, sales and use tax, and net income-based corporate taxes. State and local taxes currently make up a significant portion of many businesses' total tax burden and also consume a significant portion of the tax department's time.

Sales and use tax nexus is established through physical presence. Companies selling tangible personal property must collect sales tax from their customers (where nexus exists) and remit it to the various states. Income tax nexus requirements vary based on the type of goods or services provided by a business. Tangible personal property sales are protected from income tax nexus by Public Law 86-272 if certain criteria are met. For all other sales, nexus is created by physical presence, although some states are defining the concept of income tax nexus based on economic rather than physical presence.

Businesses subject to multijurisdictional taxation—taxation by more than one government—have many issues in common. A business located in San Diego, California, but also doing business in Tucson, Arizona, will be subject to California and Arizona tax. If it also does business in Rosarito, Mexico, it will be subject to both U.S. and Mexico taxes. State and local taxation and international taxation bring up many of the same issues. For both, businesses must determine which jurisdiction has the right to tax a transaction (nexus) and determine how to divide income among different jurisdictions. The next chapter examines multinational taxation.

Summary

LO 23-1 Describe the primary types of state and local taxes.

- The primary purpose of state and local taxes is to raise revenue.
- Like federal tax law, state tax law is composed of legislative, administrative, and judicial law.
- Judicial law plays a more important role in state tax law than federal tax law because constitutionality is a primary concern for state tax laws.
- The most important question any taxpayer must answer is whether it is subject to a state's taxing regime.
- Nexus is the connection between a business and a state sufficient to subject the business to the state's tax system.
- When a business sells tangible personal property, either sales or use tax is due. If the seller has nexus, the seller must collect and remit the tax to the state. Otherwise, the buyer is responsible for paying the use tax.
- Businesses engaged in interstate commerce that have nexus must pay income tax.

LO 23-2 Determine whether a business has sales and use tax nexus and calculate its sales tax withholding responsibilities.

- Forty-five states and the District of Columbia impose sales and use taxes.
- The items subject to sales and use tax vary from state to state.
- Businesses are required to collect sales tax on sales only if they have sales and use tax nexus with that state.
- For nondomiciliary businesses, sales and use tax nexus is created through a physical presence (having salespeople or tangible property within the state, for example).

LO 23-3 Identify whether a business has income tax nexus and determine its state income tax liabilities.

- Forty-six states impose an income tax on corporations, and 43 states tax the owners of partnerships and S corporations.
- Businesses must pay income tax in their state of commercial domicile, and nondomiciliary firms are subject to tax if they have nexus in the state.
- Businesses divide or apportion their income among the states where they have established nexus.
- Nexus requirements vary based on the nature of the business's activities: physical presence creates income tax nexus for service providers, sellers of real property, and businesses licensing intangibles; Public Law 86-272 protects solicitation of tangible personal property from nexus.
- Some states require a separate income tax return for each entity with nexus, and others require a unitary (a single) tax return for a group of related entities as long as one of the entities has established nexus in the state.

- Businesses must calculate state taxable income for each state in which they must file a tax return—this requires businesses to identify federal/state adjustments.
- Firms adjust federal taxable income to arrive at their state taxable base.
- The state taxable base of an interstate business is separated into business and nonbusiness income: business income is apportioned across states using a general formula, and nonbusiness income is allocated to specific states using specific rules.
- Business income is apportioned using some variation of sales, payroll, and property factors.

KEY TERMS

allocation (23-4)	nexus (23-2)	state tax base (23-4)
apportionment (23-4)	nonbusiness income (23-4)	throwback rule (23-19)
business income (23-4)	nondomiciliary business (23-2)	trade show rule (23-12)
commercial domicile (23-2)	Public Law 86-272 (23-10)	unitary tax return (23-15)
economic nexus (23-14)	sales tax (23-3)	use tax (23-4)
federal/state adjustments (23-17)	separate tax return (23-15)	
interstate commerce (23-4)	solicitation (23-11)	

DISCUSSION QUESTIONS

Discussion Questions are available in *Connect*®.

connect

1. Why do states and local jurisdictions assess taxes? `LO 23-1`
2. Compare and contrast the relative importance of judicial law to state and local and federal tax law. `LO 23-1`
3. Describe briefly the nexus concept and explain its importance to state and local taxation. `LO 23-1`
4. What is the difference, if any, between the state of a business's commercial domicile and its state of incorporation? `LO 23-1`
5. What types of property sales are subject to sales tax and why might a state choose to exclude the sales of certain types of property? `LO 23-1`
6. In what circumstances would a business be subject to income taxes in more than one state? `LO 23-1`
7. Describe how the failure to collect sales tax can result in a larger tax liability for a business than failing to pay income taxes. `LO 23-1`
8. Discuss why restaurant meals, rental cars, and hotel receipts are often taxed at a higher-than-average sales tax rate. `LO 23-2`
9. Compare and contrast general sales and use tax nexus and the new "Amazon" rule creating nexus in New York. `LO 23-2`
10. What is the difference between a sales tax and a use tax? `LO 23-2`
11. Renée operates Scandinavian Imports, a furniture shop in Olney, Maryland, that ships goods to customers in all 50 states. Scandinavian Imports also appraises antique furniture and has recently conducted in-home appraisals in the District of Columbia, Maryland, Pennsylvania, and Virginia. Online appraisals have been done for customers in California, Minnesota, New Mexico, and Texas. Determine where Scandinavian Imports has sales and use tax nexus. `LO 23-2`
12. Web Music, located in Gardnerville, Nevada, is a new online music service that allows inexpensive legal music downloads. Web Music prides itself on having the fastest download times in the industry. It achieved this speed by leasing server space from 10 regional servers dispersed across the country. Discuss where Web Music has sales and use tax nexus. `LO 23-2`
13. Discuss possible reasons why the Commerce Clause was included in the U.S. Constitution. `LO 23-2`

LO 23-2 14. Describe the administrative burden businesses face in collecting sales taxes.

LO 23-3 15. Compare and contrast the rules determining where domiciliary and nondomiciliary businesses must file state income tax returns.

16. Lars operates Keep Flying Incorporated, a used airplane parts business, in Laramie, Wyoming. Lars employs sales agents that visit mechanics in all 50 states to solicit orders. All orders are sent to Wyoming for approval, and all parts are shipped via common carrier. The sales agents are always on the lookout for wrecked, abandoned, or salvage aircraft with rare parts because they receive substantial bonuses for purchasing and salvaging these parts and shipping them to Wyoming. Discuss the states where Keep Flying has income tax nexus.

LO 23-3 17. Explain changes in the U.S. economy that have made Public Law 86-272 partially obsolete. Provide an example of a company that Public Law 86-272 works well for and one that it does not work well for.

LO 23-3 18. Climb Higher is a distributor of high-end climbing gear located in Paradise, Washington. Its sales personnel regularly perform the following activities in an effort to maximize sales:
   - Carry swag (free samples) for distribution to climbing shop employees.
   - Perform credit checks of new customers to reduce delivery time of first order of merchandise.
   - Check customer inventory for proper display and proper quantities.
   - Accept returns of defective goods.

   Identify which of Climb Higher's sales activities are protected and unprotected from nexus under the *Wrigley* Supreme Court decision.

LO 23-3 19. Describe a situation in which it would be advantageous for a business to establish income tax nexus in a state.

LO 23-3 20. States are arguing for economic nexus; provide at least one reason for and one against the validity of economic nexus.

LO 23-3 21. Explain the difference between separate-return states and unitary-return states.

LO 23-3 22. Explain the rationale for the factors (functional integration, centralization of management, and economies of scale) that determine whether two or more businesses form a unitary group under the *Mobil* decision.

LO 23-3 23. Compare and contrast the reasons why book/tax and federal/state adjustments are necessary for interest income.

LO 23-3 24. Compare and contrast the ways a multistate business divides business and nonbusiness income among states.

LO 23-3 25. Contrast the treatment of government sales and dock sales for the sales apportionment factor.

LO 23-3 26. Most states have increased the weight of the sales factor for the apportionment of business income. What are some possible reasons?

LO 23-3 27. Compare and contrast federal/state tax differences and book/federal tax differences.

PROBLEMS

Select problems are available in *Connect*®.   ▦ **connect**

LO 23-2 28. Crazy Eddie Incorporated manufactures baseball caps and distributes them across the northeastern United States. The firm is incorporated and headquartered in New York and sells to customers in Connecticut, Delaware, Massachusetts, New Jersey, New York, Ohio, and Pennsylvania. It has sales reps only where discussed in the scenarios below. Determine the states in which Crazy Eddie has sales and use tax nexus given the following:

a) Crazy Eddie is incorporated and headquartered in New York. It also has property, employees, salespeople, and intangibles in New York.

b) Crazy Eddie has a warehouse, personal property, and employees in Connecticut.

c) Crazy Eddie has two customers in Delaware. Crazy Eddie receives orders over the phone and ships goods to its Delaware customers using FedEx.

d) Crazy Eddie has independent sales representatives in Massachusetts who distribute baseball-related items for over a dozen companies.

e) Crazy Eddie has salespeople who visit New Jersey. They follow procedures that comply with Public Law 86-272 by sending orders to New York for acceptance. The goods are shipped to New Jersey by FedEx.

f) Crazy Eddie provides graphic design services to another manufacturer located in Ohio. While the services are performed in New York, Crazy Eddie's designers visit Ohio at least quarterly to deliver the new designs and receive feedback.

g) Crazy Eddie receives online orders from its Pennsylvania clients. Because the orders are so large, the goods are delivered weekly on Crazy Eddie's trucks.

29. Brad Carlton operates Carlton Collectibles, a rare-coin shop in Washington, D.C., that ships coins to collectors in all 50 states. Carlton also provides appraisal service upon request. During the last several years the appraisal work has been done either in the D.C. shop or at the homes of private collectors in Maryland and Virginia. Determine the jurisdictions in which Carlton Collectibles has sales and use tax nexus.   `LO 23-2`

30. Melanie operates Mel's Bakery in Foxboro, Massachusetts, with retail stores in Connecticut, Maine, Massachusetts, New Hampshire, and Rhode Island. Mel's also ships specialty breads nationwide upon request. Determine Mel's sales tax collection responsibility and calculate the sales tax liability for Massachusetts, Connecticut, Maine, New Hampshire, Rhode Island, and Texas, using the following information: `LO 23-2`

a) The Massachusetts stores earn $500,000 in sales. Massachusetts's sales tax rate is 5 percent; assume it exempts food items.

b) The Connecticut retail stores have $400,000 in sales ($300,000 from in-store sales and $100,000 from catering) and $10,000 in delivery charges for catering activities. Connecticut sales tax is 6 percent and excludes food products but taxes prepared meals (catering). Connecticut also imposes sales tax on delivery charges on taxable sales.

c) Mel's Maine retail store has $250,000 of sales ($200,000 for take-out and $50,000 of in-store sales). Maine has a 5 percent sales tax rate and a 7 percent sales tax rate on prepared food; it exempts other food purchases.

d) The New Hampshire retail stores have $250,000 in sales. New Hampshire is one of five states with no sales tax. However, it has a room and meals tax rate of 8 percent. New Hampshire considers any food or beverage served by a restaurant for consumption on or off the premises to be a meal.

e) Mel's Rhode Island stores earn $300,000 in sales. The Rhode Island sales tax rate is 7 percent and its restaurant surtax is 1 percent. Rhode Island considers Mel's a restaurant because its retail store has seating.

f) One of Mel's best customers relocated to Texas, which imposes an 8.25 percent state and local sales tax rate but exempts bakery products. This customer entertains guests regularly and ordered $5,000 of food items this year.

31. Cuyahoga County, Ohio, has a sales tax rate of 7.75 percent. Determine the state, local, and transit (a local transportation district) portions of the rate. You can find resources on the State of Ohio Web site, including the following link: http://www.tax.ohio.gov/portals/0/tax_analysis/tax_data_series/sales_and_use/ salestaxmapcolor.pdf   `LO 23-2`

 research

LO 23-2   32. Kai operates the Surf Shop in Laie, Hawaii, which designs, manufacturers, and customizes surfboards. Hawaii has a 4 percent excise tax rate, technically paid by the seller. However, the state also allows "tax on tax" to be charged, which effectively means a customer is billed 4.166 percent of the sales price. Determine the sales and use tax the Surf Shop must collect and remit—or that the customer must pay—for each of the following orders:

a) Bronco, a Utah customer, places an Internet order for a $1,000 board that will be shipped to Provo, Utah, where the local sales tax rate is 6.25 percent.

b) Nick, an Alabama resident, comes to the retail shop on vacation and has a $2,000 custom board made. Nick uses the board on vacation and then has the Surf Shop ship it to Tuscaloosa, Alabama, where the sales tax rate is 8.5 percent.

c) Brady, a Michigan resident, places an order for a $2,000 custom board at the end of his vacation. Upon completion, the board will be shipped to Ann Arbor, Michigan, where the sales tax rate is 7 percent.

d) Bo, a Nebraska resident, sends his current surfboard to the Surf Shop for a custom paint job. The customization services come to $800. The board is shipped to Lincoln, Nebraska, where the sales tax rate is 7 percent.

LO 23-2

33. Last year, Reggie, a Los Angeles, California, resident, began selling autographed footballs through Trojan Victory (TV) Incorporated, a California corporation. TV has never collected sales tax. Last year it had sales as follows: California ($100,000), Arizona ($10,000), Oregon ($15,000), New York ($50,000), and Wyoming ($1,000). Most sales are made over the Internet and shipped by common carrier. Determine how much sales tax should TV have collected in each of the following situations:

a) California treats the autographed football as tangible personal property subject to an 8.25 percent sales tax rate. Answer for California.

b) California treats the autographed football as part tangible personal property ($50,000) and part services ($50,000), and tangible personal property is subject to an 8.25 percent sales tax rate. Answer for California.

c) TV has no property or other physical presence in New York (10.25 percent) or Wyoming (5 percent). Answer for New York and Wyoming.

d) TV has Reggie deliver a few balls to fans in Arizona (5.6 percent sales tax rate) and Oregon (no sales tax) while attending football games there. Answer for Arizona and Oregon.

e) Related to part (d), can you make any suggestions that would decrease TV's Arizona sales tax liability?

LO 23-2   34. LeMond Incorporated, a Wisconsin corporation, runs bicycle tours in several states. LeMond also has a Wisconsin retail store and an Internet store that ships to out-of-state customers. The bicycle tours operate in Colorado, North Carolina, and Wisconsin, where LeMond has employees and owns and uses tangible personal property. LeMond has real property only in Wisconsin and logs the following sales:

LeMond Sales			
State	Goods	Services	Total
Arizona	$ 34,194	$ 0	$ 34,194
California	110,612	0	110,612
Colorado	25,913	356,084	381,997
North Carolina	16,721	225,327	242,048
Oregon	15,431	0	15,431
Wisconsin	241,982	877,441	1,119,423
Totals	$444,853	$1,458,852	$1,903,705

Assume the following tax rates: Arizona (5.6 percent), California (7.75 percent), Colorado (8 percent), North Carolina (6.75 percent), Oregon (8 percent), and Wisconsin (8.5 percent). How much sales and use tax must LeMond collect and remit?

35. Kashi Corporation is the U.S. distributor of fencing (sword fighting) equipment imported from Europe. It is incorporated in Virginia and headquartered in Arlington, Virginia; it ships goods to all 50 states. Kashi's employees attend regional and national fencing competitions where they maintain temporary booths to market their goods. Determine whether Kashi has income tax nexus in the following situations:

    LO 23-3

    planning

    a) Kashi is incorporated and headquartered in Virginia. It also has property, employees, salespeople, and intangibles in Virginia. Determine whether Kashi has nexus in Virginia.

    b) Kashi has employees who live in Washington, D.C., and Maryland but perform all their employment-related activities in Virginia. Does Kashi have nexus in Washington, D.C., and Maryland?

    c) Kashi has two customers in North Dakota. It receives their orders over the phone and ships goods to them using FedEx. Determine whether Kashi has nexus in North Dakota.

    d) Kashi has independent sales representatives in Illinois who distribute fencing and other sports-related items for many companies. Does Kashi have nexus in Illinois?

    e) Kashi has salespeople who visit South Carolina for a regional fencing competition for a total of three days during the year. They send all orders to Virginia for credit approval and acceptance, and Kashi ships the goods into South Carolina by FedEx. Determine whether Kashi has nexus in South Carolina.

    f) Kashi has sales reps who visit California for a national fencing competition and several regional competitions for a total of 17 days during the year. They send all orders to Virginia for credit approval and acceptance. The goods are shipped by FedEx into California. Does Kashi have nexus in California?

    g) Kashi receives online orders from its Pennsylvania client. Because the orders are so large, the goods are delivered weekly on Kashi's trucks. Does Kashi have nexus in Pennsylvania?

    h) In addition to shipping goods, Kashi provides fencing lessons in Virginia and Maryland locations. Determine whether Kashi has nexus in Virginia and Maryland.

    i) Given that Kashi ships to all 50 states, are there locations that would decrease Kashi's overall state income tax burden if nexus were created there?

36. Gary Holt LLP provides tax and legal services regarding the tax-exempt bond issues of state and local jurisdictions. Gary typically provides the services from his New York offices. However, for large issuances he and his staff occasionally travel to another state to complete the work. Determine whether the firm has income tax nexus in the following situations:

    LO 23-3

    a) Gary Holt LLP is a New York partnership and headquartered in New York. It also has property and employees in New York. Does it have income tax nexus in New York?

    b) Gary Holt LLP has employees who live in New Jersey and Connecticut and perform all their employment-related activities in New York. Does it have income tax nexus in New Jersey and/or Connecticut?

    c) Gary Holt LLP has two customers in California. Gary personally travels there to finalize the Alameda County bond issuance. Does it have income tax nexus in California?

LO 23-3   37. Root Beer Inc. (RBI) is incorporated and headquartered in Seattle, Washington. RBI runs an Internet business, makerootbeer.com, and sells bottling equipment and other supplies for making homemade root beer. It also has an Oregon warehouse from which it ships goods. Determine whether RBI has income tax nexus in the following situations:

   a) Root Beer is incorporated and headquartered in Washington and has property and employees in Oregon and Washington. Determine whether RBI has nexus in Oregon and Washington.

   b) Root Beer has hundreds of customers in California but no physical presence (no employees or property). Does it have nexus in California?

   c) Root Beer has 500 New York customers but no physical presence (no employees or property). Remember New York has the new Amazon rule. Determine whether RBI has nexus in New York.

LO 23-3   38. Rockville Enterprises manufactures woodworking equipment and is incorporated and based in Evansville, Indiana. Its real property is all in Indiana. Rockville employs a large sales force that travels throughout the United States. Determine whether each of the following is a protected activity in nondomiciliary states under Public Law 86-272:

   a) Rockville advertises in Wisconsin using television, radio, and newspapers.

   b) Rockville's employees in Illinois check the credit of potential customers.

   c) Rockville maintains a booth at an industry tradeshow in Arizona for 10 days.

   d) Sales representatives check the inventory of a Tennessee customer to make sure it has enough in stock and that the stock is properly displayed.

   e) Rockville holds a management seminar executive retreat for corporate executives over four days in Florida.

   f) Sales representatives supervise the repossession of inventory from a customer in Maine that is not making payments on time.

   g) Rockville provides automobiles to Idaho and Montana sales representatives.

   h) An Alabama sales representative accepts a customer deposit on a large order.

   i) Colorado sales reps carry display racks and promotional materials that they place in customers' retail stores without charge.

LO 23-3
research   39. Software Incorporated is a sales and use tax software vendor that provides customers with a license to download and use its software on their machines. Software retains ownership of the software. It has customers in New Jersey and West Virginia. Does Software have economic nexus in these states because of the following decisions: *Lanco, Inc. v. Director, Division of Taxation,* NJ Sup. Ct., Dkt. No.A-89-05 (2006), and *Tax Commissioner of West Virginia v. MBNA America Bank, N.A.,* 640 SE 2d 226 (WV 2006)?

LO 23-3
research   40. Peter Inc., a Kentucky corporation, owns 100 percent of Suvi Inc., a Mississippi corporation. Peter and Suvi file a consolidated federal tax return. Peter has income tax nexus in Kentucky and South Carolina; Suvi in Mississippi and South Carolina. Kentucky, Mississippi, and South Carolina are separate-return states. In which states must Pete and Suvi file tax returns? Can they file a consolidated return in any states? Explain. (Hint: Use South Carolina Form SC 1120 and the related instructions.)

LO 23-3
research   41. Use California Publication 1061 (2013) to identify the various tests California uses to determine whether two or more entities are part of a unitary group.

42. Bulldog Incorporated is a Georgia corporation. It properly included, deducted, or excluded the following items on its federal tax return in the current year:

Item	Amount	Federal Treatment
Georgia income taxes	$25,496	Deducted on federal return.
Tennessee income taxes	13,653	Deducted on federal return.
Washington gross receipts tax	3,105	Deducted on federal return.
Georgia bond interest income	10,000	Excluded from federal return.
Federal T-note interest income	4,500	Included on federal return.
Domestic production activities deduction (DPAD)	15,096	Deducted on federal return.

LO 23-3

research

tax forms

Use Georgia's Corporate Income Tax Form 600 and Instructions to determine what federal/state adjustments Bulldog needs to make for Georgia. Bulldog's federal taxable income was $194,302. Calculate its Georgia state tax base. Complete Schedule 1, Page 1, of Form 600 for Bulldog.

43. Herger Corporation does business in California, Nevada, and Oregon, and has nexus in these states as well. Herger's California state tax base was $921,023 after making the required federal/state adjustments. Herger's federal tax return contains the following items:

LO 23-3

Item	Amount
Federal T-note interest income	$ 5,000
Nevada municipal bond interest income	3,400
California municipal bond interest income	6,000
Interest expense related to T-note interest income	1,400
Royalty income	100,000
Travel expenses	9,025

Determine Herger's business income.

44. Bad Brad sells used semi-trucks and tractor trailers in the Texas panhandle. Bad Brad has sales as follows:

LO 23-3

Bad Brad	
State	Sales
Colorado	$ 234,992
Oklahoma	402,450
New Mexico	675,204
Texas	1,085,249
Totals	$2,397,895

Bad Brad is a Texas corporation. Answer the questions in each of the following alternative scenarios.

a) Bad Brad has nexus in Colorado, Oklahoma, New Mexico, and Texas. What are the Colorado, Oklahoma, New Mexico, and Texas sales apportionment factors?

b) Bad Brad has nexus in Colorado and Texas. Oklahoma and New Mexico sales are shipped from Texas (a throwback state). What are the Colorado and Texas sales apportionment factors?

c) Bad Brad has nexus in Colorado and Texas. Oklahoma and New Mexico sales are shipped from Texas (a throwback state); $200,000 of Oklahoma sales were to the federal government. What are the Colorado and Texas sales apportionment factors?

d) Bad Brad has nexus in Colorado and Texas. Oklahoma and New Mexico sales are shipped from Texas (assume Texas is a nonthrowback state). What are the Colorado and Texas sales apportionment factors?

LO 23-3   45. Nicole's Salon, a Louisiana corporation, operates beauty salons in Arkansas, Louisiana, and Tennessee. These salons' payrolls by state are as follows:

Nicole's Salon	
State	**Payroll**
Arkansas	$ 130,239
Louisiana	309,192
Tennessee	723,010
Total	$1,162,441

What are the payroll apportionment factors for Arkansas, Louisiana, and Tennessee in each of the following alternative scenarios?

a) Nicole's Salon has nexus in Arkansas, Louisiana, and Tennessee.

b) Nicole's Salon has nexus in Arkansas, Louisiana, and Tennessee, but $50,000 of the Arkansas amount is paid to independent contractors.

LO 23-3   46. Delicious Dave's Maple Syrup, a Vermont corporation, has property in the following states:

Property		
State	**Beginning**	**Ending**
Maine	$ 923,032	$ 994,221
Massachusetts	103,311	203,109
New Hampshire	381,983	283,021
Vermont	873,132	891,976
Total	$2,281,458	$2,372,327

What are the property apportionment factors for Maine, Massachusetts, New Hampshire, and Vermont in each of the following alternative scenarios?

a) Delicious Dave's has nexus in each of the states.

b) Delicious Dave's has nexus in each of the states, but the Maine total includes $400,000 of investment property that Delicious rents out (unrelated to its business).

c) Delicious Dave's has nexus in each of the states, but also pays $50,000 to rent property in Massachusetts.

LO 23-3   47. Susie's Sweet Shop has the following sales, payroll, and property factors:

	Iowa	Missouri
Sales	69.20%	32.01%
Payroll	88.00	3.50
Property	72.42	24.04

What are Susie's Sweet Shop's Iowa and Missouri apportionment factors under each of the following alternative scenarios?

a) Iowa and Missouri both use a three-factor apportionment formula.

b) Iowa and Missouri both use a four-factor apportionment formula that double-weights sales.

c) Iowa uses a three-factor formula and Missouri uses a single-factor apportionment formula (based solely on sales).

48. Brady Corporation is a Nebraska corporation, but owns business and investment property in surrounding states as well. Determine the state where each item of income is allocated.   `LO 23-3`

    a) $15,000 of dividend income.

    b) $10,000 of interest income.

    c) $15,000 of rental income for South Dakota property.

    d) $20,000 of royalty income for intangibles used in South Dakota (where nexus exists).

    e) $24,000 of royalty income from Kansas (where nexus does not exist).

    f) $15,000 of capital gain from securities held for investment.

    g) $30,000 of capital gain on real property located in South Dakota.

49. Ashton Corporation is headquartered in Pennsylvania and has a state income tax base there of $500,000. Of this amount, $50,000 was nonbusiness income. Ashton's Pennsylvania apportionment factor is 42.35 percent. The nonbusiness income allocated to Pennsylvania was $32,000. Assuming a Pennsylvania corporate tax rate of 8.25 percent, what is Ashton's Pennsylvania state tax liability?   `LO 23-3`

COMPREHENSIVE PROBLEMS

Select problems are available in *Connect*®.

50. Do you know what cloud computing is? Cloud computing is the use of hosted computer facilities through the Internet. Gmail, RIA Checkpoint, and even your iPhone are some applications of cloud computing.   **research**

    a) If HP provides a customized bundle of servers, storage, network and security software, and business application software to a customer in Washington State, how is it taxed?

    b) Is HP leasing tangible personal property, which is taxable, or providing a nontaxable service?

    c) Is the buyer of HP's product subject to Washington sales and use tax?

    d) Is HP subject to Washington's B&O tax?

51. Sharon Inc. is headquartered in State X and owns 100 percent of Carol, Josey, and Janice Corps., which form a single unitary group. Assume sales operations are within the solicitation bounds of Public Law 86-272. Each of the corporations has operations in the following states:

Domicile State	Sharon Inc. State X (throwback)	Carol Corp. State Y (throwback)	Josey Corp. State Z (nonthrowback)	Janice Corp. State Z (nonthrowback)
Dividend income	$ 1,000	$ 200	$ 300	$ 500
Business income	50,000	30,000	10,000	10,000
Sales: State X	70,000	10,000	10,000	10,000
State Y		40,000	5,000	
State Z		20,000	20,000	10,000
State A	20,000			
State B	10,000			10,000
Property: State X	50,000	20,000		10,000
State Y		80,000		
State Z			25,000	20,000
State A	50,000			
Payroll: State X	10,000	10,000		
State Y		40,000		
State Z			3,000	10,000
State A				10,000

Compute the following for State X assuming a tax rate of 15 percent.

a) Calculate the State X apportionment factor for Sharon Inc., Carol Corp., Josey Corp., and Janice Corp.

b) Calculate the business income apportioned to State X.

c) Calculate the taxable income for State X for each company.

d) Determine the tax liability for State X for the entire group.

52. Happy Hippos (HH) is a manufacturer and retailer of New England crafts headquartered in Camden, Maine. HH provides services and has sales, employees, property, and commercial domicile as follows:

Happy Hippos In-State Activities					
State	**Sales**	**Employees**	**Property**	**Services**	**Commercial Domicile**
Connecticut	✓	✓		✓	
Maine	✓	✓	✓	✓	✓
Massachusetts	✓	✓			
New Hampshire	✓				
Rhode Island	✓	✓			
Vermont	✓	✓	✓	✓	

HH's sales of goods and services by state are as follows:

Happy Hippos Sales			
State	**Goods**	**Services**	**Total**
Connecticut	$ 78,231	$ 52,321	$130,552
Maine	292,813	81,313	374,126
Massachusetts	90,238		90,238
New Hampshire	129,322		129,322
Rhode Island	98,313		98,313
Vermont	123,914	23,942	147,856
Totals	$812,831	$157,576	$970,407

HH has federal taxable income of $282,487 for the current year. Included in federal taxable income are the following income and deductions:

- $12,000 of Vermont rental income.
- City of Orono, Maine, bond interest of $10,000.
- $10,000 of dividends.
- $2,498 of state tax refund included in income.
- $32,084 of state net income tax expense.
- $59,234 of federal depreciation.

Maine state depreciation for the year was $47,923, and Maine doesn't allow deductions for state net income taxes.

The employees present in Connecticut, Massachusetts, and Rhode Island are salespeople who perform only activities protected by Public Law 86-272.

Each of the states is a separate-return state.

HH's payroll is as follows:

Payroll	
State	**Wages**
Connecticut	$ 94,231
Maine	392,195
Massachusetts	167,265
Rhode Island	92,391
Vermont	193,923
Total	$940,005

HH's property is as follows:

Property			
State	**Beginning**	**Ending**	**Rented**
Maine	$ 938,234	$ 937,652	
Vermont	329,134	428,142	$12,000
Total	$1,267,368	$1,365,794	$12,000

a) Determine the states in which HH has sales and use tax nexus.

b) Calculate the sales tax HH must remit assuming the following sales tax rates:

   • Connecticut (6 percent)
   • Maine (8 percent)
   • Massachusetts (7 percent)
   • New Hampshire (8.5 percent)
   • Rhode Island (5 percent)
   • Vermont (9 percent)

c) Determine the states in which HH has income tax nexus.

d) Determine HH's state tax base for Maine, assuming federal taxable income of $282,487.

e) Calculate business and nonbusiness income.

f) Determine HH's Maine apportionment factors using the three-factor method (assume that Maine is a throwback state).

g) Calculate HH's business income apportioned to Maine.

h) Determine HH's allocation of nonbusiness income to Maine.

i) Determine HH's Maine taxable income.

j) Calculate HH's Maine net income tax liability assuming a Maine income tax rate of 5 percent.

chapter
24 The U.S. Taxation of Multinational Transactions

Learning Objectives

Upon completing this chapter, you should be able to:

LO 24-1 Understand the basic U.S. framework for taxing multinational transactions and the role of the foreign tax credit limitation.

LO 24-2 Apply the U.S. source rules for common items of gross income and deductions.

LO 24-3 Recall the role of income tax treaties in international tax planning.

LO 24-4 Identify creditable foreign taxes and compute the foreign tax credit limitation.

LO 24-5 Distinguish between the different forms of doing business outside the United States and list their advantages and disadvantages.

LO 24-6 Comprehend the basic U.S. anti-deferral tax regime and identify common sources of subpart F income.

© Jose Luis Pelaez Inc/Blend Images LLC

Storyline Summary

Detroit Doughnut Depot

Privately held company located in Detroit, Michigan. Operated as a C corporation for U.S. tax purposes. Makes and sells fresh baked goods, homemade sandwiches, and premium coffee and tea drinks.

Lily Green
Owner of Detroit Doughnut Depot (3D)

Filing status:	Married filing jointly
Dependents:	Two children
Marginal tax rate:	28 percent

Lily Green was excited about the growth of her coffee and baked goods business since she opened her store in downtown Detroit in 2006. From its humble beginnings, the Detroit Doughnut Depot (3D) had attracted a solid base of loyal customers who appreciated the freshness and organic ingredients that set the company's products apart from its competitors. Many of Lily's customers were commuters from nearby Windsor, Canada. They often asked Lily if she ever considered opening a store in Windsor, where they thought she would find a receptive customer base.

Lily was intrigued by the idea of "going global" with her business, but she knew she needed to find someone to help her understand the U.S. and Canadian income tax implications of expanding her business to Windsor. Her first questions dealt with how and when she would be subject to Canadian tax and whether her Canadian activities also would be subject to U.S. tax.

to be continued . . .

Lily Green is about to join a growing trend of expansion by U.S. businesses into international markets. In 1983, gross receipts of non-U.S. subsidiaries of U.S. multinational corporations totaled approximately $720 billion; by 2013, that number exceeded $7 trillion, an almost tenfold increase.[1] Before-tax profits increased from $57 billion in 1983 to more than $1 trillion in 2013. Companies such as Google Inc. and Apple, Inc. report a significant amount of revenue from international operations. For example, Google Inc. reported revenue from its international operations of $24.8 billion in 2014, approximately 54 percent of its total revenue.[2] Apple, Inc. reported net sales of $233.7 billion in 2015, more than 60 percent of which came from outside the United States.

As dramatic as the outflow of investment from the United States has been, the inflow of investment by non-U.S. businesses and individuals into the United States has been just as impressive. According to the U.S. Bureau of Economic Analysis, the total amount of foreign-owned assets in the United States increased by more than 1,000 percent between 1989 and 2014 to $24.6 trillion.[3] U.S. subsidiaries of non-U.S. companies currently employ 5.8 million Americans.[4] Familiar non-U.S. headquartered companies with large U.S. operations include BP Global (United Kingdom), Toyota Motor Corporation (Japan), Honda Motor Corporation (Japan), Nissan Group (Japan), Nestle S.A. (Switzerland), Sony Corporation (Japan), GlaxoSmithKline PLC (United Kingdom), Volkswagen AG (Germany), Samsung Group (South Korea), BMW AG (Germany), Bridgestone Corporation (Japan), Bayer AG (Germany), and Philips Electronics N.V. (Netherlands).

This chapter provides a basic overview of the U.S. tax consequences related to transactions that span more than one national tax jurisdiction (in our storyline, the United States and Canada). We focus primarily on the U.S. tax rules that apply to **outbound transactions,** where a U.S. person engages in a transaction that occurs outside the United States or involves a non-U.S. person.[5] We also discuss briefly the U.S. tax rules that apply to **inbound transactions,** where a non-U.S. person engages in a transaction that occurs within the United States or involves a U.S. person. Most of the U.S. income tax rules that apply to multinational transactions are found in subchapter N of the Internal Revenue Code (IRC) (§861–§999).

 ## THE U.S. FRAMEWORK FOR TAXING MULTINATIONAL TRANSACTIONS

When a U.S. person engages in a transaction that involves a country outside the United States, there arises the issue as to which tax authority or authorities have jurisdiction (i.e., the legal right) to tax that transaction. All governments (national, state, and local) must adopt a basis on which to claim the right to tax income. The criteria they choose to assert their right to tax a person or transaction is called **nexus.** At the national level, governments most often determine nexus by either the geographic source of the income **(source-based jurisdiction)** or the taxpayer's citizenship or residence **(residence-based jurisdiction).**

Once nexus is established, a government must decide how to allocate and apportion a person's income and expenses to its tax jurisdiction. Under a residence-based approach, a country taxes the worldwide income of the person earning the income.

---

[1]Bureau of Economic Analysis, *U.S. Direct investment Abroad: Financial and Operating Data for U.S. Multinational Companies,* available at www.bea.gov.

[2]As a reference point, Google Inc. reported a *loss* of $42.3 million in 2005 from international operations.

[3]Bureau of Economic Analysis, *U.S. Net International Investment Position: End of Fourth Quarter and Year 2014.* Available at www.bea.gov.

[4]Organization for International Investment, data available at www.ofii.org.

[5]As used in this chapter, a "person" includes an individual, corporation, partnership, trust, estate, or association. Section 7701(a)(1). The "United States," as used in this context, includes only the 50 states and the District of Columbia. §7701(a)(9).

Under a source-based approach, a country taxes only the income earned within its boundaries. When applying a source-based approach, a government must develop source rules to allocate and apportion income and expenses to its jurisdiction. Within the United States, states use apportionment formulas that take into account sales, property, and payroll, or some combination of these factors, to apportion income and expenses to its tax jurisdiction.[6]

Income earned by a citizen or resident of one country that has its source in another country potentially can be taxed by both countries. The country where the taxpayer resides can assert residence-based jurisdiction, whereas the country where the income is earned can apply geographic source-based jurisdiction. To alleviate (mitigate) such double taxation and to promote international commerce, governments often allow their residents a tax credit for foreign income taxes paid on *foreign source* income. National governments also enter into income tax treaties with other national governments to mitigate the double taxation of income earned by residents of one country in the other country. Under a treaty, both countries may agree not to tax income earned within their boundaries by a resident of the other country.

The United States applies both residence-based jurisdiction and source-based jurisdiction in asserting its right to tax income. The U.S. government taxes *citizens* and *residents* on their worldwide income, regardless of source (residence-based jurisdiction).[7] In contrast, the U.S. government only taxes *nonresidents* on income that is "U.S. source" or is connected with the operation of a U.S. trade or business (source-based jurisdiction).

U.S. Taxation of a Nonresident

U.S. source income earned by a nonresident is classified into two categories for U.S. tax purposes: (1) **effectively connected income** (ECI) and (2) **fixed and determinable, annual or periodic income** (FDAP). Income that is effectively connected with a U.S. trade or business is subject to *net taxation* (i.e., gross income minus deductions) at the U.S. graduated tax rates. A nonresident reports such income and related deductions on a U.S. tax return, either a Form 1120F for a corporation or a Form 1040NR for an individual. FDAP income, which generally is passive income such as dividends, interest, rents, or royalties, is subject to a *withholding tax* regime applied to *gross income.* The payor of the FDAP income withholds the tax at the statutory rate (30 percent under U.S. tax law) or less under a treaty arrangement and remits it to the government. The recipient of the FDAP income usually does not have to file a tax return and does not reduce the FDAP income by any deductions. Most countries, including Canada, apply a similar tax regime to U.S. persons earning income within their jurisdiction.[8]

> ### THE KEY FACTS
>
> **Basic Framework for U.S. Taxation of Multinational Transactions**
>
> - The United States taxes citizens and residents on their worldwide income and nonresidents on their U.S. source income.
> - A noncitizen is treated as a U.S. resident for income tax purposes if the individual is a permanent resident (has a green card) or meets a substantial presence test.
> - Nonresident income is characterized as either ECI or FDAP income.
>   - ECI is taxed on a net basis using the U.S. graduated tax rates.
>   - FDAP is taxed on a gross basis through a flat withholding tax.
> - The U.S. allows citizens and residents a tax credit for foreign income taxes paid on foreign source income.
> - The foreign tax credit is limited to the percentage of foreign source taxable income to taxable income times the precredit income tax on total taxable income.

Example 24-1

Lily decided to open a store in Windsor, Canada, from which she will sell baked goods and sandwiches made in her U.S. store and transported daily across the border. She elected to operate the store as a **branch** (an unincorporated division) of Detroit Doughnut Depot (3D) for Canadian tax purposes. Will 3D be subject to tax in Canada on any taxable income it earns through its Windsor store?

Answer: Yes. 3D will have nexus in Canada because it operates a business there (residence-based jurisdiction). As a result, Canada and the Province of Ontario will tax the branch's Canadian-source taxable income. (*continued on page 24-4*)

---

[6]See Chapter 23 for a more thorough discussion of how states apportion income.

[7]The United States is the only country that applies full worldwide taxation based on citizenship as well as residency.

[8]Canada applies a 25 percent withholding tax rate on dividends, rents, and royalties unless reduced under a treaty. Canada does not impose a withholding tax on interest paid to a nonresident dealing at arm's length with the lender.

How will Canada tax 3D's Canadian-source taxable income?

Answer: Canada will apply the appropriate corporate tax rate(s) to the branch's taxable income (gross income less deductions). For 2016, the general Canadian corporate tax rate is a flat 15 percent after abatements. The province of Ontario also will impose an income tax between 4.5 and 11.5 percent on the branch's taxable income.

What if: Assume 3D does not operate a business in Canada but owns 5 percent of the stock in a Canadian company that pays the company a C$100 dividend each year.[9] How will Canada tax 3D on the dividend income it receives from its investment in the stock of a Canadian company?

Answer: Canada will apply a flat withholding tax on the gross amount of the dividend.[10]

Definition of a Resident for U.S. Tax Purposes

An individual who is not a U.S. citizen is characterized for U.S. tax purposes as either a **resident alien** or a **nonresident alien.** An individual becomes a U.S. resident by satisfying one of two tests found in the IRC.[11] Under the first test, sometimes referred to as the *green card test,* an individual is treated as a resident if he or she possesses a permanent resident visa ("green card") at any time during the calendar year. Under the second test, sometimes referred to as the *substantial presence test,* an individual becomes a U.S. resident when he or she is *physically present* in the United States for 31 days or more during the current calendar year, *and* the number of days of physical presence during the current calendar year plus one-third times the number of days of physical presence during the first preceding year plus one-sixth times the number of days of physical presence during the second preceding year equals or exceeds 183 days.[12] As we will discuss later in the chapter, these rules often are modified by treaties between the United States and other countries to limit instances where an individual might be taxed as a resident by more than one country.

As always, there are a number of exceptions to the physical presence test. For example, international students and teachers generally are exempt from the physical presence test for five and two years, respectively. Individuals who are present in the United States during the current year for less than 183 days and who establish that they have a "closer connection" to another country can elect to be exempt from the physical presence test.[13] Other exemptions apply to unexpected medical conditions that arise while an individual is in the United States and to commuters from Canada and Mexico who have a U.S. employer.

The residence of a corporation for U.S. tax purposes generally is determined by the entity's country of incorporation. For example, the parent company of Tyco International plc is incorporated in Ireland, although it is managed in the United States. For U.S. tax purposes, the parent company of Tyco is treated as a nonresident corporation, although its U.S. subsidiaries and U.S. branches are treated as U.S. residents. Some countries, such as the United Kingdom and Ireland, determine a corporation's residence based on where central management of the company is located. The Irish government would treat the parent company of Tyco as a U.S. resident because the company is managed in the United States.

---

[9]The national currency of Canada is the Canadian dollar, abbreviated C$.

[10]Under the U.S.-Canada income tax treaty, the withholding tax on this dividend is 15 percent.

[11]§7701(b).

[12]For purposes of this test, a full day is considered any part of a day.

[13]An individual usually satisfies the closer connection test by demonstrating that he or she has a "tax home" in another country. A "tax home" is defined as the taxpayer's regular place of business or *regular place of abode.*

Example 24-2

What if: Assume for quality control purposes that Lily decided to do all of the baking for her Windsor store in Detroit. Every morning a Windsor employee drives a van to Detroit and picks up the baked goods for sale in Windsor. One of her employees, Stan Lee Cupp, made the two-hour trip on 132 different days during 2016. He was not physically present in the United States prior to 2016. Will Stan be considered a U.S. resident in 2016 applying only the substantial presence test?

Answer: No. Although he is physically present in the United States for more than 30 days in 2016, Stan does not satisfy the 183-day test when applying the formula [132 + (1/3 × 0) + (1/6 × 0) = 132].

What if: Assume Stan continues to be physically present in the United States for 132 days in 2017 and 2018. Will Stan be considered a U.S. resident in 2017 or 2018 applying only the substantial presence test?

Answer:

2017: No. He does not satisfy the 183-day test when applying the formula [132 + (1/3 × 132) + (1/6 × 0) = 176].

2018: Yes. He now satisfies the 183-day test when applying the formula [132 + (1/3 × 132) + (1/6 × 132) = 198].

Does Stan qualify for any exceptions that allow him to avoid being treated as a U.S. resident in 2018?

Answer: Yes. Stan can avoid being a U.S. resident under the closer connection test because he was physically present in the United States for less than 183 days in 2018 and his tax home is in Canada. If Stan is in the United States for 183 days or more, he will have to rely on the U.S.-Canada income tax treaty to avoid being considered a U.S. resident for income tax purposes (to be discussed in more detail later in the chapter).

Overview of the U.S. Foreign Tax Credit System

The United States mitigates the double taxation of foreign source income by allowing citizens and residents to claim a **foreign tax credit** (FTC) for foreign income taxes paid on their *foreign source* income. The goal of the FTC is to keep a U.S. taxpayer's worldwide *effective tax rate* (total income taxes paid/taxable income) from exceeding the U.S. statutory tax rate. The United States attempts to achieve this result through the **foreign tax credit limitation,** which is computed as follows:

$$\frac{\text{Foreign source taxable income}}{\text{Total taxable income}} \times \text{Precredit U.S. tax on total taxable income}$$

Currently, the foreign tax credit limitation is computed separately for two categories of foreign source income—passive category income and general category income. (Special rules apply to income resourced by treaty and income earned in designated countries.) We discuss the type of income put in each category in more detail later in this chapter. A taxpayer can carry any unused (excess) FTC for the current year back to the previous tax year and then forward to the next ten future tax years.

Example 24-3

Lily's store in Windsor was an immediate success and reported taxable income on its Canadian operations of C$20,000 for 2016. 3D paid a combined national and provincial income tax of C$5,000 on its taxable income. Because 3D operates the Windsor store as a branch, it also must report the income on its U.S. corporate income tax return along with taxable income from its Detroit operations. Assuming a translation rate of C$1:US$1, 3D reports the Canadian taxable income on its U.S. tax return as $20,000 and reports the Canadian income taxes as $5,000. 3D reported U.S. taxable
(continued on page 24-6)

income of $80,000. The company's U.S. income tax on $100,000 of taxable income is $22,250 before any credit for the income taxes paid to Canada (see the corporate tax rate schedule on the inside back cover).

Using the above facts, what is the foreign tax credit limitation that applies to 3D's Canadian income taxes for 2016?

Answer: $4,450, computed as $20,000/$100,000 × $22,250,

where:

$20,000 = Foreign source taxable income
$100,000 = Total taxable income
$22,250 = Precredit U.S. tax on total taxable income

What is 3D's net U.S. tax after subtracting the available foreign tax credit?

Answer: $17,800, computed as $22,250 − $4,450. 3D has an excess foreign tax credit of $550 ($5,000 − $4,450) that it can carry forward for 10 years.

What is 3D's effective tax rate on its total taxable income for 2016?

Answer: 22.8 percent, computed as ($5,000 + $17,800)/$100,000.

What if: Suppose the United States did not give 3D a foreign tax credit or a deduction for the Canadian taxes it paid on the Windsor operations. What would have been 3D's effective tax rate on its total taxable income for 2016?

Answer: 27.25 percent, computed as ($5,000 + $22,250)/$100,000.

What if: Assume 3D earned all of its $100,000 taxable income in the United States and paid no Canadian income taxes. What would have been the company's effective tax rate on its total taxable income for 2016?

Answer: 22.25 percent, computed as $22,250/$100,000.

What if: Assume 3D paid Canadian income taxes of C$4,000 for 2016 (a flat tax rate of 20 percent). What would have been its net U.S. tax after subtracting the available foreign tax credit?

Answer: $18,250, computed as $22,250 − $4,000.

What would have been 3D's effective tax rate on its total taxable income for 2016?

Answer: 22.25 percent, computed as ($4,000 + $18,250)/$100,000. In this example, 3D receives a full credit for the Canadian taxes in 2016 because the Canadian tax rate is less than the average U.S. tax rate. The company's effective tax rate on its total taxable income is the same as if it had earned all of the income in the United States.

LO 24-2   U.S. SOURCE RULES FOR GROSS INCOME AND DEDUCTIONS

Many of the U.S. tax rules that apply to multinational transactions require taxpayers to determine the jurisdictional (geographic) source (U.S. or foreign) of their gross income.[14] The source rules determine whether income and related deductions are from sources within or without the United States. All developed countries have source-of-income rules, although most practitioners consider the U.S. rules to be the most complex in the world.

The U.S. source-of-income rules are important to *non-U.S. persons* because they limit the scope of U.S. taxation to only their U.S. source income. For *U.S. persons,* the primary purpose of the U.S. source-of-income rules is to calculate *foreign source taxable income* in the numerator of the foreign tax credit limitation. The United States imposes a tax on the worldwide income of U.S. persons, regardless of its source or the U.S. person's residence. The United States cedes *primary jurisdiction* to foreign

---

[14]The U.S. federal income tax source rules are found in §861–§865 and the accompanying regulations.

governments to tax U.S. persons on income earned outside the United States while retaining the *residual* right to tax foreign source income to the extent it has not been "fully taxed" by the foreign government. The net result is that the United States taxes foreign source income earned by U.S. persons at a rate that theoretically reflects the difference between the U.S. tax rate and the foreign tax rate imposed on the income.

U.S. persons must understand the source-of-income rules in other situations. For example, U.S. citizens and residents employed outside the United States may be eligible to exclude a portion of their *foreign source earned income* from U.S. taxation under §911.[15] In addition, U.S. persons that pay U.S.-source FDAP income to foreign payees (e.g., interest or dividends) usually are required to withhold U.S. taxes on such payments.[16]

The source-of-income rules are definitional in nature; they do not impose a tax liability, create income, or allow a deduction. Although the primary focus of the source rules is on where the economic activity that generates income takes place, the U.S. government also uses the source rules to advance a variety of international tax policy objectives.

Source of Income Rules

The Internal Revenue Code defines eight classes of gross income from sources within the United States[17] and eight classes of gross income from sources without the United States.[18] A summary of the general rules that apply to common sources of income follows. A detailed discussion of all of the exceptions to these rules is beyond the scope of this text.

Interest   As a general rule, the taxpayer looks to the *residence* of the party *paying* the interest (the borrower) to determine the geographic source of interest received. A borrower's residence is determined at the time the interest is paid. Factors that determine an individual's residence include the location of the individual's family; whether the person buys a home, pays foreign taxes, and becomes involved in social and community affairs; and the length of time spent in a country. Under these general rules, interest income is U.S. source if it is paid by the United States or the District of Columbia, a noncorporate U.S. resident, or a U.S. corporation. Although interest income paid by a U.S. bank to a nonresident (e.g., an international student attending your university) is U.S.-source income, such interest is exempt from U.S. withholding or other income taxation.[19] This exception is designed to attract foreign capital to U.S. banks.

> ### THE KEY FACTS
> #### Source Rules
> - The source rules determine if income or deductions are treated as U.S. source or foreign source.
> - For a U.S. taxpayer, the source rules primarily determine foreign taxable income in the calculation of the foreign tax credit limitation.
> - For a non-U.S. taxpayer, the source rules determine what income is subject to U.S. taxation.

Example 24-4

3D was dissatisfied with the 1 percent interest rate it received on its checking account at Bank of America in Detroit. Lily's investment adviser suggested the company invest $50,000 in 5-year bonds issued by the Canadian government with an interest rate of 3 percent. During 2016, 3D received C$1,500 in interest from the bonds. Per the U.S.-Canada treaty, the Canadian government did not withhold taxes on the payment. Assume the translation rate is C$1:US$1.

What is the source, U.S. or foreign, of the interest Lily receives on the bonds?

Answer: Foreign source. The source of interest income depends on the residence of the borrower at the time the interest is paid. The Canadian government is considered a resident of Canada for U.S. source rule purposes.

---

[15]If certain conditions are met, a U.S. individual can exclude up to $101,300 of earned income from U.S. taxation in 2016 plus additional earnings equal to excess "foreign housing expenses" under §911.

[16]§1441.

[17]§861(a).

[18]§862(a).

[19]§871(i)(2)(A) and §881(d).

Dividends In general, the source of dividend income is determined by the *residence* of the corporation paying the dividend. Residence usually is determined by the corporation's country of incorporation or organization (in some countries, such as the United Kingdom, a corporation's residence is determined by where its central management is located).

Example 24-5

As part of diversifying its investment portfolio, 3D purchased 200 shares of Scotiabank (Bank of Nova Scotia, Canada). In 2016, Scotiabank paid 3D dividends of C$400. Scotiabank withheld C$60 in taxes (15 percent) on the payment. Assume the translation rate is C$1:US$1.

What is the source, U.S. or foreign, of the dividend 3D receives on the stock?

Answer: Foreign source. The source of dividend income depends on the residence of the payor of the dividend. Scotiabank is headquartered in Toronto, Canada, and is a resident of Canada for U.S. source rule purposes.

Compensation for Services The source of compensation received for "labor or personal services" is determined by the *location* where the service is performed. The IRS and the courts have held that the term includes activities of employees, independent contractors, artists, entertainers, athletes, and even corporations offering "personal services" (e.g., accounting). The Code provides a limited **commercial traveler exception,** in which personal service compensation earned by nonresidents within the U.S. is *not* treated as U.S. source if the individual meets the following criteria:

- The individual was present in the United States for not more than 90 days during the current taxable year;[20]
- Compensation for the services does not exceed $3,000; and
- The services are performed for a nonresident alien, foreign corporation, or foreign partnership or for the foreign office of a domestic corporation.[21]

The United States frequently alters the limitations on length of stay and compensation through treaty agreements. In most cases, the 90-day limit is extended to 183 days, and no dollar limit is put on the amount of compensation received.

Compensation for services performed within and outside the United States must be allocated between U.S. and foreign sources. An individual who receives compensation, other than compensation in the form of fringe benefits, as an employee for labor or personal services performed partly within and partly outside the United States is required to source such compensation on a *time basis*. An individual who receives compensation as an employee for labor or personal services performed partly within and partly outside the United States in the form of fringe benefits (e.g., additional amounts paid for housing or education) is required to source such compensation on a *geographic basis* (i.e., determined by the employee's principal place of work).

Example 24-6

What if: Assume for quality control purposes that Lily decided to do all of the baking for her Windsor store in Detroit. Every morning a Windsor employee would drive a truck to Detroit and pick up the baked goods for sale in Windsor. One of her employees, Stan Lee Cupp, made the 2-hour trip on 120 different days during 2016 (240 hours spent in the U.S.). 3D paid Stan a salary of C$50,000 during 2016. He worked a total of 1,920 hours during 2016. Assume the translation rate is C$1:US$1. How much U.S. source compensation does Stan have in 2016? Base your computation on hours worked.

---

[20]For purposes of this test, a full day is considered to be any part of a day.
[21]§861(a)(3)(A)–(C).

Answer: $6,250 (C$50,000 × 240/1,920 × $1). Stan sources his salary for U.S. tax purposes based on where he performed the services. Using hours worked, Stan spent 12.5 percent of his time performing services in the United States (240/1,920).

Using only the exception found in the IRC, will Stan be subject to U.S. tax on his U.S.-source wages in 2016?

Answer: Yes. Stan fails the commercial traveler exception. He is in the United States for more than 90 days during 2016.

What if: Assume Stan limits his trips to 90 days during 2016 (180 hours spent in the U.S.). Using only the IRC exception, will Stan be subject to U.S. tax on his U.S.-source salary in 2016?

Answer: Yes. Stan still fails the commercial traveler exception. Although he is in the United States for not more than 90 days, his U.S.-source salary is $4,688 (C$50,000 × 180/1,920 × $1), which exceeds $3,000.

As we discuss later in the chapter, the U.S.-Canada income tax treaty significantly liberalizes the commercial traveler exception to allow Stan to spend more time in the U.S. without being taxed by the U.S. government on his U.S. source wages.

TAXES IN THE REAL WORLD Taxing Professional Golfers

One of the issues that the IRS has struggled with is whether to characterize fees paid to foreign professional golf and tennis players pursuant to on-court endorsement contracts (e.g., wearing a company's logo or using its equipment) as income from royalties or income from personal services, or both. Two recent Tax Court cases involving well-known professional golfers illustrate the complexities of this issue.

The first case involved Retief Goosen, a PGA tour member and winner of the 2001 U.S. Open Championship.[1] Mr. Goosen was a citizen of South Africa and a resident of the United Kingdom, but he spent most of his time competing in the United States and Europe.

Mr. Goosen entered into several endorsement and appearance agreements with sponsors that allowed the sponsor to use his name and likeness to advertise and promote the sponsor's products or in connection with advertising and promoting a specific tournament or event. The "on-course" endorsement agreements required him to wear or use the sponsor's products during golf tournaments whereas the "off-course" endorsement agreements did not have this requirement.

Mr. Goosen reported all his prize money from golf tournaments and appearance fees in the United States as "effectively connected" income taxable in the United States. He characterized his endorsement fees from on-course endorsements as 50 percent royalty income and 50 personal services income. He sourced the personal services income from the on-course endorsement fees to the United States based on the number of days he played within the United States over the total number of days he played golf for the year. Mr. Goosen characterized his endorsement fees from the off-course endorsement agreements as 100 percent royalty income. The IRS argued that the sponsors primarily paid Mr. Goosen to perform personal services, which included playing golf and carrying or wearing the sponsors' products.

The Tax Court awarded a partial victory to both parties. The Court found that Mr. Goosen's name had a value beyond his golf skills and abilities for which his sponsors paid a substantial amount of money for the right to use his name and likeness. The sponsors also valued Goosen's play at tournaments, as evidenced by the fact that the sponsors conditioned the full endorsement fee on his playing in 36 tournaments a year. The court thus held that his performance of services and the use of his name and likeness were equally important and characterized 50 percent of the endorsement fees from the on-course endorsement agreements as royalty income and 50 percent of the fees as personal services income.

The Court held that Mr. Goosen's earnings from playing golf in the United States was effectively connected U.S. source income. The

[1] *Reteif Goosen v. Commissioner,* 136 T.C. No. 27 (June 9, 2011).

(continued on page 24-10)

on-course endorsement and appearance fees and his on-course royalty income also were held to be U.S. source effectively connected income to the extent they were sourced as U.S. source income because payment depended on whether he played a specified number of tournaments. Both categories of income were taxed at the regular U.S. graduated tax rates.

The Court held that income Mr. Goosen received from off-course endorsement agreements did not depend on whether he played in golf tournaments. Thus, the income was not effectively connected with a U.S. trade or business and was thus subject to a 30 percent withholding tax to the extent it was treated as U.S. source income.

The second case involved Sergio Garcia, a Spanish citizen but a resident of Switzerland.[2] The IRS again argued that the "vast majority" of his endorsement income should be treated as personal service income and subject to U.S. taxation at the regular tax rates. Mr. Garcia characterized 85 percent of his endorsement income as royalty income, which was not subject to U.S. taxation under the U.S.-Swiss income tax treaty. The Tax Court judge held that 65 percent of the endorsement income should be characterized as royalty income. It is interesting to note that the Tax Court apportioned a higher percentage of Mr. Garcia's income as royalties because he was designated as a "Global Icon" by the golf company that paid him the endorsement fees. The same company regarded Mr. Goosen as a "brand ambassador" and paid him less than Mr. Garcia because the company valued Mr. Garcia's "flash, looks and maverick personality" more than Mr. Goosen's "cool 'Iceman' demeanor."

[2]*Sergio Garcia v. Commissioner,* 140 T.C. No 6 (March 14, 2013).

Rents and Royalties   Rent has its source where the property generating the rent is located. Royalty income has its source where the intangible property or rights generating the royalty are used. Royalties include payments related to intangibles such as patents, copyrights, secret processes and formulas, goodwill, trademarks, trade brands, and franchises. An intangible is "used" in the country that protects the owner against its unauthorized use.

Example 24-7

3D rented its Windsor store for C$2,500 per month, for a total of C$30,000 in 2016. Under the U.S.-Canada income tax treaty, 3D must withhold U.S. taxes at a 30 percent rate on rent payments that flow from the United States to Canada if the rent is U.S.-source income. Will 3D have to withhold taxes on the rent payments it makes in 2016?

Answer: No. The rent is considered foreign source income because the store that is rented is located in Canada.

Gain or Loss from Sale of Real Property   In general, gain or loss from the sale of realty has its source where the property sold is located.

Gain or Loss from Sale of Purchased Personal Property   Under the general rule, gain or loss from the sale of purchased personal (nonrealty) property[22] has its source based on the *seller's residence*. There are many exceptions to this general rule. In particular, gross income (sales minus cost of goods sold) from the sale of purchased *inventory* is sourced where *title passes*. Title is deemed to pass at the time when, and the place where, the seller's rights, title, and interest in the property are transferred to the buyer.

---

[22]Personal property under the source rules includes stock of a corporation. Sales of intangible property such as a patent, copyright, secret process, goodwill, trademark, trade brand, or franchise are subject to different source rules.

Inventory Produced within the United States and Sold Outside the United States (§863 Sales)

Taxable income derived from the production of *inventory* within the United States and the sale of that inventory outside the United States has special apportionment rules found in regulations issued by the U.S. Treasury.[23] These regulations provide taxpayers with three elective methods for apportioning gross income (defined in these regulations as sales minus cost of goods sold) between U.S. and foreign sources, the one most frequently used being the *50/50 method*.

Under the 50/50 method, the taxpayer sources one-half of the gross income from sales based on where the assets that produce the inventory are located and sources the other half based on where title passes to the inventory. Gross income from sales of inventory that is produced in the United States and sold outside the United States, with title passing outside the United States, is sourced 50 percent U.S. source and 50 percent foreign source.

The 50/50 method provides U.S. producers with the opportunity to "create" foreign source income on export sales. This foreign source income generally is not taxed by the country in which the product is sold, unless the U.S. producer has a physical presence in the foreign country. Adding zero-taxed foreign source income to the numerator of the FTC limitation ratio increases the foreign tax credit amount, which is especially helpful when the taxpayer is in an excess foreign tax credit position.

Example 24-8

Return to the facts in Example 24-3. Lily's store in Windsor reported taxable income on its Canadian operations of C$20,000 for 2016. Detroit Doughnut Depot (3D) paid a combined national and provincial income tax of C$5,000 on its taxable income. 3D reported the Canadian taxable income on its U.S. tax return as $20,000 and reported the Canadian income taxes as $5,000. 3D's Detroit operations reported U.S. taxable income of $80,000. 3D's precredit U.S. tax liability was $22,250 on taxable income of $100,000. As computed in Example 24-3, 3D's FTC is limited to $4,450 ($20,000/$100,000 × $22,250), resulting in an excess FTC of $550 in 2016. 3D's tax adviser suggested that the company could eliminate ("absorb") some of the excess credit by selling additional baked goods it produced in Detroit to grocery stores in Windsor, with shipping terms as FOB: Destination (i.e., title to the goods passes in Canada).

What if: Assume 3D is able to generate additional sales in excess of cost of goods sold of C$10,000 by selling more baked goods to Windsor grocery stores in 2016, and the sales qualify as §863(b) sales. Canada does not impose any Canadian tax on the sales because they were not made out of the Windsor store. 3D's taxable income increases to $110,000, and its precredit U.S. tax increases to $26,150. What is 3D's FTC limitation for 2016 under this change in facts?

Answer: $5,943, computed as $25,000/$110,000 × $26,150,

where:

   $25,000 = Foreign source taxable income

   $110,000 = Total taxable income

   $26,150 = Precredit U.S. tax on total taxable income

3D increases the numerator in the FTC limitation ratio by $5,000 (50% × $10,000) because title passes in Canada. The denominator increases by $10,000, the additional taxable income generated by the §863(b) sales. 3D can now claim the entire FTC of $5,000 on its 2016 tax return.

---

[23]The regulations are issued under §863(b), which is what gives these sales their name.

Source of Deduction Rules

After determining the source of gross income as being from U.S. or foreign sources, a taxpayer may be required to **allocate** and **apportion** allowable deductions to gross income from each geographical source to compute taxable income from U.S. and foreign sources. For a U.S. taxpayer, this allocation and apportionment process determines the foreign source deductions that are subtracted from foreign source gross income in computing foreign source taxable income in the numerator of the FTC limitation computation. A non-U.S. taxpayer with gross income that is effectively connected with a U.S. trade or business must determine the U.S. source deductions that are subtracted from U.S. gross income to compute U.S. taxable income.

U.S. and non-U.S. taxpayers can have different motivations in seeking to deduct (or not deduct) expenses from either foreign source or U.S. source gross income. A U.S. taxpayer seeking to maximize the foreign tax credit limitation will want to allocate as few deductions to foreign source gross income as possible, the goal being to make the ratio of foreign source taxable income to total taxable income as close to 100 percent as possible (or whatever ratio is needed to absorb any excess credits). Non-U.S. taxpayers operating in a low-tax-rate country (a tax rate less than the U.S. rate) have a tax incentive to allocate as many deductions to U.S. source income as possible to minimize their U.S. tax liability. Non-U.S. taxpayers operating in a high-tax-rate country (a tax rate greater than the U.S. rate) have a worldwide tax incentive to allocate as many deductions to foreign source income as possible to minimize their worldwide tax liability.

ETHICS

International Contractors, Inc. has been hired by the U.S. government to build roads and bridges in Irock, a country with which the United States recently signed a treaty. To facilitate the issuance of visas and licenses to begin construction, an official from the Irock government asked for 100 "facilitating payments" (otherwise known as "grease payments") of $5,000 each from the company. These payments were customary in Irock and did not violate Irock law. The company intended to deduct the $500,000 payment in its financial statements. It was not clear if these payments violated the Foreign Corrupt Practices Act. To avoid IRS and possible Department of Justice scrutiny, the company's tax director suggested that the payment be described as "taxes and licenses" on the tax return (line 17 of Form 1120) without further details. What do you think of the tax director's advice? What tax and other consequences might result from taking this advice?

General Principles of Allocation and Apportionment   The IRC provides very broad language in describing how to allocate deductions to U.S. and foreign source gross income. The regulations attempt to match deductions with the gross income such deductions were incurred to produce.[24] Matching usually is done based on the "factual relationship" of the deduction to gross income. Deductions that can be directly associated with a particular item of income (e.g., machine depreciation with manufacturing gross profit) are referred to as **definitely related deductions.** Deductions not directly associated with a particular item of gross income (e.g., medical expenses, property taxes, standard deduction) are referred to as **not definitely related deductions** and are allocated to all gross income.

---

[24]Reg. §1.861-8 provides the general rules for allocating and apportioning deductions to U.S. and foreign source gross income.

The regulations require the taxpayer to first allocate (associate) deductions to the class or classes of gross income such deductions were incurred to produce. The taxpayer then apportions the deduction between, in most cases, foreign source and U.S. source gross income. The regulations allow the taxpayer to apportion deductions using a method that reflects the factual relation between the deduction and the grouping of gross income. Examples include units sold, gross sales or receipts, and gross income.

Example 24-9

Return to the facts in Example 24-3. Lily's store in Windsor reported taxable income on its Canadian operations of C$20,000 for 2016. For U.S. tax purposes, foreign source gross income was $25,000. 3D paid a combined national and provincial income tax of C$5,000 on its taxable income (at a flat tax rate of 25 percent). The company reported the $20,000 taxable income on its U.S. corporate income tax return along with $80,000 of taxable income from its Detroit operations. 3D's U.S. income tax on $100,000 of taxable income is $22,250 before any credit for the income taxes paid to Canada. Included in the computation of taxable income was a deduction of $30,000 for advertising that 3D incurred to promote its stores in Detroit and Windsor. 3D elected to apportion the advertising deduction based on sales. For 2016, Detroit sales were $400,000 and Windsor sales were $100,000. How much of the $30,000 advertising deduction does 3D apportion to its foreign source taxable income for FTC purposes?

Answer: $6,000, computed as $100,000/$500,000 × $30,000,

where:

$100,000 = Canadian sales
$500,000 = Total sales
$30,000 = Advertising deduction

Using the above facts, what is the foreign tax credit limitation that applies to 3D's Canadian income taxes for 2016?

Answer: $4,228, computed as ($25,000 − $6,000)/$100,000 × $22,250,

where:

$25,000 = Foreign source gross income
$6,000 = Apportioned advertising deduction
$100,000 = Total taxable income
$22,250 = Precredit U.S. tax on total taxable income

Apportioning some of the advertising deduction to the numerator of 3D's FTC limitation ratio reduces the amount of foreign income taxes that are creditable in 2016.

Special Apportionment Rules Special apportionment rules apply to nine categories of deductions, most notably interest, research and experimentation, state and local income taxes, losses on property disposition, and charitable contributions.[25] These special apportionment rules are very complicated, and the details are beyond the scope of this text. The basic rules for interest expense and research and experimentation are discussed below.

Interest expense is allocated to all gross income using as a basis the assets that generated such income. Interest can be apportioned based on average tax book value or average fair market value for the year. Assets are attributed to income based on the source and type of income they generate, have generated, or may reasonably be

[25]The other deductions are stewardship expenses attributable to dividends received, supportive expenses, net operating losses, and legal and accounting fees.

expected to generate. Taxpayers may switch to the fair market value method at any time, but a switch back to the tax book value method requires permission from the commissioner. A taxpayer using the tax book value method can elect to use the alternative depreciation system on U.S. assets solely for purposes of apportioning interest expense.

Example 24-10

Expanding on the facts in Example 24-9, 3D borrowed $100,000 from Bank of America in Detroit and paid interest expense of $6,000 in 2016. 3D elected to apportion this interest expense between U.S. and foreign source income using average tax book value. 3D's U.S. assets had an average tax book value of $250,000 in 2016, and its foreign assets had an average tax book value of $50,000 in 2016. How much of the $6,000 interest deduction does 3D apportion to its foreign source taxable income for FTC purposes?

Answer: $1,000, computed as $50,000/$300,000 × $6,000,

where:

$50,000 = Average tax book value of Canadian assets

$300,000 = Total average tax book value of all of 3D's assets

$6,000 = Interest expense

Taking into account the apportioned advertising deduction and interest deduction, what is the foreign tax credit limitation that applies to 3D's Canadian income taxes for 2016?

Answer: $4,005, computed as ($25,000 − $6,000 − $1,000)/$100,000 × $22,250,

where:

$25,000 = Foreign source gross income

$6,000 = Apportioned advertising expense

$1,000 = Apportioned interest expense

$100,000 = Total taxable income

$22,250 = Precredit U.S. tax on total taxable income

Allocation of a portion of the interest expense to the numerator of 3D's FTC limitation ratio further reduces the amount of foreign taxes that are creditable in 2016.

Research and experimental (R&E) expenditures must be apportioned between U.S. and foreign source income using either a sales method or a gross income method. Taxpayers can apportion a percentage of R&E based on where the research is conducted. The amount that can be sourced under this exclusive apportionment method is 50 percent if the sales method is elected and 25 percent if the gross income method is elected.

Example 24-11

Expanding on the facts in Example 24-9 and Example 24-10, 3D incurred $8,000 of research and experimentation (R&E) expenses in developing new flavors of doughnuts and coffee. 3D incurred these expenses in its Detroit bakery and deducted the amount in computing its taxable income. 3D elected to apportion this R&E expense between U.S. and foreign source income using the sales method. For 2016, Detroit sales were $400,000 and Windsor sales were $100,000. How much of the $8,000 R&E expense does 3D apportion to its foreign source taxable income for FTC purposes?

Answer: $800, computed as $100,000/$500,000 × $4,000,

where:

$100,000 = Canadian sales

$500,000 = Total sales

$4,000   = R&E expense not exclusively apportioned to U.S. sources

3D apportions 50 percent of the $8,000 to U.S. source taxable income under the exclusive apportionment method. The remaining $4,000 is apportioned between U.S. and foreign source income based on sales.

Taking into account the apportioned advertising deduction, interest expense, and R&E expense, what is the foreign tax credit limitation that applies to 3D's Canadian income taxes for 2016?

Answer: $3,827, computed as ($25,000 − $6,000 − $1,000 − $800)/$100,000 × $22,250,

where:

$25,000   = Foreign source gross income

$6,000   = Apportioned advertising expense

$1,000   = Apportioned interest expense

$800   = Apportioned R&E expense

$100,000 = Total taxable income

$22,250 = Precredit U.S. tax on total taxable income

Allocation of a portion of the R&E expense to the numerator of 3D's FTC limitation ratio further reduces the amount of foreign taxes that are creditable in 2016.

What if: Assume 3D elected to use the gross income method to apportion R&E. For 2016, gross income from Detroit sales was $100,000 and gross income from Windsor sales was $25,000. How much of the $8,000 R&E expense does 3D apportion to its foreign source taxable income for FTC purposes?

Answer: $1,200, computed as $25,000/$125,000 × $6,000,

where:

$25,000 = Foreign source gross income

$125,000 = Total gross income

$6,000 = R&E expense not exclusively apportioned to U.S. sources

3D apportions 25 percent of the $8,000 to U.S. source taxable income under the exclusive apportionment method ($2,000). The remaining $6,000 is apportioned between U.S. and foreign source income based on gross income.

> **THE KEY FACTS**
>
> **Treaties**
>
> - Treaties are designed to encourage cross-border trade by reducing the double taxation of such income by the countries that are party to the treaty.
> - Treaties define when a resident of one country has nexus in the other country.
> - Treaties reduce or eliminate the withholding tax imposed on cross-border payments such as interest, dividends, and royalties.

The foreign tax credit limitation is computed on Form 1118 (corporations) or Form 1116 (individuals). Exhibit 24-1 presents a completed Form 1118 for the cumulative facts in Examples 24-9, 24-10, and 24-11.

TREATIES

LO 24-3

A tax treaty is a bilateral agreement between two contracting countries in which each agrees to modify its own tax laws to achieve reciprocal benefits. The general purpose of an income tax treaty is to eliminate or reduce the impact of double taxation so that residents paying taxes to one country will not have the full burden of taxes in the other country. The United States signed its first income tax treaty with France in 1939. The United States now has income tax treaties with 67 countries.

EXHIBIT 24-1   **Form 1118: Foreign Tax Credit Corporations, Schedules A, B, F, and H for 3D Corporation, cumulative facts from Examples 24-9, 24-10, and 24-11**

Form **1118**
(Rev. December 2014)
Department of the Treasury
Internal Revenue Service

Foreign Tax Credit—Corporations
▶ Information about Form 1118 and its separate instructions is at *www.irs.gov/form1118.*
▶ Attach to the corporation's tax return.

For calendar year 20____ , or other tax year beginning ____ , 20 ____ , and ending ____ , 20 ____

OMB No. 1545-0123

Name of corporation   Employer identification number

Detroit Doughnut Depot

Use a **separate** Form 1118 for each applicable category of income listed below. See **Categories of Income** in the instructions. Also, see **Specific Instructions.** Check only one box on each form.

☐ Passive Category Income
☑ General Category Income
☐ Section 901(j) Income: Name of Sanctioned Country ▶ _____
☐ Income Re-sourced by Treaty: Name of Country ▶ _____

Schedule A   **Income or (Loss) Before Adjustments** *(Report all amounts in U.S. dollars. See **Specific Instructions**.)*

1. Foreign Country or U.S. Possession (Enter two-letter code; see instructions. Use a separate line for each.) *	Gross Income or (Loss) From Sources Outside the United States (*INCLUDE* Foreign Branch Gross Income here *and* on Schedule F)								
	2. Deemed Dividends (see instructions)		3. Other Dividends		4. Interest	5. Gross Rents, Royalties, and License Fees	6. Gross Income From Performance of Services	7. Other (attach schedule)	8. Total (add columns 2(a) through 7)
	(a) Exclude gross-up	(b) Gross-up (sec. 78)	(a) Exclude gross-up	(b) Gross-up (sec. 78)					
A	CN								25,000	25,000
B										
C										
D										
E										
F										
Totals (add lines A through F)									25,000	25,000

* For section 863(b) income, NOLs, income from RICs, and high-taxed income, use a single line (see instructions).

	Deductions (*INCLUDE* Foreign Branch Deductions here *and* on Schedule F)							
	9. Definitely Allocable Deductions				10. Apportioned Share of Deductions Not Definitely Allocable (enter amount from applicable line of Schedule H, Part II, column (d))	11. Net Operating Loss Deduction	12. Total Deductions (add columns 9(e) through 11)	13. Total Income or (Loss) Before Adjustments (subtract column 12 from column 8)
	Rental, Royalty, and Licensing Expenses		(c) Expenses Related to Gross Income From Performance of Services	(d) Other Definitely Allocable Deductions	(e) Total Definitely Allocable Deductions (add columns 9(a) through 9(d))				
	(a) Depreciation, Depletion, and Amortization	(b) Other Expenses							
A				6,000	6,000	1,800		7,800	17,200
B									
C									
D									
E									
F									
Totals				6,000	6,000	1,800		7,800	17,200

For Paperwork Reduction Act Notice, see separate instructions.   Cat. No. 10900F   Form **1118** (Rev. 12-2014)

Form 1118 (Rev. 12-2014)   Page **2**

Schedule B   **Foreign Tax Credit** *(Report all foreign tax amounts in U.S. dollars.)*

Part I—Foreign Taxes Paid, Accrued, and Deemed Paid *(see instructions)*

1. Credit is Claimed for Taxes (check one):		2. Foreign Taxes Paid or Accrued (attach schedule showing amounts in foreign currency and conversion rate(s) used)							(h) Total Foreign Taxes Paid or Accrued (add columns 2(a) through 2(g))	3. Tax Deemed Paid (from Schedule C—Part I, column 12, Part II, column 8(b), and Part III, column 8)
☑ Paid ☐ Accrued		Tax Withheld at Source on:			Other Foreign Taxes Paid or Accrued on:					
Date Paid	Date Accrued	(a) Dividends	(b) Interest	(c) Rents, Royalties, and License Fees	(d) Section 863(b) Income	(e) Foreign Branch Income	(f) Services Income	(g) Other		
A	various						5,000			5,000	
B											
C											
D											
E											
F											
Totals (add lines A through F)						5,000			5,000	

Part II—Separate Foreign Tax Credit *(Complete a **separate** Part II for **each** applicable category of income.)*

1a	Total foreign taxes paid or accrued (total from Part I, column 2(h))		5,000
b	Foreign taxes paid or accrued by the corporation during prior tax years that were suspended due to the rules of section 909 and for which the related income is taken into account by the corporation during the current tax year (see instructions)		
2	Total taxes deemed paid (total from Part I, column 3)		5,000
3	Reductions of taxes paid, accrued, or deemed paid (enter total from Schedule G)	( )	
4	Taxes reclassified under high-tax kickout		
5	Enter the sum of any carryover of foreign taxes (from Schedule K, line 3, column (xiv) and from Schedule I, Part III, line 3) plus any carrybacks to the current tax year		
6	Total foreign taxes (combine lines 1a through 5)		5,000
7	Enter the amount from the applicable column of Schedule J, Part I, line 11 (see instructions). If Schedule J is **not** required to be completed, enter the result from the "Totals" line of column 13 of the applicable Schedule A		17,200
8a	Total taxable income from all sources (enter taxable income from the corporation's tax return)	100,000	
b	Adjustments to line 8a (see instructions)	0	
c	Subtract line 8b from line 8a		100,000
9	Divide line 7 by line 8c. Enter the resulting fraction as a decimal (see instructions). If line 7 is greater than line 8c, enter 1 . .		.172
10	Total U.S. income tax against which credit is allowed (regular tax liability (see section 26(b)) minus American Samoa economic development credit) . .		22,250
11	Credit limitation (multiply line 9 by line 10) (see instructions)		3,827
12	**Separate foreign tax credit** (enter the smaller of line 6 or line 11 here and on the appropriate line of Part III)		3,827

Part III—Summary of Separate Credits *(Enter amounts from Part II, line 12 for **each** applicable category of income. **Do not** include taxes paid to sanctioned countries.)*

1	Credit for taxes on passive category income	
2	Credit for taxes on general category income	3,827
3	Credit for taxes on income re-sourced by treaty (combine all such credits on this line)	
4	Total (add lines 1 through 3)	3,827
5	Reduction in credit for international boycott operations (see instructions)	
6	**Total foreign tax credit** (subtract line 5 from line 4). Enter here and on the appropriate line of the corporation's tax return	3,827

Form **1118** (Rev. 12-2014)

EXHIBIT 24-1 **Form 1118: Foreign Tax Credit Corporations, Schedules A, B, F, and H for 3D Corporation, cumulative facts from Examples 24-9, 24-10, and 24-11 (*concluded*)**

Form 1118 (Rev. 12-2014)

Schedule F Gross Income and Definitely Allocable Deductions for Foreign Branches

1. Foreign Country or U.S. Possession (Enter two-letter code from Schedule A, column 1. Use a separate line for each.)	2. Gross Income	3. Definitely Allocable Deductions
A CN	25,000	6,000
B		
C		
D		
E		
F		
Totals (add lines A through F)* ▶	25,000	6,000

* **Note:** *The Schedule F totals are not carried over to any other Form 1118 Schedule. (These totals were already included in Schedule A.) However, the IRS requires the corporation to complete Schedule F under the authority of section 905(b).*

Form 1118 (Rev. 12-2014)

Page **10**

Schedule H Apportionment of Deductions Not Definitely Allocable (*complete only once*)

Part I—Research and Development Deductions

		(a) Sales Method				(b) Gross Income Method — Check method used: ☐ Option 1 ☐ Option 2				(c) Total R&D Deductions Not Definitely Allocable (enter the sum of all amounts entered in all applicable "R&D Deductions" columns)
		Product line #1 (SIC Code:)*		Product line #2 (SIC Code:)*		Product line #1 (SIC Code:)*		Product line #2 (SIC Code:)*		
		(i) Gross Sales	(ii) R&D Deductions	(iii) Gross Sales	(iv) R&D Deductions	(v) Gross Income	(vi) R&D Deductions	(vii) Gross Income	(viii) R&D Deductions	
1	Totals (see instructions)	500,000	8,000							
2	Total to be apportioned		4,000							
3	Apportionment among statutory groupings:									
a	General category income	100,000	800							800
b	Passive category income									
c	Section 901(j) income*									
d	Income re-sourced by treaty*									
4	Total foreign (add lines 3a through 3d)	100,000	800							800

* **Important:** *See **Computer-Generated Schedule H** in instructions.*

Form **1118** (Rev. 12-2014)

Form 1118 (Rev. 12-2014)

Page **11**

Schedule H Apportionment of Deductions Not Definitely Allocable (*continued*)

Part II—Interest Deductions, All Other Deductions, and Total Deductions

		(a) Average Value of Assets—Check method used: ☐ Fair market value ☑ Tax book value ☐ Alternative tax book value		(b) Interest Deductions		(c) All Other Deductions Not Definitely Allocable	(d) Totals (add the corresponding amounts from column (c), Part I; columns (b)(iii) and (b)(iv), Part II; and column (c), Part II). Enter each amount from lines 3a through 3d below in column 10 of the corresponding Schedule A.
		(i) Nonfinancial Corporations	(ii) Financial Corporations	(iii) Nonfinancial Corporations	(iv) Financial Corporations		
1a	Totals (see instructions)	300,000		6,000			
b	Amounts specifically allocable under Temp. Regs. 1.861-10T(e)						
c	Other specific allocations under Temp. Regs. 1.861-10T						
d	Assets excluded from apportionment formula						
2	Total to be apportioned (subtract the sum of lines 1b, 1c, and 1d from line 1a)	300,000		6,000			
3	Apportionment among statutory groupings:						
a	General category income	50,000		1,000			1,000
b	Passive category income						
c	Section 901(j) income*						
d	Income re-sourced by treaty*						
4	Total foreign (add lines 3a through 3d)	50,000		1,000			1,000

* **Important:** *See **Computer-Generated Schedule H** in instructions.*

Form **1118** (Rev. 12-2014)

Exhibit 24-2 provides a list of the countries with which the United States has income tax treaties. U.S. treaties generally do not affect the U.S. taxation of U.S. citizens, residents, and domestic corporations because such taxpayers are taxed on a worldwide basis.

EXHIBIT 24-2 Countries with Which the United States Has Income Tax Treaties

Australia	India	Philippines
Austria	Indonesia	Poland
Bangladesh	Ireland	Portugal
Barbados	Israel	Romania
Belgium	Italy	Russian Federation
Bulgaria	Jamaica	Slovak Republic
Canada	Japan	Slovenia
China, People's Republic of	Kazakhstan	South Africa
Commonwealth of Independent States[a]	Korea, Republic of	Spain
Cyprus	Latvia	Sri Lanka
Czech Republic	Lithuania	Sweden
Denmark	Luxembourg	Switzerland
Egypt	Malta	Thailand
Estonia	Mexico	Trinidad and Tobago
Finland	Morocco	Tunisia
France	Netherlands	Turkey
Germany	New Zealand	Ukraine
Greece	Norway	United Kingdom
Hungary	Pakistan	Venezuela
Iceland		

[a]Armenia, Azerbaijan, Belarus, Georgia, Krygyzstan, Moldova, Takikistan, Turkmenistan, and Uzbekistan.

U.S. taxpayers can benefit from treaties that reduce the tax on designated items or classes of income. For example, most U.S. treaties provide a low withholding tax rate or an exemption from tax on various types of investment income (interest, dividends, gains from sale of stock, and royalties) that otherwise would be subject to a high withholding tax.[26] For individuals, U.S. treaties often provide exemption from taxation by the host country on wages or self-employment income earned in the treaty country, provided the individual does not spend more than 183 days in that other country. U.S. businesses generally are not taxed on business profits earned in the host treaty country unless they conduct that business through a **permanent establishment.** A permanent establishment generally is a fixed place of business such as an office or factory, although employees acting as agents can create a permanent establishment. Treaties also provide "tiebreaker" rules for determining the country in which an individual will be considered a resident for treaty purposes.

Example 24-12

What if: Lily was trying to determine if 3D would be subject to Canadian taxation under two different scenarios: (1) open a store in Windsor and operate it as a branch of 3D or (2) make the baked goods in Detroit and ship them to Windsor-area grocery stores using the company's van. Article VII of the U.S.-Canada income tax treaty states that the business profits of a U.S. resident are taxed in Canada only if the business operates in Canada through a permanent establishment. Article V defines a permanent establishment as including a place of management, a branch, an office, a factory,

[26]Absent a treaty, the United States imposes a withholding tax rate of 30 percent on payments of FDAP income to nonresidents.

and a workshop. Under the U.S.-Canada treaty, will 3D be subject to Canadian tax on taxable income earned through its Windsor store?

Answer: Yes. A branch is defined as a permanent establishment. Canada can tax 3D's Canadian-source taxable income under Article VII of the U.S.-Canada treaty.

Under the U.S.-Canada treaty, will 3D be subject to Canadian tax on taxable income earned by selling goods to grocery stores in Windsor directly?

Answer: No. 3D does not have a permanent establishment in Canada on these sales. Canada will not tax income from these sales under Article VII of the U.S.-Canada treaty.

Example 24-13

What if: Assume for quality control purposes that Lily decided to do all of the baking for her Windsor store in Detroit. Every morning a Windsor employee drives a van to Detroit and picks up the baked goods for sale in Windsor. One of her employees, Stan Lee Cupp, made the two-hour trip on 200 different days during 2016. Article IV of the U.S.-Canada income tax treaty states where an individual is considered a resident of both countries under their respective tax laws, the individual will be considered a resident of the country in which he or she has a permanent home. Stan has a home only in Canada, and Canada still considers him to be a Canadian resident. Will Stan be considered a U.S. resident in 2016 applying only the substantial presence test?

Answer: Yes. Stan is physically present in the United States for more than 30 days in 2016 and satisfies the 183-day test when applying the formula $[200 + (1/3 \times 0) + (1/6 \times 0) = 200]$.

Will Stan be considered a U.S. resident in 2016 under the U.S.-Canada treaty?

Answer: No. Under the tiebreaker rules in the U.S.-Canada treaty, Stan is considered to be a resident of Canada only for income tax purposes because that is where he has his permanent home. The United States can tax Stan only on income that is considered to be from U.S. sources.

Example 24-14

What if: Assume that Stan made the two-hour trip from Windsor to Detroit and back on 120 different days during 2016 (240 hours). 3D paid Stan a salary of C$50,000 during 2016. He worked a total of 240 days (1,920 hours) during 2016. Article XV of the U.S.-Canada income tax treaty states that a Canadian resident will be subject to U.S. tax on his or her U.S.-source compensation only if the compensation exceeds $10,000 or the individual is present in the United States for more than 183 days. Under the U.S.-Canada treaty, will Stan be subject to Canadian tax on his U.S.-source compensation in 2016?

Answer: No. Stan is exempt from U.S. tax on this compensation because under the apportionment rules for compensation discussed previously in Example 24-6, he has only $6,250 of U.S. compensation, computed as $(240/1,920) \times \$50,000$,

where:

240 = Number of hours worked in the United States

$1,920$ = Total number of hours worked

$\$50,000$ = Total compensation in U.S. dollars

What if: Assume Stan received compensation of $86,000 in 2016. Under the U.S.-Canada treaty, will Stan be subject to Canadian tax on his U.S.-source compensation in 2016?

Answer: Yes. Although Stan was in the United States for less than 184 days, his U.S. source compensation is $10,750, computed as $(240/1,920) \times \$86,000$.

LO 24-4 # FOREIGN TAX CREDITS

The United States taxes the worldwide income of U.S. corporations, partnerships, trusts and estates, U.S. citizens, and resident aliens. As we have discussed, U.S. persons earning foreign source income may be subject to multiple taxation on such income by the United States and the country in which the individual resides or where the income is earned. For example, a U.S. citizen who is a resident of Great Britain and earns income in France may be subject to tax by all three governments. Without any relief from such multiple taxation, U.S. taxpayers would have little incentive to do business outside the United States.

FTC Limitation Categories of Taxable Income

The United States alleviates the multiple taxation of foreign source income earned by U.S. persons by allowing a tax credit for income taxes paid on such foreign source income. The foreign tax credit allowed in the current year is subject to a foreign tax credit limitation,[27] computed by multiplying the ratio of foreign source taxable income to total taxable income times precredit U.S. tax, as follows:

$$\frac{\text{Foreign source taxable income}}{\text{Total taxable income}} \times \text{Precredit U.S. tax}$$

As a policy matter, the U.S. government must decide whether, and to what extent, U.S. taxpayers should segregate foreign source income subject to different tax rates and compute a separate FTC limitation for each category of income. Since 1976, the United States has required persons claiming the foreign tax credit to segregate foreign source income by category of income. Practitioners often refer to each income category as an **FTC basket.** Currently, the two primary categories of FTC income are **passive category income** and **general category income.**[28] The "basket" approach is intended to limit blending opportunities (high-tax foreign source income and low-tax foreign source income) to income that is of the same character.

Passive Category Income Passive category income generally is investment-type income that traditionally is subject to low foreign taxes (usually in the form of withholding taxes). Passive category income includes interest, certain dividends, rents, royalties, and annuities. Dividends received from 10–50 percent owned joint ventures and from more than 50 percent owned subsidiaries are subject to "look-through" rules. Under these rules, the dividend recipient characterizes the dividend for FTC basket purposes based on the source(s) of income from which the dividend is paid.

General Category Income Income not treated as passive category income is defined as general category income. General category income includes gross income from an active trade or business, financial services income, and shipping income.

The application of the FTC limitation formula can result in an excess credit if the taxpayer's creditable foreign taxes exceed the FTC limitation amount. The United States allows taxpayers to carry back an excess FTC 1 year and carry forward an excess credit 10 years. Current-year foreign tax credits are absorbed before any carryovers, which are absorbed on a first-in first-out basis.

[27]§904(d).
[28]§904(d).

Example 24-15

What if: Suppose 3D's branch operations in Windsor generated $20,000 of taxable income and paid Canadian tax of C$5,000. The branch income meets the definition of general category income for FTC purposes. In addition, 3D received a dividend of C$1,000 from its stock investment in Scotiabank. Under the U.S.-Canada treaty, Scotiabank withheld C$150 in taxes (15 percent) on the payment. The withholding tax is eligible for the foreign tax credit, and the dividend meets the definition of passive category income for FTC purposes. 3D has total taxable income of $100,000 in 2016 and has a pre-credit U.S. income tax of $22,250. In computing its FTC for 2016, can 3D combine the branch income with the dividend in calculating its FTC limitation? Assume the exchange rate is C$1:$1.

Answer: No. The branch income and dividend cannot be "blended" because they are in different income categories for FTC limitation purposes.

How much of the C$5,150 in Canadian taxes can 3D claim as an FTC in 2016?

Answer: $4,600 ($4,450 + $150).

3D must compute separate FTC limitations for the branch income and dividend, as follows:

    Branch income: $20,000/$100,000 × $22,250 = $4,450

    Dividend income: $1,000/$100,000 × $22,250 = $223

3D can take a credit for the full amount of the withholding tax on the dividend ($150) but only a partial credit on the branch income. The separate basket approach prevents 3D from blending its high-tax income with its low-tax income.

What happens to the excess credit of $550 ($5,000 − $4,450) on the branch income?

Answer: 3D can carry back the excess FTC 1 year and then carry forward any remaining FTC for 10 years.

What if: Assume the branch income and dividend are both general category income. How much of the C$5,150 of Canadian taxes can 3D take as a credit in 2016?

Answer: $4,673 computed as $21,000/$100,000 × $22,250,

where:

    $21,000 = Foreign source taxable income

    $100,000 = Total taxable income

    $22,250 = Precredit U.S. tax on total taxable income

The low tax dividend income absorbs an additional $73 of branch foreign taxes. The addition of the $1,000 dividend to the branch FTC limitation increases the FTC ratio from 20 percent to 21 percent. This 1 percent increase in the ratio increases the FTC limitation by $223 (1% × $22,250). The FTC on the dividend is $150, leaving an excess $73 to apply against the branch FTC.

Creditable Foreign Taxes

The foreign tax credit is available only for foreign taxes the United States considers to be *income* taxes "in the U.S. sense." In general, a tax "resembles" the U.S. concept of an income tax when it is applied to net income.[29] Taxes that do not qualify as income taxes include property taxes, customs taxes, sales taxes, and value-added taxes. U.S. taxpayers can deduct noncreditable foreign taxes. On an annual basis, U.S. taxpayers also can elect to deduct foreign income taxes in lieu of claiming the credit. This election might make sense if the taxpayer does not expect to be able to use the credit during the 10-year carryforward period. Foreign taxes generally are translated into U.S. dollars using the average exchange rate for the year, regardless of when the

---

[29]There has been much litigation and many IRS rulings over whether a tax paid to another country qualifies as an income tax "in the U.S. sense."

tax is actually paid.[30] U.S. taxpayers can elect to translate withholding taxes using the exchange rate on the day the tax is withheld. This election makes translation of the withholding tax consistent with the translation of the payment (dividend, interest, royalty) into U.S. dollars, which is done using the exchange rate on the date of payment (referred to as the **spot rate**).

Direct Taxes   Direct foreign income taxes are income taxes paid directly by the U.S. taxpayer.[31] For example, income taxes paid by 3D to the Canadian government on its branch operations in Windsor would be direct foreign income taxes and eligible for a credit on the company's U.S. tax return.

In Lieu of Taxes   Taxes that do not qualify as income taxes can still be creditable if they are imposed "in lieu of" an income tax.[32] The most common example is a withholding tax imposed on gross income such as dividends, interest, and royalties. These taxes technically do not meet the definition of an income tax because they are imposed on gross, rather than net, income. However, most governments impose these taxes for administrative purposes in lieu of requiring the recipient of the income to file an income tax return.

Indirect (Deemed Paid) Taxes   Indirect taxes are foreign income taxes imposed on the income of a U.S.-owned **foreign subsidiary** or **foreign joint venture**.[33] These taxes are not considered direct taxes because they are not paid by the U.S. parent company or investor. Had the U.S. corporation conducted its foreign operations through a branch, the before-tax income of the branch would be reported on the corporation's U.S. tax return and a direct FTC would be claimed for any income taxes paid by the branch. The income of a foreign subsidiary is not reported on the U.S. tax return until it is distributed to the U.S. parent as a dividend or other payment. The dividend amount is net of the foreign income taxes imposed on that income.[34]

To put the U.S. tax consequences of a dividend distribution on equal footing with branch income, the United States allows certain U.S. corporations to "impute" a foreign tax credit for the income taxes paid by the foreign subsidiary on the dividend distributed. The U.S. corporation must "gross up" the dividend by the amount of the credit.[35] This gross-up causes the U.S. corporation to report the pretax income of the subsidiary related to the dividend distributed, similar to what would have been reported had the subsidiary been operated as a branch.

Example 24-16

What if: Let's say 3D operates its Windsor operations as a branch. The branch reported taxable income of C$20,000 for 2016 on which it paid a combined national and provincial income tax of C$5,000. Not including the branch income, 3D had taxable income of $80,000 from its U.S. operations in 2016. What amount of taxable income does 3D report on its U.S. tax return in 2016? Assume a conversion exchange rate of 1C$:$1.

Answer: $100,000. 3D includes the branch income with its U.S. taxable income.

---

[30]§986(a)(1)(A).

[31]Direct foreign income taxes are creditable under §901.

[32]In lieu of income taxes are creditable under §903.

[33]Indirect foreign income taxes are creditable under §902 or §960.

[34]As discussed in Chapter 18, dividends are payments out of earnings and profits, which is after-tax economic income of a corporation.

[35]§78.

What amount of foreign taxes are creditable for foreign tax credit purposes?

Answer: $5,000. The Canadian income taxes paid on the branch operations are considered a direct FTC because 3D pays the tax directly.

What if: Suppose 3D operates its Windsor operations as a subsidiary. The subsidiary reported taxable income of C$20,000 for 2016 on which it paid a combined national and provincial income tax of C$5,000. Assume for purposes of this example only that for U.S. tax purposes the subsidiary's earnings and profits (E&P) is $15,000, computed as C$20,000 − C$5,000.[36] At the end of 2016, the subsidiary distributed all of its E&P to 3D as a dividend. Not including the dividend income, 3D had taxable income of $80,000 from its U.S. operations in 2016. Assume Canada did not impose a withholding tax on the dividend. What amount of foreign taxes are creditable for foreign tax credit purposes?

Answer: $5,000. 3D receives a deemed paid credit equal to the income taxes paid by the subsidiary on the dividend received.

What amount of taxable income does 3D report on its U.S. tax return as a result of the dividend in 2016?

Answer: $20,000. 3D grosses up the $15,000 dividend by the deemed paid credit of $5,000. The amount of taxable income reported from the dividend equals the taxable income reported from the branch operations.

Most subsidiaries and joint ventures do not pay out all of their current E&P as a dividend in the year earned. When a subsidiary distributes a portion of its total E&P as a dividend, the deemed paid credit is computed on a "blended" basis based on total income taxes paid on total E&P accumulated since 1987.[37] The amount of foreign income taxes deemed paid by the U.S. corporate shareholder on the receipt of a dividend is computed as follows:

$$\frac{\text{Dividends paid from post-1986 earnings and profits}}{\text{Total post-1986 earnings and profits}} \times \text{Post-1986 foreign taxes}$$

A foreign subsidiary or joint venture computes post-1986 E&P using its **functional currency** unless the corporation keeps its books in U.S. dollars.[38] The corporation maintains its pool of post-1986 foreign income taxes in U.S. dollars.

Example 24-17

What if: Assume 3D organized its Windsor operations as a Canadian subsidiary of 3D, Canadian Doughnut Depot Company (CDD). CDD reported taxable income of C$20,000 for 2016, on which it paid a combined national and provincial income tax of C$5,000. Because CDD operates as a Canadian corporation, its Canadian taxable income is not reported on 3D's U.S. corporate income tax return (CDD is a nonresident with no U.S.-source income). Also assume for purposes of this example only, that CDD has post-1986 E&P of C$15,000, all of which is characterized as general category income. During 2016, CDD paid a dividend of C$6,000 to 3D. Under the U.S.-Canada treaty, CDD withheld a Canadian withholding tax of C$300 (5 percent). Not including the dividend, 3D had taxable income of $142,000 in 2016. What is 3D's deemed paid credit on the dividend received from CDD in 2016?

(continued on page 24-24)

---

[36]§964 requires a U.S. parent company to compute E&P for its foreign subsidiaries under U.S. tax rules. These rules are discussed in detail in Chapter 18.

[37]This computation was changed in the Tax Reform Act of 1986. Distributions received from E&P accumulated prior to 1987 are treated as being paid out of the E&P for the year distributed assuming a LIFO assumption.

[38]§986(b). *Functional currency* is the currency in which the corporation conducts its transactions.

Answer: $2,000, computed as C$6,000/C$15,000 × $5,000,
where:

    C$6,000 = Dividend paid to 3D in CDD's functional currency

    C$15,000 = Post-1986 E&P in CDD's functional currency

    $5,000   = Post-1986 foreign taxes in U.S. dollars

What amount of creditable foreign taxes does 3D have in 2016?

Answer: $2,300, computed as $2,000 + withholding taxes of $300.

What amount of gross income does 3D report as a result of the dividend from CDD?

Answer: $8,000, computed as $6,000 + $2,000. 3D must gross up the dividend ($6,000) by the deemed paid credit ($2,000) to compute the taxable income it reports from receiving the dividend. 3D's total taxable income for 2016 is $150,000 ($142,000 + $8,000), and its precredit U.S. tax is $41,750, [($50,000 × .15) + ($25,000 × .25) + ($25,000 × .34) + ($50,000 × .39)].

Assuming no deductions are subtracted from the foreign source gross income created by the dividend, what is 3D's FTC limitation for 2016?

Answer: $2,227, computed as $8,000/$150,000 × $41,750,
where:

    $8,000   = Foreign source taxable income from the dividend

    $150,000 = Total taxable income

    $41,750   = Precredit U.S. tax on total taxable income

3D has an excess FTC of $73 ($2,300 − $2,227).

A U.S. corporation must own directly 10 percent or more of the foreign corporation paying the dividend to be eligible for the deemed paid credit.[39]

Example 24-18

What if: Assume 3D only owned 50 percent of CDD. CDD reported taxable income of C$20,000 for 2016 on which it paid a combined national and provincial income tax of C$5,000. For U.S. tax purposes, CDD has post-1986 E&P of C$15,000, all of which is characterized as general category income. During 2016 CDD paid a dividend of C$3,000 to 3D. Under the U.S.-Canada treaty, CDD withheld a Canadian withholding tax of C$150 (5 percent). Not including the dividend, 3D had taxable income of $142,000 in 2016. What is 3D's deemed paid credit on the dividend received from CDD in 2016?

Answer: $1,000, computed as C$3,000/C$15,000 × $5,000,
where:

    C$3,000 = Dividend paid to 3D in CDD's functional currency

    C$15,000 = Post-1986 E&P in CDD's functional currency

    $5,000   = Post-1986 foreign taxes in U.S. dollars

What amount of creditable foreign taxes does 3D have in 2016?

Answer: $1,150, computed as $1,000 + withholding taxes of $150.

What amount of gross income does 3D report as a result of the dividend from CDD?

Answer: $4,000, computed as $3,000 + $1,000.

[39]Dividends paid to the foreign corporation from other foreign corporations can also be eligible for the deemed paid credit if certain direct and indirect ownership tests are met. This topic is beyond the scope of this text.

PLANNING FOR INTERNATIONAL OPERATIONS   `LO 24-5`

continued from page 24-1 . . .

After operating her Windsor store as a branch for the first year, Lily began to wonder if there were more tax-efficient ways to operate her Canadian operations. She was concerned that while the branch was easy to organize and operate, it might not provide the best tax advantages. Lily's tax adviser told her that Canada imposes a 10 percent "branch profits tax" on after-tax profits that exceed $500,000. Although the Windsor operations were a long way from reaching that level of profits, she hoped one day that she would reach that level of profitability. In addition, she wondered if it might be an advantage to have her Canadian operations identified as a Canadian company. Lily's tax adviser mentioned that operating as a Canadian corporation would provide deferral of her Canadian profits from U.S. taxation and would allow for some "transfer pricing" on the "sale" of her baked goods from the United States to Canada. ■

The organizational form through which a U.S. person does business or invests outside the United States affects the timing and scope of U.S. taxation of foreign source income or loss reported by the business or investment. U.S. corporations conducting international operations directly (branch) or through a flow-through entity (partnership) are subject to U.S. tax or receive a U.S. tax benefit currently on income or loss from those operations. Foreign source income earned by a foreign corporation owned by U.S. persons (e.g., a Canadian subsidiary of a U.S. corporation) generally is not subject to U.S. taxation until such income is repatriated to the U.S. shareholder as a dividend, interest, rent, royalty, or management fee (i.e., U.S. taxation of such income is deferred to a future period).

The organizational form chosen can help a U.S. person reduce worldwide taxation through the following means:

- Defer U.S. taxation of foreign source income not repatriated to the United States.
- Maximize the foreign tax credit limitation on distributions.
- Reduce foreign taxes in high-tax jurisdictions through tax-deductible payments (e.g., rent, interest, royalties, and management fees) to lower-tax jurisdictions.
- Take advantage of tax incentives provided by host jurisdictions (e.g., a tax holiday on profits for a specified time period).
- Use transfer pricing to shift profits from a high-tax jurisdiction to a low-tax jurisdiction.
- Take advantage of tax treaties to reduce withholding taxes on cross-border payments.

Hybrid entities such as limited liability companies can provide the U.S. investor with the legal advantages of corporate form (limited liability, continuity of life, transferability of interests) and the tax advantages of partnership or branch form (flow-through of losses and flow-through of foreign taxes to individual investors).

Each organizational form offers a U.S. person investing abroad with advantages and disadvantages. Most U.S. businesses operate abroad through either a subsidiary or hybrid entity. Corporation status provides the U.S. investor with protection against liabilities of the subsidiary, entitles the subsidiary to treaty benefits in its dealings outside the country of incorporation, and insulates its business income from

U.S. taxation until such income is repatriated back to the United States. Conversely, losses incurred in the subsidiary are not currently deductible on the investor's U.S. tax return.

Check-the-Box Hybrid Entities

Through regulations, the U.S. Treasury allows U.S. taxpayers to elect the *U.S. tax status* of eligible entities by "checking the box" on Form 8832. Where the U.S. person owns 100 percent of the entity, the taxpayer can choose corporation status or branch status (the latter often is referred to as a **disregarded entity** because it is disregarded for U.S. tax purposes). Where more than one U.S. person owns the entity, the taxpayers can choose corporation status or partnership status. Such an entity is referred to as a hybrid entity. A multiple-person-owned hybrid entity for which corporation status is elected is referred to as a **reverse hybrid entity.** Certain designated "per se" foreign entities are not eligible for this elective treatment. These ineligible entities tend to be entities that can be publicly traded in their host countries (e.g., a German A.G., Dutch N.V., U.K. PLC, Spanish S.A., and a Canadian Corporation). The entire list is printed in the Instructions to Form 8832. In Canada, a U.S. corporation or individual must operate through an unlimited liability company (ULC) organized under the laws of Nova Scotia, Alberta, or British Columbia to achieve the benefits of operating through a hybrid entity.

Hybrid entities offer U.S. investors much flexibility in avoiding the U.S. "anti-deferral" rules found in subpart F, which we discuss in the next section. However, there are drawbacks to operating through a hybrid entity. In particular, a hybrid entity organized outside the United States may not be eligible for treaty benefits because it is not recognized as a resident of the United States by the host country. For example, the U.S.-Canada treaty does not extend treaty benefits to distributions from a ULC to its U.S. investors. Distributions from a Nova Scotia ULC to its U.S. parent company in the form of dividends or royalties will be subject to a 25 percent withholding tax instead of a 5 percent or 10 percent withholding tax, respectively, under the U.S.-Canada treaty. Exhibit 24-3 lists the advantages and disadvantages of operating outside the United States through different organizational forms.

Example 24-19

Lily expects her Canadian operations to be profitable for the foreseeable future. She has plans to expand her operations throughout the province of Ontario and hopefully throughout all of Canada. Lily is trying to decide whether she should change the organizational form of her Canadian operations from a branch to a corporation or perhaps a hybrid entity. Can Lily organize her Canadian operations as a hybrid entity in Ontario for U.S. tax purposes?

Answer: No. Hybrid entities (unlimited liability companies) can only be organized in Canada in the provinces of Nova Scotia, Alberta, and British Columbia.

What are the primary income tax reasons for organizing the Canadian operations as a corporation for U.S. tax purposes?

Answer: There are several. Operating as a corporation allows for deferral from U.S. taxation on income earned by the Canadian operations until it is distributed to 3D as a dividend. In addition, 3D can loan money or lease its trademarks to the Canadian corporation and transfer income from Canada to the United States in the form of tax-deductible interest or royalties.

Are there any compelling nontax reasons for organizing the Canadian operations as a corporation for U.S. tax purposes?

Answer: Yes. Corporate form limits 3D's liability in Canada to its Canadian assets. In addition, operating as a corporation allows the company to hold itself out as a Canadian business to its customers and borrow money directly from Canadian banks.

EXHIBIT 24-3   **Advantages and Disadvantages of Operating Outside the United States in Different Organizational Forms**

Branch
Advantages
- Foreign losses are currently deductible on the U.S. tax return.
- Foreign taxes imposed on income earned through the branch are eligible for the direct foreign tax credit.
- A branch qualifies as a permanent establishment and is eligible for treaty benefits.

Disadvantages
- Profits are subject to immediate U.S. taxation.
- The U.S. corporation must have 100 percent control over its international operations (joint ventures are not available).

Subsidiary
Advantages
- Separate entity status insulates the U.S. parent corporation against certain types of liabilities.
- Certain earnings are deferred from U.S. taxation until repatriation.
- Certain payments (management fees, royalties) made to the U.S. parent corporation may only be deductible in the host country if the payor is a corporation.

Disadvantages
- Losses are not deductible on the U.S. tax return for tax purposes.
- Certain foreign source income may be subject to the subpart F rules, which increases the administrative costs of operating as a subsidiary.

Hybrid entity treated as a flow-through entity
Advantages
- Foreign losses are currently deductible on the U.S. tax return.
- Foreign taxes imposed on income earned through the branch are eligible for the direct foreign tax credit.
- The U.S. corporation can operate as a joint venture.
- Certain payments (management fees, royalties, interest) made to the U.S. parent corporation are deductible in the foreign jurisdiction.

Disadvantages
- Profits are subject to immediate U.S. taxation.
- Dividend, interest, and royalty payments to the United States are not eligible for reduced treaty withholding taxes.

When drawing an organizational chart of a multinational company, the different organizational forms are often designated with different symbols. Exhibit 24-4 provides the symbols for each of the common organizational forms used by U.S. taxpayers to do business outside the United States and their tax status for U.S. tax purposes (we refer back to this exhibit in Exhibit 24-5).

U.S. ANTI-DEFERRAL RULES

LO 24-6

Deferral of U.S. taxation on all foreign source income earned through a foreign subsidiary would invite tax-planning strategies that shift income to low-tax countries to minimize worldwide taxation. U.S. individuals and corporations could transfer investment assets to subsidiaries located in low- (no-) tax countries (**tax havens**) and earn low-tax or tax-exempt income until such time as it was repatriated to the United States.

The United States has debated whether to allow full deferral on all foreign earnings since 1937, when the U.S. government enacted its first "anti-deferral" rules

EXHIBIT 24-4 **Symbols for Different Organizational Forms and Their U.S. Tax Status**

Corporation

Individual

Disregarded entity (branch)

Hybrid entity treated as a partnership

Reverse hybrid entity treated as a corporation

applying to foreign personal holding companies. Congress, with urging from President Kennedy, enacted more expansive anti-deferral rules in subpart F of subchapter N of the Internal Revenue Code in 1962.[40]

In a nutshell, subpart F requires certain *U.S. shareholders* in a **controlled foreign corporation** (CFC) to include in their gross income currently their pro rata share of specified categories of "tainted" income earned by the CFC during the current year **(subpart F income)** regardless of whether such income is repatriated as a dividend (the income is treated as if it was paid out to the shareholders as a deemed dividend at the end of the CFC's taxable year). The deemed dividend is translated into U.S. dollars using the average exchange rate for the year. The technical rules that determine the amount of the deemed dividend to be included in income are among the most complex provisions in the Internal Revenue Code.

Definition of a Controlled Foreign Corporation

A controlled foreign corporation is defined as any foreign corporation in which *U.S. shareholders* collectively own *more than* 50 percent of the total combined voting power of all classes of stock entitled to vote or the total value of the corporation's stock on *any day* during the CFC's tax year.[41] For purposes of subpart F, a *U.S. shareholder* is any *U.S. person* who owns or is deemed to own 10 percent or more of all classes of stock entitled to vote.[42] The term *United States person* means a citizen or resident of the United States, a domestic partnership, a domestic corporation, or any U.S. estate or trust, but it excludes certain residents of U.S. possessions.

Constructive ownership rules are used in the calculation of both the 50 percent test for determining CFC status and the 10 percent test for determining who is a U.S. shareholder.[43] These rules are similar to the constructive ownership rules found in subchapter C (Chapter 18) and include family attribution (spouse, children, grandchildren, and parents), entity-to-owner attribution, and owner-to-entity attribution. A detailed discussion of the other attribution rules is beyond the scope of this text.

[40]§§951–964.
[41]§957(a).
[42]§951(b).
[43]§958(b).

Example 24-20

What if: Assume Lily decided to partner with a Canadian investor, Maurice Richard, to expand her operations into Quebec through a Canadian corporation to be called Quebec Doughnut Depot (QDD). As part of the creation of QDD, Maurice contributed enough cash to the corporation to become a 50 percent shareholder in the company, with Lily owning the remaining 50 percent. Will QDD be a controlled foreign corporation (CFC) for U.S. tax purposes?

Answer: No. Lily is the only U.S. person who qualifies as a U.S. shareholder for purposes of determining if QDD is a CFC for U.S. tax purposes. Because Lily only owns 50 percent of QDD (not *more* than 50 percent), the corporation is not considered a CFC.

What if: Suppose Lily organized QDD with her husband, Red, and Maurice, with each owning one-third of the company's stock. Will QDD be a CFC for U.S. tax purposes?

Answer: Yes. Lily and Red are both U.S. persons who qualify as a U.S. shareholder for purposes of determining if QDD is a CFC for U.S. tax purposes (they each own at least 10 percent of the QDD stock). Because they collectively own more than 50 percent of QDD, the corporation is a CFC.

What if: Suppose Lily organized QDD with her husband, Red, and Maurice, with Lily owning 49 percent, Red owning 2 percent, and Maurice owning 49 percent of the company's stock. Will QDD be a CFC for U.S. tax purposes?

Answer: Yes. Lily is deemed to own Red's 2 percent stock interest in QDD under the family attribution rules, making her a U.S. shareholder owning 51 percent of QDD's stock.

Definition of Subpart F Income

Subpart F income generally can be characterized as low-taxed passive income or as "portable" income earned by a CFC. Passive income, otherwise referred to as **foreign personal holding company income,** includes interest, dividends, rents, royalties, annuities, gains from the sales of certain foreign property, foreign currency exchange rate gains, net income from certain commodities transactions, and income equivalent to interest. There are complex exceptions involving payments between CFCs in the same country, export financing interest, and rents and royalties derived in the active conduct of a trade or business. Subpart F income does not include dividends, interest, rents, and royalties received by one CFC from a related CFC to the extent the payment is attributable to non-subpart F income of the payor (the taxpayer "looks through" the payment to the income from which it was paid).

Example 24-21

What if: Assume, as in Example 24-17, that 3D organized its Windsor operations as a wholly-owned Canadian subsidiary, Canadian Doughnut Depot Company (CDD). CDD reported taxable income from its bakery operations of C$75,000 in 2016. CDD also purchased 1,000 shares of stock (less than 1 percent) in Thorntons PLC, a United Kingdom corporation that makes fine chocolate. During 2016, CDD received dividends of £1,000, which translated into C$1,500.[44] Thorntons withheld £100 (C$150) of U.K. taxes on the payment (a 10 percent withholding tax under the U.K.-Canada treaty). Does the dividend from Thorntons to CDD constitute subpart F income to 3D in 2016?

Answer: Yes. Dividends from investments in corporations that are owned less than 10 percent by 3D are considered foreign personal holding company income under subpart F.

---

[44]The currency of the United Kingdom is the pound sterling, abbreviated £.

Also included in subpart F income is foreign base company sales income, which is defined as income derived by a CFC from the sale or purchase of personal property (e.g., inventory) to (or from) a related person, and the property is manufactured and sold outside the CFC's country of incorporation.[45] Similar rules apply to foreign base company services income.

This category of subpart F income was added because many countries offer incentives to multinational corporations to locate holding companies or sales companies within their borders by imposing no or a low tax on investment income or export sales. These companies are referred to as base companies because they operate primarily as profit centers and are located in a different country than where the economic activity (manufacture, sales, or service) takes place.

Without any anti-deferral rules, a U.S. multinational corporation could shift profits to a foreign base company by selling goods to the base company at an artificially low transfer price. The base company could then resell the goods at a higher price to the ultimate customer in a different country. The profit earned by the base company would be subject to the lower (or no) tax imposed by the tax haven country. The base company thus becomes a depository for the multinational company's excess funds, which can be invested in an active business or passive investment assets outside the United States.

Example 24-22

What if: Assume in 2017 that 3D set up a corporation in the Cayman Islands through which it intended to transfer its products from the United States to its operations in Canada. Under this plan, 3D would "sell" its products, made in the United States, to the subsidiary in the Cayman Islands at a low transfer price, after which the Cayman Islands subsidiary would resell the products to CDD at a high transfer price. The goal would be to locate as much profit as possible in a low-tax country (the Cayman Islands has no corporate income tax). Will profit from the sale of goods from the Cayman Islands subsidiary to CDD constitute subpart F income to 3D in 2017?

Answer: Yes. The Cayman Islands profit is considered foreign base company sales income under subpart F because the goods are manufactured outside the Cayman Islands by a related party (3D) and sold outside the Cayman Islands to a related party (CDD). 3D will be treated has having received a deemed dividend of the profit from the Cayman Islands subsidiary.

There are several exceptions that serve to exclude all or a portion of a CFC's subpart F income from current taxation to the U.S. shareholders. A *de minimis rule* excludes all gross income from being treated as foreign base company income if the sum of the CFC's gross foreign base company income is less than the lesser of 5 percent of gross income or $1 million. A *full inclusion rule* treats all of the CFC's gross income as foreign base company income if more than 70 percent of the CFC's gross income is foreign base company income. In addition, a taxpayer can *elect* to exclude "high-tax" subpart F income from the deemed dividend rules. High-tax subpart F income is taxed at an effective tax rate that is 90 percent or more of the highest U.S. statutory rate. For a U.S. corporation, the rate currently is 31.5 percent (90% × 35%). The calculation of the effective tax rate is complex and beyond the scope of this text.

Example 24-23

Return to the facts in Example 24-21, in which CDD reported taxable income from its bakery operations of C$75,000 in 2016 and received dividends of £1,000 from Thorntons PLC, which translated into C$1,500. Assume CDD has gross income of C$125,000 in 2016. In the previous example, we determined that the dividend constitutes subpart F income for U.S. tax purposes. Will 3D have a deemed dividend of this subpart F income in 2016?

Answer: No. The dividend is less than the lesser of 5 percent of CDD's gross income ($6,250) or $1 million and is not subject to the deemed dividend rules under the *de minimis* rule.

---

[45]§954(d).

The subpart F rules apply only in years in which a corporation is a CFC for an uninterrupted period of 30 days or more during its taxable year. Only those U.S. shareholders who own stock in the CFC on the last day in the CFC's taxable year are treated as having received their pro rata share of any subpart F deemed dividend.

The computation of the deemed dividend under subpart F is exceptionally complicated and requires the CFC to allocate both deductions and taxes paid to subpart F gross income. The formula for this computation can be found in worksheets in the Instructions to Form 5471. In addition, the U.S. shareholder receives a deemed paid foreign tax credit similar to the indirect foreign tax credit available on actual dividend distributions.[46]

Earnings of the CFC treated as a deemed dividend under subpart F becomes *previously taxed income* and subsequently can be distributed to the shareholders without being included in the recipient's gross income a second time. A foreign currency gain or loss on repatriation of such income is included in (deducted from) the shareholders' income.

Non-subpart F income (that is, income otherwise eligible for deferral) that is invested in U.S. property (for example, a loan from the CFC to its U.S. shareholder or stock in the U.S. parent) can be treated as a deemed dividend under the subpart F rules. This rule is intended to prevent U.S. corporations from borrowing money from their foreign subsidiaries on an indefinite basis, which would take the form of a disguised dividend.

Planning to Avoid Subpart F Income

U.S. multinational corporations expanding outside the United States often use hybrid entities as a tax-efficient means to avoid the subpart F rules. Tax aligning a U.S. corporation's international supply chain has become a frequent objective in international tax planning. Accomplishing this goal requires the formation of a foreign holding company (Foreign HoldCo) treated as a corporation for U.S. tax purposes (and thus eligible for deferral from U.S. taxation). The holding company owns the stock of hybrid entities set up to conduct each of the components of the company's foreign operations: financing (FinanceCo), manufacturing (OpCo), distribution (DistribCo), and intellectual property (IPCo). The holding company is strategically located in a country that lightly taxes dividend income paid by the hybrid entities. The hybrid entities also are strategically located in countries that tax the income from such operations (e.g., interest or royalties paid by the operating company to the finance company or intellectual property company) at a low tax rate. For instance, Ireland taxes manufacturing and intellectual property income at 12.5 percent. By conducting these operations through hybrid entities, transactions between the entities (e.g., a payment of interest, rents, or royalties from one entity to another), which otherwise would create subpart F income, are ignored for U.S. tax purposes but respected for foreign tax purposes because the hybrid entity is treated as a corporation in the country in which it is organized. This allows for the free flow of cash between foreign operations without the intrusion of the U.S. tax laws and the reduction of taxes in high-tax countries through cross-border payments that are deductible in the country in which the hybrid entity is located. Exhibit 24-5 provides a template for such an international operation.[47]

---

[46]§960.

[47]In hearings held on May 21, 2013, Senator Carl Levin accused Apple, Inc. of avoiding billions of U.S. taxes by structuring its overseas operations to route royalty income to low-tax jurisdictions. See http://www.hsgac.senate.gov/subcommittees/investigations/hearings/offshore-profit-shifting-and-the-us-tax-code_-part-2 for more details.

EXHIBIT 24-5 **A Tax-Aligned International Supply Chain (see Exhibit 24-4 for explanation of symbols)**

TAXES IN THE REAL WORLD Setting Sail for Low-Tax Jurisdictions

In January 2012, Aon Corporation, a U.S. global corporation providing risk management and human resource services, announced it was moving its corporate residence from Delaware to London, England. The company stated that the move was motivated by the desire to achieve greater access to emerging markets and take better advantage of the strategic proximity of the London market as one of the key international hubs of insurance and risk brokerage.

In addition, the company predicted that the move also would have several near- and long-term financial benefits, in particular, lower corporate tax rates and the ability to access cash located offshore without the imposition of the U.S. tax rate on the repatriation. Specifically, the company stated they believed *"the merger should significantly improve our ability to maintain a competitive global tax rate because the U.K. has implemented a dividend exemption system that generally does not subject non-U.K. earnings to U.K. tax when such earnings are repatriated to the U.K. in the form of dividends from non-U.K. subsidiaries."* Further, the company stated that a reduction in its global tax rate over the long-term would allow it to remain competitive with their global competitors. The company's strategy appears to be working. Aon's effective tax rate in 2014 was 18.9 percent, down from 26.1 percent in 2012, the year the company inverted.

In the transaction, the Aon shareholders exchanged their common stock in Aon for common stock in a newly formed English public-limited company. Such an exchange would be tax-free if the new corporation was located in the United States. However, under the "anti-inversion" rules, this cross-border exchange is taxable to the shareholders realizing gain, but not loss, on the exchange. In addition, the U.S. can treat the U.K. corporation as a domestic corporation if the company does not have substantial business activities in its place of incorporation.

This transaction illustrates the tax incentive for U.S. companies to relocate in lower tax jurisdictions that have a dividend exemption system, which allows the company to repatriate foreign earnings without the imposition of host country taxation. It also illustrates the countermoves enacted by the U.S. government to "dissuade" domestic companies from inverting tax-free.

One of the concerns expressed by the company was the potential backlash from its U.S. customers, who might perceive the company as not paying its fair share of U.S. taxes. Apparently, the shareholders valued tax savings more than reputation, as the vote was 98 percent in favor of the move.

From 2009–2014, almost 30 U.S. corporations "expatriated" from the U.S. and set up headquarters outside the U.S. In November 2015, Pfizer, Inc. announced it was inverting its corporate residence to Ireland through a merger with Allergan plc, also a former U.S. corporation that inverted to Ireland in 2014. President Obama has denounced this activity, referring to these corporations as "corporate deserters" that are not showing "economic patriotism." The Administration and Congress continue to debate how best to take away the economic tax incentives from this "legal tax loophole."

PROPOSALS FOR CHANGE

In February 2015, President Obama proposed significant changes to the U.S. international tax laws that were intended to raise $506.4 billion in additional tax revenues over the period 2016–2025. The most significant proposals would impose a 19-percent per country minimum tax on a U.S. corporation's foreign earnings and impose a 14-percent one-time tax on earnings accumulated in controlled foreign corporations and not previously subject to U.S. tax. Analysts have estimated that U.S. companies hold more than $2 trillion of "trapped cash" off-shore.

Numerous members of Congress, both Republican and Democrat, have advanced international tax reform proposals in recent years. Tax policymakers agree that the U.S. international tax system is out of sync with the rest of the world, particularly with regard to taxing worldwide income. In addition, the U.S. statutory corporate tax rate of 35 percent exceeds that of all other G20 countries. On one end of the spectrum, proposals would convert the U.S. to a territorial tax system (that is, the U.S. would only tax U.S. source income) and lower the U.S. corporate tax rate. At the other end of the spectrum, proposals would end U.S. deferral of foreign income earned by foreign subsidiaries and treat all foreign earnings as being repatriated back to the U.S. when earned.

While the U.S. government debates U.S. international tax reform, the Organization for Economic Cooperation and Development (OECD) embarked on a "base erosion and profit shifting" (BEPS) initiative that has, as its goal, to provide "governments with solutions for closing the gaps in existing international rules that allow corporate profits to "disappear" or be artificially shifted to low/no tax environments, where little or no economic activity takes place." This initiative, which began in 2013, was prompted by estimates that governments around the world were losing between $100–$240 billion per year in tax revenues due to aggressive tax planning by multinational corporations. The OECD issued 15 "actions" in October 2015 that focus on transfer pricing, harmful tax practices, treaty shopping, and more transparent reporting ("country-by-country reporting" of income and taxes paid). Adoption of these actions by governments around the world will dramatically change how multinational corporations plan their international operations and develop their information systems and how taxing agencies audit the tax returns filed by these corporations.

CONCLUSION

In this chapter we discussed some of the important U.S. tax rules that apply to U.S. persons who expand their business operations outside the United States. As the storyline indicates, a U.S. business that wants to expand its markets outside the United States must decide on an organizational form through which to conduct its business. Establishing a physical presence in another country generally subjects the profits of the business to taxation in the host country and potentially in the United States as well. Treaties between the United States and other countries can provide beneficial tax treatment to a U.S. company's operations, employees, and cross-border payments. Where a cross-border transaction is subject to both foreign and U.S. taxation, the United States provides relief in the form of a foreign tax credit for foreign income taxes paid on foreign income that is reported on a U.S. tax return. These credits can be reduced by the foreign tax credit limitation. By operating through a foreign corporation, a U.S. business can defer U.S. taxation on foreign source income until such income is repatriated to the United States. Certain types of income are not subject to deferral if earned through a CFC. The use of hybrid entities outside the United States provides U.S. companies with the ability to shift income and move cash across jurisdictions without being subject to deemed dividends under subpart F.

Summary

LO 24-1 Understand the basic U.S. framework for taxing multinational transactions and the role of the foreign tax credit limitation.

- Countries most often determine nexus by either the geographic source of the income (source-based jurisdiction) or the taxpayer's citizenship or residence (residence-based jurisdiction).
  - Under a residence-based approach, a country taxes the worldwide income of the person earning the income.
  - Under a source-based approach, a country taxes only the income earned within its boundaries.
- The U.S. government taxes citizens and residents on their worldwide income, regardless of source (residence-based jurisdiction).
  - An individual who is not a citizen will be treated as a U.S. resident for income tax purposes if he or she is considered a permanent resident (has a green card) or satisfies a substantial presence test.
- The U.S. government only taxes nonresidents on income that is "U.S. source" or is connected with the operation of a U.S. trade or business (source-based jurisdiction).
- To alleviate (mitigate) potential double taxation and to promote international commerce, governments often allow their residents a tax credit for foreign income taxes paid on foreign source income.

LO 24-2 Apply the U.S. source rules for common items of gross income and deductions.

- The U.S. source rules determine whether income and related deductions are from sources within or without the United States.
  - The U.S. source-of-income rules are important to non-U.S. persons because they limit the scope of U.S. taxation of their worldwide income.
  - For U.S. persons, the primary purpose of the U.S. source-of-income rules is to calculate foreign source taxable income in the numerator of the foreign tax credit limitation.
- The Internal Revenue Code defines eight classes of gross income from sources within the United States and eight classes of gross income from sources without the United States.
  - As a general rule, the taxpayer looks to the borrower's residence to determine the geographic source of interest received.
  - In general, the source of dividend income is determined by the residence of the corporation paying the dividend.
  - The source of compensation received for labor or personal services is determined by the location where the service is performed.
  - Rent has its source where the property generating the rent is located.
  - Royalty income has its source where the intangible property or rights generating the royalty is used.
- After determining the source of gross income as being from U.S. or foreign sources, a taxpayer may be required to allocate and apportion allowable deductions to gross income from each geographical source to compute taxable income from U.S. and foreign sources.
  - The IRC provides very broad language in describing how to allocate deductions to U.S. and foreign source gross income.
  - The regulations attempt to match deductions with the gross income such deductions were incurred to produce, usually based on the "factual relationship" of the deduction to gross income.
  - Special apportionment rules apply to nine categories of deductions, most notably interest, research and experimentation, state and local income taxes, losses on property disposition, and charitable contributions.

Recall the role of income tax treaties in international tax planning.

LO 24-3

- A tax treaty is a bilateral agreement between two contracting countries in which each agrees to modify its own tax laws to achieve reciprocal benefits.
- The general purpose of an income tax treaty is to eliminate or reduce (mitigate) the impact of double taxation so that residents paying taxes to one country will not have the full burden of taxes in the other country.
- The United States currently has income tax treaties with 67 countries.
- Most U.S. treaties provide a low withholding tax rate or an exemption from tax on various types of investment income (interest, dividends, gains from sale of stock, and royalties) that would otherwise be subject to a high withholding tax.

Identify creditable foreign taxes and compute the foreign tax credit limitation.

LO 24-4

- The foreign tax credit is available only for foreign taxes the United States considers to be income taxes.
- Creditable foreign income taxes can be direct, indirect, or "in lieu of" income taxes.
- Taxpayers must compute a separate FTC limitation for each category ("basket") of foreign source taxable income.
  - Passive category income generally is investment-type income that traditionally is subject to low foreign taxes (usually in the form of withholding taxes).
  - Income not treated as passive category income is defined to be general category income. General category income includes gross income from an active trade or business, financial services income, and shipping income.
  - A taxpayer computes the FTC limitation by multiplying the ratio of foreign source taxable income to total taxable income times precredit U.S. tax, as follows:

$$\frac{\text{Foreign source taxable income}}{\text{Total taxable income}} \times \text{Precredit U.S. tax}$$

Distinguish between the different forms of doing business outside the United States and list their advantages and disadvantages.

LO 24-5

- A U.S. person can do business outside the United States through a branch, partnership, corporation, or hybrid entity.
- A hybrid entity is an entity that is treated as a flow-through entity for U.S. tax purposes and a corporation for foreign tax purposes (or vice versa).
- A U.S. taxpayer elects the U.S. tax status of a hybrid entity by "checking the box" on Form 8832.
  - Certain designated per se foreign entities are not eligible for this elective treatment.

Comprehend the basic U.S. anti-deferral tax regime and identify common sources of subpart F income.

LO 24-6

- Subpart F requires certain U.S. shareholders in a controlled foreign corporation (CFC) to include in their gross income currently their pro rata share of specified categories of "tainted" income earned by the CFC during the current year (*subpart F income*).
- A controlled foreign corporation is defined as any foreign corporation in which U.S. shareholders collectively own more than 50 percent of the total combined voting power of all classes of stock entitled to vote or the total value of the corporation's stock on any day during the CFC's tax year.
  - Constructive ownership rules are used in the calculation of both the 50 percent test for determining CFC status and the 10 percent test for determining who is a U.S. shareholder.
- Subpart F income generally can be characterized as low-taxed passive income or "portable" income earned by a CFC.
  - Foreign personal holding company income includes interest, dividends, rents, royalties, and gains from the sales of certain foreign property.
  - Foreign base company sales income is income derived by a CFC from the sale or purchase of personal property to (or from) a related person and the property is manufactured and sold outside the CFC's country of incorporation.

- There are several exceptions that serve to exclude all or a portion of a CFC's subpart F income from current taxation to the U.S. shareholders.
  - A *de minimis rule* excludes all gross income from being treated as foreign base company income if the sum of the CFC's gross foreign base company income is less than the lesser of 5 percent of gross income or $1 million.
  - A *full inclusion rule* treats all of the CFC's gross income as foreign base company income if more than 70 percent of the CFC's gross income is foreign base company income.

KEY TERMS

allocate (24-12)

apportion (24-12)

branch (24-3)

commercial traveler exception (24-8)

controlled foreign corporation (24-28)

definitely related deductions (24-12)

disregarded entity (24-26)

effectively connected income (24-3)

fixed and determinable, annual or periodic income (24-3)

foreign joint venture (24-22)

foreign personal holding company income (24-29)

foreign subsidiary (24-22)

foreign tax credit (24-5)

foreign tax credit limitation (24-5)

FTC basket (24-20)

functional currency (24-23)

general category income (24-20)

hybrid entity (24-26)

inbound transaction (24-2)

nexus (24-2)

nonresident alien (24-4)

not definitely related deductions (24-12)

outbound transaction (24-2)

passive category income (24-20)

permanent establishment (24-18)

residence-based jurisdiction (24-2)

resident alien (24-4)

reverse hybrid entity (24-26)

source-based jurisdiction (24-2)

spot rate (24-22)

subpart F income (24-28)

tax haven (24-27)

DISCUSSION QUESTIONS

Discussion Questions are available in *Connect*®.

LO 24-1   1. Distinguish between an outbound transaction and an inbound transaction from a U.S. tax perspective.

LO 24-1   2. What are the major U.S. tax issues that apply to an inbound transaction?

LO 24-1   3. What are the major U.S. tax issues that apply to an outbound transaction?

LO 24-1   4. How does a residence-based approach to taxing worldwide income differ from a source-based approach to taxing the same income?

LO 24-1   5. Henri is a resident of the United States for U.S. tax purposes and earns $10,000 from an investment in a French company. Will Henri be subject to U.S. tax under a residence-based approach to taxation? A source-based approach?

LO 24-1   6. What are the two categories of income that can be taxed by the United States when earned by a nonresident? How does the United States tax each category of income?

LO 24-1   7. Maria is not a citizen of the United States, but she spends 180 days per year in the United States on business-related activities. Under what conditions will Maria be considered a resident of the United States for U.S. tax purposes?

LO 24-1   8. Natasha is not a citizen of the United States, but she spends 200 days per year in the United States on business. She does not have a green card. True or False: Natasha will always be considered a resident of the United States for U.S. tax purposes because of her physical presence in the United States. Explain.

LO 24-1   9. Why does the United States allow U.S. taxpayers to claim a credit against their precredit U.S. tax for foreign income taxes paid?

10. What role does the foreign tax credit limitation play in U.S. tax policy? `LO 24-1`

11. Why are the income source rules important to a U.S. citizen or resident? `LO 24-2`

12. Why are the income source rules important to a U.S. nonresident? `LO 24-2`

13. Carol receives $500 of dividend income from Microsoft Inc., a U.S. company. True or False: Absent any treaty provisions, Carol will be subject to U.S. tax on the dividend regardless of whether she is a resident or nonresident. Explain. `LO 24-2`

14. Pavel, a citizen and resident of Russia, spent 100 days in the United States working for his employer, Yukos Oil, a Russian corporation. Under what conditions will Pavel be subject to U.S. tax on the portion of his compensation earned while working in the United States? `LO 24-2`

15. What are the potential U.S. tax benefits from engaging in a §863(b) sale? `LO 24-2`

16. True or False: A taxpayer will always prefer deducting an expense against U.S. source income and not foreign source income when filing a tax return in the United States. Explain. `LO 24-2`

17. Distinguish between *allocation* and *apportionment* in sourcing deductions in computing the foreign tax credit limitation. `LO 24-2`

18. Distinguish between a *definitely related deduction* and a *not definitely related deduction* in the allocation and apportionment of deductions to foreign source taxable income. `LO 24-2`

19. Briefly describe the two different methods for apportioning interest expense to foreign source taxable income in the computation of the foreign tax credit limitation. `LO 24-2`

20. Briefly describe the two different methods for apportioning research and experimental expenditures (R&E) to foreign source taxable income in the computation of the foreign tax credit limitation. `LO 24-2`

21. IBM incurs $250 million of R&E in the United States. How does the "exclusive apportionment" of this deduction differ depending on the R&E apportionment method chosen in the computation of the foreign tax credit limitation? `LO 24-2`

22. What is the primary goal of the United States in negotiating income tax treaties with other countries? `LO 24-3`

23. What is a *permanent establishment,* and why is it an important part of most income tax treaties? `LO 24-3`

24. Why is a treaty important to a nonresident investor in U.S. stocks and bonds? `LO 24-3`

25. Why is a treaty important to a nonresident worker in the United States? `LO 24-3`

26. Why does the United States use a "basket" approach in the foreign tax credit limitation computation? `LO 24-4`

27. True or False: All dividend income received by a U.S. taxpayer is classified as passive category income for foreign tax credit limitation purposes. Explain. `LO 24-4`

28. True or False: All foreign taxes are creditable for U.S. tax purposes. Explain. `LO 24-4`

29. What is an "indirect credit" for foreign tax credit purposes? What is the tax policy reason for allowing such a credit? `LO 24-4`

30. What is a functional currency? What role does it play in the computation of an indirect credit for foreign tax credit purposes? `LO 24-4`

31. What is a hybrid entity for U.S. tax purposes? Why is a hybrid entity a popular organizational form for a U.S. company expanding its international operations? What are the potential drawbacks to using a hybrid entity? `LO 24-5`

32. What is a "per se" entity under the check-the-box rules? `LO 24-5`

LO 24-6 33. What are the requirements for a foreign corporation to be a *controlled foreign corporation* for U.S. tax purposes?

LO 24-6 34. Why does the United States not allow deferral on all foreign source income earned by a controlled foreign corporation?

LO 24-6 35. True or False: A foreign corporation owned equally by 11 U.S. individuals can never be a controlled foreign corporation? Explain.

LO 24-6 36. What is foreign base company sales income? Why does the United States include this income in its definition of subpart F income?

LO 24-6 37. True or False: Subpart F income is always treated as a deemed dividend to the U.S. shareholders of a controlled foreign corporation. Explain.

LO 24-6 38. True or False: Non-subpart F income always qualifies for tax deferral until it is repatriated back to the United States. Explain.

PROBLEMS

Select problems are available in *Connect*®.   ▇ **connect**

LO 24-1 39. Camille, a citizen and resident of Country A, received a $1,000 dividend from a corporation organized in Country B. Which statement best describes the taxation of this income under the two different approaches to taxing foreign income?

  a) Country B will not tax this income under a residence-based jurisdiction approach but will tax this income under a source-based jurisdiction approach.

  b) Country B will tax this income under a residence-based jurisdiction approach but will not tax this income under a source-based jurisdiction approach.

  c) Country B will tax this income under both a residence-based jurisdiction approach and a source-based jurisdiction approach.

  d) Country B will not tax this income under either a residence-based jurisdiction approach or a source-based jurisdiction approach.

LO 24-1 40. Spartan Corporation, a U.S. corporation, reported $2 million of pretax income from its business operations in Spartania, which were conducted through a foreign branch. Spartania taxes branch income at 25 percent, and the United States taxes corporate income at 35 percent.

  a) If the United States provided no mechanism for mitigating double taxation, what would be the total tax (U.S. and foreign) on the $2 million of branch profits?

  b) Assume the United States allows U.S. corporations to exclude foreign source income from U.S. taxation. What would be the total tax on the $2 million of branch profits?

  c) Assume the United States allows U.S. corporations to claim a deduction for foreign income taxes. What would be the total tax on the $2 million of branch profits?

  d) Assume the United States allows U.S. corporations to claim a credit for foreign income taxes paid on foreign source income. What would be the total tax on the $2 million of branch profits? What would be your answer if Spartania taxed branch profits at 40 percent?

LO 24-1 41. Guido is a citizen and resident of Belgium. He has a full-time job in Belgium and has lived there with his family for the past 10 years. In 2014, Guido came to the United States for the first time. The sole purpose of his trip was business. He intended to stay in the United States for only 180 days, but he ended up staying for 210 days because of unforeseen problems with his business. Guido came to the United States again on business in 2015 and stayed for 180 days. In 2016 he came back to the United States on business and stayed for 70 days. Determine if Guido meets the U.S. statutory definition of a resident alien in 2014, 2015, and 2016 under the substantial presence test.

42. Use the facts in problem 41. If Guido meets the statutory requirements to be considered a resident of both the United States and Belgium, what criteria does the U.S.-Belgium treaty use to "break the tie" and determine Guido's country of residence? Look at Article 4 of the 2007 U.S.-Belgium income tax treaty, which you can find on the IRS Web site, www.irs.gov.

    LO 24-1

    research

43. How does the U.S.-Belgium treaty define a *permanent establishment* for determining nexus? Look at Article 5 of the 2007 U.S.-Belgium income tax treaty, which you can find on the IRS Web site, www.irs.gov.

    LO 24-1

    research

44. Mackinac Corporation, a U.S. corporation, reported total taxable income of $5 million. Taxable income included $1.5 million of foreign source taxable income from the company's branch operations in Canada. All of the branch income is general category income. Mackinac paid Canadian income taxes of $600,000 on its branch income. Compute Mackinac's allowable foreign tax credit. Assume a U.S. corporate tax rate of 34 percent.

    LO 24-1

45. Waco Leather Inc., a U.S. corporation, reported total taxable income of $5 million. Taxable income included $1.5 million of foreign source taxable income from the company's branch operations in Mexico. All of the branch income is general category income. Waco paid Mexican income taxes of $420,000 on its branch income. Compute Waco's allowable foreign tax credit. Assume a U.S. corporate tax rate of 34 percent.

    LO 24-1

46. Petoskey Stone Inc., a U.S. corporation, received the following sources of income during the current year. Identify the source of each item as either U.S. or foreign.

    LO 24-2

    a) Interest income from a loan to its German subsidiary.

    b) Dividend income from Granite Corporation, a U.S. corporation.

    c) Royalty income from its Irish subsidiary for use of a trademark.

    d) Rent income from its Canadian subsidiary of a warehouse located in Wisconsin.

47. Carmen SanDiego, a U.S. citizen, is employed by General Motors Corporation, a U.S. corporation. On April 1, 2016, GM relocated Carmen to its Brazilian operations for the remainder of 2016. Carmen was paid a salary of $120,000 and was employed on a 5-day week basis. As part of her compensation package for moving to Brazil, Carmen also received a housing allowance of $25,000. Carmen's salary was earned ratably over the 12-month period. During 2016 Carmen worked 260 days, 195 of which were in Brazil and 65 of which were in Michigan. How much of Carmen's total compensation is treated as foreign source income for 2016? Why might Carmen want to maximize her foreign source income in 2016?

    LO 24-2

48. Sam Smith is a citizen and bona fide resident of Great Britain (United Kingdom). During the current year, Sam received the following income:

    LO 24-2

    • Compensation of $30 million from performing concerts in the United States.

    • Cash dividends of $10,000 from a French corporation stock.

    • Interest of $6,000 on a U.S. corporation bond.

    • Interest of $2,000 on a loan made to a U.S. citizen residing in Australia.

    • Gain of $80,000 on the sale of stock in a U.S. corporation.

Determine the source (U.S. or foreign) of each item of income Sam received.

Income	Source
Income from concerts	
Dividend from French corporation	
Interest on a U.S. corporation bond	
Interest of $2,000 on a loan made to a U.S. citizen residing in Australia	
Gain of $80,000 on the sale of stock in a U.S. corporation	

LO 24-2

49. Spartan Corporation, a U.S. company, manufactures green eyeshades for sale in the United States and Europe. All manufacturing activities take place in Michigan. During the current year, Spartan sold 10,000 green eyeshades to European customers at a price of $10 each. Each eyeshade costs $4 to produce. All of Spartan's production assets are located in the United States. For each independent scenario, determine the source of the gross income from sale of the green eyeshades.

a) Spartan ships its eyeshades F.O.B., place of destination.

b) Spartan ships its eyeshades F.O.B., place of shipment.

LO 24-2

planning

50. Falmouth Kettle Company, a U.S. corporation, sells its products in the United States and Europe. During the current year, selling, general, and administrative (SG&A) expenses included:

Personnel department	$ 500
Training department	350
President's salary	400
Sales manager's salary	200
Other general and administrative	550
Total SG&A expenses	$2,000

Falmouth had $12,000 of gross sales to U.S. customers and $3,000 of gross sales to European customers. Gross income (sales minus cost of goods sold) from domestic sales was $3,000 and gross profit from foreign sales was $1,000. Apportion Falmouth's SG&A expenses to foreign source income using the following methods:

a) Gross sales.

b) Gross income.

c) If Falmouth wants to maximize its foreign tax credit limitation, which method produces the better outcome?

LO 24-2

planning

51. Owl Vision Corporation (OVC) is a North Carolina corporation engaged in the manufacture and sale of contact lenses and other optical equipment. The company handles its export sales through sales branches in Belgium and Singapore. The average tax book value of OVC's assets for the year was $200 million, of which $160 million generated U.S. source income and $40 million generated foreign source income. The average fair market value of OVC's assets was $240 million, of which $180 million generated U.S. source income and $60 million generated foreign source income. OVC's total interest expense was $20 million.

a) What amount of the interest expense will be apportioned to foreign source income under the tax book value method?

b) What amount of the interest expense will be apportioned to foreign source income under the fair market value method?

c) If OVC wants to maximize its foreign tax credit limitation, which method produces the better outcome?

52. Freon Corporation, a U.S. corporation, manufactures air-conditioning and warm-air heating equipment. Freon reported gross sales from this product group of $50,000,000, of which $10,000,000 was foreign source. The gross profit percentage for domestic sales was 15 percent, and the gross profit percentage from non-U.S. sales was 20 percent. Freon incurred R&E expenses of $6,000,000, all of which were conducted in the United States.

LO 24-2

planning

a) What amount of the R&E expense will be apportioned to foreign source income under the sales method?

b) What amount of the R&E expense will be apportioned to foreign source income under the gross income method?

c) If Freon wants to maximize its foreign tax credit limitation, which method produces the better outcome?

53. Colleen is a citizen and bona fide resident of Ireland. During the current year, she received the following income:

LO 24-3

research

- Cash dividends of $2,000 from a U.S. corporation's stock.
- Interest of $1,000 on a U.S. corporation bond.
- Royalty of $100,000 from a U.S. corporation for use of a patent she developed.
- Rent of $3,000 from U.S. individuals renting her cottage in Maine.

Identify the U.S. withholding tax rate on the payment of each item of income under the U.S.-Ireland income tax treaty and cite the appropriate treaty article. You can access the 1997 U.S.-Ireland income tax treaty on the IRS Web site, www.irs.gov.

Income	Withholding Tax Rate	Treaty Article
Cash dividends of $2,000		
Interest of $1,000		
Royalty of $100,000		
Rent of $3,000		

54. Gameco, a U.S. corporation, operates gambling machines in the United States and abroad. Gameco conducts its operations in Europe through a Dutch B.V., which is treated as a branch for U.S. tax purposes. Gameco also licenses game machines to an unrelated company in Japan. During the current year, Gameco paid the following foreign taxes, translated into U.S. dollars at the appropriate exchange rate:

LO 24-4

Foreign Taxes	Amount (in $)
National income taxes	1,000,000
City (Amsterdam) income taxes	100,000
Value-added tax	150,000
Payroll tax (employer's share of social insurance contributions)	400,000
Withholding tax on royalties received from Japan	50,000

Identify Gameco's creditable foreign taxes.

55. Sombrero Corporation, a U.S. corporation, operates through a branch in Espana. Management projects that the company's pretax income in the next taxable year will be $100,000, $80,000 from U.S. operations and $20,000 from

LO 24-4

planning

the branch. Espania taxes corporate income at a rate of 45 percent. The U.S. corporate tax rate is 35 percent.

  a) If management's projections are accurate, what will be Sombrero's excess foreign tax credit in the next taxable year? Assume all of the income is general category income.

  b) Management plans to establish a second branch in Italia. Italia taxes corporate income at a rate of 30 percent. What amount of income will the branch in Italia have to generate to eliminate the excess credit generated by the branch in Espania?

LO 24-4 56. Chapeau Company, a U.S. corporation, operates through a branch in Champagnia. The source rules used by Champagnia are identical to those used by the United States. For 2016, Chapeau has $2,000 of gross income, $1,200 from U.S. sources and $800 from sources within Champagnia. The $1,200 of U.S. source income and $700 of the foreign source income are attributable to manufacturing activities in Champagnia (general category income). The remaining $100 of foreign source income is passive category interest income. Chapeau had $500 of expenses other than taxes, all of which are allocated directly to manufacturing income ($200 of which is apportioned to foreign sources). Chapeau paid $150 of income taxes to Champagnia on its manufacturing income. The interest income was subject to a 10 percent withholding tax of $10. Assume the U.S. tax rate is 35 percent. Compute Chapeau's allowable foreign tax credit in 2016.

LO 24-4 57. Paton Corporation, a U.S. corporation, owns 100 percent of the stock of Tappan Ltd, a British corporation, and 100 percent of the stock of Monroe N.V., a Dutch corporation. Monroe has post-1986 undistributed earnings of €600 and post-1986 foreign income taxes of $400. Tappan has post-1986 undistributed earnings of £800 and post-1986 foreign income taxes of $200. During the current year, Tappan paid Paton a dividend of £100, and Monroe paid Paton a dividend of €100. The dividends were exempt from withholding tax under the U.S.-UK and U.S.-Netherlands income tax treaties. The exchange rates are as follows: €1:$1.50 and £1:$2.00.

  a) Compute Paton's deemed paid credit on the dividends it received from Tappan and Monroe.

  b) Assume this is Paton's only income and compute the company's net U.S. tax after allowance of any foreign tax credits.

LO 24-4
planning 58. Hannah Corporation, a U.S. corporation, owns 100 percent of the stock of its two foreign corporations, Red S.A. and Cedar A.G. Red and Cedar derive all of their income from active foreign business operations. Red operates in a low-tax jurisdiction (20 percent tax rate), and Cedar operates in a high-tax jurisdiction (50 percent tax rate). Red has post-1986 foreign income taxes of $200 and post-1986 undistributed earnings of 800u. Cedar has post-1986 foreign income taxes of $500 and post-1986 undistributed earnings of 500q. No withholding taxes are imposed on any dividends that Hannah receives from Red or Cedar. The exchange rate between all three currencies is 1:1. Assume a U.S. corporate tax rate of 35 percent. Under the look-through rules, all dividend income is treated as general category income.

  a) Compute the effect of an 80u dividend from Red on Hannah's net U.S. tax liability.

  b) Can you offer Hannah any suggestions regarding how it might eliminate the residual U.S. tax due on an 80u dividend from Red? Be specific in terms of the exact amounts involved in any planning opportunities you identify.

LO 24-5 59. Identify the "per se" companies for which a check-the-box election cannot be made for U.S. tax purposes in the countries listed below. Consult the Instructions to Form 8832, which can be found on the "Forms & Pubs" site on the IRS Web site, www.irs.gov.

a) Japan

b) Germany

c) Netherlands

d) United Kingdom

e) People's Republic of China

60. Eagle Inc., a U.S. corporation, intends to create a *limitada* in Brazil in 2016 to manufacture pitching machines. The company expects the operation to generate losses of US$2,500,000 during its first three years of operations. Eagle would like the losses to flow through to its U.S. tax return and offset its U.S. profits.   **LO 24-5**   research

a) Can Eagle "check the box" and treat the *limitada* as a disregarded entity (branch) for U.S. tax purposes? Consult the Instructions to Form 8832, which can be found on the "Forms & Pubs" site on the IRS Web site, www.irs.gov.

b) Assume management's projections were accurate and Eagle deducted $75,000 of branch losses on its U.S. tax return from 2016–2018. At 01/01/19, the fair market value of the *limitada*'s net assets exceeded Eagle's tax basis in the assets by US$5 million. What are the U.S. tax consequences of checking the box on Form 8832 and converting the *limitada* to a corporation for U.S. tax purposes?

61. Identify whether the corporations described below are controlled foreign corporations.   **LO 24-6**

a) Shetland PLC, a U.K. corporation, has two classes of stock outstanding, 75 shares of class AA stock and 25 shares of class A stock. Each class of stock has equal voting power. Angus owns 35 shares of class AA stock and 20 shares of class A stock. Angus is a U.S. citizen who resides in England.

b) Tony and Gina, both U.S. citizens, own 5 percent and 10 percent, respectively, of the voting stock of DaVinci S.A., an Italian corporation. Tony and Gina are also equal partners in Roma Corporation, an Italian corporation that owns 50 percent of the DaVinci stock.

c) Pierre, a U.S. citizen, owns 45 of the 100 shares outstanding in Vino S.A., a French corporation. Pierre's father, Pepe, owns 8 shares in Vino. Pepe also is a U.S. citizen. The remaining 47 shares are owned by non-U.S. individuals.

62. USCo owns 100 percent of the following corporations: Dutch N.V., Germany A.G., Australia PLC, Japan Corporation, and Brazil S.A. During the year, the following transactions took place: **LO 24-6**

a) Germany A.G. owns an office building that it leases to unrelated persons. Germany A.G. engaged an independent managing agent to manage and maintain the office building and performs no activities with respect to the property.

b) Dutch N.V. leased office machines to unrelated persons. Dutch N.V. performed only incidental activities and incurred nominal expenses in leasing and servicing the machines. Dutch N.V. is not engaged in the manufacture or production of the machines and does not add substantial value to the machines.

c) Dutch N.V. purchased goods manufactured in France from an unrelated contract manufacturer and sold them to Germany A.G. for consumption in Germany.

d) Australia PLC purchased goods manufactured in Australia from an unrelated person and sold them to Japan Corporation for use in Japan.

Determine whether the above transactions result in subpart F income to USCo.

LO 24-6 63. USCo manufactures and markets electrical components. USCo operates outside the United States through a number of CFCs, each of which is organized in a different country. These CFCs derived the following income for the current year:

a) F1 has gross income of $5 million, including $200,000 of foreign personal holding company interest and $4.8 million of gross income from the sale of inventory that F1 manufactured at a factory located within its home country.

b) F2 has gross income of $5 million, including $4 million of foreign personal holding company interest and $1 million of gross income from the sale of inventory that F2 manufactured at a factory located within its home country.

Determine the amount of income that USCo must report as a deemed dividend under subpart F in each scenario.

COMPREHENSIVE PROBLEMS

Select problems are available in *Connect*®.

64. Spartan Corporation manufactures quidgets at its plant in Sparta, Michigan. Spartan sells its quidgets to customers in the United States, Canada, England, and Australia.

Spartan markets its products in Canada and England through branches in Toronto and London, respectively. Title transfers in the United States on all sales to U.S. customers and abroad (FOB: destination) on all sales to Canadian and English customers. Spartan reported total gross income on U.S. sales of $15,000,000 and total gross income on Canadian and U.K. sales of $5,000,000, split equally between the two countries. Spartan paid Canadian income taxes of $600,000 on its branch profits in Canada and U.K. income taxes of $700,000 on its branch profits in the United Kingdom. Spartan financed its Canadian operations through a $10 million capital contribution, which Spartan financed through a loan from Bank of America. During the current year, Spartan paid $600,000 in interest on the loan.

Spartan sells its quidgets to Australian customers through its wholly-owned Australian subsidiary. Title passes in the United States (FOB: shipping) on all sales to the subsidiary. Spartan reported gross income of $3,000,000 on sales to its subsidiary during the year. The subsidiary paid Spartan a dividend of $670,000 on December 31 (the withholding tax is 0 percent under the U.S.-Australia treaty). Spartan was deemed to have paid Australian income taxes of $330,000 on the income repatriated as a dividend.

a) Compute Spartan's foreign source gross income and foreign tax (direct and withholding) for the current year.

b) Assume 20 percent of the interest paid to Bank of America is allocated to the numerator of Spartan's FTC limitation calculation. Compute Spartan Corporation's FTC limitation using your calculation from part (a) and any excess FTC or excess FTC limitation (all of the foreign source income is put in the general category FTC basket).

65. Windmill Corporation manufactures products in its plants in Iowa, Canada, Ireland, and Australia. Windmill conducts its operations in Canada through a 50 percent owned joint venture, CanCo. CanCo is treated as a corporation for U.S. and Canadian tax purposes. An unrelated Canadian investor owns the remaining 50 percent. Windmill conducts its operations in Ireland through a wholly-owned subsidiary, IrishCo. IrishCo is a controlled foreign corporation for U.S. tax purposes. Windmill conducts its operations in Australia through a wholly-owned hybrid entity (KiwiCo) treated as a branch for U.S. tax purposes and a corporation for Australian tax purposes. Windmill also owns a 5 percent interest in a Dutch corporation (TulipCo).

During 2016, Windmill reported the following foreign source income from its international operations and investments.

	CanCo	IrishCo	KiwiCo	TulipCo
Dividend income				
Amount	$45,000	$28,000		$20,000
Withholding tax	2,250	1,400		3,000
Interest income				
Amount	30,000			
Withholding tax	0	0		
Branch income				
Taxable income			$93,000	
AUS income taxes			31,000	

Notes to the table:
1. CanCo and KiwiCo derive all of their earnings from active business operations.
2. The dividend from CanCo carries with it a deemed paid credit (§78 gross-up) of $30,000.
3. The dividend from IrishCo carries with it a deemed paid credit (§78 gross-up) of $4,000.

a) Classify the income received by Windmill and any associated §78 gross-up into the appropriate FTC baskets.

b) Windmill has $1,250,000 of U.S. source gross income. Windmill also incurred SG&A of $300,000 that is apportioned between U.S. and foreign source income based on the gross income in each basket. Assume KiwiCo's gross income is $93,000. Compute the FTC limitation for each basket of foreign source income. The corporate tax rate is 35 percent.

66. Euro Corporation, a U.S. corporation, operates through a branch in Germany. During 2016 the branch reported taxable income of $1,000,000 and paid German income taxes of $300,000. In addition, Euro received $50,000 of dividends from its 5 percent investment in the stock of Maple Leaf Company, a Canadian corporation. The dividend was subject to a withholding tax of $5,000. Euro reported U.S. taxable income from its manufacturing operations of $950,000. Total taxable income was $2,000,000. Precredit U.S. taxes on the taxable income were $680,000. Included in the computation of Euro's taxable income were "definitely allocable" expenses of $500,000, 50 percent of which were related to the German branch taxable income.

 tax forms

Complete pages 1 and 2 of Form 1118 for just the general category income reported by Euro. You can use the fill-in form available on the IRS Web site, www.irs.gov.

67. USCo, a U.S. corporation, has decided to set up a headquarters subsidiary in Europe. Management has narrowed its location choice to either Spain, or Ireland, or Switzerland. The company has asked you to research some of the income tax implications of setting up a corporation in these three countries. In particular, management wants to know what tax rate will be imposed on corporate income earned in the country and the withholding rates applied to interest, dividends, and royalty payments from the subsidiary to the USCo.

 research

To answer the tax rate question, consult KPMG's *Corporate and Indirect Tax Survey 2014,* which you can access at http://www.kpmg.com/Global/en/IssuesAndInsights/ArticlesPublications/Documents/corporate-indirect-tax-rate-survey-2014.pdf. To answer the withholding tax questions, consult the treaties between the United States and Spain, Ireland, and Switzerland, which you can access at www.irs.gov (type in "treaties" as your search word).

Transfer Taxes and Wealth Planning

Learning Objectives

Upon completing this chapter, you should be able to:

LO 25-1 Outline the basic structure of federal transfer taxes and describe the valuation of property transfers.

LO 25-2 Summarize the operation of the federal gift tax and the calculation of the federal gift tax.

LO 25-3 Describe the federal estate tax, and compute taxable transfers at death and the federal estate tax.

LO 25-4 Apply fundamental principles of wealth planning and explain how income and transfer taxation interact to affect wealth planning.

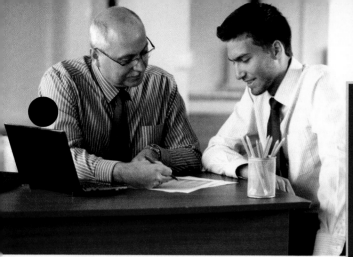

© Michal Kowalski/Shutterstock.com

Storyline Summary

Taxpayers:	Bob and Harry Smith, brothers, ages 69 and 63, respectively. Frank's Frozen Pizza Inc. (FFP) is a family business.
Description:	Bob, recently deceased, was a widower and has a son, Nate (age 28). Harry is married to Wilma, age 38, and has a daughter, Dina (age 35), a son-in-law, Steve, and a grandson, George (age 6).
Location:	Ann Arbor, Michigan
Employment status:	Bob and Harry inherited shares in FFP in 1990. Bob and Harry have been employees of FFP. Bob retired from FFP and died earlier this year. Harry is planning to retire as CEO of FFP.
Current situation:	Nate is Bob's executor.

Harry and Bob Smith were brothers and owners of a small privately held corporation, Frank's Frozen Pizzas Inc. (FFP). Their father, Frank, established the business 35 years ago, and Harry and Bob each inherited half of FFP's outstanding shares upon Frank's death. At the time of Frank's death in 1990, FFP shares were worth about $1 million, but the firm is now debt-free and has a value of $9 million. FFP's success didn't come easy. Over the years Harry and Bob were employed as executive officers and worked long, hard hours. After the death of his wife in 1995, Bob retired on his FFP pension. Over the years both Harry and Bob have transferred some of their FFP shares to other family members. Bob has given 20 percent of the shares in FFP to his son, Nate, and Harry has transferred a like amount to a trust established for Dina (his daughter) and George (his grandson).

Harry recently decided that he wants to retire from FFP and spend more time traveling and enjoying his family. Harry believes that Nate would like to assume responsibilities as CEO, and Dina has agreed to support Nate's decisions. Harry plans to begin an orderly transfer of his FFP stock to Dina to provide a future source of support for her and George. Besides his FFP stock, Harry has accumulated considerable personal assets to help maintain his lifestyle during retirement. Although Wilma, Harry's wife, owns significant assets, Harry also wants to provide for her support after his death. Finally, while Harry believes taxes and lawyers are necessary evils, he wants to avoid any unnecessary fees or taxes associated with the transfer of his assets. Hence, Harry would like advice on how to make his gifts in the most tax-efficient manner.

to be continued . . .

LO 25-1   INTRODUCTION TO FEDERAL TRANSFER TAXES

This chapter explains the structure of the federal transfer taxes. We begin by outlining transfer taxes and then proceed to describing in detail the federal gift tax. Finally, we describe the federal estate tax and introduce the principles of wealth planning.

Beginnings

In 1916 Congress imposed an estate tax on transfers of property at death. Transfers at death are dictated by the **last will and testament** of the deceased and such transfers are called **testamentary transfers.** The transfer tax system was expanded in 1924 to include a gift tax on lifetime transfers called **intervivos transfers** (from the Latin meaning "during the life of"). Eventually, a generation-skipping tax was also added to prevent tax avoidance by transferring assets to younger generations (transfers to grandchildren rather than to children).[1] Together, this trio of taxes represents one way of reducing the potential wealth society's richest families might accumulate over several generations. (Remember, neither gifts nor inheritances are included in recipients' gross income.)

TAXES IN THE REAL WORLD   Perfect Timing

Roger Milliken died on December 30, 2010, just two days before the estate tax was revived. Milliken was 95 years old and had directed his family's business for 71 years as president and CEO of Milliken & Company. Milliken's estate, estimated under $1 billion, was subject to probate in Spartanburg County, South Carolina. In his 111-page will, described by the Spartanburg *Journal Watchdog,* Milliken established multiple trusts and directed that the family business would remain privately owned. Moreover, Milliken instructed trustees that no change of tax laws would warrant deviating from his intentions. In a two-page letter, Milliken expressed the hope that income from the trust would enable his descendants to pursue careers. To qualify for income from the trusts, Milliken's children must be 40 years old at which time they will be eligible to receive 10 percent of the trust's income. The distribution increases to 50 percent at age 44 and to all of the net income by the age of 49. Milliken also expressed hope that money from the trusts would enable his children and grandchildren to achieve true self-fulfillment and happiness.

Common Features of Integrated Transfer Taxes

The two primary federal transfer taxes, the gift tax and the estate tax, were originally enacted separately and operated independently. In 1976 they were *unified* into a transfer tax scheme that applies a progressive tax rate schedule to cumulative transfers. In other words, the gift and estate taxes now are integrated into a common formula.

This integrated formula takes into account the cumulative effect of transfers in previous periods when calculating the tax on a (gift) transfer in a current period. Likewise, it takes lifetime transfers into account to determine the tax on assets transferred at death. As you'll see in the tax formulas, we add the taxable transfers in prior years to the current-year transfers and compute the tax on total (cumulative) transfers. Then, we subtract the tax on the prior-year transfers from the total tax, to avoid taxing them twice. This calculation ensures that the current transfers will be taxed at a marginal tax rate as high or higher than the rate applicable to the prior-year transfers. Exhibit 25-1 presents the unified transfer tax rate schedule for estate and gift taxes that has been in effect since 2013.

The second common feature of the integrated transfer taxes is the **applicable credit.** This credit, also known as the unified credit, was enacted in 1977, and it applies to both the gift tax and the estate tax. The credit is designed to prevent the application of transfer tax to taxpayers who either would not accumulate a relatively

---

[1]The estate tax was optional for decedents dying in 2010. In lieu of the estate tax, executors could opt to have the adjusted tax basis of the assets in gross estate carry over to the heirs of the decedent. The estate tax is back in place for decedents dying subsequent to 2010.

EXHIBIT 25-1   **Unified Transfer Tax Rates***

Tax Base equal to or over	Not over	Tentative tax	plus	of amount over
$ 0	$ 10,000	$ 0	18%	$ 0
10,000	20,000	1,800	20	10,000
20,000	40,000	3,800	22	20,000
40,000	60,000	8,200	24	40,000
60,000	80,000	13,000	26	60,000
80,000	100,000	18,200	28	80,000
100,000	150,000	23,800	30	100,000
150,000	250,000	38,800	32	150,000
250,000	500,000	70,800	34	250,000
500,000	750,000	155,800	37	500,000
750,000	1,000,000	248,300	39	750,000
1,000,000		345,800	40	1,000,000

THE KEY FACTS

Common Features of the Unified Transfer Taxes

- Property transfers, whether made by gift or at death, are subject to transfer tax using a progressive tax rate schedule.
- The unified credit exempts cumulative transfers of up to $5.45 million ($10.9 million for married taxpayers).
- Each transfer tax allows a deduction for transfers to charities and surviving spouses (the charitable and marital deductions, respectively).

large amount of property transfers during their lifetime and/or would not have a relatively large transfer passing to heirs upon their death. The amount of cumulative taxable transfers a person can make without exceeding the unified credit is called the **exemption equivalent** or, alternatively, the applicable exclusion amount.

Exhibit 25-2 presents the exemption equivalent amounts for both the estate and gift taxes since 1986. The exemption equivalent was the same amount for gift and estate tax purposes until 2004, at which time the gift tax was frozen at $1,000,000 exemption equivalent. In 2011, the exemption equivalent for the gift tax was reunified with the estate tax and, beginning in 2012, the exemption equivalent is annually adjusted for inflation.

The amount of the unified credit depends on both the transfer tax rates and the exemption equivalent that apply in the year of the transfer. Because both the tax rates and the exemption equivalent can change over time, the unified credit is best calculated by tracking the exemption equivalent and converting it into the unified tax credit using the *current* tax rate schedule. For example, the exemption equivalent was $5 million for transfers made in 2011. Consequently, when evaluating a 2011 (or prior-year) transfer for purposes of determining the current-year gift tax, the unified credit for 2011 will be $1,945,800 (no matter what the actual rates were in 2011). In contrast, the exemption equivalent is $5.45 million for transfers made in 2016 and under the current unified tax rate schedule the unified credit is $2,125,800.

EXHIBIT 25-2   **The Exemption Equivalent**

Year of Transfer	Gift Tax	Estate Tax
1986	$ 500,000	$ 500,000
1987–1997	600,000	600,000
1998	625,000	625,000
1999	650,000	650,000
2000–2001	675,000	675,000
2002–2003	1,000,000	1,000,000
2004–2005	1,000,000	1,500,000
2006–2008	1,000,000	2,000,000
2009–2010*	1,000,000	3,500,000
2011	5,000,000	5,000,000
2012	5,120,000	5,120,000
2013	5,250,000	5,250,000
2014	5,340,000	5,340,000
2015	5,430,000	5,430,000
2016	5,450,000	5,450,000

*The unified credit and exemption is zero for taxpayers who opt out of the estate tax in 2010.

A third common feature of the unified tax system is the application of two common deductions. Each transfer tax provides an unlimited charitable deduction for charitable contributions and a generous **marital deduction** for transfers to a spouse. The marital deduction allows almost unfettered transfers between spouses, treating a married couple as virtually a single taxpayer.

A final important feature of the transfer taxes is the valuation of transferred property. Property transferred via gift or otherwise is valued at fair market value. While fair market value is simple in concept, it is very complicated to apply. For purposes of the transfer taxes, fair market value is defined by the *willing-buyer, willing-seller rule* as follows:

> The price at which such property would change hands between a willing buyer and a willing seller, neither being under any compulsion to buy or to sell, and both have reasonable knowledge of the relevant facts.

Fair market value is determined based on the facts and circumstances for each individual property. Determining value is relatively simple for properties that have an active market. For example, stocks and bonds traded on exchanges or over the counter are valued at the mean of the highest and lowest selling prices. Unfortunately, the valuation of many other properties, especially realty, is very difficult. The large number of court cases resolving contentious values testifies to the difficulties in applying the willing-buyer, willing-seller rule.

LO 25-2 THE FEDERAL GIFT TAX

The gift tax is levied on individual taxpayers for all *taxable* gifts made during a calendar year. As explained shortly, each *individual* (married couples cannot elect joint filing for gift tax returns) who makes a gift in excess of the annual exclusion amount must file a gift tax return (Form 709) by April 15 of the following year.[2] Exhibit 25-3 presents the complete formula for the federal gift tax in two parts. In the first part, taxable gifts are calculated for each donee, and in the second, the gift tax is calculated using aggregate taxable gifts to all donees. We begin the first part by identifying transfers that constitute gifts.

EXHIBIT 25-3 The Federal Gift Tax Formula

	Part 1: Calculate taxable gifts for each individual donee:
	Current Gifts
Minus	½ of split gifts (included in spouse's current gifts)
Plus	½ of split gifts by spouse
Minus	Annual exclusion ($14,000 per donee)
Minus	Marital and charitable deductions
Equals	Current taxable gifts
	Part 2: Sum taxable gifts for all donees and calculate tax:
	Total Current Taxable Gifts
Plus	Prior taxable gifts
Equals	Cumulative taxable gifts
Times	Current tax rates
Equals	Cumulative tax
Minus	Tax at current rates on prior taxable gifts
Minus	Unused unified credit at current rates
Equals	Gift Tax Payable

[2]A gift tax return reporting taxable gifts must be filed by April 15th following year-end if a taxpayer has made *any* taxable gifts during the current calendar year *or wishes to elect* gift-splitting. When taxpayers request extensions for their individual income tax returns, they also receive a six-month extension for filing their gift tax returns.

Transfers Subject to Gift Tax

The gift tax is imposed on lifetime transfers of property for less than adequate consideration. Typically, a gift is made in a personal context such as between family members. The satisfaction of an obligation is not considered a gift. For example, tuition payments for a child's education satisfy a support obligation. On the other hand, transfers motivated by affection or other personal motives, including transfers associated with marriage, are gratuitous and subject to the tax. The gift tax is imposed once a gift has been completed, and this occurs when the **donor** relinquishes control of the property and the **donee** accepts the gift.[3] For example, deposits made to a joint bank account are not completed gifts because the donor (depositor) can withdraw the deposit at any time. The gift will be complete at the time the *donee* withdraws cash from the account.

> ### THE KEY FACTS
> **Gifts Excluded from the Gift Tax**
> - Incomplete and revocable gifts.
> - Payments for support obligations or debts.
> - Contributions to political parties or candidates.
> - Medical and educational expenses paid on behalf of an unrelated individual.

TAXES IN THE REAL WORLD Love and Taxes

The small claims division of the Tax Court was asked to determine whether payments between former lovers constituted gifts or compensation. Jue-Ya Yang lived with her boyfriend, Howard Shih, who was an artist and calligrapher. While they were romantically involved, Mr. Shih made payments to Ms. Yang and later deducted these payments as wages.

Ms. Yang admitted doing housekeeping and cooking, but she argued that the payments were gifts. Mr. Shih's testimony about the romantic relationship was evasive. He admitted on cross-examination that while their relationship was more than a professional one, Mr. Shih could not even recall taking Ms. Yang out on dates. The court concluded that Mr. Shih's testimony was untrue and held that the payments were gifts made because of love and affection.

Source: Jue-Ya Yang, TC Summary Opinion 2008-156 (12-15-08).

In some instances a donor may relinquish some control over transferred property but retain other powers that can influence the enjoyment or disposition of the property. If the retained powers are important, then the transfer will not be a complete gift.[4] For example, a transfer of property to a trust will not be a complete gift if the grantor retains the ability to revoke the transfer. If the grantor releases the powers, then the gift will generally be complete at that time because the property is no longer subject to the donor's control. For example, a distribution of property from a revocable trust is a completed gift because the grantor no longer has the ability to revoke the distribution.

Example 25-1

On July 12th of this year Harry transferred $250,000 of FFP stock to a new trust. He gave the trustee directions to pay income to Dina for the next 20 years and then remit the remainder to her son George. Harry named a bank as trustee but retained the power to revoke the trust in case he should need additional assets after retirement. Is the transfer of the stock a completed gift?

Answer: No. Harry retains sufficient control that the transfer of the stock to the trust is an incomplete gift.

What if: Suppose that $15,000 of trust income were distributed to Dina at year-end. Is the transfer of the cash to Dina a completed gift?

Answer: Yes. With the payment Harry has relinquished control over the $15,000, and thus, it is a completed gift.

What if: Suppose that Harry releases his power to revoke the trust at a time when the shares of FPP in the trust are valued at $225,000. Would this release cause the transfer of the stock to be a completed gift and, if so, what is the amount of the gift?

Answer: Yes. By releasing his powers Harry has relinquished control over the entire trust, and the value of the trust at that time ($225,000) would be a completed gift.

---

[3]If a donee refuses or disclaims a gift under §2518, the gift is not complete.
[4]§2514 addresses the treatment of general powers of appointment.

There are several important exceptions to the taxation of completed gifts. For example, political contributions are not gifts. Also, the payment of medical or educational expenses on behalf of another individual is not considered a gift if the payments are made directly to the health care provider or to the educational institution. To avoid confusing a division of property with a gift, a transfer of property in conjunction with a divorce is treated as nongratuitous (it is treated as a transfer for adequate consideration) if the property is transferred within three years of the divorce under a written property settlement.

In addition, special rules apply to transfers of certain types of property. To make a completed gift of a life insurance policy, the donor must give the donee all the incidents of ownership, including the power to designate beneficiaries. An individual who creates a joint tenancy (either a tenancy in common or **joint tenancy** with right of survivorship) or someone who does not provide adequate consideration is deemed to make a gift at that time. The gift is the amount necessary to pay for the other party's interest in the property. For example, suppose the donor pays $80,000 toward the purchase of $100,000 in realty held as equal tenants in common with the donee (i.e., the donee provides only $20,000 of the purchase). The donor is deemed to make a gift of $30,000 to the donee, the difference between the value of the joint interest ($100,000 ÷ 2 = $50,000) and the consideration provided by the donee ($20,000).

ETHICS

Rudy is a retired engineer who has three adult daughters and several grandchildren. This year Carol, his youngest daughter, approached Rudy for a $40,000 business loan. Although Carol had no collateral for the loan and did not sign any written promise to repay the money, Rudy still transferred the funds to her account. Do you think that Rudy should file a gift tax return for the transfer? Suppose that Rudy has no intention of demanding repayment, but has not told anyone of his intention. Any difference?

Example 25-2

This year Harry helped purchase a residence for use by Dina and her husband Steve. The price of the residence was $250,000, and the title named Harry and Steve joint tenants with the right of survivorship. Harry provided $210,000 of the purchase price and Steve the remaining $40,000. Has Harry made a completed gift and, if so, in what amount?

Answer: Yes, Harry made a complete gift to Steve of $85,000, calculated by subtracting the amount paid by Steve from the price of his ownership interest ($125,000 minus $40,000).

What if: Suppose Steve didn't provide any part of the purchase price. What is the amount of the gift?

Answer: Harry made a complete gift to Steve of half the purchase price, $125,000.

Valuation   Gifts are taxed at the fair market value of the donated property on the date the gift becomes complete. Remember, that despite the valuation of a gift at fair market value, the donee generally takes a carryover basis for income tax purposes.[5]

Valuation of remainders and other temporal interests.   Assigning value to unique property is difficult enough, but sometimes we must also assign a value to a stream of payments over time or a payment to be made in the future. The right to currently enjoy property or receive income payments from property is called a **present interest.** In contrast, the right to receive income or property in the future is called a **future interest.** A present right to possess and/or collect income from property may not be

---

[5]The carryover basis may be increased for any gift tax paid (after 1976) on the appreciation of the property.

permanent; if granted for a specific period of time or until the occurrence of a specific event, it is a **terminable interest.** For example, the right to receive income payments from property for 10 years is a terminable interest. A right to possess property and/or receive income for the duration of someone's life is called a **life estate.** The person whose life determines the duration of the life estate is called the life tenant.

At the end of a terminable interest, the property will pass to another owner, the person holding the future interest. In a **reversion,** it returns to the original owner. If it goes to a new owner, the right to the property is called a **remainder** and the owner is called a **remainderman.** For example, the right to own property after a 10-year income interest has ended is a future interest held by the remainderman. The right to property after the termination of a life estate is also called a remainder.

Future interests are common when property is placed in a trust. **Trusts** are legal entities established by a person called the **grantor.** Trusts are administered by a **trustee** and generally contain property called the trust **corpus.** The trustee has a **fiduciary duty** to manage the property in the trust for the benefit of a **beneficiary** or beneficiaries. This duty requires the trustee to administer the trust in an objective and impartial manner and not favor one beneficiary over another.

Since a future interest is essentially a promise of a future payment, we estimate the value of the remainder by discounting the future payment to a present value using a market rate of interest. For example, suppose property worth $100 is placed in a trust with the income to be paid to an income beneficiary each year for 10 years, after which time the property accumulated in the trust will be distributed. The remainder is a future interest with a value we estimate by calculating the present value of a payment of $100 in 10 years as follows:

$$\text{Value of remainder interest} = \frac{\text{Future payment}}{(1 + r)^n}$$

where r is the market rate of interest, and n is the number of years. The interest rate used for this calculation is published monthly by the Treasury as the §7520 rate.[6] If the §7520 rate is 6 percent, we calculate the value of a remainder of $100 placed in trust for 10 years as follows:

$$\text{Value of remainder interest} = \frac{\$100}{(1 + .06)^{10}} = \frac{\$100}{(1.791)} = \$55.83$$

The value of property consists of the present interest (the right to income) and the future interest (the remainder). Hence, once we have estimated the value of the remainder, we compute the value of the income interest as the difference between the value of the remainder and the total value of the property.

$$\begin{aligned}\text{Value of remainder interest} &= \text{Total value} - \text{Value of remainder}\\ &= \$100 - \$55.83\\ &= \$44.17\end{aligned}$$

If the terminable interest is a life estate, the valuation of the remainder is a bit more complicated, because payment of the remainder is delayed by the duration of the life estate. To estimate this delay, we base the calculation upon the number of years the life tenant is expected to live. To facilitate the calculation, the regulations provide a table that calculates the discount rate by including the life tenant's age. Exhibit 25-4 includes a portion of the table from the regulation with interest rates by column and the age of the life tenant by row.

[6]The §7520 rate is 120 percent of the applicable federal midterm rate in effect during the month of the transaction.

THE KEY FACTS

Valuation of Remainders and Income Interests

- Future interests are valued at present value, calculated by estimating the time until the present interest expires.
- The present value calculation uses the §7520 interest rate published by the Treasury.
- If the present interest is measured by a person's life (a life estate), then we estimate the delay by reference to the person's life expectancy as published in IRS tables.
- We value a present interest such as an income interest or life estate by subtracting the value of the remainder interest from the total value of the property.

EXHIBIT 25-4 **Discount Factors for Estimating the Value of Remainders**

	Regulation Section 20.2031-7(d)(7) Table S.—Based on Life Table 2000CM Single Life Remainder Factors Applicable After May 1, 2009 [Interest rate]									
Age	4.2%	4.4%	4.6%	4.8%	5.0%	5.2%	5.4%	5.6%	5.8%	6.0%
0	.06083	.05483	.04959	.04501	.04101	.03749	.03441	.03170	.02931	.02721
1	.05668	.05049	.04507	.04034	.03618	.03254	.02934	.02652	.02403	.02183
2	.05858	.05222	.04665	.04178	.03750	.03373	.03042	.02750	.02492	.02264
3	.06072	.05420	.04848	.04346	.03904	.03516	.03173	.02871	.02603	.02366
4	.06303	.05634	.05046	.04530	.04075	.03674	.03319	.03006	.02729	.02483
5	.06547	.05861	.05258	.04726	.04258	.03844	.03478	.03153	.02866	.02610
6	.06805	.06102	.05482	.04935	.04453	.04026	.03647	.03312	.03014	.02749
35	.19692	.18423	.17253	.16174	.15178	.14258	.13408	.12621	.11892	.11217
36	.20407	.19119	.17931	.16833	.15818	.14879	.14009	.13204	.12457	.11764
37	.21144	.19838	.18631	.17515	.16481	.15523	.14635	.13811	.13046	.12335
38	.21904	.20582	.19357	.18222	.17170	.16193	.15287	.14444	.13661	.12932
86	.79825	.79044	.78278	.77524	.76783	.76055	.75340	.74636	.73944	.73264
87	.80921	.80176	.79443	.78722	.78014	.77316	.76630	.75956	.75292	.74638
88	.81978	.81268	.80569	.79880	.79203	.78536	.77880	.77234	.76598	.75971
89	.82994	.82317	.81651	.80995	.80349	.79712	.79085	.78467	.77859	.77259

Example 25-3

Harry transferred $500,000 of FFP stock to the DG Trust, whose trustee is directed to pay income to Dina for her life and, upon Dina's death, pay the remainder to George (or his estate). At time of the gift, Dina was 35 years old and the §7520 interest rate was 5.8 percent. What are the values of the gift of the life estate and of the remainder interest?

Answer: Harry made a $59,460 gift of the remainder to George and $440,540 of the life estate to Dina. Under Table S (see Exhibit 25-4), the percentage of the property that represents the value of George's remainder is 0.11892. Thus, George's remainder is valued at $59,460 ($500,000 × 0.11892). Dina's life estate is the remaining value of $440,540 ($500,000 − $59,460).

The Annual Exclusion   One of the most important aspects of the gift tax is the **annual exclusion,** which operates to eliminate "small" gifts from the gift tax base. The amount of the exclusion has been revised upwards periodically over the years and is now indexed for inflation.[7] In 2016 it is $14,000.

The annual exclusion is available to offset gifts made to *each* donee regardless of the number of donees in any particular year. For example, a donor could give $14,000 in cash to each of 10 donees every year without exceeding the annual exclusion. One important limitation to the annual exclusion is that it applies only to gifts of *present* interests; that is, a gift of a future interest is not eligible for an annual exclusion.

---

[7]The exclusion is indexed for inflation in such a way that the amount of the exclusion only increases in increments of $1,000. The annual exclusion was $10,000 from 1981 through 2001, but was $11,000 for 2002 through 2005, $12,000 for 2006 through 2008, $13,000 for 2009 through 2012, and $14,000 since 2012.

Example 25-4

When Harry transferred $500,000 of FFP stock to the DG Trust (Example 25-3), he simultaneously made two taxable gifts, a life estate to Dina and a remainder to George. What is the amount of the taxable gift of the life estate to Dina and the remainder interest to George, after taking the exclusion amount into account?

Answer: Dina's life estate is a present interest and would qualify for the annual exclusion. However, George's remainder is a future interest and will not qualify for the annual exclusion. Harry would file a Form 709 to report total taxable gifts of $486,000 consisting of a $426,540 taxable gift to Dina ($440,540 less the annual exclusion of $14,000) and a taxable gift of $59,460 to George (no annual exclusion is available for a future interest).

	Dina	George	Harry's Gift Tax Return
Current gifts	$440,540	$59,460	$500,000
Annual exclusion	− 14,000	−0	− 4,000
Taxable gifts	$426,540	$59,460	$486,000

> **THE KEY FACTS**
> **Annual Exclusion**
> - Most gifts are eligible for an annual exclusion of $14,000 per donee per year.
> - Gifts of present interests qualify for the exclusion.
> - Gifts of future interests placed in trust for a minor can also qualify for the exclusion.

Most gifts will only qualify for an annual exclusion if the donee has a present interest (the ability to immediately use the property or the income from it). However, a special exception applies to future interests given to minors (under the age of 21). Gifts in trust for a minor are future interests if the minor does not have the ability to access the income or property until reaching the age of majority. These gifts will still qualify for the annual exclusion as long as the property can be used to support the minor and any remaining property is distributed to the child once he or she reaches age 21.[8]

Example 25-5

Harry transferred $48,500 of cash to the George Trust. The trustee of the George Trust has the discretion to distribute income or corpus (principal) for George's benefit and is required to distribute all assets to George (or his estate) not later than George's 21st birthday. Is this gift eligible for the annual exclusion? If so, what is the amount of the taxable gift?

Answer: Yes, Harry will be entitled to an annual exclusion for the transfer despite the fact that George's interest is a future one, because the gift is in trust for the support of a minor and the property must distribute the assets to George once he reaches age 21. The amount of the gift is $48,500 reduced to a taxable gift of $34,500 after application of the $14,000 annual exclusion.

Taxable Gifts

In part 1 of the formula in Exhibit 25-3, **current gifts** are accumulated for each donee, and this amount includes all gifts completed during the calendar year for each individual. Current gifts do not include transfers exempted from the tax, such as political contributions. Several adjustments are made to calculate current **taxable gifts** for each donee. As we've seen, each taxpayer is allowed an annual exclusion applied to the cumulative gifts of present interests made during the year to *each* donee. Next, if a married couple elects to split gifts (discussed below), half of each gift is included in current gifts of each spouse. The marital deduction for gifts to spouses and the charitable deduction for gifts to charity are the last adjustments to calculate taxable gifts for each donee. We discuss each in turn.

[8]The courts have created another exception to the present interest rule called *Crummey power.* A discussion of this exception is beyond the scope of this text.

Gift-Splitting Election   Married couples have the option to *split gifts,* allowing them to treat *all* gifts made in a year as if each spouse had made one-half of each gift. In a **community property state,** both spouses automatically own equal shares in most property acquired during the marriage.[9] Hence, when they make a gift of community property the transfer is divided between them equally. In **common-law states,** one spouse can own a disproportionate amount of property because he or she earns most of the income. The gift-splitting election provides a mechanism for married couples in common-law states to achieve the same result as couples receive automatically in community property states.[10]

Example 25-6

Wilma and Harry live in Michigan, a common-law state. For the holidays Wilma gave cash gifts of $30,000 to Steve and $41,000 to Dina. Wilma and Harry did not elect to split gifts. What is the amount of Wilma's taxable gifts?

Answer: $43,000. After using her annual exclusion (both gifts are present interests), Wilma has made taxable gifts of $16,000 to Steve ($30,000 − $14,000) and $27,000 to Dina ($41,000 − $14,000).

What if: Suppose Wilma and Harry elect gift-splitting this year. How would your answer change?

Answer: Both Wilma and Harry made taxable gifts of $7,500. Under gift-splitting, Wilma and Harry are each treated as making a gift of $15,000 to Steve and $20,500 to Dina. After the annual exclusion, both Wilma and Harry made a $1,000 taxable gift to Steve [($30,000 ÷ 2) − $14,000 = $1,000]. In addition, both Wilma and Harry made a $6,500 taxable gift to Dina [($41,000 ÷ 2) − $14,000 = $6,500].

What if: Suppose Wilma and Harry lived in Texas (a community property state), and Wilma made the same gifts from community property.

Answer: Both Wilma and Harry made a taxable gift of $7,500. Under state law, each spouse is automatically treated as gifting half the value of any gifts made from community property. After the annual exclusion, both Wilma and Harry made a $1,000 taxable gift to Steve [($30,000 ÷ 2) − $14,000], and each made a $6,500 taxable gift to Dina [($41,000 ÷ 2) − $14,000].

Besides increasing the application of the annual exclusion, a gift-splitting election also increases the likelihood that taxable gifts will be taxed at lower tax rates or any gift tax will be offset by unified credits. To utilize gift-splitting, each spouse must be a citizen or resident of the United States, be married at the time of the gift, and not remarry during the remainder of the calendar year. Both spouses must consent to the election by filing a timely gift tax return. Taxpayers make this election annually and can apply it to all gifts completed by either spouse during the calendar year. As a result of the election, both spouses share a joint and several liability for any gift tax due.

Marital Deduction   The marital deduction was originally enacted to equalize the treatment of spouses residing in common-law states. In community property states, the ownership of most property *acquired* during a marriage is automatically divided between the spouses. In common-law states, one spouse can own a disproportionate amount of property if he or she earns most of the income. Absent the marital deduction, in a common-law state, a transfer between the spouses to equalize the ownership of property would be treated as a taxable gift. However, because transfers to

[9]Depending upon state law, the ownership of property acquired by either spouse prior to a marriage is not automatically divided equally between the spouses. In other words, property owned prior to the marriage is not necessarily community property and continues to belong to the original owner.

[10]There are nine community property states: Arizona, California, Idaho, Louisiana, Nevada, New Mexico, Texas, Washington, and Wisconsin.

spouses are eligible for a marital deduction, no taxable gift results from such a transfer.

The marital deduction is subject to two limits. First, the amount is limited to the value of the gift after the annual exclusion. Second, transfers of **nondeductible terminable interests** do not qualify for a marital deduction. A nondeductible terminable interest is a property interest transferred to the spouse that terminates when some event occurs or after a specified amount of time, when the property is transferred to another.

Example 25-7

After his decision to retire, Harry gave Wilma a piece of jewelry that is a family heirloom valued at $50,000. What is the amount of this taxable gift?

Answer: Zero. This gift will qualify for an annual exclusion, and the value after subtracting the annual exclusion qualifies for the marital deduction. The taxable gift is calculated below:

Current gift	$50,000
Less: Annual exclusion	−14,000
Less: Marital deduction	−36,000
Taxable gift	$ 0

What if: Suppose Harry transferred $200,000 to a trust with directions to pay income to Wilma for her life (a life estate). After Wilma's death, the corpus of the trust would then pass to Dina (the remainder). What is the amount of this taxable gift if Wilma is age 38 at the time and the §7520 interest rate is 5 percent?

Answer: The total taxable gift is $186,000. This transfer is actually two gifts, a gift of a present interest to Wilma (a life estate) and a future interest to Dina (the remainder). The gift of the remainder is valued at $34,340 using Wilma's age and the §7520 interest rate from the table in Exhibit 25-4 ($200,000 × 0.17170). The remainder does not qualify for an annual exclusion because it is a future interest. The gift of the life estate is a present interest valued at $165,660 ($200,000 − $34,340), and it qualifies for the annual exclusion. The taxable gifts are calculated below:

	Dina (remainder)	Wilma (life estate)
Current gifts	$34,340	$165,660
Less: Annual exclusion (life estate)	−0	−14,000
Less: Marital deduction	−0	−0
Taxable gift	$34,340	$151,660

When the life estate is given to a spouse, it does not qualify for the marital deduction because it will terminate upon a future event (Wilma's death) and then pass to another person (Dina).

The limitation on the deductibility of terminable interests ensures that property owned by a married couple is subject to a transfer tax when the property is eventually transferred from the couple (as opposed to between the spouses).[11] If a life estate were eligible for a marital deduction, it would not be taxed at the time of the gift nor would any value be taxed upon Wilma's death (the life estate disappears with her death). Hence, a marital deduction is available only for spousal transfers that will eventually be included in the recipient spouse's estate.[12]

---

[11]Qualified terminable interest properties (QTIPs for short) are an exception to the nondeductibility of terminable interest property. A detailed discussion of this exception is beyond the scope of this text.

[12]The spouse must be entitled to all of the income from the property payable at least annually, and no person has the power to appoint any part of the property to anyone other than the spouse until the death of the spouse.

Charitable Deduction The amount of the charitable deduction is also limited to the value of the gift after the annual exclusion. Requirements for an organization to qualify for the gift tax charitable deduction are quite similar to those for the income tax deduction (the entity must be organized for religious, charitable, scientific, educational, or other public purposes, including governmental entities). Unlike the income tax deduction, however, the charitable deduction has no percentage limitation. In addition, as long as the qualifying charity receives the donor's entire interest in the property, no gift tax return need be filed (assuming the donor has no other taxable gifts). Finally, a transfer to a charity also qualifies for an income tax deduction (subject to the AGI limits on the income tax charitable deduction).

Example 25-8

Harry donated $155,000 in cash to State University. What is the amount of the taxable gift?

Answer: Zero. The gift qualifies for the charitable gift tax deduction, as calculated below.

Current gift	$155,000
Less: Annual exclusion	−14,000
Less: Charitable deduction	−141,000
Taxable gift	$ 0

Note that Harry can also claim an income tax deduction for the transfer.

Computation of the Gift Tax

Part 2 of the formula in Exhibit 25-3 provides the method of calculating the gift tax. It begins by summing the taxable gifts made for all donees during a calendar year.

Example 25-9

Harry and Wilma did not make any gifts from community property and did not elect to gift-split this year (see Example 25-6). What is the amount of Harry's current taxable gifts this year?

Answer: Harry made $591,500 of taxable gifts, calculated using Part 1 of the formula in Exhibit 25-3 as follows:

Gifted Property	Donee	Value	Explanation
1. Residence	Steve	$ 85,000	Example 25-2
Less: Annual exclusion		−14,000	
2. DG Trust—life estate	Dina	440,540	Example 25-3
Less: Annual exclusion		−14,000	
3. DG Trust—remainder	George	59,460	Example 25-3
4. George Trust	George	48,500	Example 25-5
Less: Annual exclusion		−14,000	
5. Jewelry	Wilma	50,000	Example 25-7
Less: Annual exclusion		−14,000	
Less: Marital deduction	Wilma	−36,000	
6. Donation	State University	155,000	Example 25-8
Less: Annual exclusion		−14,000	
Less: Charitable deduction	State U	−141,000	
Harry's current taxable gifts		$591,500	

The amounts of the marital and charitable deductions are limited to the value of the property included in taxable gifts.

Will Wilma be required to file a gift tax return this year? If so, what is the amount of her taxable gifts?

Answer: Wilma must also file a gift tax return this year because her current gifts exceed the annual exclusion. Wilma's taxable gifts sum to $43,000, calculated as follows:

Gifted Property	Donee	Value	Explanation
Cash gift	Steve	$30,000	Example 25-6
Less: Annual exclusion		−14,000	
Holiday gift	Dina	41,000	Example 25-6
Less: Annual exclusion		−14,000	
Wilma's current taxable gifts		$43,000	

What if: What is the amount of Harry and Wilma's taxable gifts if they elect to gift-split?

Answer: Harry and Wilma each made $310,250 of taxable gifts, calculated as follows:

	Harry	Wilma	Donee	Gift Splitting Harry	Gift Splitting Wilma
Harry's gift of a residence	85,000		Steve	42,500	42,500
Less: Annual exclusion	−14,000			−14,000	
Wilma's cash gift		30,000	Steve	15,000	15,000
Less: Annual exclusion		−14,000			−14,000
Harry's transfer to DG trust	440,540		Dina	220,270	220,270
Less: Annual exclusion	−14,000			−14,000	
Wilma's holiday gifts		41,000	Dina	20,500	20,500
Less: Annual exclusion		−14,000			−14,000
DG Trust—remainder	59,460			29,730	29,730
George Trust	48,500			24,250	24,250
Less: Annual exclusion	−14,000			−14,000	−14,000
Harry's gift of jewelry	50,000		Wilma	50,000	
Less: Annual exclusion	−14,000			−14,000	
Less: Marital deduction	−36,000			−36,000	
Donation to State U	155,000		State U	77,500	77,500
Less: Annual exclusion	−14,000			−14,000	−14,000
Less: Charitable deduction	−141,000			−63,500	−63,500
Total	591,500	43,000		310,250	310,250

Note that absent gift-splitting, Harry and Wilma made taxable gifts totaling $634,500 ($591,500 + $43,000), but under gift-splitting that reduced to $620,500 ($310,250 + $310,250) because Wilma was able to use an additional $14,000 annual exclusion for her portion of the gift to the George Trust. Neither Harry nor Wilma was able to use any additional annual exclusions for the gifts to Steve and Dina because they had already used annual exclusions to these two donees. If they elect to gift-split, Harry and Wilma will be jointly and severally liable for the gift taxes.

Tax on Current Taxable Gifts   The first step to computing the gift tax on current taxable gifts is to add prior taxable gifts to current taxable gifts. The purpose of adding gifts from previous periods is to increase the tax base and thereby increase the marginal tax rate applying to current gifts. To prevent double taxation of prior taxable gifts, the gift tax on prior taxable gifts is subtracted from the tax on total transfers. Two elements of the tax on prior taxable gifts are important to understand. First, the tax is calculated on prior taxable gifts ignoring whether any unified credit was claimed on the gifts in the prior year. Second, the tax on prior taxable gifts is computed using the *current* rate schedule (the tax rates for the year of the prior transfer are not relevant). The difference between the tax on cumulative taxable gifts and prior taxable gifts is the tax on the current taxable gifts.

Unified Credit   The last adjustment in the formula is the unused portion of the unified credit. Recall that the unified credit is determined by the current tax on the exemption equivalent, and the exemption equivalent can change over time because it is indexed for inflation (for example, the exemption equivalent is 5.45 million for 2016, see Exhibit 25-2). Hence, rather than track the unused portion of the unified credit, it is far easier to track the unused portion of the exemption equivalent and then convert that into the unified credit using current rates. Tracking the unused portion of the exemption equivalent makes sense because the exemption equivalent is ignored in calculating the tax on prior taxable gifts.

For example, suppose an individual transferred via gift $3 million in a prior year (when the exemption equivalent was $1 million) and $6 million in the current year (when the exemption equivalent increased to $5 million). This individual made cumulative transfers of $9 million and is entitled to an exemption equivalent of $5 million. Based on the gift tax formula, a transfer tax would be calculated on $9 million less the transfer tax on the prior taxable gifts on $3 million. Thus, the current taxable transfer would be $6 million, and the tax on this amount would be reduced by the tax on the unused exemption equivalent of $4 million ($5 million less $1 million used in a prior year). In sum, this individual would owe transfer tax on $2 million. This is a fair outcome because in a prior year the individual paid tax on $2 million ($3 million less the $1 million exemption equivalent in the prior year). Note that the exemption equivalent (converted into the unified credit at current rates) eliminates the gift tax for individuals who do not transfer a relatively large cumulative amount of property during their lifetime.

Also, note that a gift tax return must be filed by each individual (no joint filing) who has made taxable gifts during the calendar year or who elects to split gifts, even if no tax is due because of the unified credit.

Example 25-10

Assume that Harry made a taxable gift of $1,500,000 in 2007. At that time, the exemption equivalent for the gift tax was $1 million, so Harry paid gift taxes on $500,000. Harry has not made any taxable gifts since 2007. This year, however, Harry made taxable gifts of $591,500. What is Harry's gift tax and Harry's unused exemption equivalent (unified credit)?

Answer: Harry will report cumulative taxable gifts of $2,091,500, but he will not owe any gift tax due this year. The calculation is as follows:

Current taxable gifts	$ 591,500	
Prior taxable gifts	1,500,000	
Cumulative taxable gifts	$2,091,500	
Tax on cumulative taxable gifts		$782,400
Less: Current tax on prior taxable gifts ($1.5 million)		−545,800
Tax on current taxable gifts		$236,600
Unified credit on current taxable gifts		−236,600
Gift tax due		$ 0

Harry used $1 million of his exemption equivalent in 2007, and this year he used another $591,500. Hence, at the end of 2016, Harry has $3,858,500 of unused exemption equivalent remaining ($5,450,000 − $1,000,000 − $591,500), which translates into an unused unified credit of $1,489,200.

What if: Suppose that Harry made a taxable gift of $3,500,000 in 2007, and at that time, the exemption equivalent was $1 million. What should Harry report this year as his cumulative taxable gifts, gift tax on cumulative taxable gifts, gift tax on current taxable gifts, credit for current tax on prior taxable gifts, and gift tax due?

Answer: Harry should report cumulative taxable gifts of $4,091,500 and gift tax on cumulative gifts of $1,582,400. Harry, however, owes no gift tax. The calculation is as follows:

Current taxable gifts	$ 591,500	
Prior taxable gifts	3,500,000	
Cumulative taxable gifts	$4,091,500	
Tax on cumulative taxable gifts		$1,582,400
Less: Current tax on prior taxable gifts ($3.5 million)		−1,345,800
Tax on current taxable gifts		236,600
Unified credit on current taxable gifts		−236,600
Gift tax due		$ 0

At the end of 2016, Harry would have $3,858,500 of exemption equivalent remaining ($5,450,000 − $1,000,000 − $591,500). Note that Harry probably paid gift tax in 2007 because his taxable gifts far exceeded the exemption equivalent of $1 million in 2007. However, the amount of gift tax that was paid in 2007 is not relevant for calculating Harry's current tax. All calculations in the current year are made using the current tax rate schedule (not the one that applied in prior years).

What is Wilma's gift tax due?

Wilma's current taxable gifts	$43,000	
Prior taxable gifts	+0	
Cumulative taxable gifts	$43,000	
Tax on cumulative taxable gifts		$8,920
Less: Current tax on prior taxable gifts		−0
Tax on current taxable gifts		$8,920
Unified credit on current taxable gifts		−8,920
Gift tax due		$ 0

Wilma has used $43,000 of her exemption equivalent. Hence, at the end of 2016, Wilma has $5,407,000 of exemption equivalent remaining.

To reiterate, the gift tax requires donors to keep track of the portion of the exemption equivalent they used to generate a unified credit to offset prior taxable gifts. This prevents multiple applications of the same exemption. The gift tax on previous gifts is computed using the current tax rate schedule, but this amount does *not* represent the amount of gift tax paid—just the gifts previously subject to tax. The unused portion of the applicable credit then reduces the total gift tax to reach the gift tax due. The gift tax is calculated using the current rate schedule and ignores the amount of gift tax actually paid in prior periods. Exhibit 25-5 presents the first page of the 2015 gift tax return Form 709 for Harry Smith (Form 709 for 2016 was not available from the IRS as of press date).

EXHIBIT 25-5   Page 1 of Form 709 Gift Tax Return for Harry Smith

Form **709**

Department of the Treasury
Internal Revenue Service

United States Gift (and Generation-Skipping Transfer) Tax Return

▶ Information about Form 709 and its separate instructions is at *www.irs.gov/form709*.

(For gifts made during calendar year 2015)
▶ See instructions.

OMB No. 1545-0020

20**15**

1 Donor's first name and middle initial HARRY	**2** Donor's last name SMITH

3 Donor's social security number 000-00-0000

4 Address (number, street, and apartment number) 2813 ELMWOOD	**5** Legal residence (domicile) WASHTENAW, MICHIGAN
6 City or town, state or province, country, and ZIP or foreign postal code ANN ARBOR, MICHIGAN 48109	**7** Citizenship (see instructions) USA

Part 1—General Information

		Yes	No
8	If the donor died during the year, check here ▶ ☐ and enter date of death _____ , _____		
9	If you extended the time to file this Form 709, check here ▶ ☐		
10	Enter the total number of donees listed on Schedule A. Count each person only once ▶ FIVE		
11a	Have you (the donor) previously filed a Form 709 (or 709-A) for any other year? If "No," skip line 11b	✓	
b	Has your address changed since you last filed Form 709 (or 709-A)?		✓
12	**Gifts by husband or wife to third parties.** Do you consent to have the gifts (including generation-skipping transfers) made by you and by your spouse to third parties during the calendar year considered as made one-half by each of you? (see instructions.) (If the answer is "Yes," the following information must be furnished and your spouse must sign the consent shown below. **If the answer is "No," skip lines 13–18.**)		✓
13	Name of consenting spouse **14** SSN		
15	Were you married to one another during the entire calendar year? (see instructions)		
16	If 15 is "No," check whether ☐ married ☐ divorced or ☐ widowed/deceased, and give date (see instructions) ▶		
17	Will a gift tax return for this year be filed by your spouse? (If "Yes," mail both returns in the same envelope.)	✓	
18	**Consent of Spouse.** I consent to have the gifts (and generation-skipping transfers) made by me and by my spouse to third parties during the calendar year considered as made one-half by each of us. We are both aware of the joint and several liability for tax created by the execution of this consent.		

Consenting spouse's signature ▶   Date ▶

		Yes	No
19	Have you applied a DSUE amount received from a predeceased spouse to a gift or gifts reported on this or a previous Form 709? If "Yes," complete Schedule C		✓

Part 2—Tax Computation

1	Enter the amount from Schedule A, Part 4, line 11	**1**	591,500
2	Enter the amount from Schedule B, line 3	**2**	1,000,000
3	Total taxable gifts. Add lines 1 and 2	**3**	1,591,500
4	Tax computed on amount on line 3 (see *Table for Computing Gift Tax* in instructions)	**4**	582,400
5	Tax computed on amount on line 2 (see *Table for Computing Gift Tax* in instructions)	**5**	345,800
6	Balance. Subtract line 5 from line 4	**6**	236,600
7	Applicable credit amount. If donor has DSUE amount from predeceased spouse(s), enter amount from Schedule C, line 4; otherwise, see instructions	**7**	2,125,800
8	Enter the applicable credit against tax allowable for all prior periods (from Sch. B, line 1, col. C)	**8**	345,800
9	Balance. Subtract line 8 from line 7. Do not enter less than zero	**9**	1,780,000
10	Enter 20% (.20) of the amount allowed as a specific exemption for gifts made after September 8, 1976, and before January 1, 1977 (see instructions)	**10**	
11	Balance. Subtract line 10 from line 9. Do not enter less than zero	**11**	1,780,000
12	Applicable credit. Enter the smaller of line 6 or line 11	**12**	236,600
13	Credit for foreign gift taxes (see instructions)	**13**	
14	Total credits. Add lines 12 and 13	**14**	236,600
15	Balance. Subtract line 14 from line 6. Do not enter less than zero	**15**	0
16	Generation-skipping transfer taxes (from Schedule D, Part 3, col. H, Total)	**16**	
17	Total tax. Add lines 15 and 16	**17**	0
18	Gift and generation-skipping transfer taxes prepaid with extension of time to file	**18**	
19	If line 18 is less than line 17, enter **balance due** (see instructions)	**19**	
20	If line 18 is greater than line 17, enter **amount to be refunded**	**20**	

Sign Here

Under penalties of perjury, I declare that I have examined this return, including any accompanying schedules and statements, and to the best of my knowledge and belief, it is true, correct, and complete. Declaration of preparer (other than donor) is based on all information of which preparer has any knowledge.

▶ _____   _____
Signature of donor   Date

May the IRS discuss this return with the preparer shown below (see instructions)? ☐ Yes ☐ No

Paid Preparer Use Only

Print/Type preparer's name	Preparer's signature	Date	Check ☐ if self-employed	PTIN
Firm's name ▶			Firm's EIN ▶	
Firm's address ▶			Phone no.	

Attach check or money order here.

For Disclosure, Privacy Act, and Paperwork Reduction Act Notice, see the instructions for this form.   Cat. No. 16783M   Form **709** (2015)

continued from page 25-1...

Early this year Bob was injured in an auto accident. Unable to recover from his injuries, he died after two days in the hospital. Bob is survived by his son, Nate, who is also the executor of Bob's estate. Nate is now collecting his father's assets, and he would like help in preparing Bob's federal estate tax return. ■

THE FEDERAL ESTATE TAX

LO 25-3

The estate tax is designed to tax the value of property owned or controlled by an individual at death, the decedent. Because federal gift and estate taxes are integrated, taxable gifts affect the tax base for the estate tax. Exhibit 25-6 presents the estate tax formula.

EXHIBIT 25-6   The Federal Estate Tax Formula

	Gross estate
Minus	Expenses, debts, and losses
Equals	Adjusted gross estate
Minus	Marital and charitable deductions
Equals	Taxable estate
Plus	Adjusted taxable gifts
Equals	Cumulative taxable transfers (the tax base)
Times	Current tax rates
Equals	Tax on cumulative transfers
Minus	Gift taxes payable on adjusted taxable gifts at current rate
Equals	Tentative tax
Minus	Full unified credit calculated using current tax rate
Equals	Gross Estate Tax

The Gross Estate

Property possessed by or owned (titled) by a decedent at the time of death is generally referred to as the **probate estate,** because the transfer of this property is carried out by a probate court. **Probate** is the process of gathering property possessed by or titled in the name of a decedent at the time of death, paying the debts of the decedent, and transferring the ownership of any remaining property to the decedent's **heirs.** Property in the probate estate can include cash, stocks, jewelry, clothing, and realty owned by or titled in the name of the deceased at the time of death.

The **gross estate** is broader than the probate estate. The gross estate consists of (1) the fair market value of property possessed or owned by a decedent at death *plus* (2) the value of certain automatic property transfers that take effect at death.[13] Property transfers that take effect only at death are not in the probate estate because the transfer takes place just as death occurs. Hence, the probate court does not need to affect a transfer. However, as discussed below, property subject to certain types of automatic transfers is specifically included in the gross estate because the automatic transfer is a substitute for a testamentary transfer.

Example 25-11

What if: Nate took an inventory of his father's property in preparation for distributing assets according to Bob's will. Nate must report this preliminary inventory of personal and investment property to the probate court; it includes the following:

(continued on page 25-18)

---

[13]§2033. The principle of increasing the gross estate for transfers taking effect at death began with *gifts in contemplation of death.* So-called deathbed gifts were a device used to avoid the estate tax in the years before enactment of the gift tax.

	Fair Market Value
Auto	$ 33,000
Clothes, furniture, and personal effects	48,000
Smith painting (original cost/initial estimated value)	25,000
Checking and savings accounts	75,250
FFP stock	9,500,000
Residence	400,000
Other investments	8,200
Total	$10,089,450

What amount of this property is included in Bob's gross estate?

Answer: Bob's gross estate includes the value of *all* the above property, or $10,089,450, because he owned these assets at his death (i.e. these assets are included on Bob's probate estate).

What if: Suppose Bob was also entitled to a pension distribution of $15,000 but had not yet received the check at his time of death. Would this value also be included in Bob's probate estate and therefore gross estate?

Answer: Yes. Although Bob had not received the check, he was legally entitled to the property at the time of his death, and therefore it will be included in both his probate estate and gross estate.

Specific Inclusions   Besides property in the probate estate, the gross estate also includes property transferred automatically at the decedent's death. These automatic transfers can occur without the help of a probate court because the ownership transfers by law at the time of death.

Certain automatic property transfers are specifically included in the gross estate because, while the decedent didn't own the property at death, Congress deemed that the decedent controlled the ultimate disposition of the property. That is, the decedent effectively determined who would receive the property at the time of death. A common example is property held in **joint tenancy with right of survivorship** which legally transfers to the surviving tenant upon the joint tenant's death. Joint bank accounts are commonly owned in joint ownership with right of survivorship. In contrast, tenants in common hold divided rights to property and have the ability to transfer these rights during their life or upon death. Property held by tenants in common, such as real estate, does not automatically transfer at death and thus must be transferred via probate. Although the decedent's interest in jointly owned property (with the right of survivorship) ceases at death, the value of the interest the decedent held in this property is still included in the gross estate.[14]

Example 25-12

Nate and his father jointly own two parcels of real estate not included in the inventory above. One parcel is a vacation home in Colorado. Nate owns this property jointly with Bob and the title is held in joint ownership with the right of survivorship. Will this property be included in Bob's probate estate and/or gross estate?

Answer: The property will *not* be included in Bob's *probate* estate, but it will be included in Bob's *gross* estate. When Bob died, Nate automatically became the sole owner of the property without going through probate. However, the property will be included in Bob's gross estate because it is an automatic transfer that is specifically included in the gross estate by law.

---

[14]§2040. There are a number of other transfers that are specifically included in the gross estate. For example, §2036 to §2039 and §2041 address transfers with retained life estates, transfers taking place at death, revocable transfers, annuities, and powers of appointment. A discussion of these provisions is beyond the scope of this text.

The second parcel is real estate in west Texas that Nate and Bob hold as equal tenants in common. Will it be necessary to probate this parcel of real estate to transfer ownership of Bob's share to the beneficiary named in Bob's will?

Answer: Yes. The value of Bob's one-half interest in the west Texas real estate is also included in his gross estate.

Another example of an automatic transfer is insurance on the life of the decedent. Proceeds of life insurance paid due to the death of the decedent are specifically included in the gross estate if either of two conditions is met. The proceeds are included in the gross estate if (1) the decedent owned the policy or had "incidents" of ownership such as the right to designate the beneficiary or (2) the decedent's estate or **executor** is the beneficiary of the insurance policy (that is, the executor must use the insurance proceeds to discharge the obligations of the estate).

Example 25-13

Bob owned and paid annual premiums on an insurance policy that, on his death, was to pay the beneficiary of his choice $500,000. Bob named Nate the beneficiary, and the insurance company paid Nate $500,000 after receiving notification of Bob's death. Will Bob's gross estate include the value of the insurance proceeds paid to Nate?

Answer: Yes. The $500,000 of insurance proceeds is specifically included in Bob's estate despite the fact that it was paid directly to Nate and did not go through probate.

What if: Suppose Bob transferred ownership of the policy to Nate four years prior to his death. Nate had the power to designate the beneficiary of the policy, and he also paid the annual premiums. Will Bob's gross estate include the value of the insurance proceeds paid to Nate?

Answer: No. Bob had no incidents of ownership at his death (Nate controlled who is paid the proceeds upon Bob's death), and the proceeds were not paid to his estate.

Jointly owned property. The proportion of the value of jointly owned property included in the gross estate depends upon the type of ownership. When a decedent's interest is a **tenancy in common** (i.e., there is no right of survivorship), a proportion of the value of the property is included in the gross estate that matches the decedent's ownership interest. For example, consider a decedent who owned a one-third interest in property as a tenant in common. If the entire property is worth $120,000 at the decedent's death, then $40,000 is included in his gross estate.

The amount includible for property held as joint tenancy with the right of survivorship depends upon the marital status of the owners. When property is jointly owned by a husband and wife with the right of survivorship, *half the value* of the property is automatically included in the estate of the first spouse to die.[15] For *unmarried* co-owners, the value included in the decedent's gross estate is determined by the decedent's contribution to the total cost of the property. For example, consider a decedent who provided two-thirds of the total cost of property held as joint tenants with the right of survivorship. If the entire property is worth $240,000 at the decedent's death, then two-thirds ($160,000) is included in his gross estate.

---

[15]In some states joint tenancy with a right of survivorship between spouses is referred to as a **tenancy by the entirety.**

Bob and Nate originally purchased the Colorado vacation home seven years ago for $20,000 and held it as joint tenants with the right of survivorship. This property is not included in the list of property in Bob's probate estate because the title passes automatically to Nate upon Bob's death. Bob provided $15,000 of the purchase price, and Nate provided the remaining $5,000. The property was worth $400,000 at Bob's death. How much is included in his gross estate?

Answer: Bob's gross estate includes $300,000. For property held in joint tenancy with the right of survivorship, the amount included in the gross estate is equal to the proportion of the purchase price provided by the decedent. Bob provided 75 percent ($15,000 ÷ $20,000 = 75%). Hence, his gross estate will include $300,000 (75% × $400,000) of the value of the vacation home.

What if: Suppose Bob was married and owned the home with his wife as joint tenants with the right of survivorship. What amount would be included in Bob's gross estate?

Answer: The amount included in the estate is half the value of any property held with the surviving spouse as joint tenants with the right of survivorship, $200,000 in this case.

The west Texas land Bob and Nate owned is valued at $500,200. They owned it as tenants in common, with Bob holding a one-quarter interest and Nate holding the rest. What amount is included in Bob's gross estate?

Answer: The amount included in the estate is $125,050 ($500,200 × 25%), because Bob owned a one-quarter interest in the property.

Exhibit 25-7 summarizes the rules for determining the value of jointly owned property included in a decedent's gross estate.

EXHIBIT 25-7 **Amount of Jointly Owned Property Included in Gross Estate**

Ownership Form	Marital Status of Co-owners	Amount in Gross Estate
Community property (discussed below)	Married	Half the fair market value
Joint tenancy with right of survivorship	Married	Half the fair market value
Joint tenancy with right of survivorship	Unmarried	Percentage of fair market value determined by decedent's contribution to total cost of the property
Tenancy in common	Married or unmarried	Percentage of fair market value determined by decedent's interest in the property

Transfers within three years of death. Certain transfers, such as transfers of life insurance policies, made within three years of the decedent's death are also included in the decedent's gross estate, valued as of the time of death. Without this provision, a simple but effective estate tax planning technique would be to transfer ownership in a life insurance policy just prior to the decedent's death. This strategy, called a *deathbed gift,* would reduce the decedent's transfer taxes on the life insurance by the difference between its proceeds from the policy (the value at death) and its value on the date transferred.

Only certain transfers are specifically included under this provision, and they are often difficult to identify.

Gift taxes paid on transfers within three years of death. Gift taxes paid on any taxable gifts during the three-year period preceding the donor's death are also included in the decedent's gross estate. This inclusion provision prevents donors from escaping estate tax on the amount of gift taxes paid within three years of death.

In other words, the amount of gift taxes paid are included in the estate because these amounts would have been included in the estate had the decedent kept the property until death.

Example 25-15

What if: Suppose Bob owned a life insurance policy, and he transferred all incidents of ownership in the policy to his son one year before dying from a fatal disease. Suppose that Bob paid $40,000 of gift taxes on the transfer and the policy paid his son $3 million on Bob's death. What amount would be included in Bob's gross estate?

Answer: $3,040,000. Bob's estate would include proceeds of the policy ($3 million) because Bob transferred the incidents of ownership within three years of his death. The value of the transfer would also include the gift taxes paid ($40,000) when Bob transferred the policy.

Valuation   Property is included in the gross estate at the *fair market value* on the date of the decedent's death. Virtually all the factors (and controversies) regarding valuation that we've already discussed with the gift tax also apply to the valuation of property for estate tax purposes.

Example 25-16

At his death Bob owned an original landscape painting made in the late 1800s by one of his ancestors, Tully Smith. Bob purchased the Smith painting for $25,000 in 1980, and last year an expert estimated it was worth $210,000. Nate now has the painting appraised by another expert, who estimates its value at $250,000 based upon a painting by the same artist that sold at auction last month. What value should be placed on the painting for inclusion in the gross estate?

Answer: Nate should value the painting at $250,000 according to its specific characteristics and attributes (such as age, condition, history, authenticity, and so forth). Of course, the IRS might disagree with this value and seek to value the painting at a higher value.

> **THE KEY FACTS**
> **Valuation of Assets**
> - Property is included in the estate at its fair market value at the date of the decedent's death.
> - The executor can elect to value the estate on an alternate valuation date, six months after death, if it reduces the gross estate and estate tax.

The executor of an estate, however, can elect—irrevocably—to have all the property in the gross estate valued on an **alternative valuation date.** The alternative date for valuing the estate is six months after the date of death or on the date of sale or distribution of the property (if this occurs before the end of the six-month period). This election is available only if it reduces the value of the gross estate and the combined estate and generation-skipping taxes.[16]

Example 25-17

What if: Bob's shares of FPP are included in his estate at a value of $9.5 million. Suppose the value of the shares plummeted to $5 million several months after Bob's death. Suppose that the drop in value caused the value of Bob's estate to drop from $18 million to $13.5 million. Could Nate as executor of Bob's estate opt to value these shares at the lower cost for estate tax purposes?

Answer: Yes. Nate could elect to value the shares on the alternate valuation date, six months after Bob's death. However, to qualify for this election, he must value *all* property in the estate on the alternate date. Because the election will reduce the value of the entire gross estate, Nate could make the election to use the alternate valuation date.

---

[16]§2032A. An executor can also elect to value certain realty used in farming or in connection with a closely held business at a special use valuation. Special use valuation allows realty to be valued at a current use that does not result in the best or highest fair market value. This election is available when the business is conducted by the decedent's family, constitutes a substantial portion of the gross estate, and the property passes to a qualifying heir of the decedent.

Example 25-18

At the time of his death Bob owned a reversion in a trust he established for his niece, Dina. Under the terms of the trust, Dina is entitled to income for her life (a life estate), and Bob (or his heir) is entitled to the reversion. At the time of Bob's death, the trust assets were valued at $100,000, Dina was 35, and the §7520 interest rate was 6 percent. Should this reversion be included in Bob's gross estate and, if so, what value is placed on the future interest?

Answer: Bob's reversion interest is included in his estate because this is a property right he owned at his death. Under Table S in the regulations (Exhibit 25-4), based upon Dina's age and the current interest rate at the time of Bob's death, the percentage of the property that represents the value of Bob's reversion is 0.11217. Thus, his reversion is valued at $11,217 ($100,000 × 0.11217).

What if: Suppose the trust was established for George, age 6. Would this influence the value of Bob's reversion interest?

Answer: Yes. Under Table S in the regulations and based upon George's age and the current interest rate, the portion of the property that represents the value of Bob's reversion is 0.02749. Thus, Bob's reversion is valued at $2,749 ($100,000 × 0.02749).

Gross Estate Summary So far we've seen that the decedent's gross estate consists of the assets subject to probate as well as certain assets transferred outside probate. These latter assets include property owned by the decedent in joint tenancy with the right of survivorship as well as life insurance. The gross estate also includes certain property transferred by the decedent within three years of death and certain future interests owned by the decedent.

Example 25-19

Given previous examples, what is the value of Bob's gross estate?

Answer: It is $11,250,717, calculated as follows:

Property	Value	Explanation
Auto	$ 33,000	Example 25-11
Personal effects	48,000	Example 25-11
Smith painting	250,000	Example 25-16
Checking and savings accounts	75,250	Example 25-11
FPP shares	9,500,000	Example 25-11
Residence	400,000	Example 25-11
Other investments	8,200	Example 25-11
Life insurance proceeds	500,000	Example 25-13
Colorado vacation home	300,000	Examples 25-12 and 25-14
West Texas land	125,050	Examples 25-12 and 25-14
Reversion interest in Dina Trust	11,217	Example 25-18
Gross estate	$11,250,717	

The Taxable Estate

Referring to the estate tax formula in Exhibit 25-6, we calculate the taxable estate in two steps. The first consists of reducing the gross estate by deductions allowed for administrative expenses, debts of the decedent, and losses incurred during the administration of the estate. These deductions are allowed because Congress intends to tax the amount transferred to beneficiaries. This step results in the **adjusted gross estate.** In the second step, the adjusted gross estate is reduced for transfers to a decedent's spouse (the marital deduction) and to charities (the charitable deduction). These deductions result in the **taxable estate.** We discuss each type of deduction next.

Administrative Expenses, Debts, Losses, and State Death Taxes

Debts included in or incurred by the estate, such as mortgages and accrued taxes, are deductible. Expenses incurred in administering the estate are also deductible, such as executor's fees, attorneys' fees, and the like. Funeral expenses are deductible, including any reasonable expenditure allowed under local law. Casualty and theft losses are deductible without any floor limitation. These losses must be incurred during the administration of the estate, otherwise the deduction belongs to the new owner of the property. Finally, death taxes imposed by the state are also deductible.[17]

Example 25-20

Nate paid $6,685 in funeral expenses for his father's services, and during the administration of his father's estate he paid executor's fees of $4,032 and attorney's fees of $9,500. In addition, Nate discovered Bob owed debts totaling $100,500. Since Michigan has no state death or inheritance taxes, no amounts were owed to the state. What is Bob's adjusted gross estate (gross estate minus expenses and debts)?

Answer: It is $11,130,000, calculated as follows:

Gross estate from Example 25-19		$11,250,717
Funeral expenses	$ 6,685	
Executor's fees and expenses	4,032	
Attorney's fees	9,500	
Debts of the decedent	100,500	
Total expenses and debts		−120,717
Adjusted gross estate		$11,130,000

The estate may collect income earned during its administration and, therefore, the estate will need to file an estate *income* tax return. The executor has the option of deducting administration expenses (but not funeral expenses) and casualty and theft losses on the estate tax return or on the estate's *income* tax return. While no double deduction is available, the choice is relatively simple. If the estate owes no estate taxes, then the executor should claim the deduction on the estate income tax return. If the estate owes estate taxes, the marginal estate tax rate is likely to be higher than the marginal income tax rate. Hence, it should probably claim the deduction on the estate tax return.

What if: Suppose that during the administration of Bob's estate a storm damaged the Colorado vacation home. Bob's share of the casualty loss to the home was $25,000. Would this be deductible in calculating Bob's taxable estate?

Answer: Yes, although the executor can choose to deduct this loss on either the estate tax return or the estate's *income* tax return for the period that included the casualty. If the deduction is claimed on the estate tax return, the loss deduction is not subject to any floor limitations (such as the per casualty floor limitation and the 10 percent of AGI limits imposed on casualty losses claimed in individual income tax returns).

Marital and Charitable Deductions

To avoid taxing a married couple's estate twice, Congress provides a deduction for bequests to a surviving spouse. To qualify for the marital deduction, the transferred property must be included in the estate of

---

[17]§2053, §2054, and §2058 address expenses, losses, and state death taxes, respectively.

THE KEY FACTS

Estate Tax Deductions

- Estate tax deductions include the debts of the decedent, funeral expenses, and the costs of administering the estate, including casualty losses.
- The value of property interests bequeathed to a surviving spouse is deductible if the interest is not terminable.
- The value of property bequeathed to a qualified charity is deductible.

the deceased spouse. That is, the surviving spouse must receive the property from the decedent and control its ultimate disposition. For example, property that passes to the surviving spouse as a result of joint tenancy with the right of survivorship qualifies for the marital deduction, as would a direct bequest from the decedent. In contrast, transfers of property rights that are terminable do not generally qualify for the estate marital deduction (as discussed earlier, terminable interests are treated similarly for gift tax purposes). For example, suppose the decedent bequeaths the surviving spouse the right to occupy the decedent's residence until such time as the spouse remarries. The value of the right to possess the residence is a terminable interest and is not eligible for the marital deduction.[18]

In general, the estate tax marital deduction is unlimited in amount. Hence, no tax would be imposed on a decedent who leaves her entire estate to a spouse.[19]

Charitable contributions of property are also deductible without any limitation. Charities are defined to include the usual public organizations (corporations organized exclusively for religious, charitable, scientific, literary, or educational purposes) but exclude certain nonprofit cemetery organizations. Interestingly, foreign charities qualify for the charitable deduction under the estate and gift tax but not under the income tax. No deduction is allowed unless the charitable bequest is specified under the last will and testament or is a transfer of property by the decedent before his death that is subsequently included in the decedent's estate. The amount of any bequest must be mandatory, although another person such as the executor can be given discretion to identify the charitable organization.

Example 25-21

Not long after Bob's death, Nate gathered the Smith family for a reading of Bob's will. The will was relatively simple because Bob was unmarried at the time of his death. Bob had an adjusted gross estate of $11,130,000 and left all his property to Nate, with two exceptions. Bob bequeathed his remainder interest in the Dina Trust (value of $11,217) to Dina, and he bequeathed the Smith painting (value of $250,000) to the Midwest Museum in Ann Arbor (a qualified charity). Is either of these bequests deductible in calculating Bob's taxable estate? What is Bob's taxable estate?

Answer: The bequest to the museum qualifies for the charitable deduction because the museum is a qualified charity. Since Bob was unmarried at his death, none of the bequests qualify for the marital deduction. Bob's taxable estate is $10,880,000 calculated as follows:

Adjusted gross estate	$11,130,000
Charitable deduction	−250,000
Taxable estate	$10,880,000

What if: Suppose Bob was married at the time of his death and left a portion of his FPP stock, valued at $4.5 million, to his surviving spouse. What amount of this transfer, if any, would qualify for the marital deduction?

Answer: Bob's estate would be entitled to a marital deduction of $4.5 million, the value of the entire spousal bequest. In the extreme, if Bob had left *all his property* to his spouse, then his taxable estate would be reduced to zero.

[18]The restriction on the estate tax deduction for terminable interests is drafted consistent with the gift tax deduction. As noted previously, *Qualified terminable interest properties* (*QTIPs* for short) are an exception to the nondeductibility of terminable interest property. To qualify, the executor must agree to have qualifying terminable interests included in the estate of the surviving spouse. A detailed discussion of this exception is beyond the scope of this text.

[19]There are other credits that could also apply, but these are beyond the scope of this text. The credit for taxes on prior transfer is designed to adjust the tax for property that was subjected to estate tax within the last 10 years. There is also a credit for pre-1977 gift taxes paid on certain pre-1977 gifts that must be included in the gross estate. Both of these credits are equitable adjustments for potential multiple transfer taxes associated with sequential deaths and multiple inclusions, respectively. Prior to 2005, there was a credit for state death taxes.

Computation of the Estate Tax

Three additional steps are necessary to calculate the estate tax liability from the taxable estate. First, the taxable estate is increased by **adjusted taxable gifts** to compute cumulative lifetime transfers (the estate tax base). Next, the tax on cumulative lifetime transfers is computed and reduced by the tax payable on adjusted taxable gifts (computed using the current tax rates). This results in a tentative tax that is reduced by the applicable (unified) credit.

In contrast to the gift tax formula, the estate tax formula only allows a reduction for taxes payable on adjusted taxable gifts. Taxes payable are a hypothetical amount computed using the past amount of applicable credit but the current tax rate schedule. Another difference with the gift tax formula is that the entire applicable credit (not just the unused portion) reduces the tentative tax (because all prior transfers are included in the tax base). These differences are illustrated below.

Adjusted Taxable Gifts   Adjusted taxable gifts are taxable gifts other than transfers already included in the gross estate. For example, the value of life insurance transferred within three years of death would not be included in adjusted taxable gifts but the value of the life insurance proceeds paid at death would be included in the estate. The objective of adding previously taxed transfers to the taxable estate is to allow the estate tax base to reflect all transfers, both *inter vivos* and testamentary.

Despite increasing cumulative transfers, adjusted taxable gifts are not subject to double tax because the tentative tax on cumulative transfers is reduced by a credit for the taxes payable on adjusted taxable gifts calculated under the current tax rate schedule. It is important to note that although adjusted taxable gifts were made in prior years, all tax calculations are made using the *current* rate schedule.

Example 25-22

After reviewing all Bob's records, Nate determined Bob had made only one taxable gift of FPP stock in 2009. This transfer resulted in a taxable gift of $1 million, the tax on which was offset by the unified credit. What is the amount of cumulative transfers subject to estate tax, and what is Bob's tentative estate tax (tax prior to credits)?

Answer: Bob's estate includes $11,880,000 of cumulative taxable transfers and Bob's gross estate tax is $4,697,800 calculated as follows:

Adjusted taxable gifts	$ 1,000,000	Prior gift
Taxable estate	10,880,000	Taxable transfers in estate
Cumulative transfers	$11,880,000	Total taxable transfers
Tentative tax	$ 4,697,800	Tax prior to credits

What if: Suppose Bob had not made any taxable gifts prior to his death. Would this fact reduce his tentative tax?

Answer: Without the gift of stock Bob's tentative tax would be $4,297,800 calculated as follows:

Adjusted taxable gifts	$ 0
Taxable estate	10,880,000
Cumulative transfers	$10,880,000
Tentative tax	$ 4,297,800

Note that Bob's tentative tax has decreased by $400,000. This is the amount of tax on the $1 million 2009 gift at the top marginal rate (40%).

What if: Suppose that Bob's 2009 taxable gift was $4 million and the gift tax exemption equivalent in 2009 was $1 million. What is the amount of the reduction of taxes payable on adjusted taxable gifts?

(continued on page 25-26)

Answer: $1.2 million. The adjusted taxable gift of $4 million would result in a tax of $1,545,800 under the current rate schedule. However, because the transfer was made in 2009, the tax would be reduced by $345,800. This is the amount of the unified credit of $1 million calculated using the current tax rate schedule. The calculation would be made as follows:

Current tax on adjusted taxable gifts	$1,545,800
Unified credit ($1.0 million at current tax rate)	−345,800
Current taxes payable on adjusted taxable gifts	$1,200,000

Note that the credit is 40 percent of the gift in excess of the exemption equivalent ($4,000,000 − $1,000,000 = $3,000,000). The $4 million prior taxable transfer is included in the calculation of Bob's cumulative taxable transfers and the tentative estate tax is calculated as before.

Adjusted taxable gifts	$ 4,000,000
Taxable estate	10,880,000
Cumulative transfers	$14,880,000
Tax on cumulative transfers	$5,897,800
Taxes payable on adjusted taxable gifts	− 1,200,000
Tentative estate tax	$4,697,800

Hence, the adjusted taxable gift increases the amount of Bob's estate subject to the top estate tax rate. The adjusted taxable gift is not subject to an additional transfer tax at the time of Bob's death for two reasons. First, the tax payable on the adjusted taxable gift is deducted when computing the tentative tax. Second, the $1 million of the adjusted taxable gift that is not offset by the taxes payable will be offset by the applicable credit when computing the gross estate tax.

Applicable (Unified) Credit Besides subtracting the credit for tax on adjusted taxable gifts, we reduce the gross estate tax by several other credits.[20] The most important is the applicable credit, because it eliminates the estate tax on cumulative transfers up to the exemption equivalent (currently $5.45 million). Hence, estate taxes are only imposed on relatively large estates. The objective of the applicable credit is to prevent the application of transfer tax to taxpayers who either would not accumulate a relatively large amount of property transfers during their lifetime and/or would not have a relatively large value of assets to pass to heirs upon their death.

The applicable credit for a surviving spouse is increased by the amount of the **deceased spousal unused exclusion** (DSUE). For example, in 2016 a spouse whose deceased spouse died without using any unified credit is entitled to an exemption equivalent of $10.9 million.

Besides eliminating transfer taxes for relatively small cumulative transfers, the exemption equivalent also acts as the transfer requirement for filing an estate return. That is, an estate tax return (Form 706) must be filed if the gross estate plus adjusted taxable gifts equals or exceeds the exemption equivalent. Exhibit 25-8 presents the first page of 2016 Form 706 for Bob Smith. The deadline for the estate tax return is nine months after the decedent's death.[21]

> **THE KEY FACTS**
>
> **Adjusted Taxable Gifts and the Applicable Credit**
>
> - Adjusted taxable gifts are added to the taxable estate in calculating cumulative taxable transfers.
> - Lifetime gifts are not subject to double tax because the tax on cumulative transfers is reduced for taxes on adjusted taxable gifts.
> - The unified credit eliminates transfer taxes on estates with relatively small cumulative lifetime and testamentary transfers (total transfers under the exemption equivalent).
> - Credit is applied after reducing the total tax on cumulative transfers for taxes payable on adjusted taxable gifts.

[20]Other transfers that are required to be included in the gross estate are described in Sec. 2035(a). Discussion of these transfers are beyond the scope of this text.

[21]There is an automatic six-month extension to file the estate tax return. However, an estimate of the tax due must be paid on the due date of the return.

Example 25-23

Bob died on February 7 of this year. What amount of estate tax must be paid on his estate, given his prior taxable gift of $1 million? What is the due date for Bob's estate tax return?

Answer: Estate tax of $2,572,000 is due after applying the unified credit, computed as follows:

Tentative tax from Example 25-22	$ 4,697,800
Less: Applicable credit	2,125,800
Estate tax due	$2,572,000

Bob's executor must file the estate tax return (Form 706 in Exhibit 25-8) or request an extension of time within nine months of Bob's death (by November 7 of this year).

What if: Suppose that Bob did not make any taxable gifts during his life. What amount of estate tax would be owed upon his death?

Answer: Bob's estate would only owe $2,172,000, computed as follows:

Tentative tax	$4,297,800
Less: Applicable credit	2,125,800
Estate tax due	$2,172,000

In this case, the absence of gifts prior to Bob's death (no adjusted taxable gifts) would result in a $400,000 savings. This is because over his lifetime Bob made fewer taxable transfers ($1 million in fact).

What if: Suppose that Bob's 2009 taxable gift was $4 million (instead of $1 million) and the gift tax exemption equivalent in 2009 was $1 million. What amount of estate tax would be owed upon Bob's death?

Answer: Bob's estate would owe $2,572,000, computed as follows:

Tentative tax	$4,697,800
Less: Applicable credit	2,125,800
Estate tax due	$2,572,000

Bob's estate tax is not increased by the amount of the adjusted taxable gifts in excess of $1 million because these gifts were taxed in 2009. The taxes payable on adjusted taxable gifts eliminates the potential for double taxation. The portion of the 2009 gift that was not taxed in 2009 (recall that $1 million was offset by the applicable credit), however, is now subject to tax.

What if: Suppose that Bob was predeceased by a wife who left all of her possessions to Bob and, consequently, did not claim an exemption equivalent. What amount of estate tax would be owed upon his death?

Answer: Assuming that the executor of Bob's wife filed a estate tax return electing the DSUE, Bob's estate would be entitled to claim a unified credit based on a deceased spouse's unused exclusion. Bob's estate would not owe any estate tax computed as follows:

Tentative tax	$ 4,297,800
Less: unified credit	4,305,800
Estate tax due	$ 0

The unified credit in this case is $10.9 million ($5.45 million times 2). The unified credit is calculated using the tax rate schedule resulting in a credit of $4,305,800.

EXHIBIT 25-8   Page 1 of Form 706 Estate Tax Return for Bob Smith

Form **706**
(Rev. August 2013)

Department of the Treasury
Internal Revenue Service

United States Estate (and Generation-Skipping Transfer) Tax Return

OMB No. 1545-0015

▶ Estate of a citizen or resident of the United States (see instructions). To be filed for decedents dying after December 31, 2012.
▶ Information about Form 706 and its separate instructions is at *www.irs.gov/form706*.

Part 1—Decedent and Executor

1a Decedent's first name and middle initial (and maiden name, if any) BOB	**1b** Decedent's last name SMITH		**2** Decedent's social security no. 000 00 0000

3a City, town, or post office; county; state or province; country; and ZIP or foreign postal code.

3b Year domicile established	**4** Date of birth	**5** Date of death
1990	1940	2016

ANN ARBOR, WASHTENAW COUNTY MICHIGAN 48109

6b Executor's address (number and street including apartment or suite no.; city, town, or post office; state or province; country; and ZIP or foreign postal code) and phone no.

6a Name of executor (see instructions)
NATE SMITH

6500 TRAIL RD, ANN ARBOR, MICHIGAN 48109

6c Executor's social security number (see instructions)
000 00 0000

Phone no. (000) 000-0000

6d If there are multiple executors, check here ▢ and attach a list showing the names, addresses, telephone numbers, and SSNs of the additional executors.

7a Name and location of court where will was probated or estate administered
WASHTENAW COUNTY PROBATE COURT

7b Case number
00-12345

8 If decedent died testate, check here ▶ ▢ and attach a certified copy of the will.   **9** If you extended the time to file this Form 706, check here ▶ ▢

10 If Schedule R-1 is attached, check here ▶ ▢   **11** If you are estimating the value of assets included in the gross estate on line 1 pursuant to the special rule of Reg. section 20.2010-2T(a) (7)(ii), check here ▶ ▢

Part 2—Tax Computation

1	Total gross estate less exclusion (from Part 5—Recapitulation, item 13)	**1**	11,250,717
2	Tentative total allowable deductions (from Part 5—Recapitulation, item 24)	**2**	370,717
3a	Tentative taxable estate (subtract line 2 from line 1)	**3a**	10,880,000
b	State death tax deduction	**3b**	0
c	Taxable estate (subtract line 3b from line 3a)	**3c**	10,880,000
4	Adjusted taxable gifts (see instructions)	**4**	1,000,000
5	Add lines 3c and 4	**5**	11,880,000
6	Tentative tax on the amount on line 5 from Table A in the instructions	**6**	4,697,800
7	Total gift tax paid or payable (see instructions)	**7**	0
8	Gross estate tax (subtract line 7 from line 6)	**8**	4,697,800

9a	Basic exclusion amount	**9a**	5,450,000
9b	Deceased spousal unused exclusion (DSUE) amount from predeceased spouse(s), if any (from Section D, Part 6—Portability of Deceased Spousal Unused Exclusion).	**9b**	0
9c	Applicable exclusion amount (add lines 9a and 9b)	**9c**	5,450,000
9d	Applicable credit amount (tentative tax on the amount in 9c from Table A in the instructions)	**9d**	2,125,800
10	Adjustment to applicable credit amount (May not exceed $6,000. See instructions.)	**10**	0

11	Allowable applicable credit amount (subtract line 10 from line 9d)	**11**	2,125,800
12	Subtract line 11 from line 8 (but do not enter less than zero)	**12**	2,572,000
13	Credit for foreign death taxes (from Schedule P). (Attach Form(s) 706-CE.)	**13**	
14	Credit for tax on prior transfers (from Schedule Q)	**14**	
15	Total credits (add lines 13 and 14)	**15**	0
16	Net estate tax (subtract line 15 from line 12)	**16**	2,572,000
17	Generation-skipping transfer (GST) taxes payable (from Schedule R, Part 2, line 10)	**17**	
18	Total transfer taxes (add lines 16 and 17)	**18**	2,572,000
19	Prior payments (explain in an attached statement)	**19**	
20	Balance due (or overpayment) (subtract line 19 from line 18)	**20**	2,572,000

Under penalties of perjury, I declare that I have examined this return, including accompanying schedules and statements, and to the best of my knowledge and belief, it is true, correct, and complete. Declaration of preparer other than the executor is based on all information of which preparer has any knowledge.

Sign Here

▶ Signature of executor   Date

▶ Signature of executor   Date

Paid Preparer Use Only

Print/Type preparer's name	Preparer's signature	Date	Check ▢ if self-employed	PTIN
Firm's name ▶			Firm's EIN ▶	
Firm's address ▶			Phone no.	

For Privacy Act and Paperwork Reduction Act Notice, see instructions.   Cat. No. 20548R   Form **706** (Rev. 8-2013)

WEALTH PLANNING CONCEPTS

Wealth planning coordinates both income and transfer tax strategies with nontax objectives. Before we explore transfer tax strategies, recall the third transfer tax, the generation-skipping tax, and the potential for income taxation of fiduciary entities such as estates and trusts. While these topics are certainly not unimportant, we note them only in passing because their complexity is beyond the scope of this text.

The Generation-Skipping Tax

The **generation-skipping tax (GST)** is a supplemental tax designed to prevent the avoidance of transfer taxes (both estate and gift tax) through transfers that skip a generation of recipients. For example, a grandparent could give a life estate in property to a child, with the remainder to a grandchild. When the child dies and the grandchild inherits the property, no transfer tax is imposed because nothing remains in the child's estate (the life estate terminates at death). In this way, the grandparent pays one transfer tax (on the initial gift) to transfer the property down two generations.

The GST is triggered by the transfer of property to someone more than one generation younger than the donor or decedent—a grandchild rather than a child. A transfer to a grandchild is not subject to GST, however, if the grandchild's parents are dead. The GST is very complex and can be triggered directly by transfers or indirectly by a termination of an interest. Fortunately, the GST is not widely applicable because it does not apply to transfers that qualify for an annual gift tax exclusion and each donor/decedent is entitled to a relatively generous aggregate exemption ($5.45 million in 2016).

Income Tax Considerations

A **fiduciary** entity is a legal entity that takes possession of property for the benefit of a person. An **estate** is a fiduciary that comes into existence upon a person's death to transfer the decedent's real and personal property. Likewise, a *trust* is also a fiduciary whose purpose is to hold and administer the corpus for other persons *(beneficiaries)*. While an estate exists only temporarily (until the assets of the decedent are distributed), a trust may have a prolonged or even indefinite existence. Because fiduciaries can exist for many years, special rules govern the taxation of income realized on property they hold. These rules are complex and relate to how fiduciaries account for income under state law. A detailed discussion is beyond the scope of this text, but we can provide a useful general outline.

The trust or testamentary instrument (or, in the absence of an instrument, state law) determines how income and expenses are allocated between beneficiaries—fiduciary accounting income belongs to income beneficiaries and corpus (principal) belongs to the remainderman. For example, an instrument may allocate gains on the sale of assets to corpus and rental receipts to trust accounting income. Likewise, depreciation expense may be allocated to accounting income whereas repairs may be allocated to corpus. Accounting income is important because it determines how much income the fiduciary can (or must) distribute. Trusts and estates may have discretion whether to accumulate income within the fiduciary (for future distribution) or make current distributions.[22] Income retained by the fiduciary is taxed as income to the fiduciary, and consequently, the fiduciary must file an income tax return. In contrast, income distributed currently by the fiduciary is taxed as income to the beneficiary. To accomplish this flow-through of income, fiduciaries are granted an income tax deduction for current distributions of income and this deduction depends, in part, on accounting income.

---

[22]Regulations under §§ 651–652 make a distinction between simple trusts and complex trusts. **Simple trusts** must distribute all trust accounting income currently (and cannot make charitable contributions) whereas **complex trusts** are not required by the trust instrument to distribute income currently.

To better understand how taxable income is divided between a fiduciary and its beneficiaries, it is helpful to first summarize the formula for determining a fiduciary's taxable income.[23] With few exceptions, the formula for calculating a fiduciary's taxable income is analogous to the individual income tax formula. Gross income for a fiduciary is determined in the same manner as gross income for an individual. For example, trusts are generally taxed on realized income, but they can exclude certain items from gross income, such as municipal interest, and make elections to defer certain items, such as installment gains. A fiduciary can also deduct expenses similar to an individual. For example, a fiduciary can deduct trade or business expenses, interest, taxes, casualty losses, charitable contributions, and miscellaneous itemized deductions. Although a fiduciary is not entitled to a standard deduction (i.e., there is no distinction between deductions for AGI and itemized deductions), miscellaneous itemized deductions for a fiduciary are still subjected to a 2 percent limitation calculated using a hypothetical AGI. A fiduciary is also allowed a personal exemption, $600 for an estate and $300 for a trust that distributes all income currently, and $100 for other trusts. Lastly, a fiduciary is allowed a deduction for distributions of income to beneficiaries. It is this **distribution deduction** that operates to eliminate the potential for double taxation of income.

The maximum amount of the distribution deduction (and the maximum aggregate amount of gross income reportable by beneficiaries) is determined by reference to **distributable net income (DNI).** DNI is calculated by adjusting taxable income for the fiduciary, but unfortunately, this calculation is circular. That is, taxable income for a fiduciary depends upon the distribution deduction, which in turn depends upon DNI, which in turn depends upon taxable income. Moreover, the calculation of fiduciary taxable income is further complicated by items such as net operating losses, net capital losses, charitable contributions, multiple beneficiaries, and discretionary (versus mandatory) distributions. Suffice it to say that the calculation of income tax for a fiduciary can be a very complicated matter.

While granting a fiduciary discretion over distributions complicates the calculation of taxable income, it might appear that this discretion also provides an opportunity to split income (by creating yet another taxpayer). However, the fiduciary income tax rates are generally as high as or higher than the tax rates for individual beneficiaries. Hence, the potential income tax benefits from splitting income between fiduciaries and beneficiaries are typically negligible.

Transfer Tax Planning Techniques

Transfer tax planning strategies are the same as those employed for income tax planning: timing, shifting, and conversion. Like income tax planning, wealth planning is primarily concerned with accomplishing the client's goals in the most efficient and effective manner after considering *both* tax and nontax costs. For the most part, wealth planning is directed to maximizing after-tax wealth to be transferred from an older generation to a younger generation. A critical constraint in this process, however, is determining how tax strategies can achieve the client's ultimate (nontax) goals. Before attempting to integrate tax and nontax considerations, let's survey a few basic techniques for transfer tax planning.

Serial Gifts

A **serial gift** strategy converts a large taxable transfer into a tax-exempt transfer by dividing the transfer into multiple inter vivos gifts. As long as the gifts qualify as present interests and do not exceed the annual exclusion, the transfers are exempt from all transfer taxes. Although serial gifts are an easy and low-cost planning strategy, this technique is limited in scope because only $14,000 ($28,000 if married) can be transferred each year tax-free to any specific donee. Hence, serial gifts can move significant amounts of wealth only if employed by multiple donors over multiple years and multiple donees.

---

[23]Subchapter J (§§ 641–692) contains the provisions governing income taxation of fiduciaries.

Example 25-24

Suppose Harry and Wilma decide to begin transferring wealth to Dina and George. To what extent can serial gifts accomplish this goal without triggering gift taxes?

Answer: Harry and Wilma could make annual gifts of $14,000 each to Dina and George. These gifts would remove $56,000 per year from the Smiths' estate without triggering any transfer taxes (gift tax or generation-skipping tax). They could include any type of property as long as Dina and George can presently enjoy the property or income generated by it.

The Step-Up in Tax Basis   Timing is an important component in tax planning. Generally, a good tax strategy delays payment of tax, thereby reducing the present value of the tax paid. While deferral is important, transfer tax planning must also consider the potential appreciation of assets transferred, and the effect of the income tax that could apply if and when the appreciation is realized. Gifted property generally retains the donor's basis in the property (the donee takes a **carryover basis**), whereas inherited property takes a tax basis of fair market value. The advantage of gifting property is that the donor eliminates the transfer tax on any additional future appreciation on the gifted property. The disadvantage is that the unrealized appreciation of the gifted property will eventually be taxed (although at the donee's income tax rate). Thus, gifting appreciating property reduces future transfer taxes but at the cost of additional future income taxes imposed on the donee. In contrast, for inherited property, past appreciation (up to the date of death) will never be subject to income tax but instead is subject to transfer tax at the time of the transfer.

Example 25-25

What if: Harry currently owns 30 percent of the outstanding shares of FFP. These shares have a basis of $300,000 but are worth in excess of $2.7 million. Suppose Harry intends to transfer his FPP shares to his daughter Dina who, in turn, intends to sell them after Harry's death. To what extent should income tax considerations influence whether Harry transfers these shares via inter vivos gift or testamentary transfer? Estimate the total tax savings if Harry delays the transfer of the shares until his death three years hence. Assume that the transfer (whether by gift or inheritance) will be taxed at the top transfer rate of 40 percent, while when Dina sells the shares in three years the gain will be taxed at a capital gains tax rate of 20 percent. Let's also assume that the FPP shares will not appreciate and the prevailing interest rate is 6 percent.

Answer: The total tax savings is $686,260 if Harry delays the transfer until his death rather than gifting the shares to Dina immediately. See the following discussion and computations:

	Gift	Inheritance	Explanation
Gift tax paid	$1,080,000		40% times $2.7 million
Time value of gift tax	× 1.191		$(1.06)^3$
Future value of gift tax	$1,286,280		Value of gift tax paid
Estate tax paid		$1,080,000	40% times $2.7 million
Dina's capital gain	$ 480,000	0	Gain of $2.4 million on gift
tax 15%			due to carryover basis
Total taxes paid	$1,766,280	$1,080,000	$686,280 of tax savings

If a sale is planned, then the step-up in tax basis becomes critical to avoid being taxed on the accumulated appreciation. In this scenario, a testamentary transfer provides a step-up in tax basis and delays payment of the transfer tax for three years.

(continued on page 25-32)

What if: Suppose Dina has no interest in selling the family business and intends to eventually transfer the shares to George. Moreover, suppose Harry believes the FFP shares will appreciate to $3.5 million within three years. To what extent should income tax considerations influence whether Harry transfers these shares immediately via intervivos gift or in three years via testamentary transfer? Estimate the total tax savings if Harry transfers the shares immediately rather than delaying the transfer until his death.

Answer: The tax savings is $113,720 if Harry transfers property immediately rather than delaying the transfer until his death. See the following discussion and computations:

	Gift	Inheritance	Explanation
Gift tax paid	$1,080,000		40% times $2.7 million
Time value of gift tax	× 1.191		$(1.06)^3$
Future value of gift tax	$1,286,280		Value of gift tax paid
Estate tax paid		$1,400,000	40% times $3.5 million
Total taxes paid	$1,286,280	$1,400,000	$113,720 of tax savings

If Dina plans to hold the shares indefinitely and the property is rapidly appreciating, then an inter vivos gift avoids having future appreciation taxed in Harry's estate. Although a gift of the shares would accelerate the imposition of transfer taxes, any unused unified credit could minimize the amount of taxes due on the transfer. In this scenario, an intervivos transfer reduces total transfer taxes even though the gift tax is paid three years before an estate tax would be due.

Timing becomes critical in determining how to trade off income tax savings (the step-up in tax basis) against transfer tax costs (paying gift tax now or paying estate taxes on additional appreciation later). Most tax advisors will suggest that elderly clients sell business assets or investments with unrealized losses, because upon death the basis of these assets will be adjusted downward to fair market value. In other words, the adjustment to basis can be a step-down as well as a step-up, and a sale prevents the elimination of the loss deduction.

Integrated Wealth Plans

A client can have many nontax goals associated with the ultimate disposition of wealth, and some are very personal. It is often difficult to ascertain and prioritize them for planning purposes. However, an effective wealth plan must identify and integrate these personal objectives with tax costs. Often, the primary nontax objective of wealth planning is to preserve value during the transfer of control (management) of business assets. Thus, an essential nontax element of any effective wealth plan is to identify a safe mechanism to support the older generation in a specific lifestyle while transferring control to the younger generation.

Trusts are common vehicles for tax planning, in large part because these fiduciaries can be structured to achieve a great variety of tax and nontax objectives, including the support of specific beneficiaries.[24] The trustee is responsible for managing property in the trust, but the grantor also gives the trustee discretionary powers to provide flexibility. These powers can include the discretion to distribute income or corpus among beneficiaries. In addition grantors can retain powers, including the ability to revoke the trust, select the trustee (original or successor), terminate beneficial interests, and add to the corpus. The most important aspect of an irrevocable trust is that the provisions (including powers and guidelines for the

---

[24]Trusts are also popular because the trust property transfers outside probate, thereby avoiding both the costs and the publicity associated with probate.

exercise of discretionary powers) cannot be changed once the trust instrument has been executed.

Specific types of trusts are common to many wealth transfer plans. For example, a **life insurance trust** is funded with an irrevocable transfer of a life insurance policy, and the trustee is given the power to name beneficiaries and redesignate them in case of divorce or death. Upon the death of the grantor, the amount of the policy is paid into the trust but not included in the grantor's estate. Moreover, an immediate cash distribution from the trust is not taxable income to the beneficiaries.

Example 25-26

Harry is planning to purchase a $2 million life insurance policy. He wants to use the proceeds to support Wilma after his death and have any remaining funds paid to his surviving children. How would Harry structure a trust to accomplish these goals?

Answer: Harry should transfer the policy to an irrevocable trust that directs the trustee to hold the policy and pay the premiums until Harry's death. At that time, the trustee should be directed to invest the $2 million proceeds and pay income to Wilma for the remainder of her life or until she remarries. At Wilma's death or remarriage, the trust terminates and pays the remaining funds to Harry's surviving children or their estates.

What if: Suppose Harry transfers the policy to an irrevocable trust and dies four years later. Will the use of this trust trigger any estate taxes at that time?

Answer: Harry's transfer of the policy to the trust will be a taxable gift at the time of the transfer to the extent of the value of the transfer. However, the $2 million proceeds from the policy will not be included in Harry's estate upon his death.

Donors often use partnerships to transfer assets and for the control of a business in a systematic manner that also provides them with income and security. One specific form of partnership, the **family limited partnership,** divides a family business into various ownership interests, representing control of operations and future income and appreciation of the assets. These limited partnerships were sometimes used to transfer appreciation to members of a younger generation while allowing the older generation to effectively retain control of the business. Obviously, the intent of the estate and gift taxes is to recognize transfers of assets that also represent control of the assets. Hence, it was not surprising that Congress revised the law to restrict the ability of family limited partnerships to effectively transfer appreciation in business assets and operations to younger generations without also transferring control.

CONCLUSION

In this chapter we learned to identify taxable transfers whether made at death (testamentary transfers) or during life (inter vivos transfers). We also learned how to calculate estate and gift taxes, and we introduced some fundamental transfer tax planning techniques. The simplest and most effective wealth planning technique is serial giving. As long as the gifts are restricted to present interests under the annual exclusion, serial giving avoids all transfer taxes. Other methods, such as family limited partnerships, can also be effective under the proper circumstances. In all cases, however, wealth planning should be carefully coordinated with other needs and objectives.

Summary

LO 25-1　Outline the basic structure of federal transfer taxes and describe the valuation of property transfers.

- Congress imposes a tax on transfers of property whether the transfer is a gift or occurs at death.
- The unified transfer tax scheme provides for a progressive tax rate schedule that applies to cumulative transfers. That is, transfers in all prior periods are taken into account when calculating the tax for a transfer in a current period.
- The applicable (unified) credit offsets transfer tax on cumulative lifetime transfers (the exemption equivalent) of $5.45 million for gifts and transfers at death.
- Each transfer tax shares two common deductions, an unlimited deduction for charitable contributions and a marital deduction that allows almost unfettered transfers between spouses.
- Property transfers are valued at fair market value defined as the value paid by a willing buyer to a willing seller. The determination of fair market value often depends upon the facts and circumstances surrounding the property.

LO 25-2　Summarize the operation of the federal gift tax and the calculation of the federal gift tax.

- Lifetime transfers of property for no (or inadequate) consideration are taxed as gifts if the transfer is complete and irrevocable.
- Contributions to political parties or candidates, and medical and educational expenses paid on behalf of an unrelated individual, are excluded from gift taxation.
- Gifts are taxed at the fair market value of the donated property on the date the gift becomes complete, and small gifts are reduced by the annual exclusion ($14,000) if they are present interests.
- With gift-splitting, married couples can elect to treat all gifts made in a year as if each spouse made one-half of each gift.
- Calculate taxable gifts by adjusting current gifts for exclusions and gift-splitting, and then deducting the marital deduction (for qualifying gifts to a spouse) and the charitable deduction.
- Transfers of terminable interests in property, such as a life estate, will not generally qualify for the marital deduction.
- Compute the gift tax on cumulative taxable gifts by adding prior taxable gifts to current taxable gifts.
- Reduce the gift tax on cumulative gifts by the gift tax on prior taxable gifts calculated using the current rate schedule and ignoring any exemption equivalent used in prior years.
- Then reduce the gift tax by the *unused* portion of the exemption equivalent as converted into the unified credit using the current tax rate schedule.

LO 25-3　Describe the federal estate tax, and compute taxable transfers at death and the federal estate tax.

- The gross estate includes property owned by the decedent at death (the probate estate) and certain property transfers taking effect at death.
- Property the decedent owned jointly is included in the gross estate. The value of the decedent's interest is included when property is held in joint tenancy, whereas half the value of the property is included when held with a spouse in joint tenancy with the right of survivorship.
- Temporal interests begin or end with the passage of time. The value of a future interest, such as a remainder, can be determined from IRS tables, and the value of a present interest, such as a life estate, is calculated at the difference between the value of the future interest and the current value of the property.
- The gross estate is reduced by administrative expenses, debts of the decedent, and losses incurred during the administration of the estate, resulting in the adjusted gross estate.
- The adjusted gross estate is reduced for certain transfers to a surviving spouse (the marital deduction) and for transfers to charities (the charitable deduction), resulting in the taxable estate.

- The taxable estate is increased by adjusted taxable gifts to determine cumulative transfers.
- The tentative estate tax is calculated on cumulative transfers as reduced by the tax payable on adjusted taxable gifts calculated using the current rate schedule.
- The estate tax due is the tentative tax reduced by the unified credit.
- An estate is allowed to increase the exemption equivalent by the amount of a deceased spouse unused exclusion (DSUE).

Apply fundamental principles of wealth planning and explain how income and transfer taxation interact to affect wealth planning.

LO 25-4

- The generation-skipping tax is a supplemental tax designed to prevent the avoidance of transfer taxes (both estate and gift tax) through transfers that skip a generation of recipients.
- Trusts and estates are fiduciary taxpayers taxed on accumulated (undistributed) income via a fiduciary income tax return.
- Because fiduciary income tax rates are generally as high as or higher than the tax rates for individual beneficiaries, the income tax benefits from splitting income between fiduciaries and beneficiaries are typically negligible.
- A serial gift strategy saves gift taxes by converting a potentially large taxable transfer into a tax-exempt transfer of multiple smaller gifts that qualify for the annual exclusion of the donor.
- Testamentary transfers allow a step-up in tax basis to fair market value, thereby eliminating the income tax on unrealized appreciation. In contrast, appreciation of property transferred via inter vivos transfers may be eventually realized and taxed as income. However, a gift eliminates transfer taxes on expected future appreciation.

KEY TERMS

adjusted gross estate (25-22)
adjusted taxable gifts (25-25)
alternative valuation date (25-21)
annual exclusion (25-8)
applicable credit (25-2)
beneficiary (25-7)
carryover basis (25-31)
common-law states (25-10)
community property states (25-10)
complex trust (25-29n)
corpus (25-7)
current gifts (25-9)
deceased spousal unused
    exclusion (25-26)
distributable net income
    (DNI) (25-30)
distribution deduction (25-30)
donee (25-5)
donor (25-5)

estate (25-29)
executor (25-21n)
exemption equivalent (25-3)
family limited partnership (25-33)
fiduciary (25-29)
fiduciary duty (25-7)
future interest (25-6)
generation-skipping tax (GST) (25-29)
grantor (25-7)
gross estate (25-17)
heirs (25-17)
intervivos transfers (25-2)
joint tenancy with right of
    survivorship (25-2)
last will and testament (25-2)
life estate (25-7)
life insurance trust (25-33)
marital deduction (25-4)

nondeductible terminable
    interests (25-11)
present interest (25-6)
probate (25-17)
probate estate (25-17)
remainder (25-7)
remainderman (25-7)
reversion (25-7)
serial gift (25-30)
simple trust (25-29n)
taxable estate (25-23)
taxable gifts (25-9)
tenancy by the entirety (25-19n)
tenancy in common (25-19)
terminable interest (25-7)
testamentary transfers (25-2)
trust (25-7)
trustee (25-7)

DISCUSSION QUESTIONS

Discussion Questions are available in *Connect*®.

connect

1. Identify the features common to the gift tax formula and the estate tax formula.

LO 25-1

2. Explain why Congress felt it necessary to enact a gift tax to complement the estate tax.

LO 25-1

LO 25-1   3. Describe the unified credit and the purpose it serves in the gift and estate tax.

LO 25-1   4. Fred is retired and living on his pension. He has accumulated almost $1 million of property he would like to leave to his children. However, Fred is afraid much of his wealth will be eliminated by the federal estate tax. Explain whether this fear is well founded.

LO 25-1   5. Define fair market value for transfer tax purposes.

LO 25-2   6. Describe the requirements for a complete gift, and contrast a gift of a present interest with a gift of a future interest.

LO 25-2   7. Describe a property transfer or payment that is not, by definition, a transfer for inadequate consideration.

LO 25-2   8. Describe a situation in which a transfer of cash to a trust might be considered an incomplete gift.

LO 25-2   9. Identify two types of transfers for inadequate consideration that are specifically excluded from imposition of the gift tax.

LO 25-2   10. Under what circumstances will a deposit of cash to a bank account held in joint tenancy be considered a completed gift?

LO 25-2   11. Explain how a purchase of realty could result in a taxable gift.

LO 25-2   12. Describe the conditions for using the annual exclusion to offset an otherwise taxable transfer.

LO 25-2   13. List the conditions for making an election to split gifts.

LO 25-2   14. Describe the limitations on the deduction of transfers to charity.

LO 25-2   15. Explain the purpose of adding prior taxable gifts to current taxable gifts and show whether these prior gifts could be taxed multiple times over the years.

LO 25-3   16. Explain why the gross estate includes the value of certain property transferred by the decedent at death, such as property held in joint tenancy with the right of survivorship, even though this property is not subject to probate.

LO 25-3   17. Identify the factors that determine the proportion of the value of property held in joint tenancy with the right of survivorship that will be included in a decedent's gross estate.

LO 25-3   18. Harold owns a condo in Hawaii that he plans on using for the rest of his life. However, to ensure his sister Maude will own the property after his death, Harold deeded the remainder of the property to her. He signed the deed transferring the remainder in July 2009 when the condo was worth $250,000 and his life estate was worth $75,000. In January of this year Harold died, at which time the condo was worth $300,000. What amount, if any, is included in Harold's gross estate? Explain.

🔎 research

LO 25-3   19. Paul is a widower with several grown children. He is considering transferring his residence into a trust for his children and retaining a life estate in it. Comment on whether this plan will prevent the value of the home from being included in Paul's gross estate when he dies.

LO 25-3   20. Explain how a remainder and an income interest are valued for transfer tax purposes.

LO 25-3   21. Explain why the fair market value of a life estate is more difficult to estimate than an income interest.

LO 25-3   22. Describe a reason why transfers of terminable interests should not qualify for the marital deduction.

LO 25-3   23. True or False: Including taxable gifts when calculating the estate tax subjects these transfers to double taxation. Explain.

LO 25-3   24. People sometimes confuse the unified credit with the exemption equivalent. Describe how these terms differ and how they are related.

LO 25-4   25. Describe a reason why a generation-skipping tax was necessary to augment the estate and gift taxes.

26. Explain why an effective wealth transfer plan necessitates cooperation between lawyers, accountants, and investment advisors. `LO 25-4`

27. Describe how to initiate the construction of a comprehensive and effective wealth plan. `LO 25-4`

28. List two questions you might pose to a client to find out whether a program of serial gifts would be an advantageous wealth transfer plan. `LO 25-4`

29. A client in good health wants to support the college education of her teenage grandchild. The client holds various properties but proposes to make a gift of cash in the amount of the annual exclusion. Explain to the client why a direct gift of cash may not be advisable and what property might serve as a reasonable substitute. `LO 25-4`

30. An elderly client has a life insurance policy worth $40,000 that upon her death pays $250,000 to her sole grandchild (or his estate). The client retains ownership of the policy. Outline for her the costs and benefits of transferring ownership of the policy to a life insurance trust. `LO 25-4`

31. Identify the sections in the Internal Revenue Code that authorize the use of qualified terminable interests (QTIPs) for gift and estate tax purposes, respectively. `LO 25-4` research

32. Under what conditions can an executor or trustee elect to claim a marital deduction for a transfer of a terminable interest to a spouse? `LO 25-4` research

33. Explain how a transfer of property as a gift may have income tax implications to the donee. `LO 25-4`

PROBLEMS

Select problems are available in *Connect*®.   connect

34. Raquel transferred $100,000 of stock to a trust, with income to be paid to her nephew for 18 years and the remainder to her nephew's children (or their estates). Raquel named a bank as independent trustee but retained the power to determine how much income, if any, will be paid in any particular year. Is this transfer a complete gift? Explain. `LO 25-2`

35. This year Gerry's friend, Dewey, was disabled. Gerry paid $15,000 to Dewey's doctor for medical expenses and paid $12,500 to State University for college tuition for Dewey's son. Has Gerry made taxable gifts and, if so, in what amounts? `LO 25-2`

36. This year Dan and Mike purchased realty for $180,000 and took title as equal tenants in common. However, Mike was able to provide only $40,000 of the purchase price and Dan the remaining $140,000. Has Dan made a complete gift to Mike and, if so, in what amount? `LO 25-2`

37. Last year Nate opened a savings account with a deposit of $15,000. The account was in the name of Nate and Derrick, joint tenancy with the right of survivorship. Derrick did not contribute to the account, but this year he withdrew $5,000. Has Nate made a complete gift and, if so, what is the amount of the taxable gift and when was the gift made? `LO 25-2`

38. Barry transfers $1,000,000 to an irrevocable trust with income to Robin for her life and the remainder to Maurice (or his estate). Calculate the value of the life estate and remainder if Robin's age and the prevailing interest rate result in a Table S discount factor for the remainder of 0.27. `LO 25-2`

39. This year Jim created an irrevocable trust to provide for Ted, his 32-year-old nephew, and Ted's family. Jim transferred $70,000 to the trust and named a bank as the trustee. The trust was directed to pay income to Ted until he reaches age 35, and at that time the trust is to be terminated and the corpus is to be distributed to Ted's two children (or their estates). Determine the amount, `LO 25-2`

if any, of the current gift and the taxable gift. If necessary, you may assume the relevant interest rate is 6 percent and Jim is unmarried.

LO 25-2 40. This year Colleen transferred $100,000 to an irrevocable trust that pays equal shares of income annually to three cousins (or their estates) for the next eight years. At that time, the trust is terminated and the corpus of the trust reverts to Colleen. Determine the amount, if any, of the current gifts and the taxable gifts. If necessary, you may assume the relevant interest rate is 6 percent and Colleen is unmarried. What is your answer if Colleen is married and she elects to gift-split with her spouse?

LO 25-2 41. Sly is a widower and wants to make annual gifts of cash to each of his four children and six grandchildren. How much can Sly transfer to his children this year if he makes the maximum gifts eligible for the annual exclusion? What is the amount of the total transfer if Sly is married and elects to gift splitting, assuming his spouse makes no other gifts?

LO 25-2 42. Jack and Liz live in a community property state and their vacation home is community property. This year they transferred the vacation home to an irrevocable trust that provides their son, Tom, a life estate in the home and the remainder to their daughter, Laura. Under the terms of the trust, Tom has the right to use the vacation home for the duration of his life, and Laura will automatically own the property after Tom's death. At the time of the gift the home was valued at $500,000, Tom was 35 years old, and the §7520 rate was 5.4 percent. What is the amount, if any, of the taxable gifts? Would your answer be different if the home was not community property and Jack and Liz elected to gift-split?

LO 25-2 43. David placed $80,000 in trust with income to Steve for his life and the remainder to Lil (or her estate). At the time of the gift, given the prevailing interest rate, Steve's life estate was valued at $65,000 and the remainder at $15,000. What is the amount, if any, of David's taxable gifts?

LO 25-2 44. Stephen transferred $15,000 to an irrevocable trust for Graham. The trustee has the discretion to distribute income or corpus for Graham's benefit but is required to distribute all assets to Graham (or his estate) not later than Graham's 21st birthday. What is the amount, if any, of the taxable gift?

LO 25-2 45. For the holidays, Marty gave a watch worth $25,000 to Emily and jewelry worth $40,000 to Natalie. Has Marty made any taxable gifts this year and, if so, in what amounts? Does it matter if Marty is married to Wendy and they live in a community property state?

LO 25-2 46. This year Jeff earned $850,000 and used it to purchase land in joint tenancy with a right of survivorship with Mary. Has Jeff made a taxable gift to Mary and, if so, in what amount? What is your answer if Jeff and Mary are married?

LO 25-2 47. Laura transfers $500,000 into trust with the income to be paid annually to her spouse, William, for life (a life estate) and the remainder to Jenny. Calculate the amount of the taxable gifts from the transfers.

LO 25-2 48. Red transferred $5,000,000 of cash to State University for a new sports complex. Calculate the amount of the taxable gift.

LO 25-2 49. In 2010 Casey made a taxable gift of $5 million to both Stephanie and Linda (a total of $10 million in taxable gifts). Calculate the amount of gift tax due this year and Casey's unused exemption equivalent under the following alternatives.

   a) This year Casey made a taxable gift of $1 million to Stephanie. Casey is not married, and the 2010 gift was the only other taxable gift he has ever made.

   b) This year Casey made a taxable gift of $5 million to Stephanie. Casey is not married, and the 2010 gift was the only other taxable gift he has ever made.

   c) This year Casey made a gift worth $5 million to Stephanie. Casey is married to Helen in a common law state, and the 2010 gift was the only other taxable gift he or Helen has ever made. Casey and Helen elect to gift split.

50. Tom Hruise was an entertainment executive who had a fatal accident on a film set. Tom's will directed his executor to distribute his cash and stock to his wife, Kaffie, the real estate to his church, The First Church of Methodology, and the remainder of his assets were to be placed in trust for his three children. Tom's estate consisted of the following:

LO 25-3

tax forms

Assets:	
Personal assets	$ 800,000
Cash and stock	24,000,000
Intangible assets (film rights)	71,500,000
Real estate	15,000,000
	$111,300,000
Liabilities:	
Mortgage	$ 3,200,000
Other liabilities	4,100,000
	$ 7,300,000

a) Tom made a taxable gift of $8 million in 2011. Compute the estate tax for Tom's estate.

b) Fill out lines 1 through 12 in part 2 of Form 706 for Tom's estate.

51. Hal and Wendy are married, and they own a parcel of realty, Blackacre, as joint tenants with the right of survivorship. Hal owns an additional parcel of realty, Redacre, in his name alone. Suppose Hal should die when Blackacre is worth $800,000 and Redacre is worth $750,000. What value of realty would be included in Hal's probate estate, and what value in Hal's gross estate? **LO 25-3**

52. Walter owns a whole-life insurance policy worth $52,000 that directs the insurance company to pay the beneficiary $250,000 on Walter's death. Walter pays the annual premiums and has the power to designate the beneficiary of the policy (it is currently his son, James). What value of the policy, if any, will be included in Walter's estate upon his death? **LO 25-3**

53. Many years ago James and Sergio purchased property for $450,000. Although they are listed as equal co-owners, Sergio was able to provide only $200,000 of the purchase price. James treated the additional $25,000 of his contribution to the purchase price as a gift to Sergio. If the property is worth $900,000 at Sergio's death, what amount would be included in Sergio's estate if the title to the property was tenants in common? What if the title were joint tenancy with right of survivorship? **LO 25-3**

54. Terry transferred $500,000 of real estate into an irrevocable trust for her son, Lee. The trustee was directed to retain income until Lee's 21st birthday and then pay him the corpus of the trust. Terry retained the power to require the trustee to pay income to Lee at any time, and the right to the assets if Lee predeceased her. What amount of the trust, if any, will be included in Terry's estate? **LO 25-3**

55. Last year Robert transferred a life insurance policy worth $45,000 to an irrevocable trust with directions to distribute the corpus of the trust to his grandson, Danny, upon his graduation from college, or to Danny's estate upon his death. Robert paid $15,000 of gift tax on the transfer of the policy. Early this year, Robert died and the insurance company paid $400,000 to the trust. What amount, if any, is included in Robert's gross estate? **LO 25-3**

56. Willie purchased a whole-life insurance policy on his brother, Benny. Under the policy, the insurance company will pay the named beneficiary $100,000 upon the death of the insured, Benny. Willie names Tess the beneficiary, and upon **LO 25-3**

research

Benny's death, Tess receives the proceeds of the policy, $100,000. Identify and discuss the transfer tax implications of this arrangement.

LO 25-3 57. Jimmy owns two parcels of real estate, Tara and Sundance. Tara is worth $240,000 and Sundance is worth $360,000. Jimmy plans to bequeath Tara directly to his wife Lois and leave her a life estate in Sundance. What amount of value will be included in Jimmy's gross estate and taxable estate should he die now?

LO 25-3 58. Roland had a taxable estate of $5.5 million when he died this year. Calculate the amount of estate tax due (if any) under the following alternatives.

a) Roland's prior taxable gifts consist of a taxable gift of $1 million in 2005.

b) Roland's prior taxable gifts consist of a taxable gift of $1.5 million in 2005.

c) Explain how the tax calculation would change if Roland made a $1 million taxable gift in the year prior to his death.

LO 25-2
tax forms 59. Brad and Angelina are a wealthy couple who have three children, Fred, Bridget, and Lisa. Two of the three children, Fred and Bridget, are from Brad's previous marriages. On Christmas this year, Brad gave each of the three children a cash gift of $10,000, and Angelina gave Lisa an additional cash gift of $40,000. Brad also gave stock worth $40,000 (adjusted basis of $10,000) to the Actor's Guild (an "A" charity).

a) Brad and Angelina have chosen to split gifts. Calculate Brad's gift tax. Assume that Angelina has no previous taxable gifts, but Brad reported previous taxable gifts of $2 million in 2009 when he used $345,800 of applicable credit and paid $435,000 of gift taxes.

b) Fill out parts 1 and 4 of Form 709 for Brad.

LO 25-4
planning 60. Jones is seriously ill and has $6 million of property that he wants to leave to his four children. He is considering making a current gift of the property (rather than leaving the property to pass through his will). Assuming any taxable transfer will be subject to the highest transfer tax rate, determine how much gift tax Jones will owe if he makes the transfers now. How much estate tax will Jones save if he dies after three years, during which time the property appreciates to $6.8 million? Besides transfer taxes, what other tax and financial factors should Jones consider in making this choice?

LO 25-4 61. Angelina gave a parcel of realty to Julie valued at $210,000 (Angelina purchased the property five years ago for $88,000). Compute the amount of the taxable gift on the transfer, if any. Suppose several years later Julie sold the property for $215,000. What is the amount of her gain or loss, if any, on the sale?

LO 25-4
research 62. Several years ago Doug invested $21,000 in stock. This year he gave his daughter Tina the stock on a day it was valued at $20,000. She promptly sold it for $19,500. Determine the amount of the taxable gift, if any, and calculate the amount of taxable income or gain, if any, for Tina. Assume Doug is not married and does not support Tina, who is 28.

LO 25-4 63. Roberta is considering making annual gifts of $14,000 of stock to each of her four children. She expects to live another five years and to leave a taxable estate worth approximately $8 million. She requests that you justify the gifts by estimating her estate tax savings from making the gifts.

LO 25-4 64. Harold and Maude are married and live in a common-law state. Neither have made any taxable gifts and Maude owns (holds title to) all their property. She dies with a taxable estate of $15 million and leaves it all to Harold. He dies several years later, leaving the entire $15 million to their three children. Calculate how much estate tax is due from Harold's estate.

COMPREHENSIVE PROBLEMS

Select problems are available in *Connect*®.   ▇▇ connect

65. Suppose Vince dies this year with a gross estate of $15 million and no adjusted prior gifts. Calculate the amount of estate tax due (if any) under the following *alternative* conditions:

    a) Vince leaves his entire estate to his spouse, Millie.

    b) Vince leaves $10 million to Millie and the remainder to charity.

    c) Vince leaves $10 million to Millie and the remainder to his son, Paul.

    d) Vince leaves $10 million to Millie and the remainder to a trust whose trustee is required to pay income to Millie for her life and the remainder to Paul.

66. Hank is a single individual who possesses a life insurance policy worth $300,000 that will pay his two children a total of $800,000 upon his death. This year Hank transferred the policy and all incidents of ownership to an irrevocable trust that pays income annually to his two children for 15 years and then distributes the corpus to the children in equal shares.

    a) Calculate the amount of gift tax due (if any) on the gift. Assume that Hank has made only one prior taxable gift of $5 million in 2011.

    b) Calculate the amount of cumulative taxable transfers for estate tax purposes if Hank dies this year but after the date of the gift. At the time of his death, Hank's probate estate is $10 million divided in equal shares between his two children.

67. Jack is single and he made his first taxable gift of $1,000,000 in 2008. Jack made additional gifts in 2009, at which time he gave $1,750,000 to each of his three children and an additional $1,000,000 to State University (a charity). The annual exclusion in 2009 was $13,000. Recently Jack has been in poor health and would like you to estimate his estate tax should he die this year. Jack estimates his taxable estate (after deductions) will be worth $5.4 million at his death.

68. Montgomery has decided to engage in wealth planning and has listed the value of his assets below. The life insurance has a cash surrender value of $120,000, and the proceeds are payable to Montgomery's estate. The trust is an irrevocable trust created by Montgomery's brother 10 years ago and contains assets currently valued at $800,000. The income from the trust is payable to Montgomery's faithful butler, Walen, for his life, and the remainder is payable to Montgomery or his estate. Walen is currently 37 years old, and the §7520 interest rate is currently 5.4 percent. Montgomery is unmarried and plans to leave all his assets to his surviving relatives.

Property	Value	Adjusted Basis
Auto	$ 20,000	$ 55,000
Personal effects	75,000	110,000
Checking and savings accounts	250,000	250,000
Investments	2,500,000	770,000
Residence	1,400,000	980,000
Life insurance proceeds	1,000,000	50,000
Real estate investments	5,125,000	2,800,000
Trust	800,000	80,000

a) Calculate the amount of the estate tax due (if any), assuming Montgomery dies this year and has never made any taxable gifts.

b) Calculate the amount of the estate tax due (if any), assuming Montgomery dies this year and made one taxable gift in 2006. The taxable gift was $1 million, and Montgomery used his applicable credit to avoid paying any gift tax.

c) Calculate the amount of the estate tax due (if any), assuming Montgomery dies this year and made one taxable gift in 2006. The taxable gift was $5 million, and Montgomery used his applicable credit to avoid paying any gift tax. Montgomery plans to bequeath his investments to charity and leave his remaining assets to his surviving relatives.

Appendix A

Tax Forms

All tax forms can be obtained from the IRS website: www.irs.gov.

Form **1040**
Department of the Treasury—Internal Revenue Service   (99)
U.S. Individual Income Tax Return 2015   OMB No. 1545-0074   IRS Use Only—Do not write or staple in this space.

For the year Jan. 1–Dec. 31, 2015, or other tax year beginning _____ , 2015, ending _____ , 20 ____   **See separate instructions.**

Your first name and initial	Last name	Your social security number

If a joint return, spouse's first name and initial	Last name	Spouse's social security number

Home address (number and street). If you have a P.O. box, see instructions.   Apt. no.   ▲ **Make sure the SSN(s) above and on line 6c are correct.**

City, town or post office, state, and ZIP code. If you have a foreign address, also complete spaces below (see instructions).

Presidential Election Campaign
Check here if you, or your spouse if filing jointly, want $3 to go to this fund. Checking a box below will not change your tax or refund.   ☐ You   ☐ Spouse

Foreign country name	Foreign province/state/county	Foreign postal code

Filing Status

Check only one box.

1 ☐ Single
2 ☐ Married filing jointly (even if only one had income)
3 ☐ Married filing separately. Enter spouse's SSN above and full name here. ▶
4 ☐ Head of household (with qualifying person). (See instructions.) If the qualifying person is a child but not your dependent, enter this child's name here. ▶
5 ☐ Qualifying widow(er) with dependent child

Exemptions

6a ☐ **Yourself.** If someone can claim you as a dependent, **do not** check box 6a . . . . . .
b ☐ **Spouse** . . . .

c **Dependents:**

(1) First name Last name	(2) Dependent's social security number	(3) Dependent's relationship to you	(4) ✓ if child under age 17 qualifying for child tax credit (see instructions)
			☐
			☐
			☐
			☐

If more than four dependents, see instructions and check here ▶ ☐

Boxes checked on 6a and 6b ____
No. of children on 6c who:
• lived with you ____
• did not live with you due to divorce or separation (see instructions) ____
Dependents on 6c not entered above ____
Add numbers on lines above ▶ ____

d Total number of exemptions claimed . . . .

Income

Attach Form(s) W-2 here. Also attach Forms W-2G and 1099-R if tax was withheld.

If you did not get a W-2, see instructions.

7	Wages, salaries, tips, etc. Attach Form(s) W-2	7
8a	**Taxable** interest. Attach Schedule B if required	8a
b	**Tax-exempt** interest. **Do not** include on line 8a 8b	
9a	Ordinary dividends. Attach Schedule B if required	9a
b	Qualified dividends 9b	
10	Taxable refunds, credits, or offsets of state and local income taxes	10
11	Alimony received	11
12	Business income or (loss). Attach Schedule C or C-EZ	12
13	Capital gain or (loss). Attach Schedule D if required. If not required, check here ▶ ☐	13
14	Other gains or (losses). Attach Form 4797	14
15a	IRA distributions . 15a _____ b Taxable amount . . .	15b
16a	Pensions and annuities 16a _____ b Taxable amount . . .	16b
17	Rental real estate, royalties, partnerships, S corporations, trusts, etc. Attach Schedule E	17
18	Farm income or (loss). Attach Schedule F	18
19	Unemployment compensation	19
20a	Social security benefits 20a _____ b Taxable amount . . .	20b
21	Other income. List type and amount _____	21
22	Combine the amounts in the far right column for lines 7 through 21. This is your **total income** ▶	22

Adjusted Gross Income

23	Educator expenses 23	
24	Certain business expenses of reservists, performing artists, and fee-basis government officials. Attach Form 2106 or 2106-EZ 24	
25	Health savings account deduction. Attach Form 8889 . 25	
26	Moving expenses. Attach Form 3903 26	
27	Deductible part of self-employment tax. Attach Schedule SE . 27	
28	Self-employed SEP, SIMPLE, and qualified plans . . 28	
29	Self-employed health insurance deduction 29	
30	Penalty on early withdrawal of savings 30	
31a	Alimony paid b Recipient's SSN ▶ _____ 31a	
32	IRA deduction 32	
33	Student loan interest deduction 33	
34	Tuition and fees. Attach Form 8917 34	
35	Domestic production activities deduction. Attach Form 8903 35	
36	Add lines 23 through 35	36
37	Subtract line 36 from line 22. This is your **adjusted gross income** . . . . . ▶	37

For Disclosure, Privacy Act, and Paperwork Reduction Act Notice, see separate instructions.   Cat. No. 11320B   Form **1040** (2015)

Form 1040 (2015)   Page **2**

	38	Amount from line 37 (adjusted gross income)	38	

Tax and Credits

39a	Check if:	☐ **You** were born before January 2, 1951, ☐ Blind. ☐ **Spouse** was born before January 2, 1951, ☐ Blind.	Total boxes checked ▶ 39a	
b	If your spouse itemizes on a separate return or you were a dual-status alien, check here ▶ 39b ☐			

Standard Deduction for—

• People who check any box on line 39a or 39b **or** who can be claimed as a dependent, see instructions.

• All others:

Single or Married filing separately, $6,300

Married filing jointly or Qualifying widow(er), $12,600

Head of household, $9,250

40	**Itemized deductions** (from Schedule A) **or** your **standard deduction** (see left margin) . .	40	
41	Subtract line 40 from line 38	41	
42	**Exemptions.** If line 38 is $154,950 or less, multiply $4,000 by the number on line 6d. Otherwise, see instructions	42	
43	**Taxable income.** Subtract line 42 from line 41. If line 42 is more than line 41, enter -0- . .	43	
44	**Tax** (see instructions). Check if any from: **a** ☐ Form(s) 8814 **b** ☐ Form 4972 **c** ☐	44	
45	**Alternative minimum tax** (see instructions). Attach Form 6251	45	
46	Excess advance premium tax credit repayment. Attach Form 8962	46	
47	Add lines 44, 45, and 46 . . . . ▶	47	

48	Foreign tax credit. Attach Form 1116 if required	48	
49	Credit for child and dependent care expenses. Attach Form 2441	49	
50	Education credits from Form 8863, line 19	50	
51	Retirement savings contributions credit. Attach Form 8880	51	
52	Child tax credit. Attach Schedule 8812, if required . . .	52	
53	Residential energy credits. Attach Form 5695	53	
54	Other credits from Form: **a** ☐ 3800 **b** ☐ 8801 **c** ☐	54	

55	Add lines 48 through 54. These are your **total credits**	55	
56	Subtract line 55 from line 47. If line 55 is more than line 47, enter -0- . . . . . . ▶	56	

Other Taxes

57	Self-employment tax. Attach Schedule SE	57	
58	Unreported social security and Medicare tax from Form: **a** ☐ 4137 **b** ☐ 8919 . .	58	
59	Additional tax on IRAs, other qualified retirement plans, etc. Attach Form 5329 if required	59	
60a	Household employment taxes from Schedule H	60a	
b	First-time homebuyer credit repayment. Attach Form 5405 if required	60b	
61	Health care: individual responsibility (see instructions) Full-year coverage ☐	61	
62	Taxes from: **a** ☐ Form 8959 **b** ☐ Form 8960 **c** ☐ Instructions; enter code(s)	62	
63	Add lines 56 through 62. This is your **total tax** . . . . ▶	63	

Payments

If you have a qualifying child, attach Schedule EIC.

64	Federal income tax withheld from Forms W-2 and 1099 . .	64	
65	2015 estimated tax payments and amount applied from 2014 return	65	
66a	**Earned income credit (EIC)**	66a	
b	Nontaxable combat pay election 66b		
67	Additional child tax credit. Attach Schedule 8812	67	
68	American opportunity credit from Form 8863, line 8 . . .	68	
69	Net premium tax credit. Attach Form 8962	69	
70	Amount paid with request for extension to file	70	
71	Excess social security and tier 1 RRTA tax withheld	71	
72	Credit for federal tax on fuels. Attach Form 4136	72	
73	Credits from Form: **a** ☐ 2439 **b** ☐ Reserved **c** ☐ 8885 **d** ☐	73	

74	Add lines 64, 65, 66a, and 67 through 73. These are your **total payments** . . . . . ▶	74	

Refund

Direct deposit? See instructions.

75	If line 74 is more than line 63, subtract line 63 from line 74. This is the amount you **overpaid**	75	
76a	Amount of line 75 you want **refunded to you.** If Form 8888 is attached, check here ▶ ☐	76a	
▶ b	Routing number ☐☐☐☐☐☐☐☐☐ ▶ c Type: ☐ Checking ☐ Savings		
▶ d	Account number ☐☐☐☐☐☐☐☐☐☐☐☐☐☐☐☐☐		
77	Amount of line 75 you want **applied to your 2016 estimated tax** ▶ 77		

Amount You Owe

78	**Amount you owe.** Subtract line 74 from line 63. For details on how to pay, see instructions ▶	78	
79	Estimated tax penalty (see instructions) 79		

Third Party Designee

Do you want to allow another person to discuss this return with the IRS (see instructions)?   ☐ **Yes.** Complete below.   ☐ **No**

Designee's name ▶	Phone no. ▶	Personal identification number (PIN) ▶ ☐☐☐☐☐

Sign Here

Joint return? See instructions.
Keep a copy for your records.

Under penalties of perjury, I declare that I have examined this return and accompanying schedules and statements, and to the best of my knowledge and belief, they are true, correct, and complete. Declaration of preparer (other than taxpayer) is based on all information of which preparer has any knowledge.

Your signature	Date	Your occupation	Daytime phone number
Spouse's signature. If a joint return, **both** must sign.	Date	Spouse's occupation	If the IRS sent you an Identity Protection PIN, enter it here (see inst.) ☐☐☐☐☐☐

Paid Preparer Use Only

Print/Type preparer's name	Preparer's signature	Date	Check ☐ if self-employed	PTIN
Firm's name ▶			Firm's EIN ▶	
Firm's address ▶			Phone no.	

| SCHEDULE A
(Form 1040)

Department of the Treasury
Internal Revenue Service (99) | **Itemized Deductions**

▶ Information about Schedule A and its separate instructions is at *www.irs.gov/schedulea*.
▶ **Attach to Form 1040.** | OMB No. 1545-0074

20**15**

Attachment
Sequence No. **07** |

Name(s) shown on Form 1040 — **Your social security number**

Medical and Dental Expenses

Caution: Do not include expenses reimbursed or paid by others.

1	Medical and dental expenses (see instructions)	1
2	Enter amount from Form 1040, line 38	2	
3	Multiply line 2 by 10% (.10). But if either you or your spouse was born before January 2, 1951, multiply line 2 by 7.5% (.075) instead	3
4	Subtract line 3 from line 1. If line 3 is more than line 1, enter -0-		4

Taxes You Paid

5	State and local (**check only one box**): a ☐ Income taxes, **or** b ☐ General sales taxes	5
6	Real estate taxes (see instructions)	6
7	Personal property taxes	7
8	Other taxes. List type and amount ▶ _____	8
9	Add lines 5 through 8		9

Interest You Paid

Note:
Your mortgage interest deduction may be limited (see instructions).

10	Home mortgage interest and points reported to you on Form 1098	10
11	Home mortgage interest not reported to you on Form 1098. If paid to the person from whom you bought the home, see instructions and show that person's name, identifying no., and address ▶ _____	11
12	Points not reported to you on Form 1098. See instructions for special rules	12
13	Mortgage insurance premiums (see instructions)	13
14	Investment interest. Attach Form 4952 if required. (See instructions.)	14
15	Add lines 10 through 14		15

Gifts to Charity

If you made a gift and got a benefit for it, see instructions.

16	Gifts by cash or check. If you made any gift of $250 or more, see instructions	16
17	Other than by cash or check. If any gift of $250 or more, see instructions. You **must** attach Form 8283 if over $500 . .	17
18	Carryover from prior year	18
19	Add lines 16 through 18		19

Casualty and Theft Losses

20	Casualty or theft loss(es). Attach Form 4684. (See instructions.)		20

Job Expenses and Certain Miscellaneous Deductions

21	Unreimbursed employee expenses—job travel, union dues, job education, etc. Attach Form 2106 or 2106-EZ if required. (See instructions.) ▶ _____	21
22	Tax preparation fees	22
23	Other expenses—investment, safe deposit box, etc. List type and amount ▶ _____	23
24	Add lines 21 through 23	24
25	Enter amount from Form 1040, line 38	25	
26	Multiply line 25 by 2% (.02)	26
27	Subtract line 26 from line 24. If line 26 is more than line 24, enter -0-		27

Other Miscellaneous Deductions

28	Other—from list in instructions. List type and amount ▶ _____ _____		28

Total Itemized Deductions

29	Is Form 1040, line 38, over $154,950? ☐ **No.** Your deduction is not limited. Add the amounts in the far right column for lines 4 through 28. Also, enter this amount on Form 1040, line 40. ☐ **Yes.** Your deduction may be limited. See the Itemized Deductions Worksheet in the instructions to figure the amount to enter.	}	29
30	If you elect to itemize deductions even though they are less than your standard deduction, check here . . . . ▶ ☐	

For Paperwork Reduction Act Notice, see Form 1040 instructions.   Cat. No. 17145C   **Schedule A (Form 1040) 2015**

SCHEDULE B	Interest and Ordinary Dividends	OMB No. 1545-0074

SCHEDULE B
(Form 1040A or 1040)

Department of the Treasury
Internal Revenue Service (99)

Interest and Ordinary Dividends

▶ Attach to Form 1040A or 1040.
▶ Information about Schedule B and its instructions is at *www.irs.gov/scheduleb.*

OMB No. 1545-0074

20**15**

Attachment
Sequence No. **08**

Name(s) shown on return

Your social security number

Part I

Interest

(See instructions on back and the instructions for Form 1040A, or Form 1040, line 8a.)

Note: If you received a Form 1099-INT, Form 1099-OID, or substitute statement from a brokerage firm, list the firm's name as the payer and enter the total interest shown on that form.

		Amount
1	List name of payer. If any interest is from a seller-financed mortgage and the buyer used the property as a personal residence, see instructions on back and list this interest first. Also, show that buyer's social security number and address ▶	**1**
2	Add the amounts on line 1	**2**
3	Excludable interest on series EE and I U.S. savings bonds issued after 1989. Attach Form 8815	**3**
4	Subtract line 3 from line 2. Enter the result here and on Form 1040A, or Form 1040, line 8a . . . . ▶	**4**

Note: If line 4 is over $1,500, you must complete Part III.

Part II

Ordinary Dividends

(See instructions on back and the instructions for Form 1040A, or Form 1040, line 9a.)

Note: If you received a Form 1099-DIV or substitute statement from a brokerage firm, list the firm's name as the payer and enter the ordinary dividends shown on that form.

		Amount
5	List name of payer ▶	**5**
6	Add the amounts on line 5. Enter the total here and on Form 1040A, or Form 1040, line 9a . . . . ▶	**6**

Note: If line 6 is over $1,500, you must complete Part III.

Part III

Foreign Accounts and Trusts

(See instructions on back.)

You must complete this part if you **(a)** had over $1,500 of taxable interest or ordinary dividends; **(b)** had a foreign account; or **(c)** received a distribution from, or were a grantor of, or a transferor to, a foreign trust.

		Yes	No
7a	At any time during 2015, did you have a financial interest in or signature authority over a financial account (such as a bank account, securities account, or brokerage account) located in a foreign country? See instructions		
	If "Yes," are you required to file FinCEN Form 114, Report of Foreign Bank and Financial Accounts (FBAR), to report that financial interest or signature authority? See FinCEN Form 114 and its instructions for filing requirements and exceptions to those requirements		
b	If you are required to file FinCEN Form 114, enter the name of the foreign country where the financial account is located ▶		
8	During 2015, did you receive a distribution from, or were you the grantor of, or transferor to, a foreign trust? If "Yes," you may have to file Form 3520. See instructions on back		

For Paperwork Reduction Act Notice, see your tax return instructions.   Cat. No. 17146N   **Schedule B (Form 1040A or 1040) 2015**

SCHEDULE C **(Form 1040)** Department of the Treasury Internal Revenue Service (99)	**Profit or Loss From Business** (Sole Proprietorship) ▶ Information about Schedule C and its separate instructions is at *www.irs.gov/schedulec*. ▶ **Attach to Form 1040, 1040NR, or 1041; partnerships generally must file Form 1065.**	OMB No. 1545-0074 2015 Attachment Sequence No. 09

Name of proprietor	Social security number (SSN)

A Principal business or profession, including product or service (see instructions)

B Enter code from instructions ▶

C Business name. If no separate business name, leave blank.

D Employer ID number (EIN), (see instr.)

E Business address (including suite or room no.) ▶
City, town or post office, state, and ZIP code

F Accounting method: **(1)** ☐ Cash   **(2)** ☐ Accrual   **(3)** ☐ Other (specify) ▶

G Did you "materially participate" in the operation of this business during 2015? If "No," see instructions for limit on losses ☐ Yes ☐ No

H If you started or acquired this business during 2015, check here ▶ ☐

I Did you make any payments in 2015 that would require you to file Form(s) 1099? (see instructions) ☐ Yes ☐ No

J If "Yes," did you or will you file required Forms 1099? ☐ Yes ☐ No

Part I Income

1	Gross receipts or sales. See instructions for line 1 and check the box if this income was reported to you on Form W-2 and the "Statutory employee" box on that form was checked . . . . ▶ ☐	1	
2	Returns and allowances	2	
3	Subtract line 2 from line 1	3	
4	Cost of goods sold (from line 42)	4	
5	**Gross profit.** Subtract line 4 from line 3	5	
6	Other income, including federal and state gasoline or fuel tax credit or refund (see instructions)	6	
7	**Gross income.** Add lines 5 and 6 . . . . ▶	7	

Part II Expenses. Enter expenses for business use of your home **only** on line 30.

8	Advertising	8		18	Office expense (see instructions)	18	
9	Car and truck expenses (see instructions)	9		19	Pension and profit-sharing plans	19	
10	Commissions and fees .	10		20	Rent or lease (see instructions):		
11	Contract labor (see instructions)	11		a	Vehicles, machinery, and equipment	20a	
12	Depletion	12		b	Other business property . . .	20b	
13	Depreciation and section 179 expense deduction (not included in Part III) (see instructions)	13		21	Repairs and maintenance . . .	21	
				22	Supplies (not included in Part III) .	22	
				23	Taxes and licenses	23	
				24	Travel, meals, and entertainment:		
14	Employee benefit programs (other than on line 19) . .	14		a	Travel	24a	
15	Insurance (other than health)	15		b	Deductible meals and entertainment (see instructions) .	24b	
16	Interest:			25	Utilities	25	
a	Mortgage (paid to banks, etc.)	16a		26	Wages (less employment credits) .	26	
b	Other	16b		27a	Other expenses (from line 48) . .	27a	
17	Legal and professional services	17		b	**Reserved for future use** . . .	27b	

28	**Total expenses** before expenses for business use of home. Add lines 8 through 27a . . . . . . ▶	28	
29	Tentative profit or (loss). Subtract line 28 from line 7	29	
30	Expenses for business use of your home. Do not report these expenses elsewhere. Attach Form 8829 unless using the simplified method (see instructions). **Simplified method filers only:** enter the total square footage of: (a) your home: _____ and (b) the part of your home used for business: _____ . Use the Simplified Method Worksheet in the instructions to figure the amount to enter on line 30	30	
31	**Net profit or (loss).** Subtract line 30 from line 29. • If a profit, enter on both **Form 1040, line 12** (or **Form 1040NR, line 13**) and on **Schedule SE, line 2.** (If you checked the box on line 1, see instructions). Estates and trusts, enter on **Form 1041, line 3.** • If a loss, you **must** go to line 32.	31	
32	If you have a loss, check the box that describes your investment in this activity (see instructions). • If you checked 32a, enter the loss on both **Form 1040, line 12,** (or **Form 1040NR, line 13**) and on **Schedule SE, line 2.** (If you checked the box on line 1, see the line 31 instructions). Estates and trusts, enter on **Form 1041, line 3.** • If you checked 32b, you **must** attach **Form 6198.** Your loss may be limited.	32a ☐ All investment is at risk. 32b ☐ Some investment is not at risk.

For Paperwork Reduction Act Notice, see the separate instructions.   Cat. No. 11334P   **Schedule C (Form 1040) 2015**

Part III	**Cost of Goods Sold** (see instructions)

33 Method(s) used to
value closing inventory: **a** ☐ Cost   **b** ☐ Lower of cost or market   **c** ☐ Other (attach explanation)

34 Was there any change in determining quantities, costs, or valuations between opening and closing inventory?
If "Yes," attach explanation . . . .   ☐ **Yes**   ☐ **No**

35 Inventory at beginning of year. If different from last year's closing inventory, attach explanation . . .	**35**	
36 Purchases less cost of items withdrawn for personal use	**36**	
37 Cost of labor. Do not include any amounts paid to yourself	**37**	
38 Materials and supplies	**38**	
39 Other costs	**39**	
40 Add lines 35 through 39	**40**	
41 Inventory at end of year	**41**	
42 **Cost of goods sold.** Subtract line 41 from line 40. Enter the result here and on line 4	**42**	

Part IV	**Information on Your Vehicle.** Complete this part **only** if you are claiming car or truck expenses on line 9 and are not required to file Form 4562 for this business. See the instructions for line 13 to find out if you must file Form 4562.

43 When did you place your vehicle in service for business purposes? (month, day, year)   ▶ _____ / _____ / _____

44 Of the total number of miles you drove your vehicle during 2015, enter the number of miles you used your vehicle for:

a Business _____   **b** Commuting (see instructions) _____   **c** Other _____

45 Was your vehicle available for personal use during off-duty hours? . . . .   ☐ **Yes**   ☐ **No**

46 Do you (or your spouse) have another vehicle available for personal use? . . . .   ☐ **Yes**   ☐ **No**

47a Do you have evidence to support your deduction? . . . .   ☐ **Yes**   ☐ **No**

b If "Yes," is the evidence written? . . . .   ☐ **Yes**   ☐ **No**

Part V	**Other Expenses.** List below business expenses not included on lines 8–26 or line 30.

--		
--		
--		
--		
--		
--		
--		
--		
48 **Total other expenses.** Enter here and on line 27a	**48**	

SCHEDULE D
(Form 1040)

Department of the Treasury
Internal Revenue Service (99)

Capital Gains and Losses

▶ Attach to Form 1040 or Form 1040NR.
▶ Information about Schedule D and its separate instructions is at *www.irs.gov/scheduled*.
▶ Use Form 8949 to list your transactions for lines 1b, 2, 3, 8b, 9, and 10.

OMB No. 1545-0074

2015

Attachment
Sequence No. **12**

Name(s) shown on return

Your social security number

Part I Short-Term Capital Gains and Losses—Assets Held One Year or Less

See instructions for how to figure the amounts to enter on the lines below. This form may be easier to complete if you round off cents to whole dollars.	(d) Proceeds (sales price)	(e) Cost (or other basis)	(g) Adjustments to gain or loss from Form(s) 8949, Part I, line 2, column (g)	(h) Gain or (loss) Subtract column (e) from column (d) and combine the result with column (g)
1a Totals for all short-term transactions reported on Form 1099-B for which basis was reported to the IRS and for which you have no adjustments (see instructions). However, if you choose to report all these transactions on Form 8949, leave this line blank and go to line 1b .				
1b Totals for all transactions reported on Form(s) 8949 with **Box A** checked				
2 Totals for all transactions reported on Form(s) 8949 with **Box B** checked				
3 Totals for all transactions reported on Form(s) 8949 with **Box C** checked				

4 Short-term gain from Form 6252 and short-term gain or (loss) from Forms 4684, 6781, and 8824 .	**4**	
5 Net short-term gain or (loss) from partnerships, S corporations, estates, and trusts from Schedule(s) K-1	**5**	
6 Short-term capital loss carryover. Enter the amount, if any, from line 8 of your **Capital Loss Carryover Worksheet** in the instructions	**6**	( )
7 **Net short-term capital gain or (loss).** Combine lines 1a through 6 in column (h). If you have any long-term capital gains or losses, go to Part II below. Otherwise, go to Part III on the back	**7**	

Part II Long-Term Capital Gains and Losses—Assets Held More Than One Year

See instructions for how to figure the amounts to enter on the lines below. This form may be easier to complete if you round off cents to whole dollars.	(d) Proceeds (sales price)	(e) Cost (or other basis)	(g) Adjustments to gain or loss from Form(s) 8949, Part II, line 2, column (g)	(h) Gain or (loss) Subtract column (e) from column (d) and combine the result with column (g)
8a Totals for all long-term transactions reported on Form 1099-B for which basis was reported to the IRS and for which you have no adjustments (see instructions). However, if you choose to report all these transactions on Form 8949, leave this line blank and go to line 8b .				
8b Totals for all transactions reported on Form(s) 8949 with **Box D** checked				
9 Totals for all transactions reported on Form(s) 8949 with **Box E** checked				
10 Totals for all transactions reported on Form(s) 8949 with **Box F** checked.				

11 Gain from Form 4797, Part I; long-term gain from Forms 2439 and 6252; and long-term gain or (loss) from Forms 4684, 6781, and 8824	**11**	
12 Net long-term gain or (loss) from partnerships, S corporations, estates, and trusts from Schedule(s) K-1	**12**	
13 Capital gain distributions. See the instructions	**13**	
14 Long-term capital loss carryover. Enter the amount, if any, from line 13 of your **Capital Loss Carryover Worksheet** in the instructions	**14**	( )
15 **Net long-term capital gain or (loss).** Combine lines 8a through 14 in column (h). Then go to Part III on the back	**15**	

For Paperwork Reduction Act Notice, see your tax return instructions.   Cat. No. 11338H   Schedule D (Form 1040) 2015

Part III   **Summary**

16   Combine lines 7 and 15 and enter the result **16**

   • If line 16 is a **gain,** enter the amount from line 16 on Form 1040, line 13, or Form 1040NR, line 14. Then go to line 17 below.

   • If line 16 is a **loss,** skip lines 17 through 20 below. Then go to line 21. Also be sure to complete line 22.

   • If line 16 is **zero,** skip lines 17 through 21 below and enter -0- on Form 1040, line 13, or Form 1040NR, line 14. Then go to line 22.

17   Are lines 15 and 16 **both** gains?
   ☐ **Yes.** Go to line 18.
   ☐ **No.** Skip lines 18 through 21, and go to line 22.

18   Enter the amount, if any, from line 7 of the **28% Rate Gain Worksheet** in the instructions . . ▶   **18**

19   Enter the amount, if any, from line 18 of the **Unrecaptured Section 1250 Gain Worksheet** in the instructions . . . . ▶   **19**

20   Are lines 18 and 19 **both** zero or blank?
   ☐ **Yes.** Complete the **Qualified Dividends and Capital Gain Tax Worksheet** in the instructions for Form 1040, line 44 (or in the instructions for Form 1040NR, line 42). **Do not** complete lines 21 and 22 below.

   ☐ **No.** Complete the **Schedule D Tax Worksheet** in the instructions. **Do not** complete lines 21 and 22 below.

21   If line 16 is a loss, enter here and on Form 1040, line 13, or Form 1040NR, line 14, the **smaller** of:

   • The loss on line 16 or
   • ($3,000), or if married filing separately, ($1,500) . . . .   **21** (   )

   Note: When figuring which amount is smaller, treat both amounts as positive numbers.

22   Do you have qualified dividends on Form 1040, line 9b, or Form 1040NR, line 10b?

   ☐ **Yes.** Complete the **Qualified Dividends and Capital Gain Tax Worksheet** in the instructions for Form 1040, line 44 (or in the instructions for Form 1040NR, line 42).

   ☐ **No.** Complete the rest of Form 1040 or Form 1040NR.

Form **8949**

Department of the Treasury
Internal Revenue Service

Sales and Other Dispositions of Capital Assets

▶ Information about Form 8949 and its separate instructions is at *www.irs.gov/form8949*.

▶ **File with your Schedule D to list your transactions for lines 1b, 2, 3, 8b, 9, and 10 of Schedule D.**

OMB No. 1545-0074

20**15**

Attachment
Sequence No. **12A**

Name(s) shown on return	Social security number or taxpayer identification number

Before you check Box A, B, or C below, see whether you received any Form(s) 1099-B or substitute statement(s) from your broker. A substitute statement will have the same information as Form 1099-B. Either will show whether your basis (usually your cost) was reported to the IRS by your broker and may even tell you which box to check.

Part I   **Short-Term.** Transactions involving capital assets you held 1 year or less are short term. For long-term transactions, see page 2.

Note: You may aggregate all short-term transactions reported on Form(s) 1099-B showing basis was reported to the IRS and for which no adjustments or codes are required. Enter the totals directly on Schedule D, line 1a; you aren't required to report these transactions on Form 8949 (see instructions).

You *must* check Box A, B, *or* C below. Check only one box. If more than one box applies for your short-term transactions, complete a separate Form 8949, page 1, for each applicable box. If you have more short-term transactions than will fit on this page for one or more of the boxes, complete as many forms with the same box checked as you need.

☐ **(A)** Short-term transactions reported on Form(s) 1099-B showing basis was reported to the IRS (see **Note** above)

☐ **(B)** Short-term transactions reported on Form(s) 1099-B showing basis was **not** reported to the IRS

☐ **(C)** Short-term transactions not reported to you on Form 1099-B

1 (a) Description of property (Example: 100 sh. XYZ Co.)	(b) Date acquired (Mo., day, yr.)	(c) Date sold or disposed of (Mo., day, yr.)	(d) Proceeds (sales price) (see instructions)	(e) Cost or other basis. See the **Note** below and see *Column (e)* in the separate instructions	Adjustment, if any, to gain or loss. If you enter an amount in column (g), enter a code in column (f). See the separate instructions.		(h) Gain or (loss). Subtract column (e) from column (d) and combine the result with column (g)
					(f) Code(s) from instructions	(g) Amount of adjustment	
2 Totals. Add the amounts in columns (d), (e), (g), and (h) (subtract negative amounts). Enter each total here and include on your Schedule D, **line 1b** (if **Box A** above is checked), **line 2** (if **Box B** above is checked), or **line 3** (if **Box C** above is checked) ▶							

Note: If you checked Box A above but the basis reported to the IRS was incorrect, enter in column (e) the basis as reported to the IRS, and enter an adjustment in column (g) to correct the basis. See *Column (g)* in the separate instructions for how to figure the amount of the adjustment.

For Paperwork Reduction Act Notice, see your tax return instructions.   Cat. No. 37768Z   Form **8949** (2015)

Name(s) shown on return. Name and SSN or taxpayer identification no. not required if shown on other side	Social security number or taxpayer identification number

Before you check Box D, E, or F below, see whether you received any Form(s) 1099-B or substitute statement(s) from your broker. A substitute statement will have the same information as Form 1099-B. Either will show whether your basis (usually your cost) was reported to the IRS by your broker and may even tell you which box to check.

Part II   **Long-Term.** Transactions involving capital assets you held more than 1 year are long term. For short-term transactions, see page 1.

Note: You may aggregate all long-term transactions reported on Form(s) 1099-B showing basis was reported to the IRS and for which no adjustments or codes are required. Enter the totals directly on Schedule D, line 8a; you aren't required to report these transactions on Form 8949 (see instructions).

You *must* check Box D, E, *or* F below. Check only one box. If more than one box applies for your long-term transactions, complete a separate Form 8949, page 2, for each applicable box. If you have more long-term transactions than will fit on this page for one or more of the boxes, complete as many forms with the same box checked as you need.

- ☐ **(D)** Long-term transactions reported on Form(s) 1099-B showing basis was reported to the IRS (see **Note** above)
- ☐ **(E)** Long-term transactions reported on Form(s) 1099-B showing basis was **not** reported to the IRS
- ☐ **(F)** Long-term transactions not reported to you on Form 1099-B

1 (a) Description of property (Example: 100 sh. XYZ Co.)	(b) Date acquired (Mo., day, yr.)	(c) Date sold or disposed of (Mo., day, yr.)	(d) Proceeds (sales price) (see instructions)	(e) Cost or other basis. See the *Note* below and see *Column (e)* in the separate instructions	Adjustment, if any, to gain or loss. (f) Code(s) from instructions	(g) Amount of adjustment	(h) Gain or (loss). Subtract column (e) from column (d) and combine the result with column (g)

2 Totals. Add the amounts in columns (d), (e), (g), and (h) (subtract negative amounts). Enter each total here and include on your Schedule D, **line 8b** (if **Box D** above is checked), **line 9** (if **Box E** above is checked), or **line 10** (if **Box F** above is checked) ▶

Note: If you checked Box D above but the basis reported to the IRS was incorrect, enter in column (e) the basis as reported to the IRS, and enter an adjustment in column (g) to correct the basis. See *Column (g)* in the separate instructions for how to figure the amount of the adjustment.

Form **8949** (2015)

SCHEDULE E (Form 1040) Department of the Treasury Internal Revenue Service (99)	**Supplemental Income and Loss** (From rental real estate, royalties, partnerships, S corporations, estates, trusts, REMICs, etc.) ▶ **Attach to Form 1040, 1040NR, or Form 1041.** ▶ **Information about Schedule E and its separate instructions is at** *www.irs.gov/schedulee.*	OMB No. 1545-0074 20**15** Attachment Sequence No. **13**

Name(s) shown on return | Your social security number

Part I | **Income or Loss From Rental Real Estate and Royalties** **Note:** If you are in the business of renting personal property, use **Schedule C or C-EZ** (see instructions). If you are an individual, report farm rental income or loss from **Form 4835** on page 2, line 40.

A Did you make any payments in 2015 that would require you to file Form(s) 1099? (see instructions) ☐ Yes ☐ No
B If "Yes," did you or will you file required Forms 1099? ☐ Yes ☐ No

1a	Physical address of each property (street, city, state, ZIP code)
A	
B	
C	

1b	Type of Property (from list below)	**2**	For each rental real estate property listed above, report the number of fair rental and personal use days. Check the **QJV** box only if you meet the requirements to file as a qualified joint venture. See instructions.		**Fair Rental Days**	**Personal Use Days**	**QJV**
A				**A**			☐
B				**B**			☐
C				**C**			☐

Type of Property:
1 Single Family Residence   3 Vacation/Short-Term Rental   5 Land   7 Self-Rental
2 Multi-Family Residence   4 Commercial   6 Royalties   8 Other (describe)

Income:		Properties:		A	B	C
3	Rents received	**3**				
4	Royalties received	**4**				
Expenses:						
5	Advertising	**5**				
6	Auto and travel (see instructions)	**6**				
7	Cleaning and maintenance	**7**				
8	Commissions.	**8**				
9	Insurance	**9**				
10	Legal and other professional fees	**10**				
11	Management fees	**11**				
12	Mortgage interest paid to banks, etc. (see instructions)	**12**				
13	Other interest.	**13**				
14	Repairs.	**14**				
15	Supplies	**15**				
16	Taxes	**16**				
17	Utilities	**17**				
18	Depreciation expense or depletion	**18**				
19	Other (list) ▶ -------------------------	**19**				
20	Total expenses. Add lines 5 through 19	**20**				
21	Subtract line 20 from line 3 (rents) and/or 4 (royalties). If result is a (loss), see instructions to find out if you must file **Form 6198**	**21**				
22	Deductible rental real estate loss after limitation, if any, on **Form 8582** (see instructions)	**22**	( )	( )	( )

23a	Total of all amounts reported on line 3 for all rental properties	**23a**		
b	Total of all amounts reported on line 4 for all royalty properties	**23b**		
c	Total of all amounts reported on line 12 for all properties	**23c**		
d	Total of all amounts reported on line 18 for all properties	**23d**		
e	Total of all amounts reported on line 20 for all properties	**23e**		
24	**Income.** Add positive amounts shown on line 21. **Do not** include any losses	**24**	
25	**Losses.** Add royalty losses from line 21 and rental real estate losses from line 22. Enter total losses here	**25**	( )
26	**Total rental real estate and royalty income or (loss).** Combine lines 24 and 25. Enter the result here. If Parts II, III, IV, and line 40 on page 2 do not apply to you, also enter this amount on Form 1040, line 17, or Form 1040NR, line 18. Otherwise, include this amount in the total on line 41 on page 2	**26**	

For Paperwork Reduction Act Notice, see the separate instructions.   Cat. No. 11344L   Schedule E (Form 1040) 2015

Schedule E (Form 1040) 2015   Attachment Sequence No. **13**   Page **2**

Name(s) shown on return. Do not enter name and social security number if shown on other side. | Your social security number

Caution. The IRS compares amounts reported on your tax return with amounts shown on Schedule(s) K-1.

Part II	**Income or Loss From Partnerships and S Corporations** **Note:** If you report a loss from an at-risk activity for which **any** amount is **not** at risk, you **must** check the box in column **(e)** on line 28 and attach **Form 6198.** See instructions.

27 Are you reporting any loss not allowed in a prior year due to the at-risk, excess farm loss, or basis limitations, a prior year unallowed loss from a passive activity (if that loss was not reported on Form 8582), or unreimbursed partnership expenses? If you answered "Yes," see instructions before completing this section.   ☐ Yes ☐ No

28	(a) Name	(b) Enter P for partnership; S for S corporation	(c) Check if foreign partnership	(d) Employer identification number	(e) Check if any amount is not at risk
A			☐		☐
B			☐		☐
C			☐		☐
D			☐		☐

	Passive Income and Loss		**Nonpassive Income and Loss**		
	(f) Passive loss allowed (attach **Form 8582** if required)	**(g)** Passive income from **Schedule K-1**	**(h)** Nonpassive loss from **Schedule K-1**	**(i)** Section 179 expense deduction from **Form 4562**	**(j)** Nonpassive income from **Schedule K-1**
A					
B					
C					
D					
29a Totals					
b Totals					

30 Add columns (g) and (j) of line 29a . . . . | **30** |
31 Add columns (f), (h), and (i) of line 29b . . . . | **31** | (|) |
32 **Total partnership and S corporation income or (loss).** Combine lines 30 and 31. Enter the result here and include in the total on line 41 below . . . . | **32** |

| **Part III** | **Income or Loss From Estates and Trusts** |

33	(a) Name	(b) Employer identification number
A		
B		

	Passive Income and Loss		**Nonpassive Income and Loss**	
	(c) Passive deduction or loss allowed (attach **Form 8582** if required)	**(d)** Passive income from **Schedule K-1**	**(e)** Deduction or loss from **Schedule K-1**	**(f)** Other income from **Schedule K-1**
A				
B				
34a Totals				
b Totals				

35 Add columns (d) and (f) of line 34a . . . . | **35** |
36 Add columns (c) and (e) of line 34b . . . . | **36** | (|) |
37 **Total estate and trust income or (loss).** Combine lines 35 and 36. Enter the result here and include in the total on line 41 below . . . . | **37** |

| **Part IV** | **Income or Loss From Real Estate Mortgage Investment Conduits (REMICs)—Residual Holder** |

38	(a) Name	(b) Employer identification number	(c) Excess inclusion from Schedules Q, line 2c (see instructions)	(d) Taxable income (net loss) from Schedules Q, line 1b	(e) Income from Schedules Q, line 3b

39 Combine columns (d) and (e) only. Enter the result here and include in the total on line 41 below | **39** |

| **Part V** | **Summary** |

40 Net farm rental income or (loss) from **Form 4835.** Also, complete line 42 below . . . . . . | **40** |
41 **Total income or (loss).** Combine lines 26, 32, 37, 39, and 40. Enter the result here and on Form 1040, line 17, or Form 1040NR, line 18 ▶ | **41** |
42 **Reconciliation of farming and fishing income.** Enter your **gross** farming and fishing income reported on Form 4835, line 7; Schedule K-1 (Form 1065), box 14, code B; Schedule K-1 (Form 1120S), box 17, code V; and Schedule K-1 (Form 1041), box 14, code F (see instructions) . . | **42** |
43 **Reconciliation for real estate professionals.** If you were a real estate professional (see instructions), enter the net income or (loss) you reported anywhere on Form 1040 or Form 1040NR from all rental real estate activities in which you materially participated under the passive activity loss rules . . | **43** |

Schedule E (Form 1040) 2015

SCHEDULE SE (Form 1040)	Self-Employment Tax	OMB No. 1545-0074
Department of the Treasury Internal Revenue Service (99)	▶ Information about Schedule SE and its separate instructions is at *www.irs.gov/schedulese*. ▶ **Attach to Form 1040 or Form 1040NR.**	**20**15 Attachment Sequence No. **17**

Name of person with **self-employment** income (as shown on Form 1040 or Form 1040NR)	Social security number of person with **self-employment** income ▶

Before you begin: To determine if you must file Schedule SE, see the instructions.

May I Use Short Schedule SE or Must I Use Long Schedule SE?

Note. Use this flowchart **only if** you must file Schedule SE. If unsure, see *Who Must File Schedule SE* in the instructions.

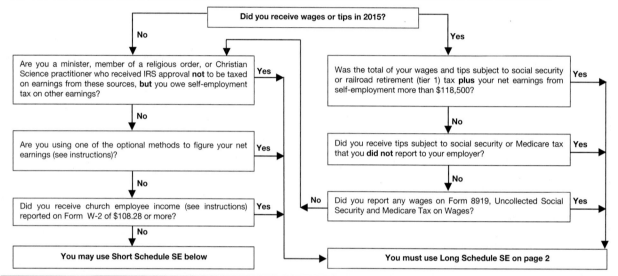

Section A—Short Schedule SE.   Caution. Read above to see if you can use Short Schedule SE.

1a	Net farm profit or (loss) from Schedule F, line 34, and farm partnerships, Schedule K-1 (Form 1065), box 14, code A	**1a**		
b	If you received social security retirement or disability benefits, enter the amount of Conservation Reserve Program payments included on Schedule F, line 4b, or listed on Schedule K-1 (Form 1065), box 20, code Z	**1b**	(	)
2	Net profit or (loss) from Schedule C, line 31; Schedule C-EZ, line 3; Schedule K-1 (Form 1065), box 14, code A (other than farming); and Schedule K-1 (Form 1065-B), box 9, code J1. Ministers and members of religious orders, see instructions for types of income to report on this line. See instructions for other income to report	**2**		
3	Combine lines 1a, 1b, and 2	**3**		
4	Multiply line 3 by 92.35% (.9235). If less than $400, you do not owe self-employment tax; **do not** file this schedule unless you have an amount on line 1b . . . . ▶	**4**		
	Note. If line 4 is less than $400 due to Conservation Reserve Program payments on line 1b, see instructions.			
5	**Self-employment tax.** If the amount on line 4 is: • $118,500 or less, multiply line 4 by 15.3% (.153). Enter the result here and on **Form 1040, line 57,** or **Form 1040NR, line 55** • More than $118,500, multiply line 4 by 2.9% (.029). Then, add $14,694 to the result. Enter the total here and on **Form 1040, line 57,** or **Form 1040NR, line 55**	**5**		
6	**Deduction for one-half of self-employment tax.** Multiply line 5 by 50% (.50). Enter the result here and on **Form 1040, line 27,** or **Form 1040NR, line 27**	**6**		

For Paperwork Reduction Act Notice, see your tax return instructions.   Cat. No. 11358Z   **Schedule SE (Form 1040) 2015**

| Name of person with **self-employment** income (as shown on Form 1040 or Form 1040NR) | Social security number of person with **self-employment** income ▶ | |

Section B—Long Schedule SE

Part I   Self-Employment Tax

Note. If your only income subject to self-employment tax is **church employee income,** see instructions. Also see instructions for the definition of church employee income.

A   If you are a minister, member of a religious order, or Christian Science practitioner **and** you filed Form 4361, but you had $400 or more of **other** net earnings from self-employment, check here and continue with Part I . . . . ▶ ☐

1a   Net farm profit or (loss) from Schedule F, line 34, and farm partnerships, Schedule K-1 (Form 1065), box 14, code A. **Note.** Skip lines 1a and 1b if you use the farm optional method (see instructions) | **1a** | |

   b   If you received social security retirement or disability benefits, enter the amount of Conservation Reserve Program payments included on Schedule F, line 4b, or listed on Schedule K-1 (Form 1065), box 20, code Z | **1b** | (|) |

2   Net profit or (loss) from Schedule C, line 31; Schedule C-EZ, line 3; Schedule K-1 (Form 1065), box 14, code A (other than farming); and Schedule K-1 (Form 1065-B), box 9, code J1. Ministers and members of religious orders, see instructions for types of income to report on this line. See instructions for other income to report. **Note.** Skip this line if you use the nonfarm optional method (see instructions) . . . . | **2** | |

3   Combine lines 1a, 1b, and 2 . . . . | **3** | |

4a   If line 3 is more than zero, multiply line 3 by 92.35% (.9235). Otherwise, enter amount from line 3 | **4a** | |
     Note. If line 4a is less than $400 due to Conservation Reserve Program payments on line 1b, see instructions. | | |

   b   If you elect one or both of the optional methods, enter the total of lines 15 and 17 here . . | **4b** | |

   c   Combine lines 4a and 4b. If less than $400, **stop;** you do not owe self-employment tax.
     Exception. If less than $400 and you had **church employee income,** enter -0- and continue ▶ | **4c** | |

5a   Enter your **church employee income** from Form W-2. See instructions for definition of church employee income . . . | **5a** | | | | |

   b   Multiply line 5a by 92.35% (.9235). If less than $100, enter -0- . . . . | **5b** | |

6   Add lines 4c and 5b . . . . | **6** | |

7   Maximum amount of combined wages and self-employment earnings subject to social security tax or the 6.2% portion of the 7.65% railroad retirement (tier 1) tax for 2015 . . . . . . | **7** | 118,500 | 00 |

8a   Total social security wages and tips (total of boxes 3 and 7 on Form(s) W-2) and railroad retirement (tier 1) compensation. If $118,500 or more, skip lines 8b through 10, and go to line 11 | **8a** | | | | |

   b   Unreported tips subject to social security tax (from Form 4137, line 10) | **8b** | | | |

   c   Wages subject to social security tax (from Form 8919, line 10) | **8c** | | | |

   d   Add lines 8a, 8b, and 8c . . . . | **8d** | |

9   Subtract line 8d from line 7. If zero or less, enter -0- here and on line 10 and go to line 11   ▶ | **9** | |

10   Multiply the **smaller** of line 6 or line 9 by 12.4% (.124) . . . . | **10** | |

11   Multiply line 6 by 2.9% (.029) . . . . | **11** | |

12   **Self-employment tax.** Add lines 10 and 11. Enter here and on **Form 1040, line 57,** or **Form 1040NR, line 55** | **12** | |

13   **Deduction for one-half of self-employment tax.**
     Multiply line 12 by 50% (.50). Enter the result here and on **Form 1040, line 27,** or **Form 1040NR, line 27** . . . . | **13** | |

Part II   Optional Methods To Figure Net Earnings (see instructions)

Farm Optional Method. You may use this method **only** if **(a)** your gross farm income[1] was not more than $7,320, **or (b)** your net farm profits[2] were less than $5,284.

14   Maximum income for optional methods . . . . | **14** | 4,880 | 00 |

15   Enter the **smaller** of: two-thirds (²⁄₃) of gross farm income[1] (not less than zero) or $4,880. Also include this amount on line 4b above . . . . | **15** | |

Nonfarm Optional Method. You may use this method **only** if **(a)** your net nonfarm profits[3] were less than $5,284 and also less than 72.189% of your gross nonfarm income,[4] **and (b)** you had net earnings from self-employment of at least $400 in 2 of the prior 3 years. **Caution.** You may use this method no more than five times.

16   Subtract line 15 from line 14 . . . . | **16** | |

17   Enter the **smaller** of: two-thirds (²⁄₃) of gross nonfarm income[4] (not less than zero) **or** the amount on line 16. Also include this amount on line 4b above . . . . | **17** | |

[1] From Sch. F, line 9, and Sch. K-1 (Form 1065), box 14, code B.

[2] From Sch. F, line 34, and Sch. K-1 (Form 1065), box 14, code A—minus the amount you would have entered on line 1b had you not used the optional method.

[3] From Sch. C, line 31; Sch. C-EZ, line 3; Sch. K-1 (Form 1065), box 14, code A; and Sch. K-1 (Form 1065-B), box 9, code J1.

[4] From Sch. C, line 7; Sch. C-EZ, line 1; Sch. K-1 (Form 1065), box 14, code C; and Sch. K-1 (Form 1065-B), box 9, code J2.

Form **1065**		**U.S. Return of Partnership Income**		OMB No. 1545-0123	
Department of the Treasury Internal Revenue Service		For calendar year 2015, or tax year beginning _____, 2015, ending _____, 20 ___. ▶ Information about Form 1065 and its separate instructions is at *www.irs.gov/form1065*.		**20**15	

A Principal business activity	Type or Print	Name of partnership	D Employer identification number
B Principal product or service		Number, street, and room or suite no. If a P.O. box, see the instructions.	E Date business started
C Business code number		City or town, state or province, country, and ZIP or foreign postal code	F Total assets (see the instructions) $

G Check applicable boxes: **(1)** ☐ Initial return **(2)** ☐ Final return **(3)** ☐ Name change **(4)** ☐ Address change **(5)** ☐ Amended return
(6) ☐ Technical termination - also check (1) or (2)

H Check accounting method: **(1)** ☐ Cash **(2)** ☐ Accrual **(3)** ☐ Other (specify) ▶ _____

I Number of Schedules K-1. Attach one for each person who was a partner at any time during the tax year ▶ _____

J Check if Schedules C and M-3 are attached . . . . ☐

Caution. *Include **only** trade or business income and expenses on lines 1a through 22 below. See the instructions for more information.*

Income

1a	Gross receipts or sales	1a		
b	Returns and allowances	1b		
c	Balance. Subtract line 1b from line 1a	1c	
2	Cost of goods sold (attach Form 1125-A)	2	
3	Gross profit. Subtract line 2 from line 1c	3	
4	Ordinary income (loss) from other partnerships, estates, and trusts (attach statement) . .	4	
5	Net farm profit (loss) (attach Schedule F (Form 1040))	5	
6	Net gain (loss) from Form 4797, Part II, line 17 (attach Form 4797)	6	
7	Other income (loss) (attach statement)	7	
8	**Total income (loss).** Combine lines 3 through 7	8	

Deductions (see the instructions for limitations)

9	Salaries and wages (other than to partners) (less employment credits)	9	
10	Guaranteed payments to partners	10	
11	Repairs and maintenance	11	
12	Bad debts	12	
13	Rent	13	
14	Taxes and licenses	14	
15	Interest	15	
16a	Depreciation (if required, attach Form 4562)	16a	
b	Less depreciation reported on Form 1125-A and elsewhere on return	16b	16c
17	Depletion **(Do not deduct oil and gas depletion.)**	17	
18	Retirement plans, etc.	18	
19	Employee benefit programs	19	
20	Other deductions (attach statement)	20	
21	**Total deductions.** Add the amounts shown in the far right column for lines 9 through 20 .	21	
22	**Ordinary business income (loss).** Subtract line 21 from line 8	22	

Sign Here

Under penalties of perjury, I declare that I have examined this return, including accompanying schedules and statements, and to the best of my knowledge and belief, it is true, correct, and complete. Declaration of preparer (other than general partner or limited liability company member manager) is based on all information of which preparer has any knowledge.

May the IRS discuss this return with the preparer shown below (see instructions)? ☐ **Yes** ☐ **No**

▶ _____ ▶ _____
Signature of general partner or limited liability company member manager | Date

Paid Preparer Use Only

Print/Type preparer's name	Preparer's signature	Date	Check ☐ if self-employed	PTIN
Firm's name ▶			Firm's EIN ▶	
Firm's address ▶			Phone no.	

For Paperwork Reduction Act Notice, see separate instructions.   Cat. No. 11390Z   Form **1065** (2015)

Schedule B   Other Information

		Yes	No
1	What type of entity is filing this return? Check the applicable box:		

a ☐ Domestic general partnership   **b** ☐ Domestic limited partnership
c ☐ Domestic limited liability company   **d** ☐ Domestic limited liability partnership
e ☐ Foreign partnership   **f** ☐ Other ▶

2 At any time during the tax year, was any partner in the partnership a disregarded entity, a partnership (including an entity treated as a partnership), a trust, an S corporation, an estate (other than an estate of a deceased partner), or a nominee or similar person? . . . .

3 At the end of the tax year:

a Did any foreign or domestic corporation, partnership (including any entity treated as a partnership), trust, or tax-exempt organization, or any foreign government own, directly or indirectly, an interest of 50% or more in the profit, loss, or capital of the partnership? For rules of constructive ownership, see instructions. If "Yes," attach Schedule B-1, Information on Partners Owning 50% or More of the Partnership . . . .

b Did any individual or estate own, directly or indirectly, an interest of 50% or more in the profit, loss, or capital of the partnership? For rules of constructive ownership, see instructions. If "Yes," attach Schedule B-1, Information on Partners Owning 50% or More of the Partnership . . . .

4 At the end of the tax year, did the partnership:

a Own directly 20% or more, or own, directly or indirectly, 50% or more of the total voting power of all classes of stock entitled to vote of any foreign or domestic corporation? For rules of constructive ownership, see instructions. If "Yes," complete (i) through (iv) below . . . .

(i) Name of Corporation	**(ii)** Employer Identification Number (if any)	**(iii)** Country of Incorporation	**(iv)** Percentage Owned in Voting Stock

b Own directly an interest of 20% or more, or own, directly or indirectly, an interest of 50% or more in the profit, loss, or capital in any foreign or domestic partnership (including an entity treated as a partnership) or in the beneficial interest of a trust? For rules of constructive ownership, see instructions. If "Yes," complete (i) through (v) below . .

(i) Name of Entity	**(ii)** Employer Identification Number (if any)	**(iii)** Type of Entity	**(iv)** Country of Organization	**(v)** Maximum Percentage Owned in Profit, Loss, or Capital

		Yes	No
5	Did the partnership file Form 8893, Election of Partnership Level Tax Treatment, or an election statement under section 6231(a)(1)(B)(ii) for partnership-level tax treatment, that is in effect for this tax year? See Form 8893 for more details		
6	Does the partnership satisfy **all four** of the following conditions?		
a	The partnership's total receipts for the tax year were less than $250,000.		
b	The partnership's total assets at the end of the tax year were less than $1 million.		
c	Schedules K-1 are filed with the return and furnished to the partners on or before the due date (including extensions) for the partnership return.		
d	The partnership is not filing and is not required to file Schedule M-3		
	If "Yes," the partnership is not required to complete Schedules L, M-1, and M-2; Item F on page 1 of Form 1065; or Item L on Schedule K-1.		
7	Is this partnership a publicly traded partnership as defined in section 469(k)(2)?		
8	During the tax year, did the partnership have any debt that was cancelled, was forgiven, or had the terms modified so as to reduce the principal amount of the debt?		
9	Has this partnership filed, or is it required to file, Form 8918, Material Advisor Disclosure Statement, to provide information on any reportable transaction?		
10	At any time during calendar year 2015, did the partnership have an interest in or a signature or other authority over a financial account in a foreign country (such as a bank account, securities account, or other financial account)? See the instructions for exceptions and filing requirements for FinCEN Form 114, Report of Foreign Bank and Financial Accounts (FBAR). If "Yes," enter the name of the foreign country. ▶		

Schedule K-1
(Form 1041)
Department of the Treasury
Internal Revenue Service

2015

For calendar year 2015,
or tax year beginning _____ , 2015,
and ending _____ , 20 ___

☐ Final K-1   ☐ Amended K-1

ᏏᏏᏏᏏᏏᏏ 661113

OMB No. 1545-0092

Beneficiary's Share of Income, Deductions, Credits, etc.

► See back of form and instructions.

Part I	Information About the Estate or Trust

A Estate's or trust's employer identification number

B Estate's or trust's name

C Fiduciary's name, address, city, state, and ZIP code

D ☐ Check if Form 1041-T was filed and enter the date it was filed

_____

E ☐ Check if this is the final Form 1041 for the estate or trust

Part II	Information About the Beneficiary

F Beneficiary's identifying number

G Beneficiary's name, address, city, state, and ZIP code

H ☐ Domestic beneficiary   ☐ Foreign beneficiary

Part III	Beneficiary's Share of Current Year Income, Deductions, Credits, and Other Items

1	Interest income	11	Final year deductions
2a	Ordinary dividends		
2b	Qualified dividends		
3	Net short-term capital gain		
4a	Net long-term capital gain		
4b	28% rate gain	12	Alternative minimum tax adjustment
4c	Unrecaptured section 1250 gain		
5	Other portfolio and nonbusiness income		
6	Ordinary business income		
7	Net rental real estate income	13	Credits and credit recapture
8	Other rental income		
9	Directly apportioned deductions		
		14	Other information
10	Estate tax deduction		

*See attached statement for additional information.

Note. A statement must be attached showing the beneficiary's share of income and directly apportioned deductions from each business, rental real estate, and other rental activity.

For IRS Use Only

For Paperwork Reduction Act Notice, see the Instructions for Form 1041.   IRS.gov/form1041   Cat. No. 11380D   Schedule K-1 (Form 1041) 2015

Form **1120**

Department of the Treasury
Internal Revenue Service

U.S. Corporation Income Tax Return

For calendar year 2015 or tax year beginning _____, 2015, ending _____, 20 _____

▶ Information about Form 1120 and its separate instructions is at *www.irs.gov/form1120.*

OMB No. 1545-0123

2015

A Check if:
1a Consolidated return (attach Form 851) ☐
 b Life/nonlife consolidated return ☐
2 Personal holding co. (attach Sch. PH) ☐
3 Personal service corp. (see instructions) ☐
4 Schedule M-3 attached ☐

TYPE OR PRINT

Name

Number, street, and room or suite no. If a P.O. box, see instructions.

City or town, state, or province, country, and ZIP or foreign postal code

B Employer identification number

C Date incorporated

D Total assets (see instructions)
$

E Check if: (1) ☐ Initial return (2) ☐ Final return (3) ☐ Name change (4) ☐ Address change

Income

1a	Gross receipts or sales	1a
b	Returns and allowances	1b
c	Balance. Subtract line 1b from line 1a	1c
2	Cost of goods sold (attach Form 1125-A)	2
3	Gross profit. Subtract line 2 from line 1c	3
4	Dividends (Schedule C, line 19)	4
5	Interest	5
6	Gross rents	6
7	Gross royalties	7
8	Capital gain net income (attach Schedule D (Form 1120))	8
9	Net gain or (loss) from Form 4797, Part II, line 17 (attach Form 4797)	9
10	Other income (see instructions—attach statement)	10
11	**Total income.** Add lines 3 through 10 ▶	11

Deductions (See instructions for limitations on deductions.)

12	Compensation of officers (see instructions—attach Form 1125-E) ▶	12
13	Salaries and wages (less employment credits)	13
14	Repairs and maintenance	14
15	Bad debts	15
16	Rents	16
17	Taxes and licenses	17
18	Interest	18
19	Charitable contributions	19
20	Depreciation from Form 4562 not claimed on Form 1125-A or elsewhere on return (attach Form 4562)	20
21	Depletion	21
22	Advertising	22
23	Pension, profit-sharing, etc., plans	23
24	Employee benefit programs	24
25	Domestic production activities deduction (attach Form 8903)	25
26	Other deductions (attach statement)	26
27	**Total deductions.** Add lines 12 through 26 ▶	27
28	Taxable income before net operating loss deduction and special deductions. Subtract line 27 from line 11.	28
29a	Net operating loss deduction (see instructions)	29a
b	Special deductions (Schedule C, line 20)	29b
c	Add lines 29a and 29b	29c

Tax, Refundable Credits, and Payments

30	**Taxable income.** Subtract line 29c from line 28 (see instructions)	30
31	Total tax (Schedule J, Part I, line 11)	31
32	Total payments and refundable credits (Schedule J, Part II, line 21)	32
33	Estimated tax penalty (see instructions). Check if Form 2220 is attached ▶ ☐	33
34	**Amount owed.** If line 32 is smaller than the total of lines 31 and 33, enter amount owed	34
35	**Overpayment.** If line 32 is larger than the total of lines 31 and 33, enter amount overpaid	35
36	Enter amount from line 35 you want: **Credited to 2016 estimated tax** ▶ Refunded ▶	36

Sign Here

Under penalties of perjury, I declare that I have examined this return, including accompanying schedules and statements, and to the best of my knowledge and belief, it is true, correct, and complete. Declaration of preparer (other than taxpayer) is based on all information of which preparer has any knowledge.

▶ _____ Signature of officer   Date   ▶ _____ Title

May the IRS discuss this return with the preparer shown below (see instructions)? ☐ Yes ☐ No

Paid Preparer Use Only

Print/Type preparer's name	Preparer's signature	Date	Check ☐ if self-employed	PTIN

Firm's name ▶   Firm's EIN ▶
Firm's address ▶   Phone no.

For Paperwork Reduction Act Notice, see separate instructions.   Cat. No. 11450Q   Form **1120** (2015)

Form **1120S**

Department of the Treasury
Internal Revenue Service

U.S. Income Tax Return for an S Corporation

▶ Do not file this form unless the corporation has filed or is
attaching Form 2553 to elect to be an S corporation.
▶ Information about Form 1120S and its separate instructions is at *www.irs.gov/form1120s.*

OMB No. 1545-0123

2015

For calendar year 2015 or tax year beginning _____ , 2015, ending _____ , 20 ____

A S election effective date	TYPE OR PRINT	Name	D Employer identification number
B Business activity code number (see instructions)		Number, street, and room or suite no. If a P.O. box, see instructions.	E Date incorporated
C Check if Sch. M-3 attached ☐		City or town, state or province, country, and ZIP or foreign postal code	F Total assets (see instructions) $

G Is the corporation electing to be an S corporation beginning with this tax year? ☐ Yes ☐ No If "Yes," attach Form 2553 if not already filed

H Check if: **(1)** ☐ Final return **(2)** ☐ Name change **(3)** ☐ Address change **(4)** ☐ Amended return **(5)** ☐ S election termination or revocation

I Enter the number of shareholders who were shareholders during any part of the tax year . . . . ▶

Caution: Include **only** trade or business income and expenses on lines 1a through 21. See the instructions for more information.

Income

1a	Gross receipts or sales	1a	
b	Returns and allowances	1b	
c	Balance. Subtract line 1b from line 1a	1c	
2	Cost of goods sold (attach Form 1125-A)	2	
3	Gross profit. Subtract line 2 from line 1c	3	
4	Net gain (loss) from Form 4797, line 17 (attach Form 4797)	4	
5	Other income (loss) (see instructions—attach statement)	5	
6	**Total income (loss).** Add lines 3 through 5 . . . . ▶	6	

Deductions (see instructions for limitations)

7	Compensation of officers (see instructions—attach Form 1125-E)	7	
8	Salaries and wages (less employment credits)	8	
9	Repairs and maintenance	9	
10	Bad debts	10	
11	Rents	11	
12	Taxes and licenses	12	
13	Interest	13	
14	Depreciation not claimed on Form 1125-A or elsewhere on return (attach Form 4562)	14	
15	Depletion **(Do not deduct oil and gas depletion.)**	15	
16	Advertising	16	
17	Pension, profit-sharing, etc., plans	17	
18	Employee benefit programs	18	
19	Other deductions (attach statement)	19	
20	**Total deductions.** Add lines 7 through 19 . . . . ▶	20	
21	**Ordinary business income (loss).** Subtract line 20 from line 6	21	

Tax and Payments

22a	Excess net passive income or LIFO recapture tax (see instructions) . .	22a	
b	Tax from Schedule D (Form 1120S)	22b	
c	Add lines 22a and 22b (see instructions for additional taxes) . . .	22c	
23a	2015 estimated tax payments and 2014 overpayment credited to 2015	23a	
b	Tax deposited with Form 7004	23b	
c	Credit for federal tax paid on fuels (attach Form 4136)	23c	
d	Add lines 23a through 23c	23d	
24	Estimated tax penalty (see instructions). Check if Form 2220 is attached . . . . . . ▶ ☐	24	
25	**Amount owed.** If line 23d is smaller than the total of lines 22c and 24, enter amount owed . .	25	
26	**Overpayment.** If line 23d is larger than the total of lines 22c and 24, enter amount overpaid . .	26	
27	Enter amount from line 26 **Credited to 2016 estimated tax ▶** **Refunded ▶**	27	

Sign Here

Under penalties of perjury, I declare that I have examined this return, including accompanying schedules and statements, and to the best of my knowledge and belief, it is true, correct, and complete. Declaration of preparer (other than taxpayer) is based on all information of which preparer has any knowledge.

▶ _____ _____ ▶ _____

Signature of officer   Date   Title

May the IRS discuss this return with the preparer shown below (see instructions)? ☐ Yes ☐ No

Paid Preparer Use Only

Print/Type preparer's name	Preparer's signature	Date	Check ☐ if self-employed	PTIN
Firm's name ▶			Firm's EIN ▶	
Firm's address ▶			Phone no.	

For Paperwork Reduction Act Notice, see separate instructions.   Cat. No. 11510H   Form **1120S** (2015)

671113

☐ Final K-1	☐ Amended K-1	OMB No. 1545-0123

Schedule K-1
(Form 1120S)
Department of the Treasury
Internal Revenue Service

2015

For calendar year 2015, or tax
year beginning _____ , 2015
ending _____ , 20 ___

Shareholder's Share of Income, Deductions, Credits, etc.
▶ **See back of form and separate instructions.**

Part I	**Information About the Corporation**

A   Corporation's employer identification number

B   Corporation's name, address, city, state, and ZIP code

C   IRS Center where corporation filed return

Part II	**Information About the Shareholder**

D   Shareholder's identifying number

E   Shareholder's name, address, city, state, and ZIP code

F   Shareholder's percentage of stock
ownership for tax year . . . . _____ %

For IRS Use Only

Part III	**Shareholder's Share of Current Year Income, Deductions, Credits, and Other Items**		
1	Ordinary business income (loss)	13	Credits
2	Net rental real estate income (loss)		
3	Other net rental income (loss)		
4	Interest income		
5a	Ordinary dividends		
5b	Qualified dividends	14	Foreign transactions
6	Royalties		
7	Net short-term capital gain (loss)		
8a	Net long-term capital gain (loss)		
8b	Collectibles (28%) gain (loss)		
8c	Unrecaptured section 1250 gain		
9	Net section 1231 gain (loss)		
10	Other income (loss)	15	Alternative minimum tax (AMT) items
11	Section 179 deduction	16	Items affecting shareholder basis
12	Other deductions		
		17	Other information

* See attached statement for additional information.

SCHEDULE M-3 (Form 1120) Department of the Treasury Internal Revenue Service	**Net Income (Loss) Reconciliation for Corporations** **With Total Assets of $10 Million or More** ▶ **Attach to Form 1120 or 1120-C.** ▶ **Information about Schedule M-3 (Form 1120) and its** separate instructions is available at *www.irs.gov/form1120.*	OMB No. 1545-0123 2015

Name of corporation (common parent, if consolidated return)	Employer identification number

Check applicable box(es):   (1) ☐ Non-consolidated return   (2) ☐ Consolidated return (Form 1120 only)

(3) ☐ Mixed 1120/L/PC group   (4) ☐ Dormant subsidiaries schedule attached

---

Part I   **Financial Information and Net Income (Loss) Reconciliation** (see instructions)

1a Did the corporation file SEC Form 10-K for its income statement period ending with or within this tax year?
　☐ **Yes.** Skip lines 1b and 1c and complete lines 2a through 11 with respect to that SEC Form 10-K.
　☐ **No.** Go to line 1b. See instructions if multiple non-tax-basis income statements are prepared.
b Did the corporation prepare a certified audited non-tax-basis income statement for that period?
　☐ **Yes.** Skip line 1c and complete lines 2a through 11 with respect to that income statement.
　☐ **No.** Go to line 1c.
c Did the corporation prepare a non-tax-basis income statement for that period?
　☐ **Yes.** Complete lines 2a through 11 with respect to that income statement.
　☐ **No.** Skip lines 2a through 3c and enter the corporation's net income (loss) per its books and records on line 4a.
2a Enter the income statement period: Beginning ___MM/DD/YYYY___   Ending ___MM/DD/YYYY___
b Has the corporation's income statement been restated for the income statement period on line 2a?
　☐ **Yes.** (If "Yes," attach an explanation and the amount of each item restated.)
　☐ **No.**
c Has the corporation's income statement been restated for any of the five income statement periods immediately preceding the period on line 2a?
　☐ **Yes.** (If "Yes," attach an explanation and the amount of each item restated.)
　☐ **No.**
3a Is any of the corporation's voting common stock publicly traded?
　☐ **Yes.**
　☐ **No.** If "No," go to line 4a.
b Enter the symbol of the corporation's primary U.S. publicly traded voting common stock . . . .
c Enter the nine-digit CUSIP number of the corporation's primary publicly traded voting common stock . . . .

4a Worldwide consolidated net income (loss) from income statement source identified in Part I, line 1 .	**4a**	
b Indicate accounting standard used for line 4a (see instructions): 　(1) ☐ GAAP (2) ☐ IFRS (3) ☐ Statutory (4) ☐ Tax-basis (5) ☐ Other (specify) _____		
5a Net income from nonincludible foreign entities (attach statement)	**5a** ( )
b Net loss from nonincludible foreign entities (attach statement and enter as a positive amount) . . .	**5b**	
6a Net income from nonincludible U.S. entities (attach statement)	**6a** ( )
b Net loss from nonincludible U.S. entities (attach statement and enter as a positive amount)	**6b**	
7a Net income (loss) of other includible foreign disregarded entities (attach statement)	**7a**	
b Net income (loss) of other includible U.S. disregarded entities (attach statement)	**7b**	
c Net income (loss) of other includible entities (attach statement)	**7c**	
8 Adjustment to eliminations of transactions between includible entities and nonincludible entities (attach statement)	**8**	
9 Adjustment to reconcile income statement period to tax year (attach statement)	**9**	
10a Intercompany dividend adjustments to reconcile to line 11 (attach statement)	**10a**	
b Other statutory accounting adjustments to reconcile to line 11 (attach statement)	**10b**	
c Other adjustments to reconcile to amount on line 11 (attach statement)	**10c**	
11 **Net income (loss) per income statement of includible corporations.** Combine lines 4 through 10 .	**11**	

Note: Part I, line 11, must equal Part II, line 30, column (a) or Schedule M-1, line 1 (see instructions).

12 Enter the total amount (not just the corporation's share) of the assets and liabilities of all entities included or removed on the following lines.

	Total Assets	Total Liabilities
a Included on Part I, line 4 . . . . ▶		
b Removed on Part I, line 5 . . . . ▶		
c Removed on Part I, line 6 . . . . ▶		
d Included on Part I, line 7 . . . . ▶		

For Paperwork Reduction Act Notice, see the Instructions for Form 1120.   Cat. No. 37961C   Schedule M-3 (Form 1120) 2015

Schedule M-3 (Form 1120) 2015 — Page **2**

Name of corporation (common parent, if consolidated return)	Employer identification number

Check applicable box(es): **(1)** ☐ Consolidated group **(2)** ☐ Parent corp **(3)** ☐ Consolidated eliminations **(4)** ☐ Subsidiary corp **(5)** ☐ Mixed 1120/L/PC group

Check if a sub-consolidated: **(6)** ☐ 1120 group **(7)** ☐ 1120 eliminations

Name of subsidiary (if consolidated return)	Employer identification number

Part II   Reconciliation of Net Income (Loss) per Income Statement of Includible Corporations With Taxable Income per Return (see instructions)

Income (Loss) Items (Attach statements for lines 1 through 12)	(a) Income (Loss) per Income Statement	(b) Temporary Difference	(c) Permanent Difference	(d) Income (Loss) per Tax Return
1 Income (loss) from equity method foreign corporations				
2 Gross foreign dividends not previously taxed				
3 Subpart F, QEF, and similar income inclusions				
4 Section 78 gross-up				
5 Gross foreign distributions previously taxed				
6 Income (loss) from equity method U.S. corporations				
7 U.S. dividends not eliminated in tax consolidation				
8 Minority interest for includible corporations				
9 Income (loss) from U.S. partnerships				
10 Income (loss) from foreign partnerships				
11 Income (loss) from other pass-through entities				
12 Items relating to reportable transactions				
13 Interest income (see instructions)				
14 Total accrual to cash adjustment				
15 Hedging transactions				
16 Mark-to-market income (loss)				
17 Cost of goods sold (see instructions)	( )			( )
18 Sale versus lease (for sellers and/or lessors)				
19 Section 481(a) adjustments				
20 Unearned/deferred revenue				
21 Income recognition from long-term contracts				
22 Original issue discount and other imputed interest				
23a Income statement gain/loss on sale, exchange, abandonment, worthlessness, or other disposition of assets other than inventory and pass-through entities				
b Gross capital gains from Schedule D, excluding amounts from pass-through entities				
c Gross capital losses from Schedule D, excluding amounts from pass-through entities, abandonment losses, and worthless stock losses				
d Net gain/loss reported on Form 4797, line 17, excluding amounts from pass-through entities, abandonment losses, and worthless stock losses				
e Abandonment losses				
f Worthless stock losses (attach statement)				
g Other gain/loss on disposition of assets other than inventory				
24 Capital loss limitation and carryforward used				
25 Other income (loss) items with differences (attach statement)				
26 **Total income (loss) items.** Combine lines 1 through 25				
27 **Total expense/deduction items** (from Part III, line 38)				
28 Other items with no differences				
29a Mixed groups, see instructions. All others, combine lines 26 through 28				
b PC insurance subgroup reconciliation totals				
c Life insurance subgroup reconciliation totals				
30 **Reconciliation totals.** Combine lines 29a through 29c				

Note: Line 30, column (a), must equal Part I, line 11, and column (d) must equal Form 1120, page 1, line 28.

Schedule M-3 (Form 1120) 2015

Schedule M-3 (Form 1120) 2015   Page **3**

Name of corporation (common parent, if consolidated return)			Employer identification number

Check applicable box(es): **(1)** ☐ Consolidated group   **(2)** ☐ Parent corp   **(3)** ☐ Consolidated eliminations   **(4)** ☐ Subsidiary corp   **(5)** ☐ Mixed 1120/L/PC group

Check if a sub-consolidated: **(6)** ☐ 1120 group   **(7)** ☐ 1120 eliminations

Name of subsidiary (if consolidated return)	Employer identification number

Part III   Reconciliation of Net Income (Loss) per Income Statement of Includible Corporations With Taxable Income per Return—Expense/Deduction Items (see instructions)

Expense/Deduction Items	(a) Expense per Income Statement	(b) Temporary Difference	(c) Permanent Difference	(d) Deduction per Tax Return
1 U.S. current income tax expense				
2 U.S. deferred income tax expense				
3 State and local current income tax expense				
4 State and local deferred income tax expense				
5 Foreign current income tax expense (other than foreign withholding taxes)				
6 Foreign deferred income tax expense				
7 Foreign withholding taxes				
8 Interest expense (see instructions)				
9 Stock option expense				
10 Other equity-based compensation				
11 Meals and entertainment				
12 Fines and penalties				
13 Judgments, damages, awards, and similar costs				
14 Parachute payments				
15 Compensation with section 162(m) limitation				
16 Pension and profit-sharing				
17 Other post-retirement benefits				
18 Deferred compensation				
19 Charitable contribution of cash and tangible property				
20 Charitable contribution of intangible property				
21 Charitable contribution limitation/carryforward				
22 Domestic production activities deduction				
23 Current year acquisition or reorganization investment banking fees				
24 Current year acquisition or reorganization legal and accounting fees				
25 Current year acquisition/reorganization other costs				
26 Amortization/impairment of goodwill				
27 Amortization of acquisition, reorganization, and start-up costs				
28 Other amortization or impairment write-offs				
29 Reserved				
30 Depletion				
31 Depreciation				
32 Bad debt expense				
33 Corporate owned life insurance premiums				
34 Purchase versus lease (for purchasers and/or lessees)				
35 Research and development costs				
36 Section 118 exclusion (attach statement)				
37 Other expense/deduction items with differences (attach statement)				
38 **Total expense/deduction items.** Combine lines 1 through 37. Enter here and on Part II, line 27, reporting positive amounts as negative and negative amounts as positive				

Schedule M-3 (Form 1120) 2015

Form **706**
(Rev. August 2013)

Department of the Treasury
Internal Revenue Service

United States Estate (and Generation-Skipping Transfer) Tax Return

► **Estate of a citizen or resident of the United States (see instructions). To be filed for decedents dying after December 31, 2012.**
► **Information about Form 706 and its separate instructions is at *www.irs.gov/form706.***

OMB No. 1545-0015

Part 1—Decedent and Executor

1a Decedent's first name and middle initial (and maiden name, if any)	**1b** Decedent's last name	**2** Decedent's social security no.

3a City, town, or post office; county; state or province; country; and ZIP or foreign postal code.	**3b** Year domicile established	**4** Date of birth	**5** Date of death

6b Executor's address (number and street including apartment or suite no.; city, town, or post office; state or province; country; and ZIP or foreign postal code) and phone no.

6a Name of executor (see instructions)

6c Executor's social security number (see instructions)

Phone no.

6d If there are multiple executors, check here ☐ and attach a list showing the names, addresses, telephone numbers, and SSNs of the additional executors.

7a Name and location of court where will was probated or estate administered	**7b** Case number

8 If decedent died testate, check here ► ☐ and attach a certified copy of the will. **9** If you extended the time to file this Form 706, check here ► ☐

10 If Schedule R-1 is attached, check here ► ☐ **11** If you are estimating the value of assets included in the gross estate on line 1 pursuant to the special rule of Reg. section 20.2010-2T(a) (7)(ii), check here ► ☐

Part 2—Tax Computation

1 Total gross estate less exclusion (from Part 5—Recapitulation, item 13)	**1**	
2 Tentative total allowable deductions (from Part 5—Recapitulation, item 24)	**2**	
3a Tentative taxable estate (subtract line 2 from line 1)	**3a**	
b State death tax deduction	**3b**	
c Taxable estate (subtract line 3b from line 3a)	**3c**	
4 Adjusted taxable gifts (see instructions)	**4**	
5 Add lines 3c and 4	**5**	
6 Tentative tax on the amount on line 5 from Table A in the instructions	**6**	
7 Total gift tax paid or payable (see instructions)	**7**	
8 Gross estate tax (subtract line 7 from line 6)	**8**	
9a Basic exclusion amount	**9a**	
9b Deceased spousal unused exclusion (DSUE) amount from predeceased spouse(s), if any (from Section D, Part 6—Portability of Deceased Spousal Unused Exclusion). .	**9b**	
9c Applicable exclusion amount (add lines 9a and 9b)	**9c**	
9d Applicable credit amount (tentative tax on the amount in 9c from Table A in the instructions)	**9d**	
10 Adjustment to applicable credit amount (May not exceed $6,000. See instructions.)	**10**	
11 Allowable applicable credit amount (subtract line 10 from line 9d)	**11**	
12 Subtract line 11 from line 8 (but do not enter less than zero)	**12**	
13 Credit for foreign death taxes (from Schedule P). (Attach Form(s) 706-CE.)	**13**	
14 Credit for tax on prior transfers (from Schedule Q)	**14**	
15 Total credits (add lines 13 and 14)	**15**	
16 Net estate tax (subtract line 15 from line 12)	**16**	
17 Generation-skipping transfer (GST) taxes payable (from Schedule R, Part 2, line 10)	**17**	
18 Total transfer taxes (add lines 16 and 17)	**18**	
19 Prior payments (explain in an attached statement)	**19**	
20 Balance due (or overpayment) (subtract line 19 from line 18)	**20**	

Under penalties of perjury, I declare that I have examined this return, including accompanying schedules and statements, and to the best of my knowledge and belief, it is true, correct, and complete. Declaration of preparer other than the executor is based on all information of which preparer has any knowledge.

Sign Here

► Signature of executor   ► Date

► Signature of executor   ► Date

Paid Preparer Use Only

Print/Type preparer's name	Preparer's signature	Date	Check ☐ if self-employed	PTIN
Firm's name ►			Firm's EIN ►	
Firm's address ►			Phone no.	

For Privacy Act and Paperwork Reduction Act Notice, see instructions.   Cat. No. 20548R   Form **706** (Rev. 8-2013)

Form 706 (Rev. 8-2013)

	Decedent's social security number

Estate of:

Part 3—Elections by the Executor

Note. For information on electing portability of the decedent's DSUE amount, including how to opt out of the election, see Part 6—Portability of Deceased Spousal Unused Exclusion.

Note. Some of the following elections may require the posting of bonds or liens.

Please check "Yes" or "No" box for each question (see instructions).

			Yes	No
1	Do you elect alternate valuation?	1		
2	Do you elect special-use valuation? If "Yes," you must complete and attach Schedule A-1	2		
3	Do you elect to pay the taxes in installments as described in section 6166? If "Yes," you must attach the additional information described in the instructions. **Note. By electing section 6166 installment payments, you may be required to provide security for estate tax deferred under section 6166 and interest in the form of a surety bond or a section 6324A lien.**	3		
4	Do you elect to postpone the part of the taxes due to a reversionary or remainder interest as described in section 6163?	4		

Part 4—General Information

Note. Please attach the necessary supplemental documents. **You must attach the death certificate.** (See instructions)

Authorization to receive confidential tax information under Reg. section 601.504(b)(2)(i); to act as the estate's representative before the IRS; and to make written or oral presentations on behalf of the estate:

Name of representative (print or type)	State	Address (number, street, and room or suite no., city, state, and ZIP code)

I declare that I am the ☐ attorney/ ☐ certified public accountant/ ☐ enrolled agent (check the applicable box) for the executor. I am not under suspension or disbarment from practice before the Internal Revenue Service and am qualified to practice in the state shown above.

Signature	CAF number	Date	Telephone number

1 Death certificate number and issuing authority (attach a copy of the death certificate to this return).

2 Decedent's business or occupation. If retired, check here ▶ ☐   and state decedent's former business or occupation.

3a Marital status of the decedent at time of death:

☐ Married   ☐ Widow/widower   ☐ Single   ☐ Legally separated   ☐ Divorced

3b For all prior marriages, list the name and SSN of the former spouse, the date the marriage ended, and whether the marriage ended by annulment, divorce, or death. Attach additional statements of the same size if necessary.

4a Surviving spouse's name	4b Social security number	4c Amount received (see instructions)

5 Individuals (other than the surviving spouse), trusts, or other estates who receive benefits from the estate (do not include charitable beneficiaries shown in Schedule O) (see instructions).

Name of individual, trust, or estate receiving $5,000 or more	Identifying number	Relationship to decedent	Amount (see instructions)

All unascertainable beneficiaries and those who receive less than $5,000 . . . . ▶

Total . . . .

If you answer "Yes" to any of the following questions, you must attach additional information as described.

		Yes	No
6	Is the estate filing a protective claim for refund? If "Yes," complete and attach two copies of Schedule PC for each claim.		
7	Does the gross estate contain any section 2044 property (qualified terminable interest property (QTIP) from a prior gift or estate)? (see instructions)		
8a	Have federal gift tax returns ever been filed? If "Yes," attach copies of the returns, if available, and furnish the following information:		
b	Period(s) covered c Internal Revenue office(s) where filed		
9a	Was there any insurance on the decedent's life that is not included on the return as part of the gross estate?		
b	Did the decedent own any insurance on the life of another that is not included in the gross estate?		

Form 706 (Rev. 8-2013)

	Decedent's social security number
Estate of:	

Part 4—General Information *(continued)*

If you answer "Yes" to any of the following questions, you must attach additional information as described.	Yes	No
10 Did the decedent at the time of death own any property as a joint tenant with right of survivorship in which **(a)** one or more of the other joint tenants was someone other than the decedent's spouse, and **(b)** less than the full value of the property is included on the return as part of the gross estate? If "Yes," you must complete and attach Schedule E		
11a Did the decedent, at the time of death, own any interest in a partnership (for example, a family limited partnership), an unincorporated business, or a limited liability company; or own any stock in an inactive or closely held corporation?		
b If "Yes," was the value of **any** interest owned (from above) discounted on this estate tax return? If "Yes," see the instructions on reporting the total accumulated or effective discounts taken on Schedule F or G		
12 Did the decedent make any transfer described in sections 2035, 2036, 2037, or 2038? (see instructions) If "Yes," you must complete and attach Schedule G		
13a Were there in existence at the time of the decedent's death any trusts created by the decedent during his or her lifetime? . .		
b Were there in existence at the time of the decedent's death any trusts not created by the decedent under which the decedent possessed any power, beneficial interest, or trusteeship?		
c Was the decedent receiving income from a trust created after October 22, 1986, by a parent or grandparent? . . . . . . If "Yes," was there a GST taxable termination (under section 2612) on the death of the decedent?		
d If there was a GST taxable termination (under section 2612), attach a statement to explain. Provide a copy of the trust or will creating the trust, and give the name, address, and phone number of the current trustee(s).		
e Did the decedent at any time during his or her lifetime transfer or sell an interest in a partnership, limited liability company, or closely held corporation to a trust described in lines 13a or 13b? . . . . If "Yes," provide the EIN for this transferred/sold item. ▶		
14 Did the decedent ever possess, exercise, or release any general power of appointment? If "Yes," you must complete and attach Schedule H		
15 Did the decedent have an interest in or a signature or other authority over a financial account in a foreign country, such as a bank account, securities account, or other financial account?		
16 Was the decedent, immediately before death, receiving an annuity described in the "General" paragraph of the instructions for Schedule I or a private annuity? If "Yes," you must complete and attach Schedule I		
17 Was the decedent ever the beneficiary of a trust for which a deduction was claimed by the estate of a predeceased spouse under section 2056(b)(7) and which is not reported on this return? If "Yes," attach an explanation		

Part 5—Recapitulation.

Note. If estimating the value of one or more assets pursuant to the special rule of Reg. section 20.2010-2T(a)(7)(ii), enter on both lines 10 and 23 the amount noted in the instructions for the corresponding range of values. (See instructions for details.)

Item no.	Gross estate		Alternate value	Value at date of death
1	Schedule A—Real Estate	1		
2	Schedule B—Stocks and Bonds	2		
3	Schedule C—Mortgages, Notes, and Cash	3		
4	Schedule D—Insurance on the Decedent's Life (attach Form(s) 712)	4		
5	Schedule E—Jointly Owned Property (attach Form(s) 712 for life insurance) .	5		
6	Schedule F—Other Miscellaneous Property (attach Form(s) 712 for life insurance)	6		
7	Schedule G—Transfers During Decedent's Life (att. Form(s) 712 for life insurance)	7		
8	Schedule H—Powers of Appointment	8		
9	Schedule I—Annuities	9		
10	Estimated value of assets subject to the special rule of Reg. section 20.2010-2T(a)(7)(ii)	10		
11	Total gross estate (add items 1 through 10)	11		
12	Schedule U—Qualified Conservation Easement Exclusion	12		
13	Total gross estate less exclusion (subtract item 12 from item 11). Enter here and on line 1 of Part 2—Tax Computation	13		

Item no.	Deductions		Amount
14	Schedule J—Funeral Expenses and Expenses Incurred in Administering Property Subject to Claims	14	
15	Schedule K—Debts of the Decedent	15	
16	Schedule K—Mortgages and Liens	16	
17	Total of items 14 through 16	17	
18	Allowable amount of deductions from item 17 (see the instructions for item 18 of the Recapitulation)	18	
19	Schedule L—Net Losses During Administration	19	
20	Schedule L—Expenses Incurred in Administering Property Not Subject to Claims	20	
21	Schedule M—Bequests, etc., to Surviving Spouse	21	
22	Schedule O—Charitable, Public, and Similar Gifts and Bequests	22	
23	Estimated value of deductible assets subject to the special rule of Reg. section 20.2010-2T(a)(7)(ii) . . .	23	
24	Tentative total allowable deductions (add items 18 through 23). Enter here and on line 2 of the Tax Computation	24	

Page 3

Form 709

Department of the Treasury
Internal Revenue Service

United States Gift (and Generation-Skipping Transfer) Tax Return

▶ Information about Form 709 and its separate instructions is at *www.irs.gov/form709*.

(For gifts made during calendar year 2015)
▶ **See instructions.**

OMB No. 1545-0020

2015

Part 1—General Information

1 Donor's first name and middle initial	2 Donor's last name	3 Donor's social security number

4 Address (number, street, and apartment number)	5 Legal residence (domicile)

6 City or town, state or province, country, and ZIP or foreign postal code	7 Citizenship (see instructions)

		Yes	No
8	If the donor died during the year, check here ▶ ☐ and enter date of death _____ , _____.		
9	If you extended the time to file this Form 709, check here ▶ ☐		
10	Enter the total number of donees listed on Schedule A. Count each person only once ▶		
11a	Have you (the donor) previously filed a Form 709 (or 709-A) for any other year? If "No," skip line 11b		
b	Has your address changed since you last filed Form 709 (or 709-A)?		
12	**Gifts by husband or wife to third parties.** Do you consent to have the gifts (including generation-skipping transfers) made by you and by your spouse to third parties during the calendar year considered as made one-half by each of you? (see instructions.) (If the answer is "Yes," the following information must be furnished and your spouse must sign the consent shown below. **If the answer is "No," skip lines 13–18.**)		
13	Name of consenting spouse	14 SSN		
15	Were you married to one another during the entire calendar year? (see instructions)		
16	If 15 is "No," check whether ☐ married ☐ divorced or ☐ widowed/deceased, and give date (see instructions) ▶		
17	Will a gift tax return for this year be filed by your spouse? (If "Yes," mail both returns in the same envelope.)		
18	**Consent of Spouse.** I consent to have the gifts (and generation-skipping transfers) made by me and by my spouse to third parties during the calendar year considered as made one-half by each of us. We are both aware of the joint and several liability for tax created by the execution of this consent.		

Consenting spouse's signature ▶ _____   Date ▶ _____

| 19 | Have you applied a DSUE amount received from a predeceased spouse to a gift or gifts reported on this or a previous Form 709? If "Yes," complete Schedule C . . . . | | |

Part 2—Tax Computation

1	Enter the amount from Schedule A, Part 4, line 11	1	
2	Enter the amount from Schedule B, line 3	2	
3	Total taxable gifts. Add lines 1 and 2	3	
4	Tax computed on amount on line 3 (see *Table for Computing Gift Tax* in instructions) . . .	4	
5	Tax computed on amount on line 2 (see *Table for Computing Gift Tax* in instructions) . . .	5	
6	Balance. Subtract line 5 from line 4	6	
7	Applicable credit amount. If donor has DSUE amount from predeceased spouse(s), enter amount from Schedule C, line 4; otherwise, see instructions	7	
8	Enter the applicable credit against tax allowable for all prior periods (from Sch. B, line 1, col. C) .	8	
9	Balance. Subtract line 8 from line 7. Do not enter less than zero	9	
10	Enter 20% (.20) of the amount allowed as a specific exemption for gifts made after September 8, 1976, and before January 1, 1977 (see instructions)	10	
11	Balance. Subtract line 10 from line 9. Do not enter less than zero	11	
12	Applicable credit. Enter the smaller of line 6 or line 11	12	
13	Credit for foreign gift taxes (see instructions)	13	
14	Total credits. Add lines 12 and 13	14	
15	Balance. Subtract line 14 from line 6. Do not enter less than zero	15	
16	Generation-skipping transfer taxes (from Schedule D, Part 3, col. H, Total)	16	
17	Total tax. Add lines 15 and 16	17	
18	Gift and generation-skipping transfer taxes prepaid with extension of time to file	18	
19	If line 18 is less than line 17, enter **balance due** (see instructions)	19	
20	If line 18 is greater than line 17, enter **amount to be refunded**	20	

Attach check or money order here.

Sign Here

Under penalties of perjury, I declare that I have examined this return, including any accompanying schedules and statements, and to the best of my knowledge and belief, it is true, correct, and complete. Declaration of preparer (other than donor) is based on all information of which preparer has any knowledge.

May the IRS discuss this return with the preparer shown below (see instructions)? ☐ Yes ☐ No

▶ _____
Signature of donor   Date

Paid Preparer Use Only

Print/Type preparer's name	Preparer's signature	Date	Check ☐ if self-employed	PTIN
Firm's name ▶			Firm's EIN ▶	
Firm's address ▶			Phone no.	

For Disclosure, Privacy Act, and Paperwork Reduction Act Notice, see the instructions for this form.   Cat. No. 16783M   Form **709** (2015)

Form 709 (2015)   Page **2**

SCHEDULE A	**Computation of Taxable Gifts** (Including transfers in trust) (see instructions)

A Does the value of any item listed on Schedule A reflect any valuation discount? If "Yes," attach explanation   . . . . . .   Yes ☐ No ☐

B ☐ ◄ Check here if you elect under section 529(c)(2)(B) to treat any transfers made this year to a qualified tuition program as made ratably over a 5-year period beginning this year. See instructions. Attach explanation.

Part 1—Gifts Subject Only to Gift Tax. Gifts less political organization, medical, and educational exclusions. (see instructions)

A Item number	**B** • Donee's name and address • Relationship to donor (if any) • Description of gift • If the gift was of securities, give CUSIP no. • If closely held entity, give EIN	**C**	**D** Donor's adjusted basis of gift	**E** Date of gift	**F** Value at date of gift	**G** For split gifts, enter ¹/₂ of column F	**H** Net transfer (subtract col. G from col. F)
1							

*Gifts made by spouse —complete **only** if you are splitting gifts with your spouse and he/she also made gifts.*

Total of Part 1. Add amounts from Part 1, column H . . . . ►

Part 2—Direct Skips. Gifts that are direct skips and are subject to both gift tax and generation-skipping transfer tax. You must list the gifts in chronological order.

A Item number	**B** • Donee's name and address • Relationship to donor (if any) • Description of gift • If the gift was of securities, give CUSIP no. • If closely held entity, give EIN	**C** 2632(b) election out	**D** Donor's adjusted basis of gift	**E** Date of gift	**F** Value at date of gift	**G** For split gifts, enter ¹/₂ of column F	**H** Net transfer (subtract col. G from col. F)
1							

*Gifts made by spouse —complete **only** if you are splitting gifts with your spouse and he/she also made gifts.*

Total of Part 2. Add amounts from Part 2, column H . . . . ►

Part 3—Indirect Skips. Gifts to trusts that are currently subject to gift tax and may later be subject to generation-skipping transfer tax. You must list these gifts in chronological order.

A Item number	**B** • Donee's name and address • Relationship to donor (if any) • Description of gift • If the gift was of securities, give CUSIP no. • If closely held entity, give EIN	**C** 2632(c) election	**D** Donor's adjusted basis of gift	**E** Date of gift	**F** Value at date of gift	**G** For split gifts, enter ¹/₂ of column F	**H** Net transfer (subtract col. G from col. F)
1							

*Gifts made by spouse —complete **only** if you are splitting gifts with your spouse and he/she also made gifts.*

Total of Part 3. Add amounts from Part 3, column H . . . . ►

(If more space is needed, attach additional statements.)   Form **709** (2015)

Part 4—Taxable Gift Reconciliation

1	Total value of gifts of donor. Add totals from column H of Parts 1, 2, and 3	**1**	
2	Total annual exclusions for gifts listed on line 1 (see instructions)	**2**	
3	Total included amount of gifts. Subtract line 2 from line 1	**3**	

Deductions (see instructions)

4	Gifts of interests to spouse for which a marital deduction will be claimed, based on item numbers _____ of Schedule A . .	**4**		
5	Exclusions attributable to gifts on line 4	**5**		
6	Marital deduction. Subtract line 5 from line 4	**6**		
7	Charitable deduction, based on item nos. _____ less exclusions .	**7**		
8	Total deductions. Add lines 6 and 7		**8**	
9	Subtract line 8 from line 3		**9**	
10	Generation-skipping transfer taxes payable with this Form 709 (from Schedule D, Part 3, col. H, Total) . .		**10**	
11	**Taxable gifts.** Add lines 9 and 10. Enter here and on page 1, Part 2—Tax Computation, line 1		**11**	

Terminable Interest (QTIP) Marital Deduction. (see instructions for Schedule A, Part 4, line 4)

If a trust (or other property) meets the requirements of qualified terminable interest property under section 2523(f), and:

a. The trust (or other property) is listed on Schedule A, and

b. The value of the trust (or other property) is entered in whole or in part as a deduction on Schedule A, Part 4, line 4,

then the donor shall be deemed to have made an election to have such trust (or other property) treated as qualified terminable interest property under section 2523(f).

If less than the entire value of the trust (or other property) that the donor has included in Parts 1 and 3 of Schedule A is entered as a deduction on line 4, the donor shall be considered to have made an election only as to a fraction of the trust (or other property). The numerator of this fraction is equal to the amount of the trust (or other property) deducted on Schedule A, Part 4, line 6. The denominator is equal to the total value of the trust (or other property) listed in Parts 1 and 3 of Schedule A.

If you make the QTIP election, the terminable interest property involved will be included in your spouse's gross estate upon his or her death (section 2044). See instructions for line 4 of Schedule A. If your spouse disposes (by gift or otherwise) of all or part of the qualifying life income interest, he or she will be considered to have made a transfer of the entire property that is subject to the gift tax. See *Transfer of Certain Life Estates Received From Spouse* in the instructions.

12 Election Out of QTIP Treatment of Annuities

◻ ◄ Check here if you elect under section 2523(f)(6) **not** to treat as qualified terminable interest property any joint and survivor annuities that are reported on Schedule A and would otherwise be treated as qualified terminable interest property under section 2523(f). See instructions. Enter the item numbers from Schedule A for the annuities for which you are making this election ▶ _____

SCHEDULE B   Gifts From Prior Periods

If you answered "Yes," on line 11a of page 1, Part 1, see the instructions for completing Schedule B. If you answered "No," skip to the Tax Computation on page 1 (or Schedules C or D, if applicable). Complete Schedule A before beginning Schedule B. See instructions for recalculation of the column C amounts. Attach calculations.

A Calendar year or calendar quarter (see instructions)	**B** Internal Revenue office where prior return was filed	**C** Amount of applicable credit (unified credit) against gift tax for periods after December 31, 1976	**D** Amount of specific exemption for prior periods ending before January 1, 1977	**E** Amount of taxable gifts

1	Totals for prior periods **1**			
2	Amount, if any, by which total specific exemption, line 1, column D is more than $30,000 . . . . . . **2**			
3	Total amount of taxable gifts for prior periods. Add amount on line 1, column E and amount, if any, on line 2. Enter here and on page 1, Part 2—Tax Computation, line 2 . . . . **3**			

(If more space is needed, attach additional statements.)

SCHEDULE C	Deceased Spousal Unused Exclusion (DSUE) Amount

Provide the following information to determine the DSUE amount and applicable credit received from prior spouses. Complete Schedule A before beginning Schedule C.

A Name of Deceased Spouse (dates of death after December 31, 2010 only)	B Date of Death	C Portability Election Made?		D If "Yes," DSUE Amount Received from Spouse	E DSUE Amount Applied by Donor to Lifetime Gifts (list current and prior gifts)	F Date of Gift(s) (enter as mm/dd/yy for Part 1 and as yyyy for Part 2)
		Yes	No			
Part 1—DSUE RECEIVED FROM LAST DECEASED SPOUSE						
Part 2—DSUE RECEIVED FROM PREDECEASED SPOUSE(S)						

TOTAL (for all DSUE amounts applied from column E for Part 1 and Part 2)			
1	Donor's basic exclusion amount (see instructions)	**1**	
2	Total from column E, Parts 1 and 2	**2**	
3	Add lines 1 and 2	**3**	
4	Applicable credit on amount in line 3 (See *Table for Computing Gift Tax* in the instructions). Enter here and on line 7, Part 2—Tax Computation	**4**	

SCHEDULE D	Computation of Generation-Skipping Transfer Tax

Note. Inter vivos direct skips that are completely excluded by the GST exemption must still be fully reported (including value and exemptions claimed) on Schedule D.

Part 1—Generation-Skipping Transfers

A Item No. (from Schedule A, Part 2, col. A)	B Value (from Schedule A, Part 2, col. H)	C Nontaxable Portion of Transfer	D Net Transfer (subtract col. C from col. B)
1			
Gifts made by spouse (for gift splitting only)			

(If more space is needed, attach additional statements.)   Form **709** (2015)

Tax Terms Glossary

§83(b) election a special tax election that employees who receive restricted stock or other property with ownership restrictions can make to accelerate income recognition from the normal date when restrictions lapse to the date when the restricted stock or other property is granted. The election also accelerates the employer's compensation deduction related to the restricted stock or other property.

§162(m) limitation the $1 million deduction limit on nonperformance-based salary paid to certain key executives.

§179 expense an incentive for small businesses that allows them to immediately expense a certain amount of tangible personal property placed in service during the year.

§197 purchased intangibles intangible assets that are purchased that must be amortized over 180 months regardless of their actual useful lives.

§263A Cost (or UNICAP) certain book expenses that must be capitalized into inventory for tax purposes.

§291 depreciation recapture the portion of a corporate taxpayer's gain on real property that is converted from §1231 gain to ordinary income.

§338 election an election by a corporate buyer of 80-percent-or-more of a corporation's stock to treat the acquisition as an asset acquisition and not a stock acquisition.

§338(h)(10) election a joint election by the corporate buyer and corporate seller of the stock of a subsidiary of the seller to treat the acquisition as a sale of the subsidiary's assets by the seller to the buyer.

§481 adjustment a change to taxable income associated with a change in accounting methods.

§1231 assets depreciable or real property used in a taxpayer's trade or business owned for more than one year.

§1231 look-back rule a tax rule requiring taxpayers to treat current year net §1231 gains as ordinary income when the taxpayer has deducted a §1231 loss as an ordinary loss in the five years preceding the current tax year.

§1245 property tangible personal property and intangible property subject to cost recovery deductions.

§1250 property real property subject to cost recovery deductions.

§7520 rate an interest rate set at 120 percent of the applicable federal midterm rate (published monthly by the Treasury) and used to calculate the value of temporal interests.

12-month rule regulation that allows prepaid business expenses to be currently deducted when the contract does not extend beyond 12 months and the contract period does not extend beyond the end of the tax year following the year of the payment.

30-day letter the IRS letter received after an audit that instructs the taxpayer that he or she has 30 days to either (1) request a conference with an appeals officer or (2) agree to the proposed adjustment.

90-day letter the IRS letter received after an audit and receipt of the 30-day letter that explains that the taxpayer has 90 days to either (1) pay the proposed deficiency or (2) file a petition in the U.S. Tax Court to hear the case. The 90-day letter is also known as the *statutory notice of deficiency.*

704(b) capital accounts partners' capital accounts maintained using the accounting rules prescribed in the Section 704(b) regulations. Under these rules, capital accounts reflect the fair market value of property contributed to and distributed property from partnerships.

A

Abandoned spouse a married taxpayer who lives apart from his or her spouse for the last six months of the year (excluding temporary absences), who files a tax return separate from his or her spouse, and who maintains a household for a qualifying child.

Accelerated Cost Recovery System (ACRS) the depreciation system enacted by Congress in 1981 that is based on the concept of set recovery periods and accelerated depreciation methods.

Accelerated death benefits early receipt of life insurance proceeds that are not taxable under certain circumstances, such as the taxpayer is medically certified with an illness that is expected to cause death within 24 months.

Accountable plan an employer's reimbursement plan under which employees must submit documentation supporting expenses to receive reimbursement and reimbursements are limited to legitimate business expenses.

Accounting method the procedure for determining the taxable year in which a business recognizes a particular item of income or deduction thereby dictating the timing of when a taxpayer reports income and deductions.

Accounting period a fixed period in which a business reports income and deductions, generally referred to as a tax year.

Accrual method a method of accounting that generally recognizes income in the period earned and recognizes deductions in the period that liabilities are incurred.

Accrued market discount a ratable amount of the market discount at the time of purchase (based on the number of days the bond is held over the number of days until maturity when the bond is purchased) that is treated as interest income when a bond with market discount is sold before it matures.

Accumulated adjustments account (AAA) an account that reflects the cumulative income or loss for the time the corporation has been an S corporation.

Accumulated earnings and profits undistributed earnings and profits from years prior to the current year.

Accumulated earnings tax a tax assessed on corporations that retain earnings without a business reason to do so.

Acquiescence issued after the IRS loses a trial-level or circuit court case when the IRS has decided to follow the court's adverse ruling in the future. It does not mean that the IRS agrees with the court's ruling. Instead, it simply means that the IRS will no longer litigate this issue.

Acquisition indebtedness debt secured by a qualified residence that is incurred in acquiring, constructing, or substantially improving the residence.

Acquisition subsidiary a subsidiary used by the acquiring corporation in a triangular merger to acquire the target corporation.

Action on decision an IRS pronouncement that explains the background reasoning behind an IRS acquiescence or nonacquiescence.

Active participant in a rental activity an individual who owns at least 10 percent of a rental property and participates in the process of making management decisions, such as approving new tenants, deciding on rental terms, and approving repairs and capital expenditures.

Ad valorem tax a tax based on the value of property.

Adjusted basis *see* adjusted tax basis.

Adjusted current earnings (ACE) a version of a corporation's current year earnings that more closely represents a corporation's economic income for the year than do regular taxable income or alternative minimum taxable income.

Adjusted gross estate gross estate reduced by administrative expenses, debts of the decedent, and losses, and state death taxes.

Adjusted gross income (AGI) gross income less deductions for AGI. AGI is an important reference point that is often used in other calculations.

Adjusted tax basis the taxpayer's acquisition basis (for example, cost) plus capital improvements less depreciation or amortization.

Adjusted taxable gifts cumulative taxable gifts from previous years other than gifts already included in the gross estate valued at date of gift values.

Affiliated group two or more "includible" corporations that are related through common stock ownership and eligible to file a U.S. consolidated tax return. An affiliated group consists of a parent corporation that owns directly 80 percent or more of the voting stock and value of another corporation and one or more subsidiary corporations that meet the 80 percent ownership requirement collectively. Includible corporations are taxable U.S. corporations, excluding real estate investment trusts, regulated investment companies, and life insurance companies.

After-tax rate of return a taxpayer's before-tax rate of return on an investment minus the taxes paid on the income from the investment. The formula for an after-tax rate of return that is taxed annually is the before-tax rate of return $\times (1 -$ marginal tax rate) [i.e., $r = R \times (1 - t)$]. A taxpayer's after-tax rate of return on an investment held form more than one tax period is $r = (FV/I)^{1/n} - 1$, where r is the after-tax rate of return, FV is the after-tax future value of the investment, I is the original investment amount, and n is the number of periods the investment is held.

Aggregate approach a theory of taxing partnerships that ignores partnerships as entities and taxes partners as if they directly owned partnership net assets.

Alimony a support payment of cash made to a former spouse. The payment must be made under a written separation agreement or divorce decree that does not designate the payment as something other than alimony, the payment must be made when the spouses do not live together, and the payments must cease no later than when the recipient dies.

All-events test requires that income or expenses are recognized when (1) all events have occurred that determine or fix the right to receive the income or liability to make the payments and (2) the amount of the income or expense can be determined with reasonable accuracy.

All-inclusive income concept a definition of income that says that gross income means all income from whatever source derived.

Allocate as used in the sourcing rules, the process of associating a deduction with a specific item or items of gross income for purposes of computing foreign source taxable income.

Allocation the method of dividing or sourcing nonbusiness income to specific states.

Allowance method bad debt expense is based on an estimate of the amount of the bad debts in accounts receivable at year-end.

Alternative minimum tax a tax on a broader tax base than the base for the "regular" tax; the additional tax paid when the tentative minimum tax (based on the alternative minimum tax base) exceeds the regular tax (based on the regular tax base). The alternative minimum tax is designed to require taxpayers to pay some minimum level of tax even when they have low or no regular taxable income as a result of certain tax breaks in the tax code.

Alternative minimum tax adjustments adjustments (positive or negative) to regular taxable income to arrive at the alternative minimum tax base.

Alternative minimum tax base (AMT base) alternative minimum taxable income minus the alternative minimum tax exemption.

Alternative minimum tax exemption a deduction to determine the alternative minimum tax base that is phased out based on alternative minimum taxable income.

Alternative minimum tax system a secondary or parallel tax system calculated on an *alternative* tax base that more closely reflects economic income than the regular income tax base. The system was designed to ensure that taxpayers generating economic income pay some *minimum* amount of income tax each year.

Alternative valuation date the date nine months after the decedent's date of death.

Amortization the method of recovering the cost of intangible assets over a specific time period.

Amount realized the value of everything received by the seller in a transaction (cash, FMV of other property, and relief of liabilities) less selling costs.

Annotated tax service a tax service arranged by code section. For each code section, an annotated service includes the code section; a listing of the code section history; copies of congressional committee reports that explain changes to the code section; a copy of all the regulations issued for the specific code section; the service's unofficial explanation of the code section; and brief summaries (called annotations) of relevant court cases, revenue rulings, revenue procedures, and letter rulings that address issues specific to the code section.

Annual exclusion amount of gifts allowed to be made each year per donee (regardless of the number of donees) to prevent the taxation of relatively small gifts ($14,000 per donee per year in 2015).

Annualized income method a method for determining a corporation's required estimated tax payments when the taxpayer earns more income later in the year than earlier in the year. Requires corporations to base their first and second required estimated tax installments on their income from the first three months of the year, their third installment based on their taxable income from the first six months of the year, and the final installment based on their taxable income from the first nine months of the year.

Annuity a stream of equal payments over time.

Applicable credit also known as the unified credit, the amount of current tax on the exemption equivalent; designed to prevent transfer taxation of smaller cumulative transfers.

Applicable tax rate the tax rate or rates used to measure a company's deferred tax asset or liability. In general, it is the enacted tax rate that is expected to apply to taxable income in the period in which the deferred tax asset or liability is expected to be recovered or settled. For U.S. tax purposes, the applicable tax rate is the regular tax rate.

Apportion as used in the sourcing rules, the process of calculating the amount of a deduction that is associated with a specific item or items of gross income for purposes of computing foreign source taxable income.

Apportionment the method of dividing business income of an interstate business among the states where nexus exists.

Arm's-length amount price in transactions among unrelated taxpayers, where each transacting party negotiates for his or her own benefit.

Arm's-length transaction transactions among unrelated taxpayers, where each transacting party negotiates for his or her own benefit.

Articles of incorporation a document, filed by a corporation's founders with the state describing the purpose, place of business, and other details of the corporation.

Articles of organization a document, filed by a limited liability company's founders with the state, describing the purpose, place of business, and other details of the company.

Asset and liability approach the approach taken by ASC Topic 740 that focuses on computing a company's current taxes payable (refundable) and deferred tax assets and liabilities on the balance sheet. The income tax provision recorded on the income statement is the amount needed to adjust the beginning of the year balance sheet amounts to the end of the year balance sheet amounts.

Assignment of income doctrine the judicial doctrine holding that earned income is taxed to the taxpayer providing the service, and that income from property is taxed to the individual who owns the property when the income accrues.

At-risk amount an investor's risk of loss in a worst-case scenario. In a partnership, an amount generally equal to a partner's tax basis exclusive of the partner's share of nonrecourse debt.

At-risk rules tax rules limiting losses flowing through to partners or S corporation shareholders to their at-risk amount.

Average tax rate a taxpayer's average level of taxation on each dollar of taxable income. Specifically,

$$\text{Average tax rate} = \frac{\text{Total tax}}{\text{Taxable income}}$$

B

Bargain element (of stock options) the difference between the fair market value of the employer's stock and the amount employees pay to acquire the employer's stock.

Barter clubs organizations that facilitate the exchange of rights to goods and services between members.

Basis a taxpayer's unrecovered investment in an asset that provides a reference point for measuring gain or loss when an asset is sold.

Before-tax rate of return a taxpayer's rate of return on an investment before paying taxes on the income from the investment.

Beneficiary person for whom trust property is held and administered.

Bond a debt instrument issued for a period of more than one year with the purpose of raising capital by borrowing.

Bond discount the result of issuing bonds for less than their maturity value.

Bond premium the result of issuing bonds for more than their maturity value.

Bonus depreciation additional depreciation allowed in the acquisition year for new tangible personal property with a recovery period of 20 years or less.

Book equivalent of taxable income a company's pretax income from continuing operations adjusted for permanent differences.

Book (financial reporting) income the income or loss corporations report on their financial statements using applicable financial accounting standards.

Book–tax difference a difference in the amount of an income item or deduction item taken into account for book purposes compared to the amount taken into account for the same item for tax purposes.

Boot property given or received in an otherwise nontaxable transaction such as a like-kind exchange that may trigger gain to a party to the transaction.

Bracket a subset (or portion) of the tax base subject to a specific tax rate. Brackets are common to graduated taxes.

Branch an unincorporated division of a corporation.

Bright line tests technical rules found in the tax law that provide the taxpayer with objective tests to determine the tax consequences of a transaction.

Brother-sister controlled group a form of controlled group consisting of two or more corporations if five or fewer individuals collectively own more than 50 percent of the voting power or stock value of the corporation on the last day of the year.

Built-in gain the difference between the fair market value and tax basis of property owned by an entity when the fair market value exceeds the tax basis.

Built-in gains tax a tax levied on S corporations that were formerly C corporations. The tax applies to net unrealized built-in gains at the time the corporation converted from a C corporation to the extent the gains are recognized during the built-in gains tax recognition period. The applicable tax rate is 35 percent.

Built-in gains tax recognition period the first 5 years a corporation operates as an S corporation after converting from a C corporation for asset sales in 2011 through 2014 (first 7 years for asset sales in 2009 and 2010; first 10 years for assets sales in other years). At press time, the built-in gains tax recognition period is scheduled to expand to 10 years for asset sales in 2015.

Built-in loss the difference between the fair market value and tax basis of property owned by an entity when the tax basis exceeds the fair market value.

Bunching itemized deductions a common planning strategy in which a taxpayer pays two year's worth of itemized expenses in one year to exceed the standard deduction in that year.

Business activity a profit-motivated activity that requires a relatively high level of involvement or effort from the taxpayer to generate income.

Business income income derived from business activities.

Business purpose doctrine the judicial doctrine that allows the IRS to challenge and disallow business expenses for transactions with no underlying business motivation.

Business tax credits nonrefundable credits designed to provide incentives for taxpayers to hire certain types of individuals or to participate in certain business activities.

Bypass provision a provision in the will of a deceased spouse that transfers property to nonspousal beneficiaries to maximize the value of the decedent's unified credit.

Bypass trust a trust used in lieu of a bypass provision to transfer property to nonspousal beneficiaries to maximize the value of the unified credit of the first spouse to die.

C

C corporation a corporate taxpaying entity with income subject to taxation. Such a corporation is termed a "C" corporation because the corporation and its shareholders are subject to the provisions of subchapter C of the Internal Revenue Code.

Cafeteria plan   an employer plan that allows employees to choose benefits from a menu of nontaxable fringe benefits or receive cash compensation in lieu of the benefits.

Capital account   an account reflecting a partner's share of the equity in a partnership. Capital accounts are maintained using tax accounting methods or other methods of accounting, including GAAP, at the discretion of the partnership.

Capital asset   in general, an asset other than an asset used in a trade or business or an asset such as an account or note receivable acquired in a business from the sale of services or property.

Capital gain property   any asset that would have generated a long-term capital gain if the taxpayer had sold the property for its fair market value.

Capital interest   an economic right attached to a partnership interest giving a partner the right to receive cash or property in the event the partnership liquidates. A capital interest is synonymous with the liquidation value of a partnership interest.

Capitalization   recording an expenditure as an asset on the balance sheet rather than expensing it immediately.

Carryover basis   the basis of an asset the transferee takes in property received in a nontaxable exchange. The basis of the asset carries over from the transferor to the transferee.

Cash method   the method of accounting that recognizes income in the period in which cash, property, or services are received and recognizes deductions in the period paid.

Cash surrender value   the amount, if any, the owner of a life insurance policy receives when the policy is cashed in before the death of the insured individual.

Cash tax rate   the tax rate computed by dividing a company's taxes paid during the year by its pretax income from continuing operations.

Cashless exercise   a technique where options are both exercised and at least a portion of the shares are sold in order to facilitate the purchase.

Casualty   an unexpected, unforeseen event driven by forces outside the control of the taxpayer (such as "fire, storm, or shipwreck" or other event or theft) that damages or destroys a taxpayer's property.

Casualty loss   a loss arising from a *sudden, unexpected,* or *unusual* event such as a "fire, storm, or shipwreck" or loss from theft.

Ceiling   limitations that are maximum amounts for adjustments to taxable income (or credits). The amounts in excess of the ceiling are either lost or carried to another tax year.

Certainty   one of the criteria used to evaluate tax systems. Certainty means taxpayers should be able to determine when, where, and how much tax to pay.

Certificate of deposit   an interest-bearing debt instrument offered by banks and savings and loans. Money removed from the CD before maturity is subject to a penalty.

Certificate of limited partnership   a document limited partnerships must file with the state to be formerly recognized by the state. The document is similar to articles of incorporation or articles or organization.

Character of income   determines the rate at which income will be taxed. Common income characters (or types of income) include tax-exempt, ordinary, and capital.

Charitable contribution limit modified taxable income   taxable income for purposes of determining the 10 percent of taxable income deduction limitation for corporate charitable contributions. Computed as taxable income before deducting (1) any charitable contributions, (2) the dividends received deduction, (3) net operating loss carrybacks, and (4) the domestic production activities deduction.

Circular 230   regulations issued by the IRS that govern tax practice and apply to all persons practicing before the IRS. There are three parts of Circular 230: Subpart A describes who may practice before the IRS (e.g., CPAs, attorneys, enrolled agents) and what practicing before the IRS means (tax return preparation, representing clients before the IRS, etc.). Subpart B describes the duties and restrictions that apply to individuals governed by Circular 230. Subparts C and D explain sanctions and disciplinary proceedings for practitioners violating the Circular 230 provisions. Subpart E concludes with a few miscellaneous provisions (such as the Circular 230 effective date).

Citator   a research tool that allows one to check the status of several types of tax authorities. A citator can be used to review the history of the case to find out, for example, whether it was subsequently appealed and overturned, and to identify subsequent cases that cite the case. Citators can also be used to check the status of revenue rulings, revenue procedures, and other IRS pronouncements.

Civil penalties   monetary penalties imposed when tax practitioners or taxpayers violate tax statutes without reasonable cause—for example, as the result of negligence, intentional disregard of pertinent rules, willful disobedience, or outright fraud.

Claim of right doctrine   judicial doctrine that states that income has been realized if a taxpayer receives income and there are no restrictions on the taxpayer's use of the income (for example, the taxpayer does not have an obligation to repay the amount).

Cliff vesting   a qualified plan provision allowing for benefits to vest all at once after a specified period of time has passed.

Collectibles   a work of art, a rug or antique, a metal or gem, a stamp or coin, an alcoholic beverage, or other similar items held for investment for more than one year.

Combined controlled group   a form of a controlled group consisting of three or more corporations each of which is a member of either a parent-subsidiary or brother-sister controlled group and one of the corporations is the parent in the parent-subsidiary controlled group and also is in a brother-sister controlled group.

Commercial domicile   the state where a business is headquartered and directs operations; this location may be different from the place of incorporation.

Commercial traveler exception   a statutory exception that exempts nonresidents from U.S. taxation of compensation from services if the individual is in the United States 90 days or less and earns compensation of $3,000 or less.

Common-law states   the 41 states that have not adopted community property laws.

Community-property states   nine states (Arizona, California, Idaho, Louisiana, Nevada, New Mexico, Texas, Washington, and Wisconsin) that automatically equally divide the ownership of property acquired by either spouse during a marriage.

Community property systems   systems in which state laws dictate how the income and property is legally shared between a husband and a wife.

Commuting   traveling from a personal residence to the place of business.

Complex trust   a trust that is not required by the trust instrument to distribute income currently.

Conglomerate   a group of corporations in different businesses under common ownership.

Consolidated tax return   a combined U.S. income tax return filed by an affiliated group of corporations.

Consolidation   the combining of the assets and liabilities of two or more corporations into a new entity.

Constructive dividend   a payment made by a corporation to a shareholder that is recharacterized by the IRS or courts as a dividend even though it is not characterized as such by the corporation.

Constructive ownership   rules that cause stock not owned by a taxpayer to be treated as owned by the taxpayer for purposes of meeting certain stock ownership tests.

Constructive receipt doctrine   the judicial doctrine that provides that a taxpayer must recognize income when it is actually or constructively received. Constructive receipt is deemed to have occurred if the income has been credited to the taxpayer's account or if the income is unconditionally available to the taxpayer, the taxpayer is aware of the income's availability, and there are no restrictions on the taxpayer's control over the income.

Continuity of business enterprise (COBE)   a judicial (now regulatory) requirement that the acquiring corporation continue the target corporation's historic business or continue to use a "significant" portion of the target corporation's historic business assets to be tax-deferred.

Continuity of interest (COI)   a judicial (now regulatory) requirement that the transferors of stock in a reorganization collectively retain a continuing ownership (equity) interest in the target corporation's assets or historic business to be tax-deferred.

Contribution to capital   a shareholder's or other person's contribution of cash or other property to a corporation without receipt of an additional equity interest in the corporation.

Controlled foreign corporation   a foreign corporation that is more than 50 percent owned by U.S. shareholders.

Controlled group   a group of corporations owned by the same individual shareholders; it can either be brother-sister corporations or parent-subsidiary corporations.

Convenience   one of the criteria used to evaluate tax systems. Convenience means a tax system should be designed to facilitate the collection of tax revenues without undue hardship on the taxpayer or the government.

Corporation   business entity recognized as separate entity from its owners under state law.

Corporation's effective tax rate   the tax rate computed by dividing a company's income tax provision (expense or benefit) for the year by its pretax income from continuing operations.

Corpus   the principal or property transferred to fund a trust or accumulated in the trust.

Correspondence examination   an IRS audit conducted by mail and generally limited to one or two items on the taxpayer's return. Among the three types of audits, correspondence audits are generally the most common, the most narrow in scope, and least complex. The IRS typically requests supporting documentation for one or more items on the taxpayer's return (e.g., documentation of charitable contributions deducted).

Cost depletion   the method of recovering the cost of a natural resource that allows a taxpayer to estimate or determine the number of units that remain in the resource at the beginning of the year and allocate a pro rata share of the remaining basis to each unit of the resource that is extracted or sold during the year.

Cost recovery   the method by which a company expenses the cost of acquiring capital assets. Cost recovery can take the form of depreciation, amortization, or depletion.

Coupon rate   the interest rate expressed as a percentage of the face value of the bond.

Covenant not to compete   a contractual promise to refrain from conducting business or professional activities similar to those of another party.

Criminal penalties   penalties commonly charged in tax evasion cases (i.e., willful intent to defraud the government). They are imposed only after normal due process, including a trial. Compared to civil cases, the standard of conviction is higher in a criminal trial (beyond a reasonable doubt). However, the penalties are also much higher, such as fines up to $100,000 for individuals plus a prison sentence.

Current earnings and profits   a year-to-year calculation maintained by a corporation to determine if a distribution is a dividend. Earnings and profits are computed for the current year by adjusting taxable income to make it more closely resemble economic income.

Current gifts   gifts completed during the calendar year that are not already exempted from the gift tax.

Current income tax expense (benefit)   the amount of taxes paid or payable (refundable) in the current year.

Current tax liability (asset)   the amount of taxes payable or refundable in the current year.

D

***De minimis* fringe benefit**   a nontaxable fringe benefit that allows employees to receive occasional or incidental benefits tax free.

Debt basis   the outstanding principal of direct loans from an S corporation shareholder to the S corporation. Once taxpayers deduct losses to the extent of their stock basis, they may deduct losses to the extent of their debt basis. When the debt basis has been reduced by losses, it is restored by income/gain allocations.

Deceased spousal unused exclusion   amount of unused unified credit from predeceased spouse.

Deductible temporary differences   book-tax differences that will result in tax deductible amounts in future years when the related deferred tax asset is recovered.

Deductions   amounts that are subtracted from gross income in calculating taxable income.

Deductions above the line   *for* AGI deductions or deductions subtracted from gross income to determine AGI.

Deductions below the line   *from* AGI deductions or deductions subtracted from AGI to calculate taxable income.

Deferral items, deferred income, or deferrals   realized income that will be taxed as income in a subsequent year.

Deferral method   recognizes income from advance payments for goods by the earlier of (1) when the business would recognize the income for tax purposes if it had not received the *advance* payment or (2) when it recognizes the income for financial reporting purposes.

Deferred like-kind exchange   a like-kind exchange where the taxpayer transfers like-kind property before receiving the like-kind property in exchange. The property to be received must be identified within 45 days and received within 180 days of the transfer of the property given up.

Deferred tax asset   the expected future tax benefit attributable to deductible temporary differences and carryforwards.

Deferred tax liability   the expected future tax cost attributable to taxable temporary differences.

Defined benefit plan   employer-provided qualified plans that spell out the specific benefit employees will receive on retirement.

Defined contribution plan   employer-provided qualified plans that specify the maximum annual contributions employers and/or employees may contribute to the plan.

Definitely related deductions   deductions that are associated with the creation of a specific item or items of gross income.

Dependency exemption   a fixed deduction allowed for each individual who qualifies as a "dependent" of the taxpayer.

Dependent   a person for whom a taxpayer may claim a dependency exemption. To qualify as a dependent a person must be a qualifying child or qualifying relative of the taxpayer.

Dependent care benefit   a nontaxable fringe benefit that allows employees to receive up to $5,000 of care for children under age 13 or for a spouse or other dependent with physical needs.

Depletion   the cost recovery method to allocate the cost of natural resources as they are removed.

Depreciation   the cost recovery method to allocate the cost of tangible personal and real property over a specific time period.

Depreciation recapture   the conversion of §1231 gain into ordinary income on a sale (or exchange) based on the amount of accumulated depreciation on the property at the time of sale or exchange.

Determination letters   rulings requested by the taxpayer, issued by local IRS directors, and generally not controversial. An example of a determination letter is the request by an employer for the IRS to rule that the taxpayer's retirement plan is a "qualified plan."

DIF (Discriminant Function) system   the DIF system assigns a score to each tax return that represents the probability that the tax liability on the return has been underreported (a higher score = a higher likelihood of underreporting). The IRS derives the weights assigned to specific tax return attributes from historical IRS audit adjustment data from the National Research Program. The DIF system then uses these (undisclosed) weights to score each tax return based on the tax return's characteristics. Returns with higher DIF scores are then reviewed to determine if an audit is the best course of action.

Direct conversion   when a taxpayer receives noncash property rather than a cash payment as a replacement for property damaged or destroyed in an involuntary conversion.

Direct write-off method   required method for deducting bad debts for tax purposes. Under this method, businesses deduct bad debt only when the debt becomes wholly or partially worthless.

Disability insurance   sometimes called sick pay or wage replacement insurance. It pays the insured for wages lost due to injury or disability.

Discharge of indebtedness   debt forgiveness.

Discount factor   the factor based on the taxpayer's rate of return that is used to determine the present value of future cash inflows (e.g., tax savings) and outflows (taxes paid).

Disproportionate distributions   partnership distributions that change the partners' relative ownership of hot assets.

Disqualifying disposition   the sale of stock acquired using incentive stock options prior to satisfying certain holding period requirements. Failing to satisfy the holding period requirements converts the options into nonqualified stock options.

Disregarded entities   incorporated entities with one owner that are treated as flow-through entities for U.S. income tax purposes.

Distributable net income (DNI)   the maximum amount of the distribution deduction by fiduciaries and the maximum aggregate amount of gross income reportable by beneficiaries.

Distribution deduction   deduction by fiduciaries for distributions of income to beneficiaries that operates to eliminate the potential for double taxation of fiduciary income.

Dividend   a distribution to shareholders of money or property from the corporation's earnings and profits.

Dividends received deduction   a corporate deduction for part or all of a dividend received from other taxable, domestic corporations.

Document perfection program   a program under which all tax returns are checked for mathematical and tax calculation errors.

Domestic production activities deduction (DPAD)   a deduction for businesses that manufacture goods in the United States.

Donee   person receiving a gift.

Donor   person making a gift.

Double taxation   the tax burden when an entity's income is subject to two levels of tax. Income of C corporations is subject to double taxation. The first level of tax is at the corporate level and the second level of tax on corporate income occurs at the shareholder level. Income of flow-through entities is generally not subject to double taxation.

DRD modified taxable income   taxable income for purposes of applying the taxable income limitation for the dividends received deduction. Computed as the dividend receiving corporation's taxable income before deducting the dividends received deduction, any net

operating loss deduction, the domestic production activities deduction, and capital loss carrybacks.

Dwelling unit   property that provides a place suitable for people to occupy (live and sleep).

Dynamic forecasting   the process of forecasting tax revenues that incorporates into the forecast how taxpayers may alter their activities in response to a tax law change.

E

Earmarked tax   a tax assessed for a specific purpose (e.g., for education).

Earned income   compensation and other forms of income received for providing goods or services in the ordinary course of business.

Earned income credit   a refundable credit designed to help offset the effect of employment taxes on compensation paid to low-income taxpayers and to encourage lower income taxpayers to seek employment.

Earnings and profits   a measure of a corporation's earnings that is similar to its economic earnings. Corporate dividends are taxable to shareholders to the extent they come from earnings and profits.

Economic nexus   the concept that businesses without a physical presence in the state may establish income tax nexus in the state through an economic presence there.

Economic performance test   the third requirement that must be met for an accrual method taxpayer to deduct an expense currently. The specific event that satisfies the economic performance test varies based on the type of expense.

Economic substance doctrine   doctrine that requires transactions to meaningfully change a taxpayer's economic position *and* to have a substantial purpose (apart from a federal income tax purpose) in order for a taxpayer to obtain tax benefits.

Economy   one of the criteria used to evaluate tax systems. Economy means a tax system should minimize its compliance and administration costs.

Educational assistance benefit   a nontaxable fringe benefit that allows an employer to provide a certain amount of education benefits on an annual basis.

Effective tax rate   the taxpayer's average rate of taxation on each dollar of total income (taxable and nontaxable income). Specifically,

$$\text{Effective tax rate} = \frac{Total\ tax}{Total\ income}$$

Effectively connected income   net income that results from the conduct of a U.S. trade or business by a nonresident.

Employee   a person who is hired to provide services to a company on a regular basis in exchange for compensation and who does not provide these services as part of an independent business.

Employment taxes   taxes consisting of the Old Age, Survivors, and Disability Insurance (OASDI) tax, commonly called the Social Security tax, and the Medical Health Insurance (MHI) tax known as the Medicare tax.

Enacted tax rate   the statutory tax rate that will apply in the current or a future period.

Entity approach   a theory of taxing partnerships that treats partnerships as entities separate from partners.

Equity   one of the criteria used to evaluate a tax system. A tax system is considered fair or equitable if the tax is based on the taxpayer's ability to pay tax; taxpayers with a greater ability to pay tax, pay more tax.

Escrow account (mortgage-related)   a holding account with a taxpayer's mortgage lender. The taxpayer makes mortgage payments to the lender that include payment for the interest and principal and payments for property taxes. The lender maintains the payments for property taxes in the escrow account and uses the funds in the account to pay the property taxes when the taxes are due.

Estate fiduciary legal entity that comes into existence upon a person's death and is empowered by the probate court to gather and transfer the decedent's real and personal property.

Estate tax the tax paid for an estate.

Estimated tax payments quarterly tax payments that a taxpayer makes to the government if the tax withholding is insufficient to meet the taxpayer's tax liability.

Excess net passive income net passive investment income × passive investment income in excess of 25 percent of the S corporation's gross receipts divided by its passive investment income.

Excess net passive income tax a tax levied on an S corporation that has accumulated earnings and profits from years in which it operated as a C corporation if the corporation reports excess net passive income.

Exchanged basis the basis of an asset received in a nontaxable exchange. An exchanged basis is generally the basis of the asset given up in a nontaxable exchange. Exchanged basis may also be referred to as a *substituted basis*.

Excise taxes taxes levied on the retail sale of particular products. They differ from other taxes in that the tax base for an excise tax typically depends on the *quantity* purchased rather than a monetary amount.

Excluded income or exclusions realized income that is exempted from income taxation.

Ex-dividend date the relevant date for determining who receives a dividend from a stock. Anyone purchasing stock before this date will receive current dividends. Otherwise, the purchaser must wait until subsequent dividends are declared before receiving them.

Executor the person who takes responsibility for collecting the assets of the decedent, paying the decedent's debts, and distributing the remaining assets to the rightful heirs.

Exemption a fixed income tax deduction a taxpayer may claim for each person who qualifies as a dependent of the taxpayer. This includes the taxpayer (and spouse on a joint return) who does not qualify as a dependent of another.

Exemption equivalent the amount of cumulative taxable transfers a taxpayer can make without exceeding the unified credit.

Exercise date the date employees use their stock options to acquire employer stock at a discounted price.

Exercise price the price at which holders of stock options may purchase stock in the corporation issuing the option.

Explicit tax a tax directly imposed by a government.

F

Face value a specified final amount paid to the owner of a coupon bond on the date of maturity. The face value is also known as the maturity value.

Facts and circumstances test a test used to make subjective determination such as whether the amount of salary paid to an employee is reasonable. The test requires the taxpayer and the IRS to consider all the relevant facts and circumstances surrounding the situation in order to make a decision. The relevant facts and circumstance are situation specific.

Family limited partnership a partnership designed to save estate taxes by dividing a family business into various ownership interests representing control of operations and future income and appreciation of the assets.

Favorable book–tax difference a book-tax difference that requires a subtraction from book income in determining taxable income.

Federal/state adjustments amounts added to or subtracted from federal taxable income when firms compute taxable income for a particular state.

Federal short-term interest rate the quarterly interest rate used to determine the interest charged for tax underpayments (federal short-term rate plus 3 percent).

FICA taxes FICA (Federal Insurance Contribution Act) taxes are a term used to denote both the Social Security and Medicare taxes upon earned income. For self-employed taxpayers, the terms "FICA tax" and "self-employment tax" are synonymous.

Fiduciary a person or legal entity that takes possession of property for the benefit of beneficiaries.

Fiduciary duty a requirement that a fiduciary act in an objective and impartial manner and not favor one beneficiary over another.

Field examination the least common audit. The IRS conducts these audits at the taxpayer's place of business or the location where the taxpayer's books, records, and source documents are maintained. Field examinations are generally the broadest in scope and most complex of the three audit types. They can last many months to multiple years and generally are limited to business returns and the most complex individual returns.

FIFO *see* first-in, first-out (FIFO) method.

Filing status filing status places taxpayers into one of five categories (married filing jointly, married filing separately, qualifying widow or widower, head of household, and single) by marital status and family situation as of the end of the year. Filing status determines whether a taxpayer must file a tax return, appropriate tax rate schedules, standard deduction amounts, and several deduction and credit limitation thresholds.

Final regulations regulations that have been issued in final form, and thus, until revoked, they represent the Treasury's interpretation of the Code.

Financial reporting income *see* book or financial reporting income.

First-in, first-out (FIFO) method an accounting method that values the cost of assets sold under the assumption that the assets are sold in the order purchased (i.e., first purchased, first sold).

Fiscal year a year that ends on the last day of a month other than December.

Fixed and determinable, annual or periodic income U.S. source passive income earned by a nonresident.

Flat tax a tax in which a single tax rate is applied throughout the tax base.

Flexible spending account a plan that allows employees to contribute before-tax dollars that may be used for unreimbursed medical expenses or dependent care.

Flipping a term used to describe the real estate investment practice of acquiring a home, repairing or remodeling the home, and then immediately, or soon thereafter, selling it (presumably at a profit).

Floor limitation a minimum amount that an expenditure (or credit or other adjustment to taxable income) must meet before any amount is allowed.

Flow-through entities legal entities like partnerships, limited liability companies, and S corporations that do not pay income tax. Income and losses from flow-through entities are allocated to their owners.

***For* AGI deductions** deductions that are subtracted from gross income to determine AGI.

For the convenience of the employer benefits   nontaxable benefits employers provide to employees and employee spouses or dependents in the form of meals or lodging if provided on the employer's premises and provided for a purpose that is helpful or convenient for the employer.

Foreign joint venture   a 50 percent or less owned foreign entity.

Foreign personal holding company income   a category of foreign source passive income that includes interest, dividends, rents, royalties, and gains from sale of assets.

Foreign subsidiary   a more than 50 percent owned foreign corporation.

Foreign tax credit   a credit for income taxes paid to a foreign jurisdiction.

Foreign tax credit limitation   the limit put on the use of creditable foreign taxes for the current year.

Form 1065   the form partnerships file annually with the IRS to report partnership ordinary income (loss) and separately stated items for the year.

Form 1120S   the form S corporations file annually with the IRS to report S corporation ordinary income (loss) and separately stated items for the year.

Form 2553   the form filed to elect S corporation status.

Form 7004   the form C corporations, partnerships, and S corporations file to receive an automatic extension to file their annual tax return.

Form W-2   used to report wages paid to employees and the taxes withheld from them. The form is also used to report FICA taxes to the Social Security Administration.

Form W-4   a form used by a taxpayer to supply her employer with the information necessary to determine the amount of tax to withhold from each paycheck.

Forward triangular merger   an acquisition in which the acquired (target) corporation merges into an acquisition subsidiary of the acquiring corporation, after which the acquired corporation becomes part of the acquisition subsidiary of the acquiring corporation.

Fringe benefits   noncash benefit provided to an employee as a form of compensation. As a general rule, fringe benefits are taxable. However, certain fringe benefits are excluded from gross income.

***From* AGI deductions**   deductions subtracted from AGI to calculate taxable income.

FTC basket   a category of income that requires a separate FTC limitation computation.

Full-inclusion method   the method for accounting for advance payments for goods that requires that businesses immediately recognize advance payments as taxable income.

Full-month convention   a convention that allows owners of intangibles to deduct an entire month's amortization in the month of purchase and month of disposition.

Functional currency   the currency of the primary economic environment in which an entity operates (i.e., the currency of the jurisdiction in which an entity primarily generates and expends cash).

Future interest   the right to receive property in the future.

G

GAAP capital accounts   partners' capital accounts maintained using generally accepted accounting principals.

General category income   foreign source income that is not considered passive category income for foreign tax credit purposes (generally income from an active trade or business).

General partnership   a partnership with partners who all have unlimited liability with respect to the liabilities of the entity.

Generation-skipping tax (GST)   supplemental transfer tax designed to prevent the avoidance of estate and gift taxes through transfers that skip a generation of recipients.

Gift   a transfer of property where no, or inadequate, consideration is paid for the property.

Gift tax   the tax paid on a gift.

Golsen rule   the rule that states that the U.S. Tax Court will abide by the circuit court's rulings that has appellate jurisdiction for a case.

Goodwill   the value of an acquired business in excess of the fair market value of identifiable assets.

Graded vesting   a qualified plan rule that requires an increasing percentage of plan benefits to vest with each additional year of employment.

Graduated taxes   taxes in which the tax base is divided into a series of monetary amounts, or brackets, where each successive bracket is taxed at a different (gradually higher or gradually lower) percentage rate.

Grant date (stock options)   the date on which employees receive stock options to acquire employer stock at a specified price.

Grantor   person creating a trust.

Gross estate   property owned by the decedent at death and certain property transfers taking effect at death.

Gross income   realized income reduced for any excluded or deferred income.

Gross receipts (for purposes of net passive investment income tax calculation)   the total amount of revenues (including passive investment income) received or accrued under the corporation's accounting method, not reduced by returns, allowances, cost of goods sold, or deductions. Gross receipts include net capital gains from the sales or exchanges of capital assets and gains from the sales or exchanges of stock or securities (losses do not offset gains).

Group-term life insurance   term life insurance provided by an employer to a group of employees.

Guaranteed payments   payments made to partners or LLC members that are guaranteed because they are not contingent on partnership profits or losses. They are economically similar to shareholder salary payments.

H

Half-year convention   a depreciation convention that allows owners of tangible personal property to take one-half of a year's worth of depreciation in the year of purchase and in the year of disposition regardless of when the asset was actually placed in service or sold.

Head of household   one of five primary filing statuses. A taxpayer may file as head of household if s/he is unmarried as of the end of the year *and* pays more than half of the cost to maintain a household for a qualifying person who lives with the taxpayer for more than half of the year; or, s/he pays more than half the costs to maintain a household for a parent who qualifies as the taxpayer's dependent.

Health and accident insurance   a fringe benefit provided to employees that provides benefits upon sickness, injury, or death.

Heirs   persons who inherit property from the deceased.

Hobby   a revenue-generating activity that is motivated by personal motives rather than profit objectives.

Home-equity indebtedness   debt (except for acquisition indebtedness) secured by the taxpayer's qualified residence to the extent it does not exceed the fair market value of the residence over the acquisition indebtedness. Interest paid on up to $100,000 of home-equity indebtedness is allowed as an itemized deduction.

Home office deduction deductions relating to the use of an office in the home. A taxpayer must meet strict requirements to qualify for the deduction.

Horizontal equity one of the dimensions of equity. Horizontal equity is achieved if taxpayers in similar situations pay the same tax.

Hot assets unrealized receivables or inventory items defined in §751(a) that give rise to ordinary gains and losses. The exact definition of hot assets depends on whether it is in reference to dispositions of a partnership interest or distributions.

Hybrid entity an entity for which an election is available to choose the entity's tax status for U.S. tax purposes.

I

Impermissible accounting method an accounting method prohibited by tax laws.

Implicit tax indirect taxes that result from a tax advantage the government grants to certain transactions to satisfy social, economic, or other objectives. They are defined as the reduced before-tax return that a tax-favored asset produces because of its tax-advantaged status.

Imputed income income from an economic benefit the taxpayer receives indirectly rather than directly. The amount of the income is based on comparable alternatives.

Inbound transaction a transaction conducted by a foreign person that is subject to U.S. taxation.

Incentive stock option a type of stock option that allows employees to defer the bargain element for regular tax purposes until the stock acquired from option exercises is sold. The bargain element is taxed at capital gains rates provided the stock is retained long enough to satisfy certain holding period requirements. Employers cannot deduct the bargain element as compensation expense.

Income effect one of the two basic responses that a taxpayer may have when taxes increase. The income effect predicts that when taxpayers are taxed more (e.g., tax rate increases from 25 to 28 percent), they will work harder to generate the same after-tax dollars.

Income tax a tax in which the tax base is income. Income taxes are imposed by the federal government and by most states.

Independent contractor a person who provides services to another entity, usually under terms specified in a contract. The independent contractor has more control over how and when to do the work than does an employee.

Indirect conversion the receipt of money or other property as a replacement for property that was destroyed or damaged in an involuntary conversion.

Individual retirement account (IRA) a tax-advantaged account in which individuals who have earned income can save for retirement.

Information matching program a program that compares the taxpayer's tax return to information submitted to the IRS from other taxpayers (e.g., banks, employers, mutual funds, brokerage companies, mortgage companies). Information matched includes items such as wages (e.g., Form W-2 submitted by employers), interest income (e.g., Form 1099-INT submitted by banks), dividend income (e.g., Form 1099-DIV submitted by brokerage companies), and so forth.

Inheritance a transfer of property when the owner is deceased (the transfer is made by the decedent's estate).

Initial public offering the first sale of stock by a company to the public.

Inside basis the tax basis of an entity's assets and liabilities.

Installment sale a sale for which the taxpayer receives payment in more than one period.

Institutional shareholders entities, such as investment companies, mutual funds, brokerages, insurance companies, pension funds, investment banks, and endowment funds, with large amounts to invest in corporate stock entities.

Intangible assets assets that do not have physical characteristics. Examples include goodwill, covenants not to compete, organizational expenditures, and research and experimentation expenses.

Internal Revenue Code of 1986 the codified tax laws of the United States. Although the Code is frequently revised, there have only been three different codes since the Code was created in 1939 (i.e., the IRC of 1939, IRC of 1954, and IRC of 1986).

Interpretative regulations the most common regulation; they represent the Treasury's interpretation of the Code and are issued under the Treasury's general authority to interpret the Code.

Interstate commerce business conducted between parties in two or more states.

Inter vivos transfers gifts made by a donor during his or her lifetime.

Inventory items (for sale of partnership interest purposes) classic inventory defined as property held for sale to customers in the ordinary course of business, but also assets that are not capital assets or §1231 assets, which would produce ordinary income if sold by the entity. There are actually two definitions of inventory items in §751. §751(a) inventory items are defined in §751(d) to include all inventory items. The §751(b) definition includes only substantially appreciated inventory.

Investment activities a profit-seeking activity that is intermittent or occasional in frequency including the production or collection of income or the management, conservation, or maintenance of property held for the production of income.

Investment expenses expenses such as safe deposit rental fees, attorney fees, and accounting fees that are necessary to produce portfolio income. Investment expenses are allowed for individuals as miscellaneous itemized deductions subject to the 2 percent of AGI floor limitation.

Investment income income received from portfolio type investments. Portfolio income includes capital gains and losses, interest, dividend, annuity, and royalty income not derived in the ordinary course of a trade or business. When computing the deductibility of investment interest expense, however, capital gains and dividends subject to the preferential tax rate are not treated as investment income unless the taxpayer elects to have this income taxed at ordinary tax rates.

Investment interest expense interest paid on borrowings or loans that are used to fund portfolio investments. Individuals are allowed an itemized deduction for qualified investment interest paid during the year.

Involuntary conversion a direct or indirect conversion of property through natural disaster, government condemnation, or accident that allows a taxpayer to defer realized gain if certain requirements are met.

IRS allocation method allocates expenses associated with rental use of the home between rental use and personal use. The percentage of total expenses allocated to rental use is the ratio of the number of rental use days for the property to the total days the property was used during the year.

Itemized deductions certain types of expenditures that Congress allows taxpayers to deduct as from AGI deductions.

J

Joint tenancy with the right of survivorship title to property that provides the co-owners with equal rights to it and that automatically transfers to the survivor(s) at the death of a co-owner.

K

Kiddie tax a tax imposed at the parent's marginal rate on a child's unearned income.

L

Last will and testament the document that directs the transfer of ownership of the decedent's assets to the heirs.

Late filing penalty a penalty assessed if a taxpayer does not file a tax return by the required date (the original due date plus extension).

Least aggregate deferral an approach to determine a partnership's required year-end if a majority of the partners don't have the same year-end and if the principal partners don't have the same year-end. As the name implies, this approach minimizes the combined tax deferral of the partners.

Legislative grace the concept that taxpayers receive certain tax benefits only because Congress writes laws that allow taxpayers to receive the tax benefits.

Legislative regulations the rarest type of regulation, issued when Congress specifically directs the Treasury Department to create regulations to address an issue in an area of law. In these instances, the Treasury is actually writing the law instead of interpreting the Code. Because legislative regulations actually represent tax law instead of an interpretation of tax law, legislative regulations have more authoritative weight than interpretative and procedural regulations.

Life estate the right to possess property and/or collect income from property for the duration of someone's life.

Life insurance trust a trust funded with an irrevocable transfer of a life insurance policy and that gives the trustee the power to re-designate beneficiaries.

LIFO last-in, first-out method; an accounting method that values the cost of assets sold under the assumption that assets are sold in the reverse order in which they are purchased (i.e., last purchased, first sold).

LIFO recapture amount the excess of a C corporation's inventory basis under the FIFO method in excess of the inventory basis under the LIFO method in its final tax year as a C corporation before it becomes an S corporation.

LIFO recapture tax a tax levied on a C corporation that elects to be taxed as an S corporation when it is using the LIFO method for accounting for inventories.

Like-kind exchange a nontaxable (or partially taxable) trade or exchange of assets that are similar or related in use.

Limited liability company (LLC) a type of flow-through entity for federal income tax purposes. By state law, the owners of the LLC have limited liability with respect to the entity's debts or liabilities. Limited liability companies are taxed as partnerships for federal income tax purposes.

Limited partnership a partnership with at least one general partner with unlimited liability for the entity's debts and at least one limited partner with liability limited to the limited partner's investment in the partnership.

Liquidating distributions a distribution that terminates an owner's interest in the entity.

Liquidation value the amount a partner would receive if the partnership were to sell all its assets, pay its debts, and distribute its remaining assets to the partners in exchange for their partnership interests.

Listed property business assets that are often used for personal purposes. Depreciation on listed property is limited to the business use portion of the asset.

Local tax taxes imposed by local governments (cities, counties, school districts, etc.).

Long-term capital gain property property that would generate long-term capital gain if it were sold. This includes capital assets held for more than a year.

Long-term capital gains or losses gains or losses from the sale of capital assets held for more than 12 months.

Luxury automobile an automobile on which the amount of annual depreciation expense is limited because the cost of the automobile exceeds a certain threshold. The definition excludes vehicles with gross vehicle weight exceeding 6,000 pounds.

M

M adjustments *see* Schedule M adjustments.

Majority interest taxable year the common tax year of a group of partners who jointly hold greater than 50 percent of the profits and capital interests in the partnership.

Marginal tax rate the tax rate that applies to the *next additional increment* of a taxpayer's taxable income (or to deductions). Specifically,

$$\text{Marginal tax rate} = \frac{\Delta\,Tax}{\Delta\,Taxable\ income}$$
$$= \frac{(New\ total\ tax - Old\ total\ tax)}{(New\ taxable\ income - Old\ taxable\ income)}$$

where "old" refers to the current tax and "new" refers to the revised tax after incorporating the additional income (or deductions) in question.

Marital deduction the deduction for transfers of qualified property to a spouse.

Market discount the difference between the amount paid for a bond in a market purchase rather than at original issuance when the amount paid is less than the maturity value of the bond.

Market premium the difference between the amount paid for a bond in a market purchase rather than at original issuance when the amount paid is greater than the maturity value of the bond.

Marriage benefit the tax savings married couples receive by filing a joint return relative to the tax they would have paid had they each filed as single taxpayers. This typically occurs when one spouse is either not working or earns significantly less than the other spouse.

Marriage penalty the extra tax cost a married couple pays by filing a joint return relative to what they would have paid had they each filed as single taxpayers. This typically occurs when both spouses earn approximately the same amount of income.

Married filing jointly one of five primary filing statuses. A taxpayer may file jointly if s/he is legally married as of the end of the year (or one spouse died during the year and the surviving spouse did not remarry) and both spouses agree to jointly file. Married couples filing joint returns combine their income and deductions and share joint and several liability for the resulting tax.

Married filing separately one of five primary filing statuses. When married couples file separately, each spouse reports the income he or she received during the year and the deductions he or she paid on a tax return separate from the other spouse.

Maturity the amount of time to the expiration date, or maturity date, of a debt instrument. The maturity of a debt instrument is generally the life of the instrument at which a payment of the face value is due or the instrument terminates.

Maturity value the amount paid to a bondholder when the bond matures and the bondholder redeems the bond for cash.

Medicare tax   the Medical Health Insurance (MHI) tax. This tax helps pay medical costs for qualifying individuals. The Medicare tax rate for employees is 1.45 percent on salary or wages up to $200,000 ($125,000 for married filing separate; $250,000 of combined salary or wages for married filing joint) and is 2.35 percent on salary or wages in excess of $200,000 ($125,000 for married filing separate; $250,000 of combined salary or wages for married filing joint). For employers, the Medicare tax rate is 1.45 percent of employee salary or wages, regardless of the amount of salary or wages. Self-employed taxpayers pay both the employee and employer Medicare tax.

Merger   the acquisition by one (acquiring) corporation of the assets and liabilities of another (target) corporation. No new entity is created in the transaction.

Mid-month convention   a convention that allows owners of real property to take one-half of a month's depreciation during the month when the property was placed in service and in the month it was disposed of.

Mid-quarter convention   a depreciation convention for tangible personal property that allows for one-half of a quarter's worth of depreciation in the quarter of purchase and in the quarter of disposition. This convention must be used when more than 40 percent of tangible personal property is placed into service in the fourth quarter of the tax year.

Minimum tax credit   credit available in certain situations for the alternative minimum tax paid. The credit can be used only when the regular tax exceeds the tentative minimum tax.

Miscellaneous itemized deductions   deductions representing the sum of certain itemized deductions, such as unreimbursed employee business expenses, investment expenses, and tax preparation fees, that are subject to a special floor limitation.

Mixed-motive expenditures   activities that involve a mixture of business and personal objectives.

Modified Accelerated Cost Recovery System (MACRS)   the current tax depreciation system for tangible personal and real property. Depreciation under MACRS is calculated by finding the depreciation method, the recovery period, and the applicable convention.

Municipal bond   the common name for state and local government debt.

Mutual fund   a diversified portfolio of securities owned and managed by a regulated investment company.

N

Negative basis adjustment   (for special basis adjustment purposes) the sum of the recognized loss and the amount of the basis increase made by an owner receiving the distribution.

Net capital gain   the net gain resulting when taxpayers combine net long-term capital gains with net short-term capital losses.

Net capital loss carryback   the amount of a corporation's net capital loss from one year that it uses to offset net capital gains in any of the three preceding tax years.

Net capital loss carryover   the amount of a corporation's or an individual's net capital loss from one year that it may use to offset net capital gains in future years.

Net earnings from self-employment   the amount of earnings subject to self-employment income taxes. The amount is 92.35 percent of the net income from a taxpayer's Schedule C (for self-employed taxpayers).

Net investment income   (for determining deductibility of investment interest expense) gross investment income reduced by deductible investment expenses.

Net investment income tax   a 3.8 percent tax on the lesser of (a) net investment income or (b) the excess of modified adjusted gross income over $250,000 for married-joint filers and surviving spouses, $125,000 for married-separate filers, and $200,000 for other taxpayers.

Net long-term capital gain   the net gain resulting when taxpayers combine long-term capital gains and losses for the year.

Net long-term capital loss   the net loss resulting when taxpayers combine long-term capital gains and losses for the year.

Net operating loss (NOL)   the excess of allowable deductions over gross income.

Net operating loss carryback   the amount of a current-year net operating loss that is carried back to offset income in a prior year.

Net operating loss carryover   the amount of a current-year net operating loss that is carried forward for up to 20 years to offset taxable income in those years.

Net passive investment income   passive investment income less any expenses connected with producing it.

Net short-term capital gain   the net gain resulting when taxpayers combine short-term capital gains and losses for the year.

Net short-term capital loss   the net loss resulting when taxpayers combine short-term capital gains and losses for the year.

Net unearned income   unearned income in excess of a specified threshold amount of a child under the age of 19 or under the age of 24 if a full-time student.

Net unrealized built-in gain   the net gain (if any) an S corporation that was formerly a C corporation would recognize if it sold each asset at its fair market value. It is measured on the first day of the corporation's first year as an S corporation.

Nexus   the connection between a business and a tax jurisdiction sufficient to subject the business to the tax jurisdiction's tax system. Also, the connection that is required to exist between a jurisdiction and a potential taxpayer such that the jurisdiction asserts the right to impose a tax.

No-additional-cost services   a nontaxable fringe benefit that provides employer services to employees with little cost to the employer (e.g., airline tickets or phone service).

Nonacquiescence   issued after the IRS loses a trial-level or circuit court case when the IRS has decided to continue to litigate this issue.

Nonbusiness income   all income except for business income—generally investment income and rental income.

Nondeductible terminable interests   transfers of property interests to a spouse that do not qualify for a marital deduction, because the interest of the spouse terminates when some event occurs or after a specified amount of time and the property is then transferred to another person.

Nondomiciliary business   a business operating in a state other than its commercial domicile.

Nonperformance based compensation   compensation paid to an employee that does not depend on the employee's performance or the corporation's performance or success. It usually is straight salary.

Nonqualified deferred compensation   compensation provided for under a nonqualified plan allowing employees to defer compensation to a future period.

Nonqualified stock option   a type of stock option requiring employees to treat the bargain element from options exercised as ordinary income in the tax year options are exercised. Correspondingly, employers may deduct the bargain element as compensation expense in the tax year options are exercised.

Nonrecaptured net §1231 losses   a net §1231 loss that is deducted as an ordinary loss in one year and has not caused subsequent §1231 gain to be taxed as ordinary income.

Nonrecognition provisions   tax laws that allow taxpayers to permanently exclude income from taxation or to defer recognizing realized income until a subsequent period.

Nonrecognition transaction   a transaction where at least a portion of the realized gain or loss is not currently recognized.

Nonrecourse debt   debt for which no partner bears any economic risk of loss. Mortgages on real property are a common form of nonrecourse debt.

Nonrefundable credits   tax credits that reduce a taxpayer's gross tax liability but are limited to the amount of gross tax liability. Any credit not used in the current year is lost.

Nonresident alien   an individual who does not meet the criteria to be treated as a resident for U.S. tax purposes.

Nonservice partner   a partner who receives a partnership interest in exchange for property rather than services.

Nontaxable fringe benefit   an employer-provided benefit that may be excluded from an employee's income.

Not definitely related deductions   deductions that are not associated with a specific item or items of gross income in computing the foreign tax credit limitation.

O

Office examination   the second most common audit. As the name suggests, the IRS conducts these audits at the local IRS office. These audits are typically broader in scope and more complex than correspondence examinations. Small businesses, taxpayers operating sole proprietorships, and middle- to high-income individual taxpayers are more likely, if audited, to have office examinations.

Operating distributions   payments from an entity to its owners that represent a distribution of entity profits. Distributions generally fall into the category of operating distributions when the owners continue their interests in the entity after the distribution.

Operating income   the annual income from a trade or business or rental activity.

Operating loss   the annual loss from a trade or business or rental activity.

Option exercise   the use of a stock option to acquire employer stock at a specified price.

Ordinary asset   an asset created or used in a taxpayer's trade or business (e.g., accounts receivable or inventory) that generates ordinary income (or loss) on disposition.

Ordinary business income (loss)   a partnership's or S corporation's remaining income or loss after separately stated items are removed. It is also referred to as nonseparately stated income (loss).

Ordinary income property   property that if sold would generate income taxed at ordinary rates.

Ordinary and necessary   an expense that is normal or appropriate and that is helpful or conducive to the business activity.

Organization costs   costs associated with legally forming a partnership (such as attorneys' and accountants' fees).

Organizational expenditures   expenses that are (1) connected directly to the creation of a corporation or partnership, (2) chargeable to a capital account, and (3) generally amortized over 180 months (limited immediate expensing may be available).

Original issue discount   a type of bond issued for less than the maturity or face value of the bond.

Outbound transaction   a transaction conducted outside the United States by a U.S. person that is subject to U.S. taxation.

Outside basis   an investor's tax basis in the stock of a corporation or the interest in a partnership or LLC.

P

PAL   an acronym for "passive activity loss." Losses allocated to partners who are not material participants in the partnership are passive activity losses.

Parent-subsidiary controlled group   a form of controlled group consisting of one corporation that owns at least 80 percent of the voting power or stock value of another corporation on the last day of the year.

Partial liquidation   a distribution made by a corporation to shareholders that results from a contraction of the corporation's activities.

Partnership agreement   an agreement among the partners in a partnership stipulating the partners' rights and responsibilities in the partnership.

Partnership interest   an intangible asset reflecting the economic rights a partner has with respect to a partnership including the right to receive assets in liquidation of the partnership called a capital interest and the right to be allocated profits and losses called a profits interest.

Passive activity   an activity in which the taxpayer does not materially participate.

Passive activity income or loss   income or loss from an activity in which the taxpayer does not materially participate.

Passive activity loss rules   tax rules designed to limit taxpayers' ability to deduct losses from activities in which they don't materially participate against income from other sources.

Passive category income   foreign source personal holding company income such as interest, dividends, rents, royalties, annuities, and gains from sale of certain assets that is combined in computing the FTC limitation.

Passive investment income (PII)   royalties, rents, dividends, interest (including tax exempt interest), annuities, and gains from the sales or exchanges of stock or securities.

Passive investments   direct or indirect investments (other than through a C corporation) in a trade or business or rental activity in which the taxpayer does not materially participate.

Payment liability   liabilities of accrual method businesses for which economic performance occurs when the business actually *pays* the liability for, among others: worker's compensation; tort; breach of contract or violation of law; rebates and refunds; awards, prizes, and jackpots; insurance, warranties, and service contracts provided *to* the business; and taxes.

Percentage depletion   a method of recovering the cost of a natural resource that allows a taxpayer to recover or expense an amount based on a statutorily determined percentage.

Permanent book–tax differences   items of income or deductions for either book purposes or for tax purposes during the year but not both. Permanent differences do not reverse over time, so over the long run, the total amount of income or deduction for the item is different for book and tax purposes.

Permanent establishment   generally, a fixed place of business through which an enterprise carries out its business. Examples include a place of management, a branch, an office, and a factory.

Permissible accounting method   accounting method allowed under the tax law. Permissible accounting methods are adopted the first time a taxpayer uses the method on a tax return.

Person   an individual, trust, estate, partnership, association, company, or corporation.

Personal exemption a fixed deduction allowed for an individual taxpayer, and spouse if filing a joint tax return.

Personal expenses expenses incurred for personal motives. Personal expenses are not deductible for tax purposes.

Personal holding companies closely held corporations generating primarily investment income.

Personal holding company tax penalty tax on the undistributed income of a personal holding company.

Personal property all tangible property other than real property.

Personal property tax a tax on the fair market value of all types of tangible and intangible property, except real property.

Phase-outs limitations that gradually eliminate deductions, credits, or other adjustments to taxable income typically done ratably over a phase-out range (based on AGI or related income measure).

Point one percent of the principal amount of a loan. A home buyer might pay points to compensate the lender for services or for a lower interest rate.

Portfolio investments investments producing dividends, interest, royalties, annuities, or capital gains.

Positive basis adjustment (for special basis adjustment purposes) the sum of the gain recognized by the owners receiving distributed property and the amount of any required basis reduction.

Post-termination transition period (PTTP) the period that begins on the day after the last day of a corporation's last taxable year as an S corporation and generally ends on the later of (a) one year after the last S corporation day, or (b) the due date for filing the return for the last year as an S corporation (including extensions).

Preferential tax rate tax rates lower than the tax rate applied to ordinary income.

Preferentially taxed income income taxed at a preferential rate such as long-term capital gains and qualified dividends.

Present interest right to presently enjoy property or receive income from the property.

Present value the concept that $1 today is worth more than $1 in the future. For example, assuming an investor can earn a 5 percent after-tax return, $1 invested today should be worth $1.05 in one year. Hence, $1 today is equivalent to $1.05 in one year.

Primary authority official sources of the tax law generated by the legislative branch (i.e., statutory authority issued by Congress), judicial branch (i.e., rulings by the U.S. District Court, U.S. Tax Court, U.S. Court of Federal Claims, U.S. Circuit Court of Appeals, or U.S. Supreme Court), or executive/administrative branch (i.e., Treasury or IRS pronouncements).

Principal partner a partner having a 5 percent interest or more in partnership capital or profits.

Principal residence the main place of residence for a taxpayer during the taxable year.

Private activity bond a bond issued by a municipality but proceeds of which are used to fund privately owned activity.

Private letter rulings IRS pronouncements issued in response to a taxpayer request for a ruling on specific issues for the taxpayer. They are common for proposed transactions with potentially large tax implications. For the requesting taxpayer, a private letter ruling has very high authority. For all other taxpayers, private letter rulings have little authoritative weight.

Private nonoperating foundations privately sponsored foundations that disburse funds to other charities.

Private operating foundations privately sponsored foundations that actually fund and conduct charitable activities.

Probate the process in the probate court of gathering property possessed by or titled in the name of a decedent at the time of death, paying the debts of the decedent and transferring the ownership of any remaining property to the decedent's heirs.

Probate estate property possessed by or titled in the name of a decedent at the time of death.

Procedural regulations regulations that explain Treasury Department procedures as they relate to administering the Code.

Production of income a for-profit activity that doesn't rise to the level of a trade or business.

Profits interest an interest in a partnership giving a partner the right to share in future profits but not the right to share in the current value of a partnership's assets. Profits interests are generally not taxable in the year they are received.

Progressive tax rate structure a tax rate structure that imposes an increasing marginal tax rate as the tax base increases. As the tax base increases, both the marginal tax rate and the taxes paid increase.

Proportional tax rate structure also known as a flat tax, this tax rate structure imposes a constant tax rate throughout the tax base. As the tax base increases, the taxes paid increase proportionally.

Proposed regulations regulations issued in proposed form; they do not carry the same authoritative weight as temporary or final regulations. All regulations are issued in proposed form first to allow public comment on them.

Public Law 86-272 federal law passed by Congress that provides additional protection for sellers of tangible personal property against income tax nexus.

Publicly state traded corporations corporations whose stock is publicly traded on a stock exchange.

Q

Qualified debt (for mortgage interest expense deduction purposes) the amount of debt on which qualified residence interest is paid. This includes debt up to $1,000,000 of acquisition indebtedness and up to $100,000 of home-equity indebtedness.

Qualified dividends paid by domestic or certain qualified foreign corporations that are eligible for lower capital gains rates.

Qualified educational expenses consist of tuition and related costs for enrolling the taxpayer, spouse, or a dependent at a post-secondary institution of higher education.

Qualified educational loans loans whose proceeds are used to pay qualified education expenses.

Qualified employee discount a nontaxable fringe benefit that provides employer goods at a discount (but not below the employer's cost) and services to employees at up to a 20 percent discount.

Qualified moving expense reimbursement a nontaxable fringe benefit that allows employers to pay moving-related expenses on behalf of employees.

Qualified nonrecourse financing nonrecourse debt secured by real property from a commercial lender unrelated to the borrower.

Qualified production activities income (QPAI) the *net* income from selling or leasing property that was manufactured in the United States.

Qualified replacement property property acquired to replace property damaged or destroyed in an involuntary conversion. It must be of a similar or related use to the original property even if the replacement property is real property (rental real estate for rental real estate).

Qualified residence the taxpayer's principal residence and one other residence.

Qualified residence interest   interest paid on acquisition indebtedness and on home-equity indebtedness that is secured by a qualified residence.

Qualified retirement accounts   plans meeting certain requirements that allow compensation placed in the account to be tax deferred until the taxpayer withdraws money from the account.

Qualified retirement plans   employer-sponsored retirement plans that meet government-imposed funding and antidiscrimination requirements.

Qualified small business stock   stock received at original issue from a corporation with a gross tax basis in its assets both before and after the issuance of no more than $50,000,000 and with 80 percent of the value of its assets used in the active conduct of certain qualified trades or businesses.

Qualified terminable interest property (QTIP)   an exception to the general prohibition against claiming a marital deduction for a transfer of a terminable interest where the surviving spouse is entitled to all of the income from the property payable at least annually and no person has the power to appoint any part of the property to anyone other than the surviving spouse until the death of the surviving spouse.

Qualified transportation fringe benefit   a nontaxable fringe benefit provided by employers in the form of mass transit passes, parking, or vanpool benefits.

Qualifying child   an individual who qualifies as a dependent of a taxpayer by meeting a relationship, age, residence, and support test with respect to the taxpayer.

Qualifying relative   an individual who is not a qualifying child of another taxpayer and who meets a relationship, support, and gross income test may qualify to be a dependent of another taxpayer.

Qualifying widow or widower   one of five primary filing statuses. Applies for up to two years after the year in which the taxpayer's spouse dies (the taxpayer files married filing jointly in the year of the spouse's death) as long as the taxpayer remains unmarried and maintains a household for a dependent child.

Question of fact   a research question that hinges upon the facts and circumstances of the taxpayer's transaction.

Question of law   a research question that hinges upon the interpretation of the law, such as interpreting a particular phrase in a code section.

R

Real property   land and structures permanently attached to land.

Real property tax   a tax on the fair market value of land and structures permanently attached to land.

Realization   gain or loss that results from an exchange of property rights in a transaction.

Realization principle   the proposition that income only exists when there is a transaction with another party resulting in a measurable change in property rights.

Realized gain or loss   the difference between the amount realized and the adjusted basis of an asset sold or otherwise disposed of.

Realized income   income generated in a transaction with a second party in which there is a measurable change in property rights between parties.

Reasonable in amount   an expenditure is reasonable when the amount paid is not extravagant nor exorbitant.

Recapture   the recharacterization of income from capital gain to ordinary income.

Recognition   gain or loss included in the computation of taxable income.

Recognized gain or loss   the gain or loss included in gross income on a taxpayer's tax return. This is usually the realized gain or loss unless a nonrecognition provision applies.

Recourse debt   debt held by a partnership for which at least one partner has economic risk of loss.

Recovery period   a length of time prescribed by statute in which business property is depreciated or amortized.

Recurring item   an election under economic performance to currently deduct an accrued liability if the liability is expected to persist in the future and is either not material or a current deduction better matches revenue.

Refinance   when a taxpayer pays off a current loan with the proceeds of a second loan.

Refundable credits   credits that are not limited to the amount of the gross tax liability. If the credit exceeds the gross tax liability, the taxpayer receives a refund for the excess credit.

Regressive tax rate structure   a tax rate structure that imposes a decreasing marginal tax rate as the tax base increases. As the tax base increases, the taxes paid increase, but the marginal tax rate decreases.

Regulations   the Treasury Department's official interpretation of the Internal Revenue Code. Regulations are the highest authority issued by the IRS.

Related-party transaction   financial activities among family members, among owners and their businesses, or among businesses owned by the same owners.

Remainder   the right to ownership of a property that transfers to a new owner, the remainderman, following a temporary interest.

Remainderman   the person entitled to a remainder interest.

Reorganization   a tax-deferred transaction (acquisition, disposition, recapitalization, or change of name or place of incorporation) that meets one of the seven statutory definitions found in §368(a)(1).

Requisite service period   the period or periods during which an employee is required to provide service in exchange for an award under a share-based payment arrangement (ASC 718, Glossary).

Research and experimentation costs   expenses for research including costs of research laboratories (salaries, materials, and other related expenses). Taxpayers can elect to amortize research and development costs over not less than 60 months from the time benefits are first derived from the research.

Residence-based jurisdiction   taxation of income based on the taxpayer's residence.

Resident alien   an individual who is not a U.S. citizen but is treated as a resident for U.S. tax purposes.

Restricted stock   stock employees receive as compensation that may only be sold after the passage of time or after certain performance targets are achieved. Because employees are not entitled to immediately sell the restricted stock they receive, the value of the stock is generally not taxable to employees or deductible by employers until the selling restrictions lapse.

Return of capital   the portion of proceeds from a sale (or distribution) representing a return of the original cost of the underlying property.

Revenue procedures   second in administrative authoritative weight after regulations. Revenue procedures are much more detailed than regulations and explain in greater detail IRS practice and procedures in administering the tax law. Revenue procedures have the same authoritative weight as revenue rulings.

Revenue rulings   second in administrative authoritative weight after regulations. Revenue rulings address the specific application of the Code and regulations to a specific factual situation. Revenue rulings have the same authoritative weight as revenue procedures.

Reverse hybrid entity   a "check-the-box" entity owned by multiple persons for which corporation status is elected.

Reverse triangular merger an acquisition in which an acquisition subsidiary of the acquiring corporation merges into the acquired (target) corporation, after which the acquired corporation becomes a subsidiary of the acquiring corporation.

Reversion terms by which ownership of property returns to the original owner following a temporary interest.

Rollover a transfer of funds from a qualified retirement plan to another qualified retirement plan, from a qualified retirement plan to a Roth or traditional IRA, or from a traditional IRA to a Roth IRA.

Roth 401(k) a type of defined contribution plan that allows employees to contribute on an after-tax basis and receive distributions tax free.

Roth IRA an individually managed retirement plan permitting individuals to contribute on an after-tax basis and receive distributions tax free.

Royalties payments taxpayers receive for allowing others to use their tangible or intangible property.

S

S corporation a corporation under state law that has elected to be taxed under the rules provided in subchapter S of the Internal Revenue Code. Under subchapter S, an S corporation is taxed as a flow-through entity.

Safe-harbor provision provision of the tax law that reduces or eliminates a taxpayer's liability under the law if the taxpayer meets certain requirements.

Salary a fixed regular payment by an employer to an employee in exchange for the employee's services which is usually paid on a monthly basis, but typically expressed as an annual amount.

Sales tax a tax imposed on the retail sales of goods (plus certain services). Retailers are responsible for collecting and remitting the tax; typically sales tax is collected at the point of sale.

Same-day sale a phrase used to describe a situation where a taxpayer exercises stock options and then immediately sells the stock received through the option exercise.

Schedule C a schedule on which a taxpayer reports the income and deductions for a sole-proprietorship.

Schedule K a schedule filed with a partnership's annual tax return listing its ordinary income (loss) and its separately stated items.

Schedule M adjustments book–tax differences that corporations report on the Schedule M-1 or M-3 of Form 1120 as adjustments to book income to reconcile to taxable income.

Schedule M-1 a schedule on Form 1120 that reconciles book income to taxable income before special deductions. Book–tax differences are reported in a general way.

Schedule M-3 a schedule on Form 1120 that reconciles book income to taxable income for corporations and partnerships with total assets of $10 million or more. The schedule M-3 includes much more detail than the Schedule M-1, including identifying whether each book–tax difference is a temporary difference or a permanent book–tax difference.

Secondary authority unofficial tax authorities that interpret and explain the primary authorities, such as tax research services, tax articles, newsletters, and textbooks. Secondary authorities may be very helpful in understanding a tax issue, but they hold little weight in a tax dispute (hence, the term *unofficial* tax authorities).

Secured loan a loan for which property is used as collateral for the loan. If the loan goes into default, the lender is only allowed to take possession of the property securing the loan.

Security a financial instrument including an equity interest in business organizations and creditor interests such as savings accounts, notes, and bonds.

Self-employment taxes Social Security and Medicare taxes paid by the self-employed on a taxpayer's net earnings from self-employment. For self-employed taxpayers, the terms "self-employment tax" and "FICA tax" are synonymous.

SEP IRA a simplified employee pension that is administered through an individual retirement account. Available to self-employed taxpayers.

Separate tax return a state tax return methodology requiring that each related entity with nexus files a separate tax return.

Separately stated items income, expenses, gains, losses, credits, and other items that are excluded from a partnership's or S corporation's operating income (loss) and disclosed to partners in a partnership or shareholders of an S corporation separately because their tax effects may be different for each partner or shareholder.

Serial gift transfer tax strategy that uses the annual exclusion to convert a potentially large taxable transfer into a tax-exempt transfer by dividing it into multiple inter vivos gifts spread over several periods or donees.

Service partner partners who receive their partnership interest by contributing services rather than cash or property.

Settlement statement a statement that details the monies paid out and received by the buyer and seller in a real estate transaction.

Short-term capital gains or losses gains or losses from the sale of capital assets held for one year or less.

Simple trust a trust that must distribute all accounting income currently and cannot make charitable contributions.

Sin taxes taxes imposed on the purchase of goods (e.g., alcohol, tobacco products, etc.) that are considered socially less desirable.

Single one of five primary statuses available. A taxpayer files as single if s/he is unmarried as of the end of the year and does not qualify for any of the other filing statuses. A taxpayer is considered single if s/he is unmarried or legally separated from his or her spouse under a divorce or separate maintenance decree.

Single member LLC a limited liability company with only one member. Single member LLCs with individual owners are taxed as sole proprietorships and as disregarded entities otherwise.

Social Security tax the Old Age, Survivors, and Disability Insurance (OASDI) tax. The tax is intended to provide basic pension coverage for the retired and disabled. Employees pay Social Security tax at a rate of 6.2 percent on the wage base (employers also pay 6.2 percent). Self-employed taxpayers are subject to a Social Security tax at a rate of 12.4 percent on their net earnings from self-employment. The base on which Social Security taxes are paid is limited to an annually determined amount of wages and/or net earnings from self-employment.

Sole proprietorship a business entity that is not legally separate from the individual owner of the business. The income of a sole proprietorship is taxed and paid directly by the owner.

Solicitation selling activities or activities ancillary to selling that are protected under Public Law 86-272.

Source-based jurisdiction taxation of income based on where the income is earned.

Special allocations allocations of income, gain, expense, or loss, etc., that are allocated to the owners of an entity in a manner out of proportion with the owners' interests in the entity. Special allocations can be made by entities treated as partnerships for federal income tax purposes.

Special basis adjustment an optional (sometimes mandatory) election to adjust the entity asset bases as a result of an owner's disposition of an interest in the entity or of distributions from the entity to its owners.

Specific identification method an elective method for determining the cost of an asset sold. Under this method, the taxpayer specifically chooses the assets that are to be sold.

Split-gift election   election that allows spouses to treat all gifts made in a year as if each spouse made one-half of each gift.

Spot rate   the foreign currency exchange rate on a specific day.

Spousal IRA   an IRA account for the spouse with the lesser amount of earned income. Contributions in this account belong to this spouse no matter where the funds for the contribution came from.

Standard deduction   a fixed deduction offered in lieu of itemized deductions. The amount of the standard deduction depends on the taxpayer's filing status.

Stare decisis   a doctrine meaning that a court will rule consistently with (a) its previous rulings (i.e., unless, due to evolving interpretations of the tax law over time, it decides to overturn an earlier decision) and (b) the rulings of higher courts with appellate jurisdiction (i.e., the courts its cases are appealed to).

Start-up costs   expenses that would be classified as business expenses except that the expenses are incurred before the business begins. These costs are generally capitalized and amortized over 180 months, but limited immediate expensing may be available.

State tax   a tax imposed by one of the 50 U.S. states.

State tax base   the federal taxable income plus or minus required state adjustments

Statements on Standards for Tax Services (SSTS)   standards of practice for tax professionals issued by the AICPA. Currently, there are seven SSTS that describe the tax professional standards when recommending a tax return position, answering questions on a tax return, preparing a tax return using data supplied by a client, using estimates on a tax return, taking a tax return position inconsistent with a previous year's tax return, discovering a tax return error, and giving tax advice to taxpayers.

Static forecasting   the process of forecasting tax revenues based on the existing state of transactions while ignoring how taxpayers may alter their activities in response to a tax law change.

Statute of limitations   defines the period in which the taxpayer can file an amended tax return or the IRS can assess a tax deficiency for a specific tax year. For both amended tax returns filed by a taxpayer and proposed tax assessments by the IRS, the statute of limitations generally ends three years from the *later* of (1) the date the tax return was actually filed or (2) the tax return's original due date.

Step-transaction doctrine   judicial doctrine that allows the IRS to collapse a series of related transactions into one transaction to determine the tax consequences of the transaction.

Stock dividend   a dividend made by a corporation of its own stock.

Stock-for-stock acquisition   an exchange of solely voting stock by the acquiring corporation in exchange for stock of the target corporation, after which the acquiring corporation controls (owns 80 percent or more of) the target corporation. Often referred to as a "Type B reorganization."

Stock redemption   a property distribution made to shareholders in return for some or all of their stock in the distributing corporation that is not in partial or complete liquidation of the corporation.

Stock split   a stock redemption in which a corporation exchanges a ratio of shares of stock (e.g., 2 for 1) for each share held by the shareholder.

Strike price   *see* exercise price.

Structural tax rate   the tax rate computed by dividing a company's income tax provision adjusted for nonrecurring permanent differences by its pretax income from continuing operations.

Student loans   loans where the proceeds are used for qualified educational expenses, but do not include home-equity loans.

Subchapter K   the portion of the Internal Revenue Code dealing with partnerships tax law.

Subchapter S   the portion of the Internal Revenue Code containing tax rules for S corporations and their shareholders.

Subpart F income   income earned by a controlled foreign corporation that is not eligible for deferral from U.S. taxation.

Substance-over-form doctrine   judicial doctrine that allows the IRS to consider the transaction's substance regardless of its form and, where appropriate, reclassify the transaction according to its substance.

Substantial authority   the standard used to determine whether a tax practitioner may recommend and a taxpayer may take a tax return position without being subject to IRS penalty under IRC §6694 and IRC §6662, respectively. A good CPA evaluates whether supporting authority is substantial or not based upon the supporting and opposing authorities' weight and relevance. Substantial authority suggests that the probability that the taxpayer's position is sustained upon audit or litigation is in the 35 to 40 percent range or above.

Substantial basis reduction   negative basis adjustment of more than $250,000 resulting from a distribution from an entity taxed as a partnership to its owners.

Substantial built-in loss   exists when a partnership's adjusted basis in its property exceeds the property's fair market value by more than $250,000 when a transfer of an interest occurs.

Substantially appreciated inventory   (for partnership disproportionate distributions purposes) inventory with a fair market value that exceeds its basis by more than 120 percent.

Substituted basis   the transfer of the tax basis of stock or other property given up in an exchange to stock or other property received in return.

Substitution effect   one of the two basic responses that a taxpayer may have when taxes increase. The substitution effect predicts that, when taxpayers are taxed more, rather than work more, they will substitute nontaxable activities (e.g., leisure pursuits) for taxable ones because the marginal value of taxable activities has decreased.

Sufficiency   a standard for evaluating a good tax system. Sufficiency is defined as assessing the aggregate size of the tax revenues that must be generated and ensuring that the tax system provides these revenues.

Syndication costs   costs partnerships incur to promote the sale of partnership interests to the public. Syndication expenses must be capitalized and are not amortizable.

T

Tacks   the adding on of the transferor's holding period of property to the transferee in a tax-deferred exchange.

Tax   a payment required by a government that is unrelated to any specific benefit or service received from the government.

Tax accounting balance sheet   a balance sheet that records a company's assets and liabilities at their tax bases instead of their financial accounting bases.

Tax avoidance   the legal act of arranging one's transactions or affairs to reduce taxes paid.

Tax base   the item that is being taxed (e.g., purchase price of a good, taxable income, etc.).

Tax basis   the amount of a taxpayer's unrecovered cost of or investment in an asset; *see also* adjusted tax basis.

Tax benefit rule   holds that a refund of an amount deducted in a previous period is only included in income to the extent that the deduction reduced taxable income.

Tax bracket   a range of taxable income taxed at a specified rate.

Tax capital accounts   partners' capital accounts initially determined using the tax basis of contributed property and maintained using tax accounting income and expense recognition principles.

Tax carryforwards tax deductions or credits that cannot be used on the current-year tax return and that can be carried forward to reduce taxable income or taxes payable in a future year.

Tax contingency reserve a company's reserve for taxes it has not paid, but it may pay in the future, for uncertain tax positions taken on the current and prior-year income tax returns.

Tax Court allocation method allocates expenses associated with rental use of the home between rental use and personal use. Property taxes and mortgage interest are allocated to rental use of the home based on the ratio of the number of rental use days to the total days in the year. All other expenses are allocated to rental use based on the ratio of the number of rental use days to total days the property was used during the year.

Tax credits items that directly reduce a taxpayer's tax liability.

Tax evasion the willful attempt to defraud the government (i.e., by not paying taxes legally owed). Tax evasion falls outside the confines of legal tax avoidance.

Tax haven generally, a country offering very favorable tax laws for foreign businesses and individuals.

Tax rate the level of taxes imposed on the tax base, usually expressed as a percentage.

Tax rate schedule a schedule of progressive tax rates and the income ranges to which the rates apply that taxpayers may use to compute their gross tax liability.

Tax shelter an investment or other arrangement designed to produce tax benefits without any expectation of economic profits.

Tax tables IRS-provided tables that specify the federal income tax liability for individuals with taxable income within a specific range. The tables differ by filing status and reflect tax rates that increase with taxable income.

Tax treaties agreements negotiated between countries that describe the tax treatment of entities subject to tax in both countries (e.g., U.S. citizens earning investment income in Spain). The U.S. president has the authority to enter into a tax treaty with another country after receiving the Senate's advice.

Tax year a fixed period in which a business reports income and deductions, generally referred to as an accounting period.

Taxable estate adjusted gross estate reduced by the marital deduction and the charitable deduction.

Taxable fringe benefit a noncash fringe benefit provided by employers to an employee that is included in taxable income (e.g., auto allowance or group-term life over $50,000).

Taxable gifts the amount left after adjusting current gifts for gift splitting, annual exclusions, the marital deduction, and the charitable deduction.

Taxable income the tax base for the individual income tax.

Taxable temporary differences book–tax differences that will result in taxable amounts in future years when the related deferred tax liability is settled.

Technical advice memorandum ruling issued by the IRS national office, requested by an IRS agent, and generally for a completed transaction.

Temporary book–tax differences book–tax differences that reverse over time such that, over the long-term, corporations recognize the same amount of income or deductions for the items on their financial statements as they recognize on their tax returns.

Temporary regulations regulations issued with a limited life (three years for regulations issued after November 20, 1988). During their life, temporary regulations carry the same authoritative weight as final regulations.

Tenancy by the entirety ownership by husband and wife similar to joint tenancy with right of survivorship.

Tenancy in common ownership in which owners hold divided rights to property and have the ability to transfer these rights during their life or upon their death.

Tentative minimum tax the tax on the AMT tax base under the alternative minimum tax system.

Terminable interest a right to property that terminates at a specified time or upon the occurrence of a specified event, such as a life estate.

Testamentary transfers transfers that take place upon the death of the donor.

Third-party intermediaries people or organizations that facilitate the transfer of property between taxpayers in a like-kind exchange. Typically, the intermediary receives the cash from selling the property received from the taxpayer and uses it to acquire like-kind property identified by the taxpayer.

Throwback rule the rule that sales into a state without nexus are included with sales from the state the property was shipped from.

Topical tax service a tax service arranged by subject (i.e., topic). For each topic, topical services identify tax issues that relate to each topic, and then explain and cite authorities relevant to the issue (code sections, regulations, court cases, revenue rulings, etc.).

Trade or business a profit-motivated activity characterized by a sustained, continuous, high level of individual involvement or effort.

Trade show rule a rule that permits businesses to have physical presence at conventions and trade shows, generally up to two weeks a year, without creating nexus.

Traditional 401(k) a popular type of defined contribution plan with before-tax employee and employer contributions and taxable distributions.

Traditional IRA an individually managed retirement account with deductible contributions and taxable distributions.

Transfer taxes taxes on the transfer of wealth from one taxpayer to another. The estate and gift taxes are two examples of transfer taxes.

Travel expenses expenditures incurred while "away from home overnight," including the cost of transportation, meals, lodging, and incidental expenses.

Treasury bond a debt instrument issued by the U.S. Treasury at face value, at a discount, or at a premium, with a set interest rate and maturity date that pays interest semiannually. Treasury bonds have terms of 30 years.

Treasury note a debt instrument issued by the U.S. Treasury at face value, at a discount, or at a premium, with a set interest rate and maturity date that pays interest semiannually. Treasury notes have terms of 2, 5, or 10 years.

Triple i agreement a 10-year agreement filed with the IRS in which the taxpayer agrees to notify the IRS that he or she has acquired a prohibited interest after waiving the family attribution rules in a complete redemption.

Trust fiduciary entity created to hold and administer the property for other persons according to the terms of a trust instrument.

Trustee the person responsible for administering a trust.

U

Uncertain tax positions a tax return position for which a corporation does not have a high degree of certainty as to its tax consequences.

Underpayment penalty the penalty that applies when taxpayers fail to adequately prepay their tax liability. The underpayment penalty is determined by multiplying the federal short-term interest rate plus three percentage points by the amount of tax underpayment per quarter.

Unearned income   income from property that accrues as time passes without effort on the part of the owner of the property.

Unemployment tax   the tax that pays for temporary unemployment benefits for individuals terminated from their jobs without cause.

Unfavorable book–tax difference   any book–tax difference that requires an add back to book income in computing taxable income. This type of adjustment is unfavorable because it increases taxable income relative to book income.

Unified credit   amount of credit based on the exemption equivalent designed to prevent transfer taxation of smaller cumulative transfers.

Uniform cost capitalization rules (UNICAP rules)   specify that inventories must be accounted for using full absorption rules to allocate the indirect costs of productive activities to inventory.

Unitary tax return   a state tax return methodology requiring the activities of a group of related entities to be reported on a single tax return. The criteria for determining whether a group of entities must file a unitary tax return are functional integration, centralization of management, and economies of scale.

Unrealized receivables   any rights to receive payment for (1) goods delivered, or to be delivered, or (2) services rendered, or to be rendered. Unrealized receivables also include other assets to the extent that they would produce ordinary income if sold for their fair market value.

Unrecaptured §1250 gain   a gain from the sale of real estate held by a noncorporate taxpayer for more than one year in a trade or business or as rental property attributable to tax depreciation deducted at ordinary tax rates. This gain is taxable at a maximum 25 percent capital gains rate.

Unrecognized tax benefit   a reserve for tax benefits related to a tax position for which the corporation does not have a high degree of certainty as to its sustainability on audit or in a court of law.

U.S. Circuit Courts of Appeal   the first level of appeals courts after the trial-level courts. There are 13 U.S. Circuit Courts of Appeal; one for the Federal Circuit and 12 assigned to hear cases that originated from a specific circuit (e.g., the 11th Circuit Court of Appeals only hears cases originating within the 11th Circuit).

U.S. Constitution   the founding law of the United States, ratified in 1789.

U.S. Court of Federal Claims   one of the three trial-level courts. It is a national court that only hears monetary claims against the federal government.

U.S. District Court   one of three trial-level courts. It is the only court that allows a jury trial. There is at least one district court in each state.

U.S. savings bonds   debt instruments issued by the U.S. Treasury at face value or at a discount, with a set maturity date. Interest earned from U.S. bonds is paid either at maturity or when the bonds are converted to cash before maturity.

U.S. Supreme Court   the highest court in the United States. The Supreme Court hears only a few tax cases a year with great significance to a broad cross-section of taxpayers or cases litigating issues in which there has been disagreement among the circuit courts. For most tax cases, the Supreme Court refuses to hear the case (i.e., the *writ of certiorari* is denied) and, thus, litigation ends with the circuit court decision.

U.S. Tax Court   a national court that only hears tax cases and where the judges are tax experts. The U.S. Tax Court is the only court that allows tax cases to be heard *before* the taxpayer pays the disputed liability and the only court with a small claims division (hearing claims involving disputed liabilities of $50,000 or less).

Use tax   a tax imposed on the retail price of goods owned, possessed, or consumed within a state that were *not* purchased within the state.

V

Valuation allowance   the portion of a deferred tax asset for which management determines it is more likely than not that a tax benefit will not be realized on a future tax return.

Value-added tax   a tax imposed on the producer of goods (and services) on the value of goods (services) added at each stage of production. Value-added taxes are common in Europe.

Vertical equity   one of the dimensions of equity. Vertical equity is achieved when taxpayers with greater ability to pay tax, pay more tax relative to taxpayers with a lesser ability to pay tax.

Vest   to become legally entitled to receive a particular benefit without risk of forfeiture; to gain ownership.

Vesting date   the date on which the taxpayer becomes legally entitled to receive a particular benefit without risk of forfeiture.

Vesting period   period of employment over which employees earn the right to own and exercise stock options.

W

Wages   a payment by an employer to an employee in exchange for the employee's services which is typically expressed in hourly, daily, or piecework rate.

Wash sale   the sale of an investment if that same investment (or substantially identical investment) is purchased within 30 days before or after the sale date. Losses on wash sales are deferred.

Wherewithal to pay   the ability or resources to pay taxes due from a particular transaction.

Withholdings   taxes collected and remitted to the government by an employer from an employee's wages.

Working condition fringe benefit   a nontaxable fringe benefit provided by employers that would be deductible as an ordinary and necessary business expense if paid by an employee (e.g., reimbursement for professional dues).

Writ of certiorari   a document filed to request the U.S. Supreme Court to hear a case.

Z

Zero coupon bond   a type of bond issued at a discount that pays interest only at maturity.

Appendix C

Comprehensive Tax Return Problems

Ten additional Comprehensive Tax Return problems—covering individual, corporation, partnership, and S corporation tax returns—can be found in the *Connect Library*.

INDIVIDUAL TAX RETURN PROBLEM 1

Required:
- Use the following information to complete Keith and Jennifer Hamilton's 2015 federal income tax return. If information is missing, use reasonable assumptions to fill in the gaps.
- Form 1040, supporting schedules, and instructions to the forms and schedules can be found at the IRS Web site (www.irs.gov).

Facts:
1. Keith Hamilton is employed as an airline pilot for Flyby Airlines in Las Vegas, Nevada. Jennifer is employed as a teacher's assistant at Small World Elementary School, in Henderson, Nevada. Keith and Jennifer live in a home they purchased this year. Keith and Jennifer have three children who lived with them all year, Joshua (17), Danielle (14), and Sara (10). Keith and Jennifer provided the following personal information:

   - Keith and Jennifer do not want to contribute to the presidential election campaign.
   - Keith and Jennifer do not claim itemized deductions.
   - Keith and Jennifer live at 3678 Blue Sky Drive, Henderson, Nevada 89052.
   - Keith's birthday is 10/12/1970 and his Social Security number is 535-22-4466.
   - Jennifer's birthday is 7/16/1973 and her Social Security number is 535-44-2255.
   - Joshua's birthday is 6/30/1998 and his Social Security number is 454-54-5454.
   - Danielle's birthday is 8/12/2001 and her Social Security number is 343-43-4343.
   - Sara's birthday is 5/13/2005 and her Social Security number is 232-32-3232.

2. Keith received the following Form W-2 for 2015 from Flyby Airlines.

22222	Void ☐	a Employee's social security number 535-22-4466	For Official Use Only ▶ OMB No. 1545-0008	
b Employer identification number (EIN) 91-0001002			**1** Wages, tips, other compensation 163,645.00	**2** Federal income tax withheld 31,000.00
c Employer's name, address, and ZIP code Flyby Airlines 375 West Flight Blvd. Las Vegas, NV 89119			**3** Social security wages $118,500.00	**4** Social security tax withheld 7,347.00
			5 Medicare wages and tips 178,645.00	**6** Medicare tax withheld 2,590.35
			7 Social security tips	**8** Allocated tips
d Control number			**9**	**10** Dependent care benefits
e Employee's first name and initial Last name Suff.			**11** Nonqualified plans	**12a** See instructions for box 12 D 15,000
Keith Hamilton 3678 Blue Sky Drive Henderson, NV 89052			**13** Statutory employee ☐ Retirement plan ☒ Third-party sick pay ☐	**12b**
			14 Other	**12c**
				12d
f Employee's address and ZIP code				

15 State Employer's state ID number	**16** State wages, tips, etc.	**17** State income tax	**18** Local wages, tips, etc.	**19** Local income tax	**20** Locality name
NV 987654321	163,645.00	0.00			

Form **W-2** Wage and Tax Statement   **2015**   Department of the Treasury—Internal Revenue Service

Copy A For Social Security Administration — Send this entire page with Form W-3 to the Social Security Administration; photocopies are **not** acceptable.

For Privacy Act and Paperwork Reduction Act Notice, see the separate instructions.

Cat. No. 10134D

Do Not Cut, Fold, or Staple Forms on This Page

3. Jennifer received the following Form W-2 for 2015 from Small World Elementary School.

22222	Void ☐	a Employee's social security number 535-44-2255	For Official Use Only ▶ OMB No. 1545-0008	
b Employer identification number (EIN) 91-0001003			**1** Wages, tips, other compensation 36,825.00	**2** Federal income tax withheld 5,524.00
c Employer's name, address, and ZIP code Small World Elementary School 333 Tiny Tot Lane Henderson, NV 89053			**3** Social security wages 39,925.00	**4** Social security tax withheld 2,469.15
			5 Medicare wages and tips 39,925.00	**6** Medicare tax withheld 577.46
			7 Social security tips	**8** Allocated tips
d Control number			**9**	**10** Dependent care benefits
e Employee's first name and initial Last name Suff.			**11** Nonqualified plans	**12a** See instructions for box 12 D 3,000
Jennifer Hamilton 3678 Blue Sky Drive Henderson, NV 89052			**13** Statutory employee ☐ Retirement plan ☒ Third-party sick pay ☐	**12b**
			14 Other	**12c**
				12d
f Employee's address and ZIP code				

15 State Employer's state ID number	**16** State wages, tips, etc.	**17** State income tax	**18** Local wages, tips, etc.	**19** Local income tax	**20** Locality name
NV 123456789	36,825.00	0.00			

Form **W-2** Wage and Tax Statement   **2015**   Department of the Treasury—Internal Revenue Service

Copy A For Social Security Administration — Send this entire page with Form W-3 to the Social Security Administration; photocopies are **not** acceptable.

For Privacy Act and Paperwork Reduction Act Notice, see the separate instructions.

Cat. No. 10134D

Do Not Cut, Fold, or Staple Forms on This Page

4. During 2015, Keith and Jennifer received $550 in interest from Las Vegas municipal bonds, $1,070 interest from U.S. Treasury bonds, and $65 from their savings account at SCD Credit Union. Keith and Jennifer are joint owners of the Las Vegas city bonds and the U.S. Treasury bonds. They have a joint savings account at SCD Credit Union.

5. On January 21, 2015, Jennifer was involved in a car accident. Because the other driver was at fault, the other driver's insurance company paid Jennifer $1,350 for medical expenses relating to her injuries from the accident and $300 for emotional distress from the accident. She received payment on March 15, 2015.

6. Keith's father died on November 15, 2014. Keith received a $100,000 death benefit from his father's life insurance policy on February 8, 2015.

7. On February 15, 2015, Keith hurt his arm on a family skiing trip in Utah and was unable to fly for two weeks. He received $4,000 for disability pay from his disability insurance policy. He received the check on March 2, 2015. Flyby Airlines paid $600 in premiums on this policy during 2015. The disability insurance policy premiums are paid for by Flyby Airlines as a fully taxable fringe benefit to Keith (the premiums paid on his behalf are included in Keith's compensation amount on his W-2).

8. Jennifer's grandmother died on March 10, 2015, leaving Jennifer with an inheritance of $30,000. (She received the inheritance on May 12, 2015.) Flyby Airlines had space available on its Long Island, New York, flight and provided Keith, Jennifer, and their three children with free flights so they could attend the funeral. The value of the ticket for each passenger was $600.

9. On April 1, 2015, Jennifer slipped in the Small World Elementary lunchroom and injured her back. Jennifer received $1,200 in worker's compensation benefits because her work-related injury caused her to miss two weeks of work. She also received a $2,645 reimbursement for medical expenses from the health insurance company. Small World Elementary pays the premiums for Jennifer's health insurance policy as a nontaxable fringe benefit.

10. On May 17, 2015, Keith and Jennifer received a federal income tax refund of $975 from their 2014 federal income tax return.

11. On June 5, 2015, Keith and Jennifer sold their home in Henderson, Nevada, for $510,000 (net of commissions). Keith and Jennifer purchased the home 11 years ago for $470,000. On July 12, 2015, they bought a new home for $675,000.

12. On July 25, 2015, Keith's aunt Beatrice gave Keith $18,000 because she wanted to let everyone know that Keith is her favorite nephew.

13. On September 29, 2015, Jennifer won an iPad valued at $500 in a raffle at the annual fair held at Joshua's high school.

14. Keith and Jennifer have qualifying insurance for purposes of the the Affordable Care Act (ACA).

INDIVIDUAL TAX RETURN PROBLEM 2

Required:
- Use the following information to complete Johnelle and Latoya Henry's 2015 federal income tax return. If information is missing, use reasonable assumptions to fill in the gaps.
- You may need the following forms to complete the project: Form 1040 and Schedule A. The forms, schedules, and instructions can be found at the IRS Web site (www.irs.gov). The instructions can be helpful in completing the forms.

Facts:
1. Johnelle Henry is employed as a human resources manager for Toys Unlimited, Inc., and Latoya is a financial planner for her mother's company, Long-term Investments, Inc., a full-service wealth-planning firm. They provide the following information:
   - They both want to contribute to the presidential election campaign.
   - They live at 9876 Old Waverly, Charleston, South Carolina.

- Johnelle's birthday is 7/17/1965 and his Social Security number is 555-12-6789.
- Latoya's birthday is 9/11/1967 and her Social Security number is 987-65-4321.
- Johnelle or Latoya do not have any foreign bank accounts or trusts.

2. Johnelle received a Form W-2 from Toys Unlimited, Inc. that contained the following information:

- Line 1 Wages, tips, other compensation: $45,000
- Line 2 Federal income tax withheld: 7,500
- Line 3 Social Security wages: 45,000
- Line 4 Social Security tax withheld: 2,790
- Line 5 Medicare wages and tips: 45,000
- Line 6 Medicare tax withheld: 653
- Line 17 State income tax: 2,200

3. Latoya received a Form W-2 from Long-term Investments, Inc. that contained the following information:

- Line 1 Wages, tips, other compensation: $85,000
- Line 2 Federal income tax withheld: 12,500
- Line 3 Social Security wages: 85,000
- Line 4 Social Security tax withheld: 5,270
- Line 5 Medicare wages and tips: 85,000
- Line 6 Medicare tax withheld: 1,233
- Line 17 State income tax: 4,200

4. Johnelle and Latoya incurred the following medical expenses for the year:

- Transportation to Chicago for Johnelle's cancer treatment: 2,000 miles
- Unreimbursed hospital charges for Johnelle: $6,500
- Unreimbursed prescription drug charges for Johnelle and Latoya: 1,750
- Unreimbursed physician charges for Johnelle and Latoya: 2,200
- Unreimbursed prescription glasses for Latoya: 150
- Laser hair treatment for Latoya (so that she will no longer need to shave her legs)   2,000

5. Johnelle and Latoya paid $12,000 of interest payments on their primary residence (acquisition debt of $225,000). They also paid $1,750 of interest expense on Latoya's car loan and $500 of interest on their Visa card.

6. Johnelle and Latoya paid $4,000 of real estate taxes on their home and $1,000 of real estate tax on a vacant lot they purchased with the hope of building their dream home in the future. They also paid $3,000 in sales tax on Latoya's car and other purchases and $1,000 of ad valorem tax on their cars.

7. Johnelle and Latoya made the following contributions this year:

- American Red Cross $ 200
- United Way   150
- St. Joseph's Catholic Church   8,000
- Food for the family of Hannah Barbara (a neighbor who suffered a tragic car accident this past year)   225
- Stock transfer to the University of South Carolina (originally purchased for $1,000 in 2005)   750

8. Johnelle incurred $4,000 of unreimbursed meals and entertainment related to his job. Latoya incurred $1,200 of expenses for investment publications, and last year they paid their CPA $500 to prepare their tax return.

9. The roof on Johnelle and Latoya's house was severely damaged in a hail storm. They had to replace the roof ($7,500), which unfortunately was not covered by insurance because of their high deductible ($10,000).

10. Johnelle won $5,000 in the state lottery. He has been playing the lottery for years [$10 in lottery tickets every week ($520 in total) that he saves to keep track of the numbers he plays].

11. Johnelle and Latoya have qualifying insurance for purposes of the Affordable Care Act (ACA).

INDIVIDUAL TAX RETURN PROBLEM 3

Required:

- Use the following information to complete Rhonda Hill's 2015 federal income tax return. If information is missing, use reasonable assumptions to fill in the gaps.
- The forms, schedules, and instructions can be found at the IRS Web site (www.irs.gov). The instructions can be helpful in completing the forms.

Facts:

1. Rhonda Hill (unmarried) is employed as an office manager at the main office of Carter and Associates CPA firm. Rhonda lives in a home she purchased 20 years ago. Rhonda's older cousin Mabel Wright lives with Rhonda in the home. Mabel is retired and receives $2,400 of Social Security payments each year. Mabel is able to save this money because Rhonda provides all of Mabel's support. Rhonda also provided the following information:
   - Rhonda does not want to contribute to the presidential election campaign.
   - Rhonda lives at 1234 Blue Ridge Way, Tulsa, Oklahoma 74101.
   - Rhonda's birthday is 12/18/1950 and her Social Security number is 335-67-8910.
   - Mabel's birthday is 11/2/1942 and her Social Security number is 566-77-8899.
   - Rhonda does not have any foreign bank accounts or trusts.
   - Rhonda has qualifying insurance for purposes of the Affordable Care Act (ACA).

2. Rhonda received a Form W-2 from Carter and Associates (her employer) that contained the following information:

   - Line 1 Wages, tips, other compensation $72,000
   - Line 2 Federal income tax withheld   9,300
   - Line 3 Social Security wages   72,000
   - Line 4 Social Security tax withheld   4,464
   - Line 5 Medicare wages and tips   72,000
   - Line 6 Medicare tax withheld   1,044
   - Line 16 State wages, tips, etc.   72,000
   - Line 17 State income tax   2,700
   - Carter and Associates address is 1234 CPA Way Tulsa, Oklahoma 74101; its FEIN is 91:0001002; and its State ID number is 123456678

3. Rhonda received $250 in interest from Tulsa City bonds, $120 interest from IBM bonds, and $15 from her savings account at UCU Credit Union. She also received a $460 dividend from Huggies Company and $500 from Bicker Corporation. Both dividends are qualified dividends.

4. Rhonda sold 200 shares of DM stock for $18 a share on June 15, 2015. She purchased the stock on December 12, 2010, for $10 a share. She also sold 50 shares of RSA stock for $15 a share on October 2, 2015. She purchased the stock for $65 a share on February 2, 2015. Stock basis amounts have been reported to the IRS.

5. The following is a record of the medical expenses that Rhonda paid for herself during the year. The amounts reported are amounts she paid in excess of insurance reimbursements. Rhonda drove 210 miles for medical purposes in 2015.

Insurance premiums	$3,700
Prescription medications	100
Over-the-counter medications	250
Doctor and dentist visits	1,450
Eyeglasses	300
Physical therapy	200

6. Rhonda paid $2,800 in mortgage interest during the year to UCU credit union (reported to her on Form 1098). She also paid $1,200 in real property taxes during the year.

7. Rhonda contributed $2,350 to Heavenly Church during the year. Heavenly Church's address is 1342 Religion Way, Tulsa, Oklahoma 74101.

INDIVIDUAL TAX RETURN PROBLEM 4

Required:
- Use the following information to complete Phillip and Claire Dunphy's 2015 federal income tax return. If information is missing, use reasonable assumptions to fill in the gaps. Ignore the alternative minimum tax for this problem.
- Any required forms, schedules, and instructions can be found at the IRS Web site (www.irs.gov). The instructions can be helpful in completing the forms.

Facts:
1. Phillip and Claire are married and file a joint return. Phillip is self-employed as a real estate agent, and Claire is a flight attendant. Phillip and Claire have three dependent children. All three children live at home with Phillip and Claire for the entire year.

   The Dunphys provide you with the following additional information:

   - The Dunphys do not want to contribute to the presidential election campaign.
   - The Dunphys live at 3701 Brighton Avenue, Los Angeles, California 90018.
   - Phillip's birthday is 11/5/1969 and his Social Security number is 321-44-5766.
   - Claire's birthday is 5/12/1972 and her Social Security number is 567-77-1258.
   - Haley's birthday is 11/6/2003 and her Social Security number is 621-18-7592.
   - Alex's birthday is 2/1/2005 and her Social Security number is 621-92-8751.
   - Luke's birthday is 12/12/2009 and his Social Security number is 621-99-9926.
   - The Dunphys do not have any foreign bank accounts or trusts.

2. Claire is a flight attendant for Western American Airlines (WAA), where she earned $57,000 in salary. WAA withheld federal income tax of $6,375, state income tax of $1,800, Los Angeles city income tax of $675, Social Security tax of $3,600, and Medicare tax of $825.

3. Phillip and Claire received $300 of interest from State Savings Bank on a joint account. They also received a qualified dividend of $395 on jointly owned stock in Xila Corporation.

4. Phillip's full-time real estate business is named "Phillip Dunphy Realty." His business is located at 645 Grove Street, Los Angeles, California 90018, and his employer identification number is 93-3488888. Phillip's gross receipts during the year were $730,000. Phillip uses the cash method of accounting for his business. Phillip's business expenses are as follows:

Advertising	$ 5,000
Professional dues	800
Professional journals	200
Employee wages	48,000
Insurance on office contents	1,120
Accounting services	2,100
Miscellaneous office expense	500
Utilities and telephone	3,360
Payroll taxes	3,600
Depreciation	To be calculated

On March 20, Phillip moved his business out of the old offices at 1103 Allium Lane into a newly constructed and equipped office on Grove Street. Phillip sold the old office building and all its furnishings. Phillip's expenditures for the new office building are as follows:

Date Acquired	Asset	Cost
3/20	Land	$ 300,000
3/20	Office building	2,500,000
3/20	Furniture	200,000
4/1	Computer system	350,000
6/1	Artwork	150,000

Phillip computes his cost recovery allowance using MACRS. He would like to use the §179 immediate expensing, but he has elected to not claim any bonus depreciation. Phillip has never claimed §179 or bonus depreciation before. The assets Phillip sold on March 20 are as follows:

Date Acquired	Asset	Sales Price	Original Cost	Accumulated Depreciation as of Beginning of the Year
5/1/09	Office building	$940,000	$900,000	$129,825
5/1/09	Land	200,000	100,000	0
7/1/09	Furniture	50,000	239,000	206,998
8/13/11	Furniture	10,000	324,000	222,782
4/12/12	Office equipment	100,000	120,000	67,524
5/13/14	Computers	30,000	50,000	10,000

Phillip has never sold any assets relating to his business before this transaction.

5. The Dunphys sold 60 shares of Fizbo Corporation common stock on September 3 for $65 a share (minus a $50 total commission). The Dunphys purchased the stock on November 8, 2014, for $90 a share. They also sold a painting for $13,000 on March 1. Claire purchased the painting for $20,050 on September 1, 2008, as an investment.

6. The Dunphys filed their 2014 federal, state, and local returns on April 13, 2015. They paid the following additional 2014 taxes with their returns: federal income taxes of $630, state income taxes of $250, and city income taxes of $75.

7. The Dunphys made timely estimated federal income tax payments of $20,000 each quarter during 2015. They also made estimated state income tax payments of $1,000 each quarter and estimated city income tax payments of $300 each

quarter. The Dunphys made all fourth-quarter payments on December 31, 2015. They would like to receive a refund for any overpayments.

8. Phillip and Clair have qualifying insurance for purposes of the Affordable Care Act (ACA).

INDIVIDUAL TAX RETURN PROBLEM 5

Required:

- Use the following information to complete Armando and Lourdes Gonzales's 2015 federal income tax return. If information is missing, use reasonable assumptions to fill in the gaps.
- You may need the following forms and schedules to complete the project: Form 1040, Schedule A, Schedule B, Schedule C, Schedule D, Schedule E, Schedule SE, Form 2106-EZ, Form 4562 (for the dental practice), Form 4562 (for the rental property), Form 4797, Form 8863, and Form 8949. The forms, schedules, and instructions can be found at the IRS Web site (www.irs.gov). The instructions can be helpful in completing the forms.

Facts:

1. Armando Z. and Lourdes K. Gonzales are married and file a joint return. Armando is self-employed as a dentist, and Lourdes is a college professor. Armando and Lourdes have three children. The oldest is Ricardo, who lives at home. Ricardo is a law student at the University of Cincinnati and worked part time during the year, earning $1,500, which he spent for his own support. Armando and Lourdes provided $6,000 toward Ricardo's support (including $4,000 for Ricardo's fall tuition). They also provided over half the support of their daughter, Selena, who is a full-time student at Edgecliff College in Cincinnati. Selena worked part time as an independent contractor during the year, earning $3,200. Selena lived at home until she was married in December 2015. She filed a joint return with her husband, Tony, who earned $20,000 during the year. Felipe is the youngest and lived in the Gonzales's home for the entire year. The Gonzaleses provide you with the following additional information:

- Armando and Lourdes would like to take advantage on their return of any educational expenses paid for their children.
- The Gonzaleses do not want to contribute to the presidential election campaign.
- The Gonzaleses live at 621 Franklin Avenue, Cincinnati, Ohio 45211.
- Armando's birthday is 3/5/1957 and his Social Security number is 333-45-6666.
- Lourdes's birthday is 4/24/1960 and her Social Security number is 566-77-8888.
- Ricardo's birthday is 11/6/1992 and his Social Security number is 576-18-7928.
- Selena's birthday is 2/1/1996 and her Social Security number is 575-92-4321.
- Felipe's birthday is 12/12/2003 and his Social Security number is 613-97-8465.
- The Gonzaleses do not have any foreign bank accounts or trusts.

2. Lourdes is a lecturer at Xavier University in Cincinnati, where she earned $30,000. The university withheld federal income tax of $3,375, state income tax of $900, Cincinnati city income tax of $375, $1,860 of Social Security tax, and $435 of Medicare tax. She also worked part of the year for Delta Airlines. Delta paid her $10,000 in salary, and withheld federal income tax of $1,125, state income tax of $300, Cincinnati city income tax of $125, Social Security tax of $620, and Medicare tax of $145.

3. The Gonzaleses received $800 of interest from State Savings Bank on a joint account. They received interest of $1,000 on City of Cincinnati bonds they bought in January with the proceeds of a loan from Third National Bank of

Cincinnati. They paid interest of $1,100 on the loan. Armando received a dividend of $540 on General Bicycle Corporation stock he owns. Lourdes received a dividend of $390 on Acme Clothing Corporation stock she owns. Armando and Lourdes received a dividend of $865 on jointly owned stock in Maple Company. All of the dividends received in 2015 are qualified dividends.

4. Armando practices under the name "Armando Z. Gonzales, DDS." His business is located at 645 West Avenue, Cincinnati, Ohio 45211, and his employer identification number is 01-2222222. Armando's gross receipts during the year were $111,000. Armando uses the cash method of accounting for his business. Armando's business expenses are as follows:

Advertising	$ 1,200
Professional dues	490
Professional journals	360
Contributions to employee benefit plans	2,000
Malpractice insurance	3,200
Fine for overbilling State of Ohio for work performed on welfare patient	5,000
Insurance on office contents	720
Interest on money borrowed to refurbish office	600
Accounting services	2,100
Miscellaneous office expense	388
Office rent	12,000
Dental supplies	7,672
Utilities and telephone	3,360
Wages	30,000
Payroll taxes	2,400

In June, Armando decided to refurbish his office. This project was completed and the assets placed in service on July 1. Armando's expenditures included $8,000 for new office furniture, $6,000 for new dental equipment (seven-year recovery period), and $2,000 for a new computer. Armando elected to compute his cost recovery allowance using MACRS. He did not elect to use §179 immediate expensing, and he chose to not claim any bonus depreciation.

5. Lourdes's mother, Maria, died on July 2, 2010, leaving Lourdes her entire estate. Included in the estate was Maria's residence (325 Oak Street, Cincinnati, Ohio 45211). Maria's basis in the residence was $30,000. The fair market value of the residence on July 2, 2010, was $155,000. The property was distributed to Lourdes on January 1, 2011. The Gonzaleses have held the property as rental property and have managed it themselves. From 2011 until June 30, 2015, they rented the house to the same tenant. The tenant was transferred to a branch office in California and moved out at the end of June. Since they did not want to bother finding a new tenant, Armando and Lourdes sold the house on June 30, 2015. They received $140,000 for the house and land ($15,000 for the land and $125,000 for the house), less a 6 percent commission charged by the broker. They had depreciated the house using the MACRS rules and conventions applicable to residential real estate. To compute depreciation on the house, the Gonzaleses had allocated $15,000 of the property's basis to the land on which the house is located. The Gonzaleses collected rent of $1,000 a month during the six months the house was occupied during the year. They incurred the following related expenses during this period:

Property insurance	$500
Property taxes	800
Maintenance	465
Depreciation (to be computed)	?

6. The Gonzaleses sold 200 shares of Capp Corporation stock on September 3, 2015, for $42 a share (minus a $50 commission). The Gonzaleses received the

stock from Armando's father on June 25, 1980, as a wedding present. Armando's father originally purchased the stock for $10 per share on January 1, 1967. The stock was valued at $14.50 per share on the date of the gift. No gift tax was paid on the gift.

7. Lourdes is required by Xavier University to visit several high schools in the Cincinnati area to evaluate Xavier University students who are doing their practice teaching. However, she is not reimbursed for the expenses she incurs in doing this. During the spring semester (January through April 2015), she drove her personal automobile 6,800 miles in fulfilling this obligation. Lourdes drove an additional 6,700 personal miles during 2015. She has been using the car since June 30, 2014. Lourdes uses the standard mileage method to calculate her car expenses.

8. Armando and Lourdes have given you a file containing the following receipts for expenditures during the year:

Prescription medicine and drugs (net of insurance reimbursement)	$ 376
Doctor and hospital bills (net of insurance reimbursement)	2,468
Penalty for underpayment of last year's state income tax	15
Real estate taxes on personal residence	4,762
Interest on home mortgage (paid to Home State Savings & Loan)	8,250
Interest on credit cards (consumer purchases)	595
Cash contribution to St. Matthew's church	3,080
Payroll deductions for Lourdes's contributions to the United Way	150
Professional dues (Lourdes)	325
Professional subscriptions (Lourdes)	245
Fee for preparation of 2014 tax return paid April 12, 2015	500

9. The Gonzaleses filed their 2014 federal, state, and local returns on April 12, 2015. They paid the following additional 2014 taxes with their returns: federal income taxes of $630, state income taxes of $250, and city income taxes of $75.

10. The Gonzaleses made timely estimated federal income tax payments of $1,500 each quarter during 2015. They also made estimated state income tax payments of $300 each quarter and estimated city income tax payments of $160 each quarter. The Gonzaleses made all fourth-quarter payments on December 31, 2015. They would like to receive a refund for any overpayments.

11. Armando and Lourdes have qualifying insurance for purposes of the Affordable Care Act (ACA).

INDIVIDUAL TAX RETURN PROBLEM 6

Required:
- Use the following information to complete Paige Turner's 2015 federal income tax return. If information is missing, use reasonable assumptions to fill in the gaps.
- Any required forms, schedules, and instructions can be found at the IRS Web site (www.irs.gov). The instructions can be helpful in completing the forms.

Facts:
1. Paige Turner is single and has two children from her previous marriage. Ali lives with Paige, and Paige provides more than half of her support. Leif lives with his father, Will (Lief lived with Will for all of 2015). Will provides more than half of Leif's support. Paige pays "alimony" of $400 per month to Will. The payments are to continue until Leif reaches age 18, when they will be reduced to $150. Paige provides you with the following additional information:

- She uses the cash method of accounting and a calendar year for reporting.
- She wishes to contribute to the presidential election campaign.
- Paige lives at 523 Essex Street, Bangor, Maine 04401.

- Paige's birthday is May 31, 1977.
- Ali's birthday is October 5, 2006.
- Leif's birthday is December 1, 2004.
- Paige's Social Security number is 007-16-4727.
- Ali's Social Security number is 005-61-7232.
- Leif's Social Security number is 004-23-3419.
- Will's Social Security number is 006-45-6333.
- She does not have any foreign bank accounts or trusts.

2. Paige is employed as a nuclear engineer with Atom Systems Consultants, Inc. (ASCI). ASCI's federal employer identification number is 79-1234466. Paige's pay stubs indicate that she had $7,230 withheld in federal taxes, $4,987 in state taxes, $4,495 in Social Security taxes, and $1,051 in Medicare taxes. ASCI has an extensive fringe benefits program for its employees.

3. Paige earned salary of $70,000 (before subtracting her 401(k) and flexible spending plan contributions). She contributed $7,000 to her 401(k) account, and she contributed $2,500 to her flexible spending account.

4. ASCI paid $397 of whole life insurance premiums to cover Paige's personal whole life insurance policy. ASCI also paid health club dues of $900 to a nearby health club on Paige's behalf.

5. Taking advantage of ASCI's educational assistance program, during the fall Paige enrolled in two graduate engineering classes at a local college. ASCI paid her tuition, fees, and other course-related costs of $2,300.

6. Paige received free parking in the company's security garage that would normally cost $200 per month.

7. Paige manages the safety program for ASCI. In recognition of her superior handling of three potential crises during the year, Paige was awarded the Employee Safety Award on December 15. The cash award was $500.

8. On January 15, 2015, Paige's father died. From her father's estate, she received stock valued at $30,000 (his basis was $12,000) and her father's house valued at $90,000 (his basis in the house was $55,000).

9. Paige owns several other investments and in February 2016 received a statement from her brokerage firm reporting the interest and dividends earned on the investments for 2015. (See Exhibit A.)

10. In addition to the investments discussed above, Paige owns 1,000 shares of Grubstake Mining & Development common stock. Grubstake is organized as an S corporation and has 100,000 shares outstanding (S corp. ID number 45-4567890). Grubstake reported taxable income of $200,000 and paid a distribution of $1.00 per share during the current year. Paige tells you that Grubstake typically does not send out its K-1 reports until late April. However, its preliminary report has been consistent with the K-1 for many years. (See Exhibit A.) Paige does not materially participate in Grubstake's activities.

11. Paige slipped on a wet spot in front of a computer store last July. She broke her ankle and was unable to work for two weeks. She incurred $1,300 in medical costs, all of which were paid by the owner of the store. The store also gave her $1,000 for pain and suffering resulting from the injury. ASCI continued to pay her salary during the two weeks she missed because of the accident. ASCI's plan also paid her $1,200 in disability pay for the time she was unable to work. Under this plan ASCI pays the premiums for the disability insurance as a taxable fringe benefit.

EXHIBIT A   Forms 1099 and 1098

This is important tax information and is being furnished to the Internal Revenue Service.

1099-Div Dividends & Distributions		
Entity	**Description**	**Amount**
General Dynamics	Gross qualified dividends	$300

1099-Int Interest		
Entity	**Description**	**Amount**
New Jersey Economic Development bonds	Gross interest	$300
IBM bonds	Gross interest	700
State of Nebraska bonds	Gross interest	700

1098-Mortgage Interest Statement		
Entity	**Description**	**Amount**
Sunbelt Credit Union	Mortgage interest	$7,100
Northeast Bank	Home-equity loan interest	435

Grubstake Mining & Development: preliminary report (preliminary K-1) to Paige for the 2015 tax year

Distribution to shareholder	$1,000
Ordinary income (1% of $200,000)	$2,000

12. Paige received a Form 1099-B from her broker for the sale of the following securities during 2015. The adjusted basis amounts were reported to the IRS.

Security	Sales Date	Purchase Date	Sales Price	Commission Paid on Sale	Her Basis
Nebraska state bonds	03/14/15	10/22/09	$2,300	$160	$1,890
Cassill Corp (500 shares)	10/20/15	02/19/14	8,500	425	9,760

13. In addition to the taxes withheld from her salary, she also made timely estimated federal tax payments of $175 per quarter and timely estimated state income tax payments of $150 for the first three quarters. The $150 fourth-quarter state payment was made on December 28, 2015. Paige would like to receive a refund for any overpayment.

14. Because of her busy work schedule, Paige was unable to provide her accountant with the tax documents necessary for filing her 2014 state and federal income tax returns by the due date (April 15, 2014). In filing her extension on April 15, 2015, she made a federal tax payment of $750. Her return was eventually filed on June 25, 2015. In August 2015, she received a federal refund of $180 and a state tax refund of $60. Her itemized deductions for 2014 were $12,430.

15. Paige found a renter for her father's house on August 1. The monthly rent is $400, and the lease agreement is for one year. The lease requires the tenant to pay the first and last months' rent and a $400 security deposit. The security deposit is to be returned at the end of the lease if the property is in good condition. On August 1, Paige received $1,200 from the tenant per the terms of the lease agreement. In November, the plumbing froze and several pipes burst. The tenant had the repairs made and paid the $300 bill. In December, he reduced his rental payment to $100 to compensate for the plumbing

repairs. Paige provides you with the following additional information for the rental in 2015.

Property taxes	$770
Other maintenance expenses	285
Insurance expense	495
Management fee	350
Depreciation (to be computed)	?

The rental property is located at 35 Harvest Street, Orono, Maine 04473. Local practice is to allocate 12 percent of the fair market value of the property to the land. (See #8.) Paige makes all decisions with respect to the property.

16. Paige paid $2,050 in real estate taxes on her principal residence. The real estate tax is used to pay for town schools and other municipal services.

17. Paige drives a 2014 Acura TL. Her car registration fee (based on the car year) is $50 and covers the period 1/1/15 through 12/31/15. In addition, she paid $280 in property tax to the state based on the book value of the car.

18. In addition to the medical costs presented in #11, Paige incurred the following unreimbursed medical costs:

Dentist	$ 310
Doctor	390
Prescription drugs	215
Over-the-counter drugs	140
Optometrist	125
Emergency room charges	440
LASIK eye surgery	2,000
Chiropractor	265

19. On March 1, Paige took advantage of low interest rates and refinanced her $75,000 home mortgage with her original lender. The new home loan is for 15 years. She paid $215 in closing costs and $1,500 in discount points (prepaid interest) to obtain the loan. The house is worth $155,000, and Paige's basis in the house is $90,000. As part of the refinancing arrangement, she also obtained a $10,000 home-equity loan. She used the proceeds from the home-equity loan to reduce the balance due on her credit cards. Paige received several Form 1098 statements from her bank for interest paid by her in 2015. Details appear below. (See also Exhibit A on page C-11.)

Primary home mortgage	$7,100
Home-equity loan	435
Credit cards	498
Car loan	390

20. On May 14, 2015, Paige contributed clothing to the Salvation Army. The original cost of the clothing was $740. She has substantiation valuing the donation at $360. The Salvation Army is located at 350 Stone Ridge Road, Bangor, Maine 04401. In addition, she made the following cash contributions and received a statement from each of the following organizations acknowledging her contribution:

Larkin College	$850
United Way	125
First Methodist Church	790
Amos House (homeless shelter)	200
Local Chamber of Commerce	100

21. On April 1, 2015, Paige's house was robbed. She apparently interrupted the burglar because all that's missing is an antique brooch she inherited from her grandmother (June 12, 2007) and $300 in cash. Unfortunately, she didn't have a separate rider on her insurance policy covering the jewelry. Therefore, the insurance company reimbursed her only $500 for the brooch. Her basis in the brooch was $6,000, and its fair market value was $7,500. Her insurance policy also limits to $100 the amount of cash that can be claimed in a theft.

22. Paige sells real estate in the evening and on weekends (considered an active trade or business). She runs her business from a rental office she shares with several other realtors (692 River Road, Bangor, Maine 04401). The name of her business is Turner Real Estate and the federal identification number is 05-8799561. Her business code is 531210. Paige has been operating in a business-like way since 2005 and has always shown a profit. She had the following income and expenses from her business:

Commissions earned	$21,250
Expenses:	
Advertising	2,200
Telephone	95
Real estate license	130
Rent	6,000
Utilities	600

She has used her Acura TL in her business since July 1, 2015. During 2015, she properly documented 6,000 business miles (1,000 miles each month). The total mileage on her car (i.e., for both business and personal use) during the year was 15,000 miles (including 200 miles commuting to and from the real estate office). In 2015, Paige elects to use the standard mileage method to calculate her car expenses. She spent $45 on tolls and $135 on parking related to the real estate business.

23. Paige's company has an accountable expense reimbursement plan for employees from which Paige receives $12,000 for the following expenses:

Airfare	$4,700
Hotel	3,400
Meals	2,000
Car rentals	600
Entertainment	900
Incidentals	400

24. During 2015, Paige also paid $295 for business publications other than those paid for by her employer and $325 for a local CPA to prepare her 2014 tax return.

25. Paige has qualifying insurance for purposes of the Affordable Care Act (ACA).

CORPORATE TAX RETURN PROBLEM 1

Required:
- Complete Alvin's Music Inc.'s (AMI) 2015 Form 1120, Schedule D, and Schedule G (if applicable) using the information provided below.
- Neither Form 4562 for depreciation nor Form 4797 for the sale of the equipment is required. Include the amount of tax depreciation and the tax gain on the equipment sale given in the problem (or determined from information given in the problem) on the appropriate lines on the first page of Form 1120.

- Assume that AMI does not owe any alternative minimum tax.
- If any information is missing, use reasonable assumptions to fill in the gaps.
- The forms, schedules, and instructions can be found at the IRS Web site (www.irs.gov). The instructions can be helpful in completing the forms.

Facts:

Alvin's Music Inc. (AMI) was formed in 2007 by Alvin Jones and Theona Smith. Alvin and Theona officially incorporated their store on June 12, 2008. AMI sells (retail) all kinds of music-related products including musical instruments, sheet music, CDs, and DVDs. Alvin owns 60 percent of the outstanding common stock of AMI and Theona owns the remaining 40 percent.

- AMI is located at 355 Music Way, East Palo Alto, California 94303.
- AMI's Employer Identification Number is 29-5748859.
- AMI's business activity is retail sales of music-related products. Its business activity code is 451140.
- Officers of the corporation are as follows:
  - Alvin is the chief executive officer and president (Social Security number 123-45-6789).
  - Theona is the executive vice president (Social Security number 978-65-4321).
  - Gwen Givens is the vice president over operations (Social Security number 789-12-3456).
  - Carlson Bannister is the secretary (Social Security number 321-54-6789).
- All officers devote 100 percent of their time to the business and all officers are U.S. citizens.
- Neither Gwen nor Carlson owns any stock in AMI.
- AMI uses the accrual method of accounting and has a calendar year-end.
- AMI made four equal estimated tax payments of $70,000 each. Its tax liability last year was $175,000. If it has overpaid its federal tax liability, AMI would like to receive a refund.
- AMI paid a dividend of $80,000 to its shareholders on December 1. AMI had ample earnings and profits (E&P) to absorb the distribution.

The following is AMI's audited income statement for 2015:

AMI Income Statement For year ending December 31, 2015	
Revenue from sales	$3,420,000
Sales returns and allowances	(40,000)
Cost of goods sold	(834,000)
Gross profit from operations	$2,546,000
Other income:	
Capital gains	$ 8,000
Gain from disposition of fixed assets	2,000
Dividend income	12,000
Interest income	15,000
Gross income	$2,583,000

AMI Income Statement For year ending December 31, 2015	
Expenses:	
Compensation	$(1,300,000)
Depreciation	(20,000)
Bad debt expense	(15,000)
Meals and entertainment	(5,000)
Maintenance	(5,000)
Charitable donations	(27,000)
Property taxes	(45,000)
State income taxes	(60,000)
Other taxes	(56,000)
Interest	(62,000)
Advertising	(44,000)
Professional services	(32,000)
Pension expense	(40,000)
Supplies	(6,000)
Other expenses	(38,000)
Total expenses	(1,755,000)
Income before taxes	828,000
Federal income tax expense	(260,000)
Net income after taxes	$ 568,000

Notes:

1. AMI has a capital loss carryover to this year from last year in the amount of $5,000.
2. AMI's inventory-related purchases during the year were $1,134,000. AMI values its inventory based on cost using the FIFO inventory cost flow method. Assume the rules of §263A do not apply to AMI.
3. Of the $15,000 interest income, $2,500 was from a City of Fremont bond that was used to fund public activities (issued in 2014), $3,500 was from a Pleasanton city bond used to fund private activities (issued in 2015), $3,000 was from a U.S. Treasury bond, and the remaining $6,000 was from a money market account.
4. AMI sold equipment for $10,000. It originally purchased the equipment for $12,000 and, through the date of the sale, had recorded a cumulative total of $4,000 of book depreciation on the asset and a cumulative total of $6,000 of tax depreciation. For tax purposes, the entire gain was recaptured as ordinary income under §1245.
5. AMI's dividend income came from Simon's Sheet Music. AMI owned 15,000 shares of the stock in Simon's Sheet Music (SSM) at the beginning of the year. This represented 15 percent of the SSM outstanding stock.
6. On July 22, 2015, AMI sold 2,500 shares of its Simon's Sheet Music Stock for $33,000. It had originally purchased these shares on April 24, 2011, for $25,000. After the sale, AMI owned 12.5 percent of Simon's Sheet Music.
7. AMI's compensation is as follows:
   - Alvin $210,000
   - Theona $190,000
   - Gwen $110,000
   - Carlson $90,000
   - Other $700,000
8. AMI wrote off $10,000 in accounts receivable as uncollectible during the year.
9. Regular tax depreciation was $31,000. None of the depreciation should be claimed on Form 1125A.

10. Of the $62,000 of interest expense, $56,000 was from the mortgage on AMI's building and the remaining $6,000 of interest is from business-related loans.
11. The pension expense is the same for both book and tax purposes.
12. Other expenses include $3,000 for premiums paid on term life insurance policies for which AMI is the beneficiary. The policies cover the lives of Alvin and Theona.

The following are AMI's audited balance sheets as of January 1, 2015, and December 31, 2015.

	2015 January 1	2015 December 31
Assets		
Cash	$ 240,000	$ 171,000
Accounts receivable	600,000	700,000
Allowance for doubtful accounts	(35,000)	(40,000)
Inventory	1,400,000	1,700,000
U.S. government bonds	50,000	50,000
State and local bonds	140,000	140,000
Investments in stock	300,000	275,000
Building and other depreciable assets	1,500,000	1,600,000
Accumulated depreciation	(200,000)	(216,000)
Land	900,000	900,000
Other assets	250,000	270,000
Total assets	$5,145,000	$5,550,000
Liabilities and Shareholders' Equity		
Accounts payable	$ 250,000	$ 220,000
Other current liabilities	125,000	120,000
Mortgage	800,000	790,000
Other liabilities	200,000	162,000
Capital stock	600,000	600,000
Retained earnings	3,170,000	3,658,000
Total liabilities and shareholders' equity	$5,145,000	$5,550,000

CORPORATE TAX RETURN PROBLEM 2

Required:
- Complete Blue Catering Service Inc.'s (BCS) 2015 Form 1120, Schedule D, and Schedule G (if applicable) using the information provided below.
- Form 4562 for depreciation is not required. Include the amount of tax depreciation given in the problem on the appropriate line on the first page of Form 1120.
- Assume that BCS does not owe any alternative minimum tax.
- If any information is missing, use reasonable assumptions to fill in the gaps.
- The forms, schedules, and instructions can be found at the IRS Web site (www.irs.gov). The instructions can be helpful in completing the forms.

Facts:
Cara Siler, Janna Funk, and Valerie Cloward each own one-third of the common stock of Blue Catering Services Inc. (BCS). BCS was incorporated on February 4, 2009. It has only one class of stock outstanding and operates as a C corporation for tax purposes. BCS caters all types of social events throughout southern California.

- BCS is located at 540 Waverly Way, San Diego, California 92101.
- BCS's Employer Identification Number is 38-4743474.

- BCS's business activity is catering food and services. Its business activity code is 722300.
- The shareholders also work as officers for the corporation as follows:
  - Cara is the chief executive officer and president (Social Security number 231-54-8976).
  - Janna is the executive vice president and chief operating officer (Social Security number 798-56-3241).
  - Valerie is the vice president of finance (Social Security number 879-21-4536).
- All officers devote 100 percent of their time to the business and all officers are U.S. citizens.
- BCS uses the accrual method of accounting and has a calendar year-end.
- BCS made four equal estimated tax payments of $20,000 each. Its tax liability last year was $70,000. If it has overpaid its federal tax liability, BCS would like to receive a refund.
- BCS paid a dividend of $30,000 to its shareholders on November 1. BCS had ample earnings and profits (E&P) to absorb the distribution.

The following is BCS's audited income statement for 2015:

BCS Income Statement For year ending December 31, 2015	
Revenue from sales	$1,800,000
Sales returns and allowances	(5,000)
Cost of goods sold	(350,000)
Gross profit from operations	$1,445,000
Other income:	
Capital loss	$ (15,000)
Dividend income	25,000
Interest income	10,000
Gross income	$1,465,000
Expenses:	
Compensation	$ (950,000)
Depreciation	(10,000)
Bad debt expense	(15,000)
Meals and entertainment	(3,000)
Maintenance	(6,000)
Property taxes	(11,000)
State income taxes	(45,000)
Other taxes	(44,000)
Rent	(60,000)
Interest	(5,000)
Advertising	(52,000)
Professional services	(16,000)
Employee benefits	(32,000)
Supplies	(5,000)
Other expenses	(27,000)
Total expenses	(1,281,000)
Income before taxes	84,000
Federal income tax expense	(62,000)
Net income after taxes	$ 122,000

Notes:

1. BCS's inventory-related purchases during 2015 were $360,000. It values its inventory based on cost using the FIFO inventory cost flow method. Assume the rules of §263A do not apply to BCS.

2. Of the $10,000 interest income, $1,250 was from a City of Irvine bond that was used to fund public activities (issued in 2013), $1,750 was from an Oceanside city bond used to fund private activities (issued in 2012), $1,000 was from a U.S. Treasury bond, and the remaining $6,000 was from a money market account.

3. BCS's dividend income came from Clever Cakes Inc. (CC). BCS owned 10,000 shares of the stock in Clever Cakes at the beginning of the year. This represented 10 percent of SSM outstanding stock.

4. On October 1, 2015, BCS sold 1,000 shares of its CC stock for $25,000. It had originally purchased these shares on April 18, 2011, for $40,000. After the sale, BCS owned 9 percent of CC.

5. BCS's compensation is as follows:

   - Cara $150,000
   - Janna $140,000
   - Valerie $130,000
   - Other $530,000

6. BCS wrote off $25,000 in accounts receivable as uncollectible during the year.

7. BCS's regular tax depreciation was $28,000. None of the depreciation should be claimed on Form 1125A.

8. The $5,000 interest expense was from a business loan.

9. Other expenses include $6,000 for premiums paid on term life insurance policies for which BCS is the beneficiary. The policies cover the lives of Cara, Janna, and Valerie.

The following are BCS's audited balance sheets as of January 1, 2015, and December 31, 2015.

	2015 January 1	2015 December 31
Assets		
Cash	$ 180,000	$ 205,000
Accounts receivable	560,000	580,000
Allowance for doubtful accounts	(60,000)	(50,000)
Inventory	140,000	150,000
U.S. government bonds	20,000	20,000
State and local bonds	120,000	120,000
Investments in stock	400,000	360,000
Fixed assets	140,000	160,000
Accumulated depreciation	(50,000)	(60,000)
Other assets	20,000	21,000
Total assets	$1,470,000	$1,506,000
Liabilities and Shareholders' Equity		
Accounts payable	$ 280,000	$ 240,000
Other current liabilities	20,000	18,000
Other liabilities	40,000	26,000
Capital stock	400,000	400,000
Retained earnings	730,000	822,000
Total liabilities and shareholders' equity	$1,470,000	$1,506,000

PARTNERSHIP TAX RETURN PROBLEM 1

Required:

- For 2015, complete Aspen Ridge limited partnership's page 1 of Form 1065; complete Schedule K on page 4 of Form 1065; complete lines 1 and 2 of the Analysis of Net Income (Loss) at the top of page 5 of Form 1065; and complete Schedules M-1 and M-2 at the bottom of page 5 of Form 1065. Finally, complete Mark Sullivan's Schedule K-1.

- Form 4562 for depreciation is not required. Include any tax depreciation or Section 179 expense on the appropriate line of page 1 of Form 1065 or Schedule K.

- If any information is missing, use reasonable assumptions to fill in any gaps.

- The forms, schedules, and instructions can be found at the IRS Web site (www.irs.gov). The instructions can be helpful in completing the forms.

Facts:

The Aspen Ridge limited partnership was formed on April 1, 2009, by Mark Sullivan, its general partner, and two other limited partners when they each contributed an equal amount of cash to start the new enterprise. Aspen Ridge is an outdoor equipment retailer selling camping, fishing, skiing, and other outdoor gear to the general public. Mark has a 33.33% profits, loss, and capital interest and the limited partners hold the remaining 66.66% of the profits, loss, and capital interests. Their profits, loss, and capital interests have remained unchanged since the partnership was formed. Mark is actively involved in managing the business while the limited partners are simply investors.

- Aspen Ridge is located at 1065 North 365 South, Ogden, Utah 84401.
- The employer identification number for Aspen Ridge is 85-8976654.
- Aspen Ridge uses the accrual method of accounting and has a calendar year-end.
- Mark's address is 543 Wander Lane, Holliday, Utah 84503 and his Social Security number is 445-27-3484.

The following is Aspen Ridge's 2015 income statement for books:

Aspen Ridge Income Statement For year ending December 31, 2015	
Sales	$965,500
Sales returns and allowances	(9,700)
Cost of goods sold	(538,200)
Gross profit from operations	$ 417,600
Other Income:	
Interest from money market account	$ 3,200
Gain from sale of photograph	34,000
Gross income	$454,800

Aspen Ridge Income Statement For year ending December 31, 2015	
Expenses:	
Employee wages	$ 95,400
Interest on accounts payable	2,700
Payroll and property taxes	10,800
Supplies	4,300
Rent on retail building	18,500
Depreciation on furniture and fixtures	4,550
Advertising	8,300
Guaranteed payments to Mark Sullivan	35,000
Utilities	6,400
Accounting and legal services	4,400
Meals and entertainment	2,240
Charitable contribution to the Sierra Club	3,300
Miscellaneous expenses	5,750
Total Expenses	(201,640)
Net income for books	$ 253,160

Notes:

1. Aspen Ridge has total assets of $1,725,800 and total liabilities of $540,300 at the beginning of the year and total assets of $2,065,300 and total liabilities of $806,640 at the end of the year.

2. Partnership liabilities consist of accounts payable, and Mark, as general partner, is legally responsible for paying these liabilities if the partnership does not.

3. Two years ago, Aspen Ridge purchased an original Ansel Adams outdoor landscape photograph with the intent to display it permanently in the retail store. This year, however, the photograph was sold to a local ski lodge where it now hangs on the wall. The $34,000 recognized gain from the sale is reflected in the income statement above.

4. For tax purposes, Aspen Ridge has consistently elected under Section 179 to expense any furniture or fixtures purchased every year since it was formed. As a result, it does not have a tax basis in any of its depreciable assets. This year, Aspen Ridge expensed $17,300 of signs and display cases for tax purposes.

5. On November 20, Aspen Ridge distributed $180,000 ($60,000 per partner) to the partners.

6. Miscellaneous expenses include a $900 fine for violating a local signage ordinance.

7. Aspen Ridge maintains its books using generally accepted accounting principles.

PARTNERSHIP TAX RETURN PROBLEM 2

Required:

- Using the information provided below, complete Arlington Building Supply's (ABS) 2015 Form 1065 and Schedule D. Also complete Jerry Johnson and Steve Stillwell's Schedule K-1.

- Form 4562 for depreciation is not required. Use the amount of tax depreciation and §179 expense provided in the income statement and the information in #4 below to complete the appropriate lines on the first page and on Schedule K of Form 1065.

- Form 4797 for the sale of trade or business property is not required. Use the amount of gain and loss from the sale of the truck and forklifts in the income statement and the information provided in #4 and #5 below to complete the appropriate lines on the first page and on Schedule K of Form 1065.
- If any information is missing, use reasonable assumptions to fill in any gaps.
- The forms, schedules, and instructions can be found at the IRS Web site (www.irs.gov). The instructions can be helpful in completing the forms.

Facts:

On January 1, 2005, two enterprising men in the community, Jerry Johnson and Steve "Swiss" Stillwell, anticipated a boom in the local construction industry. They decided to sell their small businesses and pool their resources as general partners in establishing a retail outlet for lumber and other building materials, including a complete line of specialty hardware for prefab tree-houses. Their general partnership was officially formed under the name of Arlington Building Supply and soon became a thriving business.

- ABS is located at 2174 Progress Ave., Arlington, Illinois 64888.
- ABS's Employer Identification Number is 91-3697984.
- ABS's business activity is retail construction. Its business activity code is 444190.
- Both general partners are active in the management of ABS.
  - Jerry Johnson's Social Security number is 500-23-4976. His address is 31 W. Oak Drive, Arlington, Illinois 64888.
  - Steve Stillwell's Social Security number is 374-68-3842. His address is 947 E. Linder Street, Arlington, Illinois 64888.
- ABS uses the accrual method of accounting and has a calendar year-end.

The following is ABS's 2015 income statement:

ABS Income Statement For year ending December 31, 2015		
Sales (on account)	$410,000	
Less: Sales returns	−20,000	
		$390,000
Cost of goods sold		−150,000
Gross profit on sales		$240,000
Operating expenses		
Salaries and wages (including partners' guaranteed payments)	$ 79,000	
Property taxes	1,600	
Payroll taxes	2,450	
Depreciation and 179 expense	40,062	
Advertising	2,000	
Bad debt expense	3,850	
Office expense	1,800	
Repairs	2,150	
Miscellaneous	450	
Fire insurance	4,850	138,212
Net operating income		$ 101,788

	ABS	
	Income Statement	
	For year ending December 31, 2015	
Other income		
Gain on sale of securities	$ 1,350	
Gain on sale of truck	16,399	
Dividend income	695	
Interest income	4,260	22,704
		$124,492
Other deductions		
Interest on mortgage	$ 5,400	
Interest on notes payable	2,250	
Charitable contributions	5,000	
Life insurance premiums	3,000	
Loss on sale of forklifts	466	16,116
Net income		$108,376

Notes:

1. The partnership maintains its books according to the §704(b) regulations. Under this method of accounting, all book and tax numbers are the same except for life insurance premiums and tax-exempt interest.

2. The partners' percentage ownership of original contributed capital is 30 percent for Johnson and 70 percent for Stillwell. They agree that profits and losses will be shared according to this same ratio. Any additional capital contributions and withdrawals must be made in these same ratios.

3. For their services to the company, the partners will receive the following annual guaranteed payments:

   Johnson $28,000
   Stillwell $21,000

   Johnson is expected to devote all his time to the business, while Stillwell will devote approximately 75 percent of his.

4. Two forklifts were sold in September 2015. The old lifts were purchased new four years ago. Two new forklifts were purchased on September 1, 2015, for $32,000 and the partnership intends to immediately expense them under §179 (see depreciation and 179 expense in the income statement above).

5. The truck sold this year was purchased several years ago. $16,099 of the total gain from the sale of the truck should be recaptured as ordinary income under IRC §1245.

6. The partnership uses currently allowable tax depreciation methods for both regular tax and book purposes and has adopted a policy of electing not to claim bonus depreciation. Assume alternative minimum tax depreciation equals regular tax depreciation.

7. The partners decided to invest in a small tract of land with the intention of selling it about a year later at a substantial profit. On January 1, 2015, they executed a $50,000 note with the bank to obtain the $70,000 cash purchase price. Interest on the note is payable yearly, and the principal is due in 18 months. The first interest payment of $2,250 was made on December 30, 2015 (see interest on notes payable in income statement above).

8. The note payable to the bank as well as the accounts payable are treated by the partnership as recourse debt. Assume the total recourse debt is allocated $28,776 to Jerry and $70,224 to Steve.

9. Some years after the partnership was formed, a mortgage of $112,500 was obtained on the land and warehouse from Commerce State Bank. Principal payments of $4,500 must be paid each December 31, along with 8 percent interest

on the outstanding balance (see interest on mortgage in income statement above). The holder of the note agreed therein to look only to the land and warehouse for his security in the event of default. Because this mortgage is nonrecourse debt, it should be allocated among the partners according to their profit sharing ratios.

10. The partnership values its inventory at lower of cost or market and uses the FIFO inventory method. Assume the rules of §263A do not apply to ABS.

11. During the year, the partnership bought 300 shares of ABC, Ltd., for $6,100 on February 8, 2015. All the shares were sold for $6,650 on April 2, 2015. ABS received a Form 1099-B indicating that the basis of the ABC shares was reported to the IRS.

12. Two hundred shares of XYZ Corporation were sold for $10,600 on September 13, 2015. The stock was purchased on December 1, 2009, and is not eligible for the 28 percent capital gains rate. ABS received a Form 1099-B indicating that the basis of the XYZ shares was $9,800.

13. The following dividends were received:

XYZ (qualified)	$400
ABC, Ltd. (not qualified)	295
Total	$695

14. The partnership received interest income from the following sources:

Interest on Illinois municipal bonds	$3,200
Interest on savings	560
Interest on accounts receivable	500
Total	$4,260

15. The partnership donated $5,000 cash to the Red Cross.

16. Life insurance policies on the lives of Johnson and Stillwell were purchased in the prior year. The partnership will pay all the premiums and is the beneficiary of the policy. The premiums for the current year were $3,000 (see income statement above), and no cash surrender value exists for the first or second year of the policy.

17. The partners withdrew the following cash amounts from the partnership during the year (in addition to their guaranteed payments):

Johnson	$20,000
Stillwell	35,000

The following are ABS's balance sheets as of January 1, 2015, and December 31, 2015.

		12/31/15		1/1/15
Assets				
Cash		$ 70,467		$ 43,042
Accounts receivable		76,000		57,000
Inventories		60,000		50,000
Investment in municipal bonds		50,000		50,000
Investment in XYZ common stock		40,200		50,000
Truck			$ 16,500	
Less accumulated depreciation			13,649	
				2,851
Machinery and equipment	$ 66,000		$ 50,000	
Less accumulated depreciation	58,697		34,376	
		7,303		15,624
Building	$120,000		$120,000	
Less accumulated depreciation	39,875		36,798	
		80,125		83,202
Land		90,000		20,000
Totals		$474,095		$371,719

	12/31/15	1/1/15
Liabilities and Capital		
Accounts payable	$ 49,000	$ 45,500
Notes payable	50,000	0
Mortgage payable	63,000	67,500
Capital: Jerry Johnson	94,553	82,040
Steve Stillwell	217,542	176,679
Totals	$474,095	$371,719

S CORPORATION TAX RETURN PROBLEM

Required:

- Using the information provided below, complete First Place Inc.'s (FPI) 2015 Form 1120S. Also complete Kate Kleiber's Schedule K-1.
- Form 4562 for depreciation is not required. Include the amount of tax depreciation given in the problem on the appropriate line on the first page of Form 1120S.
- If any information is missing, use reasonable assumptions to fill in the gaps.
- The forms, schedules, and instructions can be found at the IRS Web site (www.irs.gov). The instructions can be helpful in completing the forms.

Facts:

First Place Inc. (FPI) was formed as a corporation on January 5, 2012, by its two owners Kate Kleiber and James Chandler. FPI immediately elected to be taxed as an S corporation for federal income tax purposes. FPI sells mountain climbing gear to retailers throughout the Rocky Mountain region. Kate owns 70 percent of the FPI common stock (the only class of stock outstanding) and James owns 30 percent.

- FPI is located at 4200 West 400 North, Salt Lake City, Utah 84116.
- FPI's Employer Identification Number is 87-5467544.
- FPI's business activity is wholesale sales. Its business activity code is 423910.
- Both shareholders work as employees of the corporation.
- Kate is the president of FPI (Social Security number 312-89-4567). Kate's address is 1842 East 8400 South, Sandy, Utah 84094.
- James is the vice president of FPI (Social Security number 321-98-7645). James's address is 2002 East 8145 South, Sandy, Utah 84094.
- FPI uses the accrual method of accounting and has a calendar year-end.

The following is FPI's 2015 income statement:

FPI Income Statement For year ending December 31, 2015	
Revenue from sales	$ 980,000
Sales returns and allowances	(10,000)
Cost of goods sold	(110,000)
Gross profit from operations	$ 860,000
Other income:	
Dividend income	$ 15,000
Interest income	5,000
Gross income	$ 880,000
Expenses:	
Compensation	$(600,000)
Depreciation	(10,000)
Bad debt expense	(14,000)
Meals and entertainment	(2,000)
Maintenance	(8,000)
Business interest	(1,000)
Property taxes	(7,000)
Charitable contributions	(10,000)
Other taxes	(30,000)
Rent	(28,000)
Advertising	(14,000)
Professional services	(11,000)
Employee benefits	(12,000)
Supplies	(3,000)
Other expenses	(21,000)
Total expenses	(771,000)
Net income	$ 109,000

Notes:

1. FPI's purchases during 2015 were $115,000. It values its inventory based on cost using the FIFO inventory cost flow method. Assume the rules of §263A do not apply to FPI.

2. Of the $5,000 interest income, $2,000 was from a West Jordan city bond used to fund public activities (issued in 2007) and $3,000 was from a money market account.

3. FPI's dividend income comes from publicly traded stocks that FPI has owned for two years.

4. FPI's compensation is as follows:

   - Kate $120,000
   - James $80,000
   - Other $400,000.

5. FPI wrote off $6,000 in accounts receivable as uncollectible during the year.

6. FPI's regular tax depreciation was $17,000. AMT depreciation was $13,000.

7. FPI distributed $60,000 to its shareholders.

8. FPI is not required to compute the amount in its accumulated adjustments account.

The following are FPI's book balance sheets as of January 1, 2015, and December 31, 2015.

	2015 January 1	December 31
Assets		
Cash	$ 90,000	$143,000
Accounts receivable	300,000	310,000
Allowance for doubtful accounts	(60,000)	(68,000)
Inventory	45,000	50,000
State and local bonds	38,000	38,000
Investments in stock	82,000	82,000
Fixed assets	100,000	100,000
Accumulated depreciation	(20,000)	(30,000)
Other assets	20,000	21,000
Total assets	$595,000	$646,000
Liabilities and Shareholders' Equity		
Accounts payable	$ 60,000	$ 55,000
Other current liabilities	5,000	8,000
Other liabilities	10,000	14,000
Capital stock	200,000	200,000
Retained earnings	320,000	369,000
Total liabilities and shareholders' equity	$595,000	$646,000

GIFT TAX RETURN PROBLEM

Lamar Grabowski is a prosperous rancher who lives in Crawford (Cherry County), Nebraska. Lamar is 60 years old and has been married to Elouisa (58 years old) for the past 37 years. Mildred and Charles are Lamar and Elouisa's adult children, ages 32 and 36, respectively. Over the years Lamar has considered making gifts to his children. Finally, in 2007 Lamar gave $250,000 each to Mildred and Charles. This year Lamar made the following gifts to Mildred and Charles:

Property	Recipient	Market Value	Adjusted Basis
Cash from joint savings account	Mildred Jones	$1,380,000	
100 acres of ranch land near Crawford	Charles Grabowski	1,640,000	$125,000

In addition to these gifts, this year Lamar also made a gift of 20,000 shares of Acme Inc. stock to State University (a qualified educational institution). The stock is listed on a national exchange (CUSIP = 000123TP) and was valued at $800,000 on the date of the gift. Lamar purchased the Acme stock 34 years ago for $25,000, and he inherited the ranch land from his father in 1992 when it was valued at $600,000. Lamar's cash gifts are made from Lamar and Elouisa's joint savings account, and although Elouisa is a professional accountant, she has not contributed to the joint savings account.

Lamar filed a timely gift tax return for the 2007 gifts offsetting a portion of each gift with his $12,000 annual exclusion and offsetting the remaining $147,640 of gift taxes with a portion of his unified credit. Lamar has engaged you to calculate the gift tax and prepare a draft of the 2015 gift tax return (pages 1–3). Lamar and Elouisa have indicated they would like to gift split.

ESTATE TAX RETURN PROBLEM

Clark Griswold is a wealthy engineer and inventor who retired to his residence in Fort Collins (Larimer County), Colorado. Clark is married to Ellen and they have two adult children, Russell and Audrey. Clark passed away on March 22 of this year at the age of 60, and his executor, Frank Shirley, has hired you to calculate the estate tax and prepare a draft of the 2016 estate tax return (pages 1–3). Clark's estate is being administered through the Larimer County Probate Court.

Frank has inventoried Clark's assets and has listed the value of his assets below. The auto, residence, and checking account were owned jointly (with the right of survivorship) with his wife. Clark also owned a whole life insurance policy with a cash surrender value of $50,000. Ellen and Clark's estate were listed as beneficiaries on the insurance policy with Ellen receiving $1 million and the estate receiving the remainder of the proceeds. The Ajax common stock, the real estate, and the patent were all owned by Clark rather than joint ownership. Frank also noted that the real estate is subject to an $800,000 mortgage. At his death Clark also owed $1,500 on his credit card.

Property	Value	Adjusted Basis
Auto	$ 20,000	$ 55,000
Personal effects	75,000	110,000
Checking account	250,000	250,000
30,000 shares of Ajax common stock	1,200,000	270,000
Residence	6,800,000	480,000
Life insurance	4,000,000	50,000
Real estate	3,500,000	2,100,000
Patent	4,225,000	100,000

Clark's will instructs Frank to distribute Clark's property as follows: Ellen inherits Clark's personal effects, Russell inherits the patent, and Audrey inherits 10,000 shares of the Ajax stock and the real estate. The will also instructs Frank to distribute 20,000 shares of the Ajax stock to State University (an educational institution), and after paying Clark's personal debts, the residual of the estate (if any) is divided equally between Russell and Audrey. The estate paid Clark's personal debts (credit card debt) and $4,300 of funeral expenses associated with Clark's burial. Finally, the estate paid Frank $27,000 in executor's fees associated with the administration of Clark's estate.

Clark's tax records indicate that in 2007 Clark gave $500,000 of Ajax stock to Russell and $500,000 of cash to Audrey. Clark filed a timely gift tax return (Form 709) and paid no gift taxes.

Appendix D

Tax Rates

2016 Federal Tax Rate Schedule

Schedule X-Single

If taxable income is over:	But not over:	The tax is:
$ 0	$ 9,275	10% of taxable income
$ 9,275	$ 37,650	$927.50 plus 15% of the excess over $9,275
$ 37,650	$ 91,150	$5,183.75 plus 25% of the excess over $37,650
$ 91,150	$190,150	$18,558.75 plus 28% of the excess over $91,150
$190,150	$413,350	$46,278.75 plus 33% of the excess over $190,150
$413,350	$415,050	$119,934.75 plus 35% of the excess over $413,350
$415,050	—	$120,529.75 plus 39.6% of the excess over $415,050

Schedule Z-Head of Household

If taxable income is over:	But not over:	The tax is:
$ 0	$ 13,250	10% of taxable income
$ 13,250	$ 50,400	$1,325.00 plus 15% of the excess over $13,250
$ 50,400	$130,150	$6,897.50 plus 25% of the excess over $50,400
$130,150	$210,800	$26,835.00 plus 28% of the excess over $130,150
$210,800	$413,350	$49,417.00 plus 33% of the excess over $210,800
$413,350	$441,000	$116,258.50 plus 35% of the excess over $413,350
$441,000	—	$125,936.00 plus 39.6% of the excess over $441,000

Schedule Y-1-Married Filing Jointly of Qualifying Widow(er)

If taxable income is over:	But not over:	The tax is:
$ 0	$ 18,550	10% of taxable income
$ 18,550	$ 75,300	$1,855.00 plus 15% of the excess over $18,550
$ 75,300	$151,900	$10,367.50 plus 25% of the excess over $75,300
$151,900	$231,450	$29,517.50 plus 28% of the excess over $151,900
$231,450	$413,350	$51,791.50 plus 33% of the excess over $231,450
$413,350	$466,950	$111,818.50 plus 35% of the excess over $413,350
$466,950	—	$130,578.50 plus 39.6% of the excess over $466,950

Schedule Y-2-Married Filing Separately

If taxable income is over:	But not over:	The tax is:
$ 0	$ 9,275	10% of taxable income
$ 9,275	$ 37,650	$927.50 plus 15% of the excess over $9,275
$ 37,650	$ 75,950	$5,183.75 plus 25% of the excess over $37,650
$ 75,950	$115,725	$14,758.75 plus 28% of the excess over $75,950
$115,725	$206,675	$25,895.75 plus 33% of the excess over $115,725
$206,675	$233,475	$55,909.25 plus 35% of the excess over $206,675
$233,475	—	$65,289.25 plus 39.6% of the excess over $233,475

2015 Federal Tax Rate Schedule

Schedule X-Single

If taxable income is over:	But not over:	The tax is:
$ 0	$ 9,225	10% of taxable income
$ 9,225	$ 37,450	$922.50 plus 15% of the excess over $9,225
$ 37,450	$ 90,750	$5,156.25 plus 25% of the excess over $37,450
$ 90,750	$189,300	$18,481.25 plus 28% of the excess over $90,750
$189,300	$411,500	$46,075.25 plus 33% of the excess over $189,300
$411,500	$413,200	$119,401.25 plus 35% of the excess over $411,500
$413,200	—	$119,996.25 plus 39.6% of the excess over $413,200

Schedule Z-Head of Household

If taxable income is over:	But not over:	The tax is:
$ 0	$ 13,150	10% of taxable income
$ 13,150	$ 50,200	$1,315.00 plus 15% of the excess over $13,150
$ 50,200	$129,600	$6,872.50 plus 25% of the excess over $50,200
$129,600	$209,850	$26,722.50 plus 28% of the excess over $129,600
$209,850	$411,500	$49,192.50 plus 33% of the excess over $209,850
$411,500	$439,000	$115,737.00 plus 35% of the excess over $411,500
$439,000	—	$125,362.00 plus 39.6% of the excess over $439,000

Schedule Y-1-Married Filing Jointly of Qualifying Widow(er)

If taxable income is over:	But not over:	The tax is:
$ 0	$ 18,450	10% of taxable income
$ 18,450	$ 74,900	$1,845.00 plus 15% of the excess over $18,450
$ 74,900	$151,200	$10,312.50 plus 25% of the excess over $74,900
$151,200	$230,450	$29,387.50 plus 28% of the excess over $151,200
$230,450	$411,500	$51,577.50 plus 33% of the excess over $230,450
$411,500	$464,850	$111,324.00 plus 35% of the excess over $411,500
$464,850	—	$129,966.50 plus 39.6% of the excess over $464,850

Schedule Y-2-Married Filing Separately

If taxable income is over:	But not over:	The tax is:
$ 0	$ 9,225	10% of taxable income
$ 9,225	$ 37,450	$922.50 plus 15% of the excess over $9,225
$ 37,450	$ 75,600	$5,156.25 plus 25% of the excess over $37,450
$ 75,600	$115,225	$14,693.75 plus 28% of the excess over $75,600
$115,225	$205,750	$25,788.75 plus 33% of the excess over $115,225
$204,750	$232,425	$55,662.00 plus 35% of the excess over $205,750
$232,425	—	$64,998.25 plus 39.6% of the excess over $232,425

Basic Standard Deduction Amounts

Filing Status	2015 Amount	2016 Amount
Married Filing Jointly	$12,600	$12,600
Qualifying Widow or Widower	$12,600	$12,600
Married Filing Separately	$ 6,300	$ 6,300
Head of Household	$ 9,250	$ 9,300
Single	$ 6,300	$ 6,300

Amount of Each Additional Standard Deduction

	2015 Amount	2016 Amount
Married taxpayers 65 or over or blind	$1,250	$1,250
Single taxpayer or head of household who is 65 or over or blind	$1,550	$1,550

Personal and Dependency Exemption

2015 Exemption	2016 Exemption
$4,000	$4,050

Corporate Income Tax Rates

Taxable Income	Tax
< $50,000	15% of the taxable income
$50,000–$75,000	$7,500 + 25% of taxable income over $50,000
$75,000–$100,000	$13,750 + 34% of taxable income over $75,000
$100,000–$335,000	$22,250 + 39% of taxable income over $100,000
$335,000–$10,000,000	$113,900 + 34% of taxable income over $335,000
$10,000,000–$15,000,000	$3,400,000 + 35% of taxable income over $10,000,000
$15,000,000–$18,333,333	$5,150,000 + 38% of taxable income over $15,000,000
Over $18,333,333	35% of the taxable income

Code Index

Subject Index

Page numbers followed by n refer to footnotes.